D0773093

## DATE DUE

| | | | |
|---|---|---|---|
| | | | |
| | | | |
| | | | |
| | | | |
| | | | |
| | | | |
| | | | |
| | | | |
| | | | |
| | | | |
| | | | |
| | | | |
| | | | |
| | | | |
| | | | |
| | | | |

# GRANGER'S
## INDEX TO POETRY

# LIBRARIANS

Use this form to order *Granger's Index to Poetry, Seventh Edition,* and **receive at no extra charge** a desk guide to Granger's, reprinted from the actual text. It contains a complete list of all symbols used in the new Granger's, keyed to the listing of anthologies. Librarians can note call numbers in the desk guide to provide a quick response to inquiries—and maintain a personal record of the anthologies included in Granger's—without going to the volume itself.

## Order Form

**Please send me:**

___ copies of *Granger's Index to Poetry, Seventh Edition* at $124.00 net per copy. Books will be shipped **postpaid** immediately on publication in March, 1982.

$_____

One copy of the Librarians' Key to Symbols will be sent free with every copy of *Granger's Index to Poetry, Seventh Edition* you order.

Send me ___ additional copies of the Librarians' Key to Symbols at $2.00 per copy.

$_____

Total payment due

$_____

☐ Enclosed is check or money order for total payment due
☐ Purchase order is attached

**Send books to**

Name _____

Institution _____

Address _____

City _____ State _____ Zip _____

Return this form, with payment or with purchase order attached, to receive Granger's and the Librarians' Key to Symbols postpaid. Send your order in the prepaid envelope or an envelope of your own to

**Columbia University Press
136 South Broadway
Irvington, New York 10533**

Send your order by March 1, 1982 to ensure that your copies are shipped immediately upon publication.

# GRANGER'S
## INDEX TO POETRY

1970-1977

EDITED BY WILLIAM JAMES SMITH

COLUMBIA UNIVERSITY PRESS
NEW YORK 1978

Copyright © 1978 Columbia University Press
All rights reserved

Printed in the United States of America

ISBN: 231-04248-5

Library of Congress Cataloging in Publication Data

Granger, Edith.
    Granger's Index to poetry, 1970-1977.

    This volume takes the place of the usual 5-year
supplement to Granger's index. The index was first
published in 1904 under title: Index to poetry and
recitations.
    1. Poetry—Indexes.   2. English poetry—Indexes.
I. Smith, William James, 1918-     II. Title.
III. Title: Index to poetry, 1970-1977.
PN1022.G7 1978     808.81'0016     78-4097

# PREFACE

For three-quarters of a century GRANGER'S INDEX TO POETRY has guided readers to poems published in anthologies. It has provided indexes to titles and first lines, to poets' names, and an index by subjects. The practice since 1945 has been to publish a new cumulative index every ten years, with a Supplement at the five-year intervals between. The current volume marks a departure from this policy, replacing what would have been the Supplement covering the period 1970-1975. It covers instead the period 1970-1977, though it is published at approximately the same time as the Supplement would have been. The inclusive dates are not stringent. Three anthologies in the current Index have copyright dates preceding 1970, but were not previously indexed in GRANGER'S. Any 1977 anthologies not available for consideration will be considered for subsequent editions. The greater currency and inclusiveness of this volume is the result of more rapid compilation and the computerization of production. One hundred and twenty anthologies of poetry are indexed herein, all for the first time. This is a greater number than in any previous interim volume.

A second new feature of this volume is the designation of works recommended for priority acquisition by libraries. This feature is the result of requests by many librarians. Libraries which cannot acquire all or most of the anthologies indexed here may be helped by our marking eight works in the KEY TO SYMBOLS (pp. xi-xvii) with two asterisks (**) for primary acquisition, and an additional twenty-seven with one asterisk (*) for further acquisition. This is not meant as an inflexible guide, but as an aid to libraries with limited funds and no specialized requirements.

Columbia University Press was assisted in making the recommendations by a panel of experts who brought great combined library experience and a considerable array of other talents to the task. The group consisted of Wayne Gossage, Library Director, Bank Street College of Education; Stanley Kunitz, distinguished poet, editor, and teacher; and Lillian Morrison, Coordinator, Young Adult Services, New York Public Library. The panel in addition made valuable suggestions of anthologies to be indexed.

The great range of contemporary poetic interests is reflected in the anthologies of the period that have been chosen for indexing. A notable aspect of the current volume is the inclusion of a number of anthologies of poetry by women, a total of nine such volumes. Black, American Indian, and other ethnic groups are also represented as well as poetry for children. In all, more than 25,000 poems are indexed.

THE SUBJECT INDEX, in accordance with many requests, has been enlarged. This and other features of the volume reflect librarian response to extensive questionnaire surveys we have conducted. We have greatly benefited from the counsel of numerous librarians. GRANGER'S is in a real sense their creation as much as it is that of Edith Granger and her successors.

*January, 1978*

W. J. S.

# CONTENTS

# EXPLANATORY NOTES

The TITLE AND FIRST LINE INDEX is the principal index and must be used in connection with both the AUTHOR INDEX and the SUBJECT INDEX.

In the TITLE AND FIRST LINE INDEX initial capitals in the important words of the titles distinguish titles from first lines. Symbols are listed after both titles and first lines. However, more complete information as to translators, acts and scenes, abridgments, and variant titles is given in the title entries.

When the title and first line of a poem are the same, only the title entry has been indexed. When they are so nearly the same as to be adjacent, again only the title has been indexed, with the first line added in quotation marks and in parentheses to the title entry.

In the arrangement of the title entries, indention is important. Single indention indicates a selection from the work named above; double indention with parentheses indicates a variant title.

Because the Mother Goose rhymes are so much better known by first line than by the artificial and varying titles given to them in various collections, only their first lines have been included in the TITLE AND FIRST LINE INDEX.

In such titles as "Ode," "Poem," "Song," "Sonnet," too frequent to be distinctive, the first line is added to the title given in the anthology (for example, Ode: "How sleep the brave who sink to rest"). The title is then alphabeted by first line under "Ode," "Poem," etc.

Titles and first lines beginning with "O" and "Oh" have been filed, as in previous editions, as if all were spelled "O," and are alphabeted according to the words that follow.

"Mac," "Mc," and "M' " are filed as if all were spelled "Mac."

Arabic and Chinese names in the AUTHOR INDEX are filed univerted as if written in one word. Old-style Japanese names are handled in the same way as Chinese names (that is, as if written in one word), while modern Japanese names are usually inverted in the Western manner for filing purposes.

A KEY TO SYMBOLS is provided, with publishers, dates and editions added after titles of anthologies. Two asterisks (**) preceding a title are a recommendation for priority purchase by small libraries. One asterisk (*) indicates secondary recommendations. See PREFACE for a fuller explanation of this feature.

# ABBREVIATIONS

| | | | |
|---|---|---|---|
| *abr.* | abridged | *misc.* | miscellaneous |
| *ad.* | adapted | *mod.* | modernized *or* modern |
| *add.* | additional | *N.T.* | New Testament |
| *arr.* | arranged | *O.T.* | Old Testament |
| *at.* | attributed | *orig.* | original |
| *Bk.* | book | *Pt.* | part |
| *br.* | brief | *rev.* | revised |
| *c.* | copyright | *sc.* | scene |
| *ch.* | chapter | *Sec.* | section |
| *comp.* | compiled *or* compiler | *sel.* | selection |
| *comps.* | compilers | *sels.* | selections |
| *cond.* | condensed | *sl.* | slightly |
| *diff.* | different | *st.* | stanza |
| *fr.* | from | *sts.* | stanzas |
| *frag.* | fragment | *tr.* | translator, translation, *or* translated |
| *incl.* | included *or* including | | |
| *introd.* | introduction *or* introductory | *trs.* | translators *or* translations |
| *ll.* | lines | *var.* | various |
| | | *wr.* | wrong *or* wrongly |

# KEY TO SYMBOLS

*Anthologies starred with two asterisks (\*\*) are recommended for priority acquisition by small libraries, one star (\*) for further acquisition. See* PREFACE *for fuller explanation.*

o  AAS    Anchor Anthology of Sixteenth-Century Verse, The. *Richard S. Sylvester, ed.* (1974) Doubleday Anchor Books

O  AATT   Adam Among the Television Trees: An Anthology of Verse by Contemporary Christian Poets. *Virginia R. Mollenkott, ed.* (1971) Word Books

o  AIW    As I Walked Out One Evening: A Book of Ballads. *Helen Plotz, comp.* (1976) Greenwillow Books (William Morrow & Company)

PN 6101 D78

AKE    All Kinds of Everything. *Louis Dudek, ed.* (1973) Clarke, Irwin & Company

AmFP   *American Folk Poetry: An Anthology. *Duncan Emrich, ed.* (1974) Little, Brown & Company  PS593/L8E5

AmPA   American Poetry Anthology, The. *Daniel Halpern, ed.* (1975) Avon Books  PS615/A4

o  AmVN   American Verse of the Nineteenth Century. *Richard Gray, ed.* (1973) Rowman & Littlefield (Published in Great Britain by J. M. Dent & Sons)

o  AnMo   Ancients and Moderns: An Anthology of Poetry. *Stewart A. Baker, ed.* (1971) Harper & Row

PN 6110 P7ms

ANTL   America Is Not All Traffic Lights: Poems of the Midwest. *Alice Fleming, comp.* (1976) Little, Brown & Company  PN 6110/P7M5

BBGO   Being Born and Growing Older: Poems and Images. *Bruce Vance, ed.* (1971) Van Nostrand Reinhold

PR 8851 M6 1974

BIrV   *Book of Irish Verse, The: An Anthology of Irish Poetry from the Sixth Century to the Present. *John Montague, ed.* (1974) Macmillan Publishing Company (Also published as The Faber Book of Irish Verse)

BLSH   *Best Loved Songs and Hymns: Popular, Patriotic and Folk Songs, Church Hymns and Gospel Songs, Spirituals and Carols. (With music.) *James Morehead and Albert Morehead, ed.* (1965) Funk and Wagnalls

BLSo   \*\*Best Loved Songs of the American People. (With music.) *Denes Agay, ed.* (1975) Doubleday & Company  ML3551/A42 1975

BluL   *Blues Line, The: A Collection of Blues Lyrics. *Eric Sackheim, comp.* (1969, paperback 1975) Schirmer Books  PS593/L8 S24

# KEY TO SYMBOLS

BoAnP — **Book of Animal Poems, A. *William Cole, ed.* (1973) The Viking Press JUV PZ8.3/C675 Bm

*(handwritten left margin: PN6110 L6s65 1973)*

BoLoP — *Book of Love Poetry, A. *Jon Stallworthy, ed.* (1974) Oxford University Press

BoReV — *Book of Religious Verse, A. *Helen Gardner, ed.* (1972) Oxford University Press (Also published as The Faber Book of Religious Verse) PR 1191/G 33

*(handwritten left margin: PS153/B6)*

BPo — **Black Poets, The: A New Anthology. *Dudley Randall, ed.* (1971) Bantam Books

*(handwritten left margin: PS 595 H5M4)*

BTTM — Breathes There the Man: Heroic Ballads & Poems of the English Speaking Peoples. *Frank S. Meyer, ed.* (1973) Open Court Publishing Company

BuTh — Burning Thorn, The: An Anthology of Poetry. *Griselda Greaves, ed.* (1971) Macmillan Publishing Company (First published in Great Britain by Hamish Hamilton Children's Books)

*(handwritten left margin: PS615 C65 1974 have 2nd ed)*

CAAP — Contemporary American and Australian Poetry. *Thomas Shapcott, ed.* (1976) University of Queensland Press

CAPP — Contemporary American Poetry. *A. Poulin, Jr, ed.* (1971) Houghton Mifflin Company PS 613 P68 1975

CaYB — Catch Your Breath: A Book of Shivery Poems. *Lilian Moore and Lawrence Webster, comps.* (1973) Garrard Publishing Company

CDW — *Carriers of the Dream Wheel: Contemporary Native American Poetry. *Duane Niatum, ed.* (1975) Harper & Row PS591/I55N5/1975

*(handwritten left margin: PS 586 C8)*

ConAP — *Contemporary American Poetry. *Donald Hall, ed.* (2d ed., 1972) Penguin Books

CoPAm — *Contemporary Poetry in America. *Miller Williams, ed.* (1973) Random House PS 613/W5

CTBA — Crazy to Be Alive in Such a Strange World: Poems About People. *Nancy Larrick, comp.* (1977) M. Evans and Company

ECBV — Every Child's Book of Verse. *Sarah Chokla Gross, comp.* (1968) Franklin Watts, Inc.

Epi — Episodes in Five Poetic Traditions: The Sonnet; The Pastoral Elegy; The Ballad; The Ode; Masks and Voices. *R. G. Barnes, ed.* (1972) Chandler Publishing Company

ESaP — English Satiric Poetry: Dryden to Byron. *James Kinsley and James T. Boulton, eds.* (1970) University of South Carolina Press (First Published in Great Britain by Edward Arnold Publishers, 1966)

*(handwritten left margin: PR 1195 H8R56 1974)*

FaBoCo — *Faber Book of Comic Verse, The. *Michael Roberts and Janet Adam Smith, eds.* (rev. ed., 1974) Faber and Faber

Faber Book of Irish Verse, The. (1974) Faber and Faber (This book is the same as The Book of Irish Verse; see above)

Faber Book of Love Poems, The. (1975) (This book is the same as The Gambit Book of Love Poems; see below)

Faber Book of Popular Verse, The. (1971) Faber and Faber. (This

*(handwritten left margin: PR1174 G7)*

XII

# KEY TO SYMBOLS

book is the same as the Gambit Book of Popular Verse; see below)

Faber Book of Religious Verse. (1972) Faber and Faber (This book is the same as A Book of Religious Verse; see above)

FAF   Flowering After Frost: The Anthology of Contemporary New England Poetry. *Michael McMahon, ed.* (1975) Branden Press

FiCP   Fifty Contemporary Poets: The Creative Process. *Alberta T. Turner, ed.* (1977) David McKay Company

FSFS   Four Seasons Five Senses. *Elinor Parker, comp.* (1974) Charles Scribner's Sons

FSN   Favorite Songs of the Nineties: Complete Original Sheet Music for 89 Songs. *Robert A. Fremont, ed.* (1973) Dover Publications

GBL   Gambit Book of Love Poems, The. *Geoffrey Grigson, ed.* (1975) Gambit (Originally published in Great Britain by Faber and Faber as The Faber Book of Love Poems)

GBP   *Gambit Book of Popular Verse, The. *Geoffrey Grigson, ed.* (1971) Gambit (Also published as the Faber Book of Popular Verse; see above)

GrRo   Grandfather Rock: The New Poetry and the Old. *David Morse, ed.* (1972) Delacorte Press

HeIP   Heath Introduction to Poetry, The. *Joseph de Roche, ed.* (1975) D. C. Heath and Company

HeS   Heartland II: Poets of the Midwest. *Lucien Stryk, ed.* (1975) Northern Illinois University Press

IHMS   *I Hear My Sisters Saying: Poems by Twentieth-Century Women. *Carol Konek and Dorothy Walters, eds.* (1976) Thomas Y. Crowell Company

InPK   Introduction to Poetry, An. *X. J. Kennedy, ed.* (3rd ed., 1974) Little, Brown & Company

InPS   *Introduction to Poetry, An. *Louis Simpson, ed.* (2nd ed., 1972) St. Martins Press

IPWM   Introducing Poems. *Linda W. Wagner and C. David Mead, eds.* (1976) Harper and Row

JB   Jump Bad: A New Chicago Anthology. *Gwendolyn Brooks, ed.* (1971) Broadside Press

LAuP   Late Augustan Poetry. *Patricia Meyer Spacks, ed.* (1973) Prentice-Hall

LCL   Listen, Children, Listen: An Anthology of Poems for the Very Young. *Myra Cohn Livingston, ed.* (1972) Harcourt Brace Jovanovich

LoAs   *Love's Aspects: The World's Great Love Poems. *Jean Garrigue, comp.* (1975) Doubleday & Company

LP   Living Poets. *Michael Morpurgo and Clifford Simmons, comps.* (1974) John Murray

# KEY TO SYMBOLS

MAT    Messages: A Thematic Anthology of Poetry. *X. J. Kennedy, ed.* (1973) Little Brown & Company

MAuV    Map of Australian Verse, A. *James McAuley, ed.* (1975) Oxford University Press

MBPR    Major British Poets of the Romantic Period. *William Heath, ed.* (1973) Macmillan Publishing Company

MetP    Metaphysical Poets, The. *Margaret Willy, ed.* (1971) University of South Carolina Press (First published in Great Britian by Edward Arnold Publishers)

MG    *Mother Goose Nursery Rhymes. *Arthur Rackham, ed. and illus.* (1913, current edition 1975) The Viking Press

MiP    Mindscapes: Poems for the Real World. *Richard Peck, ed.* (1971) Delacorte Press

MIS    Made in Scotland: An Anthology of Fourteen Scottish Poets. *Robert Garioch, ed.* (1974) Carcanet Press

MIT    Mark in Time: Portraits and Poetry/San Francisco. *Nick Harvey, ed.* (1971) Glide Publications

MMD    Mountain Moving Day: Poems by Women. *Elaine Gill, ed.* (1973) The Crossing Press

Moon    Moonstruck: An Anthology of Lunar Poetry. *Robert Phillips, ed.* (1974) The Vanguard Press

MPo    Modern Poetry: A Selection. *John Rowe Townsend, comp.* (1974) J. B. Lippincott Company

NCSH    *New Coasts and Strange Harbors: Discovering Poems. *Helen Hill and Agnes Perkins, comps.* (1974) Thomas Y. Crowell Company

NeAC    New American and Canadian Poetry. *John Gill, ed.* (1971) Beacon Press

NMM    **No More Masks! An Anthology of Poems by Women. *Florence Howe and Ellen Bass, eds.* (1973) Doubleday Anchor Books

NoAM    *Norton Anthology of Modern Poetry, The. *Richard Ellmann and Robert O'Clair, eds.* (1973) W. W. Norton & Company

NOBA    **New Oxford Book of American Verse, The. *Richard Ellmann, ed.* (1976) Oxford University Press

NOBE    **New Oxford Book of English Verse, 1250-1950, The. *Helen Gardner, ed.* (1972) Oxford University Press

NowV    Now Voices, The: The Poetry of the Present. *Angelo Carli and Theodore Kilman, eds.* (1971) Charles Scribner's Sons

NPW    New Poets: Women. An Anthology. *Terry Wetherby, ed.* (1976) Les Femmes Publishing

NVAP    New Voices in American Poetry: An Anthology. *David Allen Evans, ed.* (1973) Winthrop Publishers

OBP    100 British Poets. *Selden Rodman, ed.* (1974) (Mentor Books) The New American Library

XIV

# KEY TO SYMBOLS

OFD    O Frabjous Day!: Poetry for Holidays and Special Occasions. *Myra Cohn Livingston, ed.* (1977) Atheneum

OLR    One Little Room, an Everywhere: Poems of Love. *Myra Cohn Livingston, ed.* (1975) Atheneum

OxBChV    Oxford Book of Children's Verse, The. *Iona and Peter Opie, eds.* (1973) Oxford University Press    JUV PN6110/C40529/1973

OxBM    Oxford Book of Medieval English Verse, The. *Celia and Kenneth Sisam, eds.* (1970) Oxford University Press

OxBTC    *Oxford Book of Twentieth-Century English Verse, The. *Philip Larkin, ed.* (1973) Oxford University Press    PR 1225/L3

PAIC    *Poetry and Its Conventions: An Anthology Examining Poetic Forms and Themes. *John T. Shawcross and Frederick R. Lapides, eds.* (1972) The Free Press

PBMP    *Premier Book of Major Poets, The: An Anthology. *Anita Dore, ed.* (1970) Fawcett Publications    PS586 D7

PCat    Poetry of Cats, The. *Samuel Carr, ed.* (1974) The Viking Press

PeBB    *Penguin Book of Ballads, The. *Geoffrey Grigson, ed.* (1975) Penguin Books    PR 1181 G74

PFD    Poems of Faith and Doubt: The Victorian Age. *R. L. Brett, ed.* (1970) University of South Carolina Press (First published in Great Britain, 1965, by Edward Arnold Publishers)

PFIr    Poems from Ireland. *William Cole, comp.* (1972) Thomas Y. Crowell Company

PiAm    Poet in America, The: 1650 to the Present. *Albert Gelpi, ed.* (1973) D. C. Heath and Company

PoBA    **Poetry of Black America, The: Anthology of the 20th Century. *Arnold Adoff, ed.* (1973) Harper & Row    PS 591/N4 A32

POL    Poems One Line and Longer. *William Cole, ed.* (1973) Grossman Publishers

PoRo    Pop/Rock Songs of the Earth. *Jerry L. Walker, ed.* (1972) Scholastic Book Services (division of Scholastic Magazines, Inc.)

PoTa    Poet's Tales. The: A New Book of Story Poems. *William Cole, ed.* (1971) World Publishing

PPoD    Poetry: Points of Departure. *Henry Taylor, ed.* (1974) Winthrop Publishers    PS586 T3

PPoe    *Pleasures of Poetry, The. *Donald Hall, ed.* (1971) Harper & Row    PR1175 H256

PPP    Poetry: Past and Present. *Frank Brady and Martin Price, eds.* (1974) Harcourt Brace Jovanovich

Prf    **Preferences: 51 American Poets Choose Poems from Their Own Work and from the Past. *Richard Howard, ed.* (1974) The Viking Press

PSN    Poems Since 1900: An Anthology of British and American Verse in the Twentieth Century. *Colin Falck and Ian Hamilton, eds.* (1975) Macdonald and Jane's (U. S. distributor: Beekman Publishers)

XV

# KEY TO SYMBOLS

PSoN
*Popular Songs of Nineteenth-Century America: Complete Original Sheet Music for 64 Songs. *Richard Jackson, ed.* (1976) Dover Publications (Published in Great Britain by Constable and Company)

Psy
Psyche: The Feminine Poetic Consciousness. An Anthology of Modern American Women Poets. *Barbara Segnitz and Carol Rainey, eds.* (1973) A Dell Laurel Edition

RAE
Round about Eight: Poems for Today. *Geoffrey Palmer and Noel Lloyd, eds.* (1972) Frederick Warne & Company

RDB
Richard Dyer-Bennet Folk Song Book, The: 50 Traditional Songs and Ballads with Guitar Accompaniments and Piano Arrangements. *Richard Dyer-Bennet, ed.* (1971) Simon and Schuster

RFM
Room for Me and a Mountain Lion: Poetry of Open Space. *Nancy Larrick, comp.* (1974) M. Evans and Co. (U. S. distributor: J. B. Lippincott Company)

RiTi
Rising Tides: 20th Century American Women Poets. *Laura Chester and Sharon Barba, eds.* (1973) (Washington Square Press) Pocket Books

RRA
Roses Race Around Her Name, The: Poems from Fathers to Daughters. *Jonathan Cott, ed.* (1974) Stonehill Publishing Company

SA
Settling America: The Ethnic Expression of 14 Contemporary Poets. *David Kherdian, ed.* (1974) Macmillan Publishing Company

SBG
Salt and Bitter and Good: Three Centuries of English and American Women Poets. *Cora Kaplan, ed.* (1975) Paddington Press

SCP 1-2
Signet Classic Poets of the 17th Century (Volumes One and Two). *John Broadbent, ed.* (1974) (A Signet Classic) New American Library

SFF
Since Feeling Is First. *James Mecklenburger and Gary Simmons, eds.* (1971) Scott, Foresman and Company

SLP
Scottish Love Poems: A Personal Anthology. *Antonia Fraser, ed.* (1976) Penguin Books (First published by Canongate Publishing, 1975)

SoSe
*Sound and Sense: An Introduction to Poetry. *Laurence Perrine, ed.* (4th ed. 1973) Harcourt Brace Jovanovich

SPo
Sports Poems. *R. R. Knudson and P. K. Ebert, eds.* (1971) (Laurel-Leaf Library) Dell

SpRo
*Speak Roughly to Your Little Boy: A Collection of Parodies and Burlesques, Together with the Original Poems, Chosen and Annotated for Young People. *Myra Cohn Livingston, ed.* (1971) Harcourt Brace Jovanovich

SS
Sounds and Silences: Poems for Performing. *Robert W. Boynton and Maynard Mack, eds.* (1975) Hayden Book Company

# KEY TO SYMBOLS

o TCP  Twentieth Century Poetry. *Carol Marshall, ed.* (1971) Houghton Mifflin Company

TH  Take Hold!: An Anthology of Pulitzer Prize Winning Poems. *Lee Bennett Hopkins, comp.* (1974) Thomas Nelson, Inc. PS 613/H6

o TSWA  To See the World Afresh. *Lilian Moore and Judith Thurman, comps.* (1974) Atheneum

o TVS  Tudor Verse Satire. *K. W. Gransden, ed.* (1970) The Athlone Press of the University of London (American distributor: Humanities Press)

TwMBP  Twenty-three Modern British Poets. *John Matthias, ed.* (1971) The Swallow Press PR 1225/M36

o VGW  *Voice That is Great Within Us, The: American Poetry of the Twentieth Century. *Hayden Carruth, ed.* (1970) Bantam Books

o VoPo  Voices of Poetry. *Allen Kirschner, ed.* (1970) (Laurel-Leaf Library) Dell

o VPC  Victorian Poetry: "The City of Dreadful Night" and Other Poems. *N. P. Messenger and J. R. Watson, eds.* (1974) Rowman & Littlefield (published in Great Britain by J. M. Dent & Sons)

VW  Voices from Wah'Kon-Tah: Contemporary Poetry of Native Americans. *Robert K. Dodge and Joseph B. McCullough, eds.* (2d ed., 1976) International Publishers Company PS 591/I55 D6

o WBN  We Become New: Poems by Contemporary American Women. *Lucille Iverson and Kathryn Ruby, eds.* (1975) Bantam Books

o WIF  Words in Flight: An Introduction to Poetry. *Richard Abcarian, ed.* (1972) Wadsworth Publishing Company

WPE  *Women Poets in English, The: An Anthology. *Ann Stanford, ed.* (1972) (A Herder and Herder Book) McGraw-Hill Book Company PR 1177/S8

# TITLE AND FIRST LINE INDEX

"A" (1-12), *sels.* Louis Zukofsky.
  "Giant sparkler,/ Lights of the river," 4. VGW
  "River that must turn full after I stop dying," 11. VGW

A, a, a, a,/ Yet I love whereso I go. A Bachelor's Life. *Unknown.* OxBM

A, a noble failure, turns his critical wits on B. Names. D. J. Enright. FaBoCo

A, an Apple, sweet and gay. A B C Objects. *Unknown.* ECBV

A Apple-pie. Mother Goose. MG

A B C, An. *Unknown.* GBP

A B C Objects. *Unknown.* ECBV

A! Dere God, what may this be. On the Death of Edward III. *Unknown.* OxBM

A dish, a dish, a green grass. Green Grass. *Unknown.* GBP

"A 11." Louis Zukofsky. *Fr.* "A." VGW

A = bh over 2. Homework for Annabelle. Phyllis McGinley. BBGO

A for action; the bull's head. Vowels. Peter West. AKE

"A 4." Louis Zukofsky. *Fr.* "A." VGW

A is for Abracadabra. Eleanor Farjeon. ECBV

A is for Angels. Alphabet of Christmas Cheer. Elizabeth Weston. ECBV

A is for axes, you very well know. The Lumberman's Alphabet. *Unknown.* AmFP

A is the aftermost part of the ship. The Sailors' Alphabet. *Unknown.* AmFP

A Quoi Bon Dire. Charlotte Mew. OxBTC

A Terre. Wilfred Owen. OxBTC

A' things created have their uses. Strictures on the Economy of Nature. George Outram. FaBoCo

A.U.C. 334: about this date. Advice to Young Ladies. A. D. Hope. SoSe

A, U, Hinny Burd. *Unknown.* GBP

A was an apple-pie. Mother Goose. ECBV

A was an archer, and shot at a frog,/ B was a blindman. *Unknown.* OxBChV

A was an archer, and [or who] shot at a frog,/ B was a butcher. *Unknown.* ECBV; MG

A Was Once an Apple Pie. Edward Lear. ECBV (Alphabet, An.). OxBChV

A was the archer who shot at a frog/ B was Bo-peep. A Nursery Rhyme Alphabet. *Unknown.* ECBV

Aardvark. Julia Fields. OFD

Aaron Burr's Wooing. Edmund Clarence Stedman. BTTM

Aaron Stark. E. A. Robinson. AmVN

Abel's Bride. Denise Levertov. VGW; WBN

Abdelazer, *sel.* Aphra Behn.
  Song: "Love in fantastic triumph sate." NOBE; WPE (Love Arm'd.) SBG

Aberdarcy: the Main Square. Kingsley Amis. OxBTC

Aberdeen, Mississippi Blues. *Unknown.* BluL

Abide, Good Men. *Unknown.* OxBM

Abide with Me, *with music.* Henry F. Lyte. BLSH

Ablow the Mune. Donald Campbell. MIS

Abnegation. Adrienne Rich. WPE

Aboard at a Ship's Helm. Walt Whitman. NOBA

Abominable Snowman, The. Ogden Nash. RAE

Aboriginal Sin. William R. Mitchell. AATT

Abortion. Mei Berssenbrugge. SA

Abortion, The. Lucille Iverson. WBN

Abortion, An. Frank O'Hara. CoPAm

Abortion, The. Anne Sexton. CAPP; IHMS; MAT; NMM; VGW

Abortions will not let you forget. The Mother. Gwendolyn Brooks. BPo; CAPP; NMM

Abou Ben Adhem. Leigh Hunt. ECBV; NOBE

About an Excavation. Charles Reznikoff. VGW

About Marriage. Denise Levertov. NMM

About mountains it is useless to argue. Alpine. R. S. Thomas. POL; RFM

About one month before my thirty-third. Thinking of You. Dick Lourie. NeAC

About suffering, about adoration, the old masters. The Old and the New Masters. Randall Jarrell. InPK

About suffering they were never wrong. Musée des Beaux Arts. W. H. Auden. AnMo; HeIP; InPK; InPS; MPo; NoAM; NOBE; OBP; PBMP; PPoD; PPP; PSN; TCP; VoPo; WIF

About That. Marvin Bell. HeS

About the Phoenix. James Merrill. NoAM

About the Shark, phlegmatical one. The Maldive Shark. Herman Melville. NOBA; PiAm

About the skull of the beloved, filled. Presentation Piece. Marilyn Hacker. AmPA

About the sweet bag of a bee. The Bag of a Bee. Robert Herrick. SCP-1

About the Teeth of Sharks. John Ciardi. CaYB

About the time that taverns shut. The Ballad of Minepit Shaw. Kipling. PoTa

About twenty years ago. Wild Oats. Philip Larkin. InPS

Above It All. Philip Levine. NOBA

Above my desk, whirring and [or but] self-important. Angel [or Another Angel]. James Merrill. ConAP; NoAM

Above Pate Valley. Gary Snyder. ConAP

Above Penmaenmawr. Tony Connor. MPo

Above the Bright Blue Sky, *sel.* Albert Midlane.
  "There's a Friend for little children." OxBChV

Above the fresh ruffles of the surf. Voyages, I. Hart Crane. NoAM; NOBA; PSN; VGW

Abraham Lincoln Walks at Midnight. Vachel Lindsay. IPWM; NoAM; NOBA; OFD; VGW

Abram Bailey he'd three sons. Sir Lionel. *Unknown.* AmFP

Absalom and Achitophel Pt. I , *sels.* Dryden.
  Achitophel: the Earl of Shaftesbury. NOBE
  "Of these the false Achitophel was first." InPS
  Zimri: the Duke of Buckingham. NOBE

Absalom and Achitophel, Pt. II, *sels.* Nahum Tate *and* John Dryden.
  "Let him rail on, let his invective Muse." Dryden. OBP
  "Next these, a troop of busy spirits press." Dryden. PPP

Absences. James Tate. CAAP

Absent, The. Edwin Muir. NoAM

Absent from thee, I languish still. Song [or Return]. Earl of Rochester. BoLoP; GBL; NOBE

Absent Lover, An. *Unknown.* OxBM

Absent-Minded Professor. Howard Nemerov. NowV

Absent One, The. Mary Queen of Scots, *tr. fr. French by* Antonia Fraser SLP

Absent, this morning. Aube Provençale. Marilyn Hacker. AmPA

Absolute, An/ patience. The Breathing. Denise Levertov. IPWM; RFM; TCP

Absolute and Abitofhell. Ronald Arbuthnott Knox. FaBoCo

Absolute zero: the locust sings. Summer. Conrad Aiken. NoAM

Abstinence. Kenneth Rosen. AmPA

Abstinence sows sand all over. Blake. GBL

Abstracted, sour, as he reaches across a dish. Scylla and Charybdis. Thomas Kinsella. OxBTC

Abt Vogler. Robert Browning. BoReV

Abu. Dudley Randall. BPo

Abyss, The. Baudelaire, tr. fr. French by Jackson Matthews. GrRo

Ac that most needen aure neighebores, and we nime good heede. Our Needy Neighbours. William Langland. Fr. The Vision of Piers Plowman. OxBM

Academic. James Reeves. MPo

Accept, my God, the praises which I bring. The Offering: Part One. Mary Lee, Lady Chudleigh. WPE

Accept, thou shrine of my dead saint. The Exequy [or Exequy on His Wife]. Henry King. BoLoP; GBL; MetP; NOBE; OBP; PAIC; PPoe; SCP-2

Acceptance. Margaret Reynolds. MIS

Acceptance Speech. Marvin Bell. AmPA

Accepting. Vassar Miller. FiCP

Accident, The. Len Gasparini. NeAC

Accident Has Occurred, The. Margaret Atwood. IPWM; NMM

Accomplices, The. Conrad Aiken. LoAs; NOBA

According to Brueghel. Landscape with the Fall of Icarus. William Carlos Williams. Pictures from Brueghel, II. BBGO; PPP; WIF

Accursed power which stands on Privilege, The. On a General Election. Hilaire Belloc. FaBoCo; NOBE; OxBTC

Accursed the man, whom fate ordains, in spite. The Pains of Education [or The Author]. Charles Churchill. ESaP; FaBoCo

Ache of Marriage, The. Denise Levertov. NoAM; NOBA; PiAm; RiTi

Achilles Tendon Coleman Barks. Fr. Body Poems. NVAP

Aching all over I believe I've got the pneumonia this time. Pneumonia Blues. Unknown. BluL

Achitophel: the Earl of Shaftesbury. Dryden. Fr. Absalom and Achitophel, Pt. I. NOBE

Achromatic Bear, The. Robert Bloom. AATT

Acis and Galatea, sel. John Gay. Song: "O ruddier than the cherry." NOBE

Acon. Hilda Doolittle ("H.D."). VGW

Acorns. Paul Mills. MIS

Acquainted with the Night. Robert Frost. IPWM; NoAM; NOBA; PPP; PSN; VGW

Acre of Grass, An. W. B. Yeats. NoAM; OBP

Acrobats. Robert Graves. PSN

Acrophobe and Lapidary. James Bonk. HeS

Across a sky suddenly mid-February blue. Cranes. J. R. S. Davies. POL

Across eternity, across her snows. Dogs and Wolves. Sorley Maclean, tr. by Iain Crichton Smith. SLP

Across the Bay. Donald Davie. PSN

Across the dinner table from me. The General's Wife. Elton Glaser. NVAP

Across the gap made by our English hinds. August. William Morris. Fr. The Earthly Paradise. VPC

Across the lonely beach we flit. The Sandpiper. Celia Thaxter. OxBChV

Across the millstream below the bridge. The Blue Swallows. Howard Nemerov. AnMo

Across the sea will come Adze-head. Adze-Head. Unknown, tr. by James Carney. BIrV

Across the sky the daylight crept. Coventry Patmore. Fr. The Angel in the House, II, x. GBL

Across the street, my aunt has lost. Emergency at 8. Geof Hewitt. NeAC

Across the tracks in Cheyenne, behind the biggest billboard. A Long Way Outside Yellowstone. Thomas McGrath. VGW

Across the Universe. John Lennon and Paul McCartney. PoRo

Across the Wide Missouri (Shenandoah). Unknown. See Shenandoah.

Across to the Peloponnese. James Welch. CDW

Across upon this undulated board of verdure chequered bright. The Five Unmistakable Marks. David Jones. In Parenthesis, VII. NoAM

Acrostic of My Sister's Name. Keats. MBPR

Act, An. Kenneth Rosen. AmPA

Act, The. William Carlos Williams. VGW

Act of Love Vernon Scannell. SFF

Acton Beauchamp, Herefordshire. Unknown. GBP

Acts passed beyond the boundary of mere wishing. Stephen Spender. OxBTC

Actual Vision of Morning's Extrusion. Alan Dugan. PPP

Ad Limina. Joseph Campbell. BIrV

Ad Vilmum Axiologum. Samuel Taylor Coleridge. MBPR

Adam and Eve in Paradise. Milton. Fr. Paradise Lost, IV. SCP-1

Adam Driven from Eden. Unknown. OxBM

Adam in the Garden. Elmer F. Suderman. AATT

Adam Lay I-bowndyn [or Y-bounden]. Unknown. InPS; LoAs; NOBE; OxBM; PPoe (O Felix Culpa!) BoReV

Adam scrivein, if ever it thee bifalle. To Adam, His Scribe. Chaucer. OxBM

Adam Smith. E. C. Bentley. Fr. Clerihews. FaBoCo

Adam, who thought himself immortal still. The Discovery. Monk Gibbon. PFIr

Adam's Apple. Coleman Barks. Fr. Body Poems. NVAP

Adam's Curse. W. B. Yeats. BIrV; LoAs; NoAM; PFIr; WIF

Adam's Song to Heaven. Edgar Bowers. ConAP

Adam's Task. John Hollander. PPP

Addict, The Anne Sexton. CTBA

Addition to the Family, An. Edwin Morgan. MPo

Address to a Child During a Boisterous Winter Evening. Dorothy Wordsworth. OxBChV

Address to the Deil. Burns. LAuP

Address to the New Tay Bridge, An, abr. William McGonagall. PPoD

Address to the Unco Guid. Burns. NOBE

Addressed to Haydon ("Great spirits now on earth are sojourning"). Keats. MBPR

Addressed to Haydon ("Highmindedness, a jealousy for good"). Keats. MBPR

Adequacy. Elizabeth Barrett Browning. SBG

Adeste Fideles. Unknown. See O Come, All Ye Faithful.

Adieu, dear object of my love's excess. Orinda to Lucasia Parting, October 1661, at London. Katherine Philips. SCP-2

Adieu, Farewell Earth's Bliss. Thomas Nashe. Fr. Summer's Last Will and Testament. HeIP; PPoe (In Time of Pestilence.) NOBE (Litany in Time of Plague, A.) PPoD; PPP (Song: "Adieu, farewell earths blisse.") OBP

Adieu, sweet Angus, Maeve and Fand. The Passing of the Shee. J. M. Synge. BIrV

Adlestrop. Edward Thomas. NOBE; OxBTC

Admetus, from my marrow's core I do. Edna St. Vincent Millay. SBG

Administration of Things, The, *sels.* Matthew Mead.
"No days but these." TwMBP
"Riot, tumult, anticipated disturbances." TwMBP
"Sword or stealth, strength or ancient blood." TwMBP

Admire Cranmer! ("Admire the old man, admire him, admire him"). Stevie Smith. NoAM

Admonitions. Lucille Clifton. BPo; InPS; NMM

Adolescence—II. Rita Dove. AmPA

Adolescent's Song. Howard Moss. LoAs

Adonais: an Elegy on the Death of John Keats. Shelley. MBPR
Mourn Not for Adonais, *sel.* BoReV; NOBE

Adorable paratroopess alights, The. Michael Silverton. POL

Adoremus. Christopher Smart. *Fr.* A Song to David. OBP

Adrian and Bardus. John Gower. *Fr.* Confessio Amantis, V. OxBM

Adrian Henri's Talking after Christmas Blues. Adrian Henri. BuTh; MPo
(Talking after Christmas Blues.) LP

Adulterers and customers of whores. Womanisers. John Press. BoLoP

Adultery. Alan Dugan. CAPP

Adultery. James Dickey. CAPP; PPoD

Adulthood. Nikki Giovanni. NMM

Advancement of Learning, An. Seamus Heaney. NCSH

Advent. *Unknown.* BoReV
(Christ's Coming.) OxBM

Advent 1966. Denise Levertov. InPS; PiAm; Prf

Adventures of Isabel. Ogden Nash. ECBV

Adventures of Master F. I., The, *sel.* George Gascoigne.
"And if I did what then?" GBL
(Farewell, A.) NOBE

Advice, The. Sir Walter Ralegh. AAS

Advice. Ruth Stone. NMM

Advice to a Prophet. Richard Wilbur. CAPP; MAT; PiAm; PPoD; PPP

Advice to a Raven in Russia. Joel Barlow. NOBA

Advice to the Lovelorn. Linda Parker-Silverman. HeS

Advice to the Old Beaux. Sir Charles Sedley. SCP-2

Advice to Young Ladies. A. D. Hope. SoSe

Adze-Head. *Unknown, tr. fr. Irish by* James Carney. BIrV

Ae Fond Kiss. Burns. OBP; PPP; SLP
(Song: "Ae fond kiss, and then we sever.") BoLoP

Aedh Thinks of Those Who Have Spoken Evil of His Beloved. W. B. Yeats. NoAM
(He Thinks of Those Who Have Spoken Evil of His Beloved.) PFIr

Aedh Wishes for the Cloths of Heaven. W. B. Yeats. NoAM
(He Wishes for the Cloths of Heaven.) OLR

Aella, *sel.* Thomas Chatterton.
Minstrel's Song, The. OBP
("O! Synge untoe mie roundelaie.") NOBE
(Song from Aella.) LoAs

Aeneas at Washington. Allen Tate. NoAM; NOBA; PiAm

Aeneid, The, *sel.* Virgil, *tr. fr. Latin by* Richard Stanyhurst.
"Now manhood and garbroyls I chaunt," *fr.* I. BIrV

Aesthetics of the Moon. Jack Anderson. Moon

Affable Irregular, An. The Road at My Door. W. B. Yeats.
Meditations in Time of Civil War, V. BIrV; NOBE

Affair of the Heart. Peter Porter. CAAP

Affinities. Adrien Stoutenburg. TSWA

Affirmed. Pent by power that holds it fast. Like a Bulwark.
Marianne Moore. PiAm

Affliction. Sir John Davies. *Fr.* Nosce Teipsum. NOBE

Affliction ("Broken in pieces all asunder"). George Herbert. SCP-1

Affliction ("When first thou didst entice to thee my heart").
George Herbert. BoReV; MetP; NOBE; SCP-1

Affliction of Margaret, The. Wordsworth. MBPR

Afoot and light-hearted I take to the open road. Song of the Open Road. Walt Whitman. NOBA; RFM

African Affair, The. Bruce McM. Wright. PoBA

African China. Melvin B. Tolson. PoBA

African Dream. Bob Kaufman. PoBA

African Elegy, An. Robert Duncan. NoAM

African Things. Victor Hernández Cruz. SA

Afro-American Fragment. Langston Hughes. PBMP

After a drifting day, visiting the bridge near Louisberg. Summer, 1960, Minnesota. Robert Bly. InPS

After a Journey. Thomas Hardy. GBL; OxBTC

After a Journey. Ken Smith. TwMBP

After All You Are Quiet. Margaret Atwood. Psy

After Apple-picking. Robert Frost. Epi; NoAM; NOBA; PPP; PSN

After Bad Dreams. George Garrett. CoPAm

After breakfast and you'd left for school. Divorce. Bink Noll. MAT

After centuries of dissecting. Lesbian Poem. Robin Morgan. IHMS

After Dark. Adrienne Rich. VGW

After dark vapours have oppress'd our plains. Keats. MBPR

After Death. Christina Rossetti. GBL

After Dilettante Concetti. Henry Duff Traill. FaBoCo

After dreaming some hours of the land of Cockaigne. Thomas Moore. *Fr.* The Fudge Family in Paris. BIrV

After Drinking Water. Daniela Gioseffi. WBN

After each quake. Crack in the Wall Holds Flowers. Adam David Miller. PoBA

After Ever Happily. Ian Serraillier. ECBV

After experience taught me that all the ordinary. W. D. Snodgrass. CAPP; PPoD; PPP

After Five Years. Augustus Young. BIrV

After Goliath. Kingsley Amis. OxBTC

After great pain, a formal feeling comes. Emily Dickinson. InPS; NOBA; PiAm; PPoe; Psy; SBG

After Greece. James Merrill. ConAP; NOBA

After Grief. Stanley Plumly. AmPA

After her pills the girl slept and counted. Tally. Josephine Miles. NoAM

After hot loveless nights, when cold winds stream. The Sisters. Roy Campbell. BoLoP

After hundreds of years of common sense. Holiday. Alan Dugan. CoPAm

After I come home from the meeting with friends. Josephine Miles. CoPAm

After I got religion and steadied down. Butch Weldy. Edgar Lee Masters. *Fr.* Spoon River Anthology. PSN

After I Had Worked All Day. Charles Reznikoff. *Fr.* Five Groups of Verse. SA; VGW

After I Have Voted. Laura Jensen. AmPA

After jump, drop and somersault. Parachutist. Samuel Hazo. SPo

After Long Silence. W. B. Yeats. BoLoP; HeIP; PPP; PSN; WIF

After Lorca. Robert Creeley. ConAP; InPS; POL

After Love. Maxine W. Kumin. NMM; RiTi; WBN

After many long months on the market. Sold. R. R. Cuscaden. ANTL

After many winters the moss. Tale. W. S. Merwin. TH

After Margrave died, nothing. History of a Literary Movement. Howard Nemerov. PSN

After Mass. "Michael Field." WPE

After Midnight. Louis Simpson. NoAM

After midnight I heard a scream. By Night. Robert Francis. POL; VGW

After Midsummer. E. J. Scovell. OxBTC

After miles of the same oasis up ahead. Truckdriver. Gary Sange. NVAP

After only a month or so—weary and. Melancholy Summer. Kris Hemensley. *Fr.* A Mile from Poetry. CAAP

After our fierce loving. The Profile on the Pillow. Dudley Randall. BPo; PoBA

After Paeschendale,/ After Katyn. Matthew Mead. *Fr.* Identities. TwMBP

After Picking Rosehips. Harley Elliott. NeAC

After Rain. Edward Thomas. NCSH

After rain, through afterglow, the unfolding fan. Train Ride. John Wheelwright. VGW

After Reading St. John the Divine. Gene Derwood. WPE

After Reading Sylvia Plath. Alta. IHMS

After Reading Takahashi. Jim Harrison. HeS

After Reading *The First Circle.* Martha Shelley. WBN

After scanning its face again and again. John Muir on Mt. Ritter. Gary Snyder. *Fr.* Myths and Texts: Burning. Epi; NOBA; TCP

After Selecting the Wedding Invitations. Diane Levenberg. NPW

After Snow. Walter Clark. NCSH

After so many victories, one. Epitaph for Goliath. David R. Slavitt. CoPAm

After some years Bohemian came to this. Epigram. J. V. Cunningham. VGW

After Swimming in the Pacific. Cathy Colman. NPW

After the agony in the guest/ bedroom. Margaret Atwood. NeAC

After the Anonymous Swedish. Jim Harrison. VGW

After the Ball, *with music.* Charles Kassell Harris. BLSo; FSN "After the ball is over," chorus. BLSH

After the Broken Arm. Ron Padgett. ConAP

After the cloud embankments. Reconnaissance. Arna Bontemps. BPo

After the cracked screams. Wife Jenné Andrews. HeS

After the Cries of the Birds. Lawrence Ferlinghetti. CAPP

After the darkness has come. Disturbances. Anthony Thwaite. MPo

After the Death of an Elder Klallam. Duane Niatum. CDW

After the doctor checked to see. First Practice. Gary Gildner. AmPA; InPK; PPoD

After the dreadful Flood was past. The Tower of Babel. Nathaniel Crouch. OxBChV

After the Engraving. David Bromige. MIT

After the entertainments of the night. The Apparition. Chris Wallace-Crabbe. MAuV

After the Fact. Grace Cavalieri. AATT

After the fiercest pangs of hot desire. Richard Duke. BoLoP

After the First Communion. Sunday Afternoon. Denise Levertov. ConAP; IHMS

After the first powerful, plain manifesto. The Express. Stephen Spender. MPo; NoAM; NowV; WIF

After the Funeral. Dylan Thomas. InPK

After the Funeral of Assam Hamady. Sam Hamod. SA

After the glass shower. Weather Report. Elaine H. Jennings. NPW

After the Industrial Revolution, All Things Happen at Once. Robert Bly. ConAP

After the "invitation" by the preacher she collapsed in the. Jim Harrison. *Fr.* Ghazals. NoAM

After the Last Bulletins. Richard Wilbur. ConAP

After the last long agate beach. Before the Dark Is Down. Mary Shumway. NVAP

After the leaves have fallen, we return. The Plain Sense of Things. Wallace Stevens. InPS

After the murder. The Last Quatrain of the Ballad of Emmett Till. Gwendolyn Brooks. CAPP; PoBA; WPE

After the Pleasure Party. Herman Melville. AmVN

After the Rain. Yannis Ritsos, *tr. fr. Greek by* Nikos Stangos. TSWA

After the rare arch-poet Jonson died. Upon Mr. Ben Jonson: Epigram. Robert Herrick. SCP-1

After the Revolution. Marilyn Hacker. AmPA

After the School-Feast. Charles Tennyson Turner. VPC

After the shot the driven feathers rock. Rainbow. Robert Huff. CoPAm

After the spring floods, after. River Road. Mary Shumway. NVAP

After the Storm. Rosalie Moore. MIT; RiTi

After the Surprising Conversions. Robert Lowell. ConAP; NoAM; PAIC; PPP

After the tiff there was stiff silence, till. The Lovers. W. R. Rodgers. BIrV

After the tornado, a dead moccasin. Heaved from the Earth. Besmilr Brigham. Psy

After the usual rounds at night. A Sense of Property. Anthony Thwaite. MPo

After the Visit. Thomas Hardy. NOBE

After the whey-faced anonymity. South Country. Kenneth Slessor. MAuV

After the Winter. Claude McKay. PoBA

After these thirty years, Mother. Mother and I. Martha Yoak. NPW

After these years of lectures heard. To a Friend on Her Examination for the Doctorate in English. J. V. Cunningham. VGW

After they passed I climbed. A Story. William Stafford. PoTa; RFM

After those first days. Death of a Bird. Jon Silkin. BoAnP

After Trinity. John Meade Falkner. OxBTC

After waking I look down across our bodies. God. Eugene Ruggles. MIT

After watching all night from a petrified. Ah, Wilderness. Peter Cooley. NVAP

After we had burned on the water a while. Voice from Danang. Thomas Dillon Redshaw. MAT

After we had torn out. For a Marriage. Erica Jong. CTBA

After weeks of watching the roof leak. Gary Snyder. *Fr.* Hitch Haiku. InPK

After Winter. Sterling A. Brown. PoBA

After Work. Gary Snyder. CoPAm

After X-Ray. Linda Pastan. POL

After Yesterday. A. R. Ammons. TSWA

After you dived from the barnacled rocks. Poem for Susan. Barbara Greenberg. RiTi

After you left me forever. Semele Recycled. Carolyn Kizer. WBN

Afterglow goldens the. The Mountain Afterglow. James Laughlin. IPWM; VGW

Aftermath. Longfellow. NOBA; PiAm

Aftermath. Sylvia Plath. SBG

Afternoon. David Sten Herrstrom. AATT

Afternoon. Desmond O'Grady. PFIr

Afternoon,/ with just enough of a breeze for him to ride it.  Robert Sund.  BoAnP

Afternoon, and the houses are quiet.  Afternoon.  Desmond O'Grady.  PFIr

Afternoon at the Beach, An.  Edgar Bowers.  PiAm

Afternoon cooking in the fall sun.  Song.  Robert Hass.  AmPA

Afternoon on a Hill.  Edna St. Vincent Millay.  PSN

Afternoons.  Philip Larkin.  PSN

Afternoons with Baedeker.  Osbert Lancaster.  FaBoCo

After-Thought.  Wordsworth.  The River Duddon, XXXIV.  MBPR
(Valediction to the River Duddon.)  NOBE

Afterwake, The.  Adrienne Rich.  NOBA; Prf

Afterward.  Mark Van Doren.  TH

Afterwards.  Thomas Hardy.  InPS; NOBE; OBP; SoSe

Afterwards, the compromise.  After Love.  Maxine W. Kumin.  NMM; RiTi; WBN

Afterwards, They Shall Dance.  Bob Kaufman.  VGW

Afterword, An: for Gwen Brooks.  Don L. Lee.  JB

Afton Water.  Burns.  HeIP; LAuP
(Flow Gently, Sweet Afton, with music.)  BLSH

Again,/ smoke starts to rise from chimneys.  The Cycle.  Stephen Dunn.  HeS

Again and then again . . . the year is born.  New Year's Day.  Robert Lowell.  ConAP; PPoe

Again, his friend's death made the man sit still.  John Berryman.  NOBA

Again last night I dreamed the dream called Laundry.  The Mad Scene.  James Merrill.  CoPAm; NoAM; NOBA

Again let me do a lot of extraordinary talking.  The Song of the Militant Romance.  Wyndham Lewis.  OxBTC

Again the ancient, meaningless.  Gary Snyder.
Myths and Texts: Logging, V.  CAPP

Again the day.  If the Stars Should Fall.  Samuel Allen.  PoBA

Again the wood, and long with-drawing vale.  To Spring.  Charlotte Smith.  WPE

Against Blame of Woman.  Gerald, Earl of Desmond, tr. fr. Late Middle Irish by the Earl of Longford.  BIrV

Against Botticelli.  Robert Hass.  AmPA

Against Constancy.  Earl of Rochester.  GBL

Against Dark's Harm.  Anne Halley.  NMM

Against Friars.  Unknown.  OxBM

Against Idleness and Mischief.  Isaac Watts.  OxBChV; SpRo

Against Love.  Katherine Philips.  SBG; WPE

Against Quarrelling and Fighting.  Isaac Watts.  OxBChV

Against Romanticism.  Kingsley Amis.  NoAM

Against Still Life.  Margaret Atwood.  NMM

Against the Friars.  Unknown.  OxBM

Against the Magpie.  Unknown.  GBP

Against the rubber tongues of cows and the hoeing hands of men.  Thistles.  Ted Hughes.  MPo; NoAM; OxBTC; PSN

Against the stone breakwater.  The Storm.  Theodore Roethke.  NCSH

Against the Sun.  George MacBeth.  TwMBP

Against Them Who Lay Unchastity to the Sex of Women.  William Habington.  MetP

Against Witches.  Unknown.  GBP

Agatha.  Nadine Major.  POL

Age?  H. R. Hays.  POL

Age.  Walter Savage Landor.  InPK

Age, The/ requires this task.  A Different Image.  Dudley Randall.  BPo; NoAM

Age and bare bone/ Are e'er allied in action.  Cyril Tourneur.  Fr. The Revenger's Tragedy, III, iv.  OBP

Age, and the deaths, and the ghosts.  He Resigns.  John Berryman.  PSN

Age demanded an image, The.  Hugh Selwyn Mauberley, II.  Ezra Pound.  PiAm; VGW

Age in her embraces passed, An.  The Mistress.  Earl of Rochester.  NOBE

Age is when to a man.  Samuel Beckett.  Fr. Words and Music.  BIrV

Age saw two quiet children.  Carpe Diem.  Robert Frost.  PAIC

Aged Aged Man, The.  "Lewis Carroll."  See White Knight's Song.

Aged in the villages, The.  War.  Miguel Hernandez, tr. by Edwin Honig.  IPWM

Aged Lover Discourses In the Flat Style, The.  J. V. Cunningham.  NoAM; PPoD

Aged man, that mows these fields.  A Dialogue betwixt Time and a Pilgrim.  Aurelian Townsend.  NOBE; SCP-2

Ageing Schoolmaster, An.  Vernon Scannell.  LP

Aghadoe.  John Todhunter.  PFIr

Agincourt Carol, The.  Unknown.  OxBM

Aging.  Erica Jong.  Psy; WBN

Agitation of the air, An.  End of Summer.  Stanley Kunitz.  VGW

Agitprop.  Marge Piercy.  MMD

Aglaura, sel.  Sir John Suckling.
Why so Pale and Wan?  Fr. IV, ii.  BuTH; NOBE
(Encouragement to a Lover.)  PBMP
(Song: "Why so pale and wan, fond lover?")  BoLoP; HeIP; InPS

Agnes.  Kathleen Fraser.  WBN

Agnosco Veteris Vestigia Flammae.  J. V. Cunningham.  VGW

Agonies confirm His hour.  Bahá'u'lláh in the Garden of Ridwan.  Robert Hayden.  PoBA

Agonies of change.  Death Takes Only a Minute.  Agnes Pratt.  VW

Agony, The.  George Herbert.  SCP-1

Agony, An. As Now.  LeRoi Jones.  BPo; IPWM; PiAm; PPP

Agony Column.  A. D. Hope.  SoSe

Agreed,/ Yesterday was terrible.  Mark This.  Sallie Chesham.  AATT

Agreed that all these birds.  All These Birds.  Richard Wilbur.  NOBA; Prf

Ah.  Greg Kuzma.  NVAP

Ah, Are You Digging on My Grave?  Thomas Hardy.  BoAnP; InPS

Ah, broken is the golden bowl! the spirit flown forever!  Lenore.  Poe.  WIF

Ah, but a good wife!  Late Abed.  Archibald MacLeish.  NCSH

Ah child, no Persian-perfect art!  From Horace.  Horace, tr. by Gerard Manley Hopkins.  Fr. Odes.  InPK

Ah, Christ, I love you rings to the wild sky.  Sonnets at Christmas, II.  Allen Tate.  VGW

Ah! dear one, we were young so long.  Alas, So Long!  Dante Gabriel Rossetti.  VPC

Ah false Amyntas, can that hour.  Song.  Aphra Behn.  Fr. The Dutch Lover.  WPE

Ah, Faustus,/ Now hast thou but one bare hour [or hower] to live.  Christopher Marlowe.  Fr. Doctor Faustus, V, ii.  HeIP; OBP; PAIC

Ah! Grandmother weaves!  Grandmother Sleeps.  Liz Sohappy Bahe.  CDW

Ah, I remember well—and how can I.  First Flame.  Samuel Daniel.  Fr. Hymen's Triumph.  VoPo

Ah—it's the skeleton of a lady's sunshade.  The Sunshade.  Thomas Hardy.  OxBTC

Ah, Lenin, you were richt. But I'm a poet.  Second Hymn to Lenin.  "Hugh MacDiarmid."  TwMBP

Ah! light lovely lady with delicate lips aglow. *Unknown, tr. fr. Irish by* Robin Flower. BIrV

Ah, look at all the lonely people! Eleanor Rigby. John Lennon *and* Paul McCartney. InPK; InPS; OBP; PPoe; WIF

Ah me! conceived in sin and born with sorrow. Childhood. Anne Bradstreet. *Fr.* The Four Ages of Man. SBG

Ah me! full sorely is my heart forlorn. The School-Mistress. William Shenstone. LAuP

Ah me, the aspidistra grows dusty behind the window pane. In North Great George's Street. "Seamas O'Sullivan." BIrV

Ah my dear angry Lord. Bitter-Sweet. George Herbert. BoReV; IPWM; NOBE

Ah my Jill loves her nakedness. Marvelous. Allan Kaplan. POL

Ah, necromancy sweet! Emily Dickinson. NOBA

Ah! no, not these! Parentage. Alice Meynell. SBG

Ah, nobody knows. Frost. Stella Benson. OxBTC

Ah, not this marble, dead and cold. Washington's Monument, February 1885. Walt Whitman. OFD

Ah nuts! It's boring reading French newspapers. Les Luths. Frank O'Hara. NoAM; NOBA

Ah! Sun-flower. Blake. *Fr.* Songs of Experience. LAuP; MBPR; PPP

Ah sweet content, where is thy mylde abode? Parthenophil and Parthenope, LXVI. Barnabe Barnes. AAS

Ah, Teneriffe! Emily Dickinson. InPS

Ah to be alone and uninhibited! American against Solitude. Alan Dugan. CAPP

Ah, wake up mama: wake up and don't sleep so sound. Sweet Patuni. *Unknown.* BluL

Ah, what avails the sceptred race! Rose Aylmer. Walter Savage Landor. BoLoP; GBL; HeIP; NOBE

Ah, what can ail thee, wretched wight [*or* knight-at-arms]. *See* O what can ail thee, knight-at-arms.

Ah! what time wilt thou come? when shall that cry. The Dawning. Henry Vaughan. BoReV

Ah, when I was a little boy, mama, 'bout 16 inches high. Stepfather Blues. *Unknown.* BluL

Ah! who can e'er forget so fair a being? Keats. MBPR

Ah, Wilderness. Peter Cooley. NVAP

Ah, Yes! I wrote the "Purple Cow." Sequel to the Purple Cow. Gelett Burgess. FaBoCo

Ah, you beast of love. Hayden Carruth. VGW

Ah, you should see Cynddylan on a tractor. Cynddylan on a Tractor. R. S. Thomas. LP; MPo

Ahab's gaily clad fisherfriends. Evil Is No Black Thing. Sarah Webster Fabio. PoBA

Aiberdeen. Donald Campbell. *Fr.* Sonnets frae Siberia. MIS

Aim get your sights and its sound. Canto 7: First Thesis. Tom Weatherly. PoBA

Aim Was Song, The. Robert Frost. SoSe

Ain't It a Sad Thing? R. Dean Taylor. PoRo

Ain't No Grave Can Hold My Body Down. *Unknown.* AmFP

Ain't No Tellin'. *Unknown.* BluL

Ainu Men, The. Gary Lawless. FAF

Air. James Rado *and* Gerome Ragni. PoRo

Air: "Cat bird singing." Robert Creeley. Prf

Air: "Love of a woman, The." Robert Creeley. VGW

Air: "Naturally it is night." W. S. Merwin. CAPP

Air and Angels. John Donne. LoAs; MetP; Prf; SCP-1

Air as the fuel of owls. Iowa. Michael Dennis Browne. ANTL

Air Force Blue, The, *with music.* Scott *and* Textor. BLSH

Air heaves at matter. Night Wind in Fall. W. R. Moses. NCSH

Air Is. John Michael Brennan. MAT

Air is thick with nerves and smoke, The. University Examinations in Egypt. D. J. Enright. NowV; OxBTC

Aire and Angells. John Donne. *See* Air and Angels.

Airstrip in Essex, 1960, An. Donald Hall. InPS

Ajax and Ulysses. James Shirley. *See* Contention of Ajax and Ulysses, The.

Akond of Swat, The. Edward Lear. FaBoCo

Al Aaraaf, *sels.* Poe.
  Song: "Young flowers were whispering in melody." NOBA
  Sonnet——to Science, *prologue.* AmVN; InPK; PAIC; PBMP; PiAm; PPoD; WIF

Al Capone in Alaska. Ishmael Reed. MIT

Al the merier is that place. The Sun of Grace. *Unknown.* OxBM

Alabama. Julia Fields. PoBA

Alabama Bound. *Unknown.* BluL

Alabama Bus. *Unknown.* BluL

Alabama Centennial. Naomi Long Madgett. BPo

Alan walks with his head upside down. Karen L. Kent. NPW

Alarm and time clock still intrude too early. And on This Shore. M. Carl Holman. PoBA

Alarm Clock, The. Mari Evans. Psy

Alas, Alack! Walter de la Mare. CaYB; OxBChV

Alas, alas the pull alas the bell alas the coach in china. Cooking. Gertrude Stein. *Fr.* Tender Buttons. RiTi

Alas, Alas, well evil [*or* Allas, allas, wel ivel] I sped! Undo! *Unknown.* BoReV; OxBM

Alas! for all the pretty women who marry dull men. Meditation at Kew. Anna Wickham. BuTH

Alas for Him Whose Sickness Is Love. Iseabal Ni Mheic Cailein, *tr. fr. Gaelic.* SLP

Alas have I not pain enough my friend. Astrophel and Stella, XIV. Sir Philip Sidney. Epi

Alas, madam, for stealing of a kiss. Sir Thomas Wyatt. BoLoP; LoAs

Alas, my brothers. Hilda Doolittle ("H.D."). *Fr.* Helen in Egypt. NOBA

Alas, my love, you [*or* ye] do me wrong. Greensleeves [*or* Lady Greensleeves]. *Unknown.* BLSo; GBL; RDB

Alas, so all things now do hold their peace. A Complaint by Night of the Lover Not Beloved. Earl of Surrey, *after* Petrarch. AAS; LoAs; PAIC

Alas, So Long! Dante Gabriel Rossetti. VPC

Alas, that I should be. To My Infant Daughter. Yvor Winters. VGW

Alas, that I should die. Song of a Woman Abandoned by the Tribe. *Unknown, tr. by* Mary Austin. WPE

Alas! what boots it that my noble steed. On a Distant Prospect of an Absconding Bookmaker. G. Rostrevor Hamilton. FaBoCo

Alas, what is the world? a sea of glass. Meditation 10. Philip Pain. NOBA; PiAm

Alas, what pleasure, now the pleasant spring. A Canzone Pastoral in Honor of Her Majesty. Edmund Bolton. PAIC

Alastor; or, The Spirit of Solitude. Shelley. MBPR

Alba. Samuel Beckett. BIrV

Alba. Ezra Pound. GBL; PiAm; VGW

Alba for Mélusine. Ramon Guthrie. LoAs

Albatross. Judy Collins. GrRo

Albert Ayler: Eulogy for a Decomposed Saxophone Player. Stanley Crouch. PoBA

Albion's most lovely daughter sat on the banks of the. Mrs. Albion You've Got a Lovely Daughter. Adrian Henri. OxBTC

Album, The. C. Day Lewis. BuTh; OxBTC

Albuquerque Indian militants. Ignacio, Colorado, for You That Time. Joy Harjo. SA

Alceste in the Wilderness. Anthony Hecht. ConAP

Alcestis on the Poetry Circuit. Erica Jong. AmPA; RiTi

Alchemist, The. Richard Church. OxBTC

Alchemist in the City, The. Gerard Manley Hopkins. IPWM

Alchemy. Diane Levenberg. NPW

Alexander and Campaspe, *sels*. John Lyly.
   Cards and Kisses, *fr*. III, v. NOBE; PBMP
      (Cupid and My Campaspe.) HeIP
      ("Cupid and my Campaspe played.") GBL
   Serving-Men's Song, A, *fr*. I, iii. NOBE
   Trico's Song: "What bird so sings, yet so does wail?" *fr*. V, i.
      OBP
      (Welcome to Spring.) NOBE

Alexander and the Gymnosophists. *Unknown*. OxBM

Alexander's Feast: or, The Power of Music. Dryden. NOBE

Alfa is nice. Her Roman eye. Safety at Forty; or, An Abecedarian
   Takes a Walk. L. E. Sissman. Prf

Alfred, a Masque, *sel*. James Thomson *and* David Mallet.
   Rule, Britannia, *fr*. II, v. Thomson. BLSH; BTTM; VoPo

Alfred Corning Clark. Robert Lowell. NoAM

Algy. *Unknown*. CaYB

Ali. Lloyd M. Corbin, Jr. PoBA

Ali Ben Shufti. Anthony Thwaite. OxBTC

Alicante. Jacques Prévert, *tr. fr. French by* Lawrence
   Ferlinghetti. BoLoP

"Alice, dear, what ails you." A Frosty Night. Robert Graves.
   LP; OxBTC

Alice Fell; or, Poverty. Wordsworth. MBPR; SpRo

Alice grown lazy, mammoth but not fat. Last Days of Alice.
   Allen Tate. NoAM; NOBA; PiAm

Alice is tall and upright as a pine. Resolution in Four Sonnets, of
   a Poetical Question Put to Me by a Friend, Concerning Four
   Rural Sisters. Charles Cotton. BoLoP; Prf

Alice's Adventures in Wonderland, *sels*. "Lewis Carroll."
   Alice's Recitation, *fr. ch*. 10. SpRo
   " Tis the voice of the Lobster; I heard him declare."
      FaBoCo
      (Lobster, The, *sl. diff.*) OxBChV
   Duchess's Lullaby, The, *fr. ch*. 6. SpRo
      ("Speak roughly to your little boy.") FaBoCo
   Evidence Read at the Trial of the Knave of Hearts, *fr. ch*. 12.
      PBMP
      (Silence in Court.) FaBoCo
      ("They told me you had been to her.") SS
   Father William, *fr. ch*. 5.) SpRo; SS
      (You Are Old, Father William.) OxBChV
      (" 'You are old, Father William,' the young man said.")
      FaBoCo
   How Doth the Little Crocodile, *fr. ch*. 2. ECBV; FaBoCo;
      LCL; SpRo
   Lobster Quadrille, The, *from ch*. 10. OxBChV
   Mad Hatter's Song, The, *fr. ch*. 7. SpRo
   Turtle Soup, *fr. ch*. 10. SpRo

Alice's Recitation. "Lewis Carroll." *Fr*. Alice's Adventures in
   Wonderland, *ch*. 10. SpRo
   " Tis the voice of the Lobster; I heard him declare," *sel*.
      FaBoCo
      (Lobster, The, *sl. diff.*) OxBChV

Alienation (To My Son). Lucille F. Travis. AATT

Alive in a brown stucco house. The Quilt. Karen Swenson.
   WBN

Alive Together. Lisel Mueller. IHMS

All, All of a Piece. Dryden. *Fr*. The Secular Masque. InPS

All alone from his dark sanctum. Mahabalipuram. Louis
   MacNeice. NoAM

All along the backwater. Ducks' Ditty. Kenneth Grahame. *Fr*.
   The Wind in the Willows. OxBTC

All along the rail. In Texas Grass. Quincy Troupe. PoBA

All along the valley, stream that flashest white. In the Valley of
   Cauteretz. Tennyson. BoLoP; NOBE

All Around Man. *Unknown*. BluL

All around the cobbler's bench. Pop! Goes the Weasel. *Unknown*.
   BLSo

All beauties vulgar eyes on earth do see. The Idea. Made of
   Alnwick, in His Expedition to Scotland with the Army, 1639.
   Lord Herbert of Cherbury. SCP-2

All beginnings start right here. The Move Continuing. Al Young
   PoBA

All Being Well. W. W. Gibson. OxBTC

All craftsmen share a knowledge. They have held. Craftsmen. V.
   Sackville-West. OxBTC

All day a strong wind blew. A Strong Wind. Austin Clarke.
   PFIr

All day and night, save winter, every weather. Aspens. Edward
   Thomas. InPS

All day beside the shattered tank he'd lain. Reconciliation. C.
   Day Lewis. NoAM

All-day Bird, the artist, The. Claritas. Denise Levertov. PiAm;
   VGW

All day he had felt her stirring. The Mermaid. Lisel Mueller.
   RiTi

All day I am before the altar. Samuel. Charles Reznikoff. *Fr*.
   Five Groups of Verses. SA

All Day I Hear the Noise of Waters. James Joyce. Chamber
   Music, XXXV. NoAM; SoSe

All Day It Has Rained. Alun Lewis. NOBE; OxBTC

All day long. Rain. "Seumas O'Sullivan." PFIr

All day long I have been working. Madonna of the Evening
   Flowers. Amy Lowell. RiTi

All day long she dials. Befriending the Weather. Helena Minton.
   FAF

All day my sheep have mingled with yours. Shepherdess.
   Norman Cameron. Three Love Poems, III. GBL; SLP

All day subdued, polite. Negro Servant. Langston Hughes.
   VGW

All day swaying in the tower.. Out from Lobster Cove. J. D.
   Reed. NeAC

All day the unnatural barking of dogs. The Dog. Valentin
   Iremonger. BIrV

All day they/ bring the face. Ceremony. Lyn Lifshin. FAF

All day to the loose tile behind the parapet. The Wasps' Nest.
   George MacBeth. OxBTC

All day we walked the streets. The Fifties. Ira Sadoff. AmPA

All dripping in tangles green. The Tuft of Kelp. Herman
   Melville. SoSe

All endeavor to be beautiful. Primer of Plato. Jean Garrigue.
   NOBA

All fathers in Western civilization must have. The Father of My
   Country. Diane Wakoski. NoAM

All gentle folks who owe a grudge. The Gadfly. Keats. MBPR

All Goats. Elizabeth J. Coatsworth. BoAnP

All God's Children Got Shoes, *with music*. *Unknown*. BLSH

All God's spades wear dark shades. Its Curtains. Ted Joans.
   PoBA

All Greece hates. Helen. Hilda Doolittle ("H. D."). NOBA;
   SBG

All Hail the Power of Jesus' Name. Edward Perronet. *See*
   Coronation.

All Hallows. Louise Glück. AmPA

All he owns is. Squirrel near Library. Genevieve Taggard.
   WPE

All his life, my father looked for money. The Game. Stuart
   Silverman. CoPAm

All human [*or* humane] things are subject to decay. MacFlecknoe.
   Dryden. ESaP; NOBE; OBP; PPP; SCP-1

All I ask of a woman is that she. D. H. Lawrence. POL

All I know is a door into the dark. The Forge. Seamus Heaney. PFIr; SoSe

All I want in this creation's. Black-eyed Susie. *Unknown.* AmFP

All I wanted/ was your/ love. To Mother and Steve. Mari Evans. BPo; PoBA; Psy

All Ignorance Toboggans into Know. E. E. Cummings. NOBA

All in a literary parleur. Bootie Black and the Seven Giants. Mike Cook. JB

All in a row, a bendy bow. Country Rhyme. *Unknown.* ECBV

All in bunches the furred leaves. Tithes. Luci Shaw. AATT

All in Green Went My Love Riding. E. E. Cummings. HeIP; InPK; NoAM
   (Song: "All in green went my love riding.") PAIC

All in the Downs. John Gay. *See* Sweet William's Farewell to Black-eyed Susan.

All-In Wrestlers. James Kirkup. SPo

All Intents. Larry Eigner. VGW

All Ireland's now one vessel's company. Fearghal Og MacWard *tr. by* the Earl of Longford. *Fr.* The Flight of the Earls, 1607. BIrV

All is best, though we oft doubt. Milton. *Fr.* Samson Agonistes. NOBE

All Is Well with the Child. Marya Zaturenska. LoAs

All joy to mortals, joy and mirth. Song. Aphra Behn. *Fr.* Emperor of the Moon. WPE

All Kinds of Shivers. Lilian Moore. CaYB

All kings, and all their favourites. The Anniversary. John Donne. BoLoP; MetP; NOBE

All La Glory. Robbie Robertson. RRA

All Legendary Obstacles. John Montague. BIrV

All look and likeness caught from earth. Phantom. Samuel Taylor Coleridge. MBPR

All men are locked in their cells. Fall Down. Calvin C. Hernton. PoBA

All Men Are . . . Socrates Is. Napoleon St. Cyr. FAF

All men are worms. But this no man. In silk. On Courtworm. Ben Jonson. SCP-1

All men,—the preacher saith,—whate'er or whence. Frederick Goddard Tuckerman. *Fr.* Sonnets. AmVN

All Morning. Terry Stokes. AmPA

All my favourite characters have been. Mythology. Lawrence Durrell. OxBTC

All my life/ they have told me. To You. Frank Horne. *Fr.* Letters Found near a Suicide. BPo

All my life I lived in a coconut. Locked In. Ingemar Gustafson, *tr. by* May Swenson. PoTa

All my past life is mine no more. Love and Life. Earl of Rochester. BoLoP; GBL; NOBE

All My Pretty Ones. Anne Sexton. NoAM

All my shortcomings, in this year of grace. Dear Uncle Stranger. Conrad Aiken. NoAM; NOBA

All Nature seems at work. Slugs leave their lair. Work Without Hope. Samuel Taylor Coleridge. AnMo; IPWM; MBPR; NOBE

All night/ you banged. To Poem. Lyn Lifshin. NeAC; Psy

All Night by the Rose. *Unknown.* HeIP
   ("All night by the rose, rose.") GBL

All night fell hammers, shock on shock. A London Fete. Coventry Patmore. VPC

All night had shout of men and cry. Easter Night. Alice Meynell. BoReV

All night I clatter upon my creed. The Wife Who Would a Wanton Be. *Unknown.* FaBoCo

All night I walked among your spirits, Richard. A Mourning Letter from Paris. Conrad Kent Rivers. BPo

All Night Long Fooling Me. *Unknown.* AmFP

All night the blind entrance of the children. Barren Poem. Michael Ryan. AmPA

All night the sound had. The Rain. Robert Creeley. CAPP; ConAP; VGW

All night the wind swept over the house. Winter Morning. William Jay Smith. NCSH

All night they whine upon their ropes and boom. Nocturne of the Wharves. Arna Bontemps. BPo

All-Night Waitress, The. Maura Stanton. AmPa

All of a row. Mother Goose. MG

All other joys of life he strove to warm. Modern Love, IV. George Meredith. PAIC

All Other Love Is Like the Moon. *Unknown.* OxBM

All our best ye have branded. 1867. Joseph Mary Plunkett. PFIr

All our roads go nowhere. On Inhabiting an Orange. Josephine Miles. NoAM

All our stones like as much sun as possible. Forecast. Josephine Miles. NoAM

All Out and Down. *Unknown.* BluL

All out for Illinois Central. Calling Trains. *Unknown.* AmFP

All out-of-doors looked darkly in at him. An Old Man's Winter Night. Robert Frost. AnMo; NoAM; PiAm; VGW

All over the blue. Vantage. Brewster Ghiselin. PPoD

"All over the world," the traveller said. The Two Travellers. C. J. Boland. PFIr

All Owners of Meat Are Hospitable. Rochelle Owens. WBN

All people that on earth do dwell. Old Hundredth. William Kethe. BLSo

All Praise to Thee, My God, This Night. Thomas Ken. BLSH, *with music*
   (Evening Hymn, An.) OxBChV

All Quiet. David Ignatow. ConAP

All Quiet Along the Potomac To-Night, *with music.* Ethel Lynn Beers. PSoN

All Revelation. Robert Frost. PiAm

All right now, listen to me right good. Unloading Rails. *Unknown.* AmFP

All right. Try this. Northern Pike. James Wright. CAAP

All saints revile her, and all sober men. The White Goddess. Robert Graves. OBP

All silence says music will follow. Onion Bucket. Lorenzo Thomas. PoBA

All Souls' Night. Frances Cornford. OxBTC

All such proclivities are tabulated. The Quiet Glades of Eden. Robert Graves. BoLoP

All Sunday I sat as lady. For Paige. Summer Brenner. RiTi

All that blazing day, swift-breasted swallows. Thunderstorm in South Dakota. Kay Boyle. WPE

All that blesses the step of the antelope. "Else a Great Prince in Prison Lies." Denise Levertov. PPP; VGW

All that I know. My Star. Robert Browning. HeIP; SoSe

All that I ran from. The Mood. Quandra Prettyman. PoBA

All that I try to save him from. Sleep-Learning. Ruth Fainlight. NMM

All that lives of legendry. Unicorn. Nicholas Stuart Gray. ECBV

All that matters is to be at one with the living God. Pax. D. H. Lawrence. BoReV

All That Time. May Swenson. RiTi

All that time wasted. Out of the Desert. Diane Levenberg. NPW

All That's Past. Walter de la Mare. NOBE; OxBTC

All the bells were ringing. Christina Rossetti. LCL

All the cages are empty. The Two Selves. Margaret Avison. NoAM

All the cautionary tales of strange girls. Mythics. Helen Chasin. IHMS

All the convicts have their roaches lit. Starry Sky. Charles Simic. POL

All the Dead Birds. Melvin Walker LaFollette. SFF

All the Dead Dears. Sylvia Plath. AnMo; CAPP; CoPAm; IHMS

All the flowers of the spring. Vanitas Vanitatum. John Webster. Fr. The Devil's Law Case. NOBE; OBP

All the hot night. Haiku. Masaoka Shiki, tr. by Kenneth Rexroth. PAIC

All the houses on drastic street. Mr. Clean. John William Corrington. PPoD

All the male poets write of orpheus. Euridice. Alta. MMD

All the Many is One. The Wild Geese. John Masefield. NoAM

All the mothers in the world. War. Miguel Hernández, tr. by James Wright. Epi

All the night in woe. The Little Girl Found. Blake. Fr. Songs of Experience. MBPR; RRA

All the night sleep came not upon my eyelids. Sapphics. Swinburne. LoAs; PAIC

All the Pretty Little Horses. Unknown. AmFP

All the sisters of mercy. Canto Llano. Anita Endrezze Probst. CDW

All the things. The objects. Cold Term. LeRoi Jones. BPo

All the Things You Are, with music. Oscar Hammerstein II. BLSo

All the Way My Saviour Leads Me, with music. Fanny Crosby. BLSH

All the World Moved. June Jordan. PoBA

All the World's a Stage. Sir Walter Ralegh. See What Is Our Life? A Play of Passion.

All the world's a stage. Shakespeare. Fr. As You Like It, II, vii. SFF

All their lives in a box! What generations. The Silkworms. Douglas Stewart. MAuV

All These Birds. Richard Wilbur. NOBA; Prf

All these illegitimate babies. Valuable. Stevie Smith. OxBTC

All these men were there inside. Fable of the Mermaid and the Drunks. Pablo Neruda, tr. by Alastair Reid. LP

All things at first was God, who dwelt alone. Joseph Beaumont. Fr. Psyche or Love's Mystery Displaying the Intercourse betwixt Christ and the Soul, Canto VI. SCP-2

"All things become thee, being thine," I think sometimes. Woman. Randall Jarrell. NoAM; NOBA

All Things Bright and Beautiful. Cecil Frances Alexander. OxBChV

All Things Can Tempt Me. W. B. Yeats. PFIr

All things come to pass. My Name Is Afrika. Keorapetse Kgositsile. PoBA

All Things Have Savour. Unknown. FaBoCo

All things uncomely and broken, all things worn out and old. The Lover Tells of the Rose in His Heart. W. B. Yeats. PFIr

All things within this fading world hath end. Before the Birth of One of Her Children. Anne Bradstreet. MAT; NOBA; PiAm; SBG; WPE

All those summers, waiting. Waiting for You to Come By. Simon J. Ortiz. CDW

All thoughts, all passions, all delights. Love. Samuel Taylor Coleridge. MBPR

All Three of Us. Carol Cox. MMD

All through October. Indian Summer: Vermont. Anne Stevenson. NCSH

All through the Night, with music. At. to David Owen. BLSH

All through the Rains. Gary Snyder. ConAP

All thru last/ year they sang. The Group. Victor Hernández Cruz. SA

All Too Late. Unknown. OxBM

All Tropic Places Smell of Mold. Karl Shapiro. VGW

All truths are half-truths. The Golden Pyramids of the Sun. Alden Nowlan. AKE

All under the leaves, the leaves of life. The Seven Virgins. Unknown. GBP; PEBB

All veiled in black, with faces hid from sight. Mourning Women. Mathilde Blind. SBG

All Watched Over by Machines of Loving Grace. Richard Brautigan. MAT

All were to little for the merchauntes hande. George Gascoigne. AAS

All wheels; a man breathed fire. The Celebration. James Dickey. VGW

All Which Isn't Singing Is Mere Talking. E. E. Cummings. VGW

All who are not just classmates. Rachel at Thirteen. Yvonne. WBN

All will die. Forecast. Sam Cornish. NVAP

All winter long I lose my poise. The Horrors. Ogden Nash. SFF

All winter long you listened for the boom. The Stoic: for Laura von Courten. Edgar Bowers. PiAm

All winter through I bow my head. The Scarecrow. Walter de la Mare. OxBTC

All women are beautiful as they rise. Poem for Easter. Robert Kelly. VGW

All worlds have halfsight, seeing either with. E. E. Cummings. PiAm

All ye young men, I pray draw near. The Gardener. Unknown. GBP

All year the flax-dam festered in the heart. Death of a Naturalist. Seamus Heaney. NCSH

All you Southerners now draw near. The Battle of Shiloh. Unknown. AIW

All you that are single and wild in your ways. Old Maids. Unknown. AmFP

All you violated ones with gentle hearts. For Malcolm X. Margaret Walker. BPo; PoBA

Allace depairting, grund of wo. Fairweill. Unknown. SLP

Allas, allas, wel ivel I sped! See Alas, alas, well evil I sped!

Allas! what shul we freres do. The Friars' Retort. Unknown. OxBM

Alle bakbiteres hi wendeth to helle. Going to Hell. Unknown. OxBM

Allegiance is assigned. Choice. J. V. Cunningham. PiAm; VGW

Allegiance to Aphrodite. Nicholas Flocos. SA

Allegory, An. David Ignatow. VGW

Allegory in Black. Carl Clark. JB

Allen said, I am searching for the true cadence. Helicon. John Hollander. NoAM

Allen-a-Dale. Sir Walter Scott. Fr. Rokeby, III. PoTa

Alley Blues. Unknown. BluL

Alligator, The. Beatrice Ravenel. WPE

Alligator, beetle, porcupine, whale. An Animal Alphabet. Unknown. ECBV

Alligator Bride, The. Donald Hall. ConAP

Allison Gross. Unknown. PeBB

Allotments: April. Bernard Spencer. PSN

All's over, then: does truth sound bitter. The Lost Mistress. Robert Browning. BoLoP; NOBE

Almighty Father, as of watery matter. 1st Week 6th Day. Joshua Sylvester. Fr. Du Bartas His Divine Weeks and Works. SCP-2

Almost Any Evening. Phyllis McGinley. *Fr.* Speaking of Television. TH

Almost at the equator. Once Only. Gary Snyder. CoPAm

Almost Human. C. Day Lewis. NoAM

Almost Persuaded, *with music.* Philip Paul Bliss. BLSH

Almost singing, she stares past the crowd and flies. Old Woman Awaiting the Greyhound Bus. Duane Niatum. CDW

Almswomen. Edmund Blunden. OxBTC

Aloft in heavenly mansions, doubleyou one. The Playboy of the Demi-World: 1938. William Plomer. OxBTC

Aloft, lightly on fingertips. Burial. Robert Francis. NCSH

Aloha Oe, *with music.* Queen Lydia Liliuokalani. BLSH

Alone. Poe. PiAm; VoPo

Alone. E. J. Scovell. GBL

Alone and Godless, stopped by the sudden edge. Patrick MacDonogh. *Fr.* Escape to Love. BIrV

Alone, at night, with all the world. Evil Nigger Waits for Lightnin'. LeRoi Jones. NoAM; NOBA

Alone at the end of green allées, alone. The Statues in the Public Gardens. Howard Nemerov. ConAP

Alone/ December/ Night. Victor Hernández Cruz. PBMP

Alone for the evening. Bringing Flowers. Roberta Spears. AmPA

Alone hunting. Deserted Farms Poem. Bruce Severy. VW

Alone I tiptoe through the stars. Star Journey. Naomi Madgett. BPo

Alone in greenwood must I roam. Hollin, Green Hollin. *Unknown.* GBP

Alone in ourselves. At midnight. And We Are Strangers to Each Other. Ruth Lisa Schechter. RiTi

Along come that F.F.V., the swiftest on the line. George Allen. *Unknown.* AmFP

Along the avenue of cypresses. Giorno Dei Morti. D. H. Lawrence. NOBE

Along the blushing borders bright with dew. Spring Flowers. James Thomson. *Fr.* The Seasons: Spring. NOBE

Along the rim of sea and sky. The Helicopter. Ian Serraillier. RAE

Along the shore the tall, thin grass. In Memory of Colonel Charles Young. Countee Cullen. PoBA

Along the streaming ground, the wet leaves. After the Storm. Rosalie Moore. MIT; RiTi

Aloof, as if a thing of mood and whim. The Schreckhorn. Thomas Hardy. OBP

Alouette, *with music. Unknown.* BLSH

Alphabet, An. Edward Lear. *See* A Was Once an Apple Pie.

Alphabet, The. Karl Shapiro. NoAM

Alphabet Calendar of Amergin, The. *Unknown, tr. fr. Irish by* Robert Graves. BIrV
(Song of Amergin) Moon

Alphabet of Christmas Cheer. Elizabeth Weston. ECBV

Alphaomegadeltasigmakappazetassssss (sing-song fashion). Greek Crazeology. Carolyn M. Rodgers. SA

Alphonso of Castile. Emerson. NOBA

Alpine. R. S. Thomas. POL; RFM

Already blushes on thy cheek. Nemesis. Emerson. NOBA

Already it's late summer. Sun-bathers go. *The Divine Insect.* John Hall Wheelock. PPoD

Already she seems bone thin. A Poem about Breasts. James Wright. CAAP

Alston Chapel. James E. Warren, Jr. AATT

Altar, The. George Herbert. AnMo; InPS; SCP-1

Altarpiece Finished, The. John Hollander. NoAM

Altars in the Street, The. Denise Levertov. CAPP

Altarwise by Owl-Light, *sels.* Dylan Thomas.
"Altarwise by owl-light in the half-way house," I. Epi; NoAM

"And from the windy West came two-gunned Gabriel," V. Epi; NoAM

"Death is all metaphors, shape in one history," II. NoAM

"First there was the lamb on knocking knees," III. Epi

"From the oracular archives and the parchment," IX. NoAM

"Let the tale's sailor from a Christian voyage," X. Epi; NoAM

"This was the crucifixion on the mountain," VIII. Epi; NoAM

Alter! When the hills do. Emily Dickinson. LoAs

Altered look about the hills, An. Emily Dickinson. PPP

Alternatives. Peter Cooley. AmPA

Although, great Queen, thou now in silence lie. In Honour of That High and Mighty Princess Queen Elizabeth of Happy Memory. Anne Bradstreet. SBG

Although he never stirs from home. Haiku. José Juan Tablada, *tr. by* Samuel Beckett. PBMP

Although I can see him still. The Fisherman. W. B. Yeats. NoAM; PSN

Although I do not hope to turn again. Ash-Wednesday, VI. T. S. Eliot. BoReV

Although I feel its shape could knit my bones. The Shirt. Jon Silkin. NoAM

Although I shelter from the rain. The Lamentation of the Old Pensioner. W. B. Yeats. InPK; PFIr

Although it is night, I sit in the bathroom, waiting. Adolescence— II. Rita Dove. AmPA

Although it's cold no clothes I wear. *Unknown.* GBP

Although my claws weaken. Sweetness. *Unknown, tr. by* John Montague. BIrV

Although my house floats on a lawn. Blues for John Coltrane, Dead at 41. William Matthews. NVAP

Although she feeds me bread of bitterness. America. Claude McKay. IPWM; NoAM; PoBA

Although the aepyornis. He "Digesteth Harde Yron." Marianne Moore. NoAM

Although the relatives in the summer house. A Poem for Bhain. John Berryman. CoPAm

Although the snow still lingers. Last Snow. Andrew Young. OxBTC

Although the summer sunlight gild. W. B. Yeats. *Fr.* Vacillation. BoReV

Although thou now put'st me in doubt. Parting with ———. Jane Barker. SCP-2

Although you see the world diff'rent from me. Child of Mine. Gerry Goffin *and* Carole King. PoRo

Always. Pablo Neruda, *tr. fr. Spanish by* Donald D. Walsh. OLR

Always Begin Where You Are. Thomas Hornsby Ferril. VGW

Always brilliant/ and all the world is queer. The Generator. Rae Desmond Jones. CAAP

Always expecting the winter. In Dream: The Privacy of Sequence. Ray A. Young Bear. CDW

Always fastidious, it removed its dying. Death of a Cat. Brian Jones. LP

Always for the first time. André Breton, *tr. fr. French by* Wallace Fowlie. LoAs

Always, from My First Boyhood. John Peale Bishop. VGW

Always I lay upon the brink of love. Judas. Vassar Miller. CoPAm

Always in that valley in Wales I hear the noise. Waterfalls. Vernon Watkins. NoAM

Always loving or blithe. Poem. Charles Senior. MIS

Always She Moves from Me. Shirley Kaufman. WPE

Always, the damage is irreparable. Cape Cod Murders, 1968. Mira Fish. FAF

Always the same, when on a fated night. The Onset. Robert Frost. PBMP; PPP

Always the setting forth was the same. Odysseus. W. S. Merwin. NOBA

Always there is this crossing. Liberation. Mary Swanson Stroh. NPW

Always this pressing for shape. Old Mill, Newton St. Cyres. Ken Smith. TwMBP

Always to want to. The Tortoise. Cid Corman. InPK; VGW

Always too eager for future, we. Next, Please. Philip Larkin. HeIP

Always when I write I wear a mask. The Mask. Valery Larbaud, *tr. by* William Jay Smith. LoAs

Always your body like a foreign country. Location. Knute Skinner. MAT

Alysoun ("Bytuene Mersh and Averil"). *Unknown.* HeIP; OxBM

Am I a stone and not a sheep. Good Friday. Christina Rossetti. OFD

Am I despised because you say. To a Gentlewoman Objecting to Him His Grey Hairs. Robert Herrick. SCP-1

Am I failing? For no longer can I cast. Modern Love, XXIX. George Meredith. GBL

Am I thy gold? Or purse, Lord, for thy wealth. Edward Taylor. *Fr.* Preparatory Meditations, First Series, VI. VoPo

Amana Colonies, The. Ken Smith. TwMBP

Amanda Barker. Edgar Lee Masters. *Fr.* Spoon River Anthology. NoAM

Amarantha sweet and fair. To Amarantha, That She Would Dishevel Her Hair. Richard Lovelace. SCP-2

Amateur Flute, The. *Unknown.* SpRo

Amateurs, we gathered mushrooms. Fall. Robert Hass. AmPA

Amazing Grace, *with music.* John Newton. BLSH; BLSo

Ambassador Puser the ambassador. Memorial Rain. Archibald MacLeish. NoAM

Ambassadors, The. Paul Lawson. PPoD

Amber husk. Sea Poppies. Hilda Doolittle ("H. D."). PiAm

Ambiguous Lines. *Unknown. See* I Saw aPeacock with a Fiery Tail.

Ambitious sir, take heed! Honour Joseph Beaumont. SCP-2

Amen. Richard W. Thomas. PoBA

Amend Me. *Unknown.* OxBM

Amends to Nature. Arthur Symons. FSFS

America. Robert Creeley. MAT

America. Henry Dumas. PoBA

America. Allen Ginsberg. CAPP; Epi; NoAM; PiAm; PPoe; PPP

America. Claude McKay. IPWM; NoAM; PoBA

America. Wendy Rose. CDW

America. Samuel Francis Smith. BLSH, *with music*; BLSo, *with music*; BTTM; PSoN, *with music*

America a Prophecy. Blake. MBPR

America Bleeds. Angelo Lewis. PoBA

America for Me. Henry van Dyke. SoSe

America Is Darken'd. R. H. W. Dillard. CoPAm

America, it is to thee. From America. James M. Whitfield. BPo

America I've given you all and now I'm nothing. America. Allen Ginsberg. CAPP; Epi; NoAM; PiAm; PPoe; PPP

America the Beautiful. Katherine Lee Bates. BLSH, *with music*; BTTM

America, you ode for reality! America. Robert Creeley. MAT

American against Solitude. Alan Dugan. CAPP

American Citizen, *sel.* Kay Boyle. Invitation in It, The. RiTi

American City. Joyce Carol Oates. IPWM

American Commencement. Aram Boyajian. NeAC

American Express called me last week. A Reason of Numbers Josephine Jacobsen. IPWM

American Farm, 1934. Genevieve Taggard. VGW

American Flag, The. Joseph Rodman Drake. BTTM

American frigate, a frigate of fame, An. *Paul Jones's Victory. Unknown.* AmFP

American Gothic, An. Dick Allen. FAF

American Gothic. Samuel Allen. *See* To Satch

American Heartbreak. Langston Hughes. BPo

American hero must triumph over, The. Eisenhower's Visit to Franco, 1959. James Wright. CAPP; PSN

American History. Michael S. Harper. BPo

American Indian, The. *Unknown.* FaBoCo

American Literature. James Russell Lowell. *Fr.* A Fable for Critics. AmVN

American muse, whose strong and diverse heart. John Brown's Body: Invocation. Stephen Vincent Benét. BTTM

American Poetry. Louis Simpson. CoPAm; NoAM; NOBA; TH

American Poets. Marvin Bell. NVAP

American poets stick together. Now Everyone Is Writing Poems about Indians. James Tipton. HeS

American Primitive. William Jay Smith. CoPAm; InPK; SFF; WIF

American Rhapsody (4). Kenneth Fearing. MiP; PAIC

American Saturday Afternoon. Ron Ikan. NVAP

American Traveller, The. "Orpheus C. Kerr." FaBoCo

Americana XIII: "Captain Patterson, the folks back home." Carl Rakosi. InPS

Americana XVII: Reminder of William Carlos Williams, A. Carl Rakosi. InPS

Americana XV: Simplicity. Carl Rakosi. InPS

Americana IX: "Your correspondent must be kidding when he says." Carl Rakosi. InPS

Amethysts and sapphires stud the sarcophagus. The Tomb of Time. Albert Howard Carter. AATT

Amid my Bale I bath in blisse. A Straunge Passion of a Lover. George Gascoigne. AAS

Amid the smoke of cities did you pass. To Joanna. Wordsworth. MBPR

Amidst the nymphs, the glory of the flood. On Mrs. E. Montague's Blushing in the Cross-bath. Thomas Flatman. SCP-2

Amish, The. John Updike. SS

Amo, Amas. John O'Keefe. GBL

Among/ of/ green. The Locust Tree in Flower. William Carlos Williams. PiAm

Among all lovely things my love had been. The Glow-Worm. Wordsworth. GBL; MBPR

Among Pelagian travellers. On the Circuit. W. H. Auden. OxBTC

Among School Children. W. B. Yeats. AnMo; Epi; NoAM; NOBE; OxBTC; PPoe; PPP; SoSe

Among Sharks. Al Lee. AmPA

Among the high-branching, leafless boughs. The View from an Attic Window. Howard Nemerov. ConAP

Among the Multitude ("Among the men and women the multitude"). Walt Whitman. LoAs

Among the orchard weeds, from every search. Hen's Nest. John Clare. AKE

Among the rain. The Great Figure. William Carlos Williams. NoAM

Among the Roman love-poets, possession. Note on Propertius 1.5. Fleur Adcock. BoLoP

Among the Shades. Thomas Campion, *after the Latin of* Propertius. NOBE (Vobiscum Est Iope.) BoLoP ("When thou must home to shades of underground.") AAS; GBL; LoAs

Among the smoke and fog of a December afternoon. Portrait of a Lady. T. S. Eliot. PSN

Among the taller wood with ivy hung. The Vixen. John Clare. BoAnP

Among them marble where the man may lie. A Thurn. John Berryman. NOBA

Among thy fancies, tell me this. The Kiss: A Dialogue. Robert Herrick. PAIC

Among twenty snowy mountains. Thirteen Ways of Looking at a Blackbird. Wallace Stevens. InPK; IPWM; NoAM; NOBA; TSWA; VoPo

Amor Vincit Omnia. Edgar Bowers. PiAm

Amores, *sel.* Ovid, *tr. fr. Latin by* Christopher Marlowe. Corinnae Concubitus, I, 5. GBL
(Elegy: "In summer's heat and mid-time of the day.") BoLoP
(Ovid's Fifth Elegy.) OBP

Amoretti Spenser. AAS
*Sels.*
I. "Happy ye leaves! when as those lily hands." LoAs; PAIC
II. "Unquiet thought, whom at the first I bred." PAIC
III. "The sovereign beauty which I do admire." PAIC
XIV. "Return again, my forces late dismayed." SoSe
XV. "Ye tradefull merchants, that with weary toyle." HeIP
XVIII. "The rolling wheel that runneth often round." Epi
LXII. "Weary year his race now having run, The." FSFS
LXVII. "Like [*or* Lyke] as a huntsman after weary chace." Epi; GBL; HeIP
LXVIII. "Most glorious Lord of life, that on this day." Epi (Easter.) BoReV; NOBE
LXXV. "One day I wrote her name upon the strand." BoLoP; GBL; HeIP; IPWM; LoAs; PBMP
LXXVIII. "Lackying my loue I go from place to place." LoAs
LXXXII. "Joy of my life, full oft for loving you." HeIP
LXXXIX. "Like as the culver on the bared bough." GBL

Amorous Neptune. Christopher Marlowe. *Fr.* Hero and Leander. NOBE

Amorous Worms' Meat, The. Petrarch, *tr. fr. Italian by* Anna Maria Armi. Sonnets to Laura: To Laura in Death, XXXVI. LoAs

Amours de Voyage. Arthur Hugh Clough.
*Sels.*
"Dear Eustatio, I write that you may write me an answer, " Canto I. VPC
"*Dulce* it is, and *decorum,* no doubt, for the country to fall," Canto II, ii. OBP
"Now supposing the French or the Neapolitan soldier," Canto II, iv. OBP
"Tell me, my friend, do you think that the grain would sprout in the furrow," Canto III, ii. OBP
"There are two different kinds, I believe, of human attraction," Canto II, xi. OBP
"There was a time, methought it was but lately departed," *fr.* Canto V, 5. OBP
"What do the people say, and what does the government do?" Canto II. VPC

Amphitryon, *sel.* Dryden.
Mercury's Song to Phaedra, *fr. IV, i. OBP*

Amputee Soldier, The. Philip Dacey. NVAP

Amusing Our Daughters. Carolyn Kizer. VGW

Amyntas led me to a grove. The Willing Mistress. Aphra Behn. *Fr.* The Dutch Lover. SBG

An' oh! the jay our rest did yield. Day's Work a-Done. William Barnes. VPC

Anacreontics: Drinking. Abraham Cowley. *See* Drinking.

Anagram, The. John Donne. Elegies, II. PAIC

Analogue of Unity in Multeity. Richard Eberhart. NoAM

Analysands. Dudley Randall. BPo

Analysis of Baseball. May Swenson. SPo

Anarchist. Norman Dugdale. BoAnP

Anarchist's Letter, An. Harald Wyndham. POL

Anathema of Cats. John Skelton. *Fr.* Phyllyp Sparowe. PCat

Anathemata, The, *sels.* David Jones.
Angle-Land, III. NoAM; TwMBP
Redriff. TwMBP

Anatomy. Gilbert Sorrentino. POL

Anatomy of Happiness, The. Ogden Nash. PAIC

Anatomy of Melancholy, The, *sel.* Robert Burton.
Author's Abstract of Melancholy, The. SCP-2
"Methinks I hear, methinks I see."
" 'Tis my sole plague to be alone."
"When I go musing all alone."

Anatomy of the World, An, *sel.* John Donne.
First Anniversary, The. SCP-1
"She, of whom the ancients seemed to prophesy."
"Some months she hath been dead (but, being dead)."

Ancestor. Thomas Kinsella. BIrV

Ancestors. Dudley Randall. BPo

Anchors Aweigh, *with music.* Alfred H. Miles. BLSH

Ancient Couple on Lu Mountain, The. Mark Van Doren. VGW

Ancient Lights. Austin Clarke. BIrV

Ancient Music. Ezra Pound. FaBoCo; HeIP; PBMP; SpRo

Ancient of Days, *with music.* William Croswell Doane. BLSH

Ancient person, for whom I. A Song of a Young Lady to Her Ancient Lover. Earl of Rochester. BoLoP; GBL

Ancient Proverb, An. Blake. *Fr.* Several Questions Answered. MBPR

Ancient to Ancients, An. Thomas Hardy. OxBTC

Ancient Wisdom, Rather Cosmic. Ezra Pound. NOBA

Ancient Yuba Miner of the Days of '49, Ye. Samuel C. Upham. AIW

And a sweet goodnight to you and you. Lights, Flowers. Judith Johnson Sherwin. WBN

And after this quick bash in the dark. Portrait of a Young Girl Raped at a Suburban Party. Brian Patten. OxBTC

And aged Tiriel stood and said: "Where does the thunder sleep?" Blake. *Fr.* Tiriel. Epi

And always through my window pane. Girl's Song. Marya Zaturenska. OLR

And among the divine paranoids old Ezra. Ezra Pound. Phyllis Webb. MMD

And as for me, though that I konne but lyte. Chaucer. *Fr.* The Legend of Good Women. HeIP

And as we came down the staircase. Valse Oubliée. John Heath-Stubbs. OxBTC

And at the last I cast my mine eye aside. Lady of the Arbour. *Fr.* The Flower and the Leaf. WPE

And because we lived in a democracy. Naming the State Bird. Keith Gunderson. HeS

And believing she was a maid. The Faithless Wife. Federico Garcia Lorca, *tr. by* A. L. Lloyd. BoLoP

And birds came crying. James Cunningham. *Fr.* The Narrator's Trance. JB

And borne with theirs, my proudest thoughts do seem. Frederick Goddard Tuckerman. *Fr.* Sonnets. AmVN

And call ye this to utter what is just. Psalm LVIII: Si Vere Utique. Countess of Pembroke. WPE

And can it be, that I should gain. Free Grace. Charles Wesley. BoReV

And can the physician make sick men well? Lily, Germander, and Sops-in-Wine. *Unknown. Fr.* Robin Goodfellow, Pt. II. ECBV

And change with hurried hand has swept these scenes. Sonnet. Frederick Goddard Tuckerman. *Fr.* Sonnets. NOBA; PiAm

And, constantly, I seek/ A poetry of facts. "Hugh MacDiarmid." *Fr.* The Kind of Poetry I Want. InPS

And Death Shall Have No Dominion. Dylan Thomas. MPo; NoAM; PPoe

And Did the Animals? Mark Van Doren. VGW

And Did Those Feet in Ancient Time. Blake. *Fr.* Milton. HeIP; InPS; MAT; MBPR; OBP
(Jerusalem.) NOBE
(New Jerusalem, A.) VoPo
(Preface.) PPoe

And does the heart grow old? You know. To My Wife. J. V. Cunningham. PiAm

And each one to the advantage of her breasts. The Girl with 18 Nightgowns. Gregory Orr. POL

And ever against eating cares. Milton. *Fr.* L'Allegro. SCP-1

And every yeare a worlde my will did deeme. George Gascoigne. AAS

And for what, except for you, do I feel love? Wallace Stevens. *Fr.* Notes Toward a Supreme Fiction. NOBA

And from the windy West came two-gunned Gabriel. Altarwise by Owl-Light, V. Dylan Thomas. Epi; NoAM

And God said, "Let the waters generate." Creation: the Fifth Day, Fishes and Birds. Milton. *Fr.* Paradise Lost, VII. SCP-1

And God stepped out on space. The Creation. James Weldon Johnson. MiP; PBMP; PoBA

And Gwydion said to Math, when it was Spring. The Wife of Llew. Francis Ledwidge. PFIr

And have we lost another friend? John Close. *Fr.* In Respectful Memory of Mr. Yarker. FaBoCo

And he passed around midnight. Nathaniel Tarn. *Fr.* A Nowhere for Vallejo. TwMBP

And He Shall Judge Among Nations. Isaiah, Bible, *O. T.* PBMP

And here face down beneath the sun. You, Andrew Marvell. Archibald MacLeish. HeIP; NoAM; NOBA; PiAm; PPP; SoSe; VoPo

And here the precious dust is laid [*or* layd]. Maria Wentworth. Thomas Carew. MetP; SCP-2

And here upon this final bed. Eschatology. Wade Hall. AATT

And how beguile you? Death has no repose. James Elroy Flecker. *Fr.* The Golden Legend of Samarkand OxBTC

And How It Goes. Anselm Hollo. TwMBP

And I a beginner. Answer to Yo/Question. Sonia Sanchez. BPo; RiTi

And I come out of it. Scenario VI. LeRoi Jones. Epi

And I have come upon this place. L'An Trentiesme de Mon Eage [*or* Age]. Archibald MacLeish. NoAM; NOBA; PAIC

And I Have Loved Thee, Ocean! Byron. *Fr.* Childe Harold's Pilgrimage, IV SPo

"And I perhaps am secret: Heav'n is high." Eve Contemplates Sharing Her Sin. Milton. *Fr.* Paradise Lost, IX. OBP

And I wanted to be inside you. Firebird. Alta. MMD

And I went down by that freight depot. Lost Lover Blues. *Unknown.* BluL

And if I did, what then? A Farewell. George Gascoigne. *Fr.* The Adventures of Master F. I. GBL; NOBE

And if sun comes. Truth. Gwendolyn Brooks. *Fr.* The Womanhood. TH

And if tonight my soul may find her peace. Shadows. D. H. Lawrence. BoReV; OxBTC

And if ye stand in doubt. Colin Clout. John Skelton. TVS

And I'm going way down. The Gone Dead Train. *Unknown.* BluL

And in the cold, bleak winter time. W. G. Vincent. *Fr.* Moonlight. ANTL

And in the frosty season, when the sun. The Skaters. Wordsworth. *Fr.* The Prelude. FSFS; SPo

And in the Hanging Gardens. Conrad Aiken. PoTa

And is it night? Are they thine eyes that shine? *Unknown.* GBL

And is there care in heaven? and is there love? Care in Heaven. Spenser. *Fr.* The Faerie Queene, II, 12. BoReV

And is this—Yarrow?—This the stream. Yarrow Visited. Wordsworth. MBPR

And it's forty miles to Nicut Hill. Prince Robert. *Unknown.* AmFP

And it's never mind, never mind, baby. Poor Man Blues *Unknown.* BluL

And Jesus Don't Have Much Use for His Old Suitcase Anymore. Tom Kryss. NeAC

And learn O voyager to walk. Seafarer. Archibald MacLeish. NoAM

And let me the canakin, clink. Shakespeare. *Fr.* Othello, II, iii. AIW

And, like a dying lady lean and pale. The Waning Moon. Shelley. Moon

And Los and Enitharmon builded Jerusalem weeping. Vala, Night the Ninth Being the Last Judgment. Blake. *Fr.* The Four Zoas. MBPR

And love hung still as crystal over the bed. Louis MacNeice. *Fr.* Trilogy for X. GBL

And no sound/and no word spoken. Three Love Poems for My Wife. George Bruce. SLP

And now another autumn morning finds me. An Ageing Schoolmaster. Vernon Scannell. LP

And now, kind friends, what I have wrote. Julia Moore. FaBoCo

And now methinks I could e'en chide myself. Cyril Tourneur. *Fr.* The Revenger's Tragedy. SCP-2

And now she cleans her teeth in the lake. Camping Out. William Empson. OxBTC

And now the dark comes on, all full of chitter noise. The Sound of Night. Maxine W. Kumin. WPE

And now the purple dusk of twilight time. Star Dust. Mitchell Parish. BLSo

"And now to God the Father," he ends. In Church. Thomas Hardy. PoTa

And now, unveiled, the toilet stands displayed. The Toilet. Pope. *Fr.* The Rape of the Lock. NOBE

And now where're he strayes. Richard Crashaw. *Fr.* Saint Mary Magdalene. FaBoCo

And of Columbus. Horace Gregory. OFD

And on This Shore. M. Carl Holman. PoBA

And one morning while in the woods. Between the World and Me. Richard Wright. MiP; NoAM; PoBA; WIF

And Our Gifts to the Seasons. Thomas Clark. SLP

And Paradise does come. Joy. Gavin Bantock. OxBTC

And prytily he wolde pant. John Skelton. *Fr.* Phyllyp Sparowe. ECBV

And semblably, though I go not upright. John Lydgate. *Fr.* The Fall of Princes: Epilogue. OxBM

And several strengths from drowsiness campaigned. The Sermon on the Warpland. Gwendolyn Brooks. BPo; NOBA; PoBA

And shall it never be again, never? Not on nights filled. To See Him Again. Gabriela Mistral, *tr.* by Doris Dana. OLR

And she, being old, fed from a mashed plate. Old Woman. Iain Crichton Smith. OxBTC; PSN

And she—her beauty never made her cold. Frederick Goddard Tuckerman. *Fr.* Sonnets. AmVN

And so deciding everything has been done. Dear Oedipus. Ann Darr. WBN

And so must I lose her whose mind. Prothalamium. Donagh MacDonagh. BIrV

And so one sees all living matter perish. Sonnet. Louise Labé, *tr.* by Frederic Prokosch. LoAS

And so the day drops by; the horizon draws. Frederick Goddard Tuckerman. *Fr.* Sonnets. AmVN

And so the scene degenerates. At the Theatre. John Williams. CoPAm

And so we too came where the rest have come. The Question. F. T. Prince. BoLoP

And some are sulky, while some will plunge. Horses. Kipling. BoAnP; POL

"And something that . . . that is theirs—no longer ours." The Dispossessed. John Berryman. VGW

And spoke: coopers, craftsmen, shepherds. Great God Paused among Men. Daniel Berrigan. MAT

And summer mornings the mute child, rebellious. Eleven. Archibald MacLeish. NCSH

And suppose the darlings get to Mantua. Purgatory. Maxine W. Kumin. CoPAm

And the Communists have nothing to offer but fat cheeks and eyeglasses and lying policemen. Kral Majales. Allen Ginsberg. PiAm

And the Days Are Not Full Enough. Ezra Pound. AKE

And "the earth under our feet." At Kenneth Burke's Place. William Carlos Williams. NOBA

And the first among them. Stony Brook Tavern. Ken Belford. NeAC

And the gud King held forth the way. Bruce Meets Three Men with a Wether. John Barbour. Fr. The Bruce. OxBM

And the next I remembered I'm on a table. The Loser. Charles Bukowski. MiP

And the Old Women Gathered. Mari Evans. PoBA

And the sun wields mercy. The Sun Wields Mercy. Charles Bukowski. MAT

And the terrible. The Vision of Felicity. William Everson. PiAm

And the voices dropped. T. C. Walter Bradford. HeS

And the way goes on in the worn earth. Prologue. Archibald MacLeish. Fr. Conquistador. NoAM

And then? Colors and names of colors. No Way of Knowing. John Ashbery. CAAP

And then he would lift this finest. Out-of-the-Body Travel. Stanley Plumly. AmPA

And Then No More. Friedrich Rückert, tr. fr. German by James Clarence Mangan. BIrV

And then went down to the ship. Canto I. Ezra Pound. NoAM; PAIC; VGW

And Then What. Dave Kelly. POL

And there he was—/ the rhinoceros! Rhinoceros. William Hart-Smith. BoAnP

And therewith kest I doun myn eye ageyne. James I, King of Scotland. Fr. The Kingis Quair. SLP

And they both lived happily ever after . . . After Ever Happily. Ian Serraillier. ECBV

And they went down into the king-city. Nathaniel Tarn. Fr. A Nowhere for Vallejo. TwMBP

And they were there in the City of Fire, enflamed. JuJu. Askia Muhammad Touré. PoBA

And this is how you live: a woman, children. A Primary Ground. Adrienne Rich. WBN

And This Is Love. Paula Reingold. IHMS

And this is the way they ring. Ringing the Bells. Anne Sexton. CAPP; VGW

And this reft house is that, the which he built. On a Ruined House in a Romantic Country [or The House That Jack Built]. Samuel Taylor Coleridge. Fr. Sonnets Attempted in the Manner of Contemporary Writers. AKE; Epi

And thou, Dalhousie, the Great God of War. Unknown. FaBoCo

And thou wert sad—yet I was not with thee. Lines on Hearing that Lady Byron Was Ill. Byron. MBPR

And through the Caribbean Sea. Margaret Danner. BPo

And thus declared that Arab lady. Solomon and the Witch. W. B. Yeats. NoAM

And Thus in Nineveh. Ezra Pound. VGW

And to Her-Without-Bounds I send. Tribal Memories. Robert Duncan. Passages, I. NOBA; PiAm

And to Private Ball it came as if a rigid beam. David Jones. Fr. In Parenthesis. TwMBP

And Was Not Improved. Lerone Bennett, Jr. PoBA

And We Are Strangers to Each Other. Ruth Lisa Schechter. RiTi

And We Conquered. Rob Penny. PoBA

And we were speaking easily and all the light stayed low. In Judgment of the Leaf. Kenneth Patchen. VGW

And What About the Children. Audre Lorde. PoBA

And what did we see, high up there. Ravenna. David Ray. HeS

And what I have learned. Duncan Spoke of a Process. LeRoi Jones. CAPP

And what is love? It is a doll dress'd up. Modern Love. Keats. LoAs; MBPR

And what is love? Misunderstanding, pain. J. V. Cunningham. CoPAm

And what is so rare as a day in June? James Russell Lowell. Fr. The Vision of Sir Launfal. FSFS

And What of Me? Liz Sohappy Bahe. CDW

And What Shall You Say? Joseph Seamon Cotter, Jr. PoBA

And when/the cold white ness. Query. Ebon Dooley. PoBA

And when I say eyes right I want to hear. Weapons Training. Bruce Dawe. CAAP

And when that ballad lady went. A Road in Kentucky. Robert Hayden. NCSH

And When the Green Man Comes. John Haines. ConAP; NCSH

And when we die at last. Heaven and Hell. Unknown, tr. by Edward Field. IPWM

And when you called. The Cry. Grace Cavalieri. AATT

And when you have forgotten the bright bedclothes. When You Have Forgotten Sunday: The Love Story. Gwendolyn Brooks. BPo

And when you try to sleep. For Bill. Geof Hewitt. NeAC

And when you walk the world lifts up its head. To a Very Beautiful Lady. Ruthven Todd. SLP

And where? it was at some moment. Home. John Blight. CAAP

And While We Are Waiting. Carolyn M. Rodgers. JB

And Who Are You? June Jordan. RiTi

And who desires, at large to know my name. George Gascoigne. Fr. The Steel Glass. TVS

And who has seen the moon, who has not seen. Moonrise. D. H. Lawrence. Moon

And who shall separate the dust. Common Dust. Georgia Douglas Johnson. PoBA

And Why Are All the Voices I Hear Divided into Colors? Alta. MMD

And will they always be so tender, her. Swift Love, Sweet Motor. Hildegarde Flanner. WPE

And wilt thou leave [or wylt thow leve] me thus? An Appeal. Sir Thomas Wyatt. AAS; NOBE

And With the Sorrows of This Joyousness. Kenneth Patchen. ECBV

And would you gather turds. A History of Love. William Carlos Williams. VGW

And wylt thow leve me thus? See And wilt thou leave me thus?

And, yeah, brothers. I Sing of Shine. Etheridge Knight. BPo

And yet a kiss (like blubber)'d blur and slip. Love and Death. John Frederick Nims. CoPAm

And yet hath prayer, the heav'n-breathing foliage of faith. Ethick. Robert Bridges. Fr. The Testament of Beauty. OxBTC

And yet the southern whale does some time come. The Whales. Marguerite Young. WPE

And yet this great wink of eternity. Voyages, II. Hart Crane. PAIC; PiAm; PPoe; PPP; VGW

And yet this is a poem. Poem for My Students. Robert L. McRoberts. HeS

And You, Helen. Edward Thomas. BoLoP

And you'll say a nation totters. G. D. H. Cole. *Fr.* Civil Riot. OxBTC

Anderson, Indiana. James L. White. HeS

Andraitx—Pomegranate Flowers. D. H. Lawrence. NoAM

Andrée Rexroth. Kenneth Rexroth. VGW

Andrew Gear of Sunderland. *Unknown.* FaBoCo

Andrew Jackson's Speech. Robert Bly. ConAP

Andrew M'Crie. Robert Fuller Murray. FaBoCo

Ane Metaphoricall Invention of a Tragedie Called Phoenix, *sel.* James I, King of England.
"For I complaine not of sic common cace." SLP

Anear the centre of that northern crest. The City's Queen. James Thomson ("B.V."). The City of Dreadful Night, XXI. NOBE; PFD

Anecdote for Fathers. Wordsworth. MBPR

Anecdote of the Jar. Wallace Stevens. InPK; NoAM; NOBA; PPP

Anemic pictures! Legend. Jules Laforgue, *tr. by* Louis Simpson. Prf

Anemones. Marion Angus. SLP

Angel, The. Blake. *Fr.* Songs of Experience. LAuP; MBPR

Angel. James Merrill. ConAP
(Another Angel.) NoAM

Angel ("Softly and gently, dearly-ransomed soul"). Cardinal Newman. *Fr.* The Dream of Gerontius. PFD

Angel and the girl are met, The. The Annunciation. Edwin Muir. BoReV

Angel came to me and stood by my bedside, An. Nightmare, with Angels. Stephen Vincent Benét. MAT

Angel in the House, The, *sels.* Coventry Patmore.
"Across the sky the daylight crept," *fr.* II, x. GBL
Cathedral Close, The, *fr.* I, i. VPC
County Ball, The, *fr.* II, iii. VPC
Kiss, The, *fr.* II, viii. BoLoP; SoSe
Love at Large, *fr.* I, ii. VPC
Perspective, *fr.* II, i. GBL
Revelation, The, *fr.* I, viii. GBL
Spirit's Epochs, The, *fr.* I, viii. GBL
" 'Twas when the spousal time of May," *fr.* II, vii. GBL
"Whirl'd off at last, for speech I sought," *fr.* II, xi. GBL

Angel of Death, The. *Unknown.* AmFP

"Angel!" said the Heavenly Father, "I have called my servant Jackson." Ascent of T. J. Jackson: a Soldier's Tale. "A. N." BTTM

Angel Surrounded by Paysans. Wallace Stevens. PPP

Angel That Presided o'er My Birth, The. Blake. InPK

Angela Honey (she wrote) I would it were not so. From Lois in London. Angela McCabe. AmPA

Angels, The. Marguerite Young. WPE

Angels are stooping, The. A Cradle Song. W. B. Yeats. LCL

Angels by one sin fell; so, man; how then. Edward Benlowes. *Fr.* Theophila, or Love's Sacrifice, Canto II. SCP-2

Angels in Winter. Nancy Willard. FiCP

Anger rises with metal fillings, The. A Man All Grown Up Is Supposed To. Terry Stokes. AmPA

Angina Pectoris. W. R. Moses. NCSH

Angle-Land David Jones. The Anathemata, III. NoAM; TwMBP

Angle of Geese. N. Scott Momaday. CDW; VW

Angle of Vision. Robert Rendall. OxBTC

Anglosaxon Street. Earle Birney. HeIP

Angola Question Mark. Langston Hughes. BPo

Angrier than my now occasional. A Preface to the Memoirs. James Merrill. NOBA

Angry nettle and the mild, The. The Plum Gatherer. Edna St. Vincent Millay. NoAM

Angry Old Men. Basil Payne. PFIr

Angry Sermon for Any Day in the Week, An. F. Eugene Warren. AATT

Anguish is always there, lurking at night. The Kingdom of Kali. May Sarton. *Fr.* The Invocation to Kali. RiTi

Animal, The. Allan Block. FAF

Animal Alphabet, An. *Unknown.* ECBV

Animal Days. Lee Harwood. TwMBP

Animal I wanted, The. Kenneth Patchen. VGW

Animal moment, when he sorted out her tail, The. John Berryman. LoAs

Animal Poems. Gwendolyn MacEwen. MMD

Animal That Drank Up Sound, The. William Stafford. VGW

Animal, Vegetable and Mineral. Louise Bogan. SBG

Animals, The. Edwin Muir. HeIP

Animals. Walt Whitman. *Fr.* Song of Myself. POL

Animals Are Passing from Our Lives. Philip Levine. NoAM; NOBA

Animals' Christmas, The. Philip Dacey. HeS; NVAP

Animals in the Ark, The. *Unknown.* GBP

Animals That Stand in Dreams, *sel.* Harley Elliott. Panda, The. NeAC

Anita, la Maldita. Teresa A. McCarthy. NPW

Ank'hor Vat. Denis Devlin. BIrV

Ann. Kaye Starbird. ECBV

Ann, Ann!/Come! quick as you can! Alas, Alack! Walter de la Mare. CaYB; OxBChV

Ann wears dresses with ruffles. Ann. Kaye Starbird. ECBV

Anna Elise. *Unknown.* ECBV

Annabel Lee, *parody.* Stanley Huntley. SpRo

Annabel Lee. Poe. AmVN; HeIP; NOBA; PiAm; SpRo

Anne and the Field-Mouse. Ian Serraillier. RAE

Anne Rutledge. Edgar Lee Masters. *Fr.* Spoon River Anthology. NoAM; NOBA; OFD

Annie appears, arrayed. Hats. R. H. W. Dillard. CoPAm

Annie Laurie, *with music.* WilliamDouglass *and* Lady John Scott. BLSH

Annihilation. Conrad Aiken. GBL

Annihilation of Nothing, The. Thom Gunn. NoAM

Anniversarie, The. John Donne. *See* Anniversary, The.

Anniversary, The. Ai. CAAP

Anniversary. Philip Dacey. HeS

Anniversary [*or* Anniversarie], The. John Donne. BoLoP; MetP; NOBE

Anniversary, An. Thomas Hardy. OxBTC

Anno Domini. E. M. Walker. POL

Annot and John, *orig. and mod. English prose. Unknown.* OxBM

Annotations of Auschwitz, *sel.* Peter Porter.
"London is full of chickens, on electric spits." OxBTC

Announced by all the trumpets of the sky. The Snow-Storm. Emerson. AmVN: FSFS; IPWM; NOBA; PiAm; PPoD; Prf; VoPo

Annunciation. John Donne. SCP-1

Annunciation, The. Edwin Muir. BoReV

Annunciation, The ("Gabriel, from Hevene-King"). *Unknown.* OxBM

Annus Mirabilis, *sels.* Dryden.
Fire of London.
"At length the crackling noise and dreadful blaze." SCP-1

London after the Great Fire, 1666.  NOBE
War.  SCP-1
Anomie.  Patricia Ramsey.  AATT
Anon out of the north-est the noys bigynes.  Jonah Is Cast into the Sea.  *Unknown.  Fr.* Patience.  OxBM
Anonymous.  Anne Hazlewood Brady.  WBN
Anonymous as cherubs.  Two Voices in a Meadow.  Richard Wilbur.  PBMP
Anonymous Drawing.  Donald Justice.  HeIP
Another ("As loving hind that, hartless, wants her deer").  Anne Bradstreet.  *See* Letter to Her Husband, Absent upon Public Employment.
Another ("Yes, every poet is a fool").  Matthew Prior.  FaBoCo
Another Angel.  James Merrill.  *See* Angel.
Another armored animal—scale.  The Pangolin.  Marianne Moore.  NoAM; NOBA
Another Attempt at the Trick.  Cynthia Macdonald.  WBN
Another cove of shale.  On the Marginal Way.  Richard Wilbur.  CAPP; NOBA
Another Epitaph on an Army of Mercenaries.  "Hugh MacDiarmid."  NoAM
Another Face.  Ray A. Young Bear.  CDW
Another Grace for a Child.  Robert Herrick.  *See* Grace for a Child.
Another hill town.  Hotel Paradiso e Commerciale.  John Malcolm Brinnin.  NoAM
Another Life, *sel.*  Derek Walcott.
Runner at Sauteurs, The.  OBP
Another Load.  William Harrold.  HeS
Another Night on the Porch Swing.  Cathleen Quirk.  NMM
Another on Her.  Robert Herrick.  SpRo
Another season centers on this place.  The Gourd Dancer.  N. Scott Momaday.  CDW
Another September.  Thomas Kinsella.  BIrV
Another shout from the wharves.  Hilda Doolittle ("H.D.").  *Fr.* Helen in Egypt.  NOBA
Another Song ("The winter of my infancy being over-past").  Ann Collins.  SCP-2
Another Song ("Merry the green, the green hill shall be merry").  Donald Justice.  ConAP; VGW
Another summer! Our Independence.  Fourth of July in Maine.  Robert Lowell.  CAPP
Another uncle/was a pathological liar.  Family 8.  Lyn Lifshin.  NeAC
Another woman: a change of tears.  Theodore Roethke.  POL
Another Year Come.  W. S. Merwin.  OFD
Answer, The.  George Herbert.  Epi
Answer [*or* Answers] to a Child's Question.  Samuel Taylor Coleridge.  ECBV; OxBChV
Answer to a Man's Question, An, "What Can I Do about Women's Liberation?"  Susan Griffin.  MMD
Answer to a Sonnet Ending Thus.  Keats.  MBPR
Answer to an Invitation to Cambridge, An.  Abraham Cowley.  PAIC
Answer to Chloe Jealous.  Matthew Prior.  NOBE
Answer to Yo/ Question.  Sonia Sanchez.  BPo; RiTi
Answering.  Robert Duncan.  PiAm
Answers.  Elizabeth Jennings.  OxBTC
Answers to a Child's Question.  Samuel Taylor Coleridge.  *See* Answer to a Child's Question.
Ant on the tablecloth, An.  Departmental.  Robert Frost.  HeIP; InPK; NOBA; WIF
Ante-Bellum Sermon, An.  Paul Laurence Dunbar.  BPo
Anthem for Doomed Youth.  Wilfred Owen.  BuTh; HeIP; NoAM; NOBE; OxBTC; PPoD; PPP; PSN; SoSe; WIF, 3 *versions*

Anthony and Cleopatra, *sel.*  Shakespeare.
"Barge she sat in, like a burnished throne, The, " *fr.* II, ii.  PPoe
Antichrist, or the Reunion of Christendom: an Ode.  G. K. Chesterton.  FaBoCo; NOBE
Anticipation of Sharks.  Diane Wakoski.  MAT
Antigone I.  Herbert Martin.  PoBA
Antigone VI.  Herbert Martin.  PoBA
Antiplatonick, The.  John Cleveland.  MetP; SCP-2
Antiquary, The.  Joseph Campbell.  OxBTC
Antiquary.  John Donne.  InPK
Antique people are down in the dungeons, The.  Goodbye and Hello.  Tim Buckley.  WIF
Anti-Semanticist, The.  Everett Hoagland.  BPo
Antisong.  Phyllis Webb.  MMD
Antlered forests, The.  Ank'hor Vat.  Denis Devlin.  BIrV
Anton Leeuwenhoek was Dutch.  The Microscope.  Maxine W. Kumin.  PoTa
Antonio's Revenge, *sel.*  John Marston.
"Being laid upon her bed she grasped my hand."  SCP-2
Antrim.  Robinson Jeffers.  BIrV; NOBA; VGW
Ants, The.  John Clare.  BoAnP
Ants and Others.  Adrien Stoutenburg.  BoAnP
Ants on inert cricket crawling.  Haiku.  José Juan Tablada, *tr. by* Samuel Beckett.  PBMP
Anxious Thought.  Thomas Hoccleve.  *Fr.* De Regimine Principum.  OxBM
Any Complaints?  Vernon Scannell.  OxBTC
Any Golf Championship.  Grantland Rice.  SPo
Any hound a porcupine nudges.  The Porcupine.  Ogden Nash.  ECBV
Any of the several names.  Eulogy for Populations.  Ron Welburn.  PoBA
Anybody Could Write This Poem. All You Have to Say Is Yes.  Alta.  MMD
Anyone Lived in a Pretty How Town.  E. E. Cummings.  AnMo; InPK; IPWM; NOBA; NowV; PAIC; VGW
Anything that promises good.  First Hymn.  John Gill.  NeAC
Anything this recognizable.  Downy Hair in the Shape of a Flame.  Coleman Barks.  *Fr.* Body Poems.  NVAP
Anywhere I look/ the water has dominion.  Dingman's Marsh.  John Moore.  NCSH
Aoibhinn, A Leabhrain, Do Thriall.  *Unknown, tr. fr. Irish by* Flann O'Brien.  BIrV
Ap Huw's Testament.  R. S. Thomas.  BuTh
Apartment House.  Gerald Raftery.  SFF
Apeneck Sweeney spreads his knees.  Sweeney Among the Nightingales.  T. S. Eliot.  HeIP; InPK; NoAM; NOBA; NOBE; PAIC; PPP
Apocalypse in Black and White.  Robert Pack.  CoPAm
Apollo and Daphne.  Yvor Winters.  PiAm
Apollo 8.  John Berryman.  Moon
Apologia pro Vita Sua.  A. R. Ammons.  NOBA
Apologia pro Vita Sua.  Samuel Taylor Coleridge.  MBPR
Apologia pro Vita Sua.  Pope.  *Fr.* Epistle to Dr. Arbuthnot.  NOBE
Apologia pro Vita Sua.  Sedulius Scottus, *tr. fr. Medieval Latin by* Helen Waddell.  BIrV
Apologue.  Tony Connor.  BoLoP
Apology.  J. V. Cunningham.  PiAm
Apology, The.  Emerson.  AmVN
Apology, An.  William Morris.  *Fr.* The Earthly Paradise.  PAIC; VPC
Apology Addressed to the Critical Reviewers, The.  Charles Churchill.  LAuP
Apology for Apostasy?  Etheridge Knight.  NeAC

Apology for Bad Dreams. Robinson Jeffers. NOBA

Apology for the Fall. E. R. Cole. AATT

Apology for Understatement. John Wain. LoAs; OxBTC

Apology. Hands shaping air. Lynn Strongin. *Fr.* First Aspen. RiTi

Apostrophe to Man. Edna St. Vincent Millay. PBMP; SBG

Apostrophe to Vincentine, The. Wallace Stevens. LoAs

Apparent Failure. Robert Browning. NOBE

Apparently with no surprise. Emily Dickinson. PPP; SoSe; WIF

Apparition, The. John Donne. GBL; HeIP; NOBE; PAIC; SCP-1

Apparition, The. Michael Heffernan. HeS

Apparition, The. Theodore Roethke. AIW; LoAs

Apparition, The. Chris Wallace-Crabbe. MAuV

Apparition of these faces in the crowd, The. In a Station of the Metro. Ezra Pound. BBGO; HeIP; InPK; NoAM; NOBA; PiAm; PPoD; VGW; WIF

Appeal, The. Samuel Daniel. OLR

Appeal, An. Sir Thomas Wyatt. NOBE ("And wylt thow leve me thus?") AAS

Appeal to Cats in the Business of Love, An. Thomas Flatman. GBL; PCat; SCP-2

Appearance, An. Sylvia Plath. CAPP

Appetite, The. Yom Kippur: Fasting. Ruth Whitman. OFD

Applauding youths laughed with young prostitutes. The Harlem Dancer. Claude McKay. BPo; IPWM; NoAM

Apple Blight. Paul Zimmer. VGW

Apple Gathering, An. Christina Rossetti. OLR

Apple-Logia. Marian Frances Brand. AATT

Apple on its bough is her desire, The. Garden Abstract. Hart Crane. PSN

Apples. Shirley Kaufman. NMM; RiTi

Apples be Ripe. *Unknown.* GBP

Apples of Sodom and Gomorrah, The. Barbara A. Holland. WBN

Apples to Keep. Frances Frost. ECBV

Applicant, The. Sylvia Plath. MAT; NMM; NOBA; Psy; SBG

Apply for the position (I've forgotten now for what) I had to marry. In Order To. Kenneth Patchen. PPoD

Appoggiatura. Donald Jeffrey Hayes. PoBA

Appointment, The. Maxine W. Kumin. NMM

Appointment, The. L.A.G. Strong. OxBTC

Appology, The. Countess of Winchilsea. SBG

Appreciate/the wide pavements. Good Morning. Layle Silbert. NPW

Apprehension this spring . . . the leaves, the leaves. Homage and Lament for Ezra Pound in Captivity. Robert Duncan. NOBA

Apprentice Painter, The. Jack Myers. AmPA

Approach to the bar, The. Pole Vaulter. David Allan Evans. NVAP

Approaches, The. W. S. Merwin. NOBA; Prf

Approve the traveler who never went. The Travelers. James Reeves. POL

April. Samuel Thompson. BIrV

April. Yvor Winters. RFM

April 1885. Robert Bridges. OxBTC

April Inventory. W. D. Snodgrass. CAPP; NoAM; NowV; PPoe; SFF; WIF

April Is in My Mistress' Face. *Unknown.* GBL; HeIP

April is the cruellest month, breeding. The Waste Land. T. S. Eliot. NoAM; NOBA; NOBE; OxBTC; PiAm; PPoe

April 1962. Paul Goodman. VGW

April Rain Song. Langston Hughes. LCL

April Rise. Laurie Lee. LP; MPo

Apron, The. Stuart Friebert. FiCP

Aprons of Silence. Carl Sandburg. NoAM; NOBA

Aquarium, San Francisco, The. V. Sackville-West. SBG

Ar ne couthe ich sorwe none. A Prisoner's Prayer. *Unknown.* OxBM

Arabesque. Fred Johnson. PoBA

Arabia. John Meade Falkner. OxBTC

Aran Islands. Irving Layton. NeAC

Arc Inside and Out, The. A. R. Ammons. NoAM

Arcades, *sel.* Milton.
  Song: "Nymphs and shepherds dance no more." LoAs

Arcadia, *sels.* Sir Philip Sidney.
  Bargain, The. NOBE
    ("My true love hath my heart, and I have his.") BoLoP; GBL; LoAs
  Sestina: "Farewell, Oh sun, Arcadia's clearest light." PAIC
  When Two Suns Do Appear. Moon
  "Ye goat-herd gods that love the grassy mountains." NOBE

Arches and Shadows. Annie Dillard. CTBA

Archie O Cawfield. *Unknown.* AmFP

Archy and Mehitabel, *sels.* Don Marquis.
  Archy Confesses. SS
  Cheerio My Deario. FaBoCo
  Freddy the Rat Perishes. MiP
  Old Trouper, The. FaBoCo

Arctic honey blabbed over the report causing darkness, The. Leaving the Atocha Station. John Ashbery. CAPP

"Arcturus" is his other name. Emily Dickinson. NOBA; WIF

Are at the end of our street. They. Donald Finkel. CoPAm

Are the desolate, dark weeks. These. William Carlos Williams. NoAM; NOBA; PBMP; TCP

Are the living so much use. At the Cenotaph. "Hugh MacDiarmid."OBP

Are Then Regalities All Gilded Masks? Keats. *Fr.* Endymion, III. Moon

Are there not twelve whole hours in every day. The Day of Denial. Jones Very. NOBA

Are there two things, of all which men possess. To Asra. Samuel Taylor Coleridge. MBPR

Are these the astronauts who carried. A Farewell to the Moon. Ed Ochester. Moon

Are these the strings that poets say. The Cat and the Lute. Thomas Master. PCat

Are they clinging to their crosses. Antichrist, or the Reunion of Christendom: an Ode. G. K. Chesterton. FaBoCo; NOBE

Are they shadows that we see? Shadows. Samuel Daniel. *Fr.* Tethys' Festival. NOBE

"Are you awake, Gemelli." Star-Talk. Robert Graves. FSFS; OXBTC

Are You Born?—I. Muriel Rukeyser. LoAs

Are you going to Scarborough Fair? Scarborough Fair. *Unknown.* BLSo

Are you going to Whittingham Fair? Whittingham Fair. *Unknown.* AIW; GBP

"Are you sad to think how often." Middle-Aged Conversation. A. S. J. Tessimond. POL

Are You the New Person Drawn Toward Me? Walt Whitman. LoAs; NoAM; PPP

Are you what your faire lookes expresse? Thomas Campion. AAS

Arethusa. Shelley. MBPR

Argument, An. Thomas Moore. BoLoP

Argument of His Book, The. Robert Herrick. HeIP; OBP

Argus and Ulysses ("Argus was a puppy"). Eleanor Farjeon. ECBV

Ariel. Sylvia Plath. AnMo; HeIP; InPK; NoAM; NOBA; PiAm; Psy

Ariel to Miranda:—Take. With a Guitar, to Jane. Shelley. MBPR

Ariel's Song: "Come unto these yellow sands." Shakespeare. *Fr.* The Tempest, I, ii. NOBE
("Come unto these yellow sands.") HeIP; SpRo

Ariel's Song: "Full fathom five thy father lies." Shakespeare. *See* Full Fathom Five Thy Father Lies.

Ariel's Song: "Where the bee sucks, there suck I." Shakespeare. *Fr.* The Tempest, V, i. NOBE; SoSe
("Where the bee sucks, there suck I.") HeIP; LCL

Aristophanes' Symposium. Rita Mae Brown. IHMS

Arizona. *Unknown.* AmFP

Arizona Highways. James Welch. CDW

Arizona Poems, *sel.* John Gould Fletcher.
Rain in the Desert, VI. NCSH

Arizona Ruins. Lyn Lifshin. RiTi

Arkansas Traveller, The, *with music.* Mose Case. PSoN

Arlo Will. Edgar Lee Masters. *Fr.* Spoon River Anthology. PBMP

Armada, 1588, The. John Wilson. OxBChV

Armadillo, The. Elizabeth Bishop. NoAM; NOBA; PiAm; VGW

Armagh. W. R. Rodgers. NoAM; PFIr

Armed we go. we are the dancers. A Tryptich for Jan Bockelson. John Oliver Simon. NeAC

Armistice. Paul Dehn. OxBTC

Arms and the Boy. Wilfred Owen. OBP; PBMP

Arms seem clumsy at first, The. The Fever Toy. Charles Wright. AmPA

Army Corps on the March, An. Walt Whitman. InPS; PiAm; PPoe

Army Goes Rolling Along, The, *with music.* Edmund L. Gruber *and* H. W. Arberg. BLSH

Army of the Lord. I'm a Soldier in the Army of the Lord. *Unknown.* AmFP

Arnold, warm with God. The Last Warmth of Arnold. Gregory Corso. NoAM; SA

Around, above my bed, the pitch-dark fly. Truth. Howard Nemerov. CoPAm

Around, around,/ All directions go around. The Direction. May Miller. PPoD

Around me roar and crash the pagan isms. The Pagan Isms. Claude McKay. BPo

Around me the images of thirty years. The Municipal Gallery Revisited. W. B. Yeats. OxBTC

Around Thanksgiving. Rolfe Humphries. OFD

Around the fire one wintry night. The Beggar Man. Lucy Aikin. OxBChV

Around the fireplace, pointing at the fire. On Falling Asleep by Firelight. William Meredith. NoAM

Around them my cleanliness stinks. At Every Gas Station There Are Mechanics. Stephen Dunn. NVAP

Arraign'd before his worldly gods. The Execution of Cornelius Vane. Sir Herbert Read. NoAM

Arraignment of a Lover, The. George Gascoigne. AAS

Arraignment of Paris, The, *sel.* George Peele.
Oenone and Paris. NOBE

Arrest of Oscar Wilde at the Cadogan Hotel, The. John Betjeman. AIW; NoAM; OxBTC

Arrival of the Bee Box, The. Sylvia Plath. PSN; TCP

Arrivals. Stuart Conn. SLP

Arrive. The Ladies from the Ladies' Betterment League. The Lovers of the Poor. Gwendolyn Brooks. CAPP; NoAM; NOBA

Arrived upon the downs of asphodel. Classic Encounter. "Christopher Caudwell." OxBTC

Arrows of the narrow moon flock down direct, The. Communion of Saints: the Poor Bastard under the Bridge. Marie Ponsot. VGW

Arroyo. Tom Weatherly. PoBA

Ars Poetica. Archibald MacLeish. HeIP; InPK; IPWM; NOBA; PAIC; PiAm; SFF; SoSe; TH; WIF

Ars Poetica: Some Recent Criticism. James Wright. CAAP

Arsonist of flesh, An. A Small Tribute. William Harrold. HeS

Art. Ambrose Bierce. InPK

Art. Denise Levertov. CAPP

Art. Herman Melville. NOBA

Art and Civilization. Robert Conquest. NoAM

Art of Enforced Deprivation, The. Alta. MMD

Art of Happiness, The. Edward Young. *Fr.* Night Thoughts, VIII. POL

Art of Poetry, The. Dennis Trudell. NowV

Art of Sinking in Poetry, The, *sel.* Pope.
"Who knocks at the door?" AnMo

Art thou a Statist in the van. A Poet's Epitaph. Wordsworth. MBPR

Art thou afraid the adorer's prayer. Walter Savage Landor. GBL

Art thou gone in haste? Love Pursued. *Unknown. Fr.* The Thracian Wonder. GBL

Art thou pale for weariness. To the Moon. Shelley. MBPR; Moon; PBMP; PPP

Art thou poor, yet hast thou golden slumbers? Thomas Dekker. *Fr.* The Pleasant Comedy of Patient Grisell, I, i. InPS

Artemis, Artemis: there is fading. The Night-Walker. Horace Gregory. Moon

Artery, The. Les A. Murray. *Fr.* Walking to the Cattle-Place. CAAP

Artery of the Sea. Napoleon St. Cyr. FAF

Arthritic farmer and a calf watch Dr. Graves, The. These Obituaries of Rattlesnakes Being Eaten by the Hogs. Roger Weingarten. AmPA

Arthur McBride. *Unknown.* GBP; PeBB

Arthur Mitchell. Marianne Moore. PiAm

Arthur O'Bower has broken his bands. *Unknown.* GBP

Arthur Ridgewood, M.D. Frank Marshall Davis. BPo

Artillery. George Herbert. InPS

Artisan didn't collect his gear and say, The. The Makers. Richard Kell. PFIr

Artist, An. Robinson Jeffers. VGW

Artist, The. William Carlos Williams. InPS

Artist is the creator of beautiful things, The. Preface to the Picture of Dorian Gray. Oscar Wilde. WIF

Arts and Sciences, *sels.* Samuel Butler.
"Nature/ leaks like a tube and not a boat." SCP-2
"Rules/ Were made for novices and fools." SCP-2

Art's Variety. David McFadden. NeAC

Arundel Tomb, An. Philip Larkin. HeIP; MPo; PPP

As a boy I collected stamps. On Seeing a Stamp from the Democratic Republic of Vietnam. Leslie Woolf Hedley. NowV

As a boy with a richness of needs I wandered. Clifford Dyment. OxBTC

As a child/I bought a red scarf. Four Sheets to the Wind and a One-Way Ticket to France. Conrad Kent Rivers. BPo; PoBA

As a child I was. Woman. Elouise Loftin. PoBA

As a child of cedar, hemlock, and the sea. No One Remembers Abandoning the Village of White Fir. Duane Niatum. CDW

As a Child Seeing a Cardinal. John Gill. NeAC

As a dare-gale skylark scanted in a dull cage. The Caged Skylark. Gerard Manley Hopkins. AnMo; SoSe

As a fond mother, when the day is o'er. Nature. Longfellow. AmVN

As a friend to the children commend me the Yak. The Yak. Hilaire Belloc. OxBChV

As a Great Prince. Edwin Honig. NoAM

As a kid I believed in democracy: I. John Berryman. PPoD

As a little fat man of Bombay. *Unknown.* OxBChV

As a pale phantom with a lamp. Moonlight. Longfellow. Moon

As a Plane Tree by the Water. Robert Lowell. NoAM; NOBA

As a rare painter draws, for pleasure, here. 1st Week 5th Day. Joshua Sylvester. *Fr.* Du Bartas His Divine Weeks and Works. SCP-2

As a white candle. The Old Woman. Joseph Campbell. OxBTC; WIF

As Adam Early in the Morning. Walt Whitman. AmVN

As an intruder I trudged with careful innocence. Old Mansion. John Crowe Ransom. NOBA

As an old traveller, I am indebted to paper-bound thrillers. Calling Spring VII-MMMC. Ogden Nash. FaBoCo

As an unperfect actor on the stage. Sonnets, XXIII. Shakespeare. OBP

As aw was gannin to Durham. Durham Old Women. *Unknown.* GBP

As Bad as a Mile. Philip Larkin. InPK

As beautiful Kitty one morning was tripping. Kitty of Coleraine. *Unknown.* PoTa

As bird to nest, when, moodily. Sarasvati. James Stephens. NoAM

As Birds Are Fitted to the Boughs. Louis Simpson. BoLoP; OLR; WIF

As cool as the pale wet leaves. Alba. Ezra Pound. GBL; PiAm

As day did darken on the dewless grass. The Wind at the Door. William Barnes. GBL

As difference blends into identity. Josephine Miles. NoAM

As down the road she wambled slow. Bessie Bobtail. James Stephens. PFIr

As down through Cupid's garden for pleasure I did walk. The 'Prentice Boy. *Unknown.* AmFP

As down through Moore's field one evening I went. The Silk Weaver's Daughter. *Unknown.* AmFP

As down thru Sally's garden one evening as I chanced to stray. Sally's Garden. *Unknown.* AmFP

As, even today, the airman, feeling the plane sweat. Icarus. Valentin Iremonger. BIrV

As fair as morn, as fresh as May. *Unknown.* GBL

As Freedom Is a Breakfastfood. E. E. Cummings. MAT; NOBA; VGW

As from an [*or* their] ancestral oak. Similes for Two Political Characters of 1819. Shelley. InPS; MBPR

As from the darkening gloom a silver dove. Keats. MBPR

As gay for you to take your father's ax. To a Young Wretch. Robert Frost. OFD

As He Lay Dying. Randolph Stow. BoAnP

As he learned the land. The Farmer. Terry Stokes. POL

As he left the ship he saw this, only this. The Descent of the Vulture. Marya Zaturenska. WPE

As he moves the mine-detector. Hunting Civil War Relics at Nimblewill Creek. James Dickey. ConAP

As he trudged along to school. The Story of Johnny Head-in-Air. Heinrich Hoffmann. OxBChV

As Hermes once took to his feathers light. On a Dream. Keats. LoAs

As I am,/ I should be able to. Missing Beat. Carolyn M. Rodgers. JB

As I am a Rhymer. On My Joyful Departure. Samuel Taylor Coleridge. FaBoCo

As I came down Talbingo Hill. Bullocky Bill. *Unknown.* MAuV

As I came down the Cano' gate. Merry May the Keel Row. *Unknown.* GBP

As I came home through Drury's woods. Cold Fear. Elizabeth Madox Roberts. WPE

As I came in by Tiviot side. The Generous Gentleman. Allan Ramsay. SLP

As I came over the humpbacked hill. The Green Fiddler. Rachel Field. PoTa

As I came to the edge of the woods. Come In. Robert Frost. NOBA

As I drive to the junction of lane and highway. At Castle Boterel. Thomas Hardy. NOBE

As I Ebb'd with the Ocean of Life. Walt Whitman. NOBA

As I in hoary winter's night stood shivering in the snow. The Burning Babe. Robert Southwell. BoReV; HeIP; InPS; NOBE; OBP; PPoe; Pfr

As I lay asleep in Italy. The Mask of Anarchy. Shelley. MBPR

As I lay in a winter's night. The Debate of the Body and the Soul. *Unknown.* PAIC

As I Lay with My Head in Your Lap Camerado. Walt Whitman. BuTh

As I lie alone. *Unknown.* SFF

As I lie here in the sun. Jonah. Randall Jarrell. CoPAm

As I looked out one May morning. The Princess and the Gypsies. Frances Cornford. PoTa

As I one evening sat before my cell. Artillery. George Herbert. InPS

As I pass through my incarnations in every age and race. The Gods of the Copybook Headings. Kipling. OBP; OxBTC

As I roved out on a May morning. Johnny's the Lad I Love. *Unknown.* AIW

As I roved out one summer's morning, speculating most curiously. Colleen Rue *Unknown.* BIrV

As I sat at the cafe, I said to myself. Spectator Ab Extra [*or* How Pleasant It Is to Have Money]. Arthur Hugh Clough. *Also in* Dipsychus. FaBoCo; NOBE; VPC

As I sat in a lonesome grove. The Little Dove. *Unknown.* AmFP

As I sat on a sunny bank. Sunny Bank. *Unknown.* GBP

As I sd to my/ friend. I Know a Man. Robert Creeley. CAPP; ConAP; CoPAm; Epi; InPK; InPS; MAT; NOBA; PPoD; PPP; TCP

As I sit looking out of a window of the building. The Instruction Manual. John Ashbery. NoAM; NOBA

As I Step over a Puddle at the End of Winter, I Think of an Ancient Chinese Governor. James Wright. CAPP; TCP

As I strole the city, oft I. Swift. *Fr.* The Legion Club. BIrV

As I strolled out one evening just as the sun went down. The Farmer and the Shanty Boy. *Unknown.* AmFP

As I talk with learned people. A Spade Is Just a Spade. Walter Everette Hawkins. PoBA

As I walked by a forest side. Stag-Hunt. *Unknown.* OxBM

As I walked out in Dublin City. The Spanish Lady in Dublin City. *Unknown.* RDB

As I Walked Out in the Streets of Laredo. *Unknown.* *See* Cowboy's Lament, The

As I Walked Out One Evening. W. H. Auden. AIW; HeIP; InPK; NOBE; PBMP; WIF

As I walked out one evening, all in the month of May. The Banks of Claudy. *Unknown.* AmFP

As I walked out one evening down by the Strawberry Lane. Captain Wedderburn's Courtship. *Unknown.* AmFP

As I walked out one May morning. The Lover Proved False. *Unknown.* AmFP

As I walked out one May morning. The Royal Fisherman. *Unknown.* GBP; PeBB

As I Walked Out One Morning. *Unknown.* AmFP

As I walked out one morning in May.  Archie O Cawfield. *Unknown.*  AmFP

As I walked out one morning, just as day was dawning.  As I Walked Out One Morning.  *Unknown.*  AmFP

As I walked out that sultry night.  Full Moon.  Robert Graves. NOBE

As I walked over London Bridge.  Georgie.  *Unknown.*  AIW

As I walked with my friend.  Columbus.  Louis Simpson.  MPo

As I wandered on the beach.  The Great Blue Heron.  Carolyn Kizer.  WPE

As I wandered through the eight hundred and eight streets of the city.  Streets.  Amy Lowell.  RiTi; SBG

As I was a-gwine down the road.  *See* As I was goin' . . .

As I was a-hoeing, a-hoeing my land.  The Six Badgers.  Robert Graves.  RAE

As I was a-roving one morning in spring.  The Mantle So Green. *Unknown.*  AmFP

As I was a-walking/ One morning in spring.  The Pretty Ploughboy.  *Unknown.*  AIW; GBP

As I was a walking one morning for pleasure.  Whoopee-Ti-Yi-Yo! *Unknown.*  BLSH

As I was a-walking to Nottingham Fair.  Nottingham Fair. *Unknown.*  AmFP

As I was fishing off Pondy Point.  Jim Desterland.  Hyam Plutzik. VGW

As I was goin' [*or* a-gwine] down the road.  Turkey in the Straw. *Unknown.*  BLSo; GBP

As I was going by Charing Cross.  King Charles the First. *Unknown.*  GBP

As I was going down the lane.  Ballad of No Proper Man.  Daniel Hoffman.  MAT

As I Was Going Out One Day.  *Unknown.*  CaYB

As I was going over Mulberry Mountain.  Mulberry Mountain. *Unknown.*  AmFP

As I was going to Derby.  The Derby Ram.  *Unknown.*  GBP

As I was going to St. Ives.  Mother Goose.  MG

As I was going up the hill.  Jack the Piper.  *Unknown.*  GBP

As I was going up the stair.  A Case.  *Unknown.*  FaBoCo

As I Was Laying on the Green.  *Unknown.*  InPK

As I was musing by myself alone.  Mirth and Melancholy. Margaret Cavendish, Duchess of Newcastle.  WPE

As I was travelling toward the city of satisfactions.  The City of Satisfactions.  Daniel Hoffman.  Prf

As I was wa'king all alone.  *See* As I was walking all alone.

As I was walking/ I came upon.  Kore.  Robert Creeley.  ConAP; InPK; InPS

As I was walking all alane.  The Twa Corbies.  *Unknown.*  AIW; Epi; InPK; PAIC; PBMP; PoTa; PPP; SoSe

As I was walking [*or* wa'king] all alone.  The Wee Wee Man. *Unknown.*  AIW; GBP; PeBB

As I was walking down by the seashore.  The Lover's Lament for Her Sailor.  *Unknown.*  AmFP

As I was walking down the street.  Buffalo Gals.  *Unknown.* BLSo

As I was washing under a span.  The Lover's Shirt.  *Unknown, tr. by* Gwyn Williams.  BuTh

As I went a-walking one fine summer's morning.  The Shoofly. Felix O'Hare.  AmFP

As I went down to Dymchurch Wall.  In Romney Marsh.  John Davidson.  OxBTC

As I went down to the huckleberry picnic.  The Kicking Mule. *Unknown.*  AmFP

As I went down to the mowin' field.  Fod.  *Unknown.*  AmFP

As I went out a crow.  The Last Word of a Bluebird.  Robert Frost.  LCL; RAE

As I went out a-walking to breathe the pleasant air.  Rolly Trudum. *Unknown.*  AmFP

As I went out one May morning.  Bird in a Cage.  *Unknown.* GBP

As I went out, so I came in.  *Unknown.*  GBP

As I went out walking for pleasure one day.  The Little Mohea. *Unknown.*  AmFP

As I went owre the Hill o' Hoos.  *Unknown.*  GBP

As I went up to Craigbilly Fair.  Craigbilly Fair.  *Unknown.*  GBP

As I were a-walking upon a fine day.  Because I Were Shy. *Unknown.*  PoTa

As I wipe the dust off my face.  The Unexpected.  Ai.  CAAP

As if a cast of grain leapt back to the hand.  An Event.  Richard Wilbur.  CoPAm

As If a Phantom Caress'd Me.  Walt Whitman.  GBL

As if engraved upon the dawn.  Storm's End.  Leonora Speyer. TH

As if I carried a charm.  Her Going.  Shirley Kaufman.  RiTi

As if I needed some means to maintain.  The Dodo.  Edward Kessler.  PPoD

As if it were a scene made-up by the mind.  Often I Am Permitted to Return to a Meadow.  Robert Duncan.  HeIP; NOBA; PiAm

As if to symptoms we may credit give.  Michael Drayton.  *Fr.* To Master George Sandys, Treasurer for the English Colony in Virginia.  SCP-2

As If Trooth.  Robert Bloom.  AATT

As imperceptibly as grief.  Emily Dickinson.  FSFS; NOBA

As in the cool-air'd road I come by.  My Love's Guardian Angel. William Barnes.  GBL

As in the house I sate.  Poverty.  Thomas Traherne.  Prf

As in the lonely night.  The Setting of the Moon.  Giacomo Leopardi, *tr. by* John Heath-Stubbs.  Moon

As in Their Time.  Louis MacNeice.  POL

As Into the Garden.  A. E. Housman.  PoTa

As it befell on a bright holiday.  The Bitter Withy.  *Unknown.* GBP; PeBB

As it fell one holy-day.  Little Musgrave and Lady Barnard. *Unknown.*  PeBB

As it fell out one May morning.  The Holy Well.  *Unknown.* GBP; PeBB

As it fell upon a day.  Philomel.  Richard Barnfield.  *Fr.* The Passionate Pilgrim.  GBL; NOBE

As It Looked Then.  E. A. Robinson.  NoAM

As It Should Be.  Tom Meschery.  SPo

As Jack, the jolly plowboy, was plowing of his land.  The Jolly Plowboy.  *Unknown.*  AmFP

As Jack walked out of London city.  Jack the Jolly Tar. *Unknown.*  AmFP

As Julia once a-slumbering lay.  The Captived Bee; or, the Little Filcher.  Robert Herrick.  SCP-1

As landscapes richen after rain, the eye.  Foliage of Vision.  James Merrill.  VGW

As late I lay in slumber's shadowy vale.  Burke.  Samuel Taylor Coleridge.  *Fr.* Sonnets on Eminent Characters.  MBPR

As late I rambled in the happy fields.  To a Friend Who Sent Me Some Roses.  Keats.  MBPR

As love and I, late harbour'd in one inn.  Michael Drayton.  GBL

As loving hind that (hartless) wants her deer.  A Letter to Her Husband, Absent upon Public Employment.  Anne Bradstreet. SBG; SCP-2; WPE

As May was opening the rosebuds.  Birth of the Foal.  Ferenc Juhász, *tr. by* David Wevill.  BoAnP

As men oft laugh at little babes when they.  Michael Drayton.  *Fr.* To My Noble Friend Master William Browne: of the Evil Time.  SCP-2

As much as he could learn has done no good.  Lesson of the Master.  William Dickey.  CoPAm

As my new life begins, I start smiling at the people around me. Farewell to Kurdistan. Rosemary Tonks. OxBTC

As night creates the sun, silence. The Roads. Stephen Stepanchev. SA

As on a dark guitar. Ballad of Love and Blood. Angel Miguel Queremel, *tr. by* Rolfe Humphries. LoAs

As on the cross, the Saviour hung. Deep Spring. *Unknown.* AmFP

As on the highway's quiet edge. The Coast: Norfolk. Frances Cornford. OxBTC

As once, if not with light regard. Ode on the Poetical Character. William Collins. LAuP

As one grows older and Caesar, Hitler. The Walk Home. Reed Whittemore. ConAP

As One Non-Combatant to Another. George Orwell. OxBTC

As praiseworthy/ the power of breathing. Lorine Niedecker. VGW

As round their dying father's bed. The Father and His Children. *Unknown.* OxBChV

As seventh sign, the antique heavens show. Feast of the Ram's Horn. Harvey Shapiro. VGW

As she jumped up to open the door. Motionless Swaying. Yannis Ritsos, *tr. by* Nikos Stangos. TSWA

As she shook her little fist. The Death of the Novel. David Young. AmPA

As ships, becalmed at eve, that lay. Qua Cursum Ventus. Arthur Hugh Clough. VPC

As silent as a mirror is believed. Legend. Hart Crane. NoAM

As simple an act. Way Out West. LeRoi Jones. PoBA

As slowly and sadly I strayed by the river. Lost Jimmie Whalen. *Unknown.* AmFP

As soft as silk, as white as milk. *Unknown.* GBP

As some brave admiral, in former war. The Disabled Debauchee. Earl of Rochester. BoLoP; PPP

As some fond virgin, whom her mother's care. Epistle to Miss Blount, on Her Leaving the Town after the Coronation. Pope. BoLoP; NOBE; PPP; SoSe

As soon as/ I speak, I. The Pattern. Robert Creeley. PPoD

As soon as I'm in bed at night. Mrs. Brown. Rose Fyleman. OxBChV

As sunbeams pierce the glass and, streaming in. The Virgin Mary. Robert Herrick. SCP-1

As sunbeams stream through liberal space. Woodnotes, II. Emerson. NOBA

"As surely as I hold your hand in mine." Brown Boy to Brown Girl. Countee Cullen. PoBA

As [*or* when] the blackbird in the spring. Aura Lea [*or* Lee]. W. W. Fosdick. BLSo

As the bull-dozer bites into the tree-ringed hill fort. Hymn to the New Omagh Road. John Montague. TwMBP

As the candle light and fire light. Cottage. "Seumas O'Sullivan." PFIr

As the car stooped, seemed to pause. Vincent Buckley. *Fr.* Golden Builders. CAAP

As the cat/ climbed over. Poem. William Carlos Williams. InPK; InPS; PiAm

As the first congress. First and Last. Bruce Severy. VW

As the gook woman howls. In the Mourning Time. Robert Hayden. BPo

As the leaves say. Free Will. Walter Clark. NCSH

As the liberty lads o'er the sea. Song for the Luddites. Byron. MBPR

As the player's breath warms the fipple the tone clears. Basil Bunting. *Fr.* Briggflatts. OBP

As the poor end of each dead day drew near. He Liked the Dead. Malcolm Lowry. OxBTC

As the Queen and Prince Albert, so buxom and all pert. Old England Forever and Do It No More. *Unknown.* GBP

As the snow falls I brush it away. A Snowfall. Richard Eberhart. FiCP

As the stars hide in the light before daybreak. Avoiding News by the River. W. S. Merwin. CoPAm

As the stores close, a winter light. February Evening in New York. Denise Levertov. InPS; NoAM

As the swamp cooler breathes. A Sale of Smoke. Roberta Spear. AmPA

As the Team's Head-Brass. Edward Thomas. OxBTC

As the wise men of old brought gifts. The Gift. William Carlos Williams. IPWM; TCP

As the Word came to prophets of old. Prophets for a New Day. Margaret Walker. BPo

As the World Turns. Larry Mollin. NeAC

As these two double verses, perfect linguists, create. In Eundem Macaronicon. John Donne. PAIC

As things be/ come. Word Poem. Nikki Giovanni. PoBA

As Thomas was cudgeled one day by his wife. Epigram. Swift. SoSe

As those who are not athletic at breakfast day by day. Nature Morte. Louis MacNeice. NoAM

As though an aged person were to wear. Elegy for the Monastery Barn. Thomas Merton. VGW

As Toilsome I Wandered Virginia's Woods. Walt Whitman. PAIC

As Tommy Snooks and Bessy Brooks. Mother Goose. MG

As two men were a-walking, down by the sea-side. The Duke of Grafton. *Unknown.* GBP; PeBB

As virtuous men pass mildly away. A Valediction Forbidding Mourning. John Donne. AnMo; HeIP; InPK; InPS; MetP; NOBE; PPoD; PPoe; PPP; SCP-1; SoSe; VoPo; WIF

As we came from the show. *Unknown.* SFF

As we get older we do not get any younger. Chard Whitlow. Henry Reed. FaBoCo; OxBTC

As we live, we are transmitters of life. We Are Transmitters. D. H. Lawrence. OxBTC

As we stand talking, his eye. An Old Acquaintance. Lewis Turco. CoPAm

As we stood on the crushed stone. A Conversation. Barbara Howes. IHMS

As we were marching to Quebec. Marching to Quebec. *Unknown.* AmFP

As Weary Pilgrim, Now at Rest. Anne Bradstreet. PiAm

As when, down some broad river dropping, we. Frederick Goddard Tuckerman. *Fr.* Sonnets. AmVN

As when far off the warbled strains are heard. La Fayette. Samuel Taylor Coleridge. *Fr.* Sonnets on Eminent Characters. MBPR

As when the moon hath comforted the night. George Chapman. *Fr.* The Conspiracy of Charles, Duke of Byron. Moon

As William and Mary stood by the seaside. William and Mary. *Unknown.* AmFP

As withereth the primrose by the river. A Palinode. Edmund Bolton. PAIC

As You Came from the Holy Land of Walsingham. *Unknown, sometimes at. to* Sir Walter Ralegh. *See* Walsingham.

As You Leave Me. Etheridge Knight. ConAP

As You Like It, *sels.* Shakespeare.
   "All the world's a stage," *fr.* II, vii. SFF
   Blow, Blow, Thou Winter Wind, *fr.* II, vii. FSFS; GBL; HeIP; InPS; NOBE; PPoe
   It Was a Lover, and His Lass, *fr.* V, iii. GBL; HeIP; InPK; InPS; NOBE; OLR; PPoe
   Under the Greenwood Tree, *fr.* II, v. ECBV; HeIP; InPS

As you read, a white bear leisurely. To the Reader. Denise Levertov. VGW

As your cream skin stretched. Poem at Semester's End. Ralph Mecklenburger. SFF

Ascending Red Cedar Moon. Duane Niatum. CDW

Ascending the hill, we saw the sun as incandescent. Vertical Is Our New Sight. Daisy Aldan. AATT

Ascension. Denis Devlin. BIrV

Ascent. Lynn Strongin. MIT

Ascent into Hell. A. D. Hope. MAuV

Ascent of T. J. Jackson: a Soldier's Tale. "A. N." BTTM

Ash and the Oak, The. Louis Simpson. ConAP

Ash-Wednesday. T. S. Eliot. VGW
  *Sels.*
  "Although I do not hope to turn again," VI. BoReV
  "At the first turning of the second stair," III. NoAM; NOBA
  "Because I do not hope to turn again," I. BoReV

Ashes, Lord. Nat Turner in the Clearing. Alvin Aubert. CoPAm

Ashland Tragedy, The, 2 *versions.* Elijah Adams. AmFP

Asia on the one side. This Narrow Stage. Theodore Weiss. NoAM

Asian Brother, Asian Sister. Lawson Fusao Inada. SA

Asian Peace Offers Rejected without Publication. Robert Bly. CAPP; NoAM

Asians Dying, The. W. S. Merwin. CAPP; NoAM

Asia's Song. Shelley. *Fr.* Prometheus Unbound, II, v. GrRo

Aside from ashcans & halljohns & pigeoncoops. Eastside Incidents. Gregory Corso. SA

Aside to Julie. Sallie Chesham. AATT

Asides and Memoranda. Elton Glaser. NVAP

Ask Me. William Stafford. FiCP

Ask me no more: the moon may draw the sea. Tennyson. *Fr.* The Princess, Pt. VI. GBL

Ask [*or* Aske] me no more where Jove bestows. Song. Thomas Carew. GBL; HeIP; InPS; NOBE; OBP; PPP; SCP-2

Ask no return for love that's given. Horace Gregory. *Fr.* Chorus for Survival. VGW

Ask of the sun. Louis Zukofsky. NoAM

Ask the Empress of the night. The Magnet. Thomas Stanley. NOBE

Ask the Mountains. Phil George. VW

Ask what kind of war it is. What Kind of War? Larry Rottman. POL

Ask you what provocation I have had? The Power of Ridicule. Pope. *Fr.* Epilogue to the Satires. NOBE

Aske me no more where Jove bestowes. *See* Ask me no more . . .

Asked me to be a woman. Wrists. Alberta Turner. HeS

Askest, "How long thou shalt stay?" The Visit. Emerson. NOBA

Asking for Ruthie. Judy Grahn. NMM

Asking little more than. Ode on Lust. Frank O'Hara. Epi

Asking what, asking what?—all a boy's afternoon. Debate: Question, Quarry, Dream. Robert Penn Warren. VGW

Asleep and Awake. David McCord. ECBV

Asleep in the Deep, *with music.* Arthur J. Lamb. FSN

Asleep! O sleep a little while, white pearl! Keats. LoAs

Asolando, *sel.* Robert Browning.
  Epilogue: "At the midnight in the silence of the sleep-time." NOBE; PAIC

Aspatia's Song. John Fletcher. *Fr.* The Maid's Tragedy, II, i. NOBE
  ("Lay a garland on my hearse.") GBL

Aspect of Love, Alive in the Ice and Fire, An. Gwendolyn Brooks. BPo; CAPP

Aspects of Robinson. Weldon Kees. AnMo

Aspects of the World Like Coral Reefs. William Bronk. VGW

Aspens. Edward Thomas. InPS

Aspen's Song, The. Yvor Winters. POL

Asphalt morning found him, The; he was dead. Raccoon on the Road. Joseph Payne Brennan. ECBV

Ass in the Lion's Skin, The. Aesop, *rhymed tr. fr. Greek by* William Ellery Leonard. ECBV

Assailant. John Raven. BPo

Assassination, The. Robert Hillyer. OFD

Assassination. Don L. Lee. NeAC; OFD; PoBA

Assassination Poems. John Ridland. MAT; OFD

Assassination Raga. Lawrence Ferlinghetti. CAPP

Assassin's Fatal Error, The. Lawrence Raab. AmPA

Assay a Friend. *Unknown.* OxBM

Assembly of Ladies, The, *sel.* Lady of the Assembly. Palace of Pleasant Regard, The. WPE

Assignment. Grace Butcher. RiTi

Assistant editor of *Crewel World,* The. The New York Woman. L. E. Sissman. MAT

Assumption. Padraic Fallon. BIrV

Assumption, The. *Unknown.* OxBM

Assyrian came down like the wolf on the fold, The. The Destruction of Sennacherib. Byron. AIW; AKE; BTTM; PBMP; SFF

Astapovo, or What Are We to Do, *sels.* Peter Whigham. TwMBP
  "Nausicaa's girls."
  "Poetry to go."
  "Violence swaddles all (love-) acts before and after."

Astigmatic, The. Philip Hobsbaum. LP

Astonished nymphs their flood's strange fate deplore, The. Richard Crashaw. *Fr.* To the Noblest and Best of Ladies, the Countess of Denbigh. OBP

Astrophel and Stella. Sir Philip Sidney. AAS
  Sonnets.
  I. "Loving in truth, and fain in verse my love to show." Epi; GBL; LoAs; OBP
  XIV. "Alas have I not pain enough my friend." Epi
  XX. "Fly, fly, my friends, I have my death wound; fly." Epi
  XXIV. "Rich fools there be, whose base and filthy heart." Epi
  XXVIII. "You that with allegory's curious frame." InPK
  XXX. "Whether the Turkish new-moon minded be." Epi
  XXXI. "With how sad steps, O Moon, thou climb'st the skies!" BoLoP; Epi; GBL; HeIP; InPK; InPS; IPWM; LoAs; MAT; Moon; OBP; PAIC; PBMP; PPoe; PPP
  (To the Sad Moon.) NOBE
  XXXIV. "Come, let me write, and to what end? to ease." Epi
  XXXVII. "My mouth doth water, and my breast doth swell." Epi
  XXXIX. "Come sleep! O sleep, the certain knot of peace." LoAs; PAIC; PPP
  (To Sleep.) NOBE
  XLI. "Having this day my horse, my hand, my lance." PPoD
  XLVII. "What, have I thus betrayed my liberty?" GBL; LoAs
  LIV. "Because I breathe not love to every one." BuTh
  LIX. "Dear, why make you more of a dog than me?" GBL; LoAs
  LXXI. "Who will in fairest book of Nature know." Epi
  LXXIV. "I never drank of Aganippe well." HeIP
  LXXXIII. "Good brother Philip, I have borne you long." Epi
  CVII. "Stella since thou so right a princess art." OBP
  CIX. "Thou blind man's mark, thou fool's self-chosen snare." *Sometimes considered part of* Astrophel and Stella. Epi; HeIP; PPP
  (Desire.) NOBE
  CX. "Leave me, O Love, which reachest but to dust." *Sometimes considered part of* Astrophel and Stella. GBL; HeIP; PPP
  (Splendidis Longum Valedico Nugis.) LoAs; NOBE

Songs.
Fourth Song: "Only joy, now here you are." GBL
Eleventh Song: "Who is it that this dark night."
(Voices at the Window.) NOBE
Aswelay. Norman Henry Pritchard, II. PoBA
Aswell within her billowed skirts. The Mad-Woman. L. A. G. Strong. PFIr
At a Bach Concert. Adrienne Rich. CoPAm
At a Bible House. Robert Lowell. SFF
At a certain hour of the morning of a certain day. Twenty Words/Twenty Days. Gael Turnbull. TwMBP
At a distance, young voices are whooping. On Returning to Teach. Marvin Bell. NowV
At a Friends' Meeting. Mary Elizabeth Coleridge. WPE
At a gay reception given in a mansion grand and old. The Moth and the Flame. George Taggart. FSN
At a Georgia Camp Meeting, with music. Kerry Mills. BLSo
At a Hasty Wedding. Thomas Hardy. PAIC
At a party of university people. Double Exposure. Ian Young. NeAC
At a pleasant evening party. Ferdinando and Elvira. W. S. Gilbert. FaBoCo
At a Solemn Music. Milton. AnMo; BoReV; HeIP; NOBE; PAIC
At a spring well under a thorn. The Virgin. Unknown. GBP
At a Summer Hotel. Isabella Gardner. RiTi
At Aberdeen. Unknown. FaBoCo
At an Exhibition of Historical Paintings, Hobart. Vivian Smith. MAuV
At Baia. Hilda Doolittle ("H.D."). NOBA; PAIC
At Barstow. Charles Tomlinson. NoAM
At Beautyes barre as I dyd stande. The Arraignment of a Lover. George Gascoigne. AAS
At Beverly Farms, a portly, uncomfortable boulder. Terminal Days at Beverly Farms. Robert Lowell. PSN
At Breakfast. May Swenson. Psy
At Brill on the Hill. Unknown. GBP
(Brill.) OBP
At Casterbridge Fair, sel. Thomas Hardy.
Former Beauties, II. NoAM
At Castle Boterel. Thomas Hardy. NOBE
At Christmas. Robert Duncan. NoAM
At court I met it, in clothes brave enough. On Something That Walks Somewhere. Ben Jonson. SCP-1
At Cove on the Crooked River. William Stafford. ConAP
At dawn, caught beneath the rim of light. Beyond Anguish. Milton Kessler. CoPAm
At dawn I squat on the garage. Sound. Jim Harrison. VGW
At dawn she lay with her profile at that angle. Daybreak. Stephen Spender. BoLoP
At dawn the ridge emerges massed and dun. Attack. Siegfried Sassoon. NOBE; OxBTC
At Dawning, with music. Nelle Richmond Eberhart. BLSo
At day's light. In Autumn. Jon Anderson. AmPA
At dinner, she is hostess, I am host. Modern Love, XVII. George Meredith. Epi; HeIP
At Dirty Dick's and Sloppy Joe's. Song of the Master and Boatswain. W. H. Auden. Fr. Sea and the Mirror. BoLoP
At Dunwich. Anthony Thwaite. MPo
At dusk/ from the island in the river. If the Owl Calls Again. John Haines. BoAnP; ConAP; HeIP; NCSH
At Eagle Farm I stand at the passenger gate. Flights. Roger McDonald. CAAP
At eighty/ reading lines. Heavy, Heavy—What Hangs Over? Kenneth Burke. POL

At eighty-six she takes to pressing flowers. Foxfire. Nancy Willard. IHMS
At Eutaw Springs the valiant died. Eutaw Springs. Philip Freneau. BTTM
"At eve should be the time," they said. The Burial Hour. Robert Stephen Hawker. VPC
At Every Gas Station There Are Mechanics. Stephen Dunn. NVAP
At every stroake his brazen finnes do take. The Whale. John Donne. Fr. The Progresse of the Soule. OBP
At first he stirs uneasily in sleep. Dog at Night. Louis Untermeyer. MiP
At first I was given centuries. Margaret Atwood. NMM
At first I was worried about you. When I Held You to My Chest, You Fit. Jack Myers. AmPA
At first nothing is. Nothing Is. Sun-Ra. PoBA
At First Sight. Alastair Reid. SLP
At five in the morning, as jolly as any. The Miner's Doom. Unknown. AmFP
At five precisely in the afternoon. Crossing. Archibald MacLeish. POL
At Flock Mass. F. R. Higgins. PFIr
At Flores in the Azores, Sir Richard Grenville lay. The Revenge. Tennyson. BTTM
At four a.m. I dreamed of myself on that beach. For You Who Didn't Know. Nancy Willard. RiTi
At four o'clock. Roosters. Elizabeth Bishop. CoPAm
At Gettysburg full anonymity. Yugoslav Cemetery. Celeste Turner Wright. WPE
At Grass. Philip Larkin. OxBTC; PSN
At Great Torrington, Devon. Unknown. FaBoCo
At Hadleigh, Suffolk. Unknown. FaBoCo
At Henry's bier let some thing fall out well. John Berryman. CAPP
At her fair hands how have I grace entreated. Ode. Walter Davison. BoLoP
At home, in my flannel gown, like a bear to its floe. 90 North. Randall Jarrell. NoAM; NOBA
At 100 Mile House the cowboys ride in rolling. The Cariboo Horses. A. W. Purdy. HeIP
At Hunegg. George MacBeth. TwMBP
At Ithaca. Hilda Doolittle ("H.D."). VGW
At Kenneth Burke's Place. William Carlos Williams. NOBA
At Kilbryde Castle. Lorn M. MacIntyre. SLP
At Last. Melvin DeBruhl. PPoD
At last I bless the hours. Rosemarie Newcombe. POL
At last I found the monastery. A young. Abstinence. Kenneth Rosen. AmPA
At last it cannot matter. What You Should Do Each Morning. Brian Patten. BuTh
At last, my old, inveterate foe. To Melancholy. Countess of Winchelsea. WPE
At last they chanced to meet upon the way. Spenser. Fr. Mother Hubberd's Tale. TVS
At last you yielded up the album, which. Lines on a Young Lady's Photograph Album. Philip Larkin. HeIP
At least at night, a streetlight. So Long. William Stafford. Epi
At Leeds. Unknown. FaBoCo
At length the crackling noise and dreadful blaze. Dryden. Fr. Annus Mirabilis: Fire of London. SCP-1
At Lindos. May Sarton. WPE
At Mass. Vachel Lindsay. VGW
At Max Gate. Siegfried Sassoon. NoAM
At meat, or hearing you deplore. Consumer's Report. X. J. Kennedy. FiCP
At Melville's Tomb. Hart Crane. NoAM; VGW

At midday the birds doze. The Hermit Picks Berries. Maxine W. Kumin. RFM

At midnight by the stream I roved. Lewti; or, The Circassian Love-Chaunt. Samuel Taylor Coleridge. MBPR

At midnight in the alley. The Tom-Cat. Don Marquis. BoAnP; SS

At midnight, in the month of June. The Sleeper. Poe. NOBA

At minus tide the music. Poke-Pole Fishing. Dennis Schmitz. AmPA

At Mrs. Tyson's farmhouse, the electricity is pumped. The Force. Peter Redgrove. MPo

At moment X. 3 Models of the Universe. May Swenson. Psy

At Mount Rushmore I looked up into one. X. J. Kennedy. *Fr.* Edgar's Story. OFD

At My Mother's Bedside. Marcia Lee Masters. WPE

At Night. Richard Eberhart. LoAs

At Night. Robley Wilson, Jr. HeS

At night all the maps grow blank. Maps. Howard Schwartz. HeS

At night, by the fire. Domination of Black. Wallace Stevens. PiAm

At night Chinamen jump. Poem. Frank O'Hara. NoAM; NOBA

At night, circling weightless, we dreamed of roses. Roses. Geoffrey Lehmann. CAAP

At night, sometimes, when I cannot sleep. The Chosen Light. John Montague. TwMBP

At night while. Black Warrior. Norman Jordan. PoBA

At nightfall, as the sea darkens. Ghost Crabs. Ted Hughes. TwMBP

At nine o'clock in the morning. Mother and Son. R. S. Thomas. BuTh

At noon in the desert a panting lizard. At the Bomb Testing Site. William Stafford. CoPAm

At one the wind rose. Night-Music. Philip Larkin. InPS

At Our House. William Stafford. Epi

At Poetry Workshop, Winter Semester. Robert A. Martin. AATT

At Potterne, Wiltshire. *Unknown.* FaBoCo

At present I still have. Exit Lines. George Jonas. NeAC

At Quincey's moat the squandering village ends. Almswomen. Edmund Blunden. OxBTC

At Rochdale. Ian Young. NeAC

At Rushy Lagoon. James McAuley. MAuV

At seven in the summer evenings. Plaza Reál with Palmtrees. Paul Blackburn. NoAM

At seven the sun that lit my world blew out. The Astigmatic. Philip Hobsbaum. LP

At 79th and Park. Barbara Howes. MiP

At 16/ I dreamed of/ a bushy beard. The Vanity of Human Wishes. John Leax. MiP

At Spearfish, S.D. once. Learning. Marie Harris. MMD

At sunset, when the night-dews fall. The Snail. James Reeves. ECBV

At ten A.M. the young housewife. The Young Housewife. William Carlos Williams. HeIP; NoAM; PiAm

At That Moment. Raymond R. Patterson. PoBA

At the age of nineteen I was digging the land. The Kerry Recruit. *Unknown.* RDB

At the age of 27. Sketch 48b.11. Ezra Pound. BBGO

At the aged. Thirteen Preludes for Pioneer Square. John Logan. CAAP

At the Airport. Evan Jones. MAuV

At the airport, ready to leave on my little trip. The Fear of Flying. Mona Van Duyn. NMM

At the Altar. Robert Lowell. Between the Porch and the Altar, IV. InPK; InPS

At the "Atlantic" Dinner. Oliver Wendell Holmes. AmVN

At the Ball Game. William Carlos Williams. NoAM; NOBA

At the Bomb Testing Site. William Stafford. CoPAm

At the bottom of the twisted. Poem for Lorry. Gerald Hausman. CTBA

At the Carnival. Anne Spencer. NoAM

At the Cenotaph. "Hugh MacDiarmid." OBP

At the Chairman's Housewarming. William Stafford. AnMo

At the corner of Wood Street, when daylight appears. The Reverie of Poor Susan. Wordsworth. MBPR

At the Crucifixion. *Unknown.* OxBM

At the Dancing School of the Sisters Schwarz. Judson Jerome. SFF

At the Dark Hour. Paul Dehn. BoLoP

At the dead end of a road twisting snakelike. Party at Bannon Brook. Alden Nowlan. NeAC

At the Drive-In: "John Wayne vs. God." A. A. Dewey. HeS

At the Eastern Front. Georg Trakl, *tr. fr. German by* Ingo Seidler. IPWM

At the end of a long-walled garden. The Cottage Hospital. John Betjeman. NOBE

At the End of the Affair. Maxine W. Kumin. CoPAm

At the end of the day. Nothing Strange. Tom Kryss. NeAC

At the end of the war I arose. The Driver. James Dickey. VGW

At the equinox when the earth was veiled in a late rain. Continent's End. Robinson Jeffers. TCP

At the field's edge. The White Hare. Lilian Bowes Lyon. OxBTC

At the first peep of dawn she roused me! Paterson—The Strike. William Carlos Williams. *Fr.* The Wanderer: A Rococo Study. Epi

At the first turning of the second stair. Ash Wednesday, III. T. S. Eliot. NoAM; NOBA

At the foot of the stairs. Hope. William Dickey. POL

At the foot of yonder mountain where the fountains do flow. The Green Briar Shore. *Unknown.* AmFP

At the ford, while grass-green frogs. Charming the Moon. James DenBoer. MAT

At the frontier the long train slows to a stop. The Frontier. John Hewitt. BIrV

At the Grave of Burns, 1803. Wordsworth. MBPR

At the Gynecologist's. Linda Pastan. RiTi

At the hour I slept. Birds in Their Title Work Freeholds of Straw. Les A. Murray. *Fr.* Walking to the Cattle-Place. CAAP

At the Indian Killer's Grave. Robert Lowell. NOBA; VGW

At the Lake's edge. Water and Light, Light and Water. Mark Perlberg. HeS

At the last moment I. Elegy for an Android. D. M. Thomas. TwMBP

At the Loom. Robert Duncan. *Fr.* Passages. PiAm; VGW

At the Manger Mary Sings. W. H. Auden. *Fr.* For the Time Being. BoReV

At the merest handshake I feel his blood. Vincent Buckley. *Fr.* Stroke. MAuV

At the Mid Hour of Night. Thomas Moore. NOBE

At the midnight in the silence of the sleep-time. Epilogue. Robert Browning. *Fr.* Asolando. NOBE; PAIC

At the Moated Grange. Shakespeare. *Fr.* Measure for Measure, IV, i. NOBE
("Take, O! take those lips away.") GBL; HeIP; InPS

At the Museum of Natural History. Poem for Explorers. Carol Bergé. MMD

At the next vacancy for God, if I am elected. In Place of a Curse. John Ciardi. NowV

At the officers' table, for half an hour afterwards, port.   Class Incident from Graves.  Alan Brownjohn.  OxBTC

At the old concert hall on the Bow'ry.   She Is More To Be Pitied, Than Censured.  William B. Gray.  FSN

At the Poem Society a black-haired man stands up to say.  Fresh Air.  Kenneth Koch.  CAPP; NoAM

At the point of shining feathers.   The Night a Sailor Came to Me in a Dream.  Diane Wakoski.  VGW

At the round earth's imagined corners blow.   Holy Sonnets, VII. John Donne.  BoReV; Epi; InPS; HeIP; NOBE; OBP; PAIC; PPoe; PPP; SCP-1

At the San Francisco Airport.  Yvor Winters.  HeIP; InPK; NOBA; RRA

At the Seaside.  Robert Louis Stevenson.  LCL; OxBChV

At the Slackening of the Tide.  James Wright.  VGW

At the Tavern.  Unknown.  OxBM

At the Theatre.  John Williams.  CoPAm

At the third hour always.  Rain.  Paul Murray.  BIrV

At the time it seemed unimportant: he was lying.  The Day.  Roy Fuller.  OxBTC

At the time there were those who said with a wink.  The Father. Desmond O'Grady.  NoAM

At the top of my street the attorneys abound.   Conversation in Craven Street, Strand.  James Smith and Sir George Rose. FaBoCo

At the top of the house the apples are laid in rows.   Moonlit Apples.  John Drinkwater.  FSFS; OxBTC

At the Ukrainian Catholic church.  One for the Album.  Rhyll McMaster.  CAAP

At the Un-National Monument along the Canadian Border. William Stafford.  HeIP; SoSe

At the very beginning of an important symphony.  Interruption at the Opera House.  Brian Patten.  LP

At the Washing of My Son.  Su Tung P'o, tr. fr. Chinese by Kenneth Rexroth.  BBGO

At the Water Zoo.  E.V. Knox.  BoAnP

At the Wax Museum.  Hollis Summers.  CoPAm

At the Wedding March.  Gerard Manley Hopkins.  LoAs

At the week-end conference on Trends.  The Subversive Sublime. Tom Buchan.  MIS

At the Western Shore.  Sarah Youngblood.  IHMS

At the Zoo.  Walter de la Mare.  BoAnP

At the Zoo.  Thackeray.  OxBChV

At this wharf there are no grand landings to speak of.  A Winter Ship.  Sylvia Plath.  PSN

At Thomas Hardy's Birthplace, 1953.  James Wright.  ConAP

At three o'clock yesterday afternoon, Jason Quidnunc.  Elderly Nobody Erases Self in Central Park.  E. S. Forgotson. NowV

"At thy door I'm knocking."  Au Clair de la Lune.  Unknown. BLSH

At Times.  Kathleen Wiegner.  MMD

At Torrey Pines State Park.  Jerome Mazzaro.  FiCP

At Tripolis.  Constance Carrier.  WPE

At Trumpingtoun, not fer fro Cantebrigge.  The Mill at Trumpington.  Chaucer.  Fr. The Canterbury Tales: The Reeve's Tale.  OxBM

At two a.m.  Truck Drivers.  Terri Haag.  CTBA

At Upton-on-Severn.  Unknown.  FaBoCo

At Veronica's.  Robert Peterson.  NeAC

At Wednesbury there was a cocking.  The Wednesbury Cocking. Unknown.  PeBB

At White River.  John Haines.  FiCP

At Woodcombe farm, wi' ground an' tree.  Hallowed Pleaces. William Barnes.  VPC

At Woodlawn I heard the dead cry.  The Lost Son.  Theodore Roethke.  VGW

At work his arms wave like a windmill.  The Secretary.  Peter Redgrove.  OxBTC

At your entreaty, I at last have writ.  Maidenhead.  "Ephelia." WPE

Atalanta in Calydon, sels.  Swinburne.
  "Before the beginning of years."  HeIP
  Chorus: "When the hounds of spring are on winter's traces." HeIP; NOBE; VPC

Atavism.  Richard Lake.  NCSH

Atavism.  Elinor Wylie.  SBG

Atheists are few; most nymph a godhead own.  Edward Young. Fr. Satire on Women.  SoSe

Athelstan King,/ Lord among Earls.  Battle of Brunanburh. Unknown, tr. by Tennyson.  BTTM

Athlete's Prayer, An.  Ed Charles.  SPo

Athol Brose.  Thomas Hood.  FaBoCo

Athwart the sky a lowly sigh.  London.  John Davidson.  NOBE

Atlantic is a stormy moat, The; and the Mediterranean.  The Eye. Robinson Jeffers.  NOBA; PiAm

Atlas.  Robert Flanagan.  HeS

Atlas' Daughter.  Polly Mann.  NPW

Atrocity, The/ Of the great elephant.  The Elephant.  Sandra Hochman.  BoAnP

Attack, The.  Leonard Clark.  RAE

Attack.  Siegfried Sassoon.  NOBE; OxBTC

Attack of the Crab Monsters.  Lawrence Raab.  AmPA

Attend ye valiant highwaymen and outlaws of disdain.  Bold Jack Donohue.  Unknown.  PeBB

Attend, Young Friends, While I Relate.  Unknown.  AmFP

Attentive eyes, fantastic heed.  A Poet.  Thomas Hardy.  NoAM

Attic Landscape, The.  Herman Melville.  NOBA

Atticus.  Pope.  Fr. Epistle to Dr. Arbuthnot.  InPK; NOBE

Attis.  George Stanley.  MIT

Attitudes, sel.  Richard Eberhart.
  New England Protestant.  TH

Au Clair de la Lune, with music.  Unknown, tr. fr. French by "C. F. M."  BLSH

Au Jardin des Plantes.  John Wain.  OxBTC

Au Tombeau de Mon Père.  Ronald McCuaig.  MAuV

Aubade: "Having bitten on life like a sharp apple."  Louis MacNeice.  PAIC

Aubade: "Hours before dawn we were woken by the quake." William Empson.  OxBTC; PAIC

Aubade: "Jane, Jane,/ Tall as a crane."  Edith Sitwell.  NoAM

Aubade: "Lark now leaves his watery nest, The."  Sir William Davenant.  NOBE
  ("Lark now leaves his watery nest, The.")  LoAs
  (Song.)  GBL

Aubade: N.Y.C.  Robert Wallace.  CoPAm

Aubade: "Stay, O sweet, and do not rise."  Unknown.  BoLoP; NOBE

Aubade: "What dawn is it?"  Karl Shapiro.  VGW

Aube Provençale.  Marilyn Hacker.  AmPA

Auden, MacNeice, Day Lewis, I have read them all.  British Leftish Poetry, 1930-40.  "Hugh MacDiarmid."  NoAM

Audubon, Drafted.  LeRoi Jones.  PPP

Augur, The.  Stephen Tudor.  HeS

Auguries of Innocence.  Blake.  LAuP; MBPR; OBP; VoPo, much abr.
  Sels.
  Robin Redbreast in a Cage, A.  AKE
  (Three Things to Remember.)  ECBV
  To See a World in a Grain of Sand.  InPK; PPoe

August.  William Everson.  PiAm

August.  William Morris.  Fr. The Earthly Paradise.  VPC

August.  Spenser.  Fr. The Shepheardes Calender.  PAIC

August/ Fresno 1973. Roberta Spear. AmPA

August Afternoon. Nancy Remaly. CTBA

August afternoon. Sunday, Guadalajara. Anthony Ostroff. MIT

August at the Lake. David Young. AmPA

August Fugue. Thomas Shapcott. CAAP

August 1914. Isaac Rosenberg. NOBE; OxBTC

August 2. Norman Jordan. PoBA

August 'twas, the twenty-fifth. Bar's Fight, August 28, 1746. Lucy Terry. BPo

August 24, 1963—1:00 A.M.—Omaha. Donna Whitewing. VW

August Weather. Katharine Tynan. FSFS

August wind rides Spain tonight in a fierce saddle, The. Casa de Pollos. Kathleen Fraser. AmPA

Augustus was a chubby lad. The Story of Augustus Who Would Not Have Any Soup. Heinrich Hoffmann, tr. fr. German. OxBChV; SpRo

Auld Daddy Darkness. James Ferguson. OxBChV

Auld Lang Syne. Burns. AKE; BLSH, with music; BLSo, with music; LAuP; NOBE

Auld Noah was at hame wi' them a'. Parley of Beasts. "Hugh MacDiarmid." BoAnP; NoAM

Auld Robin Gray. Lady Anne Lindsay. WPE

Auld sangs soored and cankered, The. The Grave of Love. Heine, tr. by Alexander Gray. SLP

Auld Seceder Cat. The. Unknown. FaBoCo

Auld wife sat at her ivied door, The. Ballad. Charles Stuart Calverley. FaBoCo; SpRo

Auld wumman cam'in, a mere rickle o' banes, An. Old Wife in High Spirits. "Hugh MacDiarmid." OxBTC

Auncient acquaintance, madam, betwen us twayn, The. John Skelton. AAS

Aunt Alice in April. William H. Matchett. CTBA

Aunt Dinah's Quilting Party. Francis Kyle. See When I Saw Sweet Nelly Home.

Aunt Jane Allen. Fenton Johnson. PoBA

Aunt Jemima of the Ocean Waves. Robert Hayden. PoBA

Aunt Jennifer's Tigers. Adrienne Rich. HeIP

Aunt Julia. Norman MacCaig. MPo

Aunt Laura Moves Toward the Open Grave of Her Father. Joseph De Roche. HeIP

Aunt Mabel. William Stafford. AnMo

Aunt Rose—now—might I see you. To Aunt Rose. Allen Ginsburg. VGW

Aunts Watching Television. John Pudney. MPo

Aura Lea [or Lee], with music. W. W. Fosdick. BLSo; PSoN

Aurora, sel. Earl of Stirling.
"Ile give thee leave my love, in beauties field," Sonnet XXVI. SLP

Auspice of Jewels. Laura Riding. NoAM

Austrian Army, An. Alaric A. Watts. FaBoCo

Aut Neutrum . . . Vel Duos. Rufinus Domesticus, tr. fr. Latin by Dudley Fitts. OLR

Authentic, The! Shadows of it. Matins. Denise Levertov. IHMS; NoAM; WIF

Authentic Tidings. Wordsworth. Fr. The Prelude, VI. BoReV

Author, The. Charles Churchill. See Pains of Education, The.

Author Apologizes to a Lady for His Being a Little Man, The. Christopher Smart. BoLoP

Author of light, revive my dying spright. Thomas Campion. AAS

Author of my talents, only you have I praised. An Athlete's Prayer. Ed Charles. SPo

Author to Her Book, The. Anne Bradstreet. InPK; NOBA; PiAm

Author to His Wife, of a Woman's Eloquence, The. Sir John Harington. BoLoP

Author's Abstract of Melancholy, The. Robert Burton. See Anatomy of Melancholy, The.

Auto Icon. John Daniel. TwMBP

Auto Mobile. A. R. Ammons. InPK

Auto Wreck. Karl Shapiro. CoPAm; VGW; VoPo

Autobiographia Literaria. Frank O'Hara. NOBA

Autobiographical Note. Vernon Scannell. LP; MPo

Autobiography. Louis MacNeice. BuTh

Autobiography: Hollywood. Charles Reznikoff. Fr. Going To and Fro and Walking Up and Down. SA

Autobiography: Last Chapter. Jim Barnes. CDW

Autobiography of a Lungworm. Roy Fuller. NoAM

Autobiography Part Two: Rock and Roll. Jessica Tarahata Hagedorn. MMD

Autocrat of the Breakfast-Table, The, sels. Oliver Wendell Holmes.
Chambered Nautilus, The, fr. ch. 4. AmVN; NOBA; PiAm; VoPo
Deacon's Masterpiece, The; or, The Wonderful "One-Hoss Shay," fr. ch. 11. NOBA; PiAm; SS

Autograph Book/ Prophecy. Anne Halley. NMM

Autolycus Sings. Shakespeare. Fr. The Winter's Tale, IV, ii. NOBE
("When daffodils begin to peer.") AIW; OBP

Autolycus' Song ("Jog on, jog on . . ."). Shakespeare. Fr. The Winter's Tale, IV, ii. SpRo

Autolycus' Song (In Basic English). Richard L. Greene. SpRo

Autumn. Roy Campbell. OxBTC; WIF

Autumn ("The thistle down's flying . . ."). John Clare. OBP

Autumn. Walter de la Mare. OxBTC

Autumn. T. E. Hulme. Moon; PAIC

Autumn ("With what a glory comes and goes the year!"). Longfellow. FSFS

Autumn. Elizabeth Madox Roberts. PoTa

Autumn. Vernon Scannell. MPo; OxBTC

Autumn. Humbert Wolfe. FSFS

Autumn; A Dirge. Shelley. FSFS

Autumn Begins in Martins Ferry, Ohio. James Wright. CAPP; InPS; POL; PPoD

Autumn Chapter in a Novel. Thom Gunn. OxBTC

Autumn Horses. Jenne Andrews. HeS

Autumn Idleness. Dante Gabriel Rossetti. The House of Life, LXIX. GBL

Autumn Journal, sels. Louis MacNeice.
"Conferences, adjournments, ultimatums." OxBTC
"Nightmare leaves fatigue." BIrV

Autumn on the Wabash. Dave Etter. CoPAm

Autumn Sequence. Adrienne Rich. VGW

Autumn Shade, sels. Edgar Bowers.
"Autumn shade is thin, The. Grey leaves lie faint," I. PiAm
"In nameless warmth, sun light in every corner," IX. PiAm
"My shadow moves, until, at noon, I stand," X. PiAm

Autumn swells over the land. Autumn Horses. Jenne Andrews. HeS

Autumn-time has come, The. My Triumph. Whittier. NOBA

Autumnal, The. John Donne. Elegies, IX. InPS

Autumnal Moon, The. James Thomson. Fr. The Seasons: Autumn. NOBE

Avalanche. Janet Emig. SPo

Ave atque Vale. Swinburne. NOBE

Ave Caesar. Robinson Jeffers. NoAM; NOBA

Ave Maria. Hart Crane. Fr. The Bridge. NoAM; NOBA

Avenge, O Lord, thy slaughtered saints, whose bones. On the Late Massacre in Piedmont. Milton. AnMo; Epi; HeIP; InPK; NOBE; OBP; PPoe; PPP; SoSe; VoPo

Avenue Bearing the Initial of Christ into the New World, The, *sel.* Galway Kinnell.
"Fishmarket closed, the fishes gone into flesh, The," II. ConAP
Average, The. W. H. Auden. BBGO
Avoid the reeking herd. The Eagle and the Mole. Elinor Wylie. PAIC
Avoidances. Ron Welburn. PoBA
Avoiding News by the River. W. S. Merwin. CoPAm
Avondale. Stevie Smith. RAE
Avondale Mine Disaster, The. *Unknown.* AmFP
Aw was young and lusty. Sair Fyel'd, Hinny. *Unknown.* GBP
Awa' wi' your witchcraft o' beauty's alarms. Hey for a Lass wi' a Tocher. Burns. SLP
Awake, Aeolian lyre, awake. The Progress of Poesy. Thomas Gray. LAuP
Awake, Arise, You Drowsy Sleeper. *Unknown.* AmFP
Awake! for Morning in the Bowl of Night. The Rubáiyát of Omar Khayyám of Naishápúr. Omar Khayyám, *tr. by* Edward Fitzgerald. HeIP
Awake, my heart, to be loved, awake, awake! Robert Bridges. NOBE
Awake, my love, who sleep into the dawn! The Lady's Farewell. Nuno Fernandez Torneol, *tr. by* Yvor Winters. AIW
Awake, my St. John! leave all meaner things. An Essay on Man, Epistle I. Pope. PAIC
Awake, oh Heaven, for (lo) the heavens conspire. Cyril Tourneur. Moon
Awake or sleeping (for I know not which). An Old-World Thicket. Christina Rossetti. SBG
Awakening. Robert Bly. ConAP
Awakening, The. *Unknown, tr. fr. French by* John Attey. NOBE ("On a time the amorous Silvy.") GBL
Award. Ray Durem. BPo; PoBA
Awareness. Don L. Lee. PoBA
Away! Robert Frost. NOBA
Away above a Harborful. Lawrence Ferlinghetti. BoLoP; SFF
Away, birds, away! In a Corn Field. *Unknown.* ECBV
Away, Delights. John Fletcher. *Fr.* The Captain, III, iv. NOBE
(Sad Song, The.) GBL
Away, for we are ready to a man! Epilogue. James Elroy Flecker. *Fr.* The Golden Journey to Samarkand. NOBE
Away in a Manger, *with music. Unknown.* BLSH
Away, Melancholy. Stevie Smith. OxBTC
Away! the moor is dark beneath the moon. Stanzas—April, 1814. Shelley. MBPR
Away, way down on the old Swanee. Yale Boola! A. M. Hirsh. FSN
Away with your fictions of flimsy romance. The First Kiss of Love. Byron. MBPR
Awful Fix. *Unknown.* BluL
Awful shadow of some unseen Power, The. Hymn to Intellectual Beauty. Shelley. BoReV; HeIP; MBPR
Axe angles, An/ from my neighbor's ashcan. Junk. Richard Wilbur. InPK; PPoD
Axe rings in the wood, The. Remembered Morning. Janet Lewis. WPE
Axes/ After whose stroke the wood rings. Words. Sylvia Plath. AnMo; ConAP
Ay, Ay, This Is the Day. *Unknown.* OxBM
Ay, besherewe yow, be my fay. Manerly Margery Mylk and Ale. John Skelton. AAS
Ay, every inch a king:/ When I do stare, see how the subject quakes. Shakespeare. *Fr.* King Lear, IV, vi. OBP
Ay me! whilst thee the shores and sounding seas. Milton. *Fr.* Lycidas. Prf

Ay, so it is in every brain. To a Young Brother. Maria Jane Jewsbury. OxBChV
Ay, tear her tattered ensign down! Old Ironsides. Oliver Wendell Holmes. BTTM
Ay! thou look'st cold on me, pomp-loving Moon. To the Moon. George Darley. Moon
"Aye! I am a poet and upon my tomb." And Thus in Nineveh. Ezra Pound. VGW
Ayii, Ayii,/ I walked on the ice of the sea. *Unknown, tr. fr. Eskimo.* RFM
Ayii, Ayii/ The great sea has set me in motion. *Unknown, tr. fr. Eskimo.* RFM
Azalea, The. Coventry Patmore. The Unknown Eros, I, vii. GBL
Azured vault, the crystal circles bright, The. Sonnet. James I, King of England. Moon

# B

B Flat. Douglas Stewart. MAuV
B. Negative. X. J. Kennedy. ConAP
Baa, baa, black sheep, have you any wool? Mother Goose. MG
Baa, baa, black sheep, where'd you leave your lamb? *Unknown.* AmFP
Babe is at peace within the womb, The. Life Rounded with Sleep. Shelley. BuTh
Babe Ruth. Damon Runyon. SPo
Babes in the Wood. *Unknown.* ECBV; OxBChV
Babies: Just Babies. Margaret Fishback. ECBV
Baby at my breast, The. Against Dark's Harm. Anne Halley. NMM
Baby did you hear about the bad luck. Bad Luck Blues. *Unknown.* BluL
Baby I can see just what's on your mind. Mind Reader Blues. *Unknown.* BluL
Baby I want to see yr. Wildflowers, Smoke. Lyn Lifshin. MMD
Baby, if you love me. Down and Out. Langston Hughes. PiAm
Baby I'm going/ down town. Sic 'Em Dogs On. *Unknown.* BluL
Baby, I'm going up town. Hunkie Tunkie. *Unknown.* BluL
Baby, I'm sick. I need. Night Thoughts. Gwen Harwood. CAAP
Baby is sleeping so cozy and fair. Rock-a-Bye Baby. Effie I. Canning. FSN
Baby Mine, *with music.* Charles Mackey. BLSo
Baby-Movements. D. H. Lawrence. RRA
Baby-Sermon, A. George MacDonald. OxBChV
Baby Toes. Carl Sandburg. LCL
Baby Tortoise. D. H. Lawrence. BoAnP
Baby you know I get high. Not Quite Spring. Lyn Lifshin. NeAC
Babylon. Ron Ikan. NVAP
Babylon; or, The Bonnie Banks o' Fordie. *Unknown.* AmFP; PAIC
Babylon Revisited. LeRoi Jones. BPo; NoAM
Baby's Dance, The. Ann Taylor. OxBChV ("Dance, little baby, dance up high.") EBCV
Baccalaureate. David McCord. SpRo
Bacchus. Emerson. NOBA; PiAm
Bacchus. William Empson. NoAM
Bachelor. William Meredith. NoAM
Bachelor Bold and Young. *Unknown.* AmFP

Bachelor's Complaint, The. *Unknown.* AmFP
Bachelor's Life, A. *Unknown.* OxBM
Back. Angela McCabe. AmPA
Back. Robert Mezey. AmPA
Back Again, Home. Don L. Lee. BPo
Back and forth, back and forth. Fall 1961. Robert Lowell. PSN; VGW
Back and Side Go Bare. *At. to* William Stevenson. *Fr.* Gammer Gurton's Needle. HeIP
Back Behind the Eyes. Leon Stokesbury. NVAP
Back from the Country. Oliver St. John Gogarty. PFIr
Back Gnawing Blues. *Unknown.* BluL
Back home the black women are all beautiful. W. W. LeRoi Jones.. HeIP; NOBA; PiAm; PoBA
Back in Black Mountain a child will smack your face. Black Mountain Blues. *Unknown.* BluL
Back Just Below the Shoulder Blades. Coleman Barks. *Fr.* Body Poems. NVAP
Back of Chicago the open fields. Evening Song. Sherwood Anderson. ANTL
Back of the dam, under. The Town of Hill. Donald Hall. FiCP
Back out of all this now too much for us. Directive. Robert Frost. MAT; NoAM; NOBA; PiAm; PPP
Back through clouds. Train Tune. Louise Bogan. ECBV
Back to Africa. Erica Jong. RiTi
Back to the roots. Vanish. John Oliver Simon. MIT
Back water at Blytheville. High Water Everywhere: 2. *Unknown.* BluL
Back Water Blues. *Unknown.* BluL
Back water done rose around Sumner, now, The. High Water Everywhere: 1. *Unknown.* BluL
Back water rising: southern people can't make no time. Rising High Water Blues. *Unknown.* BluL
Back wings, The/ of the. Between Walls. William Carlos Williams. VGW
Backgrounds to Italian Paintings: Fifteenth Century. Anne Ridler. WPE
Backlash Blues, The. Langston Hughes. BPo
Backroad leafmold stonewall chipmunk. Silent Poem. Robert Francis. FiCP
Backward Spring, A. Thomas Hardy. PPP
Bad Bishop Jegon. *Unknown.* GBP
Bad Dream. Louis MacNeice. NoAM
Bad Example. Isabella Fey. BoAnP
Bad Girl Blues. *Unknown.* BluL
Bad Luck Blues ("Baby did you hear about the bad luck"). *Unknown.* BluL
Bad Luck Blues ("I want to go home and I ain't got sufficient"). *Unknown.* BluL
Bad Man Ballad. *Unknown.* AmFP
Bad Moon Rising. John Fogerty. GrRo
Bad Morning. Langston Hughes. PiAm
Bad news has come to town, bad news is carried. Montcalm and Wolfe. *Unknown.* AmFP
Bad Old Days, The. Kenneth Rexroth. NoAM
Bad Thing, The. John Wain. BuTh
Badger, The. John Clare. InPS
Badman of the Guest Professor. Ishmael Reed. BPo
Baffled Knight, The. *Unknown.* SLP
Bag of the Bee, The. Robert Herrick. SCP-1
Bagatelle, A. James Reeves. POL
Bagel, The. David Ignatow. ConAP; PPod
Bagpipe Music. Louis MacNeice. NoAM; NOBE; OxBTC
Bags of Meat. Thomas Hardy. BoAnP
Bah! Walter de la Mare. BoAnP

Bah! I have sung women in three cities. Cino. Ezra Pound. VGW
Baha'u'llah in the Garden of Ridwan. Robert Hayden. PoBA
Bahnhofstrasse. James Joyce. NoAM
Bailiff's [*or* Bayliff's] Daughter of Islington, The. *Unknown.* AIW; AmFP; PBMP; RDB, *with music*
Bait, The. John Donne. InPK; InPS
Baked potato's, The. Diner. A. R. Ammons. POL
Baker's knuckles are bruised, The. The Town of Bricked Pathways. Roger McDonald. CAAP
Baking Day. Rosemary Joseph. MPo
Balade: "Hide, Absalon, thy gilte tresses clear." Chaucer. *Fr.* The Legend of Good Women: Prologue. GBL; NOBE ("Hide, Absalon, thy gilte tresses clere.") OxBM
Balade Simple. John Lydgate. GBL
Balalaika. Norman Dubie. AmPA
Balances. Floyd C. Stuart. FAF
Balancing 'twixt earth and sky. The Pole-Vaulter. *Unknown.* SPo
Balboa, the Entertainer. LeRoi Jones. NoAM
Bald Cavalier, The. *Unknown.* OxBChV
Bald heads forgetful of their sins. The Scholars. W. B. Yeats. WIF
Ball Game. Richard Eberhart. MiP
Ball once struck off, The. Base-Ball. John Newbery. SPo
Ball Poem, The. John Berryman. NoAM; NoBA; SPo; SoSe
Ball we bought in December, The. Handball Players. Paul Goodman. SPo
Ball will bounce, but less and less, A. Juggler. Richard Wilbur. NCSH
Ballad: "As you came from the holy land." *Unknown, sometimes at. to* Sir Walter Ralegh. *See* Walsingham.
Ballad: "Auld wife sat at her ivied door, The." Charles Stuart Calverley. FaBoCo; SpRo
Ballad: "He passed by with another." Gabriela Mistral, *tr. fr. Spanish by* Doris Dana. OLR
Ballad: "I dreamed I passed a doorway." John Hall Wheelock. AIW
Ballad for a Boy, A. William Cory. OxBChV
Ballad for Sue Ellen Westerfield, The. Robert Hayden. NoAm
Ballad Maker, A. Padraic Colum. AIW
Ballad of a Nun, A. John Davidson. PAIC
Ballad of Agincourt, The. Michael Drayton. PPoD (To the Cambro-Britons and Their Harp, His Ballad of Agincourt.) BTTM
Ballad of an Empty Table. Tom Kryss. NeAC
Ballad of Befana, The. Phyllis McGinley. AIW
Ballad of Benjamin Bones, The. Christopher Ward. BTTM
Ballad of Bigger Thomas, The. E. Curmie Price. WIF
Ballad of Billie Potts, The. Robert Penn Warren. NOBA
Ballad of Birmingham. Dudley Randall. BPo; InPK; NoAM; WIF
Ballad of Bunker Hill, The. *Unknown.* BTTM
Ballad of Chocolate Mabbie, The. Gwendolyn Brooks. CAPP
Ballad of Dead Ladies, The. Villon, *tr. fr. French by* Dante Gabriel Rossetti. PAIC
Ballad of Dead Yankees, The. Donald Petersen. HeIP
Ballad of East and West, The. Kipling. BTTM
Ballad of Father Gilligan, The. W. B. Yeats. PAIC (Father Gilligan.) AIW
Ballad of Hagensack, The. Wallace Irwin. PoTa
Ballad of Hector in Hades. Edwin Muir. NoAM; NOBE
Ballad of Hiram Hover, The. Bayard Taylor. FaBoCo
Ballad of Ira Hayes. Peter La Farge. MAT
Ballad of John Cable and Three Gentlemen. W. S. Merwin. NOBA

Ballad of Love and Blood. Angel Miguel Queremel, *tr. fr. Spanish* by Rolfe Humphries. LoAs

Ballad of Mary Baldwin, The. Stephen Sandy. MAT

Ballad of Minepit Shaw, The. Kipling. PoTa

Ballad of Mrs. Noah, The. Robert Duncan. MPo; NoAM; NOBA

Ballad of Nat Turner, The. Robert Hayden. BPo; VGW

Ballad of New Orleans. Charles G. Wilson. BTTM

Ballad of No Proper Man. Daniel Hoffman. MAT

Ballad of Orpheus, A. Maurice Lindsay. SLP

Ballad of Reading Gaol, The *sel.* Oscar Wilde.
"He did not wear his scarlet coat." NOBE

Ballad of Red Fox, The. Melvin Walker LaFollette. BoAnP

Ballad of Remembrance, A. Robert Hayden. BPo; PoBA

Ballad of the Bread Man. Charles Causley. MPo

Ballad of the Dark Ladie, The. Samuel Taylor Coleridge. MBPR

Ballad of the Goodly Fere. Ezra Pound. Epi; NoAM; OFD; PAIC

Ballad of the Harp-Weaver, The. Edna St. Vincent Millay. PBMP; PoTa

Ballad of the Landlord. Langston Hughes. NOBA

Ballad of the Long-legged Bait. Dylan Thomas. Epi

Ballad of the Man Who's Gone. Langston Hughes. AIW

Ballad of the Moon, Moon. Federico García Lorca, *tr. fr. Spanish* by Langston Hughes. Epi

Ballad of the Oedipus Complex. Lawrence Durrell. FaBoCo

Ballad of the Pigskin. Horace Spencer Fiske. SPo

Ballad of the Sleepwalker, The. Federico García Lorca. *See* Somnambulistic Ballad.

Ballad of the Three Coins. Vernon Watkins. NoAM

Ballad of Trees and the Master, A. Sidney Lanier. *See* Into the Woods My Master Went.Ballad of Villon and Fat Madge, The. Villon, *tr. fr. French by* Swinburne. LoAs

Ballad-Singer, The. Thomas Hardy. BoLoP; OLR

Ballad to a Traditional Refrain. Maurice James Craig. BIrV

Ballad upon a Wedding, A. Sir John Suckling. LoAs

Ballad Which Anne Askew Made and Sang When She Was in Newgate, The. Anne Askew. WPE

Ballade Made in Hot weather. W. E. Henley. FSFS

Ballade of Dead Actors. W. E. Henley. PPoD

Ballade of Liquid Refreshment. E. C. Bentley. FaBoCo

Ballade of Prose and Rhyme, The. Austin Dobson. PAIC

Ballade of Suicide, A. G. K. Chesterton. PAIC

Ballatetta. Ezra Pound. VGW

Balliol Rhymes. *Unknown.* FaBoCo

Ballit of de Boll Weevil, De. *Unknown.* NOBA
(Boll Weevil Song, The, *with music.*) BLSo

Balloon of the Mind, The. W. B. Yeats. POL

Balloons. Sylvia Plath. MPo; NCSH

Ballroom was filled with fashion's throng, The. A Bird in a Gilded Cage. Arthur J. Lamb. BLSo; FSN

Ballydavid Pier. Thomas Kinsella. BIrV

Ballynahinch. George Canning. FaBoCo

*Ballyshannon* foundered off the coast of Cariboo, The. Etiquette. W. S. Gilbert. FaBoCo

Balmy spring wind, A. Four Haiku. Richard Wright. NoAM

Baltimore Eclipse. Charles Plymell. MIT

Bambino. Betty Ruth Bird. AATT

Banana leaves are burning. "Containing Communism." Charlie Cobb. PoBA

Bananas ripe and green, and ginger-root. The Tropics in New York. Claude McKay. NoAM; PBMP; PoBA

Band Played On, The, *with music.* John F. Palmer. BLSH; BLSo; FSN

Bandage-white and healthy. A Gift of Trilliums. Sandra McPherson.. RiTi

Bang, bang, bang. The History of the Flood. John Heath-Stubbs. OxBTC

Banging around in a cigarette she isn't "in love." Sonnet. Ted Berrigan. CAAP

Banishment, The. Milton. *Fr.* Paradise Lost, XII. NOBE

Banker's Daughter, The. Kathryn Ruby. WBN

Banks fou, braes fou. *Unknown.* GBP

Banks o' Doon, The. Burns. BoLoP; NOBE
(Bonie Doon.) HeIP
(Ye Banks and Braes.) SLP

Banks of Champlain, The. *Unknown.* AmFP

Banks of Claudy, The. *Unknown.* AmFP

Banks of Dee, The. *Unknown.* AmFP

Banks of Newfoundland, The. *Unknown.* GBP

Banks of Sweet Dundee, The. *Unknown.* AmFP

Banks of the Condamine, The. *Unknown.* GBP;PeBB

Banks of the Gaspereaux. *Unknown.* AmFP

Bannockburn. Burns. BTTM
(Robert Bruce's March to Bannockburn.) NOBE

Banquet Song. W. S. Gilbert.. *Fr.* Patience. ECBV

Bantams in Pine-Woods. Wallace Stevens. InPS; NOBA

Baptism. Alden Nowlan. POL

Bar is closed and I come, The. Night on Clinton. Robert Mezey. AmPA

Barbara Allen. *Unknown.* RDB,*with music;* SS; WIF
(Barbara Allen's Cruelty.) AIW
(Barbara Ellen.) AIW
(Barb'ra Allen, *with music.*) BLSo
(Barb'ry Allen, *with music, ad by* James Morehead.) BLSH
(Bonny Barbara Allan) AmFP; BoLoP; HeIP; InPK; PAIC; PeBB; PPoD

Barbara Frietchie. Whittier. BTTM; NOBA

Barbarians. John Fowles. POL

Barbarians, The. Matthew Mead. TwMBP

Barbecue Blues. *Unknown.* BluL

Barber, The. Roy Fuller. NoAM

Barber, barber, shave a pig. Mother Goose. MG

Barb'ry Allen. *Unknown.* *See* Barbara Allen.

Bard. Gavin Bantock. TwMBP

Bard. William Everson. PiAm

Bard, The. Thomas Gray. LAuP; NOBE

Bards of passion and of mirth. Ode. Keats. MBPR

Bare skin is my wrinkled sack. The Shrouded Stranger. Allen Ginsberg. CoPAm

Bare that breathes the northern blast, The. *See* Bear that breathes...

Bareback in Kansas. F. Eugene Warren. AATT

Barefoot. Luís Omar Salinas. SA

Barefoot. Anne Sexton. SFF

Barely a twelvemonth after. The Horses. Edwin Muir. NoAM; NOBE; OxBTC; PPoe; SoSe; TCP

Barely did the dust settle. Taking Off. Ronald Rogers. VW

Barely literate questions it asks, The. That Bad Music. Robert Harris. CAAP

Barely tolerated, living on the margin. Soonest Mended. John Ashbery. CAAP; Prf

Bargain, The. Sir Philip Sidney. *Fr.* Arcadia. NOBE
("My true love hath my heart, and I have his.") BoLoP; GBL; LoAs

Barge she sat in, like a burnished throne, The. Shakespeare. *Fr.* Anthony and Cleopatra, II, ii. PPoe

Barges on the Hudson. Babette Deutsch. WPE

Barn Owl. Gwen Harwood. *Fr.* Father and Child. CAAP; MAuV

Barnyard, The. *Unknown.* AmFP

Baron has decided to mate the monster, The. The Bride of Frankenstein. Edward Field. HeIP

Baron of Buchlyvie. Buchlyvie. *Unknown.* GBP

Baroque Image. May Sarton. PPoD

Baroque Wall-Fountain in the Villa Sciarra, A. Richard Wilbur. CAPP; SoSe

Barrel-Organ, The, *abr.* Alfred Noyes. SoSe

Barrels of blue potato-spray, The. Spraying the Potatoes. Patrick Kavanagh. BIrV

Barren Poem. Michael Ryan. AmPA

Barren Shore, The. Coventry Patmore. GBL

Barren Spring. Dante Gabriel Rossetti. The House of Life, LXXXIII. VPC

Barricades. Michael S. Harper. PoBA

Bar's Fight, August 28, 1746. Lucy Terry. BPo

Bars on Eighth Avenue in Harlem, The. Harlem Gallery: From the Inside. Larry Neal. BPo

Barter. Sara Teasdale. SoSe

Bartley Costello, eighty years old. Gaeltacht. Pearse Hutchinson. BIrV

Base Details. Siegfried Sassoon. HeIP; SoSe

Base Stealer, The. Robert Francis. NCSH; PPoD; SPo

Base-Ball. John Newbery. SPo

Baseball and Writing. Marianne Moore. SPo

Basic themes of lyric poetry are seven, The. Seven. Nicanor Parra, *tr. by* Miller Williams. POL

Basket-weaver's Love, The. René Char, *tr. fr. French by* Jackson Mathews. LoAs

Basket-weavers ravel the Republic. Aside and Memoranda. Elton Glaser. NVAP

Basketball. Stephen Vincent. NeAC

Basking Shark. Norman MacCaig. BoAnP

Bat, The. Theodore Roethke. ECBV; RAE

Bat, The. Roberta Spear. AmPA

Bat Angels. Larry Levis. AmPA

Bat in the Monastery, A. John L'Heureux. SFF

Bat is born, A. Bats. Randall Jarrell. MPo; RAE; RFM; TSWA

Bath. Lincoln Kirstein. NoAM

Bathed in her breath I basked beside her, weak. Duo. William Keys. SLP

Bathing the Aged. Paul Monette. AmPA

Bathing with Father. Doug Fetherling. NeAC

Bathsheba! to whom none ever said scat. Epitaph [*or* For a Little Girl Mourning Her Favorite Cat]. Whittier. ECBV; POL

Bats. Randall Jarrell. MPo; RAE; RFM; TSWA

Bats. George Macbeth. NoAM

Batter my heart, three-personed God; for you. Holy Sonnets, XIV. John Donne. AnMo; BoReV; Epi; HeIP; InPK; InPS; IPWM; MetP; NOBE; OBP; PPoD; PPoe; PPP; SCP-1; WIF

Battle-brave king rested on the shore, The. Beowulf's Last Speech. *Unknown, tr. by* Burton Raffel. *Fr.* Beowulf.OBP

Battle-Cry of Freedom, The. George Frederick Root. BTTM; PSoN, *with music*

Battle Hymn of the Republic, The. Julia Ward Howe. BLSH, *with music*; BLSo, *with music*; BTTM; NOBA; PSoN, *with music*; WPE

Battle in exact though little shape, The. Gondibert, I, 5. Sir William Davenant. SCP-2

Battle of Antietam Creek, The. *Unknown.* AmFP

Battle of Aughrim, The, *sels.* Richard Murphy. BIrV
Planter.
Rapparees.

Battle of Blenheim, The. Robert Southey. AKE; PBMP

Battle of Brunanburh. *Unknown, tr. fr. Anglo-Saxon by* Tennyson. BTTM

Battle of Bull Run, The. *Unknown.* AmFP

Battle of Dunbar, The (1296). *Unknown.* OxBM

Battle of Hohenlinden, The. Thomas Campbell. *See* Hohenlinden.

Battle of Naseby, The. Macaulay. BTTM

Battle of New Orleans, The. *Unknown.* AmFP

Battle of Otterbourne, The. *Unknown.* BTTM

Battle of Shiloh, The. *Unknown.* AIW; AmFP

Battle of Sole Bay, The. *Unknown.* GBP

Battle of the Baltic. Thomas Campbell. BTTM

Battle of the Boyne, The. Captain Blacker. BTTM

Battle Picture, A. Herman Melville. PiAm

Battle Problem. William Meredith. NoAM

Battle rent a cobweb diamond-strung, The. Range-Finding. Robert Frost. NoAM; PPoD

Battle Won Is Lost. Phil George. VW

Baudelaire. Delmore Schwartz. VGW

Baudelaire in Brussels. Anthony Cronin. BIrV

Bavarian Gentians. D. H. Lawrence. InPK; InPS; NoAM; NOBE; PPoe; TCP; WIF, 2 *versions*

Bay Bridge from Portrero Hill, The. Jack Gilbert. NowV

Bay is as cold, The. Looking for Asia. R. H. W. Dillard. CoPAm

Bay of Biscay, The. *Unknown.* AmFP

Bayliff's Daughter of Islington, The. *Unknown.* *See* Bailiff's Daughter of Islington, The.

"Be alive," they say, when I. On Rape Unattempted. Alan Dugan. NoAM

Be Careful! *Unknown.* ECBV

Be Cool, Baby. Rob Penny. PoBA

Be Daedalus. Nanina Alba. PoBA

Be Frugal. Richard Church. OxBTC

Be kind and tender to the frog. The Frog. Hilaire Belloc. LCL; OxBChV

Be natural. The Name. Robert Creeley. IPWM; TCP

Be near me when my light is low. In Memoriam A. H. H., L-LVIII. Tennyson. PFD

Be not dismayed whate'er betide. God Will Take Care of You. Mrs. C. D. Martin. BLSH

Be plain in dress, and sober in your diet. Good Advice. Lady Mary Wortley Montagu. POL

Be reasonable, my pain, and think with more detachment. Inward Conversation. Baudelaire, *tr. by Robert Bly.* InPK

Be Strong. Maltbie D. Babcock. SoSe

Be this the fate. A Curse on a Closed Gate. *Unknown, tr. by* James H. Cousins. PFIr

Be thou then my beauty named. Thomas Campion. AAS

Be ware, squire, yeman, and page. Service Is No Heritage. *Unknown.* OxBM

Be with me, Luis de San Angel, now. Ave Maria. Hart Crane. *Fr.* The Bridge. NoAM; NOBA

Be you to others kind and true. Our Saviour's Golden Rule. Isaac Watts. OxBChV

Beach, The. William Hart-Smith. ECBV

Beach at Veracruz, The. George Bowering. NeAC

Beach Burial. Kenneth Slessor. MAuV

Beach in August, The. Weldon Kees. VGW

Beach is a quarter of golden fruit, The. The Beach. William Hart-Smith. ECBV

Beachy Head, *sels.* Charlotte Smith.
"I once was happy, when, when yet a child." WPE
"On thy stupendous summit, rock sublime!" SBG

Beaks of Eagles, The. Robinson Jeffers. NOBA

Beale Street. Langston Hughes. PPP

Bean Eaters, The. Gwendolyn Brooks. CAPP; CoPAm; HeIP; IPWM; MAT; PoBA

Bear, The. Robert Frost. NoAM

Bear, The. Galway Kinnell. CoPAm; RFM; VGW

Bear, The. N. Scott Momaday. CDW; VW

Bear a Horn and Blow It Not. *Unknown.* OxBM

Bear down under the cliff, A. This Poem Is for Bear. Gary Snyder. *Fr.* Myths and Texts: Hunting. NOBA

Bear me to Dictaeus. Acon. Hilda Doolittle ("H.D."). VGW

Bear on the Delhi Road, The. Earle Birney. BoAnP; HeIP

Bear part with me most straight and pleasant tree. Morea's Sonnet. Mary Sidney Wroth, Countess of Montgomery. *Fr.* Urania. WPE

Bear puts both arms around the tree above her, The. The Bear. Robert Frost. NoAM

Bear sang bass, The. The Achromatic Bear. Robert Bloom. AATT

Bear [or Bare] that breathes the northern blast, The. Upon a Wasp Chilled with Cold. Edward Taylor. NOBA; PiAm; SCP-2

Bear under the snow, A. March. James Wright. TH

Bearded goldfish move about the bowl, The. Goldfish. Howard Nemerov. BoAnP

Bearded Oaks. Robert Penn Warren. CoPAm; NoAM; NOBA; PiAm

Bearer of Evil Tidings, The. Robert Frost. NoAM

Bearing It. Carolyn Stoloff. RiTi

Bears. Adrienne Rich. NCSH

Beast Section, The. Welton Smith. PoBA

Beast, what is love? George Mackay Brown. *Fr.* Lord of the Mirrors. SLP

Beasts. Richard Wilbur. PPoe; PPP

Beasts and Birds. Adelaide O'Keeffe. OxBChV

Beasts Are Very Wise, The. Kipling. BoAnP

Beasts, cattle, have words, neither minor nor many. Death Words. Les A. Murray. *Fr.* Walking to the Cattle-Place. CAAP

Beasts in their major freedom. Beasts. Richard Wilbur. PPoe; PPP

Beat! Beat! Drums! Walt Whitman. InPK; InPS

Beat Poem by an Academic Poet. Vassar Miller. WPE

Beat the drum! beat beat the drum! A New Song Made in Honour of His Grace the Duke of Marlborough. Thomas Durfey. SCP-2

Beat the knife on the plate and the fork on the can. Going in to Dinner. Edward Shanks. OxBTC

Beating, The. Ann Stanford. WPE

Beautiful, The. W. H. Davies. BBGO

Beautiful American Word, Sure, The. Delmore Schwartz. VGW

Beautiful as the flying legend of some leopard. Judith of Bethulia. John Crowe Ransom. NoAM; NOBA; PiAm

Beautiful being, you live as do delicate blossoms in winter. To Diotima. Friedrich Hölderlin, *tr. by* Michael Hamburger. LoAs

Beautiful Black Men. Nikki Giovanni. BPo; NMM

Beautiful Black Women. LeRoi Jones. BPo

Beautiful cashier's white face has risen once more, The. Before a Cashier's Window in a Department Store. James Wright. MAT

Beautiful Changes, The. Richard Wilbur. InPS

Beautiful Contradictions, The, *Sels.* Nathaniel Tarn. "Elders at the zenith of their power look down the sky, The." TwMBP "When Caesar decided to measure the world." TwMBP

Beautiful Dreamer, *with music.* Stephen Collins Foster. BLSH; BLSo

Beautiful face of Paul Delvaux, The. Bruce Beaver. *Fr.* Lauds and Plaints. CAAP

Beautiful is fair, the just is fair, The. Fair and Unfair. Robert Francis. VGW

Beautiful Isle of Somewhere, *with music.* Jessie B. Pounds. FSN

Beautiful little children. Kyoto Born in Spring Song. Gary Snyder. RRA

Beautiful must be the mountains whence ye come. Nightingales. Robert Bridges. NOBE

Beautiful, my delight. To Be Sung on the Water. Louise Bogan. VGW

Beautiful new railway bridge of the silvery Tay. An Address to the New Tay Bridge. William McGonagall. PPoD

Beautiful railway bridge of the silvery Tay! The Railway Bridge of the Silvery Tay. William McGonagall. PPoD

Beautiful railway bridge of the silv'ry Tay! The Tay Bridge Disaster. William McGonagall. PPoD

Beautiful rain falls, the unheeded angel. In Time. Kathleen Raine. WPE

Beautiful River, *with music.* Robert Lowry. PSoN (Shall We Gather at the River?) BLSH.

Beautiful Saviour, *with music. Unknown, tr. fr. German by* J. A. Seiss. BLSH

Beautiful soup, so rich and green. Turtle Soup. "Lewis Carroll." *Fr.* Alice's Adventures in Wonderland. SpRo

Beautiful star in heav'n so bright. Star of the Evening. James M. Sayles. SpRo

Beautiful was the appearance of Cormac in that assembly. Cormac Mac Airt Presiding at Tara. *Unknown, tr. by* Douglas Hyde. BIrV

Beautiful Young Nymph Going to Bed, A. Swift. AnMo

Beautiful Youth. Gottfried Benn, *tr. fr. German by* Joachim Neugroschel. POL

Beautifully Janet slept. Janet Waking. John Crowe Ransom. InPK; NCSH; NoAM; PBMP; PiAm

Beauty. Giovanni Battista Guarini. *See* Of Beauty.

Beauty and Love. Andrew Young. GBL

Beauty Bathing. Anthony Munday. *Fr.* Primaleon of Greece. NOBE

Beauty Imposes. John Shaw Neilson. MAuV

Beauty in the old way of life. New Way, Old Way. David W. Martinez. VW

Beauty is never satisfied. Mythmaking. Kathleen Spivack. NMM

Beauty of/ the male face, The. Thanksgiving. Sharon Barba. RiTi

Beauty of manhole covers, The—what of that? Manhole Covers. Karl Shapiro. MiP; NCSH

Beauty of the world hath made me sad, The. Last Lines—1916. Padraic Pearse. PFIr; WIF

Beauty sat bathing by a spring. Beauty Bathing. Anthony Munday. *Fr.* Primaleon of Greece. NOBE

Beauty, sweet love, is like the morning dew. Samuel Daniel. *Fr.* To Delia. NOBE; PAIC

Beauty's a rose, a shining sword, a thief. A Memory, Now Distant. Eric Linklater. SLP

Beauty's Excellency. Henry Noel. SCP-2

Because. James McAuley. MAuV

Because, *with music.* Edward Teschemacher. FSN

Because he had spoken harshly to his mother. Revelation. Robert Penn Warren. NoAM

Because He Liked to Be at Home. Kenneth Patchen. CoPAm

Because he was a butcher and thereby. Reuben Bright. E. A. Robinson. IPWM; NOBA

Because I believe in the community of little children. The Massacre of the Innocents. William Jay Smith. CoPAm

Because I breathe not love to every one. Astrophel and Stella, LIV. Sir Philip Sidney. BuTh

Because I could not stop for Death. Emily Dickinson. AmVN; AnMo; BBGO; HeIP; InPK; NoAM; NOBA; PBMP; PiAm; SBG; SoSe; VoPo; WPE

Because I do not hope to turn again. Ash-Wednesday, I. T. S. Eliot. BoReV; VGW

Because I had loved so deeply. Compensation. Paul Laurence Dunbar. BPo

Because I liked you better. A. E. Housman. GBL; OxBTC

Because I Were Shy. *Unknown.* PoTa

Because in Vietnam the vision of a Burning Babe. Advent 1966. Denise Levertov. InPS; PiAm; Prf

Because it has sunk so low. Holy City. Anne Waldman. RiTi

Because of Clothes. Laura Riding. NoAM

"Because the beetle that lives in the wood." The Beetle in the Wood. Byron Herbert Reece. PoTa

Because the daughters of Zion are haughty. Isaiah, Bible, *O. T.* OBP

Because the land was shifting, dying. He Left the Pine Ridge Reservation. Carol Cox. MMD

Because the snow is deep. The Fox. Kenneth Patchen. CoPAm; LP; MPo

Because the Three Moirai Have Become the Three Maries. Constance Urdang. Moon

Because the warden is a cousin, my. Deer Hunt. Judson Jerome. CoPAm; RFM

Because there was a man somewhere in a candystripe silk shirt. Homage to the Empress of the Blues. Robert Hayden. CoPAm; PoBA

Because there was no moon. The Wedding. Roland Gant. BuTh

Because thou canst not see. The Philosopher to His Mistress. Robert Bridges. OBP

Because you come to me with naught save love. Because. Edward Teschemacher. FSN

Because you have thrown off your prelate lord. On the [New] Forcers of Conscience. Milton. PAIC; PPoD

Because your love uncurled my anxious toes. To Leonard and Kerstin, With a Gift of Books. Alberta Turner. HeS

Because your voice was at my side. James Joyce. Chamber Music, XVIII. OLR

Because You're You, *with music.* Henry Blossom. BLSo

Becket. Virginia Gilbert. NPW

Becket, *sels.* Tennyson.
    Duet: "Is it the wind of the dawn that I hear." GBL
    Prologue: "Over! the sweet summer closes." GBL

Beckett Kit, The. Linda Gregg. AmPA

Beckoned in Dream to the Unconscious. David Kherdian. FAF

Becky Deem. *Unknown.* BluL

Becoming a Nun. Erica Jong. MMD

Bed, The. A. D. Hope. NoAM

Bed, The. Dennis Saleh. NeAC

Bed by the Window, The. Robinson Jeffers. PiAm

Bed in Summer. Robert Louis Stevenson. OxBChV

Bedelia, *with music.* William Jerome. FSN

Bedtime. Denise Levertov. AnMo; IHMS

Bedtime. J. D. Whitney. NVAP

Bedtime Story. Lou Lipsitz. VGW

Bedtime Story. George Macbeth. LP; MPo; NoAM; PoTa; SoSe

Bedtime Story for My Son. Peter Redgrove. BuTh

Bee, The. James Dickey. SoSe

Bee, The ("There is a little gentleman"). *Unknown.* ECBV

Bee, A/ Interestingly. Sandra Ruth Duguid. AATT

Bee, A/ rolls/ in the yellow. A Couple. May Swenson. RiTi

Bee his burnished carriage, A. Emily Dickinson. NOBA

Bee! I'm expecting you! Emily Dickinson. BoAnP

Bee Meeting, The. Sylvia Plath. InPS; PPP; WPE

Bee, the Ant, and the Sparrow, The. Nathaniel Cotton. OxBChV

Beech Leaves. James Reeves. RAE

Bee-hive, The. Thomas Durfey. SCP-2

Beehive. Jean Toomer. PoBA

Beekeeper's Daughter, The. Sylvia Plath. IHMS

Beeny Cliff. Thomas Hardy. LoAs

Beer. Charles Stuart Calverley. FaBoCo

Bees build in the crevices, The. The Stare's Nest by My Window. W. B. Yeats. Meditations in Time of Civil War, VI. BIrV; NOBE

Beeston, the place, near Nottingham. Autobiographical Note. Vernon Scannell. LP; MPo

Beethoven's Death Mask. Stephen Spender. OxBTC

Beetle, a Bat, and a Bee, A. The Castaways. E. V. Rieu. PoTa

Beetle in the Wood, The. Byron Herbert Reece. PoTa

Beetle loves his unpretending track, The. Wordsworth. *Fr.* Liberty.FaBoCo

Beetle on the Shasta Daylight. Shirley Kaufman. WPE

Befana the Housewife, scrubbing her pane. The Ballad of Befana. Phyllis McGinley. AIW

Before/ I opened my mouth. On Reading Poems to a Senior Class at South High. D. C. Berry. SoSe

Before a Cashier's Window in a Department Store. James Wright. MAT

Before a Saint's Picture. Walter Savage Landor. OxBChV

Before/ and After. Jewel C. Latimore. JB

Before Bed. Keith Waldrop. InPK

Before Dawn. Ann Darr. MiP

Before I laughed with him. What She Said. Maturai Eruttalan Centamputan, *tr. by* A. K. Ramanujan. BoLoP

Before I melt. The Snowflake. Walter de la Mare. FSFS; LCL; NCSH

Before I see another day. The Complaint of a Forsaken Indian Woman. Wordsworth. MBPR

Before I set sail, I will not fail. Skin the Goat's Curse on Carey. *Unknown.* BIrV

Before I slept, I saw the nebula. Sea Otter, a Dream Poem to My Mother. Katherine Doak. NPW

Before man came to blow it right. The Aim Was Song. Robert Frost. SoSe

Before mine eye to feede my greedy will. George Gascoigne. AAS

Before morning you shall be here. Alba. Samuel Beckett. BIrV

Before my face the picture hangs. Upon the Image of Death. Robert Southwell. BoReV; NOBE

Before our lives divide for ever. The Triumph of Time. Swinburne. VPC

Before Parting. Swinburne. OBP

Before she has her floor swept. Portrait by a Neighbor. Edna St. Vincent Millay. TH

Before she left she took a jug of wine. Eruption. Margaret Reynolds. MIS

Before she sold her life to the asphalt. The Suicide. Joannne Casullo. NPW

Before the beginning of years. Swinburne. *Fr.* Atalanta in Calydon. HeIP

Before the Birth of One of Her Children. Anne Bradstreet. MAT; NOBA; PiAm; SBG; WPE

Before the bright sun rises over the hill. The Gleaner. Jane Taylor. OxBChV

Before the Dark is Down. Mary Shumway. NVAP

Before the Fall. Rosemary Daniell. WBN

Before the falling summer sun. Musings. William Barnes. NOBE

Before the Frost. Harley Elliot. HeS

Before the grass is out the people are out. Paterson. William Carlos Williams. PiAm

Before the moon should circlewise close both her horns in one. Medea Casts a Spell to Make Aeson Young Again. Ovid, *tr. by Arthur Golding.* *Fr.* Metamorphoses. Moon

Before the Mountain. Elizabeth Libbey. AmPA

Beside the Road   Ken Belford.   NeAC

Before the Roman came to Rye or out to Severn strode. The Rolling English Road. G. K. Chesterton. NOBE; PPoD; OxBTC

Before the Stuff Comes Down. Gary Snyder. HeIP; PiAm ✓

Before the Thaw. John Gill. NeAC

Before the War. Marilyn Hacker. AmPA

Before the war. From Our Album. Lawson Fusao Inada. AmPA

Before we shall again behold. Endimion Porter and Olivia. Sir William Davenant. NOBE

Before You're a Stranger. Raymond Fraser. AKE

Beforehand and Afterward ("Beforehand, liars studied how to lie"). Henry Tim Chambers. AATT

Befriending the Weather. Helena Minton. FAF

Beggar and Poet. Robert A. Martin. AATT

Beggar Boy, The. Cecil Frances Alexander. OxBChV

Beggar Man, The. Lucy Aikin. OxBChV

Beggarman, The, *with music. Unknown.* RDB

Beggar to Beggar Cried. W. B. Yeats. NoAM

Beggar's Opera, The, *sels.* John Gay.
  "If the heart of a man is depressed with cares," *fr.* II, i. HeIP
  "Modes of the court so common are grown, The," *fr.* III, iv. HeIP
  Over the Hills and Far Away, *fr.* I, i. BLSo, *with music;* NOBE
  Youth and Love, *fr.* II, i. NOBE

Beggar's Serenade. John Heath-Stubbs. BoLoP

Begging-bowl eyes, begging-bowl eyes. You Get Used to It. Adrian Mitchell. NowV

Begin by parting your hair. Parting: A Game. Lynn Sukenick. NMM

Begin, ephebe, by perceiving the idea. Wallace Stevens. *Fr.* Notes Toward a Supreme Fiction. NOBA

Begin with a kisse. Up Tailes All. Robert Herrick. LoAs

Begin with an unruffled lake. Short Subjects. Carolyn Stoloff. RiTi

Beginner,/ Perpetual beginner. What Can I Tell My Bones? Theodore Roethke. NOBA

Beginning. Alden Nowlan. NeAC

Beginning, A. David Steingass. CoPAm

Beginning, The. Wallace Stevens. VGW

Beginning Again As Morning. Eugene Ruggles. MIT

Beginning of an Undergraduate Poem. *Unknown.* FaBoCo

Beginning of wisdom, said the Christmas tree, The. Christmas Needles. Albert Howard Carter. AATT

Beginning the Year at Rosebud, S.D. Roberta Hill. CDW

Beginning to Squall. May Swenson. RFM

Beginnings. Robert D. Fitzgerald. MAuV

Beginnings ("Beginnings of a language"). John Montague. TwMBP

Begins the crying. Guitar. Federico García Lorca, *tr. by* Keith Waldrop. InPK

Begone, begone, my Willie, my Billy. Go from My Window. *Unknown.* AIW

Begot by butchers, but by bishops bred. On Cardinal Wolsey. *Unknown.* FaBoCo

Behind a web of bottles, bales. The Gombeen. Joseph Campbell. BIrV

Behind her not the quivering of a leaf. Circe. A. D. Hope. PPP

Behind him lay the gray Azores. Columbus. Joaquin Miller. AmVN; BTTM

Behind him the hotdogs split and drizzled. Suicide Off Egg Rock. Sylvia Plath. PPP

Behind his dinner jacket. He's Doing Natural Life. Conyus. PoBA

Behind King's Chapel what the earth has kept. At the Indian Killer's Grave. Robert Lowell. NOBA; VGW

Behind shut doors, in shadowy quarantine. The First Time. Karl Shapiro. VGW

Behind That Wall My Roomate Fucks His Girl. Geof Hewitt. NeAC; POL

Behind the Falls. William Stafford. RFM

Behind the grille that Easter noon. Reverend Mother Prioress. Betty Ruth Bird. AATT

Behold, a silly tender babe. New Prince, New Pomp. Robert Southwell. NOBE

Behold her, single in the field. The Solitary Reaper. Wordsworth. AnMo; InPS; MBPR; NOBE; PPP; SoSe

Behold, how eager this our little boy. Of the Boy and Butterfly. John Bunyan. OxBChV

Behold, love, thy power how she despiseth! Sir Thomas Wyatt. GBL

Behold the child, by Nature's kindly law. Pope. *Fr.* An Essay on Man. POL

Behold the duck. The Duck. Ogden Nash. RAE

Behold the ever-tim'rous hare. April. Samuel Thompson. BIrV

Behold the father is his daughter's son. The Nativity of Christ. Robert Southwell. BoReV

Behold the house of Sir William Forbes. The Pentland Hills. *Unknown.* GBP

Behold the worlde, how it is whirled round. Sir John Davies. *Fr.* Orchestra, or A Poem of Dauncing. OBP

Behold this little volume here enrolled. On the Bible. William Strode. SCP-2

Behold those winged images. A Legend of the Hive. Robert Stephen Hawker. VPC

Behold, within the leafy shade. The Sparrow's Nest. Wordsworth. MBPR

Being a burglar, you slip out of doors in the morning. The Burglar. David Wagoner. CoPAm

Being a mammal, I have less care than birds. Displays of Skill: The Bat. Ruth Herschberger. WBN

Being Adult. Bill Zavatsky. POL

Being kissed on the back. Knee Song. Anne Sexton. SFF

Being laid upon her bed she grasped my hand. John Marston. *Fr.* Antonio's Revenge. SCP-2

"Being no longer human, why should I." Paracelsus In Excelsis. Ezra Pound. PiAm

Being you, you cut your poetry from wood. The Egg Boiler. Gwendolyn Brooks. PoBA

Being your slave, what should I do but tend. Sonnets, LVII. Shakespeare. LoAs

Beinn Damph   Paul Mills. MIS

Belfast Lough. *Unknown, tr. fr. Irish by* John Montague. BIrV

Belief. Josephine Miles. NoAM

Believe Me, If All Those Endearing Young Charms, *with music.* Thomas Moore. BLSH

Believing What I Know. William Stafford. Epi

Bell at Midnight. May Miller. PPoD

Bell diphthonging in an atmosphere, A. A Dubious Night. Richard Wilbur. CAPP

Bell-rope that gathers God at dawn, The. The Broken Tower. Hart Crane. NoAM; NOBA; PiAm

Bell Too Heavy to Ring. Tom Kryss. NeAC

Belle of the Ball Room, The. Winthrop Mackworth Praed. FaBoCo

Bellevue. James Harrison. CoPAm

Belling the Cat. William Langland. *Fr.* The Vision of Piers Plowman. OxBM

Bells, The, *sel.* Poe.
"Hear the sledges with the bells." SpRo

Bells, The. Lucille F. Travis. AATT

Bells are booming down the bohreens. Ireland with Emily. John Betjeman. OxBTC

Bells for John Whiteside's Daughter. John Crowe Ransom. AnMo; HeIP; InPK; InPS; NoAM; NOBA; PAIC; PiAm; PPoD; PPP; PSN; RRA; SoSe; VGW; VoPo; WIF

Bells in their ears; smoke in their lungs. Diggle Mill. Glyn Hughes. LP

Bells of Heaven, The. Ralph Hodgson. NOBE; PPoD

Bells of Rhymney. Idris Davies *and* Pete Seeger. PoRo

Bells of waiting Advent ring, The. Christmas. John Betjeman. BoReV; OxBTC

Bells, Ostend, The. William Lisle Bowles. PAIC

Beloved, may your sleep be sound. Lullaby. W. B. Yeats. BoLoP

Beloved, my beloved, when I think. Sonnets from the Portuguese, XX. Elizabeth Barrett Browning. WPE

Beloved, thou hast brought me many flowers. Sonnets from the Portuguese, XLIV. Elizabeth Barrett Browning. VPC; WPE

Below the ten thousand billionth of a centimeter. The First Day. Howard Nemerov. AnMo

Ben. Thomas Wolfe. NCSH

Ben Battle was a soldier bold. Faithless Nellie Gray. Thomas Hood. FaBoCo

Ben Bolt; or, Ah! Don't You Remember, *with music.* Thomas Dunn English. PSoN

Ben Hall was out on the Lachlan side. The Death of Ben Hall. Will H. Ogilvie. PoTa

Bench of Boors, The. Herman Melville. AmVN; SoSe

Bend low again, night of summer stars. Summer Stars. Carl Sandburg. RFM

Bending down the huddle sprout grass. Rain Sleets Flat. Besmilr Brigham. Psy

Bending, I bow my head. Combing. Gladys Cardiff. CDW

Beneath a grove of stars. Gathering Gems. Ethel Green Russell. AATT

Beneath him with new wonder now he views. Milton. *Fr.* Paradise Lost. PPP

Beneath my palm-trees, by the river side. The Song of the Indian Maid. Keats. *Fr.* Endymion. NOBE

Beneath Such Rains. James E. Warren, Jr. AATT

Beneath the silent chambers of the earth. Hell. Abraham Cowley. *Fr.* Davideis, I. SCP-2

Beneath the willow wound round with ivy. Hops. Boris Pasternak, *tr. by* Jon Stallworthy *and* Peter France. BoLoP

Beneath these plains. West of Chicago. John Dimoff. RFM

Beneath these poppies buried deep. Epitaph on Robert Southey. Thomas Moore. FaBoCo

Beneath this stone in hopes of Zion. At Upton-on-Severn. *Unknown.* FaBoCo

Beneath yon birch with silver bark. The Ballad of the Dark Ladie. Samuel Taylor Coleridge. MBPR

Beneath yon larkspur's azure bells. The Blue-Bird. Herman Melville. NOBA

Benedicite! whate dreamed I this nyght? The Dream of a Lover. *Unknown.* LoAs

Benediction. Bob Kaufman. IPWM

Benediction. Stanley Kunitz. VGW

Benediction. William R. Mitchell. AATT

Benediction for Danny. William R. Mitchell. AATT

Benefits of an Education, The. John Ciardi. CoPAm

Benign Neglect/ Mississippi, 1970. Primus St. John. PoBA

Bennie Lynch died in the gutter. The Laneliest Place in the Warld. Donald Campbell. MIS

Bent and knotted as a wintered vine. The First Generation. Janice Mirikitani. MIT

Bent benches, no lockers, nor nowhere near nozzles enough. Bath. Lincoln Kirstein. NoAM

Bent double, like old beggars under sacks. Dulce et Decorum Est. Wilfred Owen. HeIP; InPK; NoAM; PPP; SFF; SoSe; VoPo; WIF

Bent over those. Watching You Draw. Carol Cox. MMD

Beowulf. Kingsley Amis. FaBoCo

Beowulf, *sels. Unknown, tr. fr. Anglo-Saxon.*
Beowulf's Last Speech, *tr. by* Burton Raffel. OBP
Grendel, *tr. by* Burton Raffel. OBP
Introductory: "That towering place, gabled and huge," *tr. by* Burton Raffel. OBP
"Oft in the hall I have heard my people," *tr. by* Charles W. Kennedy. HeIP
To the Sea, *tr. by* Burton Raffel. OBP

Beppo: a Venetian Story. Byron. MBPR
Italy and England, *sel.* PAIC
(Italy versus England.) NOBE

Bereavement. Elizabeth Barrett Browning. WPE

Bereft. Thomas Hardy. BoLoP; NoAM

Bereft Child's First Night. Frances Bellerby. POL

Berg, The. Herman Melville. AmVN; InPK; NOBA; PiAm

Bermudas. Andrew Marvell. AnMo; BoReV; MetP; NOBE

Bernard. Raymond Souster. POL

Berstein disc jockey. Ten O'Clock News. Simon Oritz. VW

Beryl. Lyn Lifshin. NeAC

Beside a chapel I'd a room looked down. Dread. J. M. Synge. BoLoP

Beside a fall there is a round wood pipe. Jean Garrigue. POL

Beside a row of gates. Stray Things. Dan Johnson. PPoD

Beside his heavy-shouldered team. Bullocky. Judith Wright. MAuV

Beside me,—in the car,—she sat. Natura Naturans. Arthur Hugh Clough. VPC

Beside the Bed. Charlotte Mew. WPE

Beside the horse troughs, General Grant. Hens. Alden Nowlan. POL

Beside the Seaside, *sels.* John Betjeman.
"Green shutters, shut your shutters! Windyridge." OxBTC
"On a secluded corner of the beach." LP

Bessie Bobtail. James Stephens. PFIr

Bessie Dreaming Bear. Marnie Walsh. VW

Bessie Smith's Funeral. Alvin Aubert. CoPAm

Best and brightest, come away. To Jane: the Invitation. Shelley. MBPR

Best Line Yet, The. Edward Allen. InPK; POL

Best Loved of Africa. Margaret Danner. PoBA

Best of thy sex! if sacred friendship can. To Philocles [*or* Phylocles], Inviting Him to Friendship. "Ephelia."SCP-2; WPE

Best of Two Worlds. Basil Boothroyd. BoAnP

Best Old Fellow in the World, The. *Unknown.* AmFP

Best slave, The. Alcestis on the Poetry Circuit. Erica Jong. AmPA; RiTi

Best thing in the world, The. Biotherm (For Bill Berkson). Frank O'Hara. CAAP

Best work is made, The. Art. Denise Levertov. CAAP

Bestiary for the Fingers of My Right Hand. Charles Simic. AmPA

Bethsabe's Song. George Peele. *Fr.* David and Bethsabe. NOBE
("Hot sun, cool fire, temper'd with sweet air.") GBL

Betjeman, 1984. Charles Causley. FaBoCo; OxBTC

Betrayal in Morninside. Donald Campbell. MIS

Betrothal, A. E. J. Scovell. GBL

Better late than never: yea, mate. Of Late and Never. John Heywood. PAIC

Better to see your cheek grown hollow. Madman's Song. Elinor Wylie. Moon

Better Way, The. Walter Leaf. FaBoCo

Betty Pringle's Pig. *Unknown.* ECBV

Between Appointments. Giles Gordon. SLP

Between distorted forests, clapped into geometry. Pastoral of the City Streets. A. M. Klein. BBGO

Between extremities. Vacillation. W. B. Yeats. NoAM

Between Me and Anyone Who Can Understand. Sharon Scott. JB

Between my finger and my thumb. Digging. Seamus Heaney. BIrV; MPo

Between painting a roof yesterday and the hay. Independence Day. Wendell Berry. OFD

Between rebellion as a private study and the public. Last Poem. Charles Donnelly. BIrV

Between the dark and the daylight. Death at Suppertime. Phyllis McGinley. PBMP

Between the Electric Rhythm and the Melodic Mind. James Schevill. MIT

Between the gardening and the cookery. A Bookshop Idyll. Kingsley Amis. OxBTC; SoSe

Between the Porch and the Altar, *sels.* Robert Lowell.
At the Altar, IV. InPK; InPS
Katherine's Dream, III. ConAP

Between the under and the upper blue. Seagulls. Robert Francis. RFM

Between the woods the afternoon. The Mirror. A. A. Milne. ECBV

Between the World and Me. Richard Wright. MiP; NoAM; PoBA; WIF

Between town and the. The Quarry Pool. Denise Levertov. VGW

Between two lines of print. Orpheus. Michael Goldman. NowV

Between Two Prisoners. James Dickey. PAIC

Between Two Wars. R. P. Kingston. NVAP

Between us, a mild river. Translation from Original. Joanne Casullo. NPW

Between Walls. William Carlos Williams. VGW

Betwene March and Averil. *See* Bytuene Mersh and Averil.

Betwixt two ridges of ploughed land sat Wat. Margaret Cavendish, Duchess of Newcastle. *Fr.* The Hunting of the Hare. SCP-2

Beulah Land, *with music* Edgar Page. BLSH

Beverly Fragments. Morgan Sanders. WBN

Beverly Hills, Chicago. Gwendolyn Brooks. VGW

Beware: Do Not Read This Poem. Ishmael Reed. BPo; Epi; IPWM; NCSH; PoBA

Beware, My Child. Shel Silverstein. CaYB

Beware of Benjamin Franklin, he is totally lacking in grace. Sonnet. Ted Berrigan. CAAP

Beware of the man who denounces ambition. Seventeen [*or* Sixteen] Warnings in Search of a Feminist Poem. Erica Jong. AmPA; NVAP; WBN

Beware! The Israelite of old, who tore. The Warning. Longfellow. PiAm

Beware the Months of Fire. Patrick Lane. NeAC

Bewick Finzer. E. A. Robinson. PPP

Bewteis of Fute-Ball, The. *Unknown.* FaBoCo

Beyond a low wall. Tortoise. Joanne de Longchamps. BoAnP

Beyond Anguish. Milton Kessler. CoPAm

Beyond Breath. Ken Smith. TwMBP

Beyond earshot of others, furtively. The Conspirators. Kenneth Burke. SFF

Beyond Logic. Adrianne Marcus. NPW

Beyond Silence (1). Andrew Taylor. CAAP

Beyond that sandbar is the river's turning. Exploration Over the Rim. William Dickey. SS

Beyond the Alps. Robert Lowell. NOBA; PiAm

Beyond the bell-post by the door. Winter Morning. Stephen Tudor. HeS

Beyond the edge of the sepia. Lament for a Cricket Eleven. Kenneth Allott. OxBTC

Beyond the End. Denise Levertov. VGW

Beyond the hour we counted rain that fell. Old Countryside. Louise Bogan. WPE

Beyond the Hunting Woods. Donald Justice. ConAP; NCSH

Beyond the Last Lamp. Thomas Hardy. NOBE

Beyond the Liss. John Montague. TwMBP

Beyond the Nigger ("Beyond the outstretched hands"). Sterling Plumpp. PoBA

Beyond the porcelain fence of the pleasure garden. A Year Passes. Amy Lowell. Moon

Beyond the Storm. James Bertolino. HeS

Beyond the sunrise. Ode to Willem de Kooning. Frank O'Hara. Epi

Beyond What. Alice Walker. WBN

Biafra. L. V. Mack. PoBA

Bible opens then closes real hard, A. Empty Streams of Autumn. Ray A. Young Bear. VW

Bibliotheca Bodleiana. Geoffrey Grigson. GBL

Bicycle Built for Two. Harry Dacre. *See* Daisy Bell...

Bicycle Rider. Eugene McCarthy. SPo

Bicycles go by in twos and threes, The. Inniskeen road: July Evening. Patrick Kavanagh. NoAM; PFIr

Bid all profane away! Ben Jonson. *Fr.* Hymenaei. SCP-1

Bid me to live, and I will live. To Anthea, Who May Command Him Anything. Robert Herrick. NOBE

Bidding Prayer, A ("Bidde we with milde stevene"). *Unknown.* OxBM

Big Apple Blues. *Unknown.* BluL

Big Bessie Throws Her Son into the Street. Gwendolyn Brooks. VGW

Big Billie Potts was big and stout. The Ballad of Billie Potts. Robert Penn Warren. NOBA

Big black Angus bull. Seventh Georgic. George Economou. POL

Big Boy came. Catch. Langston Hughes. NoAM

Big brown tin can lyin' in the black sand. Ain't It a Sad Thing? R. Dean Taylor. PoRo

Big Chief Blues. *Unknown.* BluL

Big Dog. Philip Booth. BoAnP

Big doors of the country barn stood open and ready, The. Walt Whitman. *Fr.* Song of Myself. RAE

Big Dream, Little Dream. Louis Simpson. POL

Big Hat or What, A? Pete Morgan. SLP

Big John Henry. Margaret Walker. WIF

Big Momma. Don L. Lee. BPo

Big Night Blues. *Unknown.* BluL

Big Road Blues. *Unknown.* BluL

Big Rock Candy Mountains, The, *diff. versions. Unknown.* AmFP; GBP; NOBA

Big Rock Jail. *Unknown.* BluL

Big star, and that other, The. Leaflets. Adrienne Rich. NoAM

Big Sunflower, The, *with music.* Bobby Newcomb. BLSo

Big Sur Summer. Delia Chilgren. NPW

Big Wind. Theodore Roethke. AnMo; NCSH; PiAm; PPoe; VGW

Big Woman. *Unknown.* BluL

Big young bareheaded woman, A. Proletarian Portrait. William Carlos Williams. MiP; PiAm

Bigger than your doubt, Thomas. The Ballad of Bigger Thomas. E. Curmie Price. WIF

Biggest Killing, The. Edward Dorn. VGW

Biglow Papers, The, *sels.* James Russell Lowell.
  1st Series, No. VI.
    Pious Editor's Creed, The. PiAm
  1st Series, No. VIII.
    Letter from a Candidate for the Presidency, A. PiAm
  2d Series, Introduction.
    Courtin', The. AmVN; NOBA

Bigness of Atoms, The. Margaret Cavendish, Duchess of Newcastle. SCP-2

Bilbea Carl Sandburg. PiAm

Bile Them Cabbage Down. *Unknown.* AmFP

Bill/ exists. A Personality Sketch: Bill. Ronda Davis. JB

Bill Bailey Won't You Pleases Come Home, *with music.* Hughie Cannon. BLSo; FSN

Bill of Fare, A, *sel.* William Cartwright.
  "Expect no strange or puzzling meat, no pie." SCP-2

Billy. Harry Graham. FaBoCo

Billy Boy. *Unknown.* AmFP

Billy Budd, Foretopman, *sel.* Herman Melville.
  Billy in the Darbies. NOBA

Billy goat's a handsome gent, The. The Goat. Roland Young. BoAnP

Billy Grimes. *Unknown.* AmFP

Billy, in one of his nice new sashes. Billy. Harry Graham. FaBoCo

Billy in the Darbies. Herman Melville. *Fr.* Billy Budd, Foretopman. NOBA

Billy Lyons and Stack O'Lee. *Unknown.* BluL

Bingo. *Unknown.* ECBV

Binnorie. *Unknown. See* Two Sisters, The.

Binsey Poplars. Gerard Manley Hopkins. InPS; NoAM

Biography, *sel.* John Masefield.
  "Other bright days of action have seemed great." OxBTC

Biography in the First Person. Stephen Dunn. NVAP

Biography of Southern Rain. Kenneth Patchen. VGW

Biotherm (For Bill Berkson). Frank O'Hara. CAAP

Birch ("Birch tree, you remind me"). Louis Simpson. SFF

Birches. Robert Frost. IPWM; NoAM

Bird, The. Moishe Leib Halpern, *tr. fr. Yiddish by* John Hollander. PPP

Bird, The. Charles Simic. AmPA

Bird, The. Henry Vaughan. SCP-1

Bird Calls. Cathleen Quirk. MMD

Bird calls me, A. The Bird. Charles Simic. AmPA

Bird came down the walk, A. Emily Dickinson. AmVN; IPWM; NOBA

Bird ecstatic with the spring, A. Verna Tomlinson Baker. AATT

Bird Fancier, The. James Kirkup. ECBV

Bird flying past my head said previous previous, The. Conrad Aiken. *Fr.* Time in the Rock; or, Preludes to Definition, LXII. VGW

Bird in a Cage. *Unknown.* GBP

Bird in a Gilded Cage, A, *with music.* Arthur J. Lamb. BLSo; FSN

Bird in Search of a Cage, A. Robert Pack. SFF

Bird is lost, The. Yardbird's Skull. Owen Dodson. PoBA; TCP; VGW

Bird is my neighbour, a whimsical fellow and dim, The. The Crane Is My Neighbour. John Shaw Neilson. MAuV

"Bird Lives": Charles Parker in St. Louis. Michael S. Harper. AmPA

Bird Nest Bound. *Unknown.* BluL

Bird of Night, The. Randall Jarrell. CoPAm; NCSH; RFM; TSWA

Bird on Briar. *Unknown.* OxBM

Bird on Nellie's Hat, The, *with music.* Arthur J. Lamb. FSN

Bird sighs for the air. The Lover's Song. W. B. Yeats. AnMo

Bird watchers top my honors list. Up from the Egg: The Confessions of a Nuthatch Avoider. Ogden Nash. BoAnP

Bird who for his other sins, A. A Character. Samuel Taylor Coleridge. MBPR

Birdie with a yellow bill, A. Time to Rise. Robert Louis Stevenson. OxBChV

Birds. Robinson Jeffers. VGW

Birds. D. H. Lawrence. BoAnP

Birds against the April wind, The. What the Birds Said. Whittier. NOBA

Birds and Fishes. Robinson Jeffers. PiAm; TCP

Birds and periodic blood. 5:30 A.M. Adrienne Rich. NMM; NOBA; PiAm

Birds and sunlight. Yellow. De Leon Harrison. PoBA

Birds are the life of the skies. Birds. D. H. Lawrence. BoAnP

Birds, birds, birds. Beat Poem by an Academic Poet. Vassar Miller. WPE

Birds cannot fly over it. Her Dream House. Marvin Bell. NVAP

Birds fly in the broken windows. Two Beers in Argyle, Wisconsin. Dave Etter. ANTL

Birds go fluttering in the air, The. The Silent Snake. *Unknown.* CaYB

Birds in their little nests agree. Hilaire Belloc. POL

Birds in Their Title Work Freeholds of Straw. Les A. Murray. *Fr.* Walking to the Cattle-Place. CAAP

Birds move from branch to branch. No One to Blame. Laurence Lieberman. CoPAm

Birds' Nest. Edward Thomas. HeIP

Birds of America, The. James Broughton. BoAnP

Birds of Hazard and Prey, *sel.* Nanos Valaoritis.
  "With great difficulty I managed to get out of my skin." MIT

Birds of the forest are calling for thee, The. Gypsy Love Song. Harry B. Smith. FSN

Birds Waking. W. S. Merwin. NOBA

Birdwatchers of America. Anthony Hecht. NoAM; NOBA; PPP

Birks of Invermay, The. David Mallet. SLP

Birmingham. Margaret Walker. PoBA

Birmingham Jail. *Unknown.* GBP

Birmingham 1963. Raymond R. Patterson. PoBA

Birmingham Sunday. Richard Farina. NowV

Birth, A. James Dickey. NOBA

Birth, The. Rosemary Dobson. MAuV

Birth. Amir Gilboa, *tr. fr. Hebrew by* Robert Mezey *and* Shula Starkman. OFD

Birth of a Genius Among Men. "Hugh MacDiarmid." SLP

Birth of John Henry, The. Melvin B. Tolson. *Fr.* Harlem Gallery. BPo

Birth of My Drinking Problem, The. Michael McMahon. FAF

Birth of the Foal. Ferenc Juhász, *tr. fr. Hungarian by* David Wevill. BoAnP

Birthday, The. Philip Dacey. AmPA

Birthday, The. Morley Jamieson. SLP

Birth Day. Merle Meeter. AATT

Birthday, A. Edwin Muir. LoAs

Birthday, A.   Christina Rossetti.   NOBE; OLR; VPC; WIF; WPE

Birthday Card for a Psychiatrist.   Mona Van Duyn.   IHMS

Birthday Gifts.   Herbert Asquith.   OFD

Birthday of but a single pang.   Emily Dickinson.   OFD

Birthday Verses Written in a Child's Album.   James Russell Lowell.   OxBChV

Birthdays from the ocean one desert april noon.   That "Craning of the Neck."   Isabella Gardner.   WPE

Birthing, The.   Beth Bentley.   LoAs

Birthplace, The.   Robert Frost.   OFD

Birthplace Revisited.   Gregory Corso.   SA; VGW

Birthright.   John Drinkwater.   OxBTC

Biscuits with honey running down into the deep crevices. Overweight Poem.   Diane Wakoski.   CAAP

Bishop Blougram's Apology.   Robert Browning.   PFD Unfaith and Faith, sel.   BoReV

Bishop Cody's Last Request.   Tom Paxton.   GrRo

Bishop Hatto   Robert Southey.   PoTa

Bishop of Canterbury, The.   Unknown.   AmFP

Bishop Orders His Tomb at Saint Praxed's Church, The.   Robert Browning.   AnMo; Epi; GrRo; HeIP; IPWM; PPoe; PPP

Bison Flower Days.   Anselm Hollo.   TwMBP

Bison Track, The.   Bayard Taylor.   AmVN

Bit an apple on its red.   Green Red Brown and White.   May Swenson.   VGW

Bite-lip brave and militant.   The Youngest Schizophrene. Katherine Hoskins.   TCP

Bitter for Sweet.   Christina Rossetti.   GBL

Bitter Herbs.   Alta.   NMM

Bitter is the wind tonight.   The Viking Terror.   Unknown, tr. by Kuno Meyer.   PFIr

Bitter Lemons.   Lawrence Durrell.   VoPo

Bitter morning, A.   Haiku.   J. W. Hackett.   BoAnP

Bitter Pills for the Dark Ladies.   Erica Jong.   Psy; RiTi; WBN

Bitter-Sweet.   George Herbert.   BoReV; IPWM; NOBE

Bitter the wind tonight.   The Vikings.   Unknown, tr. by John Montague.   BIrV

Bitter Withy, The.   Unknown.   GBP; PeBB

Bitter year it was, A.   What woman ever.   The Wreath.   Robert Graves.   BoLoP

Bitterness rolls off.   Antisong.   Phyllis Webb.   MMD

Bivouac on a Mountain Side.   Walt Whitman.   PiAm

Bizarre Apollo, half what Henry dreamed.   Apollo 8.   John Berryman.   Moon

Black All Day.   Raymond R. Patterson.   PoBA

Black and White.   Tom Schmidt.   NeAC

Black Angel, The.   Michael S. Harper.   NVAP

Black Art.   LeRoi Jones.   BPo; CAPP

Black Art, The.   Anne Sexton.   Psy

Black beauty, which, above that common light.   Sonnet of Black Beauty.   Lord Herbert of Cherbury.   PAIC

Black biplane crashes into the window, The.   Love Poem. Gregory Orr.   MAT

Black Book, The, sel.   John Berryman. "Grandfather, sleepless in a room upstairs."   VGW

Black Bourgeoisie.   LeRoi Jones.   BPo

Black boy/ let me get up from the white man's table of fifty sounds.   PSI.   Melvin B. Tolson.   PoBA

Black brother, think you life so sweet.   Time to Die.   Ray Garfield Dandridge.   PoBA

Black-burnin' shame is your garb, quo' they.   The Scarlet Woman. "Hugh MacDiarmid."   SLP

Black cat, sweet brother.   For James Baldwin.   Kay Boyle. NMM

Black cat yawns, The.   Cat.   Mary Britton Miller.   LCL; PCat

Black Cliffs, Ballybunion, The.   Brendan Kennelly.   PFIr

Black Clouds.   Terence Brame.   RAE

Black Cottage, The.   Robert Frost.   VGW

Black Day in July.   Gordon Lightfoot.   IPWM

Black Dog.   Ray A. Young Bear.   CDW

Black-eyed Susie.   Unknown.   AmFP

Black Finger, The.   Angelina Weld Grimké.   PoBA

Black flakes on the quiet wind, The.   A Twilight Man.   Harry Guest.   TwMBP

Black fool, why winter here? These frozen skies.   Advice to a Raven in Russia.   Joel Barlow.   NOBA

Black Forest.   Roderick Watson.   MIS

Black gal,/ she took a knife.   My Black Gal Blues.   Unknown. BluL

Black Girl, De.   Unknown.   GBP

Black girl black girl.   Blackberry Sweet [or Black Magic].   Dudley Randall.   InPS; NCSH; OLR; PoBA

Black grows the southern sky, betokening rain.   Sudden Shower. John Clare.   Epi

Black-haired girl, The.   The Yawn.   Paul Blackburn.   CTBA

Black hand supports, A.   As It Should Be.   Tom Meschery.   SPo

Black Hat, The.   Clayton Eshleman.   VGW

Black history.   The Living Truth.   Sterling Plumpp.   PoBA

Black Horse Blues.   Unknown.   BluL

Black Humor.   Archibald MacLeish.   NCSH

Black in Virginia.   Grace Cavalieri.   AATT

Black Is a Soul   Joseph White.   PoBA

Black Is Beautiful.   Philip Appleman.   SFF

Black Is Best.   Larry Thompson.   PoBA

Black is the Colour.   Unknown.   GBP

Black is the first nail I ever stepped on.   Negritude.   James A. Emanuel.   BPo

Black is what the prisons are.   The African Affair.   Bruce McM. Wright.   PoBA

Black Jack Davey.   Unknown.   MAT

Black Jackets.   Thom Gunn.   HeIP; NowV

Black Jam for Dr. Negro.   Mari Evans.   BPo; PoBA; Psy

Black Lady in an Afro Hairdo Cheers for Cassius.   R. Ernest Holmes.   PPoD

Black luggie, lammer bead.   Against Witches.   Unknown.   GBP

Black Magic.   Dudley Randall.   See Blackberry Sweet.

Black Magic.   Sonia Sanchez.   BPo

Black Mail.   Alice Walker.   AmPA

Black Majesty.   Countee Cullen.   PoBA; VGW

Black Man, A.   Sam Cornish.   PoBA

Black Man Talks of Reaping, A.   Arna Bontemps.   BPo; PoBA

Black Man's Feast.   Sarah Webster Fabio.   PoBA

Black Mother Woman.   Audré Lorde.   WBN

Black Mountain Blues.   Unknown.   BluL

Black mountains pricked with pointed pine.   The Watershed. Alice Meynell.   SBG

Black Narcissus.   Gerald W. Barrax.   PoBA

Black November Turkey, A.   Richard Wilbur.   BoAnP; CoPAm; NCSH

Black one, last as usual, swings her head, The.   Fetching Cows. Norman MacCaig.   BoAnP; LP

Black Patch on Lucasta's Face, A.   Richard Lovelace.   PAIC

Black People!   LeRoi Jones.   BPo

Black people think.   Awareness.   Don L. Lee.   PoBA

Black People: This Is Our Destiny.   LeRoi Jones.   CAPP

Black Pierrot, A.   Langston Hughes.   OLR

Black Plateau, The.   W. S. Merwin.   CAAP

Black Poet, White Critic.   Dudley Randall.   BPo; ConAP

Black poets should live—not leap.   For Black Poets Who Think of Suicide.   Etheridge Knight.   PoBA

Black Power. Nikki Giovanni. Psy

Black Power. Alvin Saxon. PoBA

Black Power Poem. Ishmael Reed. BPo

Black reapers with the sound of steel on stones. Reapers. Jean Toomer . BPo; InPK; NoAM; PoBA; PPP

Black Riders, The, *sels.*    Stephen Crane.
"Black riders came from the sea," I.  AmVN
God in Wrath, A, XIX.  AmVN; IPWM
"God lay dead in heaven," LXVII.  PiAm
I Saw a Man Pursuing the Horizon, XXIV.  MAT; NOBA; PBMP; PiAm; SFF
If I Should Cast Off This Tattered Coat, LXVI.  PBMP
In the Desert, III.  AmVN; NOBA; PiAm
(Heart, The.)  InPK
"Man saw a ball of gold in the sky, A," XXXV.  AmVN; PiAm
"Many red devils ran from my heart," XLVI.  PiAm
"Once, I knew a fine song," LXV.  PiAm
"There was, before me," XXI.  PiAm
"Well, then, I hate Thee, unrighteous picture,"XII.  AmVN
"Youth in apparel that glittered, A." XXVII.  PiAm

Black Rook In Rainy Weather. Sylvia Plath. Psy

Black sails knifing through the pitchblende night. Wooden Ships. David Crosby, Paul Kantner, *and* Stephen Stills. GrRo

Black Sheba. Jodi Braxton. WBN

Black Sketches. Don L. Lee. NeAC

Black Snake. *Unknown.* BluL

Back Spring Becomes Anonymous, The. Sotère Torregian. MIT

Black Star Line. Henry Dumas. PoBA

Black sunshine. No Dice. Kathleen Wiegner. MMD

Black Taffy. Peggy Susberry Kenner. JB

Black Tambourine. Hart Crane. InPK; NoAM; PAIC; PPP

Black Tarn. V. Sackville-West. SBG

Black Tomintoul. Ian Hamilton Finlay. SLP

Black Tower, The. W. B. Yeats. BoReV

Black Trumpeter. Henry Dumas. PoBA

Black Warrior. Norman Jordan. PoBA

Black within and red without. *Unknown.* GBP

Black Woman. Naomi Long Madgett. OLR; PoBA

Blackberries sweet and dusty. Someplace Else. Marge Piercy NeAC

Blackberry Sweet. Dudley Randall. InPS; NCSH
(Black Magic.)  OLR; PoBA

Blackberrying. Sylvia Plath. MPo; NoAM; NOBA

Blackbird. Christopher Leach. BoAnP

Blackbird, The. Humbert Wolfe. RAE

Blackbird by Belfast Lough, The. *Unknown, tr. fr. Irish by* Frank O'Connor. ECBV

Blackbird of Derrycairn, The. *Unknown, tr. fr. Irish by* Austin Clarke. BIrV

Blackbird Singing, A. R. S. Thomas. BoAnP

Blackbird singing in the tree, The. Best of Two Worlds. Basil Boothroyd. BoAnP

Blackbirds and Thrushes. *Unknown.* GBP

Blackbird's Song. *Unknown.* GBP

Blackened trees. Minneapolis. Tom Hennen. HeS

Blackfeet, Blood and Piegan Hunters. James Welch. SA

Blackfish Poem. Milton Acorn. NeAC

Blackfriars. Eleanor Farjeon. OxBChV

Blackie Thinks of His Brothers. Stanley Crouch. PoBA

Blackleg Miners, The. *Unknown.* GBP

Blacksmiths, The. *Unknown.* OxBM

Blacksmith's boy went out with a rifle, The. Legend. Judith Wright. PoTa

Blacksmith's Serenade, The. Vachel Lindsay. PoTa

Blacksmith's Song, The. *Unknown.* GBP

Blackstone Rangers, The. Gwendolyn Brooks. NoAM; NowV; PoBA

Blakeney people, The. The People of Blakeney. *Unknown.* GBP

Blame. Gavin Bantock. TwMBP

Blame not my cheeks, though pale with love they be. Thomas Campion. AAS

Blame not my lute for he must sownde. Sir Thomas Wyatt. AAS

Blanaid's Song ("Blanaid loves roses"). Joseph Campbell. PFIr

Blandly mother. Wild Orphan. Allen Ginsberg. TCP

Blank faced. Vacancy. Daniela Gioseffi. WBN

Blasted with sighs, and surrounded with tears. Twicknam Garden. John Donne. SCP-1

Bleached wood massed in bone piles. Kalaloch. Carolyn Forché. AmPA

Bless me, what damps are here! how stiff an air! The Charnel-House. Henry Vaughan. SCP-1

Blessed and Resting Uncle. Harley Elliott. NeAC

Blessed Assurance, *with music.* Fanny Crosby. BLSH

Blessed Damozel, The. Dante Gabriel Rossetti. NOBE; VPC
"Blessed damozel leaned out, The," *sel.* SpRo

Blessed Trinity have pity! Childless. Giolla Brighde MacNamee, *tr. by* Frank O'Connor. BIrV

Blessing, A. James Wright. ANTL; ConAP; InPK; NoAM; NOBA; PPP; SFF; SoSe

Blessing on the Cows, A. "Seumas O'Sullivan." BoAnP; PFIr

Blessing without Company. *Unknown.* BPo; POL

Blest Be the Tie That Binds, *with music.* John Fawcett. BLSH

Blest, blest and happy he. *Unknown.* GBL

Blest is t' bride at t' sun shines on. Wedding and Funeral. *Unknown.* GBP

Blest pair of Sirens, pledges of heaven's joy. At a Solemn Music. Milton. AnMo; BoReV; HeIP; NOBE; PAIC

B'lieve I'll take me a walk 'round the corner. Take a Walk Around the Corner. *Unknown.* BluL

Blight. Emerson. NOBA; PiAm

Blighted apples will not shine. Apple Blight. Paul Zimmer. VGW

"Blighters." Siegfried Sassoon. NoAM

Blind Adolphus. Angela McCabe. AmPA

Blind Always Come As Such a Surprise, The. Ted Kooser. HeS

Blind bald-headed blunderer. Hand. Morton Marcus. NVAP

Blind Beggar, The. *Unknown.* AmFP

Blind Boy, The. Colley Cibber. OxBChV

Blind Leading the Blind, The. Lisel Mueller. IHMS

Blind man draws his curtains for the night, The. Rooming House. Ted Kooser. POL

Blind Men and the Elephant, The. John Godfrey Saxe. ECBV; PoTa

Blind Old Woman. Clarence Major. PoBA

Blinded Bird, The. Thomas Hardy. NoAM

Blindfold. Luci Shaw. AATT

Blisful lyf, a paisible and a swete, A. The Former Age. Chaucer. OxBM

Blizzard, The. A. A. Dewey. HeS

Blk/ woman/ speaks, A. Three X Three. Sonia Sanchez. WBN

Blocks, The/ which are the buildings and walls. Comforted by Limestone. Edward Dorn. *Fr.* Oxford. NOBA

Blok: Let Me Learn the Poem. Aram Boyajian. NeAC

Blond. Joseph De Roche. HeIP

Blood. Les A. Murray. MAuV

Blood and My Brother. Richard Mathews. AATT

Blood Hound Blues. *Unknown.* BluL

Blood stains Union Street in Mississippi. May 27, 1971: No Poem. June Jordan. WBN

Blood thudded in my ears. I scuffed. First Confession. X. J. Kennedy. ConAP; CoPAm; NCSH; PPP

Blood-strained Banders, The. *Unknown.* AmFP

Bloody/ egg yolk, A. A burnt hole. Out of the Sea, Early. May Swenson. RFM

Bloody Brother, The, *sel.* John Fletcher, *and others.* Drink Today, *fr.* II, ii. PAIC

Bloom Street. Angela McCabe. AmPA

Blooms such as wither at finger-touch. Brian Coffey. *Fr.* Muse, June, Related. BIrV

Blossom, The. Blake. *Fr.* Songs of Innocence. MBPR

Blossom, The. John Donne. AnMo

Blossom blows, The/ across the step. There Are Lime Trees in Leaf on the Promenade. Tom Raworth. TwMBP

Blossom on the plum. March. Nora Hopper. FSFS

Blow, blow! The winds are so hoarse they cannot blow. The Winter Storms. Sir William Davenant. SCP-2

Blow, Blow, Thou Winter Wind! Shakespeare. *Fr.* As You Like It, II, vii. FSFS; GBL; HeIP; InPS; NOBE; PPoe

Blow, Bugle, Blow. Tennyson. *See* Splendor Falls on Castle Walls, The.

Blow Gabriel. *Unknown.* BluL

Blow, Northern Wind. *Unknown.* GBL; OxBM

"Blow out the light," they said, they said. Temper. Rose Fyleman. OxBChV

Blow softly down the valley. The King of Ireland's Cairn. "Ethna Carbery." WPE

Blow the Candle Out. *Unknown.* AmFP

Blow the Candles Out, *with music. Unknown.* RDB

Blow the Man Down. *Unknown.* AmFP; BLSH, *with music;* BLSo, *with music*

Blow the Winds, I-Ho. *Unknown.* GBP; PeBB

Blow, West Wind. Robert Penn Warren. *Fr.* Notes on a Life to Be Lived. NoAM

Blow, winds, and crack your cheeks! rage! blow! Shakespeare. *Fr.* King Lear, III, ii. OBP

Blow, Ye Winds. *Unknown.* AmFP

Blown Door, The. Malcolm Cowley. PPoD

Blows the wind today, and the sun and the rain are flying. To S. R. Crockett. Robert Louis Stevenson. NOBE

Blue and the Gray, The. Francis Miles Finch. BTTM

Blue Animals, The. Jon Anderson. AmPA

Blue-black swallowtail sits on my finger, A. Visitation. Elisavietta Ritchie. AATT

Blue Bog Children. Roger Weingarten. AmPA

Blue Booby, The. James Tate. AmPA; NoAM

Blue boughs, green fruit. The Furnished Room. James Merrill. NOBA

Blue Bowl of Plums Invention, The. Lyn Lifshin. Psy

Blue Boy on Skates (Twilight). M. L. Rosenthal. SPo

Blue-Butterfly Day. Robert Frost. RFM

Blue Coat, A. Gertrude Stein. *Fr.* Tender Buttons. RiTi

Blue Duck, The. David Ray. HeS

Blue-eyed Girl. *Unknown.* AmFP

Blue-eyed Precinct Worker, The. Henri Coulette. MAT

Blue-Fly, The. Robert Graves. NoAM

Blue-geese, white-geese, you may say. Hilda Doolittle ("H.D."). *Fr.* The Flowering of the Rod. NOBA

Blue Gift, The. David Perkins. NCSH

Blue Girls. John Crowe Ransom. GBL; NoAM; SS; VGW; VoPo

Blue Horses. Ed Roberson. PoBA

Blue jay scuffling in the bushes follows, The. On the Move. Thom Gunn. NowV; OBP; OxBTC; PPP

Blue jumped a rabbit, run him one solid mile. Rabbit Foot Blues. *Unknown.* BluL

Blue Like Death. James Welch. CDW

Blue Monday. *Unknown.* AmFP

Blue Mosque, The. Lee Harwood. TwMBP

Blue Ruth: America. Michael S. Harper. PoBA

Blue Swallows, The. Howard Nemerov. AnMo

Blue-tail Fly, The. *Unknown. See* Jim Crack Corn...

Blue Tanganyika. Lebert Bethune. PoBA

Blue Teal's Mother. James Wright. CAAP

Blue! 'Tis the life of heaven,—the domain. Answer to a Sonnet ending Thus. Keats. MBPR

Blue Whale, The. Robert Watson. MAT

Blue Wing, The. Donald Hall. ConAP

Bluebeard's Wife. Daryl Hine. NoAM

Blue-Bird, The. Herman Melville. NOBA

Blueline. Ken Belford. NeAC

Blueness of night, The. The Listening Rock. Ray A. Young Bear. VW

Blues. Derek Walcott. OBP

Blues/ Never climb a hill. Get Up, Blues. James A. Emanuel. PoBA

Blues, The: a Literary Eclogue. Byron. MBPR

Blues and Bitterness. Lerone Bennett, Jr. PoBA

Blues for a Cello Man. Carol Bergé. MMD

Blues for John Coltrane, Dead at 41. William Matthews. NVAP

Blues for Sister Sally. Lenore Kandel. NMM; RiTi

Blues meant Swiss-Up, The. Riding Across John Lee's Finger. Stanley Crouch. PoBA

Blues Note. Bob Kaufman. PoBA

Blues Today, The. Mae Jackson. PoBA

Bluff King Hal was full of beans. Henry VIII. Eleanor *and* Herbert Farjeon. PoTa

Blum. Dorothy Aldis. ECBV; LCL

Blurt, Master Constable, *sel.* Thomas Middleton. Night Sounds. RAE

Blythsome Bridal, The. *Unknown, at. to* Francis Sempill. GBP; PeBB

Boa Constrictor. Shel Silverstein. CaYB

Boar's Head, The. *Unknown.* OxBM

Boat Poem. Bernard Spencer. OxBTC

Boats sail on the rivers. The Rainbow. Christina Rossetti. OxBChV

Bob McKinney. *Unknown.* BluL

Bob Southey! You're a poet—poet-laureate. Dedication. Byron. *Fr.* Don Juan. MBPR; PPoe

Bobadil. James Reeves. LCL

Bobbily Boo and Wollypotump. Laura E. Richards. LCL

Bobbing of balloons. Greyhounds. Robert Gray. CAAP

Bobby Shaftoe. *Unknown.* GBP

Bob-ing split-able heads. Solitary Visions of a Kaufmanoid. James Cunningham. JB

Bodies lift burdens. Bearing It. Carolyn Stoloff. RiTi

Body, The. William Bronk. VGW

Body black in the rock spine of Quinag. Marry the Lass? Andrew Greig. SLP

Body full of bees. "I Don't Hear Any Melody Breathing I Hear." John Gill. NeAC

Body is like a November birch facing the full moon, The. Solitude Late at Night in the Woods. Robert Bly. IPWM; SFF; VGW

Body lies under the ground. Dirge. Gavin Bantock. OxBTC

Body Mechanics. Albert Goldbarth. NVAP

Body my house. Question. Mae Swenson. IPWM; VGW

Body of a woman, white hills, white thigh. Pablo Neruda, *tr. fr. Spanish by* Robert Bly. LoAs

Body Poems, *sels.*    Coleman Barks.   NVAP
   Achilles Tendon.
   Adam's Apple.Back Just Below the Shoulder Blades.
   Brain.
   Bruises.
   Cheek.
   Dimple.
   Downy Hair in the Shape of Flame.
   Genitals.
   Hair on the Chest.
   Liver.
   Scar.
   Semen.
   Skeleton.
   Skull.
   Tic.
   White Crescents at the Bottoms of Fingernails.
Body says, The:/ The mind: my moonlight.   The Soliloquies.
   Edward Weismiller.   PAIC
Body so carefully, The.   At the Gynecologist's.   Linda Pastan.
   RiTi
Body's products become, The.   Dido.   John Ashbery.   *Fr.* Two
   Sonnets.   CAPP; VGW
Bogart.   Nicholas Flocos.   SA
Bohannan held on to a birch branch.   The Low Road.   Tom
   Buchan.   MIS
Bolakins was a very fine mason.   Lamkin.   *Unknown.*   AmFP
Bold Fenian Men, The, *with music. Unknown.*   RDB
Bold Jack Donahue.   *Unknown.*   AmFP; PeBB
Bold Lanty was in love, you see, with lively Rosie Carey.   Lanty
   Leary.   Samuel Lover.   PFIr
Bold Pedlar and Robin Hood, The.   *Unknown.*   AIW; AmFP
Bold Robin has robed him in ghostly attire.   A Merry Jest of Robin
   Hood.   Thomas Love Peacock.   PeBB
Bold Trooper, The.   *Unknown.*   PeBB
Bold Unbiddable Child, The.   Winifrid M. Letts.   PFIr
Boll Weevil Song, The.   *Unknown.*   *See* Ballit of de Boll
   Weevil, De.
Boll-weevil's coming, and the winter's cold.   November Cotton
   Flower.   Jean Toomer.   NoAM
Bombardment of Bristol, R.I., The.   *Unknown.*   BTTM
Bombers spread out, temperature steady, The.   War and Silence.
   Robert Bly.   CAAP
Bon jour, bon jour a vous!   A Call for a Song.   *Unknown.*   OxBM
Bon Mot, A.   *Unknown.*   POL
Bonac.   John Hall Wheelock.   PPoD
Bonded.   Anne Hazlewood Brady.   WBN
Bone and Skin, two millers thin.   On Two Monopolists.   John
   Byrom.   FaBoCo
Bone Yard.   Jim Barnes.   CDW
Bones, The.   W. S. Merwin.   ConAP
Bones.   Charles Simic.   NVAP
Bones are all there waiting their hour, The.   After X-Ray.   Linda
   Pastan.   POL
Bonie Doon.   Burns.   *See* Banks o' Doon, The.
Bonie Lesley.   Burns.   *See* Bonnie Lesley
Bonnets o' Bonnie Dundee, The.   Sir Walter Scott.   *See* Bonnie
   Dundee
Bonnie Blue Flag, The.   Harry Macarthy.   BLSo, *with music;*
   BTTM; PSoN, *with music*
Bonnie Broukit Bairn, The.   "Hugh MacDiarmid."   InPS
Bonnie Dundee.   Sir Walter Scott.   *Fr.* The Doom of Devergoil,
   II, ii.   RDB, *with music*
   (Bonnets o' Bonnie Dundee, The.)   BTTM
Bonnie Earl of Morey, The.   *Unknown.*   *See* Bonny Earl of
   Murray, The.

Bonnie George Campbell.   *Unknown.*   AmFP; GBP; PeBB
   (Bonny George Campbell.)   AIW
Bonnie Lesley.   Burns.   NOBE
   (Bonie Lesley.)   SLP
Bonny at Morn.   *Unknown.*   GBP
Bonny Barbara Allan.   *Unknown.*   *See* Barbara Allen.
Bonny Earl of Murray, The.   *Unknown.*   AIW
   (Bonnie Earl of Morey, The, *with music.*)   RDB
Bonny George Campbell.   *Unknown.*   *See* Bonnie George
   Campbell.
Bonny Grey, The.   *Unknown.*   GBP
Bonny Keel Laddie, The.   *Unknown.*   GBP
Bonny Moorhen, The.   *Unknown.*   GBP
Bony.   Simon J. Ortiz.   CDW
Bonzai tree, The.   A Work of Artifice.   Marge Piercy.   IHMS
Book, The.   Adrienne Rich.   RiTi
Book Ends, Immortality Begins, The.   Adrianne Marcus.   NPW
Book of Hunting, *sels.*    Julians Barnes.   WPE
   "Time of grease beginneth at Midsummer day."
   "When ye hunt at the roe, then shall ye see there."
   "Wheresoever ye fare by frith or by fell."
Book of Kells, The.   Padraic Colum.   BIrV
Book of Lies, The.   James Tate.   PPoD
Book of the Dead, Prayer 14.   Mei Berssenbrugge.   SA
Book of Thel, The.   Blake.   LAuP; MBPR
Book of Urizen, The.   Blake.   MBPR
Book of verses underneath the bough, A.   Omar Khayyám, *tr. by*
   Edward Fitzgerald.   *Fr.* The Rubáiyát of Omar Khayyám.
   NOBE
Book was writ of late called Tetrachordon, A.   On the Detraction
   Which Followed upon My Writing Certain Treatises.   Milton.
   Epi
Book you made, The.   Love.   Patrick Lane.   NeAC
Booker T. and W. E. B.   Dudley Randall.   NoAM
Bookshop Idyll, A.   Kingsley Amis.   OxBTC; SoSe
Boom!   Howard Nemerov.   NowV
Boom above my knees lifts, and the boat, The.   Sailing to an
   Island.   Richard Murphy.   MPo
Boomerang and kangaroo, The.   Up from Down Under.   David
   McCord.   ECBV
Booth Killed Lincoln.   *Unknown.*   AmFP; OFD
Booth led boldly with his big bass drum.   General William Booth
   Enters Into Heaven.   Vachel Lindsay.   IPWM; NoAM;
   NOBA
Bootie Black and the Seven Giants.   Mike Cook.   JB
Border, The.   Edwin Muir.   BoReV
Borders slide backwards forwards.   Nathaniel Tarn.   *Fr.* A
   Nowhere for Vallejo.   TwMBP
Bored with his stall, wanting he knew not what.   On Cementing
   Level the Stable Floor at the Old Manse.   Forbes Macgregor.
   MIS
Bores hed in hands I bring, The.   The Boar's Head.   *Unknown.*
   OxBM
Borgia, thou once wert almost too august.   On Seeing a Hair of
   Lucretia Borgia.   Walter Savage Landor.   InPK
Boris is dead. The fatalist parrot.   Obituary.   Weldon Kees.
   BoAnP
Born is the quarter night, brash.   Delta Traveller.   Charles
   Wright.   AmPA
Born of my voiceless time, your steps.   The Footsteps.   Paul
   Valéry, *tr. by* C. Day Lewis.   LoAs
Born Yesterday.   Philip Larkin.   RRA
Borough, The, *sel.*   George Crabbe.
   Peter Grimes; the Outcast, *fr.* Letter XXII.   NOBE
Borrowed light went through the dark, The.   Jack Rabbit.   Adrien
   Stoutenberg.   BoAnP

Borrowing Days, The. *Unknown.* GBP

Boss he had a yaller gal. Git along Down to Town. *Unknown.* AmFP

Boston ("I come from the city of Boston"). John Collins Bossidy. FaBoCo

Boston Burglar, The. *Unknown.* AmFP

*Boston Evening Transcript,* The. T. S. Eliot. InPK; PSN

Boston has a festival. In the Public Garden. Marianne Moore. NOBA

Boston, Lincolnshire. *Unknown.* GBP

Boston Tea Tax, The. *Unknown.* BTTM

Both my child. Teitoku, *tr. fr. Japanese by* Nobuyuki Yuasa. OFD

Both Plutarch and Pausanius tell a story. Kleomedes. David Wright. NoAM

Bottled: New York. Helene Johnson. PoBA

Bottleneck. Louis MacNeice. SFF

Bottomed by tugging combs of water. The Swan. W. R. Rodgers. NoAM

Boughs, the boughs are bare enough, The. Winter with the Gulf Stream. Gerard Manley Hopkins. NoAM

Bought at the drug store, very cheap; and later pawned. Green Light. Kenneth Fearing. VGW

Bound lion, almost blind from meeting their gaze and popcorn. Riverdale Lion. John Robert Colombo. LP

Boundaries. Judith Minty. HeS

Bounty. Josephine Miles. NoAM

Bouquet has mimosas, orchids, roses, The. The Kelly Show. Charles Higham. MAuV

Bourtree, bourtree, crookit rung. The Elder, or Bourtree. *Unknown.* GBP

Bout with Burning. Vassar Miller. CoPAm

Bouzouki Music. Anselm Hollo. TwMBP

Bow down my soul in worship very low. St. Isaac's Church, Petrograd. Claude McKay. PoBA

Bowed by a torqued and weakened spine. Hunchback Pine. Ethel Green Russell. AATT

Bowed by the weight of centuries he leans. The Man with the Hoe. Edwin Markham. AmVN; WIF

Bower of Bliss, The. Spenser. *Fr.* The Faerie Queene, II, 12. NOBE

Bowery, The, *with music.* Charles Hale Hoyt. FSN

Bowery. David Ignatow. CTBA; MiP

Bowge of Courte, The. John Skelton. AAS

Bows glided down, and the coast, The. Ballad of the Long-legged Bait. Dylan Thomas. Epi

Box Comes Home, A. John Ciardi. CoPAm

Box for Tom, A. James Tate. FiCP

Boxcar Poem, The ("Boxcars drift by, The"). David Young. AmPA

Boxer. Joseph P. Clancy. SPo

Boxer bitch is pregnant, The. Geisha. Gary Gildner. POL

Boxes. Toi Derricotte. NPW

Boy. John Ciardi. SFF

Boy, The. Eugene Field. ECBV

Boy, A. Benny Graves. AKE

Boy Actor, The. Noel Coward. OxBTC

Boy and the Geese, The. Padraic Fiacc. PFIr

Boy and the Parrot, The. John Hookham Frere. OxBChV

Boy and the Snake, The. Charles *and* Mary Lamb. OxBChV

Boy at the Window. Richard Wilbur. TH

Boy Breaking Glass. Gwendolyn Brooks. NoAM; NowV

Boy can bring so much outdoors, A. Common Carrier. Richard Armour. ECBV

Boy, Cat, Canary. Stephen Spender. LP

Boy climbed up into the tree, The. The Rescue. Hal Summers. PoTa

Boy Driving His Father to Confession. Seamus Heaney. BuTh

Boy, I detest the Persian pomp. The Preference Declared. Horace, *tr. by* Eugene Field. Odes, I, 38. InPK

Boy, I hate their empty shows. Simplicity. Horace, *tr. by* William Cowper. Odes, I, 38. InPK

Boy in the Roman Zoo. Archibald MacLeish. NCSH

Boy is perplexed by the sunlight, The. Perplexed by the Sunlight. Grevel Lindop. LP

Boy is writing his first poem in a small, A. The First Poem. James Reiss. CAAP

Boy-Man. Karl Shapiro. SoSe

Boy Serving at Table, The. John Lydgate. OxBChV

Boy stoops, picking greens with his mother, A. Greens. David Ray. VGW

Boy that is good, The. The Description of a Good Boy. Henry Dixon. OxBChV

Boy tried to get killed, A. A Boy. Benny Graves. AKE

Boy Who Laughed at Santa Claus, The. Ogden Nash. PoTa

Boy Who Smells Like Cocoa, A. Robert Hershon. NeAC

Boy who was once me, The. The Characters of Forgotten Dirty Jokes. Wesley McNair. FAF

Boy with His Hair Cut Short. Muriel Rukeyser. InPK; VGW; WPE

Boys, The. Anthony Thwaite. LP

Boys/ I don't promise you nothing. Admonitions. Lucille Clifton. BPo; InPS; NMM

Boys and girls, we pledge allegiance. Dianae Sumus in Fide. Catullus, *tr. by* Horace Gregory. Moon

Boys and the Bubble, The. Samuel Wesley. SCP-2

Boys in sporadic but tenacious droves. The Horse Chestnut Tree. Richard Eberhart. BBGO

Boys of Mullabaun [Mullaghbawn], The. *Unknown.* BIrV; GBP

Boys of Sanpete County, The. *Unknown.* AmFP

Boy's Song, A. James Hogg. OxBChV

Bracken fern,/ Why are you so bent? Japanese Folk-song from Hyogo. *Unknown, tr. by* Geoffrey Bownas *and* Anthony Thwaite. RAE

Brackish reach of shoal off Madaket, A. The Quaker Graveyard in Nantucket. Robert Lowell. NoAM; NOBA; PiAm; PPoD

Brady's Bend. Martha Keller. PoTa

Brag, sweet tenor bull. Basil Bunting. *Fr.* Briggflatts. OBP; TwMBP

Brahma. Emerson. IPWM; NOBA; PAIC; PiAm; VoPo; WIF

Brahma. Andrew Lang. FaBoCo

Brahms/ stabbed me in the ear. St. Julien's Eve. James Cunningham. JB

Brain. Coleman Barks. *Fr.* Body Poems. NVAP

Brain is wider than the sky, The. Emily Dickinson. NoAM

Brain, within its groove, The. Emily Dickinson. NoAM; NOBA

Brainstorm. Howard Nemerov. NCSH; NoAM

Bramble, like barbed wire. The Thrush's Nest. Richard Ryan. PFIr

Branch swayed, swerved, The. Windy Boy in a Windswept Tree. Geoffrey Summerfield. LP

Branches Back Into. Ken Belford. NeAC

Branches ripped by a storm tide. Walking the Beach. Sarah Youngblood. IHMS

Brass Spittoons. Langston Hughes. NoAM

Brave/ they straddle the animals. Cowboys: One. Rod McKuen. MiP

Brave infant of Saguntum, clear. To the Immortal Memory and Friendship of That Noble Pair, Sir Lucius Cary, and Sir Henry Morison. Ben Jonson. NOBE; PAIC

Brave iron! brave hammer! from your sound. Thwick-a-thwack. Thomas Dekker. *Fr.* London's Tempe. SCP-2

Brave Man, The. Wallace Stevens. PBMP

Brave New World. Archibald MacLeish. NOBA; OFD

Brave weathercock, I see thou'lt set thy nose. Upon the Weathercock. John Bunyan. OxBChV

Bravely from Fairyland he rode, on furlough. The Broken Girth. Robert Graves. BIrV

Brawling of a sparrow in the eaves, The. The Sorrow of Love. W. B. Yeats. OBP

Brazil, January 1, 1502. Elizabeth Bishop. NoAm

Bread and Music. Conrad Aiken. Discordants, I. VoPo ("Music I heard with you was more than music.") NOBA

Bread in our mouths. Paradise Is Not a Place. Daniela Gioseffi. WBN

Breaded Meat, Breaded Hands. Michael S. Harper. NVAP

Break and trail home. The Girl I Left behind Me. *Unknown.* AmFP

Break, Break, Break. Tennyson. HeIP; NOBE; PPoe

Break of Day. John Donne. PAIC

Break of Day in the Trenches. Isaac Rosenberg. NOBE; PSN

Break off/ fallen Catullus. Catullus, *tr. fr. Latin by* Peter Whigham. TwMBP

Break the News to Mother, *with music.* Charles Kassel Harris. FSN

Breake now my heart and dye! Oh no, she may relent. Thomas Campion. AAS

Breakfast. W. W. Gibson. OxBTC

Breakfast Time. James Stephens. ECBV

Breaking every law except the one. Our City Is Guarded by Automatic Rockets. William Stafford. NowV

Breaking Ground in Me. Tom Kryss. NeAC

Breaking waves dashed high, The. The Landing of the Pilgrim Fathers in New England. Felicia Dorothea Hemans. BTTM; ECBV; SBG; WPE

Breakthrough. Carolyn M. Rodgers. BPo

Breasts. Tess Gallagher. AmPA

Breath of Air, A. James Wright. NOBA

Breathe In Breathe Out. Layle Silbert. NPW

Breathe in experience, breathe out poetry. Poem Out of Childhood. Muriel Rukeyser. NMM

Breathers, The. James Reiss. AmPA; CAAP; HeS

Breathes there the man, with soul so dead. This Is My Own, My Native Land. Sir Walter Scott. *Fr.* The Lay of the Last Minstrel. BTTM; NOBE; PBMP; SFF; SoSe

Breathing, The. Denise Levertov. IPWM; RFM; TCP

Breathing, at Last, in the Wichita Art Museum. D. Clinton. HeS

Breathing in morning. The Song Turning Back into Itself. Al Young. CAAP

Breathing something German at the end. The Gift to Be Simple. Howard Moss. SS

Breathless, we flung us on the windy hill. The Hill. Rupert Brooke. OxBTC

Breezes went steadily thro' the tall pines, The. Nathan Hale. *Unknown.* BTTM

Brennan on the Moor. *Unknown.* AIW; AmFP; GBP

Brewer, A. *Unknown.* FaBoCo

Brewer's Man, The. L. A. G. Strong. FaBoCo

Brian Boy Magee. "Ethna Carbery." PFIr

Bric-a-brac shelf. Still Life. Ralph Mecklenburger. SFF

Brick not used in building, A. Naomi Replansky. POL

Bricks of the wall. The Garden Wall. Denise Levertov. PiAm

Brid one brere, brid, brid one brere. Bird on Briar. *Unknown.* OxBM

Bridal Day. Compton Mackenzie. SLP

Bridal Morn, The. *Unknown. See* Maidens Came, The.

Bridal Song. Thomas Lovell Beddoes. *Fr.* Death's Jest Book, IV, iii. GBL

Bridal Song. George Chapman. *Fr.* Hero and Leander, Fifth Sestiad. NOBE

Bridal Song, A. *At. to* Shakespeare. *Fr.* The Two Noble Kinsmen, I,i. NOBE

Bride, A. Harry Fainlight. BoLoP

Bride, The. D. H. Lawrence. NoAM; OxBTC

Bride of Frankenstein, The. Edward Field. HeIP

Bride of Lammermoor, The, *sel.* Sir Walter Scott. Lucy Ashton's Song, *fr. ch.* 3. NOBE

Bride Song. Christina Rossetti. *Fr.* The Prince's Progress. WPE

Brides, The. A. D. Hope. InPK

Bridge, The, *sels.* Hart Crane.
Ave Maria. NoAM; NOBA
Cape Hatteras. PiAm
Powhatan's Daughter.
Dance, The. PiAm
Harbor Dawn, The. PiAm; PSN
Indiana. PiAm
River, The. NoAM; NOBA; PiAm
Van Winkle. PiAm
Three Songs.
National Winter Garden. InPS
To Brooklyn Bridge. InPS; NOBA
(Proem: to Brooklyn Bridge.) HeIP; NoAM; PAIC; PiAm
Tunnel, The. MAT

Bridge of Heraclitus, The. George Reavey. BIrV

Bridge says: Come across, try me; see how good I am, The. Potomac Town in February. Carl Sandburg. LCL

Brief Explanation. Claudia Dobkins. NPW

Brief Journey West, The. Howard Nemerov. NoAM

Brief, on a flying night. Chimes. Alice Meynell. SBG; WPE

Brief procession, The. Bessie Smith's Funeral. Alvin Aubert. CoPAm

Briggflatts, *sels.* Basil Bunting.
"As the player's breath warms the fipple the tone clears," IV. OBP
"Brag, sweet tenor bull," I. OBP; TwMBP
Coda TwMBP
"Grass caught in willow tells the flood's height," IV. NoAM
"Poet appointed dare not decline," II. OBP

Bright as the day, and like the morning fair. Cloë. George Granville. FaBoCo

Bright clasp of her whole hand around my finger. To My Daughter. Stephen Spender. RRA

Bright college years with pleasure rife. Yale Boola! A. M. Hirsh. FSN

Bright-coloured, mirror-plated, strung with lights. Merry-Go-Round. James McAuley. MAuV

Bright little buttercup, now you will show. Buttercup. Mary Mapes Dodge. ECBV

Bright Star! Would I Were Steadfast as Thou Art. Keats. AnMo; GBL; InPK; InPS; IPWM; LoAs; MBPR; PPoe; PPP
(Last Sonnet) NOBE
(Written on a Blank Page in Shakespeare's Poems.) OBP

Bright white street lights, The. Allegory in Black. Carl Clark. JB

Brightest morning of summer, The. Graveyard Road. Tom McKeown. HeS

Brightest of the Bright, The. Egan O'Rahilly, *tr. fr. Irish by* James Clarence Mangan. BIrV

'Brigid is a caution, sure!'—What's that ye say? Her Sister. Moira O'Neill. OxBTC

Brill. *Unknown. See* At Brill on the Hill.

Bring a Child Flowers. Nathaniel Tarn. RRA

Bring a leaf to me. Invitation Standing. Paul Blackburn. IPWM; VGW

"Bring me a long sharp knife for we are in danger." The Sunflowers. Douglas Stewart. POL

Bring me to the blasted oak. Crazy Jane and the Bishop. W. B. Yeats. AnMo

Bring me wine, but wine which never grew. Bacchus. Emerson. NOBA; PiAm

Bring now the last flower in to warm this room. At My Mother's Bedside. Marcia Lee Masters. WPE

Bring the good old bugle, boys! Marching Through Georgia. Henry Clay Work. PSoN

Bring Us in Good Ale. *Unknown.* FaBoCo; OxBM

Bringing Flowers. Roberta Spear. AmPA

Bringing in the Sheaves, *with music.* Knowles Shaw. BLSH

Brissit brawnis and broken banis. The Bewteis of the Fute-Ball. *Unknown.* FaBoCo

Britannia's Pastorals, *sels.* William Browne. SCP-2
"Glide soft, ye silver floods," *fr.* II, Song 1.
"Muses' friend, grey-eyed Aurora, yet, The," *fr.* II, Song 2.
"Now great Hyperion left his golden throne," *fr.* II, Song 1.

British Grenadiers, The. *Unknown.* BTTM

British Leftish Poetry, 1930-40. "Hugh MacDiarmid." NoAM

British Museum Reading Room, The. Louis MacNeice. NOBE

Brittle beautie, that nature made so fraile. Earl of Surrey. AAS

Broad-backed hippopotamus, The. The Hippopotamus. T.S. Eliot. AnMo; BoReV; VGW

Broad is the road that leads to death. Isaac Watts. AmFP

Broke and Hungry. *Unknown.* BluL

Broken altar, Lord, thy servant rears, A. The Altar. George Herbert. AnMo; InPS; SCP-1

Broken Appointment, A. Thomas Hardy. GBL; LoAs; NoAM

Broken Dreams. W. B. Yeats. PSN

Broken Girth, The. Robert Graves. BIrV

Broken Gull, A. John Moore. NCSH

Broken Heart, The *sels.* John Ford.
"List! what sad sounds are these? extremely." SCP-2
"Oh no more, no more, too late," *fr.* IV, iii. GBL
(Love's Martyrs.) NOBE

Broken Heart, Broken Machine. Richard E. Grant. PoBA

"Broken heart, A"...but can a heart break, now? Sonnet. John Berryman. Epi

Broken-Hearted Gardener, The. *Unknown.* GBP

Broken Home, The. James Merrill. NoAM; NOBA; PPP

Broken in pieces all asunder. Affliction. George Herbert. SCP-1

Broken pillar of the wing jags from the clotted shoulder, The. Hurt Hawks. Robinson Jeffers. NoAM; NOBA; PiAm

Broken Promise. James O. Taylor. BuTh

Broken Token, The. *Unknown.* AmFP

Broken Tower, The. Hart Crane. NoAM; NOBA; PiAm

Broken Wedding Ring, The. *Unknown.* AIW

Bronxomania. Victor Hernández Cruz. SA

Bronze David of Donatello, The. Randall Jarrell. WIF

Bronzeville Man with a Belt in the Back. Gwendolyn Brooks. PoBA

Brooding. David Ignatow. PBMP; TCP

Brooklyn Heights. John Wain. OxBTC

Brooklyn Theater Fire, The. *Unknown.* AmFP

Broom out the floor now, lay the fender by. June. Frances Ledwidge. BIrV

Broomfield Hill, The. *Unknown.* AmFP; PeBB

Brooms. Charles Simic. AmPA

Brother, The. Thomas Hardy. AIW

Brother. Jewel C. Latimore. JB

Brother at One Week. Carole Oles. NPW

Brother, Can You Spare a Dime? E.Y. Harburg. AIW

Brother, come! And What Shall You Say? Joseph Seamon Cotter, Jr. PoBA

Brother Fire. Louis MacNeice. NoAM; NOBE

Brother Green. *Unknown.* AmFP

Brother to the firefly. Morning Light (The Dew-Drier). Effie Lee Newsome. PoBA

Brother, today I sit on the brick bench outside the house. To My Brother Miguel: In Memoriam. César Vallejo, *tr. by* John Knoepfle *and* James Wright. MiP

Brother told me, A. Untitled. Michele Wallace. WBN

Brothers, The. Edwin Muir. HeIP

Brothers, The. Wordsworth. MBPR

Brothers/ brothers/ everywhere. Utopia. Jewel C. Latimore. BPo

Brothers! between you and me. To the Republicans of North America. Shelley. MBPR

Brother's cradle/ doesn't rock. Brother at One Week. Carole Oles. NPW

Brothers Together in Winter. Harley Elliott. NeAC

Brought here in slave ships and pitched overboard. Love Your Enemy. Yusef Iman. BPo

Brown and furry. Caterpillar. Christina Rossetti. OxBChV

Brown Boy to Brown Girl. Countee Cullen. PoBA

Brown Bug, The. Michael R. Brown. SFF

Brown Circles. Melvin DeBruhl. PPoD

Brown enormous odor he lived by, The. The Prodigal. Elizabeth Bishop. CoPAm; PPP

Brown-faced nurse has murmured something unintelligible, The. Microscosmos. Susan Miles. OxBTC

Brown from the sun's mid-afternoon caress. Spectrum. William Dickey. SoSe

Brown girl chanting Te Deums on Sunday. Ruth. Pauli Murray. NMM

Brown is my love, but graceful. *Unknown, tr. fr. Italian.* GBL

Brown lived at such a lofty farm. Brown's Descent. Robert Frost. PoTa

Brown old man with a green thumb, A. He Was. Richard Wilbur. NCSH; SS

Brown owl sits in the ivy bush, The. The Great Brown Owl. Jane Euphemia Browne. OxBChV

Brown Penny. W. B. Yeats. BoLoP; OLR; PFIr

Brown River, Smile. Jean Toomer. PoBA

Brown Robin. *Unknown.* PeBB

Brown Robyn's Confession. *Unknown.* GBP; PeBB

Brown Skin Girl. *Unknown.* BluL

Brown's Descent. Robert Frost. PoTa

Brownsville Blues. *Unknown.* BluL

Bruadar and Smith and Glinn. *Unknown, tr. fr. Irish by* Douglas Hyde. PFIr
(Curse, A.) BIrV

Bruce, The, *sel.* John Barbour.
Bruce Meets Three Men with a Wether. OxBM

Bruckner. James Camp. MAT

Brueghel's Winter. Walter de la Mare. WIF

Bruised by the masseur's final whack. Health and Fitness. J. B. Morton. FaBoCo

Bruises. Coleman Barks. *Fr. Body Poems.* NVAP

Brushing back the curls from your famous brow. The Copulating Gods. Carolyn Kizer. Prf

Brussels in Winter. W. H. Auden. OxBTC

Brut, The, *sel.* Layamon.
Death of Arthur, The, *orig. and mod. English prose.* OxBM

Bryan O'Lynn. *Unknown.* GBP

Bryan's Last Battle. *Unknown.* AmFP

Bryant. James Russell Lowell. *Fr.* A Fable for Critics. AmVN; NOBA

Bubba Smith. Ogden Nash. SPo

Buchlyvie. *Unknown.* GBP

Buck in the Snow, The. Edna St. Vincent Millay. BoAnP

Buckdancer's Choice. James Dickey. NoAM; NOBA

Bucking Bronco. *Unknown.* AmFP

Buckingham Palace. A. A. Milne. OxBChV

Buckinghamshire. *Unknown.* GBP

Bucolic Eclogues, *sel.* Ethel Anderson.
"Waking, child, while you slept, your mother took." WPE

Buddha. Herman Melville. HeIP; PiAm

Buddha's Birthday: April 8, 1819. Issa, *tr. fr. Japanese by* Nobuyuki Yuasa. *Fr.* Oraga Haru. OFD

Buddha's Death Day: February 15, 1815. Issa, *tr. fr. Japanese by* Nobuyuki Yuasa. *Fr.* Oraga Haru. OFD

Buffalo. Henry Dumas. PoBA

Buffalo Bill's. E. E. Cummings. GrRo; InPK; NOBA; PiAm; PPoD; VGW
(Portrait.) HeIP; InPS

Buffalo Boy. *Unknown.* AmFP

Buffalo breathed quietly inside, The. The Crow-Children Walk My Circles in the Snow. Ray A. Young Bear. CDW

Buffalo Dusk. Carl Sandburg. MiP; RFM; TH

Buffalo Girls. *Unknown.* AmFP; ECBV
(Buffalo Gals, *with music.*) BLSH; BLSo

Buffalo—Isle of Wight Power Cable. Anselm Hollo. TwMBP

Buffalo, Our Sacred Beast, The. Tom McKeown. NVAP

Buffalo Skinners, The. *Unknown.* AmFP; GBP; PeBB

Buffaloes are gone, The. Buffalo Dusk. Carl Sandburg. MiP; RFM; TH

Bugler's First Communion, The ("A bugler boy from barrack"). Gerard Manley Hopkins. NoAM

Buik of Alexander, The, *sel. Unknown, at. to* John Barbour.
"When I see hir forrow me." SLP

Building, The. Philip Larkin. PSN

Building of the Ship, The, *sel.* Longfellow.
Republic, The. BTTM

Bulb, A. Richard Kendall Munkittrick. POL

Bulkeley, Hunt, Willard, Hosmer, Meriam, Flint. Hamatreya. Emerson. AmVN; HeIP; IPWM; MAT; NOBA; PiAm

Bull, A. Babette Deutsch. BoAnP

Bull, The. Ralph Hodgson. OxBTC

Bull, The. V. Sackville-West. WPE

Bull, The. Judith Wright. MAuV

Bull Calf, The. Irving Layton. InPK

Bullfrog. Ted Hughes. RFM; TSWA

Bullfrog Blues. *Unknown.* BluL

Bullocky. Judith Wright. MAuV

Bullocky Bill. *Unknown.* MAuV

Bull's Eye: the water cries out. Stone and the Obliging Pond. Felix Pollak. POL

Bully Song, The, *with music.* Charles E. Trevathan. BLSo

Bumi. LeRoi Jones. PoBA

Bummer, A. Michael Casey. TSWA

Bums are the spirit of us parked in ratty old hotels. Bowery. David Ignatow. CTBA; MiP

Bums, on Waking. James Dickey. TSWA

Bunch of Grapes, The. George Herbert. AnMo

Bunches of Grapes. Walter de la Mare. LCL; OxBChV

Bunker Hill, *with music.* Nathaniel Niles. BLSo

Bunky Boy Bunky Boy Who's My Little Bunky Boy. Larry Mollin. NeAC

Buoy like a man in a red sou'wester, A. Beginning to Squall. May Swenson. RFM

Burden of Tyre, The, *sel.* Christopher Brennan.
Epilogue: "O life, O radiance, love, delight." MAuV

Burglar, The. Sonya Dorman. SFF

Burglar, The. David Wagoner. CoPAm

Burglar came, jimmied a window, A. The Burglar. Sonya Dorman. SFF

Burial. Robert Francis. NCSH

Burial. Alice Walker. AmPA; WBN

Burial Hour, The. Robert Stephen Hawker. VPC

Burial in the Country, A. Paul Clause. AATT

Burial of an Irish President. Austin Clarke. BIrV

Burial of Sir John Moore after [*or* at] Corunna, The. Charles Wolfe. BTTM; NOBE

Burial of the Linnet, The. Juliana Horatia Ewing. OxBChV

Buried Lake, The. Allen Tate. PiAm

Buried Life, The. Matthew Arnold. PFD

Buried under a flat stone, but beside. Patty, 1949-1961. Sharon Mayer Libera. IHMS

Burke. Samuel Taylor Coleridge. *Fr.* Sonnets on Eminent Characters. MBPR

Burlesque of Lope De Vega. Samuel Johnson. FaBoCo
(Deduction.) ECBV

Burlesque upon the Great Frost, *sel.* Charles Cotton.
"Maid compelled to be a gadder, A." SCP-2

Burly, dozing humble-bee. The Humble-Bee. Emerson. FSFS; NOBA

Burn drowns steadily in its own downpour, The. Waterfall. Seamus Heaney. NoAM

Burn Ovid with the rest. Lovers will find. Penal Law. Austin Clarke. BoLoP; NoAM

Burned Bridge, The. Ruth Stone. WPE

Burning. Galway Kinnell. CoPAm

Burning. Gary Snyder. *See* Myths and Texts.

Burning/ burning/ burning. Crow's Last Stand. Ted Hughes. InPS

Burning Babe, The. Robert Southwell. BoReV; HeIP; InPS; NOBE; OBP; PPoe; Prf

Burning of Paper Instead of Children, The. Adrienne Rich. PiAm

Burning of the Leaves, The. Laurence Binyon. FSFS; NOBE; OxBTC
"Now is the time for the burning of the leaves," *sel.* PSN

Burning the Christmas Greens. William Carlos Williams. NoAM; NOBA; PiAm

Burning the Letters. Randall Jarrell. CoPAm

Burning the Small Dead. Gary Snyder. CAPP

Burning the Tomato Worms. Carolyn Forché. AmPA

Burning with zeal, whole villages. Theologia Germanica. David Malouf. CAAP

Burnt Norton. T. S. Eliot. *Fr.* Four Quartets. HeIP

Burnt Ship, A. John Donne. InPK

Burst, A/ of confidence. Confiding. Answering. Robert Duncan. PiAm

Burst of iris so that, A. Iris. William Carlos Williams. InPS

Burst of steam from the pipes in the morning startles me, A. The Two of Cups. Emmett Jarrett. NeAC

Bury her deep, down deep. Cat's Funeral. E. V. Rieu. ECBV

Bury Me in a Free Land. Frances E. W. Harper. BPo

Bury this old Illinois farmer with respect. Illinois Farmer. Carl Sandburg. ANTL

Bury your heart in some deep green hollow. Saturday Market. Charlotte Mew. WPE

Burying Blues for Janis. Marge Piercy. NeAC; WBN

Bus, The. Leonard Cohen. HeIP

Bus Ride. Lenore Kandel. NMM

Bus Stop. Donald Justice. TCP

Bushes quiver. Shivers. Aileen Fisher. CaYB

Bushrangers, The. Edward Harrington. PoTa

Busie old foole, unruly Sunne. *See* Busy old fool, unruly Sun.

Business, The. Robert Creeley. CAPP

Business of the lambing ewes would make me, The. Eagles Over the Lambing Paddock. Ernest Moll. MAuV

Busses are bright yellow and have brought, The. The Dream about Junior High School in America. Dick Lourie. NeAC

Bustle in a house, The. Emily Dickinson. HeIP; IPWM

Busy, curious, thirsty fly. The Fly. William Oldys. PAIC

Busy in study be thou, child. Demeanour. *Unknown.* OxBChV

Busy Man Speaks, A. Robert Bly ConAP

Busy [*or* Busie] old fool, unruly sun. The Sun [*or* Sunne] Rising. John Donne. AnMo; BoLoP; GBL; HeIP; InPS; IPWM; MetP; NOBE; PPP; SCP-1; SoSe

Busy with love, the bumble bee. Meleager, *tr. fr. Greek by* Peter Whigham. BoLoP

But/ he" i/ staring. E. E. Cummings. NoAM

But are these landscapes to be imagined. Letters to Walt Whitman, IX. Ronald Johnson. VGW

But as she sat allone and thoughte thus. Criseyde Sees Troilus Return from Battle. Chaucer. *Fr.* Troilus and Criseyde, II. OxBM

But black is the colour of my true love's hair. Black is the Colour. *Unknown.* GBP

But for a brief. A Grasshopper. Richard Wilbur. CoPAm

But for Lust. Ruth Pitter. OxBTC

But He Was Cool; or, He Even Stopped for Green Lights. Don L. Lee. BPo; NoAM; PoBA

But how shall we this union well express? The Soul and the Body. Sir John Davies. *Fr.* Nosce Teipsum. NOBE

But I Am Growing Old and Indolent. Robinson Jeffers. NoAM; NOBA

But I Do Not Need Kindness. Gregory Corso. CoPAm

But if I look the ice is gone from the lake. Spring of the Thief. John Logan. CAPP

But in the crowding darkness not a word did they say. The Old-Marrieds. Gwendolyn Brooks. PoBA

But in the end one tires of the high-flown. About the Phoenix. James Merrill. NoAM

But, John, have you seen the world, said he. Angle of Vision. Robert Rendall. OxBTC

But, knowing now that they would have her speak. The Defence of Guenevere. William Morris. PAIC; VPC

But let my due feet never fail. Milton. *Fr.* Il Penseroso. SCP-1

But, lo! from forth a copse that neighbours by. Courser and Jennet. Shakespeare. *Fr.* Venus and Adonis. NOBE

But man finds means, grant him but place and room. Sonnet. Frederick Goddard Tuckerman. *Fr.* Sonnets. PiAm

But most by numbers judge a poet's song. Pope. *Fr.* An Essay on Criticism. WIF

But no, the familiar symbol, as that the. Time in the Rock, XCII. Conrad Aiken. VGW

But Not Forgotten. Luci Shaw. AATT

But now at thirty years my hair is grey. Growing Old. Byron. *Fr.* Don Juan, I. NOBE

But she had seen the cattle drop their young. The Birthing. Beth Bentley. LoAs

But, soft! What light through yonder window breaks. Shakespeare. *Fr.* Romeo and Juliet, II, ii. Moon

But That Is Another Story. Donald Justice. CoPAm

"But that was nothing to what things came out." Welsh Incident. Robert Graves. NOBE; OxBTC

But the kitten, how she starts. Wordsworth. *Fr.* The Kitten and Falling Leaves. PCat

But the light returns. Dreams. André Breton, *tr. by* Robert Duncan. InPS

But the whole thing is a miracle. Black Power. Nikki Giovanni. Psy

But Then. Ben King. PoTa

But Then and There the Sun Bore Down. N. Scott Momaday. CDW

But this, so feminine? Donald Davie. *Fr.* The Forests of Lithuania. OxBTC

But thou my deere sweet-sounding lute be still. Diella, XVI. Richard Lynche. AAS

But to reach the archimedean point. "Mysticism Has Not the Patience to Wait for God's Revelation." Richard Eberhart. NoAM

But what does it mean? this harmonica. What Does It Mean? This Harmonica. Virginia Gilbert. NVAP

But What I'm Trying to Say Mother Is. Ai. CAAP

But when I waked, I saw that I saw not. A Storm at Sea. John Donne. NOBE

But when it was my turn to wrestle with the angel. Under the Ladder to Heaven. Elizabeth Fenton. NMM

But why,/ O fatal Time. George Wither. *Fr.* Rhomboidal Dirge. SCP-2

But You, My Darling, Should Have Married the Prince. Kathleen Spivack. AmPA; NMM

But you, Thomas Jefferson. Brave New World. Archibald MacLeish. NOBA; OFD

"But, you're so/ different," they said of. The Photograph the Cat Licks. Beatrice Walter. NMM

Butch Weldy. Edgar Lee Masters. *Fr.* Spoon River Anthology. PSN

Butcher, The. Hugo Williams. OxBTC

Butcher, a bald guy, The. Kicking from Centre Field. David McFadden. NeAC

Butcherboy. Tom Schmidt. NeAC

Butcher Boy, The. *Unknown.* AmFP

Butcher carves veal for two, The. The Butcher. Hugo Williams. OxBTC

Butcher Shop. Charles Simic. AmPA; NVAP

Buteo Regalis. N. Scott Momaday. VW

Butter. Tom Schmidt. NeAC

Buttercup. Mary Mapes Dodge. ECBV

Buttercups and Daisies. Mary Howitt. OxBChV

Butterflies. Clive Sansom. BoAnP

Butterflies on an Illinois Road. Helena Minton. FAF

Butterfly in the Fields. Joseph Campbell. BoAnP; PFIr

Butterfly the ancient Grecians made, The. Psyche. Samuel Taylor Coleridge. MBPR; PBMP

Butterfly's Ball, The. William Roscoe. OxBChV

Butterfly's Ball and the Grasshopper's Feasts, The. The Peacock "At Home." Catherine Ann Dorset. OxBChV

Buy me an ounce and I'll sell you a pound. E. E. Cummings. NCSH

Buy the paper, take it home. Coming and Going. Mitchell Goodman. VGW

Buying Lilies. Stephen Stepanchev. SA

Buzz saw snarled and rattled in the yard, The. "Out, Out." Robert Frost. AnMo; BuTh; MiP; NowV; PiAm; PPoe; SoSe; VGW; WIF

Buzzing Doubt, The. Donald L. Hill. NCSH

Bwagamoyo. Lebert Bethune. PoBA

By a Chapel as I Came. *Unknown.* GBP; OxBM

By a flat rock on the shore of the sea. The Rock. *Unknown, tr. by* Geoffrey Grigson. GBL

By a forrest as I gan fare. The Hare. *Unknown.* OxBM

By a route obscure and lonely. Dream-Land. Poe. NOBA

By all the laws. The Tree Is Father to the Man. Lou Lipsitz. NCSH

By blind meanders and by crankled ways. Thomas Nashe. *Fr.* The Choice of Valentines; or, The Merry Ballad of Nashe His Dildo. SCP-2

By Blue Ontario's Shore, *sels.*    Walt Whitman.
  "I swear I begin to see the meaning of these things!"  *fr.* XV.
    (Marches Now the War Is Over.)  InPS
  "I will confront these shows of the day and the night!"  *fr.*
    XVIII.
    (Marches Now the War Is Over.)  InPS
  "Rhymes and rhymers pass away,"  *fr.* XIII.
    (Marches Now the War Is Over.)  InPS
By Candlelight.  Sylvia Plath.  SBG
By dark severance the apparition head.  Painted Head.  John
  Crowe Ransom.  NoAM; NOBA; PiAm
By day the bat is cousin to the mouse.  The Bat.  Theodore
  Roethke.  ECBV; RAE
By Derwent's side my father's cottage stood.  The Female Vagrant.
  Wordsworth.  MBPR
By dint of color.  A Dab of Color.  Theodore Weiss.  VGW
By fate, not option, frugal Nature gave.  Xenophanes.  Emerson.
  NOBA
By Ferry to the Island.  Iain Crichton Smith.  MPo
By Her Aunt's Grave   Thomas Hardy.  Satires of Circumstance,
  III.  SFF
By landscape reminded once of his mother's figure.  Prologue.  W.
  H. Auden.  NoAM
By love was my eye opened.  How Beautiful You Are: 3.  Elaine
  Edelman.  IHMS
By mid-century there were two quaggas left.  The Quagga.  D. J.
  Enright.  MPo
By mid-day it was warm enough; she climbed.  Aunt Alice in April.
  William H. Matchett.  CTBA
By Night.  Robert Francis.  POL; VGW
By night they haunted a thicket of April mist.  Spectral Lovers.
  John Crowe Ransom.  GBL; HeIP; LoAs; PiAm
By our first strange and fatal interview.  On His Mistress [*or* Elegy
  on His Mistress].  John Donne.  Elegies, XVI.  BoLoP;
  GBL; NOBE; OBP
By Rail Through Istria.  Robert Conquest.  NoAM
By Saint [*or* Saynt] Mary, my lady.  To Mistress [*or* Maystres]
  Isabel Pennell.  John Skelton.  *Fr.* The Garlande of Laurell.
  AAS; NOBE; RRA
By some derision of wild circumstance.  Reunion.  E. A.
  Robinson.  NoAM; NOBA
By sundown we came to a hidden village.  Conquerors.  Henry
  Treece.  MPo
By that dejected city, Arno runs.  To My Daughter.  Walter
  Savage Landor.  RRA
By the Bivouac's Fitful Flame.  Walt Whitman.  NoAM
By the city dead-house by the gate.  The City Dead-House.  Walt
  Whitman.  InPK
By the Denali road, facing.  Denali Road.  John Haines.  PPoD
By the dry road the fathers cough and spit.  The Brief Journey
  West.  Howard Nemerov.  NoAM
By the Exeter River.  Donald Hall.  AIW; MPo
By the flow of the inland river.  The Blue and the Gray.  Francis
  Miles Finch.  BTTM
By the gate with star and moon.  Medallion.  Sylvia Plath.  HeIP
By the highway the stream downslope.  Runoff.  A. R. Ammons.
  PPP
By the impulse of my will.  Magnetism.  Emma Lazarus.  SBG
By the Isar, in the twilight.  River Roses.  D. H. Lawrence.
  GBL
By the new Boot's, a tool-chest with flagpoles.  Aberdarcy: the
  Main Square.  Kingsley Amis.  OxBTC
By the newly bulldozed logging road, for a hundred yards.  Working
  against Time.  David Wagoner.  MAT
By the North Gate, the wind blows full of sand.  Lament of the
  Frontier Guard.  Li Po, *tr. by* Ezra Pound.  PiAm; VGW

By the old Moulmein Pagoda, lookin' lazy at the sea.  Mandalay.
  Kipling.  NOBE; PBMP
By the public hook for the private eye.  River Song.  Weldon
  Kees.  NoAM; PPP
By the Road.  Geoffrey Grigson.  OxBTC
By the road to the contagious hospital.  Spring and All.  William
  Carlos Williams.  NoAM; NOBA; PiAm; PPoe; PSN; TCP
By the rude bridge that arched the flood.  Concord Hymn.
  Emerson.  AmVN; BTTM; HeIP; NOBA; PPoD
By the sad waters of separation.  Exile.  Ernest Dowson.  BoLoP
By the sand between my toes.  Summer Song.  John Ciardi.
  ECBV
By the secret that holds the forest up.  Reporting Back.  William
  Stafford.  CoPAm
By the shore [*or* shores] of Gitche Gumee.  Old Nokomis Sings.
  Longfellow.  *Fr.* The Song of Hiawatha.  ECBV; SpRo
By the side of a murmuring stream an elderly gentleman sat.  The
  Elderly Gentleman.  George Canning.  ECBV
By the Statue of King Charles at Charing Cross.  Lionel Johnson.
  NOBE
By the Swimming.  Robert Sward.  SPo
By the time you swear you're his.  Unfortunate Coincidence.
  Dorothy Parker.  SBG
By the Waters of Babylon, *sels.*       Emma Lazarus.  WPE
  Currents.
  Exodus, The (August 3, 1492).
By the Waters of Minnetonka, *with music.*  J. M. Cavanass.
  BLSo
By this he knew she wept with waking eyes.  Modern Love, I.
  George Meredith.  Epi; HeIP; LoAs; PAIC; PBMP; VPC
By this low fire I often sit to woo.  Frederick Goddard
  Tuckerman.  *Fr.* Sonnets.  AmVN
By those soft tods of wool.  A Conjuration, to Electra.  Robert
  Herrick.  GBL
By two black eyes my heart was won.  Rondeau.  *Unknown.*
  FaBoCo
By Way of Preface.  Edward Lear.      *See* How Pleasant to
  Know Mr. Lear.
By what sends.  Children's Rhymes.  Langston Hughes.  BPo
By yon bonnie banks, and by yon bonnie braes.  Loch Lomond.
  *Unknown.*  BLSH
By your unnumbered charities.  Hospital for Defectives.  Thomas
  Blackburn.  OxBTC
Bye baby bunting.  Rhyme for Astronomical Baby.  Joseph Cook.
  SpRo
Bye, baby bunting./ Daddy's gone a-hunting.  Mother Goose.
  MG; SpRo
Bye Bye Baby Blues.  *Unknown.*  BluL
Byre.  Norman MacCaig.  BoAnP
Byrnies, The.  Thom Gunn.  NoAM; OxBTC
Byron! how sweetly sad thy melody!  To Lord Byron.  Keats.
  MBPR
Byron vs. DiMaggio.  Peter Meinke.  SPo
Bytuene Mersh [*or* Betwene March] and Averil.  Alysoun.
  *Unknown.*  HeIP; OxBM
Byzantium.  W. B. Yeats.  InPS; NoAm; NOBE; OxBTC; PPP

## C

C44.  Karen L. Kent.  NPW
C. L. M.  John Masefield.  OxBTC
C was papa's gray cat.  Edward Lear.  PCat
Cabin Creek Flood, The.  *Unknown.*  AmFP
Cabin in the Clearing, A.  Robert Frost.  PiAm
Cabin North of It All, The.  James McMichael.  AmPA

Cable Hymn, The.  Whittier.  PiAm
Cactus Tree.  Joni Mitchell.  GrRo
Cadaver.  John Stone.  CoPAm
Caelica, *sels.*  Fulke Greville.
  "Caelica, I overnight was finely used."  AAS
  "Caelica, when I did see you every day."  AAS
  "Cynthia, because your horns look diverse ways."  Moon
  "Downe in the depth of mine iniquity."  PPoe
  "Earth with thunder torne, with fire blasted, The."  AAS
  "Farewell sweet boy, complain not of my truth."  GBL
  "I offer wrong to my beloved saint."  PAIC
  "I, with whose colours Myra dress'd her head."  GBL
    (Myra.)  NOBE
  "In night when colours all to blacke are cast."  AAS
  "Love is the peace, whereto all thoughts doe strive."  AAS
  "Man, dream no more of curious mysteries."
    (Vain Learning.)  BoReV
  "Merlin, they say, an English prophet borne."  OBP
  "Nurse-life wheat within his greene huske growing, The."
    AAS; PAIC
  "O false and treacherous Probability."  AAS
  "Whenas man's life, the light of human lust."  SCP-2
    (Memento Mori.)  BoReV
Caesar.  W. S. Merwin.  PPoD
Caesar is dead, and cannot see the sun.  Nominis Umbra.  J. A. R.
  McKellar.  MAuV
Cage, The.  George Garrett.  SS
Cage, The.  James Stephens.  OxBTC
Caged Skylark, The.  Gerard Manley Hopkins.  AnMo; SoSe
Cairo Hotel.  J. R. Rowland.  MAuV
Caissons Go Rolling Along, The.  Edmund L. Gruber.  BLSo,
  *with music;* BTTM
Calais, August, 1802.  Wordsworth.  MBPR
Calais, August 15, 1802.  Wordsworth.  MBPR
Calculating Female.  Jill Hellyer.  POL
Caldwell of Springfield.  Bret Harte.  BTTM
Calico Pie.  Edward Lear.  LCL; RAE
Calidore.  Keats.  MBPR
California Phrasebook, The.  Dennis Schmitz.  AmPA
Californian, The.  *Unknown.*  AmFP
Call for a Song, A.  *Unknown.*  OxBM
Call for the Robin Redbreast and the Wren.  John Webster.  *Fr.*
  The White Devil, V, iv.  HeIP
  (Cornelia's Song.)  InPS
  (Dirge, A: "Call for the robin-redbreast and the wren.")
    NOBE; OBP
Call him drunken Ira Hayes, he won't answer any more.  Ballad of
  Ira Hayes.  Peter La Farge.  MAT
Call Him the Lover and call me the Bride.  The Song the Body
  Dreamed in the Spirit's Mad Behest.  William Everson.
  PiAm
Call It a Good Marriage  Robert Graves.  BoLoP; LoAs; NowV
Call it a louse—I'm.  Cid Corman.  VGW
Call it neither love nor spring madness.  Without Name.  Pauli
  Murray.  PoBA
Call me the Valiant heading west on Fourteen into the frozen.
  Ford Pickup.  David Allan Evans.  NVAP
Call not thy wanderer home as yet.  Germinal.  "Æ."  BIrV
Call of green things to his hand.  Nathaniel Tarn.  *Fr.* A Nowhere
  for Vallejo.  TwMBP
Call of the old cock pheasant breaks, The.  Boundaries.  Judith
  Minty.  HeS
Call out. Call loud: "I'm ready! Come and find me!"  Hide and
  Seek.  Vernon Scannell.  LP
Call the roller of big cigars.  The Emperor of Ice Cream.  Wallace
  Stevens.  AnMo; InPK; NoAM; NOBA; PAIC; PiAm
Call to Arms.  James Welch.  SA

Call to the Wild, A.  Lord Dunsany.  PFIr
Call to worship said, The.  Worship.  Elmer F. Suderman.
  AATT
Called Proud.  Walter Savage Landor.  GBL
Caller haar fae lift tae lan', A.  Furst Snaw.  Billy Kay.  MIS
Calling black people.  SOS.  LeRoi Jones.  BPo; PoBA
Calling in the Cat.  Elizabeth J. Coatsworth.  BoAnP; PCat
Calling Spring VII-MMMC.  Ogden Nash.  FaBoCo
Calling to mind[e], mine eye [*or* eie] long went about.  The
  Excuse.  Sir Walter Ralegh.  AAS; LoAs
Calling to mind since first my love begun.  Michael Drayton.  *Fr.*
  Idea.  NOBE
Calling Trains.  *Unknown.*  AmFP
Callypso Speaks.  Hilda Doolittle ("H. D.").  PiAm; RiTi; SBG
Calm as that second summer which precedes.  Charleston.  Henry
  Timrod.  AmVN; NOBA
Calm down, my sorrow, we must move with care.  Meditation.
  Baudelaire, *tr. by* Robert Lowell.  InPK
Calm is the landscape when the storm has passed.  Peace in the
  Welsh Hills.  Vernon Watkins.  OxBTC
Calm is the morn without a sound.  In Memoriam A. H. H., XI.
  Tennyson.  NOBE
Calm is unceasing, The.  The Old Man in the Autumn.  John
  Shaw Neilson.  MAuV
Calm [*or* Calme] was the day, and through the trembling air [*or*
  ayre].  Prothalamion.  Spenser.  AAS; PPoe; PPP
Calvary.  E. A. Robinson.  OFD
Calverly's.  E. A. Robinson.  NoAM
Calvinist in Love, A.  Jack R. Clemo.  LoAs
Calypsos, *sels.*  William Carlos Williams.  TH
  "Love the sun," II.
  "We watched/ a red rooster," III.
Calypso's Island.  Archibald MacLeish.  PiAm
Calypso's Song to Ulysses.  Adrian Mitchell.  GBL
Cam Ye By the Salmon Fishers.  *Unknown.*  GBP
Camas Tuath.  Tom Buchan.  MIS
Cambridge Ladies Who Live in Furnished Souls, The.  E. E.
  Cummings.  *Fr.* Sonnets—Realities.  Epi; HeIP; InPK;
  NoAM; NOBA; WIF
Came to lakes; came to dead water.  A Field of Light.  Theodore
  Roethke.  PiAm
Came to me.  Rudaki, *tr. fr. Persian by* Basil Bunting.  BoLoP
Came up that cold sea at Cromer like a running grave.  On a
  Friend's Escape from Drowning off the Norfolk Coast.  George
  Barker.  MPo
Came You Not from Newcastle.  *Unknown.*  GBP
Camel.  Jon Stallworthy.  BoAnP
Camel's Complaint, The.  Charles Edward Carryl.  OxBChV
Camel's hump is an ugly lump, The.  The Hump.  Kipling.
  OxBChV
Cameo, The.  Edna St. Vincent Millay.  WPE
Cameo, A.  Swinburne.  LoAs
Cameo No. II.  June Jordan.  BPo; WBN
Camera records, The.  Poem.  Diane Kruchkow.  FAF
Camerados.  Bayard Taylor.  PAIC
Camp in the Prussian Forest, A.  Randall Jarrell.  NowV; TCP
Camp meeting took place, in a wide open space, A.  At a Georgia
  Camp Meeting.  Kerry Mills.  BLSo
Campaign, The.  Josephine Miles.  WPE
Campaign for Peace in Our Time, The.  Jon Anderson.  CAAP
Campbells Are Comin', The.  *Unknown.*  BLSH, *with music;*
  BTTM
Camping Out.  William Empson.  OxBTC
Camping Out on Rainy Mountain.  Jim Barnes.  CDW
Camptown Races, The [*or* De], *with music.*  Stephen Collins
  Foster.  BLSH; PSoN

Campus on the Hill, The. W. D. Snodgrass. NoAM; NowV; WIF

Can death be faithful, or the grave be just? The Resurrection. Nathaniel Wanley. SCP-2

Can flame beget white steel. She Contrasts with Herself Hippolyta. Hilda Doolittle ("H. D."). SBG

Can I easily say. Sisters. Adrienne Rich. IHMS

Can I explain this to you? Your eyes. The Knife. Keith Douglas. LoAs

Can I not sing but "hoy." The Jolly Shepherd Wat. *Unknown.* NOBE; OxBM

Can—I—poet. For Some Poets. Mae Jackson. PoBA

Can I see anothers woe. On Anothers Sorrow. Blake. *Fr.* Songs of Innocence. MBPR

Can I, who have for others oft compiled. Of My Dear Son, Gervase Beaumont. Sir John Beaumont. NOBE

Can u walk away from ugly. Positives for Sterling Plumpp. Don L. Lee. JB; PoBA

Can ye see the mune, my love? She drives. Ablow the Mune. Donald Campbell. MIS

Can you/ own land, can you. Revolutionary Letter #21. Diane DiPrima. RiTi

Can you keep it so. Starlings. Norman MacCaig. BoAnP

Can you make me a cambric shirt. Proofs of Love. *Unknown.* ECBV

Can you remember the times. Now That the Buffalo's Gone. Buffy Sainte-Marie. PoRo

Canada-I-O. *Unknown.* AmFP

Canadian Boat-Song. *Unknown, at. to* John Galt, *and also to* "Christopher North." AIW

Canal Bank Walk. Patrick Kavanagh. NoAM

Canary, The. Elizabeth Turner. OxBChV

Canary-birds feed on sugar and seed. The Camel's Complaint. Charles Edward Carryl. OxBChV

Cancelled Stanza of the Ode on Melancholy. Keats. MBPR

Cancer's a Funny Thing. J. B. S. Haldane. OxBTC

Candidate, The. Thomas Gray. PPP

Candle lit in darkness of black waters, A. On the Lake. V. Sackville-West. SBG

Candle takes the first desperate, The. Homage to Chagall. Duane Niatum. CDW

Candles. Peter Meinke. AATT

Candles. Sylvia Plath. NMM; PSN

Candy/ Is dandy. Reflections on Ice-Breaking. Ogden Nash. FaBoCo; SFF

Candy Man Blues. *Unknown.* BluL

Canedolia. Edwin Morgan. FaBoCo

Canibolos de la Montana. Renée Roper. NPW

Cannas shiny as slag. Flower Dump. Theodore Roethke. PiAm

Canned Heat Blues. *Unknown.* BluL

Cannibal Flea, The. Tom Hood. SpRo

Cannibalee: A Po'em of Passion. C. F. Lummis. SpRo

Canonization, The. John Donne. AnMo; Epi; IPWM; LoAs; MetP; NOBE; PPoe; PPP; SCP-1

Canst thou bind the cluster of the Pleiades. Job, Bible, *O. T.* OBP

Canst work i' th' ground so fast? Anarchist. Norman Dugdale. BoAnP

Can't tell my future/ I can't tell my past. Future Blues. *Unknown.* BluL

Can't you hear that rooster crowin'? New Morning. Bob Dylan. GrRo

Cantares, *sels.* Leonora Speyer. TH
  "I lied—trusting you knew."
  "Sweet, my sweet!"

Canterbury Tales, The, *sels.* Chaucer.
  Prologue, *abr.* PPP
  Clerk of Oxford, The. OxBM
    ("Clerk ther was of Oxenford also, The.") InPs
  "Knyght ther was, and that a worthy man, A." InPS
  Persons in the Prologue, *mod. version by* Nevill Coghill. OBP
  Poor Parson, A. BoReV
  Prioress, The. OxBM
    (Madame Eglantine.) NOBE
  Reeve, The. OxBM
  Wanton Merry Friar, A. BoReV
  "Whan that Aprill with his shoures soote." InPS
  Wife of Bath, The. OxBM
    ("Good Wif was ther of biside Bathe, A.") InPS; PPoe
  Friar's Tale, The. PAIC
  Knight's Tale, The.
    "In the third hour after Palamon," *mod. version by* Nevill Coghill. OBP
  Manciple's Tale, The.
    Controlling the Tongue. OxBChV
    Mice before Milk. PCat
  Pardoner's Tale, The.
    Three Revellers Search for Death. OxBM
  Reeve's Tale, The.
    Mill at Trumpington, The. OxBM
  Wife of Bath's Prologue, The.
    "If there were no authority on earth," *mod. version by* Nevill Coghill. OBP
  Wife's Fifth Husband, The. OxBM

Canticle. John Norris. SCP-2

Canticle of the Rose, The. Edith Sitwell. NoAM

Canticle to the Waterbirds, A. William Everson. PiAm

Canto Amor. John Berryman. PAIC; VGW

Canto del Señor Segovia. David Sten Herrstrom. AATT

Canto Llano. Anita Endrezze Probst. CDW

Cantos, *sels.* Ezra Pound.
  "And then went down to the ship," I. NoAM; PAIC; VGW
  "Eleanor (she spoiled in a British climate)," VII. NoAM; NOBA
  " 'From the colour the nature,' " XC. VGW
  "Hang it all, Robert Browning," II. NoAM; NOBA; PiAm
  "I sat on the Dogana's steps," III. Epi
  "Kung walked/ by the dynastic temple," XIII. PiAm
  "What thou lovest well remains," *fr.* LXXXI. InPS; NOBE
  "Who even dead, yet hath his mind entire!" XLVII. PiAm; VGW
  "With Usura," XLV. NOBA; PiAm
  "Zeus lies in Ceres' bosom," LXXXI. NoAm; NOBA; VGW

Cantos, *sels.* Tom Weatherly. PoBA
  Coon Fire, 5.
  First Thesis, 7.
  Gullfish, 4.

Canzone Pastoral in Honor of Her Majesty, A. Edmund Bolton. PAIC

Cap and Bells, The. W. B. Yeats. NoAM

Cape Ann, *with music. Unknown.* BLSo

Cape Cod girls they've got no combs. The Codfish Shanty. *Unknown.* GBP

Cape Code Murders, 1968. Mira Fish. FAF

Cape Cornwall. Paul Mills. MIS

Cape Hatteras. Hart Crane. *Fr.* The Bridge. PiAm

Cape Horn Gospel—1 (" 'I was in a hooker once,' said Karlssen"). John Masefield. PoTa

Caprice. Dorothy Stott Shaw. PoTa

Caprice of the strokes, The. Heirloom. Robert Flanagan. HeS

Captain, The, *sel.* John Fletcher.
  Away, Delights, *fr.* III, iv. NOBE
  (Sad Songs, The.) GBL

Captain/ what are you doing. George Simic. Charles Simic. CAAP

Captain bold in Halifax, that dwelt in country quarters, A. Unfortunate Miss Bailey. George Colman the Younger. GBP; PeBB

Captain Bover. *Unknown.* GBP

Captain Bunker. *Unknown.* AmFP

Captain Captain. *Unknown.* BluL

Captain, captain, what will you give me. The *Turkish Revery.* *Unknown.* RDB

Captain Carpenter. John Crowe Ransom. Epi; NoAM; NOBA; PPoe

Captain Fox was padding along sociably. The Fox and the Goat. La Fontaine, *tr. by* Marianne Moore. AKE

Captain Hall. *Unknown.* GBP

Captain Jinks, *with music.* William Horace Lingard. BLSo

Captain Kidd. *Unknown.* AmFP
    (Captain Robert Kidd.) PeBB

Captain or Colonel, or Knight in Arms. Milton. PAIC

Captain Patterson, the folks back home. Americana XIII. Carl Rakosi. InPS

Captain Quiros and Mr. William Lane. Terra Australis. Douglas Stewart. MAuV

Captain Robert Kidd. *Unknown. See* Captain Kidd.

Captain stood on the carronade, The. The Old Navy. Frederick Marryat. PoTa

Captain! we often heretofore. To Our House-Dog Captain. Walter Savage Landor. OBP

Captain Wedderburn's Courtship. *Unknown.* AmFP; SLP

Captive, The. Rochelle Ratner. WBN

Captive Stone, The. Jim Barnes. CDW

Captived Bee, The: or, the Little Filcher. Robert Herrick. SCP-1

Captive of Major André, The. *Unknown.* BTTM

Caput apri refero. The Boar's Head. *Unknown.* OxBM

Car has pulled up outside, A. Alta. MMD

Card-Players, The. David Ray. VGW

Cardinal Ideograms. May Swenson. Psy

Cards and Kisses. John Lyly. *Fr.* Alexander and Campaspe, III, v. NOBE; PBMP
    (Cupid and My Campaspe.) HeIP
    ("Cupid and my Campaspe played.") GBL

Care Away! *Unknown.* OxBM

Care away, away, away. I Am Forsaken. *Unknown.* OxBM

Care-Charmer Sleep. Samuel Daniel. *Fr.* To Delia. IPWM
    ("Care-charmer sleep, son of the sable night.") Epi; InPS; NOBE; PAIC
    ("Care-charmer sleepe, sonne of the sable night.") AAS

Care-charmer sleepe, sweet ease in restles miserie. Fidessa, More Chaste than Kind, XV. Bartholomew Griffin. AAS

Care in Heaven. Spenser. *Fr.* The Faerie Queene, II, 12. BoReV

Careful Angler, The. Robert Louis Stevenson. SPo

Careful observers may foretell the hour. A Description of a City Shower. Swift. AnMo; HeIP; MAT; PCat; PPoD; PPP

Careless and still. The Rabbit Hunter. Robert Frost. SPo; TH

Careless Love. *Unknown.* BLSH, *with music;* BLSo, *with music;* BluL

Carentan O Carentan. Louis Simpson. MPo; NOBA

Cares o' Love, The. Burns. PBMP

Cargoes. John Masefield. NOBE; WIF

Carhop floated up, The. Chicken. Dave Etter. MAT

Cariboo Horses, The. A. W. Purdy. HeIP

Carious Exposure. Gladys Cardiff. CDW

Carmel Point. Robinson Jeffers. PiAm

Carmen. Victor Hernandez Cruz. PoBA

Carmen Bellicosum. Guy Humphreys McMaster. BTTM

Carmen Saeculare. John Taylor. NowV

Carmina Burana, *sel. Unknown, tr. fr. Latin by* George F. Whicher.
    In the Balance. OLR

Carnal Knowledge. Thom Gunn. BoLoP

Carnation, The. Paul Hannigan. POL

Carol: "My lady went to Canterbury." *Unknown.* FaBoCo

Carol: "There was a boy bedded in bracken." John Short. MPo

Carol of the Brown King. Langston Hughes. LCL

Carol of the Numbers. *Unknown.* AmFP
    (Dilly Song, The.) GBP

Carol Took Her Clothes Off. Bill Messenger. CTBA

Caroline and Her Young Sailor Bold. *Unknown.* AmFP

Caroline of Edinboro' Town. *Unknown.* AmFP

Carousel, The. Gloria C. Oden. PoBA

Carpe Diem. Robert Frost. PAIC

Carpenter, The. Michael Perkins. POL

Carpenter's made a hole, The. A Hole in the Floor. Richard Wilbur. NoAM; NOBA

Carpenter's Son, The. A. E. Housman. PBMP; SoSe; SpRo

Carpets cover many floors where I come from. To Vietnam. Charlie Cobb. PoBA

Carriage from Sweden, A. Marianne Moore. SoSe

Carrickfergus. Louis MacNeice. NoAM

Carried her unprotesting out the door. The Rites for Cousin Vit. Gwendolyn Brooks. *Fr.* The Womanhood. BPo; WPE

Carrier Letter. Hart Crane. BoLoP

Carriers of the Dream Wheel. N. Scott Momaday. CDW

Carrion Comfort. Gerard Manley Hopkins. AnMo; BoReV; HeIP; InPK; NoAM; PFD; PPP

Carrion crow sat on an oak, A. Mother Goose. MG

Carrion-eater's nobility calls back from God, The. A Dreamed Realization. Gregory Corso. VGW

Carrots are disappointing. Garden Report. Greg Kuzma. HeS

Carry Me Back to Old Virginny, *with music.* James A. Bland. BLSo; PSoN

Carry me back to Ole Virginny. First Families Move Over! Ogden Nash. FaBoCo

Carry your garden. The Serpent Muses. Peggy Henderson. NMM

Carrying a bunch of marigolds. A Negro Woman. William Carlos Williams. IPWM

Carrying a hammer on a quiet street. The Planting. Harley Elliott. NeAC

Carrying Food Home in Winter. Margaret Atwood. TSWA

Cars/ In the park. Central Park Tourney. Mildred Weston. MiP

Cars collide and erupt luggage and babies. In Laughter. Ted Hughes. InPS

Cars once steel and green, now old. Louis Zukofsky. VGW

Carson, turn your coat collar up, throw the cigarette from your hand. The Invitation in It. Kay Boyle. *Fr.* American Citizen. RiTi

Caruso: a voice. Sleeping with Women. Kenneth Koch. NoAM

Caryatid. Léonie Adams. LoAs

Caryophyllaceae, The. Spring Coming. A. R. Ammons. InPK

Casa de Pollos. Kathleen Fraser. AmPA

Casabianca. Elizabeth Bishop. LoAs

Casanova. Richard Usborne. POL

Cascadilla Falls. A. R. Ammons. CoPAm; NOBA

Case, A. *Unknown.* FaBoCo

Casey at the Bat. Ernest Lawrence Thayer. PPoD; SPo

Casey Jones ("Driving that train, high on cocaine"). Robert Hunter. GrRo

Casey Jones ("Come, all you rounders, if you want to hear").
T. Lawrence Seibert.  AIW; BLSH, *with music*

Casey Jones ("Come all you muckers and gather here").
*Unknown.*  AmFP

Casey would waltz with the strawberry blonde.  The Band Played
On.  John E. Palmer.  BLSH

Casey's Daughter at the Bat.  Al Graham.  SPo

Cash on the barrelhead.  Hair on the Chest.  Coleman Barks.  *Fr.*
Body Poems.  NVAP

Cashel of Munster.  *Unknown, at. to* William English, *tr. fr. Irish
by* Sir Samuel Ferguson.  BIrV; GBL; PFIr

Casino.  W. H. Auden.  PSN

Cassandra.  Louise Bogan.  RiTi; SBG; VGW

Cassandra.  Robinson Jeffers.  HeIP

Cassandra.  E. A. Robinson.  NoAM; PiAm

Cassinus and Peter.  Swift.  PPP

Cassius Hueffer.  Edgar Lee Masters.  *Fr.* Spoon River
Anthology.  NoAM

Castara, you too fondly court.  A Dialogue between Araphil and
Castara.  William Habington.  SCP-2

Castaway, The.  William Cowper.  HeIP; LAuP; NOBE; PPoe;
PPP

Castaways, The.  E. V. Rieu.  PoTa

Casting a Vote.  James DenBoer.  PPoD

Castle of Indolence, The, *sel.*  James Thomson.
"O mortal Man, who livest here by toil," Canto I.  LAuP

Castle of Thorns, The.  Yvor Winters.  NoAM

Castles and Candlelight.  James Reeves.  PoTa

Castoff Skin.  Ruth Whitman.  InPK

Casual at the wheel, blinding rainstorm.  Nobody Dies Like
Humphrey Bogart.  Norman Rosten.  PPoD

Cat, The.  Richard Church.  BoAnP; PCat

Cat, The.  W. H. Davies.  NOBE; PCat

Cat.  Eleanor Farjeon.  RAE

Cat, The.  William Matthews.  AmPA

Cat.  Mary Britton Miller.  LCL; PCat

Cat.  Lytton Strachey.  PCat

Cat, A.  Edward Thomas.  BoAnP

Cat.  J. R. R. Tolkien.  ECBV

Cat, The.  Helen Wolfert.  RiTi

Cat, A/ I keep, that plays about my.  Robert Herrick.  PCat

Cat!/ Scat!  Cat.  Eleanor Farjeon.  RAE

Cat and the Bird, The.  George Canning.  ECBV

Cat and the Lute, The.  Thomas Master.  PCat

Cat and the Moon, The.  W. B. Yeats.  PCat; PFIr

Cat and the Rain, The.  Swift.  *Fr.* A Description of a City
Shower.  PCat

Cat and the Weather.  May Swenson.  MiP

Cat as Cat, The.  Denise Levertov.  NOBA; PiAm

Cat at the Cream.  *Unknown.*  GBP; POL

Cat bird singing.  Air.  Robert Creeley.  Prf

Cat, Caged and Shrunken, The.  Arthur Freeman.  BoAnP

Cat Came Back, The, *with music.*  Harry S. Miller.  FSN

Cat came fiddling, A.  The Fiddling Cat.  *Unknown.*  ECBV

Cat Heard the Cat-bird, The.  John Ciardi.  ECBV

Cat in the cold, so eager to come in.  Will You, Won't You.
Mark Van Doren.  NCSH

Cat into Lady.  La Fontaine, *tr. fr. French by* Edmund Marsh.
PCat

Cat of Cats, The.  William Brighty Rands.  *Fr.* The White
Princess.  OxBChV

Cat of the House, The.  Ford Madox Ford.  PCat

Cat on Couch.  Barbara Howes.  NCSH

Cat on my bosom, The.  The Cat as Cat.  Denise Levertov.
NOBA; PiAm

Cat runs races with her tail, The.  The dog.  Signs of Winter.
John Clare.  Epi

Cat said, A.  Vietnam #4.  Clarence Major.  PoBA

Cat sits on the pavement by the house, A.  The Lonely Man.
Randall Jarrell.  MPo

Cat takes a look at the weather.  Cat and the Weather.  May
Swenson.  MiP

Cat went here and there, The.  The Cat and the Moon.  W. B.
Yeats.  PCat; PFIr

Cat! who has[t] past thy grand climacteric.  To a Cat.  Keats.
MBPR; PCat

Catachism, 1958.  W. M. Ransom.  CDW

Cataract.  Margoret J. Smith.  PPoD

Cataract at Lodore, The.  Helen Bevington.  SpRo

Cataract of Lodore, The.  Robert Southey.  OxBChV; SpRo

Catch.  Robert Francis.  InPK; NCSH; WIF

Catch.  Langston Hughes.  NoAM

Catch him coming off the thing after a state of the union.
Strategies.  Welton Smith.  PoBA

Catch him, crow!  Carry him, kite!  Swinging the Baby.  *Unknown.*
ECBV

Catch me!  Love in the Middle of the Air.  Lenore Kandel.  *Fr.*
Circus.  RiTi

Catch of Shy Fish, A.  Gwendolyn Brooks.  CAPP

Catch What You Can.  Jean Garrigue.  VGW

Caterpillar.  Christina Rossetti.  OxBChV

Caterpillar, The.  Miller Williams.  CoPAm

Cathedral Close, The.  Coventry Patmore.  *Fr.* The Angel in the
House, I, i.  VPC

Cathexis.  F. J. Bryant, Jr.  PoBA

Cathleen.  *Unknown, tr. fr. Irish by* Thomas MacIntyre.  BIrV

Catholic Bells, The.  William Carlos Williams.  NOBA

Catkins, like caterpillars slung arow.  Lost Lane.  Dorothy
Wellesley.  WPE

Cats.  Eleanor Farjeon.  ECBV; PCat

Cats.  Francis Scarfe.  BoAnP
"Those who love cats which do not even purr," *sel.*  PCat

Cats.  A. S. J. Tessimond.  BoAnP; PCat

Cat's electric fur, The.  The Cat, Caged and Shrunken.  Arthur
Freeman.  BoAnP

Cat's Eyes.  Francis Scarfe.  PCat

Cat's Funeral.  E. V. Rieu.  ECBV

Cats I scorn, who sleek and fat.  A True Cat.  Anna Seward.
PCat

Cat's Life, A.  Eleanor Struthers.  CaYB

Cats, no less liquid than their shadows.  Cats.  A. S. J. Tessimond.
BoAnP; PCat

Cats prowl late at night.  A Cat's Life.  Eleanor Struthers.  CaYB

Cat's purr, A.  At the Loom.  Robert Duncan.  *Fr.* Passages.
PiAm; VGW

Cats sleep/ Anywhere.  Cats.  Eleanor Farjeon.  ECBV; PCat

Cat's Song, The.  *Unknown.*  GBP

Cattails for Bennett.  Mary Shumway.  HeS

Cattle Ghosts, The.  David Allan Evans.  NVAP

Cattle huddle together.  The Blizzard.  A. A. Dewey.  HeS

Cattle Show.  "Hugh MacDiarmid."  OxBTC

Caught at hanger's ends the limp.  Goodwill, Inc.  Dennis Schmitz.
AmPA

Caught between two streams of traffic, in the gloom.  T. S. Eliot.
Robert Lowell.  NoAM; NOBA

Caught in the centre of a soundless field.  Myxomatosis. Philip
Larkin.  NoAM

Caught off first, he leaped to run to second, but.  Ball Game.
Richard Eberhart.  MiP

Caught without wife and mother, child.  Getting Drunk with
Daughter.  Robert Huff.  CoPAm

Cauld Cornwood. *Unknown.* GBP

Cauliflower, The. John Haines. InPK

Cauliflower-eared Spartan. Reading and Talking. Louis Zukofsky. VGW

Caulker, The. M. A. Lewis. PoTa

Cause nobody deals with Aretha—a mother with four children. Poem for Aretha. Nikki Giovanni. BPo; PoBA

Cautionary Verses to Youth of Both Sexes. Theodore Hook. OxBChV

Cautious Gunslinger, The. An Idle Visitation. Edward Dorn. *Fr.* Gunslinger. NOBA

Cavalier Lyric. James Simmons. InPK; POL

Cavalier Tunes. Robert Browning. BTTM

Cavalry Crossing a Ford. Walt Whitman. AmVN; HeIP; InPK; InPS; NoAM; PiAm; PPoD; PPP

Cave, The. Glenn W. Dresbach. RFM

Cave of Despair, The. Spenser. *Fr.* The Faerie Queene, I, 9. NOBE

Cave Where Night Sleeps, The. T. Alan Broughton. FAF

Caw, caw, caw. Poem/Ditty-Bop. Carolyn M. Rodgers. JB

Cean Dubh Deelish. *Unknown. See* Dear Dark Head.

Cease rude Boreas blust'ring railers. The Tempest. *Unknown.* AmFP

Cecil County. Ron Welburn. PoBA

Ceiling, The. Theodore Roethke. ECBV; LCL

Celandine. Edward Thomas. OxBTC

Celebration, The. James Dickey. VGW

Celebration. Ray A. Young Bear. CDW

Celebration for a Young Priest. Barbara Earl Thomson. AATT

Celebration for My Mother. Wendy Rose. CDW

Celebration of Charis, A, *sel.* Ben Jonson.
Triumph of Charis, The. InPS; NOBE
(Her Triumph.) LoAs

Celemene, pray tell me. A New Dialogue, Sung by a Boy and Girl at the Playhouse. Thomas Durfey. SCP-2

Celery. Gertrude Stein. *Fr.* Tender Buttons. RiTi

Celestial choir, enthron'd in realms of light. To His Excellency, General Washington. Phillis Wheatley. OFD; SBG; WPE

Celestial City, The. Giles Fletcher the Younger. Christ's Victory and Triumph, IV. BoReV; NOBE

Celia. Ellen Bass. NMM

Celia Bleeding: to the Surgeon. Thomas Carew. SCP-2

Celia, Celia, your name is like cilia. Celia. Ellen Bass. NMM

Cell Song. Etheridge Knight. PoBA

Cells Breathe in the Emptiness. Galway Kinnell. VGW

"Cemetery stone New England autumn, The." Voice of Heroes. Horace Gregory. OFD

Cenci, The. Shelley. MBPR

Cenotaph, The. Charlotte Mew. WPE

Censorship. Arthur Waley. OxBTC

Centaur, The. May Swenson. NMM

Centaur Overheard, The. Edgar Bowers. ConAP

Centaur Song. Hilda Doolittle ("H.D."). VGW

Centaurs, The. James Stephens. PFIr

Centenary Ode, A: Inscribed to Little Crow, Leader of the Sioux Rebellion. James Wright. CoPAm

Centennial Hymn. Whittier. BTTM

Centipede was happy quite, A. Sad Results of Thinking. *Unknown.* SFF

Central Park Tourney. Mildred Weston. MiP

Century and eight more years, A. The Four Directions. Emerson Blackhorse Mitchell. VW

Ceremony. Lyn Lifshin. FAF

Ceremony. Richard Wilbur. NoAM

Ceremony/ Judy upstairs. Bedtime. J. D. Whitney. NVAP

Cerne Giant, The. Paul Mills. MIS

Certain dark underground eyes. Picture of Loot. Alan Sillitoe. OxBTC

Certain great statesman, whom all of us know, A. Ballynahinch. George Canning. FaBoCo

Certain portions of the heart. Anatomy. Gilbert Sorrentino. POL

Certain presuppositions are altered. Upland. A. R. Ammons. NOBA

Certain World, A. Ruth Herschberger. WBN

Cervantes, Dostoievsky, Poe. A Poem Intended to Incite the Utmost Depression. Samuel Hoffenstein. FaBoCo

'Cession's stahted on de gospel way, De. A Spiritual. Paul Laurence Dunbar. BPo

C'est un grand Monsieur Pussy-cat. Monsieur Pussy-cat, Blackmailer. Stevie Smith. PCat

Cethegrande is a fis. The Whale. *Unknown.* OxBM

Cézanne's Ports. Allen Ginsberg. WIF

Cha Till Maccruimein. E. A. Mackintosh. SoSe

Chad. Edward Brathwaite. MPo

Chaff, The. W. S. Merwin. PPP

Chain Gang Trouble. *Unknown.* BluL

Chain of Pearl, A, *sel.* Lady Diana Primrose.
Fourth Pearl, The: Temperance. WPE

Chains, my good lord: in your raised brows I read. Tennyson. *Fr.* Columbus. OFD

Chair, The. Theodore Roethke. AnMo

Chalk Blue Butterfly, The. Stephen Spender. LP

Chalk mark sex of the nation, on walls we drummers. Three Modes of History and Culture. LeRoi Jones. NoAM

Challenge, The. Longfellow. PiAm

Chamber Music. James Joyce. *Poems indexed separately by titles and first lines.*

Chamber-pot Rhyme. *Unknown.* GBP

Chambered Nautilus, The. Oliver Wendell Holmes. *Fr.* The Autocrat of the Breakfast-Table, *ch.* 4. AmVN; NOBA; PiAm; VoPo

Chambermaid's First Song, The. W. B. Yeats. AnMo

Chambermaid's Second Song, The. W. B. Yeats. AnMo

Chameleons feed on light and air. An Exhortation. Shelley. MBPR

Chameleons saw an arc of color, The. The Lord's Chameleons. Peter Klappert. AmPA

Champagne Charlie, *with music.* At. to George Leybourne. BLSo; PSoN

Championing heights. Plato. Sandra Ruth Duguid. AATT

Chance adjustment of my car mirror, A. In a Mirror. Marcia Stubbs. MAT

Chancery Suit, A. Sir George Rose. FaBoCo

Chances, The, *sel.* John Fletcher.
"Merciless love, whom nature hath denied," III, ii. GBL

Chances, The. Wilfred Owen. OxBTC

Chandeliers hemorrhage, Tritons, The. Figures in a Ruined Ballroom. George Hitchcock. VGW

Change, The. Michael Dransfield. CAAP

Change. Robert Graves. OxBTC

Change, The. David O'Bruadair, *tr. fr. Irish by* Austin Clarke. BIrV

Change./ like if u were a match I wd light u. A Poem to Complement Other Poems. Don L. Lee. BPo; NoAM

Change, move, dead clock, that this fresh day. Small Prayer. Weldon Kees. VGW

Change of Address. Kathleen Fraser. WBN

Change-Up. Don L. Lee. PoBA

Changeling, The. Charlotte Mew. SoSe

Changing a Tire by the Missouri River. Harley Elliott. HeS

Changing of the Guard.   Charles G. Ballard.   VW
Channel Firing.   Thomas Hardy.   HeIP; InPK; NoAM; OBP; OxBTC; PPoD; VoPo
Chansons Innocentes, *sels.*   E. E. Cummings.
  "In Just-/ Spring when the world is mud," I.   BBGO; HeIP; InPK; NowV; PiAm
  "Little tree," II.   LCL
Chant for Dark Hours.   Dorothy Parker.   SBG
Chant for Young/Brothas and Sistuhs, A.   Sonia Sanchez.   BPo
Chapel's cowbell, The.   Crusoe's Island.   Derek Walcott.   NoAM
Chaplinesque.   Hart Crane.   NoAM; NOBA; VGW
Character, A.   Samuel Taylor Coleridge.   MBPR
Character of a Happy Life, The.   Sir Henry Wotton.   NOBE
Character of Charles Brown.   Keats.   MBPR
Character of Love Seen as a Search for the Lost, The.   Kenneth Patchen.   VGW
Character of the Happy Warrior.   Wordsworth.   MBPR
Characteristics of a Child Three Years Old.   Wordsworth.   MBPR; RRA
Characters of Forgotten Dirty Jokes, The.   Wesley McNair.   FAF
Chard Whitlow.   Henry Reed.   FaBoCo; OxBTC
Charge, The.   Anselm Hollo.   TwMBP
Charge of the gallant Three Hundred, the Heavy Brigade, The. The Charge of the Heavy Brigade.   Tennyson.   BTTM
Charge of the Grid Brigade.   George S. Applegarth.   SPo
Charge of the Heavy Brigade, The.   Tennyson.   BTTM
Charge of the Light Brigade, The.   Tennyson.   BTTM; PBMP; PPoD; SFF
Charitas Nimia; or, The Dear Bargain.   Richard Crashaw.   BoReV
Charles Cavendish to His Posterity.   Ben Jonson.   SCP-1
Charles Guiteau, 2 *versions. Unknown.*   AmFP
Charles Harpur in his journals long ago.   Extinct Birds.   Judith Wright.   MAuV
Charles river reaps here like a sickle, The.   Professor Kelleher and the Charles River.   Desmond O'Grady.   NoAm
Charles XII of Sweden.   Samuel Johnson.   *Fr.* The Vanity of Human Wishes.   NOBE
Charles used to watch Naomi, taking heart.   Laboratory Poem. James Merrill.   InPK; MAT; PPoD
Charleston.   Henry Timrod.   AmVN; NOBA
Charleston Blues ("Charleston, South Carolina, baby is where I was born"). *Unknown.*   BluL
Charlie Cherry. *Unknown.*   BluL
Charlie Is My Darling, *with music.*   Lady Caroline Nairne.   RDB
Charlie Two-Head.   Marnie Walsh.   VW
Charlie Wolf used to whittle skinning knives.   Halcyon Days.   Jim Barnes.   CDW
Charm against the Toothache, A.   John Heath-Stubbs.   InPK
Charm against Wens, *orig. and mod. English prose. Unknown.* OxBM
Charm'd with a drink which Highlanders compose.   Athol Brose. Thomas Hood.   FaBoCo
Charmed as a brown wicker nest.   Reflections on a Womb Which Is Called "Vacant."   Jeanine Hathaway.   IHMS
Charming Beauty Bright. *Unknown.*   AmFP
Charming the Moon.   James DenBoer.   MAT
Charming Woman, The.   Helen Selina Sheridan.   WPE
Charms, that call down the moon from out her sphere.   To Music, to Becalm a Sweet-Sick Youth.   Robert Herrick.   SCP-1
Charnel-House, The.   Henry Vaughan.   SCP-1
Chase, The.   J. V. Cunningham.   NoAM
Chaste Florimel.   Matthew Prior.   BoLoP
Chat/ shah shah.   French Persian Cats Having a Ball.   Edwin Morgan.   MPo
Chatterers in Church. *Unknown.*   OxBM

Chaucer.   Longfellow.   AmVN; HeIP; NOBA; PAIC
Cheap Rent.   Carl Sandburg.   PiAm
Cheating Droone.   "T. M."Micro-Cynicon, Satire IV.   TVS
Check to Song.   Owen Meredith.   FaBoCo
Cheek.   Coleman Barks.   *Fr.* Body Poems.   NVAP
Cheer Leader, The.   Carl Sandburg.   SPo
Cheerio My Deario.   Don Marquis.   *Fr.* Archy and Mehitabel. FaBoCo
Cheers.   Eve Merriam.   SPo
Chelsea Morning.   Joni Mitchell.   GrRo; PoRo; WIF
Chenille.   James Dickey.   NoAm
Cherry-ripe.   Thomas Campion.
  *See* There Is a Garden in Her Face.
Cherry Robbers.   D. H. Lawrence.   OBP
Cherry-Tree Carol, The (*diff. versions*).   *Unknown.*   AmFP (4 versions); GBP; HeIP; IPWM; OFD; PeBB
Cherrylog Road.   James Dickey.   CoPAm; InPK; InPS
Cheshire for men.   English Counties.   *Unknown.*   POL
Chester, *with music.*   William Billings.   BLSo
Chestnut Casts His Flambeaux, The.   A. E. Housman.   NoAM; PPP
Chestnut tree stands in the line of sight, A.   St. Asaph's.   Kingsley Amis.   OxBTC
Chevy Chase.   *Unknown.*   PeBB
Chewing Chawing Gum.   *Unknown.*   AmFP
Chez Jane.   Frank O'Hara.   NoAM; NOBA
Chic Freedom's Reflection.   Alice Walker.   NMM
Chicago.   Carl Sandburg.   IPWM; NoAM; NOBA; PiAm; VGW
Chicago/ 3 Hours.   Victor Hernández Cruz.   ANTL
Chicago *Defender* Sends a Man to Little Rock, The.   Gwendolyn Brooks.   PoBA; Psy
Chicago: Near West-Side Renewal.   Dennis Schmitz.   AmPA
Chicago Picasso, The.   Gwendolyn Brooks.   *Fr.* Two Dedications. BPo; Psy
Chicken.   Dave Etter.   MAT
Chicken. How shall I tell you what it is.   A Presentation of Two Birds to My Son.   James Wright.   PPP
Chickens, The.   *Unknown.*   ECBV
Chickens a-crowin' on Sourwood Mountain.   Sourwood Mountain. *Unknown.*   GBP
Chief Leschi of the Nisqually.   Duane Niatum.   CDW
Chief of organic numbers!   Lines on Seeing a Lock of Milton's Hair.   Keats.   MBPR
Chief Petty Officer.   Charles Causley.   OxBTC
Chieftain Iffucan of Azcan in caftan.   Bantams in Pine-Woods. Wallace Stevens.   InPS; NOBA
Child, The.   Donald Hall.   NCSH
Child, The.   W. S. Merwin.   NoAM
Child at Winter Sunset, The.   Mark Van Doren.   NCSH
Child, dreamer, that I may wind.   A Fan for His Daughter. Stéphane Mallarmé, *tr. by* David Paul.   RRA
Child Half-Asleep, A.   Tony Connor.   BuTh
Child, I suffered them, A.   Doubts.   Elizabeth Jennings.   LP
Child, I warn thee in all wise.   Symon's Lesson of Wisdom for All Manner of Children.   *Unknown.*   OxBChV
Child in Adam's field I dreamed away, A.   Edwin Muir.   *Fr.* Variations on a Time Theme.   NoAM
"Child Is Father to the Man, The."   Gerard Manley Hopkins. FaBoCo
Child is on my shoulders, The.   Laughing Child.   Carl Sandburg. CTBA
Child Is Singing, A.   Adrian Mitchell.   BuTh; LP
Child Next Door, The.   Robert Penn Warren.   TCP
Child of Mine.   Gerry Goffin *and* Carole King.   PoRo
Child of my winter, born.   Heart's Needle.   W. D. Snodgrass. CAPP; ConAP; PiAm; RRA

Child of patient industry. Invitation to the Bee. Charlotte Smith. OxBChV

Child of the clouds! remote from every taint. The River Duddon, II. Wordsworth. MBPR

Child of the Romans. Carl Sandburg. PiAm

Child on Top of a Greenhouse. Theodore Roethke. BuTh; NCSH; PiAm; VGW

Child saw the bombers skate, The. Come to the Stone. Randall Jarrell. VGW

Child should always say what's true, A. Whole Duty of Children. Robert Louis Stevenson. OxBChV

Child, the current of your breath is six days long. Unknown Girl in the Maternity Ward. Anne Sexton. NoAM

Child Unborn, The. Humbert Wolfe. BuTh

Child Waters. *Unknown.* PeBB

Child with Six Fingers. Carol Muske. AmPA

Child, you were conceived in my upstairs room. To a Child Born in Time of Small War. Helen Sorrells. WPE

Childcity, Aprilcity. Paris. Gregory Corso. VGW

Childe Harold's Pilgrimage, *sels.* Byron.
  And I Have Loved Thee, Ocean! *fr.* IV. SPo
  Dying Gladiator, The, *fr.* IV. NOBE
  Eve of Waterloo, *fr.* III. NOBE
    (Waterloo.) PPoD
  "Is thy face like thy mother's, my fair child!" III. MBPR
  "Lake Leman woos me with its crystal face," *fr.* III. InPS
  "Stop!—for thy tread is on an empire's dust!" *fr.* III. InPS
    (Field of Waterloo, The.) BTTM
  Venice and Sunset, *fr.* IV. PAIC

"Childe Roland to the Dark Tower Came." Robert Browning. PPP

Childhood. Anne Bradstreet. *Fr.* The Four Ages of Man. SBG

Childhood. Frances Cornford. OxBTC

Childhood. Jewel C. Latimore. JB

Childhood. Lisel Mueller. RiTi

Childhood. Edwin Muir. HeIP

Childhood. Henry Vaughan. SCP–1

Childhood. Margaret Walker. IHMS; PoBA

Childhood and School-Time. Wordsworth. *Fr.* The Prelude, I. NOBE

Childhood games. The Black Angel. Michael S. Harper. NVAP

Childhood of an Equestrian, The. Russell Edson. AmPA

Childhood remembrances are always a drag. Nikki-Rosa. Nikki Giovanni. IHMS; IPWM; NoAM; PBMP; PoBA; RiTi

Childless. Giolla Brighde MacNamee, *tr. fr. Irish by* Frank O'Connor. BIrV

Childlessness. James Merrill. ConAP

Children. Russell Edson. AmPA

Children, The. Susan MacDonald. IHMS

Children, The. Constance Urdang. IHMS

Children, The. William Carlos Williams. BBGO

Children are dumb to say how hot the day is. The Cool Web. Robert Graves. NoAM; OxBTC

Children are singing, The. Singing. Peter Shelton. AKE

Children begin at green dawn nimbly to build. The Altars in the Street. Denise Levertov. CAPP

Children go forward with their little satchels, The. The School Children. Louise Glück. AmPA

Children of Darkness. Robert Graves. NoAM

Children of Night. Richard Shelton. FiCP

Children of the future age. A Little Girl Lost. Blake. *Fr.* Songs of Experience. MBPR; RRA

Children of the Poor, The. Gwendolyn Brooks. *Fr.* The Womanhood. WPE

Children they move stand, The. Clear. Angelo Lewis. PoBA

Children tumbling about the yard, The. On the Knowledge of Things. Alexander Taylor. NowV

Children Visit the Island. Diane Wakoski. CAAP

Children walk. City. Jane Stembridge. NMM

Children, you are very little. Good and Bad Children. Robert Louis Stevenson. OxBChV

Children's Rhymes. Langston Hughes. BPo; InPS

Children's Runes and Omens. *Unknown.* MAT

Child's Drawing. Allan Block. FAF

Child's Evening Prayer, A. Samuel Taylor Coleridge.          *See* Pains of Sleep, The.

Child's face at the window, The. The Revenant. Margaret Atwood. Psy

Child's Present, A. Robert Herrick. OxBChV

Child's Sight, The. Hy Sobiloff. VGW

Child's Song. Thomas Moore. ECBV

Child's Song in Spring. Edith Nesbit. OxBChV

Child's Umbrella, The. Raymond Souster. AKE

Child's Visit to the Biology Lab, A. Kathleen Spivack. AmPA

Child's wisdom is in saying, The. The Child's Sight. Hy Sobiloff. VGW

Chilled by the Present, its gloom and its noise. Sonnets from China, XVIII. W. H. Auden. PPP

Chimes. Longfellow. PiAm

Chimes. Alice Meynell. SBG; WPE

Chimney Sweeper, The ("A little black thing among the snow"). Blake. *Fr.* Songs of Experience. LAuP; MBPR; PPoe; PPP

Chimney Sweeper, The ("When my mother died I was very young"). Blake. *Fr.* Songs of Innocence. AnMo; HeIP; InPK; LAuP; MBPR; OxBChV; PPoe; PPP; SoSe

Chimney Sweeper, The. *Unknown.* AmFP

Chimneys, rank on rank, The. Evening. Richard Aldington. Moon

China Shop Vigil. Christopher Middleton. TwMBP

Chinese Baby Asleep. Dorothy Donnelly. NCSH

Chinese Winter. F. R. Higgins. BIrV

Chinoiserie. Charles Wright. AmPA

Chipmunk's Day, The. Randall Jarrell. NCSH
  ("In and out the bushes, up the ivy.") BoAnP

Chloe. Pope. *Fr.* Moral Essays. NOBE

Chloe found Amyntas lying. A Rondelay. Dryden. PAIC

Chloe, why wish you that your years. To Chloe Who Wish'd Her Self Young Enough for Me. William Cartwright. MetP

Chloris, *sels.* William Smith.
  "Some in their harts their mistris colours bears," XXIX. AAS
  To the Most Excellent and Learned Shepheard Collin Cloute, *dedication.* AAS

Chloris' Charms Dissolved by Eudora, *sel.* Anne Killigrew.
  "Press on till thou descry." SCP–2

Chloris, forbear a while. Song. Henry Bold. GBL

Chloris in the Snow. William Strode.          *See* On Chloris Walking in the Snow.

Chock House Blues. *Unknown.* BluL

Chocolate Soldiers, The. Calvin Forbes. MAT

Choice. J. V. Cunningham. PiAm; VGW

Choice, The. Winifrid M. Letts. PFIr

Choice, The. W. B. Yeats. NoAM; OxBTC

Choice of Valentines: or, The Merry Ballad of Nashe His Dildo, The *sels.* Thomas Nashe. SCP–2
  "By blind meanders and by crankled ways."
  "Sweeping she comes, as she would brush the ground."

Choice of Weapons, A. Stanley Kunitz. VGW

Choice of Weapons, A. Phyllis McGinley. SS

Choirs of Heaven are tokened in a harp-string, The. The Counsels of O'Riordan, the Rann Maker. T. D. O'Bolger. PFIr

Chomei at Toyama. Basil Bunting. OxBTC; TwMBP

Choose me your valentine. To His Mistresse. Robert Herrick. OFD

Choose now among this fairest number. Song. William Browne. GBL

Choose the darkest part o' the grove. Incantation to Oedipus. Dryden. *Fr.* Oedipus, III, i. OFD

Choosing a Name. Charles *and* Mary Lamb. OxBChV

Choosing a Name. Anne Ridler. NOBE

Choosing Their Names. Thomas Hood. PCat

Chops. Alan Dixon. BoAnP

Choristers Training, *orig. and mod. English prose. Unknown.* OxBM

Chorus: "Dharma law". Jack Kerouac. Mexico City Blues, 66. PiAm

Chorus: "Long ago, the Mountain Mother." Euripides, *tr. fr. Greek by* Richmond Lattimore. *Fr.* Helen. RRA

Chorus: "Praised be man, he is existing in milk." Jack Kerouac. Mexico City Blues, 228. PiAm

Chorus: "Songs that erupt, The." Jack Kerouac. Mexico City Blues, 195. PiAm

Chorus: "Summer holds, The: upon its glittering lake." W. H. Auden. *Fr.* The Dog Beneath the Skin. OxBTC

Chorus: "They were singing Old MacDonald in the schoolbus." John Ciardi. SS

Chorus: "We do not wish anything to happen." T. S. Eliot. *Fr.* Murder in the Cathedral. OxBTC

Chorus: "We have not been happy, my Lord, we have not been too happy." T. S. Eliot. *Fr.* Murder in the Cathedral. OxBTC

Chorus: "When the hounds of spring are on winter's traces." Swinburne. *Fr.* Atalanta in Calydon. HeIP; NOBE; VPC

Chorus: "You are the town and we are the clock." W. H. Auden. *Fr.* The Dog Beneath the Skin. OxBTC

Chorus for Survival, *sel.* Horace Gregory.
"Ask no return for love that's given." VGW

Chorus Sacerdotum. Fulke Greville. *Fr.* Mustapha. NOBE; PPP

Chosen. W. B. Yeats. BoLoP

Chosen, The. Thomas Hardy. LoAs

Chosen Light, The. John Montague. TwMBP

Christ, *sel.* Gavin Bantock.
"Rolleth the seventh wave." TwMBP

Christ Climbed Down. Lawrence Ferlinghetti. TCP; VGW

Christ in Alabama. Langston Hughes. PoBA

Christ in the Universe. Alice Meynell. BoReV; NOBE

Christ is a nigger. Christ in Alabama. Langston Hughes. PoBA

Christ Walking on the Water. W. R. Rodgers. NoAM

Christ, wha'd ha'e been Chief Rabbi gin he lik't. Up to Date. "Hugh MacDiarmid." FaBoCo

Christ, whose glory fills the skies. Morning Hymn. Charles Wesley. BoReV

Christabel. Samuel Taylor Coleridge. MBPR
" 'Tis the middle of night by the castle clock," I. OBP

Christening-Day Wishes for My God-child. Robert P. Tristam Coffin. OFD

Christians awake, salute the happy morn. A Hymn for Christmas Day. John Byrom. BoReV

Christina. Louis MacNeice. BoLoP

Christmas. Daisy Aldan. AATT

Christmas. John Betjeman. BoReV; OxBTC

Christmas. Grace Cavalieri. AATT

Christmas at Sea. Robert Louis Stevenson. PoTa

Christmas Carol, A: "In the bleak mid-winter." Christina Rossetti. BoReV
"What can I give Him," *st.* 5. LCL

Christmas Comes to Moccasin Flat. James Welch. CDW; MAT; SA; SFF

Christmas day. Robert Dana. *Fr.* Natural Odes/American Elegies. HeS

Christmas Day. John Meade Falkner. OxBTC

Christmas Eve. Anne Sexton. RiTi

Christmas Eve, and twelve of the clock. The Oxen. Thomas Hardy. InPK; IPWM; NoAM; NOBE; OxBTC; PPoe; PPP; VoPo

Christmas Eve under Hooker's Statue. Robert Lowell. CAPP; ConAP; PiAm

Christmas Hymn, A. Richard Wilbur. MPo; OFD

Christmas is in the air. Five Days Old. Francis Webb. MAuV

Christmas is my name, for have I gone, have I gone, have I gone. A Song Bewailing the Time of Christmas. *Unknown.* SCP-2

Christmas Letter Home. G. S. Fraser. OxBTC; SLP

Christmas Morning, I. Carol Freeman. PoBA

Christmas Mourning. Vassar Miller. CoPAm

Christmas Needles. Albert Howard Carter. AATT

Christmas 1959 Et Cetera. Gerald William Barrax. OFD

Christmas: 1924. Thomas Hardy. BuTh

Christmas Prayer, A. William R. Mitchell. AATT

Christmas Tree, A. William Burford. SoSe

Christmas was in the air and all was well. Karma. E. A. Robinson. HeIP; IPWM; NoAM; OFD; PiAm

Christofo Colombo was a hungry man. Mysterious Biography. Carl Sandburg. OFD

Christopher St. Liberation Day, June 28, 1970. Fran Winant. MMD

Christ's Coming. *Unknown. See* Advent.

Christ's Descent into Hell. Rainer Maria Rilke, *tr. fr. German by* James Wright *and* Sarah Youngblood. Prf

Christ's Love-Song. *Unknown.* BoReV; OxBM

Christ's Plea to Mankind. *Unknown.* OxBM

Christ's Victory and Triumph, *sels.* Giles Fletcher the Younger.
Christ's Triumph after Death, IV.
Celestial City, The. BoReV; NOBE
Christ's Triumph over Death, III.
Palm Sunday: Good Friday. BoReV
Christ's Victory in Heaven, I.
He Was Made Man. BoReV
Christ's Victory on Earth, II.
"Therefore above the rest Ambition sat." SCP-2

Chromis! Mnasil! None appear? Ben Jonson. *Fr.* Oberon the Fairy Prince. SCP-1

Chronicle, *sel.* Robert of Gloucester.
Town Against Gown at Oxford. OxBM

Chronicles: Numbers One and Two. Mei Berssenbrugge. SA

Chronicles: Number Three. Mei Berssenbrugge. SA

Chronos, Chronos, mend thy pace. The Secular Masque. Dryden. OBP; PAIC

Chrysalides. Thomas Kinsella. BIrV; NoAM

Chuck Will's Widow Song. *Unknown.* BPo

Chums, The. Theodore Roethke. NoAM

Chunk off and float she thought. Hibernating in an Old Lost Neighbourhood. Laura Chester. RiTi

Church at little Winwick, The. Winwick, Lancashire. *Unknown.* GBP

Church bells toll a melancholy round, The. Written in Disgust of Vulgar Superstition. Keats. MBPR

Church Burning: Mississippi. James A. Emanuel. PoBA

Church Going. Philip Larkin. InPK; NoAm; PPP; PSN; SoSe

Church is a business, and the rich, The. After Lorca. Robert Creeley. ConAP; InPS; POL

Church Monuments. George Herbert. SCP-1

Church Mouse, The. Gerald Bullett. BoAnP

Church on Comiaken Hill, The. Richard Hugo. Prf

Church Romance, A. Thomas Hardy. NOBE; OxBTC

Church's One Foundation, The, *with music.* Samuel J. Stone. BLSH

Churchyard on the Sands, The. Lord de Tabley. GBL

Cicada. Adrien Stoutenburg. RFM

Cider and Vesalius. John Peck. AmPA

Cielito Lindo, *with music*. Carlos Fernandez, *tr. fr. Spanish by* James Morehead. BLSH

Cigales. Richard Wilbur. NoAM; NOBA

Cigarette Poem, The. Faye Kicknosway. IHMS

Cinderella. Anne Sexton. Psy

Cindy, *with music*. *Unknown*. BLSo

Cinéma Vérité. Dorothy Walters. IHMS

Cino. Ezra Pound. VGW

Circe. A. D. Hope. PPP

Circle, The. Alan Riddell. SLP

Circles. Harry Behn. LCL

Circling. Carole Oles. NPW

Circumference thou bride of awe. Emily Dickinson. PiAm

Circus, *sels*. Lenore Kandel.
    Freak Show and Finale. RiTi
    Love in the Middle of the Air. RiTi

Circus Animals' Desertion, The. W. B. Yeats. MAT; NoAM;
    — NOBE; OxBTC; PPoD; PSN

Circus Lion. C. Day Lewis. BoAnP; MPo

Cistercians in Germany. Robert Lowell. NowV

Citadels. Richard Kell. PFIr

Cities and Thrones and Powers. Kipling. *Fr.* Puck of Pook's Hill. NOBE; OxBTC

Cities are washed into time, The. John Oliver Simon. NeAC

Citizen, A. Charles Reznikoff. *Fr.* Five Groups of Verse. SA

Citizen. Peter Schjeldahl. CAAP

Citizen Paine. James Daugherty. ECBV

Citizens' Complaint, The. David Allan Evans. HeS

City. Joseph Bruchac. CDW

City. Roy Fisher. TwMBP

City. Langston Hughes. ECBV; LCL

City. Jane Stembridge. NMM

City, The. James Thomson ("B. V.").
    The City of Dreadful Night, *proem*. NOBE

City Afternoon. Barbara Howes. PPoD

City Bird. Theda Kenyon. ECBV

City Boy, The. Stephen Dunn. HeS

City Child, The. Tennyson. OxBChV

City Dead-House, The. Walt Whitman. InPK

City in the Sea, The. Poe. AmVN; MAT; NOBA; PiAm

City Is Falling Apart, The. Diane Kruchkow. FAF

City Life. D. H. Lawrence. SoSe

City Limits, The. A. R. Ammons. NoAM; NOBA

City of Dreadful Night, The. James Thomson ("B. V."). VPC
    *Sels.*
       "Anear the centre of that northern crest," XXI. PFD
       (City's Queen, The.) NOBE
       City, The, *proem*. NOBE

City of Satisfactions, The. Daniel Hoffman. Prf

City planners. To the New Annex to the Detroit County Jail. Richard W. Thomas. PoBA

City Psalm. Denise Levertov. PiAm

City Rain. Rachel Field. ECBV

City Rises, The. James Cunningham. JB

City rises, The. A Poem for Democrats. LeRoi Jones. CAPP

City's Queen, The. James Thomson ("B. V."). The City of Dreadful Night, XXI. NOBE
    ("Anear the centre of that northern crest.") PFD

Civil Riot, *sel*. G. D. H. Cole.
    "And you'll say a nation totters." OxBTC

Civil Servant, A. Robert Graves. InPK

Civilian. Josephine Miles. WPE

Civilization. Tom Schmidt. NeAC

Civilization and Its Discontents. John Ashbery. CAPP

Civilization is hooped together, brought. Meru. W. B. Yeats. InPS; NoAM

Civilized, crying how to be human again: this will tell you how. Signpost. Robinson Jeffers. TCP

Civilizing the Child. Lisel Mueller. CTBA

Clack your beaks you cormorants and kittiwakes. A Canticle to the Waterbirds. William Everson. PiAm

Clair de Lune. Paul Verlaine, *tr. fr. French by* Arthur Symons. Moon

Clamb ape mountain backwards. To Be Quicker. Don L. Lee. JB

Clamming. Reed Whittemore. IPWM

Clamour of the wind making music. Saint Columcille, *tr. fr. Irish by* John Montague. BIrV

Clancy of the Overflow. Andrew Barton Paterson. MAuV

Clari, the Maid of Milan, *sel*. John Howard Payne.
    Home, Sweet Home. BLSH; BLSo; PSoN

Clarinda's Indifference at Parting with Her Beauty. Countess of Winchilsea. SBG

Claritas. Denise Levertov. PiAm; VGW

Claritas. Gerrye Payne. NWP

Clarity of spring, The. Verna Tomlinson Baker. AATT

Clark Colven. *Unknown*. *See* Clerk Colvill.

Clark Sanders. *Unknown*. *See* Clerk Saunders.

Class Incident from Graves. Alan Brownjohn. OxBTC

Class is judging swine, The. Two for the Hampton Institute. David Young. CAAP

Class of thirty student engineers, A. The Pay Is Good. Richard Kell. MPo

Classes. Keith Wilson. NowV

Classic. A. R. Ammons. NOBA

Classic Encounter. "Christopher Caudwell." OxBTC

Classic landscapes of dreams are not, The. The Snowfall. Donald Justice. CoPAm; VGW

Classic Waits for Me, A. E. B. White. SpRo

Classical Quatrain, A. Paul Goodman. VGW

Claude Allen. *Unknown*. AmFP

Clay Comes Out to Meet Terrell. Muhammed Ali. SPo

Clay is the word and clay is the flesh. Patrick Kavanagh. *Fr.* The Great Hunger. NoAM; OxBTC

Clean birds by sevens. The Dove. *Unknown*. GBP

Clean the spittoons, boy. Brass Spittoons. Langston Hughes. NoAM

Clean thin hollow of breast. Reflections. Anita Barrows. NMM

Cleanliness. Charles *and* Mary Lamb. OxBChV

Cleanly, sir, you went to the core of the matter. A Correct Compassion. James Kirkup. OxBTC

Clear. Angelo Lewis. PoBA

Clear Air of October, The. Robert Bly. NoAM

Clear and cool, clear and cool. The Tide River. Charles Kingsley. *Fr.* The Water Babies. OxBChV

Clear bright morning, with its scented air, The. The Fair Morning. Jones Very. NOBA

Clear cool note of the cuckoo which has ousted the legitimate nest holder, The. Sincere Flattery of W. W. (Americanus). J. K. Stephen. SpRo

Clear ocean seems, The. The Double Vision of Manannan. *Unknown, tr. by* John Montague. BIrV

Clearing the Air. Nancy Willard. RiTi

Cleator Moor. Norman Nicholson. MPo

Clement Attlee. Michael Benedikt. CAAP; InPS

Clementine. *Unknown*. *See* Oh, My Darling Clementine.

Clerihews, *sels*. E. C. Bentley.
    "Adam Smith." FaBoCo

"George the Third." FaBoCo

"John Stuart Mill." FaBoCo

"Sir Christopher Wren." FaBoCo; InPk

"Sir Humphry Davy." FaBoCo

Clerimont's Song. Ben Jonson. *See* Simplex Munditiis.

Clerk Colvill. *Unknown.* GBP
(Clark Colven, *with music.*) Epi

Clerk of Oxford, The. Chaucer. *Fr.* The Canterbury Tales:
Prologue. OxBM
("Clerk ther was of Oxenford, A.") InPS

Clerk Saunders. *Unknown.* LoAs; SLP
(Clark Sanders.) PeBB

Clerk ther was of Oxenford also, A. The Clerk of Oxford.
Chaucer. *Fr.* The Canterbury Tales: Prologue. InPS;
OxBM

Clerks, The. E. A. Robinson. PiAm; VoPo

Clerk's Song II. Norman H. Russell. VW

Clerk's Twa Sons O Owsenford, The. *Unknown.* PeBB

Clever Chinese say they read, The. Cat's Eyes. Francis Scarfe.
PCat

Clever Skipper, The. *Unknown.* AmFP

Click Go the Shears, Boys. *Unknown.* MAuV

Clickety-Clack. Paul Blackburn. NoAM

Client meeting at twelve, that lot of layabouts. Nine O'Clock
Thoughts on the 73 Bus. Peter Porter. POL

Cliff, The. David Rowbotham. CAAP

Cliff Klingenhagen. E. A. Robinson. PAIC; PiAm

Climate of Paradise, The. Louis Simpson. NOBA

Climbed from the road and found. Latitude, Longitude. George
Oppen. CAAP

Climbing from the Lethal dead. Orpheus. Yvor Winters.
NOBA; PiAm; VGW

Climbing the last steps to your house, I knew. Light Dying.
Brendan Kennelly. PFIr

Climbing the staircase. Simplicity. Louis Simpson. InPS; Prf

Climbing the stairway gray with urban midnight. Effort at Speech.
William Meredith. Prf

Climbing through the January snow, into the Lobo Canyon.
Mountain Lion. D. H. Lawrence. BoAnP; OxBTC; RFM

Climbs hobbling. A Very Old Woman. Clayton Eshleman.
MAT

Clinging to my breast, no stronger. Spinster's Lullaby. Vassar
Miller. NMM; RiTi

Clipper *Dunbar* to the clipper *Cutty Sark,* The. Ethel Anderson.
PoTa

Clock in the Square, A. Adrienne Rich. HeIP

Clock of my days winds down, The. The Alligator Bride. Donald
Hall. ConAP

Clock stopped, A. Emily Dickinson. AmVN

Clock-a-clay (The Ladybird). John Clare. OBP

Clod and the Pebble, The. Blake. *Fr.* Songs of Experience.
AnMo; InPS; LAuP; LoAs; MBPR; NOBE; SS

Cloë. George Granville. FaBoCo; POL

Cloe, by your command, in verse I write. A Letter from Artemisia
in the Town to Cloe in the Country. Earl of Rochester.
ESaP

Cloe's the wonder of her sex. Cloe. George Granville. POL

Clogged ashtray a dead lung, A. Grass, Grass. George Bowering.
NeAC

Clonmel Jail. *Unknown, tr. fr. Irish by* Valentin Iremonger.
BIrV

Clorinda and Damon. Andrew Marvell. PAIC

Cloris, I cannot say your eyes. To Cloris. Sir Charles Sedley.
BoLoP

Close to the west the great ocean is singing. Two Rain Songs.
*Unknown.* AKE

Close up the casement, draw the blind. Shut Out That Moon.
Thomas Hardy. NoAM; NOBE

Close Your Eyes! Arna Bontemps. IPWM; PoBA

Closed window looks down, A. Ka 'Ba. LeRoi Jones. BPo;
CAPP; PiAm

Closer First to Earth. Anne Hazlewood-Brady. IHMS

Closet, The. Dave Smith. HeS

Closing of the Rodeo, The. William Jay Smith. PPoD

Cloth was laid in the Vorkhouse hall, The. The Workhouse Boy.
*Unknown.* GBP; PeBB

Clothes. Elizabeth Jennings. RAE

Clothes Maketh the Man. Theodore Weiss. NoAM

Clothes Pit, The. Douglas Dunn. OxBTC

Clothesline, The. John Stevens Wade. FAF

Cloud, The. Shelley. MBPR
Orbed Maiden,*sel.* Moon

Cloud moved close, A. The bulk of the wind shifted. The Visitant.
Theodore Roethke. PPoe

Cloud of witnesses, A. To whom? To what? A Fanfare for the
Makers. Louis MacNeice. NOBE

Cloud-puffball, torn tufts, tossed pillows. That Nature is a
Heraclitean Fire and of the Comfort of the Resurrection.
Gerard Manley Hopkins. AnMo; Epi

Cloud Shadows. John Updike. VoPo

Cloudburst and Soaring Moon. "Hugh MacDiarmid." NoAM

Clouded Morning, The. Jones Very. NOBA

Clouds. Rupert Brooke. OxBTC

Clouds, The. William Carlos Williams. VGW

Clouds are electric in this university, The. Ghazals: Homage to
Ghalib. Adrienne Rich. CAAP

Clouds, lingering yet, extend in solid bars. Composed by the Side
of Grasmere Lake. Wordsworth. MBPR

Clouds prophesy; the sky portends. Year's End. Jim Barnes.
HeS

Clouds spout upon her. Rain on a Grave. Thomas Hardy.
LoAs

Clouds swollen with rain. Door to the Sun. Ralph J. Molls, Jr.
HeS

Clove As Ego. Daniel Halpern. CAAP

Clove, salmon knocking. For Lerida. David St. John. AmPA

Clownlike, happiest on your hands. You're. Sylvia Plath.
NCSH

Clutter of Mothers, A. Edwin Brock. IPWM

Clydesdale New Town Walk. Duncan Glen. MIS

"C'mon, get out." Sunflower Rock. Paul Blackburn. NoAM

Coal. Audre Lorde. PoBA

Coal black woman fry no meat for me. Seven Sister Blues.
*Unknown.* BluL

Coal Diggin' Blues. *Unknown.* AmFP

Coal Loadin' Blues. *Unknown.* AmFP

Coal Miner's Goodbye, A. *Unknown.* AmFP

Coarse/jocosity. Archy Confesses. Don Marquis. *Fr.* Archy
and Mehitabel. SS

Coast, The: Norfolk. Frances Cornford. OxBTC

Coat, A. W. B. Yeats. NoAM

Coax Me, *with music.* Andrew Sterling. FSN

Cobbled with rough stone which rings my tread. Allotments: April.
Bernard Spencer. PSN

Cocaine Lil. *Unknown.* MAT; MiP
(Cocaine Lil and Morphine Sue.) GBP; PeBB

Cock, The. A. Buttigieg. RAE

Cock-a-doodle-doo! Mother Goose. MG

Cock-a-doodle-doo the brass-lined rooster goes. Dog. John
Crowe Ransom. InPS

Cock-a-Hoop. Isabella Gardner. WPE

Cock and the Bull, The. Charles Stuart Calverley. FaBoCo

Cock Crow. Rosemary Dobson. MAuV

Cock-Crow. Kenneth Slessor. MAuV

Cock-Crowing. Henry Vaughan. SCP-1

Cock Crowing in a Poulterer's Shop, A. John Ferguson. BoAnP

Cock doth crow, the wind doth blow, The. Mother Goose. GBP

Cock is crowing, The. Written in March. Wordsworth. MBPR; PBMP

Cock Lorell's Boat. *Unknown.* TVS

Cock Robin he got a neat tippet at spring. The Red Robin. John Clare. RAE

Cockerel. *Unknown. See* I Have a Gentle Cock.

Cockles and Mussels (Molly Malone), *with music. Unknown, ad. by* James Morehead. BLSH

Cockleshells. *Unknown. See* Waly, Waly ("When cockleshells turn silver bells").

Cock's far cry, The. Cock-Crow. Kenneth Slessor. MAuV

Cocky's Calendar, *sel.* David Campbell. To a Ground-lark. MAuV

Coconut for Katerina, A. Sandra McPherson. FiCP

Coda. Basil Bunting. *Fr.* Briggflatts. TwMBP

Coda. Dorothy Parker. SBG

Coda. Ezra Pound. NOBA

Coda. James Tate. AmPA

Coda. William Carlos Williams. NOBA

Code, The. Robert Frost. InPS

Code of Morals, A. Kipling. FaBoCo

Codfish Shanty, The. *Unknown.* GBP

Codicil. Alvin Aubert. CoPA⌐

Codicil. Derek Walcott. NoAM

Co-ed protester named Lil, A. Ogden Nash. SFF

Coelia, *sels.* William Percy. "It shall be sayd I dy'de for Coelia," XIX. AAS "Relent, my deere, yet unkind Coelia," XVII. AAS

Coffee. J. V. Cunningham. VGW

Coin from B.C. Nicholas Flocos. SA

Cold, The. Lance Henson. CDW

Cold. Glyn Hughes. LP

Cold and Married War, A. Marge Piercy. Psy

Cold Are the Crabs. Edward Lear. Epi

Cold before the Moonrise, The. W. S. Merwin. CoPAm

Cold blood or warm, crawling or fluttering. Pet Shop. Louis MacNeice. BoAnP

Cold-blooded Creatures. Elinor Wylie. SBG

Cold-blooded in warm waters, my Nurse. Among Sharks. Al Lee. AmPA

Cold blows the wind to my true-love. The Unquiet Grave. *Unknown.* WIF

Cold Coffee. John Williams. CoPAm

Cold, cold! A Song of Winter. *Unknown, tr. by* Kuno Meyer. PFIr

"Cold coming we had of it, A." Journey of the Magi. T. S. Eliot. BoReV; HeIP; OxBTC; PBMP; PPoe; TCP

Cold earth slept below, The. To ——. Shelley. MBPR

Cold Fall. Richard Eberhart. PAIC

Cold Fear. Elizabeth Madox Roberts. WPE

Cold grey walls. San Francisco County Jail Cell B-6. Conyus. PoBA

Cold has put blue horses where lambs were, The. Blue Horses. Ed Roberson. PoBA

Cold Heaven, The. W. B. Yeats. NoAM

Cold in the earth, and the deep snow piled above thee! Remembrance. Emily Brontë. BoLoP; NOBE; OBP; WPE

Cold Irish Earth, The. Knute Skinner. InPK

Cold moon hangs to the sky by its horn, The. The Night of the Dance. Thomas Hardy. OBP

Cold morning early. Two Mornings. Lawrence McGaugh. PoBA

Cold rises around, The. Midwinter, Presolstice. Margaret Atwood. Psy

Cold slope is standing in darkness, The. December Night. W. S. Merwin. CAPP

Cold Snap, A. Robert Tait. SLP

Cold Spring, The. Denise Levertov. CAAP; Psy

Cold Term. LeRoi Jones. BPo

Cold was the night wind, drifting fast the snow fell. The Widow, Sapphics. Robert Southey. ESaP

Cold Water. Donald Hall. NCSH

Cold Water Flat. Philip Booth. NowV

Cold Wave Blues. *Unknown.* BluL

Colder. Erica Jong. MMD

Coldness that falls upon the hours, The. Cold Fall. Richard Eberhart. PAIC

Cole Younger. *Unknown.* AmFP

Coleman lantern light poses the parameter of darkness. Big Sur Summer. Delia Chilgren. NPW

Coleridge received the person from Porlock. Thoughts about the Person from Porlock. Stevie Smith. FaBoCo

Colette, Poor Clare. Colette Inez. AATT

Colin Barnes, Drums. John Smith. *Fr.* Jazz for Five. MPo

Colin Clout, *abr.* John Skelton. TVS

Colin Clout's Come Home Again, *sel.* Spenser. "Why, Colin, since thou found'st such grace." TVS

Colin my dear when shall it please thee sing. November. Spenser. *Fr.* The Shepheardes Calendar. Epi

Coliseum, The. Poe. NOBA

Collaborations. Cathleen Quirk. MMD

Collage for Richard Davis, A—Two Short Forms. De Leon Harrison. PoBA

Collar, The. George Herbert. AnMo; BoReV; HeIP; InPS; IPWM; MetP; NOBE; OBP; PPoD; PPoe; PPP; SCP-1

Collar-Bone of a Hare, The. W. B. Yeats. OxBTC

Collector of lost beads, buttons, bird bones. The Pack Rat. Robert Pack. CoPAm; PPP

Colleen Rue. *Unknown.* BIrV

Colley's Run-I-O. *Unknown.* AmFP

Collier, The. Vernon Watkins. MPo

Collier's Wife, The. D. H. Lawrence. OxBTC

Collin my deere and most entire beloved. To the Most Excellent and Learned Shepheard Collin Cloute. William Smith. Chloris: Dedication. AAS

Colloquy in Black Rock. Robert Lowell. CAPP; NoAM; PiAm

Colm had a cat. The Pets. Robert Farren. ECBV

Colma—It is night. James Macpherson. *Fr.* The Songs of Selma. SLP

Cologne. Samuel Taylor Coleridge. MBPR; PBMP

Colonel Cold strode up the line. Winter Warfare. Edgell Rickword. OxBTC

Colonel Martin. W. B. Yeats. Epi

Colonus' Praise. Sophocles, *tr. by* W. B. Yeats. *Fr.* Oedipus at Colonus. Epi

Colophon for Lan-t'ing Hsiu-Hsi. John Peck. AmPA

Color—caste—denomination. Emily Dickinson. PBMP

Colored folks work on the Mississippi. Ol' Man River. Oscar Hammerstein II. BLSo

Colored pictures/ of all things to eat: dirty. The Songs of Maximus. Charles Olson. CoPAm; NoAM

Colours. Frances Evans. RAE

Colors for Mama. Barbara Mahone. PoBA

Colossi. Albert De Pietro. AATT

Colossus, The. Sylvia Plath. AnMo; CAPP; CoPAm; NoAM; NOBA; Psy

Colt, The. Raymond Knister. AKE

Coltrane must understand how. Soul. D. L. Graham. PoBA

Columbia ("Thus down a lone valley with cedars o'erspread"). *Unknown.* AmFP

Columbia, the Gem of the Ocean. David T. Shaw. BTTM

Columbiad, The, *sel.* Joel Barlow.
"Now had Columbus well enjoy'd the sight," *fr.* VIII. PiAm

Columbian poet, whom we've all respected. Letter to an American Visitor. Alex Comfort. OxBTC

Columbine, The. Jones Very. NOBA; PiAm

Columbus. Joaquin Miller. AmVN; BTTM

Columbus. Ogden Nash. OFD

Columbus. Louis Simpson. MPo

Columbus. Schiller, *tr. fr. German by* Erika Gathmann Koessler. OFD

Columbus, *sel.* Tennyson.
"Chains, my good lord: in your raised brows I read." OFD

Columbus discovered America. A Concise History of the World. Ira Sadoff. AmPA

Columbus is remembered by young men. And of Columbus. Horace Gregory. OFD

Columns and Caryatids. Carolyn Kizer. WPE

Com my swete, com my flowr. The Assumption. *Unknown.* OxBM

Com out, Lazer, what-so befalle! Come out Lazurus! *Unknown.* OxBM

Combat, The. Edwin Muir. NOBE

Combing. Gladys Cardiff. CDW

Come. Bob Kaufman. MIT

Come again to the place. After the Visit. Thomas Hardy. NOBE

Come, all my good people, and listen to my song. Tittery-Irie-Aye. *Unknown.* AmFP

Come all my jolly seamen, likewise the landsmen, too. The *Cumberland* and the *Merrimac. Unknown.* AmFP

Come all New England men. Giles Corey and Goodwyfe Corey—A Ballad of 1692. *Unknown.* PAIC

Come all ye bold undaunted ones who brave the winter's frost. Fifteen Ships on Georges Banks. *Unknown.* AmFP

Come all ye bould Free Staters now and listen to my lay. The Lay of Oliver Gogarty. William Dawson. PeBB

Come All Ye Fair and Tender Ladies. *Unknown.* AmFP

Come all ye gentle Christians, wherever you may be. Charles Guiteau. *Unknown.* AmFP

Come, all ye good people, my story to hear. Poor Ellen Smith. *Unknown.* AmFP

Come all ye jolly boatsman boys. Blow the Candle Out. *Unknown.* AmFP

"Come all ye jolly fellows, who delight in a gun." Polly Vaughn (Molly Bawn). *Unknown.* AmFP

Come all ye Knights, ye Knights of Molites. The Sons of Levi. *Unknown.* AmFP

Come all ye Lewiston fac'try girls. The Factory Girl's Come-All-Ye. *Unknown.* AmFP

Come all ye young fellows that follow the sea. Blow the Man Down. *Unknown.* BLSH; BLSo.

Come all ye young people and all my relations. Mr. Davis's Experience. *Unknown.* AmFP

Come all you brave Americans and unto me give ear. The Capture of Major André. *Unknown.* BTTM

Come all you cockers, far and near. The Bonny Grey. *Unknown.* GBP

Come all you fair gallants, fair gallants attend. Pretty Polly of Topsham. *Unknown.* AmFP

Come all you gallant heroes, I'd have you lend an ear. Major André. *Unknown.* AmFP

Come all you girls and all you boys. Kitty Morey. *Unknown.* AmFP

Come all you good people. Lula Vires. *Unknown.* AmFP

Come all you heroes, where'er you be. The Dying Sergeant. *Unknown.* AmFP

Come all you jolly cowboys and listen to my song. The Buffalo Skinners. *Unknown.* GBP; PeBB

Come all you jolly fellows, come listen to my song. The Shanty Boys and the Pine. *Unknown.* AmFP

Come all you jolly freighters that ever hit the road. Freighting from Wilcox to Globe. *Unknown.* AmFP

Come all you jolly-hearted sailors. False Nancy. *Unknown.* AmFP

Come all you jolly highwaymen and outlaws of the land. Bold Jack Donahue. *Unknown.* AmFP

Come all you jolly lumbermen, and listen to my song. Colley's Run-I-O. *Unknown.* AmFP

Come all you jolly lumbermen, I'd have you for to know. The Banks of the Gaspereaux. *Unknown.* AmFP

Come all you jolly railroad men, and I'll sing you if I can. Way Out in Idaho. *Unknown.* AmFP

Come all you jolly seamen who plough that restless deep. Jimmy Judge. *Unknown.* AmFP

Come all you jolly shanty boys that work the shanty and go. Turner's Camp on the Chippewa. *Unknown.* AmFP

Come all you loyal Unionists, wherever you may be. Virginia's Bloody Soil. *Unknown.* AmFP

Come all you men and maidens. Rufus Mitchell's Confession. *Unknown.* AmFP

Come all you muckers and gather here. Casey Jones. *Unknown.* AmFP

Come all you people from every land. Ellen Flannery. *Unknown.* AmFP

Come all you pretty fair maids. Green Willow, Green Willow. *Unknown.* AmFP

Come all you pretty fair maids, I pray you attend. My New Garden Field. *Unknown.* AmFP

Come, all you rounders, if you want to hear. Casey Jones. T. Lawrence Seibert. AIW; BLSH

Come all you sailors bold. The Death of Admiral Benbow. *Unknown.* GBP; PeBB

Come all you sons of freedom and listen to my theme. Once More a-Lumbering Go. *Unknown.* AmFP

Come all you true-born shanty boys, wherever ye may be. The Jam on Gerry's Rocks. *Unknown.* AmFP

Come all you young and handsome ladies. Little Sparrow. *Unknown.* AmFP

Come all you young fellows that follow the gun. Young Molly Ban. *Unknown.* PeBB

Come, all young men, taking warning by me. Married and Single Life. *Unknown.* AmFP

Come all you young people/ That live far and near. The Murder of Goins. *Unknown.* AmFP

Come all you young people, a story I will tell. Naomi Wise. *Unknown.* AmFP

Come all young men and ladies, fathers and mothers, too. The Rowan County Crew. James William Day. AmFP

Come all young men and maidens, come listen to my rhyme. Caroline of Edinboro' Town. *Unknown.* AmFP

Come along get you ready. A Hot Time in the Old Town [*or* There'll Be a Hot Time]. Joe Hayden. BLSo; FSN

Come Anthea, let us two. The Wake. Robert Herrick. PAIC

Come away, come away, death. Shakespeare. *Fr.* Twelfth Night, II, iv. AIW; GBL; NOBE

Come away, come, sweet love. To His Love. *Unknown.* GBL

Come Away, My Love. Joseph Kariuki. BuTH

Come Back Blues. Michael S. Harper. PoBA

Come Back, Paddy Reilly. Percy French. PFIr

Come balmy sleep! tired nature's soft resort. To Sleep. Charlotte Smith. WPE

Come, brethren of the water. The Powte's Complaint. *Unknown.* GBP

Come, brother, come. Lets lift it. Cotton Song. Jean Toomer. BPo

Come buy my fine wares. Market Women's Cries. Swift. LoAs; PFIr

Come, chearfull day, part of my life, to mee. Thomas Campion. AAS

Come, come, my love, the bush is growing. With Garments Flowing. John Clare. GBL

"Come, come," said Tom's father, "at your time of life." A Joke Versified. Thomas Moore. FaBoCo

Come Dance with Kitty Stobling. Patrick Kavanagh. NoAM

Come darling/ be my scapegoat. Lying Down Hungry. Carol Bergé. MMD

Come dear sisters and brothers. Ol' Tim Legion. Rubee Dreher Moxley. NPW

Come down from the Cross, my soul, and save thyself. Descent from the Cross. "Michael Field." WPE

Come, follow me by the smell. Onyons. Swift. *Fr.* Market Women's Cries. BIrV

Come forth, you workers! Reveille. Lola Ridge. WPE

Come, friends, if you will listen, a story I will tell. The Sherman Cyclone. *Unknown.* AmFP

Come from thy palace, beauteous Queen of Greece. Invocation. Thomas Randolph. Moon

Come, gaze with me upon this dome. E. E. Cummings. NoAM

Come, gentle Spring, ethereal mildness, come. Spring. James Thomson. *Fr.* The Seasons. LAuP

Come here/ Come near. Phrases for Everyday Use by the British in India. John Daniel. TwMBP

Come hither all sweet maidens soberly. On a Leander Gem. Keats. MBPR

Come hither, Evan Cameron. The Execution of Montrose. William Edmonstoune Aytoun. BTTM

Come hither my sparrows. The Fairy. Blake. MBPR

Come In. Robert Frost. NOBA

Come into Animal Presence. Denise Levertov. AnMo; HeIP; InPK

Come into the garden, Maud. Tennyson. *Fr.* Maud, Pt. I. NOBE

Come join hand in hand brave Americans all. The Liberty Song. John Dickinson. BLSo

Come lasses and lads. The Rural Dance about the Maypole. *Unknown.* GBP

Come, lecturer on love, resume your rostrum. Last Letter to the Scholar. Jean Garrigue. LoAs

Come, let me write, and to what end? to ease. Astrophel and Stella, XXXIV. Sir Philip Sidney. Epi

Come! let us draw the curtains. Autumn. Humbert Wolfe. FSFS

Come let us journey to. Come. Bob Kaufman. MIT

Come, let us pity those who are better off than we are. The Garret. Ezra Pound. PSN

Come, let's to bed. Mother Goose. GBP; MG

Come, list and hark! the bell doth toll. Thomas Heywood. *Fr.* The Rape of Lucrece. SCP-2

Come listen a while and give ear to my song. Hard Times. *Unknown.* AmFP

Come, listen, all you gals and boys. Jump Jim Crow. Thomas D. Rice. BLSo

Come, listen to another song. The Old Scottish Cavalier. William Edmonstoune Aytoun. BTTM

Come listen to me, you gallants so free. Robin Hood and Allen a Dale. *Unknown.* GBP; PEBB

Come, listen to my tragedy, good people, young and old. Mary Wyatt and Henry Green. *Unknown.* AmFP

Come, Little Babe. Nicholas Breton. *See* Cradle Song: "Come, little babe . . ."

Come little infant, love me now. Young Love. Andrew Marvell. RRA

Come, live with me and be my love. C. Day Lewis. BoLoP

Come live with me and be my love. The Bait. John Donne. InPK; InPS

Come live with me and be my love. The Passionate Shepherd to His Love. Christopher Marlowe. AAS; BoLoP; Epi; HeIP; InPK; InPS; IPWM; LoAs; NOBE; OLR; PAIC; PBMP; PPoD; PPoe; PPP

Come live with me and be my love. Love under the Republicans (or Democrats.) Ogden Nash. IPWM; PBMP

Come, love, for now the night and day. Song for Autumn. Andrew Young. GBL

Come, madam, come, all rest my powers defy. Going to Bed [*or* To His Mistress Going to Bed]. John Donne. *Fr.* Elegies. AnMo; BoLoP; GBL; OBP; PPP

Come, melt thy soul in mine, that when unite. Song. Sir William Davenant. *Fr.* The Temple of Love. SCP-2

Come, my brothers. The Only Tourist in Havana Turns His Thoughts Homeward. Leonard Cohen. NoAM

Come, My Celia. Ben Jonson. *Fr.* Volpone, III, vii. HeIP; IPWM

Come, my little Robert, near. Cleanliness. Charles *and* Mary Lamb. OxBChV

Come, my Lucasia, since we see. Friendship's Mystery, to My Dearest Lucasia. Katherine Philips. SCP-2

Come, my sweet, whiles every strain. William Cartwright. *Fr.* The Royal Slave. SCP-2

Come Not Near My Songs. *Unknown, tr. fr. Shoshone Indian by* Mary Austin. OLR; WPE

Come Not, When I Am Dead. Tennyson. BBGO; GBL

Come, O thou traveller unknown. Wrestling Jacob. Charles Wesley. BoReV; NOBE

Come on Home. Sharon Scott. JB

Come On in My Kitchen. *Unknown.* BluL

Come on in now and get in this hip shaking contest. Hip Shakin' Strut. *Unknown.* BluL

Come on, mama/ Out to the edge of town. Bird Nest Bound. *Unknown.* BluL

Come on, my fellow pilgrims, come. At. to Sarah Lancaster. AmFP

Come on out of there with your hands up, Charlie. Patriotic Ode on the Fourteenth Anniversary of the Persecution of Charlie Chaplin. Bob Kaufman. PoBA

Come out come out come out. Moon Eclipse Exorcism. *Unknown, tr. by* Armand Schwerner. Moon

Come out, Lazarus! *Unknown.* BoReV; OxBM

Come out, 'tis now September. The Ripe and Bearded Barley. *Unknown.* GBP

Come play with me. To a Squirrel at Kyle-Na-No. W. B. Yeats. LCL

Come praise Colonus' horses, and come praise. Colonus' Praise. Sophocles, *tr. by* W. B. Yeats. *Fr.* Oedipus at Colonus. Epi

Come, radishes, rosy against your green. Three from the Market. Sandra McPherson. RiTi

Come 'round by my side and I'll sing you a song. Birmingham Sunday. Richard Farina. NowV

"Come saddle me my fastest steed." Geordie. *Unknown.* AmFP

Come, Said My Soul. Walt Whitman. NOBA

"Come!" said Old Shellover. Old Shellover. Walter de la Mare. LCL; OxBChV

Come sleep! O sleep, the certain knot of peace.  Astrophel and Stella, XXXIX.  Sir Philip Sidney.  LoAs; NOBE; PAIC; PPP

Come small creatures of low estate, friskily moving.  To the Field Mice.  Richard Eberhart.  BoAnP

Come sons of France, march on to victory.  La Marseillaise.  Claude Joseph Rouget de Lisle, *tr. by* Albert Morehead.  BLSH

Come, sons of summer, by whose toil.  The Hock-Cart, or Harvest Home.  Robert Herrick.  Epi; SCP-1

Come spring, when clouds.  Sailing.  Susan Murray.  NowV

Come, spur away.  An Ode to Master Anthony Stafford to Hasten Him into the Country.  Thomas Randolph.  NOBE; SCP-2

Come, stack arms, men! Pile on the rails.  Stonewall Jackson's Way.  John Williamson Palmer.  BTTM

Come take up your hats, and away let us haste.  The Butterfly's Ball.  William Roscoe.  OxBChV

Come, Thou Almighty King, *with music*.  *Unknown*.  BLSH

Come, Thou Fount of Every Blessing, *with music*.  Robert Robinson.  BLSH

Come to a Wedding.  Grace Cavalieri.  AATT

Come to conquer.  Cold Water Flat.  Philip Booth.  NowV

Come to me broken dreams and all.  The Still Voice of Harlem.  Conrad Kent Rivers.  PoBA

Come to me in the silence of the night.  Echo.  Christina Rossetti.  BoLoP; GBL; NOBE; VPC

Come to me, my borrowed love.  A Poem for One Who Bares a Pome.  Richard Bastian.  AATT

Come to my door, baby.  Janis Ian.  Society's Child.  WIF

Come to my Sunny Prestatyn.  Sunny Prestatyn.  Philip Larkin.  NoAM

Come to term the started child shocks.  Mustipara: Gravida 5.  Marie Ponsot.  VGW

Come to the Stone.  Randall Jarrell.  VGW

Come to your heaven, you heavenly choirs!  New Heaven, New War.  Robert Southwell.  BoReV; NOBE

Come touch me baby in his waking dream.  John Berryman.  *Fr.* Dream Songs.  RRA

Come unto these yellow sands.  Paul Dehn.  SpRo

Come unto these yellow sands.  Ariel's Song.  Shakespeare.  *Fr.* The Tempest, I, ii.  HeIP; NOBE; SpRo

Come Up from the Fields Father.  Walt Whitman.  PPP

Come, we shepherds, whose blest sight.  An Hymn of the Nativity, Sung as by the Shepherds.  Richard Crashaw.  BoReV

Come when you're called.  Mother Goose.  MG

Come with Me.  Robert Bly.  CAPP; CoPAm; NoAM; NOBA; SFF

Come, worthy Greek! Ulysses, come.  Ulysses and the Siren.  Samuel Daniel.  NOBE; PAIC

Come Ye Sinners, Poor and Needy, *with music*.  Joseph Hart.  BLSH

Come ye that love the Lord.  We're Marching to Zion.  Isaac Watts.  BLSH

Come you masters of war.  Masters of War.  Bob Dylan.  GrRo

Comes a crackling noise, a kind of chirping.  From the Direction of the State Mental Institution.  Carol Cox.  MMD

Comes it will come.  When the Revolution Really.  Peter Michelson.  HeS

Comes the time when it's later.  A Wicker Basket.  Robert Creeley.  CAPP; NoAM

Comes a cry from Cuban water.  Cuba Libre.  Joaquin Miller.  BTTM

Comet at Yell'ham, The.  Thomas Hardy.  GBL

Comfort From Arcadia.  Nicholas Flocos.  SA

Comfort to a Youth That Had Lost His Love.  Robert Herrick.  NOBE

Comforted by Limestone.  Edward Dorn.  *Fr.* Oxford.  NOBA

Comic Adventures of Old Mother Hubbard and Her Dog, The.  Sarah Catherine Martin.  OxBChV

Comin' Thro' the Rye.  Burns.  BLSH, *with music;* SLP; SpRo

Coming.  Philip Larkin.  OxBTC; PSN

Coming and Going.  Mitchell Goodman.  VGW

Coming around the Horn.  John A. Stone.  AmFP

Coming Back.  Joseph Bruchac.  CDW

Coming Back Home.  Ray A. Young Bear.  CDW

Coming back over the col between.  Strength Through Joy.  Kenneth Rexroth.  VGW

Coming by evening through the wintry city.  At a Bach Concert.  Adrienne Rich.  CoPAm

Coming by night, furtively, one by one.  The Invaders.  A. D. Hope.  CAAP

Coming Down Cleveland Avenue.  James Tate.  PPoD; SFF

Coming Fall, The, *sel*.  Denise Levertov.
"Down by the fallen fruit in the old orchard."  TSWA

Coming from —— in a Dark Night.  Jane Barker.  SCP-2

Coming from the south.  Six Ten Sixty-Nine.  Conyus.  PoBA

Coming in again, you know the town by boards it makes eyes touch.  Autobiography: Last Chapter.  Jim Barnes.  CDW

Coming into the store at first angry.  The Man Who Finds That His Son Has Become a Thief.  Raymond Souster.  BBGO

Coming of the Plague, The.  Weldon Kees.  VGW

Coming of Wisdom with Time, The.  W. B. Yeats.  POL; SoSe

Coming on to Winter.  Doug Flaherty.  HeS

Coming Out.  Jacqueline Lapidus.  IHMS

Coming out of you.  Out of You.  Rodney Phillips.  POL

Coming to cottonwoods, an.  Prospecting.  A. R. Ammons.  ConAP

Coming Up and Falling Down.  Stephen Vincent.  NeAC

Coming up Buchanan Street, quickly, on a sharp winter evening.  Trio.  Edwin Morgan.  MPo

Commander Lowell.  Robert Lowell.  VGW

Commemoration, The.  Edwin Muir.  SLP

Commencement.  Constance Carrier.  WPE

Commendation of Music, The.  William Strode.  SCP-2

Comments.  Peggy Susberry Kenner.  JB

Commercial Bank.  A. M. Klein.  BBGO

Commission.  Ezra Pound.  BoLoP

Commitment in a City.  Margaret Tsuda.  CTBA

Committee's fat, The.  Un-American Investigators.  Langston Hughes.  BPo

Common Bill.  *Unknown*.  AmFP

Common Carrier.  Richard Armour.  ECBV

Common Cormorant, The.  Christopher Isherwood.  FaBoCo; RAE
(Shag, The.)  ECBV

Common Dust.  Georgia Douglas Johnson.  PoBA

Common Sense.  Ogden Nash.  SFF

Common Woman, The.  Judy Grahn.  RiTi
Ella, in a Square Apron, along Highway 80, *sel*.  NMM

Commons' Petition to Charles II, The.  Earl of Rochester.  FaBoCo

Communication in Whi-te.  Don L. Lee.  BPo

Communion of Saints: the Poor Bastard under the Bridge.  Marie Ponsot.  VGW

Commuters.  E. B. White.  FaBoCo; SFF

Companion, The.  E. A. Robinson.  NoAM

Companions.  Charles Stuart Calverley.  FaBoCo

Company of vessels on the sea, A.  Battle Problem.  William Meredith.  NoAM

Comparison of the Sonnet and the Epigram.  Sir John Harington.  PAIC

Comparisons.  Christina Rossetti.  OxBChV

Compassionate Fool, The.  Norman Cameron.  OxBTC; WIF

Compelled by calamity's magnet. Aftermath. Sylvia Plath. SBG

Compensation. Paul Laurence Dunbar. BPo

Compensation. Emerson. NOBA

Compensation. Robinson Jeffers. PAIC

Competing not so much with one another. Watching Gymnasts. Robert Francis. SPo

Complacencies of the peignoir, and late. Sunday Morning. Wallace Stevens. HeIP; NOBA; PiAm; PPoD; PPoe; PSN

Complaint. Ian Hamilton. NoAM

Complaint. Rufinus Domesticus, tr. fr. Greek by Dudley Fitts. OLR

Complaint. William Carlos Williams. TCP

Complaint, A. Wordsworth. NOBE

Complaint. James Wright. CoPAm; NOBA; VGW

Complaint, The. Edward Young. See Night Thoughts.

Complaint by Night of the Lover Not Beloved, A. Earl of Surrey, after Petrarch. LoAs; PAIC
("Alas so all thinges nowe doe holde their peace.") AAS

Complaint of a Forsaken Indian Woman, The. Wordsworth. MBPR

Complaint of Chaucer to His Purse, The. Chaucer. InPK; OxBM; PAIC; PPoD

Complaint of the Absence of Her Lover Being upon the Sea. Earl of Surrey. GBL
("O happie dames, that may embrace.") AAS
(Seafarer, The.) NOBE

Complaint of Troilus, The. Chaucer. Fr. Troilus and Criseyde. NOBE

Complicity killed you. I know. I know. Closer First to Earth. Anne Hazlewood-Brady. IHMS

Composed by the Sea-Side, near Calais, August 1802. Wordsworth. MBPR

Composed by the Side of Grasmere Lake. Wordsworth. MBPR

Composed in the Tower before his execution. "More Light! More Light!" Anthony Hecht. ConAP; NoAM; NOBA; SFF; SoSe; VGW

Composed in the Valley near Dover, on the Day of Landing. Wordsworth. MBPR

Composed near Calais, on the Road Leading to Ardres. Wordsworth. MBPR

Composed on a May Morning, 1838. Wordsworth. FSFS

Composed Upon Westminster Bridge, September 3, 1802. Wordsworth. AnMo; Epi; HeIP; InPK; InPS; IPWM; MBPR; OBP; PAIC; PBMP; PPoD; PPP
(Upon Westminster Bridge.) NOBE

Composing scales beside the rails. The Harmonious Heedlessness of Little Boy Blue. Guy Wetmore Carryl. BoAnP

Composition. Cathleen Quirk. MMD

Compozishun—to James Herndon and Others. Ronald J. Goba. NCSH

Compromised by sorrow. Elegy for Chief Sealth. Duane Niatum. CDW

Computer's First Christmas Card, The. Edwin Morgan. FaBoCo; MPo; SFF

Comrades, with music. Felix McGlennon. FSN

Comrades, leave me here a little, while as yet 'tis early morn. Locksley Hall. Tennyson. PFD

Comrades, you may pass the rosy. The Lay of the Lovelorn. William E. Aytoun and Sir Theodore Martin. FaBoCo

Comus, sels. Milton.
Comus Speaks. NOBE
("Star that bids the shepherd fold, The.") PPoe
Lady Sings, The. NOBE
Sabrina. NOBE
Spirit Epiloguizes, The. NOBE

Concealment, The: Ishi, the Last Wild Indian. William Stafford. TCP

Concerning One Responsible Negro with Too Much Power. Nikki Giovanni. BPo

Concerning the Dead Women: The Munitions Plant Explosion: June, 1918. Elizabeth Libbey. AmPA

Concerning your letter in which you ask. With Mercy for the Greedy. Anne Sexton. CAPP

Concert. Robert Sward. VGW

Concert Scene. John Logan. CoPAm

Concise History of the World, A. Ira Sadoff. AmPA

Conclusion: "High in front advanc'd/ The brandisht sword of God before them blaz'd." Milton. Fr. Paradise Lost, XII. OBP

Concord Hymn. Emerson. AmVN; BTTM; HeIP; NOBA; PPoD

Concrete Cat. Dorthi Charles. InPK

Concrete cold face cased in steel. Pictures of a City. Robert Fripp and Peter Sinfield. GrRo

Condemned to Hope's delusive mine. On the Death of Mr. Robert Levet, a Practiser in Physic. Samuel Johnson. BoReV; HeIP; InPS; LAuP; NOBE; PPP

Coney Island of the Mind, A, sels. Lawrence Ferlinghetti.
"Constantly risking absurdity." CAPP; NowV; PAIC; SoSe; WIF
"Frightened/ by the sound of my own voice." NoAM
"In Golden Gate Park That Day." BBGO; NoAM
"In Goya's Greatest Scenes." BBGO; PBMP; HeIP; NoAM
In Woods Where Many Rivers Run. BBGO
"Pennycandystore beyond the El, The." BBGO; CAPP; CoPAm; CTBA; HeIP; IPWM; SS
"See/ it was like this when." CoPAm
"Sometime during eternity." CAPP; NoAM
"This life is not a circus where." PPP
"What could she say to the fantastic foolybear." CAPP
"Wounded Wilderness of Morris Graves." WIF

Confab. Kenneth Rosen. AmPA

Conferences, adjournments, ultimatums. Louis MacNeice. Fr. Autumn Journal. OxBTC

Confessio Amantis, sels. John Gower.
Adrian and Bardus, fr. V. OxBM
Ceix and Alceone, fr. IV. OxBM
Medea's Magic, fr. V. OxBM

Confessio Fidei. Dryden. See Revelation.

Confession, The. Peter Cooley. AmPA

Confession, The. Gary Lawless. FAF

Confession, A. Robert Mezey. AmPA

Confession of a Young Hegelian. Ellen McEvilley Griffin. NPW

Confession of Faith. Elinor Wylie. SBG

Confession to J. Edgar Hoover. James Wright. CAPP; ConAP

Confessional, The ("It is a lie—their Priests, their Pope"). Robert Browning. OBP

Confessions ("What is he buzzing in my ears?"). Robert Browning. NOBE

Confirmation, The. Edwin Muir. SLP

Conflict of Convictions, The. Herman Melville. NOBA

Confrontation. John Hart. MIT; POL

Congo, The. Vachel Lindsay. NoAM; NOBA

Conjugation of the Verb, "To Hope." Lou Lipsitz. FiCP

Conjuration, to Electra, A. Robert Herrick. GBL

Connecticut, with much at stake. The Customs of the Country. Phyllis McGinley. Fr. New England Pilgrimage. TH

Conn-Eda hid himself in horse's hide. Dreaming of Conn-Eda. Diane Levenberg. NPW

Connoisseur of pearl, A. African China. Melvin B. Tolson. PoBA

Conqueror Worm, The. Poe. Fr. Ligeia, prose tale. NOBA; PiAm

Conquerors, The. Phyllis McGinley. PBMP

Conquerors. Henry Treece. MPo

Conquistador. A. D. Hope. PPoD

Conquistador, *sel.* Archibald MacLeish.
Prologue: "And the way goes on in the worn earth." NoAM

Conscience, The. Anna Wickham. POL

Conscience Is Instinct Bred in the House. Henry David Thoreau. *Fr.* A Week on the Concord and Merrimack Rivers. HeIP; PiAm

Conscientious Objector. Edna St. Vincent Millay. VoPo

Conscious am I in my chamber. Emily Dickinson. PiAm

Consciousness/ in itself. Who Shall Doubt. George Oppen. CAAP

Consecration, A. John Masefield. NoAM

Consequence, The. Roger McDonald. CAAP

Consequences. William Meredith. NoAM

Conserving the Magnitude of Uselessness A. R. Ammons. NoAM

Consider ("Consider this and in our time."). W. H. Auden. OBP

Considerable Speck, A. Robert Frost. PBMP; PPP

Consideration for Others. Christopher Smart. OxBChV

Considered Reply to a Child, A. Jonathan Price. BoLoP

Consolatio Nova: for Alan Swallow. J. V. Cunningham. PiAm

Consolation. Earl of Surrey. NOBE
("When ragyng love with extreme payne.") AAS

Consolations of Philosophy. Derek Mahon. BIrV

Consorting with Angels. Anne Sexton. NMM

Conspiracy of Charles, Duke of Byron, The, *sel.* George Chapman.
"As when the moon hath comforted the night," *fr.* III, i. Moon

Conspirators, The. Kenneth Burke. SFF

Constancy to an Ideal Object. Samuel Taylor Coleridge. MBPR; OBP

Constant I will be. She Vowed Him This. William Box. BuTh

Constant Labor, A. James W. Thompson. BPo

Constant Love in All Conditions. James I, King of England. SLP

Constant Lover, The. Sir John Suckling. HeIP; NOBE; OLR; PBMP; SoSe
(Out Upon It! I Have Loved.) BoLoP; IPWM
(Song: "Out upon it! I have lov'd.") MetP

Constant North, The. J. F. Hendry. SLP

Constant Penelope sends to thee, careless Ulysses. Ovid, *tr. fr. Latin* GBL

Constant to none, but ever false to me. An Elegye. Thomas Campion. AAS

Constantly near you, I never in my entire. The Horse Show. William Carlos Williams. NOBA; VGW

Constantly risking absurdity. Lawrence Ferlinghetti. *Fr.* A Coney Island of the Mind. CAPP; NowV; PAIC; SoSe; WIF

*Constitution* and the *Guerrière*, The. Unknown. AmFP

*Constitution's* Last Fight, The. James Jeffrey Roche. BTTM

Construction #13. Judith Johnson Sherwin. NoAM

Constructions: Upper East Side. Sandra Hochman. NowV

Consumed. James Tate. MAT

Consumer's Report. X. J. Kennedy. FiCP

Consumer's Report, A. Peter Porter. FaBoCo

Container, The. Cid Corman. VGW

"Containing Communism." Charlie Cobb. PoBA

Containment. Howard Schwartz. HeS

Contemplations, *abr.* Anne Bradstreet. WPE

Contemporary Fear. Don Ober. NowV

Contemporary Nursery Rhyme. Unknown. SpRo

Contemptuous of his home beyond. A Frog's Fate. Christina Rossetti. VPC

Contend in a sea which the land partly encloses. The Yachts. William Carlos Williams. HeIP; NoAM; NOBA; PiAm; PPP; SPo

Content. George Herbert. SCP-1

Content in her skin she does not challenge. Nude. Robert Siegel. FAF

Contention of Ajax and Ulysses, The, *sel.* James Shirley.
Glories of Our Blood and State, The, *fr.* sc. iii. PPP; SCP-2; SoSe
(Death the Leveller.) NOBE; PBMP
(Dirge: "Glories of our blood and state, The.") OBP

Contentment. Nathaniel Cotton. OxBChV

Continent o Venus. Alexander Scott. SLP

Continent's End. Robinson Jeffers. TCP

Continuing. Madeline Bass. WBN

Continuing Story of Bungalow Bill, The. John Lennon *and* Paul McCartney. GrRo

Contrapuntalist, A—/ composer of chorales. Melchior Vulpius. Marianne Moore. PiAm

Contrite Heart, The. William Cowper. WIF

Controlling the Tongue. Chaucer. *Fr.* The Canterbury Tales: The Manciple's Tale. OxBChV

Conundrum. Carl Clark. JB

Convalescence. J. V. Cunningham. PiAm

Convent, The. "Seumas O'Sullivan." PFIr; POL

Convent of Pleasure, The, *sel.* Margaret Cavendish, Duchess of Newcastle.
"My cabinets are oyster-shells." SCP-2
(Song: "My cabinets are oyster-shells.") WPE

Conventionalist, The. Stevie Smith. BBGO

Convergence of the Twain, The. Thomas Hardy. AKE; HeIP; InPK; OxBTC; NoAM; PAIC; PBMP

Conversation. Nikki Giovanni. CTBA

Conversation, A. Barbara Howes. IHMS

Conversation, A. Dylan Thomas. RFM

Conversation brings us so close! Opening. Looking into a Face. Robert Bly. NOBA; TSWA

Conversation confers a sacrament. Life, the Eternal Sacrament. Virginia Floyd. AATT

Conversation in Craven Street, Strand. James Smith *and* Sir George Rose. FaBoCo

Conversation in the Eighth Street Bookstore. Honor Moore. WBN

Conversation with a Giraffe at Dusk in the Zoo. Douglas Livingstone. LP; MPo

Conversation with Washington. Myra Cohn Livingston. OFD

Conversion. Geof Hewitt. NeAC

Convert, The. Margaret Danner. BPo

Convict, The. Wordsworth. MBPR

Convict of Clonmel, The. Unknown, *tr. fr. Modern Irish by* Jeremiah Joseph Callanan. PFIr

Cook, The. Ray A. Young Bear. CDW

Cooking. Myra Cohn Livingston. ECBV

Cooking. Gertrude Stein. *Fr.* Tender Buttons. RiTi

Cook-out. Dan Masterson. CoPAm

Cool black nights thru redwoods. First Party at Ken Keseys with Hell's Angels. Allen Ginsberg. ConAP

Cool it Mag. Margaret Are You Drug. George Starbuck. MAT

Cool shades, air-fanning groves. Ex M. Antonio Flaminio, Ad Agellum Suum. John Ashmore. SCP-2

Cool shades and dews are round my way. A Scene on the Banks of the Hudson. Bryant. PiAm

Cool shadows blanked dead cities, falling. Falling. Bob Kaufman. PoBA

Cool Tombs. Carl Sandburg. HeIP; NoAM; NOBA; PAIC; PiAm

Cool Web, The. Robert Graves. NoAM; OxBTC

Coole Park and Ballylee, 1931. W. B. Yeats. NoAM; PPP; PSN

Coon Song. A. R. Ammons. NOBA; NoAM

Cooney Potter. Edgar Lee Masters. *Fr.* Spoon River Anthology. CTBA

Cooper. James Russell Lowell. *Fr.* A Fable for Critics. NOBA

Cooper & Bailey Great London Circus, The. Robert Hershon. MAT

Cooper's Hill, *sel.* Sir John Denham.
   "My eye descending from the hill, surveys." PAIC

Cop, The/ with a cold. High-cool/2. James Cunningham. JB

Cop holds me up like a fish, The. Fish. Larry Levis. AmPA

Cophetua. "Hugh MacDiarmid." POL

Coptic Poem. Lawrence Durrell. FaBoCo

Copulating Gods, The. Carolyn Kizer. Prf

Copy. Richard Armour. BBGO

Copying Architecture in an Old Minster. Thomas Hardy. OBP

Coquetry. Eugene Field. ECBV

Cora Punctuated with Strawberries. George Starbuck. NCSH

Cordate head meanders through himself, The. Pit Viper. N. Scott Momaday. CDW; VW

Corinna in Vendome. Pierre de Ronsard, *tr. fr. French by* Robert Mezey. BoLoP

Corinna, pride of Drury Lane. A Beautiful Young Nymph Going to Bed. Swift. AnMo

Corinna, to Tanagra, from Athens. Walter Savage Landor. *Fr.* Pericles and Aspasia, XLIV. NOBE

Corinnae Concubitus. Ovid, *tr. fr. Latin by* Christopher Marlowe. Amores, I, 5. GBL
   (Elegy: "In summer's heat and mid-time of the day.") BoLoP
   (Ovid's Fifth Elegy.) OBP

Corinna's Going a-Maying. Robert Herrick. AnMo; Epi; NOBE; PPP

Cormac Mac Airt Presiding at Tara. *Unknown, tr. fr. Irish by* Douglas Hyde. BIrV

Cormorant still screams, The. Late. Louise Bogan. VGW

Corn. Sidney Lanier. AmVN

Corn Harvest, The. William Carlos Williams. Pictures from Brueghel, VII. PPP

Corn Rigs Are Bonie. Burns. *See* Rigs o' Barley, The.

Corn-Song, A. Paul Laurence Dunbar. AmVN

Corn swaying in the rhythm of the wind. Death in the Woods. Harold Bird ("Littlebird"). VW

Corncrake, The. James H. Cousins. BoAnP; PFIr

Cornelia's Song. John Webster. *See* Call for the Robin Redbreast . . .

Cornered and trapped, The. For Mack C. Parker. Pauli Murray. PoBA

Cornhusk bag. Talking Designs. Liz Sohappy Bahe. CDW

Cornish Cliffs. John Betjeman. MPo; PAIC

Cornwallis' Country Dance. *Unknown.* BTTM

Coronation, *with music.* Edward Perronet. BLSo
   (All Hail the Power of Jesus' Name.) BLSH

Coroner's Jury. L. A. G. Strong. OxBTC

Coroner's jury yesterday, A. MD Sewed Wrong Section of Colon. F. R. Scott. AKE

Coronet, The. Andrew Marvell. BoReV; MetP

Corposant. Peter Redgrove. OxBTC

Corps d'Esprit. Heather McHugh. AmPA

Corpus Christi Carol, The ("Heron flew east, the heron flew west, The"). *Unknown.* GBP

Corpus Christi Carol ("Lully, lullay, lully, lullay"). *Unknown.* BoReV; GBP; NOBE; OxBM

Corpus Christi Carol, The ("Over yonder's a park, which is newly begun"). *Unknown.* GBP

Correct Compassion, A. James Kirkup. OxBTC

Correspondence School Instructor Says Goodbye to His Poetry Students, The. Galway Kinnell. NOBA

Corridor, The. Thom Gunn. NowV; PPP

Corrupt Man in the French Pub, The. Brian Higgins. OxBTC

Corruption. Henry Vaughan. Prf; SCP-1

Corsons Inlet. A. R. Ammons. NoAM; NOBA; PPP

Cossante. Pero Meogo, *tr. fr. Medieval Galician by* Yvor Winters. AIW

Cosy Cat Nap. James Kirkup. RAE

Cottage. "Seumas O'Sullivan." PFIr

Cottage Hospital, The. John Betjeman. NOBE

Cottager to Her Infant, The. Dorothy Wordsworth. OxBChV

Cotter's Saturday Night, The. Burns. LAuP

Cotton Song. Jean Toomer. BPo

Cottonwood, willow, and briar. Leaves Like Fish. Gladys Cardiff. CDW

Cougait Revisited. Donald Campbell. MIS

Could Man Be Drunk For Ever. A. E. Housman. PPP

Could we but see men as they are! A Window in the Breast. *Unknown, tr. by* Walter Headlam. ECBV

Councell Given to Master Bartholmew Withipoll. George Gascoigne. AAS

Councils. Marge Piercy. NeAC; RiTi; TSWA

Counsel to Girls. Robert Herrick. *See* To the Virgins, to Make Much of Time.

Counsels of O'Riordan, the Rann Maker, The. T. D. O'Bolger. PFIr

Count Arnaldos. *Unknown, tr. fr. Spanish by* W. S. Merwin. Epi

Count not his broken pledges as a crime. Lloyd George. *Unknown.* FaBoCo

Count this among my heartfelt wishes. Fish Story. Richard Armour. SPo

Countdown takeoff. To the Moon and Back. William Plomer. Moon

Counterpoint, A. Robert Creeley. CoPAm

Counting. Harry Behn. ECBV

Counting Out Rhyme ("Round about, round about"). *Unknown.* SpRo

Counting Sheep. Russell Edson. FiCP

Counting Small-Boned Bodies. Robert Bly. CAPP; PPoD; TSWA

Counting the Beats. Robert Graves. GBL; OxBTC

Counting the Mad. Donald Justice. ConAP; LP

Country, The/ was back in the hands of the patriots. Poem. Fred Levinson. AmPA

Country Air. Mike Love *and* Brian Wilson. PoRo

Country Bedroom, The, *sel.* Frances Cornford.
   "My room's a square and candle-lighted boat." RAE

Country Clergy, The. R. S. Thomas. BoReV; OxBTC; PSN

Country Club Sunday. Phyllis McGinley. WIF

Country Dance. Edith Sitwell. NoAM

Country Dance, The. Charles Tennyson Turner. VPC

Country Fiddler, The. John Montague. TwMBP

Country Girl. George Mackay Brown. SLP

Country House, The. Louis Simpson. NOBA

Country Midwife, The: A Day. Ai. CAAP

Country Morning. Rosemary Dobson. MAuV

Country Mouse and the City Mouse, The. Richard Scrafton Sharpe. OxBChV

Country of Water. Bernice Ames. WPE

Country Press. Rosemary Dobson. MAuV

Country Rhyme. *Unknown.* ECBV

Country Road. James Taylor. PoRo

Country Singer, The. Carl Rakosi. HeS

Country surrounds the city, The. Revolution in the Revolution in the Revolution. Gary Snyder. PiAm

Country rings around with loud alarms, The. Lines on a Paid Militia. Dryden. *Fr.* Cymon and Iphigenia. SoSe

Country Towns. Kenneth Slessor. MAuV

Countryman's Return, The. Dylan Thomas. OxBTC

Country's Crisis, The. Brian Merriman, *tr. fr. Modern Irish by* David Marcus. *Fr.* The Midnight Court. BIrV

County Ball, The. Coventry Patmore. *Fr.* The Angel in the House, II, iii. VPC

County Mayo, The. Anthony Raftery, *tr. fr. Irish by* James Stephens. PFIr

County of Mayo, The. *Unknown, tr. fr. Irish by* George Fox. BIrV

Coup de Grâce. A. D. Hope. PPP

Couple, The. Sandra Hochman. CTBA

Couple, A. May Swenson. RiTi

Couple Overhead, The. William Meredith. CoPAm; NoAM

Couple Upstairs, The. Hugo Williams. POL

Coupling. Cynthia Macdonald. WBN

Courage, my soul, now learn to wield. A Dialogue between the Resolved Soul and Created Pleasure. Andrew Marvell. BoReV; PAIC

Courage: your tongue has left. Stutterer. Alan Dugan. CAPP

Course of a Particular, The. Wallace Stevens. PPoe

Courser and Jennet. Shakespeare. *Fr.* Venus and Adonis. NOBE

Court considered the country's crisis, The. The Country's Crisis. Brian Merriman, *tr. by* David Marcus. *Fr.* The Midnight Court. BIrV

Courtin', The. James Russell Lowell. *Fr.* The Biglow Papers, 2d series, *introd.* AmVN; NOBA

Cousin Jack Song. *At. to* Charley Tregonning. AmFP

Covenant, The. James Cunningham. JB

Coventry Carol. *Unknown.* OFD

Cover me over, clover. Richard Eberhart. CoPAm

Covetousness. Peter Idley. OxBChV

Cow, The. James Stephens. ECBV

Cow, The. Robert Louis Stevenson. OxBChV

Cow, The. Ann *or* Jane Taylor. OxBChV

Cow Ate the Piper, The. *Unknown.* GBP; PeBB

Cow, cow. The Cow. James Stephens. ECBV

Cow in Apple Time, The. Robert Frost. PSN

Cow Slips Away, The. Ben King. ECBV

Coward, The. Stephen Spender. NoAM

Cowboy Song. Charles Causley. MiP

Cowboy with his sweetheart stood beneath a starlit sky, A. The Broken Wedding Ring. *Unknown.* AIW

Cowboy's Lament, The. *Unknown.* BLSo, *with music*; GBP; PeBB
(As I Walked Out in the Streets of Laredo.) AIW
(Streets of Laredo, The.) AmFP

Cowboy's Life Is a Very Dreary Life, The. *Unknown.* AmFP

Cowboys: One ("Brave/ they straddle the animals"). Rod McKuen. MiP

Cowboys: Three ("They wade through beer cans"). Rod McKuen. MiP

Cowboys: Two ("Huddled in the pits"). Rod McKuen. MiP

Cowled with a news-sheet in his asphalt cage. At the Zoo. Walter de la Mare. BoAnP

Cows bring in the last light, The. The Black Plateau. W. S. Merwin. CAAP

Coyote, The. A. A. Dewey. HeS

Cozy above us a little airplane chugs. Mail from Home in the Sky. Ernest Sandeen. HeS

Crab, The. Conrad Aiken. BoAnP

Crabbed Age and Youth. Shakespeare. The Passionate Pilgrim, XII. InPS
("Crabbed age and youth cannot live together.") GBL

Crack in the Wall Holds Flowers. Adam David Miller. PoBA

Crack of Doom. Albert Howard Carter. AATT

Crack ran through our hearthstone long ago, A. The Refugees. Edwin Muir. NoAM

Cracked cedar, The. Elephants. Patrick Lane. NeAC

Cracked Looking Glass. Jean Garrigue. LoAs

Cracked Record Blues. Kenneth Fearing. SFF

Cracks, The. Robert Creeley. ConAP

Cracks on the walls, The. Star Blanket. Ray A. Young Bear. CDW

Cradle Hymn. Isaac Watts. OxBChV

Cradle Song, A: "Angels are stooping, The." W. B. Yeats. LCL

Cradle Song, A: "Come, little babe, come, silly soul." Nicholas Breton. NOBE
(Come, Little Babe.) PPoe

Cradle Song, A: "Golden slumbers kiss your eyes." Thomas Dekker. *Fr.* The Pleasant Comedy of Patient Grissell. OxBChV

Cradle Song: "Lullaby and good-night," *with music. Unknown, tr. fr. German by* Natalia Macfarren. BLSH

Cradle Song, A: "Sweet dreams form a shade." Blake. *Fr.* Songs of Innocence. LAuP; MBPR

Cradle Song: "What does little birdie say." Tennyson. OxBChV

Craftsmen. V. Sackville-West. OxBTC

Crafty Farmer, The. *Unknown.* AmFP

Craigbilly Fair. *Unknown.* GBP

Cranberry Song, The. Barney Reynolds. AmFP

Crane Is My Neighbour, The. John Shaw Neilson. MAuV

Cranes. J. R. S. Davies. POL

Cranes, The. Po Chü-i , tr. tr. Chinese by Arthur Waley. ECBV

Crapshooters. Carl Sandburg. VGW

Crash, bang! Noisy Boys. Jack Castiglione. BBGO

Craving of Samuel Rouse for clearance to create, The. The Slave and the Iron Lace. Margaret Danner. BPo

Crawl, laugh. Issa, *tr. fr. Japanese by* Nobuyuki Yuasa. OFD

Craw's Killed the Poussie, O, The! *Unknown.* BoAnP

Crazed Girl, The. W. B. Yeats. InPS

Crazed Moon, The ("Crazed through much child-bearing"). W. B. Yeats. Moon

Crazy/ to be alive in such a strange. Lawrence Ferlinghetti. CTBA

Crazy Arithmetic. D'Arcy Thompson. FaBoCo

Crazy Horse Returns to South Dakota. Harley Elliott. NeAC

Crazy Jane and the Bishop. W. B. Yeats. AnMo

Crazy Jane on God. W. B. Yeats. Epi; OxBTC

Crazy Jane Talks with the Bishop. W. B. Yeats. AnMo; BoLoP; InPK; NoAM; PPP

Created, The. Jones Very. AmVN; PiAm

Creation, The. James Weldon Johnson. MiP; PBMP; PoBA

Creation, The. Patricia Ramsey. AATT

Creation, The: According to Coyote. Simon J. Ortiz. CDW

Creation of Anguish. Howard Nemerov. AnMo

Creation of the Moon, The. *Unknown, tr. fr. Amazonian Indian by* W. S. Merwin. Moon

Creation: the Fifth Day, Fishes and Birds. Milton. *Fr.* Paradise Lost, VII. SCP-1

Creator Spirit, by whose aid. Veni Creator Spiritus. *Unknown, paraphrased by* Dryden. BoReV

Creatures. Maxine W. Kumin. BoAnP

Credibility. John Ciardi. InPK; WIF

Credo. Georgia Douglas Johnson. PoBA

Credo. E. A. Robinson. PiAm; VoPo

Creek Mother Poem. Joy Harjo. SA

Creep into thy narrow bed. The Last Word. Matthew Arnold. NOBE; PBMP

Creeper, The. Tom Schmidt. NeAC

Cremation of Sam McGee, The. Robert W. Service. PoTa

Crescent Moon, The. *Unknown.* Moon ("In Mornigan's park there is a deer.") GBP

Crew-cuts. Donald Hall. MAT

Cricket, The. Frederick Goddard Tuckerman. NOBA; PiAm

Cricket and the greshope wenten hem to fight, The. Nonsense. *Unknown.* OxBM

Crickets. Aram Saroyan. MAT; SFF

Cried the Lip. Wallace Carroll. SPo

Cried the navy-blue ghost. Four in the Morning. Edith Sitwell. NoAM

Crier, The. Michael Drayton. PAIC

Crime Club. Weldon Kees. AnMo

Crimes of Lizzie Borden, The. *Unknown.* FaBoCo

Crimes of Passion: The Phone Caller. Terry Stokes. AmPA

Crimes of Passion: The Slasher. Terry Stokes. AmPA

Crimson lute that comest in the dawn. Sister Juana Inés de la Cruz, *tr. fr. Spanish by* Samuel Beckett. Epi

Crimson nor yellow roses, nor. Eros D'Aute. Theodore Wratislaw. GBL

Cripple Creek. *Unknown.* AmFP

Cripple for Life, The; or, The Poor Volunteer. *Unknown.* AmFP

Cripples. J. D. Reed. NeAC

Cripples. Kathleen Spivack. SFF

Criseyde Sees Troilus Return from Battle. Chaucer. *Fr.* Troilus and Criseyde, II. OxBM

Crisis, The. Robert Creeley. PPP

Crisis is a hair. Emily Dickinson. PiAm

Crispus Attucks McCoy. Sterling A. Brown. BPo

Crist made to man a fair present. Divine Love. *Unknown.* OxBM

Criteria. Ruthe T. Spinnanger. AATT

Critic advises, A. Black Poet, White Critic. Dudley Randall. BPo; ConAP

Critics and Connoisseurs. Marianne Moore. NoAM; NOBA; PSN

Critics cry unfair, The. In Defense of Black Poets. Conrad Kent Rivers. BPo

Critique for Our Times. Albert Howard Carter. AATT

Critter. W. M. Ransom. CDW

Croak of a raven hoar, The! A Mammon-Marriage. George Macdonald. BoLoP

Crocodile ("Once a haughty crocodile left his home upon the Nile"). Kornei Chukovsky, *tr. fr. Russian by* Babette Deutsch. ECBV

Crocodile ("Once there was a crocodile"). Kornei Chukovsky, *tr. fr. Russian by* Richard Coe. ECBV

Crois was made al of reed, A. Prologue to a Translation. John Trevisa. OxBM

Cromwell, our chief of men, who through a cloud. To the Lord General Cromwell, May 1652 [*or* To Oliver Cromwell]. Milton. Epi; OBP

Cromwell. Paul Mills. MIS

Cronos, Cronos, mend thy pace. Dryden. *Fr.* The Secular Masque. SCP-1

Crooked/ beneath a denim. Dreams. Charles Cooper. PoBA

Crooked Carol. Norma Farber. POL

Croppy Boy, The. *Unknown.* AmFP

Crops are all in and the peaches are rotting, The. Plane Wreck at Los Gatos (Deportee). Woody Guthrie. InPK

Croquet in Childhood. Helena Minton. FAF

Cross. Langston Hughes. CoPAm; PoBA; SoSe

Cross and the Weathercock, The. James Nolan. AATT

Cross-eyed Lover, The. Donald Finkel. Prf

Cross of boy with man within is an, The. On a Prize Crucifix by a Student Sculptor. Robert Logan. CAPP

Cross of Snow, The. Longfellow. AmVN; HeIP; IPWM; NOBA; PiAm

Cross Patch/ Lift the latch. Mother Goose. GBP; MG

Cross Ties. X. J. Kennedy. CoPAm

Crossed Apple, The. Louise Bogan. HeIP

Crossing. Archibald MacLeish. POL

Crossing alone the nighted ferry. A. E. Housman. NOBE

Crossing Brooklyn Ferry. Walt Whitman. NoAM; NOBA; PiAm
"Crowds of men and women attired in the usual costumes," *sel.* CTBA

Crossing into the Prairies. Bruce Severy. HeS

Crossing Kansas by Train. Donald Justice. ANTL

Crossing the Atlantic. Anne Sexton. NoAM

Crossing the Bar. Tennyson. HeIP; InPK; NOBE; PBMP; PFD; VoPo

Crossing the Plains. Joaquin Miller. AmVN

Crossing the shallow holdings high above sea. Hungry Grass. Donagh MacDonagh. BIrV

Crossing the street. The Broken Home. James Merrill. NoAM; NOBA; PPP

Crosspatch. *See* Cross Patch.

Crotchet Castle, *sel.* Thomas Love Peacock. Priest and the Mulberry Tree, The, *fr. ch.* 18 PoTa

Crow, The. James Reaney. AKE

Crow and the Birds. Ted Hughes. OBP

Crow-Children Walk My Circles in the Snow, The. Ray A. Young Bear. CDW

Crow flies between your phone and mine, The. Poem. Cathleen Quirk. MMD

Crowd, The. John Masefield. OxBTC

Crowd at the ball game, The. At the Ball Game. William Carlos Williams. NoAM; NOBA

Crowd fear: blown paper and uprooted ferns. The Spring Festival on the River. John Peck. AmPA

Crowdieknowe. "Hugh MacDiarmid." InPS; NoAM

Crowds of men and women attired in the usual costumes. Walt Whitman. *Fr.* Crossing Brooklyn Ferry. CTBA

Crown of Windflowers, A. Christina Rossetti. OxBChV

Crown Prince of Dullness, The. Dryden. *Fr.* MacFlecknoe. NOBE
("All human things are subject to decay.") SCP-1

Crowning a bluff where gleams the lake below. Pontoosuce. Herman Melville. NOBA

Crows, The. Louise Bogan. SBG

Crows, The. Zulfikar Ghose. BoAnP

Crows. David McCord. RFM

Crows. William Witherup. POL

Crow's Ditty. *Unknown.* GBP

Crow's First Lesson. Ted Hughes. InPS; NoAM

Crow's Last Stand. Ted Hughes. InPS

Crow's Way. Duane Niatum. CDW

Crows will stick their beaks into anything. The Crows. Zulfikar Ghose. BoAnP

Crowsfeet Splaying Round His Eyes. L. Paul Lloyd-Evans. BuTh

Crucified upon this cross is black, The. Ebony: Contemporary. Marian Frances Brand. AATT

Crucifix, The. Robert Lowell. NowV

Crucifixion. *Unknown.* BPo

Crucifixus Pro Nobis. Patrick Carey. SCP-2

Cruel arrows gone, The. Fleche. Larry Eigner. VGW

Cruel Brother, The. *Unknown.* AmFP; PeBB

Cruel, but composed and bland. Matthew Arnold. *Fr.* Matthias. POL

Cruel Frederick. Heinrich Hoffmann, *tr. fr. German.* SpRo

Cruel girls we loved, The. Mothers and Daughters. David Campbell. POL

Cruel Mother, The. *Unknown.* AmFP; InPK; PeBB

Cruelty has a human heart. A Divine Image. Blake. MBPR

Crumbling is not an instant's act. Emily Dickinson. NOBA; PPP

Crush the manroot, swallow what you desire. Learning the Spells: A Diptych. Anita Endrezze Probst. CDW

Crusoe's Island. Derek Walcott. NoAM

Crustaceans. Roy Fuller. NoAM

Cry, The. Grace Cavalieri. AATT

Cry, A!—someone is knocked. At 79th and Park. Barbara Howes. MiP

Cry, baby, cry,/ Put your finger in your eye. Mother Goose. MG

Cry of an Aged One, The. Ray Fraser. NeAC

Cry of the Children, The. Elizabeth Barrett Browning. VPC

Cry of the High Hurdlers, The. Horace Spencer Fiske. SPo

Cry of those being eaten by America, The. Those Being Eaten By America. Robert Bly. PPoD

Cryin' ain't goin' down this big road by myself. Big Road Blues. *Unknown.* BluL

Cryin' canned heat. Canned Heat Blues. *Unknown.* BluL

Cryin' I ain't goin' down the dark road by myself. Dark Road Blues. *Unknown.* BluL

Cryin', who's that yonder. Maggie Campbell Blues. *Unknown.* BluL

Crystal. Faye Kicknosway. IHMS

Crystal Cabinet, The. Blake. AIW; MBPR ("Maiden caught me in the wild, The.") Epi

Crystal Moment. Robert P. Tristram Coffin. ECBV

Crystals like Blood. "Hugh MacDiarmid." InPS

Cu Chuimne in youth. *Unknown, tr. fr. Irish by* John V. Kelleher. BIrV

Cuba Libre. Joaquin Miller. BTTM

Cuba, 1962. Ai. AmPA

Cucaracha, La, *with music. Unknown, tr. fr. Spanish.* BLSH

Cuckoo, The. Patrick Reginald Chalmers. BoAnP

Cuckoo. R. P. Lister. BoAnP

Cuckoo, The ("The cuckoo is a bonny bird"), *diff. versions. Unknown.* AmFP; GBP; RAE

"Cuckoo! The," cried my child, the while I slept. The Oocuck. Justin Richardson. BoAnP

Cuckoo Song. *Unknown.* NOBE; PBMP; SpRo (Sumer Is Icumen In.) GBP; HeIP; InPS; OxBM

Cuckoo, when the lambkins bleat, The. The Cuckoo. Patrick Reginald Chalmers. BoAnP

Cuckoo's double note, The. Wiltshire Downs. Andrew Young. OxBTC

Culbin Sands. Andrew Young. OxBTC

Culprit, The. A. E. Housman. AIW

Cultivation of Christmas Trees, The. T. S. Eliot. OFD

Cultural Exchange. Langston Hughes. BPo; PoBA

*Cumberland* and the *Merrimac,* The, 2 *versions. Unknown.* AmFP

*Cumberland's* Crew, The. *Unknown.* AmFP

Cup of tea on a God-swept evening, A. Knell for Insularity. Merle Meeter. AATT

Cupid and My Campaspe. John Lyly. *See* Cards and Kisses.

Cupid and Venus. Mark Alexander Boyd. *See* Fra Bank to Bank, Fra Wood to Wood I Rin.

Cupid as he lay among. The Wounded Cupid. Robert Herrick. OFD

Cupid's Call. James Shirley. SCP-2

Curfew. Paul Eluard, *tr. fr. French by* Quentin Stevenson. BoLoP

Curfew tolls the knell of parting day, The. Elegy Written in a Country Churchyard. Thomas Gray. HeIP; InPK; InPS; LAuP; NOBE; OBP; PAIC; PBMP; PPoD; PPoe; PPP; WIF

Curio, aye me, thy mistress' monkey's dead! Inamorato Curio. John Marston. *Fr.* The Scourge of Villainy. TVS

Curiosity. Alastair Reid. SoSe

Curious business, A. Petty Murder. Albert MacLean, Jr. SFF

Curiously, I still remember. After Reading *The First Circle.* Martha Shelley. WBN

Curiously Young Like a Freshly-dug Grave. Richard Brautigan. MIT

Curly locks! curly locks! wilt thou be mine? Mother Goose. MG

Currants on a bush. Fruits. Christina Rossetti. ECBV

Currents. Emma Lazarus. *Fr.* By the Waters of Babylon. WPE

Curricle and hansom, The. The Great Garret, or 100 Wheels. James McMichael. AmPA

Curriculum Vitae: Incomplete. Elisavietta Ritchie. AATT

Curse, The. J. M. Synge. FaBoCo

Curse, A. *Unknown. See* Bruadar and Smith and Glinn.

Curse for a Nation, A. Elizabeth Barrett Browning. SBG; WPE

Curse of Cromwell, The. W. B. Yeats. BIrV

Curse on a Closed Gate, A. *Unknown, tr. fr. Irish by* James H. Cousins. PFIr

Curse upon that faithless maid, A. Song. Aphra Behn. *Fr.* Emperor of the Moon. WPE

Cursor Mundi, *sel. Unknown.* Pound of Flesh, The. OxBM

Curst be the verse, how well so'er it flow. Pope. *Fr.* Epistle to Dr. Arbuthnot. OBP

Curst Wife, The. *Unknown.* AIW

Curtain World. Heather Morse. CaYB

Curtains drawn back, the door ajar. Robinson at Home. Weldon Kees. AnMo

Curtains were half drawn, the floor was swept, The. After Death. Christina Rossetti. GBL

Cushy Cow, Bonny. *Unknown.* GBP

Cusp/ the little word. How One Thing Leads to Another. David Smith. NVAP

Custom of the World, The. Louis Simpson. BoLoP; SFF

Customarily Autumn. F. Eugene Warren. AATT

Customs Change. *Unknown.* OxBChV

Customs of the Country, The. Phyllis McGinley. *Fr.* New England Pilgrimage. TH

Cut. Sylvia Plath. CAPP; InPK; PiAm

Cut the Grass. A. R. Ammons. PPP

Cutting shade, cool spades and a little last beds. Pastry. Gertrude Stein. *Fr.* Tender Buttons. RiTi

Cutting the Jewish Bride's Hair. Ruth Whitman. RiTi

Cuttings ("Sticks-in-a-drowse droop over sugary loam"). Theodore Roethke. AnMo; NoAM; NOBA; PiAM

Cuttings ("This urge, wrestle, resurrection of dry sticks"). Theodore Roethke. AnMo; NoAM; NOBA; PiAM; PPoe

Cutty Wren, The. *Unknown.* GBP

Cy Est Pourtraicte, Madame Ste. Ursule, et les Unze Mille Vierges. Wallace Stevens. LoAs

Cycads, The. Judith Wright. MAuV

Cycle, The. Stephen Dunn. HeS

Cycle, A. John Leax. AATT

Cycle of Women, A. Sharon Barba. RiTi

Cycles, Cycles. Suzanne Berger Rioff. NMM

Cyclists, The. Amy Lowell. WPE

Cymbeline, *sels.* Shakespeare. Fear No More the Heat o' the Sun, *fr.* IV, ii. AIW; GBL; HeIP; InPK; InPS; OBP; PBMP; PPoe; SoSe

(Dirge for Fidele.) NOBE
"Hark, hark! the lark at heaven's gate sings," *fr.* II, iii. HeIP; OBP; PAIC
Cymon and Iphigenia, *sel.* Dryden.
Lines on a Paid Militia. SoSe
Cynddylan on a Tractor. R. S. Thomas. LP; MPo
Cynic Satyre, A. John Marston. *Fr.* The Scourge of Villainy, VII. TVS
Cynthia. Edward Benlowes. *Fr.* Theophila; or, Love's Sacrifice. Moon
Cynthia, because your horns look diverse ways. Fulke Greville. *Fr.* Caelica. Moon
Cynthia in the Snow. Gwendolyn Brooks. LCL
Cynthia's Revels, *sels.* Ben Jonson.
Echo's Lament of Narcissus, *fr.* I, ii. SoSe
("Slow, slow, fresh fount, keep time with my salt tears.") InPK
Hymn to Diana, *fr.* V, vi. Moon; NOBE
("Queen and huntress, chaste and fair." HeIP; PAIC
"Thou more than most sweet glove," *fr.* IV. GBL
Cypress Grove Blues. *Unknown.* BluL
Cyrano De Bergerac, *sel.* Edmond Rostand, *tr. fr. French by* Brian Hooker.
"Love, I love beyond," *fr.* Act III. OLR
Cyriac, this three years' day these eyes, though clear. To Mr. Cyriac Skinner upon His Blindness. Milton. SCP-1
Cyriack, Whose Grandsire on the Royal Beach. Milton. PAIC

# D

D Blues. Calvin C. Hernton. PoBA
D-day Minus. Edwin Brock. BBGO
D.O.M., A.D. 2167. John Frederick Nims. CoPAm
D-Y Bar. James Welch. CDW
Dab of Color, A. Theodore Weiss. VGW
Dachau, Now: "Roses Grow There, Fat with Blood." Elisavietta Ritchie. AATT
Daddy. Sylvia Plath. AnMo; CAPP; InPK; InPS; NMM; NoAM; NOBA; PiAm; Psy; RiTi
Daddyboy/ trickster hero. Daring. Carol Konek. IHMS
Daedalus. Alastair Reid. NCSH
Daemon Lover, The. *Unknown. See* Demon Lover, The.
Daffodils. Wordsworth. NOBE
Daffy-Down-Dilly has come up to town. Mother Goose. MG
Dago shovelman sits by the railroad track, The. Child of the Romans. Carl Sandburg. PiAm
Dainty little maiden, whither would you wander? The City Child. Tennyson. OxBChV
Dainty young heiress of Lincoln's Inn Fields, The. Charles Sackville. POL
Daisies. Alden Nowlan. NeAC
Daisies. John Stevens Wade. FAF
Daisy, The. Marya Zaturenska. LoAs
Daisy Bell; or, A Bicycle Built for Two, *with music.* Harry Dacre. BLSH; BLSo; FSN
Dallán Dé! Dallán Dé! Butterfly in the Fields. Joseph Campbell. BoAnP; PFIr
Dalliance of the Eagles, The. Walt Whitman. BoAnP; HeIP; InPK; LoAs; PiAm; POL; PPoe; PPP
Dam, The. Patric Dickinson. PoTa

Dame Wiggins of Lee. *Unknown.* OxBChV
Dames of France are fond and free, The. The Girl I Left behind Me. Thomas Osborne Davis. BTTM
Damisel, rest thee wel. A Student Courting. *Unknown.* OxBM
Damn it all! all this our South stinks peace. Sestina: Altaforte. Ezra Pound. NOBA
Damned Women. Baudelaire, *tr. fr.* French by Roy Campbell. BoLoP
Damon, come drive thy flocks this way. Clorinda and Damon. Andrew Marvell. PAIC
Damon the Mower. Andrew Marvell. AnMo
Damsels of Time, the hypocritic Days. *See* Daughters of Time. . .
Dan Ellis's Boys. *Unknown.* AmFP
Danäe. Barbara Howes. RiTi; WPE
Dance, The. Hart Crane. *Fr.* The Bridge: Powhatan's Daughter. PiAm
Dance, The. LeRoi Jones. PiAm
Dance, The. William Carlos Williams. HeIP; InPK; NCSH; NoAM; NOBA; PAIC; PiAm; POL; SoSe; WIF
Dance, The/ (held up for me by). The Dance. LeRoi Jones. PiAm
Dance and Eye Me (Wicked)ly My Breath a Fixed Sphere. Rochelle Owens. NMM
Dance Figure. Ezra Pound. HeIP
Dance for Ma Rainey, A. Al Young. SA
Dance for Militant Dilettantes, A. Al Young. PiAm; PoBA; PPoD; SA
Dance, little baby, dance up high. The Baby's Dance. Ann Taylor. ECBV; OxBChV
Dance of the Infidels. Al Young. PoBA
Dance of the Macabre Mice. Wallace Stevens. NOBA
Dance Steps. *Unknown.* ECBV
Dance there upon the shore. To a Child Dancing in the Wind. W. B. Yeats. BBGO; PFIr
Dance, Thumbkin, dance. *Unknown.* MG
Dance to your daddy. Mother Goose. MG
Dancer, The. Al Young. PiAm; PoBA; SA
Dancer from the Dance, The. Suzanne Juhasz. IHMS
Dancers at the Moy. Paul Muldoon. BIrV
Dancers of Colbek, The. Robert Mannyng. *Fr.* Handlyng Synne. OxBM
Dancing/ to the sound of the night. Sabinas Hidalgo. Diane Kruchkow. FAF
Dancing, bright lady, then began to be. The Praise of Dancing. Sir John Davies. *Fr.* Orchestra; or, A Poem of Dancing. NOBE
Dancing in the Street. Al Young. SA
Dancing Teepees. Calvin O'John. VW
Dancing the Shout to the True Gospel; or, The Song Movement Sisters Don't Want Me to Sing. Rita Mae Brown. NMM; WBN
Dandelions. Gerda Mayer. POL
Dane-Geld. Kipling. OxBTC
Danger stalks on such nights, the moon is dangerous. The Lunar Tides. Marya Zaturenska. Moon
Dangling Conversation. Paul Simon. NowV
Daniel at Breakfast. Phyllis McGinley. BBGO
Danny Deever. Kipling. AIW; BTTM; Epi; InPS; NOBE; OxBTC; PeBB; PBMP; SFF
Danse Russe. William Carlos Williams. InPK; InPS; NOBA; PPP
Dante Etudes, *sel.* Robert Duncan.
Etude from the Third Epistle, III. CAAP
Danty, baby, diddy. Mother Goose. MG

Danube orchards, The. The Peachtree. Denise Levertov. *Fr.* During the Eichmann Trial. CAPP

Daphnis. Theocritus, *tr. fr. Greek by* Dryden. *Fr.* Idylls, XXVII. SCP-1

Dar was ole Mister Johnson, he had trouble of his own. The Cat Came Back. Harry S. Miller. FSN

Darest Thou Now O Soul. Walt Whitman. PAIC

Daring. Carol Konek. IHMS

Darius Green and His Flying-Machine. John Townsend Trowbridge. OxBChV

Dark accurate plunger down the successive knell. The Subway. Allen Tate. NoAM; NOBA; PiAm

Dark an' stormy may come de wedder. Slave Marriage Ceremony Supplement. *Unknown.* BPo; POL

Dark and the Fair, The. Stanley Kunitz. LoAs

Dark and Wrinkled. Arthur Rimbaud, *tr. fr. French by* Wallace Fowlie. LoAs

Dark Angel, The. Lionel Johnson. BoReV; NOBE; PFD

Dark as wells, his eyes. Long Person. Gladys Cardiff. CDW

Dark, black robe. Invitation (To the Night and All Other Things Dark). Ronda Davis. JB

Dark brown is the river. Where Go the Boats? Robert Louis Stevenson. LCL; OxBChV

Dark cliff towered up to the stars that flickered, The. The Passage at Night—The Blaskets. Robin Flower. PFIr

Dark Country, A. Derek Mahon. BIrV

Dark, deeply. A red. Inside the River. James Dickey. SPo

Dark Exciting Days, The. Karl Shapiro. CoPAm

Dark eyed,/ O woman of my dreams. Dance Figure. Ezra Pound. HeIP

Dark Eyes, *with music. Unknown, tr. fr. Russian by* Albert Morehead. BLSH

Dark figures, lunged ahead, The. The Moral. Theodore Weiss. Prf

Dark Glass, The. Dante Gabriel Rossetti. The House of Life, XXXIV. VPC

Dark-haired girl, who holds my thoughts entirely, The. Peggy Browne. Turlough O'Carolan, *tr. by* Austin Clarke. BIrV

Dark Hills, The. E. A. Robinson. NoAM

Dark Hope. Wade Hall. AATT

Dark house, by which once more I stand. In Memoriam A. H. H., VII. Tennyson. InPK; NOBE; PPoe; SoSe

Dark Lady, The. *Unknown.* OxBM

Dark Road Blues. *Unknown.* BluL

Dark Rosaleen. *At. to* Owen Roe MacWard, *tr. fr. Irish by* James Clarence Mangan. BIrV; LoAs; PFIr

Dark Song. A. R. Ammons. MAT

Dark streets are deserted, The. After Midnight. Louis Simpson. NoAM

Dark thoughts are my companions. I have wined. Epigram. J. V. Cunningham. VGW

Dark Was the Night. *Unknown.* AmFP

Darkened farmhouse is asleep, The. Saving the Harvest. Geoffrey Lehmann. MAuV

Darkling Thrush, The. Thomas Hardy. BoReV; FSFS; InPS; NoAM; NOBE; PPP; SoSe; VoPo

Darkness. Joseph Campbell. BIrV

Darkness Comes to the Woods. Norbert Krapf. HeS

Darkness crumbles away, The. Break of Day in the Trenches. Isaac Rosenberg. NOBE; PSN

Darkness dwells around Dunlathmon. Oithona: a Poem. James Macpherson. LAuP

Darkness falls like a wet sponge. The Picture of Little J.A. in a Prospect of Flowers. John Ashbery. ConAP; PPP

Darkness has called to darkness, and disgrace. As a Plane Tree by the Water. Robert Lowell. NoAM; NOBA

Darkness is not dark, nor sunlight the light of the sun. Foal. Vernon Watkins. OxBTC

Darkness lifts, imagine, in your lifetime, The. The Undertaking. Louise Glück. NVAP

Darkness surrounds us; seeking, we are lost. Uncertainty. Wordsworth. *Fr.* Ecclessiastical Sonnets. MBPR

Darkness wears off and, dawning into daylight. The Figures on the Frieze. Alastair Reid. SLP

Darling, at the beautician's you buy. A Valentine for a Lady. Lucillius, *tr. by* Dudley Fitts. OFD

Darling Cory. *Unknown.* AmFP

Darling, each morning a blooded rose. Corinna in Vendome. Pierre de Ronsard, *tr. by* Robert Mezey. BoLoP

Darling, I am growing old. Silver Threads among the Gold. Eben Eugene Rexford. BLSH; BLSo; PSoN

Darling Nelly Gray, *with music.* Benjamin Russel Hanby. BLSo; PSoN

Darling of Gods and Men, beneath the gliding stars. Basil Bunting. NoAM

Dar'st thou amid the varied multitude. The Solitary. Shelley. MBPR

Dart, The. *Unknown.* GBP

Dart, here's a man. The River Dart. *Unknown.* GBP

Dart of Love, The. *Unknown, tr. fr. Gaelic by* G.R.D. McLean. SLP

Das Schloss. Lincoln Kirstein. NoAM

Dash back that ocean with a pier. Tennyson. *Fr.* Mechanophilus. FaBoCo

Dashing thro' the snow in a one-horse open sleigh. Jingle Bells [*or* The One Horse Open Sleigh]. James S. Pierpont. BLSH; BLSo; PSoN

Dated Valmont 10-16/ october 1849. Eugene Delacroix Says. Edward Dorn. NoAM

Dates on bridges, The. History and Abstraction. Thomas Lux. AmPA

Daughters of Beulah! Muses who inspire the poets song. Milton. Blake. MBPR

Daughters of the Seraphim led round their sunny flocks. The Book of Thel. Blake. LAuP; MBPR

Daughters [*or* Damsels] of Time, the hypocritic Days. Days. Emerson. AmVN; HeIP; IPWM; NOBA; PAIC; PiAm; SoSe; VoPo

David. Josephine Miles. MIT

David and Bethsabe, *sel.* George Peele.
 Bethsabe's Song, *fr. sc. i.* NOBE
 ("Hot sun, cool fire, temper'd with sweet air.") GBL

David and Goliath. Nathaniel Crouch. OxBChV

David Hume ate a swinging great dinner. On the Author of the *Treatise of Human Nature.* James Hay Beattie. FaBoCo

David the king was grieved and moved. David's Lamentation. William Billings. AmFP

David, we must have looked comic, sitting. Elegy for David Beynon. Leslie Norris. LP

Davideis, *sel.* Abraham Cowley.
 Hell, *fr.* I. SCP-2
 Music, *fr.* I. SCP-2

David's Harp. Gwen Harwood. MAuV

David's Lamentation. William Billings. AmFP

Davy and the Goblin, *sel.* Charles Edward Carryl.
 Robinson Crusoe's Story, *fr. ch.* 11. ECBV

Dawn. Octavio Paz. TSWA

Dawn, The. W. B. Yeats. GrRo

Dawn and a high film; the sun burned it. We in the Fields. William Everson. PiAm

Dawn cried out: the brutal voice of a bird. In All These Acts. William Everson. PiAm

Dawn in January. Lance Henson. CDW

Dawn is a Feeling. Mike Pinder. GrRo

Dawn is, in essence, sinister as fire. Dew. Jennifer Maiden. CAAP

Dawn on the East Coast. Alun Lewis. PSN

Dawn was apple-green, The. Green. D. H. Lawrence. GBL

Dawndrizzle ended dampness steams from. Anglosaxon Street. Earle Birney. HeIP

Dawning, The. Henry Vaughan. BoReV

Dawning of morn, the daylight's sinking. Thee, Thee, Only Thee. Thomas Moore. GBL

Day, The. Roy Fuller. OxBTC

Day after day, alone on a hill. The Fool on the Hill. John Lennon *and* Paul McCartney. GrRo; PPoe

Day and Night Handball. Stephen Dunn. AmPA

Day arrives of the autumn fair, The. A Sheep Fair. Thomas Hardy. Prf

Day before the houses sank beneath the waves, The. The Day the Houses Sank. Constance Urdang. MAT

Day Begins, A. Denise Levertov. AnMo; CoPAm

Day by day I float my paper boats. Rabindranath Tagore. *Fr.* Paper Boats. RAE

Day dawns with scent of must and rain, The. Mirror in February. Thomas Kinsella. NoAM

Day has been washed clean, and so have I, The. Washed in Water. Rayne Mackinnon. MIS

Day I rode throught Devonshire, The. Beneath Such Rains. James E. Warren, Jr. AATT

Day I Stopped Dreaming About Barbara Steele, The. R. H. W. Dillard. PPoD

Day in the Life, A. John Lennon *and* Paul McCartney. PPoe; WIF

Day Is Done, The. Longfellow. NOBA

Day is gone, and all its sweets are gone, The! Keats. LoAs; MBPR

Day is past and gone, The. Evening Shade. John Leland. AmFP

Day is past, the sun is set, The. Evening. Thomas Miller. OxBChV

Day Jayne Mansfield died, The. Bison Flower Days. Anselm Hollo. TwMBP

Day Lady Died, The. Frank O'Hara. CAPP; NoAM; NOBA

Day of Denial, The. Jones Very. NOBA

Day of hunting done. Twilight in California. Philip Dow. AmPA

Day of Judgement, The. Swift. BIrV; ESaP; InPK; NOBE; PPP

Day of Judgement, The. Isaac Watts. NOBE; PAIC

Day of sunny face and temper, A. Big Bessie Throws Her Son into the Street. Gwendolyn Brooks. VGW

Day of the Pancreas, The. David McFadden. NeAC

Day Sailing. David R. Slavitt. CoPAm

Day she visited the dissecting room, The. Two Views of a Cadaver Room. Sylvia Plath. AnMo

Day Sleeper. James L. White. HeS

Day that I left my home for the rolling sea, The. La Paloma. Sebastian Yradier. BLSH

Day the fat woman, The. The Beach in August. Weldon Kees. VGW

Day the Houses Sank, The. Constance Urdang. MAT

Day the Weather Broke, The. Alastair Reid. SLP

Day They Ate the Baritone, The. Samuel Hazo. PPoD

Day They Busted the Grateful Dead, The. Richard Brautigan. MAT

Day Thou Gavest, Lord, Is Ended, The, *with music.* John Ellerton. BLSH

Day Time Sequence/ November. Dalene Stowe. NPW

Day waits quietly, The. Still Branches. Jack Simcock. BuTh

Day was here when it was his to know, The. The New Tenants. E. A. Robinson. NoAM

Day was so bright, The. Miroslav Holub, *tr. by* George Theiner *and* Ian Milner. *Fr.* A Dog in the Quarry. BoAnP

Day with the Foreign Legion, A. Reed Whittemore. ConAP

Day worth losing, A. The Line. Dan Gerber. HeS

Day you appeared I began to speak, The. To Your Question. Duane Niatum. CDW

Day you came, The. Breasts. Tess Gallagher. AmPA

Day, you have bruised and beaten me. The New Moon. Sara Teasdale. Moon

Daybreak. Stephen Spender. BoLoP

Daybreak: the household slept. Barn Owl. Gwen Harwood. *Fr.* Father and Child. CAAP; MAuV; WPE

Day-breakers, The. Arna Bontemps. PoBA

Day-Dream, A. Samuel Taylor Coleridge. MBPR

Day-Dream from an Emigrant to His Absent Wife, The. Samuel Taylor Coleridge. MBPR

Daylight falls upon the path, the forest falls behind. I Think I Understand. Joni Mitchell. GrRo

Day-long cold hard rain drove, The. Surviving. James Welch. CDW; SA

Daylong this tomcat lies stretched flat. Esther's Tomcat. Ted Hughes. PCat

Days. Emerson. AmVN; HeIP; IPWM; NOBA; PAIC; PiAm; SoSe; VoPo

Days, The. Donald Hall. CoPAm

Days. Philip Larkin. LP; PSN

Days are cold, the nights are long, The. The Cottager to Her Infant. Dorothy Wordsworth. OxBChV

Day's grown old, the fainting sun, The. Evening. Charles Cotton. SCP-2

Days Like This. John Stevens Wade. FAF

Days of Re-entry. Patricia Henley. NPW

Day's Ration, The. Emerson. PiAm

Day's Work a-Done. William Barnes. VPC

Dazzled thus with height of place. Upon the Sudden Restraint of the Earl of Somerset, Then Falling from Favour. Sir Henry Wotton. NOBE; SCP-2

De Aegypto. Ezra Pound. VGW

De Clerico et Puella. *Unknown.* OxBM

"De Gustibus." Robert Browning. InPS

De Profundis. Thomas Campion. BoReV

De Regimine Principum, *sels.* Thomas Hoccleve.
Anxious Thought. OxBM
Lament for Chaucer and Gower. OxBM

Deacon's Masterpiece, The; or, The Wonderful "One-Hoss Shay." Oliver Wendell Holmes. *Fr.* The Autocrat of the Breakfast-Table, *ch.* 11. NOBA; PiAm; SS

Dead, The. Mathilde Blind. SBG

Dead, The. Mark Strand. HeIP

Dead, The. Jones Very. AmVN; NOBA; PAIC

Dead abide with us, The! Though stark and cold. The Dead. Mathilde Blind. SBG

Dead at Clonmacnoise, The. *Unknown, tr. fr. Irish by* Thomas William Rolleston. PFIr

Dead at the pasture edge. The Dead Calf. Wendell Berry. PiAm

Dead beast, turned up, The. The Well-travelled Roadway. John Newlove. NeAC

Dead birds fell, but no one had seen them fly, The. Some Dreams They Forgot. Elizabeth Bishop. NoAM

Dead Boy. John Crowe Ransom. NoAM; PiAm

Dead boy living among men as a man, A. A Head. James Schuyler. NoAM

Dead brood over Europe, the cloud and vision descends over chearful France, The. The French Revolution. Blake. MBPR

Dead Calf, The. Wendell Berry. PiAm

Dead Drunk Blues. *Unknown.* BluL

Dead Hand. W. S. Merwin. CAPP; InPK

Dead heat and windless air. August Weather. Katharine Tynan. FSFS

Dead in the cold, a song-singing thrush. Last Rites. Christina Rossetti. OxBChV

Dead Lady Canonized, The. LeRoi Jones. CAPP

Dead Love. Swinburne. LoAs

Dead Man Creek. Van K. Brock. NVAP

Dead Man Dragged from the Sea, The. Carl Gardner. PoBA

Dead! One of them shot by the sea in the east. Mother and Poet. Elizabeth Barrett Browning. SBG

Dead poets, philosophs, priests. Walt Whitman. *Fr.* Starting from Paumanok. InPS

Dead Ponies. Brenda Chamberlain. WPE

Dead scents I couldn't bear bore. Year of the Bird. Brian Swann. AmPA

Dead Seal. A. W. Purdy. NoAM

Dead Shall Be Raised Incorruptible, The. Galway Kinnell. CAAP; NOBA

Dead Sparrow, The. William Cartwright. BoAnP

Dead Still. Andrei Voznesensky, *tr. fr. Russian by* Richard Wilbur. BoLoP

Deader they die here, or at least. Fall Comes in Back-Country Vermont. Robert Penn Warren. VGW

Deadfall. Martha Keller. ECBV

Deadly destructive to my man and me. The Conscience. Anna Wickham. POL

Deaf, giddy, helpless, left alone. On His Own Deafness. Swift. AnMo; BIrV

Deafening tic-tic-tic of the clock, The. Loneliness. Loyal Shegonee. VW

Deafness. Richard Ryan. BIrV

Dean of Paul's did search for his wife, The. Fragment of a Song on the Beautiful Wife of Dr. John Overall. *Unknown.* BoLoP

Dear America. Robert Peterson. SFF

Dear Black Head. *Unknown. See* Dear Dark Head.

Dear boy, you will not hear me speak. Pangloss's Song. Richard Wilbur. NoAM

Dear child of nature, let them rail! To a Young Lady. Wordsworth. MBPR

Dear child, these words which briefly I declare. The Maiden's Best Adorning. *Unknown.* OxBChV; RRA

Dear Chloe, how blubbered is that pretty face! Answer to Chloe Jealous. Matthew Prior. NOBE

Dear Colette. Erica Jong. MMD

Dear creature by the fire a-purr. Cat. Lytton Strachey. PCat

Dear critic, who my lightness so deplores. To a Captious Critic. Paul Laurence Dunbar. BPo

Dear Dark Head. *Unknown, tr. fr. Irish by* Sir Samuel Ferguson. LoAs; PFIr
(Cean Dubh Deelish.) GBL
(Dear Black Head.) BIrV

Dear Emily, my tears would burn your page. To Emily Dickinson. Yvor Winters. PiAm

Dear Eustatio, I write that you may write me an answer. Amours de Voyage, Canto I. Arthur Hugh Clough. VPC

Dear father, mother, sister, come listen while I tell. The Ashland Tragedy. Elijah Adams. AmFP

Dear fellow castaway, the cruise ships. Weathering the Depths. Al Lee. AmPA

Dear friend, be silent and with patience see. Michael Drayton. *Fr.* To My Noble Friend Master William Browne: of the Evil Time. SCP-2

Dear friends/ (and how). Mr. Whitman to His Friends in the Antipodes. Kris Hemensley. *Fr.* The Poem of the Clear Eye. CAAP

Dear gentle soul, who went so soon away. Luís Camoës, *tr. fr. Portuguese by* Roy Campbell. BoLoP

Dear Girl. Gregory Corso. NoAM

Dear Girl, The. Sylvia Townsend Warner. AIW

Dear God, the Day Is Grey. Anne Halley. NowV

Dear, if unsocial privacies obsess me. Epigram. J. V. Cunningham. VGW

Dear, if you change, I'll never choose again. *Unknown.* LoAs

Dear ——, I'll gie ye some advice. To an Artist. Burns. PBMP

Dear John, Dear Coltrane. Michael S. Harper. AmPA; NVAP

Dear Kong. Fay Wray to the King. Judith Rechter. NMM

Dear, let us two each other spy. Love's Vision. William Cavendish, Duke of Newcastle. SCP-2

Dear Lord and Father of Mankind, *with music.* Whittier. BLSH

Dear Mamma, if you just could be. A Lesson for Mamma. Sydney Dayre. OxBChV

Dear March, come in. Emily Dickinson. FSFS

Dear me! what signifies a pin. The Pin. Ann Taylor. OxBChV

Dear Men and Women. John Hall Wheelock. Prf

Dear miss, not with a lie to cheat ye. Samuel Wesley. *Fr.* To My Gingerbread Mistress. SCP-2

Dear Mister Congressman. Bob Dylan. MAT

Dear Mother. Emmett Jarrett. NeAC

Dear mother, dear mother, the Church is cold. The Little Vagabond. Blake. *Fr.* Songs of Experience. MBPR

Dear native brook! wild streamlet of the west! Sonnet to the River Otter. Samuel Taylor Coleridge. MBPR

Dear Oedipus. Ann Darr. WBN

Dear Old Girl, *with music.* Richard Henry Buck. BLSH; FSN

Dear parents,/ I forgive you my life. Sorry. R. S. Thomas. LP

Dear Rat,/ Never in all my life have I seen. Letters from an Irishman to a Rat. Christopher Logue. BoAnP

Dear Reynolds, as last night I lay in bed. To J. H. Reynolds, Esq. Keats. MBPR

Dear Ron: hello. Your name is now a household name. Sonnet. Ted Berrigan. CAAP

Dear Sir,—You wish to know my notions. A Letter from a Candidate for the Presidency. James Russell Lowell. *Fr.* The Biglow Papers: 1st Series, No. VII. PiAm

Dear Sir, your astonishment's odd. A Reply. *Unknown.* FaBoCo

Dear, though the night is gone. W. H. Auden. BoLoP

Dear Uncle Stranger. Conrad Aiken. NoAM; NOBA

Dear, when on some distant planet. Love in a Space-suit. James Kirkup. MPo

Dear Whoever-You-Are-That-You-Are. A Letter from the Pygmies. Theodore Weiss. VGW

Dear, why make you more of a dog than me? Astrophel and Stella, LIX. Sir Philip Sidney. GBL; LoAs

Dear, why should you command me to my rest. Michael Drayton. *Fr.* Idea. AAS; NOBE

Deare Friend, sit down, the tale is long and sad. Love Unknown. George Herbert. Prf

Deare love, for nothing lesse than thee. The Dreame. John Donne. LoAs

Dearest Evelyn, I often think of you. The Jungle Husband. Stevie Smith. BuTh

Dearest love, do you remember. When This Cruel War Is Over. *Unknown.* AmFP

Dear Man-in-the-Moon. Erica Jong. MMD; Moon

Death. Roy Fuller. NoAM

Death. George Herbert. SCP-1

Death. Keats. *Fr.* The Fall of Hyperion. OBP

Death. L. E. Jones. POL

Death. Lynn Sukenick. RiTi

Death. William Carlos Williams. VGW

Death. Charles Wright. FiCP

Death!/ Plop. A Tragedy. Théophile Marzials. PPoD

Death and Co. Sylvia Plath. ConAP

Death and Disfiguration. Judy Grahn. *Fr.* A Woman Is Talking to Death. WBN

Death and Love. Ben Jonson. *Fr.* The Sad Shepherd, I, v. NOBE

Death and the Arkansas River. Frank Stanford. FiCP

Death and the Lover. *Unknown, tr. fr. Spanish by* W. S. Merwin. Epi

Death and the Plowman. Sidney Keyes. OxBTC

Death As History. Jay Wright. PoBA

Death at Suppertime. Phyllis McGinley. PMBP

Death at Winson Green, A. Francis Webb. MAuV

Death, Be Not Proud. Holy Sonnets, X. John Donne. AnMo; BoReV; Epi; HeIP; MetP; NOBE; OBP; PAIC; PBMP; PPoe; PPP; SCP-1; VoPo

Death be not proud, thy hand gave not this blow. Elegy. Lucy Harington, Countess of Bedford. WPE

Death-bed, The. Thomas Hood. NOBE

Death-Bed Song. *Unknown.* AmFP

Death Bells. *Unknown.* BluL

Death by Aesthetics. Mona Van Duyn. RiTi

Death Dance, The. Marge Piercy. WBN

Death designs swirl high above faces that are of disbelief. War Walking Near. Ray A. Young Bear. CDW

Death devours all lovely things. Passer Mortuus Est. Edna St. Vincent Millay. RiTi

Death for the Dark Stranger. Thomas McGrath. VGW

Death, I repent. Two Invocations of Death. Kathleen Raine. OxBTC

Death in the Desert, A. Charles Tomlinson. TwMBP

Death in the Woods. Harold Bird ("Littlebird"). VW

Death in Yorkville. Langston Hughes. PoBA

Death Insurance. Wade Hall. AATT

Death Invited. May Swenson. BoAnP; WPE

Death Is a Door. John Allcock. BuTh

Death is all metaphors, shape in one history. Altarwise by Owl-Light, II. Dylan Thomas. NoAM

Death is another milestone on their way. The Funeral. Stephen Spender. NoAM

Death Is Awful. *Unknown.* BluL

Death Is Not Evil, Evil is Mechanical. D. H. Lawrence. PBMP

Death is stronger than all the governments. Death Snips Proud Men. Carl Sandburg. BBGO

Death is the cook of nature, and we find. Margaret Cavendish, Duchess of Newcastle. *Fr.* Nature's Cook. SCP-2

Death is the supple suitor. Emily Dickinson. AnMo

Death-Lace. David Ray. MAT

Death makes me love you. Allegiance to Aphrodite. Nicholas Flocos. SA

Death News. Allen Ginsberg. NoAM

Death of a Bird. Jon Silkin. BoAnP

Death of a Cat. Brian Jones. LP

Death of a Cat, The, *sels.* Louis MacNeice.
    "For he was our puck, our miniature lar." PCat
    "To begin with he was a beautiful object." PCat

Death of a Friend. Pauli Murray. PoBA

Death of a Naturalist. Seamus Heaney. NCSH

Death of a Negro Poet, The. Conrad Kent Rivers. BPo

Death of a Poet. Charles Causley. OxBTC

Death of a Soldier, The. Wallace Stevens. OFD

Death of a Son. Jon Silkin. BBGO; IPWM; NoAM; OxBTC; PPoD

Death of a Toad, The. Richard Wilbur. AnMo; NoAM

Death of a Vermont Farm Woman. Barbara Howes. CoPAm

Death of Admiral Benbow, The. *Unknown.* GBP; PeBB

Death of Arthur, The. Layamon. *Fr.* The Brut. OxBM

Death of Ben Hall, The. Will H. Ogilvie. PoTa

Death of Dr. King. Sam Cornish. OFD; PoBA

Death of Justice, The. Walter Everette Hawkins. PoBA

Death of King George V. John Betjeman. NOBE

Death of Kings, The. Shakespeare. *Fr.* King Richard II, III, ii. GrRo
    ("Let's talk of graves, of worms, and epitaphs.") PPoe

Death of mine honor, with the city's fool! Ben Jonson. *Fr.* Volpone, II, iii. SCP-1

Death of Queer Jane, The, 2 *versions. Unknown.* AmFP

Death of Robin Hood, The. Eugene Field. PoTa

Death of Samuel Adams, The. *Unknown.* AmFP

Death of Sir Nihil, book the *n*th. Tywater. Richard Wilbur. ConAP

Death of the Ball Turret Gunner, The. Randall Jarrell. CoPAm; InPK; IPWM; NoAM; NOBA; NowV; PPP; PSN; SoSe; VGW; WIF

Death of the Bird, The. A. D. Hope. MAuV

Death of the Craneman, The. Alfred Hayes. NCSH

Death of the Epileptic Poet Yesenin, The. Aram Boyajian. NeAC

Death of the Hired Man, The. Robert Frost. IPWM

Death of the Novel, The. David Young. AmPA

Death of the Sports-car Driver, The. Jonathan Aaron. MiP

Death of Venus, The. Robert Creeley. NOBA; PiAm

Death of Warren, The. Epes Sargent. BTTM

Death Snips Proud Men. Carl Sandburg. BBGO

Death Songs. L. V. Mack. PoBA

Death stands above me, whispering low. On Death. Walter Savage Landor. BBGO; NOBE

Death Sting Me Blues. *Unknown.* BluL

Death Takes Only a Minute. Agnes Pratt. VW

Death Terrible in Countenance. Thomas Dekker. *Fr.* Dekker His Dream. SCP-2

Death the Leveller. James Shirley. *See* Glories of Our Blood and State, The.

Death, thou wast once an uncouth hideous thing. Death. George Herbert. SCP-1

Death, though I see him not, is near. Age. Walter Savage Landor. InPK

Death to Van Gogh's Ear! Allen Ginsberg. VGW

Death Valley Blues. *Unknown.* BluL

Death, where is thy victory! To Death. Shelley. MBPR

Death Words. Les A. Murray. *Fr.* Walking to the Cattle-Place. CAAT

Deaths and Pretty Cousins. David Campbell. CAAP

Death's Jest Book, *sels.* Thomas Lovell Beddoes.
    Bridal Song ("We have bathed, . . ."), *fr.* IV, iii. GBL
    Sibilla's Dirge, *fr.* V, iv. NOBE
    Song from the Waters, *fr.* I, iv. NOBE
    Song: "Old Adam, the carrion crow," *fr.* V, iv. OBP
    Wolfram's Dirge, *fr.* II, ii. NOBE

Deaths of Paragon, The. John Woods. IPWM

Deathward. John Lyle Donaghy. BIrV

Deathwatch. Michael S. Harper. AmPA; PoBA

Debate of the Body and the Soul, The, *abr. Unknown.* PAIC

Debate: Question, Quarry, Dream. Robert Penn Warren. VGW

Debt, The. Paul Laurence Dunbar. SS

Deceased. Cid Corman. VGW

Deceitful Brownskin Blues. *Unknown.* BluL

December. James Schuyler. NoAM

December. Gary Snyder. InPS

December 18th. Anne Sexton. *Fr.* Eighteen Days without You. CAPP

December 15, 1811. Poem for My Family: Hazel Griffin and Victor Hernandez Cruz. June Jordan. BPo; RiTi

December Night. W. S. Merwin. CAPP

December Sky, The. A. G. Sobin. HeS

Decidedly the crocus. For the Spring Being. Albert Howard Carter. AATT

Decision. Theodore Roethke. VGW

Deck the Halls, *with music. Unknown.* BLSH

Decline and Fall. John Frederick Nims. CoPAm

Decorate the carcass. Song to Be Attached. Hollis Summers. CoPAm

Decorating Problem. Sonya Dorman. RiTi

Decrepit old gas man named Peter, A. Limerick. *Unknown.* SoSe

Dede's Return to New Mexico. Summer Brenner. RiTi

Dedicated Dancing Bull and the Water Maid, The, *sel.* Stevie Smith.
  "Hop hop, thump thump." WPE

Dedication: "Bob Southey! You're a poet—poet-laureate." Byron. *Fr.* Don Juan. MBPR
  ("Bob Southey! You're a poet—poet-laureate.") PPoe

Dedication: "Memory of one particular hour, The." Wordsworth. *Fr.* The Prelude, IV. BoReV

Dedication to a Book of Stories Selected from the Irish Novelists, The. W. B. Yeats. OBP

Dedication to Leigh Hunt, Esq. Keats. MBPR

Dedication to My Wife, A. T. S. Eliot. BoLoP

Dedication to the Final Confrontation. Lloyd M. Corbin, Jr. PoBA

Dedicatory: "Somewhere, sometime, in an April twilight." Willa Cather. WPE

Deduction. *Unknown. See* Burlesque of Lope de Vega.

Dee dee dee dee dee wee weee eeeeee wee we. Communication in Whi-te. Don L. Lee. BPo

Deedle, deedle, dumpling, my son John. Mother Goose. MG

Deep in Deering Oaks. Hard Edge of Beauty. Floyd C. Stuart. FAF

Deep in the back ways of my mind I see them. My Great-Grandfather's Slaves. Wendell Berry. TCP

Deep in the forest there is a pond. After the Anonymous Swedish. Jim Harrison. VGW

Deep in the leafy fierceness of the wood. Apollo and Daphne. Yvor Winters. PiAm

Deep in the shady sadness of a vale. Hyperion; a Fragment. Keats. MBPR

Deep in the winter plain, two armies. Two Armies. Stephen Spender. OxBTC

Deep in their roots, all flowers keep the light. Theodore Roethke. POL

Deep in Winter. Ted Kooser. HeS

Deep in your cheeks. Origins. Keorapetse Kgositsile. PoBA

Deep River ("Deep river, my home is over Jordan"). *Unknown.* BLSH, *with music;* BPo

Deep Spring. *Unknown.* AmFP

Deep-Sworn Vow, A. W. B. Yeats. PSN; TCP

Deeper than sleep but not so deep as death. Night Feeding. Muriel Rukeyser. NMM; WPE

Deepest Sensuality, The. D. H. Lawrence. NoAM

Deer among Cattle. James Dickey. TCP; TSWA

Deer carcass hangs from a rafter, The. Gathering the Bones Together. Gregory Orr. AmPA

Deer feed on. Upon Leaving the Parole Board Hearing. Conyus. PoBA

Deer Hunt. Judson Jerome. CoPAm; RFM

Deer Isle. Philip Booth. VGW

Deer Lay Down Their Bones, The. Robinson Jeffers. PiAm

Deere to my soule, then leave me not forsaken. Henry Constable. *Fr.* Diana. AAS

Defeated Victor, The. Horst Bienek, *tr. fr. German.* LP

Defence of Guenevere, The. William Morris. PAIC; VPC

Defence of the Alamo, The. Joaquin Miller. BTTM

Defiled Is My Name Full Sore. *At. to* Anne Boleyn. WPE

Definition for Blk/ Children. Sonia Sanchez. PoBA

Definition of Blue. John Ashbery. Epi

Definition of Love, The. Andrew Marvell. AnMo; BoLoP; GBL; InPK; InPS; LoAs; MetP; NOBE

Definition of Nature. Eugene Redmond. PoBA

Deftly admiral, cast your fly. Song. W. H. Auden. PSN

Degas. Paul Monette. AmPA

Deirdre. James Stephens. NoAM

Dejection; an Ode. Samuel Taylor Coleridge. Epi; MBPR, 3 *versions;* NOBE; PPP
  New Moon, The, *sel.* FSFS

Dekker His Dream, *sels.* Thomas Dekker.
  Death Terrible in Countenance. SCP-2
  Extremities of Cold in Hell, The. SCP-2

Delay. Elizabeth Jennings. InPK; OxBTC

Delia. Samuel Daniel. *See* To Delia.

Delia Holmes ("Delia, Delia, why didn't you run?). *At. to* "Whistling Bill" Ruff. AmFP

Delicate Bird Who is Flying Up Our Asses, The. Marvin Bell. NVAP

Delicate young Negro stands, A. Anonymous Drawing. Donald Justice. HeIP

Delight in Disorder. Robert Herrick. AnMo; HeIP; InPK; InPS; NOBE; PBMP; PPoe; PPP

Delight Song of Tsoai-Talee, The. N. Scott Momaday. CDW

Delightful, book, your trip. Aoibhinn, A Leabhrain, Do Thriall. *Unknown, tr. by* Flann O'Brien. BIrV

Delineaments of the Giants, The. William Carlos Williams. *Fr.* Paterson. NoAM

Delirium in Vera Cruz. Malcolm Lowry. OxBTC

Delirium of arms. Apology for the Fall. E. R. Cole. AATT

Deliver us for thy descent. John Donne. *Fr.* A Litany. SCP-1

Deliverance, The. Ralph Knevet. SCP-2

Delivering Lambs. David Campbell. MAuV

Delivery, The. Hollis Summers. CoPAm

Delta Traveller. Charles Wright. AmPA

Demeanour. *Unknown.* OxBChV

Demon Lover, The. Adrienne Rich. IHMS

Demon Lover, The. *Unknown.* AIW; MAT; PBMP
  (Daemon Lover, The.) SLP
  (House Carpenter, The.) AmFP; RDB, *with music;* WIF
  (James Harris.) PeBB

Demonstration, The, *sel.* Thomas Traherne.
  "Highest things are easiest to be shown, The." SCP-2

Denali Road. John Haines. PPoD

Denial, A. Elizabeth Barrett Browning. GBL

Denial. George Herbert. BoReV; NOBE

Denied the shelter of air and the power. A Broken Gull. John Moore. NCSH

Dented spider like a snow drop white, A. In White. Robert Frost. WIF

Dentist, A. *Unknown.* FaBoCo

Dentists continue to water their lawns even in the rain.   The Great Society.   Robert Bly.   NoAM

Deo Gracias.   *Unknown.*   OxBM

Deo gracias, Anglia.   The Agincourt Carol.   *Unknown.*   OxBM

Deor.   *Unknown, tr. fr. Anglo-Saxon by* Kemp Malone.   PAIC

Depairt, depairt, depairt.   Lament of the Master of Erskine.   Alexander Scott.   GBL

Departmental   Robert Frost.   HeIP; InPK; NOBA; WIF

Departure.   Elizabeth Hanson.   NPW

Departure.   Coventry Patmore.   The Unknown Eros, I, viii.   NOBE

Departure of the Women, The.   Nancy Mairs.   NPW

Departure's Girl-Friend.   W. S. Merwin.   ConAP

Depot Blues ("Standing at the station").   *Unknown.*   BluL

Depot Blues ("Well look a-here, honey").   *Unknown.*   AmFP

Depressed by a Book of Bad Poetry, I Walk Toward an Unused Pasture and Invite the Insects to Join Me.   James Wright.   ConAP; TH

Depression, *sel.*   Charles Reznikoff.
   "Simple soul, who so early in the morning."   CTBA

Depression.   William Witherup.   NowV

Depression: My Father Speaks to My Mother.   Dick Allen.   FAF

Deprived of his enemy, shrugged to a standstill.   John Berryman.   *Fr.* Dream Songs.   CAPP; PiAm

Der Deitcher's Dog, *with music.*   Septimus Winner.   PSoN

Deranged.   Padraic Fiacc.   PFIr

Derby Ram, The.   *Unknown.*   AmFP; GBP

Dere's No Hidin' Place Down Dere.   *Unknown.*   BPo

Derricks.   R. R. Cuscaden.   ANTL

Des plu sages de la tere.   Four Wise Men on Edward II's Reign.   *Unknown.*   OxBM

Descend, silent spirit.   Prayer to the Snowy Owl.   John Haines.   BoAnP

Descent, The.   William Carlos Williams.   PiAm

Descent from the Cross.   "Michael Field."   WPE

Descent of Odin, The; an Ode from the Norse Tongue.   Thomas Gray.   LAuP

Descent of the Vulture, The.   Marya Zaturenska.   WPE

Descent of Winter, The (Section 10/30).   William Carlos Williams.   InPK

Deschutes River.   Raymond Carver.   NVAP

Description of a City Shower, A.   Swift.   AnMo; HeIP; MAT; PPoD; PPP;
   Cat and the Rain, The, 4 *ll.*   PCat

Description of a Good Boy, The.   Henry Dixon.   OxBChV

Description of an Author's Bedchamber, A.   Goldsmith.   BIrV

Description of the Contrarious Passions in a Lover.   Petrarch, *tr. fr. Italian by* Sir Thomas Wyatt.   Sonnets to Laura: To Laura in Life, CIV.   PAIC
   ("I find [*or* fynde] no peace, and all my war is done.")   AAS; PPoe

Description of the Morning, A.   Swift.   AnMo; HeIP; InPS; NOBE; PAIC; PPP; Prf; SoSe

Desert.   Del Marie Rogers.   NPW

Desert in the Sea.   Brian Swann.   AmPA

Desert moves out on half the horizon, The.   The Supper after the Last.   Galway Kinnell.   NOBA

Desert Places.   Robert Frost.   IPWM; PiAm; PPoD; PPP; NCSH; NoAM; NOBA

Deserted Farms Poem.   Bruce Severy.   VW

Deserted House, The.   Mary Elizabeth Coleridge.   RAE

Deserted Mountain, The.   *Unknown, tr. fr. Irish by* John Montague.   BIrV

Deserted Village, The.   Goldsmith.   LAuP
   *Sels.*

   "O luxury! Thou curst by Heaven's decree."   BIrV
   Sweet Auburn.   NOBE

Deserted Village, The.   Robin Hyde.   WPE

Design.   Robert Frost.   AnMo; HeIP; InPK; InPS; NoAM; NOBA; PBMP; PiAm; PPP; SoSe; WIF

Design, The.   Clarence Major.   PoBA

Desire.   Samuel Taylor Coleridge.   MBPR

Desire.   Sir Philip Sidney.   *See* Astrophel and Stella: Sonnet CIX

Desk, The.   Cid Corman.   VGW

Desolation Row.   Bob Dylan.   InPS; WIF

Despair.   Denise Levertov.   RiTi

Despair is big with friends I love.   Consequences.   William Meredith.   NoAM

Desperate Measure, A.   Nigel Dennis.   WIF

Despisals.   Muriel Rukeyser.   NMM; Prf

Despot's heel is on thy shore, The.   Maryland, My Maryland!   James Ryder Randall.   BTTM; PSoN

Destinations.   Josephine Jacobsen.   WPE

Destruction of Letters.   Babette Deutsch.   WPE

Destruction of Sennacherib, The.   Byron.   AIW; AKE; BTTM; PBMP; SFF

Destruction of the Bastille.   Samuel Taylor Coleridge.   MBPR

Determination.   John Henrik Clarke.   PoBA

Determinism.   *Unknown.*   FaBoCo

Detestable race, continue to expunge yourself, die out.   Apostrophe to Man.   Edna St. Vincent Millay.   PBMP; SBG

Detroit.   Donald Hall.   ANTL

Developing Curious Survival Patterns against Winter Saltwinds The.   Lyn Lifshin.   FAF

Devil Got My Woman.   *Unknown.*   BluL

Devil, having nothing else to do, The.   On Lady Poltagrue, a Public Peril.   Hilaire Belloc.   FaBoCo; POL

Devil, Maggot and Son.   *Unknown, tr. fr. Irish by* Frank O'Connor.   SoSe

Devilish Mary.   *Unknown.*   AmFP

Devil's Advice to Story-Tellers, The.   Robert Graves.   NoAM

Devil's Bag, The.   James Stephens.   PFIr; PoTa

Devil's Law-Case, The *sel.*   John Webster.
   Vanitas Vanitatum, *fr.* V, iv.   NOBE; OBP

Devil's Nine Questions, The.   *Unknown.*   AmFP

Devil's Thoughts, The.   Robert Southey *and* Samuel Taylor Coleridge.   FaBoCo

Devoide of reason, thrale to foolish ire.   Thomas Lodge, *after* Pierre de Ronsard.   Phillis XXXI.   AAS

Devotion   Thomas Campion.   NOBE
   ("Follow your saint, follow with accents sweet.")   AAS

Devouring Time, blunt thou the lion's paw.   Sonnets, XIX.   Shakespeare.   Epi; MAT

Dew.   Jennifer Maiden.   CAAP

Dew-Bite.   *Unknown.*   ECBV

Dew was falling fast, the stars began to blink, The.   The Pet Lamb.   Wordsworth.   OxBChV

Dey is times in life when Nature.   When de Co'n Pone's Hot.   Paul Laurence Dunbar.   AmVN

Dey was talkin' in de cabin, dey was talkin' in de hall.   When Dey 'Listed Colored Soldiers.   Paul Laurence Dunbar.   BPo

Dey's a so't o' threatenin' feelin' in de blowin' of de breeze.   Soliloquy of a Turkey.   Paul Laurence Dunbar.   BPo

Dharma law.   Chorus.   Jack Kerouac.   *Fr.* Mexico City Blues.   PiAm

Dial Tone, The.   Howard Nemerov.   NowV

Dialogue.   Agathias Scholasticus, *tr. fr. Greek by* Dudley Fitts.   OLR

Dialogue.   George Herbert.   BoReV

Dialogue, A.   Pope.   POL

Dialogue. James Tipton. HeS

Dialogue after Enjoyment. Abraham Cowley. BoLoP

Dialogue between Araphil and Castara, A. William Habington. SCP-2

Dialogue between the Resolved Soul and Created Pleasure, A. Andrew Marvell. BoReV; PAIC

Dialogue between the Soul and Body, A. Andrew Marvell. MetP; PAIC; PPP; SCP-1

Dialogue betwixt [or between] Time and a Pilgrim, A. Aurelian Townsend. NOBE; SCP-2

Dialogue 4 1 Voice Only. Doug Fetherling. NeAC

Dialogue of Absence 'twixt Lucasia and Orinda, A. Katherine Philips. SCP-2

Dialogue of Self and Soul, A. W. B. Yeats. NoAM; PAIC

Dialogue of Watching, A. Kenneth Rexroth. MiP

Diamond, The. Daniel Moore. MIT

Diamond Body. "Hugh MacDiarmid." TwMBP

Diamond Cut Diamond. Ewart Milne. ECBV; PCat

Diamond of a morning, A. Morning Song. Sara Teasdale. Moon

Diana, *sels*. Henry Constable.
"Deere to my soule, then leave me not forsaken." AAS
"My lady's presence makes the roses red." WIF
"To live in hell, and heaven to behold." AAS
"Whilst eccho cryes, what shall become of mee." AAS

Dianae Sumus in Fide. Catullus, *tr. fr. Latin by* Horace Gregory. Moon

Diane. Stewart McIntosh. SLP

Diapered in hospital linen. The Recovery Room: Lying-in. Helen Chasin. IHMS

Diaphenia. Henry Chettle. NOBE

Diary of a Church Mouse. John Betjeman. OxBTC

Dick and Jane. Judith Kroll. AmPA

Dick and Will and Charles and I. Autumn. Elizabeth Madox Roberts. PoTa

Dick is the one with the weenie. Dick and Jane. Judith Kroll. AmPA

Dick Swash. John Taylor. SCP-2

Dick Szymanski. Ogden Nash. SPo

Dick Turpin and Black Bess. *Unknown.* AmFP

Dictionary Is an *His*torian, The: A Found Political Poem. Judith McCombs. IHMS

Dictum: For a Masque of Deluge. W. S. Merwin. NoAM

Did all the lets and bars appear. The March into Virginia. Herman Melville. PiAm

Did ever lord such noble house maintain. Edward Taylor. Preparatory Meditations: First Series, IX. SCP-2

Did he strike soundings off Vecta Insula? Angle-Land. David Jones. The Anathemata, III. NoAM; TwMBP

Did I, my lines intend for publick view. The Introduction. Countess of Winchilsea. SBG

Did Not. Thomas Moore. BoLoP

Did our best moment last. Emily Dickinson. NOBA

Did the harebell loose her girdle. Emily Dickinson. PiAm

Did the people of Viet Nam. What Were They Like? Denise Levertov. HeIP; PPoD; TCP; VGW; WPE

"Did they dare, did they dare to slay Eoghan Ruadh O'Neill?" Lament for the Death of Eoghan Ruadh O'Neill. Thomas Osborne Davis. PFIr

Did they send me away from my cat and my wife. Gunner. Randall Jarrell. OFD

Did you ever, ever, ever. *Unknown.* GBP

Did you ever hear about Cocaine Lil? Cocaine Lil and Morphine Sue. *Unknown.* GBP; MAT; MiP; PeBB

Did you ever hear of good Earl Brand. Earl Brand. *Unknown.* PeBB

Did you ever hear tell of sweet Betsy from Pike. Sweet Betsy From Pike. *Unknown.* PeBB

Did you ever see an alligator. Arlo Will. Edgar Lee Masters. *Fr.* Spoon River Anthology. PBMP

Did you ever see two Yankees. Give My Regards to Broadway. George M. Cohan. BLSo; FSN

Did you go at all to Chicago? The Stockyard. J. C. Squire. OxBTC

Did you hear? The Old Warrior Terror. Alice Walker. NVAP

Did you hear of the curate who mounted his mare. The Priest and the Mulberry Tree. Thomas Love Peacock. *Fr.* Crotchet Castle. PoTa

Did you see the sun blotted from sky. Baltimore Eclipse. Charles Plymell. MIT

Did You See the *Times* Today? Louis Wyse. SFF

Did you think you could hide from me? A Song for Sigmund Freud. Kelly Cherry. PPoD

Diddie Wa Diddie. *Unknown.* BluL

Diddlety, diddlety, dumpty. *Unknown.* MG

Didn't I teach you that? To My Former Student on the Occasion of Birth. Madeline Bass. WBN

Didn't My Lord Deliver Daniel? *Unknown.* WIF

Dido. John Ashbery. *Fr.* Two Sonnets. CAPP; VGW

Didymus. Louis MacNeice. LoAs

Diella, *sels*. Richard Lynche. AAS
"But thou my deere sweet-sounding lute be still," XVI.
"What sugred termes, what all-perswading arte," IV.

Difference, The. Tadhg Dall O'Huiginn, *tr. fr. Irish by* Robin Flower. BIrV

Difference between despair, The. Emily Dickinson. NoAM

Difference of Zoos, A. Gregory Corso. VGW

Different Image, A. Dudley Randall. BPo; NoAM

Different Persuasions. Marge Piercy. *See* Nothing More Will Happen.

Difficult achievement for true lovers, A. The Starred Coverlet. Robert Graves. BuTh; LoAs

"Difficult ordinary happiness." In the Woods. Adrienne Rich. PiAm

Difficult to recall an emotion that is dead. The Patient Is Rallying. Weldon Kees. AnMo

Difficulty to think at the end of day, The. A Rabbit As King of the Ghosts. Wallace Stevens. PBMP

Dig My Grave. *Unknown.* AmFP

Digging. Seamus Heaney. BIrV; MPo

Digging. Edward Thomas. FSFS; OxBTC

Digging for China. Richard Wilbur. BuTh; NCSH; PiAm; TH

Digging for Indians. Gary Gildner. AmPA

Diggle Mill. Glyn Hughes. LP

Dilemma. David Ignatow. VGW

Diligent in the burnt fields above the sea. Find. Josephine Miles. WPE

Dill. Marie Harris. MMD

Dillar, a dollar, A,/ A ten o'clock scholar. Mother Goose. MG

Dilly Song, The. *Unknown. See* Carol of the Numbers.

Dim as the borrowed beams of moon and stars. Reason and Religion. Dryden. *Fr.* Religio Laici. BoReV

Dimple. Colman Barks. *Fr.* Body Poems. NVAP

Dimpling in his cheeks. Smile at the Birdie. Polly Mann. NPW

Dinah and Villikens, *with music. Unknown.* RDB

Dinch me, dark God, having smoked me out. John Berryman. *Fr.* Dream Songs. CAPP

Diner. A. R. Ammons. POL

Diner, The. Gloria Bussel Koster. NPW

Ding, Dong, Bell. Eve Merriam. *Fr.* The Inner-City Mother Goose. IPWM

Ding, dong, bell/ Pussy's in the well! Mother Goose. MG

Dingman's Marsh. John Moore. NCSH

Dingy donkey, formal and unchanged, A. A Fable. John Hookham Frere. FaBoCo

Dinner, The. Gregory Orr. POL

Dinner Guest: Me. Langston Hughes. BPo; SS

Dinoland. Thomas Reiter. PPoD

Dinosaur Bones, The. Carl Sandburg. TH

Dinosaur Tracks in Beit Zayit. Shirley Kaufman. FiCP

Dip, dip, allebadar. *Unknown.* GBP

Dip, dip, dip. *Unknown.* GBP

Dipsychus, *sels.* Arthur Hugh Clough.
  "As I sat at the café, I said to myself," *fr.* Pt. II, sc. ii; *also in* Spectator ab Extra. VPC
  (How Pleasant It Is to Have Money.) NOBE
  " 'There is no God,' the wicked saith," *fr.* Pt. I, sc. v. VPC
  (There Is No God.) NOBE

Diptych. Velma West Sykes. IHMS

Dirce. Walter Savage Landor. *Fr.* Pericles and Aspasia, CCXXX. GBL; NOBE

Dirdum drum. The Cat's Song. *Unknown.* GBP

Direction. Barbara Guest. WPE

Direction. Roberta Hill. CDW

Direction. Alonzo Lopez. VW

Direction, The. May Miller. PPoD

Direction/ is in you. The Tree. E. R. Cole. AATT

Directions. William Matthews. AmPA

Directions that you took. Old Haven. Jean Garrigue. WPE

Directions to the Nomad. James Welch. CDW

Directive. Robert Frost. MAT; NoAm; NOBA; PiAm; PPP

Director of the Museum, The. Roderick Watson. MIS

Dirge: "Body lies under the ground." Gavin Bantock. OxBTC

Dirge, A: "Call for the robin-redbreast and the wren." John Webster. *See* Call for the Robin Redbreast. . .

Dirge: "Glories of our blood and state, The." James Shirley. *See* Glories of Our Blood and State.

Dirge: "I make this dirge for you Miss Mary Binning I miss you." *Unknown, tr. fr. Hawaiian by* Armand Schwerner. RRA

Dirge: "It is the endless dance of the dead." Quincy Troupe. PoBA

Dirge: "1-2-3 was the number he played but today the number came 3-2-1." Kenneth Fearing. HeIP; InPK

Dirge, A: "Rough wind, that moanest loud." Shelley. GrRo; InPK; NOBE; VoPo

Dirge, A: "Why were you born when the snow was falling?" Christina Rossetti. SBG; VPC

Dirge for Fidele. Shakespeare. *See* Fear No More the Heat O' the Sun.

Dirge for the Year. Shelley. FSFS

Dirge in "Cymbeline." William Collins.
  *See* Song from Shakespeare's Cymbelyne, A.

Dirge without Music. Edna St. Vincent Millay. NoAM; SBG

Dirt Road. Tom Hennen. HeS

Dirty Colours of Her Kiss Have Just, The. E. E. Cummings. Epi

Dirty Dozens, The. *Unknown.* BluL

Dirty socks in dirty sneakers. Sorting, Wrapping, Packing, Stuffing. James Schuyler. NoAM

Dirty Word, The. Karl Shapiro. InPK

Dis sun are hot. This Sun Is Hot. *Unknown.* BPo

Disabled. Wilfred Owen. InPS; NoAM; OxBTC; PoTa; PSN; VoPo

Disabled Debauchee, The. Earl of Rochester. BoLoP; PPP

Disappointment, The. Aphra Behn. SBG; SCP-2

Disaster. Charles Stuart Calverley. SpRo

Disasters numb within us, The. Life at War. Denise Levertov. NMM; VGW

Discipline. George Herbert. BoReV; NOBE; PAIC; SCP-1

Disconnection, The. Rita Mae Brown. IHMS

Disconsolate I/ from the thinning line. Witness to Death. Richmond Lattimore. VGW

Discontented Satyre, The. Thomas Lodge. TVS

Discontents in Devon. Robert Herrick. PAIC; POL

Discordants, *sel.* Conrad Aiken.
  "Music I heard with you was more than music, " I. NOBA (Bread and Music.) VoPo

Discovered an old rocking-horse in Woolworth's. You'd Better Believe Him. Brian Patten. LP

Discoveries of Fire, The. Lucille Clifton. TSWA

Discovering. Sharon Scott. JB

Discovering Parts of a Body. Rhyll McMaster. CAAP

Discovery, The. Monk Gibbon. PFir

Discovery. Myra Cohn Livingston. LCL

Discovery, The. J. C. Squire. OFD

Discovery of the Pacific, The. Thom Gunn. HeIP; MIT

Disdaining butterflies. The Woman Who Loved Worms. Colette Inez. AATT; NMM; RiTi; WBN

Diseases of the Moon. Doug Fetherling. NeAC; POL

Dishonest Mailmen, The. Robert Creeley. PiAm

Dishonest Miller, The. *Unknown.* AmFP

Disillusionment of Ten O'Clock. Wallace Stevens. InPK; InPS; PPod; PPoe; SFF

Dismantled Ship, The. Walt Whitman. NoAM

Dismissing reports and men, he put pressure on the wax. Offa's Laws. Geoffrey Hill. *Fr.* Mercian Hymns. PSN

Dispatch Number Nine. Doug Fetherling. NeAC

Dispatch Number Sixteen. Doug Fetherling. NeAC

Dispatch Number Sixty. Doug Fetherling. NeAC

Display thy breasts, my Julia: there let me. Upon Julia's Breasts. Robert Herrick. SCP-1

Displays of Skill: The Bat. Ruth Herschberger. WBN

Dispossessed, The. John Berryman. VGW

Dispraise of Absalom, The. *Unknown, tr. fr. Irish by* Robin Flower. BIrV

Disqualification. Elizabeth Brewster. MMD

Disquieting Muses, The. Sylvia Plath. NMM; SBG

Distance back is greater, The. Return. Michael Anania. HeS

Distance brings proportion. From here. Tao in the Yankee Stadium Bleachers. John Updike. SPo

Distance comes between us like a knife. Leaving the Prison. Joseph Bruchac. FAF

Distance decieves. Novelists mistake. Day Sailing. David R. Slavitt. CoPAm

Distance doesn't matter, Francisco. Extracts: from the Journal of Elisa Lynch. Maura Stanton. AmPA

Distance from the Sea, A. Weldon Kees. NoAM

Distance is swept by the smooth. Radar. Alan Ross. NowV

Distances, The. W. S. Merwin. NOBA

Distances, The. Charles Olson. PiAm

Distances. Linda Pastan. RiTi

Distances They Keep, The. Howard Nemerov. BoAnP

Distant Drum, The. Calvin C. Hernton. CTBA

Distant Orgasm, The. James Tate. AmPA

Distant Winter, The. Philip Levine. VGW

District, The: Both Sides of Chandler River. Ted Enslin. FAF

Disturbances. Anthony Thwaite. MPo

Disturbing the Tarantula. Christopher Middleton. TwMBP

Disused Temple, The. Norman Cameron. OxBTC

Dithyramb, A. John Hall. SCP-2

Ditty. Roger Hecht. NowV

Dive for dreams. E. E. Cummings. OLR

Diver. Robert Francis. SPo

Diver, The. Robert Hayden. BPo

Diversions for an Unhappy Princess. *Unknown. Fr.* The Squyer of Lowe Degre. OxBM

Diverting History of John Gilpin, The. William Cowper. LAuP

Dives and Lazarus. *Unknown.* AmFP

Divided. Jean Ingelow. SpRo

Divina Commedia, *sels.* Dante, *tr. fr. Italian.*
  Inferno.
    Guido da Montefeltro, *fr.* XXVII, *tr. by* Longfellow. Epi.
    "Like fire-flies that the peasant on the hill," *fr.* XXVI, *tr. by* Laurence Binyon. Prf
    Ulysses, *fr.* XXVI, *tr. by* Longfellow. Epi

Divina Commedia (*poems introductory to* Longfellow's *tr. of the* Divine Comedy, I–VI), *sel.* Longfellow.
  "Oft have I seen at some cathedral door," I. IPWM; PAIC

Divine Image, A ("Cruelty has a human heart"). Blake. MBPR

Divine Image, The ("To mercy pity peace and love"). Blake. *Fr.* Songs of Innocence. BoReV; LAuP; MBPR; NOBE; PPP

Divine Insect, The. John Hall Wheelock. PPoD

Divine Love. Michael Benedikt. AmPA; ConAP

Divine Love. *Unknown.* OxBM

Divine Lover, The. Phineas Fletcher. *Fr.* The Divine Wooer. BoReV

Divine Thalia, strike the harmonious lute. On the Soft and Gentle Motions of Eudora. Anne Killigrew. SCP-2

Divine Wooer, The, *sel.* Phineas Fletcher.
  Divine Lover, The. BoReV

Divinely Superfluous Beauty. Robinson Jeffers. HeIP; PiAm

Diviners, The. Mary Oliver. WPE

Diving. Shiro Murano, *tr. fr. Japanese by* Ichiro Kono *and* Rikutaro Fukuda. SPo

Diving into the Wreck. Adrienne Rich. NoAM; NOBA

Divorce. Bink Noll. MAT

Divorce. Siv Widerberg, *tr. fr. Swedish by* Verne Moberg. CTBA

Divorce of a Lover, The ("Divorce me nowe good death"). George Gascoigne. AAS

Dixie ("I wish I was in the land of cotton"), *with music.* Daniel Decatur Emmett. BLSH; BLSo
  (Dixie's Land.) PSoN

Dixie ("Southrons, hear your country call you!"). Albert Pike. BTTM

Do as they do in the Isle of Man. The Isle of Man. *Unknown.* GBP

Do I sleep? do I dream? Further Language from Truthful James. Bret Harte. FaBoCo

Do Li A. *Unknown.* GBP

Do, Lord, Remember Me. *Unknown.* AmFP

Do not account that for thine own. Isabella Whitney. *Fr.* A Sweet Nosegay, or Pleasant Posy. WPE

Do not bathe her in blood. An Abortion. Frank O'Hara. CoPAm

Do not be a lost dog. Dogs of Santiago. Eugene McCarthy. BoAnP

Do not conceal thy radiant eyes. To Cynthia: On Concealment of Her Beauty. Sir Francis Kynaston. NOBE

Do Not Dream. Natan Zach, *tr. fr. Hebrew by* Jon Silkin. BuTh

Do Not Expect Again. C. Day Lewis. NoAM
  ("Do not expect again a phoenix hour.") OxBTC

Do Not Go Gentle into That Good Night. Dylan Thomas. BuTh; HeIP; InPK; InPS; IPWM; NoAM; NOBE; OxBTC; PAIC; PBMP; PPoD; SoSe; TCP; WIF

Do not hold my few years. So We've Come at Last to Freud. Alice Walker. IHMS

Do not let any woman read this verse! Deirdre. James Stephens. NoAM

Do not lift him from the bracken. William Aytoun. *Fr.* The Widow of Glencoe. SLP

Do not look for him. Elegy. Leonard Cohen. HeIP

Do not think I am not grateful for your small. Gratitude. Louise Glück. CAAP

Do not weep, maiden, for war is kind. War is Kind, I. Stephen Crane. NOBA; PAIC; PiAm; VoPo; WIF

Do Nothing Till You Hear from Me. David Henderson. PoBA

Do skyscrapers ever grow tired. Skyscrapers. Rachel Field. ECBV

Do the Dead Know What Time It Is? Kenneth Patchen. CoPAm; PAIC

Do ye hear the children weeping, O my brothers. The Cry of the Children. Elizabeth Barrett Browning. VPC

Do ye ken hoo to fush for the salmon? Master and Man. Sir Henry Newbolt. OxBTC

Do you/ dig ray/ charles. Ray Charles. Sam Cornish. NVAP

Do you ask me what I think of. What I Think of Hiawatha. J. W. Morris. SpRo

Do you ask what the birds say? Answer to a Child's Question. Samuel Taylor Coleridge. ECBV; OxBChV

Do you ever think of me, Kitty Kline? Kitty Kline. *Unknown.* AmFP

Do you hear, sir? John Webster. *Fr.* The White Devil. SCP-2

Do you know, I would quietly. Rainer Maria Rilke, *tr. fr. German by* M. D. Herter Norton. OLR

Do you know that your soul is of my soul such part. To My Son. Margaret Johnston Griffin. SoSe

Do you know what. Fancy. Robert Creeley. NOBA

Do you look for a rainbow, Love, in this wet weather. Wet Weather. Patricia Low. VGW

Do You Love Me? Robert Watson. POL

"Do you not find something very strange about him?" The Assassination. Robert Hillyer. OFD

Do you remember/ How you won. To James. Frank Horne. *Fr.* Letters Found Near a Suicide. BPo; PAIC

Do you remember an inn. Tarantella. Hilaire Belloc. SpRo

Do You Remember That Night? *Unknown, tr. fr. Irish by* Eugene O'Curry. BIrV; PFIr

Do you remember, when you were first a child. Message from Home. Kathleen Raine. WPE

Docker. Seamus Heaney. NoAM

Dockery and Son (" 'Dockery was junior to you' "). Philip Larkin. NoAM

Doctor Black. John Blight. CAAP

Doctor, doctor, it fits real fine. Vet's Rehabilitation. Ray Durem. PoBA

Doctor Faustus, *sels.* Christopher Marlowe.
  "Ah, Faustus,/ Now hast thou but one bare hour [*or* hower] to live." HeIP; OBP; PAIC
  "Was this the face that launched a thousand ships?" GBL; HeIP

Doctor Faustus was a good man. Mother Goose. MG

Doctor Fell. Thomas Brown, *after the Latin of* Martial. FaBoCo

Doctor Foster went to Glo'ster. Mother Goose. MG

Doctor loves the patient, The. The Bed. A. D. Hope. NoAM

Dr. Potatohead Talks to Mothers. Judith Johnson Sherwin. NoAM

Dr. Sigmund Freud Discovers the Sea Shell. Archibald MacLeish. SoSe

Dr. Unlikely, we love you so. Horror Movie. Howard Moss. MiP

Doctor Who Sits at the Bedside of a Rat, The. Josephine Miles. CoPAm; VGW

Doctor's Story, The. Will M. Carleton. PoTa

Document, A. Judith Wright. MAuV

Documentary on Airplane Glue, A. David Henderson. MAT

Dodger, The. *Unknown.* AmFP; GBP

Dodo, The. Edward Kessler. PPoD

Dodo, The. Edward Lucie-Smith. POL

Dodona's Oaks Were Still.  Patrick MacDonogh.  PFIr

Does It Matter?  Siegfried Sassoon.  VoPo

Does man love Art? Man visits Art, but squirms.  The Chicago Picasso.  Gwendolyn Brooks.  *Fr.* Two Dedications.  BPo; Psy

Does nature bear a tyrant's breast?  John Langhorne.  *Fr.* Owen of Carron.  FaBoCo

Does the road wind up-hill all the way?  Up-Hill.  Christina Rossetti.  ECBV; IPWM; NOBE; PPP; SS; VPC; WPE

Does the typewriter type.  Truth.  Susan Fromberg Schaeffer.  IHMS

Dog, The.  A. Buttigieg.  RAE

Dog.  Lawrence Ferlinghetti.  CoPAm

Dog, The.  Valentin Iremonger.  BIrV

Dog.  John Crowe Ransom.  InPS

Dog Alive.  Harold Witt.  BoAnP

Dog and Tiger.  Eliezer Greenberg, *tr. fr. Yiddish by* Stanley Kunitz.  BoAnP

Dog at Night.  Louis Untermeyer.  MiP

Dog Beneath the Skin, The, *sels.*  W. H. Auden.  OxBTC
  Chorus: "The Summer holds: upon its glittering lake."
  Chorus: "You are the town and we are the clock."

Dog Creek Mainline.  Charles Wright.  AmPA

Dog-Days.  Amy Lowell.  FSFS

Dog fox rolls on his lolling tongue, The.  The Hunt.  Louis Kent.  SoSe

Dog Hospital.  Peter Wild.  AmPA

Dog howled and howled, The.  Alison Prince.  POL

Dog in the Quarry, A, *sel.*  Miroslav Holub, *tr. fr. Czech by* George Theiner *and* Ian Milner.
  "Day was so bright, The."  BoAnP

Dog is cousin to the wolf, but more acceptable, The.  Dog and Tiger.  Eliezer Greenberg, *tr. by* Stanley Kunitz.  BoAnP

Dog means dog. And cat means cat.  Blum.  Dorothy Aldis.  ECBV; LCL

Dog of Art, The.  Denise Levertov.  NoAM

Dog Parade, The.  Arthur Guiterman.  BoAnP

Dog Sacrifice at Lake Ronkonkoma.  William Heyen.  AmPA

Dog stops barking after Robinson has gone, The.  Robinson.  Weldon Kees.  AnMo; NoAM

Dog Talk.  Albert De Pietro.  AATT

Dog, the lightning frightened us, dark house and both of us.  Jim Harrison.  *Fr.* Ghazals.  InPS

Dog-Tired.  D. H. Lawrence.  BuTh

Dog-tired, suisired, will now my body down.  The Poet's Final Instructions.  John Berryman.  VGW

Dog trots freely in the street, The.  Dog.  Lawrence Ferlinghetti.  CoPAm

Dog will come when he is called, The.  Beasts and Birds.  Adelaide O'Keeffe.  OxBChV

Dogget Gap.  *Unknown.*  AmFP

Doggin' Me Around Blues.  *Unknown.*  BluL

Dogs and Wolves.  Sorley Maclean, *tr. fr. Gaelic by* Iain Crichton Smith.  SLP

Dogs Are Shakespearean, Children Are Strangers.  Delmore Schwartz.  NoAM

Dog's Best Friend Is His Illiteracy, A.  Ogden Nash.  BoAnP

Dog's Cold Nose, The.  Arthur Guiterman.  ECBV; PoTa

Dogs of Santiago.  Eugene McCarthy.  BoAnP

Dogwood flakes.  Variations Done for Gerald van de Wiele.  Charles Olson.  NoAM; NOBA

Doing, a Filthy Pleasure Is, and Short.  Petronius Arbiter, *tr. fr. Latin by* Ben Jonson.  BoLoP; WIF
  (Fragment of Petronius Translated, A.)  LoAS
  (Fragmentum Petronius Arbiter, Translated.)  HeIP

Doing my wash.  Wash Day.  Larry Mollin.  NeAC

Dolgelley Hotel, The.  Thomas Hughes.  FaBoCo

Doll, The.  Gregory Orr.  AmPA

Doll in the doll-maker's house, A.  The Dolls.  W. B. Yeats.  NoAM

Doll Poem ("Doll is sitting in a box").  Toi Derricotte.  NPW

Doll Thy Ale.  *Unknown.*  OxBM

Dolls, The.  W. B. Yeats.  NoAM

Doll's hair concealing, A.  Partial Resemblance.  Denise Levertov.  CoPAm

Dolls' Wash, The.  Juliana Horatia Ewing.  OxBChV

Dolor.  Theodore Roethke.  AnMo; CoPAm; HeIP; InPK; InPS; NoAM; PBMP; PPoD; SFF; TCP

Dolorous kno.  Koko Oloro.  Wole Soyinka.  BuTh

Dolphin.  Robert Lowell.  NOBA

Dolphin See Alone.  Richmond Lattimore.  BoAnP

*Dom Pedro,* The.  *Unknown.*  AmFP

Dome of Sunday, The.  Karl Shapiro.  NoAM

Domestic Duties.  Richard Emil Braun.  NoAM

Domestic Scene.  Michael Hartnett.  BIrV

Domination of Black.  Wallace Stevens.  PiAm

Don Juan.  Byron.  MBPR, *abr.*
  *Sels.*
  Dedication: "Bob Southey! You're a poet—poet-laureate."  MBPR
  ("Bob Southey! You're a poet—Poet laureate.")  PPoe
  Fragment: "I would to heaven that I were so much clay."  MBPR; OBP
  Growing Old, *fr.* I.  NOBE
  "I want a hero: an uncommon want," I.  MBPR
  Isles of Greece, The, *fr.* III.  BTTM; NOBE
  Modern Discoveries, *fr.* I.  OBP
  Moon Shot, *fr.* X.  OBP
  Race, fr. XIV.  OBP
  Seduction of Juan, The, *fr.* I.  OBP
  Sun Set, and Up Rose the Yellow Moon, The, *fr.* I.  Moon
  "To our theme.—The man who has stood on the Acropolis," *fr.* XI.  InPS
  " 'Twas on a summer's day—the sixth of June," *fr.* I.  PPP

Don Larsen's Perfect Game.  Paul Goodman.  SPo

Don 1958.  Alta.  MMD

Don Quixote, *sel.*  Thomas Durfey.
  "Sleep, sleep, poor youth! sleep, sleep in peace."  SCP-2

Donal Oge: Grief of a Girl's Heart.  *Unknown, tr. fr. Modern Irish by* Lady Gregory.  GBL; PFIr
  (Grief of a Girl's Heart, The, *shorter version.*)  OLR

Done is a battell on the dragon blak.  The Lord Is Risen.  William Dunbar.  BoReV; NOBE

Dong with a Luminous Nose, The.  Edward Lear.  FaBoCo

Donkey, The.  Gertrude Hinde.  ECBV

Donkey.  Vasko Popa, *tr. fr. Serbian by* Anne Pennington.  TSWA

Donkey, The.  Theodore Roethke.  ECBV

Donkey Riding.  *Unknown.*  RAE

Donkey sat down on the roadside, The.  Time Out.  John Montague.  BoAnP; PFIr

Donkeys.  Edward Field.  BoAnP

Don's Holiday.  G. Rostrevor Hamilton.  FaBoCo

Don't ask a geologist about rocks.  No More Soft Talk.  Diane Wakoski.  IHMS

Don't ask me if these knives are real.  Dreaming Winter.  James Welch.  VW

Don't Ask Me Who I Am.  James A. Randall, Jr.  BPo

Don't bother a bit, you are only a dream you are having.  A Real Question Calling for a Solution.  Robert Penn Warren.  PPP

Don't-Care.  *Unknown.*  ECBV; GBP

Don't care when you go.  Someday Baby.  *Unknown.*  BluL

Don't drive me out of my mind. Second Honeymoon. *Unknown, tr. by* Augustus Young. BIrV

Don't ever grab/ old crusty crab. The Crab. Conrad Aiken. BoAnP

Don't Fish in My Sea. *Unknown.* BluL

"Don't get the cart before the horse." Horseplay by Reverse Descartes. Merle Meeter. AATT

Don't know why I. Angola Question Mark. Langston Hughes. BPo

Don't let me lose you. How Tuesday Began. Kathleen Fraser. CTBA

Don't Let That Horse. Lawrence Ferlinghetti. TCP

Don't let them die out. Now Poem. For Us. Sonia Sanchez. PoBA

Don't lock me in wedlock, I want. About Marriage. Denise Levertov. NMM

Don't Look Now. J. C. Fogerty. PoRo

Don't love me, my sweet. Song of a Common Lover. Flavien Ranaivo, *tr. by* Alan Ryder. BuTh

Don't Put Me. Stanley Kiesel. HeS

Don't Steal. Ambrose Bierce. POL

Don't step/ so lightly. Break. The Cracks. Robert Creeley. ConAP

Don't talk to me no words. Relocation. Simon Ortiz. VW

Don't Tell Bad Dreams Says Tita's Mother. John Oliver Simon. NeAC

Don't Want No Hungry Woman. *Unknown.* BluL

Don't worry/ One night we'll find that deserted kinema. If Life's a Lousy Picture, Why Not Leave Before the End. Roger McGough. OxBTC

Don't worry baby. Broken Heart, Broken Machine. Richard E. Grant. PoBA

Don't you care for my love? she said bitterly. Intimates. D. H. Lawrence. BoLoP; PoTa

Don't you ever. Plaint Against the Fog. *Unknown.* AKE

Don't you let my good girl catch you here. Ain't No Tellin'. *Unknown.* BluL

Don'ts. D. H. Lawrence. NoAM

Dooley Is a Traitor. James Michie. OxBTC

Doom is dark and deeper than any sea-dingle. The Wanderer. W. H. Auden. NoAM

Doom of Devergoil, The, *sel.* Sir Walter Scott. Bonnie Dundee, *fr.* II, ii. RDB, *with music* (Bonnets o' Bonnie Dundee, The.) BTTM

Dooms menace from tumults. Who's immune. John Berryman. CAAP

Door, The. Robert Creeley. NoAM; VGW

Door, The. Miroslav Holub, *tr. fr. Czech by* Ian Milner *and* George Theiner. LP

Door, The. Mark Strand. NoAM

Door, The. Lewis Turco. CoPAm

Door, A: Per L'Universo. Idyll. Charles Tomlinson. TwMBP

Door a maze, The. Disturbing the Tarantula. Christopher Middleton. TwMBP

Door is before you again and the skrieking, The. The Door. Mark Strand. NoAM

Door it opened slowly, The. Story of Isaac. Leonard Cohen. GrRo; WIF

Door still swinging to, and girls revive, The. A Dream of Fair Women. Richard Wilbur. NoAM

Door sunk in a hillside, with a bolt, A. The Icehouse in Summer. Howard Nemerov. NoAM

Door to the Sun. Ralph J. Mills, Jr. HeS

Doors. Tom Clark. ConAP

Doors have opened and, The. Feature Time. Jerry Hammond. PPoD

Doors open, The/ and the heat undoes itself. In the Beach House. Anne Sexton. PPP

Doretha wore the short blue lace last night. The Reception. June Jordan. NMM

Dorlan's Home Walk. Arthur Guiterman. PoTa

Dorothy Q. Oliver Wendell Holmes. NOBA; PiAm

Dorset. John Betjeman. MPo

"Dorset Nose," The. Clive Sansom. MPo

Dossier, The. Michael McMahon. FAF

Dost thou know who made thee? The Lamb. Blake. *Fr.* Songs of Innocence. InPS

Double Axe, The. Anne Hazlewood-Brady. IHMS

Double-conscious sister in the veil. Madimba: Gwendolyn Brooks. Michael S. Harper. MIT

Double Exposure. Ian Young. NeAC

Double Lent has this your absence been, A. In the Wilderness. Albert Howard Carter. AATT

Double Monologue. Adrienne Rich. Psy

Double Shame, The. Stephen Spender. LoAs

Double Vision, The. C. Day Lewis. NoAM

Double Vision of Manannan, The. *Unknown, tr. fr. the Irish by* John Montague. BIrV

Doubt of Future Foes, The. Elizabeth I, Queen of England. WPE

Doubt of Martyrdom, A. Sir John Suckling. BoLoP; NOBE ("O for some honest lover's ghost.") SCP-2

Doubtless, sweet girl! the hissing lead. Lines Addressed to a Young Lady. Byron. MBPR

Doubts. Elizabeth Jennings. LP

Dough Roller Blues. *Unknown.* BluL

Douglas Tragedy, The. *Unknown.* IPWM; PeBB (Earl Brand.) AmFP; PeBB

Douglass was someone who. Frederick Douglass: 1817-1895. Langston Hughes. BPo

Dove, The. *Unknown.* GBP

Dove returns, The; it found no resting place. Where We Must Look for Help. Robert Bly. ConAP

Dover Beach. Matthew Arnold. AnMo; Epi; GrRo; HeIP: InPK; InPS; IRWM; MAT; NOBE; OBP; PAIC; PMBP; PFD; PPoD; PPoe; PPP; Prf; SFF; SoSe; VoPo

Dover Bitch, The. Anthony Hecht. MAT; NOBA; NowV; PAIC; PPP; SFF; VGW

Down/ Down into the fathomless depths. Black Is a Soul Joseph White. PoBA

Down a blackened alley. La Llorona. Greg Pape. AmPA

Down a broad river of the western wilds. Indian Woman's Death-Song. Felicia Dorothea Hemans. SBG

Down and Out. Langston Hughes. PiAm

Down at the Docks. Kenneth Koch. VGW

Down by the fallen fruit in the old orchard. Denise Levertov. *Fr.* The Coming Fall. TSWA

Down by the ocean side where ships were sailing. The Nightingales of Spring. *Unknown.* AmFP

Down by the Salley Gardens. W. B. Yeats. NoAM; RDB, *with music;* SoSe

Down by the waterside stand a house and a plat. *Unknown.* GBP

Down by the weeping willow. Florella; or, The Jealous Lover. *Unknown.* AmFP

Down by the Wild Mustard River. The Wild Mustard River. *Unknown.* AmFP

Down every passage of the cloister hung. Upon the Death of George Santayana. Anthony Hecht. CoPAm

Down flew the shaft of the god. A Love Affair. Arnold Bennett. OxBTC

Down in a Coal Mine. J. B. Geoghegan. AmFP

Down in Alabam'; or, Aint I Glad I Got Out de Wilderness. *At. to* J. Warner. PSoN

Down in Carlisle there lived a lady. The Lady of Carlisle. *Unknown.* AmFP

Down in Dallas. X. J. Kennedy. IPWM; OFD

Down in front of Casey's. The Sidewalks of New York. Charles B. Lawlor *and* James W. Blake. BLSo; FSN

Down in some lonesome piney grove. Lonesome Dove. *Unknown.* AmFP

Down in the hole we go, boys. Lament While Descending a Shaft. *Unknown.* AmFP

Down in the jungle [or jungles] lived a maid. Under the Bamboo Tree. Bob Cole. BLSo; FSN

Down in the Lonesome Garden. *Unknown.* BPo

Down in the mine, in the dark, dismal drift. Only a Miner. *Unknown.* AmFP

Down in the Valley, *with music. Unknown.* BLSH; BLSo; RDB (Birmingham Jail.) GBP, *without music*

Down mountain roads like scars across a fist. At Tripolis. Constance Carrier. WPE

Down the assembly line they roll and pass. The Brides. A. D. Hope. InPK

Down the blue night the unending columns press. Clouds. Rupert Brooke. OxBTC

Down the close, darkening lanes they sang their way. The Send-off. Wilfred Owen. InPS; OxBTC; PSN; SoSe

Down the deep sea, full fourscore fathoms down. The Fatal Ship. Robert Stephen Hawker. VPC

Down the hall a bookcase. Lyn Lifshin. *Fr.* Walking thru Audley End Mansion Late Afternoon. RiTi

Down the long hall she glistens like a star. Venus of the Louvre. Emma Lazarus. SBG

Down the road someone is practicing scales. Sunday Morning. Louis MacNeice. HeIP

Down the rock chute into the tombs of the kings. This Is the Life. Louis MacNeice. NoAM

Down the sky in file the wild geese tack. Harold Stewart. *Fr.* A Flight of Wild Geese. MAuV

Down through the snow-drifts in the street. The Boy. Eugene Field. ECBV

Down to the Puritan marrow of my bones. Puritan Sonnet. Elinor Wylie. Wild Peaches, IV. PAIC; VoPo

Down valley a smoke haze. Mid-August at Sourdough Mountain Lookout. Gary Snyder. MAT; NCSH

Down, Wanton, Down! Robert Graves. BoLoP; HeIP, NoAM

Down Went McGinty, *with music.* Joseph Flynn. FSN

Downe in the depth of mine iniquity. Fulke Greville. *Fr.* Caelica. PPoe

Downe lay the shepherd swaine. Hye Nonny Nonny Noe. *Unknown.* FaBoCo

Downfall of Charing Cross, The. *Unknown.* FaBoCo

Downhill I came, hungry, and yet not starved. The Owl. Edward Thomas. NoAm; NOBE; PPoe

Downstairs Two Old Lovers Meet. Lyn Lifshin. Psy

Downtown Roanoke. R. H. W. Dillard. PPoD

Downwind, he caught the scent. Hunter, Prey. Dabney Stuart. NVAP

Downy Hair in the Shape of a Flame. Coleman Barks. *Fr.* Body Poems. NVAP

Dow's Flat. Bret Harte. PoTa

Dozen clocks of this courthouse, The. State Message: A Midwestern Small Town. Robert Flanagan. HeS

Dozens of girls would storm up. Embraceable You. Ira Gershwin. BLSo

Draft Dodger Rag. Phil Ochs. WIF

Draft Horse, The. Robert Frost. HeIP; PiAm

Dragged through doorways of fragrance. The Lynching. Milton Kessler. CoPAm

Dragging in Winter. David McElroy. AmPA

Dragon Country: To Jacob Boehme. Robert Penn Warren. PPP

Dragon Skate. Gladys Cardiff. CDW

Dragonfly, The. Louise Bogan. HeIP

Dragon-fly strives patiently, The. Haiku. José Juan Tablada, *tr. by* Samuel Beckett. PBMP

Dragons. John Ciardi. SFF

Drake, who the world hast conquered like a scroll. To the Noble Sir Francis Drake. Thomas Beedome. SCP-2

Drama's vitallest expression is the common day. Emily Dickinson. NOBA

Draw me nere, draw me nere. The Juggler and the Baron's Daughter. *Unknown.* OxBM

Draw near, young men, and learn of me. McAfee's Confession. *Unknown.* AmFP

Drawn from his refuge in some lonely elm. Squirrel in Sunshine. William Cowper. BoAnP

Dread. J. M. Synge. BoLoP

Dread of Death. John Audelay. *See* Passion of Christ Strengthen Me.

"Dreadful Has Already Happened, The." Mark Strand. NoAM

*Dreadnought,* The. *Unknown.* AmFP

Dream, The [*or* A]. William Allingham. BIrV; PFIr; PoTa

Dream, A. Matthew Arnold. GBL

Dream, A. Blake. *Fr.* Songs of Innocence. LAuP; MBPR

Dream, The. Louise Bogan. MAT; SBG

Dream, The, *sel.* Byron. "Our life is two-fold: Sleep hath its own world," I. GrRo

Dream, The. Stephen Dunn. HeS

Dream, The. Robert Herrick. LoAs; SCP-1

Dream, The. David Ignatow. MAT

Dream, The. Ben Jonson. NOBE

Dream. Emilio Prados, *tr. fr. Spanish by* Eleanor L. Turnbull. LoAs

Dream, A, *sels.* Rachel Speght. WPE "I sought, I found, she asked me what I would." "My grief, quoth I, is called Ignorance." "Quoth she, I wish I could prescribe your help." "Upon a sudden, as I gazing stood."

Dream, A. *Unknown. Fr.* Mum and the Sothsegger. OxBM

Dream about Junior High School in America, The. Dick Lourie. NeAC

Dream Barker. Jean Valentine. VGW

Dream Deferred. Langston Hughes. *See* Harlem ("What happens to a dream deferred.")

Dream in a dream the heavy soul somewhere. Canto Amor. John Berryman. PAIC; VGW

Dream in Cold, A. Besmilr Brigham. Psy

Dream is that you are half crow, The. The Night You Got Back from the Mountains. Holly Prado. NPW

Dream is vague, The. Beale Street. Langston Hughes. PPP

Dream-Land. Poe. NOBA

Dream of a Baseball Star. Gregory Corso. NoAM; VGW

Dream of a Boy Who Lived at Nine Elms, The. William Brighty Rands. OxBChV

Dream of a Girl Who Lived at Sevenoaks, The. William Brighty Rands. OxBChV

Dream of a Lover, The. *Unknown.* LoAs

Dream of Ascent. James Applewhite. NVAP

Dream of Death, A. W. B. Yeats. GBL

Dream of Fair Women, A. Kingsley Amis. NoAM

Dream of Gerontius, The, *sel.* Cardinal Newman. Angel ("Softly and gently, dearly-ransom'd soul"). PFD

Dream of Hanging, A. Patricia Beer. MPo

Dream of Lakes, A.   Laurence Lieberman.   HeS

Dream of Rebirth.   Roberta Hill.   CDW

Dream of the Rood, The.   *Unknown, tr. fr. Anglo-Saxon by* Helen Gardner.   BoReV

Dream of Washed Hair, A.   Rhyll McMaster.   CAAP

Dream of Women, A.   Carolyn Maisel.   IHMS

Dream-Pedlary.   Thomas Lovell Beddoes.   LoAs, NOBE
   "(If there were dreams to sell," *st.* 1.)   LCL

Dream Record: June 8, 1955.   Allen Ginsberg.   ConAP; NOBA

Dream Sequence, Part 9.   Naomi Long Madgett.   BPo

Dream Song.   Lewis Alexander.   PoBA

Dream Songs.   John Berryman.   *Poems indexed separately by titles and first lines.*

Dream time, The.   Out.   Ted Hughes.   TwMBP

Dream Variation [*or* Variations].   Langston Hughes.   MiP; NOBA; PiAm; PoBA

Dream Vision.   J. V. Cunningham.   PiAm

Dream within a Dream, A.   Poe.   AmVN; GBL; NOBA; PiAm

Dreame, The.   John Donne.   LoAs

Dreamed Grail found as if in dreams, The.   On Finding the Meaning of "Radiance."   Alan Dugan.   PAIC

Dreamed Realization, A.   Gregory Corso.   VGW

Dreamed-Up for Winter.   Arthur Rimbaud, *tr. fr. French by* William Mead.   LoAs

Dreamers.   Siegfried Sassoon.   NoAM

Dreaming/ I saw a butterfly in the night.   God Bless Us.   Gaston Bart-Williams.   BuTh

Dreaming in the Shanghai Restaurant.   D. J. Enright.   MPo; PSN

Dreaming of Conn-Eda.   Diane Levenberg.   NPW

Dreaming Winter.   James Welch.   VW

Dreams.   André Breton, *tr fr. French by* Robert Duncan.   InPS

Dreams.   Charles Cooper.   PoBA

Dreams.   Nikki Giovanni.   PoBA

Dreams.   Thomas Traherne.   SCP-2

Dreams come from circular longings.   After Drinking Water.   Daniela Gioseffi.   WBN

Dreams fled away, this country bedroom, raw.   Another September.   Thomas Kinsella.   BIrV

Dreams from War.   Marilyn Krysl.   NPW

Dreams of Eurydice.   Margaret Ryan.   NPW

Dreams of the Wars.   David Young.   CAAP

Dreamscape.   Philip Booth.   FiCP

Dreary Black Hills, The.   *Unknown.*   AmFP

Dress of clouds opens like a flower, The.   Diving.   Shiro Murano, *tr. by* Ichiro Kono *and* Rikutaro Fukuda.   SPo

Dressed As I Am, a Young Man Once Called Me Names in Spanish.   Judy Grahn.   *Fr.* A Woman Is Talking to Death.   WBN

Dresses.   Kathleen Fraser.   NMM

Dressing Stations, The.   Norman Dubie.   AmPA

Drifters.   Bruce Dawe.   MAuV

Drifting, A.   Robert Hutchinson.   LoAs

Drifting.   Kathleen Spivack.   IHMS

Drifting and innocent and like snow.   Christmas Letter Home.   G. S. Fraser.   OxBTC; SLP

Drifting night in the Georgia pines.   O Daedalus, Fly Away Home.   Robert Hayden.   NCSH; PoBA

Drifting outside in a pall of smoke.   The Wall.   Raymond Carver.   NVAP

Drifting The.   Lyn Lifshin.   MMD

Driftwood.   Daniel Smythe.   RFM

Drill Man Blues.   George Sizemore.   AmFP

Drill, Ye Tarriers, Drill!   *Unknown.*   *See* Tarrier's Song.

Drink to Me Only with Thine Eyes.   Ben Jonson.   *See* To Celia ("Drink to me only. . .").

Drink Today.   John Fletcher, *and others.*   *Fr.* The Bloody Brother, II, ii.   PAIC

Drinker, The.   Robert Lowell.   SoSe

Drinking.   Abraham Cowley, *after the Greek of* Anacreon.   NOBE; PAIC
   (Anacreontics: Drinking.)   HeIP; OBP

Drinking hot saké.   Gary Synder.   *Fr.* Hitch Haiku.   InPK

Drinking Song ("Tappster, fill another ale").   *Unknown.*   OxBM

Drinking Song, A.   W. B. Yeats.   BoLoP; LoAs; POL

Drinking Time.   D. J. O'Sullivan.   PFIr

Drinking While Driving.   Raymond Carver.   NVAP

Dripping locker room, A.   Liver.   Coleman Barks.   *Fr.* Body Poems.   NVAP

Dripping Tap, The.   James Kirkup.   RAE

Drive Away Blues.   *Unknown.*   BluL

Drive In Movie.   Gary Sange.   NVAP; SFF

Drive-ins are out, to start with. One must always be.   Movie-Going.   John Hollander.   PPoD; PPP

Driver, The.   James Dickey.   VGW

Driver rubbed at his nettly chin, The.   To the Four Courts, Please.   James Stephens.   BIrV; PFIr

"Driver, what stream is it?" I asked, well knowing.   The Lordly Hudson.   Paul Goodman.   VGW

Driving along the eastern shore of Lake Michigan.   An Impossibility.   Robert Vas Dias.   HeS

Driving at Night.   John Calvin Rezmerski.   HeS

Driving down the concrete vein.   The White Man Pressed the Locks   James C. Kilgore.   InPK

Driving east.   Returning from the Funeral.   Patricia Henley.   NPW

Driving home from the school.   All three of Us.   Carol Cox.   MMD

Driving late at night I pass.   Sleep.   Dana Naone.   CDW

Driving that train, high on cocaine.   Casey Jones.   Robert Hunter.   GrRo

Driving the Mule.   *Unknown.*   *See* My Sweetie's a Mule in the Mine.

Driving to Town Late to Mail a Letter.   Robert Bly.   InPK; SFF; TSWA; VGW

Driving toward the Lac Qui Parle River.   Robert Bly.   ConAP; NCSH

Driving Wheels, The.   G. E. Murray.   HeS

Drizzle shifted, The.   The Day I Stopped Dreaming about Barbara Steele.   R. H. W. Dillard.   PPoD

Droit de Seigneur.   Richard Murphy.   PFIr

Dromedary.   François Dodat, *tr. fr. French by* Bert and Odette Meyers.   BoAnP

Droning a drowsy syncopated tune.   The Weary Blues.   Langston Hughes.   InPK; NoAM; NOBA

Drop.   George MacBeth.   TwMBP

Drop, Drop, Slow Tears.   Phineas Fletcher.   NOBE; SCP-2
   (Hymn, A: "Drop, drop slow tears.")   BoReV

Drop the Wires.   Hugh Seidman.   AmPA

Dropping Toward Stillness.   Sharon Barba.   RiTi

Drought.   David Holbrook.   OxBTC

Drove away I/ know I'll never go.   Leaving Them, letting the Farm Swallow,   Lyn Lifshin.   FAF

Drove-Road, The.   W. W. Gibson.   OxBTC

Drover, A.   Padraic Colum.   PFIr

Drowning in Spanish.   Tom Schmidt.   NeAC

Drug Store.   Karl Shapiro.   NowV; TCP

Drugs are a tuition.   Going to School in France or America.   Tom Clark.   ConAP

Drum, The.   John Scott of Amwell.   NOBE

Drum Songs.   Joseph Bruchac.   TSWA

Drumdelgie.   *Unknown.*   GBP

Drumdrumdrum, A. The Wall. Gwendolyn Brooks.. *Fr.* Two Dedications. PoBA

Drumlin Woodchuck, A. Robert Frost. NoAM; NOBA

Drummer Boy of Shiloh, The. *Unknown.* AmFP

Drummer Hodge. Thomas Hardy. InPS; NoAM

Drums. Martha Chosa. VW

Drunk as drunk on turpentine. Pablo Neruda, *tr fr. Spanish by* Christopher Logue. BoLoP

Drunk I have been. And drunk I was that night. To Laura Phelan: 1880-1906 Leon Stokesbury. NVAP

Drunk in the Furnace, The. W. S. Merwin. CAPP; MAT; NoAM

Drunk last night. A Dry Day just before the Rainy Season. Gary Snyder. MIT

Drunkard, A. *Unknown.* OxBM

Drunkard cannot meet a cork, A. Emily Dickinson. InPS

Drunkard's Last Market, The. Charles Tennyson Turner. VPC

Drunken Fisherman, The. Robert Lowell. AnMo; CoPAm; NOBA; VGW

Drunken night in my house with a, A. Dream Record: June 8, 1955. Allen Ginsberg. ConAP; NOBA

Dry brown coughing beneath their feet, The. Beverly Hills, Chicago. Gwendolyn Brooks. VGW

Dry Day just before the Rainy Season, A. Gary Snyder. MIT

Dry Land Blues. *Unknown.* BluL

Dry Loaf. Wallace Stevens. NOBA

Dry Salvages, The. T. S. Eliot. *Fr.* Four Quartets. PiAm

Dry tree with an empty honeycomb, A. The Tomb of Heracles. James McAuley. *Fr.* The Hero and the Hydra. MAuV

Dry vine leaves burn in an angle of the wall. The Thousand Things. Christopher Middleton. TwMBP

Drynaun, Dhun, The. *Unknown.* GBP

Dtah Dtah. David Kherdian. SA

Du Bartas His Divine Weeks and Works, *sels.* Joshua Sylvester. SCP-2
     1st Week 5th Day.
     1st Week 6th Day.

Dual Site, The  Michael Hamburger. AIW; NowV

Duality. Dannie Abse. NoAM

Dubious Night, A. Richard Wilbur. CAPP

Dublin. Louis MacNeice. OxBTC; PFIr

Dublin Made Me. Donagh MacDonagh. OxBTC; PFIr

Duchess of Malfi, The, *sels.* John Webster.
     Hark, Now Everything Is Still, *fr.* IV, ii. InPS
     (Shrouding of the Duchess of Malfi, The) NOBE
     "I am come to make thy tomb," *fr.* IV, ii. OBP
     "O let us howl some heavy note," *fr.* IV, ii. SCP-2

Duchess Potatoes, The. Diane Wakoski. CAAP

Duchess's Lullaby, The. "Lewis Carroll." *Fr.* Alice's Adventures in Wonderland. SpRo
     ("Speak roughly to your little boy.") FaBoCo

Duck. John Lyle Donaghy. BIrV

Duck, The. Ogden Nash. RAE

Duck and the Kangaroo, The. Edward Lear. OxBChV

Duck-Chasing. Galway Kinnell. VGW

Duck Pond at Mini's Pasture, a Dozen Years Later, The. Philip Dow. AmPA

Duck who had got such a habit of stuffing, A. The Notorious Glutton. Ann Taylor. OxBChV

Ducks. Phoebe Hesketh. BoAnP

Ducks' Ditty. Kenneth Grahame. *Fr.* The Wind in the Willows. OxBChV

Duel, The. Eugene Field. FCBV

Duet. Tennyson. *Fr.* Becket GBL

Duke of Buckingham, The. Pope. *Fr.* Moral Essays. NOBE

Duke of Grafton, The. *Unknown.* GBP; PeBB

Duke upon Duke. Pope. Epi

Duke's Song, The. Mary Sidney Wroth, Countess of Montgomery. *Fr.* Urania. WPE

Dulce et Decorum Est. Wilfred Owen. HeIP; InPK; NOAM; PPP; SFF; SoSe; VoPo; WIF

*Dulce* it is, and *decorum,* no doubt, for the country to fall. Arthur Hugh Clough. *Fr.* Amours De Voyage, II, ii. OBP

Dull as I was to think that a court fly. A Black Patch on Lucasta's Face. Richard Lovelace. PAIC

Dull Love, no more thy senseless arrows prize. An Ode to Love. Aphra Behn. SCP-2

Dull unwashed windows of eyes. A Poem Some People Will Have to Understand. LeRoi Jones. BPo; NOBA; PiAm

Dumb,/ Bloodied, the severed. A Grafted Tongue. John Montague. BIrV

Dumb Soldier, The. Robert Louis Stevenson. OxBChV

Dumb World, The. W. H. Davies. BoAnP; OxBTC

Dump, The. Donald Hall. TCP

Dunbarton. Robert Lowell. MPo

Duncan Spoke of a Process. LeRoi Jones. CAPP

Dunciad, The, *sel.* Pope.
     Triumph of Dullness, The. NOBE

Duns Scotus's Oxford. Gerard Manley Hopkins. Epi; NoAM; OBP

Duo. William Keys. SLP

Durban, Birmingham. Question and Answer. Langston Hughes. BPo

Dürer would have seen a reason for living. The Steeple-Jack. Marianne Moore. *Fr.* Part of a Novel, Part of a Poem, Part of a Play. NoAM; NOBA; SBG; WPE

Durham Old Women. *Unknown.* GBP

During the Eichmann Trial, *sel.* Denise Levertov.
     Peachtree, The. CAPP

During the Pageant at Medicine Lodge. Charles G. Ballard. VW

During the season of cut organs we. Initiation. Jayne Cortez. PoBA

During the Tet offensive, U.S. marines in Hue. News. Robin Morgan. WBN

During Wind and Rain. Thomas Hardy. InPK; OxBTC; PPP

Dusk. Ken Belford. NeAC

Dusk/ no dawns, and silver linings. No Dawns. Julianne Perry. PoBA

Dusk is in the cat. Affinities. Adrien Stroutenberg. TSWA

Dust. Rupert Brooke. OxBTC

Dust of Snow. Robert Frost. FSFS; IPWM; SoSe; SS; TSWA

Dustless Chalk. James Rankin. MIS

Dusty black beetle, A. Robert Sund. BoAnP

Dutch Lover, The, *sels.* Aphra Behn.
     Song: "Ah false Amyntas, can that hour." WPE
     Willing Mistress, The. SBG

Dutch Proverb, A. Matthew Prior. POL

Duty. Arthur Hugh Clough. VPC

Dvonya. Louis Simpson. NOBA

Dwarf barefooted, chanting, The. The Peasants. Alun Lewis. PPP

D'ye ken the big village of Balmaquhapple. The Village of Balmaquhapple. James Hogg. FaBoCo

Dying Californian, The. *Unknown.* AmFP

Dying Father's Farewell, The. *Unknown.* AmFP

Dying firelight slides along the quirt, A. The End of the Weekend. Anthony Hecht. ConAP; PSN

Dying Gaul, The. Desmond O'Grady. BIrV

Dying Gladiator, The. Byron. *Fr.* Childe Harold's Pilgrimage, IV. NOBE

Dying Goddess, The. Carolyn Kizer. WBN

Dying Hobo, The. *Unknown.* AmFP

Dying Mine Brakeman, The.  Orville Jenks.  AmFP

Dying Off Egg Island Bar.  David Smith.  NVAP

Dying Sergeant, The.  *Unknown.*  AmFP

Dying Speech of an Old Philosopher.  Walter Savage Landor.
*See* On His Seventy-Fifth Birthday.

Dylan Thomas.  T. O. Maglow.  InPK

Dylan, Who Is Dead.  Samuel Allen.  PoBA

Dynamite Song.  *Unknown.*  AmFP

Dyvers dother use as I have hard and kno.  Sir Thomas Wyatt.
AAS

Dyvers thy death doo dyverslye bemone.  Earl of Surrey.  AAS


# E


E=mc²: Einstein at Princeton.  David Rowbotham.  CAAP

E. P. Ode pour l'Election de Son Sepulchre.  Ezra Pound.  Hugh
Selwyn Mauberley, I.  InPS; NoAm; NOBA; PiAm; VGW

È, the Feasting Florentines.  Daniel Hoffman.  VGW

'E was warned agin 'er.  The Sergeant's Weddin'.  Kipling.
OxBTC

Each and All.  Emerson.  AmVN; NOBA; PiAm

Each day brings its toad, each night its dragon.  Jerome.  Randall
Jarrell.  PPP

Each day I live, each day the sea of light.  Poem against the Rich.
Robert Bly.  CAPP; NoAM; NOBA

Each dusk I saw, while those I loved the most.  The Owl.  V.
Sackville-West.  SBG

Each for himself is still the rule.  In the Great Metropolis.  Arthur
Hugh Clough.  VPC

Each is beautiful.  Tell Our Daughters.  Besmilr Brigham.
IHMS

Each known mile comes late.  The Train Runs Late to Harlem.
Conrad Kent Rivers.  PoBA

Each Morning.  LeRoi Jones.  *Fr.* Hymn for Lanie Poo.  PoBA

Each night/ just before dusk.  Elaine H. Jennings.  NPW

Each one had defenses, they said.  Continuing.  Madeline Bass.
WBN

Each prisoner is so sad in the glare.  The Line-up.  Joan Swift.
FiCP

Each year, the court expands.  The Old Pro's Lament.  Paul
Petrie.  SPo

Eachie, peachie, pearie, plum.  *Unknown.*  GBP

Eadwacer.  *Unknown, tr. fr. Anglo-Saxon.*  WPE

Eager note on my door said, "Call me," The.  Poem.  Frank
O'Hara.  NoAM; NOBA

Eagerly/ Like a woman hurrying to her lover.  Four Glimpses of
Night.  Frank Marshall Davis.  PoBA

Eagle, The.  Tennyson.  HeIP; InPK; IPWM; OBP; PPoe; SoSe;
SS

Eagle and the Mole, The.  Elinor Wylie.  PAIC

Eagle Converses with Chaucer, The.  Chaucer.  *Fr.* The House of
Fame.  OxBM

Eagle-feather Fan, The ("The Eagle is my power").  N. Scott
Momaday.  CDW

Eagle Sings, The.  *Unknown, tr. fr. Papago Indian.*  AKE

Eagle That Is Forgotten, The.  Vachel Lindsay.  NOBA; VoPo

Eagle's eye is the strongest eye, The.  The Great Way of the Man.
Norman H. Russell.  VW

Eagle's nest on the head of an old redwood, An.  The Beaks of
Eagles.  Robinson Jeffers.  NOBA

Eagles on a Half.  *Unknown.*  BluL

Eagles Over the Lambing Paddock  Ernest Moll.  MAuV

Eagle's shadow runs across the plain, The.  Zebra.  "Isak
Dinesen."  MiP; RFM

Earl Brand.  *Unknown.*  *See* Douglas Tragedy, The.

Earl Richard.  *Unknown.*  SLP

Earlier in the evening the moon.  The Moon.  Robert Creeley.
VGW

Early before the day doth spring.  Of Astraea  Sir John Davies.
*Fr.* Hymns of Astraea.  PAIC

Early Copper.  Carl Sandburg.  HeIP; PiAm

Early, early in the spring.  Early in the Spring.  *Unknown.*
AmFP

Early Electric! With what radiant hope.  The Metropolitan Railway.
John Betjeman.  OxBTC

Early Ella  Lynn Sukenick.  RiTi

Early in the Dawning.  Thomas Durfey.  SCP-2

Early in the Morning.  Louis Simpson.  ConAP

Early in the Spring  *Unknown.*  AmFP

Early in the spring when the snow is all gone.  A Trip to The
Grand Banks  Amos Hanson.  AmFP

Early January.  W.S. Merwin.  VGW

Early Morning, The.  Hilaire Belloc.  ECBV

Early morning over Rouen, hopeful.  Rouen.  May Wedderburn
Cannan.  OxBTC

Early Morning Song: The Snowstorm.  Gloria Bussel Koster.
NPW

Early, my God, without delay.  Isaac Watts.  AmFP

Early one morning.  Voodoo on the Un-Assing of Janis Joplin.
Carolyn M. Rodgers.  JB

Early one morning just about 4 o'clock.  Titanic Blues.  *Unknown.*
BluL

Early Purges, The.  Seamus Heaney.  NCSH

Early Supper.  Barbara Howes.  NCSH

Early this morning when you knocked upon my door.  Me and the
Devil Blues.  *Unknown.*  BluL

Early thou goest forth, to put to rout.  To a "Tenting" Boy.
Charles Tennyson Turner.  VPC

Early Thoughts of Marriage.  Nathaniel Cotton.  OxBChV

Early to bed, and early to rise.  *Unknown.*  MG

Early Warning.  George MacBeth.  TwMBP

Earlye, Earlye, in the Spring.  *Unknown.*  AmFP

Earth.  Oliver Herford.  MiP

Earth ("'A planet doesn't explode'").  John Hall Wheelock.
SFF; SoSe

Earth, The/ is a wonderful.  Poem for Friends.  Quincy Troupe.
PoBA

Earth and I Gave You Turquoise.  N. Scott Momaday.  CDW;
VW

Earth does not understand her child.  The Return.  Edna St.
Vincent Millay.  NoAM

Earth grows green; the flowers bloom, The.  Song to the Ninth
Grade.  Pamela Crawford Holahan.  AIW

Earth has not any thing to show more fair.  Composed Upon
Westminster Bridge, September 3, 1802.  Wordsworth.
AnMo; Epi; HeIP; InPK; InPS; IPWM; MBPR; NOBE;
OBP; PAIC; PBMP; PPoD; PPP

Earth is a beautiful place, The.  The Third Sermon on the
Warpland.  Gwendolyn Brooks.  BPo

Earth keeps some vibration going, The.  Fiddler Jones.  Edgar Lee
Masters.  *Fr.* Spoon River Anthology.  NoAM

Earth, ocean, air, beloved brotherhood!  Alastor; or, the Spirit of
Solitude.  Shelley.  MBPR

Earth Psalm.  Denise Levertov.  PPP

Earth rais'd up her head.  Earth's Answer.  Blake.  *Fr.* Songs of
Experience.  InPS; LAuP; MBPR

Earth Sings Mi-fa-mi, The.  Pat Lowther.  MMD

Earth smells different here, The.  War.  Patricia Ramsey.  AATT

Earth, The: To Marilyn. Judith Johnson Sherwin. WBN

Earth Walk. William Meredith. MAT; PPoD

Earth was green, the sky was blue, The. A Green Cornfield. Christina Rossetti. RAE

Earth was my home, but even there I was a stranger. The Flight of Apollo. Stanley Kunitz. Moon

Earth with thunder torne, with fire blasted, The. Fulke Greville. Fr. Caelica. AAS

Earth Worm, The. Denise Levertov. NOBA

Earthly Paradise, The, sels. William Morris.
   Apology, An. PAIC; VPC
   August. VPC
   February. VPC
   L'Envoi: "Here we are for the last time face to face." VPC
   October. VPC
   Outlanders, The. VPC
   Wanderers, The. VPC

Earth's Answer. Blake. Fr. Songs of Experience. InPS; LAuP; MBPR

Earth's Bondman. Betty Page Dabney. ECBV

Earthy Anecdote. Wallace Stevens. RFM

Eartly nourris sits and sings, An. The Great Silkie of Sule Skerry. Unknown. GBP; MAT; PeBB

Ease It to Me Blues. Unknown. BluL

East Bronx. David Ignatow. ConAP; IPWM

East Coker. T. S. Eliot. Fr. Four Quartets. PPP; VGW

East St. Louis Blues. Unknown. AmFP

East side, west side, all around the town. The Sidewalks of New York. James W. Blake. BLSH

East to west. Our little township is a lesion. Eyre All Alone. Francis Webb. CAAP

Easter ("I got me flowers to straw thy way"). George Herbert. NOBE

Easter ("Rise, heart! thy Lord is risen"). George Herbert. SCP-1

Easter. Spenser. See Amoretti, LXVIII.

Easter Bunny Blues Or All I Want for Xmas Is the Loop, The. Ebon Dooley. PoBA

Easter Communion. Gerard Manley Hopkins. OFD

Easter Day. Richard Crashaw. MetP
   (Upon Easter Day.) SCP-1

Easter Day, Naples, 1849. Arthur Hugh Clough. PFD; VPC

Easter Day II. Arthur Hugh Clough. PFD; VPC

Easter Eve. Muriel Rukeyser. VGW

Easter has come around. W.D. Snodgrass. Fr. Heart's Needle. ConAP

Easter Hymn. A. E. Housman. BoReV; OFD

Easter Night. Alice Meynell. BoReV

Easter 1916. W. B. Yeats. Epi; InPS; NoAM; NOBE; OBP; OxBTC; PAIC; PPoe; PPP

Easter Song, An. Unknown. OxBM

Easter Sunday. Sedulius Scottus, tr. fr. Latin by Helen Waddell. OFD

Easter Sunday: Not the Artist. Ralph Adamo. CoPAm

Easter Wings. George Herbert. AnMo; HeIP; InPK; InPS; PAIC; PPP; WIF

Eastern guard tower. Haiku. Etheridge Knight. BPo; NeAC; NoAM

Eastside Chick with Drive. Albert Spector. CTBA

Eastside Incidents. Gregory Corso. SA

Eastward to Eden. Edgar Bogardus. POL

Easy Decision, An. Kenneth Patchen. CTBA; SFF

Easy Rider Blues. Unknown. BluL

Eat, eat, while there is bread. Tewa Song of War. Unknown, tr. by Daniel G. Brinton. PBMP

Eat 'Em Up Smith Tells All in South Africa. Judith Johnson Sherwin. NoAM

'Eathen, The. Kipling. OxBTC

Eating fire. First Element. Margaret Atwood. MMD

Eating Poetry. Mark Strand. CoPAm; MAT; NoAM; PPP

Eau-Forte. F. S. Flint. OxBTC

Ebb slips from the rock, the sunken, The. Night. Robinson Jeffers. NOBA

Ebb tide has come for me. The Hag of Beare. Unknown, tr. by John Montague. BIrV

Ebb-tide to me as of the sea! The Lament of the Old Woman of Beare. Unknown, tr. by Kuno Meyer. Epi

Ebony: Contemporary. Marian Frances Brand. AATT

Ecce Homo. David Gascoyne. BoReV

Ecce Puer. James Joyce. BIrV; NoAM

Ecchoing Green, The. Blake. See Echoing Green, The.

Ecclesiastes Derek Mahon. BIrV

Ecclesiastes, sels. Bible, O.T.
   "I returned, and saw under the sun," IX: 11-12. Prf
   "Remember also thy Creator in the days of thy youth," XII: 1-7. OBP
   To Everything There Is a Season, III: 1-8. PBMP
   Vanity of Vanities, I: 2-11. PBMP

Ecclesiastical Sonnets, sels. Wordsworth.
   "I, who accompanied with faithful pace," Introd. MBPR
   Mutability, Pt. III, Sonnet XXXIV. HeIP; InPK; MBPR; NOBE; PPoD
   Uncertainty. MBPR
   "Why sleeps the future, as a snake enrolled," Conclusion. MBPR

Ech, Sic a Pairish. Unknown. FaBoCo

Eche man me telleth I chaunge moost my devise. Sir Thomas Wyatt. AAS

Echo. Sara Asheron. CaYB

Echo. Walter de la Mare. AKE

Echo. Christina Rossetti. BoLoP; GBL; NOBE; VPC

Echo Canyon. Unknown. AmFP

Echo Elf Answers, The. Thomas Hardy. LoAs

Echo, I ween, will in the wood reply. A Gentle Echo on Woman. Swift. FaBoCo; OLR

Echo to a Rock. Lord Herbert of Cherbury. PAIC

Echoes. W. E. Henley. Poems indexed separately by titles and first lines.

Echoes. Emma Lazarus. SBG

Echoing [or Ecchoing] Green, The. Blake. Fr. Songs of Innocence. FSFS; LAuP; MBPR

Echo's Lament of Narcissus. Ben Jonson. Fr. Cynthia's Revels, I, ii. SoSe
   ("Slow, slow, fresh fount, keep time with my salt tears.") InPK

Eclogue: The Common a-Took In. William Barnes. VPC

Eclogue for Christmas, An. Louis MacNeice. NoAM

Eclogues. Dennis Schmitz. NVAP

Ecole St. Luc. Ray Fraser. NeAC

Eclipse. Anita Endrezze Probst. CDW

Ecologue. Allen Ginsberg. CAAP

Ecology X. J. Kennedy. BoAnP

Ecstasy, The. Abraham Cowley. SCP-2

Ecstasy, The. John Donne. BoLoP; InPs; NOBE; PPoe; SCP-1
   (Exstasie, The.) MetP
   (Extasie,The.) LoAS; OBP

Ecstasy. John Leland. AmFP

Eddington's universe goes phut. Richard Tolman's Universe. Leonard Bacon. PAIC

Eddystone Light, The. Unknown. PoTa

Eden. D. M. Thomas. NCSH

Eden Is a Zoo. Margaret Atwood. WPE

Edgar's Story, *sel.* X. J. Kennedy.
"At Mount Rushmore I looked up into one." OFD

Edge. Sylvia Plath. PSN; RiTi

Edge of/ a coat-of-arms, The. White Crescents at the Bottoms of Fingernails. Coleman Barks. *Fr.* Body Poems. NVAP

Edge of town disappears, The. The Dream. Stephen Dunn. HeS

Edith Sitwell Assumes the Role of Luna. Robert Francis. Moon

Editor Whedon. Edgar Lee Masters. *Fr.* Spoon River Anthology. NoAM; NOBA

Edmonton, thy cemetery. Stevie Smith. OxBTC

Edna St. Vincent Millay Exhorts Little Boy Blue. Louis Untermeyer. PAIC

Edom O Gordon. *Unknown.* PeBB

Education. Kenneth Rexroth. NowV

Educators, The. D. M. Black. MPo

Edward *Unknown.* AmFP; InPK; IPWM; PeBB; PPoe; RDB,*with music*; SoSe
(Edward,Edward.) AIW; InPS; NOBE

Edward Hicks: "The Peaceable Kingdom." Ann Stanford. PPoD

Edwardian Hat Betty Parvin. POL

Edwardus Comes Clarendoniae. Bibliotheca Bodleiana. Geoffrey Grigson. GBL

Edwin in the Lowlands Low. *Unknown.* AmFP

Edy be thou, Hevene-Quene. Queen of Heaven. *Unknown.* OxBM

Eee wah-wah-wah-wah-wah. Talking to Myself. *Unknown.* BluL

E'en so the nipping wind in May doth come. Upon the Decease of My Infant Lady. Clement Barksdale. SCP-2

Eena, deena, dina, duss. *Unknown.* MG

Effect, The. Siegfried Sassoon. BuTh

Effect of Light, An. Vivian Smith. MAuV

Effendi. Michael S. Harper. PoBA

Efficiency Apartment. Gerald W. Barrax. PoBA

Effort at Speech. William Meredith. Prf

Effort at Speech between Two People. Muriel Rukeyser. VoPo

Eftsoones they heard a most melodious sound. The Bower of Bliss. Spenser. *Fr.* The Faerie Queene, II, 12. NOBE

Egan O Rahilly. Egan O'Rahilly, *tr. fr. Irish by* James Stephens. NoAM

Egg, The. George Bowering. NeAC

Egg Boiler, The. Gwendolyn Brooks. PoBA

Egg sat on the workbench, The. The Egg. George Bowering. NeAC

Eggs and Marrowbone,*with music. Unknown.* RDB

Ego. Robert Siegel. FAF

Ego Tripping. Nikki Giovanni. NoAM

Egotist, The. H. A. C. Evans. POL

Egrets. Judith Wright. NCSH

Egyptian Book of the Dead David Henderson. MIT

Egyptian Pulled Glass Bottle in the Shape of a Fish, An. Marianne Moore. PiAm

Eichmann before his death. Construction #13. Judith Johnson Sherwin. NoAM

Eight hands across, form a ring. Mississippi Sawyer. *Unknown.* AmFP

Eight Lines for a Script Girl. George Jonas. NeAC

Eight Oars and a Coxswain. Arthur Guiterman. SPo

Eight O'Clock. A. E. Housman. InPK; NoAM

Eight years ago this May. A Spring Night in Shokoku-Ji. Gary Snyder. VGW

Eight young pigs in a row look at me from the trough. The Laughing Faces of Pigs. Fred Lape. BoAnP

Eighteen Days without You, *sel.* Anne Sexton.
December 18th. CAPP

1887. A. E. Housman. BTTM; VoPo

Eighteen-Forty-Three. *Unknown.* FaBoCo

1867. Joseph Mary Plunkett. PFIr

1867. Coventry Patmore. *Fr.* The Unknown Eros. VPC

1867: Last Sounds. Gerry O'Egan. POL

Eighth Air Force. Randall Jarrell. NoAM; NOBA

Einstein's eyes. Relative Sadness. Colin Rowbotham. BuTh

Eire. David O'Bruadair, *tr. fr. Irish by* Austin Clarke. BIrV

Eisenhower's Visit to Franco, 1959. James Wright. CAPP; PSN

Either you will. Prospective Immigrants Please Note. Adrienne Rich. VGW

El Bosco. Mei Berssenbrugge. SA

Elder, or Bourtree, The. *Unknown.* GBP

Elderly Gentleman, The. George Canning. ECBV

Elderly Nobody Erases Self in Central Park. E. S. Forgotson. NowV

Elders at the zenith of their power look down the sky, The. Nathaniel Tarn. *Fr.* The Beautiful Contradictions. TwMBP

Eldorado. Poe. AmVN; IPWM; NOBA; PiAm; SS

El Dorado. Richard Ryan. BIrV

Eleanor (she spoiled in a British climate). Ezra Pound. Cantos, VII. NoAM; NOBA

Eleanor Rigby. John Lennon *and* Paul McCartney. InPK; InPS; OBP; PPoe; WIF

Elected silence, sing to me. The Habit of Perfection. Gerard Manley Hopkins. NoAM; SoSe

Elective Affinities. David Malouf. CAAP

Electric Cop, The. Victor Hernandez Cruz. PoBA

Electrocution. Lola Ridge. WPE

Elegiac Stanzas Suggested by a Picture of Peele Castle, in a Storm. Wordsworth. MBPR

Elegiac Verses. Wordsworth. MBPR

Elegie: Autumnal, The. John Donne. *See* Elegies.

Elegies, *sels.* John Donne.
Anagram, The. II. PAIC
Autumnal, The, IX. InPS
Elegy: "Nature's lay idiot, I taught thee to love," VII. SCP-1
Going to Bed, XIX. GBL; PPP
(To His Mistress [*or* Mistris] Going to Bed.) AnMo; BoLoP; OBP
Love's Progress, XVIII. SCP-1
On His Mistress, XVI. BoLoP
(Elegy on His Mistress.) GBL
(On His Mistris.) OBP
(To His Mistress Desiring to Travel with Him As His Page.) NOBE

Elegies for the Hot Season. Sandra McPherson. AmPA; CAAP; RiTi

Elegy: "Death be not proud, thy hand gave not this blow." Lucy Harington, Countess of Bedford. WPE

Elegy: "Do not look for him." Leonard Cohen. HeIP

Elegy: "Her face like a rain-beaten stone on the day she rolled off." Theodore Roethke. CTBA; NCSH; PSN

Elegy: "Here where the elm trees were." Constance Carrier. FAF

Elegy: "I know but will not tell." Alan Dugan. CAPP

Elegy: "I stood between two mirrors when you died." William Jay Smith. CoPAm

Elegy: "In summer's heat and mid-time of the day." Ovid. *See* Corinnae Concubitus.

Elegy, An: "Let me be what I am, as Virgil cold," *abr.* Ben Jonson. SCP-1

Elegy: "Let them bury your big eyes." Edna St. Vincent Millay. Memorial to D.C., V. LoAs

Elegy: "Me happy, night, night full of brightness." Ezra Pound. *Fr.* Homage to Sextus Propertius. PAIC

Elegy: "My comrade is dead." Salomon de la Selva, *tr. fr. Spanish by* Donald Walsh. LoAs
Elegy: "My mother in the witness box." Virginia Scott. NPW
Elegy: "My prime of youth is but a frost of cares." Chidiock Tichborne. NOBE; PPoD
  (Elegy, Written with His Own Hand in the Tower before His Execution.) InPK; WIF
  (His Elegy.) PPoe
  (On the Eve of His Execution.) OBP
  (Tichborne's Elegy.) HeIP; InPS
  (Written the Night before His Execution.) PAIC
Elegy: "Nature's lay idiot, I taught thee to love." John Donne. Elegies, VII. SCP-1
Elegy, An: "Noon is beautiful, The: the perfect wheel." Yvor Winters. VGW
Elegy: "Our hammock swung between Americas." Derek Walcott. OBP
Elegy for a Cricket. J. V. Cunningham. NoAM
Elegy for a Dead Soldier, *sel.* Karl Shapiro.
  Epitaph: "Underneath this wooden cross there lies." OFD
Elegy for a Diver. Philip Booth. SPo
Elegy for a Nature Poet. Howard Nemerov. CoPAm
Elegy for a Polish Grandaunt. James Bonk. HeS
Elegy for a Puritan Conscience. Alan Dugan. CAPP; CoPAm; NoAM
Elegy for a School Friend.
  Augustus Young. BIrV
Elegy for Alfred Hubbard. Tony Connor. MPo; SoSe
Elegy for an Android. D. M. Thomas. TwMBP
Elegy for Chief Sealth. Duane Niatum. CDW
Elegy for D. H. Lawrence, An. William Carlos Williams. Epi; NoAM
Elegy for David Beynon. Leslie Norris. LP
Elegy for Jack Bowman. Joseph Bruchac. CDW
Elegy for Jane. Theodore Roethke. CoPAm; InPK; InPS; IPWM; PAIC; PPoe; PSN; RRA; TCP; VoPo; WIF
Elegy for My Father. Mark Strand. CAAP; NVAP
  Your Shadow, *sel.* Prf
Elegy for the Monastery Barn. Thomas Merton. VGW
Elegy in a Presbyterian Burying-Ground. R. N. D. Wilson. BIrV
Elegy on Herakleitos. Callimachus, *tr. fr. Greek by* Dudley Fitts. InPK
Elegy on His Mistress. John Donne. *See* On His Mistress.
Elegy on That Glory of Her Sex, Mrs. Mary Blaize, An. Goldsmith. LAuP
  (Mrs. Mary Blaize.) FaBoCo
Elegy on the Death of a Mad Dog, An. Goldsmith. *Fr.* The Vicar of Wakefield, *ch.* 17. AIW; FaBoCo; LAuP; SS
Elegy on the Death of Her Husband. Anne Howard, Duchess of Arundel. WPE
Elegy on the Dust. Thom Gunn. NoAM
Elegy over a Tomb. Lord Herbert of Cherbury. NOBE
Elegy to the Memory of an Unfortunate Lady. Pope. NOBE; PAIC
Elegy upon the Death of the Most Illustrious Prince Henry, An, *sel.* John Hagthorpe.
  "I do not grieve when some unwholesome air." SCP-2
Elegy Written in a Country Churchyard. Thomas Gray. HeIP; InPK; InPS; LAuP; NOBE; OBP; PAIC; PBMP; PPoD; PPoe; PPP; WIF
Elegy, Written with His Own Hand in the Tower before His Execution. Chidiock Tichborne. *See* Elegy: "My prime of youth is but a frost of cares."
Elegye, An: "Constant to none, but ever false to me." Thomas Campion. AAS
Elementary School Classroom [*or* Class Room ]in a Slum, An. Stephen Spender. MPo; PPoD; WIF

Elements have merged into solicitude, The. The Racer's Widow. Louise Glück. AmPA
Elements of Geometry, The. David Malouf. CAAP
Elements of Night Arthur Gregor. LoAs
Elephant, The. John Donne. *Fr.* The Progresse of the Soule. OBP
Elephant, The. Sandra Hochman. BoAnP
Elephant in the Moon, The: a Satire, *sel.* Samuel Butler. "Learn'd society of late, A." SCP-2
Elephant Is Slow to Mate, The. D.H. Lawrence. InPK; NoAM; PPP
Elephant of long service to a circus, An. The Retirement of the Elephant. Russell Edson. AmPA
Elephant Rock. Primus St. John. PoBA
Elephant, the huge old beast, The. The Elephant Is Slow to Mate. D.H. Lawrence. InPK; NoAM; PPP
Elephants. Patrick Lane. NeAC
Elephants from the Sea. Ian Young. NeAC
Elephants in the Circus. D.H. Lawrence. BoAnP
Eletelephony. Laura E. Richards. ECBV; OxBChV
Elevator Landscapes, *sels.* Stephen Vincent. NeAC
  Floor: Five.
  Floor: O.
Elevator Man Adheres to Form, The. Margaret Danner. PoBA
Eleven. Archibald MacLeish. NCSH
Eleven Addresses to the Lord, *sels.* John Berryman.
  "Fearful I peer upon the mountain path," X. PiAm
  Prayer for the Self, A, VIII. PiAm; PPP
  "Sole watchman of the flying stars, guard me," III. PiAm
"1100 Exposition." Newsletter from My Mother. Michael S. Harper. PoBA
Elfin Knight, The. *Unknown.* *See* Lady Isabel and the Elf-Knight.
Elgonyi say, there are big dreams and little dreams, The. Big Dream, Little Dream. Louis Simpson. POL
El-Hajj Malik El-Shabazz. Robert Hayden. PoBA
Elinda's Glove. Richard Lovelace. SCP-2
Elinoure and Juga Thomas Chatterton. LAuP
Elisabeth, Elspeth, Betsy, and Bess. *See* Elizabeth, Elspeth, Betsy, and Bess.
Elisha wroth wi sin and sloth. Jezebel. Forbes Macregor. MIS
Elizabeth. Robert Lowell. *Fr.* Harriet. LoAs
Elizabeth, Elspeth, Betsy, and Bess. Mother Goose. ECBV; MG
Elizabeth, frigidly stretched. This Houre Her Vigill. Valentin Iremonger. OxBTC; PFIr
Elizabeth in Italy Richard Weber. BoLoP
Elizabeth of Bohemia. Sir Henry Wotton. *See* On His Mistress, the Queen of Bohemia.
Ella, in a Square Apron, along Highway 80. Judy Grahn. *Fr.* The Comman Woman. NMM
Ella Speed. *Unknown.* AmFP
Ellen Flannery. *Unknown.* AmFP
Elm. Sylvia Plath. NoAM; NOBA
Elm Buds. Carl Sandburg. PiAm
Elsa Wertman. Edgar Lee Masters. *Fr.* Spoon River Anthology. NoAM
"Else a Great Prince in Prison Lies." Denise Levertov. PPP; VGW
Elsie Marley has grown so fine. *Unknown.* MG
Elvin's Blues. Michael S. Harper. BPo
Elwha River, The. Gary Snyder. NoAM
Elysee. Larry Eigner. VGW
Elysium is as far as to. Emily Dickinson. LoAs; OLR; WPE
Embankment, The. T. E. Hulme. OxBTC; PPoD
Embarrassing Episode of Little Miss Muffet, The. Guy Wetmore Carryl. PoTa

Emblem of Two Foxes, An  Barry Spacks.  CoPAm

Emblems, *sels.*  Francis Quarles.
  Epigram: "My soul, thy love is dear: 'twas thought a good," V, 4.  SCP-2
  Epigram: "What makes thee, fool, so fat? Fool, thee so bare?" I, 12.  SCP-2
  "Ev'n like two little bank-dividing brooks," V, 3.  PAIC
  (My Beloved Is Mine and I Am His.)  NOBE
  "Here's your right ground. Wag gently o'er this black," I, 10.  SCP-2
  "Like to the arctic needle that doth guide," V, 4.  SCP-2
  "What, never filled? Be thy lips screwed so fast," I, 12.  SCP-2
  Why Dost Thou Shade Thy Lovely Face? III, 7.  BoReV

Emblems.  Allen Tate.  VGW

Embraceable You, *with music.*  Ira Gershwin.  BLSo

Embracing low-falutin.  The Countryman's Return.  Dylan Thomas.  OxBTC

Embro my ain, ye are aye meant.  Betrayal in Morninside.  Donald Campbell.  MIS

Embroidery, An.  Denise Levertov.  NMM; RiTi

Embryos.  Marge Piercy.  RiTi

Emerald is as green as grass, An.  Flint.  Christina Rossetti.  OxBChV

Emergency at 8.  Geof Hewitt.  NeAC

Emerges daintily, the skunk.  The Wood Weasel.  Marianne Moore.  PiAm

Emerson.  James Russell Lowell.  *Fr.* A Fable for Critics.  AmVN; NOBA; PAIC

Emigration.  Anita Barrows.  NMM

Emily Dickinson Postage Stamp.  Lynn Strongin.  NMM

Emma in My Third Eye.  Renée Roper.  NPW

Emmet Kills-Warrior Turtle Mountain Reservation.  Marnie Walsh.  VW

Emmett Till.  James A. Emanuel.  PoBA; WIF

Emmiline, you were there even before they were cold.  Flowers for the Grangerford Girl.  William Harrold.  HeS

Empathy.  Agnes Pratt.  VW

Empedocles came coughing through the smoke.  To the Thoughtful Reader.  William Meredith.  NoAM

Empedocles on Etna, *sel.*  Matthew Arnold.
  Song of Callicles, The, *fr.* II.  NOBE

Emperor Nap he would set off, The.  The March to Moscow.  Robert Southey.  FaBoCo

Emperor of Ice-Cream, The.  Wallace Stevens.  AnMo; InPK; NoAM; NOBA; PAIC; PiAm

Emperor of the Moon, *sels.*  Aphra Behn.  WPE
  Song: "All joy to mortals, joy and mirth."
  Song: "Curse upon that faithless maid, A."

Emperors and kings! in vain you strive.  The Republican Genius of Europe.  Philip Freneau.  VoPo

Employed.  James Bertolino.  HeS

Empress in the Mirror.  Colette Inez.  WBN

Emptiness, An.  Passage.  Warren Slesinger.  HeS

Empty ashtray, An.  In Place of a Phone Call to Arabia.  Diane Wakoski.  Psy

Empty carousel in a deserted place, An.  The Carousel.  Gloria C. Oden.  PoBA

Empty Holds a Question.  Pat Folk.  NowV

Empty house,The—the empty country—the empty sky.  Plato was Right Though.  Lee Harwood.  TwMBP

Empty lap, an hour to tea, An.  Anno Domini.  E. M. Walker.  POL

Empty sky, a world of heather, An.  Divided.  Jean Ingelow.  SpRo

Empty Streams of Autumn  Ray A. Young Bear.  VW

Empty Threat, An.  Robert Frost.  RFM

Empty Vessel.  "Hugh MacDiarmid."  SLP

Empty Woman, The.  Gwendolyn Brooks.  IHMS

Emus.  Mary Fullerton.  BoAnP

En route to the picnic they drive through their history.  Picnic: The Liberated.  M. Carl Holman.  PoBA

Enacting somone's notion of themselves.  Aunt Jemima of the Ocean Waves.  Robert Hayden.  PoBA

Enamoured of the Miniscule.  Michael Hartnett.  BIrV

Encase your legs in nylons.  Inexpensive Progress.  John Betjeman.  LP

Enchanted Shirt, The.  John Hay.  PoTa

Enchantment.  Lewis Alexander.  PoBA

Enchantress Circe, with a potent wine, The.  To a Lady.  J. B. Morton.  POL

Encompass me, my lover.  The Constant North.  J. F. Hendry.  SLP

Encounter.  Denis Devlin.  BIrV

Encounter.  Geraldine Hammond.  IHMS

Encounter, The.  Edgell Rickword.  OxBTC

Encounter in the Cage Country.  James Dickey.  CAPP

Encouragement to a Lover.  Sir John Suckling.  *See* Why So Pale and Wan?

End, The.  Allen Ginsberg.  ConAP

End, An.  Christina Rossetti.  GBL

End came as I drove it down the road, The.  Last of the Poet's Car.  Tony Connor.  OxBTC

End came easy for most of us, The.  The Man from Washington  James Welch.  CDW; SA; VW

End of a long stillness.  Dawn in January.  Lance Henson.  CDW

End of Love, The.  Kathleen Raine.  BuTh

End of Summer.  Stanley Kunitz.  VGW

End of Summer, The.  Judith Minty.  FiCP; HeS

End of the Affair.  Geoffrey Grigson.  GBL

End of the Weekend, The.  Anthony Hecht.  ConAP; PSN

End of the World, The.  Archibald MacLeish.  InPK; MAT; NoAM; NCSH; NOBA; PAIC; PBMP; PiAM; SS; VGW

End was quick and bitter, The.  Quick and Bitter.  Yehuda Amichai, *tr. by* Assia Gutmann.  BoLoP

Endimion Porter and Olivia.  Sir William Davenant.  NOBE

Endings.  Daniel Halpern.  CAAP

Endlessly searching, we look for the meaning.  Acceptance.  Margaret Reynolds.  MIS

Ends in a house.  His Third Decade.  Dabney Stuart.  NVAP

Endymion [a Poetic Romance], *sels.*  Keats.
  Are Then Regalities All Gilded Masks? *fr.* III.  Moon
  Song of the Indian Maid, The, *fr.* IV.  NOBE
  "Thing of beauty is a joy for ever, A," I.  MBPR; VoPo, 24 *ll.*

Energetic Women.  D. H. Lawrence.  InPS

Energy.  Victor Hernández Cruz.  PoBA; SA

Enfranchising cable, silvered by the sea.  Granite and Steel.  Marianne Moore.  PiAm

Engaged.  Octavio Paz, *tr. fr. Spanish by* Muriel Rukeyser.  PBMP

Engine and transmission and the wheels, The.  The Great Society, Mark X.  Howard Nemerov.  AnMo

England.  Marianne Moore.  Psy

England ("This royal throne of Kings").  Shakespeare.  *See* This England ("This royal throne...").

England in 1819.  Shelley.  GrRo; MAT; MBPR; NOBE; PBMP; PPoD
  (Sonnet: England in 1819.)  PPP

England, unlike junior nations.  Remember Suez?  Adrian Mitchell.  OxBTC

England's lads are miniature men.  Boy-Man.  Karl Shapiro.  SoSe

English, The.  *Unknown.*  GBP

English Bards, and Scotch Reviewers. Byron. MBPR
English Counties. *Unknown.* POL
English Elegy, An. Daryl Hine. NoAM
English Flag, The. Kipling. BTTM
English Retort, The. *Unknown.* OxBM
English Succession, The. *Unknown.* OxBChV
Engraved on the Collar of a Dog Which I Gave to His Royal
     Highness. Pope. *See* Epigram Engraved on the Collar of a
     Dog.
Enkindled Spring, The. D. H. Lawrence. NoAM
Enmeshed in steel stands a stone. The Captive Stone. Jim
     Barnes. CDW
Enormous Sleep. Tom Crawford. NVAP
Enough. Marianne Moore. NOBA
Enquiry. Denise Levertov. *Fr.* Two Variations. RiTi
Enraptured I Gaze,*with music.* Francis Hopkinson. BLSo
Enriching the Earth. Wendell Berry. PiAm
Ensign and a lady gay, An. Clerk Saunders.     *Unknown.*
     SLP
Enslav'd, the daughters of Albion weep: a trembling lamentation.
     Visions of the Daughters of Albion. Blake. MBPR
Enslaved. Claude McKay. BPo
Enter Harlem. Walk with de Mayor of Harlem. David
     Henderson. PoBA
Enter the dream-house, brothers and sisters, leaving. Newsreel.
     C. Day Lewis. PPoD
Enthusiast, The; or, The Lover of Nature. Joseph Warton.
     LAuP
Enticer. Richard Armour. SoSe
Entire country is overrun with private property, The. Gypsy.
     Josephine Miles. NoAM
Entrance and exit wounds are silvered clean. Recalling War.
     Robert Graves. NoAM; OBP
Entrapped inside a submarine. H. C. Canfield. *Fr.* On the Loss
     of U.S. Submarine S4. FaBoCo
Entrepreneur chicken shed his tail feathers, surplus, The.
     Josephine Miles. NoAM
Enueg II. Samuel Beckett. NoAM
Envoi: "Hear me, whom I betrayed." J. V. Cunningham. VGW
Envoi: "Take of me what is not my own." Kathleen Raine.
     NOBE
Envoi: "What has want to give." Kathleen Raine. WPE
Envoi (1919). Ezra Pound. *Fr.* Hugh Selwyn Mauberly. InPS;
     NoAM; NOBA; VGW
Envoy. Robert Duncan. *Fr.* Passages. VGW
Envy. Charles *and* Mary Lamb. OxBChV
Envy the Old. Mark Van Doren. Prf
Eolian Harp, The. Samuel Taylor Coleridge. MBPR
Epic. Patrick Kavanagh. BIrV
Epicoene; or, The Silent Woman, *sel.* Ben Jonson.
     Simplex Munditiis, *fr.* I, i, *tr. fr. the Latin of* Jean Bonnefons.
     NOBE; OBP; PBMP
     (Clerimont's Song.) InPS; PPP
     ("Still to be neat, still to be dressed [*or* drest].") GBL; HeIP
Epicure, Dining at Crewe, An. *Unknown.*    AKE
Epicure, The, Sung by One in the Habit of a Town Gallant.
     Thomas Jordan. NOBE
Epidermal Macabre. Theodore Roethke. NoAM
Epigram: "After some years Bohemian came to this." J. V.
     Cunningham. VGW
Epigram: "As Thomas was cudgeled one day by his wife." Swift.
     SoSe
Epigram: "Dark thoughts are my companions. I have wined." J. V.
     Cunningham. VGW
Epigram: "Dear, if unsocial privacies obsess me." J. V.
     Cunningham. VGW

Epigram: For a Woman with Child. J. V. Cunningham. PiAm
Epigram: "Golden casket I designed, A." John Swanick Drennan.
     BIrV
Epigram: "Homer was poor. His scholars live at ease." J. V.
     Cunningham. VGW
Epigram: "How we desire desire! Joy of surcease." J. V.
     Cunningham. VGW
Epigram: "I am his Highness' dog at Kew." Pope. *See* Epigram
     Engraved on the Collar of a Dog.
Epigram: "I who by day am function of the light." J. V.
     Cunningham. *See* Motto for a Sun Dial.
Epigram: "If wisdom, as it seems it is." J. V. Cunningham.
     PiAm
Epigram: "In digging up your bones, Tom Paine." Byron. MBPR
Epigram: "In the neat parlor of their honeymoon." Max Halpern.
     SFF
Epigram: "In whose will is our peace? Thou happiness." J. V.
     Cunningham. VGW
Epigram: "King George, observing with judicious eyes." Joseph
     Trapp. FaBoCo
Epigram: "King to Oxford sent a troop of horse, The." William
     Browne. FaBoCo
Epigram: "Life flows to death as rivers to the sea." J. V.
     Cunningham. VGW
     ("Life flows to death as rivers to the sea.") POL
Epigram: "Love signed the contract blithe and leal." John
     Swanick Drennan. BIrV
Epigram: "My Soul, sit thou a patient looker-on." Francis
     Quarles. NOBE
Epigram: "My soul, thy love is dear: 'twas thought a good."
     Francis Quarles. *Fr.* Emblems, V, 4. SCP-2
Epigram: "Naked I came, naked I leave the scene." J. V.
     Cunningham. VGW
Epigram: Night-piece. J. V. Cunningham. PiAm
Epigram: "Oh, God of dust and rainbows." Langston Hughes.
     SoSe
Epigram: On Sir Roger Phillimore. *Unknown.*    FaBoCo
Epigram: "Scaurus hates Greek, and is become." *Unknown.*
     PiAm
Epigram: "Swans sing before they die." Samuel Taylor Coleridge.
     *See* Swans Sing before They Die.
Epigram: "This Humanist whom no beliefs constrained." J. V.
     Cunningham. VGW
Epigram: "Time heals not: it extends a sorrow's scope." J. V.
     Cunningham. VGW
Epigram: "To John I ow'd great obligation." Matthew Prior.
     FaBoCo
Epigram: "What makes thee, fool, so fat? Fool, thee so bare?"
     Francis Quarles. *Fr.* Emblems, I, 12. SCP-2
Epigram: "Within this mindless vault." J. V. Cunningham.
     VGW
Epigram: "World is full of care, much like unto a bubble, The."
     Nathaniel Ward. POL
Epigram Engraved on the Collar of a Dog Given to His Royal
     Highness. Pope. FaBoCo; InPK
     (Engraved on the Collar of a Dog Which I Gave to His
     Highness.) AnMo
     (Epigram: "I am his Highness' dog at Kew.") PAIC
Epigram on John Bull. Byron. FaBoCo
Epigram on Miltonicks Samuel Wesley. POL
Epigram on the Unknown Inventor of Scissors. L. E. Jones. POL
Epigram on Two Ladies. Sophia Burrell. POL
Epigram on Voltaire. Edward Young. FaBoCo
Epigrams. Phillip Hey. NVAP
Epigraph to the Theme of Love. Margaret Cavendish, Duchess of
     Newcastle. SCP-2

Epilogue: "At the midnight in the silence of the sleep-time."
Robert Browning. *Fr.* Asolando NOBE; PAIC

Epilogue: "Away, for we are ready to a man!" James Elroy
Flecker. *Fr.* The Golden Journey to Samarkand. NOBE

Epilogue: "I have just joined a raggedy line." Dennis Trudell.
NVAP

Epilogue, An: "I have seen flowers come in stony places." John
Masefield. OxBTC

Epilogue: "I, too, sing America." Langston Hughes. *See* I, Too.

Epilogue: "O life, O radiance, love, delight." Christopher
Brennan. *Fr.* The Burden of Tyre. MAuV

Epilogue: "So she went into the garden." Samuel Foote. *See*
Great Panjandrum, The.

Epilogue: "There's something in a stupid ass." Byron. PAIC

Epilogue Spoken at Mithridates King of Pontus, *sel.* Dryden
"Pox on this playhouse! 'Tis an old tired jade." SCP-1

Epilogue to the Satires, *sels.* Pope. NOBE
Power of Ridicule, The.
Triumph of Vice, The.

Epiphany on a Plot of Moonlight William R. Mitchell. AATT

Epipsychidion. Shelley. MBPR

Epistemology Richard Wilbur. NoAM; NOBA

Epistle An: "Whether these lines do find you out." Sir John
Suckling. PAIC

Epistle, An, Containing the Strange Medical Experience of
Karshish, the Arab Physician. Robert Browning. PFD

Epistle from Mr. Pope, to Dr. Arbuthnot, An. Pope. *See* Epistle
to Dr. Arbuthnot.

Epistle to a Friend (Mr. Colby) to Persuade Him to the Wars, An,
*sel.* Ben Jonson.
"Wake, friend, from forth thy lethargy! the drum." SCP-1

Epistle to a Young Lady, on Her Leaving the Town after the
Coronation. Pope. *See* Epistle to Miss Blount, on Her
Leaving the Town after the Coronation.

Epistle to Augusta. Byron. MBPR

Epistle to Be Left in the Earth. Archibald MacLeish. NOBA;
PAIC

Epistle to Dr. Arbuthnot. Pope. InPS
(Epistle from Mr. Pope, to Dr. Arbuthnot, An.) ESaP; PAIC
*Sels.*
Apologia pro Vita Sua. NOBE
Atticus. InPK; NOBE
"Curst be the verse, how well so'er it flow." OBP
Sporus. NOBE

Epistle to Katherine, Lady Aubigny, *sel.* Ben Jonson.
"'Tis grown almost a danger to speak true." SCP-1

Epistle to Miss Blount, on Her Leaving the Town after the
Coronation. Pope. BoLoP; NOBE; PPP
(Epistle to a Young Lady, on Her Leaving the Town after the
Coronation.) SoSe

Epistle to Peter Pindar. William Gifford. ESaP

Epi-Strauss-ium. Arthur Hugh Clough. PAIC; PFD; VPC

Epitaph: "Bathsheba! to whom none ever said scat." Whittier.
ECBV
(Epitaph for Bathsheba.) PCat
(For a Little Girl Mourning Her Favorite Cat.) POL

Epitaph: "Even such is Time, which takes in trust." Sir Walter
Ralegh. AKE; BoReV; NOBE
(Even Such Is Tyme.) BuTh
(Verses Made the Night before He Dyed.) AAS

Epitaph: "For this she starred her eyes with salt." Elinor Wylie.
SBG

Epitaph, An: "He worshipped at the altar of Romance." Colin
Ellis. OxBTC

Epitaph: "Here Johnson lies—a sage by all allow'd." William
Cowper. LAuP

Epitaph: "Here lies a poet, briefly known as Hecht." Anthony
Hecht. POL

Epitaph: "Here lies fierce Strephon, whose poetic rage." Anthony
Hecht. PPoD

Epitaph: "Here lies Sir Tact, a diplomatic fellow." Timothy
Steele. InPK

Epitaph: "I am old." Christopher Logue. OxBTC

Epitaph, An: Inscription on a Monument at Newstead Abbey.
Byron. BoAnP

Epitaph: "Mr. Heath-Stubbs as you must understand." John
Heath-Stubbs. MPo; OxBTC

Epitaph: "My brother is skull and skeleton now." William
Montgomerie. POL

Epitaph: "Roots of mankind are tangled in my hair, The." Wendy
Rose. CDW

Epitaph: "Sir, you should notice me: I am the Man." Lascelles
Abercrombie. BBGO

Epitaph: "Stavro's dead. A truant vine." Lawrence Durrell.
FaBoCo

Epitaph: "Stop, Christian passer-by!—Stop, child of God." Samuel
Taylor Coleridge. MBPR

Epitaph: "They hanged him on a clement morning, swung."
Dennis Scott. SFF

Epitaph: "Underneath this wooden cross there lies." Karl Shapiro.
*Fr.* Elegy for a Dead Soldier. OFD

Epitaph: "When I shall be without regret." J. V. Cunningham.
InPK

Epitaph for a Horse Thief *Unknown.* ECBV

Epitaph for Bathsheba Whittier. *See* Epitaph: "Bathsheba!..."

Epitaph for Goliath David R. Slavitt. CoPAm

Epitaph for Mr. Partridge *Unknown.* AKE

Epitaph for the Tomb of Adolfo Baez Bone. Ernesto Cardenal, *tr.
fr. Spanish by* Janet Brof. POL

Epitaph for the Unknown Soldier. W. H. Auden. FaBoCo

Epitaph for William Pitt. Byron. MBPR

Epitaph in St. Olave's, Southwark, on Mr. Munday. *Unknown.*
FaBoCo

Epitaph on a Dog.*Unknown, tr. fr. Greek by* Forrest Reid. ECBV

Epitaph on a Dormouse. *Unknown.* OxBChV

Epitaph on a Hare William Cowper. HeIP

Epitaph on a Schoolmaster. Burns. FaBoCo

Epitaph on a Tuft-Hunter. Thomas Moore. FaBoCo

Epitaph on a Tyrant. W. H. Auden. HeIP; MiP; SFF

Epitaph on an Army of Mercenaries A. E. Housman. BTTM;
NoAM; NOBE; OBP; OxBTC; PPP; PSN

Epitaph on an Infant. Samuel Taylor Coleridge. MBPR

Epitaph on an Infant Eight Months Old. *Unknown.* SoSe

Epitaph on Any Man A. S. J. Tessimond. POL

Epitaph on Charles I. James Graham, Marquess of Montrose.
NOBE

Epitaph on Charles II. Earl of Rochester. FaBoCo; OBP

Epitaph on Elizabeth, L. H. Ben Jonson. HeIP; SCP-1

Epitaph on Floyd. *Unknown.* POL

Epitaph on Holy Willie Burns. ESaP

Epitaph on John Dove. Burns. FaBoCo

Epitaph on Robert Southey. Thomas Moore. FaBoCo

Epitaph on S. P., a Child of Queen Elizabeth's Chapel. Ben
Jonson. HeIP; PPP
(On Solomon Pavy, a Child of Queen Elizabeth's Chapel.)
NOBE

Epitaph on the Countess Dowager of Pembroke. William Browne.
*See* On the Countess Dowager of Pembrooke.

Epitaph on the Earl of Strafford. John Cleveland. NOBE; SCP-2

Epitaph on the Lady Mary Villiers. Thomas Carew. SCP-2
(On the Lady Mary Villiers.) NOBE

Epitaph on the Monument of Sir William Dyer At Colmworth,
1641. Lady Catherine Dyer. *Fr.* Sir William Dyer, Knight.
BoLoP
("My dearest dust, could not thy hasty day.") SCP-2

Epitaph on the Secretary to the Muses.  Jane Barker.  FaBoCo
Epitaph on the World.  Henry David Thoreau.  HeIP
Epitaph upon Husband and Wife Who Died and Were Buried Together, An.  Richard Crashaw.  NOBE
Epitaph upon the Right Honorable Sir Philip Sidney, An.  Fulke Greville.  Prf
Epitaphs  Glyn Hughes.  LP
Epithalamion: "Kingfisher falls through the dry air, The."  Charles Wright.  CoPAm
Epithalamion: "Thou art reprieved old year, thou shalt not die," abr.  John Donne.  SCP-1
Epithalamion: "Ye learned sisters which have oftentimes."  Spenser.  AAS; BoLoP; Epi; InPS; LoAs; NOBE; PAIC
"Wake, now my love, awake; for it is time," sel.  GBL
Epithalamion Made at Lincoln's Inn.  John Donne.  PAIC
Epithalamion, An; or, Marriage-Song on the Lady Elizabeth and Count Palatine Being Married on St. Valentine's Day, abr.  John Donne.  SCP-1
"Hail, Bishop Valentine, whose day this is," sel.  OFD
Epithalamium: "When first my beloved came to my bed."  John Peale Bishop.  PAIC
Epochs.  Emma Lazarus.  SBG
Eppie Morrie  Unknown.  PeBB
Equestrian fell from his horse, An.  The Childhood of an Equestrian.  Russell Edson.  AmPA
Equilibrists, The.  John Crowe Ransom.  LoAs; NoAM; NOBA; PPP
Ere I go hence and be no more.  My Daughter's Dowry.  Robert Herrick.  RRA
Ere long they come, where that same wicked wight.  The Cave of Despair.  Spenser.  Fr. The Faerie Queene.  NOBE
Ere on my bed my limbs I lay.  The Pains of Sleep [or A Child's Evening Prayer].  Samuel Taylor Coleridge.  MBPR; OxBChV
Ere the cock has crowed.  The Forsaken Girl.  Randall Jarrell.  OLR
Ere You Were Queen of Sheba.  Sir Arthur Shipley.  FaBoCo
Erie Canal, The, with music.  Unknown.  BLSo
Erith, on the Thames.  Unknown.  GBP
Erl-King's Daughter, The.  Johann Gottfried Herder, tr. fr. German by James Clarence Mangan.  PoTa
Eros.  Robert Bridges.  NOBE
Ερος δ'αμτε  Theodore Wratislaw.  GBL
Eros Turannos.  E. A. Robinson.  GBL; IPWM; NoAM; NOBA; PiAm; PPoe
Erotion's Death.  Peter Whigham.  TwMBP
Errata,  Charles Simic.  NVAP
Eruption.  Margaret Reynolds.  MIS
Es war einmal . . . No, it's too heavy.  Märchenbilder.  John Ashbery.  NOBA
Escape.  Georgia Douglas Johnson.  PoBA
Escape to Love, sel.  Patrick MacDonogh.
"Alone and Godless, stopped by the sudden edge."  BIrV
Escapist's Song.  Theodore Spencer.  POL; SFF
Eschatology  Wade Hall.  AATT
Eskimo Chant.  Unknown, tr. fr. Eskimo by Knud Rasmussen.  RFM
Esope, mine author, makis mentioun.  The Two Mice.  Robert Henryson.  OxBM
Especially he loves.  God Poem.  Stanley Moss.  VGW
Especially I like the bit where.  Sleight-of-Hand.  Bruce Dawe.  CAAP
Especially when the October wind.  Dylan Thomas.  OxBTC
Esplumeoir.  "Hugh MacDiarmid."  TwMBP
Essay on Criticism, An, sels.  Pope.
"But most by numbers judge a poet's song," fr. Pt.II  WIF
Little Learning, A, fr. Pt. II.  NOBE

"Of all the causes which conspire to blind," fr. Pt.II.  PPoD; PPoe
Sound and Sense ("True ease in writing comes from art, not chance"), fr. Pt. II.  SoSe
Essay on Man, An, sels.  Pope.
"Awake, my St. John! leave all meaner things," Epistle I.  PAIC
"Behold the child, by Nature's kindly law," fr. Epistle II.  POL
"For forms of government let fools contest," fr. Epistle III.  POL
"Know then thyself, presume not God to scan," Epistle II.  PPoe
(Know Thyself.)  NOBE
"What would this Man? Now upward will he soar," fr. Epistle I.  HeIP
Essential Beauty.  Philip Larkin.  NowV
Essential oils are wrung.  Emily Dickinson.  AmVN; PBMP; PiAm; SBG
Essential poem at the centre of things, The.  A Primitive Like an Orb.  Wallace Stevens.  NOBA
Esther's Tomcat.  Ted Hughes.  PCat
Esthete in Harlem  Langston Hughes.  BPo; SS
Esthetique du Machiavel.  George Starbuck.  PAIC
Esthétique du Mal, sels.  Wallace Stevens.  NOBA
"He was at Naples writing letters home."
"How red the rose that is the soldier's wound."
"Sun, in clownish yellow, but not a clown, The."
Estrich, thou feathered fool and easy prey.  Lucasta's Fan, with a Looking-glass in It.  Richard Lovelace.  SCP-2
Et Incarnatus Est.  William Langland.  Fr. The Vision of Piers Plowman.  BoReV; NOBE
Eternal Dice, The.  César Vallejo, tr. fr. Spanish by James Wright.  IPWM
Eternal Father! strong to save.  The Navy Hymn.  William Whiting.  BLSH
Eternal Female groand, The! it was heard over all the Earth.  A Song of Liberty.  Blake.  MBPR
Eternal gates' terrific porter lifted the northern bar, The.  The Secrets of the Earth.  Blake.  NOBE
Eternal Image, The.  Ruth Pitter.  OxBTC
Eternal Spirit of the chainless mind!  Sonnet on Chillon.  Byron.  Fr. The Prisoner of Chillon.  PAIC; PBMP
Eternity ("He who binds [or bends] to himself a joy").  Blake.  Fr. Several Questions Answered.  BoReV; LAuP; MBPR; NOBE; WIF
Eternity is passion, girl or boy.  Whence Had They Come?  W. B. Yeats.  BoLoP
Ethan Boldt.  Roger Weingarten.  AmPA
Ethelstan, sel.  George Darley.
Runilda's Chant.  PFIr
Ethereal minstrel! pilgrim of the sky!  To a Skylark.  Wordsworth.  MBPR
Ethick.  Robert Bridges.  Fr. The Testament of Beauty.  OxBTC
Ethnic Life, The.  Daniel Halpern.  AmPA
Ethnogenesis  Henry Timrod.  NOBA
Etienne de Silhouette  Cornelius J. Ter Maat.  InPK
Etiquette.  W. S. Gilbert.  FaBoCo
Ettrick.  Lady John Scott.  SLP; WPE
Etude.  Carlos Pellicer, tr. fr. Spanish by H. R. Hays.  LoAs
Etude from the Third Epistle.  Robert Duncan.  Fr. Dante Etudes.  CAAP
Euch, are you having your period?  Alta.  NMM
Euclid.  Vachel Lindsay.  SFF
Eugene Delacroix Says.  Edward Dorn.  NoAM
Eulogy for Populations.  Ron Welburn.  PoBA

Eupheme, *sels.*    Ben Jonson.
   "I sing the just and uncontrolled descent."   SCP-1
   "Truly honoured lady, the Lady Venetia Digby, The."   SCP-1
Euridice.   Alta.   MMD
Europe and America.   David Ignatow.   PBMP
Europe overwhelms me!   Traveling.   Anne Waldman.   RiTi
European Shoe, The.   Michael Benedikt.   AmPA; ConAP
Eurydice   Hilda Doolittle ("H.D.").   VGW
Eustace and Edith.   Charles Tennyson Turner.   VPC
Eutaw Springs.   Philip Freneau.   BTTM
Evacuee, The.   R. S. Thomas.   MPo
Evadne.   Hilda Doolittle ("H.D.").   LoAs; RiTi
Evangeline, *sel.*   Longfellow.
   "This is the forest primeval. The murmuring pines and the hemlocks," *fr.* Prologue.   SpRo
Evaporation Poems.   Kathleen Norris.   IHMS
Evasive souls, of whom the wise lose track.   The Imaginative Life.   Geoffrey Hill.   NoAM
Eve.   Ralph Hodgson.   PAIC; PoTa; SoSe
Eve.   *Unknown.*   *See* Eve's Lament.
Eve Contemplates Sharing Her Sin.   Milton.   *Fr.* Paradise Lost, IX.   OBP
Eve: Night Thoughts.   Judson Jerome.   CoPAm
Eve of July Fourth.   James Bertolino.   HeS
Eve of St. Agnes, The.   Keats.   AnMo; MBPR; PAIC
Eve of Saint Mark, The.   Keats.   MBPR
Eve of Waterloo, The.   Byron.   *See* Waterloo.
Eve Speaks to Adam ("With thee conversing I forget all time").   Milton.   *Fr.* Paradise Lost, IV.   GBL
Eve to Her Daughters.   Judith Wright.   MPo
Eve, with her basket, was.   Eve.   Ralph Hodgson.   PAIC; PoTa; SoSe
Even as a dragon's eye that feels the stress.   Wordsworth.   MBPR
Even as children they were late sleepers.   The Undead.   Richard Wilbur.   CAPP; ConAP
Even as we kill.   On the Birth of My Son, Malcolm Coltrane.   Julius Lester.   PoBA
Even for the wind there was no room.   The Way the Bird Sat.   Ray A. Young Bear.   CDW
Even from the beach I could sense it.   Attack of the Crab Monsters.   Lawrence Raab.   AmPA
Even if the geraniums are artificial.   The Geraniums.   Genevieve Taggard.   VGW
Even if there'd been prayers.   Vincent Buckley.   *Fr.* Golden Builders.   CAAP
Even in bed I pose: desire may grow.   Carnal Knowledge.   Thom Gunn.   BoLoP
Even in the cemetery.   Fitzroy, Carlton.   Vincent Buckley.   *Fr.* Golden Builders.   CAAP
Even in the moment of our earliest kiss.   Edna St. Vincent Millay.   VGW
Even is come; and from the dark Park, hark.   A Nocturnal Sketch.   Thomas Hood.   FaBoCo
Even [or Ev'n] like two little bank-dividing brooks.   My Beloved is Mine and I Am His.   Francis Quarles.   Emblems, V, 3.   NOBE
Even now this landscape is assembling.   All Hallows.   Louise Glück.   AmPA
Even on clear nights, lead the most supple children.   The Great Bear.   John Hollander.   CoPAm; NoAM
Even So.   Dante Gabriel Rossetti.   NOBE
Even Such Is Time [or Tyme].   Sir Walter Ralegh.   *See* Epitaph: "Even such is Time, which takes in trust."
Even the sun-clouds this morning cannot manage such skirts.   Poppies in October.   Sylvia Plath.   NoAM

Even the sun, still warm.   August/ Fresno 1973.   Roberta Spear.   AmPA
Even the tips of their fingers.   The Loss.   Stephen Dunn.   NVAP
Even the train is taller than those shacks.   Homecoming.   John Thompson.   MAT
Even the walls are flowing, even the ceiling.   Variation on Heraclitus.   Louis MacNeice.   NoAM
Even There.   Lyn Lifshin.   IHMS
Even though/ a cat has a kitten.   Scat! Skitten!   David McCord.   ECBV
Even with its own ax to grind, sometimes.   The Mind, Intractable Thing.   Marianne Moore.   Psy
Evenen in the Village.   William Barnes.   VPC
Evening.   Richard Aldington.   Moon
Evening.   Charles Cotton.   SCP-2
Evening.   Hilda Doolittle, ("H. D.").   IPWM; VGW; WPE
Evening.   Thomas Miller.   OxBChV
Evening.   Edith Sitwell.   AIW
Evening.   James Wright.   NOBA
Evening Before Rain.   L. A. G. Strong.   OxBTC
Evening comes early, and soon discovers.   Master's in the Garden Again.   John Crowe Ransom.   NoAM
Evening cracks.   Days of Re-entry.   Patricia Henley.   NPW
Evening drooped toward owl-call, The.   In Italian They Call the Bird Civetta.   Robert Penn Warren.   PiAm
Evening Ebb.   Robinson Jeffers.   NoAM; PSN
Evening gathers everything.   James Stephens.   *Fr.* Hesperus.   LCL
Evening Gown, The.   Karen Swenson.   WBN
Evening Hymn.   John Keble.   PFD
Evening Hymn, An.   Thomas Ken.   *See* All Praise To Thee, My God, This Night.
Evening in Eden.   Milton.   *Fr.* Paradise Lost, IV.   OBP
   (Evening in Paradise.)   NOBE
   (Moon and the Nightingale, The.)   Moon.
Evening in Harvest Time, An.   Charles Tennyson Turner.   VPC
Evening in Paradise.   Milton.   *See* Evening in Eden.
Evening in the Sanitarium.   Louise Bogan.   IHMS; SBG
Evening is clogged with gnats as the light fails.   Alceste in the Wilderness.   Anthony Hecht.   ConAP
Evening isnt so much a playland as it is.   Groupie.   Al Young.   NVAP
Evening: Ponte a Mare, Pisa.   Shelley.   MBPR
Evening Shade.   John Leland.   AmFP
Evening Song.   Sherwood Anderson.   ANTL
Evening Song.   Jean Toomer.   BPo
Evening: to Harriet   Shelley.   MBPR
Evening Walk, An.   Wordsworth.   MBPR
Evening without Angels.   Wallace Stevens.   VGW
Event.   Sylvia Plath.   NOBA
Event, An.   Richard Wilbur.   CoPAm
Ever been Kidnapped.   Kidnap Poem.   Nikki Giovanni.   BPo; InPK; NoAM
Ever-fixed Mark, An.   Kingsley Amis.   NoAM
Ever let the fancy roam.   Fancy.   Keats..   MBPR
Ever since my daughters started to walk.   The Green Tree.   James Reiss.   AmPA
Ever since our lunch of cheese.   Dearest Man-in-the-Moon.   Erica Jong.   MMD; Moon
Everlasting Mercy, The, *sel.*   John Masefield.
   "From '41 to '51."   NoAM
Everlasting Teamwork in Basketball.   H. Victory.   SPo
Everlasting universe of things, The.   Mont Blanc.   Shelley.   MBPR
Every afternoon at four.   Quail Walk.   Heather Ross Miller.   BoAnP

Every branch big with it. Snow in the Suburbs. Thomas Hardy. IPWM; OxBTC; PPP

Every child who has gardening tools. Garden Lore. Juliana Horatia Ewing. OxBChV

Every critic in the town. Robert Fuller Murray. POL

Every day I see from my window. Wild Oats. Norman MacCaig. OxBTC

"Every day I wake up the world," said the cock. The Cock. A. Buttigieg. RAE

Every day I work a little on my biceps. Muscle Building. Dalene Stowe. NPW

Every day our bodies separate. Villanelle. Marilyn Hacker. AmPA

Every day that their sky droops down. Moles. William Stafford. RFM

Every day, walking the city streets. The Nature of Jungles. W. R. Moses. NCSH

Every evening, down into the hardweed. Hardweed Path Going. A. R. Ammons. VGW

Every little nail. Sleepy Song. Arthur Guiterman. ECBV

Every man in the world thinks his banner the best. Pat's Opinion of Flags. Fred Emerson Brooks. InPK

Every man spins a web of light circles. Webs. Carl Sandburg. TH

Every morning at seven o'clock. Tarrier's Song [or Drill, Ye Terriers, Drill!]. Unknown. AIW; RDB

Every morning at six o'clock. Everybody Works but Father. Charles W. McClintock. FSN

Every morning I forget how it is. Poem. Charles Simic. NVAP

Every morning I went to her charity and learned. To a Red-headed Do-good Waitress. Alan Dugan. CAPP; NowV

Every night in the town. Shooting at the Moon. Kim Yo-sop, tr. by Ko Won. Moon

Every October millions of little fish come along the shore. Birds and Fishes. Robinson Jeffers. PiAm; TCP

Every planet is a small plane. The Plane: Earth. Sun-Ra. PoBA

Every stinking son of a bitch. Peace, So That. Greg Kuzma. InPK

Every time I nudge that spring. The Experiment with a Rat. Carl Rakosi. POL

Every time she tugs the sun across the sky. She Doesn't Want to Bring the Tides in Any More. Ruth Whitman. RiTi

Every time the bucks went clattering. Earthy Anecdote. Wallace Stevens. RFM

Every time you hear me sing this song. The Railroad Blues. Unknown. AmFP

Every two hours they broke. The Slaughter-Room Picture. David Steingass. CoPAm

Every year without knowing it I have passed the day. For the Anniversary of My Death. W. S. Merwin. CAPP; CoPAm; InPK; NOBA

Everybody loved Chick Lorimer in our town. Gone. Carl Sandburg. NOBA

Everybody Ought to Make a Change. Unknown. BluL

Everybody wants an intelligent son. At the Washing of My Son. Su Tung P'o, tr. by Kenneth Rexroth. BBGO

Everybody wants to know why I sing the blues. Why I Sing the Blues. B. B. King. MAT

Everybody went to bat three times. Don Larsen's Perfect Game. Paul Goodman. SPo

Everybody Works but Father, with music. Charles W. McClintock. FSN

Everyone Begs for Mercy. John Biguenet. CoPAm

Everyone in class two at the Grammar School. The French Master. Dannie Abse. LP

Everyone in me is a bird. In Celebration of My Uterus. Anne Sexton. CAPP; RiTi

Everyone is after me to jump through hoops. Fear. Pablo Neruda, tr. by Nathanial Tarn. IPWM

Everyone now is crowding everyone. Robert Lowell. Fr. Long Summer CAPP

Everyone Sang ("Everyone suddenly burst out singing"). Siegfried Sassoon. FSFS; NOBE; OxBTC

Everything as before: blown snow. The Guest. Anna Akhmatova, tr. byRichard McKane. LoAs

Everything: Eloy, Arizona, 1956. Ai. AmPA

Everything in Its Place. Arthur Guiterman. ECBV

Everything is a large box--you can't see into it. To Start With. J. S. Harry. CAAP

Everything is, once was not. Life After Death. Richard W. Thomas. PoBA

Everything Is Possible. Robert Pack. PPP

Everything is stuck together. What Holds the Universe Together. James Broughton. MIT

Everything Must Go. Tom Crawford. NVAP

Everything That Acts Is Actual. Denise Levertov. NoAM

Everytime I leave you. Mother. Stephen Vincent. NeAC

Everywhere, everywhere, following me. Camerados. Bayard Taylor. PAIC

Everywhere in constancy, He is intoning, Look! Look! Daisy Aldan. AATT

Everywhere of silver, An. Emily Dickinson. SoSe

Eve's Lament. Unknown, tr. fr. Old Irish by Kuno Meyer. Epi; PFIr
(Eve, tr. by Thomas MacDonagh.) BIRv

Eviction, The. William Allingham. Fr. Laurence Bloomfield in Ireland BIrV

Evidence, The. Van K. Brock. NVAP

Evidence, like the weather, is from, The. In the Giving Vein. Peter Porter. CAAP

Evidence Read at the Trial of the Knave of Hearts. "Lewis Carroll." Fr. Alice's Adventures in Wonderland. PBMP
(Silence in Court.) FaBoCo
("They told me you had been to her.") SS

Evil Devil Woman. Unknown. BluL

Evil does not go always. Lines for a Hard Time. Gena Ford. IHMS

Evil Eye, The. John Ciardi. CoPAm

Evil Is No Black Thing. Sarah Webster Fabio. PoBA

Evil Nigger Waits for Lightnin'. LeRoi Jones. NoAM; NOBA

Evil spirit, your beauty haunts me still, An. Michael Drayton. Fr. Idea. AAS; GBL; NOBE

Evin Dead Behold I Breathe, sel. Alexander Montgomerie. "Evin dead behold I breathe!" SLP

Ev'n like two little bank-dividing brooks. See Even like two little . . .

Evolution. Edwin Brock. MPo

Evolution. May Swenson. TCP

Evolution from the Fish. Robert Bly. NoAM; NOBA

Evolution, though a good thing, has. Bathing with Father. Doug Fetherling. NeAC

Ev'ry Saturday, Willie got his pay. The Bird on Nellie's Hat. Arthur J. Lamb. FSN

Ev'rything is over and I'm feeling bad. My Gal Sal. Paul Dresser. BLSo; FSN

Ewes and lambs, loving the far hillplaces, The. Ad Limina. Joseph Campbell. BIrV

Ex and Squary. Unknown. GBP

Ex-Basketball Player. John Updike. BBGO; CTBA; MiP; SPo

Ex M. Antonio Flaminio, Ad Agellum Suum. John Ashmore. SCP-2

Ex Ore Infantium. Francis Thompson. OxBChV

Exactitude: to memorize. From the Bridge. Albert Goldbarth. NVAP

Examination, The. W. D. Snodgrass. CAPP; ConAP

Excelente Balade of Charitie, An. Thomas Chatterton. LAuP

Excelsior Longfellow. SpRo

Except for me, nobody remembers Clement Attlee. Clement Attlee. Michael Benedikt. CAAP; InPS

Except ourselves, we have no other prayer. Without Ceremony. Vassar Miller. CoPAm

Excepting the diner. Poem to Be Read at 3 A.M. Donald Justice. CoPAm; MiP

Excerpts from a Diary of a War (1-3). John Daniel. TwMBP

Exchange in greed the ungraceful signs. Thrust. The Violent Space. Etheridge Knight. BPo

Excuse, The. Sir Walter Ralegh. AAS; LoAs

Excuse me. Do not speak of nerves. To the Upright. Stephen Dunn. NVAP

Excuse me, isn't that you I see concealed underneath there. Thoughts. Michael Benedikt. ConAP

Excuses. Mary Swanson Stroh. NPW

Exeat. Stevie Smith. NoAM

Execution James A. Randall, Jr. BPo

Execution of Cornelius Vane, The. Sir Herbert Read. NoAM

Execution of Montrose, The. William Edmonstoune Aytoun. BTTM

Exequy, The. Henry King. GBL; MetP; PAIC; PPoe (Exequy on [or upon] His Wife.) BoLoP; NOBE; OBP (Exequy, An: To His Matchless Never-to-be-forgotten Friend.) SCP-2

Exercise. W. S. Merwin. NOBA

Exercise No. 2. William Carlos Williams. TH

Exert thy voice, sweet harbinger of Spring! To the Nightingale. Countess of Winchilsea. PAIC; SBG; WPE

Exeunt. Richard Wilbur. HeIP; NCSH

Exhaust the little moment. Soon it dies. Gwendolyn Brooks. Fr. The Womanhood. TH

Exhortation, An. Shelley. MBPR

Exhortation of a Father to His Children, The. Robert Smith. OxBChV

Exigent Gymnastic, An. Merle Meeter. AATT

Exile. Ernest Dowson. BoLoP

Exiles. "Æ." BIrV

Exiles, The. W. H. Auden. OxBTC

Exile's Letter. Li Po, tr. fr. Chinese by Ezra Pound. TCP

Existence egotistically formed. Homily: Contemporary. Marian Frances Brand. AATT

Exit Lines George Jonas. NeAC

Exit Molloy. Derek Mahon. PFIr; POL

Exit, Pursued by a Bear. James Tipton. HeS

Exodus George Oppen. RRA

Exodus Anita Endrezze Probst. CDW

Exodus, The (August 3, 1492). Emma Lazarus. Fr. By the Waters of Babylon. WPE

Exorcism, The. Theodore Roethke. NoAM

Expect no strange or puzzling meat, no pie. William Cartwright. Fr. A Bill of Fare SCP-2

Expect Nothing. Alice Walker. AmPA

Expense of spirit in a waste of shame, The [or Th]. Sonnets, CXXIX. Shakespeare. Epi; GBL; HeIP; InPS; LoAs; NOBE; OBP; PPoD; PPoe; PPP

Experience. James Simmons. BIrV

Experiment with a Rat, The. Carl Rakosi. POL

Expiration, The. John Donne. LoAs

Explanation. Geof Hewitt. NeAC

Explanations of Love. Carl Sandburg. SFF

Exploration Over the Rim. William Dickey. SS

Explosion of a bomb, The. Perhaps. Stephen Spender. NoAM

Explosions are nearer this evening, The. You Were Wearing Blue. Tom Raworth. TwMBP

Expose yourself! Freak Show and Finale. Lenore Kandel. Fr. Circus. RiTi

Expostulation, An. Isaac Bickerstaffe. FaBoCo; PFIr

Expostulation and Reply. Wordsworth. MBPR

Exposure Wilfred Owen. InPS; NoAM

Express, The. Stephen Spender. MPo; NoAM; NowV; WIF

Exstasie [or Extasie], The. John Donne. See Ecstasy, The.

Extempore Effusion upon the Death of James Hogg. Wordsworth. MBPR; NOBE

Extempore Verses Intended to Allay the Violence of Party-Spirit. John Byrom. See Jacobite Toast.

Extensions of Linear Mobility. Jeanine Hathaway. IHMS

External Element, The. David McFadden. NeAC

Extinct Birds Judith Wright. MAuV

Extracts: from the Journal of Elisa Lynch. Maura Stanton. AmPA

Extraordinary patience of things, The! Carmel Point. Robinson Jeffers. PiAm

Extravagantly your stone gestures. Sentence for Konarak. John Montague. TwMBP

Extreme Unction. Ernest Dowson. BoReV

Extremes. James Whitcomb Riley. ECBV

Extremities of Cold in Hell, The. Thomas Dekker. Fr. Dekker His Dream. SCP-2

Exultation is the going. Emily Dickinson. AmVN

Eye, The. Michael Benedikt. ConAP

Eye, The. Robinson Jeffers. NOBA; PiAm

Eye, The. Richard Wilbur. FiCP

Eye and Tooth. Robert Lowell. CAPP

Eye can hardly pick them out, The. At Grass. Philip Larkin. OxBTC; PSN

Eye is lion of these wastes, The. Whose vision. Tears of St. Francis. Robert Duncan. CAAP

Eye-aya/ I call to mind. Ulivfak's Song of the Caribou. Unknown. AKE

Eyeglasses. Tom Clark. ConAP

Eyeglasses, The. William Carlos Williams. NoAM

Eyeless labourer in the night, The. Woman to Man. Judith Wright. MAuV; WPE

Eyelids fall, the star-charts, The. The Invention of Astronomy. William Matthews. POL

Eyelids glowing, some chill morning, The. Monet: "Les Nymphéas." W. D. Snodgrass. ConAP; TCP

Eyelids meet, The. He'll catch a little nap. In the Smoking Car. Richard Wilbur. ConAP

Eyes and Tears. Andrew Marvell. MetP

Eyes, hide my love, and do not show. Secrecy. Samuel Daniel. Fr. Hymen's Triumph. OLR

Eyes of darkest hue. Dark Eyes. Unknown, tr. fr. Russian. BLSH

Eyes of despair, eyes of fire. Ophelia's Song. Marya Zaturenska. OLR

Eyes of Flesh, The. Sandra Hochman. NMM

Eyes of the Child Do Not See Me, The. Norman H. Russell. VW

Eyes of the Garden. Laura Chester. RiTi

Eyes open to a cry of pulleys, The. Love Calls Us to the Things of This World. Richard Wilbur. AnMo; CAPP; HeIP; InPS; NoAM; PiAm; PPP; TCP; VGW; WIF

Eyes that last I saw in tears. T. S. Eliot. NOBE

Eyes that mock me sign the way, The. Bahnhofstrasse. James Joyce. NoAM

Eyre All Alone. Francis Webb. CAAP

Ezra Pound. Robert Lowell. NoAM; NOBA

Ezra Pound. Jonathan Price. CoPAm
Ezra Pound. Phyllis Webb. MMD
Ezra Shank. *Unknown.* CaYB
Ezry. Archibald MacLeish. NOBA


# F

Fa, mi, fa, re, la, mi. *Unknown.* InPK
Fa saw the Forty-Second. The Forty-Second. *Unknown.* GBP
Fable, A: "Dingy donkey, formal and unchanged, A." John Hookham Frere. FaBoCo
Fable: "Mountain and the squirrel, The." Emerson. PiAm
Fable for Critics, A, *sels.* James Russell Lowell.
  American Literature. AmVN
  Bryant. AmVN; NOBA
  Cooper. NOBA
  Emerson. AmVN; NOBA; PAIC
  Hawthorne. NOBA
  Holmes. NOBA
  Lowell. AmVN; NOBA
  Poe and Longfellow. AmVN; NOBA
  Whittier. AmVN; NOBA
Fable for When There's No Way Out. May Swenson. MiP
Fable of the Mermaid and the Drunks. Pablo Neruda, *tr. fr. Spanish by* Alastair Reid. LP
Fable of the Piece of Glass and the Piece of Ice, The. John Hookham Frere. OxBChV
Fable of the Talented Mockingbird. Scott Bates. BoAnP
Fable of the Transcendent Tannenbaum. Scott Bates. PoTa
Fables, *sel.* John Gay.
  Poet and the Rose, The. PAIC
Fables, The. David Malouf. CAAP
Fabrication of Ancestors. Alan Dugan. NoAM
Face, A. Robert Browning. LoAs
Face, A. Marianne Moore. PiAm; Psy
Face as It Might Be of Love, The. Toi Derricotte. NPW
Face in the Mirror, The. Robert Graves. LP
Face Lift. Sylvia Plath. InPK; PPoD
Face of the precipice is black with lovers, The. Salvador Dali. David Gascoyne. OxBTC
Face sings, alone, The. A Poem for Willie Best. LeRoi Jones. CAPP
Faceless miner. For Laurence Jones. Gary Kizer. CTBA
Faces everwhere! Beautiful ones. Idolatry. Ralph Mecklenburger. SFF
Faces irresolute and unperplexed. In the National Gallery. Siegfried Sassoon. NoAM
Facing West From California's Shore. Walt Whitman. PPoD
Facing you/ I am not jealous. Always. Pablo Neruda, *tr. by* Donald D. Walsh. OLR
Fact of this man having made, The. The Lift. Raymond Souster. POL
Factories are pretending to be closed down for eternity, The. Babylon. Ron Ikan. NVAP
Factory Girl's Come-All-Ye, The. *Unknown.* AmFP
Facts. Ken Smith. TwMBP
Facts have no eyes. One must. Observation of Facts. Charles Tomlinson. TwMBP
Facts of Winter. Marie Harris. MMD
Fade in the sound of summer music. Notes for a Movie Script. M. Carl Holman. PoBA
Faerie Queen, The, *sel.* Spenser.
  Bower of Bliss, The, *fr.* II, 12. NOBE

Care in Heaven, *fr.* II, 8. BoReV
Cave of Despair, The, *fr.* I, 9. NOBE
Garden of Adonis, The, *fr.* III, 6. NOBE
Guyon's Temptation, *fr.* II, 12. OBP
Hill of the Graces, *fr.* VI, 10. NOBE
"Lo! I the man, whose Muse whylome did maske," I, *induction.* PAIC
Masque of Cupid, The, *fr.* III, 12. NOBE
Nature's Reply to Mutability, *fr.* VIII, 7. NOBE
"Right well I wrote, most mighty Soveraine," II, *induction.* PAIC
"Sudden upriseth from her stately place," I, iv. PPP
Failure, A. C. Day Lewis. NOBE
Fain would I change that note. No Other Choice. *Unknown.* GBL; NOBE
Fain would I kiss my Julia's dainty leg. Her Leg [*or* Legs]. Robert Herrick. LoAs; SpRo
Faint Yet Pursuing. Coventry Patmore. The Unknown Eros, I, xii PFD
Fair/ Boy Christian Takes a Break. Jim Harrison. NoAM
Fair and fair, and twice so fair. Oenone and Paris. George Peele. *Fr.* The Arraignment of Paris. NOBE
Fair and Unfair. Robert Francis. VGW
Fair Annie. *Unknown.* PeBB
Fair at Windgap, The. Austin Clarke. OxBTC
Fair Beauty Bride, The. *Unknown.* AmFP
Fair Cassidy. *Unknown, tr. fr. Irish by* Donagh MacDonagh. BIrV
Fair Circassian. Richard Garnett. PoTa
Fair daffodils, we weep to see. To Daffodils. Robert Herrick. AKE; FSFS; InPS; NOBE; PAIC; PPP; SCP-1; WIF
Fair Damsel from London, The. *Unknown.* AmFP
Fair flower, that dost so comely grow. The Wild Honey Suckle. Philip Freneau. AmVN; NOBA; PiAm
Fair, great, and good: since seeing you we see. To the Countess of Salisbury. John Donne. SCP-1
Fair Iris I love, and hourly I die. Mercury's Song to Phaeda. Dryden. *Fr.* Amphitryon. PBMP
Fair is my love, and cruel as she's fair. Samuel Daniel. *Fr.* To Delia. AAS; NOBE
Fair is my love that feeds among the lilies. Bartholomew Griffin. *Fr.* Fidessa, More Chaste Than Kind. GBL
Fair Isabel, poor simple Isabel! Isabella; or, The Pot of Basil. Keats. MBPR
Fair Isle Pattern. James Rankin. MIS
Fair lady Isabel sits in her bower sewing. Lady Isobel and the Elf-Knight. *Unknown.* PeBB
Fair lady, will you travel. The Wooing of Etain. *Unknown, tr. by* John Montague. BIrV
Fair little girl sat under a tree, A. Good Night and Good Morning. Richard Monckton Milnes. OxBChV
Fair lovely maid, or if that title be. To the Fair Clarinda, Who Made Love to Me, Imagin'd More than Woman. Aphra Behn. SBG
Fair Lucy was sitting in her own cabin door. Lizie Wna. *Unknown.* AmFP
Fair Maid by the Shore, The. *Unknown.* AmFP
Fair maid who, the first of May, The. Mother Goose. MG
Fair maiden, white and red. The Voice from the Well. George Peele. *Fr.* The Old Wife's Tale. NOBE
Fair Margaret and Sweet William. *Unknown.* AmFP
Fair Mary sat at her father's castle gate. Willie of Winsbury. *Unknown.* AmFP
Fair Morning, The. Jones Very. NOBA
Fair Phoebe and Her Dark-eyed Sailor. *Unknown.* AmFP
Fair Phyllis I saw sitting all alone. *Unknown.* GBL

Fair seed-time had my soul, and I grew up.  Childhood and School-Time.  Wordsworth.  *Fr.* The Prelude, I.  NOBE

Fair Singer, The.  Andrew Marvell.  LoAs; NOBE

Fair star of evening, splendour of the west.  Composed by the Sea-Side, near Calais, August, 1802.  Wordsworth.  MBPR

Fair stood the wind for France.  The Ballad of Agincourt.  Michael Drayton.  BTTM; PPoD

Fair Summer droops, droop men and beast therefore.  Thomas Nashe.  *Fr.* Summer's Last Will and Testament.  SCP-2

Fair Virtue, *sel.*  George Wither.
   Lover's Resolution, A.  NOBE

Fair Weather.  Dorothy Parker.  SGB

Faire daffadills, we weep to see.  *See* Fair daffodils. . .

Faire is my love, and cruell as she's faire.  *See* Fair is my love. . .

Fairest action of our human life, The.  Lady Elizabeth Carey.  *Fr.* Mariam, IV.  WPE

"Fairest, The!" Aphrodite laughed, and caught.  Apple-Logia.  Marian Frances Brand.  AATT

Fairest day that ever yet has shone, The.  The Lost.  Jones Very.  PiAm; NOBA

Fairest Flower, The.  John Audelay.  OxBM

Fairest flower, all flowers excelling.  To a Child Five Years Old.  Nathaniel Cotton.  OxBChV

Fairest Lord Jesus, *with music.  Unknown, tr. fr. German.*  BLSH

Fairest of stars, that with your persant light.  Balade Simple.  John Lydgate.  GBL

Fairground.  W. H. Auden.  LP

Fairies, The.  William Allingham.  ECBV; LCL; NOBE; OxBChV

Fairies.  Rose Fyleman.  OxBChV

Fairies Break Their Dances, The.  A. E. Housman.  NoAM

Fairies' Farewell, The.  Richard Corbet.  NOBE
   "Farewell, rewards and fairies," *sel.* SCP-2

Fairies Have Never a Penny to Spend, The.  Rose Fyleman.  OxBChV

Fairweill.  *Unknown.*  SLP

Fairy, The.  Blake.  MBPR

Fairy Went A-Marketing, A.  Rose Fyleman.  OxBChV

Faith Healing.  Philip Larkin.  NoAM

Faith, Hope, and Charity.  Giovanni Battista Guarini, *tr. fr. Italian by* Samuel Taylor Coleridge.  MBPR

"Faith" is a fine invention.  Emily Dickinson.  NOBA; PiAm

Faith of Our Fathers, *with music.*  Frederick W. Faber.  BLSH

Faith Unfaithful.  Siegfried Sassoon.  BoReV

Faithful, The.  Jane Cooper.  CoPAm

Faithful messinger, which is the nicht, The.  *At. to* James I, King of Scotland.  *Fr.* Sang on Absence.  SLP

Faithful Shepherdess, The, *sels.*  John Fletcher.
   Hymn to Pan, *fr.* I, ii.  NOBE
   "Shepherds all, and maidens fair," II, i.  SCP-2

Faithless Nellie Gray.  Thomas Hood.  FaBoCo

Faithless Wife, The.  Federico García Lorca, *tr. fr. Spanish by* A. L. Lloyd.  BoLoP

Faithlesse and fond mortality.  Upon the Death of a Gentleman.  Richard Crashaw.  MetP

Fake,/ I am a thief an honest thief, I lead none.  Judas Before.  Lucille F. Travis.  AATT

Falcon, The.  The Knight of Kürenberg, *tr. fr. German by* Margarete Münsterberg.  LoAs

Falcon Woman, The.  Robert Graves.  BuTh; LoAS

Falconers.  Lady Luck.  Ann Gottlieb.  NMM

Fall.  Robert Francis.  VGW

Fall.  Robert Hass.  AmPA

Fall, The.  Edmund Waller.  SCP-2

Fall, The: a Song.  Earl of Rochester.  SCP-2

Fall Again, The.  Howard Nemerov.  ConAP

Fall Comes in Back-Country Vermont.  Robert Penn Warren.  VGW

Fall Down.  Calvin C. Hernton.  PoBA

Fall In.  Lincoln Kirstein.  NoAM

Fall in Massachusetts.  Isabella Gardner.  RiTi

Fall, Leaves, Fall.  Emily Brontë.  FSFS

Fall 1961.  Robert Lowell.  PSN; VGW

Fall none but angels suddenly to hell?  Fulke Greville.  *Fr.* Mustapha.  SCP-2

Fall of Hyperion, The: a Dream.  Keats.  MBPR
   Death, *sel.* OBP

Fall of J. W. Beane, The.  Oliver Herford.  PoTa

Fall of Princes, The, *sel.*  John Lydgate.
   "And semblably, though I go not upright," *fr.* Epilogue.  OxBM

Fall of Rome, The.  W. H. Auden.  AnMo; InPS; MAT; OxBTC

Fall of the House of Usher, The, *sel.*  Poe.
   Haunted Palace, The.  NOBA; PiAm

Fall of the House of Usher, The.  Reed Whittemore.  InPK

Fall Practice.  Dabney Stuart.  CoPAm

Fallen flowers rise.  Haiku.  Arakida Moritake.  SoSe

Falling.  James Dickey.  CAAP

Falling.  Bob Kaufman.  PoBA

Falling Asleep.  Siegfried Sassoon.  FSFS; OxBTC

Falling Asleep over the Aeneid.  Robert Lowell.  NoAM

Falling flower, The.  Haiku.  Arakida Moritake.  SoSe

Falling in Love.  David Perkins.  NCSH

Falling In Love with Tygers.  Thomas Brush.  NVAP

Falling Moon.  Roberta Hill.  CDW

Falling Out.  Helen Chasin.  IHMS

Falling separate into the dark.  Late at Night.  William Stafford.  POL; RFM

Fallingstars/ "a field of/ buttercups."  Treblinka Gas Chamber.  Phyllis Webb.  MMD

Fallow Deer at the Lonely House, The.  Thomas Hardy.  BoAnP

False Fox, The.  *Unknown.*  GBP; OxBM

False Gallop of Analogies, A.  Warham St. Leger.  FaBoCo

False Knight upon the Road, The.  *Unknown.*  AmFP; GBP; PeBB

False life! a foil and no more, when.  Quickness.  Henry Vaughan.  BoReV; NOBE; SCP-1

False Luve, and Hae Ye Played Me This?  *Unknown.*  GBP; POL

False Nancy.  *Unknown.*  AmFP

False Security.  John Betjeman.  BBGO; LP

False Sir John a-wooning came.  May Colvin.  *Unknown.*  PBMP

False though she be to me and love.  Song.  Congreve.  BoLoP; NOBE; POL

Fame.  Charlotte Mew.  SBG

Fame, like a wayward girl, will still be coy.  On Fame.  Keats.  MBPR

Famed ship *California*, a ship of high renown, The.  The Girls around Cape Horn.  *Unknown.*  AmFP

Familiar Epistle, A.  Ann Murry.  WPE

Families, when a child is born.  On the Birth of His Son.  Su Tung-Po, *tr. by* Arthur Waley.  BuTh; OFD

Family crowded, The.  Blood and My Brother.  Richard Mathews.  AATT

Family 8.  Lyn Lifshin.  NeAC

Family Game.  Morton Marcus.  NVAP

Family Goldschmitt, The.  Henri Coulette.  NowV

Family Man, A.  Maxine W. Kumin.  CoPAm; IHMS

Family portrait not too stale to record, A.  Father and Son: 1939.  William Plomer.  NoAM

Family Prime.  Mark Van Doren.  VGW

Famine Year, The.  Lady Wilde.  PFIr

"Famous bard, he comes, The! The vision nears!" Visiting Poet. John Frederick Nims. InPK

Famous Hot Pepper Eating Contest, The. Sam Hamod. SA

Famously she descended, her red hair. A Recollection. John Peale Bishop. LoAs; PPoD

Fan for His Daughter, A. Stéphane Mallarmé, *tr. fr. French by* David Paul. RRA

Fanaticism? No. Writing is exciting. Baseball and Writing. Marianne Moore. SPo

Fanatics have their dreams, wherewith they weave. The Fall of Hyperion: a Dream. Keats. MBPR

Fancy. Robert Creeley. NOBA

Fancy. Keats. MBPR

Fane Wald I Luve. John Clerk. SLP

Fanfare for the Makers, A, *abr.* Louis MacNeice. NOBE

Fantasia. Winifrid M. Letts. PFIr

Fantasies of old age. Merced. Adrienne Rich. NOBA

Far back when I went zig-zagging. Orion. Adrienne Rich. NoAM; WPE

Far Cry from Africa, A. Derek Walcott. NoAM

"Far enough down is China," somebody said. Digging for China. Richard Wilbur. BuTh; NCSH; PiAm; TH

Far, far down. City Afternoon. Barbara Howes. PPoD

Far far from gusty waves, these children's faces. An Elementary School Class Room in a Slum. Stephen Spender. MPo; PPoD; WIF

Far from Africa: Four Poems. Margaret Danner. PoBA
Garnishing the Aviary, I. BPo

Far from far. Bobadil. James Reeves. LCL

Far from my dearest friend, 'tis mine to rove. An Evening Walk. Wordsworth. MBPR

Far from the trouble and toil of town. Old Man Platypus. A. B. Paterson. BoAnP

Far from the vulgar haunts of men. On the Same. Roy Campbell. OxBTC

Far in the background a blue mountain waits. Venus and the Lute Player. Paul Engle. WIF

Far out of sight forever stands the sea. The Slow Pacific Swell. Yvor Winters. HeIP; NoAM; NOBA; PiAm

Far Rockaway. Delmore Schwartz. NoAM

Far to sea, west from Spain. The Land of Cockaigne. *Unknown, tr. by* John Montague. BIrV

Fara Diddle Dyno. *Unknown.* FaBoCo; SCP-2

Fare Thee well. Byron. MBPR

Fare Thee Well. *Unknown, tr. fr. Chippewa by* Frances Densmore. PBMP

Fare Thee Well Blues. *Unknown.* BluL

Fare thee well. The time is come. Fare Thee Well. *Unknown, tr. by* Frances Densmore. PBMP

Fare wel Advent! Christemas is cum. Farewell Advent. *At. to* James Ryman. OxBM

Fare Well. Walter de la Mare. NOBE

Fare you well, my blue-eyed girl. Blue-eyed Girl. *Unknown.* AmFP

Fare You Well, My Darling. *Unknown.* AmFP

Farewell, A: "And if I did, what then?" George Gascoigne. *Fr.* The Adventures of Master F. I. GBL; NOBE

Farewell, A: "Farewell, thou little nook of mountain-ground." Wordsworth. MBPR

Farewell, A: "My fairest child, I have no song to give you." Charles Kingsley. OxBChV

Farewell, A: "Oft have I mused, but now at length I find." Sir Philip Sidney. GBL; NOBE

Farewell, A: "Partner in the corner bar is high, a grin." Stanley Kiesel. HeS

Farewell: "We were gone from each other." Iain Crichton Smith. SLP

Farewell: "What should I say." Sir Thomas Wyatt. NOBE ("What should I say.") LoAs; NOBE

Farewell, A: "With all my will, but much against my heart." Coventry Patmore. The Unknown Eros, I, xvi. BoLoP; NOBE

Farewell: "You sang round-dance songs." Liz Sohappy Bahe. CDW

Farewell, a Welcome, A. Lisel Mueller. Moon

Farewell Advent. *At. to* James Ryman. OxBM

Farewell, all my welfare. Sir Thomas Wyatt. GBL

Farewell, dear babe, my heart's too much content. In Memory of My Dear Grandchild Elizabeth Bradstreet. Anne Bradstreet. WPE

Farewell, dear scenes, for ever closed to me. Lines Written on a Window Shutter at Weston. William Cowper. LAuP

Farewell false love, the oracle of lies. A Farewell to false Love. Sir Walter Ralegh. BoLoP; LoAs

Farewell! If Ever Fondest Prayer. Byron. VoPo

Farewell, love and all thy laws for ever. A Renoucing of Love. Sir Thomas Wyatt. AAS; GBL; SoSe

Farewell, O eyes which I ne'er saw before. Coming from——in a Dark Night. Jane Barker. SCP-2

Farewell, Oh sun, Arcadia's clearest light. Sestina. Sir Philip Sidney. *Fr.* Arcadia. PAIC

Farewell Poem. Sandra Hochman. RiTi

Farewell, rewards and fairies. The Fairies' Farewell. Richard Corbet. NOBE; SCP-2

Farewell sweet boy, complain not of my truth. Fulke Greville. *Fr.* Caelica. GBL

"Farewell, sweet Jane, for I must go across the flowing sea." Sweet Jane. *Unknown.* AmFP

Farewell, Sweet Mary. *Unknown.* AmFP

Farewell this World! *Unknown.* OxBM

Farewell! thou art too dear for my possessing. Sonnets, LXXXVII. Shakespeare. InPS; LoAs; NOBE; PPoD

Farewell, thou child of my right hand, and joy. On My First Son. Ben Jonson. HeIP; IPWM; LoAs; NOBE; OBP; PAIC; PBMP; PPoe; SCP-1; VoPo

Farewell, thou little nook of mountain-ground. A Farewell. Wordsworth. MBPR

Farewell to Arms. George Peele. *See* His Golden Locks Time Hath to Silver Turned.

"Farewell to barn and stack and tree." A. E. Housman. AIW

Farewell to Bath. Lady Mary Wortley Montagu. WPE

Farewell to False Love, A. Sir Walter Ralegh. BoLoP; LoAs

Farewell to Juliet. Wilfrid Blunt. *Fr.* The Love Sonnets of Proteus. BoLoP
("I see you, Juliet, still, with your straw hat.") OxBTC

Farewell to Kingsbridge. *Unknown.* AIW

Farewell to Kurdistan. Rosemary Tonks. OxBTC

Farewell to Love. Michael Drayton. *Fr.* Idea. VoPo
("Since there's no help, come let us kiss and part.") AAS; BoLoP; Epi; GBL; HeIP; InPK; InPS; LoAs; NOBE; PAIC; PBMP; PPoD; PPoe; SoSe

Farewell to Love. Sir John Suckling. SCP-2

Farewell to the Moon, A. Ed Ochester. Moon

Farewell, too little and too lately known. To the Memory of Mr. Oldham. Dryden. HeIP; InPK; InPS; NOBE; PAIC; PPoe; PPP; Prf

Farewell, Ungrateful Traitor. Dryden. *Fr.* The Spanish Friar, V, i. BoLoP; NOBE

Farewell with a Mischeife. George Gascoigne. AAS

Farm, The. Vassar Miller. NCSH

Farm Boy after Summer. Robert Francis. NCSH

Farm boys wild to couple. The Sheep Child. James Dickey. CAPP; CoPAm; NoAM; NOBA; Prf

Farm on the Great Plains, The. William Stafford. VGW

Farm Picture, A.  Walt Whitman.  InPS; PPoe

Farm was abandoned, The.  North Dakota Gothic.  Mark Vinz. HeS

Farmer, The.  Terry Stokes.  POL

Farmer and the Shanty Boy, The.  *Unknown.*  AmFP

Farmer had a daughter whose beauty ne'er was told, A.  The Banks of Sweet Dundee.  *Unknown.*  AmFP

Farmer in Bungleton, A.  Mary Mapes Dodge.  ECBV

Farmer went riding [*or* trotting] upon his gray mare, A.  Mother Goose.  ECBV; MG

Farmer's Bride, The.  Charlotte Mew.  BoLoP; OxBTC; SBG; WPE

Farmer's Complaint, The, *orig. and mod. English prose..  Unknown.* OxBM

Farmer's Curst Wife, The.  *Unknown.*  AIW; AmFP

Farmer's Life, A.  *Unknown.*  RAE

Farmer's Point of View.  Alan Brownjohn.  BuTh

Farmer's Wife, The.  Anne Sexton.  CoPAm

Farmer's Wife, The.  Mary Swanson Stroh.  NPW

Farrell O'Reilly.  Oliver St. John Gogarty.  OxBTC

Farther and farther from the three Pa Roads.  On New Year's Eve. Ts'uei T'u, *tr. by* Witter Bynner.  OFD

Farther east it wouldn't be on the map.  Midwest Town.  Ruth De Long Peterson.  ANTL

Farther in summer than the birds.  Emily Dickinson.  AmVN

Farwell, A: "And if I did, what then?"  George Gascoigne.  *See* And If I Did, What Then?

Fascination of What's Difficult, The.  W. B. Yeats.  BIrV; Epi

Fashionable Poet Reading.  Tony Connor.  PPoD

Fast rode the knight.  War Is Kind, VIII.  Stephen Crane.  PiAm

Faster than fairies, faster than witches.  From a Railway Carriage. Robert Louis Stevenson.  OxBChV

Fastidious Serpent, The.  Henry Johnstone.  ECBV

Fat black bucks in a wine-barrel room.  The Congo.  Vachel Lindsay.  NoAM; NOBA

Fat cat on the mat, The.  Cat.  J. R. R. Tolkien.  ECBV

Fat-kneed god! Feeder of mangy leopards!  You Also, Gaius Valerius Catullus.  Archibald MacLeish.  NoAM

Fat Man in the Mirror, The.  Robert Lowell.  AnMo

Fat mothering boy that won't.  Won't Go to School.  James Rankin.  MIS

Fat White Woman Speaks, The.  G. K. Chesterton.  SpRo

Fatal Love.  Matthew Prior.  FaBoCo

Fatal Ship, The.  Robert Stephen Hawker.  VPC

Fatal Sisters, The.  Thomas Gray, *after the Icelandic.*  LAuP

Father, The.  Desmond O'Grady.  NoAM

Father,/ Where do giants go to cry?  A Small Discovery.  James A. Emanuel.  LCL

Father and Child.  Gwen Harwood.  WPE
    Barn Owl, *sel.*  CAAP

Father and Child.  W. B. Yeats.  RRA; TCP

Father and Daughter.  Joanne Casullo.  NPW

Father and His Children, The.  *Unknown.*  OxBChV

Father and I went down to camp.  Yankee Doodle.  *Unknown, at. to* Richard Shuckburg.  AIW; AmFP; BLSo; BTTM

Father and Son.  F. R. Higgins.  BIrV; PFIr

Father and Son.  Stanley Kunitz.  NoAM

Father and Son: 1939.  William Plomer.  NoAM

Father, be with me still.  From Thursday.  Barbara Earl Thomson.  AATT

Father, father, where are you going.  The Little Boy Lost.  Blake. *Fr.* Songs of Innocence.  LAuP; MPBR

Father Gilligan.  W. B. Yeats.  *See* Ballad of Father Gilligan, The.

Father Grumble.  *Unknown.*  AmFP

Father, I expect your eyes.  Before the Mountain.  Elizabeth Libbey.  AmPA

Father is hard to live with.  Old Storm.  David Phillips.  NeAC

Father Is Home.  *Unknown.*  ECBV

Father Missouri takes his own.  Foreclosure.  Sterling A. Brown. PoBA

Father of heaven, after squandered days.  Petrarch, *tr. by* R. G. Barnes.  Sonnets to Laura: To Laura in Life, LXII.  Epi

Father of lights! what sunny seed.  Cock-Crowing.  Henry Vaughan.  SCP-1

Father of My Country, The.  Diane Wakoski.  NoAM

Father of Night.  Bob Dylan.  GrRo

Father of Women, A.  Alice Meynell.  SBG; WPE

Father O'Flynn.  Alfred Perceval Graves.  PFIr

Father, on the first day on the Hunting Moon.  The First Day of the Hunting Moon.  Patricia Low.  VGW

Father Out, an' Mother Hwome, A.  William Barnes.  VPC

Father qua Father.  Celebration for a Young Priest.  Barbara Earl Thomson.  AATT

Father Son and Holy Ghost.  Audre Lorde.  PoBA

Father, the Year Is Fallen.  Audre Lorde.  PoBA

Father, this year's jinx rides us apart.  All My Pretty Ones.  Anne Sexton.  NoAM

"Father, what is truelove."  Truelove.  Mark Van Doren.  AIW

Father William.  "Lewis Carroll".  *Fr.* Alice's Adventure's in Wonderland, *ch.* 5.  SpRo; SS
    (You Are Old, Father William.)  OxBChV
    ("You are old, Father William," the young man said.) FaBoCo

Fatherless and motherless.  *Unknown.*  GBP

Fatherless, 250 people.  Verigin, Moving in Alone.  John Newlove.  NeAC

Fathers, The.  Siegfried Sassoon.  NoAM

Fathers: naked, you stand for their big faces.  This Is a Poem for the Dead.  Michael Ryan.  AmPA

Fathers told us, The.  Raspberries.  Doug Flaherty.  HeS

Father's voice.  William Stafford.  RFM

Fatigue.  Hilaire Belloc.  FaBoCo; OxBTC

Fatigue, regrets. The lights.  The Demon Lover.  Adrienne Rich. IHMS

Fatted/ on herbs, swollen on crabapples.  The Porcupine.  Galway Kinnell.  CoPAm; NOBA

Faust's Servant.  Roy Fuller.  OxBTC

Fawn's Foster-Mother.  Robinson Jeffers.  NoAm; NOBA

Fay Wray to the King.  Judith Rechter.  NMM

Fear.  Pablo Neruda, *tr. fr. Spanish by* Nathanial Tarn.  IPWM

Fear, The.  Margaret Reynolds.  MIS

Fear death?—to feel the fog in my throat.  Prospice.  Robert Browning.  PAIC; PFD; VoPo

Fear me, virgin whosoever.  After the Pleasure Party.  Herman Melville.  AmVN

Fear No More the Heat o' the Sun.  Shakespeare.  *Fr.* Cymbeline, IV, ii.  AIW; GBL; HeIP; InPK; InPS; OBP; PBMP; PPoe; SoSe
    (Dirge for Fidele.)  NOBE

Fear of Flying, The.  Mona Van Duyn.  NMM

Fearful Finale of the Irascible Mouse, The.  Guy Wetmore Carryl. ECBV

Fearful I peer upon the mountain path.  Eleven Addresses to the Lord, X.  John Berryman.  PiAm

Fears in solitude.  Samuel Taylor Coleridge.  MBPR

Feast is o'er—the music and the stir, The.  After the School-Feast. Charles Tennyson Turner.  VPC

Feast of the Ram's Horn.  Harvey Shapiro.  VGW

Feather plucked out and tossed away, A.  Dirt Road.  Tom Hennen.  HeS

Feathers and Moss. Jean Ingelow. SpRo

Feathers blacken against the sun. Manifest Destiny. Anita Endrezze Probst. CDW

Feathers of Snow. *Unknown.* GBP

Feathers of the willow, The. Song. Richard Watson Dixon. NOBE

Feathers up fast, and steeples; then in clods. The Fountain. Donald Davie. OxBTC

Featherstone's Doom. Robert Stephen Hawker. VPC

Feathery forests are blown back, frost rends, The. Winter. John Lyle Donaghy. BIrV

Feature Time. Jerry Hammond. PPoD

February. John Clare. *Fr.* The Shepherd's Calendar. NOBE

February. William Morris. *Fr.* The Earthly Paradise. VPC

February Afternoon. Edward Thomas. NoAM

February Evening in New York. Denise Levertov. InPS; NoAM

February I Turn off the Porch Light and Go Outside. James Tipton. HeS

February Loves. Richmond Lattimore. LoAS

Feckless Dinner Party, The. Walter de la Mare. PoTa

Fee, Fi, Fo, Fum. Eve Merriam. *Fr.* The Inner-City Mother Goose. IPWM

Feeding Cycle of the Catfish, The. Tom Crawford. NVAP

Feeding the Lions. Norman Jordan. CTBA; PoBA

Feel free. To Bobby Seale. Lucille Clifton. PoBA

Feel Like a Bird. May Swenson. SoSe

Feel of Hands, The. Thom Gunn. PSN

Feeling, The. William Bronk. VGW

Feeling so up into the air, The. Some Feelings. Michael Benedikt. ConAP

Feelings I don't have I don't have, The. To Women, as Far as I'm Concerned. D. H. Lawrence. InPS

Feelings of a Republican on the Fall of Bonaparte. Shelley. MBPR

Feigned Courage. Charles *and* Mary Lamb. OxBChV

Feliks Skrzynecki. Peter Skrzynecki. CAAP

Felix Randal. Gerard Manley Hopkins. BoReV; Epi; InPS; NoAM; NOBE; OBP

Felixstowe, or The Last of Her Order. Sir John Betjeman. OxBTC

Felled at a Word? Nathaniel Wanley. SCP-2

Fellows up in Personnel, The. The Perforated Spirit. Morris Bishop. MiP

Felo De Se. Thomas Blackburn. OxBTC

Female Friend, The. Cornelius Whur. FaBoCo

Female Vagrant, The. Wordsworth. MBPR

Fence beyond fence from breakfast. The Names of the Humble. Les A. Murray. *Fr.* Walking to the Cattle-Place. CAAP

Fence Wire. James Dickey. VGW

Fer in see by west Spaygne. The Land of Cockayne. *Unknown.* OxBM

Feral Pioneers, The. Ishmael Reed. PoBA

Ferdinando and Elvira. W. S. Gilbert. FaBoCo

Fern Hill. Dylan Thomas. BBGO; FSFS; HeIP; InPK; InPS; IPWM; NoAM; NOBE; NowV; OxBTC; PPoD; PPoe; PPP; TCP; VoPo; WIF

Ferry Me across the Water. Christina Rossetti. ECBV; OxBChV

Fertile Valley of the Nile, The. Eve Merriam. IHMS

Feste's Song ("O mistress mine"). Shakespeare. *Fr.* Twelfth Night, II, iii. BoLoP

("O mistress mine, where are you roaming?") GBL; HeIP; InPS; NOBE; OLR

(Sweet-and-Twenty.) GrRo

Festivals have I seen that were not names. Calais, August 15, 1802. Wordsworth. MBPR

Fetching Cows. Norman MacCaig. BoAnP; LP

Fete confused me, The. Guest played the part of gods. Sigismundo. Linda Gregg. AmPA

Fever 103°. Sylvia Plath. AnMo; NoAM; NOBA; PiAm; VGW

Fever Toy, The. Charles Wright. AmPA

Feverish room and that white bed, The. White Heliotrope. Arthur Symons. BoLoP; InPS

Few light flakes of snow, A. Kyoto: March. Gary Snyder. PPP

Few rape men or kill coons so I bat them, A! Mess Occupations. Ted Berrigan. CAAP

Few years later, A. Endings. Daniel Halpern. CAAP

Fhairshon swore a feud. The Massacre of the Macpherson. William Edmonstoune Aytoun. FaBoCo

Fiametta. John Peale Bishop. LoAs

Fiascherino. Charles Tomlinson. NoAM

Fickle One, The. Pablo Neruda, *tr. fr. Spanish by* Donald D. Walsh. OLR

Fiction of relationship, The. New Potatoes. Ken Belford. NeAC

Fiddle-de-dee, fiddle-de-dee. *Unknown.* MG

Fiddlehead, The. David McFadden. NeAC

Fiddle-I-Fee. *Unknown.* AmFP

Fiddler Jones. Edgar Lee Masters. *Fr.* Spoon River Anthology. NoAM

Fiddler's Song. George Mackay Brown. SLP

Fiddling Cat, The. *Unknown.* ECBV

Fidessa, More Chaste than Kind, *sels.* Bartholomew Griffin.

"Care-charmer sleepe, sweet ease in restles miserie," XV. AAS

"Fair is my love that feeds among the lilies," XXXVII. GBL

"Fly [*or* Flye] to her heart; hover about her heart," XXIII. AAS; LoAs

"I have not spent the April of my time," XXXV. AAS; LoAs

"My ladies haire is threeds of beaten gold," XXXI. AAS

Fie on Eastern Luxury! ("Persicos odi"). Horace, *tr. fr. Latin by* Hartley Coleridge. Odes, I, 38. InPK

(From Horace, *tr. by* Gerard Manley Hopkins.) InPK

(Preference Declared, The, *tr. by* Eugene Field.) InPK

(Simplicity, *tr. by* William Cowper.) InPK

Field and Forest. Randall Jarrell. VGW

Field Day. W. R. Rodgers. BIrV

Field Full of Folk, The. William Langland.. *See* Prologue: "In a summer season, when soft was the sun."

Field of Autumn. Laurie Lee. NCSH

Field of corn and a bird in flight, A. Sensible People. James Stephens. RAE

Field of Light, A. Theodore Roethke. PiAm

Field of Waterloo, The. Byron. *Fr.* Childe Harold's Pilgrimage, III. BTTM

("Stop—for thy tread is on an empire's dust.") InPS

Field with Figurations. Warren Slesinger. HeS

Fieldmouse, The. Cecil Frances Alexander. OxBChV

Fieldmouse, A/ crouches low. Robert Sund. BoAnP

Field from Islington to Marybone, The. To the Jews. Blake. *Fr.* Jerusalem. MBPR

Fiend, The. James Dickey. CoPAm; PPP

Fierce musical cries of a couple of sparrowhawks, The. Birds. Robinson Jeffers. VGW

Fiery mountains answer each other, The. Liberty. Shelley. MBPR

Fifteen Boys. Bella Akhmadulina, *tr. fr. Russiam by* George Reavey. BuTh

Fifteen churches lie here. At Dunwich. Anthony Thwaite. MPo

Fifteen Million Plastic Bags. Adrian Mitchell. OxBTC

Fifteen nights I have lain awake and called you. Elegy for a Cricket. J. V. Cunningham. NoAM

Fifteen Ships on Georges Banks. *Unknown.* AmFP

Fifteen years ago and twenty. To an Athlete Turned Poet. Peter Meinke. SPo

Fifteen years in the coal mine. Coal Diggin' Blues. *Unknown.* AmFP

Fifth Day. Robert D. Fitzgerald. MAuV

Fifth-Floor Window, The. Lola Ridge. WPE

Fifties, The. Ira Sadoff. AmPA

50-50. Langston Hughes. NoAM; NOBA

59th Street Bridge Song, The. Paul Simon. TCP

Fifty years and three. My Dad and Mam They Did Agree. *Unknown.* POL

Fig for Momus, A, *sel.* Thomas Lodge.
"In every land from Gades to Ganges flood." TVS

Fight, The. Sam Hamod. SA

Fight your little fight, my boy. Don'ts. D. H. Lawrence. NoAM

Fighting Her. David Phillips. NeAC

Fight my dependency. Alta. MMD

Fighting Talk. Tom Buchan. MIS

Figure. Marcia Lee Masters. HeS

Figure of Plain Force, A. Michael Heffernan. HeS

Figurehead, The. Léonie Adams. WPE

Figurehead, The. Crosbie Garstin. PoTa

Figures and Ground. Robert Leverant. MIT

Figures in a Ruined Balloon. George Hitchcock. VGW

Figures on the Frieze, The. Alastair Reid. SLP

Filing-cabinet of human lives, A. Apartment House. Gerald Raftery. SFF

Fill High the Bowl. John Keble. PFD

Fill the Bowl, Butler. *Unknown.* OxBM

Fill your dark glasses with water and toast. Rip-off #1: Hippie Capitalism. Geof Hewitt. NeAC

Filling her compact and delicious body. John Berryman. *Fr.* Dream Songs. BoLoP; CAPP; LoAs; PSN

Filling the mind. The Clouds. William Carlos Williams. VGW

Filtres. Andrew Hoyem. MIT

Final Soliloquy of the Interior Paramour. Wallace Stevens. PiAm

Final Solstice, The. Robert Adamson. CAAP

Final tiny gnash snapped strand from claw, A. Mus Ridiculus Non. Marie De L. Welch. BoAnP

Finale. Carl Sandburg. *Fr.* Prairie. ANTL

Finally. Bruce Severy. HeS

Finally, from your house, there is no view. Water Island. Howard Moss. Prf

Finally retired pensionless. Big Momma. Don L. Lee. BPo

Finally the problem is my meaning. Guevara with Minutes to Go. John William Corrington. CoPAm

Finally, to forgo love is to kiss a leaf. Rescue the Dead. David Ignatow. ConAP; VGW

Finch-notes and swallow-notes tell the new year. Spring Thoughts. Huang-fu Jan, *tr. by* Witter Bynner. OFD

Finches, The. Thomas W. Shapcott. BoAnP

Find. Josephine Miles. WPE

Finding a Poem. Eve Merriam. RFM

Finding is the first act. Emily Dickinson. NOBA; Psy

Finding Roots. Judith Minty. HeS

Finding the hotel was not the real problem. The Peddler. Hollis Summers. CoPAm

Finding the Pistol. Gibbons Ruark. MAT

Finding Words in Winter. John Judson. HeS

Finding You. Virginia Gilbert. IHMS; NVAP

Fine feelings under blockade! Cargoes just in from Kamschatka! Winter Coming On. Martin Bell. OxBTC

Fine Flowers in the Valley, *with music. Unknown.* RDB

Fine knacks for ladies, cheap, choice, brave and new! A Pedlar. *Unknown.* NOBE

Fine young folly, though you were. Pretty Sport. William Habington. NOBE

Finesse be first, whose elegance deplores. Six Poets in Search of a Lawyer. Donald Hall. SoSe

Finger Points to the Moon, A. R. D. Laing. Moon

Finished at last, he escaped from that hideous. Christ's Descent into Hell. Rainer Maria Rilke, *tr. by* James Wright *and* Sarah Youngblood. Prf

Finnegans Wake, *sel.* James Joyce.
Ondt and the Gracehoper, The. BIrV

Fire. Anita Barrows. RiTi

Fire, The. Robert Creeley. NOBA

Fire, The. Robert Duncan. *Fr.* Passages. VGW

Fire, The. Louise Glück. CAAP

Fire. Langston Hughes. NoAM; NOBA; PiAm

Fire and brimstone have been modified, The. Seventy. Margaret Reynolds. MIS

Fire and Ice. Robert Frost. AnMo; HeIP; InPK; LoAs; MiP; NoAM; NOBA; PPP; SoSe

Fire and Rain. James Taylor. WIF

Fire at Alexandria, The. Theodore Weiss. NoAM

Fire burns down on winter nights, The. Dark Hope. Wade Hall. AATT

Fire, fire. Song. Henry Bold. GBL

Fire! Fire! says the town crier. *Unknown.* GBP

Fire, Hair, Meat and Bone. Fred Johnson. PoBA

Fire in Enfield. Wesley McNair. FAF

Fire in leaf and grass, The. Living. Denise Levertov. VGW; WPE

Fire Island. Rita Mae Brown. IHMS

Fire of Despair Has Been Our Saviour, The. Robert Bly. CoPAm

Fire of Drift-wood, The. Longfellow. NOBA; PiAm; VoPo

Fire of London, *sel.* Dryden. *Fr.* Annus Mirabilis.
"At length the crackling noise and dreadful blaze." SCP-1

Fire-Truck, A. Richard Wilbur. NCSH

"Fire, water, woman, are man's ruin!" A Dutch Proverb. Matthew Prior. POL

Firebird. Alta. MMD

Firebombing, The. James Dickey. CAPP

Fired Pot, The. Anna Wickham. OxBTC

Fireflies. Helena Minton FAF

Firefly. Kamimura Hajime, *tr. fr. Japanese by* Harry *and* Lynn Guest *and* Kajima Shozo. TSWA

Firefly. Elizabeth Madox Roberts. LCL

Firefly, The. *Unknown, tr. fr. Italian.* RAE

Firelight. E. A. Robinson. NoAM

Fireman enters, A. He entertains us. Grief. Sandra Hochman. NowV

Fireworks. Babette Deutsch. OFD

1st, The. Lucille Clifton. CAAP; InPS; TSWA

First and Last. Bruce Severy. VW

First Anniversary, The. John Donne. *See* Anatomy of the World, An.

First, are you our sort of a person? The Applicant. Sylvia Plath. MAT; NMM; NOBA; Psy; SBG

First Aspen, *sels.* Lynn Strongin.
"Apology. Hands shaping air." RiTi
"Sapphic Love! Sculptress of far more than stone." RiTi
"Sensuous Latin poet, now I will go off with a thermos, A." IHMS; RiTi

First Blood. Jon Stallworthy. BoAnP

First blow caught me sideways, my jaw, The. The Beating. Ann Stafford. WPE

First Camp. Greg Kuzma. NVAP

First cocks begin clearing the throat of morning, The.   A Valley Where I Don't Belong.   Marge Piercy.   IHMS

First come I, my name is Jowett.   Balliol Rhymes.   *Unknown.*   FaBoCo

First comes love and then comes marriage.   Autograph Book/Prophecy.   Anne Halley.   NMM

First Confession.   X. J. Kennedy.   ConAP; CoPAm; NCSH; PPP

First Corinthians, *sel.*   Bible, *N.T.*
Though I Speak with the Tongues of Men and Angels, XIII: 1-13.   PBMP

First Day, The.   Howard Nemerov.   AnMo

First Day, The.   Christina Rossetti.   *Fr.* Monna Innominata.   BoLoP; OLR

First Day at School   Michael Ivens.   OxBTC

First day I shot dope, The.   Summer Words of a Sistuh Addict.   Sonia Sanchez.   BPo

First day of Christmas my true love sent to me, The.   The Twelve Days of Christmas.   *Unknown.*   AmFP

First Day of the Hunting Moon, The.   Patricia Low.   VGW

First-Day Thoughts.   Whittier.   AmVN; IPWM; PPoD

First day's night had come, The.   Emily Dickinson.   Psy

First Death.   Donald Justice.   FiCP

First Death in Nova Scotia.   Elizabeth Bishop.   NCSH; NOBA

First Element.   Margaret Atwood.   MMD

First Families Move Over!   Ogden Nash.   FaBoCo

First, feel, then feel, then.   Young Soul.   LeRoi Jones.   BPo; TSWA

First Fig.   Edna St. Vincent Millay.   BBGO; NoAM; TH

First Fight. Then Fiddle. Ply the Slipping String.   Gwendolyn Brooks.   InPK

First Flame.   Samuel Daniel.   *Fr.* Hymen's Triumph.   VoPo

First forget what time it is.   Exercise.   W. S. Merwin.   NOBA

First Frost.   E. Margaret Clarkson.   AATT

First Generation, The.   Janice Mirikitani.   MIT

First, Goodbye.   John Smith.   MPo

First having read the book of myths.   Diving into the Wreck.   Adrienne Rich.   NoAM; NOBA

First hear the story of Kaspar the rosy-cheeked.   Fraulein Reads Instructive Rhymes.   Maxine W. Kumin.   SpRo

First Hymn.   John Gill.   NeAC

First, I put my.   The Power of Love He Wants Shih (Everything).   Rochelle Owens.   NMM; Psy

First I saw the white bear, then I saw the black.   At the Zoo.   Thackeray.   OxBChV

First idea was not our own, The.   Wallace Stevens.   *Fr.* Notes Toward a Supreme Fiction.   NOBA

First in the North. The black sea-tangle beaches.   The Mythical Journey.   Edwin Muir.   NoAM

First Invasion of Ireland.   *Unknown, tr. fr. Irish by* John Montague.   BIrV

First Kiss of Love, The.   Byron.   MBPR

First Lawcase, The.   *Unknown, tr. fr. Irish by* John Montague.   BIrV

First Lecture.   James Whitehead.   CoPAm

First Lesson.   Philip Booth.   IPWM; SFF

First Light.   Thomas Kinsella.   BIrV; NoAm

First Love.   John Clare.   BoLoP; GBL

First Love.   "Hugh MacDiarmid."   SLP

First Love.   *Unknown, tr. fr. Latin by* George F. Whicher.   OLR

First Maccabees, *sel.*   Bible, Apocrypha.
"Then they took whole stones according to the law," IV: 47-59.   OFD

First, make a letter like a monument.   The Book of Kells.   Padraic Colum.   BIrV

First Meditation.   Theodore Roethke.   *Fr.* Meditations of an Old Woman.   NOBA

First Monday Scottsboro Alabama.   Tom Weatherly.   PoBA

First night when I came home, The.   Our Goodman.   *Unknown.*   AmFP

First Nowell, The, *with music.*   *Unknown.*   BLSH

"First of all, it's all true."   The Creation: According to Coyote.   Simon J. Ortiz.   CDW

First of All My Dreams Was of, The.   E. E. Cummings.   VGW

First of God by whom all grace is spread.   Sources of Good Counsel.   Peter Idley.   OxBChV

First Party at Ken Keseys with Hell's Angels.   Allen Ginsberg.   ConAP

First Person Demonstrative.   Phyllis Gotlieb.   MiP

First person I loved, The.   Coming Out.   Jacqueline Lapidus.   IHMS

First Poem, The.   James Reiss.   CAAP

First Practice.   Gary Gildner.   AmPA; InPK; PPoD

First Praise.   William Carlos Williams.   VGW

First Prayer.   Margaret Atwood.   MMD

First Pregnancy.   Alta.   NMM

First Satire of the Second Book of Horace, The.   Pope.   PPP

First Shaman Song.   Gary Snyder.   *Fr.* Myths and Texts: Hunting, I.   NOBA

First shot out of that sling, The.   After Goliath.   Kingsley Amis.   OxBTC

First Sight.   Philip Larkin.   NCSH; TSWA

First sign was your hair, The.   I'm just a Stranger Here, Heaven Is My Home.   Carole Gregory Clemmons.   PoBA

First Snow of the Year, The.   Mark Van Doren.   NCSH

First Song.   Galway Kinnell.   CTBA; NCSH

First Star.   *Unknown.*   ECBV

First Steps Up Parnassus.   Michael Drayton.   *Fr.* To My Most Dearly Loved Henry Reynolds.   NOBE

First Test, The.   Susan Fromberg Schaeffer.   IHMS

First the canoe.   Portage Poem.   Louis Jenkins.   HeS

First, the dodo disappeared.   The Last Monster.   John Montague.   WIF

First the falls, then the cave.   Behind the Falls.   William Stafford.   RFM

First the heel.   Dance Steps.   *Unknown.*   ECBV

First the melody, clean and hard.   How High the Moon.   Lance Jeffers.   PoBA

First the soul of our house left, up the chimney.   Tornado.   William Stafford.   AnMo

First their eyes.   Pulling Out.   Lyn Lifshin.   NeAC

First there was the lamb on knocking knees.   Altarwise by Owl-Light, III.   Dylan Thomas.   Epi

First Time, The.   John Newlove.   NeAC

First Time, The.   Karl Shapiro.   VGW

First time death struck her criticism, The.   The Slabs of Her Eyes.   Patricia Goedicke.   Psy

First time he kissed me, he but only kissed.   Sonnets from the Portuguese, XXXVIII.   Elizabeth Barrett Browning.   LoAs

First time I met the blues, mama they came walking through the wood, The.   The First Time I Met You.   *Unknown.*   BluL

First Time I Met You, The.   *Unknown.*   BluL

First time that the sun rose on thine oath, The.   Sonnets from the Portuguese, XXXII.   Elizabeth Barrrett Browning.   WPE

First to fight for the right.   The Army Goes Rolling Along.   Edmund L. Gruber *and* H. W. Arberg.   BLSH

First, to the feet, as they bear what you have grown to live in.   Praise.   William Matthews.   AmPA; NVAP

First Tooth, The.   Charles *and* Mary Lamb.   OxBChV

First Vision, *sel.*   Tadhg Dall O'Huiginn, *tr. fr. Irish by* the Earl of Longford.
"Vision of a Queen of Fairyland, A."   BIrV

First Walk in the Park.   Ruth Herschberger.   WBN

First was Fancy, like a lovely boy, The. The Masque of Cupid. Spenser. *Fr.* The Faerie Queene, III, 12. NOBE

1st Week 5th Day. Joshua Sylvester. *Fr.* Du Bartas His Divine Weeks and Works. SCP-2

1st Week 6th Day. Joshua Sylvester. *Fr.* Du Bartas His Divine Weeks and Works. SCP-2

First week the soil was clean, The. Digging for Indians. Gary Gildner. AmPA

First whimper of the storm, The. A Local Storm. Donald Justice. NCSH

First white hair coils in my hand, The. Sign. Marge Piercy. Psy

First woman I loved, he said, The. Escapist's Song. Theodore Spencer. POL; SFF

First you bite your fingernails. American Rhapsody (4). Kenneth Fearing. MiP; PAIC

First, you think they are dead. Lobsters in the Window. W. D. Snodgrass. BoAnP; HeIP; NCSH; PiAm

First, you will say goodbye. You will turn. First, Goodbye. John Smith. MPo

Fish. Elizabeth Bishop. CoPAm; HeIP; InPK; NoAM; NOBA

Fish. Daniel Halpern. AmPA

Fish. Larry Levis. AmPA

Fish, The. Paul Mills. MIS

Fish, The. Marianne Moore. NoAM; PBMP; PiAm

Fish. William Carlos Williams. NoAM

Fish/ fowl/ flood. Paean to Place. Lorine Niedecker. RiTi

Fish, The/ that fly. Seals. David R. Slavitt. CoPAm

Fish and Swimmers and Lonely Birds Sweep Past Us. Mei Berssenbrugge. SA

Fish at Mass, The. *Unknown, tr. fr. Latin by* J. F. Webb. BIrV

Fish Does . . . Hip! The. Mba Sholé, *tr. fr. Gabon Pygmy.* AKE

Fish (fly-replete, in depth of June). Heaven. Rupert Brooke. NOBE

Fish in the unruffled lakes. W. H. Auden. BoLoP; NoAm

Fish Story. Richard Armour. SPo

Fishbowl. Margaret Atwood. MMD

Fisherman. Philip Booth. SPo

Fisherman. William Pitt Root. NVAP

Fisherman, The. Dabney Stuart. NVAP; SPo

Fisherman, The. W. B. Yeats. NoAM; PSN

Fisher's Life, The. *Unknown.* GBP

Fishes, The. *Unknown.* GBP

Fishing Blues. *Unknown.* BluL

Fishing Harbour towards Evening. Richard Kell. LP; MPo

Fishmarket closed, the fishes gone into flesh, The. Galway Kinnell. *Fr.* The Avenue Bearing the Initial of Christ into the New World. ConAP

Fishy Square Dance, A. Eve Merriam. ECBV

Fisk is/ a/ negroid/ institution. Sharon Scott. JB

Fisted, bitten by blizzards. Lava Bed. William Everson. PiAm

Fit of Rime against Rime, A. Ben Jonson. MAT; PAIC

Fitly so named since it doth waste. *Unknown.* SCP-2

Fitting, The. Edna St. Vincent Millay. LoAs

Fitting the labels. Cadaver. John Stone. CoPAm

Fitz Hugh Lane Goes to the Masthead. Wesley McNair. FAF

Fitzroy, Carlton. Vincent Buckley. *Fr.* Golden Builders. CAAP

Five. Weldon Kees. PPP

Five, The. Swift. ECBV

Five A.M. on East Fourteenth I'm out to eat. Sonnet. Tom Clark. Epi

Five Bells. Kenneth Slessor. MAuV

.05. Ishmael Reed. InPK

Five Days Old. Francis Webb. MAuV

Five Dreams, The. John Woods. FiCP

Five Eyes. Walter de la Mare. PCat

515 Madison Avenue. Rhapsody. Frank O'Hara. NoAM

Five for the Grace of Man. Winfield Townley Scott. VGW

Five Groups of Verse, *sels.* Charles Reznikoff.
"After I had worked all day at what I earn my living." SA
Citizen, A, 29. SA
Ghetto Funeral, 17. SA
"God saw Adam in a town." SA
"How difficult for me is Hebrew." SA
"How shall we mourn you who are killed and wasted." SA
Samuel. SA
"Showing a torn sleeve, with stiff and shaking fingers the old man." SA

Five Hens, The. *Unknown.* GBP

Five hours (and who can do it less in?). The Lady's Dressing Room. Swift. AnMo

Five Joys, The. *Unknown.* OxBM

Five Men I Know. Thomas Lux. NVAP

Five Minutes after the Air Raid. Miroslav Holub, *tr. fr. Czech by* Ian Milner *and* George Theiner. BuTh

Five o'clock closes in on another Sunday. View of Vienna from Schonbrunn. Peggy Ruse. NPW

Five Psalms of Common Man. Christopher Middleton. TwMBP

Five Reasons, The. Henry Aldrich. FaBoCo

Five soldiers fixed by Mathew Brady's eye. Looking into History. Richard Wilbur. VGW

Five summer days, five summer nights. The Blue-Fly. Robert Graves. NoAM

5:30 A.M. Adrienne Rich. NMM; NOBA; PiAm

5:32, The. Phyllis McGinley. *Fr.* I Know a Village. NMM; WPE

Five times a day is what he really likes. A Young Lover. Elizabeth Sargent. WBN

Five Unmistakable Marks, The. David Jones. In Parenthesis, VII. NoAM

Five Vignettes. Jean Toomer. PoBA

Five Ways to Kill a Man. Edwin Brock. IPWM; SFF; TSWA

Five years. Anniversary. Philip Dacey. HeS

Five years have passed; five summers, with the length. Lines Composed [*or* Written] A Few Miles Above Tintern Abbey. Wordsworth. AnMo; HeIP; InPS; IPWM; MBPR; PPP; VoPo

Fix me on some bleak precipice. William Habington. *Fr.* Quoniam Ego in Flagella Paratus Sum. David. SCP-2

Fixing to Die. *Unknown.* BluL

Fixture, A. May Swenson. RiTi

Flag Goes By, The. Henry Holcomb Bennett. BTTM

Flag/ is folded,/ The. The Lowering. May Swenson. TCP

Flagon in the backyard, A. March Fugue. Thomas Shapcott. CAAP

Flame burns in the morning, A. Le Chariot. John Wieners. VGW

Flame of a Candle, The. Howard Nemerov. AnMo

Flaming Heart, The, *sels.* Richard Crashaw.
"O Heart! the equal poise of love's both parts." OBP
"O thou undaunted daughter of desires!" BoReV
(Upon the Book and the Picture of the Seraphical Saint Teresa.) NOBE

Flammonde. E. A. Robinson. NoAM

Flannan Isle. W. W. Gibson. PoTa

Flannery O'Connor. Dorothy Walters. IHMS

Flashlight, A. Brain. Coleman Barks. NVAP

Flat on the bank I parted. The Trout. John Montague. BoAnP; PFIr; SFF

Flat One, A. W. D. Snodgrass. CAPP

Flattered Lightning Bug, The. Don Marquis PoTa

Flaubert wanted to write a novel.  Style.  Howard Nemerov. NoAM

Flavour the days, tobacco.  Tobacco.  Robert Harris.  CAAP

Flea, The.  John Donne.  AnMo; BoLoP; MAT; PAIC; PPoe; SCP-1

Flea and the Fly, The ("A flea and a fly in a flue").  *Unknown.* ECBV

Fleas, The.  Augustus De Morgan.  FaBoCo

Fleche.  Larry Eigner.  VGW

Flee from the press [*or* fro the prees], and dwell with soothfastness.  Truth.  Chaucer.  BoReV; OxBM

Fleeing from threatened flood, they sailed.  The First Invasion of Ireland.  *Unknown, tr. by* John Montague.  BIrV

Fleeting birds may soon in ocean swim, The.  To Miss Laetitia Van Lewen.  Constantia Grierson.  WPE

Flesh-and-blood does not wear pain.  Thoughts on Pain.  Sallie Chesham.  AATT

Flesh and the Spirit, The.  Anne Bradstreet.  NOBA

Flies in the buttermilk, skip to my Lou.  Skip to My Lou.  *Unknown.*  ECBV

Flight, The.  Lisel Mueller.  RiTi

Flight.  Mary Shumway.  HeS

Flight.  James Tate.  InPK

Flight in the Desert, The.  William Everson.  VGW

Flight of Apollo, The.  Stanley Kunitz.  Moon

Flight of the Earls, The, 1607, *sel.*  Fearghal Og MacWard, *tr. fr. Irish by* the Earl of Longford.  "All Ireland's now one vessel's company."  BIrV

Flight of the Roller Coaster.  Raymond Souster.  PoTa

Flight of Wild Geese, A, *sel.*  Harold Stewart.  "Down the sky in file the wild geese tack."  MAuV

Flight to Italy, *sel.*  C. Day Lewis.  "Winged bull trundles to the wired perimeter, The."  OxBTC

Flights.  Roger McDonald.  CAAP

Fling this useless book away.  Written in a Lady's Prayer Book.  Earl of Rochester.  BoLoP

Flint.  Christina Rossetti.  OxBChV

Flip, clack! The windscreen wipers clear.  Seven Rainy Months.  William Plomer.  OxBTC

Flitcraft's Woods.  Warren Woessner.  HeS

Floating across the lake.  Not Thinking of America.  Judith Kroll.  AmPA

Floating Bridge.  *Unknown.*  BluL

Floating Coathangers.  Peter Cooley.  NVAP

Floating off to Timor.  Edwin Morgan.  SLP

Floating thru chairs.  Nice.  Lyn Lifshin.  Psy

Flock of birds, soaring, twisting, turning, A.  Love Is.  Ann Darr.  MiP

Flock of winds came winging from the North, A.  The Roaring Frost.  Alice Meynell.  WPE

Flooding with a brilliant mist.  To the Moon.  Goethe, *tr. by* John Frederick Nims.  Moon

Floodtide.  Askia Muhammad Touré.  PoBA

Flood-tide below me! I see you face to face!  Crossing Brooklyn Ferry.  Walt Whitman.  NOBA; NoAM; PiAm

Floor: Five.  Stephen Vincent.  *Fr.* Elevator Landscapes.  NeAC

Floor: O.  Stephen Vincent.  *Fr.* Elevator Landscapes.  NeAC

Flora.  Ray Fraser.  NeAC

Florella; or, The Jealous Lover.  *Unknown.*  AmFP

Florida Road Workers.  Langston Hughes.  CTBA; SFF

Floris nad Blaunchefiour, *sel.*  *Unknown.*  Lover's Stratagem, A.  OxBM

Flotsam and Jetsam.  E. E. Cummings.  NOBA

Flow Gently, Sweet Afton.  Burns.  *See* Afton Water.

Flower, The.  Robert Creeley.  CAPP

Flower, The.  George Herbert.  BoReV; MetP; NOBE; PPP; SCP-1

Flower.  Peter Schjeldahl.  CAAP

Flower, The/ fallen.  The Loving Dexterity.  William Carlos Williams.  TH

Flower and the Leaf, The, *sel.*  Lady of the Arbour.  "And at the last I cast my mine eye aside."  WPE

Flower Dump.  Theodore Roethke.  PiAm

Flower-fed Buffaloes, The.  Vachel Lindsay.  NOBA; RFM; VGW

Flower Given to My Daughter, A.  James Joyce.  RRA

Flower Herding on Mount Monadnock.  Galway Kinnell.  HeIP; NOBA

(Flower Herding Pictures on Mount Monadnock.)  ConAP

Flower in the Crannied Wall.  Tennyson.  InPK; IPWM; PBMP; VoPo

Flower of the flock.  On Sweet Killen Hill.  Tom MacIntyre.  NCSH

Flower that smiles to-day, The.  Mutability.  Shelley.  MBPR

Flower was offered to me, A.  My Pretty Rose Tree.  Blake.  *Fr.* Songs of Experience.  BoLoP; LAuP; MBPR

Flowering jungle, where all fauna meet.  Commercial Bank.  A. M. Klein.  BBGO

Flowering of the Rod, The, *sel.*  Hilda Doolittle ("H. D.").  "Blue-geese, white-geese, you may say."  NOBA

Flowering Plum.  Louise Glück.  CAAP

Flowers are beautiful: This opinion.  Flower.  Peter Schjeldahl.  CAAP

Flowers are dead, The.  Scenery.  Ted Joans.  PoBA

Flowers by the Sea.  William Carlos Williams.  NoAM

Flowers for the Grangerford Girl.  William Harrold.  HeS

Flowers in the Valley.  *Unknown.*  ECBV; OLR

Flowers left thick at nightfall in the wood, The.  In Memoriam (Easter, 1915).  Edward Thomas.  NOBE; OxBTC

Flowers of Darkness.  Frank Marshall Davis.  PoBA

Flowers of the forest, The; or, The Battle of Flodden.  Jane Elliot.  BTTM; SLP; WPE

Flowers of the willow-herb are wool.  Seed-Time.  George Meredith.  FSFS

Flowers That Bloom in the spring, The, *with music.*  William S. Gilbert.  *Fr.* The Mikado.  BLSo

Floyd has died and few have sobb'd.  Epitaph on Floyd.  *Unknown.*  POL

Flukum couldn't stand the strain.  2 Poems for Black Relocation Centers.  Etheridge Knight.  NoAM

Flush with the pond the lurid furnace burn'd.  The Steam Threshing-Machine.  Charles Tennyson Turner.  VPC

Flutes, and the harp on the plain.  Home on the Range, February 1962.  Edward Dorn.  ConAP

Flux.  Richard Eberhart.  CoPAm; VGW

Fly, The.  Blake.  *Fr.* Songs of Experience.  LAuP; MBPR; OBP; PBMP

Fly.  W. S. Merwin.  CoPAm

Fly, The.  William Oldys.  PAIC

Fly, The.  Karl Shapiro.  CoPAm; NoAM; NowV; PBMP

Fly, envious Time, till thou run out thy race.  On Time.  Milton.  BoReV

Fly, fly, my friends, I have my death wound; fly.  Astrophel and Stella, XX.  Sir Philip Sidney.  Epi

Fly is dying hard, The.  Mayday.  Ed Roberson.  PoBA

Fly[e] to her heart; hover about her heart.  Bartholomew Griffin.  *Fr.* Fidessa, more Chaste Than Kind, XXIII.  AAS; LoAs

Fly to the desert, fly with me.  Thomas Moore.  *Fr.* Lalla Rookh.  BIrV

Flye to her heart, hover about her heart.  *See* Fly to her heart . . .

*Flying Cloud*, The.  *Unknown.*  AmFP

Flying Crow. *Unknown.* BluL

Flying Dutchman, The. E. A. Robinson. PiAm

Flying Home from Utah. May Swenson. WPE

Flying Trapeze, The. George Leybourne. *See* The Man on the Flying Trapeze

Foal. Vernon Watkins. OxBTC

Focus. Adrienne Rich. PiAm

Fod. *Unknown.* AmFP

Foetal Song. Joyce Carol Oates. IHMS

Fog ("The fog comes/ on little cat feet"). Carl Sandburg. HeIP; InPK; PiAm; RAE; SoSe

Fog and snow for New Year's greeting. Rhyming Prophecy for a New Year. Leonard Cooper. FaBoCo

Fog over the base: the beams ranging. A Front. Randall Jarrell. VGW

Foggy, Foggy Dew, The. *Unknown.* BLSH, *with music*; GBP; RDB, *with music*
(Foggy Dew, The, *diff. version*) PeBB

Fog-Horn. W. S. Merwin. TCP; TSWA

Fogless morning but black. Early Morning Song: The Snowstorm. Gloria Bussel Koster. NPW

Folded Skyscraper, A, *sel.* William Carlos Williams. Hemmed-in Males MAT

Folding Fan, The. Grey Cohoe. VW

Foliage of Vision. James Merrill. VGW

Folk group chopped its last note clean, The. Spring Revue. Charlotte Mortimer. NowV

Folk remedy, A. Skull. Coleman Barks. *Fr.* Body Poems. NVAP

Folk Tune. Richard Wilbur. AIW

Follow a shadow, it still flies you. That Women are but Men's Shadows [*or* The Shadow]. Ben Jonson. InPS; NOBE

Follow me, follow me, follow and find me! Night Riddle. *Unknown.* ECBV

Follow my Bangelory Man. My Bangelory Man. *Unknown.* ECBV

Follow the Drinkin' Gourd. *Unknown.* WIF

Follow Thy Fair Sun. Thomas Campion. NOBE

Follow your saint, follow with accents sweet. Devotion. Thomas Campion. AAS; NOBE

Follow your saint, follow with accents sweet. Devotion. Thomas Campion AAS; NOBE

Followe Thy Faire Sunne. Thomas Campion. AAS; Prf

Followed by his lodge, shabby men stumbling over the cobblestones. Ghetto Funeral. Charles Rezikoff. *Fr.* Five Groups of Verse. SA

Follower. Seamus Heaney. LP; PFIr

Folly and error, avarice and vice. To the Reader. Baudelaire, *tr. by* Roy Campbell. GrRo

Folly of Being Comforted, The. W. B. Yeats. GBL; HeIP; LoAs; SoSe

Fond man, that canst believe her blood. Celia Bleeding: to the Surgeon. Thomas Carew. SCP-2

Fondle me. Marrow of My Bone. Mari E. Evans. BPo

Font, The. Clive Sansom. BuTh

Food drops off a fork, The. Michael Silverton. POL

Fool on the Hill, The. John Lennon *and* Paul McCartney. GrRo; PPoe

Fool once caught a crow, A. The Crow. James Reaney. AKE

Fooled me once and you fooled me bad. All Night Long Fooling Me. *Unknown.* AmFP

Foolish Boy, The. *Unknown.* RAE

Foolish rhythm turns in my idle head, A. A Tune. Arthur Symons. BoLoP

Fool's Blues. *Unknown.* BluL

Football. F. Scott Fitzgerald. SPo

Football. Walt Mason. SPo

Footballer in the Small Room, The. Janet Frame. SPo

Foote-Ball. Sebastian Brant. SPo

Foot-folk, The. The Battle of Dunbar (1296). *Unknown.* OxBM

Footnote to a Gray Bird's Pause, A. James Cunningham. JB

Footnote to Howl. Allen Ginsberg. CAPP

Footnote upon the Construction of the Masses. Charles Bukowski. CoPAm

Footprint in the Night. Elizabeth Coatsworth. CaYB

Footprints on the Glacier. W. S. Merwin. NoAM

Footsteps, The. Paul Valéry, *tr. fr. French by* C. Day Lewis. LoAs

For a Child Expected. Anne Ridler. BuTh

For a College Yearbook. J. V. Cunningham. NoAM

For a Coming Extinction. W. S. Merwin. TSWA

For a Dead Lady. E. A. Robinson. HeIP; LoAs; NoAM; NOBA; PiAm

For a Fatherless Son. Sylvia Plath. TSWA

For a fresh start. Issa, *tr. fr. Japanese by* Nobuyuki Yuasa. *Fr.* Oraga Haru. OFD

For a Friend. Lyn Lifshin. NeAC; Psy

For a good decade. The Drunk in the Furnace. W. S. Merwin. CAPP; MAT; NoAM

For a Homecoming. Julia Randall. NMM

For a Junior School Poetry Book. Christopher Middleton. BBGO; MPo

For a Lady I Know. Countee Cullen. HeIP; InPK; WIF

For a Little Girl Mourning Her Favorite Cat. Whittier. *See* Epitaph: "Bathsheba! to whom none ever said scat."

For a long time I've thought about this body of mine. The Vases of Wombs. Daniela Gioseffi. RiTi

For a long time you looked stuffed. Lizard. Alan McLean. BoAnP

For a man that is almost blind. For Sore Eyes. *Unknown.* OxBM

For a Marriage. Erica Jong. CTBA

For a moment pause. The Mound. Thomas Hardy. OxBTC

For a Mouthy Woman. Countee Cullen. PoBA

For A' That and A' That, *parody.* Shirley Brooks. FaBoCo

For A' That, and A' That. Burns. BTTM; LAuP
("Is there, for honest poverty.") OBP

For a Wine Festival. Vernon Watkins. OxBTC

For a Winnebago Brave. Joseph Bruchac. CDW

For a Woodscolt Miscarried. John William Corrington. CoPAm

For Alan Blanchard. John Oliver Simon. NeAC

For Andy Goodman—Michael Schwerner—and James Chaney. Margaret Walker. BPo

For Angela. Zack Gilbert. PoBA

For Anna. Irving Layton. NeAC

For Anne. Leonard Cohen. TCP

For Anne Gregory. W. B. Yeats. BuTh; Epi; InPK; PFIr; SFF; SS

For Anne, Who Doesn't Know. Gail Fox. IHMS

For Annie. Poe. NOBA; PiAm; VoPo

For Anybody's Martyr's Song. Jean Garrigue. LoAs

For as the honey of heaven's lovely hives. Joseph Beaumont. *Fr.* Psyche or Love's Mystery. SCP-2

For authorities whose hopes. The Paper Nautilus. Marianne Moore. VGW

For, before Cythna loved it, had my song. Shelley. *Fr.* The Revolt of Islam, II. MBPR

For, Behold the Day Cometh. Rochelle Owens. Psy

For best work. Lorine Niedecker. VGW

For Bill. Geof Hewitt. NeAC

For Bill Hawkins, a Black Militant.  William J. Harris.  PoBA
For Black Poets Who Think of Suicide.  Etheridge Knight.
  PoBA
For Bonny Elspeth.  Hamish Macbride.  SLP
For Both of Us at Fisk.  Sharon Scott.  JB
For C.  Philip Whalen.  VGW
For Cal.  James Cunningham.  JB
For Cynara.  Charles Plymell.  RRA
For Dan Berrigan.  Etheridge Knight.  NeAC
For days I have been walking around.  Letter to a Friend in an
  Unknown Place.  Anita Barrows.  NMM; RiTi
For days these curious cardboard buds have lain.  Gunpowder Plot.
  Vernon Scannell.  MPo
For de Lawd.  Lucille Clifton.  PoBA; PPoD
For dear life some do.  Portrait of an Artist.  Barbara Howes.
  IHMS
For Delphine.  James Simmons.  POL
For E. C. J.  Emmett Jarrett.  NeAC
For E. J. P.  Leonard Cohen.  NoAM
For Eleanor and Bill Monahan.  William Carlos Williams.  VGW
For Eleanor Boylan Talking with God.  Anne Sexton.  InPK
For Ellen.  Richard Wilbur.  RRA
For Eusi, Ayi Kwei and Gwen Brooks.  Keorapetse Kgositsile.
  PoBA
For every bird there is this last migration.  The Death of the Bird.
  A. D. Hope.  MAuV
For Every Sister in the White Man's Jail.  Rita Mae Brown.
  WBN
For Fear.  Robert Creeley.  NoAM; PiAm
For fifty thousand years man has been dreaming of power.
  Unnatural Powers.  Robinson Jeffers.  PBMP
For first the abiding.  Bruce Beaver.  Fr. Lauds and Plaints.
  CAAP
For forms of government let fools contest.          Pope.  Fr. Essay
  on Man, Epistle III.  POL
For Freckle-faced Gerald.  Etheridge Knight.  BPo; NeAC
For Fyodor.  Phyllis Webb.  MMD
For George Santayana.  Robert Lowell.  VGW
  (George Santayana.)  CoPAm
For God while Sleeping.  Anne Sexton.  CAPP; CoPAm
For Godsake [or God's sake] hold your tongue, and let me love.
  The Canonization.  John Donne.  AnMo; Epi; IPWM;
  LoAs; MetP; NOBE; PPoe; PPP; SCP-1
For God's sake mark that fly!  Nulla Fides.  Patrick Carey.  SCP-
  2
For H. W. Fuller.  Carolyn M. Rodgers.  BPo
For he was our puck, our miniature lar.  Louis MacNeice.  Fr.
  The Death of a Cat.  PCat
For He's a Jolly Good Fellow, with music.  Unknown.  BLSo
For Hettie.  LeRoi Jones.  NoAM; NOBA; SS
For his religion, it was fit.  Samuel Butler.  Fr. Hudibras, I, 1.
  SCP-2
For I am not without authority in my jeopardy.  Christopher Smart.
  Fr. Jubilate Agno.  LAuP; OBP
For I bless the Prince of Peace and pray that all the guns may be
  nail'd up.  Christopher Smart.  Fr. Jubilate Agno.  InPS
For I complaine not of sic common cace.  James I, King of
  England.  Fr. Ane Metaphoricall Invention of a Tragedie
  Called Phoenix.  SLP
For I have founde you folk faithful of speche.  Alexander and the
  Gymnosophists.  Unknown.  OxBM
For I inhabit a wood.  Marban, a Hermit Speaks.  Unknown, tr. by
  Michael Hartnett.  BIrV
For I will consider my cat Jeoffry.  Christopher Smart.  Fr.
  Jubilate Agno.  AnMo; HeIP; InPK; LAuP; PCat; PPP; Prf

For instance/ if the sea should break.  If Something Should
  Happen.  Lucille Clifton.  MAT
For J. A. R. McKellar.  Geoffrey Lehmann.  MAuV
For James Baldwin.  Kay Boyle.  NMM
For Jan, in Bar Maria.  Carolyn Kizer.  RiTi; VGW
For Jane.  Charles Bukowski.  CoPAm
For Jane Myers.  Louise Glück.  CAAP
For John Berryman.  Virginia Gilbert.  NPW
For John Berryman, I.  Robert Lowell.  NOBA
For Kelley.  Ken Belford.  NeAC
For Kenneth and Miriam Patchen.  Al Young.  CoPAm
For Kenneth Patchen.  Wayne Miller.  MIT
For Laurence Jones.  Gary Kizer.  CTBA
For Lerida.  David St. John.  AmPA
For Life I Had Never Cared Greatly.  Thomas Hardy.  NoAM
For lo! the new Moon winter-bright.  The New Moon.  Samuel
  Taylor Coleridge.  Fr. Dejection; an Ode.  FSFS
For Love.  Robert Creeley.  ConAP; NOBA; PiAm
For love—I would.  The Warning.  Robert Creeley.  CoPAm;
  VGW
For Mack C. Parker.  Pauli Murray.  PoBA
For Malcolm: After Mecca.  Gerald W. Barrax.  OFD; PoBA
For Malcolm Who Walks in the Eyes of Our Children.  Quincy
  Troupe.  PoBA
For Malcolm X.  Nanina Alba.  PoBA
For Malcolm X.  Margaret Walker.  BPo; PoBA
For Malcolm's eyes, when they broke.  A Poem for Black Hearts.
  LeRoi Jones.  CAPP; PoBA; SFF
For Mama Streek.  Colette Inez.  AATT
For many, many days together.  Riding Together.  William
  Morris.  NOBE
For Marianne Moore's Birthday.  Kay Boyle.  RiTi
For Mary.  Kenneth Rexroth.  SFF
For Masturbation.  Alan Dugan.  CAPP; NoAM
For Me  and My Gal.  Edgar Leslie and E. Ray Goetz.  BLSo
For me, the naked and the nude.  The Naked and the Nude.
  Robert Graves.  OBP; SoSe; WIF
For "Mr. Dudley," a Black Spy.  James A. Emanuel.  BPo
For My Contemporaries.  J. V. Cunningham.  CoPAm; PiAm
For My Daughter.  David Ignatow.  RRA
For My Daughter.  Weldon Kees.  RRA
For My Daughter in Reply to a Question.  David Ignatow.  RRA
For My Daughter's 20th Birthday.  Walter Lowenfels.  RRA
For My Funeral.  A. E. Housman.  BoReV
For My Grandfather in Greenfield Center.  Joseph Bruchac.
  FAF
For My Grandmother.  Countee Cullen.  Four Epitaphs, 1.
  VGW
For My Grandmother, Bridgid Halpin.  Michael Hartnett.  BIrV
For My Lover, Returning to His Wife.  Anne Sexton.  IHMS;
  NMM; RiTi; WPE
For My Mother.  Louise Glück.  CAAP
For My Mother.  June Jordan.  NMM
For My People.  Wendy Rose.  CDW
For My People.  Margaret Walker.  PBMP; POBA
For My Sister Molly Who in the Fifties.  Alice Walker.  WBN
For My Son.  Alan Brownjohn.  LP
For My Son on the Highways of His Mind.  Maxine W. Kumin.
  CoPAm; MAT
For My Unborn and Wretched Children.  A. B. Spellman.  PoBA
For Natalya Correia.  Irving Layton.  NeAC
For nations vague as weed.  Nothing to Be Said.  Philip Larkin.
  OxBTC
For Nature daily through her grand design.  Frederick Goddard
  Tuckerman.  Fr. Sonnets.  AmVN; PiAm

For No Clear Reason. Robert Creeley. VGW

For Once, Then, Something. Robert Frost. NoAM; NOBA; PiAm

For one long term, or e'er her trial came. Inscription. George Canning *and* John Hookham Frere. FaBoCo

For One Moment. David Ignatow. TCP

For Our Lady. Sonia Sanchez. IHMS

For "Our Lady of the Rocks." Dante Gabriel Rossetti. PFD

For Paige. Summer Brenner. RiTi

For physic and farces his equal there scarce is. On Sir John Hill, M.D., Playwright. David Garrick. FaBoCo

For Poets. Al Young. PoBA; RFM

For Prodigal Read Generous. E. E. Cummings. NoAM; PBMP

For Proserpine. Stanley Kunitz. PAIC

For rage and dignity no words compare. A Classical Quatrain. Paul Goodman. VGW

For Randie. Geof Hewitt. NeAC

For Real. Jayne Cortez. PoBA

For Robert Frost. Galway Kinnell. NOBA; VGW

For Rosa Yen, Who Lived Here. Greg Pape. AmPA

For Sale. Robert Lowell. ConAP; PSN

For Sale. Shel Silverstein. CTBA

For Sammy Younge. Charlie Cobb. PoBA

For Saturday. Christopher Smart. *Fr.* Hymns for the Amusement of Children. LAuP
(Hymn for Saturday.) OxBChV

For Saundra. Nikki Giovanni. BPo; Psy; RiTi; WIF

For Scholars and Pupils. George Wither. OxBChV

For seven days it rained that June. Wash. John Updike. TSWA

For several days I have been under. The Prisoner. Derek Mahon. PFIr

For several months. P.C. Plod Versus the Dale St. Dog Strangler. Roger McGough. NoAM

For shame, thou everlasting wooer. The Antiplatonick. John Cleveland. MetP; SCP-2

For so long/ We looked into mirrors. Us. Julius Lester. PoBA

For solidarity. South American Sway. Margaretta Byers. ECBV

For Some Poets. Mae Jackson. PoBA

For Some Weeks. Robert Creeley. RRA

For Sore Eyes. *Unknown.* OxBM

For Steph. Wendy Rose. CDW

For Stephen Dixon. Zack Gilbert. PoBA

For the air is purified by prayer which is made aloud. Christopher Smart. *Fr.* Jubilate Agno. Prf

For the Anniversary of My Death. W. S. Merwin. CAAP; CoPAm; InPK; NOBA

For the Book of Love. Jules Laforgue, *tr. fr. French by* Jethro Bithell. LoAs

For the bumps bangs and scratches of. Auto Mobile. A. R. Ammons. InPK

For the Coming Year. Peter Everwine. OFD

For the Country. Larry Levis. NVAP

For the Crêche. G. K. Chesterton. *Fr.* Songs of Education. FaBoCo

For the dim regions whence my fathers came. Outcast. Claude McKay. PoBA

For the doubling of flowers is the improvement of the gardners talent. Christopher Smart. *Fr.* Jubilate Agno. LAuP

For the El Paso Weather Bureau. Peter Wild. MAT

For the Fallen. Laurence Binyon. NOBE; OxBTC

For the Far Edge. Mark Vinz. HeS

For the 5th time. Poem. Diane Kruchkow. FAF

For the first time. A Poem for Positive Thinkers. Barbara Mahone. PoBA

For the Good. Orders, Passages 24. Robert Duncan. CAAP

For the Lord's Day Evening. Isaac Watts. OxBChV

For the Marriage of Faustus and Helen. Hart Crane. InPS; NoAM; NOBA

For the Minority. Robert Peterson. NeAC

For the Moment. Richard Weber. PFIr

For the Night-Mare. *Unknown.* OxBM

For the One Who Would Take Man's Life in His Hands. Delmore Schwartz. NoAM; VGW

For the Opening of the Hunting Season. Morris Bishop. BoAnP; SPo

For the Record. R. S. Thomas. LP; MPo

For the Sleepless. Stephen Dunn. HeS

For the Spring Being. Albert Howard Carter. AATT

For the Suicide's Daughter. Carolyn Stoloff. RiTi

For the Time Being, *sels.* W. H. Auden.
At the Manger Mary Sings. BoReV
Voice of Caesar, The. AnMo

For the Union Dead. Robert Lowell. HeIP; InPS; NoAM; NOBA; PiAm; PPoe; PPP; PSN

For the Unknown Goddess. Elizabeth Brewster. MMD

For the Waiter at Jhonny Pavlovs. Luís Omar Salinas. SA

For the Woman Who Asked Me If I Believed in God and If I Pray. Kathleen Wiegner. MMD

For the Word Is Flesh. Stanley Kunitz. VGW

For thirst of power that heaven disowns. Ode on the Installation of His Royal Highness Prince Albert. Wordsworth. MBPR

For this is not the road against which stand enemy lines. Piyyut for Rosh Hashana. Chaim Guri, *tr. by* Ruth Finer Mintz. OFD

For this she starred her eyes with salt. Epitaph. Elinor Wylie. SBG

For this your mother sweated in the cold. To Jesus on His Birthday. Edna St. Vincent Millay. VoPo

For those my unbaptisèd rhymes. His Prayer for Absolution. Robert Herrick. SCP-1

For those who worship Thee there is no death. The Trees of Life. Jones Very. NOBA

For those with empirical. 24 December. John Judson. HeS

For thou art with men here upon the banks. Wordsworth. *Fr.* Lines Composed a Few Miles above Tintern Abbey. Prf

For three days/ I've wanted to get married. Gerrye Payne. NPW

For three years, out of key with his time. E. P. Ode pour l'Election de Son Sepulchre. Ezra Pound.　Hugh Selwyn Mauberley, I. InPS; NoAM; NOBA; PiAm; VGW

For Tinkers Who Travel on Foot. Margaret Avison. NoAM

For to torche or to a taper the Trinité is likened. The Trinity. William Langland. *Fr.* The Vision of Piers Plowman. OxBM

For two days her lineage is in doubt. Childhood. Lisel Mueller. RiTi

For Walter Lowenfels. Wendy Rose. CDW

For want of a nail, the shoe was lost. Mother Goose. ECBV; MG

For weeks I thought of you. Beyond Logic. Adrianne Marcus. NPW

For weeks, of course, the phone still rang for you. One Year Later. Eric Torgerson. POL

For What It's Worth. Stephen Stills. PoRo; WIF

For what the world admires I'll wish no more. The Resolve. Mary Lee, Lady Chudleigh. WPE

For when they meet, the tensile air. The Paradigm. Allen Tate. NOBA

For whom the possessed sea littered, on both shores. Requiem for the Plantagenet Kings. Geoffrey Hill. NoAM

For Whosoever Will Save His Life Shall Lose It. St Matthew, XVI: 25-26. Bible, *N.T..* PBMP

For why? the gaines doth seldome quitte the charge.   George Gascoigne.   AAS

For William Edward Burghardt Du Bois on His Eightieth Birthday.   Bette Darcie Latimer.   PoBA

For Witches.   Susan Sutheim.   NMM

For X.   Louis MacNeice.   BoLoP

For years I have been a coal miner.   A Coal Miner's Goodbye. *Unknown.*   AmFP

For years she smiled.   The Metamorphosis of Aunt Jemima. William Childress.   MAT

For you I have emptied the meaning.   Louis Zukofsky.   NoAM

For you, I will be less desperate.   Dialogue.   James Tipson.   HeS

For you . . . if you live to retire."   How I Cancelled My Life Insurance.    Joseph Bruchac.   FAF

For You, Who Didn't Know.   Nancy Willard.   RiTi

Force, The.   Peter Redgrove.   MPo

Force That Through the Green Fuse Drives the Flower, The. Dylan Thomas.   AnMo; InPS; NoAM; NOBE; PAIC; PBMP; PPP; OxBTC

Forcing House.   Theodore Roethke.   PiAm

Ford Pickup.   David Allan Evans.   NVAP

Foreboding, The.   Robert Graves.   GBL

Foreboding.   John Haines.   ConAP

Foreboding.   Rainer Maria Rilke, *tr. fr. German by* Lori Weistein. InPK

Forecast.   Sam Cornish.   NVAP

Forecast.   Josephine Miles.   NoAM

Foreclosure.   Sterling A. Brown.   PoBA

Forefathers.   Edmund Blunden.   NOBE; OxBTC

Foreign country of the river, The.   Poem for Nancy.   Stephen Tudor.   HeS

Foreign Policy Commitments; or, You Get Into the Catamaran First, Old Buddy.   Paul Blackburn.   NowV

Foreign Student.   Barbara B. Robinson.   CTBA

Forerunners, The.   George Herbert.   BoReV; SCP-1

Foresight.   Lincoln Kirstein.   NoAM

Forest.   Jean Garrigue.   NOBA

Forest, The.   Judith Wright.   MAuV

Forest beyond the Glass, The.   Lewis Turco.   CoPAm

Forester, The.   *Unknown.   See* I Have Been a Foster.

Forests are branches of a tree lying down.   Flying Home from Utah.   May Swenson.   WPE

Forests of Lithuania, The, *sel.*   Donald Davie. "But this, so feminine?"   OxBTC

Forever—is composed of nows.   Emily Dickinson.   AnMo

Forever over now, forever, forever gone.   The Cameo.   Edna St. Vincent Millay.   WPE

Foreword to New Numbers.   Christopher Logue.   OxBTC

Forge, The.   Seamus Heaney.   PFIr; SoSe

Forge me a tool, my Seamus.   His Request.   Owen Roe O'Sullivan, *tr. by* John Keefe.   BIrV

Forget about us.   Leave Us Alone.   Tadeusz Rozewicz, *tr. by* Czeslaw Milosz.   BuTh

Forget Not Yet.   Sir Thomas Wyatt.   AAS; LoAs (Lover Beseecheth His Mistress Not to Forget His Steadfast Faith and True Intent, The.)   PAIC (Steadfastness.)   NOBE

Forget six counties overhung with smoke.   The Wanderers. Will:.m Morris.   *Fr.* The Earthly Paradise.   VPC

Forgive?   José Montoya.   MIT

Forgive/ my sadness.   Barefoot.   Luís Omar Salinas.   SA

Forgive me that I pitch your praise too low.   Apology for Understatement.   John Wain.   LoAs; OxBTC

Forgive, O Lord.   Robert Frost.   AnMo

Forgiven Past, The.   Laura Riding.   NoAM

Fork.   Charles Simic.   AmPA

Forlorn and glum the couples go.   The Houses.   Eden Phillpotts. OxBTC

Form is in the woods: the beast.   Poem.   Jim Harrison.   VGW

Form of Women, A.   Robert Creeley.   CAPP

Form Rejection Letter.   Philip Dacey.   AmPA

Formal Application.   Donald W. Baker.   SoSe

Former Age, The.   Chaucer.   OxBM

Former Beauties.   Thomas Hardy.   At Casterbridge Fair, II. NoAM

Former Love, A.   Giles Gordon.   SLP

Formerly the individual work of a Nuremburg artificer.   Watch. John Daniel.   TwMBP

Forming Child Poems.   Simon J. Ortiz.   CDW

Forms of the Earth at Abiquiu.   N. Scott Momaday.   CDW

Forms of the Human.   Richard Eberhart.   TH

Forsaken, The.   Duncan Campbell Scott.   PoTa

Forsaken.   *Unknown.*   AmFP

Forsaken Garden, A.   Swinburne.   NOBE

Forsaken Girl, The.   Randall Jarrell.   OLR

Fort of Rathangan, The.   *Unknown, tr. fr. Irish by* Kuno Meyer. PFIr

Fort or Castle of Hope, The,   *sel.*   Margaret Cavendish, Duchess of Newcastle. "Some with sharp swords, to tell O most accursed!"   SCP-2

Fort over against the oak-wook, The.   The Fort of Rathangan. *Unknown, tr. by* Kuno Meyer.   PFIr

Forte: for Tina.   David Meltzer.   MIT

Forth from the dark and dismal cell.   Mad Tom of Bedlam. *Unknown.*   SCP-2

Forth, to the alien gravity.   The Launch.   Alice Meynell.   WPE

Forties Flick.   John Ashbery.   CAAP

Fortitude, endurance, amana: remain faithful.   The Amana Colonies.   Ken Smith.   TwMBP

Fortnight before Christmas Gypsies were everywhere, A.   The Gypsy.   Edward Thomas.   HeIP; NoAM

Fortress, The.   Louise Glück.   NVAP

Fortunate,/ Being articulate.   Nocturne of the Self-evident Presence.   Thomas MacGreevy.   BIrV

Fortunate Isles, and Their Union, The,   *sel.*   Ben Jonson. "Now turn, and view the wonders of the deep."   SCP-1

Fortune.   Lawrence Ferlinghetti.   BBGO; SFF

Fortunes of War, The.   *Unknown.*   InPK; POL

Forty-five Minutes from Broadway, *with music.*   George M. Cohan. FSN

45 Pistol Blues.   *Unknown.*   BluL

40-Love.   Roger McGough.   NoAM

Forty-Second, The.   *Unknown.*   GBP

46 and Recalling.   Allan Block.   FAF

Forty viziers saw I go.   The Fair Circassian.   Richard Garnett. PoTa

Forward abrupt.   Night and a Distant Church.   Russell Atkins. PoBA

Forward youth that would appear, The.   An Horatian Ode upon Cromwell's Return from Ireland.   Andrew Marvell.   Epi; InPS; NOBE; OBP; PAIC

Foster-Mother's Tale, The.   Samuel Taylor Coleridge.   MBPR

Foul ill spirit hath possessed her, A.   Ben Jonson.   *Fr.* The Sad Shepherd; or, A Tale of Robin Hood.   SCP-1

Foul Shot.   Edwin A. Hoey.   SPo

"Foul vermin they."   Rats.   Walter de la Mare.   BoAnP

Found.   Carol Muske.   AmPA

Found a family, build a state.   Fragments of a Lost Gnostic Poem of the 12th Cetruy.   Herman Melville.   NOBA

Found in a Storm.   William Stafford.   RFM

Found in the garden—dead in his beauty.   The Burial of the Linnet.   Juliana Horatia Ewing.   OxBChV

Found out in left hayfield. Poet. Robert Siegel. FAF

Found Poem with Grafts 1866. Christopher Middleton. TwMBP

Founding Fathers, Nineteenth-Century Style. Robert Penn Warren. Promises, VIII. NoAM

Fountain, The. Donald Davie. OxBTC

Fountain. Elizabeth Jennings. WPE

Fountain, The. Wordsworth. MBPR

Fountain, a Bottle, a Donkey's Ears and Some Books, A. Robert Frost. VGW

Fountain in the Park, The. Ed Haley. *See* While Strolling through the Park.

Fountains, The. W. R. Rodgers. PFIr; POL

Fountains mingle with the river, The. Love's Philosophy. Shelley. BoLoP; MBPR; OLR; PBMP: VoPo

Fountains that frisk and sprinkle. Ballade Made in the Hot Weather. W. E. Henley. FSFS

Four Ages of Man, The, *sel.* Anne Bradstreet. Childhood. SBG

Four Ages of Man, The. W. B. Yeats. BoReV

Four and Twenty. Stephen Stills. GrRo

Four-and-twenty Highland men. Eppie Morrie. *Unknown.* PeBB

Four and twenty tailors went to kill a snail. Mother Goose. GBP; MG

Four and twenty white bulls. *Unknown.* GBP

Four and twenty years ago a-comin to this life. Four and Twenty. Stephen Stills. GrRo

Four Directions, The. Emerson Blackhorse Mitchell. VW

Four ducks on a pond. A Memory. William Allingham. FSFS

Four Epitaphs. Countee Cullen. PoBA
　For My Grandmother, I. VGW

Four feet up, under the bruise-blue. Small Woman on Swallow Street. W. S. Merwin. ConAP

Four for Sir John Davies. Theodore Roethke. NoAM; NOBA; PiAm

Four gents up and swing Sally Goodin. Sally Goodin. *Unknown.* AmFP

Four Glimpses of Night. Frank Marshall Davis. PoBA

Four Haiku. Richard Wright. NoAM

Four Homages. Allan Block. FAF

Four horsemen rode out from the heart of the range. The Bushrangers. Edward Harrington. PoTa

400-Meter Freestyle. Maxine W. Kumin. SPo

Four in the Morning. Edith Sitwell. NoAM

4 in 2 goes twice as fast. Crazy Arithmetic. D'Arcy Thompson. FaBoCo

Four little children. The Lost Angel. Philip Levine. NOBA

Four Little Foxes. Lew Sarett. RFM

Four miles out the tide curls in. Poem. Mira Fish. FAF

Four O'Clock Flower Blues. *Unknown.* AmFP

Four Poems. Ray A. Young Bear. Epi

Four Poems for Robin. Gary Snyder. NoAM; NOBA

Four Preludes on Playthings of the Wind. Carl Sandburg. NOBA; PAIC; PiAm

Four Quartets, *sels.* T. S. Eliot.
　Burnt Norton. HeIP
　Dry Salvages, The. PiAm
　East Coker. PPP; VGW
　Little Gidding. BoReV; NoAM; NOBA; NOBE

Four seasons fill the measure of the year. Keats. MBPR

Four Sheets to the Wind and a One-Way Ticket to France. Conrad Kent Rivers. BPo; PoBA

Four-square Gospel. Roderick Hartigh Jellema. AATT

Four stiff standers. *Unknown.* GBP

Four sweaters are woven upon me. Springer Mountain. James Dickey. CAPP

Four times now I have seen you as another. Boy Driving His Father to Confession. Seamus Heaney. BuTh

Four Translations from the English of Robert Hershon. Robert Hershon. NeAC

Four Untitled Poems. Kathleen Wiegner. MMD

Four white heifers with sprawling hooves. The Orotava Road. Basil Bunting. NoAM

Four Wise Men on Edward II's Reign. *Unknown.* OxBM

Four Women. Nina Simone. MAT

Four-Word Lines. May Swenson. WPE

Four Zoas, The, *sels.* Blake.
　"I am made to sow the thistle for wheat." Prf
　Vala, Night the Ninth Being the Last Judgment. MBPR

1492. Emma Lazarus. WPE

Fourteen-year-old, why must you giggle and dote. The Conventionalist. Stevie Smith. BBGO

Fourth Dance Poem. Gerald W. Barrax. PoBA

Fourth of July Fireworks. Liz Lochhead. MIS

Fourth of July in Maine. Robert Lowell. CAPP

Fourth of July Night. Carl Sandburg. OFD

Fourth Pearl, The: Temperance. Lady Diana Primrose. *Fr.* A Chain of Pearl. WPE

Fourth Psalm: The Cerements. W. S. Merwin. CAAP

Fourth Song. Sir Philip Sidney. *Fr.* Astrophel and Stella. GBL

Fourth Song the Night Nurse Sang. Robert Duncan. VGW

Foveran Sands. Roderick Watson. MIS

Fox, The. John Clare. BoAnP

Fox, The. C. Day Lewis. BoAnP

Fox, The. Kenneth Patchen. CoPAm; LP; MPo

Fox, The. *Unknown. See* Fox and the Geese, The.

Fox and the Crow, The. La Fontaine, *tr. fr. French by* Marianne Moore. PPP

Fox and the Geese, The. *Unknown.* RDB, *with music*
　(Fox, The.) PoTa
　("Fox started out in a hungry plight, A.") MG

Fox and the Goat, The. La Fontaine, *tr. fr. French by* Marianne Moore. AKE

Fox and the Goose, The (" 'Pax vobis,' quod the fox"). *Unknown.* OxBM

Fox and the Wolf, The. *Unknown.* OxBM

Fox at your neck and snakeskin on your feet, A. Leaving Something Behind. David Wagoner. CoPAm

Fox [he] came lolloping, lolloping, The. Hunting Song. Donald Finkel. NCSH; SoSe; SPo

Fox Court, Winter. Cathy Colman. NPW

Fox gan out of the wode go, A. The Fox and the Wolf. *Unknown.* OXBM

Fox Song. Katherine Doak. NPW

Fox started out in a hungry plight, A. *Unknown.* MG

Fox went out on a chilly night, The. The Fox [and the Geese]. *Unknown.* PoTa; RDB

Fox woman/ dances, string of blue beads. Second Skins—a Peyote Song. Joseph Bruchac. CDW

Foxes, The. Janet Frame. WPE

Foxfire. Nancy Willard. IHMS

Fra Bank to Bank, Fra Wood to Wood I Rin. Mark Alexander Boyd. InPK; PPoe
　(Cupid and Venus.) SLP
　(Sonet: "Fra bank to bank, fra wood to wood I rin.") OBP
　(Sonnet: "Fra banc to banc, fra wod to wod, I rin.") GBL; NOBE
　(Venus and Cupid.) Prf

Fra Lippo Lippi, *sel.* Robert Browning. Prf
　"I shall paint/ God in the midst."

Fragment: "I would to heaven that I were so much clay." Byron. *Fr.* Don Juan. MBPR; OBP

Fragment: "Locke sank into a swoon." W. B. Yeats. NoAM; SoSe

Fragment: "Strike, churl; hurl, cheerless wind, then; heltering hail." Gerard Manley Hopkins. OBP

Fragment: To Byron. Shelley. MBPR

Fragment, The: "Towards the evening of her splendid day." Hilaire Belloc. POL

Fragment: "Welcome joy, and welcome sorrow." Keats. MBPR

Fragment: "Where's the poet? show him! show him." Keats. MBPR

Fragment from the Elizabethans. W. Bridges-Adams. FaBoCo

Fragment of a Character. Thomas Moore. FaBoCo

Fragment of a Greek Tragedy. A. E. Housman. SpRo

Fragment of a Love Lament. Unknown. OxBM

Fragment of a Song on the Beautiful Wife of Dr. John Overall. Unknown. BoLoP

Fragment of an Ode to Maia. Keats. OBP
(Ode to May, Fragment.) MBPR

Fragment of Petronius Translated, A. Petronius Arbiter. See Doing, a Filthy Pleasure Is, and Short.

Fragment 113. Hilda Doolittle ("H.D."). PiAm

Fragment Reflection I. Doris Turner. JB

Fragment Thirty-Six. Hilda Doolittle ("H.D."). VGW

Fragments of a Lost Gnostic Poem of the 12th Century. Herman Melville. NOBA

Fragmentum Pertronius Arbiter, Translated. Petronius Arbiter. See Doing, a Filthy Pleasure Is, and Short.

Frail the white rose and frail are. A Flower Given to My daughter. James Joyce. RRA

Frames on Bright Faces. Bruce Severy. HeS

France: an Ode. Samuel Taylor Coleridge. MBPR

France Blues. Unknown. BluL

Francesca. Ezra Pound. PSN

Francis Marion nudges himself gently into the big blue sky. Sonnet. Ted Berrigan. CAAP

Frank Drummer. Edgar Lee Masters. Fr. Spoon River Anthology. NoAM

Frank James, the Roving Gambler. Unknown. AmFP

Frankie and Johnny [or Johnnie]. Unknown. AmFP; BLSo, with music; InPK; NOBA
(Frankie.) BluL
(Frankie and Albert.) PeBB

Frankie and Johnny [or Johnnie] were lovers. Frankie and Johnny [or Johnnie]. Unknown. AmFP; BLSo; NOBA

Frankie she was a good woman, Johnny he was her man. Frankie and Johnny. Unknown. InPK

Frankie Silvers. Frances Silvers. AmFP

Frankie was a good girl. Frankie. Unknown. BluL

Frankie wuz a good woman. Frankie and Albert. Unknown. PeBB

Franz Kafka had a nightmare. Kafka's Other Metamoprhosis. Len Gasparini. NeAC

"Frater Ave atque Vale." Tennyson. InPS

Frau Bauman, Frau Schmidt, and Frau Schwartze. Theodore Roethke. InPK; NoAM; NOBA; PiAm; PSN

Fräulein Reads Instructive Rhymes. Maxine W. Kumin. SpRo

Freak Show, The. Nancy Willard. RiTi

Freak Show and Finale. Lenore Kandel. Fr. Circus. RiTi

"Fred, where is north?" West-running Brook. Robert Frost. NOBA; PAIC; PiAm; SoSe

Freddy the Rat Perishes. Don Marquis. Fr. Archy and Mehitabel. MiP

Frederick Douglass. Sam Cornish. NVAP; PoBA

Frederick Douglass. Paul Laurence Dunbar. PoBA

Frederick Douglass. Robert Hayden. CoPAm; PBMP; PoBA

Frederick Douglass: 1817-1895. Langston Hughes. BPo

Free America. At. to Joseph Warren. BTTM

Free at las'—free at las'. I Thank God I'm Free at Las'. Unknown. BPo; PBMP

Free evening fades, outside the windows, The. Evening in the Sanitarium. Louise Bogan. IHMS; SBG

Free Grace. Charles Wesley. BoReV

Free Kirk, The. Eighteen-Forty-Three. Unknown. FaBoCo

Free Little Bird. Unknown. AmFP

Free Silver. Unknown. AmFP

Free Thoughts on Several Eminent Composers. Charles Lamb. FaBoCo

Free Will. Walter Clark. NCSH

Freedom. Langston Hughes. PoBA; WIF

Freedom ("Men! whose boast it is that ye"). James Russell Lowell. VoPo

Freedom. William Stafford. MiP

Freedom of the Moon, The. Robert Frost. Moon

Freedom will not come. Freedom. Langston Hughes. PoBA; WIF

Freighting from Wilcox to Globe. Unknown. AmFP

French. Osbert Lancaster. FaBoCo

French Master, The. Dannie Abse. LP

French Persian Cats Having a Ball. Edwin Morgan. MPo

French Revolution, The. Blake. MBPR

Frenzy. George Crabbe. Fr. Sir Eustace Grey. NOBE

Fresh Air. Kenneth Koch. CAPP; NoAM

Fresh day cacks, goat's milkspurt. Six-forty-two Farm Commune Struggle Poem. Jay Leifer. MAT

Fresh from the dewy hill, the merry year. Song. Blake. MBPR

Fresh I'm cum fra Sandgate Street. Do Li A. Unknown. GBP

Fresh peaches, large balls that glow for a princess at night. To Bed. Diane Wakoski. CAAP

Freshet springs from woodland cleft, The. Postscript to Die Schöne Müllerin. R. P. Lister. POL

Freshmen. Barry Spacks. CoPAm

Fretful ladybirds complain, The. The Ladybirds. Edward Lucie-Smith. BoAnP

Friar and the Nun, The. Unknown. GBP

Friar had said his paternosters duly, The. Necrological. John Crowe Ransom. PiAm

Friar of Rubygill, The. Thomas Love Peacock. Fr. Maid Marian. PeBB

Friar there was, a wanton and a merry, A. A Wanton Merry Friar. Chaucer. Fr. The Canterbury Tales: Prologue. BoReV

Friars' Retort, The. Unknown. OxBM

Friar's Tale, The. Chaucer. Fr. The Canterbury Tales. PAIC

Friday afternoon: chicken eggs. Alchemy. Diane Levenberg. NPW

Friday Morning. Sydney Carter. LP

Friday. Wet Dusk. Christopher Logue. OxBTC

Friend, The. Marge Piercy. IPWM; NMM; RiTi

Friend, A. Marguerite Power. FaBoCo

Friend, A. W. D. Snodgrass. MAT

Friend in the Garden, A. Juliana Horatia Ewing. OxBChV

Friend of Humanity and the Knife-Grinder, The. George Canning and John Hookham Frere. ESaP; FaBoCo

Friend of Ronsard, Nashe and Beaumont. On a Birthday. J. M. Synge. GBL

Friend of the albatross. Maidenhead. Michael McMahon. FAF

Friend of the wise! and teacher of the good! To William Wordsworth. Samuel Taylor Coleridge. MBPR

Friend, on this scaffold Thomas More lies dead. J. V. Cunningham. InPK

Friend with Spinning Rod. Napoleon St. Cyr. FAF

Friendless and faint, with martyred steps and slow. Calvary. E. A. Robinson. OFD

Friendly Beasts, The. *Unknown.* RAE

Friendly cow, all red and white, The. The Cow. Robert Louis Stevenson. OxBChV

Friends, The. Robert Creeley. Epi

Friends. Ray Durem. PoBA

Friends. Elizabeth Jennings. LP

Friends. W. B. Yeats. NoAM

Friends Departed. Henry Vaughan. *See* They Are All Gone into the World of Light.

Friends recommmended the new Polish film. A Night Out. Dannie Abse. BuTh

Friendship's Mystery, to My Dearest Lucasia. Katherine Philips. SCP-2

Frigate Pelican, The. Marianne Moore. Psy

Frightened/ by the sound of my own voice. Lawrence Ferlinghetti. *Fr.* Coney Island of the Mind. NoAM

Frightened Man, The. Louise Bogan. SBG

'Frisco Town. *Unknown.* BluL

Frisco Whistle Blues. *Unknown.* BluL

Frog, The. Hilaire Belloc. LCL; OxBChV

Frog, The. *Unknown.* ECBV

Frog and the Crow, The. *Unknown.* GBP

Frog and the Toad, The. Christina Rossetti. RAE

Frog he would a wooing go, A. *Unknown.* MG

Frog Plague, The. Bruce Dawe. CAAP

Frog Went a-Courting. *Unknown.* RDB, *with music* (Froggie Went a-Courting.) AmFP; BLSo, *with music*

Frogs. Norman MacCaig. BoAnP; SFF

Frogs. Louis Simpson. BoAnP; InPS; TH

Frogs and the serpents each had a football team, The. Cheers. Eve Merriam. SPo

Frog's Fate, A. Christina Rossetti. VPC

Frogs sit more solid. Frogs. Norman MacCaig. BoAnP; SFF

From a Brother Dreaming in the Rye. James Cunningham. JB

From a Cheerful Alphabet. John Updike. FaBoCo

From a Correct Address in a Suburb of a Major City. Helen Sorrells. WPE

From a Distance. Marvin Bell. HeS

From a distance, I watch. Practical Concerns. William J. Harris. PoBA

From a green sack on a green hill. Here and There. Jon Stallworthy. NoAM

From a Litany. Mark Strand. PPP

From a magician's midnight sleeve. Late Air. Elizabeth Bishop. LoAs

From a Museum Man's Album. John Hewitt. OxBTC

From a Railway Carriage. Robert Louis Stevenson. OxBChV

From a Survivor. Adrienne Rich. LoAs

From America. James M. Whitfield. BPo

From an old man. Dusk. Ken Belford. NeAC

From Arranmore the weary miles I've come. Mavrone. Arthur Guiterman. SpRo

From being anxious, or secure. Good Lord, Deliver Us! John Donne. *Fr.* The Litany. BoReV

From childhood's hour I have not been. Alone. Poe. PiAm; VoPo

From Clee to heaven the beacon burns. 1887. A. E. Housman. BTTM; VoPo

From deep sleep. Nightmare. James A. Emanuel. BPo

From Eastertide to Eastertide. A Ballad of a Nun. John Davidson. PAIC

From Far, from Eve and Morning. A. E. Housman. HeIP

From '41 to '51. John Masefield. *Fr.* The Everlasting Mercy. NoAM

From four walls of/ ivory. Ellen Cooney. NPW

From garden to garden, ridge to ridge. John Muir. RFM

From ghoulies and ghosties. *Unknown, tr. fr. Cornish.* OFD

From Gloucester Out. Edward Dorn. NoAM; NOBA

From Grant's grave Galena. Old Dubuque. Dave Etter. ANTL

From Greenland's Icy Mountains, *with music.* Reginald Heber. BLSH

From harmony, from heavenly harmony. A Song for St. Cecilia's Day, 1687. Dryden. AnMo; InPS; PPP; SCP-1

From here through tunnelled gloom the track. The Railway Junction. Walter de la Mare. OxBTC

From his brimstone bed at break of day. The Devil's Thoughts. Robert Southey *and* Samuel Taylor Coleridge. FaBoCo

From his shoulder Hiawatha. Hiawatha's Photographing. "Lewis Carroll." FaBoCo; SpRo

From Horace ("Persicos odi"). Horace. *See* Fie on Eastern Luxury!

From inside the bird a dream hums itself out and turns. These Horses Came. Ray A. Young Bear. CDW

From life's grim nightmare he is now released. Jacob Epstein. *Unknown.* FaBoCo

From Lois in London. Angela McCabe. AmPA

From low to high doth dissolution climb. Mutability. Wordsworth. *Fr.* Ecclesiastical Sonnets. HeIP; InPK; MBPR; NOBE; PPoD

From Montauk Point. Walt Whitman. RFM

From my front wheels the scared rabbits. Iowa, June. Michael Dennis Browne. AmPA

From my mother's sleep I fell into the State. The Death of the Ball Turret Gunner. Randall Jarrell. CoPAm; InPK; IPWM; NoAM; NOBA; NowV; PPP; PSN; SoSe; VGW; WIF

From my personal album. For Malcolm X. Nanina Alba. PoBA

From Now On. *Unknown.* BluL

From one shaft at Cleator Moor. Cleator Moor. Norman Nicholson. MPo

From Orford Ness to Shingle Street. Dawn on the East Coast. Alun Lewis. PSN

From Our Album. Lawson Fusao Inada. AmPA

From Pent-up Aching Rivers. Walt Whitman. BoLoP; NOBA

From pitch and catch. Fungo. Stanley Plumly. AmPA

From pleasure of the bed. The Chambermaid's Second Song. W. B. Yeats. AnMo

From point A a wind is blowing to point B. After the Broken Arm. Ron Padgett. ConAP

From Rome, for More Public fountains in New York City. Alan Dugan. Prf

From St. Luke's Hospital. Madeleine L'Engle. CTBA

From Sappho to myself, consider the fate of women. Pro Femina, I. Carolyn Kizer. NMM; Psy; RiTi; WBN

From scars where kestrels hover. Missing. W. H. Auden. OxBTC

From stainless steel basins of water. The Operation. W. D. Snodgrass. InPK

From Stirling castle we had seen. Yarrow Unvisited. Wordsworth. MBPR

From Sunset to Star Rise. Christina Rossetti. SGB

From that last acre on oblivion's heap. Edna St. Vincent Millay Exhorts Little Boy Blue. Louis Untermeyer. PAIC

From that last mountain's track. The Last View. Ruthe T. Spinnanger. AATT

From that they found most lovely, most abhorred. Beginning. Alden Nowlan. NeAC

From the bonny bells of heather. Heather Ale. Robert Louis Stevenson. PoTa

From the Bridge. Albert Goldbarth. NVAP

"From the colour the nature." Ezra Pound. Cantos, XC. VGW

From the commandant's quarters on Westchester height. Aaron Burr's Wooing. Edmund Clarence Stedman. BTTM

From the Dark Tower. Countee Cullen. BPo; PoBA

From the depth of the dreamy decline of the dawn. Nephelidia. Swinburne. *Fr.* The Heptalogia. FaBoCo; SpRo

From the Direction of the State Mental Institution. Carol Cox. MMD

From the Flats. Sidney Lanier. NOBA

From the forests and highlands. Hymn of Pan. Shelley. MBPR

From the French. Sir Walter Scott. SLP

From the Gallows Hill to the Tineton Copse. John Masefield. *Fr.* Reynard the Fox, II. OBP From the great Atlantic Ocean, to the wide Pacific shore. Wabash Cannonball. *Unknown.* BLSo

From the hag [*or* hagg] and hungry [*or* hungrie] goblin. Tom o' Bedlam's Song. *Unknown.* Moon; NOBE; OBP

From the Halls of Montezuma. The Marines' Hymn. *Unknown.* BLSH; BLSo; BTTM

From the Hazel Bough. Earle Birney. HeIP

From the heart of a flower. Leave It to Me Blues. Joel Oppenheimer. VGW

From the high deck of Santa Fe's El Capitan. A Siding near Chillicothe. Richmond Lattimore. ANTL

From the hodge porridge. The Farmer's Wife. Anne Sexton. CoPAm

From the Night-Window. Douglas Dunn. SLP

From the oracular archives and the parchment. Altarwise by Owl-Light, IX. Dylan Thomas. NoAM

From the quarters of the compass. Catullus, *tr. fr. Latin by* Peter Whigham. TwMBP

From the tawny light. Everything That Acts Is Actual. Denise Levertov. NoAM

From the television set comes shots and cries. Goodbye, Old Paint, I'm leaving Cheyenne. George Garrett. PPoD

From the Underworld. Howard Blaikley. GrRo

From the Wash the Laundress Sends. A. E. Housman. InPK; NoAM

From the very first coming down. The Letter. W. H. Auden. NoAM

From these bare trees. Chinese Winter. F. R. Higgins. BIrV

From this moment/ and hence backwards. Joanne Kyger. RiTi

From this mountain's edge, clouds crowd. Beinn Damph. Paul Mills. MIS

From this valley they say you are going. Red River Valley. *Unknown.* BLSH; BLSo

From three dark places Christ came forth this day. Upon Christ's Nativity; or, Christmas. Rowland Watkyns. SCP-2

From Thursday. Barbara Earl Thomson. AATT

From Travancore to Tripoli. Ballad of the Oedipus Complex. Lawrence Durrell. FaBoCo

From Tuscan cam my ladies worthi race. Earl of Surrey. AAS

From Venice Was That Afternoon. Jean Garrigue. NOBA

From Venus' breast a bit of greenery grows. On a Statue of Venus. *Unknown.* LoAs

From what great sleep. Watts. Alvin Saxon. PoBA

From what strange country do you come, then? Poem. Siv Cedering Fox. NVAP

From whence cometh song? Song. Theodore Roethke. NCSH

From where I live, from windows on four sides. Juniper. Robert Francis. VGW

From where I sit I see the stars. Midnight. Archibald Lampman. AKE

From which flow destructions of the Constitution. The Law I Love Is Major Mover. Robert Duncan. PiAm

From witty men and mad. The Poet. Thomas Randolph. POL

From you have I been absent in the spring. Sonnets, XCVIII. Shakespeare. FSFS; NOBE

From you, Ianthe, little troubles pass. Ianthe's Troubles. Walter Savage Landor. *Fr.* Ianthe. GBL; NOBE

From your lips I will pluck. Love's Flowers. William Cavendish, Duke of Newcastle. SCP-2

Fronleichnam. D. H. Lawrence. GBL

Front, A. Randall Jarrell. VGW

Frontier, The. John Hewitt. BIrV

Frontispiece. May Swenson. WPE

Frost. Stella Benson. OxBTC

Frost/ lacing/ late summer. Peter Whigham. *Fr.* Love Poems of the VIth Dalai Lama. TwMBP

Frost at Midnight. Samuel Taylor Coleridge. IPWM; MBPR; NOBE; PPP
  "Therefore all seasons shall be sweet to thee," *sel.* FSFS

Frost-fallen are the leaves. Insight. Ruthe T. Spinnanger. AATT

Frost is here, The. Winter. Tennyson. FSFS

Frost on the ground, so still and white. First Frost. E. Margaret Clarkson. AATT

Frost performs its secret ministry, The. Frost at Midnight. Samuel Taylor Coleridge. IPWM; MBPR; NOBE; PPP

Frost's nimble silk. Trahison des Clercs; Against the Perversion of Language. Ezra Pound. PAIC

Frosty Night, A. Robert Graves. LP; OxBTC

Froward Maymond ("Froward knave plainly to descrive, A"). John Lydgate. OxBM

Frozen Hands. Joseph Bruchac. CDW

Frozen Zone, The; or Julia Disdainful. Robert Herrick. SCP-1

Fruit and Vegetables. Erica Jong. CAAP

Fruit rolled by all day, The. Pickle Belt. Theodore Roethke. AnMo

Fruits. Christina Rossetti. ECBV

Fruits of the Earth. Christopher Smart. *Fr.* A Song to David. OBP

Frying Pan Skillet Blues. *Unknown.* BluL

Fudge Family in Paris, The, *sel.* Thomas Moore.
  "After dreaming some hours of the land of Cockaigne." BIrV

Fueled. Marcie Hans. MiP

Full deep green. On Driving Behind a School Bus for Mentally Retarded Children. Grace Butcher. RiTi

Full Fathom Five Thy Father Lies. Shakespeare. *Fr.* The Tempest, I, ii. InPK; InPS; OBP; PPoe; WIF
  (Ariel's Song.) AKE; NOBE
  ("Full fadom five thy father lies.") HeIP

Full many a dreary hour have I past. To My Brother George. Keats. MBPR

Full many a gem of purest ray serene. A "Prize" Poem. Shirley Brooks. FaBoCo

Full many a glorious morning have I seen. Sonnets, XXXIII. Shakespeare. PPP

Full many sing to me and thee. The Barren Shore. Coventry Patmore. GBL

Full Moon. Walter de la Mare. ECBV

Full Moon. Robert Graves. NOBE

Full Moon. Robert Hayden. BPo

Full Moon. Elinor Wylie. Psy; SBG; VGW

Full moon half way up the sky, The. Gulls. E. A. Muir. NCSH

Full moon rising on the waters of my heart. Evening Song. Jean Roomer. BPo

Full Moonlight in Spring. W. S. Merwin. TH

Full of a nitty-gritty anxiety. Paraders for the Bomb. Sidney Bernard. NowV

Full of her long white arms and milky skin. The Equilibrists. John Crowe Ransom. LoAs; NoAM; NOBA; PPP

Full often as I rove by path or stile. Wind on the Corn. Charles Tennyson Turner. VPC

Full rage of Kansas, The. Outside Abilene. Harley Elliott. HeS

Full roses with all their petals like the wrinkles of laughter, The. In Gratitude to Beethoven. Diane Wakoski. Psy

Full year since, I took this eager city, A. An Irishman in Coventry. John Hewitt. BIrV

Fuller and Warren. *At. to* Moses Whitecotton. AmFP

Fumes from all kinds, The. Coming Down Cleveland Avenue. James Tate. PPoD; SFF

Function Room, The. Patrice Phillips MAT

Funeral, The. John Donne. BoLoP; HeIP

Funeral, The. Stephen Spender. NoAM

Funeral of Martin Luther King, Jr., The. Nikki Giovanni. BPo

Funeral Oration for a Mouse. Alan Dugan. NoAM; PPP

Fungo. Stanley Plumly. AmPA

Funny thing about a chair, A. The Chair. Theodore Roethke. AnMo

Funny thing is that he's reading a paper, The. The Sandwich Man. Ron Padgett. ConAP

Furies sink upon their iron beds, The. Pope. *Fr.* Ode on St. Cecilia's Day. FaBoCo

Furl back black walls with shook Fire! The Diamond. Daniel Moore. MIT

Furnished Lives. Jon Silkin. NoAM

Furnished Room, The. James Merrill. NOBA

Furniture of a Woman's Mind, The. Swift. PPoe

Furniture of the Poem, The. Dennis Saleh. NeAC

Furst Snaw. Billy Kay. MIS

Further in summer than the birds. Emily Dickinson. NOBA

Further Language from Truthful James. Bret Harte. FaBoCo

Further Notice. Philip Whalen. VGW

Fury of Aerial Bombardment, The. Richard Eberhart. CoPAm; HeIP; InPK; IPWM; NoAM; PPoD; PSN; TCP; VGW; VoPo; WIF

Fury this Friday broke through my wall, The. In Memory of a Friend. George Barker. OxBTC

Fuscara; or, the Bee-Errant. John Cleveland. SCP-2

Futility. Wilfred Owen. BuTh; NoAM; PSN

Future Blues. *Unknown.* BluL

Fuzzy-Wuzzy. Kipling. BTTM

Fy let us a to the bridal. The Blythsome Bridal. *Unknown, at. to* Frances Sempill. GBP; PeBB


# G

G stands for gnu, whose weapons of defense. The Gnu. Hilaire Belloc. BoAnP

Gabriel. Adrienne Rich. Psy; VGW

Gabriel, from Hevene-King. The Annunciation. *Unknown.* OxBM

Gadfly, The. Keats. MBPR

Gaeltacht. Pearse Hutchinson. BIrV

Gaily bedight,/ A gallant knight. Eldorado. Poe. AmVN; IPWM; NOBA; PiAm; SS

Gaily into Ruislip Gardens. Middlesex. John Betjeman. OxBTC

Gaily the Troubadour, *with music.* Thomas Haynes Bayly. BLSo

Gal, I'm tellin' you, I'm tired fo' true. Lament of the Banana Man. Evan Jones. MPo

Gallop apace, you fiery-footed steeds. Shakespeare. *Fr.* Romeo and Juliet, III, ii. GBL

Galloping collection of boards, The. Somewhere. Robert Creeley. NoAM

Gallows, The. Edward Thomas. InPS; NoAM; SFF

Gallows in my garden, people say, The. A Ballade of Suicide. G. K. Chesterton. PAIC

Galveston with a seawall. Wasn't That a Mighty Storm? *Unknown.* AmFP

Gambler's life I do admire, du-da, du-da. The Gambler. *Unknown.* AmFP

Game, The. Stuart Silverman. CoPAm

Game After Supper. Margaret Atwood. Psy

Game at Salzburg, A. Randall Jarrell. NoAM

Game Called. Grantland Rice. SPo

Game Resumed. Richmond Lattimore. SPo

Game was ended, and the noise, The. Football. Walt Mason. SPo

Gammer Gurton's Needle, *sel. At. to* William Stevenson. Back and Side Go Bare. HeIP

Gang wanted to give Oedipus Rex a going away present, The. Oedipus. Josephine Miles. WPE

Gangrene. Philip Levine. VGW

Gangster's Death, The. Ishmael Reed. PoBA

Gaol Song, The. *Unknown.* GBP

Garbage Disposal Truck, The. Galway Kinnell. AKE

Garden, The, *sel.* Hilda Doolittle ("H.D."). Heat, II. FSFS; HeIP; InPK; NoAM; PiAm

Garden. Minou Drouet, *tr. fr. French by* Margaret Crosland. ECBV

Garden, The. Louise Glück. AmPA; FiCP

Garden, The ("How vainly men themselves amaze"). Andrew Marvell. AnMo; InPS; NOBE; PAIC; PPoD; PPoe; PPP; SCP-1
"What wondrous life is this I lead!" *sel.* FSFS

Garden, The. Ezra Pound. HeIP; PiAm; PPP; PSN

Garden, The. Stuart Silverman. CoPAm

Garden, The. Jones Very. AmVN; PiAm

Garden Abstract. Hart Crane. PSN

Garden Blooms. Nicholas Flocos. SA

Garden by the Sea, A. William Morris. *Fr.* The Life and Death of Jason, IV. NOBE

Garden Fancies, *sel.* Robert Browning. Sibrandus Schafnaburgensis. OBP

Garden flew round with the angel, The. The Pleasures of Merely Circulating. Wallace Stevens. MAT

Garden Hose, The. Beatrice Janosco. POL

Garden is a lovesome thing, God wot, A! My Garden. Thomas Edward Brown. InPK

Garden is a *lovesome* thing, A? What rot! My Garden. J. A. Lindon. InPK; POL

Garden Lore. Juliana Horatia Ewing. OxBChV

Garden of Adonis, The. Spenser. *Fr.* The Faerie Queene, III, 6. NOBE

Garden of Appleton House, The. Andrew Marvell. *Fr.* Upon Appleton House NOBE

Garden of Eden has vanished they say, The. Come Back, Paddy Reilly. Percy French. PFIr

Garden of Love, The. Blake. *Fr.* Songs of Experience. GBL; IPWM; LAuP; LoAs; MAT; MBPR; OBP; PPoe; SS; WIF

Garden of mouthings, A. Purple, scarlet-speckled, black. The Beekeeper's Daughter. Sylvia Plath. IHMS

Garden of Proserpine, The. Swinburne. NOBE

Garden Report. Greg Kuzma. HeS

Garden Wall, The. Denise Levertov. PiAm

Garden Where the Praties Grow, The, *with music. Unknown.* RDB

Gardener, The. *Unknown.* GBP

Gardener to His God, The. Mona Van Duyn. WPE

Gare du Midi W. H. Auden. PSN

Gargoyle. Carl Sandburg. NoAM; NOBA

Garlande of Laurell, The, *sels.* John Skelton. To Maystres Jane Blenner-Haiset. AAS

To Mistress [or Maystres] Isabell Pennell. AAS; NOBE; RRA

To Mistress [or Maystres] Margaret Hussey. AAS; HeIP; LoAs; NOBE; PAIC; PPoe; PPP

To Mistress Margery Wentworth. NOBE

Garnishing the Aviary. Margaret Danner. Far from Africa,I. BPo

Garret, The. Ezra Pound. PSN

Gas flaring on the yellow platform. The Night-Ride. Kenneth Slessor. MAuV

Gas-lamps abandoned by the night burn on. Baudelaire in Brussels. Anthony Cronin. BIrV

Gascoignes Good Morrow. George Gascoigne. AAS

Gascoigne's Memories. George Gascoigne. See Memories.

Gascoignes Woodmanship. George Gascoigne. AAS

Gascoygnes Good Night. George Gascoigne. AAS

Gasoline makes game scarce. Written on the Stub of the First Paycheck. William Stafford. Fr. The Move to California AnMo; InPK

Gate was open, The; the fence under the aspens, fallen. Mountain Corral. Helen Sorrells. WPE

Gateway, The. A. D. Hope. BoLoP

Gather kittens while you may. Song. Oliver Herford. AKE; SpRo

Gather while you may. Rose. Kathleen Raine. WPE

Gather ye rosebuds while ye may. To the Virgins, to Make Much of Time. Robert Herrick. AKE, 1 st.; AnMo; BoLoP; GBL; HeIP; InPK; InPS; IPWM; NOBE; OLR; PAIC; PBMP; PPoe; SFF; SoSe; SpRo

Gathering Gems. Ethel Green Russell. AATT

Gathering Leaves. Robert Frost. VGW

Gathering Song of Donald the Black. Sir Walter Scott. BTTM

Gathering the Bones Together. Gregory Orr. AmPA

Gathers/ and gathers. The Gypsy Motorcycle Club of South Minneapolis. Keith Gunderson. Hes

Gauguin's Menhir, Tahiti ("Gauguin's Museum in Papeari bay"). A. D. Hope. CAAP

Gaunt in gloom. Nightpiece. James Joyce. NoAM

Gaunt kept house with her child for the old man. Montana Fifty Years Ago. J. V. Cunningham. Prf

Gaunt thing, The. Babylon Revisited. LeRoi Jones. BPo; NoAM

Gave me things I. Swallow the Lake. Clarence Major. PoBA

Gave proof through the night. Poem to My Sister, Ethel Ennis, Who Sang "The Star-spangled Banner" at the Second Inauguration of Richard Milhous Nixon. June Jordan. WBN

Gawain and the Lady of the Castle, orig. and mod. English prose. Unknown. Fr. Sir Gawain and the Green Knight. OxBM

Gawain and the Temptress. Unknown, tr. fr. Middle English by Burton Raffel. Fr. Sir Gawain and the Green Knight. OBP

Gay go up and gay go down. Unknown. MG

Gay Goshawk, The. Unknown, at. to Anna Gordon Brown. PeBB; WPE

Gay little Girl-of-the-Diving-Tank. At the Carnival. Anne Spencer. NoAM

Gay Old Hag, The. Unknown. BIrV

Gaze North-east. Unknown, tr. fr. Irish by John Montague. BIrV

Gaze not on swans, in whose soft breast. Beauty's Excellency. Henry Noel. SCP-2

Gazelle Calf, The. D. H. Lawrence. OxBTC

Gazing down upon you I am made aware. The Sleeper William Soutar. SLP

Gazing upon him now, severe and dead. Edna St. Vincent Millay. SBG

Gecko Noel Lloyd. RAE

Gee, but it's tough to be broke, kid. I Can't Give You Anything But Love. Dorothy Fields. BLSo

Geiger, geiger, ticking slow. Paul Dehn. SpRo

Geisha. Gary Gildner. POL

Gemini Robert Creeley. PiAm

Gemwood. Marvin Bell. FiCP

General, The. Siegfried Sassoon. OxBTC

General Communion, A. Alice Meynell. WPE

General Prologue. Chaucer. See Canterbury Tales, The: Prologue.

General Song of Praise to Almighty God, A. John Mason. SCP-2

General William Booth Enters into Heaven. Vachel Lindsay. IPWM; NoAM; NOBA

General's Wife, The. Elton Glaser. NVAP

Generations. Evan Jones. MAuV

Generations 1. Sam Cornish. NVAP

Generations 2. Sam Cornish. NVAP

Generator, The. Rae Desmond Jones. CAAP

"Generosity of her love provides, The." The Grand Guignols of Love. Michael Benedikt. AmPA

Generous Gentleman, The. Allan Ramsay. SLP

Genesis. Harold Witt. SFF

Genitals. Coleman Barks. Fr. Body Poems. NVAP

Genius Loci of the Morning. Doug Fetherling. NeAC

Gentle Alice Brown. W. S. Gilbert. FaBoCo; PeBB

Gentle Ambush, The. George Macadam. SLP

Gentle and smiling as before. The Wheel. Robert Hayden. BPo

Gentle at last, and as clean as ever. Grandfather in the Old Men's Home W. S. Merwin. ConAP; TCP

Gentle blondness and the moray eel go at the same time. On Giving a Son to the Sea. James Dickey. TCP

Gentle Breeze, A. Thomas Durfey. SCP-2

Gentle Echo on Woman, A. Swift. FaBoCo; OLR

Gentle Jesus, Meek and Mild. Charles Wesley. OxBChV

Gentle lady, do not sing. James Joyce. Chamber Music, XXVIII. OLR

"Gentle, modest little flower." To Phoebe. W. S. Gilbert. OLR; WIF

Gentle of hand, the Dean of St. Patrick's guided. A Sermon on Swift. Austin Clarke. BIrV

"Gentle youth, forbear." Hero Feels the Shaft of Love. Christopher Marlowe. Fr. Hero and Leander. GBL

Gentlemen, as we take our seats. The Rehearsal. Horace Gregory. VGW

Gentlemen-Rankers. Kipling. BTTM

Gentleness of rain was in the wind, The. Rain Shelley. POL

Gentlest of women, put your weapons by. Lay Your Arms Aside. Pierce Ferriter, tr. by Eilean Ni Chuilleanain. BIrV

Gently. Christina Rossetti. See Hurt No Living Thing.

Gently dip, but not too deep. George Peele. Fr. The Old Wives' Tale. InPS

Gently, O gently, father, do not bruise. On the Circumcision: for the King's Music. William Cartwright. SCP-2

Gently, years, gently! Ralph Hodgson. POL

Geograpy. Michael Dransfield. CAAP

Geograpy. Kenneth Koch. NoAM

Geography Lesson. Zulfikar Ghose. LP; MPo

Geordie, 2 versions. Unknown. AmFP

George. Dudley Randall. BPo; ConAP; NoAM

George Allen. Unknown. AmFP

George Collins came home last Saturday night. Lady Alice. Unknown. AmFP

George Crabbe. E. A. Robinson. NOBA

George Santayana. Robert Lowell. See For George Santayana.

George Simic. Charles Simic. CAAP

George the First was always reckon'd. On the Four Georges. Walter Savage Landor. FaBoCo

George the Third. E. C. Bentley. *Fr.* Clerihews. FaBoCo

George the Third's Soliloquy. Philip Freneau. NOBA

George used to say we all need an hour a day. Morningside Heights: Fragment of a Film James Reiss. CAAP

George Washington Goes to a Girlie Movie. Aram Boyajian. NeAC

George Washington Whistler, chief engineer. Whistler's Father. Margaret Ryan. NPW

George Washington, your name is on my lips. Patriotic Poem. Diane Wakoski. OFD; VGW

Georgia Dusk. Jean Toomer. BPo; NoAM; PoBA

Georgia dusk/ And the turpentine woods. Mulatto. Langston Hughes. PAIC

Georgia O'Keeffe as a child. Ready. Lynn Strongin. RiTi

Georgiad, The, *sel.* Roy Campbell.
  "Next him Jack Squire through his own tear-drops sploshes." OxBTC

Georgics, *sel.* Vergil, *tr. fr. Latin by* Dryden.
  "When, after such a length of rolling years," *fr.* III. SCP-1

Georgie. *Unknown.* AIW

Georgie Porgie, pudding and pie. Mother Goose. MG

Georgie Wedlock. *Unknown.* AmFP

Geraldines, The. Thomas Osborne Davis. BTTM

Geranium The. Theodore Roethke. MPo

Geranium, The. Sheridan. BoLoP

Geraniums, The. Genevieve Taggard. VGW

Gerard de Nerval. Thomas Brush. NVAP

German Shepherd. Myra Cohn Livingston. RFM

German steel built like a water-drop. The Death of the Sports-car Driver. Jonathan Aaron. MiP

Germans in Greek, The. Posrson on German Scholarship. Richard Porson. FaBoCo

Germinal. "Æ." BIrV

Gerontion. T. S. Eliot. AnMo; InPS; NoAM; NOBA; PPP

Gesture. Donald Finkel. InPK

Gesture by a Lady with an Assumed Name, A. James Wright. ConAP

"Get down, get down, lovin' Henry," she cried. Young Hunting. *Unknown.* AmFP

Get enough food to eat. Karma Repair Kit: Items 1-4. Richard Brautigan. IPWM

Get off my oriental rug, dust I can't shake! Poem for a Hustler. Kathleen Fraser. RiTi

Get on Board, Little Children. *Unknown. See* Gospel Train, The.

Get the children of America out of Troy, New York! Going and Coming: Two Poems. Michael Benedikt. CAAP

Get the Gasworks. David Ignatow. InPK; InPS

Get Up! Joseph Skipsey. InPK

Get Up and Bar the Door. *Unknown.* AIW; AmFP; HeIP; PAIC; PBMP; PoTa

Get Up, Blues. James A. Emanuel. PoBA

Get up, get up for shame, the blooming morn. Corinna's Going a-Maying. Robert Herrick. AnMo; Epi; NOBE; PPP

Get Up or You'll Be Late for School, Silly! John Ciardi. ECBV

"Get up!" the caller calls, "Get up!" Get Up! Joseph Skipsey. InPK

Get up under a mule. The Mule. Coleman Barks. POL

Get Your tongue. Poem. Ted Kooser. POL

Getting a Poem in the Rain. Dick Lourie. NeAC

Getting Drunk with Daughter. Robert Huff. CoPAm

Getting into Focus. Miriam Palmer. RiTi

Getting tired of sleeping in this: : low down lonesome cE-Ell. Prison Cell Blues. *Unknown.* BluL

Geve place, ye lovers, here before. Earl of Surrey. AAS

Ghazals, *sels.* Jim Harrison.
  "After the 'invitation' by the preacher she collapsed in the." NoAM
  "Dog, the lightning frightened us, dark house and both of us." InPS
  "He sings from the bottom of a well but she can hear him up." NoAM
  "I imagined her dead, killed by some local maniac who." InPS
  "She climbed the ladder looking over the wall at the party." InPS

Ghazals: Homage to Ghalib. Adrienne Rich. CAAP

Ghetto Funeral. Charles Reznikoff. *Fr.* Five Groups of Verse. SA

Ghetto Lovesong—Migration. Carole Gregory Clemmons. NMM
  (Migration.) PoBA

Ghost, The. Walter de la Mare. NOBE; OxBTC

Ghost Crabs. Ted Hughes. TwMBP

Ghost of a mouldy larder is one thing, A: whiskery bread. Corposant. Peter Redgrove. OxBTC

Ghost of Ninon would be sorry now, The. Veteran Sirens. E. A. Robinson. NoAM; NOBA; PiAm

Ghost Poem Five. Mary Norbert Körte. IHMS

Ghostly Story. Milton Acorn. NeAC

Ghost's Song, The. *Unknown.* RAE

Giant Decorative Dahlia. Molly Holden. OxBTC; PSN

Giant Norway spruce from Podunk, The. December. James Schuyler. NoAM

Giant sparkler, Lights of the river. "A 4." Louis Zukofsky. VGW

Giant Tortoise, The. Edward Lucie-Smith. BoAnP
  ("Giant tortoise had a look, The.") POL

Giaour, The: a Fragment of a Turkish Tale. Byron. MBPR

Gift. Leonard Cohen. NoAM

Gift, The. Robert Creeley. NOBA

Gift, The. Dick Lourie. NeAC

Gift,The. J. D. Whitney. NVAP

Gift, The. William Carlos Williams. IPWM; TCP

Gift for Mary MacLane, A. T. Alan Broughton. FAF

Gift of Fire, The. Lisel Mueller. NowV

Gift of Trilliums, A. Sandra McPherson. RiTi

Gift Outright, The. Robert Frost. IPWM; NoAM; NOBA; PPP

Gift to be Simple, The. Howard Moss. SS

Gifts/ And words. We'll Never Be the Same (Until Later). Grace Cavalieri. AATT

Gigantic mass, the hard material, The. Shore Leave Lorry. Roy Fuller. NoAM

Gigantic mills stand stark against the sky. Steel Mills. Rachel Albright. ANTL

Gil Brenton. *Unknown.* PeBB

Gilderoy, *sel.* Thomas Campbell.
  "Last, the fatal hour is come, The." SLP

Giles Corey and Goodwyfe Corey—A Ballad of 1692. *Unknown.* PAIC

Giles Johnson, Ph.D. Frank Marshall Davis. BPo; PoBA

Gilgamesh, *sel. Unknown, tr. fr. Babylonian by* E. A. Speiser.
  "Gilgamesh washed his grimy hair, polished his weapons." Prf

Gin a body meet a body. Rigid Body Sings. James Clerk Maxwell. FaBoCo; SpRo

Gin I Were a Doo. *Unknown.* GBP

Ginger Bread Mama. Doughtry Long. BPo; PoBA

Gingham dog and the calico cat, The. The Duel. Eugene Field. ECBV

Giorno dei Morti. D. H. Lawrence. NOBE

Giovanni Da Fiesole on the Sublime; or, Fra Angelico's "Last Judgment." Richard Howard. Prf

Gipsies. *See also* Gypsies.

Gipsies ("The snow falls deep; the forest lies alone"). John Clare. Epi; OBP

Giraffe. Stanley Plumly. AmPA

Giraffes, The. Roy Fuller. NoAM

Giraffes already had sea legs, The. In Noah's Wake. Allan Block. FAF

Giraffes: The American Version. Stephen Dunn. HeS

Girl. A. W. Purdy. NoAM

Girl at the Center of Her Life, A. Joyce Carol Oates. CoPAm

Girl at the Seaside. Richard Murphy. BIrV

Girl, Boy, Flower, Bicycle. M. K. Joseph. MiP

Girl Friends. Rosemary Daniell. WBN

Girl goes dancing there, The. Sweet Dancer. W. B. Yeats. AnMo

Girl Held without Bail. Margaret Walker. BPo; PoBA

Girl I Call Alma, The. Linda Gregg. AmPA

Girl I left behind Me, The ("Dames of France are fond and free, The"). Thomas Osborne Davis. BTTM

Girl I Left behind Me, The ("Break and trail home"). *Unknown.* AmFP

Girl I Left Behind Me, The ("I'm lonesome since I cross'd the hill"), *with music. Unknown.* BLSo

Girl I left behind Me, The ("My parents raised me tenderly"). *Unknown.* AmFP

Girl in a Library, A. Randall Jarrell. NoAM; NOBA

Girl in our village makes love in the churchyard, A. RIP. Alan Garner. BuTh

Girl in the lane, that couldn't speak plain, The. *Unknown.* MG

Girl in the tea shop, The. The Tea Shop. Ezra Pound. BBGO; HeIP

Girl in the Willow Tree, The. Carolyn Maisel. IHMS

Girl in trousers wheeling a red baby, The. Metamorphoses. Roy Fuller. OxBTC

Girl Marcher. John Frederick Nims. SFF

Girl who felt my stare and raised her eyes, The. The Invisible Man. T. S. Matthews. POL

Girl with Car and Guitar. Ralph Mecklenburger. SFF

Girl with Coffee Tray. John Fuller. LP

Girl with 18 Nightgowns, The. Gregory Orr. POL

Girl with the Green Skirt. Dana Naone. CDW

Girls. Pablo Neruda, *tr. fr. Spanish by* Donald D. Walsh. OLR

Girls. Kenneth Rosen. AmPA

Girls and boys, come out to play. Mother Goose. MG

Girls are simply the prettiest things. My Cat and I. Roger McGough. OxBTC; POL

Girls around Cape Horn, The. *Unknown.* AmFP

Girls buck the wind in the grooves toward work. The Morning Half-Life Blues. Marge Piercy. WBN

Girl's far treble, muted to the heat, The. Milkmaid. Laurie Lee. BoLoP; MPo

Girls in their Seasons. Derek Mahon. BoLoP

Girls scream,/ Boys shout. School's Out. W. H. Davies. BBGO

Girl's Song. W. B. Yeats. SS

Girl's Song. Marya Zaturenska. OLR

Girls' Voices. Brendan Gill. POL

Girls Who Wave at Cars from Bridges. Harold Bond. NVAP

Girls with fat thighs and no breasts. Before Bed. Keith Waldrop. InPK

Girtonian Funeral, A. *Unknown.* FaBoCo

Git Along Down to Town. *Unknown.* AmFP

Git on Board, Little Chillen. *Unknown. See* Gospel Train, The.

Give a man his. Wait for Me. Robert Creeley. NOBA; PPP

Give All to Love. Emerson. NOBA; PAIC

Give beauty all her right. Thomas Campion. AAS

Give him the darkest inch your shelf allows. George Crabbe. E. A. Robinson. NOBA

Give me a color. America. Wendy Rose. CDW

Give me a death like Buddha's, let me fall. Prayer. Stanley Moss. POL

Give me a harsh land to wring music from. This Land. Ian Mudie. BuTh

Give Me Jesus. *Unknown.* BPo

Give me leave, fairest Cynthia, to envy. To Cynthia, on Her Looking-glass. Sir Francis Kynaston. SCP-2

Give me leave to rail at you. Song. Earl of Rochester. LoAs

Give me more love or more disdain. Song: Mediocrity in Love Rejected. Thomas Carew. GBL

"Give me my bow," said Robin Hood. The Death of Robin Hood. Eugene Field. PoTa

Give me my scallop shell of quiet. The Passionate Man's Pilgrimage. Sir Walter Ralegh. AAS; BoReV; IPWM; MetP; NOBE; OBP

Give me O indulgent Fate! The Petition for an Absolute Retreat. Countess of Winchilsea. SBG; WPE

Give me one kiss. To Dianeme. Robert Herrick. SoSe

Give Me Peace ("Give me quietness and peace"). Andrei Voznesensky, *tr. fr. Russian by* Jean Garrigue *and* Max Hayward. BuTh

Give me that old-time religion. That Old-time Religion. *Unknown.* BLSH

Give Me the Splendid Silent Sun. Walt Whitman. IPWM; NOBA; VoPo

Give me time i cannot think. These Dreamings Mine. James O. Taylor. BuTh

Give me truths. Blight. Emerson. NOBA; PiAm

Give me women, wine and snuff. Keats. MBPR

Give me your hand at once. Garden. Minou Drouet, *tr. by* Margaret Crosland. ECBV

Give me your patience sister while I frame. Acrostic of My Sister's Name. Keats. MBPR

Give My Regards to Broadway, *with music.* George M. Cohan. BLSo; FSN

Give names to sounds. Out of Blindness. Leslie B. Blades. NowV

Give them my regards when you go to the school reunion. More of a Corpse Than a Woman. Muriel Rukeyser. NMM

Give to Our God Immortal Praise, *with music.* Isaac Watts. BLSH

"Give us a song!" the soldiers cried. The Song of the Camp. Bayard Taylor. BTTM

Give us another poem, he said. Prelude. Patrick Kavanagh. NoAM

Giveaway, The. Phyllis McGinley. PBMP

Given Note, The. Seamus Heaney. NCSH

Giving the Moon a New Chance. Terry Stokes. Moon

Gladdest spaniel who prancing brings the ball, The. Dog Alice. Harold Witt. BoAnP

Gladstone gave his name to the gladstone bag. Christopher Reid. POL

Glance, The. George Herbert. SCP-1

Glance at this fabled page straight from. Historical Society Exhibit: Old Programme. Felix Pollak. HeS

Glanced down at Shannon from the sky-way. Irish-American Dignitary. Austin Clarke. BIrV; PFIr

Glasgerion. *Unknown.* PeBB

Glasgow. Alexander Smith. VPC

Glasgow Botanic Gardens. James Rankin. MIS

Glass Eaters, The. George Jonas. NeAC

Glass Falling ("Glass is going down, The"). Louis MacNeice. PFIr; RAE

Glass of Beer, A. James Stephens, *after the Irish of* David O'Bruaidar. FaBoCo; NCSH; NoAM; OxBTC; SoSe

Glass World. Dorothy Donnelly. NCSH

Glaze, The. You try to see. Jonathan Price. CoPAm

Gleaming in silver are the hills. Washed in Silver. James Stephens. Moon

Gleaner, The. Jane Taylor. OxBChV

Glencoe. Billy Kay. MIS

Glenlogie, *with music*. Unknown. Epi

Glide soft, ye silver floods. William Browne. *Fr.* Britannia's Pastorals, II, Song 1. SCP-2

Glimpse. Pearl Cleage Lomax. PoBA

Glimpse, A. Walt Whitman. PPP

Glittering rises in flocks, The. The Approaches. W. S. Merwin. NOBA; Prf

Glooms of the live-oaks, beautiful-braided and woven. The Marshes of Glynn. Sidney Lanier. AmVN; NOBA; PiAm; VoPo

Gloomy night embraced the place. The Shepherds' Hymn. Richard Crashaw. *Fr.* In the Holy Nativity of Our Lord God. NOBE; SCP-1

Gloomy thought, Ben Bulben, A. The Deserted Mountain. *Unknown, tr. by* John Montague. BIrV

Gloria. Christopher Smart. *Fr.* A Song to David OBP

Gloria Patri, *with music*. *At. to* St. Thomas Aquinas, *ad. by* John Mason Neale. BLSH

Glories of Our Blood and State, The. James Shirley. *Fr.* The Contention of Ajax and Ulysses. PPP; SCP-2; SoSe (Death the Leveller.) NOBE; PBMP (Dirge.) OBP

Glorious it is/ to see long-haired winter caribou. *Unknown, tr. fr. Eskimo.* RFM

Glorious people vibrated again, A. Ode to Liberty. Shelley. MBPR

Glorious the sun in mid career. Gloria. Christopher Smart. *Fr.* A Song to David. OBP

Glorious World. Hermann Hesse, *tr. fr. German by* James Wright. IPWM

Glory. Harvey Shapiro. POL

Glory, The. Edward Thomas. OxBTC

Glory and a glory, A. Somewhere. James E. Warren, Jr. AATT

Glory and loveliness have passed away. Dedication to Leigh Hunt, Esq. Keats. MBPR

Glory be to God for dappled things. Pied Beauty. Gerard Manley Hopkins. AKE; AnMo; BoReV; Epi; HeIP; InPK; InPS; NoAM; NOBE; PAIC; PBMP; PPoD; PPP; SS; VoPo; WIF

Glory be to the Father, and to the Son, and to the Holy Ghost. Gloria Patri. *At. to* St. Thomas Aquinas. BLSH

Glory of evening was spread through the west, The. The Convict. Wordsworth. MBPR

Glory of the beauty of the morning, The. The Glory. Edward Thomas. OxBTC

Glory of the Day Was in Her Face, The. James Weldon Johnson. PoBA

Glory Trail, The. Badger Clark. PoTa

Glory's given to the first. Honorable Mention. Rebecca Stutsman. SPo

Gloucester Moors. William Vaughn Moody. AmVN; NOBA

Glove Glue. Ken Belford. NeAC

Glowing gloom of eventide, The. The Monarch's Funeral. Shelley. MBPR

Glowworm. David McCord. ECBV

Glow Worm, *with music*. Lila Cayley Robinson. BLSo

Glow-Worm, The. Wordsworth. MBPR ("Among all lovely things my love had been.") GBL

Glucose. Dabney Stuart. CoPAm

Glutton, The. John Oakman. OxBChV

Glutton in the Tavern. William Langland. *Fr.* The Vision of Piers Plowman OxBM

Gnarled old apple-tree. Old Sinner. Derek Bowman. MIS

Gnat, The. Joseph Beaumont. SCP-2

Gnat-Psalm. Ted Hughes. NoAM

Gnome. Samuel Beckett. BIrV

Γνωθι σεαυτον!—and is this the prime. Self-Knowledge. Samuel Taylor Coleridge. MBPR

Gnu, The. Hilaire Belloc. BoAnP

Gnu, The. Theodore Roethke. ECBV

Go and ask Robin to bring the girls over. Vision by Sweetwater. John Crowe Ransom. NOBA

Go [*or* Goe,] and catch a falling star. Song. John Donne. AnMo; BuTh; HeIP; InPK; InPS; NOBE; OBP; PBMP; PPoD; PPoe; SoSe; VoPo

Go and dig my grave both long and narrow. Dig My Grave. *Unknown.* AmFP

Go and open the door. The Door. Miroslav Holub, *tr. by* Ian Milner *and* George Theiner. LP

Go back, old Devil and look up on your shelf. Old Devil. *Unknown.* BluL

Go Back to the Country. *Unknown.* BluL

Go bet, peny, go bet, go! Penny Is a Hardy Knight. *Unknown.* OxBM

Go down Death. James Weldon Johnson. PoBA

Go Down, Moses. *Unknown.* BPo; NOBA; RDB, *with music*

Go Down, Old Hannah. *Unknown.* AmFP

Go, dumb-born book. Envoi (1919). Ezra Pound. *Fr.* Hugh Selwyn Mauberly. VGW

Go fetch to me a pint o'wine. The Silver Tassie. Burns. NOBE

Go, for they call you, shepherd, from the hill. The Scholar-Gipsy. Matthew Arnold. HeIP; NOBE

Go friendly, Go lovely, Go naked. Jealousy. Stephen Vincent. NeAC

Go from me, summer friends, and tarry not. From Sunset to Star Rise. Christina Rossetti. SBG

Go from My Window. *Unknown.* AIW

Go Heart, Hurt with Adversity. *Unknown.* OxBM

Go, ill-sped book, and whisper to her or. John Berryman.* BoLoP; LoAs

Go, let the fatted calf be killed. The Welcome. Abraham Cowley. *Fr.* The Mistress. BoLoP

Go, Little Book ("Go, litel book, go, litel myn tragedy"). Chaucer. *Fr.* Troilus and Criseyde, V. OxBM ("Go, little book, go, my little tragedy.") OBP

Go, Lovely Rose. Edmund Waller. BoLoP; HeIP; InPK; NOBE; OLR (Song: "Go lovely rose.") GBL; OBP; PAIC; PPoe

Go, my songs, to the lonely and the unsatisfied. Commission. Ezra Pound. BoLoP

Go out with a small flashlight and a star chart. Things to Do around a Ship at Sea. Gary Snyder. CAPP

Go pretty child, and bear this flower. A Child's Present. Robert Herrick. OxBChV

Go, said old Lyce, senseless lover, go. Lyce. William Walsh. BoLoP

Go, Soul [*or* Goe soule], the body's guest. The Lie. Sir Walter Ralegh. AAS; NOBE; PPoD; PPoe

Go tell Aunt Rhody [*or* Nancy]. The Old Gray Goose. *Unknown.* AmFP; GBP

"Go tell him to clear me one acre of ground." The Elfin Knight. *Unknown.* AmFP

Go through the gates with closed eyes. Close Your Eyes! Arna Bontemps. IPWM; PoBA

Go to Bed First. *Unknown.* GBP

Go to Old Ireland. *Unknown.* AmFP

Go to sleep, go to sleepy. All the Pretty Little Horses. *Unknown.* AmFP

Go to the western gate, Luke Havergal. Luke Havergal. E. A. Robinson. AmVN; GBL; LoAs; NoAM; NOBA; PiAm

Go 'way from dat window, "My Honey, My Love." Song to the Runaway Slave. *Unknown.* BPo

Goals. Elisavietta Ritchie. AATT

Goat. Siddie Joe Johnson. ECBV

Goat, The. Roland Young. BoAnP

Goblin Market. Christina Rossetti. SBG; VPC

God. Eugene Ruggles. MIT

God—/they fear you, they hold you so. Testimony   Carolyn M. Rodgers. BPo

God almighty's colly cow. The Ladybird. *Unknown.* GBP

God and Saint [*or* Sanct] Peter was gangand be the way. How the First Hielandman [of God] Was Made. *Unknown.* FaBoCo; GBP

God and the devil still are wrangling. For a Mouthy Woman. Countee Cullen. PoBA

God and Yet a Man, A? *Unknown.* IPWM (Wit Wonders.) BoReV

God banish from your house. Benediction. Stanley Kunitz. VGW

God be with trewthe wher he be! Truth. *Unknown.* OxBM

God Be with You Till We Meet Again, *with music.* J. E. Rankin. BLSH

God bless all policemen. Goodbat Nightman. Roger McGough. BBGO; NoAM

God Bless America, *with music.* Irving Berlin. BLSo

God bless Henry. He lived like a rat. John Berryman. *Fr.* Dream Songs. CAPP

God bless little Danny, where his spirit runs. Benediction for Danny. William R. Mitchell. AATT

God bless our good and gracious King. Impromptu on Charles II. Earl of Rochester. InPK

God Bless the Child. Arthur Herzog, Jr., *and* Billie Holiday. WIF

God bless the field and bless the furrow. The Robin's Song. *Unknown, at. to* Richard Honeywood. ECBV; RAE

God bless the King!—I mean the Faith's Defender. A Jacobite Toast [*or* Extempore Verses...]. John Byrom. FaBoCo; PPoD

God Bless Us. Gaston Bart-Williams. BuTh

God Don't Never Change. *Unknown.* BluL

God gave all men all earth to love. Sussex. Kipling. BTTM

God Give to Men ("God give the yellow man"). Arna Bontemps. BPo

God has a brown voice. For Eleanor Boylan Talking with God. Anne Sexton. InPk

God! how they plague his life, the three damned sisters. The Little Brother. James Reeves. LoAs; OxBTC

God in Wrath, A. Stephen Crane. Black Riders, XIX. AmVN; IPWM

God is indeed a jealous God. Emily Dickinson. NOBA

God is no botcher, but when God wrought you two. On Botching. John Heywood. FaBoCo

God is the Old Repair Man. The Old Repair Man   Fenton Johnson. MiP

God knows how our neighbor managed to breed. Sow. Sylvia Plath. AnMo; CoPAm

God knows it, I am with you. To a Republican Friend, 1848. Matthew Arnold. PAIC

God knows what it is about Town Halls. Vincent Buckley. *Fr.* Golden Builders CAAP

God lay dead in heaven. The Black Riders, LXVII. Stephen Crane. PiAm

God love you now, if no one else will ever. Ode for the American Dead in Korea. Thomas McGrath. VGW

God made the wicked grocer. The Song Against Grocers. G. K. Chesterton. FaBoCo

God makes sech nights, all white an' still. The Courtin'. James Russell Lowell. *Fr.* The Biglow Papers. AmVN; NOBA

God moves in a mysterious way. Light Shining Out of Darkness. William Cowper. BoReV; HeIP; NOBE

God of mine, I am weeping for the life that I live. The Eternal Dice. César Vallejo, *tr. by* James Wright. IPWM

God of our fathers, known of old. Recessional. Kipling. BLSH; BTTM; NOBE

God of our fathers, what is man! The Ways of God. Milton. *Fr.* Samson Agonistes BoReV

God of the golden bow. Hymn to Apollo. Keats. MBPR

God of the Meridian. Keats. MBPR

God Poem   Stanley Moss. VGW

God prosper long our noble king. Chevy Chase. *Unknown.* PeBB

God Rest You Merry, Gentlemen, *with music.* *Unknown.* BLSH

God Save the King [*or* Queen] ("God save our gracious King [*or* Queen]"). *Unknown, at. to* Henry Carey. BLSH, *with music;* BTTM, *sl. diff.*

God saw Adam in a town. Charles Reznikoff. *Fr.* Five Groups of Verse. SA

God send every priest a wife. *Unknown.* TVS

God shepherds me, I have. Psalm XXIII. *Paraphrased by* Harry H. Mayer. SFF

God Speed the Plough! *Unknown.* OxBM

God strengthen me to bear myself. Who Shall Deliver Me? Christina Rossetti. BoReV; PFD

God, That Madest All Things. *Unknown.* SoSe

God, the Port of Peace. John Walton. OxBM

God to Be First Served. Robert Herrick. OxBChV

God told Noah about the rainbow sign. Lining Track. *Unknown.* AmFP

God tried to teach Crow how to talk. Crow's First Lesson. Ted Hughes. InPS; NoAM

God Walks among the Dust. Henry Tim Chambers. AATT

God Will Take Care of You, *with music.* Mrs. C. D. Martin. BLSH

God Wills It. Gabriela Mistral, *tr. fr. Spanish by* K. G. C. LoAs

God with a Roll of Honour in His hand. The Investiture. Siegfried Sassoon. NoAM

God with honour hang your head. At the Wedding March. Gerard Manley Hopkins. LoAs

God, Woman, Egg. Helena Minton. FAF

God, you could grow to love it. Ecclesiastes. Derek Mahon. BIrV

Goddess, The. Denise Levertov. NOBA

Goddess Fortune be praised (on her toothed wheel), The. The Unpredicted. John Heath-Stubbs. BoLoP

Goddess of light, renewer of the mind. Sportsfield. A. D. Hope. MAuV

Goddess of poetry. To the Moon. Yvor Winters. HeIP

Goddess stands in front of her cave, The. On the Occasion of Becoming an Echo. Anselm Hollo. TwMBP

Godly Dream, A, *sels.* Elizabeth Melvill, Lady Culross. WPE
　"I looked down and saw a pit most black."
　"Into that pit when I did enter in."
　"Then up I rose, and made no more delay."
　"This pit is Hell where through thou now must go."
　"Weary I was, and thought to sit at rest."

Godolphin Horne. Hilaire Belloc. FaBoCo

God's collage. Lesson from Jim Crane. Barbara Earl Thomson. AATT

God's Determinations, *sels.*    Edward Taylor.
   Our Insufficiency to Praise God Suitably, for His Mercy.   PiAm
   Preface, The: "Infinity, when all things it beheld."   NOBA; PiAm

God's Education.   Thomas Hardy.   OBP

God's Grandeur.   Gerard Manley Hopkins.   AnMo; BoReV; Epi; InPK; IPWM; NoAM; NOBE; OBP; PAIC; PPP; SoSe; VoPo

Gods have taken alien shapes upon them, The.   Exiles."Æ."   BIrV

God's head for a paperweight, A.   The Desk.   Cid Corman.   VGW

Gods in Vietnam.   Eugene Redmond.   PoBA

Gods, men in straw hats, girls in calico.   For J. A. R. McKellar.   Geoffrey Lehmann.   MAuV

Gods of the Copybook Headings, The.   Kipling.   OBP; OxBTC

God's World.   Edna St. Vincent Millay.   VoPo

Gods would have chastened us through confusion, The.   The Outrageously Blessed.   Barry Spacks.   CoPAm

Goe, and catche a falling starre.   *See* Go and catch a falling star.

Goe soule, the bodies guest.   *See* Go, Soul, the body's guest.

Goggled yellow, the cyclist's face.   Stoplight.   William Pitt Root.   SFF

Goin' 'cross the Mountain.   *Unknown.*   AmFP

Goin' down to Cripple Creek, goin' at a run.   Cripple Creek.   *Unknown.*   AmFP

Goin' down to the delta.   Mississippi Blues.   *Unknown.*   AmFP

Goin' up State Street, comin' down Main.   Take a Whiff on Me.   *Unknown.*   NOBA

Going, The.   Thomas Hardy.   NOBE

Going.   Philip Larkin.   NowV; PSN

Going and Coming: Two Poems.   Michael Benedikt.   CAAP

Going and Staying.   Thomas Hardy.   NoAM

Going Away Blues.   *Unknown.*   BluL

Going backward.   In the Pocket.   James Dickey.   SPo

Going Fishing.   Lexie Griffiths.   RAE

Going Home.   Thomas Lux.   NVAP

Going Home.   Tim Reynolds.   NowV

Going Home.   Renée Roper.   NPW

Going in to Dinner.   Edward Shanks.   OxBTC

Going into a church my prayers to say.   On a Melting Beauty.   Margaret Cavendish, Duchess of Newcastle.   SCP-2

Going into Breeches.   Charles *and* Mary Lamb.   OxBChV

Going into the Woods.   Tom Hennen.   HeS

Going the Rounds: A Sort of Love Poem.   Anthony Hecht.   BoLoP

Going Through.   Bruce P. Woodford.   MAT

Going Through Changes.   Jean Tepperman.   NMM

Going To and Fro and Walking Up and Down, *sels.*   Charles Reznikoff.   SA
   Autobiography: Hollywood.
   Kaddish: "In her last sickness, my mother took my hand in hers."

Going to Bed.   John Donne.   Elegies, XIX.GBL;PPP
   (To His Mistress [*or* Mistris] Going to Bed.)   AnMo; BoLoP; OBP

Going to Cythera.   Chris Wallace-Crabbe.   CAAP

Going to Germany.   *Unknown.*   BluL

Going to Hell.   *Unknown.*   OxBM

Going to Mass Last Sunday.   Donagh MacDonagh.   BIrV

Going to Remake This World.   James Welch.   CDW; SA

Going to School in France or America.   Tom Clark.   ConAP

Going to Sleep in the Country.   Howard Moss.   PPoD

Going to the Wars.   Richard Lovelace.   *See* To Lucasta, Going to the Wars.

Going up for the jump shot.   The Poet Tries to Turn in His Jock.   David Hilton.   NowV

Going Up the River.   *Unknown.*   AIW

Going up the river, or down, their tuneless look.   Barges on the Hudson.   Babette Deutsch.   WPE

Going Uptown to Visit Miriam.   Victor Hernandez Cruz.   MAT

Gold.   Donald Hall.   ConAP; InPS

Gold-coloured skin of my Lebanese friends, The.   A Trip to Four or Five Towns.   John Logan.   ConAP

Gold Leaves.   G. K. Chesterton.   OxBTC

Gold savours well, though it be got.   Isabella Whitney.   *Fr.* A Sweet Nosegay, or Pleasant Posy.   WPE

Gold Watch, The.   John Blight.   CAAP

Golden.   Gérard de Nerval, *tr. fr. French by* Andrew Hoyem.   Epi

Golden Age Restored, The, *sel.*   Ben Jonson.
   "We come!/ We come!"   SCP-1

Golden bridle of Bellerephon.   The Fourth Pearl: Temperance.   Lady Diana Primrose.   *Fr.* A Chain of Pearl.   WPE

Golden Builders, *sels.*   Vincent Buckley.   CAAP
   "As the car stooped, seemed to pause," XXVII.
   "Even if there'd been prayers," III.
   Fitzroy, Carlton, IX.
   "God knows what it is about Town Halls," II.
   "Hammers of iron glow down Faraday, The," I.
   "Here, though, the fine cool air," VI.
   "Purblind walls," V.
   Telephones, Muzak, XXV.
   "They are digging everywhere. From street to street," IV.
   "Timid and hot-tempered," VIII.
   "Traffic glitters towards dull junction, The," XXVI.
   "With the spring rains, small spiders," VII.

Golden casket I designed, A.   Epigram.   John Swanick Drennan.   BIrV

Golden-eyed Crossbow, The.   Claude Pélieu.   MIT

Golden gift that nature did thee geve, The.   Earl of Surrey.   AAS

Golden Glove, The.   *Unknown.*   AmFP

Golden Journey to Samarkand, The, *sels.*   James Elroy Flecker.
   "And how beguile you? Death has no repose," II.   OxBTC
   Epilogue: "Away, for we are ready to a man!"   NOBE
   Prologue: "We who with songs beguile your pilgrimage."   OxBTC

Golden Moonrise.   William Stanley Braithwaite.   PoBA

Golden Net, The.   Blake.   MBPR

Golden Pyramids of the Sun, The.   Alden Nowlan.   AKE

Golden Shower, The, *sel.*   Roy Campbell.
   "Here, where relumed by changing seasons, burn."   OxBTC

Golden slumbers kiss your eyes.   A Cradle Song.   Thomas Dekker.   *Fr.* The Pleasant Comedy of Patient Grissell.   OxBChV

*Golden Vanity*, The.   *Unknown.*   AIW; PBMP; RDB, *with music*

Golden Witch, The.   Alan Dienstag.   MIT

Golden, within this golden hive.   Danaë.   Barbara Howes.   RiTi; WPE

Goldfish.   Howard Nemerov.   BoAnP

Goldfish Floats, The.   Ted Kooser.   HeS

Goldfish Wife, The.   Sandra Hochman.   RiTi

Goliath stood up clear in the assumption of status.   David.   Josephine Miles.   MIT

Gombeen, The.   Joseph Campbell.   BIrV

Gondibert, *sels.*   Sir William Davenant.   SCP-2
   "Battle in exact though little shape, The," I, 5.
   "Verona by the port's pencil drawn," II, 1.

Gondoliers, The, *sel.*   W. S. Gilbert.
   There Lived a King.   PoTa

Gone.   Carl Sandburg.   NOBA

Gone are the days when my heart was young and gay. Old Black Joe. Stephen Collins Foster. PSoN

Gone Dead Train, The. *Unknown.* BluL

Gone, I say, and walk from church. The Truth the Dead Know. Anne Sexton. CoPAm; NoAM; Psy

Gone now the baby's nurse. Home after Three Months Away. Robert Lowell. PBMP; PSN; RRA

Gone the three ancient ladies. Frau Bauman, Frau Schmidt, and Frau Schwartze. Theodore Roethke. InPK; NoAM; NOBA; PiAm; PSN

Gone were but the winter. Spring Quiet. Christina Rossetti. FSFS; VoPo; WPE

"Goneys an' gullies an' all o' the birds o' the sea." Sea Change. John Masefield. PoTa

Gonna Lay My Head Down on Some Railroad Line. *Unknown.* AmFP

Gonna sit around for a while. I Don't Know. *Unknown.* BluL

Goober Peas, *with music. Unknown.* PSoN

Good Advice. Lady Mary Wortley Montagu. POL

Good aged Bale, that with thy hoary hairs. To Doctor Bale. Barnabe Googe. PAIC

Good and Bad Children. Robert Louis Stevenson. OxBChV

Good and Clever. Elizabeth Wordsworth. OxBTC

Good and great God! can I not think of Thee. To Heaven. Ben Jonson. PPoe

Good are attracted by mens perceptions, The. Motto to the Songs of Innocence and of Experience. Blake. MBPR

Good brother Philip, I have borne you long. Astrophel and Stella, LXXXIII. Sir Philip Sidney. Epi

Good-By on an All Day Bean Planter. Nathan Whiting. HeS

Good-bye. Emerson. VoPo

Goodbye. Alun Lewis. BoLoP; MPo; OxBTC; PSN

Good-bye,/ try to stay awake now you're dead. Book of the Dead, Prayer 14. Mei Berssenbrugge. SA

Goodbye and Hello. Tim Buckley. WIF

Goodbye David Tamunoemi West. Margaret Danner. BPo

Goodbye, goodbye to summer! Robin Redbreast. William Allingham. OxBChV

Goodbye, he waved, entering the apple. Fruit and Vegetables. Erica Jong. CAAP

Goodbye, lady in Bangor, who sent me. The Correspondence School Instructor Says Goodbye to His Poetry Students. Galway Kinnell. NOBA

Goodbye, Little Bonny Blue Eyes. *Unknown.* AmFP

Good Bye, My Lady Love, *with music.* Joseph E. Howard. FSN

Goodbye, Old Paint, I'm Leaving Cheyenne. George Garrett. PPoD

Goodbye pale cold inconstant. A Farewell, a Welcome. Lisel Mueller. Moon

Good-bye, proud world! I'm going home. Good-bye. Emerson. VoPo

Goodbye, Sally. James Simmons. BIrV

Good-Bye to the Mezzogiorno. W. H. Auden. OxBTC

Goodbye to the town!—goodbye! July. Austin Dobson. RAE

Goodbye, winter. Prognosis. Louis MacNeice. NOBE

Good children, refuse not these lessons to learn. A Schoolmaster's Admonition. *Unknown.* OxBChV

Good Christians all, both great and small. The Avondale Mine Disaster. *Unknown.* AmFP

Good folk, for gold or hire. The Crier. Michael Drayton. PAIC

Good folks ever will have their way. The Doctor's Story. Will M. Carleton. PoTa

Good Frend, *sel.* Hilda Doolittle ("H.D.").
"Time has an end, they say." NOBA

Good Friday. Richard Bastian. AATT

Good Friday. Christina Rossetti. OFD

Good Friday./ Miss Booker's beauty parlor. Rachel and the Truth (c.1945). Yvonne. WBN

Good Friday Explosives. E. R. Cole. AATT

Good Friday, 1613. Riding Westward. John Donne. AnMo; PPP

Good Friday was the day. The Martyr. Herman Melville. VoPo

Good God, what a night that was. Petronius Arbiter, *tr. fr. Latin by* Kenneth Rexroth. BoLoP

Good Gossips Mine. *Unknown.* OxBM

Good grey guardians of art, The. Museum Piece. Richard Wilbur. ConAP; WIF

Good Harbor Bay, Leland, Michigan. Ellen McEvilley Griffin. NPW

Good Heav'n, I thank thee, since it was design'd. On Myselfe. Countess of Winchilsea. SBG

Good King Wenceslas, *with music. Unknown, tr. fr. Latin by* John Mason Neale. BLSH

Good Kosciusko, thy great name alone. To Kosciusko. Keats. MBPR

Good Lord, Deliver Us! John Donne. *Fr.* The Litany. BoReV

Good Lord, what a wicked world is this. *Unknown.* TVS

Good Luck. Robert Herrick. ECBV

Good Luck to You Kafka/ You'll Need It Boss. Henry Graham. NowV

Good man was there of religion, A. A Poor Parson. Chaucer. *Fr.* The Canterbury Tales: Prologue. BoReV

Good morn t'ye, John. How b'ye? how b'ye? Eclogue: The Common a-Took In. William Barnes. VPC

Good Mornin', Blues. *Unknown.* InPK

Good Morning. Langston Hughes. WIF

Good Morning. Layle Silbert. NPW

Good morning, Algernon: Good morning, Percy. On Mundane Acquaintances. Hilaire Belloc. OxBTC

Good Morning America, *sel.* Carl Sandburg.
"Now it's Uncle Sam sitting on top of the world," XIV. OFD

"Good-morning; good-morning!" the General said. The General. Siegfried Sassoon. OxBTC

Good morning, Judge what may be my fine. Judge Harsh Blues. *Unknown.* BluL

Good Morning Love! Paul Blackburn. NoAM

Good morning, man; good morning, child. World, Hold Me Close. Virginia Floyd. AATT

Good-Morrow, The. John Donne. AnMo; BoLoP; InPS; LoAs; MetP; OLR; PAIC; PPP; SCP-1; SoSe

Good morrow to the day so fair. The Mad Maid's Song. Robert Herrick. SCP-1

Good news. It seems he loved them after all. A Song about Major Eatherly. John Wain. NowV; OxBTC

Good news! Nilda Is Back. Colette Inez. RiTi

Goodnight, The. Louis Simpson. MPo; PBMP

Good Night and Good Morning. Richard Monckton Milnes. OxBChV

Good Night, at last. Envoy. Robert Duncan. *Fr.* Passages. VGW

Good-night; ensured release. Parta Quies. A. E. Housman. NOBE

Good-night to the Season. Winthrop Mackworth Praed. NOBE

Good of the Chaplain to enter Lone Bay. Billy in the Darbies. Herman Melville. *Fr.* Billy Budd, Foretopman. NOBA

Good people all, of every sort. An Elegy on the Death of a Mad Dog. Goldsmith. *Fr.* The Vicar of Wakefield. AIW; FaBoCo; LAuP; SS

Good people all, with one accord. An Elegy on That Glory of Her Sex, Mrs. Mary Blaize. Goldsmith. FaBoCo; LAuP

Good Sportsmanship. Richard Armour. SPo

Good sword and a trusty hand! A The Song of the Western Men. Robert Stephen Hawker. BTTM

Good Taste. Christopher Logue. RAE

Good Times. Lucille Clifton. AmPA; BPo; CAAP; InPS; NCSH; PoBA

"Good weather for hay." Vermont Conversation. Patricia Hubbell. CTBA

Good Wif was ther of biside Bathe, A. The Wife of Bath. Chaucer. *Fr.* The Canterbury Tales: Prologue. InPS; OxBM; PPoe

Goodbat Nightman. Roger McGough. BBGO; NoAM

Goodby. *See* Good-by.

Goodbye. *See* Good-bye.

Goodly Child, A. *Unknown.* OxBChV

Goodly host one day was mine, A. Mine Host of the "Golden Apple." Thomas Westwood. ECBV

Goodwill, Inc. Dennis Schmitz. AmPA

Goody Blake, and Harry Gill. Wordsworth. MBPR

Goose. Richard Emil Braun. NoAm

Goose, The. Tennyson. ECBV

Goose and the Gander, The. *Unknown.* GBP

Goose Fish, The. Howard Nemerov. HeIP; InPK; LoAs; NoAM

Goose, Moose, and Spruce. David McCord. ECBV

Gooseberry Wine. Mary Shumway. NVAP

Goosegirl, your feet are slow. The New Leda. Barbara Howes. RiTi

Goosey, goosey, gander,/ Whither shall I wander? Mother Goose. MG

Gorilla at Twenty Nine Years, The. J. D. Reed. NeAC

Gorilla Gorilla. Bruce Dawe. CAAP

Gorilla lay on his back, The. Au Jardin des Plantes. John Wain. OxBTC

Gospel Train, The. *Unknown.* BLSo, *with music*
  (Get on Board, Little Children.) PBMP
  (Git on Board, Little Chillen.) BPo

Gosport Tragedy, The. *Unknown.* AmFP

Gossip. Nicholas Flocos. SA

Gossip grows like weeds. Hitomaro, *tr. fr. Japanese by* Kenneth Rexroth. OLR

Got a little bitty mama, and a big mama too. Big Woman. *Unknown.* BluL

"Got any boys?" the Marshal said. The Puzzled Census Taker. John Godfrey Saxe. PoTa

Got the Blues, Can't Be Satisfied. *Unknown.* BluL

Got three womens: yellow, brown and black. Three Women Blues. *Unknown.* BluL

Got up this morning/ The blues, walking like a man. Preaching Blues. *Unknown.* BluL

Gothic looks solemn, The. Lines Rhymed in a Letter Received from Oxford. Keats. MBPR

Gourd Dancer, The. N. Scott Momaday. CDW

Government of your body, sweet, The. The United States. William Carlos Williams. LoAs

Governor your husband lived so long, The. John Berryman. *Fr.* Homage to Mistress Bradstreet. NoAM; NOBA

Governor's Palace, The. Linda Pastan. *Fr.* Williamsburg. RiTi

Gowa! Gowa! Crow's Ditty. *Unknown.* GBP

Gowan glitters on the sward, The. The Trysting Bush. Joanna Baillie. WPE

Grace. Michael Sheridan. HeS

Grace for a Child. Robert Herrick. InPS
  (Another Grace for a Child.) HeIP; InPK; OxBChV

Grace for Children, A. Robert Herrick. OxBchV

Grace-note. The. Denise Levertov. ConAP

Grace of Cynthia's Maidenhood, The. Vinnie-Marie D'Ambrosio. IHMS

Grace to Be Said at the Supermarket. Howard Nemerov. AnMo; MPo

Graceful and sure with youth, the skaters glide. The Skaters. John Williams. CoPAm

Gracie. Faye Kicknosway. NMM

Gracious Goodness. Marge Piercy. BoAnP

Gradually growing fur. Traveling North. John Woods. POL

Graduate Assistant Tells about His Visit, The. Leon Stokesbury. NVAP

Grafted Tongue, A. John Montague. BIrV

Grain of space holds suns which move like flecks, A. God Walks among the Dust. Henry Tim Chambers. AATT

Grains of snow ride down here as bits. Letter from a Black Soldier. Bill Anderson. VGW

Grammer's Shoes. William Barnes. VPC

Grand Guignols of Love, The. Michael Benedikt. AmPA

Grand Inquisitor Continues, The. John William Corrington. CoPAm

Grand Slammer. R. R. Knudson. SPo

Grandad, I didn't burn it, I. Legacy. Gena Ford. IHMS

Grandeurs of the crazy man alone, The. Theodore Roethke. POL

Grandfather. Michael S. Harper. FiCP

Grandfather. Lance Henson. CDW

Grandfather. John Leax. AATT

Grandfather. Derek Mahon. LP

Grandfather in the Old Men's Home. W. S. Merwin. ConAP; TCP

Grandfather Poem, A. William J. Harris. PoBA

Grandfather, sleepless in a room upstairs. John Berryman. *Fr.* The Black Book. VGW

Grandfather Watts's Private Fourth. H. C. Bunner. PoTa

Grandfathers, The. Donald Justice. NCSH; PPoD

Grandfather's Clock, *with music.* Henry Clay Work. BLSo; PSoN

Grandma and the children left at night. My Polish Grandma. Edward Field. Prf

Grandma sleeps with. Medicine. Alice Walker. NMM

Grandmither, Think Not I Forget. Willa Cather. WPE

Grandmother Came Down to Visit Us, The. Joseph Bruchac. CDW

Grandmother Sleeps. Liz Sohappy Bahe. CDW

Grandmother Watching at Her Window. W. S. Merwin. VGW

Grandmothers, The. Mary Oliver. WPE

Grandmother's mother: her age, I guess. Dorothy Q. Oliver Wendell Holmes. NOBA; PiAm

Grandpa. James Rankin. MIS

Grandparents. Robert Lowell. PiAm

Grandpa's .45. W. M. Ransom. CDW

Granite and Steel. Marianne Moore. PiAm

Granny and I with dear Dadu. A Very Odd Fish. D'Arcy Wentworth Thompson. OxBChV

Grant, I thee pray, such heat into mine heart. A Prayer. Sir Thomas More. BoReV

Grape is my mulatto mother. Wino. Ted Hughes. NoAM

"Graphemics," *sels.* Jack Spicer. VGW
  "Like a scared rabbit running over and," 1.
  "Love is not mocked whatever use," 10.
  "Walden Pond/ All those noxious gases rising from it," 7.

Grasmere Sonnets. David Wright. NoAM

Grass. Carl Sandburg. NoAM; NOBA; PiAm

Grass, The. Helen Wolfert. RiTi

Grass bends, The: blades crack from a wind. Camping Out on Rainy Mountain. Jim Barnes. CDW

Grass caught in willow tells the flood's height. Briggflatts, IV. Basil Bunting. NoAM

Grass clutches at the dark dirt with finger holds. Grassroots. Carl Sandburg. RFM

Grass cropped to grass-roots, and a few ewes go down. Lambing. David Campbell. *Fr.* Works and Days. MAuV

Grass cuts our feet as we wend our way, The. The Young Prince and the Young Princess. John Ashbery. ConAP

Grass, Grass. George Bowering. NeAC

Grass Is a Reasonable Colour, The. John Newlove. NeAC

Grass is half-covered with snow, The. Snowfall in the Afternoon. Robert Bly. CAPP; NOBA

Grass is very green, my friend, The. A Unison. William Carlos Williams. Epi; NOBA

Grass people bow, The. To Turn Back. John Haines. ConAP

Grasse: The Olive Trees. Richard Wilbur. NoAM; NOBA

Grasses, ancient enemies, The. Syria. Keith Douglas. PSN

Grasshopper, The. Richard Lovelace. NOBE; PPP; SCP-2

Grasshopper. Roger McDonald. CAAP

Grasshopper, A. Richard Wilbur. CoPAm

Grasshopper and the Cricket, The. Keats. *See* On the Grasshopper and Cricket.

Grasshopper clings crazily, A. Grasshopper Roger McDonald. CAAP

Grassroots. Carl Sandburg. RFM

Gratitude. Louise Glück. CAAP

Gratitude. Christopher Smart. *Fr.* Hymns for the Amusement of Children. LAuP

Gratitude to Mother Earth, sailing through night and day. Prayer for the Great Family. Gary Snyder. OFD

Grave, A. Marianne Moore. HeIP; InPK; NoAM; NOBA; PPoe; WPE

Grave, The. Yvor Winters. NoAM

Grave charge in Mayfair bathroom case. Headline History. William Plomer. FaBoCo

Grave of Love, The. Heine, *tr. fr. German by* Alexander Gray. SLP

Grave wise man that had a great rich lady, A. Of an Heroical Answer of a Great Roman Lady to Her Husband. Sir John Harington. BoLoP

Gravelly Run. A. R. Ammons. Prf

Graves grow deeper, The. The Dead. Mark Strand. HeIP

Graves of a Household, The. Felicia Dorothea Hemans. WPE

Graveyard, The. Jane Cooper. CoPAm

Grave-Yard, The. Jones Very. NOBA

Graveyard Road, The. Tom McKeown. HeS

Gravities. Seamus Heaney. NoAM

Gray. *See also* Grey.

Gray and dusty daylight flows, A. Christopher Brennan. *Fr.* The Quest of Silence. MAuV

Gray-eyed huntress in whose hair. Hymn to Artemis, the Destroyer. Marya Zaturenska. Moon

Gray gossamer day, A. Afternoon. David Sten Herrstrom. AATT

Gray his head goes his feet green. Sonnet. Ted Berrigan. CAAP

Gray maidservant lets me in, A. Matinees. James Merrill. NOBA; Prf

Gray Mare, The. *Unknown.* AmFP

Gray sea and the long black land, The. *See* Grey sea ...

Gray Silk Twisting. Patrick Lane. NeAC

Gray smoke rose from the morning ground. Actual Vision of Morning's Extrusion. Alan Dugan. PPP

Gray steel, cloud-shadow-stained. Watch the Lights Fade. Robinson Jeffers. NoAM; NOBA

Gray Weather. Robinson Jeffers. NoAM

Gray Whale. For a Coming Extinction. W. S. Merwin. TSWA

Gray's Anatomy. David Malouf. CAAP

Greasy oysters on friday nights. Cycles, Cycles. Suzanne Berger Rioff. NMM

Greasy Spoon Blues. Len Gasparini. NeAC

Great A, little a. Mother Goose. MG

Great Alexander sailing was from his true course turned. The Speaking Tree. Muriel Rukeyser. VGW

Great-Aunts. Seán O'Críadáin. PFIr

Great Bacchus: from the Greek. Matthew Prior. FaBoCo

Great Bear, The. John Hollander. CoPAm; NoAM

Great Blue Heron, The. Carolyn Kizer. WPE

Great Brown Owl, The. Jane Euphemia Browne. OxBChV

Great Canzon, The. Kenneth Rexroth. NoAM

Great Day, The. W. B. Yeats. BIrV; WIF

Great dream stinks like a whale gone aground, The. Why the Soup Tastes like the Daily News. Marge Piercy. MAT

Great-enough both accepts and subdues. Phenomena. Robinson Jeffers. NoAM; NOBA

Great eucalypti, black amid the flame. The Grave. Yvor Winters. NoAM

Great Explosion, The. Robinson Jeffers. IPWM

Great Figure, The. William Carlos Williams. NoAM

Great fleas have little fleas. The Fleas. Augustus De Morgan. FaBoCo

Great freight truck, A. Gary Snyder. *Fr.* Hitch Haiku. InPK

Great Garret, or 100 Wheels, The. James McMichael. AmPA

Great God, attend while Zion sings. Isaac Watts. AmFP

Great God! I Ask Thee for No Meaner Pelf. Henry David Thoreau. NOBA; PiAm
(My Prayer.) AmVN

Great God, let all my tuneful pow'rs. Ottiwell Heginbothom. AmFP

Great God Paused among Men. Daniel Berrigan. MAT

Great, good and just, could I but rate. Epitaph on Charles I. James Graham, Marquess of Montrose. NOBE

Great Hunger, The, *sels.* Patrick Kavanagh.
"Clay is the word and clay is the flesh." NoAM; OxBTC
"He gave himself another year." BIrV

Great iron throats offering. The Bells. Lucille F. Travis. AATT

Great is the folly of a feeble brain. Joseph Hall. *Fr.* Virgidemiarum, Bk. I, Satire VII. TVS

Great men have been among us; hands that penned. Wordsworth. MBPR

Great Merchant, Dives Pragmaticus, Cries His Wares, The, *sel.* Thomas Newbery.
"What lack you, sir? What seek you? What will you buy?" OxBChV

Great Moth, The. Robert Gittings. OxBTC

Great Nature clothes the soul, which is but thin. The Soul's Garment. Margaret Cavendish, Duchess of Newcastle. WPE

Great Nebula in Andromeda, The. Hugh Seidman. AmPA

Great Northern. Dave Etter. CoPAm

Great Panjandrum, The. Samuel Foote. FaBoCo
(Epilogue: "So she went into the garden.") ECBV

Great queen of shadows, you are pleased to speak. Beaumont *and* Fletcher. *Fr.* The Maid's Tragedy. SCP-2

Great Santa Barbara Oil Disaster OR, The. Conyus. AmPA

Great Silkie of Sule Skerry, The. *Unknown.* GBP; MAT; PeBB

Great Society, The. Robert Bly. NoAm

Great Society, Mark X, The. Howard Nemerov. AnMo

Great spirits now on earth are sojourning. Addressed to Haydon. Keats. MBPR

Great Things. Thomas Hardy. NOBE

Great *Titanic. Unknown.* AmFP

Great Wave, The: Hokusai. Donald Finkel. WIF

Great Way of the Man, The. Norman H. Russell. VW

Great, wide, beautiful, wonderful World. The World. William Brighty Rands. OxBChV

Great wrought-iron gates have been, The.   Twilight at the Zoo. Alex Rodger.   NCSH

Greate Macedon that out of Persy chased, The.   Earl of Surrey. AAS

Greater cities are, The.   Poem.   Victor Hernández Cruz.   SA

Greater Love.   Wilfred Owen.   NoAm; OBP; PSN

Greatly shining,/ The autumn moon floats in the thin sky.   Wind and Silver.   Amy Lowell.   IPWM; Moon; RiTi; SoSe

Greed, sel.   Diane Wakoski. Turtle, The.   NoAm

Greedy Jane.   Unknown.   ECBV; OxBChV

Greedy Richard.   Jane Taylor.   OxBChV

Greedy the People, The.   E. E. Cummings.   SoSe

Greek Crazeology.   Carolyn M. Rodgers.   SA

Greek Room, The.   James W. Thompson.   BPo

Greek ship, A/ Sails on the sea.   The Couple.   Sandra Hochman. CTBA

Green.   D. H. Lawrence.   GBL

Green Afternoon, The.   Henry Rago.   VGW

Green and silent spot, amid the hills, A.   Fears in Solitude. Samuel Taylor Coleridge.   MBPR

Green arsenic smeared on an egg-white cloth.   L'Art, 1910.   Ezra Pound.   HeIP

Green as I would have you green.   The Ballad of the Sleepwalker. Federico García Lorca, tr. by Langston Hughes.   Epi

Green at Colmar.   Daisy Aldan.   AATT

Green Bed, The.   Unknown.   AmFP

Green Beginning, The.   Warren Slesinger.   HeS

Green Briar Shore, The.   Unknown.   AmFP

Green Broom.   Unknown.   PoTa

Green Bushes, The.   Unknown.   AIW

Green catalpa tree has turned, The.   April Inventory.   W. D. Snodgrass.   CAPP; NoAM; NowV; PPoe; SFF; WIF

Green Cornfield, A.   Christina Rossetti.   RAE

Green elm with the one great bough of gold, The.   October. Edward Thomas.   NoAM

Green enravishment of human life.   Sister Juana Inés de la Cruz, tr. fr. Spanish by Samuel Beckett.   Epi

Green Fiddler, The.   Rachel Field.   PoTa

Green Gnome, The.   Robert Buchanan.   PoTa

Green Grass.   Unknown.   GBP

Green Grass Growing All Around, The.   Unknown.   ECBV

Green, green, I want you green.   Somnambulistic Ballad. Federico García Lorca, tr. by.   Roy and Mary Campbell. TCP

Green, Green Is El Aghir.   Norman Cameron.   OxBTC

Green Grows the Rashes [or Rushes], O.   Burns.   LAuP; PBMP; PPoe; PPP; SS

Green Grows the Rashes.   Unknown.   GBP

Green lady, green lady, come doon for thy tea.   Unknown.   GBP

Green lamp flares on the table, The.   This Life.   Rita Dove. AmPA

Green lawn/ a picket fence.   Alice Walker.   Fr. Once.   PoBA

Green leaf that will outlast the winter, The.   Louis Zukofsky. VGW

Green Light.   Kenneth Fearing.   VGW

Green Mountain Boy.   Florida Watts Smyth.   ECBV

Green points on the shrub.   An Elegy for D. H. Lawrence. William Carlos Williams.   Epi; NoAM

Green Red Brown and White.   May Swenson.   VGW

Green River.   Bryant.   NOBA

Green Roads, The.   Edward Thomas.   NoAM

Green Room, The.   Paul Mills.   MIS

Green rushes with red shoots.   Plucking the Rushes.   Unknown, tr. by Arthur Waley.   BoLoP; BuTh; OLR

Green rustlings, more-than-regal charities.   Royal Palm.   Hart Crane.   NoAM

Green Shepherd, The.   Louis Simpson.   NoAM; PAIC

Green shutters, shut your shutters! Windyridge.   John Betjeman. Fr. Beside the Seaside.   OxBTC

Green Sleeves ("Green sleeves and tartan ties").   Unknown.   GBP

Green Snake, when I hung you round my neck.   To the Snake. Denise Levertov.   NMM; Psy; SFF

Green Tree, The.   James Reiss.   AmPA

Green Willow, Green Willow.   Unknown.   AmFP

Green Willow Tree, The.   Unknown.   AIW

Greenback Dollar, The.   Unknown.   AmFP

Greene's Mourning Garment, sel.   Robert Greene. Hexametra Alexis in Laudem Rosamundi.   GBL

Greenland, 850 A.D.   Lyn Lifshin.   MMD

Greenland Whale, The.   Unknown.   GBP; PeBB

Greenland Whale Fishery, The.   Unknown.   AmFP

Greens.   Greg Kuzma.   HeS

Greens.   David Ray.   VGW

Greensleeves, with music.   Unknown.   BLSo; RDB (Lady Greensleeves.)   GBL

Grenadier, The.   Unknown.   GBP

Grenadine.   Susan Griffin.   MMD

Grendel.   Unknown, tr. fr. Anglo-Saxon by Burton Raffel.   Fr. Beowulf.   OBP

Gresford Disaster, The.   Unknown.   AIW; GBP; PeBB

Gretel in Darkness.   Louise Glück.   AmPA; NVAP

Grey.   See also Gray.

Grey as a mouse.   Oliphaunt.   J. R. R. Tolkien.   LCL

Grey brick upon brick.   Dublin.   Louis MacNeice.   OxBTC; PFIr

Grey Goose and Gander.   Unknown.   GBP

Grey haunted eyes, absent-mindedly glaring.   The Face in the Mirror.   Robert Graves.   LP

Grey horse, Death, in profile bears the young Titus, The.   The Polish Rider.   Derek Walcott.   OBP

Grey [or Gray] sea and the long black land, The.   Meeting at Night.   Robert Browning.   BoLoP; GBL; HeIP; InPS; LoAs; NOBE; OLR; PAIC; SoSe; SS

Grey sheep came, The. I ran.   The Exorcism.   Theodore Roethke. NoAM

Grey Woman.   Gladys Cardiff.   CDW

Greyhounds.   Robert Gray.   CAAP

Grief.   Elizabeth Barrett Browning.   HeIP; InPK; SBG; WPE

Grief.   Sandra Hochman.   NowV

Grief, have I denied thee?   A Lamentation.   Denise Levertov. PiAm

Grief of a Girl's Heart, The.   Unknown.   See Donal Oge: Grief of a Girl's Heart.

Grief Streams Down My Chest.   Lance Jeffers.   PoBA

Griesly Wife, The.   John Manifold.   SoSe

Griffin.   Richard Mathews.   AATT

Grim was fishere swithe good   .Havelok at Grimsby and Lincoln. Unknown.   Fr. Havelok.   OxBM

Grinder, who serenely grindest.   Lines on Hearing the Organ. Charles Stuart Calverley.   FaBoCo

Grinders, The; or, The Saddle on the Right Horse.   Unknown. GBP

Grinning, the foreman asked them for a vote.   In the Jury Room. Hodding Carter.   MAT

Grizzly Bear.   Mary Austin.   ECBV; RAE

Grizzly Bear is huge and wild, The.   Infant Innocence.   A. E. Housman.   FaBoCo

Grocery Shopping.   John Leax.   AATT

Grongar Hill.   John Dyer.   LAuP; PAIC

Groom's Lament, The.   Robert Peterson.   NeAC

Groping along the tunnel, step by step. The Rear-Guard. Siegfried Sassoon. NoAM

Grotesque, jumping out. Sky Diver. Adrien Stoutenberg. SPo; TSWA

Grotesque, the line of trees, pronged. Outside. Phyllis Beauvais. IHMS

Grotto, The. Ray Fraser. NeAC

Ground is white with snow, The. Resolution. Ted Berrigan. OFD

Ground-Mist, The. Denise Levertov. PiAm

Ground twitches and the noble head, The. The Second Coming. Dannie Abse. NoAM

Groundhog, The. Richard Eberhart. CoPAm; NoAM; PPoe; VoPo

Group, The. Victor Hernández Cruz. SA

Groupie. Al Young. NVAP

Grow old along with me! *Rabbi Ben Ezra.* Robert Browning. PBMP

Growing Old. Matthew Arnold. VoPo

Growing Old. Byron. *Fr.* Don Juan, I. NOBE

Growing Together. Joyce Carol Oates. IHMS

Growing weather; enough rain. The Satisfactions of the Mad Farmer. Wendell Berry. PiAm

Grown too big for his skin. Fable for When There's No Way Out. May Swenson. MiP

Grown-up. Edna St. Vincent Millay. NoAM; TH

Grown-ups are all safe, The. Hard Cheese. Justin St. John. LP

Growth of Love, The, *sels.* Robert Bridges. NoAM
"Man that sees by chance his picture, made, A," XXXIX.
"They that in play can do the thing they would," I.

Gr-r-r—there go, my heart's abhorrence! Soliloquy of the Spanish Cloister. Robert Browning. AnMo; Epi; FaBoCo; InPK; OBP; PAIC

Grünewald knew that green. Green at Colmar. Daisy Aldan. AATT

Grunion. Myra Cohn Livingston. RFM

Grunion. Wendy Rose. CDW

Guarded Wound, The. Adelaide Crapsey. WPE

Guerrilla Handbook, A. LeRoi Jones. PoBA

Guest, The. Anna Akhmatova, *tr. fr. Russian by* Richard McKane. LoAs

Guest, The. *Unknown.* ECBV

Guests are gathered, The. Fourth of July Fireworks. Liz Lochhead. MIS

Guests in their summer colors have fled, The. The Last Picnic. Stanley Kunitz. NoAM

Guevara with Minutes to Go. John William Corrington. CoPAm

Guid day now, bonnie robin. Robin Redbreast's Testament. *Unknown.* GBP

Guide Me, O Thou Great Jehovah, *with music.* William Williams, *tr. fr. Welsh by* Peter Williams *and* John Williams. BLSH

Guide to Familiar American Incest, A, *sel.* Dennis Saleh. Inventing a Family. NeAC

Guide to the Symphony. Weldon Kees. VGW

Guido da Montefeltro. Dante, *tr. fr. Italian by* Longfellow. *Fr.* Divina Commedia: Inferno, XXVII. Epi

Guilt. Wordsworth. *Fr.* The Prelude, I. BoReV

Guinea-pig Song, A. *Unknown.* OxBChV
(Precise Guinea-Pig, The.) ECBV

Guitar. Federico García Lorca, *tr. fr. Spanish by* Keith Waldrop. InPK

Guitarist Tunes Up, The. Frances Cornford. SoSe

Gull, ballast of its wings. Stabilities. Anne Stevenson. NCSH

Gulling Sonnets, *sels.* Sir John Davies.
"Lover, under burden of his mistress' love, The,"I. Epi; PAIC
"Mine eye, mine ear, my will, my wit, my heart,"V. Epi

"My case is this, I love Zepheria bright,"VIII. Epi
"Sacred muse that first made love divine,The,"VI. PAIC

Gullion, The. Duncan Glen. MIS

Gulliver. Sylvia Plath. NOBA

Gulls. Barbara Howes. BoAnP

Gulls. E. A. Muir. NCSH

Gulls. Leonora Speyer. *Fr.* Sand-pipings. TH

Gully, The. Douglas Stewart. MAuV

Gun full swing the swimmer catapults and cracks, The. 400-Meter Freestyle. Maxine W. Kumin. SPo

Gun Teams. Gilbert Frankau. OxBTC

Gunfighter. Phillip Hey. NVAP

Gunga Din. Kipling. BTTM

Gunner. Randall Jarrell. OFD

Gunpowder Plot. Vernon Scannell. MPo

Guns know what is what, but underneath, The. Memories of a Lost War. Louis Simpson. VGW

Guns spell money's ultimate reason, The. Ultima Ratio Regum. Stephen Spender. LP; MPo; SFF

Gunslinger, *sels.* Edward Dorn.
"I met in Mesilla." NoAM
Idle Visitation, An. NOBA

Gup, Scot. John Skelton. OBP

Gus is the Cat at the Theatre Door. Gus: The Theatre Cat. T. S. Eliot. OxBTC

Gus the Greek is a short-order cook. Greasy Spoon Blues. Len Gasparini. NeAC

Gus: the Theatre Cat. T. S. Eliot. OxBTC

Gut eats all day and lechers all the night. On Gut. Ben Jonson. SCP-1

Guy. Emerson. NOBA

Guyon's Temptation. Spenser. *Fr.* The Faerie Queene, II, 12. OBP

G'way an' quit dat noise, Miss Lucy. When Malindy Sings. Paul Laurence Dunbar. PoBA

Gwendolyn Brooks. Don L. Lee. NoAM

Gyges Ring they bear about them still, A. Lovers How They Come and Part. Robert Herrick. GBL

Gypsies. *See also* Gipsies.

Gypsies. Alden Nowlan. NeAC

Gypsies they came to my lord Cassilis' yett, The. The Gypsy Laddie. *Unknown.* PeBB

Gypsy. Josephine Miles. NoAM

Gypsy, The. Edward Thomas. HeIP; NoAM

Gypsy Davy, The. *Unknown.* AmFP

Gypsy Eyes. Jimi Hendrix. GrRo

Gypsy Laddie, The. *Unknown.* PeBB

Gypsy Love Song, *with music.* Harry B. Smith. FSN

Gypsy Motorcycle Club of South Minneapolis, The. Keith Gunderson. HeS

Gypsy woman told my mother, The. Hoochie Coochie. *Unknown.* BluL

Gyres, The. W. B. Yeats. NoAM

Gyre's Galax. Norman Henry Pritchard, II. PoBA

Gyres, The! the gyres! Old Rocky Face, look forth. The Gyres. W. B. Yeats. NoAM

# H

H. M. S. *Hero.* Michael Roberts. OxBTC

H——, thou return'st from Thames, whose Naiads long. An Ode on the Popular Superstitions of the Highlands of Scotland. William Collins. LAuP

Ha ha! Ha ha! This world doth pass. Fara Diddle Dyno. *Unknown.* FaBoCo; SCP-2

Ha! Original Sin. Ogden Nash. FaBoCo

Ha' we lost the goodliest fere o' all. Ballad of the Goodly Fere. Ezra Pound. Epi; NoAM; OFD; PAIC

Ha! whare ye gaun, ye crowlin' ferlie? To a Louse. Burns. PBMP

Habit of Perfection, The. Gerard Manley Hopkins. NoAM; SoSe

Habits of the Hippopotamus. Arthur Guiterman. BoAnP

Habla Usted Español? James Reiss. AmPA

Had a whole dream once. Some Words. Judith Wright. CAAP

"Had he and I but met." The Man He Killed. Thomas Hardy. HeIP; InPS; IPWM; PBMP; SFF; SoSe; VoPo; WIF

Had I a Golden Pound. Francis Ledwidge, *after the Irish.* PFIr

Had I a man's fair form, then might my sighs. To——. Keats. MBPR

Had I but gone some forty days or more. William R. Mitchell. AATT

Had I but plenty of money, money enough and to spare. Up at a Villa—Down in the City. Robert Browning. NOBE; PPP

Had I lived till now. Poem for the Year Twenty Twenty. Al Lee. AmPA

Had I the Choice. Walt Whitman. SoSe

Had I the heavens' embroidered cloths. Aedh [*or* He] Wishes for the Cloths of Heaven. W. B. Yeats. NoAM; OLR

Had me a cat, the cat pleased me. Fiddle-I-Fee. *Unknown.* AmFP

Had she come all the way for this. The Haystack in the Floods. William Morris. OBP; PAIC

Had we but world enough, and time. To His Coy Mistress. Andrew Marvell. AnMo; BoLoP; Epi; GBL; HeIP: InPK; InPS; IPWM; LoAs; MAT; MetP; NOBE; OBP; PAIC; PBMP; PPoD; PPoe; PPP; SCP-1; SoSe; VoPo; WIF

Had you come to me. Regrets. Vassar Miller. RiTi

Had you died when we were together. The Fire. Louise Glück. CAAP

Hadst thou liv'd in days of old. To —— . Keats. MBPR

Hag of Beare, The. *Unknown.* See Lament of the Old Woman of Beare, The.

Hag-ridden. Robert Graves. BIrV

Haiku: "All the hot night." Masaoka Shiki, *tr. fr. Japanese by* Kenneth Rexroth. PAIC

Haiku: "Although he never stirs from home." José Juan Tablada, *tr. fr. Spanish by* Samuel Beckett. PBMP

Haiku: "Ants on inert cricket crawling." José Juan Tablada, *tr. fr. Spanish by* Samuel Beckett. PBMP

Haiku: "Bitter morning, A," J. W. Hackett. BoAnP

Haiku: "Dragon-fly strives patiently, The." José Juan Tablada, *tr. fr. Spanish by* Samuel Beckett. PBMP

Haiku: "Eastern guard tower." Etheridge Knight. BPo; NeAC; NoAM

Haiku: "Falling flower, The." Arakida Moritake, *tr. fr. Japanese by* Babette Deutsch. SoSe
(Haiku: "Fallen flowers rise.") SoSe

Haiku: "Halo of the moon, The." Buson, *tr. fr. Japanese.* Moon

Haiku: "Lightning gleam, A." Basho, *tr. fr. Japanese by* Harold G. Henderson. SoSe
(Haiku: "Lightning flashes, The!") SoSe

Haiku: "Lumps of mud, the toads." José Juan Tablada, *tr. fr. Spanish by* Samuel Beckett. PBMP

Haiku: "New moon in the sky." Basho, *tr. fr. Japanese by* Nobuyuki Yuasa. PAIC

Haiku: "Red cold." José Juan Tablada, *tr. fr. Spanish by* Samuel Beckett. PBMP

Haiku: "This broken bottle." Elisavietta Ritchie. AATT

Haiku: "Tiny monkey looks at me, The." José Juan Tablada, *tr. fr. Spanish by* Samuel Beckett. PBMP

Haiku Ambulance. Richard Brautigan. InPK

Haiku, you ku, he. The Traditional Grammarian as Poet. Ted Hipple. POL

Hail and beware the dead who will talk life until you are blue. A Newly Discovered "Homeric" Hymn. Charles Olson. CoPAm; NoAM

Hail be thou, Mary, maiden bright. The Five Joys. *Unknown.* OxBM

Hail Bishop Valentine, whose day this is! An Epithalamion; or, Marriage-Song on the Lady Elizabeth and Count Palatine Being Married on St. Valentine's Day. John Donne. OFD; SCP-1

Hail! blessed Virgin, full of heavenly grace. On the Infancy of Our Saviour. Francis Quarles. SCP-2

Hail, Columbia. Joseph Hopkinson. BLSo, *with music;* BTTM

Hail, Dionysos. Dudley Randall. BPo

Hail, happy day, when, smiling like the morn. To the Right Honourable William, Earl of Dartmouth. Phillis Wheatley. SBG

Hail, holy light, offspring of Heaven first-born. Holy Light [*or* The Poet's Blindness]. Milton. *Fr.* Paradise Lost, III. NOBE; OBP

Hail, lofty,/ necking quizzically. Conversation with a Giraffe at Dusk in a Zoo. Douglas Livingstone. LP; MPo

Hail Mary!/ Ich am sary. *Unknown.* OxBM

Hail Saint Michael with thy longe spere! An Irish Satire. *Unknown.* OxBM

Hail, sister springs! Saint Mary Magdalene; or, The Weeper. Richard Crashaw. SCP-1

Hail to thee. The Carnation. Paul Hannigan. POL

Hail to thee, blithe spirit. To a Skylark [*or* Ode to a Skylark]. Shelley. BoAnP; InPS; MBPR; NOBE; PBMP; VoPo

Hail wedded love, mysterious law, true source. Milton. *Fr.* Paradise Lost, IV. PAIC

Hain't no use to weep, hain't no use to moan. Down in Lonesome Garden. *Unknown.* BPo

Hair. Gregory Corso. SFF

Hair/ like heather, father would boast. Song. Marie Harris. MMD

Hair and nose and eyes like mine. Living with a Voodoo Doll. John Stone. CoPAm

Hair is heaven's water flowing eerily over us. Hair Poem. William Knott. PPoD

Hair on the Chest. Coleman Barks. *Fr.* Body Poems. NVAP

Hair Poem. William Knott. PPoD

Hairs in My Nose, The. Aram Boyajian. NeAC

Hairy Dog, The. Herbert Asquith. ECBV

Halcyon Days. Jim Barnes. CDW

Halem dud. For "Mr. Dudley," a Black Spy. James A. Emanuel. BPo

Half a league, half a league. The Charge of the Light Brigade. Tennyson. BTTM; PBMP; PPoD; SFF

Half a yard, half a yard. Charge of the Grid Brigade. George S. Applegarth. SPo

Half asleep on top this bleak landscape. Hunter. Raymond Carver. NVAP

Half Black, Half Blacker. Sterling Plumpp. PoBA

Half close your eyelids, loosen your hair. Aedh [*or* He] Thinks of Those Who Have Spoken Evil of His Beloved. W. B. Yeats. NoAM; PFIr

"Half-cracked" to Higginson, living. "I Am in Danger— Sir." Adrienne Rich. NOBA; PiAm; Psy

Half-door, hall door. Purgatory. W. B. Yeats. PAIC

Half-hidden in a graveyard. The Stranger. Walter de la Mare. OxBTC

Half hour for coffee, and at night, A.  To What Strangers, What Welcome, X.  J. V. Cunningham.  PiAm

Half in the dim light from the hall.  To——.  William Stanley Braithwaite.  PoBA

Half loving-kindliness and half disdain.  To My Cat.  Rosamund Marriott Watson.  PCat

Half Moon.  Federico García Lorca, tr. fr. Spanish by W. S. Merwin.  RFM

Half Moon Shows a Face of Plaintive Sweetness, The.  Christina Rossetti.  Moon

Half of his/ body hung in.  Spirits.  Victor Hernandez Cruz.  PoBA

Half of my life is gone, and I have let.  Mezzo Cammin.  Longfellow.  AmVN

Half spirit, the older.  The Jest.  Austin Clarke.  BIrV

Half the year has hot nights, like this.  Elegies for the Hot Season.  Sandra McPherson.  AmPA; CAAP; RiTi

Halfway Down.  A. A. Milne.  LCL

Halidon Hill.  Laurence Minot.  OxBM

Hallelujah: A Sestina.  Robert Francis.  PPoD

Hallelujah, Bum Again.  Unknown.  GBP

Hallowed be the Sabbaoth.  Epitaph in St. Olave's, Southwark, on Mr. Munday.  Unknown.  FaBoCo

Hallowed Pleaces.  William Barnes.  VPC

Halloween.  Myra Cohn Livingston.  OFD

Hallowe'en 1971.  Michael Dennis Browne.  AmPA

Halo of the moon, The.  Haiku.  Buson.  Moon

Halt! Shoulder arms! Recover! As you were!  Sonnet to Britain.  William Edmonstoune Aytoun.  FaBoCo

Ham Hound Crave.  Unknown.  BluL

Hamatreya.  Emerson.  AmVN; HeIP; IPWM; MAT; NOBA; PiAm

Hambone Blues.  Unknown.  BluL

Hamelin Town's in Brunswick.  The Pied Piper of Hamelin.  Robert Browning.  OxBChV

Hamilton Greene.  Edgar Lee Masters.  Fr. Spoon River Anthology.  NoAM

"Hamlet."  Emmett Jarrett.  NeAC

Hamlet, sels.  Shakespeare.
    "How should I your true love know," fr. IV, v.  AIW (Ophelia's Song.)  GBL
    "Some say that ever 'gainst that season comes," fr. I, i.  OFD
    Tomorrow Is Saint Valentine's Day, fr. IV, v.  LCL; OFD; WIF

Hamlet's Soliloquy Imitated.  Richard Jago.  FaBoCo

Hammer, Ring.  Unknown.  AmFP

Hammers, The.  Ralph Hodgson.  NOBE; OxBTC

Hammers of iron glow down Faraday.  Vincent Buckley.  Fr. Golden Builders.  CAAP

Ha'nacker Mill.  Hilaire Belloc.  OxBTC

Hand.  Morton Marcus.  NVAP

Hand a shade of moonlight on the pillow, The.  Non Ti Fidar.  Louis Zukofsky.  VGW

Hand and Foot, The.  Jones Very.  AmVN; PiAm

Hand by Hand We Shall Us Take.  Unknown.  OxBM

Hand Me Down My Walking Cane, with music.  Unknown, ad. by James Morehead.  BLSH

Hand, The: Spread against the cloudless night.  Body Mechanics.  Albert Goldbarth.  NVAP

Hand That Signed the Paper Felled a City, The.  Dylan Thomas.  NoAM; NOBE; PBMP

Handball Players.  Paul Goodman.  SPo

Handcart Song, The.  Unknown.  AmFP

Handlyng Synne, sel.  Robert Mannyng.
    Dancers of Colbek, The.  OxBM

Hands.  Donald Finkel.  MAT

Hands.  Siv Cedering Fox.  NVAP

Hands, do what you're bid.  The Balloon of the Mind.  W. B. Yeats.  POL

Hands explore tentatively, The.  The Feel of Hands.  Thom Gunn.  PSN

Hands folded like napkins in my lap.  Robert Peterson.  NeAC

Hands must touch and handle many things, The.  The New Man.  Jones Very.  NOBA

Hands were yours, the arms were yours, The.  Elegy for My Father.  Mark Strand.  CAAP; NVAP

Handsome young rodent named Gratian, A.  Ogden Nash.  SFF

Handwriting on the Wall.  Unknown.  AmFP

Hang it all, Robert Browning.  Ezra Pound.  Cantos, II.  NoAM; NOBA; PiAm

Hang It on the Wall.  Unknown.  BluL

Hang Me, O Hang Me, and I'll Be Dead and Gone.  Unknown.  AmFP

Hangar Nine.  Ann Darr.  WBN

Hanged man, please grow wild and luminous.  To Her Dead Mate, Montana, 1966.  Elizabeth Libbey.  AmPA

Hanging from fresh trees.  Lemons, Lemons.  Al Young.  HeIP; PiAm

Hanging from the beam.  The Portent.  Herman Melville.  AmVN; NOBA

Hanging Johnny.  Unknown.  GBP

Hanging of Sam Archer, The.  Unknown.  AmFP

Hangman.  Ai.  AmPA

Hangman at Home, The.  Carl Sandburg.  AKE

"Hangman, hangman, slack on the line."  The Maid Freed from the Gallows.  Unknown.  AmFP

Hangman's Love Song, The.  Stanley Moss.  VGW

Hans Breitmann's Barty.  Charles Godfrey Leland.  FaBoCo

Hap.  Thomas Hardy.  NoAM; PBMP; PPP

Happened like this: it was hot as hell.  The Death of the Craneman.  Alfred Hayes.  NCSH

Happened when he was yawning.  The Man Who Swallowed a Bird.  David Young.  CAAP

Happiness.  Carl Sandburg.  TH; VoPo

Happiness Is a Charlie Chaplin Movie.  Luís Omar Salinas.  SA

Happiness of a Flea, The.  Tasso, tr. fr. Italian by William Drummond of Hawthornden.  LoAs

Happiness of hedgehogs, The.  The Happy Hedgehog.  E. V. Rieu.  ECBV

Happy are men who yet before thay are killed.  Insensibility.  Wilfred Owen.  InPS; OxBTC

Happy Day (or Independence Day).  James Cunningham.  JB

Happy Hedgehog, The.  E. V. Rieu.  ECBV

Happy is England! I could be content.  Keats.  MBPR

Happy is he that from all business clear.  The Praises of a Country Life.  Ben Jonson.  SCP-1

Happy Life, The.  Martial, tr. fr. Latin.  NOBE, tr. by Earl of Surrey; PAIC, tr. by Sir Edward Sherburne.

Happy Marriage.  Thomas Blacklock.  SLP

Happy Nightingale, The.  Unknown.  OxBChV

Happy people die whole, they are all dissolved in a moment.  Post Mortem.  Robinson Jeffers.  PiAm

Happy the man who, void of cares and strife.  The Splendid Shilling.  John Philips.  PAIC

Happy the man whose wish and care.  Ode on Solitude [or Solitude, an Ode].  Pope.  Epi; HeIP; IPWM; PAIC; PBMP; PPoe; PRF

Happy those early days [or dayes]! when I.  The Retreat[e].  Henry Vaughan.  HeIP; InPS; MetP; NOBE; OBP; PPP; SCP-1

Happy Thought.  Robert Louis Stevenson.  OxBChV

Happy ye leaves! when as those lily hands. Amoretti, I. Spenser. AAS; LoAs; PAIC

Harbingers are come, The. See, see their mark. The Forerunners. George Herbert. BoReV; SCP-1

Harbor. Nancy Price. IHMS

Harbor, The. Carl Sandburg. NCSH

Harbor Dawn, The. Hart Crane. *Fr.* The Bridge: Powhatan's Daughter. PiAm; PSN

Hard Cheese. Justin St. John. LP

Hard Edge of Beauty. Floyd C. Stuart. FAF

Hard Journey, A. Yes. Hayden Carruth. VGW

Hard Questions. Margaret Tsuda. RFM

Hard Rain's a-Gonna Fall, A. Bob Dylan. PoRo

Hard Rock Returns to Prison from the Hospital for the Criminal Insane. Etheridge Knight. ConAP; NoAM

Hard sand breaks, The. Hermes of the Ways. Hilda Doolittle ("H.D."). WPE

Hard Time Killin' Floor Blues. *Unknown.* BluL

Hard Times ("Come listen a while"). *Unknown.* AmFP

Hard times here every, where you go. Hard Time Killin' Floor Blues. *Unknown.* BluL

Hard-working Miner, The ("The hard-working miners"). *Unknown.* AmFP

Hard-working Miner, The ("To the hard-working miner"). *Unknown.* AmFP

Harden now thy tyred hart with more then flinty rage. Thomas Campion. AAS

Hardest thing to imagine is, The. A Valentine for Marianne Moore. Elder Olson. PAIC

Hardest work I ever did, The. Bile Them Cabbage Down. *Unknown.* AmFP

Hardship of Accounting, The. Robert Frost. FaBoCo

Hardweed Path Going. A. R. Ammons. VGW

Hare, The. *Unknown.* OxBM

Hare in Winter. Marge Piercy. NeAC

Hark! ah, the nightingale. Philomela. Matthew Arnold. PPP

Hark, All You Ladies. Thomas Campion. Epi, *with music*; SCP-2
    ("Harke, al you ladies that do sleep.") AAS

Hark Back. Richard Eberhart. TH

Hark, Celia, hark! but lay thou close thine ear. The Secret. *Unknown.* SCP-2

Hark! from the tombs a doleful sound. Plenary. *Unknown.* AmFP

Hark, hark!/ Bow-wow. Song. Shakespeare. *Fr.* The Tempest, I, ii. SoSe

Hark, hark, the dogs do bark. Mother Goose. GBP; MG

Hark! hark! the lark at heaven's gate sings. Shakespeare. *Fr.* Cymbeline, II, iii. HeIP; OBP; PAIC

Hark how the mower Damon sung. Damon the Mower. Andrew Marvell. AnMo

Hark my soul! it is the Lord. Lovest Thou Me? William Cowper. BoReV

Hark, Now Everything Is Still. John Webster. *Fr.* The Duchess of Malfi, IV, ii. InPS
    (Shrouding of the Duchess of Malfi, The.) NOBE

Hark! She is calling to her cat. The Cat. Richard Church. BoAnP; PCat

Hark! the cock proclaims the morning. St. Matthias. Christopher Smart. *Fr.* Hymns and Spiritual Songs. LAuP

Hark, the Herald Angels Sing, *with music.* Charles Wesley. BLSH

Hark! through the quiet evening air, their song. Emma Lazarus. *Fr.* In Memoriam Rev. J. J. Lyons. SBG

Hark to the story of Willie the Weeper. Willy the Weeper. *Unknown.* GBP; PeBB

Hark to the welkin ringing at Shea! September Valentine. Frank Sullivan. SPo

Hark to the whimper of the sea-gull. The Sea-Gull. Ogden Nash. SoSe

Hark, ye sighing sons of sorrow. The Mouldering Vine. *Unknown.* AmFP

Harke, Al You Ladies That Do Sleep. Thomas Campion. *See* Hark, All You Ladies.

Harke how the birds doe sing, and marke then how. Sir John Davies. *Fr.* Orchestra, or A Poeme of Dauncing. OBP

Harlem ("Here on the edge of hell"). Langston Hughes. PPP

Harlem ("What happens to a dream defferred"). Langston Hughes. *Fr.* Lenox Avenue Mural. HeIP; InPS; PBMP (Dream Deferred.) InPK; PoBA; PPP; SoSe; WIF

Harlem Dancer, The. Claude McKay. BPo; IPWM; NoAM

Harlem Freeze Frame. Lebert Bethune. PoBA

Harlem Gallery, *sels.* Melvin B. Tolson.
    Birth of John Henry, The. BPo
    Sea-Turtle and the Shark, The. PoBA

Harlem Gallery: From the Inside. Larry Neal. BPo

Harlem is vicious. Return of the Native. LeRoi Jones. BPo

Harlem, Montana: Just Off the Reservation. James Welch. CDW; SA; VW

Harlem Riot, 1943. Pauli Murray. PoBA

Harlot's House, The. Oscar Wilde. InPK; PPoD

Harmonious Heedlessness of Little Boy Blue, The. Guy Wetmore Carryl. BoAnP

Harold. Stephen Tudor. HeS

Harp That Once through Tara's Halls, The. Thomas Moore. BTTM

Harper, The. *Unknown, tr. fr. Early Modern Irish by* Frank O'Connor. PFIr

Harpkin. *Unknown.* GBP; PeBB

Harriet, *sel.* Robert Lowell.
    "Unaccustomed ripeness in the wood, An." CAPP
    (Elizabeth.) LoAs

Harriet Beecher Stowe. Paul Laurence Dunbar. AmVN; BPo

Harriet! thy kiss to my soul is dear. To Harriet. Shelley. MBPR

Harry Parry. *Unknown.* GBP

Harry Semen. "Hugh MacDiarmid." NoAM; OBP

Harsh entry I had of it, Grasud, A. Missionary. D. M. Thomas. MPo

Hart [He] Loves the High Wood, The. *Unknown.* ECBV; GBP

Harum-scarum haze on the Pollock streets. Sonnet. Ted Berrigan. CAAP

Harvest falls, The. The Upper Meadows. Yvor Winters. PiAm

Harvest Home. Sir Herbert Read. RAE

Harvest Hymn. John Betjeman. PAIC

Harvest Song. Joseph Campbell. OFD

Has a gold tooth, sits long hours. Black Bourgeoisie. LeRoi Jones. BPo

Has anybody seen. Lost—A Lizard. Irene Gough. ECBV

Has not altered. Spenser's Ireland. Marianne Moore. NOBA; NoAM; PAIC

Has thrust his nose under every board. Ego. Robert Siegel. FAF

Hast thou a charm to stay the morning-star. Hymn before Sunrise, in the Vale of Chamouni. Samuel Taylor Coleridge. BoReV; MBPR

Hast thou from the caves of Golconda, a gem. On Receiving a Curious Shell, and a Copy of Verses. Keats. MBPR

Hast thou given the horse his might? Job, Bible, *O.T.* OBP

Hast thou seen reversed the prophet's miracle. Frederick Goddard Tuckerman. *Fr.* Sonnets. NOBA

Hasty Pudding, The. Joel Barlow. PiAm
    "Ye Alps audacious, thro' the Heavens that rise," I. NOBA

Hate. James Stephens. VoPo

Hate in the world's hand. A Proud Lady. Elinor Wylie. SBG

Hate-Song, A. Shelley. MBPR

Hateful is the dark blue sky. Tennyson. *Fr.* The Lotus Eaters. GrRo

Hater he came and sat by a ditch, A. A Hate-Song. Shelley. MBPR

Hath not the morning dawned with added light? Ethnogenesis. Henry Timrod. NOBA

Hatred. Gwendolyn B. Bennett. PoBA

Hatred and vengeance, my eternal portion. Lines Written During a Period of Insanity. William Cowper. PPP; Prf

Hats. R. H. W. Dillard. CoPAm

Hats off!/ Along the street there comes. The Flag Goes By. Henry Holcomb Bennett. BTTM

Hatshepsut, old girl, old friend. Sister Pharaoh. Ruth Whitman. MAT

Hatteras Calling. Conrad Aiken. NoAM; NOBA

Haul Away, My Rosy. *Unknown.* AmFP

Haunted Palace, The. Poe. *Fr.* The Fall of the House of Usher. NOBA; PiAm

Haunter, The. Thomas Hardy. LoAs; NOBE

Haunting, The. Irving Layton. NeAC

Have done, you men and women all! The Animals in the Ark. *Unknown.* GBP

Have I a wife? Bedam I have! The Brewer's Man. L. A. G. Strong. FaBoCo

Have I, this moment, led thee from the beach. Walter Savage Landor. GBL

Have learned to burn my hands with fire. Breaking Ground in Me. Tom Kryss. NeAC

Have no accidents. They loop. Bats. George Macbeth. NoAM

Have over the Water to Florida. *Unknown.* AIW

Have Thine Own Way, Lord! *with music.* Adelaide A. Pollard. BLSH

Have thou no other gods but me. The Ten Commandments. *Unknown.* OxBChV

Have ye beheld (with much delight). Upon the Nipples of Julia's Breasts. Robert Herrick. SCP-1

Have You Been at Carrick. *Unknown, tr. fr. Irish by* Edward Walsh. BIrV

Have you ever been in love, me boys. The Garden Where the Praties Grow. *Unknown.* RDB

Have You Ever Had a Witch Bloom Like a Highway. Richard Brautigan. InPK

Have you ever heard of Betty Pringle's Pig? Betty Pringle's Pig. *Unknown.* ECBV

Have you ever heard of the Sugar-Plum Tree? The Sugar-Plum Tree. Eugene Field. OxBChV

Have you ever heard the sun the sky. Shake Keane, Trumpet. John Smith. *Fr.* Jazz for Five. MPo

Have your ever held hands with a woman? A Mock Interrogation. Judy Grahn. *Fr.* A Woman Is Talking to Death. WBN

Have You Ever Seen the Rain? J. C. Fogerty. PoRo

Have you ever took a trip, baby, on the Mobile Line. France Blues. *Unknown.* BluL

Have you ever woke up with them. Bullfrog Blues. *Unknown.* BluL

Have you heard about that bully. The Bully Song. Charles E. Trevathan. BLSo

Have you heard of the wonderful one-hoss shay. The Deacon's Masterpiece; or, The Wonderful "One-Hoss Shay." Oliver Wendell Holmes. *Fr.* The Autocrat of the Breakfast-Table. NOBA; PiAm; SS

Have you listened for the things I have left out? Unsaid. A. R. Ammons. NOBA

Have you lived long, sir, in these parts? An Interview. K. W. Grandsen. OxBTC

Have you met Miss Mabel Green. If It Looks Like Jelly, Shakes Like Jelly, It Must Be Gel-a-tine. *Unknown.* BluL

Have you no eyes for me? The Intruder. Marya Zaturenska. OLR

Have you seen me at all. Before the Thaw. John Gill. NeAC

Havelok, *sel. Unknown.*

Havelok at Grimsby and Lincoln. OxBM

Having a fine new suit. Apologue. Tony Connor. BoLoP

Having attained success in business. Robert Whitmore. Frank Marshall Davis. BPo; PoBA

Having been tenant long to a rich Lord. Redemption. George Herbert. BoReV; InPS; MetP; NOBE; SCP-1; SoSe

Having bitten on life like a sharp apple. Aubade. Louis MacNeice. PAIC

Having confused me. A Voice from the Roses. Maxine W. Kumin. NMM

Having interred her infant-birth. An Ode, Upon a Question Moved, Whether Love Should Continue Forever? Lord Herbert of Cherbury. NOBE; SCP-2

Having learned to play the guitar. On Learning to Play the Guitar. Ray Fraser. NeAC

Having left hard ground behind. The Insular Celts. Ciaran Carson. BIrV

Having lost my leather purse. My Son. Ruth Stone. WPE

Having put yourself on the way. Spirits, Dancing. Arthur Gregor. VGW

Having so rich a treasury, so fine a hoard. The Daisy. Marya Zaturenska. LoAs

Having stood before the upraised wing of the male fruit fly. On Sunday, the Beginning of the Week, I Make a Religion. Albert Goldbarth. NVAP

Having this day my horse, my hand, my lance. Astrophel and Stella, XLI. Sir Philip Sidney. PPoD

Having tried to use the/ witch cord. It Is Deep. Carolyn M. Rodgers. SA

Having used every subterfuge. A Renewal. James Merrill. CoPAm

Hawk, The. Robert Bloom. AATT

Hawk, A/ (I am a hawk). Memoir. David Schaff. MIT

Hawk free of jess. Elegy for a Diver. Philip Booth. SPo

Hawk has haven that is not of man, The. The Hawk. Robert Bloom. AATT

Hawk Is a Woman. Hildegarde Flanner. WPE

Hawk Roosting. Ted Hughes. HeIP; MPo; OxBTC; PPP; PSN

Hawk's sudden weight. Balances. Floyd C. Stuart. FAF

Hawthorn, The. *Unknown.* GBP; OxBM

Hawthorn Hedge, The. Judith Wright. WPE

Hawthorn White. Charles Causley. BuTh

Hawthorne. James Russell Lowell. *Fr.* A Fable for Critics. NOBA

Hay, ay, hay, ay. Now Is Yule Come. *Unknown.* OxBM

Hay for the Horses. Gary Snyder. ConAP; CTBA; InPS

Hay, hay, by this day. A Schoolboy's Complaint. *Unknown.* OxBM

Hay Hotel, The. Oliver St. John Gogarty. BIrV

Haydon! forgive me that I cannot speak. To B. R. Haydon. Keats. MBPR

Haystack, The. Andrew Young. POL

Haystack in the Floods, The. William Morris. OBP; PAIC

Haze. Henry David Thoreau. *Fr.* A Week on the Concord and Merrimack Rivers. HeIP; PiAm

Haze, char, and the weather of All Souls'. In the Elegy Season. Richard Wilbur. InPK

He. Stanley Kunitz. VGW

He/ and she, A.   A Pair.   May Swenson.   RFM

He angled the bright shield.   Baroque Image.   May Sarton.
PPod

He appears from afar.   To Wilt Chamberlain.   Tom Meschery.
SPo

He as O, A.   E. E. Cummings.   InPS

He asked me what was I fantasizing.   Alta.   MMD

He awoke this morning from a strange dream.   Chief Leschi of
the Nisqually.   Duane Niatum.   CDW

He brought our Saviour to the western side.   Political Power.
Milton.   *Fr.* Paradise Regained, IV.   SCP-1

He came apart in the open.   Martin's Blues.   Michael S. Harper.
PoBA

He came back and shot. He shot him. When he came.   Incident.
LeRoi Jones.   NoAM

He came from Malta; and Eumelus says.   The Maltese Dog.
*Unknown, tr. by* Edmund Blunden.   ECBV

He came in silvern armor, trimmed with black.   Sonnet.
Gwendolyn B. Bennett.   PoBA

He came like ashes in the burnt leaf fall.   Oh, Do You Know the
Muffin Man?   Richard Mathews.   AATT

He came to his love's window at the dead of the night.   The Little
Drummer.   *Unknown.*   AmFP

He came to Washington secure in tweeds.   Curriculum Vitae:
Incomplete.   Elisavietta Ritchie.   AATT

He chants a boy-chant.   The Grace of Cynthia's Maidenhood.
Vinnie-Marie D'Ambrosio.   IHMS

He clasps the crag with crooked hands.   The Eagle.   Tennyson.
HeIP; InPK; IPWM; OBP; PPoe; SoSe; SS

He climbs the stair.   Waterchew!   Gregory Corso.   VGW

He comes through the door.   The Assassin's Fatal Error.
Lawrence Raab.   AmPA

He could not breathe in a crowded place.   The Pioneer.   William
B. Ruggles.   ECBV

He could reduce all things to acts.   Samuel Butler.   *Fr.* Hudibras,
I, 1.   SCP-2

He counts his blessings who.   Dustless Chalk.   James Rankin.
MIS

He crawls to the edge of the foaming creek.   Meeting the
Mountains.   Gary Snyder.   NoAM; PiAm

He darkens the boxes of desired characteristics.   The Lecturer
Seeks a Wife.   Gary Lawless.   FAF

He debated whether.   Arthur Ridgewood, M.D.   Frank Marshall
Davis.   BPo

He did not come to woo U Nu.   Just Dropped In.   William Cole.
POL

He did not wear his scarlet coat.   Oscar Wilde.   *Fr.* The Ballad
of Reading Gaol.   NOBE

He "Digesteth Harde Yron."   Marianne Moore.   NoAM

He dines alone surrounded by reflections.   Witch Doctor.   Robert
Hayden.   MAT; NoAM

He disappeared in the dead of winter.   In Memory of W. B.
Yeats.   W. H. Auden.   Epi; HeIP; NoAM; NOBE; OxBTC;
PAIC; PPoe; PPP; TCP; WIF

He discovers himself on an old airfield.   The Old Pilot's Death.
Donald Hall.   MPo

He does not have the experiences.   The Poster.   Lynn Sukenick.
RiTi

He does not think that I haunt here nightly.   The Haunter.
Thomas Hardy.   LoAs; NOBE

He doesn't like it, of course.   His Body.   Sandra McPherson.
AmPA; CAAP

He Don't Know the Inside Feel.   Herbert R. Adams.   MiP

He drives onto the grassy shoulder and unfastens.   Earth Walk.
William Meredith.   MAT; PPoD

He eats of the fruits of the great Speckle.   Real Life.   Ted
Berrigan.   NoAM

He ended; and thus Adam last replied.   Milton.   *Fr.* Paradise
*Lost, XII.*   HeIP

He erupts from our soil: a grenade.   Quaker Hero, Burning.
Bink Noll.   TCP

He examined the length of his thin body.   The Twelve Hotels.
George MacBeth.   TwMBP

He Fell Among Thieves.   Sir Henry Newbolt.   OxBTC

He fell in a sweeping arc.   Malfunction.   Richard E. Albert.
MiP

He felt the wild beast in him betweenwhiles.   Modern Love IX.
George Meredith.   LoAs

He first deceased; she for a little tried.   Upon the Death of Sir
Albert Morton's Wife.   Sir Henry Wotton.   BoLoP

He floats a burnt auburn blur.   The Animal.   Allan Block.   FAF

He followed me up and he followed me down.   Lady Isabel and
the Elf Knight (Pretty Polly).   *Unknown.*   AmFP

He found a rope and picked it up.   Epitaph for a Horse Thief.
*Unknown.*   ECBV

He found her by the ocean's moaning verge.   Modern Love,
XLIX.   George Meredith.   LoAS; PAIC; VPC

He gave himself another year.   Patrick Kavanagh.   *Fr.* The Great
Hunger.   BIrV

He had a name.   Generations 1.   Sam Cornish.   NVAP

He had been coming a very long time.   For Malcolm Who Walks
in the Eyes of Our Children.   Quincy Troupe.   PoBA

He had driven half the night.   Hay for the Horses.   Gary Snyder.
ConAP; CTBA; InPS

He had got, finally.   A Poem for Speculative Hipsters.   LeRoi
Jones.   NoAM; NOBA

He had no past and he certainly.   Pity Ascending with the Fog.
James Tate.   NoAM

He had smiled at us.   Maximus, to Gloucester, Letter 19.
Charles Olson.   PAIC

He hands/ down the gift.   The Gift.   Robert Creeley.   NOBA

He has been walking toward me for a thousand miles.   The
Mailman.   Thomas Brush.   NVAP

He has been washed and locked in.   Someone Gone Away
Downstairs.   Jeanette Nichols.   RiTi

He has finished a day's work.   The Pornographer.   Robert Hass.
CAAP

He has forgone the razor for a year.   Fashionable Poet Reading.
Tony Connor.   PPoD

He has gone.   Last Journey.   Enrique Gonzales Martinez, *tr. by*
Samuel Beckett.   PBMP

He has hanged himself—the Sun.   November.   F. W. Harvey.
OxBTC

He has never heard of tides.   German Shepherd.   Myra Cohn
Livingston.   RFM

He has not woo'd, but he has lost his heart.   A Country Dance.
Charles Tennyson Turner.   VPC

He has only to pass by a tree moodily walking head down.   The
Fiend.   James Dickey.   CoPAm; PPP

He has the full moon on his breast.   The Smoker Parrot.   John
Shaw Neilson.   MAuV

He has the sign.   Portrait of Malcolm X.   Etheridge Knight.
PoBA

He hated them all one by one but wanted to show them.   A
Teacher.   Reed Whittemore.   NCSH

He Hears the Cry of the Sedge.   W. B. Yeats.   OxBTC

He hears the summer at a distance.   Vanishing Point.   Peter
Cooley.   AmPA

He Held Radical Light.   A. R. Ammons.   NoAM

He is a tower unleaning. But how will he not break.   Vaunting
Oak.   John Crowe Ransom.   VGW

He is always right.   The Interrogator.   Elizabeth Jennings.   WPE

He Is Far.   *Unknown.*   OxBM

He is found with the homeless dogs.  Kid.  Robert Hayden.  NCSH

He is in his room sulked shut.  The small.  Boy.  John Ciardi.  SFF

He is leading his grandfather under the sun to market.  Niño Leading an Old Man to Market.  Leonard Nathan.  CTBA; NCSH

He is mad. He is filthy.  Jonah: A Report.  David R. Slavitt.  CoPAm

He is making love with his wife on the roof.  The Roof of the World.  Michael Dennis Browne.  AmPA

He is murdered upright in the day.  Vaticide.  Myron O'Higgins.  PoBA

He is my love/ my sweet nutgrove.  *Unknown, tr. fr. Irish by* Michael Hartnett.  BirV

He is not ded that somtyme hath a fall.  Sir Thomas Wyatt.  AAS

He is not here, the old sun.  No Possum, No Sop, No Taters.  Wallace Stevens.  VGW

He is not John the gardener.  A Friend in the Garden.  Juliana Horatia Ewing.  OxBChV

He is older than the naval side of British history.  Chief Petty Officer.  Charles Causley.  OxBTC

He is quick, thinking in clear images.  In Broken Images.  Robert Graves.  PPoe

He is that fallen lance that lies as hurled.  The Soldier.  Robert Frost.  OFD

He is the pond's old father, its brain.  The Snapper.  William Heyen.  AmPA

He is to weet a melancholy carle.  Character of Charles Brown.  Keats.  MBPR

He is trying to think.  Teechur.  Dick Higgins.  MiP

He is very busy with his looking.  Young Heroes.  Gwendolyn Brooks.  BPo

He is wasted now.  Dylan, Who Is Dead.  Samuel Allen.  PoBA

He jumped me while I was asleep.  Assailant.  John Raven.  BPo

"He Killed Many of My Men."  John Bennett.  BuTh

He [*or* When he] killed the [noble] Mudjokivis.  The Modern Hiawatha.  George A. Strong.  AKE; ECBV; FaBoCo; SpRo

He larved ond he larved on he merd such a nauses.  The Ondt and the Gracehoper.  James Joyce.  *Fr.* Finnegans Wake.  BIrV

He lay upon his dying bed.  The Sword of Bunker Hill.  William Ross Wallace.  BTTM

He Leadeth Me, *with music.*  Joseph H. Gilmore.  BLSH

He leaned.  Treaty-trip from Shulus Reservation.  Patrick Lane.  NeAC

He Left the Pine Ridge Reservation.  Carol Cox.  MMD

He lifted up, among the actuaries.  So Long? Stevens.  John Berryman.  NOBA

He Liked the Dead.  Malcolm Lowry.  OxBTC

He Lived amidst th' Untrodden Ways.  Hartley Coleridge.  FaBoCo

He lives among a dog.  The Child.  Donald Hall.  NCSH

He lives near a grain elevator, farms.  The City Boy.  Stephen Dunn.  HeS

He lives unsociable, aloof.  The Liftman.  H. A. C. Evans.  POL

He lives, who last night flopped from a log.  Burning.  Galway Kinnell.  CoPAm

He looked and saw a spacious plain, whereon.  Vision of the Future; the Flood.  Milton.  *Fr.* Paradise Lost, XI.  SCP-1

He looks like a fat little old man.  Dead Seal.  A. W. Purdy.  NoAM

He looks out the window.  In Flight.  Patrick Smith.  MIT

He loved her and she loved him.  Lovesong.  Ted Hughes.  OBP

He loved her, and through many years.  Then and Now.  Paul Laurence Dunbar.  PBMP

He made his master to cutte his hore.  Ipomadon Plays the Fool at Court.  *Unknown. Fr.* Ipomadon.  OxBM

He May Be Envied, Who with Tranquil Breast.  Charlotte Smith.  SBG

He met a lady.  From the Hazel Bough.  Earle Birney.  HeIP

He motions me over with a question.  Kidnaper.  Tess Gallagher.  AmPA

He must be coyote.  Lame Deer.  Joy Harjo.  SA

He Never Expected Much.  Thomas Hardy.  NoAM; OxBTC

He never felt twice the same about the flecked river.  This Solitude of Cataracts.  Wallace Stevens.  PiAm

He never spoke a word to me.  Simon the Cyrenian Speaks.  Countee Cullen.  BPo

He never talk enough.  Blues for a Cello Man.  Carol Bergé.  MMD

He, of that greater dread.  Dog talk.  Albert De Pietro.  AATT

He once did love with fond affection.  Forsaken.  *Unknown.*  AmFP

He outstripped Time with but a bout.  Emily Dickinson.  PiAm

He owns no car.  Drum Songs.  Joseph Bruchac.  TSWA

He Paid Me Seven.  *Unknown.*  BPo

He passed by with another.  Ballad.  Gabriela Mistral, *tr. by* Doris Dana.  OLR

He paused on the sill of a door ajar.  The Newcomer's Wife.  Thomas Hardy.  BoLoP; OxBTC

He picks up what he thinks is.  My Father: October 1942.  William Stafford.  CoPAm

He placed the medicine.  Wrong Kind of Love.  Ray A. Young Bear.  VW

He played by the river when he was young.  Washington.  Nancy Byrd Turner.  ECBV

He Praises the Trees.  *Unknown, tr. fr. Irish by* Robin Skelton.  BIrV

He preached upon "breadth" till it argued him narrow.  Emily Dickinson.  PAIC; PPoD

He preaches to the crowd that power is lent.  Vox Populi.  Dryden.  *Fr.* The Medal.  NOBE

He proposed to me on the Ferris wheel.  Arches and Shadows.  Annie Dillard.  CTBA

He pushes behind the words.  Waiting.  Robert Creeley.  VGW

He Puts Me to Rest.  David Ignatow.  VGW

He ran the course and as he ran he grew.  Innocence.  Thom Gunn.  NoAM

He rang me up/ In a dream.  A Dream of Hanging.  Patricia Beer.  MPo

He Resigns.  John Berryman.  PSN

He roars in the swamp.  The Alligator.  Beatrice Ravenel.  WPE

He rocked the boat.  Ezra Shank.  *Unknown.*  CaYB

He rose at dawn and, fired with hope.  The Sailor Boy.  Tennyson.  AIW

He runs before the wise men: he.  He.  Stanley Kunitz.  VGW

He said:/ "Let's stay here."  Party Piece.  Brian Patten.  BoLoP

He said everything is a struggle.  The Augur.  Stephen Tudor.  HeS

He said, I want to be wrapped.  Warrior Dreams.  Ray A. Young Bear.  VW

He said this/ he said that.  Your Friend.  Anselm Hollo.  TwMBP

He sang of life, serenely sweet.  The Poet.  Paul Laurence Dunbar.  BPo

He sat in a wheeled chair, waiting for dark.  Disabled.  Wilfred Owen.  InPS; NoAM; OxBTC; PoTa; PSN; VoPo

He sat upon the rolling deck.  Sailor.  Langston Hughes.  ECBV

He saw her from the bottom of the stairs.  Home Burial.  Robert Frost.  PiAm

He saw my/ picture in a/ magazine. Tentacles, Leaves. Lyn Lifshin. RiTi

He scarce had ceased when the superior Fiend. Satan and the Fallen Angels. Milton. *Fr.* Paradise Lost, I. SCP-1

He sd please/ take it. Here. J. D. Whitney. NVAP

He sees the heat give a surge under its tight canopy. The Starer. Rhyll McMaster. CAAP

He sees the ocean. For the Waiter at Jhonny Pavlovs. Luís Omar Salinas. SA

He Sees Through Stone. Etheridge Knight. ConAP; PoBA

He served his master well from youth to age. Old Stephen. Charles Tennyson Turner. VPC

He shall not hear the bittern cry. Lament for Thomas MacDonagh. Frances Ledwidge. BIrV

He She Because How. Anselm Hollo. TwMBP

He shuddered briefly and stared down the long valley. The Return of Robinson Jeffers. Robert Hass. AmPA

He shudders . . . feeling on the shaven spot. Electrocution. Lola Ridge. WPE

He sings from the bottom of a well but she can hear him up. Jim Harrison. *Fr.* Ghazals. NoAM

He sipped at a weak hock and seltzer. The Arrest of Oscar Wilde at the Cadogan Hotel. John Betjeman. AIW; NoAM; OxBTC

He sits at the bar in the Alhambra. Simple. Naomi Long Madgett. PoBA

He sits in the chair and does not move. Medicine. Louis Jenkins. HeS

He sleeps in the next room. Nightwalker. Delia Chilgren. NPW

He sleeps on the top of a mast. The Unbeliever. Elizabeth Bishop. NoAM

He slid out of the skin, leaving it. Summer. Diane Wakoski. IPWM; VGW

He slides the cut paper out. The Paper Cutter. David Ignatow. CTBA

He slowly paced his distance off, and turned. The High Jump. *Unknown.* SPo

He snuggles his fingers. After Winter. Sterling A. Brown. PoBA

He spake no dream, for as his words had end. Temptation of the Magic Banquet. Milton. *Fr.* Paradise Regained, II. SCP-1

He Spends Time in Southern California. Jonathan Cott. RRA

He squats there stolid, brown, and small. Toad School. Merle Meeter. AATT

He stared at ruin. Ruin stared straight back. John Berryman. *Fr.* Dream Songs. CAPP

He stares upward at a monstrous face. The Pieta, Rhenish, 14th C., The Cloisters. Mona Van Duyn. Prf

He stood among a crowd at Drumahair. The Man Who Dreamed of Faeryland. W. B. Yeats. NoAM

He stood, and heard the steeple. Eight O'Clock. A. E. Housman. InPK; NoAM

He stood still by her bed. The Goodnight. Louis Simpson. MPo; PBMP

He stoops down, and crawls on hands and knees. Soil Searcher. J. Joyce. CTBA

He stopped on the irreproachable sidewalk. Elysee. Larry Eigner. VGW

He swings down like the flourish of a pen. Skier. Robert Francis. NCSH; RFM

He talked, and as he talked. The Story-Teller. Mark Van Doren. CTBA; ECBV; TH

He talked of Delhi brothels half the night. Long Tom. W. W. Gibson. OxBTC

He tells many bad things. Young Training. Lawrence McGaugh. PoBA

He that had come that morning. Ballad of John Cable and Three Gentlemen. W. S. Merwin. NOBA

He that hath no mistress, must not wear a favour. *Unknown.* GBL

He that is down needs fear no fall. The Shepherd Boy Sings in the Valley of Humiliation. Bunyan. *Fr.* The Pilgrim's Progress. NOBE

He That Ne'er Learns His ABC. *Unknown.* GBP

He That Never Read a Line. *Unknown, tr. fr. Old Irish by* Robin Flower. PFIr

He Thinks of Those Who Have Spoken Evil of His Beloved. W. B. Yeats. *See* Aedh Thinks of Those Who Have Spoken Evil of His Beloved.

He thought he kept the universe alone. The Most of It. Robert Frost. PiAm; PPoe

He thought he saw an Elephant. The Mad Gardener's Song. "Lewis Carroll." *Fr.* Sylvie and Bruno. FaBoCo; OxBChV; PBMP

He thrust his joy against the weight of the sea. The Surfer. Judith Wright. WPE

He told me I drive. Soursobs. Richard Tipping. CAAP

He told the barmaid he had things to do. Dodona's Oaks Were Still. Patrick MacDonogh. PFIr

He Understands the Great Cruelty of Death. Petrarch, *pr. tr. fr. Italian by* J. M. Synge. Sonnets to Laura: To Laura in Death, XLVII. BIrV

He usually managed to be there when. Because He Liked to Be at Home. Kenneth Patchen. CoPAm

He waits perpetually crouched, teeth. Mean Rufus Throw-Down. David Smith. NVAP

He wakes to a confused dream of boats, gulls. Murphy in Manchester. John Montague. PFIr

He walks on rubber knees. Oh Lord! Tarzan, Old. Allan Block. FAF

He wanted to pat. A Kind of Love. Jeanette Nichols. RiTi

He Was. Richard Wilbur. NCSH; SS

He was a mighty hunter in his youth. The White Cat of Trenarren. A. L. Rowse. OxBTC; PCat

He was a plain man. Royalty. Luci Shaw. AATT

He was a rat and she was a rat. The Two Rats [*or* What Became of Them?]. *Unknown.* ECBV; OxBChV

He was at Naples writing letters home. Wallace Stevens. *Fr.* Esthétique du Mal. NOBA

He was born in Alabama. Of De Witt Williams on His Way to Lincoln Cemetery. Gwendolyn Brooks. ANTL; CAPP; NoAM; NOBA

He was found by the Bureau of Statistics to be. The Unknown Citizen. W. H. Auden. BuTh; HeIP; InPK; IPWM; LP; PAIC; PPoD; SFF; SoSe; WIF

He was in logick a great critick. Sir Hudibras, His Passing Worth. Samuel Butler. *Fr.* Hudibras, 1. FaBoCo

He was just a young aviator. Lindbergh. *Unknown.* AmFP

He was just back. Vietnam. Clarence Major. PoBA

He Was Made Man. Giles Fletcher the Younger. *Fr.* Christ's Victory and Triumph, I. BoReV

He was not bad, as emperors go, not really. Two Pieces After Suetonius. Robert Penn Warren. NOBA

He was reading late, at Richard's, down in Maine. Henry's Understanding. John Berryman. NoAM; NOBA

He was really her favorite. In Spite of His Dangling Pronoun. Lyn Lifshin. IHMS; Psy

He was the doctor up to Combe. Coroner's Jury. L. A. G. Strong. OxBTC

He went down to the woodshed. No One Heard Him Call. Dorothy Aldis. CaYB

He went out/ the snow was hard packed. And Our Gift to the Seasons. Thomas Clark. SLP

He went to the wood and caught it. Riddle. *Unknown.* GBP

He which hath no stomach to this fight. King Henry the Fifth before Agincourt. Shakespeare. *Fr.* King Henry V. BTTM

He who binds [*or* bends] to himself a joy. Eternity. Blake. *Fr.* Several Questions Answered. BoReV; LAuP; MBPR; NOBE; WIF

He, who once was my brother, is dead by his own hand. Justice Is Reason Enough. Diane Wakoski. AmPA

He will not see the East catch fire again. A Cock Crowing in a Poulterer's Shop. John Ferguson. BoAnP

He will watch the hawk with an indifferent eye. Icarus. Stephen Spender. NoAM

He Wishes for the Cloths of Heaven. W. B. Yeats. *See* Aedh Wishes for the Cloths of Heaven.

He with body waged a fight. The Four Ages of Man. W. B. Yeats. BoReV

He worshipped at the altar of Romance. An Epitaph. Colin Ellis. OxBTC

He would declare and could himself believe. Never Again would Birds' Song Be the Same. Robert Frost. InPK; NoAM; VGW

He yelled at me in Greek. John Berryman. *Fr.* Dream Songs. PiAm

Head, A. James Schuyler. NoAM

Head Byzantine or from, The. Resting Figure. Denise Levertov. AnMo

Head: egg of all, The. Right Thinking Man. Marge Piercy. RiTi

Head like a snake, a neck like a drake, A. How a Good Greyhound Is Shaped. *Unknown.* BoAnP

Head or Tail, A—which does he lack? The Hippo. Theodore Roethke. VGW

Head thrust in as for the view, A. All Revelation. Robert Frost. PiAm

Headless fountains/ running loose. The Preponderance. William Meredith. PBMP

Headless squirrel, some blood, A. A Day Begins. Denise Levertov. AnMo; CoPAm

Headline History. William Plomer. FaBoCo

Heads, impenetrable, The. Oxen: Ploughing at Fiesole. Charles Tomlinson. OxBTC

Health and Fitness. J. B. Morton. FaBoCo

Health to the Birds, A. Seumas MacManus. PFIr

Hear me/ don't you hear me. Tambourine. James Cunningham. JB

Hear me, Melissus; I will tell you a dream. The Terror by Night. Giacomo Leopardi, *tr. by* John Heath-Stubbs. Moon

Hear me, O God! A Hymn to God the Father. Ben Jonson. BoReV

Hear me, whom I betrayed. Envoi. J. V. Cunningham. VGW

Hear the fluter with his flute. The Amateur Flute. *Unknown.* SpRo

Hear the sledges with the bells. Poe. *Fr.* The Bells. SpRo

Hear the Voice of the Bard (*Introd. to* Songs of Experience). Blake. NOBE; OBP
(Introduction: "Hear the voice of the bard!") InPS; LAuP; MBPR

Hear what Highland Nora said. Nora's Vow. Sir Walter Scott. SLP

Hear, Ye Ladies. John Fletcher. *Fr.* The Tragedy of Valentinian. NOBE

Heard in a Violent Ward. Theodore Roethke. NoAM

Heard in the Cougate. Robert Garioch. OxBTC

Heard'st thou yon universal cry. Destruction of the Bastille. Samuel Taylor Coleridge. MBPR

Hearing a sound that may be thy return. Hildegarde Flanner. *Fr.* Sonnets in Quaker Language. WPE

Hearing Men Shout at Night on Macdougal Street. Robert Bly. TCP

Hearing of you, I never lost a brother. Stepping Outside. Tess Gallagher. AmPA

Hearing one saga, we enact the next. Remembering the 'Thirties. Donald Davie. OxBTC

Hearing that you would come who by my love. Incantatory Poem. Jean Garrigue. LoAs

Hearing your words, and not a word among them. Edna St. Vincent Millay. NoAM; PSN; VGW

Hearken, thou craggy ocean pyramid! To Ailsa Rock. Keats. MBPR

Hears not my Phyllis how the birds. Phyllis Knotting. Sir Charles Sedley. NOBE

Hearse Song, The. *Unknown.* SFF

Heart, The. Stephen Crane. *See* In the Desert.

Heart and Mind. Edith Sitwell. OxBTC

Heart asks pleasure first, The. Emily Dickinson. NOBA; PPP; SBG; WPE

Heart Burial. Geoffrey Grigson. POL

Heart has need of some deceit, The. Only the Polished Skeleton. Countee Cullen. VGW

Heart of cleft gold. Pond Lily. E. Margaret Clarkson. AATT

Heart of Midlothian, The, *sel.* Sir Walter Scott.
Proud Maisie, *fr. ch.* 38. AIW; Epi; InPK
(Madge Wildfire's Song.) NOBE; SLP

Heart of my day holds no, The. Oh, Say, Mr. Toffler. Mira Fish. FAF

Heart of the heartless world. Huesca [*or* To Margot Heinemann]. John Cornford. BoLoP; OxBTC

Heart, that hideous bear, The. Falling in Love. David Perkins. NCSH

Heart! We will forget him! Emily Dickinson. OLR

Heartbreak Camp. Roy Campbell. OxBTC

Hearts and Flowers, *with music.* Mary D. Brine. FSN

Heart's Compass. Dante Gabriel Rossetti. The House of Life, XXVII. PAIC

Heart's Ease. *Unknown. Fr.* Misogonus. WIF

Heart's Needle. W. D. Snodgrass. CAPP; RRA
*Sels.*
"Child of my winter born," I. ConAP; PiAm
"Easter has come around," VI. ConAP
"Here in the scuffled dust," VII. NCSH; PiAm
"I thumped on you the best I could," VIII. NoAM
"Late April and you are three; today," II. CoPAm
"No one can tell you why," IV. ConAP; CoPAm
"Vicious winter finally yields, The," X. PSN

Hearts of Gold. Ogden Nash. AKE

Heat. Hilda Doolittle ("H.D."). The Garden, II. FSFS; HeIP; InPK; NoAM; PiAm

Heat of the oven, The. Breaded Meat, Breaded Hands. Michael S. Harper. NVAP

Heathen Chinee, The. Bret Harte. FaBoCo
(Plain Language from Truthful James.) AmVN

Heathen Pass-ee, The, *parody.* A. C. Hilton. FaBoCo

Heather Ale. Robert Louis Stevenson. PoTa

Heat's on the hooker, The. Translations from the English. George Starbuck. VGW

Heaved from the Earth. Besmilr Brigham. Psy

Heaven. Rupert Brooke. NOBE

Heaven. Langston Hughes. NOBA

Heaven and Hell. *Unknown, tr. fr. Eskimo by* Edward Field. IPWM

Heaven-haven. Gerard Manley Hopkins. BuTh; HeIP; NoAM; NOBE; SoSe

Heaven is/ The place where. Heaven. Langston Hughes. NOBA

Heaven is so far of the mind. Emily Dickinson. PiAm

Heaven-murdered one. Poem of Solitude at Columbia University. Federico García Lorca, *tr. by* Ben Belitt. PBMP

Heaven of Animals, The. James Dickey. CAPP; CoPAm; HeIP; NCSH; NoAM; NOBA; TCP

Heavenly Eloquence. Samuel Daniel. *Fr. Musophilus.* NOBE

"Heavenly Father"—take to thee. Emily Dickinson. PiAm

Heavenly Grass. Tennessee Williams. ECBV

Heavenly Vision. William Billings. AmFP

Heavens declare the glory of God, The. Psalms, XIX, Bible, *O.T.* OBP

Heaven's Queene. Sir Walter Ralegh. Moon

Heaving the Lead Line. *Unknown.* AmFP

Heavy Bear Who Goes with Me, The. Delmore Schwartz. NoAM; NOBA

Heavy breathing fills all my chamber. August 24, 1963—1:00 A.M.—Omaha. Donna Whitewing. VW

Heavy glacier and the terrifying Alps, The. Long Lines. Paul Goodman. VGW

Heavy, Heavy—What Hangs Over? Kenneth Burke. POL

Hebrew of Your Poets, Zion, The. Charles Reznikoff. VGW

Hector Protector was dressed all in green. Mother Goose. ECBV

Hector the Collector. Shel Silverstein. CTBA

"He'd never seen so many dead before." The Effect. Siegfried Sassoon. BuTh

He'd never wrung the. The Husband. Barbara Greenberg. RiTi

Hedge before me, one behind, A. *Unknown, tr. fr. Irish by* Flann O'Brien. BIrV

Hedgehog. Paul Muldoon. BIrV

Hedges Freaked with Snow. Robert Graves. OxBTC

Heedless o' My Love. William Barnes. GBL

Heh Nonny No! *Unknown.* BuTh

Heifer Clambers Up, A. Gary Snyder. NoAM; NOBA

Heigh-ho on a Winter Afternoon. Donald Davie. OxBTC

Heir, The. *Unknown.* RAE

Heir to the office of a man not dead. A Miltonic Sonnet for Mr. Johnson on His Refusal of Peter Hurd's Official Portrait. Richard Wilbur. CAPP

Heirloom. Robert Flanagan. HeS

Hekatompathia; or, Passionate Century of Love, *sels.* Thomas Watson. AAS
  "Some that reporte great Alexanders life."
  "Speake gentle heart, where is thy dwelling place?"

Held between wars. Käthe Kollwitz. Muriel Rukeyser. NMM; RiTi

Helen. Hilda Doolittle ("H.D."). NOBA; SBG

Helen, *sels.* Euripides, *tr. fr. Greek by* Richmond Lattimore. Chorus: "Long ago, the Mountain Mother." RRA

Helen in Egypt, *sels.* Hilda Doolittle ("H.D.").
  "Alas, my brothers." NOBA
  "Another shout from the wharves." NOBA
  "Thetis is the moon-goddess." Moon

Helen, thy beauty is to me. To Helen. Poe. AmVN; BoLoP; GBL; HeIP; InPS; NOBA; PAIC; PBMP; PiAm; WIF

Helicon. John Hollander. NoAM

Helicopter, The. Ian Serraillier. RAE

Helicopter in the sky, A. Street Scene. Peter Suffolk. PoTa

Hell. Abraham Cowley. *Fr. Davideis, I.* SCP-2

Hell freezing over. To keep sane. Mandelstam. David Young. AmPA

Hell Gate. A. E. Housman. NoAM

Hell is a city much like London. Shelley. *Fr. Peter Bell the Third.* OBP

Hellas, *sels.* Shelley.
  World's great age begins anew, The." HeIP; NOBE
  "Worlds on worlds are rolling ever." HeIP

Hellenics, The, *sel.* Walter Savage Landor. Ternissa. NOBE

Hellhound on My Trail. *Unknown.* BluL

Hello!/ hello! Echo. Sara Asheron. CaYB

Hello darkness my old friend. The Sound of Silence. Paul Simon. PBMP; WIF

"Hello! Good luck: the trip out west." Letter Back to Oregon. Albert Goldbarth. HeS

Hello, Ma Baby, *with music.* Joseph E. Howard *and* Ida Emerson. BLSo; FSN

Hell's Pavement. John Masefield. PoTa

Helmet now an hive for bees becomes, The. The Vote. Ralph Knevet. SCP-2

Helmeted, booted, numbered, horsed, and always at a distance. Polo Match. John Ciardi. SPo

Help me now. Song. Emmett Jarrett. NeAC

Help[e] me to seek [*or* seke], for I lost it there. Rondeau. Sir Thomas Wyatt. AAS; PAIC

Helpe me! helpe me! now I call. To His Mistresses. Robert Herrick. LoAs

Helves Surling Out of Eakspeasies Per (Reel) hapsingly. E. E. Cummings. Epi

Hemmed-in Males. William Carlos Williams. *Fr.* A Folded Skyscraper. MAT

Hen: Cock, cock, I have la-a-a-yd. Hen and cock. *Unknown.* GBP

Hen Dying. Alasdair MacLean. BoAnP

Hen Flower, The. Galway Kinnell. CAAP

Hen Under Bay-Tree. Ruth Pitter. OxBTC

Hence burgundy, claret, and port. Song. Keats. MBPR

Hence Cupid! with your cheating toys. Against Love. Katherine Philips. SGB; WPE

Hence curiosity me led. Thomas Heyrick. *Fr.* The Submarine Voyage: a Pindaric Poem in Four Parts. SCP-2

Hence loathèd Melancholy. L'Allegro. Milton. PPP

Hence vain deluding Joys. Il Penseroso. Milton. PPP

Henceforth, from the Mind. Louise Bogan. WPE

Henceforth I will not set my love. Sir Arthur Gorges. GBL

Hendescasyllabics. Tennyson. FaBoCo

Henpecked Husband, A. *Unknown.* OxBM

Henry VIII. Eleanor *and* Herbert Farjeon. PoTa

Henry got me with child. Amanda Barker. Edgar Lee Masters. *Fr.* Spoon River Anthology. NoAM

Henry in transition, transient Henry. John Berryman. *Fr.* Dream Songs. RRA

Henry K. Sawyer. *Unknown.* AmFP

Henry was every morning fed. The Boy and the Snake. Charles *and* Mary Lamb. OxBChV

Henry's Confession. John Berryman. *Fr.* Dream Songs. NoAM

Henry's mind grew blacker the more he thought. John Berryman. *Fr.* Dream Songs. NOBA

Henry's pelt was put on sundry walls. John Berryman. *Fr.* Dream Songs. NoAM

Henry's Secret. Dorothy Kilner. OxBChV

Henry's Understanding. John Berryman. NoAM; NOBA

Hens. Alden Nowlan. POL

Hens, The. Elizabeth Madox Roberts. LCL

Hens in Winter. Robert P. Tristram Coffin. TH

Hen's Nest. John Clare. AKE

Heptalogia, The, *sels.* Swinburne.

Higher Pantheism in a Nutshell, The. PAIC; SpRo

Nephelidia. FaBoCo; SpRo

Her ambition is to be more shiny. The Common Woman. Judy Grahn. RiTi

Her angel looked upon God's face. The Eternal Image. Ruth Pitter. OxBTC

Her Application to Elysium. Kathleen Norris. IHMS

Her Apron through the Trees. Roger Weingarten. AmPA

Her body is not so white as. Queen-Ann's Lace. William Carlos Williams. LoAs; NoAM; NOBA

Her Chinese lamps. Just After the Widow's Death. Barbara Greenberg. RiTi

Her day out from the workhouse-ward, she stands. The Ice. W. W. Gibson. OxBTC

Her Dream House. Marvin Bell. NVAP

Her Dwarf. George P. Elliott. MAT

Her eyes are wild, her head is bare. The Mad Mother. Wordsworth. MBPR

Her Eyes Don't Shine Like Diamonds, *with music.* David Marion. FSN

Her eyes' flood licks his feet's fair stain. Luke VII: She Began to Wash His Feet with Tears. Richard Crashaw. SCP-1

Her eyes were gentle; her voice was for soft singing. An Old Woman Remembers. Sterling A. Brown. PoBA

Her face/ Betrays the darkness of storms. Kornelia Woloszczuk. Peter Skrzynecki. CAAP

Her face her tongue her wit. *At. to* Sir Arthur Gorges. GBL

Her face like a rain-beaten stone on the day she rolled off. Elegy. Theodore Roethke. CTBA; NCSH; PSN

Her face with bones. Welthistorische Perpekitven. Roderick Watson. MIS

Her Going. Shirley Kaufman. RiTi

Her grandmother called her from the playground. Legacies. Nikki Giovanni. CTBA

Her hands established, last time she left my room. Winter Bouquet. W. D. Snodgrass. NowV

Her health is good. She owns to forty-one. Occupation: Housewife. Phyllis McGinley. *Fr.* I Know a Village. WPE

Her heart a bruise on the Christ-flesh suffered out of locked agonies of rebirth. The Rose of Solitude. William Everson. PiAm

Her intentions are to see that blue. Kindergarten Teacher. Stanley Kiesel. NowV

Her Irish maids could never spoon out mush. Mary Winslow. Robert Lowell. PPP

Her iron beats. Domestic Scene. Michael Hartnett. BIrV

Her Kind. Anne Sexton. HeIP; PPP

Her—"last poems." Emily Dickinson. SBG

Her Leg [*or* Legs]. Robert Herrick. LoAs; SpRo

Her Lips Are Copper Wire. Jean Toomer. NoAM

Her lips they are redder than coral. *Unknown.* FaBoCo

Her long brown fingers. Creek Mother Poem. Joy Harjo. SA

Her lovely skin is white, like curds new pressed. *Unknown.* SCP-2

Her mind is a stone dull. Dropping Toward Stillness. Sharon Barba. RiTi

Her mind lives in a quiet room. Interior. Dorothy Parker. SBG

Her mindful breast perfumes with frankincense. *Unknown.* SCP-2

Her mother died when she was young. Kemp Owyne. *Unknown.* PeBB

Her mouth an O. The Poetess Kō Ōgimi. Helen Chasin. NMM

Her Muff. Richard Lovelace. SCP-2

Her paps like two fair apples in their prime. *Unknown.* SCP-2

Her Reply. Sir Walter Ralegh. *See* Nymph's Reply to the Shepherd, The.

Her Reticence. Theodore Roethke. AnMo; LoAs

Her scarf à la Bardot. Twice Shy. Seamus Heaney. NCSH

Her sense of humor has no gold stop. Telephonist. Janet Frame. WPE

Her shoulder is in your mouth. Some Oral Stanzas. Thomas Lux. NVAP

Her Sister. Moira O'Neill. OxBTC

Her smiling eyes in the glass. Calculating Female. Jill Hellyer. POL

Her stiffening captor lies in wait. Mercedes, Her Aloneness. Colette Inez. IHMS

Her Story. Naomi Long Madgett. IHMS; PoBA

Her Strong Enchantments Failing. A. E. Housman. MAT; NOBE

Her Triumph. Ben Jonson. *See* Triumph of Charis, The.

Her veins run Mogen David. Lane Is the Pretty One. Lucille Clifton. CAAP

Her voice/ slips through our ears. Early Ella. Lynn Sukenick. RiTi

Her Whole Life Is an Epigram. Blake. InPK

Her window looks upon the lane. Launcelot With Bicycle. Phyllis McGinley. SS

Her Words. Theodore Roethke. LoAs

Hera, Hung from the sky. Carolyn Kizer. NMM; WPE

Heraclitus. William Johnson Cory, *paraphrased fr. the Greek of* Callimachus. InPK; NOBE

Heralitus dwelled. Artery of the Sea. Napoleon St. Cyr. FAF

Herberie. Forbes Macgregor. MIS

Herbert White. Frank Bidart. AmPA

Herdmen, The. *Unknown.* NOBE

Here. Marvin Bell. AmPA

Here. Robert Creeley. NOBA

Here. R. S. Thomas. PSN

Here. J. D. Whitney. NVAP

Here/ I am cutting you. For Kenneth and Miriam Patchen. Al Young. CoPAm

Here a little child I stand. Grace [*or* Another Grace] for a Child. Robert Herrick. HeIP; InPK; InPS; OxBChV

Here a pretty baby lies. Upon a Child. Robert Herrick. SCP-1

Here, above,/ cracks in the buildings are filled with battered moonlight. The Man-Moth. Elizabeth Bishop. MAT; NoAM; NOBA; PPP

Here am I, a shape under a cedar. Sitting in the Woods: A Contemplation. W. R. Moses. NCSH

Here am I, little jumping Joan. Mother Goose. MG

Here among long-discarded cassocks. Diary of a Church Mouse. John Betjeman. OxBTC

Here, and here only in an age of iron. Terra Australis. Chris Wallace-Crabbe. MAuV

Here and There. Jon Stallworthy. NoAM

Here and there in the searing beam. Deer Among Cattle. James Dickey. TCP; TSWA

Here are people and sports of all sizes and sorts. The Mountebank Song. Thomas Durfey. SCP-2

Here are weeds about his mouth. Wide Empty Landscape with a Death in the Foreground. N. Scott Momaday. CDW

Here at the Super Duper, in a glass tank. Lobsters. Howard Nemerov. AnMo; PBMP

Here at the Vespasian-Carlton, it's just one. Boom! Howard Nemerov. NowV

Here at the wayside station, as many a morning. The Wayside Station. Edwin Muir. PSN

Here come two swans below the Roman bridge. Swans. Morley Jamieson. SLP

Here Comes.  Erica Jong.  PPoD

Here comes Old Man Adkins with a battle-ax.  Coal Loadin' Blues.  *Unknown.*  AmFP

Here comes the shadow not looking where it is going.  Sire.  W. S. Merwin.  VGW

Here corpse and soul go bare.  The Leader's headpiece.  Cistercians in Germany.  Robert Lowell.  NowV

Here evening comes without a welcome.  Reilly.  Rayne Mackinnon.  MIS

Here, ever since you went abroad.  What News.  Walter Savage Landor.  BoLoP

Here further up the mountain slope.  The Birthplace.  Robert Frost.  OFD

Here goes a poor old chimney sweeper.  The Chimney Sweeper.  *Unknown.*  AmFP

Here Holy Willie's sair worn clay.  Epitaph on Holy Willie.  Burns.  ESaP

Here I am,/ Novice of many years.  Two Roads, Etc.  Dorothy Walters.  IHMS

Here I am, an industry without chimneys.  The Perfection of Dentistry.  Marvin Bell.  AmPA

Here I am, an old man in a dry month.  Gerontion.  T. S. Eliot.  AnMo;  InPS;  NoAM;  NOBA;  PPP

Here I am and forth I must.  Prayer for the Journey.  *Unknown.*  OxBM

Here I am sitting like a side of beef in the middle of Kansas.  Three Weeks in the State of Loneliness.  Marge Piercy.  MMD

Here I am, troubling the dream coast.  In California.  Louis Simpson.  NoAM;  NowV

Here I go again.  Starting from San Francisco.  Lawrence Ferlinghetti.  CAPP;  PiAm

Here I sit.  Bad Morning.  Langston Hughes.  PiAm

Here I sit in my infested cubicle.  Theresa Greenwood.  CTBA

Here I sit in this quiet place.  Fair Isle Pattern.  James Rankin.  MIS

Here I slept with my face turned.  Prospect Beach.  Lou Lipsitz.  VGW

Here I stand/ For centuries watching.  Ask the Mountains.  Phil George.  VW

Here in a crumbled corner of the wall.  The Church Mouse.  Gerald Bullett.  BoAnP

Here in a distant place I hold my tongue.  Egan O Rahilly.  Egan O'Rahilly, *tr. by* James Stephens.  NoAM

Here, in a field.  In a Field.  Robert Pack.  CoPAm;  MAT

Here in Katmandu.  Donald Justice.  ConAP;  HeIP;  RFM

Here, in late spring, the summer is on us already.  Hot Afternoons Have Been in West 15th Street.  Paul Blackburn.  VGW

Here in my head, the home that is left for you.  Burning the Letters.  Randall Jarrell.  CoPAm

Here in Nantucket does the tiny soul.  Phenomenal Survivals of Death in Nantucket.  Louise Glück.  AmPA

Here in our cloud we talk.  Quiet Town.  William Stafford.  MAT

Here in Polynia.  Tom Raworth.  TwMBP

Here in the ancient floor.  The Self-Unseeing.  Thomas Hardy.  NOBE

Here, in the darkness, where this plaster saint.  Madeleine in Church.  Charlotte Mew.  SBG

Here, in the most Unchristian basement.  The Men's Room in the College Chapel.  W. D. Snodgrass.  PPP

Here in the newspaper—the wreck of the East Bound.  It's Here in The.  Russell Atkins.  PoBA

Here in the scuffled dust.  W. D. Snodgrass.  Heart's Needle, VII.  NCSH;  PiAm

Here, in the thick Carolina darkness.  1965.  Gibbons Ruark.  NowV

Here in the wind-shave of prairie land.  Inland Sea.  Franklin Brainard.  HeS

Here in this car is surcease from a thousand dead.  Surcease.  Patrick Lane.  NeAC

Here, in this little Bay.  Magna Est Veritas.  Coventry Patmore.  *Fr.* The Unknown Eros.  NOBE;  VPC

Here is a place that is no place.  Madhouse [*or* The Patient: Rockland County Sanitarium].  Calvin C. Hernton.  PoBA;  TCP

Here is a poem for the two of us to play.  The Newly Pressed Suit.  Roger McGough.  NoAM

Here is a ship you made.  The Ship.  J. F. Hendry.  SLP

Here is a symbol in which.  Rock and Hawk.  Robinson Jeffers.  IPWM;  NoAM;  NOBA

Here is another poem in a picture.  Untitled.  Daryl Hine.  NoAM

Here is cruel Frederick, see!  Cruel Frederick.  Heinrich Hoffmann, *tr. fr. German.*  SpRo

Here Is Little Effie's Head.  E. E Cummings.  AnMo

Here is the doctor, an abstracted lover.  Death by Aesthetics.  Mona Van Duyn.  RiTi

Here is the place; right over the hill.  Telling the Bees.  Whittier.  NOBA

Here is where people.  Library.  Richard Armour.  ECBV

Here its like that.  Blue Tanganyika.  Lebert Bethune.  PoBA

Here Johnson lies—a sage by all allow'd.  Epitaph.  William Cowper.  LAuP

Here lay a fair fat land.  Culbin Sand.  Andrew Young.  OxBTC

Here lie I, Martin Elgibrodde.  At Aberdeen.  *Unknown.*  FaBoCo

Here lie Willie Michie's banes.  Epitaph on a Schoolmaster.  Burns.  FaBoCo

Here lies a clerk who half his life had spent.  The Volunteer.  Herbert Asquith.  OxBTC

Here lies a Doctor of Divinity.  On a Doctor of Divinity.  Richard Porson.  FaBoCo

Here Lies a Lady.  John Crowe Ransom.  NoAM;  VGW

Here lies a man who was killed by lightning.  At Great Torrington, Devon.  *Unknown.*  FaBoCo

Here lies a poet, briefly known as Hecht.  Epitaph.  Anthony Hecht.  POL

Here lies dust confusèdly hurled.  On Sight of Some Martyrs' Sepulchres.  Nahum Tate.  SCP-2

Here lies factotum Ned at last.  Fragment of a Character.  Thomas Moore.  FaBoCo

Here lies fierce Strephon, whose poetic rage.  Epitaph.  Anthony Hecht.  PPoD

Here lies Fred.  On Prince Frederick.  *Unknown.*  FaBoCo

Here lies John Bun.  John Bun.  *Unknown.*  FaBoCo

Here lies Johnny Pidgeon.  Epitaph on John Dove.  Burns.  FaBoCo

Here lies Mary, the wife of John Ford.  At Potterne, Wiltshire.  *Unknown.*  FaBoCo

Here lies my wife.  At Leeds.  *Unknown.*  FaBoCo

Here lies our Sovereign Lord the King.  Epitaph on Charles II.  Earl of Rochester.  FaBoCo;  OBP

Here lies poor Burton.  A Brewer.  *Unknown.*  FaBoCo

Here lies resting, out of breath.  Little Elegy.  X. J. Kennedy.  ConAP;  NCSH

Here lies Sir Tact, a diplomatic fellow.  Epitaph.  Timothy Steele.  InPK

Here lies the body of Andrew Gear.  Andrew Gear of Sunderland.  *Unknown.*  FaBoCo

Here lies the body of Richard Hind.  On Richard Hind.  *Unknown.*  FaBoCo

Here lies the body of this world.  Epitaph on the World.  Henry David Thoreau.  HeIP

Here lies the Devil—ask no other name.  On a Lord.  Samuel Taylor Coleridge.  FaBoCo

Here lies the preacher, judge and poet, Peter.  On Peter Robinson.  Francis Jeffrey.  FaBoCo

Here lies [or lyes] to each her parents' ruth.  On My First Daughter.  Ben Jonson.  NOBE; RRA

Here lies, whom hound did ne'er pursue.  Epitaph on a Hare.  William Cowper.  HeIP

Her lies Will Smith—and, what's something rarish.  On Will Smith.  Unknown.  ECBV; FaBoCo

Here lies wise and valiant dust.  Epitaph on the Earl of Strafford.  John Cleveland.  NOBE; SCP-2

"Here lieth One whose name was writ on water!"  On Keats.  Shelley.  MBPR

Here love delights the wandering thought.  Unknown.  SCP-2

Here luxury's the common lot.  The light.  Grasse: The Olive Trees.  Richard Wilbur.  NoAM; NOBA

Here lyes to each her parents ruth.  See Here lies to each...

Here, on our native soil, we breathe once more.  Composed in the Valley near Dover, on the Day of Landing.  Wordsworth.  MBPR

Here on the edge of hell.  Harlem.  Langston Hughes.  PPP

Here or there, some one among the waiting tourists.  Going to Cythera.  Chris Wallace-Crabbe.  CAAP

Here she lies, a pretty bud.  Upon a Child That Died.  Robert Herrick.  InPK; SCP-1

Here sits a shepherd and a shepherdess.  The Green Shepherd.  Louis Simpson.  NoAM; PAIC

Here something stubborn comes.  Seed Leaves.  Richard Wilbur.  NCSH; PiAm

"Here the hangman stops his cart."  The Carpenter's Son.  A. E. Housman.  PBMP; SoSe; SpRo

Here the jack-hammer jabs into the ocean.  Colloquy in Black Rock.  Robert Lowell.  CAPP; NoAm; PiAm

Here. The silence echoes. Here.  In His Poems Are El Greco's Hands.  Robert Leverant.  MIT

Here the whitest birds.  Morning in Gainesville.  Karen Whitehill.  NPW

Here they are. The soft eyes open.  The Heaven of Animals.  James Dickey.  CAPP; CoPAm; HeIP; NCSH; NoAM; NOBA; TCP

Here they come back again, the harriers.  Person to Person.  Lorine Parks.  NowV

Here they lie mottled to the ground unseen.  Partidges.  John Masefield.  OxBTC

Here they went with smock and crook.  Forefathers.  Edmund Blunden.  NOBE; OxBTC

Here, though, the fine cool air.  Vincent Buckley.  Fr. Golden Builders.  CAAP

Here to the leisured side of life.  The Lamplighter.  "Seamas O'Sullivan."  BIrV

Here was raised.  The Plain of Adoration.  Unknown, tr. by John Montague.  BIrV

Here was the sound of water falling only.  The Owl.  Robert Penn Warren.  CoPAm

"Here we are at the river" I said to no one.  The Gift.  Dick Lourie.  NeAC

Here we are for the last time face to face.  L'Envoi.  William Morris.  Fr. The Earthly Paradise.  VPC

Here We Are in the Years.  Neil Young.  PoRo

Here we bring new water from the well so clear.  New Year's Water.  Unknown.  GBP; OFD; POL

Here we broached the Christmas barrel.  The House of Hospitalities.  Thomas Hardy.  NoAM

Here we go around this ring.  Marriage.  Unknown.  AmFP

Here we go round the mulberry bush.  Mother Goose.  MG

Here we go the jingo-ring.  The Merry-ma-Tanzie.  Unknown.  GBP

Here we have thirst.  An Egyptian Pulled Glass Bottle in the Shape of a Fish.  Marianne Moore.  PiAm

Here We March All Around in a Ring.  Unknown.  AmFP

Here where by all, all saints invoked are.  A Letter to the Lady Carey and Mrs. Essex Rich.  John Donne.  SCP-1

Here Where Coltrane Is.  Michael S. Harper.  PoBA

Here where Gary Cooper's figure stands.  At the Wax Museum.  Hollis Summers.  CoPAm

Here, where relumed by changing seasons, burn.  Roy Campbell.  Fr. The Golden Shower.  OxBTC

Here where the elm trees were.  Elegy.  Constance Carrier.  FAF

Here where the parrots come down.  Thomas and Charlie.  Peter Wild.  AmPA

Here, where the red man swept the leaves away.  Frederick Goddard Tuckerman.  Fr. Sonnets.  NOBA

Here where the wind is always north-north-east.  New England.  E. A. Robinson.  HeIP; NOBA; PiAm

Here, where the world is quiet.  The Garden of Proserpine.  Swinburne.  NOBE

Heredity.  Thomas Hardy.  IPWM

Herefor and therefor and therefor I cam.  This Pretty Woman.  Unknown.  OxBM

"Here's a fine bag of meat."  Bags of Meat.  Thomas Hardy.  BoAnP

Here's a health to the birds one and all!  A Health to the Birds.  Seumas MacManus.  PFIr

Here's a health to the blacksmith, the best of all fellows.  The Blacksmith's Song.  Unknown.  GBP

Here's a man knows what he's going to shoot.  Gunfighter.  Phillip Hey.  NVAP

Here's a song.  Scel Lem Duib.  Unknown, tr. by Flann O'Brien.  BIrV

Here's an old lady, almost ninety-one.  Two Old Ladies.  Siegfried Sassoon.  OxBTC

Here's Cooper, who's written six volumes to show.  Cooper.  James Russell Lowell.  Fr. A Fable for Critics.  NOBA

Here's Death.  Rhyll McMaster.  CAAP

Here's flowers for you.  Shakespeare.  Fr. The Winter's Tale, IV, iii.  GBL

Here's no more news than virtue: I may as well.  To Sir Henry Wotton.  John Donne.  PAIC

Here's the spot. Look around you. Above on the height.  Caldwell of Springfield.  Bret Harte.  BTTM

Here's the Tender Coming.  Unknown.  GBP

Here's your right ground. Wag gently o'er this black.  Emblems, I, 10.  Francis Quarles.  SCP-2

Hereto I come to view a voiceless ghost.  After a Journey.  Thomas Hardy.  GBL; OxBTC

Heritage.  Gwendolyn B. Bennett.  PoBA

Heritage.  Countee Cullen.  BPo; NoAM; PoBA; WIF

Herkens to my tale that I shall here shewe.  Marvels.  Unknown.  OxBM

Herman Melville.  Conrad Aiken.  NoAM; NOBA

Hermes of the Ways.  Hilda Doolittle ("H.D.").  WPE

Hermetic Bird.  Philip Lamantia.  VGW

Hermit, The.  Hsü Pên, tr. fr. Chinese by Henry H. Hart.  RFM

Hermit hoar, in solemn cell.  Imitation of the Style of * * * *.  Samuel Johnson.  FaBoCo

Hermit Picks Berries, The.  Maxine W. Kumin.  RFM

Hermit's Song, A.  Unknown, tr. fr. Irish by James Simmons.  BIrV

Hero.  Ronald Gross.  SPo

Hero, The.  Marianne Moore.  Fr. Part of a Novel, Part of a Poem, Part of a Play.  NOBA

Hero and Leander.   Christopher Marlowe, (First *and* Second Sestiads), *completed by* George Chapman.  AAS
*Sels.*
Amorous Neptune.  Marlowe.  NOBE
Bridal Song, *fr.* Fifth Sestiad.  Chapman.  NOBE
Hero Feels the Shaft of Love.  Marlowe.  GBL
Love at First Sight, *fr.* First Sestiad.  Marlowe.  NOBE
Hero and the Hydra, The, *sel.*  James McAuley.
Tomb of Heracles, The.  MAuV
Hero Feels the Shaft of Love.  Christopher Marlowe.  *Fr.* Hero and Leander.  GBL
Heroes.  Robert Creeley.  NOBA; PPP
Heroes paused upon the plain, The.  The Byrnies.  Thom Gunn.  NoAM; OxBTC
Heroes screamed from my fingertips.  Bard.  Gavin Bantock.  TwMBP
Heroic good, target for which the young.  Faint Yet Pursuing.  Coventry Patmore.  *Fr.* The Unknown Eros.  PFD
Heron, The.  Philip Murray.  BoAnP
Heron.  Stanley Plumly.  AmPA
Heron, The.  Theodore Roethke.  BoAnP; RFM
Heron flew east, the heron flew west, The.  The Corpus Christi Carol.  *Unknown.*  GBP
Heron stands in water where the swamp, The.  The Heron.  Theodore Roethke.  BoAnP; RFM
Herr Privatdozent, it is not my way.  1907, A Proposal from Paris.  Richard Howard.  CAAP
Herrick's Julia.  Helen Bevington.  SpRo
Herring Is King.  Alfred Perceval Graves.  PFIr
Hervordshir, shild and spere.  The Shires.  *Unknown.*  OxBM
He's dead/ the dog won't have to.  Death.  William Carlos Williams.  VGW
He's Doing Natural Life.  Conyus.  PoBA
He's gone, and Fate admits of no return.  Epitaph on the Secretary to the Muses.  Jane Barker.  FaBoCo
He's Got the Whole World in His Hands, *with music.*  *Unknown.*  BLSo
He's Known His Lesson for Years.  R. P. Kingston.  NVAP
He's no Apollo Belvedere.  Babe Ruth.  Damon Runyon.  SPo
He's nothing much but fur.  A Kitten.  Eleanor Farjeon.  RAE
Hesitant door chain, The.  Into Blackness Softly.  Mari Evans.  PoBA
Hesperus, *sel.*  James Stephens.
"Evening gathers everything."  LCL
Hev ye seen owt o' maw bonnie lad.  Maw Bonnie Lad.  *Unknown.*  GBP
Hexameters.  Samuel Taylor Coleridge.  MBPR
Hexametra Alexis in Laudem Rosamundi.  Robert Greene.  *Fr.* Greene's Mourning Garment.  GBL
Hey, boys, joint ahead.  Track-lining Song.  *Unknown.*  AmFP
Hey brassy baby whose switched-on hair.  The Earth: To Marilyn.  Judith Johnson Sherwin.  WBN
Hey, Bungalow Bill.  The Continuing Story of Bungalow Bill.  John Lennon *and* Paul McCartney.  GrRo
Hey daddy/ hey daddy/ don't let me cry in vain.  Oh Ambulance Man.  *Unknown.*  BluL
Hey! diddle, diddle,/ The cat and the fiddle.  Mother Goose.  MG
Hey diddle dinketty, poppetty pet.  The Merchants of London.  *Unknown.*  GBP
Hey for a Lass wi' a Tocher.  Burns.  SLP
Hey! hey! by this day!  The Unhappy Schoolboy.  *Unknown.*  OxBChV
Hey, hey, hey, hey/ I will have the whetstone.  I Will Have the Whetstone.  *Unknown.*  GBP
Hey-ho Knave: A Catch.  *Unknown.*  GBP

Hey, how!/ Sely men, God helpe you!  An Old Man and His Wife.  *Unknown.*  OxBM
Hey, mama/ Tell me what have I.  Awful Fix.  *Unknown.*  BluL
Hey Mom!  Assignment.  Grace Butcher.  RiTi
Hey Nellie.  Smokey's Gettin' Old.  Jessica Tarahata Hagedorn.  MMD
Hey, this little kid gets roller skates.  74th Street.  Myra Cohn Livingston.  CTBA
Hiawatha and Mudjekeewis.  Longfellow.  The Song of Hiawatha, IV.  AKE
Hiawatha's Photographing.  "Lewis Carroll."  FaBoCo; SpRo
Hibernating in an Old Lost Neighbourhood.  Laura Chester.  RiTi
Hibiscus on the Sleeping Shores.  Wallace Stevens.  InPS
Hickety, Pickety,/ My black hen.  Mother Goose.  MG
Hickety pickety i sillickety.  *Unknown.*  GBP
Hickory, dickory, dock.  Mother Goose.  MG
Hide, Absalon, thy gilte tresses clear.  Balade.  Chaucer.  *Fr.* The Legend of Good Women: Prologue.  GBL; NOBE; OxBM
Hide and Seek.  Vernon Scannell.  LP
Hide Thou Me.  *Unknown.*  AmFP
Hiding in the church of an abandoned stone.  Confession to J. Edgar Hoover.  James Wright.  CAPP; ConAP
Hie upon Hielands [*or* High up on highland].  Bonnie [*or* Bonny] George Campbell.  *Unknown.*  AIW; AmFP; GBP; PeBB
Hierusalem, My Happy Home.  *Unknown.*  BoReV; NOBE
Higgledy-piggledy.  Twilight's Last Gleaming.  Arthur W. Monks.  OFD
High Are the Winter Rivers.  Dave Smith.  HeS
High Chair and Low Spirits.  Richard Armour.  BBGO
High ding a ding, and ho ding a ding.  The Parliament Soldiers.  *Unknown.*  GBP
High Frequency.  Marge Piercy.  MMD
High in front advanc'd/ The brandisht sword of God before them blaz'd.  Conclusion.  Milton.  *Fr.* Paradise Lost, XIII.  OBP
High in the breathless hall the minstrel sate.  Song at the Feast of Brougham Castle.  Wordsworth.  MBPR
High in the jacaranda shines the gilded thread.  The 90th Year.  Denise Levertov.  FiCP
High in the pine, the soft winds sough.  The Pine Assessor.  Prentice Baker.  AATT
High is our calling, friend!—creative art.  To B. R. Haydon.  Wordsworth.  MBPR
High Jump, The.  *Unknown.*  SPo
High-cool/ 2.  James Cunningham.  JB
High on a ridge of tiles.  Poem.  Maurice James Craig.  BoAnP
High on a slope in New Guinea.  The Man in the Dead Machine.  Donald Hall.  CoPAm
High on his stockroom ladder like a dunce.  Playboy.  Richard Wilbur.  NoAM; NOBA
High on the thrilling strand he dances.  Tightrope Walker.  Vernon Scannell.  NCSH
High overhead.  Looking Up at Airplanes, Always.  Rolfe Humphries.  PAIC
High Price Blues.  *Unknown.*  BluL
High-riding kites appear to range quite freely.  Gravities.  Seamus Heaney.  NoAM
High School Band, The.  Reed Whittemore.  MiP; NCSH
High sheriff been here, The.  Big Rock Jail.  *Unknown.*  BluL
High Sheriff Blues.  *Unknown.*  BluL
High spirited friend.  An Ode.  Ben Jonson.  PAIC
High Summer on the Mountain.  Idris Davies.  OxBTC
High summer's sheen upon all things.  The Web.  Theodore Weiss.  NoAM

High Tension Wires. Allan Block. FAF
High-Toned Old Christian Woman, A. Wallace Stevens. NoAM; NOBA; PAIC; PiAm; PPP; SoSe
High up on highland. *See* Hie upon Hielands.
High walls...of stones. Aran Islands. Irving Layton. NeAC
High Water Everywhere: 1 ("The back water done rose around Sumner, now"). *Unknown.* BluL
High Water Everywhere: 2 ("Back water at Blytheville"). *Unknown.* BluL
Higher ("The shadows of night were a-comin' down swift"). *Unknown.* SpRo
Higher Pantheism, The. Tennyson. PAIC; SpRo
Higher Pantheism in a Nutshell, The, *parody.* Swinburne. *Fr.* The Heptalogia. PAIC; SpRo
Higher than gull's nest, higher than children go. Rock Climbing. Jane Cooper. NMM
Higher than the handsomest hotel. The Building. Philip Larkin. PSN
Highest things are easiest to be shown, The. Thomas Traherne. *Fr.* The Demonstration. SCP-2
Highmindedness, a jealousy for good. Addressed to Haydon. Keats. MBPR
Highway Blues. *Unknown.* BluL
Highway of blood/ volkswagens crushed up. Megalopolis. Victor Hernández Cruz. SA
Highway 101, Seal Beach. Curtis Zahn. NowV
Highway Patrol Stops Me, Going Too Slow. Robert Peterson. NeAC
Highwayman's Ghost, The. Richard Garnett. PoTa
Hiking. Joseph Bruchac. CDW
Hilda Lay in Hospital. Judith McCombs. WBN
Hilda's Pelt. Judith McCombs. WBN
Hill, The. Rupert Brooke. OxBTC
Hill, The. Robert Creeley. ConAP; NoAM
Hill, The. Edgar Lee Masters. *Fr.* Spoon River Anthology. NoAM; NOBA
Hill Farmer Speaks, The. R. S. Thomas. MPo
Hill flank overlooking the Axe valley, A. Watching Post. C. Day Lewis. MPo
Hill of the Graces, The. Spenser. *Fr.* The Faerie Queene, VI, 10. NOBE
Hill of Zion yields, The. Mount Zion. *Unknown.* AmFP
Hill was higher every year, The. Model T. Adrien Stoutenburg. CTBA
HIll Wife, The, *sels.* Robert Frost.
   Impulse, The. AIW; NoAM
   "One ought not to have to care." VGW
Hillcrest. E. A. Robinson. PPoe
Hills, The. Rachel Field. LCL
Hills moved. I watched their shadows. Beetle on the Shasta Daylight. Shirley Kaufman. WPE
Hills step off into whiteness, The. Sheep in Fog. Sylvia Plath. PSN
Hills where I grew up had learned to hide, The. The Hughesville Scythe. Henry Taylor. PPoD
Himself is all he'll talk about to you. The Egotist. H. A. C. Evans. POL
Hind and the Panther, The, *sel.* Dryden.
   Revelation, *fr.* I. BoReV
   (Confessio Fidei.) NOBE
Hind Etin. *Unknown.* PeBB
Hind Horn. *Unknown.* AmFP
Hinx! minx!/ The old witch winks! Children's Runes and Omens. *Unknown.* MAT
Hip Shakin' Strut. *Unknown.* BluL
Hippo, The. Theodore Roethke. VGW

Hippolytus Temporizes. Hilda Doolittle ("H.D."). SBG
Hippopotamus, The. Hilaire Belloc. InPK
Hippopotamus, The. T. S. Eliot. AnMo; BoReV; VGW
Hippopotamus is strong, The. Habits of the Hippopotamus. Arthur Guiterman. BoAnP
Hips and ass go to an' fro on this good good earth. All Owners of Meat Are Hospitable. Rochelle Owens. WBN
"Hiram, I think the sump is backing up." Mending Sump. Kenneth Koch. InPK; NoAM
Hiram Powers' "Greek Slave." Elizabeth Barrett Browning. SBG
Hiroshima, *sel.* Gavin Bantock.
   "There were many of us at the time." TwMBP
His aging widow dreams of youth. Memorial Service. Ursula Vaughan Williams. POL
His art is eccentricity, his aim. Pitcher. Robert Francis. SPo; WIF
His Body. Sandra McPherson. AmPA; CAAP
His brother after dinner. Uncle Bull-Boy. June Jordan. PoBA
His Coming. Irene Dayton. AATT
His compassionate face, slightly wan. On the Street. C. P. Cavafy, *tr. by* Rae Dalven. BoLoP
His daughter Charlotte said to Mr. Brontë. Sampler from Haworth. Frances Minturn Howard. WPE
His desires, growing. Black Man's Feast. Sarah Webster Fabio. PoBA
His drifter swung in the night. Uncle Roderick. Norman McCaig. MPo
His Elegy. Chidiock Tichborne. *See* Elegy: "My prime of youth is but a frost of cares."
His eyes locked in a stare. Griffin. Richard Mathews. AATT
His father gave him a box of truisms. The Truisms. Louis MacNeice. NOBE
His father said that he had grown. All the Dead Birds. Melvin Walker LaFollette. SFF
His finger resembled. The Accident. Len Gasparini. NeAC
His flesh/ fish underwater. The Death of the Epileptic Poet Yesenin. Aram Boyajian. NeAC
His frailty discrete, the rodent turns, looks. Buteo Regalis. N. Scott. Momaday. VW
His friends drudged in an airplane factory. Icarus. Irving Layton. BBGO
His Golden Locks Time Hath to Silver Turned. George Peele. *Fr.* Polyhymnia. HeIP; PPoe
   (Farewell to Arms.) NOBE
   (Sonnet, A: "His golden locks time hath to silver turned.") InPS
His Grace! impossible! what dead! A Satirical Elegy on the Death of a Late Famous General. Swift. ESaP; PAIC; PBMP; SS
His great bald head, trembling weightiness. Stone Age. Floyd C. Stuart. FAF
His hair was yellow and long. A Tale of Last Stands. Fred Red Cloud. VW
His headstone said. The Funeral of Martin Luther King, Jr. Nikki Giovanni. BPo
His high-boned, young face is so brown. White Pass Ski Patrol. John Logan. CAPP
His job was. Branches Back Into. Ken Belford. NeAC
His last days linger in that low attic. The Old Jockey. F. R Higgins. OxBTC
His Late Wife's Wedding-Ring. George Crabbe. *See* Marriage Ring, A.
His Litany to the Holy Spirit. Robert Herrick. BoReV
His lordship's steed. Riding. William Allingham. OxBChV
His mother's eyes. Copy. Richard Armour. BBGO
His name is/ Rubin. Rubin. Charles Cooper. PoBA

His paper propped against the electric toaster.  Daniel at Breakfast.  Phyllis McGinley.  BBGO

His peasant parents killed themselves with toil.  The Average.  W. H. Auden.  BBGO

His Prayer for Absolution.  Robert Herrick.  SCP-1

His pride/ Had cast him out from Heaven, with all his host.  Milton.  *Fr. Paradise Lost, I.*  PPoe

His Remedie for Love.  Michael Drayton.  *Fr. Idea.*  AAS

His Request.  Owen Roe O'Sullivan, *tr. fr. Irish by* Joan Keefe.  BIrV

His sad brown bulk rears patient as the hills.  A Bull.  Babette Deutsch.  BoAnP

His self-conceit's so swollen by inflation.  Positive, a Coxcomb.  William Plomer.  POL

His spirit in smoke ascended to high heaven.  The Lynching.  Claude McKay.  PoBA; WIF

His spirit went into the television.  When Daddy Died.  Duane Ackerson.  POL

His sullen kinsmen, by the winter sea.  Santa Claus.  Dom Moraes.  NoAM

His Sweetheart Slain.  *Unknown.*  OxBM

His Third Decade.  Dabney Stuart.  NVAP

His tundra'd mind sprouts leaflets.  Senile.  Pat Folk.  NowV

His wet fur, velvet-smooth, was sleek as reeds.  Otters.  William Hart-Smith.  BoAnP

Hist Whist.  E. E. Cummings.  OFD; RAE

Historian, The.  Christopher Middleton.  TwMBP

Historical Society Exhibit: Old Programme.  Felix Pollak.  HeS

History.  Robert Penn Warren.  NoAM

History and Abstraction.  Thomas Lux.  AmPA

History Lesson, A.  Miroslav Holub, *tr. fr. Czech by* Ian Milner *and* George Theiner.  BuTh

History Lesson for My Son.  Ted Kooser.  POL

History of a Literary Movement.  Howard Nemerov.  PSN

History of blacklife is put down in the motions, The.  The Sound of Afroamerican History Chapt I.  S. E. Anderson.  PoBA

History of Love, A.  William Carlos Williams.  VGW

History of My Feeling, The.  Kathleen Fraser.  WBN (Love Poem.)  RiTi

History of Samson, The, *sel.*  Francis Quarles.  "When lusty diet and the frolic cup."  SCP-2

History of the Father, A.  Charles Buckmaster.  CAAP

History of the Flood, The.  John Heath-Stubbs.  OxBTC

History of the Opera, A.  Sandra Hochman.  RiTi

History she (Zelda) said stops here.  Inside History.  Angela McCabe.  AmPA

Hit a huge drive.  Hero.  Ronald Gross.  SPo

Hit it on the rock.  Test.  Jonathan Price.  CoPAm

Hit me! Jab me!  Third Degree.  Langston Hughes.  BPo; BuTh

Hit wes upon a Scere-thorsday that ure loverd aros.  Judas.  *Unknown.*  Epi

Hitch Haiku, *sels.*  Gary Snyder.  InPK
"After weeks of watching the roof leak."
"Drinking hot saké."
"Great freight truck, A."
"Over the Mindanao Deep."
"They didn't hire him."

Hither thou com'st. The busy wind all night.  The Bird.  Henry Vaughan.  SCP-1

Hits and Runs.  Carl Sandburg.  SPo

Hitting Fungoes.  Michael Ryan.  HeS

Ho, Androcles!  One Lion, Once.  Robert Canzoneri.  CoPAm

Ho! brother Teague, dost hear the decree.  Lilli Burlero.  *Unknown.*  RDB

Ho, Brother Teig.  *Unknown.*  GBP

Ho! cupid calls, come, lovers, come.  Cupid's Call.  James Shirley.  SCP-2

Ho! in the dawn.  Side by Side.  Adrienne Rich.  CoPAm

Ho! Westward Ho! *with music.*  Ossian E. Dodge.  BLSo

Ho! who comes here along with bagpipe and drumming?  The Morris Dance.  *Unknown.*  RAE

Hobbes, 1651.  John Hollander.  NoAM

Hobthrush, The.  *Unknown.*  GBP

Hock-Cart, or Harvest Home, The.  Robert Herrick.  Epi; SCP-1

Hoeing.  John Updike.  TSWA

Hoelderlin's Old Age.  Stephen Spender.  NoAM

Hog Butcher for the World.  Chicago.  Carl Sandburg.  IPWM; NoAM; NOBA; PiAm; VGW

Hog Drovers.  *Unknown.*  AmFP

Hogan.  Archie Washburn.  VW

Hogyn.  *Unknown.*  GBP

Hohenlinden.  Thomas Campbell.  NOBE
(Battle of Hohenlinden, The.)  BTTM

Hoise up the sail, cried they who understand.  A Sea-Voyage from Tenby to Bristol.  Katherine Philips.  SBG; WPE

Hokku Poems.  Richard Wright.  PoBA

Hold a glass of pure water to the eye of the sun.  Robin Fulton.  *Fr.* Hung Red.  MIS

"Hold Back the Edges of Your Gowns, Ladies, We Are Going through Hell."  Cathleen Quirk.  MMD

Hold the Wind.  *Unknown.*  GBP

Holdfast, The.  George Herbert.  Epi

Holding black whips.  Thoughts of Chairman Mao.  David Young.  AmPA; CAAP

Holding Pattern.  Sandra McPherson.  RiTi

Holding the Sky.  William Stafford.  RFM

Hole in the Floor, A.  Richard Wilbur.  NoAM; NOBA

Holes in my arms.  For Real.  Jayne Cortez.  PoBA

Holiday.  Alan Dugan.  CoPAm

Hollin, Green Hollin.  *Unknown.*  GBP

Hollo, My Fancy!  *Unknown.*  SCP-2

Hollow-feeling, empty of sleep and as yet unbreakfasted.  Morning.  Harry Fainlight.  POL

Hollow Men, The.  T. S. Eliot.  AnMo; InPS; PBMP; TCP

Hollow sea-shell which for years hath stood, The.  Sea-Shell Murmurs.  Eugene Lee-Hamilton.  SoSe

Hollow Thesaurus, The.  Roger McDonald.  CAAP

Hollow Wood, The.  Edward Thomas.  RAE

Holly and His Merry Men.  *Unknown.*  OxBM

Holly and Ivy ("Holver and Hivy made a gret party").  *Unknown.*  OxBM

Holly and the Ivy, The ("The holly and the ivy,/ When they are both full grown").  *Unknown.*  GBP; OFD

Holmes.  James Russell Lowell.  *Fr.* A Fable for Critics.  NOBA

Holstein cows parked.  Black and White.  Tom Schmidt.  NeAC

Holver and Hivy made a gret party.  Holly and Ivy.  *Unknown.*  OxBM

Holy Baptism ("Since, Lord, to thee/ A narrow way and little gate").  George Herbert.  SCP-1

Holy City.  Anne Waldman.  RiTi

Holy Eye is Blind, The.  Stephen Stepanchev.  SA

Holy Fair, The.  Burns.  LAuP

Holy, Holy, Holy! *with music.*  Reginald Heber.  BLSH

Holy! Holy! Holy! Holy! Holy! Holy!  Footnote to Howl.  Allen Ginsberg.  CAPP

Holy Innocents, The.  Robert Lowell.  ConAP; NowV

Holy Light.  Milton.  *Fr.* Paradise Lost, III.  NOBE
(Poet's Blindness, The.)  OBP

Holy Office, The.  James Joyce.  NoAM; OxBTC

Holy Scriptures, The, I.  George Herbert.  Epi

"Holy Socrates, why always with deference." Socrates and
    Alcibiades. Friedrich Hölderlin, *tr.* by Michael Hamburger.
    LoAs
Holy Sonnets, *sels.*    John Donne.
    "At the round earth's imagined [*or* imagin'd] corners, blow,"
        VII.    BoReV; Epi; HeIP; InPS; NOBE; OBP; PAIC; PPoe;
        PPP; SCP-1
    "Batter my heart, three-personed [*or* person'd] God; for you,"
        XIV.    AnMo; BoReV; Epi; HeIP; InPK; InPS; IPWM;
        MetP; NOBE; OBP; PPod; PPoe; PPP; SCP-1; WIF
    "Death, be not proud, though some have called thee," X.
        AnMo; BoReV; Epi; HeIP; MetP; NOBE; OBP; PAIC;
        PBMP; PPoe; PPP; SCP-1; VoPo
    "If poisonous minerals, and if that tree," IX.    Epi; PPP
    "O, to vex me contraries meet in one," XIX.    BoReV
    "Show me, dear Christ, thy spouse, so bright and clear," XVIII.
        SCP-1
    "Since she whom I loved hath paid her last debt," XVII.    SCP-
        1
    "Thou hast made me, and shall thy work decay?" I.    BoReV;
        NOBE
    "What if this present were the world's last night?" XIII.
        BoReV; HeIP; InPS
Holy Thursday ("Is this a holy thing to see").    Blake.    *Fr.* Songs
    of Experience.    InPS; LAuP; MBPR
Holy Thursday ("'Twas on a Holy Thursday").    Blake.    *Fr.*
    Songs of Innocence.    BoReV; InPS; LAuP; MBPR; NOBE;
    OFD
Holy Well, The.    *Unknown.*    GBP; PeBB
Holy Willie's Prayer.    Burns.    BoReV; ESaP; InPS; LAuP; OBP;
    PPP
    (Prayer of Holy Willie, The.)    Epi
Holyhead, Sept. 25th, 1727.    Swift.    BIrV
Homage and Lament for Ezra Pound in Captivity.    Robert
    Duncan.    NOBA
Homage to Chagall.    Duane Niatum.    CDW
Homage to Chagall.    Kathleen Teague.    MIT
Homage to Hieronymus Bosch.    Thomas MacGreevy.    BIrV
Homage to Mistress Bradstreet, *sels.*    John Berryman.
    "Governor your husband lived so long, The."    NoAM; NOBA
    "I trundle the bodies, on the iron bars."    NOBA
    "O all your ages at the mercy of my loves."    NOBA
    "Winters close, Springs open, no child stirs, The."    NoAM
Homage to Sextus Propertius, *sels.*    Ezra Pound.
    "Me happy, night, night full of brightness."    VGW
    (Elegy VII: "Me happy, night, night full of brightness.")
        PAIC
    Now if ever it is time to cleanse Helicon."    Epi; VGW
    "Shades of Callimachus, Coan ghosts of Philetas."    NoAM;
        NOBA
    "When, when, and whenever death closes our eyelids."    NoAM
    "Who, who will be the next man to entrust his girl to a friend?"
        NoAM
Homage to the Empress of the Blues.    Robert Hayden.    CoPAm;
    PoBA
Home, The.    Susan Axelrod.    NMM
Home ("Home's home, although it reachèd be").    Joseph
    Beaumont.    SCP-2
Home.    John Blight.    CAAP
Home after Three Months Away.    Robert Lowell.    PBMP; PSN;
    RRA
Home at Grasmere.    Wordsworth.    *See* Recluse, The.
Home Burial.    Robert Frost.    PiAm
Home for Thanksgiving.    W. S. Merwin.    NoAM
Home is mysterious: a place to die, a place to breed.
    Destinations.    Josephine Jacobsen.    WPE
Home Is So Sad.    Philip Larkin.    PSN
Home late, one lamp turned low.    At Our House.    William
    Stafford.    Epi

Home on the Range, *with music.*    *Unknown.*    BLSH; BLSo
Home on the Range, February 1962.    Edward Dorn.ConAP
Home, Sweet Home, *with music.*    John Howard Payne.    *Fr.* Clari,
    The Maid of Milan.    BLSH; BLSo; PSoN
Home Thoughts from Abroad.    Robert Browning.    HeIP;
    IPWM; NOBE; OBP; PBMP; VoPo
Home Thoughts from the Sea.    Robert Browning.    NOBE; OBP
Home Town.    W. D. Snodgrass.    NowV
Homecoming, The.    James B. Allen.    HeS
Homecoming.    Dan Gerber.    HeS
Homecoming.    Sonia Sanchez.    PoBA
Homecoming.    John Thompson.    MAT
Homecoming Singer, The.    Jay Wright.    PoBA
Homeless Blues.    *Unknown.*    BluL
Homeowners unite.    The Firebombing.    James Dickey.    CAPP
Homer was poor. His scholars live at ease.    Epigram.    J. V.
    Cunningham.    VGW
Homeric Hexameter Described and Exemplified, The.    Schiller, *tr.*
    *fr. German by* Samuel Taylor Coleridge.    MBPR
Home's home, although it reachèd be.    Home.    Joseph
    Beaumont.    SCP-2
Homes of England, The.    Felicia Dorothea Hemans.    SBG; WPE
Homework for Annabelle.    Phyllis McGinley.    BBGO
Homily: Contemporary.    Marian Frances Brand.    AATT
Homo Sapiens.    Earl of Rochester.    *Fr.* A Satire against
    Mankind.    NOBE
    ("Were I who to my cost already am.")    SCP-2
Homosexuality.    Frank O'Hara.    CoPAm
Honeeeeeeeey, I'm all out and down.    All Out and Down.
    *Unknown.*    BluL
Honey/ When de man.    Sister Lou.    Sterling A. Brown.    PoBA
Honey Bee, The.    Don Marquis.    BoAnP
Honey from silk-worms who can gather.    Lines to a Critic.
    Shelley.    MBPR
Honey from the white rose, honey from the red.    Sing a Song of
    Honey.    Barbara Euphan Todd.    FSFS
Honey-hued beauty, you are.    Black Lady in an Afro Hairdo
    Cheers for Cassius.    R. Ernest Holmes.    PPoD
Honey people murder mercy U.S.A.    In Memoriam: Martin
    Luther King, Jr.    June Jordan.    PoBA
Honey, you been gone all day that you may make whoopee all
    night.    Whoopee Blues.    *Unknown.*    BluL
Honeyflowing moon is on every madman's tongue, The.
    Moonlight.    Guillaume Apollinaire, *tr. by* William Meredith.
    Moon
Honeystain/ the rhetoricians of blackness.    The Anti-Semanticist.
    Everett Hoagland.    BPo
Honeysuckle, nightshade.    Poem for L. C.    Peter Klappert.
    AmPA
Honky.    Charles Cooper.    PoBA
Honour ("Ambitious sir, take heed!").    Joseph Beaumont.    SCP-2
Honour.    Abraham Cowley.    BoLoP
Honour is so sublime perfection.    To the Countess of Bedford.
    John Donne.    SCP-1
Honour thy parents; but good manners call.    God to Be First
    Served.    Robert Herrick.    OxBChV
Honourable Entertainment Given to the Queen's Majesty in
    Progress at Elvetham, The, 1591, *sel.*    Nicholas Breton.
    Ploughman's Song, The.    NOBE
Honorable Mention.    Rebecca Stutsman.    SPo
Honored Dead, The.    Thomas Doulis.    NowV
Hoo, Suffolk.    *Unknown.*    GBP
Hoochie Coochie.    *Unknown.*    BluL
Hood.    C. K. Williams.    InPK
Hook.    Erica Jong.    RiTi

Hooked for two years now on wrinkle creams.   Aging.   Erica Jong.   Psy; WBN

Hop hop, thump thump.   Stevie Smith.   *Fr.* The Dedicated Dancing Bull and the Water Maid.   WPE

Hop-poles stand in cones, The.   The Midnight Skaters.   Edmund Blunden.   NOBE; PSN

Hope.   William Dickey.   POL

Hope and Joy.   Christina Rossetti.   OxBChV

Hope for Those Separated by War, A.   Sidney Keyes.   BuTh

Hope I dreamed of was a dream, The.   Mirage.   Christina Rossetti.   BoLoP

Hope is a strange invention.   Emily Dickinson.   WIF

Hope is a subtle glutton.   Emily Dickinson.   WIF

Hope is like a harebell trembling from its birth.   Comparisons.   Christina Rossetti.   OxBChV

"Hope" is the thing with feathers.   Emily Dickinson.   NOBA; SBG; WIF

Hope, whose weak being ruined is.   On Hope by Way of Question and Answer between Abraham Cowley and Richard Crashaw.   Abraham Cowley *and* Richard Crashaw.   NOBE

Hopi Woman Talking, A.   Joy Harjo.   SA

Hopping frog, hop here and be seen.   The Frog and the Toad.   Christina Rossetti.   RAE

Hoppy.   Edwin S. Godsey.   PPoD

Hops.   Boris Pasternak, *tr. fr. Russian by* Jon Stallworthy *and* Peter France.   BoLoP

Hopscotch/ Through patches.   Mercedes.   Barbara Howes.   CoPAm; RiTi

Hop't She.   *Unknown.*   GBP

Horae Canonica, *sel.*   W. H. Auden.   Sext.   TCP

Horatian Ode upon Cromwell's Return from Ireland, An.   Andrew Marvell.   Epi; InPS; NOBE; OBP; PAIC

Horatio, of ideal courage vain.   Feigned Courage.   Charles *and* Mary Lamb.   OxBChV

Horatius.   Macaulay..   *Fr.* Lays of Ancient Rome.   BTTM

Horizon of Holland, The.   Ian Hamilton Finlay.   InPK

Horizontal in a deckchair on the bleak ward [*or* Horizontal on a deckchair in the Ward].   Ezra Pound.   Robert Lowell.   NoAM; NOBA

Horrible crime was committed, A.   Pearl Bryan.   *Unknown.*   AmFP

Horror Comic.   Robert Conquest.   OxBTC

Horror Movie.   Howard Moss.   MiP

Horrors, The.   Ogden Nash.   SFF

Horse, The.   A. E. Coppard.   BoAnP

Horse.   Jim Harrison.   BoAnP

Horse, The.   Naomi Royde Smith.   FaBoCo

Horse and hattock.   Witch's Broomstick Spell.   *Unknown.*   GBP

Horse and the Mule, The.   John Huddlestone Wynne.   OxBChV

Horse Chestnut Tree, The.   Richard Eberhart.   BBGO

Horse in the Drugstore, The.   Tess Gallagher.   AmPA

Horse Show, The.   William Carlos Williams.   NOBA; VGW

Horse Trader's Song, The.   *Unknown.*   AmFP

Horseplay by Reverse Descartes.   Merle Meeter.   AATT

Horses, The.   Ted Hughes.   NoAM

Horses.   Kipling.   BoAnP; POL

Horses, The ("Barely a twelvemonth after").   Edwin Muir.   NoAM; NOBE; OxBTC; PPoe; SoSe; TCP

Horses.   Dorothy Wellesley.   OxBTC

Horses Aboard ("Horses in horsecloths stand in a row").   Thomas Hardy.   BoAnP

Horses move sideways to start.   Here in Polynia.   Tom Raworth.   TwMBP

Horses of the sea, The.   Christina Rossetti.   LCL

Horsey Gap.   *Unknown.*   GBP

Hose and Iron.   Greg Kuzma.   MAT; NVAP

Hospital, The.   Patrick Kavanagh.   BIrV

Hospital.   Karl Shapiro.   VGW

Hospital for Defectives.   Thomas Blackburn.   OxBTC

Hospital/ Poem.   Sonia Sanchez.   BPo; PoBA

Hospital smell, The.   Visiting Hour.   Norman MacCaig.   LP

Hospital Window, The.   James Dickey.   HeIP

Hospitality.   John Banister Tabb.   ECBV

Hosting of the Sidhe, The ("The host is riding from Knocknarea").   W. B. Yeats.   NoAM

Hot Afternoons Have Been in West 15th Street.   Paul Blackburn.   VGW

Hot cross buns!   Mother Goose.   MG

Hot Day at the Races.   Tom Raworth.   TwMBP

Hot days/ the farm does not.   Memory of Kuhre.   Wesley McNair.   FAF

Hot in June a narrow winged.   A Nameless One.   Margaret Avison.   HeIP

Hot midsummer night on Water Street, A.   Hot Night on Water Street.   Louis Simpson.   NowV; SFF

"Hot night makes us keep our bedroom windows open, The."   "To Speak of Woe That Is in Marriage."   Robert Lowell.   CAPP; NoAM

Hot Night on Water Street.   Louis Simpson.   NowV; SFF

Hot sun, cool fire, tempered with sweet air.   Bethsabe's Song.   George Peele.   *Fr.* David and Bethsabe.   GBL; NOBE

Hot Time in the Old Town, A, *with music.*   Joe Hayden.   FSN (There'll Be a Hot Time.)   BLSo

Hotel Paradiso e Commerciale.   John Malcolm Brinnin.   NoAM

Hottest Brand Goin'.   *Unknown.*   BluL

Hound, The.   Robert Francis.   SoSe

Hound bays in the blood again, A.   Flight.   Mary Shumway.   HeS

Hound twitches, A.   Eve of July Fourth.   James Bertolino.   HeS

Hour at last come round, The.   The Dying Gaul.   Desmond O'Grady.   BIrV

Hour-glass whispers to the lion's roar, The.   Our Bias.   W. H. Auden.   NoAM

Hour of Feeling, The.   Louis Simpson.   FiCP

Hour of the Parting, The.   John Shaw Neilson.   MAuV

Hour with Thee, An.   Sir Walter Scott.   BoLoP

Hours, The.   Calvin Forbes.   CoPAm

Hours after fate had brot us 2gether in.   She Employed the Familiar "Tu" Form.   Doug Fetherling.   NeAC

Hours before dawn we were woken by the quake.   Aubade.   William Empson.   OxBTC; PAIC

Hours I spent with thee, dear heart, The.   The Rosary.   Robert Cameron Rogers.   BLSH; BLSo; FSN

House, The.   William Carlos Williams.   VGW

House Beautiful, The.   Robert Louis Stevenson.   NOBE

House Carpenter, The.   *Unknown.*   *See* Demon Lover, The.

House catch on fire and ain't no water 'round.   Southern Blues.   *Unknown.*   BluL

House Guest.   Elizabeth Bishop.   CoPAm; NCSH

House Guest, The.   Laura Chester.   RiTi

House had gone to bring again, The.   The Need of Being Versed in Country Things.   Robert Frost.   NoAM; NOBA; PiAm

House in Chicago, The.   Marcia Lee Masters.   HeS

House is crammed, The: tier beyond tier they grin.   "Blighters."   Siegfried Sassoon.   NoAM

House is filled, The. The last heartthrob.   Near the Ocean.   Robert Lowell.   NOBA

House o' the Mirror, The.   Helen Adam.   MAT; NMM

House of Fame, The, *sels.*   Chaucer.   OxBM
   Eagle Converses with Chaucer, The.
   Jove's Eagle Carries Chaucer into Space.

House of Hospitalities, The.   Thomas Hardy.   NoAM

House of Life, The, *sels.*   Dante Gabriel Rossetti.
  Autumn Idleness, LXIX.   GBL
  Barren Spring, LXXXIII.   VPC
  Dark Glass, The, XXXIV.   VPC
  Heart's Compass, XXVII.   PAIC
  Severed Selves, XL.   BoLoP; VPC
  Silent Noon, XIX   OBP
  Sonnet, The ("A sonnet is a moment's monument"), *introd.*
    HeIP; PAIC; SoSe
  Superscription, A, XCVII.   VPC
  Without Her, LIII.   GBL

House on the Hill, The.   E. A. Robinson.   AmVN; TH; VoPo

House That Jack Built, The.   Samuel Taylor Coleridge.   *See* On
  a Ruined House in a Romantic Country.
SpRo

House-Top, The.   Herman Melville.   AmVN; NOBA; Prf

House Was Quiet and the World Was Calm, The.   Wallace
  Stevens.   VGW

House was shaken by a rising wind, The.   Brainstorm.   Howard
  Nemerov.   NCSH; NoAM

House where every, A.   Louis Zukofsky.   *Fr.* Light.   NoAM

House You Looked For, The.   William Pitt Root.   NVAP

Housed in each other's arms.   Song for a Marriage.   Vassar
  Miller.   PAIC

Houses, The.   Eden Phillpotts.   OxBTC

Houses are haunted, The.   Disillusionment of Ten O'Clock.
  Wallace Stevens.   InPK; InPS; PPoD; PPoe; SFF

Housewife.   Josephine Miles.   RiTi

Housewife.   Susan Fromberg Schaeffer.   IHMS; WBN

Housewife.   Anne Sexton.   NMM; Psy

Housewife's Lament, The.   *Unknown.*   MAT

Housewife's Letter: to Mary.   Anne Halley.   NMM

Housing Shortage.   Naomi Replansky.   NMM

Hovering and huge, dark, formless sway, The.   The Virgin Mary.
  Edgar Bowers.   PiAm

How/ Then,/ Distinguish.   Query.   Mildred Weston.   POL

How a Good Greyhound Is Shaped.   *Unknown.*   BoAnP

How Annandale Went Out.   E. A. Robinson.   NoAM; NOBA;
  PAIC; PPoD

How badly and how beautifully she speaks.   A Bagatelle.   James
  Reeves.   POL

"How bare! How all the lion-desert lies."   Macrinus against
  Trees.   "Michael Field."WPE

How Beastly the Bourgeois Is.   D. H. Lawrence.   NoAM

How beautiful are thy feet in sandals, O prince's daughter!   Song
  of Solomon, VII: 1-9, Bible, *O.T.*   OBP

How beautiful is the rain!   Rain in Summer.   Longfellow.   FSFS

How beautiful their feet.   Martin Tupper.   *Fr.* The Train of
  Religion.   FaBoCo

How Beautiful You Are: 3.   Elaine Edelman.   IHMS

How Bill Went East.   George S. Bryan.   PoTa

How blest [*or* bless'd] art thou, canst love the country, Wroth.   To
  Sir Robert Wroth.   Ben Jonson.   SCP-1; TVS

How blest was the created state.   The Fall: a Song.   Earl of
  Rochester.   SCP-2

How brittle are the piers.   Emily Dickinson.   PiAm

How, butler, how! Bevis a tout!   Fill the Bowl, Butler.   *Unknown.*
  OxBM

How came this ranger.   The Chambermaid's First Song.   W. B.
  Yeats.   AnMo

How can I care whether you sigh for me.   Song: How Can I
  Care?   Robert Graves.   GBL

How can I choose but love, and follow her.   Another on Her.
  Robert Herrick.   SpRo

How Can I Keep My Maidenhead.   Burns.   LoAs

How Can I Leave Thee? *with music.*   Friedrich Wilhelm Küken,
  *tr. fr. German.*   BLSH

How can I sing you when I cannot find you?   To Sing the People.
  Lucille F. Travis.   AATT

How can I sustain.   Private Pain in Time of Trouble.   Kathleen
  Spivack.   AmPA

How can I, that girl standing there.   Politics.   W. B. Yeats.
  HeIP; InPS; OBP; OxBTC; PFIr; POL

How can I turn this wheel that turns my life.   The Wheel.
  Edwin Muir.   NoAM

How can it be thought?   The Six Days of Creation.   James
  McAuley.   CAAP

How can people stand to be around me? I'm always babbling.
  Alta.   MMD

How can you know, or understand, our loss.   Navajo Signs.
  Winifred Fields Walters.   VW

How can you live, how exist.   The Likeness.   Arthur Gregor.
  VGW

How can you set to the table a-dining?   The Lost Baby.
  *Unknown.*   AmFP

How changed is here each spot man makes or fills.   Thyrsis.
  Matthew Arnold.   Epi; NOBE

How Come?   Sara Asheron.   CaYB

How come nobody is being bombed today?   All Quiet.   David
  Ignatow.   ConAP

How comes this blood on thy shirt sleeve?   Edward.   *Unknown.*
  RDB

How dark to my mind are the scenes of my childhood.   The Old,
  Filthy Beer Pail.   Katie V. Hall.   InPK

How dear to my [*or* this] heart are the scenes of my childhood.
  The Old Oaken Bucket.   Samuel Woodworth.   BLSo; PSoN

How dear to my heart was the old-fashioned hurler.   The Old-
  Fashioned Pitcher.   George E. Phair.   SPo

How dear to this heart are the scenes of my childhood.   *See* How
  dear to my heart...

How did he die/ O if I told you.   The Gangster's Death.
  Ishmael Reed.   PoBA

How did the Devil come? When first attack?   Norfolk.   John
  Betjeman.   BBGO

How did the party go in Portman Square.   Juliet.   Hilaire Belloc.
  BoLOP

How did they fume, and stamp, and roar, and chafe.   Atticus.
  Pope.   *Fr.* Epistle to Dr. Arbuthnot.   InPK

How did your father come down at Lodore?   The Cataract at
  Lodore.   Helen Bevington.   SpRo

How difficult for me is Hebrew.   Charles Reznikoff.   *Fr.* Five
  Groups of Verse.   SA

How do I know it was a fox?   Blue Teal's Mother.   James
  Wright.   CAAP

How do I love thee? Let me count the ways.   Sonnets from the
  Portuguese, XLIII.   Elizabeth Barrett Browning.   BoLoP;
  HeIP; InPS; IPWM; LoAS; OLR; PAIC; SFF; VPC; WPE

How do we know, by the bank-high river.   The Last Lap.
  Kipling.   OxBTC

How Do You Do, *Alabama*!   Fred Wilson.   AIW

How do you know that the pilgrim track.   The Year's Awakening.
  Thomas Hardy.   OxBTC

How do you like to go up in a swing.   The Swing.   Robert Louis
  Stevenson.   LCL

How does my royal lord? How fares your Majesty?   Shakespeare.
  *Fr.* King Lear, IV, vii.   Prf

How does one tell.   Innocence.   Irving Layton.   BBGO

How does the water.   The Cataract of Lodore.   Robert Southey.
  OxBChV; SpRo

How doth the little busy bee.   Against Idleness and Mischief.
  Isaac Watts.   OxBChV; SpRo

How Doth the Little Crocodile. "Lewis Carroll." *Fr.* Alice's Adventures in Wonderland, *ch.* 2. ECBV; FaBoCo; LCL; SpRo

How dry time screaks in its fat axle-grease. The Crucifix. Robert Lowell. NowV

How easily the ripe grain. The Widow. W. S. Merwin. VGW

How everything gets tamed. Mountain, Fire, Thornbush. Harvey Shapiro. VGW

How Everything Happens. May Swenson. Psy; RFM

"How farest thou?" quod he to me. The Eagle Converses with Chaucer. Chaucer. *Fr.* The House of Fame. OxBM

How fever'd is the man, who cannot look. On Fame. Keats. MBPR

How fresh, O Lord, how sweet and clean. The Flower. George Herbert. BoReV; MetP; NOBE; PPP; SCP-1

How funny you are today New York. Steps. Frank O'Hara. CAPP; ConAP

How! gossip mine, gossip mine. Good Gossips Mine. *Unknown.* OxBM

How Grand and How Bright. *Unknown.* GBP

How happier is that flea. The Happiness of a Flea. Tasso, *tr. by* William Drummond of Hawthornden. LoAs

How happy is he born and taught. The Character of a Happy Life. Sir Henry Wotton. NOBE

How hard is my fortune. The Convict of Clonmel. *Unknown, tr. by* Jeremiah Joseph Callanan. PFIr

How hard it is, we say. Clothes Maketh the Man. Theodore Weiss. NoAM

How he thought. Drop the Wires. Hugh Seidman. AmPA

How, hey! It is none les. A Henpecked Husband. *Unknown.* OxBM

How High the Moon. Lance Jeffers. PoBA

How I Brought the Good News from Aix to Ghent. R. J. Yeatman *and* W. C. Sellar. SpRo

How I Cancelled My Life Insurance. Joseph Bruchac. FAF

How I Escaped from the Labyrinth. Philip Dacey. POL

How I go courting a charming beauty bright. Charming Beauty Bright. *Unknown.* AmFP

How I Got Myself Trapped. Felix Pollak. HeS

How is it that I am so careless here. Meditation 62. Philip Pain. NOBA; PiAm

How is man parcelled out! how every hour. The Tempest. Henry Vaughan. SCP-1

How is't, my soul, that thou giv'st eyes their sight. To My Soul in Its Blindness. Phineas Fletcher. SCP-2

How it feels to be touching. We Become New. Marge Piercy. WBN

How It Goes On. Maxine W. Kumin. FiCP

"How like a well-kept garden is your soul." The Nineteenth Century As a Song. Robert Hass. CAAP

How like a winter hath my absence been. Sonnets, XCVII. Shakespeare. NOBE

How like an angel came I down! Wonder. Thomas Traherne. BoReV; PPoe; SCP-2

How long ago she planted the hawthorn hedge. The Hawthorn Hedge. Judith Wright. WPE

How long, dear Savior, O how long. Isaac Watts. AmFP

"How Long Hast Thou Been a Gravemaker?" David Perkins. NCSH

How long have the cows been gone. Until the Cows Come Home. Michael McMahon. FAF

How long have you been living here? The Arkansas Traveller. Mose Case. PSoN

How long shall I endure without reply. Thomas Shadwell. *Fr.* The Medal of John Bays: a Satire against Folly and Knavery. SCP-2

How long shall I pine for love? Pining for Love. Francis Beaumont. POL

"How long shall man be nature's fool?" Man cries. The Sakiyeh. Mathilde Blind. SBG

How Man Learned to Walk—and Run. Louis Dudek. AKE

How many bards gild the lapses of time! Keats. MBPR

How many bullets does it take. Death in Yorkville. Langston Hughes. PoBA

How many dawns, chill from his rippling rest. To Brooklyn Bridge [*or* Proem]. Hart Crane. *Fr.* The Bridge. HeIP; InPS; NoAM; NOBA; PAIC; PiAm

How many days has my baby to play? Mother Goose. MG

How may doors will this man open. Death. Roy Fuller. NoAM

How many miles to Babylon. Mother Goose. GBP; MG

How Many Nights. Galway Kinnell. MAT

How many paltry, foolish, painted things. Michael Drayton. *Fr.* Idea. AAS; Epi; GBL; HeIP

How much are they deceived who vainly strive. Love and Jealousy. William Walsh. BoLoP

How much longer will I be able to inhabit the divine sepulcher. John Ashbery. NoAM

How much of me is sandwiches radio beer? Lonesome in the Country. Al Young. MAT; SA

How much shall I love her? The Echo Elf Answers. Thomas Hardy. LoAs

How mutable is every thing that here. Meditation 29. Philip Pain. NOBA

How, my dear Mary,—are you critic-bitten. The Witch of Atlas. Shelley. MBPR

How oft have I, my dere and cruell foo. Sir Thomas Wyatt. AAS

How oft when thou, my music, music play'st. Sonnets, CXXVIII. Shakespeare. Epi

How Old's the Moon? *Unknown, tr. fr. Japanese by* Graehme Wilson. Moon

How One Thing Leads to Another. David Smith. NVAP

How Pleasant It Is to Have Money. Arthur Hugh Clough. *Fr.* Dipsychus. NOBE
("As I sat at the café, I said to myself.") VPC

How Pleasant to Know Mr. Lear. Edward Lear. FaBoCo; NOBE; SpRo
(By Way of Preface.) InPS

How pure, how beautiful, how fine. Reflections Dental. Phyllis McGinley. *Fr.* Speaking of Television. TH

How quickly the dandelions. Americana XVII: A Reminder of William Carlos Williams. Carl Rakosi. InPS

How rare to be born a human being! Gary Snyder. Myths and Texts: Hunting, XVI. CAPP

How red the rose that is the soldier's wound. Wallace Stevens. *Fr.* Esthétique du Mal. NOBA

How rewarding to know Mr. Smith. Mr. Smith/ (with Nods to Mr. Lear and Mr. Eliot.) William Jay Smith. SpRo

How rich the wave, in front, imprest. Lines Written Near Richmond, upon the Thames, at Evening. Wordsworth. MBPR

How right that you should rise. New York Skyline. Ruthe T. Spinnanger. AATT

How Robin Hood Rescued the Widow's Sons. *Unknown.* PoTa

How sad I was then! "Many Brave Hearts Are Asleep in the Deep." Morgan Sanders. WBN

How sad it must be. A Poem for My Father. Sonia Sanchez. BPo; IHMS; RiTi

How sad, they think, to see him homing nightly. Academic. James Reeves. MPo

How shall I sing that majesty. A General Song of Praise to Almighty God. John Mason. SCP-2

How shall I withhold my soul so that. Lovesong. Rainer Maria Rilke, *tr. by* M. D. Herter Norton. LoAs; OLR

How shall the wine be drunk, or the woman known? A Voice from under the Table. Richard Wilbur. NOBA

How shall we adorn. Angle of Geese. N. Scott Momaday. CDW; VW

How Shall We Mourn You Who Are Killed and Wasted. Charles Reznikoff. InPK; SA

How should I describe you—eternal. Koala. Alan Ross. BoAnP

How should I praise thee, Lord! The Temper. George Herbert. BoReV

How Should I Rule Me? *Unknown.* OxBM

How should I your true love know. Ophelia's Song. Shakespeare. *Fr.* Hamlet, IV, v. AIW; GBL

"How should I your true love know." An Old Song Ended. Dante Gabriel Rossetti. BoLoP; VPC

How silly that soldier is pointing his gun at the wood. Russians. Keith Douglass. OxBTC

How Sleep the Brave. William Collins. NOBE
  (Ode: "How sleep the brave, who sink to rest.") WIF
  (Ode Written in 1746.) PAIC
  (Ode, Written in the Beginning of the Year 1746.) HeIP; LAuP; PBMP
  (Ode, Written in the Year 1746.) BTTM

How smartly the quarters of the hour march by. Copying Architecture in an Old Minster. Thomas Hardy. OBP

How smooth that lake expands its ample breast! Stanzas. Anne Radcliffe. WPE

How soon doth man decay! Mortification. George Herbert. SCP-1

How Soon Hath Time the Subtle Thief of Youth. Milton. HeIP; InPS; IPWM; PAIC; PBMP; PPoe

How still. Sea Calm. Langston Hughes. CaYB

How Still, How Happy. Emily Brontë. FSFS

How straight it flew, how long it flew. Seaside Golf. John Betjeman. SPo

How strange at night to wake. Night and Sleep. Coventry Patmore. VPC

How strange it seems! These Hebrews in their graves. The Jewish Cemetery at Newport. Longfellow. HeIP; NOBA; PiAm

How strange the pride of many Irishmen! The New Style. David O'Bruadair, *tr. by* John Montague. BIrV

How strange to awake in a city. Hearing Men Shout at Night on Macdougal Street. Robert Bly. TCP

How strange to be gone in a minute! A man. Sonnet. Ted Berrigan. CAAP

How strange to think of giving up all ambition! Watering the Horse. Robert Bly. NCSH

How strong does my passion flow. On Her Loving Two Equally. Aphra Behn. SBG

How struts my love my cavalier. Cock-a-Hoop. Isabella Gardner. WPE

How sweet a Lord is mine? If any should. Edward Taylor. *Fr.* Preparatory Meditations: First Series, III. PiAm

How sweet I roamed from field to field. Song [or The Prince of Love]. Blake. LoAS; MBPR; NOBE; OLR

How sweet is the shepherds sweet lot. The Shepherd. Blake. *Fr.* Songs of Innocence. MBPR

How sweet the birds of Avondale. Avondale. Stevie Smith. RAE

How sweet the name of Jesus sounds. The Name of Jesus. John Newton. BoReV

How sweet the tuneful bells' responsive peal! The Bells, Ostend. William Lisle Bowles. PAIC

How swift along the winding way. Upon Boys Diverting Themselves in the River. Thomas Foxton. OxBChV

How the days went. Now That I Am Forever with Child. Audre Lorde. PoBA

How the elements solidify! Event. Sylvia Plath. NOBA

How the First Hielandman [of God] Was Made. *Unknown.* FaBoCo; GBP

How the Indians Lost the Hot Springs. Carol Cox. MMD

How the Invalids Make Love. Susan Feldman. AmPA

How the Ploughman Learned His Paternoster. *Unknown.* OxBM

How the red road stretched before us, mile on mile. Independence. Nancy Cato. WPE

How the waters closed above him. Emily Dickinson. WIF

How there is anything so old. Dinosaur Tracks in Beit Zayit. Shirley Kaufman. FiCP

How They Brought the Good News from Ghent to Aix. Robert Browning. BTTM; ECBV; PAIC; SpRo

How thin and sharp is the moon tonight. Winter Moon. Langston Hughes. PAIC

How this year of years do I best see. May Trees in a Storm. Geoffrey Grigson. GBL

How time reverses. For My Contemporaries. J. V. Cunningham. CoPAm; PiAm

How to Be Old. May Swenson. MAT

How to behold what cannot be held? Giovanni Da Fiesole on the Sublime; or, Fra Angelico's "Last Judgment." Richard Howard. Prf

How to Catch Tiddlers. Brian Jones. LP

How to Cure Your Fever. Thomas Lux. NVAP

How to do it from the beginning. Let Me Tell You. Miller Williams. CoPAm

How to Get On in Society. John Betjeman. OxBTC

How to keep—is there any any, is there none such. The Leaden Echo and the Golden Echo. Gerard Manley Hopkins. PAIC

How to Kill. Keith Douglas. NOBE

How to Sing or Read. Robert Louis Stevenson. ECBV

How to Tell the Wild Animals, *sel.* Carolyn Wells.
  "If strolling forth, a beast you view." CaYB

How to Write a Letter. Elizabeth Turner. OxBChV

How totally unpredictable we are to one another. Robert Sward. POL

How Tuesday Began. Kathleen Fraser. CTBA

How unpleasant to meet Mr. Eliot! Lines for Cuscuscaraway and Mirza Murad Ali Beg. T. S. Eliot. SpRo

How vainly men themselves amaze. The Garden. Andrew Marvell. AnMo; InPS; NOBE; PAIC; PPoD; PPoe; PPP; SCP-1

How we desire desire! Joy of surcease. Epigram. J. V. Cunningham. VGW

How we envy their not caring. The Card-Players. David Ray. VGW

How We Heard the Name. Alan Dugan. NoAM

How we lived through that. Depression: My Father Speaks to My Mother. Dick Allen. FAF

How well I remember those days of danger. The Road to Pengya. Tu Fu, *tr. by* Rewi Alley *and* Edward Field. Prf

How well these frozen floods now represent. Sliding on Skates in Very Hard Frost. Nahum Tate. SCP-2

How well you served me above ground. Spirit's Song. Louise Bogan. LoAs

"How will he hear the bell at school." Mutterings over the Crib of a Deaf Child. James Wright. CoPAm

How wisely nature did decree. Eyes and Tears. Andrew Marvell. MetP

However we wrangled with Britain awhile. Literary Importation. Philip Freneau. AmVN

Howl. Allen Ginsberg. CAPP
  "I saw the best minds of my generation destroyed by madness,"
    I. AnMo; CoPAm; InPS, *ll.* 1-30; NoAM
Howling of Wolves, The. Ted Hughes. OxBTC
Hubbard is dead, the old plumber. Elegy for Alfred Hubbard.
  Tony Connor. MPo; SoSe
Huddled in the pits. Cowboys: Two. Rod McKuen. MiP
Hudibras, *sels.* Samuel Butler.
  "For his religion, it was fit," *fr.* I, 1. SCP-2
  "He could reduce all things to acts," *fr.* I, 1. SCP-2
  Independent Squire, *fr.* I, 1. NOBE
  Presbyterian Knight, *fr.* I, 1. NOBE
    ("When civil fury first grew high.") PAIC; SCP-2
  Sir Hudibras, His Passing Worth, *fr.* I, Argument. FaBoCo;
    SCP-2
Huesca. John Cornford. BoLoP
  (To Margot Heinemann). OxBTC
Huff the talbot and our cat Tib. The Wars of the Roses.
  *Unknown.* GBP
Huffy Henry hid the day. John Berryman. *Fr.* Dream Songs.
  CAPP; PiAm
Hug me closer, closer, mother. Little Bessie. *Unknown.* AmFP
Huge/ when she comes back to me. The Mouth That Is a
  Wound. Holly Prado. NPW
Huge commentators grace my learned shelves. James Bramston.
  *Fr.* The Man of Taste. FaBoCo
Huge doll of my body, The. My Life. Mark Strand. CAAP
Huge-headed oak. He Praises the Trees. *Unknown, tr. by* Robin
  Skelton. BIrV
Huge red-buttressed mesa over yonder, The. Rain in the Desert.
  John Gould Fletcher. *Fr.* Arizona Poems. NCSH
Huge wound in my head began to heal, The. The Wound.
  Thom Gunn. PSN
Hugging the ground by the lilac tree. Man and Beast. Clifford
  Dyment. BoAnP
Hugh Selwyn Mauberley (Life and Contacts). Ezra Pound.
  InPS; NoAM, *complete with* Mauberley; NOBA, *complete*
  *with* Mauberley
  "Age demanded an image, The," II. PiAm; VGW
  E. P. Ode Pour l'Election de Son Sépulchre. PiAm; VGW
  Envoi (1919). VGW
  "Tea-rose tea-gown, etc., The." NOBE
  "There died a myriad." NOBE; PiAm; TCP
  "These fought in any case." HeIP; NOBE; PiAm; PPoe; VGW
Hughie at the Inn. Elinor Wylie. WPE
Hughsville Scythe, The. Henry Taylor. PPoD
Hulk, three masted once, three stubbed now, A. The Benefits of
  an Education. John Ciardi. CoPAm
Hulling peas. Seeding. Mary Moore. NPW
Human Abstract, The. Blake. *Fr.* Songs of Experience. LAuP;
  MBPR; PPP
Human Condition, The. Howard Nemerov. CoPAm; NowV
Human Form Divine, The ("The human contours are so easily
  lost."). Kathleen Raine. WPE
Human Life: on the Denial of Immortality. Samuel Taylor
  Coleridge. IPWM; MBPR
Human Needs. *Unknown.* POL
Human Relations. Emmett Jarrett. NeAC
Human Relations. C. H. Sisson. POL
Human Tragedy, The, *sel.* Alfred Austin.
  "When with staid mothers' milk and sunshine warmed."
  FaBoCo
Humble-Bee, The. Emerson. FSFS; NOBA
Humble Petition of Frances Harris, The. Swift. Epi
Humidity. R. P. Dickey. HeS
Humming bee purrs softly o'er his flower, The. The Cricket.
  Frederick Goddard Tuckerman. NOBA; PiAm

Hummingbird. E. Margaret Clarkson. AATT
Hummingbird. D. H. Lawrence. InPS; PPP
Hump, The. Kipling. OxBChV
Humpty Dumpty sat on a wall. Mother Goose. MG
Humpty Dumpty's Song [*or* Recitation]. "Lewis Carroll." *Fr.*
  Through the Looking Glass. FaBoCo; OxBChV
Hunchback in the Park, The. Dylan Thomas. TCP
Hunchback on the corner, with gum and shoelaces, The. Pursuit.
  Robert Penn Warren. CoPAm; PPP
Hunchback Pine. Ethel Green Russell. AATT
Hunchbacked/ by his heart. The Life. Philip Dow. AmPA
Hunchbacked and corrected. Ken Belford. NeAC
Hunchbacked woman, The. Textures. Carol Bergé. MMD
Hunched, The. Douglas Dunn. LP
Hundred buffalo, A. Bone Yard. Jim Barnes. CDW
Hundred-gated Thebes. George Darley. *Fr.* Nepenthe. NOBE
Hundreds of yards of woodland. The Forest beyond the Glass.
  Lewis Turco. CoPAm
Hung from a stone branch of city wall. Beware the Months of
  Fire. Patrick Lane. NeAC
Hung Red, *sel.* Robin Fulton.
  "Hold a glass of pure water to the eye of the sun," III. MIS
Hunger. Laurence Binyon. OxBTC
Hunger. Lennart Bruce. MiP
Hunger. *Unknown, tr. fr. Eskimo by* Edward Field. IPWM
Hunger Artist, The. Shirley Kaufman. RiTi
Hungry Black Child, The. Adam David Miller. PoBA
Hungry Grass. Donagh MacDonagh. BIrV
Hunkie Tunkie. *Unknown.* BluL
Hunt, The. Walter de la Mare. BoAnP
Hunt, The. Louis Kent. SoSe
Hunt is up, The. *Unknown.* GBP
Hunter. Raymond Carver. NVAP
Hunter, The. Ogden Nash. SPo
Hunter, Prey. Dabney Stuart. NVAP
Hunters. Sonya Dorman. RiTi
Hunters are back, The. The Woman Thing. Audre Lorde.
  NMM
Hunters in the Snow: Brueghel. Joseph Langland. WIF
Hunters of Kentucky, The. Samuel Woodworth. BLSo, *with*
  *music;* BTTM
Hunting. Gary Snyder. *See* Myths and Texts.
Hunting Civil War Relics at Nimblewill Creek. James Dickey.
  ConAP
Hunting Dragons with Fire Tongues and Deep Smoky Throats.
  J. S. Harry. CAAP
Hunting for Blueberries. Thomas James. AmPA
Hunting Fragment. Gary Lawless. FAF
Hunting of Cupid, The, *sel.* George Peele.
  What Thing Is Love? LoAs; NOBE
Hunting of the Hare, The, *sel.* Margaret Cavendish, Duchess of
  Newcastle.
  "Betwixt two ridges of ploughed land sat Wat." SCP-2
Hunting Pheasants in a Cornfield. Robert Bly. ConAP
Hunting season. Long Hair. Gary Snyder. NOBA; PiAm
Hunting Song. Donald Finkel. NCSH; SoSe; SPo
Huntsman, What Quarry? Edna St. Vincent Millay. RiTi
Huron, The. Ruth Herschberger. WPE
Hurrah for revolution and more cannon-shot! The Great Day.
  W. B. Yeats. BIrV; WIF
Hurrah! Hurrah!/ Have you heard? Christmas. Grace
  Cavalieri. AATT
Hurrahing in Harvest. Gerard Manley Hopkins. AnMo; OBP
Hurricane. Archibald MacLeish. NCSH
Hurrying Away from the Earth. Robert Bly. CoPAm

Hurrying thru eternity. After the Cries of the Birds. Lawrence Ferlinghetti. CAPP

Hurt./ U worried abt a. To All Sisters. Sonia Sanchez. PoBA

Hurt Hawks. Robinson Jeffers. NoAM; NOBA; PiAm

Hurt No Living Thing. Christina Rossetti. RAE (Gently.) ECBV

Hurled under the lover-sundering river. Traveling Boy. William Meredith. NoAM

Husband, The. Barbara Greenberg. RiTi

Hush and Baloo. *Unknown.* GBP

Hush, hush,/ Nobody cares! Now We Are Sick. J. B. Morton. SpRo

Hush, hush! tread softly! hush, hush, my dear! Song. Keats. MBPR

Hush is over all the teeming lists, A. Frederick Douglass. Paul Lawrence Dunbar. PoBA

Hush Little Baby, *with music. Unknown.* BLSo

Hush! my dear, lie still and slumber. Cradle Hymn. Isaac Watts. OxBChV

Hush up, baby,/ Don't say a word. The Mocking Bird. *Unknown.* AmFP

Hush, woman, do not speak to me! The Tryst after Death. *Unknown, tr. by* Kuno Meyer. Epi

Hush-a-ba, Burdie. *Unknown.* GBP

Hush-a-bye, baby, on the tree top. Mother Goose. MG

Hush'd are the winds, and still the evening gloom. On the Death of a Young Lady, Cousin to the Author. Byron. MBPR

Huswifery. Edward Taylor. NOBA; SoSe

Huzza! Hodgson, we are going. Lines to Mr. Hodgson. Byron. MBPR

Hyde stamps, and straight upon the ground the swarms. Andrew Marvell. *Fr.* The Last Instructions to a Painter. SCP-1

Hye Nonny Nonny Noe. *Unknown.* FaBoCo

Hyena. Carol Muske. AmPA

Hymenaei, *sel.* Ben Jonson.
"Bid all profane away!" SCP-1

Hymeneal Dialogue, An. Thomas Carew. SCP-2

Hymen's Triumph, *sels.* Samuel Daniel.
First Flame. VoPo
Love Is a Sickness. NOBE
Secrecy. OLR

Hymn, A: "Drop, drop, slow tears." Phineas Fletcher. *See* Drop, Drop, Slow Tears.

Hymn: "I know if I find you I will have to leave the earth." A. R. Ammons. ConAP; CoPAm

Hymn: "Lord, when the wise men came from far." Sidney Godolphin. BoReV
(Wise Men and Shepherds.) NOBE

Hymn: "To those who know the Lord I speak." William Cowper. PAIC

Hymn: "Whilst I beheld the neck o' the dove." Patrick Carey. SCP-2

Hymn, A: "Wilt thou forgive that sin where I begun." John Donne. *See* Hymn to God the Father, A.

Hymn before Sunrise in the Vale of Chamouni. Samuel Taylor Coleridge. BoReV; MBPR

Hymn for Christmas Day, A. John Byrom. BoReV

Hymn for Lanie Poo, *sel.* LeRoi Jones.
Each Morning. PoBA

Hymn for Saturday. Christopher Smart. *See* For Saturday.

Hymn of Apollo. Shelley. MBPR

Hymn of Pan. Shelley. MBPR

Hymn of the City. Bryant. PiAm

Hymn of the Nativity, Sung as by the Shepherds, An. Richard Crashaw. BoReV

Hymn on the Morning of Christ's Nativity. Milton. *Fr.* On the Morning of Christ's Nativity. NOBE

Hymn on the Seasons, A. James Thomson. *Fr.* The Seasons. LAuP

Hymn to Apollo. Keats. MBPR

Hymn to Artemis, the Destroyer. Marya Zaturenska. Moon

Hymn to Christ, at the Author's Last Going into Germany, A. John Donne. BoReV

Hymn to Diana. Ben Jonson. *Fr.* Cynthia's Revels, V, vi. Moon; NOBE
("Queen and huntress, chaste and fair.") HeIP; PAIC

Hymn to God My God, in My Sickness. John Donne. AnMo; HeIP; PPP; SCP-1; SoSe
(Hymne to God My God.) MetP

Hymn to God the Father, A. John Donne. BoReV; InPK; PAIC; PPoe; WIF
(Hymn: "Wilt Thou forgive that sin where I begun.") NOBE
(Hymne To God the Father.) MetP

Hymn to God the Father, A. Ben Jonson. BoReV

Hymn to Intellectual Beauty. Shelley. BoReV; HeIP; MBPR

Hymn to Moloch. Ralph Hodgson. OxBTC

Hymn to My God in a Night of My Late Sickness, A. Sir Henry Wotton. BoReV

Hymn to Pan. John Fletcher. *Fr.* The Faithful Shepherdess, I, ii. NOBE

Hymn to Proserpine. Swinburne. PFD; VPC

Hymn to the Evening, An. Phillis Wheatley. WPE

Hymn to the Name and Honour of the Admirable Saint Teresa, A. Richard Crashaw. BoReV; NOBE; SCP-1

Hymn to the New Omagh Road. John Montague. TwMBP

Hymn to the Night. Longfellow. AmVN; NOBA

Hymn to the Sun. Michael Roberts. OxBTC

Hymn to the 10,000 Who Die Each Year on the Abortionist's Table in Amerika. Rita Mae Brown. WBN

Hymn to the Virgin. *At. to* William of Shoreham. OxBM

Hymn Written after Jeremiah Preached to Me in a Dream. Owen Dodson. PAIC

Hymne to God My God, in My Sicknesse. John Donne. *See* Hymn to God My God, in My Sickness.

Hymne to God the Father, A. John Donne. *See* Hymn to God the Father.

Hymmnn. Allen Ginsberg. NOBA

Hymns and Spiritual Songs, *sels.* Christopher Smart.
Nativity of Our Lord and Saviour Jesus Christ, The. BoReV; LAuP; NOBE; OBP
St. Mark, XII. LAuP
St. Matthias, VIII. LAuP

Hymns for the Amusement of Children, *sels.* Christopher Smart.
For Saturday, XXXIII. LAuP
(Hymn for Saturday.) OxBChV
Gratitude, XXII. LAuP
Long-Suffering of God, XXIX. LAuP
Mirth, XXV. LAuP; OxBChV

Hymns of Astraea, *sel.* Sir John Davies.
Of Astraea. PAIC

Hyperborean wind, whose rough hand flings, The. The Extremities of Cold in Hell. Thomas Dekker. *Fr.* Dekker His Dream. SCP-2

Hyperion; a Fragment. Keats. MBPR

Hypnopompic Poem. William Cole. POL

Hypocrite. Ann M. Craig. PPoD

Hypocrite Swift. Louise Bogan. SBG

Hypocrite Women. Denise Levertov. AnMo; CAPP; Epi; MAT; NMM; Psy

Hypothesis. Jennifer Maiden. CAAPs, The. The Extremities of

# I

I/ am going to rise. Vive Noir! Mari Evans. IHMS; PoBA; Psy

I,/ at one time. The Self-Hatred of Don L. Lee. Don L. Lee. BPo

I/ is the total black, being spoken. Coal. Audre Lorde. PoBA

I/ never liked/ white folks. Alice Walker. *Fr.* Once. PoBA

I/ was five/ when/ mom and dad got married. Black Sketches. Don L. Lee. NeAC

I abdicate my daily self that bled. Vita Nuova. Stanley Kunitz. VGW

I abide and abide and better abide. Sir Thomas Wyatt. BoLoP

I ache to touch distance into center of light. Versions of Sunlight. James Applewhite. NVAP

I address you only. Letter to My Mother. Dom Moraes. NoAM

I adore you darling. Complaint. Rufinus Domesticus, *tr. by* Dudley Fitts. OLR

I advocate a semi-revolution. A Semi-Revolution. Robert Frost. WIF

I advocate a total revolution. A Total Revolution. Oscar Williams. WIF

I ain't gonna tell no body 34 have done for me-e-e. 34 Blues. *Unknown.* BluL

I ain't never been to heaven but Ah been told. Swing Low, Sweet Chariot. *Unknown.* GBP

I ain't never loved but three womens in my life. Back Gnawing Blues. *Unknown.* BluL

I almost know you now. You are your name. Eight Lines for a Script Girl George Jonas. NeAC

I, Alphonso, live and learn. Alphonso of Castile. Emerson. NOBA

I always like summer. Knoxville, Tennessee. Nikki Giovanni. BPo; InPS; PoBA

I always see—I don't know why. The Knowledgeable Child. L. A. G. Strong. PFIr

I always think of a coffin's quiet. A Poem for a Poet. Audre Lorde. NMM

I always was afraid of Somes's Pond. Atavism. Elinor Wylie. SBG

I Am. John Clare. IPWM; NOBE; PRF
(Written in Northampton County Asylum.) PBMP

I am a beetle in the cabbage soup they serve up for geniuses. For Fyodor. Phyllis Webb. MMD

I am a bonded highwayman, Cole Younger is my name. Cole Younger. *Unknown.* AmFP

I am a black Pierrot. A Black Pierrot. Langston Hughes. OLR

I Am a Black Woman. Mari Evans. NMM

I Am a Cowboy in the Boat of Ra. Ishmael Reed. Epi; InPK; PoBA

I am a feather on the bright sky. The Delight Song of Tsoai-Talee. N. Scott Momaday. CDW

I am a flag by distant space surrounded. Foreboding. Rainer Maria Rilke, *tr. by* Lori Weinstein. InPK

I am a fool, I can no good. Love. *Unknown.* OxBM

I am a gentleman in a dustcoat trying. Piazza Piece. John Crowe Ransom. BoLoP; HeIP; NoAM; NOBA; PAIC; PiAm; SFF

I am a jolly forester. The Jolly Forester. *Unknown.* RAE

I am a jovial collier lad, as blithe as blithe can be. Down in a Coal Mine. J.B. Geohegan. AmFP

I am a man now. Here. R. S. Thomas. PSN

I am a miner. The light burns blue. Nick and the Candlestick. Sylvia Plath. CAPP

I Am a Parcel of Vain Strivings Tied. Henry David Thoreau. NOBA
(Sic Vita.) AmVN

I Am a Peach Tree. Li Po, *tr. fr. Chinese by* Shigeyoshi Obata. OLR

I Am a Poor Wayfaring Stranger. *Unknown.* BLSH, *with music* (Poor Wayfaring Stranger, A.) AmFP; BLSo, *with music*

I am a rich widow, I live all alone. The Rich Widow. *Unknown.* AmFP

I am a river. No More. Carl Clark. JB

I am a roving shanty boy, love to sing and dance. The Roving Shanty Boy. *Unknown.* AmFP

I am a soul in the world: in. The Invention of Comics. LeRoi Jones. CAPP; PBMP; PoBA

I am a stag: of seven tines. The Alphabet Calendar of Amergin [*or* Song of Amergin]. *Unknown, tr. by* Robert Graves. BIrV; Moon

I am a sundial, turned the wrong way round. Hilaire Belloc. POL

I am a turtle. The Marriage. James Bertolino. HeS

I am afraid these verses will not please you, but. Sonnet to Byron. Shelley. MBPR

I am afraid to own a body. Emily Dickinson. PiAm

I am alive at night. Moon Song, Woman Song. Anne Sexton. Moon; PPP

I am alive—I guess. Emily Dickinson. NOBA

I am alone tonight. Report of Health. John Updike. PBMP

I am an ancient reluctant conscript. Old Timers. Carl Sandburg. NoAM

I am an old man. Crossing into the Prairies. Bruce Severy. HeS

I am as light as any roe. A Woman Is a Worthy Thing. *Unknown.* GBP; OxBM

I am, as you know, Walter Llywarch. Walter Llywarch. R. S. Thomas. PSN

I am become a frightful bloody murtherer. Fragment from the Elizabethans. W. Bridges-Adams. FaBoCo

I am becoming a god! Everything Is Possible. Robert Pack. PPP

I am beside you, now. The Shadow's Song. Yvor Winters. POL

I am black and I have seen black hands. I Have Seen Black Hands. Richard Wright. NoAM; PoBA

I am Brian Boy Magee. Brian Boy Magee. "Ethna Carbery." PFIr

I am broke and hungry. Broke and Hungry. *Unknown.* BluL

I am called by name of man. *Unknown.* GBP

I am called Chyldhod, in play is all my mynde. Pageant Verses. Sir Thomas More. AAS

I am caught in the act. The Captive. Rochelle Ratner. WBN

I am caught up in her. Woman. Jane Chambers. IHMS

I Am Christmas *Unknown.* OxBM

I am closing my window. Tears silence the wind. Sonnet. Ted Berrigan. Epi

I am come to make thy tomb. John Webster. *Fr.* The Duchess of Malfi, IV, ii OBP

I Am Crying from Thirst. Alonzo Lopez. VW

I am Death, all bone and hair. Pardoner's Tale Blues. Patricia Beer. AIW

I Am Disquieted when I See Many Hills. Hyam Plutzik. VGW

I am dreaming about trains, perhaps. Lines Written in Objection, or the Limpopo Express. Philip Hey. SFF

I am dressed in my old grey running suit. The Work-out. Geoffrey Movius. MAT

I am driving; it is dusk; Minnesota. Driving toward the Lac Qui Parle River. Robert Bly. ConAP; NCSH

I am drunk. Love Poem Beginning with I. David Steingass. CoPAm

I am Eve, great Adam's wife. Eve's Lament [or Eve]. *Unknown.* BIrV; Epi; PFIr

I am filled with fire oaths and utterances. Interpretation. Gloria Bussel Koster. NPW

I Am Forsaken. *Unknown.* OxBM

I am Giuletta, the bird woman. I married. The Freak Show. Nancy Willard. RiTi

I am gloomy; I am the widower. Spook Sheep. Gérard de Nerval, *tr. by* Andrew Hoyem. Epi

I Am Going to California. *Unknown.* AIW

I am going to make up a legend. The Writer's House. Dick Allen. FAF

I am going to sing you a song, full of muskrats, and guinea hens. Song for Everybody. Robert Paul Smith. ECBV

I am he as you are he as you are me and we are all together. I Am the Walrus. John Lennon *and* Paul McCartney. PPoe

I am hearing the shape of the rain. In the Mountain Tent. James Dickey. CAPP

I am here with my beautiful bountiful womanful child. At a Summer Hotel. Isabella Gardner. RiTi

I am his Highness' dog at Kew. Epigram Engraved on the Collar of a Dog Which I Gave to His Royal Highness. Pope. AnMo; FaBoCo; InPK; PAIC

I am holding this turquoise. The Serenity in Stones. Simon J. Ortiz. CDW

I am I, old Father Fisheye that begat the ocean, the worm. The End. Allen Ginsberg. ConAP

"I am Imagination," he said, "I am never idle." The Poet, Rebuked, Responds. William Langland, *tr. by* Selden Rodman *Fr.* The Vision of Piers Plowman, Passus XII. OBP

"I Am in Danger—Sir." Adrienne Rich. NOBA; PiAm; Psy

I am in love with the laughing sickness. Zizi's Lament. Gregory Corso. Epi; VGW

I am in the corner of your eye all day. A Stranger in Your Town. Michael McMahon. FAF

I am inside someone. An Agony. As Now. LeRoi Jones. BPo; IPWM; PiAm; PPP

I am just a weary pilgrim. When the Saints Come Marching In. Edward C. Redding. BLSo

I am leaving. South Wind. Mary Logue. NPW

I am listening here in Rome. A Song for the Ragged Schools of London. Elizabeth Barrett Browning. SBG

I am listening to the silence. Sticks and Stones Paulette Dusdall Zachariou. NPW

I am locked in a very expensive suit. The Suit. Leonard Cohen. BBGO

"I am Lot's pillar, caught in turning." Columns and Caryatids. Carolyn Kizer. WPE

I am made to sow the thistle for wheat. Blake. *Fr.* The Four Zoas. Prf

I Am Moved by a Necessity from Within. Daisy Aldan. RiTi

I am my mammie's ae bairn. I'm Owre Young to Marry Yet. Burns. LoAs

I am my prison. Conundrum. Carl Clark. JB

I am no shepherd of a child's surmises. Montana Pastoral. J. V.. Cunningham. CoPAm; MAT; PPoD; VGW

I am nobody/ A red sinking autumn sun. Hokku Poems. Richard Wright. PoBA

I am not a metaphor or symbol. The Distant Drum. Calvin C. Hernton. CTBA

I am not a painter, I am a poet. Why I Am Not a Painter. Frank O'Hara. ConAP; CoPAm; NoAM; NOBA

I Am Not as I Wish. Richard Brathwaite. *Fr.* Nature's Embassy. SCP-2

I am not blind. For Steph. Wendy Rose. CDW

I am not going to invite you. Blond. Joseph De Roche. HeIP

I am not one who much or oft delight. Personal Talk. Wordsworth. MBPR; NOBE

I am not resigned to the shutting away of loving hearts. Dirge Without Music. Edna St. Vincent Millay. NoAM; SBG

"I am not treacherous, callous, jealous, superstitious." A Face. Marianne Moore. PiAm; Psy

I am not yet born; O hear me. Prayer before Birth. Louis MacNeice. BuTh; MPo; PBMP; PFIr

"I Am Not Yours." Sara Teasdale. VGW

I Am of Ireland *Unknown.* GBP (Irish Dancer, The.) BuTh; NOBE; OxBM

"I Am of Ireland." W. B. Yeats. PFIr

I am of puritan and loyalist ancestry. Disqualification. Elizabeth Brewster. MMD

I Am of These. David Curry. HeS

I am old. Epitaph. Christopher Logue. OxBTC

I am on the way. Song of a Child's Spirit. *Unknown.* AKE

I am, outside. Incredible panic rules. John Berryman. *Fr.* Dream Songs. CAPP

"I am Pancho Villa," says the truck. Pancho Villa Lou Lipsitz. NCSH

I am pounding the faces of gods back into the red clay they. The Runner at Sauteurs. Derek Walcott. *Fr.* Another Life. OBP

I am Prytherch. Forgive me. I don't know. Invasion on the Farm. R. S. Thomas. POL

I Am Raftery. Anthony Raftery, *tr. fr. Irish by* James Stephens. PFIr

I am reading. The Distant Orgasm. James Tate. AmPA

I am reminded, by the tan man who wings. The Elevator Man Adheres to Form. Margaret Danner. PoBA

I am riding a lion. Elaine H. Jennings. NPW

I am riding on a limited express, one of the crack trains of the nation. Limited. Carl Sandburg. PSN

I am rooted to a cliff. Lighthouse Keeper. Gary Sange. NVAP

I am scorned by patterns which hold. Moon at Three A.M. Lance Henson. CDW

I am seeing/ other men now. "Hold Back the Edges of Your Gowns, Ladies, We Are Going through Hell." Cathleen Quirk. MMD

I am silver and exact. I have no preconceptions. Mirror. Sylvia Plath. SoSe

I am sitting here. The Poor Girl's Meditation. *Unknown, tr. by* Padraic Colum. BIrV; OLR; PFIr

I am sitting in Mike's Place trying to figure out. One Thousand Fearful Words for Fidel Castro. Lawrence Ferlinghetti. VGW

I am sitting on your Indian rock watching the third. The Wake. Madeline DeFrees. RiTi

I am telling you this Blue Ruth: America. Michael S. Harper. PoBA

I am so fragile this morning. The U.S. Coast and Geodetic Survey Ship *Pioneer*. Robert Hershon. NeAC

I am so lonely, I am so blue. Somebody's Sweetheart I Want To Be. Will D. Cobb. FSN

I am the American heartbreak. American Heartbreak. Langston Hughes. BPo

I am the cat of cats, I am. The Cat of Cats. William Brighty Rands. *Fr.* The White Princess OxBChV

I am the child of the Yei-ie. Yei-ie's Child. Charles C. Long. VW

I Am the Duke of Norfolk. *Unknown.* GBP

I am the family face. Heredity. Thomas Hardy. IPWM

I am the farmer, stripped of love. The Hill Farmer Speaks. R. S. Thomas. MPo

I Am the Great Sun. Charles Causley. BuTh

I am the man crouched behind a bush. The Rapist. Stephen Dunn. POL

I am the man who. The Carpenter. Michael Perkins. POL

I am the man who looked for peace and found. War Poet. Sidney Keyes. BuTh

I am the mother of sorrows. The Paradox. Paul Laurence Dunbar. PoBA

I Am the One. Thomas Hardy. OxBTC

I Am the Only Being Whose Doom. Emily Brontë. MAT

I am the rose of Sharon, and the lily of the valleys. Song of Solomon, II, Bible, *O.T.* BoLoP; GBL; OLR

I am the seller and the sold. Criteria. Ruthe T. Spinnanger. AATT

I am the smoke king. The Song of the Smoke. W. E. B. DuBois. PoBA

I am the sorrow in the wheat fields. Ellen Bass. NMM

I am the teacher of athletes. Song of Myself, XLVII Walt Whitman. AnMo

I am the seventh son of the son. Malcolm X—An Autobiography. Larry Neal. BPo

I am the unnoticed, the unnoticeable man. The Man in the Bowler Hat. Peter Black. BuTh

I Am the Walrus. John Lennon *and* Paul McCartney. PPoe

I am thin as nail parings. Light as dandruff. Embryos Marge Piercy. RiTi

I am thinking of Iowa. The Driving Wheels. G. E. Murray. HeS

I am thinking today of that beautiful land I shall reach when the sun goeth down. Will There Be Any Stars in My Crown? E. E. Hewitt. BLSH

I am 32 years old. Writ on the Eve of My 32nd Birthday. Gregory Corso. SA

I am tired of work; I am tired of building up somebody else's civilization. Tired. Fenton Johnson. PoBA

I am too young to grow a beard. Street Song. Thom Gunn. HeIP

I am trying/ to learn to walk again. Walk. Frank Horne. BPo

I am 25. Gregory Corso. CoPAm

I am 25 years old. My Poem Nikki Giovanni. BPo; PoBA

I am two fools I know. The Triple Fool John Donne. GBL

I am unhappy that I am not God. He Puts Me to Rest David Ignatow. VGW

I Am Waiting. Lawrence Ferlinghetti. *Fr.* Oral Messages. CAPP

I am waiting by the canal. The Governor's Palace. Linda Pastan. *Fr.* Williamsburg. RiTi

I am walking rapidly through striations of light and dark. I Dream I'm the Death of Orpheus Adrienne Rich. NMM; NoAM

I am watching them churn the last milk. The Mad Yak Gregory Corso. NoAM

I am weary of these times and their dull burden. Quid Restat Lucius Beebe. RFM

I am within as white as snow. *Unknown.* GBP

I am wondering how I could have changed her blood. Marlow and Nancy. Sandra McPherson. AmPA

I am wondering how these first words will look. American Saturday Afternoon Ron Ikan. NVAP

I am: yet what I am none [*or* who] cares or knows. I Am [*or* Written in Northampton County Asylum]. John Clare. IPWM; NOBE; PBMP; Prf

I am yours and you are mine so. Michael Silverton. POL

I and Pangur Ban, my cat. Pangur Ban. *Unknown, tr. by* Robin Flower. PFIr

I and the other intruders. Of Objects Considered as Fortresses in a Baleful Place Hyam Plutzik. VGW

I arise from dreams of thee. The Indian Serenade Shelley. MBPR

I arrive/ Langston. Do Nothing Till You Hear from Me David Henderson. PoBA

I asked a thief to steal me a peach Blake. LAuP; MBPR

I asked if I got sick and died, would you. A Question J. M. Synge. OxBTC; PFIr

I asked if I should pray. Mohini Chatterjee W. B. Yeats. NoAM

I asked no other thing. Emily Dickinson. NOBA; PBMP

I asked professors who teach the meaning. Happiness Carl Sandburg. TH; VoPo

I awakened to dryness and the ferns were dead. The Tragedy of Leaves Charles Bukowski. CoPAm

I awoke in profuse sweat, arms aching. Hag-ridden Robert Graves. BIrV

I awoke in the Midsummer not-to-call night. Moonrise, Gerard Manley Hopkins. Moon

I Awoke with the Room Cold. Marge Piercy. NeAC

I banked the five in the side. Kelly. Robert Hershon. NeAC

I bear, in sign of love. Francis Andrewes. *Fr.* Shepherdess' Valentine. OFD

I been drifting and rolling along the road. Rolling Log Blues. *Unknown.* BluL

I been scarred and battered. Still Here. Langston Hughes. BPo

I been t'inkin' 'bout de preachah; whut he said de othah night. Philosophy Paul Laurence Dunbar. BPo

I Been Treated Wrong. *Unknown.* BluL

I been walking all day and all night too. No Job Blues *Unknown.* BluL

I beheld, and lo a great multitude, which no man could number. Heavenly Vision. William Billings. AmFP

I begin with the hills. This House Ray A. Young Bear. CDW

I begin with words of air but delightful ones. Sappho, *tr. fr Greek by* Bill Zavatsky. POL

I, being a woman and distressed. Edna St. Vincent Millay. BoLoP; SBG

I believe a leaf of grass is no less than the journey-work of the stars. Walt Whitman. *Fr.* Song of Myself, XXXI. InPS

I Believe I'll Dust My Broom. *Unknown.* BluL

I believe in the flesh and the appetites. Walt Whitman *Fr.* Song of Myself, XXIV. Prf

I believe in the ultimate justice of Fate. Credo. Georgia Douglas Johnson. PoBA

I believe in you my soul. Walt Whitman. *Fr.* Song of Myself, V. Prf

I believe that if I had my sweet woman's heart in my hand. Drive Away Blues. *Unknown.* BluL

I believe we came together. Past Time. Harvey Shapiro. POL

I bellowed to the ferryman, methought. Death Terrible in Countenance. Thomas Dekker. *Fr.* Dekker His Dream. SCP-2

I bend over the woman. The Country Midwife: A Day Ai. CAAP

I bless thee, Lord, because I grow. Paradise. George Herbert. PAIC

I bought a dishmop. Youth and Beauty. William Carlos Williams. RRA

I Break the Sky. Owen Dodson. PoBA

I breathed enough to take the trick. Emily Dickinson. NoAM

I bring fresh showers for the thirsting flowers. The Cloud. Shelley. MBPR

I bring myself back from the streets that open like long. Home for Thanksgiving. W. S. Merwin. NoAM

I called him to come in. Evening. James Wright. NOBA

I called you. You called me. Dream. Emilio Prados, *tr. by* Eleanor L. Turnbull. LoAs

I came/ in the blinding sweep. To Mother. Frank Horne. *Fr.* Letters Found near a Suicide. BPo

I came as a shadow. Nocturne Varial. Lewis Alexander. PoBA

I came from Alabama wid my banjo on my knee. *See* I come from Alabama...

I come to tell you that my son is dead.  The Prince.  Edgar Bowers.  ConAP

I come to the garden alone.  In the Garden.  C. Austin Miles.  BLSH

I come to town the other night.  Old Dan Tucker.  Daniel Decatur Emmett.  BLSo; PSoN

I come to you from a lonely place.  And Why Are All the Voices I Hear Divided into Colors?  Alta.  MMD

I could have said makes love.  Behind That Wall My Roommate Fucks His Girl.  Geof Hewitt.  NeAC; POL

I could I might.  Come to a Wedding.  Grace Cavalieri.  AATT

I could look at.  Joy.  Robert Creeley.  PPP

I could replace.  Earth Psalm.  Denise Levertov.  PPP

I could ride the Disneyland sky ride forever.  He Spends Time in Southern California.  Jonathan Cott.  RRA

I could take the Harlem night.  Juke Box Love Song.  Langston Hughes.  OLR; PoBA

I could tell you.  The Farmer's Wife.  Mary Swanson Stroh.  NPW

I couldnt ever tell you.  Paris.  Al Young.  CoPAm

I couldn't find my playground.  Letter to My Father.  Delia Chilgren.  NPW

I couldn't touch a stop and turn a screw.  Thirty Bob a Week.  John Davidson.  InPS; NoAM; NOBE; OBP; OxBTC

I count black-lipped.  Come Back Blues.  Michael S. Harper.  PoBA

I cross'd pynot, an't' pynot cross'd me.  Against the Magpie.  *Unknown.*  GBP

I crouch among the arbor's swollen tongues.  Spider in the Grapes.  Thomas James.  HeS

I crouch over my radio.  Speech.  Henry Taylor.  MAT

I crushed the brown bug in a blood rage.  The Brown Bug.  Michael R. Brown.  SFF

I Cry Your Mercy.  Keats.  *See* To Fanny.

I Dance and I Have a Fast Hook.  Muhammed Ali.  SPo

"I dance on all the mountains."  This Poem Is for Deer.  Gary Snyder.  *Fr.* Myths and Texts: Hunting.  CAPP; NOBA

I danced in the morning.  Lord of the Dance.  Sydney Carter.  LP

I demand a thatched house.  The Poet's Request.  *Unknown, tr. by* John Montague.  BIrV

I desire that my body be.  When I Am Dead.  George MacBeth.  OxBTC

I did not live until this time.  To My Excellent Lucasia, on Our Friendship.  Katherine Philips.  SBG; SCP-2; WPE

I Did Not Lose My Heart.  A. E. Housman.  PPoD

I did not think that I should find them there.  The Clerks.  E. A. Robinson.  PiAm

I Did Not See a Mermaid?  Siddie Joe Johnson.  LCL

I did not want to be old Mr.  Uncle Dog: the Poet at 9.  Robert Sward.  VGW

I did not want to go.  Speaking: The Hero.  Felix Pollak.  CTBA

I did not know the laws of the land.  Trailing My Balloon.  Stephen Stepanchev.  SA

I did not think that I should find them there.  The Clerks.  E. A. Robinson.  VoPo

I didn't make you know how glad I was.  A Servant to Servants.  Robert Frost.  Epi

I didn't want you cosy and neat and limited.  To Anybody At All.  Margaret Tait.  SLP

I died for beauty—but was scarce.  Emily Dickinson.  AnMo; NOBA; PBMP; SBG

I do confess, in many a sigh.  Lying.  Thomas Moore.  PFIr

I do confess thou'rt smooth and fair.  Inconstancy Reproved.  Sir Robert Ayton.  GBL

I do not come alone.  The Defeated Victor.  Horst Bienek.  *tr. fr. German.*  LP

I do not count the hours I spend.  Waldeinsamkeit.  Emerson.  NOBA

I do not grieve when some unwholesome air.  John Hagthorpe.  *Fr.* An Elegy upon the Death of the Most Illustrious Prince Henry.  SCP-2

I do not know much about gods; but I think that the river.  The Dry Salvages.  T. S. Eliot.  *Fr.* Four Quartets.  PiAm

I do not like my state of mind.  Symptom Recital.  Dorothy Parker.  SBG

I do not look for love that is a dream.  Christina Rossetti.  GBL

I do not love thee, Doctor Fell.  Doctor Fell.  Thomas Brown, *after* Martial.  FaBoCo

I do not sleep at night.  Night-Piece.  Raymond R. Patterson.  PoBA

I do not think of you lying in the wet clay.  In Memory of My Mother.  Patrick Kavanagh.  NoAM

I do not think the ending can be right.  But That Is Another Story.  Donald Justice.  CoPAm

I do not want a plain box, I want a sarcophagus.  Last Words.  Sylvia Plath.  RiTi

I do not want to be reflective any more.  Wolves.  Louis MacNeice.  NoAM; OxBTC

I do not want to stand.  My Own Hallelujahs.  Zack Gilbert.  PoBA

I do remember an apothecary.  Drug Store.  Karl Shapiro.  NowV

I do seem to zee Grammer as she did use.  Grammer's Shoes.  William Barnes.  VPC

I do tricks in order to know.  With My Crowbar Key.  William Stafford.  ConAP

I done lose all-a my money.  Frying Pan Skillet Blues.  *Unknown.*  BluL

I don't believe the sleepers in this house.  A Cabin in the Clearing.  Robert Frost.  PiAm

I don't bother with rhymes.  Alberto Caeiro, *tr. fr. Portuguese by* Jonathan Griffin.  TSWA

I Don't Care, *with music.*  Jean Lenox.  FSN

I don't dream anymore about arthritic spiders.  Succubi.  John Newlove.  NeAC

I Don't Eat Animals (And They Don't Eat Me.)  Melanie Safka.  PoRo

"I Don't Hear Any Melody Breathing I Hear."  John Gill.  NeAC

I Don't Know.  *Unknown.*  BluL

I don't know.  A Poem Against Rats.  Fred Levinson.  AmPA

I don't know about anything sometimes.  Between Me and Anyone Who Can Understand.  Sharon Scott.  JB

I don't know about you, whiteman all dressed in black.  For Dan Berrigan.  Etheridge Knight.  NeAC

I don't know any greatest treat.  The Parterre.  E. Harriet Palmer.  FaBoCo

I don't know if he is rare on these northern lakes.  The Pelican.  Greg Kuzma.  AmPA

I don't know my real name I don't know when I was born.  I Been Treated Wrong.  *Unknown.*  BluL

I don't know somehow it seems sufficient.  Gravelly Run.  A. R. Ammons.  Prf

I Don't Let the Girls Worry My Mind.  *Unknown.*  AmFP

I Don't Like Beetles.  Rose Fyleman.  OxBChV

I don't pretend to drink.  A Welcome for Etheridge.  James Cunningham.  JB

I don't think it important.  The Beast Section.  Welton Smith.  PoBA

I don't use chemical sprays.  Note to a New Lesbian.  Martha Shelley.  WBN

I don't want no woman if her hair ain't no longer'n mine.  Short Haired Woman.  *Unknown.*  BluL

I Don't Want to Play in Your Yard, *with music.* Philip Wingate. FSN

I don't want your greenback dollar. The Greenback Dollar. *Unknown.* AmFP

I doubt not God is good, well-meaning, kind. Yet Do I Marvel. Countee Cullen. BPo; IPWM; NoAM; PBMP; PoBA; SS

I drank,/ my arteries filled with fat. Organ Transplant. J. D. Reed. POL

I dreaded that first robin, so. Emily Dickinson. AnMo

I Dream I'm the Death of Orpheus. Adrienne Rich. NMM; NoAM

I dream millions of buffalo. The Buffalo, Our Sacred Beast. Tom McKeown. NVAP

I dream of Jeanie with the light brown hair. Jeanie, with the Light Brown Hair. Stephen Collins Foster. BLSH; BLSo

I dream of whales. I feel upon my skin. The Suicides. George Macbeth. NoAM

I dream'd that, as I wander'd by the way. The Question. Shelley. FSFS

I dream'd that I walk'd in Italy. Check to Song. Owen Meredith. FaBoCo

I dream'd we both were in a bed. The Vision to Electra. Robert Herrick. LoAs

I dreamed a dream the other night, when everything was still. Prospecting Dream. *Unknown.* AmFP

I dreamed I passed a doorway. Ballad. John Hall Wheelock. AIW

I dreamed I saw the crescent moon. *Unknown.* POL

I dreamed last night I dreamed, and in that sleep. Le Rêve. Edgar Bowers. ConAP

I dreamed of a shark following us two. Sharks. Dick Lourie. NeAC

I dreamed of Ted Williams. Dream of a Baseball Star. Gregory Corso. NoAM; VGW

I dreamed that one had died in a strange place. A Dream of Death. W. B. Yeats. GBL

I dreamed there would be spring no more. In Memoriam A. H. H., LXIX. Tennyson. NOBE

I dreamt a dream the other night. Lowlands. *Unknown.* AIW

I dreamt a dream! what can it mean? The Angel. Blake. *Fr.* Songs of Experience. LAuP; MBPR

I dreamt her sensual proportions. The Death of Venus. Robert Creeley. NOBA; PiAm

I dreamt last night. For No Clear Reason. Robert Creeley. VGW

I dreamt last night of you, John-John. John-John. Thomas MacDonagh. PFIr; PoTa

I drink to forget, but whenever I think. Alan Bold. POL

I drive my car to supermarket. Superman. John Updike. BBGO; LP

I drive Westward. Tumble and loco weed. To What Strangers, What Welcome. J. V. Cunningham. NoAM

I drove to Little Hunger promontory. Little Hunger. Richard Murphy. BIrV

I du believe in Freedom's cause. The Pious Editor's Creed. James Russell Lowell. *Fr.* The Biglow Papers. PiAm

I dwell apart. The Hermit. Hsü Pên, *tr.* by Henry H. Hart. RFM

I dwell in Possibility. Emily Dickinson. NoAM; NOBA

I eat my cereal with a sliced peach. Getting a Poem in the Rain. Dick Lourie. NeAC

I employ the blind mandolin player. A Music. Wendell Berry. VGW

I empty myself of the names of others. I empty my pockets. The Remains. Mark Strand. PPP

I entreat you, Alfred Tennyson. To Alfred Tennyson. Walter Savage Landor. POL

I envy e'en the fly its gleams of joy. Written in Prison. John Clare. Epi

I envy seas, whereon he rides. Emily Dickinson. OLR

I, even I, am he who knoweth the roads. De Aegypto. Ezra Pound. VGW

I examine my wound. The December Sky. A. G. Sobin. HeS

I fasted three canonical hours. The Maiden's Plight. Brian Merriman, *tr.* by Frank O'Connor. *Fr.* The Midnight Court. BIrV

I fear it's very wrong of me. Friends. Elizabeth Jennings. LP

I feared the fury of my wind. Blake. MBPR

I feel I know what you have worked through, you. For John Berryman. Robert Lowell. NOBA

I feel it again and again, no matter. Glorious World. Hermann Hesse, *tr.* by James Wright. IPWM

I feel my face being bitten by the tides. The Knowledge That Comes through Experience. Jane Cooper. NMM

I feel remorse for all that time has done. Love's Remorse. Edwin Muir. OxBTC

I feel so awful blue. Teasing; or, I Was Only, Only Teasing You. Cecil Mack. FSN

I feel so lonesome you can hear me when I moan. Terraplane Blues. *Unknown.* BluL

I felt a cleaving in my mind. Emily Dickinson. NOBA

I felt a funeral, in my brain. Emily Dickinson. NOBA; PiAm; Psy

I felt no pain when they cut it off. Child with Six Fingers. Carol Muske. AmPA

I felt that glance. "The Strength of That Food." Jane Marie Luecke. AATT

I figure her. Takes All Kinds. R. P. Dickey. POL

I figured you as nude between. The Apostrophe to Vincentine. Wallace Stevens. LoAs

I finally found a way of using the tree. The Beckett Kit. Linda Gregg. AmPA

I finally ran into me one night. And Then What? Dave Kelly. POL

I find [*or* fynde] no peace, and all my war is done. Description of the Contrarious Passions in a Lover. Petrarch, *tr.* by Sir Thomas Wyatt. Sonnets to Laura: To Laura in Life, CIV. AAS; PAIC; PPoe

I first adventure, with foolhardy might. Prologue. Joseph Hall. *Fr.* Virgidemiarum, Bk. I. TVS

I first tasted under Apollo's lips. Evadne. Hilda Doolittle ("H.D."). LoAs; RiTi

I follow the scent of a woman. Dancing the Shout to the True Gospel or The Song Movement Sisters Don't Want Me to Sing. Rita Mae Brown. NMM; WBN

I followed the narrow cliffside trail half way up the mountain. The Deer Lay Down Their Bones. Robinson Jeffers. PiAm

I forgotten who. Bumi. LeRoi Jones. PoBA

I found a/ hummingbird. The Container. Cid Corman. VGW

I found a ball of grass among the hay. Mouse's Nest. John Clare. InPK; SoSe

I found a dimpled spider, fat and white. Design. Robert Frost. AnMo; HeIP; InPK; InPS; NoAM; NOBA; PBMP; PiAm; PPP; SoSe; WIF

I Found Her Out There. Thomas Hardy. LoAs; NoAM; NOBE

I found his wool face, I went away. Reading Walt Whitman. Calvin Forbes. PoBA

I found in Munster, unfettered of any. *Unknown, tr.* by James Clarence Mangan. *Fr.* Prince Alfrid's Itinerary. BIrV

I found that consciousness itself betrays. Convalescence. J. V. Cunningham. PiAm

I found the phrase to every thought. Emily Dickinson. AmVN

I found them there today. Mementos, 2. W. D. Snodgrass. CoPAm

I found you on a rainy morning. Nansen. Gary Snyder. InPS

I fynde no peace and all my warr is done. *See* I find no peace...

I gave my heart to a tin pan bitch. Judas. Andrew Baster. BuTh

I gave my life to learning how to live. Postscript. Sandra Hochman. NMM

I Gave My Love a Cherry (The Riddle), *with music. Unknown.* BLSH

(Riddle Song, The.) BLSo

I Gave You My Love. *Unknown, tr. fr. Gaelic by* Derick Thomson. SLP

I gaze where August's sunbeam falls. Newark Abbey. Thomas Love Peacock. NOBE

I Gazed upon the Cloudless Moon. Emily Brontë. Moon

I gently touched her hand: she gave. *Unknown.* BoLoP

I give praise to thee God for thy kingfisher creeks. One Fragment for God. William Everson. MIT

I go digging for clams once every two or three years. Clamming. Reed Whittemore. IPWM

I go out like a ghost. Home Town. W. D. Snodgrass. NowV

I go out to totem street. Knock on Wood. Henry Dumas. PoBA

I go through hollyhocks. Las Trampas U.S.A. Charles Tomlinson. TwMBP

I go to concert, party, ball. My Rival. Kipling. OxBTC

I go to say goodbye to the Cailleach. The Wild Dog Rose. John Montague. BIrV

I go to see my parents. Generations. Evan Jones. MAuV

I got a gal/ She's got a baker's shop. High Price Blues. *Unknown.* BluL

I Got a Home in Dat Rock. *Unknown.* BPo

I got a woman in West Helena, Arkansas. West Helena Blues. *Unknown.* BluL

I got me flowers to straw thy way. Easter. George Herbert. NOBE

I got one good look. Coon Song. A. R. Ammons. NoAM; NOBA

I Got So Old. *Unknown.* BluL

I got stones in my passway. Stones in My Passway. *Unknown.* BluL

I got the blues for my baby. My Crime. *Unknown.* BluL

I got those sad old weary blues. Too Blue. Langston Hughes. SFF

I got up this morning. I Got So Old. *Unknown.* BluL

I got-a shoes, you got-a shoes. All God's Children Got Shoes. *Unknown.* BLSH

I grant indeed that fields and flocks have charms. Rural Life. George Crabbe. *Fr.* The Village. NOBE

I grew up on Humphrey Bogart movies; it was like church. Bogart. Nicholas Flocos. SA

I grieve and dare not show my discontent. On Monsieur's Departure. Elizabeth I, Queen of England. WPE

I grieved for Buonaparté, with a vain. Wordsworth. MBPR

I grind the hoofs of broken animals. In the Glue Factory. Allan Block. FAF

I guess because it was Key West. Meeting the Reincarnation Analyst. Gary Gildner. AmPA

I had/ a dream of women, dark. A Dream of Women. Carolyn Maisel. IHMS

I had a chair at every hearth. The Lamentation of the Old Pensioner [*or* The Old Pensioner]. W. B. Yeats. InPK; NoAM

I had a dog like a love. Penny Trumpet. Raphael Rudnick. MAT

I had a donkey, that was all right. The Donkey. Theodore Roethke. ECBV

I had a dream of purity. Salome. George Garrett. CoPAm; PPoD

I Had a Future. Patrick Kavanagh. BIrV; NoAM

I had a little nut tree. Mother Goose. ECBV; GBP, 2 *sts.*

I had a little pony. Mother Goose. MG

I had a silver penny. Nursery Rhyme of Innocence and Experience. Charles Causley. LP

I had a sister once, an island sister. A Drifting. Robert Hutchinson. LoAs

I had an uncle once who kept a rock in his pocket. I've Got a Home in That Rock. Raymond R. Patterson. PoBA

I had been hungry, all the years. Emily Dickinson. SBG

I had been sitting for days. Long Distance. Dana Naone. CDW

I had come to the house, in a cave of trees. Medusa. Louise Bogan. RiTi; WPE

I had eight birds hatcht in one nest. In Reference to Her Children, 23 June, 1656. Anne Bradstreet. SBG

I had finished my dinner. An Easy Decision. Kenneth Patchen. CTBA; SFF

I had four brothers over the sea. The Tokens of Love. *Unknown.* GBP

I had heard/ before, of an. Mr. Brodsky. Charles Tomlinson. NoAM; TwMBP

I had no thought of violets of late. Sonnet. Alice Dunbar Nelson. PoBA

I had nothing to do with it. I was not here. A Centenary Ode: Inscribed to Little Crow, Leader of the Sioux Rebellion. James Wright. CoPAm

I had the blues/ Last night. Never Let Your Left Hand Know. *Unknown.* BluL

I had thought of the bear in his lair as fiercely free. Part of the Darkness. Isabella Gardner. ANTL; BoAnP

I had to kick their law into their teeth in order to save them. Negro Hero. Gwendolyn Brooks. CAPP

I had walked since dawn and lay down to rest on a bare hillside. Vulture. Robinson Jeffers. BoAnP; NOBA; PiAm

I had written him a letter which I had, for want of better. Clancy of the Overflow. Andrew Barton Paterson. MAuV

I had written to Aunt Maud. Waste Harry Graham. FaBoCo

I Hae a Wife o' My Ain. Burns.. LAuP

I hand you:/ stars, nearer than ever. A Gift for Mary MacLane. T. Alan Broughton. FAF

I hang by my heels from the sky. Hera, Hung from the Sky. Carolyn Kizer. NMM; WPE

I hardly know you, and already I say to myself. Étude. Carlos Pellicer, *tr. by* H. R. Hays. LoAs

"I hate my verses, every line, every word." Love the Wild Swans. Robinson Jeffers. HeIP; InPS; PiAm

I hate that drum's discordant sound. The Drum. John Scott of Amwell. NOBE

I hate the man who builds his name. The Poet and the Rose. John Gay. *Fr.* Fables. PAIC

I hate to see de ev'nin' sun go down. Saint Louis Blues. W. C. Handy. BLSo

I hated thee, fallen tyrant! I did groan. Feelings of a Republican on the Fall of Bonaparte. Shelley. MBPR

I Haue a Youg Suster. *Unknown. See* I Have a Young Sister.

I have a bottle and a pen. Thoughts from a Bottle. Carl Clark. JB

I have a boy of five years old. Anecdote for Fathers. Wordsworth. MBPR

I have a copper penny and another copper penny. Logic. *Unknown.* ECBV

I have a desk job. Shawano Lake, Wisconsin. Robert Gillespie. NVAP

I have a fifth of therapy. Interview with Doctor Drink. J. V. Cunningham. VGW

I have a friend, she says. The Cross-eyed Lover. Donald Finkel. Prf

I have a garden here, shaped. Letter from an Institution: III. Michael Ryan. AmPA

I have a garden of my own. Child's Song. Thomas Moore. ECBV

I Have a Gentle Cock. *Unknown.* NOBE; OxBM (Cockerel.) GBP

I have a gold watch, willed to me by a. The Gold Watch. John Blight. CAAP

I have a house where I go. Solitude. A. A. Milne. LCL

I have a life of my own. Maxine W. Kumin. *Fr.* Song for Seven Parts of the Body. POL

I have a little brain. My Brain. Annabel Laurance. AKE

I have a little shadow that goes in and out with me. My Shadow. Robert Louis Stevenson. OxBChV

I have a love is Heven-King. The Love of God. John Audelay. OxBM

I have a new garden and new is begun. The Pear-Tree. *Unknown.* GBP

I Have a Rendezvous with Death. Alan Seeger. BTTM

I have a song to sing, O! The Merryman Sings. W. S. Gilbert. ECBV

I have a vague remembrance. The Challenge. Longfellow. PiAm

I have a white cat whose name is Moon. Moon. John Ciardi. CaYB

I Have a Young Sister. *Unknown.* OxBM
(I Haue a Yong Suster.) InPS
(Tokens of Love, The.) GBP

I have allowed myself. For Masturbation. Alan Dugan. CAPP; NoAM

I Have Always Heard of These Old Men. *Unknown.* AmFP

I Have Always Known. Narihira, *tr. fr. the Japanese by* Kenneth Rexroth. BBGO

I have always known. The Way It Is. Gloria Oden. IHMS

I have appropriated the windy twittering of aspen leaves. Plunder. A. R. Ammons. NoAM

I have awakened from the unknowing to the knowing. For William Edward Burghardt Du Bois on His Eightieth Birthday. Bette Darcie Latimer. PoBA

I have been a. Homecoming. Sonia Sanchez. PoBA

I have been a censor for fifteen months. Censorship. Arthur Waley. OxBTC

I Have Been a Foster. *Unknown.* GBP
(Forester, The.) OxBM

I have been asked to write a poem about. A Non Poem About Vietnam. Carolyn M. Rodgers. SA

I have been cruel to a fat pigeon. Fly. W. S. Merwin. CoPAm

I have been having an affair. Affair of the Heart. Peter Porter. CAAP

I have been here before. Sudden Light. Dante Gabriel Rossetti. BoLoP; NOBE; VPC

I have been here. Dispersed in meditation. Agnosco Veteris Vestigia Flammae. J. V. Cunningham. VGW

I have been in this garden of unripe fruit. First Love. "Hugh MacDiarmid." SLP

I have been my arm. Margo Taft. NMM

I have been one acquainted with the night. Acquainted with the Night. Robert Frost. IPWM; NoAM; NOBA; PPP; PSN; VGW

I have been treading on leaves all day until I am autumn tired. A Leaf Treader. Robert Frost. BBGO

I have been walking today. Furnished Lives. Jon Silkin. NoAM

I have been warned. It is more than thirty years since I wrote. But I Am Growing Old and Indolent. Robinson Jeffers. NoAM; NOBA

I have been wondering. A Letter. Anthony Hecht. CoPAm

I have been young, and now am not too old. Report on Experience. Edmund Blunden. NOBE

I have begun my freedom and it hurts. Stability Before Departure. Alan Dugan. NowV

I have begun to die. The Sentry. Alun Lewis. PSN

I have beheld two lovers, in a night. Mr. Robert Herrick, His Farewell unto Poetry. Robert Herrick. SCP-1

I have burst into. The Ritual. Marge Piercy. MMD

I have but one story. Summer Is Gone. *Unknown, tr. by* Sean O'Faolain. PFIr

I have carried my pillow to the windowsill. Summer Near the River. Carolyn Kizer. VGW

I have changed nothing but coins. A Pavement Artist. G. E. Murray. HeS

I have come all this way. Ways of Day. Robert Penn Warren. *Fr.* Notes on a Life to Be Lived. NoAM

I have come at last to the short. The Great Canzon. Kenneth Rexroth. NoAM

I have come far enough. A Form of Women. Robert Creeley. CAPP

I have come far to have found nothing. Cid Corman. VGW

I have come to claim. Judy Grahn. RiTi

I have come to the borders of sleep. Lights Out. Edward Thomas. NOBE

I have come to understand my love for you. A Quiet Place. Louis Jenkins. HeS

I have desired to go. Heaven-Haven. Gerard Manley Hopkins. BuTh; HeIP; NoAM; NOBE; SoSe

I have discovered that most of. January Morning. William Carlos Williams. InPS

I have done it again. Lady Lazarus. Sylvia Plath. AnMo; CAPP; ConAP; Epi; InPK; MAT; NoAM; NOBA; PiAm; PPoe; Psy; VGW

I have done one braver thing. The Undertaking. John Donne. NOBE

I have done what I could but you avoid me. My Life by Somebody Else. Mark Strand. CAAP

I have dreamed so much of you. Poem to the Mysterious Woman. Robert Desnos, *tr. by* Wallace Fowlie. LoAs

I have eaten/ the plums. This Is Just to Say. William Carlos Williams. Epi; InPK; InPS; NOBA; PBMP; PiAm; SoSe; SpRo; SS

"I have finished another year," said God. New Year's Eve. Thomas Hardy. NoAM

I Have Folded My Sorrows. Bob Kaufman. PoBA

I have followed you model. Ode to a Model. Vladimir Nabokov. SFF

I have forsworn it while I life. The Wake at the Well. *Unknown.* GBP

I have found, my dear Miss Ware, a new way of coloring the glass. The Stained Glass Man. Cynthia Macdonald. FiCP

I have found out a gift for my Erin. A Pastoral Ballad by John Bull. Thomas Moore. BIrV

I have found out a gig-gig-gift for my fuf-fuf-fair. An Invitation to the Zoological Gardens. *Unknown.* BoAnP

I have gone into the tin can. The Tin Can. William Jay Smith. CoPAm

I have gone out, a possessed witch. Her Kind. Anne Sexton. HeIP; PPP

I have got a new-born sister. Choosing a Name. Charles *and* Mary Lamb. OxBChV

I have grete marvel of a brid. Fragment of a Love Lament. *Unknown.* OxBM

I have grown past hate and bitterness. Nationality. Mary Gilmore. MAuV

I have had asthma for a.  Visitors.  Tu Fu, *tr. by* Kenneth Rexroth.  IPWM

I have had playmates, I have had companions.  The Old Familiar Faces.  Charles Lamb.  GrRo; NOBE; PAIC

I have had to learn the simplest things.  Maximus, to Himself.  Charles Olson.  CoPAm; NOBA; VGW

I have had to stop answering yes and no.  Diseases of the Moon.  Doug Fetherling.  NeAC

I have heard some jealous women say.  Romantic.  George Garrett.  CoPAm

I have heard that hysterical women say.  Lapis Lazuli.  W. B. Yeats.  AnMo; InPK; InPS; MAT; NoAM; NOBE; OBP; PPoe; WIF

I have heard the pigeons of the Seven Woods.  In the Seven Woods.  W. B. Yeats.  NoAM

I have heard your voice floating, royal and real.  To Dinah Washington.  Etheridge Knight.  PoBA

I have her name, here in my hand, to riddle.  The Apples of Sodom and Gomorrah.  Barbara A. Holland.  WBN

I have just been to the Milo.  A Thank You Poem For The Andersons.  Phillip Hey.  NVAP

I have just come down from my father.  The Hospital Window.  James Dickey.  HeIP

I have just joined a raggedy line.  Epilogue.  Dennis Trudell.  NVAP

I have just now.  The Young Girl's Song.  Alvin J. Gordon.  MiP

I have just realized that the stakes are myself.  Revolutionary Letter # 1.  Diane DiPrima.  RiTi

I have just seen a most beautiful thing.  The Black Finger.  Angelina Weld Grimké.  PoBA

I have known it from the beginning.  Aristophanes' Symposium.  Rita Mae Brown.  IHMS

I have known the inexorable sadness of pencils.  Dolor.  Theodore Roethke.  AnMo; CoPAm; HeIP; InPK; InPS; NoAM; PBMP; PPoD; SFF; TCP

I have known the strange nurses of Kindness.  But I Do Not Need Kindness.  Gregory Corso.  CoPAm

I have led her home, my love, my only friend.  Tennyson..  *Fr.* Maud.  LoAs

I have lived in important places, times.  Epic.  Patrick Kavanagh.  BIrV

I have lived long enough, having seen one thing, that love hath an end.  Hymn to Proserpine.  Swinburne.  PFD; VPC

I Have Longed to Move Away.  Dylan Thomas.  WIF

I have looked at the Roubaix Cemetery.  Roubaix Cemetery.  Franklin Brainard.  HeS

I have looked him round and looked him through.  Nora Criona.  James Stephens.  PFIr

I have loved colours, and not flowers.  Amends to Nature.  Arthur Symons.  FSFS

I have met them at close of day.  Easter, 1916.  W. B. Yeats.  Epi; InPS; NoAM; NOBE; OBP; OxBTC; PAIC; PPoe; PPP

I have mislaid the torment and the fear.  Success.  William Empson.  OxBTC

I have moved to Dublin to have it out with you.  John Berryman.  NoAM

I have named you queen.  The Queen.  Pablo Neruda, *tr. by* Donald D. Walsh.  OLR

I have never seen that beast.  Rhinoceros.  Adrien Stoutenburg.  BoAnP

I have no brother,—they who meet me now.  Thy Brother's Blood.  Jones Very.  AmVN; NOBA

I have no name.  Infant Joy.  Blake.  *Fr.* Songs of Innocence.  LAuP; MBPR

I Have No Pain.  *Unknown.*  FaBoCo

I have not ever seen my father's grave.  Father Son and Holy Ghost.  Audre Lorde.  PoBA

I have not so much emulated the birds that musically sing.  To Soar in Freedom and in Fullness of Power.  Walt Whitman.  RFM

I have not spent the April of my time.  Fidessa, More Chaste than Kind, XXXV.  Bartholomew Griffin.  AAS; LoAs

I have not the purity.  Light.  Jon Silkin.  NoAM

I have not yet begun to relate.  Lune Concrete.  Raymond Federman.  Moon

I have nothing new to ask of you.  Another Year Come.  W. S. Merwin.  OFD

I have put my time into the ground.  Melons.  Greg Kuzma.  HeS

I have said, "Dear God," under my breath a thousand times.  Raingatherer.  Franklin Brainard.  HeS

I have said I will marry the moon.  The One-Eyed Bridegroom.  Constance Urdang.  Moon

I Have Seen Black Hands.  Richard Wright.  NoAM; PoBA

I have seen flowers come in stony places.  An Epilogue.  John Masefield.  OxBTC

I have seen the smallest minds of my generation.  Problem in Social Geometry—the Inverted Square!  Ray Durem.  PoBA

I have seen the soft light flicker.  Message from Ohanapecosh Glacier.  W. M. Ransom.  CDW

I have seen the young Negroes and Puerto Ricans.  A Documentary on Airplane Glue.  David Henderson.  MAT

I have seen them at many hours.  Poems: Birmingham 1962-1964.  Julia Fields.  PoBA

I Have Set My Heart so High  *Unknown.*  OxBM

I have something to tell you.  Two Friends.  David Ignatow.  PBMP

I have sown beside all waters in my day.  A Black Man Talks of Reaping.  Arna Bontemps.  BPo; PoBA

I have thoughts that are fed by the sun. Wordsworth.  MBPR

I Have Three Daughters.  Ruth Stone.  NMM

I have to stop answering yes and no.  Diseases of the Moon.  Doug Fetherling.  POL

I have told you.  Tenth Symphony.  John Ashbery.  NOBA

I have tossed hours upon the tides of fever.  Bout with Burning.  Vassar Miller.  CoPAm

I have travell'd this wide world over.  Old Rosin the Beau.  *Unknown.*  PSoN

I have turned to the landscape because men disappoint me.  The Ram's Horn   John Hewitt.  BIrV

I Have Twelve Oxen.  *Unknown.*  GBP

I have visited Men's Rooms.  The Repeated Shapes.  Donald Hall.  CoPAm

I have walked a great while over the snow.  The Witch.  Mary Elizabeth Coleridge.  WPE

I have watched you.  Saying Goodbye.  Suzanne Juhasz.  IHMS

I have wrought these words together out of a wryed existence.  The Wife's Complaint.  Unknown, *tr. by* Michael Alexander.  BoLoP

I hear a bull blaring.  Near Midnight.  Norman MacCaig.  SLP

I hear a sudden cry of pain!  The Snare.  James Stephens.  ECBV

I hear a whistling.  Emmett Till.  James A. Emanuel.  PoBA; WIF

I Hear America Singing.  Walt Whitman.  IPWM; PBMP

I Hear an Army Charging upon the Land.  James Joyce.  Chamber Music, XXXVI.  InPK; LoAs; NoAM; NOBE; OBP; OxBTC; SoSe

I hear April's shudder of gutter lakes.  The Same Lady.  Jeanette Nichols.  RiTi

I hear ghosts of grouse.  Opening Day.  Bruce Severy.  VW

I Hear It Was Charged against Me.  Walt Whitman.  PBMP; PPP

I hear leaves drinking rain.  The Rain.  W. H. Davies.  FSFS; OxBTC

I hear the buckles rattle from his bed.  Tyger! Tyger!  James Nolan.  AATT

I hear the clattering of an armed troop.  Psychozoia or the First Part of the Song of the Soul, Canto III.  Henry More.  SCP-2

I hear the doctor's loud success.  Waiting for the Doctor.  Colette Inez.  IHMS

I hear the shadowy horses, their long manes a-shake.  Michael Robartes Bids His Beloved Be at Peace.  W. B. Yeats.  NoAM

I heard a bird at dawn.  The Rivals.  James Stephens.  NoAM; RAE

I Heard a Bird Sing.  Oliver Herford.  LCL

I heard a cow low, a bonnie cow low.  The Queen of Elfan's Nourice.  *Unknown.*  AIW

I heard a fly buzz—when I died.  Emily Dickinson.  AmVN; AnMo; InPK; NoAM; NOBA; PiAm; PPP; Psy

I heard a mither baing her bairn.  Sealchie Song.  *Unknown.*  PeBB

I heard a thousand blended notes.  Lines Written in Early Spring.  Wordsworth.  MBPR; PBMP

I heard a voice from Etna's side.  The Mad Monk.  Samuel Taylor Coleridge.  MBPR

I heard a woman's voice that wailed.  In Ruin Reconciled.  Aubrey Thomas De Vere.  BIrV

I heard an angel speak last night.  A Curse for a Nation.  Elizabeth Barrett Browning.  SBG; WPE

I heard Andrew Jackson say, as he closed his Virgil.  Andrew Jackson's Speech.  Robert Bly.  ConAP

I Heard Christ Sing.  "Hugh MacDiarmid."  NoAM

I heard him faintly, far away.  The Corncrake.  James H. Cousins.  BoAnP; PFIr

I heard of gold at Sutter's Mill.  When I Went Off to Prospect.  *Unknown.*  AmFP

I heard one who said: "Verily."  Cassandra.  E. A. Robinson.  NoAM

I heard the cock at morning crow.  Country Morning.  Rosemary Dobson.  MAuV

I heard the dogs howl in the moonlight night.  The Dream.  William Allingham.  BIrV; PFIr; PoTa

I heard the old, old men say.  The Old Men Admiring Themselves in the Water.  W. B. Yeats.  MiP

I heard the trailing garments of the night.  Hymn to the Night.  Longfellow.  AmVN; NOBA

I heard them say I'm ugly.  The Ugly Child.  Elizabeth Jennings.  RAE

I heard thy fate without a tear.  Stanzas  Byron.  PBMP

I Held a Shelley Manuscript.  Gregory Corso.  VGW

I herde a carping of a clerk.  Robin and Gandelein.  *Unknown.*  OxBM

I Hid My Love.  John Clare.  GBL; MAT

I hoist the mummy, an armful of frozen plaster.  Floating Coathangers.  Peter Cooley.  NVAP

I hold him wise and wel y-taught.  Bear a Horn and Blow It Not.  *Unknown.*  OxBM

I hold in my hands.  Look Closely.  Morton Marcus.  SFF

I hoped/ —the night came anyway.  Conjugation of the Verb, "To Hope."  Lou Lipsitz.  FiCP

I hug you there, moccasins of worn buckskin.  The Moccasins of an Old Man.  Ramona Carden.  VW

I hung like a man on a trapeze, my arms stiffening.  Dying off Egg Island Bar.  David Smith.  NVAP

I, Icarus.  Alden Nowlan.  NCSH

I imagine him still with heavy brow.  Beethoven's Death Mask.  Stephen Spender.  OxBTC

I imagine the time of our meeting.  Forms of the Earth at Abiquiu.  N. Scott Momaday.  CDW

I imagine this midnight moment's forest.  The Thought-Fox  Ted Hughes.  HeIP; NCSH; NoAM

I imagined her dead, killed by some local maniac who.  Jim Harrison.  *Fr.* Ghazals.  InPS

I inherited forty acres from my father.  Cooney Potter.  Edgar Lee Masters.  *Fr.* Spoon River Anthology.  CTBA

I intended an Ode.  Urceus Exit.  Austin Dobson.  *Fr.* Rose-Leaves.  PAIC

I invited Mozart to dinner.  The Dinner.  Gregory Orr.  POL

I is uh revolutionist.  Yeah, I Is uh Shootin Off at the Mouth.  Carolyn M. Rodgers.  SA

I journeyed on a winter's day.  Jane Smith.  Kipling.  SpRo

I jump with terror seeing him.  Modes of Pleasure.  Thom Gunn.  PPP

I just want to get back to Birmingham.  Third Alley Blues.  *Unknown.*  BluL

I keep my parents in a garden.  Eden Is a Zoo.  Margaret Atwood.  WPE

I keep to myself such.  Robert Creeley.  NoAM

I ken these islands each inhabited.  Harry Semen.  "Hugh MacDiarmid."  NoAM; OBP

I kening through astronomy divine.  Edward Taylor.  *Fr.* Preparatory Meditations: First Series, VIII.  NOBA; PAIC; PiAM; SCP-2

I kept my answers small and kept them near.  Answers.  Elizabeth Jennings.  OxBTC

I kissed them in fancy as I came.  Two Lips.  Thomas Hardy.  BoLoP

I knew a man who used to say.  The Statesman.  Hilaire Belloc.  NOBE

I Knew a Woman.  Theodore Roethke.  AnMo; BoLoP; CoPAm; HeIP; InPK; IPWM; MAT; NoAM; NOBA; PPoe; SoSe; TCP

("I knew a woman, lovely in her bones.")  LoAs

I knew an old wife lean and poor.  The Goose.  Tennyson.  ECBV

I knew not 'twas so dire a crime.  Last Words.  Emily Brontë.  WPE

I knew that porcupines liked to eat trees.  Porcupines.  Robert Huff.  CoPAm

I knew the dignity of the words.  My Grandfather's Funeral.  James Applewhite.  NVAP

I know a little garden-close.  A Garden by the Sea.  William Morris.  *Fr.* The Life and Death of Jason.  NOBE

I know a little what it is like, once here at high tide.  Seaweed.  Sandra McPherson.  AmPA

I Know a Man.  Robert Creeley.  CAPP; ConAP; CoPAm; Epi; InPK; InPS; MAT; NOBA; PPoD; PPP; TCP

I Know a Spot Just over the Hill.  William Mills.  CoPAm

I Know a Village, sel.  Phyllis McGinley.
    5:32, The.  NMM; WPE
    Occupation: Housewife.  WPE

I know but will not tell.  Elegy.  Alan Dugan.  CAPP

I Know de Moonlight.  *Unknown.*  BPo

I know him;/ He'll give no horse for a poem.  *Unknown, tr. fr. Irish by* Vivian Mercier.  BIrV

I know I am/ The Negro Problem.  Dinner Guest: Me.  Langston Hughes.  BPo; SS

I know, I know—though the evidence.  Blow, West Wind.  Robert Penn Warren.  *Fr.* Notes on a Life to Be Lived.  NoAM

I know if I find you I will have to leave the earth.  Hymn.  A. R. Ammons.  ConAP; CoPAm

I Know I'm Not Sufficiently Obscure.  Ray Durem.  BPo; PoBA

I know it is dark; and though I have lain.  An Ode to the Rain.  Samuel Taylor Coleridge.  MBPR

I know little about bushes and trees.  A Citizen.  Charles Reznikoff.  *Fr.* Five Groups of Verse.  SA

I Know My Soul. Claude McKay. BPo

I know not how it may be with others. Old Furniture. Thomas Hardy. OxBTC

I know not of my forefathers. Lost. Bruce Ignacio. VW

I know not of what we ponder'd. Companions. Charles Stuart Calverley. FaBoCo

I know not what to do. Fragment Thirty-Six. Hilda Doolittle ("H.D."). VGW

I know that He exists. Emily Dickinson. PiAm: Psy

I know that I shall meet my fate. An Irish Airman Foresees His Death. W. B. Yeats. Epi; HeIP; NoAM; NOBE; PPP

I Know That My Redeemer Lives, *with music*. Charles Wesley. BLSH

I know the barn where they got you. For a Woodscolt Miscarried. John William Corrington. CoPAm

I know the bottom, she says. I know it with my great tap root. Elm. Sylvia Plath. NoAM; NOBA

I know the injured pride of sleep. Night and Morning. Austin Clarke. NoAM

I know the thing that's most uncommon. On a Certain Lady at Court. Pope. NOBE

I know the tops of shoes now. The Plant Rhythms. G. E. Murray. HeS

I know the ways of learning: both the head. The Pearl. George Herbert. SCP-1

I know there is a worm in the human heart. John Clare. Jon Anderson. AmPA

I know there is someone. Poem to Be Read And Sung. César Vallejo, *tr. by* James Wright *and* Robert Bly. LoAs

I know this road like the back of my hand. Ballad of the Three Coins. Vernon Watkins. NoAM

I know two things about the horse. The Horse. Naomi Royde Smith. FaBoCo

I know two women. The Wife. Robert Creeley. VGW

I know very well, goddess, she is not beautiful. Calypso's Island. Archibald MacLeish. PiAm

I know what the caged bird feels, alas! Sympathy. Paul Laurence Dunbar. PoBA

I Know Where I'm Going. *Unknown.* GBP; OLR

I know you got some good apples. Big Apple Blues. *Unknown.* BluL

I knowed a man, which he lived in Jones. Thar's More in the Man Than Thar Is in the Land. Sidney Lanier. NOBA

I knows a gal that you don't know. Li'l Liza Jane. *Unknown.* BLSo

I lack the braver mind. Confession of Faith. Elinor Wylie. SBG

I laid me down beside the sea. Lassitude. Mathilde Blind. SBG

I laid me down upon a bank. Blake. GBL; MBPR

I laks yo' kin' of lovin'. Long Gone. Sterling A. Brown. BPo

I lately vow'd, but 'twas in haste. Song. John Oldmixon. POL

I laughed at sweethearts I met at schools. My Heart Stood Still. Lorenz Hart. BLSo

I lay at the edge of a well. The Underground Stream. James Dickey. NOBA

I lay down. Children of Night. Richard Shelton. FiCP

I lay my hand. Tribal Cemetery. Janet Campbell Hale. VW

I lay with my heart under me. Cicada. Adrien Stoutenburg. RFM

I lean on a lighthouse rock. Girl at the Seaside. Richard Murphy. BIrV

I leant upon a coppice gate. The Darkling Thrush. Thomas Hardy. BoReV; FSFS; InPS; NoAM; NOBE; PPP; SoSe; VoPo

I learned in my credulous youth. Why, Some of My Best Friends Are Women. Phyllis McGinley. NMM

I leave here I'm gonna catch that M and O. M & O Blues. *Unknown.* BluL

I leave mortality, and things below. The Ecstasy. Abraham Cowley. SCP-2

I leave my heart in the doorway. Thank You for the Valentine. Diane Wakoski. CoPAm

I leave this at your ear for when you wake. W. S. Graham. LoAs

I left my prayers and the kneeling pilgrims. Fair Cassidy. *Unknown, tr. by* Donagh MacDonagh. BIrV

I left old Lake Chemo a long way behind me. Lake Chemo. James Wilton Rowe. AmFP

I let him find, but never what he sought. Epitaph on Any Man. A. S. J. Tessimond. POL

I let my soul drift with the thistledown. Soul-Drift. Mathilde Blind. SBG

I lie in bed. The Way It Is. Mark Strand. CAAP

I lied—trusting you knew. Leonora Speyer. *Fr.* Cantares. TH

I lift—lift you five States away your glass. Sonnet. John Berryman. Epi

I lift my head and watch. Thoughts in Exile. Su Tung P'o, *tr. by* Kenneth Rexroth. IPWM

I like/ dead residue. Let Us Honor Them. Rochelle Owens. Psy

I like a church; I like a cowl. The Problem. Emerson. NOBA

I like a look of agony. Emily Dickinson. AmVN; INPS

I like it here just fine. Girl Held without Bail. Margaret Walker. BPo; PoBA

I like [*or* love] little pussy, her coat is so warm. Pussy. *Unknown, at. to* Jane Taylor. OxBChV

I Like My Body When It Is with Your Body. E. E. Cummings. *Fr.* Sonnets—Actualities. AnMo; BoLoP; SFF; VGW

I like not tears in tune, nor will I prize. On the Memory of Mr. Edward King, Drowned in the Irish Seas. John Cleveland. SCP-2

I like that poem, Win. There's a green world in it. To W. T. Scott. John Ciardi. NowV

I like the streets of New York City, where I was born. Autobiography: Hollywood. Charles Reznikoff. *Fr.* Going To and Fro and Walking Up and Down. SA

I like the wind. Wind Secrets. Diane Wakoski. AmPA

I like to beat people up. Sonnet. Ted Berrigan. CAAP

I like to find. Pleasures. Denise Levertov. CAPP; NoAM; NOBA

I like to see it lap the miles. Emily Dickinson. AmVN; InPK; NOBA; PPoD; SoSe; WIF

I like to see the cowboys ride. Silver Screen. Leonard Clarke. RAE

I like to think (and/ the sooner the better!). All Watched Over by Machines of Loving Grace. Richard Brautigan. MAT

I Like to Think of Harriet Tubman. Susan Griffin. NMM; RiTi

I like to walk/ And hear the black crows talk. Crows. David McCord. RFM

I likes a woman. Preference. Langston Hughes. NOBA

I listened to the man and he. Psychometrist. James Stephens. NoAM

I live for the good of my nation. Old Rosin the Beau. *Unknown.* BLSo

I live quietly and go nowhere. My Father's House. Calvin Forbes. CoPAm

I Live Up Here. W. S. Merwin. CAPP

I live with the mad woman. The Life. George Chambers. HeS

I lived among great houses. The Statesman's Holiday. W. B. Yeats. OxBTC

"I lived with Mr. Punch, they said my name was Judy." Variations. Randall Jarrell. VGW

I long had rack'd my brains to find. A New Simile in the Manner of Swift. Goldsmith. LAuP

I long to talk with some old lover's ghost. Love's Deity. John Donne. GBL; LoAs

I look down the montainside. Just below my window. In a
Mountain Cabin in Norway. Robert Bly. RFM

I look into my glass. Thomas Hardy. NOBE

I look into the eyes of the child. The Eyes of the Child Do Not
See Me. Norman H. Russell. VW

I look out at the white sleet covering the still streets. Sleet Storm
on the Merritt Parkway. Robert Bly. ConAP; NOBA

I looked and I saw. Who But the Lord? Langston Hughes. BPo

I looked for that which is not, nor can be. A Pause of Thought.
Christina Rossetti. NOBE

I looked down and saw a pit most black. Elizabeth Melvill, Lady
Culross. Fr. A Godly Dream WPE

I looked in the first glass. The Three Mirrors. Edwin Muir.
NoAM

I Looked Over Jordan. Lane Dunlop. NowV

I looked over Jordan and what did I see. Swing Low, Sweet
Chariot. Unknown. BLSH; BLSo; WIF

I looked to find Spring's early flowers. The Lament of the Flowers.
Jones Very. NOBA

I looked to the east, I looked to the west. Pull Off Your Old Coat.
Unknown. RDB

I lost my pardner, what'll I do? Skip to My Lou. Unknown.
AmFP

I lost the love of heaven above. A Vision. John Clare. PPP

I Love. Stevie Smith. FaBoCo

I love crows. Crows. William Witherup. POL

"I love, I love, and whom love ye?" Roses. Unknown. OxBM

I love it, I love it! and who shall dare. The Old Arm-Chair. Eliza
Cook. InPK

I Love Life, with music. Irwin M. Cassel. BLSo

I love little pussy, her coat is so warm. See I like little pussy...

I Love My Jean. Burns. LAuP

I love my little son, and yet when he was ill. The Two Parents.
"Hugh MacDiarmid." OxBTC

I Love My Love. Helen Adam. NMM

"I love my love with an M," said I. Fantasia. Winifrid M. Letts.
PFIr

I love my work and my children. God. Ovid in the Third Reich.
Geoffrey Hill. NoAM; POL

I love sixpence, pretty little sixpence. Mother Goose. ECBV;
MG

I love somebody. Unknown. AmFP

I love the country air. Mother Pin a Rose on Me. David Lewis,
Paul Schindler, and Bob Adams. FSN

I love the English country scene. I Love. Stevie Smith. FaBoCo

I love the jocund dance. Song. Blake. MBPR

I love the old melodious lays. Proem. Whittier. AmVN

"I love the sea because it has drowned me." Sea Shanty. Clifford
Dyment. POL

I loved thee ere I loved a woman, Love. To Art. Dante Gabriel
Rossetti. POL

I love to rise in a summer morn. The School Boy. Blake. Fr.
Songs of Experience. MBPR

I love to see boards lying on the ground in early spring. Old
Boards. Robert Bly. CAPP

I love to see those loving and beloved. Lonely Love. Edmund
Blunden. OxBTC

I love to see, when leaves depart. Autumn. Roy Campbell.
OxBTC; WIF

I Love to Tell the Story, with music. Katherine Hankey. BLSH

I love you/ with my linen heart. The Rag Doll to the Heedless
Child. David Harsent. LP

I love you as a sheriff searches for a walnut. To You. Kenneth
Koch. CAPP

I love you, as I never loved before. When You Were Sweet
Sixteen. James Thornton. BLSH

I love you first because your face is fair. V-Letter. Karl Shapiro.
NoAM

I love you for your brownness. To a Dark Girl. Gwendolyn B.
Bennett. PoBA

I love you ginger bread mama. Ginger Bread Mama. Doughtry
Long. BPo; PoBA

I Love You Truly, with music. Carrie Jacobs Bond. BLSH;
BLSo; FSN

"I love you," you said between two mouthfuls of pudding. A
Considered Reply to a Child. Jonathan Price. BoLoP

I love your hands. Your Hands. Angelina Weld Grimké. PoBA

I loved a child of this countrie. Unknown. GBL

I Loved a Lass. George Wither. NOBE
(Love Sonnet, A.) GBL

I loved my country. Ars Poetica: Some Recent Criticism. James
Wright. CAAP

I loved thee, though I told thee not. The Secret. John Clare.
GBL

I loved to talk of home. Pacific Epitaphs. Dudley Randall.
NoAM

I loved you; even now I may confess. Pushkin, tr. fr. Russian by
Reginald Mainwaring Hewitt. BoLoP

I loved you. I loved your face, like a wellspring. The Basket-
weaver's Love. René Char, tr. by Jackson Mathews. LoAs

I made my song a coat. A Coat. W. B. Yeats. NoAM

I made up my mind for to change my way. The Trail to Mexico.
Unknown. AmFP

I make a pact with you, Walt Whitman. A Pact. Ezra Pound.
NoAM; NOBA; PAIC; PiAm; PSN

I make a simple assertion. Working with Tools. A. R. Ammons.
NoAM

I make all the poetic pauses. Dana Naone. CDW

I make seven circles, my love. Country Girl. George Mackay
Brown. SLP

I make this dirge for you Miss Mary Binning I miss you. Dirge.
Unknown, tr. by Armand Schwerner RRA

I make this song about me full sadly. The Wife's Lament.
Unknown, tr. fr. Anglo-Saxon. IPWM; WPE

I marvell'd why a simple child. Only Seven. Henry Sambrooke
Leigh. SpRo

I may be dead to-morrow, uncaressed. For the Book of Love.
Jules Laforgue, tr. by Jethro Bithell. LoAs

I May, I Might, I Must. Marianne Moore. PSN; SoSe

I, Maximus of Gloucester, to You. Charles Olson. NoAM;
NOBA

I mean/ if I didn't know. Discovering. Sharon Scott. JB

I mean/ the fiddleheads have forced their babies. May 10th.
Maxine W. Kumin. RFM

I mean by atoms small as small can be. The Bigness of Atoms.
Margaret Cavendish, Duchess of Newcastle. SCP-2

I mean, I'm a no shoes hillbilly an' home. Gracie. Faye
Kicknosway. NMM

I mean to penetrate the particular. The Medium IV: Sights. Carl
Rakosi. InPS

I meant to have but modest needs. Emily Dickinson. Psy

I Meant to Tell You. Sean Haldane. POL

I meet Mother on the street. Poem. Lennart Bruce. POL

I meet you in an evil time. An Eclogue for Christmas. Louis
MacNeice. NoAM

I met a traveller from an antique land. Ozymandias Revisited.
Morris Bishop. PAIC; SpRo

I met a traveller from an antique land. Ozymandias. Shelley.
Epi; HeIP; InPK; IPWM; MBPR; NOBE; OBP; PAIC;
PPoD; SFF; SoSe; SpRo

I met an adolescent kitten on Lexington Ave. Eastside Chick with
Drive. Albert Spector. CTBA

I met ayont the cairney. Empty Vessel. "Hugh MacDiarmid." SLP

I met in Mesilla. Edward Dorn. *Fr.* Gunslinger NoAM

I met Louisa in the shade. Louisa. Wordsworth. GBL

I met Murder on the way. Shelley. *Fr.* The Mask of Anarchy. OBP

I met the Bishop on the road. Crazy Jane Talks with the Bishop. W. B. Yeats. AnMo; BoLoP; InPK; NoAM; PPP

I met the Love-Talker one eve in the glen. The Love-Talker. "Ethna Carbery." PFIr; PoTa; WPE

I met with the gnat. The Confession. Gary Lawless. FAF

I mind as 'ow the night afore that show. The Chances. Wilfred Owen. OxBTC

I miss the peace and quiet of Chicago. Poem after Apollinaire. Ira Sadoff. AmPA

I move among my pots and pans. Trimming the Sails. Vassar Miller. NMM

I move each fall. Mover. James L. White. HeS

I move on feeling and have learned to distrust those who don't. Poem of Angela Yvonne Davis. Nikki Giovanni. PoBA

I move the curtain back. After I Have Voted. Laura Jensen. AmPA

I Move to Random Consolations. William Heyen. AmPA

I moved to the window to wait for somebody. A Suicide. Tom Kryss. NeAC

I murder hate by field or flood. Burns. OBP

I Must Ask. James E. Warren, Jr.. AATT

I must be mad, or very tired. Meeting-House Hill. Amy Lowell. PSN; SBG

I must complain, yet doe enjoy my love. Thomas Campion. AAS

I must explain why it is that at night, in my own house. Still Life. Reed Whittemore. ConAP

I must find a slut tonight. What a Way to Lose the War. Luís Omar Salinas. SA

I must go back to winter. Two Decisions. Vernon Watkins. OxBTC

I must go down to the seas again, to the lonely sea and the sky. Sea Fever. John Masefield. IPWM; OxBTC; SFF

I must hide him in my innermost veins. Totem. Léopold Sédar Senghor, *tr. by* Gerald Moore *and* Ulli Beier. BuTh

I must lie down with them all soon and sleep. Thomas Kinsella. *Fr.* Nightwalker. BIrV

I must not grieve my love, whose eyes would read. Sonnet. Samuel Daniel. *Fr.* To Delia. LoAs

I must not think of thee; and, tired yet strong. Renouncement. Alice Meynell. BoLoP; NOBE; WPE

I myself saw furious with blood. Aeneas at Washington. Allen Tate. NoAM; NOBA; PiAm

I nail Picasso's girl with a mirror. Notes from an Analyst's Couch. Anita Endrezze Probst. CDW

I Need Not Go. Thomas Hardy. NOBE; OxBTC

I ne'er was struck before that hour. First Love. John Clare. BoLoP; GBL

I never cast a flower away. Partings. Maria Jane Jewsbury. OxBChV

I never drank of Aganippe well. Astrophel and Stella, LXXIV. Sir Philip Sidney. HeIP

I never gave a lock of hair away. Sonnets from the Portuguese, XVIII. Elizabeth Barrett Browning. VPC

I never felt so much. A Birthday. Edwin Muir. LoAs

I never hear the word "escape." Emily Dickinson. NOBA

I never let you come to the games. I never. Basketball. Stephen Vincent. NeAC

I never lost as much but twice. Emily Dickinson. AmVN; NOBA; PiAm

I never loved a dear gazelle. Tèma Con Variazióni. "Lewis Carroll." SpRo

"I never nursed a dear gazelle." Thomas Moore. *Fr.* Lalla Rookh. SpRo

I never rear'd a young gazelle. 'Twas Ever Thus. Henry Sambrooke Leigh. FaBoCo; SpRo

I never saw a moor. Emily Dickinson. HeIP; LCL

I never saw a purple cow. The Purple Cow. Gelett Burgess. FaBoCo

I never saw a wild thing. Self-Pity. D. H. Lawrence. BoAnP; OxBTC

I never saw the man whom you describe. The Foster-Mother's Tale. Samuel Taylor Coleridge. MBPR

I never saw you, madam, lay apart. Earl of Surrey. AAS; LoAs

I never wake up well. Collaborations. Cathleen Quirk. MMD

I never would 'ave done it if I'd known what it would be. Mules. C. Fox-Smith. BoAnP

I, now at Carthage. He, shot dead at Rome. Vale from Carthage. Peter Viereck. CoPAm; SS

I offer my back to the silken net. An Allegory. David Ignatow. VGW

I offer you the chance to forgive your wounds. Songs from the Maker of Totems. Duane Niatum. VW

I offer wrong to my beloved saint. Fulke Greville. *Fr.* Caelica. PAIC

I once believed a single line. For E. J. P. Leonard Cohen. NoAM

I once did an hour-long TV show reading. Osip Mandelshtam. Irving Layton. NeAC

I once did court a damsel most beautiful and bright. A Lover's Lament. *Unknown.* AmFP

I once had a girl. Norwegian Wood. John Lennon *and* Paul McCartney. OBP

I once had a sweet little doll, dears. The Lost [*or* Little] Doll. Charles Kingsley. *Fr.* The Water Babies. ECBV; OxBChV

I once knew a fellow named Arthur McBride. Arthur McBride. *Unknown.* GBP; PeBB

I once knew a lass and I loved her to [*or* I've oft heard her] tell. So I Let Her Go. *Unknown.* AmFP

I once knew a little girl, a charming beauty bright. The Rejected Lover. *Unknown.* AmFP

I once knowed an ole Sexion Boss but he done been laid low. The Old Section Boss. *Unknown.* BPo

I Once Loved a Young Man. *Unknown.* AmFP

I once loved a young man as dear as my life. I'm Going to Georgia. *Unknown.* AmFP

I once may see when yeares shall wreck my wrong. Samuel Daniel. *Fr.* To Delia. AAS

I once spent an evening in a village. The Man Upright. Thomas MacDonagh. BIrV

I once was a seaman stout and bold. Jolly Soldier. *Unknown.* AmFP; OFD

I once was happy, when, while yet a child. Charlotte Smith. *Fr.* Beachy Head. WPE

I once wrote a letter as follows. The Invoice. Robert Creeley. VGW

I Only Am Escaped Alone to Tell Thee. Howard Nemerov. HeIP; NoAM

I only knew her as a spouse. At Flock Mass. F. R. Higgins. PFIr

I open the door and walk in. Pop. David McFadden. NeAC

I opened my door to this nutty witch. I've been suicidal. After Reading Sylvia Plath. Alta. IHMS

I opened my eyes at the foot of a grey mountain. Gavin Bantock. *Fr.* Ichor TwMBP

I ordered this, this clean wood box. The Arrival of the Bee Box. Sylvia Plath. PSN; TCP

I own certain acre-scraps of woodland, scattered. Farmer's Point of View. Alan Brownjohn. BuTh

I own, the match, you recommend. To a Friend, Who Recommended a Wife to Him. *Unknown.* PiAm

I painted her a gushing thing. My Fancy. "Lewis Carroll." FaBoCo

I parted from my life last night. On the Death of His Wife. Muireadach O'Dalaegh, *tr. by* Frank O'Connor. BIrV

I passed along the water's edge below the humid trees. The Indian upon God. W. B. Yeats. IPWM

I picked some flowered weeds. A Visit to My Father-In-Law on Memorial Day. Peggy Ruse. NPW

I picked up a leaf. Les Etiquettes Jaunes. Frank O'Hara. CAPP

I pitied one whose tattered dress. The Vesture of the Soul. "AE." PFIr

I placed a jar in Tennessee. Anecdote of the Jar. Wallace Stevens. InPK; NoAM; NOBA; PPP

I planned to have a border of lavender. Paul Goodman. VGW

"I play for seasons; not eternities!" Modern Love, XIII. George Meredith. PFD; VPC

I play it cool. Motto. Langston Hughes. PoBA

I pledge allegiance to the flag. The Pledge to the Flag. Francis Bellamy. BLSH

I pledge myself through thick and thin. Tory Pledges. Thomas Moore. FaBoCo

I plucked my soul out of its secret place. I Know My Soul. Claude McKay. BPo

I plucked pink blossoms from mine apple-tree. An Apple Gathering. Christina Rossetti. OLR

I polish, cook, or clean my nest. Bruce Holsapple. FAF

I pondered the cold simplicity. Rejoinder. Albert De Pietro. AATT

I pray that the great world's flowering stay as it is. The Gardener to His God. Mona Van Duyn. WPE

I pray thee leave, love me no more. To His Coy Love. Michael Drayton. LoAs

I pray you all with one thought. Amend Me. *Unknown.* OxBM

"I pray you, cum kiss me." My Little Pretty Mopsy. *Unknown.* OxBM

I pray you, M, to me be trew. Letter to "M." *Unknown.* OxBM

I Promise Nothing. A. E. Housman. PPP

I promised I would but I can't. Alta. MMD

I promised once if I got hold of. Written in a Copy of Swift's Poems, for Wayne Burns. James Wright. NOBA

I promised to look out for the child. The Delivery. Hollis Summers. CoPAm

I Put My Hand on His Head. Ted Kooser. HeS

I put my nickel. Midnight Raffle. Langston Hughes. PiAm

I quit my job this morning. Employed. James Bertolino. HeS

I raced to the bluff to drown in the sea. Tarred Gull. Elisavietta Ritchie. AATT

I raised a noble falcon. The Falcon. The Knight of Kürenberg, *tr. by* Margarete Münsterberg. LoAs

I ran from you to danger. Round Trip to Chicago. Martha Shelley. WBN

I ran onto Mehitabel again. The Old Trouper. Don Marquis. *Fr.* Archy and Mehitabel. FaBoCo

I rasp like a sick dog. Theodore Roethke. POL

I Read a Tight-Fisted Poem Once. Nancy Woods. RFM

I read my sentence—steadily. Emily Dickinson. NoAM

I read or write, I teach or wonder what is truth. Apologia pro Vita Sua. Sedulius Scottus, *tr. by* Helen Waddell. BIrV

I read the news today, oh boy. A Day in the Life. John Lennon *and* Paul McCartney. PPoe; WIF

I really do not like that cat. What Could It Be? William Cole. BoAnP

I reckon—when I count at all. Emily Dickinson. PiAm

I recognized you because when I saw the print. Poetry. Juan Ramón Jiménez. LoAs; OLR

I Remember. Mae Jackson. PoBA

I Remember. Stevie Smith. BoLoP; InPK

I remember a house where all were good. The Valley of Elwy. Gerard Manley Hopkins. LoAs

I remember back in hi school. The Art of Enforced Deprivation. Alta. MMD

I remember how, long ago, I found. Crystals like Blood. "Hugh MacDiarmid." InPS

I Remember How She Sang. Rob Penny. PoBA

I Remember, I Remember. Thomas Hood. NOBE

I remember Longwood. Blind Adolphus. Angela McCabe. AmPA

I remember my mother, the day that we met. For the Crèche. G. K. Chesterton. *Fr.* Songs of Education. FaBoCo

I remember one September. Billy Lyons and Stack O'Lee. *Unknown.* BluL

I remember the August afternoon. August Afternoon. Nancy Remaly. CTBA

I remember the Chillicothe ball players. Hits and Runs. Carl Sandburg. SPo

I remember the day when I learned to whistle. When I Learned to Whistle. Gordon Lea. AKE

I remember the dread with which I at a quarter past four. False Security. John Betjeman. BBGO; LP

I remember the evening. The Swarming Bees. James Laughlin. VGW

I remember the neckcurls, limp and damp as tendrils. Elegy for Jane. Theodore Roethke. CoPAm; InPK; InPS; IPWM; PAIC; PPoe; PSN; RRA; TCP; VoPo; WIF

I remember the night. Somebody Call. Carolyn M. Rodgers. JB

I remember the old joke. The Cliff. David Rowbotham. CAAP

I remember the Roman Emperor, one of the cruellest of them. Exeat. Stevie Smith. NoAM

I remember the United States of America. A Box Comes Home. John Ciardi. CoPAm

I remember to this day. Me and You and a Dog Named Boo. Kent LaVoie. PoRo

I remember Wednesday was the day. Two Lean Cats. Myron O'Higgins. PoBA

I remember when a Sunday friend and I. Letter to My Mother. Anita Skeen. IHMS

I remember you as you were that final autumn. Pablo Neruda, *tr. fr. Spanish by* Robert Bly. LoAs

I remember zoot-suited pimps. 6th and Walnut Street. Rubee Dreher Moxley. NPW

I reside at Table Mountain and my name is Truthful James. Plain Language from Truthful James. Bret Harte. FaBoCo

I returned, and saw under the sun. Ecclesiastes, Bible, *O. T.* Prf

I Ride an Old Paint. *Unknown.* AmFP; RDB

I ride through Queens. An Invitation to Madison County. Jay Wright. PoBA

I rip off/ bobtail. Skinning a Rabbit. Norbert Krapf. HeS

I rise at 2 a.m. these mornings, to. The Feral Pioneers. Ishmael Reed. PoBA

I rise from the sun-deck. Cook-out. Dan Masterson. CoPAm

I rise, I rise I who [*or whose tread*] makes the earth to rumble. The Rising of the Buffalo Men. *Unknown.* ANTL; SFF

I rise in the dawn, and I kneel and blow. The Song of the Old Mother. W. B. Yeats. IPWM; PFIr

I rode one evening with Count Maddalo. Julian and Maddalo. Shelley. MBPR

I Rode Southern, I Rode L. & N. *Unknown.* AmFP

I rode till I reached the House of Wealth. Rest Only in the Grave. James Clarence Mangan. BIrV

I rode to church last Sunday. My Love She Passed Me By. *Unknown.* AmFP

I rub the one bullet. Snake Dance. Lyn Lifshin. FAF; RiTi

I sagh Him with flesh al bi-spred: He cam from Est. *See* I saw him with flesh all be-spread...

I said:/ Now will the poets sing. Scottsboro, Too, Is Worth Its Song. Countee Cullen. PoBA

I said I splendidly loved you; it's not true. Sonnet. Rupert Brooke. BuTh

I said I'd get her a towel and ran. Girls. Kenneth Rosen. AmPA

I said—Then, dearest, since 'tis so. The Last Ride Together. Robert Browning. BoLoP

I said, "This horse, sir, will you shoe?" Logical English. *Unknown.* ECBV

I Said to Love. Thomas Hardy. GBL; NoAM

I said to my baby. Same in Blues. Langston Hughes. *Fr.* Lenox Avenue Mural. InPS; WIF

I sat all morning in the college sick bay. Mid-term Break. Seamus Heaney. NCSH

I sat by a stream in a. Classic. A. R. Ammons. NOBA

I sat next the duchess at tea. Limerick. *Unknown.* SoSe

I sat on the Dogana's steps. Cantos, III. Ezra Pound. Epi

I sat wi' my love, and I drank wi' my love. *Unknown.* GBP

I sat with John Brown. That night moonlight framed. Narrative. Russell Atkins. PoBA

I sate beside the steersman then, and gazing. The Revolt of Islam, VIII. Shelley. MBPR

I saw/ a specialist a cook. To the Heart. Tadeusz Rozewicz, *tr. by* Victor Contoski. POL

I Saw a Chapel All of Gold. Blake. AnMo; LAuP; MBPR

I saw a donkey. The Donkey. Gertrude Hinde. ECBV

I saw a doo flee our the dam. *Unknown.* GBP

I saw a famous man eating soup. Soup. Carl Sandburg.. AKE; NOBA; TH

I Saw a Fish Pond. *Unknown.* ECBV; GBP

I saw a gardener with a watering can. The Progress of Poetry. "Christopher Caudwell." OxBTC

I saw a hawk devour a screaming bird. Hawk Is a Woman. Hildegarde Flanner. WPE

I Saw a Jolly Hunter. Charles Causley. BoAnP; LP

I saw a little tailor sitting stitch, stitch, stitching. Tailor. Eleanor Farjeon. OxBChV

I Saw a Man Pursuing the Horizon. Stephen Crane. The Black Riders, XXIV. MAT; NOBA; PBMP; PiAm; SFF

I saw a mouth jeering. Gargoyle. Carl Sandburg. NoAM; NOBA

I Saw a Peacock with a Fiery Tail. *Unknown.* GBP; OBP (Ambiguous Lines.) ECBV

I saw a ship a-sailing. Mother Goose. ECBV; MG

I saw a ship a-sailing, a-sailing, a-sailing. An Old Song Re-sung. John Masefield. ECBV

I saw a ship of martial build. The Berg. Herman Melville. AmVN; InPK; NOBA; PiAm

I saw a stable, low and very bare. Salus Mundi. Mary Elizabeth Coleridge. BoReV

I saw a staring virgin stand. Two Songs from a Play, I. W. B. Yeats. *Fr.* The Resurrection. NOBE; OBP; PPoe; PPP

I saw a vision yesternight. To the State of Love, or the Senses' Festival. John Cleveland. SCP-2

I saw a young snake glide. Snake. Theodore Roethke. AKE; ECBV; NOBA; RFM

I saw a youth and maiden on a lonely city street. Take Back Your Gold. Louis W. Pritzkow. FSN

I saw again in a dream the other night. Two Girls. Howard Nemerov. AnMo

I saw an aged beggar in my walk. The Old Cumberland Beggar. Wordsworth. MBPR

I Saw an Army. George Abbe. FAF

I saw each soul as light, each single body. Night of Souls. Ann Stanford. WPE

I saw Eternity the other night. The World. Henry Vaughan. BoReV; HeIP; MetP; NOBE; OBP; PPoe; PPP; SCP-1

I saw fair Chloris walk alone. On Chloris Walking in the Snow. William Strode. NOBE; SCP-2

I saw five birds all in a cage. Riddle. *Unknown.* GBP

I Saw from the Beach. Thomas Moore. PFIr

I saw God! Do You doubt it? What Tomas Said in a Pub. James Stephens. NoAM

I saw her amid the dunghill debris. Tinker's Wife. Patrick Kavanagh. NoAM

I saw her once, one little while, and then no more. And Then No More. Friedrich Rückert, *tr. by* James Clarence Mangan. BIrV

I saw him brought into Emergency. Empty Holds a Question. Pat Folk. NowV

I saw him in the Airstrip Gardens. Betjeman, 1984. Charles Causley. FaBoCo; OxBTC

I saw him once before. The Last Leaf. Oliver Wendell Holmes. AmVN; PiAm; VoPo

I saw him steal the light away. God's Education. Thomas Hardy. OBP

I saw [or sagh] him with flesh all be-spread: He came from East. Advent [or Christ's Coming]. *Unknown.* BoReV

I saw in a poet's song. Symbols. John Drinkwater. WIF

I Saw in Louisiana a Live-Oak Growing. Walt Whitman. AmVN; InPK; IPWM; MAT; NoAM; NOBA

I saw it all, Polly, how when you had call'd for sop. Poor Poll. Robert Bridges. OxBTC

I saw it in an empty window. In an Empty Window. Ray Fraser. NeAC

I saw it jerking as I drove by. The Coyote. A. A. Dewey. HeS

I saw it rise, a stunted, soot-encrusted. The Honored Dead. Thomas Doulis. NowV

I saw magic on a green country road. Sonnet. Michael Hartnett. BIrV

I saw my grandmother grow weak. First Death. Donald Justice. FiCP

I saw my lady weep. My Lady's Tears. *Unknown.* NOBE

I saw my love, younger than primroses. In a Wood. E. J. Scovell. GBL

I saw myself leaving. Reflections. Carl Gardner. PoBA

I saw new worlds beneath the water lie. On Leaping over the Moon. Thomas Traherne. Moon

I saw no way—the heavens were stitched. Emily Dickinson. PiAm

I saw old Autumn in the misty morn. Ode: Autumn. Thomas Hood. FSFS

I saw the best minds of my generation destroyed by madness, starving hysterical naked. Howl. Allen Ginsberg. AnMo; CAPP; CoPAm; InPS; NoAM

I saw the best parts of Iowa covered with New Jersey tea. Touring the Hawkeye State. Gary Gildner. HeS

I saw the black trees leaning. Trees and Evening Sky. N. Scott Momaday. CDW

I saw the Devil walking down the lane. The Devil's Bag. James Stephens. PFIr; PoTa

I Saw the Light Yesterday. Galina V. Ogilvie-Laing. SLP

I saw the midlands. Kisses in the Train. D. H. Lawrence. OBP

I saw the spiders marching through the air. Mr. Edwards and the Spider. Robert Lowell. AnMo; CAPP; HeIP; InPS; NOBA; PSN

I saw the spot where our first parents dwelt. The Garden. Jones Very. AmVN; PiAm

I saw the tall bush burn. Fall in Massachusetts. Isabella Gardner. RiTi

I saw the throng, so deeply separate. A General Communion. Alice Meynell. WPE

I Saw the Wind Today. Padraic Colum. Reminiscence, II. CaYB; ECBV; RAE

I saw them at games every. Seven Mexican Children. Tom Schmidt. NeAC

I Saw Them Lynch. Carole Freeman. NMM; PoBA; WIF

I saw three ships come sailing by. Mother Goose. MG

I saw two trees embracing. All That Time. May Swenson. RiTi

I saw with open eyes. Studpidity Street. Ralph Hodgson. OxBTC

I saw you/ on my walk last. Glimpse. Pearl Cleage Lomax. PoBA

I saw you/ peeking out thru the flower pots. As the World Turns. Larry Mollin. NeAC

I saw you arise from your bed, I saw your door open. All Is Well with the Child. Marya Zaturenska. LoAs

"I saw you take his kiss!" " 'Tis true." The Kiss. Coventry Patmore. The Angel in the House, II, viii. BoLoP; SoSe

I say I woke up this morning, baby so dark I couldn't hardly see. Y M & V Blues. Unknown. BluL

I say now, Fernando, that on that day. Hibiscus on the Sleeping Shores. Wallace Stevens. InPS

I say the women don't sleep right. Explanation. Geof Hewitt. NeAC

I scarce believe my love to be so pure. Love's Growth; or, Spring. John Donne. SCP-1

I see a bad moon rising. Bad Moon Rising. John Fogerty. GrRo

I see a rabbit drinking at a stream. The Rabbit. Philip McIntyre, Jr. AKE

I see before me now a traveling army halting. Bivouac on a Mountain Side. Walt Whitman. PiAm

I see before me the gladiator lie. The Dying Gladiator. Byron. Fr. Childe Harold's Pilgrimage, IV. NOBE

I see black dragons mount the sky. Shapes and Signs. James Clarence Mangan. PFIr

I see her against the pearl sky of Dublin. My Mother's Sister. C. Day Lewis. OxBTC

I see her seventeen. Arizona Highways. James Welch. CDW

I see I've come a pilgrimage. I didn't. The Weepers Tower in Amsterdam. Paul Goodman. VGW

I see the children running out of school. The Poet Laments the Coming of Old Age Edith Sitwell. NoAM

I See the Moon. Unknown. GBP

I see the thin bell-ringer standing at corners. The Jew at Christmas Eve. Karl Shapiro. VGW

I see them/ Puerto Ricans. You're Nothing But a Spanish Colored Kid. Felipe Luciano. PoBA

I see them, crowd on crowd they walk the earth. The Dead. Jones Very. AmVN; NOBA; PAIC

I see them illumine. Fireflies. Helena Minton. FAF

I see them working in old rectories. The Country Clergy. R. S. Thomas. BoReV; OxBTC; PSN

I see you, a child. The Album. C. Day Lewis. BuTh; OxBTC

I see you, Juliet, still, with your straw hat. Farewell to Juliet. Wilfrid Blunt. Fr. The Love Sonnets of Proteus. BoLoP; OxBTC

I see you lizard. What Might Pass a Man As a Survivor. J. S. Harry. CAAP

I see your breath. Going into the Woods. Tom Hennen. HeS

I see'd her in de springtime. She Hugged Me and Kissed Me. Unknown. BPo

I seek about this world unstable. Of the Changes of Life. William Dunbar, tr. by Andrew Glaze. OBP

I seem to see. Queer. David McCord. CaYB

I send my poisoned candies through the mail. End of the Affair. Geoffrey Grigson. GBL

I send these wild roses. Bruce Holsapple. FAF

I serve a mistress whiter than the snow. Anthony Munday. LoAs

I shall begin by learning to throw. Formal Application. Donald W. Baker. SoSe

I shall die, but that is all that I shall do for Death. Conscientious Objector. Edna St. Vincent Millay. VoPo

I shall go among red faces and virile voices. Cattle Show. "Hugh MacDiarmid." OxBTC

I shall go as my father went. The Tenancy. Mary Gilmore. MAuV

I shall hate you. Hatred. Gwendolyn B. Bennett. PoBA

I shall kneel weeping when you say. Letter to Her Son's Commanding Officer. Ethel Green Russell. AATT

I shall know why—when time is over. Emily Dickinson. NoAM

I shall lie hidden in a hut. Prophecy. Elinor Wylie. RiTi; VGW

I shall never get you put together entirely. The Colossus. Sylvia Plath. AnMo; CAPP; CoPAm; NoAM; NOBA; Psy

I shall not linger in that draughty square. French. Osbert Lancaster. FaBoCo

I shall paint/ God in the midst. Robert Browning. Fr. Fra Lippo Lippi. Prf

I shall say what inordinate love is. Inordinate Love. John Lydgate. LoAs

I shall write of the old men I knew. In These Dissenting Times. Alice Walker. PoBA

I shipped on board of a Liverpool liner. Sally Brown. Unknown. AmFP

I shiver, spirit fierce and bold. At the Grave of Burns, 1803. Wordsworth. MBPR

I shoot the hippopotamus. The Hippopotamus. Hilaire Belloc. InPK

I shot an arrow into the air. A Shot at Random. D. B. Wyndham Lewis. FaBoCo

I should have thought. At Baia. Hilda Doolittle ("H.D."). NOBA; PAIC

I shudder thinking  The Cold Irish Earth. Knute Skinner. InPK

I Sigh When I Sing ("I sike al when I singe"). Unknown. OxBM

I Sing No New Songs. Frank Marshall Davis. PoBA

I sing of a captain who's well known to fame. A Nautical Ballad. Keighley Goodchild. ECBV

I sing of a hero, unsung, unrecorded. Crispus Attucks McCoy. Sterling A. Brown. BPo

I Sing of a Maiden That Is Makeless. Unknown. BoReV; InPK; InPS; NOBE; OxBM

(Maiden That Is Makeless, A.) OFD

I sing of brooks, of blossoms, birds, and bowers. The Argument of His Book. Robert Herrick. HeIP; OBP

I Sing of Olaf Glad and Big. E. E. Cummings. HeIP; NoAM; NOBA; PAIC; VGW; VoPo; WIF

I Sing of Shine. Etheridge Knight. BPo

I sing of the decline of Henry Clay. Conquistador. A. D. Hope. PPoD

I sing the brave adventures of two wights. The Voyage Itself. Ben Jonson. TVS

I sing the sofa. I who lately sang. The Sofa. William Cowper. Fr. The Task. LAuP

I sing the just and uncontrolled descent. Ben Jonson. Fr. Eupheme SCP-1

I, singularly moved. Winter. Coventry Patmore. NOBE

I sink my soft butt in an easy chair. News. Marnie Pomeroy. POL

I Sit and Look Out. Walt Whitman. CTBA; SFF

I sit at a gold table with my girl. At the Altar. Robert Lowell. Between the Porch and the Altar, IV. InPK; InPS

I sit back in the city. Wearing Breasts. Daniela Gioseffi. RiTi

I sit clumsy in my flesh, my legs. The Cigarette Poem. Faye Kicknosway. IHMS

I sit down at a table and open a book of poems. Library. Louis Jenkins. HeS

"I sit here in these stocks." In Weatherbury Stocks. Thomas Hardy. AIW

I sit here with the wind is in my hair. To Helen (of Troy, N.Y.). Peter Viereck. CoPAm

I sit in a huge auditorium. The Return. Dennis Saleh. NeAC

I sit in the marsh. River and Light. Siv Cedering Fox. RiTi

I sit in the top of the wood, my eyes closed. Hawk Roosting. Ted Hughes. HeIP; MPo; OxBTC; PPP; PSN;

I sit musing, ten minutes from the Jap. A Letter for Marian. Thomas McGrath. VGW

I sit poking a small fire. In Memory of Francis Webb. Thomas Shapcott. CAAP

I slam the door. Outside I find the day. John Nobody. Dom Moraes. NoAM

I sleep with thee, and wake with thee. To Mary: I Sleep with Thee, and Wake with Thee. John Clare. GBL

I slept alone last nite but when you know you dont have to. Alta. MMD

I slept under rhododendron. Four Poems for Robin. Gary Snyder. NoAM; NOBA

I snum I am a Yankee lad, and I guess I'll sing a ditty. The Boston Tea Tax. Unknown. BTTM

I So Liked Spring. Charlotte Mew. OxBTC

I sometimes fear the younger generation will be deprived. Hoeing. John Updike. TSWA

I sometimes sleep with other girls. Cavalier Lyric. James Simmons. InPK; POL

I sometimes think. Did You See the Times Today? Lois Wyse. SFF

I sometimes think I'd rather crow. To Be or Not to Be [or Rooster Be? Or a Crow?]. Unknown. ECBV; FaBoCo

I sought a theme and sought for it in vain. The Circus Animals' Desertion. W. B. Yeats. MAT; NoAM; NOBE; OxBTC; PPoD; PSN

I sought, I found, she asked me what I would. Rachel Speght. Fr. A Dream. WPE

I sowed the seeds of love. The Seeds of Love. Unknown, at. to Mrs. Fleetwood Habergham. AIW; GBP

I speak for Erin. The Muse of Amergin. Unknown, tr. by John Montague. BIrV

I speak from ignorance. Last of the Chiefs. Nathaniel Tarn. TwMBP

I speak of that great house. Beyond the Hunting Woods. Donald Justice. ConAP; NCSH

I speak skimpily to. Personal Letter No. 2. Sonia Sanchez. WBN

I spent a nicht amang the cognoscenti. I Was Fair Beat. Robert Garioch. OxBTC

I spent a night turning in bed. The Whip. Robert Creeley. NoAM

I spied a very small brown duck. Duck-Chasing. Galway Kinnell. VGW

I spied John Mouldy in his cellar. John Mouldy. Walter de la Mare. NCSH; OxBChV

I spoke without caring. Investigation. Julia Vinograd. IHMS

I spot the hills. Theme in Yellow. Carl Sandburg. LCL

I sprang to the rollocks and Jorrocks and me. How I Brought the Good News from Aix to Ghent. R. J. Yeatman and W. C. Sellar. SpRo

I sprang to the stirrup, and Joris, and he. How They Brought the Good News from Ghent to Aix. Robert Browning. BTTM; ECBV; PAIC; SpRo

I stand and watch for minutes by the pond. This, That & the Other. Howard Nemerov. AnMo

I stand as on some mighty eagle's beak. From Montauk Point. Walt Whitman. RFM

I stand before you. Position. Carol Bergé. MMD

I stand in my door and look over the low field of Drynam. The Widow of Drynam. Patrick MacDonogh. PFIr

I stand in the dark light in the dark street. Birthplace Revisited. Gregory Corso. SA; VGW

I stand mute in the moonshine and lights of the moon. The Preparation of the Body. Helen Wolfert. Fr. Woman Against the Moon. RiTi

I stand on the ledge where rock runs into the river. The Wreck of the Thresher. William Meredith. CoPAm

I stand on the mark beside the shore. The Runaway Slave at Pilgrim's Point. Elizabeth Barrett Browning. SBG

I stand on the wharf. Voyage. Stephen Stepanchev. SA

I stand there slapping a house. The Apprentice Painter. Jack Myers. AmPA

I stand upon my miracle hill. Miracle Hill. Emerson Blackhorse Mitchell. VW

I stand within the willowing shadows of Memp-ch-ton. On Hearing the Marsh Bird's Water Cry. Duane Niatum. CDW

I standing on a hill of fancies high. Margaret Cavendish, Duchess of Newcastle. Fr. Nature's Landskip. SCP-2

I stared at the printed words. Printed Words. Liz Sohappy Bahe. CDW

I start awake at night afraid of death. Sonnet 21. Paul Goodman. VGW

I started early, took my dog. Emily Dickinson. AmVN; InPK; Psy; SBG

I started picking up the stones. Apologia pro Vita Sua. A. R. Ammons. NOBA

I stay;/ But it isn't as if. An Empty Threat. Robert Frost. RFM

I stayed in jail and worked for thirty long days. Nashville Stonewall Blues. Unknown. BluL

I stayed the night for shelter at a farm. The Witch of Coös. Robert Frost. Fr. Two Witches. NoAM; NOBA; PAIC

I step around a gate of bushes. Cold Water. Donald Hall. NCSH

I stepped from plank to plank. Emily Dickinson. NOBA; Psy

I stick my tongue in you. Gray Silk Twisting. Patrick Lane. NeAC

I Still Feel You. Marge Piercy. Psy

I stole forth dimly in the dripping pause. Moon Compasses. Robert Frost. LoAs; Moon

I stood and marveled. About my head. The Washer-Widows. Paul Clause. AATT

I stood between two mirrors when you died. Elegy. William Jay Smith. CoPAm

I stood by the stone sea-wall at Depoe Bay. The Sprouting Horn. Nelson Bentley. LoAs

I stood in the shelter of a great tree. Tumbleweed. Ramona Carden. VW

I stood in Venice on the Bridge of Sighs. Venice and Sunset. Byron. Fr. Childe Harold's Pilgrimage. PAIC

I stood on Brocken's sovran height, and saw. Lines Written in the Album at Elbingerode. Samuel Taylor Coleridge. MBPR

I stood one day by the breezy bay. A Nautical Extravaganza. Wallace Irwin. PoTa

I stood still and was a tree amid the wood. The Tree. Ezra Pound. PBMP; PiAm

I Stood Tiptoe upon a Little Hill.  Keats.  MBPR
On a Summer's Day *sel.*  FSFS

I stood within the city disinterred.  Ode to Naples.  Shelley.
PAIC

I stopped the doctor busy with his hemps.  Lines for a Fifty-fifth
Birthday.  Jeanne McGahey.  MIT

I stopped to pick up the bagel.  The Bagel.  David Ignatow.
ConAP; PPoD

I strolled across/ An open field.  The Waking.  Theodore
Roethke.  RFM

I strove with none, for none was worth my strife.  On His Seventy-
Fifth Birthday [*or* Dying Speech of an Old Philosopher].
Walter Savage Landor.  *Fr.* The Last Fruit off an Old Tree.
HeIP; NOBE; PBMP

I struck the board, and cried: No more.  The Collar.  George
Herbert.  AnMo; BoReV; HeIP; InPS; IPWM; MetP;
NOBE; OBP; PPoD; PPoe; PPP; SCP-1

I study out a dark similitude.  The Swan.  Theodore Roethke.
VGW

I study the lives on a leaf: the little.  The Minimal.  Theodore
Roethke.  NoAM; NOBA

I subside like a trick cushion.  Sleep.  Rhyll McMaster.  CAAP

I Substitute for the Dead Lecturer.  LeRoi Jones.  NOBA

I summon to the winding ancient stair.  A Dialogue of Self and
Soul.  W. B. Yeats.  NoAM; PAIC

I suppose it's because we're on foot I'm reminded.  Kyran's
Christening.  Alden Nowlan.  NeAC

I suppose it's myself that you're making allusion to.  At the
"Atlantic" Dinner.  Oliver Wendell Holmes.  AmVN

I swam the Huron of love, and am not ashamed.  The Huron.
Ruth Herschberger.  WPE

I swear I begin to see the meaning of these things.  Walt Whitman.
*Fr.* By Blue Ontario's Shore, XV.  InPS

I swing round the corner, still alone.  Montage.  Harry Guest.
TwMBP

I switch on the light. Crickets tick.  Sleep in the Heat.  Laura
Jensen.  AmPA

I swore I would go back.  O Lyric Love.  Winfield Townley Scott.
VGW

I take as my theme, "The Independent Woman."  Pro Femina, II.
Carolyn Kizer.  MAT; NMM; Psy; RiTi

I take my Aunt out in her pram.  My Aunt.  Peggy Wood.  POL

I take my pen in hand.  The Letter.  Elizabeth Riddell.  BuTh

I take my son outside.  What I Tell Him.  Simon J. Ortiz.  CDW

I take off my shirt, I show you.  Taking Off My Clothes.  Carolyn
Forché.  AmPA

I take their hands.  They.  R. S. Thomas.  OxBTC

I take you as I take the moon rising.  Death.  Charles Wright.
FiCP

I talked to old Lem.  Old Lem.  Sterling A. Brown.  BPo; PoBA

I taste a liquor never brewed.  Emily Dickinson.  AmVN; AnMo;
HeIP; IPWM; NOBA; PBMP; PiAm; SBG; VoPo; WPE

I Tell Her She Is Lovely.  Monk Gibbon.  PFIr

I tell thee, Dick, where I have been.  A Ballad upon a Wedding.
Sir John Suckling.  LoAs

I tell Therese.  Therese.  Alden Nowlan.  NeAC

I tell you, hopeless grief is passionless.  Grief.  Elizabeth Barrett
Browning.  HeIP; InPK; SBG; WPE

I tell you how dat hypocrite do.  That Hypocrite.  *Unknown.*  BPo

I tell you that I see her still.  I Only Am Escaped Alone to Tell
Thee.  Howard Nemerov.  HeIP; NoAM

I Thank God I'm Free at Las'  *Unknown.*  BPo; PBMP

I Thank You God for Most This Amazing.  E. E. Cummings.
IPWM; PiAm; VoPo

I that in health was, and gladness.  Lament for the Poets.  William
Dunbar, *tr. by* Andrew Glaze *and* Selden Rodman.  OBP

I that in heill wes and gladnes.  Timor Mortis Conturbat Me.
William Dunbar.  NOBE

I, the poet William Yeats.  To Be Carved on a Stone at Thoor
Ballylee.  W. B. Yeats.  NoAM

I, therefore, will begin. Soul of the age!  Ben Jonson.  *Fr.* To the
Memory of My Beloved Mr. William Shakespeare.  NOBE

I think all this is somewhere in myself.  The Room.  W. S.
Merwin.  NOBA

I think before they saw me the giraffes.  The Giraffes.  Roy
Fuller.  NoAM

I Think Continually of Those Who Were Truly Great.  Stephen
Spender.  NOBE; OBP; OxBTC; VoPo

I think I could turn and live with animals.  Animals.  Walt
Whitman.  *Fr.* Song of Myself.  POL

I think I grow tensions.  The Flower.  Robert Creeley.  CAPP

I think I hear the angels sing.  Shew! Fly Don't Bother Me.  *At.
to* Billy Reeves, *and to* T. Brigham Bishop.  PSoN

I think I heard the belle.  The Old Lady's Lament for Her Youth.
Villon, *tr. by* Robert Lowell.  BoLoP

I think I see her sitting bowed and black.  Oriflamme.  Jessie
Redmond Fauset.  PoBA

I think I shall live for a while a bit gamely.  The Poet Loves from
Afar.  Desmond O'Grady.  NoAM

I think I sing that little song.  Union Man.  Albert Morgan.
AmFP

I Think I Understand.  Joni Mitchell.  GrRo

"I think I want some pies this morning."  Greedy Richard.  Jane
Taylor.  OxBChV

I think I will learn some beautiful language, useless for commercial.
Intention to Escape from Him.  Edna St. Vincent Millay.
SBG

I think if you had loved me when I wanted.  Success.  Rupert
Brooke.  OxBTC

I think I'll get a paper.  Nerves.  "Sagittarius."  OxBTC

I think it better that in times like these.  On Being Asked for a
War Poem.  W. B. Yeats.  PFIr

I think it is in Virginia, that place.  Low Fields and Light.  W. S.
Merwin.  ConAP

I think it most peculiar.  What a Coincidence?  *Unknown.*  AKE

I think it must be lonely to be God.  The Preacher: Ruminates
behind the Sermon.  Gwendolyn Brooks.  PBMP

I think it's worth it today.  Souster.  Ray Fraser.  NeAC

I think not on the state, nor am concerned.  Upon the Double
Murther of King Charles I.  Katherine Philips.  SBG

I think of all the women behind locked doors.  Winter Mornings.
Nancy Mairs.  NPW

I think of corner shots, the ball.  Day and Night Handball.
Stephen Dunn.  AmPA

I think of God.  The Hairs in My Nose.  Aram Boyajian.  NeAC

I think of the twenty thousand poems of Li Po.  Word Drunk.  Jim
Harrison.  IPWM

I think of things like the shadow of a branch.  The Shadow of a
Branch.  Edith Marcombe Shiffert.  WPE

I think, old bone, the world's not with us much.  To William
Wordsworth from Virginia.  Julia Randall.  NMM; WPE

"I think," she said, "we shall not see again."  The Shadows.  Iain
Crichton Smith.  SLP

I think she sleeps: it must be sleep, when low.  Modern Love, XV.
George Meredith.  Epi

I think that I shall never see.  Trees.  Joyce Kilmer.  AKE

I think that I shall never see.  Song of the Open Road.  Ogden
Nash.  AKE; FaBoCo

I think that night's our balance.  Suite to Fathers.  Jim Harrison.
AmPA

I think the dead are tender. Shall we kiss?  She.  Theodore
Roethke.  BoLoP

I think we are being given the same messages. On Reading Another Poet. Elizabeth Brewster. MMD

I thirst for violins, as drunkards thirst. Ideal and Reality. Joseph Campbell. BIrV

I thought he was dumb. Tortoise Shout. D. H. Lawrence. NoAM

I thought of thee, my partner and my guide. After-Thought. Wordsworth. The River Duddon, XXXIV. MBPR; NOBE

I thought once how Theocritus had sung. Sonnets from the Portuguese, I. Elizabeth Barrett Browning. GBL; NOBE; PAIC; VPC; WPE

I thought they stood. I Know a Spot Just over the Hill. William Mills. CoPAm

"I thought you loved me." "No, it was only fun." In the Orchard. Muriel Stuart. OxBTC

I threat'ned to observe the strict decree. The Holdfast. George Herbert. Epi

I threw the inside of my gizzard out, splashing. Zimmer Drunk and Alone, Dreaming of Old Football Games. Paul Zimmer. MAT

I thumped on you the best I could. Heart's Needle, VIII. W. D. Snodgrass. NoAM

I tiptoed into her sleep. Mirru. Kenneth Patchen. RRA

I Told Jesus. Sterling Plumpp. PoBA

I told my captain that old Maude was dead. Captain Captain. Unknown. BluL

I told the sun that I was glad. The Sun. John Drinkwater. LCL

I told you to make me some crazy. Structure. Alberta Turner. HeS

I, Too. Langston Hughes. HeIP; PiAm
(Epilogue; "I, too, sing America.") VGW
(I, Too, Sing America.) VGW

I, too, at the mid-point, in a well-lit wood. Ascent into Hell. A. D. Hope. MAuV

I, too, dislike it: there are things that are important beyond all this fiddle. Poetry. Marianne Moore. AnMo; HeIP; IPWM; NoAM; NOBA; PAIC; PiAm; Psy; TSWA; WIF

I, too, have plucked a stalk of grass. Letters to Walt Whitman, V. Ronald Johnson. VGW

I, Too, Sing America. Langston Hughes. See I, Too.

I too was born out of a lion's mouth. Let Heroes Account to Love. Alan Dugan. NoAM

I took/ a coney island of the mind. Clickety-Clack. Paul Blackburn. NoAM

I took away the ocean once. The Shell. David McCord. LCL

I took her to the river. The Unfaithful Married Woman Federico García Lorca, tr. by Rolfe Humphries. LoAs

I took my heart in my hand. Twice. Christina Rossetti. BoReV; GBL; NOBE

I took my mind a walk. An Ordinary Day. Norman MacCaig. LP

I took my oath I would inquire. The Inquest. W. H. Davies. NOBE; OxBTC

I took the embankment path. An Advancement of Learning. Seamus Heaney. NCSH

I touch your face. Poems of Night. Galway Kinnell. LoAs

I touch your nose. The Face as It Might Be of Love. Toi Derricotte. NPW

I touched the nothingness of air once. I Read a Tight-Fisted Poem Once. Nancy Woods. RFM

I traded a girl. Trader. Jim Harrison. NoAM

I travel'd thro' a land of men. The Mental Traveller. Blake. Epi; GrRo; LAuP; MBPR

I Traveled among Unknown Men. Wordsworth. AnMo; MBPR

I traveled on, seeing the hill, where lay. The Pilgrimage. George Herbert. SoSe

I traveled to the ocean. Prayer to the Pacific. Leslie Silko. CDW

I travelled the land from Leap to Corbally. The Volatile Kerryman. Owen Roe O'Sullivan, tr. by Sean O'Riada. BIrV

I tried to live small. Housing Shortage. Naomi Replansky. NMM

I trundle the bodies, on the iron bars. John Berryman. Fr. Homage to Mistress Bradstreet. NOBA

I Try to Waken and Greet the World Once Again. James Wright. InPS

I turn on all the lights. My Mother Tries to Visit Me in the Dead of Night. Diane Wakoski. CAAP

I turn round. The Lady's First Song. W. B. Yeats. PSN

I turn you out of doors. Alain Chartier, tr. fr. French by Edward Lucie-Smith. BoLoP

I turned to speak to God. Not All There. Robert Frost. FaBoCo

I understand the large heart of heroes. Walt Whitman. Fr. Song of Myself, XXXIII. InPS

I understand the ties that are between us. The Summing Up. James Simmons. POL

I upon the first creation. Gratitude. Christopher Smart. Fr. Hymns for the Amusement of Children. LAuP

I used to be a drill man. Drill Man Blues. George Sizemore. AmFP

I Used to Love My Garden. C. P. Sawyer. FaBoCo

I used to see her in the door. Paul. James Wright. WIF

I used to think that grown-up people chose. Childhood. Frances Cornford. OxBTC

I used to walk the morning stream. Walk. Brian Merriman, tr. by Brendan Behan. Fr. The Midnight Court. BIrV

I Used to Wrap My White Doll Up in. Mae Jackson. PoBA

I usta wonder who i'd be. Adulthood. Nikki Giovanni. NMM

I Visit My Brother. Greg Kuzma. NVAP

I wad ha'e gi'en him my lips tae kiss. Mary's Song. Marion Angus. SLP

I wade through sea-green grass. Epitaphs. Glyn Hughes. LP

I wait for her who restores my fingertips. Song of Expectancy. George Hitchcock. MIT

I wait in the cafe for my wife like a gorilla. Waiting in the Cafe. Stan Rice. MIT

I wait to tangle fear around my hand. Night along the Mackinac Bridge. Roberta Hill. CDW

I wake/ when lightning cracks. Night Storm. Jane Sherman. CaYB

I Wake and Feel the Fell of Dark, Not Day. Gerard Manley Hopkins. BoReV; NoAM; NOBE; PPoe; PPP

I wake and hear it raining. Morning Worship. Mark Van Doren. LoAs

I Wake, My Friend, I. Faye Kicknosway. IHMS

I wake to sleep, and take my waking slow. The Waking. Theodore Roethke. HeIP; InPS; NoAM; NOBA; PiAm; PPP; SoSe; TCP; VoPo

I wake up back aching from soft bed Pat. Sonnet. Ted Berrigan. CAAP

I wake up first and with a sense of. Genius Loci of the Morning. Doug Fetherling. NeAC

I wake up in a morning. Unknown. SFF

I wake up in a room that seems to be snowing. The White Room. Peter Cooley. NVAP

I wakened on my hot, hard bed. The Watch. Frances Cornford. InPK; OxBTC

I walk beside the prisoners to the road. A Camp in the Prussian Forest. Randall Jarrell. NowV; TCP

I walk by the sea-shore. Psychology. Duncan Glen. MIS

I walk down the garden paths. Patterns. Amy Lowell. GrRo; PBMP; VoPo

I walk facing against the wind. Walking without Snowshoes. Elizabeth Hanson. NPW

I walk in the old street. Louis Zukofsky. VGW

I walk into your house, a friend. A Friend. W. D. Snodgrass. MAT

I walk Main Street, a pelican. Small Town: The Friendly. Stephen Dunn. POL

I Walk Out into the Country at Night. Lu Yu, *tr. fr. Chinese by* Kenneth Rexroth. IPWM

I walk through the long schoolroom questioning. Among School Children. W. B. Yeats. AnMo; Epi; NoAM; NOBE; OxBTC; PPoe; PPP; SoSe

I walk uphill through the snow. Carrying Food Home in Winter. Margaret Atwood. TSWA

I walked abroad on a snowy day. Soft Snow. Blake. FSFS; SoSe

I walked all the way from East St. Louis. East St. Louis Blues. *Unknown.* AmFP

I walked on the banks of the tincan banana dock. Sunflower Sutra. Allen Ginsberg. MAT; NOBA; PiAm

I walked over the grave of Henry James. Richard Eberhart. VGW

I walked, the first, into a world of whiteness. White Worlds. Jane Marie Luecke. AATT

I walked through Ballinderry in the spring-time. Lament for the Death of Thomas Davis. Sir Samuel Ferguson. BIrV

I walked, when love was gone. A Breath of Air. James Wright. NOBA

I wander by the edge. He Hears the Cry of the Sedge. W. B. Yeats. OxBTC

I wander through each chartered street. London. Blake. *Fr.* Songs of Experience. AnMo; GrRo; HeIP; InPK; InPS; LAuP; MAT; MBPR; NOBE; OBP; PAIC; PBMP; PPoD; VoPo; WIF

I wandered angry as a cloud. Paul Dehn. SpRo

I Wandered Lonely As a Cloud. Wordsworth. InPK; IPWM; MBPR; NOBE; SpRo

I wandered today to the hill, Maggie. When You and I Were Young, Maggie. George W. Johnson. BLSH; BLSo; PSoN

I Want. Rosemary Daniell. WBN

I want a hero: an uncommon want. Don Juan, I. Byron. MBPR

I want a job as a low cloud. Job Hunting. Tom Hennen. HeS

I want all you women to listen to my tale of woe. Death Sting Me Blues. *Unknown.* BluL

I want it to be clear for us. On My Stand. Sharon Scott. JB

I want my house with open doors. My House. Saint-Denys Garneau, *tr. by* John Glassco. AKE

I want the grave to be six by six. One Song. Stanley Plumly. HeS

"I want to fight you," he said in a Belfast accent. Experience. James Simmons. BIrV

I want to give my babies to the moon. Giving the Moon a New Chance. Terry Stokes. Moon

I want to go home and I ain't got sufficient. Bad Luck Blues. *Unknown.* BluL

I want to hear pitter patter. All La Glory. Robbie Robertson. RRA

I want to help you. The Friends. Robert Creeley. Epi

I want to leave him. Dreams of Eurydice. Margaret Ryan. NPW

I want to see the slim palm-trees. Heritage. Gwendolyn B. Bennett. PoBA

I wanta say just gotta say something. Beautiful Black Men. Nikki Giovanni. BPo; NMM

I wanted so ably. The World. Robert Creeley. NoAM

I wanted to be a cauliflower. The Cauliflower. John Haines. InPK

I wanted to be more human. Forms of the Human. Richard Eberhart. TH

I wanted to bring you this Jap iris. For C. Philip Whalen. VGW

I wanted to know my mother when she sat. Leroy. LeRoi Jones. BPo; PiAm; PoBA

I wanted to write. For Saundra. Nikki Giovanni. BPo; Psy; RiTi; WIF

I warn ye all, ye gay ladies. Child Waters. *Unknown.* PeBB

I was/ the girl of the chain letter. Love Song. Anne Sexton. NCSH

I was a girl waiting by the roadside for my boyfriend to come. The Elwha River. Gary Snyder. NoAM

I was a lady of high renown. Jamie Douglas. *Unknown. See* Waly, Waly ("When cockle shells turn silver bells").

I was a peasant girl from Germany. Elsa Wertman. Edgar Lee Masters. *Fr.* Spoon River Anthology. NoAM

I was a traveller then upon the moor. Wordsworth. *Fr.* Resolution and Independence. SpRo

I was about to go, and said so. Loneliness. Brooks Jenkins. CTBA

I was all self-righteous. Shirley 4 Years Later. Alta. MMD

I was alone then looking at the picture of a child. Six Days. Tom Raworth. TwMBP

I was angry with my friend. A Poison Tree. Blake. *Fr.* Songs of Experience. AnMo; IPWM; LAuP; MBPR; PBMP; PPoD; PPoe; PPP; SFF; WIF

I was born conscious, I can't remember. Rino's Song. Lynne Lawner. IHMS

I was born in August, 1942—conceived on a Christmas leave. Requiem of a War-Baby. Joan Watton. PFIr

I was born in Belfast between the mountain and the gantries. Carrickfergus. Louis MacNeice. NoAM

I was born in Boston, a city you all know well. The Boston Burglar. *Unknown.* AmFP

I was born in the congo. Ego Tripping. Nikki Giovanni. NoAM

I was born in the desert. New Minglewood Blues. *Unknown.* BluL

I was born on a street named Joy. Lines on His Birthday. John Logan. CAPP

I was born the year of the loon. Chronicles: Number Three. Mei Berssenbrugge. SA

I was broke and out of a job in the city of London. Paddy, Get Back. *Unknown.* AmFP

I was brought up in Sheffield, all of a high degree. The Sheffield 'Prentice. *Unknown.* AmFP

I was brought up with a myth in my mind. Confession of a Young Hegelian. Ellen McEvilley Griffin. NPW

I was but seven year auld. The Laily Worm and the Machrel of the Sea. *Unknown.* PeBB

I was directed by my grandfather. Direction. Alonzo Lopez. VW

I was down and I cried. Tin Cup Blues. *Unknown.* BluL

I Was Driving across the Island. Dennis Trudell. NVAP

I Was Fair Beat. Robert Garioch. OxBTC

I was far forward on the plain, the burning swamp. The Little Girl with Bands on Her Teeth. Genevieve Taggard. VGW

I was going to say something. Ancestor. Thomas Kinsella. BIrV

I was happy I was bubbly drunk. Second Night in N.Y.C. after 3 Years. Gregory Corso. BuTh

"I was in a hooker once," said Karlssen. Cape Horn Gospel—1. John Masefield. PoTa

I was just thinkin' 'bout the way it's s'posed to be. I Don't Eat Animals (And They Don't Eat Me). Melanie Safka. PoRo

I was led into captivity by the bitch business. Money. C. H. Sisson. POL

I was myself blown. For My People. Wendy Rose. CDW

I was never the light lad. The Spawn of Slums. James W. Thompson. BPo

I was no taller than a seedling then. All Men Are...Socrates Is. Napoleon St. Cyr. FAF

I was on holiday in August. The Director of the Museum. Roderick Watson. MIS

I was out in the country one beautiful night. The Widow's Old Broom. *Unknown.* AmFP

I was over in Aberdeen on my way to New Orleans. Aberdeen, Mississippi Blues. *Unknown.* BluL

I Was Proud. Jim Harrison. HeS

I was raised up in Louisville, a town you all knew well. Frank James, the Roving Gambler. *Unknown.* AmFP

I Was Riding to Poughkeepsie. Mary Ann Hoberman. ECBV

I was round and small like a pearl. *Unknown.* GBP

I was sick. Jesus Was Crucified or: It Must Be Deep. Carolyn M. Rodgers. PoBA; SA

I Was Sick and in Prison. Jones Very. NOBA

I was sinking deep in sin. Love Lifted Me. James Rowe. BLSH

I was sitting in mcsorley's. E. E. Cummings. NoAM

I was six when I first saw kittens drown. The Early Purges. Seamus Heaney. NCSH

I was sixteen years of age. Song Ballet. *Unknown.* AmFP

I was sleeping. A Translation from. Fred Levinson. AmPA

I was so sick last night I. Morning After. Langston Hughes. NoAM

I was the last passenger of the day. The Bus. Leonard Cohen. HeIP

I was the Mooress, Morayma. The Mooress Morayma. *Unknown, tr. by W. S. Merwin.* Epi

I was the only child of Frances Harris of Virginia. Hamilton Greene. Edgar Lee Masters. *Fr.* Spoon River Anthology. NoAM

I was the patriarch of the shining land. John Sutter. Yvor Winters. NoAM; NOBA

I was thinking of a son. Menstruation at Forty. Anne Sexton. CAPP

I was thy neighbour once, thou rugged pile! Elegiac Stanzas Suggested by a Picture of Peele Castle, in a Storm. Wordsworth. MBPR

I was tired of being a woman. Consorting with Angels. Anne Sexton. NMM

I was traveling fast. Highway Blues. *Unknown.* BluL

I was traveling through South Americas. Travelin' Blues. *Unknown.* BluL

I was walking along, reciting the Lord's Prayer. The Orange Tree. Ellen Pearce. IHMS

I was walking in a government warehouse. Fifteen Million Plastic Bags. Adrian Mitchell. OxBTC

I was Willie Metcalf. Willie Metcalf. Edgar Lee Masters. *Fr.* Spoon River Anthology. IPWM

I was wrapped in black. Us. Anne Sexton. CAPP

I washed my face in water. *Unknown.* GBP

I watch the Indians dancing to help the young corn at Taos pueblo. New Mexico Mountain. Robinson Jeffers. InPS; NoAM

I watch the roses float. Requiem. Stephen Vincent. NeAC

I watched for years a sidehill farm that died. The Blown Door. Malcolm Cowley. PPoD

I watched old squatting chimpanzee: he traced. Sporting Acquaintances. Siegfried Sassoon. OxBTC

I watched the house, and barked agreeably, and. Sudden Assertion. Kenneth Leslie. BoAnP; POL

I watched the moon around the house. Emily Dickinson. Moon

I watched thee when the foe was at our side. Love and Death. Byron. MBPR; NOBE

I weave the night, I cross the weft with stars. In the Flight of the Blue Heron: To Montezuma. Anita Endrezze Probst. CDW

I weep for Adonais—he is dead! Adonais: an Elegy on the Death of John Keats. Shelley. MBPR

I weep when the gay are around me. Mary and Her Dead Canary. Alexander Kerr. InPK

I wende to dede, a king y-wis. I Went to Death. *Unknown.* OxBM

I went down a narrow, narrow road, and I lost my cap. The Firefly. *Unknown, tr. fr. Italian.* RAE

I went down by Cascadilla. Cascadilla Falls. A. R. Ammons. CoPAm; NOBA

I went down in Death Valley. Death Valley Blues. *Unknown.* BluL

I went down to malcolmland. Half Black, Half Blacker. Sterling Plumpp. PoBA

I went down to Saint James this morning. St. James Infirmary. *Unknown.* AmFP

I went for a walk over the dunes again this morning. Corsons Inlet. A. R. Ammons. NoAM; NOBA; PPP

I went into a public-'ouse to get a pint o' beer. Tommy. Kipling. BTTM; OxBTC

I went into my [or the ] stable, to see what I might [or could] see. Old Wichet. *Unknown.* GBP; PoTa

I went into the flea circus. Small Talk. Don Marquis. PoTa

I Went into the Maverick Bar. Gary Snyder. MAT

I went on Friday afternoons. Au Tombeau de Mon Père. Ronald McCuaig. MAuV

I went out alone. Girl's Song. W. B. Yeats. SS

I went out at daybreak and stood on Primrose Hill. Birds Waking. W. S. Merwin. NOBA

I went out on. Saying. A. R. Ammons. TSWA

I went out to the hazel wood. The Song of Wandering Aengus. W. B. Yeats. AKE; MAT; OBP; PBMP; WIF

I Went to Death. *Unknown.* OxBM

I went to Frankfort and got drunk. Porson's Visit to the Continent. Richard Porson. FaBoCo

I Went to Nole. *Unknown.* GBP

I went to the dance. Vickie. Marnie Walsh. VW

I went to the dances at Chandlerville. Lucinda Matlock. Edgar Lee Masters. *Fr.* Spoon River Anthology. IPWM; NoAM; NOBA; PBMP; VoPo

I went to the garden of love. The Garden of Love. Blake. *Fr.* Songs of Experience. GBL; IPWM; LAuP; LoAs; MAT; MBPR; OBP; PPoe; SS; WIF

I went to the Hotel Broog. A Difference of Zoos. Gregory Corso. VGW

I Went to the Market, *with music. Unknown.* AKE

I went to the river: couldn't get across. Keep It Clean. *Unknown.* BluL

I went to turn the grass once after one. The Tuft of Flowers. Robert Frost. IPWM

I went uptown last Saturday night. Blue Monday. *Unknown.* AmFP

I were unkind unless that I did shed. Lines on His Companions Who Died in the Northern Seas. Thomas James. SCP-2

I, when exposed, will pass the letter on to you. The Rendezvous. Steven Graves. PPoD

I whispered, "I am too young." Brown Penny. W. B. Yeats. BoLoP; OLR; PFIr

I, who accompanied with faithful pace. Ecclesiastical Sonnets: Introduction. Wordsworth. MBPR

I who by day am function of the light. Motto for a Sun Dial. J. V. Cunningham. InPK; VGW

I will arise and go now, and go to Innisfree. The Lake Isle of Innisfree. W. B. Yeats. AKE; InPS; IPWM; NoAM; NOBE; OxBTC

I Will Be. E. E. Cummings. VGW

I will be the gladdest thing. Afternoon on a Hill. Edna St. Vincent Millay. PSN

I will confront these shows of the day and night! Walt Whitman. Fr. By Blue Ontario's Shore, XVIII. InPS

I will consider the outnumbering dead. Merlin. Geoffrey Hill. POL

I will draw you. Indian Warrior. Mary Logue. NPW

I will enjoy thee now my Celia, come. A Rapture. Thomas Carew. LoAs; SCP-2

I Will Give My Love an Apple. Unknown. PBMP

I will go back to the great sweet mother. Swinburne. Fr. The Triumph of Time. SoSe

I Will Go into the Ghetto. Charles Reznikoff. VGW

I Will Go with My Father a-Ploughing. Joseph Campbell. OFD

I will grieve alone. In Response to a Rumor That the Oldest Whorehouse in Wheeling, West Virginia, Has Been Condemned. James Wright. CAPP

I Will Have the Whetstone. Unknown. GBP

I will kneel at thine altar, will crown thee with bays. Shelley. MBPR

I will live Ringsend. Ringsend. Oliver St. John Gogarty. OxBTC

I Will Make You Brooches. Robert Louis Stevenson. SLP (My Valentine.) OFD

I will never more deceive you. You Naughty, Naughty Men. T. Kennick. BLSo

I will not be inhabited. The Turtle's Belly. Ellen Pearce. IHMS

I will not kiss you, country fashion. A Calvinist in Love. Jack R. Clemo. LoAs

I will not toy with it nor bend an inch. The White City. Claude McKay. BPo; NoAM

I will remember you on Bloom Street. Bloom Street. Angela McCabe. AmPA

I will sing no more songs! O'Bruadair. David O'Bruadair, tr. by James Stephens. BIrV

I Will Sing the Wondrous Story, with music. Francis H. Rowley. BLSH

I will sing you a song. Streets of Cairo; or The Poor Little Country Maid. James Thornton. FSN

I will speak about women of letters, for I'm in the racket. Pro Femina, III. Carolyn Kizer. MAT; NMM; Psy; RiTi

I will stuff a small rag of. Winter. Larry Levis. NVAP

I will teach you my townspeople. Tract. William Carlos Williams. MiP; NoAM; NOBA; PPoD; TCP; VGW

I will tell you of a gallan soldier. The Soldier's Wooing. Unknown. AmFP

I will track you down the years. Quest. Naomi Long Madgett. BPo

I Will Turn Your Money Green. Unknown. BluL

I will twine and will mingle my raven black hair. Wildwood Flower Unknown. BLSo

I Will Write Songs Against you. Charles Reznikoff. VGW

I wish I could proclaim. The Commemoration. Edwin Muir. SLP

I wish I could remember the [or that] first day. The First Day. Christina Rossetti. Fr. Monna Innominata. BoLoP; GBL; OLR

I wish I could teach you how ugly. On Flunking a Nice Boy Out of School. John Ciardi. NowV; SFF

I wish I had the voice of Homer. Cancer's a Funny Thing. J. B. S. Haldane. OxBTC

I wish I knew the names of all the stars. Stars. Alden Nowlan. POL

I wish I lived in a caravan. The Pedlar's Caravan. William Brighty Rands. OxBChV

I wish I loved an honest girl. A Song for an Able Bastard. Eric Linklater. SLP

I wish I loved the Human Race. The Wishes of an Elderly Man. Sir Walter Alexander Raleigh. FaBoCo

I Wish I Was a Mole in the Ground. Unknown. AmFP

I wish I was in the [or de] land of [or ob] cotton. Dixie. Daniel Decatur Emmet. BLSH; BLSo; PSoN

I Wish I Was Single, 2 versions. Unknown. AmFP

I wish I were a jelly fish. Triolet. G. K. Chesterton. LCL

I wish I were close. Yamabe No Akahito. OLR

I Wish I Were Single Again. Unknown. AmFP

I wish sometimes, although a worthlesse thing. Licia, XII. Giles Fletcher the Elder. AAS

I wish that when you died last May. May and Death. Robert Browning. NOBE

I wish there were a touch of these boats about my life. Boat Poem. Bernard Spencer. OxBTC

I wish they would hurry up their trip to Mars. A Projection. Reed Whittemore. WIF

I wish to God my child was born. Lullaby. Unknown. AmFP

I wish to make a positive statement. Peace. George Jonas. NeAC

I wish you triumphs that are yours already. For Marianne Moore's Birthday. Kay Boyle. NMM; RiTi

I wish you were not flying, and I wish. For a Homecoming. Julia Randall. NMM

I, with whose colours Myra dressed her head. Myra. Fulke Greville. Fr. Caelica. GBL; NOBE

I woke before the day, when the night bird. Thomas Iron-Eyes. Marnie Walsh. VW

I woke up this mornin'. Sylvester's Dying Bed. Langston Hughes. NoAM

I woke up this mornin' with the blues all round my bed. Good Mornin', Blues. Unknown. InPK

I woke up this morning feeling around for my shoes. Walking Blues. Unknown. BluL

I woke up this morning, four o'clock. Kassie Jones. Unknown. BluL

I woke up this morning my good gal was gone. No No Blues. Unknown. BluL

I woke up this morning with the blues all 'round my bed. You'll Never Miss Your Jelly. Unknown. BluL

I wonder about/ the brother. Come on Home. Sharon Scott. JB

I wonder about the trees. The Sound of Trees. Robert Frost. NoAM

I wonder, by my troth, what thou and I. The Good-Morrow. John Donne. AnMo; BoLoP; InPS; LoAs; MetP; OLR; PAIC; PPP; SCP-1; SoSe

I wonder do you feel to-day. Two in the Campagna. Robert Browning. LoAs; NOBE

I wonder how many old men last winter. The Minneapolis Poem. James Wright. NoAM

I wonder if the elephant. Pete at the Zoo. Gwendolyn Brooks. ECBV

I wonder, since we are both travelling out. The Traveling Out. Lucile Adler. IHMS

I wonder what to mean by sanctuary, if a real or. Triphammer Bridge. A. R. Ammons. NOBA

"I won't go with you. I want to stay with Grandpa!" My Last Afternoon with Uncle Devereux Winslow. Robert Lowell. VGW

I worked all the winter. Tired As I Can Be. Unknown. BluL

I worship the greatest first. Hippolytus Temporizes. Hilda Doolittle ("H.D."). SBG

I wot not how the world's degenerate. Joseph Hall. *Fr.* Virgidemiarum. TVS

I would be ignorant as the dawn. The Dawn. W. B. Yeats. GrRo

I would be wandering in distant fields. In Bondage. Claude McKay. PoBA

I would be wearing. Wistful Butch Poem. Rochelle Owens. WBN

I would be with the wind. Theodore Roethke. POL

I would in rich and golden coloured raine. Thomas Lodge, *after* Pierre de Ronsard. Phillis, XXXIV. AAS

I would like/ to make. Oh---Yeah. Sharon Scott. JB

I would like my love to die. Samuel Beckett. BIrV

I would like to be as mobile as my mind. Evaporation Poems. Kathleen Norris. IHMS

I would like to be that elderly Chinese gentleman. Dreaming in the Shanghai Restaurant. D. J. Enright. MPo; PSN

I Would Like to Describe. Zbigniew Herbert, *tr. fr. Polish by* Czeslaw Milosz. BuTh

I would like to scream but there is no one to hear. Setting/ Slow Drag. Carolyn Rodgers. JB

I Would Like You for a Comrade. Edward Abbott Parry. OxBChV

I would not be the moon, the sickly thing. In Dispraise of the Moon. Mary Elizabeth Coleridge. Moon

I would not feign a single sigh. Song. John Clare. GBL

I would not have gotten in this boat with you. Revolution Susan Griffin. RiTi

I would not marry a blacksmith. Soldier Boy for Me. *Unknown.* AmFP

I would not paint—a picture. Emily Dickinson. NOBA; PiAm

I would not tell them why I had smashed the window. "In This House, There Shall Be No Idols." Carolyn M. Rodgers. JB

I would not wish to sit. Between Two Prisoners. James Dickey. PAIC

I would play, plucking flowers by the gate. Two Letters from Chang-Kan. Li Po, *tr. by* Shigeyoshi Obata. OLR

I would prefer to live quietly in silks. Running Through Sleep. Kathleen Norris. IHMS

I would rather be buried/ in some cypress grove. Cypress Grove Blues. *Unknown.* BluL

I would to heaven that I were so much clay. Fragment. Byron. *Fr.* Don Juan. MBPR; OBP

I Wouldn't. John Ciardi. ECBV

I wouldn't give a damn if some rum. Whatfor to 3 Who Stole My Shovel. Phyllis Gotlieb. BBGO

I wouldn't marry a bachelor. Old Maid's Song. *Unknown.* AmFP

I write what I know on one side of the paper. Paper II. Carl Sandburg. TH

I wrung my hands under my dark veil. Anna Akhmatova, *tr. fr. Russian by* Max Hayward *and* Stanley Kunitz. BoLoP

I years had been from home. Emily Dickinson. NOBA; Psy

Iambicum Trimetrum. Spenser. BoLoP

Ianthe, *sels.* Walter Savage Landor.
  "From you, Ianthe, little troubles pass." NOBE
  (Ianthe's Troubles.) GBL
  "My hopes retire; my wishes as before." GBL
  "Proud word you never spoke, but you will speak." GBL
  "Thou has not rais'd, Ianthe, such desire." GBL
  Your Name upon the Sand. BuTh

Ibby Damsel. *Unknown.* AmFP

Icarus. Valentin Iremonger. BIrV

Icarus Irving Layton. BBGO

Icarus. Stephen Spender. NoAM

Ice, The. W. W. Gibson. OxBTC

Ice comes undone. Thaw. Lyn Lifshin. FAF

Ice Eagle, The. Diane Wakoski. InPS

Ice tinkled in glasses Blues and Bitterness. Lerone Bennett, Jr. PoBA

Icehouse in Summer, The. Howard Nemerov. NoAM

Ich am of Irlaunde. I am of Ireland [ *or* The Irish Dancer]. *Unknown.* BuTh; GBP; OxBM

Ich herde men upon mold make muche mone. The Farmer's Complaint. *Unknown.* OxBM

Ich was in one sumere dale. Owl against Nightingale. *Unknown. Fr.* The Owl and the Nightingale. OxBM

Ichabod. Whittier. NOBA; PBMP; VoPo

Ichor, *sel.* Gavin Bantock.
  "I opened my eyes at the foot of a grey mountain." TwMBP

Ich'ot a burde in a bowr as breyl so bright. Annot and John. *Unknown.* OxBM

Icy evil that struck his father down, The. El-Hajj Malik El-Shabazz. Robert Hayden. PoBA

I'd a dream to-night. The Mother's Dream. William Barnes. NOBE

I'd been away a year, a year. The Ballad of Hagensack. Wallace Irwin. PoTa

I'd cut the warp. Where It Appears. Robert Duncan. *Fr.* Passages. PiAm

I'd fill up the house with guests this minute. A Revel. Donagh MacDonagh. PFIr

I'd like to have a word. The Book of Lies. James Tate. PPoD

I'd Like to Mark Myself. Milton Acorn. NeAC

I'd rather/ heave half a brick than say. First Person Demonstrative. Phyllis Gotlieb. MiP

I'd rather be the devil. Devil Got My Woman. *Unknown.* BluL

I'd rather be the devil. Evil Devil Woman. *Unknown.* BluL

I'd rather listen to a flute. Samuel Hoffenstein. POL

I'd wed you without herds, without money, or rich array. Cashel of Munster. *At. to* William English, *tr. by* Sir Samuel Ferguson. BIrV; GBL; PFIr

Ida, Sweet as Apple Cider, *with music.* Eddie Leonard. BLSo; FSN

Idaho. *Unknown.* GBP

Idea, *sels.* Michael Drayton.
  "Calling to mind since first my love begun." NOBE
  "Deare [ *or* Dear], why should you command me to my rest." AAS; NOBE
  "Evil [ *or* Evill] spirit, your beauty, haunts me still, An." AAS; GBL; NOBE
  "How many paltry, foolish, painted things." AAS; Epi; GBL; HeIP
  "If he, from heav'n that filch'd that living fire." AAS
  "Into these loves, who but for passion lookes," *introd. sonnet.* (To the Reader of These Sonnets.) AAS
  "Nothing but no and I, and I and no," GBL
  "Since there's [ *or* ther's] no help, come let us kiss[e] and part. AAS; BoLoP; Epi; GBL; HeIP; InPK; InPS; LoAs; NOBE; PAIC; PBMP; PPoD; PPoe; SoSe
  (Farewell to Love.) VoPo
  "Since to obtaine thee, nothing me will sted." (His Remedie for Love.) AAS
  "There's nothing grieves me, but that age should haste." AAS
  "Whilst thus my pen strives to eternize thee." AAS; PAIC
  "Witeless gallant, a young wench that woo'd, A." AAS

Idea can be glazed, captured, brought down, An. The Blue Duck. David Ray. HeS

Idea, The. Made of Alnwick, in His Expedition to Scotland with the Army, 1639. Lord Herbert of Cherbury. SCP-2

Idea of Ancestry, The. Etheridge Knight. BPo; ConAP; PoBA; PPoe

Idea of Order at Key West, The. Wallace Stevens. AnMo; HeIP; NoAM; NOBA; PiAm; PPoD; PPP

Idea was that Little Louey, The. The Little Louey Comic. Wesley McNair. FAF

Ideal and Reality. Joseph Campbell. BIrV

Ideal Landscape. Adrienne Rich. NoAM

Idealism. Ronald Arbuthnott Knox. FaBoCo

Idea's Mirror. Michael Drayton. *See* Idea.

Identities, *sels.* Matthew Mead.
 "After Paeschendale/ After Katyn." TwMBP
 "My verses, Ochkasty, and your music." TwMBP
 "We stand here." TwMBP

Identity. A. R. Ammons. CoPAm

Identity, that spectator. To What Strangers, What Welcome, XV. J. V. Cunningham. PiAm

Idiot, The John Ashbery. *Fr.* Two Sonnets. VGW

Idiot, The. Dudley Randall. BPo

Idiot Boy, The. Wordsworth. MBPR

Idle poet, here and there, An. The Revelation. Coventry Patmore. *Fr.* The Angel in the House. GBL

Idle Visitation, An. Edward Dorn. *Fr.* Gunslinger. NOBA

Idolatry. Ralph Mecklenburger. SFF

Idyll: "A door:/ Per L'Universo." Charles Tomlinson. TwMBP

Idylls, *sels* Theocritus, *tr. fr. Greek.*
 Daphnis, *fr.* XXVII, *tr. by* Dryden. SCP-1
 "Whisper of the wind in, The," I, *tr. by* William Carlos Williams. Epi

Idylls of the King, *sel.* Tennyson.
 Morte D'Arthur. PAIC

If. Haroldo de Campos. BBGO

If. Kipling. OxBChV; OxBTC

If a body meet a body. Comin' through the Rye. Burns. BLSH

If a clear fountain still keeping a sad course. The Duke's Song. Mary Sidney Wroth, Countess of Montgomery. *Fr.* Urania WPE

If a large heart joined with a noble mind. Lady Catherine Dyer. *Fr.* Sir William Dyer, Knight. SCP-2

If all be true that I do think. The Five Reasons. Henry Aldrich. FaBoCo

If all the good people were clever. Good and Clever. Elizabeth Wordsworth. OxBTC

If all the seas were one sea. Mother Goose. MG

If all the world and love were young. The Nymph's Reply to the Shepherd. Sir Walter Ralegh. AAS; BoLoP; Epi; HeIP; IPWM; LoAs; NOBE; OLR; PPoD; PPP

If all the world was apple-pie. Mother Goose. MG

If All the World were Paper. *Unknown.* FaBoCo; GBP; OBP

If an eagle be imprisoned. America. Henry Dumas. PoBA

If angels sung a Savior's birth. *At. to* John Stephenson. AmFP

If any man sits up suddenly in the dark at night. Blame. Gavin Bantock. TwMBP

If apples were pears. To My Valentine. *Unknown.* ECBV

If aught can teach us aught, Affliction's looks. Affliction. Sir John Davies. *Fr.* Nosce Teipsum. NOBE

If aught [*or* ought] of oaten stop, or pastoral song. Ode to Evening. William Collins. Epi; LAuP; NOBE; OBP; PPP

If Blood Is Black Then Spirit Neglects My Unborn Son. Conrad Kent Rivers. PoBA

If but some vengeful god would call to me. Hap. Thomas Hardy. NoAM; PBMP; PPP

If by dull rhymes our English must be chain'd. On the Sonnet. Keats. MBPR; PAIC

If "compression is the first grace of style." To a Snail. Marianne Moore. PiAm

If could some Delius with divided hands. Daniel Cudmore. SCP-2

If dead, we cease to be; if total gloom. Human Life: on the Denial of Immortality. Samuel Taylor Coleridge. IPWM; MBPR

If death were nothing. Waking to Snowfall. Roderick Hartigh Jellema. AATT

If death were truly conquered, there would be. Death. L. E. Jones. POL

If, doubtful of your fate. The Mark. Robert Graves. LoAs

If doughty deeds my ladye please. O Tell Me How to Woo Thee. Robert Graham. SLP

If Ever Hapless Woman Had a Cause. Countess of Pembroke. WPE

If ever I am an old lady. Survival. Barbara Greenberg. RiTi

If ever I had dreamed of my dead name. To My Friend. Wilfred Owen. OBP

If ever I saw blessing in the air. April Rise. Laurie Lee. LP; MPo

If ever there lived a Yankee lad. Darius Green and His Flying-Machine. John Townsend Trowbridge. OxBChV

If ever two were one, then surely we. To My Dear and Loving Husband. Anne Bradstreet. HeIP; NOBA; PiAm; SBG; VoPo; WPE

If ever you go to Dolgelley. The Dolgelley Hotel. Thomas Hughes. FaBoCo

If Ever You Go to Dublin Town. Patrick Kavanagh. MPo

If Everything Happens That Can't Be Done. E. E. Cummings. SoSe; TCP

If fansy would favor. Sir Thomas Wyatt. AAS

If from the public way you turn your steps. Michael: A Pastoral Poem. Wordsworth. MBPR

If he, from heav'n that filch'd that living fire. Michael Drayton. *Fr.* Idea. AAS

If hope grew on a bush. Hope and Joy. Christina Rossetti. OxBChV

If hours be years the twain are blest. At a Hasty Wedding. Thomas Hardy. PAIC

If I am proud, you surely know. Called Proud. Walter Savage Landor. GBL

If I Ask Whether the Islands. Ellen McEvilley Griffin. NPW

If I believed that my reply were made. Guido da Montefeltro. Dante, *tr. by* Longfellow. *Fr.* Divina Commedia: Inferno. Epi

If I bring back. For My Unborn and Wretched Children. A. B. Spellman. PoBA

If I could, I'd write. Housewife's Letter: to Mary. Anne Halley. NMM

If I Could Meet God. Dennis Schmitz. NVAP

If I Could Only Live at the Pitch That Is Near Madness. Richard Eberhart. MAT

If I could reach you now, in any way. Letter to a Mute. Thomas James. AmPA

If I could send him only. Her Reticence. Theodore Roethke. AnMo; LoAs

If I Could Tell You. W. H. Auden. PSN

If I die let my widow go. Jacques Audiberti, *tr. fr. French by* William Mead. LoAs

If I do not look up. The Student. Frederick Eckman. IPWM

If I had a girl child I would tell her to eat. To the Mother from Scarsdale Who Asked About Publishing Her Daughter's Poems. Madeline Bass. WBN

If I had a nickel. .05. Ishmael Reed. InPK

If I Had My Way. *Unknown.* BluL

If I Have Made, My Lady, Intricate. E. E. Cummings. LoAs; NOBA

If I love you. Thread. Catherine Lucy Czerkawska. SLP

If I only had something to drink. The Rime of the Ancient Mariner. Bruce Haley. PPoD

If I profane with my unworthiest hand. Shakespeare. *Fr.* Romeo and Juliet, II, v. SoSe

If I Ride This Train. Joe Johnson. PoBA

If I say to you: "I have given up everything." The One for All Time. Paul Eluard, *tr. by* Wallace Fowlie. LoAs

If I Should Cast Off This Tattered Coat. Stephen Crane. The Black Riders, LXVI. PBMP

If I should die, think only this of me. The Soldier. Rupert Brooke. 1914, V. BTTM; HeIP; NOBE; OxBTC; PAIC; VoPo

If I Should Ever by Chance. Edward Thomas. OxBChV; RAE

If I should go away. Postscript: For Gweno. Alun Lewis. BoLoP

If I should pass the tomb of Jonah. Losers. Carl Sandburg. NoAM

If I Should Sleep with a Lady Called Death. E. E. Cummings. BoLoP; VGW

If I should touch her she would shriek and weeping. Secretary. Ted Hughes. InPK; SFF

If I sing because I must. Signature. Hannah Kahn. IHMS

If I Stand in My Window. Lucille Clifton. BPo; CAAP; RiTi

If I stare at you. The Straits. Valerie Gillies. SLP

If I want to go to pieces. Occupational Hazards. David Young. FiCP

If I were asked to play the part. If I Were on the Stage; or Kiss Me Again. Henry Blossom. FSN

If I were fierce, and bald, and short of breath. Base Details. Siegfried Sassoon. HeIP; SoSe

If I Were in Charge of Epiphanies. Stephen Dunn. NVAP

If I were Lord of Tartary. Tartary. Walter de la Mare. OxBChV

If I Were on the Stage. Henry Blossom. *See* Kiss Me Again.

If I were only dafter. Witter Bynner. Spectra: Opus 6. InPK

If I were Sophocles, brave with truth. Kaire. Richard Eberhart. NoAM

If I when my wife is sleeping. Danse Russe. William Carlos Williams. InPK; InPS; NOBA; PPP

If I'd as much money as I could spend. Mother Goose. ECBV; MG

If, in an odd angle of the hutment. Eighth Air Force. Randall Jarrell. NoAM; NOBA

If in his study he hath so much care. Antiquary. John Donne. InPK

If in that Syrian garden, ages slain. Easter Hymn. A. E. Housman. BoReV; OFD

If, in the month of dark December. Written after Swimming from Sestos to Abydos. Byron. MBPR

If it/ Were lighter touch. The guarded Wound. Adelaide Crapsey. WPE

If It Comes. Philip Booth. NCSH

If it form the one landscape that we, the inconstant ones. In Praise of Limestone. W. H. Auden. NoAM; PPP

If it is a poem. Sandra Ruth Duguid. AATT

If it is spring, an early warm spring. Photo of a Retired Farmer, Big Bend, Wisconsin. Robert L. McRoberts. HeS

If It Looks Like Jelly, Shakes Like Jelly, It Must Be Gel-a-tine. *Unknown.* BluL

If it were not for these things. The Grand Inquisitor Continues. John William Corrington. CoPAm

If It Were Winter. Barry MacSweeney. LP

If It's Ever Spring Again. Thomas Hardy. OxBTC

If Langour Makis Men Licht. Lord Darnley. SLP

If life is here how stealthily. The Gully. Douglas Stewart. MAuV

If Life's a Lousy Picture, Why Not Leave Before the End. Roger McGough. OxBTC

If love be strong, hot, mighty and fervent. The Measure of Love. Sir Thomas More. BoReV

If Man Him Bethought. *Unknown.* OxBM

If Mary came would Mary. A Penitent Considers Another Coming of Mary. Gwendolyn Brooks. NoAM

If musique and sweet poetrie agree. Richard Barnfield. AAS

If My Head Hurt a Hair's Foot. Dylan Thomas. NoAM

If Nancy Hanks came back as a ghost. Nancy Hanks. Rosemary Benét *and* Stephen Vincent Benét. ECBV

If nature, for a favourite child. Matthew. Wordsworth.. MBPR

If no love is, O God, what fele I so. Chaucer. *Fr.* Troilus and Criseyde. LoAs

If No One Ever Marries Me. Laurence Alma-Tadema. OxBChV

If not necessary, is essential. Love. Anne Stevenson. NCSH

If one could have that little head of hers. A Face. Robert Browning. LoAs

If one were to describe him, one. The Man. Lucille Iverson. WBN

If Only. David Gladish. SFF

If only we'd been strangers. Floating off to Timor. Edwin Morgan. SLP

If only you/ Were night sky. If Only. David Gladish. SFF

If ought of oaten stop, or pastoral song. *See* If aught of oaten stop, or pastoral song.

If out of a dire suspicion. Wet Hair: If Now His Mother Should Come. Robert Penn Warren. *Fr.* Penological Study: Southern Exposure. NoAM

If poisonous minerals, and if that tree. Holy Sonnets, IX. John Donne. Epi; PPP

If shame can on a soldier's vein-swoll'n front. King Stephen: a Fragment of a Tragedy. Keats. MBPR

If she had been beautiful, even. Of a Woman, Dead Young. Dorothy Parker. SBG

If she would come to me here. Dog-Tired. D. H. Lawrence. BuTh

If so it hap, this of-spring of my care. Samuel Daniel. *Fr.* To Delia. AAS

If someone said, Escape. Longface Mahoney Discusses Heaven. Horace Gregory. VGW

If someone was walking across. A Confession. Robert Mezey. AmPA

If Something Should Happen. Lucille Clifton. MAT

If strolling forth, a beast you view. Carolyn Wells. *Fr.* How to Tell the Wild Animals. CaYB

If the autumn would. Winter Is Another Country. Archibald MacLeish. NCSH

If the Black Frog Will Not Ring. Ed Roberson. PoBA

If the butterfly courted the bee. Topsy-Turvy World. William Brighty Rands. ECBV; OxBChV

If the heart of a man is depressed with cares. John Gay. *Fr.* The Beggar's Opera, II, i. HeIP

If the kissing cashier. Peter. Albert Howard Carter. AATT

If the man who turnips cries. Burlesque of Lope De Vega [*or* Deduction]. Samuel Johnson. ECBV; FaBoCo

If the Owl Calls Again. John Haines. BoAnP; ConAP; HeIP; NCSH

If the quick spirits in your eye. Persuasions to Enjoy. Thomas Carew. NOBE; PAIC

If the red slayer think he slays. Brahma. Emerson. IPWM; NOBA; PAIC; PiAM; VoPo; WIF

If the shack get raided ain't no body run. Charlie Cherry. *Unknown.* BluL

If the Stars Should Fall. Samuel Allen. PoBA

If the time ever came. Poem for Ben Barney. Leslie Silko. CDW

If the victors were magnificent. The Barbarians. Matthew Mead. TwMBP

If the wild bowler thinks he bowls. Brahma. Andrew Lang. FaBoCo

If there are any heavens my mother will (all by herself) have.  E. E. Cummings.  PiAm

If There Be Sorrow.  Mari Evans.  PBMP

If there is no change in the ocean.  No Change in Me.  *Unknown.*  AmFP

If there must be a god in the house, must be.  Less and Less Human, O Savage Spirit.  Wallace Stevens.  IPWM; VGW

If there was a broken whispering by night.  Parting at Dawn.  John Crowe Ransom.  LoAs

If there were dreams to sell.  Dream-Pedlary.  Thomas Lovell Beddoes.  LCL; LoAs; NOBE

If there were no authority on earth.  Chaucer, tr. by Nevill Coghill.  *Fr.* The Canterbury Tales: The Wife of Bath's Prologue.  OBP

If they had cursed the man.  A Part-Sequence for Change.  Robert Duncan.  VGW

If this be love, to drawe a wearie breath.  Samuel Daniel.  *Fr.* To Delia.  AAS; GBL

If this country were a sea (that is solid rock).  Pennines in April.  Ted Hughes.  PPP

If this little world tonight.  Earth.  Oliver Herford.  MiP

If thou a reason dost desire to know.  To Cynthia.  Sir Francis Kynaston.  GBL

If thou must love me, let it be for nought.  Sonnets from the Portuguese, XIV.  Elizabeth Barrett Browning..  HeIP; LoAs; NOBE; PBMP; WPE

If thou wert here, these tears were tears of light!  The Day-Dream from an Emigrant to His Absent Wife.  Samuel Taylor Coleridge.  MBPR

If thou wilt ease thine heart.  Wolfram's Dirge.  Thomas Lovell Beddoes.  *Fr.* Death's Jest Book.  NOBE

If thy soul check thee that I come so near.  Sonnets, CXXXVI.  Shakespeare.  Epi

If to demands of others I agree.  Resolving Doubts.  William Dickey.  CoPAm

If waker care, if sodayne pale coulor.  Sir Thomas Wyatt.  AAS

If We Cannot Live As People.  Charles Lynch.  PoBA

If we meet a gorilla.  Carl Sandburg.  *Fr.* We Must Be Polite.  CaYB

If We Must Die.  Claude McKay.  BPo; NoAM; PoBA; PPP

If we must part.  A Valediction.  Ernest Dowson.  BoLoP

If we raced a century over hills.  Blackfeet, Blood and Piegan Hunters.  James Welch.  SA

If we shall live, we live.  Meeting.  Christina Rossetti.  GBL

If we were in Talisker on the shore.  Shores.  Sorley MacLean, *tr. by* Iain Crichton Smith.  SLP

If what you want is jobs.  Revolutionary Letter # 9.  Diane Di Prima.  IHMS

If when my wife is sleeping.  *See* If I when my wife is sleeping.

If, whittler and dumper, gross carver.  The Arc Inside and Out.  A. R. Ammons.  NoAM

If wisdom, as it seems it is.  Epigram.  J. V. Cunningham.  PiAm

If wishes were horses.  Mother Goose.  MG

If You.  Robert Creeley.  NoAM; NOBA

If You/ have seen her.  Woman with Finger.  Tom McKeown.  NVAP

If you and I could ever meet.  Monkey.  Syliva Read.  RAE

If you and I should chance to meet.  The Ordinary Man.  Robert Service.  BBGO

If you are/ in Spain.  Drowning in Spain.  Tom Schmidt.  NeAC

If you are merry sing away.  Mirth.  Christopher Smart.  *Fr.* Hymns for the Amusement of Children.  LAuP; OxBChV

If you can keep your head when all about you.  If.  Kipling.  OxBChV; OxBTC

If you c'n keep alive when li'l bleeders.  A London Sparrow's If.  J. A. Lindon.  BoAnP

If you desire to paralyze.  The Better Way.  Walter Leaf.  FaBoCo

If You Don't Like My Apples.  *Unknown.*  GBP

If you ever, ever, ever meet a grizzly bear.  Grizzly Bear.  Mary Austin.  ECBV; RAE

If You Had Known.  Thomas Hardy.  GBL

If you had not heard of the northward migration.  Visitors.  Marie Harris.  MMD

If you have seen the long lean hound.  Aboriginal Sin.  William R. Mitchell.  AATT

If you listen, I'll sing you a sweet little song.  My Wild Irish Rose  Chauncey Olcott.  BLSo; FSN

If you make a revolution, make it for fun.  A Sane Revolution.  D. H. Lawrence.  SFF

If you never do anything for anyone else.  The Immoral Proposition.  Robert Creeley.  PiAm

If you offer your bag of butterflies.  El Bosco.  Mei Berssenbrugge.  SA

If you press a stone with your finger.  Natural Law.  Babette Deutsch.  RiTi

If You Saw a Negro Lady.  June Jordan.  IHMS; NMM

If You See This Man  Thomas Lux.  AmPA; NVAP

If you should meet a crocodile.  Be Careful!  *Unknown.*  CaYB; ECBV

If you visit American city.  Pollution.  Tom Lehrer.  PoRo; WIF

If you wake at midnight, and hear a horse's feet.  A Smuggler's Song.  Kipling.  *Fr.* Puck of Pook's Hill.  OxBChV; PoTa

If you wander far enough.  Oh No.  Robert Creeley.  InPK

If you want to go to heaven.  The Blood-strained Banders.  *Unknown.*  AmFP

If You Want to Go to Heben.  *Unknown.*  GBP

If you watch it long enough you can see the clock move.  Cracked Record Blues.  Kenneth Fearing.  SFF

If you were coming in the fall.  Emily Dickinson.  NOBA

If you were going to get a pet.  If You.  Robert Creeley.  NoAM

If you will tell me why the fen.  I May, I Might, I Must.  Marianne Moore.  PSN; SoSe

If you would learn.  The Antiquary.  Joseph Campbell.  OxBTC

If your eyes fall.  In Bhaudanath.  Mei Berssenbrugge.  SA

If your man gets personal.  Traveling Riverside Blues.  *Unknown.*  BluL

If you're not home, where.  Numbers, Letters.  LeRoi Jones.  BPo; NOBA

If you've ever been in a car.  Stun.  James Schuyler.  MAT

If you've got to if after tying to.  Bitter Pills for the Dark Ladies.  Erica Jong.  Psy; RiTi; WBN

Ignacio, Colorado, for You That Time.  Joy Harjo.  SA

Ignorance of Death.  William Empson.  NoAM

Ignorant dawn of William Butler Yeats, The.  We Love You the Way You Are.  David McFadden.  NeAC

Ignorant two, we glide.  On Minding One's Own Business.  James Wright.  CoPAm

Il Pastor Fido, *sel.*  Giovanni Battista Guarini, *tr. fr. Italian by* Sir Richard Fanshawe.
Of Beauty.  BoLoP
(Beauty.  GBL

Il Penseroso.  Milton.  PPP
*Sels.*
"But let my due feet never fail."  SCP-1
"Sweet bird, that shunn'st the noise of folly."  SCP-1

Ile give thee leave my love, in beauties field.  Sonnet.  Earl of Stirling.  *Fr.* Aurora  SLP

Iliad, The, *sels.*  Homer, *tr. fr. Greek by* Christopher Logue.  TwMBP
"Now hear this," *fr.* XVI.
"Rat,/ pearl,/ onion,/ honey," *fr.* XIX.

I'll be an otter, and I'll let you swim. River-Mates. Padraic Colum. LoAs; PFIr

I'll Be Fourteen Next Sunday. *Unknown.* AmFP; OLR

I'll be going home today. Bunky Boy Bunky Boy Who's My Little Bunky Boy. Larry Mollin. NeAC

I'll do so much for my sweetheart. The Unquiet Grave. *Unknown.* Epi

"Ill fares the land to hastening ills a prey." On Vital Statistics. Hilaire Belloc. POL

"I'll give to you a paper of pins." Paper of Pins. *Unknown.* AmFP; BLSo

I'll go among the dead to see my friend. An Afternoon at the Beach. Edgar Bowers. PiAm

I'll go into the bedroom silently and lie down between the bridegroom and the bride. Love Poem on Theme by Whitman. Allen Ginsberg. CAPP

I'll Go with Her Blues. *Unknown.* BluL

Ill Government. Robert Herrick. PAIC

I'll hang/ them by the neck. The Consequence. Roger McDonald. CAAP

I'll lay you five hundred pounds. The Broomfield Hill. *Unknown.* AmFP

I'll Never Love Thee More. James Graham, Marquess of Montrose. GBL; NOBE
To His Mistress, *sel.* SLP

I'll Not Marry at All. *Unknown.* AmFP

I'll not weep that thou art going to leave me. Stanzas. Emily Brontë. IPWM; WPE

I'll prop her, I swear, ankle, butt and chin. The Nude on the Bathroom Wall. Gena Ford. IHMS

I'll Sail Upon the Dog-star. Thomas Durfey. RAE

I'll sing you a one-O. Carol of the Numbers [*or* The Dilly Song]. *Unknown.* AmFP; GBP

I'll sing you a song and it'll be a sad one. The Sioux Indians. *Unknown.* AmFP

I'll sing you a song of peace and love. Whack Fol the Diddle. Peadar Kearney. PFIr

I'll sing you one O. *See* I'll sing you a one-O.

I'll Take You Home Again, Kathleen, *with music.* Thomas P. Westendorf. BLSH; PSoN

I'll tell thee everything I can. The White Knight's Song [*or* The Aged Aged Man]. "Lewis Carroll." *Fr.* Through the Looking-Glass. ECBV; FaBoCo; InPS; NOBE; OBP; OxBChV; SpRo

I'll tell you a story. Mother Goose. ECBV; MG

I'll tell you of a come-lye young lady fair. Fair Phoebe and Her Dark-eyed Sailor. *Unknown.* AmFP

I'll tell you of a sailor now, a tale that can't be beat. The Story of Samuel Jackson. Charles Godfrey Leland. PoTa

I'll tell you of a wild Colloina boy. The Wild Colloina Boy. *Unknown.* AmFP

I'll tell you the story of Jimmy Jet. Jimmy Jet and His TV Set. Shel Silverstein. CTBA

I'll Wear Me a Cotton Dress. *Unknown.* BPo

Illinois Farmer. Carl Sandburg. ANTL

Illinois, Iowa. Inventory/ Itinerary. Ken Smith. TwMBP

Illustration, The/ is nothing to you. To a Steam Roller. Marianne Moore. Psy; VGW

Illustrious Ancestors. Denise Levertov. NoAM; NOBA; VGW

I'm a broken-hearted gardener, and don't know what to do. The Broken-Hearted Gardener. *Unknown.* GBP

I'm a heartbroken raftsman, from Greenville I came. Jack Haggerty. *Unknown.* AmFP

I'm a peevish old man with a penny-whistle. Beggar's Serenade. John Heath-Stubbs. BoLoP

I'm a poor boy, I'm a poor boy. Payday at Coal Creek. *Unknown.* RDB

I'm a poor little girl. The Wagoner's Lad. *Unknown.* AmFP

I'm a riddle in nine syllables. Metaphors. Sylvia Plath. InPK; SoSe

I'm a snake doctor man. Snake Doctor Blues. *Unknown.* BluL

I'm a Soldier in the Army of the Lord. *Unknown.* AmFP

I'm a stranger here just blowed in your town. Doggin' Me Around Blues. *Unknown.* BluL

I'm all alone in this world, she said. 50—50. Langston Hughes. NoAM; NOBA

I'm as free a little bird as I can be. Free Little Bird. *Unknown.* AmFP

I'm Captain Jinks of the Horse Marines. Captain Jinks. William Horace Lingard. BLSo

I'm ceded—I've stopped being theirs. Emily Dickinson. PiAm; SBG

I'm cold in hand can't get nothing here. No Woman No Nickel. *Unknown.* BluL

"I'm corrupt, " he said to me in the French. The Corrupt Man in the French Pub. Brian Higgins. OxBTC

I'm dead drunk this morning, daddy. Dead Drunk Blues. *Unknown.* BluL

I'm determined to be an old maid. I'll Marry Not at All. *Unknown.* AmFP

I'm discontented with homes that are rented. Tea for Two. Irving Caesar. BLSo

I'm dreaming now of Hally [*or* Hallie]. Listen to the Mocking Bird. Septimus Winner. BLSo; PSoN

I'm driving my car back to you filled. The Furniture of the Poem. Dennis Saleh. NeAC

I'm driving straight and my irons are good. Any Golf Championship. Grantland Rice. SPo

I'm eating alone lately. Things of Late. David Phillips. NeAC

I'm flagging to South Carolina. Long Distance Moan. *Unknown.* BluL

I'm getting old and feeble and I cannot work no more. The Old Miner's Refrain. *Unknown.* AmFP

I'm glad that I am born to die. Shout for Joy. *Unknown.* AmFP

I'm goin' away baby take me seven long months to ride. Big Chief Blues. *Unknown.* BluL

I'm goin' get up in the morning. I Believe I'll Dust My Broom. *Unknown.* BluL

I'm going away. Going Away Blues. *Unknown.* BluL

I'm going back where I come f'm. Old Dog Blue. *Unknown.* BluL

I'm Going Down to the River of Jordan, *with music.* *Unknown.* BLSH

I'm going home/ friends, sitdown. That's No Way to Get Along. *Unknown.* BluL

I'm going out to clean the pasture spring. The Pasture. Robert Frost. LCL; NOBA; NowV; RAE

I'm going over to 3rd Alley lord, but I'm gonna carry my 45. 45 Pistol Blues. *Unknown.* BluL

I'm going to be a pirate with a bright brass pivot-gun. The Tarry Buccaneer. John Masefield. PoTa

I'm going to be just like you, Ma. A Dance for Ma Rainey. Al Young. SA

I'm going to Georgia. *Unknown.* AIW; AmFP

I'm going to Germany—I'll be back some day. Going to Germany. *Unknown.* BluL

I'm Going to Rocky Island. *Unknown.* AmFP

I'm gonna get up in the morning do like Buddy Brown. 98 Degree Blues. *Unknown.* BluL

I'm Gonna Move to the Outskirts of Town. *Unknown.* BluL

I'm Gonna Run to the City of Refuge. *Unknown.* BluL

I'm gonna stay around this town. 'Tain't Nobody's Business. *Unknown.* BluL

I'm happy/ could a pome be a cup.   Anybody Could Write This Poem. All You Have to Say Is Yes. Alta.   MMD

I'm having an affair with Hamlet. "Hamlet." Emmett Jarrett. NeAC

I'm Here. Theodore Roethke. *Fr.* Meditations of an Old Woman   Epi

I'm in a nice bit of trouble, I confess.   Waiting at the Church; or, My Wife Won't Let Me.   Fred W. Leigh.   FSN

I'm just a poor wayfaring stranger.   Poor Wayfaring Stranger. *Unknown.* BLSo

I'm Just a Stranger Here, Heaven Is My Home.   Carole Gregory Clemmons.   PoBA

I'm just a typical American boy.   Draft Dodger Rag.   Phil Ochs. WIF

I'm just like an old rooster.   Looking Up at Down.   *Unknown.* BluL

I'm lonesome since I cross'd the hill.   The Girl I Left Behind Me. *Unknown.* BLSo

I'm looking funny in my eye, and I.   Fixing to Die.   *Unknown.* BluL

I'm looking mighty seedy while holding down my claim.   Little Old Sod Shanty.   *Unknown.* AmFP

I'm lost in my name.   Theodore Roethke.   POL

I'm made in sport by nature when.   On an Indian Tomineios, the Least of Birds.   Thomas Heyrick.   SCP-2

I'm makin' a road.   Florida Road Workers.   Langston Hughes. CTBA; SFF

"I'm 92," Joe said.   Tom Weber.   CTBA

I'm nobody! Who are you?   Emily Dickinson.   IPWM; NOBA; SBG; SS; WPE

I'm not scared of dyin.   And When I Die.   Laura Nyro.   WIF

I'm not sure why I touched it.   Last Patch of Snow.   George Abbe.   FAF

I'm on Highway 28 facing the morning.   Meditations on Frost's "Stopping by Woods."   Albert De Pietro.   AATT

I'm Only a Broken-down Miner.   *Unknown.* AmFP

I'm Owre Young to Marry Yet.   Burns.   LoAs

I'm quiet as an old leather belt lapped snakewise.   Quiet.   Brian Swann.   AmPA

I'm quite the opposite of my clever master.   Faust's Servant.   Roy Fuller.   OxBTC

I'm ready now to cat-chase those porcelain people, get after them. Imprecation for an Aesthetics Society with Newts, Warts, Waxes and Pins.   Rosalie Moore.   RiTi

"I'm rising five," he said.   Rising Five.   Norman Nicholson. MPo

I'm sister and brotherless.   Remember Way Back.   *Unknown.* BluL

I'm sitting down here wondering would a, would a matchbox hold my clothes.   Packin' Trunk Blues.   *Unknown.* BluL

I'm so glad good whiskey have made it through.   More Good Whiskey Blues.   *Unknown.* BluL

I'm speaking again.   Speaking.   Michael Ryan.   AmPA

I'm the kid that's all the candy.   The Yankee Doodle Boy.   George M. Cohan.   BLSo; FSN

I'm tired of love: I'm still more tired of rhyme.   Fatigue.   Hilaire Belloc.   FaBoCo; OxBTC

I'm trav'ling to my grave.   The Traveler.   *Unknown.* AmFP

I'm wearin' awa', John.   The Land o' the Leal.   Lady Nairne. SLP

I'm "wife"—I've finished that.   Emily Dickinson.   PiAm

I'm yours, dearest, as are the winter towns.   Marceline, to Her Husband.   Elizabeth Libbey.   AmPA

Image, The.   Roy Fuller.   OxBTC

Image.   T. E. Hulme.   InPK; OxBTC

Image comes, An.   Laser.   A. R. Ammons.   NOBA

Image in the Mirror.   Peggy Susberry Kenner.   JB

Images.   Alastair Campbell.   Moon

Images drip down my back like sweat.   On the Morning of the Third Night above Nisqually.   W. M. Ransom.   CDW

Imaginative Life, The.   Geoffrey Hill.   NoAM

Imagine a lost language, imagine a shadow.   A Northern Habitat. Robin Fulton.   MIS

Imagine it, a Sophocles complete.   The Fire at Alexandria. Theodore Weiss.   NoAM

Imitation of Spenser.   Keats.   MBPR

Imitation of the Style of * * * *.   Samuel Johnson.   FaBoCo

Immeasurable haze.   To the Holy Spirit.   Yvor Winters.   PiAm; VGW

Immense hope, and forbearance, The.   Spring Day.   John Ashbery.   NOBA

Immensity, cloistered in thy dear womb.   Nativity.   John Donne. SCP-1

Immersed in night, my senses sharpen, hear.   Porch.   Alden Nowlan.   NeAC

Immoral Proposition, The.   Robert Creeley.   PiAm

Immorality, An.   Ezra Pound.   NOBA; OLR; VoPo

Immortal Hate.   Milton.   *Fr.* Paradise Lost, I.   NOBE

Immured in thickening walls.   The Old Ones.   R. E. Sebenthall. HeS

Impact of a dollar upon the heart, The.   War Is Kind, XX. Stephen Crane.   PiAm

Impartial Law enrolled a name, The.   My Name and I.   Robert Graves.   NoAM

Impatiently she tampered with the locks.   Bluebeard's Wife. Daryl Hine.   NoAM

Imperfect Enjoyment, The.   Earl of Rochester.   BoLoP; SCP-2

Imperfect enough once for all at thirty.   Last Things, Black Pines at 4 a.m.   Robert Lowell.   NOBA

Imperfect pine, An.   On Restoring Verticals.   Sandra Ruth Duguid.   AATT

Imperfect Sympathies.   Clarice Short.   PPoD

Imperial Adam.   A. D. Hope.   MAuV; NoAM

Imperial Thumbprint.   Tom Weatherly.   PoBA

Imperialists in Retirement.   Edward Lucie-Smith.   MPo

Imperiously he leaps, he neighs, he bounds.   Shakespeare.   *Fr.* Venus and Adonis.   BoAnP

Imponderable the dinosaur.   Cape Hatteras.   Hart Crane.   *Fr.* The Bridge.   PiAm

Importance of Mirrors, The.   Helga Sandburg.   IHMS

Importer, An.   Robert Frost.   FaBoCo

Impossibilities to His Friend.   Robert Herrick.   OLR

Impossibility, An.   Robert Vas Dias.   HeS

Impossible Dream, The, *with music*   Joe Darion.   BLSo

Imposture, The, *sel.*   James Shirley.
    "You virgins that did late despair."   SCP-2
    (Piping Peace.)   NOBE

Impotence.   Marvin Bell.   AmPA

Imprecation for an Aesthetics Society with Newts, Warts, Waxes and Pins.   Rosalie Moore.   RiTi

Imprimis: I forgot all day your face.   Sonnet.   Conrad Aiken. LoAs

Impromptu on Charles II.   Earl of Rochester.   InPK

Improved Farm Land.   Carl Sandburg.   RFM

Impulse, The.   Robert Frost.   *Fr.* The Hill Wife.   AIW; NoAM

Impulse of October, The.   W. R. Moses.   NCSH

In/ The/ Space/ Between.   Separation.   Duane Niatum.   VW

In a Bar.   Ruth Herschberger.   WBN

In a Bar Near Shibuya Station, Tokyo.   Paul Engle.   SFF

In a Bye-Canal.   Herman Melville.   AmVN

In a cavern [or cabin], in a canyon. Oh, My Darling Clementine. *Unknown, at. to* Percy Montross. AIW; AmFP; BLSo; PSoN

In a chariot of light from the regions of day. Liberty Tree. Thomas Paine. BTTM

In a Chinese window. Elephants from the Sea. Ian Young. NeAC

In a chirche ther I con knel. Deo Gracias. *Unknown.* OxBM

In a Churchyard. Richard Wilbur. HeIP; PiAm

In a coign of the cliff between lowland and highland. A Forsaken Garden. Swinburne. NOBE

In a Corn Field. *Unknown.* ECBV

In a dark, dark wood there was a dark, dark house. In a Dark Wood. *Unknown.* RAE

In a Dark Time. Theodore Roethke. HeIP; IPWM; MAT; NoAM; NOBA; PBMP; PiAm; PPoD; PPP

In a Dark Wood. *Unknown.* RAE

In a dream I returned to the river of bees. The River of Bees. W. S. Merwin. HeIP

In a Dream, the Automobile. Adrian Marcus. SFF

In a Drear-Nighted December. Keats. MBPR; NOBE; PBMP

In a fashionable suburb of Santa Barbara. In Montecito. Randall Jarrell. MAT; VGW

In a few moments. The Death of a Negro Poet. Conrad Kent Rivers. BPo

In a Field. Robert Pack. CoPAm; MAT

In a field. Keeping Things Whole. Mark Strand. CoPAm; NoAM; PPP; SFF

In a frith as I can fare fremede. The Lady in the Wood. *Unknown.* OxBM

In a frosty sunset. Winter: East Anglia. Edmund Blunden. OxBTC

In a Gondola, *sel.* Robert Browning. "Moth's kiss, first, The!" BoLoP; GBL

In a Grave-Yard. William Stanley Braithwaite. PoBA

In a grey rectory a clergyman was reading. Droit de Seigneur. Richard Murphy. PFIr

In a gym in Spanish Harlem. To a Fighter Killed in the Ring. Lou Lipsitz. SPo

In a herber green, asleep whereas I lay. In Youth Is Pleasure. Robert Wever. *Fr.* Lusty Juventus. GBL; NOBE

In a Hotel Writing-Room. John Cowper Powys. OxBTC

In a long room that voices sundered. Cold Coffee. John Williams. CoPAm

In a loose robe of tinsel forth she came. George Chapman. *Fr.* Ovid's Banquet of Sense. SCP-2

In a melancholy fancy. Hollo, My Fancy! *Unknown.* SCP-2

In a Mental Hospital Sitting Room. Elizabeth Jennings. LP

In a Mirror. Marcia Stubbs. MAT

In a Moonlit Hermit's Cabin. Allen Ginsberg. Moon

In a Mountain Cabin in Norway. Robert Bly. RFM

In a noon-tide of a sumers day. Turn Again. *Unknown.* OxBM

In a pine tree. I Try to Waken and Greet the World Once Again. James Wright. InPS

In a Prominent Bar in Secaucus One Day. X. J. Kennedy. ConAP; NowV; PAIC; PPP

In a quiet water'd land, a land of roses. The Dead at Clonmacnoise. *Unknown. tr. by* Thomas William Rolleston. PFIr

In a Remote Cloister Bordering the Empyrean. Joel Sloman. VGW

In a Roman tram, where the famous Roman mob. The Thief. Stanley Kunitz. VGW

In a salt ring of moonlight. Moorings. Norman MacCaig. OxBTC

In a season/ the shoots we planted. Peter Whigham. *Fr.* Love Poems of the VIth Dalai Lama. TwMBP

In a shoe box stuffed in an old nylon stocking. The Meadow Mouse. Theodore Roethke. HeIP; InPk; IPWM; PPoe; PSN; TSWA

In a sick shade of spruce, moss-webbed, rock-fed. As It Looked Then. E. A. Robinson. NoAM

In a snug little cot lived a fat little mouse. The Country Mouse and the City Mouse. Richard Scrafton Sharpe. OxBChV

In a solitude of the sea. The Convergence of the Twain. Thomas Hardy. AKE; HeIP; InPK; NoAM; OxBTC; PAIC; PBMP

In a somer seson whenne softe was the sunne. The Field Full of Folk. William Langland. *Fr.* The Vision of Piers Plowman. OxBM

In a Spring Still Not Written of. Robert Wallace. CoPAm; WIF

In a square case. Museum Item 237. Polly Mann. NPW

In a stable of boats I lie still. The Lifeguard. James Dickey. NowV

In a Station of the Metro. Ezra Pound. BBGO; HeIP; InPK; NoAM; NOBA; PiAm; PPoD; VGW; WIF

In a summer season, when soft was the sun. Prologue. William Langland, *tr. by* Selden Rodman. *Fr.* The Vision of Piers Plowman. OBP

In a tea-garden overhanging Rotha. Grasmere Sonnets. David Wright. NoAM

In a thousand years, if there's History. Ecologue. Allen Ginsberg. CAAP

In a time of damnation. The Gift of Fire. Lisel Mueller. NowV

In a Train. Robert Bly. CAPP; POL

In a universe infinitely subdividable. Candles. Peter Meinke. AATT

In a wee cot hoose far across the muir. Kate Dalrymple. *Unknown.* GBP

In a white gully among fungus red. Native Born. Eve Langley. WPE

In a Wood. E. J. Scovell. GBL

In Adam' fall. An ABC. *Unknown.* GBP

In Aeternum. James McAuley. MAuV

In Agypt's land contaygious to the Nile. Pharao's Daughter. Michael Moran. BIrV

In all humanity, we crave. The Commons' Petition to Charles II. Earl of Rochester. FaBoCo

In All the Days of My Childhood. Russell Edson. AmPA

In all the Eastern hemisphere. The Fall of J. W. Beane. Oliver Herford. PoTa

In all the good Greek of Plato. Survey of Literature. John Crowe Ransom. VGW

In All These Acts. William Everson. PiAm

In all those stories the hero. Heroes. Robert Creeley. NOBA; PPP

"In America," began. The Student. Marianne Moore. NowV

In an Artist's Studio. Christina Rossetti. OBP

In an Empty Window. Ray Fraser. NeAC

In an envelope marked. Personal. Langston Hughes. NOBA

In an instant, by instinct, I apprehended. An Act. Kenneth Rosen. AmPA

In an island of bitter lemons. Bitter Lemons. Lawrence Durrell. VoPo

In an upper room at midnight. The Love Feast. W. H. Auden. SFF

In ancient Egypt. The Fertile Valley of the Nile. Eve Merriam. IHMS

In and out of the streets. Bruce Beaver. *Fr.* Lauds and Plaints. CAAP

In and out the bushes, up the ivy. The Chipmunk's Day. Randall Jarrell. BoAnP; NCSH

In Answer to a Request to Write a Poem on World Peace. Elisavietta Ritchie. AATT

In Antarctica drooping their little shoulders. The View from Here. William Stafford. RFM

In April we will pierce his body. Letters to a Stranger. Thomas James. AmPA

In Aprill the koocoo can sing her song by rote. The Koocoo. *Unknown.* GBP

In Arizona/ (how many years in the mountains). Louis Zukofsky. NoAM

In Autumn. Jon Anderson. AmPA

In autumn down the beechwood path. Beech Leaves. James Reeves. RAE

In autumn, the bats. The Bat. Roberta Spear. AmPA

In Autumpne, whan the sonne in vyrgyne. The Bowge of Courte. John Skelton. AAS

In Back of the Real. Allen Ginsberg. HeIP; InPK

In Baltimore there lived a boy. The Boy Who Laughed at Santa Claus. Ogden Nash. PoTa

In bed./ My hand on Mark's bare chest. At Rochdale. Ian Young. NeAC

In bed/ with my friend's young brother. A Sugar-Candy Bird. Ian Young. NeAC

In bed I muse on Tenier's boors. The Bench of Boors. Herman Melville. AmVN; SoSe

In bed with the stranger who had picked him up. A Bride. Harry Fainlight. BoLoP

In Bertram's Garden. Donald Justice. BoLoP; InPK; SFF; VGW

In Bhaudanath. Mei Berssenbrugge. SA

In birth we're fired from our hole. Fox Song. Katherine Doak. NPW

In black core of night, it explodes. African Dream. Bob Kaufman. PoBA

In Blessed Weather. Michael Heffernan. HeS

In Bloemfontein. Alan Ross. BoLoP

In Bondage. Claude McKay. PoBA

In Breughel's great picture, The Kermess. The Dance. William Carlos Williams. HeIP; InPK; NCSH; NoAM; NOBA; PAIC; PiAm; POL; SoSe; WIF

In Broken Images. Robert Graves. PPoe

In California. Louis Simpson. NoAM; NowV

In calm and cool and silence, once again. First-Day Thoughts. Whittier. AmVN; IPWM; PPoD

In calm fellowship they sleep. In a Grave-Yard. William Stanley Braithwaite. PoBA

In came her sister. Janet (Lady Maisry). *Unknown.* PeBB

In canary grass insects. Ethan Boldt. Roger Weingarten. AmPA

In Celebration. Ellen Bass. NMM

In Celebration of My Uterus. Anne Sexton. CAPP; RiTi

In Charles the Second's golden days. *See* In good King Charles's golden days.

In childhood you think. Thanksgiving. John N. Morris. OFD

In Church. Thomas Hardy. PoTa

In Cipres springes (wheras dame Venus dwelt). Earl of Surrey. AAS

In Come de Animuls Two by Two. *Unknown.* GBP

In Commendation of a Solitary Life. Thomas Lodge. TVS

In Commendation of the Female Sex. Jane Barker. SCP-2

In crow's-foot patterns, like deltas. January Thaw. Allan Block. FAF

In Danger from the Outer World. Robert Bly. CAPP

In daydream fantasies of self-indulgence. Personal Column. William Price Turner. SLP

In days of yore from Britain's shore. The Maple Leaf Forever. Alexander Muir. BLSH

In dear old New York it's remarkable. The Streets of New York. Henry Blossom. FSN

In Defense of Black Poets. Conrad Kent Rivers. BPo

In Dessexshire as It Befel. *Unknown.* GBP; PeBB

In Detroit, I walk out Woodward Avenue. R. R. Cuscaden. POL

In digging up your bones, Tom Paine. Epigram. Byron. MBPR

In Dispraise of the Moon. Mary Elizabeth Coleridge. Moon

In distant countries I have been. The Last of the Flock. Wordsworth. MBPR

In Distrust of Merits. Marianne Moore. VoPo

In Dives' Dive. Robert Frost. VGW

In Dream: The Privacy of Sequence. Ray A. Young Bear. CDW

In Dublin's fair city, where girls are so pretty. Cockles and Mussels (Molly Malone). *Unknown.* BLSH

In Due Season. W. H. Auden. Prf

In early morning twilight, raw and chill. The Eviction. William Allingham. *Fr.* Laurence Bloomfield in Ireland. BIrV

In early youth's unclouded scene. Thirty-Eight. Charlotte Smith. SBG

In 1876/ The Cooper & Bailey Great London Circus. The Cooper & Bailey Great London Circus. Robert Hershon. MAT

In Eternum. Sir Thomas Wyatt. NOBE ("In eternum I was ons determed.") AAS

In Eundem Macaronicon. John Donne. PAIC

In every brain there do loose atoms lie. Of Loose Atoms. Margaret Cavendish, Duchess of Newcastle. SCP-2

In every dream thy lovely features rise. Sonnet. William Barnes. BoLoP

In every land from Gades to Ganges flood. Thomas Lodge. *Fr.* A Fig for Momus. TVS

In Exile. Emma Lazarus. SBG

In fair London city a woman did dwell. The Bold Trooper. *Unknown.* PeBB

In Fargo, North Dakota, a man. To Flood Stage Again. James Wright. NOBA; Prf

In fear of the rich mouth. The Frightened Man. Louise Bogan. SBG

In February there are days. When. Dorothy Aldis. ECBV

In Fields of Summer. Galway Kinnell. RFM; VGW

In fifty-seeven the sweet guitars rang. Minding. Donald Campbell. *Fr.* Sonnets frae Siberia. MIS

In five-score summers! All new eyes. 1967. Thomas Hardy. NoAM

In Flanders Fields. John McCrae. BTTM

In Flight. Patrick Smith. MIT

In former days we'd both agree. Bhartrihari, *tr. fr. Sanskrit by* John Brough. BoLoP

In former times, when Israel's ancient creed. Absolute and Abitofhell. Ronald Arbuthnott Knox. FaBoCo

In fragrant Dixie's arms. Church Burning: Mississippi. James A. Emanuel. PoBA

In frames as large as rooms that face all ways. Essential Beauty. Philip Larkin. NowV

In France, (to baffle thieves and murderers). The Paris Railway-Station. Dante Gabriel Rossetti. VPC

In from the roundup and dressed to kill. Love and an Old Western at the Starlite Drive-In Theater. Philip Legler. PPoD

In front of the sombre mountains. On the Balcony. D. H. Lawrence. GBL

In Fur. William Stafford. RFM

In futurity/ I prophetic see. The Little Girl Lost. Blake. *Fr.* Songs of Experience. MBPR; RRA

In Glasgow. Edwin Morgan. SLP

In Glencullen. J. M. Synge. PFIr; RAE

In Golden Gate Park That Day. Lawrence Ferlinghetti. *Fr.* A Coney Island of the Mind. BBGO; NoAM

In good King Charles's [*or* In Charles the Second's] golden days. The Vicar of Bray. *Unknown.* AIW; ESaP; GBP; NOBE; RDB

In good old colony times. Old Colony Times. *Unknown.* BLSo

In Gosport of late a young damsel did dwell. The Gosport Tragedy. *Unknown.* AmFP

In Goya's Greatest Scenes. Lawrence Ferlinghetti. *Fr.* A Coney Island of the Mind. BBGO; HeIP; NoAM; PAIC; PBMP

In Gratitude to Beethoven. Diane Wakoski. Psy

In Hans' old mill his three black cats. Five Eyes. Walter de la Mare. PCat

In Hardin County, 1809. Lulu E. Thompson. PoTa

In Harmony with Nature. Matthew Arnold. PFD

In haste, post haste, when first my wandering mind. Memories, IV. George Gascoigne. AAS; PAIC

In Heaven a spirit doth dwell. Israfel. Poe. AmVN; NOBA; PiAm

In heaven queene is she among the spheares. Heaven's Queene. Sir Walter Ralegh. Moon

In heaven, too. Heard in a Violent Ward. Theodore Roethke. NoAM

In Heavenly Realms of Hellas Dwelt. E. E. Cummings. NOBA; SoSe

In her last sickness, my mother took my hand in hers. Kaddish. Charles Reznikoff. *Fr.* Going To and Fro And Walking Up and Down. SA

In Her Praise. Robert Graves. BIrV

In her room that night she looks at herself in the mirror. Randall Jarrell. *Fr.* "The Night before the Night Before Christmas." MiP

In his chamber, weak and dying. A Strike Among the Poets. *Unknown.* FaBoCo

In His Poems Are El Greco's Hands. Robert Leverant. MIT

In hollows of the land. The Ground-mist. Denise Levertov. PiAm

In Hollywood, the air was quiet. Trying to Forget. John Wieners. MIT

In Honour of That High and Mighty Princess Queen Elizabeth of Happy Memory. Anne Bradstreet. SBG

In Hospital. James Elroy Flecker. OxBTC

In Hospital. W. E. Henley. VPC

In Imago Dei: Fiat Lux. Roderick Hartigh Jellema. AATT

In Ireland they were put in foundling homes. Orphans. David Ray. FiCP

In Italian They Call the Bird Civetta. Robert Penn Warren. PiAm

In Jersey City where I did dwell. The Butcher Boy. *Unknown.* AmFP

In Jerusalem. Elisavietta Ritchie. AATT

In Joe Brainard's collage its white arrows. Sonnet. Ted Berrigan. Epi

In Judgment of the Leaf. Kenneth Patchen. VGW

In july of 19 somethin. With All Deliberate Speed. Don L. Lee. JB

In jumping and tumbling. Tumbling. *Unknown.* OxBChV

In June, amid the golden fields. The Groundhog. Richard Eberhart. CoPAm; NoAM; PPoe; VoPo

In Just-/ Spring. E. E. Cummings. Chansons Innocentes, I. BBGO; HeIP; InPK; NCSH; NowV; PiAm

In Kerry. J. M. Synge. GBL

In Köhln, a town of monks and bones. Cologne. Samuel Taylor Coleridge. MBPR; PBMP

In late autumn the hound. Old Man, Phantom Dog. Frederick Eckman. ANTL

In late winter/ I sometimes glimpse bits of steam. The Bear. Galway Kinnell. RFM; VGW

In Laughter. Ted Hughes. InPS

In Little Rock the people bear. The Chicago "Defender" Sends a Man to Little Rock. Gwendolyn Brooks. PoBA; Psy

In London Town. Mary Elizabeth Coleridge. RAE

In Love for Long. Edwin Muir. BoLoP; LoAs

In Love with You. Kenneth Koch. CAPP

In loving, each one hath free choice. Isabella Whitney. *Fr.* A Sweet Nosegay or Pleasant Posy. WPE

In lungs fresh like honeycomb. Indian. Laura Jensen. AmPA

In Madurai,/ city of temples and poets. A River. A. K. Ramanujan. MPo

In Manchester Square. Alice Meynell. SBG

In marble halls as white as milk. *Unknown.* GBP

In Marion, the honey locust trees are falling. Two Poems about President Harding. James Wright. NoAM

In matters of commerce the fault of the Dutch. A Political Despatch. George Canning. FaBoCo

In May, his last time over, he drank too much. Statement and Vision, Two Signs of History. James Whitehead. CoPAm

In May, when sea-winds pierced out solitudes. The Rhodora. Emerson. HeIP; NOBA; PiAm

In me (the worm) clearly. Hilda Doolittle ("H.D."). *Fr.* The Walls Do Not Fall. NoAM

In Memoriam. Max Adeler. FaBoCo

In Memoriam A. H. H., *sels.* Tennyson.
 "Be near me when my light is low," L-LVIII. PFD
 "Calm is the morn without a sound," XI. NOBE
 "Dark house, by which once more I stand," VII. InPK; NOBE; PPoe; SoSe
 "I dreamed there would be spring no more," LXIX. NOBE
 "Love is and was my lord and king," CXXVI. NOBE
 "Now fades the last long streak of snow," CXV. FSFS; NOBE
 "O yet we trust that somehow good," LIV. BoReV; VoPo
 "Old Yew, which graspest at the stones," II NOBE
 Ring Out, Wild Bells, CVI. OFD
 " 'So careful of the type?' but no," LVI. BoReV
 "Strong Son of God, immortal Love," Proem. BoReV; PFD
 "That which we dare invoke to bless," CXXIV. BoReV
 "There rolls the deep where grew the tree," CXXIII. BoReV; NOBE
 "Time draws near the birth of Christ, The," XXVIII. SoSe
 "To-night the winds began to rise," XV. FSFS; NOBE
 "Wish, that of the living whole, The," LV. BoReV

In Memoriam (Easter, 1915). Edward Thomas. NOBE; OxBTC

In Memoriam: Gertrude Kolmar, 1943. A. D. Hope. CAAP

In Memoriam James Joyce, *sel.* "Hugh MacDiarmid."
 "World is fast bound in the snares of Varuna, The." TwMBP

In Memoriam: Martin Luther King, Jr. June Jordan. PoBA

In Memoriam: Rev. J. J. Lyons, *sel.* Emma Lazarus.
 "Hark! through the quiet evening air, their song." SBG

In Memory of a Friend. George Barker. OxBTC

In Memory of Arthur Winslow. Robert Lowell. PAIC

In Memory of Colonel Charles Young. Countee Cullen. PoBA

In Memory of Eva Gore-Booth and Con Markiewicz. W. B. Yeats. NoAM; OxBTC

In Memory of Francis Webb. Thomas Shapcott. CAAP

In Memory of G. K., for 50 Years the College Carpenter. Robert A. Martin. AATT

In Memory of Jane Fraser. Geoffrey Hill. NoAM; OxBTC

In Memory of My Cat Domino: 1951-1966. Roy Fuller. PSN

In Memory of My Dear Grandchild Elizabeth Bradstreet. Anne Bradstreet. WPE

In Memory of My Mother. Patrick Kavanagh. BIrV; NoAM

In Memory of the Circus Ship *Euzkera*. Walter Gibson. NCSH

In Memory of W. B. Yeats. W. H. Auden. Epi; HeIP; NoAM; NOBE; OxBTC; PAIC; PPoe: PPP; TCP; WIF

In merry old England, it once was a rule. On the New Laureate. *Unknown.* FaBoCo

In Mexico. Robert Sward. NowV

In midnight sleep of many a face of anguish. Old War-Dreams. Walt Whitman. WIF

In midst of the city celestial. The Celestial City. Giles Fletcher, the Younger. *Fr.* Christ's Victory and Triumph, IV. BoReV; NOBE

In Mind. Denise Levertov. Epi; InPS; NMM; RiTi

In Missing. Ray A. Young Bear. CDW

In Mississippi/ balloons of hunger. No New Music. Stanley Crouch. PoBA

In Missoula, Montana, where the townsfolk water. Pendant Watch. Madeline DeFrees. NMM

In Montecito. Randall Jarrell. MAT; VGW

In More's Hotel. Robert Nye. SLP

In Mornigan's park there is a deer. The Crescent Moon. *Unknown.* GBP; Moon

In moss-prankt dells which the sunbeams flatter. Lovers, and a Reflection. Charles Stuart Calverley. FaBoCo; SpRo

In moving-slow he has no Peer. The Sloth. Theodore Roethke. SS

In Murasaki's time. Tale of Genji. Hugh Seidman. AmPA

In my beginning is my end. East Coker. T. S. Eliot. *Fr.* Four Quartets. PPP; VGW

In my childhood trees were green. Autobiography. Louis MacNeice. BuTh

In My Craft or Sullen Art. Dylan Thomas. BoLoP; HeIP; IPWM; LoAs; MAT; NoAM; NowV; OBP; PAIC; WIF

In my dreams I always speak Spanish. Sueños. James Reiss. FiCP

In my dreams I hear my tribe. Then and Now. Kath Walker. IHMS

In my dry cell. The Riven Quarry. Gloria C. Oden. PoBA

In My First Hard Springtime. James Welch. AmPA; CDW

In my grandmother's house there was always chicken soup. A Story about Chicken Soup. Louis Simpson. NoAM

In my kindergarten class. Kindergarten. Ronald Rogers. VW

In My Life. John Lennon *and* Paul McCartney. GrRo

In my life there will be U.S. famine. Good-by on an All Day Bean Planter. Nathan Whiting. HeS

In My Lifetime. James Welch. CDW

In My Merry Oldsmobile, *with music.* Vincent Bryan. FSN

In my paintings for they are present. Sonnet. Ted Berrigan. CAAP

In my prison cell I sit, thinking Mother, dear, of you. Tramp! Tramp! Tramp! George F. Root. BLSo

In my sleep I was fain of their fellowship, fain. Sunrise. Sidney Lanier. PiAm

In my smoochy corner. In Glasgow. Edwin Morgan. SLP

In my younger years. Dreams. Nikki Giovanni. PoBA

In nameless warmth, sun light in every corner. Autumn Shade, IX. Edgar Bowers. PiAM

In "nature" there's no choice. Beyond the End. Denise Levertov. VGW

In Neglect. Robert Frost. VGW

In night when colours all to blacke are cast. Caelica, C. Fulke Greville. AAS

In 1915 my grandfather's. Grandfather. Michael S. Harper. FiCP

In 1939 the skylark had nothing to say to me. The Ninth of July. John Hollander. CoPAm

In no country. No Offence. D. J. Enright. OxBTC

In No Strange Land. Francis Thompson. NOBE

In Noah's Wake. Allan Block. FAF

In North Great George's Street. "Seumas O'Sullivan." BIrV

In Northern Tasmania. James McAuley. MAuV

In November, in the days to remember the dead. St. Malachy. Thomas Merton. VGW

In Obitum M. S. x Maij, 1614. William Browne. NOBE

In Obitum Promi. Henry Parrot. FaBoCo

In Ohio, where these things happen. The Breathers. James Reiss. AmPA; CAAP; HeS

In One Battle. LeRoi Jones. BPo

In Orangeburg My Brothers Did. A. B. Spellman. BPo; PoBA

In orchard under the hawthorne. Vergier. *Unknown, tr. by* Ezra Pound. GBL

In Order to. Kenneth Patchen. PPoD

In order to escape you. Love. Jaime Torres Bodet, *tr. by* Muna Lee de Munoz Marín. LoAs

In our country, in our country. The Merry Haymakers; or, Pleasant Pastime Between the Young Men and Maids in the Pleasant Meadows. *Unknown.* SCP-2

In our old shipwrecked days there was an hour. Modern Love, XVI. George Meredith. BoLoP; LoAs

In our tin-roofed house in the big war's summer. War Summer. James Applewhite. NVAP

In our town, people live in rows. The Fired Pot. Anna Wickham. OxBTC

In Oxford there lived a merchant by trade. The Crafty Farmer. *Unknown.* AmFP

In paper case. Epitaph on a Dormouse. *Unknown.* OxBChV

In Parenthesis, *sels.* David Jones.
   "And to Private Ball it came as if a rigid beam." TwMBP
   Five Unmistakable Marks, The. NoAM
   King Pellam's Launde. NoAM
   "Lift gently Dai, gentleness befits his gun-shot wound." TwMBP
   "You drop apprehensively—the sun gone out." TwMBP

In Paths Untrodden. Walt Whitman. AmVN; NOBA

In Pennsylvania; it's sort of like losing. Another Night on the Porch Swing. Cathleen Quirk. NMM

In Pilsen,/ Twenty-six Station Road. Five Minutes after the Air Raid. Miroslav Holub, *tr. by* Ian Milner *and* George Theiner. BuTh

In pity for man's darkening thought. Two Songs from a Play. W. B. Yeats. *Fr.* The Resurrection. NOBE; PPP

In Place of a Curse. John Ciardi. NowV

In Place of a Phone Call to Arabia. Diane Wakoski. Psy

In placid hours well-pleased we dream. Art. Herman Melville. NOBA

In Pliny, Phoenice, Phoenicians. What Day Is. Robert Penn Warren. PiAm

In poems, our earth's wonders. Poems. Peter Kelso. AKE

In Praise of BIC Pens. David Hilton. NowV

In Praise of Lichen. Mark Perlberg. HeS

In Praise of Limestone. W. H. Auden. NoAM; PPP

In Praise of Mary. *Unknown.* BoReV; NOBE

In Praise of Neptune. Thomas Campion. NOBE

In Praise of Winchester. *Unknown.* OxBM

In Progress. Christina Rossetti. WPE

In Pursuit of the Family. Jenne Andrews. HeS

In Reference to Her Children, 23 June, 1656. Anne Bradstreet. SBG

In Respectful Memory of Mr. Yarker, *sel.* John Close.
   "And have we lost another friend?" FaBoCo

In Response to a Rumor That the Oldest Whorehouse In Wheeling, West Virginia, Has Been Condemned. James Wright. CAPP

In restaurants we argue. They Eat Out. Margaret Atwood. NeAC; Psy

In Romney Marsh. John Davidson. OxBTC

In rosy-fingered dawn they go. Jersey Cattle. R. N. Currey. OxBTC

In Ruin Reconciled. Aubrey Thomas De Vere. BIrV

In Sabbath quiet, a street. The Grace-note. Denise Levertov. ConAP

In sad and ashy weeds I sigh. Elegy on the Death of Her Husband. Anne Howard, Duchess of Arundel. WPE

In St. Louis as at Fountainbleau there is. Letter to Belden. Rosalie Moore. NPW

In Salem. Lucille Clifton. AmPA

In Scarlet Town, where I was born. Barbara Allen [or Barb'ra Allen]. *Unknown.* BLSo; RDB; WIF

In Scarlet Town, where I was bound. Barbara Allen's Cruelty. *Unknown.* AIW

In School Days. Whittier. OxBChV

In Scotland I was bred and born. Barbara Ellen. *Unknown.* AIW

In Scotland town where I was borned. Hind Horn. *Unknown.* AmFP

In secret/ the out's in. Robert Creeley. PiAm

In secret place where once I stood. The Flesh and the Spirit. Anne Bradstreet. NOBA

In September she appeared. Foreign Student. Barbara B. Robinson. CTBA

In serious jest and jesting seriousness. John Marston. *Fr.* The Scourge of Villainy, Proemium, Bk. III. TVS

In seventeen hundred and forty-four. The Kilruddery Hunt. Thomas Mozeen. BIrV

In seventeen hundred seventy-five. The Bombardment of Bristol, R.I. *Unknown.* BTTM

In Shadow. Hart Crane. NOBA

In shadows fishing sycamores. Autumn on the Wabash. Dave Etter. CoPAm

In Shame and Humiliation. James Wright. CAPP

In shards the sylvan vases lie. The Ravaged Villa. Herman Melville. NOBA; PiAm

In Siberia's wastes. Siberia. James Clarence Mangan. BIrV

In silence I lie. Buddha's Death Day: February 15, 1815. Issa, *tr. by* Nobuyuki Yuasa. *Fr.* Oraga Haru. OFD

In silence I must take my seat. Table Rules for Little Folks. *Unknown.* OxBChV

In silent night when rest I took. Upon the Burning of Our House, July 10th, 1666. Anne Bradstreet. NOBA; PiAm; SBG; WPE

In Small Townlands. Seamus Heaney. NoAM

In smoky outhouses of the court of love. In the Queen's Room. Norman Cameron. OxBTC

In sober mornings do not thou rehearse. When He Would Have His Verses Read. Robert Herrick. NOBE

In some places the color. Lyn Lifshin. *Fr.* Walking thru Audley End Mansion Late Afternoon. RiTi

In some unused lagoon, some nameless bay. The Dismantled Ship. Walt Whitman. NoAM

In southeastern Ohio there are porches. Porches. Stanley Plumly. HeS

In spite of all the learned have said. The Indian Burying Ground. Philip Freneau. HeIP; IPWM; NOBA; PiAm

In Spite of His Dangling Pronoun. Lyn Lifshin. IHMS; Psy

In Split: Diocletian's Palace. Stephen Stepanchev. SA

In spots/ it is warm enough. Ken Belford. NeAC

In spring from the black branches of the flowering plum tree. Flowering Plum. Louise Glück. CAAP

In stagnant pools, by disused tennis-courts. The Frog Plague. Bruce Dawe. CAAP

In Stamford, at the edge of town, a giant statue stands. The Best Line Yet. Edward Allen. InPK; POL

In such a night, when every louder wind. A Nocturnal Reverie. Countess of Winchilsea. SBG; WPE

In such an armor he may rise and raid. Bronzeville Man with a Belt in the Back. Gwendolyn Brooks. POBA

In summer/ this red-patch. Peter Whigham. *Fr.* Love Poems of the VIth Dalai Lama. TwMBP

In summer-colored dresses, six young girls. Baptism. Alden Nowlan. POL

In summer-time it was a paradise. The Seaside. Charles Tennyson Turner. VPC

In summer time when leaves grow green. Under the Greenwood Tree. *Unknown.* GBP

In summer time, when leaves grew green. King Edward the Fourth and a Tanner of Tamworth. *Unknown.* PeBB

In summer's heat and mid-time of the day. Corinnae Concubitus [or Elegy]. Ovid, *tr. by,* Christopher Marlowe. *Fr.* Amores BoLoP; GBL; OBP

In summer's mellow midnight. The Night-Wind. Emily Brontë. FSFS

In Sylvia Plath Country. Erica Jong. IHMS

In Tenebris. Thomas Hardy. NOBE
    "When the clouds' swoln bosoms echo back the shouts," II. NoAM; OxBTC

In Texas Grass. Quincy Troupe. PoBA

In that age, the great anagram of God. The Incarnation of Sirius. James McAuley. MAuV

In that building, long and low. The Ropewalk. Longfellow. PiAm

In that corner, where we slept together. Trilce. César Vallejo, *tr. by* James Wright. LoAs

In that November off Tehuantepec. Sea Surface Full of Clouds. Wallace Stevens. VGW

In that same gardin all the goodly flowres. The Garden of Adonis. Spenser. *Fr.* The Faerie Queene, III, 6. NOBE

In that town were hard spaces. Town I Left. Helen Sorrells. IHMS

In the afternoon, while the wind. Views from the High Camp. W. S. Merwin. ConAP

In the alley he lay on what was. Contemporary Fear. Don Ober. NowV

In the back yard. The Clothesline. John Stevens Wade. FAF

In the Baggage Coach Ahead, *with music.* Gussie L. Davis. FSN

In the Balance. *Unknown, tr. fr. Latin by* George F. Whicher. *Fr.* Carmina Burana. OLR

In the barn stallions stand. Summer Solstice. Marilyn Krysl. NPW

In the bars, the gambling rooms. The Price of Breast in Las Vegas. Carole Oles. NPW

In the Beach House. Anne Sexton. PPP

In the bedroom dense with feathers and smell of sex. The Death Dance. Marge Piercy. WBN

In the beginning was the/ Kickoff. Lillian Morrison. SPo

In the bell toll of a clang. Salt. Ruth Stone. NMM

In the black forge. The Cerne Giant. Paul Mills. MIS

In the black winter morning. Bereft. Thomas Hardy. BoLoP; NoAM

In the bleak mid-winter. A Christmas Carol. Christina Rossetti. BoReV

In the blue hubbub of the same-through-wealth sky. Geography. Kenneth Koch. NoAM

In the blue night. Pine Tree Tops. Gary Snyder. NOBA; Prf

In the bramble bush shelley slowly eats a lark's heart. Hot Day at the Races. Tome Raworth. TwMBP

In the Cabin of Lost Fir Smells. Mary Moore. NPW

In the Cage. Robert Lowell. NOBA; PPoD

In the Canyon of Echo, ther's a railroad begun. Echo Canyon. *Unknown.* AmFP

In the Carolinas. Wallace Stevens. VGW

In the center of the field a Lamb. At Christmas. Robert Duncan. NoAM

In the city, as soon as you fall someone is there to catch you. Not Having a History. John Vernon. PPoD

In the city of fire the eyes. The Pens. W. S. Merwin. TH

In the city of St. Francis. Afterwards, They Shall Dance. Bob Kaufman. VGW

In the close covert of a grove. The Geranium. Sheridan. BoLoP

In the cold, cold parlor. First Death in Nova Scotia. Elizabeth Bishop. NCSH; NOBA

In the cold compassion. Forgive? José Montoya. MIT

In the cold static of air. Looking for a Place to be Comfortable. Virginia Gilbert. NVAP

In the coolness of the day. Jesus Inter Ubera Mariae. Joseph Beaumont. SCP-2

In the country down below. Old Dolores. *Unknown.* MiP

In the County Tyrone, in the town of Dungannon. Old Orange Flute. *Unknown.* GBP

In the cowslip pips I lie. Clock-a-clay (The Ladybird). John Clare. OBP

In the crept hours of our street. The Summons in Indiana. William Stafford. AnMo

In the dark aisles of Bruckner's symphonies. Bruckner. James Camp. MAT

In the dark womb where I began. C. L. M. John Masefield. OxBTC

In the darkness/ of the house of the white brother. Indian School. Norman H. Russell. MAT

In the days of Caesar Augustus. Christmas Day. John Meade Falkner. OxBTC

In the Days of Prismatic Color. Marianne Moore. PiAm

In the Dead of the Night. Norman Dubie. AmPA

In the dead screen. While the TV Is Shut Off. Diane Kruchkow. FAF

In the Deep Museum. Anne Sexton. Prf

In the Desert. Stephen Crane. The Black Riders, III. AmVN; NOBA; PiAm;
(Heart, The.) InPK

In the Desert. Herman Melville. PiAm

In the deserted village, sunken down. The Deserted Village. Robin Hyde. WPE

In the Dordogne. John Peale Bishop. VGW

In the Dumps. *Unknown.* FaBoCo
(We're All in the Dumps.) GBP

In the dust are my father's beautiful hands. At Night. Richard Eberhart. LoAs

In the earth—the earth—thou shalt be laid. Warning and Reply. Emily Brontë. WPE

In the Elegy Season. Richard Wilbur. InPK

In the Embers at Midnight. Paulette Dusdall Zachariou. NPW

In the empty lot—a place. The Wild. Wendell Berry. VGW

In the end, Keats's stone will go. Revelation. Peter Meinke. AATT

In the end you are tired of those places. Locations. Jim Harrison. AmPA

In the evening/ my griefs come to me. Old Woman. Linda Pastan. FiCP

In the evening/ Quiet of the country town. Tanka. Noin Hoshi, *tr. by* Nobuyuki Yuasa. PAIC

In the Evening as from a Cradle. Robert Bloom. AATT

In the Evening by the Moonlight, *with music.* James A. Bland. PSoN

In the evening, just before. For Mary. Kenneth Rexroth. SFF

In the evening the dusk. The Poet Is Dead. William Everson. PiAm

In the evening there is a snail. Talking to the Mule. Laura Jensen. AmPA

In the evening when I sit alone a-dreaming. Sweet Adeline. Richard H. Gerard. FSN

In the evenings the old country old take. In the Gazebo. Nicholas Flocos. SA

In the eyes of the brown bear. Casting a Vote. James DenBoer. PPoD

In the faint blue light. Vincent Buckley. *Fr.* Stroke. MAuV

In the far corner. The Blackbird. Humbert Wolfe. RAE

In the Field. Phyllis Janik. IHMS

In the Fields. Charlotte Mew. LoAs

In the fields, the silos open their mouths. Hangman. Ai.. AmPA

In the first. Ezra Pound. Jonathan Price. CoPAm

In the first ruder age, when love was wild. Love's Force. Thomas Carew. SCP-2

In the first taxi he was alone, tra-la. The Taxis. Louis MacNeice. OxBTC

In the Fleeting Hand of Time. Gregory Corso. SA

In the Flight of the Blue Heron: To Montezuma. Anita Endrezze Probst. CDW

In the foreground we see time and life. Cézanne's Ports. Allen Ginsberg. WIF

In the forest hearing. The World Has Many Places Many Ways. Norman H. Russell. VW

In the forest of noyous hevynesse. Lost. Charles d'Orléans. OxBM

In the furrows of the world. Nation. Charlie Cobb. PoBA

In the Garden, *with music.* C. Austin Miles. BLSH

In the Garden. Tom Schmidt. NeAC

In the garden there strayed. *Unknown.* SoSe

In the Gazebo. Nicholas Flocos. SA

In the Giving Vein. Peter Porter. CAAP

In the Gloaming, *with music.* Meta Orred. BLSH; BLSo

In the Glorious Epiphany of Our Lord God, *sel.* Richard Crashaw. "We who strangely went astray." SCP-1

In the Glue Factory. Allan Block. FAF

In the golden glade the chestnuts are fallen all. North Wind in October. Robert Bridges. FSFS

In the Good Old Summertime, *with music.* Ren Shields. BLSo; FSN

In the gray evening. The Garden Hose. Beatrice Janosco. POL

In the great gardens, after bright spring rain. The Innocent Spring. Edith Sitwell. *Fr.* The Sleeping Beauty. NOBE; OxBTC

In the Great Metropolis. Arthur Hugh Clough. VPC

In the great place the great house is gone from. Slave Quarters. James Dickey. CAPP

In the great snowfall before the bomb. Lorine Niedecker. RiTi

In the green light of water, like the day. The Swans. Edith Sitwell. WPE

In the greenest of our valleys. The Haunted Palace. Poe. *Fr.* The Fall of the House of Usher. NOBA; PiAm

In the groves of Africa from their natural wonder. An African Elegy. Robert Duncan. NoAM

In the halls, in the universities. Cripples. Kathleen Spivack. SFF

In the hazy shape of my mind. Squall. John Moore. NCSH

In the heat of the day a funnel cloud. For the El Paso Weather Bureau. Peter Wild. MAT

In the heat-locked room. As a Child Seeing a Cardinal. John Gill. NeAC

In the heavens' universal alphabet. Joseph Hall. *Fr.* Virgidemiarum. TVS

In the hexemeter rises the fountain's silvery column. The Ovidian Elegiac Metre Described and Exemplified. Schiller, *tr. by* Samuel Taylor Coleridge. MBPR

In the heydays of 'forty-five. For George Santayana. Robert Lowell. CoPAm; VGW

In the high/ clear air. Joanne Kyger. RiTi

In the high jungle where Assam meets Tibet. Moschus Moschiferus. A. D. Hope. MAuV

In the high leaves of a walnut. Walnut-Leaf Scent. Laurence Binyon. BBGO

In the Holy Nativity of Our Lord God, *sel.* Richard Crashaw. "Gloomy night embraced the place." SCP-1 (Shepherds' Hymn, The.) NOBE

In the Home. Marvin Bell. NVAP

In the Hospital. Laura Jensen. AmPA

In the Hospital of the Holy Physician. Nancy Willard. IHMS

In the hour of my distress. His Litany to the Holy Spirit. Robert Herrick. BoReV

In the House of the Dying. Jane Cooper. CoPAm; NMM

In the house of the hangman. The Hangman's Love Song. Stanley Moss. VGW

In the house with the tortoise chair. Poem to Ease Birth. *Unknown, tr. by* Anselm Hollo. IPWM

In the human cities, never again to. Despisals. Muriel Rukeyser. NMM; Prf

In the Huon Valley. James McAuley. MAuV

In the inner city. Lucille Clifton. CAAP; TSWA

In the Jury Room. Hodding Carter. MAT

In the kitchen/ making dishes with a brush. A Plea to My Sister. James Cunningham. JB

In the Kitchen of the Old House. Donald Hall. MPo

In the land of God. Cecil County. Ron Welburn. PoBA

In the land of turkeys in turkey weather. Dance of the Macabre Mice. Wallace Stevens. NOBA

In the landscape that was a saga. Regenerate. Robert Bloom. AATT

In the Last Few Moments Came the Old German Cleaning Woman. Jane Cooper. CoPAm

In the late night listening from bed. Thinking for Berky. William Stafford. PPoD; RRA

In the late winter. The Bear. Galway Kinnell. CoPAm

In the licorice fields at Pontefract. The Licorice Fields at Pontefract. John Betjeman. SS

In the life we live together every paradise is lost. Against Botticelli. Robert Hass. AmPA

In the lisping drizzle. Elegy for a Polish Grandaunt. James Bonk. HeS

In the lonesome latter years. The Promissory Note. Bayard Taylor. SpRo

In the long journey out of the self. Journey to the Interior. Theodore Roethke. VGW

In the long, sleepless watches of the night. The Cross of Snow. Longfellow. AmVN; HeIP; IPWM; NOBA; PiAm

In the Madison Zoo. Roberta Hill. CDW

In the Men's Room(s). Marge Piercy. MMD

In the merry month of May. The Ploughman's Song. Nicholas Breton. *Fr.* The Honorable Entertainment Given to the Queen's Majesty in Progress at Elvetham, 1591. NOBE

In the middle of the night. Silver Wedding. Ralph Hodgson. OxBTC

In the monethe of Maye when mirthes been fele. The Poacher. *Unknown. Fr.* The Parlement of the Thre Ages. OxBM

In the Moonlight. Thomas Hardy. NoAM

In the Morning. Paul Laurence Dunbar. BPo

In the Morning. Paulette Dusdall Zachariou. NPW

In the morning cool and slender, you. The Hours. Calvin Forbes. CoPAm

In the morning, in the dark. The Night Hunt. Thomas MacDonagh. PFIr

In the Morning, in the Morning. A. E. Housman. InPK

In the morning light a line. The Morning Light. Louis Simpson. NoAM

In the morning the city. City. Langston Hughes. ECBV; LCL

In the Mountain Cabin. Del Marie Rogers. NPW

In the Mountain Tent. James Dickey. CAPP

In the Mountains, *sel.* Robert Penn Warren. Skiers. SPo; TCP

In the mountains of the Peloponnesus. Gossip. Nicholas Flocos. SA

In the Mourning Time. Robert Hayden. BPo

In the museum of antiquities. Glory. Harvey Shapiro. POL

In the Naked Bed, in Plato's Cave. Delmore Schwartz. NoAM; NOBA; PAIC; VGW

In the name of all the gods, tell me, Lydia, why. Horace, *tr. by* C. E. Bennett. Odes, I, 8. LoAs

In the narrow/ closet under the stairs, its curved. For the Suicide's Daughter. Carolyn Stoloff. RiTi

In the National Gallery. Siegfried Sassoon. NoAM

In the nativity of time. Love Made in the First Age: to Chloris. Richard Lovelace. SCP-2

In the neat parlor of their honeymoon. Epigram. Max Halpern. SFF

In the news that sails through the air. Los New Yorks. Victor Hernández Cruz. SA

In the North. The Reach of Winter. Jenne Andrews. HeS

In the northern hemisphere. Kangeroo. D. H. Lawrence. InPS; OxBTC

In the oasis of the day. Peter Whigham. *Fr.* Love Poems of the VIth Dalai Lama. TwMBP

In the old days either the plaintiff or the defendant won or lost. Poem. Alan Dugan. NowV

In the old days with married women's stockings. The Libertine. Louis MacNeice. NoAM

In the olive darkness of the sally-trees. The Bull. Judith Wright. MAuV

In the Orchard. Muriel Stuart. OxBTC

In the Orchard. Swinburne. BoLoP

In the palm. A Guerilla Handbook. LeRoi Jones. PoBA

In the Pantry. "Hugh MacDiarmid." NoAM

In the Park. Gwen Harwood. MAuV

In the Past. Trumbull Stickney. NOBA

In the Penile Colony. Erica Jong. MMD

In the Pines. *Unknown.* AmFP

In the pleasant pastime of temple viewing. Manners. Edith Marcombe Shiffert. WPE

In the Pocket. James Dickey. SPo

In the prison cell I sit. Tramp! Tramp! Tramp! or, The Prisoner's Hope. George Frederick Root. PSoN

In the Public Garden. Marianne Moore. NOBA

In the purple light, heavy with redwood, the slopes drop seaward. Apology for Bad Dreams. Robinson Jeffers. NOBA

In the Quarter of the Negroes. Cultural Exchange. Langston Hughes. BPo; PoBA

In the Queen's Room. Norman Cameron. OxBTC

In the quiet before cockcrow when the cricket's. Dear Men and Women. John Hall Wheelock. Prf

In the Radiotherapy Unit. Margaret Stanley Wrench. SFF

In the red water. New Spring. Juan Ramón Jiménez, *tr. by* H. R. Hays. OLR

In the region where the roses always bloom. Ida, Sweet as Apple Cider. Eddie Leonard. BLSo; FSN

In the Room of the Bride-Elect. Thomas Hardy. BuTh

In the rude age when scyence was not so rife. Earl of Surrey. AAS

In the Second-Best Hotel in Tokyo. Karl Shapiro. TCP

In the Seminole darkness of your singing eyes. Poem to a Redskin. Wendy Rose. CDW

In the Seven Woods. W. B. Yeats. NoAM

In the Shade of the Old Apple Tree, *with music.* Harry H. Williams. FSN

In the shoppes. Gemwood. Marvin Bell. FiCP

In the Shreve High football stadium. Autumn Begins in Martins Ferry, Ohio. James Wright. CAPP; InPS; POL; PPoD

In the Silence. Stephany Fuller. BPo

In the silence that prolongs the span. Black Jackets. Thom Gunn. HeIP; NowV

In the sky the bright stars glittered. When I Saw Sweet Nelly Home. Francis Kyle. BLSH; PSoN

In the Sly Gardens. Sonya Dorman. RiTi

In the Smoking Car. Ruth Whitman. RiTi

In the Smoking Car. Richard Wilbur. ConAP

In the Snake Park. William Plomer. NoAM; OxBTC

In the Soul Hour. Robert Mezey. AmPA

In the south, sleeping against. Legacy. LeRoi Jones. NoAM; NOBA; PoBA

In the Spring. William Barnes. GBL

In the spring woods, how good it is to see. Aspects of the World Like Coral Reefs. William Bronk. VGW

In the state of old Kentucky. The Death of Samuel Adams. *Unknown.* AmFP

In the street two children sharpen. East Bronx. David Ignatow. ConAP; IPWM

In the streetcar conductor's uniform. Portrait: The Freedom Fighter. George Jonas. NeAC

In the Suburbs. Louis Simpson. CoPAm; MAT; SFF; TH

In the swamp in secluded recesses. Walt Whitman. *Fr.* When Lilacs Last in the Dooryard Bloom'd. RFM

In the Sweet Bye-and-bye, *with music.* Sanford Fillmore Bennett. BLSH
(Sweet By and By.) PSoN

In the sweet shire of Cardigan. Simon Lee. Wordsworth. MBPR

In the Tail of the Scorpion. Genevieve Taggard. VGW

In the Tank. Thom Gunn. NoAM

In the third-class seat sat the journeying boy. Midnight on the Great Western. Thomas Hardy. NOBE; OBP

In the third hour after Palamon. Chaucer, *tr. by* Nevill Coghill. *Fr.* The Canterbury Tales: The Knight's Tale. OBP

In the third month, a sudden flow of blood. The Vow. Anthony Hecht. ConAP; CoPAm; Prf

In the thirtieth year of life. J. V. Cunningham. POL

In the Time of Revolution, *sels.* Julius Lester.
"It cannot be/ reasoned with," V. PoBA
"One needs a lyric poet in these," IV. PoBA
"One needs a lyric poet in this, " VI. PoBA

In the town of Odessa. Dvonya. Louis Simpson. NOBA

In the town where every man is king. Josephine Miles. CoPAm

In the town where I was born. Yellow Submarine. John Lennon *and* Paul McCartney. PPoe

In the tunnel of woods, as the road. Last Things. William Meredith. NoAM

In the 2 A.M. Club, a working man's bar. Robert Peterson. NeAC

In the vale [*or* vaile] of restless mind. Quia Amore Langueo. *Unknown.* BoReV; OxBM; NOBE

In the Valley of Cauteretz. Tennyson. BoLoP; NOBE

In the Vaulted Way. Thomas Hardy. BoLoP; OLR

In the very earliest time. Magic Words. *Unknown, tr. fr. Eskimo.* IPWM

In the village of the dead. First Shaman Song. Gary Snyder. *Fr.* Myths and Texts: Hunting. NOBA

In the village the children. Then. Gary Gildner. FiCP

In the violet country. Dont Tell Bad Dreams Says Tita's Mother. John Oliver Simon. NeAC

In the Waiting Room. Elizabeth Bishop. NOBA; Prf

In the waiting room of the psychiatric ward. To a Student Poet, Hospitalized, Having "Broken with Reality." Roderick Hartigh Jellema. AATT

In the water cave, below the root. Howard Nemerov. *Fr.* The Scales of the Eyes. NoAM

In the Week When Christmas Comes. Eleanor Farjeon. LCL

In the well-fed cage-sound of diesels. Them, Crying. James Dickey. NowV

In the Wilderness. Albert Howard Carter. AATT

In the winding folds of old capitals. The Little Old Women. Baudelaire, *tr. by* Barbara Gibbs. LoAs

In the Winter of My Thirty-Eighth Year. W. S. Merwin. NOBA

In the wintertime. Toe'osh: A Laguna Coyote Story. Leslie Silko. CDW

In the winter time we go. White Fields. James Stephens. ECBV

In the Woods. Adrienne Rich. PiAm

In the world which He has created. Hymmnn. Allen Ginsberg. NOBA

In the worst inn's worst room, with mat half-hung. The Duke of Buckingham. Pope. *Fr.* Moral Essays. NOBE

In the wracks of Walsingham. A Lament for the Priory of Walsingham. *Unknown.* GBP

In the year ninety-eight, when our troubles were great. The Cow Ate the Piper. *Unknown.* GBP; PeBB

In the year of the great crime. 1867. Coventry Patmore. *Fr.* The Unknown Eros. VPC

In the zócalo. Three Portraits. George Hitchcock. VGW

In their/ limousines the/ teachers come. The Educators. D. M. Black. MPo

In their long/ Arabesque, wings ferrying the steady. Gulls. Barbara Howes. BoAnP

In their ragged regimentals. Carmen Bellicosum. Guy Humphreys McMaster. BTTM

In These Dissenting Times. Alice Walker. PoBA

In these prayers let us not forget our bodies. First Prayer. Margaret Atwood. MMD

In this bankers' town of course art would depend. The Elements of Geometry. David Malouf. CAAP

In this book I see your face and in your face. Frontispiece. May Swenson. WPE

In this café Durruti. The Midget. Philip Levine. NoAM

In this country I planted not one seed. Sailing from the United States. Stanley Moss. VGW

In this crush around us of a cruel city. Metropole. Forrest Anderson. AATT

In this factory, here the axe-grinders. University Curriculum. William Price Turner. POL

In this green month when resurrected flowers. Memorial Wreath. Dudley Randall. PoBA

"In This House, There Shall Be No Idols." Carolyn M. Rodgers. JB

In this imperfect, gloomy scene. The Female Friend. Cornelius Whur. FaBoCo

In this little urn is laid. Upon Prew His Maid. Robert Herrick. InPK

In this most foreign of all places. Stateside. R. P. Kingston. NVAP

In this motel where I was told to wait. The Human Condition. Howard Nemerov. CoPAm; NowV

In this poem I am fast asleep in bed. Back Behind the Eyes. Leon Stokesbury. NVAP

In this stoned and. Definition of Nature. Eugene Redmond. PoBA

In this world. Flannery O'Connor. Dorothy Walters. IHMS

In this world a tablecloth need not be laid. Tea in a Space-ship. James Kirkup. MPo

In this world (the Isle of Dreams). The White Island: Or the Place of the Blest. Robert Herrick. BoReV; SCP-1

In this Year of Grace. John Hewitt. PFIr

In those cold regions which no summers cheer. Prologue to His Royal Highness. Dryden. SCP-1

In those old days which poets say were golden. Beer. Charles Stuart Calverley. FaBoCo

In thriving arts long time had Holland grown. War. Dryden. *Fr.* Annus Mirabilis. SCP-1

In thy western halls of gold. Ode to Apollo. Keats. MBPR

In tight pants, tight skirts. The Young Ones, Flip Side. James A. Emanuel. SS

In Time. Kathleen Raine. WPE

In Time of Pestilence. Thomas Nashe. *See* Adieu, Farewell Earth's Bliss.

In Time of "The Breaking of Nations." Thomas Hardy. BoLoP; NoAM; NOBE; POL; PPoD; PPP; PSN; VoPo

In Time's concatenation and/ Carnal conventicle. Mortmain, I. Robert Penn Warren. NOBA; Prf

In times of calm or hurricane, in days of sun or shower. The Dog Parade. Arthur Guiterman. BoAnP

In toaster and rotisserie. Try Brillo on the Slimy Stove. Phyllis Gotlieb. BBGO

In town, your friends play hide-and-seek. September. W. D. Snodgrass. PSN

In trellised shed with clustering roses gay. The White Doe of Rylstone; or, The Fate of the Nortons. Wordsworth. MBPR

In Tupelo, Mississippi. The Tupelo Destruction. *Unknown.* AmFP

In tyme the strong and statelie turrets fall. Licia, XXVIII. Giles Fletcher the Elder. AAS

In unexperienced infancy. Shadows in the Water. Thomas Traherne. BoReV; MetP; SCP-2

In us and into us and ours. For Eusi, Ayi Kwei and Gwen Brooks. Keorapetse Kgositsile. PoBA

In using there are always two. Song of the Fucked Duck. Marge Piercy. NMM

In vain, in vain,—the all-composing hour. The Triumph of Dullness. Pope. *Fr.* The Dunciad. NOBE

In vain to me the smiling mornings shine. Sonnet on the Death of [Mr.] Richard West. Thomas Gray. LAuP; NOBE; PAIC

In vain would man his mighty patent show. In Commendation of the Female Sex. Jane Barker. SCP-2

In Virgyne the sweltrie sun gan sheene. An Excelente Balade of Charitie. Thomas Chatterton. LAuP

In Weather. Robert Hass. AmPA

In Weatherbury Stocks. Thomas Hardy. AIW

In Westminster Abbey. John Betjeman. BoReV; FaBoCo; InPK

In Westminster not long ago. The Ratcatcher's Daughter. *Unknown.* GBP

In wet and cloudy mists I slowly rise. Night's Song. Sir William Davenant. *Fr.* Luminalia. SCP-2

In wet green midspring, midnight and the wind. Mrs. Walpurga. Muriel Rukeyser. NMM

In what state that ever I be. The Sparrow-Hawk's Complaint. *Unknown.* OxBM

In what torn ship soever I embark. A Hymn to Christ, at the Author's Last Going into Germany. John Donne. BoReV

In White. Robert Frost. WIF

In whose will is our peace? Thou happiness. Epigram. J. V. Cunningham. VGW

In William Rufus's hall the galleries reached. Fifth Day. Robert D. Fitzgerald. MAuV

In Windsor Castle. Earl of Surrey. NOBE ("So crewell prison, howe could betyde, alas.") AAS

In winter I get up at night. Bed in Summer. Robert Louis Stevenson. OxBChV

In winter in my room. Emily Dickinson. NoAM; NOBA

In Winter in the Woods Alone. Robert Frost. HeIP; PiAm

In winter my mother goes away. Desert. Del Marie Rogers. NPW

In winter twilight on a side street. Ghostly Story. Milton Acorn. NeAC

In winter, when the fields are white. Humpty Dumpty's Song [*or* Recitation]. "Lewis Carroll." *Fr.* Through the Looking-Glass. FaBoCo; OxBChV

In winters just returne, when Boreas gan his raigne. Earl of Surrey. AAS

In Woods Where Many Rivers Run. Lawrence Ferlinghetti. *Fr.* A Coney Island of the Mind. BBGO

In Worcester, Massachusetts. In the Waiting Room. Elizabeth Bishop. NOBA; Prf

In Xanadu did Kubla Khan. Kubla Khan. Samuel Taylor Coleridge. AKE; AnMo; ECBV; HeIP; InPK; InPS; MAT; MBPR; NOBE; OBP; PBMP; PPoD; PPoe; SoSe; VoPo

In yonder grave a Druid lies. Ode Occasion'd by the Death of Mr. Thomson. William Collins. LAuP

In yonder marble hero's shade. Afternoons with Baedeker. Osbert Lancaster. FaBoCo

In your next letter I wish you'd say. Letter to N. Y. Elizabeth Bishop. TH

In Youth Is Pleasure. Robert Wever. *Fr.* Lusty Juventus. NOBE ("In a herber green, asleep whereas I lay.") GBL

Inamorato Curio. John Marston. The Scourge of Villainy, VIII. TVS

Incantation to Oedipus. Dryden. *Fr.* Oedipus, III, i. OFD

Incantatory Poem. Jean Garrigue. LoAs

Incarnatio Est Maximum Dei Donum. William Alabaster. BoReV

Incarnation of Sirius, The. James McAuley. MAuV

Incident. Countee Cullen. BPo; CTBA; NoAM; NowV; PoBA; SFF; SoSe; VGW

Incident. LeRoi Jones. NoAM

Incident here and there, An. Hilda Doolittle ("H.D."). *Fr.* The Walls Do Not Fall. NoAM

Incident in a Rose Garden. Donald Justice. NCSH

Incident in the Early Life of Ebenezer Jones, Poet, 1828, An. John Betjeman. NoAM

Incident of the French Camp. Robert Browning. AKE; BTTM

Incident on a Journey. Thom Gunn. MPo

Incidental Pieces to a Walk. James Cunningham. JB

Incidents in the Life of My Uncle Arly. Edward Lear. OBP

Incoherent in the midst of men. The New Lost Feminist. Rita Mae Brown. WBN

Inconstancy Reproved. Sir Robert Ayton. GBL

Inconvenience, An. John Raven. BPo

Indelicate is he who loathes. Epidermal Macabre. Theodore Roethke. NoAM

Independence. Nancy Cato. WPE

Independence Day. Wendell Berry. OFD

Independent Squire. Samuel Butler. *Fr.* Hudibras, I, 1. NOBE

Indian. Laura Jensen. AmPA

Indian at the Burial-Place of His Fathers, An. Bryant. HeIP; PiAm

Indian Burying Ground, The. Philip Freneau. HeIP; IPWM; NOBA; PiAm

Indian Love Letter. Soge Track. VW

Indian riding. In the Embers at Midnight. Paulette Dusdall Zachariou. NPW

Indian Rock, Bainbridge Island, Washington. Duane Niatum. CDW

Indian School. Norman H. Russell. MAT

Indian Serenade, The. Shelley. MBPR

Indian Song: Survival. Leslie Silko. CDW

Indian Summer. Barbara Howes. IHMS

Indian Summer Day on the Prairie, An. Vachel Lindsay. RFM

Indian Summer: Montana, 1956. W. M. Ransom. CDW

Indian-summer-sun. October-November. Hart Crane. PSN

Indian Summer: Vermont. Anne Stevenson. NCSH

Indian to His Love, The. W. B. Yeats. PBMP

Indian upon God, The. W. B. Yeats. IPWM

Indian Warrior. Mary Logue. NPW

Indian Woman's Death-Song. Felicia Dorothea Hemans. SBG

Indiana. Hart Crane. *Fr*. The Bridge: Powhatan's Daughter. PiAm

Indiana: no blustering summit or coarse gorge. Midwest. John Frederick Nims. ANTL

Indians Come Down from Mixco, The. Miguel Angel Asturias, *tr. fr. Spanish by* Donald Devenish Walsh. TSWA

Indifferent, The. John Donne. AnMo; BoLoP; PBMP

Indignant at the fumbling wits, the obscure spite. Paudeen. W. B. Yeats. InPS

Individual spider web, An. Identity. A. R. Ammons. CoPAm

Induction to "A Mirror for Magistrates." Thomas Sackville. *See* Mirror for Magistrates, The.

Inexorable. William Drummond of Hawthornden. NOBE

Inexpensive Progress. John Betjeman. LP

Infant Innocence. A. E. Housman. FaBoCo

Infant Joy. Blake. *Fr*. Songs of Innocence. LAuP; MBPR

Infant Sorrow. Blake. *Fr*. Songs of Experience. InPS; LAuP; MBPR

Inferno, The, *sel*. Dante,*tr. fr. Italian by* Laurence Binyon. *Fr*. Divina Commedia.
"Like fire-flies that the peasant on the hill," *fr*. XXVI. Prf

Infinite cosanguinity it bears. Voyages, III. Hart Crane. LoAs

Infinity, with all things it beheld. The Preface. Edward Taylor. *Fr*. God's Determinations. NOBA; PiAm

Ingathering of Love, The, *sel*. Peter Whigham.
"It was in one of those old houses in Monmouthshire." TwMBP

Ingestion. Barry McDonald. POL

Inglorious friend! most confident I am. Sonnet to a Clam. John Godfrey Saxe. BoAnP

Ingoldsby Legends, The, *sels*. "Thomas Ingoldsby." FaBoCo
Jackdaw of Rheims, The.
Not a Sous Had He Got. *Fr*. The Cynotaph.

Inis Fal. Egan O'Rahilly, *tr. fr. Irish by* James Stephens. BIrV

Initiation. Jayne Cortez. PoBA

Injured Moon, The. Baudelaire, *tr. fr. French by* Robert Lowell. Moon

Injury to Insured. John Daniel. TwMBP

Ink runs from the corners of my mouth. Eating Poetry. Mark Strand. CoPAm; MAT; NoAM; PPP

Inland Lighthouse, The. James McMichael. AmPA

Inland Sea. Franklin Brainard. HeS

Inland, within a hollow vale, I stood. September, 1802. Near Dover. Wordsworth. MBPR

Inner-City Mother Goose, The, *sels*. Eve Merriam. IPWM
Ding, Dong, Bell.
Fee, Fi, Fo, Fum.
Wino Will.

Inner Part, The. Louis Simpson. InPS; PBMP; SFF

Inner Temple Masque, *sel*. William Browne.
Sirens' Song, The. NOBE
(Syrens' Song, The.) GBL

Inniskeen Road: July Evening. Patrick Kavanagh. NoAM; PFIr

Innocence, The. Robert Creeley. NoAM

Innocence. Thom Gunn. NoAM

Innocence. Irving Layton. BBGO

Innocence?/ In a sense. A Life. Howard Nemerov. AnMo; PBMP

Innocent Spring, The. Edith Sitwell. *Fr*. The Sleeping Beauty. NOBE
("In the great gardens, after bright spring rain." OxBTC

Innocent to innocent. To What Strangers, What Welcome, IX. J. V. Cunningham. PiAm

Innocent's Song. Charles Causley. MPo

Innominatus. Sir Walter Scott. *See* This Is My Own, My Native Land.

Inordinate Love. John Lydgate. LoAs

Inquest, The. W. H. Davies. NOBE; OxBTC

Inquisition, The. Thomas Beedome. SCP-2

Insatiable Baby, The. Cynthia Macdonald. WBN

Inscription. George Canning *and* John Hookham Frere. FaBoCo

Inscription for a Fountain on a Heath. Samuel Taylor Coleridge. MBPR

Inscription for a Headstone. Austin Clarke. BIrV

Inscription for the Entrance to a Wood. Bryant. AmVN; PiAm; PPoD

Inscription on the Monument of a Newfoundland Dog. Byron. MBPR

Insect Hunter, The, *sel*. Edward Newman.
"Take thy hat, my little Laura." PPoD

Insensibility. Wilfred Owen. InPS; OxBTC

Inseparable. Philip Bourke Marston. BoLoP

Inseparable from the fire. Coda. William Carlos Williams. NOBA

Inside at the green cafe. Over Coffee. Jennifer Maiden. CAAP

Inside History. Angela McCabe. AmPA

Inside or out, the key is pain. It holds. Hospital. Karl Shapiro. VGW

Inside that figure rides opaque malice. The Picador Bit. Bink Noll. SFF

Inside the child. Night Watch. Margo Magid. NMM

Inside the coconut is Katerina's baby. A Coconut for Katerina. Sandra McPherson. FiCP

Inside the River. James Dickey. SPo

Inside the veins there are navies setting forth. Waking from Sleep. Robert Bly. CAPP; InPS; NoAM; NOBA

Insight. Ruthe T. Spinnanger. AATT

Insistently through sleep—a tide of voices. The Harbor Dawn. Hart Crane. *Fr*. The Bridge: Powhatan's Daughter. PiAm; PSN

Insomnia. Elizabeth Bishop. TH

Inspiration. Henry David Thoreau. NOBA

Inspire our sons to seek their man-shadows. If We Cannot Live People as People. Charles Lynch. PoBA

Instalment, The, *sel*. Edward Young.
"Since Brunswick's smile has authoris'd my muse." FaBoCo

Instances. Anselm Hollo. TwMBP

Instead of you, I choose the blood. The Unwanted. Mary Gordon. IHMS

Instruction from Bly. Cynthia Macdonald. NMM

Instruction Manual, The. John Ashbery. NoAM; NOBA

Instructions. Anita Skeen. IHMS

Instructions for the Erection of a Statue to Myself in Central Park. Colette Inez. RiTi

Instructions of King Cormac, The, *sel*. *Unknown, tr. fr. Irish by* Kuno Meyer.
" 'O Cormac, grandson of Conn,' said Carbery." BIrV

Instructions to a Princess. Ishmael Reed. PoBA

Instructor said, The. Theme for English B. Lanston Hughes. NoAM; NOBA

Insular Celts, The. Ciaran Carson. BIrV

Insusceptibles, The. Adrienne Rich. ConAP; HeIP; InPK

Integer Vitae. Thomas Campion. NOBE
("Man of life upright, The.") AAS

Intellect of man is forced to choose, The. The Choice. W. B. Yeats. NoAM; OxBTC

Intellectuals, The. Dudley Randall. PoBA

Intended for Sir Isaac Newton. Pope. InPK
("Nature, and Nature's laws, lay hid in night.") FaBoCo

Intention to Escape from Him. Edna St. Vincent Millay. SBG

Interests of a black man in a cellar, The. Black Tambourine. Hart Crane. NoAM; PAIC; PPP

Interior. Padraic Colum. PFIr

Interior. Dorothy Parker. SBG

Interlude. Karl Shapiro. PBMP

Interlude. Welton Smith. PoBA

Interpretation. Gloria Bussel Koster. NPW

Interrogator, The. Elizabeth Jennings. WPE

Interruption at the Opera House. Brian Patten. LP

Interview, An. K. W. Grandsen. OxBTC

Interview with a Tourist. Margaret Atwood. IHMS

Interview with Doctor Drink. J. V. Cunningham. VGW

Intimates. D. H. Lawrence. BoLoP; PoTa

Intimations at the Lake, 1963. Helena Minton. FAF

Intimations of Immortality. Wordsworth. *See* Ode: Intimations of Immortality...

Intimations of Immortality, Cuttingsville, Vermont, 1880. Constance Carrier. FAF

Into Battle. Julian Grenfell. OcBTC

Into Blackness Softly. Mari Evans. PoBA

Into her mother's bedroom to wash the ballooning body. Jessie Mitchell's Mother. Gwendolyn Brooks. NMM

Into love and out again. Theory. Dorothy Parker. SBG

Into my empty head there come. Morning Swim. Maxine W. Kumin. NVAP; WPE

Into My Heart an Air That Kills. A. E. Housman. BBGO; NoAM; NOBE; OxBTC; POL

Into that pit when I did enter in. Elizabeth Melvill, Lady Culross. *Fr.* A Godly Dream. WPE

Into the clouds the devil lately got. Michael Drayton. *Fr.* To My Noble Friend Master William Browne: of the Evil Time. SCP-2

Into the Dark. Paul Monette. AmPA

Into the Devil tavern. The Three Troopers. George Walter Thornbury. BTTM

Into the night. The Inland Lighthouse. James McMichael. AmPA

Into the playground we went. Black Clouds. Terence Brame. RAE

Into the pool of silence our tears made. The Ancient Couple on Lu Mountain. Mark Van Doren. VGW

Into the Sky. Sallie Chesham. AATT

Into the spacious bay the sun of the afternoon. Players. Josephine Miles. RiTi

Into the Woods My Master Went. Sidney Lanier. BLSH, *with music*
(Ballad of Trees and the Master, A). NOBA

Into these loves, who but for passion lookes. To the Reader of These Sonnets. Michael Drayton. Idea, *introd.* AAS

Into your arms I came. To the Anxious Mother. Valente Malangatana, *tr. by.* Dorothy Guedes *and* Philippa Rumsey. BBGO

Introduction, The: "Did I, my lines intend for publick view." Countess of Winchilsea. SBG

Introduction: "Hear the voice of the bard!" Blake. *See* Hear the Voice of the Bard.

Introduction: "Piping down the valleys wild." Blake. *See* Piping Down the Valleys Wild.

Introduction: "Romance, who loves to nod and sing." Poe. NOBA

Introduction: "Should you ask me, whence these stories?" Longfellow. *Fr.* The Song of Hiawatha. NOBA; PiAm

Introductory: "That towering place, gabled and huge." *Unknown, tr. fr. Anglo-Saxon by* Burton Raffel. *Fr.* Beowulf. OBP

Intruder. Susan Feldman. AmPA

Intruder, The. Carolyn Kizer. RiTi

Intruder, The. Marya Zaturenska. OLR

Intry, mintry, cutry corn. Mother Goose. ECBV

Invaders, The. A. D. Hope. CAAP

Invaders, The. Yvor Winters. PiAm

Invariably when wine redeems the sight. The Wine Menagerie. Hart Crane. NoAM; NOBA; VGW

Invasion on the Farm. R. S. Thomas. POL

Inventing a Family. Dennis Saleh. *Fr.* A Guide to Familiar American Incest. NeAC

Inventing a story with grass. A Birth. James Dickey. NOBA

Invention of Astronomy, The. William Matthews. POL

Invention of Comics, The. LeRoi Jones. CAPP; PBMP; PoBA

Invention of New Jersey, The. Jack Anderson. InPS

Invention of the Telephone, The. Peter Klappert. AmPA

Inventory/ Itinerary. Ken Smith. TwMBP

Inversely, as the Square of Their Distances Apart. Kenneth Rexroth. TSWA

Inversnaid. Gerard Manley Hopkins. InPK; NoAM

Investigation. Julia Vinograd. IHMS

Investiture, The. Siegfried Sassoon. NoAM

Investment. Norman Nathan. MiP

Invictus. W. E. Henley. *See* Out of the Night That Covers Me.

Invisible Man, The. T. S. Matthews. POL

Invisible Tree. Ryuichi Tamura, *tr. fr. Japanese by* Thomas Fitzsimmons. TSWA

Invisible Woman, The. Robin Morgan. IHMS; NMM

Invitation, The. Nathaniel Wanley. BoReV

Invitation in It, The. Kay Boyle. *Fr.* American Citizen. RiTi

Invitation Standing. Paul Blackburn. IPWM; VGW

Invitation to Lubberland, An. *Unknown.* GBP

Invitation to Madison County, An. Jay Wright. PoBA

Invitation to the Bee. Charlotte Smith. OxBChV

Invitation (To the Night and All Other Things Dark). Ronda Davis. JB

Invitation to the Zoological Gardens, An. *Unknown.* BoAnP

Inviting a Friend to Supper. Ben Jonson, *after the Latin of* Martial. NOBE; PPP; TVS

Invocation: "American muse, whose strong and diverse heart." Stephen Vincent Benét. *Fr.* John Brown's Body. BTTM

Invocation: "Come from thy palace, beauteous Queen of Greece." Thomas Randolph. Moon

Invocation: "Of mans first disobedience, and the fruit." Milton. *Fr.* Paradise Lost, I. OBP
("Of man's first disobedience, and the fruit.") PAIC

Invocation: "Ten bloody years with this quill lying." Valentin Iremonger. BIrV

Invocation: "Unwinding the spool of the morning." Vassar Miller. NCSH

Invocation to Kali, The, *sels.* May Sarton. RiTi
"It is time for the invocation."
Kingdom of Kali, The.
"There are times when."

Invocation to Sappho. Elsa Gidlow. IHMS

Invocation to the Goddess, An. David Wright. NoAM

Invoice, The. Robert Creeley. VGW

Involuntary flex. Jeanetta Jones. MIT

Inward Conversation. Baudelaire, *tr. fr. French by* Robert Bly. InPK

Inward Morning, The. Henry David Thoreau. AmVN; PiAm

Iolanthe, *sel.* W. S. Gilbert.
Nightmare. PBMP

Iowa. Michael Dennis Browne. ANTL

Iowa, June. Michael Dennis Browne. AmPA

Ipomadon, *sel. Unknown.*
Ipomadon Plays the Fool at Court. OxBM

Ireland Lake. Robert Hershon. NeAC

Ireland Never Was Contented. Walter Savage Landor. FaBoCo

Ireland with Emily. John Betjeman. OxBTC

Iris. William Carlos Williams. InPS

Irish Airman Foresees His Death, An. W. B. Yeats. Epi; HeIP; NoAM; NOBE; PPP

Irish-American Dignitary. Austin Clarke. BIrV; PFIr

Irish Cliffs of Moher, The. Wallace Stevens. NOBA; VGW

Irish Curse on the Occupying English. *Unknown, tr. fr. Modern Irish by* Máire MacEntee. PFIr

Irish Dancer, The. *Unknown. See* I Am of Ireland.

Irish Lake, An. W. R. Rodgers. BIrV

Irish Marriage Night, An. Brian Merriman, *tr. fr. Modern Irish by* Frank O'Connor. *Fr.* The Midnight Court. BIrV

Irish Satire, An. *Unknown.* OxBM

Irishman in Coventry, An. John Hewitt. BIrV

Iron horse draweth nigh, with its smoke nostrils high, The. The Utah Iron Horse. *Unknown.* AmFP

Iron Lung, The. Stanley Plumly. AmPA

Iron, sulphur, steam: the wastes. Saratoga Ending. Weldon Kees. AnMo

Irondale. Stephen Stepanchev. SA

Irresponsive silence of the land, The. Christina Rossetti. *Fr.* The Thread of Life. NOBE

Is/ red beans. Energy. Victor Hernandez Cruz. PoBA; SA

Is an enchanted thing. The Mind Is an Enchanting Thing. Marianne Moore. PiAm; PPP

"Is anybody there?" said the Traveller. *See* "Is there anybody there?"...

Is anything central? The One Thing That Can Save America. John Ashbery. NOBA

I's born in Louisiana. Nothing in Rambling. *Unknown.* BluL

Is drunken,/ Drunken, drunken. A Drunkard. *Unknown.* OxBM

Is 5, *sel.* E. E. Cummings.
My Sweet Old Etcetera, III. AnMo; HeIP; InPS; PPP

Is Football Playing? A. E. Housman. *Fr.* Is My Team Ploughing? SPo

Is Is Like Is. Adrien Stoutenburg. TSWA

Is it a dream, or not? During my fever. The Blue Gift. David Perkins. NCSH

Is it a Martian creature. Martian. Eve Merriam. CaYB

Is It a Month. J. M. Synge. BIrV; PFIr

Is it a reed that's shaken by the wind. Calais, August, 1802. Wordsworth. MBPR

Is it any better in Heaven, my friend Ford. To Ford Madox Ford in Heaven. William Carlos Williams. NoAM; NOBA

Is it enough? I'm Here. Theodore Roethke. *Fr.* Meditations of an Old Woman. Epi

Is It Far to Go? C. Day Lewis. AIW; BBGO

Is it no dream that I am he. Walter Savage Landor. GBL

Is it not better at an early hour. On Living Too Long. Walter Savage Landor. PAIC

Is it not fine to fling against loaded dice. Hughie at the Inn. Elinor Wylie. WPE

Is it possible [*or* Ys yt possyble]. Sir Thomas Wyatt. AAS; GBL

Is it the wind of the dawn that I hear. Duet. Tennyson. *Fr.* Becket. GBL

Is it time now to go away? Death of a Vermont Farm Woman. Barbara Howes. CoPAm

Is it true, ye gods, who treat us. Arthur Hugh Clough. VPC

Is it Ulysses that approaches from the east. The World as Meditation. Wallace Stevens. HeIP; PiAm; PPP

Is it you? Are you there. Poem Wondering If I'm Pregnant. Kathleen Fraser. IHMS; NMM

Is like a dull dream. From time to time. Summer in Fairbanks. Leon Stokesbury. NVAP

Is my favourite. Who flies. Owl. George MacBeth. MPo

Is My Team Ploughing? A. E. Housman. NoAM; PAIC; SoSe; SS
Is Football Playing? *sel.* SPo

Is poetry always worthy when it's old. Kalidasa, *tr. fr. Sanskrit by* John Brough. BuTh

Is premature as a dead white cat. Black in Virginia. Grace Cavalieri. AATT

Is something like the rest. The Politics of Rich Painters. LeRoi Jones. VGW

Is tell you my mind, Annes Tayliur: Dame. At the Tavern. *Unknown.* OxBM

Is that dance slowing in the mind of man. Four for Sir John Davies. Theodore Roethke. NoAM; NOBA; PiAm

Is the Moon Tired? Christina Rossetti. Moon

Is the slide. Relicts. Layle Silbert. NPW

Is then no nook of English ground secure. Sonnet on the Projected Kendal and Windermere Railway. Wordsworth. MBPR

Is there a Baltimore fan alive. Tom Matte. Ogden Nash. SPo

Is there any good man here. A Call for a Song. *Unknown.* OxBM

Is There Any Reward? Hilaire Belloc. BuTh

"Is there anybody [*or* Is anybody] there?" said the Traveller. The Listeners. Walter de la Mare. InPK; NCSH; NoAM; NOBE; PPoD; SFF; SoSe; SS

Is there anything I can do. The Key to Everything. May Swenson. IHMS; Psy

Is there, for honest poverty. For A' That and A' That. Burns. BTTM; LAuP; OBP

Is There No Love Can Link Us? Mervyn Peake. BuTh

Is this a fast, to keep. To Keep a True Lent [*or* A True Lent]. Robert Herrick. BoReV; OFD

Is this a holy thing to see. Holy Thursday. Blake. *Fr.* Songs of Experience. InPS; LAuP; MBPR

Is this pain, when my heart. Gavin Bantock. *Fr.* Person. TwMBP

Is this the object. Sestina. Judith Kroll. AmPA

Is this the region, this the soil, the clime. Satan As Rebel-Liberator. Milton. *Fr.* Paradise Lost, I. OBP

Is thy face like thy mother's, my fair child! Childe Harold's Pilgrimage, III. Byron. MBPR

Is without world. The Howling of Wolves. Ted Hughes. OxBTC

Is you eye so empty. Signals. Jewel C. Latimore. PoBA

Isabel met an enormous bear. Adventures of Isabel. Ogden Nash. ECBV

Isabella; or, the Pot of Basil. Keats. MBPR

Isaiah, *sels.* Bible, *O. T.*
And He Shall Judge among Nations, II:4. PBMP
"Because the daughters of Zion are haughty," III:16-26. OBP

I'se got a gal in the Sourwood Mountain. Sourwood Mountain. *Unknown.* AmFP

I'se got a little baby, but she's out of sight. Hello! Ma Baby. Joseph E. Howard *and* Ida Emerson. FSN

I'se wild Nigger Bill. Wild Negro Bill. *Unknown.* BPo

Island, The. Dorothy Aldis. ECBV

Island dreams under the dawn, The. The Indian to His Love. W. B. Yeats. PBMP

Island Letter. Charles Senior. MIS

Island Quarry. Hart Crane. PPP; PSN

Islands move inward. The Name of Our Country. Dennis Schmitz. AmPA

Isle of Man, The. *Unknown.* GBP

Isle of Man Shore, The. *Unknown.* AmFP

Isles of Greece, The. Byron. *Fr.* Don Juan, III. BTTM; NOBE

"Isn't the violet a dear little flower? And the daisy, too." The Lay Preacher Ponders. Idris Davies. OxBTC

Israfel. Poe. AmVN; NOBA; PiAm

It all began so easy. Christina. Louis MacNeice. BoLoP

It all fails now. Anderson, Indiana. James L. White. HeS

It all happened so fast. Fenya was in the straight chair. Pastoral. Norman Dubie. AmPA

It appears to be the pampas. The Man in the Dream Is Death. Lynne Butler. IHMS

It baffles the foreigner like an idiom. Drug Store. Karl Shapiro. TCP

It beats me. The way. Old People. Myra Cohn Livingston. CTBA

It begins to trickle. Darkness Comes to the Woods. Norbert Krapf. HeS

It bends far over Yell'ham Plain. The Comet at Yell'ham. Thomas Hardy. GBL

It burns in the void. The World. Kathleen Raine. OxBTC

It bursts and holds. Roman Candle. Neil Weiss. LoAs

It came/ Out of the blackness of the spaces between galaxies. The Second Coming. Carl Clark. JB

It Came upon a Midnight Clear, *with music.* Edmund Hamilton Sears. BLSH

It cannot be/ reasoned with. Julius Lester. *Fr.* In the Time of Revolution. PoBA

It cannot come. Balboa, the Entertainer. LeRoi Jones. NoAM

It can't be a pocket. The District: Both Sides of Chandler River. Ted Enslin. FAF

It can't happen to me. Age? H. R. Hays. POL

It chanced that Cupid on a season. From the French. Sir Walter Scott. SLP

It comes back. Deceased. Cid Corman. VGW

It consisted of 8 to 10 pages of short essays. Her Application to Elysium. Kathleen Norris. IHMS

It Did Not Last. J. C. Squire. InPK ("It did not last: the Devil howling Ho.") FaBoCo

It does, it does, I have seen it. America Bleeds. Angelo Lewis. PoBA

It does not happen. That love, removes. Audubon, Drafted. LeRoi Jones. PPP

It does not matter. Moonshot. Robert Kelly. Moon

It dropped so low—in my regard. Emily Dickinson. InPK; PBMP

It embarrasses. Personal Poem. Ingrid Wendt. NMM

It ended, and the morrow brought the task. Modern Love, II. George Meredith. PAIC

It feels good as it is without the giant. Wallace Stevens. *Fr.* Notes Toward a Supreme Fiction. NOBA

It fell about the Lammas tide. The Battle of Otterbourne. *Unknown.* BTTM

It fell about the Martinmas. Edom O Gordon. *Unknown.* PeBB

It fell about the Martinmas time. Get Up and Bar the Door. *Unknown.* AIW; HeIP; PBMP; PoTa

It fell about the Martinmas tyde. Jamie Telfer of the Fair Dodhead. *Unknown.* PeBB

It fell in the ancient periods. Uriel. Emerson. AmVN; NOBA; PiAm

It fell upon a holy eve. August. Spenser. *Fr.* The Shepheardes Calender. PAIC

If fell upon a Wodensday. Brown Robyn's Confession. *Unknown.* GBP; PeBB

It flows through old hushed Egypt and its sands. The Nile. Leigh Hunt. NOBE

It had been a good evening. The Lovers. Karen Swenson. WBN

It hangs from heaven to earth. Tapestry. Charles Simic. NVAP

It happened in Jacksboro in the year of 'seventy-three. The Buffalo Skinners. *Unknown.* AmFP

It happened, it happened all on a Saturday night. Johnny Dyers. *Unknown.* AmFP

It happens through the blond window, the trees. Ascension. Denis Devlin. BIrV

It has a name. Sleep. Greg Kuzma. NVAP

It has all/ come back today. From Gloucester Out. Edward Dorn. NoAM; NOBA

It has all to be experienced. Between Appointments. Giles Gordon. SLP

It has been/ a long flight. The Pilot. Lewis Turco. CoPAm

It has been well said that quietness. A Dog's Best Friend Is His Illiteracy. Ogden Nash. BoAnP

It has to be the end of the day. Surf-Casting W. S. Merwin. NOBA

It Is a Beauteous Evening, Calm and Free. Wordsworth. AnMo; Epi; HeIP; IPWM; MBPR; PPP; RRA; WIF

It is a beauteous morning, calm and free. Country Club Sunday. Phyllis McGinley. WIF

It is a cave of red stone. The Cave Where Night Sleeps. T. Alan Broughton. FAF

It is a clearing deep in a forest: overhanging boughs. Johnson's Cabinet Watched by Ants. Robert Bly. NoAM; NOBA

It is a cold and snowy night. The main street is deserted. Driving to Town Late to Mail a Letter. Robert Bly. InPK; SFF; TSWA; VGW

It is a cramped little state with no foreign policy. Shame. Richard Wilbur. ConAP; PPoD

It is a delusion. Solitary Confinement. Phyllis Webb. *Fr.* The Kropotkin Poems. MMD

It is a God-damned lie to say that these. Another Epitaph on an Army of Mercenaries. "Hugh MacDiarmid." NoAM

It is a good plan, and began with childhood. Monologue of a Deaf Man. David Wright. NoAM; NowV

It is a human universe: and I. Sonnet. Ted Berrigan. Epi

It is a lie—their priests, their pope. The Confessional. Robert Browning. OBP

It is a lost road into the air. An Airstrip in Essex, 1960. Donald Hall. InPS

It is a new America. Brown River, Smile. Jean Toomer. PoBA

It is a normal day. Poem Found Emptying Out My Pockets. Al Young. CoPAm

It is a summer evening. Lullaby. Anne Sexton. NoAM

It is a tide pool, shallow. Looking into a Tide Pool. Robert Bly. MAT

It is a universal network. High Tension Wires. Allan Block. FAF

It is a willow when summer is over. Willow Poem. William Carlos Williams. NCSH

It is all here. The Shad-Blow Tree. Louise Glück. NVAP

It Is Almost the Year Two Thousand. Robert Frost. TH

It is always a temptation to an armed and agile nation. Dane-Geld. Kipling. OxBTC

It is always handled. George Macbeth. *Fr.* A Riddle. TSWA

It is always morning. The fields of Europe begin to dissolve. Gerard de Nerval. Thomas Brush. NVAP

It is an ancient Mariner. The Rime of the Ancient Mariner. Samuel Taylor Coleridge. Epi; InPS; MBPR; NOBE; PPoD

It is an old stove. Stove. Ken Belford. NeAC

It is August. Drinking while Driving. Raymond Carver. NVAP

It is because the sea is blue. The Great Wave: Hokusai. Donald Finkel. WIF

It is blue-butterfly day here in spring. Blue-Butterfly Day. Robert Frost. RFM

It is cold here. The Moths. W. S. Merwin. HeIP

It is colder now. Epistle to Be Left in the Earth. Archibald MacLeish. NOBA; PAIC

It is common knowledge to every schoolboy. Portrait of the Artist as a Prematurely Old Man. Ogden Nash. SoSe

It is dangerous for a woman to defy the gods. Letter to My Sister. Anne Spencer. PoBA

It Is Dangerous to Read Newspapers. Margaret Atwood. HeIP; Psy

It is dark now. Route 40—Ohio, U.S.A. Milton Kessler. CoPAm

It is day's end; I am thinking of weight. At Night. Robley Wilson, Jr. HeS

It Is Deep. Carolyn M. Rodgers. SA

It is deep summer. Far out. There. Robert Mezey. TSWA

It is difficult now to speak of poetry. George Oppen. *Fr.* Of Being Numerous. MIT

It is down/ makes/ up seem/ taller. Of Consolation. Luci Shaw. AATT

It is easy enough to love flowers but these. Giant Decorative Dahlias. Molly Holden. OxBTC; PSN

It is easy to be young. How to Be Old. May Swenson. MAT

It is equal to living in a tragic land. Dry Loaf. Wallace Stevens. NOBA

It is essential I remember. Man White, Brown Girl and All That Jazz. Gloria C. Oden. PoBA

It is far to Assisi. The Mental Hospital Garden. William Carlos Williams. PiAm

It is finished. The enormous dust-cloud over Europe. Armistice. Paul Dehn. OxBTC

It is fitting that you be here. On Seeing Two Brown Boys in a Catholic Church. Frank Horne. PoBA

It is 5 A.M. everything is the same as it was. Some Lines after the Razing of the Sioux City Armour's Plant. David Allan Evans. HeS

It is from the lips. Sonsito. Victor Hernandez Cruz. MIT

It is hard going to the door. The Door. Robert Creeley. NoAM; VGW

It is hard to be a man. The Falcon Woman. Robert Graves. BuTh; LoAs

It is hunter's magic to perform. Magic. Rex Veeder. HeS

It Is Impossible. Ross Falconer. BuTh

It is impossible to see anything. Inversely, as the Square of Their Distances Apart. Kenneth Rexroth. TSWA

It is June, it is June. Andraitx—Pomegranate Flowers. D. H. Lawrence. NoAM

It is late at night and still I am losing. In Divés' Dive. Robert Frost. VGW

It is late last night the dog was speaking of you. The Grief of a Girl's Heart. *Unknown, tr. by* Lady Gregory. OLR

It is like the plot of an ol. Instructions to a Princess. Ishmael Reed. PoBA

It is midnight. Poem at Thirty. Sonia Sanchez. BPo; NMM; PoBA

It is midnite. The room is blue. Death Songs. L. V. Mack. PoBA

It is Monday morning. The Goldfish Wife. Sandra Hochman. RiTi

It is morning darling look the sun. Aubade: N.Y.C. Robert Wallace. CoPAm

It is morning, Senlin says, and in the morning. Morning Song. Conrad Aiken. *Fr.* Senlin; a Biography. NoAM; SoSe

It Is Na, Jean, Thy Bonie Face. Burns. SLP

It is New Year's Day. Best Loved of Africa. Margaret Danner. PoBA

It is night and it is the ice storm. February I Turn Off The Porch Light and Go Outside. James Tipton. HeS

It is night. You are asleep. And beautiful tears. Sonnet. Ted Berrigan. CAAP

It is not enough. The Prophet's Warning or Shoot to Kill. Ebon Dooley. PoBA

It is not growing like a tree. The Noble Nature. Ben Jonson. *Fr.* To the Immortal Memory and Friendship of That Noble Pair, Sir Lucius Cary and Sir Henry Morison. HeIP; SoSe; VoPo

It is not in the books. The Three Movements. Donald Hall. NowV

It is not love knowledge to thee. Love Charm. *Unknown, tr. fr. Gaelic.* SLP

It is not so much/ Cooking. Outrage. Lucille Iverson. WBN

It is not so much the image of the man. Photograph of Haymaker, 1890. Molly Holden. OxBTC; PSN

It is not to be thought of that the flood. Wordsworth. MBPR; NOBE

It is not youth that intrigues me but suppleness. Michael McClure. MIT

It is of a fearless Irishman a story I will tell. Brennan on the Moor. *Unknown.* AmFP

It Is Oregon, The Highway Looms. Harold Bond. NVAP

It is out in the flimsy suburbs. Sunday in Glastonbury. Robert Bly. ConAP

It is past midnight in a thick fog when sirens. Street Fire. Daniel Halpern. AmPA

It is patience and stalks in the wide house of cattle. The Artery. Les A. Murray. *Fr.* Walking to the Cattle-Place. CAAP

It is pleasant enough here. Voice. Claudia Dobkins. NPW

It is portentous, and a thing of state. Abraham Lincoln Walks at Midnight. Vachel Lindsay. IPWM; NoAM; NOBA; OFD; VGW

It is reported. Sharks in Shallow Water. Fred Levinson. AmPA

It is rough. Poem about a Seashell. Ranice Henderson Crosby. NMM

It is said that certain orientational concepts of an ontological sort. Maxim. Josephine Miles. RiTi

It is said they feed at night. The Feeding Cycle of the Catfish. Tom Crawford. NVAP

It is scary the way I am dreaming of flowers. Van Gogh. Lynn Strongin. RiTi

It is so long since my heart has been with yours. E. E. Cummings. NoAM

It is so much easier to forget than to have been Mr. Whittier. Mr. Whittier. Winfield Townley Scott. VGW

It is so pure, so complete. Aesthetics of the Moon. Jack Anderson. Moon

It is sometime since I have been. The Hill. Robert Creeley. ConAP; NoAM

It is spring once more in the Coast Range. Yin and Yang. Kenneth Rexroth. MIT

"It is such a beautiful day I had to write you a letter." Thoughts of a Young Girl. John Ashbery. ConAP; RRA; VGW

It is that dream world Anaïs speaks of. A Cycle of Women. Sharon Barba. RiTi

It is the best thing. Pregnancy. Sandra McPherson. NMM

It is the effort of the lie. Upon the Intimations of Love's Mortality. Jean Garrigue. LoAs

It is the endless dance of the dead. Dirge. Quincy Troupe. PoBA

It is the evening hour. To Mary: It Is the Evening Hour. John Clare. BoLoP; GBL

It is the first mild day of March. To My Sister [or Lines Written at a Small Distance from My House]. Wordsworth. FSFS; LoAs; MBPR

It is the football season once more. Autumn. Vernon Scannell. MPo; OxBTC

It is the Greek waiter. Garden Blooms. Nicholas Flocos. SA

It is the morning of our love. An Aspect of Love, Alice in the Ice and Fire. Gwendolyn Brooks. BPo; CAPP

It is the Negro's tragedy I feel. The Negro's Tragedy. Claude McKay. BPo

It is the Old Man through the sleeping town. The Fall Again. Howard Nemerov. ConAP

It is the pain, it is the pain, endures. Villanelle. William Empson. LoAs; NoAM

It is the picnic with Ruth in the spring. The Picnic. John Logan. ConAP; CTBA; LP; NCSH

It is the sea's edge lubbers love. Sailing, Sailing. Gray Burr. SPo

It is the season of the sweet wild rose. Modern Love, XLV. George Meredith. GBL

It is the silver seeking salvation. The Plight. James W. Thompson. BPo

It is the sinners' dust-tongued bell claps me to churches. Dylan Thomas. OxBTC

It is the snow-gum silently. The Snow-Gum. Douglas Stewart. MAuV

It is the spot I came to seek. An Indian at the Burial-Place of His Fathers. Bryant. HeIP; PiAm

It is the whales that drive. Fish. William Carlos Williams. NoAM

It is this deep blankness is the real thing strange. Let It Go. William Empson. OxBTC; PSN

It is three o'clock in the morning. Trials of a Tourist. Anne Tibble. FaBoCo

It Is Time. Ted Joans. PAIC

It is time for the invocation. May Sarton. Fr. The Invocation to Kali. RiTi

It is time for the United States to spend money on education. It Is Time. Ted Joans. PAIC

It is time to be old. Terminus. Emerson. NOBA; PAIC; PiAm

It is time to re-invent life. Moon Walk. Ben Belitt. PPoD

It is to a goodly child well fitting. A Goodly Child. Unknown. OxBChV

It is tomorrow now. Morning Star. Thomas Hornsby Ferril. VGW

It is too simple to turn to the sound. The Cold before the Moonrise. W. S. Merwin. CoPAm

It Is True. Federico García Lorca, tr. fr. Spanish by Harriet de Onís. OLR

It is true-/ I've always loved. Alice Walker. Fr. Once NMM; NVAP; PoBA

It is true that, older than man and ages to oulast him. Gray Weather. Robinson Jeffers. NoAM

It is 12:20 in New York a Friday. The Day Lady Died. Frank O'Hara. CAPP; NoAM; NOBA

It is Ulysses that approaches from the east. The World as Meditation. Wallace Stevens. IPWM

It is well to plant balm about places where bees are. Lemon Balm. Marie Harris. MMD

It is what he does not know. On a Squirrel Crossing the Road in Autumn, in New England. Richard Eberhart. HeIP; TH; VoPo; WIF

It is whatever day, whatever time it is. Sunday Morning. Wayne Moreland. PoBA

It is when I hear Mozart. Deafness. Richard Ryan. BIrV

It isn't the thing you do. The Sin of Omission. Margaret Elizabeth Munson Sangster. SoSe

It keeps eternal whisperings around. On the Sea. Keats. MBPR

It little profits that an idle king. Ulysses. Tennyson. AnMo; Epi; HeIP; InPK; InPS; IPWM; NOBE; PAIC; PPoe; PPP; SoSe

It lives on mere banks and drifts of air. In Praise of Lichen. Mark Perlberg. HeS

It looked extremely rocky for the Mudville five that nite. Lucky Louie Makes a Goal. H. Van Arsdale. SPo

It matters not. Be lean as Bengal beef. Poets of My Epoch. Irwin Stark. PAIC

It may be good, like it who list. Sir Thomas Wyatt. AAS

It may be so, my lord./ Hear, Nature, hear! Shakespeare. Fr. King Lear, I, iv. OBP

It may that a strange dream. Max Jacob, tr. fr. French by Wallace Fowlie. LoAs

It may indeed be phantasy, when I. To Nature. Samuel Taylor Coleridge. MBPR

It may not always be so; and I say. E. E. Cummings. Fr. Sonnets—Unrealities. BoLoP

It might be good to gather. I Must Ask. James E. Warren, Jr. AATT

It must be done, my soul; but 'tis a strange. The Meditation. John Norris. SCP-2

It must have been a Friday. I could hear. Katherine's Dream. Robert Lowell. Fr. Between the Porch and the Altar. ConAP

It must have been a year. Fire, Hair, Meat and Bone. Fred Johnson. PoBA

It must have been one or one-thirty. To Remain. C. P. Cavafy, tr. by Nikos Stangos and Stephen Spender. BoLoP

It never gets dark. Crickets suffocate with little. Luxury Apt. Marie Harris. MMD

It occurred to Marshall. Marshall. George Macbeth. NoAM

It oft times has been told, that the British seamen bold. The Constitution and the Guerriére. Unknown. AmFP

"It Out-Herods Herod. Pray You, Avoid It." Anthony Hecht. CoPAm; NCSH; NoAM; NOBA

It rained quite a lot that spring. Metropolitan Nightmare. Stephen Vincent Beñet. PAIC

It Rains. Edward Thomas. OxBTC

It rains? you knot that goddam gawdy. A Big Hat or What? Pete Morgan. SLP

It rains and nothing stirs within the fence. It Rains. Edward Thomas. OxBTC

It seemed that out of battle I escaped. Strange Meeting. Wilfred Owen. HeIP; NoAM; NOBE; OBP

It seems a day. Nutting. Wordsworth. MBPR

It seems a frail mathematics, and ancient. Robin Fulton. Fr. The Voice of the Surbahar, I. MIS

It seems now far off and foolish, a memory. Lot Later. Howard Nemerov. CoPAm

It seems there should be someplace in a poem for black camels. The Loss of Black Camels. Sam Hamod. SA

"It seems to me," said Booker T. Booker T. and W. E. B. Dudley Randall. NoAM

It seems vainglorious and proud. The Conquerors. Phyllis McGinley. PBMP

It seems wrong that out of this bird. A Blackbird Singing. R. S. Thomas. BoAnP

It shall be sayd I dy'de for Coelia. Coelia, XIX. William Percy. AAS

It sifts from leaden sieves. Emily Dickinson. SoSe; SS

It snowed hard. Poem for My Great Grandfather. Michael Van Walleghen. HeS

It sounds unconvincing to say "When I was young." In the Winter of My Thirty-Eighth Year. W. S. Merwin. NOBA

It starts out. The Light Year. John Ridland. OFD

It struck me every day. Emily Dickinson. PPP

It sushes. Cynthia in the Snow. Gwendolyn Brooks. LCL

It takes a long time to hear what the sands. The Bones. W. S. Merwin. ConAP

It tried to get from out the cage. The Cage. James Stephens. OxBTC

It used to be said that love is a bird. The Wishbone. Fred Bornhauser. PPoD

It was a big boxy wreck of a house. The Fall of the House of Usher. Reed Whittemore. InPK

It was a bird of Paradise. In London Town. Mary Elizabeth Coleridge. RAE

It was a chilly winter's night. A Winter Night. William Barnes. NOBE

It was a dim October day. Thomas Caulfield Irwin. *Fr.* Swift. BIrV

It was a dismal and a fearful night. Abraham Cowley. *Fr.* On the Death of Mr. William Harvey. NOBE

It Was A' for Our Rightfu' King. Burns. AIW

It was a friar of orders free. The Friar of Rubygill. Thomas Love Peacock. *Fr.* Maid Marian. PeBB

It Was a Funky Deal. Etheridge Knight. BPo; PoBA

It was a great pleasure. Spitting on Ira Rosenblatt. Robert Hershon. NeAC

It was a kind and northern face. Praise for an Urn. Hart Crane. NoAM; NOBA; PPP

It was a little captive cat. The Singing Cat. Stevie Smith. OxBTC; PCat

It Was a Lover, and His Lass. Shakespeare. *Fr.* As You Like It, V, iii. GBL; HeIP; InPK; InPS; NOBE; OLR; PPoe

It was a maid of brenten arse. A Maid of Brenten Arse. *Unknown.* GBP

It was a Maine lobster town. Water. Robert Lowell. HeIP; NOBA; PiAm

It was a miniature country once. Japan. Anthony Hecht. InPK

It was a miracle he glimpsed owl swaying. Owl Seen In Rearview Mirror. Duane Niatum. VW

It was a place of force. The Rabbit Catcher. Sylvia Plath. SBG

It was a quiet night, you will remember. To My Wife. Edwin Brock. BuTh

It was a robber's daughter, and her name was Alice Brown. Gentle Alice Brown. W. S. Gilbert. FaBoCo; PeBB

It was a summer evening. The Battle of Blenheim. Robert Southey. AKE; PBMP

It was a yearlong bloodbath it was. With. Carol Bergé. MMD

It was after a day's rain. Night Herons. Judith Wright. MAuV

It was all technicolor. Reel One. Adrien Stoutenburg. MiP

It Was All Very Tidy. Robert Graves. OxBTC

It was always. Hose and Iron. Greg Kuzma. MAT; NVAP

"It was an amazing discovery, like the inside of your head." Esplumeoir. "Hugh MacDiarmid." TwMBP

It was at the very date to which we have come. An Anniversary. Thomas Hardy. OxBTC

It was better when we were. For My Mother. Louise Glück. CAAP

It was bright day and all the trees were still. Silence. W. J. Turner. FSFS

It was but now their sounding clamours sung. Palm Sunday: Good Friday. Giles Fletcher the Younger. *Fr.* Christ's Victory and Triumph, III. BoReV

It was December. Even There. Lyn Lifshin. IHMS

It was early, early in the spring. The Croppy Boy. *Unknown.* AmFP

It was early in the season, the fall of 'sixty-three. Michigan-I-O. *Unknown.* AmFP

It was early Monday morning Willie Leonard arose. Willie Leonard; or, The Lake of Cold Finn. *Unknown.* AmFP

It was early Sunday mornin. Stagolee. *Unknown.* MAT

It was easy. How I Escaped from the Labyrinth. Philip Dacey. POL

It was easy. How I Got Myself Trapped. Felix Pollak. HeS

It was in and about the Martinmas time. Bonny Barbara Allan. *Unknown.* BoLoP; HeIP; InPK; PAIC; PeBB; PPoD; SS

It was in October, a favorite season. Elegy for a Nature Poet. Howard Nemerov. CoPAm

It was in one of those old houses in Monmouthshire. Peter Whigham. *Fr.* The Ingathering of Love. TwMBP

It was in the city of Expert. The Oxford Girl; or, Expert Town. *Unknown.* AmFP

It was just before the last fierce charge, two soldiers drew a-rein. The Last Fierce Charge. *Unknown.* AmFP

It was justice to see her nude haunches. The Return. Stanley Moss. POL

It was late last night when my lord come home. The Gypsy Davy. *Unknown.* AmFP

It was late, we. Man and Wife. Mitchell Goodman. VGW

It was Leroy Smith we meant to find. The Young Deputy. James Whitehead. CoPAm

It was like this once: sprinklers mixed. Memo to the 21st Century. Philip Appleman. SFF

It was Mabbie without the grammar school gates. The Ballad of Chocolate Mabbie. Gwendolyn Brooks. CAPP

It was many and many a year ago. The Cannibal Flea. Tom Hood. SpRo

It was many and many a year ago. Cannibalee: A Po'em of Passion. C. F. Lummis. SpRo

It was many and many a year ago. Andrew M'Crie. Robert Fuller Murray. FaBoCo

It was many and many a year ago. Annabel Lee. Poe. AmVN; HeIP; NOBA; PiAm; SpRo

It was my bridal night I remember. I Remember. Stevie Smith. BoLoP; InPK

It was my desert army. no fuss. no incidents. North Africa Breakdown. Tom Raworth. TwMBP

It was my thirtieth year to heaven. Poem in October. Dylan Thomas. FSFS; MPo; OBP; SoSe

It was near evening, the room was cold. The Oath. Allen Tate. NoAM; VGW

It was 1912 when the awful news got around. Sinking of the Titanic. *Unknown.* PAIC

It was no costume jewellery I sent. With a Gift of Rings. Robert Graves. GBL

It was not death, for I stood up. Emily Dickinson. InPK; NOBA

It was not I who began it. Eve to Her Daughters. Judith Wright. MPo

It was not like your great and gracious ways! Departure. Coventry Patmore. *Fr.* The Unknown Eros. NOBE

It was not meant for human eyes. The Combat. Edwin Muir. NOBE

It was not quite winter. Robert Dana. *Fr.* Natural Odes/ American Elegies. HeS

It was on a Friday morning that they took me from the cell. Friday Morning. Sydney Carter. LP

It was on a May, on a midsummer's day. Sir Hugh; or, The Jew's Daughter. *Unknown.* AmFP

It was on a Wednesday night, the moon was shining bright. Jesse James. *Unknown.* AIW

It was on one Monday morning. Lisbon. *Unknown.* AmFP

It was on one Monday morning just about one o'clock. The *Titanic. Unknown.* AmFP

It was on the twenty-first day of December. Ella Speed. *Unknown.* AmFP

It was one afternoon when I was young. The Tale the Hermit Told. Alastair Reid. PoTa

It was one Sunday morning of June the eighth day. Henry K. Sawyer. *Unknown.* AmFP

It was only a film. Two Deaths. Elizabeth Jennings. LP

It was only a small dream of the golden world. John Berryman. *Fr.* Dream Songs. RRA

It was only important. The Moss of His Skin. Anne Sexton. CoPAm; IHMS

It was roses, roses, all the way. The Patriot. Robert Browning. PBMP

It was said at the/ flirting creekwater's birth. To an Imaginary Father. Wendy Rose. CDW

It was six men of Indostan. The Blind Men and the Elephant. John Godfrey Saxe. ECBV; PoTa

It was somewhere in September, and the sun was going down. Sweeney. Henry Lawson. MAuV

It was summer on Boulevard Raspail. A History of the Opera. Sandra Hochman. RiTi

It was the beginning of me. Look at My Face, a Collage. Carolyn M. Rodgers. JB

It was. The breech smelling of oil. First Blood. Jon Stallworthy. BoAnP

It was the dingiest bird. Robin Redbreast. Stanley Kunitz. Prf

It was the night of hardly anyone. The No-Night. Irving Feldman. NoAM

It was the rainbow gave thee birth. The Kingfisher. W. H. Davies. NOBE

It was the *Stately Southerner*, that carried the Stripes and Stars. The *Stately Southerner*. *Unknown.* AmFP

It was the time when lilies blow. Lady Clare. Tennyson. PBMP; PoTa

It was the west wind caught her up, as. The Ring of. Charles Olson. NOBA; VGW

It was the winter wild. Hymn on the Morning of Christ's Nativity. Milton. *Fr.* On the Morning of Christ's Nativity. NOBE

It was the wrong office. Life and Death Among the Xerox People. Olga Cabral. WBN

It was Tiny's habit. Sketches of Harlem. David Henderson. PAIC

It was too lonely for her there. The Impulse. Robert Frost. *Fr.* The Hill Wife. AIW; NoAM

It was upon a Cristemesse night. The Dancers of Colbek. Robert Mannyng. *Fr.* Handlyng Synne. OxBM

It was upon a Lammas night. The Rigs o' Barley [or Corn Rigs Are Bonie *or* Song]. Burns. BoLoP; LoAs; OBP; SLP

It was upon a Shere Thorsday that oure Loverd aras. Judas. *Unknown.* OxBM

It was very late at an empty table. Ballad of an Empty Table. Tom Kryss. NeAC

It was water I was trying to think of all the time. Appoggiatura. Donald Jeffrey Hayes. PoBA

It was wild. Assassination. Don L. Lee. NeAC; OFD; PoBA

It was with resolution that she gave up the. The Ice Eagle. Diane Wakoski. InPS

It was you:/ I could have crawled. Watching Salmon Jump. Simon J. Ortiz. CDW

It wasn't always this way for us. A Poem with a Conclusion. Walter Bradford. HeS

It wasn't intended that the cow should find the poppies. Caprice. Dorothy Stott Shaw. PoTa

It went many years. The Lockless Door. Robert Frost. NOBA

It went off in his face. $E = mc^2$: Einstein at Princeton. David Rowbotham. CAAP

It will be like this. Pax Romana. Virginia Gilbert. NPW

It will darken, stars glimmering, repeating. Tides. Fred Ostrander. MIT

It will not hurt me when I am old. Moonlight. Sara Teasdale. VGW

It will not resemble the sea. The New Poem. Charles Wright. CoPAm

"It would be—/ a mercy if." Phone Call to Rutherford. Paul Blackburn. CTBA

It would have starved a gnat. Emily Dickinson. SBG

Italia, Io Ti Saluto. Christina Rossetti. WPE

Italian Extravaganza. Gregory Corso. SA

Italian women in the back room, The. Excuses. Mary Swanson Stroh. NPW

Italy and England. Byron. *Fr.* Beppo. PAIC (Italy versus England.) NOBE

Iter Boreale, *sel.* Richard Corbet. "There we crossed Trent and on the other side." SCP-2

It's a Different Story When You're Going into the Wind. David McFadden. NeAC

It's a little Walden. You All Know the Story of the Other Woman. Anne Sexton. InPK

It's a low it's a low low. Eagles on a Half. *Unknown.* BluL

It's a still life water color. Dangling Conversation. Paul Simon. NowV

It's a Terrible Thing! Everett Hoagland. BPo

It's a wonderful world. This Wonderful World. Mary Britton Miller. ECBV

It's about/ the ball,/ the bat,/ and the mitt. Analysis of Baseball. May Swenson. SPo

It's all a trick, quite easy when you know it. Villanelle. W. W. Skeat. FaBoCo

It's all mostly on the ropes now. TKO. Richard Peck. SPo

It's all very well to dream of a dove that saves. Birdwatchers of America. Anthony Hecht. NoAM; NOBA; PPP

It's as though/ I had been very happy. When Snow Falls. Katherine Hoskins. TCP

It's autumn in the country I remember. Mnemosyne. Trumbull Stickney. NOBA; PAIC

Its balmy lips the infant blest. Epitaph on an Infant. Samuel Taylor Coleridge. MBPR

It's been a long time comin'. Long Time Gone. David Crosby. WIF

It's been like fixing a clock, jamming the wheels. Making Up for a Soul. David Wagoner. VGW

It's been so long. Alone/ December/ Night. Victor Hernandez Cruz. PBMP

It's been ten years since you tried to kill me. Clearing the Air. Nancy Willard. RiTi

It's Cold in China Blues. *Unknown.* BluL

It's cold, wind gusty. Woman Crossing the Road. Rhyll McMaster. CAAP

Its Curtains. Ted Joans. PoBA

It's dark on purpose. Visiting the Oracle. Lawrence Raab. AmPA

It's 8:54 a.m. Brooklyn it's the 28th of July and. Sonnet. Ted Berrigan. CAAP

It's fine to have a blow-out in a fancy restaurant. The Reckoning. Robert Service. BBGO

It's four long years since I reached this land. Lousy Miner. *Unknown.* AmFP

It's getting to the point. Suite: Judy Blue Eyes. Stephen Stills. WIF

It's going to be a thick night tonight. Officers' Mess. Gavin Ewart. OxBTC

It's going to rain. The Watchers. Paul Blackburn. PAIC

It's grey/ today. The Time Is Open. Joanne Kyger. RiTi

It's hard to make a j. A Jamboree for J. Eve Merriam. ECBV

It's hard to see but think of a sea. Louis Zukofsky. VGW

It's Here in The. Russell Atkins. PoBA

It's just no use. Execution. James A. Randall, Jr. BPo

It's Lamkin was a mason good. Lamkin. *Unknown.* PeBB

It's late. Dark. A swatch of moonlight. For the Sleepless. Stephen Dunn. HeS

It's like the riddle Tolstoy. Slow Dance. David St. John. AmPA

It's Little for Glory I Care. Charles Lever. PFIr

It's me/ bathed and ashy. Me, in Kulu Se and Karma. Carolyn M. Rodgers. PoBA

Its metal top refused my father's twisting. The Soup Jar. Dabney Stuart. CoPAm

It's mostly people. Mostly People. Jeanette Nichols. SFF

It's much like stopping travellers to ask directions. Good Harbor Bay, Leland, Michigan. Ellen McEvilley Griffin. NPW

It's my lunch hour, so I go. A Step Away from Them. Frank O'Hara. ConAP; VGW

It's narrow, narrow, make your bed. Fair Annie. *Unknown.* PeBB

It's natural the Boys should whoop it up for. Moon Landing. W. H. Auden. Moon

It's no go the merrygoround, it's no go the rickshaw. Bagpipe Music. Louis MacNeice. NoAM; NOBE; OxBTC

It's No Good! D. H. Lawrence. InPS

It's no good/ being an actor. Ian Young. NeAC

It's no use trying to find again. The Hunger Artist. Shirley Kaufman. RiTi

It's not celestial music it's the girl in the bathroom singing. Ode on Celestial Music. Brian Patten. OxBTC

It's not exciting to have a bar of soap. Living with Chris. Ted Berrigan. NoAM

It's not my world, I grant, but I made it. Ride. Josephine Miles. RiTi

It's not that/ unlikely that. Downstairs Two Old Lovers Meet. Lyn Lifshin. Psy

It's not that I usually try for much. Love. Robert Pack. CoPAm

It's Not the Heat So Much as the Humidity. James Tate. NoAM

It's November. The Song of This House. Stephen Vincent. NeAC

It's O! but aw ken well. A, U, Hinny Burd. *Unknown.* GBP

It's of a famous highwayman a story I will tell. Brennan on the Moor. *Unknown.* AIW; GBP

It's of flash packet, a packet of fame. The *Dom Pedro. Unknown.* AmFP

It's of a rich squire in Bristol I'll tell. Squire and Milkmaid; or, Blackberry Fold. *Unknown.* InPK

It's one of those storybook days. "You Get th Groceries, I'll Guard the Crib." Dennis Trudell. NVAP

It's Over a (See Just). E. E. Cummings. VGW

Its quick soft silver bell beating, beating. Auto Wreck. Karl Shapiro. CoPAm; VGW; VoPo

It's quiet for me, now that I have buried the child. Ritual Three. David Ignatow. ConAP

It's right to call you son. That cursing alcoholic. Letter to an Absent Son. Madeline DeFrees. NMM; RiTi

It's so cold in China birds can't hardly sing. It's Cold in China Blues. *Unknown.* BluL

It's so pure in the cemetery. Not Like That. Adrienne Rich. CoPAm

It's the anarchy of poverty. The Poor. William Carlos Williams. IPWM; PPP

It's to possess more than the skin. Cutting the Jewish Bride's Hair. Ruth Whitman. RiTi

It's too dark to see black. A Mother Speaks: The Algiers Motel Incident, Detroit. Michael S. Harper. AmPA; BPo

It's too good for them. Sex and the Over Forties. Peter Porter. CAAP

It's too late, too late. T.B. Blues. Leadbelly (Huddie Ledbetter). BluL

It's true Mattie Lee. Unidentified Flying Object. Robert Hayden. NCSH

It's true that days are longer in the country. Romantic Poem. Anne Waldman. RiTi

It's wonderful how I jog. Animals Are Passing from Our Lives. Philip Levine. NoAM; NOBA

Itum Paradisum all clothed in green. *Unknown.* GBP

I've a letter from thy sire. Baby Mine. Charles Mackey. BLSo

I've always thought Polonius a dry. Lines to His Son on Reaching Adolescence. John Logan. CAPP

I've always wanted one. Wanting a Mummy. Sandra McPherson. AmPA

I've been a woman. Poem. Sonia Sanchez. WBN

I've been after the exotic. The Ethnic Life. Daniel Halpern. AmPA

I've been driving for hours. Looking for a Rest Area. Stephen Dunn. AmPA

I've been going around everywhere without any skin. Josephine Miles. IHMS

I've been in jail from slander. The Rocky Mountains. *Unknown.* AmFP

I've been in love for long. In Love for Long. Edwin Muir. BoLoP; LoAs

I've been scarred and battered. Still Here. Langston Hughes. BuTh

I've Been Workin' [or Working] on the Railroad, *with music. Unknown.* BLSH; BLSo

I've come this far to freedom and I won't turn back. Midway. Naomi Long Madgett. BPo

I've come to close your door, my handsome, my darling. Bereft Child's First Night. Frances Bellerby. POL

I've come to give you fruit from out my orchard. The Crossed Apple. Louise Bogan. HeIP

I've come to see Miss Jennian Jones. Miss Jennian Jones. *Unknown.* AmFP

I've come to town to see you all. Long Tail Blue. *Unknown.* BLSo

I've done what I could. My boys run wild now. Complaint. Ian Hamilton. NoAM

I've ever lost were. For Both of Us at Fisk. Sharon Scott. JB

I've found a small dragon in the woodshed. A Small Dragon. Brian Patten. LP

I've Gone and Stained with the Color of Love. Milton Acorn. NeAC

I've Got a Home in That Rock. Raymond R. Patterson. PoBA

I've got a little baby, but she's out of sight. Hello, Ma Baby. Joseph E. Howard *and* Ida Emerson. BLSo

I've got a mule, her name is Sal. The Erie Canal. *Unknown.* BLSo

I've got nasty habits. Live with Me. Mick Jagger *and* Keith Richard. InPK

I've Got No Use for the Women. *Unknown.* AmFP

I've Got the World on a String, *with music.* Ted Koehler. BLSo

I've got to keep moving. Hellhound on My Trail. *Unknown.* BluL

I've had all of the apple, she said. Once When She Thought Aloud. Dorothea MacKellar. MAuV

I've had tangled feelings lately. Breakthrough. Carolyn M. Rodgers. BPo

I've heard them lilting at loom and belting. Two Songs. C. Day Lewis. NoAM

I've heard them [*or* the] lilting at our yowe-milking [*or* the ewe-milking]. The Flowers of the Forest. Jane Elliot. BTTM; SLP; WPE

I've just got here, through Paris, from the sunny southern shore. The Man Who Broke the Bank at Monte Carlo. Fred Gilbert. FSN

I've known her too long. A Sequence of Women. James Harrison. CoPAm

I've known rivers. The Negro Speaks of Rivers. Langston Hughes. BPo; CoPAm; HeIP; NoAM; NOBA; PiAm; PoBA; TSWA

I've learned to recognize angels. Propeller Sleep. Mei Berssenbrugge. SA

I've never seen an abominable snowman. The Abominable Snowman. Ogden Nash. RAE

I've oft been told by learned friars. An Argument. Thomas Moore. BoLoP

I've often heard my mother say. The Unknown Color. Countee Cullen. ECBV

I've only sailed through the Mediterranean. Notes to a Biographer. Peter Porter. CAAP

I've poached a pickle paitricks. Poaching *in Excelsis.* G. K. Menzies. FaBoCo

I've reached the land of corn and wine. Beulah Land. Edgar Page. BLSH

I've rode the Southern, I've rode the L. & N. I Rode Southern, I Rode L & N. *Unknown.* AmFP

I've seen a deal of gaiety through out my noisy life. Champagne Charlie. *At. to* George Leybourne. PSoN

I've seen a dying eye. Emily Dickinson. NOBA

Ive seen all the sunrises since u left me. Sex Play in Four Acts. Doug Fetherling. NeAC

I've stayed in the front yard all my life. A Song in the Front Yard. Gwendolyn Brooks. IPWM; NoAM; NOBA; PoBA

I've thought of names. Labour of the Brain, Ballad of the Body. Nicole Forman. NMM

I've tried the new moon tilted in the air. The Freedom of the Moon. Robert Frost. Moon

I've watched you now a full half-hour. To a Butterfly. Wordsworth. MBPR

Ivory Masks in Orbit. Keorapetse Kgositsile. PoBA

Ivry. Macaulay. BTTM

Ivy, Chief of Trees. *Unknown.* OxBM

# J

Jabberwocky. "Lewis Carroll." *Fr.* Through the Looking-Glass, *ch.* 1. AnMo; FaBoCo; HeIP; InPK; InPS; NOBE; OBP; OxBChV; PPoe; PPP; SpRo; WIF

Jack. Charles Henry Ross. OxBChV

Jack and Dinah Want Freedom. *Unknown.* BPo

Jack and His Pony, Tom. Hilaire Belloc. BoAnP

Jack and Jill went up the hill. Mother Goose. MG

Jack be nimble. Mother Goose. MG

Jack, eating rotten cheese, did say. Quatrain. Benjamin Franklin. SoSe

Jack had a little pony—Tom. Jack and His Pony, Tom. Hilaire Belloc. BoAnP

Jack Haggerty. *Unknown.* AmFP

Jack Monroe. *Unknown.* AmFP

Jack of Diamonds. *Unknown.* AmFP

Jack Rabbit. Adrien Stoutenburg. BoAnP

Jack Sprat could eat no fat. Mother Goose. MG

Jack the Jolly Tar. *Unknown.* AmFP

Jack the Piper. *Unknown.* GBP

Jackdaw. Tom Earley. BoAnP

Jackdaw of Rheims, The. "Thomas Ingoldsby." *Fr.* The Ingoldsby Legends. FaBoCo

Jacke and Jone, they thinke no ill. Thomas Campion. AAS

Jacket it winsomely in primrose yellow! Ultimate Anthology. Martin Bell. POL

Jackie's gone a-sailing with trouble on his mind. Jack Monroe. *Unknown.* AmFP

Jacksonville Blues. *Unknown.* BluL

Jacob Epstein. *Unknown.* FaBoCo

Jacobite Toast, A. John Byrom. FaBoCo
(Extempore Verses Intended to Allay the Violence of Party-Spirit.) PPoD

Jacobite's Epitaph, A. Macaulay. NOBE

Jacob's Ladder, The. Denise Levertov. AnMo; CoPAm; IPWM; PPP

Jagg'd mountain peaks and skies ice-green. Brueghel's Winter. Walter de la Mare. WIF

Jailhouse Blues. *Unknown.* BluL

Jake Hates All the Girls. E. E. Cummings. CTBA

Jam Fish, The. Edward Abbott Parry. OxBChV

Jam on Gerry's Rocks, The. *Unknown.* AmFP

Jamaican Bus Ride. A. S. J. Tessimond. OxBTC

Jamboree for J, A. Eve Merriam. ECBV

James Alley. *Unknown.* BluL

James Bird. *Unknown.* AmFP

James Harris. *Unknown. See* Demon Lover, The.

James Powell on Imagination. Larry Neal. BPo

James Watt. W. H. Auden. InPK

Jamie Douglas. *Unknown. See* Waly, Waly ("When cockle shells...").

Jamie Telfer of the Fair Dodhead. *Unknown.* PeBB

Jane, Jane,/ Tall as a crane. Aubade. Edith Sitwell. NoAM

Janet (Lady Maisry). *Unknown.* PeBB

Jane looks down at her organdy skirt. In Bertram's Garden. Donald Justice. BoLoP; InPK; SFF; VGW

Jane Smith. Kipling. SpRo

Janet Waking. John Crowe Ransom. InPK; NCSH; NoAM; PBMP; PiAm

Jangle of the jeering crows, The. Black Humor. Archibald MacLeish. NCSH

Jankin. *Unknown. See* Jolly Jankin.

Januar: by this fire I warme my handes. *See* January. By this fire I warm my hands.

Januaries, Nature greets our eyes. Brazil, January 1, 1502. Elizabeth Bishop. NoAM

January bring the snow. The Months. Sara Coleridge. OxBChV

January. [*or* Januari:] By this fire I warm my hands. The Months. *Unknown.* GBP; OxBM

January, heat. Raw saplings stand like cattle. SMLE. Les A. Murray. CAAP

January Morning. William Carlos Williams. InPS

January 1919. Christopher Middleton. TwMBP

January Sky, The. A. G. Sobin. HeS

January sky is deep and calm, The. Reason for Not Writing Orthodox Nature Poetry. John Wain. PAIC

January Thaw. Allan Block. FAF

January 3, 1970. Mae Jackson. PoBA

Japan. Gavin Bantock. TwMBP

Japan. Anthony Hecht. InPK

Japanese Children. James Kirkup. RAE

Japanese Folk-song from Hyogo. *Unknown, tr. fr. Japanese by* Geoffrey Bownas *and* Anthony Thwaite. RAE

Japanese next to me at the bar, The. In a Bar Near Shibuya Station, Tokyo. Paul Engle. SFF

Jazz. Carolyn M. Rodgers. JB

Jazz for Five, *sels.* John Smith. MPo
  Colin Barnes, Drums, III.
  Shake Keane, Trumpet, V.

Jazzonia. Langston Hughes. CoPAm

"Je Ne Sais Quoi," The. William Whitehead. SoSe

Je t'adore. Thomas Kinsella. NoAM

Jealous Brothers, The. *Unknown.* AmFP

Jealousy. Mary Elizabeth Coleridge. WPE

Jealousy. Stephen Vincent. NeAC

Jean, Jean, Jean. Cat at the Cream. *Unknown.* GBP; POL

Jean Richepin's Song. Herbert Trench. ECBV; PFIr; PoTa

Jeanie with the Light Brown Hair, *with music.* Stephen Collins Foster. BLSH; BLSo

Jefferson Valley. John Hollander. PPP

Jellicle cats are black and white. The Song of the Jellicles. T. S. Eliot. LCL; PCat; OxBChV

Jellon Grame. *Unknown.* PeBB

Jelly roll/ Jelly roll/ Jelly roll is so hard to find. Hambone Blues. *Unknown.* BluL

Jellyfish, The. William Pitt Root. BoAnP; NVAP

Jenny. Dante Gabriel Rossetti. VPC

Jenny cold, Jenny darkness. October Ghosts. James Wright. CAAP

Jenny Kiss'd [*or* Kissed] Me. Leigh Hunt. SFF; SpRo
  (Rondeau: "Jenny kissed me when we met.") InPK; NOBE; PAIC

Jenny kiss'd me in a dream. Such Stuff as Dreams. Franklin P. Adams. SpRo

Jenny kiss'd me when we met. Paul Dehn. *Fr.* A Leaden Treasury of English Verse. SpRo

Jerome. Randall Jarrell. PPP

Jersey Belle Blues. *Unknown.* BluL

Jersey Cattle. R. N. Currey. OxBTC

Jerusalem, *sels.* Blake. MBPR
  "Of the sleep of Ulro! and of the passage through," *ch.* 1.
  "There is a void, outside of existence, which if enterd into."
  To the Jews.

Jerusalem. Blake. *Fr.* Milton. *See* And Did Those Feet in Ancient Time.

Jesse James. William Rose Benét. ANTL; PoTa

Jesse James ("It was on a Wednesday night, the moon was shining bright"). *Unknown.* AIW

Jesse James ("Jesse James was a lad that killed many a man"). *Unknown.* AmFP

Jesse James was a two-gun man. Jesse James. William Rose Benét. ANTL; PoTa

Jessie Mitchell's Mother. Gwendolyn Brooks. NMM

Jessie, my cousin, remembers there were gypsies. Gypsies. Alden Nowlan. NeAC

Jest, The. Austin Clarke. BIrV

Jester walked in the garden, The. The Cap and Bells. W. B. Yeats. NoAM

Jesu Christ, My Leman Swete. *Unknown.* OxBM

Jesu, sweete [*or* swete] sone dear [*or* dere]. The Virgin's Song. *Unknown.* BoReV; NOBE; OxBM

Jesus and His Mother. Thom Gunn. MPo

Jesus Borned in Bethlea. *Unknown.* AmFP

Jesus Calls Us, *with music.* Cecil Frances Alexander. BLSH

Jesús, Estrella, Esperanza, Mercy. Middle Passage. Robert Hayden. PAIC

Jesus got mad one day. A Pun for Al Gelpi. Jack Kerouac. PiAm

Jesus, grant us all a blessing. Shouting Song. *Unknown.* AmFP

Jesus Inter Ubera Mariae. Joseph Beaumont. SCP-2

Jesus Is Coming Soon. *Unknown.* BluL

Jesus, Lover of My Soul, *with music.* Charles Wesley. BLSH

Jesus Make Up My Dying Bed. *Unknown.* BluL

Jesus our brother, strong and good. The Friendly Beasts. *Unknown.* RAE

Jesus, thou art the sinner's friend. 'Tis Sweet to Rest in Lively Hope. *Unknown.* AmFP

Jesus Was Crucified or: It Must Be Deep. Carolyn M. Rodgers. PoBA; SA

Jet Must Be Hunting for Something, The. Robert Penn Warren. CoPAm

Jew. James A. Randall, Jr. BPo

Jew at Christmas Eve, The. Karl Shapiro. VGW

Jewel, The. James Wright. CAPP

Jewel Stairs' Grievance, The ("The jewelled steps are already quite white with dew"). Li Po, *tr. fr. Chinese by* Ezra Pound. InPK; NOBA; PiAm

Jewels, The. Baudelaire, *tr. fr. French by* Roy Campbell. BoLoP

Jewish Cemetery at Newport, The. Longfellow. HeIP; NOBA; PiAm

Jezebel. Forbes Macgregor. MIS

Jig. C. Day Lewis. PFIr

Jig Tune: Not for Love. Thomas McGrath. VGW

Jim and I as children played together. Oh Lucky Jim. *Unknown.* GBP

Jim Crack Corn; or, the Blue Tail Fly. *Unknown.* PSoN, *with music*
  (Blue-tail Fly, The.) BLSH, *with music*; BLSo, *with music*; GBP

Jim Desterland. Hyam Plutzik. VGW

Jim Jones at Botany Bay. *Unknown.* GBP; PeBB

Jim, Who Ran Away from His Nurse, and Was Eaten by a Lion. Hilaire Belloc. OxBChV

Jimmy Jet and His TV Set. Shel Silverstein. CTBA

Jimmy Judge. *Unknown.* AmFP

Jimson lives in a new. A Call to the Wild. Lord Dunsany. PFIr

Jindrichuv Hradec. Christopher Middleton. TwMBP

Jingle Bells, *with music.* James S. Pierpont. BLSH; BLSo
  (One Horse Open Sleigh, The.) PSoN

Jinnie Jinkins. *Unknown.* AmFP

Jinny the Just. Matthew Prior. NOBE

Jinx Blues, The. *Unknown.* BluL

Jitterbugging in the Streets. Calvin C. Hernton. PoBA

Job, *sels.* Bible, *O.T.* OBP
  "Canst thou bind the cluster of the Pleiades," XXXVIII: 31-34.
  "Hast thou given the horse his might?" XXXIX: 19-25.

Job Hunting. Tom Hennen. HeS

Joe Bowers. *Unknown.* AmFP

Joe Was the Best of Them. Judith McCombs. WBN

Jog on, Jog on, the Footpath Way. *Unknown.* GBP

Jog on, jog on the footpath way. Autolycus' Song. Shakespeare. *Fr.* The Winter's Tale, IV, ii. SpRo

Johannes Milton, Senex. Robert Bridges. BoReV; OBP

John Adkins' Farewell. *Unknown.* AmFP

John Anderson. Keith Douglas. SoSe

John Anderson, My Jo ("John Anderson my jo, John,/ When we were first acquent"). Burns. BoLoP; HeIP; InPK; IPWM; LAuP; LoAs; NOBE; SLP

John Anderson My Jo ("John Anderson my jo, John,/ I wonder what you mean"). *At. to* Burns. LAuP

John Barleycorn [a Ballad]. Burns. AIW; Epi

John Brown's Body, *sels.*    Stephen Vincent Benét.
Invocation: "American muse, whose strong and diverse heart."
BTTM
Melora's Song.    AIW
John Brown's Body.    *Unknown.*    BLSo, *with music*; BTTM
John Bun.    *Unknown.*    FaBoCo
John Cabot, out of Wilma, once a Wycliffe.    Riot.    Gwendolyn
Brooks.    BPo; CAPP; PoBA; Psy
John Cherokee.    *Unknown.*    GBP
John Clare.    Jon Anderson.    AmPA
John Coltrane: an Impartial Review.    A. B. Spellman.    PoBA
John Doe and Mary Smith.    Podunk, 1941.    Dick Allen.
CoPAm
John Gilpin was a citizen.    The Diverting History of John Gilpin.
William Cowper.    LAuP
John Gorham.    E. A. Robinson.    NoAM
John Grumlie.    *Unknown.*    GBP
John Hardy.    *Unknown.*    AmFP
John Henry, *with music.*    Unknown, ad. by James Morehead.
BLSH
John Henry (*diff.* versions).    *Unknown.*    AIW; AmFP; BPo;
NOBA; PeBB; WIF
John Hielandman.    *Unknown.*    GBP
John in the desert.    Bellevue.    James Harrison.    CoPAm
John J. Curtis.    Joseph Gallagher.    AmFP
John-John.    Thomas MacDonagh.    PFIr; PoTa
John Keats.    Byron.    MBPR
John Littlehouse the redhead was a large ruddy man.    The
Blacksmith's Serenade.    Vachel Lindsay.    PoTa
John Mouldy.    Walter de la Mare.    NCSH; OxBChV
John Muir on Mt. Ritter.    Gary Snyder.    Myths and Texts:
Burning, VIII.    Epi; NOBA; TCP
John Nobody.    Dom Moraes.    NoAM
John Oswald McGuffin he wanted to die.    But Then.    Ben King.
PoTa
John Stuart Mill.    E. C. Bentley.    *Fr.* Clerihews.    FaBoCo
John Sutter.    Yvor Winters.    NoAM; NOBA
John, Tom, and James ("John was a bad boy").    Charles Henry
Ross.    OxBChV
John Without Heaven.    John Malcolm Brinnin.    NoAM
Johnie Cam to Our Toun.    *Unknown.*    GBP
Johnnie Crack and Flossie Snail.    Dylan Thomas.    *Fr.* Under
Milk Wood.    LCL; RAE
Johnny Carroll's Camp.    *Unknown.*    AmFP
Johnny Dow.    *Unknown.*    FaBoCo
Johnny Dyers.    *Unknown.*    AmFP
Johnny Gallagher.    *Unknown.*    AmFP
Johnny Germany.    *Unknown.*    AmFP
Johnny Get Your Gun, *with music.*    Monroe H. Rosenfeld.
PSoN
Johnny, I Hardly Knew Ye.    *Unknown.*    BIrV; GBP; InPK;
OBP; PeBB
Johnny is a long-haired Blue.    Three Cheers for the Black, White
and Blue.    Ruth Pitter.    BoAnP
Johnny Sands.    *Unknown.*    AmFP
Johnny shall have a new bonnet.    Mother Goose.    MG
Johnny Thomson, so they say.    Mrs. Vickers' Daughter.
*Unknown.*    AmFP
Johnny's in the basement.    Subterranean Homesick Blues.    Bob
Dylan.    InPK
Johnny's the Lad I Love.    *Unknown.*    AIW
John's my name, John Everyone, citizen.    John Without Heaven.
John Malcolm Brinnin.    NoAM
Johnshaven.    *Unknown.*    GBP
Johnson, he was riding along, as fast as he could ride.    Johnson-
Jinkson.    *Unknown.*    AmFP

Johnson's Cabinet Watched by Ants.    Robert Bly.    NoAM;
NOBA
Johny he has risen up i' the morn.    Johny Cock.    *Unknown.*
PeBB
Joke Versified, A.    Thomas Moore.    FaBoCo
Jolly Beggars, The.    Burns.    LAuP
Jolly Forester, The.    *Unknown.*    RAE
Jolly Jankin.    *Unknown.*    GBP; OxBM
(Jankin.)    NOBE
Jolly old sow once lived in a sty, A.    The Three Little Pigs.    Sir
Alfred Scott Gatty.    OxBChV
Jolly Plowboy, The.    *Unknown.*    AmFP
Jolly Shepherd Wat, The.    *Unknown.*    NOBE; OxBM
Jolly soldier ("I once was a seaman stout and bold").    *Unknown.*
AmFP; OFD
Jolly Soldier, The (" 'Tis of a jolly soldier that lately came from
war").    *Unknown.*    AmFP
Jolly Thresherman, The.    *Unknown.*    AmFP
Jollymerry/ hollyberry.    The Computer's First Christmas Card.
Edwin Morgan.    FaBoCo; MPo; SFF
Jonah.    Randall Jarrell.    CoPAm
Jonah: A Report.    David R. Slavitt.    CoPAm
Jonah Is Cast into the Sea.    *Unknown.*    *Fr.* Patience.    OxBM
Jonathan Swift/ Had the gift.    Lines on Swift's Ancestors.    Pope.
FaBoCo
Jones! as from Calais southward you and I.    Composed near
Calais, on the Road Leading to Ardres.    Wordsworth.
MBRP
Jordan ("When first my lines of heavenly joy made mention").
George Herbert.    PPP
Jordan ("Who says that fictions only and false hair").    George
Herbert.    OBP; PAIC; PPP
Joseph and Mary walked one day.    The Cherry-Tree Carol.
*Unknown.*    AmFP
Joseph Mica.    *Unknown.*    GrRo
Joseph was an old man.    The Cherry-Tree Carol.    *Unknown.*
AmFP; GBP; HeIP; IPWM; OFD; PeBB
Joseph were a young man, a young man were he.    The Cherry-
Tree Carol.    *Unknown.*    AmFP
Joshua Fit De Battle of [*or* ob] Jericho.    *Unknown.*    BPo; NOBA
Journal for My Daughter.    Stanley Kunitz.    RRA
Journal of the Storm.    Greg Kuzma.    AmPA
Journey.    Diane Wakoski.    IHMS
Journey of a Poem Compared to all the Sad Variety of Travel,
The.    Delmore Schwartz.    NowV
Journey of the Magi.    T. S. Eliot.    BoReV; HeIP; OxBTC;
PBMP; PPoe; TCP
Journey to the Interior.    Theodore Roethke.    VGW
Jousting of Jesus, The.    William Langland.    *Fr.* The Vision of
Piers Plowman.    BoReV
Jove for Europa's [*or* Europaes] love, took shape of bull.
Parthenophil and Parthenophe, LXIII.    Barnabe Barnes.
AAS; Epi; LoAs
Jove, grant me length of life, and years' good store.    Juvenal, *tr.*
*fr. Latin by* Dryden.    *Fr.* Satires, X.    SCP-1
Jove's Eagle Carries Chaucer into Space.    Chaucer.    *Fr.* The
House of Fame.    OxBM
Jovial Hunter of Bromsgrove, The.    *Unknown.*    PeBB
Joy.    Gavin Bantock.    OxBTC
Joy.    Robert Creeley.    PPP
Joy—a beginning. Anguish, ardor.    Relearning the Alphabet.
Denise Levertov.    NOBA
Joy, I did lock thee up, but some bad man.    The Bunch of
Grapes.    George Herbert.    AnMo
Joy of my life, full oft for loving you.    Amoretti, LXXXII.
Spenser.    HeIP

Joy of the springtime! How the sun. Sisyphus. Robert J. Burdette. PoTa

Joy, Shipmate, Joy. Walt Whitman. VoPo

Joy to Philip, he this day. Going into Breeches. Charles *and* Mary Lamb. OxBChV

Joy to the bridegroom and the bride. The Milkmaid's Epithalamium. Thomas Randolph. BoLoP

Joy to the World, *with music.* Isaac Watts. BLSH

Joyful ants nest on the roof of my tree. Sonnet. Ted Berrigan. CAAP

Joyless/ what have I done. Liadan Laments Cuirithir. *Unknown, tr. by* John Montague. BIrV

Joys of Mary, The. *Unknown.* AmFP

Juan, the moron next door. Report from the Correspondent They Fired. David McElroy. AmPA

Juanita, *with music.* Caroline Norton. BLSH

Jubilate Agno, *sels.* Christopher Smart.
  "For I am not without authority in my jeopardy." LAuP; OBP
  "For I bless the Prince of Peace and pray that all the guns may be nail'd up." InPS
  "For I will consider my Cat Jeoffry." AnMo; HeIP; InPK; LAuP; PCat; PPP; Prf
  "For the air is purified by prayer which is made aloud." Prf
  "For the doubling of flowers is the improvement of the gardners talent." LAuP
  "Rejoice in god, O ye tongues; give the glory to the Lord, and the Lamb." LAuP

Judas. Andrew Baster. BuTh

Judas. Vassar Miller. CoPAm

Judas. *Unknown.* Epi; OxBM

Judas Before. Lucille F. Travis. AATT

Judeebug's Country. Joe Johnson. PoBA

Judge gimme life this morning. Parchman Farm Blues. *Unknown.* BluL

Judge Harsh Blues. *Unknown.* BluL

Judge said "Stand up, boy, and dry up your tears," The. Twenty-one Years. *Unknown.* AmFP

Judging Distances. Henry Reed. Lessons of the War, II. BoLoP; NOBE; PSN; SoSe

Judith of Bethulia. John Crowe Ransom. NoAM; NOBA; PiAm

Judith Recalls Holofernes. Maura Stanton. AmPA

Jug-jug! Fair fall the nightingale. I Am Not as I Wish. Richard Brathwaite. *Fr.* Nature's Embassy. SCP-2

Juggler. Richard Wilbur. NCSH

Juggler and the Baron's Daughter, The. *Unknown.* OxBM

JuJu Askia Muhammad Touré. PoBA

Juju of My Own, A. Lebert Bethune. InPS; PoBA

Juke Box Love Song. Langston Hughes. OLR; PoBA

Julian and Maddalo. Shelley. MBPR

Julia's Petticoat. Robert Herrick. SCP-1

Juliet. Hilaire Belloc. BoLoP

Julius Caesar. *Unknown.* InPK

July. John Clare. *See* The Shepherd's Calendar.

July. Austin Dobson. RAE

July in Indiana. Robert Fitzgerald. ANTL

July in Washington. Robert Lowell. Prf

July the first, in Oldbridge town, there was a grievous battle. The Battle of the Boyne. Captain Blacker. BTTM

July 31. Norman Jordan. PoBA

Jumblies, The. Edward Lear. OxBChV; SS

Jump bigness upward. Mwilu/ or Poem for the Living. Don L. Lee. JB

Jump Jim Crow, *with music.* Thomas D. Rice. BLSo

Jump Shot. Richard Peck. MiP; SPo

Jump stone hand leaf shadow sun. The Fire. Robert Duncan. *Fr.* Passages. VGW

June. Francis Ledwidge. BIrV

June. Bink Noll. TCP

June. Spenser. *Fr.* The Shepheardes Calender. PAIC

June Bracken and Heather. Tennyson. PPoe

June Fugue. Thomas Shapcott. CAAP

June Is Bustin' Out All Over, *with music.* Oscar Hammerstein II. BLSo

June Thunder ("Junes were free and full"). Louis MacNeice. MPo

Jungle Husband, The. Stevie Smith. BuTh

Junglegrave. S. E. Anderson. PoBA

Junior Addict. Langston Hughes. BPo; TCP

Juniper. Robert Francis. VGW

Juniper ("Juniper, Juniper/ Green in the snow"). *Unknown.* RAE

Junk. Richard Wilbur. InPK; PPoD

Junkman's Obbligato. Lawrence Ferlinghetti. WIF

Just a little more. Mythistorema. George Seferis, *tr. by* Rex Warner. BuTh

Just a little rain falling all around. What Have They Done to the Rain. Malvina Reynolds. PoRo

Just a Smack at Auden. William Empson. FaBoCo

Just a worried old rounder. Lowdown Rounder's Blues. *Unknown.* BluL

Just about now. To a Woman Half a World Away. Dick Allen. CoPAm

Just after the Widow's Death. Barbara Greenberg. RiTi

Just as I Am, *with music.* Charlotte Elliot. BLSH

Just as my fingers close about the pen. The Spider. Kenneth Mackenzie. BoAnP

Just as my fingers on these keys. Peter Quince at the Clavier. Wallace Stevens. AnMo; InPK; InPS; LoAs; NOBA; PAIC; PPP; SoSe; TCP

Just at that moment the Wolf. Coup de Grâce. A. D. Hope. PPP

Just Because. David McCord. ECBV

Just because you wear a natural baby. Dancing in the Street. Al Young. SA

Just Before the Battle, Mother, *with music.* George Frederick Root. PSoN

Just broke from school, pert, impudent, and raw. The Modern Fine Gentleman. Soame Jenyns. ESaP

Just down around the corner of the street where I reside. Sweet Rosie O'Grady. Maude Nugent. FSN

Just Dropped In. William Cole. POL

Just for a handful of silver he left us. The Lost Leader. Robert Browning. BTTM; PBMP; PPoD

Just inside the bark the tree's charm slides. Tree Animals. Laurence Lieberman. CoPAm

Just Italian, The, *sel.* Sir William Davenant.
  "This lady, ripe and calm and fresh." SCP-2

Just like a penitent that doth prepare. Love's Preparation. William Cavendish, Duke of Newcastle. SCP-2

Just lookee here mama don't treat pigmeat the way you do. Pigmeat. *Unknown.* BluL

Just lost, when I was saved! Emily Dickinson. NOBA; Prf

Just now/ Out of the strange. The Warning. Adelaide Crapsey. WPE

Just now the lilac is in bloom. The Old Vicarage, Grantchester. Rupert Brooke. OxBTC

Just off the highway to Rochester, Minnesota. A Blessing. James Wright. ANTL; ConAP; InPK; NoAM; NOBA; PPP; SFF; SoSe

Just out of San Francisco one cold December day. The Dying Hobo. *Unknown.* AmFP

Just so it goes—the day, the night. An Ordinary evening in Cleveland. Lewis Turco. ANTL

Just Taking Note. Sharon Scott. JB

Just Tell Them That You Saw Me, *with music.* Paul Dresser. FSN

Just this morning I signed the contract. Pearl Harbor Day 1970. Dick Lourie. NeAC

Just three days old. The New Moon. Issa, *tr. by* Harold G. Henderson. Moon

Just weeks ago dead. Poppies. Greg Kuzma. HeS

Just when you're able to admit. Corps d'Esprit. Heather McHugh. AmPA

Just yesterday morning they let me know you were gone. Fire and Rain. James Taylor. WIF

Justice. Langston Hughes. BPo

Justice Denied in Massachusetts. Edna St. Vincent Millay. RiTi; SBG

Justice Had Become a Woman. Anne Hazlewood Brady. WBN

Justice Is Reason Enough. Diane Wakoski. AmPA

Justice is the Man's statue. Justice Has Become a Woman. Anne Hazlewood Brady. WBN

Justshakeityoucanbreakityoucan-hangitonthewall. Hang It on the Wall. *Unknown.* BluL

# K

Ka 'Ba. LeRoi Jones. BPo; CAPP; PiAm

Kaddish, *sel.* Allen Ginsberg. "Strange now to think of you, gone without corsets & eyes." NOBA

Kaddish: "In her last sickness, my mother took my hand in hers." Charles Reznikoff. *Fr.* Going To and Fro and Walking Up and Down. SA

Kaddish: "Upon Israel and upon the rabbis." Charles Reznikoff. *Fr.* Separate Way. SA

Kafka's Other Metamorphosis. Len Gasparini. NeAC

Kag the Porcupine (The Misanthrope). Arthur Guiterman. ECBV

Kaire. Richard Eberhart. NoAM

Kalaloch. Carolyn Forché. AmPA

Kangeroo. D. H. Lawrence. InPS; OxBTC

Kangaroo, The. *Unknown.* ECBV

Kansa, The. Victor Contoski. HeS

Kansas Boy. Ruth Lechlitner. ANTL

Karl Marx. Al Lee. AmPA

Karma. E. A. Robinson. HeIP; IPWM; NoAM; OFD; PiAm

Karma Repair Kit: Items 1-4. Richard Brautigan. IPWM

Karshish, the picker-up of learning's crumbs. An Epistle Containing the Strange Medical Experience of Karshish, the Arab Physician. Robert Browning. PFD

Kassie Jones. *Unknown.* BluL

Kate and the Cowhide. *Unknown.* AmFP

Kate Being Pleased. Sir John Davies. POL

Kate Dalrymple. *Unknown.* GBP

Kate meets me at the top of the stairs. At Veronica's. Robert Peterson. NeAC

Käthe Kollwitz. Muriel Rukeyser. NMM; RiTi

Katherine's Dream. Robert Lowell. *Fr.* Between the Porch and the Altar. ConAP

Katie May. *Unknown.* BluL

Kato's Poem. David Kherdian. FAF

Katrina. Bruce Dawe. CAAP

Katzenjammer Kids, The. James Reaney. AKE

Kayumangi. Jessica Tarahata Hagedorn. MMD

Kearney at Seven Pines. Edmund Clarence Stedman. BTTM

Keen, fitful gusts are whisp'ring here and there. Keats. MBPR

Keep It Clean. *Unknown.* BluL

Keep It under Your Hat. Gary Margolis. CoPAm

Keep me clean. Chamber-pot Rhyme. *Unknown.* GBP

Keep on Pushing. David Henderson. PoBA

Keep the Sea. *Unknown.* *Fr.* The Libelle of Englyshe Polycye. OxBM

Keep thy tunge, thy tunge, thy tunge. Wicked Tongues. *Unknown.* OxBM

Keep to yourself your kisses. Taisigh Agat Fein Do Phog. *Unknown, tr. by* Maire Cruise O'Brien. BIrV

Keep your back door locked baby, keep your windows pinned. Keep Your Windows Pinned. *Unknown.* BluL

Keep your eyes open when you kiss: do: when. John Berryman. BoLoP

Keep Your Windows Pinned. *Unknown.* BluL

Keeper of the Eddystone Light, The. *Unknown.* PeBB

Keeping Things Whole. Mark Strand. CoPAm; NoAM; PPP; SFF

Kelly. Robert Hershon. NeAC

Kelly Show, The. Charles Higham. MAuV

Kelly's kept an unlicensed bull, well away. The Outlaw. Seamus Heaney. NoAM

Kemp Owyne. *Unknown.* PeBB

Kenst doo hoo. The Miller's Wife's Lullaby. *Unknown.* GBP

Kent State, May 4, 1970. Paul Goodman. MAT; TSWA

Kentish Sir Byng stood for his King. Cavalier Tunes. Robert Browning. BTTM

Kentucky Babe, *with music.* Richard Henry Buck. BLSH; FSN

Kentucky Belle. Constance Fenimore Woolson. PoTa

Kentucky Blues. *Unknown.* BluL

Kentucky water, clear springs: a boy fleeing. The Swimmers. Allen Tate. InPS; NOBA

Kerry Recruit, The, *with music.* *Unknown.* RDB

Key of the Kingdom, The. Ed Reed. BBGO

Key to Everything, The. May Swenson. IHMS; Psy

Keys of Canterbury, The. *Unknown.* AmFP

Khwa! Ye! O! Rainbow, O rainbow! The Rainbow. *Unknown.* AKE

Kick at the rock, Sam Johnson, break your bones. Epistemology. Richard Wilbur. NoAM; NOBA

Kicking from Centre Field. David McFadden. NeAC

Kicking Mule, The. *Unknown.* AmFP

Kid. Robert Hayden. NCSH

Kid Stuff. Frank Horne. PoBA

Kidnap Poem. Nikki Giovanni. BPo; InPK; NoAM

Kidnaper. Tess Gallagher. AmPA

Kids are asleep, The. It's a Different Story When You're Going into the Wind. David McFadden. NeAC

Kids are left out late tonight, The. New Year 1974. Rae Desmond Jones. CAAP

Kid's Last Fight, The. *Unknown.* SPo

Kilcash. *Unknown, tr. fr. Irish by* Frank O'Connor. BIrV; PFIr

Killer Diller. *Unknown.* BluL

Killigrew Wood, The. Norman Dubie. AmPA

Killing a Whale. David Gill. BoAnP

Killing Kiss, The. Thomas Stanley. SCP-2

Killings continue, each second, The. City Psalm. Denise Levertov. PiAm

Kilruddery Hunt, The. Thomas Mozeen. BIrV

Kind[e] are her answers [*or* answeres]. Thomas Campion. BoLoP; LoAs; SCP-2

Kind Friends, you must pity my horrible tale. The Dreary Black Hills. *Unknown.* AmFP

Kind o'er the kinderbank leans Myfanwy. Myfanwy. John Betjeman. BoLoP

Kind of change came in my fate, A. Byron. *Fr.* The Prisoner of Chillon. NOBE

Kind of Love, A. Jeanette Nichols. RiTi

Kind of Poetry I Want, The, *sels.* "Hugh MacDiarmid." InPS
"And, constantly, I seek/ A poetry of facts."
"Poetry of one the Russians call 'a broad nature,' The."

Kind old face, the egg-shaped head, The. On a Portrait of a Deaf Man. John Betjeman. NoAM

Kind pity chokes my spleen; brave scorn forbids. Satires, III. John Donne. PAIC; SCP-1

Kinde are her answeres. *See* Kind are her answers.

Kindergarten. Ronald Rogers. VW

Kindergarten children first come forth, The. The May Day Dancing. Howard Nemerov. NoAM

Kindergarten Teacher. Stanley Kiesel. NowV

Kindness. Sylvia Plath. Psy

Kindred. Douglas Stewart. MAuV

King, The. Douglas Livingstone. BoAnP

King Arthur Growing Very Tired Indeed. Mortimer Collins. FaBoCo

King asked, The. The King's Breakfast. A. A. Milne. OxBChV

King but an his nobles a', The. Brown Robin. *Unknown.* PeBB

King Charles the First. *Unknown.* GBP

King Edward the Fourth and a Tanner of Tamworth. *Unknown.* PeBB

King George, observing with judicious eyes. Epigram. Joseph Trapp. FaBoCo

King had three little sons, The. Lanzarote. *Unknown, tr. by* W. S. Merwin. Epi

King he hath been a prisoner, The. Willie O Winsbury. *Unknown.* PeBB

King he sits in Dumferling town, The. *See* King sits in Dunfermline town, The.

King he wrote a love-letter, The. Lord Derwentwater. *Unknown.* AmFP

King Henry V, *sels.* Shakespeare.
King Henry the Fifth before Agincourt, *fr.* IV, iii. BTTM
King Henry the Fifth before Harfleur, *fr.* III, i. BTTM
("Once more unto the breach, dear friends, once more.") PPoe

King Henry VIII, *sel.* Shakespeare *and probably* John Fletcher.
Sweet Music's Power, *fr.* III, i. Fletcher. NOBE

King I Sit. *Unknown.* OxBM

King Lear, *sels.* Shakespeare.
"Ay, every inch a king:/ When I do stare, see how the subject quakes," *fr.* IV, vi. OBP
"Blow, winds, and crack your cheeks! rage! blow! *fr.* III, ii. OBP
"How does my royal lord? How fares your Majesty?" *fr.* IV, vii. Prf
"It may be so, my lord./ Hear, Nature, hear!" *fr.* I, iv. OBP
"Let it be so; thy truth then be thy dower," *fr.* I, i. OBP
"No, no, no, no! Come, let's away to prison," *fr.* V, iii. OBP
"Thou art a lady;/ If only to go warm were gorgeous," *fr.* II, iv. OBP
"Thou thinkst 'tis much that this contentious storm," *fr.* III, iv. OBP

King Midas Has Asses' Ears. Donald Finkel. CoPAm

King Must Die, The. Bernie Taupin. GrRo

King of China's Daughter, The. Edith Sitwell. RAE

King of Ireland's Cairn, The, *abr.* "Ethna Carbery." WPE

King Oliver of New Orleans. Satchmo. Melvin B. Tolson. BPo

King Pellam's Launde. David Jones. In Parenthesis, IV. NoAM

King Richard II, *sels.* Shakespeare.
Death of Kings, The, *fr.* III, ii. GrRo
("Let's talk of graves, of worms, and epitaphs.") PPoe
This England ("This royal throne of kings, this sceptered isle"), *fr.* II, i. VoPo
(England.) BTTM

King sent his lady on the first Yule day, The. The Yule Days. *Unknown.* GBP

King Siegfried sat in his lofty hall. The Three Songs. Bayard Taylor. PoTa

King [he] sits in Dunfermline [*or* Dumferling] town [*or* toune], The. Sir Patrick Spens [*or* Spence]. *Unknown.* AIW; AmFP; Epi; InPK; InPS; NOBE; PAIC; PBMP; PeBB; PPP

King Stephen: a Fragment of a Tragedy. Keats. MBPR

King to Oxford sent a troop of horse, The. Epigram. Sir William Browne. FaBoCo

King was not to think of other days, The. Larder. John Blight. CAAP

King was sick, The. His cheek was red. The Enchanted Shirt. John Hay. PoTa

King William Was King George's Son. *Unknown.* AmFP

King Wind. Mark Van Doren. NCSH

Kingdom Coming, *with music.* Henry Clay Work. BLSo; PSoN

Kingdom of Kali, The. May Sarton. *Fr.* The Invocation to Kali. RiTi

Kingdoms. Oliver St. John Gogarty. RAE

Kingfisher, The. W. H. Davies. NOBE

Kingfisher falls through the dry air, The. Epithalamion. Charles Wright. CoPAm

Kingfishers, The. Charles Olson. NOBA; PiAm

Kingis Quair, The, *sels.* James I, King of Scotland.
"An therewith kest I doun myn eye ageyne." SLP
Nightingale's Song, The. OxBM

Kings/ like golden gleams. A History Lesson. Miroslav Holub, *tr. by* Ian Milner *and* George Theiner. BuTh

King's Breakfast, The. A. A. Milne. OxBChV

King's Dochter Lady Jean, The. *Unknown.* AmFP

Kings kill their messengers. Song to Accompany the Bearer of Bad News. David Wagoner. PPoD

King's Son, The. Thomas Boyd. AIW

Kinmont Willie. *Unknown.* PeBB

Kirk of the Birds, Beasts and Fishes, The. *Unknown.* GBP

Kirov was shot, Solon will rot in jail. Once More. George Jonas. NeAC

Kiss, A. Austin Dobson. *Fr.* Rose-Leaves. PPoD

Kiss, The. Coventry Patmore. *Fr.* The Angel in the House, II, viii. BoLoP; SoSe

Kiss. Al Young. PoBA

Kiss, The: A Dialogue. Robert Herrick. PAIC

"Kiss Grandpa!" you said. Grandpa. James Rankin. MIS

Kiss in the Morning Early, A. *Unknown.* GBP

Kiss Me Again, *with music.* Henry Blossom. BLSo
(If I Were on the Stage, *longer version.*) FSN

Kiss me Quick and Go, *with music.* Silas S. Steele. BLSo

Kiss'd Yestreen. *Unknown.* GBP; POL; SLP

Kisses in the Train. D. H. Lawrence. OBP

Kissie Lee. Margaret Walker. NMM

Kissing and Bussing. Robert Herrick. SoSe

Kissing her hair I sat against her feet. Rondel. Swinburne. PAIC

Kissing of My Dame. *Unknown.* GBP

Kit Carson might be surprised. Imperfect Sympathies. Clarice Short. PPoD

Kitchen patio in snowy, The. One A.M. Denise Levertov. CAPP

Kitchenette Building. Gwendolyn Brooks. BPo

Kite, The. Adelaide O'Keeffe. OxBChV

Kite Is a Victim, A. Leonard Cohen. AKE

Kitten, A. Eleanor Farjeon. RAE

Kitten and Falling Leaves, The, sels. Wordsworth. PCat
"But the kitten, how she starts."
"See the kitten on the wall."

Kitten can, A. Where Knock Is Open Wide. Theodore Roethke. VGW

Kittens have paws they don't have pawses. Just Because. David McCord. ECBV

Kitty Kline. Unknown. AmFP

Kitty Morey. Unknown. AmFP

Kitty of Coleraine. Unknown. PoTa

Kleomedes. David Wright. NoAM

Klunder, people of sensibility. A Necessary Bucket. Peter Meinke. AATT

Knave of darkness, limber in the leaves, The. Death for the Dark Stranger. Thomas McGrath. VGW

Knedneuch land. In the Pantry. "Hugh MacDiarmid." NoAM

Knee Song. Anne Sexton. SFF

Kneegrows niggas. Be Cool, Baby. Rob Penny. PoBA

Kneeling Here, I Feel Good. Marge Piercy. NeAC

Kneeling in the sheepshit. Mountain Oysters. Patrick Lane. NeAC

Knell for Insularity. Merle Meeter. AATT

Knew a poet. W. C. W. David Ray. POL

Knife, The. Keith Douglas. LoAs

Knife and Sap. Kenneth Leslie. POL

Knight, The. Adrienne Rich. PiAm

Knight and a Lady, A. Unknown. ECBV

Knight and the Lady, The. William Cornish. NOBE

Knight and the Shepherd's Daughter, The. Unknown. AmFP

Knight knocked at the castle gate, The. The Knight and the Lady. William Cornish. NOBE

Knight of the Sad Face, The. Rafael Jesús González. MIT

Knight rides into the noon, A. The Knight. Adrienne Rich. PiAm

"Knight there is, A," a lady said. Reward of Service. Unknown, tr. by F. C. Nicholson. LoAs

Knight's Leap, The. Charles Kingsley. PoTa

Knight's Tale, The, sel. Chaucer, tr. fr. Middle English by Nevill Coghill. Fr. The Canterbury Tales.
"In the third hour after Palamon." OBP

Knight's Tomb, The. Samuel Taylor Coleridge. MBPR

Knock last night's softness. Loving. Kathleen Fraser. WBN

Knock on Wood. Henry Dumas. PoBA

Knolege, aquayntance, resort, favour with grace. John Skelton. AAS

Know, that I would accounted be. To Ireland in the Coming Times. W. B. Yeats. NoAM

Know then, my brethren, heaven is clear. Song. Unknown. Fr. The Song of Anarchus. FaBoCo

Know Thyself. Pope. Fr. An Essay on Man, Epistle II. NOBE
("Know then thyself, presume not God to scan.") PPoe

Knowing her is not knowing her. An Afterword: for Gwen Brooks. Don L. Lee. JB

Knowledge of Light, The. Henry Rago. VGW

Knowledge That Comes through Experience, The. Jane Cooper. NMM

Knowledgeable Child, The. L. A. G. Strong. PFIr

Knoxville, Tennessee. Nikki Giovanni. BPo; InPS; PoBA

Knuckles over the flame. Paradigms of Fire. Brian Swann. AmPA

Knyght ther was, and that a worthy man, A. Chaucer. Fr. The Canterbury Tales: Prologue. InPS

Koala. Alan Ross. BoAnP

Koko Oloro. Wole Soyinka. BuTh

Koocoo, The. Unknown. GBP

Kore. Robert Creeley. ConAP; InPK; InPS

Kornelia Woloszczuk. Peter Skrzynecki. CAAP

Kral Majales. Allen Ginsberg. PiAm

Kropotkin Poems, The, sel. Phyllis Webb.
Solitary Confinement. MMD

Ku Klux. Langston Hughes. BPo

Kubla Kahn; or, A Vision in a Dream. Samuel Taylor Coleridge. AKE; AnMo; ECBV; HeIP; InPK; InPS; MAT; MBPR; NOBE; OBP; PBMP; PPoD; PPoe; SoSe; VoPo

Kung walked/ by the dynastic temple. Canto XIII. Ezra Pound. PiAm

Kyoto Born in Spring Song. Gary Snyder. RRA

Kyoto: March. Gary Snyder. PPP

Kyran's Christening. Alden Nowlan. NeAC

"Kyrie," so "Kyrie." Jolly Jankin. Unknown. GBP; NOBE; OxBM

# L

L(a. E. E. Cummings. BBGO

La Bella Bona Roba. Richard Lovelace. LoAs; OBP; SCP-2

La Belle Confidante. Thomas Stanley. SCP-2

La Belle Dame sans Merci. Keats. AIW; AnMo; Epi; InPK; InPS; IPWM; LoAs; MBPR; NOBE; OLR; PAIC; PBMP; PPoD; PPoe; Prf

La Chute. Charles Olson. InPK

La Condition Botanique. Anthony Hecht. NoAM

La Divina Commedia. David Malouf. CAAP

La Figlia Che Piange. T. S. Eliot. AnMo; BuTh; GBL; HeIP; MAT; OxBTC; PiAm; PSN; VGW

La Llorona. Greg Pape. AmPA

La Marche des Machines. A. S. J. Tessimond. MPo

La Paloma, with music. Sebastian Yradier, tr. fr. Spanish. BLSH

La Selva. Cid Corman. VGW

La Vie En Rose. Peter Schjeldahl. CAAP

La Vita Nuova. Weldon Kees. VGW

Label, The. Ruthe T. Spinnanger. AATT

Labour of the Brain, Ballad of the Body. Nicole Forman. NMM

Laboratory, The: Ancien Régime. Robert Browning. LoAs

Laboratory Poem. James Merrill. InPK; MAT; PPoD

Laboring men, please all attend. Free Silver. Unknown. AmFP

Labours of the Months. Unknown. See Months, The.

Labyrinth, The. Edwin Muir. NoAM

Lace grows in her eyes like. Waiting, the Hallways under Her Skin Thick with Dreamchildren. Lyn Lifshin. FAF; NeAC

Lack of Steadfastness. Chaucer. PBMP

Lackying my loue I go from place to place. Amoretti, LXXVIII. Spenser. LoAs

Lacrimas or There Is a Need to Scream. K. Curtis Lyle. PoBA

Lad came to the door at night, The. The True Lover. A. E. Housman. LoAs

Ladder sticking up at the open window, A. Dog-Days. Amy Lowell. FSFS

Ladies and gentlemen/ This is our final word. Nicanor Parra, tr. by Miller Williams. Fr. Manifesto. TSWA

Lads in their hundreds to Ludlow come in for the fair, The. A. E. Housman. OxBTC

Lady Alice, *4 versions*. *Unknown*. AmFP

Lady and the Bear, The. Theodore Roethke. ECBV

Lady and Tiger. *Unknown*. ECBV

Lady-Bird. *See* Ladybird.

Lady-Bug. *See* Ladybug.

Lady, by yonder blessed moon I swear. Shakespeare. *Fr.*
Romeo and Juliet, II, ii. Moon

Lady came to a bear by a stream, A. The Lady and the Bear.
Theodore Roethke. ECBV

Lady Clare. Tennyson. PBMP; PoTa

Lady Comes to an Inn, A. Elizabeth J. Coatsworth. PoTa

Lady comes to the gate, The. Albatross. Judy Collins. GrRo

Lady Diamond. *Unknown*. PeBB

Lady Feeding the Cats, *sel.* Douglas Stewart.
"Shuffling along in her broken shoes from the slums." BoAnP

Lady Fortune, The. *Unknown*. HeIP

Lady Greensleeves. *Unknown*. *See* Greensleeves

Lady, help! Jesu, [*or* Hesu] mercy! Passion of Christ Strengthen
Me [*or* Dread of Death]. John Audelay. BoReV; OxBM

Lady, I Thank Thee. *Unknown*. OxBM

Lady in a Distant Face. James Welch. AmPA

Lady in the Wood, The. *Unknown*. OxBM

Lady Isabel and the Elf-Knight. *Unknown*. PeBB; SLP
(Elfin Knight, The.) AmFP; GBP; PeBB

Lady Isabel and the Elf-Knight (Pretty Polly). *Unknown*. AmFP

Lady Isabella's Tragedy, The. *Unknown*. GBP

Lady, Lady. Anne Spencer. PoBA

Lady, lady, lady fair. The Suffolk Miracle. *Unknown*. AmFP

Lady Lazarus. Sylvia Plath. AnMo; CAPP; ConAP; Epi;
InPK; MAT; NoAM; NOBA; PiAm; PPoe; Psy; VGW

Lady lived in Lancaster, A. Kate and the Cowhide. *Unknown*.
AmFP

Lady Luck. Ann Gottlieb. NMM

Lady Maisery, *with music*. *Unknown*. Epi

Lady Mary Villiers lies, The. Epitaph on the Lady Mary Villiers.
Thomas Carew. NOBA; SCP-2

Lady Moon. Richard Monckton Milnes. OxBChV

Lady Moon. Christina Rossetti. *See* O Lady Moon.

Lady Moon, Lady Moon, where are you roving? Lady Moon.
Richard Monckton Milnes. OxBChV

Lady My Treasure. Sir Philip Sidney. GBL

Lady, of anonymous flesh and face. J. V. Cunningham. CoPAm

Lady of Carlisle, The. *Unknown*. AmFP

Lady of dusk-wood fastnesses. First Praise. William Carlos
Williams. VGW

Lady of light, I would admit a dream. The Burried Lake. Allen
Tate. PiAm

Lady of Shalott, The. Tennyson. NOBE

Lady of the bright coils and curlings. Eire. David O'Bruadair,
*tr. by* Austin Clarke. BIrV

Lady of the crescent moon. Indian Love Letter. Soge Track.
VW

Lady of the Lake, The, *sel.* Sir Walter Scott.
Soldier, Rest! *fr.* I. NOBE

Lady of the Manor, The. George Crabbe. *Fr.* The Parish
Register: Burials, Pt. III. NOBE

Lady Prayeth the Return of Her Lover Abiding on the Seas, The.
*Unknown*. GBL

Lady Sings, The. Milton. *Fr.* Comus. NOBE

Lady stands in her bower door, The. The Twa Magicians.
*Unknown*. GBP; PeBB

Lady, take care; for in the diamond eyes. Light and Dark.
Barbara Howes. CoPAm; RiTi

Lady, the unknown goddess. For the Unknown Goddess.
Elizabeth Brewster. MMD

Lady, this measure of time accept with serene eye. To Eliza, with
a Tulip-fashioned Watch. Robert Baron. SCP-2

Lady Weeping at the Crossroads. W. H. Auden. AIW

Lady, When I Behold the Roses Sprouting. *Unknown*. InPK

Lady Who Loved a Swine, The. *Unknown*. RDB, *with music*
(There Was a Lady Loved a Swine.) GBP

Ladybird, The, *sel.* John Clare.
"Ladybird! Ladybird! Where art thou gone?" RAE

Ladybird, The. *Unknown*. GBP

Lady bird, lady bird, fly away home. Mother Goose. MG

Ladybird! Ladybird! Where art thou gone? John Clare. *Fr.* The
Ladybird. RAE

Ladybirds, The. Edward Lucie-Smith. BoAnP

Ladybug. François Dodat, *tr. fr.* French by Bert *and* Odette
Meyers. BoAnP

Lady's Dressing Room, The. Swift. AnMo

Lady's Farewell, The. Nuño Fernández Torneol, *tr. fr. Medieval
Galician by* Yvor Winters. AIW

Lady's First Song, The. W. B. Yeats. PSN

Lady's Policy, The, *with music*. *Unknown*. RDB

Lady's song in Leap Year, The. *Unknown*. GBP

La Fayette. Samuel Taylor Coleridge. *Fr.* Sonnets on Eminent
Characters. MBPR

Laid in My Quiet Bed. Earl of Surrey. RBMP

Laily Worm and the Machrel of the Sea, The. *Unknown*. PeBB

Laird o' Cockpen, The. Lady Nairne. PoTa; WPE

"Lake, The/ is not encumbered by the swan." The Mutabilities.
Vincent McHugh. MIT

Lake Chemo. James Wilton Rowe. AmFP

Lake Flies of Winnebago, The. Doug Flaherty. HeS

Lake is sky, The. To the Other Side. T. Alan Broughton. FAF

Lake Isle, The. Ezra Pound. FaBoCo

Lake Isle of Innisfree, The. W. B. Yeats. AKE; InPS; IPWM;
NoAM; NOBE; OxBTC

Lake Leman woos me with its crystal face. Byron. *Fr.* Childe
Harold's Pilgrimage, III. InPS

Lake Michigan. David Kherdian. FAF

Lake Michigan Blues. *Unknown*. BluL

Lake of Gaube, The. Swinburne. VPC

Lake on the map of Canada, A. Believing What I Know.
William Stafford. Epi

Lake sunken among, A. Woman Skating. Margaret Atwood.
IHMS

Lalla Rookh, *sels*. Thomas Moore.
"Fly to the desert, fly with me," *fr.* The Story of the Sultana
Nourmahal. BIrV
" 'I never nursed a dear gazelle,' " *fr.* The Fire-Worshippers.
SpRo

Lalla Rookh/ Is a naughty book. On T. Moore's Poems.
*Unknown*. FaBoCo

L'Allegro. Milton. PPP
*Sels.*
"And ever against eating cares." SCP-1
"While the cock with lively din." SCP-1

Lama, The. Ogden Nash. RAE

Lamb, The. Blake. *Fr.* Songs of Innocence. HeIP; InPS;
LAuP; LCL; MBPR; OxBChV; PAIC; RAE; SoSe

Lamb. James Rankin. MIS

Lamb, The. Theodore Roethke. LCL

Lambing. David Campbell. *Fr.* Works and Days. MAuV

Lambs Frolicking Home. Fred Lape. BoAnP

Lambs that learn to walk in snow. First Sight. Philip Larkin.
NCSH; TSWA

Lambton Worm, The. *Unknown*. PeBB

Lame Deer. Joy Harjo. SA

Lament: "My man is a bone ringed with weed." Brenda Chamberlain. WPE

Lament, A: "O world! O life! O time!" Shelley. MBPR; NOBE

Lament: "Someone is dead." Anne Sexton. ConAP; WPE

Lament: "We who are left, how shall we look again." W. W. Gibson. OxBTC

Lament: "What face, in the water." William Carlos Williams. VGW

Lament: "When I was a windy boy and a bit." Dylan Thomas. PPP

Lament City. Thomas Lux. AmPA

Lament for a Cricket Eleven. Kenneth Allott. OxBTC

Lament for Adonis. Bion, *tr. fr. Greek by* John Addington Symonds. Epi

Lament for Art O'Leary. Eibhlin Dubh O'Connell, *tr. fr. Irish by* Eilis Dillon *and* John Montague. BIrV

Lament for Chaucer and Gower. Thomas Hoccleve. *Fr.* De Regimine Principum. OxBM

Lament for Lost Lodgings. Phyllis McGinley. SpRo

Lament for the Death of Eoghan Ruadh O'Neill. Thomas Osborne Davis. PFIr

Lament for the Death of Thomas Davis. Sir Samuel Ferguson. BIrV

Lament for the Great Music, *sel.* "Hugh MacDiarmid." "Yet there is no great problem in the world today." OxBTC

Lament for the Poets. William Dunbar. *See* Timor Mortis Conturbat Me.

Lament for the Priory of Walsingham, A. *Unknown.* GBP

Lament for Thomas MacDonagh. Francis Ledwidge. BIrV

Lament, lament, Sir Isaac Heard. Epitaph on Tuft-Hunter. Thomas Moore. FaBoCo

Lament my losse, my labor, and my payne. Sir Thomas Wyatt. AAS

Lament of My Father, Lakota. Paula Gunn Allen. VW

Lament of the Banana Man. Evan Jones. MPo

Lament of The Border Widow, The. *Unknown.* GBP; PeBB; SLP

Lament of the Cherokee Reservation Indian, The. John D. Loudermilk. PoRo

Lament of the Flowers, The. Jones Very. NOBA

Lament of the Frontier Guard. Li Po, *tr. fr. Chinese by* Ezra Pound. PiAm; VGW

Lament of the Master of Erskine. Alexander Scott. GBL

Lament of the Old Woman of Beare, The. *Unknown, tr. fr. Irish by* Kuno Meyer. Epi
(Hag of Beare, The, *tr. by* John Montague.) BIrV

Lament While Descending a Shaft. *Unknown.* AmFP

Lamentation, A: "Grief, have I denied thee?" Denise Levertov. PiAm

Lamentation of Glumdalclitch, The. Pope. Epi

Lamentation of the Old Pensioner, The. W. B. Yeats. InPK; NoAM; PFIr
(Old Pensioner, The, *diff. version.*) InPK

Lamentations of an Au Pair Girl. Susan Feldman. AmPA

Lamia. Keats. MBPR

L'Amitié et l'Amour. John Swanick Drennan. BIrV

Lamkin ("Bolakins was a very fine mason"). *Unknown.* AmFP

Lamkin ("It's Lamkin was a mason good"). *Unknown.* PeBB

Lammermuir Lilt, The. Forbes Macgregor. MIS

Lamp, The. A. Buttigieg. RAE

Lamp must be replenished, but even then, The. Manfred: a Dramatic Poem. Byron. MBPR

Lamplighter, The. "Seumas O'Sullivan." BIrV

Lamplighter, The. Robert Louis Stevenson. OxBChV

L'An Trentiesme de Mon Eage [*or* Age]. Archibald MacLeish. NoAM; NOBA; PAIC

Lana Turner has collapsed! Poem. Frank O'Hara. CAPP; CoPAm; VGW

Lancashire Born. *Unknown.* GBP

Lancashire Winter. Tony Connor. OxBTC

Lancaster County Tragedy. W. Lowrie Kay. CaYB

Lancelot of the Laik, *sel. Unknown.*
Lancelot's Soliloquy in Prison. SLP

Land and sea. Wordsworth. *Fr.* Ode: Intimations of Immortality from Recollections of Early Childhood. FSFS

Land has sunk to black, The. Pilot. Floyd C. Stuart. FAF

Land I came thro' last was dumb with night, The. Christopher Brennan. *Fr.* The Wanderer. MAuV

Land is an ark, full of things waiting, The. A Wet Time. Wendell Berry. PiAm

Land lies in water; it is shadowed green. The Map. Elizabeth Bishop. NOBA

Land o' the Leal, The. Lady Nairne. SLP

Land of Cockayne, The. *Unknown.* OxBM
(Land of Cockaigne, The, *tr. fr. Middle English by* John Montague.) BIrV

Land of Counterpane, The. Robert Louis Stevenson. ECBV; OxBChV

Land of leaning ice, A. North Labrador. Hart Crane. POL

Land of the Silver Birch, *with music. Unknown.* AKE

Land was ours before we were the land's, The. The Gift Outright. Robert Frost. NoAM; NOBA; PPP

Landing, The. Daniel Halpern. AmPA

Landing of the Pilgrim Fathers in New England, The. Felicia Dorothea Hemans. BTTM; ECBV; SBG; WPE

Landing on the Moon. May Swenson. Moon

Landlady, The. Margaret Atwood. Psy

Landlord, landlord. Ballad of the Landlord. Langston Hughes. NOBA

Land's End. Daniel J. Langton. MIT

Landscape, Deer Season. Barbara Howes. MiP; POL

Landscape 4. Robert Gray. CAAP

Landscape near an Aerodrome, The. Stephen Spender. IPWM; NoAM; OxBTC

Landscape was, The. Canto 5: Coon Fire. Tom Weatherly. PoBA

Landscape with Pervert. Bink Noll. PPoD

Landscape with the Fall of Icarus. William Carlos Williams. Pictures from Brueghel, II. BBGO; PPP; WIF

Lane Is the Pretty One. Lucille Clifton. CAAP

Laneliet Place in the Warld, The. Donald Campbell. MIS

Language, The. Robert Creeley. CAPP; IPWM; LoAs; PiAm

Lanky hank of a she in the inn over there, The. A glass of Beer. James Stephens, *after* O'Bruaidair. FaBoCo; NCSH; NoAM; OxBTC; SoSe

Lantern Out of Doors, The. Gerard Manley Hopkins. AnMo

Lanty Leary. Samuel Lover. PFIr

Lanzarote. *Unknown, tr. fr. Spanish by* W. S. Merwin. Epi

Laodamia. Wordsworth. MBPR

Lapis Lazuli. W. B. Yeats. AnMo; InPK; InPS; MAT; NoAM; NOBE; OBP; PPoe; WIF

Lapsus Linguae. Richard Howard. NoAM

Larder. John Blight. CAAP

Largest stock of armaments allows me, The. Civilian. Josephine Miles. WPE

Lariat snaps, The; the cowboy rolls. The Closing of the Rodeo. William Jay Smith. PPoD

Lark, The ("Liverockie, liverockie lee"). *Unknown.* GBP

Lark, The ("Malisons, malisons more than ten"). *Unknown.* GBP

Lark now leaves his watery [*or* wat'ry] nest, The. Aubade [*or* Song]. Sir William Davenant. GBL; LoAs; NOBE

Lars Porsena of Clusium. Horatius. Macaulay. *Fr.* Lays of Ancient Rome. BTTM

L'Art, 1910. Ezra Pound. HeIP

Las Trampas U.S.A. Charles Tomlinson. TwMBP

LaSalle Street. Rachel Albright. ANTL

Laser. A. R. Ammons. NOBA

Lashes of my eye are clipped away, The. Cataract. Margoret J. Smith. PPoD

Lass from Bally-na-Lee, The. Anthony Raftery, *tr. fr. Irish by* Desmond O'Grady. BIrV

Lass of Richmond Hill, The, *with music.* Leonard McNally. BLSo

Lass of Roch Royal, The. *Unknown.* AmFP

Lass That Made the Bed to Me, The. Burns. OBP

Lassitude. Mathilde Blind. SBG

Last and greatest herald of Heaven's King. Saint John Baptist. William Drummond of Hawthornden. NOBE; OBP

Last Confession, A. W. B. Yeats. BoLoP

Last Day and the First, The. Theodore Weiss. LoAs; VGW

Last Days of Alice. Allen Tate. NoAM; NOBA; PiAm

Last decent man alive, The. Across to the Peloponnese. James Welch. CDW

Last Drink, A. *Unknown.* OxBM

Last Easter I was married, that night I went to bed. The Lowlands of Holland. *Unknown.* AmFP

Last Fierce Charge, The. *Unknown.* AmFP

Last Fruit off an Old Tree, The, *sel.* Walter Savage Landor. On His Seventy-Fifth Birthday. PBMP
(Dying Speech of an Old Philosopher.) HeIP
("I strove with none, for none was worth my strife.") NOBE

Last Gangster, The. Gregory Corso. CoPAm; SA

Last Instructions to a Painter, The, *sels.* Andrew Marvell. SCP-1
"Hyde stamps, and straight upon the ground the swarms."
"Monk from the bank the dismal sight does view."
"Paint Castlemain in colours that will hold."
"Ruyter the while, that had our ocean curbed."

Last Journey. Enrique Gonzales Martinez, *tr. fr. Spanish by* Samuel Beckett. PBMP

Last Lap, The. Kipling. OxBTC

Last Lauch. Douglas Young. FaBoCo

Last Leaf, The. Oliver Wendell Holmes. AmVn; PiAm; VoPo

Last Letter to the Scholar. Jean Garrigue. LoAs

Last Light. Robert Kelly. VGW

Last light muffles itself in cloud and goes, The. Mise en Scène. Robert Fitzgerald. VGW

Last Lines. Emily Brontë. BoReV; NOBE; OBP
(No Coward Soul Is Mine.) HeIP; PFD; VoPo

Last Lines—1916. Padraic Pearse. PFIr; WIF

Last Look at La Plata, Missouri. Jim Barnes. CDW

Last Look Round St. Martin's Fair. Thomas Hardy. OBP

Last Love. Fyodor Tyutchev, *tr. fr. Russian by* Vladimir Nabokov. BoLoP

Last Monster, The. John Montague. WIF

Last Month. John Ashbery. CAPP

Last month in your little Roman house, The. On the Death of Keats. John Logan. Prf

Last Night. David Ignatow. VGW

Last night. After Selecting the Wedding Invitations. Diane Levenberg. NPW

Last night a freezing cottontail. Twin Lakes Hunter. A. B. Guthrie, Jr. PoTa

Last night, ah, yesternight, betwixt her lips and mine. Non Sum Qualis Eram Bonae Sub Regno Cynarae. Ernest Dowson. BoLoP; GBL; HeIP; LoAs; NOBE; VoPo

Last night and the night before. Robbers. *Unknown.* ECBV

Last night did Christ the Sun rise from the dark. Easter Sunday. Sedulius Scottus, *tr. by* Helen Waddell. OFD

Last night I dreamed. The Night-Apple. Allen Ginsberg. NoAM

Last night I dreamed a dream. Death and the Lover. *Unknown, tr. by* W. S. Merwin. Epi

Last night I heard wolves howling. Wolves. John Haines. BoAnP

Last night I licked. In Celebration. Ellen Bass. NMM

Last night I spoke to a dead woman with green face. Last Night. David Ignatow. VGW

Last night I watched my brother play. The Brothers. Edwin Muir. HeIP

Last Night in Calcutta. Allen Ginsberg. NoAM

Last night it rained. Amy Lowell. TH

Last night we sat with the stereopticon. Readings of History. Adrienne Rich. ConAP

Last night we slept in Miami in the house of. September 30. Dick Lourie. NeAC

Last night we started with some dry vermouth. Ballade of Liquid Refreshment. E. C. Bentley. FaBoCo

Last night you would not come. Love Poem. John Logan. CAPP; CoPAm

Last November in a Field. James Wright. CAPP

Last of the Chiefs. Nathaniel Tarn. TwMBP

Last of the Flock, The. Wordsworth. MBPR

Last of the Light Brigade, The. Kipling. BTTM

Last of the Poet's Car. Tony O'Connor. OxBTC

Last of the poets, first of the undead. The Mole. Dennis Schmitz. AmPA

Last on legs, last on sax. "Bird Lives": Charles Parker in St. Louis. Michael S. Harper. AmPA

Last One, The. W. S. Merwin. CoPAm; NoAM; VGW

Last out in the raining weather, a girl and I. The Day the Weather Broke. Alastair Reid. SLP

Last Patch of Snow. George Abbe. FAF

Last Picnic, The. Stanley Kunitz. NoAM

Last Poem. Charles Donnelly. BIrV

Last Quarter. John Hollander. Moon

Last Quatrain of the Ballad of Emmet Till, The. Gwendolyn Brooks. CAPP; PoBA; WPE

Last Refuge, The. Augustus Young. BIrV

Last Ride Together, The. Robert Browning. BoLoP

Last Ride Together, The. James Kenneth Stephen. FaBoCo

Last Rites. Christina Rossetti. OxBChV

Last seeds, The. Flitcraft's Woods. Warren Woessner. HeS

Last settlement scraggled out with a barbed wire fence, The. The Flight in the Desert. William Everson. VGW

Last Snow. Andrew Young. OxBTC

Last Sonnet. Keats. *See* Bright Star! Would I Were Steadfast as Thou Art.

Last summer, in the blue heat. La Vita Nuova. Weldon Kees. VGW

Last Sunday petrified. Wingwalking in Oregon. Robert Peterson. MIT; NeAC

Last Supper, The. Rainer Maria Rilke, *tr. fr. German by* M. D. Herter Norton. OFD

Last, the fatal hour is come, The. Thomas Campbell. *Fr.* Gilderoy. SLP

Last Things. William Meredith. NoAM

Last Things, Black Pines at 4 a.m. Robert Lowell. NOBA

Last time I saw Donald Armstrong, The. The Performance. James Dickey. ConAP; NoAM; NOBA

Last time i was home, The. Mothers. Nikki Giovanni. CTBA

Last View, The. Ruthe T. Spinnanger. AATT

Last Warmth of Arnold, The. Gregory Corso. NoAM; SA

Last week a new dentist.  Loyal Citizen.  Richard Lyons.  HeS

Last Week I Took a Wife, *with music.*  M. Kelly.  BLSo

Last Will and Testament.  Alvin Aubert.  CoPAm

Last Word, The.  Matthew Arnold.  NOBE; PBMP

Last Word, The.  Peter Davison.  InPK

Last Word, A.  W. R. Rodgers.  Epi

Last Word of a Bluebird, The.  Robert Frost.  LCL; RAE

Last Words.  Emily Brontë.  WPE

Last Words.  Sylvia Plath.  RiTi

Last Words, 1968.  Lance Henson.  CDW

Last words of Shaw, The: "I'm going to die."  Alan Bold.  POL

Last Words to a Dumb Friend.  Thomas Hardy.  PCat

Lastly, stood War, in glittering arms yclad.  The Shield of War.  Thomas Sackville.  *Fr.* Mirror for Magistrates.  NOBE

Lat take a cat and fostre hym wel with milk.  Mice before Milk.  Chaucer.  *Fr.* The Canterbury Tales: The Manciple's Tale.  PCat

Late.  Louise Bogan.  VGW

Late Abed.  Archibald MacLeish.  NCSH

Late Air.  Elizabeth Bishop.  LoAs

Late April and you are three; today.  W. D. Snodgrass.  *Fr.* Heart's Needle.  CoPAm

Late at night.  First Camp.  Greg Kuzma.  NVAP

Late at Night.  William Stafford.  POL; RFM

Late Aubade, A.  Richard Wilbur.  PAIC; SoSe

Late August.  Margaret Atwood.  MMD

Late-born and woman-souled I dare not hope.  Echoes.  Emma Lazarus.  SBG

Late-Flowering Lust.  John Betjeman.  PAIC

Late lark twitters from the quiet skies, A.  Margaritae Sorori.  William Ernest Henley.  *Fr.* Echoes.  NOBE

Late Last Night.  Arthur Gregor.  VGW

Late Last Night.  Langston Hughes.  NoAM

Late last night I killed my wife.  Necessity.  Harry Graham.  FaBoCo

Late last night I was a-making my rounds.  Bad Man Ballad.  *Unknown.*  AmFP

Late lies the wintry sun a-bed.  Winter Time.  Robert Louis Stevenson.  OxBChV

Late Miss H. came to us Wednesday at four, The.  Swansong.  Carol Muske.  AmPA

Late, my grandson! half the morning have I paced these sandy tracts.  Locksley Hall, Sixty Years After.  Tennyson.  PFD

Late Saturday afternoons in Emeryville.  Butcherboy.  Tom Schmidt.  NeAC

Late Spring: a Heaving, a Turning.  John Gill.  NeAC

Late Spring Day in My Life, A.  Robert Bly.  NCSH

Late Visitor, The.  Ann Stanford.  PPoD

Lately I become.  Names.  Lyn Lifshin.  FAF

Lately, I've become accustomed to the way.  Preface to a Twenty Volume Suicide Note.  LeRoi Jones.  CAPP; InPK; InPS; IPWM; PAIC; PoBA; PPP; TCP

Later there would be miles, hills, a country, a world.  Under Way.  Bruce Dawe.  CAAP

Latest Decalogue, The.  Arthur Hugh Clough.  BoReV; FaBoCo; IPWM; NOBE; PBMP; PPP; SoSe; SS; VPC

Latest poems, like the most recent, The.  Dispatch Number Sixteen.  Doug Fetherling.  NeAC

Latitude, Longitude.  George Oppen.  CAPP

Lauds and Plaints, *sels.*  Bruce Beaver.  CAAP
  "Beautiful face of Paul Delvaux, The."
  "For first the abiding."
  "In and out of the streets."

Laughing Child.  Carl Sandburg.  CTBA

Laughing Faces of Pigs, The.  Fred Lape.  BoAnP

Laughing god born of a startling answer, The.  Bacchus.  William Empson.  NoAM

Laughing Song.  Blake.  *Fr.* Songs of Innocence.  LAuP; MBPR; OxBChV
  (Laughter.)  ECBV

Laughs not the heart, when giants, big with pride.  The Apology Addressed to the Critical Reviewers.  Charles Churchill.  LAuP

Laughter.  Blake.  *See* Laughing Song.

Laughter of children brings.  Early Supper.  Barbara Howes.  NCSH

Launcelot with Bicycle.  Phyllis McGinley.  SS

Launch, The.  Alice Meynell.  WPE

Laundrette.  Liz Lochhead.  MIS

Laura.  Thomas Campion.  *See* Rose-cheeked Laura, Come.

Laureate, The.  Robert Graves.  BIrV

Laurence Bloomfield in Ireland, *sel.*  William Allingham.  Eviction, The.  BIrV

Lava Bed.  William Everson.  PiAm

Lavender Kitten, The.  Alonzo Lopez.  VW

Lavinia at Church.  Edward Young.  *Fr.* Love of Fame, the Universal Passion.  BoReV

Law Against Lovers, The, *sel.*  Sir William Davenant.  "Wake all the dead! what ho! what ho!"  OBP; SCP-2

Law I Love Is Major Mover, The.  Robert Duncan.  PiAm

Law in the Country of the Cats.  Ted Hughes.  NowV

Law Like Love.  W. H. Auden.  PBMP

Law makes long spokes of the short stakes of men.  Legal Fiction.  William Empson.  InPK; NoAM

Law of Falling and Catching Up, The.  Cathleen Quirk.  MMD

Law, say the gardeners, is the sun.  Law Like Love.  W. H. Auden.  PBMP

Law there is of ancient fame, A.  Tit for Tat: A Tale.  John Aikin.  OxBChV

Lawd, I'm broke and hungry, ragged and dirty, too.  Ragged and Dirty.  *Unknown.*  AmFP

Lawn, The.  Robert Herrick.  LoAs

Lawrence—not the bearded one—the one.  Any Complaints?  Vernon Scannell.  OxBTC

Laws of God, The.  A. E. Housman.  PPP
  ("Laws of God, the laws of man, The.")  OBP

Laws of the bronze gods, The.  Cheap Rent.  Carl Sandburg.  PiAm

Lawyer Clark Blues.  *Unknown.*  BluL

Lawyer Dickinson's spinsterly daughter.  Occupation: Spinster.  Olga Cabral.  WBN

Lay a garland on my hearse of the dismal yew.  Aspatia's Song.  Beaumont *and* Fletcher.  *Fr.* The Maid's Tragedy.  GBL; NOBE

Lay down these words.  Riprap.  Gary Snyder.  NOBA; PPoD

Lay her and lea her here i the gantan grund.  The Shepherd's Dochter.  Douglas Young.  SLP

Lay of Oliver Gogarty, The.  William Dawson.  PeBB

Lay of the Honeysuckle, The.  Marie de France, *tr. fr. French by* Robin Johnson.  WPE

Lay of the Last Minstrel, The, *sel.*  Sir Walter Scott.
  "Breathes there the man, with soul so dead," *fr.* VI  SoSe
  (Innominatus.)  PBMP
  (Native Land.)  SFF
  (Patriotism.)  NOBE
  (This Is My Own, My Native Land.)  BTTM

Lay of the Lovelorn, The.  William E. Aytoun *and* Sir Theodore Martin.  FaBoCo

Lay Preacher Ponders, The.  Idris Davies.  OxBTC

Lay to Eliza, The.  Spenser.  *Fr.* The Shepheardes Calendar: April.  NOBE

Lay Your Arms Aside. Pierce Ferriter, *tr. fr. Irish by* Eilean Ni Chuilleanain. BIrV

Lay your sleeping head, my love. Lullaby. W. H. Auden. BoLoP; NoAM; NOBE; OxBTC; PPP; PSN

Lays of Ancient Rome, *sel.* Macaulay. Horatius. BTTM

Laziness and Silence. Robert Bly. PPP

Lazy laughing languid Jenny. Jenny. Dante Gabriel Rossetti. VPC

Lazy Mary. *Unknown.* AmFP

Lazy sheep, pray tell me why. The Sheep. Ann *or* Jane Taylor. OxBChV

Le Chariot. John Wieners. VGW

Le Rêve. Edgar Bowers. ConAP

Le Monocle de Mon Oncle. Wallace Stevens. NoAM

Lead. Jayne Cortez. PoBA

Lead, Kindly Light. Cardinal Newman. *See* Pillar of the Cloud, The.

Leaden Echo and the Golden Echo, The. Gerard Manley Hopkins. PAIC

Leaden-eyed, The. Vachel Lindsay. PBMP; SFF

Leaden Treasury of English Verse, A, *sel.* Paul Dehn. "Jenny kiss'd me when we met." SpRo

Leaders of the Crowd, The. W. B. Yeats. SFF

Leads nowhere, cannot be entered. The Street. Ken Smith. TwMBP

Leaf Out of a Rhyming Diary. Hugh McCrae. MAuV

Leaf Treader, A. Robert Frost. BBGO

Leafing through. Looking for Lola. Morgan Sanders. WBN

Leaflets. Adrian Mitchell. NowV

Leaflets. Adrienne Rich. NoAM

Leaflight. Dorothy Donnelly. NCSH

Leafy-with-love banks and the green waters of the canal. Canal Bank Walk. Patrick Kavanagh. NoAM

Leaning into the edge of the earth. Summer's Darkness. Elizabeth Hanson. NPW

Leaning on the Everlasting Arms, *with music.* Elisha A. Hoffman. BLSH

Lear. William Carlos Williams. NOBA

Learn'd lapidaries say the diamond. To Cynthia: Learn'd Lapidaries. Sir Francis Kynaston. SCP-2

Learn'd society of late, A. Samuel Butler. *Fr.* The Elephant in the Moon: a Satire. SCP-2

Learning. Marie Harris. MMD

Learning By Doing. Howard Nemerov. NowV

Learning the Spells: A Diptych. Anita Endrezze Probst. CDW

Leather belt white shirt black pants. Telegram. Dick Lourie. NeAC

Leathery, wry and rough. Rodeo. Edward Lueders. SPo

Leave go my hands, let me catch breath and see. In the Orchard. Swinburne. BoLoP

Leave it for the papers. Keep It under Your Hat. Gary Margolis. CoPAm

Leave It to Me Blues. Joel Oppenheimer. VGW

Leave Me, O Love. Sir Philip Sidney. *Sometimes considered Sonnet CX of* Astrophel and Stella. HeIP; PPP ("Leave me, O Love, which reachest but to dust.") GBL (Splendidis Longum Valedico Nugis.) BoReV; LoAs; NOBE

Leave my eyes. And Who Are You? June Jordan. RiTi

Leave-taking, A. Swinburne. NOBE

Leave the bars lying in the grass. Fall. Robert Francis. VGW

Leave Us Alone. Tadeusz Rozewicz, *tr. fr. Polish by* Czeslaw Milosz. BuTh

Leaves. Sam Hamod. SA

Leaves bed the woods. Near Caledonia. Patricia Henley. NPW

Leaves Compared with Flowers. Robert Frost. NOBA

Leaves from the ancient forest gleam. The Princes' Land. Les A. Murray. MAuV

Leaves hang like fruit in your eyes, autumn cat, The. The Cat. Helen Wolfert. RiTi

Leaves Like Fish. Gladys Cardiff. CDW

Leaving beer and apples. For a Friend. Lyn Lifshin. Psy; NeAC

Leaving Something Behind. David Wagoner. CoPAm

Leaving the Atocha Station. John Ashbery. CAPP

Leaving the bird house. Responses. Robert Hershon. POL

Leaving the Country House to the Landlord, Five Years Later. Wesley McNair. FAF

Leaving the Flag Out All Night. Napoleon St. Cyr. FAF

Leaving the Motel. W. D. Snodgrass. PiAm

Leaving the Prison. Joseph Bruchac. FAF

Leaving Them, Letting the Farm Swallow. Lyn Lifshin. FAF

Leaving them, running. 28 VIII 69. Laura Chester. IHMS

Leaving, to where it was that. The Way it Happens to You. Harold Bond. NVAP

Leaving Town Blues. *Unknown.* BluL

Leavings. Barbara A. Holland. WBN

Lecture before a Lecture on Pushkin. George M. Young, Jr. FAF

Lecture Hall. Patrick Kavanagh. NoAM

Lecture Upon the Shadow, A. John Donne. Epi; InPK

Lecture with Slides, Film Clips and Tape. Marilyn Krysl. NPW

Lecturer Seeks a Wife, The. George M. Young, Jr. FAF

Lectures on the Biology of the Shadow. George M. Young, Jr. FAF

Leda. Mona Van Duyn. NMM

Leda and the Swan. W. B. Yeats. AnMo; Epi; HeIP; InPK; NoAM; NOBE; NowV; OBP; PAIC; PPoD; PPoe; PPP; PSN; SoSe; TCP

Leda Reconsidered. Mona Van Duyn. NMM

L'Education Sentimentale. David Malouf. CAAP

Lee-ers of Hew. James Cunningham. JB

Leering across Pearl Street. Trouble. James Wright. InPK

Leesome Brand. *Unknown.* PeBB

Left/ Forward! He's the leanest in the shower. Soccer. Andrei Voznesensky, *tr. by* Anselm Hollo. SPo

Left Folkestone 5 p.m. Excerpts from a Diary of a War. John Daniel. TwMBP

Left leg flung out, head cocked to the right. Poet. Karl Shapiro. NoAM

Left like water in glasses overnight. Love from My Father. Carole Gregory Clemmons. PoBA

Left side of her world is gone, The. Strokes. William Stafford. ConAP

Left to themselves people. Revolutionary Letter # 4. Diane DiPrima. RiTi

Leg over leg. *Unknown.* MG

Legacies. Nikki Giovanni. CTBA

Legacy. Gena Ford. IHMS

Legacy. LeRoi Jones. NoAM; NOBA; PoBA

Legacy: My South. Dudley Randall. PoBA

Leg-acy of a Blue Capricorn. James Cunningham. JB

Legal children of a literary man, The. Relationships. Mona Van Duyn. RiTi

Legal Fiction. William Empson. InPK; NoAM

Legend. Hart Crane. NoAM

Legend. Jules Laforgue, *tr. fr. French by* Louis Simpson. Prf

Legend. Judith Wright. PoTa

Legend of Good Women, The: Prologue, *sels.* Chaucer. "And as for me, though that I konne but lyte." HeIP

Balade: "Hide, Absalon [or Absalom], thy gilte tresses clear."
GBL
("Hide, Absalon, thy gilte tresses clere.") OxBM
Old Books. OxBM
Legend of Lake Okeefinokee, The. Laura E. Richards. ECBV
Legend of Paper Plates, The. John Haines. PPoD
Legend of the Hive, A. Robert Stephen Hawker. VPC
Legend of Versailles, A. Melvin B. Tolson. BPo
Legende. Hart Crane. PSN
Legion Club, The, sel. Swift.
"As I strole the city, oft I." BIrV
Legs, The. Robert Graves. NoAM
Legs!/ How we have suffered each other. Poem in Which My
Legs Are Accepted. Kathleen Fraser. AmPA; NMM; RiTi
Legs of the elk punctured the snow's crust, The. To Christ Our
Lord. Galway Kinnell. InPK; MiP; RFM
Legsby, Lincolnshire. Unknown. GBP
Leisure. W. H. Davies. ECBV; NOBE; WIF
L'Elisir d'Amore. Dallas E. Wiebe. MAT
Lemmings, The. John Masefield. NoAM
Lemon Balm. Marie Harris. MMD
Lemonade. Unknown. GBP
Lemons. Patricia Hubbell. ECBV
Lemons, Lemons. Al Young. HeIP; PiAm
Lemuel's Blessing. W. S. Merwin. CAPP; TCP
L'Enfant Glacé. Harry Graham. FaBoCo
Lenore, 3 versions. Poe. WIF
Lenox Avenue is a big street. Keep on Pushing. David
Henderson. PoBA
Lenox Avenue Mural. Langston Hughes. CoPAm
Sels.
Harlem ("What happens to a dream deferred"). HeIP; InPS;
PBMP
(Dream Deferred.) InPK; PoBA; PPP; SoSe; WIF
Same in Blues. InPS; WIF
Lent Lily, The. A. E. Housman. FSFS
Lenten is come with love to towne. Spring. Unknown. OxBM
L'Envoi: "Here we are for the last time face to face." William
Morris. Fr. The Earthly Paradise. VPC
Lepanto. G. K. Chesterton. BTTM
Leper, The. Swinburne. GBL
Leroy. LeRoi Jones. BPo; PiAm; PoBA
Les Etiquettes Jaunes. Frank O'Hara. CAPP
Les Luths. Frank O'Hara. NoAM; NOBA
Les Sylphides. Louis MacNeice. BoLoP; BuTh; PSN
Lesbia loads me night and day with her curses. Catullus, tr. fr.
Latin by Peter Whigham. BoLoP
Lesbian Poem. Robin Morgan. IHMS
Lesbia's sparrow. Catullus, tr. fr. Latin by Peter Whigham.
TwMBP
Lesbos. Sylvia Plath. RiTi
Less and Less Human, O Savage Spirit. Wallace Stevens.
IPWM; VGW
Less Nonsense. A. P. Herbert. OxBTC
Less Passionate the long war throws. The Long War. Laurie
Lee. BuTh
Less said the better. Missing. John Pudney. OxBTC
Less than Love. Aileen Campbell Nye. SLP
Lesson, The. Miroslav Holub, tr. fr. Czech by Ian Milner and
George Theiner. LP
Lesson, The. Edward Lucie-Smith. BuTh; LP; MPo; NCSH;
OxBTC
Lesson for Mamma, A. Sydney Dayre. OxBChV
Lesson from Jim Crane. Barbara Earl Thomson. AATT
Lesson in Love, A. Philip Hobsbaum. OxBTC
Lesson of the Master. William Dickey. CoPAm

Lessons of the War. Henry Reed. HeIP
Sels.
Judging Distances, II. BoLoP; NOBE; PSN; SoSe
Naming of Parts, I. InPK; InPS; MPo; NOBE; OxBTC;
PPoD; SoSe; VoPo
Lest men suspect your tale to be untrue. The Devil's Advice to
Story-Tellers. Robert Graves. NoAM
Let all the fish that swim the sea. Herring Is King. Alfred
Perceval Graves. PFIr
Let all who will. Militant. Langston Hughes. PoBA
Let Bachus to Venus libations pour forth. "Vive La Compagnie."
Unknown. PSoN
Let By Rain. Edward Taylor. NOBA
Let dogs delight to bark and bite. Against Quarrelling and
Fighting. Isaac Watts. OxBChV
"Let Earth give thanks," the deacon said. Simon Sogg's
Thanksgiving. W. A. Croffut. PoTa
Let go of the present and death. Once Again. Liz Sohappy
Bahe. CDW; VW
Let Heroes Account to Love. Alan Dugan. NoAM
Let him answer as he will. The Companion. E. A. Robinson.
NoAM
Let him rail on, let his invective Muse. Dryden. Fr. Absalom
and Achitophel, Pt. II. OBP
Let him who may. To Be Recited to Flossie on Her Birthday.
William Carlos Williams. VGW
Let holy saints, now safely out. After Bad Dreams. George
Garrett. CoPAm
Let it be alleys. Let it be a hall. A Lovely Love. Gwendolyn
Brooks. BPo
Let it be so; thy truth then be thy dower. Shakespeare. Fr.
King Lear, I, i. OBP
Let it disturb no more at first. Fountain. Elizabeth Jennings.
WPE
Let It Go. William Empson. OxBTC; PSN
Let man's soul be a sphere, and then in this. Good Friday, 1613.
Riding Westward. John Donne. AnMo; PPP
Let me alone, I prithee, in this cell. Everard Guilpin. Fr.
Skialetheia. TVS
Let me be at the place of the castle. Psalm Concerning the
Castle. Denise Levertov. PiAm; WPE
Let me be formed with stone. Instructions for the Erection of a
Statue of Myself in Central Park. Colette Inez. RiTi
Let Me Be Held When the Longing Comes. Stephany Fuller.
BPO
Let me be my own fool. A Counterpoint. Robert Creeley.
CoPAm
Let me be the mane that swings. Poem for a Singer. Milton
Acorn. NeAC
Let me be what I am as Virgil cold. An Elegy. Ben Jonson.
SCP-1
Let me be your wiggler until your wobbler comes. Jacksonville
Blues. Unknown. BluL
Let me call a ghost. Song of Three Smiles. W. S. Merwin.
NOBA; VGW
Let me celebrate you. A Dialogue of Watching. Kenneth
Rexroth. MiP
Let Me Die a Youngman's Death. Roger McGough. BuTh; LP
Let Me Enjoy. Thomas Hardy. NoAM
Let me not die for ever, when I'm gone. A Wish. Fanny
Kemble. WPE
Let me not go anywhere. Poem Composed in Rogue River Park...
Tom Wayman. POL
Let me not to the marriage of true minds. Sonnets, CXVI.
Shakespeare. Epi; GBL; HeIP; InPK; InPS; IPWM;
NOBE; OBP; PBMP; PPoe; PPP; SoSe; VoPo
Let Me Out. Michael Benedikt. CAAP

Let me pour [*or* powre] forth. A Valediction: Of Weeping. John Donne. HeIP; MetP; SCP-1

Let me put it this way. George Jonas. NeAC

Let me say (in anger) that since the day we were married. The Crisis. Robert Creeley. PPP

Let me see if Philip can. The Story of Fidgety Philip. Heinrich Hoffmann, *tr. fr. German.* OxBChV

Let me take this other glove off. In Westminster Abbey. John Betjeman. BoReV; FaBoCo; InPK

Let me take you down. Strawberry Fields Forever. John Lennon *and* Paul McCartney. GrRo

Let Me Tell You. Miller Williams. CoPAm

Let me tell you a little story. Miss Gee. W. H. Auden. OxBTC

Let No Charitable Hope. Elinor Wylie. Psy; SBG; VGW

Let no man boste of cunning nor vertù. Like a Midsummer Rose. John Lydgate. OxBM

Let not young souls be smothered out before. The Leaden-eyed. Vachel Lindsay. PBMP; SFF

Let observation with extensive view. The Vanity of Human Wishes: The Tenth Satire of Juvenal, Imitated. Samuel Johnson. ESaP; HeIP; LAuP

Let Other People Come as Streams. Charles Reznikoff. VGW

Let others sing of knights and palladin[e]s. Samuel Daniel. *Fr.* To Delia. AAS; NOBE

Let school-masters puzzle their brain. Song. Goldsmith. *Fr.* She Stoops to Conquer. BIrV

Let sleep take her, let sleep take her, let sleep. Fourth Song the Night Nurse Sang. Robert Duncan. VGW

Let Sporus tremble—"What? That thing of silk." Sporus. Pope. *Fr.* Epistle to Dr. Arbuthnot. NOBE

Let the bird of loudest lay. The Phoenix and the Turtle. Shakespeare. NOBE

Let the boy try along this bayonet-blade. Arms and the Boy. Wilfred Owen. OBP; PBMP

Let the Brothels of Paris Be Opened. Blake. Epi; MBPR

Let the crows go by hawking their caw and caw. River Roads. Carl Sandburg. VGW

Let the damned ride their earwigs to Hell, but let me not join them. Rock Pilgrim. Herbert Palmer. OxBTC

Let the day glare: O memory, your tread. Ode to Fear. Allen Tate. PAIC

Let the rain kiss you. April Rain Song. Langston Hughes. LCL

Let the rain plunge radiant. The Way Through. Denise Levertov. CoPAm

Let the shark keep to the shelves and closets of coral. From a litany. Mark Strand. PPP

Let the sloughs back up and history. Spring for all Seasons. James Welch. SA

Let the tale's sailor from a Christian voyage. Altarwise by Owl-Light, X. Dylan Thomas. Epi; NoAM

Let the wealthy and great. A Farmer's Life. *Unknown.* RAE

Let them bestow on every airth a limb. On Himself, upon Hearing What Was His Sentence. James Graham, Marquis of Montrose. SCP-2

Let them bury your big eyes. Elegy. Edna St. Vincent Millay. *Fr.* Memorial to D.C. LoAs

Let them count scalps under the barroom wall. Lying in a Yuma Saloon. Jim Barnes. CDW

Let them keep it. And Was Not Improved. Lerone Bennett, Jr. PoBA

Let there be light in all the nightmare places. Benediction. William R. Mitchell. AATT

Let those whose low delights to earth are given. Faith, Hope, and Charity. Giovanni Battista Guarini, *tr. by* Samuel Taylor Coleridge. MBPR

Let tyrants shake their iron rod. Chester. William Billings. BLSo

Let uh revolution come. uh. U Name This One. Carolyn M. Rodgers. NMM; PoBA

Let us abandon then our gardens and go home. Justice Denied in Massachusetts. Edna St. Vincent Millay. RiTi; SBG

Let Us All be Unhappy on Sunday. Lord Neaves. FaBoCo

Let us begin and portion out these sweets. A Girtonian Funeral. *Unknown.* FaBoCo

Let Us Believe. Hildegarde Flanner. WPE

Let us consider the skeleton inside the body. Three Lectures on the Skeleton. George M. Young, Jr. FAF

Let us drink and be merry, dance, joke, and rejoice. The Epicure, Sung by One in the Habit of a Town Gallant. Thomas Jordan. NOBE

Let us for this love. Paradox. Tom McGrath. SLP

Let us forgive Ty Kendricks. Southern Cop. Sterling A. Brown. WIF

Let us give up our trips. Direction. Barbara Guest. WPE

Let us go hence, my songs; she will not hear. A Leave-taking. Swinburne. NOBE

Let us go then, you and I. The Love Song of J. Alfred Prufrock. T. S. Eliot. AnMo; Epi; HeIP; InPK; InPS; IPWM; NoAM; NOBA; NOBE; OxBTC; PAIC; PPP; PSN; SoSe; WIF

Let us have winter loving that the heart. Winter Love. Elizabeth Jennings. BoLoP

Let Us Honor Them. Rochelle Owens. Psy

Let us leave this place, brother. The Romanies in Town. Anne Beresford. LP; MPo

Let us make death masks. Hymn to the 10,000 Who Die Each Year on the Abortionist's Table in Amerika. Rita Mae Brown. WBN

Let us not live with Lear. Ripeness Is All. J. V. Cunningham. PiAm

Let us not make apologies. Instructions. Anita Skeen. IHMS

Let us quit the leafy arbour. The Longest Day. Wordsworth. RRA

Let us say my drinking problem hangs. The Birth of My Drinking Problem. Michael McMahon. FAF

Let us sing of the unsung hero. Mel Allen, Mel Allen, Lend Me Your Cliché. Ogden Nash. SPo

Let us stiffen. The Covenant. James Cunningham. JB

Let us suppose the mind. Barbara Moraff. IHMS

Let us suppose, valley and such ago. John Berryman. *Fr.* Dream Songs. PPP

Let us tunnel. Letters to Walt Whitman, I. Ronald Johnson. VGW

Let us use it while we may. Of Beauty [*or* Beauty]. Giovanni Battista Guarini, *tr. by* Sir Richard Fanshawe. *Fr.* Il Pastor Fido. BoLoP; GBL

Let us walk in the white snow. Velvet Shoes. Elinor Wylie. FSFS

Let wits contest. The Posy. George Herbert. SCP-1

Let your song be delicate. Song Be Delicate. John Shaw Neilson. MAuV

Lethe. Hilda Doolittle ("H.D."). PiAm; VGW

Let's All Meet and Have a Party Sometime. John Birkby. BuTh

Let's count the bodies over again. Counting Small-Boned Bodies. Robert Bly. CAPP; PPoD; TSWA

Let's go/ Come on. Junkman's Obbligato. Lawrence Ferlinghetti. WIF

Let's go—much as that dog goes. Overland to the Islands. Denise Levertov. ConAP

Let's go see Old Abe. Lincoln Monument: Washington. Langston Hughes. OFD

Let's go up to the hillside today.  Play Song.  Peter Kumalo. SPo

Let's have less nonsense from the friends of Joe.  Less Nonsense. A. P. Herbert.  OxBTC

Let's let the good man sign the bill.  The Man of Property. Charles G. Ballard.  VW

Let's step on daddy's head shout.  Step on His Head.  James Laughlin.  VGW

Let's talk of graves, of worms, and epitaphs.  The Death of Kings. Shakespeare.  King Richard II, fr. III, ii.  GrRo; PPoe

Let's think of eggs.  The Poultries.  Ogden Nash.  RAE

Letter, The.  W. H. Auden.  NoAM

Letter, A.  Anthony Hecht.  CoPAm

Letter, The.  Elizabeth Riddell.  BuTh

Letter, A.  Burns Singer.  SLP

Letter.  Mark Strand.  NoAM

Letter Back to Oregon.  Albert Goldbarth.  HeS

Letter V.  W. S. Graham.  OxBTC

Letter for Marian, A.  Thomas McGrath.  VGW

Letter from a Black Soldier.  Bill Anderson.  VGW

Letter from a Candidate for the Presidency, A.  James Russell Lowell.  Fr. The Biglow Papers, 1st Series, No. VII.  PiAm

Letter from a Death Bed.  John Ciardi.  NCSH

Letter from a Friend, A.  Carolyn Maisel.  1HMS

Letter from a Girl to Her Own Old Age, A.  Alice Meynell. SBG

Letter from an Institution: III.  Michael Ryan.  AmPA

Letter from Artemisia in the Town to Cloe in the Country, A. Earl of Rochester.  ESaP

Letter from Berlin, A.  Jon Stallworthy.  NoAM

Letter from Brooklyn, A.  Derek Walcott.  OxBTC

Letter from Li Po, A, sel.  Conrad Aiken. "Winds of doctrine blow both ways at once, The."  VGW

Letter form the North Atlantic.  John Williams.  CoPAm

Letter from the Pygmies, A.  Theodore Weiss.  VGW

Letter from Town: The Almond Tree.  D. H. Lawrence.  PAIC

Letter in my mailbox says you've made it, A.  To a Girl Who Lives in a Tree.  Audré Lorde.  WBN

Letter in Winter.  Raymond R. Patterson.  PoBA

Letter Reaching Out to My Sister, 1600 Miles.  Sharon Barba. RiTi

Letter 6.  Charles Olson.  Fr. The Maximus Poems.  PiAm

Letter to a Conceivable Great-Grandson.  Earle Birney.  BBGO

Letter to a Friend.  Jon Stallworthy.  NoAM

Letter to a Friend in an Unknown Place.  Anita Barrows. NMM; RiTi

Letter to a Librarian.  Irving Layton.  MAT

Letter to a Mute.  Thomas James.  AmPA

Letter to a Teacher of English, A.  Robert Hillyer.  PAIC

Letter to a Young Father in Exile.  John Logan.  CAPP

Letter to a Young Friend.  Alden Nowlan.  AKE

Letter to an Absent Son.  Madeline DeFrees.  NMM; RiTi

Letter to an American Visitor.  Alex Comfort.  OxBTC

Letter to Be Disguised As a Gas Bill.  Marge Piercy.  MMD; WPE

Letter to Belden.  Rosalie Moore.  NPW

Letter to Dafnis, A.  Countess of Winchilsea.  SBG

Letter to E. Franklin Frazier.  LeRoi Jones.  BPo; PoBA

Letter to Eve.  Alan Dugan.  PAIC

Letter to Her Husband, Absent upon Public Employment, A ("As loving hind...").  Anne Bradstreet.  SCP-2; WPE (Another.)  SBG

Letter to Her Husband, Absent upon Publick Employment, A ("My head, my heart, mine eyes,...").  Anne Bradstreet. HeIP; PiAm

Letter to Her Son's Commanding Officer.  Ethel Green Russell. AATT

Letter to Kafka.  Maura Stanton.  AmPA

Letter to Lady Margaret Cavendish Holles-Harley, When a Child, A.  Matthew Prior.  See Letter to the Honourable Lady Miss Margaret Cavendish Holles-Harley.

Letters to Live Poets, sel.  Bruce Beaver. Letter XII.  MAuV

Letter to "M."  Unknown.  OxBM

Letter to Maria Gisborne.  Shelley.  MBPR To Maria Gisborne in England, from Italy, sel.  NOBE

Letter to My Father.  Delia Chilgren.  NPW

Letter to My Mother.  Dom Moraes.  NoAM

Letter to My Mother.  Anita Skeen.  IHMS

Letter to My Sister.  Anne Spencer.  PoBA

Letter to N.Y.  Elizabeth Bishop.  TH

Letter to Robert.  Mary Fabilli.  IHMS

Letter to Sara Hutchinson, A.  Samuel Taylor Coleridge.  See Dejection: an Ode.

Letter to the Child Lady Margaret Cavendish Holles-Harley, A. Matthew Prior.  See Letter to the Honourable Lady Miss Margaret Cavendish Holles-Harley.

Letter to the Countess of Denbigh against Irresolution and Delay in Matters of Religion, A.  Richard Crashaw.  See To the Noblest and Best of Ladyes.

Letter to the Honourable Lady Miss Margaret Cavendish Holles-Harley, A.  Matthew Prior.  PAIC (Letter to Lady Margaret Cavendish Holles-Harley, When a Child, A.)  NOBE (Letter to the Child Lady Margaret Cavendish Holles-Harley, A.)  OxBChV

Letter to the Lady Carey and Mrs. Essex Rich, A, sel.  John Donne. "Here where by all, all saints invokèd are."  SCP-1

Letter to Three Irish Poets, A.  Michael Longley.  BIrV

Letters [or Notes] Found near a Suicide.  Frank Horne.  PoBa Sels. To "Chick."  BPo To James.  BPo; PAIC To Mother.  BPo To You.  BPo

Letters from an Irishman to a Rat.  Christpher Logue.  BoAnP

Letters of the Jews as strict as flames, The.  The Alphabet.  Karl Shapiro.  NoAM

Letters, Returned.  Adrianne Marcus.  NPW

Letters she left to clutter up the desk.  A Gesture by a Lady with an Assumed Name.  James Wright.  ConAP

Letters to a Stranger.  Thomas James.  AmPA

Letters to Walt Whitman, sels.  Ronald Johnson.  VGW "But are these landscapes to be imagined," IX. "I, too, have plucked a stalk of grass," V. "Let us tunnel," I. "Slant sheen/ wrinkled silver," II.

Letting his wisdom be the whole of love.  The World and the Child.  James Merrill.  CoPAm; PAIC

Letting of Humour's Blood in the Head-Vein, The, sels.  Samuel Rowlands.  TVS "Melfluvious, sweet, rose-watered eloquence," Satire IV. "Oh let the gentlewoman have the wall," Satire III. "Who have we here? Behold him and be mute!" Satire I.

Levedy, ich thanke thee.  Lady, I Thank Thee.  Unknown. OxBM

Levee Camp Moan.  Unknown.  BluL

Levelled Churchyard, The.  Thomas Hardy.  OBP

Leviathan.  W. S. Merwin.  ConAP; NoAM; NOBA; TCP

Lewis Carrol.  Eleanor Farjeon.  OxBChV

Lewti; or, The Circassian Love-Chaunt.  Samuel Taylor Coleridge.  MBPR

Li Po. Mary Moore. NPW

Liadan Laments Cuirithir. *Unknown, tr. fr. Irish by* John Montague. BIrV

Liar, The. LeRoi Jones. NOBA; WIF

Liard Hot Springs. Gordon Massman. CTBA

'Lias! 'Lias! Bless de Lawd! In the Morning. Paul Laurence Dunbar. BPo

Libelle of Englyshe Polycye, The, *sel. Unknown.* Keep the Sea. OxBM

Liberal, blue-eyed, shivering, trying not. The Blue-eyed Precinct Worker. Henri Coulette. MAT

Liberation. Mary Swanson Stroh. NPW

Libertine, The. Louis MacNeice. NoAM

Liberty. Shelley. MBPR

Liberty, *sel.* Wordsworth. "Beetle loves his unpretending track, The." FaBoCo

Liberty and Peace. Phillis Wheatley. SBG

Liberty Song, The, *with music.* John Dickinson. BLSo

Liberty Tree. Thomas Paine. BTTM

Library. Richard Armour. ECBV

Library. Louis Jenkins. HeS

Licia, *sels.* Giles Fletcher the Elder. AAS "I wish sometimes, although a worthlesse thing," XII. "In tyme the strong and statelie turrets fall," XXVIII. "Lyke Memnons rocke toucht, with the rising sunne," XLVII.

Licorice Fields at Pontefract, The. John Betjeman. MPo; SS

Lie, The. Al Lee. AmPA

Lie, The. Sir Walter Ralegh. AAS; NOBE; PPoD; PPoe

Lie back, daughter, let your head. First Lesson. Philip Booth. IPWM; SFF

Lie Closed, My Lately Loved. John Woods. ConAP

"Lie still, my newly married wife." The Griesly Wife. John Manifold. SoSe

Lie up nearer, brother, nearer, for my limbs are growing cold. The Dying Californian. *Unknown.* AmFP

Lie where you fell and longed. Letter V. W. S. Graham. OxBTC

Liefer would I turn and love. Deranged. Padraic Fiacc. PFIr

Lies. Yevgeny Yevtushenko, *tr. fr. Russian by* Robin Milner-Gulland *and* Peter Levi. LP

Lif of this world, The. The Life of This World. *Unknown.* OxBM

Life, The. George Chambers. HeS

Life, The. Philip Dow. AmPA

Life, A. Howard Nemerov. AnMo; PBMP

Life, A. Sylvia Plath. NOBA

Life. Grace Treasone. InPK

Life/ is at 2 playing. Childhood. Jewel C. Latimore. JB

Life After Death. Richard W. Thomas. PoBA

Life and Death Among the Xerox People. Olga Cabral. WBN

Life and Death of Jason, The, *sel.* William Morris. Garden by the Sea, A, IV. NOBE

Life at War. Denise Levertov. NMM; VGW

Life breathes its first in gasps. Birth Day. Merle Meeter. AATT

Life contracts and death is expected. The Death of a Soldier. Wallace Stevens. OFD

Life-Cycle. Bruce Dawe. MAuV

Life Cycle of Common Man. Howard Nemerov. MPo

Life flows to death as rivers to the sea. Epigram. J. V. Cunningham. POL; VGW

Life, friends, is boring. We must not say so. John Berryman. *Fr.* Dream Songs. CAPP; HeIP; InPK; IPWM; NoAM; NOBA; PPoD

Life has loveliness to sell. Barter. Sara Teasdale. SoSe

Life in a day: he took his girl to the ballet. Les Sylphides. Louis MacNeice. BoLoP; BuTh; PSN

Life is like a jagged tooth. Life. Grace Treasone. InPK

Life is ours like the real. Theme One: The Variations. August Wilson. PoBA

Life is suspended over foreign countries, A. Over Asia. Anne Waldman. RiTi

Life of an offensive center, The. Dick Szymanski. Ogden Nash. SPo

Life of Life! thy lips enkindle. Shelley. *Fr.* Prometheus Unbound. NOBE

Life of the snail is a fight against odds, The. The Snail. A. P. Herbert. BoAnP

Life of the Wolf, The. Gary Gildner. AmPA

Life of This World, The. *Unknown.* OxBM

Life on the Ocean Wave, A, *with music.* Epes Sargent. BLSH

Life pours out images, the accidental. The Rokeby Venus. Robert Conquest. NoAM

Life Rounded with Sleep. Shelley. BuTh

Life Style, The. Edwin Brock. IPWM

Life, the Eternal Sacrament. Virginia Floyd. AATT

Life the hound. The Hound. Robert Francis. SoSe

Life with yon lambs, like day, is just begun. Composed on a May Morning, 1838. Wordsworth. FSFS

Lifeguard, The. James Dickey. NowV

Lifeguard is a man of brawn, The. Seasonal Phenomenon. Richard Armour. BBGO

Lifeless solitude—an angry waste, A. On the Telescopic Moon. John Swanick Drennan. BIrV

Lifers file into the hall, The. In the Cage. Robert Lowell. NOBA; PPoD

Lifesize in a car. Drive In Movie. Gary Sange. NVAP; SFF

Lift, The. Raymond Souster. POL

Lift gently Dai, gentleness befits his gunshot wound. David Jones. *Fr.* In Parenthesis. TwMBP

Lift latch, step in, be welcome, Sir. A Luncheon. Max Beerbohm. FaBoCo; OxBTC

Lift not the painted veil which those who live. Sonnet. Shelley. MBPR

Lifting, both hands pulling whitely. Grandpa's .45. W. M. Ransom. CDW

Lifting his slowly trickling jaws. Tête-á-Tête. Edwin Honig. NoAM

Lifting my fingers. Frozen Hands. Joseph Bruchac. CDW

Liftman, The. H. A. C. Evans. POL

Ligeia, *prose tale, sel.* Poe. Conqueror Worm, The. NOBA; PiAm

Light. Jon Silkin. NoAM

Lights, *sels.* Louis Zukofsky. NoAM "House where every, A." "These are not my sentiments."

Light, The/ drains me of what I might be. A Nude by Edward Hopper. Lisel Mueller. RiTi

Light across the courtyard. Saint's Bridge. Lola Ridge. WPE

Light and Dark. Barbara Howes. CoPAm; RiTi

Light are the spinning favours, intangible tonight. An English Elegy. Daryl Hine. NoAM

Light as petals, white as daisies. Butterflies. Clive Sansom. BonAnP

Light became her grace and dwelt among, The. Ballatetta. Ezra Pound. VGW

Light Breaks Where No Sun Shines. Dylan Thomas. OxBTC; PAIC

Light comes into the house and a few flies, The. In Blessed Weather. Michael Heffernan. HeS

Light Dying. Brendan Kennelly. PFIr

Light exists in spring, A.  Emily Dickinson.  FSFS; NOBA; VoPo

Light falling into my kitchen.  Words from Storms and Geese in the Morning.  Jenne Andrews.  HeS

Light feet, dark violet eyes, and parted hair.  Keats.  MBPR

Light flows our war of mocking words, and yet.  The Buried Life.  Matthew Arnold.  PFD

Light foot hears you and the brightness begins, The.  A Poem Beginning with a Line by Pindar.  Robert Duncan.  ConAP; Epi

Light, glinting off the bracelet, The.  Claritas.  Gerrye Payne.  NPW

Light glows bright, The.  The Parade.  Liz Sohappy Bahe.  VW

Light going out in the forehead, A.  Swimming By Night.  James Merrill.  VGW

Light in he window seemed perpetual, The.  The Room above the Square.  Stephen Spender.  NOBE

Light into the olive entered.  After Greece.  James Merrill.  ConAP; NOBA

Light is around the petals, and behind them.  Looking at Some Flowers.  Robert Bly.  NOBA

Light Listened.  Theodore Roethke.  AnMo; NowV

Light little zephyr came flitting, A.  Morning Compliments.  Sydney Dayre.  OxBChV

Light making patterns.  The Creation.  Patricia Ramsey.  AATT

Light of evening, Lissadell, The.  In Memory of Eva Gore-Booth and Con Markiewicz.  W. B. Yeats.  NoAM; OxBTC

Light of Other Days, The.  Thomas Moore.  See Oft in the Stilly Night.

Light on his pins.  Roethke Plain.  John Malcolm Brinnin.  NoAM

Light passes, The.  Evening.  Hilda Doolittle ("H.D.").  IPWM; VGW; WPE

Light rides the wings of heron.  Passage.  Mary Shumway.  NVAP

Light Shining Out of Darkness.  William Cowper.  BoReV; HeIP; NOBE

Light, so low upon earth.  Marriage Morning.  Tennyson.  GBL

Light the first light of evening, as in a room.  Final Soliloquy of the Interior Paramour.  Wallace Stevens.  PiAm

Light the prime work of God to me is extinct.  Milton.  Fr. Samson Agonistes.  SCP-1

Light white, a disgrace, an ink spot, a rosy charm.  A Petticoat.  Gertrude Stein.  Fr. Tender Buttons.  RiTi

Light-Winged Smoke, Icarian Bird.  Henry David Thoreau.  See Smoke.

Light Year, The.  John Ridland.  OFD

Lighthouse.  Merle Meeter.  AATT

Lighthouse Keeper.  Gary Sange.  NVAP

Lighthouses.  Dorothy Wellesley.  WPE

Lightning and thunder, The.  A Baby-Sermon.  George MacDonald.  OxBChV

Lightning bug got, A.  The Flattered Lightning Bug.  Don Marquis.  PoTa

Lightning Flash, The.  Unknown.  AmFP

Lightning flashes, The!  Haiku.  Basho.  SoSe

Lightning gleam, A.  Haiku.  Basho.  SoSe

Lightning is a yellow fork, The.  Emily Dickinson.  InPK

Lights are burning.  Bus Stop.  Donald Justice.  TCP

Lights, Flowers.  Judith Johnson Sherwin.  WBN

Lights in the Hallway, The.  James Wright.  CAPP

Lights in the Sky Are Stars, The.  Kenneth Rexroth.  RRA

Lights Out.  Edward Thomas.  NOBE

Like a Bulwark.  Marianne Moore.  PiAm

Like a drummer's brush.  Rain.  Emanuel diPasquale.  InPK; POL

Like a dry fish flung inland far from shore.  Lost Anchors.  E. A. Robinson.  PiAm

Like a first coat of whitewash when it's wet.  Twelfth Morning; or What You Will.  Elizabeth Bishop.  PSN

Like a fishbone in my throat.  I Still Feel You.  Marge Piercy.  Psy

Like a fruit wine with earth.  Cider and Vesalius.  John Peck.  AmPA

Like a glum cricket.  Flight.  James Tate.  InPK

Like a lizard in the sun, though not scuttling.  The Laureate.  Robert Graves.  BIrV

Like a lone Arab, old and blind.  Love's Apparition and Evanishment.  Samuel Taylor Coleridge.  MBPR

Like a Midsummer Rose.  John Lydgate.  OxBM

Like a rainstorm, he said, the braided colors.  Worsening Situation.  John Ashbery.  NOBA

Like a river she was.  The Memory.  Robert Creeley.  CAPP; VGW

Like a sacred rabbit running over and.  "Graphemics," 1.  Jack Spicer.  VGW

Like a skein of loose silk blown against a wall.  The Garden.  Ezra Pound.  HeIP; PiAm; PPP; PSN

Like a sleeping swine upon the skyline.  Muckish Mountain (The Pig's Back).  Shane Leslie.  PFIr

Like America, his art consists.  Politics of a Pornographer.  Robert Hass.  CAAP

Like apoplectic fur balloons.  Babies: Just Babies.  Margaret Fishback.  ECBV

Like [or Lyke] as a huntsman after weary chace.  Amoretti, LXVII.  Spenser.  Epi; GBL; HeIP

Like as the armed knight.  The Ballad Which Anne Askew Made and Sang When She Was in Newgate.  Anne Askew.  WPE

Like as the culver on the bared bough.  Amoretti, LXXXIX.  Spenser.  GBL

Like as the fountain of all light created.  Incarnatio Est Maximum Dei Donum.  William Alabaster.  BoReV

Like as the waves make toward the pebbled shore.  Sonnets, LX.  Shakespeare.  Epi; NOBE

Like drunken seamen bunched upon the ground.  They Slept While Jesus Prayed.  Henry Tim Chambers.  AATT

Like eyes coming out of the wood.  Some Knots.  Edwin Honig.  NoAM

Like fire-flies that the peasant on the hill.  Dante, tr. by Laurence Binyon.  Fr. Divina Commedia: Inferno.  Prf

Like lamps between the trees.  Firefly.  Kamimura Hajime, tr. by Harry and Lynn Guest and Kajima Shozo.  TSWA

Like mail order brides.  Seedlings in the Mail.  Marge Piercy.  MMD

Like Mistress, Like Maid.  Samuel Rowlands.  SCP-2

Like Musical Instruments.  Tom Clark.  PPoe (Poem.)  ConAP

Like one who in her third widowhood doth profess.  To Mr. Rowland Woodward.  John Donne.  PAIC

Like snooker balls thrown on the table's faded green.  A Poet's Progress.  Michael Hamburger.  WIF

Like the beat, beat, beat of the tom-tom.  Night and Day.  Cole Porter.  BLSo

Like the Idalian queen.  Madrigal.  William Drummond of Hawthornden.  GBL; NOBE; SCP-2

Like the Touch of Rain.  Edward Thomas.  BoLoP; GBL

Like the universe.  Science As Art.  Hugh Seidman.  AmPA

Like the wild organs of winter storms.  At the Eastern Front.  Georg Trakl, tr. by Ingo Seidler.  IPWM

Like This Together.  Adrienne Rich.  PiAm; VGW

Like to a Hermit Poor.  At. to Sir Walter Ralegh.  GBL

Like to Diana in her summer weed.  Samela.  Robert Greene.  Fr. Menaphon.  GBL; NOBE

Like to the arctic needle that doth guide. Emblem V, 4. Francis Quarles. SCP-2

Like to the falling of a star. Sic Vita. Henry King. BBGO; NOBE; WIF

Like to these unmesurable montayns. Jacopo Sannazaro, tr. fr. Italian by Sir Thomas Wyatt. AAS

Like trains of cars on tracks of plush. Emily Dickinson. PiAm

Like two cathedral towers these stately pines. My Cathedral. Longfellow. PBMP

Like two somnambulists we entered the dawn sun. Hunting for Blueberries. Thomas James. AmPA

Likeness, A. Robert Browning. InPS

Likeness, The. Arthur Gregor. VGW

Li'l Liza Jane, with music. Unknown. BLSo

Lilacs, sel. Amy Lowell. "May is lilac here in New England." FSFS

Lilacs wither in the Carolinas, The. In the Carolinas. Wallace Stevens. VGW

Lilies of the Valley. Jon Silkin. NoAM

Lilith, sel. Christopher Brennan. "She is the night: all horror is of her." MAuV

Lilli Burlero, with music. Unknown. RDB

Lilly, The. Blake. Fr. Songs of Experience. MBPR

Lilly Dale, with music. H. S. Thompson. BLSo

Lily, Germander, and Sops-in-Wine. Unknown. Fr. Robin Goodfellow, Pt. II. ECBV

Lily of the West, The. Unknown. AmFP

Limbo. Samuel Taylor Coleridge. MBPR; OBP

Lime condensed on the ceiling, or maybe. Living in the Boneyard. John Oliver Simon. NeAC

Lime-Tree, The. Edward Lucie-Smith. BuTh

Limerick: "Decrepit old gas man named Peter, A." Unknown. SoSe

Limerick: "I sat next the duchess at tea." Unknown. SoSe

Limerick: "There was a young lady of Lynn/ Who was so uncommonly thin." Unknown. SoSe

Limerick: "There was a young maid who said, 'Why'." Unknown. SoSe

Limerick: "There was an Old Man of Hong Kong." Edward Lear. FaBoCo

Limerick: "There was an old man of Peru." Unknown. SoSe

Limerick: "There was an old man who said, 'Hush!' " Edward Lear. FaBoCo; OxBChV

Limerick: "There was an old man with a beard,/ Who said, 'It is just as I feared!' " Edward Lear. FaBoCo; OxBChV (Nesting.) ECBV

Limerick: "There was an Old Person of Anerley." Edward Lear. FaBoCo

Limerick: "Tutor who tooted the flute, A." Carolyn Wells. SoSe

Limerick: "Well, it's partly the shape of the thing." Unknown. SoSe

Limestone and pine: a dry country. By Rail Through Istria. Robert Conquest. NoAM

Limited. Carl Sandburg. PSN

Limpopo and Tugela churned. The Scorpion. William Plomer. NoAM

Lincoln, sel. John Gould Fletcher. "There was a darkness in this man," II. OFD

Lincoln Monument: Washington. Langston Hughes. OFD

Lincoln, the Man of the People, sel. Edwin Markham. "Up from the log cabin to the capitol." OFD

Lincolnshire Poacher, The. Unknown. GBP

Linda. John Stone. CoPAm

Lindamira's Complaint. Mary Sidney Wroth, Countess of Montgomery. Fr. Urania. WPE

Lindbergh. Unknown. AmFP

Line, The. Dan Gerber. HeS

Line in long array where they wind betwixt green islands, A. Cavalry Crossing a Ford. Walt Whitman. AmVN; HeIP; InPK; InPS; NoAM; PiAm; PPoD; PPP

Line-Up, The. Joan Swift. FiCP

Lineage. Margaret Walker. NMM; PoBA

Linear, encircled youth, The. On Alexander and Aristotle, on a Black-on-Red Greek Plate. Alan Dugan. PPP

Lines: Inspired by the Controversy on the Value or Otherwise of Old English Studies. Anthony Burgess. FaBoCo

Lines: "Lines which are the imitation of imagined veins." Anne Waldman. CAAP

Lines: "Singularly and in pairs the decade has been ripped by bullets." Herbert Martin. PoBA

Lines: "Unfelt, unheard, unseen." Keats. MBPR

Lines: "We meet not as we parted." Shelley. MBPR

Lines: "When the lamp is shattered." Shelley. See When the Lamp Is Shattered.

Lines: "Wheresoe'er I turn my view." Samuel Johnson. See Lines Written in Ridicule of Certain Poems Published in 1777.

Lines Addressed to a Young Lady. Byron. MBPR

Lines are keen against today's bad sky, The. The Church on Comiaken Hill. Richard Hugo. Prf

Lines Composed a Few Miles above Tintern Abbey. Wordsworth. HeIP; InPS; IPWM; PPP; VoPo (Lines Written a Few Miles above Tintern Abbey.) AnMo; MBPR "For thou art with me here upon the banks," sel. Prf

Lines for a Christmas Card. Hilaire Belloc. SFF; SoSe

Lines for a Fifty-fifth Birthday. Jeanne McGahey. MIT

Lines for a Hard Time. Gena Ford. IHMS

Lines for a President. Robert Watson. PPoD

Lines for an Interment. Archibald MacLeish. NOBA

Lines for Cuscuscaraway and Mirza Murad Ali Beg. T. S. Eliot. SpRo

Lines for Marking Time. Roberta Hill. CDW

Lines for Michael in the Picture. John Logan. CAPP

Lines for Those to Whom Tragedy Is Denied. Joyce Carol Oates. CoPAm; IHMS

Lines Found on an Envelope. Adrianne Marcus. NPW

Lines in Ridicule of Certain Poems Published in 1777. Samuel Johnson. See Lines Written in Ridicule of Certain Poems Published in 1777.

Lines Inscribed upon a Cup Formed from a Skull. Byron. InPK; MBPR

Lines Left upon a Seat in a Yew-Tree. Wordsworth. MBPR

Lines of this new song are nothing, The. Louis Zukofsky. VGW

Lines on a Paid Militia. Dryden. Fr. Cymon and Iphigenia. SoSe

Lines on a Young Lady's Photograph Album. Philip Larkin. HeIP

Lines on Hearing that Lady Byron Was Ill. Byron. MBPR

Lines on Hearing the Organ. Charles Stuart Calverley. FaBoCo

Lines on His Birthday. John Logan. CAPP

Lines on His Companions Who Died in the Northern Seas. Thomas James. SCP-2

Lines on Seeing a Lock of Milton's Hair. Keats. MBPR

Lines on Swift's Ancestors. Pope. FaBoCo

Lines on the Back of a Leary Bailfund Card. Mary Norbert Körte. MIT

Lines on the Mermaid Tavern. Keats. MBPR

Lines parallel. The Room. De Leon Harrison. PoBA

Lines Printed under the Engraved Portrait of Milton. Dryden. HeIP; InPK

Lines Rhymed in a Letter Received from Oxford. Keats. MBPR

Lines Supposed to Have Been Addressed to Fanny Brawne. Keats. *See* This Living Hand, Now Warm and Capable.

Lines to a Critic. Shelley. MBPR

Lines to a Don. Hilaire Belloc. FaBoCo

Lines to García Lorca. LeRoi Jones. TCP

Lines to His Son on Reaching Adolescence. John Logan. CAPP

Lines to Mr. Hodgson. Byron. MBPR

Lines to My Father. Sam Hamod. SA

Lines which are the imitation of imagined veins. Lines. Anne Waldman. CAAP

Lines Written a Few Miles Above Tintern Abbey. Wordsworth. *See* Lines Composed a Few Miles above Tintern Abbey.

Lines Written Among the Euganean Hills. Shelley. MBPR

Lines Written at a Small Distance from my House. Wordsworth. *See* To My Sister.

Lines Written Beneath an Elm in the Churchyard of Harrow. Byron. MBPR

Lines Written During a Period of Insanity. William Cowper. PPP; Prf

Lines Written in Early Spring. Wordsworth. MBPR; PBMP

Lines Written in Objection, or the Limpopo Express. Philip Hey. SFF

Lines Written in Ridicule of Certain Poems Published in 1777. Samuel Johnson. PAIC
(Lines: "Wheresoe'er I turn my view.") PPoD
(Lines in Ridicule of Certain Poems Published in 1777.) FaBoCo

Lines Written in the Album at Elbingerode. Samuel Taylor Coleridge. MBPR

Lines Written in the Bay of Lerici. Shelley. MBPR

Lines Written in the Highlands after a Visit to Burns's Country. Keats. MBPR

Lines Written Near Richmond, upon the Thames, at Evening. Wordsworth. MBPR

Lines Written on a Seat on the Grand Canal. Patrick Kavanagh. BIrV

Lines Written on a Window Shutter at Weston. William Cowper. LAuP

Lines Written on Hearing the News of the Death of Napoleon. Shelley. MBPR

Lingam and the Yoni, The. A. D. Hope. MAT; NoAM

Linger longer, Olga. Molly Fitton. POL

Lining Track. *Unknown.* AmFP

Lion, The. Lord Alfred Douglas. ECBV

Lion and lioness are intractable, The. Letter to Eve. Alan Dugan. PAIC

Lion and the unicorn, The. Mother Goose. MG

Lion Hunts. Patricia Beer. OxBTC

Lion is an awful bore, The. The Lion. Lord Alfred Douglas. ECBV

Lion is never a lion in a royal hunt, A. Lion Hunts. Patricia Beer. OxBTC

Lions. Sandra McPherson. CAAP

Lions of fire, The. Kenneth Patchen. VGW

Lions who ate the Christians on the sands of the arena, The. Sunt Leones. Stevie Smith. SBG

Lip which had once been stolid, now moving, A. Divine Love. Michael Benedikt. AmPA; ConAP

Lips of the one I love are my perpetual pleasure, The. Hafiz, *tr. fr. Persian by* Peter Avery *and* John Heath-Stubbs. BoLoP

Lisbon. *Unknown.* AmFP

List! what sad sounds are these? extremely. John Ford. *Fr.* The Broken Heart. SCP-2

Listen,/ listen to me, fellow members of the company. An Angry Sermon for Any Day in the Week. F. Eugene Warren. AATT

Listen.../ With faint dry sound. November Night. Adelaide Crapsey. PAIC

Listen, and when thy hand this paper presses. A Letter from a Girl to Her Own Old Age. Alice Meynell. SBG

Listen Children. Lucille Clifton. PoBA

"Listen, children, listen, won't you come into the night?" Who Calls? Frances Clarke. LCL

Listen! I will tell the most treasured of dreams. The Dream of the Rood. *Unknown, tr. by* Helen Gardner. BoReV

Listen, let me explain, it was not the fire. The Late Visitor. Ann Stanford. PPoD

Listen listen/ There's walking in the world. Colin Barnes, Drums. John Smith. *Fr.* Jazz for Five. MPo

Listen, Lord—a Prayer. James Weldon Johnson. BPo

Listen, my children, and you shall hear. Paul Revere's Ride. Longfellow. *Fr.* Tales of a Wayside Inn. BTTM

Listen natives of a dry place. The Old Boast. W. S. Merwin. NOBA

Listen, the hay-bells tinkle as the cart. The Holy Innocents. Robert Lowell. ConAP; NowV

Listen. The wind is still. Spring Thunder. Mark Van Doren. TH

Listen to me, as when ye heard our father. Canadian Boat-Song. *Unknown, at. to* John Galt. AIW

Listen to me there have. Freddy the Rat Perishes. Don Marquis. *Fr.* Archy and Mehitabel. MiP

Listen to the Mocking Bird, *with music.* Septimus Winner. BLSo; PSoN

Listen, you drawing men. Snapshots of the Cotton South. Frank Marshall Davis. PoBA

"Listen," you said. Rainbow. Liz Lochhead. MIS

Listenen to Big Black at S. F. State. Sonia Sanchez. BPo

Listeners, The. Walter de la Mare. InPK; NCSH; NoAM; NOBE; PPoD; SoSe; SS; SFF

Listening. William Stafford. RFM; TSWA

Listening Rock, The. Ray A. Young Bear. VW

Listening to Foxhounds. James Dickey. InPS; PPoD

Litany, A, *sels.* John Donne.
"Deliver us for thy descent." SCP-1
Good Lord, Deliver Us! BoReV
"O Holy Ghost, whose temple I." SCP-1

Litany in Time of Plague, A. Thomas Nashe. *See* Adieu, Farewell Earth's Bliss.

Litel wot it any mon. An Unfortunate Lover. *Unknown.* OxBM

Literary Importation. Philip Freneau. AmVN

Lithe, quicker than the ball itself. Jump Shot. Richard Peck. MiP; SPo

Little Annie Rooney, *with music.* Michael Nolan. FSN

Little Bessie. *Unknown.* AmFP

Little Betty Blue. Mother Goose. MG

Little Billee. Thackeray. ECBV; FaBoCo

Little Billy. *Unknown.* GBP

Little bird whispers in their ear, A. Parable for Our Time. Peter Michelson. HeS

Little Black Boy, The. Blake. *Fr.* Songs of Innocence. AnMo; HeIP; InPK; LAuP; MBPR; OBP; OxBChV

Little Black Rose, The. Aubrey Thomas De Vere. BIrV

Little black thing among the snow, A. The Chimney Sweeper. Blake. *Fr.* Songs of Experience. LAuP; MBPR; PPoe; PPP

Little Black Train. *Unknown.* AmFP

Little boat at anchor, The. Fourth of July Night. Carl Sandburg. OFD

Little Bo-Peep has lost her sheep. Mother Goose. MG; SpRo

Little bo-peepals. Rhyme for Botanical Baby. Joseph Cook. SpRo

Little boy, The. Junior Addict. Langston Hughes. BPo; TCP

Little Boy Blue. Eugene Field. SoSe

Little Boy Blue. *Unknown.* BluL

Little boy blue, come, blow up your horn. Mother Goose. MG

Little Boy Found, The. Blake. *Fr.* Songs of Innocence. LAuP; MBPR

Little boy kneels at the foot of the bed. Vespers. A. A. Milne. OxBChV; SpRo

Little boy, little boy, where wast thou born? Lancashire Born. *Unknown.* GBP

Little Boy Lost, The ("Father, father, where are you going"). Blake. *Fr.* Songs of Innocence. LAuP; MBPR

Little Boy Lost, A ("Nought loves another as itself"). Blake. *Fr.* Songs of Experience. MBPR; OBP

Little Boy lost in the lonely fen, The. The Little Boy Found. Blake *Fr.* Songs of Innocence. LAuP; MBPR

Little boy once played so loud, A. Extremes. James Whitcomb Riley. ECBV

Little boy stopped in the middle of the haystack, The. Railroad Reverie. E. R. Young. ECBV

Little boys and little maidens. Little Catkins. Alexander Blok, *tr. by* Babette Deutsch. OFD

Little Brother, The. James Reeves. LoAs; OxBTC

Little brown boy. Poem. Helene Johnson. PoBA

Little Brown Bulls, The. *Unknown.* AmFP

Little Brown Church in the Vale, The, *with music.* William S. Pitts. BLSH

Little Brown Jug, *with music.* At. to Joseph E. Winner. BLSH; BLSo; PSoN

Little bunches of/ grass pretend they are bushes. Stories from Kansas. William Stafford. RFM

Little Bush. Elizabeth Madox Roberts. LCL

Little Catkins. Alexander Blok, *tr. fr. Russian by* Babette Deutsch. OFD

Little child, I counsel you that ye. Customs Change. *Unknown.* OxBChV

Little children here ye may lere. Manners at Table When Away from Home. *Unknown.* OxBChV

Little circle/ big circle. Blue Boy on Skates (Twilight). M. L. Rosenthal. SPo

Little cock-sparrow sat on a green tree, A. Mother Goose. MG

Little cousin is dead, by foul subtraction, The. Dead boy. John Crowe Ransom. NoAM; PiAm

Little Cradle Rocks Tonight in Glory, The. *Unknown.* AmFP

Little Dame Crump. *Unknown.* RAE

Little Dancers, The. Laurence Binyon. BBGO; OxBTC

Little Doll, The. Charles Kingsley. *See* Lost Doll, The.

Little Dove, The. *Unknown.* AmFP

Little drops of water. Little Things. Julia A. Carney. OxBChV

Little Drummer, The. *Unknown.* AmFP

Little Dunkeld. *Unknown.* GBP

Little Elegy. X. J. Kennedy. ConAP; NCSH

Little Elegy. Elinor Wylie. LoAs

Little Exercise. Elizabeth Bishop. NCSH

Little Fish. D. H. Lawrence. AKE; OxBTC

Little fish swim in the river, big fish swim in the sea. I Don't Let the Girls Worry My Mind. *Unknown.* AmFP

Little fly/ Thy summers play. The Fly. Blake. *Fr.* Songs of Experience. LAuP; MBPR; OBP; PBMP

Little Gidding. T. S. Eliot. *Fr.* Four Quartets. BoReV; NoAM; NOBA; NOBE; OxBTC

Little girl dressed, The. Celebration. Ray A. Young Bear. CDW

Little Girl Found, The. Blake. *Fr.* Songs of Experience. MBPR; RRA

Little girl I'd known, The. Flora. Ray Fraser. NeAC

Little Girl Lost, A ("Children of the future age"). Blake. *Fr.* Songs of Experience. MBPR; RRA

Little Girl Lost, The ("In futurity/ I prophetic see"). Blake. *Fr.* Songs of Experience. MBPR; RRA

Little Girl, My String Bean, My Lovely Woman. Anne Sexton. RiTi; WBN

Little Girl Saw Her First Troop Parade, The. Carl Sandburg. PBMP

Little Girl with Bands on Her Teeth, The. Genevieve Taggard. VGW

Little goat/ crops/ new grass lying down, The. April. Yvor Winters. RFM

Little gold in law will make, A. Isabella Whitney. *Fr.* A Sweet Nosegay, or Pleasant Posy. WPE

Little Grenade, The. J. S. Harry. CAAP

Little hedge-row birds, The. Old Man Travelling; Animal Tranquillity and Decay, a Sketch. Wordsworth. MBPR

Little Horse. W. S. Merwin. TH

Little Hunger. Richard Murphy. BIrV

Little Ink More or Less, A. War Is Kind, II. Stephen Crane. VoPo

Little Jack Horner/ Sat in a corner. Mother Goose. MG; SoSe

Little Jesus, wast Thou shy. Ex Ore Infantium. Francis Thompson. OxBChV

Little joe gould has lost his teeth and doesn't know where. E. E. Cummings. NoAM

Little Johnny's Final Letter. Brian Patten. LP

Little Johnny's Foolish Invention. Brian Patten. BuTh

Little Keats' Soliloquy. Leon Stokesbury. NVAP

Little Lamb, who made thee? The Lamb. Blake. *Fr.* Songs of Innocence. HeIP; LAuP; LCL; MBPR; OxBChV; PAIC; RAE; SoSe

Little-League Baseball Fan. W. R. Moses. NCSH

Little League Women. Deena Metzger. RiTi

Little Learning, A. Pope. *Fr.* An Essay on Criticism, Pt. II. NOBE

Little Lemlem was married, at last. The Marital Journey. Hailu Araaya. MiP

Little light is going by, A. Firefly. Elizabeth Madox Roberts. LCL

Little Louey Comic, The. Wesley McNair. FAF

Little maiden climbed an old man's knee, A. After the Ball. Charles K. Harris. BLSo; FSN

Little Marg'et sitting in her high hall door. Fair Margaret and Sweet William. *Unknown.* AmFP

Little Mary Bell had a fairy in a nut. Long John brown and Little Mary Bell. Blake. InPK

Little Militant, The. John Shaw Neilson. MAuV

Little Miss and Her Parrot. John Marchant. OxBChV

Little Miss Muffett. Mother Goose. MG

Little Miss Muffet discovered a tuffet. The Embarrassing Episode of Little Miss Muffet. Guy Wetmore Carryl. PoTa

Little Mohea, The. *Unknown.* AmFP

Little More About the Brothers and Sisters, A. Sharon Scott. JB

Little moths are creeping, The. Interior. Padraic Colum. PFIr

Little Musgrave and Lady Barnard, *diff. versions. Unknown.* AmFP; PeBB

Little Nancy Etticoat. Mother Goose. MG

Little Old Sod Shanty. *Unknown.* AmFP

Little Old Women, The. Baudelaire, *tr. fr. French by* Barbara Gibbs. LoAs

Little Orphant Annie. James Whitcomb Riley. OxBChV

Little Piggy. Thomas Hood. ECBV

Little Pigs Lie in the Best of Straw, *with music. Unknown.* RDB

Little Polly Flinders. Mother Goose. MG

Little ragged girl, our ball-boy, A. A Game at Salzburg. Randall Jarrell. NoAM

Little Raindrops. Jane Euphemia Browne. OxBChV

Little robber girl, you sleep. The Story of Good. Phyllis Janik. IHMS

Little saint best fits a little shrine, A. A Ternarie of Littles, Upon a Pipkin of Jelly Sent to a Lady. Robert Herrick. ECBV

Little Sally Waters, 2 versions. Unknown. AmFP

Little Scraping, A. Robinson Jeffers. NoAM

Little Shon a Morgan, shentleman of Wales. Shon a Morgan. Unknown. GBP

Little Sleep's-Head Sprouting Hair in the Moonlight. Galway Kinnell. RRA

Little Sparrow. Unknown. AmFP

Little Star, The. Unknown. SpRo

Little Stone in the Middle of the Road, in Florida, A. Muriel Rukeyser. RiTi

Little Things. Julia A. Carney. OxBChV

Little Things. James Stephens. ECBV

Little thinks, in the field, yon red-cloaked clown. Each and All. Emerson. AmVN; NOBA; PiAm

Little think'st thou, poor flower. The Blossom. John Donne. AnMo

Little to write about. Sea Variations. R. A. Simpson. CAAP

Little Tom Tucker. Mother Goose. MG

Little Tommy Tittlemouse. Unknown. MG

Little toy dog is covered with dust, The. Little Boy Blue. Eugene Field. SoSe

Little train called 29, A. Number 29. Unknown. BluL

Little tree. E. E. Cummings. Chansons Innocentes, II. LCL; RAE

Little Turtle, The. Vachel Lindsay. LCL; RAE

Little Vagabond, The. Blake. Fr. Songs of Experience. MBPR

Little Wind. Kate Greenaway. RAE

Little Wren of tender mind, The. The Wren. Unknown. OxBChV

Little Yellow Leaf. James Tate. NoAM

Liu Ch'e. Ezra Pound. VGW

Live fowl squatting on the grapefruit and bananas, The. Jamaican Bus Ride. A. S. J. Tessimond. OxBTC

Live, live with me, and thou shalt see. To Phillis to Love, and Live with Him. Robert Herrick. LoAs

Live Man's Epitaph. Francis Hope. BuTh

Live thy life,/ Young and old. The Oak. Tennyson. SoSe

Live with Me. Mick Jagger and Keith Richard. InPK

Liver. Coleman Barks. Fr. Body Poems. NVAP

Liverockie, liverockie lee. The Lark. Unknown. GBP

Liverpool. Unknown. AmFP

Lives of the Saints. Jon Anderson. FiCP

Living, A. D. H. Lawrence. RFM

Living. Denise Levertov. VGW; WPE

Living ahead of people—a dangerous habit. In the Evening as from a Cradle. Robert Bloom. AATT

Living in an old house. Great-Aunts. Seán O'Criádáin. PFIr

Living in Sin. Adrienne Rich. IHMS; RiTi

Living in the Boneyard. John Oliver Simon. NeAC

Living room walks softly on Bukara, The. Oriental. Napoleon St. Cyr. FAF

Living someplace else in wrong. The Spring Offensive of the Snail. Marge Piercy. WBN

Living Tenderly. May Swenson. BoAnP

Living Truth, The. Sterling Plumpp. PoBA

Living with a Voodoo Doll. John Stone. CoPAm

Living with Chris. Ted Berrigan. NoAM

Lizard. D. H. Lawrence. BoAnP

Lizard. Alan McLean. BoAnP

Lizard. Paul Mills. MIS

Lizard, lover of heat, of high. The Old Man to the Lizard. Archibald MacLeish. PiAm

Lizard ran out on a rock and looked up, listening, A. Lizard. D. H. Lawrence. BoAnP

Lizards and Snakes. Anthony Hecht. NCSH; PPoD

Lizie Wan. Unknown. AmFP; PeBB

Lizzie Borden with an axe. The Crimes of Lizzie Borden. Unknown. FaBoCo

Lloyd George. Unknown. FaBoCo

Lloyd George and Woodrow Wilson and Clemenceau. A Legend of Versailles. Melvin B. Tolson. BPo

Lo, as a careful housewife runs to catch. Sonnets, CXLIII. Shakespeare. InPK

Lo as I pause in the alien vale of the airport. Twenty-Third Flight. Earle Birney. HeIP

Lo, Collin, here the place whose pleasaunt syte. June. Spenser. Fr. The Shepheardes Calender. PAIC

Lo! Death has reared himself a throne. The City in the Sea. Poe. AmVN; MAT; NOBA; PiAm

Lo freedom comes. Th' prescient muse foretold. Liberty and Peace. Phillis Wheatley. SBG

Lo here I sit at holy head. Holyhead, Sept. 25th, 1727. Swift. BIrV

Lo, how it gleams and glistens in the sun. The New Cake of Soap. Ezra Pound. PAIC

Lo! I am come to autumn. Gold Leaves. G. K. Chesterton. OxBTC

Lo! I must tell a tale of chivalry. Specimen of an Induction to a Poem. Keats. MBPR

Lo! I the man, whose Muse whylome did maske. The Faerie Queene, I, Induction. Spenser. PAIC

Lo! in the middle of the wood. Tennyson. Fr. The Lotus Eater. GrRo

Lo! lemman swete, now may thou see. Christ's Plea to Mankind. Unknown. OxBM

Lo, quhat it is to love. See Lo! what it is to lufe.

Lo, the moon's self! Phases of the Moon. Robert Browning. Fr. One Word More. Moon

Lo, thus, as prostrate, "In the dust I write." The City of Dreadful Night. James Thomson ("B. V."). NOBE; VPC

Lo! 'tis a gala night. The Conqueror Worm. Poe. Fr. Ligeia. NOBA; PiAm

Lo! what [or quhat] it is to lufe [or love]. A Rondel of Luve [or Love]. Alexander Scott. BoLoP; SLP

Lo! where the rosy-bosom'd hours. Ode on the Spring. Thomas Gray. LAuP

Loaded questions, The. Genitals. Coleman Barks. Fr. Body Poems. NVAP

Lobster, The. "Lewis Carroll." See Alice's Recitation.

Lobster Quadrille, The. "Lewis Carroll." Fr. Alice's Adventures in Wonderland, ch. 10. OxBChV

Lobsters. Howard Nemerov. AnMo; PBMP

Lobsters in the Window. W. D. Snodgrass. BoAnP; HeIP; NCSH; PiAm

Local Man Remembers the Killing Ground, A. James Whitehead. CoPAm

Local Storm, A. Donald Justice. NCSH

Locate I/ love you. The Language. Robert Creeley. CAPP; IPWM; LoAs; PiAm

Location. Knute Skinner. MAT

Locations. Jim Harrison. AmPA

Loch Achray was a clipper tall, The. The Yarn of the Loch Achray. John Masefield. PoTa

Loch Lomond, with music. Unknown. BLSH

Loch Ness Monster, The. Tom Buchan. SLP

Lochinvar. Sir Walter Scott. *Fr.* Marmion, V. AIW; BTTM; ECBV; NOBE; PoTa; SLP

Lock, The. Pope. *Fr.* The Rape of the Lock, V. Moon

Locke sank into a swoon. Fragment. W. B. Yeats. NoAM; SoSe

Locked arm in arm they cross the way. Tableau. Countee Cullen. PoBA

Locked In. Ingemar Gustafson, *tr. fr. Swedish by* May Swenson. PoTa

Locked in a Home for Les Enfants Dérangés en Dieu. James Nolan. AATT

Lockless Door, The. Robert Frost. NOBA

Locksley Hall. Tennyson. PFD

Locksley Hall, Sixty Years After. Tennyson. PFD

Locus, The. Cid Corman. VGW

Locust Tree in Flower, The. William Carlos Williams. PiAm

Locusts or Appolyonists, The, *sel.* Phineas Fletcher. "Now are they met: this armèd with a spade." SCP-2

Lodged firmly in my jaw a little tombstone, memorial. Gray's Anatomy. David Malouf. CAAP

Lodged in a flake of bone. Songs. David Steingass. HeS

Loftiest spirit that ever flamed in flesh, The. Paul Clause. AATT

Lofty ship from Salcombe came, A. The Salcombe Seaman's Flaunt to the Proud Pirate. *Unknown.* PeBB

Lofty young squire from Portsmouth he came, A. The Golden Glove. *Unknown.* AmFP

Logging. Gary Snyder. *See* Myths and Texts.

Logic. *Unknown.* ECBV

Logic does well at school. Scholars. Walter de la Mare. NoAM

Logical English. *Unknown.* ECBV

Loitering with a Vacant Eye. A. E. Housman. SoSe

Lollay, Lollay, Little Child! *Unknown.* OxBM

London ("I wander through each chartered street"). Blake. *Fr.* Songs of Experience. AnMo; GrRo; HeIP; InPK; InPS; LAuP; MAT; MBPR; NOBE; OBP; PAIC; PBMP; PPoD; VoPo; WIF

London. John Davidson. NOBE

London: a Poem in Imitation of the Third Satire of Juvenal. Samuel Johnson. LAuP

London after the Great Fire, 1666. Dryden. *Fr.* Annus Mirabilis. NOBE

London Bridge Is a-Burning Down. *Unknown.* AmFP

London Bridge [is broken down]. *Unknown.* GBP; MG

London Bridge was built. Stranger Than the Worst. Babette Deutsch. WPE

London, 1802 ("Milton! thou shouldst be living..."). Wordsworth. Epi; HeIP; IPWM; MBPR; OBP; PAIC; PBMP

London Fete, A. Coventry Patmore. VPC

London, hast thow accused me. Earl of Surrey. AAS

London is full of chickens, on electric spits. Peter Porter. *Fr.* Annotations of Auschwitz. OxBTC

"London: John Lane, The Bodley Head." On the Imprint of the First English Edition of "The Works of Max Beerbohm." Max Beerbohm. InPK

London Lickpenny. *Unknown.* OxBM

London Rain. Louis MacNeice. HeIP

London Snow. Robert Bridges. FSFS; NoAM; NOBE; OxBTC

London Sparrow's If, A. J. A. Lindon. BoAnP

London Tom-Cat. Michael Hamburger. BoAnP

London's Tempe; or, The Field of Happiness, *sel.* Thomas Dekker. Thwick-a-thwack. SCP-2

Loneliness. Hayden Carruth. FiCP

Loneliness. Brooks Jenkins. CTBA

Loneliness. Loyal Shegonee. VW

Loneliness. Al Young. NVAP; PoBA

Loneliness leapt in the mirrors, but all week. Departure's Girl-Friend. W. S. Merwin. ConAP

Lonely and big. First Pregnancy. Alta. NMM

Lonely Love. Edmund Blunden. OxBTC

Lonely Man, The. Randall Jarrell. MPo

Lonely, save for a few faint stars, the sky. The Little Dancers. Laurence Binyon. BBGO; OxBTC

Lonely Scarecrow, The. James Kirkup. RAE

Lonesome Dove ("Down in some lonesome piney grove"), 3 *versions. Unknown.* AmFP

Lonesome Dove, The ("Ye weary, heavy laden souls"). *Unknown.* AmFP

Lonesome in the Country. Al Young. MAT; SA

Lonesome scenes of winter incline to frost and snow, The. The Rejected Lover. *Unknown.* AmFP

Lonesome Valley, The, *with music. Unknown.* RDB

Long after you have swung back. Losing Track. Denise Levertov. AnMo; HeIP; NoAM; NOBA; SoSe

Long afterward, Oedipus, old and blinded. Myth. Muriel Rukeyser. IHMS

Long ago he had walked. Rimbaud in Abyssinia. Ellen McEvilley Griffin. NPW

Long ago, the Mountain Mother. Chorus. Euripides, *tr. by* Richmond Lattimore. *Fr.* Helen. RRA

Long beardes heartles. The English. *Unknown.* GBP

Long before morning they waked me to say. The Lunar Probe. Maxine W. Kumin. Moon

Long curved room, the walls, The. Monet's Les Nymphéas. Lyn Lifshin. FAF

Long Distance. Dana Naone. CDW

Long Distance. William Stafford. CoPAm

Long distance information, get me Memphis, Tennessee. Memphis, Tennessee. Chuck Berry. RRA

Long Distance Moan. *Unknown.* BluL

Long, Dodington, in debt, I long have sought. Edward Young. *Fr.* Love of Fame, the Universal Passion: Satire III. LAuP

Long-expected one and twenty. A Short Song of Congratulation. Samuel Johnson. InPK; InPS; LAuP; NOBE

Long Gone. Sterling A. Brown. BPo

Long Hair. Gary Snyder. NOBA; PiAm

Long hair tangled. Sedna. Lyn Lifshin. MMD

Long-haired preachers come out ev'ry night. Pie in the Sky. *Unknown.* GBP

Long have I beat with timid hands upon life's leaden doors. The Suppliant. Georgia Douglas Johnson. PoBA

Long I Thought That Knowledge Alone Would Suffice. Walt Whitman. NOBA

Long John Brown and Little Mary Bell. Blake. InPK

Long-legged Fly. W. B. Yeats. AnMo; InPK; InPS; NoAM; NOBE; PPoe; PSN

Long legs, crooked thighs. Mother Goose. GBP; MG

Long Lines. Paul Goodman. VGW

Long live our dear and noble Queen. Edward Edwin Foot. *Fr.* On the Inauguration of the Memorial Statue. FaBoCo

Long Live the Weeds. Theodore Roethke. NoAM; NOBA

Long, Long Ago, *with music.* Thomas Haynes Bayly. BLSH; BLSo; PSoN

Long, Long Ago. *Unknown.* RAE

Long long ago when the world was a wild place. Bedtime Story. George MacBeth. LP; MPo; NoAM; PoTa; SoSe

Long[e] love, that in my thought doth harbour, The. The Lover for Shamefastnesse Hideth His Desire within His Faithfull Hart. Petrarch, *tr. by* Sir Thomas Wyatt. Sonnets to Laura: To Laura in Life, CIX. AAS; Epi

Long Overdue Thankyou Note to the Girl Who Taught Me Loving, A. Tom Schmidt. NeAC

Long Person. Gladys Cardiff. CDW

Long red underwear of Randolph Scott, The. Ride the High Country. David Slavitt. PPoD

Long River, The. Donald Hall. ConAP

Long schoolroom days, drowsy with chanting voices. Photograph of an Actress, c. 1860 Nan McDonald. MAuV

Long straggling lines. Wild Geese. William Hart-Smith. BoAnP

Long Summer, sel. Robert Lowell.
"Everyone now is crowding everyone." CAPP

Long-Suffering of God. Christopher Smart. Fr. Hymns for the Amusement of Children. LAuP

Long Tail Blue, with music. Unknown. BLSo

Long Time Ago, A. Unknown. AmFP

Long Time Gone. David Crosby. WIF

Long time he lay upon the sunny hill. Childhood. Edwin Muir. HeIP

Long Tom. W. W. Gibson. OxBTC

Long, Too Long America. Walt Whitman. NoAM

Long Voyage, The. Malcolm Cowley. SoSe

Long War, The. Laurie Lee. BuTh

Long Way Outside Yellowstone, A. Thomas McGrath. VGW

Long ways, A. A Remembrance of a Color inside a Forest. Ray A. Young Bear. CDW

Long white barn, A. Unknown. GBP

Long Will in London. William Langland. Fr. The Vision of Piers Plowman. OxBM

Longe love that in my thought doth harbour, The. See Long love...

Longest Day, The. Wordsworth. RRA

Longface Mahoney Discusses Heaven. Horace Gregory. VGW

Longford Legend, A. Unknown. PoTa

Longing, The. Theodore Roethke. PiAm

Look at him there in his stovepipe hat. American Primitive. William Jay Smith. CoPAm; InPK; SFF; WIF

Look at it! The Photo. Lennart Bruce. MIT

Look at me 8th. Poem. Sonia Sanchez. PoBA

Look at me move. The Amputee Soldier. Philip Dacey. NVAP

Look at My Face, a Collage. Carolyn M. Rodgers. JB

Look at the gentle savage, monstrous gentleman. London Tom-Cat. Michael Hamburger. BoAnP

Look at the stars! look, look up at the skies! The Starlight Night. Gerard Manley Hopkins. InPS; PPP

Look between the bow and the bowstring, beneath. Backgrounds to Italian Paintings: Fifteenth Cnetury. Anne Ridler. WPE

Look Closely. Morton Marcus. SFF

Look, Delia, how we 'steem the half-blown rose. Samuel Daniel. Fr. To Delia. HeIP

Look down Fair Moon. Walt Whitman. Moon

Look Down That Lonesome Road, with music. Unknown. BLSo

Look! From my window there's a view. There Is. Louis Simpson. ConAP

Look how he shakes for cold! Crucifixus Pro Nobis. Patrick Carey. SCP-2

Look how the pale Queen of the silent night. A Sonnet of the Moon. Charles Best. Moon; SoSe

Look in my face; my name is Might-have-been. A Superscription. Dante Gabriel Rossetti. The House of Life, XCVII. NOBE; VPC

"Look, it's a fox!"—their two hearts spoke. The Fox. C. Day Lewis. BoAnP

Look, it's morning, and a little water gurgles in the tap. Morning Song. Alan Dugan. NowV

Look, Loig, behind. The Only Jealousy of Emer. Unknown, tr. by John Montague. BIrV

Look, look! rejoice and wonder! The Return of Astraea. Ben Jonson. NOBE

Look, my love, on the wall, and here, at this Eastern picture. Morning. Henry Reed. LoAs

Look not thou on beauty's charming. Lucy Ashton's Song. Sir Walter Scott. Fr. The Bride of Lammermoor, ch. 3. NOBE

Look one way and the sun is going down. The Mockingbird. Randall Jarrell. RFM

Look out how you use proud words. Primer Lesson. Carl Sandburg. SFF; TH

Look, stranger, on this island now. On This Island. W. H. Auden. InPS; MPo; PSN

Looking at Models in the Sears Catalogue. Philip Dacey. HeS

Looking at Pictures to Be Put Away. Gary Snyder. CoPAm; InPS

Looking at Some Flowers. Robert Bly. NOBA

Looking Both Ways before Crossing. John Woods. ConAP; IPWM

Looking by chance in at the open window. The Foreboding. Robert Graves. GBL

Looking for a Place to be Comfortable. Virginia Gilbert NVAP

Looking for a Rest Area. Stephen Dunn. AmPA

Looking for Asia. R. H. W. Dillard. CoPAm

Looking for Lola. Morgan Sanders. WBN

Looking for love, she read cookbooks. The Woman Who Loved to Cook. Erica Jong. WBN

Looking for Mountain Beavers. David Wagoner. VGW

Looking for Mushrooms at Sunrise. W. S. Merwin. NOBA

Looking Forward. Robert Louis Stevenson. OxBChV

Looking into a Face. Robert Bly. NOBA; TSWA

Looking into a Tide Pool. Robert Bly. MAT

Looking into History. Richard Wilbur. VGW

Looking into my daughter's eyes I read. For My Daughter. Weldon Kees. RRA

Looking Out. Helen Chasin. NMM

Looking to the sea, it is a line. The Innocence. Robert Creeley. NoAM

Looking Up. John Allcock. BuTh

Looking up/ I find myself written. The Paisley Ceiling. Lila Arnold. IHMS

Looking Up at Airplanes, Always. Rolfe Humphries. PAIC

Looking Up at Down. Unknown. BluL

Lopsided love in hotel rooms. Adolescent's Song. Howard Moss. LoAs

Lord/ forgive me/ if I twist the sunset. The Hungry Black Child. Adam David Miller. PoBA

Lord/ We come. A Maze of the Magi. Sandra Ruth Duguid. AATT

Lord Apollo, who has never died, The. Many Are Called. E. A. Robinson. PiAm

Lord Arnaldos. James Elroy Flecker. PoTa

Lord Bateman. Unknown. AmPF

Lord Bless You and Keep You, the, with music. Numbers, Bible, O.T. BLSH

Lord, confound this surly sister. The Curse. J. M. Synge. FaBoCo

Lord Cozens Hardy. John Betjeman. OxBTC

Lord Derwentwater. Unknown. AmPF

Lord, dub my tongue with a new tier of words. Edward Taylor. Preparatory Meditations: Second Series, XIX. SCP-2

Lord Finchley. Hilaire Belloc. FaBoCo

Lord Fluting Dreams of America on the Eve of His Departure from Liverpool. Paul Zimmer. VGW

Lord god of wings, forgive this hand. Early Warning. George MacBeth. TwMBP

Lord Gorbals. Harry Graham. FaBoCo

Lord, heavy hip mama she done moved to piney wood. Piney Wood Money Mama. *Unknown.* BluL

Lord, how can man preach thy eternal word? The Windows. George Herbert. AnMo; SCP-1

Lord, how delightful 'tis to see. For the Lord's Day Evening. Isaac Watts. OxBChV

Lord, how sholde I roule me. How Should I Rule Me? *Unknown.* OxBM

Lord I can't see how these hungry women please. Don't Want No Hungry Woman. *Unknown.* BluL

Lord I hate to hear that Frisco whistle blow. Frisco Whistle Blues. *Unknown.* BluL

Lord, I have leaped my zenith, passed my noon. The Old Tiger and the God of the Water-hole. Margaret Reynolds. MIS

Lord, I lie here. Prayer from a Stryker Frame. E. Margaret Clarkson. AATT

Lord, I'm Troublin', *with music. Unknown.* BLSH

Lord is my external-internal integrative mechanism, The. The Twenty-third Psalm. Alan Simpson. SFF

Lord is my shepherd, The; I shall not want. Psalms, XXIII, Bible, *O.T.* SFF

Lord Is Risen, The. William Dunbar. BoReV; NOBE

Lord Jesus bring your peace to fathers with no luck. A Christmas Prayer. William R. Mitchell. AATT

Lord Lovel. *Unknown.* AmFP

Lord Lundy. Hilaire Belloc. FaBoCo; OBP

Lord of Rosslyn's daughter gaed through the wud her lane, The. Captain Wedderburn's Courtship. *Unknown.* SLP

Lord of the Dance. Sydney Carter. LP

Lord of the Isles, The, *sel.* Sir Walter Scott.
"No! sum thine Edith's wretched lot." SLP

Lord of the Mirrors, *sel.* George Mackay Brown.
"Beast, what is love?" SLP

Lord Rameses of Egypt sighed. Birthright. John Drinkwater. OxBTC

Lord Randal. *Unknown.* AIW; AmFP; HeIP; PAIC; SLP
(Lord Randall.) WIF
(Lord Rendal, *with music.*) RDB

Lord, serene on your symbol. Accepting. Vassar Miller. FiCP

Lord, shall I find it in Thy Holy Church. Truth. Claude McKay. BPo

Lord, she won't pick cotton girl won't pull no corn. No More Women Blues. *Unknown.* BluL

Lord, the Roman hyacinths are blooming in bowls. A Song for Simeon. T. S. Eliot. BuTh

Lord they accused me of murder. Levee Camp Moan. *Unknown.* BluL

Lord Thomas and Fair Annet, *diff. versions. Unknown.* AmFP; PeBB
(Lord Thomas and Fair Ellender.) AmFP

Lord, Thou hast given me a cell. A Thanksgiving to God, for His House. Robert Herrick. OFD
Lord, thou hast made this world below the shadow of a dream. McAndrew's Hymn. Kipling. OXBTC

Lord Waterford. *Unknown.* GBP

Lord, what a thoughtless wretch was I. *Unknown.* AmFP

Lord, what is man? why should he cost thee. Charitas Nimia: or, The Dear Bargain. Richard Crashaw. BoReV

Lord, what unvalued pleasures crowned. The Invitation. Nathaniel Wanley. BoReV

Lord, when I look at lovely things which pass. In the Fields. Charlotte Mew. LoAs

Lord, when the sense of thy sweet grace. A Song. Richard Crashaw. IPWM

Lord, when the wise men came from far. Hymn [*or* Wise Men and Shepherds]. Sidney Godolphin. BoReV; NOBE

Lord, who createdst man in wealth and store. Easter Wings. George Herbert. AnMo; HeIP; InPK; InPS; PPP; WIF

Lord, who hast formed me out of mud. Trinity Sunday. George Herbert. PAIC

Lord will happiness divine, The. The Contrite Heart. William Cowper. WIF

Lord, with what care hast Thou begirt us round! Sin. George Herbert. Epi

Lordly Hudson, The. Paul Goodman. VGW

Lord's Chameleons, The. Peter Klappert. AmPA

Lords, knights, and squires, the numerous band. To a Child of Quality Five Years Old. Matthew Prior. NOBE; RRA

Lord's lost Him His mockingbird. Mourning Poem for the Queen of Sunday. Robert Hayden. PoBA

Lorelei, The, *with music.* Heine, *tr. fr. German by* James Morehead. BLSH

Lorena, *with music.* Henry De Lafayette Webster. PSoN

Los Alamos: Manhattan. David Rowbotham. CAAP

Los New Yorks. Victor Hernández Cruz. SA

Loser, The. Charles Bukowski. MiP

Losers. Carl Sandburg. NoAM

Losing Track. Denise Levertov. AnMo; HeIP; NoAM; NOBA; SoSe

Loss. A. R. Ammons. ConAP

Loss, The. Stephen Dunn. NVAP

Loss, my molester, at last patient be. Pamphilia's Sonnet. Mary Sidney Wroth, Countess of Montgomery. *Fr.* Urania. WPE

Loss of Black Camels, The. Sam Hamod. SA

Loss of the *Due Dispatch*, The. *Unknown.* AmFP

Loss of the *New Columbia*, The. *Unknown.* AmFP

Lost. Bruce Ignacio. VW

Lost. Charles d' Orléans. OxBM

Lost, The. Jones Very. NOBA; PiAm

Lost—A Lizard. Irene Gough. ECBV

Lost Acres. Robert Graves. NoAM

Lost Anchors. E. A. Robinson. PiAm

Lost Angel, The. Philip Levine. NOBA

Lost Baby, The. *Unknown.* AmFP

Lost Baby Poem, The. Lucille Clifton. InPK; RiTi; WPE

Lost Children, The. Randall Jarrell. PBMP; RRA

Lost Contact. William Cole. POL

Lost Country. Warren Woessner. HeS

Lost Dancer, The. Jean Toomer. PoBA

Lost Deer, The. Joseph Bruchac. FAF

Lost Desire. Meleager, *tr. fr. Greek by* William M. Hardinge. LoAs

Lost Doll, The. Charles Kingsley. *Fr.* The Water Babies. ECBV
(Little Doll, The.) OxBChV

Lost Egg, The. Percy Illot. ECBV

Lost Heifer, The. Austin Clarke. BIrV

Lost in Oregon, hunting my bearings. Atlas. Robert Flanagan. HeS

Lost Jewel, A. Robert Graves. LoAs

Lost Jimmie Whalen. *Unknown.* AmFP

Lost Johnny. *Unknown.* AmFP

Lost Lane. Dorothy Wellesley. WPE

Lost Leader, The. Robert Browning. BTTM; PBMP; PPoD

Lost Love. Andrew Lang. SLP

Lost Lover Blues. *Unknown.* BluL

Lost manor where I walk continually. The Pier-Glass. Robert Graves. NoAM

Lost Mistress, The. Robert Browning. BoLoP; NOBE

Lost Moment. Hoyt W. Fuller. PoBA

Lost Occasion, The. Whittier. NOBA

Lost Picture. Ray Fraser. NeAC

Lost Son, The. Theodore Roethke. VGW

Lost Weekend Bar, The. Joy Harjo. SA

Lot Later. Howard Nemerov. CoPAm

Lot of love is chosen, The. I learnt that much. Chosen. W. B. Yeats. BoLoP

Lotos-Eaters, The, sels. Tennyson.
  "Hateful is the dark blue sky." GrRo
  "Lo! in the middle of the wood." GrRo
  Song of the Lotos-Eaters. NOBE
  ("There is sweet music here that softer falls.") HeIP

Lots of truisms don't have to be repeated. The Anatomy of Happiness. Ogden Nash. PAIC

Lotus Eaters, The. Tennyson. See Lotos-Eaters, The.

Loud is the summer's busy song. John Clare. Fr. The Shepherd's Claendar: July. FSFS

Loudest thing in our car, The. Vacation Trip. William Stafford. CTBA

Lough Derg. Denis Devlin. BIrV

Louisa. Wordsworth. GBL

Louisburg. Unknown. BTTM

Louise. Stevie Smith. SBG

Louisiana Weekly # 4, The. David Henderson. PoBA

Louse Hunting. Isaac Rosenberg. OxBTC

Lousy Miner. Unknown. AmFP

Love. Jaime Torres Bodet, tr. fr. Spanish by Muna Lee de Munoz Marín. LoAs

Love. Samuel Taylor Coleridge. MBPR

Love. George Granville. BoLoP

Love. Pauline Hanson. LoAs

Love ("Love bade me welcome; yet my soul drew back"). George Herbert. BoReV; HeIP; InPK; LoAs; MAT; MetP; NOBE; PBMP; PPP; Prf; SCP-1; VoPo

Love. Patrick Lane. NeAC

Love. Pablo Neruda, tr. fr. Spanish by Alastair Reid. LP

Love. Robert Pack. CoPAm

Love. Shelley. MBPR

Love. Anne Stevenson. NCSH

Love ("I am a fool, I can no good"). Unknown. OxBM

Love ("My love is no short year's sentence"). Unknown, tr. fr. Irish by John Montague. BIrV

Love ("She stood in her snood and arasaid"). Unknown, tr. fr. Gaelic by G. R. D. McLean. SLP

Love ("There's the wonderful love of a beautiful maid.") Unknown. SFF; SoSe

Love, sel. Alice Walker.
  "Old man in White, An." NMM

Love a woman? You're an ass! Song. Earl of Rochester. GBL

Love Affair, A. Arnold Bennett. OxBTC

Love among the Ruins. Robert Browning. NOBE

Love and a Question. Robert Frost. LoAs

Love and Age. Walter Savage Landor. GBL

Love and an Old Western at the Starlite Drive-In Theater. Philip Legler. PPoD

Love and Death. Byron. MBPR; NOBE

Love and Death. John Frederick Nims. CoPAm

Love and harmony combine. Song. Blake. MBPR

Love and Jealousy. William Walsh. BoLoP

Love and Liberty (The Jolly Beggars), sel. Burns.
  "See the smoking bowl before us." OBP

Love and Life. Earl of Rochester. BoLoP; GBL; NOBE

Love and Poetry. Louis Simpson. PPoe

Love and Sleep. Swinburne. BoLoP; LoAs

Love Arm'd. Aphra Behn. See Song: "Love in fantastic triumph sate."

Love at First Sight. Christopher Marlowe. Fr. Hero and Leander, First Sestiad. NOBE

Love at Large. Coventry Patmore. Fr. The Angel in the House, I, ii. VPC

Love at Stress-Point. Ruthe T. Spinnanger. AATT

Love at the closing of our days. Last Love. Fyodor Tyutchev, tr. by Valdimir Nabokov. BoLoP

Love at the lips was touch. To Earthward. Robert Frost. LoAs; NoAM; NOBA; PPoe

Love bade me welcome; yet my soul drew back. Love. George Herbert. BoReV; HeIP; InPK; LoAs; MAT; MetP; NOBE; PBMP; PPP; Prf; SCP-1; VoPo

Love brought by night a vision to my bed. Lost Desire. Meleager, tr. by William M. Hardinge. LoAs

Love Calls Us to the Things of This World. Richard Wilbur. AnMo; CAPP; HeIP; InPS; NoAM; PiAm; PPP; TCP; VGW; WIF

Love came by from the riversmoke. Melora's Song. Stephen Vincent Benét. Fr. John Brown's Body. AIW

Love Charm. Unknown, tr. fr. Gaelic. SLP

Love-Charms. Thomas Campion. See Thrice Toss These Oaken Ashes in the Air.

Love Child—a Black Aesthetic. Everett Hoagland. BPo

Love comes back to his vacant dwelling. Rondel: The Wanderer. Austin Dobson. PAIC

Love Divine, with music. Charles Wesley. BLSH

Love ere he bleeds, an eagle in high skies. Modern Love, XXVI. George Meredith. PAIC

Love Feast, The. W. H. Auden. SFF

Love flies with bow unstrung when Time appears. Love and Age. Walter Savage Landor. GBL

Love from My Father. Carole Gregory Clemmons. PoBA

Love God—/ my mother said. The Will's Love. Besmilr Brigham. IHMS

Love goddess, alas, grows frailer, The. The dying Goddess. Carolyn Kizer. WBN

Love, I love beyond. Edmond Rostand, tr. by Brian Hooker. Fr. Cyrano de Bergerac, Act III. OLR

Love I love whose lips I love, A. The Accomplices. Conrad Aiken. LoAs; NOBA

Love? I'd rather be condemned to Grand Opera. Do You Love Me? Robert Watson. POL

Love, if nothing solid rises like wood. Song: The Organic Years. Marvin Bell. NVAP

Love in a Life. Robert Browning. NOBE

Love in a Space-suit. James Kirkup. MPo

Love in a Village, sel. Isaac Bickerstaffe.
  Song: "There was a jolly miller once." PFIr

Love in Edinburgh. Nicholas Fairbairn. SLP

Love in fantastic [or fantastique] triumph sate. Song [or Love Arm'd]. Aphra Behn. Fr. Abdelazer. NOBE; SBG; WPE

Love in Labrador. Carl Sandburg. VGW

Love in my bosom like a bee. Rosalind's Madrigal. Thomas Lodge. Fr. Rosalynde; or, Euphues' Golden Legacy. NOBE

Love in the Asylum. Dylan Thomas. LoAs

Love in the Middle of the Air. Lenore Kandel. Fr. Circus. RiTi

Love in the Valley. George Meredith. NOBE; VPC

Love Is. Ann Darr. MiP

Love is a circle that doth restless move. Love What It Is. Robert Herrick. GBL

"Love is a law, a discord of such force." Unknown, at. to John Webster and William Rowley. Fr. The Thracian Wonder. GBL

Love is a place. E. E. Cummings. OLR

Love is a queer little elfin sprite. Because You're You. Henry Blossom. BLSo

Love Is a Sickness. Samuel Daniel. *Fr.* Hymen's Triumph. NOBE

Love is a universal migraine. Symptoms of Love. Robert Graves. BoLoP

Love is and was my lord and king. In Memoriam A. H. H., CXXVI. Tennyson. NOBE

Love is begot by fancy, bred. Love. George Granville. BoLoP

Love Is Life, *orig. and mod. English prose.* Richard Rolle of Hampole. OxBM

Love Is Like a Dizziness. James Hogg. SLP

Love Is More Thicker than Forget. E. E. Cummings. AnMo

Love is no more. Amor Vincit Omnia. Edgar Bowers. PiAm

Love is not all; it is not meat nor drink. Edna St. Vincent Millay. NoAM

Love is not blind. I see with single eye. Edna St. Vincent Millay. SBG

Love is not mocked whatever use. "Graphemics," 10. Jack Spicer. VGW

Love is not worth so much. Coda. James Tate. AmPA

Love is soft, love is swete, love is good sware. Love is Weal, Love is Wo. *Unknown.* OxBM

Love is something some people do not know about. *Unknown.* SFF

Love is the peace, whereto all thoughts doe strive. Fulke Greville. *Fr.* Caelica. AAS

Love is the plant of peace and most precious of virtues. Et Incarnatus Est. William Langland. *Fr.* Vision of Piers Plowman. BoReV; NOBE

Love is too young to know what conscience is. Sonnets, CLI. Shakespeare. HeIP

Love Is Weal, Love Is Wo. *Unknown.* OxBM

Love Letter. Sylvia Plath. NOBA

Love Lifted Me, *with music.* James Rowe. BLSH

Love lives beyond. John Clare. NOBE

Love, love, a lily's my care. Words for the Wind. Theodore Roethke. LoAs; NoAM; NOBA

Love Made in the First Age: to Chloris. Richard Lovelace. SCP-2

Love Me and Never Leave Me. Ronald McCuaig. POL

Love me brought[e]. Christ's Love-Song. *Unknown.* BoReV; OxBM

Love Me Little, Love Me Long. Robert Herrick. LoAs

Love me, love my dog: by love to agree. Of Loving a Dog. John Heywood. PAIC

Love, oh, love, oh, careless love. Careless Love. *Unknown.* BLSH; BluL; BLSo

Love, oh my love, it will come. Geoffrey Hill. *Fr.* The Songbook of Sebastian Arrurruz. PSN

Love of a woman, The. Air. Robert Creeley. VGW

Love of Fame, The Universal Passion, *sels.* Edward Young. Lavinia at Church, *fr.* Satire VI. BoReV
   "Long, Dodington, in debt, I long have sought," Satire III. LAuP

Love of God, The. John Audelay. OxBM

Love on the Farm. D. H. Lawrence. OBP

Love Poem: "Black biplane crashes into the window, The." Gregory Orr. MAT

Love Poem: "History of My Feeling, The." Kathleen Fraser. *See* History of My Feeling, The.

Love Poem: "Last night you would not come." John Logan. CAPP; CoPAm

Love Poem: "My clumsiest dear, whose hands shipwreck vases." John Frederick Nims. CoPAm; InPK; SoSe; TCP; VoPo

Love Poem: "She coils her body around me." Howard Schwartz. HeS

Love Poem: "Six o'clock and/ the sun rises..." Miller Williams. MAT

Love Poem: "These words are all of me." Lewis Turco. NowV

Love Poem: "When we are in love, we love the grass." Robert Bly. InPS

Love Poem Beginning with I. David Steingass. CoPAm

Love Poem on Theme by Whitman. Allen Ginsberg. CAPP

Love Poem 3. Laughton Johnston. SLP

Love Poems of the VIth Dalai Lama, *sels.* Peter Whigham. TwMBP
   "Frost/ lacing/ late summer."
   "In a season/ the shoots we planted."
   "In summer/ this reed-patch."
   "In the oasis of the day."
   "Old dog, The/ at the west poster."
   "Pattern of birds, A."
   "This country girl."
   "Why does this pretty boy from Kong-po."

Love Pursued. *Unknown. Fr.* The Thracian Wonder. GBL

Love Rejected. Lucille Clifton. BPo

"Love seeketh not itself to please." The Clod and the Pebble. Blake. *Fr.* Songs of Experience. AnMo; InPS; LAuP; LoAs; MBPR; NOBE; SS

Love sells off a wilderness in which. About That. Marvin Bell. HeS

Love set you going like a fat gold watch. Morning Song. Sylvia Plath. HeIP; IHMS; InPK; InPS; LoAs; NOBA; PSN; SBG

Love should grow up like a wild iris in the fields. Susan Griffin. RiTi

Love signed the contract blithe and leal. Epigram. John Swanick Drennan. BIrV

Love Song. Gavin Ewart. OxBTC

Lovesong. Ted Hughes. OBP

Love Song. Edward Lear. *Fr.* The Owl and the Pussy-cat. PCat

Love Song. Joseph Macleod. SLP

Lovesong. Rainer Maria Rilke, *tr. fr. German by* M. D. Herter Norton. LoAs; OLR

Love Song. Anne Sexton. NCSH

Love Song for the Future. Vassar Miller. NCSH

Love Song: I and Thou. Alan Dugan. BuTh; CAPP; CoPAm; InPK; LoAs; NoAM; SFF; SoSe

Love Song of J. Alfred Prufrock, The. T. S. Eliot. AnMo; Epi; HeIP; InPK; InPS; IPWM; NoAM; NOBA; NOBE; OxBTC; PAIC; PPP; PSN; SoSe; WIF

Love Songs. Mina Loy. VGW; WPE, *abr.*

Love Songs in Age. Philip Larkin. PPP; PSN

Love Sonnet, A. George Wither. *See* I Loved a Lass.

Love Sonnets of Proteus, The, *sels.* Wilfrid Scawen Blunt.
   Farewell to Juliet ("I see you, Juliet, still, with your straw hat), XLVIII. BoLoP; OxBTC
   St. Valentine's Day, LV. LoAs

Love still has something of the sea. Song. Sir Charles Sedley. GBL; NOBE

Love, strong as death, is dead. An End. Christina Rossetti. GBL

Love-Talker, The. "Ethna Carbery." PFIr; PoTa; WPE

Love That Doth Reign and Live within My Thought. Petrarch, *tr. fr. Italian by* the Earl of Surrey. Sonnets to Laura: To Laura in Life, CIX. HeIP
   ("Love that doth raine and live within my thought.") AAS
   ("Love that liveth and reigneth in my thought.") Epi

Love that is not pardoned, A. Doors. Tom Clark. ConAP

Love, the delight of all well-thinking minds. Fulke Greville. GBL

Love the sun. William Carlos Williams. *Fr.* Calypsos. TH

Love the Wild Swan. Robinson Jeffers. HeIP; InPS; PiAm

Love, thou art absolute, sole Lord. A Hymn to the Name and Honour of the Admirable Saint Teresa. Richard Crashaw. BoReV; NOBE; SCP-1, *abr.*

Love to My Electric Handmixer. Diane Wakoski. CoPAm

Love twists. The Pressures. LeRoi Jones. BPo

Love Undeclared. *Unknown.* OxBM

Love under the Republicans (or Democrats.) Ogden Nash. IPWM; PBMP

Love Unfeigned. Chaucer. *Fr.* Troilus and Criseyde. BoReV; NOBE
    (O Yonge Freshe Folkes.) OxBM

Love Unknown. George Herbert. Prf

Love, we are a small pond. We Are. Maxine W. Kumin. WBN

Love, we curve downwards, we are set to night. After Midsummer. E. J. Scovell. OxBTC

Love we define for ourselves, The. Prothalamion. Michael Ryan. AmPA

Love What It Is. Robert Herrick. GBL

Love who points the swallow home. Who Points the Swallow. David Campbell. MAuV

Love Will Find Out the Way. *Unknown.* GBL

Love without Hope. Robert Graves. BoLoP; GBL

Love Your Enemy. Yusef Iman. BPo

Loveliest of Trees. A. E. Housman. FSFS; HeIP; InPK; IPWM; NoAM; OxBTC; PPoD; VoPo; WIF

Lovely Big Cow. J. B. Morton. RAE

Lovely form there sate beside my bed, A. Phantom or Fact. Samuel Taylor Coleridge. MBPR

Lovely Love, A. Gwendolyn Brooks. BPoLovely Shall Be
*Lovely Shall Be Choosers, The. Robert Frost. NOBA*

Lovely Tear of Lovely Eye. *Unknown.* OxBM

Lovely whore though. Cathleen. *Unknown, tr. by* Thomas MacIntyre. BIrV

Lovelye William, 2 *versions. Unknown.* AmFP

Lover Beseecheth His Mistress Not to Forget His Steadfast Faith and True Intent, The. Sir Thomas Wyatt. *See* Forget Not Yet.

Lover Compareth His State to a Ship in Perilous Storm Tossed on the Sea, The. Petrarch, *tr. fr. Italian by* Sir Thomas Wyatt. Sonnets to Laura: To Laura in Life, CLVI. GBL; HeIP; PAIC
    (My Galley Charged with Forgetfulness.) Epi; PPP
    ("My galy charged with forgetfulnes.") AAS

Lover Complaineth the Unkindness of His Love, The. Sir Thomas Wyatt. GBL
    ("My lute, awake! perform the last.") AAS; LoAs
    (To His Lute.) BoLoP; NOBE

Lover Deceived Writes to His Lady, The, *sel.* Thomas Howell. "Who would have thought that face of thine." POL

Lover for Shamefastnesse Hideth His Desire within His Faithfull Hart, The. Petrarch, *tr. fr. Italian by* Sir Thomas Wyatt. Sonnets to Laura: To Laura in Life, CIX. AAS, 2 *versions*
    ("Long love that in my thought doth harbour, The.") Epi

Lover Having Dreamed Enjoying of His Love, Complaineth That the Dream Is Not either Longer or Truer. Sir Thomas Wyatt. AAS, 2 *versions*

Lover in Winter Plaineth for the Spring, The. *Unknown. See* Western Wind.

Lover of swamps. To the Snipe. John Clare. Epi

Lover of the Lord. *Unknown.* AmFP

Lover Proved False, The. *Unknown.* AmFP

Lover Showeth [*or* Sheweth] How He Is Forsaken of Such as He Sometime Enjoyed, The. Sir Thomas Wyatt. AAS, 2 *versions*; GBL; InPS
    (Remembrance.) BoLoP; NOBE
    (They Flee from Me That Sometime Did Me Seek [*or* Seke].) HeIP; InPK; LoAS; PPP; SoSe
    (Vixi Puellis Nuper Idoneus.) OBP

Lover Tells of the Rose in His Heart, The. W. B. Yeats. PFIr

Lover That I Hope You Are. Milton Acorn. NeAC

Lover to Himself, The. David Phillips. NeAC

Lover to His Lady, The. *At. to* Plato, *tr. fr. Greek by* George Turberville. LoAs

Lover under burden of his mistress' love, The. Gulling Sonnets, I. Sir John Davies. Epi; PAIC

Loverd, thou clepedest me. Wait a Little! *Unknown.* BoReV; OxBM

Lovers, The. Conrad Aiken. LoAs

Lovers, The. W. R. Rodgers. BIrV

Lovers, The. Karen Swenson. WBN

Lovers, and a Reflection. Charles Stuart Calverley. FaBoCo; SpRo

Lover's Confession, A. Charles d'Orléans. *See* My Ghostly Father, I Me Confess.

Lovers everywhere are bringing babies into the world. Make Love Not War. Howard Nemerov. NoAM

Lover's eyes will gaze an eagle blind, A. Shakespeare. *Fr.* Love's Labour's Lost, IV, iii. GBL

Lovers Go Fly a Kite, The. W. D. Snodgrass. NowV

Lovers How They Come and Part. Robert Herrick. GBL

Lovers in ladies' magazines. Song. Thomas McGrath. VGW

Lovers in the act dispense. The Thieves. Robert Graves. BoLoP

Lover's Lament, A, 3 *versions. Unknown.* AmFP

Lover's Lament for Her Sailor, The. *Unknown.* AmFP

Lovers of pleasure more than God. Lover of the Lord. *Unknown.* AmFP

Lovers of the Poor, The. Gwendolyn Brooks. CAPP; NoAM; NOBA

Lover's Plea, A. Thomas Campion. NOBE
    ("Shall I come sweet love to thee.") AAS; GBL; LoAs

Lover's Resolution, A. George Wither. *Fr.* Fair Virtue. BoLoP; NOBE
    ("Shall I wasting in despair.") PAIC; SS

Lover's Shirt, The. *Unknown, tr. fr. Welsh by* Gwyn Williams. BuTh

Lover's Song, The. W. B. Yeats. AnMo

Lover's Stratagem, A. *Unknown. Fr.* Floris and Blauncheflour. OxBM

Lovers who/ came to me. Ghost Poem Five. Mary Norbert Körte. IHMS

Lovers whose lifted hands are candles in winter. For a Child Expected. Anne Ridler. BuTh

Love's Alchemy. John Donne. AnMo

Love's Apparition and Evanishment. Samuel Taylor Coleridge. MBPR

Love's Commission. William Cavendish, Duke of Newcastle. SCP-2

Love's Deity [*or* Deitie]. John Donne. GBL; LoAs

Love's Emblems. John Fletcher. *Fr.* The Tragedy of Valentinian, II, iv. BoLoP; NOBE

Love's Flowers. William Cavendish, Duke of Newcastle. SCP-2

Love's Force. Thomas Carew. SCP-2

Love's Good-morrow. Thomas Heywood. *Fr.* The Rape of Lucrece. LoAs
    ("Pack, clouds, away, and welcome, day!") GBL

Love's Growth; or, Spring. John Donne. SCP-1

Love's Immaturity. E. J. Scovell. GBL

Love's Labour's Lost, *sels.* Shakespeare.
"Lover's eyes will gaze an eagle blind, A," *fr.* IV, iii. GBL
Spring, *fr.* V, ii. FSFS; SoSe
("When daisies pied and violets blue.") HeIP; InPK; IPWM; NOBE; OBP
When Icicles Hang by the Wall, *fr.* V, ii. HeIP; InPK; InPS; NOBE; OBP
(Winter.) AKE; FSFS; IPWM; SoSe
Love's Martyrs. John Ford. *Fr.* The Broken Heart, IV, iii. NOBE
("Oh no more, no more, too late.") GBL
Love's Matrimony. William Cavendish, Duke of Newcastle. SCP-2
Love's night and a lamp. Meleager, *tr. fr. Greek by* Peter Whigham. BoLoP
Loves of the Puppets. Richard Wilbur. LoAs
Love's Old Sweet Song, *with music.* G. Clifton Bingham. BLSH; BLSo; FSN
Love's own form. R. G. Vliet. POL
Love's Philosophy. Shelley. BoLoP; MBPR; OLR; PBMP; VoPo
Love's Preparation. William Cavendish, Duke of Newcastle. SCP-2
Love's Progress. John Donne. Elegies, XVIII. SCP-1
Love's Remorse. Edwin Muir. OxBTC
Love's Secret. Blake. OLR; PPoe
(Never Seek to Tell Thy Love.) InPS; LoAs; NOBE; OBP
Love's the boy stood on the burning deck. Casabianca. Elizabeth Bishop. LoAs
Love's Vision. William Cavendish, Duke of Newcastle. SCP-2
Loves who many years held all my mind, The. Walter Savage Landor. GBL
Lovest Thou Me? William Cowper. BoReV
Loving. Kathleen Fraser. WBN
Loving. Jane Stembridge. NMM
Loving and Liking. Dorothy Wordsworth. OxBChV
Loving Dexterity, The. William Carlos Williams. TH
Loving in truth, and fain in verse my love to show. Astrophel and Stella, I. Sir Philip Sidney. AAS; Epi; GBL; LoAs; OBP
Loving Mad Tom. *Unknown. See* Tom o' Bedlam's Song.
Loving me with my shoes off. Barefoot. Anne Sexton. SFF
Loving she is, and tractable, though wild. Characteristics of a Child Three Years Old. Wordsworth. MBPR; RRA
Loving She Stood Apart. Patrick Lane. NeAC
Loving you is a warm room. A Cold And Married War. Marge Piercy. Psy
Lovingly I turn me down. After Mass. "Michael Field." WPE
Low along the River. Ralph Adamo. CoPAm
Low Barometer. Robert Bridges. NoAM
Low Fields and Light. W. S. Merwin. ConAP
Low Road, The. Tom Buchan. MIS
Low...the Violence Begins Low. Ann Darr. WBN
Low was our pretty cot: our tallest rose. Reflections on Having Left a Place of Retirement. Samuel Taylor Coleridge. MBPR
Lowdown Dirty Blues. *Unknown.* AmFP
Lowdown Rounder's Blues. *Unknown.* BluL
Lowell. James Russell Lowell. *Fr.* A Fable for Critics. AmVN; NOBA
Lower the flags. Special Bulletin. Langston Hughes. PoBA
Lower the Standard: That's My Motto. Karl Shapiro. NoAM
Lowering, The. May Swenson. TCP
Lowest trees have tops, the ant her gall, The. A Silent Love. Sir Edward Dyer. BoLoP; NOBE
Lowlands ("I dreamt a dream the other night") *Unknown.* AIW

Lowlands Away ("Lowlands, Lowlands away, my John"). *Unknown.* GBP; PeBB
Lowlands of Holland, The ("Last Easter I was married"). *Unknown.* AIW; AmFP, *diff. version*
Lowson. John Blight. CAAP
Loyal Citizen. Richard Lyons. HeS
Lucas Park (Saint Louis). Paul Southworth Bliss. ANTL
Lucasta Taking the Waters at Tunbridge: Ode. Richard Lovelace. SCP-2
Lucasta's Fan, With a Looking-glass in It. Richard Lovelace. SCP-2
Lucifer in Starlight. George Meredith. Epi; InPK; IPWM; NOBE; OBP; PAIC; PBMP; PPoe; SoSe; VCP
Lucinda Matlock. Edgar Lee Masters. *Fr.* Spoon River Anthology. IPWM; NoAM; NOBA; PBMP; VoPo
Luck. W. W. Gibson. ECBV; RAE
Luck of Edenhall, The. Longfellow. PoTa
Luckes, my faire falcon, and your fellowes all. Sir Thomas Wyatt. AAS
Lucky Chance, The, *sel.* Aphra Behn.
Song: "Oh! Love, that stronger art than wine." WPE
Lucky Louie Makes a Goal. H. Van Arsdale. SPo
Lucky the husband. Mabel Kelly. Turlough O'Carolan, *tr. by* Austin Clarke. BIrV
Lucy, *complete, in 5 parts.* Wordsworth. AnMo; MBPR; NOBE Sels.
I Traveled Among Unknown Men. AnMo; MBPR; NOBE
She Dwelt among the Untrodden Ways. AnMo; BoLoP; HeIP; MBPR; NOBE; PPP; SpRo; WIF, 2 versions
Slumber Did My Spirit Seal, A. *AnMo; HeIP; InPK; InPS;* MBPR; NOBE; PAIC; PBMP; PPP
Strange Fits of Passion I Have Known. AnMo; Epi; GBL; LoAs; MBPR; NOBE; PPP; SoSe
Three Years She Grew in Sun and Shower. AnMo; MBPR; NOBE
Lucy Ashton's song. Sir Walter Scott. *Fr.* The Bride of Lammermoor, *ch.* 3. NOBE
Lucy Gray; or, Solitude. Wordsworth. Epi; MBPR; OxBChV
Lucy Lake. Newton Mackintosh. SpRo
Ludwig's Death Mask. Ted Hughes. NoAM
Luini in porcelain! Medallion. Ezra Pound. PSN
Luke and John. Handwriting on the Wall. *Unknown.* AmFP
Luke XI: Blessed Be the Paps Which Thou Hast Sucked. Richard Crashaw. SCP-1
Luke Havergal. E. A. Robinson. AmVN; GBL; LoAs; NoAM; NOBA; PiAm
Luke VII: She Began to Wash His Feet with Tears. Richard Crawshaw. SCP-1
Lula Vires. *Unknown.* AmFP
Lullabie of a Lover, The. George Gascoigne. AAS
Lullaby: "Beloved, may your sleep be sound." W. B. Yeats. BoLoP
Lullaby: "I wish to God my child was born." *Unknown.* AmFP
Lullaby: "It is a summer evening." Anne Sexton. NoAM
Lullaby: "Lay your sleeping head, my love." W. H. Auden. NoAM; NOBE; OxBTC; PPP; PSN
("Lay your sleeping head, my love.") BoLoP
Lullaby and good-night. Cradle Song. *Unknown.* BLSH
Lullaby for Ann-Lucian. Calvin Forbes. PoBA
Lullaby of an Infant Chief. Sir Walter Scott. OxBChV
Lullay, By-by, Lullay. *Unknown.* OxBM
Lullay, Lullay, Little Child. *Unknown.* BoReV
Lullay, My Child. *Unknown.* OxBM
Lully, lulla, thou little tiny child. Coventry Carol. *Unknown.* OFD
Lully, lullay, lully, lullay. Corpus Christi Carol. *Unknown.* BoReV; GBP; NOBE; OxBM

Lumber of a London-going dray, The.  An Incident in the Early Life of Ebenezer Jones, Poet, 1828.  John Betjeman.  NoAM

Lumbering haunches, pussyfoot tread, a pride of.  Circus Lion. C. Day Lewis.  BoAnP; MPo

Lumberman's Alphabet, The.  *Unknown.*  AmFP

Lumberyard, The.  Ruth Herschberger.  WPE

Luminalia, *sel.*  Sir William Davenant.
  Night's Song.  SCP-2

Lumps of mud, the toads.  Haiku.  José Juan Tablada, *tr. by* Samuel Beckett.  PBMP

Lunar Baedeker.  Mina Loy.  VGW

Lunar Paraphrase.  Wallace Stevens.  Moon

Lunar Probe, The.  Maxine W. Kumin.  Moon

Lunar Tides, The.  Marya Zaturenska.  Moon

Lunatic, the Lover, and the Poet, The.  Shakespeare.  *Fr.* A Midsummer Night's Dream, V, i.  PAIC

Luncheon, A.  Max Beerbohm.  FaBoCo; OxBTC

Lune Concrete.  Raymond Federman.  Moon

Lusty Juventus, *sel.*  Robert Wever.
  In Youth Is Pleasure.  NOBE
    ("In a herber green, asleep whereas I lay.")  GBL

Lutra, The Fisher.  James McMichael.  AmPA

Luxurious man, to bring his vice in use.  The Mower Against Gardens.  Andrew Marvell.  AnMo; PPP

Luxury.  Donald Justice.  HeIP

Luxury Apt.  Marie Harris.  MMD

Luxury, then, is a way of.  Political Poem.  LeRoi Jones. NoAM

Lyarde Is an Old Horse.  *Unknown.*  OxBM

Lyce.  William Walsh.  BoLoP

Lycidas.  Milton.  AnMo; Epi; InPK; InPS; NOBE; OBP; PAIC; PPoD; PPoe; PPP; SCP-1
  *"Ay me! whilst thee the shores and sounding seas," sel.*  Prf

Lycoris darling, once I burned for you.  Martial, *tr. fr. Latin by* Peter Porter.  BoLoP

Lydlinch Bells.  William Barnes.  VCP

Lyell's Hypothesis Again.  Kenneth Rexroth.  NoAM

Lying.  Thomas Moore.  PFIr

Lying apart now, each in a separate bed.  One Flesh.  Elizabeth Jennings.  MPo; OxBTC

Lying asleep between the strokes of night.  Love and Sleep. Swinburne.  BoLoP; LoAs

Lying Down Hungry.  Carol Bergé.  MMD

Lying here, everything in me.  Margaret Atwood.  NeAC

Lying in a Hammock at William Duffy's Farm.  James Wright. ANTL; CAPP; ConAP; InPS; IPWM; NOBA; PSN; SFF

Lying in a Yuma Saloon.  Jim Barnes.  CDW

Lying in bed in the dark, I hear the bray.  Weather Ear. Norman Nicholson.  MPo

Lying is an occupation.  Song.  Laetitia Pilkington.  WPE

Lying On a Bridge.  Van K. Brock.  NVAP

Lyke as a huntsman, after weary chace.  *See* Like as a huntsman. . .

Lyke Memnons rocke toucht, with the rising sunne.  Lucia, XLVII.  Giles Fletcher the Elder.  AAS

Lyke-Wake Dirge, The.  *Unknown.*  GBP; NOBE

Lynching, The.  Claude McKay.  PoBA; WIF

Lynching, The.  Milton Kessler.  CoPAm

Lynching and Burning.  Primus St. John.  PoBA

Lyrebirds.  Judith Wright.  BoAnP

Lyve thowe gladly, yff so thowe may.  Sir Thomas Wyatt.  AAS

# M

M and A, R and I.  *Unknown.*  OxBM

M & O Blues.  *Unknown.*  BluL

MD Sewed Wrong Section of Colon.  F. R. Scott.  AKE

Ma Canny Hinny.  *Unknown.*  GBP

Mabel Kelly.  Turlough O'Carolan, *tr. fr. Irish by* Austin Clarke. BIrV

Mabel—when is the bomb set to.  An Anarchist's Letter. Harald Wyndham.  POL

Macadam, gun-grey as the tunny's belt.  Van Winkle.  Hart Crane.  *Fr.* The Bridge: Powhatan's Daughter.  PiAm

McAfee's Confession.  *Unknown.*  AmFP

McAndrew's Hymn.  Kipling.  OxBTC

Macavity: The Mystery Cat.  T. S. Eliot.  FaBoCo; InPS; OxBChV

Macbeth, *sels.*  Shakespeare.
  "She should have died hereafter," *fr.* V, v.  SoSe
  "Thrice the brinded cat hath mew'd," *fr.* IV, i.  OFD

MacFlecknoe; or, A Satire upon the True-Blue Protestant Poet T. S. Dryden.  ESaP; PPP
  *Sels.*
  "All human things are subject to decay."  SCP-1
    (Crown Prince of Dullness, The.)  NOBE
  "Now Empress Fame had published the renown."  SCP-1
  Shadwell Anatomized.  OBP

Machu Picchu, Peru.  Fred Red Cloud.  VW

Macrinus against Trees.  "Michael Field."  WPE

Macy's Poem, The.  James Reiss.  POL

Mad Answer of a Madman, A.  Robert Hayman.  SoSe

Mad Dog.  Robert Siegel.  FAF

Mad Gardener's Song, The.  "Lewis Carroll."  *Fr.* Sylvie and Bruno.  FaBoCo; OxBChV; PBMP

Mad girl with the staring eyes and long white fingers, The. Cassandra.  Robinson Jeffers.  HeIP; PiAm

Mad Hatter's Song.  "Lewis Carroll."  *Fr.* Alice's Adventures in Wonderland, *ch.* 7.  SpRo

Mad have black roots in their brains, The.  Sequence.  James Harrison.  CoPAm

Mad Lover, The, *sels.*  John Fletcher.
  "O divine star of heaven," *fr.* IV, i.  GBL
  "Orpheus I am, come from the deeps below," *fr.* IV, i.  GBL

Mad Maid's Song, The.  Robert Herrick.  SCP-1

Mad male-hearted woman in a prouder age, A.  Desmond O'Grady.  NoAM

Mad Meg on my mantelpiece.  Three Women.  Liz Lochhead. MIS

Mad Monk, The.  Samuel Taylor Coleridge.  MBPR

Mad Mother, The.  Wordsworth.  MBPR

Mad paper, stay! and grudge not here to burn.  To Mrs. Magdalen Herbert.  John Donne.  SCP-1

Mad Poem Addressed to My Nephews and Nieces, A.  Po Chu-i, *tr. fr. Chinese by* Arthur Waley.  BBGO; BuTh

Mad Scene, The.  James Merrill.  CoPAm; NoAM; NOBA

Mad Song.  Blake.  MBPR

Mad Song.  Denise Levertov.  Psy

Mad Tom of Bedlam.  *Unknown.*  SCP-2

Mad-Woman, The.  L. A. G. Strong.  PFIr

Mad Yak, The.  Gregory Corso.  NoAM

Madam and the Minister.  Langston Hughes.  NOBA

Madam Eglantine.  Chaucer.  *See* Prioress, The.

Madam Life's a Piece in Bloom.  W. E. Henley.  InPK

Madam, your beauty and your lovely parts.  Platonic Love. Lord Herbert of Cherbury.  SCP-2

Madame, I Have Come a-Courting.  *Unknown.*  AmFP

Madame, withouten many wordes.  Sir Thomas Wyatt.  AAS; LoAS

Madam's Past History.  Langston Hughes.  NoAM

Made Shine.  Josephine Miles.  NoAM

Madeleine in Church.  Charlotte Mew.  SBG

Mademoiselle from Armentières, *with music*.  *Unknown*.  BLSo

Madge Wildfire's Song.  Sir Walter Scott.  *See* Proud Maisie.

Madhouse.  Calvin C. Hernton.  TCP
  (The Patient: Rockland County Sanitarium.)  PoBA

Madimba: Gwendolyn Brooks.  Michael S. Harper.  MIT

Madman's Song.  Elinor Wylie.  Moon

Madness is my sidekick.  Whats My Name if Not Everyone Elses.  Luís Omar Salinas.  SA

Madonna and Daughter.  Carol Bergé.  MMD

Madonna of the Evening Flowers.  Amy Lowell.  RiTi

Madonna over the pool table.  Locked in a Home for Les Enfants Dérangés en Dieu.  James Nolan.  AAT

Madrigal: "Like the Idalian queen."  William Drummond of Hawthornden.  GBL; NOBE

Madrigal: "My love in her attire doth show her wit."  *Unknown*.  *See* My Love in Her Attire.

Madrigal: "Your love is dead, lady, your love is dead."  R. S. Thomas.  BoLoP

Mag.  Patricia Hubbell.  CaYB

Magalu.  Helene Johnson.  PoBA

Magdalene, Afterward.  Karen Whitehill.  NPW

Magdalene Silver Mine, The.  Gene Frumkin.  CoPAm

Magellan braved all seas that roll.  The Windham Thaw.  Arthur Guiterman.  ECBV

Maggie and Milly and Molly and May.  E. E. Cummings.  BuTh; NOBA

Maggie Campbell Blues.  *Unknown*.  BluL

Maggie Lauder.  At. to Francis Sempill of Beltrees.  SLP

*Maggie Mac.*  *Unknown*.  AmFP

Magi, The.  W. B. Yeats.  InPK; InPS; NoAM; OFD; PPoe; PSN

Magic.  Rex Veeder.  HeS

Magic/ my man.  Black Magic.  Sonia Sanchez.  BPo

Magic Fox.  James Welch.  CDW

Magic Seeds, The.  James Reeves.  ECBV

Magic Words.  *Unknown, tr. fr. Eskimo*.  IPWM

Magician, The.  Diane Wakoski.  Psy

Magna Est Veritas.  Coventry Patmore.  *Fr*. The Unknown Eros.  NOBE; VCP

Magnet, The.  Thomas Stanley.  NOBE

Magnetism.  Emma Lazarus.  SBG

Magnets.  Countee Cullen.  PBMP

Magpie Rhyme, Northumberland, A.  *Unknown*.  GBP

Magus, A.  John Ciardi.  CoPAm; MAT

Mahabalipuram.  Louis MacNeice.  NoAM

Mahler, *sel*.  Jonathan Williams.
  Symphony No. 3, in D Minor.  VGW

Maid and the Palmer, The.  *Unknown*.  PeBB

Maid compelled to be a gadder, A.  Charles Cotton.  *Fr*. Burlesque upon the Great Frost.  SCP-2

Maid Freed from the Gallows, The.  *Unknown*.  AIW; AmFP, 2 *versions*; ECBV

Maid in the Mill, The, *sel*.  John Fletcher *and* William Rowley.  "Now having leisure, and a happy wind," *fr*. V, i.

Maid Marian, *sel*.  Thomas Love Peacock.
  Friar of Rubygill, The.  PeBB

Maid Mars Me, A.  *Unknown*.  OxBM

Maid of Athens Ere We Part.  Byron.  MBPR

Maid of Brenten Arse, A.  *Unknown*.  GBP

Maid of Monterey, The.  *Unknown*.  AmFP

Maid of Neidpath, The.  Sir Walter Scott.  SLP

Maid of the Moor, The.  *Unknown*.  NOBE; OxBM

Maid shee went to the well to washe, The.  The Maid and the Palmer.  *Unknown*.  PeBB

Maiden caught me in the wild, The.  The Crystal Cabinet.  Blake.  AIW; Epi; MBPR

Maiden in the moor lay.  The maid of the Moor.  *Unknown*.  NOBE; OxBM

Maiden That Is Makeless, A.  *Unknown*.  *See* I Sing of a Maiden That Is Makeless.

Maidenhead.  "Ephelia."  WPE

Maidenhead.  Michael McMahon.  FAF

Maiden's Best Adorning, The.  *Unknown*.  OxBChV; RRA

Maidens Came, The.  *Unknown*.  BuTh; GBL
  (Bridal Morn, The.)  NOBE

Maiden's Complaint, The.  *Unknown*.  OLR

Maiden's Plight, The.  Brian Merriman, *tr. fr. Modern Irish by* Frank O'Connor.  *Fr*. The Midnight Court.  BIrV

Maidens shall weep at merry morn.  The Summer Malison.  Gerard Manley Hopkins.  NoAM

Maid's Tragedy, The, *sels*.  Beaumont *and* Fletcher.
  Aspatia's Song, *fr*. II, i.  NOBE
  ("Lay a garland on my hearse.")  GBL
  "Great queen of shadows, you are pleased to speak."  SCP-2

Mail from Home in the Sky.  Ernest Sandeen.  HeS

Mailman, The.  Thomas Brush.  NVAP

Main Problem in Portraiture, The.  Elisavietta Ritchie.  AATT

Maine Sea Gulls.  Russell Hoban.  BoAnP

Major abstraction is the idea of man, The.  Wallace Stevens.  *Fr*. Notes Toward a Supreme Fiction.  NOBA

Major André.  *Unknown*.  AmFP

Major Macroo.  Stevie Smith.  SBG

Make a joyful noise unto the Lord, all ye lands.  Psalm C, Bible, *O.T.*  OFD

Make Love Not War.  Howard Nemerov.  NoAM

Make me a grave where'er you will.  Bury Me in a Free Land.  Frances E. W. Harper.  BPo

Make Me a Pallet on Your Floor.  *Unknown*.  BluL

Make me, O Lord, thy spinning wheel complete.  Huswifery.  Edward Taylor.  NOBE; SoSe

Make no mistake. This is not.  The Seven-Year Body Cycle: To My Cells Replacing Themselves for the Fourth Time.  David Steingass.  NVAP

Make this assumption.  Rearrangement for the Brain.  Gary Margolis.  CoPAm

Make we mery, both more and lass.  Now Is the Time of Christmas.  *Unknown*.  OxBM

Maker-of-Sevens in the scheme of things.  The Wife-Woman.  Anne Spencer.  NoAM

Makers, The.  Richard Kell.  PFIr

Making his advances.  Tortoise Gallantry.  D. H. Lawrence.  NoAM

Making It Simple December 8, 1969.  David McElroy.  AmPA

Making of Color, The.  Hugh Seidman.  AmPA

Making of the Cross, The.  William Everson.  VGW

Making Out.  Leatrice W. Emeruwa.  RiTi

Making Up for a Soul.  David Wagoner.  VGW

Malaga.  Pearse Hutchinson.  BIrV

Malcolm.  Welton Smith.  BPo

Malcolm X.  Gwendolyn Brooks.  NowV; OFD; PoBA

Malcolm X—An Autobiography.  Larry Neal.  BPo

Maldive Shark, The.  Herman Melville.  NOBA; PiAm

Malediction.  Barry Spacks.  InPK

Malfunction.  Richard E. Albert.  MiP

Malison of the Stone-chat.  *Unknown*.  GBP

Malisons, malisons more than ten.  The Lark.  *Unknown*.  GBL

Mallow evenings on the shallow lake. The Heron. Philip Murray. BoAnP

Maltese Dog, The. *Unknown, tr. fr. Greek by* Edmond Blunden. ECBV

Malum Opus. James Appleton Morgan. FaBoCo

Malvern Hill. Herman Melville. AmVN

Malvolio in San Francisco. Jack Gilbert. NowV

Mama,/ papa,/ and us. An Inconvenience. John Raven. BPo

Mama Knows. Sharon Scott. JB

Mama was a friendly mountain. For Mama Streek. Colette Inez. AATT

Mama writes. Under Your Voice, Among Legends. Phyllis Beauvais. NMM

Mamma! Frank Horne. BPo

Mamma sent me to the spring, she told me not to stay. Chewing Chawing Gum. *Unknown.* AmFP

Mammon-Marriage, A. George Macdonald. BoLoP

Man. George Herbert. MetP

Man, The. Lucille Iverson. WBN

Man. Henry Vaughan. MetP; NOBE; SCP-1

"Man, a man, a kingdom for a man, A." A Cynic Satyre. John Marston. *Fr.* The Scourge of Villainy, VII. TVS

Man adrift on a slim spar, A. Stephen Crane. AmVN

Man All Grown Up Is Supposed To, A. Terry Stokes. AmPA

Man and a woman, A. The Origin of Hot and Cold According to the Delawares. Lyn Lifshin. FAF

Man and Bat. D. H. Lawrence. BoAnP

Man and Beast. Clifford Dyment. BoAnP

Man and Wife. Mitchell Goodman. VGW

Man and Wife. Robert Lowell. BoLoP; ConAP; PSN

Man and Wife. Anne Sexton. CAPP

Man and Woman. Robert Conquest. OxBTC

Man and Woman. Don L. Lee. NeAC

Man, be ware and wise in dede. Assay a Friend. *Unknown.* OxBM

Man behind the counter is young and blond, The. Conversation in the Eighth Street Bookstore. Honor Moore. WBN

Man bent over his guitar, The. The Man with the Blue Guitar. Wallace Stevens. NoAM

Man builds boxes, A. Boxes. Toi Derricotte. NPW

Man-brained and man-handed ground-ape, physically, The. Original Sin. Robinson Jeffers. PiAm

Man cut his throat and left his head there, The. The Creation of the Moon. *Unknown, tr. by* W. S. Merwin. Moon

Man, dream no more of curious mysteries. Vain Learning. Fulke Greville. *Fr.* Caelica. BoReV

Man Flammonde, from God knows where, The. Flammonde. E. A. Robinson. NoAM

Man, free-thinker, think you yourself alone possessed of thought? Golden. Gérard de Nerval, *tr. by* Andrew Hoyem. Epi

Man from Snowy River, The. Andrew Barton Paterson. MAuV

Man from the finance company, The. Good Luck to You Kafka/ You'll Need It Boss. Henry Graham. NowV

Man from Washington, The. James Welch. CDW; SA; VW

Man growing old is going, A. Shalom. Denise Levertov. NoAM

Man has been standing, A. The Tunnel. Mark Strand. HeIP

Man He Killed, The. Thomas Hardy. HeIP; InPS; IPWM; PBMP; SFF; SoSe; VoPo; WIF

Man, if you gonna love your woman. You Got to Love Her with a Feeling. *Unknown.* BluL

Man in armor, A. Touch. Erica Jong. RiTi

Man in the Bowler Hat, The. Peter Black. BuTh

Man in the Dead Machine, The. Donald Hall. CoPAm

Man in the Dream Is Death, The. Lynne Butler. IHMS

Man in the feed store called them mountain beavers, The. Looking for Mountain Beavers. David Wagoner. VGW

Man in the Moon, The ("Man in the moone stand and strit."), *orig. and mod. English prose. Unknown.* OxBM

Man in the moon came tumbling down, The. *Unknown.* Moon

Man in the moon was caught in a trap, The. *Unknown.* Moon

Man in the moone stand and strit. The Man in the Moon. *Unknown.* OxBM

Man in the wilderness asked me, The. Mother Goose. ECBV; FaBoCo; GBP; MG

Man in the womb is but a zoophyte. The Progress. Ralph Knevet. SCP-2

Man, introverted man, having crossed. Science. Robinson Jeffers. WIF

Man is clothed, The. And When the Green Man Comes. John Haines. ConAP; NCSH

Man is killing time—there's nothing else, The. The Drinker. Robert Lowell. SoSe

Man is mind. Progress. Peter Meinke. POL

Man laughing on the steep hill, The. Trifles. William Everson. CoPAm

Man lies down to sleep, A. Pull of the Earth. Stanley Plumly. HeS

Man looking into the sea. A Grave. Marianne Moore. HeIP; InPK; NoAM; NOBA; PPoe; WPE

Man, Man, Man is for the Woman Made. *Unknown.* PAIC; Prf

Man-Moth, The. Elizabeth Bishop. MAT; NoAM; NOBA; PPP

Man, My Father, The. Marcia Lee Masters. HeS

Man of Calvary, The, *sel.* "Sin-Killer" Griffin. "Roman soldiers come riding in full speed." AmFP

Man of Experience, A. Laoiseach Mac an Bhaird, *tr. fr. Irish by* Frank O'Connor. PFIr

Man of himself's a little world, but join'd. The Microcosm. Giovanni Battista Guarini, *tr. by* Sir Edward Sherburne. LoAs

Man of life upright, The. Integer Vitae. Thomas Campion. AAS; NOBE

Man of massive meditation, A. Analogue of Unity in Multeity. Richard Eberhart. NoAM

Man of Property, The. Charles G. Ballard. VW

Man of Taste, The, *sel.* James Bramston. "Huge commentators grace my learned shelves." FaBoCo

Man of Thessaly, The. *Unknown.* FaBoCo ("There was a man of Thessaly.") MG

Man of Words, A. *Unknown.* ECBV

Man on his own in a car, A. Meditation on the A30. John Betjeman. BBGO

Man on My Back, The. Pradip Sen. BuTh

Man on the Flying Trapeze, The. George Leybourne. BLSH, *with music*; BLSo, *with music*; PoTa (The Flying Trapeze.) PSoN

Man one out of his head, A. A Week in Paradise. John Ridland. NowV

Man out walking alone in the snow, A. Winter Exercise. Howard Nemerov. NowV

Man possessed a cat on which he doted, A. Cat into Lady. La Fontaine, *tr. by* Edmund Marsh. PCat

Man proposes, God in His time disposes. On a Dead Child. Richard Middleton. SoSe

Man riding on the meaning of rivers, A. Are You Born?—I. Muriel Rukeyser. LoAs

Man said to me at the fair, A. The Market. James Stephens. AIW

Man said to the universe, A. War Is Kind, XXI. Stephen Crane. AmVN; PiAm; SFF

Man sat in the felon's tank, alone, A.   In the Tank.   Thom Gunn.   NoAM

Man saw a ball of gold in the sky, A.   The Black Riders, XXXV. Stephen Crane.   AmVN; PiAm

Man say I had someting look like new, A.   Stew Meat Blues. *Unknown.*   BluL

Man should never earn his living, A.   A Living.   D. H. Lawrence.   RFM

Man sits in a timelessness, The.   The Rescue.   Robert Creeley. CAPP

Man, standing in the shadows of a, A.   For H. W. Fuller. Carolyn M. Rodgers.   BPo

Man stood in the laurel tree, A.   Things.   Louis Simpson.   TCP

Man that hails you Tom or Jack, The.   William Cowper.   *Fr.* On Friendship.   POL

Man that sees by chance his picture made, A.   The Growth of Love, XXXIX.   Robert Bridges.   NoAM

Man, the egregious egoist.   Cold-blooded Creatures.   Elinor Wylie.   SBG

Man, them revolutionary niggers is all.   Just Taking Note. Sharon Scott.   JB

Man Thinking about Woman.   Don L. Lee.   IPWM; NoAM

Man Under the Bed, The.   Erica Jong.   AmPA; NVAP

Man Upright, The.   Thomas MacDonagh.   BIrV

Man walks quietly through the bank, A.   Papa Doc Is Dead. Carol Cox.   MMD

Man was sitting underneath a tree, A.   Seumas Beg.   James Stephens.   OxBTC

Man went forth with gifts, A.   Martin Luther King, Jr. Gwendolyn Brooks.   PoBA; WIF

Man White, Brown Girl and All That Jazz.   Gloria C. Oden. PoBA

Man Who Broke the Bank at Monte Carlo, The, *with music.*   Fred Gilbert.   FSN

Man Who Closes Himself, The.   Peter Cooley.   NVAP

Man Who Dreamed of Faeryland, The.   W. B. Yeats.   NoAM

Man Who Finds That His Son Has Become a Thief, The. Raymond Souster.   BBGO

Man Who Had Fallen among Thieves, A.   E. E. Cummings. NoAM; NOBA; NowV; PiAm

Man who loves hiking, A.   Hiking.   Joseph Bruchac.   CDW

Man Who Married Magdalene, The.   Louis Simpson.   NoAM

Man Who Prayed, The.   John Shaw Neilson.   MAuV

Man who sold his lawn to standard oil, The.   The War Against the Trees.   Stanley Kunitz.   NoAM

Man Who Swallowed a Bird, The.   David Young.   CAAP

Man whose height his fear improved he, The.   Medgar Evers. Gwendolyn Brooks.   NowV; PoBA

Man Whose Pharynx Was Bad, The.   Wallace Stevens.   PiAm

Man with the Blue Guitar, The, *sel.*   Wallace Stevens. "Man bent over his guitar, The."   NoAM

Man with the Hoe, The.   Edwin Markham.   AmVN; WIF

Man you know, assured and kind, The.   Almost Human.   C. Day Lewis.   NoAM

Manchester by Night.   Mathilde Blind.   SBG

Manciple's Tale, The, *sel.*   Chaucer.   *Fr.* The Canterbury Tales. Controlling the Tongue.   OxBChV Mice before Milk.   PCat

Mandalay.   Kipling.   NOBE; PBMP

Mandarin/ in a silent film.   The Yellow Bird.   James W. Thompson.   PoBA

Mandelstam.   David Young.   AmPA

Mandrake Hairt, The.   Sydney Goodsir Smith.   SLP

Manerly Margery Mylk and Ale.   John Skelton.   AAS

Manfred: A Dramatic Poem.   Byron.   MBPR

Mango on the Mango Tree, The.   Robert Penn Warren.   Mexico Is a Foreign Country: Four Studies in Naturalism, IV. NoAM

Manhattan is no island, it.   Under.   George Bowering.   NeAC

Manhole Covers.   Karl Shapiro.   MiP; NCSH

MANICdepressant.   Kim Dammers.   POL

Manichaeans, The.   Gary Snyder.   VGW

Manifest Destiny.   Anita Endrezze Probst.   CDW

Manifesto, *sel.*   Nicanor Parra, *tr. fr. Spanish by* Miller Williams. "Ladies and gentlemen/ This is our final word."   TSWA

Manners.   Elizabeth Bishop.   CTBA; NCSH

Manners.   Edith Marcombe Shiffert.   WPE

Manners at Table When Away from Home.   *Unknown.*   OxBChV

Manor Water.   *Unknown.*   GBP

Manresa and the mango trees and the sterile landscape.   St. Ignatius Loyola, Founder of the Jesuits: His Autobiography. John L'Heureux.   PAIC

Man's been pitying himself all Sunday long, The.   The Apron. Stuart Friebert.   FiCP

Man's Days.   Eden Phillpotts.   OxBTC

Man's life is like a rose, that in the spring.   Meditation 9.   Philip Pain.   NOBA

Man's work, A.   The Stone Poems.   Ken Smith.   TwMBP

Mantis with translucent grin, The.   Confontation.   John Hart. MIT; POL

Mantle So Green, The.   *Unknown.*   AmFP

Many a curious mortal have I seen.   The Aquarium, San Francisco.   V. Sackville-West.   SBG

Many a green isle needs must be.   Lines Written among the Euganean Hills.   Shelley.   MBPR

Many Are Called.   E. A. Robinson.   PiAm

"Many Brave Hearts Are Asleep in the Deep."   Morgan Sanders. WBN

Many-clothed and smelling of cheap soap.   A Clutter of Mothers. Edwin Brock.   IPWM

Many desire, but few or none deserve.   The Advice.   Sir Walter Ralegh.   AAS

Many ingenious lovely things are gone.   Nineteen Hundred and Nineteen.   W. B. Yeats.   BIrV

Many liberals don't just.   Respectabilities.   Jon Silkin.   NoAM

Many-maned scud-thumper, tub.   Winter Ocean.   John Updike. InPK; SoSe

Many, many welcomes.   The Snowdrop.   Tennyson.   FSFS

Many red devils ran from my heart.   The Black Riders, XLVI. Stephen Crane.   PiAm

Many the wonders I this day have seen.   To My Brother George. Keats.   MBPR

Many things I might have said today.   Aprons of Silence.   Carl Sandburg.   NoAM; NOBA

Manzanita, The.   Yvor Winters.   VGW

Map, The.   Elizabeth Bishop.   NOBA

Map of Places, The.   Laura Riding.   NoAM

Map of the Western Part of he County of Essex in England, A. Denise Levertov.   ConAP

Maple buds were blossoming reddish tufts, The.   The Grotto. Ray Fraser.   NeAC

Maple in November.   Ethel Green Russell.   AATT

Maple Leaf Forever, The, *with music.*   Alexander Muir.   BLSH

Maple Leaf Rag, *with music.*   Sydney Brown.   BLSo

Maps.   Robert Hass.   CAAP

Maps.   Howard Schwartz.   HeS

Maratea Porto: Saying Goodbye to the Vitolos.   Richard Hugo. MAT

Marban, a Hermit Speaks.   *Unknown, tr. fr. Irish by* Michael Hartnett.   BIrV

Marceline, to Her Husband.   Elizabeth Libbey.   AmPA

March. Nora Hopper. FSFS

March, The ("Under the too white marmorial Lincoln Memorial"). Robert Lowell. NowV

March, The ("Where two or three were heaped together, or fifty"). Robert Lowell. NowV

March. *Unknown.* GBP

March. William Carlos Williams. NCSH

March. James Wright. TH

March Fugue. Thomas Shapcott. CAAP

March into Virginia, The. Herman Melville. PiAM

March on the Delta. Art Berger. NowV

March Rite: Getting It Up. A. G. Sobin. HeS

March said to Averil. The Borrowing Days. *Unknown.* GBP

March to Moscow, The. Robert Southey. FaBoCo

March went out like a lion. June Is Bustin' Out All Over. Oscar Hammerstein II. BLSo

March winds and April showers. *Unknown.* MG

March yeans the lammie. March. *Unknown.* GBP

Märchenbilder. John Ashbery. NOBA

Marches Now the War Is Over. Walt Whitman. *See* By Blue Ontario's Shore.

Marching 'round the Levee. *Unknown.* AmFP

Marching Through Georgia, *with music.* Henry Clay Work. PSoN

Marching To Quebec. *Unknown.* AmFP

Marching to Utah. *Unknown.* AmFP

Mare, dead since November, is still, The. The January Sky. A. G. Sobin. HeS

Mare lathers the wind, The. Bareback in Kansas. F. Eugene Warren. AATT

Margaret Are You Drug. George Starbuck. MAT

Margaret, are you grieving. Spring and Fall. Gerard Manley Hopkins. AnMo; BBGO; HeIP; InPK; InPS; MAT; NOBE; PAIC; PPoe; PPP; VoPo; WIF

Margaritae Sorori. W. E. Henley. *Fr.* Echoes. NOBE

Maria intended a letter to write. How to Write a Letter. Elizabeth Turner. OxBChV

Maria Wentworth. Thomas Carew. MetP; SCP-2

Mariam, *sel.* Lady Elizabeth Carey.
    "Fairest action of our human life, The," *fr.* IV. WPE
    " 'Tis not enough for one that is a wife," *fr.* III. WPE

Mariana. Tennyson. InPS; NOBE

Marigold. Richard Garnett. PCat

Marigold. John Haines. POL

Marigolds. Bliss Carman. AKE

Marijuana Patch on the State Hospital's Former Grounds. Nathan Whiting. HeS

Marilyn Monroe. Paul Ramsey. PPoD

Marina. T. S. Eliot. BoReV; HeIP; NOBE; PiAm; PSN; RRA; TCP

Marines' Hymn, The. *Unknown.* BLSH, *with music*; BLSo, *with music*; BTTM

Marital Journey, The. Hailu Arraya. MiP

Mark, The. Robert Graves. LoAs

Mark Anthony. John Cleveland. SCP-2

Mark but this flea, and mark in this. The Flea. John Donne. AnMo; BoLoP; MAT; PAIC; PPoe; SCP-1

Mark the note that rises, mark the notes that fall. How to Sing or Read. Robert Louis Stevenson. ECBV

Mark This. Sallie Chesham. AATT

Mark where the pressing wind shoots javelin-like. Modern Love, XLIII. George Meredith. GBL; NOBE; OBP; VPC

Marker slants, flowerless, day's almost done, The. John Berryman. *Fr.* Dream Songs. CAPP

Market, The. James Stephens. AIW

Market Women's Cries. Swift. LoAs; PFIr
    Onyons, *sel.* BIrV

Marl white road, the Dorée rushing cool, The. Tales of the Islands. Derek Walcott. OxBTC

Marlin. Brewster Ghiselin. PPoD

Marlow and Nancy. Sandra McPherson. AmPA

Marmion, *sel.* Sir Walter Scott.
    Lochinvar, *fr.* V. AIW; BTTM; ECBV; NOBE; PoTa; SLP

Marriage, The. James Bertolino. HeS

Marriage. Austin Clarke. BIrV

Marriage. Gregory Corso. CoPAm; InPS; NoAM; PPoD; PPP

Marriage. Marianne Moore. NOBA; RiTi

Marriage, The. Mark Strand. NoAM

Marriage ("Here we go around this ring"). *Unknown.* AmFP

Marriage ("Put your hand in the creel"). *Unknown.* GBP

Marriage. William Carlos Williams. IPWM

Marriage à la Mode, *sels.* Dryden.
    Song: "Why should a foolish marriage vow," *fr.* I, i. BuTh; LoAs
    (Why Should a Foolish Marriage Vow.) HeIP
    "Whil'st Alexis lay prest," *fr.* IV, ii. LoAs
    (Song: "Whilst Alexis lay pressed.") BoLoP

Marriage Amulet. Nancy Willard. RiTi

Marriage Morning. Tennyson. GBL

Marriage of Heaven and Hell, The. Blake. LAuP; MBPR

Marriage Ring, A. George Crabbe. BoLoP
    (His Late Wife's Wedding-Ring.) NOBE

Marriage Wig, The. Ruth Whitman. IHMS

Marrie dear. When in Rome. Mari Evans. SoSe

Married and Single Life. *Unknown.* AmFP

Married for one year. Making It Simple December 8, 1969. David McElroy. AmPA

Married Man Blues. *Unknown.* BluL

Married man who begs his friend, A. Enticer. Richard Armour. SoSe

Marrow of My Bone. Mari Evans. BPo

Marry and love thy Flavia, for she. The Anagram. John Donne. *Fr.* Elegies. PAIC

Marry the Lass? Andrew Greig. SLP

Mars is braw in crammasy. The Bonnie Broukit Bairn. "Hugh MacDiarmid." InPS

Marseillaise, La, *with music.* Claude Joseph Rouget de Lisle, *tr. fr. French by* Albert Morehead. BLSH

Marsh, The. W. D. Snodgrass. PiAm

Marsh Song—At Sunset. Sidney Lanier. NOBA

Marshall. George Macbeth. NoAM

Marshes of Glynn, The. Sidney Lanier. AmVN; NOBA; PiAm; VoPo

Marten flew to the finch's nest, The. Feathers and Moss. Jean Ingelow. SpRo

Martha/ Mary passed this morning. Mary Passed This Morning. Owen Dodson. PoBA

Martial Cadenza. Wallace Stevens. VGW

Martial, the things for to attain. The Happy Life. Martial, *tr. by* Earl of Surrey. NOBE

Martial, thou gavest far nobler epigrams. To the Ghost of Martial. Ben Jonson. PAIC

Martian. Eve Merriam. CaYB

Martin Luther King, Jr. Gwendolyn Brooks. PoBA; WIF

Martin's Blues. Michael S. Harper. PoBA

Martyr, The. Herman Melville. VoPo

Martyrdom. Richard W. Thomas. PoBA

Martyrdom of Saint Sebastian, The. Rosemary Dobson. MAuV

Martyred Earth, The. Ewart Milne. BIrV

Maru Mori brought me. Ode to My Socks. Pablo Neruda, *tr. by* Robert Bly. Epi

Marvaill no more all tho. Sir Thomas Wyatt. AAS

Marvel of Marvels. Christina Rossetti. BoReV; NOBE

Marvelous. Allan Kaplan. POL

Marvels. *Unknown.* OxBM

Marvoil. Ezra Pound. Epi

Marx the Sign Painter. Edgar Lee Masters. *Fr.* The New Spoon River. NoAM

Mary. Blake. MBPR

Mary—A Reminiscence. Charles Tennyson Turner. VPC

Mary and Her Dead Canary. Alexander Kerr. InPK

Mary and Her Son Alone. *At. to* James Ryman. OxBM

Mary and the Baby, Sweet Lamb. *Unknown.* AmFP

Mary Ann. *Unknown.* FaBoCo

Mary Arnold the Female Monster. *Unknown.* GBP; PeBB

Mary had a baby. Crooked Carol. Norma Farber. POL

Mary had a little bird. The Canary. Elizabeth Turner. OxBChV

Mary had a little lamb. Mary's Lamb. Sara Joseph Hale. MG; OxBChV

Mary Hamilton. *Unknown.* AIW; AmFP; NOBE; PAIC; PeBB

Mary hath born alone. Mary and Her Son Alone. *At. to* James Ryman. OxBM

Mary Hines. Padraic Fallon, *after the Irish of* Anthony Raftery. SoSe

Mary, Mary. Peter Viereck. CoPAm

Mary, Mary, quite contrary. Mother Goose. MG

Mary Passed This Morning. Owen Dodson. PoBA

Mary sat musing on the lamp-flame at the table. The Death of the Hired Man. Robert Frost. IPWM

Mary sat on a long brown bench. Song About Mary. Adrian Mitchell. PeBB

Mary stood in the kitchen. Ballad of the Bread Man. Charles Causley. MPo

Mary, will you ever grow? Water, blessed by bishops. Song for Healing. Roberta Hill. CDW

Mary Winslow. Robert Lowell. PPP

Mary Wyatt and Henry Green. *Unknown.* AmFP

Marye, maide milde and free. Hymn to the Virgin. *At. to* William of Shoreham. OxBM

Maryland Battalion, The. John Williamson Palmer. BTTM

Maryland, My Maryland! James Ryder Randall. PSoN, *with music*

(My Maryland.) BTTM

Maryland, Virginia, Caroline. Emblems. Allen Tate. VGW

Mary's a Grand Old Name, *with music.* George M. Cohan. BLSo; FSN

Mary's Ghost. Thomas Hood. PoTa

Mary's Lamb. Sarah Josepha Hale. OxBChV

Mary's Song. Marion Angus. SLP

Mary's Song. Sylvia Plath. CAPP

Masai warrior is not, The. Outbreak. Bill Anderson. VGW

Mask, The. Valery Larbaud, *tr. fr. French by* William Jay Smith. LoAs

Mask of Anarchy, The. Shelley. MBPR
 "I met Murder on the way," *sel.* OBP

Masks. Elizabeth Fenton. NMM

Masochist, The. Maxine W. Kumin. IHMS

Masons, when they start upon a building. Scaffolding. Seamus Heaney. LP

Masque of Cupid, The. Spenser. *Fr.* The Faerie Queene, III, 12. NOBE

Masque of Flowers, The, *sel. Unknown.*
 "Thrice happy flowers!" SCP-2

Masque of Queens, The, *sels.* Ben Jonson.
 "What our Dame bids us do." OFD

Witches' Charm, The. NOBE
 ("Owl is abroad, the bat and the toad, The.") SCP-1

Mass media I adore you. To R—— Before Leaving to Fight in Unknown Terrain. Nina Serrano. MIT

Massacre of the Innocents, The. William Jay Smith. CoPAm

Massacre of the Macpherson, The. William Edmonstoune Aytoun. FaBoCo

Massive engines lift beautifully from the deck. The Teeth Mother Naked at Last. Robert Bly. CAAP

Massive trembling of late dusk air, The. Night Riders. Jean Farley. NowV

Master and Man. Sir Henry Newbolt. OxBTC

Master of discords John. The Harper. *Unknown, tr. by* Frank O'Connor. PFIr

Master, the swabber, the boatswain and I, The. Shakespeare. *Fr.* The Tempest, II, ii. OBP

Masters, be kind to the old house that must fall. Rockland. Julia Randall. WPE

Master's in the Garden Again. John Crowe Ransom. NoAM

Masters of War. Bob Dylan. GrRo

Materialism. C. E. M. Joad. FaBoCo

Maternity. Alice Meynell. BBGO

Maternity Gown. David Holbrook. OxBTC

Matilda Who Told Lies, and Was Burned to Death. Hilaire Belloc. NOBE; OxBChV; PoTa

Matinees. James Merrill. NOBA; Prf

Mating Swans. James McAuley. MAuV

Martins. Denise Levertov. IHMS; NoAM; NOBA

Matisse: "The Red Studio." W. D. Snodgrass. WIF

Matrilineal Descent. Robin Morgan. WBN

Matsushima. Harry Guest. TwMBP

Matt Casey formed a social club that beat the town for style. The Band Played On. John F. Palmer. BLSo; FSN

Matthew. Wordsworth. MBPR

Matthew and Mark and Luke and holy John. Epi-Strauss-ium. Arthur Hugh Clough. PAIC; PFD; VPC

Matthew, Mark, Luke and John. The White Paternoster. *Unknown.* GBP; MG

Matthias, *sels.* Matthew Arnold.
 "Cruel, but composed and bland." POL
 "Rover, with the good brown head." PCat

Mauberley. Ezra Pound. *See* Hugh Selwyn Mauberley.

Maud, *sels.* Tennyson.
 "Come into the garden, Maud," Pt. I, xxii. NOBE
 "I have led her home, my love, my only friend," Pt. I, xviii. LoAs
 "Oh! that 'twere possible," Pt. II, iv. BoLoP; NOBE

Maud went to college. Sadie and Maud. Gwendolyn Brooks. CoPAm; NoAM; NOBA

Maude Clare. Christina Rossetti. VPC

Mavrone. Arthur Guiterman. SpRo

Maw Bonnie Lad. *Unknown.* GBP

Maxim. Josephine Miles. RiTi

Maximus, to Himself. Charles Olson. CoPAm; NOBA; VGW

Maximus, to Gloucester, Letter 19. Charles Olson. PAIC

Maximus, to Gloucester, Letter 6. Charles Olson. PiAm

Maximus, to Gloucester, Letter 2. Charles Olson. NoAM

Maximus to Gloucester, Letter 27. Charles Olson. NOBA

Maxwelton's braes are bonnie. Annie Laurie. William Douglas *and* Lady John Scott. BLSH

May. John Shaw Neilson. MAuV

May. Christina Rossetti. GBL

May All Earth Be Clothed in Light. George Hitchcock. VGW

May all my enemies go to hell. Lines for a Christmas Card. Hilaire Belloc. SFF; SoSe

May and Death. Robert Browning. NOBE

May, and the air is light. The Road's End. John Montague. TwMBP

May! Be thou never graced with birds that sing. In Obitum M. S. x Maij, 1614. William Browne. NOBE

May Colvin. *Unknown.* PBMP

May Day Carol, A. *Unknown.* RDB, *with music* ("Moon shines bright, The.") GBL

May Day Dancing, The. Howard Nemerov. NoAM

May Day Rounds: Renfrew County, *sel.* Joan Finnigan. "The stoop on the log-house is brown with sweet rain-rot." IPWM; WPE

May-Fly. John Heath-Stubbs. SoSe

May have killed the cat; more likely. Curiosity. Alastair Reid. SoSe

May he have new life like the fall. John Coltrane: an Impartial Review. A. B. Spellman. PoBA

May I Ask You a Question. Kenneth Patchen. CoPAm

May I Feel Said He. E. E. Cummings. BoLoP; HeIP; NOBE; SFF

May I for my own self song's truth reckon. The Seafarer. *Unknown, tr. by* Ezra Pound. HeIP

May I slobber over you. Third Day in a Strange City. Carol Bergé. MMD

May is lilac here in New England. Amy Lowell. *Fr.* Lilacs. FSFS

May Margret stood in her bouer door. Hind Etin. *Unknown.* PeBB

May Mobilization. Allen Ginsberg. MIT

May No Man Sleep in Your Hall. *Unknown.* GBP

May Poem ("O lusty May with Flora quene"). *Unknown.* SLP

May Poem ("When flora had ourfret the firth"). *Unknown.* SLP

May 10th. Maxine W. Kumin. RFM

May they stumble, stage by stage. Traveller's Curse after Misdirection. Robert Graves. NCSH

May Trees in a Storm. Geoffrey Grigson. GBL

May 27, 1971: No Poem. June Jordan. WBN

May we never taste of death nor quit this vale of tears. Irish Curse on the Occupying English. *Unknown, tr. fr. Modern Irish by* Máire MacEntee. PFIr

Maya. E. A. Robinson. PiAm

Mayakovsky was right. Kiss. Al Young. PoBA

Maybe it is true we have to return. Obsessions. Denise Levertov. PAIC

Maybe it was the way. Finding You. Virginia Gilbert. IHMS; NVAP

Maybe morning lightens over. For My Grandfather, Bridgid Halpin. Michael Hartnett. BIrV

Maybe the Birds. June Jordan. TSWA

Maybe you ranted in the grove. Ezry. Archibald MacLeish. NOBA

Mayday. Ed Roberson. PoBA

Mayers' Song, The. *Unknown.* AIW; GBP

Maze of the Magi, A. Sandra Ruth Duguid. AATT

Me and My Chauffeur Blues. *Unknown.* BluL

Me and the Devil Blues. *Unknown.* BluL

Me and You and a Dog Named Boo. Kent LaVoie. PoRo

Me father was the keeper of the Eddystone Light. The Eddystone Light. *Unknown.* PoTa

Me from myself—to banish. Emily Dickinson. NoAM; SBG

Me happy, night, night full of brightness. Elegy VII. Ezra Pound. *Fr.* Homage to Sextus Propertius. PAIC; VGW

Me Imperturbe. Walt Whitman. NOBA

Me, in Kulu Se and Karma. Carolyn M. Rodgers. PoBA

Me liketh ever the lengere the bet. In Praise of Winchester. *Unknown.* OxBM

Me list no more to sing. Sir Thomas Wyatt. AAS

Me, Lord? Canst thou mispend. The Divine Lover. Phineas Fletcher. *Fr.* The Divine Wooer. BoReV

Me nappy hair dream child. Image in the Mirror. Peggy Susberry Kenner. JB

Me Rueth, Mary. *Unknown.* GBP ("Now goeth sun under wood.") BoReV

Me thinks, I see, with what a busie hast. On Zacheus. Frances Quarles. MetP

Me thought I was in wildernesse walking al one. A Dream. *Unknown. Fr.* Mum and the Sothsegger. OxBM

Me thought, (last night) love in an anger came. *See* Methought (last night)

Meadow Mouse, The. Theodore Roethke. HeIP; InPK; IPWM; PPoe; PSN; TSWA

Meal Piece. Elton Glaser. NVAP

Mean grimy houses, shades drawn. May I Ask You a Question. Kenneth Patchen. CoPAm

Mean Mistreater Mama. *Unknown.* BluL

Mean Old Twister. *Unknown.* BluL

Mean Rufus Thrown-Down. David Smith. NVAP

Mean Song. Eve Merriam. CaYB

Meanwhile, the Baron Albert. At Hunegg. George MacBeth. TwMBP

Meares' milk, and deers' milk. Witch's Milking Charm. *Unknown.* GBP

Measles in the Ark. "Susan Coolidge." OxBChV

Measure for Measure, *sel.* Shakespeare. At the Moated Grange, *fr.* IV, i. NOBE ("Take, O take those lips away,") GBL; HeIP; InPS

Measure of Love, The. Sir Thomas More. BoReV

Meat Epitaph, The. Michael Benedikt. FiCP

Meat Works, The. Robert Gray. CAAP

Mechanic, The. Diane Wakoski. AmPA

Mechanical/ Oracles dot the sky. Gods in Vietnam. Eugene Redmond. PoBA

Mechanophilus, *sel.* Tennyson. "Dash back that ocean with a pier." FaBoCo

Medal, The, *sel.* Dryden. Vox Populi. NOBE

Medal of John Bays, The: A Satire against Folly and Knavery, *sel.* Thomas Shadwell. "How long shall I endure without reply." SCP-2

Medallion. Sylvia Plath. HeIP

Medallion. Ezra Pound. PSN

Meddlesome Matty. Ann Taylor. OxBChV

Medea Casts a Spell to Make Aeson Young Again. Ovid, *tr. fr. Latin by* Arthur Golding. *Fr.* Metamorphoses, VII. Moon

Medea's Magic. John Gower. *Fr.* Confessio Amantis. OxBM

Medgar Evers. Gwendolyn Brooks. NowV; PoBA

Medicine. Louis Jenkins. HeS

Medicine. Alice Walker. NMM

Meditatio. Ezra Pound. PBMP

Meditation. Baudelaire, *tr. fr. French by* Robert Lowell. InPK

Meditation, The. John Norris. SCP-2

Meditation at Kew. Anna Wickham. BuTh

Meditation 8 ("Scarce do I pass a day but that I hear"). Philip Pain. NOBA; PiAm

Meditation for a Pickle Suite. R. H. W. Dillard. CoPAm

Meditation for His Mistress, A. Robert Herrick. NOBE

Meditation in My Favorite Position. Marge Piercy. *Fr.* Walking into Love. RiTi

Meditation 9 ("Man's live is like a rose, that in the spring"). Philip Pain. NOBA

Meditation on a Bone. A. D. Hope. MAuV

Meditation on Statistical Method. J. V. Cunningham. VGW

Meditation on the A30. John Betjeman. BBGO

Meditation 62 ("How is it that I am so careless here").  Philip Pain.  NOBA; PiAm

Meditation 10 ("Alas, what is the world? A sea of glass").  Philip Pain.  NOBA; PiAm

Meditation 29 ("How mutable is every thing that here").  Philip Pain.  NOBA

Meditations.  Edward Taylor.  *See* Proparatory Meditations.

Meditations in Time of Civil War, *sels.*  W. B. Yeats.
Road at My Door, The, V.  BIrV; NOBE
Stare's Nest by My Windows, The, VI.  BIrV; NOBE

Meditations of an Old Woman, *sels.*  Theodore Roethke.  First Meditation.  NOBA
I'm Here.  Epi

Meditations on Frost's "Stopping by Woods."  Albert De Pietro.  AATT

Mediterranean, The.  Allen Tate.  VGW

Medium IV, The: Sights.  Carl Rakosi.  InPS

Medora, N.D.  Richard Lyons.  HeS

Medusa.  Louise Bogan.  RiTi; WPE

Medusa.  Sylvia Plath.  CAPP

Meek, sang the crickets, wheat, meet, creek.  A Small Score.  Delmore Schwartz.  PBMP

Meet Me in St. Louis, Louis, *with music.*  Andrew B. Sterling.  FSN

Meet was at 'The Cock and Pye,' The.  John Masefield.  *Fr.* Reynard the Fox.  OxBTC

Meeting.  Christina Rossetti.  GBL

Meeting, The.  Kathleen Spivack.  NMM

Meeting at Night.  Robert Browning.  BoLoP; GBL; HeIP; InPS; LoAs; NOBE; OLR; PAIC; SoSe; SS

Meeting-House Hill.  Amy Lowell.  PSN; SBG

Meeting-house is not what it used to be, The.  Elegy in a Presbyterian Burying-Ground.  R. N. D. Wilson.  BIrV

Meeting the Mountains.  Gary Snyder.  NoAM; PiAm

Meeting the Reincarnation Analyst.  Gary Gildner.  AmPA

Meeting when all the world was in the bud.  Loves of the Puppets.  Richard Wilbur.  LoAs

Meetings meetings meetings.  Yuh Lookin Good.  Carolyn M. Rodgers.  BPo

Meg Merrilies.  Keats.  OxBChV
("Old Meg she was a gipsey.")  MBPR

Megalopolis.  Victor Hernández Cruz.  SA

Mel Allen, Mel Allen, Lend Me Your Cliché.  Ogden Nash.  SPo

Melancholy Summer.  Kris Hemensley.  *Fr.* A Mile from Poetry.  CAAP

Melchoir Vulpius.  Marianne Moore.  PiAm

Melfluvious, sweet, rose-watered eloquence.  Samuel Rowlands.  *Fr.* The Letting of Humour's Blood in the Head-Vein.  TVS

Mellow the moonlight to shine is beginnning.  The Spinning Wheel.  John Francis Waller.  PFIr; PoTa

Mellow year is hastening to its close, The.  November.  Hartley Coleridge.  FSFS

Melody For Lute and Ocarina.  Morris Bishop.  ECBV

Melons.  Greg Kuzma.  HeS

Melora's Song.  Stephen Vincent Benét.  *Fr.* John Brown's Body.  AIW

Melting Pot, The.  Dudley Randall.  BPo

Members of the Family.  Derek Bowman.  MIS

Memento Mori.  Fulke Greville.  *Fr.* Caelica.  BoReV
("Whenas man's life, the light of human lust.")  SCP-2

Mementos, 1 ("Sorting out letters and piles of my old").  W. D. Snodgrass.  CoPAm; HeIP; PiAm; PPP

Mementos, 2 ("I found them there today").  W. D. Snodgrass.  CoPAm

Memo.  Charles Lynch.  PoBA

Memo to the 21st Century.  Philip Appleman.  SFF

Memoir.  David Schaff.  MIT

Memoranda.  William Dickey.  CoPAm

Memorial Pillar, The.  Felicia Dorothea Hemans.  SBG

Memorial Rain.  Archibald MacLeish.  NoAM

Memorial Service.  Ursula Vaughan Williams.  POL

Memorial to D. C., *sel.*  Edna St. Vincent Millay.
Elegy: "Let them bury your big eyes," V.  LoAs

Memorial Wreath.  Dudley Randall.  PoBA

Memories, *sel.*  George Gascoigne.
"In haste, post haste, when first my wandering mind," IV.  AAS; PAIC

Memories of a Lost War.  Louis Simpson.  VGW

Memories of President Lincoln.  Walt Whitman.  *See* When Lilacs Last in the Dooryard Bloomed *and* O Captain, My Captain!

Memories of West Street and Lepke.  Robert Lowell.  CAPP; ConAP; CoPAm; InPS; NOBA; PiAm; PSN

Memory, A.  William Allingham.  FSFS

Memory, The.  Robert Creeley.  CAPP; VGW

Memory.  Michael Hamburger.  OxBTC

Memory, A.  L. A. G. Strong.  FaBoCo; PFIr

Memory, A.  Mona Van Duyn.  *Fr.* Recovery.  RiTi

Memory.  W. B. Yeats.  BIrV

Memory: farfields of morning.  Persephone.  Robert Duncan.  NoAM; NOBA

Memory, hither come.  Song.  Blake.  MBPR

Memory, Now Distant, A.  Eric Linklater.  SLP

Memory of a Porch.  Donald Justice.  NCSH

Memory of Kreisler once, A.  The Musician.  R. S. Thomas.  BoReV

Memory of Kuhre.  Wesley McNair.  FAF

Memory of one particular hour, The.  Dedication.  Wordsworth.  *Fr.* The Prelude, IV.  BoReV

Memory of the Players in a Mirror at Midnight, A.  James Joyce.  NoAM

Memory pales in the face of the moon.  On Leaving Baltimore.  Duane Niatum.  CDW

Memphis Minnie-Jitis Blues.  *Unknown.*  BluL

Memphis, Tennessee.  Chuck Berry.  RRA

Men/ dropped children.  After the Fact.  Grace Cavalieri.  AATT

Men and women long ago, The.  Old Laughter.  Gwendolyn Brooks.  TH

Men Are Coming Back, The.  Barry Cole.  OxBTC

Men are running across a field.  Letter.  Mark Strand.  NoAm

Men at Forty.  Donald Justice.  Prf; PPP

Men, bloody, approach the house.  Dreams from War.  Marilyn Krysl.  NPW

Men en masse.  Observation.  Richard Weber.  POL

Men heard this roar of parleying starlings, saw.  February Afternoon.  Edward Thomas.  NoAM

Men in her department envied her, The.  Sayre.  Lynn Strongin.  IHMS; RiTi

Men lean toward the wood.  Lynching and Burning.  Primus St. John.  PoBA

Men Loved Wholly Beyond Wisdom.  Louise Bogan.  VGW

Men Made Out of Words.  Wallace Stevens.  NOBA; VGW

Men may leve all games.  Pilgrims to St. James.  *Unknown.*  OxBM

Men might put their hands.  This Woman Will Not Bear Children.  Toi Derricotte.  NPW

Men of England, wherefore plough.  Song to the Men of England.  Shelley.  InPS; MBPR; PBMP; SFF

Men of the East, The.  Feathers of Snow.  *Unknown.*  GBP

Men trample the earth, The.  The Departure of the Women.  Nancy Mairs.  NPW

Men! whose boast it is that ye.  Freedom.  James Russell Lowell.  VoPo

Men with crew-cuts.  Crew-cuts.  Donald Hall.  MAT

Men with ventilators of black straw, The.  Confab.  Kenneth Rosen.  AmPA

Men would never have come to need an attic.  Up There.  W. H. Auden.  OxBTC

Menaphon, *sels.*    Robert Greene.
   Samela.  GBL; NOBE
   Sephestia's Song to Her Childe.  OBP
      (Sephestia's Lullaby.)  NOBE

Mendelian Theory.  *Unknown.*  FaBoCo

Mending Sump.  Kenneth Koch.  InPK; NoAM

Mending Wall.  Robert Frost.  InPS; IPWM; NoAM; NOBA; NowV; PiAm; PPoD; VGW

Meningitis killing me, The.  Memphis Minnie-Jitis Blues.  *Unknown.*  BluL

Men's Room in the College Chapel, The.  W. D. Snodgrass.  PPP

Menstruation at Forty.  Anne Sexton.  CAPP

Mental Cases.  Wilfred Owen.  NoAM

Mental Hospital Garden, The.  William Carlos Williams.  PiAm

Mental Traveller, The.  Blake.  Epi; GrRo; LAuP; MBPR

Mercado.  Greg Pape.  AmPA

Merced.  Adrienne Rich.  NOBA

Mercedes.  Barbara Howes.  CoPAm; RiTi

Mercedes, Her Aloneness.  Colette Inez.  IHMS

Merchant Marine.  Josephine Miles.  VGW

Merchant of Venice, The, *sels.*    Shakespeare.
   "Moon shines bright, The. In such a night as this," *fr.* V, i.  GBL
   Quality of Mercy, The, *fr.* IV, i.  AKE

Merchants of London, The.  *Unknown.*  GBP

Mercian Hymns, *sel.*  Geoffrey Hill.
   Offa's Laws, XIV.  PSN

Merciless Beauty.  Chaucer.  OxBM; PAIC
   "Your eyen two will slay me suddenly,"  *sel.* BoLoP

Merciless love, whom nature hath denied.  John Fletcher.  *Fr.* The Chances.  GBL

Mercury's Song to Phaedra.  Dryden.  *Fr.* Amphitryon, IV, i.  PBMP

Mercy.  *Unknown.*  OxBM

Mercy is hendest where sinne is mest.  Mercy.  *Unknown.*  OxBM

Mercy is whiter than laundry.  Angels in Winter.  Nancy Willard.  FiCP

Mercy Mercy Me.  Marvin Gaye.  PoRo

Mercy of God may often come to a homeless hermit, The.  The Wanderer.  *Unknown, tr. by* Andrew Hoyem.  Epi

Merlin (I-II).  Emerson.  AmVN; NOBA; PiAm

Merlin.  Geoffrey Hill.  POL

Merlin, they say, an English prophet borne.  Caelica, XXIII.  Fulke Greville.  OBP

Mermaid.  Helena Minton.  FAF

Mermaid, The.  Lisel Mueller.  RiTi

Mermaid, The, *sel.* Tennyson.
   "Who would be/ A mermaid fair."  LCL

Mermaid, The, 2 *versions.*  *Unknown.*  AmFP

Mermaidens' Vesper-Hymn, The.  George Darley.  *Fr.* Syren Songs, VI.  GBL
   (Siren Chorus.)  BIrV

Merry-Go-Round.  Langston Hughes.  CTBA

Merry-Go-Round.  James McAuley.  MAuV

Merry Haymakers, The; or, Pleasant Pastimes Between the Young Men and Maids in the Pleasant Meadows.  *Unknown.*  SCP-2

Merry [*or* Mery] it is in May morning.  By a Chapel as I Came.  *Unknown.*  GBP; OxBM

Merry Jest of Robin Hood, A.  Thomas Love Peacock.  PeBB

Merry-ma-Tanzie, The.  *Unknown.*  GBP

Merry [*or* Mirry] Margaret,/ As midsummer flower.  To Mistress Margaret Hussey.  John Skelton.  *Fr.* The Garlande of Laurell.  AAS; HeIP; LoAs; NOBE; PAIC; PPoe; PPP

Merry May the Keel Row.  *Unknown.*  GBP

Merry merry sparrow.  The Blossom.  Blake.  *Fr.* Songs of Innocence.  MBPR

Merry month of May, sunny skies of blue.  I've Got the World on a String.  Ted Koehler.  BLSo

Merry the green, the green hill shall be merry.  Another Song.  Donald Justice.  ConAP; VGW

Merry world did on a day, The.  The Quip.  George Herbert.  SCP-1

Merryman Sings, The.  W. S. Gilbert.  ECBV

Merthe of all this land, The.  God Speed the Plough!  *Unknown.*  OxBM

Meru.  W. B. Yeats.  InPS; NoAM

Mery Gest How a Sergeaunt Wolde Lerne to Be a Frere, A.  Sir Thomas More.  AAS

Mery it is in May morning.  *See* Merry it is in May morning.

Mery it is while sumer y-last.  Winterfall.  *Unknown.*  OxBM

Mess Occupations.  Ted Berrigan.  CAAP

Message, The.  John Donne.  PAIC

Message.  Allen Ginsberg.  ConAP; VGW

Message from Home.  Kathleen Raine.  WPE

Message from Ohanapecosh Glacier.  W. M. Ransom.  CDW

Messed Damozel, The.  Charles Hanson Towne.  SpRo

Messengers.  Louise Glück.  CAAP

Metal smokestack, The.  Exercise No. 2.  William Carlos Williams.  TH

Metamorphoses.  Roy Fuller.  OxBTC

Metamorphoses.  Vassar Miller.  RiTi

Metamorphoses, *sels.*  Ovid, *tr. fr. Latin.*
   Medea casts a Spell to Make Aeson Young Again, *fr.* VII, *tr. by* Arthur Golding.  Moon
   Orpheus and Eurydice, *fr.* X, *tr. by* Rolfe Humphries.  GrRo

Metamorphosis.  Peter Porter.  OxBTC

Metamorphosis.  Wallace Stevens.  InPK; VGW

Metamorphosis of Aunt Jemima, The.  William Childress.  MAT

Metaphors.  Sylvia Plath.  InPK; SoSe

Metaphysical Amorist, The.  J. V. Cunningham.  VGW

Methinks already from this chymic flame.  London after the Great Fire, 1666.  Dryden.  *Fr.* Annus Mirabilis.  NOBE

Methinks I hear, methinks I see.  Robert Burton.  *Fr.* The Anatomy of Melancholy: The Author's Abstract of Melancholy.  SCP-2

Method must be purest meat, The.  On Burroughs' Work.  Allen Ginsberg.  NoAM; NOBA

Methought I saw my late espoused saint.  On His Deceased Wife.  Milton.  BoLoP; Epi; GBL; LoAs; NOBE; OBP; PPP; SCP-1

Methought [*or* Me thought,] (last night), love in an anger came.  The Dream.  Robert Herrick.  LoAs; SCP-1

Meticulous, past midnight in clear rime.  Voyages, V.  Hart Crane.  PSN

Metonymy as an Approach to a Real world.  William Bronk.  VGW

Metre Columbian, The.  *Unknown.*  SpRo

Metric Figure.  William Carlos Williams.  AKE

Metrical Feet.  Samuel Taylor Coleridge.  OxBChV

Metropole.  Forrest Anderson.  AATT

Metropolitan Nightmare.  Stephen Vincent Benét.  PAIC

Metropolitan Railway, The.  John Betjeman.  OxBTC

Mexican/ Flea powder. In Mexico. Robert Sward. NowV

Mexico City Blues, *sels.* Jack Kerouac.
Chorus: "Dharma law," 66. PiAm
Chorus: "Praised be man, he is existing in milk," 228. PiAm
Chorus: "Songs that erupt, The," 195. PiAm

Mexico Is a Foreign Country: Four Studies in Naturalism, *sel.* Robert Penn Warren.
Mango on the Mango Tree, The, IV. NoAM

Mezzo Cammin. Longfellow. AmVN

Mice before Milk. Chaucer. *Fr.* The Canterbury Tales: The Manciple's Tale. PCat

Mice in the garbage. For Rosa Yen, Who Lived Here. Greg Pape. AmPA

Michael: A Pastoral Poem. Wordsworth. MBPR

Michael from Mountains. Joni Mitchell. WIF

Michael Robartes Bids His Beloved Be at Peace. W. B. Yeats. NoAM

Michael, Row the Boat Ashore, *with music.* Unknown. BLSo

Michael wakes you up with sweets. Michael from Mountains. Joni Mitchell. WIF

Michigan-I-O. *Unknown.* AmFP

Mick. James Reeves. RAE

Microcosm, The. Giovanni Battista Guarini, *tr. fr. Italian by* Sir Edward Sherburne. LoAs

Microcosmos. Susan Miles. OxBTC

Micro-Cynicon, *sel.* "T. M."
Cheating Droone, Satire IV. TVS

Microscope, The. Maxine W. Kumin. PoTa

Mid-August at Sourdough Mountain Lookout. Gary Snyder. MAT; NCSH

Mid pleasures and palaces though we may roam. Home, Sweet Home. John Howard Payne. *Fr.* Clari, the Maid of Milan. BLSH; BLSo; PSoN

Middleged. 40-Love. Roger McGough. NoAM

Middle . . . aged Conversation. A. S. J. Tessimond. POL

Middle Passage. Robert Hayden. BPo; CoPAm; NoAM; PAIC; PoBA

Middleness of the Road, The. Robert Frost. NOBA

Middlesex. John Betjeman. OxBTC

Middleton's Rouseabout. Henry Lawson. MAuV

Midget, The. Philip Levine. NoAM

Midnight. Weldon Kees. NoAM

Midnight. Archibald Lampman. AKE

Midnight Court, The, *sels.* Brian Merriman, *tr. fr. Modern Irish.*
Country's Crisis, The, *tr. by* David Marcus. BIrV
Irish Marriage Night, An, *tr. by* Frank O'Connor. BIrV
Maiden's Plight, The, *tr. by* Frank O'Connor. BIrV
Now God Stand Up for Bastards, *tr. by* Arland Ussher. BIrV
Old Man's Tale, The, *tr by* David Marcus. BIrV
Solution, The, *tr. by* Arland Ussher. BIrV
Walk, *tr. by* Brendan Behan. BIrV

Midnight Lamentation. Harold Monro. OxBTC

Midnight on Front Street. Roberta Hill. CDW

Midnight on my ladders, FM blasting, and three beers. Painting an Old Apartment. James Bonk. HeS

Midnight on the Great Western. Thomas Hardy. NOBE; OBP

Midnight Raffle. Langston Hughes. PiAm

Midnight Skaters, The. Edmund Blunden. NOBE; PSN

Midnight Special. Kenneth Patchen. VGW

Midnight Tennis Match, The. Thomas Lux. AmPA

Midnight. The words start out, walking. Tracks. Peter Cooley. HeS

Midnight's bell goes ting, ting, ting, ting, ting. Night Sounds. Thomas Middleton. *Fr.* Blurt, Master Constable. RAE

Mid-term Break. Seamus Heaney. NCSH

Midstream they met. Challenger and champion. The Swan. Clifford Dyment. BoAnP

Midsummer Night's Dream, A, *sel.* Shakespeare.
Lunatic, the Lover, and the Poet, The, *fr.* V, i. PAIC
"Over hill, over dale," *fr.* II, i. NOBE
Puck's Night Song, *fr.* V, ii. ECBV
("Now the hungry lion roars.") OBP
"You spotted snakes with double tongue," *fr.* II, ii. ECBV; NOBE

Midway. Naomi Long Madgett. BPo

Midweek. Josephine Miles. RiTi

Midwest. John Frederick Nims. ANTL

Midwest Town. Ruth De Long Peterson. ANTL

Midwest U. F. O. David Steingass. NVAP

Midwinter, Presolstice. Margaret Atwood. Psy

Midwinter spring is its own season. Little Gidding. T. S. Eliot. *Fr.* Four Quartets. BoReV; NoAM; NOBA; NOBE; OxBTC

Might have been. This Place Rumord to Have Been Sodom. Robert Duncan. NOBA; PPP

Might I, if you can find it, be given. Saint Nicholas. Mariannne Moore. WPE

Might souls converse with souls by angel-way. Edward Benlowes. *Fr.* Theophila; or, Love's Sacrifice, Canto I. SCP-2

Mighty Fortress, A, *with music.* Martin Luther, *tr. fr. German by* Frederick H. Hedge. BLSH

Mighty Lak' a Rose, *with music.* Frank L. Stanton. BLSo; FSN

Migrant Hostel. Peter Skrzynecki. CAAP

Migration. Carole Gregory Clemmons. *See* Ghetto Lovesong— Migration.

Migration of the Grey Squirrels, The. William Howitt. OxBChV

Mikado, The, *sels.* William S. Gilbert.
Flowers That Bloom in the Spring, The, *with music.* BLSo
"Wandering minstrel I, A." AIW

Mike 65. Lennox Raphael. PoBA

Mild yoke of Christ, most harsh to me not bearing. Paradox. Vassar Miller. WIF

Mile behind is Glouster town, A. Gloucester Moors. William Vaughn Moody. AmVN; NOBA

Mile from Poetry, A, *sel.* Kris Hemensley.
Melancholy Summer. CAAP

Mile out in the marshes, under a sky, A. The Town Dump. Howard Nemerov. MAT

Miles and miles of giraffes galloping. Serengeti Sunset. Andrew Oerke. POL

Miles and miles of pasture. The Lavender Kitten. Alonzo Lopez. VW

Militant. Langston Hughes. PoBA

Military officers from Prussia. The Dossier. Michael McMahon. FAF

Milk for the Cat. Harold Monro. PCat

Milkcow Blues. *Unknown.* BluL

Milkcow's Calf Blues. *Unknown.* BluL

Milken Time. William Barnes. VPC

Milking Time. Elizabeth Madox Roberts. RAE

Milkmaid. Laurie Lee. BoLoP; MPo

Milkmaid, The. *Unknown.* AmFP

Milkmaid's Epithalamium, The. Thomas Randolph. BoLoP

Milkweed. James Wright. NOBA

Mill, A. William Allingham. POL

Mill, The. E. A. Robinson. NoAM; SoSe

Mill at Trumpington, The. Chaucer. *Fr.* The Canterbury Tales: The Reeve's Tale. OxBM

Mill Valley. Myra Cohn Livingston. RFM

Miller of Dee, The. *Unknown.* GBP

Miller's Daughter, The. *Unknown.* PeBB

Miller's mill-dog lay at the mill door, The. Bingo. *Unknown.* ECBV

Miller's wife had waited long, The. The Mill. E. A. Robinson. NoAM; SoSe

Miller's Wife's Lullaby, The. *Unknown.* GBP

Mill-stream, now that noises cease, The. A. E. Housman. GBL

Milton. Blake. MBPR
 *Sels.*
  And Did Those Feet in Ancient Time, *fr.* Preface. HeIP; InPS; MAT; OBP
  (Jerusalem.) NOBE
  (New Jerusalem, A.) VoPo
  (Preface: "And did those feet in ancient time.") PPoe
  Vision of Beulah, The, *fr.* II. NOBE

Milton. Tennyson. Epi; PAIC

Milton by Firelight. Gary Snyder. CAPP; ConAP; InPK; InPS; PPP

Milton! thou shouldst be living at this hour. London, 1802. Wordsworth. Epi; HeIP; IPWM; MBPR; OBP; PAIC; PBMP

Miltonic Sonnet for Mr. Johnson on His Refusal of Peter Hurd's Official Portrait, A. Richard Wilbur. CAPP

Milwaukee Fire, The. *Unknown.* AmFP

Mimnermus in Church. William Cory. NOBE

Min. *Unknown.* ECBV

Mind. Richard Wilbur. CoPAm; NCSH; PPP

Mind and Matter. *Unknown.* FaBoCo

Mind has shown itself at times, The. For the Marriage of Faustus and Helen. Hart Crane. InPS; NoAM; NOBA

Mind in its purest play is like some bat. Mind. Richard Wilbur. CoPAm; NCSH; PPP

Mind, Intractable Thing, The. Marianne Moore. Psy

Mind Is an Ancient and Famous Capital, The. Delmore Schwartz. NoAM

Mind Is an Enchanting Thing, The. Marianne Moore. PiAm; PPP

Mind Reader Blues. *Unknown.* BluL

Mind would like to get out of here, The. Winter Insomnia. Raymond Carver. NVAP

Minding. Donald Campbell. *Fr.* Sonnets frae Siberia. MIS

Mine be a cot beside the hill. A Wish. Samuel Rogers. NOBE

Mine—by the right of the white election. Emily Dickinson. LoAs

Mine enemy is growing old. Emily Dickinson. WIF

Mine eye, mine ear, my will, my wit, my heart. Gulling Sonnets, V. Sir John Davies. Epi

Mine eyes have seen the glory of the coming of the Lord. The Battle Hymn of the Republic. Julia Ward Howe. BLSH; BLSo; BTTM; NOBA; PSoN; WPE

Mine eyes have seen the guru. *Unknown.* POL

Mine eyes were dim with tears unshed. To Mary Wollstonecraft Godwin. Shelley. MBPR

Mine Host of the "Golden Apple." Thomas Westwood. ECBV

Mine owne good Bat, before thou hoyse up saile. Councell Given to Master Bartholmew Withipoll. George Gascoigne. AAS

Mine was a Midwest home—you can keep your world. One Home. William Stafford. IPWM; VGW

Miner Boy, The. *Unknown.* AmFP

Miner Coming Home One Night, A. *Unknown.* GBP

Miners. Wilfred Owen. NOBE

Miners. James Wright. ConAP; CTBA; TCP

Miner's Doom, The. *Unknown.* AmFP

Miner's Helmet, The. George MacBeth. OxBTC

Miner's Lament, The. *Unknown.* AmFP

Mines/ concealed/ in the flesh. Good Friday Explosions. E. R. Cole. AATT

Mingled the moonlight with daylight. Thomas Hardy. Walter de la Mare. NoAM

Mingram Mo. David McCord. ECBV

Mingus. Bob Kaufman. PoBA

Miniatures IV. Lynn Strongin. IHMS

Minimal, The. Theodore Roethke. NoAM; NOBA

Minister said it wad dee, The. Last Lauch. Douglas Young. FaBoCo

Miniver Cheevy. E. A. Robinson. HeIP; NoAM; NOBA; PiAm; SpRo; SS; WIF

Miniver Cheevy, Jr. David Fisher Parry. SpRo

Minneapolis. Tom Hennen. HeS

"Minneapolis, Midwest." Wisconsin Farm Auction. David Steingass. NVAP

Minneapolis Poem, The. James Wright. NoAM

Minneapolis White Castle, Winter '72. James L. White. HeS

Minnie and Winnie. Tennyson. OxBChV

Minstrel's Song, The. Thomas Chatterton. *Fr.* Aella. OBP
  ("O! Synge untoe mie roundelaie.") NOBE
  (Song from Aella.) LoAs

Minute flowers harden. Depend. Lilies of the Valley. Jon Silkin. NoAM

Minutes are flying swiftly, and as yet. On Receiving a Laurel Crown from Leigh Hunt. Keats. MBPR

Mirabeau Bridge, The. Guillaume Apollinaire, *tr. fr. French by* Quentin Stevenson. BoLoP

Miracle Hill. Emerson Blackhorse Mitchell. VW

Miracle of the children the brilliant. Exodus. George Oppen. RRA

Miracle Worker. Claudia Dobkins. NPW

Miracles ("Why, who makes much of a miracle?"). Walt Whitman. PBMP

Mirage. Christina Rossetti. BoLoP

Miramichi Fire, The. *Unknown.* AmFP

Mirror, The. A. A. Milne. ECBV

Mirror for Magistrates, A, *sel.* William Baldwin *and others.*
  Induction, The. Thomas Sackville. AAS; PAIC, 56 *ll.*
  Shield of War, The. NOBE

Mirror. Sylvia Plath. SoSe

Mirror for the Barnyard. Jack Myers. AmPA

Mirror in February. Thomas Kinsella. NoAM

Mirror in Which Two Are Seen As One, The. Adrienne Rich. RiTi; WBN

Mirru. Kenneth Patchen. RRA

Mirry Margaret,/ As mydsomer flowre. *See* Merry Margaret...

Mirth. Christopher Smart. *Fr.* Hyms for the Amusement of Children. LAuP; OxBChV

Mirth and Melancholy. Margaret Cavendish, Duchess of Newcastle. WPE

Misapprehension. Paul Laurence Dunbar. BPo

Miscarriage. Michael Longley. POL

Miscegenous Zebra, The. Roland Young. BoAnP

Mischievous, they say, as a monkey. Jackdaw. Tom Earley. BoAnP

Mise en Scène. Robert Fitzgerald. VGW

Miser and the Mouse, The. Christopher Smart. RAE

Miserable Catullus, stop being foolish. Catullus, *tr. fr. Latin by* Louis Zukofsky. NoAM

Misericordia. Teresa A. McCarthy. NPW

Misery of Mechanics, The. Philip Booth. MAT

Misfortunes of Elphin, The, *sel.* Thomas Love Peacock.
  War Song of Dinas Vawr, The. NOBE; PoTa

Misgivings. Herman Melville. NOBA; PiAm

Mishnah says I blind you with my hair, The. The Marriage Wig. Ruth Whitman. IHMS

Misogonus, *sel. Unknown.*
  Heart's Ease. WIF
Miss Gee. W. H. Auden. OxBTC
Miss J. Hunter Dunn, Miss J. Hunter Dunn. A Subaltern's Love-Song. John Betjeman. BoLoP; OxBTC; PPoD
Miss Jennian Jones. *Unknown.* AmFP
Miss Loo. Walter de la Mare. OxBTC
Miss Maime. Jodi Braxton. WBN
Miss Rosie. Lucille Clifton. AmPA; CAPP; NMM; PoBA; RiTi
Misshapen, black, unlovely to the sight. A Bulb. Richard Kendall Munkittrick. POL
Missing. W. H. Auden. OxBTC
Missing. John Pudney. OxBTC
Missing Beat. Carolyn M. Rodgers. JB
Missing Dates. William Empson. NoAM; NOBE; PAIC; PSN
Missing My Daughter. Stephen Spender. RRA
Mission. *Unknown.* AmFP
Mission Uncontrolled. Richard Peck. MiP
Missionary. D. M. Thomas. MPo
Missionary from the Mau Mau told me, A. A Magus. John Ciardi. CoPAm; MAT
Mississippi Blues. *Unknown.* AmFP
Mississippi Sawyer. *Unknown.* AmFP
Mist came up thick this morning, The. November Birthday. Mary Swanson Stroh. NPW
Mist-moist, past the rainbow, we make a small row. Niagara. Richard Emil Braun. NoAM
Mistaken Identity. Joanne Casullo. NPW
Mr. and Mrs. Spikky Sparrow. Edward Lear. OxBChV
Mr. Artesian's Conscientiousness. Ogden Nash. SS
Mister Backlash, Mister Backlash. The Backlash Blues. Langston Hughes. BPo
Mister Beedle Baddlebug. Tea Party. Harry Behn. LCL
Mr. Bleaney. Philip Larkin. BuTh; InPS; PPoe
Mr. Brodsky. Charles Tomlinson. NoAM; TwMBP
Mister Charlie. *Unknown.* BluL
Mr. Clean. John William Corrington. PPoD
"Mr. Colwell"/ says Sharon the nurse. The Cry of an Aged One. Ray Fraser. NeAC
Mr. Con, Mr. Can. *Unknown.* ECBV
Mr. Cooper. Anthony Thwaite. OxBTC
Mr. Davis's Experience. *Unknown.* AmFP
Mr. Edwards and the Spider. Robert Lowell. AnMo; CAPP; HeIP; InPS; NOBA; PSN
Mr. Finney's Turnip. *Unknown.* ECBV
Mr. Flood's Party. E. A. Robinson. InPK; IPWM; MAT; MiP; NoAM; NOBA; PAIC; PiAm; PoTa; PPoD; PPoe; PPP; SoSe
Mr. Heath-Stubbs as you must understand. Epitaph. John Heath-Stubbs. MPo; OxBTC
Mr. Housman's Message. Ezra Pound. PAIC
Mr. Jones. Harry Graham. FaBoCo
Mr. Leach made a speech. A Chancery Suit. Sir George Rose. FaBoCo
Mr. Macklin's Jack-o'-Lantern. David McCord. CaYB
Mr. Mine. Anne Sexton. SFF
"Mr. Nowlan, are you asleep?" Semi-Private Room. Alden Nowlan. NeAC
Mr. P.—I have heard it rumored. Letter to a Librarian. Irving Layton. MAT
Mr. Pope. Allen Tate. NoAM; NOBA; PAIC; VGW
Mr. Pratt, your sheep are very fat. The Norfolk Rebellion. *Unknown.* GBP
Mr. Punchinello. *Unknown.* ECBV
Mr. Rhind is very kind. The Schoolmaster. *Unknown.* GBP

Mr. Robert Herrick, His Farewell unto Poetry. Robert Herrick. SCP-1
Mr. Roosevelt Regrets. Pauli Murray. PoBA
Mr. Smith/ (With Nods to Mr. Lear and Mr. Eliot.) William Jay Smith. SpRo
Mr. T./ bareheaded. The Artist. William Carlos Williams. InPS
Mr. U Will Not Be Missed. E. E. Cummings. VGW
Mr. Walter de la Mare Makes the Little Ones Dizzy, *sel.* Samuel Hoffenstein.
  "Speckled with glints of star and moonshine." SpRo
Mr. Whitman to His Friends in the Antipodes. Kris Hemensley.
  *Fr.* The Poem of the Clear Eye. CAAP
Mr. Whittier. Winfield Townley Scott. VGW
Mr. Z. M. Carl Holman. SoSe
Mistress, The. Joan Barton. OxBTC
Mistress, The, *sels.* Abraham Cowley.
  Spring, The. MetP
  Welcome, The. BoLoP
  Wish, The. NOBE
Mistress, The. Earl of Rochester. NOBE
Mrs. Albion You've Got a Lovely Daughter. Adrian Henri. OxBTC
Mrs. Alfred Uruguay. Wallace Stevens. InPS; PiAm
Mrs. Brown. Rose Fyleman. OxBChV
Mrs. Busk. Sir Osbert Sitwell. OxBTC
Mrs. Coley's three-flat brick. The Vacant Lot. Gwendolyn Brooks. NoAM; NOBA
Mrs. Hamer. Jane Stembridge. NMM
Mrs. Lombardi's month-old son is dead. Italian Extravaganza. Gregory Corso. SA
Mrs. Malone. Eleanor Farjeon. OxBChV
Mrs. Mary Blaize. Goldsmith. *See* Elegy on That Glory of Her Sex ...
Mistress Murphy gave a party just about a week ago. Who Threw the Overalls in Mistress Murphy's Chowder? George L. Geifer. FSN
Mrs. Noah in the Ark. The Ballad of Mrs. Noah. Robert Duncan. MPo; NoAM; NOBA
Mrs. Saunder's Experience. *Unknown.* AmFP
Mrs. Snipkin and Mrs. Wobblechin. Laura E. Richards. OxBChV
Mrs. Someone's been to Asia. An Importer. Robert Frost. FaBoCo
Mrs. Vickers' Daughter. *Unknown.* AmFP
Mrs. Walpurga. Muriel Rukeyser. NMM
Misty-Moisty Was the Morn. *Unknown.* GBP
Mithras, God of the Morning, our trumpets waken the wall! A Song to Mithras. Kipling. BTTM
Mithridates. Emerson. NOBA
Mix a pancake. Christina Rossetti. LCL
Mixed Sketches. Don L. Lee. BPo
Mmenson. Edward Brathwaite. MPo
Mmmmmmmm lordy lordy lord. Savannah Mama. *Unknown.* BluL
Mnemosyne. Trumbull Stickney. NOBA; PAIC
Moccasins of an Old Man, The. Ramona Carden. VW
Mock Interrogation, A. Judy Grahn. *Fr.* A Woman Is Talking to Death. WBN
Mock On, Mock On, Voltaire, Rousseau. Blake. AnMo; BoReV; LauP; MBPR; PPoe; PPP
Mockingbird, The. Randall Jarrell. RFM
Mocking Bird, The. *Unknown.* AmFP
Model T. Adrien Stoutenburg. CTBA
Modern Discoveries. Byron. *Fr.* Don Juan. OBP
Modern Fine Gentleman, The. Soame Jenyns. ESaP

Modern Hiawatha, The, *parody*. George A. Strong. AKE; ECBV; FaBoCo; SpRo

Modern Love. J. V. Cunningham. POL

Modern Love. Keats. LoAs; MBPR

Modern Love, *sels.* George Meredith.
  "All other joys of life he strove to warm," IV. PAIC
  "Am I failing? For no longer can I cast," XXIX. GBL
  "At dinner, she is hostess, I am host," XVII. Epi; HeIP
  "By this he knew she wept with waking eyes," I. Epi; HeIP; LoAs; PAIC; PBMP; VPC
  "He felt the wild beast in him betweenwhiles," IX. LoAs
  "He found her by the ocean's moaning verge," XLIX. LoAs; PAIC; VPC
  "I play for seasons; not eternities!" XIII. PFD; VPC
  "I think she sleeps; it must be sleep, when low," XV. Epi
  "In our old shipwrecked days there was an hour," XVI. BoLoP; LoAs
  "It ended, and the morrow brought the task," II. PAIC
  "It is the season of the sweet wild rose," XLV. GBL
  "Love ere he bleeds, an eagle in high skies," XXVI. PAIC
  "Mark where the pressing wind shoots javelin-like," XLIII. GBL; NOBE; OBP; VPC
  "My lady unto madam makes her bow," XXXVI. VPC
  "Not solely that the future she destroys," XII. GBL; VPC
  "Out in the yellow meadows, where the bee," XI. GBL
  "Their sense is with their senses all mixed in," XLVIII. LoAs
  "This was the woman; what now of the man?" III. PAIC
  "Thus piteously love closed what he begat," L. NOBE; PAIC; PFD; VPC
  " 'Tis Christmas weather, and a country house," XXIII. PAIC
  "We saw the swallows gathering in the sky," XLVII. NOBE
  "What are we first? First, animals; and next," XXX. GBL; VPC
  "What soul would bargain for a cure that brings," XIV. PAIC
  "Yet it was plain she struggled, and that salt," VIII. LoAs

Modern Poetry. Anita Skeen. IHMS

Modes of Pleasure. Thom Gunn. PPP

Modes of the court so common are grown, The. John Gay. *Fr.* The Beggar's Opera, III, iv. HeIP

Modest Couple, The. W. S. Gilbert. PoTa

Modest rose puts forth a thorn, The. The Lilly. Blake. *Fr.* Songs of Experience. MBPR

Modifications. Ron Koertge. MiP

Mohini Chatterjee. W. B. Yeats. NoAM

Mojo Hiding Woman. *Unknown.* BluL

Mole, The. John Haines. NCSH

Mole, The. Dennis Schmitz. AmPA

Moles. William Stafford. RFM

Molly Brannigan, *with music. Unknown.* RDB

Molly Means. Margaret Walker. NMM; PoTa; SS

Moloney Remembers the Resurrection of Kate Finucane. Brendan Kennelly. PoTa

Moly. Thom Gunn. NoAM

Moment. Howard Nemerov. CoPAm

Moment of silence, first, then there it is, A. The Dial Tone. Howard Nemerov. NowV

Moment Please, A. Samuel Allen. PoBA; SS

Monarch of gods and daemons, and all spirits. Prometheus Unbound. Shelley. MBPR

Monarch's Funeral, The. Shelley. MBPR

Monday Night in Winter. Ellen Cooney. NPW

Monday's child [*or* bairn] is fair of face. Mother Goose. ECBV; MG

Monet: "Les Nymphéas." W. D. Snodgrass. ConAP; TCP

Monet's Les Nymphéas. Lyn Lifshin. FAF

Money. C. H. Sisson. POL

Monk from the bank the dismal sight does view. Andrew Marvell. *Fr.* The Last Instructions to a Painter. SCP-1

Monkey. Sylvia Read. RAE

Monkeys. Padraic Colum. OxBTC

Monkeys, The. Marianne Moore. NoAM; NOBA

Monkeys on Mt. Hiei. Edith Marcombe Shiffert. WPE

Monkshood. Marie Harris. MMD

Mona Innominata, *sels.* Christina Rossetti.
  First Day, The, I. BoLoP
    ("I wish I could remember that first day.") GBL
  "Youth gone, and beauty gone if ever there," XIV. GBL

Monody on a Tea-Kettle. Samuel Taylor Coleridge. MBPR

Monody on the Death of Chatterton. Samuel Taylor Coleridge. MBPR

Monogamy, *sel.* Gerald Gould.
  "You were young—but that was scarcely to your credit." OxBTC

Monologue of a Deaf Man. David Wright. NoAM; NowV

Monologue of Two Moons, Nudes with Crests. 1938. Norman Dubie. FiCP

Monsieur Etienne de Silhouette. Some Frenchmen. John Updike. FaBoCo

Monsieur Pussy-cat, Blackmailer. Stevie Smith. PCat

Monsieur qui Passe. Charlotte Mew. SBG

Monster, The. Greg Kuzma. AmPA

Mont Blanc. Shelley. MBPR

Montage. Harry Guest. TwMBP

Montalbert, *sel.* Charlotte Smith.
  "Swift fleet the billowy clouds along the sky." WPE

Montana Fifty Years Ago. J. V. Cunningham. Prf

Montana Pastoral. J. V. Cunningham. CoPAm; MAT; PPoD; VGW

Montcalm and Wolfe. *Unknown.* AmFP

Montezuma. A. F. Alderson. ECBV

Montgomery. Sam Cornish. PoBA

Month or twain to live on honeycomb, A. Before Parting. Swinburne. OBP

Months, The. Sara Coleridge. OxBChV

Months, The. *Unknown.* OxBM
  (Labours of the Months.) GBP

Monument. Milton Acorn. NeAC

Monument, The. Elizabeth Bishop. NoAM; NOBA; PPoe

Monumentum Aere, Etc. Ezra Pound. NOBA

Moo! Robert Hillyer. TH

Mood, The. Quandra Prettyman. PoBA

Moon. Elizabeth Brewster. MMD

Moon, The. Robert Creeley. VGW

Moon, The. Robert Duncan. *Fr.* Passages. PiAm

Moon, The. Donald Hall. NCSH

Moon. William Jay Smith. CaYB

Moon, The. Charles Upton. MIT

Moon. Derek Walcott. NoAM

Moon, The/ is a white/ bull. Images. Alastair Campbell. Moon

Moon and the Night and the Men, The. John Berryman. VGW

Moon and the Nightingale, The. Milton. *See* Evening in Eden.

Moon and the Yew Tree, The. Sylvia Plath. Moon; MPo; PPP; VGW; WPE

Moon as Medusa. Vinnie-Marie D'Ambrosio. IHMS

Moon at Three A.M. Lance Henson. CDW

Moon beams and yams. Rapping Along with Ronda Davis. James Cunningham. JB

Moon came to the forge, The. Ballad of the Moon, Moon. Fererico García Lorca, *tr. by* Langston Hughes. Epi

Moon Compasses. Robert Frost. LoAs; Moon

Moon dangling wet like a half-plucked eye, The. Summer Night. Leonard Cohen. TCP

Moon Deer, how near.  By the Waters of Minnetonka.  J. M. Cavanass.  BLSo

Moon Exlipse Exorcism.  *Unknown, tr. fr. American Indian by* Armand Schwerner.  Moon

Moon-faced baby with cocaine arms.  Blues for Sister Sally.  Lenore Kandel.  NMM; RiTi

Moon goes over the water, The.  Half Moon.  Federico García Lorca, *tr. by* W. S. Merwin.  RFM

Moon Going Down.  *Unknown.*  BluL

Moon Ground, The.  James Dickey.  Moon

Moon had climbed the highest hill, The.  The Banks of Dee.  *Unknown.*  AmFP

Moon had risen on the eastern hill, The.  The Sailor and His Bride.  *Unknown.*  AmFP

Moon hangs in the air, A.  Starting from Central Station.  David Campbell.  MAuV

Moon holds nothing in her arms, The.  Target.  R. P. Lister.  SoSe

Moon, in her pride, once glanced aside, The.  The Moon Sings.  *Unknown.*  Moon

Moon in the bureau mirror, The.  Insomia.  Elizabeth Bishop.  TH

Moon in your eyes is best, The.  Tracking Rabbits: Night.  Jim Barnes.  CDW

Moon is a sow, The.  Song for Ishtar.  Denise Levertov.  AnMo; NMM; NoAM; PiAm; Psy

Moon is an eye under pondweed of trees, The.  The Fish.  Paul Mills.  MIS

Moon is an usurer, whose gain.  Upon Moon.  Robert Herrick.  Moon

Moon is balking its bleached skin from the November night, The.  Sunday Evening with Elizabeth, Age 5.  Martha Yoak.  NPW

Moon is so high it is, The.  I Walk Out into the Country at Night.  Lu Yu, *tr. by* Kenneth Rexroth.  IPWM

Moon is the mother of pathos and pity, The.  Lunar Paraphrase.  Wallace Stevens.  Moon

Moon, The? It is a griffin's egg.  Yet Gentle Will the Griffin Be.  Vachel Lindsay.  ECBV; Moon

Moon Landing.  W. H. Auden.  Moon

Moon like a flower, The.  Blake.  *Fr.* Songs of Innocence: Night.  Moon

Moon made a double circle around itself, The.  Christmas.  Daisy Aldan.  AATT

Moon Man.  Jean Valentine.  Moon

Moon Mattress.  Diane Di Prima NMM

Moon mentions, The.  Grunion.  Myra Cohn Livingston.  RFM

Moon more indolently dreams tonight, The.  The Sadness of the Moon.  Baudelaire, *tr. by* F. P. Trurm.  Moon

Moon on the one hand, the dawn on the other, The.  The Early Morning.  Hilaire Belloc.  ECBV

Moon Poems.  John Wieners.  VGW

Moon Rock.  E. Louise Mally.  POL

Moon, The: she shakes off her cloaks.  Promontory Moon.  Galway Kinnell.  Moon

Moon shines bright, The. In such a night as this.  Shakespeare.  *Fr.* The Merchant of Venice.  GBL

Moon shines bright, The; [and] the stars give a light.  A May Day Carol.  *Unknown.*  GBP; RDB

Moon Shot.  Byron.  *Fr.* Don Juan, X.  OBP

Moonshot.  Robert Kelly.  Moon

Moon Sings, The.  *Unknown.*.  Moon

Moon, Son of Heaven.  Miyazawa Kenji, *tr. fr. Japanese by* Gary Snyder.  Moon

Moon Song, Woman Song.  Anne Sexton.  Moon; PPP

Moon that is a cow, being horned like her.  Because the Three Moirai Have Become the Three Maries.  Constance Urdang.  Moon

Moon Tiger.  Denise Levertov.  Moon

Moon Walk.  Ben Belitt.  PPoD

Moon Was Waning, The.  James Hogg.  SLP

Moon was born grey, and Beethoven was weeping, The.  Nudes.  Juan Ramón Jiménez.  LoAs

Moon was but a chin of gold, The.  Emily Dickinson.  Moon

Moon was shining brightly upon the battle plain, The.  The Maid of Monterey.  *Unknown.*  AmFP

Moon, worn thin to the width of a quill.  Moon's Ending.  Sara Teasdale.  Moon

Moonlight.  Guillaume Apollinaire, *tr. fr. French by* William Meredith.  Moon

Moonlight.  Longfellow.  Moon

Moonlight.  Sara Teasdale.  VGW

Moonlight, *sel.*  W. G. Vincent.
  "And in the cold, bleak winter time."  ANTL

Moonlight, The: Juice flowing from an overripe pomegranate.  Enchantment.  Lewis Alexander.  PoBA

Moonlight through my gauze curtains.  The Skein.  Carolyn Kizer.  LoAs; VGW

Moonlit Apples.  John Drinkwater.  FSFS; OxBTC

Moonmoth and grasshopper that flee our page.  A Name for All.  Hart Crane.  VGW

Moonrise.  Gerard Manley Hopkins.  Moon

Moonrise.  D. H. Lawrence.  Moon

Moon's a steaming chalice, The.  What Semiramis Said.  Vachel Lindsay.  Moon

Moon's Ending.  Sara Teasdale.  Moon

Moon's glow by seven fold multiplied, turned red.  After Reading St. John the Divine.  Gene Derwood.  WPE

Moon's the North Wind's Cooky, The.  Vachel Lindsay.  LCL

Moon's up-riding makes a line, The.  Night Scenes.  Robert Duncan.  VGW

Moonsheep, The.  Christian Morgenstern, *tr. fr. German by* E. M. Valk.  Moon

Moonshine.  *Unknown.*  BluL

Moonwalk.  John Engels.  MAT

Moored wes i Cornwale and somnede cnihtes feole:  The Death of Arthur. Layamon.  *Fr.* The Brut.  OxBM

Mooress Morayma, The.  *Unknown, tr. fr. Spanish by* W. S. Merwin.  Epi

Moorhen Pond, The.  Tom Earley.  BoAnP

Moorings.  Norman MacCaig.  OxBTC

Moorish King Who Lost Granada, The.  *Unknown, tr. fr. Spanish by* W. S. Merwin.  Epi

Moral, The.  Theodore Weiss.  Prf

Moral Essays, *sels.*    Pope.
  Chloe, *fr.* Epistle II.  NOBE
  Duke of Buckingham, The, *fr.* Epistle III.  NOBE
  Sad Story, A, *fr.* Epistle III.  BoReV
  To Richard Boyle, Earl of Bulington: Of the Use of Riches, Epistle IV.  PPP

Moral Poem, A.  J. V. Cunningham.  VGW

Moralists, The.  Yvor Winters.  PiAm

Morality Play.  Pat Lowther.  MMD

More beautiful and soft than any moth.  The Landscape Near an Aerodrome.  Stephen Spender.  IPWM; NoAM; OxBTC

More beautiful than any gift you gave.  The Token.  F. T. Prince.  OxBTC

More Clues.  Muriel Rukeyser.  IHMS

More discontents I never had.  Discontents in Devon.  Robert Herrick.  PAIC; POL

More gaily, dance.  Quick-Step.  Robert Creeley.  VGW

More Good Whiskey Blues. *Unknown.* BluL

More grotesque than a row of laundromats. The Novelty Shop. Duane Niatum. CDW

More I chew this stuff, The. O'Connor the Bad Traveler. Peter Klappert. FiCp

"More Light! More Light!" Anthony Hecht. ConAP; NoAM; NOBA; SFF; SoSe; VGW

More luck to honest poverty. For A' That and A' That. Shirley Brooks. FaBoCo

More of a Corpse Than a Woman. Muriel Rukeyser. NMM

More Power. Egan O'Rahilly, *tr. fr. Irish by* John Montague. BIrV

More shower than shine. Valentines to My Mother, 1880. Christina Rossetti. OFD

More than the ash stays you from nothingness! The Phoenix. J. V. Cunningham. NoAM

Morea's Sonnet. Mary Sidney Wroth, Countess of Montgomery. *Fr.* Urania. WPE

Morels. William Jay Smith. MAT; PPoD; RFM

Morley's light went out. Power Failure. Michael Dennis Browne. AmPA

Mormons, led by Colonel Cooke, The. On the Road to California; or, The Buffalo Bullfight. *Unknown.* AmFP

Morning. Harry Fainlight. POL

Morning. Henry Reed. LoAs

Morning After, The. Walter Clark. NCSH

Morning After. Langston Hughes. NoAM

Morning and evening. Goblin Market. Christina Rossetti. SBG; VPC

Morning and the snow might fall forever. Going to Remake This World. James Welch. CDW; SA

Morning at the Window. T. S. Eliot. PiAm; PSN

Morning comes, and thickening clouds prevail, The. The Clouded Morning. Jones Very. NOBA

Morning comes with milk and bread. Morning Voluntary. James McAuley. MAuV

Morning Compliments. Sydney Dayre. OxBChV

Morning Dialogue. Conrad Aiken. NoAM

Morning-glory, climbing the morning long, The. Indiana. Hart Crane. *Fr.* The Bridge: Powhatan's Daughter. PiAm

Morning Half-Life Blues, The. Marge Piercy. WBN

Morning Has No House. Rosemarie Waldrop. MAT

Morning Hymn, A. Christopher Smart. OxBChV

Morning Hymn. Charles Wesley. BoReV

Morning in Gainesville. Karen Whitehill. NPW

Morning in Spring. Louis Ginsberg. ECBV

Morning Light, The. Louis Simpson. NoAM

Morning Light (The Dew-Drier). Mary Effie Lee Newsome. PoBA

Morning mists still haunt the stony street, The. In Hospital. W. E. Henley. VPC

Morning opened/ Like a rose. Song. Donald Justice. NCSH

Morning Prayer. Ogden Nash. OxBChV

Morning Song. Conrad Aiken. *Fr.* Senlin; a Biography, II, ii. SoSe
("It is morning, Senlin says, and in the morning.") NoAM

Morning Song. Alan Dugan. NowV

Morning Song. Sylvia Plath. HeIP; IHMS; InPK; InPS; LoAs; NOBA; PSN; SBG

Morning Song. Sara Teasdale. Moon

Morning spreads over. May All Earth Be Clothed in Light. George Hitchcock. VGW

Morning Star. Thomas Hornsby Ferril. VGW

Morning Star, The. Primus St. John. PoBA

Morning Swim. Maxine W. Kumin. NVAP; WPE

Morning: the soft release. Meditation for a Pickle Suite. R. H. W. Dillard. CoPAm

Morning to Remember, A; or, E Pluribus Unum. Edward Dorn. NoAM

Morning uptown, quiet on the street. Song Form. LeRoi Jones. CTBA

Morning Voluntary. James McAuley. MAuV

Morning-Watch, The. Henry Vaughan. BoReV; GrRo; MetP; PiAm; SCP-1

Morning Worship. Mark Van Doren. LoAs

Mornings/ I got up early. The Way It Was. Lucille Clifton. WPE

Mornings/ of an Impossible Love. Alice Walker. NVAP

Mornings everything is grey. Morning Has No House. Rosemarie Waldrop. MAT

Morningside Hights: Fragment of a Film. James Reiss. CAAP

Morns are meeker than they were, The. Emily Dickinson. FSFS

Morrigan, The. *Unknown, tr. fr. Irish by* Thomas Kinsella. BIrV

Morris Dance, The. *Unknown.* RAE

Mort Aux Chats. Peter Porter. CAAP

Mortal mixed of middle clay. Guy. Emerson. NOBA

Morality. Naomi Long Madgett. PoBA

Mortality, behold, and fear. On the Tombs in Westminster Abbey. *At. to* Francis Beaumont. NOBE; OBP

Morte D'Arthur. Tennyson. *Fr.* Idylls of the King. PAIC

Mortification. George Herbert. SCP-1

Mortmain, *sel.* Robert Penn Warren.
"In Time's concatenation and/ Carnal conventicle," I. NOBA; Prf

Moschus Moschiferus. A. D. Hope. MAuV

Mosquito, The. D. H. Lawrence. BoAnP

Mosquito. John Updike. BoAnP

Mosquito Knows, The. D. H. Lawrence. OxBTC

Moss-Gathering. Theodore Roethke. PiAm; RFM; VGW

Moss of His Skin, The. Anne Sexton. CoPAm; IHMS

Mossbawn Sunlight. Seamus Heaney. BIrV

Most Days. Elisavietta Ritchie. AATT

Most days/ the barn stands. Fire in Enfield. Wesley McNair. FAF

Most glorious Lord of life [or lyfe], that on this day. Amoretti, LXVIII [or Easter]. Spenser. BoReV; Epi; NOBE

Most is your name the name of this dark stone. Rainy Mountain Cemetery. N. Scott Momaday. CDW

Most kissed, The. Back Just Below the Shoulder Blades. Coleman Barks. *Fr.* Body Poems. NVAP

Most men use/ their eyes. The Mechanic. Diane Wakoski. AmPA

Most near, most dear, most loved and most far. Sonnet to My Mother. George Barker. LoAs; LP; NCSH; OxBTC; PAIC

Most of It, The. Robert Frost. PiAm; PPoe

Most of them worked around the slaughtering. The Meat Works. Robert Gray. CAAP

Most people, of which I am. The Graduate Assistant Tells About His Visit. Leon Stokesbury. NVAP

Most stupendous show they ever gave, The. In Memory of the Circus Ship *Euzkera*. Walter Gibson. NCSH

Mostly, I remember all the books. The House in Chicago. Marcia Lee Masters. HeS

Mostly People. Jeanette Nichols. SFF

Moth, The. Prentice Baker. AATT

Moth and the Flame, The, *with music*. George Taggart. FSN

Mother, The. Gwendolyn Brooks. BPo; CAPP; NMM

Mother, The. Babette Deutsch. RiTi

Mother. Sharon Mayer Libera. IHMS

Mother. Stephen Vincent. NeAC

Mother and child! whose blending tears. The Memorial Pillar. Felicia Dorothea Hemans. SBG

Mother and daughter German refugees. Schwiegermutterlieder. Tony Harrison. InPS

Mother and I. Martha Yoak. NPW

Mother and listener she is, but she does not listen. The Question. Muriel Rukeyser. IHMS

Mother and Poet. Elizabeth Barrett Browning. SBG

Mother and Son. Allen Tate. PiAm

Mother and Son. R. S. Thomas. BuTh

Mother and the Moon. Martha Yoak. NPW

Mother at her novenas. Puritan Poet Reel. Vincent Buckley. MAuV

Mother, because you never spoke to me. More Clues. Muriel Rukeyser. IHMS

"Mother dear, may I go downtown." Ballad of Birmingham. Dudley Randall. BPo; InPK; NoAM; WIF

Mother Hubberd's Tale, sel. Spenser. "At last they chanced to meet upon the way." TVS

Mother, I am something more. Looking Out. Helen Chasin. NMM

Mother, I Cannot Mind My Wheel. Walter Savage Landor, first st. par. fr. the Greek of Sappho. BoLoP; GBL; InPK; NOBE

Mother, I have loved you long. Misericordia. Teresa A. McCarthy. NPW

Mother, I long to get married. Whistle, Daughter, Whistle. Unknown. AmFP

Mother, I may do violence to you. Mother. Sharon Mayer Libera. IHMS

Mother, I won't be home this evening, so. Little Johnny's Final Letter. Brian Patten. LP

Mother, is this the darkness of the end. For "Our Lady of the Rocks." Dante Gabriel Rossetti. PFD

Mother, mother, what illbred aunt. The Disquieting Muses. Sylvia Plath. NMM; SBG

Mother of God! no lady thou. Our Lady. Mary Elizabeth Coleridge. WPE

Mother of God! Our Lady! For Eleanor and Bill Monahan. William Carlos Williams. VGW

"Mother of heaven, regina of the clouds." Le Monocle de Mon Oncle. Wallace Stevens. NoAM

Mother of Hermes! and still youthful Maia! Fragment of an Ode to Maia. Keats. MBPR; OBP

Mother of musings, contemplation sage. The Pleasures of Melancholy. Thomas Warton, the Younger. LAuP

Mother Pin a Rose on Me, with music. David Lewis, Paul Schindler, and Bob Adams. FSN

Mother Rosarine. Maxine W. Kumin. RiTi

Mother said to call her if the H bomb exploded. Belief. Josephine Miles. NoAM

Mother Speaks, A: The Algiers Motel Incident, Detroit. Michael S. Harper. AmPA; BPo

Mother Tabbyskins. Elizabeth Anna Hart. OxBChV

Mother the Wardrobe Is Full of Infantrymen. Roger McGough. BuTh; MAT

Mother, they say you looked Irish. Summer Brenner. RiTi

Mother to Son. Langston Hughes. CTBA; IPWM

Mother Was a Lady; or, If Jack Were Only Here, with music. Edward B. Marks. FSN

Mother your children give you. Karen L. Kent. NPW

Motherless Child Blues. Unknown. BluL

Motherless Children. Unknown. BluL

"Motherless mite," the women bill. Lamb. James Rankin. MIS

Mothers. Nikki Giovanni. CTBA

Mothers. Anne Sexton. IPWM

Mother's Advice. Unknown. AmFP

Mothers and Daughters. David Campbell. POL

Mothers are waiting in the yard, The. For a Junior School Poetry Book. Christopher Middleton. BBGO; MPo

Mothers, Daughters. Shirley Kaufman. NMM; RiTi

Mother's Day. Sam Hamod. SA

Mother's Dream, The. William Barnes. NOBE

Mothers of sailors, I hope you will draw nigh. Johnny Gallagher. Unknown. AmFP

Moths, The. W. S. Merwin. HeIP

Moth's kiss, first, The! Robert Browning. Fr. In a Gondola. BoLoP; GBL

Motionless Swaying. Yannis Ritsos, tr. fr. Greek by Nikos Stangos. TSWA

Motor Bus. Alfred Denis Godley. FaBoCo

Motorcycle Irene. Skip Spence. MAT

Motorcyclist's Song, The. DeWitt Bell. MiP

Motto. Langston Hughes. PoBA

Motto for a Sun Dial. J. V. Cunningham. InPK
(Epigram: "I who by day am function of the light.") VGW

Motto to the Songs of Innocence and of Experience. Blake. MBPR

Moulded in cobweb, horse-hair, cow-hair. The Wagtail's Nest. Kenneth Mackenzie. MAuV

Mouldering Vine, The. Unknown. AmFP

Mound, The. Thomas Hardy. OxBTC

Mount Vernon. Unknown. AmFP; OFD

Mount Zion. Unknown. AmFP

Mountain, The. W. S. Merwin. VGW

Mountain Afterglow, The. James Laughlin. IPWM; VGW

Mountain and the squirrel, The. Fable. Emerson. PiAm

Mountain Cemetery, The. Edgar Bowers. ConAP

Mountain Corral. Helen Sorrells. WPE

Mountain, Fire, Thornbush. Harvey Shapiro. VGW

Mountain is streaked white, the air is cold, The. St. John's Park. James McAuley. MAuV

Mountain Lion. D. H. Lawrence. BoAnP; OxBTC; RFM

Mountain moving day is coming, The. Yosano Akiko and Naomi Weisstein. MMD

Mountain Oysters. Patrick Lane. NeAC

Mountain road ends here, The. Lyell's Hypothesis Again. Kenneth Rexroth. NoAM

Mountain sheep are sweeter, The. The War song of Dinas Vawr. Thomas Love Peacock. Fr. The Misfortune of Elphin. NOBE; PoTa

Mountain Whippoorwill, The. Stephen Vincent Benét. PoTa

Mountains. Besmilr Brigham. RiTi

Mountains are moving, rivers. The Redwoods. Louis Simpson. TH

Mountain's green and shining, The. Summer Solstice. Alan Garner. BuTh

Mountains have gathered in the distance. Sleep on the Fraser. Patrick Lane. NeAC

Mountains high seem to hide the sky. Cielito Lindo. Carlos Fernandez. BLSH

Mountains of Mourne, The. Percy French. PFIr

Mountains stand, and stare around, The. The Paps of Dana. James Stephens. NoAM

Mountebank Song, The. Thomas Durfey. SCP-2

Mourn for Yourself. Geoffrey Keating, tr. fr. Irish by Sean Lucy. BIrV

Mourn Not for Adonais. Shelley. Fr. Adonais. BoReV; NOBE

Mournful Dove, The. Unknown. AmFP

Mourning. Andrew Marvell. SCP-1

Mourning Dove, The. Myra Cohn Livingston. ECBV

Mourning Letter from Paris, A. Conrad Kent Rivers. BPo

Mourning Letter, March 29 1963. Edward Dorn. ConAP

Mourning Poem for the Queen of Sunday. Robert Hayden. PoBA

Mourning Women. Mathilde Blind. SBG

Mouse and the Cake, The. Eliza Cook. OxBChV

Mouse in the cupboard repeats himself, The. A Ritual Mouse. William Meredith. PBMP

Mouse Night: One of Our Games. William Stafford. NCSH

Mouse, the Frog, and the Little Red Hen, The. *Unknown.* ECBV

Mousemeal. Howard Nemerov. NCSH; NowV

Mouse's Courting Song, The. *Unknown.* AIW

Mouse's Nest. John Clare. InPK; SoSe

Mouse's Petition, The. Anna Laetitia Barbauld. OxBChV

Mouth, A. Can blow or breathe. Cardinal Ideograms. May Swenson. Psy

Mouth of a girl who had been lying, The. Beautiful Youth. Gottfried Benn, *tr. by* Joachim Neugroschel. POL

Mouth of the Hudson, The. Robert Lowell. PSN

Mouth That Is a Wound, The. Holly Prado. NPW

Mouth to mouth joined we lie, her naked breasts. Tantalos. Paulus Silentarius, *tr. by* Dudley Fitts. LoAs

Mouths of the Poor, The. Jon Anderson. CAAP

Move Continuing, The. Al Young. PoBA

Move him into the sun. Futility. Wilfred Owen. BuTh; NoAM; PSN

Move to California, The, *sel.* William Stafford. Written on the Stub of the First Paycheck. AnMo; InPK

Move your head and the view undulates. Through Old Farmhouse Windows. Allan Block. FAF

Moved to forward position at Lovidina. Excerpts from a Diary of a War (2). John Daniel. TwMBP

Movement. Gary Lawless. FAF

Movement of Fish, The. James Dickey. VGW

Mover. James L. White. HeS

Movie-Going. John Hollander. PPoD; PPP

Movie House. John Updike. PPoD

Movies, she told me, The. Grenadine. Susan Griffin. MMD

Movin amang thae stanes, I ken. Cougait Revisited. Donald Campbell. MIS

Moving. James Harrison. CoPAm

Moving. William Matthews. POL

Moving from Cheer to Joy, from Joy to All. Next Day. Randall Jarrell. NoAM; PPoD

Moving sun-shapes on the spray, The. Going and Staying. Thomas Hardy. NoAM

Moving through the Silent Crowd. Stephen Spender. LP; MPo; NOBE

Mower Against Gardens, The. Andrew Marvell. AnMo; PPP

Mower to the Glow-Worms, The. Andrew Marvell. AnMo; NOBE; PPP

Mower's Song, The. Andrew Marvell. AnMo; PPP

Mowing. Robert Frost. NOBA; PPP; VGW

Much Ado about Nothing, *sel.* Shakespeare. "Sigh no more, ladies, sigh no more," *fr.* II, iii. SS

Much as he left it when he went from us. Why He Was There. E. A. Robinson. NOBA

Much have I traveled in the realms of gold. On First Looking into Chapman's Homer. Keats. AnMo; HeIP; InPK; MBPR; NOBE; OBP; PAIC; PPoD; PPoe; PPP; SoSe; WIF

Much madness is divinest sense. Emily Dickinson. AmVN; HeIP; MAT; NoAM; NOBA; PBMP; PiAm; SS; WPE

Much on my early youth I love to dwell. To a Young Lady with a Poem on the French Revolution. Samuel Taylor Coleridge. MBPR

Much suspected by me. Written with a Diamond on Her Window at Woodstock. Elizabeth I, Queen of England. WPE

Muckers. Carl Sandburg. CTBA

Muckish Mountain (The Pig's Back). Shane Leslie. PFIr

Mud turkle settin' on de end of a log. The Turtle's Song. *Unknown.* BPo

Mulatto. Langston Hughes. PAIC

Mulberry Mountain. *Unknown.* AmFP

Mule, The. Coleman Barks. POL

Mules. C. Fox-Smith. BoAnP

Mulligan Guard, The, *with music.* Ned Harrigan. BLSo

Multipara: Gravida 5. Marie Ponsot. VGW

Multitude of masts in the harbour, A. The Victim of Aulis. Dannie Abse. NoAM

Mum and the Sothsegger, *sel. Unknown.* Dream, A. OxBM

Mummy of a Lady Named Jemutesonekh XXI Dynasty. Thomas James. AmPA

Municipal Gallery Revisited, The. W. B. Yeats. OxBTC

Murder in the Cathedral, *sels.* T. S. Eliot. OxBTC
Chorus: "We do not wish anything to happen."
Chorus: "We have not been happy, my Lord, we have not been too happy."

Murder of Goins, The. *Unknown.* AmFP

Murder self slowly. And die like ants shuffling up under. Reckoning A.M. Thursday. Doris Turner. JB

Murderers/ of Emmett Till. Salute. Oliver Pitcher. PoBA

Murderous owls off Malo bay, The. Owls. John Fuller. POL

Murphy in Manchester. John Montague. PFIr

Mus Ridiculus Non. Marie De L. Welch. BoAnP

Muscle Building. Dalene Stowe. NPW

Muse, The. Barry Spacks. MAT; POL

Muse, disgusted at an age and clime, The. On the Prospect of Planting Arts and Learning in America. George Berkeley. OPB; PAIC; PPoD

Muse, June, Related, *sel.* Brian Coffey. "Blooms such as wither at finger-touch." BIrV

Muse of Amergin, The. *Unknown, tr. fr. Irish by* John Montague. BIrV

Muse of Water, A. Carolyn Kizer. NMM

Muse! twang the powerful harp and brush each string. Edward Benlowes. *Fr.* Theophila; or, Love's Sacrifice, Canto III. SCP-2

Musée des Beaux Arts. W. H. Auden. AnMo; HeIP; InPK; InPS; MPo; NoAM; NOBE; OBP; PBMP; PPoD; PPP; PSN; TCP; VoPo; WIF

Muses' friend, grey-eyed Aurora, yet, The. William Browne. *Fr.* Britannia's Pastorals, II, Song 2. SCP-2

Muses' garden, with pedantic weeds, The. On the Death of Donne. Thomas Carew. NOBE

Museum Item 237. Polly Mann. NPW

Museum Piece. Richard Wilbur. ConAP; WIF

Musgrove. *Unknown.* AmFP

Mushrooms. Sylvia Plath. PBMP; Psy; SS

Music, A. Wendell Berry. VGW

Music. Abraham Cowley. *Fr.* Davideis, I. SCP-2

Music. Amy Lowell. RiTi

Music and Drum. Archibald MacLeish. TH

Music and its harmony, The. The Design. Clarence Major. PoBA

Music I heard with you was more than music. Bread and Music. Conrad Aiken. Discordants, I. NOBA; VoPo

Music, when soft voices die. To ——. Shelley. HeIP; MBPR; NOBE

Musical Instrument, A.   Elizabeth Barrett Browning.   OBP; VPC; WPE

Musical poet, collector of basset-horns, A.   An Addition to the Family.   Edwin Morgan.   MPo

Musician, The.   R. S. Thomas.   BoReV

Music's Duel.   Richard Crashaw.   SCP-1

Musing on roses and revolution.   Roses and Revolutions. Dudley Randall.   BPo; ConAP; NoAM; PoBA

Musing upon the restless bisynesse.   Anxious Thought.   Thomas Hoccleve.   Fr. De Regimine Principum.   OxBM

Musings.   William Barnes.   NOBE

Musings.   Patty Harjo.   VW

Musk-ox smells, The.   The Long River.   Donald Hall.   ConAP

Muskrats, The.   Winter Pond.   Mary Logue.   NPW

Musophilus, sel.   Samuel Daniel.
      Heavenly Eloquence.   NOBE

Must I shoot me.   Watts.   Conrad Kent Rivers.   PoBA

Must I then see, alas! eternal night.   Elegy over a Tomb.   Lord Herbert of Cherbury.   NOBE

Must then my crimes become thy scandal too?   To Antenor. Katherine Philips.   SBG

Must we part, Von Hügel, though much alike, for we.   W. B. Yeats.   Fr. Vacillation.   BoReV

Mustapha, sels.      Fulke Greville.
      Chorus Sacerdotum.   NOBE; PPP
      "Fall none but angels suddenly to hell?"   SCP-2

Mutabilities, The.   Vincent McHugh.   MIT

Mutability ("The flower that smiles to-day").   Shelley.   MBPR

Mutability ("We are as clouds that veil the midnight moon.") Shelley.   MBPR

Mutability.   Wordsworth.   Fr. Ecclesiastical Sonnets, Pt. III, Sonnet XXXIV.   HeIP; InPK; MBPR; NOBE; PPoD

Mutant, The.   Anita Barrows.   RiTi

Mute/ the hand moves from the heart.   Miniatures IV.   Lynn Strongin.   IHMS

Mute Is Thy Wild Harp, Now, O Bard Sublime!   Charlotte Smith.   SBG

Mute, with signs I speak.   Faith Unfaithful.   Siegfried Sassoon. BoReV

Mutes, The.   Denise Levertov.   AnMo; IHMS; NOBA; Psy; RiTi

Mutterings over the Crib of a Deaf Child.   James Wright. CoPAm

Mutual Problem.   William Cole.   POL

Mwilu/ or Poem for the Living.   Don L. Lee.   JB

My/ father/ dreams.   The Eyes of Flesh.   Sandra Hochman. NMM

My Alba.   Allen Ginsberg.   NoAM; NOBA

My annals have it so.   Emus.   Mary Fullerton.   BoAnP

My arm sweeps down.   Gesture.   Donald Finkel.   InPK

My arms smell good.   Think.   Please Forward.   James Welch. CDW

My aspen dear, whose airy cages quelled.   Binsey Poplars. Gerard Manley Hopkins.   InPS; NoAM

My Atlas Poet.   George Bowering.   NeAC

My Auld Wife.   Unknown.   GBP

My Aunt.   Peggy Wood.   POL

My aunt she died a month ago.   The Heir.   Unknown.   RAE

My Aunt's Spectre.   Mortimer Collins.   PoTa

My Babe My Babe.   Unknown.   BluL

My baby ain't good looking and she don't dress fine.   Robbing and Stealing Blues.   Unknown.   BluL

My baby done quit me.   Squabbling Blues.   Unknown.   BluL

My baby's face is a.   To the White Critics.   Carolyn M. Rodgers. SA

My bands of silk and miniver.   Full Moon.   Elinor Wylie.   Psy; SBG; VGW

My Bangelory Man.   Unknown.   ECBV

My Baselard.   Unknown.   OxBM

My beautiful hair is dead.   Hair.   Gregory Corso.   SFF

My Beloved Is Mine and I Am His.   Francis Quarles.   Emblems, V, 3.   NOBE
      ("Ev'n like two little bank-dividing brooks.")   PAIC

My black-eyed lover broke my back.   The Masochist.   Maxine W. Kumin.   IHMS

My Black Gal Blues.   Unknown.   BluL

My black hills have never seen the sun rising.   Shancoduff. Patrick Kavanagh.   BIrV

My Black Mama.   Unknown.   BluL

My Blackness Is the Beauty of This Land.   Lance Jeffers.   PoBA

My blessed Lord, art thou a lilly flower?   Edward Taylor.   Fr. Prepatory Meditations: First Series, V.   PiAm

My blessing on the patient cows.   A Blessing on the Cows. Seumas O'Sullivan.   BoAnP; PFIr

My body a rounded stone.   Living Tenderly.   May Swenson. BoAnP

My body being dead, my limbs unknown.   The Preparative. Thomas Traherne.   SCP-2

My body holds its shape.   The genius is intact.   Mummy of a lady Named Jemutesonekh XXI Dynasty.   Thomas James. AmPA

My body I give.   Auto Icon.   John Daniel.   TwMBP

My body is weary to death of my mischievous brain. Nebuchadnezzar.   Elinor Wylie.   SBG

My Bonnie Lies over the Ocean, with music.   Unknown.   BLSH

My bonny keel laddie, my canny keel laddie.   The Bonny Keel Laddie.   Unknown.   GBP

My bonny moorhen, my bonny moorhen.   The Bonny Moorhen. Unknown.   GBP

My boy was scarcely ten years auld.   Leesome Brand.   Unknown. PeBB

My Brain.   Annabel Laurance.   AKE

My Brother Ben's face, thought Eugene.   Ben.   Thomas Wolfe. NCSH

My brother came home from a Princeton club.   Eastward to Eden.   Edgar Bogardus.   POL

My brother is skull and skeleton now.   Epitaph.   William Montgomerie.   POL

My brother stands among his friends.   I Visit My Brother.   Greg Kuzma.   NVAP

My bully boys of Liverpool.   The Banks of Newfoundland. Unknown.   GBP

My Buried Firends.   Unknown.   AmFP

My Busconductor.   Roger McGough.   LP

My business is words.   Words are like labels.   Said the Poet to the Analyst.   Anne Sexton.   Psy

My cabinets are oyster-shells.   Song.   Margaret Cavendish, Duchess of Newcastle.   Fr. The Convent of Pleasure.   SCP-2; WPE

My candle burns at both ends.   First Fig.   Edna St. Vincent Millay.   BBGO; NoAM; TH

My case is this, I love Zepheria bright.   Gulling Sonnets, VIII. Sir John Davies.   Epi

My Cat.   Lesley Syrett.   RAE

My Cat and I.   Roger McGough.   OxBTC; POL

My cat is a blackish-brown Persian.   My Cat.   Lesley Syrett. RAE

My cat jumps to the window sill.   Waiting for It.   May Swenson. BoAnP

My cat, washing her tail's tip, is a whorl.   Cat on Couch. Barbara Howes.   NCSH

My Cathedral.   Longfellow.   PBMP

My child and I hold hands on the way to school. September, the First Day of School. Howard Nemerov. PPoD

My clumsiest dear, whose hands shipwreck vases. Love Poem. John Frederick Nims. CoPAm; InPK; SoSe; TCP; VoPo

My clutch and your clutch. Gary Snyder. Myths and Texts: Burning, VI. Epi

My comforts drop and melt away like snow. The Answer. George Herbert. Epi

My comrade is dead. Elegy. Salomón de la Selva, *tr. by* Donald Walsh. LoAs

My country, 'tis of thee. America. Samuel Francis Smith. BLSH; BLSo; BTTM; PSoN

My Country 'Tis of Thy People You're Dying. Buffy Sainte-Marie. WIF

My countrymen have now become too base. April 1962. Paul Goodman. VGW

My cousin Max is being married. Plan. Rod McKuen. MiP

My Crime. *Unknown.* BluL

My Dad and Mam They Did Agree. *Unknown.* POL

My daddy come home this morning drunk as he could be. Don't Fish in My Sea. *Unknown.* BluL

My Daddy has paid the rent. Good Times. Lucille Clifton. AmPA; BPo; CAAP; InPS; NCSH; PoBA

My daddy's fingers move among the couplers. Lucille Clifton. CAAP

My Dark Fathers. Brendan Kennelly. BIrV

My Darling Dear, My Daisy Flower. John Skelton. LoAs ("With, Lullay, lullay, lyke a chylde.") AAS

My Darling's on the Deep Blue Sea. *Unknown.* AmFP

My Daughter. Robert Pack. CoPAm

My daughter, at eleven. Little Girl, My String Bean, My Lovely Woman. Anne Sexton. RiTi; WBN

My Daughter Very Ill. Paul Goodman. RRA

My Daughter's Dowry. Robert Herrick. RRA

My daughter' heavier. Light leaves are flying. John Berryman. *Fr.* Dream Songs. CAPP; RRA

My dear,/ Today a letter from Berlin. A Letter from Berlin. Jon Stallworthy. NoAM

My dear and only love, I pray. I'll Never Lover Thee More. James Graham, Marquess of Montrose. GBL; NOBE; SLP

My dear child, first thyself enable. The Boy Serving at Table. John Lydgate. OxBChV

My dear deaf father, how I loved him then. John Betjeman. *Fr.* Summoned by Bells. OxBTC

My dear, deare, Lord I do thee Saviour call. Edward Taylor. *Fr.* Preparatory Meditations: First Series, II. PiAm

My dear [*or* dears], do you know. The Babes in the Wood. *Unknown.* ECBV; OxBChV

My dear, do you remember that country. Remember That Country. Jean Garrigue. VGW

My dear, my dear, I know. To a Young Girl. W. B. Yeats. OLR; PSN; SoSe

My dear, when I was very young. To a Lady on Her Marriage. William Bell. PAIC

My dearest dust, could not thy hasty day. Epitaph on the Monument of Sir William Dyer at Colmworth, 1641. Lady Catherine Dyer. *Fr.* Sir William Dyer, Knight. BoLoP; SCP-2

My dearly loved friend, how oft have we. First Steps Up Parnassus. Michael Drayton. *Fr.* To My Most Dearly Loved Henry Reynolds. NOBE

My dears, do you know. *See* My dear, do you know.

My dears, 'tis said in days of old. The Bee, the Ant, and the Sparrow. Nathaniel Cotton. OxBChV

My Death. Mark Strand. CAAP

My death was arranged by special plans in Heaven. A New England Bachelor. Richard Eberhart. NoAM

My delight and thy delight. Robert Bridges. NOBE

"My deth I love, my lif ich hate, for levedy shene." De Clerico et Puella. *Unknown.* OxBM

My dog lay dead five days without a grave. The Pardon. Richard Wilbur. NoAM; NOBA

My dog's so furry, I've not seen. The Hairy Dog. Herbert Asquith. ECBV

My Dolphin, you only guide my by surprise. Dolphin. Robert Lowell. NOBA

My dream a drink with Lonnie Johnson. Sonnet. Ted Berrigan. CAAP; NoAM

My drum, hollowed out thru the thin slit. La Chute. Charles Olson. InPK

My eight spring in England I walk among. This Landscape, These People. Zulfikar Ghose. MPo

My Elbow Ancestry. Larry Mollin. NeAC

My electric handmixer of 87 bloodstone finches. Love to My Electric Handmixer. Diane Wakoski. CoPAm

My enemy came nigh. Hate. James Stephens. VoPo

My enemy had bidden me as guest. The Compassionate Fool. Norman Cameron. OxBTC; WIF

My eye descending from the hill, surveys. Sir John Denham. *Fr.* Cooper's Hill. PAIC

My eyes make pictures, when they are shut. A Day-Dream. Samuel Taylor Coleridge. MBPR

My eyes welcome high grass. Some Good Things Left after the War with the Sioux. John Calvin Rezmerski. HeS

My eyes went away from me. The Fickle One. Pablo Neruda, *tr. by* Donald D. Walsh. OLR

My Face. *Unknown.* RAE

My face is black. See the moon? My eyes. Crystal. Faye Kicknosway. IHMS

My face isn't pretty. My Face. *Unknown.* RAE

My fairest child, I have no song to give you. A Farewell. Charles Kingsley. OxBChV

My Faith Looks Up to Thee, *with music.* Ray Palmer. BLSH; BLSo

My Faither. Duncan Glen. MIS

My faithful friend, if you can see. Impossibilities to His Friend. Robert Herrick. OLR

My family, in Christian pantomime. Grace. Michael Sheridan. HeS

My Fancy. "Lewis Carroll." FaBoCo

My Father. Judy Collins. WIF

My Father. David Kherdian. SA

My father always promised us. My Father. Judy Collins. WIF

My father and his muscles. My Father Toured the South. Jeanette Nichols. RiTi

My father and my mother never quarrelled. Because. James McAuley. MAuV

My father brought that dog home. Bony. Simon J. Ortiz. CDW

My father brought the emigrant bundle. Europe and America. David Ignatow. PBMP

My father by some strange conjuction had mice for sons. In All the Days of My Childhood. Russell Edson. AmPA

My father could go down a mountain faster than I. The Dark Other Mountain. Robert Francis. NCSH

My father could hear a little animal step. Listening. William Stafford. RFM; TSWA

My father died, and I cannot tell how. The Foolish Boy. *Unknown.* RAE

My Father Dreams of Baseball. Laurence Lieberman. SPo

My father hurried. Chronicles: Numbers One and Two. Mei Berssenbrugge. SA

My father in his. Beryl. Lyn Lifshin. NeAC

My Father in the Night Commanding No. Louis Simpson. ConAP; HeIP; NoAM; NOBA; VGW

My Father is watching over his Mosque, silently. Lines To My Father. Sam Hamod. SA

My Father Kept a Horse. *Unknown.* GBP

My father lies black and hushed. The worker. Richard W. Thomas. PoBA

My Father Moved Through Dooms of Love. E. E. Cummings. AnMo; IPWM; NoAM; NOBA; WIF

My father moves through the South hunting duck. Treetops. Marvin Bell. AmPA

My father: October 1942. William Stafford. CoPAm

My Father Paints the Summer. Richard Wilbur. NCSH; NOBA

"My father planted those fields." The Wheat District. Ted Enslin. FAF

My Father Toured the South. Jeanette Nichols. RiTi

My father used to say. Silence. Marianne Moore. NOBA; PiAm; PSN; Psy; SBG

My father was a farmer gay. One-and-Twenty. *Unknown.* AmFP

My father was a working man. Red-Herring. D. H. Lawrence. NoAM

My father was the keeper of the Eddystone Light. The Keeper of the Eddystone Light. *Unknown.* PeBB

My father wore it working coal at Shotts. The Miner's Helmet. George MacBeth. OxBTC

My father worked with a horse plough. Follower. Seamus Heaney. LP; PFIr

My Father's House. Calvin Forbes. CoPAm

My Father's Leaving. Ira Sadoff. AmPA

My feet have felt the sands. Determination. John Henrik Clarke. PoBA

My feet taste funny. Why I Didn't Go to Delphi. James Welch. CDW

My feet took a walk in heavenly grass. Heavenly Grass. Tennessee Williams. ECBV

My feets is so sore can't hardly wear my shoes. Big Night Blues. *Unknown.* BluL

My fiftieth year had come and gone. W. B. Yeats. *Fr.* Vacillation. BoReV

My First Cigar. Robert J. Burdette. PoTa

My first thought was, he lied in every word. "Childe Roland to the Dark Tower Came." Robert Browning. PPP

My flowery and green age was passing away. He Understands the Great Cruelty of Death. Petrarch, *tr. by* J. M. Synge. Sonnets to Laura: To Laura in Death, XLVII. BIrV

My Folk, What Have I Done Thee? William Herebert. OxBM

My freshmen/ settle in. Achilles. Freshmen. Barry Spacks. CoPAm

My Friend, the Doctor. George Abbe. FAF

My friend who married the girl I. Watts. Shirley Kaufman. NMM

My friends,/ I am amazed. Acceptance Speech. Marvin Bell. AmPA

My Gal Sal, *with music.* Paul Dresser. BLSo; FSN

My Galley Charged with Forgetfulness. Petrarch. *See* Lover Compareth His State to a Ship

My Garden. Thomas Edward Brown. InPK

My Garden, *parody.* J. A. Lindon. InPK; POL

My gentle child, behold this horse. The Racing-Man. A. P. Herbert. BoAnP

My gentle father. Feliks Skrzynecki. Peter Skrzynecki. CAAP

My Ghostly Father, I Me Confess. Charles d'Orléans. BoLoP; SoSe
    (Lover's Confession, A.) NOBE; OxBM
    ("My ghostly fadir I me confess.") GBL

My girl the voluptuous creature. Love and Poetry. Louis Simpson. PPoe

My girl, thou gazest much. The Lover to His Lady. *At. to* Plato, *tr. by* George Turberville. LoAs

My girlfriend, at my urging. Domestic Duties. Richard Emil Braun. NoAM

My god,/ the joke's on you. Good Friday. Richard Bastian. AATT

My God, how gracious art thou! The Relapse. Henry Vaughan. PAIC

My God, I heard this day. Man. George Herbert. MetP

My God most glad to look, most prone to hear. Psalm LV: Exaudi, Deus. Countess of Pembroke. WPE

My God, my God, what queer corner am I in? In the Deep Museum. Anne Sexton. Prf

My God, when I walk in those groves. Religion. Henry Vaughan. BoReV

My gracious Lord, I would thee glory doe. Edward Taylor. *Fr.* Preparatory Meditations: Second Series, IV. PiAm

My Grandfather/ the Hajj Abbass Habhab. The Fight. Sam Hamod. SA

My grandfather said to me. Manners. Elizabeth Bishop. CTBA; NCSH

My grandfather's clock was too large for the shelf. Grandfather's Clock. Henry Clay Work. BLSo; PSoN

My Grandfather's Funeral. James Applewhite. NVAP

My Grandmother. Elizabeth Jennings. LP; MPo

My Grandmother. Karl Shapiro. VGW

My Grandmother Green ("My grandmother lived on yonder green"). *Unknown.* AmFP

My grandmother moves to my mind in context of sorrow. My Grandmother. Karl Shapiro. VGW

My Grandmother's Love Letters. Hart Crane. NoAM; NOBA; PSN

My grandmothers were strong. Lineage. Margaret Walker. NMM; PoBA

My great brother. A Psalm Praising the Hair of Man's Body. Denise Levertov. AnMo; CAPP

My Great-Grandfather's Slaves. Wendell Berry. TCP

My grief, quoth I, is called Ignorance. Rachel Speght. *Fr.* A Dream. WPE

My growning up. Enormous Sleep. Tom Crawford. NVAP

My hair has dried. Self Dirge. Wendy Rose. CDW

My hair is grey, but not with years. The Prisoner of Chillon. Byron. MBPR

My hair is springy like the forest grasses. Black Woman. Naomi Long Madgett. OLR; PoBA

My hand has a pain from writing. *Unknown, tr. fr. Irish by* Flann O'Brien. BIrV

My hands/ Open the curtains of your being. Touch. Octavio Paz, *tr. by* Charles Tomlinson. BoLoP

My hands are in the garden. Song of Ceres. Katherine Doak. NPW

My hands are tender feathers. Calypso's Song to Ulyssess. Adrian Mitchell. GBL

My hands did numb to beauty. I Held a Shelley Manuscript. Gregory Corso. VGW

My hands have developed eyes! Conversion. Geof Hewitt. NeAC

My hands have not touched water since your hands. Carrier Letter. Hart Crane. BoLoP

My hands, my fists, my small bells. Oh Yes. William Matthews. AmPA

My hazard wouldn't be yours, not ever. Advice. Ruth Stone. NMM

My head aches. Going Through Changes. Jean Tepperman. NMM

My head is bald, my breath is bad. Late-Flowering Lust. John Betjeman. PAIC

My head, my heart, mine eyes, my life, nay more. A Letter to Her Husband, Absent upon Publick Employment. Anne Bradstreet. HeIP; PiAm

My heart aches, and a drowsy numbness pains. Ode to a Nightingale. Keats. AnMo; Epi; HeIP; InPK; InPS; IPWM; MBPR; NOBE; OBP; PAIC; PPoe; PPP; SoSe; SpRo; VoPo

My heart beating, my blood running. Time's Dedication. Delmore Schwartz. VGW

My heart grows sick before the wide-spread death. The Grave-Yard. Jones Very. NOBA

My heart has grown rich with the passing of years. The Solitary. Sara Teasdale. IPWM

My heart has thank'd thee, Bowles! for those soft strains. To the Rev. W. L. Bowles. Samuel Taylor Coleridge. MBPR

My heart is like a singing bird. A Birthday. Christina Rossetti. NOBE; OLR; VPC; WIF; WPE

My heart is like one asked to dine. An Unexpected Pleasure. *Unknown.* FaBoCo

My Heart Is Set upon a Lusty Pin. Queen Elizabeth of York. WPE

My Heart Is Woe. *Unknown. See* O, My Heart Is Woe!

My Heart Leaps Up When I Behold. Wordsworth. AKE; InPK; NOBE; PBMP (Rainbow, The.) MBPR

My heart stirs quietly now to think. A Hermit's Song. *Unknown, tr. by* James Simmons. BIrV

My Heart Stood Still, *with music.* Lorenz Hart. BLSo

My Heart's in the Highlands. Burns. BTTM

My home over there, my home over there. That Mountain Far Away. *Unknown, tr. by* Herbert Joseph Spinden. PBMP

My Home's Across the Smoky Mountains. *Unknown.* AmFP

My Hope, My Love. *Unknown, tr. fr. Irish by* Edward Walsh. BIrV

My hopes retire; my wishes as before. Walter Savage Landor. *Fr.* Ianthe. GBL

My House. Saint-Denys Garneau, *tr. fr. French by* John Glassco. AKE

My house was an infinite series of houses. Poem to my Twin Possibility. Dalene Stowe. NPW

My humanoid friend, myself, a limited animal. The Week-end Naturalist. Tom Buchan. MIS

My innocent my animal. Before the Fall. Rosemary Daniell. WBN

My kid says I. Playing. Philip Dow. MIT

My kite is three feet broad, and six feet long. The Kite. Adelaide O'Keeffe. OxBChV

My Knees Go before the Firing Squad at Dawn. Diane Wakoski. CAAP

My ladies haire is threeds of beaten gold. Fidessa, More Chaste than Kind, XXXI. Bartholomew Griffin. AAS

My lady/ fair with. A Token. Robert Creeley. VGW

My lady unto madam makes her bow. Modern Love, XXXVI. George Meredith. VPC

My lady went to Canterbury. Carol. *Unknown.* FaBoCo

My Lady Wind. *Unknown.* ECBV

My lady's presence makes the roses red. Henry Constable. *Fr.* Diana. WIF

My Lady's Tears. *Unknown.* NOBE

My Last Afternoon with Uncle Devereux Winslow. Robert Lowell. VGW

My last defense. Old Mary. Gwendolyn Brooks. CoPAm

My Last Duchess. Robert Browning. InPS; IPWM; MAT; NOBE; PAIC; PBMP; PPoD; PPP; SoSe; SS; WIF

My lefe is faren in londe. Separated Lovers. *Unknown.* OxBM

My left eye is blind and jogs like. Sketch for a Job Application Blank. Jim Harrison. AmPA; NoAM

My Life. Mark Strand. CAAP

My life/ is/ a/ bald headed match. Black Taffy. Peggy Susberry Kenner. JB

My Life by Somebody Else. Mark Strand. CAAP

My life closed twice before its close. Emily Dickinson. BoLoP; GBL; HeIP; NoAM; NOBA; OLR; PAIC; PPP; SBG

My life had stood—a loaded gun. Emily Dickinson. PiAm; Psy; SBG; SoSe

My life is measured by this glass, this glass. On an Hour-glass. John Hall. SCP-2

My light will tip tankards of fire in the sky. A Costant Labor. James W. Thompson. BPo

My little bird, how canst thou sit. Of the Child with the Bird on the Bush. John Bunyan. OxBChV

My little cousin, if you'll be. To My Youngest Kinsman, R. L. Abraham Chear. OxBChV

My little darling looked so pale today. My Daughter Very Ill. Paul Goodman. RRA

My little dears, who learn to read. Cautionary Verses to Youth of Both Sexes. Theodore Hook. OxBChV

My Little Pretty Mopsy. *Unknown.* OxBM

My little scholar, to thy book inclined. A Schoolmaster's Precepts. John Penkethman. OxBChV

My little son, I have cast you out. Choosing a Name. Anne Ridler. NOBE

My little son, who looked from thoughtful eyes. The Toys. Coventry Patmore. *Fr.* The Unknown Eros. BoReV; PAIC; SoSe; VPC

My little stone. Letters [*or* Notes] Found near a Suicide. Frank Horne. PoBA

My lizard, my lively writher. Wish for a Young Wife. Theodore Roethke. AnMo; LoAs; NoAM

My locker, green steel. Game Resumed. Richmond Lattimore. SPo

My long strong bamboo fishing pole. Goals. Elisavietta Ritchie. AATT

My long two-pointed ladder's sticking through a tree. After Apple-Picking. Robert Frost. Epi; NoAM; NOBA; PPP; PSN

My Lord: Poor wretched states, pressed by extremities. To the Right Honourable the Lord High Treasurer. Ben Jonson. SCP-1

My Lost Youth. Longfellow. AmVN; IPWM; NOBA

My loud machine for making hay. An Old Field Mowed for Appearances' Sake. William Meredith. PPoD

My lov'd, my honor'd, much respected friend. The Cotter's Saturday Night. Burns. LAuP

My Love. E. E. Cummings. VGW

My love came back to me. All Souls' Night. Frances Cornford. OxBTC

My love forever! Lament for Art O'Leary. Eibhlin Dubh O'Connell, *tr. by* Eilis Dillon *and* John Montague. BIrV

My love has left me has gone from me. Souvenirs. Dudley Randall. BPo

My love he built me a bonny bower. Lament of the Border Window. *Unknown.* GBP; PeBB; SLP

My love he is fairer than a summer day. The Drynaun Dhun. *Unknown.* GBP

My Love I Gave for Hate. *Unknown, tr. fr. Irish by* George Hay. BIrV

My love, I have betrayed you seventy times. Sonnet. Conrad Aiken. LoAs

My Love in Her Attire. *Unknown.* HeIP (Madrigal: "My love in her attire doth show her wit.") BoLoP; NOBE; PAIC

My Love Is Like a Red, Red Rose. Burns. *See* Red, Red Rose, A.

My love is living. South of the Great Sea. *Unknown, tr. by* Arthur Waley. OLR

My love is no short year's sentence. Love. *Unknown, tr. by* John Montague. BIrV

My love is o' comely height, an' straight. White an' Blue. William Barnes. GBL

My love is of a birth as rare. The Definition of Love. Andrew Marvell. AnMo; BoLoP; GBL; InPK; InPS; LoAs; MetP; NOBE

My love is the maid ov all maidens. In the Spring. William Barnes. GBL

My Love Is to the Light of Lights. "Hugh MacDiarmid." SLP

My love lies in the gates of foam. The Churchyard on the Sands. Lord De Tabley. GBL

My love looks like a girl tonight. The Bride. D. H. Lawrence. NoAM; OxBTC

My Love Must Be As Free. Henry David Thoreau. PiAm

My Love, She Passed Me By. *Unknown.* AmFP

My love to you is so much—nay, 'tis more. The Unexpressible Love. William Cavendish, Duke of Newcastle. SCP-2

My Love When This Is Past. Stephany Fuller. BPo

My lovely friend, that long hast been content. Prosopopoeia Corporis Animae Valedicturi: Adios: Arrivederci. William Lathum. SCP-2

My lover's a cowboy, wild broncos he breaks. Bucking Bronco. *Unknown.* AmFP

My lovers suffocate me. Walt Whitman. *Fr.* Songs of Myself, XLV. LoAs

My Love's Guardian Angel. William Barnes. GBL

My love's manners in bed. The Way. Robert Creeley. BoLoP; PPP

My Lucia in the dew did go. Upon Lucia Dabbled in the Dew. Robert Herrick. SCP-1

My lute, awake! perform the last. The Lover Complaineth the Unkindness of His Love [*or* To His Lute]. Sir Thomas Wyatt. AAS; BoLoP; GBL; LoAs; NOBE

My Luve Is Like a Red, Red Rose. Burns. *See* Red, Red Rose, A.

My madness is dear to me. Mad Song. Denise Levertov. Psy

My Mall, I mark that when you mean to prove me. The Author to His Wife, of a Woman's Eloquence. Sir John Harington. BoLoP

My Mama Moved among the Days. Lucille Clifton. CAAP; PoBA

My mamma is dead and she's buried. My Darling's on the Deep Blue Sea. *Unknown.* AmFP

My mammy she told me to open the door. Old Gray Beard a-Shaking. *Unknown.* AmFP

My man is a bone ringed with weed. Lament. Brenda Chamberlain. WPE

My Maryland. James Ryder Randall. *See* Maryland, My Maryland!

My mattress floats in an ocean of newspapers. Depression. William Witherup. NowV

My mind is so evil and unjust. Human Relations. C. H. Sisson. POL

My mind is stuffed with tablecloths. Poland/ 1931. Jerome Rothenberg. Prf

My Mind to Me a Kingdom Is. Sir Edward Dyer. NOBE

My Mind to Me a Kingdom Is. Antonia Fraser. SLP

My mind was once the true survey. The Mower's Song. Andrew Marvell. AnMo; PPP

My mistress' eyes are nothing like the sun. Sonnets, CXXX. Shakespeare. BoLoP; Epi; InPK; InPS; IPWM; PBMP; PPoD; PPP; SoSe; VoPo; WIF

My mistress is a hive of bees in yonder flowery garden. The Bee-hive. Thomas Durfey. SCP-2

My misunderstandings: for years I thought "muso bello" meant. Taking a Walk with You. Kenneth Koch. CAPP

My mither sent me to the well. Whistle o'er the Lave o't. *Unknown.* GBP

My Morose Master-Sergeants. Ray Holt. PPoD

My most distinguished guest and learnèd friend. Edna St Vincent Millay. VGW

My most honoured father. William Cartwright. *Fr.* The Siege; or, Love's Convert. SCP-2

My Mother. Ann Taylor. OxBChV

My mother/ a snail in black velvet. That Life, on Film. Lynn Sukenick. RiTi

My Mother and the Americans. David Kherdian. FAF; SA

My mother bore me in the heat of summer. On Approaching My Birthday. Vassar Miller. IHMS; NMM

My mother bore me in the southern wild. The Little Black Boy. Blake. *Fr.* Songs of Innocence. AnMo; HeIP; InPK; LAuP; MBPR; OBP; OxBChV

My Mother came again, her. Mother's Day. Sam Hamod. SA

My mother groaned! my father wept. Infant Sorrow. Blake. *Fr.* Songs of Experience. InPS; LAuP; MBPR

My mother had a maid call'd Barbara. Shakespeare. *Fr.* Othello, IV, iii. AIW

My mother in the witness box. Elegy. Virginia Scott. NPW

My mother keeps on telling me. Clothes. Elizabeth Jennings. RAE

My mother never forgave my father. The Portrait. Stanley Kunitz. CTBA

My mother—preferring the strange to the tame. The Intruder. Carolyn Kizer. RiTi

My Mother Said. *Unknown.* RAE

My mother said. Warning. *Unknown.* ECBV

My mother said I'd inherit a moustache and I did. My Mother's Moustache. Honor Moore. WBN

My mother saw the green tree toad. Lorine Niedecker. VGW

My mother sliced the south for us. Lullaby for Ann-Lucian. Calvin Forbes. PoBA

My Mother Takes My Wife's Side. David Kherdian. SA

My mother told me just before she died. Motherless Child Blues. *Unknown.* BluL

My mother took care of my father's shirts. Tracing Back. Jane Mayhall. WBN

My Mother Tries to Visit Me in the Dead of Night. Diane Wakoski. CAAP

My mother twice in her life on worn feet. Frederick Douglass. Sam Cornish. NVAP; PoBA

My mother was a romantic girl. Papa Love Baby. Stevie Smith. SBG

My mother, who. My Mother and the Americans. David Kherdian. FAF; SA

My Mother Would Be a Falconress. Robert Duncan. CAAP

My mother-in-law hates. Li Po. Mary Moore. NPW

My Mother's/ My/ Death/ Birthday. Patricia Goedicke. Psy

My mother's brother hauled me to the big-boys' club. Fall In. Lincoln Kirstein. NoAM

My mother's fingers that have decorated cakes. I Am of These. David Curry. HeS

My mother's maids [*or* maydes], when they did sew and spin [*or* sowe and spynne]. Sir Thomas Wyatt. Satires, II. AAS; TVS

My Mother's Moustache. Honor Moore. WBN

My mother's name was Mary. Mary's a Grand Old Name. George M. Cohan. BLSo; FSN

My Mother's Sister. C. Day Lewis. OxBTC

My mournful Muse Melpomene, draw near.   Truth's Complaint over England.   Thomas Lodge.   TVS

My mouth doth water, and my breast doth swell.   Astrophel and Stella, XXXVII.   Sir Philip Sidney.   Epi

My naked foot was sheeted with blood.   My Friend, the Doctor.   George Abbe.   FAF

My Name and I.   Robert Graves.   NoAM

My Name Is Afrika.   Keorapetse Kgositsile.   PoBA

My name is Captain Hall.   Captain Hall.   *Unknown.*   GBP

My name is Edward Hollander, as you may understand.   The *Flying Cloud. Unknown.*   AmFP

My name is Frank Taylor, a bachelor I am.   Starving to Death on a Government Claim.   *Unknown.*   AmFP

My name is John J. Curtis.   John J. Curtis.   Joseph Gallagher.   AmFP

My name is Johnson.   Madam's Past History.   Langston Hughes.   NoAm

My name is Peter Emily, as you might understand.   Peter Amberley.   *Unknown.*   AmFP

My name is Phyllis Janik.   In the Field.   Phyllis Janik.   IHMS

My name is Samuel Hall, Samuel Hall.   Sam Hall.   *Unknown.*   AmFP

My name is Sanford Barney, and I came from Little Rock town.   Sanford Barney.   *Unknown.*   AmFP

My name is sweet Jenny, my age is sixteen.   A Song.   *Unknown.*   POL

My name it is Joe Bowers, I have a brother Ike.   Joe Bower.   *Unknown.*   AmFP

My neighbor, a scientist and art-collector, telephones me in a.   The Burning of Paper Instead of Children.   Adrienne Rich.   PiAm

My New Garden Field.   *Unknown.*   AmFP

My nights is so lonely days is so doggone long.   Jersey Belle Blues.   *Unknown.*   BluL

My noble, lovely, little Peggy.   A Letter to the Honourable Lady Miss Margaret Cavendish Holles-Harley.   Matthew Prior.   NOBE; OxBChV; PAIC

My normal dwelling is the lungs of swine.   Autobiography of a Lungworm.   Roy Fuller.   NoAM

My Old Cat.   Hal Summers.   OxBTC; PCat

My old flame, my wife!   The Old Flame.   Robert Lowell.   BoLoP; NoAM; NOBA

My Old Kentucky Home, *with music.*   Stephen Collins Foster.   BLSH; BLSo; PSoN

My old man's a white old man.   Cross.   Langston Hughes.   CoPAm; PoBA; SoSe

My old massa he's got the dropser.   Down in Alabam'; or, Aint I Glad I Got Out de Wilderness.   *At.* to J. Warner.   PSoN

My old Mistiss promise me.   Promises of Freedom.   *Unknown.*   BPo

My Olson Elegy.   Irving Feldman.   Prf

My once dear love; hapless that I no more.   The Surrender.   Henry King.   BoLoP; SCP-2

My only son, more God's than mine.   Jesus and His Mother.   Thom Gunn.   MPo

My Own Hallelujahs.   Zack Gilbert.   PoBA

My Own Heart Let Me More Have Pity On.   Gerard Manley Hopkins.   InPS

My own musk.   The Tropics.   Holly Prado.   NPW

My Packard Bell was set up in the vacant lot near the stump.   The Campaign.   Josephine Miles.   WPE

My Papa's Waltz.   Theodore Roethke.   AnMo; CTBA; HeIP; InPK; InPS; NCSH; NoAM; NOBA; NowV; PBMP; PPoe; PPP; PSN; VGW

My Parents Kept Me.   Stephen Spender.   BBGO (Rough.)   LP; NoAM; PBMP

My parents raised me tenderly.   The Girl I Left behind Me.   *Unknown.*   AmFP

My passion is as mustard strong.   A New Song of New Similies.   John Gay.   FaBoCo

My pensive Sara! thy soft cheek reclined.   The Eolian Harp.   Samuel Taylor Coleridge.   MBPR

My People.   Margery Himel.   IHMS

My people grew potatoes.   The Duchess Potatoes.   Diane Wakoski.   CAAP

My pillow won't tell me.   The Apparition.   Theodore Roethke.   AIW; LoAs

My plaid awa, my plaid awa.   Lady Isabel and the Elf-Knight [*or* The Elfin Knight].   *Unknown.*   GBP; SLP

My Playmate.   Whittier.   NOBA

My Poem.   Nikki Giovanni.   BPo; PoBA

My poem is full of joy.   My Poem.   Ethel Hewell.   AKE

My poem would eat nothing.   The Poem You Asked For.   Larry Levis.   AmPA; NVAP

My poems/ are the sounds.   Poems.   Bruce Severy.   VW

My Poetry.   Kotaro Takamura.   IPWM

My Polish Grandma.   Edward Field.   Prf

My poor old bones—I've only two.   The Lonely Scarecrow.   James Kirkup.   RAE

My Prayer.   Henry David Thoreau   *See* Great God, I ask Thee for No Meaner Pelf.

My Pretty Pink.   *Unknown.*   AmFP

My Pretty Rose Tree.   Blake.   *Fr.* Songs of Experience.   BoLoP; LAuP; MBPR

My prime of youth is but a frost of cares.   Elegy [*or* On the Eve of His Execution].   Chidiock Tichborne.   HeIP; InPK; InPS; NOBE; OBP; PAIC; PPoD; PPoe; WIF

My Purse.   *Unknown.*   OxBM

My quiet kin, must I affront you.   Preliminary to Classroom Lecture.   Josephine Miles.   NoAM

My Ratclif, when thy retchlesse youth offendes.   Earl of Surrey.   AAS

My Rival.   Kipling.   OxBTC

My roof is covered wtih pigeon bones.   Bones.   Charles Simic.   NVAP

My room's a square and candle-lighted boat.   Frances Cornford.   *Fr.* The Country Bedroom.   RAE

My room's bigger than a coffin.   On Saint-Urbain Street.   Milton Acorn.   NeAC

My Sad Captains.   Thom Gunn.   InPS

My Sad Self.   Allen Ginsberg.   IPWM; NoAM

My Sadness Sits around Me.   June Jordan.   BPo

My scarlet coat lies on the ground.   The Martyrdom of Saint Sebastian.   Rosemary Dobson.   MAuV

My secrets cry aloud.   Open House.   Theodore Roethke.   AnMo; NoAM; NOBA

My serious son! I see thee look.   Before a Saint's Picture.   Walter Savage Landor.   OxBChV

My Shadow.   Robert Louis Stevenson.   OxBChV

My shadow moves, until, at noon, I stand.   Autumn Shades, X.   Edgar Bowers.   PiAm

My shattred phancy stole away from mee.   Edward Taylor.   *Fr.* Preparatory Meditations: First Series, XXIX.   PiAm

My shoes are almost dead.   Caesar.   W. S. Merwin.   PPoD

My signs are a rain-proof coat, good shoes, and a staff cut from the woods.   Walt Whitman.   *Fr.* Song of Myself, XLVI.   Prf

My Silks and Fine Array.   Blake.   *See* Song: "My silks and fine array."

My sister/ we are lying in a large bed by the sea.   Monday Night in Winter.   Ellen Cooney.   NPW

My sister Betty.   Charlie Two-Head.   Marnie Walsh.   VW

My sister! my sweet sister! if a name.   Epistle to Augusta.   Byron.   MBPR

My sister was quicker at everything than I.   The Paper Lantern. Tennessee Williams.   *Fr.* Recuerdo.   CTBA

My skin is black, my arms are long.   Four Women.   Nina Simone.   MAT

My Son.   Ruth Stone.   WPE

My Son.   Rex Veeder.   HeS

My son as a child saying.   Little Stone in the Middle of the Road, in Florida.   Muriel Rukeyser.   RiTi

My Son, Forsake Your Art.   Mahon O'Heffernan, *tr. fr. Irish by* Maire Cruise O'Brien.   BIrV

My son has birds in his head.   Daedalus.   Alastair Reid.   NCSH

My son invites me to witness with him.   Mousemeal.   Howard Nemerov.   NCSH; NowV

My son, keep well thy tongue, and keep thy friend.   Controlling the Tongue.   Chaucer.   *Fr.* The Canterbury Tales: The Manciple's Tale.   OxBChV

My son kept wanting a snake.   The Evidence.   Van K. Brock.   NVAP

My Son, My Executioner.   Donald Hall.   CoPAm; InPK

My son tells his aunt.   A San Diego Poem.   Simon J. Ortiz.   CDW

My Song Is Love Unknown.   Samuel Crossman.   OxBChV

My song today is the storm-cock's song.   The Storm-Cock's Song. "Hugh MacDiarmid."   OxBTC

My sons/ sometimes I can.   Efficiency Apartment.   Gerald W. Barrax.   PoBA

My Soul is an enchanted boat.   Asia's Song.   Shelley.   *Fr.* Prometheus Unbound, II, v.   GrRo

My soul looked down from a vague height, with Death.   The Show.   Wilfred Owen.   NoAM; OBP; OxBTC

My soul, sit thou a patient looker-on.   Epigram.   Francis Quarles.   NOBE

My soul, there is a country.   Peace.   Henry Vaughan.   BoReV; IPWM; NOBE

My soul, thy love is dear: 'twas thought a good.   Epigram. Francis Quarles.   *Fr.* Emblems, V, 4.   SCP-2

My soul was an old horse.   Pegasus.   Patrick Kavanagh.   PFIr

My Soul Was as if free and.   Etude from the Third Epistle. Robert Duncan.   *Fr.* Dante Etudes.   CAAP

My Specialty Is Living Said.   E. E. Cummings.   NOBA

My spirit is too weak—mortality.   On Seeing the Elgin Marbles. Keats.   MBPR; PAIC

My Spirit Longeth for Thee.   John Byrom.   BoReV; NOBE

My Spring Thing.   Everett Hoagland.   BPo

My Star.   Robert Browning.   HeIP; SoSe

My Stars.   Abraham Ibn Ezra, *tr. fr. Spanish by* Robert Mezey. OFD

My straying thoughts, reduced stay.   Song.   Anne Collins.   WPE

My street is holy.   The Street Where I Live.   Virginia Floyd. AATT

My stutter, my cough, my unfinished sentences.   The Second-fated.   Robert Graves.   NoAM

My sweet, let me tell you about the Shark.   The Shark.   John Ciardi.   MiP

My Sweet Old Etcetera.   E. E. Cummings.   *Fr.* Is 5.   AnMo; HeIP; InPS; PPP

My Sweetest Lesbia [Let Us Live and Love].   Thomas Campion, *after the Latin of* Catullus.   AAS; GBL; HeIP; LoAs; PAIC

My Sweetie's a Mule in the Mine.   *Unknown.*   AmFP (Driving the Mule.)   GBL

My swirling wants. Your frozen lips.   A Valediction Forbidding Mourning.   Adrienne Rich.   NoAM

My tea is nearly ready and the sun has left the sky.   The Lamplighter.   Robert Louis Stevenson.   OxBChV

My teacher fish!   He Don't Know the Inside Feel.   Herbert R. Adams.   MiP

My temples throb, my pulses boil.   To Minerva.   Thomas Hood. FaBoCo

My tender age in sorrow did begin.   Easter Wings.   George Herbert.   PAIC

My tender parents brought me here.   The Wexford Girl. *Unknown.*   AmFP

My thoughts are winged with hopes, my hopes with love.   *At. to* Sir Walter Ralegh.   GBL

My thoughts hold mortal strife.   Inexorable.   William Drummond of Hawthornden.   NOBE

My three sisters are sitting.   Women.   Adrienne Rich.   NMM; Psy

"My towers at last!"   Herman Melville   Conrad Aiken.   NoAM; NOBA

My towers at last! These rovings end.   The Return of the Sire de Nesle A. D. 16—.   Herman Melville.   NOBA

My trade takes me frequently into decaying houses.   From a Museum Man's Album.   John Hewitt.   OxBTC

My trembling song, awake! arise!   A Song on New Year's Day before the King.   Thomas Flatman.   SCP-2

My Trewth is Plicht.   Sir John Fethy.   SLP

My Triumph.   Whittier.   NOBA

"My True Love Hath My Heart and I Have His."   Mary Elizabeth Coleridge.   BoLoP

My true love hath my heart, and I have his.   The Bargain.   Sir Philip Sidney.   *Fr.* Arcadia.   BoLoP; GBL; LoAs; NOBE

My Twelve Oxen.   *Unknown.*   OxBM

My Ulick.   Charles J. Kickham.   PFIr

My uncle died a month ago.   My Uncle.   *Unknown.*   ECBV

My Uncle Jehoshaphat.   Laura E. Richards.   OxBChV

My uncle played the fiddle—more elegantly the violin.   The Country Fiddler.   John Montague.   TwMBP

My urine smells of smoke.   Desert in the Sea.   Brian Swann. AmPA

My Valentine.   Robert Louis Stevenson.   *See* I Will Make You Brooches.

"My verses, Ochkasty, and your music."   Matthew Mead.   *Fr.* Identities.   TwMBP

My verses will never stop bombs.   Most Days.   Elisavietta Ritchie.   AATT

My wavering mind resembles.   In the Balance.   *Unknown, tr. by* George Whicher.   *Fr.* Carmina Burana.   OLR

My well-beloved was stripped. Knowing my whim.   The Jewels. Baudelaire, *tr. by* Roy Campbell.   BoLoP

My whole eye was sunset red.   Eye and Tooth.   Robert Lowell. CAPP

My whole life coming to this place.   Port Jefferson.   Louis Simpson.   IPWM

My whole life has been a chronology of—changes.   For Malcolm: After Mecca.   Gerald W. Barrax.   OFD

My wife and I have asked a crowd of craps.   Vers de Société. Philip Larkin.   PSN

My wife and I lived all alone.   Little Brown Jug.   *At. to* Joseph E. Winner.   BLSH; BLSo; PSoN

My wife is left-handed.   For Hettie.   LeRoi Jones.   NoAM; NOBA; SS

My Wife Is My Shirt.   Stephen Tropp.   InPK

My wife saw it first.   Balckbird.   Christopher Leach.   BoAnP

My Wife Who Is American.   John Daniel.   TwMBP

My Wild Irish Rose, *with music.*   Chauncey Olcott.   BLSH, *chorus only;* BLSo; FSN

My window opens out into the trees.   Solace.   Clarissa Scott Delany.   PoBA

My window shows the travelling clouds.   The Alchemist in the City.   Gerard Manley Hopkins.   IPWM

My wives do not write.   Memory.   Michael Hamburger. OxBTC

My Woman/ she look at me. Brown Circles. Melvin DeBruhl. PPoD

My woorthy Lord, I pray you wonder not. Gascoignes Woodmanship. George Gascoigne. AAS

My young comrade. Letter to a Young Friend. Alden Nowlan. AKE

My young love said to me, "My brothers won't mind." She Moved through the Fair. Padraic Colum. AIW; BIrV

My Young Mother. Jane Cooper. NMM

Mye love toke skorne my servise to retaine. Sir Thomas Wyatt. AAS

Myfanwy. John Betjeman. BoLoP

Myne owne John Poyntz, sins ye delight to know. Sir Thomas Wyatt. Satires, I. AAS

Myra. Fulke Greville. *Fr.* Caelica. NOBE ("I, with whose colours Myra dress'd her head.") GBL

Myrtilla, early on the lawn. Sweet Slug-a-Bed. *Unknown.* FaBoCo

Myrtle. Theodore Roethke. RAE

Myrtle bush grew shady, The. Jealousy. Mary Elizabeth Coleridge. WPE

Myself unto myself will give. The Holy Office. James Joyce. NoAM; OxBTC

Myself When I Am Real. Al Young. PoBA

Mysteries Remain, The. Hilda Doolittle ("H.D."). NOBA; VGW

Mysterious Biography. Carl Sandburg. OFD

Mysterious Night! when our first parent knew. To Night. Joseph Blanco White. SoSe

" 'Mystery boy' Looks for Kin in Nashville." Robert Hayden. NoAM

Mystery of a kind, A. Planting a Magnolia. W. D. Snodgrass. NoAM

Mystic in the morning, half asleep, A. Bachelor. William Meredith. NoAM

Mystic Lake. R. P. Kingston. NVAP

Mysticism, but let us have no words. Conrad Aiken. *Fr.* Time in the Rock, XI. VGW

"Mysticism Has Not the Patience to Wait for God's Revelation." Richard Eberhart. NoAM

Myth. Muriel Rukeyser. IHMS

Myth lilies. A smog-edge sky blurs his eyes. Crow's Way. Duane Niatum. CDW

Myth of the Blaze. George Oppen. CAAP

Mythical Journey, The. Edwin Muir. NoAM

Mythics. Helen Chasin. IHMS

Mythistorema. George Seferis, *tr. fr. Modern Greek by* Rex Warner. BuTh

Mythmaking. Kathleen Spivack. NMM

Mythology. Lawrence Durrell. OxBTC

Myths and Texts, *sels.*    Gary Snyder.
  Burning.
    John Muir on Mt. Ritter, VIII. Epi; NOBA; TCP
    "My clutch and your clutch," VI. Epi
    Second Shaman Song, I. NOBA
    ("Squat in swamp shadows.") Epi
    Text, The, XVII. Epi
  Hunting.
    First Shaman Song, I. NOBA
    "How rare to be born a human being! XVI. CAPP
    This Poem Is for Bear, VI. NOBA
    This Poem Is for Deer, VIII. CAPP; NOBA
  Logging.
    "Again the ancient, meaningless," V. CAPP
    "Stood straight/ holding the choker high," III. NOBA

Myxomatosis. Philip Larkin. NoAM

**N**

N. B. A. Prelim, Boston Garden. Thomas Whitbread. PPoD

Naighbour Playmeates. William Barnes. VPC

Naked all night the field. Sports Field. Judith Wright. MAuV

Naked and the Nude, The. Robert Graves. OBP; SoSe; WIF

Naked earth is warm with Spring, The. Into Battle. Julian Grenfell. OxBTC

Naked house, a naked moor, A. The House Beautiful. Robert Louis Stevenson. NOBE

Naked I came, naked I leave the scene. Epigram. J. V. Cunningham. VGW

Naked I came, when I began to be. Nudus Redibo. Thomas Flatman. SCP-2

Naked in snowdrifts, we've made love. Windy Nights. David Campbell MAuV

Naked she lay, clasped in my longing arms. The Imperfect Enjoyment. Earl of Rochester. BoLoP; SCP-2

Nakedness of women, The. Blake. POL

Name, The. Robert Creeley. IPWM; TCP

Name for All, A. Hart Crane. VGW

Name—of it—is "Autumn," The. Emily Dickinson. InPS

Name of Jesus, The. John Newton. BoReV

Name of Our Country, The. Dennis Schmitz. AmPA

Name of the product I test is "Life," The. A Consumer's Report. Peter Porter. FaBoCo

Name of this poem is, The. Cameo No. II. June Jordan. BPo; WBN

Nameless Doon, The. William Larminie. BIrV

Nameless One, A. Margaret Avison. HeIP

Nameless One, The. James Clarence Mangan. BIrV

Names. D. J. Enright. FaBoCo

Names. Lyn Lifshin. FAF

Names for everything I touch. The Hollow Thesaurus. Roger McDonald. CAAP

Names of the Humble, The. Les A. Murray. *Fr.* Walking to the Cattle-Place. CAAT

Naming of Cats, The. T. S. Eliot. AnMo

Naming of Parts. Henry Reed. Lessons of the War, I. InPK; InPS; MPo; NOBE; OxBTC; PPoD; SoSe; VoPo; WIF

Naming the State Bird. Keith Gunderson. HeS

Nancy Hanks. Rosemary Benét *and* Stephen Vincent Benét. ECBV

Nancy Lee, *with music.* Frederick E. Weatherly. BLSH

Nancy, the hogs don't know us. Mirror for the Barnyard. Jack Myers. AmPA

Nansen. Gary Snyder. InPS

Naomi Wise. *Unknown.* AmFP

Napoleon. Walter de la Mare. NOBE

Napoleon hoped that all the world would fall beneath his sway. *Unknown.* FaBoCo

Napoleon is standing with his pants upon the floor. The Poor Old Prurient Interest Blues. John Hartford. MAT

Nappy Head Blues. *Unknown.* BluL

Narcissist's eye is blue, fringed with white and covered, The. The Eye. Michael Benedikt. ConAP

Narrative. Russell Atkins. PoBA

Narrator's Trance, The, *sels.*    James Cunningham. JB
  "And birds came crying."
  "Song thumbed down a cruiser for a ride, A."
  "There were blood spots on the skirt."
  "Woods are overhead over everywhere, The."

Narrow Door, The. Charlotte Mew. SBG

Narrow fellow in the grass, A. Emily Dickinson. AnMo; IPWM; NOBA; PBMP; PiAm; PPoe; PPP; VoPo

Nashville Stonewall Blues. *Unknown.* BluL

Nat Turner in the Clearing. Alvin Aubert. CoPAm

Nathan Hale. Francis Miles Finch. BTTM

Nathan Hale. *Unknown.* BTTM

Nation. Charlie Cobb. PoBA

Nation Wrapped in Stone, A. Roberta Hill. CDW

National Cold Storage Company. Harvey Shapiro. MAT; VGW

National Miner, The. *Unknown.* AmFP

National Shrine. X. J. Kennedy. CoPAm

National Winter Garden. Hart Crane. *Fr.* The Bridge: Three Songs. InPS

Nationality. Mary Gilmore. MAuV

Native Born. Eve Langley. WPE

Native Land. Sir Walter Scott. *See* This Is My Own, My Native Land.

Nativity. John Donne. SCP-1

Nativity, The. William Drummond of Hawthornden. SCP-2

Nativity of Christ, The. Robert Southwell. BoReV

Nativity of Our Lord and Saviour Jesus Christ, The. Christopher Smart. *Fr.* Hymns and Spiritual Songs. BoReV; LAuP; NOBE; OBP

Natura Naturans. Arthur Hugh Clough. VPC

Natural Law. Babette Deutsch. RiTi

Natural Odes/ American Elegies, *sel.* Robert Dana. HeS
"Christmas day," 39.
"It was not quite winter," 42
"We had known from the beginning this could happen," 38.

Natural Order of Things, The. Harley Elliott. NeAC

Natural pussy. Bitter Herbs. Alta. NMM

Naturalist, The. Margaret Reynolds. MIS

Naturally it is night. Air. W. S. Merwin. CAPP

Nature. Longfellow. AmVN

Nature/ leaks like a tub and not a boat. Samuel Butler. *Fr.* Arts and Sciences. SCP-2

Nature and Nature's laws lay hid in night. Intended for Sir Isaac Newton. Pope. FaBoCo; InPK

Nature had made them hide in crevices. New Hampshire, February. Richard Eberhart. SS

Nature Lover. John Frederick Nims. CoPAm

Nature Morte. Louis MacNeice. NoAM

Nature of Jungles, The. W. R. Moses. NCSH

Nature that washt her hands in milke. A Poem of Sir Walter Rawleighs. Sir Walter Ralegh. AAS

Nature, which is the vast creation's soul. To Mr. Henry Lawes. Katherine Philips. SBG; WPE

Nature's confectioner, the bee. Fuscara; or, the Bee-Errant. John Cleveland. SCP-2

Nature's Cook, *sel.* Margaret Cavendish, Duchess of Newcastle. "Death is the cook of nature, and we find." SCP-2

Nature's Dessert, *sel.* Margaret Cavendish, Duchess of Newcastle.
"Sweet marmalade of kisses newly gathered." SCP-2

Nature's Embassy, *sel.* Richard Brathwaite.
I Am Not as I Wish. SCP-2

Nature's first green is gold. Nothing Gold Can Stay. Robert Frost. AnMo; NCSH; NOBA; PPP; TSWA; VGW

Nature's great masterpiece, an elephant. The Elephant. John Donne. *Fr.* The Progresse of the Soule. OBP

Nature's Landskip, *sel.* Margaret Cavendish, Duchess of Newcastle.
"I standing on a hill of fancies high." SCP-2

Nature's lay idiot, I taught thee to love. Elegy VII. John Donne. *Fr.* Elegies. SCP-1

Nature's Prospect. Margaret Cavendish, Duchess of Newcastle. SCP-2

Nature's Questioning. Thomas Hardy. IPWM; PBMP

Nature's Reply to Mutability. Spenser. *Fr.* The Faerie Queene, VII, 7. NOBE

Naughty Boy. Robert Creeley. NoAM; NOBA

Nausicaa's girls. Peter Whigham. *Fr.* Astapovo, or What Are We to Do. TwMBP

Nautical Ballad. Keighley Goodchild. ECBV

Nautical Extravaganza, A. Wallace Irwin. PoTa

Nautilus Island's hermit. Skunk Hour. Robert Lowell. CAPP; ConAP; HeIP; InPK; NoAM; NOBA; PiAm; PPP; TCP

Navajo Girl of Many Farms. Charles G. Ballard. VW

Navajo Poem. Warren Woessner. HeS

Navajo Signs. Winifred Fields Walters. VW

Navy Hymn, The, *with music.* William Whiting. BLSH

Nay but you, who do not love her. Song. Robert Browning. VoPo

Nay, Ivy, nay, it shal not be y-wis. Holly and His Merry Men. *Unknown.* OxBM

Nay, nay, my boy—'tis not for me. Fie on Eastern Luxury! Horace, *tr. by* Hartley Coleridge. Odes, I, 38. InPK

Nay, traveller! rest. This lonely yew-tree stands. Lines Left upon a Seat in a Yew-Tree. Wordsworth. MBPR

Ne Plus Ultra. Samuel Taylor Coleridge. MBPR

Neaps are ow'er champit, The. Love in Edinburgh. Nicholas Fairbairn. SLP

Near. William Stafford. ConAP

Near and Far. Harry Behn. LCL

Near Caledonia. Patricia Henley. NPW

Near Lanivet, 1872. Thomas Hardy. NoAM

Near Midnight. Norman MacCaig. SLP

Near the Death of Ovid. Robert Conquest. NoAM

Near the Ocean. Robert Lowell. NOBA

Near the Old Slave Fort. Joseph Bruchac. FAF

Near this spot. An Epitaph: Inscription on a Monument at Newstead Abbey. Byron. BoAnP

Near to the silver Trent. Michael Drayton. *Fr.* The Shepherd's Sirena. SCP-2

Nearer, My God, to Thee, *with music.* Sarah Flower Adams. BLSH

Nearer the pulse than other themes. A True Picture Restored. Vernon Watkins. NoAM

Nearing the Snow-line. Oliver Wendell Holmes. PiAm

Nebraska. Jon Swan. RFM

Nebraskan Childhood. Daniel Halpern. CAAP

Nebuchadnezzar. Elinor Wylie. SBG

Necessary Bucket, A. Peter Meinke. AATT

Necessities of Life. Adrienne Rich. NoAM; NOBA; Psy

Necessity. Harry Graham. FaBoCo

Necessity. Langston Hughes. NOBA

Necrological. John Crowe Ransom. PiAm

Neddy Nibble'm and Biddy Finn. *Unknown.* GBP

Need of Being Versed in Country Things, The. Robert Frost. NoAM; NOBA; PiAm

Needles and pins, needles and pins. Mother Goose. MG

Needle's Eye, The. *Unknown.* AmFP

"Needy Knife-grinder! whither are you going?" The Friend of Humanity and the Knife-Grinder. George Canning *and* John Hookham Frere. FaBoCo

Negritude. James A. Emanuel. BPo

Negro Dreams. Doughtry Long. PoBA

Negro Hero. Gwendolyn Brooks. CAPP

Negro in a Chesterfield, A. Street Scenes from All Over. Elisavietta Ritchie. AATT

Negro Servant. Langston Hughes. VGW

Negro Soldier's Civil War Chant. *Unknown.* BPo

Negro Soldier's Viet Nam Diary, A. Herbert Martin. PoBA

Negro Speaks of Rivers, The. Langston Hughes. BPo; CoPAm; HeIP; NoAM; NOBA; PiAm; PoBA; TSWA

Negro sprouts from the pavement like an asparagus, A. Stumpfoot on 42nd Street. Louis Simpson. TCP; VGW

Negro Woman. Lewis Alexander. PoBA

Negro Woman, A. William Carlos Williams. IPWM

Negroes/ Sweet and docile. Warning. Langston Hughes. BPo

Negro's Tragedy, The. Claude McKay. BPo

Negrun. Lucille F. Travis. AATT

Nehi Blues. *Unknown.* BluL

Neighbor thought that they, A. The Planetary Arc-Light. August Derleth. ECBV

Neighbour sits in his window and plays the flute, The. Music. Amy Lowell. RiTi

Neighbors. David Allan Evans. HeS

Neither on horseback nor seated. Walt Whitman at Bear Mountain. Louis Simpson. ConAP

Neither our vices nor our virtues. Poetry, a Natural Thing. Robert Duncan. NoAM; NOBA

Neither Out Far nor In Deep. Robert Frost. NoAM; NOBA; PSN

Nemesis. Emerson. NOBA

Nepenthe, *sels.* George Darley.
  Hundred-Gated Thebes. NOBE
  "O blest unfabled incense tree." BIrV
  (Phoenix, The.) NOBE

Nephelidia. Swinburne. *Fr.* The Heptalogia. FaBoCo; SpRo

Neptune and Mars in council sate. Louisburg. *Unknown.* BTTM

Neptune—Polka. Edith Sitwell. NOBE

Neptune sat in his chariot high. Thomas Heyrick. *Fr.* The Submarine Voyage: A Pindaric Poem in Four Parts. SCP-2

Nerves. "Sagittarius" OxBTC

Nervous hose is dribbling on the tar, A. The Roof Garden. Howard Moss. MAT

Nervous poet sings again, The. Ode to Mexican Experience. Luís Omar Salinas. SA

Nervy with neons, the main drag. At Barstow. Charles Tomlinson. NoAM

Nesting. Edward Lear. *See* Limerick: "There was an old man with a beard."

Nesting. Dennis Saleh. NeAC

Nesting Time. Arthur Guiterman. ECBV

Nesting Time. Douglas Stewart. BoAnP

Net, The. W. R. Rodgers. BoLoP

Neutral Tones. Thomas Hardy. HeIP; InPK; LoAs; NoAM; PPP; SS

Never. George Reavey. BIrV

Never a careworn wife but shows. Wives in the Sere. Thomas Hardy. NOBE

Never Again Would Birds' Song Be the Same. Robert Frost. InPK; NoAM; VGW

Never ask of money spent. The Hardship of Accounting. Robert Frost. FaBoCo

Never Give All the Heart. W. B. Yeats. BoLoP; LoAs

Never in This World You Will Drop a Yellow Sponge. Rochelle Owens. WBN

Never Let Your Left Hand Know. *Unknown.* BluL

Never love unlesse you can. Thomas Campion. AAS

Never May the Fruit Be Plucked. Edna St. Vincent Millay. SBG

Never pain to tell thy love. Blake. MBPR

Never Pharaoh's night. In the Desert. Herman Melville. PiAm

Never said/ a word. Adam's Apple. Coleman Barks. *Fr.* Body Poems. NVAP

Never Said a Mumbalin' Word. *Unknown.* GBP

Never Seek to Tell Thy Love. Blake. *See* Love's Secret.

"Never shall a young man." For Anne Gregory. W. B. Yeats. BuTh; Epi; InPK; PFIr; SFF; SS

Never Such Love. Robert Graves. BoLoP

Never take her away. Song. Vinícius de Moraes, *tr. by* Richard Wilbur. RRA

Never talk down to a glowworm. Glowworm. David McCord. ECBV

Never think you fortune can bear the sway. On Fortune. Elizabeth I, Queen of England. WPE

Never to fight unless from a pure motive. Bottleneck. Louis MacNeice. SFF

Never until the mankind making. A Refusal to Mourn the Death, by Fire, of a Child in London. Dylan Thomas. AnMo; BuTh; HeIP; MPo; NoAM; NOBE; OxBTC; VoPo

Never was there a man much uglier. Vain Gratuities. E. A. Robinson. SS

Never weather-beaten sail more willing bent to shore. O Come Quickly! Thomas Campion. BoReV; NOBE

New Antigone, The, *sel.* Thomas Parkinson.
  "Twenty five years of the endless war." MIT

New Approach Needed. Kingsley Amis. OxBTC

New Arm, The. Tom Hennen. HeS

New Birth, The. Jones Very. AmVN; NOBA; PiAm

New Block. Patric Dickinson. LP

New Cake of Soap, The. Ezra Pound. PAIC

New Colossus, The. Emma Lazarus. SBG; WPE

New Dialogue, Sung by a Boy and Girl at the Playhouse, A. Thomas Durfey. SCP-2

New diet, A. Figures and Ground. Robert Leverant. MIT

New Direction, The. Emerson Blackhorse Mitchell. VW

New Emigration, The. Kay Boyle. WPE

New England. E. A. Robinson. HeIP; NOBA; PiAm

New England Bachelor, A. Richard Eberhart. NoAM

New England Pilgrimage, *sel.* Phyllis McGinley.
  Customs of the Country, The. TH

New England Protestant. Richard Eberhart. *Fr.* Attitudes. TH

New Excavations. Leonora Speyer. *Fr.* Pompeii. TH

New Farm Tractor. Carl Sandburg. AKE

New Hampshire, February. Richard Eberhart. SS

New Heaven, New War. Robert Southwell. BoReV; NOBE

New House, The. Edward Thomas. NOBE

New Houses, New Clothes. D. H. Lawrence. BBGO

New Jail. *Unknown.* AmFP

New Jerusalem, A. Blake. *See* And Did Those Feet in Ancient Time.

New Kelso. Roderick Watson. MIS

New Leda, The. Barbara Howes. RiTi

New Little Boy, The. Harry Behn. LCL

New Lost Feminist, The. Rita Mae Brown. WBN

New Man, The. Jones Very. NOBA

New man flies in from Manchester, A. A New Poet Arrives. Gavin Ewart. OxBTC

New Mexican Mountain. Robinson Jeffers. InPS; NoAM

New Minglewood Blues. *Unknown.* BluL

New Mistress, The. A. E. Housman. SoSe

New Moon, The. Samuel Taylor Coleridge. *Fr.* Dejection; an Ode. FSFS

New Moon, The. Issa, *tr. fr. Japanese by* Harold G. Henderson. Moon

New Moon, The. Sara Teasdale. Moon

New moon in the sky. Haiku. Basho, *tr. by* Nobuyuki Yuasa. PAIC

New Morality, *sel.* George Canning, *and* John Hookham Frere.
  "Sweet sensibility, that dwells enshrined." ESaP
New Morning. Bob Dylan. GrRo
New Pietà, The: For the Mothers and Children of Detroit. Clarence Major. PoBA
New Poem, The. Charles Wright. CoPAm
New Poet Arrives, A. Gavin Ewart. OxBTC
New Potatoes. Ken Belford. NeAC
New Prince, New Pomp. Robert Southwell. NOBE
New road runs into, The. Directions. William Matthews. AmPA
New Simile in th Manner of Swift, A. Goldsmith. LAuP
New Song Made in Honour of His Grace the Duke of Marlborough, A. Thomas Durfey. SCP-2
New Song of New Similies, A. John Gay. FaBoCo
New Spoon River, The, *sels.* Edgar Lee Masters. NoAM
  Marx the Sign Painter.
  Rhoda Pitkin.
  Unknown Soldiers.
New Spring. Juan Ramón Jiménez, *tr. fr. Spanish by* H. R. Hays. OLR
New Style, The. David O'Bruadair, *tr. fr. Irish by* John Montague. BIrV
New Tenants, The. E. A. Robinson. NoAM
New Vestments, The. Edward Lear. RAE
New Way, Old Way. David W. Martinez. VW
New World, The. LeRoi Jones. NoAM
New World, The. Jones Very. AmVN
New Year Letter, *sel.* W. H. Auden.
  "O Unicorn among the cedars." BoReV; NoAM
New Year 1974. Rae Desmond Jones. CAAP
New Year's. Charles Reznikoff. VGW
  "This is the autumn and our harvest," *sel.* OFD
New Year's Day. Robert Lowell. ConAP; PPoe
New Year's Eve. Thomas Hardy. NoAM
New Year's Eve. D. H. Lawrence. BoLoP
New Year's Song. Ted Hughes. OFD
New Year's Water. *Unknown.* GBP; OFD; POL
New York Skyline. Ruthe T. Spinnanger. AATT
New York Woman, The. L. E. Sissman. MAT
Newark Abbey. Thomas Love Peacock. NOBE
Newark, for Now (68). Carolyn M. Rodgers. PoBA
Newberry. *Unknown.* AmFP
Newborn, on the naked sand. Song for the Newborn. *Unknown, tr. by* Mary Austin. OFD; WPE
Newcomer's Wife, The. Thomas Hardy. BoLoP; OxBTC
Newest Banana Plant Leaf, The. Ingrid Wendt. NMM
Newly Born, The. *Unknown. Fr.* The Pricke of Conscience. OxBM
Newly Discovered "Homeric" Hymn, A. Charles Olson. CoPAm; NoAM
Newly Pressed Suit, The. Roger McGough. NoAM
News. Robin Morgan. WBN
News. Marnie Pomeroy. POL
News. Thomas Traherne. *Fr.* The Third Century. NOBE
  (On News.) BoReV; MetP
News for the Delphic Oracle. W. B. Yeats. NoAM
News from a foreign [*or* forrein] country came. News. Thomas Traherne. *Fr.* The Third Century. BoReV; MetP; NOBE
Newsletter from My Mother. Michael S. Harper. PoBA
Newsreel. C. Day Lewis. PPoD
Next Day. Randall Jarrell. NoAM; PPoD
Next died the Lady who yon Hall possessed. The Lady of the Manor. George Crabbe. *Fr.* The Parish Register: Burials, Pt. III. NOBE

Next Heaven, my vows to thee, O sacred Muse! Upon the Saying That My Verses Were Made by Another. Anne Killigrew. WPE
Next him Jack Squire through his own tear-drops sploshes. Roy Campbell. *Fr.* The Georgiad. OxBTC
Next, Please. Philip Larkin. HeIP
Next these, a troop of busy spirits press. Dryden. *Fr.* Absalom and Achitophel, Pt. II. PPP
Next to of Course God America I. E. E. Cummings. Epi; InPK; IPWM; NCSH; NowV; OFD; PPoD; VGW
Next-door Mother Rosarine. Mother Rosarine. Maxine W. Kumin. RiTi
Niagara. Richard Emil Braun. NoAM
Niagara Falls Nocturne. Len Gasparini. NeAC
Nice. Lyn Lifshin. Psy
Nice place ya got here. Instances. Anselm Hollo. TwMBP
Nichols, my better self, forbear. An Answer to an Invitation to Cambridge. Abraham Cowley. PAIC
Nicht we stood on Snawdon Hill, The. Snawdon Wood. Forbes Macgregor. MIS
Nick and the Candlestick. Sylvia Plath. CAPP
Nigerian Unity/ or Little Niggers Killing Little Niggers. Don L. Lee. NeAC
Nigga Section, The. Welton Smith. BPo
Nigger. Sonia Sanchez. BPo
Nigger/ Can you kill. The True Import of Present Dialogue, Black vs. Negro. Nikki Giovanni. BPo; PoBA
Nigger Song: An Odyssey. Rita Dove. AmPA
Night. Blake. *Fr.* Songs of Innocence. MBPR; OxBChV
Night. Robinson Jeffers. NOBA
Night. Anne Radcliffe. WPE
Night. Sara Teasdale. FSFS
Night, The ("Through that pure virgin shrine"). Henry Vaughan. BoReV; MetP; NOBE; SCP-1
Night/ and in the warm blackness. Upon Your Leaving. Etheridge Knight. NeAC
Night a Sailor Came to Me in a Dream, The. Diane Wakoski. VGW
Night after summer night the drift of pipe-talk. Figure. Marcia Lee Masters. HeS
Night along the Mackinac Bridge. Roberta Hill. CDW
Night and a Distant Church. Russell Atkins. PoBA
Night and Day, *with music.* Cole Porter. BLSo
Night and Morning. Austin Clarke. NoAM
Night and Sleep. Coventry Patmore. VPC
Night and the hood. Prelude. Conrad Kent Rivers. PoBA
Night-Apple, The. Allen Ginsberg. NoAM
Night attendant, a B.U. sophomore, The. Waking in the Blue. Robert Lowell. CoPAm; PiAm; PPP; PSN
Night before Larry Was Stretched. *Unknown.* BIrV; GBP; PeBB
"Night before the Night before Christmas," *sel.* Randall Jarrell.
  "In her room that night she looks at herself in the mirror." MiP
Night Blessing. Phil George. VW
Nigth breaths, short ones. In the Hospital. Laura Jensen. AmPA
Night Catch. Heather McHugh. AmPA
Night Clouds. Amy Lowell. TH
Night covers the pond with its wing. The Pond. Louise Glück. CAAP
Night Crow. Theodore Roethke. CoPAm; InPK; NCSH; VGW
Night, Death, Mississippi. Robert Hayden. VGW
Night Duty. Kenneth Mackenzie. MAuV
Night Feeding. Muriel Rukeyser. NMM; WPE

Night filled, A:/ Light pinning the dark. Verna Tomlinson Baker. AATT

Night folded itself about me like a woman's hair, The. Birth of a Genius Among Men. "Hugh MacDiarmid." SLP

Night Funeral in Harlem. Langston Hughes. InPS

Night has a thousand eyes, The. Francis William Bourdillon. BoLoP

Night has come on like a woman sleeping, The. Moon Poems. John Wieners. VGW

Night has secreted us. Amen. Richard W. Thomas. PoBA

Night he died, earth's images all came, The. Poet. Peter Viereck. CoPAm

Night Herons. Judith Wright. MAuV

Night his/ house I don't remember. The Blue Bowl of Plumbs Invention. Lyn Lifshin. Psy

Night Hunt, The. Thomas MacDonagh. PFIr

Night, I know you are powerful and artistic. For Bill Hawkins, a Black Militant. William J. Harris. PoBA

Night in a rainbow pool. Rachel at Twenty-three. Yvonne. WBN

Night in June, a lovely moon, A. Coax Me. Andrew Sterling. FSN

Night in the Forest. Galway Kinnell. CoPAm

Night is dark and stormy, and the sky is clouded o'er, The. The Sandy Maranoa. At. to A. W. Davis. MAuV

Night Is Darkening Round Me. Emily Brontë. VoPo (Spellbound.) NOBE

Night is still, The. The unfailing surf. To What Strangers, What Welcome, VIII. J. V. Cunningham. PiAm

Night is very dark, The. Assassination Poems. John Ridland. MAT; OFD

Night it was horribly dark, The. Measles in the Ark. "Susan Coolidge." OxBChV

Night John Henry is born an ax, The. The Birth of John Henry. Melvin B. Tolson. Fr. Harlem Gallery. BPo

Night Journey. Theodore Roethke. ECBV; InPS

Night Letter. Marge Piercy. NMM

Night lies beside me. Amy Lowell. TH

Night Mail. W. H. Auden. OxBTC

Night-March, The. Herman Melville. PiAm

Night Mirror, The. John Hollander. Prf

Night-Music. Philip Larkin. InPS

Night music slanted. Cell Song. Etheridge Knight. PoBA

Night my father got me, The. The Culprit. A. E. Housman. AIW

Night of Dreams. Laura Beausoleil. NPW

Night of Souls. Ann Stanford. WPE

Night of the Dance, The. Thomas Hardy. OBP

Night on Clinton. Robert Mezey. AmPA

Night on Hatchet Cove. Denise Levertov. PiAm; Psy

Night on the Prairies, sel. Walt Whitman. "Night on the prairies." RFM

Night Out, A. Dannie Abse. BuTh

Nightpiece. James Joyce. NoAM

Night-Piece. Raymond R. Patterson. PoBA

Nightpiece. Judith Johnson Sherwin. WBN

Night-Piece, A. Wordsworth. Moon

Night rattles with nightmares, The. From the Night-Window. Douglas Dunn. SLP

Night Riddle. Unknown. ECBV

Night-Ride, The. Kenneth Slessor. MAuV

Night Riders. Jean Farley. NowV

Night, say all, was made for rest, The. Upon Visiting His Lady by Moonlight. "A. W." Moon

Night Scenes. Robert Duncan. VGW

Night sea quickens, The. On the shoal or rock. Lighthouses. Dorothy Wellesley. WPE

Night sends this white eye. Full Moonlight in Spring. W. S. Merwin. TH

Night Shift at the Plating Division of Keeler Brass. James B. Allen. HeS

Night-sky bird's world. Myth of the Blaze. George Oppen. CAAP

Night-sky red, crackle and roar of flame, The. In This Year of Grace. John Hewitt. PFIr

Night Sounds. Thomas Middleton. Fr. Blurt, Master Constable. RAE

Night Sowing. David Campbell. MAuV

Night still lingers. To My Wife. Jack Simcock. BuTh

Night Storm. Jane Sherman. CaYB

Night Sweat. Robert Lowell. VGW

Night that ends so soon. The Short Night. Buson, tr. by Harold G. Henderson. Moon

Night that has no star lit up by God, The. The New World. Jones Very. AmVN

Night, the black summer, simplifies her smells. Nights in the Gardens of Port of Spain. Derek Walcott. OBP

Night Thoughts. Richard Bastian. AATT

Night Thoughts. Gwen Harwood. CAAP

Night Thoughts [The Complaint], sels. Edward Young. Art of Happiness, The, fr. VIII. Night the First ("Tir'd nature's sweet restorer, balmy Sleep!") LAuP

Nightwalker. Delia Chilgren. NPW

Night-Walker, The. Horace Gregory. Moon

Nightwalker, sel. Thomas Kinsella. "I must lie down with them all soon and sleep." BIrV

Night was coming very fast, The. The Hens. Elizabeth Madox Roberts. LCL

Night Was Smooth, The. James Bertolino. POL

Night was thick and hazy, The. Robinson Crusoe's Story. Charles Edward Carryl. Fr. Davy and the Goblin. ECBV

Night Watch. Margo Magid. NMM

Night we went up into the rising hills, The. The Moon. Charles Upton. MIT

Night Will Never Stay, The. Eleanor Farjeon. OxBChV

Night-Wind, The. Emily Brontë. FSFS

Night Wind in Fall. W. R. Moses. NCSH

Night without Sleep. Robinson Jeffers. PiAm

Night you got away, I dreamed you rose, The. To a Fugitive. James Wright. TH

Night You Got Back from the Mountains, The. Holly Prado. NPW

Nightbreak. Adrienne Rich. IHMS; PiAm

Nighthawks circle/ through the midwestern elms. For a Winnebago Brave. Joseph Bruchac. CDW

Nightingale, The. Samuel Taylor Coleridge. MBPR

Nightingale, The ("One morning, one morning, one morning in May"). Unknown. See One Morning in May.

Nightingale, as soon as April bringeth, The. Philomela. Sir Philip Sidney. NOBE

Nightingale has a lyre of gold, The. To A. D. W. E. Henley. Echoes, XVIII. LoAs

Nightingale, in dead of night, The. The Happy Nightingale. Unknown. OxBChV

Nightingale, whose happy noble hart, The. The Steele Glas. George Gascoigne. AAS

Nightingales. Robert Bridges. NOBE

Nightingales of Spring, The. Unknown. AmFP

Nightingale's Song, The. James I, King of Scotland. Fr. The Kingis Quair. OxBM

Nightlines. Paul Clause. AATT

Nightlong you lie and mock the idle moon. Moon Rock. E. Louise Mally. POL

Nightmare. James A. Emanuel. BPo

Nightmare. W. S. Gilbert. *Fr.* Iolanthe. PBMP

Nightmare Factory, The. Maxine W. Kumin. NVAP

Nightmare leaves fatigue. Louis MacNeice. *Fr.* Autumn Journal. BIrV

Nightmare of beasthood, snorting, how to wake. Moly. Thom Gunn. NoAM

Nightmare, with Angels. Stephen Vincent Benét. MAT

Nightmares have told me. 46 and Recalling. Allan Block. FAF

Nights and days we stumble over each other. Stumbling. Dick Lourie. NeAC

Nights in the Gardens of Port of Spain. Derek Walcott. OPB

Nights Passed on Ward's Island, Toronto Harbour. Doug Fetherling. NeAC

Night's Song. Sir William Davenant. *Fr.* Luminalia. SCP-2

Night we spent apart. Hook. Erica Jong. RiTi

Nighttime. The faithful prison guard. Bedtime Story. Lou Lipsitz. VGW

Nikki-Rosa. Nikki Giovanni. IHMS; IPWM; NoAM; PoBA; RiTi
(Nikki-Roasa.) PBMP

Nil Pejus Est Caelibe Vita. Samuel Taylor Coleridge. MBPR

Nile, The. Leigh Hunt. NOBE

Nimphs Reply to the Sheepheard, The. Sir Walter Ralegh. *See* Nymph's Reply to the Shepherd, The.

Nine adulteries, 12 liaisons, 64 fornications and something approaching a rape. The Temperaments. Ezra Pound. BoLoP; NoAM; NOBA

Nine Bean-Rows on the Moon. A. W. Purdy. Moon

Nine drops of water bead the jessamine. A Wet August. Thomas Hardy. PPP

Nine grenadiers, with bayonets in their guns. The Dream of a Boy Who Lived at Nine Elms. William Brighty Rands. OxBChV

Nine meshes of the net enclose. Jonathan Price. CoPAm

Nine O'Clock Thoughts on the 73 Bus. Peter Porter. POL

Nine Parts of Speech, The. *Unknown.* ECBV

Nine swallows sat on a telephone wire. The Swallows. Elizabeth J. Coatsworth. LCL

Nine white chickens come. A Black November Turkey. Richard Wilbur. BoAnP; CoPAm; NCSH

1915: A Pre Raphaelite Ending, London. Richard Howard. NoAM

1945. Sir Herbert Read. OxBTC

1914, *sels.* Rupert Brooke.
Peace, I. BTTM
Soldier, The, V. BTTM; HeIP; NOBE; OxBTC; PAIC; VoPo

19??. Dan Georgakas. NowV

Nineteen Hundred and Nineteen. W. B. Yeats. BIrV

1907, A Proposal from Paris. Richard Howard. CAAP

1965. Gibbons Ruark. NowV

1967. Thomas Hardy. NoAM

1939. Alan Brownjohn. LP

1937 Ford Convertible. Tom McKeown. NVAP

Nineteenth Century as a Song, The. Robert Hass. CAAP

90th Year, The. Denise Levertov. FiCP

Ninety and Nine, The, *with music.* Elizabeth Cecilia Clephane. BLSH

90 North. Randall Jarrell. NoAM; NOBA

98 Degree Blues. *Unknown.* BluL

Ninety-fifth. Isaac Watts. AmFP

Niño Leading an Old Man to Market. Leonard Nathan CTBA; NCSH

Ninth, The; last half; the score was tied. Dorlan's Home Walk. Arthur Guiterman. PoTa

Ninth of July, The. John Hollander. CoPAm

No! Thomas Hood. PBMP

No/ No/ No/ I am not doing. Our Lives. Sharon Scott. JB

No argument, no anger, no remorse. Hedges Freaked with Snow. Robert Graves. OxBTC

No Bargains Today. Peggy Susberry Kenner. JB

No bars are set too close, no mesh too fine. The Sparrow in the Zoo. Howard Nemerov. NoAM

No bitterness: our ancestors did it. Ave Caesar. Robinson Jeffers. NoAM; NOBA

No bottom,/ Mark four. *Unknown.* AmFP

No breath of air to break the wave. The Giaour: a Fragment of a Turkish Tale. Byron. MBPR

No butler, no second maid, no blood upon the stair. Crime Club. Weldon Kees. AnMo

No cedar dares a roothold in the stone. LaSalle Street. Rachel Albright. ANTL

No Change in Me. *Unknown.* AmFP

No Change of Place. W. H. Auden. OxBTC

No changes of support—only. Last Month. John Ashbery. CAPP

No closer the glove clings to the sweaty hand. Little-League Baseball Fan. W. R. Moses. NCSH

No cloud, no relique of the sunken day. The Nightingale. Samuel Taylor Coleridge. MBPR

No Coward Soul Is Mine. Emily Brontë. *See* Last Lines.

No crooked leg, no bleared eye. Written in Her French Psalter. Elizabeth I, Queen of England. WPE

No crowd that has occurred. Emily Dickinson. PiAm

No Dawns. Julianne Perry. PoBA

No days but these. Matthew Mead. *Fr.* The Administration of Things. TwMBP

No Dice. Kathleen Wiegner. MMD

No Difference. Keats. *See* Song about Myself.

No doubt this way is best. No Use. W. D. Snodgrass. BoLoP

No doubt to-morrow I will hide. At Mass. Vachel Lindsay. VGW

No egg on Friday Alph will eat. Of Alphus. John Parkhurst, *tr. by* Timothe Kendall. SoSe

No fabulous warrior came hunting. The Gentle Ambush. George Macadam. SLP

No "fan is in his hand" for these. The Threshing-Machine. Alice Meynell. WPE

No, for I'll save it! Seven years since. Apparent Failure. Robert Browning. NOBE

No Great Matter. David Lawson. VGW

No haste but good, where wisdom makes the waye. George Gascoigne. AAS

No hesitation. Mourning Letter, March 29 1963. Edward Dorn. ConAP

No Hiding Place Down There. *Unknown.* GBP

"No home, no home," cried an orphan girl. The Orphan Girl. *Unknown.* AmFP

No, I would not like to meet Bob Dylan. Citizen. Peter Schjeldahl. CAAP

No—I'll endure ten thousand deaths. Chaste Florimel. Matthew Prior. BoLoP

No Images. Waring Cuney. MAT

No. It's an impudent falsehood. Men did not. On a Vulgar Error. C. S. Lewis. OxBTC

No Job Blues. *Unknown.* BluL

No light except the stars, but from the cliff. The Sea Birds. Van K. Brock. NVAP

No Loath[e]someness in Love. Robert Herrick. GBL; PBMP

No longer can we sit. The Transparent Closet. Martha Shelley. WBN

No longer itself. Six Kisses. Nancy Sullivan. LoAs

No longer mourn for me when I am dead. Sonnets, LXXI. Shakespeare. Epi; GBL; PPoe; SoSe

No longer throne of a goddess to whom we pray. Full Moon. Robert Hayden. BPo

No longer will I close an opaque door. Daisy Aldan. AATT

No man e'er found a happy life by chance. The Art of Happiness. Edward Young. *Fr.* Night Thoughts, VIII. POL

No Man, If Men Are Gods. E. E. Cummings. VGW

"No man may him hyde." Sun. Marianne Moore. PiAm

No man's a jester playing Shakespeare. The King Must Die. Bernie Taupin. GrRo

No Man's Good Bull. James Seay. PPoD

No Matter How Her Thighs. James Mecklenburger. SFF

No Matter If You Remain Unaffected by. Brian Patten. BuTh

No Mean City. Patrick MacDonogh. BIrV

No Meaning. Terence Brame. RAE

No mo meetings. Listenen to Big Black at S. F. State. Sonia Sanchez. BPo

No money to bury him. Ballad of the Man Who's Gone. Langston Hughes. AIW

No More. Carl Clark. JB

No More Auction Block. *Unknown.* BPo

No More Good Water. *Unknown.* BluL

No more let Greece her bolder fables tell. On the Famous Voyage. Ben Jonson. PAIC; TVS

No more my visionary soul shall dwell. Pantisocracy. Samuel Taylor Coleridge. MBPR; PAIC

No more no more to be. I Want. Rosemary Daniell. WBN

No More Soft Talk. Diane Wakoski. IHMS

No More Than Five. Fred Levinson. AmPA

No more violets. Pastroale. Hart Crane. PSN

No more wine? Then we'll push back chairs and talk. Bishop Blougram's Apology. Robert Browning. PFD

No more with overflowing light. For a Dead Lady. E. A. Robinson. HeIP; LoAs; NoAm; NOBA; PiAm

No More Women Blues. *Unknown.* BluL

No name but a number. Number 1 by Jackson Pollack (1948). Nancy Sullivan. WIF

"No need to get home early." Father's Voice. William Stafford. RFM

No new delights to our desire. Singers to Come. Alice Meynell. WPE

No new moon in its arms. Last Quarter. John Hollander. Moon

No New Music. Stanley Crouch. PoBA

No New Thing. Vincent Buckley. MAuV

No-Night, The. Irving Feldman. NoAM

No No Blues. *Unknown.* BluL

No, no, don't, please. Crimes of Passion: The Phone Caller. Terry Stokes. AmPA

No, no; for my virginity. A True Maid. Matthew Prior. FaBoCo

No, no! Go from me. I have left her lately. A Virginal. Ezra Pound. NoAM; NOBA

No, no, go not to Lethe, neither twist. Ode on Melancholy. Keats. Epi; InPS; MAT; MBPR; NOBE; OBP; PPP

No, no, no I know I was not important as I moved. Come Dance with Kitty Stobling. Patrick Kavanagh. NoAM

No, no, no, no! Come, let's away to prison. Shakespeare. *Fr.* King Lear, V, iii. OBP

No noise is here, or none that hinders thought. William Cowper. *Fr.* The Robin in Winter. BoAnP

No Offence. D. J. Enright. OxBTC

No one but him. Swimmer in the Rain. Robert Wallace. FiCP

No one can die twice of the same fever? Twice of the Same Fever. Robert Graves. LoAs

No one can tell you why. Heart's Needle, IV. W. D. Snodgrass. ConAP; CoPAm

No one could find his grave for relic-plunder. Casanova. Richard Usborne. POL

No one could have a blacker tail. Othello Jones Dresses for Dinner. Ed Roberson. PoBA

No One Heard Him Call. Dorothy Aldis CaYB

No one kept count. Migrant Hostel. Peter Skrzynecki. CAAP

No One Remembers Abandoning the Village of White Fir. Duane Niatum. CDW

No One So Much as You. Edward Thomas. GBL; PSN

No One to Blame. Laurence Lieberman. CoPAm

No one told them about the disease. How the Indians Lost the Hot Springs. Carol Cox. MMD

No one was in the fields. Tom's Angel. Walter de la Mare. AIW

No one's going to read. A Dance for Militant Dilettantes. Al Young. PiAm; PoBA; PPoD; SA

No Other Choice. *Unknown.* NOBE ("Fain would I change that note.") GBL

No pavement chalks the plain with memories. Beginning the Year at Rosebud, S. D. Roberta Hill. CDW

No photographs exist. This man. Crazy Horse Returns to South Dakota. Harley Elliott. NeAC

No Platonic Love. William Cartwright. GBL; SCP-2

No Possum, No Sop, No Taters. Wallace Stevens. VGW

No Remedy. Drummond Allison. OxBTC

No room for mourning: he's gone out. William Wordsworth. Sidney Keyes. OxBTC

No rooster wakes them. A donkey brays. In the Madison Zoo. Roberta Hill. CDW

No saint on a disc of snow. Emily Dickinson Postage Stamp. Lynn Strongin. NMM

No Second Troy. W. B. Yeats. NoAM; NOBE; OxBTC; PPP

No, she's not lying down there now for love. In the Radiotherapy Unit. Margaret Stanley Wrench. SFF

No, Sir, No. *Unknown.* AmFP

No sleep. The sultriness pervades the air. The House-Top. Herman Melville. AmVN; NOBA; Prf

No sleep tonight. Summary. Sonia Sanchez. BPo

No sound of any storm that shakes. Hillcrest. E. A. Robinson. PPoe

No Speech from the Scaffold. Thom Gunn. OxBTC

No spot of earth where men have so fiercely for ages of time. Antrim. Robinson Jeffers. BIrV; NOBA; VGW

No spring, nor summer beauty hath such garce. The Autumnal. John Donne. Elegies, IX. InPS

No! sum thine Edith's wretched lot. Sir Walter Scott. *Fr.* The Lord of the Isles. SLP

No sun—no moon! No! Thomas Hood. PBMP

No, the serpent did not. Theology. Ted Hughes. NoAM

No, the serpent was not. Reveille. Ted Hughes. PPP

No thing/ no-thing. Cathexis. F. J. Bryant, Jr. PoBA

No this time it is not the Avon Lady. The Sacred Heart of Jesus Bleeds for You. Elton Glaser. NVAP

No! those days are gone away. Robin Hood. Keats. MBPR

No, thou hast never griev'd but I griev'd too. Walter Savage Landor. GBL

No time, no time. The Suburb. Anne Stevenson. NMM

No Use. W. D. Snodgrass. BoLoP

No use waiting for it to stop. Apples. Shirley Kaufman. NMM; RiTi

No water is still, on top. The Movement of Fish. James Dickey. VGW

No Way of Knowing. John Ashbery. CAAP

No woman has ever lost her man. Nine Bean-Rows on the Moon. A. W. Purdy. Moon

No Woman No Nickel. *Unknown.* BluL

No Worst, There Is None. Gerard Manley Hopkins. BoReV; HeIP; InPS; NoAM; NOBE; PFD; PPP (Sonnet.) OBP

No You. Robert Tait. SLP

Noah's Ark. Marguerite Young. WPE

Noble lady, in whose light. With an Antique Crystal Cup and Ring. John Sobieski Stuart. SLP

Noble Nature, The. Ben Jonson. *Fr.* To the Immortal Memory and Friendship of That Noble Pair, Sir Lucius Cary, and Sir Henry Morison. VoPo ("It is not growing like a tree.") HeIP; SoSe

Noble Soldier, The, *sel.* Thomas Dekker. "O Sorrow, Sorrow, say where dost thou dwell?" SCP-2

Noblest bodies are but gilded clay. Samuel Harding. *Fr.* Sicily and Naples; or, The Fatal Union: A Tragedy. SCP-2

Nobly, nobly Cape Saint Vincent to the North-West died away. Home-Thoughts, from the Sea. Robert Browning. NOBE; OBP

Nobody Dies Like Humphrey Bogart. Norman Rosten. PPoD

Nobody else makes doors like the poet's wife. The Poet's Wife Makes Him a Door So He Can Find the Way Home. Nancy Willard. RiTi

Nobody ever told my grandmother Eleni. Comfort From Arcadia. Nicholas Flocos. SA

Nobody heard him, the dead man. Not Waving but Drowning. Stevie Smith. BuTh; HeIP; NoAM; NOBE; OxBTC; POL; PPP; SS

Nobody in the lane, and nothing, nothing but blackberries. Blackberrying. Sylvia Plath. MPo; NoAM; NOBA

Nobody interfered. My two uncles stood. The Life Style. Edwin Brock. IPWM

Nobody know what i got inside. Emmet Kills-Warrior Turtle Mountain Reservation. Marnie Walsh. VW

Nobody Knows the Trouble I've Seen, *with music. Unknown.* BLSH; BLSo

Nobody Loses All the Time. E. E. Cummings. FaBoCo; IPWM; NOBA

Nobody noggers the shaff of a sloo. On a Flimmering Floom You Shall Ride. Carl Sandburg. ECBV

Nobody planted roses, he recalls. "Summertime and the Living." Robert Hayden. BPo; NCSH; PoBA; PPP

Nobody Riding the Roads Today. June Jordan. BPo

Nobody told her it was time to go. Time Out. Patricia Henley. NPW

Nobody would have guessed. Sixes and Sevens. Roderick Hartigh Jellema. AATT

Nocturnal Reverie, A. Countess of Winchilsea. SBG; WPE

Nocturnal Sketch, A. Thomas Hood. FaBoCo

Nocturnal[l] upon St Lucy's [*or* S. Lucies] Day, Being the Shortest Day, A. John Donne. AnMo; GBL; MetP; NOBE; OBP; PPP; SCP-1

Nocturne: "Three-toed tree toad, The." Arthur Guiterman. ECBV

Nocturne of the Self-evident Presence. Thomas MacGreevy. BIrV

Nocturne of the Wharves. Arna Bontemps. BPo

Nocturne Varial. Lewis Alexander. PoBA

Nod. Walter de la Mare. OxBTC

Nodding, its great head rattling like a gourd. Original Sin: A Short Story. Robert Penn Warren. CoPAm; PPP

Nofretete. Felix Pollak. HeS

Noise of hammers once I heard. The Hammers. Ralph Hodgson. NOBE; OxBTC

Noise of water teased his literal ear, The. Persistent Explorer. John Crowe Ransom. PiAm

Noiseless Patient Spider, A. Walt Whitman. HeIP; InPK; IPWM; NOBA; PAIC; PBMP; PiAm; SoSe; VoPo; WIF, 2 *versions*

Noise from underground made gibber some. John Berryman. *Fr.* Dream Songs. CAPP

Noises of the harbour die, the smoke is petrified, The. The Statue. Roy Fuller. NOBE

Noisy Boys. Jack Castiglione. BBGO

Nominis Umbra. J. A. R. McKellar. MAuV

Non Poem About Vietnam, A. Carolyn M. Rodgers. SA

Non Sum Qualis Eram Bonae Sub Regno Cynarae. Ernest Dowson. BoLoP; GBL; HeIP; NOBE; VoPo ("Last night ah, yesternight, betwixt her lips and mine.") LoAs

Non Ti Fidar. Louis Zukofsky. VGW

Nona poured oil on the water and saw the eye. The Evil Eye. John Ciardi. CoPAm

Nondescript express in from the South, A. Gare du Midi. W. H. Auden. PSN

None. Josephine Miles. VGW

None ever was in love with me but grief. "My True Love Hath My Heart and I Have His." Mary Elizabeth Coleridge. BoLoP

None other fame mine unambitious muse. Samuel Daniel. *Fr.* To Delia. AAS

None Other Lamb, None Other Name. Christina Rossetti. PFD

Nonsense ("The cricket and the greshop..."). *Unknown.* OxBM

Nonsense Rhyme. Elinor Wylie. PBMP; Psy

Noon—and the north-west sweeps the empty road. February. William Morris. *Fr.* The Earthly Paradise. VPC

Noon Hour. Joan Finnigan. BuTh

Noon is beautiful, The: the perfect wheel. An Elegy. Yvor Winters. VGW

Noon of the Sunbather. Marge Piercy. NMM

Noon. The luminous tide. Ballydavid Pier. Thomas Kinsella. BIrV

Nor happiness, nor majesty, nor fame. Sonnet: Political Greatness. Shelley. OBP

Nor looks that backward life so bare to me. Frederick Goddard Tuckerman. *Fr.* Sonnets. AmVN

Nor shall you for your fields neglect your stock. Young Stock. V. Sackville-West. OxBTC

Nor skin nor hide nor fleece. Lethe. Hilda Doolittle ("H.D."). PiAm; VGW

Nor, will anyone dare say to. Sharon Will Be No/Where on Nobody's Best-Selling List. Sharon Scott. JB

Nor yet do I, your knowing lover. Portrait. John Lyle Donaghy. BIrV

Nora. Fran Winant. WBN

Nora Criona. James Stephens. PFIr

Nora's Vow. Sir Walter Scott. SLP

Norfolk. John Betjeman. BBGO

Norfolk Rebellion, The. *Unknown.* GBP

Norfolk sprang thee, Lambeth holds thee dead. Earl of Surrey. AAS

Normal Lives. Dick Allen. FAF

Norman conquest all historians fix, The. The English Succession. *Unknown.* OxBChV

Norman Morrison. David Ferguson. NowV

Norman Morrison. Adrian Mitchell. NowV

North Africa Breakdown. Tom Raworth. TwMBP

North Coast Town. Robert Gray. CAAP

North Dakota Gothic. Mark Vinz. HeS

North Labrador. Hart Crane. POL

North Pole Story, A. Menella Bute Smedley. OxBChV

North wind doth blow, The. Mother Goose. MG

North Wind in October. Robert Bridges. FSFS

Northern Habitat, A. Robin Fulton. MIS

Northern Pike. James Wright. CAAP

Norwegian Wood. John Lennon *and* Paul McCartney. OBP

Nosce Teipsum, *sels.* Sir John Davies. NOBE
Affliction.
Soul and the body, The.

Noses are running at our house, The. A Winter Scene. Reed Whittemore. NCSH

Not a drum was heard, not a funeral note. The Burial of Sir John Moore after [*or* at] Corunna. Charles Wolfe. BTTM; NOBE

Not a line of her writing have I. Thoughts of Phena. Thomas Hardy. OxBTC

Not a Sous Had He Got. "Thomas Ingoldsby." *Fr.* The Ingoldsby Legends: The Cynotaph. FaBoCo

Not a thing on the river McCluskey did fear. The Little Brown Bulls. *Unknown.* AmFP

Not a tree but the tree. There Is Only One of Everything. Margaret Atwood. MMD

Not Aladdin magian. On Visiting Staffa. Keats. MBPR

Not all of them were human. The Village of Tudda. Kenneth Patchen. VGW

Not All There. Robert Frost. FaBoCo

Not all thy flushing suns are set. An Ode to Master Endymion Porter, upon His Brother's Death. Robert Herrick. SCP-1

Not an unhappy man. Norman Morrison. David Ferguson. NowV

Not at midnight, not at morning, O sweet city. Caryatid. Léonie Adams. LoAs

Not because your body is lovely or your hair. To X. Tom Scott. SLP

Not believing that igneous dream. Nothing Inside and Nothing Out. Ray Amorosi. FiCP

Not but they die, the teasers and the dreams. The Teasers. William Empson. OxBTC

Not by hammering the furious word. Harlem Riot, 1943. Pauli Murray. PoBA

Not by lost killers stranded. The Biggest Killing. Edward Dorn. VGW

Not, Celia, that I juster am. To Celia. Sir Charles Sedley. NOBE

Not easy to state the change you made. Love Letter. Sylvia Plath. NOBA

Not envying Latin shades—if yet they throw. The River Duddon, I. Wordsworth. MBPR

Not even dried-up leaves. Thesis, Antithesis, and Nostalgia. Alan Dugan. NowV

Not even for a moment. He knew, for one thing, what he was. Leda. Mona Van Duyn. NMM

Not even my pride will suffer much. Theme and Variations. Edna St. Vincent Millay. SBG

Not even when the early birds. The Rabbit. W. H. Davies. BoAnP

Not ever to talk when merely requested. For My Son. Alan Brownjohn. LP

Not every man has gentians in his house. Barvarian Gentians. D. H. Lawrence InPK; InPS; NoAM; NOBE; PPoe; TCP; WIF, 2 *versions*

Not for the promise of the laboured field. Ode to the Poppy. Henrietta Oneil. WPE

Not for these lovely blooms that prank your chambers did I come. Rendezvous. Edna St. Vincent Millay. RiTi

Not Fortune's worshipper, nor Fashion's fool. Apologia pro Vita Sua. Pope. *Fr.* Epistle to Dr. Arbuthnot. NOBE

Not guns, not thunder, but a flutter of clouded drums. Fireworks. Babette Deutsch. OFD

Not Having a History. John Vernon. PPoD

Not having spoken for years now. Matrilineal Descent. Robin Morgan. WBN

Not honey,/ not the plunder of the bee. Fragment 113. Hilda Doolittle ("H.D."). PiAm

Not I myself know all my love for thee. The Dark Glass. Dante Gabriel Rossetti. The House of Life, XXXIV. VPC

Not I, not I, but the wind that blows through me! The Song of a Man Who Has Come Through. D. H. Lawrence. InPS; NoAM; OxBTC

Not, I'll not, carrion comfort, Despair, not feast on thee. Carrion Comfort. Gerard Manley Hopkins. AnMo; BoReV; HeIP; InPK; NoAM; PFD; PPP

Not in a silver casket cool with pearls. Edna St. Vincent Millay. VGW

Not in my saddle, but above it. Indian Summer: Montana, 1956. W. M. Ransom. CDW

Not in our time, O Lord. Hilda Doolittle ("H.D."). *Fr.* Tribute to the Angels. NOBA

Not in the crises of events. The Spirit's Epochs. Coventry Patmore. *Fr.* The Angel in the House. GBL

Not in the days of Adam and Eve, but when Adam. In the Days of Prismatic Color. Marianne Moore. PiAm

Not in the solitude. Hymn of the City. Bryant. PiAm

Not just one night but all the nights. Land's End. Daniel J. Langton. MIT

Not Leaving the House. Gary Snyder. IPWM

Not Like That. Adrienne Rich. CoPAm

Not like the brazen giant of Greek fame. The New Colossus. Emma Lazarus. SBG; WPE

"Not Marble nor the Gilded Monuments." Archibald MacLeish. BoLoP; WIF

Not marble, not the gilded monuments. Sonnets, LV. Shakespeare. Epi; HeIP; InPK; NOBE; PAIC; PPoe; WIF

Not mine own fears nor the prophetic soul. Sonnets, CVII. Shakespeare. PPoe

Not Now. Robert Creeley. Epi

Not of the princes and prelates with periwigged charioteers. A Consecration. John Masefield. NoAM

Not Often. Ray Fraser. NeAC

Not often *con brio,* but *andante, andante.* Stanley Matthews. Alan Ross. OxBTC

Not only how far away, but the way that you say it. Judging Distances. Henry Reed. Lessons of the War, II. BoLoP; NOBE; PSN; SoSe

Not Palaces. Stephen Spender. NoAM

Not proud of station nor in worldly pelf. Frederick Goddard Tuckerman. *Fr.* Sonnets. AmVN

Not-Quiet touchable air, A. The State in Indian Language was Called "Running Water." Besmilr Brigham. Psy

Not quite/ spherical. At Breakfast. May Swenson. Psy

Not Quite Spring. Lyn Lifshin. NeAC

Not so long ago my Lord a child lay manger-cradled. Bambino. Betty Ruth Bird. AATT

Not solely that the future she destroys. Modern Love, XII. George Meredith. GBL; VPC

Not that by this disdain. The Repulse. Thomas Stanley. MetP

Not that he promised not to windowshop. One Man's Wife. Philip Booth. VGW

Not that I cared about the other women. Colder. Erica Jong. MMD

Not that the pines were darker there. The Long Voyage. Malcolm Cowley. SoSe

Not the divine rising up from earth as dew. Forte: For Tina. David Meltzer. MIT

Not the round natural world, not the deep mind. Frederick Goddard Tuckerman. *Fr.* Sonnets. AmVN; PiAm; PPoD

Not Thinking of America. Judith Kroll. AmPA

Not those who have lived here and gone. Moving. James Harrison. CoPAm

Not time in a rush but whole time. June. Bink Noll. TCP

Not to be the mother of solitude will I give myself. A Busy Man Speaks. Robert Bly. ConAP

Not to have known the hard-bitten. Beginnings. Robert D. Fitzgerald. MAuV

Not to Sleep. Robert Graves. BuTh

Not to touch, she said to me, anything sticky. Nightpiece. Judith Johnson Sherwin. WBN

Not under a stone. Breathe In Breathe Out. Layle Silbert. NPW

Not under Holly or Green Boughs. Tom Raworth. TwMBP

Not upon earth, as you suppose. Tu Non Se' in Terra, Si Come Tu Credi. Kathleen Raine. WPE

Not Waving but Drowning. Stevie Smith. BuTh; HeIP; NoAM; NOBE; OxBTC; POL; PPP; SBG; SS

No weaned yet, without comprehension loving. Love's Immaturity. E. J. Scovell. GBL

Not with more glories, in the ethereal plain. The Voyage on the Thames. Pope. *Fr.* The Rape of the Lock. NOBE

Not yet can she bear the yoke on submissive neck. Odes II, 5. Horace, *tr. by* C. E. Bennett. LoAs

Not yet dawn. Asian Brother, Asian Sister. Lawson Fusao Inada. SA

Not yet forsaken (gentle muse) draw near. In Commendation of a Solitary Life. Thomas Lodge. TVS

Not yet, not yet. The Tree. Joel Sloman. VGW

Not yet will those measureless fields be green again. The Cenotaph. Charlotte Mew. WPE

Not you, lean quarterlies and swarthy periodicals. To the Film Industry in Crisis. Frank O'Hara. CAAP; NoAM; NOBA

Note Delivered by a Female Impersonator. Heather McHugh. AmPA

Note on Local Flora. William Empson. PSN

Note on Master Crow, A. Jean Garrigue. BoAnP

Note on Propertius 1.5. Fleur Adcock. BoLoP

Note on the Latin Gerunds, A. Richard Porson. FaBoCo

Note to a New Lesbian. Martha Shelley. WBN

Note to Olga (1966), A. Denise Levertov. CAPP

Notes for a Movie Script. M. Carl Holman. PoBA

Notes Found near a Suicide. Frank Horne. *See* Letters Found near a Suicide.

Notes from an Analyst's Couch. Anita Endrezze Probst. CDW

Notes from the Delivery Room. Linda Pastan. RiTi

Notes on a Life to Be Lived, *sels.* Robert Penn Warren. NoAM
    Blow, West Wind.
    Small White House.
    Ways of Day.

Notes on a Long Evening. David Phillips. NeAC

Notes to a Biographer. Peter Porter. CAAP

Notes toward a Supreme Fiction, *sels.* Wallace Stevens. NOBA
    "And for what, except for you, do I feel love?"

    "Begin, ephebe, by perceiving the idea."
    "First idea was not our own, The. Adam."
    "It feels good as it is without the giant."
    "Major abstraction is the idea of man, The."

Nothin very bad happen to me lately. Henry's Confession. John Berryman. *Fr.* Dream Songs. NoAM

Nothing. Walter de la Mare. ECBV

Nothing but no and I, and I and no. Michael Drayton. *Fr.* Idea. GBL

Nothing could/ prevent her from being photographed. Rested near Nefertete. Carol Bergé. MMD

Nothing False and Possible Is Love. E. E. Cummings. Epi

Nothing Gold Can Stay. Robert Frost. AnMo; NCSH; NOBA; PPP; TSWA; VGW

Nothing in Heaven Functions As It Ought. X. J. Kennedy. CoPAm

Nothing in Rambling. *Unknown.* BluL

Nothing in the sky is high. Asleep and Awake. David McCord. ECBV

Nothing in thick clothes is. In the Home. Marvin Bell. NVAP

Nothing Inside and Nothing Out. Ray Amorosi. FiCP

Nothing Is. Sun-Ra. PoBA

Nothing is better, I well think. The Leper. Swinburne. GBL

Nothing is easy! Pity then. Variations: # 21. James Stephen. WIF

Nothing is getting up now in my life. Packer City Poem. Peter Cooley. HeS

Nothing is happening after all. Codicil. Alvin Aubert. CoPAm

Nothing Is Lost. Anne Ridler. WPE

Nothing is plumb, level or square. Love Song: I and Thou. Alan Dugan. BuTh; CAPP; CoPAm; InPK; LoAs; NoAM; SFF; SoSe

Nothing is so beautiful as spring. Spring. Gerard Manley Hopkins. FSFS; NoAM; NOBE; OBP; SoSe

Nothing is the same to anyone. After Reading Takahashi. Jim Harrison. HeS

Nothing More Will Happen. Marge Piercy. NeAC (Different Persuasions.) InPK

"Nothing moves," you say, and stare across the lawn. The Recruits. Ian Hamilton. NoAM

Nothing out of which to create a new, A. None. Josephine Miles. VGW

Nothing remained: Nothing, the wanton name. The Annihilation of Nothing. Thom Gunn. NoAM

Nothing Strange. Tom Kryss. NeAC

Nothing! thou elder brother even to Shade. Upon Nothing. Earl of Rochester. SCP-2

Nothing to Be Said. Philip Larkin. OxBTC

Nothing to do but work. The Pessimist. Ben King. FaBoCo

Nothing Will Die. Tennyson. PBMP

Nothing will fill the salt caves our youth wore. Alone. E. J. Scovell. GBL

Nothing will keep. Personal Letter # 3. Sonia Sanchez. RiTi

Nothing would sleep in that cellar, dank as a ditch. Root Cellar. Theodore Roethke. HeIP; PiAm; PPP

Notice how he has numbered the blue veins. Mr. Mine. Anne Sexton. SFF

Notice the Convulsed Orange Inch of Moon. E. E. Cummings. VGW

Noticing winter I can't stop thinking. Winter Sonnet. Anne Waldman. CAAP

Notify someone of authority. If You See This Man. Thomas Lux. AmPA; NVAP

Notorious Glutton, The. Ann Taylor. OxBChV

Nottingham Fair. *Unknown.* AmFP

Nought loves another as itself. A Little Boy Lost. Blake. *Fr.* Songs of Experience. MBPR; OBP

Novel, The. Denise Levertov. NoAM

Novella. Adrienne Rich. PPP

Novelty Shop, The. Duane Niatum. CDW

November. John Clare. FSFS

November. Hartley Coleridge. FSFS

November. F. W. Harvey. OxBTC

November. Spenser. *Fr.* The Shepheardes Calendar. Epi

November. Frederick Goddard Tuckerman. NOBA

November Birthday. Mary Swanson Stroh. NPW

November Cotton Flower. Jean Toomer. NoAM

November Night. Adelaide Crapsey. PAIC

November 1968. Adrienne Rich. NMM

November on Lake Michigan. Tom McKeown. HeS

November Through a Giant Copper Beech. Edwin Honig. NoAM

Novembers, half a stalk high. Cattails for Bennett. Mary Shumway. HeS

Novus Ordo Seclorum. Grace Cavalieri. AATT

Now,/ asked sweet mama, let me. Milkcow Blues. *Unknown.* BluL

Now/ Change in the ocean. Everybody Ought to Make a Change. *Unknown.* BluL

Now/ Got offices in town. Lawyer Clark Blues. *Unknown.* BluL

Now/ I know the people. Street Car Blues. *Unknown.* BluL

Now, after a party with the consul and our best friend. Summer, 1970. Daniel Halpern. AmPA

Now, age came on, and all the dismal traine. Clarinda's Indifference at Parting with Her Beauty. Countess of Winchilsea. SBG

Now Ain't That Love? Carolyn M. Rodgers. BPo

Now air is air and thing is thing: no bliss. E. E. Cummings. PBMP

Now all the wind and rain. The Watercress Seller. Thomas Miller. OxBChV

Now all day long the man who is not dead. Mother and Son. Allen Tate. PiAm

Now almost everything I ever imagined. My Mother's/ My/ Death/ Birthday. Patricia Goedicke. Psy

Now and it's moon shine. Moonshine. *Unknown.* BluL

Now and Then. Ian Hamilton. NoAM

Now another day is breaking. Morning Prayer. Ogden Nash. OxBChV

Now are they met: this armed with a spade. Phineas Fletcher. *Fr.* The Locusts or Appolyonists. SCP-2

Now as at all times I can see in the mind's eye. The Magi. W. B. Yeats. InPK; InPS; NoAM; OFD; PPoe; PSN

Now as I was young and easy under the apple boughs. Fern Hill. Dylan Thomas. BBGO; FSFS; HeIP; InPK; InPS; IPWM; NoAM; NOBE; NowV; OxBTC; PPoD; PPoe; PPP; TCP; VoPo; WIF

Now as the train bears west. Night Journey. Theodore Roethke. ECBV; InPS

Now at the end I smell the smells of spring. Exit Molloy. Derek Mahon. PFIr; POL

Now at the road's quick turn. Edwin Muir. *Fr.* Variations on a Time Theme. SCP-2

Now *Ban the Bomb*! I'm with you, though we fail. Girl Marcher. John Frederick Nims. SFF

Now be ye lords or commoners. The Tod's Hole. *Unknown.* GBP

Now bethink thee, gentilman. Adam Driven from Eden. *Unknown.* OxBM

Now biginneth Glotoun for to go to shrifte. Glutton in the Tavern. William Langland. *Fr.* The Vision of Piers Plowman. OxBM

Now burst above the city's cold twilight. Six O'Clock. Trumbull Stickney. PPoD

Now, by the verdure on thy thousand hills. Adequacy. Elizabeth Barrett Browning. SGB

Now came still evening on, and twilight gray. Evening in Eden [*or* The Moon and the Nightingale]. Milton. *Fr.* Paradise Lost, IV. Moon; NOBE; OBP

Now can you see the monument? It is of wood. The Monument. Elizabeth Bishop. NoAM; NOBA; PPoe

Now cometh alle ye that been y-brought. God, the Port of Peace. John Walton. OxBM

Now corn pushes past the foam. Ode to a Dead Dodge. David McElroy. AmPA

Now do you suppose that bee. The Buzzing Doubt. Donald L. Hill. NCSH

Now doeth disdainfull Saturne sadd and olde. Constant Love in All Conditions. James I, King of England. SLP

Now Empress Fame had published the renown. Dryden. *Fr.* MacFlecknoe; or, A Satire upon the True-Blue Protestant Poet. SCP-1

Now every day the braken browner grows. September. Mary Elizabeth Coleridge. FSFS

Now Everyone Is Writing Poems about Indians. James Tipton. HeS

Now ev'ning fades! her pensive step retires. Night. Anne Radcliffe. WPE

Now fades the last long streak of snow. In Memoriam A. H. H., CXV. Tennyson. FSFS; NOBE

Now first, as I shut the door. The New House. Edward Thomas. NOBE

Now from the dark, a deeper dark. Calling in the Cat. Elizabeth J. Coatsworth. BoAnP; PCat

Now glory to the Lord of Hosts, from whom all glories are! Ivry. Macaulay. BTTM

Now, God be thanked Who has matched us with His hour. Peace. Rupert Brooke. 1914, I. BTTM

Now God Stand Up for Bastards. Brian Merriman, *tr. fr. Modern Irish by* Arland Ussher. *Fr.* The Midnight Court. BIrV

Now goth son [*or* goeth sun under wod [*or* wood]. Me Rueth, Mary. *Unknown.* BoReV; GBP

Now great Hyperion left his golden throne. William Browne. *Fr.* Birtannia's Pastorals. SCP-2

Now had Columbus well enjoy'd the sight. Joel Barlow. *Fr.* The Columbiad, Book VIII. PiAm

Now handy high and handy low. So Handy, Me Boys, So Handy. *Unknown.* AmFP

Now hardly here and there a hackney-coach. A Description of the Morning. Swift. AnMo; HeIP; InPS; NOBE; PAIC; PPP; Prf: SoSe

Now have good day, now have good day! I Am Christmas. *Unknown.* OxBM

Now having leisure, and a happy wind. John Fletcher *and* William Rowley. *Fr.* The Maid in the Mill. GBL

Now he is dead. The End of Love. Kathleen Raine. BuTh

Now he roars through an unlit stadium of silence. The Footballer in the Small Room. Janet Frame. SPo

Now hear this. Homer, *tr. by* Christopher Logue. *Fr.* The Iliad, XVI. TwMBP

Now his nose's bridge is broken, one eye. On Hurricane Jackson. Alan Dugan. MiP; NCSH; NowV; POL; PPoD; SPo

Now homing tradesmen scatter through the streets. Place Pigalle. Richard Wilbur. HeIP

Now how I came to get this hat 'tis very strange and funny. Where Did You Get That Hat? Joseph J. Sullivan. FSN

Now I ain't no butcher. All Around Man. *Unknown.* BluL

Now I am slow and placid, fond of sun. With Child. Genevieve Taggard. LoAs

Now I can be sure of my sleep. On the Hill Below the Lighthouse. James Dickey. PAIC

Now I can straighten your wires. Brownsville Blues. *Unknown.* BluL

Now I come home to you. The Homecoming. James B. Allen. HeS

Now I got a brown skin girl. Brown Skin Girl. *Unknown.* BluL

Now I Have Nothing. Stella Benson. OxBTC

Now I Lay Me Down to Sleep. *Unknown.* GBP

Now I lay (with everywhere around). E. E. Cummings. PiAm

Now I never will forget that floating bridge. Floating Bridge. *Unknown.* BluL

Now I out walking. Away! Robert Frost. NOBA

Now I tell you mama now I'm sure gonna leave this town. Leaving Town Blues. *Unknown.* BluL

Now I woke up this morning, mama. You Can't Keep No Brown. *Unknown.* BluL

Now ich see blostme springe. Of Jesu Christ I Sing. *Unknown.* OxBM

Now if ever it is time to cleanse Helicon. Ezra Pound. *Fr.* Homage to Sextus Propertius. Epi; VGW

Now I'm going to sing to you. Sheep-skin and Beeswax. *Unknown.* RAE

Now in the dawn before it dies, the eagle swings low. The Story of a Well-made Shield. N. Scott Momaday. CDW

Now in the suburbs and the falling light. Father and Son. Stanley Kunitz. NoAM

Now in the summer of life sweet-heart. Will You Love Me in December as You Do in May? J. J. Walker. FSN

Now in the window. Four Untitled Poems. Kathleen Wiegner. MMD

Now is Albano's marriage-bed new hung. John Marston. *Fr.* What You Will: A Comedy. SCP-2

Now is Ingland all in fight. On the Times. *Unknown.* OxBM

Now is my misery full, and namelessly. Pieta. Rainer Maria Rilke, *tr. by* M. D. Herter Norton. OFD

Now is the season when myriad leaves are. Maple in November. Ethel Green Russell. AATT

Now is the time for the burning of the leaves. The Burning of the Leaves. Laurence Binyon. FSFS; NOBE; OxBTC; PSN

Now Is the Time of Christmas. *Unknown.* OxBM

Now is the time when all the lights wax dim. To Anthea. Robert Herrick. SCP-1

Now Is Yule Come. *Unknown.* OxBM

Now it is autumn and the falling fruit. The Ship of Death. D. H. Lawrence. NoAM

Now is fifteen years you have lain in the meadow. Lines for an Interment. Archibald MacLeish. NOBA

Now it was that the Morrigan settled in bird shape. The Morrigan. *Unknown, tr. by* Thomas Kinsella. BIrV

Now It's Happened. D. H. Lawrence. OBP

Now it's stingy mama. Mojo Hiding Woman. *Unknown.* BluL

Now it's Uncle Sam sitting on top of the world. Carl Sandburg. *Fr.* Good Morning America. OFD

Now Jack he had a ship in the North Counterie. The *Golden Vanity. Unknown.* AIW

Now Jentil Belly Down. *Unknown.* GBP

Now Jones had left his new-wed bride. A Code of Morals. Kipling. FaBoCo

Now let no charitable hope. Let No Charitable Hope. Elinor Wylie. Psy; SBG; VGW

Now let the cycle sweep us here and there. Sigil. Hilda Doolittle ("H.D."). VGW

Now let the wife look up from her stove, the husband. The Voice of Caesar. W. H. Auden. *Fr.* For the Time Being. AnMo

"Now life alone is left me, to maintain." Near the Death of Ovid. Robert Conquest. NoAM

Now light the candles; one; two; there's a moth. Repression of War Experience. Siegfried Sassoon. NoAM

Now Little Billy is gone to the kirk. Little Billy. *Unknown.* GBP

Now manhood and garbroyls I chaunt. Vergil, *tr. by* Richard Stanyhurst. *Fr.* The Aeneid, I. BIrV

Now may we turn aside and dry our tears. Inis Fal. Egan O'Rahilly, *tr. by* James Stephens. BIrV

Now me and my baby we talked last night. Welfare Store. *Unknown.* BluL

Now, miners, if you'll listen, I'll tell you quite a tale. Coming around the Horn. John A. Stone. AmFP

Now morning from her orient chamber came. Imitation of Spenser. Keats. MBPR

Now must I lerne to lyve at rest. Sir Thomas Wyatt. AAS

Now must I these three praise. Friends. W. B. Yeats. NoAM

"Now, my dear friend, what is our plan?" America is Darken'd. R. H. W. Dillard. CoPAm

Now my legs begin to walk. Thaw in the City. Lou Lipsitz. MAT; NCSH

Now, My Usefulness Over. Edwin Honig. NoAM

Now 'neath the silver moon. Santa Lucia. Teodoro Cottrau. BLSH

Now, not a tear begun. A Woman Mourned by Daughters. Adrienne Rich. IHMS; NCSH; Psy

Now on this out of season afternoon. Original Sin on the Sussex Coast. John Betjeman. BBGO

Now our joy. A Sad Song, This Time. Rolfe Humphries. PAIC

Now Poem. For Us. Sonia Sanchez. PoBA

Now prompts the muse poetic lays. Monody on the Death of Chatterton. Samuel Taylor Coleridge. MBPR

Now rock the boat to a fare-thee-well. Rite of Passage. Audre Lorde. PoBA

Now roses grow there, fat with blood. Dachau, Now: "Roses Grow There, Fat with Blood." Elisavietta Ritchie. AATT

Now Sam McGee was from Tennessee, where the cotton blooms. The Cremation of Sam McGee. Robert W. Service. PoTa

Now shall the adventurous muse attempt a theme. Philip Freneau. *Fr.* The Rising Glory of America. AmVN

Now Shrinketh Rose and Lily-Flower. *Unknown.* OxBM

Now sinks another day to rest. The Bull. V. Sackville-West. WPE

Now Sleeps the Crimson Petal. Tennyson. *Fr.* The Princess, Pt. VII. BoLoP; GBL; LoAs; NOBE; PPoe; PPP

Now Snow Descends. Jean Garrigue. WPE

Now so many people that are in this place. *Unknown, tr. by* Richard Johnny John. *Fr.* Thank You, Part I. IPWM

Now spears lift them by their ribs. Dog Sacrifice at Lake Ronkonkoma. William Heyen. AmPA

Now Springs the Spray. *Unknown.* OxBM

Now, starflake frozen on the windowpane. Moment. Howard Nemerov. CoPAm

Now, suddenly, they show up. My Morose Master-Sergeants. Ray Holt. PPoD

Now supposing the French or the Neapolitan soldier. Arthur Hugh Clough. *Fr.* Amours de Voyage. OBP

Now tell me where my easy rider gone. Easy Rider Blues. *Unknown.* BluL

Now That I Am Forever with Child. Audre Lorde. PoBA

Now that I have lighted my smoke. Smoking My Prayers. Simon Ortiz. VW

Now that I have your face by heart, I look. Song for the Last Act. Louise Bogan. LoAs; WPE

Now that I, tying thy glass mask tightly. The Laboratory: Ancien Régime. Robert Browning. LoAs

Now that I've nearly done my days. The Things That Matter. Edith Nesbit. OxBTC

Now that I've taken a wife. The Groom's Lament. Robert Peterson. NeAC

Now that I've wasted. My Alba. Allen Ginsberg. NoAM; NoBA

Now that my father telephones long distance. Grocery Shopping. John Leax. AATT

Now that the barbarians have got as far as Picra. Translation. Roy Fuller. NOBE; OxBTC

Now That the Buffalo's Gone. Buffy Sainte-Marie. PoRo

Now that the day is done. Centaur Song. Hilda Doolittle ("H.D."). VGW

Now that the days are growing light and long. Cuckoo. R. P. Lister. BoAnP

Now that the holidays have come. Here We Are in the Years. Neil Young. PoRo

Now that the winter's gone, the earth hath lost. The Spring. Thomas Carew. OBP; PPoe

Now that your big eyes have finally opened. My Country 'Tis of Thy People You're Dying. Buffy Sainte-Marie. WIF

Now the bat circles on the breeze of eve. Sonnet. Anne Radcliffe. WPE

Now the bright morning star, day's harbinger. Song on May Morning. Milton. FSFS

Now the Day Is Over. Sabine Baring-Gould. OxBChV

Now the golden morn aloft. Ode on the Pleasure Arising from Vicissitude. Thomas Gray. LAuP

Now the heart sings with all its thousand voices. The Gateway. A. D. Hope. BoLoP

Now the Holy Lamp of Love. Patrick MacDonogh. BIrV

Now the hungry lion roars. Puck's Night Song. Shakespeare. Fr. A Midsummer Night's Dream, V, ii. ECBV; OBP

Now the ice lays its smooth claw on the sill. Scotland's Winter. Edwin Muir. OxBTC

Now the last day of many days. To Jane: the Recollection. Shelley. MBPR

Now the late fruits are in. For a Wine Festival. Vernon Watkins. OxBTC

Now the light o' the west is a-turn'd to gloom. Evenen in the Village. William Barnes. VPC

Now the lusty spring is seen. Love's Emblems. John Fletcher. Fr. The Tragedy of Valentinian, II, iv. BoLoP; NOBE

Now the People Have the Light. Charles G. Ballard. VW

Now the pines lift. Burning the Tomato Worms. Carolyn Forché. AmPA

Now the snow/ lies on the ground. Winter. William Carlos Williams. NCSH

Now the storm begins to lower. The Fatal Sisters. Thomas Gray. LAuP

Now the time of year has come for the leaves to be burning. October 1954. Kay Boyle. RiTi

Now then, for love of Crist and of His joye. Keep the Sea. Unknown. Fr. The Libelle of Englyshe Polycye. OxBM

Now there comes/ The Christmas rose. New Year's Song. Ted Hughes. OFD

Now they're ready, now they're waiting. Football. F. Scott Fitzgerald. SPo

Now this dark cloud is rising. Mean Old Twister. Unknown. BluL

Now this particular girl. Spinster. Sylvia Plath. CoPAm

Now to be clean he must abandon himself. The Swan Bathing. Ruth Pitter. BoAnP

Now to the banquet we press. Banquet Song. W. S. Gilbert. Fr. Patience. ECBV

Now to the dry hillside. Education. Kenneth Rexroth. NowV

Now turn, and view the wonders of the deep. Ben Jonson. Fr. The Fortunate Isle, and their Union. SCP-1

Now upon this piteous year. The Stranger. Jean Garrigue. NOBA

Now war is all the world about. An Ode upon Occasion of His Majesty's Proclamation in the Year 1630 [or Ode on His Majesty's Proclamations]. Sir Richard Fanshawe. Fr. Il Pastor Fido. NOBE; SCP-2

Now was there maid fast by the towris wall. The Nightingale's Song. James I, King of Scotland. Fr. The Kingis Quair. OxBM

Now watch this autumn that arrives. Song at the Beginning of Autumn. Elizabeth Jennings. OxBTC

Now we are at peaceful war. Testimonies for a School Prayer. Serge Gavronsky. NowV

Now We Are Sick. J. B. Morton. SpRo

Now we enter a strange world, where the Hessian Christmas. After the Industrial Revolution, All Things Happen at Once. Robert Bly. ConAP

Now we have in our group a lot. Should We Legalize Abortion? Frank O'Hara. NoAM

Now we must get up quickly. Two Lines from the Brothers Grimm. Gregory Orr. AmPA

Now Welcome, Summer. Chaucer. Fr. The Parliament of Fowls. OxBM

Now we're stuck there. Heaving the Lead Line. Unknown. AmFP

Now westward Sol had spent the richest beams. Music's Duel. Richard Crashaw. SCP-1

Now we've made a child. And What About the Children. Audre Lorde. PoBA

Now what is he after below in the street? The bold Unbiddable Child. Winifrid M. Letts. PFIr

Now when I walk around at lunchtime. Personal Poem. Frank O'Hara. CAPP

Now, while the birds thus sing a joyous song. Wordsworth. Fr. Ode: Intimations of Immortality from Recollections of Early Childhood. Prf

Now Winter as a shrivelled scroll. Winter. Katharine Tynan. FSFS

Now winter downs the dying of the year. Year's End. Richard Wilbur. CAPP; HeIP

Now Winter Nights Enlarge. Thomas Campion. AAS; HeIP; NOBE; PPoD

Now with the coming in of the spring the days will stretch a bit. The County Mayo. Anthony Raftery, tr. by James Stephens. PFIr

Now, with your palms on the blades of my shoulders. Dead Still. Andrei Voznesenky, tr. by Richard Wilbur. BoLoP

Now wolde I faine sum merthes make. An Absent Lover. Unknown. OxBM

Not yet half-drest. To a Late Poplar. Patrick Kavanagh. PFIr

Now you/ tell me mama, do you. Saturday Blues. Unknown. BluL

Now you are dead. Broken Promise. James O. Taylor. BuTh

Now you are the gay familiar. Island Letter. Charles Senior. MIS

Now you clown with your grocery man. Go Back to the Country. Unknown. BluL

Now you done spent all my 1940 rent. Working Man Blues. Unknown. BluL

Now you take ol Rufus. He beat drums. For Freckle-faced Gerald. Etheridge Knight. BPo; NeAC

Nowhere are we safe. Hymn Written after Jeremiah Preached to Men in a Dream. Owen Dodson. PAIC

Nowhere around him. The Perfectionist. Philip Dacey. NVAP

Nowhere for Vallejo, A, *sels.*    Nathaniel Tarn.  TwMBP
  "And he passed around midnight."
  "And they went down into the king-city."
  "Borders slide backwards forwards."
  "Call of green things to his hand."
  "On the train to the ruins."

Now's the time for mirth and play.  For Saturday.  Christopher Smart.  *Fr.* Hymns for the Amusement of Children.  LAuP; OxBChV

Nox Nocti Indicat Scientiam.  William Habington.  NOBE

Nude.  Robert Siegel.  FAF

Nude bodies like pelled logs.  Sonnet in Search of an Author.  William Carlos Williams.  Epi

Nude by Edward Hopper, A.  Lisel Mueller.  RiTi

Nude Descending a Staircase.  X. J. Kennedy.  ConAP; HeIP; POL; PPoD; WIF

Nude on the Bathroom Wall, The.  Gena Ford.  IHMS

Nude Swim, The.  Anne Sexton.  WPE

Nudes.  Juan Ramón Jiménez, *tr. fr. Spainish.*  LoAs

Nudes—stark and glistening.  Louse Hunting.  Isaac Rosenberg.  OxBTC

Nudus Redibo.  Thomas Flatman.  SCP-2

Nulla Fides.  Patrick Carey.  SCP-2

Number Four.  Doughtry Long.  PoBA

Number 14.  Keith Bosley.  LP

Number 1 by Jackson Pollock (1948).  Nancy Sullivan.  WIF

Number One Daughter of the Wang Family, The.  Chen Hsieh, *tr. fr. Chinese by* C. H. Kwock.  MIT

Number 29.  *Unknown.*  BluL

Numbers, *sel.* Bible, *O.T.*
  Lord Bless You and Keep You, The, VI: 24-26.  BLSH

Numbers.  Elizabeth Madox Roberts.  LCL

Numbers, Letters.  LeRoi Jones.  BPo; NOBA

Numbers of employees them.  Richard Hofstadter and Michael Wallace, a Documentary History of American Violence.  Jim Rosenberg.  Epi

Numerous Celts.  J. C. Squire.  SpRo

Numerous host of dreaming Saints succeed, A.  Zimri: the Duke of Buckingham.  Dryden.  *Fr.* Absalom and Achitophel, Pt. I.  NOBE

Nun walked on her prayer, The.  The Friar and the Nun.  *Unknown.*  GBP

Nunc Viridant Segetes.  Sedulius Scottus, *tr. fr. Medieval Latin by* Helen Waddell.  BIrV

Nunnery.  Katherine Doak.  NPW

Nuns at Eve.  John Malcolm Brinnin.  PPoD

Nuns fret not at their convent's narrow room.  Wordsworth.  MBPR; OBP; PAIC

Nuptial Song, or Epithalamy, on Sir Clipesby Crew and His Lady, A.  Robert Herrick.  SCP-1
  "To bed, to bed, kind turtles, now, and unite," *sel.* OBP

Nuremberg.  Kenneth Slessor.  MAuV

Nurse carried him up the stair, The.  At Thomas Hardy's Birthplace, 1953.  James Wright.  ConAP

Nurse-life wheat withing his green husk growing, The.  Fulke Greville.  *Fr.* Caelica.  AAS; PAIC

Nurse No Long Grief.  Mary Gilmore.  MAuV

Nurse Sharks.  William Matthews.  FiCP

Nurse, who is neither young nor pretty, The.  Rivalry.  Alden Nowlan.  POL

Nursey Rhyme Alphabet, A.  *Unknown.*  ECBV

Nursery Rhyme of Innocence and Experience.  Charles Causley.  LP

Nursery Song in Pidgin English.  *Unknown.*  SpRo

Nurse's Song ("When the voices of children are heard on the green/ And laughing is heard on the hill")  Blake.  *Fr.* Songs of Innocence.  LAuP; MBPR; OxBChV

Nurse's Song ("When the voices of children are heard on the green/ And whisprings are in the dale").  Blake.  *Fr.* Songs of Experience.  LAuP; MBPR

Nursing Home.  Linda Parker-Silverman.  HeS

Nursing your nerves.  The Afterwake.  Adrienne Rich.  NOBA; Prf

Nutting.  Wordsworth.  MBPR

Nymph Complaining for the Death of Her Fawn, The.  Andrew Marvell.  Epi; HeIP; PAIC; SCP-1

Nymph, nymph, what are your beads?  Overheard on [*or* in] a Saltmarsh.  Harold Monro.  ECBV; LCL

Nymph of the downward smile, and sidelong glance.  To G. A. W.  Keats.  MBPR

Nymphs and shepherds dance no more.  Song.  Milton.  *Fr.* Arcades.  LoAs

Nymph's Reply to the Shepherd, The.  Sir Walter Ralegh.  Epi; HeIP; IPWM; LoAs; NOBE; OLR; PPoD; PPP
  (Her Reply.)  BoLoP
  (Nimphs Reply to the Sheepheard, The.)  AAS


# O

Oh a high holiday, on a high holiday.  Little Musgrave and Lady Barnard.  *Unknown.*  AmFP

Oh, a ship she was rigged and ready for sea.  The Fishes.  *Unknown.*  GBP

O a year from tomorrow I left my own people.  Clonmel Jail.  *Unknown, tr. by* Valentin Iremonger.  BIrV

Oh Achilles of the moleskins.  To "Chick."  Frank Horne.  *Fr.* Letters Found near a Suicide.  BPo

O all ye fair ladies with your colours and your graces.  The Revenant.  Walter de la Mare.  GBL

O all ye who pass by, whose eyes and mind.  The Sacrifice.  George Herbert.  SCP-1

O all your ages at the mercy of my loves.  John Berryman.  *Fr.* Homage to Mistress Bradstreet.  NOBA

O Allison Gross, that lives in yon towr.  Allison Gross.  *Unknown.*  PeBB

Oh Ambulance Man.  *Unknown.*  BluL

Oh, answer me a question, love, I pray.  The Sweetest Story Ever Told.  R. M. Stults.  BLSo; FSN, *with music*

O apple into ant and beard.  And With the Sorrows of This Joyousness.  Kenneth Patchen.  ECBV

Oh, as I went down to Derby Town.  The Derby Ram.  *Unknown.*  AmFP

O Autumn, laden with fruit, and stained.  To Autumn.  Blake.  FSFS; MBPR

Oh, away down South where I was born.  Roll the Cotton Down.  *Unknown.*  AmFP

O beautiful for spacious skies.  America the Beautiful.  Katherine Lee Bates.  BLSH; BTTM

Oh Beverly, do you remember.  September 7.  Ellen Bass.  NMM

O Black and Unknown Bards.  James Weldon Johnson.  BPo; HeIP; PAIC; PoBA

O blessed body! Whither art thou thrown?  Sepulchre.  George Herbert.  SCP-1

O blest unfabled incense tree.  The Phoenix.  George Darley.  *Fr.* Nepenthe.  BIrV; NOBE

O blithe new-comer! I have heard.  To the Cuckoo.  Wordsworth.  MBPR

O blush not so! O blush not so!  Song.  Keats.  MBPR

Oh blythely shines the bonnie sun.  We'll Go to Sea No More.  *Unknown.*  GBP

Oh Book! infinite sweetness! let my heart.  The Holy Scriptures, I. George Herbert.  Epi

Oh, Boston, Boston, thou hast nought to boast on.  Boston, Lincolnshire.  *Unknown.*  GBP

O Boswell, Bozzy, Bruce, what'er thy name.  A Poetical and Congratulatory Epistle to James Boswell, Esq.  "Peter Pindar."  ESaP

Oh, bow your head, Tom Dooley.  Tom Dooley.  *Unknown.*  AmFP

O Boys! O Boys!  Oliver St. John Gogarty.  PFIr

"Oh, brother, oh, brother, can you play ball."  The Two Brothers. *Unknown.*  AmFP

"O! bury me not in the deep, deep sea."  The Ocean Burial. Edwin H. Chapin.  PSoN

O Bury Me Not on the Lone Prairie, *with music.*  *Unknown.* BLSH

O Cambridge, attend.  Satire upon the Heads.  Thomas Gray. FaBoCo

O Canada! *with music.*  Adolphe Routhier, *tr. fr. French by* Robert Stanley Weir.  BLSH

O Captain! My Captain!  Walt Whitman.  *Fr.* Memories of President Lincoln.  BTTM; InPK; PBMP

O Carib Isle!  Hart Crane.  NoAM; VGW

O Catch Miss Daisy Pinks.  Alistair Campbell.  MiP

Oh, Charlie's sweet and Charlie's neat.  Weevily Wheat. *Unknown.*  AmFP

O Chatterton! how very sad thy fate!  To Chatterton.  Keats. MBPR

O child's tremble.  Forming Child Poems.  Simon J. Ortiz. CDW

O Columbia, the gem of the ocean.  Columbia, the Gem of the Ocean.  David T. Shaw.  BTTM

O Come, All Ye Faithful, *with music.*  *Unknown, at. to* John Francis Wade, *tr. fr. Latin by* Frederic Oakeley.  BLSH (Adeste Fideles.)  PSoN

O Come Quickly!  Thomas Campion.  BoReV; NOBE

O! Come, soft rest of cares, come Night.  Bridal Song.  George Chapman.  *Fr.* Hero and Leander, Fifth Sestiad.  NOBE

O come to me, my brother Green, for I am shot and bleeding. Brother Green.  *Unknown.*  AmFP

O commemorate me where there is water.  Lines Written on a Seat on the Grand Canal.  Patrick Kavanagh.  BIrV

O comrades, come gather and join in my ditty.  The *Cumberland*'s Crew.  *Unknown.*  AmFP

"O Cormac, grandson of Conn," said Carbery.  *Unknown, tr. by* Kuno Meyer.  *Fr.* The Instructions of King Cormac.  BIrV

Oh, could we weep.  Nurse No Long Grief.  Mary Gilmore. MAuV

O Country People.  John Hewitt.  PFIr

"O cruel day, accusour of the joie."  Chaucer.  *Fr.* Trolius and Criseyde, III.  PAIC

Oh Cruel Was the Press-gang.  *Unknown.*  GBP

O Daedalus, Fly Away Home.  Robert Hayden.  NCSH; PoBA

Oh, de ole sheep, dey know de road.  De Ole Sheep Dey Know De Road.  *Unknown.*  BPo

Oh, de white gal ride in a automobile.  De Black Girl.  *Unknown.* GBP

Oh! Death.  *Unknown.*  AmFP

O Death, Rock Me Asleep.  *At. to* Anne Boleyn.  WPE

Oh, Dem Golden Slippers!, *with music.*  James A. Bland.  PSoN

O depth sufficient to desire.  Adam's Song to Heaven.  Edgar Bowers.  ConAP

Oh, dey whupped him up de hill, up de hill, up de hill.  Never Said a Mumbalin' Word.  *Unknown.*  GBP

Oh, did you go to see the show.  The Orange Lily.  *Unknown.* GBP

O divine star of heaven.  John Fletcher.  *Fr.* The Mad Lover, IV, i.  GBL

Oh do not wanton with those eyes.  Song.  Ben Jonson.  LoAs

Oh, Do You Know the Muffin Man?  Richard Mathews.  AATT

Oh, do [*or* don't] you remember sweet Betsy from Pike.  Sweet Betsy from Pike.  *Unknown.*  AmFP; BLSo

O Doctor Dear My Love.  Anne Halley.  NMM

O Donal Oge, if you go across the sea.  Donal Oge: Grief of a Girl's Heart.  *Unknown, tr. by* Lady Gregory.  GBL; PFIr

O don't, don't ever ask me for alms.  Death and the Plowman. Sidney Keyes.  OxBTC

Oh! don't you remember sweet Alice, Ben Bolt.  Ben Bolt; or, Ah! Don't You Remember.  Thomas Dunn English.  PSoN

Oh, don't you remember sweet Betsey from Pike.  *See* Oh, do you remember . . .

Oh, early in the evenin', just after dark.  The Blackleg Miners. *Unknown.*  GBP

O early one morning I walked out like Agag.  The Streets of Laredo.  Louis MacNeice.  AIW; MPo; PeBB

O Earth, lie heavily upon her eyes.  Rest.  Christina Rossetti. NOBE

Oh, East is East, and West is West, and never the twain shall meet.  The Ballad of East and West.  Kipling.  BTTM

Oh effervescent palisades of ferns in drippage.  From Rome, for More Public Fountains in New York City.  Alan Dugan. Prf

Oh, factious viper! whose envenom'd tooth.  On the Death of Mr. Fox.  Byron.  MBPR

Oh, Fair to See.  Christina Rossetti.  ECBV

O fair young land, the youngest, fairest far.  On Leaving California.  Bayard Taylor.  AmVN

O false and treacherous Probability.  Fulke Greville.  *Fr.* Caelica. AAS

O fare ye weel, my auld wife!  My Auld Wife.  *Unknown.*  GBP

Oh, fare you well, my darling.  Fare You Well, My Darling. *Unknown.*  AmFP

"O fare you well, my darling."  Ten Thousand Miles.  *Unknown.* AmFP

O fare you well, sweet Ireland, whom I shall see no more.  The Sons of Liberty.  *Unknown.*  AIW

Oh Father.  Wendy Rose.  CDW

O Father, God! to whom, in happier days.  Frederick Goddard Tuckerman.  *Fr.* Sonnets.  AmVN

O Felix Culpa!  *Unknown.*  *See* Adam Lay I-bowndyn.

Oh flame falling, as shaken, as the stories.  The Fire.  Robert Creeley.  NOBA

O fond, but fickle and untrue.  Walter Savage Landor.  GBL

O! for a bowl of fat canary.  A Serving-Men's Song.  John Lyly. *Fr.* Alexander and Campaspe.  NOBE

Oh! for a closer walk with God.  Walking with God.  William Cowper.  BoReV

O for some honest lover's ghost.  A Doubt of Martyrdom.  Sir John Suckling.  BoLoP; NOBE; SCP-2

Oh forlorn fancy, whereto dost thou live.  A Solemn Farewell to the World.  Nicholas Breton.  TVS

Oh fortune, thy wresting wavering state.  Written on a Wall at Woodstock.  Elizabeth I, Queen of England.  WPE

O Friend! I Know Not Which Way I Must Look.  Wordsworth. BBGO; VoPo
(Written in London, September, 1802.)  MBPR

O friends! who have accompanied thus far.  Walter Savage Landor.  GBL

O Friendship! Friendship! the shell of Aphrodite.  Walter Savage Landor.  GBL

Oh, Frog Prince, Frog Prince.  The Princess Addresses the Frog Prince.  Elizabeth Brewster.  MMD

Oh, Froggie went a'courtin' and he did ride. Froggie Went a Courtin'. *Unknown.* BLSo

Oh Galuppi, Baldassaro, this is very sad to find! A Toccata of Galuppi's. Robert Browning. NOBE; PAIC

O generation of the thoroughly smug. Salutation. Ezra Pound. HeIP; NOBA; PiAm; VGW

Oh Genevieve, I'd give the world. Sweet Genevieve. George Cooper. BLSH; BLSo; PSoN

O gentle, gentle land. Night Sowing. David Campbell. MAuV

O gentle sleep! do they belong to thee. To Sleep. Wordsworth. MBPR

"Oh, Georgie Wedlock is my name." Georgie Wedlock. *Unknown.* AmFP

Oh gin I were a doo. Gin I Were a Doo. *Unknown.* GBP

O Gin My Love Were Yon Red Rose. *Unknown.* GBP; SLP

Oh, give me a home, where the buffalo roam. Home on the Range. *Unknown.* BLSH; BLSo

Oh, Give Me the Hills. *Unknown.* AmFP

Oh, give us pleasure in the flowers today. A Prayer in Spring. Robert Frost. SoSe

Oh, go to old Ireland and then you will know. Go to Old Ireland. *Unknown.* AmFP

O God, in the dream the terrible horse began. The Dream. Louise Bogan. MAT; SBG

O God! O Montreal! Samuel Butler. FaBoCo

O God, O Venus, O Mercury, patron of thieves. The Lake Isle. Ezra Pound. FaBoCo

Oh, God of dust and rainbows, help us see. Epigram. Langston Hughes. SoSe

Oh God, she said. Song My. Susan Griffin. NMM

O Goddess! hear these tuneless numbers, wrung. Ode to Psyche. Keats. InPS; MBPR; NOBE; PPP

O golden tongued romance, with serene lute! On Sitting Down to Read King Lear Once Again. Keats. MBPR

Oh! Good, good, good, my Lord. What more love yet. Edward Taylor. Preparatory Meditations: Second Series, CXII. NOBA

"O good Lord Judge, and sweet Lord Judge." The Maid Freed From the Gallows. *Unknown.* ECBV

"Oh, hangman, hangman, slacken your rope." The Sycamore Tree. *Unknown.* AmFP

O happy [or happie] dames, that may embrace. Complaint of the Absence of Her Lover Being upon the Sea. Earl of Surrey. AAS; GBL; NOBE

O Happy Day, *with music.* Philip Doddridge. BLSH

O, happy is the craw. The Lammermuir Lilt. Forbes Macgregor. MIS

Oh happy shades—to me unblest. The Shrubbery. William Cowper. NOBE

Oh, hark the dogs are barking, love. The Banks of the Condamine. *Unknown.* GBP; PeBB

O have ye na heard o the fause Sakelde? Kinmont Willie. *Unknown.* PeBB

O have you caught the tiger? A. E. Housman. SpRo

Oh, have you heard de lates'. De Ballit of de Boll Weevil. *Unknown.* NOBA

"Oh, have you heard the gallant news." Stephen Vincent Benét. *Fr.* Western Star. AIW

Oh, he was old and he was spare. The Swagman. C. J. Dennis. ECBV

O hear a pensive prisoner's prayer. The Mouse's Petition. Anna Laetitia Barbauld. OxBChV

O Heart! the equal poise of love's both parts. Richard Crashaw. *Fr.* The Flaming Heart. OBP

"Oh hell, what do mine eyes." Milton by Firelight. Gary Snyder. CAPP; ConAP; InPK; InPS; PPP

O helpless few in my country. The Rest. Ezra Pound. NoAM; NOBA

Oh he's God. God Don't Never Change. *Unknown.* BluL

O hideous little bat, the size of snot. The Fly. Karl Shapiro. CoPAm; NoAM; NowV; PBMP

O Holy Ghost, whose temple I. John Donne. *Fr.* A Litany. SCP-1

Oh how comely it is and how reviving. Milton. *Fr.* Samson Agonistes. BoReV; NOBE; SCP-1

Oh, how I love, on a fair summer's eve. Keats. MBPR

O how this sullen, careless world. The Idiot. John Ashbery. *Fr.* Two Sonnets. VGW

O hurry where by water among the trees. The Ragged Wood. W. B. Yeats. GBL

O hush thee, my baby, thy sire was a knight. Lullaby of an Infant Chief. Sir Walter Scott. OxBChV

Oh, I am a Texas cowboy, just off the Texas plains. The Texas Cowboy. *Unknown.* AmFP

Oh, I am the living God. Novus Ordo Seclorum. Grace Cavalieri. AATT

Oh I do love thee, meek Simplicity! To Simplicity. Samuel Taylor Coleridge. *Fr.* Sonnets Attempted in the Manner of Contemporary Writers. Epi

O I forbid you, maidens a'. Tam Lin. *Unknown.* AIW; Epi; NOBE; PeBB

Oh, I had a bird and the bird pleased me. The Barnyard. *Unknown.* AmFP

O I had a future. I Had a Future. Patrick Kavanagh. BIrV; NoAM

Oh, I never had but one true love. The Unquiet Grave. *Unknown.* AmFP

O I remember in Duncan's Mills. Kato's Poem. David Kherdian. FAF

Oh! I vu'st know'd o' my true love. Heedless o' My Love. William Barnes. GBL

Oh, I was born in Mobile town. I've Been Workin' on the Railroad. *Unknown.* BLSH

O I will sing to you a sang. The Clerk's Twa Sons O Owsenford. *Unknown.* PeBB

Oh, I Wish I Were Single Again. *Unknown.* AmFP

Oh, I wonder where my lost Johnny's gone. Lost Johnny. *Unknown.* AmFP

O if all the young maidens was blackbirds and thrushes. Blackbirds and Thrushes. *Unknown.* GBP

Oh I'm being eaten by a boa constrictor. Boa Constrictor. Shel Silverstein. CaYB

Oh, I'm goin' to sing a song, and I won't detain you long. How Do You Do, *Alabama!* Fred. Wilson. AIW

Oh, I'm gonna get me a religion. Preachin' the Blues. *Unknown.* BluL

Oh, in the merry month of May. Bonny Barbara Allan. *Unknown.* AmFP

O It's Nice to Get Up in, the Slipshod Mucous Kiss. E. E. Cummings. Epi

Oh, It's Nine Years Ago I Was Digging in the Land. *Unknown.* AmFP

Oh, I've got no use for the women. I've Got No Use for the Women. *Unknown.* AmFP

O jay betide the dear wold mill. Naighbour Playmeates. William Barnes. VPC

O Jean Baptiste, pourquoi. Pourquoi? *Unknown.* ECBV

O Jean, my Jean, when the bell ca's the congregation. Tam I' the Kirk. Violet Jacob. GBL; SLP

O Jellon Grame sat in Silver Wood. Jellon Grame. *Unknown.* PeBB

O Jenny, don't sobby! vor I shall be true. A Zong. William Barnes. BoLoP

O Joy of Love's Renewing. Andrew Lang. SLP

O Joyes! Infinite sweetness! with what flowres. *See* O joys! Infinite sweetness! with what flowers.

Oh, Joyous House. Richard Janzen. AKE

O joys! Infinite sweetness! with what flowers. The Morning-Watch. Henry Vaughan. BoReV; GrRo; MetP; SCP-1

O King of the Friday. *Unknown, tr. fr. Irish by* Douglas Hyde. BIrV

O kiss me yet again, O kiss me over. Sonnet. Louise Labé. *tr. by* Frederic Prokosch. LoAs

O know you what I have done. The Brother. Thomas Hardy. AIW

O! Lady dear, fair is thy noon. The Song. James Hogg. *Fr.* The Queen's Wake. SLP

O Lady Moon. Christina Rossetti. Moon (Lady Moon.) OxBChV

O lady, rock never your young son young. Young Hunting. *Unknown.* PeBB

O, land of mud and mist, where man is wet and shivers. Such Is Holland! Petrus Augustus de Genestet, *tr. by* Adriaan Barnouw. POL

Oh last Thursday morning while playing at ball. Willie. *Unknown.* AmFP

Oh Lawd have mussy now upon us. Blessing without Company. *Unknown.* BPo; POL

Oh Leaden heeld. Lord, give, forgive I pray. Edward Taylor. *Fr.* Preparatory Meditations: Second Series, I. PiAm

Oh leave his body broken on the rocks. On a Dying Boy. William Bell. WIF

Oh let the gentlewoman have the wall. Samuel Rowlands. *Fr.* The Letting of Humour's Blood in the Head-Vein. TVS

O let us howl some heavy note. John Webster. *Fr.* The Duchess of Malfi. SCP-2

O life, O radiance, love, delight. Epilogue. Christopher Brennan. *Fr.* The Burden of Tyre. MAuV

O listen for a moment, lads. Jim Jones at Botany Bay. *Unknown.* GBP; PeBB

O Little Town of Bethlehem, *with music.* Phillips Brooks. BLSH

O Living Always, Always Dying. Walt Whitman. NOBA

O living pine, be still! Sleep. Yvor Winters. POL

O lonely bay of Trinity. The Cable Hymn. Whittier. PiAm

O lonely workman, standing there. In the Moonlight. Thomas Hardy. NoAM

Oh look outside the window. Outside of a Small Circle of Friends. Phil Ochs. NowV

Oh Lord Cozens Hardy. Lord Cozens Hardy. John Betjeman. OxBTC

O Lord, I been a-working. Trifling Women. *Unknown.* AmFP

O Lord in me there lieth nought. Psalm CXXXIX: Domine, Probasti. Countess of Pembroke. WPE

O Lord, it was all night. Sun. James Dickey. CAPP

O Lord, our Lord, how excellent is thy name. Psalm VIII, Bible, *O.T.* AKE; PBMP

O Lord, we come this morning. Listen, Lord—a Prayer. James Weldon Johnson. BPo

Oh lordy, lord, oh lordy, lord. Worried Life Blues. *Unknown.* AmFP

O Love, be fed with apples while you may. Sick Love. Robert Graves. BoLoP; NoAM; NOBE

O Love, bringer of fire. Aut Neutrum . . . Vel Duos. Rufinus Domesticus, *tr. by* Dudley Fitts. OLR

O love, how thou art tired out with rhyme! Epigraph to the Theme of Love. Margaret Cavendish, Duchess of Newcastle. SCP-2

O, Love, love, love! Love is Like a Dizziness. James Hogg. SLP

O love, love, love! O withering might! Fatima. Tennyson. GBL

Oh! Love, that stronger art than wine. Song. Aphra Behn. *Fr.* The Lucky Chance. WPE

O Love That Wilt Not Let Me Go, *with music.* George Matheson. BLSH

O love, turn from the unchanging sea, and gaze. October. William Morris. *Fr.* The Earthly Paradise. VPC

O lovely O most charming pug. A Sonnet. Marjory Fleming. FaBoCo

O lovely pussy! O pussy my love. Love Song. Edward Lear. *Fr.* The Owl and the Pussy-cat. PCat

Oh, Lovely Rock. Robinson Jeffers. NoAM

O lovers' eyes are sharp to see. The Maid of Neidpath. Sir Walter Scott. SLP

Oh Lucky Jim. *Unknown.* GBP

O, lucky poet tone-deaf. Poet. Conrad Hilberry. PPoD

O luely, luely, cam she in. The Tryst [*or* Trysting Place]. William Soutar. BoLoP; SLP

O lusty May with Flora quene. May Poem. *Unknown.* SLP

O luxury! Thou curst by Heaven's decree. Goldsmith. *Fr.* The Deserted Village. BIrV

O Lyric Love. Winfield Townley Scott. VGW

O madam, I will give to you the keys of Canterbury. The Keys of Canterbury. *Unknown.* AmFP

O maister deer and fader reverent! Lament for Chaucer and Gower. Thomas Hoccleve. *Fr.* De Regimine Principum. OxBM

Oh, make me, sphere-descended Queen. A Wykehamist's Address to Learning. P. N. Shuttleworth. FaBoCo

"Oh, Mammy, Mammy, now I'm married." Will the Weaver. *Unknown.* AmFP

O Man Unkind. *Unknown.* OxBM

Oh, many a day have I made good ale in the glen. The Outlaw of Loch Lene. *Unknown, tr. by* Jeremiah Joseph Callanan. BIrV; GBL; PFIr

O many-petaled light where. Lament of My Father, Lakota. Paula Gunn Allen. VW

Oh, Mary and the Baby, sweet Lamb. Mary and the Baby, Sweet Lamb. *Unknown.* AmFP

O Mary Hamilton to the kirk is gane. Mary Hamilton. *Unknown.* NOBE

Oh, Mary, this London's a wonderful sight. The Mountains of Mourne. Percy French. PFIr

O Mary's lovelier than anything that grows. Prisoner's Song. Horace Gregory. OLR

O May I Join the Choir Invisible. "George Eliot." PFD

Oh, meet me tonight in the moonlight. New Jail. *Unknown.* AmFP

"O 'Melia, my dear, this does everything crown!" The Ruined Maid. Thomas Hardy. BoLoP; HeIP; InPK; OPB; OxBTC; PPoD; PPoe; WIF

O Memory, could I but loose thee now. Lindamira's Complaint. Mary Sidney Wroth, Countess of Montgomery. *Fr.* Urania. WPE

O merciful God, hear this our request. A Prayer to Be Said When Thou Goest to Bed. Francis Seager. OxBChV

O might/ I but touch. On the Daughter of Lykambes. Archilochos, *tr. by* Jonathan Cott. RRA

O mighty mind, in whose deep stream this age. Fragment: To Byron. Shelley. MBPR

O mighty-mouth'd inventor of harmonies. Milton. Tennyson. Epi; PAIC

Ohhhhhhh Mister Charlie your rolling mill is burning down. Mister Charlie. *Unknown.* BluL

O mistress mine, where are you roaming?  Feste's Song [or Sweet-and-Twenty].  Shakespeare.  *Fr.* Twelfth Night, II, iii.  BoLoP; GBL; GrRo; HeIP; InPS; NOBE; OLR

Oh, Molly, oh, Molly, I've told you before.  Red Whiskey.  *Unknown.*  AmFP

Oh Moon, discreetly worshipped by our sires.  The Injured Moon.  Baudelaire, *tr. by* Robert Lowell.  Moon

O Moon, When I Gaze on Thy Beautiful Face.  *Unknown.*  InPK

O mortal Man, who livest here by toil.  The Castle of Indolence, Canto I.  James Thomson.  LAuP

Oh mother,/ here in your lap.  Mothers.  Anne Sexton.  IPWM

Oh, Mother, I shall be married to Mr. Punchinello.  Mr. Punchinello.  *Unknown.*  ECBV

Oh mother my mouth is full of stars.  Song of the Dying Gunner A.A.1.  Charles Causley.  AIW

O muse who sangest late another's pain.  Monody on a Tea-Kettle.  Samuel Taylor Coleridge.  MBPR

Oh, Musgrove, he persuaded me.  Musgrove.  *Unknown.*  AmFP

O my aged Uncle Arly.  Incidents in the Life of My Uncle Arly.  Edward Lear.  OBP

O My America.  D. M. Thomas.  TwMBP

O My Belly.  *Unknown.*  GBP; POL

Oh! my boat can swiftly float.  The Queen of Connemara.  Francis A. Fahy.  PFIr

O My Bonny, Bonny May.  *Unknown.*  GBP

O my brother I heard u.  Before/ and After.  Jewel C. Latimore.  JB

O my dark Rosaleen.  Dark Rosaleen.  *Unknown, at. to* Owen Roe MacWard, *tr. by* James Clarence Mangan.  BIrV; LoAs; PFIr

Oh, My Darling Clementine.  *Unknown, at. to* Percy Montross.  AIW; PSoN, *with music*
(Clementine.)  AmFP; BLSo, *with music*

O my first love! You are in my life forever.  Of My First Love.  "Hugh MacDiarmid."  SLP

Oh, my golden slippers am laid away.  Oh, Dem Golden Slippers.  James A. Bland.  PSoN

O, My Heart Is Woe!  *Unknown.*  BoReV
(My Heart Is Woe.)  OxBM

O my life is so simple and the world.  The Fiddlehead.  David McFadden.  NeAC

O my love/ The pretty towns.  Kenneth Patchen.  VGW

O, My Luve Is Like a Red, Red Rose.  Burns.  *See* Red, Red Rose, A.

Oh my name it is Benjamin Bones.  The Ballad of Benjamin Bones.  Christopher Ward.  BTTM

Oh, my name it is Sam Hall, it is Sam Hall.  Sam Hall.  *Unknown.*  PeBB

Oh My People I Remember.  Wendy Rose.  CDW

O my songs.  Coda.  Ezra Pound.  NOBA

O my thoughts' sweet food, my only owner.  Lady My Treasure.  Sir Philip Sidney.  GBL

Oh never in this hard world was such an absurd.  Nesting Time.  Douglas Stewart.  BoAnP

O! Never say that I was false of heart.  Sonnets, CIX.  Shakespeare.  NOBE

O Night! O jealous Night, repugnant to my pleasures!  To Night.  *Unknown.*  Moon

Oh nimber, nimber Will-o!  Chuck Will's Widow Song.  *Unknown.*  BPo

Oh No.  Robert Creeley.  InPK

Oh no more, no more! too late.  Love's Martyrs.  John Ford.  *Fr.* The Broken Heart, IV, iii.  GBL; NOBE

"Oh, now I've come back to you, Mother."  The Cripple for Life; or, The Poor Volunteer.  *Unknown.*  AmFP

O now you come in rut.  To Frighten a Storm.  Gladys Cardiff.  CDW

O nuclear wind, when wilt thou blow.  Paul Dehn.  SpRo

Oh - ohh/ Smokestack lightnin'.  Smokestack Lightnin'.  *Unknown.*  BluL

Oh Oh Blues.  *Unknown.*  BluL

Oh—oh: death is awful.  Death Is Awful.  *Unknown.*  BluL

O ole Zip Coon he is a larned skoler.  Zip Coon.  *Unknown.*  PSoN

Oh, on an early morning I think I shall live forever!  Poem in Three Parts.  Robert Bly.  CAPP; ConAP; NOBA

Oh, once I lived in Cottonwood and owned a little farm.  Once I Lived in Cottonwood.  *Unknown.*  AmFP

Oh, once I was happy but now I'm forlorn.  The Man on the Flying Trapeze.  George Leybourne.  BLSH; BLSo

O only Source of all our light and life.  Qui Laborat, Orat.  Arthur Hugh Clough.  VPC

Oh, open the door, my hinnie, my heart.  The Padda Song.  *Unknown.*  GBP

"O opportunity! thy guilt is great."  An Outcry upon Opportunity.  Shakespeare.  *Fr.* The Rape of Lucrece.  NOBE

Oh our Mother the Earth oh our Father the Sky.  Song of the Sky Loom.  *Unknown, tr. by* Herbert J. Spinden.  TSWA

O Paddy, dear, and did you hear the news that's going 'round?  The Wearing of [or Wearin' o'] the Green.  *Unknown.*  AIW; BLSH; BTTM; GBP

"O palace, whilom crown of houses all."  The Complaint of Troilus.  Chaucer.  *Fr.* Troilus and Criseyde.  NOBE

O parent of each lovely Muse.  Ode to Fancy.  Joseph Warton.  PAIC

"O Passenger, pray list and catch."  The Levelled Churchyard.  Thomas Hardy.  OBP

O peace! and dost thou with thy presence bless.  On Peace.  Keats.  MBPR

O, Pioneers!  John Peale Bishop.  VGW

O, po' sinner, O, now is yo' time.  What Yo' Gwine to Do When Yo' Lamp Burn Down?  *Unknown.*  BPo

O poet strutting from the sandbagged portal.  As One Non-Combatant to Another.  George Orwell.  OxBTC

O prairie mother, I am one of your boys.  Finale.  Carl Sandburg.  *Fr.* Prairie.  ANTL

O praise God in his holiness: praise him.  Psalm CL, Bible, *O.T.*  RAE

Oh, Promise Me, *with music.*  Clement Scott.  BLSH; BLSo; FSN

Oh, pure is the poppy on the prairie.  Melody for Lute and Ocarina.  Morris Bishop.  ECBV

O rare circle.  Americana XV: Simplicity.  Carl Rakosi.  InPS

O rare Harry Parry.  Harry Parry.  *Unknown.*  GBP

O reapers and gleaners.  Harvest Song.  Joseph Campbell.  OFD

O rich red wheat! thou wilt not long defer.  To a Red-Wheat Field.  Charles Tennyson Turner.  VPC

Oh Roberta honey where you been so long.  Roberta.  *Unknown.*  BluL

O, Rose, thou art sick!  The Sick Rose.  Blake.  *Fr.* Songs of Experience.  BoLoP; HeIP; InPK; InPS; LAuP; MBPR; NOBE; PAIC; PPP

O ruddier than the cherry.  Song.  John Gay.  *Fr.* Acis and Galatea.  NOBE

O ruined father dead, long sweetly rotten.  For the Word Is Flesh.  Stanley Kunitz.  VGW

Oh, San-ty Ana won th' day.  Santy Ana.  *Unknown.*  AIW

O saw ye bonnie [or bonie] Lesley.  Bonnie Lesley.  Burns.  NOBE; SLP

Oh say! can you see, by the dawn's early light.  The Star-spangled Banner.  Francis Scott Key.  BLSH; BLSo; BTTM

Oh, Say, Mr. Toffler.  Mira Fish.  FAF

O, Say My Jolly Fellow.  *Unknown.*  AIW

O say, what is that thing called light. The Blind Boy. Colley Cibber. OxBChV

O scapegoats! How you grew chaste. Poem for my Hands. Carole Oles. NPW

O sea born and obscene. An Invocation to the Goddess. David Wright. NoAM

Oh sharp diamond my mother! Christmas Eve. Anne Sexton. RiTi

Oh, she walked unaware of her own increasing beauty. She Walked Unaware. Patrick MacDonogh. BoLoP; PFIr

"O she was the handsome corpse," he said. Moloney Remembers the Resurrection of Kate Finucane. Brendan Kennelly. PoTa

Oh, Shenandoah, I long to hear you. Shenandoah [or Across the Wide Missouri]. *Unknown.* BLSH; BLSo

O shut your bright eyes that mine must endanger. At the Manger Mary Sings. W. H. Auden. *Fr.* For the Time Being. BoReV

"Oh, sick I am to see you, will you never let me be?" The New Mistress. A. E. Housman. SoSe

Oh, silver tree! Jazzonia. Langston Hughes. CoPAm

Oh, sing a song of phosphates. Rhyme for a Chemical Baby. Joseph Cook. SpRo

Oh! sing unto my roundelay [or O! Synge untoe mie roundelaie]. The Minstrel's Song. Thomas Chatterton. *Fr.* Aella. LoAs; NOBE; OBP

O singer of Persephone! Theocritus. Oscar Wilde. NOBE

Oh, sister Phoebe, how merry were we. Tom Jones's Plum Tree. *Unknown.* AmFP

Oh, sleep forever in the Latmian cave. Edna St. Vincent Millay. NoAM

O sleepy city of reeling wheelchairs. The Wheelchair Butterfly. James Tate. NoAM

O small-feac'd flow'r that now dost bloom. The Water Crowvoot. William Barnes. VPC

O soft embalmer of the still midnight. To Sleep. Keats. MBPR; OBP

"O soldier, O soldier, won't you marry me now." Soldier, Won't You Marry Me? *Unknown.* AmFP; OLR

O Sole Mio, *with music.* Eduardo di Capua, *tr. fr. Italian by* James Morehead. BLSH

O solitude! if I must with thee dwell. Keats. MBPR

O Sorrow, Sorrow, say where dost thou dwell? Thomas Dekker. *Fr.* The Noble Soldier. SCP-2

Oh, Stormy's dead an' gone to rest. Stormalong. *Unknown.* AIW

O suitably-attired-in-leather-boots. Fragment of a Greek Tragedy. A. E. Housman. SpRo

Oh! Susanna, *with music.* Stephen Collins Foster. BLSH; BLSo; PSoN

O Sweet Spontaneous Earth. E. E. Cummings. NoAM; PAIC

O sweetheart, hear you. James Joyce. GBL

O Sylvia, Sylvia. Sylvia's Death. Anne Sexton. WBN

O! Synge untoe mie roundelaie. *See* Oh! sing unto my roundelay.

O. T.'s Blues. Waring Cuney. MAT

O Taste and See. Denise Levertov. PiAm; PPP

Oh, Teddy wants a nine-dollar shawl. I Wish I Was a Mole in the Ground. *Unknown.* AmFP

O Tell Me How to Woo Thee. Robert Graham. SLP

Oh, tell me the reason I sorrow. The Lorelei. Heine. BLSH

O terrible is the highest thing. Kenneth Patchen. VGW

O Terry why is sex so quick. Ruth Herschberger. POL

O, That I Had Some Secret Place. *Unknown.* AmFP

Oh, that last day in Lucknow fort! The Relief of Lucknow. Robert Traill Spence Lowell. BTTM; PoTa

Oh that moon is going down, baby. Moon Going Down. *Unknown.* BluL

Oh that my lungs could bleat like butter'd pease. Odd But True. *Unknown.* FaBoCo

Oh that my soul a marrow-bone might seize! Sonnet Found in a Deserted Mad-House. *Unknown.* FaBoCo

Oh! that 'twere possible. Tennyson. *Fr.* Maud, Pt. II, iv. BoLoP; NOBE

Oh, the boll weevil is a little black bug. The Boll Weevil Song. *Unknown.* BLSo

Oh, the bosses' tricks of '76. Two-Cent Coal. *Unknown.* AmFP

O the cuckoo she's a pretty bird. The Cuckoo. *Unknown.* GBP

O the French are on the sea. The Shan Van Vocht. *Unknown.* GBP

Oh, the full-back bows to the cheering crowd. To the Men Who Hold the Line. W. F. Barron. SPo

O the goose and the gander walk'd over the green. The Goose and the Gander. *Unknown.* GBP

O, the grand old Duke of York. Mother Goose. GBP; MG

Oh! The King's gane gyte. Cophetua. "Hugh MacDiarmid." POL

Oh, the moonlight's fair tonight along the Wabash. On the Banks of the Wabash. Paul Dresser. BLSH

Oh! the night that I struck New York. The Bowery. Charles Hale Hoyt. FSN

Oh, the old gray mare, she ain't what she used to be. Old Gray Mare. *Unknown.* GBP

O the opal and the sapphire of that wandering western sea. Beeny Cliff. Thomas Hardy. LoAs

Oh, the outlook isn't pretty for the Orioles today. Ode to the New York Mets. John Vliet Lindsay. SPo

O the Raggedy Man! He works fer Pa. The Raggedy Man. James Whitcomb Riley. OxBChV

Oh, the revenue men is riding. Revenue Man Blues. *Unknown.* BluL

Oh! the time that is past. *Unknown.* BoLoP

Oh, the train's off the track. The Train Is off the Track. *Unknown.* AmFP

O the vexation. Lost Contact. William Cole. POL

Oh the white seagull, the wild seagull. The Seagull. Mary Howitt. OxBChV

O the wonder man rides his space ship. African Things. Victor Hernández Cruz. SA

Oh! There are spirits of the air. To ——. Shelley. MBPR

O there is blessing in this gentle breeze. The Prelude; or, Growth of a Poet's Mind. Wordsworth. MBPR

Oh there was a woman and she was a widow. Flowers in the Valley. *Unknown.* ECBV; OLR

Oh, there was a youth and a noble youth. The Bailiff's Daughter of Islington. *Unknown.* AmFP

Oh, this is the tale of John Cherokee. John Cherokee. *Unknown.* GBP

O thou bright sun! beneath the dark blue line. Evening: To Harriet. Shelley. MBPR

O thou by Nature taught. Ode to Simplicity. William Collins. LAuP; NOBE

O thou great Power, in whom I move. A Hymn to My God in a Night of My Late Sickness. Sir Henry Wotton. BoReV

O Thou my monster, Thou my guide. Prayer in Mid-Passage. Louis MacNeice. BoReV

O thou that from thy mansion. For My Funeral. A. E. Housman. BoReV

O thou that [or who] in the heavens does [or dost] dwell! Holy Willie's Prayer [or The Prayer of Holy Willie]. Burns. BoReV; Epi; ESaP; InPS; LAuP; OBP; PPP

O thou that sit'st upon a throne. A Song to David. Christopher Smart. BoReV; LAuP; NOBE

O thou that swing'st upon the waving hair. The Grasshopper. Richard Lovelace. NOBE; PPP; SCP-2

O thou, the friend of man assign'd. Ode to Pity. William Collins. LAuP

O thou undaunted daughter of desires! Upon the Book and Picture of the Seraphical Saint Teresa. Richard Crashaw. *Fr.* The Flaming Heart. BoReV; NOBE

O thou, wha in the heavens does dwell. *See* O thou that in the heavens does dwell!

O thou, whatever title suit thee! Address to the Deil. Burns. LAuP

O thou who didst furnish. Hymn to Moloch. Ralph Hodgson. OxBTC

O thou, who lately closed my eyes. A Morning Hymn. Christopher Smart. OxBChV

O thou, who passest thro' our vallies in. To Summer. Blake. LAuP; MBPR

O thou, who plumed with strong desire. The Two Spirits: An Allegory. Shelley. MBPR; Prf

O thou, who sit'st a smiling bride. Ode to Mercy. William Collins. LAuP

O thou whom Poetry abhors. On Elphinston's Translation of Martial. Burns. FaBoCo

O thou whose face hath felt the winter's wind. What the Thrush Said. Keats. MBPR; OBP

O thou! whose fancies from afar are brought. To H. C. Wordsworth. MBPR

O thou, whose radiant eyes and beamy smile. Sonnet to Harriet on Her Birthday. Shelley. MBPR

O thou, with dewy locks, who lookest down. To Spring. Blake. LAuP; MBPR; PPP

Oh! 'tis of a bold major a tale I'll relate. A Longford Legend. *Unknown.* PoTa

Oh to be at Crowdieknowe. Crowdieknowe. "Hugh MacDiarmid." InPS; NoAM

Oh, to be in England. Home-Thoughts, from Abroad. Robert Browning. HeIP; IPWM; NOBE; OBP; PBMP; VoPo

O to be "in the news" again—now as fashion runs. Sonnets to Be Written from Prison. Robert Adamson. CAAP

O to break loose, like the chinook. Waking Early Sunday Morning. Robert Lowell. NOBA

Oh, to those who know no better. That Little Lump of Coal. *Unknown.* AmFP

O, to vex me contraries meet in one. Holy Sonnets, XIX. John Donne. BoReV

Oh 'twas a poor country, in autumn it was bare. The Poor, Poor Country. John Shaw Neilson. MAuV

O Unicorn among the cedars. W. H. Auden. *Fr.* New Year Letter. BoReV; NoAM

O Waly, Waly, up the Bank. *Unknown. See* Waly, Waly.

O, we loved long and happily, God knows! The Custom of the World. Louis Simpson. BoLoP; SFF

Oh wearisome condition of humanity! Chorus Sacerdotum. Fulke Greville. *Fr.* Mustapha. NOBE; PPP

Oh well it's our Father who art in Heaven. You Shall. *Unknown.* BluL

"O well's me o my gay goss-hawk." The Gay Goshawk. *Unknown, at. to* Anna Gordon Brown. PeBB; WPE

Oh were I at the moss house, where the birds do increase. The Streams of Bunclody. *Unknown.* BIrV

O, Were I on Parnassus Hill Burns. SLP

O Were My Love Yon Lilac Fair. Burns. GBL

O, Wert Thou in the Cauld Blast. Burns. HeIP; NOBE

O Western Wind. *Unknown.* SLP; SpRo

O wha my babie-clouts will buy. The Rantin Dog the Daddie O't. Burns. PPP

"O whare are ye gaun?" The False Knight Upon the Road. *Unknown.* GBP; PeBB

O Wha's the Bride? "Hugh MacDiarmid." BoLoP; NoAM; TwMBP

Oh, what a dreary place this was when first the Mormons found it. St. George. Charlie Walker. AmFP

O what a lovely poem, Mrs. Jones. The Teacher of Poetry. William Packard. PPoD

O what a physical effect it has on me. In Love with You. Kenneth Koch. CAPP

Oh! What a thing is man? Lord, who am I? Edward Taylor. *Fr.* Preparatory Meditations: First Series, XXXVIII. NOBA; PiAM

Oh, what an effort it is. It is True. Federico García Lorca, *tr. by* Harriet de Onís. OLR

O what are heroes, prophets, men. Pan. Emerson. PiAm

O [*or* Ah,] what can ail thee, knight-at-arms. La Belle Dame sans Merci. Keats. AIW; AnMo; Epi; InPK; InPS; IPWM; LoAs; MBPR; NOBE; OLR; PAIC; PBMP; PPoD; PPoe; Prf

O what could be more nice. Light Listened. Theodore Roethke. AnMo; NowV

O What Is That Sound. W. H. Auden. AIW; MPo; SS (Quarry, The.) MiP

"Oh, what will you give me?" say the sad bells of Rhymney. Bells of Rhymney. Idris Davies *and* Pete Seeger. PoRo

"Oh, what's that stain on your shirt sleeve?" Edward. *Unknown.* AmFP

Oh! what's the matter? what's the matter? Goody Blake, and Harry Gill. Wordsworth. MBPR

O What's the Rhyme to Porringer. *Unknown.* GBP

Oh, when I come to die. Give Me Jesus. *Unknown.* BPo

Oh when I think of my long-suffering race. Enslaved. Claude McKay. BPo

Oh, When I Was in Love with You. A. E. Housman. BoLoP; MiP; OLR

Oh, when I was single, oh then, oh then! I Wish I Were Single Again. *Unknown.* AmFP

Oh, when I'm in trouble. Do, Lord, Remember Me. *Unknown.* AmFP

O, when our clergy, at the dreadful day. On Those That Deserve It. Francis Quarles. BoReV

Oh, when shall I see Jesus. Ecstasy. John Leland. AmFP

Oh! when shall the grave hide for ever my sorrow? To Caroline. Byron. MBPR

"Oh, when we going to marry, to marry, to marry." Buffalo Boy. *Unknown.* AmFP

"Oh whence do you come, my dear friend, to me." The Poor Ghost. Christina Rossetti. GBL

O Where Are You Going? W. H. Auden. *Fr.* The Orators. NOBE; OBP

"Oh, where are you going, my kind old husband." The Best Old Fellow in the World. *Unknown.* AmFP

"Oh, where are you going, my little maiden fair." The Milkmaid. *Unknown.* AmFP

"O where are you going?" said reader to rider. O Where Are You Going? W. H. Auden. *Fr.* The Orators. NOBE; OBP

O where are you going? says Milder to Melder. The Cutty Wren. *Unknown.* GBP

Oh, where do you come from. Little Raindrops. Jane Euphemia Browne. OxBChV

"O where ha[e] you been, Lord Randal, my son?" *See* "O where have you been, Lord Randal my son?"

'O where hae ye been, my long, long love. *See* "O where have you been . . ."

"Oh, where have you been, Billy boy, Billy boy?" Billy Boy. *Unknown.* AmFP

"O where have [*or* ha *or* hae] you been, Lord Randal my son?" Lord Randal. *Unknown.* AmFP; HeIP; PAIC; SLP; WIF

Oh, where have you been, my blue-eyed son? A Hard Rain's a-Gonna Fall. Bob Dylan. PoRo

"O where have you [or hae ye] been, my dear, dear [or long, long] love." The Demon [or Daemon] Lover [or James Harris]. *Unknown.* AIW; MAT; PBMP; PeBB; SLP

O where is the dwelling I love the most. Ruth Pitter. LoAs

Oh where, Oh where ish mine little dog gone. Der Deitcher's Dog. Septimus Winner. PSoN

O, where, where are the winter grounds of angels. The Angels. Marguerite Young. WPE

O! Wherefore. Robert Peter. PPoD

Oh! wherefore come ye forth in triumph from the north. The Battle of Naseby. Macaulay. BTTM

O! wherefore pensive heaves that sigh? O! Wherefore. Robert Peter. PPoD

Oh, whisky here, and whisky there. Whisky Johnny. *Unknown.* AmFP

O whisper, O my soul! The afternoon. The Tired Worker. Claude McKay. BPo

O Whistle, and I'll Come to You, My Lad. Burns. InPS (Song: "O whistle, and I'll come to ye, my lad.") BoLoP

"O whither are you faring to, my sweetheart?" The Tryst. Walter de la Mare. AIW

Oh! who is there of us that has not felt. November. Frederick Goddard Tuckerman. NOBA

O who shall, from this dungeon, raise. A Dialogue between the Soul and [the] Body. Andrew Marvell. MetP; PAIC; PPP; SCP-1

"O who will shoe my little feet." The Lass of Roch Royal. *Unknown.* AmFP

"Oh, who will shoe your feet, my love." The Mournful Dove. *Unknown.* AmFP

Oh, who will shoe your pretty little foot. Kenneth Rexroth. AIW

O why do you walk through the field in gloves. To a Fat Lady Seen from the Train. Frances Cornford. SpRo

Oh, why don't I work like other men do? Hallelujah, Bum Again. *Unknown.* GBP

O why was I born with a different face? Blake. POL

O Wilberforce! thou man of black renown. Race. Byron. *Fr.* Don Juan, XIV. OBP

O wild West Wind, thou breath of autumn's being. Ode to the West Wind. Shelley. Epi; FSFS; HeIP; InPS; IPWM; MBPR; NOBE; OBP; PAIC; PBMP; PPoe; PPP; VoPo

Oh, will you wear red? I'll Wear Me a Cotton Dress. *Unknown.* BPo

O wind, rend open the heat. Heat. Hilda Doolittle ("H.D."). *Fr.* The Garden. FSFS; HeIP; InPK; NoAM; PiAm

O Winter! bar thine adamantine doors. To Winter. Blake. MBPR

Oh, with the hunger of the sea, forever born anew. Song. John Hall Wheelock. LoAs

O with what key. Skeleton Key. John Hollander. InPK

O woe, woe,/ People are born and die. Mr. Housman's Message. Ezra Pound. PAIC

O woman of Three Cows, agra! don't let your tongue thus rattle! The Woman of Three Cows. *Unknown, tr. by* James Clarence Mangan. PFIr

O Woman, Shapely As the Swan. *Unknown, tr. fr. Irish by* Padraic Colum. BIrV

O world, I cannot hold thee close enough! God's World. Edna St. Vincent Millay. VoPo

O world invisible, we view thee. In No Strange Land. Francis Thompson. NOBE

O world! O life! O time! A Lament. Shelley. MBPR; NOBE

O ye that put your trust and confidence. A Rueful Lamentation. Sir Thomas More. AAS

O ye wha are sae guid yoursel. Address to the Unco Guid. Burns. NOBE

Oh---Yeah! Sharon Scott. JB

O year, grow slowly. Exquisite, holy. Slow Spring. Katharine Tynan. FSFS

Oh Yes. William Matthews. AmPA

Oh yes/ We got Mr. President Roosevelt. President Roosevelt. *Unknown.* BluL

Oh yesterday I was married, last night I went to bed. The Lowlands of Holland. *Unknown.* AIW

O yet we trust that somehow good. In Memoriam A. H. H., LIV. Tennyson. BoReV; VoPo

O Yonge Freshe Folkes. Chaucer. *See* Love Unfeigned.

O You among Women. F. R. Higgins. BIrV

O you chorus of indolent reviewers. Hendecasyllabics. Tennyson. FaBoCo

O you clouds. Callypso Speaks. Hilda Doolittle ("H. D."). PiAm; RiTi; SBG

Oh, you come along, boys, you listen to my tale. The Old Chisholm Trail. *Unknown.* AmFP

"Oh, you must answer my questions nine." The Devil's Nine Questions. *Unknown.* AmFP

Oh you used to told me you could drive me like a cow. From Now On. *Unknown.* BluL

O, young Lochinvar is come out of the west. Lochinvar. Sir Walter Scott. *Fr.* Marmion, V. AIW; BTTM; ECBV; NOBE; PoTa; SLP

O younge [or yonge] freshe folkes, he or she. Love Unfeigned. Chaucer. *Fr.* Troilus and Criseyde. BoReV; NOBE; OxBM

Oa! hoy! awe! ba! mey! Canedolia. Edwin Morgan. FaBoCo

Oak, The. Tennyson. SoSe

Oak is called the king of trees, The. Trees. Sara Coleridge. OxBChV

Oak leaf fell from the tree, An. The One Leaf. Leslie Norris. LP

Oaks, how subtle and marine, The. Bearded Oaks. Robert Penn Warren. CoPAm; NoAM; NOBA; PiAm

Oath, The. Joseph Beaumont. SCP-2

Oath, The. Allen Tate. NoAM; VGW

Oberon the Fairy Prince, *sel.* Ben Jonson. "Chromis! Mnasil! None appear?" SCP-1

Oberon's Feast. Robert Herrick. SCP-1

Obituary. Kenneth Fearing. VGW

Obituary. Weldon Kees. BoAnP

Object among dreams, you sit here with your shoes off, An. A Girl in a Library. Randall Jarrell. NoAM; NOBA

Objets d'Art. Cynthia Macdonald. NMM; WBN

O'Bruadair. David O'Bruadair, *tr. fr. Irish by* James Stephens. BIrV

Obscene Caller, The. Philip Dacey. AmPA

Obscurely yet most surely called to praise. Praise in Summer. Richard Wilbur. CAPP

Obscurest night involved the sky. The Castaway. William Cowper. HeIP; LAuP; NOBE; PPoe; PPP

Obscuring the hieroglyphs. Poem while Reading *The Naked Lunch* by William Burroughs. Charles Senior. MIS

Obscurity has its tale to tell. Focus. Adrienne Rich. PiAm

Observant of the way she told. Tact. E. A. Robinson. NoAM

Observation, The. Donovan Leitch. GrRo

Observation. Richard Weber. POL

Observation Car. A. D. Hope. NoAM

Observation of Facts. Charles Tomlinson. TwMBP

Obsessions. Denise Levertov. PAIC

Occasion. Roger Pfingston. SFF

Occasional mornings when an early fog. Housewife. Josephine Miles. RiTi

Occupation: Housewife. Phyllis McGinley. *Fr.* I Know a Village. WPE

Occupation: Spinster. Olga Cabral. WBN

Occupational Hazards. David Young. FiCP

Ocean Burial, The, *with music.* Edwin H. Chapin. PSoN

Ocean has not been so quiet for a long while, The. Evening Ebb. Robinson Jeffers. NoAM; PSN

Ocean, mother of all living. Riptide. Marge Piercy. MMD

Och, we shall never want, witch, you and I. We Shall Never Want. Sydney Goodsir Smith. SLP

Och, what was it got me at all that time. The Rachray Man. Moira O'Neill. PFIr

Och! what will we do for linen? What Will We Do for Linen? *Unknown.* GBP

O'Connor the Bad Traveler. Peter Klappert. FiCP

October. William Morris. *Fr.* The Earthly Paradise. VPC

October. Greg Pape. AmPA

October. Edward Thomas. NoAM

October and November. Robert Lowell. MAT

October Dawn. Ted Hughes. TwMBP

October Ghosts. James Wright. CAAP

October is marigold, and yet. October Dawn. Ted Hughes. TwMBP

October Journey. Margaret Walker. PoBA

October nights, wild geese string. The Impulse of October. W. R. Moses. NCSH

October 1954. Kay Boyle. RiTi

October-November. Hart Crane. PSN

October 16: The Raid. Langston Hughes. PoBA

Octobers. Christopher Middleton. TwMBP

Octopus. A. C. Hilton. FaBoCo

Octopus. Sam Reavin. CaYB

Odd But True. *Unknown.* FaBoCo

Odd, friendless boy raised by four aunts, The. Thumb. Philip Dacey. POL

Odd way you comb your hair, The. Lady in a Distant Face. James Welch. AmPA

Ode: "At her fair hands how have I grace entreated." Walter Davison. BoLoP

Ode: Autumn. Thomas Hood. FSFS

Ode: "Bards of passion and of mirth." Keats. MBPR

Ode, An: "High spirited friend." Ben Jonson. PAIC

Ode: "How sleep the brave, who sink to rest." William Collins. *See* How Sleep the Brave.

Ode: Intimations of Immortality from Recollections of Early Childhood. Wordsworth. HeIP; MBPR; NOBE; OBP; PAIC; PBMP; PPoD; PPoe; PPP
  *Sels.* "Land and sea." FSFS
  "Now, while the birds thus sing a joyous song." Prf
  "O joy! that in our embers." Prf

Ode: Of Wit. Abraham Cowley. PAIC

Ode: "Sleep sweetly in your humble graves." Henry Timrod. AmVN; NOBA

Ode: "Spacious firmament on high, The." Joseph Addison. BoReV; HeIP; IPWM

Ode: "We are the music-makers." Arthur O'Shaughnessy. PFIr; WIF

Ode for the American Dead in Korea. Thomas McGrath. VGW

Ode Inscribed to W. H. Channing. Emerson. NOBA; PAIC; PiAm

Ode Occasion'd by the Death of Mr. Thomson. William Collins. LAuP

Ode of Odium on Aquariums. Arthur Guiterman. BoAnP

Ode on a Distant Prospect of Eton College. Thomas Gray. HeIP; LAuP; NOBE; PAIC

Ode on a Grecian Urn. Keats. AnMo; HeIP; InPK; InPS; MBPR; NOBE; OBP; PAIC; PBMP; PPoD; PPoe; PPP; SoSe; WIF

Ode on a Jar of Pickles. Bayard Taylor. SpRo

Ode on Celestial Music. Brian Patten. OxBTC

Ode on His Majesty's Proclamation, Commanding the Gentry to Reside on Their Estates. Sir Richard Fanshawe. *See* Ode, An, upon Occasion of His Majesty's Proclamation in the Year 1630.

Ode on Indolence. Keats. MBPR

Ode on Lust. Frank O'Hara. Epi

Ode on Melancholy. Keats. Epi; InPS; MAT; MBPR; NOBE; OBP; PPP

Ode on St. Cecilia's Day, *sel.* Pope.
  "Furies sink upon their iron beds, The." FaBoCo

Ode on Solitude. Pope. HeIP; IPWM; PAIC; PPoe; Prf (Solitude, an Ode.) Epi; PBMP

Ode on the Death of a Favourite Cat, Drowned in a Tub of Gold Fishes. Thomas Gray. Epi; LAuP; NOBE; PCat; PPP (On a Favorite Cat Drowned in a Tub of Goldfishes.) FaBoCo; PBMP

Ode on the Installation of His Royal Highness Prince Albert. Wordsworth. MBPR

Ode on the Morning of Christ's Nativity. Milton. *See* On the Morning of Christ's Nativity.

Ode on the Pleasure Arising from Vicissitude. Thomas Gray. LAuP

Ode on the Poetical Character. William Collins. LAuP

Ode on the Popular Superstitions of the Highlands of Scotland, An. William Collins. LAuP
  Stormy Hebrides, The, *sel.* NOBE

Ode on the Spring. Thomas Gray. LAuP

Ode Recited at the Harvard Commemoration. James Russell Lowell. NOBA; PiAm

Ode to a Beautiful Woman. Carl Clark. JB

Ode to a Dead Dodge. David McElroy. AmPA

Ode to a Fat Cat. Annabel Farjeon. PCat

Ode to a Model. Vladimir Nabokov. SFF

Ode to a Nightingale. Keats. AnMo; Epi; HeIP; InPK; InPS; IPWM; MBPR; NOBE; OBP; PAIC; PPoe; PPP; SoSe; SpRo; VoPo
  "I cannot see what flowers are at my feet," *sel.* FSFS

Ode to a Skylark. Shelley. *See* To a Skylark.

Ode to a Violin. Luís Omar Salinas. SA

Ode to Anactoria. Sappho, *tr. fr. Greek by* William Ellery Leonard. LoAs

Ode to Apollo. Keats. MBPR

Ode to Duty. Wordsworth. MBPR

Ode to Evening. William Collins. Epi; LAuP; NOBE; OBP; PPP

Ode to Fancy. Joseph Warton. PAIC

Ode to Fanny. Keats. MBPR

Ode to Fear. William Collins. LAuP; PAIC

Ode to Fear. Allen Tate. PAIC

Ode to Himself, An ("Where dost thou careless lie"). Ben Jonson. Epi; NOBE; PAIC; SCP-1

Ode to Joy. Miroslav Holub, *tr. fr. Czech by* Ian Milner *and* George Theiner. BuTh

Ode to Joy. Frank O'Hara. PPP

Ode to Liberty. Shelley. MBPR

Ode to Love, An. Aphra Behn. SCP-2

Ode to Master Anthony Stafford to Hasten Him into the Country, An. Thomas Randolph. NOBE; SCP-2

Ode to Master Endymion Porter, upon His Brother's Death, An. Robert Herrick. SCP-1

Ode to May. Fragment. Keats. *See* Fragment of an Ode to Maia.

Ode to Mercy. William Collins. LAuP

Ode to Mexican Experience. Luís Omar Salinas. SA

Ode to My Socks. Pablo Neruda, tr. fr. Spanish by Robert Bly. Epi

Ode to Naples. Shelley. PAIC

Ode to Napoleon Buonaparte. Byron. MBPR

Ode to Pity. William Collins. LAuP

Ode to Psyche. Keats. InPS; MBPR; NOBE; PPP

Ode to Simplicity. William Collins. LAuP; NOBE

Ode to Spring. Burns. OBP

Ode to the Confederate Dead. Allen Tate. HeIP; NoAM; NOBA

Ode to the Departing Year. Samuel Taylor Coleridge. MBPR

Ode to the Maguire. Eochaidh O'Hussey, tr. fr. Irish by James Clarence Mangan. BIrV

Ode to the New York Mets. John Vliet Lindsay. SPo

Ode to the Poppy. Henrietta Oneil. WPE

Ode to the Rain, An. Samuel Taylor Coleridge. MBPR

Ode to the West Wind. Shelley. Epi; FSFS; HeIP; InPS; IPWM; MBPR; NOBE; OBP; PAIC; PBMP; PPoe; PPP; VoPo

Ode to Tobacco. Charles Stuart Calverley. FaBoCo

Ode to Tranquillity. Samuel Taylor Coleridge. MBPR

Ode to Willem de Kooning. Frank O'Hara. Epi

Ode upon a Question Moved, Whether Love Should Continue Forever? Lord Herbert of Cherbury. NOBE; SCP-2

Ode, An, upon Occasion of His Majesty's Proclamation in the Year 1630. Sir Richard Fanshawe. SCP-2
(Ode on His Majesty's Proclamation, Commanding the Gentry to Reside on Their Estates.) NOBE

Ode Written in the Beginning of the Year 1746. William Collins. See How Sleep the Brave.

Odes, sels. Horace, tr. fr. Latin.
I, 4. Solvitur Acris Hiems, tr. by Louis MacNeice. Epi
I, 5. "What slender youth bedewed with liquid odours" ("Quis multa gracilis"), tr. by Milton. SCP-1
(To Pyrrha.) LoAs
I, 8. "In the name of all the gods, tell me, Lydia, why ("Lydia, dic, per omnes"), tr. by C. E. Bennett. LoAs
I, 23. To Chloe ("Vitas hinnuleo"), tr. by Austin Dobson. LoAs
I, 25. Ribald Romeos Less and Less Berattle ("Parcius iunctas quatiunt fenestras"), tr. by John Frederick Nims. MAT
("Young bloods come round less often now, The.") BoLoP
I, 38. Fie on Eastern Luxury! ("Persicos odi"), tr. by Hartley Coleridge. InPK
(From Horace, tr. by Gerard Manley Hopkins.) InPK
(Preference Declared, The, tr. by Eugene Field.) InPK
(Simplicity, tr. by William Cowper.) InPK
II, 5. "Not yet can she bear the yoke on submissive neck" ("Nondum subacta"), tr. by C. E. Bennett. LoAs
III, 30. This Monument Will Outlast ("Exegi monumentum aere perennius"), tr. by Ezra Pound. Epi
IV, 2. The Praise of Pindar ("Pindarum quisquis studet aemulari"), tr. by Abraham Cowley. Epi; PAIC
IV, 7. "The snow dissolv'd no more is seen" (Diffugere nives"), tr. by Samuel Johnson. LAuP

Odes, sel. Pindar, tr. fr. Greek.
Seventh Olympic Hymn, tr. by Robin Blaser. Epi

Odiham. John Gray. FaBoCo

Odor of Limp Leaves, The. My Daughter. Robert Pack. CoPAm

Odysseus. W. S. Merwin. NOBA

Odysseus/ once I was ready to split. Penelope. Karen Whitehill. NPW

Odysseus was/ ein Sitzriese. Bouzouki Music. Anselm Hollo. TwMBP

Odyssey, The, sel. Homer, tr. by Robert Fitzgerald.
The Sirens' Song, fr. XII. GrRo

Oedipus, sel. Dryden.
Incantation to Oedipus, fr. III, i. OFD

Oedipus. Josephine Miles. WPE

Oedipus at Colonus, sel. Sophocles, tr. fr. Greek.
Colonus' Praise, tr. by W. B. Yeats. Epi

Oedipus Tyrannus; or, Swellfoot the Tyrant. Shelley. MBPR

Oenone and Paris. George Peele. Fr. The Arraignment of Paris. NOBE

O'er the wild gannet's bath. Runilda's Chant. George Darley. Fr. Ethelstan. PFIr

O'er this huge town, rife with intestine wars. Manchester by Night. Mathilde Blind. SBG

Of a pendulum's mildness, with her feet up. A Timepiece. James Merrill. NoAM

Of a Rose, a Lovely Rose. Unknown. OxBM

Of a sudden and sharp I arise from the loam. Where the Mind Meets the Body in Revolt. Helen Wolfert. Fr. Woman Against the Moon. RiTi

Of a' the airts the wind can blaw. I Love My Jean. Burns. LAuP

Of a Woman, Dead Young. Dorothy Parker. SBG

Of all the causes which conspire to blind. Pope. Fr. An Essay on Criticism, Pt. I. PPoD, PPoe

Of all the girls that are so smart. Sally in Our Alley. Henry Carey. BLSo; BoLoP; NOBE

Of all the rides since the birth of time. Skipper Ireson's Ride. Whittier. NOBA

Of all the souls that stand create. Emily Dickinson. LoAs

Of all the tales of human struggle, hear this one from Tennessee. Bryan's Last Battle. Unknown. AmFP

Of all the tales was ever told. Mary Arnold the Female Monster. Unknown. GBP; PeBB

Of all the weathers wind is kind. King Wind. Mark Van Doren. NCSH

Of all the wives as e'er you know. Nancy Lee. Frederick E. Weatherly. BLSH

Of Alphus. John Parkhurst, tr. fr. Latin by Timothe Kendall. SoSe

Of an Heroical Answer of a Great Roman Lady to Her Husband. Sir John Harington. BoLoP

Of Astraea. Sir John Davies. Fr. Hymns of Astraea. PAIC

Of Battel: whereat Michael bid sound. War in Heaven. Milton. Fr. Paradise Lost, VI. OBP

Of Beauty. Sir Richard Fanshawe. BoLoP

Of Being Numerous, sel. George Oppen.
"It is difficult now to speak of poetry." MIT

Of bricks . . . Who built it? Like some crazy balloon. Our Youth. John Ashbery. CAPP; ConAP; VGW

Of bronze and blaze. Emily Dickinson. AmVN

Of Commerce and Society. Geoffrey Hill. PPoe

Of Consolation. Luci Shaw. AATT

Of course I tried to tell him. Poets Hitchhiking on the Highway. Gregory Corso. NoAM

Of course when someone leaves you forever. Back. Angela McCabe. AmPA

Of De Witt Williams on His Way to Lincoln Cemetery. Gwendolyn Brooks. ANTL; CAPP; NoAM; NOBA

Of Eden lost, in ancient days. Rondeau. George Ellis. PAIC

Of Edenhall, the youthful Lord. The Luck of Edenhall. Longfellow. PoTa

Of English Verse. Edmund Waller. OBP

Of every kinne [or everykune] tree, of every kinne tree. The Hawthorn. Unknown. GBP; OxBM

Of Heaven or Hell I have no power to sing. An Apology. William Morris. Fr. The Earthly Paradise. PAIC; VPC

Of Jeoffry, His Cat. Christopher Smart. See For I Will Consider My Cat Jeoffry.

Of Jesu Christ I Sing. *Unknown.* OxBM

Of Kings and Things. Lillian Morrison. NCSH

Of Late. George Starbuck. NowV; VGW

Of Late and Never. John Heywood. PAIC

Of lead and emerald. A Note to Olga (1966). Denise Levertov. CAPP

Of Loose Atoms. Margaret Cavendish, Duchess of Newcastle. SCP-2

Of Loving a Dog. John Heywood. PAIC

Of M, A, R, I,/ Sing I will a new song. M and A, R and I. *Unknown.* OxBM

Of mans first disobedience, and the fruit. Invocation. Milton. *Fr.* Paradise Lost, I. OBP; PAIC

Of Modern Poetry. Wallace Stevens. NoAM; PAIC; WIF

Of My Dear Son, Gervase Beaumont. Sir John Beaumont. NOBE

Of My First Love. "Hugh MacDiarmid." SLP

Of Nelson and the North. Battle of the Baltic. Thomas Campbell. BTTM

Of Neptune's empire let us sing. In Praise of Neptune. Thomas Campion. NOBE

Of 91 Men Leaving an Underground Station. John Daniel. TwMBP

Of Objects Considered as Fortresses in a Baleful Place. Hyam Plutzik. VGW

Of old, when Scarron his companions invited. Retaliation. Goldsmith. ESaP

Of one that is so fair and bright. In Praise of Mary. *Unknown.* BoReV; NOBE; OxBM

Of people running down the street. A Picture. Howard Nemerov. NowV

Of priests we can offer a charmin' variety. Father O'Flynn. Alfred Perceval Graves. PFIr

Of Robert Frost. Gwendolyn Brooks. NoAM; NOBA

Of Suicide. John Berryman. NoAM

Of that world, having returned from it, I may say. Voyage to the Moon. William Dickey. CoPAm; Moon

Of the Boy and Butterfly. John Bunyan. OxBChV

Of the Changes of Life. William Dunbar, *tr. fr. Middle English by* Andrew Glaze. OBP

Of the Child with the Bird on the Bush. John Bunyan. OxBChV

Of the dark past. Ecce Puer. James Joyce. BIrV; NoAM

Of the Elmira Wood. Her Apron through the Trees. Roger Weingarten. AmPA

Of the first paradise there's nothing found. Edmund Waller. *Fr.* On St. James's Park as Lately Improved by His Majesty. SCP-2

Of the Last Verses in the Book. Edmund Waller. MetP; PAIC; SCP-2

    Old Age ("The seas are quiet"), *sel.* NOBE

Of the Moon. Charles Best. *See* Sonnet of the Moon, A.

Of the primeval priests assum'd power. The Book of Urizen. Blake. MBPR

Of the Progress of the Soul; the Second Anniversary, *sels.* John Donne.

    "Think further on thyself, my soul, and think." SCP-1

    "Think then, my soul, that Death is but a groom." BoReV

Of the sleep of Ulro! and of the passage through. Blake. Jerusalem, *ch.* 1. MBPR

Of the three Wise Men. Carol of the Brown King. Langston Hughes. LCL

Of these the false Achitophel was first. Dryden. *Fr.* Absalom and Achitophel, Pt. I. InPS

Of this blot. Spiritus Sanctus. Betty Ruth Bird. AATT

Of this house I know the backwindow. Eyeglasses. Tom Clark. ConAP

Of Treason. Sir John Harington. InPK

    (Treason.) InPK

Of Tyndarus, That Frumped a Gentlewoman. *Unknown, tr. fr. Latin by* Richard Stanyhurst. BIrV

Of waterbirds that in my youth I did admire. The Little Militant. John Shaw Neilson. MAuV

Of your lives and of your love. Love. Pauline Hanson. LoAs

Off Crane's Neck the sun. The Spirit of Wrath. William Heyen. AmPA

Off Highway 106. Cherrylog Road. James Dickey. CoPAm; InPK; InPS

Off that landspit of stony mouth-plugs. Medusa. Sylvia Plath. CAPP

Off the Ground. Walter de la Mare. PoTa

Off the track/ I blew. Phoenix. Carolyn M. Rodgers. JB

Off with your shoes, forget those blues. Walking through the Country. Dennis Provisor. PoRo

Offa's Laws. Geoffrey Hill. Mercian Hymns, XIV. PSN

Offering, The: Part One. Mary Lee, Lady Chudleigh. WPE

Officers' Mess. Gavin Ewart. OxBTC

Offshore Breeze. Milton Acorn. NeAC

Off-shore, by islands hidden in the blood. I, Maximus of Gloucester, to You. Charles Olson. NoAM; NOBA

Oft have I brooded on defeat and pain. Success. Emma Lazarus. SBG

Oft have I heard my lief Corydon. Hexametra Alexis in Laudem Rosamundi. Robert Greene. *Fr.* Greene's Mourning Garment. GBL

Oft have I mused, but now at length I find. A Farewell. Sir Philip Sidney. GBL; NOBE

Oft have I played at cards and dice. The Rantin Laddie. *Unknown.* AmFP

Oft have I seen at some cathedral door. Divina Commedia, I. Longfellow. IPWM; PAIC

Oft have I seen, when that renewing breath. Resurrection and Immortality. Henry Vaughan. SCP-1

Oft have you seen a swan superbly frowning. To Charles Cowden Clarke. Keats. MBPR

Oft I had heard of Lucy Gray. Lucy Gray; or, Solitude. Wordsworth. Epi; MBPR; OxBChV

Oft I string the Lydian lyre. To Sylvia. An Imitation of Anacreon. *Unknown.* PiAm

Oft in the hall I have heard my people. *Unknown, tr. fr. Anglo-Saxon by* Charles W. Kennedy. *Fr.* Beowulf. HeIP

Oft, in the Stilly Night. Thomas Moore. PFIr; Prf; RDB, *with music*

    (Light of Other Days, The.) NOBE

Often beneath the wave, wide from this ledge. At Melville's Tomb. Hart Crane. NoAM; VGW

Often I Am Permitted to Return to a Meadow. Robert Duncan. HeIP; NOBA; PiAm

Often I think of my Jewish friends. The Pripet Marshes. Irving Feldman. NoAM

Often I think of the beautiful town. My Lost Youth. Longfellow. AmVN; IPWM; NOBA

Often, in these blue meadows. Pursuit from Under. James Dickey. PPP

Often I've wished that I'd been born a woman. A Wish. Laurence Lerner. OxBTC

Often when the moon is full. Wife of the Moon Man Who Never Came Back. Grace Butcher. RiTi

Oftener seen, the more I lust, The. Out of Sight, Out of Mind. Barnabe Googe. InPS

Ogres and Pygmies. Robert Graves. NoAM

Ohms. Irving Layton. NeAC

Oithona: a Poem. James Macpherson. LAuP

Okay. Sharon Scott. JB

Okay, my starsick beauty! Unknown Shores. D. M. Thomas, *after* Théophile Gautier. MPo

Okay "Negroes." June Jordan. BPo; RiTi

Okay, so the wheel bit was a grinding bore. Eve: Night Thoughts. Judson Jerome. CoPAm

Ol' Bunk's Band. William Carlos Williams. NOBA

Ol' Hannah. *Unknown.* BluL

Ol' Man River, *with music.* Oscar Hammerstein II. BLSo

Ol' Tim Legion. Rubee Dreher Moxley. NPW

Old Acquaintance, An. Lewis Turco. CoPAm

Old Adam, the carrion crow. Song. Thomas Lovell Beddoes. *Fr.* Death's Jest Book, V, iv. OBP

Old Age. E. E. Cummings. BBGO

Old Age. Edmund Waller. *Fr.* Of the Last Verses in the Book. NOBE

Old age is. To Waken an Old Lady. William Carlos Williams. InPK; PSN

Old Age Sticks. E. E. Cummings. InPS

Old, and abandon'd by each venal friend. On Lord Holland's Seat near Margate, Kent. Thomas Gray. LAuP

Old and longhairs in crome light. Minneapolis White Castle, Winter '72. James L. White. HeS

Old and the New Masters, The. Randall Jarrell. InPK

Old Arm-Chair, The. Eliza Cook. InPK

Old bitch labrador swims, The. The End of Summer. Judith Minty. FiCP; HeS

Old Black Joe, *with music.* Stephen Collins Foster. PSoN

Old Black ladies. Weeksville Women. Elouise Loftin. PoBA

Old Black Men. Georgia Douglas Johnson. PoBA

Old Black Men Say. James A. Emanuel. PoBa

Old Boards. Robert Bly. CAPP

Old Boast, The. W. S. Merwin. NOBA

Old Books. Chaucer. *Fr.* The Legend of Good Women: Prologue. OxBM

Old Chartist, The. George Meredith. VPC

Old Chisholm Trail, The. *Unknown.* AmFP; BLSH, *with music*

Old Codger's Lament, The. Carl Rakosi. HeS

Old Colony Times, *with music. Unknown.* BLSo

Old cottonwood has jeweled, my piece, An. Pietas: The Petrified Wood. Dave Smith. HeS

Old Countryside. Louise Bogan. WPE

Old Couple, The. F. Pratt Green. OxBTC

Old Cumberland Beggar, The. Wordsworth. MBPR

Old Dan Tucker, *with music.* Daniel Decatur Emmett. BLSo; PSoN

Old Davis owned a solid mica mountain. A Fountain, a Bottle, a Donkey's Ears and Some Books. Robert Frost. VGW

Old Devil. *Unknown.* BluL

Old Devil he came to a woodsman one day, The. The Curst Wife. *Unknown.* AIW

Old Dog, The. Alasdair MacLean. LP

Old Dog. William Stafford. BoAnP

Old dog, The/ at the west postern. Peter Whigham. *Fr.* Love Poems of the VIth Dalai Lama. TwMBP

Old dog barks backward without getting up, The. The Span of Life. Robert Frost. SoSe

Old Dog Blue. *Unknown.* BluL

Old Dog lay in the summer sun. Sunning. James S. Tippett. ECBV

Old Dolores. *Unknown.* MiP

Old Dubuque. Dave Etter. ANTL

Old Eben Flood, climbing alone one night. Mr. Flood's Party. E. A. Robinson. InPK; IPWM; MAT; MiP; NoAM; NOBA; PAIC; PiAm; PoTa; PPoD; PPoe; PPP; SoSe

Old Egyptians hid their wit, The. On Mr. Nash's Picture at Full Length. Jane Brereton. WPE

Old England Forever and Do it no More. *Unknown.* GBP

Old Ernie Anderson eating peanuts. Peanuts. Ken Belford. NeAC

Old Euclid drew a circle. Euclid. Vachel Lindsay. SFF

Old fabulous rendering up. The Flame of a Candle. Howard Nemerov. AnMo

Old Familiar Faces, The. Charles Lamb. GrRo; NOBE; PAIC

Old Farmer and His Young Wife, The. *Unknown. See* Old Wichet.

Old farmer, nearing death, asked, The. Field Day. W. R. Rodgers. BIrV

Old-Fashioned Pitcher, The. George E. Phair. SPo

Old Fence Post. Leigh Hanes. ECBV

Old Field Mowed For Appearances' Sake, An. William Meredith. PPoD

Old, Filthy Beer Pail, The. Katie V. Hall. InPK

Old Flame, The. Robert Lowell. BoLoP; NoAM; NOBA

Old Florist. Theodore Roethke. CTBA; NCSH; PiAm

Old Folks at Home, The, *with music.* Stephen Collins Foster. BLSH; BLSo; PSoN

Old Folks Home. Tom Hennen. HeS

Old friend, kind friend! lightly down. To My Old Schoolmaster. Whittier. NOBA

Old Fritz, on this rotating bed. A Flat One. W. D. Snodgrass. CAPP

Old Furniture. Thomas Hardy. OxBTC

Old Grandpaw Yet. *Unknown.* AmFP

Old Gray Beard a-Shaking. *Unknown.* AmFP

Old Gray Goose, The. *Unknown.* GBP ("Go tell Aunt Rhody.") AmFP

Old gray hearse goes rolling by, The. The Hearse Song. *Unknown.* SFF

Old gray hen is dying, The. Hen Dying. Alasdair MacLean. BoAnP

Old Gray Mare. *Unknown.* GBP

Old Grey. Fred Lape. BoAnP

Old greybeard dozing, The. On the Death of God. Roderick Hartigh Jellema. AATT

Old guy put down his beer, The. Do the Dead Know What Time It Is? Kenneth Patchen. CoPAm; PAIC

Old Haven. Jean Garrigue. WPE

Old house with trees and twisting river, An. A Visit to Bridge House. Richard Weber. BIrV

Old houses were scaffolding once. Images. T. E. Hulme. InPK; OxBTC

Old Humpy. *Unknown.* AmFP

Old Hundredth, *with music.* William Kethe. BLSo

Old Ironsides. Oliver Wendell Holmes. BTTM

Old Jockey, The. F. R. Higgins. OxBTC

Old John is foolish. Epigrams. Phillip Hey. NVAP

Old Jumpety-Bumpety-Hop-and-Go-One. The Kangaroo. *Unknown.* ECBV

Old Kimball. *Unknown.* AmFP

Old King, The. Walter de la Mare. AIW

Old King Cole. Mother Goose. MG

Old Ladies, The. Colin Ellis. OxBTC

Old Lady of London, The. *Unknown.* AmFP

Old Lady Sitting in the Dining Room. *Unknown.* AmFP

Old lady writes me in a spidery style, An. A Letter from Brooklyn. Derek Walcott. OxBTC

Old Lady's Lament for Her Youth, The. Villon, *tr. fr.* French by Robert Lowell. BoLoP

Old Laughter. Gwendolyn Brooks. *Fr.* The Womanhood. TH

Old Lem. Sterling A. Brown. BPo; PoBA

Old, mad, blind, despised, and dying king, An. England in 1819. Shelley. GrRo; MAT; MBPR; NOBE; PBMP; PPoD; PPP

Old Maids. *Unknown.* AmFP

Old Maid's Song. *Unknown.* AmFP

Old Man. Edward Thomas. PSN

Old man/ man black man. Tony Get the Boys. D. L. Graham. PoBA

Old man, The/ sits. Navajo Poem. Warren Woessner. HeS

Old man alone in the dark, muttering, An. Girls' Voices. Brendan Gill. POL

Old Man and His Wife, An. *Unknown.* OxBM

Old Man and Jim, The. James Whitcomb Riley. PoTa

Old man bending I come among new faces, An. The Wound-Dresser. Walt Whitman. NOBA

Old man in a lodge within a park, An. Chaucer. Longfellow. AmVN; HeIP; NOBA; PAIC

Old Man in the Autumn, The. John Shaw Neilson. MAuV

Old man in white, An. Alice Walker. *Fr.* Love. NMM

Old man never had much to say. The Old Man and Jim. James Whitcomb Riley. PoTa

Old Man Jeremy. James K. Baxter. ECBV

Old Man Know-All. *Unknown.* BPo

Old Man Let's Go Fishing in the Yellow Reeds of the Bay. Mei Berssenbrugge. SA

Old man, listening to the careful, The. The First Snow of the Year. Mark Van Doren. NCSH

Old Man, or Lad's-love, —in the name there's nothing. Old Man. Edward Thomas. PSN

Old Man, Phantom Dog. Frederick Eckman. ANTL

Old Man Platypus. A. B. Paterson. BoAnP

Old Man, the Sweat Lodge. Phil George. VW

Old Man to the Lizard, The. Archibald MacLeish. PiAm

Old Man Travelling; Animal Tranquillity and Decay, a Sketch. Wordsworth. MBPR

Old man who seined. Lorine Niedecker. VGW

Old man whose black face, An. The Rainwalkers. Denise Levertov. CTBA; PPP

Old Man's Comforts and How He Gained Them, The. Robert Southey. OxBChV; SpRo

Old Man's Tale, The. Brian Merriman, *tr. fr. Modern Irish by* David Marcus. *Fr.* The Midnight Court. BIrV

Old Man's Winter Night, An. Robert Frost. AnMo; NoAM; PiAm; VGW

Old Mansion. John Crowe Ransom. NOBA

Old-Marrieds, The. Gwendolyn Brooks. PoBA

Old Mary. Gwendolyn Brooks. CoPAm

Old Meg she was a gipsy. Meg Merrilies. Keats. MBPR; OxBChV

Old Men. Ogden Nash. SFF

Old men/ in Lucas Park. Lucas Park (St. Louis). Paul Southworth Bliss. ANTL

Old Men Admiring Themselves in the Water, The. W. B. Yeats. MiP

Old men in blue: and heavily encumbered. Pihsien Road. Robin Hyde. WPE

Old Men Working Concrete. Phil Hey. FiCP

Old Mill, Newton St. Cyres. Ken Smith. TwMBP

Old Miner's Refrain, The. *Unknown.* AmFP

Old Mr. Hardy, upright in his chair. At Max Gate. Siegfried Sassoon. NoAM

Old Molly Means was a hag and a witch. Molly Means. Margaret Walker. NMM; PoTa; SS

Old moon is tarnished. Sea Lullaby. Elinor Wylie. PBMP

Old moon my eyes are new moon with human footprint. Poem Rocket. Allen Ginsberg. CoPAm; VGW

Old Mother Goose, when. Mother Goose. MG

Old Mother Hubbard. The Comic Adventures of Old Mother Hubbard and Her Dog. Sarah Catherine Martin. MG; OxBChV

Old Mother turns blue and from us. Lorine Niedecker. RiTi

Old Navy, The. Frederick Marryat. PoTa

Old Noah he had an ostrich farm and fowls. Wine and Water. G. K. Chesterton. FaBoCo

Old Nokomis Sings. Longfellow. *Fr.* The Song of Hiawatha. ECBV

("By the shores of Gitche Gumee.") SpRo

Old Oaken Bucket, The, *with music.* Samuel Woodworth. BLSo; PSoN

Old One and the Wind, The. Clarice Short. IHMS

Old Ones, The. R. E. Sebenthall. HeS

Old one's to the side. Psalm. Charles Simic. AmPA

Old Orange Flute. *Unknown.* GBP

Old Penobscot Indian, The. Flux. Richard Eberhart. CoPAm; VGW

Old Pensioner, The. W. B. Yeats. *See* Lamentation of the Old Pensioner, The.

Old People. Myra Cohn Livingston. CTBA

Old Peter led a wretched life. The Perils of Invisibility. W. S. Gilbert. PoTa

Old Photo in an Old Life, An. Daniel Hoffman. SoSe

Old Photographs. David Harsent. POL

Old Pilot's Death, The. Donald Hall. MPo

Old priest Peter Gilligan, The. The Ballad of Father Gilligan [or Father Gilligan]. W. B. Yeats. AIW; PAIC

Old Prison, The. Judith Wright. MAuV

Old Pro's Lament, The. Paul Petrie. SPo

Old Repair Man, The. Fenton Johnson. MiP

Old Roger. *Unknown.* RAE

Old Rosin the Beau, *with music. Unknown.* BLSo; PSoN

Old Rugged Cross, The, *with music.* George Bennard. BLSH

Old Ruralities. Charles Tennyson Turner. VPC

Old rusty-belly thing will soon be gone. The Sappa Creek. Gary Snyder. NCSH

Old Scottish Cavalier, The. William Edmonstoune Aytoun. BTTM

Old sea dog on a sailor's log, An. The Powerful Eyes o' Jeremy Tait. Wallace Irwin. PoTa

Old Section Boss, The. *Unknown.* BPo

Old Shellover. Walter de la Mare. LCL; OxBChV

Old Shepherd's Prayer. Charlotte Mew. OxBTC; WPE

Old Shoe, an old pot, an old skin, An. Autumn Sequence. Adrienne Rich. VGW

Old Sinner. Derek Bowman. MIS

Old Sir Robert Bolton had three sons. The Jovial Hunter of Bromsgrove. *Unknown.* PeBB

Old smiling woman, you have had all the lessons. Salt. Nicholas Flocos. SA

Old Smoky. *Unknown.* AmFP

Old Song Ended, An. Dante Gabriel Rossetti. BoLoP; VPC

Old Song Re-sung, A. John Masefield. ECBV

Old South Boston Aquarium stands, The. For the Union Dead. Robert Lowell. HeIP; InPS; NOBA; NoAM; PiAm; PPoe; PPP; PSN

Old Stephen. Charles Tennyson Turner. VPC

Old Stoic, The. Emily Brontë. NOBE

Old Stone Cross, The. W. B. Yeats. PBMP

Old Storm. David Phillips. NeAC

Old Story, The. Louis MacNeice. GBL

Old Story, An. E. A. Robinson. TH

Old Tailor, The. Walter de la Mare. ECBV

Old Tawny's mane is moth. The King. Douglas Livingstone. BoAnP

Old Tiger and the God of the Water-hole, The. Margaret Reynolds. MIS

Old Timbrook Blues. *Unknown.* BluL

Old Timers. Carl Sandburg. NoAM

Old Trouper, The. Don Marquis. *Fr.* Archy and Mehitabel. FaBoCo

Old Uncle Fred could squint along forty-foot beams. Four-square Gospel. Roderick Hartigh Jellema. AATT

Old Upright I Did Not Learn to Play, The. Nicholas Flocos. SA

Old Vicarage, Grantchester, The. Rupert Brooke. OxBTC

Old Walking Song, The. J. R. R. Tolkien. RFM

Old Walt. Langston Hughes. HeIP; PiAm

Old War-Dreams. Walt Whitman. WIF

Old Warrior Terror, The. Alice Walker. NVAP

Old watch, The: their. Vapor Trail Reflected in the Frog Pond. Galway Kinnell. VGW

Old Wichet. *Unknown.* PoTa
(Old Farmer and His Young Wife, The.) GBP

Old Wife and the Ghost, The. James Reeves. ECBV; RAE

Old Wife in High Spirits. "Hugh MacDiarmid." OxBTC

Old Wife's Tale, The. George Peele. *See* Old Wives' Tale, The.

Old Witherington. Dudley Randall. ConAP; NoAM

Old Wives' [*or* Wife's] Tale, The, *sels.* George Peele.
"Gently dip, but not too deep." InPS
Summer Song, A. NOBE
("When as the rye reach to the chin.") GBL
Voice from the Well, The. NOBE

Old Woman, The. Joseph Campbell. OxBTC; WIF

Old Woman. Elizabeth Jennings. BuTh

Old Woman. Linda Pastan. FiCP

Old Woman, An. Charles Henry Ross. OxBChV

Old Woman. Iain Crichton Smith. OxBTC; PSN

Old Woman. *Unknown.* AmFP

Old woman across the way, The. The Whipping. Robert Hayden. MiP; NCSH; POBA; SFF

Old Woman Awaiting the Greyhound Bus. Duane Niatum. CDW

Old woman, naked, An. Near the Old Slave Fort. Joseph Bruchac. FAF

"Old woman, old woman, are you fond of carding?" Old Woman. *Unknown.* AmFP

"Old woman, old woman, shall we go shearing?" Mother Goose. ECBV

Old Woman on a Broom. *Unknown.* ECBV

Old Woman Remembers, An. Sterling A. Brown. PoBA

Old woman sits, The. Leasa Davis. CTBA

Old woman sits on a bench before the door and quarrels, The. Fawn's Foster-Mother. Robinson Jeffers. NoAM; NOBA

Old Woman Speaks of the Moon, An. Ruth Pitter. WPE

Old woman was sweeping her house, An. *Unknown.* MG

Old-World Thicket, An. Christina Rossetti. SBG

Old wound in my ass, The. Fabrication of Ancestors. Alan Dugan. NoAM

Old yellow stucco, The. Winter Nightfall. J. C. Squire. OxBTC

Old Yew, which graspest at the stones. In Memoriam, A. H. H., II. Tennyson. NOBE

Old Young who sleeps by day by night. Night Duty. Kenneth Mackenzie. MAuV

Ole Abe (God bless 'is ole soul!). Negro Soldier's Civil War Chant. *Unknown.* BPo

Ole Aunt Dinah, she's jes lak me. Jack and Dinah Want Freedom. *Unknown.* BPo

Ole Sheep Dey Know De Road, De. *Unknown.* BPo

Oliphaunt. J. R. R. Tolkien. LCL

Olive, The. A. E. Housman. NoAM

Omen of Victory Mina Loy. InPK

Omnes gentes plaudite. A Last Drink. *Unknown.* OxBM

On a Bicycle, *sel.* Yevgeny Yevtushenko, *tr. fr. Russian by* Robin Milner-Gulland *and* Peter Levi.
"Under the dawn I wake my two-wheel friend." SPo

On a Birthday. J. M. Synge. GBL

On a Bright and Summer's Morning. *Unknown.* AmFP

On a Certain Lady at Court Pope. NOBE

On a Clergyman's Horse Biting Him. *Unknown.* FaBoCo; SoSe

On a Cock at Rochester. Sir Charles Sedley. POL

On a Country Road. Harley Elliott. NeAC

On a dark/and lonely street. Witch? Sam Reavin. CaYB

On a dark and stormy night. The Wreck of the Royal Palm. *Unknown.* AmFP

On a dark stormy night, as the train rattled on. In the Baggage Coach Ahead. Gussie L. Davis. FSN

On a day when smoke lies down in alleys. Looking Both Ways before Crossing. John Woods. ConAP; IPWM

On a Dead Child. Robert Bridges. NoAM; NOBE

On a Dead Child. Richard Middleton. SoSe

On a Distant Prospect of an Absconding Bookmaker. G. Rostrevor Hamilton. FaBoCo

On a Doctor of Divinity. Richard Porson. FaBoCo

On a Dream. Keats. LoAs

On a Drop of Dew. Andrew Marvell. AnMo; BoReV; MetP; PAIC

On a Dying Boy. William Bell. WIF

On a Favorite Cat Drowned in a Tub of Goldfishes. Thomas Gray. *See* Ode on the Death of a Favourite Cat . . .

On a flat road runs the well-train'd runner. The Runner. Walt Whitman. InPS; MiP; PPoD; SPo

On a Flimmering Floom You Shall Ride. Carl Sandburg. ECBV

On a Friend's Escape from Drowning off the Norfolk Coast. George Barker. MPo

On a General Election. Hilaire Belloc. FaBoCo; NOBE; OxBTC

On a Girdle. Edmund Waller. HeIP; InPK; SoSe

On a Great Hollow Tree William Strode. SCP-2

On a green island in the Main Street traffic. Pro Patria. Constance Carrier. WPE

On a hill far away stood an old rugged cross. The Old Rugged Cross. George Bennard. BLSH

On a hill there grows a flower. A Pastoral of Phillis and Coridon. Nicholas Breton. PAIC

On a holy day when sails were blowing southward. The Straying Student. Austin Clarke. BIrV

On a ladder, in an old checkered shirt. Washing Windows. Barry Spacks. NCSH

On a Leander Gem. Keats. MBPR

On a Little Boy's Endeavouring to Catch a Snake Thomas Foxton. OxBChV

On a little piece of wood. Mr. and Mrs. Spikky Sparrow. Edward Lear. OxBChV

On a Lord Samuel Taylor Coleridge. FaBoCo

On a Mandrake. Thomas Heyrick. SCP-2

On a Melting Beauty. Margaret Cavendish, Duchess of Newcastle. SCP-2

On a mid-December day. Since. W. H. Auden. InPS

On a Monday morning early as my wandering steps did lead me. The Boys of Mullabaun [*or* Mullaghbawn]. *Unknown.* BIrV; GBP

On a morning such as this. Veteran Lola Ridge. WPE

On a Painted Woman. Shelley. FaBoCo

On a Painting by Patient B of the Independence State Hospital for the Insane. Donald Justice. ConAP

On a Photo of Sgt. Ciardi a Year Later. John Ciardi. CoPAm

On a Portrait of a Deaf Man. John Betjeman. NoAM

On a Portrait of Wordsworth by B. R. Haydon. Elizabeth Barrett Browning. HeIP

On a Prize Crucifix by a Student Sculptor. Robert Logan. CAPP

On a Ruined House in a Romantic Country. Samuel Taylor Coleridge. *Fr.* Sonnets Attempted in the Manner of Contemporary Writers. Epi
(House That Jack Built, The.) AKE

On a Saturday afternoon in the football season. Laziness and Silence. Robert Bly. PPP

On a secluded corner of the beach. John Betjeman. *Fr.* Beside the Seaside. LP

On a Soldier Fallen in the Philippines. William Vaughn Moody. AmVN; NOBA

On a squeaking cart, they push the usual stuff. A Removal from Terry Street. Douglas Dunn. LP; POL

On a Squinting Poetess. Thomas Moore. FaBoCo

On a Squirrel Crossing the Road in Autumn, in New England. Richard Eberhart. HeIP; TH; VoPo; WIF

On a starred [*or* starr'd] night Prince Lucifer uprose. Lucifer in Starlight. George Meredith. Epi; InPK; IPWM; NOBE; OBP; PAIC; PBMP; PPoe; SoSe; VPC

On a Statue of Sir Arthur Sullivan. G. Rostrevor Hamilton. FaBoCo

On a Statue of Venus. *Unknown.* LoAs

On a summer day in the month of May. The Big Rock Candy Mountains. *Unknown.* NOBA

On a Summer's Day. Keats. *Fr.* I Stood Tiptoe upon a Little Hill. FSFS

On a Sunday Afternoon, *with music.* Andrew B. Sterling. FSN

On a Sunday morn, sat a maid forlorn. Wait Till the Sun Shines, Nellie. Andrew B. Sterling. BLSo; FSN

On a Sundial. Hilaire Belloc. POL

On a time the amorous Silvy. The Awakening. *Unknown, tr. by* John Attey. GBL; NOBE

On a Vulgar Error. C. S. Lewis. OxBTC

On a Windy Day. Gene Frumkin. CoPAm

On Alexander and Aristotle, on a Black-on-Red Greek Plate. Alan Dugan. PPP

On all the channels,/ Nothing but panels! Almost Any Evening. Phyllis McGinley. *Fr.* Speaking of Television. TH

On all the whole nacyon. Anathema of Cats. John Skelton. *Fr.* Phyllyp Sparowe. PCat

On an Anniversary. J. M. Synge. POL

On an Hour-glass. John Hall. SCP-2

On an Indian Tomineios, the Least of Birds. Thomas Heyrick. SCP-2

On an Island, *abr.* "Ethna Carbery." WPE

On an Island. J. M. Synge. BIrV

On an oak in autumn. Survivor. Archibald MacLeish. NCSH

On Anothers Sorrow. Blake. *Fr.* Songs of Innocence. MBPR

On Approaching My Birthday. Vassar Miller. IHMS; NMM

On Being Asked for a War Poem. W. B. Yeats. PFIr

On Being Brought from Africa to America. Phillis Wheatley. HeIP; IPWM; NOBA; PiAm; SBG; WPE

On black bare trees a stale cream moon. Eau-Forte. F. S. Flint. OxBTC

On Botching. John Heywood. FaBoCo

On Burroughs' Work. Allen Ginsberg. NoAM; NOBA

On Cardinal Wolsey. *Unknown.* FaBoCo

On Cementing Level the Stable Floor at the Old Manse. Forbes Macgregor. MIS

On Certain Ladies. Pope. FaBoCo

On Children. Kahlil Gibran. *Fr.* The Prophet. SFF

On Chloris Walking in the Snow. William Strode. SCP-2
(Chloris in the Snow.) NOBE

On Christmas Day I weep. Christmas Mourning. Vassar Miller. CoPAm

On Christopher Wordsworth, Master of Trinity. Benjamin Hall Kennedy. FaBoCo

On Christ's Birth (To Sisters). Jane Marie Luecke. AATT

On clear May evenings the old sheep. Lambs Frolicking Home. Fred Lape. BoAnP

On cold days/it is easy to be reasonable. Becoming a Nun. Erica Jong. MMD

On Courtworm. Ben Jonson. SCP-1

On Cromek. Blake. FaBoCo

On Death. Walter Savage Landor. BBGO
("Death stands above me, whispering low.") NOBE

On Dr. Isaac Letsome. *Unknown.* FaBoCo

On Dr. Samuel Ogden. R. P. Arden. FaBoCo

On Donne's Poetry. Samuel Taylor Coleridge. MBPR; PAIC; PPoD

On Dreams. Swift. BIrV

On Driving Behind a School Bus for Mentally Retarded Children. Grace Butcher. RiTi

On dull mornings. Mrs. Busk. Sir Osbert Sitwell. OxBTC

On Edges. Adrienne Rich. Psy

On either side the river lie. The Lady of Shalott. Tennyson. NOBE

On Elphinston's Translation of Martial. Burns. FaBoCo

On eyes embarked for sleep the only light. For Ellen. Richard Wilbur. RRA

On fair Augusta's towers and trees. A Tale of Drury Lane. Horace Smith. FaBoCo

On Falling Asleep by Firelight. William Meredith. NoAM

On Fame ("Fame, like a wayward girl, will still be coy"). Keats. MBPR

On Fame ("How fever'd is the man, who cannot look"). Keats. MBPR

On Finding the Meaning of "Radiance." Alan Dugan. PAIC

On First Looking into Chapman's Homer. Keats. AnMo; HeIP; InPK; MBPR; NOBE; OBP; PAIC; PPoD; PPoe; PPP; SoSe; WIF

On Flunking a Nice Boy Out of School. John Ciardi. NowV; SFF

On Forelands High in Heaven. A. E. Housman. InPS

On Fortune. Elizabeth I, Queen of England. WPE

On Friendship. William Cowper
"Man that hails you Tom or Jack, The." POL

On getting a card. Poem. William Carlos Williams. VGW

On Getting a Natural. Dudley Randall. PoBA

On Giving a Son to the Sea. James Dickey. TCP

On glossy wires artistically bent. Waspish. Robert Frost. BoAnP

On goes the age with footsteps fleet and strong. An Evening in Harvest Time. Charles Tennyson Turner. VPC

On Gut. Ben Jonson. SCP-1

On gypsum slabs of preternatural whiteness. Animal, Vegetable and Mineral. Louise Bogan. SBG

On Hardscrabble Mountain Galway Kinnell. RFM

On Harting Down. T. Sturge Moore. OxBTC

On Hearing a Symphony of Beethoven. Edna St. Vincent Millay. VoPo

On Hearing That the Students of Our New University Have Joined the Agitation Against Immoral Literature. W. B. Yeats. NoAM

On Hearing the Airlines Will Use a Psychological Profile to Catch Potential Skyjackers. Stephen Dunn. AmPA

On Hearing the Marsh Bird's Water Cry. Duane Niatum. CDW

On Hellespont guiltie of true-loves blood. Hero and Leander. Christopher Marlowe. AAS

On Her Loving Two Equally. Aphra Behn. SBG

On her side, reclining on her elbow. So-and-so Reclining on Her Couch. Wallace Stevens. NOBA

On Himself. Swift. PFIr

On Himself, upon Hearing What Was His Sentence. James Graham, Marquis of Montrose. SCP-2

On his airy perch among the branches. The Fox and the Crow. La Fontaine, *tr. by* Marianne Moore. PPP

On His Blindness. Milton. BoReV; Epi; HeIP; InPS; IPWM; NOBE; PBMP; PPoe; SoSe; WIF
(Sonnet: "When I consider how my light is spent.") AnMo; SCP-1
(When I Consider How My Light Is Spent.) InPK; MAT; OBP; PAIC; PPoD; PPP

On His Books. Hilaire Belloc. FaBoCo

On His Deceased Wife. Milton. Epi; LoAs
("Methought I saw my late espoused saint.") BoLoP; OBP; PPP
(On His Dead Wife.) GBL; NOBE
(Sonnet: "Methought I saw my late espoused saint.") SCP-1

On His Mistress [*or* Mistris]. John Donne. Elegies, XVI. BoLoP; OBP
(Elegy on His Mistress.) GBL
(To His Mistress Desiring to Travel with Him as His Page.) NOBE

On His Mistress, [*or* Mistris], the Queen of Bohemia. Sir Henry Wotton. GBL; MetP
(Elizabeth of Bohemia.) BoLoP; NOBE

On His Own Deafness. Swift. AnMo; BIrV

On His Queerness Christopher Isherwood. OxBTC

On His Seventy-Fifth Birthday. Walter Savage Landor. *Fr.* The Last Fruit off an Old Tree. PBMP
(Dying Speech of an Old Philosopher.) HeIP
("I strove with none, for none was worth my strife.") NOBE

On Hope by Way of Question and Answer between Abraham Cowley and Richard Crashaw. Abraham Cowley *and* Richard Crashaw. NOBE

On Hot Days. James Reiss. AmPA

On hot September nights, when sleep is scarce. My Father Dreams of Baseball. Laurence Lieberman. SPo

On Hurricane Jackson. Alan Dugan. MiP; NCSH; NowV; POL; PPoD; SPo

On Inclosures. *Unknown.* FaBoCo

On Inhabiting an Orange. Josephine Miles. NoAM

On Its Way. May Swenson. WPE

On Jordan's stormy banks I stand. The Promised Land. Samuel Stennett. AmFP

On Keats. Shelley. MBPR

On Lady Poltagrue, a Public Peril. Hilaire Belloc. FaBoCo; POL

On Lake Michigan—1972. John Matthias. HeS

On Leaping over the Moon. Thomas Traherne. Moon

On Learning to Play the Guitar. Ray Fraser. NeAC

On Leaving Baltimore. Duane Niatum. CDW

On Leaving California. Bayard Taylor. AmVN

On Leaving London for Wales. Shelley. MBPR

On Leaving Newstead Abbey. Byron. MBPR

On Linden, when the sun was low. Hohenlinden [*or* The Battle of Hohenlinden]. Thomas Campbell. BTTM; NOBE

On Listening to a Death-of-God Theologian Lecture in the Chapel. Elmer F. Suderman. AATT

On Listening to the Spirituals. Lance Jeffers. PoBA

On Living Too Long. Walter Savage Landor. PAIC

On London fell a clearer light. Summer in England, 1914. Alice Meynell. SBG; WPE

On Longer evenings. Coming. Philip Larkin. OxBTC; PSN

On Looking at a Copy of Alice Meynell's Poems. Amy Lowell. SBG

On Lord Chesterfield and His Son. *Unknown.* FaBoCo

On Lord Holland's Seat near Margate, Kent. Thomas Gray. LAuP

On love's worst ugly day. First Meditation. Theodore Roethke. *Fr.* Meditations of an Old Woman. NOBA

On Minding One's Own Business. James Wright. CoPAm

On Mr. Nash's Picture at Full Length. Jane Brereton. WPE

On Mrs. E. Montague's Blushing in the Cross-bath. Thomas Flatman. SCP-2

On Monsieur's Departure. Elizabeth I, Queen of England. WPE

On moonlit heath and lonesome bank. A. E. Housman. SoSe

On Mundane Acquaintances. Hilaire Belloc. OxBTC

On my desk lies a photo. Surfer and Others. Sonya Dorman. SPo

On My 18th Birthday. John William Corrington. CoPAm

On My First Daughter. Ben Jonson. NOBE; RRA

On My First Son [*or* Sonne]. Ben Jonson. HeIP; IPWM; LoAs; OBP; PAIC; PBMP; PPoe; SCP-1; VoPo
(On My Son.] NOBE

On My Joyful Departure. Samuel Taylor Coleridge. FaBoCo

On my knees. In the Garden. Tom Schmidt. NeAC

On My Son. Ben Jonson. *See* On My First Son.

On My Stand. Sharon Scott. JB

On My Thirty-third Birthday. Byron. BBGO

On my way home from school. The Testing-Tree. Stanley Kunitz. MAT

On my way to Mass. The Lass from Bally-na-Lee. Anthony Raftery, *tr. by* Desmond O'Grady. BIrV

On Myselfe. Countess of Winchilsea. SBG

On New Year's Eve. Ts'uei T'u, *tr. fr. Chinese by* Witter Bynner. OFD

On News Thomas Traherne. *See* News.

On November 2nd 1965. Norman Morrison. Adrian Mitchell. NowV

On ochre walls in ice-formed caves shaggy Neanderthals. To My Son Parker, Asleep in the Next Room. Bob Kaufman. PoBA; VGW

On old slashed spruce boughs. On Hardscrabble Mountain. Galway Kinnell. RFM

On one fixed point all nature moves. On the Uniformity and Perfection of Nature. Philip Freneau. IPWM

On one of the steep slopes. City. Roy Fisher. TwMBP

On one of those days with the Legion. A Day with the Foreign Legion. Reed Whittemore. ConAP

On one summer [*or* summer's] day, sun was shining fine. Bill Bailey, Won't You Please Come Home. Hughie Cannon. BLSo; FSN

On Our Crucified Lord, Naked and Bloody. Richard Crashaw. SCP-1

On Paunch, a Parasite. Hilaire Belloc. POL

On Peace. Keats. MBPR

On Peter Robinson. Francis Jeffrey. FaBoCo

On Prince Frederick. *Unknown.* FaBoCo

On Pure Sudden Days Like Innocence. Richard Brautigan. MIT

On Rachmaninoff's Birthday. Frank O'Hara. CAPP

On rainy days alone I dine. On Himself. Swift. PFIr

On Rape Unattempted. Alan Dugan. NoAM

On Reading Another Poet. Elizabeth Brewster. MMD

On Reading Poems to a Senior Class at South High. D. C. Berry. SoSe

On Receiving a Curious Shell, and a Copy of Verses. Keats. MBPR

On Receiving a Laurel Crown from Leigh Hunt. Keats. MBPR

On Restoring Verticals. Sandra Ruth Duguid. AATT

On Returning to Teach. Marvin Bell. NowV

On Richard Hind. *Unknown.* FaBoCo

On Richmond Hill there lives a lass. The Lass of Richmond Hill. Leonard McNally. BLSo

On Roofs of Terry Street. Douglas Dunn. OxBTC

On St. James's Park as Lately Improved by His Majesty, *sels.* Edmund Waller.
"Of the first paradise there's nothing found." SCP-2

On St. Martin's evening green. Nuns at Eve. John Malcolm Brinnin. PPoD

On Saint-Urbain Street. Milton Acorn. NeAC

On sale everywhere: Spicer's Instant Poetry. Spicer's Instant Poetry. James Reeves. MPo

On Sannazar's Being Honoured, *sel.* Richard Lovelace.
"There is not in my mind one sullen fate." SCP-2

On Saturday on Saturday. Saturday in New York. Anne Beresford. MPo

On Scott's "The Field of Waterloo." Thomas, Lord Erskine. FaBoCo

On Seeing a Hair of Lucretia Borgia. Walter Savage Landor. InPK

On Seeing a Stamp from the Democratic Republic of Vietnam. Leslie Woolf Hedley. NowV

On Seeing a Torn Out Coin Telephone. Martin Robbins. MAT

On Seeing Films of the War. Louis Coxe. PPoD

On Seeing the Elgin Marbles. Keats. MBPR; PAIC

On Seeing Two Brown Boys in a Catholic Church. Frank Horne. PoBA

On shadowy back porches. Old Folks Home. Tom Hennen. HeS

On shallow straw, in shadeless glass. Take One Home for the Kiddies. Philip Larkin. OxBTC

On Shiloh's dark and bloody ground. The Drummer Boy of Shiloh. *Unknown.* AmFP

On Sight of Some Martyrs' Sepulchres. Nahum Tate. SCP-2

On Sir John Hill, M.D., Playwright. David Garrick. FaBoCo

On Sir John Vanbrugh, Architect. Abel Evans. FaBoCo

On Sir Voluptuous Beast. Ben Jonson. SCP-1

On Sitting Down to Read King Lear Once Again. Keats. MBPR

On Solomon Pavy, a Child of Queen Elizabeth's Chapel. Ben Jonson. *See* Epitaph on S.P., a Child of . . .

On some island I long to be. SaintColumcille, *tr. fr. Irish by* John Montague. BIrV

On Some South African Novelists. Roy Campbell. FaBoCo; InPK; OxBTC

On Something That Walks Somewhere. Ben Jonson. SCP-1

On Springfield Mountain[s] there did dwell. Springfield Mountain. *Unknown.* AIW; AmFP; BLSo

On starry heights. The Conflict of Convictions. Herman Melville. NOBA

On Stella's Birthday. Swift. InPK
(Stella's Birthday.) SoSe

On Sunday Afternoons. Sunday Afternoons. Anthony Thwaite. OxBTC

On Sunday, the Beginning of the Week, I Make a Religion. Albert Goldbarth. NVAP

On Sweet Killen Hill. Tom MacIntyre. NCSH

On T. Moore's Poems. *Unknown.* FaBoCo

On Teaching the Young. Yvor Winters. NoAM; NOBA

On the Author of the *Treatise of Human Nature.* James Hay Beattie. FaBoCo

On the back porch. The Passport. Luis Garcia. MIT

On the Balcony D. H. Lawrence. GBL

On the Banks of Salee. *Unknown.* AmFP

On the Banks of the Little Eau Pleine. *Unknown.* AmFP

On the banks of the Potomac there's an army so grand. The Red, White and Red. *Unknown.* AmFP

On the Banks of the Wabash, Far Away, *with music.* Paul Dresser. BLSH; BLSo; FSN

On the Beach. Frances Cornford. BoAnP

On the Beach at Fontana. James Joyce. SoSe

On the Beach at Night. Walt Whitman. InPS; NOBA

On the beach where we had been idly. Gracious Goodness. Marge Piercy. BoAnP

On the Bible. William Strode. SCP-2

On the Birth of His Son. Su Tung-Po, *tr fr. Chinese by* Arthur Waley. BuTh; OFD

On the Birth of My Son, Malcolm Coltrane. Julius Lester. PoBA

On the bog road the blackthorn flowers, the turf-stacks. Anthony Cronin. *Fr.* R.M.S. *Titanic.* BIrV

On the Border of Impossibility. Laura Beausoleil. NPW

On the Circuit. W. H. Auden. OxBTC

On the Circumcision: for the King's Music. William Cartwright. SCP-2

On the corner—116th and Lenox. Harlem Freeze Frame. Lebert Bethune. PoBA

On the Countess Dowager of Pembroke. William Browne. OBP
(Epitaph on the Countess Dowager of Pembrooke.) NOBE
(On the Death of Mary, Countess of Pembroke.) SCP-2

On the Daughter of Lykambes. Archilochos, *tr. fr. Greek by* Jonathan Cott. RRA

On the day I was born. My Stars. Abraham Ibn Ezra, *tr. by* Robert Mezey. OFD

On the Death of a Cat. Christina Rossetti. PCat

On the Death of a Metaphysician. George Santayana. PAIC

On the Death of a Young Lady, Cousin to the Author. Byron. MBPR

On the Death of Anne Brontë. Charlotte Brontë. WPE

On the Death of Dr. Robert Levet. Samuel Johnson. *See* On the Death of Mr. Robert Levet.

On the Death of Donne. Thomas Carew. NOBE

On the Death of Echo. Hartley Coleridge. BoAnP

On the Death of Edward III. *Unknown.* OxBM

On the Death of Friends in Childhood. Donald Justice. ConAP; NCSH

On the Death of God. Roderick Hartigh Jellema. AATT

On the Death of His Wife. Muireadach O'Dalaigh, *tr. fr. Irish by* Frank O'Connor. BIrV

On the Death of Keats. John Logan. Prf

On the Death of Mary, Countess of Pembroke. William Browne. *See* On the Countess Dowager of Pembroke.

On the Death of Mr. Fox. Byron. MBPR

On the Death of Mr. [*or Dr.*] Robert Levet, a Practiser in Physic. Samuel Johnson. BoReV; HeIP; InPS; LAuP; NOBE; PPP

On the Death of Mr. William Harvey, *sel.* Abraham Cowley.
"It was a dismal and a fearful night." NOBE

On the Death of Mrs. Throckmorton's Bullfinch. William Cowper. PPP
(On the Lamented Death of Mrs. Throckmorton's Bullfinch.) LAuP

On the Death of Richard West. Thomas Gray. *See* Sonnet on the Death of Richard West.

On the Death of William Edward Burghardt Du Bois by African Moonlight and Forgotten Shores. Conrad Kent Rivers. PoBA

On the Debt My Mother Owed to Sears Roebuck. Edward Dorn. ConAP

On the deck of Patrick Lynch's boat I sat in woeful plight. The County of Mayo. *Unknown, tr. by* George Fox. BIrV

On the Departure Platform. Thomas Hardy. NOBE; OxBTC

On the Detraction Which Followed upon My Writing Certain Treatises. Milton. Epi

On the distant prairie, where the heather wild. Rosalie, the Prairie Flower. George Frederick Root. BLSo

On the Eclipse of the Moon of October 1865. Charles Tennyson Turner. VPC

On the Emigration to America. Philip Freneau. PiAm

On the Eve of His Execution. Chidiock Tichborne. *See* Elegy: "My prime of youth is but a frost of cares."

On the Extinction of the Venetian Republic. Wordsworth. MBPR; NOBE; OBP; PPoD

On the Famous Voyage. Ben Jonson. PAIC; TVS

On the far edge of a plain. The Watcher. John Peck. AmPA

On the Farm. R. S. Thomas. OxBTC

On the 15th day of November in the year of the motorcar. Sonnet. Ted Berrigan. VW

On the Fifth Anniversary of Bluma Sach's Death. Vinnie-Marie D'Ambrosio. IHMS

On the Fine Arts Garden, Cleveland. Russell Atkins. PoBA

On the fine wire of his whine he walked. Mosquito. John Updike. BoAnP

On the first day/ malcolm. The Easter Bunny Blues Or All I Want for Xmas Is the Loop. Ebon Dooley. PoBA

On the first day of Christmas. The Twelve Days of Christmas. *Unknown.* BLSH

On the first of March. The Rooks. *Unknown.* GBP

On the Fly-Leaf of Pound's Cantos. Basil Bunting. NoAM; OxBTC

On the Forcers of Conscience. Milton. PAIC
(On the New Forcers of Conscience.) PPoD

On the Four Georges. Walter Savage Landor. FaBoCo

On the front of the envelope. Lines Found on an Envelope. Adrianne Marcus. NPW

On the Grasshopper and Cricket. Keats. Epi; FSFS; MBPR; OBP
(Grasshopper and the Cricket, The.) ECBV

On the ground there was a tree. The Tree in the Wood. *Unknown.* AmFP

On the Hall at Stowey. Charles Tomlinson. NoAM

On the Happy Corydon and Phyllis. *At. to* Sir Charles Sedley. BoLoP; SCP-2
("Young Caridon and Phillis.) SFF

On the headland's grassed and sheltered side. Storm. Judith Wright. WPE

On the Hill Below the Lighthouse. James Dickey. PAIC

On the hills behind the dunes. November on Lake Michigan. Tom McKeown. HeS

On the hilltop, close to the house of the empress. The Mother. Babette Deutsch. RiTi

On the idle hill of summer. A. E. Housman. NOBE

On the Imprint of the First English Edition of "The Works of Max Beerbohm." Max Beerbohm. InPK

On the Inauguration of the Memorial Statue, *sel.* Edward Edwin Foot.
"Love live our dear and noble Queen." FaBoCo

On the Infancy of Our Saviour. Francis Quarles. SCP-2

On the Isle of Man shore, I carelessly wandered. The Isle of Man Shore. *Unknown.* AmFP

On the kitchen wall a flash. The World Outside. Denise Levertov. ConAP

On the Knowledge of Things. Alexander Taylor. NowV

On the Lady Mary Villiers. Thomas Carew. *See* Epitaph on the Lady Mary Villiers.

On the Lake. V. Sackville-West. SBG

On the lake-bottom near. Petoskey Stone. Robert Vas Dias. HeS

On the Lakes of Ponchartrain. *Unknown.* AmFP

On the Lamented Death of Mrs. Throckmorton's Bullfinch. William Cowper. *See* On the Death of Mrs. Throckmorton's Bullfinch.

On the Late Massacre in Piedmont. Milton. Epi; HeIP; InPK; NOBE; OBP; PPoe; PPP; SoSe; VoPo
(Sonnet: On the Late Massacre in Piedmont.) AnMo

On the Lawn at the Villa. Louis Simpson. PPoD; PPP

On the Life of Man. Sir Walter Ralegh. *See* What Is Our Life? A Play of Passion.

On the long shore, lit by the moon. The Goose Fish. Howard Nemerov. HeIP; InPK; LoAs; NoAM

On the Loss of the Royal George. William Cowper. NOBE

On the Loss of U.S. Submarine S4, *sel.* H. C. Canfield. "Entrapped inside a submarine." FaBoCo

On the Marginal Way. Richard Wilbur. CAPP; NOBA

On the Marriage of T. K. and C. C., the Morning Stormy. Thomas Carew. BoLoP

On the Memory of Mr. Edward King, Drowned in the Irish Seas. John Cleveland. SCP-2

On the Morning of Christ's Nativity. Milton. Epi; SCP-1
(Ode on the Morning of Christ's Nativity.) BoReV
Hymn on the Morning of Christ's Nativity, *sel.* NOBE

On the Morning of the Third Night above Nisqually. W. M. Ransom. CDW

On the morning you woke beside me. Mornings/of an Impossible Love. Alice Walker. NVAP

On the most westerly Blasket. The Given Note. Seamus Heaney. NCSH

On the Move. Thom Gunn. NowV; OBP; OxBTC; PPP

On the New Forcers of Conscience. Milton. *See* On the Forcers of Conscience.

On the New Laureate. *Unknown.* FaBoCo

On the New Road. Lyn Lifshin. FAF; NeAC; RiTi

On the night of the Belgian surrender the moon rose. The Moon and the Night and the Men. John Berryman. VGW

On the ninth of November by the dawning of the day. Farewell to Kingsbridge. *Unknown.* AIW

On the Occasion of Becoming an Echo. Anselm Hollo. TwMBP

On the other side/ of my world. To the Man I Live With. Ann Menebroker. IHMS

On the Passion. *Unknown.* OxBM

On the path. Under the Maud Moon. Galway Kinnell. CAAP

On the path winding. The Path among the Stones. Galway Kinnell. NOBA; Prf

On the Prospect of Establishing a Pantisocracy in America. Samuel Taylor Coleridge. MBPR

On the Prospect of Planting Arts and Learning in America. George Berkeley. OBP
(Verses on the Prospect of Planting Arts and Learning in America.) PAIC; PPoD

On the prow. The Landing. Daniel Halpern. AmPA

On the Road to California; or, The Buffalo Bullfight. *Unknown.* AmFP

On the Same. Roy Campbell. OxBTC

On the Saviour's Wounds. Richard Crashaw. PAIC

On the Sea. Keats. MBPR

On the secret map the assassins. Rivers and Mountains. John Ashbery. NoAM; NOBA

On the sidewalk the people are bustling. The Observation. Donovan Leitch. GrRo

On the sixteenth day of September, nineteen twenty-eight. The West Palm Beach Storm. *Unknown.* AmFP

On the smooth brow and clustering hair. Walter Savage Landor. GBL

On the snow I found prints. Invisible Tree. Ryuichi Tamura, *tr. by* Thomas Fitzsimmons. TSWA

On the Soft and Gentle Motions of Eudora. Anne Killigrew. SCP-2

On the Sonnet. Keats. MBPR; PAIC

On the southwest side of Capri. The Nude Swim. Anne Sexton. WPE

On the southwest up-escalator. The Macy's Poem. James Reiss. POL

On the stage, mirrored many times. The Stripper. Anita Endrezze Probst. CDW

On the steep road. Dreamscape. Philip Booth. FiCP

On the steps of the bright madhouse. In the Fleeting Hand of Time. Gregory Corso. SA

On the stiff twig up there. Black Rook In Rainy Weather. Sylvia Plath. Psy

On "The Story of Rimini." Keats. MBPR

On the Street. C. P. Cavafy. *tr. fr. Greek by* Rae Dalven. BoLoP

On the street-corner. What It Means, Living in the City. William Dickey. POL

On the street we two pass. Commitment in a City. Margaret Tsuda. CTBA

On the Suicide of a Friend. Reed Whittemore. ConAP

On the summer road that ran by our front porch. Lizards and Snakes. Anthony Hecht. NCSH; PPoD

On the Telescopic Moon. John Swanick Drennan. BIrV

On the third day after her unexpected death. A Ballad of Orpheus. Maurice Lindsay. SLP

On the threshold of heaven, the figures in the street. To an Old Philosopher in Rome. Wallace Stevens. NoAM; NOBA

On the Times. *Unknown.* OxBM

On the Tombs in Westminster Abbey. *At. to* Francis Beaumont. NOBE; OBP

On the train/ old ladies playing football. Going Uptown to Visit Miriam. Victor Hernandez Cruz. MAT

On the train to the ruins. Nathaniel Tarn. *Fr.* A Nowhere for Vallejo. TwMBP

On the Triumph of Rationalism. Alfred Ainger. FaBoCo

On the Uniformity and Perfection of Nature. Philip Freneau. IPWM

On the Vanity of Earthly Greatness. Arthur Guiterman. InPK

On the Wall. *Unknown.* BluL

On the way down. The Way Down. Philip Levine. NOBA

On the wet sand the queen emerged from forest. Theseus: a Trilogy. Yvor Winters. NOBA

On the Wide Heath. Edna St. Vincent Millay. WPE

On the wide level of a mountain's head. Time, Real and Imaginary. Samuel Taylor Coleridge. MBPR; NOBE; PBMP

On the wide veranda white. A Corn-Song. Paul Laurence Dunbar. AmVN

On the Wing. Christina Rossetti. SBG

On their highest bluff. The Citizen's Complaint. David Allan Evans. HeS

On things asleep, no balm. The Longing. Theodore Roethke. PiAm

On Third Street there's a naked spot. The Ballad of Mary Baldwin. Stephen Sandy. MAT

On This Day I Complete My Thirty-Sixth Year. Byron. MBPR

On this feast day, oh, cursed day and hour! Love at First Sight. Christopher Marlowe. *Fr.* Hero and Leander, First Sestiad. NOBE

On this floor. Floor: O. Stephen Vincent. *Fr.* Elevator Landscapes. NeAC

On This Island. W. H. Auden. InPS; MPo; PSN

On this jungle gym. Skeleton. Coleman Barks. *Fr.* Body Poems. NVAP

On this side of the tapestry. The Tapestry. Howard Nemerov. Prf

On this tree thrown up. Spindrift. Galway Kinnell. IPWM

On Thomas, Second Earl of Onslow. *Unknown.* FaBoCo

On Those That Deserve It. Francis Quarles. BoReV

On thy stupendous summit, rock sublime! Charlotte Smith. *Fr.* Beachy Head. SBG

On Time. Milton. BoReV

On Tintock-Tap there is a mist. Tintock. *Unknown.* GBP

On to the beach the quiet waters crept. The Quiet Tide near Ardrossan. Charles Tennyson Turner. VPC

On top of old smoky. Old Smoky. *Unknown.* AmFP; BLSH, *with music;* BLSo, *with music;* InPK

On Two Monopolists. John Byrom. FaBoCo

On Venus, time passes slowly because. Here. Marvin Bell. AmPA

On Visiting My Son, Port Angeles, Washington. Duane Niatum. CDW

On Visiting Staffa. Keats. MBPR

On Visiting the Tomb of Burns. Keats. MBPR

On Vital Statistics. Hilaire Belloc. POL

On wan dark night on Lac St. Pierre. The Wreck of the *Julie Plante.* William Henry Drummond. PoTa

On warm days in September the high school band. The High School Band. Reed Whittemore. MiP; NCSH

On Waterloo's ensanguined plain. On Scott's "The Field of Waterloo." Thomas, Lord Erskine. FaBoCo

On Wednesday night. Wednesday Night Prayer Meeting. Jay Wright. PoBA

On Wenlock Edge the wood's in trouble. A. E. Housman. NOBE; OxBTC

On Westwell Downs. William Strode. SCP-2

On what foundation stands the warrior's pride. Charles XIII of Sweden. Samuel Johnson. *Fr.* The Vanity of Human Wishes. NOBE

On what pure mission do the seagulls fly. On the Beach. Frances Cornford. BoAnP

On Will Smith. *Unknown.* ECBV; FaBoCo

On windy days the mill. The Unfortunate Miller. A. E. Coppard. PoTa

On yonder hill there is a red deer. *Unknown.* GBP

On Zacheus. Francis Quarles. MetP

Once, *sels.* Alice Walker.
  "Green lawn/ a picket fence." PoBA
  "I/ never liked/white folks." PoBA
  "It is true—/ I've always loved." NMM; NVAP; PoBA

Once a dream did weave a shade. A Dream. Blake. *Fr.* Songs of Innocence. LAuP; MBPR

Once a haughty crocodile left his home upon the Nile. Crocodile. Kornei Chukovsky, *tr. by* Babette Deutsch. ECBV

Once a jolly swagman camped by a billabong. Waltzing Matilda. Andrew Barton Paterson. GBP; PeBB; PoTa; RDB

Once a man is born he has to die. All Intents. Larry Eigner. VGW

Once a mouse, a frog, and a little red hen. The Mouse, the Frog, and the Little Red Hen. *Unknown.* ECBV

Once, after a rotten day at school. The Place's Fault. Philip Hobsbaum. LP; MPo

Once Again. Liz Sohappy Bahe. CDW; VW

Once an old man was an only. Something Like an Apple. James Reiss. CAAP

Once as I travelled through a quiet evening. Egrets. Judith Wright. NCSH

Once as methought Fortune me kissed. Sir Thomas Wyatt. BoLoP
("One as me thought fortune me Kyst.") AAS

Once, as old Lord Gorbals motored. Lord Gorbals. Harry Graham. FaBoCo

Once as we were sitting by. Spring 1942. Lawrence Durrell. OxBTC

Once at imagination's windows I. Nature's Prospect. Margaret Cavendish, Duchess of Newcastle. SCP-2

Once by a mountain lake high in the wilds. Mystic Lake. R. P. Kingston. NVAP

Once by mishap two poets fell a-squaring. Comparison of the Sonnet and the Epigram. Sir John Harrington. PAIC

Once by the Pacific. Robert Frost. HeIP; NOBA; PiAM; VGW

Once did she hold the gorgeous east in fee. On the Extinction of the Venetian Republic. Wordsworth. MBPR; NOBE; OBP; PPoD

Once, far over the breakers. Tanka. Akiko No Yosano, *tr. by* Kenneth Rexroth. PAIC

Once Fondly Lov'd. Burns. SLP

Once I am sure there's nothing going on. Church Going. Philip Larkin. InPK; NoAM; PPP; PSN; SoSe

Once I courted a fair beauty bride. The Fair Beauty Bride. *Unknown.* AmFP

Once I cried for new songs to sing. I Sing No New Songs. Frank Marshall Davis. PoBA

Once I heard an old bachelor say. The Bachelor's Complaint. *Unknown.* AmFP

Once, I knew a fine song. The Black Riders, XLV. Stephen Crane. PiAM

Once I Lived in Cottonwood. *Unknown.* AmFP

Once I lived with my brothers, images. The Centaur Overheard. Edgar Bowers. ConAP

Once I loved a maiden fair. A Ballad Maker. Padraic Colum. AIW

Once I loved a spider. The Spider and the Ghost of the Fly. Vachel Lindsay. VGW

Once I Pass'd through a Populous City. Walt Whitman. MiP

Once I saw a wolf tread a circle in his cage. Traverse City Zoo. Jim Harrison. BoAnP

Once I stood in a green bough. Portrait of the Father. Lindy Hough. IHMS

Once I was good like the Virgin Mary and the Minister's wife. The Scarlet Woman. Fenton Johnson. PoBA

Once I was happy, but now I'm forlorn. The Man on the Flying Trapeze [*or* The Flying Trapeze]. George Leybourne. PoTa; PSoN

Once in a dream (for once I dreamed of you). On the Wing. Christina Rossetti. SBG

Once in a hundred years the Lemmings come. The Lemmings. John Masefield. NoAM

Once in a while. The Children. William Carlos Williams. BBGO

Once in an adolescent sweat. The Campaign for Peace in Our Time. Jon Anderson. CAAP

Once, in finesse of fiddles found I ecstasy. The Embankment. T. E. Hulme. OxBTC; PPoD

Once in Love With Amy, *with music.* Frank Loesser. BLSo

Once in Royal David's City. Cecil Frances Alexander. OxBChV

Once in the dear dead days beyond recall. Love's Old Sweet Song. G. Clifton Bingham. BLSH; BLSo; FSN

Once in the Jurassic, about 150 million years ago. Smokey the Bear Sutra. *Unknown.* MAT

Once in the winter. The Forsaken. Duncan Campbell Scott. PoTa

Once, Lily and I fell from a ladder. Monologue of Two Moons, Nudes with Crests. 1938. Norman Dubie. FiCP

Once made a fairy rooster from. For My Sister Molly Who in the Fifties. Alice Walker. WBN

Once More. George Jonas. NeAC

Once More a-Lumbering Go. *Unknown.* AmFP

Once more around should do it, the man confided. Flight of the Roller Coaster. Raymond Souster. PoTa

Once more I came to Sarum Close. The Cathedral Close. Coventry Patmore. *Fr.* The Angel in the House. VPC

Once more, if you want, make many. Landscape with Pervert. Bink Noll. PPoD

Once more, listening to the wind and rain. The Return. Arna Bontemps. PoBA; WIF

Once more the changed year's turning wheel returns. Barren Spring. Dante Gabriel Rossetti. The House of Life, LXXXIII. VPC

Once more the storm is howling, and half hid. A Prayer for My Daughter. W. B. Yeats. NoAM; OxBTC; RRA; SoSe

Once more unto the breach, dear friends, once more. King Henry the Fifth before Harfleur. Shakespeare. King Henry V, *fr.* III, i. BTTM; PPoe

Once neighbor to the dinosaur. The Star-nosed Mole. Robert Wallace. BoAnP

Once on a time, it came to pass. The Fable of the Piece of Glass and the Piece of Ice. John Hookham Frere. OxBChV

Once on a time there lived a man. Peter Gray. *Unknown.* BLSo

Once on a time—'twas long ago. The Youth and the Northwind. John Godfrey Saxe. PoTa

Once Only. Gary Snyder. CoPAm

Once only by the garden gate. Youth and Love. Robert Louis Stevenson. SLP

Once or twice this side of death. Crystal Moment. Robert P. Tristram Coffin. ECBV

Once people believed the blood. Why Fires Are Lit December 21st. Michael McMahon. FAF

Once riding in old Baltimore. Incident. Countee Cullen. BPo; CTBA; NoAM; NowV; PoBA; SoSe; SFF; VGW

Once the basic skills have been mastered. Another Attempt at the Trick. Cynthia Macdonald. WBN

Once the poet goes behind the shades. For Cynara. Charles Plymell. RRA

Once there lived side by side. I Don't Want to Play in Your Yard. Philip Wingate. FSN

Once there was a crocodile. Crocodile. Kornei Chukovsky, *tr. by* Richard Coe. ECBV

Once there was a house with the ceiling on the floor. Time Upon a Once. Robert Paul Smith. ECBV

Once there was a man named Mr. Artesian and his. Mr. Artesian's Conscientiousness. Ogden Nash. SS

Once there was a Quaker lover. The Quaker Lover. *Unknown.* RDB

Once there was an elephant. Eletelephony. Laura E. Richards. ECBV; OxBChV

Once there would have been the woman standing. The Railings. Alan Brownjohn. LP

Once to the verge of yon steep barrier came. The Recluse; or, Home at Grasmere. Wordsworth. MBPR

Once up u hurl a stone. Mike 65. Lennox Raphael. PoBA

Once upon a midnight dreary, while I pondered, weak and weary. The Raven. Poe. NOBA; PiAM

Once upon a time I spent a summer. Remembering Kevan MacKenzie. Henry Taylor. InPK

Once upon a time there was an Italian. Columbus. OFD

Once upon a time there were three little foxes. The Three Foxes. A. A. Milne. OxBChV

Once we rode. The Number One Daughter of the Wang Family. Chen Hsieh, *tr. by* C. H. Kwock. MIT

Once we'd packed up your clothes. Partial Eclipse. W. D. Snodgrass. Moon; PSN

Once When She Thought Aloud. Dorothea MacKellar. MAuV

Once when the snow of the year was beginning to fall. The Runaway. Robert Frost. ECBV; VGW

Once, when their hearts were wild with joy. On Harting Down. T. Sturge Moore. OxBTC

Once when you were a star. A Poem for Foster. Walter Bradford. HeS

Once, with a whirl of thought oppressed. The Day of Judgment. Swift. InPK

Once you said joking slyly. The Faithful. Jane Cooper. CoPAm

Oncoming Industrial Revolution, The. George Crabbe. *Fr.* The Village. OBP

Ondt and the Gracehoper, The. James Joyce. *Fr.* Finnegans Wake. BIrV

One. Carolyn M. Rodgers. BPo

One A.M. Denise Levertov. CAPP

One a.m./ and she has been sleeping. He She Because How. Anselm Hollo. TwMBP

One-and-Twenty. *Unknown.* AmFP

One arch of the sky. Love in Labrador. Carl Sandburg. VGW

One asked a madman if a wife he had. A Mad Answer of a Madman. Robert Hayman. SoSe

One blindfold went upon the narrow ridge. The Deliverance. Ralph Knevet. SCP-2

One block away from my house is an office building. Tie Your Tongue, Sir? Robert Paul Smith. ECBV

One brought me the news of your death, O Herakleitos my friend. Elegy on Herakleitos. Callimachus, *tr. by* Dudley Fitts. InPK

One by one they appear in. My Sad Captains. Thom Gunn. InPS

One can do one begins to one can only. Reincarnation (II). James Dickey. CAPP

One cannot now help thinking. Now It's Happened. D. H. Lawrence. OBP

One chance, The. Scar. Coleman Barks. *Fr.* Body Poems. NVAP

One Chip of Human Bone. Ray A. Young Bear. VW

One chop uncovered. Chops. Alan Dixon. BoAnP

One Christmas eve my lovers and I. Death and Disfiguration. Judy Grahn. *Fr.* A Woman Is Talking to Death. WBN

One cop holds the spic delicately between thumb and forefinger. The Jet Must Be Hunting for Something. Robert Penn Warren. CoPAm

One day/ Marilyn marched. Chic Freedom's Reflection. Alice Walker. NMM

One day/ two people decide to build a bed. The Bed. Dennis Saleh. NeAC

One day/ while playing with old junk in the attic. Little Johnny's Foolish Invention. Brian Patten. BuTh

One day/ You gonna walk in this house. Seduction. Nikki Giovanni. NMM; RiTi

One day, a fine day, a high-flying-sky day. The Cat Heard the Cat-bird. John Ciardi. ECBV

One day a wag—what would the wretch be at? Art. Ambrose Bierce. InPK

One day across the lake where echoes come now. The Animal that Drank Up Sound. William Stafford. VGW

One day as I was a-rambling around. Will Bill Jones. *Unknown.* AmFP

One day as I was sitting still. The Battle of Sole Bay. *Unknown.* GBP

One-Day Diary. John Biguenet. CoPAm

One day I complained about the periphery. Periphery. A. R. Ammons. NOBA

One day I was out walking on the mountain. The Wild Lumberjack. *Unknown.* AIW

One day I was walking, I heard a complaining. The Housewife's Lament. *Unknown.* MAT

One day I went down in the golden harvest field. *Unknown.* GBP

One day I wrote her name upon the strand. Amoretti, LXXV. Spenser. BoLoP; GBL; HeIP; IPWM; LoAs; PBMP

One day Mamma said "Conrad dear." The Story of Little Suck-a-Thumb. Heinrich Hoffmann, *tr. fr. German.* SpRo

One day ringing men will be a race gone. The Ringers. John Peck. AmPA

One day soon he'll tell her it's time to start packing. Drifters. Bruce Dawe. MAuV

One day the amorous Lysander. The Disappointment. Aphra Behn. SBG; SCP-2

One day the Nouns were clustered in the street. Permanently. Kenneth Koch. CAPP; PPP

One day the sun was rising high. The Peddler and His Wife. *Unknown.* AmFP

One day when I was a child, long ago. Grace Paley. NMM

One day, while in a lonesome grove. Newberry. *Unknown.* AmFP

One dolphin./ Strongly curved, watertight. Dolphin Seen Alone. Richmond Lattimore. BoAnP

One dot/ Grainily shifting. The Bee. James Dickey. SoSe

One dream of passion and of beauty more! Properzia Rossi. Felicia Dorothea Hemans. SBG

One-Eleven Grape Street. Dan Masterson. CoPAm

One evenin' in de month of May. Johnny Get Your Gun. Monroe H. Rosenfeld. PSoN

One evening a young lady fair, her estate rode out to see. On the Banks of Salee. *Unknown.* AmFP

One evening as the sun went down. The Big Rock Candy Mountains. *Unknown.* AmFP

One evening bright stars they were shining. The Brooklyn Theater Fire. *Unknown.* AmFP

One evening, coming home when I should. Winter Evening. Harry Behn. CaYB

One evening in November I happened for to stray. Johnny Carroll's Camp. *Unknown.* AmFP

One evening last June as I rambled. On the Banks of the Little Eau Pleine. *Unknown.* AmFP

One evening (surely I was led by her). Guilt. Wordsworth. *Fr.* The Prelude, I. BoReV

One evening when the sun was low. The Big Rock Candy Mountains. *Unknown.* GBP

One Eyed Black Man in Nebraska. Sam Cornish. PoBA

One-Eyed Bridegroom, The. Constance Urdang. Moon

One face looks out from all his canvases. In an Artist's Studio. Christina Rossetti. OBP

One feather is a bird. The Voice. Theodore Roethke. NowV; VGW

One Flesh. Elizabeth Jennings. MPo; OxBTC

One Foot in Eden. Edwin Muir. BoReV; NoAM; NOBE

One foot in front of the other, heel to toe. Highway Patrol Stops Me, Going Too Slow. Robert Peterson. NeAC

One for All Time, The. Paul Eluard, *tr. fr. French by* Wallace Fowlie. LoAs

One for the Album. Rhyll McMaster. CAAP

One Fragment for God. William Everson. MIT

One granite ridge. Piute Creek. Gary Snyder. CAPP; ConAP; NOBA

One had a lovely face. Memory. W. B. Yeats. BIrV

One has a feeling it is all coming to an end. The Feeling. William Bronk. VGW

One has fallen drunk. Five Men I Know. Thomas Lux. NVAP

One Home. William Stafford. IPWM; VGW

One-Horned Ewe, The. *Unknown.* GBP

One Horse Open Sleigh, The. James S. Pierpont. *See* Jingle Bells.

One hundred feet from off the ground. Long-Suffering of God. Christopher Smart. *Fr.* Hymns for the Amusement of Children. LAuP

One Kingfisher and One Yellow Rose. Eileen Brennan. PFIr

One-l lama, The. The Lama. Ogden Nash. RAE

One Leaf, The. Leslie Norris. LP

One Lion, Once. Robert Canzoneri. CoPAm

One little noise of life remain'd—I heard. On the Eclipse of the Moon of October 1865. Charles Tennyson Turner. VPC

One looks from the train. The Orient Express. Randall Jarrell. NOBA

One Man's Wife. Philip Booth. VGW

One misty, moisty morning. Mother Goose. MG

One more march. March on the Delta. Art Berger. NowV

One More New Botched Beginning. Stephen Spender. NoAM

One More Time. James Welch. VW

One morn before me were three figures seen. Ode on Indolence. Keats. MBPR

One morning as I rambled. The Miner Boy. *Unknown.* AmFP

One morning, as we travelled in the fields. The Riders Held Back. Louis Simpson. ConAP

One Morning in May. *Unknown.* AIW (Nightingale, The.) AmFP

One Morning in May; or, The Young Girl Cut Down in Her Prime. *Unknown.* AmFP

One morning in St. Thomas, when I tried. The Eye. Richard Wilbur. FiCP

One Morning, Oh, So Early! Jean Ingelow. OxBChV

One morning, one morning, one morning in May. One Morning in May [*or* The Nightingale]. *Unknown.* AIW; AmFP

One morning, one morning, one morning in Spring. I'll Be Fourteen Next Sunday. *Unknown.* AmFP; OLR

One Morning We Brought Them Order. Al Lee. WIF

One morning when I went downtown. Morning in Spring. Louis Ginsberg. ECBV

One must have a mind of winter. The Snow Man. Wallace Stevens. HeIP; InPK; MAT; PiAm

One need not be a chamber—to be haunted. Emily Dickinson. AmVN; PiAm; Psy

One needs a lyric poet in these. Julius Lester. In the Time of Revolution, IV. PoBA

One needs a lyric poet in this. Julius Lester. In the Time of Revolution, VI. PoBA

One night, all tired with the weary day. The Gnat. Joseph Beaumont. SCP-2

One night as Dick lay half asleep. Full Moon. Walter de la Mare. ECBV

One night, being pressed by his old friend Chubb. The Undertakers' Club. *Unknown.* GBP

One night came on a hurricane. The Sailor's Consolation. William Pitt, *wr. at. to* Charles Dibdin. FaBoCo

One night he dreamed he was a. The Young Man Who Loved the Girl Who Took Care of Her Aged Father. Greg Kuzma. AmPA

One night I reached a cave: I slept, my head. Incident on a Journey. Thom Gunn. MPo

One of the numb ones, hating. Fighting Talk. Tom Buchan. MIS

One of them undid your blouse, then. For the Country. Larry Levis. NVAP

One ought not to have to care. Robert Frost. *Fr.* The Hill Wife. VGW

One Perfect Rose. Dorothy Parker. OLR; PAIC

One person present steps on his pedal of speech. The Talker. Mona Van Duyn. POL

One Saturday night as we set sail. The Mermaid. *Unknown.* AmFP

One scene as I bow to pour her coffee. Vacation. William Stafford. POL; SFF

One should not neglect one's chin-ups. An Exigent Gymnast. Merle Meeter. AATT

One Sided Shoot-out. Don L. Lee. BPo; PoBA

One sister for sale! For Sale. Shel Silverstein. CTBA

One Song. Stanley Plumly. HeS

One sound. Then the hiss and whir. The Garden. Louise Glück. AmPA; FiCP

One still dark night I sat alone and wrote. Sonnet. Frederick Goddard Tuckerman. *Fr.* Sonnets. PiAm

One stood still, looking stupid. The other. The Willets. May Swenson. WPE

One Summer Evening. Wordsworth. *Fr.* The Prelude, I. OBP

One Sunday mornin' Lambton went. The Lambton Worm. *Unknown.* PeBB

One sure hand. Skipping Stones. Allan D. Farber. SoSe

One that is ever kind said yesterday. The Folly of Being Comforted. W. B. Yeats. GBL; HeIP; LoAs; SoSe

One, The Other, And. Wendy Wieber. NMM

One thing has a shelving bank. A Drumlin Woodchuck. Robert Frost. NoAM; NOBA

One Thing That Can Save America, The. John Ashbery. NOBA

One thing that literature would be greatly the better for. Very Like a Whale. Ogden Nash. InPK

One thing you left with us, Jack Johnson. Strange Legacies. Sterling A. Brown. PoBA

One thousand eight hundred and twenty-four. The Greenland Whale Fishery. *Unknown.* AmFP

One Thousand Fearful Words for Fidel Castro. Lawrence Ferlinghetti. VGW

One Time Henry Dreamed the Number. Doughtry Long. BPo; PoBA

One to make ready. *Unknown.* MG

One translucent magenta leaf on a hot house plant is. Filtres. Andrew Hoyem. MIT

One tree might take seventy years to produce this round. Acorns. Paul Mills. MIS

One, two/ Buckle my shoe. Mother Goose. MG

One, two, three, four. Mother Goose. MG

One, two, three, four, five. *Unknown.* MG

1-2-3 was the number he played but today the number came 3-2-1. Dirge. Kenneth Fearing. HeIP; InPK

One ugly trick has often spoiled. Meddlesome Matty. Ann Taylor. OxBChV

One wading a Fall meadow finds on all sides. The Beautiful Changes. Richard Wilbur. InPS

One wants a Teller in a time like this. Gwendolyn Brooks. *Fr.* The Womanhood. WPE

One wants to be sitting in. The Sky-Splitting Pink Rubber Bistro. Rochelle Owens. RiTi

One was kicked in the stomach. Gangrene. Philip Levine. VGW

One wave/ sucking the shingle. Evolution. Edwin Brock. MPo

One Way Gal. *Unknown.* BluL

One wept whose only child was dead. Maternity. Alice Meynell. BBGO

One, who is not, we see: but one, whom we see not, is. The Higher Pantheism in a Nutshell. Swinburne. *Fr.* The Heptalogia. PAIC; SpRo

One winter afternoon. E. E. Cummings. NCSH

One without looks in to-night. The Fallow Deer at the Lonely House. Thomas Hardy. BoAnP

One word is too often profaned. To ——. Shelley. BoLoP; MBPR; NOBE; PPP

One Word More, *sel.* Robert Browning. Phases of the Moon. Moon

One Year Later. Eric Torgerson. POL

One's grand flights, one's Sunday baths. The Sense of the Sleight-of-hand Man. Wallace Stevens. NOBA

One's-Self I Sing. Walt Whitman. NOBA

Ones who hammer the air with fists, The. Cripples. J. D. Reed. NeAC

Onion Bucket. Lorenzo Thomas. PoBA

Only/ a little/ yellow/ school bus. Snow Country. David Etter. SFF

Only a dish of blueberries could pull me. It's Not the Heat So Much as the Humidity. James Tate. NoAM

Only a few top-heavy hollyhocks, wilting in arid beds. The Public Gardens. Alun Lewis. PSN

Only a few will really understand. One Sided Shoot-out. Don L. Lee. BPo; PoBA

Only a green hill. A Last Word. W. R. Rodgers. Epi

Only a man harrowing clods. In Time of "The Breaking of Nations." Thomas Hardy. BoLoP; NoAM; NOBE; POL; PPoD; PPP; PSN; VoPo

Only a Miner. *Unknown.* AmFP

Only Bar in Dixon, The. James Welch. AmPA

Only brooms. Brooms. Charles Simic. AmPA

Only for Me. Mark Van Doren. NCSH

Only head in the sky, The. Giraffe. Stanley Plumly. AmPA

Only Jealousy of Emer, The. *Unknown, tr. fr. Irish by* John Montague. BIrV

Only joy, now here you are. Fourth Song. Sir Philip Sidney. *Fr.* Astrophel and Stella. GBL

Only last week, walking the hushed fields. Father and Son. F. R. Higgins. BIrV; PFIr

Only on the rarest occasions, when the blue air. The Mountain. W. S. Merwin. VGW

Only response, The. Poem. William Knott. InPK

Only Seven. Henry Sambrooke Leigh. SpRo

Only Sign, The/advertises Tire Ale. Thinking about Carnevale's Wife. Wesley McNair. FAF

Only teaching on Tuesdays, book-worming. Memories of West Street and Lepke. Robert Lowell. CAPP; ConAP; CoPAm; InPS; NOBA: PiAM; PSN

Only the city's people understand four-thirty. American City. Joyce Carol Oates. IPMW

Only the deep well. I Break the Sky. Owen Dodson. PoBA

Only the human being, absolved from kissing and strife. Death Is Not Evil, Evil Is Mechanical. D. H. Lawrence. PBMP

Only the Illegitimate are beautiful. Thesis. Edward Dorn. NOBA

Only the Polished Skeleton. Countee Cullen. VGW

Only the Sky. Pete Winslow. MIT

Only their hands are living, to the wheel attracted. Casino. W. H. Auden. PSN

Only thing that can be relied on, The. The Snow on Saddle Mountain. Kenji Miyazawa, *tr. by* Gary Snyder. IPWM; NoAM; NOBA

Only this evening I saw again low in the sky. Martial Cadenza. Wallace Stevens. VGW

Only Tourist in Havana Turns His Thoughts Homeward, The. Leonard Cohen. NoAM

Onne Ruddeborne bank twa pynynge maydens sate. Elinoure and Juga. Thomas Chatterton. LAuP

Ons as me thought fortune me kyst. Sir Thomas Wyatt. *See* Once as methought Fortune me kissed.

Onset, The. Robert Frost. PBMP; PPP

Onward, Christian Soldiers, *with music.* Sabine Baring-Gould. BLSH

Onward led the road again. Hell Gate. A. E. Housman. NoAM

Onyons. Swift. *Fr.* Market Women's Cries. BIrV

Oo oo ah, mercy mercy me. Mercy Mercy Me. Marvin Gaye. PoRo

Oocuck, The. Justin Richardson. BoAnP

Ootower the grey-broon mairs. Glencoe. Billy Kay. MIS

Opal. Josephine Miles. PAIC

Open Door, The. Elizabeth J. Coatsworth. ECBV

Open House. Theodore Roethke. AnMo; NoAM; NOBA

Open, love. Unclench Yourself. Marge Piercy. NeAC

Open me. Close me. The Swimming Pool. Sandra Hochman. RiTi

Open me like a meadow lily. The Seduction. Suzanne Berger Rioff. NMM

Open Sea, The. William Meredith. CoPAm

Open the door, who's there within? *Unknown.* GBL

Opened, clear as a child's geography. The Summer Countries. Henry Rago. VGW

Opening Day. Bruce Severy. VW

Opening of Eyes. Laura Riding. NoAM

Operation, The. W. D. Snodgrass. InPK

Ophelia's Song. Shakespeare. *Fr.* Hamlet, IV, v. GBL ("How Should I your true love know.") AIW

Ophelia's Song. Marya Zaturenska. OLR

Opportunity. Harry Graham. FaBoCo

Opposites. Carolyn Stoloff. RiTi

Opulent oracle—it's a terrible thing! It's a Terrible Thing! Everett Hoagland. BPo

Opusculum paedagogum. Study of Two Pears. Wallace Stevens. InPK; InPS

Or/ did he make the estuary? Redriff. David Jones. *Fr.* The Anathemata. TwMBP

Or/ hoodoo ecology vs. the judeo. Al Capone in Alaska. Ishmael Reed. MIT

Or scorn or pity on me take. The Dream. Ben Jonson. NOBE

Oracles, The. A. E. Housman. BTTM

Oraga Haru, *sels.* Issa, *tr. fr. Japanese by* Nobuyuki Yuasa. OFD
Buddha's Birthday: April 8, 1819.
Buddha's Death Day: February 15, 1815.
"For a fresh start."

Oral Messages, *sel.* Lawrence Ferlinghetti. I Am Waiting. CAPP

Orange Bears, The. Kenneth Patchen. IPWM

Orange in the middle of a table. Against Still Life. Margaret Atwood. NMM

Orange Juice Song. David Phillips. NeAC

Orange Lily, The. *Unknown.* GBP

Orange on its way. On Its Way. May Swenson. WPE

Orange on the table, An. Alicante. Jacques Prévert, *tr. by* Lawrence Ferlinghetti. BoLoP

Orange Tree, The. John Shaw Neilson. MAuV

Orange Tree, The. Ellen Pearce. IHMS

Orange Tree Dream. Judith Serin. NPW

Orators, The, *sel.* W. H. Auden. O Where Are You Going? NOBE; OBP

Orbed Maiden. Shelley. *Fr.* The Cloud. Moon

Orchard Is Not Cut Down, The ("The orchard is gone. A space"). Peter Whigham. TwMBP

Orchestra, or A Poeme of Dauncing, *sels.* Sir John Davies. "Behold the worlde, how it is whirled round." OBP "Harke how the birds doe sing, and marke then how." OBP Praise of Dancing, The. NOBE

Orchids. Theodore Roethke. AnMo; PiAm; PPoe

Orders, Passages 24. Robert Duncan. CAAP

Ordinary Day, An. Norman MacCaig. LP

Ordinary Evening in Cleveland, An. Lewis Turco. ANTL

Ordinary Man, The. Robert Service. BBGO

Oread. Hilda Doolittle ("H.D."). NoAM; NOBA; PiAm; RiTi; SBG

Oregon Message, An. William Stafford. Moon

Organ Transplant. J. D. Reed. POL

Organizer's Bogeymen, The. Marge Piercy. Psy

Orgasm completely, The. Sonnet. Tom Clark. PPoD

Orient Express, The. Randall Jarrell. NOBA

Oriental. Napoleon St. Cyr. FAF

Oriflamme. Jessie Redmond Fauset. PoBA

Origin of Baseball, The. Kenneth Patchen. IPWM

Origin of Hot and Cold According to the Delawares, The. Lyn Lifshin. FAF

Original./ Ragged-round. Malcolm X. Gwendolyn Brooks. NowV; OFD; PoBA

Original Sequence. Philip Booth. SFF

Original Sin. Robinson Jeffers. PiAm

Original Sin: A Short Story. Robert Penn Warren. CoPAm; PPP

Original Sin on the Sussex Coast. John Betjeman. BBGO

Origins. Keorapetse Kgositsile. PoBA

Orinda to Lucasia Parting, October 1661, at London. Katherine Philips. SCP-2

"Oriole, questing." Nesting Time. Arthur Guiterman. ECBV

Oriole with joy was sweetly singing, The. In the Shade of the Old Apple Tree. Harry H. Williams. FSN

Orion. Adrienne Rich. NoAM; WPE

Orison to the Blessed Virgin, An. William Herebert. BoReV

Ornithology. Siv Cedering Fox. NVAP

Ornithology in Florida. Arthur Guiterman. BoAnP

Orotava Road, The. Basil Bunting. NoAM

O'Rourke's Feast ("O'Rourke's revel rout let no person forget"). Hugh MacGowran, *tr. fr. Irish by* Charles Wilson. BIrV

Orphan Girl, The. *Unknown.* AmFP

Orphan hours, the year is dead. Dirge for the Year. Shelley. FSFS

Orphan, or the Unhappy Marriage, The, *sels.* Thomas Otway. SCP-2 "Then thus let's go together," *fr.* IV, ii. "Where am I? Sure I wander 'midst enchantment," *fr.* V, ii.

Orphan, yes, An. But not. Fragment Reflection I. Doris Turner. JB

Orphans. David Ray. FiCP

Orpheus. Michael Goldman. NowV

Orpheus. Yvor Winters. NOBA; PiAm; VGW

Orpheus and Eurydice. Ovid, *tr. fr. Latin by* Rolfe Humphries. *Fr.* Metamorphoses. GrRo

Orpheus I am, come from the deeps below. John Fletcher. *Fr.* The Mad Lover, IV, i. GBL

Orpheus in Greenwich Village. Jack Gilbert. POL

Orpheus with his lute made trees. Sweet Music's Power. John Fletcher. *Fr.* King Henry VIII (*by* Shakespeare). NOBE

Orthodoxy's staunch adherent. To Dr. Kipling. Richard Porson. FaBoCo

Oscar Robertson: Peripheral Vision. William Matthews. PPoD

Osip Mandelstam. Irving Layton. NeAC

Othello, *sels.* Shakespeare. AIW "And let me the canakin clink, clink," *fr.* II, iii. "My mother had a maid call'd Barbara," *fr.* IV, iii.

Othello Jones Dresses for Dinner. Ed Roberson. PoBA

Other bright days of action have seemed great. John Masefield. *Fr.* Biography. OxBTC

Other night while I was sparking sweet. Terlina Spray, The. Kiss Me Quick and Go. Silas S. Steele. BLSo

Other props are gone, The. Je t'adore. Thomas Kinsella. NoAM

Others always skip over the word. In Praise of BIC Pens. David Hilton. NowV

Others because you did not keep. A Deep-Sworn Vow. W. B. Yeats. PSN; TCP

Others, I am not the first. A. E. Housman. OBP; OxBTC; PPP

Others taunt me with having knelt at well-curbs. For Once, Then, Something. Robert Frost. NoAM; NOBA; PiAm

Otter, An. Ted Hughes. NoAM

Otter is known, The. Lutra, The Fisher. James McMichael. AmPA

Otters. William Hart-Smith. BoAnP

Our band is few, but true and tried. Song of Marion's Men. Bryant. BTTM

Our Bias. W. H. Auden. NoAM

Our Bodies. Denise Levertov. AnMo; PPP

Our brains ache, in the merciless iced east winds that knive us. Exposure. Wilfred Owen. InPS; NoAM

Our captain stood upon the deck, a spyglass in his hand. Captain Bunker. *Unknown.* AmFP

Our City Is Guarded by Automatic Rockets. William Stafford. NowV

Our day was composed of resemblances, take. Sail Away. Robert Adamson. CAAP

"Our Fadder, Which are in Heaben!" He Paid Me Seven. *Unknown.* BPo

Our Family. Leonard Clark. RAE

Our father works in us. A Father of Women. Alice Meynell. SBG; WPE

Our fathers' God! from out whose hand. Centennial Hymn. Whittier. BTTM

Our Fear. Zbigniew Herbert, *tr. fr. Polish by* Czeslaw Milosz. BuTh

Our flat bottomed boat. Old Man Let's go Fishing in the Yellow Reeds of the Bay. Mei Berssenbrugge. SA

Our glances spin silver threads. Empathy. Agnes Pratt. VW

Our God, Our Help in Ages Past. Isaac Watts. BLSH, *with music;* BoReV

Our golden age was then, when lamp and rug. Family Prime. Mark Van Doren. VGW

Our Goodman. *Unknown.* AmFP

Our hammock swung between Americas. Elegy. Derek Walcott. OBP

Our hearts knelt down in wonder. Alston Chapel. James E. Warren, Jr. AATT

Our Hunting Fathers. W. H. Auden. NoAM

Our Insufficiency to Praise God Suitably, for His Mercy. Edward Taylor. *Fr.* God's Determinations. PiAm

Our journey had advanced. Emily Dickinson. AmVN; GrRo

Our King went forth to Normandy. The Agincourt Carol. *Unknown.* OxBM

Our Lady. Mary Elizabeth Coleridge. WPE

Our last free summer we mooned about at odd hours. Chrysalides. Thomas Kinsella. BIrV; NoAM

Our last morning in that long room. In the Last Few Moments Came the Old German Cleaning Woman. Jane Cooper. CoPAm

Our life is not life, save in the fleeting. Responding Voice. Francisco A. De Icaza, *tr. by* Samuel Beckett. PBMP

Our life is two-fold: Sleep hath its own world. The Dream, I. Byron. GrRo

Our little fleet in July first. The Armada, 1588. John Wilson. OxBChV

Our Lives. Sharon Scott. JB

Our lives are Swiss. Emily Dickinson. NOBA; POL

Our love was conceived in silence and must live silently. At the Dark Hour. Paul Dehn. BoLoP

Our moulting days are in their twilight stage. Garnishing the Aviary. Margaret Danner. Far from Africa, I. BPo; PoBA

Our mournful Philomel. Michael Drayton. *Fr.* The Shepherd's Sirena. SCP-2

Our Needy Neighbours. William Langland. *Fr.* The Vision of Piers Plowman. OxBM

Our Norman betters. Lines: Inspired by the Controversy on the Value or Otherwise of Old English Studies. Anthony Burgess. FaBoCo

Our objections to the war. For the Minority. Robert Peterson. NeAC

Our old cat has kittens three. Choosing Their Names. Thomas. Hood. PCat

Our passions are most like to floods and streams. Sir Walter Ralegh to the Queen. Sir Walter Ralegh. AAS

Our portion of fire. The Manichaeans. Gary Snyder. VGW

Our purple tongues that testify. For Proserpine. Stanley Kunitz. PAIC

Our roads are ridden. For Sammy Younge. Charlie Cobb. PoBA

"Our saints are poets, Milton and Blake." Encounter. Denis Devlin. BIrV

Our sardine fishermen work at night in the dark of the moon. The Purse-Seine. Robinson Jeffers. NoAM; NOBA

Our Saviour's Golden Rule. Isaac Watts. OxBChV

Our short fat, lord bishop. Bad Bishop Jegon. *Unknown.* GBP

Our single purpose was to walk through snow. Polar Exploration. Stephen Spender. NoAM

Our Smoke Has Gone Four Ways. Lance Henson. CDW

Our Sobbing Must Be Heard. Grace Cavalieri. AATT

Our Sunday morning when dawn-priests were applying. Sonnet. John Berryman. BoLoP; Epi

Our Vegetable Love Shall Grow. Elaine Feinstein. POL

Our whistling son called his canary Hector. Boy, Cat, Canary. Stephen Spender. LP

Our Youth. John Ashbery. CAPP; ConAP; VGW

Out. Ted Hughes. TwMBP

Out amongst the flowers sweet. Hearts and Flowers. Mary D. Brine. FSN

Out beside the highway, first thing in the morning. North Coast Town. Robert Gray. CAAP

Out Fishing. Barbara Howes. PPoD; WPE

Out for a walk, after a week in bed. An Urban Convalescence. James Merrill. NOBA; NowV

Out from Lobster Cove. J. D. Reed. NeAC

Out in the Dark. Edward Thomas. NOBE

Out in the far distance away. Unknown Smoke. Archie Washburn. VW

Out in the late amber afternoon. In Shadow. Hart Crane. NOBA

Out in the sun the goldfinch flits. The Hollow Wood. Edward Thomas. RAE

Out in the yellow meadows, where the bee. George Meredith. *Fr.* Modern Love. GBL

Out in this desert we are testing bombs. Trying to Talk with a Man. Adrienne Rich. RiTi; WBN

Out-island once, on a South slope. Deer Isle. Philip Booth. VGW

Out of a cell into this darkened space. Frank Drummer. Edgar Lee Masters. *Fr.* Spoon River Anthology. NoAM

Out of a fired ship which by no way. A Burnt Ship. John Donne. InPK

Out of a gothic North, the pallid children. Good-Bye to the Mezzogiorno. W. H. Auden. OxBTC

Out of Blindness. Leslie B. Blades. NowV

Out of burlap sacks, out of bearing butter. They Feed They Lion. Philip Levine. MAT; NoAM; NOBA; Prf

Out of childhood into manhood. Hiawatha and Mudjekeewis. Longfellow. The Song of Hiawatha, IV. AKE

Out of every hundred of us. American Commencement. Aram Boyajian. NeAC

Out of friendship and a slow retreat of the blood. Ascending Red Cedar Moon. Duane Niatum. CDW

Out of me unworthy and unknown. Anne Rutledge. Edgar Lee Masters. *Fr.* Spoon River Anthology. NoAM; NOBA; OFD

Out of my heart, one day, I wrote a song. Misapprehension. Paul Laurence Dunbar. BPo

Out of my soul's depth to thee my cries have sounded. De Profundis. Thomas Campion. BoReV

Out of Sight, Out of Mind. Barnabe Googe. InPS

Out-of-the-Body Travel. Stanley Plumly. AmPA

Out of the bosom of the air. Snow-Flakes. Longfellow. FSFS; NOBA

Out of the broken/ morning. To Redistort a Weltanschauung. Matthew Mead. TwMBP

Out of the church she followed them. Maude Clare. Christina Rossetti. VPC

Out of the Cradle Endlessly Rocking. Walt Whitman. AmVN; Epi; HeIP; IPWM; NOBA; PiAm; PPoe

Out of the dark. The Open Door. Elizabeth J. Coatsworth. ECBV

Out of the dark raw earth. Alabama. Julia Fields. PoBA

Out of the Desert. Diane Levenberg. NPW

Out of the earth, out of the air, out of the water. Rapparees. Richard Murphy. *Fr.* The Battle of Aughrim. BIrV

Out of the hurt left standing in his eyes. A Requiem for Innocence. William R. Mitchell. AATT

Out of the land of shadows and darkness. From the Underworld. Howard Blaikley. GrRo

Out of the mud two strangers came. Two Tramps in Mud Time. Robert Frost. NoAM

Out of the night that covers me. W. E. Henley. NOBE

Out of the Past. Robert Wallace. POL

Out of the rolling ocean the crowd came a drop gently to me." Walt Whitman. LoAs

Out of the Sea, Early. May Swenson. RFM

Out of the shadow, I am come in to you whole a black holy man. Study Peace. LeRoi Jones. PoBA

Out of their slumber Europeans spun. Snow in Europe. David Gascoyne. LP; MPo

Out of You. Rodney Phillips. POL

Out on Santa Fe—Blues. *Unknown.* BluL

Out on the board the old shearer stands. Click Go the Shears, Boys. *Unknown.* MAuV

Out on the Hillside. Mary Gilmore. MAuV

Out on the lawn I lie in bed. A Summer Night. W. H. Auden. PSN

Out on the ocean, great wide ocean. Great *Titanic. Unknown.* AmFP

"Out, Out." Robert Frost. AnMo; BuTh; MiP; NowV; PiAm; PPoe; SoSe; VGW; WIF

Out through the fields and the woods. Reluctance. Robert Frost. NOBA

Out Upon It! I Have Loved. Sir John Suckling. *See* Constant Lover, The.

Out walking in the frozen swamp one gray day. The Wood-Pile. Robert Frost. AnMo; NoAM; VGW

Out walking ties left over from a track. Cross Ties. X. J. Kennedy. CoPAm

Out with the mountain moon, stinging clear. Mill Valley. Myra Cohn Livingston. RFM

Outbreak. Bill Anderson. VGW

Outcast. Claude McKay. PoBA

Outcry upon Opportunity, An. Shakespeare. *Fr.* The Rape of Lucrece. NOBE

Outlanders, The. William Morris. *Fr.* The Earthly Paradise. VPC

Outlaw, The. Seamus Heaney. NoAM

Outlaw of Loch Lene, The. *Unknown, tr. fr. Modern Irish by* Jeremiah Joseph Callanan. BIrV; GBL; PFIr

Outlook wasn't brilliant for the Mudville nine that day, The. Casey at the Bat. Ernest Lawrence Thayer. PPoD; SPo

Outlook wasn't brilliant for the Mudvillettes, it seems; The. Casey's Daughter at the Bat. Al Graham. SPo

Outposts. J. S. Harry. CAAP

Outrage. Lucille Iverson. WBN

Outrageously Blessed, The. Barry Spacks. CoPAm

Outside. Phyllis Beauvais. IHMS

Outside Abilene. Harley Elliott. HeS

Outside, affectionate eyes. Ursula. David Ray. VGW

Outside it is cold. Inside. Winter: For an Untenable Situation. Alan Dugan. NowV

Outside my cheap candle. To Myself, Late, in a Myrtle Grove. Robert Peterson. NeAC

Outside of a Small Circle of Friends. Phil Ochs. NowV

Outside soft and sidling, white as June, snow. At Poetry Workshop, Winter Semester. Robert A. Martin. AATT

Outside the cold, the rain, the happy dogs. This is Not a Poem. Luís Omar Salinas. SA

Outside, the landlord undertakes the landscape. Leaving the Country House to the Landlord, Five Years Later. Wesley McNair. FAF

Outside, the last kids holler. Leaving the Motel. W. D. Snodgrass. PiAm

Outside the plasma supermarket. Leaflets. Adrian Mitchell. NowV

Outside the U.S. Consulate. The Earth Sings Mi-fa-mi. Pat Lowther. MMD

Outspoken buttocks in pink beads. National Winter Garden. Hart Crane. *Fr.* The Bridge: Three Songs. InPS

Oven Bird, The. Robert Frost. HeIP; NoAM; NOBA; PiAm; PPP; VoPo

Over an ash-fawn beach fronting a sea which keeps. Fiascherino. Charles Tomlinson. NoAM

Over and back. At Ithaca. Hilda Doolittle ("H.D."). VGW

Over Asia. Anne Waldman. RiTi

Over Coffee. Jennifer Maiden. CAAP

Over deep cushions, drenched with drowsy scents. Damned Women. Baudelaire, *tr. by* Roy Campbell. BoLoP

Over hill, over dale. Shakespeare. *Fr.* A Midsummer Night's Dream, II, i. NOBE

Over hill, over dale, we have hit the dusty trail. The Caissons Go Rolling Along. Edmund L. Gruber. BLSo; BTTM

Over my head, I see the bronze butterfly. Lying in a Hammock at William Duffy's Farm. James Wright. ANTL; CAPP; ConAP; InPS; IPWM; NOBA; PSN; SFF

Over that morn hung heaviness, until. Seascape. Francis Brett Young. OxBTC

Over the barbered lawn a great. Glasgow Botanic Gardens. James Rankin. MIS

Over the bleak and barren snow. Tony O. Colin Francis. FaBoCo

Over the fence. Emily Dickinson. SBG

Over the half-finished houses. The Roofwalker. Adrienne Rich. PiAm; PPP; Psy

Over the hearth with my 'minishing eyes I muse. The Cat of the House. Ford Madox Ford. PCat

Over the hill and over the dale. Keats. MBPR

Over the Hills and Far Away. John Gay. *Fr.* The Beggar's Opera, I, i. BLSo, *with music;* NOBE

Over the land freckled with snow half-thawed. Thaw. Edward Thomas. OxBTC

Over the Mindanao Deep. Gary Snyder. *Fr.* Hitch Haiku. InPK

Over the monstrous shambling sea. Marsh Song—At Sunset. Sidney Lanier. NOBA

Over the mountains. Love Will Find Out the Way. *Unknown.* GBL

Over the river, and through the woods. Thanksgiving Day. Lydia Maria Child. ECBV

Over! the sweet summer closes. Prologue. Tennyson. *Fr.* Becket. GBL

Over the warts on the bumpy. Sadie's Playhouse. Margaret Danner. PoBA

Over the west side of the mountain. Lyrebirds. Judith Wright. BoAnP

Over 2000 Illustrations and a Complete Concordance. Elizabeth Bishop. NoAM

Over yonder's a park, which is newly begun. The Corpus Christi Carol. *Unknown.* GBP

Over your body the clouds go. Gulliver. Sylvia Plath. NOBA

Overheard in a Saltmarsh. Harold Monro. ECBV; LCL

Overland to the Islands. Denise Levertov. ConAP

Overnight, very. Mushrooms. Sylvia Plath. PBMP; Psy; SS

Overweight Poem. Diane Wakoski. CAAP

Ovid in the Third Reich. Geoffrey Hill. NoAM; POL

Ovidian Elegiac Metre Described and Exemplified, The. Schiller, *tr. fr. German by* Samuel Taylor Coleridge. MBPR

Ovid's Banquet of Sense, sel. George Chapman.
"In a loose robe of tinsel forth she came." SCP-2

Ovid's Fifth Elegy. Ovid. *See* Corinnae Concubitus.

Owen of Carron, sel. John Langhorne.
"Does nature bear a tyrant's breast?" FaBoCo

Owl. George MacBeth. MPo

Owl, The. W. S. Merwin. PPP

Owl, The. V. Sackville-West. SBG

Owl, The. Tennyson. ECBV

Owl, The. Edward Thomas. NoAM; NOBE; PPoe

Owl, The. Robert Penn Warren. CoPAm

Owl, The. David Young. CAAP

Owl and the Nightingale, The, *sel. Unknown, at. to* Nicholas de Guildford.
Owl against Nightingale, *orig. and mod. English prose.* OxBM

Owl and the Pussy-cat, The. Edward Lear. NOBE; OxBChV; SFF
Love Song, sel. PCat

Owl-Critic, The. James Thomas Fields. ECBV; PoTa

Owl is abroad, the bat, and the toad, The. The Witches' [3rd] Charm. Ben Jonson. *Fr.* The Masque of Queens. NOBE; SCP-1

Owl Seen In Rearview Mirror. Duane Niatum. VW

Owls. John Fuller. POL

Owls. W. D. Snodgrass. BoAnP

Owner of My Face, The, *sel.* Rodney Hall.
   "You are coming to me in the rain." CAAP
Ox, long fed with musty hay, An. Recantation Illustrated in the Story of the Mad Ox. Samuel Taylor Coleridge. MBPR
Oxen, The. Thomas Hardy. InPK; IPWM; NoAM; NOBE; OxBTC; PPoe; PPP; VoPo
Oxen: Ploughing at Fiesole. Charles Tomlinson. OxBTC
Oxford, *sel.* Edward Dorn.
   Comforted by Limestone. NOBA
Oxford Canal. James Elroy Flecker. OxBTC
Oxford Girl, The; or, Expert Town. *Unknown.*
Oystering. Richard Howard. NoAM
Ozymandias. Shelley. Epi; HeIP; InPK; IPWM; MBPR; NOBE; OBP; PAIC; PPoD; SFF; SoSe; SpRo
Ozymandias Revisited. Morris Bishop. PAIC; SpRo

**P**

P. C. Plod Versus the Dale St Dog Strangler. Roger McGough. NoAM
P.S. 42. Gregory Corso. SA
Pa, Pa, Build Me a Boat. *Unknown.* AmFP
Pa would often have to fetch you home. To My Sister. David Kherdian. SA
Pacific Epitaphs. Dudley Randall. NoAM
Pack, clouds, away! and welcome day! Love's Good-morrow. Thomas Heywood. *Fr.* The Rape of Lucrece. GBL; LoAs
Pack Rat, The. Robert Pack. CoPAm; PPP
Packed in my mind lie all the clothes. The Inward Morning. Henry David Thoreau. AmVN; PiAm
Packer City Poem. Peter Cooley. HeS
Packin' Trunk Blues. *Unknown.* BluL
Pact, A. Ezra Pound. NoAM; NOBA; PAIC; PiAm; PSN
Pact that we made was the ordinary pact, The. From a Survivor. Adrienne Rich. LoAs
Padda Song, The. *Unknown.* GBP
Paddy, Get Back. *Unknown.* AmFP
Paddy O'Rafther. Samuel Lover. PFIr; PoTa
Padraic O'Conaire, Gaelic Storyteller. F. R. Higgins. PFIr
Padstow Night Song, The. *Unknown.* GBP
Paean to Place. Lorine Niedecker. RiTi
Pagan Isms, The. Claude McKay. BPo
Page from a Diary. Desmond O'Grady. NoAM
Pageant Verses. Sir Thomas More. AAS
Pain—expands the time. Emily Dickinson. PiAm
Pain has an element of blank. Emily Dickinson. PPP; SBG
Pain of loving you, The. A Young Wife. D. H. Lawrence. PBMP; VoPo
Pain visits me. My Knees Go before the Firing Squad at Dawn. Diane Wakoski. CAAP
Pains of Education, The. Charles Churchill. FaBoCo (Author, The.) ESaP
Pains of insecurity surround me. Back Again, Home. Don L. Lee. BPo
Pains of Sleep, The. Samuel Taylor Coleridge. MBPR (Child's Evening Prayer, A.) OxBChV
Paint Castlemaine in colours that will hold. Andrew Marvell. *Fr.* The Last Instructions to a Painter. SCP-1
Paint me a cavernous waste shore. Sweeney Erect. T. S. Eliot. AnMo; OxBTC; VGW

Paint samples. Bruises. Coleman Barks. *Fr.* Body Poems. NVAP
Painted Head. John Crowe Ransom. NoAm; NoBA; PiAm
Painted Lady, The. Margaret Danner. BPo
Painter, The. John Ashbery. NOBA
Painting an Old Apartment. James Bonk. HeS
Paintings with stiff. Primitives. Dudley Randall. BPo
Pair, A. May Swenson. RFM
Pair of black swans on the lake, A. Mating Swans. James McAuley. MAuV
Paisley Ceiling, The. Lila Arnold. IHMS
Paiute Ponies. Jim Barnes. CDW
Pal, in the Pals of Death Club. This Is a Poem for the Fathers and for Michael Ryan. Thomas Lux. AmPA
Palace of Pleasant Regard, The. Lady of the Assembly. *Fr.* The Assembly of Ladies. WPE
Pale Blue Casket, The. Oliver Pitcher. PoBA
Pale brown Moses went down to Egypt land. Benediction. Bob Kaufman. IPWM
Pale faced, tight laced. Margaret Southgate. POL
Pale gold of the walls, gold. Gold. Donald Hall. ConAP; InPS
Pale grey, her guns hooded, decks clear of all impediment. H. M. S. *Hero.* Michael Roberts. OxBTC
Pale moon was rising above the green mountain, The. The Rose of Tralee. C. Mordaunt Spencer. BLSH
Palindrome. Lisel Mueller. IHMS
Palinode, A. Edmund Bolton. PAIC
Palinode, A. Matthew Arnold. PPP
Palm Sunday: Good Friday. Giles Fletcher the Younger. *Fr.* Christ's Victory and Triumph, III. BoReV
Palomino Stallion, The. Alden Nowlan. BoAnP; POL
Pampered steed, of swiftness proud. The. The Horse and the Mule. John Huddlestone Wynne. OxBChV
Pamphilia to Amphilanthus. Mary Sidney Wroth, Countess of Montgomery. *Fr.* Urania. WPE
Pamphilia's Sonnet. Mary Sidney Wroth, Countess of Montgomery. *Fr.* Urania. WPE
Pan. Emerson. PiAm
Pan, grant that I may never prove. Song by the Wavering Nymph. Aphra Behn. SBG
Panama Limited, The. *Unknown.* BluL
Pancho Villa. Lou Lipsitz. NCSH
Panda, The. Harley Elliott. *Fr.* Animals That Stand in Dreams. NeAC
Panegyric to My Lord Protector, A, *sel.* Edmund Waller.
   "While with a strong and yet a gentle hand." SCP-2
Pangloss's Song. Richard Wilbur. NoAM
Pangolin, The. Marianne Moore. NoAM, NOBA
Pangur Ban. *Unknown, tr. fr. Old Irish by* Robin Flower. PFIr
Pan's/ spring rain. Symphony No. 3, in D Minor. Jonathan Williams. *Fr.* Mahler. VGW
Pansies, lilies, kingcups, daisies. To the Small Celandine. Wordsworth. MBPR
Panther. Sam Cornish. PoBA
Panther Man. James A. Emanuel. BPo
Pantisocracy. Samuel Taylor Coleridge. MBPR; PAIC
Papa above! Emily Dickinson. PiAM
Papa Doc Is Dead. Carol Cox. MMD
Papa finally left us. Divorce. Siv Widerberg, *tr. by* Verne Moberg. CTBA
Papa . . . here are the $7. Happiness is a Charlie Chaplin Movie. Luis Omar Salinas. SA
Papa Love Baby. Stevie Smith. SBG
Paper Boats, *sel.* Rabindranath Tagore.
   "Day by day I float my paper boats." RAE

Paper come out—done strewed de news. Scottsboro. *Unknown.* InPK

Paper Cutter, The. David Ignatow. CTBA

Paper Lantern, The. Tennessee Williams. *Fr.* Recuerdo. CTBA

Paper Nautilus, The. Marianne Moore. VGW

Paper of Pins. *Unknown.* AmFP; BLSo, *with music*

Paper tiger throw H-bomb in south pole. Pepsi Generation. Walasse Ting. MAT

Paper II. Carl Sandburg. TH

Papers that clear him tucked in his inside pocket, The. Two Figures from the Movies. William Meredith. PPoD

Paps of Dana, The. James Stephens. NoAM

Parable. W. H. Auden. FaBoCo

Parable for Our Time. Peter Michelson. HeS

Parable of the Old Man [*or* Men] and the Young. The. Wilfred Owen. GrRo; OBP; WIF

Paracelsus In Excelsis. Ezra Pound. PiAM

Parachutist, The. Jon Anderson. AmPA

Parachutist. Samuel Hazo. SPo

Parade, The. Liz Sohappy Bahe. VW

Paraders for the Bomb. Sidney Bernard. NowV

Paradigm, The. Allen Tate. NOBA

Paradigms of Fire. Brian Swann. AmPA

Paradise. George Herbert. PAIC

Paradise Is Not a Place. Daniela Gioseffi. WBN

Paradise Lost, *sels.* Milton.
  Adam and Eve in Paradise, Bk. IV, *ll.* 223-319, 736-775. SCP-1
  Banishment, The, Bk. XII, *ll.* 624-649. NOBE
  "Beneath him with new wonder now he views," Bk. IV, *ll.* 205-268. PPP
  Conclusion: "High in front advanc'd/ The brandisht sword of God before them blaz'd," Bk. XII, *ll.* 632-649. OBP
  Creation: the Fifth Day, Fishes and Birds, Bk. VII, *ll.* 387-449. SCP-1
  Eve Contemplates Sharing Her Sin, Bk. IX, *ll.* 811-833. OBP
  Eve Speaks to Adam, Bk. IV, *ll.* 639-656. GBL
  Evening in Paradise, Bk. IV, *ll.* 598-656. NOBE
    (Evening in Eden, *ll.* 598-609.) OBP
    (Moon and the Nightingale, The, *ll.* 598-609.) Moon
  "Hail wedded love, mysterious law, true source," Bk. IV, *ll.* 750-770. PAIC
  "He ended; and thus Adam last replied," Bk. XII, *ll.* 552-649. HeIP
  "His pride/ Had cast him out from Heaven, with all his host," Bk. I, *ll.* 37-236, *abr.* PPoe
  Holy Light, Bk. III, *ll.* 1-55. NOBE
    (Poet's Blindness, The.) OBP
  Immortal Hate, Bk. I, *ll.* 76-124. NOBE
  "Of man's first disobedience, and the fruit," Bk. I, *ll.* 1-83. PAIC
    (Invocation, *ll.* 1-26.) OBP
  Satan and the Fallen Angels, Bk. I, *ll.* 283-376, 492-507. SCP-1
  Satan as Rebel-Liberator, Bk. I, *ll.* 242-262. OBP
  Satan Flies to the Sun, Bk. III, *ll.* 552-630. SCP-1
  Vision of the Future; the Flood, Bk. XI, *ll.* 556-700, 738-756, 829-835. SCP-1
  War in Heaven, Bk. VI, *ll.* 202-219. OBP

Paradise Regained, *sels.* Milton. SCP-1
  Political Power, Bk. IV, *ll.* 25-143.
  Temptation of the Magic Banquet, Bk. II, *ll.* 337-392.

Paradox. Benjamin K. Bennett. POL

Paradox, The. Paul Laurence Dunbar. PoBA

Paradox. Tom McGrath. SLP

Paradox. Vassar Miller. WIF

Paralytic man has dropped in death, The. In Manchester Square. Alice Meynell. SBG

Paranoia. Michael Dennis Browne. AmPA

Parasitosis. Ronda Davis. JB

Parchman Farm Blues. *Unknown.* BluL

Parchment and paper left clean. The Making of Color. Hugh Seidman. AmPA

Pardon, The. Richard Wilbur. NoAM; NOBA

Pardoner's Tale Blues. Patricia Beer. AIW

Pare a willow. Peeled Wand. Derek Bowman. MIS

Parentage. Alice Meynell. SBG

Parents are sinful now, for they must whisper. Marriage. Austin Clarke. BIrV

Paring the Apple. Charles Tomlinson. OxBTC, TwMBP

Paris. Gregory Corso. VGW

Paris. Al Young. CoPAm

Paris Railway-Station, The. Dante Gabriel Rossetti. VPC

Parish Register, The, *sel.* George Crabbe.
  Burials, Pt. III.
  Lady of the Manor, The. NOBE

Park, the heart, you see at town's center is soft, The. Last Look at La Plata, Missouri. Jim Barnes. CDW

Park's beautiful, The. On the Fine Arts Garden, Cleveland. Russell Atkins. PoBA

Parlement of the Thre Ages, The, *sel. Unknown.*
  Poacher, The, *orig. and mod. English prose.* OxBM

Parley of Beasts. "Hugh MacDiarmid." BoAnP; NoAM

Parliament Hill Fields. John Betjeman. NOBE

Parliament of England, Ye. *Unknown. See* Ye Parliament of England.

Parliament of Fowls, The, *sel.* Chaucer.
  Now Welcome, Summer. OxBM

Parliament Soldiers, The. *Unknown.* GBP

Parlour Piece. Ted Hughes. BuTH

Parrot, The. Edward Lucie-Smith. BoAnP

Parrot, The/ Is eating a carrot. Who Killed Lawless Lean? Stevie Smith. BBGO

Parrot Fish, The. James Merrill. NOBA

Parrot, if I had your wings. The Boy and the Parrot. John Hookham Frere. OxBChV

Parrot is a thief, The. The Parrot. Edward Lucie-Smith. BoAnP

Part of a Novel, Part of a Poem, Part of a Play, *sels.* Marianne Moore.
  Hero, The. NOBA
  Steeple-Jack, The. NoAM; NOBA; SBG; WPE

Part of Plenty. Bernard Spencer. GBL

Part of the Darkness. Isabella Gardner. ANTL; BoAnP

Part of the Doctrine. LeRoi Jones. PiAM

Part of the Vigil. James Merrill. NoAM

Part-Sequence for Change, A. Robert Duncan. VGW

Parta Quies. A. E. Housman. NOBE

Parterre, The. E. Harriet Palmer. FaBoCo

Parthenophil and Parthenophe, *sels.* Barnabe Barnes.
  "Ah sweet content, where is thy mylde abode?" LXVI. AAS
  "Jove for Europaes [*or* Europa's] love took[e] shape of bull," LXIII. AAS; Epi; LoAs
  "Write! write! help! help, sweet Muse! and never cease!" XVIII. Epi
  "Yea, but uncertain hopes are anchors feeble," XXI. Epi

Partholan went out one day. The First Lawcase. *Unknown, tr. by* John Montague. BIrV

Partial Comfort. Dorothy Parker. FaBoCo

Partial Eclipse. W. D. Snodgrass. Moon, PSN

Partial Explanation, The. Charles Simic. FiCP

Partial Resemblance. Denise Levertov. CoPAm

Parting. Lady Heguri, *tr fr. Japanese by* Geoffrey Bownas *and* Anthony Thwaite. OLR
  ("Thousand years, you said, A.") BoLoP
Parting: A Game. Lynn Sukenick. NMM
Parting as Descent. John Berryman. CoPAm
Parting at Dawn. John Crowe Ransom. LoAs
Parting at Morning. Robert Browning. HeIP; LoAs; NOBE; PAIC; SoSe
Parting with——. Jane Barker. SCP-2
Parting, without a Sequel. John Crowe Ransom. SoSe
Partings. Maria Jane Jewsbury. OxBChV
Partly to My Cat. Ellen Bass. NMM
Partner in the corner bar is high, a grin. A Farewell. Stanley Kiesel. HeS
Partners. Jaime Castiello. ECBV
Partridge and quail, of course. Occasional woodcock. The Sportsman. David McCord. SPo
Partridges. John Masefield. OxBTC
Party, The. W. R. Rodgers. BIrV
Party, The. Reed Whittemore. BBGO; ConAP; LP; NCSH
Party at Bannon Brook. Alden Nowlan. NeAC
Party is going strong, The. Tribute to Kafka for Someone Taken. Alan Dugan. CAPP; CoPAm; NoAM
Party Piece. Brian Patten. BoLoP
Pascal's abyss went with him, yawned in the air. The Abyss. Baudelaire, *tr. by* Jackson Matthews. GrRo
Paso por Aqui. Wade Hall. AATT
Pass Me Not, O Gentle Saviour, *with music.* Fanny Crosby. BLSH
Pass of Kirkstone, The. Wordsworth. MBPR
Passage. Hart Crane. NoAM; NOBA
Passage. Mary Shumway. NVAP
Passage. Warren Slesinger. HeS
Passage at Night, The—The Blaskets. Robin Flower. PFIr
Passage over Water. Robert Duncan. NoAM; NOBA
Passages, *sels* Robert Duncan.
  At the Loom. PiAM; VGW
  Envoy. VGW
  Fire, The. VGW
  Moon, The. PiAm
  Tribal Memories. NOBA; PiAM
  Where It Appears. PiAM
Passer Mortuus Est. Edna St. Vincent Millay. RiTi
Passer-By, A. Robert Bridges. OxBTC
Passes are blocked by snow, The. Persia. V. Sackville-West. WPE
Passing Away. Christina Rossetti. WPE
Passing By. *Unknown. See* There Is a Lady Sweet and Kind.
Passing of the Shee, The. J. M. Synge. BIrV
Passing Stockyards Where They Killed the Buffalo. Harley Elliott. HeS
Passing stranger! you do not know how longingly I look upon you. To a Stranger. Walt Whitman. NoAM; NOBA
Passing through huddled and ugly walls. The Harbor. Carl Sandburg. NCSH
"Passion o' me!" cried Sir Richard Tyrone. The Sally from Coventry. George Walter Thornbury. BTTM
Passion of Christ Strengthen Me. John Audelay. BoReV
  (Dread of Death.) OxBM
Passionate Man's Pilgrimage, The. Sir Walter Ralegh. AAS; BoReV; IPWM; MetP; NOBE; OBP
Passionate Pilgrim, The, *sels.* Shakespeare, *and others.*
  Crabbed Age and Youth, XII. Shakespeare. InPS
    ("Crabbed age and youth cannot live together.") GBL
  Philomel. Richard Barnfield. NOBE
    ("As it fell upon a day.") GBL

"Venus, with young Adonis sitting by her," XI. Bartholomew Griffin. LoAs
Passionate Shepherd to His Love, The, 6 *sts.* Christopher Marlowe. AAS; BoLoP; Epi; HeIP; InPK; InPS; IPWM; LoAs; NOBE; OLR; PAIC; PBMP; PPoD; PPoe, 7 *sts.;* PPP
Passions, The; an Ode to Music. William Collins. LAuP
Passport, The. Luis Garcia. MIT
Past and present wilt, The. Song of Myself, LI. Walt Whitman. AnMo
Past comes back, The. Ralph Hodgson. POL
Past crag and scarp. History. Robert Penn Warren. NoAM
Past Mogollon River. Arizona Ruins. Lyn Lifshin. RiTi
Past Ruined [*or* Ruin'd] Ilion Helen Lives. Walter Savage Landor. GBL; HeIP; POL
  (To Ianthe.) NOBE
Past the school and down. Directions to the Nomad. James Welch. CDW
Past Time. Harvey Shapiro. POL
Pastel the flowers, the wreaths in the pastel gardens. Moon Mattress. Diane Di Prima. NMM
Pastoral: "It all happened so fast. Fenya was in the straight chair." Norman Dubie. AmPA
Pastoral: "Shuddering geography pulls the dead sentences, A." James Tipton. HeS
Pastoral: "Today in Peru, this first day of summer." Lawrence Raab. AmPA
Pastoral Ballad by John Bull, A. Thomas Moore. BIrV
Pastoral Dialogue, A. Thomas Carew. GBL; SCP-2
Pastoral of Phillis and Coridon, A. Nicholas Breton. PAIC
Pastoral of the City Streets. A. M. Klein. BBGO
Pastorale: "No more violets." Hart Crane. PSN
Pastorals, *sel.* Robert Hillyer.
  "So soft in the hemlock wood." PAIC
Pastorals, *sels.* Pope.
  Summer.
    Sylvan Delights. NOBE
  Winter. PAIC
Pastry. Gertrude Stein. *Fr.* Tender Buttons. RiTi
Pasture, The. Robert Frost. LCL; NOBA; NowV; RAE
Pasture, stone wall, and steeple. Question in a Field. Louise Bogan. SBG
Pat-a-cake, pat-a-cake, baker's man! Mother Goose. MG
Patch-Shaneen. J. M. Synge. PFIr
Paternosters/ flow from facile worshipers. Thy Kingdom Come. Elmer F. Suderman. AATT
Pater's Bathe. Edward Abbott Parry. OxBChV
Paterson, *sels.* William Carlos Williams.
  Delineaments of the Giants, The. NoAM
  Preface: "To make a start." NoAM; NOBA
Paterson ("Before the grass is out the people are out"). William Carlos Williams. PiAM
Paterson lies in the valley under the Passaic Falls. The Delineaments of the Giants. William Carlos Williams. *Fr.* Paterson. NoAM
Paterson—The Strike. William Carlos Williams. *Fr.* The Wanderer: A Rococo Study. Epi
Path, The. Edward Thomas. NoAM
Path among the Stones, The. Galway Kinnell. NOBA; Prf
Path I Must Travel, The. Emerson Blackhorse Mitchell. VW
Patience, *sel.* W. S. Gilbert.
  Banquet Song. ECBV
Patience. Frank Horne. BPo
Patience, *sel. Unknown.*
  Jonah Is Cast into the Sea, *orig. and mod. English prose.* OxBM
Patience Hard Thing. Gerard Manley Hopkins. Prf
Patience . . . patience. Patience Frank Horne. BPo

Patient Is Rallying, The.  Weldon Kees.  AnMo
Patient, The: Rockland County Sanitarium.  Calvin C. Hernton. *See* Madhouse.
Patriot, The.  Robert Browning.  PBMP
Patriotic Ode on the Fourteenth Anniversary of the Persecution of Charlie Chaplin.  Bob Kaufman.  PoBA
Patriotic Poem.  Diane Wakoski.  OFD; VGW
Patriotism.  Sir Walter Scott.  *See* This Is My Own, My Native Land.
Pat's Opinion of Flags.  Fred Emerson Brooks.  InPK
Pattern, The.  Robert Creeley.  PPoD
Pattern of birds, A.  Peter Whigham.  *Fr.* Love Poems of the VIth Dalai Lama.  TwMBP
Patterns.  Amy Lowell.  GrRo; PBMP; VoPo
Patty, 1949-1961.  Sharon Mayer Libera.  IHMS
Paudeen.  W. B. Yeats.  InPS
Paul.  James Wright.  WIF
Paul grounded at Braga, a gull on his shoulder.  Shipwreck.  George Mackay Brown.  LP
Paul Jones's Victory.  *Unknown.*  AmFP
Paul Revere's Ride.  Longfellow.  *Fr.* Tales of a Wayside Inn: The Landlord's Tale, Pt. I.  BTTM
Paul Robeson.  Gwendolyn Brooks.  PoBA
Paunch talks against good liquor to excess.  On Paunch, a Parasite.  Hilaire Belloc.  POL
Pause of Thought, A.  Christina Rossetti.  NOBE
Pavane for the Passing of a Child.  Laura Chester.  FiCP
Pavement Artist, A.  G. E. Murray.  HeS
Pavlov.  Naomi Long Madgett.  BPo
Pawnbroker, The.  Maxine W. Kumin.  NVAP
Pawn-shop man knows hunger, The.  Street Window.  Carl Sandburg.  SFF
Pax.  D. H. Lawrence.  BoReV
Pax Romana.  Virginia Gilbert.  NPW
Pax vobis', quod the fox.  The Fox and the Goose.  *Unknown.*  OxBM
Pay Is Good, The.  Richard Kell.  MPo
Payday at Coal Creek.  *Unknown.*  AmFP; RDB, *with music*
Peabody Bird, The.  Rachel Field.  ECBV
Peace.  Rupert Brooke.  1914, I.  BTTM
Peace.  Langston Hughes.  BPo
Peace.  George Jonas.  NeAC
Peace.  Henry Vaughan.  BoReV; IPWM; NOBE
Peace, Be at Peace, O Thou My Heaviness.  Baudelaire, *tr. fr. French by* Lord Alfred Douglas.  InPK
Peace in the Welsh Hills.  Vernon Watkins.  OxBTC
Peace is made with a warlike man.  *Unknown, tr. fr. Irish by* John Montague.  BIrV
Peace, muttering thoughts! and do not grudge to keep.  Content.  George Herbert.  SCP-1
Peace of Wild Things, The.  Wendell Berry.  HeIP; IPWM; PiAM; VGW
Peace, peace! he is not dead, he doth not sleep.  Mourn Not for Adonais.  Shelley.  *Fr.* Adonais.  BoReV; NOBE
Peace Prospect.  Daniela Gioseffi.  RiTi
Peace, So That.  Greg Kuzma.  InPK
Peace, the wild valley streaked with torrents.  The Straw.  Robert Graves.  OxBTC
Peace to all such! But were there one whose fires.  Atticus.  Pope.  *Fr.* Epistle to Dr. Arbuthnot.  NOBE
"Peace upon earth!" was said.  We sing it.  Christmas: 1924.  Thomas Hardy.  BuTH
Peace, war, religion.  This Tokyo.  Gary Snyder.  CAPP
Peace, we have arrived.  Meditation in My Favorite Position.  Marge Piercy.  *Fr.* Walking into Love.  RiTi
Peach Orchard Mama.  *Unknown.*  BluL

Peachtree, The.  Denise Levertov.  *Fr.* During the Eichmann Trial.  CAPP
Peacock "At Home," The.  Catherine Ann Dorset.  OxBChV
"Peacock colored tears and rotten oranges."  Midnight on Front Street.  Roberta Hill.  CDW
Peanuts.  Ken Belford.  NeAC
Pear Tree.  Hilda Doolittle ("H.D.")..  NOBA
Pear-Tree, The.  *Unknown.*  GBP
Pearl, The.  Hans Christian Andersen, *tr. fr. Danish by* Charles Wharton Stork.  LoAs
Pearl, The.  George Herbert.  SCP-1
Pearl, *sels.*  *Unknown.*
   "Pearl all-pleasing, prince's treasure," *sts.* 1-32, *tr. fr. Middle English by* Sir Israel Gollancz.  RRA
   "Perle, plesaunte to prynces paye," *sts.* 1-15, *orig. and mod. English prose.*  OxBM
Pearl Avenue runs past the high-school lot.  Ex-Basketball Player.  John Updike.  BBGO; CTBA; MiP; SPo
Pearl Bryan, 2 *versions.*  *Unknown.*  AmFP
Pearl Harbor Day 1970.  Dick Lourie.  NeAC
Peasants, The.  Alun Lewis.  PPP
Pease-pudding hot.  Mother Goose.  MG
Pebbles.  Herman Melville.  AmVN
Peddler, The.  Hollis Summers.  CoPAm
Peddler and His Wife, The.  *Unknown.*  AmFP
Pedigree of honey, The.  Emily Dickinson.  NoAM; NOBA
Pedlar, A.  *Unknown.*  NOBE
Pedlar's Caravan, The.  William Brighty Rands.  OxBChV
Peeled Wand.  Derek Bowman.  MIS
Peepers in Our Meadow, The.  Archibald MacLeish.  NCSH
Peer of the golden gods is he to Sappho.  Ode to Anactoria.  Sappho, *tr. by* William Ellery Leonard.  LoAs
Pegasus.  Patrick Kavanagh.  PFIr
Peggy Browne.  Turlough O'Carolan.  BIrV
Pelican, The.  Greg Kuzma.  AmPA
Penal Law.  Austin Clarke.  BoLoP; NoAM
Pendant Watch.  Madeline DeFrees.  NMM
Pendulum.  John Updike.  BBGO
Penelope.  Mary Gilmore.  MAuV
Penelope.  Karen Whitehill.  NPW
Penitent Considers Another Coming of Mary, A.  Gwendolyn Brooks.  NoAM
Pennines in April.  Ted Hughes.  PPP
Pennsylvania Dutch Mouse.  Lancaster County Tragedy.  W. Lowrie Kay.  CaYB
Penny Fiddle, The.  Robert Graves.  ECBV
Penny Is a Hardy Knight.  *Unknown.*  OxBM
Penny Trumpet.  Raphael Rudnick.  MAT
Pennycandystore beyond the El, The.  Lawrence Ferlinghetti.  *Fr.* A Coney Island of the Mind.  BBGO; CAPP; CoPAm; CTBA; HeIP; IPWM; SS
Penological Study: Southern Exposure, *sel.*  Robert Penn Warren.  Wet Hair: If Now His Mother Should Come.  NoAM
Pens, The.  W. S. Merwin.  TH
Pensive they sit, and roll their languid eyes.  Keats.  MBPR
Pentagonia.  G. E. Bates.  SpRo
Pentland Hills, The.  *Unknown.*  GBP
Penus envy, they call it.  Alta.  NMM
People, The.  Robert Creeley.  VGW
People, The.  Joy Harjo.  SA
People along the sand, The.  Neither Out Far nor In Deep.  Robert Frost.  NoAM; NOBA; PSN
People are putting up storm windows now.  Storm Windows.  Howard Nemerov.  ConAP
People Cannot Speak, The.  T. Aian Broughton.  FAF

People chained to aurora, A. Civilization and Its Discontents. John Ashbery. CAPP

People die from loneliness. One. Carolyn M. Rodgers. BPo

People expect old men to die. Old Men. Ogden Nash. SFF

People Hide Their Love. Emperor Wu Ti, *tr. fr. Chinese by* Arthur Waley. OLR

People know, The. A Little More about the Brothers and Sisters. Sharon Scott. JB

People living round the place. Thief Jones. Robert P. Tristram Coffin. MiP

People of Blakeney, The. *Unknown.* GBP

People say they have a hard time. For de Lawd. Lucille Clifton. PoBA; PPoD

People who have no children can be hard. The Children of the Poor. Gwendolyn Brooks. *Fr.* The Womanhood. WPE

People who remain flabergasting for a lifetime. Staying Married. Dick Allen. FAF

People, Yes, The, *sels.* Carl Sandburg.
"People will live on, The," Sec. 107. NoAM; NOBA; PiAM
"People, yes, the people, The," *fr.* Secs. 86-107. WIF

Pepita, my paragon, bright star of Arragon. Saragossa. Henry Sambrooke Leigh. FaBoCo

Pepsi Generation. Walasse Ting. MAT

Perambulator Poem. David McCord. OFD

Perception of an object costs. Emily Dickinson. NOBA

Perfect Day, A, *with music.* Carrie Jacobs Bond. BLSo

Perfect little body, without fault or stain on thee. On a Dead Child. Robert Bridges. NoAM; NOBE

Perfect Poem Trumpets, The. James E. Warren, Jr. AATT

Perfection, of a kind, was what he was after. Epitaph on a Tyrant. W. H. Auden. HeIP; MiP; SFF

Perfection of Dentistry, The. Marvin Bell. AmPA

Perfectionist, The. Philip Dacey. NVAP

Perforated Spirit, The. Morris Bishop. MiP

Performance, The. James Dickey. ConAP; NoAM; NOBA

Performance at Hog Theater, A. Russell Edson. AmPA

Performances, assortments, résumés. The Tunnel. Hart Crane. *Fr.* The Bridge. MAT

Perhaps. Stephen Spender. NoAM

Perhaps/ This is the way. Antigone I. Herbert Martin. PoBA

Perhaps/ You will remember/ John Brown. October 16: The Raid. Langston Hughes. PoBA

"Perhaps I may allow, the Dean." Swift. *Fr.* Verses on the Death of Doctor Swift. NOBE

Perhaps I'll find God someday. Search. Elisavietta Ritchie. AATT

Perhaps it makes more. Letter to a Conceivable Great-Grandson. Earle Birney. BBGO

Perhaps it was usual. Into the Sky. Sallie Chesham. AATT

Perhaps they wonder who the tall man is. Riding with Some North Vietnamese Students in a Polish Elevator, 1966. Roger Mitchell. PAIC

Pericles and Aspasia, *sels.* Walter Savage Landor.
Corinna, to Tanagra, from Athens, *fr.* XLIV. NOBE
Dirce, *fr.* CCXXX. GBL; NOBE

Perils of Invisibility, The. W. S. Gilbert. PoTa

Periphery. A. R. Ammons. NOBA

Perle, plesaunte to prynces paye. *Unknown. Fr.* Pearl. OxBM

Permanently. Kenneth Koch. CAPP; PPP

Permitted to assist you, let me see. St. Valentine. Marianne Moore. OFD

Perplexed by the Sunlight. Grevel Lindop. LP

Persephone. Robert Duncan. NoAM; NOBA

Persia. V. Sackville-West. WPE

Persian Version, The. Robert Graves. FaBoCo; NoAM

Persimmon Tree, The. *Unknown.* GBP

Persistent Explorer. John Crowe Ransom. PiAm

Persistent Narrative. Ken Smith. TwMBP

Person, *sel.* Gavin Bantock.
"Is this pain, when my heart." TwMBP

Person after person. Buddha's Birthday: April 8, 1819. Issa, *tr. by* Nobuyuki Yuasa. *Fr.* Oraga Haru. OFD

Person to Person. Lorine Parks. NowV

Person who can do, The. Poem. Alan Dugan. NoAM

Personal. Langston Hughes. NOBA

Personal Column. William Price Turner. SLP

Personal Letter No. 3. Sonia SanchezRiTi

Personal Letter No. 2. Sonia Sanchez. WBN

Personal Poem Frank O'Hara. CAPP

Personal Poem. Ingrid Wendt. NMM

Personal Talk. Wordsworth. MBPR; NOBE

Personality Sketch, A: Bill. Ronda Davis. JB

"Personals." Leatrice W. Emeruwa. RiTi

Persons of the Prologue. Chaucer, *tr. fr. Middle English by* Nevill Coghill. *Fr.* The Canterbury Tales: Prologue. OBP

Perspective. Adrianne Marcus. MIT

Perspective. Coventry Patmore. *Fr.* The Angel in the House, II, i. GBL

Persuasions to Enjoy. Thomas Carew. NOBE; PAIC

Perversion interests me. Note Delivered by a Female Impersonator. Heather McHugh. AmPA

Pessimist, The. Ben King. FaBoCo

Pet Lamb, The. Wordsworth. OxBChV

Pet Shop. Louis MacNeice. BoAnP

Pet was never mourned as you. Last Words to a Dumb Friend. Thomas Hardy. PCat

Pete at the Zoo. Gwendolyn Brooks. ECBV

Pete Petersen, before this bit, a professional entertainer. Vaudeville. Lincoln Kirstein. NoAM

Peter. Albert Howard Carter. AATT

Peter Amberley. *Unknown.* AmFP

Peter Bell. Wordsworth. MBPR

Peter Bell the Third. Shelley. MBPR
"Hell is a city much like London," *sel.* OBP

Peter Gray, *with music. Unknown.* BLSo

Peter Grimes; the Outcast. George Crabbe. *Fr.* The Borough, Letter XXII. NOBE

Peter Piper picked a peck of pickled pepper. Mother Goose. MG

Peter Quince at the Clavier. Wallace Stevens. AnMo; InPK; InPS; LoAs; NOBA; PAIC; PPP; SoSe; TCP

Peter's Little Daughter Dies. Kenneth Patchen. RRA

Peter's not friendly. He gives me sideways looks. John Berryman. *Fr.* Dream Songs. CAPP

Petit, the Poet. Edgar Lee Masters. *Fr.* Spoon River Anthology. InPK; NoAM; NOBA

Petition for an Absolute Retreat, The. Countess of Winchilsea. SBG; WPE, *abr.*

Petoskey Stone. Robert Vas Dias. HeS

Pets, The. Robert Farren. ECBV

Petticoat, A. Gertrude Stein. *Fr.* Tender Buttons. RiTi

Pettigrew Museum. John Calvin Rezmerski. HeS

Petty Murder. Albert McLean, Jr. SFF

Petty sneaking knave I knew, A. On Cromek. Blake. FaBoCo

Petulance is purple. Spectrum. Mari Evans. BPo

Pew, The/ across from mine. On Listening to a Death-of-God Theologian Lecture in Chapel. Elmer F. Suderman. AATT

Pew, pew,/My minny me slew. Song of the Murdered Child. *Unknown.* GBP

Phaedra. Hilda Doolittle ("H. D."). SBG

Phantom. Samuel Taylor Coleridge. MBPR

Phantom Horsewoman, The. Thomas Hardy. LoAs; NOBE

Phantom or Fact. Samuel Taylor Coleridge. MBPR

Phantom to me. Second Sapphic Fragment/Fainetai Moi. Sappho, *tr. by* Harvey Bialy. MIT

Pharao's Daughter. Michael Moran. BIrV

Pharisees come bloom. Egyptian book of the Dead. David Henderson. MIT

Phases of the Moon. Robert Browning. *Fr.* One Word More. Moon.

Pheasant, The. Robert P. Tristram Coffin. TH

Phenomena. Robinson Jeffers. NoAM; NOBA

Phenomenal Survivals of Death in Nantucket. Louise Glück. AmPA

Philadelphia ("Philadelphia is a handsome town"). *Unknown.* AmFP

Philatelist Royal. Robert Graves. FaBoCo

Philip Sparrow. John Skelton. *See* Phyllyp Sparowe.

Phillis, *sels.* Thomas Lodge. AAS
     "Devoide of reason, thrale to foolish ire, XXXI, *after the French of* Pierre de Ronsard.
     "I would in rich and golden coloured raine," XXXIV, *after the French of* Pierre de Ronsard.

Phillis was a fair maid. The Maiden's Complaint. *Unknown.* OLR

Philomel. Richard Barnfield. *Fr.* The Passionate Pilgrim. NOBE
     ("As it fell upon a day.") GBL

Philomela. Matthew Arnold. PPP

Philomela. John Crowe Ransom. NoAM; NOBA

Philomela. Sir Philip Sidney. NOBE

Philon the Shepherd. *Unknown.* NOBE

Philosopher and the Lover, The: To a Mistress Dying. Sir William Davenant. NOBE; Prf

Philosopher to His Mistress, The. Robert Bridges. OBP

Philosophers have measured mountains. The Agony. George Herbert. SCP-1

Philosophy. Paul Laurence Dunbar. BPo

Phineas Within and Without. Paul Zimmer. VGW

Phoebus with Admetus. George Meredith. NOBE

Phoenix, The. J. V. Cunningham. NoAM

Phoenix, The. George Darley. *Fr.* Nepenthe. NOBE
     ("O blest unfabled incense tree.") BIrV

Phoenix. Carolyn M. Rodgers. JB

Phoenix and the Turtle, The. Shakespeare. NOBE

Phone Call to Rutherford. Paul Blackburn. CTBA

Phone duet over the radio, A. The Louisiana Weekly #4. David Henderson. PoBA

Phone for the fish-knives, Norman. How to Get On in Society. John Betjeman. OxBTC

Phoning My Son Long Distance. Ted Kooser. HeS

Photo, The. Lennart Bruce. MIT

Photo of a Retired Farmer, Big Bend, Wisconsin. Robert L. McRoberts. HeS

Photograph. Quandra Prettyman. PoBA

Photograph at the Cloisters: April 1972. Helen Chasin. NMM

Photograph of an Actress, c. 1860. Nan McDonald. MAuV

Photograph of Haymaker, 1890. Molly Holden. OxBTC; PSN

Photograph of Myself, The. Jon Anderson. AmPA

Photograph of the Back of My House. Del Marie Rogers. NPW

Photograph the Cat Licks, The. Beatrice Walter. NMM

Photographs: A Vision of Massacre. Michael S. Harper. PoBA

Phrases for Everyday Use by the British in India. John Daniel. TwMBP

Phyllis. Thomas Lodge. *See* Phillis.

Phyllis. Thomas Randolph. BoLoP

Phyllis Corydon clutched to him. Catullus, *tr. fr. Latin by* Peter Whigham. BoLoP

Phyllis Knotting. Sir Charles Sedley. NOBE

Phyllyp Sparowe [*or* Philip Sparrow]. John Skelton. AAS
*Sels.*
     Anathema of Cats. PCat
     "And prytily he wolde pant." ECBV
     "Pla ce bo! Who is there, who?" NOBE

Physical Imperfections of Old Films, The. Paul Ramsey. PPoD

Physician Nature! let my spirit blood! Ode to Fanny. Keats. MBPR

Piano. D. H. Lawrence. HeIP; InPK; NoAM; NOBE; PPP

Piano hums, The. Effendi. Michael S. Harper. PoBA

Piazza di Spagna, Early Morning. Richard Wilbur. InPS; PSN; VGW

Piazza Piece. John Crowe Ransom. BoLoP; HeIP; NoAM; NOBA; PAIC; PiAm; SFF

Pibroch. Ted Hughes. TwMBP

Pibroch of Donuil Dhu, pibroch of Donuil. Gathering Song of Donald the Black. Sir Walter Scott. BTTM

Picador Bit, The. Bink Noll. SFF

Pickety Fence. David McCord. ECBV

Pickle Belt. Theodore Roethke. AnMo

Picnic, The. John Logan. ConAP; CTBA; LP; NCSH

Picnic. Adrienne Rich. CoPAm

Picnic: The Liberated. M. Carl Holman. PoBA

Picture, The. Robert Lowell. NoAM

Picture, A. Howard Nemerov. NowV

Picture and book remain. An Acre of Grass. W. B. Yeats. NoAM; OBP

Picture-frame for you to fill, A. To Minnie. Robert Louis Stevenson. SLP

Picture of a Nativity. Geoffrey Hill. NoAM

Picture of J. T. in a Prospect of Stone, The. Charles Tomlinson. PPP

Picture of Little J. A. in a Prospect of Flowers, The. John Ashbery. ConAP; PPP

Picture of Little T. C. in a Prospect of Flowers, The. Andrew Marvell. NOBE; PPP

Picture of Loot. Alan Sillitoe. OxBTC

Picture of the Times, A. Philip Freneau. PiAm

Picture, The; or, the Lover's Resolution. Samuel Taylor Coleridge. MBPR

Pictures from Brueghel, *sels.* William Carlos Williams.
     Corn Harvest, The, VII. PPP
     Landscape with the Fall of Icarus, II. BBGO; PPP; WIF

Pictures of a City. Robert Fripp *and* Peter Sinfield. GrRo

Pie in the Sky. *Unknown.* GBP

Pie sat on a pear tree, A. Hop't She. *Unknown.* GBP

Piece by piece I seem. Necessities of Life. Adrienne Rich. NoAM; NOBA; Psy

Piece of flesh gives off, A. The Dead Shall Be Raised Incorruptible. Galway Kinnell. CAAP; NOBA

Piece of green pepper, A. Haiku Ambulance. Richard Brautigan. InPK

Piecemeal the summer dies. Exeunt. Richard Wilbur. HeIP; NCSH

Pied Beauty. Gerard Manley Hopkins. AKE; AnMo; BoReV; Epi; HeIP; InPK; InPS; NoAM; NOBE; PAIC; PBMP; PPoD; PPP; SS; VoPo; WIF

Pied Piper of Hamelin, The. Robert Browning. OxBChV

Pier-Glass, The. Robert Graves. NoAM

Piercing, The. Pat Lowther. MMD

Piercing Chill I Feel, The. Buson, *tr. fr. Japanese by* Harold G. Henderson. InPK

Pierrot le Fou. Adrienne Rich. PiAm

Piers are pummelled by the waves, The.  The Fall of Rome. W. H. Auden.  AnMo; InPS; MAT; OxBTC

Piers Plowman.  William Langland.  *See* Vision of Piers Plowman, The.

Pietà.  James McAuley.  MAuV

Pieta.  Rainer Maria Rilke, *tr. fr. German by* M. D. Herter Norton.  OFD

Pieta, The, Rhenish, 14th C., The Cloisters.  Mona Van Duyn. Prf

Pietas: The Petrified Wood.  Dave Smith.  HeS

Pig-crowds in successive, screaming pens.  Blood.  Les A. Murray.  MAuV

Pig lay on a barrow dead, The.  View of a Pig.  Ted Hughes. BoAnP; OxBTC; SoSe

Pig Tale, The, *abr.*  "Lewis Carroll."  *Fr.* Sylvie and Bruno. RAE

Pigeons.  Richard Kell.  BoAnP

Pigeons.  James Mecklenburger.  SFF

Pigmeat.  *Unknown.*  BluL

Pigs.  John Cotton.  BoAnP

Pigs o' Pelton.  *Unknown.*  GBP

Pihsien Road.  Robin Hyde.  WPE

Pike.  Ted Hughes.  HeIP; MAT; MPo; NCSH; OBP; OxBTC; PSN

"Pikes him/ And dikes him."  The English Retort.  *Unknown.* OxBM

Pile the bodies high at Austerlitz and Waterloo.  Grass.  Carl Sandburg.  NoAM; NOBA; PiAm

Pilgrim Fathers, The.  John Pierpont.  BTTM

Pilgrimage, The.  George Herbert.  SoSe

Pilgrimage Song.  *Unknown, tr. fr. Pueblo Indian by* Mary Austin. WPE

Pilgrim's Progress, The, *sel.*  Bunyan. Shepherd Boy Sings in the Valley of Humiliation, The.  NOBE

Pilgrims to St. James.  *Unknown.*  OxBM

Pill Versus the Springhill Mine Disaster, The.  Richard Brautigan. NowV

Pillar of the Cloud, The.  Cardinal Newman.  PFD (Lead, Kindly Light, *with music.*)  BLSH

Piller pearisht is whearto I lent, The.  Sir Thomas Wyatt.  AAS

Pilot.  Floyd C. Stuart.  FAF

Pilot, The.  Lewis Turco.  CoPAm

Pin, The.  Ann Taylor.  OxBChV

Pindar is imitable by none.  The Praise of Pindar.  Horace, *tr. by* Abraham Cowley.  Odes, IV, 2.  Epi; PAIC

Pindaric Ode, A.  Ben Jonson.  *See* To the Immortal Memory and Friendship of That Noble Pair, Sir Lucius Cary and Sir Henry Morison.

Pine Assessor, The.  Prentice Baker.  AATT

Pine Needles.  Warren Slesinger.  HeS

Pine Tree Tops.  Gary Snyder.  NOBA; Prf

Pine trees were stripped red, The.  Black Forest.  Roderick Watson.  MIS

Pines were dark on Ramoth hill, The.  My Playmate.  Whittier. NOBA

Piney Woods Money Mama.  *Unknown.*  BluL

Pining for Love.  Francis Beaumont.  POL

Pink confused with white.  The Pot of Flowers.  William Carlos Williams.  PiAm

Pink sand and sandpipers pink in the setting.  Camas Tuath. Tom Buchan.  MIS

Pinkletinks.  Grace Elisabeth Allen.  ECBV

Pioneer, The.  William B. Ruggles.  ECBV

Pioneers, The.  Charlotte Mortimer.  NowV

Pious Editor's Creed, The.  James Russell Lowell.  *Fr.* The Biglow Papers, 1st Series, No. VI.  PiAm

Pious Selinda.  Congreve.  *See* Song: "Pious Selinda goes to prayers."

Piper, The.  Blake.  *See* Piping Down the Valleys Wild.

Piper, A.  "Seumas O'Sullivan."  PFIr

Piper's Progress, The.  Francis Sylvester Mahony.  PFIr

Pipes in the street were playing bravely, The.  Cha Till Maccruimein.  E. A. Mackintosh.  SoSe

Piping Down the Valleys Wild (*Introd. to* Songs of Innocence). Blake.  NOBE (Introduction: "Piping down the Valleys Wild.")  InPS; LAuP; MBPR (Piper, The.)  LCL; OxBChV (Songs of Innocence: Introduction.)  HeIP

Piping Peace.  James Shirley.  *Fr.* The Imposture.  NOBE ("You virgins that did late despair.")  SCP-2

Pippa Passes, *sels.*  Robert Browning. Year's at the Spring, The, *fr.* sc. i.  InPK (Pippa's Song.)  LCL (Song: "Year's at the spring, The.")  GrRo You'll Love Me Yet! *fr.* sc. iii.  OLR

Pisan Cantos, The.  Ezra Pound.  *See* Cantos.

Pisces Child.  Sandra McPherson.  NMM

Pistol Slapper Blues.  *Unknown.*  BluL

Pit Viper.  N. Scott Momaday.  CDW; VW

Pitch pine/ often stops.  Developing Curious Survival Patterns against Winter Saltwinds The.  Lyn Lifshin.  FAF

Pitch was lowered, slowed, decoded, The.  Whale Song.  Francis Maguire.  BoAnP; POL

Pitcher.  Robert Francis.  SPo; WIF

Pittsburgh.  Peggy Ruse.  NPW

Pity.  William Mills.  CoPAm

Pity Ascending with the Fog.  James Tate.  NoAM

Pity beyond all telling, A.  The Pity of Love.  W. B. Yeats. PBMP

Pity for him who suffers from his waste.  Suffer the Children. Audre Lorde.  PoBA

Pity of Love, The.  W. B. Yeats.  PBMP

Pity This Busy Monster, Manunkind.  E. E. Cummings.  NOBA; PPP

Pity this girl.  The Stranger.  William Everson.  CoPAm

Pity, A; We Were Such a Good Invention.  Yehuda Amichai, *tr. fr. Hebrew by* Assia Gutmann.  BoLoP, LoAs

Pity would be no more.  The Human Abstract.  Blake.  *Fr.* Songs of Experience.  LAuP; MBPR; PPP

Piute Creek.  Gary Snyder.  CAPP; ConAP; NOBA

Piyyut for Rosh Hashana.  Chaim Guri, *tr. fr. Hebrew by* Ruth Finer Mintz.  OFD

Place, The.  Robert Wallace.  CoPAm

Place a custard stand in a garden.  The Invention of New Jersey. Jack Anderson.  InPS

Place in Kansas, A.  Ted Kooser.  HeS

Place Pigalle.  Richard Wilbur.  HeIP

". . . place your name in a time."  Hangar Nine.  Ann Darr. WBN

Pla ce bo,/ Who is there, who?  Phyllyp Sparowe.  John Skelton. AAS; NOBE

Place's Fault, The.  Philip Hobsbaum.  LP; MPo

Placid Pew, The.  Elmer F. Suderman.  AATT

Plague of Dead Sharks.  Alan Dugan.  NoAM

Plague take all your pedants, say I!  Sibrandus Schafnaburgensis. Robert Browning.  *Fr.* Garden Fancies.  OBP

Plain as the Glistering Planets Shine.  Robert Louis Stevenson. SLP

Plain Language from Truthful James  ("I reside at Table Mountain").  Bret Harte.  FaBoCo

Plain Language from Truthful James ("Which I wish to remark"). Bret Harte. *See* Heathen Chinee, The.

Plain of Adoration, The. *Unknown, tr. fr. Irish* by John Montague. BIrV

Plain Sense of Things, The. Wallace Stevens. InPS

Plaint Against the Fog. *Unknown, tr. fr. Nootka Indian.* AKE

Plainview: 3. N. Scott Momaday. CDW

Plan. Rod McKuen. MiP

Plane, The: Earth. Sun-Ra. PoBA

Plane Geometry. Emma Rounds. SpRo

Plane meets, The. Arrivals. Stuart Conn. SLP

Plane tilts in to Nashville, The. The Homecoming Singer. Jay Wright. PoBA

Plane Wreck at Los Gatos (Deportee). Woody Guthrie. InPK

"Planet doesn't explode of itself, A," said drily. Earth. John Hall Wheelock. SFF; SoSe

Planet Dream. T. Alan Broughton. FAF

Planetarium. Adrienne Rich. NoAM; NOBA; RiTi

Planetary Arc-Light, The. August Derleth. FCBV

Plant Rhythms, The. G. E. Murray. HeS

Plant without moisture sweet, A. Rising in the Morning. Hugh Rhodes. OxBChV

Planter. Richard Murphy. *Fr.* The Battle of Aughrim. BIrV

Planter's Daughter, The. Austin Clarke. OxBTC; PFIr

Planting, The. Harley Elliott. NeAC

Planting a Magnolia. W. D. Snodgrass. NoAM

Plato. Sandra Ruth Duguid. AATT

Plato, despair! Meditation on Statistical Method. J. V. Cunningham. VGW

Plato Told Him. E. E. Cummings. AnMo; NoAM; NOBA

Plato Was Right Though. Lee Harwood. TwMBP

Platonic Love. Lord Herbert of Cherbury. SCP-2

Play of Nature underground, The. On a Mandrake. Thomas Heyrick. SCP-2

Play Song. Peter Kumalo. SPo

Playboy. Richard Wilbur. NoAM; NOBA

Playboy of the Demi-World, The: 1938. William Plomer. OxBTC

Players. Josephine Miles. RiTi

Playground, The. Michael Bedard. BBGO

Playing. Philip Dow. MIT

Playing upon the hill three centaurs were! The Centaurs. James Stephens. PFIr

Plaza Reál with Palmtrees. Paul Blackburn. NoAM

Plea for a Captive. W. S. Merwin. NoAM

Plea to My Sister, A. James Cunningham. JB

Plea to Those Who Matter. James Welch. AmPA; SA

Pleasant Changes. Jane Euphemia Browne. OxBChV

Pleasant Comedy of Patient Grissell, The, *sels.* Thomas Dekker, *and others.*
"Art thou poor, yet hast thou golden slumbers?" *fr.* I, i. InPS
Cradle Song, A: "Golden slumbers kiss your eyes," *fr.* IV, ii. OxBChV

Pleasant it was, when woods were green. Prelude. Longfellow. *Fr.* Voices of the Night. FSFS

Pleasant the House. *Unknown, tr. fr. Irish by* John Montague. BIrV

Please Forward. James Welch. CDW

Pleased am I, and more than willing. The Lay of the Honeysuckle. Marie de France, *tr. by* Robin Johnson. WPE

Pleasures. Denise Levertov. CAPP; NoAM; NOBA

Pleasures newly found are sweet. To the Same Flower. Wordsworth. MBPR

Pleasures of Melancholy, The. Thomas Warton, the Younger. LAuP

Pleasures of Merely Circulating, The. Wallace Stevens. MAT

Pledge to the Flag, The, *with music.* Francis Bellamy. BLSH

Plenary. *Unknown.* AmFP

Plentiful people went to the Cadillac drawing. Midweek. Josephine Miles. RiTi

Plight, The. James W. Thompson. BPo

Ploughing on Sunday. Wallace Stevens. NCSH; RAE

Ploughman, The. *Unknown.* GBP

Ploughman's Song, The. Nicholas Breton. *Fr.* The Honourable Entertainment Given to the Queen's Majesty in Progress at Elvetham, 1591. NOBE

Plucking Out a Rhythm. Lawson Fusao Inada. AmPA

Plucking the Rushes. *Unknown, tr. fr. Chinese by* Arthur Waley. BoLoP; BuTh; OLR

Plum Gatherer, The. Edna St. Vincent Millay. NoAM

Plunder. A. R. Ammons. NoAM

Pneumonia Blues. *Unknown.* BluL

Po Chu-i, balding old politician. As I Step Over a Puddle at the End of Winter, I Think of an Ancient Chinese Governor. James Wright. CAPP; TCP

Poacher, The. *Unknown. Fr.* The Parlement of the Thre Ages. OxBM

Poaching *in Excelsis.* G. K. Menzies. FaBoCo

Pobble Who Has No Toes, The. Edward Lear. ECBV; FaBoCo; OxBChV

Pockets of our greatcoats full of barley, The. Requiem for the Croppies. Seamus Heaney. BIrV

Pocomania. Derek Walcott. NoAM

Podunk, 1941. Dick Allen. CoPAm

Poe and Longfellow. James Russell Lowell. *Fr.* A Fable for Critics. AmVN; NOBA

Poem: "Always loving or blithe." Charles Senior. MIS

Poem: "As the cat." William Carlos Williams. InPK; InPS; PiAm

Poem: "At night Chinamen jump." Frank O'Hara. NoAM; NOBA

Poem: "Camera records, The." Diane Kruchkow. FAF

Poem: "Country, The/ was back in the hands of the patriots." Fred Levinson. AmPA

Poem: "Crow flies between your phone and mine, The." Cathleen Quirk. MMD

Poem: "Eager note, The, on my door said, 'Call me'." Frank O'Hara. NoAM; NOBA

Poem: "Every morning I forget how it is." Charles Simic. NVAP

Poem: "For the 5th time." Diane Kruchkow. FAF

Poem: "Form is the woods: the beast." Jim Harrison. VGW

Poem: "Four miles out the tide curls in." Mira Fish. FAF

Poem: "From what strange country do you come, then?" Siv Cedering Fox. NVAP

Poem: "Get your tongue." Ted Kooser. POL

Poem: "Greater cities are, The." Victor Hernández Cruz. SA

Poem: "High on a ridge of tiles." Maurice James Craig. BoAnP

Poem: "I meet Mother on the street." Lennart Bruce. POL

Poem: "In the old days either the plaintiff or the defendant won or lost." Alan Dugan. NowV

Poem: "I've been a woman." Sonia Sanchez. WBN

Poem: "Lana Turner has collapsed!" Frank O'Hara. CAPP; CoPAm; VGW

Poem: "Like musical instruments." Tom Clark. *See* Like Musical Instruments.

Poem: "Little brown boy." Helene Johnson. PoBA

Poem: "Look at me 8th." Sonia Sanchez. PoBA

Poem: "On getting a card." William Carlos Williams. VGW

Poem: "Only response, The." William Knott. InPK

Poem: "Person who can do, The." Alan Dugan. NoAM

Poem: "She didn't know it yet." Diane Kruchkow. FAF

Poem: "So many pigeons at Columbus." Arthur Gregor. VGW

Poem: "Something broke the dream." John Gill. NeAC

Poem: "Thing, The/ To do/ Is organize." Kenneth Koch. CAPP

Poem: "This life like no other." Gregory Orr. AmPA

Poem: "Tiny new emotions, The." Tom Clark. ConAP

Poem: "What's the balm." Alan Dugan. CAPP

Poem: "When he came home." Sonia Sanchez. WBN

Poem: "Yo/ smile." Sonia Sanchez. WBN

Poem: "You can look into my face." Mike Todachine. CTBA

Poem: "You jam your arm into the white air." Mira Fish. FAF

Poem: "Your face,/so pale now it is blue." David St. John. AmPA

Poem, The/ exists. A Cycle. John Leax. AATT

Poem about a Poem about a Poem. Robert Conquest. WIF

Poem about a Seashell. Ranice Henderson Crosby. NMM

Poem about Breasts, A. James Wright. CAAP

Poem about Poems about Vietnam, A. Jon Stallworthy. NoAM

Poem after Apollinaire. Ira Sadoff. AmPA

Poem against Rats, A. Fred Levinson. AmPA

Poem Against the British. Robert Bly. ConAP; InPS

Poem Against the Rich. Robert Bly. CAPP; NoAM; NOBA

Poem as Mask, The. Muriel Rukeyser. RiTi

Poem at Semester's End. Ralph Mecklenburger. SFF

Poem at Thirty. Sonia Sanchez. BPo; NMM; PoBA

Poem Before Birth. George MacBeth. SLP

Poem before Departure. Jean Burden. WPE

Poem Beginning with a Line by Pindar, A. Robert Duncan. ConAP; Epi

Poem Beginning with a Line Memorized at School. Roderick Hartigh Jellema. AATT

Poem Composed in Rogue River Park . . . Tom Wayman. POL

Poem/ Ditty-Bop. Carolyn M. Rodgers. JB

Poem for a Goodbye. Norman MacCaig. SLP

Poem for a Hustler. Kathleen Fraser. RiTi

Poem for a Poet, A. Don L. Lee. PoBA

Poem for a Poet, A. Audre Lorde. NMM

Poem for a Singer. Milton Acorn. NeAC

Poem for Aretha. Nikki Giovanni. BPo; PoBA

Poem for Ben Barney. Leslie Silko. CDW

Poem for Bhain, A. John Berryman. CoPAm

Poem for Black Boys. Nikki Giovanni. BPo

Poem for Blackboys in Floppy Tie-Dye Hats. Jodi Braxton. WBN

Poem for Black Hearts, A. LeRoi Jones. CAPP; PoBA; SFF

Poem for Democrats, A. LeRoi Jones. CAPP

Poem for Diane Wakoski, A. Ray A. Young Bear. CDW

Poem for Easter. Robert Kelly. VGW

Poem for Etheridge. Sonia Sanchez. BPo

Poem for Explorers. Carol Bergé. MMD

Poem for Flora. Nikki Giovanni. PoBA

Poem for Foster, A. Walter Bradford. HeS

Poem for Friends. Quincy Troupe. PoBA

Poem for Half White College Students. LeRoi Jones. BPo; CAPP

Poem for Integration, A. Alvin Saxon. PoBA

Poem for Jan. Joseph Bruchac. CDW

Poem for L. C. Peter Klappert. AmPA

Poem for Lorry. Gerald Hausman. CTBA

Poem for Mother's Day. Stanley Kiesel. HeS

Poem for My Family. June Jordan. BPo; RiTi

Poem for My Father, A. Sonia Sanchez. BPo; IHMS; RiTi

Poem for My Great Grandfather. Michael Van Walleghen. HeS

Poem for my Hands. Carole Oles. NPW

Poem for My Students. Robert L. McRoberts. HeS

Poem for Nancy. Stephen Tudor. HeS

Poem for One Who Bares a Pome, A. Richard Bastian. AATT

Poem for Positive Thinkers, A. Barbara Mahone. PoBA

Poem for Richard Speck, A. Michael McMahon. FAF

Poem for Speculative Hipsters, A. LeRoi Jones. NoAM; NOBA

Poem for Susan. Barbara Greenberg. RiTi

Poem for the Year Twenty Twenty. Al Lee. AmPA

Poem for Willie Best, A. LeRoi Jones. CAPP

Poem Found Emptying Out My Pockets. Al Young. CoPAm

Poem from the Empire State. June Jordan. BPo

Poem in October. Dylan Thomas. FSFS; MPo; OBP; SoSe

Poem in Three Parts. Robert Bly. CAPP; ConAP; NOBA

Poem in which My Legs Are Accepted. Kathleen Fraser. AmPA; NMM; RiTi

Poem Intended to Incite the Utmost Depression, A. Samuel Hoffenstein. FaBoCo

Poem makes truth a little more disturbing, The. Hands. Donald Finkel. MAT

Poem moves down a page, A. Richard Meltzer. POL

Poem moves forward, A. The Journey of a Poem Compared to All the Sad Variety of Travel. Delmore Schwartz. NowV

Poem of Angela Yvonne Davis. Nikki Giovanni. PoBA

Poem of Sir Walter Rawleighs, A. Sir Walter Ralegh. AAS

Poem of Solitude at Columbia University. Federico García Lorca, tr. fr. Spanish by Den Delitt. PBMP

Poem of the Clear Eye, The, sel. Kris Hemensley.
Mr. Whitman to His Friends in the Antipodes. CAAP

Poem of the mind in the act of finding, The. Of Modern Poetry. Wallace Stevens. NoAM; PAIC; WIF

Poem, or Beauty Hurts Mr. Vinal. E. E. Cummings. InPS; PAIC; PiAm, PPoe

Poem Out of Childhood. Muriel Rukeyser. NMM

Poem Rocket. Allen Ginsberg. CoPAm; VGW

Poem should be palpable and mute, A. Ars Poetica. Archibald MacLeish. HeIP; InPK; IPWM; NOBA; PAIC; PiAm; SFF; SoSe; TH; WIF

Poem Some People Will Have to Understand, A. LeRoi Jones. BPo; NOBA; PiAm

Poem That Took the Place of a Mountain, The. Wallace Stevens. PiAm

Poem to a Mule, Dead Twenty Years. Guy Owen. BoAnP; POL

Poem to a Redskin. Wendy Rose. CDW

Poem to Be Read and Sung. César Vallejo, tr. fr. Spanish by James Wright and Robert Bly. LoAs

Poem to Be Read at 3 A.M. Donald Justice. CoPAm; MiP

Poem to Complement Other Poems, A. Don L. Lee. BPo; NoAM

Poem to Ease Birth. Unknown, tr. fr. Aztec by Anselm Hollo. IPWM

Poem to My New Jacket. Fran Winant. MMD

Poem to My Sister, Ethel Ennis, Who Sang "The Star-spangled Banner" at the Second Inauguration of Richard Milhous Nixon. June Jordan. WBN

Poem to My Twin Possibility. Dalene Stowe. NPW

Poem to the Mysterious Woman. Robert Desnos, tr. fr. French by Wallace Fowlie. LoAs

Poem While Reading "The Naked Lunch" by William Burroughs. Charles Senior. MIS

Poem with a Conclusion, A. Walter Bradford. HeS

Poem without a Metaphor. David Allan Evans. NVAP

Poem Wondering If I'm Pregnant. Kathleen Fraser. IHMS; NMM

Poem Written after Contemplating the Adverb "Primarily." Christopher Middleton. TwMBP

Poem You Asked For, The. Larry Levis. AmPA; NVAP

Poems. Peter Kelso. AKE

Poems. Bruce Severy. VW

Poems about Playmates. Ronda Davis. JB

Poems are bullshit unless they are. Black Art. LeRoi Jones. BPo; CAPP

Poems: Birmingham 1962–1964. Julia Fields. PoBA

Poems for My Brother Kenneth, *sel.* Owen Dodson. "Sleep late with your dream." PoBA

Poems for the New. Kathleen Fraser. IHMS; NMM; RiTi

Poems of Night. Galway Kinnell. LoAs

Poems to My Father. Rae Desmond Jones. CAAP

Poet, The. Paul Laurence Dunbar. BPo

Poet, A. Thomas Hardy. NoAM

Poet. Conrad Hilberry. PPoD

Poet, The. Thomas Randolph. POL

Poet. Karl Shapiro. NoAM

Poet. Robert Siegel. FAF

Poet. Peter Viereck. CoPAm

Poet and the Rose, The. John Gay. *Fr.* Fables. PAIC

Poet appointed dare not decline. Basil Bunting. *Fr.* Briggflatts. OBP

Poet because his hand goes first, A. Spitballer. Fred Chappell. PPoD

Poet doesn't speak in paradigms, A. Critique for Our Times. Albert Howard Carter. AATT

Poet in his lone yet genial hour, The. Apologia Pro Vita Sua. Samuel Taylor Coleridge. MBPR

Poet in Need, A. John Heath-Stubbs. SFF

Poet is Dead, The. William Everson. PiAm

Poet is Priest. Death to Van Gogh's Ear! Allen Ginsburg. VGW

Poet is the dreamer, The. Loneliness. Al Young. NVAP; PoBA

Poet Laments the Coming of Old Age, The. Edith Sitwell. NoAM

Poet Loves from Afar, The. Desmond O'Grady. NoAM

Poet of nature, thou hast wept to know. To Wordsworth. Shelley. MBPR

Poet of One Mood, A. Alice Meynell. SBG

Poet, Rebuked, Responds, The. William Langland, *tr. fr. Middle English by* Selden Rodman. *Fr.* The Vision of Piers Plowman, Passus XII. OBP

Poet Recognizing the Echo of the Voice, A. Diane Wakoski. Psy

Poet told me if I was serious, The. Instruction from Bly. Cynthia Macdonald. NMM

Poet Tries to Turn in His Jock, The. David Hilton. NowV

Poet was busted by a topless judge, A. Sermonette. Ishmael Reed. PoBA

Poetess Kō Ōgimi, The. Helen Chasin. NMM

Poetical and Congratulatory Epistle to James Boswell, Esq., A. "Peter Pindar." ESaP

Poetical and Philosophical Essay on the French Revolution . . ., A, *sel.* John Courtenay. "Ye Nuns and Capuchins, begin the song." ESaP

Poetical Economy. Harry Graham. FaBoCo

Poetry. Juan Ramón Jiménez, *tr. fr. Spanish.* LoAs ("I recognized you because when I saw the print.") OLR

Poetry. Marianne Moore. AnMo; HeIP; IPWM; NoAM; NOBA; PAIC; PiAm; Psy; TSWA; WIF

Poetry, a Natural Thing. Robert Duncan. NoAM; NOBA

Poetry and Revolution. William Pitt Root. NVAP

Poetry is a projection across silence. Ten Definitions of Poetry. Carl Sandburg. WIF

Poetry is a way of counting. Holding Pattern. Sandra McPherson. RiTi

Poetry is in the Darkness. Aram Boyajian. NeAC

Poetry is the supreme fiction, madame. A High-Toned Old Christian Woman. Wallace Stevens. NoAM; NOBA; PAIC; PiAm; PPP; SoSe

Poetry? It's a hobby. What the Chairman Told Tom. Basil Bunting. OxBTC; TwMBP

Poetry of Departures. Philip Larkin. HeIP; LP; NowV; SS

Poetry of earth is never dead, The. On the Grasshopper and Cricket. Keats. ECBV; Epi; FSFS; MBPR; OBP

Poetry of one the Russians call "a broad nature," The. "Hugh MacDiarmid." *Fr.* The Kind of Poetry I Want. InPS

Poetry to go. Peter Whigham. *Fr.* Astapovo, or What Are We to Do. TwMBP

Poetry Today. John Heath-Stubbs. POL

Poetry's a tree. Yes, the Secret Mind Whispers. Al Young. PoBA

Poets Agree to Be Quiet by the Swamp, The. David Wagoner. CoPAm; VGW

Poet's Blindness, The. Milton. *See* Holy Light.

Poet's cat, sedate and grave, A. The Retired Cat. William Cowper. PCat

Poet's Complaint of His Muse, The, *sel.* Thomas Otway. "To a high hill where never yet stood tree." SCP-2

Poet's Epitaph, A. Wordsworth. MBPR

Poet's Final Instructions, The. John Berryman. VGW

Poets Hitchhiking on the Highway. Gregory Corso. NoAM

Poet's Household, A. Carolyn Kizer. POL

Poets light but lamps, The. Emily Dickinson. HeIP; PiAm

Poets may boast, as safely vain. Of English Verse. Edmund Waller. OBP

Poets of My Epoch. Irwin Stark. PAIC

Poet's Progress, A. Michael Hamburger. WIF

Poet's Request, The. *Unknown, tr. fr. Irish by* John Montague. BIrV

Poet's Welcome to His Love-Begotten Daughter, A. Burns. RRA

Poet's Wife, A. Amy Lowell. RiTi

Poet's Wife Makes Him a Door So He Can Find the Way Home, The. Nancy Willard. RiTi

Poet's Wish. Valery Larbaud, *tr. fr. French by* William Jay Smith. LoAs

Poggio. Lawrence Durrell. OxBTC

Point of Love, The. Alan Bold. SLP

Point of No Return. Robert Graves. BIrV

Poised between going on and back, pulled. The Base Stealer. Robert Francis. NCSH; PPoD; SPo

Poised impossibly on the high tight-rope. Acrobats. Robert Graves. PSN

Poised, relaxed, as a cat that waits. Boxer. Joseph P. Clancy. SPo

Poison. Nancy Mairs. NPW

Poison Tree, A. Blake. *Fr.* Songs of Experience. AnMo; IPWM; LAuP; MBPR; PBMP; PPoD; PPoe; PPP; SFF; WIF

Poke-Pole Fishing. Dennis Schmitz. AmPA

Poland/ 1931. Jerome Rothenberg. Prf

Polar DEW has just warned that, The. Your Attention Please. Peter Porter. LP; OxBTC

Polar Expedition. George M. Young, Jr. FAF

Polar Exploration. Stephen Spender. NoAM

Pole Vaulter. David Allan Evans. NVAP

Pole-Vaulter, The. *Unknown.* SPo

Polemical Elegy for Reinhardt Heydrich. Tom Buchan. MIS

Police are dragging for the bodies, The. Miners. James Wright. ConAP; CTBA; TCP

Policeman, A/ is a pig. Definition for Blk/Children. Sonia Sanchez. PoBA

Policemen Laughing. Ray Fraser. NeAC

Polis is/ yes. Maximus, to Gloucester, Letter 6. Charles Olson. PiAm

Polish Rider, The. Derek Walcott. OBP

Political Despatch, A. George Canning. FaBoCo

Political Poem. LeRoi Jones. NoAM

Political Power. Milton. Fr. Paradise Regained, IV. SCP-1

Politician, A. E. E. Cummings. InPK

Politician, The. Michael McMahon. FAF

Politics. W. B. Yeats. HeIP; InPS; OBP; OxBTC; PFIr; POL

Politics of a Pornographer. Robert Hass. CAAP

Politics of Rich Painters, The. LeRoi Jones. VGW

Poll. Ed Roberson. PoBA

Pollution. Tom Lehrer. PoRo; WIF

Polly put the kettle on. Mother Goose. MG

Polly Vaughn (Molly Bawn). Unknown. AmFP

Polo Match. John Ciardi. SPo

"Polo season would start early in April, The." Animal Days. Lee Harwood. TwMBP

Polyhymnia, sels. George Peele.
  His Golden Locks Time Hath to Silver Turned. HeIp; PPoe (Farewell to Arms.) NOBE
  (Sonnet, A: "His golden locks time hath to silver turned.") InPS

Pompeii, sel. Leonora Speyer.
  New Excavations. TH

Pond, The. Louise Glück. CAAP

Pond, The. Anthony Thwaite. LP; MAT

Pond Lily. E. Margaret Clarkson. AATT

Ponder, darling, these busted statues. E. E. Cummings. NoAM

Pont and Blyth. Unknown. GBP

Pontoosuce. Herman Melville. NOBA

Pony Blues, The. Unknown. BluL

Pool-Shootin' Roy. Damon Runyon. SPo

Poor, The. William Carlos Williams. IPWM; PPP

Poor, and the dazed, and the idiots, The. Hurrying Away from the Earth. Robert Bly. CoPAm

Poor Boy Blues. Unknown. BluL

Poor Can Feed the Birds, The. John Shaw Neilson. MAuV

Poor clerk, "Arnaut the less" they call me, A. Marvoil Ezra Pound. Epi

Poor credulous and simple maid! Phyllis. Thomas Randolph. BoLoP

Poor drunkards, poor drunkards, take warning by me. John Adkins' Farewell. Unknown. AmFP

Poor Ellen Smith. Unknown. AmFP

Poor Ghost, The. Christina Rossetti. GBL

Poor Girl's Meditation, The. Unknown, tr. fr. Irish by Padraic Colum. BIrV; PFIr; OLR

Poor Hal caught his death standing under a spout. Fatal Love. Matthew Prior. FaBoCo

Poor have hands, and feet, and eyes, The. The Poor Man and His Parish Church. Robert Stephen Hawker. VPC

Poor in spirit on their rosary rounds, The. Lough Derg. Denis Devlin. BIrV

Poor john, who joined in make of wrong. Welcome the Wrath. Stanley Kunitz. VGW

Poor lad once and a lad so trim, A. Jean Richepin's Song. Herbert Trench. ECBV; PFIr; PoTa

Poor little foal of an oppressed race! To a Young Ass. Samuel Taylor Coleridge. MBPR

Poor Little Johnny. Unknown. AmFP

Poor Lucy Lake was overgrown. Lucy Lake. Newton Mackintosh. SpRo

Poor malkin, why hast thou been left behind? To a Scarecrow; or, Malkin Left Long after Harvest. Charles Tennyson Turner. VPC

Poor Man, The. Unknown, tr. fr. Swahili. SFF

Poor Man and His Parish Church, The. Robert Stephen Hawker. VPC

Poor Man Blues. Unknown. BluL

Poor man knows not how to eat with the rich man, The. The Poor Man. Unknown, tr. fr. Swahili. SFF

"Poor man, oh, poor man, come tell to me true." The Jolly Thresherman. Unknown. AmFP

Poor man's sins are glaring, The. Rich and Poor; or, Saint and Sinner. Thomas Love Peacock. FaBoCo; NOBE

Poor Old Prurient Interest Blues, The. John Hartford. MAT

Poor old Reuben Ranzo. Reuben Ranzo. Unknown. AmFP

Poor old Robinson Crusoe! Mother Goose. MG

Poor Parson, A. Chaucer. Fr. The Canterbury Tales: Prologue. BoReV

Poor Poll. Robert Bridges. OxBTC

Poor, Poor Country, The. John Shaw Neilson. MAuV

Poor rocking-horse! Eustace, and Edith too. Eustace and Edith. Charles Tennyson Turner. VPC

Poor sheepish plaything. For Sale. Robert Lowell. ConAP; PSN

Poor soul, the centre [or center] of my sinful earth. Sonnets, CXLVI. Shakespeare. Epi; InPK; NOBE; OBP; PPoe; PPP

Poor South! Her books get fewer and fewer. J. Gordon Coogler. FaBoCo

Poor tired Tim! It's sad for him. Tired Tim. Walter de la Mare. LCL

"Poor wanderer," said the leaden sky. The Subalterns. Thomas Hardy. NoAM; PPP

Poor Wayfaring Stranger, A. Unknown. See I Am a Poor Wayfaring Stranger.

Poor wayside white. Queen Anne's Lace. Ruthe T. Spinnanger. AATT

Pop. David McFadden. NeAC

Pop! Goes the [or de] Weasel, with music. Unknown. BLSo; PSoN

Pope He Leads a Happy Life, The. Charles Lever. PFIr

Poplar-Field, The ("The poplars are felled, farewell to the shade"). William Cowper. LAuP; NOBE; VoPo

Poplars are standing there still as death. Southern Mansion. Arna Bontemps. PoBA; SoSe

Poppies. Greg Kuzma. HeS

Poppies in October. Sylvia Plath. NoAM

Porch. Alden Nowlan. NeAC

Porch, The. Philip Pain. PiAm

Porches. Stanley Plumly. HeS

Porcupine, The. Galway Kinnell. CoPAm; NOBA

Porcupine, The. Ogden Nash. ECBV

Porcupines. Robert Huff. CoPAm

Porno Love. Philip Dacey. NVAP

Pornographer, The. Robert Hass. CAAP

Porphyria's Lover. Robert Browning. AnMo; LoAs

Porson on German Scholarship. Richard Porson. FaBoCo

Porson on His Majesty's Government. Richard Porson. FaBoCo

Porson's Visit to the Continent. Richard Porson. FaBoCo

Port Jefferson. Louis Simpson. IPWM

Portage Poem. Louis Jenkins. HeS

Portent, The. Herman Melville. AmVN; NOBA

Portentous change when history can appear.  Sonnet in Allusion to Various Recent Histories and Notices of the French Revolution.  Wordsworth.  MBPR

Porter thoughte what to rede, The.  A Lover's Stratagem.  *Unknown.*  *Fr.* Floris and Blaunchefluor.  OxBM

Portion of this yew.  Transformations.  Thomas Hardy.  NoAM; PPP

Portrait.  E. E. Cummings.  *See* Buffalo Bill's.

Portrait, A.  Walter de la Mare.  NoAM

Portrait.  John Lyle Donaghy.  BIrV

Portrait, The.  Robert Graves.  LoAs; PBMP

Portrait, The.  Stanley Kunitz.  CTBA

Portrait by a Neighbor.  Edna St. Vincent Millay.  TH

"Portrait de Femme."  Irving Feldman.  NoAM

Portrait d'une Femme.  Ezra Pound.  NoAM; NOBA; PPP; SoSe

Portrait of a Girl with Comic Book.  Phyllis McGinley.  CTBA; IPWM

Portrait of a Lady.  T. S. Eliot.  PSN

Portrait of a Lady.  William Carlos Williams.  NoAM; NOBA

Portrait of a Machine.  Louis Untermeyer.  MiP

Portrait of a Marriage.  Dannie Abse.  NoAM

Portrait of a Woman.  Kathryn Ruby.  WBN

Portrait of a Young Girl Raped at a Suburban Party.  Brian Patten.  OxBTC

Portrait of an Artist.  Barbara Howes.  IHMS

Portrait of Malcolm X.  Etheridge Knight.  PoBA

Portrait of the Artist as a Prematurely Old Man.  Ogden Nash.  SoSe

Portrait of the Father.  Lindy Hough.  IHMS

Portrait: The Freedom Fighter.  George Jonas.  NeAC

Position.  Carol Bergé.  MMD

Position is where you.  The Window.  Robert Creeley.  CAPP; CoPAm; NoAM; NOBA; VGW

Positive, a Coxcomb.  William Plomer.  POL

Positives.  Jewel C. Latimore.  PoBA

Positives for Sterling Plumpp.  Don L. Lee.  JB; PoBA

Possession.  Marie Ponsot.  VGW

Possession palls.  Prophecy of the Grecian Urn.  Ruthe T. Spinnanger.  AATT

Possessions.  Ai.  CAAP

Possible/ that I lift this hand.  Pavane for the Passing of a Child.  Laura Chester.  FiCP

Possibility of New Poetry, The.  Robert Bly.  ConAP

Possum Tree, The.  Irene Gough.  ECBV

Post-boy drove with fierce career, The.  Alice Fell.  Wordsworth.  MBPR; SpRo

Post Mortem.  Robinson Jeffers.  PiAm

Post-Mortem, A.  Siegfried Sassoon.  PBMP

Postcard to Send to Sumer, A.  William Bronk.  VGW

Poster, The.  Lynn Sukenick.  RiTi

Poster with my picture on it, The.  Unwanted.  Edward Field.  SS

Postman comes when I am still in bed, The.  A Sick Child.  Randall Jarrell.  VGW

Postscript.  Sandra Hochman.  NMM

Postscript: For Gweno.  Alun Lewis.  BoLoP

Postscript to Die Schöne Müllerin.  R. P. Lister.  POL

Posy, The.  George Herbert.  SCP-1

Pot of Flowers, The.  William Carlos Williams.  PiAm

Potato.  Richard Wilbur.  CAPP

Potomac Town in February.  Carl Sandburg.  LCL

Potted fern, A.  Two Takes from Love in Los Angeles.  Al Young.  CoPAm

Poultries, The.  Ogden Nash.  RAE

Pound of Flesh, The.  *Unknown.*  *Fr.* Cursor Mundi.  OxBM

Pour, O pour that parting soul in song.  Song of the Son.  Jean Toomer.  PoBA

Pourquoi?  *Unknown.*  ECBV

Poverty.  Margaret Reynolds.  MIS

Poverty.  Charles Simic.  MAT

Poverty.  Thomas Traherne.  Prf

Power above powers, O heavenly Eloquence.  Heavenly Eloquence.  Samuel Daniel.  *Fr.* Musophilus.  NOBE

Power Failure.  Michael Dennis Browne.  AmPA

Power Failure.  Dabney Stuart.  NVAP

Power of armies is a visible thing, The.  Wordsworth.  MBPR

Power of Love He Wants Shih (Everything), The.  Rochelle Owens.  NMM; Psy

Power of Prayer, The.  Samuel Johnson.  *Fr.* The Vanity of Human Wishes.  NOBE
(Prayer: "Where then shall Hope and Fear their objects find?")  BoReV

Power of Ridicule, The.  Pope.  *Fr.* Epilogue to the Satires.  NOBE

Power of the Dog, The.  Kipling.  BoAnP

Power Station, The.  James Merrill.  ConAP

Power to the People.  Howard Nemerov.  POL

Powerful Eyes o' Jeremy Tait, The.  Wallace Irwin.  PoTa

Powhatan's Daughter.  Hart Crane.  *See* Bridge, The.

Powte's Complaint, The.  *Unknown.*  GBP

Pox on this playhouse! 'Tis an old tired jade.  Dryden.  *Fr.* Epilogue Spoken at Mithridates King of Pontus.  SCP-1

Practical Concerns.  William J. Harris.  PoBA

Prairie, *sel.*  Carl Sandburg.
Finale.  ANTL

Prairie grass:/ new sprouts.  Struggle for the Roads.  Bruce Severy.  VW

Prairie Sunset, A.  Walt Whitman.  PiAm

Prairie Town.  William Stafford.  PPoD

Prairie wind blew harder than it could, The.  Swallows.  Thomas Hornsby Ferril.  RFM

Prairies, The.  Bryant.  AmVN; NOBA; PiAm

Praise.  William Matthews.  AmPA; NVAP

Praise.  Christopher Smart.  OxBChV

Praise above all—for praise prevails.  Adoremus.  Christopher Smart.  *Fr.* A Song to David.  OBP

Praise for an Urn.  Hart Crane.  NoAM; NOBA; PPP

Praise God for this little scrap of light.  Epiphany on a Plot of Moonlight.  William R. Mitchell.  AATT

Praise in Summer.  Richard Wilbur.  CAPP

Praise of Dancing, The.  Sir John Davies.  *Fr.* Orchestra; or, A Poem of Dancing.  NOBE

Praise of Pindar, The.  Horace, *tr. by* Abraham Cowley.  Odes, IV, 2.  Epi; PAIC

"Praise ye the Lord!" The psalm to-day.  The Thanksgiving in Boston Harbor.  Hezekiah Butterworth.  BTTM

Praised be man, he is existing in milk.  Chorus.  Jack Kerouac.  *Fr.* Mexico City Blues.  PiAm

Praisers of women in their proud and beautiful poems, The.  "Not Marble nor the Gilded Monuments."  Archibald MacLeish.  BoLoP; WIF

Praises, The.  Charles Olson.  VGW

Praises of a Country Life, The.  Ben Jonson.  SCP-1

Pray but one prayer for me 'twixt thy closed lips.  Summer Dawn.  William Morris.  NOBE

Pray for you, my darling?  Aside to Julie.  Sallie Chesham.  AATT

Pray in May.  James J. Metcalfe.  SoSe

Prayer: "Give me a death like Buddha's, let me fall."  Stanley Moss.  POL

Prayer, A: "Grant, I thee pray, such heat into mine heart." Sir Thomas More. BoReV

Prayer: "Prayer the church's [or churches] banquet, angels' age." George Herbert. BoReV; Epi; InPS; NOBE; PAIC

Prayer, A: "Sun, my relative." *Unknown, tr. fr. Havasupai Indian.* AKE

Prayer: "Where then shall Hope and Fear their objects find?" Samuel Johnson. *See* Power of Prayer, The.

Prayer, The: "Wilt thou not visit me?" Jones Very. AmVN

Prayer after World War. Carl Sandburg. VGW

Prayer before Birth. Louis MacNeice. BuTh; MPo; PBMP; PFIr

Prayer for Fine Weather. Shane Leslie. PFIr; POL

Prayer for Good Dreams. *Unknown.* OxBM

Prayer for My Daughter, A. W. B. Yeats. NoAM; OxBTC; RRA; SoSe

Prayer for Rain. *Unknown, tr. fr. Zuni Indian.* AKE

Prayer for the Great Family. Gary Snyder. OFD

Prayer for the Journey. *Unknown.* OxBM

Prayer for the Self, A. John Berryman. Eleven Addresses to the Lord, VIII. PiAm; PPP

Prayer from a Stryker Frame. E. Margaret Clarkson. AATT

Prayer in Mid-Passage. Louis MacNeice. BoReV

Prayer in Spring, A. Robert Frost. SoSe

Prayer of Holy Willie, The. Burns. *See* Holy Willie's Prayer.

Prayer of Thanksgiving, *with music. Unknown, tr. fr. Dutch by* Theodore Baker. BLSo

Prayer the church's [or churches] banquet, angels' age. Prayer. George Herbert. BoReV; Epi; InPS; NOBE; PAIC

Prayer to Be Said When Thou Goest to Bed, A. Francis Seager. OxBChV

Prayer to St. Helena. *Unknown.* OxBM

Prayer to the Mothers. Diane DiPrima. RiTi

Prayer to the Pacific. Leslie Silko. CDW

Prayer to the Snowy Owl. John Haines. BoAnP

Prayer unsaid, and Mass unsung. The Sea-Ritual. George Darley. Syren Songs, V. BIrV

Preacher Considers His Sermon, The. Elmer F. Suderman. AATT

Preacher, The: Ruminates behind the Sermon. Gwendolyn Brooks. PBMP

Preacher, Said the General. Peter Meinke. AATT

Preachin' the Blues. *Unknown.* BluL

Preaching Blues. *Unknown.* BluL

Precise Guinea-Pig, The. *Unknown. See* Guinea-Pig Song, A.

Predicter of Famine, The. William Carlos Williams. VGW

Prediction, The. Mark Strand. NVAP

Preest ne monk ne yet canoun. Against Friars. *Unknown.* OxBM

Preface: "And did those feet in ancient time." Blake. *See* And Did Those Feet in Ancient Time.

Preface, The: "Infinity, when all things it beheld." Edward Taylor. *Fr.* God's Determinations. NOBA; PiAm

Preface: " 'Sonja Henie,' the young girl." Theodore Weiss. VGW

Preface: "To make a start." William Carlos Williams. *Fr.* Paterson. NoAM; NOBA

Preface to a Twenty Volume Suicide Note. LeRoi Jones. CAPP; InPK; InPS; IPWM; PAIC; PoBA; PPP; TCP

Preface to the Memoirs, A. James Merrill. NOBA

Preface to the Picture of Dorian Gray. Oscar Wilde. WIF

Preference. Langston Hughes. NOBA

Preference. Elinor Wylie. Psy

Preference Declared, The ("Persicos odi"). Horace. *See* Fie on Eastern Luxury!

Pregnancy. Mira Fish. FAF

Pregnancy. Sandra McPherson. NMM

Pregnant girl, under sorrow's sign, A. Under Sorrow's Sign. Gofraidh Fionn O'Dalaigh, *tr. by* John Montague. BIrV

Prejudice. Georgia Douglas Johnson. PoBA

Preliminary to Classroom Lecture. Josephine Miles. NoAM

Prelude, The [or, Growth of a Poet's Mind]. Wordsworth. MBPR

*Sels.*

"And in the frosty season, when the sun," *fr.* I. FSFS (Skaters, The.) SPo

Authentic Tidings, *fr.* VI. BoReV

Childhood and School-Time, *fr.* I. NOBE

Dedication: "Memory of one particular hour, The," *fr.* IV. BoReV

Guilt, *fr.* I. BoReV

One Summer Evening, *fr.* I. OBP

"Thus did my days pass on, and now at length," *fr* II. BoReV

"Wisdom and Spirit of the universe!" *fr.* I. NOBE

Prelude: "Give us another poem, he said." Patrick Kavanagh. NoAM

Prelude: "Night and the hood." Conrad Kent Rivers. PoBA

Prelude: "Pleasant it was, when woods were green." Longfellow. *Fr.* Voices of the Night. FSFS

Preludes (I–IV). T. S. Eliot. HeIP; InPS; PPoD; PPP; PSN; VGW

Preludes for Memnon, *sels.* Conrad Aiken. NoAM

"Rimbaud and Verlaine, precious pair of poets," LVI.

"Two coffees in the Español, the last," II.

Preludes to Definition. Conrad Aiken. *See* Time in the Rock.

Prenegard, prenegard! My Baselard. *Unknown.* OxBM

'Prentice Boy, The. *Unknown.* AmFP

Preparation of the Body, The. Helen Wolfert. *Fr.* Woman Against the Moon. RiTi

Preparations. *Unknown.* NOBE

Preparative, The. Thomas Traherne. SCP-2

Preparatory Meditations, *sels.* Edward Taylor.

*First Series.*

"Am I thy gold? Or purse, Lord, for thy wealth," VI. VoPo

"Did ever lord such noble house maintain," IX. SCP-2

"How sweet a Lord is mine? If any should," III. PiAm

"I kenning [or kening] through astronomy divine," VIII. NOBA; PiAm; SCP-2

(Sacramental Meditations.) PAIC

"My blessed Lord, art thou a lilly flower?" V. PiAm

"My dear, deare Lord I do thee Savior call," II. PiAm

"My shattred phancy stole away from mee," XXIX. PiAm

"Oh! What a thing is man? Lord, who am I?" XXXVIII. NOBA; PiAm

"Thy humane frame, my glorious Lord, I spy," VII. PiAm

"What love is this of thine, that cannot bee," I. PiAm

"Would God I in that Golden City were," XXIII. PiAm

*Second Series.*

"Lord, dub my tongue with a new tier of words," XIX. SCP-2

"My gracious Lord, I would thee glory doe," IV. PiAm

"Oh! Good, good, good, my Lord. What more love yet," CXII. NOBA

"Oh leaden heeld. Lord, give, forgive I pray," I. PiAm

"Ye angells bright, pluck from your wings a quill," LX. PiAm

Preparing for Exile. Derek Walcott. OBP

Preponderance, The. William Meredith. PBMP

Preposterous is that government, and rude. Ill Government. Robert Herrick. PAIC

Presbyterian Knight. Samuel Butler. *Fr.* Hudibras, I, 1. NOBE ("When civil fury first grew high.") PAIC; SCP-2

Presence, The. Maxine W. Kumin. RFM; TSWA; WPE

Presence, The. Dana Naone. CDW

Presence among us. Voyage to the Moon. Archibald MacLeish. Moon; PBMP

Present, The. Dick Allen. FAF

Present day we cannot spend, The. Isabella Whitney. *Fr.* A Sweet Nosegay, or Pleasant Posy. WPE

Present is such a lovely place, The. The Present. Dick Allen. FAF

Present of Butter, A. Tadhg Dall O'Huiginn, *tr. fr. Irish by* the Earl of Longford. BIrV

Presentation of Two Birds to My Son, A. James Wright. PPP

Presentation Piece. Marilyn Hacker. AmPA

Preserve thy sighs, unthrifty girl. The Soldier [*or* Souldier] Going to the Field. Sir William Davenant. MetP; NOBE

President Roosevelt. *Unknown.* BluL

President says, The/eat fish. Virginia Scott. NPW

Press on till thou descry. Anne Killigrew. *Fr.* Chloris' Charms Dissolved by Eudora. SCP-2

Press'd by the Moon, Mute Arbitress of Tides. Charlotte Smith. SBG
(Sonnet Written in the Church-yard at Middleton, in Sussex.) WPE

Pressure. Anne Waldman. CAAP

Pressures, The. LeRoi Jones. BPo

Prestidigitator, The. Al Young. MIT

Preston. *Unknown.* GBP

Pretending Not to Sleep. Ian Hamilton. NoAM

Prettiest girl, The. Sucking Cider Through a Straw. *Unknown.* GBP

Pretty fair maid all in the garden, A. The Broken Token. *Unknown.* AmFP

Pretty Ploughboy, The. *Unknown.* AIW; GBP

Pretty Polly, 2 *versions. Unknown.* AmFP

Pretty Polly of Topsham. *Unknown.* AmFP

Pretty prating poll. Little Miss and Her Parrot. John Marchant. OxBChV

Pretty Saro. *Unknown.* AmFP

"Pretty, say when." The Dear Girl. Sylvia Townsend Warner. AIW

Pretty Sport. William Habington. NOBE

Pretty Woman, A. Simon J. Ortiz. CDW

Previsioning death in advance, our doom is delayed. Foresight. Lincoln Kirstein. NoAM

Priapus and the Pool, *sels.* Conrad Aiken.
"This is the shape of the leaf, and this of the flower," IV. NOBA
"When trout swim down Great Ormond Street," III. NoAM; NOBA

Price of Beast in Las Vegas, The. Carole Oles. NPW

Price seemed reasonable, location, The. Telephone Conversation. Wole Soyinka. SSF; SoSe

Pricke of Conscience, The, *sel. Unknown.*
Newly Born, The. OxBM

Pride of Ladies, A. Anne Halley. NMM

Priest and the Mulberry Tree, The. Thomas Love Peacock. *Fr.* Crotchet Castle. PoTa

Priestley. Samuel Taylor Coleridge. *Fr.* Sonnets on Eminent Characters. MBPR

Primaleon of Greece, *sel.* Anthony Munday.
Beauty Bathing. NOBE

Primary Ground, A. Adrienne Rich. WBN

Primary Lesson: The Second Class Citizens. Sun-Ra. PoBA

Prime. Langston Hughes. PoBA

Primer Lesson. Carl Sandburg. SFF; TH

Primer of Plato. Jean Garrigue. NOBA

Primitive, The. Don L. Lee. BPo

Primitive Like an Orb, A. Wallace Stevens. NOBA

Primitives. Dudley Randall. BPo

Primrose, Being at Montgomery Castle, The. John Donne. GBL

Primula Scotica. Charles Senior. MIS

Prince, The. Edgar Bowers. ConAP

Prince Absalom and Sir Rotherham Redde. Evening. Edith Sitwell. AIW

Prince Alfrid's Itinerary, *sel. Unknown, tr. fr. Irish by* James Clarence Mangan.
"I found in Munster, unfettered of any." BIrV

Prince of Love, The. Blake. *See* Song: "How sweet I roamed from field to field."

Prince Robert. *Unknown.* AmFP

Princes' Land, The. Les A. Murray. MAuV

Prince's Progress, The, *sel.* Christina Rossetti.
Bride Song. WPE

Princess, The, *sels.* Tennyson.
"Ask me no more: the moon may draw the sea," *fr.* Pt. VI. GBL
"Now sleeps the crimson petal, now the white," *fr.* Pt. VII. BoLoP; GBL; LoAs; NOBE; PPoe; PPP
Splender Falls on Castle Walls, The, *fr.* Pt. III. HeIP; InPK (Blow, Bugle, Blow.) NOBE
Sweet and Low, *fr.* Pt. II. BLSH; OxBChV
"Tears, idle tears, I know not what they mean," *fr.* Pt. IV. InPK; InPS; NOBE; PPoe; PPP; VoPo

Princess Addresses the Frog Prince, The. Elizabeth Brewster. MMD

Princess and the Gypsies, The. Frances Cornford. PoTa

Printed Words. Liz Sohappy Bahe. CDW

Printing Jenny ("Printing Bibles is Jenny's daily chore"). Matthew Mitchell. OxBTC

Prioress, The. Chaucer. *Fr.* The Canterbury Tales: Prologue OxBM
(Madam Eglantine.) NOBE

Pripet Marshes, The. Irving Feldman. NoAM

Prison Cell Blues. *Unknown.* BluL

Prisoner, The. Emily Brontë. BoReV; NOBE

Prisoner, The. Keith Douglas. PSN

Prisoner, The. Derek Mahon. PFIr

Prisoner of Chillon, The. Byron. MBPR
*Sels.*
"Kind of change came in my fate, A." NOBE
Sonnet on Chillon. PAIC; PBMP

Prisoner's Prayer, A. *Unknown.* OxBM

Prisoner's Song. Horace Gregory. OLR

Prithee forgive me,/ I did but chide in jest. Thomas Middleton. *Fr.* Women Beware Women: a Tragedy. SCP-2

Prithee, say aye or no. The Resolute Courtier. Thomas Shipman. GBL

Prithee stand awhile and view this tree. On a Great Hollow Tree. William Strode. SCP-2

Private Pain in Time of Trouble. Kathleen Spivack. AmPA

Privately, your pencil makes. Snapshot of a Pedant. George Garrett. WIF

Prize Cat, The. E. J. Pratt. NoAM

"Prize" Poem, A. Shirley Brooks. FaBoCo

Pro Basketball Players. Tom Meschery. SPo

Pro Femina, *sels.* Carolyn Kizer.
"From Sappho to myself, consider the fate of women," I. NMM; Psy; RiTi; WBN
"I take as my theme, 'The Independent Woman,' " II. MAT; NMM; Psy; RiTi; WBN
"I will speak about women of letters, for I'm in the racket," III. MAT; NMM; Psy; RiTi; WBN

Pro Patria, *abr.* Constance Carrier. WPE

Problem, The. Emerson. NOBA

Problem in Social Geometry—The Inverted Square! Ray Durem. PoBA

Problem With Dreams, The. Thomas Brush. NVAP

Proclamation/ From Sleep, Arise. Carolyn M. Rodgers. JB

Proclitic in the wind he walks.  Prophet.  Henry Tim Chambers. AATT

Procne, Philomela, and Itylus.  Philomela.  John Crowe Ransom. NoAM; NOBA

Prodigal, The.  Elizabeth Bishop.  CoPAm; PPP

Proem: "I love the old melodious lays."  Whittier.  AmVN

Proem: "Strong Son of God, immortal Love."  Tennyson.  *See* In Memoriam A.H.H.: "Strong Son of God. . ."

Proem: To Brooklyn Bridge.  Hart Crane.  *See* To Brooklyn Bridge.

Professor Kelleher and the Charles River.  Desmond O'Grady. NoAM

Professor Robinson each summer beats.  Don's Holiday.  G. Rostrevor Hamilton.  FaBoCo

Professor's Song, A.  John Berryman.  HeIP; NoAM; NOBA

Profile of a Day.  Ruthe T. Spinnanger.  AATT

Profile on the Pillow, The.  Dudley Randall.  BPo; PoBA

Profoundest of all sensualities, The.  The Deepest Sensuality. D. H. Lawrence.  NoAM

Prognosis.  Louis MacNeice.  NOBE

Progress, The.  Ralph Knevet.  SCP-2

Progress.  Peter Meinke.  POL

Progress of Beauty, The.  Swift.  AnMo

Progress of Learning, The, *sel.*  Sir John Denham. "Then darkness Europe's face did overspread."  SCP-2

Progress of Poesy, The.  Thomas Gray.  LAuP

Progress of Poetry, The.  "Christopher Caudwell."  OxBTC

Progress of the Soul, The ("Nothing could make me sooner to confess").  John Donne.  *See* Of the Progress of the Soul; the Second Anniversary.

Progresse of the Soule, The ("I sing the progress of a deathless soul"), *sels.*  John Donne.  OBP
Elephant, The.
Whale, The.

Projection, A.  Reed Whittemore.  WIF

Projectionist's Nightmare, The.  Brian Patten.  LP

Projections for an Eagle Escaped in This City, March 1965. Nathaniel Tarn.  TwMBP

Proletarian Portrait.  William Carlos Williams.  MiP; PiAm

Prologue: "And the way goes on in the worn earth."  Archibald MacLeish.  *Fr.* Conquistador.  NoAM

Prologue: "By landscape reminded once of his mother's figure." W. H. Auden.  NoAM

Prologue: "I first adventure, with foolhardy might."  Joseph Hall. *Fr.* Virgidemiarum, Bk. I.  TVS

Prologue: "In a summer season, when soft was the sun."  William Langland, *tr. fr. Middle English by* Selden Rodman.  *Fr.* The Vision of Piers Plowman.  OBP
(Field Full of Folk, The.)  OxBM

Prologue: "Over! the sweet summer closes."  Tennyson.  *Fr.* Becket.  GBL

Prologue, The: "To sing of wars, of captain[e]s, and of kings." Anne Bradstreet.  NOBA; SBG; WPE

Prologue: "We who with songs beguile your pilgrimage.  James Elroy Flecker.  *Fr.* The Golden Journey to Samarkand. OxBTC

Prologue: "Whan that April with his showres soote."  Chaucer. *See* Canterbury Tales, The.

Prologue Spoken at the Opening of the Theatre in Drury-Lane, 1747.  Samuel Johnson.  LAuP

Prologue to a Translation.  John Trevisa.  OxBM

Prologue to His Royal Highness.  Dryden.  SCP-1

Prologue to "The Canterbury Tales."  Chaucer.  *See* Canterbury Tales, The.

Promenading their/ skirted galleons of sex.  The Return to Work. William Carlos Williams.  CTBA

Prometheus.  Byron.  InPS; MBPR; NOBE

Prometheus Unbound.  Shelley.  MBPR
*Sels.*
Asia's Song, *fr.* II, v.  GrRo
"Life of Life! thy lips enkindle," *fr.* II, v.  NOBE

Promised Land, The.  Samuel Stennett.  AmFP

Promises, *sel.*  Robert Penn Warren.
Founding Fathers, Nineteenth-Century Style, VIII.  NoAM

Promises of Freedom.  *Unknown.*  BPo

Promissory Note, The.  Bayard Taylor.  SpRo

Promontory Moon.  Galway Kinnell.  Moon

Promptress of unnumber'd sighs.  To Fortune on Buying a Ticket in the Irish Lottery.  Samuel Taylor Coleridge.  MBPR

Prone couple still sleeps, A.  First Light.  Thomas Kinsella. BIrV; NoAM

Proofs of Love.  *Unknown.*  ECBV

Prope ripam fluvii solus.  Malum Opus.  James Appleton Morgan.  FaBoCo

Propeller Sleep.  Mei Berssenbrugge.  SA

Properties of the Shires of England, The ("The properte of every shire").  *Unknown.*  GBP

Properzia Rossi.  Felicia Dorothea Hemans.  SBG

Prophecy.  Elinor Wylie.  RiTi; VGW

Prophecy of the Grecian Urn.  Ruthe T. Spinnanger.  AATT

Prophecy of this Present Year 1600, A.  John Weever.  TVS

Prophet.  Henry Tim Chambers.  AATT

Prophet, The, *sel.*  Kahlil Gibran.
On Children.  SFF

Prophet of the body's.  Walt Whitman.  Edwin Honig.  PAIC

Prophet speaks, The.  Saint Malcolm.  Jewel C. Latimore.  BPo

Prophets for a New Day.  Margaret Walker.  BPo

Prophet's Warning or Shoot to Kill, The.  Ebon Dooley.  PoBA

Propped boughs are heavy with apples.  In the Huon Valley. James McAuley.  MAuV

Prosopopoeia-Corporis Animae Valedicturi: Adios: Arrivederci. William Lathum.  SCP-2

Prospect Beach.  Lou Lipsitz.  VGW

Prospecting.  A. R. Ammons.  ConAP

Prospecting Dream.  *Unknown.*  AmFP

Prospective Immigrants Please Note.  Adrienne Rich.  VGW

Prospice.  Robert Browning.  PAIC; PFD; VoPo

Prostitutes at Les Halles, The.  Jane Mayhall.  WBN

Protective Grigri, The.  Ted Joans.  PoBA

Proteus.  Kathleen Wiegner.  MMD

Prothalamion.  Spenser.  AAS; PPoe; PPP

Prothalamion.  Michael Ryan.  AmPA

Prothalamium.  Donagh MacDonagh.  BIrV

Protocols.  Randall Jarrell.  VGW

Proud Lady, A.  Elinor Wylie.  SBG

Proud Maisie.  Sir Walter Scott.  *Fr.* The Heart of Midlothian, *ch.* 38.  AIW; Epi; InPK
(Madge Wildfire's Song.)  NOBE; SLP

Proud of his hump.  Dromedary.  François Dodat, *tr. by* Bert *and* Odette Meyers.  BoAnP

Proud Preston, poor people.  Preston.  *Unknown.*  GBP

Proud Songsters.  Thomas Hardy.  NoAM

Proud word you never spoke, but you will speak.  Walter Savage Landor.  *Fr.* Ianthe.  GBL

Proudly swept the rain cloud by the cliff.  Aloha Oe.  Queen Lydia Liliuokalani.  BLSH

Proust's Madeleine.  Kenneth Rexroth.  NoAM

Proverbial Philosophy: Of Reading.  Charles Stuart Calverley. FaBoCo

Proverbs.  Morton Marcus.  NVAP

Proverbs of Alfred, The, *sel.*  *At. to* Alfred, King of England. Wealth and Wisdom.  OxBM

Provide, Provide. Robert Frost. InPK; IPWM; NoAM; NOBA; PPP; SS

Provisions. Margaret Atwood. IHMS

Pruners and quick and cruel, The. Knife and Sap. Kenneth Leslie. POL

Psalm. Charles Simic. AmPA

Psalm Concerning the Castle. Denise Levertov. PiAm; WPE

Psalm of Life, A. Longfellow. AmVN; PiAm

Psalm of Onan for Harp, Flute and Tambourine, A. Alden Nowlan. NeAC

Psalm Praising the Hair of Man's Body, A. Denise Levertov. AnMo; CAPP

Psalm III: "To God: to illuminate all men. Beginning with Skid Row." Allen Ginsberg. CAPP

Psalmen Gezangen. Irene Dayton. AATT

Psalms, sels. Bible, O.T.
Psalm VIII ("O Lord, our Lord, how excellent is thy name"). AKE; PBMB
Psalm XIX ("The Heavens declare the glory of God"). OBP
Psalm XXIII ("The Lord is my shepherd; I shall not want."). SFF
(Psalm XXIII: "God shepherds me," paraphrased by Harry H. Mayer.) SFF
(Psalm XXIII: "Yahweh is my shepherd," Jerusalem Bible.) SFF
Psalm LV ("Give ear to my prayer. . ."). 
(Psalm LV: Exaudi, Deus: "My God most glad to look, most prone to hear," paraphrased by the Countess of Pembroke.) WPE
Psalm LVIII ("Do ye indeed speak righteousness . . ."). 
(Psalm LVIII: Si Vere Utique: "And call ye this to utter what is just," paraphrased by the Countess of Pembroke.) WPE
Psalm C ("Make a joyful noise unto the Lord, all ye lands"). OFD
Psalm CXXXIX ("O Lord, thou hast searched me . . ."). 
(Psalm CXXXIX: Domine, Probasti: "O Lord in me there lieth nought," paraphrased by the Countess of Pembroke.) WPE
Psalm CL ("Praise ye the Lord . . .")
(Psalm CL: "O praise God in his holiness: praise him," Book of Common Prayer.) RAE

PSI. Melvin B. Tolson. PoBA

Psychathanasia; or, the Second Part of the Song of the Soul, sel. Henry More.
"World's great soul knows by protópathy, The," Bk. III. SCP-2

Psyche. Samuel Taylor Coleridge. MBPR; PBMP

Psyche or Love's Mystery, sels. Joseph Beaumont. SCP-2
"All things at first was God, who dwelt alone," fr. Canto VI
"For as the honey of heaven's lovely hives," fr. Canto II.
"Stately mirror's all-enamelled case, A," fr. Canto V.

Psychology. Duncan Glen. MIS

Psychometrist. James Stephens. NoAM

Psychozoia; or, the First Part of the Song of the Soul, sels. Henry More. SCP-2
"I hear the clattering of an armèd troop," Canto III.
"There you may see the eyelids of the morn," Canto I.

Public Bar. D. J. Enright. LP

Public Gardens, The. Alun Lewis. PSN

Public-House Confidence. Norman Cameron. BBGO

Puck of Pook's Hill, sels. Kipling.
Cities and Thrones and Powers. NOBE; OxBTC
Puck's Song ("See you the ferny ride that steals"). OxBChV
Smuggler's Song, A. OxBChV

Puck's Night Song ("Now the hungry lion"). Shakespeare. Fr. A Midsummer Night's Dream. ECBV

Puck's Song ("See you the ferny ride that steals"). Kipling. Fr. Puck of Pook's Hill. OxBChV

"Pudding and pie." Greedy Jane. Unknown. ECBV; OxBChV

Puddy and the Mouse, The. Unknown. GBP

Puerto Ricans in New York, I. Charles Reznikoff. CTBA

Puerto Ricans in New York, II. Charles Reznikoff. CTBA

Pu-Heter Pu-Huligan. Unknown. ECBV

Pull my arm back, Seymour. Seymour and Chantelle or Un Peu de Vice. Stevie Smith. SBG

Pull of the Earth. Stanley Plumly. HeS

Pull Off Your Old Coat, with music. Unknown. RDB

Pull up the bell-flow'rs of the spring. St. Mark. Christopher Smart. Fr. Hymns and Spiritual Songs. LAuP

Pull your bed aside and dig. How to Cure Your Fever. Thomas Lux. NVAP

Pulley, The. George Herbert. HeIP; InPK; InPS; MetP; NOBE; PPP

Pullin me in off the corner to wash my face an. Black Jam for Dr. Negro. Mari Evans. BPo; PoBA; Psy

Pulling Out. Lyn Lifshin. NeAC

Pulling up in my car, I went into the cottage. After Five Years. Augustus Young. BIrV

Pumpkin, The. Robert Graves. CaYB

Pun for Al Gelpi, A. Jack Kerouac. PiAM

Punctual as bad luck. The Family Goldschmitt. Henri Coulette. NowV

Punctually at Christmas the soft plush. White Christmas. W. R. Rodgers. PFIr

Puppy. Fred Lape. BoAnP

Purblind walls. Vincent Buckley. Fr. Golden Builders. CAAP

Purcell in many victories of his. Bounty. Josephine Miles. NoAM

Pure/ Every day there's the bridge. The Bay Bridge from Portrero Hill. Jack Gilbert. NowV

Pure blood domestic, guaranteed. The Prize Cat. E. J. Pratt. NoAM

Pure fasted faces draw unto this feast. Easter Communion. Gerard Manley Hopkins. OFD

Pure gold, they said in her praise. Around Thanksgiving. Rolfe Humphries. OFD

Pure products of America, The. To Elsie. William Carlos Williams. InPS; NOBA

Pure? What does it mean? Fever 103°. Sylvia Plath. AnMo; NoAM; NOBA; PiAM; VGW

Pure white bodies of my friends, The. Verigin 3. John Newlove. NeAC

Purgatory. Maxine W. Kumin. CoPAm

Purgatory. W. B. Yeats. PAIC

Puritan Poet Reel. Vincent Buckley. MAuV

Puritan Sonnet. Elinor Wylie. Wild Peaches, IV. PAIC ("Down to the Puritan marrow of my bones.") VoPo

Purity/ Is obscurity. Reflection On a Wicked World. Ogden Nash. SFF

Purple blot against the dead white door, A. Monsieur qui Passe. Charlotte Mew. SBG

Purple Cow, The. Gelett Burgess. FaBoCo

Purple Indians pas de bourrée. Lord Fluting Dreams of America on the Eve of His Departure from Liverpool. Paul Zimmer. VGW

Purse-Seine, The. Robinson Jeffers. NoAM; NOBA

Pursuit. Hilda Doolittle ("H.D."). WPE

Pursuit. Robert Penn Warren. CoPAm; PPP

Pursuit from Under. James Dickey. PPP

Pussy. Unknown. OxBChV

Pussy-cat, pussy-cat, where have you been? Mother Goose. MG

Pussy-kitten, pussy-cat. Cosy Cat Nap. James Kirkup. RAE

Put down the pen. The Tale. Charles Simic. CAAP

Put his head. Odiham. John Gray. FaBoCo

Put on the skillet, put on the led. Short'nin' Bread. *Unknown.* BLSo

Put your arms on your back. Bird Calls. Cathleen Quirk. MMD

Put your hand in the creel. Marriage. *Unknown.* GBP

Put your hand on my heart, say that you love me as. A Betrothal. E. J. Scovell. GBL

Put your head, darling, darling, darling. Dear Dark Head [*or* Cean Dubh Deelish]. *Unknown, tr. by* Sir Samuel Ferguson. BIrV; GBL; LoAs; PFIr

Putting in the Seed. Robert Frost. NoAM

Putting the Croutons Back into the Jar. Diane Kruchkow. FAF

Puzzle faces in the dying elms. " 'Mystery Boy' Looks for Kin in Nashville." Robert Hayden. NoAM

Puzzled Census Taker, The. John Godfrey Saxe. PoTa

Pygmalion. Kathryn Ruby. WBN

Pylons, The. Stephen Spender. LP; NoAM

Pythagoras planned it. Why did the people stare? The Statues. W. B. Yeats. NoAM

Python, The. Hilaire Belloc. OxBChV

# Q

Qua Cursum Ventus. Arthur Hugh Clough. VPC

Quadroon mermaids, Afro angels, black saints. A Ballad of Remembrance. Robert Hayden. BPo; PoBA

Quagga, The. D. J. Enright. MPo

Quail and rabbit hunters with tawny hounds. Hunters in the Snow: Brueghel. Joseph Langland. WIF

Quail Walk. Heather Ross Miller. BoAnP

Quaker Graveyard in Nantucket, The. Robert Lowell. NoAM; NOBA; PiAm; PPoD

Quaker Hero, Burning. Bink Noll. TCP

Quaker Lover, The, *with music. Unknown.* RDB

Quaker Widow, The. Bayard Taylor. AmVN

Quality of Mercy, The. Shakespeare. *Fr.* The Merchant of Venice, IV, i. AKE

Quarrel, The. Conrad Aiken. LoAs

Quarrel, The. Diane DiPrima. NMM; RiTi

Quarrel of the sparrows in the eaves, The. The Sorrow of Love. W. B. Yeats. NoAM

Quarry, The. W. H. Auden. *See* O What Is That Sound.

Quarry, The. Vassar Miller. WPE

Quarry Pool, The. Denise Levertov. VGW

Quarter horse, no rider, A. Horse. Jim Harrison. BoAnP

Quarter less four,/ Half twain. *Unknown.* AmFP

Quatrain: "Jack, eating rotten cheese, did say." Benjamin Franklin. SoSe

Quavering cry, A. Screech-owl? Night, Death, Mississippi. Robert Hayden. VGW

Quechua Song: When You Find Yourself Alone. *Unknown, tr. fr. Spanish by* Ruth Stephan. RRA

Queen, The  Pablo Neruda, *tr. fr. Spanish by* Donald D. Walsh. OLR

Queen [*or* Queene] and huntress, chaste and fair. Hymn to Diana. Ben Jonson. *Fr.* Cynthia's Revels, V, vi. HeIP; Moon; NOBE; PAIC

Queen Anne's Lace. Ruthe T. Spinnanger. AATT

Queen-Ann's-Lace. William Carlos Williams. LoAs; NoAM; NOBA

Queen Elenor's Confession. *Unknown.* PeBB

Queen Jane sat at her window one day. The King's Dochter Lady Jean. *Unknown.* AmFP

Queen Jane was in labor. The Death of Queen Jane. *Unknown.* AmFP

Queen of Connemara, The. Francis A. Fahy. PFIr

Queen of Elfan's Nourice, The. *Unknown.* AIW

Queen of Hearts, The/ She made some tarts. Mother Goose. MG

Queen of Heaven. *Unknown.* OxBM

Queen of Paphos, Erycine, The. *Unknown.* GBL

Queen of the silver bow!—by thy pale beam. To the Moon. Charlotte Smith. Moon

Queen Victoria and Me. Leonard Cohen. NoAM

Queen was in the parlour, The. Contemporary Nursery Rhyme. *Unknown.* SpRo

Queene and huntress, chaste and faire. *See* Queen and huntress. . .

Queens. J. M. Synge. GBR

Queen's Wake, The, *sel.* James Hogg. Song, The: "O! lady dear, fair is thy noon." SLP

Queer. David McCord. CaYB

Queer are the ways of a man I know. The Phantom Horsewoman. Thomas Hardy. LoAs; NOBE

Queer thing about those waters, A: there are no. Across the Bay. Donald Davie. PSN

Quem Queritis. Albert Howard Carter. AATT

Query. Ebon Dooley. PoBA

Query. Mildred Weston. POL

Quest. Naomi Long Madgett. BPo

Quest of Silence, The, *sel.* Christopher Brennan. "Gray and dusty daylight flows, A." MAuV

Question, The. James Beattie. FaBoCo

Question, A. William Cole. BoAnP

Question. Norma Craig. POL

Question, A. Robert Frost. TH

Question, The. F. T. Prince. BoLoP

Question, The. Muriel Rukeyser. IHMS

Question, The ("I dream'd that, as I wander'd by the way"). Shelley. FSFS

Question. May Swenson. IPWM; VGW

Question, A. J. M. Synge. OxBTC; PFIr

Question. Lucille F. Travis. AATT

Question and Answer. Langston Hughes. BPo

Question Answer'd, The. Blake. *Fr.* Several Questions Answered. GBL
("What is it men in women do require?") MBPR

Question in a Field. Louise Bogan. SBG

Questioning Faces. Robert Frost. NCSH

Questions of Travel. Elizabeth Bishop. NOBA

Qui Laborat, Orat. Arthur Hugh Clough. VPC

Quia Amore Langueo ("In the vale of restless mind"). *Unknown.* BoReV; NOBE; OxBM

Quick! a last poem before I go. On Rachmaninoff's Birthday. Frank O'Hara. CAPP

Quick and Bitter. Yehuda Amichai, *tr. fr. Hebrew by* Assia Gutmann. BoLoP

Quick cold hands. Dawn. Octavio Paz. TSWA

Quick, Henry, the Flit! James Schuyler. NoAM

Quick-Step. Robert Creeley. VGW

Quick, woman, in your net. The Net. W. R. Rodgers. BoLoP

Quickness. Henry Vaughan. BoReV; NOBE; SCP-1

Quid Restat, *abr.* Lucius Beebe. RFM

Quiet. Brian Swann. AmPA

Quiet Days in Sutherland. Robin Fulton. MIS

Quiet faces. Bruce Holsapple. FAF

Quiet Glades of Eden, The. Robert Graves. BoLoP

Quiet House, The. Charlotte Mew. SBG

Quiet Place, A. Louis Jenkins. HeS

Quiet Tide near Ardrossan, The. Charles Tennyson Turner. VPC

Quiet Town. William Stafford. MAT

Quieter the people are, The. The Signboard. Robert Creeley. ConAP

Quilt, The. Karen Swenson. WBN

Quinquireme of Nineveh from distant Ophir. Cargoes. John Masefield. NOBE; WIF

Quintana Lay in the Shallow Grave of Coral. Karl Shapiro. VGW

Quip, The. George Herbert. SCP-1

Quite a country, back and forth. The U.S.A. Grantland Rice. SPo

Quite unexpectedly as Vasserot. The End of the World. Archibald MacLeish. InPK; MAT; NCSH; NoAM; NOBA; PAIC; PBMP; PiAm; SS; VGW

Quitting is out of the question yet. Dispatch Number Sixty. Doug Fetherling. NeAC

Quondam was I in my leady's grace. Sir Thomas Wyatt. GBL

Quoniam Ego in Flagella Paratus Sum. David, *sel.* William Habington.
"Fix me on some bleak precipice." SCP-2

Quotations from Charwoman Me. Robin Morgan. WBN

Quoth she, I wish I could prescribe your help. Rachel Speght. *Fr.* A Dream. WPE

# R

RIP. Alan Garner. BuTh

R.M.S. *Titanic, sel.* Anthony Cronin.
"On the bog road the blackthorn flowers, the turf-stacks." BIrV

Rabbi Ben Ezra. Robert Browning. PBMP

Rabbinic/ The cynic. Sandra Ruth Duguid. AATT

Rabbit, The. Alan Brownjohn. MPo

Rabbit, The. W. H. Davies. BoAnP

Rabbit, The. Philip McIntyre, Jr.. AKE

Rabbit, The. *Unknown.* FaBoCo

Rabbit as [*wr.* Is] King of the Ghosts, A. Wallace Stevens. PBMP

Rabbit Catcher, The. Sylvia Plath. SBG

Rabbit crossed and dodged and turned, The. The Chase. J. V. Cunningham. NoAM

Rabbit Foot Blues. *Unknown.* BluL

Rabbit has a charming face, The. The Rabbit. *Unknown.* FaBoCo

Rabbit Hunter, The. Robert Frost. SPo; TH

Rabbit Leaves, The. Dennis Schmitz. NVAP

Rabbits. Dennis Schmitz. FiCP

Rabid or dog dull. Let me tell you how. A Professor's Song. John Berryman. HeIP; NoAM; NOBA

Raccoon on the Road. Joseph Payne Brennan. ECBV

Raccoon Poem. Miriam Palmer. NMM

Raccoon Skeleton at Long Plain Creek. Helena Minton. FAF

Raccoons are selectively polygamous. Raccoon Poem. Miriam Palmer. NMM

Race. Byron. Don Juan, XIV. OBP

Race Question, The. Naomi Long Madgett. BPo

Racer's Widow, The. Louise Glück. AmPA

Racetrack, The. Jane Cooper. LoAs

Rachel and the Truth (c.1945). Yvonne. WBN

Rachel at Thirteen. Yvonne. WBN

Rachel at Twenty-three. Yvonne. WBN

Rachray Man, The. Moira O'Neill. PFIr

Racialism. John Blight. CAAP

Racing-Man, The. A. P. Herbert. BoAnP

Racoon up the 'simmon tree. The Persimmon Tree. *Unknown.* GBP

Radar. Alan Ross. NowV

Radiance of that star that leans on me, The. Delay. Elizabeth Jennings. InPK; OxBTC

Radiant Heat. Rochelle Owens. WBN

Radiant soda of the seashore fashions, The. Far Rockaway. Delmore Schwartz. NoAM

Radio brings whole cities, The. Driving at Night. John Calvin Rezmerski. HeS

Raffaele Minichiello. Sandra McPherson. CAAP

Rag Doll to the Heedless Child, The. David Harsent. LP

Ragged and Dirty. *Unknown.* AmFP

Ragged, unheeded, stooping, meanly shod. The Poor Can Feed the Birds. John Shaw Neilson. MAuV

Ragged Wood, The. W. B. Yeats. GBL

Raggedy Man, The. James Whitcomb Riley. OxBChV

Raid, The. William Everson. NoAM; PiAm; TCP

Rail Splitting. Gary Lawless. FAF

Railings, The. Alan Brownjohn. LP

Railroad Blues, The. *Unknown.* AmFP

Railroad Reverie. E. R. Young. ECBV

Railroad suddenly hops out of the, A. Machu Picchu, Peru. Fred Red Cloud. VW

Railroad yard in San Jose. In Back of the Real. Allen Ginsberg. HeIP; InPK

Railroader for Me, A. *Unknown.* AmFP

Railway Bridge of the Silvery Tay, The. William McGonagall. PPoD

Railway Junction, The. Walter de la Mare. OxBTC

Rain, The. Robert Creeley. CAPP; ConAP; VGW

Rain, The. W. H. Davies. FSFS; OxBTC

Rain. Emanuel diPasquale. InPK; POL

Rain. Paul Murray. BIrV

Rain. "Seumas O'Sullivan." PFIr

Rain. Shelley. POL

Rain. Adrian Keith Smith. AKE

Rain. Robert Louis Stevenson. ECBV

Rain. Edward Thomas. OxBTC

Rain, The ("The rain it raineth every day"). *Unknown.* ECBV; FaBoCo

Rain, / Million-footed requiem of the rain. Atavism. Richard Lake. NCSH

Rain in Summer. Longfellow. FSFS

Rain in the city! City Rain. Rachel Field. ECBV

Rain in the Desert. John Gould Fletcher. *Fr.* Arizona Poems. NCSH

Rain is over, The. Birth. Amir Gilboa, *tr. by* Robert Mezey *and* Shula Starkman. OFD

Rain is plashing on my sill, The. The Unknown Dead. Henry Timrod. AmVN

Rain is raining all around, The. Quick, Henry, the Flit! James Schuyler. NoAM

Rain is raining all around, The. Rain. Robert Louis Stevenson. ECBV

Rain it raineth every day, The. The Rain. *Unknown.* ECBV; FaBoCo

Rain makes little cuts on the window, The. Dialogues 4 1 Voice Only. Doug Fetherling. NeAC

Rain, midnight rain, nothing but the wild rain. Rain. Edward Thomas. OxBTC

Rain of a night and a day and a night, The. After Rain. Edward Thomas. NCSH

Rain of London pimples, The. London Rain. Louis MacNeice. HeIP

Rain on a Grave. Thomas Hardy. LoAs

Rain Poem. Elizabeth J. Coatsworth. ECBV

Rain, rain, go to Spain. *Unknown.* MG

Rain Rain on the Splintered Girl. Ishmael Reed. PoBA

Rain screws up its face, The. Rain. Adrian Keith Smith. AKE

Rain set early in tonight, The. Porphyria's Lover. Robert Browning. AnMo; LoAs

Rain Sleets Flat. Besmilr Brigham. Psy

Rain sweeps in as the gale begins to blow. Wet Day. James McAuley. MAuV

Rain was like a little mouse, The. Rain Poem. Elizabeth J. Coatsworth. ECBV

Rain was raining cheerfully, The. The Vulture and the Husbandman. A. C. Hilton. FaBoCo

Rainbow. Robert Huff. CoPAm

Rainbow. Liz Lochhead. MIS

Rainbow, The. Christina Rossetti. OxBChV

Rainbow, The. *Unknown, tr. fr. Gabon Pygmy.* AKE

Rainbow, The. Wordsworth. *See* My Heart Leaps Up When I Behold.

Rainbow at Night. *Unknown.* ECBV

Raingatherer. Franklin Brainard. HeS

Rain's all right. The boys who physic. Biography of Southern Rain. Kenneth Patchen. VGW

Rainwalkers, The. Denise Levertov. CTBA; PPP

Rainy Mountain Cemetery. N. Scott Momaday. CDW

Rainy Pleiads Wester, The. A. E. Housman. BoLoP; NoAM

Rainy Summer, The. Alice Meynell. OxBTC; SBG

Raise a "Rucus" To-Night. *Unknown.* BPo

Raise Me Up, Lord. Miguel de Guevara, *tr. fr. Spanish by Samuel Beckett.* PBMP

Raise the race raise the rays the raze raise it race raise. Part of the Doctrine. LeRoi Jones. PiAm

Raise the Shade. E. E. Cummings. VGW

Raising the blind, she said. The Green Room. Paul Mills. MIS

Rake. Dorothy Una Ratcliffe. BoAnP

Raleigh Was Right. William Carlos Williams. NoAM

Ram, the Bull, the Heavenly Twins, The. The Zodiac Rhyme. *Unknown.* GBP

Ramble, The: an Anti-Heroic Poem, *much abr.* Alexander Radcliffe. SCP-2

Ram's Horn, The. John Hewitt. BIrV

Ramshackles, archipelagoes, loose constellations. The Unifying Principle. A. R. Ammons. NOBA

Ran out of tear gas and became panicky. Kent State, May 4, 1970. Paul Goodman. MAT; TSWA

Range-Finding. Robert Frost. NoAM; PPoD

Range in the Desert, The. Randall Jarrell. NOBA

Ransomed from darkness and released in Time. Edwin Muir. *Fr.* Variations on a Time Theme. NoAM

Rantin Dog the Daddie O't, The. Burns. PPP

Rantin Laddie, The. *Unknown.* AmFP

Rape of Lucrece, The. *sels.* Thomas Heywood.
 "Come, list and hark! the bell doth toll." SCP-2
 "Pack, clouds, away, and welcome, day!" GBP (Love's Good-morrow.) LoAs
 Outcry upon Opportunity, An. NOBE

Rape of the Lock, The. Pope. AnMo
 *Sels.*
 Lock, The, *Fr.* V. Moon
 Toilet, The, *Fr.* I. NOBE
 Voyage on the Thames, The, *Fr.* II. NOBE

Rapidly cruising or lying on the air there is a bird. The Frigate Pelican. Marianne Moore. Psy

Rapist, The. Stephen Dunn. POL

Rapparees. Richard Murphy. *Fr.* The Battle of Aughrim. BIrV

Rapping Along with Ronda Davis. James Cunningham. JB

Rapture, A. Thomas Carew. LoAs; SCP-2

Rapunzel. Anne Sexton. RiTi

Rapunzel, Rapunzel. Mark Van Doren. AIW

Rare Willie Drowned in Yarrow. *Unknown.* AIW; GBP; PeBB

Rarely, rarely, comest thou. Song. Shelley. MBPR

Raspberries. Doug Flaherty. HeS

Raspberries splash, redly. What He Says. Robert Wallace. CoPAm

Rat, The. W. H. Davies. OxBTC

Rat,/ pearl,/ onion,/ honey. Homer, *tr. by* Christopher Logue. *Fr.* The Iliad, XIX. TwMBP

Ratcatcher's Daughter, The. *Unknown.* GBP

Rather notice, mon cher. To a Solitary Disciple. William Carlos Williams. VGW

Ration Card, The. Liz Sohappy Bahe. CDW

Rats. Walter de la Mare. BoAnP

Rats Away! *Unknown.* OxBM

Rats, Ducks, Dogs, Cats, Pigs. *Unknown.* *See* Three Young Rats.

Rattlesnakes have begun to come out, The. Snakes. Peter Wild. AmPA

Rav, The/ of Northern White Russia declined. Illustrious Ancestors. Denise Levertov. NoAM; NOBA; VGW

Ravaged Villa, The. Herman Melville. NOBA; PiAM

Raven, The. Poe. NoBA; PiAm

Raven sat upon a tree, A. The Sycophantic Fox and the Gullible Raven. Guy Wetmore Carryl. PBMP

Ravenna. David Ray. HeS

Raving warre, begot. Thomas Campion. AAS

Ravished arms. Boy in the Roman Zoo. Archibald MacLeish. NCSH

Ray Charles. Sam Cornish. NVAP

Ray Charles is the black wind of Kilimanjaro. Blues Note. Bob Kaufman. PoBA

Ray John. Honky. Charles Cooper. PoBA

Razors pain you. Résumé. Dorothy Parker. InPK; SS

Razorsharp wind, A. Valentine. Len Gasparini. NeAC

Re. Vito Hannibal Acconci. PAIC

Reach for arrows of falling light. A man once sang. Falling Moon. Roberta Hill. CDW

Reach like you never reached before past Night's somber robes. Tauhid. Askia Muhammad Touré. PoBA

Reach of Winter, The. Jenne Andrews. HeS

Re-act for Action ("Re-act to Animals"). Don L. Lee. BPo

Read me a lesson, muse, and speak it loud. Sonnet Written upon Ben Nevis. Keats. MBPR

Read not Milton, for he is dry; no Shakespeare. Proverbial Philosophy: Of Reading. Charles Stuart Calverley. FaBoCo

Read yr/ exile. A Poem for a Poet. Don L. Lee. PoBA

Readers of the *Boston Evening Transcript.* The *Boston Evening Transcript.* T. S. Eliot. InPK; PSN

Reading about Machado. Facts. Ken Smith. TwMBP

Reading and Talking. Louis Zukofsky. VGW

Reading how even the Swiss had thrown the sponge. Beyond the Alps. Robert Lowell. NOBA; PiAm

Reading the shorthand on a barber's sheet. The Barber. Roy Fuller. NoAM

Reading Walt Whitman. Calvin Forbes. PoBA

Readings of History. Adrienne Rich. ConAP

Ready. Lynn Strongin. RiTi

Real Life. Ted Berrigan. NoAM

Real People Loves One Another, The. Rob Penny. PoBA

Real Question Calling for Solution, A.  Robert Penn Warren. PPP

Realities.  Shirley Kaufman.  MIT

Really, what a shocking scene!  A Man of Experience. Laoiseach Mac an Bhaird, *tr. by* Frank O'Connor.  PFIr

Reaper, The.  L. H. Allen.  MAuV

Reapers.  Mathilde Blind.  SBG; WPE

Reapers.  Jean Toomer.  BPo; InPK; NoAM; PoBA; PPP

Reaping.  Amy Lowell.  SBG

Rear-Guard, The.  Siegfried Sassoon.  NoAM

Rearmament.  Robinson Jeffers.  PSN

Rearrangement for the Brain.  Gary Margolis.  CoPAm

Reason.  Josephine Miles.  InPK; NCSH; NoAM; PPoD; SS

Reason and Nature.  J. V. Cunningham.  PiAm

Reason and Religion.  Dryden.  *Fr.* Religio Laici.  BoReV

Reason for Not Writing Orthodox Nature Poetry.  John Wain. PAIC

Reason I Stay on Job So Long.  *Unknown.*  GBP

Reason is our soul's left hand, faith her right.  To the Countess of Bedford.  John Donne.  PAIC

Reason of Numbers, A.  Josephine Jacobsen.  IPWM

Reasons.  Tom McGrath.  SLP

Reasons for Attendance.  Philip Larkin.  NowV; OBP

Reasons for Music.  Archibald MacLeish.  PiAm

Rebel, The.  Mari Evans.  IHMS; PoBA

Rebolushinary X-mas.  Carolyn M. Rodgers.  JB

Recalling War.  Robert Graves.  NoAM; OBP

Recantation Illustrated in the Story of the Mad Ox.  Samuel Taylor Coleridge.  MBPR

Recently I heard a friend was mad.  First Lecture.  James Whitehead.  CoPAm

Reception, The.  June Jordan.  NMM

Recessional.  Kipling.  BLSH, *with music*; BTTM; NOBE

Recipe for Toothache.  *Unknown.*  SCP-2

Reciprocity.  Vassar Miller.  IHMS

Reckoning, The.  Robert Service.  BBGO

Reckoning A. M. Thursday.  Doris Turner.  JB

Reclaimed Area.  Jon Silkin.  NoAM

Reclining Figure.  Donald Hall.  ConAP

Recluse, The.  Lisel Mueller.  RiTi

Recluse, The; or, Home at Grasmere.  Wordsworth.  MBPR

Recognition, The.  Denise Levertov.  VGW

Recollection, A.  John Peale Bishop.  LoAs; PPoD

Recollection.  Dorothy Donnelly.  NCSH

Recollection of First Love.  William Soutar.  SLP

Reconciliation.  C. Day Lewis.  NoAM

Reconnaissance.  Arna Bontemps.  BPo

Recovery, *sel.*  Mona Van Duyn. Memory, A.  RiTi

Recovery Room, The: Lying-in.  Helen Chasin.  IHMS

Recruiting Drive.  Charles Causley.  OxBTC

Recruits, The.  Ian Hamilton.  NoAM

Rector's pallid neighbor at The Firs, The.  The Villagers and Death.  Robert Graves.  HeIP

Recuerdo.  Edna St. Vincent Millay.  CTBA; NoAM

Recuerdo, *sel.*  Tennessee Williams. Paper Lantern, The.  CTBA

Red and blue and delicate green.  *Unknown.*  GBP

Red as the guardroom lamp.  Heartbreak Camp.  Roy Campbell. OxBTC

Red brick in the suburbs, white horse on the wall.  Ballad to a Traditional Refrain.  Maurice James Craig.  BIrV

Red brick monastery in, The.  The Semblables  William Carlos Williams.  NOBA

Red carpet-ing, The.  While Cecil Snores: Mom Drinks Cold Milk.  James Cunningham.  JB

Red cold.  Haiku.  José Juan Tablada, *tr. by* Samuel Beckett. PBMP

Red Dress, The.  James Bertolino.  HeS

Red eyes of rabbits, The.  The Springtime.  Denise Levertov. ConAP

Red for danger and for rage.  No Meaning.  Terence Brame. RAE

Red fox, the vixen, The.  Abnegation.  Adrienne Rich.  WPE

Red head, red head.  Blackbird's Song.  *Unknown.*  GBP

Red-Herring.  D. H. Lawrence.  NoAM

Red is death, for people who are dying.  Colours.  Frances Evans.  RAE

Red lips are not so red.  Greater Love.  Wilfred Owen.  NoAM; OBP; PSN

Red Movie.  John Tranter.  CAAP

Red, Red Rose, A.  Burns.  BoLoP; GBL; IPWM; LAuP; NOBE; OBP; OLR; PAIC; SLP; SoSe; WIF (O, My Luve Is Like a Red, Red Rose.)  InPS

Red River Valley, *with music.*  *Unknown.*  BLSH; BLSo

Red Robin, The.  John Clare.  RAE

Red Rock Ceremonies.  Anita Endrezze Probst.  CDW

Red Rose, proud Rose, sad Rose of all my days!  To the Rose upon the Rood of Time.  W. B. Yeats.  NoAM

Red rose whispers of passion, The.  A White Rose.  John Boyle O'Reilly.  SoSe

Red sky at night is a shepherd's delight, A.  *Unknown.*  MG

Red sumac presses.  On the New Road.  Lyn Lifshin.  FAF; NeAC; RiTi

Red-tiled ships you see reflected, The.  Five Vignettes.  Jean Toomer.  PoBA

Red Wheelbarrow, The.  William Carlos Williams.  InPK; NoAM; NOBA; NowV; PiAm; SFF; TSWA; WIF

Red Whiskey.  *Unknown.*  AmFP

Red, White and Red, The.  *Unknown.*  AmFP

Redemption.  George Herbert.  BoReV; InPS; MetP; NOBE; SCP-1; SoSe

Redriff.  David Jones.  *Fr.* The Anathemata.  TwMBP

Redwing, The.  Patric Dickinson.  BoAnP

Redwoods, The.  Louis Simpson.  TH

Reeds give, The.  Small Song.  A. R. Ammons.  POL

Reel One.  Adrien Stoutenburg.  MiP

Reeve, The.  Chaucer.  *Fr.* The Canterbury Tales: Prologue. OxBM

Reeving.  Michael Anania.  HeS

Reflection in a Green Arena.  Gregory Corso.  VGW

Reflection Kiss, one given, The.  Some Kisses from *The Kama Sutra.*  Hugo Williams.  BoLoP

Reflection on a Wicked World.  Ogden Nash.  SFF

Reflections.  Anita Barrows.  NMM

Reflections.  Carl Gardner.  PoBA

Reflections Dental.  Phyllis McGinley.  *Fr.* Speaking of Television.  TH

Reflections on a Womb Which Is Called "Vacant."  Jeanine Hathaway.  IHMS

Reflections on Having Left a Place of Retirement.  Samuel Taylor Coleridge.  MBPR

Reflections on Ice-Breaking.  Ogden Nash.  FaBoCo; SFF

Reflections on Limitations.  Albert Howard Carter.  AATT

Reflexions on suicide, and on my father, possess me.  Of Suicide. John Berryman.  NoAM

Reformer to His Father, A.  James Simmons.  BIrV

Refugees, The.  Edwin Muir.  NoAM

Refusal, A.  Thomas Hardy.  FaBoCo

Refusal to Mourn the Death, by Fire, of a Child in London, A. Dylan Thomas. AnMo; BuTh; HeIP; MPo; NoAM; NOBE; OxBTC; VoPo

Refusing to fall in love with God, he gave. Didymus. Louis MacNeice. LoAs

Regard to Neruda. Pat Lowther. MMD

Regarding Wave, II. Gary Snyder. CAAP

Regenerate. Robert Bloom. AATT

Regeneration. Henry Vaughan. SCP-1

Regiment of Princes, The. Thomas Hoccleve. *See* De Regimine Principum.

Regret. Vassar Miller. RiTi

Rehearsal, The. Horace Gregory. VGW

Reilly. Rayne Mackinnon. MIS

Reincarnation (I). James Dickey. CoPAm

Reincarnation (II). James Dickey. CAPP

Reincarnation. Mae Jackson. PoBA

Reindeer and Engine. Josephine Jacobsen. WPE

Rejected Lover, The ("I once knew a little girl"). *Unknown.* AmFP

Rejected Lover, The ("The lonesome scenes of winter"). *Unknown.* AmFP

Rejoice in God, O ye tongues; give the glory to the Lord, and the Lamb. Christopher Smart. *Fr.* Jubilate Agno. LAuP

Rejoice in the Lamb. Christopher Smart. *See* Jubilate Agno.

Rejoinder. Albert De Pietro. AATT

Relapse, The. Henry Vaughan. PAIC

Relating to Robinson. Weldon Kees. AnMo

Relationship, The. Stephen Vincent. NeAC

Relationships. Mona Van Duyn. RiTi

Relative Sadness. Colin Rowbotham. BuTh

Relatives are leaning over, staring expectantly, The. "The Dreadful Has Already Happened." Mark Strand. NoAM

Relativity. *Unknown.* FaBoCo

Relearning the Alpahabet. Denise Levertov. NOBA

Released from the noise of the butcher and baker. Jinny the Just. Matthew Prior. NOBE

Relent, my deere, yet unkind Coelia. Coelia, XVII. William Percy. AAS

Relic, The. John Donne. GBL; NOBE; PPP; SCP-1 (Relique, The.) MetP

Relicts. Layle Silbert. NPW

Relief of Lucknow, The. Robert Traill Spence Lowell. BTTM; PoTa

Relieved, I let the book fall behind a stone. Depressed by a Book of Bad Poetry. James Wright. ConAP; TH

Religio Laici, *sel.* Dryden.    Reason and Religion. BoReV

Religion. Henry Vaughan. BoReV

Religious Musings. Samuel Taylor Coleridge. MBPR

Relique, The. John Donne. *See* Relic, The.

Relish of the Muse, The. Sir John Beaumont. POL

Relocation. Simon Ortiz. VW

Reluctance. Robert Frost. NOBA

Remains, The. Mark Strand. PPP

Remains of blue bog children, The. Blue Bog Children. Roger Weingarten. AmPA

Remember. Christina Rossetti. BoLoP; IPWM; NOBE; PAIC; SBG; VPC

Remember/ when the skin of your fingers healed. The Discoveries of Fire. Lucille Clifton. TSWA

Remember also thy Creator in the days of thy youth. Ecclesiastes, Bible, *O. T.* OBP

Remember always to eat with both eyes open. Meal Piece. Elton Glaser. NVAP

Remember me? I was the one. Hood. C. K. Williams. InPK

Remember me when I am dead. Simplify Me When I'm Dead. Keith Douglas. OxBTC

Remember me when I am gone away. Remember. Christina Rossetti.. BoLoP; IPWM; NOBE; PAIC; SBG; VPC

Remember Suez? Adrian Mitchell. OxBTC

Remember That Country. Jean Garrigue. VGW

Remember thee! remember Thee! Byron. BoLoP

Remember those X-ray machines in shoe stores. On Hot Days. James Reiss. AmPA

Remember Times for Sandy. Carolyn M. Rodgers. JB

Remember us poor Mayers all. The Mayers' Song. *Unknown.* AIW; GBP

Remember Way Back. *Unknown.* BluL

Remembered Morning. Janet Lewis. WPE

Remembering How. Pat Lowther. MMD

Remembering Kevan MacKenzie. Henry Taylor. InPK

Remembering Nat Turner. Sterling A. Brown. PoBA

Remembering the 'Thirties. Donald Davie. OxBTC

Remembrance. Emily Brontë. BoLoP; NOBE; OBP; WPE

Remembrance. Sir Thomas Wyatt. *See* Lover Showeth How He Is Forsaken...

Remembrance of a Color inside a Forest, A. Ray A. Young Bear. CDW

Reminiscence, A. Anne Brontë. WPE

Reminiscence, *sel.* Padraic Colum.    "I saw the wind to-day, " II. CaYB; ECBV

Reminiscent Reflection. Ogden Nash. FaBoCo

Remonstrance. Philodemos the Epicurean, *tr. fr. Greek by* Dudley Fitts. OLR

Remorse for Time, The. Howard Nemerov. NCSH

Remorse is memory awake. Emily Dickinson. NOBA; Psy

Remote and ineffectual don. Lines to a Don. Hilaire Belloc. FaBoCo

Remote House. Hans Enzenberger. LP

Remote, unfriended, melancholy, slow. The Traveller. Goldsmith. BIrV; LAuP

Removal, The. W. S. Merwin. TCP

Removal from Terry Street, A. Douglas Dunn. LP; POL

Remove away that blackning church. An Ancient Proverb. Blake. *Fr.* Several Questions Answered. MBPR

Rendezvous, The. Steven Graves. PPoD

Rendezvous. Edna St. Vincent Millay. RiTi

Rendez-vous Manqué dans la Rue Racine. J. M. Synge. BIrV

Renegade Wants Words, The. James Welch. CDW; SA

Renewal, A. James Merrill. CoPAm

Renewal, The. Theodore Roethke. VGW

Renouncement. Alice Meynell. BoLoP; NOBE; WPE

Renouncing of Love, A. Sir Thomas Wyatt. GBL ("Farewell, love, and all thy laws for ever.") AAS; SoSe

Renunciation—is a piercing virtue. Emily Dickinson. PiAm

Repeated Shapes, The. Donald Hall. CoPAm

Reply. Victoria McCabe. POL

Reply, A. *Unknown.* FaBoCo

Report from the Correspondent They Fired. David McElroy. AmPA

Reply to Dipsychus. Arthur Hugh Clough. FaBoCo

Report of Health. John Updike. PBMP

Report on Experience. Edmund Blunden. NOBE

Report Song in a Dream, A. Nicholas Breton. GBL (Wooing in a Dream.) NOBE

Reporting Back. William Stafford. CoPAm,

Reportless subjects, to the quick. Emily Dickinson. NOBA

Repose of Rivers. Hart Crane. NoAM; NOBA

Repose they know in storefronts, The. The Village of the Presents. James McMichael. AmPA

Repression of War Experience.  Siegfried Sassoon.  NoAM

Reproaches.  William Price Turner.  SLP

Reptilian green the wrinkled throat.  Sir Gawaine and the Green Knight.  Yvor Winters.  NoAM; PAIC; VGW

Republic, The.  Longfellow.  *Fr.* The Building of the Ship.  BTTM

Republican Genius of Europe, The.  Philip Freneau.  VoPo

Repulse, The.  Thomas Stanley.  MetP

Requiem.  Robert Louis Stevenson.  NOBE

Requiem.  Stephen Vincent.  NeAC

Requiem for a Personal Friend.  Eavan Boland.  PFIr

Requiem for a River.  Kim Williams.  RFM

Requiem for Innocence, A.  William R. Mitchell.  AATT

Requiem for the Croppies.  Seamus Heaney.  BIrV

Requiem for the Plantagenet Kings.  Geoffrey Hill.  NoAM

Requiem of a War-Baby.  Joan Watton.  PFIr

Requiescat.  Matthew Arnold.  HeIP; NOBE; PBMP

Rescue, The.  Robert Creeley.  CAPP

Rescue, The.  Hal Summers.  PoTa

Rescue the Dead.  David Ignatow.  ConAP; VGW

Resembles life what once was deem'd of light.  What Is Life?  Samuel Taylor Coleridge.  MBPR

Resident Stranger, The.  Harley Elliott.  HeS

Residue of Song.  Marvin Bell.  AmPA

Resisting Each Other.  Anne Waldman.  RiTi

Resisting poetry I am becoming a poem.  Moon.  Derek Walcott.  NoAM

Resolute Courtier, The.  Thomas Shipman.  GBL

Resolution.  Ted Berrigan.  OFD

Resolution and Independence.  Wordsworth.  InPS; MAT; MBPR; NOBE; PPP; SoSe

"I was a traveller then upon the moor," *sel.*  SpRo

Resolution in Four Sonnets, of a Poetical Question Put to me by a Friend, Concerning Four Rural Sisters.  Charles Cotton.  Prf Two Rural Sisters, *sel.*  BoLoP

Resolve, The.  Mary Lee, Lady Chudleigh.  WPE

Resolve, The.  Denise Levertov.  RFM

Resolving Doubts.  William Dickey.  CoPAm

Resound my voyse, ye wodes that here me plain.  Sir Thomas Wyatt.  AAS

Respect the dreams of old men, said the cricket.  Song for September.  Robert Fitzgerald.  VGW

Respectabilities.  Jon Silkin.  NoAM

Respectable Burgher, The.  Thomas Hardy.  NoAM

Respectable Folks, The.  Henry David Thoreau.  AmVN

Respondez!  Walt Whitman.  NoAM

Responding Voice.  Francisco A. de Icaza, *tr. fr. Spanish by* Samuel Beckett.  PBMP

Responses.  Robert Hershon.  POL

Responsory, 1948, A.  Thomas Merton.  VGW

Rest.  Mathilde Blind.  SBG

Rest, The.  Ezra Pound.  NoAM; NOBA

Rest.  Christina Rossetti.  NOBE

Rest Only in the Grave.  James Clarence Mangan.  BIrV

Rested near Nefertete.  Carol Bergé.  MMD

Resting Figure.  Denise Levertov.  AnMo

Restless water of sound, The.  War Requiem.  Del Marie Rogers.  NPW

Results of the Polo Game.  Grace Butcher.  RiTi

Résumé.  Dorothy Parker.  InPK; SS

Resurrection.  Frank Horne.  OFD; PoBA

Resurrection, The.  Nathaniel Wanley.  SCP-2

Resurrection, The, *sel.*  W. B. Yeats.
  Two Songs from a Play.  NOBE; OBP; PPoe; PPP

Resurrection and Immortality.  Henry Vaughan.  SCP-1

Resurrection Song.  Thomas Lovell Beddoes.  InPK

Retaliation.  Goldsmith.  ESaP

Retired Cat, The.  William Cowper.  PCat

Retired this hour from wondering crowds.  Walter Savage Landor.  GBL

Retirement, *sel.*  William Cowper.
  Statesman in Retirement, The.  PPoD

Retirement of the Elephant, The.  Russell Edson.  AmPA

Retreat[e], The.  Henry Vaughan.  HeIP; InPS; MetP; NOBE; OBP; PPP; SCP-1

Return.  Michael Anania.  HeS

Return, The.  Arna Bontemps.  PoBA; WIF

Return.  C. P. Cavafy, *tr. fr. Modern Greek by* Rae Dalven.  LoAs

Return.  Seamus Deane.  BIrV

Return, The.  Edna St. Vincent Millay.  NoAM

Return, The.  Stanley Moss.  POL

Return, The.  Ezra Pound.  NoAM; NOBA; PPoe; PSN; VGW

Return.  Earl of Rochester.  *See* Song, A: "Absent from thee, I languish still."

Return, The.  Dennis Saleh.  NeAC

Return again, my forces late dismayed.  Amoretti, XIV.  Spenser.  SoSe

Return of Astraea, The.  Ben Jonson.  NOBE

Return of Robinson Jeffers, The.  Robert Hass.  AmPA

Return of the Native.  LeRoi Jones.  BPo

Return of the Sire de Nesle A. D. 16—, The.  Herman Melville.  NOBA

Return often and take me.  Return.  C. P. Cavafy, *tr. by* Rae Dalven.  LoAs

Return to Work, The.  William Carlos Williams.  CTBA

Returne Thee, Hairt.  Alexander Scott.  SLP

Returned from the opera, as lately I sat.  A Bon Mot.  *Unknown.*  POL

Returned to Say.  William Stafford.  ConAP

Returning after dark, I thought.  Traditional Red.  Robert Huff.  CoPAm

Returning at Night.  Jim Harrison.  VGW

Returning from the Funeral.  Patricia Henley.  NPW

Reuben and Rachel, *with music.*  Harry Birch.  PSoN

Reuben Bright.  E. A. Robinson.  IPWM; NOBA

Reuben, I have long been thinking.  Reuben and Rachel.  Harry Birch.  PSoN

Reuben Ranzo.  *Unknown.*  AmFP

Reunion.  E. A. Robinson.  NoAM; NOBA

Reve was a slendre colerik man, The.  The Reeve.  Chaucer.  *Fr.* The Canterbury Tales: Prologue.  OxBM

Reveille.  A. E. Housman.  SoSe

Reveille.  Ted Hughes.  PPP

Reveille.  Lola Ridge.  WPE

Revel, A.  Donagh MacDonagh.  PFIr

Revelation.  Dryden.  *Fr.* The Hind and the Panther, I.  BoReV (Confessio Fidei.)  NOBE

Revelation.  Peter Meinke.  AATT

Revelation, The.  Coventry Patmore.  *Fr.* The Angel in the House, I, viii.  GBL

Revelation.  Robert Penn Warren.  NoAM

Revenant, The.  Margaret Atwood.  Psy

Revenant, The.  Peter Cooley.  HeS

Revenant, The.  Walter de la Mare.  GBL

*Revenge*, The.  Tennyson.  BTTM

Revenger's Tragedy, The, *sel.*  Cyril Tourneur.
  "Age and bare bone/ Are e'er allied in action," *Fr.* III, iv.  OBP
  "And now methinks I could e'en chide myself."  SCP-2

Revenue Man Blues.  *Unknown.*  BluL

Reverend Butler came by. Madam and the Minister. Langston Hughes. NOBA

Reverend Mother Prioress. Betty Ruth Bird. AATT

Reverie of Poor Susan, The. Wordsworth. MBPR

Review from Staten Island. Gloria C. Oden. PoBA; PPP

Reviewing me without undue elation. A Choice of Weapons. Stanley Kunitz. VGW

Revival, The. Henry Vaughan. BoReV

Revive Us Again, *with music*. William Paton Mackay. BLSH

Revolt of Islam, The, *sels.* Shelley. MBPR
  "For, before Cythna loved it, had my song," *Fr.* II
  "I sate beside the steersman then, and gazing, " VIII.

Revolution. Susan Griffin. RiTi

Revolution in the Revolution in the Revolution. Gary Snyder. PiAm

Revolution is the pod. Emily Dickinson. WIF

Revolutionary, The/ element remained. Mrs. Hamer. Jane Stembridge. NMM

Revolutionary Letter # 1. Diane DiPrima. RiTi

Revolutionary Letter # 4. Diane DiPrima. RiTi

Revolutionary Letter # 19. Diane DiPrima. IHMS

Revolutionary Letter # 21. Diane DiPrima. RiTi

Reward of Service. *Unknown, tr. fr. German by* F. C. Nicholson. LoAS

Reynard the Fox, *sels.* John Masefield.
  "From the Gallows Hill to the Tineton Copse," *Fr.* .II  OBP
  "Meet was at 'The Cock and Pye,' The." OxBTC

Rhapsody. Frank O'Hara. NoAM

Rhapsody on a Windy Night. T. S. Eliot. HeIP

Rhinoceros. William Hart-Smith. BoAnP

Rhinoceros. Adrien Stoutenburg. BoAnP

Rhoda Pitkin. Edgar Lee Masters. *Fr.* The New Spoon River. NoAM

Rhodora, The. Emerson. HeIP; NOBA; PiAm

Rhomboidal Dirge, *sel.* George Wither.
  "But why,/ O fatal Time." SCP-2

Rhyme. Louise Bogan. LoAs

Rhyme for a Chemical Baby. Joseph Cook. SpRo

Rhyme for a Geological Baby. Joseph Cook. SpRo

Rhyme for Astronomical Baby. Joseph Cook. SpRo

Rhyme for Botanical Baby. Joseph Cook. SpRo

Rhyme of the Fishermen's Children. *Unknown.* GBP

Rhyme of the poet, The. Merlin, II. Emerson. AmVN; NOBA; PiAm

Rhymes and rhymers pass away. Walt Whitman. *Fr.* By Blue Ontario's Shore, XIII. InPS

Rhyming Prophecy for a New Year. Leonard Cooper. FaBoCo

Rhythm and blues. The Blues Today. Mae Jackson. PoBA

Rhythm it is we. Spirits Unchained. Keorapetse Kgositsile. PoBA

Ribald Romeos Less and Less Berattle. Horace, *tr. fr. Latin by* John Frederick Nims. Odes, I, 25. MAT
  ("Young bloods come round less often now, The," *tr. by* James Michie.) BoLoP

Ribbe ne rele ne spinne ich ne may. A Servant-girl's Holiday. *Unknown.* OxBM

Ribh Considers Christian Love Insufficient. W. B. Yeats. BoReV

Rice. Carol Muske. AmPA

Rich and Poor; or, Saint and Sinner. Thomas Love Peacock. FaBoCo; NOBE

Rich Days. W. H. Davies. FSFS

Rich fools there be, whose base and filthy heart. Astrophel and Stella, XXIV Sir Philip Sidney. Epi

Rich Irish Lady, A, 2 *versions. Unknown.* AmFP

Rich Lady over the Sea, The. *Unknown.* AIW

Rich Man, The. Franklin P. Adams. SoSe

Rich Morning. Robert Farren. PFIr

Rich Old Miser, A. *Unknown.* AmFP

Rich Widow, The. *Unknown.* AmFP

Richard Cory. E. A. Robinson. AmVN; BBGO; InPK; IPWM; MiP; NOBA; PAIC; PoTa; SFF; SoSe; TH; WIF

Richard Cory. Paul Simon. InPK; WIF

Richard Hofstadter and Michael Wallace, a Documentary History of American Violence. Jim Rosenberg. Epi

Richard Tolman's Universe. Leonard Bacon. PAIC

Riches I hold in light esteem. The Old Stoic. Emily Brontë. NOBE

Riddle: "He went to the wood and caught it." *Unknown.* GBP

Riddle: "I saw five birds all in a cage." *Unknown.* GBP

Riddle: "Stiff standing on the bed." *Unknown.* POL

Riddle: "Their tongues are knives, their forks are hands and feet." Adrian Mitchell. GBL

Riddle, A: "There is one that has a head without an eye." Christina Rossetti. OxBChV

Riddle, The: "What it is, the literal size." Robert Creeley. PiAm

Riddle, The: "White men's children spread over the earth." Georgia Douglas Johnson. PoBA

Riddle, A: "Why is a pump like V-sc-- nt C--stl-r-gh?" Thomas Moore. FaBoCo

Riddle, A (for Ponge) *sel.* George MacBeth.
  "It is always handled." TSWA

Riddle Song, The, *with music. Unknown.* BLSo

Riddles Wisely Expounded. *Unknown.* GBP; PeBB

Riddling Knight, The. *Unknown.* AIW; PBMP

"Riddling world, A!" one cried. The Two Questions. Alice Meynell. WPE

Ride. Josephine Miles. RiTi

Ride a cock-horse to Banbury Cross. Mother Goose. MG

Ride 'Im Cowboy. A. L. Freebairn. SPo

Ride the High Country. David Slavitt. PPoD

Rider, The. Ann Stanford. WPE

Riders Held Back, The. Louis Simpson. ConAP

Riding. William Allingham. OxBChV

Riding Across John Lee's Finger. Stanley Crouch. PoBA

Riding by there every day. Dog Hospital. Peter Wild. AmPA

Riding Double. Peter Wild. AmPA

Riding in the Rain. Maxine W. Kumin. RFM

Riding Together. William Morris. NOBE

Riding with Some North Vietnamese Students in a Polish Elevator, 1966. Roger Mitchell. PAIC

Riflemen's Song at Bennington. *Unknown.* BTTM

Rigged poker-stiff on her back. All the Dead Dears. Sylvia Plath. AnMo; CAPP; CoPAm; IHMS

Right down the shocked street with a siren-blast. A Fire-Truck. Richard Wilbur. NCSH

Right On: White America. Sonia Sanchez. PoBA

Right Thinking Man. Marge Piercy. RiTi

Right well I wote, most mighty Soveraine. The Faerie Queen, II, induction. Spenser. PAIC

Rigid Body Sings. James Clerk Maxwell. FaBoCo; SpRo

Rigorists. Marianne Moore. SBG

Rigs o' Barley, The. Burns. LoAs
  (Corn Riggs.) SLP
  (Corn Rigs are Bonie.) OBP
  (Song: "It was upon a Lammas night.") BoLoP

Rilke, my river, I know your locked look of a poet. Visions. Kathleen Spivack. AmPA

Rimbaud and Verlaine, precious pair of poets. Conrad Aiken. Preludes for Memnon, LVI. NoAM

Rimbaud in Abyssinia. Ellen McEvilley Griffin. NPW

Rime Intrinsica, Fontmell Magna, Sturminster Newton and Melbury Bubb. Dorset. John Betjeman. MPo

Rime of the Ancient Mariner, The. Samuel Taylor Coleridge. Epi; InPS; MBPR; NOBE; PPoD
  "Sun now rose upon the right, The," II. OBP

Rime of the Ancient Mariner, The. Bruce Haley. PPoD

Rime, the rack of finest wits. A Fit of Rime against Rime. Ben Jonson. MAT; PAIC

Ring-a-ring-a-roses. Unknown. MG
  (Ring-a-ring o' roses.) SpRo

Ring-a-ring o' neutrons. Paul Dehn. SpRo

Ring-a-ring o' roses. See Ring-a-ring-a-roses.

Ring around a rosey. Squat Down, Josey. Unknown. AmFP

Ring Of, The. Charles Olson. NOBA; VGW

Ring Out, Wild Bells. In Memoriam A.H.H., CVI. Tennyson. OFD

Ring out your bells, let mourning shows be spread. Sir Philip Sidney. GBL

Ring, sing! ring, sing! pleasant Sabbath bells! The Green Gnome. Robert Buchanan. PoTa

Ring so worn as you behold, The. A Marriage Ring [or His Late Wife's Wedding-Ring]. George Crabbe. BoLoP; NOBE

Ring the bell! Unknown. MG

Ring—ting! I wish I were a primrose. Wishing. William Allingham. OxBChV

Ringers, The. John Peck. AmPA

Ringing the Bells. Anne Sexton. CAPP; VGW

Ringing tire iron, A. Some Good Things to Be Said for the Iron Age. Gary Snyder. CoPAm

Ringless. Diane Wakoski. Prf

Ringleted Youth of My Love. Unknown, tr. fr. Modern Irish by Douglas Hyde. PFIr

Ringsend. Oliver St. John Gogarty. OxBTC

Rino's Song. Lynne Lawner. IHMS

Rintrah roars and shakes his fires in the burdened air. The Marriage of Heaven and Hell. Blake. LAuP; MBPR

Riot. Gwendolyn Brooks. BPo; CAPP; PoBA; Psy

Riot, tumult, anticipated disturbances. Matthew Mead. Fr. The Administration of Things. TwMBP

Riots and Rituals. Richard W. Thomas. PoBA

Ripe and Bearded Barley, The. Unknown. GBP

Ripeness. Ruth Whitman. TSWA

Ripeness Is All. J. V. Cunningham. PiAm

Ripeness is all; her in her cooling planet. To an Old Lady. William Empson. Moon; NoAM; NOBE

Ripley or not. A Street in Kaufman-ville. James Cunningham. JB

Rip-off # 1: Hippie Capitalism. Geof Hewitt. NeAC

Riprap. Gary Snyder. NOBA; PPoD

Riptide. Marge Piercy. MMD

Rise at 7:15. Good Morning Love! Paul Blackburn. NoAM

Rise, heart! thy Lord is risen. Sing His praise. Easter. George Herbert. SCP-1

Rise, heir[e] of fresh eternity. Easter Day. Richard Crashaw. MetP; SCP-1

Rise of capitalism parallels the advance of romanticism, The. Definition of Blue. John Ashbery. Epi

Rise, rise from sluggishness, fly fast my dear. The Verses of the Talkative Knight. Mary Sidney Wroth, Countess of Montgomery. Fr. Urania. WPE

"Rise up, rise up, now, Lord Douglas, " she says. The Douglas Tragedy. Unknown. IPWM; PeBB

Rise You Up, My True Love. Unknown. AmFP

Rising at dawn to pee, I thought I saw you. In Memory of My Cat Domino: 1951-1966. Roy Fuller. PSN

Rising Five. Norman Nicholson. MPo

Rising from bed. Poem Before Birth. George MacBeth. SLP

Rising Glory of America, The, sel. Philip Freneau.
  "Now shall the adventurous muse attempt a theme." AmVN

Rising High Water Blues. Unknown. BluL

Rising in lamplight dying at dawn. Voices Answering Back: The Vampires. Lawrence Raab. AmPA

Rising in the Morning. Hugh Rhodes. OxBChV

Rising of the Buffalo Men. Unknown, tr. fr. American Indian. SFF
  ("I rise, I rise/ I who makes the earth to tremble.") ANTL

Rising of the Moon, The, with music. Unknown. RDB

Rising sun complies with our weak sight, The. Edmund Waller. Fr. To the King, upon His Majesty's Happy Return. SCP-2

Rising through sky. Planet Dream. T. Alan Broughton. FAF

Rites for Cousin Vit, The. Gwendolyn Brooks. Fr. The Womanhood. BPo; WPE

Rites of Passage. Audre Lorde. PoBA

Ritual, The. Marge Piercy. MMD

Ritual, The. E. J. Pratt. NoAM

Ritual Mouse, A. William Meredith. PBMP

Ritual Three. David Ignatow. ConAP

Rivalry. Alden Nowlan. POL

Rivals, The. James Stephens. NoAM; RAE

Riven Quarry, The. Gloria C. Oden. PoBA

River, The. Sam Cornish. PoBA

River, The. Hart Crane. Fr. The Bridge: Powhatan's Daughter. NoAM; NOBA; PiAm

River, A. A. K. Ramanujan. MPo

River, The. James Stephens. ECBV

River and Light. Siv Cedering Fox. RiTi

River at its brim, The. Landscape 4. Robert Gray. CAAP

River brought down, The. How We Heard the Name. Alan Dugan. NoAM

River Dart, The. Unknown. GBP

River Don, The. Unknown. GBP

River Duddon, The, sels. Wordsworth.
  After-Thought, XXXIV. MBPR
  (Valediction to the River Duddon.) NOBE
  "Child of the clouds! remote from every taint," II. MBPR
  "Not envying Latian shades—if yet they throw," I. MBPR

River-march-drowse. Lorine Niedecker. RiTi

River-Mates. Padraic Colum. LoAs; PFIr

River-Merchant's Wife, The: a Letter. Li Po, tr. fr. Chinese by Ezra Pound. BoLoP; InPK; InPS; IPWM; LoAs; NoAM; NOBA; NOBE; PAIC; PPoe; PPP

River of Bees, The. W. S. Merwin. HeIP

River of Dart, O river of Dart. The Dart. Unknown. GBP

River of Rivers in Connecticut, The. Wallace Stevens. NOBA; VGW

River rattles its money, A. Sleeping Out In Vermont. Conrad Hilberry. PPoD

River Road. Stanley Kunitz. NoAm

River Road. Mary Shumway. NVAP

River Roads. Carl Sandburg. VGW

River Roses. D. H. Lawrence. GBL

Riversong. Michael Anania. HeS

River Song. Weldon Kees. NoAM; PPP

River Swelleth More and More, The. Henry David Thoreau. NOBA

River that must turn full after I stop dying. "A 11." Louis Zukofsky. Fr. "A." VGW

River this November afternoon, The. The Double Vision. C. Day Lewis. NoAM

Riverdale Lion. John Robert Colombo. LP

Rivers and Mountains. John Ashbery. NoAM; NOBA

Rivers Arise; Whether Thou Be the Son. Milton. InPK

Rizpah.  Tennyson.  PAIC

Roach, The.  John Raven.  BPo

Road at My Door, The.  W. B. Yeats.  Meditations in Time of Civil War, V.  BIrV; NOBE

Road at the top of the rise, The.  The Middleness of the Road.  Robert Frost.  NOBA

Road beneath the giant original trees, The.  Sanctuary.  Judith Wright.  WPE

Road ends with the hills, The.  Black Tarn.  V. Sackville-West.  SBG

Road goes ever on and on, The.  The Old Walking Song.  J. R. R. Tolkien.  RFM

Road in Kentucky, A.  Robert Hayden.  NCSH

Road is a crayon line, A. One bus.  Child's Drawing.  Allan Block.  FAF

Road Not Taken, The.  Robert Frost.  HeIP; NoAM; RFM; SoSe; VoPo

Road runs straight with no turning, the circle, The.  Black People: This Is Our Destiny.  LeRoi Jones.  CAPP

Road to Pengya, The.  Tu Fu, tr. fr. Chinese by Rewi Alley and Edward Field.  Prf

Road to your house leads past the motley plane trees, The.  I Am Moved by a Necessity from Within.  Daisy Aldan.  RiTi

Road was one she saw each day, The.  The Sacrament.  Robert P. Tristram Coffin.  TH

Road winds down through autumn hills, The.  Tour 5.  Robert Hayden.  PPP

Roads, The.  Stephen Stepanchev.  SA

Road's End, The.  John Montague.  TwMBP

Roaring alongside he takes for granted, The.  Sandpiper.  Elizabeth Bishop.  HeIP; PiAM

Roaring company that festive night, A.  The Dark and the Fair.  Stanley Kunitz.  LoAs

Roaring Frost, The.  Alice Meynell.  WPE

Robbers.  Unknown.  ECBV

Robbers came to our house, The.  Unknown.  GBP

Robbing and Stealing Blues.  Unknown.  BluL

Robbing the Tree Hive.  Ernest G. Moll.  PoTa

Robene and Makyne ("Robene sat on gud grene hill").  Robert Henryson.  BoLoP

Robert.  Lucille Clifton.  CAAP

Robert Bruce's March to Bannockburn.  Burns.  See Bannockburn.

Robert Frost.  Robert Lowell.  NoAM

Robert Whitmore.  Frank Marshall Davis.  BPo; PoBA

Roberta.  Unknown.  BluL

Robertin Tush.  Unknown.  GBP

Robin, The.  Thomas Hardy.  RAE

Robin and Gandelein.  Unknown.  OxBM

Robin and Richard were two pretty men.  Mother Goose.  MG

Robin and the wren, The.  Robin, Wren, Martin, Swallow.  Unknown.  GBP

Robin Hood.  Gray Burr.  NCSH

Robin Hood.  Keats.  MBPR

Robin Hood and Allen a Dale.  Unknown.  GBP; PeBB

Robin Hood and Little John.  Unknown.  AmFP

Robin Hood and the Bishop of Hereford.  Unknown.  PeBB

Robin Hood and the Sheriff ("Robin Hood's gone to Nottinghame gane").  Unknown.  PeBB

Robin Goodfellow, sel  Unknown.
Lily, Germander, and Sops-in-Wine, fr. Pt. II.  ECBV

Robin in Winter, The, sel.  William Cowper.
"No noise is here, or none that hinders thought."  BoAnP

Robin Redbreast.  William Allingham.  OxBChV

Robin Redbreast.  Stanley Kunitz.  Prf

Robin Redbreast in a Cage, A, abr.  Blake..  Fr. Auguries of Innocence.  AKE
(Three Things to Remember, 6 ll.)  ECBV

Robin Redbreast's Testament.  Unknown.  GBP

Robin, Wren, Martin, Swallow.  Unknown.  GBP

Robin's Song, The.  Unknown, at. to Richard Honeywood.  ECBV; RAE

Robinson.  Weldon Kees.  AnMo; NoAM

Robinson at cards at the Algonquin; a thin.  Aspects of Robinson.  Weldon Kees.  AnMo

Robinson at Home.  Weldon Kees.  AnMo

Robinson Crusoe's Story.  Charles Edward Carryl.  Fr. Davy and the Goblin, ch. 11.  ECBV

Robyn, A/ Joly Robyn.  Sir Thomas Wyatt.  AAS

Rock, The.  Unknown, tr. fr. Welsh by Geoffrey Grigson.  GBL

Rock, a leaf, mud, even the grass, A.  The Concealment: Ishi, the Last Wild Indian.  William Stafford.  TCP

Rock and Hawk.  Robinson Jeffers.  IPWM; NoAM; NOBA

Rock Climbing.  Jane Cooper.  NMM

Rock Island Line, The.  Unknown.  AmFP

Rock of Ages, with music.  Augustus Montague Toplady.  BLSH; BLSo

Rock Pilgrim.  Herbert Palmer.  OxBTC

Rock swallows the snake, The.  Kindred.  Douglas Stewart.  MAuV

Rock-a-Bye Baby, with music.  Effie I. Canning.  FSN

Rock-a-bye, baby, thy cradle is green.  Mother Goose.  MG

Rock'd in the Cradle of the Deep, with music.  Emma Hart Willard.  PSoN

Rocking Hymn, A.  George Wither.  OxBChV

Rockland.  Julia Randall.  WPE

Rocks have been my pillow, baby.  Homeless Blues.  Unknown.  BluL

Rocky Acres.  Robert Graves.  NoAM

Rocky Island, The.  Unknown.  AmFP

Rocky Mountains, The.  Unknown.  AmFP

Rodeo.  Edward Lueders.  SPo

Roethke Plain.  John Malcolm Brinnin.  NoAM

Rokeby, sels.  Sir Walter Scott.
Allen-a-Dale, fr. III.  PoTa
Rover's Farewell, The, fr. III.  NOBE

Rokeby Venus, The.  Robert Conquest.  NoAM

Roll, Alabama, Roll.  Unknown.  AIW

Roll forth, my song, like the rushing river.  The Nameless One.  James Clarence Mangan.  BIrV

Roll on, sad world! not Mercury or Mars.  Sonnet.  Frederick Goddard Tuckerman.  Fr. Sonnets.  PiAm

Roll on the Ground.  Unknown.  AmFP

Roll the Cotton Down.  Unknown.  AmFP

Rolleth onward the seventh wave.  Gavin Bantock.  Fr. Christ.  TwMBP

Rolling away from Chicago.  Derricks.  R. R. Cuscaden.  ANTL

Rolling English Road, The.  G. K. Chesterton.  NOBE; OxBTC; PPoD

Rolling from St. Patrick's, The.  Burial of An Irish President.  Austin Clarke.  BIrV

Rolling Log Blues.  Unknown.  BluL

Rolling wheel that runneth often round, The.  Amoretti, XVIII.  Spenser.  Epi

Rolly Trudum.  Unknown.  AmFP

Roman Candle.  Neil Weiss.  LoAs

Roman Fountain.  Louise Bogan.  SBG

Roman Kamin grunted through art class.  In Imago Dei: Fiat Lux.  Roderick Hartigh Jellema.  AATT

Roman Road, The.  Thomas Hardy.  NOBE

Roman soldiers come riding in full speed.  "Sin-Killer" Griffin.  Fr. The Man of Calvary.  AmFP

Romance. Walter James Turner. NOBE

Romance, who loves to nod and sing. Introduction. Poe. NOBA

Romanies in Town, The. Anne Beresford. LP; MPo

Romans Angry about the Inner World. Robert Bly. NoAM; NOBA; PPoe

Romans, rheumatic, gouty, came. La Condition Botanique. Anthony Hecht. NoAM

Romantic, The. Colin Ellis. POL

Romantic. George Garrett. CoPAm

Romantic Age, The. Ogden Nash. SFF

Romantic Poem. Anne Waldman. RiTi

Rome Ryme. Joseph Hall. *Fr.* Virgidemiarum, Bk. IV, Satire VII. TVS

Romeo and Juliet, *sels.*    Shakespeare.
   "But, soft! What light through yonder window breaks?" *fr.* II, ii. Moon
   "Gallop apace, you fiery-footed steeds," *fr.* III, ii. GBL
   "If I profane with my unworthiest hand," *fr.* II, v. SoSe
   "Lady, by yonder blessed moon I swear," *fr.* II, ii. Moon
   "Wilt thou be gone? it is not yet near day," *fr.* III, v. PAIC

Romping. John Ciardi. CTBA; NCSH

Rondeau: "By two black eyes my heart was won." *Unknown.* FaBoCo

Rondeau: "Help me to seek, for I lost it there." Sir Thomas Wyatt. PAIC
   ("Helpe me to seke for I lost it there.") AAS

Rondeau: "Jenny kissed me when we met." Leigh Hunt. *See* Jenny Kiss'd Me.

Rondeau: "Of Eden lost, in ancient days." George Ellis. PAIC

Rondel: "Kissing her hair I sat against her feet." Swinburne. PAIC

Rondel of Love [*or* Luve], A. Alexander Scott. BoLoP; SLP

Rondel; The Wanderer. Austin Dobson. PAIC

Rondelay, A: "Chloe found Amyntas lying." Dryden. PAIC

Roof Garden, The. Howard Moss. MAT

Roof is shattered, the bone house splintered, The. In Memory of G. K., for 50 Years the College Carpenter. Robert A. Martin. AATT

Roof of the World, The. Michael Dennis Browne. AmPA

Roofs are lit with rain, The. Vincent Buckley. *Fr.* Stroke. MAuV

Roof's peak is eye. Sitting Here. Robert Creeley. RRA

Roofwalker, The. Adrienne Rich. PiAm; PPP; Psy

Rooks, The. Jane Euphemia Browne. OxBChV

Rooks, The. *Unknown.* GBP

Rooks above the convent walls, The. The Convent. "Seumas O'Sullivan." PFIr; POL

Rooks are building on the trees, The. The Rooks. Jane Euphemia Browne. OxBChV

Room, The. Conrad Aiken. NOBA

Room, The. Duncan Glen. MIS

Room, The. De Leon Harrison. PoBA

Room. Shirley Kaufman. NMM

Room, The. W. S. Merwin. NOBA

Room above the Square, The. Stephen Spender. NOBE

Room after room. Love in a Life. Robert Browning. NOBE

Room must be warmer than, The. How the Invalids Make Love. Susan Feldman. AmPA

Room the size of a warehouse, A. Cairo Hotel. J. R. Rowland. MAuV

Room was a, The/ red glow. We Dance Like Ella Riffs. Carolyn M. Rodgers. PoBA

Room was suddenly rich and the great bay-window was, The. Snow. Louis MacNeice. NoAM; NOBE; OxBTC

Rooming House. Ted Kooser. POL

Rooster Be? Or a Crow? *Unknown.*    *See* To Be or Not to Be.

Roosters. Elizabeth Bishop. CoPAm

Root Cellar. Theodore Roethke. HeIP; PiAm; PPP

Root-Crops. Derek Bowman. MIS

Root Eater, The. Ai. CAAP

Root Hog or Die. *Unknown.* AmFP

Roots and Branches. Robert Duncan. VGW

Roots around your soul and eyes, The. Sweating It Out on Winding Stair Mountain. Jim Barnes. CDW

Roots of fern, The. In Split: Diocletian's Palace. Stephen Stepanchev. SA

Roots of mankind are tangled in my hair, The. Epitaph. Wendy Rose. CDW

Ropewalk, The. Longfellow. PiAm

Rorate coeli desuper. Unto Us a Child Is Born. William Dunbar. BoReV

Rosalie, the Prairie Flower, *with music.* George Frederick Root. BLSo

Rosalynde; or, Euphues' Golden Legacy, *sel.* Thomas Lodge. Rosalind's Madrigal. NOBE

Rosary, The, *with music.* Robert Cameron Rogers. BLSH; BLSo; FSN

Rose, The. Thomas Howell. FSFS

Rose. Kathleen Raine. WPE

Rose, The. Theodore Roethke. InPS; NOBA; PiAm; PPoe

Rose, The. William Carlos Williams. NOBA

Rose Aylmer. Walter Savage Landor. BoLoP; HeIP; NOBE

Rose-cheeked Laura, Come. Thomas Campion. InPK; InPS; PAIC
   (Laura.) NOBE
   ("Rose-cheekt Lawra, come.") AAS

Rose Connoley. *Unknown.* AmFP

Rose Family, The. Robert Frost. SoSe

Rose, harsh rose. Sea Rose. Hilda Doolittle ("H.D."). NoAM

Rose in the Garden. *Unknown.* AmFP

Rose is a rose, The. The Rose Family. Robert Frost. SoSe

Rose kissed me today. A Kiss. Austin Dobson. *Fr.* Rose-Leaves. PPoD

Rose-Leaves, *sels.*    Austin Dobson.
   Kiss, A. PPod
   Urceus Exit. PAIC

Rose of Solitude, The. William Everson. PiAm

Rose of Tralee, The, *with music.* C. Mordaunt Spencer. BLSH

Rose Red's hair is brown as fur. An Embroidery. Denise Levertov. NMM; RiTi

Rose That Bore Jesu, The. *Unknown.* OxBM

Rose upon the wall, The. The Canticle of the Rose. Edith Sitwell. NoAM

Roseberry to his lady says. Supper Is Na Ready. *Unknown.* GBP

Rosebud. Jon Anderson. CAAP

Roses. Geoffrey Lehmann. CAAP

Roses. *Unknown.* OxBM

Roses and Revolutions. Dudley Randall. BPo; ConAP; NoAM; PoBA

Roses are red, diddle diddle, lavender's blue. The Lady's Song in Leap Year. *Unknown.* GBP

Roses, their sharp spines being gone. A Bridal Song. *At. to* Shakespeare. *Fr.* The Two Noble Kinsmen, I, i. NOBE

Rosy Apple, Lemon or Pear. *Unknown.* POL

Roubaix Cemetery. Franklin Brainard. HeS

Rou-cou spoke the dove. Song of Fixed Accord. Wallace Stevens. InPS

Rouen. May Wedderburn Cannan. OxBTC

Rough. Stephen Spender. *See* My Parents Kept Me.

Rough fir, hauled from the hills. The Making of the Cross. William Everson VGW

Rough wind, that moanest loud. A Dirge. Shelley. GrRo; InPK; NOBE; VoPo

Rough winds do shake/ do shake/ the darling buds of May. Song: "Rough Winds Do Shake the Darling Buds of May." Louis Simpson. SFF

Roughly figured, this man of moderate habits. Life Cycle of Common Man. Howard Nemerov. MPo

Round, The. Philip Booth. NCSH

Round. Weldon Kees. NoAM

Round a cleft in the cliffs to come upon. Venus of the Salty Shell. Denis Devlin. BIrV

Round about, round about. Counting Out Rhyme. *Unknown.* SpRo

Round and round and round I spin. Discovery. Myra Cohn Livingston. LCL

Round, calm faces rosy with the cold, The. Japanese Children. James Kirkup. RAE

'Round my Indiana homestead wave the cornfields. On the Banks of the Wabash, Far Away. Paul Dresser. BLSo; FSN

Round Table, The. Peggy Susberry Kenner. JB

Round the cape of a sudden came the sea. Parting at Morning. Robert Browning. HeIP; LoAs; NOBE; PAIC; SoSe

Round Trip to Chicago. Martha Shelley. WBN

Route 40—Ohio, U.S.A. Milton Kessler. CoPAm

Route of evanescence, A. Emily Dickinson. AmVN

Routes. Peter Everwine. FiCP

Rover, with the good brown head. Matthew Arnold. *Fr.* Matthias. PCat

Rover's Farewell, The. Sir Walter Scott. *Fr. Rokeby, III.* NOBE

Roving breezes come and go, The. The Traveling Post Office. Andrew Barton Paterson. PoTa

Roving Shanty Boy, The. *Unknown.* AmFP

Row after row with strict impunity. Ode to the Confederate Dead. Allen Tate. HeIP; NoAM; NOBA

Row of pearls, A. Seeds. James Reeves. ECBV

Row us out from Desenzano, to your Sirmione row! "Frater Ave atque Vale." Tennyson. InPS

Rowan County Crew, The. James William Day. AmFP

Rows of cells are unroofed, The. The Old Prison. Judith Wright. MAuV

Rows of Cold Trees, The. Yvor Winters. NoAM; NOBA

Royal Fisherman, The. *Unknown.* GBP; PeBB

Royal Palm. Hart Crane. NoAM

Royal Slave, The, *sel.* William Cartwright. "Come, my sweet, whiles every strain." SCP-2

Royalty. Luci Shaw. AATT

R-P-O-P-H-E-S-S-A-G-R. E. E. Cummings. InPK; PiAm; PPP

Rub a dub dub,/ Three men in a tub. Mother Goose. MG

Rubáiyát of Omar Khayyám of Naishápúr, The. Omar Khayyám, *tr. fr. Persian by* Edward Fitzgerald. HeIP *Sels.* "Book of verses underneath the bough, A." NOBE "Wake! For the sun, who scattered into flight." OBP

Rubber penis, the wig, false breasts, The. Poggio. Lawrence Durrell. OxBTC

Rubin. Charles Cooper. PoBA

Rueful Lamentation, A. Sir Thomas More. AAS

Rufus Mitchell's Confession. *Unknown.* AmFP

"Ruin seize thee, ruthless King." The Bard. Thomas Gray. LAuP; NOBE

Ruined Cottage, The. Wordsworth. MBPR

Ruined Maid, The. Thomas Hardy. BoLoP; HeIP; InPK; OBP; OxBTC; PPoD; PPoe; WIF

Ruins Under the Stars, *sel.* Galway Kinnell. "Sometimes I see them." RFM

Rule, Britannia. James Thomson. *Fr.* Alfred, a Masque, II, v (*by* Thomson *and* David Mallet). BLSH, *with music*; BTTM; VoPo

Rule of the road is a paradox quite, The. Mother Goose. MG

Rules/ Were made for novices and fools. Samuel Butler. *Fr.* Arts and Sciences. SCP-2

Rumbling under blackened girders, Midland, bound for Cricklewood. Parliament Hill Fields. John Betjeman. NOBE

Rumination. Richard Eberhart. CoPAm

Rummaging through childhood. Snapshot. Colette Inez. AATT

Rumors open up. The Morning Star. Primus St. John. PoBA

Rumpled sheet, A. The Term. William Carlos Williams. TSWA

Run, Nigger, Run! *Unknown.* BPo

Run on, run on, in a way causing shaking motion on the sidewalk. Autolycus' Song. Richard L. Greene. SpRo

Run out the boat, my broken comrades. Thalassa. Louis MacNeice. BIrV; NOBE

Run, shepherds, run where Bethlehem blest appears. The Nativity. William Drummond of Hawthornden. SCP-2

Runagate Runagate. Robert Hayden. BPo; PoBA

Runaway, The. Robert Frost. ECBV; VGW

Runaway Slave at Pilgrim's Point, The. Elizabeth Barrett Browning. SBG

Runilda's Chant. George Darley. *Fr.* Ethelstan. PFIr

Runnable Stag, A. John Davidson. OxBTC

Runner, The. Walt Whitman. InPS; MiP; PPoD; SPo

Runner at Sauteurs, The. Derek Walcott. *Fr.* Another Life. OBP

Running. Richard Wilbur. NCSH

Running across to the lot. Lucille Clifton. CAAP

Running along a bank, a parapet. The Path. Edward Thomas. NoAM

Running through Sleep. Kathleen Norris. IHMS

Running Water Music. Gary Snyder. PiAm

Running your apartment. Getting into Focus. Miriam Palmer. RiTi

Runoff. A. R. Ammons. PPP

Runs falls rises stumbles on from darkness into darkness. Runagate Runagate. Robert Hayden. BPo; PoBA

Rural Dance about the Maypole, The. *Unknown.* GBP

Rural Life. George Crabbe. *Fr.* The Village. NOBE

Rushing. Ray A. Young Bear. CDW

Russia. William Carlos Williams. VGW

Russians. Keith Douglas. OxBTC

Rust, a little pile of western color, lies, The. We Continue. W. S. Merwin. CAPP

Rusted and without tires. 1937 Ford Convertible. Tom McKeown. NVAP

Rustling of Grass, The. Alfred Noyes. FSFS

Rustling of the silk is discontinued, The. Liu Ch'e. Ezra Pound. VGW

Ruth. Laura Freedgood. SFF

Ruth. Thomas Hood. BoLoP; NOBE

Ruth. Pauli Murray. NMM

Ruth. Wordsworth. MBPR

Ruyter the while, that had our ocean curbed. Andrew Marvell. *Fr.* The Last Instructions to a Painter. SCP-1

Rythm. Iain Crichton Smith. LP; MPoA Rustling of the silk is

## S

SOS. LeRoi Jones. BPo; PoBA

Sabidi, I love thee not, nor why I wot. Translated out of Martial. Martial, *tr. by* John Weever. PAIC

Sabinas Hidalgo. Diane Kruchkow. FAF

Sabrina. Milton. *Fr.* Comus. NOBE

Sacrament, The. Robert P. Tristram Coffin. TH

Sacramental Meditations. Edward Taylor. *See* Preparatory Meditations.

Sacred Heart of Jesus Bleeds for You, The. Elton Glaser. NVAP

Sacred muse that first made love divine, The. Gulling Sonnets, VI. Sir John Davies. PAIC

Sacred to the Memory of Maria (To Say Nothing of Jane and Martha) Sparks. Max Adeler. FaBoCo

Sacrifice, The, *much abr.* George Herbert. SCP-1

Sacsahuamán, you know, where they drag out. Visit Peru: Of Stoned Incas' Land. Teresa A. McCarthy. NPW

Sad and mournful history, A. The Cabin Creek Flood. *Unknown.* AmFP

Sad for those without sweet Anglo-Saxon. The Change. David O'Bruadair, *tr. by* Austin Clarke. BIrV

Sad lot, to have no hope! Though lowly kneeling. The Visionary Hope. Samuel Taylor Coleridge. MBPR

Sad Results of Thinking. *Unknown.* SFF

Sad seamstress, The. House Guest. Elizabeth Bishop. CoPAm; NCSH

Sad Shepherd, The, *sels.* Ben Jonson.
Death and Love, *fr.* I, v. NOBE
"Foul ill spirit hath possessed her, A," *fr.* II, ii. SCP-1

Sad Song, The. John Fletcher. *See* Away, Delights.

Sad Song, This Time, A. Rolfe Humphries. PAIC

Sad Story, A. Pope. *Fr.* Moral Essays, Epistle III. BoReV

Sad Tale of Mr. Mears, The. *Unknown.* PoTa

Saddest place that e'er I saw, The. Screaming Tarn. Robert Bridges. PoTa

Sadie/ the cleaning lady. "Personals." Leatrice W. Emeruwa. RiTi

Sadie and Maud. Gwendolyn Brooks. CoPAm; NoAM; NOBA

Sadies's Playhouse. Margaret Danner. PoBA

Sadness. William Cartwright. SCP-2

Sadness in the human visage stares, The. At an Exhibition of Historical Paintings, Hobart. Vivian Smith. MAuV

Sadness, of course, and confusion. My Death. Mark Strand. CAAP

Sadness of our lives, The. Brooding. David Ignatow. PBMP; TCP

Sadness of the Moon, The. Baudelaire, *tr. fr. French by* F. P. Trurm. Moon

Safari to Bwagamoyo. Bwagamoyo. Lebert Bethune. PoBA

Safari West. John A. Williams. InPS

Safe Flights. Barbara Guest. RiTi

Safe in the magic of my woods. The Voice. Rupert Brooke. BuTh

Safe in their alabaster chambers. Emily Dickinson. NOBA; PiAm; WPE

Safe upon the solid rock the ugly houses stand. Second Fig. Edna St. Vincent Millay. TH

Safe where I cannot lie yet. Christina Rossetti. BoReV

Safety at Forty; or, An Abecedarian Takes a Walk. L. E. Sissman. Prf

Safety pin on the floor. Fox Court, Winter. Cathy Colman. NPW

Said/ a hip/ lip-ful. Leg-acy of a Blue Capricorn. james Cunningham. JB

Said a snake to a frog with a wrinkled skin. Hospitality. John Banister Tabb. ECBV

Said a woman and a dollar a bout the same. Out on Santa Fe—Blues. *Unknown.* BluL

Said Abner, "At last thou art come! Ere I tell, ere thou speak." Saul. Robert Browning. PFD

Said Hanrahan. P. J. Hartigan. MAuV

Said Jerome K. Jerome to Ford Madox Ford. Mutual Problem. William Cole. POL

Said, Pull her up a bit will you, Mac, I want to unload there. Reason. Josephine Miles. InPK; NCSH; NoAM; PPoD; SS

Said the bird in search of a cage. A Bird in Search of a Cage. Robert Pack. SFF

Said the birds of America. The Birds of America. James Broughton. BoAnP

Said the Duck to the Kagaroo. The Duck and the Kangaroo. Edward Lear. OxBChV

Said the first little chicken. The Chickens. *Unknown.* ECBV

Said the grave dean of Westminster. A Refusal. Thomas Hardy. FaBoCo

Said the Lion to the Lioness—"When you are amber dust." Heart and Mind. Edith Sitwell. OxBTC

Said the little warbling vireo. Fable of the Talented Mockingbird. Scott Bates. BoAnP

Said the Poet to the Analyst. Anne Sexton. Psy

Said the sun, "I'm about to sink and disappear." The Lamp. A. Buttigieg. RAE

Said the trout to the fluke. Johnshaven. *Unknown.* GBP

Said the Wind to the Moon, "I will blow you out." George MacDonald. *Fr.* Th Wind and the Moon. CaYB; LCL

Sail Away. Robert Adamson. CAAP

Sail, Monarchs, rising and falling. Roots and Branches. Robert Duncan. VGW

Sailing. Susan Murray. NowV

Sailing from the United States. Stanley Moss. VGW

Sailing Home from Rapallo. Robert Lowell. NoAM

Sailing in Crosslight. Anita Skeen. IHMS

Sailing in the boat when the tide runs high. Rose in the Garden. *Unknown.* AmFP

Sailing, Sailing. Gray Burr. SPo

Sailing to an Island. Richard Murphy. MPo

Sailor. Langston Hughes. ECBV

Sailor and His Bride, The. *Unknown.* AmFP

Sailor at Midnight, A. E. N. Sargent. NMM; WBN

Sailor Boy, The. Tennyson. AIW

Sailor tells the children, The. Kingdoms. Oliver St. John Gogarty. RAE

Sailor to His Parrot, The. W. H. Davies. BoAnP

"Sailorman, I'll give to you." The Silver Penny. Walter de la Mare. WIF

Sailors' Alphabet, The. *Unknown.* AmFP

Sailor's Consolation, The. William Pitt, *wr. at. to* Charles Dibdin. FaBoCo

Sailor's trade is a weary life, A. The Rocky Island. *Unknown.* AmFP

Sails flashing to the wind like weapons. Middle Passage. Robert Hayden. BPo; CoPAm; NoAM; PoBA

St. Agnes' Eve—Ah, bitter chill it was! The Eve of St. Agnes. Keats. AnMo; MBPR; PAIC

St. Asaph's. Kingsley Amis. OxBTC

Saint Bridget was. The Giveaway. Phillis McGinley. PBMP

Saint Elène, I thee pray. Prayer to St. Helena. *Unknown.* OxBM

St. George. Charlie Walker. AmFP

Saint Harmony my patroness. Paul Goodman. VGW

Saint-Henri Spring. Milton Acorn. NeAC

St. Ignatius Loyola, Founder of the Jesuits: His Autobiography. John L'Heureux. PAIC

St. Isaac's Church, Petrograd. Claude McKay. PoBA

St. James Infirmary. *Unknown.* AmFP

Saint John Baptist. William Drummond of Hawthornden. NOBE; OBP

St. John was staring skyward. Wormwood. James E. Warren, Jr. AATT

St. John's Park. James McAuley. MAuV

Saint Jorge, our Lady knight. For the Night-Mare. *Unknown.* OxBM

Saint Joseph, let you send me a comrade true and kind. The Choice. Winifrid M. Letts. PFIr

Saint Joseph, Saint Peter, Saint Paul! Prayer for Fine Weather. Shane Leslie. PFIr; POL

Saint Judas. James Wright. ConAP; NOBA; TCP

St. Julien's Eve. James Cunningham. JB

Saint Louis Blues, *with music.* W. C. Handy. BLSo

St. Malachy. Thomas Merton. VGW

Saint Malcolm. Jewel C. Latimore. BPo

St. Mark. Christopher Smart. *Fr.* Hymns and Spiritual Songs. LAuP

Saint Mary Magdalene; or, The Weeper. Richard Crashaw. SCP-1

"And now where're he strayes." FaBoCo

St. Matthew, *sel.* Bible, *N.T.*. For Whosoever Will Save His Life Shall Lose It. XVI: 25-26. PBMP

St. Matthias. Christopher Smart. *Fr.* Hymns and Spiritual Songs. LAuP

Saint Nicholas. Marianne Moore. WPE

Saint Patrick's Day, 1973. Wendy Rose. CDW

Saint Peter sat by the celestial gate. The Vision of Judgment. Byron. ESaP; MBPR

St. Peter's Day was celebrated by St. Brendan at sea. The Fish at Mass. *Unknown, tr. by* J. F. Webb. BIrV

St. Peter's, that old angelic church. The Cross and the Weathercock. James Nolan. AATT

Saint Steven [*or* Seynt Stevene] was a clerk in King Herowdes halle. Saint Stephen and Herod. *Unknown.* OxBM; PeBB

St. Valentine. Marianne Moore. OFD

St. Valentine. William Carlos Williams. LoAs

St. Valentine is gone with his sweet arts. February Loves. Richmond Lattimore. LoAs

St. Valentine's Day. Wilfred Scawen Blunt. The Love Sonnets of Proteus, LV. LoAs

Saint Vesta! Oh thou sanctifying saint. To Vesta. Thomas Middleton. Moon

Sainted isle of old, The. The Shan Van Vocht. *Unknown.* BTTM

Saint's Bridge. Lola Ridge. WPE

Sair Fyel'd, Hinny. *Unknown.* GBP

Sakiyeh, The. Mathilde Blind. SBG

Salami. Philip Levine. NOBA

Salcombe Seaman's Flaunt to the Proud Pirate, The. *Unknown.* PeBB

Sale. Josephine Miles. POL; WPE

Sale began—young girls were there, The. The Slave Auction. Frances E. W. Harper. BPo

Sale of Smoke, A. Roberta Spear. AmPA

Salesman, The. Mary Moore. NPW

Salesman is an it that stinks Excuse, A. E. E. Cummings. NoAM

Sally Brown. Thomas Hood. FaBoCo

Sally Brown. *Unknown.* AmFP

Sally from Coventry, The. George Walter Thornbury. BTTM

Sally Goodin. *Unknown.* AmFP

Sally in Our Alley. Henry Carey. BLSo, *with music*; BoLoP; NOBE

Sally is gone that was so kindly. Ha'nacker Mill. Hilaire Belloc. OxBTC

Sally is the laundress, and every Saturday. The Dolls' Wash. Juliana Horatia Ewing. OxBChV

Sally's Garden. *Unknown.* AmFP

Salome. George Garrett. CoPAm; PPoD

Saloon is gone up the creek, The. Hemmed-in Males. William Carlos Williams. *Fr.* A Folded Skyscraper. MAT

Salt. Nicholas Flocos. SA

Salt. Ruth Stone. NMM

Salt creek mouths unflushed by the sea. The South Coast. William Everson. PiAm

Salt grass silent of hooves, the lake stinks. Vestiges. Basil Bunting. TwMBP

Salt of the Earth. D. H. Lawrence. NoAM

Salt Pork, The. Robert Clayton Casto. HeIP

Salted chips, The. In the Morning. Paulette Dusdall Zachariou. NPW

Saltlick, A. Dimple. Coleman Barks. *Fr.* Body Poems. NVAP

Salus Mundi. Mary Elizabeth Coleridge. BoReV

Salutation. Ezra Pound. HeIP; NOBA; PiAm; VGW

Salutation, The. Thomas Traherne. MetP

Salutation the Second. Ezra Pound. NOBA

Salute! Lawrence Ferlinghetti. MIT

Salute. Oliver Pitcher. PoBA

Salute Your Partner. *Unknown.* AmFP

Salvador Dali. David Gascoyne. OxBTC

Salvaging Spikes. Robert Vas Dias. HeS

Salvation Army lass, The. Lola Ridge. *Fr.* Ward X. WPE

Salvation to all that will is nigh. Annunciation. John Donne. SCP-1

Sam Bass. *Unknown.* AmFP

Sam Hall. *Unknown.* AmFP; PeBB

Same Gesture, The. John Montague. BIrV

Same in Blues. Langston Hughes. *Fr.* Lenox Avenue Mural. InPS; WIF

Same Lady, The. Jeanette Nichols. RiTi

Same old souvenirs, The. Niagra Falls Nocturne. Len Gasparini. NeAC

Samela. Robert Greene. *Fr.* Menaphon. GBL; NOBE

Sampler from Haworth. Frances Minturn Howard. WPE

Samson Agonistes, *sels.* Milton. "All is best, though we oft doubt." NOBE

"Light the prime work of God to me is extinct." SCP-1

"Oh how comely it is and how reviving." BoReV; NOBE; SCP-1

Ways of God, The. BoReV

"While their hearts were jocund and sublime." SCP-1

Samuel. Charles Reznikoff. *Fr.* Five Groups of Verse. SA

Samuel Allen. *Unknown.* AmFP

Samuel Sewall. Anthony Hecht. ConAP

San Diego Poem, A. Simon J. Ortiz. CDW

San Francisco Company, The. *Unknown.* AmFP

San Francisco County Jail Cell B-6. Conyus. PoBA

San Joaquin. William Everson. CoPAm

Sanctioned by eagles, this house. Here they'd met. National Shrine. X. J. Kennedy. CoPAm

Sanctity. Patrick Kavanagh. BIrV

Sanctuary. Judith Wright. WPE

Sanctuary. Elinor Wylie. Psy

Sanctuary should exist on earth. To Any M. F. H. V. Sackville-West. SBG

Sand. Charles Higham. LP

Sand Dunes. Robert Frost. RFM

Sand: the crystalline children. Kneeling Here, I Feel Good. Marge Piercy. NeAC

Sandhill Crane, The. Mary Austin. ECBV

Sandpiper. Elizabeth Bishop. HeIP; PiAm

Sandpiper, The. Celia Thaxter. OxBChV

Sand-pipings, sel. Leonora Speyer. Gulls. TH

Sandra and that boy that's going to get her in trouble. Cora Punctuated with Strawberries. George Starbuck. NCSH

Sandstone carriage, A. For Cal. James Cunningham. JB

Sandwich Man, The. Ron Padgett. ConAP

Sandy Maranoa, The. At. to A. W. Davis. MAuV

Sane Revlolution, A. D. H. Lawrence. SFF

Sanford Barney. Unknown. AmFP

Sang: "There's a reid lowe in yer cheek." Robert McLellan. SLP

Sang on Absence, sel. At. to James I, King of Scotland. "Faithful messinger, which is the nicht, The." SLP

Sank through easeful. The Diver. Robert Hayden. BPo

Sanskrit. Les A. Murray. Fr. Walking to the Cattle-place. CAAP

Santa Ana came storming, as a storm might come. The Defence of the Alamo. Joaquin Miller. BTTM

Santa Barbara Earthquake, The. Unknown. AmFP

Santa Claus. Christopher Hassall. OxBTC

Santa Claus. Dom Moraes. NoAM

Santa Claus. Howard Nemerov. NowV

Santa Lucia, with music. Teodoro Cottrau, tr. fr. Italian. BLSH

Santy Ana. Unknown. AIW

Sap rises from the sodden ditch. For Jane Myers. Louise Glück. CAAP

Sappa Creek, The. Gary Snyder. NCSH

Sapphic Love! Sculptress of far more than stone. Alex. Lynn Strongin. Fr. First Aspen. RiTi

Sapphics. Swinburne. LoAs; PAIC

Sappho. Olga Cabral. WBN

Sappho/ Sister/Mother. Invocation to Sappho. Elsa Gidlow. IHMS

Saragossa. Henry Sambrooke Leigh. FaBoCo

Sarasvati. James Stephens. NoAM

Saratoga Ending. Weldon Kees. AnMo

Saris go by me from the embassies, The. The Woman at the Washington Zoo. Randall Jarrell. PSN

Sasha and the Poet. Jean Valentine. VGW

Sassafras Tea. Mary Effie Lee Newsome. ECBV

Sat in the sun. Virginia. Elouise Loftin. PoBA

Sat up all night and lugged at the moon. Critter. W. M. Ransom. CDW

Satan and the Fallen Angels. Milton. Fr. Paradise Lost, I. SCP-1

Satan as Rebel-Liberator. Milton. Fr. Paradise Lost, I. OBP

Satan Flies to the Sun. Milton. Fr. Paradise Lost, III. SCP-1

Satan is on your tongue, sweet singer, with. Secular Elegies, III. George Barker. PAIC

Satchmo. Melvin B. Tolson. BPo

Satire: "Kind pity chokes my spleen; brave scorn forbids. John Donne. Satires, III. PAIC; SCP-1

Satire III: "Long, Dodington, in debt, I long have sought." Edward Young. Fr. Love of Fame, the Universal Passion. LAuP

Satire: "Well, I may now receive, and die: my sin." John Donne. Satires, IV. TVS

Satire: "Where I who to my cost already am." Earl of Rochester. See Satire against Mankind, A.

Satire against Mankind, A. Earl of Rochester. PAIC

"Were I (who to my cost already am)." SCP-2 (Homo Sapiens.) NOBE

Satire Entitled the Witch, A, sel. Unknown. "She with whom troops of bustuary slaves." SCP-2

Satire on Women, sel. Edward Young. "Atheists are few; most nymph a godhead own." SoSe

Satire upon the Heads. Thomas Gray. FaBoCo

Satires, sels. John Donne. "Kind pity chokes my spleen; brave scorn forbids," III. PAIC; SCP-1 "Well, I may now receive, and die: my sin," IV. TVS

Satires, sel. Horace, tr. fr. Latin. TVS "Some think my satyre's too too tart," II, 1, tr. by Thomas Drant. ("There are, to whom I seem excessive sour," tr. by Ben Jonson.)

Satires, sel. Juvenal, tr. fr. Latin by Dryden. "Jove, grant me length of life, and years' good store," fr. X. SCP-1

Satires, sel. Persius, tr. fr. Latin by Dryden. SCP-1 "Thus fares the drudge; but thou, whose life's a dream," fr. IV. "Yawning youth, scarce half awake, essays, The," fr. III.

Satires, sels. Sir Thomas Wyatt. "My mother's maids [or maydes], when they did sew and spin [or sowe and spynne], II. AAS; TVS "Myne owne John Poyntz, sins ye delight to know," I. AAS "Spending hand that always poureth out [or powreth owte], A," III. AAS; TVS

Satires of Circumstance, sel. Thomas Hardy. By Her Aunt's Grave, III. SFF

Satirical Elegy on the Death of a Late Famous General, A. Swift. ESaP; PAIC; PBMP; SS

Satisfaction—is the agent. Emily Dickinson. NOBA

Satisfactions of the Mad Farmer, The. Wendell Berry. PiAm

Saturday Blues. Unknown. BluL

Saturday in New York. Anne Beresford. MPo

Saturday Market. Charlotte Mew. WPE

Saturday morning. I rehearse. David's Harp. Gwen Harwood. MAuV

Saturday Night. Rubee Dreher Moxley. NPW

Saturday: The Small Pox. Lady Mary Wortley Montagu. WPE

Saturdays/ I am telling Anne. What Is There? Ruth Lisa Schechter. RiTi

Saturday's Child. Countee Cullen. InPK; OFD; PoBA

Sauchs in the Reuch Heuch Hauch, The. "Hugh MacDiarmid." NoAM

Saul. Robert Browning. PFD

Saul, Afterward, Riding East. John Malcolm Brinnin. Prf

Savage lion in the zoo. Supper for a Lion. Dorothy Aldis. CaYB

Savannah Mama. Unknown. BluL

Save it all; you do not know. 1915: A Pre-Raphelite Ending, London. Richard Howard. NoAM

Save on the rare occasion when the sun. On a Sundial. Hilaire Belloc. POL

Saved. Yet not saved. The Starface. Madeline Gleason. MIT

Saving Tallow. Barbara Guest. RiTi

Saving the Harvest. Geoffrey Lehmann. MAuV

Saviour, Like a Shepherd Lead Us, with music. Dorothy Ann Thrupp. BLSH

Saw the last of my Spanish shampoo. Today. Liz Lochhead. SLP

Saw ye owt o' ma' lad. The Waggoner. Unknown. GBP

Saxophone turned into a dolphin, The. Albert Ayler: Eulogy for a Decomposed Saxophone Player. Stanley Crouch. PoBA

Say "Au Revoir," but not "Good-Bye," *with music.* Harry Kennedy. FSN

Say, darkeys [*or* darkies] hab you seen de massa. Kingdom Coming. Henry Clay Work. BLSo; PSoN

Say, dear Maria! is the modish life. A Familiar Epistle. Ann Murry. WPE

Say, ma'am dear, did ye never hear. Molly Brannigan. *Unknown.* RDB

Say me, wight in the brom. Wight in the Broom. *Unknown.* OxBM

Say, my Orinda, why so sad? A Dialogue of Absence 'twixt Lucasia and Orinda. Katherine Philips. SCP-2

Say Not the Struggle Nough Availeth. Arthur Hugh Clough. NOBE; VPC

Say of them/ They Knew no Spanish. To the Veterans of the Abraham Lincoln Brigade. Genevieve Taggard. OFD

Say that the men of the old back tower. The Black Tower. W. B. Yeats. BoReV

Say that We Saw Spain Die. Edna St. Vincent Millay. SBG

Say you talking 'bout your red ripe tomato. T-Bone Steak Blues. *Unknown.* BluL

Saying. A. R. Ammons. TSWA

Saying Goodbye. Suzanne Juhasz. IHMS

Sayre. Lynn Strongin. IHMS; RiTi

Says I went to Lake Michigan. Lake Michigan Blues. *Unknown.* BluL

Says the Miner to the Mucker. *Unknown.* AmFP

Says the Pont to the Blyth. Pont and Blyth. *Unknown.* GBP

Says Tweed to Till. Tweed and Till. *Unknown.* GBP

Says William to Henry, "I cannot conceive." Henry's Secret. Dorothy Kilner. OxBChV

Scaffolding. Seamus Heaney. LP

Scalded cat. Night Letter. Marge Piercy. NMM

Scales of the Eyes, The, *sel.* Howard Nemerov. "In the water cave, below the root." NoAM

Scar. Coleman Barks. *Fr.* Body Poems. NVAP

Scarborough Fair, *with music. Unknown.* BLSo

Scarce do I pass a day, but that I hear. Meditation 8. Philip Pain. NOBA; PiAm

Scarecrow, The. Walter de la Mare. OxBTC

Scared?/ are responsible negros running. Concerning One Responsible Negro with Too Much Power. Nikki Giovanni. BPo

Scarlet Woman, The. Fenton Johnson. PoBA

Scarlet Woman, The. "Hugh MacDiarmid." SLP

Scars take us back to places we have been, The. Memoranda. William Dickey. CoPAm

Scat! Scitten. David McCord. ECBV

Scaurus hates Greek, and is become. Epigram. *Unknown.* PiAm

Scel Lem Duib. *Unknown, tr. fr. Irish by* Flann O'Brien. BIrV

Scenario VI. LeRoi Jones. Epi

Scene on the Banks of the Hudson, A. Bryant. PiAm

Scenery. Ted Joans. PoBA

Scenes from the Fall of Troy. William Morris. PAIC

Scent of unseen jasmine on the warm night beach, The. Malaga. Pearse Hutchinson. BIrV

Schizophrenic, wrenched by two styles. Codicil. Derek Walcott. NoAM

Schloss Voss, built between 1600 and 1650. Das Schloss. Lincoln Kirstein. NoAM

Scholar-Gipsy, The. Matthew Arnold. HeIP; NOBE

Scholars. Walter de la Mare. NoAM

Scholars, The. W. B. Yeats. WIF

Scholar's Life, The. Samuel Johnson. *Fr.* The Vanity of Human Wishes. NOBE

School Children, The. Louise Glück. AmPA

School Days, *with music.* Will D. Cobb. BLSH

School that looks like an army barracks, A. Ecole St. Luc. Ray Fraser. NeAC

School of Beauty's a tavern now, The. A Street in Bronzeville: Southeast Corner. Gwendolyn Brooks. VGW

School Boy, The. Blake. *Fr.* Songs of Experience. MBPR

Schoolboy's Complaint, A. *Unknown.* OxBM

Schoolboy's Lot, A. *Unknown.* OxBM

Schoolmaster, The. *Unknown.* GBP

Schoolmaster's Admonition, A. *Unknown.* OxBChV

Schoolmaster's Precepts, A. John Penkethman. OxBChV

Schoolmistress. Clive Sansom. LP; MPo

School-Mistress, The. William Shenstone. LAuP

School's Out. W. H. Davies. BBGO

Schooner *Fred Dunbar*, The. Amos Hanson. AmFP

Schreckhorn, The. Thomas Hardy. OBP

Schwiegermutterlieder. Tony Harrison. InPS

Science. Robinson Jeffers. WIF

Science As Art. Hugh Seidman. AmPA

Science, that simple saint, cannot be bothered. Dr. Sigmund Freud Discovers the Sea Shell. Archibald MacLeish. SoSe

Science! true daughter of Old Time thou art! Sonnet—To Science. Poe. Al Aaraaf: Prologue. AmVN; InPK; PAIC: PBMP; PiAm; PPoD; WIF

Scientist, The. Janet Burroway. SoSe

Scientist has a test tube full of sheep, A. Counting Sheep. Russell Edson. FiCP

Scintillate, scintillate, globule orific. The Little Star. *Unknown.* SpRo

Scorn Not the Sonnet. Wordsworth. Epi; HeIP ("Scorn not the sonnet; critic, you have frowned.") MBPR; OBP

Scorpion, The. Hilaire Belloc. BoAnP

Scorpion, The. William Plomer. NoAM

Scorpion is black as soot, The. The Scorpion. Hilaire Belloc. BoAnP

Scot, a Welsh and an Irish Man, A. *Unknown.* GBP

Scotland's Winter. Edwin Muir. OxBTC

Scots in Berwick (1296), The. *Unknown.* OxBM

Scots, wha hae wi' Wallace bled. Bannockburn [*or* Robert Bruce's March to Bannockburn]. Burns. BTTM; NOBE

Scottes out of Berwik and of Abirdene. Halidon Hill. Laurence Minot. OxBM

Scottsboro. *Unknown.* InPK

Scottsboro, Too, Is Worth Its Song. Countee Cullen. PoBA

Scourge of Villainy, The, *sels.* John Marston. TVS Cynic Satyre, A, VII. "In serious jest and jesting seriousness," Proemium, Bk. III. Inamorato Curio, VIII.

Scrape no more your hairless chins. Advice to the Old Beaux. Sir Charles Sedley. SCP-2

Scrawny yank of kid, A. The Evening Gown. Karen Swenson. WBN

Screaming Tarn. Robert Bridges. PoTa

Screendoor whines, clacks, The. Night on Hatchet Cove. Denise Levertov. PiAm; Psy

Scrubbed pink/ They look the most naked of animals. Pigs. John Cotton. BoAnP

Scrunched down in the seats. Winter. D. W. Donzella. FAF

Scrutiny [*or* Scrutinie], The. Richard Lovelace. BoLoP; GBL; LoAs

Scylla and Charybdis. Thomas Kinsella. OxBTC

Sea and the Hills, The. Kipling. OBP

Sea and the Mirror, *sel.* W. H. Auden.
Song of the Master and Boatswain. BoLoP

Sea at evening moves across the sand, The. Soldiers bathing. F. T. Prince. OxBTC

Sea Birds, The. Van K. Brock. NVAP

Sea Boy on the Giddy Mast, A. John Clare. PPP

Sea Calm. Langston Hughes. CaYB

Sea Change. John Masefield. PoTa

Sea cries wih its meaningless voice, The. Pibroch. Ted Hughes. TwMBP

Sea-Fever. John Masefield. IPWM; OxBTC; SFF

Seagull, The. Mary Howitt. OxBChV

Sea-Gull, The. Ogden Nash. SoSe

Sea-Gull, The. *Unknown.* GBP

Seagulls. Robert Francis. RFM

Seagulls inland, The. The Natural Order of Things. Harley Elliott. NeAC

Sea-Hawk. Richard Eberhart. BoAnP

Sea is calm tonight, The. Dover Beach. Matthew Arnold. AnMo; Epi; GrRo; HeIP; InPK; InPS; IPWM; MAT; NOBE; OBP; PAIC; PBMP; PFD; PPoD; PPoe; PPP; Prf; SFF; SoSe; VoPo

Sea is enormous, but calm with evening, The. Whale at twilight. Elizabeth J. Coatsworth. BoAnP

Sea is obsidian, The. Fire Island. Rita Mae Brown. IHMS

Sea laying it down, the sea saying it, The. The Wheel. Rosalie Moore. RiTi

Sea Legs. Susan Feldman. AmPA

Sea Love. Charlotte Mew. OxBTC

Sea Lullaby. Elinor Wylie. PBMP

Sea of stretch'd ground-swells. Walt Whitman. *Fr.* Song of Myself, XXII. GrRo

Sea Otter, Dream Poem to My Mother. Katherine Doak. NPW

Sea Poppies. Hilda Doolittle ("H.D."). PiAm

Sea-preserved, heaped with sea-spoils. Picture of a Nativity. Geoffrey Hill. NoAM

Sea-Ritual, The. George Darley. Syren Songs, V. BIrV

Sea Rose. Hilda Doolittle ("H.D."). NoAM

Sea runs back against itself, The. Winter Seascape. John Betjeman. SS

Sea Shanty. Clifford Dyment. POL

Sea Shell. Amy Lowell. LCL

Sea-Shell Murmurs. Eugene Lee-Hamilton. SoSe

Sea-Sonnet. V. Sackville-West. SBG

Sea Surface Full of clouds. Wallace Stevens. VGW

Sea-Turtle and the Shark, The. Melvin B. Tolson. *Fr.* Harlem Gallery. PoBA

Sea Variations. R. A. Simpson. CAAP

Sea-Voyage from Tenby to Bristol, A. Katherine Philips. SBG; WPE

Sea Waves are green and wet. Sand Dunes. Robert Frost. RFM

Seafarer. Archibald MacLeish. NoAM

Seafarer, The. Earl of Surrey. *See* Complaint of the Absence of Her Lover. . .

Seafarer, The ("May I for my own self song's truth reckon"). *Unknown, tr. fr. Anglo-Saxon by* Ezra Pound. HeIP

Seal. William Jay Smith. RFM

Seal in the Lowry Park Zoo, The. Richard Mathews. AATT

Sealchie Song. *Unknown.* PeBB

Seals. David R. Slavitt. CoPAm

Sean the hunchback, sadly. Beyond the Liss. John Montague. TwMBP

Search. Elisavietta Ritchie. AATT

Searching for souvenirs among some rubble. Post-Mortem, A. Siegfried Sassoon. PBMP

Searching for the Desert Blues. *Unknown.* BluL

Seas are quiet when the winds give o'er, The. Old Age. Edmund Waller. *Fr.* Of the Last Verses in the Book. NOBE

Seascape. Elizabeth Bishop. PPP

Seascape. Francis Brett Young. OxBTC

Seaside, The. Charles Tennyson Turner. VPC

Seaside Golf. John Betjeman. SPo

Season of mists and mellow fruitfulness. To Autumn. Keats. AnMo; Epi; FSFS; IPWM; MBPR; NOBE; OBP; PBMP; PPoD; PPoe; PPP; Prf; SoSe; WIF

Seasonal Phenomenon. Richard Armour. BBGO

Seasons, The, *sels.* James Thomson.
  Autumn.
    Autumnal Moon, The. NOBE
  Hymn on the Seasons, A. LAuP
  Spring. LAuP
    Spring Flowers. NOBE
  Winter.
    Winter Night, A. NOBE

Seasons, The. *Unknown.* ECBV

Seat Was Up, The. Judith McCombs. WBN

Seated on a metal folding chair. Dtah Dtah. David Kherdian. SA

Seated statue of himself he seems, A. Farm Boy after Summer. Robert Francis. NCSH

Seaweeds. Sandra McPherson. AmPA

Second Anniversary, The. John Donne. *See* Of the Progress of the Soul.

Second class is the second grade, The. Primary Lesson: The Second Class Citizens. Sun-Ra. PoBA

Second Coming, The. Dannie Abse. NoAM

Second Coming, The. Carl Clark. JB

Second Coming, The. W. B. Yeats. AnMo; BIrV; GrRo; HeIP; InPK; InPS; IPWM; MAT; NoAM; NOBE; OBP; OxBTC; PBMP; PPoD; PPoe; PPP; PSN; TCP; VoPo; WIF, 2 *versions*

Second-fated, The. Robert Graves. NoAM

Second Fig. Edna St. Vincent Millay. TH

Second Glance at a Jaguar. Ted Hughes. NoAM

Second-hand sights, like crumpled. Newark, for Now (68). Carolyn M. Rodgers. PoBA

Second Honeymoon. *Unknown, tr. fr. Irish by* Augustus Young. BIrV

Second Hymn to Lenin. "Hugh MacDiarmid." TwMBP

Second man I love, The. Spring. Carole Gregory Clemmons. PoBA

Second Night in N.Y.C. after 3 Years. Gregory Corso. BuTh

Second Psalm: The Signals. W. S. Merwin. CAAP

Second Sapphic Fragment/ Fainetai Moi. Sappho, *tr. fr. Greek by* Harvey Bialy. MIT

Second Sermon on the Warpland, The. Gwendolyn Brooks. BPo; NOBA; PoBA

Second Shaman Song. Gary Snyder. Myths and Texts: Burning, I. NOBA
  ("Squat in swamp meadows.") Epi

Second Skins—A Peyote Song. Joseph Bruchac. CDW

Secrecy. Samuel Daniel. *Fr.* Hymen's Triumph. OLR

Secret, The. John Clare. GBL

Secret, The. Robert P. Tristram Coffin. FSFS

Secret, The. Denise Levertov. AnMo; PBMP; Psy; SFF

Secret, The ("Hark, Celia, hark!). *Unknown.* SCP-2

Secret, The ("We have a secret, just we three"). *Unknown.* ECBV

Secret is a secret, any size, A. The Secret. Robert P. Tristram Coffin. FSFS

Secret love or two, I must confesse, A. Thomas Campion. AAS

Secret of these hills was stone, and cottages, The.  The Pylons.
  Stephen Spender.  LP; NoAM

Secret People, The.  G. K. Chesterton.  OxBTC

Secret Sits, The.  Robert Frost.  InPK; TH

Secret they are, sealed, annealed, and brainless.  Oystering.
  Richard Howard.  NoAM

Secretaries drive by the factory, The.  Night Shift at the Plating
  Division of Keeler Brass.  James B. Allen.  HeS

Secretary.  Ted Hughes.  InPK; SFF

Secretary, The.  Peter Redgrove.  OxBTC

Secrets of the Earth, The.  Blake.  NOBE

Secular Elegies, sel.  George Barker.
  "Satan is on your tongue, sweet singer, with," III  PIAC

Secular Masque, The.  Dryden.  OBP; PAIC
  *Sels.*
  All, All of a Piece.  InPS
  "Cronos, Cronos, mend thy pace."  SCP-1
  "With horns and with hounds I waken the day."  NOBE

Sedna.  Lyn Lifshin.  MMD

Seduced Girl.  Hedylos, *tr. fr. Greek by* Louis Untermeyer.
  BoLoP

Seduction.  Nikki Giovanni.  NMM; RiTi

Seduction, The.  Suzanne Berger Rioff.  NMM

Seduction of Juan, The.  Byron.  *Fr.* Don Juan.  OBP

See/ it was like this when.  Lawrence Ferlinghetti.  *Fr.* A Coney
  Island of the Mind.  CoPAm

See a pin and pick it up.  *Unknown.*  MG

See an old unhappy bull.  The Bull.  Ralph Hodgson.  OxBTC

See here the diving beetle is split.  Creatures.  Maxine W.
  Kumin.  BoAnP

"See, here's the workbox, little wife."  The Workbox.  Thomas
  Hardy.  InPK

See how he dives.  Seal.  William Jay Smith.  RFM

See how like twilight slumber falls.  Charles Cotton.  SCP-2

See how the orient dew.  On a Drop of Dew.  Andrew Marvell.
  AnMo; BoReV; MetP; PAIC

See how the willing earth gave way.  The Fall.  Edmund Waller.
  SCP-2

See, saw, Margery Daw,/ Johnny shall have a new master.
  Mother Goose.  MG

See, saw, Margery Daw/ Sold her bed and lay upon straw.
  *Unknown.*  MG

See-saw sacradown,/ which is the way to London town?  Mother
  Goose.  MG

Seesaw, sacradown, sacradown.  To Boston Town.  *Unknown.*
  ECBV

See, see the mighty hunter, fiercely bland.  For the Opening of the
  Hunting Season.  Morris Bishop.  BoAnP; SPo

See that brave and trembling motorman.  The Dying Mine
  Brakeman.  Orville Jenks.  AmFP

See that [or the] building which, when my mistress living.  A
  Well-Wishing to a Place of Pleasure.  *Unknown.*  GBL; SCP-
  2

See the chariot at hand here of Love.  The Triumph of Charis.
  Ben Jonson.  *Fr.* A Celebration of Charis.  InPS; LoAs;
  NOBE

See the fountain opened wide.  Zion's Sons and Daughters.
  *Unknown.*  AmFP

See the kitten on the wall.  Wordsworth.  *Fr.* The Kitten and
  Falling Leaves.  PCat

See the smoking bowl before us!  Burns.  *Fr.* The Jolly Beggars.
  OBP

See there the taper's dim and doleful light.  Verses on the Snuff of
  a Candle, Made in Sickness.  Anne Wharton.  SCP-2

See, they return; ah, see the tentative.  The Return.  Ezra Pound.
  NoAM; NOBA; PPoe; PSN; VGW

See this air, how empty it is of angels.  Five for the Grace of
  Man.  Winfield Towley Scott.  VGW

See what delights in sylvan scenes appear!  Sylvan Delights.
  Pope.  *Fr.* Pastorals: Summer.  NOBE

See where 'tis fallen, among a ring of boys.  The Boys and the
  Bubble.  Samuel Wesley.  SCP-2

See, whilst thou weep'st, fair Cloe, see.  To Cloe Weeping.
  Matthew Prior.  PAIC

See with what simplicity.  The Picture of Little T. C. in a
  Prospect of Flowers.  Andrew Marvell.  NOBE; PPP

See you that beauteous queen, which no age tames?  To Etesia
  Looking from Her Casement at the Full Moon.  Henry
  Vaughan.  Moon

See you the ferny ride that steals.  Punk's Song.  Kipling.  *Fr.*
  Puck of Pook's Hill.  OxBChV

Seed Journey.  Gregory Corso.  VGW

Seed Leaves.  Richard Wilbur.  NCSH; PiAm

Seed of Nimrod, The.  De Leon Harrison.  PoBA

Seed-potatoes, staring their eyes.  Root-crops.  Derek Bowman.
  MIS

Seeding.  Mary Moore.  NPW

Seedlings in the Mail.  Marge Piercy.  MMD

Seeds.  James Reeves.  ECBV

Seeds in a dry pod, tick, tick, tick.  Petit, the Poet.  Edgar Lee
  Masters.  *Fr.* Spoon River Anthology.  InPK; NoAM;
  NOBA

Seeds of Love, The.  *Unknown, at. to* Mrs. Fleetwood Habergham.
  AIW; GBP, *longer version*

Seed-Time.  George Meredith.  FSFS

Seedy Henry rose up shy in de world.  John Berryman.  *Fr.*
  Dream Songs.  PiAm

Seeing me weary.  Back to Africa.  Erica Jong.  RiTi

Seeing the Elephant.  *Unknown.*  AIW

Seeing the snowman standing all alone.  Boy at the Window.
  Richard Wilbur.  TH

Seeing you/ in the laundromat.  Thinking Twice in the
  Laundromat.  Harley Elliott.  NeAC

Seek love/ Without the light-low night.  Love at Stress-Point.
  Ruthe T. Spinnanger.  AATT

Seek not man to please, for that.  Isabella Whitney.  *Fr.* A Sweet
  Nosegay, or Pleasant Posy.  WPE

Seek out reality, leave things that seem.  W. B. Yeats.  *Fr.*
  Vacillation.  BoReV

Seek the Lord!  Thomas Campion.  BoReV

Seek True Religion!  John Donne.  *Fr.* Satires, III.  BoReV;
  NOBE

Seeking necessity, he only found.  Live Man's Epitaph.  Francis
  Hope.  BuTh

Seeking the words.  Poem for Jan.  Joseph Bruchac.  CDW

Seems like a long time.  The Partial Explanation.  Charles Simic.
  FiCP

Seen through the Trees behind Which You're Walking.  Brian
  Patten.  BuTh

Self.  Norman Henry Pritchard, II.  PoBA

Self-Dependence.  Matthew Arnold.  IPWM; PBMP

Self Dirge.  Wendy Rose.  CDW

Self-Hatred of Don L. Lee, The.  Don L. Lee.  BPo

Self-Knowledge.  Samuel Taylor Coleridge.  MBPR

Self-Pity.  D. H. Lawrence.  BoAnP; OxBTC

Self-Unseeing, The.  Thomas Hardy.  NOBE

Selfsame surface that billowed once with, The.  Skin Flick.  Fred
  Chappell.  PPoD

Semblables, The.  William Carlos Williams.  NOBA

Semele Recycled.  Carolyn Kizer.  WBN

Semele to Jupiter.  Congreve.  LoAs
  (Song: "With my frailty don't upbraid me.")  POL

Semen. Coleman Barks. *Fr.* Body Poems. NVAP

Semi-Private Room. Alden Nowlan. NeAC

Semi-Revolution, A. Robert Frost. WIF

Seminar. Erica Jong. RiTi

Send cards send. Notes on a Long Evening. David Phillips. NeAC

Send home my long-strayed eyes to me. The Message. John Donne. PAIC

Send me no flowers, for they will die before they leave America. Junglegrave. S. E. Anderson. PoBA

Send-off, The. Wilfred Owen. InPS; OxBTC; PSN; SoSe

Send soldiers again to kill you, García. Lines to García Lorca. LeRoi Jones. TCP

Senile. Pat Folk. NowV

Senlin, Biography, *sel.* Conrad Aiken.
    "It is morning, Senlin says, and in the morning," II, ii. NoAM (Morning Song.) SoSe

Señor Torres. Luis Omar Salinas. SA

Sense of Coolness, A. Quincy Troupe. PoBA

Sense of Property, A. Anthony Thwaite. MPo

Sense of the Sleight-of-hand Man, The. Wallace Stevens. NOBA

Senseless school, where we must give, A. A Young Man's Epigram on Existence. Thomas Hardy. NoAM

Sensible People. James Stephens. RAE

Sensitive Plant, The. Shelley. MBPR

Sensuous Latin poet, now I will go off with a thermos, A. Lynn Strongin. *Fr.* First Aspen. IHMS; RiTi

Sentence for Konarak. John Montague. TwMBP

Sentimental Ode. Tom Buchan. MIS

Sentry, The. Alun Lewis. PSN

Sepal, petal, and a thorn, A. Emily Dickinson. PiAm

Separate place between the thought and felt, A. The Corridor. Thom Gunn. NowV; PPP

Separate Way, *sel.* Charles Reznikoff.
    Kaddish: "Upon Israel and upon the rabbis." SA

Separated Lovers. *Unknown.* OxBM

Separation. Samuel Taylor Coleridge. MBPR

Separation. Duane Niatum. VW

Separation. Gary Sange. NVAP

Sephestia's Song to Her Childe. Robert Greene. *Fr.* Menaphon. OBP
    (Sephestia's Lullaby.) NOBE

September. Mary Elizabeth Coleridge. FSFS

September. Ted Hughes. BoLoP; OLR

September. W. D. Snodgrass. PSN

September, 1819. Wordsworth. MBPR

September 1802. Near Dover. Wordsworth. MBPR

September 1, 1802. Wordsworth. MBPR

September 1957 summoned by my vision-agent. Vision of Rotterdam. Gregory Corso. NoAM

September 1913. W. B. Yeats. NoAM; PPoe

September 7. Ellen Bass. NMM

September, the First Day of School. Howard Nemerov. PPoD

September 30. Dick Lourie. NeAC

September twenty-second, Sir: today. After th Surprising Conversions. Robert Lowell. ConAP; NoAM; PAIC; PPP

September Valentine. Frank Sullivan. SPo

September was when it began. The Coming of the Plague. Weldon Kees. VGW

Sepulchre. George Herbert. SCP-1

Sequel to the Purple Cow. Gelett Burgess. FaBoCo

Sequence. James Harrison. CoPAm

Sequence for a Young Widow Passing. Deborah Munro. IHMS

Sequence of Women, A. James Harrison. CoPAm

Seravazza. Hoyt W. Fuller. PoBA

Serenade: "Stars of the summer night." Longfellow. *Fr.* The Spainish Student, I, iii. PAIC

Serenade: "Thou moon, like a white Christus hanging." Kenneth Slessor. POL

Serenade: "Tin-type tune the locusts make, The." Dorothy Donnelly. NCSH

Serenade of a Loyal Martyr. George Darley. NOBE

Serene Art. Lewis Warsh. MIT

Serengeti Sunset. Andrew Oerke. POL

Serenity in Stones, The. Simon J. Ortiz. CDW

Sgt. stands so fluently in leather, The. On a Photo of Sgt. Ciardi a Year Later. John Ciardi. CoPAm

Sergeant's Weedin', The. Kipling. OxBTC

Sermon on Swift, A. Austin Clarke. BIrV

Sermon on the Warpland, The. Gwendolyn Brooks. BPo; NOBA; PoBA

Sermonette. Ishmael Reed. PoBA

Serpent, The. Theodore Roethke. ECBV

Serpent is shut out from paradise, The. To Edward Williams. Shelley. MBPR

Serpent Muses, The. Peggy Henderson. NMM

Servant-girl's Holiday, A. *Unknown.* OxBM

Servant Man, The. *Unknown.* AmFP

Servant to Servants, A. Robert Frost. Epi

Service is joy, to see or swing. Allow. Tennis. Margaret Avison. NoAM

Service Is No Heritage. *Unknown.* OxBM

Serving-Men's Song, A. John Lyly. *Fr.* Alexander and Campaspe, I, iii. NOBE

Sestina. Judith Kroll. AmPA

Sestina: Altaforte. Ezra Pound. NOBA

Sestina: "Farewell, Oh sun, Arcadia's clearest light." Sir Philip Sidney. *Fr.* Arcadia. PAIC

Sestina from the Home Gardener. Diane Wakoski. NoAM

Sestina in a Cantina. Malcolm Lowry. PAIC

Sestina of the Lady Pietra degli Scrovigni. Dante, *tr. fr. Italian by* Dante Gabriel Rossetti. LoAs

Sestina of the Tramp-Royal. Kipling. PAIC

Set me whereas the sun doth parch the green. A Vow to Love Faithfully, Howsoever He Be Rewarded. Petrarch, *tr. by the* Earl of Surrey. Sonnets to Laura: To Laura in Life, CXIII. AAS; PAIC

Set of phrases learnt by rote, A. The Furniture of a Woman's Mind. Swift. PPoe

Set out at any hour, from behind. L'Education Sentimentale. David Malouf. CAAP

Set the foot down with distrust upon the crust of the world—it is thin. Underground System. Edna St. Vincent Millay. SBG

Set where the upper streams of Simois flow. Palladium. Matthew Arnold. PPP

Seth compton died, and by that alone. Rhoda Pitkin. Edgar Lee Masters. *Fr.* The New Spoon River. NoAM

Seth Dismounts Thrice. Marnie Walsh. VW

Setting/ Slow Drag. Carolyn M. Rodgers. JB

Setting, The/ had no special theme. Slow Riff for Billy. James Cunningham. JB

Setting of the Moon, The. Giacomo Leopardi, *tr. fr. Italian by* John Heath-Stubbs. Moon

Settling Some Old Football Scores. Morris Bishop. SPo

Seumas Beg. James Stephens. OxBTC

Seven. Nicanor Parra, *tr. fr. Spanish by* Miller Williams. POL

Seven Black Friars sitting back to back. Blackfriars. Eleanor Farjeon. OxBChV

Seven candles in silver sticks. Planter. Richard Murphy. *Fr.* The Battle of Aughrim. BIrV

Seven dog-days we let pass. Queens. J. M. Synge. GBL

Seven, frog-legged among the boys. Linda. John Stone. CoPAm

Seven Mexican Children. Tom Schmidt. NeAC

Seven Rainy Months. William Plomer. OxBTC

Seven Seals. D. H. Lawrence. LoAs

Seven Sins, The. *Unknown.* OxBM

Seven Sister Blues. *Unknown.* BluL

Seven sweet singing birds up in a tree. The Dream of a Girl Who Lived at Sevenoaks. William Brighty Rands. OxBChV

Seven Virgins, The. *Unknown.* GBP; PeBB

Seven-Year Body Cycle, The: To My Cells Replacing Themselves for the Fourth Time. David Steingass. NVAP

Seventeen Warnings in Search of a Feminist Poem. Erica Jong. AmPA; WBN
(Sixteen Warnings in Search of a Feminist Poem.) NVAP

Seventeen years ago you said. A Quoi Bon Dire. Charlotte Mew. OxBTC

Seventh Georgic. George Economou. POL

Seventh Olympic Hymn. Pindar, *tr. by* Robin Blaser. *Fr.* Odes. Epi

Seventh robin, The. Poem Without a Metaphor. David Allan Evans. NVAP

Seventh Son. Ed Roberson. PoBA

Seventy. Margaret Reynolds. MIS

74th Street. Myra Cohn Livingston. CTBA

Seventy Six Trombones, *with music.* Meredith Wilson. BLSo

Several Questions Answered, *sels.* Blake.
Ancient Proverb, A. MBPR
Eternity ("He who binds [*or* bends] to himself a joy"). BoReV; LAuP; MBPR; NOBE; WIF
Question Answer'd, The. GBL
("What is it men in women do require?") MBPR

Severed at the hip, Howard. He's Known His Lesson for Years. R. P. Kingston. NVAP

Severed Selves. Dante Gabriel Rossetti. The House of Life, XL. BoLoP; VPC

Sevier County Runaway, The. Besmilr Brigham. Psy

Sex and the Over Forties. Peter Porter. CAAP

Sex, as they harshly call it. Two Songs. Adrienne Rich. NOBA; Psy

Sex fingers toes. Dear John, Dear Coltrane. Michael S. Harper. AmPA; NVAP

Sex Play in Four Acts. Doug Fetherling. NeAC

Sext. W. H. Auden. *Fr.* Horae Canonica. TCP

Sexton stood one Sabbath eve, A. Those Wedding Bells Shall Not Ring Out! Monroe H. Rosenfeld. FSN

Seymour and Chantelle or Un Peu de Vice. Stevie Smith. SBG

Seynt Stevene was a clerk. *See* Saint Steven was a clerk. . .

Shack and a few trees, The. After Work. Gary Snyder. CoPAm

Shacked Up at the Ritz. Doug Fetherling. NeAC

Shakley-Hay. *Unknown.* GBP

Shad-Blow Tree, The. Louise Glück. NVAP

Shades of Callimachus, Coan ghosts of Philetas. Ezra Pound. *Fr.* Homage to Sextus Propertius. NaAM; NOBA

Shades of night were falling fast, The. A. E. Housman. SpRo

Shades of night were falling fast, The. Excelsior. Longfellow. SpRo

Shadow, The. Ben Jonson. *See* That Women Are but Men's Shadows.

Shadow/ flutters/ through/ the forest, A. Family Game. Morton Marcus. NVAP

Shadow, The/ ran before it lengthening. Up at La Serra. Charles Tomlinson. TwMBP

Shadow and Shade. Allen Tate. VGW

Shadow is floating through the moonlight, A. The Bird of Night. Randall Jarrell. CoPAm; NCSH; RFM; TSWA

Shadow of a Branch, The. Edith Marcombe Shiffert. WPE

Shadow of Cain, The. Edith Sitwell. OxBTC

Shadow of the little fishing launch, The. The Parrot Fish. James Merrill. NOBA

Shadow of the Venetian blind on the painted wall. Forties Flick. John Ashbery. CAAP

Shadow streamed into the wall, The. Shadow and Shade. Allen Tate. VGW

Shadowboxing. James Tate. CAAP

Shadows. Samuel Daniel *Fr.* Tethys' Festival. NOBE

Shadows. D. H. Lawrence. BoReV; OxBTC

Shadows, The. Iain Crichton Smith. SLP

Shadows in the Water. Thomas Traherne. BoReV; MetP; SCP-2

Shadows of night were a-comin' down swift, The. Higher. *Unknown.* SpRo

Shadows, shadows,/ Hug me round. Escape. Georgia Douglas Johnson. PoBA

Shadow's Song, The. Yvor Winters. POL

Shadowy daughter of Urthona stood before red orc, The. America a Prophecy. Blake. MBPR

Shadwell Anatomized. Dryden. *Fr.* MacFlecknoe. OBP

Shadwell and Settle are both fools to Bays. *At. to* Thomas Shadwell. *Fr.* The Tory Poets: a Satire. SCP-2

Shag, The. Christopher Isherwood. *See* Common Cormorant, The.

Shake Keane, Trumpet. John Smith. *Fr.* Jazz for Five. MPo

Shaken already, I know. Goodbye, Sally. James Simmons. BIrV

Shakespeare would have savored his coarse, irate. "How Long Hast Thou Been a Gravemaker?" David Perkins. NCSH

"Shakin like the." On a Country Road. Harley Elliot. NeAC

Shaking in White streetlight in. Our Vegetable Love Shall Grow. Elaine Feinstein. POL

Shall I abide this jesting? *Unknown.* GBL

Shall I connect for this world's eyes. The Dumb World. W. H. Davies. BoAnP

Shall I come, sweet love, to thee. A Lover's Plea. Thomas Campion. AAS; GBL; LoAs; NOBE

Shall I campare thee to a summer's day? Sonnets, XVIII. Shakespeare. BoLoP; GBL; HeIP; InPK; InPS; IPWM; MAT; NOBE; OLR; PAIC; PBMP; PPoe

Shall I dwell in my shell? The Snail's Monologue. Christian Morgenstern, *tr. by* Max Knight. BoAnP

Shall I strew on thee rose or rue or laurel. Ave atque Vale. Swinburne. NOBE

Shall I then hope when faith is fled? Thomas Campion. AAS

Shall I thus ever long, and be no whit the near. The Lady Prayeth the Return of Her Lover Abiding on the Seas. *Unknown.* GBL

Shall I Wasting in Despair. George Wither. *Fr.* Fair Vitue. PAIC; SS
(Lover's Resolution, A.) BoLoP; NOBE

Shall we assult the pain? The Hour of the Parting. John Shaw Neilson. MAuV

Shall We Gather at the River? Robert Lowry. *See* Beautiful River.

Shall we go dance the hay? The hay? A Report Song in a Dream [*or* Wooing in a Dream]. Nicholas Breton. GBL; NOBE

Shall we have a family born. For Walter Lowenfels. Wendy Rose. CDW

Shall we sit here some more. August at the Lake. David Young. AmPA

Shalom. Denise Levertov. NoAM

Shaman Songs 12. Gene Fowler. MIT

Shame. Richard Wilbur. ConAP; PPoD

Shan Van Vocht, The. *Unknown.* BTTM; GBP

Shancoduff. Patrick Kavanagh. BIrV

Shandon Bells, The. Francis Sylvester Mahony. PFIr

Shane O'Neill's Cairn. Robinson Jeffers. NoAM; NOBA

Shaneen and Maurya Prendergast. Patch-Shaneen. J. M. Synge. PFIr

Shanty Boys and the Pine, The. *Unknown.* AmFP

Shanty Man's Life, A. *Unknown.* AmFP

Shapcot, to thee the fairy state. Oberon's Feast. Robert Herrick. SCP-1

Shape of Death, The. May Swenson. LoAs

Shapes and Signs. James Clarence Mangan. PFIr

Shark, The. John Ciardi. MiP

Shark flopped on the porch, The. The Shark's Parlor. James Dickey. MiP

Sharks. Dick Lourie. NeAC

Sharks in Shallow Water. Fred Levinson. AmPA

Shark's Parlor, The. James Dickey. MiP

Sharon Will Be No/ Where on Nobody's Best-Selling List. Sharon Scott. JB

Shattered water made a misty din, The. Once by the Pacific. Robert Frost. HeIP; NOBA; PiAm; VGW

Shawano Lake, Wisconsin. Robert Gillespie. NVAP

Shazam. R. P. Dickey. HeS

She. Vicente Huidobro, *tr. fr. Spanish by* Dudley Fitts. LoAs

She. Theodore Roethke. BoLoP

She. Richard Wilbur. AnMo; ConAP

She asked me twice. Pity. William Mills. CoPAm

She Being Brand. E. E. Cummings. NOBA; SFF

She brings that breath, and music too. The Visitor. W. H. Davies. GBL

She came from country closed. Decorating Problem. Sonya Dorman. RiTi

She cannot see. Nursing Home. Linda Parker-Silverman. HeS

She clasps a jewel. Words. David Phillips. NeAC

She climbed the ladder looking over the wall at the party. Jim Harrison. *Fr.* Ghazals. InPS

She coils her body around me. Love Poem. Howard Schwartz. HeS

She comes on at night. From St. Luke's Hospital. Madeleine L'Engle. CTBA

She Contrasts with Herself Hippolyta. Hilda Doolittle ("H.D."). SBG

She danced, near nude, to tom-tom beat. Zalka Peetruza. Ray Garfield Dandridge. PoBA

She didn't know it yet. Poem. Diane Kruchkow. FAF

She didn't know she was beautiful. On Getting a Natural. Dudley Randall. PoBA

She died in June, while yet the woodbine sprays. Mary—A Reminiscence. Charles Tennyson Turner. VPC

She does not know. No Images. Waring Cuney. MAT

She does not talk. Floor: Five. Stephen Vincent. *Fr.* Elevator Landscapes. NeAC

She Doesn't Want to Bring the Tides in Any More. Ruth Whitman. RiTi

She doesn't wear/ costume jewelry. Gwendolyn Brooks. Don L. Lee. NoAM

She dreams of the desert again. Magdalene, Afterward. Karen Whitehill. NPW

She drew back; he was calm. The Subverted Flower. Robert Frost. NoAM; NOBA

She Dwelt among the Untrodden Way. Wordsworth. AnMo; BoLoP; HeIP; MBPR; PBMP; PPP; SpRo; WIF, 2 *versions*

She Employed the Familiar "Tu" Form. Doug Fetherling. NeAC

She enters the bus demurely. Puerto Ricans in New York, I. Charles Reznikoff. CTBA

She even thinks that up in heaven. For a Lady I Know. Countee Cullen. HeIP; InPK; WIF

She fears him, and will always ask. Eros Turannos. E. A. Robinson. GBL; IPWM; NoAM; NOBA; PiAm; PPoe

She finds grief, her meat. Hyena. Carol Muske. AmPA

She found herself 7 no less. Snow White. Robert Gillespie. NVAP

She goes but softly, but she goeth sure. Upon the Snail [or a Snail]. Bunyan. OxBChV; SCP-2

She grew from the crowd. A Former Love. Giles Gordon. SLP

She grew up in bedeviled southern wilderness. The Ballad of Sue Ellen Westerfield. Robert Hayden. NoAM

She had a little time to think. Leda Reconsidered. Mona Van Duyn. NMM

She had a name among the children. A Cat. Edward Thomas. BoAnP

She had a way with comedy and men. Marilyn Monroe. Paul Ramsey. PPoD

She had thought the studio would keep itself. Living in Sin. Adrienne Rich. IHMS; RiTi

She has a husband, he a wife. Modern Love. J. V. Cunningham. POL

She has finished and sealed the letter. Parting, without a Sequel. John Crowe Ransom. SoSe

She has the immaculate look of the new. Chinese Baby Asleep. Dorothy Donnelly. NCSH

She hears me strike the board and say. Father and Child. W. B. Yeats. RRA; TCP

She hovered hooded, blue-eyed. Catechism, 1958. W. M. Ransom. CDW

She Hugged Me and Kissed Me. *Unknown.* BPo

She hung away her years, her eyes grew young. Waiting for the Bus. D. J. Enright. OxBTC

She, in dowdy dress and dumpy. Still Life: Lady with Birds. Quandra Pettyman. PoBA

She in whose lipservice. The Goddess. Denise Levertov. NOBA

She is a weak sister, that ocean. Finding Roots. Judith Minty. HeS

She is all there. For My Lover, Returning to His Wife. Anne Sexton. IHMS; NMM; RiTi; WPE

She is as in a field a silken tent. The Silken Tent. Robert Frost. InPK; NOBA; PAIC; PiAm; PPoD; SoSe; WIF

She Is More To Be Pitied, Than Censured, *with music.* William B. Gray. FSN

She is most fair. The Unknown. Edward Thomas. GBL

She is Queen Nofretete translated into. Nofretete. Felix Pollak. HeS

She is the night: all horror is of her. Christopher Brennan. *Fr.* Lilith. MAuV

She is the one you call sister. The Mirror in Which Two Are Seen As One. Adrienne Rich. RiTi; WBN

She is the woman I follow. Why I Died. Erica Jong. RiTi

She is washed by whit-water, white if she looked up. Fish. Daniel Halpern. AmPA

She kept an antique shop—or it kept her. My Grandmother. Elizabeth Jennings. LP; MPo

She kept her songs, they took so little space. Love Songs in Age. Philip Larkin. PPP; PSN

She lay all naked in her bed. *Unknown.* BoLoP

She lay down beneath a thorn. Fine Flowers in the Valley. *Unknown.* RDB

She lay in her girlish sleep at ninety-six. Castoff Skin. Ruth Whitman. InPK

She left me at the silent time. Lines Written in the Bay of Lerici. Shelley. MBPR

She lies ablow my body's lust and love. Continent o Venus. Alexander Scott. SLP

She looked over his shoulder. The Shield of Achilles. W. H. Auden. AnMo; NOBE; SoSe

She loves, and she confesses too. Honour. Abraham Cowley. BoLoP

She loves the wind. The Old One and the Wind. Clarice Short. IHMS

She made him a roof with her hands. Fourth Psalm: The Cerements. W. S. Merwin. CAAP

She marries him in mid-air. The Flight. Lisel Mueller. RiTi

She May Have Seen Better Days, *with music.* James Thornton. FSN

She Moved through the Fair. Padraic Colum. AIW; BIrV

She moved through the garden in glory, because. Marigold. Richard Garnett. PCat

She never asked to lose innocence. God, Woman, Egg. Helena Minton. FAF

She, of whom the ancients seemed to prophesy. John Donne. *Fr.* An Anatomy of the World: The First Anniversary. SCP-1

She peered through the curtain, and courteous. Gawain and the Temptress. *Unknown, tr. by* Burton Raffel. *Fr.* Sir Gawain and the Green Knight. OBP

She pulled me out the kitchen door. Monkshood. Marie Harris. MMD

She Rebukes Hippolyta. Hilda Doolittle ("H.D."). SBG

She remembers seasons. Poison. Nancy Mairs. NPW

She said, if tomorrow my world were torn in two. The 5:32. Phyllis McGinley. *Fr.* I Know a Village. NMM; WPE

She sang beyond the genius of the sea. The Idea of Order at Key West. Wallace Stevens. AnMo; HeIP; NoAM; NOBA; PiAm; PPoD; PPP

She sat and sang alway. Song. Christina Rossetti. GBL

She sat down below a thorn. The Cruel Mother. *Unknown.* InPK; PeBB

She says how/ is it when you. John Knoepfle. *Fr.* "The Ten-Fifteen Community Poems." MAT

She should have died hereafter. Shakespeare. *Fr.* Macbeth, V, v. SoSe

She sits in the park. Her clothes are out of date. In the Park. Gwen Harwood. MAuV

She speaks always in her own voice. The Portrait. Robert Graves. LoAs; PBMP

She Speaks the Morning's Filigree. Philip Lamantia. VGW

She spoke to me gently with words of sweet meaning. Song. Patrick MacDonogh. PFIr

She staked her feathers—gained an arc. Emily Dickinson. PiAm

She stands/ In the quiet darkness. Troubled Woman. Langston Hughes. CTBA

She stepped two paces forward. She. Vincente Huidobro, *tr. by* Dudley Fitts. LoAs

She stole my pencil-case, red leather. The Thief. Josephine Jacobsen. WPE

She stood breast high amid the corn. Ruth. Thomas Hood. BoLoP; NOBE

She stood hanging wash before sun. Ghetto Lovesong— Migration. Carole Gregory Clemmons. NMM; PoBA

She stood in her snood and arasaid. Love. *Unknown, tr. fr. Gaelic.* SLP

She stoops to Conquer, *sel.* Goldsmith. Song: "Let school-masters puzzle their brain," *fr.* I, ii. BIrV

She suffers like a red stone, small as a carat. Sisters. Sandra McPherson. AmPA

She swam smiling in the river. Waiting to Be Fed. Ray A. Young Bear. CDW

She tells Her Love While Half Asleep. Robert Graves. BoLoP; GBL; NOBE; OxBTC

She that holds me under the laws of love. Sir Arthur Gorges. GBL

She, the sensual creature, the green singer. Slow Dancer That No One Hears but You. Duane Niatum. CDW

She, to Him. Thomas Hardy. OxBTC

She told me. A Hopi Woman Talking. Joy Harjo. SA

She told the story, and the whole world wept. Harriet Beecher Stowe. Paul Laurence Dunbar. AmVN; BPo

She took her name beneath according skies. The Ritual. E. J. Pratt. NoAM

She tosses, one midnight so close. Midwest U. F. O. David Steingass. NVAP

She turned in the high pew, until her sight. A Church Romance. Thomas Hardy. NOBE; OxBTC

She Vowed Him This. William Box BuTh

She Walked Unaware. Patrick MacDonogh. BoLoP; PFIr

She walks a beach assaulted by the sea. Thanksgiving 1963. Philip Booth. IPWM

She walks down the road. Girl with the Green Skit. Dana Naone. CDW

She Walks in Beauty. Byron. BoLoP; HeIP; InPS; IPWN; MBPR; NOBE; PBMP; SLP; WIF

She walks—the lady of my delight. The Shepherdess. Alice Meynell. SBG

She Wandered Through the Garden Fence. Keith Reid. GrRo

She Was a Phantom of Delight. Wordsworth. HeIP; MBPR; PBMP; VoPo

She was all around me. The Blue Wing. Donald Hall. ConAP

She Was Bred in Old Kentucky, *with music.* Harry Braisted. FSN

She was eager to be heard and nibbled on memories. One-Eleven Grape Street. Dan Masterson. CoPAm

She was lyin face down in her face. Song. William Knott. MAT

She was no armored cruiser of twice six thousand tons. The Warship of 1812. *Unknown.* BTTM

She Was Poor But She Was Honest. *Unknown.* FaBoCo; GBP; PeBB

She was so small and pretty. Art's Variety. David McFadden. NeAC

She was urgent to speak of the moon: she offered delight. An Old Woman Speaks of the Moon. Ruth Pitter. WPE

She wears her middle age like a cowled. From a Correct Address in a Suburb of a Major City. Helen Sorrells. WPE

She Wept, She Railed. Stanley Kunitz. VGW

She who has power to call her man. An Unsaid Word. Adrienne Rich. NMM

She who is always in my thoughts perfers. Bhartrihari, *tr. fr. Sanskrit by* John Brough. BoLoP

She who was burned more than half her body. The Praises. Charles Olson. VGW

She wiped his face and brought away. The Sixth Station. Jean Marie Luecke. AATT

She with whom troops of bustuary slaves. *Unknown. Fr.* A Satire Entitled the Witch. SCP-2

She woke up under a loose quilt. The Evacuee. R. S. Thomas. MPo

She wore a new "terra-cotta" dress. A Thunderstorm in Town. Thomas Hardy. BoLoP; GBL

She wouldn't like Agnes to be. Agnes. Kathleen Fraser. WBN

Sheaves, The. E. A. Robinson. NoAM; NOBA; PiAm

Sheep. W. H. Davies. PoTa; RAE

Sheep, The. Ann *or* Jane Taylor. OxBChV

Sheep-boy whistled loud, and lo, The! Elegiac Verse. Wordsworth. MBPR

Sheep Child, The. James Dickey. CAPP; CoPAm; NoAM; NOBA; Prf

Sheep Fair, A. Thomas Hardy. Prf

Sheep get up and make their many tracks, The. Sheep in Winter. John Clare. BoAnP

Sheep in Fog. Sylvia Plath. PSN

Sheep in Winter. John Clare. BoAnP

Sheep on these hills, The. Judith Serin. NPW

Sheepdog Trials in Hyde Park. C. Day Lewis. NoAM; OxBTC

Sheep's in the meadow, The. Bonny at Morn. *Unknown.* GBP

Sheep-skin and Beeswax. *Unknown.* RAE

Sheet of writing paper, The. The Alchemist. Richard Church. OxBTC

Sheets were frozen hard, and they cut the naked hand, The. Christmas at Sea. Robert Louis Stevenson. PoTa

Sheffield grinder's a terrible blade, The. The Grinders; or, The Saddle on the Right Horse. *Unknown.* GBP

Sheffield 'Prentice, The. *Unknown.* AmFP

Shell, The. George MacBeth. SLP

Shell, The. David McCord. LCL

She'll Be Comin' 'round the Mountain, *with music.* *Unknown.* BLSH; BLSo

Shelter this candle from the wind. To the Wife of a Sick Friend. Edna St. Vincent Millay. SBG

Shelter was possible. Instead. Elements of Night. Arthur Gregor. LoAs

Shelving slimy river Don, The. The River Don. *Unknown.* GBP

Shenandoah, *with music.* *Unknown.* BLSo (Across the Wide Missouri.) BLSH

Shepheard, what's Loue, I pray thee tell? The Shepherd's Description of Love. *At. to* Sir Walter Ralegh. LoAs

Shepheardes Calendar, The, *sels.* Spenser.
  April.
    Lay to Eliza, The. NOBE
  August. PAIC
  June. PAIC
  November. Epi

Shepherd, The. James K. Baxter. ECBV

Shepherd, The. Blake. *Fr.* Songs of Innocence. MBPR

Shepherd Boy Sings in the Valley of Humiliation, The. Bunyan. *Fr.* The Pilgrim's Progress. NOBE

Shepherd on his journey heard when nigh, The. The Fox. John Clare. BoAnP

Shepherd Paris bore the Spartan bride, The. Daphnis. Theocritus, *tr. by* Dryden. *Fr.* Idylls, XXVII. SCP-1

Shepherd shrieves in Egyptian light, De. Pocomania. Derek Walcott. NoAM

Shepherd stands at one end of the arena, A. Sheepdog Trials in Hyde Park. C. Day Lewis. NoAM; OxBTC

Shepherdess. Norman Cameron. Three Love Poems, III. GBL; SLP

Shepherdess, The. Alice Meynell. SBG

Shepherdess' Valentine, *sel.* Francis Andrewes.
  "I bear, in sign of love." OFD

Shepherds all, and maidens fair. John Fletcher. *Fr.* The Faithful Shepherdess, II, i. SCP-2

Shepherd's Calendar, The, *sels.* John Clare.
  February. NOBE
  July.
    "Loud is the summer's busy song." FSFS

Shepherd's daughter watching sheep, A. The Knight and the Shepherd's Daughter. *Unknown.* AmFP

Shepherd's Description of Love, The. *At. to* Sir Walter Ralegh. LoAs

Shepherd's Dochter, The. Douglas Young. SLP

Shepherd's Hut, The. Andrew Young. OxBTC

Shepherds' Hymn, The. Richard Crashaw. *Fr.* In the Holy Nativity of Our Lord God. NOBE
  ("Gloomy night embraced the place.") SCP-1

Shepherd's Sirena, The, *sels.* Michael Drayton. SCP-2
  "Near to the silver Trent."
  "Our mournful Philomel."
  "Verdant meads are seen, The."
  "When she looks out by night."

Shepherd's Tale, The. Raoul Ponchon, *tr. fr. French by* James Kirkup. PoTa

Sheridan's Ride. Thomas Buchanan Read. BTTM

Sherman Cyclone, The. *Unknown.* AmFP

She's a copperheaded waitress. Ella, in a Square Apron, along Highway 80. Judy Grahn. *Fr.* The Common Woman. NMM

She's Gone Blues. *Unknown.* BluL

She' gone. She was my love, my moon or more. Complaint. James Wright. CoPAm; NOBA; VGW

She's Leaving Home. John Lennon *and* Paul McCartney. RRA

She's little and she's low she's right down on the ground. She's Mine. *Unknown.* BluL

She's taen her petticoat by the band. Tam Lin. *Unknown.* AIW

Shetland funeral. James Rankin. MIS

Shew! Fly, Don't Bother Me, *with music.* *At. to* Billy Reeves *and to* T. Brigham Bishop. PSon

Shield of Achilles, The. W. H. Auden. AnMo; NOBE; SoSe

Shield of War, The. Thomas Sackville. *Fr.* Mirror for Magistrates. NOBE

Shilling life will give you all the facts, A. Who's Who. W. H. Auden. BBGO; NoAM

Shiloh; a Requiem. Herman Melville. AmVN; NOBA

Shine on, Harvest Moon, *with music.* Nora Bayes *and* Jack Norworth. BLSH

Shine, Perishing Republic. Robinson Jeffers. IPWM; MAT; NoAM; NOBA; PiAm; PPoD; VGW; VoPo; WIF

Shining children in the fog. The Swimming Lesson. Robert Hershon. NeAC

Shiny record albums scattered over. As You Leave Me. Etheridge Knight. ConAP

Ship, The. J. F. Hendry. SLP

Ship of Death, The. D. H. Lawrence. NoAM

Shipwreck. George Mackay Brown. LP

Shires, The. *Unknown.* OxBM

Shirley 4 Years Later. Alta. MMD

Shirley standing on the table. Stockton State Mental Hospital 1962. Alta. MMD

Shirt, The. Jon Silkin. NoAM

Shiva. Robinson Jeffers. NoAM; NOBA

Shivers. Aileen Fisher. CaYB

Shlup, shlup, the dog. Denise Levertov. *Fr.* Six Variations. HeIP; InPK

Shoes instead of slippers down the stairs. The Couple Upstairs. Hugo Williams. POL

Shon a Morgan. *Unknown.* GBP

Shoofly, The. Felix O'Hare. AmFP

Shooting at the Moon. Kim Yo-sop, *tr. by* Ko Won. Moon

Shooting Song, A. William Brighty Rands. OxBChV

Shopping for Meat in Winter. Oscar Williams. MiP

Shore Leave Lorry. Roy Fuller. NoAM

Shore of Life, The. Robert Fitzgerald. VGW

Shores   Sorley MacLean, *tr. fr. Gaelic by* Iain Crichton Smith. SLP

Short cut, A.   Bruce Holsapple.   FAF

Short cut home lay through the cemetery, The.   The Mistress. Joan Barton.   OxBTC

Short Haired Woman.   *Unknown.*   BluL

Short Night, The.   Buson, *tr. fr. Japanese by* Harold G. Henderson.   Moon

Short Pastoral.   Leonard E. Nathan.   MIT

Short Song of Congratulation, A.   Samuel Johnson.   InPK; InPS; LAuP; NOBE

Short Subjects.   Carolyn Stoloff.   RiTi

Short'nin' Bread, *with music. Unknown.*   BLSo

Shot at Random, A.   D. B. Wyndham Lewis.   FaBoCo

Shot gold, maroon and violet, dazzling silver, emerald, fawn.   A Prairie Sunset.   Walt Whitman.   PiAm

Shot with a Hot Rot Gun.   Michael Goode.   NowV

Should all the world so wide to atoms fall.   Our Insufficiency to Praise God Suitably, for His Mercy.   Edward Taylor.   *Fr.* God's Determinations.   PiAm

Should auld acquaintance be forgot.   Auld Lang Syne.   Burns. AKE; BLSH; BLSo; LAuP; NOBE

Should I get married? Should I be good?   Marriage.   Gregory Corso.   CoPAm; InPS; NoAM; PPoD; PPP

Should I say, my people? I turned stone.   Maratea Porto: Saying Goodbye to the Vitolos.   Richard Hugo.   MAT

Should I speak unthinkingly.   At First Sight.   Alastair Reid. SLP

Should no man write, say you, but such as do excel?   That No Man Should Write but Such as do Excel.   George Turberville.   PPoD

Should We Legalize Abortion?   Frank O'Hara.   NoAM

Should you ask me, whence these stories?   The Song of Hiawatha: Introduction.   Longfellow.   NOBA; PiAm

Should you, my lord, while you pursue my song.   Phillis Wheatley.   *Fr.* To the Right Honorable William, Earl of Dartmouth.   BPo

Should you revisit us.   New Approach Needed.   Kingsley Amis. OxBTC

Shout for Joy.   *Unknown.*   AmFP

Shout, Little Lulu.   *Unknown.*   AmFP

Shouting Song.   *Unknown.*   AmFP

Shovelling Iron Ore.   *Unknown.*   GBP

Show, The.   Wilfred Owen.   NoAM; OBP; OxBTC

Show me, dear Christ, thy spouse, so bright and clear.   Holy Sonnets, XVIII.   John Donne.   SCP-1

Show me thy feet: show me thy legs, thy thighs.   To Dianeme. Robert Herrick.   POL

Showing a torn sleeve, with stiff and shaking fingers the old man. Charles Reznikoff.   *Fr.* Five Groups of Verse.   SA

Shredded Wheat.   Louis Dudek.   AKE

Shriek said the saw smile said the mice.   To the Age's Insanities. Maire Ponsot.   VGW

Shrinking to enter, did. Your heart.   Part of the Vigil.   James Merrill.   NoAM

Shropshire Lad, A.   A. E. Housman.   *Poems indexed separately by first lines.*

Shroud keeps scratching my eyes my nuts my, The.   Breathing, at Last, in the Wichita Art Museum.   D. Clinton.   HeS

Shrouded Stranger, The.   Allen Ginsberg.   CoPAm

Shrouding of the Duchess of Malfi.   John Webster.   *See* Hark, Now Everything Is Still.

Shrubbery, The.   William Cowper.   NOBE

Shuddering geography pulls the dead sentences, A.   Pastoral. James Tipton.   HeS

Shuffle and reshuffle. Still the times will stack.   Carmen Saeculare. John Taylor.   NowV

Shuffling along in her broken shoes from the slums.   Douglas Stewart.   *Fr.* Lady Feeding the Cats.   BoAnP

Shut not so soon; the dull-eyed [*or* dull-ey'd] night.   To Daisies, Not to Shut so Soon.   Robert Herrick.   GBL; InPK

Shut Not Your Doors.   Walt Whitman.   NOBA

Shut off the radio.   Putting the Croutons Back into the Jar. Diane Kruchkow.   FAF

Shut Out That Moon.   Thomas Hardy.   NoAM; NOBE

Shut, shut the door, good John!   Epistle to Dr. Arbuthnot [*or* An Epistle from Mr. Pope, to Dr. Arbutnot].   Pope.   ESaP; InPS; PAIC

Shyly the silver-hatted mushrooms make.   May.   John Shaw Neilson.   MAuV

Siberia.   James Clarence Mangan.   BIrV

Sibilla's Dirge.   Thomas Lovell Beddoes.   *Fr.* Death's Jest Book. NOBE

Sibrandus Schafnaburgensis.   Robert Browning.   *Fr.* Garden Fancies.   OBP

Sic 'Em Dogs On.   *Unknown.*   BluL

Sic Vita.   Henry King.   BBGO; NOBE; WIF

Sic Vita.   Henry David Thoreau.   *See* I Am a Parcel of Vain Strivings Tied.

Sicily and Naples; or, The Fatal Union: a Tragedy, *sel.*   Samuel Harding.
   "Noblest bodies are but gilded clay."   SCP-2

Sick Child, A.   Randall Jarrell.   VGW

Sick Love.   Robert Graves.   BoLoP; NoAM; NOBE

Sick Rose, The.   Blake.   *Fr.* Songs of Experience.   BoLoP; HeIP; InPK; InPS; LAuP; MBPR; NOBE; PAIC; PPP

Side by Side.   Adrienne Rich.   CoPAm

Side by side, their faces blurred.   An Arundel Tomb.   Philip Larkin.   HeIP; MPo; PPP

Sidewalk Restoration.   Ron Ikan.   NVAP

Sidewalks of New York, The, *with music.*   James W. Blake. BLSH; BLSo; FSN

Siding Near Chillicothe, A.   Richmond Lattimore.   ANTL

Siege of Rhodes, The, *sel.*   Sir William Davenant.
   "These are court-monsters, cormorants of the crown."   SCP-2

Siege; or, Love's Convert, The, *sel.*   William Cartwright.
   "My most honoured father."   SCP-2

Siesta of a Hungarian Snake.   Edwin Morgan.   InPK   Sigh no more, ladies, sigh no more.   Shakespeare.   *Fr.* Much Ado About Nothing, II, iii.   SS

Sight in Camp in the Daybreak Gray and Dim, A.   Walt Whitman.   NoAM; OFD

Sighted a black tornado of.   Comments.   Peggy Susberry Kenner. JB

Sigil.   Hilda Doolittle ("H.D.").   VGW

Sigismundo.   Linda Gregg.   AmPA

Sign.   Marge Piercy.   Psy

"Sign there." I signed, but uneasily.   A Document.   Judith Wright.   MAuV

Signals.   Jewel C. Latimore.   PoBA

Signature.   Hannah Kahn.   IHMS

Signature.   Larry Mollin.   NeAC

Signature, A.   F. Eugene Warren.   AATT

Signature for Tempo.   Archibald MacLeish.   VGW

Signatures.   Daniel Hoffman.   VGW

Signboard, The.   Robert Creeley.   ConAP

Signpost.   Robinson Jeffers.   TCP

Signs of the Seasons.   *Unknown.*   ECBV

Signs of Winter.   John Clare.   Epi

Silence. Thomas Hood.   NOBE

Silence.   Edward Lucie-Smith.   LP

Silence.   Marianne Moore.   NOBA; PiAm; PSN; Psy; SBG

Silence.   W. J. Turner.   FSFS

Silence, and stealth of days! 'Tis now.  Since Thou Art Gone. Henry Vaughan.  SCP-1

Silence augmenteth grief, writing increaseth rage.  An Epitaph upon the Right Honorable Sir Philip Sidney.  Fulke Greville. Prf

Silence hovers over the earth, A.  A Late Spring Day in My Life. Robert Bly.  NCSH

Silence in Court.  "Lewis Carroll."  *See* Evidence Read at the Trial of the Knave of Hearts.

Silence of a city, how awful at midnight, The.  Samuel Taylor Coleridge.  MBPR

Silence: one would willingly consume it.  Silence.  Edward Lucie-Smith.  LP

Silence slipping around like death, A.  A Winter Twilight. Angelina Weld Grimké.  PoBA

Silent at last, beneath the silent ground.  On the Death of Echo. Hartley Coleridge.  BoAnP

Silent is the house: all are laid asleep.  The Visionary.  Emily Brontë.  BoReV; NOBE

Silent Love, A.  Sir Edward Dyer.  BoLoP; NOBE

Silent Night! Holy Night! *with music.*  Joseph Mohr, *tr. fr. German.*  BLSH

Silent Noon.  Dante Gabriel Rossetti.  The House of Life, XIX, OBP

Silent nymph, with curious eye!  Grongar Hill.  John Dyer. LAuP; PAIC

Silent, O Moyle, be the roar of thy water.  The Song of Fionnuala.  Thomas Moore.  BIrV

Silent Poem.  Robert Francis.  FiCP

Silent silent night.  Blake.  MBPR

Silent Slain, The.  Archibald MacLeish.  POL

Silent Snake, The.  *Unknown.*  CaYB

Silent Tower of Bottreau, The.  Robert Stephen Hawker.  VPC

Silent, you say, I'm grown of late.  Walter Savage Landor.  GBL

Silently grave as voyeurs in a powder room.  At the Dancing School of the Sisters Schwartz.  Judson Jerome.  SFF

Silhouettes, they lean against a ringed moon.  Paiute Ponies.  Jim Barnes.  CDW

Silk Weaver's Daughter, The.  *Unknown.*  AmFP

Silked, or smoked from that field.  Whether Firelocked.  Mary Shumway.  HeS

Silken Tent, The.  Robert Frost.  InPK; NOBA; PAIC; PiAm; PPoD; SoSe; WIF

Silkworms, The.  Douglas Stewart.  MAuV

Silly. All giggles and ringlets and never.  Romping.  John Ciardi. CTBA; NCSH

Silly boy 'tis full moon yet, thy night as day shines clearly. Thomas Campion.  GBL

Silver.  Walter de la Mare.  IPWM; SS

Silver birch is a dainty lady, The.  Child's Song in Spring.  Edith Nesbitt.  OxBChV

Silver Dagger, The.  *Unknown.*  AmFP

Silver Dollar.  Kathleen Wiegner.  MMD

Silver dust.  Pear Tree.  Hilda Doolittle ("H.D.").  NOBA

Silver Lucifer, A.  Lunar Baedeker.  Mina Loy.  VGW

Silver Penny, The.  Walter de la Mare.  WIF

Silver Screen.  Leonard Clark.  RAE

Silver spoons/ were warbling, The.  Here Comes.  Erica Jong. PPoD

Silver Swan, The.  *Unknown.*  HeIP; InPK

Silver Tassie, The.  Burns.  NOBE

Silver tetradrachm of King Antigónos, The.  Coin From B.C. Nicholas Flocos.  SA

Silver Threads among the Gold, *with music*  Eben Eugene Rexford.  BLSH; BLSo; PSoN

Silver watch you've worn for years, A.  Some Slippery Afternoon. Daniela Gioseffi.  WBN

Silver Wedding.  Ralph Hodgson.  OxBTC

Silvery Tide, The.  *Unknown.*  AmFP

Simile.  N. Scott Momaday.  CDW

Simile for Her Smile, A.  Richard Wilbur.  InPK; OLR; WIF

Similes for Two Political Characters of 1819.  Shelley.  InPS (To Sidmouth and Castlereagh.)  MBPR

Simon Lee.  Wordsworth.  MBPR

Simon Soggs' Thanksgiving.  W. A. Croffut.  PoTa

Simon the Cyrenian Speaks.  Countee Cullen.  BPo

Simple.  Naomi Long Madgett.  PoBA

Simple Beast.  Mark Van Doren.  TH

Simple child, A.  We Are Seven.  Wordsworth.  MBPR; OxBChV; SpRo

Simple Simon met a pieman.  Mother Goose.  MG

Simple nosegay, A! was that much to ask?  The Troll's Nosegay. Robert Graves.  SoSe

Simple-Song.  Marge Piercy.  CTBA; Psy; TSWA

Simple soul, who so early in the morning.  Charles Reznikoff. *Fr.* Depression.  CTBA

Simplex Munditiis.  Ben Jonson, *tr. fr. the Latin of* Jean Bonnefons.  *Fr.* Epicoene; or, The Silent Woman, I, i. NOBE; OBP; PBMP
(Clerimont's Song.)  InPS; PPP
("Still to be neat, still to be dressed.")  GBL; HeIP

Simplicity ("Persicos odi").  Horace.  *See* Fie on Eastern Luxury!

Simplicity.  Louis Simpson.  InPS; Prf

Simplicity assuages.  Apology.  J. V. Cunningham.  PiAm

Simplicity so graven hurts the sense.  So Graven.  Josephine Miles.  NoAM

Simplify Me When I'm Dead.  Keith Douglas.  OxBTC

Simply to breath.  An Emblem of Two Foxes.  Barry Spacks. CoPAm

Simultaneously.  David Ignatow.  NCSH; POL

Sin.  George Herbert.  Epi

Sin of Omission, The.  Margaret Elizabeth Munson  Sangster. SoSe

Since.  W. H. Auden.  InPS

Since/ Malcolm died.  Aardvark.  Julia Fields.  OFD

Since all that beat about in nature's range.  Constancy to an Ideal Object.  Samuel Taylor Coleridge.  MBPR; OBP

Since brass, nor stone, nor earth, nor boundless sea.  Sonnets, LXV.  Shakespeare.  Epi; InPS; NOBE

Since Brunswick's smile has authoris'd my muse.  Edward Young. *Fr.* The Instalment.  FaBoCo

Since Christmas they have lived with us.  Balloons.  Sylvia Plath. MPo; NCSH

Since feeling is first.  E. E. Cummings.  SFF

Since I am coming to that holy room.  Hymn to God My God, in My Sickness.  John Donne.  AnMo; HeIP; MetP; PPP; SCP-1; SoSe

Since I believe in God the Father Almighty.  Johannes Milton, Senex.  Robert Bridges.  BoReV; OBP

Since I emerged that day from the labyrinth.  The Labyrinth. Edwin Muir.  NoAM

Since I have been so quickly done for.  Epitaph on an Infant Eight Months Old.  *Unknown.*  SoSe

Since I must love your north.  To My Mountain.  Kathleen Raine.  SLP

Since I noo mwore do zee your feace.  The Wife a-Lost.  William Barnes.  BoLoP; VPC

Since Jesus Came into My Heart, *with music.*  R. H. McDaniel. BLSH

Since, Lord, to thee/ A narrow way and little gate.  Holy Baptism.  George Herbert.  SCP-1

Since me and Jesus got: married. Jesus Make Up My Dying Bed. *Unknown.* BluL

Since most sharks have no flotation bladders and must swim. Nurse Sharks. William Matthews. FiCP

Since my old friend is grown so great. A Dialogue. Pope. POL

Since of no creature living the last breath. Edna St. Vincent Millay. VGW

Since Reverend Doctors now declare. The Respectable Burgher. Thomas Hardy. NoAM

Since she whom I loved hath paid her last debt. Holy Sonnets, XVII. John Donne. SCP-1

Since the shell came and took you in its arms. The Shell. George MacBeth. SLP

Since the storm two night ago. The Recognition. Denise Levertov. VGW

Since there's no help [*or* helpe], come let us kiss [*or* kisse] and part. Farewell to Love. Michael Drayton. *Fr.* Idea. AAS; BoLoP; Epi; GBL; HeIP; InPK; InPS; LoAs; NOBE; PAIC; PBMP; PPoD; PPoe; SoSe; VoPo

Since this is the last night I keep you home. Seven Seals. D. H. Lawrence. LoAs

Since Thou Art Gone. Henry Vaughan. SCP-1

Since Time began, such alphabets begin. From a Cheerful Alphabet. John Updike. FaBoCo

Since to obtain thee, nothing me will sted. His Remedie for Love. Michael Drayton. *Fr.* Idea. AAS

Since we had changed. Message. Allen Ginsberg. ConAP; VGW

Since you ask, most days I cannot remember. Wanting to Die. Anne Sexton. ConAP; IHMS; NoAM

Since you wrote a poem. What Color is Lonely. Carolyn M. Rodgers. BPo

Sincere Flattery of W. W. (Americanus) J. K. Stephen. SpRo

Sinful to Flirt. *Unknown.* AmFP

Sing a Song of Honey. Barbara Euphan Todd. FSFS

Sing a Song of Juniper. Robert Francis. ECBV; NCSH

Sing a song of sixpence. Mother Goose. MG; SpRo

Sing, ballad-singer, raise a hearty tune. The Ballad-Singer. Thomas Hardy. BoLoP; OLR

Sing care away, with sport and play. Heart's Ease. *Fr.* Misogonus. *Unknown.* WIF

Sing his praises that doth keep. Hymn to Pan. John Fletcher. *Fr.* The Faithful Shepherdess, I, ii. NOBE

Sing it. Utter the phrase, the fine word. Bard. William Everson. PiAm

Sing jigmijole the pudding-bowl. Kissing of My Dame. *Unknown.* GBL

Sing lullaby, as women doe. The Lullabie of a Lover. George Gascoigne. AAS

Sing Me a New Song. John Henrik Clarke. PoBA

Sing Me a Song. Robert Louis Stevenson. AIW; NOBE

Sing me at morn but only with your laugh. Song of Songs. Wilfred Owen. OBP

"Sing me to sleep." The Snake and the Snake-Charmer. E. V. Rieu. ECBV

Sing, Poet, 'tis a merry world. Glasgow. Alexander Smith. VPC

Sing praise/ Sing praise. Canto del Señor Segovia. David Sten Herrstrom. AATT

Sing, sing, what shall I sing? Mother Goose. MG

Sing softly, Muse, the Reverend Henry White. B Flat. Douglas Stewart. MAuV

Sing them over again to me. Wonderful Words of Life. Philip Paul Bliss. BLSH

Sing We and Chant It. Thomas Morley. WIF

Sing we for love and idleness. An Immorality. Ezra Pound. NOBA; OLR; VoPo

Singe we alle and say we thus. My Purse. *Unknown.* OxBM

Singee a songee sick a pence. Nursery Song in Pidgin English. *Unknown.* SpRo

Singers to Come. Alice Meynell. WPE

Singing. Peter Shelton. AKE

Singing Aloud. Carolyn Kizer. IHMS

Singing Cat, The. Stevie Smith. OxBTC; PCat

Singing of Niagara, and the Huron squaws. The Possibility of New Poetry. Robert Bly. ConAP

Single clover plank, A. Emily Dickinson. PiAm

Single flow'r he sent me, since we met, A. One Perfect Rose. Dorothy Parker. OLR; PAIC

Single man stands like a bird-watcher, A. The Mouth of the Hudson. Robert Lowell. PSN

Single naked wire at ground level, A. George Jonas. *Fr.* To Christian Montpelier. NeAC

Sing-Song: A Nursery Rime Book. Christina Rossetti. *Poem indexed separately by titles and first lines.*

Singular Metamorphosis, A. Howard Nemerov. ConAP

Singular Self, The. Charles Bukowski. CoPAm

Singularly and in pairs the decade has been ripped by bullets. Lines. Herbert Martin. PoBA

Sinking of the *Titanic. Unknown.* PAIC

Sinner man sat on the gates of hell, A. No Hiding Place Down There. *Unknown.* GBP

Sins of Kalamazoo, The. Carl Sandburg. VGW

Sioux Indians, The. *Unknown.* AmFP

Sipping whiskey and gin. Analysands. Dudley Randall. BPo

Sir Andrew Barton, 2 *versions. Unknown.* AmFP

Sir Beelzebub. Edith Sitwell. OBP; OxBTC

Sir Christopher Wren. E. C. Bentley. *Fr.* Clerihews. FaBoCo; InPK

Sir Edward Michael Pakenham. Ballad of New Orleans. Charles G. Wilson. BTTM

Sir Edward, that was by este tho mid power gret ynow. Town Against Gown at Oxford. Robert of Gloucester. *Fr.* Chronicle. OxBM

Sir Eglamour. Samuel Rowlands. ECBV

Sir Eustace Grey, *sel.* George Crabbe. Frenzy. NOBE

Sir Francis Drake; or Eighty-Eight. *Unknown.* GBP

Sir Gawain and the Green Knight, *sels. Unknown.* Gawain and the Lady of the Castle, *orig. and mod. English prose.* Gawain and the Temptress, *tr. fr. Middle English by* Burton Raffel. OBP

Sir Gawaine and the Green Knight. Yvor Winters. NoAM; PAIC; VGW

Sir George and Lady Cepheus of Upper Slaughter. Agony Column. A. D. Hope. SoSe

Sir Hudibras, His Passing Worth. Samuel Butler. *Fr.* Hudibras, I. FaBoCo; SCP-2

Sir Hugh; or, The Jew's Daughter. *Unknown.* AmFP

Sir Humphry Davy. E. C. Bentley. *Fr.* Clerihews. FaBoCo

Sir, I encountered Death. Incident in a Rose Garden. Donald Justice. NCSH

Sir Joshua Reynolds. Blake. FaBoCo

Sir Lionel. *Unknown.* AmFP

Sir Marmaduke. George Colman the Younger. PeBB

Sir, more than kisses letters mingle souls. To Sir Henry Wotton. John Donne. TVS

Sir Olf rode fast toward Thurston's walls. The Erl-King's Daughter. Johann Gottfried Herder, *tr. by* James Clarence Mangan. PoTa

Sir Orfeo. *Unknown.* OxBM

Sir Patrick Spens [*or* Spence]. *Unknown.* AIW; AmFP; Epi, *with music;* InPK; InPS; NOBE; PAIC; PBMP; PeBB; PPP

Sir Rider Haggard.  W. H. Auden.  FaBoCo

Sir, say no more.  Trumbull Stickney.  InPK

Sir Thomas Becket wore a gray sackcloth.  Becket.  Virginia Gilbert.  NPW

Sir Walter Ralegh to the Queen.  Sir Walter Ralegh.  AAS

Sir William Dyer, Knight, *sels.*  Lady Catherine Dyer.
"If a large heart joined with a noble mind."  SCP-2
"My dearest dust, could not thy hasty day."  SCP-2
(Epitaph on the Monument of Sir William Dyer at Colmworth, 1641.)  BoLoP

Sir, you should notice me: I am the Man.  Epitaph.  Lascelles Abercrombie.  BBGO

Sire.  W. S. Merwin.  VGW

Sired by old hearts.  Colette, Poor Clare.  Colette Inez.  AATT

Siren Chorus.  George Darley.  *See* Mermaiden's Vesper-Hymn, The.

Siren sang, and Europe turned away, A.  To the Western World. Louis Simpson.  ConAP; CoPAm; NOBA

Sirens' Song, The.  William Browne.  *Fr.* Inner Temple Masque. NOBE
(Syrens' Song, The.)  GBL

Sirens' Song, The.  Homer, *tr. fr.* Greek by Robert Fitzgerald. *Fr.* The Odyssey, XII.  GrRo

Sister, Awake!  *Unknown.*  NOBE

Sister Lou.  Sterling A. Brown.  PoBA

Sister of love-lorn poets, Philomel!  To the Nightingale.  Samuel Taylor Coleridge.  MBPR

Sister Pharaoh.  Ruth Whitman.  MAT

Sister was wedged beside the wicker basket.  The Burned Bridge. Ruth Stone.  WPE

Sisters, The.  Roy Campbell.  BoLoP

Sisters, The.  Amy Lowell.  SBG

Sisters.  Sandra McPherson.  AmPA

Sisters.  Adrienne Rich.  IHMS

Sisters.  Alberta Turner.  HeS

Sisters are always drying their hair.  Triolet Against Sisters. Phyllis McGinley.  MiP

Sisyphus.  Robert J. Burdette.  PoTa

Sit down by the side of you mother, my boy.  Mother's Advice. *Unknown.*  AmFP

Sit on the bed. I'm blind, and three parts shell.  A Terre. Wilfred Owen.  OxBTC

Sith that you both are like in life.  To a Married Couple That Could Not Agree.  Timothy Kendall.  PAIC

Sitteth alle stille and herkneth to me.  The Song of Lewes. *Unknown.*  OxBM

Sitting at a window.  Mother Tabbyskins.  Elizabeth Anna Hart. OxBChV

Sitting at the kitchen table.  Going Home.  Thomas Lux. NVAP

Sitting between the sea and the buildings.  The Painter.  John Ashbery.  NOBA

Sitting by the roadside on a summer day.  Goober Peas. *Unknown.*  PSoN

Sitting Here.  Robert Creeley.  RRA

Sitting in the Woods: A Contemplation.  W. R. Moses.  NCSH

Sitting straightbacked, a modest Irish miss.  A Lesson in Love. Philip Hobsbaum.  OxBTC

Six Badgers, The.  Robert Graves.  RAE

Six Days.  Tom Raworth.  TwMBP

Six Days of Creation, The.  James McAuley.  CAAP

Six days on snowshoes.  Hunting Fragment.  Gary Lawless. FAF

Six disorderly bears.  Bad Example.  Isabella Fey.  BoAnP

Six-foot nest of the sea-hawk, The.  Sea-Hawk.  Richard Eberhart.  BoAnP

Six-forty-two Farm Commune Struggle Poem.  Jay Leifer.  MAT

Six Kisses.  Nancy Sullivan.  LoAs

Six lessons.  Ode to a Violin.  Luís Omar Salinas.  SA

Six O'Clock.  Trumbull Stickney.  PPoB

Six o'clock and/ the sun rises across the river.  Love Poem. Miller Williams.  MAT

Six of them climbed aboard.  The Boys.  Anthony Thwaite.  LP

6 p.m./ middle of south Dakota.  After the Funeral of Assam Hamady.  Sam Hamod.  SA

Six Poets in Search of a Lawyer.  Donald Hall.  SoSe

Six Reveilles to Match My Self-Indulgence, *sel.*  Wilder Bentley.
"Up, up, old Benedict, the bard who would," IV.  MIT

Six Statues in a Park.  Floyd C. Stuart.  FAF

Six Ten Sixty-Nine.  Conyus.  PoBA

Six Variations.  Denise Levertov.  ConAP
"Shlup, shlup, the dog," *sel.*  HeIP; InPK

Six Week Old Blues.  *Unknown.*  BluL

Sixes and Sevens.  Roderick Hartigh Jellema.  AATT

"Sixpence a week," says the girl to her lover.  By Aunt's Grave. Thomas Hardy.  Satires of Circumstance, III.  SFF

16/53.  Marge Piercy.  NeAC

Sixteen Warnings in Search of a Feminist Poem.  Erica Jong. *See* Seventeen Warnings in Search of a Feminist Poem.

Sixteen years old and beautiful.  Girl.  A. W. Purdy.  NoAM

6th and Walnut Street.  Rubee Dreher Moxley.  NPW

Sixth Station, The.  Jane Marie Luecke.  AATT

Skaters, The.  John Williams.  CoPAm

Skaters, The.  Wordsworth.  *Fr.* The Prelude, I.  SPo
("And in the frosty season, when the sun.")  FSFS

'Skeeters are [*or* am] a-hummin' on the [*or* de] honeysuckle vine. Kentucky Babe.  Richard Henry Buck.  BLSH; FSN

Skein, The.  Carolyn Kizer.  LoAs; VGW

Skeleton.  Coleman Barks.  *Fr.* Body Poems.  NVAP

Skeleton is hiding in the closet as it should, The.  Everything in Its Place.  Arthur Guiterman.  ECBV

Skeleton Key.  John Hollander.  InPK

Sketch for a Job Application Blank.  Jim Harrison.  AmPA; NoAM

Sketch 48b.11.  Ezra Pound.  BBGO

Sketch of His Own Character.  Thomas Gray.  LAuP

Sketches of Harlem.  David Henderson.  PAIC

Skialetheia, *sel.*  Everard Guilpin.
"Let me alone, I prithee, in this cell," Satire V.  TVS

Skier.  Robert Francis.  NCSH; RFM

Skiers.  Robert Penn Warren.  *Fr.* In the Mountains.  SPo; TCP

Skies they were ashen and sober, The.  Ulalume—A Ballad.  Poe. NOBA; PiAm

Skiing champs, The.  Hunger.  Lennart Bruce.  MiP

Skill in Killing, A.  George Abbe.  FAF

Skimbleshanks: The Railway Cat.  T. S. Eliot.  FaBoCo

Skimming lightly, wheeling still.  Shiloh; a Requiem.  Herman Melville.  AmVN; NOBA

Skin-and-Bone Lady, The.  *Unknown.*  AmFP

Skin Divers, The.  George Starbuck.  SPo

Skin Flick.  Fred Chappell.  PPoD

Skin Man.  *Unknown.*  BluL

Skin of/ elm ebony eucalyptus.  Emma in My Third Eye.  Renée Roper.  NPW

Skin of the sea, The.  In Sylvia Plath Country.  Erica Jong. IHMS

Skin quickens to noises, The.  One Eyed Back Man in Nebraska. Sam Cornish.  PoBA

Skin Song.  Laurence Lieberman.  CoPAm

Skin that is a closed curtain.  Poll.  Ed Roberson.  PoBA

Skin the Goat's Curse on Carey.  *Unknown.*  BIrV

Skinfull of bowls, he bowls them. Second Glance at a Jaguar. Ted Hughes. NoAM

Skinning a Rabbit. Norbert Krapf. HeS

Skinny Mrs. Snipkin. Mrs. Snipkin and Mrs. Wobblechin. Laura E. Richards. OxBChV

Skinny Salvador went in first, a diamond. Intimations at the Lake, 1963. Helena Minton. FAF

Skins hang on fence-wires, purple, blue and green. Delivering Lambs. David Campbell. MAuV

Skip to My Lou. *Unknown.* AmFP; ECBV

Skipper Ireson's Ride. Whittier. NOBA

Skipping Stones. Allan D. Farber. SoSe

Skirting the river road (my forenoon walk, my rest). The Dalliance of the Eagles. Walt Whitman. BoAnP; HeIP; InPK; LoAs; PiAm; POL; PPoe; PPP

Skull. Coleman Barks. *Fr.* Body Poems. NVAP

Skull, The. Ian Young. NeAC

Skull closes like a closet, The. The Closet. Dave Smith. HeS

Skunk cabbage, bloodroot. The Round. Philip Booth. NCSH

Skunk Hour. Robert Lowell. CAPP; ConAP; HeIP; InPK; NoAM; NOBA; PiAm; PPP; TCP

Skunks, *sel.* Robinson Jeffers.
"We have little animals here." BoAnP

Sky, The. Susan Griffin. RiTi

Sky can't get in, The. Room. Shirley Kaufman. NMM

Sky Diver. Adrien Stoutenburg. SPo; TSWA

Sky Diving. Richmond Lattimore. SPo

Sky droops like the lapel on a corpse, The. Mother and the Moon. Martha Yoak. NPW

Sky hangs heavy tonight, The. Negro Woman. Lewis Alexander. PoBA

Sky is blue, or something, The. Anyway, it's there. Words, for E. Tom Leonard. SLP

Sky is low, the clouds are mean, The. Emily Dickinson. FSFS; PBMP

Sky is overcast, The. A Night-Piece. Wordsworth. Moon

Sky, lazily disdaining to pursue, The. Georgia Dusk. Jean Toomer. BPo; NoAM; PoBA

Sky-Splitting Pink Rubber Bistro, The. Rochelle Owens. RiTi

Sky walks into the florist's shop, The. Buying Lilies. Stephen Stepanchev. SA

Sky Was Candy Luminous, The. E. E. Cummings. AKE

Sky was the white soil you. Drop. George MacBeth. TwMBP

Skyline of New York does not excite me, The. Review from Staten Island. Gloria C. Oden. PoBA; PPP

Skyscrapers. Rachel Field. ECBV

Skyscrapers Stand Proud. Carl Sandburg. PiAm

Slabs of Her Eyes, The. Patricia Goedicke. Psy

"Slack your rope, hangs-a-man." The Maid Freed from the Gallows. *Unknown.* AIW

Slant of sun on dull brown walls, A. War Is Kind, XIV. Stephen Crane. AmVN; PiAm

Slant sheen/ wrinkled silver. Letters to Walt Whitman, II. Ronald Johnson. VGW

Slashed clouds leak gold. Along the slurping wharf. Fishing Harbour towards Evening. Richard Kell. LP; MPo

Slaughter-House, The. Alfred Hayes. NowV

Slaughter-Room Picture, The. David Steingass. CoPAm

Slave and the Iron Lace, The. Margaret Danner. BPo

Slave Auction, The. Frances E. W. Harper. BPo

Slave Marriage Ceremony Supplement. *Unknown.* BPo; POL

Slave Quarters. James Dickey. CAPP

Slavery. Robert Herrick. PAIC

Sleep. Greg Kuzma. NVAP

Sleep. Rhyll McMaster. CAAP

Sleep. Dana Naone. CDW

Sleep. Yvor Winters. POL

Sleep and Poetry. Keats. MBPR
"What is more gentle than a wind in summer?" *sel.* FSFS

Sleep at noon. Window blind. Hurricane. Archibald MacLeish. NCSH

Sleep, baby mine, Desire, nurse Beauty singeth. Sir Philip Sidney. NOBE

Sleep, Darling. Sappho, *tr. fr. Greek by* Mary Barnard. IPWM

Sleep half sleep half silence and with reasons. Sonnet. Ted Berrigan. CAAP; Epi

Sleep in the Heat. Laura Jensen. AmPA

Sleep is a country of water. Country of Water. Bernice Ames. WPE

Sleep late with your dream. Owen Dodson. *Fr.* Poems for My Brother Kenneth. PoBA

Sleep-Learning. Ruth Fainlight. NMM

Sleep, my child, and peace attend thee. All through the Night. *At. to* David Owen. BLSH

Sleep now, O sleep now. James Joyce. GBL

Sleep on the Fraser. Patrick Lane. NeAC

Sleep only with strangers. George Jonas. NeAC

Sleep plays hide-and-seek with darkness. Night Blessing. Phil George. VW

Sleep, sleep, poor youth! sleep, sleep in peace. Thomas Durfey. *Fr.* Don Quixote. SCP-2

Sleep softly. . .eagle forgotten. . .under the stone. The Eagle That Is Forgotten. Vachel Lindsay. NOBA; VoPo

Sleep sweetly in your humble graves. Ode. Henry Timrod. AmVN; NOBA

Sleep was only a dream. Chicago: Near West-Side Renewal. Dennis Schmitz. AmPA

Sleeper, The. Edward Field. SPo

Sleeper, The. Poe. NOBA

Sleeper, The. William Soutar. SLP

Sleeping at Last. Christina Rossetti. HeIP

Sleeping Beauty, The, *sel.* Edith Sitwell.
"In the great gardens, after bright spring rain." OxBTC
(Innocent Spring, The.) NOBE

Sleeping Fury, The. Louise Bogan. IHMS; RiTi

Sleeping Giant, The. Donald Hall. NCSH

Sleeping in fever, I am unfit. For God while Sleeping. Anne Sexton. CAPP; CoPAm

Sleeping Out in Vermont. Conrad Hilberry. PPoD

Sleeping with Foxes. Roberta Hill. CDW

Sleeping with Women. Kenneth Koch. NoAM

Sleepless hours who watch me as I lie, The. Hymn of Apollo. Shelley. MBPR

Sleepmonger,/ deathmonger. The Addict. Anne Sexton. CTBA

Sleepy little village, The. Mendora, N.D.. Richard Lyons. HeS

Sleepy Man Blues. *Unknown.* BluL

Sleepy Song. Arthur Guiterman. ECBV

Sleet Storm on the Merritt Parkway. Robert Bly. ConAP; NOBA

Sleight-of-Hand. Bruce Dawe. CAAP

Slice of Wedding Cake, A. Robert Graves. BoLoP; BuTh; NOBE; OxBTC

Slicing Button Mushrooms. Derek Bowman. MIS

Sliding on Skates in Very Hard Frost. Nahum Tate. SCP-2

Sliding Two Mirrors. Tom Raworth. TwMBP

Slight Confusion, A. James Reiss. AmPA

Slim and singing copper girl, A. Early Copper. Carl Sandburg. HeIP; PiAm

Slim dragonfly. Arthur Mitchell. Marianne Moore. PiAm

Slim in Hell ("Slim Greer went to heaven"). Sterling A. Brown. BPo

Slimy obscene creatures, insane. The Nigga Section. Welton Smith. BPo

Slipping, she fell into the sitting-room. Girl with Coffee Tray. John Fuller. LP

Sloped-down shark nose. Regarding Wave, II. Gary Snyder. CAAP

Sloping at a 45° angle. Umbaji Park. David Kherdian. SA

Sloth, The. Isabella Gardner. BoAnP

Sloth, The. Theodore Roethke. SS

Slovenly Peter. Heinrich Hoffmann. *Poems indexed separately by titles and first lines.*

Slow Dance. David St. John. AmPA

Slow Dancer That No One Hears but You. Duane Niatum. CDW

Slow down,/ You move too fast. The 59th Street Bridge Song. Paul Simon. TCP

Slow, heavy, deadly was my pace: the cold. Death. Keats. *Fr.* The Fall of Hyrerion. OBP

Slow Mama Slow. *Unknown.* BluL

Slow May. Spring in These Hills. Archibald MacLeish. NCSH

Slow moves the acid breath of noon. Field of Autumn. Laurie Lee. NCSH

Slow Pacific Swell, The. Yvor Winters. HeIP; NoAM; NOBA; PiAm

Slow Riff for Billy. James Cunningham. JB

Slow, slow, fresh fount, keep time with my salt tears. Echo's Lament of Narcissus. Ben Jonson. *Fr.* Cynthia's Revels. InPK; SoSe

Slow Spring. Katharine Tynan. FSFS

Slow Starter, The. Louis MacNeice. MPo; PBMP

Slow the Kansas sun was setting o'er the wheat fields far away. Towser Shall Be Tied Tonight. *Unknown.* BoAnP

Slow toiling upward from the misty vale. Nearing the Snow-line. Oliver Wendell Holmes. PiAm

Slowly, O so slowly, longing rose up. Christ Walking on the Water. W. R. Rodgers. NoAM

Slowly, silently, now the moon. Silver. Walter de la Mare. IPWM; SS

Slowly the night blooms, unfurling. Flowers of Darkness. Frank Marshall Davis. PoBA

Slowly the poison the whole blood stream fills. Missing Dates. William Empson. NoAM; NOBE; PAIC; PSN

Slowly the salt of the earth becomes salt of the sea. Salt of the Earth. D. H. Lawrence. NoAM

Slowly the women file to where he stands. Faith Healing. Philip Larkin. NoAM

Slowness ("Slowness, says Rodin, is beauty"). Gibbons Ruark. SFF

Sluggard, The. Isaac Watts. OxBChV; SpRo

Slumber Did My Spirit Seal, A. Wordsworth. AnMo; HeIP; InPK; InPS; MBPR; NOBE; PAIC; PBMP; PPP

Slumbersong. Rainer Maria Rilke, *tr. fr. German by* M. D. Herter Norton. LoAs

Slurped/ and waters moved. Lee-ers of Hew. James Cunningham. JB

Small/ bottle/ of blackish, A. Death. Lynn Sukenick. RiTi

Small boy, four years, A. Terminal. D. J. Enright. LP

Small, busy flames play through the fresh laid coals. To My Brothers. Keats. MBPR

Small Celandine, The. Wordsworth. MBPR

Small Discovery, A. James A. Emanuel. LCL

Small Dragon, A. Brian Patten. LP

Small eyes water on the branch. Another Face. Ray A. Young Bear. CDW

Small jeweled creatures. Hummingbirds. E. Margaret Clarkson. AATT

Small metal box I was given. The Charge. Anselm Hollo. TwMBP

Small Prayer. Weldon Kees. VGW

Small procession waddles single file, A. Ducks. Phoebe Hesketh. BoAnP

Small Score, A. Delmore Schwartz. PBMP

Small service is true service while it lasts. Written in the Album of a Child. Wordsworth. OxBChV

Small, significant bumps would appear on your skin. If I Were in Charge of Epiphanies. Stephen Dunn. NVAP

Small Song. A. R. Ammons. POL

Small Talk. Don Marquis. PoTa

Small Town: The Friendly. Stephen Dunn. POL

Small Tribute, A. William Harrold. HeS

Small White House. Robert Penn Warren. *Fr.* Notes on a Life to Be Lived. NoAM

Small Woman on Swallow Street. W. S. Merwin. ConAP

Smaller role for peanut butter, A. Being Adult. Bill Zavatsky. POL

Smaller than molehills their breasts. A View Toward Wife Trading. Robert Gillespie. NVAP

Smart and stylish girl and you see, A. Ta-Ra-Ra Boom-De-Ay! *Unknown.* FSN

Smear of blue peat smoke, The. The Shepherd's Hut. Andrew Young. OxBTC

Smell of Wood, The. John Stevens Wade. FAF

Smell of woodyards in the rain is strong, The. Woodyards in the Rain. Anne Marriott. AKE

Smelling a Stone in the Middle of Winter. Tom Hennen. HeS

Smelling coffee. The Salesman. Mary Moore. NPW

Smile, The. Blake. MBPR

Smile/ to see the lake. Lorine Niedecker. VGW

Smile at the Birdie. Polly Mann. NPW

Smile at us, pay us, pass us; but do not quiet forget. The Secret People. G. K. Chesterton. OxBTC

Smile, Death. Charlotte Mew. WPE

Smile of iceboxes annihilates me, The. An Appearance. Sylvia Plath. CAPP

Smiling girls, rosy boys. Mother Goose. ECBV

Smiling morn, the breathing spring, The. The Birks of Invermay. David Mallet. SLP

Smith at the organ is like an anvil being. The Sound of Afroamerican History Chapt II. S. E. Anderson. PoBA

Smle. Les A. Murray. CAAP

Smoke. Henry David Thoreau. AmVN; IPWM (Light-Winged Smoke, Icarian Bird.) NOBA

Smoke-color; haze thinly over the hills, low hanging. August. William Everson. PiAm

Smoke of Birds, A. Malcolm Cowley. TSWA

Smoked Herring, The. Charles Cros, *tr. fr. French by* A. L. Lloyd. PoTa

Smoker Parrot, The. John Shaw Neilson. MAuV

Smokestack Lightnin'. *Unknown.* BluL

Smokey the Bear Sutra. *Unknown.* MAT

Smokey's Gettin' Old. Jessica Tarahata Hagedorn. MMD

Smoking Drugs wtih Strangers. George Bowering. NeAC

Smoking Prayers. Simon Ortiz. VW

Smoky rain riddles the ocean plains, A. My Father Paints the Summer. Richard Wilbur. NCSH; NOBA

Smoldering dry fern. And What of Me? Liz Sohappy Bahe. CDW

Smooth lake, The. Wilderness. Ralph Mecklenburger. SFF

Smooth smell of Manhattan taxis, The. Dance of the Infidels. Al Young. PoBA

Smudging. Diane Wakoski. AmPA

Smuggler's Song, A. Kipling. *Fr.* Puck of Pook's Hill. OxBChV; PoTa

Snail. John Drinkwater. LCL; RAE

Snail, The. A. P. Herbert. BoAnP

Snail, The. Richard Lovelace. SCP-2

Snail, The. James Reeves. ECBV

Snail moves like a, The. Hedgehog. Paul Muldoon. BIrV

Snail upon the wall. Snail. John Drinkwater. LCL; RAE

"Snails lead slow idyllic lives." The Widow's Yard. Isabella Gardner. RiTi

Snail's Monologue, The. Christian Morgenstern, *tr. fr. German by* Max Knight. BoAnP

Snake. D. H. Lawrence. HeIP; NoAM; NOBE; PPP

Snake. David McCord. CaYB

Snake. Theodore Roethke. AKE; ECBV; NOBA; RFM

Snake and the Snake-Charmer, The. E. V. Rieu. ECBV

Snake came to my water-trough, A. Snake. D. H. Lawrence. HeIP; NoAM; NOBE; PPP

Snake climbs. Snake Poem I. Joy Harjo. SA

Snake Dance. Lyn Lifshin. FAF; RiTi

Snake Doctor Blues. *Unknown.* BluL

Snake Eyes. LeRoi Jones. VGW

Snake horse stops at bronx clouds. Bronxomania. Victor Hernández Cruz. SA

Snake Poem I. Joy Harjo. SA

Snake Yarn, A. W. T. Goodge. ECBV

Snakes. Peter Wild. AmPA

Snapper, The. William Heyen. AmPA

Snapshot. Colette Inez. AATT

Snapshot of a Pedant. George Garrett. WIF

Snapshots of a Daughter-in-Law. Adrienne Rich. NMM
  "You, once a belle in Shreveport," *sel.* I NCSH

Snapshots of the Cotton South. Frank Marshall Davis. PoBA

Snare, The. James Stephens. ECBV

Snaw, snaw, coom faster. Snow. *Unknown.* GBP

Snawdon Woods. Forbes Macgregor. MIS

Sneaked about here. By the Road. Geoffrey Grigson. OxBTC

Sneeze on a Monday, sneeze for danger. Mother Goose. MG

Snickles and podes. Mean Song. Eve Merriam. CaYB

Sniffed, dilating my nostrils. Elvin's Blues. Michael S. Harper. BPo

Snorting Bedmate, The. *Unknown, tr. fr. Irish by* John V. Kelleher. BIrV

Snorting his pleasure in the dying sun. Landscape, Deer Season. Barbara Howes. MiP; POL

Snow. Louis MacNeice. NoAM; NOBE; OxBTC

Snow. *Unknown.* GBP

Snow/ on insulated roofs. Reflections on Limitations. Albert Howard Carter. AATT

Snow Chant. T. Alan Broughton. FAF

Snow Country. David Etter. SFF

Snow Country Weavers. James Welch. CDW

Snow dissolv'd no more is seen, The. Horace. Odes, IV, 7. LAuP

Snow drifts melt in the streets, pock-marked at the curb. What Train Will Come? William Jay Smith. PPoD

Snow falling and night falling fast, oh, fast. Desert Places. Robert Frost. IPWM; NCSH; NoAM; NOBA; PiAm; PPoD; PPP

Snow falling outside, The. Written on a Paper Napkin. Len Gasparini. NeAC

Snow falls deep, The; the forest lies alone. Gipsies. John Clare. Epi; OBP

Snow falls like wedding rice. Coming on to Winter. Doug Flaherty. HeS

Snow-Gum, The. Douglas Stewart. MAuV

Snow has left the cottage top, The. February. John Clare. *Fr.* The Shepherd's Calendar. NOBE

Snow in Europe. David Gascoyne. LP; MPo

Snow in Summer. Daisy Aldan. RiTi

Snow in the City. Rachel Field. ECBV

Snow in the Suburbs. Thomas Hardy. IPWM; OxBTC; PPP

Snow is out of fashion. Snow in the City. Rachel Field. ECBV

Snow Lies Sprinkled on the Beach, The. Robert Bridges. NoAM

Snow Man, The. Wallace Stevens. HeIP; InPK; MAT; PiAm

Snow on Saddle Mountain, The. Kenji Miyazawa, *tr. fr. Japanese by* Gary Snyder. IPWM; NoAM; NOBA

Snow that never drifts, The. Emily Dickinson. SoSe

Snow White. Robert Gillespie. NVAP

Snow-white clouds did float on high, The. A Father Out, an' Mother Hwome. William Barnes. VPC

Snow-Bound; a Winter Idyl. Whittier. AmVN, *abr.*; PiAm; NOBA
  "Sun that brief December day, The," *sel.* FSFS

Snowdrop, The. Tennyson. FSFS

Snowfall, A. Richard Eberhart. FiCP

Snowfall, The. Donald Justice. CoPAm; VGW

Snowfall in the Afternoon. Robert Bly. CAPP; NOBA

Snow-flake, The. Walter de la Mare. FSFS; LCL; NCSH

Snow-flakes. Longfellow. FSFS; NOBA

Snows of yesteryear, The? Polar Expedition. George M. Young. FAF

Snow-Storm, The. Emerson. AmVN; FSFS; IPWM; NOBA; PiAm; PPoD; Prf; VoPo

Snowy Night. John Haines. NCSH

Snub nose, the guts of twenty mules. New Farm Tractor. Carl Sandburg. AKE

Snuffboxes, The. *Unknown.* PoTa

Snug at the club two fathers sat. The Fathers. Siegfried Sassoon. NoAM

So Abram rose, and clave the wood, and went. The Parable of the Old Men [*or* Man] and the Young. Wilfrid Owen. GrRo; OBP; WIF

So all day long the noise of battle roll'd. Morte D'Arthur. Tennyson. *Fr.* Idylls of the King. PAIC

So be it. I am. Hayden Carruth. VGW

So black great great grandmomma. Black Sheba. Jodi Braxton. WBN

So, bored with dragons, he lay down to sleep. Beowulf. Kingsley Amis. FaBoCo

"So careful of the type?" but no. In Memoriam A.H.H., LVI. Tennyson. BoReV

So cold the wintry winds do blow. The Unquiet Grave. *Unknown.* AIW

So crewell prison, howe could betyde, alas. *See* So Cruel prison. . .

So Crow found Proteus—steaming in the sun. Truth Kills Everybody. Ted Hughes. InPS

So cruel [*or* crewell] prison how could betide, alas. In Windsor Castle. Earl of Surrey. AAS; NOBE

So Cynthia seems star chamber's president. Cynthia. Edward Benlowes. *Fr.* Theophila; or, Love's Sacrifice. Moon

So different, this man. Marriage. William Carlos Williams. IPWM

So earth's inclined toward the one invisible. Winter Scene. Marguerite Young. WPE

So fallen! so lost! the light withdrawn. Ichabod. Whittier. NOBA; PBMP; VoPo

So Good Luck came, and on my roof did light. Good Luck. Robert Herrick. ECBV

So Graven. Josephine Miles. NoAM

So Handy, Me Boys, So Handy. *Unknown.* AmFP

So having ended, silence long ensewed. Nature's Reply to Mutability. Spenser. *Fr.* The Faerie Queene, VII, 7. NOBE

So he sits down. His host will play for him. Concert Scene. John Logan. CoPAm

So humble things thou hast borne for us, O God. Veni Creator. Alice Meynell. WPE

So I am your "darling girl!" Remonstrance. Philodemos the Epicurean, *tr. by* Dudley Fitts. OLR

So I cut my hair; so I'm shorn. Song of the Strange Young Duckling. Deborah Munro. IHMS

So I Let Her Go, 2 *versions. Unknown.* AmFP

So I Said I Am Ezra. A. R. Ammons. NoAM; NOBA

So I would hear out those lungs. Buckdancer's Choice. James Dickey. NoAM; NOBA

So In Love, *with music.* Cole Porter. BLSo

So in the sinful streets, abstracted and alone. Easter Day II. Arthur Hugh Clough. PFD; VPC

So it is, my dear. Even So. Dante Gabriel Rossetti. NOBE

So light no one noticed. The Song. Edward Dorn. VGW

So Long. William Stafford. Epi

So long,/ So far away. Afro-American Fragment. Langston Hughes. PBMP

So long as we speak the same language. Useless Words. Carl Sandburg. PBMP; PPoD

So Long Solon. Jack Myers. AmPA

So Long? Stevens. John Berryman. NOBA

So looks Anthea when in bed she lies. To Anthea Lying in Bed. Robert Herrick. AnMo; SCP-1

So Lucky I was in being born. Yankee Cradle. Robert P. Tristram Coffin. ECBV

So many days, oh so many days. Love. Pablo Neruda, *tr. by* Alastair Reid. LP

So many pigeons at Columbus. Poem. Arthur Gregor. VGW

So many wagons they have cut that good road down. Chock House Blues. *Unknown.* BluL

So Miss Myrtle is going to marry? The Charming Woman. Helen Selina Sheridan. WPE

So much depends. The Red Wheelbarrow. William Carlos Williams. InPK; NoAM; NOBA; NowV; PiAm; SFF; TSWA; WIF

So much she caused she cannot now account for. Old Woman. Elizabeth Jennings. BuTh

So much that is weak has survived. The Weak. Greg Kuzma. HeS

So, my sweet thing, a little tighter yet. Scenes from the Fall of Troy. William Morris. PAIC

So, on the bloody sand, Sohrab lay dead. Sohrab Dead. Matthew Arnold. *Fr.* Sohrab and Rustum. NOBE

So once again, hearing the tired aunts. In the House of the Dying. Jane Cooper. CoPAm; NMM

So pleasing a light. The Moon. Robert Duncan. *Fr.* Passages. PiAm

So proud she was to die. Emily Dickinson. NOBA

So Quietly. Leslie Pinckney Hill. PoBA

So quiet it was in that high, sun-steeped room. Nuremberg. Kenneth Slessor. MAuV

So several factions from this first ferment. Achitophel: the Earl of Shaftsbury. Dryden. *Fr.* Absalom and Achitophel, Pt. I. NOBE

So she took up a number twelve crewel needle. Agatha. Nadine Major. POL

So she went into the garden. The Great Panjandrum. Samuel Foote. ECBV; FaBoCo

So, since your heart is set on those sweet fields. To Colman Returning. *At. to* Colman, *tr. by* Helen Waddell. BIrV

So smell those odours that do rise. To the Most Fair and Lovely Mistress Anne Soame, Now Lady Abdie. Robert Herrick. NOBE

So smooth, so sweet, so silv'ry is thy voice. Upon Julia's Voice. Robert Herrick. AnMo; InPK; NOBE; SCP-1; SoSe

So, so, breake off this last lamenting kisse. The Expiration. John Donne. LoAs

So soft in the hemlock wood. Robert Hillyer. *Fr.* Pastorals. PAIC

So, some tempestuous morn in early June. Matthew Arnold. *Fr.* Thyrsis. FSFS

So spake our mother Eve, and Adam heard. The Banishment. Milton. *Fr.* Paradise Lost, XII. NOBE

So summer comes in the end to these few stains. The Beginning. Wallace Stevens. VGW

So swete a kis yestrene [*or* yistrene] fra thee I reft. To His Mistress [*or* Maistres]. Alexander Montgomerie. GBL; SLP

So that soldierly legend is still on its journey. Kearney at Senven Pines. Edmund Clarence Stedman. BTTM

So the distances are Galatea. The Distances. Charles Olson. PiAm

So the foemen have fired the gate, men of mine. The Knight's Leap. Charles Kingsley. PoTa

So the Seeds Are Growing. Joe South. PoRo

"So then you won't fight?" Dooley Is a Traitor. James Michie. OxBTC

So there stood Matthew Arnold and this girl. The Dover Bitch. Anthony Hecht MAT; NOBA; NowV; PAIC; PPP; SFF; VGW

So they laid oars. Against the Sun. George MacBeth. TwMBP

So they went, leaving a picnic-litter of talk. The Party. W. R. Rodgers. BIrV

So this is the dust that passes through porcelain. The Iron Lung. Stanley Plumly. AmPA

So through that unripe day you bore your head. Philip Larkin. NoAM

So through the sun-laced woods they went. The Sphere of Glass. John Lehmann. LoAs

So thus he sorrowed till it was day. King Pellam's Launde. David Jones. In Parenthesis, IV. NoAM

So Tired Are All My Thoughts. Thomas Campion. SCP-2

So, to the mind long brooding but on it. Frederick Goddard Tuckerman. *Fr.* Sonnets. AmVN

So we are taking off our masks, are we, and keeping. Homosexuality. Frank O'Hara. CoPAm

"So we diverted the river," he said. Requiem for a River. Kim Williams. RFM

So we lay down and made our love. One-Day Diary. John Biguenet. CoPAm

So we must say goodbye, my darling. Goodbye. Alun Lewis. BoLoP; MPo; OxBTC; PSN

So we reveal our status. Hilda Doolittle ("H.D"). *Fr.* The Walls Do Not Fall. NoAM

So We'll Go No More a-Roving. Byron. BoLoP; HeIP; LoAs; MBPR; NOBE; OLR; SLP; SoSe
(We'll Go No More a-Roving.) Moon

So well I love thee as without thee I. Verses Made the Night before He Died. Michael Drayton. GBL; NOBE

So, we're estranged again—how it goes on! Drought. David Holbrook. OxBTC

So We've Come at Last to Freud. Alice Walker. IHMS

So what said the others and the sun went down. Mrs. Alfred Uruguay. Wallace Stevens. InPS; PiAm

So you dance with me. Ellen Cooney. NPW

So you have swept me back. Eurydice. Hilda Doolittle ("H.D."). VGW

So you said you'd go home to work on your father's farm.  To a Young Poet Who Died.  John Logan.  CAPP

So you're going away.  Good Bye, My Lady Love.  Joseph E. Howard.  FSN

So zestfully canst thou sing?  The Blinded Bird.  Thomas Hardy.  NoAM

So-and-so Reclining on Her Couch.  Wallace Stevens.  NOBA

Sober, he thinks of her; so he gets drunk.  Man and Woman.  Robert Conquest.  OxBTC

Soccer.  Andrei Voznesensky, tr. fr. Russian by Anselm Hollo.  SPo

Social Studies.  Mary Neville.  POL

Society's Child.  Janis Ian.  WIF

Sock left by the road, A.  Judith Serin.  NPW

Socrates and Alcibiades.  Friedrich Hölderlin, tr. fr. German by Michael Hamburger.  LoAs

Sodenly afraid, half waking, half sleeping.  A Woman Sat Weeping.  Unknown.  OxBM

Sofa, The.  William Cowper.  Fr. The Task.  LAuP

Soft as the voice of an angel.  Whispering Hope.  Septimus Winner.  PSoN

Soft as the wind your hair.  Love Song.  Joseph Macleod.  SLP

Soft light, low.  Finding Words in Winter.  John Judson.  HeS

Soft morning. Sycamores. In this one some women pass.  Lecture with Slides, Film Clips and Tape.  Marilyn Krysl.  NPW

Soft o'er the fountain.  Juanita.  Caroline Norton.  BLSH

Soft rainbows, tumbling fleeces of grey cloud.  In Aeternum.  James McAuley.  MAuV

Soft Snow.  Blake.  FSFS; SoSe

Soft sodden fields. The new lambs cry.  In Northern Tasmania.  James McAuley.  MAuV

Soft songs, like birds, die in poison air.  Apology for Apostasy?  Etheridge Knight.  NeAC

Softened by time's consummate plush.  Emily Dickinson.  NOBA

Softly along the road of evening.  Nod.  Walter de la Mare.  OxBTC

Softly and gently, dearly-ransom'd soul.  Angel.  Cardinal Newman.  Fr. The Dream of Gerontius.  PFD

Softly and humbly to the Gulf of Arabs.  Beach Burial.  Kenneth Slessor.  MAuV

Softly and Tenderly Jesus Is Calling, with music.  Will L. Thompson.  BLSH

Softly, in the dusk, a woman is singing to me.  Piano.  D. H. Lawrence.  HeIP; InPK; NoAM; NOBE; PPP

Softly the crane's foot crumples a star.  Recollection.  Dorothy Donnelly.  NCSH

Sohrab and Rustum, sel.  Matthew Arnold.  Sohrab Dead.  NOBE

Soil now gets a rumpling soft and damp, The.  The Strong Are Saying Nothing.  Robert Frost.  AnMo

Soil Searcher.  J. Joyce.  CTBA

Soil was deep and the field well-sited, The.  A Failure  C. Day Lewis.  NOBE

Sojourn in the Whale.  Marianne Moore.  SBG

Solace.  Clarissa Scott Delany.  PoBA

Solar Creation.  Charles Madge.  OxBTC

Sold.  R. R. Cuscaden.  ANTL

Soldier, The.  Rupert Brooke.  1914, V.  BTTM; HeIP; NOBE; OxBTC; PAIC; VoPo

Soldier, The.  Robert Frost.  OFD

Soldier Boy for Me.  Unknown.  AmFP

Soldier [or Souldier] Going to the Field, The.  Sir William Davenant.  MetP; NOBE

Soldier is, The/ all alone.  Glove Glue.  Ken Belford.  NeAc

Soldier, Rest!  Sir Walter Scott.  Fr. The Lady of the Lake, I.  NOBE

Soldier, Won't You Marry Me?  Unknown.  AIW; AmFP; OLR

Soldiers.  Unknown.  GBP

Soldiers are citizens of death's grey land.  Dreamers.  Siegfried Sassoon.  NoAM

Soldiers Bathing.  F. T. Prince.  OxBTC

Soldiers from town to the foot of the hill, The.  The Ballad of Bunker Hill.  Unknown.  BTTM

Soldiers who wish to be a hero.  Soldiers.  Unknown.  GBP

Soldier's Wooing, The, 2 versions.  Unknown.  AmFP

Sole positive of night.  Ne Plus Ultra.  Samuel Taylor Coleridge.  MBPR

Sole true something—This! In Limbo's den, The.  Limbo.  Samuel Taylor Coleridge.  MBPR; OBP

Sole watchman of the flying stars, guard me.  Eleven Addresses to the Lord, III.  John Berryman.  PiAm

Solemn Farewell to the World, A.  Nicholas Breton.  TVS

Solemn plain-faced child stands gazing there, A.  A Portrait.  Walter de la Mare.  NoAM

Solid houses in the mist, The.  New Year's.  Charles Reznikoff.  VGW

Solid Mountain.  George Bowering.  NeAC

Soliloquies, The.  Edward Weismiller.  PAIC

Soliloquy of a Turkey.  Paul Laurence Dunbar.  BPo

Soliloquy of the Spanish Cloister.  Robert Browning.  AnMo; Epi; FaBoCo; InPK; OBP; PAIC

Solitary, The.  Shelley.  MBPR

Solitary, The.  Sara Teasdale.  IPWM

Solitary Confinement.  Phyllis Webb.  Fr. The Kropotkin Poems.  MMD

Solitary prospector, A.  Sunstrike.  Douglas Livingstone.  MPo

Solitary Reaper, The.  Wordsworth.  AnMo; InPS; MBPR; NOBE; PPP; SoSe

Solitary Visions of a Kaufmanoid.  James Cunningham.  JB

Solitude.  A. A. Milne.  LCL

Solitude, an Ode.  Pope.  See Ode on Solitude.

Solitude Late at Night in the Woods.  Robert Bly.  IPWM; SFF; VGW

Solitude that unmakes me one of men.  Compensation.  Robinson Jeffers.  PAIC

Solomon and the Witch.  W. B. Yeats.  NoAM

Solomon Grundy.  Mother Goose.  MG

Solution, The.  Brian Merriman, tr. fr. Modern Irish by Arland Ussher.  Fr. The Midnight Court.  BIrV

Solvitur Acris Hiems.  Horace, tr. by Louis MacNeice.  Odes, I, 4.  Epi

Sombre and rich, the skies.  By the Statue of King Charles at Charing Cross.  Lionel Johnson.  NOBE

Some after a night of sex, some hungover.  Fall Practice.  Dabney Stuart.  CoPAm

Some Are Born.  Stevie Smith.  FaBoCo

Some are in prison; some are dead.  The Chumbs.  Theodore Roethke.  NoAM

Some are teethed on a silver spoon.  Saturday's Child.  Countee Cullen.  InPK; OFD; PoBA

Some autumn leaves a painter took.  The Sumach Leaves.  Jones Very.  NOBA

Some Boys.  John Penkethman.  OxBChV

Some cry up Haydn, some Mozart.  Free Thoughts on Several Eminent Composers.  Charles Lamb.  FaBoCo

Some day I will go to Aarhus.  The Tollund Man.  Seamus Heaney.  BIrV

Some day, when I lose you.  Slumbersong.  Rainer Maria Rilke, tr. by M. D. Herter Norton.  LoAs

Some day, when trees have shed their leaves.  After the Winter.  Claude McKay.  PoBA

Some Days/ Out Walking Above.  De Leon Harrison.  PoBA

Some days, I'm sorely tempted to throw out the baby. Lamentations of an Au Pair Girl. Susan Feldman. AmPA

Some Days the Blood is Warm and Certain. Gene Frumkin. CoPAm

Some die too late and some too soon. The Lost Occasion. Whittier. NOBA

Some Dreams They Forgot. Elizabeth Bishop. NoAM

Some Eyes Condemn. Edward Thomas. NoAM

Some Feelings. Michael Benedikt. ConAP

Some food, some sun. Human Needs. *Unknown.* POL

Some Frenchmen. John Updike. FaBoCo

Some girls wear short dresses. Nehi Blues. *Unknown.* BluL

Some Good Things Left after the War with the Sioux. John Calvin Rezmerski. HeS

Some Good Things to Be Said for the Iron Age. Gary Snyder. CoPAm

Some in the Godspeed, the Susan C. Enough. Marianne Moore. NOBA

Some in their harts their mistris colours bears. Chloris, XXIX. William Smith. AAS

Some keep the Sabbath going to church. Emily Dickinson. IPWM; PBMP; PiAm

Some Kind of Giant. Sheila Pritchard. BoAnP

Some Kind of Toughguy. Gene Frumkin. CoPAm

Some Kisses from "The Kama Sutra." Hugo Williams. BoLoP

Some Knots. Edwin Honig. NoAM

Some Last Questions. W. S. Merwin. CAPP

Some lines after the Razing of the Sioux City Armour's Plant. David Allan Evans. HeS

Some little mice sat in a barn to spin. Mother Goose. MG

Some look at nature for the surface: eye. Nature Lover. John Frederick Nims. CoPAm

Some men sayen that I am blac. The Dark Lady. *Unknown.* OxBM

Some men, some men. Chant for Dark Hours. Dorothy Parker. SBG

Some months she hath been dead (but, being dead). John Donne. *Fr.* An Anatomy of the World: The First Anniversary. SCP-1

Some morning, while you and I are dozing. Intruder. Susan Feldman. AmPA

Some of my best friends are white boys. Friends. Ray Durem. PoBA

Some of us/ these days. Resurrection. Frank Horne. OFD; PoBA

Some "old Robin Down" they call me. Ibby Damsel. *Unknown.* AmFP

Some Oral Stanzas. Thomas Lux. NVAP

Some people are born. For Kenneth Patchen. Wayne Miller. MIT

Some people are young and nothing. Footnote upon the Construction of the Masses. Charles Bukowski. CoPAm

Some people cannot endure. Going the Rounds: A Sort of Love Poem. Anthony Hecht. BoLoP

Some people hang portraits up. A Likeness. Robert Browning. InPS

Some people long to have plenty money. Ease It to Me Blues. *Unknown.* BluL

Some people tell me God takes care of old folks and fools. Fool's Blues. *Unknown.* BluL

Some say my love has proved unfaithful. The Weeping Willow. *Unknown.* AmFP

Some say that ever 'gainst that season comes. Shakespeare. *Fr.* Hamlet, I, i. OFD

Some say the world will end in fire. Fire and Ice. Robert Frost. AnMo; HeIP; InPK; LoAs; MiP; NoAM; NOBA; PPP; SoSe

Some Slippery Afternoon. Daniela Gioseffi. WBN

Some Syrian rainmaker. Assumption. Padraic Fallon. BIrV

Some talk of Alexander, and some of Hercules. The British Grenadiers. *Unknown.* BTTM

Some that have deeper digged love's mine than I. Love's Alchemy. John Donne. AnMo

Some that reporte great Alexanders life. Thomas Watson. *Fr.* Hekatompathia. AAS

Some there are who are present at such occasions. On the Suicide of a Friend. Reed Whittemore. ConAP

Some they will talk of bold Robin Hood. Robin Hood and the Bishop of Hereford. *Unknown.* PeBB

Some thing is lost in me. Man Thinking about Woman. Don L. Lee. IPWM; NoAM

Some things are very dear to me. Sonnet. Gwendolyn B. Bennett. PoBA

Some think my satyre's too too tart. Satires, II, 1. Horace, *tr. by* Thomas Drant. TVS

Some think that in the Christian scheme. Consideration for Others. Christopher Smart. OxBChV

Some thought it mounted to the Lunar sphere. The Lock. Pope. *Fr.* The Rape of the Lock. Moon

Some Thoughts. Gary Simmons. SFF

Some time now past in the autumnal tide. Contemplations. Anne Bradstreet. WPE, *abr.*

Some time when the river is ice ask me. Ask Me. William Stafford. FiCP

Some Trees. John Ashbery. CAPP; ConAP

Some twenty years of marital agreement. J. V. Cunningham. POL

Some tyme I fled the fyre that me brent. Sir Thomas Wyatt. AAS

Some Verses upon the Burning of Our House July 10th, 1666. Anne Bradstreet. *See* Upon the Burning of Our House, July 10th, 1666.

Some with sharp swords, to tell O most accursed! Margaret Cavendish, Duchess of Newcastle. *Fr.* The Fort or Castle of Hope. SCP-2

Some women marry houses. Housewife. Anne Sexton. NMM; Psy

Some Words. Judith Wright. CAAP

Some years of late, in 'Eighty-Eight, as I do well remember-a. Sir Francis Drake; or Eighty-Eight. *Unknown.* GBL

Somebody/ Cut his hair. Young Poet. Myron O'Higgins. PoBA

Somebody Call. Carolyn M. Rodgers. JB

Somebody has given my. Proust's Madeleine. Kenneth Rexroth. NoAM

Somebody just keep on calling me. Stocking Feet Blues. *Unknown.* BluL

Somebody knocked. Who's There? Frances Frost. ECBV

Somebody loses whenever somebody wins. Crapshooters. Carl Sandburg. VGW

Somebody told me I wouldn't know how to choose. Song: Paper. Keith Waldrop. MAT

Somebody under my window. Leaf Out of a Rhyming Diary. Hugh McCrae. MAuV

Somebody who should have been born. The Abortion. Anne Sexton. CAPP; IHMS; MAT; NMM; VGW

Somebody's/ house is on fire. Fire. Anita Barrows. RiTi

Somebody's hiding. Cheek. Coleman Barks. *Fr.* Body Poems. NVAP

Somebody's knockin' at th' door. The Collier's Wife. D. H. Lawrence. OxBTC

Somebody's Sweetheart I Want To Be, *with music.* Will D. Cobb. FSN

Someday Baby. *Unknown.* BluL

Somedays now/ I can squash a cockroach. Wendy G. Rickert. NMM

Somehow/ I cannot think of god. Hypnopompic Poem. William Cole. POL

Somehow it should have been. Masks. Elizabeth Fenton. NMM

Some One. Walter de la Mare. LCL

Someone. Sam Reavin. CaYB

Someone approaches to say his life is ruined. The Dream. David Ignatow. MAT

Some one came knocking. Some One. Walter de la Mare. LCL

Someone Gone Away Downstairs. Jeanette Nichols. RiTi

Someone had been walking in and out. The Orgin of Baseball. Kenneth Patchen. IPWM

Someone has just. Where Are You Now? Mary Britton Miller. ECBV

Someone has shut the shining eyes, straightened and folded. Beside the Bed. Charlotte Mew. WPE

Someone I know—and he's very near. Get Up or You'll Be Late for School, Silly. John Ciardi. ECBV

Someone Is Beating a Woman. Andrei Voznesensky, *tr. fr. Russian by* Jean Garrigue *and* Max Hayward. BuTh

Someone is breathing in the room. Waking. Hugh Maxton. BIrV

Someone is Dead. Lament. Anne Sexton. ConAP; WPE

Someone must make out the cards. What Was Her Name? John Ciardi. MiP

Someone passes. Lady Murasaki Shikibu, *tr. fr. Japanese by* Kenneth Rexroth. OLR

Someone told me long ago. Have You Ever Seen the Rain? J. C. Fogerty. PoRo

Someplace Else. Marge Piercy. NeAC

Something broke the dream. Poem. John Gill. NeAC

Something broken Something. Nightbreak. Adrienne Rich. IHMS; PiAm

Something disturbs your big pale limbs among. For Delphine. James Simmons. POL

Something forgotten twenty years: though my fathers. A Map of the Western Part of the County of Essex in England. Denise Levertov. ConAP

Something hangs in back of me. The Wings. Denise Levertov. CAPP

Something happened the other day that never happened before. Shovelling Iron Ore. *Unknown.* GBP

Something has ceased to come along with me. Death of a Son. Jon Silkin. BBGO; IPWM; NoAM; OxBTC; PPoD

Something has snapped. A Cold Snap. Robert Tait. SLP

Something I want to communicate to you. With the Door Open. David Ignatow. CTBA

Something immense and lonely. Foreboding. John Haines. ConAP

Something inspires the only cow of late. The Cow in Apple Time. Robert Frost. PSN

Something is happening. Last Will and Testament. Alvin Aubert. CoPAm

Something Like an Apple. James Reiss. CAAP

Something, the sandwich and the coffee. Young Woman in Apathy. Christopher Middleton. TwMBP

Something there is that doesn't love a wall. Mending Wall. Robert Frost. InPS; IPWM; NoAM; NOBA; NowV; PiAm; PPoD; VGW

Something went crabwise. The Presence. Maxine W. Kumin. RFM; TSWA; WPE

Something you said—I found it written down. A Postcard to Send to Sumer. William Bronk. VGW

Sometime during eternity. Lawrence Ferlinghetti. *Fr.* A Coney Island of the Mind. CAPP; NoAM

Sometime I Loved. *Unknown.* OxBM

Sometime in Fraunce dwelled a plowman. How the Ploughman Learned His Paternoster. *Unknown.* OxBM

Sometime this world was so steadfast and stable. Lack of Steadfastness. Chaucer. PBMP

Sometimes/ I cool out. Spacin. Ronda Davis. JB

Sometimes/ the poems. Sharon Scott. JB

Sometimes a lantern moves along the night. The Lantern Out of Doors. Gerard Manley Hopkins. AnMo

Sometimes at night when the wind blows hard. The Loch Ness Monster. Tom Buchan. SLP

Sometimes he brays. Donkey. Vasko Popa, *tr. by* Anne Pennington. TSWA

Sometimes he walked to occupy. Generation 2. Sam Cornish. NVAP

Sometimes I catch a glimpse of it. The Presence. Dana Naone. CDW

Sometimes I envy those. The Mole. John Haines. NCSH

Sometimes I Feel Like a Motherless Child. *Unknown.* BLSo, *with music;* WIF

Sometimes I feel like I will never stop. To Satch [*or* American Gothic]. Samuel Allen. BuTh; CTBA; PoBA; SoSe; SPo

Sometimes I get the feeling that I have been here before. Reincarnation. Mae Jackson. PoBA

Sometimes I Go to Camarillo and Sit in the Lounge. K. Curtis Lyle. PoBA

Sometimes I see them. Galway Kinnell. *Fr.* Ruins Under the Stars. RFM

Sometimes I stare into an awning of spirit. Sometimes I Go to Camarillo and Sit in the Lounge. K. Curtis Lyle. PoBA

Sometimes I think the hills. The Hills. Rachel Field. LCL

Sometimes I walk where the deep water dips. Fredrich Goddard Tuckerman. *Fr.* Sonnets. NOBA; PiAm

Sometimes I'm happy. MANICdepressant. Kim Dammers. POL

Sometimes in the over-heated house, but not for long. Fame. Charlotte Mew. SBG

Sometimes in weariness I stop. Years. Jon Anderson. AmPA

Sometimes it is inconceivable that I should be the age I am. The Child. W. S. Merwin. NoAM

Sometimes it seems. The Children. Susan MacDonald. IHMS

Sometimes just being alone seems the bad thing. The Bad Thing. John Wain. BuTh

Sometimes, riding in a car, in Wisconsin. Three Kinds of Pleasures. Robert Bly. ANTL

Sometimes the night echoes to prideless wailing. Sonnet. John Berryman. NoAM

Sometimes the sea lays. Dragging in Winter. David McElroy. AmPA

Sometimes they smear the evening on the air. Bat Angels. Larry Levis. AmPA

Sometimes this quiet settles in like a stone. A Letter from a Friend. Carolyn Maisel. IHMS

Sometimes thou seemest not as thyself alone. Heart's Compass. Dante Gabriel Rossetti. The House of Life, XXVII. PAIC

Sometimes walking late at night. Butcher Shop. Charles Simic. AmPA; NVAP

Sometimes we meet like old lovers. Dede's return to New Mexico. Summer Brenner. RiTi

Sometimes when my eyes are red. My Sad Self. Allen Ginsberg. IPWM; NoAM

Sometimes When Night. V. Sackville-West. SBG; WPE

Sometimes when the boy was troubled he would go. The Cave. Glenn W. Dresbach. RFM

Sometimes, when winding slow by brook and bower.  Frederick Goddard Tuckerman.  *Fr.* Sonnets.  AmVN

Sometimes when you watch the fire.  Long Distance.  William Stafford.  CoPAm

Sometimes, when you're called a bastard.  When Something Happens.  James A. Randall, Jr.  BPo

Sometimes with One I Love.  Walt Whitman.  GBL

Sometimes you almost get a punch in.  Shadowboxing.  James Tate.  CAAP

Sometimes you hear, fifth-hand.  Poetry of Departures.  Philip Larkin.  HeIP; LP; NowV; SS

Somewhere.  Robert Creeley.  NoAM

Somewhere.  James E. Warren, Jr.  AATT

Somewhere/ a niche.  Wish.  Lance Henson.  CDW

Somewhere between our nervousness and.  "Portrait de Femme."  Irving Feldman.  NoAM

Somewhere, farther even than the Sahara.  Clove As Egg.  Daniel Halpern.  CAAP

Somewhere Friendly.  Bruce Dawe.  CAAP

Somewhere I Have Never Travelled, Gladly Beyond.  E. E. Cummings.  BoLoP; InPS; LoAs; VGW

Somewhere, I think in Dakota.  A Sound from the Earth.  William Stafford.  RFM

Somewhere in all this mess.  Pettigrew Museum.  John Calvin Rezmerski.  HeS

Somewhere in California miners rise.  Fitz Hugh Lane Goes to the Masthead.  Wesley McNair.  FAF

Somewhere in Chelsea, early summer.  Relating to Robinson.  Weldon Kees.  AnMo

Somewhere in Kansas, a friend found.  A Place in Kansas.  Ted Kooser.  HeS

Somewhere in the quiet lakes.  A Dream of Lakes.  Laurence Lieberman.  HeS

Somewhere inside me.  Coming Back Home.  Ray A. Young Bear.  CDW

Somewhere near here a new-loosed creek sloughs down.  A Walk in March.  Tim Reynolds.  MAT

Somewhere now she takes off the dress I am putting.  Palindrome.  Lisel Mueller.  IHMS

Somewhere nowhere in Utah, a boy by the roadside.  Utah.  Anne Stevenson.  NCSH

Somewhere on his travels the strange child.  Santa Claus.  Howard Nemerov.  NowV

Somewhere on these bare rocks in some bare hall.  For A College Yearbook.  J. V. Cunningham.  NoAM

Somewhere or Other.  Christina Rossetti.  NOBE

Somewhere outside your window.  A Sense of Coolness.  Quincy Troupe.  PoBA

Somewhere, sometime, in an April twilight.  Dedicatory.  Willa Cather.  WPE

Somewhere the lines were down.  Power Failure.  Dabney Stuart.  NVAP

Somewhere the sun is shining.  Beautiful Isle of Somewhere.  Jessie B. Pounds.  FSN

Somnambulistic Ballad.  Federico García Lorca, *tr. fr. Spanish by* Roy *and* Mary Campbell.  TCP
(Ballad of the Sleepwalker, The, *tr. by* Langston Hughes.)  Epi

Son o' ol' Miz McAuliffe, the widder o' Box-Car Jack.  Pool-Shootin' Roy.  Damon Runyon.  SPo

Son of the King of the Moy, The.  *Unknown, tr. fr. Irish by* John Montague.  BIrV

Son of the old moon-mountains African!  To the Nile.  Keats.  MBPR

"Son," said my mother.  The Ballad of the Harp-Weaver.  Edna St. Vincent Millay.  PBMP; PoTa

Son, upon whose shoulders hung the world one dark Friday.  The Vinedresser Yearns over His Vineyard.  Irene Dayton.  AATT

Son, you have two more months.  D-day Minus.  Edwin Brock.  BBGO

Sonet:"Fra bank to bank, fra wood to wood I rin."  Mark Alexander Boyd.  *See* Fra Bank to Bank,. . .

Sonet Written in Prayse of the Browne Beautie, A.  George Gascoigne.  AAS

Song, A: "Absent from thee, I languish still."  Earl of Rochester.  BoLoP; GBL
(Return.)  NOBE

Song: "Adieu, farewell earths blisse."  Thomas Nashe.  *See* Adieu, Farewell Earth's Bliss.

Song: "Ae fond kiss, and then we sever."  Burns.  *See* Ae Fond Kiss.

Song: "Afternoon cooking in the fall sun."  Robert Hass.  AmPA

Song: "Ah false Amyntas, can that hour."  Aphra Behn.  *Fr.* The Dutch Lover.  WPE

Song: "All in green went my love riding."  E. E. Cummings.  *See* All in Green Went My Love Riding.

Song: "All joy to mortals, joy and mirth."  Aphra Behn.  *Fr.* Emperor of the Moon.  WPE

Song, A: "Ask me no more where Jove bestows."  Thomas Carew.  GBL; HeIP; InPS; NOBE; OBP; PPP
(Ask Me No More.)  SCP-2

Song: "Chloris, forbear a while."  Henry Bold.  GBL

Song: "Choose now among this fairest number."  William Browne.  GBL

Song: "Come, melt thy soul in mine, that when unite."  Sir William Davenant.  *Fr.* The Temple of Love.  SCP-2

Song: "Curse upon that faithless maid, A."  Aphra Behn.  *Fr.* Emperor of the Moon.  WPE

Song: "Deftly, admiral, cast your fly."  W. H. Auden.  PSN

Song:  "False through she be to me and love."  Congreve.  POL
("False through she be to me and love.")  BoLoP; NOBE

Song: "Feathers of the willow, The."  Richard Watson Dixon.  NOBE

Song: "Fire, fire."  Henry Bold.  GBL

Song: "Fresh from the dewy hill, the merry year."  Blake.  MBPR

Song: "From whence cometh song?"  Theodore Roethke.  NCSH

Song: "Gather kittens while you may."  Oliver Herford.  AKE; SpRo

Song: "Give me leave to rail at you."  Earl of Rochester.  LoAs

Song: "Go and catch a falling star."  John Donne.  AnMo; HeIP; InPK; InPS; NOBE; PBMP; PPoD; PPoe; SoSe; VoPo
(Song: "Goe, and catche a falling starre.")  BuTh; OBP

Song: "Go lovely rose."  Edmund Waller.  *See* Go, Lovely Rose.

Song: "Goe, and catche a falling starre."  John Donne.  *See* Song: "Go and catch a falling star."

Song: "Hair/ like heather, father would boast."  Marie Harris.  MMD

Song: "Hark, hark!/ Bow-wow."  Shakespeare.  *Fr.* The Tempest, I, ii.  SoSe

Song: "Help me now."  Emmett Jarrett.  NeAC

Song: "Hence burgundy, claret, and port."  Keats.  MBPR

Song: How can I Care?  Robert Graves.  GBL

Song: "How sweet I roamed [*or* roam'd] from field to field."  Blake.  LoAs; MBPR; OLR
(Prince of Love, The.)  NOBE

Song: "Hush, hush! tread softly! hush, hush, my dear!"  Keats.  MBPR

Song: "I lately vow'd, but 'twas in haste."  John Oldmixon.  POL

Song: "I love the jocund dance."  Blake.  MBPR

Song: "I would not feign a single sigh."  John Clare.  GBL

Song: "It was upon a Lammas night." Burns. *See* Rigs O' Barley, The.

Song: "Know then, my brethren, heaven is clear." *Unknown.* Fr. The Song of Anarchus. FaBoCo

Song: "Lark now leaves his wat'ry nest, The." Sir William Davenant. *See* Aubade: "Lark now leaves. . ."

Song, A: "Lord, when the sense of thy sweet grace." Richard Crashaw. IPWM

Song: "Love a woman? You're an ass!" Earl of Rochester. GBL

Song: "Love and harmony combine." Blake. MBPR

Song: "Love in fantastic triumph sate." Aphra Behn. *Fr.* Abdelazer. NOBE; WPE
(Love Arm'd) SBG

Song: "Love still has something of the sea." Sir Charles Sedley. GBL; NOBE

Song: "Lovers in ladies' magazines." Thomas McGrath. VGW

Song: "Lying is an occupation." Laetitia Pilkington. WPE

Song: Mediocrity in Love Rejected. Thomas Carew. GBL

Song: "Memory, hither come." Blake. MBPR

Song: "Morning opened/ Like a rose. Donald Justice. NCSH

Song: "My cabinets are oyster-shells." Margaret Cavendish, Duchess of Newcastle. *Fr.* The Convent of Pleasure. WPE
("My cabinets are oyster-shells.") SCP-2

Song, A: "My name is sweet Jenny, my age is sixteen." *Unknown.* POL

Song: "My silks and fine array." Blake. LAuP; MBPR
(My Silks and Fine Array.) GBL

Song: "My straying thoughts, reduced stay." Anne Collins. WPE

Song: "Nay but you, who do not love her." Robert Browning. VoPo

Song: "Never take her away." Vinícius de Moraes, *tr. fr. Portuguese by* Richard Wilbur. RRA

Song: "Nymphs and shepherds dance no more." Milton. *Fr.* Arcades. LoAs

Song: "O blush not so! O blush not so! Keats. MBPR

Song, A: "Oh do not wanton with those eyes." Ben Jonson. LoAs

Song, The: "O! Lady dear, fair is thy noon." James Hogg. *Fr.* The Queen's Wake. SLP

Song: "Oh! Love, that stronger art than wine." Aphra Behn. *Fr.* The Lucky Chance. WPE

Song: "O ruddier than the cherry." John Gay. *Fr.* Acis and Galatea. NOBE

Song: "Oh, with the hunger of the sea, forever born anew." John Hall Wheelock. LoAs

Song: "O whistle, and I'll come to ye, my lad." Burns. *See* O Whistle, and I'll Come to You, My Lad.

Song: "Old Adam, the carrion crow." Thomas Lovell Beddoes. *Fr.* Death's Jest Book, V, iv. OBP

Song: Organic Years, The. Marvin Bell. NVAP

Song: "Out upon it, I have lov'd." Sir John Suckling. *See* Constant Lover, The.

Song: Paper. Keith Waldrop. MAT

Song: "Pious Selinda goes to prayers." Congreve. BoLoP; FaBoCo
(Pious Selinda.) NOBE

Song: "Rarely, rarely, comest thou." Shelley. MBPR

Song: "Rough Winds Do Shake the Darling Buds of May." Louis Simpson. SFF

Song: "She sat and sang alway." Christina Rossetti. GBL

Song: "She spoke to me gently with words of sweet meaning." Patrick MacDonogh. PFIr

Song: "She was lyin face down in her face." William Knott. MAT

Song, The: "So light no one noticed." Edward Dorn. VGW

Song: "Spirit haunts the year's last hours, A." Tennyson. HeIP

Song: "Stranger lighted from his steed, The." Keats. SS

Song: "Sweet beast, I have gone prowling." W. D. Snodgrass. SoSe

Song: "Sweetest love, I do not go." John Donne. BoLoP; HeIP; NOBE
(Sweetest Love, I Do Not Go.) VoPo

Song: "Sylvia the fair, in the bloom of fifteen." Dryden. LoAs

Song, The: "That day, in the slipping of torsos and straining flanks." Lola Ridge. WPE

Song, A: "There is a blue sky." Edward Dorn. ConAP

Song: "There was a jolly miller once." Isaac Bickerstaffe. *Fr.* Love in a Village. PFIr

Song: "Those rivers run from that land." Robert Creeley. VGW

Song: To Celia ("Drink to me, only, with thine eyes"). Ben Jonson. *See* To Celia ("Drink to me only. . .").

Song: To My Inconstant Mistress. Thomas Carew. *See* To My Inconstant Mistress.

Song: "We Raise de Wheat." *Unknown.* BPo

Song: "What do you/ want, love. To be." Robert Creeley. TCP

Song: "When early morn walks forth in sober grey." Blake. MBPR

Song: "When I am dead, my dearest." Christina Rossetti. AKE; BoLoP; GBL; NOBE; WPE
(When I Am Dead, My Dearest.) PBMP

Song: "When lovely woman stoops to folly." Goldsmith. *Fr.* The Vicar of Wakefield, ch. 24. BoLoP; LAuP; NOBE
(When Lovely Woman Stoops to Folly.) HeIP

Song: "Where I walk out." Yvor Winters. BoAnP; POL

Song: "Whilst Alexis lay pressed." Dryden. *Fr.* Marriage à la Mode, IV, ii. BoLoP
("Whil'st Alexis lay prest.") LoAs

Song: "Who can say." Tennyson. BBGO

Song: "Why should a foolish marriage vow." Dryden. *See* Why Should a Foolish Marriage Vow.

Song: "Why should your face so please me." Edwin Muir. SLP

Song: "Why so pale and wan, fond lover?" Sir John Suckling. *See* Why So Pale and Wan?

Song: "Widow bird sate mourning for her love, A." Shelley. NOBE

Song: "Whith my frailty don't upbraid me." Congreve. *See* Semele to Jupiter.

Song: "Year's at the spring, The." Robert Browning *See* Year's at the Spring, The.

Song: "Young flowers were whispering in melody." Poe. *Fr.* Al Aaraaf. NOBA

Song about Major Eatherly, A. John Wain. NowV; OxBTC

Song About Mary. Adrian Mitchell. PeBB

Song About Myself. Keats. MBPR
(No Difference, *st.* 4.) ECBV
(There Was a Naughty Boy.) FaBoCo, *st.* 4; OxBChV, *sts.* 1 *and* 4

Song Against Grocers, The. G. K. Chesterton. FaBoCo

Song at the Beginning of Autumn. Elizabeth Jennings. OxBTC

Song at the Feast of Bougham Castle. Wordsworth. MBPR

Song Ballet (I Was Sixteen Years of Age). *Unknown.* AmFP

Song Be Delicate. John Shaw Neilson. MAuV

Song Bewailing the Time of Christmas, A. *Unknown.* SCP-2

Song by the Wavering Nymph. Aphra Behn. SBG

Song for a Dark Girl. Langston Hughes. PoBA

Song for a Marriage. Vassar Miller. PAIC

Song for Afterwards. Francisco Lopez Merina, *tr. fr. Spanish by* Richard O'Connell. LoAs

Song for an Able Bastard, A. Eric Linklater. SLP

Song for Autumn. Andrew Young. GBL

Song For Everybody. Robert Paul Smith. ECBV

Song for Healing. Roberta Hill. CDW

Song for Ishtar. Denise Levertov. AnMo; NMM; NoAM;
PiAm; Psy

Song for Saint Cecilia's Day, 1687, A. Dryden. AnMo; InPS;
PPP; SCP-1
 "Trumpet's loud clangour, The," sel. RAE

Song for September. Robert Fitzgerald. VGW

Song for Seven Parts of the Body, sels. Maxine W. Kumin.
POL
 "I have a life of my own," III.
 "These nubbins/ these hangers-on," VII.
 "They have eyes that see not," V.

Song for Sigmund Freud, A. Kelly Cherry. PPoD

Song for Simeon, A. T. S. Eliot. BuTh

Song for the Cisco Kid; or, Singing for the Face. K. Curtis Lyle.
PoBA

Song for the Last Act. Louise Bogan. LoAs; WPE

Song for the Luddites. Byron. MBPR

Song for the Newborn. Unknown, tr. fr. Grande Pueblo Indian by
Mary Austin. OFD; WPE

Song for the Ragged Schools of London, A. Elizabeth Barrett
Browning. SBG

Song for the unsung heroes who rose in the country's need, A.
The Unsung Heroes. Paul Laurence Dunbar. BPo

Song Form. LeRoi Jones. CTBA

Song from Aella. Thomas Chatterton. See Minstrel's Song, The.

Song from Shakespear's Cymbelyne, A. William Collins. LAuP
(Dirge in "Cymbeline.") NOBE

Song from the Waters. Thomas Lovell Beddoes. Fr. Death's
Jest Book. NOBE

Song in Autumn. Robert D. Fitzgerald. MAuV

Song in Passing, A. Yvor Winters. VGW

Song in the Front Yard, A. Gwendolyn Brooks. IPWM;
NoAM; NOBA; PoBA

Song Mt. Tamalpais Sings, The. Lew Welch. MIT

Song My. Susan Griffin. NMM

Song of a Child's Spirit. Unknown, tr. fr. Pueblo Indian. AKE

Song of a Common Lover. Flavien Ranaivo, tr. fr. French by
Alan Ryder. BuTh

Song of a Man Who Has Come Through, The. D. H. Lawrence.
InPS; NoAM; OxBTC

Song of a Woman Abandoned by the Tribe. Unknown, tr. fr.
Shoshone Indian by Mary Austin. WPE

Song of a Young Lady to Her Ancient Lover, A. Earl of
Rochester. BoLoP; GBL

Song of Amergin. Unknown. See Alphabet Calendar of
Amergin.

Song of Anarchus, The, sel. Unknown.
 Song: "Know then, my brethern, heaven is clear." FaBoCo

Song of Callicles, The. Matthew Arnold. Fr. Empedocles on
Etna, II. NOBE

Song of Ceres. Katherine Doak. NPW

Song of Cove Creek Dam, The. Unknown. AmFP

Song of Crede, The. Unknown, tr. fr. Irish by Alfred Perceval
Graves. BIrV

Song of Expectancy. George Hitchcock. MIT

Song of Fionnuala, The. Thomas Moore. BIrV

Song of Fixed Accord. Wallace Stevens. InPS

Song of Hiawatha, The, sels. Longfellow.
 Hiawatha and Mudjekeewis, IV. AKE
 Introduction: "Should you ask me, whence these stories?"
 NOBA; PiAm
 Old Nokomis Sings, fr. III. ECBV
 ("By the shores of Gitche Gumee.") SpRo

Song of Lewes, The. Unknown. OxBM

Song of Liberty. Blake. MBPR

Song of Marion's Men. Bryant. BTTM

Song of Myself. Walt Whitman. AmVN; NOBA; PiAm; VoPo,
much abr.
Sels.
 Animals, fr. XXXII. POL
 "Big doors of the country barn stood open and ready, The," IX.
 RAE
 "I am the teacher of athletes," XLVII. AnMo
 "I believe a leaf of grass is no less than the journey-work of the
 stars," fr. XXXI. InPS
 "I believe in the flesh and the appetites," fr. XXIV. Prf
 "I believe in you my soul," V. Prf
 "I celebrate myself and sing myself," I. AnMo
 "I understand the large heart of heroes," fr. XXXIII. InPS
 "My lovers suffocate me," fr. XLV. LoAs
 "My signs are a rain-proof coat, good shoes, a staff cut from the
 woods," fr. XLVI. Prf
 "Past and present wilt, The," LI. AnMo
 "Sea of stretch'd ground-swells," fr. XXII. GrRo
 "Spotted hawk swoops by and accuses me, The," LII. AnMo
 "Trippers and askers surround me," fr. IV. InPS
 "Twenty-eight young men bathe by the shore," XI. LoAs
 "Walt Whitman, a kosmos, of Manhattan the son," XXIV.
 AnMo
 ("Walt Whitman, an American, one of the roughs, a kosmos,"
 11 ll.) GrRo

Song of Seyd Nimetollah of Kuhistan. Emerson. NOBA

Song of Solomon, The, sels. Bible, O.T.
 "How beautiful are thy feet in sandals, O prince's daughter!"
 VII: 1-9. OBP
 "I am the rose of Sharon, and the lily of the valleys," II.
 BoLoP; GBL
 (Song of Songs.) OLR
 "Voice of my beloved, The," II: 8-17. PBMP

Song of Songs, The. Bible, O.T. See Song of Solomon, The.

Song of Songs. Wilfred Owen. OBP

Song of the Banana Man. Evan Jones. MPo

Song of the Battery Hen. Edwin Brock. LP; MPo

Song of the Camp, The. Bayard Taylor. BTTM

Song of the Cauld Lad of Hylton. Unknown. GBP

Song of the Death of Mr. Thewlis, The, abr. Unknown. SCP-2

Song of the Degrees, A, sel. Ezra Pound.
 "Wind moves above the wheat, The." AKE

Song of the Dying Gunner A.A.1. Charles Causley. AIW

Song of the Freedman. Unknown. PBMP

Song of the Fucked Duck. Marge Piercy. NMM

Song of the Galley-Slaves. Kipling. OBP

Song of the Happy Shepherd, The. W. B. Yeats. NoAM

Song of the Indian Maid, The. Keats. Fr. Endymion. NOBE

Song of the Jellicles, The. T. S. Eliot. LCL; OxChV; PCat

Song of the Lotos-Eaters, The. Tennyson. Fr. The Lotos-Eaters.
NOBE
 ("There is sweet music here that softer falls.") HeIP

Song of the Mad Prince, The. Walter de la Mare. NoAM;
NOBE; OxBChV

Song of the Master and Boatswain. W. H. Auden. Fr. Sea and
the Mirror. BoLoP

Song of the Mean Mary Jean Machine, The. James Baker Hall.
FiCP

Song of the Militant Romance, The. Percy Wyndham Lewis.
OxBTC

Song of the Murdered Child. Unknown. GBP

Song of the Old Mother, The. W. B. Yeats. IPWM; PFIr

Song of the Open Road. Ogden Nash. AKE; FaBoCo

Song of the Open Road. Walt Whitman. NOBA
 "Afoot and light-hearted I take to the open road," sel. RFM

Song of the Reed Sparrow, The. *Unknown.* OxBChV
Song of the Shirt, The, *sel.* Thomas Hood.
  "Work—work—work." VoPo
Song of the Sky Loom. *Unknown, tr. fr. Tewa Indian by* Herbert
  J. Spinden. TSWA
Song of the Smoke, The. W. E. B. DuBois. PoBA
Song of the Son. Jean Toomer. PoBA
Song of the Strange Young Duckling. Deborah Munro. IHMS
Song of the Western Men, The. Robert Stephen Hawker.
  BTTM
Song of This House, The. Stephen Vincent. NeAC
Song of Three Smiles. W. S. Merwin. NOBA; VGW
Song of Wandering Aengus, The. W. B. Yeats. AKE; MAT;
  OBP; PBMP; WIF
Song of Winter, A. *Unknown, tr. fr. Old Irish by* Kuno Meyer.
  PFIr
Song on May Morning. Milton. FSFS
Song on New Year's Day before the King, A. Thomas Flatman.
  SCP-2
Song the Body Dreamed in the Spirit's Mad Behest, The.
  William Everson. PiAm
Song thumbed down a cruiser for a ride, A. James Cunningham.
  *Fr.* The Narrator's Trance. JB
Song to Accompany the Bearer of Bad News. David Wagoner.
  PPoD
Song to Be Attached. Hollis Summers. CoPAm
Song to David, A. Christopher Smart. BoReV, *abr.*; LAuP;
  NOBE, *abr.*
  *Sels.*
  Adoremus. OBP
  Fruits of the Earth. OBP
  Gloria. OBP
Song to Mithras, A. Kipling. BTTM
Song to the Men of England. Shelley. InPS; MBPR; PBMP;
  SFF
Song to the Ninth Grade. Pamela Crawford Holahan. AIW
Song to the Runaway Slave. *Unknown.* BPo
Song Turning Back into Itself, The. Al Young. CAAP
Song will deceive you, the scent will incite you to sing, The. You
  Cannot Go Down to the Spring. John Shaw Neilson.
  MAuV
Song Written at Sea in the First Dutch War. Charles Sackville.
  NOBE.
Songbook of Sebastian Arrurruz, The, *sel.* Geoffrey Hill.
  "Love, oh my love, it will come." PSN
Song-ily. *Unknown.* ECBV
Songs. David Steingass. HeS
Songs for the Cisco Kid; or, Singing: Song # 2. K. Curtis Lyle.
  PoBA
Songs from the Maker of Totems. Duane Niatum. VW
Songs My Mother Taught Me, *with music. Unknown, tr. fr.*
  *German by* Natalia Macfarren. BLSH
Songs of Education, *sel.* G. K. Chesterton.
  For the Crèche. FaBoCo
Songs of Experience, *sel.* Blake.
  Ah! Sun-flower. LAuP; MBPR; PPP
  Angel, The. LAuP; MBPR
  Chimney Sweeper, The ("A little black thing among the snow").
    LAuP; MBPR; PPoe; PPP
  Clod and the Pebble, The. AnMo; InPS; LAuP; LoAs; MBPR;
    NOBE; SS
  Earth's Answer. InPS; LAuP; MBPR
  Fly, The. LAuP; MBPR; OBP; PBMP
  Garden of Love, The. GBL; IPWM; LAuP; LoAs; MAT;
    MBPR; OBP; PPoe; SS; WIF
  Hear the Voice of the Bard, *Introd.* NOBE; OBP
    (Introduction: "Hear the voice of the bard!") InPS; LAuP;
    MBPR

Holy Thursday ("Is this a holy thing to see"). InPS; LauP;
  MBPR
Human Abstract, The. LAuP; MBPR; PPP
Infant sorrow. InPS; LauP; MBPR
Little Boy Lost, A ("Nought loves another as itself"). MBPR;
  OBP
Little Girl Found, The. MBPR; RRA
Little Girl Lost, A ("Children of the future age"). MBPR;
  RRA
Little Girl Lost, The ("In futurity/ I prophetic see"). MBPR;
  RRA
Little Vagabond, The. MBPR
Lilly, The. MBPR
London ("I wander thro' each charter'd street"). AnMo;
  GrRo; HeIP; InPK; InPS; LauP; MAT; MBPR; NOBE;
  OBP; PAIC; VoPo; WIF
My Pretty Rose Tree. BoLoP; LAuP; MBPR
Nurse's Song ("When the voice of children are heard on the
  green/ And whisprings are in the dale"). LAuP; MBPR
Poison Tree, A. AnMo; IPWM; LAuP; MBPR; PBMP;
  PPoD; PPoe; PPP; SFF; WIF
School Boy, The. MBPR
Sick rose, The. BoLoP; HeIP; InPK: InPS; LAuP; MBPR;
  NOBE; PAIC; PPP
Tiger, The. InPS; NOBE; PBMP; SoSe; SpRo; WIF, 3
  *versions*
  (Tyger, The.) BoReV; HeIP; InPK; IPWM; LAuP; MBPR;
    OBP; PPoD; PPoe; PPP
To Tizrah. BoReV; MBPR; NOBE
Voice of the Ancient Bard, The. MBPR
Songs of Innocence, *sels.* Blake.
  Blossom, The. MBPR
  Chimney Sweeper, The ("When my mother died I was very
    young"). AnMo; HeIP; InPK; LAuP; MBPR; OxBChV;
    PPoe; PPP; SoSe
  Cradle Song, A: "Sweet dreams form a shade." LAuP; MBPR
  Divine Image, The ("To mercy pity peace and love"). BoReV;
    LAuP; MBPR; NOBE; PPP
  Dream, A. LAuP; MBPR
  Echoing [*or* Ecchoing] Green, The. FSFS; LAuP; MBPR
  Holy Thursday (" 'Twas on a Holy Thursday, their innocent
    faces clean"). BoReV; InPS; LAuP; MBPR; NOBE; OFD
  Infant Joy. LAuP; MBPR
  Lamb, The. HeIP; InPS; LAuP; LCL; MBPR; OxBChV;
    PAIC; RAE; SoSe
  Laughing Song. LAuP; MBPR; OxBChV
    (Laughter.) ECBV
  Little Black Boy, The. AnMo; HeIP; InPK; LAuP; MBPR;
    OBP; OxBChV
  Little Boy Found, The. LAuP; MBPR
  Little Boy Lost, The ("Father, father, where are you going?").
    LAuP; MBPR
  Night. MBPR; OxBChV
  Nurse's Song ("When the voices of children are heard on the
    green/ And laughing"). LAuP; MBPR; OxBChV
  On Anothers Sorrow. MBPR
  Piping Down the Valleys Wild. HeIP; NOBE
    (Introduction: "Piping down the valleys wild.") InPS; LAuP;
    MBPR
    (Piper, The.) LCL; OxBChV
  Shepherd, The. MBPR
  Spring. FSFS; LCL; MBPR
Songs of Maximus, The. Charles Olson. CoPAm
  *Sels.*
  "All/ wrong," II. NoAM
  "Colored pictures," I. NoAM
  "This morning of the small snow," III. PPP
Songs of Selma, The, *sel.* James Macpherson.
  "Colma—It is night." SLP
Songs of tears. To the Spirit of Carlos Gardel. Victor
  Hernández Cruz. SA

Songs that erupt, The. Chorus. Jack Kerouac. *Fr.* Mexico City Blues. PiAm

Songs to Survive the Summer. Robert Hass. AmPA

"Sonja Henie," the young girl. Preface. Theodore Weiss. VGW

Sonne hath twyse brought forthe the tender grene, The. Earl of Surrey. AAS

Sonnet: "And change with hurried has swept these scenes." Frederick Goddard Tuckerman. *Fr.* Sonnets; II, xviii. PiAm

Sonnet: "And so one sees all living matter perish." Louise Labé, *tr. fr.* French by Frederic Prokosch. LoAs

Sonnet: "As an unperfect actor on the stage." Shakespeare. *See* Sonnets, XXIII.

Sonnet: "Azured vault, the crystal circles bright, The." James I, King of England. Moon

Sonnet: "Banging around in a cigarette she isn't 'in love.'" Ted Berrigan. CAAP

Sonnet: "Batter my heart, three-personed God; for you." John Donne. Holy Sonnets, XIV. IPWM

Sonnet: "Being your slave, what should I do but tend." Shakespeare. *See* Sonnets, LVII.

Sonnet: "Beware of Benjamin Franklin, he is totally lacking in grace." Ted Berrigan. CAAP

Sonnet: " 'Broken heart,' A. . .but can a heart break, now?" John Berryman. Epi

Sonnet: "But man finds means, grant him but place and room." Frederick Goddard Tuckerman. *Fr.* Sonnets; V, iv. PiAm

Sonnet: "Dear Ron: hello. Your name is now a household name." Ted Berrigan. CAAP

Sonnet: "Devouring Time, blunt thou the lion's paws." Shakespeare. *See* Sonnets, XIX.

Sonnet: England in 1819. Shelley. *See* England in 1819.

Sonnet: "Expense of spirit in a waste of shame, The." Shakespeare. *See* Sonnets, CXXIX.

Sonnet: "Farewell! thou art too dear for my possessing." Shakespeare. *See* Sonnets, LXXXVII.

Sonnet: "Five A.M. on East Fourteenth I'm out to eat." Tom Clark. Epi

Sonnet: "For Nature daily through her grand design." Frederick Goddard Tuckerman. *Fr.* Sonnets; I, xxvi. PiAm

Sonnet: "Fra banc to banc, fra wod to wod, I rin." Mark Alexander Boyd. *See* Fra Bank to Bank, . . .

Sonnet: "Francis Marion nudges himself gently into the big blue sky." Ted Berrigan. CAAP

Sonnet: "From you have I been absent in the spring." Shakespeare. *See* Sonnets, XCVIII.

Sonnet: "Full many a glorious morning have I seen." Shakespeare. *See* Sonnets, XXXIII.

Sonnet: "Gray his head goes his feet green." Ted Berrigan. CAAP

Sonnet: "Harum-scarum haze on the Pollock streets." Ted Berrigan. CAAP

Sonnet: "He came in silvern armor, trimmed with black." Gwendolyn B. Bennett. PoBA

Sonnet, A: "His golden locks time hath to silver turned." George Peele. *See* His Golden Locks. . .

Sonnet: "How do I love thee? Let me count the ways." Elizabeth Barrett Browning. *See* Sonnets from the Portuguese: "How do I love thee. . ."

Sonnet: "How like a winter hath my absence been." Shakespeare. *See* Sonnets, XCVII.

Sonnet: "How oft when thou, my music, music play'st." Shakespeare. *See* Sonnets, CXXVIII.

Sonnet: "How strange to be gone in a minute." Ted Berrigan. CAAP

Sonnet: "How strange to be gone in a minute! A man! Ted Berrigan. CAAP

Sonnet: "I am closing my window. Tear silence the wind." Ted Berrigan. Epi

Sonnet: "I had no thought of violets of late." Alice Dunbar Nelson. PoBA

Sonnet: "I lift—lift you five States away your glass." John Berryman. Epi

Sonnet: "I like to beat people up." Ted Berrigan. CAAP

Sonnet: "I must not grieve my love, whose eyes would read." Samuel Daniel. *Fr.* To Delia. LoAs

Sonnet: "I said I splendidly loved you; it's not true." Rupert Brooke. BuTh

Sonnet: "I saw magic on a green country road." Michael Hartnett. BIrV

Sonnet: "I wake up back aching from soft bed Pat." Ted Berrigan. CAAP

Sonnet: "If thy soul check thee that I come so near." Shakespeare. *See* Sonnets, CXXXVI.

Sonnet: "Ile give thee leave my love, in beauties field." Earl of Stirling. *Fr.* Aurora. SLP

Sonnet: "Imprimis: I forgot all day your face." Conrad Aiken. LoAs

Sonnet: "In every dream thy lovely features rise." William Barnes. BoLoP

Sonnet: "In Joe Brainard's collage its white arrows." Ted Berrigan. Epi

Sonnet: "In my paintings for they are present." Ted Berrigan. CAAP

Sonnet: "It is a human universe: and I. Ted Berrigan. Epi

Sonnet: "It is night. You are asleep. And beautiful tears." Ted Berrigan. CAAP

Sonnet: "It's 8:54 a.m. Brooklyn it's the 28th of July and." Ted Berrigan. CAAP

Sonnet: "Joyful ants nest on the roof of my tree." Ted Berrigan. CAAP

Sonnet: "Lackying my loue I go from place to place." Spenser. *See* Amoretti, LXXVIII.

Sonnet: "Let me not to the marriage of true minds." Shakespeare. *See* Sonnets, CXVI.

Sonnet: "Lift not the painted veil which those who live." Shelley. MBPR

Sonnet: "Like as the waves make towards the pebbled shore." Shakespeare. *See* Sonnets, LX.

Sonnet: "Lo, as a careful housewife runs to catch." Shakespeare. *See* Sonnets, CXLIII.

Sonnet: "Love is too young to know what conscience is." Shakespeare. *See* Sonnets, CLI.

Sonnet: "Methought I saw my late espoused saint." Milton. *See* On His Deceased Wife.

Sonnet: "My dream a drink with Lonnie Johnson." Ted Berrigan. CAAP; NoAM

Sonnet: "My love, I have betrayed you seventy times." Conrad Aiken. LoAs

Sonnet: "My mistress' eyes are nothing like the sun." Shakespeare. *See* Sonnets, CXXX.

Sonnet: "No longer mourn for me when I am dead." Shakespeare. *See* Sonnets, LXXI.

Sonnet: "No worst, there is none. Pitched past pitch of grief." Gerard Manley Hopkins. *See* No Worst, There Is None.

Sonnet: "Not marble, not the gilded monuments." Shakespeare. *See* Sonnets, LV

Sonnet: "Not mine own fears nor the prophetic soul." Shakespeare. *See* Sonnets, CVII.

Sonnet: "Not the round natural world, not the deep mind." Frederick Goddard Tuckerman. *Fr.* Sonnets; I, xxviii. PiAm

Sonnet: "Now the bat circles on the breeze of eve."  Anne Radcliffe.  WPE

Sonnet: "O kiss me yet again, O kiss me over."  Louise Labé, *tr. fr. French by* Frederic Prokosch.  LoAs

Sonnet, A: "O lovely O most charming pug."  Marjory Fleming.  FaBoCo

Sonnet: "O! Never say that I was false of heart."  Shakespeare. *See* Sonnets, CIX

Sonnet: "Oh the 15th day of November in the year of the motorcar."  Ted Berrigan.  VW

Sonnet: On the Late Massacre in Piedmont.  Milton.  *See* On the Late Massacre in Piedmont.

Sonnet: "One day I wrote her name upon the strand."  Spenser. *See* Amoretti, LXXV.

Sonnet: "One still dark night I sat alone and wrote."  Frederick Goddard Tuckerman.  *Fr.* Sonnets; II, xxxiii.  PiAm

Sonnet: "Orgasm completely, The."  Tom Clark.  PPoD

Sonnet: "Our Sunday morning when dawn-priests were applying." John Berryman.  Epi
("Our Sunday morning when dawn-priests were applying.") BoLoP

Sonnet: Political Greatness.  Shelley.  OBP

Sonnet: "Poor soul, the center of my sinful earth."  Shakespeare. *See* Sonnets, CXLVI.

Sonnet: Rapture Concerning His Lady, A.  Guido Cavalcanti, *tr. fr. Italian by* Dante Gabriel Rossetti.  LoAs

Sonnet: "Roll on, sad world! not Mercury or Mars."  Frederick Goddard Tuckerman.  *Fr.* Sonnets, II, xvii.  PiAm

Sonnet: "Shall I compare thee to a summer's day?"  Shakespeare. *See* Sonnets, XVIII.

Sonnet: "Since brass, nor stone, nor earth, nor boundless sea." Shakespeare.  *See* Sonnets, LXV.

Sonnet: "Sleep half sleep half silence and with reasons."  Ted Berrigan.  CAAP; Epi

Sonnet: "Some things are very dear to me."  Gwendolyn B. Bennett.  PoBA

Sonnet: "Sometimes I walk where the deep water dips." Frederick Goddard Tuckerman.  *Fr.* Sonnets; III, x.  PiAm

Sonnet: "Sometimes the night echoes to prideless wailing."  John Berryman.  NoAM

Sonnet, A: "Sonnet is a moment's monument, A."  Dante Gabriel Rossetti.  The House of Life, *introd.*  HeIP; PAIC; SoSe

Sonnet: "Summer so histrionic, marvelous dirty days."  Ted Berrigan.  CAAP; Epi

Sonnet: "That time of year thou mayst in me behold." Shakespeare.  *See* Sonnets, LXXIII.

Sonnet: "Then hate me when thou wilt; if ever, now." Shakespeare.  *See* Sonnets, XC.

Sonnet: "They basted his caption on top of the fat sheriff, 'The Pig.'"  Ted Berrigan.  CAAP

Sonnet: "They that have power to hurt and will do none." Shakespeare.  *See* Sonnets, XCIV.

Sonnet: "Thy bosom is endearèd with all hearts."  Shakespeare. *See* Sonnets, XXXI.

Sonnet: "Tired with all these, for restful death I cry." Shakespeare.  *See* Sonnets, LXVI.

Sonnet: "To me, fair friend, you never can be old."  Shakespeare. *See*  Sonnets, CIV.

Sonnet: "Today as I passed through the market-place."  Robert Hillyer.  *Fr.* A Sonnet Sequence.  TH

Sonnet: "Too many fucking mosquitoes under the blazing sun." Ted Berrigan.  CAAP

Sonnet: "Two loves have I of comfort and despair."  Shakespeare. *See* Sonnets, CXLIV.

Sonnet, A: "Two voices are there: one is of the deep."  James Kenneth Stephen.  FaBoCo; PPoD; SpRo

Sonnet: "Under the mountain, as when first I knew."  Frederick Goddard Tuckerman.  *Fr.* Sonnets; II, xvi.  PiAm

Sonnet: "Unthrifty loveliness, why dost thou spend." Shakespeare.  *See* Sonnets, IV.

Sonnet: "Upon a day, came sorrow in to me."  Dante, *tr. fr. Italian by* Dante Gabriel Rossetti.  LoAs

Sonnet: "Wan as pale thighs making apple belly strides."  Ted Berrigan.  CAAP

Sonnet: "Weary year his race now having run, The."  Spenser. *See* Amoretti, LXII.

Sonnet: "What thwarts this fear I love."  Ted Berrigan.  CAAP

Sonnet: "What was ashore, then?. . .Cargoed with forget."  John Berryman.  Epi

Sonnet: "When I consider how my light is spent."  Milton.  *See* On His Blindness.

Sonnet: "When I do count the clock that tells the time." Shakespeare.  *See* Sonnets, XII.

Sonnet: "When I have seen by Time's fell hand defaced." Shakespeare.  *See* Sonnets, LXIV.

Sonnet: "When in disgrace with fortune and men's eyes." Shakespeare.  *See* Sonnets, XXIX.

Sonnet: "When in the chronicle of wasted time."  Shakespeare. *See* Sonnets, CVI.

Sonnet: "When my love swears that she is made of truth." Shakespeare.  *See* Sonnets, CXXXVIII.

Sonnet: "When to the sessions of sweet silent thought." Shakespeare.  *See* Sonnets, XXX.

Sonnet: "Where are we to go when this is done?"  Alfred A. Duckett.  PoBA

Sonnet: "Whoever hath her wish, thou hast thy Will." Shakespeare.  *See* Sonnets, CXXXV.

Sonnet: "Wind has blown the rain away and blown, A."  E. E. Cummings.  PAIC

Sonnet: "With how sad steps, Oh Moon."  Sir Philip Sidney.  *See* Astrophel and Stella, XXXI.

Sonnet: "Withered leaves fly higher than dolls can see, The."  Ted Berrigan.  CAAP

Sonnet: "Woman is singing the song and summer."  Ted Berrigan.  CAAP

Sonnet Found in a Deserted Mad-House.  *Unknown.*  FaBoCo

Sonnet in Allusion to Various Recent Histories and Notices of the French Revolution.  Wordsworth.  MBPR

Sonnet in Search of an Author.  William Carlos Williams.  Epi

Sonnet is a moment's monument, A.  A Sonnet.  Dante Gabriel Rossetti.  The House of Life, *introd.*  HeIP; PAIC; SoSe

Sonnet of Black Beauty.  Lord Herbert of Cherbury.  PAIC

Sonnet of the Moon, A.  Charles Best.  SoSe
(Of the Moon.)  Moon

Sonnet on Chillon.  Byron.  *Fr.* The Prisoner of Chillon.  PAIC; PBMP

Sonnet on Launching Some Bottles Filled with Knowledge into the Bristol Channel.  Shelley.  MBPR

Sonnet on the Death of [Mr.] Richard West.  Thomas Gray.  LAuP; PAIC
(On the Death of Richard West.)  NOBE

Sonnet on the Projected Kendal and Windermere Railway. Wordsworth.  MBPR

Sonnet Sequence, A, *sel.*  Robert Hillyer.
"Today as I passed through the market-place," VIII.  TH

Sonnet—Silence.  Poe.  NOBA; PiAm

Sonnet to a Clam.  John Godfrey Saxe.  BoAnP

Sonnet to Britain.  William Edmonstoune Aytoun.  FaBoCo

Sonnet To Byron.  Shelley.  MBPR

Sonnet to Harriet on Her Birthday.  Shelley.  MBPR

Sonnet to My Mother.  George Barker.  LoAs; PAIC

Sonnet to Negro Soldiers.  Joseph Seamon Cotter, Jr.  PoBA

Sonnet—To Science. Poe. Al Aaraaf: Prologue. AmVN; InPK; PAIC; PBMP; PiAm; PPoD; WIF

Sonnet to the Prince Regent. Byron. MBPR

Sonnet to the River Otter. Samuel Taylor Coleridge. MBPR

Sonnet 21. Paul Goodman. VGW

Sonnet Written in the Church-yard at Middleton, in Sussex. Charlotte Smith. See Press'd by the Moon, Mute Arbitress of Tides.

Sonnet Written in the Cottage Where Burns Was Born. Keats. MBPR

Sonnet Written upon Ben Bevis. Keats. MBPR

Sonnets, sel. Shakespeare.
 IV. "Unthrifty loveliness, why dost thou spend." GrRo
 XII. "When I do count the clock that tells the time." InPS; VoPo
 XVIII. "Shall I compare thee to a summer's day?" BoLoP; GBL; HeIP; InPS; InPK; IPWM; MAT; NOBE; OLR; PAIC; PBMP; PPoe
 XIX. "Devouring Time blunt thou the lion's paws." Epi; MAT
 XXIII. "As an unperfect actor on the stage." OBP
 XXIX. "When in disgrace with fortune and men's eyes." Epi; GBL; HeIP; NOBE; OBP; PAIC; PPoe; PPP; Prf
 XXX. "When to the sessions of sweet silent thought." Epi; GBL; InPS; NOBE; PAIC; PPP; VoPo; WIF
 XXXI. "Thy bosom is endeared with all hearts." NOBE
 XXXIII. "Full many a glorious morning have I seen." PPP
 LV. "Not marble, nor the gilded monuments." Epi; HeIP; InPK; NOBE; PAIC; PPoe: WIF
 LVII. "Being your slave, what should I do but tend." LoAs
 LX. "Like as the waves make towards the pebbled shore." Epi; NOBE
 LXIV. "When I have seen by Time's fell hand defaced." HeIP; NOBE; PAIC; PPoe
 LXV. "Since brass, nor stone, nor earth, nor boundless sea." Epi; InPS; NOBE
 LXVI. "Tired with all these, for restful death I cry." InPS; NOBE
 LXXI. "No longer mourn for me when I am dead." Epi; GBL; PPoe; SoSe
 LXXIII. "That time of year thou may'st in me behold." BoLoP; Epi; FSFS; GBL; HeIP; InPK; InPS; IPWM; LoAs; NOBE; OBP; PBMP; PPoD; PPP; SoSe
 LXXXVII. "Farewell! thou art too dear for my possessing." InPS; LoAs; NOBE; PPoD
 XC. "Then hate me when thou wilt; if ever, now." NOBE
 XCIV. "They that have power to hurt, and will do none." Epi; InPS; LoAs; NOBE; PPoe; PPP
 XCVII. "How like a winter hath my absence been." NOBE
 XCVIII. "From you I have been absent in the spring." FSFS; NOBE
 CIV. "To me, fair friend, you never can be old." GBL; HeIP; LoAs; Prf
 CVI. "When in the chronicle of wasted time." NOBE; PPoe
 CVII. "Not mine own fears nor the prophetic soul." PPoe
 CIX. "O! Never say that I was false of heart." NOBE
 CXVI. "Let me not to the marriage of true minds." Epi; GBL; HeIP; InPK; InPS; IPWM; NOBE; OBP; PBMP; PPoe; PPP; SoSe; VoPo
 CXXVIII. "How oft when thou, my music, music play'st." Epi
 CXXIX. "Expense of spirit in a waste of shame, The." Epi; GBL; HeIP; InPS; LoAs; NOBE; OBP; PPoe; PPoD; PPP
 CXXX. "My mistress' eyes are nothing like the sun." BoLoP; Epi; InPK; InPS; IPWM; PBMP; PPoD; PPP; SoSe; VoPo; WIF
 CXXXV. "Whoever hath her wish, thou hast thy Will." Epi
 CXXXVI. "If thy soul check thee that I come so near." Epi
 CXXXVIII. "When my love swears that she is made of truth." Epi; LoAs; OBP; PPoD; PPP; SoSe
 CXLIII. "Lo, as a careful housewife runs to catch." InPK
 CXLIV. "Two loves have I of comfort and despair." Epi

 CXLVI. "Poor soul the centre of my sinful earth." Epi; InPK; NOBE; OBP; PPoe; PPP
 CLI. "Love is too young to know what conscience is." HeIP
Sonnets, sels. Frederick Goddard Tuckerman.
 "All men,—the preacher saith,—whate'er or whence," I, xvii. AmVN
 "And borne with theirs, my proudest thoughts do seem," I, iii. AmVN
 "And change with hurried hand has swept these scenes," II, xviii. NOBA; PiAm
 "And she—her beauty never made her cold," I, xv. AmVN
 "And so the day drops by; the horizon draws," I, v. AmVN
 "As when, down some broad river dropping, we," I, viii. AmVN
 "But man finds means, grant him but place and room," V, iv. PiAm
 "By this low fire I often sit to woo," I, xxv. AmVN
 "For Nature daily through her grand design," I, xxvi. AmVN; PiAm
 "Hast thou seen reversed the prophet's miracle," IV, x. NOBA
 "Here, where the red man swept the leaves away," IV, ix. NOBA
 "Nor looks that backward life so bare to me," I, iv. AmVN
 "Not proud of station, nor in worldly pelf," I, xiv. AmVN
 "Not the round natural world, not the deep mind," I, xxviii. AmVN; PiAM; PPoD
 "O Father, God! to whom, in happier days," I, xxi. AmVN
 "One still dark night I sat alone and wrote," II, xxxiii. PiAm
 "Roll on, sad world! not Mercury or Mars," II, xix. PiAm
 "Sometimes I walk where the deep water dips," III, x. NOBA; PiAm
 "Sometimes, when winding slow by brook and bower," I, i. AmVN
 "So, to the mind long brooding but on it," I, xxvii. AmVN
 "Still craves the spirit: never Nature solves," I, xx. AmVN
 "Still pressing through these weeping solitudes," II, xi. NOBA
 "Under the mountain, as when first I knew," II, xvi. PiAm
 "Upper chamber in a darkened house, An," I, x. AmVN; NOBA; PiAm
 "What profits it to me, though here allowed," I, xi. AmVN
 "Wherefore, with this belief, held like a blade," I, ii. AmVN
 "Yet Nature, where the thunder leaves its trace," I, xvi. AmVN
 "Yet wear we on; the deep light disallowed," I, ix. AmVN
Sonnets—Actualities, sel. E. E. Cummings.
 I Like My Body When It Is with Your Body. AnMo; BoLoP; SFF; VGW
Sonnets at Christmas (I-II). Allen Tate. NoAM; NOBA; PAIC; VGW
Sonnets Attempted in the Manner of Contemporary Writers, sels. Samuel Taylor Coleridge.
 On a Ruined House in a Romanitc Country. Epi
 (House That Jack Built, The.) AKE
 To Simplicity. Epi
Sonnets frae Siberia, sel. Donald Campbell.
 Aiberdeen. MIS
 Minding. MIS
Sonnets from China, sel. W. H. Auden.
 "Chilled by the present, its gloom and its noise," XVIII. PPP
Sonnets from the Portuguese, sels. Elizabeth Barrett Browning.
 "Beloved, my beloved, when I think," XX. VPC; WPE
 "Beloved, thou hast brougth me many flowers," XLIV. WPE
 "First time he kissed me, he but only kissed," XXXVIII. LoAs
 "First time that the sun rose on thine oath, The," XXXII. WPE
 "How do I love thee? Let me count the ways," XLIII. BoLoP; HeIP; InPS; IPWM; LoAs; OLR; PAIC; SFF; VPC; WPE
 "I never gave a lock of hair away," XVIII. VPC
 "I thought once how Theocritus had sung," I. GBL; NOBE; PAIC; VPC; WPE

"If thou must love me, let it be for nought," XIV.   HeIP;
LoAs; NOBE; PBMP; WPE

"When our two souls stand up erect and strong," XXII.
NOBE; SBG; WPE

Sonnets in Quaker Language, sels.   Hildegarde Flanner.
"Hearing a sound that may be thy return," VI.   WPE
"Thee sets a bell to swinging in my soul," II.   WPE

Sonnets on Eminent Characters, sels.   Samuel Taylor Coleridge.
Burke.   MBPR
La Fayette.   MBPR
Priestley.   MBPR

Sonnets on the Seasons, sel.   Hartley Coleridge.
November.   FSFS

Sonnets—Realities, sel.   E. E. Cummings.
Cambridge Ladies Who Live in Furnished Souls.   Epi; HeIP;
InPK; NOAM; NOBE; WIF

Sonnets to Be Written from Prison.   Robert Adamson.   CAAP

Sonnets to Delia.   Samuel Daniel.   See To Delia.

Sonnets to Idea.   Michael Drayton.   See Idea.

Sonnets to Laura, sels.   Petrarch, tr. fr. Italian.
To Laura in Death.
"My flowery and green age was passing away," XLVII, prose
tr. by J. M. Synge.
(He Understands the Great Cruelty of Death.)   BIrV
"When my heart was the amorous worms' meat," XXXVI, tr.
by Anna Maria Armi.
(Amorous Worms' Meat, The.)   LoAs
To Laura in Life.
"Father of heaven, after squandered days," LXII, tr. by   R. G.
Barnes.   Epi
"I find [or fynde] no peace and all my war[r] is done," CIV, tr.
by Sir Thomas Wyatt.   AAS; PPoe
(Description of the Contrarious Passions in a Lover.)
PAIC
"Long love that in my thought doth harbour, The," CIX, tr.
by Sir Thomas Wyatt.   Epi
(Lover for Shamefastnesse Hideth His Desire within His
Faithfull Hart, The.)   AAS, 2 versions
"Love that liveth and reigneth in my thought," CIX, tr. by the
Earl of Surrey.   Epi
("Love that doth raine and live within my thought.")   AAS
(Love That Doth Reign and Live within My Thought.)   HeIP
"My galley [or galy] charged with forgetfulness," CLVI, tr. by
Sir Thomas Wyatt.   AAS; Epi; PPP
(Lover Compareth His State to a Ship in Perilous Storm
Tossed on the Sea, The.)   GBL; HeIP; PAIC
"Set me wheras the sonne dothe perche the grene," CXIII, tr. by
the Earl of Surrey.   AAS
(Vow to Love Faithfully, Howsoever He Be Rewarded, A.)
PAIC
"White doe appeared to me over green, A," CLVII, tr. by R. G.
Barnes.

Sonnets—Unrealities, sel.   E. E. Cummings.
"It may not always be so; and I say."   BoLoP

Sons, sel.   Kathleen Lubeck.
"Through the noonday sun."   NPW

Sons, my sons.   Black Star Line.   Henry Dumas.   PoBA

Sons of freedom, listen to me, and ye daughters, too, give ear.
James Bird.   Unknown.   AmFP

Sons of Levi, The.   Unknown.   AmFP

Sons of Liberty, The.   Unknown.   AIW

Sons, seek not me among these polished stones.   Charles
Cavendish to His Posterity.   Ben Jonson.   SCP-1

Sonsito.   Victor Hernandez Cruz.   MIT

Soon as Glumdalclitch mist her pleasing care.   The Lamentation
of Glumdalclitch.   Pope.   Epi

Soon as the sun forsook the eastern main.   An Hymn to the
Evening.   Phillis Wheatley.   WPE

Soon the advertisements.   The Table.   Jennifer Maiden.   CAAP

Soonest Mended.   John Ashbery.   CAAP; Prf

Soote Season, The.   Earl of Surrey, after Petrarch.   AAS; HeIP
(Spring.)   NOBE

Sophistication.   Vassar Miller.   NCSH

Soraidh Slan Don Oidhche Areir.   Niall Mor MacMuireadach, tr.
fr. Irish by Maire Cruise O'Brien.   BIrV

Sorrow.   D. H. Lawrence.   PSN

Sorrow how high it is.   Dark Song.   A. R. Ammons.   MAT

Sorrow is my own yard.   The Widow's Lament in Springtime.
William Carlos Williams.   IPWM; NoAM; NOBA; PSN

Sorrow Is the Only Faithful One.   Owen Dodson.   PoBA

Sorrow of Love, The.   W. B. Yeats.   NoAM; OBP

Sorrowing nymph, oh why display.   On a Statue of Sir Arthur
Sullivan.   G. Rostrevor Hamilton.   FaBoCo

Sorrows of Werther, The.   Thackeray.   FaBoCo

Sorry.   R. S. Thomas.   LP

Sorting out letters and piles of my old.   Mementos, 1.   W. D.
Snodgrass.   CoPAm; HeIP; PiAm; PPP

Sorting, Wrapping, Packing, Stuffing.   James Schuyler.   NoAM

So-shu dreamed.   Ancient Wisdom, Rather Cosmic.   Ezra Pound.
NOBA

Soul.   D. L. Graham.   PoBA

Soul and race.   Here Where Coltrane Is.   Michael S. Harper.
PoBA

Soul and the Body, The.   Sir John Davies.   Fr. Nosce Teipsum.
NOBE

Soul-drift.   Mathilde Blind.   SBG

Soul has bandaged moments, The.   Emily Dickinson.   PiAm

Soul is a region without definite boundaries, The.   Terrain.   A.
R. Ammons.   ConAP

Soul is lonely, The.   La Selva.   Cid Corman.   VGW

Soul of my soul! it cannot be.   The Sympathy.   Owen Felltham.
SCP-2

Soul selects her own society, The.   Emily Dickinson.   AmVN;
InPK; InPS; NoAM; NOBA; PAIC; Psy; SBG; WPE

Souldier Going to the Field, The.   Sir William Davenant.   See
Soldier Going to the Field, The.

Soul's Garment, The.   Margaret Cavendish, Duchess of
Newcastle.   WPE

Souls from Purgatory they come.   Negrun.   Lucille F. Travis.
AATT

Souls of poets dead and gone.   Lines of the Mermaid Tavern.
Keats.   MBPR

Sound.   Jim Harrison.   VGW

Sound and Sense.   Pope.   Fr. An Essay on Criticism, Pt. II.
SoSe

Sound and sweet in the big gray barrels.   Apples to Keep.
Frances Frost.   ECBV

Sound from the Earth, A.   William Stafford.   RFM

Sound like I can hear this morning.   Death Bells.   Unknown.
BluL

Sound of Afroamerican History Chapt I, The.   S. E. Anderson.
PoBA

Sound of Afroamerican History Chapt II, The.   S. E. Anderson.
PoBA

Sound of faint thunder, The.   At the Drive-In: "John Wayne vs.
God."   A. A. Dewey.   HeS

Sound of Night, The.   Maxine W. Kumin.   WPE

Sound of Silence, The.   Paul Simon.   PBMP; WIF

Sound of Trees, The.   Robert Frost.   NoAM

Sound of water running, The.   Civilization.   Tom Schmidt.
NeAC

Sound, Sound the Clarion.   Thomas Osbert   Mordaunt.   Fr.
Verses Written During the War, 1756-1763.   NOBE

Sound the flute!   Spring.   Blake.   Fr. Songs of Innocence.
FSFS; LCL; MBPR

Sound variegated through beneath lit.  Gyre's Galax.  Norman Henry Pritchard, II.  PoBA

Sounding.  Jenne Andrews.  HeS

Sounds like big.  Walking from a Nap on the Beach.  May Swenson.  RFM

Sounds of us, The.  Our Sobbing Must Be Heard.  Grace Cavalieri.  AATT

Soup.  Carl Sandburg.  AKE; NOBE; TH

Soup Jar, The.  Dabney Stuart.  CoPAm

Soup of Venus, The.  James Tate.  AmPA

Sour daylight cracks through my sleep-caked lids, The.  The Distant Winter.  Philip Levine.  VGW

Sources of Good Counsel.  Peter Idley.  OxBChV

Sourdough french bread and pinot chardonnay.  Maps.  Robert Hass.  CAAP

Sourdough mountain called a fire in.  The Text.  Gary Snyder.  Fr. Myths and Texts: Burning.  Epi

Soursobs.  Richard Tipping.  CAAP

Sourwood Mountain.  Unknown.  AmFP; GBP

Souster.  Ray Fraser.  NeAC

South American Sway.  Margaretta Byers.  ECBV

South Atlantic clouds rode low, The.  Safari West.  John A. Williams.  InPS

South Coast, The.  William Everson.  PiAm

South Country.  Kenneth Slessor.  MAuV

South of My Days.  Judith Wright.  WPE

South of the Great Sea.  Unknown, tr. fr. Chinese by Arthur Waley.  OLR

South Wind.  Mary Logue.  NPW

South-wind brings, The.  Threnody.  Emerson.  PAIC

South-wind strengthens to a gale, The.  Low Barometer.  Robert Bridges.  NoAM

Southbound on the Freeway.  May Swenson.  BBGO

Southeast, and storm, and every weathervane.  Hatteras Calling.  Conrad Aiken.  NoAM; NOBA

Souther, wind, souther!  Rhyme of the Fishermen's Children.  Unknown.  GBP

Southern Blues.  Unknown.  BluL

Southern Cop.  Sterling A. Brown.  WIF

Southern Mansion.  Arna Bontemps.  PoBA; SoSe

Southern Road.  Sterling A. Brown.  BPo; PoBA

Southern Road, The.  Dudley Randall.  PAIC; PoBA

Southrons, hear your country call you!  Dixie.  Albert Pike.  BTTM

Southward through Eden went a river large.  Adam and Eve in Paradise.  Milton.  Fr. Paradise Lost, IV.  SCP-1

Souvenir.  E. A. Robinson.  NoAM

Souvenirs.  Dudley Randall.  BPo

Sovereign beauty which I do admire, The.  Amoretti, III.  Spenser.  PAIC

Sow.  Sylvia Plath.  AnMo; CoPAm

Sower, The.  Mathilde Blind.  SBG; WPE

Sowing in the morning, sowing seeds of kindness.  Bringing in the Sheaves.  Knowles Shaw.  BLSH

Sow's Ear, A.  Theodore Weiss.  NoAM

Space.  X. J. Kennedy.  Moon

Space Being (Don't Forget to Remember) Curved.  E. E. Cummings.  Epi; NoAM

Space is too full. Did nothing happen here?  American Farm, 1934.  Genevieve Taggard.  VGW

Spacin.  Ronda Davis.  JB

Spacious firmament on high, The.  Ode.  Joseph Addison.  BoReV; HeIP; IPWM

Spade Is Just a Spade, A.  Walter Everette Hawkins.  PoBA

Spades take up leaves.  Gathering Leaves.  Robert Frost.  VGW

Span of Life, The.  Robert Frost.  SoSe

Spanish expression Cuando yo era muchacho, The.  Habla Usted Español?  James Reiss.  AmPA

Spanish Friar, The, sel.  Dryden.  Farewell, Ungrateful Traitor, fr. V, i.  BoLoP; NOBE

Spanish Is the Loving Tongue, with music.  Unknown.  RDB

Spanish Lady in Dublin City, The, with music.  Unknown.  RDB

Spanish noon is a blaze of azure fire, and the dusty pilgrims, The.  The Exodus (August 3, 1492).  Emma Lazarua.  Fr. By the Waters of Babylon.  WPE

Spanish Student, The, sel.  Longfellow.  Serenade: "Stars of the summer night," fr. I, iii.  PAIC

Spark of Laurel, A.  Stanley Kunitz.  NoAM

Sparkles from the Wheel.  Walt Whitman.  AmVN

Sparrow, The.  William Carlos Williams.  InPS; PiAm; VGW

Sparrow-Hawk's Complaint, The.  Unknown.  OxBM

Sparrow in the Zoo, The.  Howard Nemerov.  NoAM

Sparrow's Nest, The.  Wordsworth.  MBPR

Spatial depths of being survive.  The Lost Dancer.  Jean Toomer.  PoBA

Spawn of fantasies.  Love Songs.  Mina Loy.  VGW; WPE

Spawn of Slums, The.  James W. Thompson.  BPo

Spawning in Northern Minnesota.  David McElroy.  AmPA

Speak Gently.  David Bates.  SpRo

Speak gently, Spring, and make so sudden sound.  Four Little Foxes.  Lew Sarett.  RFM

Speak not ill of womankind.  Against Blame of Woman.  Gerald, Earl of Desmond, tr. by the Earl of Longford.  BIrV

Speak roughly to your little boy.  The Duchess's Lullaby.  "Lewis Carroll."  Fr. Alice's Adventures in Wonderland.  FaBoCo; SpRo

Speak to me. Take my hand. What are you now?  Effort at Speech between Two People.  Muriel Rukeyser.  VoPo

Speak to us who.  Tiresias.  George Garrett.  CoPAm

Speake gentle heart, where is thy dwelling place?  Thomas Watson.  Fr. Hekatompathia.  AAS

Speaker opens his mouth, The.  Persistent Narrative.  Ken Smith.  TwMBP

Speakin' in general, I'ave tried 'em all.  Sestina of the Tramp-Royal.  Kipling.  PAIC

Speaking.  Michael Ryan.  AmPA

Speaking like wind.  Swimmer.  Gladys Cardiff.  CDW

Speaking of marvels, I am alive.  Alive Together.  Lisel Mueller.  IHMS

Speaking of Television, sels.  Phyllis McGinley.
Almost Any Evening.  TH
Reflections Dental.  TH

Speaking: the Hero.  Felix Pollak.  CTBA

Speaking Tree, The.  Muriel Rukeyser.  VGW

Special Bulletin.  Langston Hughes.  PoBA

Special Rider Blues.  Unknown.  AmFP

Specimen of an Induction to a Poem.  Keats.  MBPR

Speck that would have been beneath my sight, A.  A Considerable Speck.  Robert Frost.  PBMP; PPP

Speckled with glints of star and moonshine.  Samuel Hoffenstein.  Fr. Mr. Walter de la Mare Makes the Little Ones Dizzy.  SpRo

Spectator Ab Extra.  Arthur Hugh Clough.  FaBoCo

Spectra, sel.  Witter Bynner.
"If I were only dafter," Opus 6.  InPK

Spectral Lovers.  John Crowe Ransom.  GBL; HeIP; LoAs; PiAm

Spectre is haunting America—the spectre of hoodooism, A.  Black Power Poem.  Ishmael Reed.  BPo

Spectrum.  William Dickey.  SoSe

Spectrum.  Mari Evans.  BPo

Speech.  Henry Taylor.  MAT

Speech after long silence; it is right.  After Long Silence.  W. B. Yeats.  BoLoP; HeIP; PPP; PSN; WIF

Speed of Darkness, The.  Muriel Rukeyser.  WBN

Spell, THe.  LeRoi Jones.  PiAm

Spellbound.  Emily Brontë  See Night Is Darkening Round Me.

Spelling Bee at Angels, The.  Bret Harte.  PoTa

Spend the years of learning squandering.  Gnome.  Samuel Beckett.  BIrV

Spending hand that alway poureth out [or powreth owte], A.  Sir Thomas Wyatt.  Satires, III.  AAS; TVS

Spenser! a jealous honourer of thine.  Keats.  MBPR

Spenser's Ireland.  Marianne Moore.  NoAM; NoBA; PAIC

Sphere of Glass, The.  John Lehmann.  LoAs

Sphinx, The.  Emerson.  NOBA

Spicer's Instant Poetry.  James Reeves.  MPo

Spider, The.  Kenneth Mackenzie.  BoAnP

Spider and the Fly, The.  Mary Howitt.  ECBV; OxBChV

Spider and the Ghost of the Fly, The.  Vachel Lindsay.  VGW

Spider as an artist, The.  Emily Dickinson.  PiAm

Spider bite the size of a dinner plate, A.  Into the Dark.  Paul Monette.  AmPA

Spider holds a silver ball, The.  Emily Dickinson.  PiAm

Spider in the bath, A. The image noted.  The Image.  Roy Fuller.  OxBTC

Spider in the Grapes.  Thomas James.  HeS

Spider sewed at night, A.  Emily Dickinson.  PiAm

Spider spreads her webs, whether she be.  Letter to Maria Gisborne.  Shelley.  MBPR

Spike Driver Blues.  *Unknown.*  BluL

Spilled from a mildewed box.  Grandfather.  John Leax.  AATT

Spin the ball! I reel, I burn.  Song of Seyd Nimetollah of Kuhistan.  Emerson.  NOBA

Spindrift.  Galway Kinnell.  IPWM

Spinning Wheel, The.  John Francis Waller.  PFIr; PoTa

Spinster.  Sylvia Plath.  CoPAm

Spinster's Lullaby.  Vassar Miller.  NMM; RiTi

Spirit.  Mei Berssenbrugge.  SA

Spirit Epiloguizes, The.  Milton.  *Fr.* Comus.  NOBE

Spirit haunts the year's last hours, A.  Song.  Tennyson.  HeIP

Spirit of Wrath, The.  William Heyen.  AmPA

Spirit who sweepest the wild harp of time.  Ode to the Departing Year.  Samuel Taylor Coleridge.  MBPR

Spirits.  Victor Hernandez Cruz.  PoBA

Spirits, Dancing.  Arthur Gregor.  VGW

Spirit's Epochs, The.  Coventry Patmore.  *Fr.* The Angel in the House, I, viii.  GBL

Spirits of well-shot woodcock, partridge, snipe.  Death of King George V.  John Betjeman.  NOBE

Spirit's Song.  Louise Bogan.  LoAs

Spirits Unchained.  Keorapestse Kgositsile PoBA

Spiritual, A.  Paul Laurence Dunbar.  BPo

Spiritus Sanctus.  Betty Ruth Bird.  AATT

Spitballer.  Fred Chappell.  PPoD

Spits of glitter in lowgrade ore.  Conserving the Magnitude of Uselessness.  A. R. Ammons.  NoAM

Spittal wiver are no' very nice.  The Wives of Spittal.  *Unknown.*  GBP

Spitting on Ira Rosenblatt.  Robert Hershon.  NeAC

Splendid Shilling, The.  John Philips.  PAIC

Splendidis Longum Valedico Nugis.  Sir Philip Sidney.  *See* Leave Me, O Love.

Splendor Falls on Castle Walls, The.  Tennyson.  *Fr.* The Princess, Pt. III.  HeIP; InPK
(Blow, Bugle, Blow.)  NOBE

Splinter.  Carl Sandburg.  SoSe

Spontaneous Requiem for the American Indian.  Gregory Corso.  MAT

Spook Sheep.  Gérard de Nerval, *tr. fr. French by* Andrew Hoyem.  Epi

Spool, The.  Ben Belitt.  PPoD

Spoon River Anthology, *sels.*      Edgar Lee Masters.
    Amanda Barker.  NoAM
    Anne Rutledge.  NoAM; NoBA; OFD
    Arlo Will.  PBMP
    Butch Weldy.  PSN
    Cassius Hueffer.  NoAM
    Cooney Potter.  CTBA
    Editor Whedon.  NoAM; NOBA
    Elsa Wertman.  NoAM
    Fiddler Jones.  NoAM
    Frank Drummer.  NoAM
    Hamilton Greene.  NoAM
    Hill, The.  NoAM; NOBA
    Lucinda Matlock.  IPWM; NoAM; NOBA; PBMP; VoPo
    Petit, the Poet.  InPK; NoAM; NOBA
    Willie Metcalf.  IPWM

Spooning in gravy.  The Diner.  Gloria Bussel Koster.  NPW

Sports Field.  Judith Wright.  MAuV

Sportsfield.  A. D. Hope.  MAuV

Sporting Acquaintances.  Siegfried Sassoon.  OxBTC

Sportsman, The.  David McCord.  SPo

Sporus.  Pope.  *Fr.* Epistle to Dr. Arbuthnot.  NOBE

Spot of my youth! whose hoary branches sigh.  Lines Written Beneath an Elm in the Churchyard of Harrow.  Byron.  MBPR

Spotlights had you covered, The.  A Poem about Poems about Vietnam.  Jon Stallworthy.  NoAM

Spotted hawk swoops by and accuses me, The.  Song of Myself, LII.  Walt Whitman.  AnMo

Spots on black skin.  Blind Old Woman.  Clarence Major.  PoBA

Spouting Horn, The.  Nelson Bentley.  LoAs

Sprawled/ on our faces in the spring.  The Hen Flower.  Galway Kinnell.  CAAP

Sprawled on the crates and sacks in the rear of the truck.  Green, Green Is El Aghir.  Norman Cameron.  OxBTC

Spraying the Potatoes.  Patrick Kavanagh.  BIrV

Spread on the roadway.  The Cyclists.  Amy Lowell.  WPE

Spring.  Blake.  *Fr.* Songs of Innocence.  FSFS; LCL; MBPR

Spring, The.  Thomas Carew.  OBP; PPoe

Spring.  Carole Gregory Clemmons.  PoBA

Spring, The.  Abraham Cowley.  *Fr.* The Mistress.  MetP

Spring.  Gerard Manley Hopkins.  FSFS; NoAM; NOBE; OBP; SoSe

Spring.  Edna St. Vincent Millay.  BuTh

Spring.  Thomas Nashe.  *Fr.* Summer's Last Will and Testament.  NOBE; RAE
(Spring, the Sweet Spring.)  HeIP

Spring.  Lola Ridge.  WPE

Spring.  Shakespeare.  *Fr.* Love's Labour's Lost, V, ii.  FSFS; IPWM; SoSe
("When daisies pied and violets blue,")  HeIP; InPK; NOBE; OBP

Spring.  Earl of Surrey.  *See* Soote Season, The.

Spring.  James Thomson.  *Fr.* The Seasons.  LAuP

Spring.  Ruth Whitman.  IHMS

Spring ("Lenten is come with love to towne.")  *Unknown.*  OxBM

Spring and All ("By the road to the contagious hospital").  William Carlos Williams.  NoAM; NOBA; PiAm; PPoe; TCP

Spring and Fall.  Gerard Manley Hopkins.  AnMo; HeIP; InPK; InPS; MAT; NOBE; PAIC; PPoe; PPP; VoPo; WIF

Spring, and the Blind Children. Alfred Noyes. OxBTC

Spring comes in with all her hues and smells, The. A Spring Morning. John Clare. GBL

Spring Day. John Ashbery. NOBA

Spring Coming. A. R. Ammons. InPK

Spring Festival on the River, The. John Peck. AmPA

Spring Flowers. James Thomson. *Fr.* The Seasons: Spring. NOBE

Spring for All Seasons. James Welch. SA

Spring Goeth All in White. Robert Bridges. FSFS

Spring has darkened with activity, The. Time and the Garden. Yvor Winters. NoAM; VGW

Spring I remember wild canaries. Saint-Henri Spring. Milton Acorn. NeAC

Spring Images. James Wright. TH

Spring in Iowa comes in three days. March Rite: Getting It Up. A. G. Sobin. HeS

Spring in New Hampshire. Claude McKay. BPo

Spring in These Hills. Archibald MacLeish. NCSH

Spring is a shock to winter's placid senses. A Time: A Season. Patricia Ramsey. AATT

Spring Is Like a Perhaps Hand. E. E. Cummings. IPWM; PiAm; VGW

Spring is showery, flowery, bowery. The Seasons. *Unknown.* ECBV

Spring Morning, A. John Clare. GBL

Spring Night. Su Tung-P'o, *tr. fr. Chinese by* Burton Watson. Prf

Spring Night in Shokoku-Ji, A. Gary Snyder. VGW

Spring night—one hour worth a thousand gold coins. Spring Night. Su Tung-P'o, *tr. by* Burton Watson. Prf

Spring 1942. Roy Fuller. OxBTC

Spring of the Thief. John Logan. CAPP

Spring Offensive of the Snail, The. Marge Piercy. WBN

Spring Pools. Robert Frost. NoAM; NOBA; PiAm; TCP

Spring Quiet. Christina Rossetti. FSFS; VoPo; WPE

Spring Revue. Charlotte Mortimer. NowV

Spring Stops Me Suddenly. Valentin Iremonger. PFIr

Spring sun bends down between the branches, The. Stephen's Green Revisited. Richard Weber. PFIr

Spring, the sweet spring, is the year's pleasant king. Spring. Thomas Nashe. *Fr.* Summer's Last Will and Testament. HeIP; NOBE; RAE

Spring Thoughts. Huang-fu Jan, *tr. fr. Chinese by* Witter Bynner. OFD

Spring Thunder. Mark Van Doren. TH

Spring was a month late, autumn a month early. Robin Fulton. *Fr.* The Voice of the Surbahar, IV. MIS

Spring wind on the Bowery, A. Spring. Lola Ridge. WPE

Springer Mountain. James Dickey. CAPP

Springfield Mountain. *Unknown.* AIW; AmFP; BLSO, *with music*

Spring-Heeled Jack. James K. Baxter. ECBV

Springtime, The. Denise Levertov. ConAP

Springtime, Summer and Fall: days to behold a world. In Due Season. W. H. Auden. Prf

Sprinkle Me, Just. Patricia Goedicke. Psy

Spruce Macaronis, and pretty to see. The Maryland Battalion. John Williamson Palmer. BTTM

Spur, The. W. B. Yeats. SoSe

Squabbling Blues. *Unknown.* BluL

Squad of soldiers lies beside a river, A. An Old Photo in an Old Life. Daniel Hoffman. SoSe

Squalid, empty-headed hen, A. Hen Under Bay-Tree. Ruth Pitter. OxBTC

Squall. John Moore. NCSH

Square at Dawn, The. James Tate. NoAM

Square sheets—they saw the marble into. Island Quarry. Hart Crane. PPP; PSN

Squat Down, Josey. *Unknown.* AmFP

Squat, granular skinned. Toad. John Cotton. BoAnP

Squat in swamp shadows. Second Shaman Song. Gary Snyder. *Fr.* Myths and Texts: Burning. Epi; NOBA

Squinting against neon signs. Eclipse. Anita Endrezze Probst. CDW

Squire and Mildmaid; or, Blackberry Fold. *Unknown.* InPK

Squire he had whose name was Ralph, A. Independent Squire. Samuel Butler. *Fr.* Hudibras, I, 1. NOBE

Squirrel in Sunshine. William Cowper. BoAnP

Squirrel near Library. Genevieve Taggard. WPE

Squirrels. Al Young. NVAP

Squirrels in Wind Pine. David Kherdian. FAF

Squyer of Lowe Degre, The, *sel. Unknown.* Diversions for an Unhappy Princess. OxBM

Stable-lamp is lighted, A. A Christmas Hymn. Richard Wilbur. MPo; OFD

Stabilities. Anne Stevenson. NCSH

Stability before Departure. Alan Dugan. NowV

Stack o'Dollars. *Unknown.* BluL

Stack up the sky wth strata of rose shale. Theoria in Early Morning. William R. Mitchell. AATT

Stag-Hunt. *Unknown.* OxBM

Stagolee. *Unknown.* MAT

Stained Glass Man, The. Cynthia Macdonald. FiCP

Staircase, The ("Stairs mount to his eternity, The"). Samuel Allen. PoBa

Stairway is not, The. The Jacob's Ladder. Denise Levertov. AnMo; CoPAm; IPWM; PPP

Stalls were empty in the shed, The. Afterward. Mark Van Doren. TH

Stamp Blues. *Unknown.* BluL

Stand close around, ye Stygian set. Dirce. Walter Savage Landor. *Fr.* Pericles and Aspasia. GBL; NOBE

Stand Navy down the field. Anchors Aweigh. Alfred H. Miles. BLSH

Stand on the highest pavement of the stair. La Figlia Che Piange. T. S. Eliot. AnMo; BuTh; GBL; HeIP; MAT; PiAm; OxBTC; PSN; VGW

Stand still, and I will read to thee. A Lecture upon the Shadow. John Donne. Epi; InPK

Stand! the ground's your own, my braves! Warren's Address. John Pierpont. BTTM

Stand Up! ("Stand up, but not for Jesus"). D. H. Lawrence. OxBTC

Stand Up! Stand Up for Jesus, *with music.* George Duffield. BLSH

Stand wel, moder, under roode. At the Crucifixion. *Unknown.* OxBM

Standing aloof in giant ignorance. To Homer. Keats. MBPR

Standing at the station. Depot Blues. *Unknown.* BluL

Standing corn is green, the wild in flower, The. Nunc Viridant Segetes. Sedulius Scottus, *tr. by* Helen Waddell. BIrV

Standing here in the pulpit primly. The Preacher Considers His Sermon. Elmer F. Suderman. AATT

Standing in the 14th st snack place. Poem to My New Jacket. Fran Winant. MMD

Standing on my head makes. Ingestion. Barry McDonald. POL

Standing under the shower. a Dream of Washed Hair. Rhyll McMaster. CAAP

Standing with raised arms before. Edwardian Hat. Betty Parvin. POL

Stane-chack! Malison of the Stone-chat. *Unknown.* GBP

Stanley Matthews. Alan Ross. OxBTC

Stanzas: "How smooth that lake expands its ample breast!" Anne Radcliffe. WPE

Stanzas: "I heard thy fate without a tear." Byron. PBMP

Stanza: "I'll not weep that thou art going to leave me." Emily Brontë. IPWM; WPE

Stanzas: "In a drear-nighted December." Keats. MBPR; NOBE Stanzas: "You say you love; but with a voice." Keats. MBPR

Stanzas—April, 1814. Shelley. MBPR

Stanzas for My Daughter. Horace Gregory. RRA

Stanzas to ——: "Well, some may hate, and some may scorn." Emily Brontë. WPE

Stanzas to a Lady, on Leaving England. Byron. MBPR

Stanzas, Written in Dejection, near Naples. Shelley. MBPR; PBMP

Stanzas Written in My Pocket-Copy of Thomson's "Castle of Indolence." Wordsworth. MBPR

Star, The. Jane Taylor. ECBV; OxBChV; SpRo

Star,/ If you are. A Christmas Tree. William Burford. SoSe

Star Blanket. Ray A. Young Bear. CDW

Star Dust, *with music.* Mitchell Parish. BLSo

Star in the Hills, The. William Stafford. SFF

Star Journey. Naomi Long Madgett. BPo

Star light, star bright. First Star. *Unknown.* ECBV

Star-nosed Mole, The. Robert Wallace. BoAnP

Star of Empire poet say, The. Ho! Westward Ho! Ossian E. Dodge. BLSo

Star of the Evening. James M. Sayles. SpRo

Star Quality. Chris Wallace-Crabbe. CAAP

Star Quilt. Roberta Hill. CDW

Star Song, The: A Carol to the King. Robert Herrick. SCP-1

Star-Spangled Banner, The. Francis Scott Key. BLSH, *with music*; BLSo, *with music*; BTTM

Star-Splitter, The. Robert Frost. PAIC

Star-Talk. Robert Graves. FSFS; OxBTC

Star that bids the shepherd fold, The. Comus Speaks. Milton. *Fr.* Comus. NOBE; PPoe

Stared, astonied all. È, the Feasting Florentines. Daniel Hoffman. VGW

Starer, The. Rhyll McMaster. CAAP

Stare's Nest by My Window, The. W. B. Yeats. Meditations in Time of Civil War, VI   BIrV; NOBE

Starface, The. Madeline Gleason. MIT

Stargazer, The. *Unknown.* OxBChV

Starlight Night, The. Gerard Manley Hopkins. InPS; PPP

Starling, The. John Heath-Stubbs. MPo

Starlings. Norman MacCaig. BoAnP

Starlings descend at nightfall. A Smoke of Birds. Malcolm Cowley. TSWA

Starred Coverlet, The. Robert Graves. BuTh; LoAs

Starry Night, The. Anne Sexton. NoAM

Starry Sky. Charles Simic. POL

Stars. Alden Nowlan. POL

Stars Climb Girders of Light. Bert Meyers. MAT

Stars, I have seen them fall. A. E. Housman. SoSe; VoPo

Stars in your face, The. In Missing. Ray A. Young Bear. CDW

Stars of the summer night. Serenade. Longfellow. *Fr.* The Spanish Student. PAIC

Stars over snow. Night. Sara Teasdale. FSFS

Stars Stand Up in the Air, The. *Unknown, tr. fr. Irish by* Thomas MacDonagh. BIrV

Stars, the stars everlasting are fugitives also, The. Emerson. POL

Stars walk downhill. Concert. Robert Sward. VGW

Stars Wheel in Purple. Hilda Doolittle ("H.D."). NOBA

Start and Goal. Christina Rossetti. VoPo

Start not—or deem my spirit fled. Lines Inscribed upon a Cup Formed from a Skull. Byron. InPK; MBPR

Start with a simple room. Plucking Out a Rhythm. Lawson Fusao Inada. AmPA

Starting again. A Dark Country. Derek Mahon. BIrV

Starting from Central Station. David Campbell. MAuV

Starting from Paumanok, *sel.* Walt Whitman. "Dead poets, philosophs, priests." InPS

Starting from San Francisco. Lawrence Ferlinghetti. CAPP; PiAm

Startling to observe on the face of a Dorset yeoman. The "Dorset Nose." Clive Sansom. MPo

Starved old gelding, blind and lamed, A. An Irish Marriage Night. Brian Merriman, *tr. by* Frank O'Connor. *Fr.* The Midnight Court. BIrV

Starving to Death on a Government Claim. *Unknown.* AmFP

Stasis in darkness. Ariel. Sylvia Plath. AnMo; HeIP; InPK; NoAM; NOBA; PiAm; Psy

State in Indian Language Was Called "Running Water," The. Besmilr Brigham. Psy

State Message: A Midwestern Small Town. Robert Flanagan. HeS

State Street is lonely today. Aunt Jane Allen has driven her chariot to heaven. Aunt Jane Allen. Fenton Johnson. PoBA

State Street's cold mingling. Chicago/ 3 Hours. Victor Hernandez Cruz. ANTL

Stately homes of England, The. The Homes of England. Felicia Dorothea Hemans. SBG; WPE

Stately, kindly, lordly friend. To a Cat. Swinburne. PCat

Stately mirror's all-enamelled case, A. Joseph Beaumont. *Fr.* Psyche or Love's Mystery Displaying the Intercourse betwixt Christ and the Soul. SCP-2

*Stately Southerner, The. Unknown. See* Yankee Man-of-War, The.

Statement and Vision, Two Signs of History. James Whitehead. CoPAm

Statement on Our Higher Education. W. M. Ransom. CDW

States when they black out and lie there rolling, The. Falling. James Dickey. CAAP

Statesboro Blues. *Unknown.* BluL

Stateside. R. P. Kingston. NVAP

Statesman, The. Hilaire Belloc. NOBE

Statesman in Retirement, The. William Cowper. *Fr.* Retirement. PPoD

Statesman is an easy man, A. The Old Stone Cross. W. B. Yeats. PBMP

Statesman's Holiday, The. W. B. Yeats. OxBTC

Stations. Ted Hughes. NoAM

Statue, The. Hilaire Belloc. POL

Statue, The. Roy Fuller. NOBE

Statues, The. W. B. Yeats. NoAM

Statues in the Public Gardens, The. Howard Nemerov. ConAP

Staunin noo aside his braw bress-haunled coffin. My Faither. Duncan Glen. MIS

Stavro's dead. A truant vine. Epitaph. Lawrence Durrell. FaBoCo

Stay All Night, Stay a Little Longer. *Unknown.* AmFP

Stay beautiful/ but dont stay down underground too long. For Poets. Al Young. PoBA; RFM

Stay near me—do not take thy flight! To a Butterfly. Wordsworth. MBPR

Stay, O sweet, and do not rise. Aubade. *Unknown.* BoLoP; NOBE

Stay silent/ keep away from sharks. Anticipation of Sharks. Diane Wakoski. MAT

Staying Alive. David Wagoner. CoPAm; IPWM; MiP; RFM; TSWA

Staying Married. Dick Allen. FAF

Steadfast Cross. *Unknown.* OxBM

Steadfastness. Sir Thomas Wyatt. *See* Forget Not Yet.

Steady heart, which in its steadiness, The. Angina Pectoris. W. R. Moses. NCSH

Steal Away to Jesus. *Unknown.* BLSH, *with music;* BPo

Stealing white from the withered moon. Halloween. Myra Cohn Livingston. OFD

Stealthily parting the small-hours silence. A Child Half-Asleep. Tony Connor. BuTh

Steam Threshing-Machine, The. Charles Tennyson Turner. VPC

Steamfitter had no notion of buying an opal, The. Opal. Jospehine Miles. PAIC

Steddefast cross, inmong alle other. Steadfast Cross. *Unknown.* OxBM

Steed bit his master, The. On a Clergyman's Horse Biting Him. *Unknown.* FaBoCo; SoSe

Steel Mills. Rachel Albright. ANTL

Steel print, A: two stags with antlers locked. New Kelso. Roderick Watson. MIS

Steel snaps and stabs. Strawberry-bright. Jennifer Maiden. CAAP

Steel Glass [*or* Steele Glas], The. George Gascoigne. AAS "And who desires, at large to know my name," *sel.* TVS

Steely train in the stupid green, The. Train: Abstraction. Genevieve Taggard. WPE

Steeple-Jack, The. Marianne Moore. *Fr.* Part of a Novel, Part of a Poem, Part of a Play. NoAM; NOBA; SBG; WPE

Steer hither, steer, your winged pines. The Sirens' Song. William Browne. *Fr.* Inner Temple Masque. GBL; NOBE

Steer on, courageous sailor! Columbus. Schiller, *tr. by* Erika Gathmann Koessler. OFD

Stella at Wood-Park. Swift. BIrV

Stella since thou so right a princess art. Astrophel and Stella, CVII. Sir Philip Sidney. OBP

Stella this day is thirty-four. On Stella's Birthday. Swift. InPK; SoSe

Step Away from Them, A. Frank O'Hara. ConAP; VGW

Step in, young man, I know your face. The Gaol Song. *Unknown.* GBP

Step on His Head. James Laughlin. VGW

Step on the path, A. Ireland Lake. Robert Hershon. NeAC

Stepfather Blues. *Unknown.* BluL

"Stephen Smith, University of Iowa sophomore, burned what he said was his draft card." Of Late. George Starbuck. NowV; VGW

Stephen's Green Revisited. Richard Weber. PFIr

Stepping out of the bath. Discovering Parts of a Body. Rhyll McMaster. CAAP

Stepping Outside. Tess Gallagher. AmPA

Stepping Westward. Denise Levertov. CAPP; NMM; Psy; VGW; WBN

Stepping Westward. Wordsworth. MBPR

Steps. Frank O'Hara. CAPP; ConAP

Stereo. Don L. Lee. POL

Stern daughter of the voice of God! Ode to Duty. Wordsworth. MBPR

Stern mouth, lid eyes, green body. Lizard. Paul Mills. MIS

Stew Meat Blues. *Unknown.* BluL

Stick of Incense, A. W. B. Yeats. AnMo

Stick the finger inside. Black Mail. Alice Walker. AmPA

Stick your patent name on a signboard. The River. Hart Crane. *Fr.* The Bridge: Powhatan's Daughter. NoAM; NOBA; PiAm

Sticks and Stones. Paulette Dusdall Zachariou. NPW

Sticks and stones are hard on bones. A choice of Weapons. Phyllis McGinley. SS

Sticks-in-a-drowse droop over sugary loam. Cuttings. Theodore Roethke. AnMo; NoAM; NOBA; PiAm

Stiff in a white coat. A Child's Visit to the Biology Lab. Kathleen Spivack. AmPA

Stiff Shirts. Derek Bowman. MIS

Stiff spokes of this wheel, The. July in Washington. Robert Lowell. Prf

Stiff standing on the bed. *Unknown.* GBL; POL

Still. Lucille Clifton. CAAP; InPS

Still/ our breath our sun. Joanne Kyger. MIT

Still a bit dazed. Saul, Afterward, Riding East. John Malcolm Brinnin. Prf

Still accelerating,/ my right foot useless, the needle passes. In a Dream, the Automobile. Adrian Marcus. SFF

Still, after all, the kelp remain. At the Western Shore. Sarah Youngblood. IHMS

Still Branches. Jack Simcock. BuTh

Still, Citizen Sparrow. Richard Wilbur. AnMo; CoPAm; NoAM

Still craves the spirit: never Nature solves. Frederick Goddard Tuckerman. *Fr.* Sonnets. AmVN

Still creeping, still degenerous soul. A Dithyramb. John Hall. SCP-2

Still Falls the Rain. Edith Sitwell. BoReV; NoAM; NOBE; OBP

Still Growing, *with music. Unknown.* InPK

Still Here. Langston Hughes. BPo; BuTh

"Still, let my tyrants know, I am not doomed to wear." The Prisoner. Emily Brontë. BoReV; NOBE

Still-Life. Elizabeth Daryush. WPE

Still Life. Claudia Dobkins. NPW

Still Life. Rosemary Dobson. MAuV

Still Life. Ralph Mecklenburger. SFF

Still Life. Reed Whittemore. ConAP

Still Life: Lady with Birds. Quandra Prettyman. PoBA

Still must I hear?—shall hoarse Fitzgerald bawl. English Bards, and Scotch Reviewers. Byron. MBPR

Still night. The old clock ticks. Last Night in Calcutta. Allen Ginsberg. NoAM

Still, passed through the spokes of an old wheel. Reincarnation (I). James Dickey. CoPAm

Still pressing through these weeping solitudes. Frederick Goddard Tuckerman. *Fr.* Sonnets. NOBA

Still round the world triumphant discord flies. A Picture of the Times. Philip Freneau. PiAm

Still scene scintillates, The. Glass World. Dorothy Donnelly. NCSH

Still silver in their polished myth. Crack of Doom. Albert Howard Carter. AATT

Still sits the school-house by the road. In School Days. Whittier. OxBChV

Still, still my eye will gaze long fixed on thee. The Columbine. Jones Very. NOBA; PiAm

Still to be neat, still to be dressed [*or* drest]. Simplex Munditiis [*or* Clerimont's Song]. Ben Jonson. *Fr.* Epicoene; or, The Silent Woman, I, i. GBL; HeIP; InPS; NOBE; OBP; PBMP; PPP

Still Voice of Harlem, The. Conrad Kent Rivers. PoBA

Stillborn Silence. Richard Flecknoe. SCP-2

Stillness and moonlight, with.  Loneliness.  Hayden Carruth.  FiCP

Stillness of the rose, The.  The Rose.  William Carlos Williams.  NOBA

Stingier your suppers, The.  Karl Marx.  Al Lee.  AmPA

Stirling's Hotel.  *Unknown.*  AmFP

Stockdoves, The.  Andrew Young.  BoAnP

Stocking and Shirt.  James Reeves.  ECBV

Stocking Feet Blues.  *Unknown.*  BluL

Stockton State Mental Hospital 1962.  Alta.  MMD

Stocky woman at the door, The.  The Last Day and the First.  Theodore Weiss.  LoAs; VGW

Stockyard, The.  J. C. Squire.  OxBTC

Stoic, The: for Laura von Courten.  Edgar Bowers.  PiAm

Stolen base, metaphor.  Grand Slammer.  R. R. Knudson.  SPo

Stomach of goat, crushed.  Salami.  Philip Levine.  NOBA

Stond who so list upon the slipper toppe.  Seneca, *tr. by* Sir Thomas Wyatt.  *Fr.* Thyestes.  AAS

Stone, The/ would like to be.  Evolution.  May Swenson.  TCP

Stone Age.  Floyd C. Stuart.  FAF

Stone and the Obliging Pond.  Felix Pollak.  POL

Stone/ cold/ daylight.  Poem for Etheridge.  Sonia Sanchez.  BPo

Stone-cutters fighting time with marble, you foredefeated.  To the Stone-Cutters.  Robinson Jeffers.  NOBA; PiAm

Stone Giant.  Joseph Bruchac.  CDW

Stone goes straight, The.  Washington Monument by Night.  Carl Sandburg.  OFD

Stone Gullets.  May Swenson.  InPK

Stone Poems, The.  Ken Smith.  TwMBP

Stones, The.  Sylvia Plath.  CAPP; SBG

Stones in My Passway.  *Unknown.*  BluL

Stonewall Jackson's Way.  John Williamson Palmer.  BTTM

Stony Brook Tavern.  J. D. Reed.  NeAC

Stony Lonesome.  Langston Hughes.  NOBA; PiAm

Stood straight/ holding the choker high.  Gary Snyder.  Myths and Texts: Logging, III.  NOBA

Stoop on the log-house is brown wih sweet rain-rot, The.  Joan Finnigan.  *Fr.* May Day Rounds: Renfrew County.  IPWM; WPE

Stop, Christian passer-by!—Stop, child of God.  Epitaph.  Samuel Taylor Coleridge.  MBPR

Stop! for thy tread is on an empire's dust!  The Field of Waterloo.  Byron.  *Fr.* Childe Harold's Pilgrimage.  BTTM; InPS

Stop, stop and listen for the bough top.  The Blackbird of Derrycairn.  *Unknown, tr. by* Austin Clarke.  BIrV

Stop the Alabama bus I don't wanna ride.  Alabama Bus.  *Unknown.*  BluL

Stoplight.  William Pitt Root.  SFF

Stopping by Woods on a Snowy Evening.  Robert Frost.  ECBV; FSFS; HeIP; InPK; InPS; IPWM; NoAM; NOBA; PiAm; PPoD; PSN; SoSe

Stopping Near Highway 80.  David Ray.  HeS

Stops.  Lucille Clifton.  CAAP

Stories.  Jon Anderson.  HeS

Stories In Kinsman's Park.  Margaret Atwood.  Psy

Stories from Kansas.  William Stafford.  RFM

Stories of the Street.  Leonard Cohen.  GrRo

Storm, The, *sel.*  John Donne.
   Storm at Sea, A.  NOBE

Storm, The.  Theodore Roethke.  NCSH

Storm.  Judith Wright.  WPE

Storm at Sea, A.  John Donne.  *Fr.* The Storm.  NOBE

Storm broke, and it rained, The.  Frogs.  Louis Simpson.  BoAnP; InPS; TH

Storm-Cock's Song, The.  "Hugh MacDiarmid."  OxBTC

Storm Cone,The.  Kipling.  OxBTC

Storm-dances of gulls, the barking game of seals, The.  Divinely Superfluous Beauty.  Robinson Jeffers.  HeIP; PiAm

Storm End.  Jonathan Griffin.  TSWA

Storm Fear.  Robert Frost.  IPWM

Storm has come again today, The.  Beyond the Storm.  James Bertolino.  HeS

Storm House, The.  Elizabeth Jennings.  WPE

Storm is over, lady, The.  Fiddler's Song.  George Mackay Brown.  SLP

Storm on the Island.  Seamus Heaney.  NCSH

Storm that needed a mountain, A.  Found in a Storm.  William Stafford.  RFM

Storm Tide on Mejit.  *Unknown, tr. fr. Micronesian by* Augustin Krämer *and* Willard Trask.  RFM

Storm-Wind, The.  William Barnes.  NOBE

Storm Windows.  Howard Nemerov.  ConAP

Stormalong.  *Unknown.*  AIW

Storm's End.  Leonora Speyer.  TH

Stormy Hebrides, The.  William Collins.  *Fr.* An Ode on the Popular Superstitions.  NOBE

Stormy Scenes of Winter, The, 2 *versions.*  *Unknown.*  AmFP

Stormy the night and the waves roll high.  Asleep in the Deep.  Arthur J. Lamb.  FSN

Story.  Dennis Saleh.  NeAC

Story, A.  William Stafford.  PoTa; RFM

Story, a story, a story anon, A.  The Bishop of Canterbury.  *Unknown.*  AmFP

Story about Chicken Soup, A.  Louis Simpson.  NoAM

Story about Indians, A.  The Climate of Paradise.  Louis Simpson.  NOBA

Story of a Hotel Room.  Rosemary Tonks.  OxBTC

Story of a Well-made Shield, The.  N. Scott Momaday.  CDW

Story of Augustus Who Would Not Have Any Soup, The.  Heinrich Hoffmann, *tr. fr. German.*  OxBChV; SpRo

Story of Fidgety Philip, The.  Heinrich Hoffmann, *tr. fr. German.*  OxBChV

Story of Flying Robert, The.  Heinrich Hoffmann, *tr. fr. German.*  SpRo

Story of Good, The.  Phyllis Janik.  IHMS

Story of Isaac.  Leonard Cohen.  GrRo; WIF

Story of Johnny Head-in-Air, The.  Heinrich Hoffmann, *tr. fr. German.*  OxBChV

Story of Little Suck-a-Thumb, The.  Heinrich Hoffmann, *tr. fr. German.*  SpRo

Story of Prince Agib, The.  W. S. Gilbert.  FaBoCo

Story of Samuel Jackson, The.  Charles Godfrey Leland.  PoTa

Story of the Rose, The, *with music.*  "Alice."  FSN

Story of the Zeros, The.  Victor Hernandez Cruz.  PoBA

Story-Teller, The.  Mark Van Doren.  CTBA; ECBV; TH

Story Which Should Have Happened.  Peter Porter.  CAAP

Stout poet tiptoes, The.  A Poet's Household.  Carolyn Kizer.  POL

Stove.  Ken Belford.  NeAC

Stowed away in a Montreal lumber room.  O God! O Montreal!  Samuel Butler.  FaBoCo

Strahan, Tonson, Lintot of the times.  To Mr. Murray.  Byron.  FaBoCo; PAIC

Straight-backed as a Windsor chair.  Schoolmistress.  Clive Sansom.  MPo; LP

Straight, the swift, the debonair, The.  Magnets.  Countee Cullen.  PBMP

Straits, The.  Valerie Gillies.  SLP

Strand on the Green.  *Unknown.*  GBP

Strange,/ That in this nigger place. Esthete in Harlem. Langston Hughes. BPo; SS

Strange beauty, eight-limbed and eight-handed. Octopus. A. C. Hilton. FaBoCo

Strange but true is the story. The Sea-Turtle and the Shark. Melvin B. Tolson. *Fr.* Harlem Gallery. PoBA

Strange creeper. The Creeper. Tom Schmidt. NeAC

Strange, dear, but true, dear. So In Love. Cole Porter. BLSo

Strange Fits of Passion I Have Known. Wordsworth. AnMo; Epi; GBL; LoAs; MBPR; NOBE; PPP; SoSe

Strange Hells. Ivor Gurney. OxBTC

Strange how our failures shine in memory. The Old Upright I Did Not Learn to Play. Nicholas Flocos. SA

Strange Kind (II). J. D. Reed. Moon

Strange Legacies. Sterling A. Brown. PoBA

Strange Meeting. Wilfred Owen. HeIP; NoAM; NOBE; OBP

Strange now to think of you, gone without corsets & eyes. Allen Ginsberg. *Fr.* Kaddish. NOBA

Strange that I did not know him then. An Old Story. E. A. Robinson. TH

Strange Visitor, The. *Unknown.* GBP

Strangely/ my mother's sad eyes. X-Ray. David Ray. IPWM

Stranger, The. Walter de la Mare. OxBTC

Stranger, The. William Everson. CoPAm

Stranger, The. Jean Garrigue. NOBA

Stranger! Approach this spot with gravity! A Dentist. *Unknown.* FaBoCo

Stranger came to the door at eve, A. Love and a Question. Robert Frost. LoAs

Stranger has come, A. Love in the Asylum. Dylan Thomas. LoAs

Stranger, if thou hast learned a truth which needs. Inscription for the Entrance to a Wood. Bryant. AmVN; PiAm; PPoD

Stranger in Your Town, A. Michael McMahon. FAF

Stranger lighted from his steed, The. Song. Keats. SS

Stranger, pause and drop a tear. Sacred to the Memory of Maria (To Say Nothing of Jane and Martha) Sparks. Max Adeler. FaBoCo

Stranger! Tell the people of Spoon River two things. Unknown Soldiers. Edgar Lee Masters. *Fr.* The New Spoon River. NoAM

Stranger Than the Worst. Babette Deutsch. WPE

"Stranger are we and pilgrims here!" At a Friends' Meeting. Mary Elizabeth Coleridge. WPE

Strangers ask. The Tower. Philip Booth. PAIC

Strangest of adventures, The. Lord Arnaldos. James Elroy Flecker. PoTa

Strangled child, forty years old, old, The. Madonna and Daughter. Carol Bergé. MMD

Strapped down. Notes from the Delivery Room. Linda Pastan. RiTi

Strapped to my seat, I turn. Above It All. Philip Levine. NOBA

Strapped to the roof rack of her. The Song of the Mean Mary Jean Machine. James Baker Hall. FiCP

Strategies. Welton Smith. PoBA

Straunge Passion of a Lover, A. George Gascoigne. AAS

Straw, The. Robert Graves. OxBTC

Strawberries. Edwin Morgan. BoLoP

Strawberries that in gardens grow. Wild Strawberries. Robert Graves. FSFS

Strawberry-bright. Jennifer Maiden. CAAP

Strawberry Fields Forever. John Lennon *and* Paul McCartney. GrRo

Straws like tame lightnings lie about the grass. Summer Farm. Norman MacCaig. OxBTC

Stray Animals. James Tate. NoAM

Stray Things. Dan Johnson. PPoD

Straying Student, The. Austin Clarke. BIrV

Streams of Bunclody, The. *Unknown.* BIrV

Street, The. Ken Smith. TwMBP

Street Car Blues. *Unknown.* BluL

Street Demonstration. Margaret Walker. BPo

Street Fire. Daniel Halpern. AmPA

Street in Bronzeville, A: Southeast Corner. Gwendolyn Brooks. VGW

Street in Kaufman-ville, A. James Cunningham. JB

Street Scene. Peter Suffolk. PoTa

Street Scenes from All Over. Elisavietta Richie. AATT

Street Song. Thom Gunn. HeIP

Street Sounds to the Soldiers' Tread, The. A. E. Housman. PPP

Street Where I Live, The. Virginia Floyd. AATT

Street Window. Carl Sandburg. SFF

Streetlights blink Dont Walk Walk, The. Downtown Roanoke. R. H. W. Dillard. PPoD

Streets. Amy Lowell. RiTi; SBG

Streets of Cairo; or, The Poor Little Country Maid, *with music.* James Thornton. FSN

Streets of Laredo, The. Louis MacNeice. AIW; MPo; PeBB

Streets of Laredo, The. *Unknown. See* Cowboy's Lament.

Streets of New York, The, *with music.* Henry Blossom. FSN

Streets of the roaring town. On a Soldier Fallen in the Philippines. William Vaughn Moody. AmVN; NOBA

Streetsinger is sick, The. Three. Gregory Corso. SA

"Strength of That Food, The." Jane Marie Luecke. AATT

Strength Through Joy. Kenneth Rexroth. VGW

Strengthened to live, strengthened to die for. In Distrust of Merits. Marianne Moore. VoPo

Stretched out on the grass. Engaged. Octavio Paz, *tr. by* Muriel Rukeyser. PBMP

Strew on her roses, roses. Requiescat. Matthew Arnold. HeIP; NOBE; PBMP

Strictures on the Economy of Nature. George Outram. FaBoCo

Strike Among the Poets, A. *Unknown.* FaBoCo

Strike, churl; hurl, cheerless wind, then; heltering hail. Fragment. Gerard Manley Hopkins. OBP

Strike the concertina's melancholy string! The Story of Prince Agib. W. S. Gilbert. FaBoCo

Strike the tent! the sun has risen; not a vapor streaks the dawn. The Bison Track. Bayard. Taylor. AmVN

String-chewing bass players. Mingus. Bob Kaufman. PoBA

Strings lay all about. The Disconnection. Rita Mae Brown. IHMS

Striped blouse in a clearing by Bazille, A. Ceremony. Richard Wilbur. NoAM

Striped philistine with quick, A. Requiem for a Personal Friend. Eavan Boland. PFIr

Stripped/ you're beginning to float free. November 1968. Adrienne Rich. NMM

Stripper, The. Anita Endrezze Probst. CDW

Strive not, vain lover, to be fine. Richard Lovelace. SCP-2

Striving brothers, students in the communtiy colleges of the world. The Voice of the Future. Michele Wallace. WBN

Stroke, *sels.* Vincent Buckley.
    "At the merest handshake I feel his blood," VII. MAuV
    "In the faint blue light," I. MAuV
    "Roofs are lit with rain, The," VI. MAuV

Strokes. William Stafford. ConAP

Strong ankled, sun burned, almost naked. Vitamins and Roughage. Kenneth Rexroth. NoAM

Strong Are Saying Nothing, The. Robert Frost. AnMo

Strong imagination from my youth has been combined, A. The Caulker. M. A. Lewis. PoTa

Strong Men. Sterling A. Brown. BPo; PoBA

Strong men keep coming on, The. Upstream. Carl Sandburg. MiP; PiAm

Strong Men, Riding Horses. Gwendolyn Brooks. PoBA

Strong Son of God, immortal Love. In Memoriam A. H. H., Proem. Tennyson. BoReV; PFD

Strong song tows, A. Coda. Basil Bunting. *Fr.* Briggflatts. TwMBP

Strong Wind, A. Austin Clarke. PFIr

Strong wings in the stormy weather. Gulls. Leonora Speyer. *Fr.* Sand-pipings. TH

Strongest creature for his size, The. Weary Will. A. B. Paterson. BoAnP

Strongly it bears us along in swelling and limitless billows. The Homeric Hexameter Described and Exemplified. Schiller, *tr. by* Samuel Taylor Coleridge. MBPR

Structure. Alberta Turner. HeS

Struggle for the Roads. Bruce Severy. VW

Strut for Roethke, A. John Berryman. NOBA

Student, The. Frederick Eckman. IPWM

Student, The. Marianne Moore. NowV

Student, The. Dabney Stuart. NowV

Student Courting, A. *Unknown.* OxBM

Study in Aesthetics, The. Ezra Pound. InPS; NOBA

Study of Reading Habits, A. Philip Larkin. PPP; SoSe

Study of Two Pears. Wallace Stevens. InPK; InPS

Study Peace. LeRoi Jones. PoBA

Stuffed birds in a/ cage. Lyn Lifshin. *Fr.* Walking thru Audley End Mansion Late Afternoon. RiTi

Stumbling. Dick Lourie. NeAC

Stump, The. Donald Hall. MiP

Stumpfoot on 42nd Street. Louis Simpson. TCP; VGW

Stun. James Schuyler. MAT

Stunned cabin boy, A. Miscarriage. Michael Longley. POL

Stunt Flier, The. John Updike. BBGO

Stupidity Street. Ralph Hodgson. OxBTC

Sturdie plowman lustie, strong and bold, The. Foote-ball. Sebastian Brant. SPo

Sturdy tutsan strikes out, The. Tutsan. Charles Senior. MIS

Stutterer. Alan Dugan. CAPP

Style. Howard Nemerov. NoAM

Suave and paltry man, my enemy, A. In the Tail of the Scorpion. Genevieve Taggard. VGW

Subalterns, The. Thomas Hardy. NoAM; PPP

Subaltern's Love-Song, A. John Betjeman. BoLoP; OxBTC; PPoD

Subject. Marie Ponsot. VGW

Submarine Voyage, The: a Pindaric Poem in Four Parts, *sels.* Thomas Heyrick.
   "Hence curiosity me led." SCP-2
   "Neptune sat in his chariot high." SCP-2
   "There two that struggling into the deep." SCP-2

Subterranean Homesick Blues. Bob Dylan. InPK

Suburb, The. Anne Stevenson. NMM

Suburban Dream. Edwin Muir. OxBTC

Suburbs are known only to dogs and children. We Told You So. Nancy Kessing. MAuV

Subversive Sublime. Tom Buchan. MIS

Subverted Flower, The. Robert Frost. NoAM; NOBA

Subway, The. Allen Tate. NoAM; NOBA; PiAm

Subway messes me up, The. Tubes. Larry Mollin. NeAC

Subway Witnesses, The. Lorenzo Thomas. PoBA

Success. Rupert Brooke. OxBTC

Success. William Empson. OxBTC

Success. Emma Lazarus. SBG

Success is counted sweetest. Emily Dickinson. AmVN; AnMo; InPS; NOBA; PPoD; SBG; SPo; WPE

Succubi. John Newlove. NeAC

Such brazen slatterns. Dandelions. Gerda Mayer. POL

Such easy, easy hours. Moon as Medusa. Vinnie-Marie D'Ambrosio. IHMS

Such Is Holland! Petrus Augustus de Genestet, *tr. fr. Dutch by* Adriaan Barnouw. POL

Such poor folk as to law do go. Isabella Whitney. *Fr.* A Sweet Nosegay, or Pleasant Posy. WPE

Such should this day be, so the sun should hide. On the Marriage of T. K. and C. C., the Morning Stormy. Thomas Carew. BoLoP

Such Stuff as Dreams. Franklin P. Adams. SpRo

Such time as from her mother's tender lap. The Discontented Satyre. Thomas Lodge. TVS

Such was God's poem, this world's new essay. Music. Abraham Cowley. *Fr.* Davideis, I. SCP-2

Suche waywarde wais hath love, that moste parte in discorde. Earl of Surrey. AAS

Such wonder seized, though after Heaven seen. Satan Flies to the Sun. Milton. *Fr.* Paradise Lost, III. SCP-1

Sucking Cider Through a Straw. *Unknown.* GBP

Sudden and from horizon to horizon driven steady. Storm End. Jonathan Griffin. TSWA

Sudden Assertion. Kenneth Leslie. BoAnP; POL

Sudden blow, A: the great wings beating still. Leda and the Swan. W. B. Yeats. AnMo; Epi; HeIP; InPK; NoAM; NOBE; NowV; OBP; PAIC; PPoD; PPoe; PPP; PSN; SoSe; TCP

Sudden Gale in Spring. Martha Banning Thomas. ECBV

Sudden Light. Dante Gabriel Rossetti. BoLoP; NOBE; VPC

Sudden Shower. John Clare. Epi

Sudden upriseth from her stately place. Spenser. *Fr.* The Faerie Queene, I, iv. PPP

Sudden wakin', a sudden weepin', A. Man's Days. Eden Phillpotts. OxBTC

Suddenly, after the quarrel, while we waited. The Quarrel. Conrad Aiken. LoAs

Suddenly all the fountains in the park. The Fountains. W. R. Rodgers. PFIr; POL

Suddenly her breast has never been larger. Impotence. Marvin Bell. AmPA

Suddenly his mouth filled with sand. Death of a Poet. Charles Causley. OxBTC

Suddenly his poor body. Stations. Ted Hughes. NoAM

Suddenly I saw the cold and rook-delighting heaven. The Cold Heaven. W. B. Yeats. NoAM

Suddenly, in my world of you. You Went Away. Norman MacCaig. SLP

Suddenly it was quiet as a Sunday. The Wave. Daryl Hine. Prf

"Suddenly she slapped me, hard across the face." Elizabeth in Italy. Richard Weber. BoLoP

Sue works in a shop. John's driving a bus. Our Family. Leonard Clark. RAE

Sueños. James Reiss. FiCP

Suffer the Children. Audre Lorde. PoBA

Suffolk Miracle, The, 2 *versions. Unknown.* AmFP

Sugar-Candy Bird, A. Ian Young. NeAC

Sugar-Plum Tree, The. Eugene Field. OxBChV

Sugarfields. Barbara Mahone. PoBA

Suicide, The. Joanne Casullo. NPW

Suicide, A. Tom Kryss. NeAC

Suicide Off Egg Rock. Sylvia Plath. PPP

Suicides, The. George MacBeth. NoAM

Suit, The. Leonard Cohen. BBGO

Suite: Judy Blue Eyes. Stephen Stills. WIF

Suite to Fathers. Jim Harrison. AmPA

Sumach Leaves, The. Jones Very. NOBA

Sumer is comen and winter gon. An Easter Song. *Unknown.* OxBM

Sumer Is Icumen In. *Unknown. See* Cuckoo Song.

Summa is i-cumen in. Baccalaureate. David McCord. SpRo

Summary. Sonia Sanchez. BPo

Summer. Conrad Aiken. NoAM

Summer. Josephine Miles. WPE

Summer. Christina Rossetti. FSFS; PBMP

Summer. Diane Wakoski. IPWM; VGW

Summer!/ the painting is organized. The Corn Harvest. William Carlos Williams. *Fr.* Pictures from Brueghel. PPP

Summer and autumn had been so wet, The. Bishop Hatto. Robert Southey. PoTa

Summer comes/ The ziczac hovers. Magalu. Helene Johnson. PoBA

Summer Countries, The. Henry Rago. VGW

Summer Dawn. William Morris. NOBE

Summer ends now; now, barbarous in beauty, the stooks arise. Hurrahing in Harvest. Gerard Manley Hopkins. AnMo; OBP

Summer Farm. Norman MacCaig. OxBTC

Summer holds me here, The. The Aspen's Song. Yvor Winters. POL

Summer holds, The: upon its glittering lake. Chorus. W. H. Auden. *Fr.* The Dog Beneath the Skin. OxBTC

Summer Holiday. Robinson Jeffers. MiP

Summer in England, 1914. Alice Meynell. SBG; WPE

Summer in Fairbanks. Leon Stokesbury. NVAP

Summer is all a green air. Summer Music. May Sarton. NCSH

Summer is fading. Afternoons. Philip Larkin. PSN

Summer Is Gone. *Unknown, tr. fr. Early Irish by* Sean O'Faolain. PFIr

Summer is gone with all its roses. Bitter for Sweet. Christina Rossetti. GBL

Summer Is Icumen In. *Unknown. See* Cuckoo Song.

Summer is over, the old cow said. Moo! Robert Hillyer. TH

Summer Malison, The. Gerard Manley HopkinsNoAM

Summer Music. May Sarton. NCSH

Summer Near the River. Carolyn Kizer. VGW

Summer nests uncovered by autumn wind, The. Birds' Nests. Edward Thomas. HeIP

Summer Night, A. W. H. Auden. PSN

Summer Night. Leonard Cohen. TCP

Summer, 1970. Daniel Halpern. AmPA

Summer, 1960, Minnesota. Robert Bly. InPS

Summer of nineteen eighteen, The. The Bad Old Days. Kenneth Rexroth. NoAM

Summer of 'sixty-three, sir, and Conrad was gone away. Kentucky Belle. Constance Fenimore Woolson. PoTa

Summer Oracle. Audre Lorde. PoBA

Summer so histrionic, marvelous dirty days. Sonnet. Ted Berrigan. CAAP; Epi

Summer Solstice. Alan Garner. BuTh

Summer Solstice. Marilyn Krysl. NPW

Summer Song. John Ciardi. ECBV

Summer Song, A. George Peele. *Fr.* The Old Wife's Tale. NOBE
("When as the rye reach to the chin.") GBL

Summer Stars. Carl Sandburg. RFM

Summer that I was ten, The. The Centaur. May Swenson. NMM

Summer was dry, dry the garden. On the Debt My Mother Owed to Sears Roebuck. Edward Dorn. ConAP

Summer will come with its warm, clear light. Out on the Hillside. Mary Gilmore. MAuV

Summer Words of a Sistuh Addict. Sonia Sanchez. BPo

Summer's Darkness. Elizabeth Hanson. NPW

Summer's Last Will and Testament, *sels.* Thomas Nashe.
Adieu, Farewell Earth's Bliss. HeIP; PPoe
(In Time of Pestilence.) NOBE
(Litany in Time of Plague, A. ) PPoD; PPP
(Song: "Adieu, farewell earths blisse.") OBP
"Fair Summer droops, droop men and beast therefore." SCP-2
Spring, the Sweet Spring. HeIP; NOBE; RAE
"This is the last stroke my tongue's clock must strike." SCP-2

Summer's sun is warm and bright. Pleasant Changes. Jane Euphemia Browne. OxBChV

"Summertime and the Living." Robert Hayden. BPo; NCSH; PoBA; PPP

Summing Up, The. James Simmons. POL

Summon now the king of the forest. Mmenson. Edward Brathwaite. MPo

Summoned by Bells, *sel.* John Betjeman.
"My dear deaf father, how I loved him then." OxBTC

Summons in Indiana, The. William Stafford. AnMo

Sun. James Dickey. CAPP

Sun, The. John Drinkwater. LCL

Sun. Marianne Moore. PiAm

Sun appearing, The: a pendant. Plainview: 3. N. Scott Momaday. CDW

Sun Came, The. Etheridge Knight. NeAC; PoBA

Sun came up, The. Rain Rain on the Splintered Girl. Ishmael Reed. PoBA

Sun descending in the west, The. Night. Blake. *Fr.* Songs of Innocence. MBPR; OxBChV

Sun does arise, The. The Ec[c]hoing Green. Blake. *Fr.* Songs of Innocence. FSFS; LAuP; MBPR

Sun drops below the elms. Routes. Peter Everwine. FiCP

Sun eyed fire-macaw sits in a white tree, The. A Dream in Cold. Besmilr Brigham. Psy

Sun-flower, The. Dora Greenwell. WPE

Sun has long been set, The. Wordsworth. MPBR

Sun Heals, A. Jewel C. Latimore. JB

Sun, in clownish yellow, but not a clown, The. Wallace Stevens. *Fr.* Esthétique du Mal. NOBA

Sun is a huntress young, The. An Indian Summer Day on the Prairie. Vachel Lindsay. RFM

Sun is always in the sky, The. Breakfast Time. James Stephens. ECBV

Sun is blue and scarlet on my page, The. Falling Asleep over the Aeneid. Robert Lowell. NoAM

Sun is eclipsed, The; and one by one. Poetry Today. John Heath-Stubbs. POL

Sun is folding, cars stall and rise, The. The New World. LeRoi Jones. NoAM

Sun is like an open furnace door, The. Last Look Round St. Martin's Fair. Thomas Hardy. OBP

Sun is lord and god, sublime, serene, The. The Lake of Gaube. Swinburne. VPC

Sun is set, The; the swallows are asleep. Evening: Ponte a Mare, Pisa. Shelley. MBPR

Sun is shining in my backdoor, The. Myself When I Am Real. Al Young. PoBA

Sun is warm, the sky is clear, The. Stanzas, Written in Dejection, near Naples. Shelley. MBPR; PBMP

Sun, my relative. A Prayer. *Unknown.* AKE

Sun now rose upon the right, The.  Samuel Taylor Coleridge.  *Fr.* The Rime of the Ancient Mariner.  OBP

Sun of Grace, The.  *Unknown.*  OxBM

Sun of July beats down on the small white house, The.  Small White House.  Robert Penn Warren.  *Fr.* Notes on a Life to Be Lived.  NoAM

Sun of the Sleepless!  Byron.  Moon

Sun, of whose terrain we creatures are, The.  Solar Creation.  Charles Madge.  OxBTC

Sun rises, The.  In Fields of Summer.  Galway Kinnell.  RFM; VGW

Sun [*or* Sunne] Rising, The.  John Donne.  AnMo; BoLoP; GBL; HeIP; InPS; IPWM; MetP; NOBE; PPP; SCP-1; SoSe

Sun rushed up the sky, The; the taxi flew.  Parting as Descent.  John Berryman.  CoPAm

Sun Set, and Up Rose the Yellow Moon, The.  Byron.  *Fr.* Don Juan, I.  Moon

Sun shines bright in the old Kentucky home, The.  My Old Kentucky Home.  Stephen Collins Foster.  BLSH; BLSo; PSoN

Sun Shines over the Mountain, The.  *Unknown.*  AmFP

Sun shines through you, The.  Triptych.  Luci Shaw.  AATT

Sun streaked the coffee urn.  The Death of Paragon.  John Woods.  IPWM

Sun struts over the asphalt world, The.  Noon of the Sunbather.  Marge Piercy.  NMM

Sun-tanned men and women, toiling there together.  Reapers.  Mathilde Blind.  SBG; WPE

Sun, that brave man, The.  The Brave Man.  Wallace Stevens.  PBMP

Sun that brief December day, The.  Snow-Bound; a Winter Idyl.  Whittier.  AmVN; FSFS; NOBA; PiAm

Sun, the moon, the stars, the seas, the hills and the plains, The.  The Higher Pantheism.  Tennyson.  PAIC; SpRo

Sun was shining on the sea, The.  The Walrus and the Carpenter.  "Lewis Carroll."  *Fr.* Through the Looking Glass.  AKE; FaBoCo; OxBChV

Sun Wields Mercy, The.  Charles Bukowski.  MAT

Sunbeams in the east are spread, The.  Epithalamion Made at Lincoln's Inn.  John Donne.  PAIC

Sunday.  Laura Beausoleil.  NPW

Sunday Afternoon.  Denise Levertov.  ConAP; IHMS

Sunday Afternoons.  Anthony Thwaite.  OxBTC

Sunday dreamer's Guide to Yarrow, Missouri, A.  Jim Barnes.  HeS

Sunday Evening with Elizabeth, Age 5.  Martha Yoak.  NPW

Sunday in Glastonbury.  Robert Bly.  ConAP

Sunday in Inwood Park.  Picnic.  Adrienne Rich.  CoPAm

Sunday, Guadalajara.  Anthony Ostroff.  MIT

Sunday lamb cracks in its fat, The.  Mary's Song.  Sylvia Plath.  CAAP

Sunday Morning.  Louis MacNeice.  HeIP

Sunday Morning.  Wayne Moreland.  PoBA

Sunday Morning.  Wallace Stevens.  HeIP; NOBA; PiAm; PPoD; PPoe; PSN

Sunday morning and her mother's hands.  Birmingham 1963.  Raymond R. Patterson.  PoBA

Sunday morning just at nine.  Down Went McGinty.  Joseph Flynn.  FSN

Sunday shuts down on this twentieth-century evening.  Boy with His Hair Cut Short.  Muriel Rukeyser.  InPK; VGW; WPE

Sunday strollers along a sewage-chocked Schuylkill.  To Some Millions Who Survive Joseph E. Mander, Sr.  Sarah E. Wright.  PoBA

Sunday the only day we don't work.  A Walk.  Gary Snyder.  NoAM; NOBA

Sundays too my father got up early.  Those Winter Sundays.  Robert Hayden.  CoPaM; CTBA; IPWM; NoAM; PoBA; PPP

Sunflower Rock.  Paul Blackburn.  NoAM

Sunflower Sutra.  Allen Ginsberg.  MAT; NOBA; PiAm

Sunflowers, The.  Douglas Stewart.  POL

Sunglare and sea pale as tears.  Blackfish Poem.  Milton Acorn.  NeAC

Sunjuice.  Erica Jong.  MMD

Sunlight inches down.  The White Piano.  Ralph J. Mills, Jr.  HeS

Sunlight lies along my table.  The Weather of Six Mornings.  Jane Cooper.  IHMS

Sunlight on the Garden, The.  Louis MacNeice.  NoAM; NOBE; OxBTC; PPoe

Sunlight on the water, The.  Riversong.  Michael Anania.  HeS

Sunne Rising, The.  John Donne.  *See* Sun Rising, The.

Sunning.  James S. Tippett.  ECBV

Sunny Bank.  *Unknown.*  GBP

Sunny Prestatyn.  Philip Larkin.  NoAM

Sunrise.  Sidney Lanier.  PiAm

Sun's rays, The.  The Eagle Sings.  *Unknown.*  AKE

Sunset and evening star.  Crossing the Bar.  Tennyson.  HeIP; InPK; NOBE; PBMP; PFD; VoPo

Sunshade, The.  Thomas Hardy.  OxBTC

Sunshine of Paradise Alley, The, *with music.*  Walter H. Ford.  FSN

Sunshine on paddocks backyards.  August Fugue.  Thomas Shapcott.  CAAP

Sunshiny shower, A.  *Unknown.*  MG

Sunstrike.  Douglas Livingstone.  MPo

Sunt Leones.  Stevie Smith.  SBG

Super-cool/ ultrablack.  But He Was Cool or: He Even Stopped for Green Lights.  Don L. Lee.  BPo; NoAM; PoBA

Superman.  John Updike.  BBGO; LP

Supermarket in California, A.  Allen Ginsberg.  ConAP; CoPAm; HeIP; NOBA; PiAm; PBMP; PPoD; TCP

Superscription, A.  Dante Gabriel Rossetti.  The House of Life, XCVII.  NOBE; VPC

Supper after the Last, The.  Galway Kinnell.  NOBA

Supper for a Lion.  Dorothy Aldis.  CaYB

Supper is Na Ready.  *Unknown.*  GBP

Suppliant, The.  Georgia Douglas Johnson.  PoBA

Suppose he had been tabled at thy teats.  Luke XI; Blessed Be the Paps Which Thou Hast Sucked.  Richard Crashaw.  SCP-1

Suppose me dead; and then suppose.  Swift.  *Fr.* Verses on the Death of Doctor Swift.  NOBE

Suppose the ceiling went outside.  The Ceiling.  Theodore Roethke.  ECBV; LCL

Suppose the dead could crown their wit.  A Responsory, 1948.  Thomas Merton.  VGW

Suppose they had cheated me out of my.  Remember Times for Sandy.  Carolyn M. Rodgers.  JB

Suppose those/ who made/ wars.  Nigerian Unity/ or Little Niggers Killing Little Niggers.  Don L. Lee.  NeAC

Suppose you screeve? or go cheap-jack?  Villon's Straight Tip to All Cross Coves.  W. E. Henley.  FaBoCo

Suppose you stood facing.  Pierrot Le Fou.  Adrienne Rich.  PiAm

Suppose you were dreaming about your family.  Benign Neglect/ Mississippi, 1970.  Primus St. John.  PoBA

Supremacy.  E. A. Robinson.  NoAM

Surcease.  Patrick Lane.  NeAC

Sure an' twas a/ fine st. patrick's day.  Saint Patrick's Day, 1973.  Wendy Rose.  CDW

Sure as hell. Blueline. Ken Belford. NeAC

Sure the night was smooth. The Night Was Smooth. James Bertolino. POL

Sure, it was so. Man in those early days. Corruption. Henry Vaughan. Prf; SCP-1

Surely I know that. Phoning My Son Long Distance. Ted Kooser. HeS

Surely in my eyes that light is now lost. The Photograph of Myself. Jon Anderson. AmPA

Surely it is death to come here. Tlanusi' yi, the Leech Place. Gladys Cardiff. CDW

Surely that moan is not the thing. Fog-Horn. W. S. Merwin. TCP; TSWA

Surf-Casting. W. S. Merwin. NOBA

Surfer, The. Judith Wright. WPE

Surfer and Others. Sonya Dorman. SPo

Surfers at Santa Cruz. Paul Goodman. SPo

Surprised by Evening. Robert Bly. CAPP; VGW

Surprised by Joy—Impatient as the Wind. Wordsworth. BoLoP; LoAs; MBPR; NOBE; OBP; RRA

Surreal morning grey. The Change. Michael Dransfield. CAAP

Surrender, The. Henry King. BoLoP; SCP-2

Surrounded by tigers. The Life of the Wolf. Gary Gildner. AmPA

Survey of Literature. John Crowe Ransom. VGW

Survival. Albert Goldbarth. NVAP

Survival. Barbara Greenberg. RiTi

Survival This Way. Simon J. Ortiz. CDW

Surviving. James Welch. CDW; SA

Survivor. Archibald MacLeish. NCSH

Susan, we meet in late fall. The Meeting. Kathleen Spivack. NMM

Susan would meet with Richard and with Ned. Like Mistress, Like Maid. Samuel Rowlands. SCP-2

Susanna and the Elders. Adelaide Crapsey. PAIC; WPE

Susannah and the Elders. Unknown. OLR

Susannah the fair. Susannah and the Elders. Unknown. OLR

Susie Asado. Gertrude Stein. RiTi

Sussex. Kipling. BTTM

Suzanne Takes You Down. Leonard Cohen. GrRo; InPK; SFF; TCP; WIF

Swagman, The. C. J. Dennis. ECBV

Swallow, The. Lucy Aikin. OxBChV

Swallow leaves her nest, The. Song from the Waters. Thomas Lovell Beddoes. Fr. Death's Jest Book. NOBE

Swallow, that on rapid wing. The Swallow. Lucy Aikin. OxBChV

Swallow the Lake. Clarence Major. PoBA

Swallows, The. Elizabeth J. Coatsworth. LCL

Swallows. Thomas Hornsby Ferril. RFM

Swallows flap in waves against the house, The. Late Spring: a Heaving, a Turning. John Gill. NeAC

Swam too far out: the swell took him. Elegy for a School-Friend. Augustus Young. BIrV

Swampstrife and spatterdock. The Marsh. W. D. Snodgrass. PiAm

Swan, The. W. R. Rodgers. NoAM

Swan, The. Theodore Roethke. VGW

Swan Bathing, The. Ruth Pitter. BoAnP

Swans. Morley Jamieson. SLP

Swans, The. Edith Sitwell. WPE

Swan's Feet, The. E. J. Scovell. OxBTC

Swans in their grey and silver park. An Effect of Light. Vivian Smith. MAuV

Swan rise up with their wings in day, The. The Boys and the Geese. Padraic Fiacc. PFIr

Swans Sing before They Die. Samuel Taylor Coleridge. FaBoCo

(Epigram: "Swans sing before they die.") AKE

Swansong. Carol Muske. AmPA

Swapping Song, with music. Unknown. RDB

Swarm off the cool water. The Lake Flies of Winnebago. Doug Flaherty. HeS

Swarming Bees, The. James Laughlin. VGW

Swarte smeked smithes smatered with smoke. The Blacksmiths. Unknown. OxBM

Swear by what the sages spoke. Under Ben Bulben. W. B. Yeats. NoAM; OxBTC

Sweat like drops of blood run down, The. Dark Was the Night. Unknown. AmFP

Sweating It Out on Winding Stair Mountain. Jim Barnes. CDW

Sweeney. Henry Lawson. MAuV

Sweeney Among the Nightingales. T. S. Eliot. HeIP; InPK; NoAM; NOBA; NOBE; PAIC; PPP

Sweeney Erect. T. S. Eliot. AnMo; OxBTC; VGW

Sweeping she comes, as she would brush the ground. Thomas Nashe. Fr. The Choice of Valentines, or the Merry Ballad of Nashe His Dildo. SCP-2

Sweet, acidulous, down-reaching thrill, A. Ode on a Jar of Pickles. Bayard Taylor. SpRo

Sweet Adeline, with music. Richard Gerard. BLSH; FSN

Sweet and Low. Tennyson. Fr. The Princess, Pt. II. OxBChV; BLSh, with music

Sweet-and Twenty. Shakespeare. See Feste's Song.

Sweet are the pleasures that to verse belong. To George Felton Mathew. Keats. MBPR

Sweet Auburn, loveliest village of the plain. The Deserted Village. Goldsmith. LAuP; NOBE

Sweet baby, sleep: what ails my dear? A Rocking Hymn. George Wither. OxBChV

Sweet baked apple dappled cinnamon speckled sin of mine. Love Child—a Black Aestetic. Everett Hoagland. BPo

Sweet, be not proud of those two eyes. To Dianeme. Robert Herrick. NOBE; SCP-1

Sweet beast, I have gone prowling. Song. W. D. Snodgrass. SoSe

Sweet beats of jazz impaled on slivers of wind. Walking Parker Home. Bob Kaufman. PoBA

Sweet Benedict, whilst thou art young. To His Little Son Benedict from the Tower of London. John Hoskyns. OxBChV

Sweet Betsy from Pike, with music. Unknown. AmFP; BLSo; PeBB

Sweet bird, that shunn'st the noise of folly. Milton. Fr. Il Penseroso. SCP-1

Sweet By and By. Sanford Filmore Bennett. See In the Sweet Bye-and-Bye.

Sweet chimes! that in the loneliness of night. Chimes. Longfellow. PiAm

Sweet cyder is a great thing. Great Things. Thomas Hardy. NOBE

Sweet Dancer. W. B. Yeats. AnMo

Sweet day, so cool, so calm, so bright. Virtue. George Herbert. HeIP; NOBE; PPP; SCP-1; SoSe

Sweet disorder in the dress, A. Delight in Disorder. Robert Herrick. AnMo; HeIP; InPK; InPS; NOBE; PBMP; PPoe; PPP

Sweet dreams form a shade. A Cradle Song. Blake. Fr. Songs of Innocence. LAuP; MBPR

Sweet Echo, sweetest nymph, that liv'st unseen.   The Lady Sings. Milton.   *Fr.* Comus.   NOBE

Sweet empty sky of June without a stain.   Epochs.   Emma Lazarus.   SBG

Sweet flower! belike one day to have.   To the Daisy. Wordsworth.   MBPR

Sweet Genevieve, *with music.*   George Cooper.   BLSH; BLSo; PSoN

Sweet Highland girl, a very shower.   To a Highland Girl. Wordsworth.   MBPR

Sweet Hour of Prayer, *with music.*   William W. Walford.   BLSH

Sweet in her green cell the flower of beauty slumbers.   Serenade of a Loyal Martyr.   George Darley.   NOBE

Sweet Is the Budding Spring of Love, *with music.*   John Hippisley. BLSo

Sweet Jane.   *Unknown.*   AmFP

Sweet Jesu.   *Unknown.*   OxBM

Sweet, Let Me Go.   *Unknown.*   BuTh

Sweet marmalade of kisses newly gathered.   Margaret Cavendish, Duchess of Newcastle.   *Fr.* Nature's Dessert.   SCP-2

Sweet Mary the first time she ever was there.   Mary.   Blake. MBPR

Sweet Muse, Descend.   Isaac Watts.   BoReV; NOBE

Sweet Music's Power.   John Fletcher.   King Henry VIII, *fr.* III, i. NOBE

Sweet, my sweet.   Leonora Speyer.   *Fr.* Cantares.   TH

Sweet Nosegay, A, or Pleasant Posy, *sels.*        Isabella Whitney. WPE

    "Do not account that for thine own."
    "Gold savours well, though it be got."
    "In loving, each one hath free choice."
    "Little gold in law will make, A."
    "Present day we cannot spend, The."
    "Seek not man to please, for that."
    "Such poor folk as to law do go."

Sweet one I love you.   Reasons.   Tom McGrath.   SLP

Sweet Patuni.   *Unknown.*   BluL

Sweet Rosie O'Grady, *with music.*   Maude Nugent.   FSN

Sweet sensibility, that dwells enshrin'd.   George Canning *and* John Hookham Frere.   *Fr.* New Morality.   ESaP

Sweet Slug-a-Bed.   *Unknown.*   FaBoCo

Sweet sounds, oh, beautiful music, do not cease!   On Hearing a Symphony of Beethoven.   Edna St. Vincent Millay.   VoPO

Sweet spirit! Sister of that orphan one.   Epipsychidion.   Shelley. MBPR

"Sweet spring is your."   E. E. Cummings.   NCSH; PiAm

Sweet summer breeze, whispering trees.   Kiss Me Again.   Henry Blossom.   BLSo

Sweet, sweet is the greeting of eyes.   Keats.   MBPR

Sweet, sweet, sweet, let me go.   *Unknown.*   GBL

Sweet sweet sweet sweet sweet tea.   Susie Asado.   Gertrude Stein. RiTi

Sweet trees who shade this mould.   *Unknown, tr. fr. Spanish by* James Mabbe.   GBL

Sweet Trinity, The.   *Unknown.*   AmFP

Sweet Tuxedo girl you see, A.   Ta-ra-ra Boom-der-é.   Henry J. Sayers.   BLSo

Sweet William he married a wife.   The Wife Wrapt in Wether's Skin.   *Unknown.*   AIW; AmFP

Sweet William rode up to the old man's gate.   Earl Brand. *Unknown.*   AmFP

Sweet William's Farewell to Black-eyed Susan.   John Gay. BoLoP

    (All in the Downs, *folk version.*)   AmFP

Sweet William's Ghost, A *version.   Unknown.*   AIW

Sweet Woodley! oh! how fresh an' gay.   Woodley.   William Barnes.   VPC

Sweetening of the Year, The.   John Shaw Neilson.   MAuV

Sweetest li'l' feller, ev'rybody knows.   Mighty Lak' a Rose. Frank L. Stanton.   BLSo; FSN

Sweetest Love, I Do Not Go.   John Donne.   *See* Song: "Sweetest love, I do not go."

Sweetest Saviour, if my soul.   Dialogue.   George Herbert. BoReV

Sweetest Story Ever Told, The, *with music.*   R. M. Stults.   BLSo; FSN

Sweetness.   *Unknown, tr. fr. Irish by* John Montague.   BIrV

Sweit rois of vertew and of gentilnes.   To a Lady.   William Dunbar.   GBL; SLP

Swete were the sauce would please ech kind of tast.   Walter Rawely of the Middle Temple, in Commendation of the Steele Glasse.   Sir Walter Ralegh.   AAS

Swift, *sel.*   Thomas Caulfield Irwin.
    "It was a dim October day."   BIrV

Swift as a spirit hastening to his task.   The Triumph of Life. Shelley.   MBPR

Swift boomerang, come get!   December 18th.   Anne Sexton.   *Fr.* Eighteen Days without You.   CAPP

Swift fleet the billowy clouds along the sky.   Charlotte Smith. *Fr.* Montalbert.   WPE

Swift Love, Sweet Motor.   Hildegarde Flanner.   WPE

Swift red flesh, a winter king, The.   The Dance.   Hart Crane. *Fr.* The Bridge: Powhatan's Daughter.   PiAm

Swifter than hail.   Tanka.   Akiko No Yosano, *tr. by* Kenneth Rexroth.   PAIC

Swiftly walk over the western wave.   To Night.   Shelley.   MBPR

Swim in Ohuira Bay, A.   Robert Peterson.   NeAC

Swim on your back.   Avalanche.   Janet Emig.   SPo

Swimmer.   Gladys Cardiff.   CDW

Swimmer in the Rain.   Robert Wallace.   FiCP

Swimmers, The.   Allen Tate.   InPS; NOBA

Swimming By Night.   James Merrill.   VGW

Swimming Chenango Lake.   Charles Tomlinson.   NoAM

Swimming down to us.   Moon Man.   Jean Valentine.
    MoonSwimming Lesson, The.   Robert Hershon.   NeAC

Swimming Pool, The.   Sandra Hochman.   RiTi

Swine com jingling doun Pelton lonin, The.   Pigs o' Pelton. *Unknown.*   GBP

Swineherd.   Eilean Ni Chuilleanain.   BIrV; PFIr

Swing, The.   Robert Louis Stevenson.   LCL

Swing dat hammer—hunh.   Southern Road.   Sterling A. Brown. BPo; PoBA

Swing Low, Sweet Chariot ("I ain't never been to heaven"). *Unknown.*   GBP

Swing Low, Sweet Chariot ("I looked over Jordan and what did I see").   *Unknown.*   BLSH, *with music;* BLSo, *with music;* WIF

Swing Swong.   *Unknown.*   ECBV

Swinging Chick.   Ern Alpaugh *and* Dewey G. Pell.   InPK

Swinging the Baby.   *Unknown.*   ECBV

Swirl sleeping in the waterfall!   Chomei at Toyama.   Basil Bunting.   OxBTC; TwMBP

Switzerland, *sel.*   Matthew Arnold.
    To Marguerite—Continued, V.   BoLoP; NOBE; PFD; PPP

Swoon on noon, a trance of tide, A.   In a Bye-Canal.   Herman Melville.   AmVN

Swooning swim to less and less.   Buddha.   Herman Melville. HeIP; PiAm

Sword of Bunker Hill, The.   William Ross Wallace.   BTTM

Sword or stealth, strength or ancient blood.   Matthew Mead.   *Fr.* The Administration of Things.   TwMBP

Sword in his right hand, a stone in his left hand, A.   The Bronze David of Donatello.   Randall Jarrell.   WIF

Sworded man whose trade is blood, A.  Separation.  Samuel Taylor Coleridge.  MBPR

Sybil of months, and worshipper of winds.  November.  John Clare.  FSFS

Sycamore Tree, The.  *Unknown.*  AmFP

Sycophantic Fox and the Gullible Raven, The.  Guy Wetmore Carryl.  PBMP

Sylvan Delights.  Pope.  *Fr.* Pastorals: Summer.  NOBE

Sylvan slopes with corn-clad fields, The.  September, 1819.  Wordswoth.  MBPR

Sylvester's Dying Bed.  Langston Hughes.  NoAM

Sylvia the fair, in the bloom of fifteen.  Song.  Dryden.  LoAs

Sylvia's Death.  Anne Sexton.  WBN

Sylvie and Bruno, *sels.*  "Lewis Carroll."
  Mad Gardener's Song, The.  FaBoCo; OxBChV; PBMP
  Pig Tale, The, *abr.* RAE

Symbol inside this poem is my father's feet, The.  The Pawnbroker.  Maxine W. Kumin.  NVAP

Symbols.  John Drinkwater.  WIF

Symon's Lesson of Wisdom for All Manner of Children.  *Unknown.*  OxBChV

Sympathy.  Paul Laurence Dunbar.  PoBA

Sympathy, The.  Owen Felltham.  SCP-2

Symphony No. 3, in D Minor.  Jonathan Williams.  *Fr.* Mahler.  VGW

Symptom Recital.  Dorothy Parker.  SBG

Symptoms of Love.  Robert Graves.  BoLoP

Syren Songs, *sels.*   George Darley.
  Mermaidens' Vesper-Hymn, The, VI.  GBL
    (Siren Chorus.)  BIrV
  Sea-Ritual, The, V.  BIrV

Syrens' Song, The.  William Browne.  *See* Sirens' Song, The.

Syria.  Keith Douglas.  PSN


# T

T.B. Blues.  Leadbelly (Huddie Ledbetter).  BluL

T-bone Steak Blues.  *Unknown.*  BluL

T. C.  Walter Bradford.  HeS

TKO.  Richard Peck.  SPo

T of the pole is someone, The.  In Pursuit of the Family.  Jenne Andrews.  HeS

T. S. Eliot   Robert Lowell.  NoAM; NOBA

Table, The.  Jennifer Maiden.  CAAP

Table Rules for Little Folks.  *Unknown.*  OxBChV

Tableau.  Countee Cullen.  PoBA

Tables Turned, The.  Wordsworth.  IPWM; MBPR

Tact.  E. A. Robinson.  NoAM

Tadlow.  Abel Evans.  FaBoCo

Taffy was a Welshman, Taffy was a thief.  Mother Goose.  GBP; MG

Tagus, fare well, that westward with thy stremes.  Sir Thomas Wyatt.  AAS

Tailor.  Eleanor Farjeon.  OxBChV

Tain't Nobody's Business.  *Unknown.*  BluL

Taisigh Agat Fiein Do Phog.  *Unknown, tr. fr. Irish by* Maire Cruise O'Brien.  BIrV

Take a look, i/ sd.  For Kelley.  Ken Belford.  NeAC

Take a pound of butter made in May.  Recipe for Toothache.  *Unknown.*  SCP-2

Take a Walk Around the Corner.  *Unknown.*  BluL

Take a Whiff on Me.  *Unknown.*  NOBA

Take Back Your Gold, *with music.*  Louis W. Pritzkow.  FSN

Take heed of loving me.  John Donne.  GBL

Take Him away, he's dead as they die.  Obituary.  Kenneth Fearing.  VGW

Take in prospering hand a shining cup.  Seventh Olympic Hymn.  Pindar, *tr. by* Robin Blaser.  *Fr.* Odes.  Epi

Take it from me kiddo.  Poem, or Beauty Hurts Mr. Vinal.  E. E. Cummings.  InPS; PAIC; PiAm; PPoe

Take Me Out to the Ball Game, *with music.*  Jack Norworth.  BLSH

Take my hand.  There are two of us in this cave.  The Blind Leading the Blind.  Lisel Mueller.  IHMS

Take My Life and Let It Be, *with music.*  Frances Ridley Havergal.  BLSH

Take, O! take those lips away.  At the Moated Grange.  Shakespeare.  *Fr.* Measure for Measure, IV, i.  GBL; HeIP; InPS; NOBE

Take of me what is not my own.  Envoi.  Kathleen Raine.  NOBE

Take One:/ They are next to each other.  Two Pennies Found on the Gravel.  David Kherdian.  FAF

Take One Home for the Kiddies.  Philip Larkin.  OxBTC

Take the Name of Jesus with You, *with music.*  Lydia Baxter.  BLSH

Take, then, this image for what it is worth.  The Cage.  George Garrett.  SS

Take this hammer and carry it to my captain.  Spike Driver Blues.  *Unknown.*  BluL

Take this kiss upon the brow!  A Dream within a Dream.  Poe.  AmVN; GBL; NOBA; PiAm

Take this solemn tip.  Octopus.  Sam Reavin.  CaYB

Take thy hat, my little Laura.  Edward Newman.  *Fr.* The Insect Hunters.  PPoD

Take to the highway.  Country Road.  James Taylor.  PoRo

Take up the White Man's burden.  The White Man's Burden.  Kipling.  BTTM

Take your time kind mama I'm gonna do it just as slow as I can.  Slow Mama Slow.  *Unknown.*  BluL

Taken from the.  The Primitive.  Don L. Lee.  BPo

Taken Town, The.  Constance Carrier.  FAF

Takes All Kinds.  R. P. Dickey.  POL

Taking a shell he had never seen.  Outposts.  J. S. Harry.  CAAP

Taking a Walk with You.  Kenneth Koch.  CAPP

Taking Leave of the Old.  Clarice Short.  PPoD

Taking Off.  Ronald Rogers.  VW

Taking Off My Clothes.  Carolyn Forché.  AmPA

Taking Out Jim.  John Walsh.  RAE

Taking pity on this scrag-end of the city.  One Kingfisher and One Yellow Rose.  Eileen Brennan.  PFIr

Taking us by and large, we're a queer lot.  The Sisters.  Amy Lowell.  SBG

Tale.  W. S. Merwin.  TH

Tale, The.  Charles Simic.  CAAP

Tale of Drury Lane, A.  Horace Smith.  FaBoCo

Tale of Genji.  Hugh Seidman.  AmPA

Tale of Last Stands, A.  Fred Red Cloud.  VW

Tale the Hermit Told, The.  Alastair Reid.  PoTa

Tales of a Wayside Inn, *sel.*  Longfellow.
  Paul Revere's Ride (The Landlord's Tale), *fr.* Pt. I.  BTTM

Tales of Brave Ulysses.  Eric Clapton *and* Martin Sharp.  GrRo

Tales of the Islands.  Derek Walcott.  OxBTC

Talisman, A.  Marianne Moore.  NCSH

Talisman for the New Year, A.  Deena Metzger.  RiTi

Talk about killing.  In a life.  A Sow's Ear.  Theodore Weiss.  NoAM

Talk about your harbor girls around the corner, Sally. Haul Away, My Rosy. *Unknown.* AmFP

Talk like a jellyfish can ruin a party. At the Chairman's Housewarming. William Stafford. AnMo

Talk to me. Tic. Coleman Barks. *Fr.* Body Poems. NVAP

Talker, The. Mona Van Duyn. POL

Talking after Christmas Blues. Adrian Henri. *See* Adrian Henri's Talking after Christmas Blues.

Talking along in this not quite prose way. Near. William Stafford. ConAP

Talking Designs. Liz Sohappy Bahe. CDW

Talking in Bed. Philip Larkin. BoLoP

Talking to Myself. *Unknown.* BluL

Talking to the Mule. Laura Jensen. AmPA

Talks with Himself. Bruce Severy. HeS

Tall among the corn stalks. Ruth. Laura Freedgood. SFF

Tall and freckled and sandy. Middleton's Rouseabout. Henry Lawson. MAuV

Tall and singularly dark you pass among the breakers. Louis Zukofsky. NoAM

Tall camels of the spirit, The. "A World without Objects Is a Sensible Emptiness." Richard Wilbur. ConAP; NoAM; NOBA; PiAm

Tall Figures of Giacometti, The. May Swenson. WIF

Tall glass, round loaf and tumbled cloth. Still Life. Rosemary Dobson. MAuV

Tall pines pine, The. The Cow Slips away. Ben King. ECBV

Tall timber stood here once. Improved Farm Land. Carl Sandburg. RFM

Tallest poet for his height. Arroyo. Tom Weatherly. PoBA

Tally. Josephine Miles. NoAM

Tallyho! Tallyho!/Echo faints far astray. The Hunt. Walter de la Mare. BoAnP

Tam i' the Kirk. Violet Jacob. GBL; SLP

Tam Lin. *Unknown.* AIW, *2 versions;* Epi; NOBE; PeBB

Tambourine. James Cunningham. JB

Tamed by Miltown, we lie on Mother's bed. Man and Wife. Robert Lowell. BoLoP; ConAP; PSN

Tamping Ties ("Tamp 'em up solid"). *Unknown.* AmFP

Tanagra! think not I forget. Corinna, to Tanagra, from Athens. Walter Savage Landor. *Fr.* Pericles and Aspasia. NOBE

Tanglid I was yn loves snare. Sir Thomas Wyatt. AAS

Tanka: "In the evening/ Quiet of the country town." Noin Hoshi, *tr. fr. Japanese by* Nobuyuki Yuasa. PAIC

Tanka: "Once, far over the breakers." Akiko No Yosano, *tr. fr. Japanese by* Kenneth Rexroth. PAIC

Tanka: "Swifter than hail." Akiko No Yosano, *tr fr. Japanese by* Kenneth Rexroth. PAIC

Tannen-/ baum/ whose secret, A. Fable of the Transcendent Tannenbaum. Scott Bates. PoTa

Tantalos. Paulus Silentiarius, *tr. fr. Greek by* Dudley Fitts. LoAs

Tao in the Yankee Stadium Bleachers. John Updike. SPo

Taped to the wall of my cell are 47 pictures: 47 black. The Idea of Ancestry. Etheridge Knight. BPo; ConAP; PoBA; PPoe

Taper wastes within yon window-pane, The. The Drunkard's Last Market. Charles Tennyson Turner. VPC

Tapestry, The. Howard Nemerov. Prf

Tapestry. Charles Simic. NVAP

Tappster, fill another ale. Drinking Song. *Unknown.* OxBM

Tara Is Grass. *Unknown, tr. fr. Irish by* Padraic Pearse. POL

Tarantella. Hilaire Belloc. SpRo

Tarantula rattling at the lily's foot, The. O Carib Isle! Hart Crane. NoAM; VGW

Ta-ra-ra Boom-der-é, *with music.* Henry J. Sayers. BLSo (Ta-Ra-Ra Boom-De-Ay!, *diff. version.*) FSN

Target. R. P. Lister. SoSe

Tarred Gull. Elisavietta Ritchie. AATT

Tarrier's Song. *Unknown.* AIW (Drill, Ye Tarriers, Drill!) RDB, *with music*

Tarry Buccaneer, The. John Masefield. PoTa

Tartary. Walter de la Mare. OxBChV

Tarzan, Old. Allan Block. FAF

Task, The. John Ashbery. CAAP

Task, The, *sels.* William Cowper. LAuP
    Sofa, The, I.
    Winter Morning Walk, The, V.

"Taste of Honey, A." King D. Kuka. VW

Taught early that his mother's skin was the sign of error. Mr. Z. M. Carl Holman. SoSe

Tauhid. Askia Muhammad Touré. PoBA

Taxis, The. Louis MacNeice. OxBTC

Tay Bridge Disaster, The, *abr.* William McGonagall. PPoD

Tea for Two, *with music.* Irving Caesar. BLSo

Tea in a Space-ship. James Kirkup. MPo

Tea Party. Harry Behn. LCL

Tea-rose tea-gown, etc., The. Ezra Pound. *Fr.* Hugh Selwyn Mauberley. NOBE

Tea Shop, The. Ezra Pound. BBGO; HeIP

Teach the Rover. *Unknown.* PeBB

Teacher, A. Bruce McGregor. AKE

Teacher, A. Reed Whittemore. NCSH

Teacher of Poetry, The. William Packard. PPoD

Teacher's got a temper, A. A Teacher. Bruce McGregor. AKE

Tears. Elizabeth Barrett Browning. WPE

Tears. *Unknown. See* Weep You No More, Sad Fountains.

Tears, Idle Tears. Tennyson. *Fr.* The Princess, Pt. IV. InPK; InPS; NOBE; PPoe; PPP; VoPo

Tears of Rage. Bob Dylan. RRA

Tears of St. Francis. Robert Duncan. CAAP

Tears, the firebursts and the vows, The. Cracked Looking Glass. Jean Garrigue. LoAs

Teasers, The. William Empson. OxBTC

Teasing; or, I Was Only, Only Teasing You, *with music.* Cecil Mack. FSN

Teechur. Dick Higgins. MiP

Te-ell me milkcow. Milkcow's Calf Blues. *Unknown.* BluL

Teeth bare to the wind. Bicycle Rider. Eugene McCarthy. SPo

Teeth Mother Naked at Last, The. Robert Bly. CAAP

Telegram. Dick Lourie. NeAC

Telephone, The. Robert Frost. LoAs

Telephone Arguin' Blues. *Unknown.* BluL

Telephone Conversation. Wole Soyinka. SFF; SoSe

Telephone line goes cold, A. The Farm on the Great Plains. William Stafford. VGW

Telephone poles, The. Crossing Kansas by Train. Donald Justice. ANTL

Telephones, Muzak. Vincent Buckley. *Fr.* Golden Builders. CAAP

Telephonist. Janet Frame. WPE

Television/ radio sunday benevolent sunday. They Are Killing All the Young Men. David Henderson. PoBA

Television aerials, Chinese characters. On Roofs of Terry Street. Douglas Dunn. OxBTC

Tell all the truth but tell it slant. Emily Dickinson. HeIP; NoAM; NOBA; PiAm; PPP; Psy

Tell her I love. Stanzas for My Daughter. Horace Gregory. RRA

Tell, if thou canst, and truly, whence doth come. Upon Julia's Unlacing Herself. Robert Herrick. SCP-1

Tell me, daughter, my pretty daughter. Cossante. Pero Meogo, *tr. by* Yvor Winters. AIW

Tell Me Man Blues. *Unknown.* BluL

Tell me, my friend, do you think that the grain would sprout in the furrow. Arthur Hugh Clough. *Fr.* Amours de Voyage, III, ii   OBP

Tell me, my love, since Hymen tied. An Hymeneal Dialogue. Thomas Carew. SCP-2

Tell me no more of constancy. Against Constancy. Earl of Rochester. GBL

Tell me no more of minds embracing minds. No Platonic Love. William Cartwright. GBL; SCP-2

Tell me not here, it needs not saying. A. E. Housman. NOBE; OxBTC; PSN

Tell me not in joyous numbers. Stephen Crane. AmVN

Tell me not, in mournful numbers. A Psalm of Life. Longfellow. AmVN; PiAm

Tell me not of joy; there's none. The Dead Sparrow. William Cartwright. BoAnP

Tell me not, sweet, I am unkind. To Lucasta, Going to the Wars. Richard Lovelace. BuTh; GBL; HeIP; InPK; InPS; NOBE; OBP; PBMP; SoSe; VoPo; WIF

Tell me now in what hidden way is. The Ballad of Dead Ladies. Villon, *tr. by* Dante Gabriel Rossetti. PAIC

Tell me, O tell, what kind of thing is wit. Ode: Of Wit. Abraham Cowley. PAIC

Tell Me Pretty Maiden; or, English Girls and Clerks, *with music.* Owen Hall. FSN

Tell Me, Tell Me. Marianne Moore. Psy

Tell me, tell me, gentle robin. The Cat and the Bird. George Canning. ECBV

Tell me, tell me, Sean O'Farrell, tell me why you hurry so? The Rising of the Moon. *Unknown.* RDB

Tell me the tales that to me were so dear. Long, Long Ago. Thomas Haynes Bayly. BLSH; BLSo; PSoN

Tell me what time do the trains come through your town. Black Horse Blues. *Unknown.* BluL

"Tell me what you're doing over here, John Gorham." John Gorham. E. A. Robinson. NoAM

Tell Our Daughters. Besmilr Brigham. IHMS

Tell tale, tit! Mother Goose. MG

Tell us, thou clear and heavenly tongue. The Star Song: a Carol to the King. Robert Herrick. SCP-1

Tell you? ha! who. Maximus, to Gloucester, Letter 2. Charles Olson. NoAM

Tell you I chyll. The Tunnyng of Elynour Rummyng. John Skelton. AAS

Telling lies to the young is wrong. Lies. Yevgeny Yevtushenko, *tr. by* Robin Milner-Gulland *and* Peter Levi. LP

Telling the Bees. Whittier. NOBA

Tèma Con Variazioni. "Lewis Carroll." SpRo

Temper. Rose Fyleman. OxBChV

Temperaments, The. Ezra Pound. BoLoP; NoAM; NOBA

Temperance Billiards Rooms, The. P. J. Kavanagh. OxBTC

Tempest, The ("How should I praise thee, Lord!"). George Herbert. BoReV

Tempest, The, *sels.* Shakespeare.
     Ariel's Song: "Come unto these yellow sands," *fr.* I, ii. NOBE ("Come unto these yellow sands.") HeIP; SpRo
     Ariel's Song: "Full fathom five thy father lies," *fr.* I, ii. AKE; NOBE
     (Full Fathom [*or* Fadom] Five Thy Father Lies.) HeIP; InPK; InPS; OBP; PPoe; WIF
     Ariel's Song: "Where the bee sucks, there suck I," *fr.* V, i. NOBE; SoSe
     ("Where the bee sucks, there suck I.") HeIP; LCL
     "Master, the swabber, the boatswain and I, The," *fr.* II, ii. OBP
     Song: "Hark, hark!/ Bow-wow," *fr.* I, ii. SoSe

Tempest, The ("Cease rude Boreas blust'ring railers"). *Unknown.* AmFP

Tempest, The. Henry Vaughan. SCP-1

Temple, The. C. H. Sisson. OxBTC

Temple of Love, The, *sel.* Sir William Davenant.
     Song: "Come, melt thy soul in mine, that when unite." SCP-2

Temple of the Animals, The. Robert Duncan. NOBA

Temptation of the Magic Banquet. Milton. *Fr.* Paradise Regained, II. SCP-1

Temptations still nest in it like basilisks. Dead Hand. W. S. Merwin. CAPP; InPK

Ten bloody years with this quill lying. Invocation. Valentin Iremonger. BIrV

Ten Commandments, The ("Have thou no other gods but me"). *Unknown.* OxBChV

Ten Definitions of Poetry. Carl Sandburg. WIF

"Ten-Fifteen Community Poems, The," *sel.* John Knoepfle. "She says how/ is it when you." MAT

Ten O'Clock News. Simon Ortiz. VW

Ten Thousand Miles. *Unknown.* AmFP

Ten years ago it seemed impossible. In Progress. Christina Rossetti. WPE

Ten years ago this minute, he possibly sat. The Days. Donald Hall. CoPAm

Ten years together without yet a cloud. Firelight. E. A. Robinson. NoAM

Tenancy, The. Mary Gilmore. MAuV

Tender Buttons, *sels.* Gertrude Stein. RiTi
     Blue Coat, A.
     Celery.
     Cooking.
     Pastry.
     Petticoat, A.
     Water Raining.

Tender each to the other, gentle. Imperialists in Retirement. Edward Lucie-Smith. MPo

Tenebrae. Austin Clarke. BIrV

Tenebris. Angelina Weld Grimké. PoBA

Tennessee. *Unknown.* AmFP

Tennis. Margaret Avison. NoAM

Tennis Court Oath, The. John Ashbery. NoAM

Tentacles, Leaves. Lyn Lifshin. RiTi

Tenth Pastoral, The; or, Gallus. Vergil, *tr. fr. Latin by* Dryden. Epi

Tenth Symphony. John Ashbery. NOBA

Tenting on the Old Camp Ground, *with music.* Walter Kittredge. PSoN
     (Tenting Tonight.) BLSo

Tenuous and Precarious. Stevie Smith. OxBTC

Terence, This Is Stupid Stuff. A. E. Housman. HeIP; InPK; NoAM; SoSe

Term, The. William Carlos Williams. TSWA

Terminal. D. J. Enright. LP

Teminal Days at Beverly Farms. Robert Lowell. PSN

Terminus. Emerson. NOBA; PAIC; PiAm

Ternarie of Littles, upon a Pipkin of Jelly Sent to a Lady, A. Robert Herrick. ECBV

Ternissa. Walter Savage Landor. *Fr.* The Hellenics. NOBE

Terra Australis. Douglas Stewart. MAuV

Terra Australis. Chris Wallace-Crabbe. MAuV

Terra Incognita. D. H. Lawrence. OBP

Terraces rise and fall, The. Going to Sleep in the Country. Howard Moss. PPoD

Terrain. A. R. Ammons. ConAP

Terraplane Blues. *Unknown.* BluL

"Terre des Hommes." Ruth Lisa Schechter. RiTi

Terrible/ a horse at night. Lawrence Ferlinghetti. CoPAm

Terrible Door, The. Harold Monro. BoLoP

Terrible is my plight this night. Wolves for Company. *Unknown.* BIrV

Terrifying are the attent sleek thrushes on the lawn. Thrushes. Ted Hughes. TwMBP

Terror by Night, The. Giacomo Leopardi, *tr. fr. Italian by* John Heath-Stubbs. Moon

Terry is sitting in the kafeneion writing letters to all his friends. Human Relations. Emmett Jarrett. NeAC

Test. Jonathan Price. CoPAm

Testament of Beauty, The, *sel.* Robert Bridges. Ethick, *fr.* IV. OxBTC

Testament of Cresseid, The, *sel.* Robert Henryson. "Wha wait if all that Chauceir wrait was trew?" SLP

Testimonies for a School Prayer. Serge Gavronsky. NowV

Testimony. Carolyn M. Rodgers. BPo

Testing-Tree, The. Stanley Kunitz. MAT

Tête-à-Tête. Edwin Honig. NoAM

Tethys' Festival, *sel.* Samuel Daniel. Shadows. NOBE

Tewa Song of War. *Unknown, tr. fr. Mayan by* Daniel G. Brinton. PBMP

Texas Cowboy, The ("Oh, I am a Texas Cowboy"). *Unknown.* AmFP

Text, The. Gary Snyder. Myths and Texts:Burning, XVII. Epi

Textures. Carol Bergé. MMD

Thack church and a wooden steeple, A. Legsby, Lincolnshire. *Unknown.* GBP

Thalassa. Louis MacNeice. BIrV; NOBE

Than (By Yon Sunset's Wintry Glow). E. E. Cummings. VGW

Thanatopsis. Bryant. AmVN; NOBA; PiAm; VoPo

Thank God, bless God, all ye who suffer not. Tears  Elizabeth Barrett Browning. WPE

Thank Heaven! the crisis. For Annie. Poe. NOBA; PiAm; VoPo

Thank You, *sel. Unknown, tr. fr. Seneca Indian by* Richard Johnny John. "Now so many people that are in this place," Part I. IPWM

Thank you for asking this question. What Is Salt? John Vernon. PPoD

Thank You for the Valentine. Diane Wakoski. CoPAm

Thank you for your recent letter. Dear Mother. Emmett Jarrett. NeAC

Thank You Poem for the Andersons, The. Phillip Hey. NVAP

Thank you, pretty cow, that made. The Cow. Ann *or* Jane Taylor. OxBChV

Thanks to Industrial Essex. Donald Davie. OxBTC

Thanksgiving. Sharon Barba. RiTi

Thanksgiving. Robert Herrick. OFD

Thanksgiving. Kenneth Koch. VGW

Thanksgiving. John N. Morris. OFD

Thanksgiving Day. Lydia Maria Child. ECBV

Thanksgiving for a former, doth invite. Thanksgiving. Robert Herrick. OFD

Thanksgiving in Boston Harbor, The. Hezekiah Butterworth. BTTM

Thanksgiving 1963. Philip Booth. IPWM

Thanksgiving to God, for His House, A. Robert Herrick. OFD

Thar's More in the Man Than Thar Is in the Land. Sidney Lanier. NOBA

Thassyryans king, in peas with fowle desyre. Earl of Surrey. AAS

That Bad Music. Robert Harris. CAAP

That beauty I ador'd before. Westminster Drollery, 1671. Aphra Behn. SBG

That blacksnake across the furrows. The Motorcyclist's Song. DeWitt Bell. MiP

That Black Snake Moan. *Unknown.* BluL

That Chinese restaurant was a joke. The Will to Change. Adrienne Rich. NMM

That civilisation may not sink. Long-Legged Fly. W. B. Yeats. AnMo; InPK; InPS; NoAM; NOBE; PPoe; PSN

"That cop was powerful mean." The Idiot. Dudley Randall. BPo

That "Craning of the Neck." Isabella Gardner. WPE

That Crawling Baby Blues. *Unknown.* BluL

That crazed girl improvising her music. The Crazed Girl. W. B. Yeats. InPS

That Dark Other Mountain. Robert Francis. NCSH

That Day. John Leax. AATT

That Day. Anne Sexton. ConAP

That day, in the slipping of torsos and straining flanks. The Song. Lola Ridge. WPE

That day the/ words/ formed. That Day. John Leax. AATT

That day when oats were reaped, and wheat was ripe. When Oats Were Reaped. Thomas Hardy. OxBTC

That Death should thus from hence our Butler catch. In Obitum Promi. Henry Parrot. FaBoCo

That dog with daisies for eyes. The Dog of Art. Denise Levertov. NoAM

That Familiar way the Bowmans have always had. Members of the Family. Derek Bowman. MIS

That flower unseen, that gem of purest ray. In a Churchyard. Richard Wilbur. HeIP; PiAm

That force is lost. Snake Eyes. LeRoi Jones. VGW

That God of ours, the Great Geometer. Grace to Be Said at the Supermarket. Howard Nemerov. AnMo; MPo

That hatless chewed woman sending me messages. In the Smoking Car. Ruth Whitman. RiTi

That her serene influence should spread. Two Loves. Richard Eberhart. LoAs

That hobnailed goblin, the bobtailed Hob. Country Dance. Edith Sitwell. NoAM

That house you took me to. Number 14. Keith Bosley. LP

That hump of a man bunching chrysanthemums. Old Florist. Theodore Roethke. CTBA; NCSH; PiAm

That Hypocrite. *Unknown.* BPo

That I went to warm my self in Lady Betty's chamber, because I was cold. The Humble Petition of Frances Harris. Swift. Epi

That is no country for old men. Sailing to Byzantium. W. B. Yeats. AnMo; HeIP; InPK; InPS; NoAM; NOBE; OxBTC; PAIC; PPoD; PPoe: PPP; PSN; SoSe; WIF

That it should end in an Albert Pick hotel. At the End of the Affair. Maxine W. Kumin. CoPAm

That it will never come again. Emily Dickinson. NOBA

That Justice is a blind goddess. Justice. Langston Hughes. BPo

That king spent fifty years or more. Citadels. Richard Kell. PFIr

That Life, on Film. Lynn Sukenick. RiTi

That 'lil girl that Daddy loved. Ted Kooser. *Fr.* Themes for Country-Western Singers. POL

That Little Black Cat. D'Arcy Wentworth Thompson. OxBChV

That Little Lump of Coal. *Unknown.* AmFP

That Lonesome Train Took My Baby Away. *Unknown.* BluL

That love is all there is. Emily Dickinson. NOBA

That lovely spot which thou dost see. Upon a Mole in Celia's Bosom. Thomas Carew. SCP-2

That lover of a night. Crazy Jane on God. W. B. Yeats. Epi; OxBTC

That mare stood in the field. All through the Rains. Gary Snyder. ConAP

That matter of the murder is hushed up. The Cenci. Shelley. MBPR

That motion which doth from the mouth proceed. What Makes Echo. Margaret Cavendish, Duchess of Newcastle. SCP-2

That Mountain Far Away. *Unknown, tr. fr. Tewa by* Herbert Joseph Spinden. PBMP

That mountain there. Pilgrimage Song. *Unknown, tr. by* Mary Austin. WPE

That Nature Is a Heraclitean Fire and of the Comfort of the Resurrection. Gerard Manley Hopkins. AnMo; Epi

That night the dog let night in. Mad Dog. Robert Siegel. FAF

That night the moon drifted over the pond. The Prediction. Mark Strand. NVAP

That Night When Joy Began. W. H. Auden. OxBTC; PPoD; SoSe

That night your great guns, unawares. Channel Firing. Thomas Hardy. HeIP; InPK; NoAM; OBP; OxBTC; PPoD; VoPo

That No Man Should Write But Such As Do Excel. George Turberville. PPoD

That old 'Frisco train left a mile a minute. 'Frisco Town. *Unknown.* BluL

That old nineteenth-century hold. Salvaging Spikes. Robert Vas Dias. HeS

That Old-time Religion, *with music. Unknown.* BLSH

That once which pained to think of. The Forgiven Past. Laura Riding. NoAM

That orbéd maiden with white fire laden. Orbed Maiden. Shelley. *Fr.* The Cloud. Moon

That practising bird is sharpening his call. Before Dawn. Ann Darr. MiP

That raft we rigged up, under the water. A Distance from the Sea. Weldon Kees. NoAM

"That red fox." The Trap. William Beyer. PoTa

That sculptor we know, the passionate-eyed son of a quarryman. An Artist. Robinson Jeffers. VGW

That seat of science, Athens. Free America. *At. to* Joseph Warren. BTTM

That Sharp Knife. Thomas Wolfe. NCSH

That she must change so soon her curving city. Peter's Little Daughter Dies. Kenneth Patchen. RRA

That shore, with its seagulls. Lake Michigan. David Kherdian. FAF

That soldier with a machinegun bolted. Two Summers in Moravia. Roger McDonald. CAAP

That sound like the scratch. One, The Other, And. Wendy Wieber. NMM

That summer nothing would do. Herbert Scott. POL

That Sunday, on my oath, the rain was a heavy overcoat. Mary Hines. Padraic Fallon, *after* Anthony Raftery. SoSe

That the war would be over before they got to you. When You Have Forgotten Sunday: The Love Story. Gwendolyn Brooks. VoPo

That time/ we all heard it. Paul Robeson. Gwendolyn Brooks. PoBA

That time of year thou mayst in me behold. Sonnets, LXXIII. Shakespeare. BoLoP; Epi; GBL; HeIP; InPK; InPS; IPWM; LoAs; NOBE; OBP; PBMP; PPoD; PPP; SoSe

That time of year you may in me behold. The Winter Twilight, Glowing Black and Gold. Delmore Schwartz. NoAM

That towering place, gabled and huge. Introductory. *Unknown, tr. by* Burton Raffel. *Fr.* Beowulf. OBP

That way the moonflower and the sunflower this. Morning Dialogue. Conrad Aiken. NoAM

That We Head Towards. Stephany Fuller. BPo

That which her slender waist confined. On a Girdle. Edmund Waller. HeIP; InPK; SoSe

That which we dare invoke to bless. In Memoriam A.H.H., CXXIV. Tennyson. BoReV

That white coconut, the sun. Cloud Shadows. John Updike. VoPo

That Whitsun, I was late getting away. The Whitsun Weddings. Philip Larkin. NoAM; OxBTC; PSN

That winter love spoke and we raised no objection. Jig. C. Day Lewis. PFIr

That within me. Anomie. Patricia Ramsey. AATT

That woman there is almost dead. The Rat. W. H. Davies. OxBTC

That woman, vacuum in her mouth. The Great Nebula in Andromeda. Hugh Seidman. AmPA

That Women Are but Men's Shadows. Ben Jonson. InPS (Shadow, The.) NOBE

That year of the cloud, when my marriage failed. River Road. Stanley Kunitz. NoAM

That you worked. Poems to My Father. Rae Desmond Jones. CAAP

That your little finger. The Wishbone. Rae Desmond Jones. CAAP

Thatched roof rings like heaven where mice, The. Byre. Norman MacCaig. BoAnP

That's Ethan Allen on the monument. Green Mountain Boy. Florida Watts Smyth. ECBV

That's Jack. Jack. Charles Henry Ross. OxBChV

That's my last Duchess painted on the wall. My Last Duchess. Robert Browning. InPS; IPWM; MAT; NOBE; PAIC; PBMP; PPoD; PPP; SoSe; SS; WIF

That's No Way to Get Along. *Unknown.* BluL

That's the way Tod Johnson signed. X. R. P. Dickey. HeS

Thaw. Lyn Lifshin. FAF

Thaw. Edward Thomas. OxBTC

Thaw in the City. Lou Lipsitz. MAT; NCSH

Thee finds me in the garden, Hannah, —come in! The Quaker Widow. Bayard Taylor. AmVN

Thee for my recitative. To A Locomotive in Winter. Walt Whitman. InPK; NoAM; WIF

Thee sets a bell to swinging in my soul. Hildegarde Flanner. *Fr.* Sonnets in Quaker Language. WPE

Thee, Thee, Only Thee. Thomas Moore. GBL

Their attendant nuns spare the tourists well. Bathing the Aged. Paul Monette. AmPA

Their Attitudes Differ. Margaret Atwood. Psy

Their black truck rattled up the dusty hill. The Diviners. Mary Oliver. WPE

Their calendars are based on rice. Rice. Carol Muske. AmPA

Their idiom, their dimension. Intimations of Immortality, Cuttingsville, Vermont, 1880. Constance Carrier. FAF

Their intuition/ Was as elegant as the stars above the mesa. Los Alamos: Manhattan. David Rowbotham. CAAP

Their rugs are sodden, their heads are down. Gun Teams. Gilbert Frankau. OxBTC

Their sense is with their senses all mixed in. Modern Love, XLVIII. George Meredith. LoAs

Their smooth dark flames flicker at time's own root. The Cycads. Judith Wright. MAuV

Their spare, fanatic sentry comes. Ants and Others. Adrien Stoutenburg. BoAnP

Their time past, pulled down. Burning the Christmas Greens. William Carlos Williams. NoAM; NOBA; PiAm

Their tongues are knives, their forks are hands and feet. Riddle. Adrian Mitchell. GBL

Their voices heard, I stumble suddenly. One More New Botched Beginning. Stephen Spender. NoAM

Them, Crying. James Dickey. NowV

Them that's got shall have.  God Bless the Child.  Arthur Herzog, Jr. and Billie Holiday.  WIF

Theme and Variations.  Edna St. Vincent Millay.  SBG

Theme for English B.  Langston Hughes.  NoAM; NOBA

Theme in Yellow.  Carl Sandburg.  LCL

Theme One: The Variations.  August Wilson.  PoBA

Themes for Country-Western Singers, sel.  Ted Kooser.  "That 'lil girl that Daddy loved."  POL

Then.  Walter de la Mare.  RAE

Then.  Gary Gildner.  FiCP

Then and Now.  Paul Laurence Dunbar.  PBMP

Then and Now.  Kath Walker.  IHMS

Then call me traitor if you must.  To Certain Critics.  Countee Cullen.  BPo

Then came one with two bulldogs at his tail.  Cock Lorell's Boat.  Unknown.  TVS

Then cease fond satyres, quipping epigrammatists.  A Prophecy of This Present Year 1600.  John Weever.  TVS

Then darkness Europe's face did overspread.  Sir John Denham.  Fr. The Progress of Learning.  SCP-2

Then did he friendly leave.  The Song of the Death of Mr. Thewlis.  Unknown.  SCP-2

Then find me some World Peace!  In Answer to a Request to Write a Poem on World Peace.  Elisavietta Ritchie.  AATT

Then fled, O brethren, the wicked juba.  The Ballad of Nat Turner.  Robert Hayden.  BPo; VGW

Then has a man less might than a beste.  The Newly Born.  Unknown.  Fr. The Pricke of Conscience.  OxBM

Then hate me when thou wilt; if ever, now.  Sonnets, XC.  Shakespeare.  NOBE

Then it was dusk in Illinois, the small boy.  First Song.  Galway Kinnell.  CTBA; NCSH

Then leave old regret.  A Moral Poem.  J. V. Cunningham.  VGW

Then of the antique flame the greater horn.  Ulysses.  Dante, tr. by Longfellow.  Fr. Divina Commedia: Inferno.  Epi

Then ran ther a route of ratones, as it were.  Belling the Cat.  William Langland.  Fr. The Vision of Piers Plowman.  OxBM

Then sent the King Constantine.  The Pound of Flesh.  Unknown.  Fr. Cursor Mundi.  OxBM

Then Strip Lads, and To It.  Sir Walter Scott.  SPo

Then the air was perfect. And his descent.  The Parachutist.  Jon Anderson.  AmPA

Then the band of Geats, young and brave.  To the Sea.  Unknown, tr. by Burton Raffel.  Fr. Beowulf.  OBP

Then the knee of the wave.  Reclining Figure.  Donald Hall.  ConAP

Then the long sunlight lying on the sea.  The Insusceptibles.  Adrienne Rich.  ConAP; HeIP; InPK

Then there is this civilising love of death, by which.  Ignorance of Death.  William Empson.  NoAM

Then they took whole stones according to the law.  First Maccabees, Bible, Apocrypha.  OFD

Then this poor woman's blind.  Oh Oh Blues.  Unknown.  BluL

Then thus let's go together.  Thomas Otway.  Fr. The Orphan, or the Unhappy Marriage, IV, ii.  SCP-2

Then up I rose, and make no more delay.  Elizabeth Melvill, Lady Culross.  Fr. A Godly Dream.  WPE

Then was I cast from out my state.  Frenzy.  George Crabbe.  Fr. Sir Eustace Grey.  NOBE

Theocritus.  Oscar Wilde.  NOBE

Theologia Germanica.  David Malouf.  CAAP

Theological Limerick.  T. Lindsay.  FaBoCo

Theology.  Ted Hughes.  NoAM

"Theon to his father Theon greetings. Another."  To Theon from His Son Theon.  C. A. Trypanis.  NCSH

Theophila; or, Love's Sacrifice, sels.  Edward Benlowes.  "Angels by one sin fell: so, man; how then," fr. Canto II.  SCP-2

Cynthia.  Moon.  "Might souls converse with souls by angel-way," fr. Canto I.  SCP-2

"Muse! twang the powerful harp and brush each string," fr. Canto III.  SCP-2

Theoria in Early Morning.  William R. Mitchell.  AATT

Theory.  Dorothy Parker.  SBG

Ther is no rose of swich vertu.  The Rose That Bore Jesu.  Unknown.  OxBM

Ther was also a Nonne, a Prioresse.  See There was also a nun, a Prioress.

There.  Mary Elizabeth Coleridge.  BoReV

There.  Robert Mezey.  TSWA

There/ is someone I can bear.  W. S. Landor.  Marianne Moore.  Psy

There ain't but three men who really can spend my dough.  Three Men.  Unknown.  BluL

There ain't nothing special about me.  The Country Singer.  Carl Rakosi.  HeS

There all the golden codgers lay.  News for the Delphic Oracle.  W. B. Yeats.  NoAM

There are also the dark exciting days of.  The Dark Exciting Days.  Karl Shapiro.  CoPAm

There are different ways of dying without.  After the Revolution.  Marilyn Hacker.  AmPA

"There are dreams that need rest."  Okay.  Sharon Scott.  JB

There are 86,400 seconds in every 24 hours.  A Desperate Measure.  Nigel Dennis.  WIF

There are fairies at the bottom of our garden!  Fairies.  Rose Fyleman.  OxBChV

There are fish that we never quite catch swimming.  The Final Solstice.  Robert Adamson.  CAAP

There are four men mowing down by the Isar.  A Youth Mowing.  D. H. Lawrence.  NoAM

There are four verses to put down.  Ap Huw's Testament.  R. S. Thomas.  BuTh

There are half-naked men who stand.  The Glass Eaters.  George Jonas.  NeAC

There are (I scarce can think it, but am told.)  The First Satire of the Second Book of Horace.  Pope.  PPP

There Are Lime Trees in Leaf on the Promenade.  Tom Raworth.  TwMBP

There are lots of places to go.  White Collar Ballad.  Weldon Kees.  AnMo

There are many cumbersone ways to kill a man.  Five Ways to Kill a Man.  Edwin Brock.  IPWM; SFF; TSWA

There are men in the village of Erith.  Erith, on the Thames.  Unknown.  GBP

There are no angels yet.  Gabriel.  Adrienne Rich.  Psy; VGW

There are no crosses.  A Death in the Desert.  Charles Tomlinson.  TwMBP

There are no nightmares now. Only when memory settles.  Seravezza.  Hoyt W. Fuller.  PoBA

There are no rules for so much sadness.  "Woman with Tongue in Cheek."  Daniela Gioseffi.  RiTi

There are no stars to-night.  My Grandmother's Love Letters.  Hart Crane.  NoAM; NOBA; PSN

There are only two things now.  New Year's Eve.  D. H. Lawrence.  BoLoP

There are, perhaps, whom passion gives a grace.  The Aged Lover Discourses in the Flat Style.  J. V. Cunningham.  NoAM; PPoD

There are places I'll remember all my life.  In My Life.  John Lennon and Paul McCartney.  GrRo

There are portraits and still-lifes. Paring the Apple. Charles Tomlinson. OxBTC; TwMBP

There are Roughly Zones. Robert Frost. PPP

There are seeds within the tide. City. Joseph Bruchac. CDW

There are several attitudes towards Christmas. The Cultivation of Christmas Trees. T. S. Eliot. OFD

There are so many lies in nature. Degas. Paul Monette. AmPA

There are so many roots to the tree of anger. Who Said It Was Simple. Audré Lorde. WBN

There are some/ secrets. July 31. Norman Jordan. PoBA

There are some heights in Wessex, shaped as if by a kindly hand. Wessex Heights. Thomas Hardy. IPWM

There are some people who are very resourceful. Hearts of Gold. Ogden Nash. AKE

There are some qualities—some incorporate things. Sonnet—Silence. Poe. NOBA; PiAm

There are some things in life. Unknown. SFF

There are some things which, left unsaid, are true. Paradox. Benjamin K. Bennett. POL

There are strange Hells within the minds war made. Strange Hells. Ivor Gurney. OxBTC

There are the Alps. What is there to say about them? On the Fly-Leaf of Pound's Cantos. Basil Bunting. NoAM; OxBTC

There are these small cliffs. The Singular Self. Charles Bukowski. CoPAm

There are things to be said. No doubt. Cid Corman. VGW

There are those to whom place is unimportant. The Rose. Theodore Roethke. InPS; NOBA; PiAm; PPoe

There are times when. May Sarton. Fr. The Invocation to Kali. RiTi

There are, to whom I seem excessive sour. Satire, II, 1. Horace, tr. by Ben Jonson. TVS

There are too many waterfalls here. Questions of Travel. Elizabeth Bishop. NOBA

There are truths you Americans need to be told. American Literature. James Russell Lowell. Fr. A Fable for Critics. AmVN

There are twelve months in all the year. How Robin Hood Rescued the Widow's Sons. Unknown. PoTa

There are two different kinds, I believe, of human attraction. Arthur Hugh Clough. Fr. Amours de Voyage, II, xi. OBP

There are two facing peacocks. Chenille. James Dickey. NoAM

There are two Mays. Emily Dickinson. NOBA

There are vast realms of consciousness still undreamed of. Terra Incognita. D. H. Lawrence. OBP

There are voices, voices. Light's dying. Birds have quit. John Berryman. Fr. Dreams Songs. CAPP

There are wolves in the next room waiting. The Wolves. Allen Tate. NoAM; NOBA; PiAm

There are words like freedom. Words Like Freedom. Langston Hughes. BPo

There arent. Untitled Requiem for Tomorrow. Conyus. PoBA

There blows a cold wind today, today. To Keep the Cold Wind Away. Unknown. OxBM

There came a day at summer's full. Emily Dickinson. LoAs; NoAM; NOBA; PiAm

There came a ghost to Margret's door. Sweet Williams's Ghost. Unknown. AIW

There came a wind like a bugle. Emily Dickinson. NoAM; NOBA

There came you wishing me. José Garcia Villa, tr. fr. Spanish by Ben F. Carruthers. LoAs

There chanced to be a pedlar bold. The Bold Pedlar and Robin Hood. Unknown. AIW

There comes Emerson first, whose rich words, every one. Emerson. James Russell Lowell. Fr. A Fable for Critics. AmVN; NOBA; PAIC

There comes Poe, with his raven, like Barnaby Rudge. Poe and Longfellow. James Russell Lowell. Fr. A Fable for Critics. AmVN; NoBA

There died a myriad. Ezra Pound. Fr. Hugh Selwyn Mauberley. NOBE; PiAm; TCP

There dewlt a miller hale and bold. The Miller of Dee. Unknown. GBP

There Gowans are Gay. Unknown. GBP

There has been a light snow. In a Train. Robert Bly. CAPP; POL

There Has to Be a Jail for Ladies. Thomas Merton. VGW

There, in that other world, what waits for me? There. Mary Elizabeth Coleridge. BoReV

There, in the corner, staring at his drink. Docker. Seamus Heaney. NoAM

There in the hard light. An Irish Lake. W. R. Rodgers. BIrV

There, in the market, with Mrs. Peters. Journal of the Storm. Greg Kuzma. AmPA

There Is. Louis Simpson. ConAP

There is/ A welcome at the door to which no one comes? Angel Surrounded by Paysans. Wallace Stevens. PPP

There is a bale of hay. Beside the Road. Ken Belford. NeAC

There is a bird in the poplars! Metric Figure. William Carlos Williams. AKE

There is a blue sky. A Song. Edward Dorn. ConAP

There is a blue star, Janet. Baby Toes. Carl Sandburg. LCL

There is a change—and I am poor. A Complaint. Wordsworth. NOBE

There is a charm I can't explain. The Big Sunflower. Bobby Newcomb. BLSo

There is a charm in footing slow across a silent plain. Lines Written in the Highlands after a Visit to Burns's Country. Keats. MBPR

There is a cheater by profession. Cheating Droone. "T. M." Fr. Micro-Cynicon. TVS

There is a child unborn. The Child Unborn. Humbert Wolfe. BuTh

There is a cool river. Detroit. Donald Hall. ANTL

There is a door. The Door. Lewis Turco. CoPAm

There is a drear and lonely tract of hell. Supremacy. E. A. Robinson. NoAM

There is a fine stuffed chavender. A False Gallop of Analogies. Warham St. Leger. FaBoCo

There is a flower, the lesser celandine. The Small Celandine. Wordsworth. MBPR

There is a flower within my heart. Daisy Bell; or, A Bicycle Built for Two. Harry Dacre. BLSo; FSN

There is a flowr sprung of a tree. The Fairest Flower. John Audelay. OxBM

There Is a Garden in Her Face. Thomas Campion. AAS; HeIP; InPK (Cherry-ripe.) BoLoP; NOBE; PPoe

There is a great amount of poetry in unconscious/ fastidiousness. Critics and Connoisseurs. Marianne Moore. NoAM; NOBA; PSN

There is a great river this side of Stygia. The River of Rivers in Connecticut. Wallace Stevens. NOBA; VGW

There Is a Green Hill. Cecil Frances Alexander. OxBChV

There is a green spell stolen from Birmingham. A Death at Winson Green. Francis Webb. MAuV

There is a hawk that is picking the birds out of our sky. Shiva. Robinson Jeffers. NoAM; NOBA

There is a heigh-ho in these glowing coals. Heigh-ho on a Winter Afternoon. Donald Davie. OxBTC

There is a joyful night in which we lose.  When the Dumb Speak. Robert Bly.  CAPP; NoAM; NOBA

There Is a Lady Sweet and Kind.  *Unknown, at. to* Thomas Ford. GBL; HeIP; LoAs, *abr.* (Passing By, *abr.*)  NOBE

There is a land of pure delight.  Isaac Watts.  BoReV

There is a light in the snow.  The Revenant.  Peter Cooley.  HeS

There is a little gentleman.  The Bee.  *Unknown.*  ECBV

There is a little lightning in his eyes.  Of Robert Frost. Gwendolyn Brooks.  NoAM; NOBA

There is a magic melting pot.  The Melting Pot.  Dudley Randall.  BPo

There is a man walking.  The People.  Joy Harjo.  SA

There is a meadow.  Last Light.  Robert Kelly.  VGW

There is a myth, a tale men tell.  The Pearl.  Hans Christian Andersen, *tr. by* Charles Wharton Stork.  LoAs

There is a pain—so utter.  Emily Dickinson.  NOBA

There is a place in Montana where the grass stands up two feet. Rosebud.  Jon Anderson.  CAAP

There is a place where love begins and a place.  Explanations of Love.  Carl Sandburg.  SFF

There is a secret room.  The Same Gesture.  John Montague. BIrV

There is a silence where hath been no sound.  Silence.  Thomas Hood.  NOBE

There is a singer everyone has heard.  The Oven Bird.  Robert Frost.  HeIP; NoAM; NOBA; PiAm; PPP; VoPo

There is a smile of love.  The Smile.  Blake.  MBPR

There is a spell, for instance.  Hilda Doolittle ("H.D.").  *Fr.* The Walls Do Not Fall.  NoAM

There is a story in my book.  Witchcraft.  Siddie Joe Johnson. ECBV

There is a stream which rises.  Joseph Bruchac.  CDW

There Is a Tavern in the Town, *with music. Unknown, at. to* William H. Hills.  BLSH; BLSo; PSoN

There is a thorn; it looks so old.  The Thorn.  Wordsworth. MBPR

There is a through-otherness about Armagh.  Armagh.  W. R. Rodgers.  NoAM; PFIr

There is a Tide.  Sydney Goodsir Smith.  SLP

There is a time of notation.  Lines on the Back of a Leary Bailfund Card.  Mary Norbert Körte.  MIT

There is a tree, by day.  Tenebris.  Angelina Weld Grimké. PoBA

There is a tree native in Turkestan.  Note on Local Flora. William Empson.  PSN

There is a void, outside of existence, which if entered into.  Blake. *Fr.* Jerusalem.  MBPR

There is a white mare that my love keeps.  Alex Comfort.  LoAs

There is a wind where the rose was.  Autumn.  Walter de la Mare.  OxBTC

There is a window stuffed with hay.  The Hay Hotel.  Oliver St. John Gogarty.  BIrV

There is a wolf in me . . . fangs pointed for tearing .  Wilderness. Carl Sandburg.  PiAm

There is a woman climbing a glass hill.  Two Women.  Naomi Replansky.  NMM

There is a woman in a white or blue.  An American Gothic. Dick Allen.  FAF

There is a word at heart for the next of death.  Written in Exile. Kathleen Raine.  WPE

There is a young lady, whose nose.  Edward Lear.  OxBChV

There is an evening coming in.  Going.  Philip Larkin.  NowV; PSN

There is Bryant, as quiet, as cool, and as dignified.  Bryant. James Russell Lowell.  *Fr.* A Fable for Critics.  AmVN; NOBA

There is death enough in Europe without these.  Dead Ponies. Brenda Chamberlain.  WPE

There is Gray in My Eyebrows.  Karl Shapiro.  CoPAm

There is grey in your hair.  Broken Dreams.  W. B. Yeats.  PSN

There is Hawthorne, with genius so shrinking and rare. Hawthorne.  James Russell Lowell.  *Fr.* A Fable for Critics. NOBA

There is joy in/ Feeling the warmth.  Eskimo Chant.  *Unknown, tr. by* Knud Rasmussen.  RFM

There is Lowell, who's striving Parnassus to climb.  Lowell. James Russell Lowell.  *Fr.* A Fable for Critics.  AmVN; NOBA

There is naught for thee by thy haste to gain.  The Created. Jones Very.  AmVN; PiAm

There is no frigate like a book.  Emily Dickinson.  ECBV; SoSe; WIF

"There is no God," the wicked saith.  Arthur Hugh Clough.  *Fr.* Dipsychus, Pt. I, sc. v.  NOBE; VPC

There is no happy life.  Love's Matrimony.  William Cavendish, Duke of Newcastle.  SCP-2

There is no harmony in victory.  Cromwell.  Paul Mills.  MIS

There is no more good water.  No More Good Water.  *Unknown.* BluL

There is no one here.  Matisse: "The Red Studio."  W. D. Snodgrass.  WIF

There Is No Time.  Elaine H. Jennings.  NPW

There is no time.  XXth Century.  Robert Hillyer.  TH

There is not in my mind one sullen fate.  Richard Lovelace.  *Fr.* On Sannazar's Being Honoured.  SCP-2

There is nothing at all pretty about death.  Esthetique du Machiavel.  George Starbuck.  PAIC

There is nothing now. To learn.  The Fortress.  Louise Glück. NVAP

There is one story and one story only.  To Juan at the Winter Solstice.  Robert Graves.  NoAM; OBP

There is one that has a head without an eye.  A Riddle. Christina Rossetti.  OxBChV

There Is Only One of Everything.  Margaret Atwood.  MMD

There is so much potential.  Wheels.  Vicki Viidikas.  CAAP

There is something suspicious about the spring.  The Green Beginning.  Warren Slesinger.  HeS

There is sorrow enough in the natural way.  The Power of the Dog.  Kipling.  BoAnP

There is sweet music here that softer falls.  Song of the Lotos-Eaters.  Tennyson.  *Fr.* The Lotos-Eaters.  HeIP; NOBE

There is the star bloom of the moss.  Forest.  Jean Garrigue. NOBA

There is this cave.  The Jewel.  James Wright.  CAPP

There is unknown dust that is near us.  Surprised by Evening. Robert Bly.  CAPP; VGW

There is Whittier, whose swelling and vehement heart.  Whittier. James Russell Lowell.  *Fr.* A Fable for Critics.  AmVN; NOBA

There is your brain.  The Resident Stranger.  Harley Elliott. HeS

There isn't much a man can do.  The Jellyfish.  William Pitt Root.  BoAnP; NVAP

There it was, word for word.  The Poem That Took the Place of a Mountain.  Wallace Stevens.  PiAm

There lies a somnolent lake.  In the Past.  Trumbull Stickney. NOBA

There livd a man in yonder glen.  Get Up and Bar the Door. *Unknown.*  PAIC

There lived a fat old lady, in London she did dwell.  The Old Lady of London.  *Unknown.*  AmFP

There Lived a King.  W. S. Gilbert.  *Fr.* The Gondoliers.  PoTa

There lived a lady, a lady gay. The Wife of Usher's Well. *Unknown.* AIW

There lived a Puddy in a well. The Puddy and the Mouse. *Unknown.* GBP

There lived a sage in days of yore. A Tragic Story. Adelbert von Chamisso, *tr. by* Thackeray. ECBV

There lived a wife at Usher's well. The Wife of Usher's Well. *Unknown.* AIW; Epi; NOBE; PeBB; SoSe

There Lived among the Untrodden Ways. Hartley Coleridge. SpRo

There lived an old lord by the northern sea. The Two Sisters. *Unknown.* AIW

There lived an old man in the kingdom of Tess. The New Vestments. Edward Lear. RAE

There lived an old woman at Lynn. *Unknown.* OxBChV

There may be some way back. A Girl at the Center of Her Life. Joyce Carol Oates. CoPAm

There on the top of the down. June Bracken and Heather. Tennyson. PPoe

There once was a day when. Shot with a Hot Rot Gun. Michael Goode. NowV

There once was a frog. A Legend of Lake Okeefinokee. Laura E. Richards. ECBV

There once was a girl named Myrtle. Myrtle. Theodore Roethke. RAE

There once was a man who said, "God." Idealism. Ronald Arbuthnott Knox. FaBoCo

There once was a Willow, and he was very old. The Willow-Man. Juliana Horatia Ewing. OxBChV

There once were some people called Sioux. The American Indian. *Unknown.* FaBoCo

There once were three brothers from merry Scotland. Sir Andrew Barton *Unknown.* AmFP

There ought to be capital punishment for cars. Thoughts on Capital Punishment. Rod McKuen. InPK

There rolls the deep where grew the tree. In Memoriam A. H. H., CXXIII. Tennyson. BoReV; NOBE

There sat down, once, a thing on Henry's heart. John Berryman. *Fr.* Dream Songs. CAPP; PiAm; PPoD; PSN

There shall be no more songs. Black Power. Alvin Saxon. PoBA

There she sits a'-smokin'. Motorcycle Irene. Skip Spence. MAT

There She Stands a Lovely Creature. *Unknown.* AmFP; OLR

There should have been the Old Manse under creeper. Story Which Should Have Happened. Peter Porter. CAAP

There sits a fair couple courting. The Jealous Brothers. *Unknown.* AmFP

There, spring lambs jam the sheepfold. Watercolor of Grantchester. Sylvia Plath. SBG

There stand three mills on Manor Water. Manor Water. *Unknown.* GBP

There the black river, boundary to hell. The Southern Road. Dudley Randall. PAIC; PoBA

There the companions of his fall, o'erwhelmed. Immortal Hate. Milton. *Fr.* Paradise Lost, I. NOBE

There the most daintie Paradise on ground. Guyon's Temptation. Spenser. *Fr.* The Faerie Queene. OBP

There, there is no mountain within miles. Nebraska. Jon Swan. RFM

There they are/ Thirty at the corner. The Blackstone Rangers. Gwendolyn Brooks. NoAM; NowV; PoBA

There they are now. Three Sentences for a Dead Swan. James Wright. NoAM; NOBA

There they go. Seed Journey. Gregory Corso. VGW

There two that struggling into the deep. Thomas Heyrick. *Fr.* The Submarine Voyage: a Pindaric Poem in Four Parts. SCP-2

There was a boy bedded in bracken. Carol. John Short. MPo

There was a boy whose name was Jim. Jim, Who Ran Away from His Nurse, and Was Eaten by a Lion. Hilaire Belloc. OxBChV

There was a bridge that Rozinante would not cross. The Bridge of Heraclitus. George Reavey. BIrV

There Was a Child Went Forth. Walt Whitman. InPS; PBMP; SoSe

"There was a child went forth every day, *sel.* RFM

There was a clever skipper, in Akron he did dwell. The Clever Skipper. *Unknown.* AmFP

There was a clock in Grandad's house. Two Clocks. John Daniel. LP

There was a crooked man, and he went a crooked mile. Mother Goose. MG

There was a darkness in this man. John Gould Fletcher. *Fr.* Lincoln. OFD

There was a fair maiden who lived on the shore. The Fair Maid by the Shore. *Unknown.* AmFP

There was a fair young creature who lived by the seaside. The Silvery Tide. *Unknown.* AmFP

There was a faith-healer of Deal. Mind and Matter. *Unknown.* FaBoCo

There was a farmer's son kept sheep upon a hill. The Lady's Policy. *Unknown.* RDB

There was a gallant lady all in her tender youth. Canada-I-O. *Unknown.* AmFP

There was a gallant ship, a gallant ship was she. The *Golden Vanity. Unknown.* PBMP

There was a graven image of desire. A Cameo. Swinburne. LoAs

There was a great white wall—bare, bare, bare. The Smoked Herring. Charles Cros, *tr. by* A. L. Lloyd. PoTa

There was a green branch hung with many a bell. The Dedication to a Book of Stories Selected from the Irish Novelists. W. B. Yeats. OBP

There was a jolly fat frog that did in the river swim O. The Frog and the Crow. *Unknown.* GBP

There was a jolly miller once. Song. Isaac Bickerstaffe. *Fr.* Love in a Village. PFIr

There was a king, and a very great king. Lady Diamond. *Unknown.* PeBB

There was a knicht riding frae the east. Riddles Wisely Expounded. *Unknown.* GBP; PeBB

There was a Knight, a most distinguished man. Persons of the Prologue. Chaucer, *tr. by* Nevill Coghill. *Fr.* The Canterbury Tales. OBP

There was a knight and a lady bright. The Broomfield Hill. *Unknown.* PeBB

There was a knight, and he was young. The Baffled Knight. *Unknown.* SLP

There was a lady all skin and bone. The Skin-and-Bone Lady. *Unknown.* AmFP

There was a lady lived in York. The Cruel Mother. *Unknown.* AmFP

There Was a Lady Loved a Swine. *Unknown. See* Lady Who Loved a Swine, The

There was a lady of beauty rare. The Wife of Usher's Well. *Unknown.* AmFP

There was a lady who loved a swine. The Lady Who Loved a Swine. *Unknown.* RDB

There was a little boy and a little girl. Mother Goose. MG

There Was a Little Girl, *1 st. At. to* Longfellow. OxBChV

There was a little guinea-pig. A Guinea-Pig Song [*or* The Precise Guinea-Pig]. *Unknown.* ECBV; OxBChV

There was a little man/ And he had a little gun. Mother Goose. ECBV; MG, *longer version*

There was a little mouse who lived on a hill. The Mouse's Courting Song. *Unknown.* AIW

There was a little ship in South Amerikee. The Sweet Trinity. *Unknown.* AmFP

There was a little turtle. The Little Turtle. Vachel Lindsay. LCL; RAE

There was a lizard kept me company. Gecko. Noel Lloyd. RAE

There was a lord of worthy fame. The Lady Isabella's Tragedy. *Unknown.* GBP

There Was a Maid Went to the Mill. *Unknown.* GBP

There was a man a-coming from the south. Trooper and Maid. *Unknown.* AmFP

There Was a Man and He Was Mad. *Unknown.* GBP

There was a man, and his name was Dob. Whose Dog? Whose Cat? *Unknown.* ECBV

There was a man in olden times. Dives and Lazarus. *Unknown.* AmFP

There was a man made a thing. *Unknown.* GBP

There was a man named Johnny Sands, who married Betty Hague. Johnny Sands. *Unknown.* AmFP

There was a man named Mingram Mo. Mingram Mo. David McCord. ECBV

There Was a Man of Double Deed. *Unknown.* GBP; InPK

There was a man of Thessaly. The Man of Thessaly. *Unknown.* FaBoCo; MG

There was a man who had a clock. The Sad Tale of Mr. Mears. *Unknown.* PoTa

There was a man who married a maid. She laughed as he led her home. I Love My Love. Helen Adam. NMM

There was a man with tongue of wood. War Is Kind, XVI. Stephen Crane. PiAm

There Was a Monkey. *Unknown.* ECBV; RAE

There was a most odious yak. The Yak. Theodore Roethke. ECBV; LCL

There Was a Naughty Boy. Keats. *See* Song about Myself.

There was a noted hero, Jack Dolan was his name. The Wild Colonial Boy. *Unknown.* AIW

There was a Pig, that sat alone. The Pig Tale. "Lewis Carroll." *Fr.* Sylvie and Bruno. RAE

There was a Presbyterian cat. The Auld Seceder Cat. *Unknown.* FaBoCo

There was a professor of Beaulieu. Materialism. C. E. M. Joad. FaBoCo

There was a rich lady, from London she came. A Rich Irish Lady. *Unknown.* AmFP

There was a rich lady lived over the sea. The Rich Lady over the Sea. *Unknown.* AIW

There was a rich merchant in London did dwell. Dinah and Villikens. *Unknown.* RDB

There was a river that rose. The River. James Stephens. ECBV

There was a river under First and Main. Prairie Town. William Stafford. PPoD

There was a roaring in the wind all night. Resolution and Independence. Wordsworth. InPS; MAT; MBPR; NOBE; PPP; SoSe

There Was a Sang. Helen B. Cruickshank. SLP

There was a serpent who had to sing. The Serpent. Theodore Roethke. ECBV

There was a shepherd's son. Blow the Winds, I-Ho. *Unknown.* GBP; PeBB

There was a ship a-sailing off North America. The Green Willow Tree. *Unknown.* AIW

There was a ship that sailed upon the lowland sea. The *Golden Vanity. Unknown.* RDB

There was a sick man of Tobago. *Unknown.* OxBChV

There was a snake that dwelt in Skye. The Fastidious Serpent. Henry Johnstone. ECBV

There was a sound of revelry by night. Waterloo [*or* The Eve of Waterloo]. Byron. *Fr.* Childe Harold's Pilgrimage, III. NOBE; PPoD

There was a stunted handpost just on the crest. Near Lanivet, 1872 Thomas Hardy. NoAM

There was a sunlit absence. Mossbawn Sunlight. Seamus Heaney. BIrV

There was a time for discoveries. Voyage West. Archibald MacLeish. VGW

There was a time, methought it was but lately departed. Arthur Hugh Clough. *Fr.* Amours de Voyage, V, 5. OBP

There was a time when I could fly, I swear it. I, Icarus. Alden Nowlan. NCSH

There was a time when meadow, grove, and stream. Ode: Intimations of Immortality from Recollections of Early Childhood. Wordsworth. HeIP; MBPR; NOBE; OBP; PAIC; PBMP; PPoD; PPoe; PPP

There was a time when we all were dancers. Gerrye Payne. NPW

There was a tree stood in the ground. The Green Grass Growing All Around. *Unknown.* ECBV

There was a wealthy merchant. The Wars of Santa Fe. *Unknown.* AmFP

There was a weasel lived in the sun. The Gallows. Edward Thomas. InPS; NoAM; SFF

There was a whispering in my hearth. Miners. Wilfred Owen. NOBE

There was a young curate of Salisbury. *Unknown.* FaBoCo

There was a young doctor, from London he came. The Fair Damsel from London. *Unknown.* AmFP

There was a young lady named Bright. Relativity. *Unknown.* FaBoCo

There was a young lady named Min. Min. *Unknown.* ECBV

There was a young lady of Lynn/ Who was so uncommonly thin. Limerick. *Unknown.* SoSe

There was a young lady of Niger. Lady and Tiger. *Unknown.* ECBV

There was a young lady of Riga. *Unknown.* FaBoCo

There was a young lady of Spain. *Unknown.* FaBoCo

There was a young maid who said "Why." Limerick. *Unknown.* SoSe

There was a young man from Trinity. *Unknown.* SFF

There was a young man of Japan. *Unknown.* FaBoCo

There was a young man of Mauritius. Theological Limerick. T. Lindsay. FaBoCo

There was a young man of Quebec. *Unknown, at to* Kipling. FaBoCo

There was a young man of St. Bees. *Unknown, at. to* W. S. Gilbert. FaBoCo

There was a young man so benighted. The Guest. *Unknown.* ECBV

There was a young man who said, "Damn!" Determinism. *Unknown.* FaBoCo

There was a young woman called Starkie. Mendelian Theory. *Unknown.* FaBoCo

There was a youth, and a well belovd youth. The Bailiff's Daughter of Islington. *Unknown.* AIW; PBMP; RDB

There was airy music and sport at the fair. The Fair at Windgap. Austin Clarke. OxBTC

There [*or* Ther] was also a nun [*or* Nonne], a Prioress. The Prioress [*or* Madam Eglantine]. Chaucer. *Fr.* The Canterbury Tales: Prologue. NOBE; OxBM

There was always the river or the train. Grandmother Watching at Her Window. W. S. Merwin. VGW

There was an ancient carver that carved of a saint. The Figurehead. Crosbie Garstin. PoTa

There was an ancient spring inside the glacier. Found, Carol Muske. AmPA

There was an Indian, who had known no change. The Discovery. J. C. Squire. OFD

There was an old farmer in Sussex did dwell. The Farmer's Curst Wife. *Unknown.* AIW

There was an old lady of Chertsey. Edward Lear. OxBChV

There was an old lady of France. Edward Lear. LCL

There was an old man/ And he had a calf. *Unknown.* ECBV

There was an old man and for begging he was bound. The Beggarman. *Unknown.* RDB

There was an old man at the foot of the hill. The Farmer's Curst Wife. *Unknown.* AmFP

There was an old man in a tree. Edward Lear. OxBChV

There was an old man in a trunk. Ultimate Reality. Ogden Nash. FaBoCo

There was an old man lived out in the wood. Green Broom. *Unknown.* PoTa

There was an old man of Boulogne. *Unknown.* FaBoCo

There was an old man of Cape Race. *Unknown.* FaBoCo

There was an old man of Dumbree. Edward Lear. OxBChV

There was an old man of Hong Kong. Limerick. Edward Lear. FaBoCo

There was an old man of Peru. Limerick. *Unknown.* SoSe

There was an old man on the Border. Edward Lear. LCL

There was an old man who liv'd in Middle Row. The Five Hens. *Unknown.* GBP

There was an old man who lived in the wood. Father Grumble. *Unknown.* AmFP

There was an old man who made his will. The Dishonest Miller. *Unknown.* AmFP

There was an old man who said, "How." Edward Lear. OxBChV

There was an old man who said, "Hush!" Limerick. Edward Lear. FaBoCo: OxBChV

There was an old man with a beard,/ Who said, "It is just as I feared!" Limerick [*or* Nesting]. Edward Lear. ECBV; FaBoCo; OxBChV

There was an old miser at Reading. *Unknown.* OxBChV

There was an old party of Lyme. *Unknown.* FaBoCo

There was an old person of Anerley. Limerick. Edward Lear. FaBoCo

There was an old person of Gretna. Edward Lear. OxBChV

There was an old person of Ware. Edward Lear. LCL

There was an old soldier of Bicester. *Unknown.* OxBChV

Ther was an old wife and she lived all alone. The Old Wife and the Ghost. James Reeves. ECBV; RAE

There was an old woman/ Lived under a hill. Mother Goose. MG

There was an old woman, and what do you think? Mother Goose. MG

There was an old woman, as I've heard tell. Mother Goose. ECBV; MG; PoTa

There was an old woman as ugly as sin. An Old Woman. Charles Henry Ross. OxBChV

There was an old woman called Nothing-at-all. Mother Goose. MG

There was an old woman in our town. Eggs and Marrowbone. *Unknown.* RDB

There was an old woman in Surrey. *Unknown.* OxBChV

There was an old woman lived on the seashore. The Two Sisters. *Unknown.* AmFP

There was an old woman named Towl. *Unknown.* OxBChV

There was an old woman tossed up in a basket. Mother Goose. ECBV; MG

There was an old woman who lived in a shoe. Mother Goose. MG

There was an old woman who rode on a broom. Old Woman on a Broom. *Unknown.* ECBV

There was an old woman who sowed a corn seed. The Magic Seeds. James Reeves. ECBV

There was an owd yowe wi' only one horn. The One-Horned Ewe. *Unknown.* GBP

There was an ox, there was a flea. Partners. Jaime Castiello. ECBV

There was ance a may, and she lo'ed na men. Werena My Heart Licht. Lady Grizel Baillie. SLP

There was, before me. The Black Riders, XXI. Stephen Crane. PiAm

There was Dai Puw. He was no good. On the Farm. R. S. Thomas. OxBTC

There was movement at the station. The Man from Snowy River. Andrew Barton Paterson. MAuV

There was never a sound beside the wood but one. Mowing. Robert Frost. NOBA; PPP; VGW

There was never nothing more me pained [*or* payned]. Sir Thomas Wyatt. AAS; GBL

There was once a hog theater where hogs performed. A Performance at Hog Theater. Russell Edson. AmPA

There was once an old tailor of Hickery Mo. The Old Tailor. Walter de la Mare. ECBV

There was one among us who rose. Death of a Friend. Pauli Murray. PoBA

There was scurrying and scrimmage. When the Animals Left the Ark. *Unknown.* RAE

There was six jovial tradesmen, they all sat down to drinking. When Jones's Ale Was New. *Unknown.* AmFP

There was such speed in her little body. Bells for John Whiteside's Daughter. John Crowe Ransom. AnMo; HeIP; InPK; InPS; NoAM; NOBA; PAIC; PiAm; PPoD; PPP; PSN; RRA; SoSe; VGW; VoPo; WIF

There was that horse. The White Stallion. Pete Morgan. SLP

There was this road. The Legs. Robert Graves. NoAM

There was three kings into the east. John Barleycorn. Burns. AIW; Epi

There was three ladies playd at the ba. The Cruel Brother. *Unknown.* PeBB

There we crossed Trent and on the other side. Richard Corbet. *Fr.* Iter Boreale. SCP-2

There were always five. Sisters. Alberta Turner. HeS

There Were an Old and Wealthy Man. *Unknown.* AmFP

There were blood spots on the skirt. James Cunningham. *Fr.* The Narrator's Trance. JB

There were many of us at the time. Gavin Bantock. *Fr.* Hiroshima TwMBP

There were miners from Bisbee. Tramp Miner's Song. *Unknown.* AmFP

There were never strawberries. Strawberries. Edwin Morgan. BoLoP

There were ninety and nine that safely lay. The Ninety and Nine. Elizabeth Cecilia Clephane. BLSH

There were no antelope on the balcony. Midnight Special. Kenneth Patchen. VGW

There were no drawings on the page. Water Poems. Sandra McPherson. CAAP

There were no undesirables or girls in my set. Commander Lowell. Robert Lowell. VGW

There were six and six nobles. Glenlogie. *Unknown.* Epi

There were the roses, in the rain. The Act. William Carlos Williams. VGW

There were thirty million English who talked of England's might. The Last of the Light Brigade. Kipling. BTTM

There were three crows sat on a tree. *See* There were three ravens sat on a tree.

There were three in the meadow by the brook. The Code. Robert Frost. InPS

There Were Three Jovial Welshman. *Unknown.* GBP

There were three ladies [*or* maids] lived in a bower [*or* barn]. Babylon; or, The Bonnie Banks o' Fordie. *Unknown.* AmFP; PAIC

There were three ravens [*or* crows] sat on a tree. The Three Ravens. *Unknown.* AIW; AmFP; Epi; GBP; HeIP; InPK; PeBB; RDB

There were three sailors of Bristol city. Little Billee. Thackeray. ECBV; FaBoCo

There were three sisters fair and bright. The Riddling Knight. *Unknown.* AIW; PBMP

There were twa brethren in the North. The Twin Brothers. *Unknown.* PBMP

There were twa sisters sat in a bour. Binnorie. *Unknown.* AIW

There, where the sun shines first. The Azalea. Coventry Patmore. *Fr.* The Unknown Eros. GBL

There will be no Holyman crying out this year. Jitterbugging in the Streets. Calvin C. Hernton. PoBA

There will be no more cats. Mort aux Chats. Peter Porter. CAAP

There will be no speech from. No Speech from the Scaffold. Thom Gunn. OxBTC

There will be the cough before the silence, then. Dictum: For a Masque of Deluge. W. S. Merwin. NoAM

There you may see the eyelids of the morn. Henry More. *Fr.* Psychozoia, or the First Part of the Song of the Soul, Canto I. SCP-2

Therefore above the rest Ambition sat. Giles Fletcher the Younger. *Fr.* Christ's Victory and Triumph. SCP-2

Therefore all seasons shall be sweet to thee. Samuel Taylor Coleridge. *Fr.* Frost at Midnight. FSFS

There'll Be a Hot Time. Joe Hayden. *See* Hot Time in the Old Town.

There's a barrel-organ carolling across a golden street. The Barrel-Organ. Alfred Noyes. SoSe

There's a breathless hush in the Close tonight. Vitaï Lampada. Sir Henry Newbolt. BTTM

There's a brown 'cross town and she's. Deceitful Brownskin Blues. *Unknown.* BluL

There's a certain slant of light. Emily Dickinson. AmVN; FSFS; HeIP; NoAM; NOBA; PiAm; PPP; SBG; VoPo; WPE

There's a charming Irish lady with a roguish winning way. Bedelia. William Jerome. FSN

There's a church in the valley by the wildwood. The Little Brown Church in the Vale. William S. Pitts. BLSH

There's a day we feel gay. On a Sunday Afternoon. Andrew B. Sterling. FSN

There's a fairmer up in Cairnie. Drumdelgie. *Unknown.* GBP

There's a feeling comes a stealing. You're a Grand Old Flag. George M. Cohan. FSN

There's a Friend for little children. Albert Midlane. *Fr.* Above the Bright Blue Sky. OxBChV

There's a glen in Aghadoe, Aghadoe, Aghadoe. Aghadoe. John Todhunter. PFIr

There's a great mystery. Diddie Wa Diddie. *Unknown.* BluL

There's a grey wind wails on the clover. Numerous Celts. J. C. Squire. SpRo

There's a land that is fairer than day. In the Sweet Bye-and-bye. Sanford Fillmore Bennett. BLSH; PSoN

There's a little black train a-coming. Little Black Train. *Unknown.* AmFP

There's a little side street such as often you meet. The Sunshine of Paradise Alley. Walter H. Ford. FSN

There's a long funny shiver. All Kinds of Shivers. Lilian Moore. CaYB

There's a low green valley on the old Kentucky shore. Darling Nelly Gray. Benjamin Russel Hanby. BLSo; PSoN

There's a man going 'round taking names. The Angel of Death. *Unknown.* AmFP

There's a man who's been out sailing. Cactus Tree. Joni Mitchell. GrRo

There's a mean black snake been suckin' my rider's tongue. Black Snake. *Unknown.* BluL

There's a mouse house. I Wouldn't. John Ciardi. ECBV

There's a pretty spot in Ireland I always claim for my land. Where the River Shannon Flows. James I. Russell. FSN

There's a reid lowe in yer cheek. Sang. Robert McLellan. SLP

There's a saucy, wild packet and a packet of fame. The *Dreadnought. Unknown.* AmFP

There's a small café off the Avenue. Wardour Street. Humbert Wolfe. OxBTC

There's a thrush that sings in a shadowy wood. City Bird. Theda Kenyon. ECBV

There's a time in each year that we always hold dear. In the Good Old Summertime. Ren Shields. BLSo; FSN

"There's a tree in father's garden, lovelye William," says she. Lovelye William. *Unknown.* AmFP

There's a whisper down the line at 11: 39. Skimbleshanks: The Railway Cat. T. S. Eliot. FaBoCo

There's a yellow rose of Texas that I am going to see. The Yellow Rose of Texas. *Unknown.* BLSo; PSoN

There's a yel-;low sponge. Never in This World You Will Drop a Yellow Sponge. Rochelle Owens. WBN

There's all sorts of fowl and fish. An Invitation to Lubberland. *Unknown.* GBP

There's been a death in the opposite house. Emily Dickinson. AmVN; InPS

"There's been an accident," they said. Mr. Jones. Harry Graham. FaBoCo

There's Holmes, who is matchless among you for wit. Holmes. James Russell Lowell. *Fr.* A Fable for Critics. NOBA

There's in my mind a woman. In Mind. Denise Levertov. Epi; InPS; NMM; RiTi

There's little in taking or giving. Coda. Dorothy Parker. SBG

There's little joy in life for me. On the Death of Anne Brontë. Charlotte Brontë. WPE

There's more in words than I can teach. Loving and Liking. Dorothy Wordsworth. OxBChV

There's More Pretty Girls than One. *Unknown.* AmFP

There's much afoot in heaven and earth this year. The Rainy Summer. Alice Meynell. OxBTC; SBG

There's Music in the Air, *with music.* Fanny Crosby. BLSo

There's my old man. The Famous Hot Pepper Eating Contest. Sam Hamod. SA

There's naught but care on every hand. *See* There's nought but care on ev'ry han'.

There's nawbody comes near my hoose ony mair. Herberie. Forbes Macgregor. MIS

There's no better dog nor Hardcastle's Rake. Rake. Dorothy Una Ratcliffe. BoAnP

There's no smoke in the chimney. The Deserted House. Mary Elizabeth Coleridge. RAE

There's no way out. In the Suburbs. Louis Simpson. CoPAm; MAT; SFF; TH

There's nothing grieves me, but that age should haste. Michael Drayton. *Fr.* Idea. AAS

"There's nothing mysterious about the skull." The Scientist. Janet Burroway. SoSe

There's nought [or naught] but care on ev'ry han'. Green Grow the Rashes [or Rushes], O. Burns. LAuP; PBMP; PPP

There's old Molly Hogan who cooks from a book. Stirling's Hotel. *Unknown.* AmFP

There's one in every city. Passing Stockyards Where They Killed the Buffalo. Harley Elliott. HeS

There's one rides very sagely on the road. Upon the Horse and His Rider. Bunyan. OxBChV

There's one thing I like about that gal of mine. One Way Gal. *Unknown.* BluL

There's snow in every street. Winter. J. M. Synge. OxBTC; POL

There's something happenin' here. For What It's Worth. Stephen Stills. PoRo; WIF

There's something in a flying horse. Peter Bell. Wordsworth. MBPR

There's something in a stupid ass. Epilogue. Byron. PAIC

There's something to think about. The Smell of Wood. John Stevens Wade. FAF

There's teuch sauchs growin' i' the Reuch Heuch Hauch. The Sauchs in the Reuch Heuch Hauch. "Hugh MacDiarmid." NoAM

There's that mirk room I ken. The Room. Duncan Glen. MIS

There's the story of me sitting in the grass in the dark. In the Dead of the Night. Norman Dubie. AmPA

There's the wonderful love of a beautiful maid. Love. *Unknown.* SFF; SoSe

There's this to remember about the gnu. The Gnu. Theodore Roethke. ECBV

There's three fair maids went to play at ball. The Cruel Brother. *Unknown.* AmFP

There's two white horses in a line. Two White Horses in a Line. *Unknown.* BluL

Therese. Alden Nowlan. NeAC

Thermometer is not to be believed, The. Facts of Winter. Marie Harris. MMD

Therwith, when he was ware and gan beholde. Troilus Laments Criseyde's Absence. Chaucer. *Fr.* Troilus and Criseyde, V. OxBM

These. William Carlos Williams. NoAM; NOBA; PBMP; TCP

These acres, always again lost. Lost Acres. Robert Graves. NoAM

These are amazing: each. Some Trees. John Ashbery. CAPP; ConAP

These are court-monsters, cormorants of the crown. Sir William Davenant. *Fr.* The Siege of Rhodes. SCP-2

These are men! the gaunt, unforesold, the vocal. Ol' Bunk's Band. William Carlos Williams. NOBA

These are my legs. I don't have to tell them, legs. Walter Jenks' Bath. William Meredith. CoPAm

These are not my sentiments. Louis Zukofsky. *Fr.* Light. NoAM

These are notes to lightning in my bedroom. Star Quilt. Roberta Hill. CDW

These are our immortals. Looking at Models in the Sears Catalogue. Philip Dacey. HeS

These are the arrows that murder sleep. The Song of Crede. *Unknown, tr. by* Alfred Perceval Graves. BIrV

These are the days when birds come back. Emily Dickinson. FSFS; PBMP; PiAm

These are the dog days. Songs to Survive the Summer. Robert Hass. AmPA

These are the dream machines. The Nightmare Factory. Maxine W. Kumin. NVAP

These are the gardens of the desert, these. The Prairies. Bryant. AmVN; NOBA; PiAm

These are the last crumbs of winter. Winter Flowers. Wade Hall. AATT

These, as they change, Almighty Father, these. A Hymn on the Seasons. James Thomson. *Fr.* The Seasons LAuP

These be/ Three silent things. Triad. Adelaide Crapsey. PAIC; WPE

These chairs they have no words to utter. Wordsworth. MBPR

These Damned Trees Crouch. Jim Barnes. CDW

These Days. Charles Olson. TSWA

These Days the Papers in the Street. Charles Reznikoff. VGW

These Dreamings Mine. James O. Taylor. BuTh

These dried-out paint brushes which fell from my lips. Sestina from the Home Gardener. Diane Wakoski. NoAM

These exquisite rags carry. A Box For Tom. James Tate. FiCP

These eyes of timid cherubim. Primula Scotica. Charles Senior. MIS

These fell miasmic rings of mist, with ghoulish menace bound. Prejudice. Georgia Douglas Johnson. PoBA

These flowers are I, poor Fanny Hurd. Voices from Things Growing in a Churchyard. Thomas Hardy. OxBTC

These fought in any case. Ezra Pound. *Fr.* Hugh Selwyn Mauberley. HeIP; NOBE; PiAm; PPoe; VGW

These grand and fatal movements toward death. Rearmament. Robinson Jeffers. PSN

These Horses Came. Ray A. Young Bear. CDW

These, in the day when heaven was falling. Epitaph on an Army of Mercenaries. A. E. Housman. BTTM; NoAM; NOBE; OBP; OxBTC; PPP; PSN

These Indians once imitated life. The Only Bar in Dixon. James Welch. AmPA

These islands gathering images. Matsushima. Harry Guest. TwMBP

These Lacustrine Cities. John Ashbery. CAPP

These little limmes. The Salutation. Thomas Traherne. MetP

These market-dames, mid-aged, with lips thin-drawn. Former Beauties. Thomas Hardy. At Casterbridge Fair, II. NoAM

These massacres of the superior peoples. John Berryman. *Fr.* Dream Songs. CAPP

These men were kings, albeit they were black. Black Majesty. Countee Cullen. PoBA; VGW

These new night. Ivory Masks in Orbit. Keorapetse Kgositsile. PoBA

These nubbins/ these hangers-on. Maxine W. Kumin. *Fr.* Song for Seven Parts of the Body. POL

These Obituaries of Rattlesnakes Being Eaten by the Hogs. Roger Weingarten. AmPA

These plaintive verse, the postes of my desire. Samuel Daniel. *Fr.* To Delia AAS

These poems are too much tangled with the error. To the Reader. Edgar Bowers. PiAm

These pools that, though in forests, still reflect. Spring Pools. Robert Frost. NoAM; NOBA; PiAm; TCP

These riotoures three, of which I telle. Three Revellers Search for Death. Chaucer. *Fr.* The Canterbury Tales: The Pardoner's Tale. OxBM

These royall kinges, that reare up to the skye. Thomas Sackevyll in Commendation of the Worke to the Reader. Thomas Sackville. AAS

These seven houses have learned to face one another. On a Painting by Patient B of the Independence State Hospital for the Insane. Donald Justice. ConAP

These sticks I am holding. This Preparation. Simon Ortiz. VW

These suggestions by Asians are not taken seriously. Asian Peace Offers Rejected without Publication. Robert Bly. CAPP; NoAM

These the dread days which the seers have foretold. The Death of Justice. Walter Everette Hawkins. PoBA

These things bear the brain's fruiit. High Are the Winter Rivers. Dave Smith. HeS

These to me are beautiful people. Preference. Elinor Wylie. Psy

"These tourists, heaven preserve us! needs must live." The Brothers. Wordsworth. MBPR

These Trees Stand. W. D. Snodgrass. NoAM; PPP

These two great men battling like lovers. All-In Wrestlers. James Kirkup. SPo

These Women All. —— Heath. FaBoCo

These women have no language and so they chatter. Lines for Those to Whom Tragedy Is Denied. Joyce Carol Oates. CoPAm; IHMS

These woods are one of my great lies. The Owl. W. S. Merwin. PPP

These words are all of me. Love Poem. Lewis Turco. NowV

These words we have swallowed. Your Eyes, Your Name. William Matthews. NVAP

Theseus: a Trilogy. Yvor Winters. NOBA

Thesis. Edward Dorn. NOBA

Thesis, Antithesis, and Nostalgia. Alan Dugan. NowV

Thetis is the moon-goddess. Hilda Doolittle ("H.D."). *Fr.* Helen in Egypt. Moon

They. Donald Finkel. CoPAm

They. R. S. Thomas. OxBTC

They/ say/ you/ went/ abroad. Incidental Pieces to a Walk James Cunningham. JB

They aint no use a-telling, boy, what's for you to do. Dan Ellis's Boys. *Unknown.* AmFP

They All Want To Play Hamlet. Carl Sandburg. NOBA

They amputated/ Your thighs off my hips. A Pity; We Were Such a Good Invention. Yehuda Amichai, *tr. by* Assia Gutmann. BoLoP; LoAs

They are aging in attic. Advice to the Lovelorn. Linda Parker-Silverman. HeS

They are all dying. Death as History. Jay Wright. PoBA

They Are All Gone. Henry Vaughan. *See* They Are All Gone into the World of Light.

They are all gone away. The House on the Hill. E. A. Robinson. AmVN; TH; VoPo

They Are All Gone into the World of Light. Henry Vaughan. HeIP; InPS; MetP; NOBE; SCP-1 (Friends Departed.) BoReV

They are always living. The Animal's Christmas. Philip Dacey. HeS; NVAP

They are coming through the bright fields. Falling in Love with Tygers. Thomas Bush. NVAP

They are cutting down the great plane-trees at the end of the gardens. The Trees Are Down. Charlotte Mew. WPE

They are digging everywhere. From street to street. Vincent Buckley. *Fr.* Golden Builders. CAAP

They are gathered, astounded and disturbed. The Last Supper. Rainer Maria Rilke, *tr. by* M. D. Herter Norton. OFD

They Are Killing All the Young Men. David Henderson. PoBA

They are not here. And we, we are the Others. The Absent. Edwin Muir. NoAM

They are not long, the weeping and the laughter. Vitae Summa Brevis Spem Nos Vetat Incohare Longam. Ernest Dowson. NOBE

They are not silent like workhorses. Donkeys. Edward Field. BoAnP

They are out-of-date. Normal Lives. Dick Allen. FAF

They are preparing to begin again. The Task. John Ashbery. CAAP

They are pulling down that London hotel. Reproaches. William Price Turner. SLP

They are rattling breakfast plates in basement kitchens. Morning at the Window. T. S. Eliot. PiAm; PSN

They are taking all my letters, and they. The Dishonest Mailmen. Robert Creeley. PiAm

They are the clean boys from the midwest. Seminar. Erica Jong. RiTi

They are the last romantics, these candles. Candles. Sylvia Plath. NMM; PSN

They are with us always, but they have the wit. The Distances They Keep. Howard Nemerov. BoAnP

They basted his caption on top of the fat sheriff, "The Pig." Sonnet. Ted Berrigan. CAAP

They began to sway to the. When These Old Barns Lost Their Inhabitants. David Kherdian. FAF

They brought him in on a stretcher from the world. Grandfather. Derek Mahon. LP

They brought it alone and they slipped it in. Heart Burial. Geoffrey Grigson. POL

They call me and I go. Complaint. William Carlos Williams. TCP

They call me Hanging Johnny. Hanging Johnny. *Unknown.* GBP

"They called it Annandale—and I was there." How Annandale Went Out. E. A. Robinson. NoAM; NOBA; PAIC; PPoD

They called it sin. The Label. Ruthe T. Spinnanger. AATT

They came hurrying across the mountain highway. Monkeys on Mt. Hiei. Edith Marcombe Shiffert. WPE

They came out of the sun undetected. The Raid. William Everson. NoAM; PiAm; TCP

They came running over the perilous sands. 1945. Sir Herbert Read. OxBTC

"They carry on." Floodtide. Askia Muhammad Touré. PoBA

They clear the left side for him. Oscar Robertson: Peripheral Vision. William Matthews. PPoD

They climbed the upward path, through absolute silence. Orpheus and Eurydice. Ovid, *tr. by* Rolfe Humphries. *Fr.* Metamorphoses. GrRo

They come into. Feeding the Lions. Norman Jordan. CTBA; PoBA

They cross the frontier as their names cross your pages. The New Emigration. Kay Boyle. WPE

They crossed her face with blood. A Hope for Those Separated by War. Sidney Keyes. BuTh

They crucified my Lord, an' He never said a mumbalin' word. Crucifixion. *Unknown.* BPo

They did it George. They did it. Conversation with Washington. Myra Cohn Livingston. OFD

They didn't hire him. Gary Synder. *Fr.* Hitch Haiku. InPK

They do not come with furred caps. Barbarians. John Fowles. POL

They do not live in the world. The Animals. Edwin Muir. HeIP

They done took Cordelia. Stony Lonesome. Langston Hughes. NOBA; PiAm

They don't get anywhere. The Couple Overheard. William Meredith. CoPAm; NoAM

They don't have gibbons in Nebraska. Nebraskan Childhood. Daniel Halpern. CAAP

They don't hold grudges. First Monday Scottsboro Alabama. Tom Weatherly. PoBA

They dragged you from homeland. Strong Men. Sterling A. Brown. BPo; PoBA

They Dream Only of America. John Ashbery. CAPP

They dunno how it is.  Rythm.  Ian Crichton Smith.  LP; MPo

They eat beans mostly, this old yellow pair.  The Bean Eaters.
Gwendolyn Brooks.  CAPP; CoPAm; HeIP; IPWM; MAT;
PoBA

They Eat Out.  Margaret Atwood.  Psy
("In restaurants we argue.")  NeAC

They Feed They Lion.  Philip Levine.  MAT; NoAM; NOBA;
Prf

They Flee from Me That Sometime Did Me Seek [or Seke].  Sir
Thomas Wyatt.  See Lover Showeth How He Is Forsaken...

They formed the ritual circle.  A Local Man Remembers the
Killing Ground.  James Whitehead.  CoPAm

They gave me the wrong name, in the first place.  Her Story.
Naomi Long Madgett.  IHMS; PoBA

They grew in beauty side by side.  The Graves of a Household.
Felicia Dorothea Hemans.  WPE

They had been there a month; the water had begun to tear them
apart.  A Negro Soldier's Viet Nam Diary.  Herbert Martin.
PoBA

They had secured their beauty to the dock.  The Crowd.  John
Masefield.  OxBTC

They had supposed their formula was fixed.  The White Troops
Had Their Orders, But the Negroes Looked Like Men.
Gwendolyn Brooks.  PBMP

They hanged him on a clement morning, swung.  Epitaph.
Dennis Scott.  SFF

They haul away our nights in manure trucks.  Another Load.
William Harrold.  HeS

They had chiseled on my stone the words.  Cassius Hueffer.
Edgar Lee Masters.  Fr. Spoon River Anthology.  NoAM

They have come by carloads.  Surfers at Santa Cruz.  Paul
Goodman.  SPo

They have connived at those jewelled fascinations.  Auspice of
Jewels.  Laura Riding.  NoAM

They have dreamed as young men dream.  Old Black Men.
Georgia Douglas Johnson.  PoBA

They have eyes that see not.  Maxine W. Kumin.  Fr. Song for
Seven Parts of the Body.  POL

They have fenced in the dirt road.  Burial.  Alice Walker.
AmPA; WBN

They have forgotten that wolves.  The Villages.  R. E.
Sebenthall.  HeS

They have left thee naked, Lord. O that they had!  On Our
Crucified Lord, Naked and Bloody.  Richard Crashaw.
SCP-1

They have loved the shadows.  The Seal in the Lowry Park Zoo.
Richard Mathews.  AATT

They have sed.  Hospital/Poem.  Sonia Sanchez.  BPo; PoBA

They have stood long in the sun.  Greens.  Greg Kuzma.  HeS

They have turned, and say that I am dying. That.  I Substitute for
the Dead Lecturer.  LeRoi Jones.  NOBA

The have won out at last and laid us bare.  The Invaders.  Yvor
Winters.  PiAm

They hold their hands over their mouths.  The Poets Agree to Be
Quiet by the Swamp.  David Wagoner.  CoPAm; VGW

They hurt no one. They rove the North.  In Fur.  William
Stafford.  RFM

They keep coming at me.  Stops.  Lucille Clifton.  CAAP

They killed you and didn't tell us where they.  Epitaph for the
Tomb of Adolfo Baez Bone.  Ernesto Cardenal, tr. by Janet
Brof.  POL

They lean against the cooling car, backs pressed.  The Discovery
of the Pacific.  Thom Gunn.  HeIP; MIT

They lean over the path.  Orchids.  Theodore Roethke.  AnMo;
PiAm; PPoe

They leaned a good stout rail against the tree.  Robbing the Tree
Hive.  Ernest G. Moll.  PoTa

They leave us so to the way we took.  In Neglect.  Robert Frost.
VGW

They left him behind.  Mission Uncontrolled.  Richard Peck.
MiP

They left the primrose glistening in its dew.  Spring, and the Blind
Children.  Alfred Noyes.  OxBTC

They lied about.  Strange Kind (II).  J. D. Reed.  Moon

They live alone.  Neighbors.  David Allan Evans.  HeS

They looked so good.  The Young Fenians.  Padraic Fallon.
BIrV

They make it plain.  The Recluse.  Lisel Mueller.  RiTi

They meet but with unwholesome springs.  Against Them Who
Lay Unchastity to the Sex of Women.  William Habington.
MetP

They mouth love's language.  A Memory of the Players in a
Mirror at Midnight.  James Joyce.  NoAM

They moved like rivers in their mended stockings.  The
Grandmothers.  Mary Oliver.  WPE

They mowed the meadow down below.  The Island.  Dorothy
Aldis.  ECBV

They must to keep their certainty accuse.  The Leaders of the
Crowd.  W. B. Yeats.  SFF

They named the huge one Grendel.  Grendel.  Unknown, tr. by
Burton Raffel.  Fr. Beowulf.  OBP

They paddle with staccato feet.  Pigeons.  Richard Kell.  BoAnP

They pointed me out on the highway, and they said.  The
Traveller.  John Berryman.  VGW

They rest: the cat curls next the sleeping wife.  Night Thoughts.
Richard Bastian.  AATT

They rode north.  Blackie Thinks of His Brothers.  Stanley
Crouch.  PoBA

They rose up in a twinkling cloud.  The Stockdoves.  Andrew
Young.  BoAnP

They said, "Wait." Well, I waited.  Alabama Centennial.  Naomi
Long Madgett.  BPo

They said, "You are no longer a lad."  Battle Won Is Lost.  Phil
George.  VW

They sat. They stood about.  Of Commerce and Society.
Geoffrey Hill.  PPoe

They say ideal beauty cannot enter.  Hiram Powers' "Greek
Slave."  Elizabeth Barrett Browning.  SBG

They say I'm crazy got no sense.  I Don't Care.  Jean Lenox.
FSN

They say it's just a pumpkin.  How Come?  Sara Asheron.
CaYB

They Say My Verse Is Sad: No Wonder.  A. E. Housman.
NoAM

They say "Son."  Old Black Men Say.  James A. Emanuel.
PoBA

They say that Richard Cory owns.  Richard Cory.  Paul Simon.
InPK; WIF

They say that trees scream.  High Frequency.  Marge Piercy.
MMD

They say the men are.  The Men Are Coming Back!  Barry Cole.
OxBTC

They say the sea is cold, but the sea contains.  Whales Weep Not!
D. H. Lawrence.  OBP; PPoe

They say there is a land.  Idaho.  Unknown.  GBP

They say there is a sweeter air.  A Carriage from Sweden.
Marianne Moore.  SoSe

They say 'tis sinful to flirt.  Sinful to Flirt.  Unknown.  AmFP

They say you lurk here still, perhaps.  Prayer to the Mothers.
Diane DiPrima.  RiTi

They served tea in the sandpile, together with.  The Party.  Reed
Whittemore.  BBGO; ConAP; LP; NCSH

They shall go down unto life's borderland.  Sonnet to Negro
Soldiers.  Joseph Seamon Cotter, Jr.  PoBA

They shook the green leaves down. Magic Fox. James Welch. CDW

They should be held in the open. Classes. Keith Wilson. NowV

They shut me up in prose. Emily Dickinson. InPS; NOBA; SBG

They shut the road through the woods. The Way through the Woods. Kipling. NOBE; OxBChV; OxBTC; RFM

They sing their dearest songs. During Wind and Rain. Thomas Hardy. InPK; OxBTC; PPP

They sit among music of waterfall leaves. Six Statues in a Park. Floyd C. Stuart. FAF

They Slept While Jesus Prayed. Henry Tim Chambers. AATT

They slip on to the bus, hair piled up high. The Young Ones. Elizabeth Jennings. OxBTC

They Sometimes Call Me. Wendy Rose. CDW

They splay at a bend of the road, rifles slung, the. The Spool. Ben Belitt. PPoD

They started with his best guitar. The Day They Ate the Baritone. Samuel Hazo. PPoD

They step from the high plane and begin to tumble. Sky Diving. Richmond Lattimore. SPo

They tell me (but I really can't). My Aunt's Spectre. Mortimer Collins. PoTa

They tell me she's crazy. Going Home. Renée Roper. NPW

They tell us: We are the barren who give. On Christ's Birth (To Sisters). Jane Marie Luecke. AATT

They that have power to hurt, and will do none. Sonnets, XCIV. Shakespeare. Epi; InPS; LoAs; NOBE; PPoe; PPP

They that in play can do the thing they would. The Growth of Love, I. Robert Bridges. NoAM

They throw in Drummer Hodge, to rest. Drummer Hodge. Thomas Hardy. InPS; NoAM

They told me. Witch. Jean Tepperman. NMM

They told me, Heraclitus, they told me you were dead. Heraclitus. William Johnson Cory, *after* Callimachus. InPK; NOBE

They told me you had been to her. Evidence Read at the Trial of the Knave of Hearts. "Lewis Carroll." *Fr.* Alice's Adventures in Wonderland. FaBoCo; PBMP; SS

They took me out. Ku Klux. Langston Hughes. BPo

They took the blue from the skies. The Air Force Blue. Scott *and* Textor. BLSH

They took the whole Cherokee nation. The Lament of the Cherokee Reservation Indian. John D. Loudermilk. PoRo

They trace their ancestry. The Legend of Paper Plates. John Haines. PPoD

They used to tell me I was building a dream. Brother, Can You Spare a Dime? E. Y. Harburg. AIW

They wade through beer cans. Cowboys: Three. Rod McKuen. MiP

They wait like darkness not becoming stars. The New Pietà: For the Mothers and Children of Detroit. June Jordan. PoBA

They walk dangerously. The Home. Susan Axelrod. NMM

They walked in straitened ways. The Old Ladies. Colin Ellis. OxBTC

They watch the big vats bubbling over. Octobers. Christopher Middleton. TwMBP

They Went Home. Maya Angelou. IHMS

They went to sea in a Sieve, they did. The Jumblies. Edward Lear. OxBChV; SS

They were human, they suffered. Founding Fathers, Nineteenth-Century Style. Robert Penn Warren. *Fr.* Promises. NoAM

They were like fish meal. Lead. Jayne Cortez. PoBA

They were singing Old MacDonald in the schoolbus. Chorus. John Ciardi. SS

They were so mean they could not between them. As in Their Time. Louis MacNeice. POL

They who in folly or mere greed. Where Are the War Poets? C. Day Lewis. OxBTC

They will catch me. On Hearing the Airlines Will Use a Psychological Profile to Catch Potential Skyjackers. Stephen Dunn. AmPA

They will come for you in morning. Whispers. Roberta Hill. CDW

They will not leave me, the lives of other people. The Hunched. Douglas Dunn. LP

They wore light dresses and their arms were bare. A Pride of Ladies. Anne Halley. NMM

They work in an iron mill. Irondale. Stephen Stepanchev. SA

They're altogether otherworldly now. Grandparents. Robert Lowell. PiAm

They're changing guard at Buckingham Palace. Buckingham Palace. A. A. Milne. OxBChV

They're selling postcards of the hanging. Desolation Row. Bob Dylan. InPS; WIF

They're taking down a tree at the front door. Learning By Doing. Howard Nemerov. NowV

They've killed you. Martyrdom. Richard W. Thomas. PoBA

They've paid the last respects in sad tobacco. Padraic O'Conaire, Gaelic Storyteller. F. R. Higgins. PFIr

Thick water laps. The Fisherman. Dabney Stuart. NVAP; SPo

Thief, The. Josephine Jacobsen. WPE

Thief, The. Stanley Kunitz. VGW

Thief in me is running a, The. Zapata and the Landlord. A. B. Spellman. PoBA

Thief Jones. Robert P. Tristram Coffin. MiP

Thieves, The. Robert Graves. BoLoP

Thin and graceful. The Tightrope Walker. Rochelle Ratner. WBN

Thine Am I. Burns. VoPo

Thine eyes shall see the light of distant skies. To Cole, the Painter, Departing for Europe. Bryant. PiAm

Thine Eyes Still Shined. Emerson. NOBA

Thing, The/ To do/ Is organize. Poem. Kenneth Koch. CAPP

Thing about a shark is—teeth, The. About the Teeth of Sharks. John Ciardi. CaYB

Thing could barely stand, The. Yet taken. The Bull Calf. Irving Layton. InPK

Thing of beauty is a joy for ever, A. Endymion, a Poetic Romance, I. Keats. MBPR; VoPo, 24 *ll.*

Thing to do is try for that sweet skin, The. Catch What You Can. Jean Garrigue. VGW

Things. Louis Simpson. TCP

Things I have and. Drifting the. Lyn Lifshin. MMD

Things I'm told, I could raise your hair, The. The Old Man's Tale. Brian Merriman, *tr. by* David Marcus. *Fr.* The Midnight Court. BIrV

Things Made by Iron. D. H. Lawrence. BBGO

Things Men Have Made. D. H. Lawrence. NoAM

Things might not be so bad. The Historian. Christopher Middleton. TwMBP

Things of Late. David Phillips. NeAC

Things That Matter, The. Edith Nesbit. OxBTC

Things to Do around a Lookout. Gary Snyder. CAPP

Things to Do around a Ship at Sea. Gary Snyder. CAPP

Things to Do in New York (City). Ted Berrigan. NoAM

Things to draw with compasses, The. Circles. Harry Behn. LCL

Think back now to that cleft. The Power Station. James Merrill. ConAP

Think further on thyself, my soul, and think. John Donne. *Fr.* Of the Progress of the Soul: The Second Anniversary. SCP-1

Think me not unkind and rude. The Apology. Emerson. AmVN

Think not, nor for a moment let your mind. Edna St. Vincent Millay. VGW

Think, O my soul. Phaedra. Hilda Doolittle ("H.D."). SBG

Think of it little, a fib. The Lie. Al Lee. AmPA

Think of the storm roaming the sky uneasily. Little Exercise. Elizabeth Bishop. NCSH

Think on Yesterday. *Unknown.* OxBM

Think that this world against the wind of time. Signature for Tempo. Archibald MacLeish. VGW

Think then, my soul, that death is but a groom. John Donne. *Fr.* Of the Progress of the Soul: The Second Anniversary. BoReV

Think well of those whose fortune fell. Anonymous. Anne Hazlewood Brady. WBN

Think you I am not fiend and savage too? To the White Fiends. Claude McKay. PoBA

Thinking about Carnevale's Wife. Wesley McNair. FAF

Thinking Back Seven Years and Being Here Now. Daved Curry. HeS

Thinking for Berky. William Stafford. PPoD; RRA

Thinking of her had saddened me at first. Celandine. Edward Thomas. OxBTC

Thinking of the Lost World. Randall Jarrell. NoAM; NOBA

Thinking of You. Dick Lourie. NeAC

Thinking of you. Love Poem 3. Laughton Johnston. SLP

Thinking the unthinkable. 19??. Dan Georgakas. NowV

Thinking to take on the power. The Wives of Mafiosi. Erica Jong. AmPA

Thinking Twice in the Laundromat. Harley Elliott. NeAC

Thinking we were safe—insanity! Story of a Hotel Room. Rosemary Tonks. OxBTC

Think'st thou I saw thy beauteous eyes. To Caroline. Byron. MBPR

Thinner now/ we are together. Air Is. John Michael Brennan. MAT

Third Alley Blues. *Unknown.* BluL

Third Avenue in Sunlight. Anthony Hecht. CoPAm; PPP

Third Century, The, *sel.* Thomas Traherne.
News. NOBE
(On News.) BoReV; MetP

Third Child. Peter Meinke. AATT

Third Day in a Strange City. Carol Bergé. MMD

Third Degree. Langston Hughes. BPo; BuTh

Third Dimension, The. Denise Levertov. NoAM

Third Sermon on the Warpland, The. Gwendolyn Brooks. BPo

Third Thing, The. D. H. Lawrence. AKE

Third World, The. Lawrence Ferlinghetti. TCP

Thirsty earth soaks up the rain, The. Drinking. Abraham Cowley, *after* Anacreon. HeIP; NOBE; OBP; PAIC

Thirteen Preludes for Pioneer Square. John Logan. CAAP

—Thirteen Ways of Looking at a Blackbird. Wallace Stevens. InPK; IPWM; NoAM; NOBA; TSWA; VoPo

Thirteen's no age at all. Portrait of a Girl with Comic Book. Phyllis McGinley. CTBA; IPWM

Thirty Bob a Week. John Davidson. InPS; NoAM; NOBE; OBP; OxBTC

Thirty candles and one. The Birthday. Philip Dacey. AmPA

Thirty days hath September. Mother Goose. MG

Thirty days in jail with my back turned to the wall. Jailhouse Blues. *Unknown.* BluL

Thirty-Eight. Charlotte Smith. SBG

Thirty eighth year, The. Lucille Clifton. AmPA; CAAP

34 Blues. *Unknown.* BluL

Thirty generations have stood and listened. The Font. Clive Sansom. BuTh

Thirty-nine thousand. Dennis Trudell. NVAP

"Thirty," the doctor said, "three grains, each one." Felo De Se. Thomas Blackburn. OxBTC

Thirty-three Triads. *Unknown. See* Triads.

This ae nighte [*or* ean night], this ae nighte. The Lyke-Wake Dirge. *Unknown.* GBP; NOBE

This afternoon as I sat. Elegy for Jack Bowman. Joseph Bruchac. CDW

This afternoon, darling, when you were here. Letter from a Death Bed. John Ciardi. NCSH

This almost bare tree is racing. November through a Giant Copper Beech. Edwin Honig. NoAM

This be the meed, that thy song creates a thousand-fold echo! Ad Vilmum Axiologum. Samuel Taylor Coleridge. MBPR

This beast that rends me in the sight of all. Edna St. Vincent Millay. VGW

This bond of the prelates I pray you revoke. Now God Stand Up for Bastards. Brian Merriman, *tr. by* Arland Ussher. *Fr.* The Midnight Court. BIrV

This book was written in order to change the world. Foreword to New Numbers. Christopher Logue. OxBTC

This bridal day with gold I will enchain. Bridal Day. Compton Mackenzie. SLP

This broken bottle. Haiku. Elisavietta Ritchie. AATT

This burning in the eyes, as we open doors. In Danger from the Outer World. Robert Bly. CAPP

This celestial seascape, with white herons got up as angels. Seascape. Elizabeth Bishop. PPP

This country girl. Peter Whigham. *Fr.* Love Poems of the VIth Dalai Lama. TwMBP

This country might have. Right On: White America. Sonia Sanchez. PoBA

This Cross-Tree Here. Robert Herrick. OFD; PAIC

This cup has touched. The Wine Cup. Meleager, *tr. by* Dudley Fitts. OLR

This darksome burn, horseback brown. Inversnaid. Gerard Manley Hopkins. InPK; NoAM

This Day. Hildegarde Flanner. WPE

This day the children of Speakthunder. In My Lifetime. James Welch. CDW

This day when I lay my hope aside. This Day. Hildegarde Flanner. WPE

This day will be remembered by America's noble sons. The Battle of Bull Run. *Unknown.* AmFP

This dread is like a calm. Winter Holding Off the Coast of North America. N. Scott Momaday. CDW

This dreadful, dark and dismal day. Frankie Silvers. Frances Silvers. AmFP

This dry and lusty wind has stirred all night. Dream Vision. J. V. Cunningham. PiAm

This dry night nothing unusual. The War Horse. Eavan Boland. BIrV

This ean night, this ean night. *See* This ae nighte, this ae nighte.

This Easter, Arthur Winslow, less than dead. In Memory of Arthur Winslow. Robert Lowell. PAIC

This egle, of which I have you told. Jove's Eagle Carries Chaucer into Space. Chaucer. *Fr.* The House of Fame. OxBM

This endris night. Lullay, By-by, Lullay. *Unknown.* OxBM

This England ("This royal throne of kings, this sceptered isle"). Shakespeare. King Richard II, *fr.* II, i. VoPo (England.) BTTM

This Excellent Machine. John Lehmann. OxBTC

This face had no use for light, took none of it. Made Shine. Josephine Miles. NoAM

This finde I write in Poesie. Ceix and Alceone. John Gower. *Fr.* Confessio Amantis, IV. OxBM

This gentleman the charming duck. A Trueblue Gentleman. Kenneth Patchen. RAE

This girl/ Waits at the corner. Girl, Boy, Flower, Bicycle. M. K. Joseph. MiP

This grandson of fishes holds inside him. Evolution from the Fish. Robert Bly. NoAM; NOBA

This guy on t.v. The Electric Cop. Victor Hernandez Cruz. PoBA

This Hand. Elinor Wylie. Psy

This handless clock stares blindly from its tower. A Clock in the Square. Adrienne Rich. HeIP

This here's a tale of a sho-nuff man. Big John Henry. Margaret Walker. WIF

This Houre Her Vigill. Valentin Iremonger. OxBTC; PFIr

This House. Ray A. Young Bear. CDW

This house has been far out at sea all night. Wind. Ted Hughes. LP; MPo; SoSe

This Humanist whom no beliefs constrained. Epigram. J. V. Cunningham. VGW

This institution,/ perhaps one should say enterprise. Marriage. Marianne Moore. NOBA; RiTi

This is a damned inhuman sort of war. Unseen Fire. R. N. Currey. MPo; OxBTC

This is a morning to say something. A Morning to Remember, or, E Pluribus Unum. Edward Dorn. NoAM

This Is a Poem. Hilary-Anne Farley. AKE

This Is a Poem for the Dead. Michael Ryan. AmPA

This Is a Poem for the Fathers and for Michael Ryan. Thomas Lux. AmPA

This is a silence. Arabesque. Fred Johnson. PoBA

This is a slice of the oldest. Tree. Daniel Hoffman. IPWM

This is a story declining, as landscape. Stories. Jon Anderson. HeS

This is a white. Imperial Thumbprint. Tom Weatherly. PoBA

This is a wild land, country of my choice. Rocky Acres. Robert Graves. NoAM

This is about the summer and the wheels of sleep. The Salt Pork. Robert Clayton Casto. HeIP

This is about the women of that country. The Women in Vietnam. Grace Paley. NMM

This is an/ ignominious tale about the naming. My Mother Takes My Wife's Side. David Kherdian. SA

This Is an African Worm. Margaret Danner. BPo

This is before electricity. Game After Supper. Margaret Atwood. Psy

This is dying, to cut off a part of yourself. Attis. George Stanley. MIT

This is earthquake. Today. Langston Hughes. VGW

This is enchanted country, lies under a spell. Bonac. John Hall Wheelock. PPoD

This is everyone's marriage. Nesting. Dennis Saleh. NeAC

This is how to come in. Welcome. Harvey Feinberg. POL

This Is Just to Say. William Carlos Williams. Epi; InPK; InPS; NOBA; PBMP; PiAm; SoSe; SpRo; SS

This is like a place. Snowy Night. John Haines. NCSH

This is my coliseum. The Womb Is Ruins. Helena Minton. FAF

This is my last cry. For Stephen Dixon. Zack Gilbert. PoBA

This is my letter to the world. Emily Dickinson. AmVN; NoAM; NOBA; PAIC; WPE

This Is My Own, My Native Land. Sir Walter Scott. *Fr.* The Lay of the Last Minstrel, VI. BTTM
("Breathes there the man, with soul so dead.") SoSe
(Innominatus.) PBMP

(Native Land.) SFF
(Patriotism.) NOBE

This is my wolf. He sits. The Appointment. Maxine W. Kumin. NMM

This is no poet's heaven. Colophon for Lan-t'ing Hsiu-Hsi. John Peck. AmPA

This is Not a Poem. Luís Omar Salinas. SA

This is not sorrow, this is work: I build. The Tomb of Lieutenant John Learmonth, A.I.F. J. S. Manifold. MAuV

This is not the man that women choose. Act of Love. Vernon Scannell. SFF

This is not the way I am. Biography in the First Person. Stephen Dunn. NVAP

This is the autumn and our harvest. Charles Reznikoff. *Fr.* New Year's. OFD

This is the beauty of being alone. Stray Animals. James Tate. NoAM

This is the black sea-brute bulling through wave-wrack. Leviathan. W. S. Merwin. ConAP; NoAM; NOBA; TCP

This is the bricklayer; hear the thud. Sanctuary. Elinor Wylie. Psy

This is the chapel of the holy. Jindrichuv Hradec. Christopher Middleton. TwMBP

This is the church of giraffes. Survival. Albert Goldbarth. NVAP

This is the city where men are mended. The Stones. Sylvia Plath. CAPP; SBG

This is the day His hour of life draws near. Sonnets at Christmas, I. Allen Tate. NoAM; NOBA; PAIC; VGW

This is the debt I pay. The Debt. Paul Laurence Dunbar. SS

This is the desk I sit at. That Day. Anne Sexton. ConAP

This is the dragon's country, and these his own streams. Dragon Country: To Jacob Boehme. Robert Penn Warren. PPP

This is the easy time, there is nothing doing. Wintering. Sylvia Plath. NMM

This is the field where the battle did not happen. At the Un-National Monument along the Canadian Border. William Stafford. HeIP; SoSe

This is the football hero's moment of fame. Settling Some Old Football Scores. Morris Bishop. SPo

This is the forest primeval. The murmuring pines and the hemlocks. Longfellow. *Fr.* Evangeline: Prologue. SpRo

This is the gay cliff of the nineteenth century. Brooklyn Heights. John Wain. OxBTC

This is the horror that, night after night. Gerald Gould. OxBTC

This is the hour that we must mourn. Tenebrae. Austin Clarke. BIrV

This is the house of Bedlam. Visits to St. Elizabeths. Elizabeth Bishop. VGW

This is the house that Jack built. Mother Goose. AKE, *abr*; MG; SpRo

This Is the Key of the Kingdom *Unknown.* ECBV; Prf

This is the kind/ of marriage they live in. The Way Sun Keeps Falling Away from Every Window. Lyn Lifshin. NeAC

This is the lair of the landlady. The Landlady. Margaret Atwood. Psy

This is the last place, there is nowhere else to go. The Song Mt. Tamalpais Sings. Lew Welch. MIT

This is the last stroke my tongue's clock must strike. Thomas Nashe. *Fr.* Summer's Last Will and Testament. SCP-2

This Is the Life. Louis MacNeice. NoAM

This is the light of the mind, cold and planetary. The Moon and the Yew Tree. Sylvia Plath. Moon; MPo; PPP; VGW; WPE

This is the meadow of the mind. A Way of Keeping. Nancy Willard. IHMS

This is the metre Columbian. The soft-flowing trochees and dactyls. The Metre Columbian. *Unknown.* SpRo

This is the midnight—let no star. The Storm Cone. Kipling. OxBTC

This is the month, and this the happy morn. On the Morning of Christ's Nativity. Milton. BoReV; Epi; SCP-1

This is the most ridiculous womb! Womb Song. Susan Fromberg Schaeffer. IHMS

This is the moth that came inside. The Moth. Prentice Baker. AATT

This is the night mail crossing the border. Night Mail. W. H. Auden. OxBTC

This is the nunnery. Nunnery. Katherine Doak. NPW

This is the Pentagon building. Pentagonia. G. E. Bates. SpRo

This is the plaza of Paradise. Marigold. John Haines. POL

This is the plum season, the nights. Late August. Margaret Atwood. MMD

This is the possum's tree. The Possum Tree. Irene Gough. ECBV

This is the projectionist's nightmare. The Projectionist's Nightmare. Brian Patten. LP

This is the rain on Mozart's grave. Lives of the Saints. Jon Anderson. FiCP

This is the room. Those windows. Poem Written after Contemplating the Adverb "Primarily." Christopher Middleton. TwMBP

This is the shape of the leaf, and this of the flower. Conrad Aiken. *Fr.* Priapus and the Pool. NOBA

This is the ship of pearl, which, poets feign. The Chambered Nautilus. Oliver Wendell Holmes. *Fr.* The Autocrat of the Breakfast-Table. AmVN; NOBA; PiAm; VoPo

This is the story of/ The brawny Brady riflemen. Brady's Bend. Martha Keller. PoTa

This is the sum of it. On My 18th Birthday. John William Corrington. CoPAm

This is the surest death. Mortality. Naomi Long Madgett. PoBA

This is the tale of how Tim one. Aileen Fisher. *Fr.* The Witch in the Wintry Wood. CaYB

This is the terminal: the light. At the San Francisco Airport. Yvor Winters. HeIP; InPK; NOBA; RRA

This is the time of year. The Armadillo. Elizabeth Bishop. NoAM; NOBA; PiAm; VGW

This is the time, when most divine to hear. Religious Musings. Samuel Taylor Coleridge. MBPR

This is the truth what I now tell you. The Miramichi Fire. *Unknown.* AmFP

This is the urgency: Live! The Second Sermon on the Warpland. Gwendolyn Brooks. BPo; NOBA; PoBA

This is the way it was at Uncle Rob's. History Lesson for My Son. Ted Kooser. POL

This is the way the ladies ride:/ Tri, tre, tre, tree. Mother Goose. MG

This is the way we come. Riding in the Rain. Maxine W. Kumin. RFM

This is the week when Christmas comes. In the Week When Christmas Comes. Eleanor Farjeon. LCL

This is the Wheel of Dreams. Carriers of the Dream Wheel. N. Scott Momaday. CDW

This is winter, this is night, small love. By Candlelight. Sylvia Plath. SBG

This is the world we wanted. Gretel in Darkness. Louise Glück. AmPA; NVAP

This Is Today. David W. Martinez. VW

This is where we're at the gate. Photograph at the Cloisters: April 1972. Helen Chasin. NMM

This Italian square. Dancers at the Moy. Paul Muldoon. BIrV

This Kansas boy who never saw the sea. Kansas Boy. Ruth Lechlitner. ANTL

This knot I knit. To Know Whom One Shall Marry. *Unknown.* GBP

This lady, ripe and calm and fresh. Sir William Davenant. *Fr.* The Just Italian. SCP-2

This Lady She Wears a Dark Green Shawl. *Unknown.* AmFP

This lake was clean (we used to swim in it once). The Moorhen Pond. Tom Earley. BoAnP

This Land. Ian Mudie. BuTh

This land was ours before we were the land's. The Gift Outright. Robert Frost. IPWM

This Landscape, These People. Zulfikar Ghose. MPo

This Last Pain. William Empson. NoAM

This lean commuter busies. Pendulum. John Updike. BBGO

This level reach of blue is not my sea. Fair Weather. Dorothy Parker. SBG

This Life. Rita Dove. AmPA

This life is not a circus where. Lawrence Ferlinghetti. *Fr.* A Coney Island of the Mind. PPP

This life like no other. Poem. Gregory Orr. AmPA

This life which seems so fair. William Drummond of Hawthornden. SCP-2

This Lime-Tree Bower My Prison. Samuel Taylor Coleridge. HeIP; MBPR; PAIC

This little bride and groom are. E. E. Cummings. PiAm

This little house is sugar. Winter Sweetness. Langston Hughes. ECBV

This little pig went to market. Mother Goose. MG

This Living Hand, Now Warm and Capable. Keats. BoLoP; InPK; InPS; MBPR
    (Lines Supposed to Have Been Addressed to Fanny Brawne.) LoAs
    (To Fanny Brawne.) NOBE

This lonely figure of not much fun. Absent-Minded Professor. Howard Nemerov. NowV

This long straight line of elegant limousines highly polished. A Burial in the Country. Paul Clause. AATT

This, Lord, was an anxious brother and. Funeral Oration for a Mouse. Alan Dugan. NoAM; PPP

This loud morning. The Third World. Lawrence Ferlinghetti. TCP

This lovely flower fell to seed. For My Grandmother. Countee Cullen. Four Epitaphs, 1. PoBA; VGW

This Lunar Beauty. W. H. Auden. OxBTC

This man contrived (but yet no glory won). Epigram on the Unknown Inventor of Scissors. L. E. Jones. POL

This man, this poet, said. A Spark of Laurel. Stanley Kunitz. NoAM

This man, this stranger in my arms. Indian Summer. Barbara Howes. IHMS

This man who seems to be my husband. Orange Tree Dream. Judith Serin. NPW

This meeting has gone on with small interruptions. The Organizer's Bogeymen. Marge Piercy. Psy

This might be nature—twenty stories high. The Picture. Robert Lowell. NoAM

This might have been a place for sleep. Thistledown. Harold Monro. OxBTC

This Monument Will Outlast. Horace, *tr. by* Ezra Pound. Odes, III, 30. Epi

This morn my friend Al mentioned his wife had taken a job. The Day of the Pancreas. David McFadden. NeAC

This Morning. Muriel Rukeyser. IPWM; NMM

This morning/ a gun held at a man's ear. "He Killed Many of My Men." John Bennett. BuTh

This morning/ my child dances naked.   Variations on a Theme. Mark Vinz.   HeS

This morning/ with a class of girls outdoors, I saw.   In a Spring Still Not Written of.   Robert Wallace.   CoPAm; WIF

This morning I threw the windows.   Jay Wright.   PAIC

This morning of the small snow.   The Songs of Maximus, III. Charles Olson.   PPP

This morning, when he looked at me.   Black All Day.   Raymond R. Patterson.   PoBA

This mortal body of a thousand days.   Sonnet Written in the Cottage Where Burns Was Born.   Keats.   MBPR

This mossy bank they press'd.   A Pastoral Dialogue.   Thomas Carew.   GBL; SCP-2

This Narrow Stage.   Theodore Weiss.   NoAM

This new Daks suit, greeny-brown.   Metamorphosis.   Peter Porter.   OxBTC

This Night Sees Ireland Desolate.   Aindrais MacMarcuis, *tr. fr. Irish by* Robin Flower.   BIrV

This old hen, she laid an egg.   The Lost Egg.   Percy Illot. ECBV

This old soul, you know, time she left Chicago.   The Panama Limited.   *Unknown.*   BluL

This one is entering her teens.   The Romantic Age.   Ogden Nash. SFF

This one was put in a jacket.   Counting the Mad.   Donald Justice.   ConAP; LP

This other speaks of bones, blood wet.   Fair/ Boy Christian Takes a Break.   Jim Harrison.   NoAM

This painful love dissect to the last shred.   The Lovers.   Conrad Aiken.   LoAs

This piston's infinite recurrence is.   La Marche des Machines.   A. S. J. Tessimond.   MPo

This pit is Hell where through thou now must go.   Elizabeth Melvill, Lady Culross.   *Fr.* A Godly Dream.   WPE

This place is cold.   Three Poems for the Indian Steelworkers. Joseph Bruchac.   CDW

This place moves from me.   Poem before Departure.   Jean Burden.   WPE

This Place Rumord to Have Been Sodom.   Robert Duncan. NOBA; PPP

This pleasant tale is like a little copse.   Keats.   MBPR

This poem I write to teach the reader.   Writing In England Now. Philip O'Connor.   OxBTC

This Poem Is for Bear.   Gary Snyder.   Myths and Texts: Hunting, VI.   NOBA

This Poem Is for Deer.   Gary Snyder.   Myths and Texts: Hunting, VIII.   CAPP; NOBA

This pool in a pure frame.   Reason and Nature.   J. V. Cunningham.   PiAm

This Preparation.   Simon Ortiz.   VW

This pretty bird, oh, how she flies and sings!   Upon the Swallow. Bunyan.   OxBChV

This Pretty Woman.   *Unknown.*   OxBM

This quiet morning light.   To Mark Anthony in Heaven. William Carlos Williams.   NOBA

This ration card, once shocking pink.   The Ration Card.   Liz Sohappy Bahe.   CDW

This road is so fuzzy.   Cinéma Vérité.   Dorothy Walters.   IHMS

This rose tree is not made to bear.   Envy.   Charles *and* Mary Lamb.   OxBChV

This royal throne of kings, this sceptered isle.   This England. Shakespeare.   *Fr.* King Richard II.   BTTM; VoPo

This sacred lake/ is the soul/ of the world.   Chad. Edward Brathwaite.   MPo

This Shell.   Mark Van Doren.   SPo

This ship is the ship of butchery and increase.   Songs for the Cisco Kid: or Singing: Song #2.   K. Curtis Lyle.   PoBA

This sky, for instance.   Deschutes River.   Raymond Carver. NVAP

This sky is to be opened.   Hermetic Bird.   Philip Lamantia. VGW

"This small lodge is now."   Old Man, the Sweat Lodge.   Phil George.   VW

This Solitude of Cataracts.   Wallace Stevens.   PiAm

This song of journeys into sorrow.   A Woman's Message. *Unknown, tr. by* Burton Raffel.   OBP

This soup is cold.   The Soup of Venus.   James Tate.   AmPA

This sparrow/ who comes to sit at my window.   The Sparrow. William Carlos Williams.   InPS; PiAm; VGW

This spoonful of chocolate tapioca.   Thinking of the Lost World. Randall Jarrell.   NoAM; NOBA

This spring as it comes bursts up in bonfires green.   The Enkindled Spring.   D. H. Lawrence.   NoAM

This still life of cups mocking the table.   Still Life.   Claudia Dobkins.   NPW

This strange thing must have crept.   Fork.   Charles Simic. AmPA

This straw horse and this crabshell.   Spirit.   Mei Berssenbrugge. SA

This Subway Station.   Charles Reznikoff.   LP

This Summer and Last.   Thomas Hardy.   OxBTC

This Sun Is Hot.   *Unknown.*   BPo

This sunlight shames November where he grieves.   Autumn Idleness.   Dante Gabriel Rossetti.   *Fr.* The House of Life. GBL

This sycamore, oft musical with bees.   Inscription for a Fountain on a Heath.   Samuel Taylor Coleridge.   MBPR

This, That and the Other.   Howard Nemerov.   AnMo

This that is washed with weed and pebblestone.   The Figurehead. Léonie Adams.   WPE

This, the twentieth day of March.   A Letter to Three Irish Poets. Michael Longley.   BIrV

This they know well: the Goddess yet abides.   In Her Praise. Robert Graves.   BIrV

This to the crown, and blessing of my life.   A Letter to Dafnis. Countess of Winchilsea.   SBG

This Tokyo.   Gary Snyder.   CAPP

This town is haunted by some good deed.   Aunt Mabel.   William Stafford.   AnMo

This Train Don't Carry No Gamblers.   *Unknown.*   AmFP

This Unimportant Morning.   Lawrence Durrell.   BoLoP; OxBTC

This urge, wrestle, resurrection of dry sticks.   Cuttings.   Theodore Roethke.   AnMo; NoAM; NOBA; PiAm; PPoe

This vale of teargas.   Unlawful Assembly.   D. J. Enright. OxBTC

This valley after the storms can be beautiful.   San Joaquin. William Everson.   CoPAm

This vanishing old road.   The New Direction.   Emerson Blackhorse Mitchell.   VW

This wall-paper has lines that rise.   Missing My Daughter. Stephen Spender.   RRA

This was a poet—it is that.   Emily Dickinson.   NOBA

This was a rich morning.   Rich Morning.   Robert Farren.   PFIr

This was childhood.   The Worms.   Carolyn Kizer.   IPWM

"This was Mr Bleaney's room. He stayed."   Mr Bleaney.   Philip Larkin.   BuTh; InPS; PPoe

This was our valley, yes.   The Dam.   Patric Dickinson.   PoTa

This was the crucifixion on the mountain.   Altarwise by Owl-Light, VIII.   Dylan Thomas.   Epi; NoAM

This was the peaceable kingdom: the river flows.   Edward Hicks: "The Peaceable Kingdom."   Ann Stanford.   PPoD

This was the woman: what now of the man?   Modern Love, III. George Meredith.   PAIC

This way, oh turn your bows. The Sirens' Song. Homer, *tr. by* Robert Fitzgerald. *Fr.* The Odyssey. GrRo

This what it was. The Meat Epitaph. Michael Benedikt. FiCP

This will be a chocolate cake. Cooking. Myra Cohn Livingston. ECBV

This will really try you. Mamma! Frank Horne. BPo

This Wind. Tom Kryss. NeAC

This winter in a rosy railroad car. Dreamed-Up for Winter. Arthur Rimbaud, *tr. by* William Mead. LoAs

This Woman Will Not Bear Children. Toi Derricotte. NPW

This Wonderful World. Mary Britton Miller. ECBV

This world a hunting is. William Drummond of Hawthornden. SCP-2

This World Fares as a Fantasy. *Unknown.* OxBM

This world is gradually becoming a place. John Berryman. *Fr.* Dream Songs. NoAM; NOBA

This world is not conclusion. Emily Dickinson. IPWM

This world is very odd we see. Reply to Dipsychus. Arthur Hugh Clough. FaBoCo

This world of ours thus runneth upon wheels. Michael Drayton. *Fr.* To My Noble Friend Master William Browne: of the Evil Time. SCP-2

This year I intended children Margaret Atwood. NeAC

"This year she has changed greatly"—meaning you. Change. Robert Graves. OxBTC

Thistledown. Harold Monro. OxBTC

Thistledown blows over the poisoned fields. The Martyred Earth. Ewart Milne. BIrV

Thistle down's flying, though the winds are all still, The. Autumn. John Clare. OBP

Thistles. Ted Hughes. MPo; NoAM; OxBTC; PSN

Tho' grief and fondness in my breast rebel. London. Samuel Johnson. LAuP

Tho' I'm no Catholic. The Catholic Bells. William Carlos Williams. NOBA

Thomas and Charlie. Peter Wild. AmPA

Thomas Hardy. Walter de la Mare. NoAM

Thomas Iron-Eyes. Marnie Walsh. VW

Thomas Rymer. *Unknown. See* Thomas the Rhymer.

Thomas Sackevyll in Commendation of the Worke to the Reader. Thomas Sackville. AAS

Thomas the Rhymer. *Unknown.* InPS; NOBE; Prf
(Thomas Rymer.) AIW; PeBB
(Thomas the Rimer.) InPK
(True Thomas.) PoTa

Thorn, The. Wordsworth. MBPR

Those awful words " 'Till death do part." Early Thoughts of Marriage. Nathaniel Cotton. OxBChV

Those Being Eaten By America. Robert Bly. PPoD

Those Boys That Ran Together. Lucille Clifton. PoBA

Those buffalo, white, that gather in the bean field. Winter in Elwell. James Tipton. HeS

Those calm swamp-green eyes. Pisces Child. Sandra McPherson. NMM

Those, Cynthia, that do taste the honey-dew. To Cynthia, on Sugar and Her Sweetness. Sir Francis Kynaston. SCP-2

Those days, the angry persons were the old. Angry Old Men. Basil Payne. PFIr

Those days when it was all right. Letter to E. Franklin Frazier. LeRoi Jones. BPo; PoBA

Those dreams that on the silent night intrude. On Dreams. Swift. BIrV

Those famous men of old, the Ogres. Ogres and Pygmies. Robert Graves. NoAM

Those five or six young guys. Blues. Derek Walcott. OBP

Those four black girls blown up. American History. Michael S. Harper. BPo

Those groans men use. The Mutes. Denise Levertov. AnMo; IHMS; NOBA; Psy; RiTi

Those legs you left here still stick. Leavings. Barbara A. Holland. WBN

Those moments, tasted once and never done. Cornish Cliffs. John Betjeman. MPo; PAIC

Those mothers down there off the hill. Seventh Son. Ed Roberson. PoBA

Those my friendships most obtain. Contentment. Nathaniel Cotton. OxBChV

Those red men you offended were my brothers. In My First Hard Springtime. James Welch. AmPA; CDW

Those rivers run from that land. Song. Robert Creeley. VGW

Those things which make life truly blest. The Happy Life. Martial, *tr. by* Sir Edward Sherburne. PAIC

Those vitreous vivariums. Ode of Odium on Aquariums. Arthur Guiterman. BoAnP

Those Wedding Bells Shall Not Ring Out! *with music.* Monroe H. Rosenfeld. FSN

Those who cannot love the heavens or the earth. The Chaff. W. S. Merwin. PPP

Those who love cats which do not even purr. Cats. Francis Scarfe. BoAnP; PCat

Those Winter Sundays. Robert Hayden. CoPAm; CTBA; IPWM; NoAM; PoBA; PPP

Thou are not, Penshurst, built to envious show. *See* Thou art not...

Thou art a lady;/ If only to go warm were gorgeous. Shakespeare. *Fr.* King Lear, II, iv. OBP

Thou Art Indeed Just, Lord, If I Contend. Gerard Manley Hopkins. NoAM; NOBE; WIF

Thou art not faire, for all thy red and white. Thomas Campion. AAS

Thou art [*or are*] not, Penshurst, built to envious show. To Penshurst. Ben Jonson. PAIC; PPP; SCP-1; TVS

Thou art reprieved old year, thou shalt not die. Epithalamion. John Donne. SCP-1

Thou art so fair, and young withal. Youth and Beauty. Aurelian Townsend. GBL

Thou Blind Man's Mark. Sir Philip Sidney. *Sometimes considered Sonnet CIX of* Astrophel and Stella. Epi; HeIP; PPP
(Desire.) NOBE

Thou blossom bright with autumn dew. To the Fringed Gentian. Bryant. FSFS; PiAm

Thou cursed cock, with thy perpetual noise. On a Cock at Rochester. Sir Charles Sedley. POL

Thou damn'd antipodes to common sense. To Mr. Edward Howard, on His Plays. Charles Sackville. ESaP

Thou fair-hair'd angel of the evening. To the Evening Star. Blake. LAuP; MBPR; PPP

Thou foul-mouthed wretch! Why dost thou choose. The Sailor to His Parrot. W. H. Davies. BoAnP

Thou genius of connubial love, attend. Happy Marriage. Thomas Blacklock. SLP

Thou grimmest far o grusome tykes. To a Hedgehog. Samuel Thompson. BIrV

Thou hast made me, and shall thy work decay? Holy Sonnets, I. John Donne. BoReV; NOBE

Thou hast not left the rough-barked tree to grow. I Was Sick and in Prison. Jones Very. NOBA

Thou hast not rais'd, Ianthe, such desire. Walter Savage Landor. *Fr.* Ianthe. GBL

Thou hearest the nightingale begin the song of spring. The Vision of Beulah. Blake. *Fr.* Milton, II. NOBE

Thou heaven-threatening rock, gentler than she! Echo to a Rock. Lord Herbert of Cherbury. PAIC

Thou ill-formed offspring of my feeble brain. The Author to Her Book. Anne Bradstreet. InPK; NOBA; PiAm

Thou in Whose Swordgreat Story Shine the Deeds. E. E. Cummings. Epi

Thou mastering me. The Wreck of the *Deutschland.* Gerard Manley Hopkins. BoReV; NoAM; NOBE; PFD

Thou miserable city! where the gloom. On Leaving London for Wales. Shelley. MBPR

Thou moon, like a white Christus hanging. Serenade. Kenneth Slessor. POL

Thou more than most sweet glove. Ben Jonson. *Fr.* Cynthia's Revels. GBL

Thou, paw-paw-paw; thou, glurd; thou, spotted. Adam's Task. John Hollander. PPP

Thou shalt have one God only; who. The Latest Decalogue. Arthur Hugh Clough. BoReV; FaBoCo; IPWM; NOBE; PBMP; PPP; SoSe; SS; VPC

Thou snowy farm with thy five tenements! Elinda's Glove. Richard Lovelace. SCP-2

Thou sorrow, venom elfe. Upon a Spider Catching a Fly. Edward Taylor. NOBA

Thou speckled little trout so fair. The Trout of the Well. *Unknown, tr. by* G. R. D. McLean. SLP

Thou still unravished bride of quietness. Ode on a Grecian Urn. Keats. AnMo; HeIP; InPK; InPS; MBPR; NOBE; OBP; PAIC; PBMP; PPoD; PPoe; PPP; SoSe; WIF

Thou supreme Goddess! by whose power divine. Oeidipus Tyrannus; or Swellfoot the Tyrant. Shelley. MBPR

Thou that sellest the word of God. Against the Friars. *Unknown.* OxBM

Thou thinkst 'tis much that this contentious storm. Shakespeare. *Fr.* King Lear, III, iv. OBP

Thou, to whom the world unknown. Ode to Fear. William Collins. LAuP; PAIC

Thou, too, sail on, O Ship of State! The Republic. Longfellow. *Fr.* The Building of the Ship. BTTM

Thou two-faced year, Mother of Change and Fate. 1492. Emma Lazarus. WPE

Thou wast that all to me, love. To One in Paradise. Poe. BoLoP; PiAm

Thou who hast slept all night upon the storm. To the Man-of-War Bird. Walt Whitman. BoAnP

Thou who, when fears attack. Ode to Tobacco. Charles Stuart Calverley. FaBoCo

Thou woman bute fere. An Orison to the Blessed Virgin. William Herebert. BoReV

Thou youngest virgin-daughter of the skies. To the Pious Memory of the Accomplished Young Lady Mrs. Anne Killigrew. Dryden. SCP-1

Though come down in the world to. Camel. Jon Stallworthy. BoAnP

Though conscience void of all offence. Praise. Christopher Smart. OxBChV

Though I am young, and cannot tell. Death and Love. Ben Jonson. *Fr.* The Sad Shepherd, I, v. NOBE

Though I regarded not. Earl of Surrey. AAS

Though I Speak with the Tongues of Men and Angels. Bible, *N. T..* *Fr.* First Corinthians. PBMP

Though I Thy Mithridates Were. James Joyce. NoAM

Though it's true we were young girls when we met. For Jan, in Bar Maria. Carolyn Kizer. RiTi; VGW

Though knowledge must be got with pain. For Scholars and Pupils. George Wither. OxBChV

Though leaves are many, the root is one. The Coming of Wisdom with Time. W. B. Yeats. POL; SoSe

Though loath to grieve. Ode Inscribed to W. H. Channing. Emerson. NOBA; PAIC; PiAm

Though naughty flesh will multiply. No Mean City. Patrick MacDonogh. BIrV

Though no kin to those fine glistening. Christening-Day Wishes for My God-child. Robert P. Tristram Coffin. OFD

Though riders be thrown in black disgrace. *Unknown, tr. fr. Irish by* Douglas Hyde. BIrV

Though rous'd by that dark Vizir Riot rude. Priestley. Samuel Taylor Coleridge. *Fr.* Sonnets on Eminent Characters. MBPR

Though the barn is so warm. The Palomino Stallion. Alden Nowlan. BoAnP; POL

Though the Clerk of the Weather insist. Pebbles. Herman Melville. AmVN

Though the crocuses poke up their heads in the usual places. Vernal Sentiment. Theodore Roethke. VoPo

Though three men dwell on Flannan Isle. Flannan Isle. W. W. Gibson. PoTa

Though truth and falsehood be. Seek True Religion! John Donne. *Fr.* Satires, III. BoReV; NOBE

Though we have put. Song in Autumn. Robert D. Fitzgerald. MAuV

Though you be absent here, I needs must say. The Spring. Abraham Cowley. *Fr.* The Mistress. MetP

Though you should build a bark of dead men's bones. Cancelled Stanza of the Ode on Melancholy. Keats. MBPR

Though your strangenesse frets my hart. Thomas Campion. AAS

Thought-Fox, The. Ted Hughes. HeIP; NCSH; NoAM

Thought looking out on thought. Opening of Eyes. Laura Riding. NoAM

Thought of a Briton on the Subjugation of Switzerland. Wordsworth. MBPR; PBMP; SpRo

Thoughts. Michael Benedikt. ConAP

Thoughts about the Person from Porlock. Stevie Smith. FaBoCo

Thoughts for You (When She Came Back from the Mountains). Ranice Henderson Crosby. NMM

Thoughts from a Bottle. Carl Clark. JB

Thoughts in Exile. Su Tung P'o, *tr. fr. Chinese by* Kenneth Rexroth. IPWM

Thoughts of a Young Girl. John Ashbery. ConAP; RRA; VGW

Thoughts of Chairman Mao. David Young. AmPA; CAAP

Thoughts of Phena. Thomas Hardy. OxBTC

Thoughts on Capital Punishment. Rod McKuen. InPK

Thoughts on Pain. Sallie Chesham. AATT

Thou's welcome, wean! Mishanter fa' me. A Poet's Welcome to His Love-Begotten Daughter. Burns. RRA

Thousand doors ago, A. Young. Anne Sexton. MPo; NCSH

Thousand gloomy walks the bower contains, A. Aphra Behn. *Fr.* A Voyage to the Island of Love. SCP-2

Thousand Martyrs I Have Made, A. Aphra Behn. SBG

Thousand Things, The. Christopher Middleton. TwMBP

Thousand times have I herd men telle, A. Old Books. Chaucer. *Fr.* The Legend of Good Women: Prologue. OxBM

Thousand years, you said, A. Parting. Lady Heguri, *tr. by* Geoffrey Bownas *and* Anthony Thwaite. BoLoP; OLR

Thousands/ of weird little figurines. Semen Coleman Barks. NVAP

Thracian Wonder, The, *sels.* *Unknown, at. to* John Webster *and* William Rowley. GBL
  "Love is a law, a discord of such force," I, i.
  Love Pursued, I, i.
  "Whither shall I go," II, i.

Thread. Catherine Lucy Czerkawska. SLP

Thread, A/ of meaning. Meaning light. The Dead Lady Canonized. LeRoi Jones. CAPP

Thread/ without cloth. Poverty. Margaret Reynolds. MIS

Thread of Life, The, *sel.* Christina Rossetti. "Irresponsive silence of the land, The." NOBE

Thread the nerves through the right holes. Resurrection Song. Thomas Lovell Beddoes. InPK

Three. Gregory Corso. SA

Three a.m.—a far bell. December. Gary Snyder. InPS

Three anti-depressants and one diuretic a day. Letter XII. Bruce Beaver. *Fr.* Letters to Live Poets. MAuV

Three black boys. Panther. Sam Cornish. PoBA

Three blind mice. Mother Goose. MG

Three Cheers for the Black, White and Blue. Ruth Pitter. BoAnP

Three Colts Exercising in a Six-Acre. Joseph Campbell. BoAnP; PFIr

Three days rain and. Short Pastoral. Leonard E. Nathan. MIT

Three excellent qualities in narration. Triads [*or* Thirty-three Triads]. *Unknown, tr. by* Thomas Kinsella. BIrV; PFIr

Three faces.../mirrored in the muddy streams of living. For Andy Goodman—Michael Schwerner—and James Chaney. Margaret Walker. BPo

Three flutes, two oboes, English horn, violins. Guide to the Symphony. Weldon Kees. VGW

Three Foxes, The. A. A. Milne. OxBChV

Three from the Market. Sandra McPherson. RiTi

Three gooses: geese. Goose, Moose, and Spruce. David McCord. ECBV

Three grey boys tracked us to an old house. In One Battle. LeRoi Jones. BPo

Three Grey Geese. *Unknown.* SoSe

Three hugest dinosaurs do not outweigh. The Blue Whale. Robert Watson. MAT

Three hundred fillings high. New Block. Patric Dickinson. LP

Three hundred from one village. 1867: Last Sounds. Gerry O'Egan. POL

Three Hundred Thousand More. James Sloan Gibbons. BTTM

"Three in heaven I hope" said old Jane to Henry. John Berryman. *Fr.* Dream Songs. RRA

Three jolly farmers. Off the Ground. Walter de la Mare. PoTa

Three Kinds of Pleasures. Robert Bly. ANTL

Three Lectures on the Skeleton. George M. Young, Jr. FAF

Three little kittens they lost their mittens. *Unknown, at. to* Eliza Lee Follen *and to* Eliza Cook MG

Three little lads were seated one day. Her Eyes Don't Shine Like Diamonds. David Marion. FSN

Three Little Pigs, The. Sir Alfred Scott Gatty. OxBChV

Three little ponies who didn't like their hay. Three Ponies. Arthur Guiterman. ECBV

Three little words we often use. The Nine Parts of Speech. *Unknown.* ECBV

Three Love Poems, *sel.* Norman Cameron. Shepherdess, III. GBL; SLP

Three Love Poems for My Wife. George Bruce. SLP

Three matches in a folder, you and me. Epigram: Night-piece. J. V. Cunningham. PiAm

Three Men. *Unknown.* BluL

Three men coming down the winter hill, The. Winter Landscape. John Berryman. CoPAm; WIF

Three Mirrors, The. Edwin Muir. NoAM

3 Models of the Universe. May Swenson. Psy

Three Modes of History and Culture. LeRoi Jones. NoAM

Three mounted buglers laced in gold. A Battle Picture. Herman Melville. PiAm

Three Movements, The. Donald Hall. NowV

Three Moves. John Logan. CAPP

Three of us in the bar. Jazz. Carloyn M. Rodgers. JB

Three of us went to the top of the city. Poem from the Empire State. June Jordan. BPo

3 of Washingtons heads. George Washington Goes to a Girlie Movie. Aram Boyajian. NeAC

Three Old Brothers. Frank O'Connor. PFIr

Three Poems for the Indian Steelworkers. Joseph Bruchac. CDW

Three poets, in three distant ages born. Lines Printed under the Engraved Portrait of Milton. Dryden. HeIP; InPK

Three Ponies. Arthur Guiterman. ECBV

Three Portraits. George Hitchcock. VGW

Three Ravens, The ("There were three ravens [*or* crows] sat on a tree"). *Unknown.* AIW; AmFP; Epi, *with music;* GBP; HeIP; InPK; PeBB; RDB, *with music*

Three Revellers Search for Death. Chaucer. *Fr.* The Canterbury Tales: The Pardoner's Tale. OxBM

Three Riddles. Brian Swann. TSWA

Three roads were shadowy and the sky over. Vanessa Vanessa. Ewart Milne. BIrV

Three Sentences for a Dead Swan. James Wright. NoAM; NOBA

Three Songs, The. Bayard Taylor. PoTa

3 Stanzas about a Tree. Marvin Bell. Prf

3 Stones. Roderick Watson. MIS

Three strange men came to the Inn. A Lady Comes to an Inn. Elizabeth J. Coatsworth. PoTa

Three strings, a neck of almond, and the heart. Balalaika. Norman Dubie. AmPA

Three summers since I chose a maid. The Farmer's Bride. Charlotte Mew. BoLoP; OxBTC; SBG; WPE

Three things seek my death. Devil, Maggot and Son. *Unknown.* SoSe

Three things there are more beautiful. The Beautiful. W. H. Davies. BBGO

Three things there be that prosper all apace. To His Son. Sir Walter Ralegh. InPS; PPoe

Three Things to Remember. Blake. *See* Robin Redbreast in a Cage, A.

Three X Three. Sonia Sanchez. WBN

Three-toed tree toad, The. Nocturne. Arthur Guiterman. ECBV

Three Troopers, The. George Walter Thornbury. BTTM

Three Valentines to the Wide World, *sel.* Mona Van Duyn. "When, in the middle of my life, the earth stalks me." RiTi

Three virgins at the break of day. The Golden Net. Blake. MBPR

Three weeks, and now I hear! My Olson Elegy. Irving Feldman. Prf

Three weeks gone and the combatants gone. Vergissmeinicht. Keith Douglas. InPS; OxBTC; SoSe

Three Weeks in the State of Loneliness. Marge Piercy. MMD

Three wise men of Gotham. Mother Goose. MG

Three Wise Old Women. Elizabeth T. Corbett. OxBChV

Three Women. Liz Lochhead. MIS

Three Women Blues. *Unknown.* BluL

Three Years She Grew in Sun and Shower. Wordsworth. AnMo; MBPR; NOBE

Three Young Rats ("Three young rats with black felt hats"). *Unknown.* ECBV (Rats, Ducks, Dogs, Cats, Pigs.) GBP

Threnody: "South-wind brings, The." Emerson. PAIC

Threshing-Machine, The. Alice Meynell. WPE

Threw a woman's shoe. My Atlas Poet. George Bowering. NeAC

Thrice happy flowers! *Unknown. Fr.* The Masque of Flowers. SCP-2

Thrice the brinded cat hath mew'd. Shakespeare. *Fr.* Macbeth, IV, i. OFD

Thrice Toss These Oaken Ashes in the Air. Thomas Campion. MAT
(Love-Charms.) NOBE

Thriftles thred which pampred beauty spinnes, The. A Sonet Written in Prayse of the Browne Beautie. George Gascoigne. AAS

Thro elm and maple and syringa branches. Commencement. Constance Carrier. WPE

Throbbing—all I can hear! Drums. Martha Chosa. VW

Through a blue-buoyant lake of air wavers. Dream of Ascent. James Applewhite. NVAP

Through an ascending emptiness. Maya. E. A. Robinson. PiAm

Through autumn evening, water whirls thin blue. The Castle of Thorns. Yvor Winters. NoAM

Through every age, eternal God. Isaac Watts. AmFP

Through every night we hate. Mothers, Daughters. Shirley Kaufman. NMM; RiTi

Through lane or black archway. The Young Woman of Beare. Austin Clarke. NoAM

Through life's dull road, so dim and dirty. On My Thirty-third Birthday. Byron. BBGO

Through Old Farmhouse Windows. Allan Block. FAF

Through our laced and latticed windows. Shacked Up at the Ritz. Doug Fetherling. NeAC

Through Ruddy Orchards. Mary Oliver. WPE

Through swamps and alligators I wend my weary way. On the Lakes of Ponchartrain. *Unknown.* AmFP

Through that pure virgin shrine. The Night. Henry Vaughan. BoReV; MetP; NOBE; SCP-1

Through that window—all else being extinct. The Room. Conrad Aiken. NOBA

Through the ample open door of the peaceful country barn. A Farm Picture. Walt Whitman. InPS; PPoe

Through the black, rushing smoke-bursts. The Song of Callicles. Mattew Arnold. *Fr.* Empedocles on Etna, II. NOBE

Through the gate. The Colt. Raymond Knister. AKE

Through the great sinful streets of Naples as I past. Easter Day, Naples, 1849. Arthur Hugh Clough. PFD; VPC

Through the hanging turkey's mouth. A Skill in Killing. George Abbe. FAF

Through the house what busy joy. The First Tooth. Charles *and* Mary Lamb. OxBChV

Through the Looking-Glass, *sels.* "Lewis Carroll."
Humpty Dumpty's Song, *fr.* ch. 6. OxBChV
(Humpty Dumpty's Recitation.) FaBoCo
Jabberwocky, *fr.* ch. 1. AnMo; FaBoCo; HeIP; InPK; InPS; NOBE; OBP; OxBChV; PPoe; PPP; SpRo; WIF
Walrus and the Carpenter, The, *fr.* ch. 4. AKE; FaBoCo; OxBChV
White Knight's Song, The, *fr.* ch. 8. FaBoCo; InPS; NOBE; OBP
(Aged Aged Man, The.) OxBChV; SpRo
(Ways and Means.) ECBV

Through the night on fire with my blood. She Speaks the Morning's Filigree. Philip Lamantia. VGW

Through the noonday sun. Kathleen Lubeck. *Fr.* Sons. NPW

Through the open French window the warm sun. Still-Life. Elizabeth Daryush. WPE

Through the white winter palace. At Kilbryde Castle. Lorn M. MacIntyre. SLP

Through this indifferent winter's gaze. Beggar and Poet. Robert A. Martin. AATT

Through thy battlements, Newstead, the hollow winds whistle. On Leaving Newstead Abbey. Byron. MBPR

Through weeds and thorns, and matted underwood. The Picture; or, the Lover's Resolution. Samuel Taylor Coleridge. MBPR

Through woods, Mme Une Telle, a trifle ill. Autumn Chapter in a Novel. Thom Gunn. OxBTC

Throughout the World If It Were Sought. Sir Thomas Wyatt. MAT

Throw away thy rod. Discipline. George Herbert. BoReV; NOBE; PAIC; SCP-1

Throw Him Down M'Closkey; or, M'Closkey's Great Fight, *with music.* John W. Kelly. FSN

Throwing stone perhaps its surface carved, A. 3 Stones. Roderick Watson. MIS

Thrown backwards first, head over heels in the wind. To My Friend Whose Parachute Did Not Open. David Wagoner. SFF

Thrush before Dawn, A. Alice Meynell. WPE

Thrush, linnet, stare, and wren. In Glencullen. J. M. Synge. PFIr; RAE

Thrushes. Ted Hughes. TwMBP

Thrushes sing as the sun is going, The. Proud Songsters. Thomas Hardy. NoAM

Thrush's Nest, The. John Clare. BoAnP

Thrush's Nest, The. Richard Ryan. PFIr

Thumb. Philip Dacey. POL

Thumb, The. Dennis Saleh. MAT; NeAC

Thumb, loose tooth of a horse. Bestiary for the Fingers of My Right Hand. Charles Simic. AmPA

Thumbing through someone else's book. Thinking Back Seven Years and Being Here Now. David Curry. HeS

Thumping old tunes give a voice to its whereabouts. Fairground. W. H. Auden. LP

Thunderstorm in South Dakota. Kay Boyle. WPE

Thunderstorm in Town, A. Thomas Hardy. BoLoP; GBL

Thurn, A. John Berryman. NOBA

Thursday was baking day in our house. Baking Day. Rosemary Joseph. MPo

Thus by himself compelled to live each day. Peter Grimes; the Outcast. George Crabbe. *Fr.* The Borough, Letter XXII. NOBE

Thus did my days pass on, and now at length. Wordsworth. *Fr.* The Prelude, II. BoReV

Thus down a lone valley with cedars o'er spread. Columbia. *Unknown.* AmFP

Thus fares the drudge; but thou, whose life's a dream. Persius, *tr. fr. Latin by* Dryden. *Fr.* Satires, IV. SCP-1

Thus have I shunned the fire for fear of burning. Shakespeare. *Fr.* The Two Gentlemen of Verona, I, iii. GBL

Thus I awakede, wot God, when I wonede in Cornehille. Long Will in London. William Langland. *Fr.* The Vision of Piers Plowman. OxBM

Thus it befell upon a night. Medea's Magic. John Gower. *Fr.* Confessio Amantis, V. OxBM

Thus laykes this lorde by lynde-wodes eves. Gawain and the Lady of the Castle. *Unknown. Fr.* Sir Gawain and the Green Knight. OxBM

Thus piteously Love closed what he begat. Modern Love, L. George Meredith. NOBE; PAIC; PFD; VPC

Thus queth Alfred. Wealth and Wisdom. *At. to* Alfred, King of England. *Fr.* The Proverbs of Alfred. OxBM

Thus saith my Chloris bright. Giovanni Battista Guarini, *tr. fr. Italian* GBL

Thus should have been our travels. Over 2000 Illustrations and a Complete Concordance. Elizabeth Bishop. NoAM

Thus sung Orpheus to his strings. *Unknown.* GBL

Thwick-a-thwack. Thomas Dekker. *Fr.* London's Tempe. SCP-2

Thy azure robe I did behold.  Julia's Petticoat.  Robert Herrick.
  SCP-1

Thy bosom is endearèd with all hearts.  Sonnets, XXXI.
  Shakespeare.  NOBE

Thy Brother's Blood.  Jones Very.  AmVN; NOBA

Thy byrth, thy beautie, nor thy brave attyre.  Farewell with a
  Mischeife.  George Gascoigne.  AAS

Thy country's curse is on thee, darkest crest.  To the Lord
  Chancellor.  Shelley.  MBPR

Thy fingers make early flowers of.  E. E. Cummings.  LoAs

Thy friendship oft has made my heart to ache.  To William
  Hayley.  Blake.  FaBoCo

Thy humane frame, my glorious Lord, I spy.  Edward Taylor.
  Fr. Preparatory Meditations: First Series, VII.  PiAm

Thy Kingdom Come.  Elmer F. Suderman.  AATT

Thy look of love has power to calm.  To Harriett.  Shelley.
  MBPR

Thy praise or dispraise is to me alike.  To Fool, or Knave.  Ben
  Jonson.  SoSe

Thy sacred succour, Arethusa, bring.  The Tenth Pastoral; or,
  Gallus. Vergil, tr. by Dryden.  Epi

Thy summer voice, Musketaquit.  Two Rivers.  Emerson.
  NOBA

Thy trivial harp will never please.  Merlin, I.  Emerson.
  AmVN; NOBA; PiAm

Thy voice slow rising like a spirit, lingers.  To Constantia Singing.
  Shelley.  MBPR

Thyestes, sel.  Seneca, tr. fr. Latin by Sir Thomas Wyatt.
  "Stond who so list upon the Slipper toppe."  AAS

Thyme.  Unknown.  AmFP

Thyrsis.  Matthew Arnold.  Epi; NOBE
  "So, some tempestuous morn in early June,"  sel.  FSFS

Thyrsis and Milla, arm in arm together  Unknown.  GBL

Thyrsis, the music of that murmuring spring.  Winter.  Pope.
  Fr. Pastorals.  PAIC

Tic.  Coleman Barks.  Fr. Body Poems.  NVAP

Tichborne's Elegy.  Chidiock Tichborne.  See Elegy: "My prime
  of youth is but a frost of cares."

Tickled,/my thoughts wander.  Celebration for My Mother.
  Wendy Rose.  CDW

Tiddle-de-dumpty, tiddle-de-dee.  Coquetry.  Eugene Field.
  ECBV

Tide be runnin' the great world over.  Sea Love.  Charlotte Mew.
  OxBTC

Tide Rises, the Tide Falls, The.  Longfellow.  AmVN; NOBA;
  PBMP; PiAM; RAE; VoPo

Tide River, The.  Charles Kingsley.  Fr. The Water Babies.
  OxBChV

Tides.  Fred Ostrander.  MIT

Tides, The.  Quiet Days in Sutherland.  Robin Fulton.  MIS

Tides shape the sides of the agate mountain.  On Visiting My
  Son, Port Angeles, Washington.  Duane Niatum.  CDW

Tie Your Tongue, Sir?  Robert Paul Smith.  ECBV

Ties.  Dabney Stuart.  CoPAm; SPo

Tiger, The.  Blake.  Fr. Songs of Experience.  InPS; NOBE;
  PBMP; SoSe; SpRo; WIF, 3 versions
  (Tyger, The.)  BoReV; HeIP; InPK; IPWM; LAuP; MBPR;
  OBP; PPoD; PPoe; PPP

Tiger.  Claude McKay.  BPo

Tiger at Play.  Joanna Baillie.  PCat

Tiger Christ unsheathed his sword.  For the One Who Would
  Take Man's Life in His Hands.  Delmore Schwartz.
  NoAM; VGW

Tiger! Tiger! [or Tyger! Tyger!] burning bright.  The Tiger [or
  Tyger].  Blake.  Fr. Songs of Experience.  BoReV; HeIP;
  InPK; InPS; IPWM; LAuP; MBPR; NOBE; OBP; PBMP;
  PPoD; PPoe; PPP; SoSe; SpRo; WIF

Tight,—proof, unavailable.  Falling Out.  Helen Chasin.  IHMS

Tightly-folded bud.  Born Yesterday.  Philip Larkin.  RRA

Tightrope Walker, The.  Rochelle Ratner.  WBN

Tightrope Walker.  Vernon Scannell.  NCSH

Tihuitkli.  Luís Omar Salinas.  SA

Tiki.  Forrest Anderson.  AATT

Tilda Tidbury.  Unknown.  RAE

Till the slow daylight pale.  The Sun-flower.  Dora Greenwell.
  WPE

Timbuctu.  Edward Brathwaite.  MPo

Time.  John Huddlestone Wynne.  OxBChV

Time, A: A Season.  Patricia Ramsey.  AATT

Time admires ruin. The wonders of collapse.  Colossi.  Albert De
  Pietro.  AATT

Time and again I've longed for adventure.  All the Things You
  Are.  Oscar Hammerstein II.  BLSo

Time and the Garden.  Yvor Winters.  NoAM; VGW

Time began in time begotten—this night.  His Coming.  Irene
  Dayton.  AATT

Time came, The.  For John Berryman.  Virginia Gilbert.  NPW

Time changeth still, and we are changed with time.  Time's
  Metamorphosis.  Richard Middleton.  TVS

Time draws near the birth of Christ, The.  In Memoriam A.H.H.,
  XXVIII.  Tennyson.  SoSe

Time feels so vast that were it not.  Emily Dickinson.  PiAm

Time has an end, they say.  Hilda Doolittle ("H.D.").  Fr. Good
  Frend.  NOBA; VGW

Time heals not: it extends a sorrow's scope.  Epigram.  J. V.
  Cunningham.  VGW

Time I dropped your almost body down, The.  The Lost Baby
  Poem.  Lucille Clifton.  InPK; RiTi; WPE

Time in the Rock; or, Preludes to Definition, sels.      Conrad
  Aiken.
  "Bird flying past my head said previous previous, The," LXII.
    VGW
  "But no, the familiar symbol, as that the," XCII.  VGW
  "Mysticism, but let us have no words," XI.  VGW
  "What face she put on it, we will not discuss," LXXXIV.
    VGW
  "Where we were walking in the day's light, seeing," XXXVII.
    VGW

Time is divided into.  Time Is the Mercy of Eternity.  Kenneth
  Rexroth.  VGW

Time is not remote when I, The.  Swift.  Fr. Verses on the Death
  of Doctor Swift.  NOBE

Time Is Open, The.  Joanne Kyger.  RiTi

Time is swiftly rolling on, The.  The Dying Father's Farewell.
  Unknown.  AmFP

Time Is the Mercy of Eternity.  Kenneth Rexroth.  VGW

Time it took he could have, The.  The Invention of the
  Telephone.  Peter Klappert.  AmPA

Time I've Lost in Wooing, The.  Thomas Moore.  PFIr; VoPo

Time of Change, A.  Egan O'Rahilly, tr. fr. Irish by Eavan
  Boland.  BIrV

Time of grease beginneth at Midsummer day.  Julians Barnes.
  Fr. Book of Hunting.  WPE

Time of year has grown indifferent.  The Man Whose Pharynx
  Was Bad.  Wallace Stevens.  PiAm

Time Out.  Patricia Henley.  NPW

Time Out.  John Montague.  BoAnP; PFIr

Time Passing, Beloved.  Donald Davie.  BoLoP

Time present and time past.  Burnt Norton.  T. S. Eliot.  Fr.
  Four Quartets.  HeIP

Time, Real and Imaginary.  Samuel Taylor Coleridge.  MBPR;
  NOBE; PBMP

Time that is moved by little fidget wheels.  Five Bells.  Kenneth
  Slessor.  MAuV

Time to Die. Ray Garfield Dandridge. PoBA

Time to put off the world and go somewhere. Beggar to Beggar Cried. W. B. Yeats. NoAM

Time to Rise. Robert Louis Stevenson. OxBChV

Time to Talk, A. Robert Frost. NCSH

Time to tell you things are well, A. Snow Country Weavers. James Welch. CDW

Time Upon a Once. Robert Paul Smith. ECBV

Time was the apple Adam ate. Original Sequence. Philip Booth. SFF

Time Was the Trail Went Deep. Charles G. Ballard. VW

Time was when his half million drew. Bewick Finzer. E. A. Robinson. PPP

Time will assuage. To the Reader. J. V. Cunningham. NoAM

Time will say nothing but I told you so. If I Could Tell You. W. H. Auden. PSN

Time you won your town the race, The. To an Athlete Dying Young. A. E. Housman. BTTM; HeIP; InPK; IPWM; MiP; NoAM; PBMP; PPoD; PPoe; SoSe; SPo; WIF

Timepiece, A. James Merrill. NoAM

Times ain't now nothing like they used to be, The. James Alley. *Unknown.* BluL

Times's an hand's-breadth; 'tis a tale. Time. John Huddlestone Wynne. OxBChV

Times are swiftly drawing nigh. When You and I Must Part. *Unknown.* AmFP

Time's Dedication. Delmore Schwartz. VGW

Time's Fool. Ruth Pitter. OxBTC; WPE

Time's Metamorphosis. Richard Middleton. TVS

Time's sea hath been five years at its slow ebb. To——. Keats. MBPR

Timid and hot-tempered. Vincent Buckley. *Fr.* Golden Builders. CAAP

Timmy Pimmy. *Unknown.* ECBV

Timon of Athens, the Man-hater, *sel.* Thomas Shadwell. "Well, babbling philosophical rascal." SCP-2

Timor Mortis Conturbat Me. William Dunbar. NOBE, *abr.* (Lament for the Poets, *tr. fr. Middle English by* Andrew Glaze *and* Selden Rodman.) OBP

Timothy. Thomas James. HeS

Timothy Winters. Charles Causley. MPo

Tin Can, The. William Jay Smith. CoPAm

Tin Cup Blues. *Unknown.* BluL

Tin shack, where my baby sleeps on his back. Everything: Eloy, Arizona, 1956. Ai. AmPA

Tinker's Wife. Patrick Kavanagh. NoAM

Tintadgel bells ring o'er the tide. The Silent Tower of Bottreau. Robert Stephen Hawker. VPC

Tintock. *Unknown.* GBP

Tin-type tune the locusts make, The. Serenade. Dorothy Donnelly. NCSH

Tiny Baby Lizard, The. Besmilr Brigham. RiTi

Tiny fish enjoy themselves, The. Little Fish. D. H. Lawrence. AKE; OxBTC

Tiny island, A. Ladybug. Francois Dodat, *tr. by* Bert *and* Odette Meyers. BoAnP

Tiny monkey looks at me, The. Haiku. José Juan Tablada, *tr. by* Samuel Beckett. PBMP

Tiny new emotions, The. Poem. Tom Clark. ConAP

Tiny spill of bird-things in a swirl, A. The Finches. Thomas W. Shapcott. BoAnP

Tiny, turreted occurrence, The. Profile of a Day. Ruthe T. Spinnanger. AATT

Tip-burning wings. Vita-Sheet. Ruth Weiss. MIT

Tirade. Honor Moore. WBN

Tir'd nature's sweet restorer, balmy sleep! Edward Young. Night Thoughts: Night the First. LAuP

Tired. Fenton Johnson. PoBA

Tired and dejected hair dripping. Diane. Stewart McIntosh. SLP

Tired As I Can Be. *Unknown.* BluL

Tired Tim. Walter de la Mare. LCL

Tired with all these, for restful death I cry. Sonnets, LXVI. Shakespeare. InPS; NOBE

Tired Worker, The. Claude McKay. BPo

Tiresias. George Garrett. CoPAm

Tiriel, *sel.* Blake. "And aged Tiriel stood and said: 'Where does the thunder sleep?' " Epi

'Tis a new life;—thoughts move not as they did. The New Birth. Jones Very. AmVN; NOBA; PiAm

'Tis advertised in Boston, New York and Buffalo. Blow, Ye Winds. *Unknown.* AmFP

'Tis affection but dissembled. Sidney Godolphin. SCP-2

'Tis bad enough in man or woman. On Inclosures. *Unknown.* FaBoCo

'Tis Christmas weather, and a country house. Modern Love, XXIII. George Meredith. PAIC

'Tis done—and shivering in the gale. Stanzas to a Lady, on Leaving England. Byron. MBPR

'Tis done—but yesterday a king. Ode to Napoleon Buonaparte. Byron. MBPR

'Tis eight o'clock,—a clear March night. The Idiot Boy. Wordsworth. MBPR

'Tis fine to see the Old World, and travel up and down. America for Me. Henry van Dyke. SoSe

'Tis gone, that bright and orbèd blaze. Evening Hymn. John Keble. PFD

'Tis goodbye then to last night. Soraidh Slan Don Oidhche Areir. Niall Mor MacMuireadach, *tr. by* Maire Cruise O'Brien. BIrV

'Tis grown almost a danger to speak true. Ben Jonson. *Fr.* Epistle to Katherine, Lady Aubigny. SCP-1

'Tis known, at least it should be, that throughout. Beppo: a Venetian Story. Byron. MBPR

'Tis liberty to serve one lord. Slavery. Robert Herrick. PAIC

'Tis love's commission—justly it may call. Love's Commission. William Cavendish, Duke of Newcastle. SCP-2

'Tis morning; and the sun with ruddy orb. The Winter Morning Walk. William Cowper. *Fr.* The Task. LAuP

'Tis mute, the word they went to hear on high Dodona mountain. The Oracles. A. E. Housman. BTTM

'Tis my sole plague to be alone. Robert Burton. *Fr.* The Anatomy of Melancholy: The Author's Abstract of Melancholy. SCP-2

'Tis near the morning watch: the dim lamp burns. The Morning Watch. Jones Very. PiAm

" 'Tis no sin for a man to labour in his vocation." The Ballad of Villon and Fat Madge. Villon, *tr. by* Swinburne. LoAs

'Tis not enough for one that is a wife. Lady Elizabeth Carey. *Fr.* Mariam, III. WPE

'Tis not that I am weary grown. Upon His Leaving His Mistress. Earl of Rochester. GBL; OBP

'Tis not the world nor what can please. *Unknown.* SCP-2

'Tis of a blind beggar who a long time was blind. The Blind Beggar. *Unknown.* AmFP

'Tis of a gallant Yankee ship that flew the stripes and stars. The Yankee Man-of-War. *Unknown.* BTTM

'Tis of a jolly soldier that lately came from war. The Jolly Soldier. *Unknown.* AmFP

'Tis of a lady both fair and handsome. The Servant Man. *Unknown.* AmFP

'Tis of a pedlar, a pedlar trim. The Bold Pedlar and Robin Hood. *Unknown.* AmFP

'Tis of a rich merchant who in London did dwell. Villikins and His Dinah. Sam Cowell. PoTa

'Tis of a sad and dismal story that happened off the fatal rock. The Loss of the *New Columbia. Unknown.* AmFP

'Tis of a wild Colonial boy, Jack Doolan was his name. The Wild Colonial Boy. *Unknown.* PeBB

'Tis sad to see the sons of learning. He That Never Read a Line. *Unknown, tr. by* Robin Flower. PFIr

'Tis said, that some have died for love. Wordsworth. MBPR

'Tis spring: come out to ramble. The Lent Lily. A. E. Housman. FSFS

'Tis strange! I saw the skies. Dreams. Thomas Traherne. SCP-2

'Tis strange, the miser should his cares employ. To Richard Boyle, Earl of Burlington: Of the Use of Riches. Pope. Moral Essays, Epistle IV. PPP

'Tis summer time on Bredon. Hugh Kingsmill. FaBoCo

'Tis Sweet to Rest in Lively Hope. *Unknown.* AmFP

'Tis the middle of night by the castle clock. Christabel. Samuel Taylor Coleridge. MBPR; OBP

'Tis the voice of the Lobster: I heard him declare. Alice's Recitation [*or* The Lobster]. "Lewis Carroll" *Fr.* Alice's Adventures in Wonderland, *ch.* 10. FaBoCo; OxBChV; SpRo

'Tis the voice of the sluggard: I heard him complain. The Sluggard. Isaac Watts. OxBChV; SpRo

'Tis "the witching time of night." Keats. MBPR

'Tis the year's [*or* yeares] midnight, and it is the day's [*or* dayes]. A Nocturnal[l] upon Saint Lucy's [*or* S. Lucies] Day, Being the Shortest Day. John Donne. AnMo; GBL; MetP; NOBE; OBP; PPP; SCP-1

'Tis time this heart should be unmoved. On This Day I Complete My Thirty-Sixth Year. Byron. MBPR

'Tis to yourself I speak; you cannot know. Yourself. Jones Very. AmVN; NOBA

'Tis true I write and tell me by what rule. The Appology. Countess of Winchilsea. SBG

'Tis true—they shut me in the cold. Emily Dickinson. SBG

'Tis true, 'tis day, what though it be? Break of Day. John Donne. PAIC

Tit for Tat: A Tale. John Aikin. OxBChV

Tit-tat-toe. *Unknown.* MG

Titan! to whose immortal eyes. Prometheus. Byron. InPS; MBPR; NOBE

*Titanic,* The. *Unknown.* AmFP

*Titanic* Blues. *Unknown.* BluL

Tithes. Luci Shaw. AATT

Tithonus. Tennyson. NOBE; OBP; PPP

Title divine—is mine! Emily Dickinson. NOBA; PAIC; PiAm

Titmouse, The. Emerson. PiAm

Tittery-Irie-Aye. *Unknown.* AmFP

Titus reads neither prose nor rhyme. The Writer. Hildebrand Jacob. FaBoCo

Tlanusi' yi, the Leech Place. Gladys Cardiff. CDW

To——: "Cold earth slept below, The." Shelley. MBPR

To——: "Had I a man's fair form, then might my sighs." Keats. MBPR

To——: "Hadst thou liv'd in days of old." Keats. MBPR

To——: "Half in the dim light from the hall." William Stanley Braithwaite. PoBA

To——: "Music, when soft voices die." Shelley. HeIP; MBPR ("Music, when soft voices die.") NOBE

To——: "Oh! There are spirits of the air." Shelley. MBPR

To——: "One word is too often profaned." Shelley. BoLoP; MBPR; NOBE; PPP

To——: "Time's sea hath been five years at its slow ebb." Keats. MBPR

To——: "What can I do to drive away." Keats. MBPR

To——: "When passions's trance is overpast." Shelley. MBPR

To a Baseball. *Unknown.* SPo

To a Butterfly ("I've watched you now a full half-hour"). Wordsworth. MBPR

To a Butterfly ("Stay near me—do not take thy flight!"). Wordsworth. MBPR

To a Calvinist in Bali. Edna St. Vincent Millay. NoAM

To a Captious Critic. Paul Laurence Dunbar. BPo

To a Cat. Keats. PCat
(To Mrs. Reynold's Cat.) MBPR

To a Cat. Swinburne. PCat

To a Child Born in Time of Small War. Helen Sorrells. WPE

To a Child Dancing in the Wind. W. B. Yeats. BBGO; PFIr

To a Child Five Years Old. Nathaniel Cotton. OxBChV

To a Child of Quality [Five Years Old]. Matthew Prior. NOBE; RRA

To a Child Running with Outstretched Arms in the Canyon de Chelly. N. Scott Momaday. CDW

To a Child Trapped in a Barber Shop. Philip Levine. InPK; NoAM; NOBA; VGW

To A. D. W. E. Henley. Echoes, XVIII. LoAs

To a Dark Girl. Gwendolyn B. Bennett. PoBA

To a Family Man in His Family Room. Rosemary Daniell. WBN

To a Fat Lady Seen from the Train. Frances Cornford. SpRo

To a Fighter Killed in the Ring. Lou Lipsitz. SPo

To a 14 Year Old Girl in Labor and Delivery. John Stone. CoPAm

To a Friend. Matthew Arnold. PAIC

To a Friend. William Carlos Williams. LoAs

To a Friend Concerning Several Ladies. William Carlos Williams. VGW

To a Friend, on Her Examination for the Doctorate in English. J. V. Cunningham. VGW

To a Friend, Who Recommended a Wife to Him. *Unknown.* PiAm

To a Friend Who Sent Me Some Roses. Keats. MBPR

To a Fugitive. James Wright. TH

To a Gentlewoman Objecting to Him His Grey Hairs. Robert Herrick. SCP-1

To a Girl Who Lives in a Tree. Audré Lorde. WBN

To a good man of most dear memory. Written after the Death of Charles Lamb. Wordsworth. MBPR

To a Ground-Lark. David Campbell. *Fr.* Cocky's Calendar. MAuV

To a Hedgehog. Samuel Thompson. BIrV

To a high hill where never yet stood tree. Thomas Otway. *Fr.* The Poet's Complaint of His Muse. SCP-2

To a Highland Girl. Wordsworth. MBPR

To a Husband. Maya Angelou. IHMS

To a Lady [*or* Ladye]. William Dunbar. GBL; SLP

To a Lady. J. B. Morton. POL

To a Lady on Her Marriage. William Bell. PAIC

To a Lady that Forbade to Love before Company. Sir John Suckling. SCP-2

To a Late Poplar. Patrick Kavanagh. PFIr

To a Locomotive in Winter. Walt Whitman. InPK; NoAM; WIF

To a Lost Sweetheart. Don Marquis. POL

To a Louse. Burns. PBMP

To a Married Couple That Could Not Agree. Timothy Kendall. PAIC

To a Mouse [on Turning Her Up in Her Nest, with the Plough, November 1785]. Burns. HeIP; InPS; LAuP; PAIC; PPP

To a Mouse says a Miser, "My dear Mr. Mouse." The Miser and the Mouse. Christopher Smart. RAE

To a Nightingale. Keats. *See* Ode to a Nightingale

To a Poet I Knew. Jewel C. Latimore. PoBA

To a Poet, Who Would Have Me Praise Certain Bad Poets, Imitators of His and Mine. W. B. Yeats. PFIr

To a Portuguese Man-o-War. Four Homages. Allan Block. FAF

To a Proud Old Woman Watching the Tearing Down of the Hurricane Shed. Kay Boyle. MIT

To a Red-headed Do-good Waitress. Alan Dugan. CAPP; NowV

To a Red-Wheat Field. Charles Tennyson Turner. VPC

To a Republican Friend, 1848. Matthew Arnold. PAIC

To a Romantic. Allen Tate. PiAm

To a Scarecrow; or, Malkin, Left Long after Harvest. Charles Tennyson Turner. VPC

To a Single Shadow Without Pity. Sam Cornish. PoBA

To a Skylark. Shelley. BoAnP, *abr.*; InPS; MBPR; PBMP; VoPo
(Ode to a Skylark.) NOBE

To a Skylark. Wordsworth. MBPR

To a Snail. Marianne Moore. PiAm

To a Snow-flake. Francis Thompson. FSFS

To a Solitary Disciple. William Carlos Williams. VGW

To a Squirrel at Kyle-Na-No. W. B. Yeats. LCL

To a Steam Roller. Marianne Moore. Psy; VGW

To a Stranger. Walt Whitman. NoAM; NOBA

To a Student Poet, Hospitalized, Having "Broken with Reality." Roderick Hartigh Jellema. AATT

To a "Tenting" Boy. Charles Tennyson Turner. VPC

To a Very Beautiful Lady. Ruthven Todd. SLP

To a Waterfowl. Bryant. AmVN; IPWM; NOBA; PiAm; SoSe

To a Woman Half a World Away. Dick Allen. CoPAm

To a Woman Who Wants Darkness and Time. Gerald W. Barrax. PoBA

To a Young Ass. Samuel Taylor Coleridge. MBPR

To a Young Brother. Maria Jane Jewsbury. OxBChV

To a Young Girl. W. B. Yeats. OLR; PSN; SoSe

To a Young Lady. Wordsworth. MBPR

To a Young Lady with a Poem on the French Revolution. Samuel Taylor Coleridge. MBPR

To a Young Poet Who Fled. John Logan. CAPP

To a Young Wretch. Robert Frost. OFD

To Adam, His Scribe. Chaucer. OxBM

To Age. Walter Savage Landor. SoSe

To Ailsa Rock. Keats. MBPR

To Alfred Tennyson. Walter Savage Landor. POL

To All Brothers. Sonia Sanchez. BPo

To All Sisters. Sonia Sanchez. PoBA

To all you ladies now at Bath. Farewell to Bath. Lady Mary Wortley Montagu. WPE

To all you ladies now at land. Song, Written at Sea in the First Dutch War. Charles Sackville. NOBE

To Althea, from Prison. Richard Lovelace. GBL; HeIP; InPS; MetP; NOBE

To Amarantha, That She Would Dishevel Her Hair. Richard Lovelace. SCP-2

To an Artist. Burns. PBMP

To an Athlete Dying Young. A. E. Housman. BTTM; HeIP; InPK; IPWM; MiP; NoAM; PBMP; PPoD; PPoe; SoSe; SPo; WIF, 3 *versions*

To an Athlete Turned Poet. Peter Meinke. SPo

To an Author. Philip Freneau. AmVN; NOBA

To an Imaginary Father. Wendy Rose. CDW

To an Old Lady. William Empson. Moon; NoAM; NOBE

To an Old Philosopher in Rome. Wallace Stevens. NoAM; NOBA

To Antenor. Katherine Philips. SBG

To Anthea. Robert Herrick. SCP-1

To Anthea Lying in Bed. Robert Herrick. AnMo; SCP-1

To Anthea, Who May Command Him Anything. Robert Herrick. NOBE

To Any M. F. H. V. Sackville-West. SBG

To Any Member of My Generation. George Barker. PAIC

To Anybody At All. Margaret Tait. SLP

To Art. Dante Gabriel Rossetti. POL

To Arthur's court, when men began. A Scot, a Welsh and an Irish Man. *Unknown.* GBP

To Asra. Samuel Taylor Coleridge. MBPR

To Aunt Rose. Allen Ginsberg. VGW

To Autumn. Blake. FSFS; MBPR

To Autumn. Keats. AnMo; Epi; FSFS; IPWM; MBPR; NOBE; OBP; PBMP; PPoD; PPoe; PPP; Prf; SoSe; WIF

To B. R. Haydon. Keats. MBPR

To B. R. Haydon. Wordsworth. MBPR

To be a poet and not know the trade. Sanctity. Patrick Kavanagh. BIrV

To be a successful and competent vet. The Vet. Guy Boas. BoAnP

To be able to see every side of every question. Editor Whedon. Edgar Lee Masters. *Fr.* Spoon River Anthology. NoAM; NOBA

To be alive—is power. Emily Dickinson. PiAm

To Be Carved on a Stone at Thoor Ballylee. W. B. Yeats. NoAM

To Be in Love. Gwendolyn Brooks. IHMS; OLR

To be in love is like going out. The Business. Robert Creeley. CAPP

To be married. The Relationship. Stephen Vincent. NeAC

To be my own Messiah to the. The Rows of Cold Trees. Yvor Winters. NoAM; NOBA

To Be Or Not to Be. *Unknown.* FaBoCo
(Rooster Be? Or a Crow?) ECBV

To be put on the train and kissed and given my ticket. Observation Car. A. D. Hope. NoAM

To Be Quicker. Don L. Lee. JB

To Be Recited to Flossie on Her Birthday. William Carlos Williams. VGW

To Be Sung on the Water. Louise Bogan. VGW

To be ten and skinny. Exodus. Anita Endrezze Probst. CDW

To be the father of the fatherless. Sonnet to the Prince Regent. Byron. MBPR

To Bed. Diane Wakoski. CAAP

To bed, to bed, kind turtles, now, and write. Robert Herrick. *Fr.* A Nuptiall Song, or Epithalamie, on Sir Clipsey Crew and His Lady. OBP

To begin with he was a beautiful object. Louis MacNeice. *Fr.* The Death of a Cat. PCat

To Blok/ words that had stuck together. Blok: Let Me Learn the Poem. Aram Boyajian. NeAC

To Bobby Seale. Lucille Clifton. PoBA

To Boston Town. *Unknown.* ECBV

To brave and to know the unknown. The Unknown. John Davidson. PAIC

To Brooklyn Bridge. Hart Crane. *Fr.* The Bridge. InPS; NOBA
(Proem: To Brooklyn Bridge.) HeIP; NoAM; PAIC; PiAm

To call a bird a bird, a tree a tree. The Naturalist. Margaret Reynolds. MIS

To Caroline ("Oh! when shall the grave hide for ever my sorrow"). Byron. MBPR

To Caroline ("Think'st thou I saw thy beauteous eyes"). Byron. MBPR

To Carry the Child. Stevie Smith. NoAM

To Castara ("Why should we fear to melt away in death"). William Habington. SCP-2

To Castara: of True Delight. William Habington. SCP-2

To Castara: of What We Were before Our Creation. William Habington. SCP-2

To Castara: the Reward of Innocent Love. William Habington. SCP-2

To cause accord or to aggre. Sir Thomas Wyatt. AAS

To Celia ("Drink to me only with thine eyes"). Ben Jonson. AKE; BoLoP; InPK; NOBE
(Drink to Me Only with Thine Eyes, *with music*.) BLSH; BLSo
(Song: To Celia.) GBL; HeIP

To Celia. Sir Charles Sedley. NOBE

To Certain Critics. Countee Cullen. BPo

To Charles Cowden Clarke. Keats. MBPR

To Chatterton. Keats. MBPR

To Cheer Our Minds. William Ronksley. OxBChV

To "Chick" Frank Horne. *Fr.* Letters Found near a Suicide. BPo

To Children. Lawrence McGaugh. PoBA

To Chloe ("Vitas hinnuleo"). Horace, *tr. fr. Latin by* Austin Dobson. Odes, I, 23. LoAs

To Chloe Who Wish'd Her Self Young Enough for Me. William Cartwright. MetP

To Christ Our Lord. Galway Kinnell. InPK; MiP; RFM

To Christian Montpelier, *sel.* George Jonas.
"Single naked wire at ground level, A." NeAC

To Cloe Weeping. Matthew Prior. PAIC

To Cloris ("Cloris, I cannot say your eyes"). Sir Charles Sedley. BoLoP

To Cole, the Painter, Departing for Europe. Bryant. PiAm

To Colman Returning. *At. to* Colman, *tr. fr. Medieval Latin by* Helen Waddell. BIrV

To come back from the sweet South, to the North. Italia, Io Ti Saluto. Christina Rossetti. WPE

To come to the river. The Resolve. Denise Levertov. RFM

To come up behind you. Agitprop. Marge Piercy. MMD

To Constantia Singing. Shelley. MBPR

To cut a shape out in form of a man. What Is She Trying to Do, to Pattern Love. Besmilr Brigham. RiTi

To Cynthia. Sir Francis Kynaston. GBL

To Cynthia: Learn'd Lapidaries. Sir Francis Kynaston. SCP-2

To Cynthia: On Concealment of Her Beauty. Sir Francis Kynaston. NOBE

To Cynthia, on Her Looking-glass. Sir Francis Kynaston. SCP-2

To Cynthia, on Sugar and Her Sweetness. Sir Francis Kynaston. SCP-2

To Daffodils [*or* Daffadills]. Robert Herrick. AKE; FSFS; InPS; NOBE; PAIC; PPP; SCP-1; WIF

To Daisies, Not To Shut So Soon. Robert Herrick. GBL; InPK

To David, about His Education. Howard Nemerov. NowV; SFF

To deal with death, ignore it. La Vie En Rose. Peter Schjeldahl. CAAP

To Death. Shelley. MBPR

To Delia, *sels.* Samuel Daniel.
"Beauty, sweet love, is like the morning dew," XLII. NOBE; PAIC
"Care-charmer sleep [*or* sleepe], son [*or* sonne] of the sable night," XXXV. AAS; Epi; InPS; IPWM; NOBE; PAIC

"Fair [*or* Faire] is my love, and cruel [*or* cruell] as she's fair," VI. AAS; NOBE
"I once may see when yeares shall wreck my wrong," XXXIV. AAS
"If so it hap, this of-spring of my care," III. AAS
"If this be love, to draw [*or* drawe] a weary [*or* wearie] breath," IX. AAS; GBL
"Let others sing of knights and paladins [*or* palladines], XLVI." AAS; NOBE
"Look, Delia, how we 'steem the half-blown rose," XXXI. HeIP
"None other fame mine unambitious muse." AAS
Sonnet: "I must not grieve my love, whose eyes would read," XLVI. LoAs
"These plaintive verse, the postes of my desire," VI. AAS
"When men shall find thy flower, thy glory, pass," XXXVI. NOBE

To Delmore Schwartz. Robert Lowell. NoAM

To Dianeme. Robert Herrick. NOBE; POL; SCP-1; SoSe

To die—takes just a little while. Emily Dickinson. PBMP

To Dinah Washington. Etheridge Knight. PoBA

To Diotima. Friedrich Hölderlin, *tr. fr. German by* Michael Hamburger. LoAs

To Doctor Bale. Barnabe Googe. PAIC

To Dr. Kipling. Richard Porson. FaBoCo

To draw no envy, Shakespeare, on thy name. To the Memory of My Beloved, the Author, Mr. William Shakespeare, and What He Hath Left Us. Ben Jonson. HeIP; OBP

To dream the impossible dream. The Impossible Dream. Joe Darion. BLSo

To drum-beat and heart-beat a soldier marches by. Nathan Hale. Francis Miles Finch. BTTM

To Earthward. Robert Frost. LoAs; NoAM; NOBA; PPoe

To Edward Williams. Shelley. MBPR

To Eliza, with a Tulip-fashioned Watch. Robert Baron. SCP-2

To Elsie. William Carlos Williams. InPS; NOBA

To Emily Dickinson. Hart Crane. NoAM; NOBA

To Emily Dickinson. Yvor Winters. PiAm

To end it all, the people elected a thumb. The Thumb. Dennis Saleh. MAT; NeAC

To enrich the earth I have sowed clover and grass. Enriching the Earth. Wendell Berry. PiAm

To Etesia Looking from Her Casement at the Full Moon. Henry Vaughan. Moon

To every animal who eats or shoots his own kind. Salute. Lawrence Ferlinghetti. MIT

To every man. The Treehouse. James A. Emanuel. BPo; PoBA

To everything. Turn! Turn! Turn! Pete Seeger. WIF

To Everything There Is a Season. Bible, *O. T. Fr.* Ecclesiastes. PBMP

To fair Fidele's grassy tomb. A Song from Shakespear's Cymbelyne. William Collins. LAuP; NOBE

To Fanny. Keats. LoAs
(I Cry Your Mercy.) BoLoP; LoAs; MBPR; PPP

To Fanny Brawne. Keats. *See* This Living Hand, Now Warm and Capable.

To feed the baby's quite a chore. High Chair and Low Spirits. Richard Armour. BBGO

To fight aloud is very brave. Emily Dickinson. WPE

To find, he'd like to say, the god. Star Quality. Chris Wallace-Crabbe. CAAP

To fling my arms wide. Dream Variation. Langston Hughes. MiP; NOBA; PiAm; PoBA

To Flood Stage Again. James Wright. NOBA; Prf

To Flossie. William Carlos Williams. TH

To Fool, or Knave. Ben Jonson. SoSe

To Ford Madox Ford in Heaven. William Carlos Williams. NoAM; NOBA

To Fortune on Buying a Ticket in the Irish Lottery. Samuel Taylor Coleridge. MBPR

To free me from domestic strife. At Hadleigh, Suffolk. *Unknown.* FaBoCo

To freight cars in the air. The Descent of Winter (Section 10/30). William Carlos Williams. InPK

To Frighten a Storm. Gladys Cardiff. CDW

To G. A. W. Keats. MBPR

To gallop horses (or eat buns). Poem about a Poem about a Poem. Robert Conquest. WIF

To George Felton Mathew. Keats. MBPR

To George Sand. Elizabeth Barrett Browning. SBG

To God: to illuminate all men. Beginning with Skid Road. Psalm III. Allen Ginsberg. CAPP

To H. C. Wordsworth. MBPR

To Harriet ("Harriet! thy kiss to my soul is dear"). Shelley. MBPR

To Harriett ("Thy look of love has power to calm"). Shelley. MBPR

To have found at last that noble, candid speech. William Butler Yeats. A. D. Hope. MAuV

To have gold in your back yard and not know it. Tom O' Bedlam among the Sunflowers. Thomas James. HeS

To have stepped lightly among European marbles. Hark Back. Richard Eberhart. TH

To Heaven. Ben Jonson. PPoe

To Helen ("Helen, thy beauty is to me"). Poe. AmVN; BoLoP; GBL; HeIP; InPS; NOBA; PAIC; PBMP; PiAm; WIF

To Helen (of Troy, N.Y.). Peter Viereck. CoPAm

To Hell With Your Fertility Cult. Gary Snyder. PPoD

To Henrietta, on Her Departure for Calais. Thomas Hood. OxBChV

To Her Dead Mate: Montana, 1966. Elizabeth Libbey. AmPA

To him who in the love of Nature holds. Thanatopsis. Bryant. AmVN; NOBA; PiAm; VoPo

To His Child. William Bullokar. OxBChV

To His Coy Love. Michael Drayton. LoAs

To His Coy Mistress. Andrew Marvell. AnMo; BoLoP; Epi; GBL; HeIP; InPK; InPS; IPWM; LoAs; MAT; MetP; NOBE; OBP; PAIC; PBMP; PPoD; PPoe; PPP; SCP-1; SoSe; VoPo; WIF

To His Dead Body. Siegfried Sassoon. NoAM

To His Excellency George Washington. Phillis Wheatley. OFD; SBG; WPE

To His Little Son Benedict from the Tower of London. John Hoskyns. OxBChV

To His Love. *Unknown.* GBL

To His Lute. Sir Thomas Wyatt. *See* Lover Complaineth the Unkindness...

To His Mistress. James Graham, Marquess of Montrose. *See* I'll Never Love Thee More.

To His Mistress [*or* Maistres]. Alexander Montgomerie. GBL; SLP

To His Mistress ("Your husband will be with us at the treat"). Ovid, *tr. fr. Latin by* Dryden. BoLoP

To His Mistress. Earl of Rochester. LoAs

To His Mistress Desiring to Travel with Him As His Page. John Donne. *See* On His Mistress.

To His Mistress Going to Bed. John Donne. *See* Going to Bed.

To His Mistresse. Robert Herrick. OFD

To His Mistresses. Robert Herrick. LoAs

To His Mistris Going to Bed. John Donne. *See* Going to Bed.

To His Son. Sir Walter Ralegh. InPS; PPoe

To His Son, Vincent Corbet. Richard Corbet. OxBChV

To His Watch When He Could Not Sleep. Lord Herbert of Cherbury. NOBE

To Homer. Keats. MBPR

To Hope. Keats. MBPR

To hurt the Negro and avoid the Jew. University. Karl Shapiro. NowV

To Ianthe ("Past ruined Ilion Helen lives"). Walter Savage Landor. *See* Past Ruined Ilion...

To Inez Milholland. Edna St. Vincent Millay. WPE

To Insure Survival. Simon J. Ortiz. CDW

To interpret the wood you first must fall. The Fables. David Malouf. CAAP

To Ireland in the Coming Times. W. B. Yeats. NoAM

To J. H. Reynolds, Esq. Keats. MBPR

To James. Frank Horne. *Fr.* Letters Found Near a Suicide. BPo; PAIC

To Jane: the Invitation. Shelley. MBPR

To Jane: the Recollection. Shelley. MBPR

To Jesus on His Birthday. Edna St. Vincent Millay. VoPo

To Joanna. Wordsworth. MBPR

To John I ow'd great obligation. Epigram. Matthew Prior. FaBoCo

To Juan at the Winter Solstice. Robert Graves. NoAM; OBP

To Kate, Skating Better Than Her Date. David Daiches. CTBA; SPo

To Keep a True Lent. Robert Herrick. BoReV (True Lent, A.) OFD

To Keep the Cold Wind Away. *Unknown.* OxBM

To keep your marriage brimming. A Word to Husbands. Ogden Nash. POL

To Know Whom One Shall Marry. *Unknown.* GBP

To Kosciusko. Keats. MBPR

To L. Julianne Perry. PoBA

To Lake Aghmoogenegamook. The American Traveller. "Orpheus C. Kerr." FaBoCo

To Laura Phelan: 1880-1906. Leon Stokesbury. NVAP

To Leonard and Kerstin, With a Gift of Books. Alberta Turner. HeS

To Lindsay. Allen Ginsberg. ConAP

To live illusionless, in the abandoned mine. Double Monologue. Adrienne Rich. Psy

To live in/ myself. Drifting. Kathleen Spivack. IHMS

To live in hell, and heaven to behold. Henry Constable. *Fr.* Diana AAS

To live in Wales is to be conscious. Welsh Landscape. R. S. Thomas. LP; MPO

To live's a gift, to dye's a debt that we. The Porch. Philip Pain. PiAm

To London once my stepps I bent. London Lickpenny. *Unknown.* OxBM

To Look at Any Thing. John Moffitt. RFM; SFF

To loosen with all ten fingers held wide and limber. Moss-Gathering. Theodore Roethke. PiAm; RFM; VGW

To Lord Byron. Keats. MBPR

To lordings proud I tune my lay. Duke upon Duke. Pope. Epi

To Lucasta, [on] Going to the Wars. Richard Lovelace. BuTh; GBL; HeIP; InPK; InPS; NOBE; OBP; PBMP; SoSe; WIF (Going to the Wars.) VoPo

To Luve Unluvit. Alexander Scott. SLP

To make a final conquest of all me. The Fair Singer. Andrew Marvell. LoAs; NOBE

To make a juju of my own. A Juju of My Own. Lebert Bethune. InPS; PoBA

To Make a Play. May Swenson. Psy

To make a prairie it takes a clover and one bee. Emily Dickinson. ANTL; HeIP

To make a start. Preface. William Carlos Williams. *Fr.* Paterson. NoAM; NOBA

To Margaret. Gerard Manley Hopkins. BbGO

To Margot Heinemann. John Cornford. *See* Huesca.

To Marguerite ("Yes! in the sea enisled"). Matthew Arnold. *Fr.* Switzerland. NOBE
(To Marguerite—Continued.) BoLoP; PFD; PPP

To Maria Gisborne in England, from Italy. Shelley. *Fr.* Letter to Maria Gisborne. NOBE

To Mark Anthony in Heaven. William Carlos Williams. NOBA

To market, to market/ To buy a plum cake. Mother Goose. MG

To market, to market, to buy a fat pig. Mother Goose. MG

To Mary. William Cowper. LAuP; PAIC

To Mary: I Sleep with Thee, and Wake with Thee. John Clare. GBL

To Mary: It Is the Evening Hour. John Clare. BoLoP; GBL

To Mary Wollstonecraft Godwin. Shelley. MBPR

To Master George Sandys, Treasurer for the English Colony in Virginia, *sel.* Michael Drayton.
"As if to symptoms we may credit give." SCP-2

To Maystres Isabell Pennell. John Skelton. *See* To Mistress Isabel Pennell.

To Maystres Jane Blenner-Haiset. John Skelton. *Fr.* The Garlande of Laurell. AAS

To Maystres Margaret Hussey. John Skelton. *See* To Mistress Margaret Hussey.

To me, fair friend, you never can be old. Sonnets, CIV. Shakespeare. GBL; HeIP; LoAs; Prf

To me, one silly task is like another. Cassandra. Louise Bogan. RiTi; SBG; VGW

To Meadows. Robert Herrick. NOBE

To Meath of the pastures. A Drover. Padraic Colum. PFIr

To Melancholy. Countess of Winchelsea. WPE

To Mercy, Pity, Peace, and Love. The Divine Image. Blake. *Fr.* Songs of Innocence. BoReV; LAuP; MBPR; NOBE; PPP

To Minerva. Thomas Hood. FaBoCo

To Minnie. Robert Louis Stevenson. SLP

To Miss Laetitia Van Lewen. Constantia Grierson. WPE

To Mr. Cyriac Skinner upon His Blindness. Milton. SCP-1

To Mr. Edward Howard, on His Plays. Charles Sackville. ESaP

To Mr. Henry Lawes. Katherine Philips. SBG; WPE

To Mr. Murray. Byron. FaBoCo

To Mr. Rowland Woodward. John Donne. PAIC

To Mistress [*or* Maystres] Isabel[l] Pennell. John Skelton. *Fr.* The Garlande of Laurell. AAS; NOBE; RRA

To Mrs. Magdalen Herbert, *sel.* John Donne.
"Mad paper, stay! and grudge not here to burn." SCP-1

To Mistress [*or* Maystres] Margaret Hussey. John Skelton. *Fr.* The Garlande of Laurell. AAS; HeIP; LoAs; NOBE; PAIC; PPoe; PPP

To Mistress Margery Wentworth. John Skelton. *Fr.* The Garlande of Laurell. NOBE

To Mrs. Reynolds's Cat. Keats. *See* To a Cat.

To Mother. Frank Horne. *Fr.* Letters Found near a Suicide. BPo

To Mother and Steve. Mari Evans. BPo; PoBA; Psy

To Music, to Becalm a Sweet-Sick Youth. Robert Herrick. SCP-1

To musicke bent is my retyred minde. Thomas Campion. AAS

To My Admired and Soul-loved Friend, Master of All Essentials and True Knowledge, Mr. Harriots, *sel.* George Chapman.
"To you, whose depth of soul measures the height." SCP-2

To My Brother George ("Full many a dreary hour have I past"). Keats. MBPR

To My Brother George ("Many the wonders I this day have seen"). Keats. MBPR

To My Brother Miguel: In Memoriam. César Vallejo, *tr. fr.* Spanish by John Knoepfle *and* James Wright. MiP

To my Brothers. Keats. MBPR

To My Cat. Rosamund Marriott Watson. PCat

To My Daughter. Walter Savage Landor. RRA

To My Daughter. Stephen Spender. RRA

To My Dear and Loving Husband. Anne Bradstreet HeIP; NOBA; PiAm; SBG; VoPo; WPE

To My Excellent Lucasia, on Our Friendship. Katherine Philips. SBG; SCP-2; WPE

To My Father on Pearl Harbor Day. D. W. Donzella. FAF

To My Former Student on the Occasion of Birth. Madeline Bass. WBN

To My Friend. Wilfred Owen. OBP

To My Friend Whose Parachute Did Not Open. David Wagoner. SFF

To My Gingerbread Mistress, *sel.* Samuel Wesley.
"Dear miss, not with a lie to cheat ye." SCP-2

To My Inconstant Mistris[s]. Thomas Carew. MetP; NOBE
(Song: To My Inconstant Mistress.) GBL

To My Infant Daughter: "Alas, that I should be." Yvor Winters. VGW

To My Most Dearly Loved Henry Reynolds, *sel.* Michael Drayton.
First Steps Up Parnassus. NOBE

To My Mother. George Barker. LP; NCSH; OxBTC

To My Mountain. Kathleen Raine. SLP

To My Ninth Decade. Walter Savage Landor. PAIC

To My Noble Friend Master William Browne: of the Evil Time, *sels.* Michael Drayton. SCP-2
"As men oft laugh at little babes when they."
"Dear friend, be silent and with patience see."
"Into the clouds the devil lately got."
"This world of ours thus runneth upon wheels."

To My Old Schoolmaster. Whittier. NOBA

To my people it's as though he gave them a sacrifice. Eadwacer. *Unknown.* WPE

To My Sister. David Kherdian. SA

To My Sister. Wordsworth. LoAs
(Lines Written at a Small Distance from My House.) MBPR
"It is the first mild day of March," *sel.* FSFS

To My Son. Margaret Johnston Griffin. SoSe

To My Son Parker, Asleep in the Next Room. Bob Kaufman. PoBA; VGW

To My Soul in Its Blindness. Phineas Fletcher. SCP-2

To my true king I offered free from stain. A Jacobite's Epitaph. Macaulay. NOBE

To my twin who lives in a cruel country. The Dual Site. Michael Hamburger. AIW; NowV

To My Valentine. *Unknown.* ECBV

To My Wife. Edwin Brock. BuTh

To My Wife. J. V. Cunningham. PiAm

To My Wife. Jack Simcock. BuTh

To My Youngest Kinsman, R. L. Abraham Chear. OxBChV

To Myself, Late, in a Myrtle Grove. Robert Peterson. NeAC

To Nature. Samuel Taylor Coleridge. MBPR

To Ned. Herman Melville. NOBA

To Night. Shelley. MBPR

To Night. *Unknown.* Moon

To Night. Joseph Blanco White. SoSe

To no longer taste like the taste of whiskey. Safe Flights. Barbara Guest. RiTi

To no one Muse does she her glance confine. On a Squinting Poetess. Thomas Moore. FaBoCo

To Nobodaddy. Blake. MBPR

To Nowhere. David Ignatow. NCSH

To O. E. A. Claude McKay. BPo

To Oliver Cromwell. Milton. *See* To the Lord General Cromwell.

To One in Paradise. Poe. BoLoP; PiAm

To One Who Has Been Long in City Pent. Keats. MBPR; VoPo

To onpreise womene it were a shame. A Woman Is a Worthy Thing. *Unknown.* FaBoCo

To Our House-Dog Captain. Walter Savage Landor. OBP

To our ruined vineyard come. Love Song for the Future. Vassar Miller. NCSH

To our theme—The man who has stood on the Acropolis. Byron. *Fr.* Don Juan, XI. InPS

To Penshurst. Ben Jonson. PAIC; PPP; SCP-1, *abr.*; TVS

To Persuade a Lady. Michael Benedikt. CAAP

To Phillis to Love, and Live with Him. Robert Herrick. LoAs

To Philocles [*or* Phylocles], Inviting Him to Friendship. "Ephelia." SCP-2; WPE

To Phoebe. W. S. Gilbert. OLR; WIF

To Ping-Ku, Asleep. Lawrence Durrell. RRA

To Poem. Lyn Lifshin. NeAC; Psy

To prinke me up and make me higher plaste. George Gascoigne. AAS

To print, or not to print—that is the question. Hamlet's Soliloquy Imitated. Richard Jago. FaBoCo

To Pyrrha ("Quis multa gracilis"). Horace, *tr. fr. Latin by* Milton. Odes, I, 5. LoAs
("What slender youth bedewed with liquid odours") SCP-1

To R——Before Leaving to Fight in Unknown Terrain. Nina Serrano. MIT

To R. K. James Kenneth Stephen. FaBoCo

To Rail or Jest, Ye Know I Use It Not. Sir Thomas Wyatt. Epi

To Redistort a Weltanschauung. Matthew Mead. TwMBP

To Remain. C. P. Cavafy, *tr. fr. Greek by* Nikos Stangos *and* Stephen Spender. BoLoP

To Richard Boyle, Earl of Burlington: Of the Use of Riches. Pope. Moral Essays, Epistle IV. PPP

To Richard Wright. Conrad Kent Rivers. PoBA

To Roses in the Bosom of Castara. William Habington. SCP-2

To S. R. Crockett. Robert Louis Stevenson. NOBE

To Satch. Samuel Allen. CTBA; PoBA; SoSe; SPo (American Gothic.) BuTh

To save your world, you asked this man to die. Epitaph for the Unknown Soldier. W. H. Auden. FaBoCo

To Scotland came the tall American. Black Tomintoul. Ian Hamilton Finlay. SLP

To see a world in a grain of sand. Auguries of Innocence. Blake. InPK; LAuP; MBPR; OBP; PPoe; VoPo

To see both blended in one flood. Upon the Infant Martyrs. Richard Crashaw. PAIC

To See Him Again. Gabriela Mistral, *tr. fr. Spanish by* Doris Dana. OLR

To shoot, to shoot, would be my delight. A Shooting Song. William Brighty Rands. OxBChV

To shred them: a narrow labor, and simply toss. Destruction of Letters. Babette Deutsch. WPE

To Sidmouth and Castlereagh. Shelley. *See* Similes for Two Political Characters of 1819.

To Simplicity. Samuel Taylor Coleridge. *Fr.* Sonnets Attempted in the Manner of Contemporary Writers. Epi

To sing of wars, of captains [*or* captaines], and of kings. The Prologue. Anne Bradstreet. NOBA; SBG; WPE

To Sing the People. Lucille F. Travis. AATT

To Sir Henry Wotton ("Here's no more news than virtue"). John Donne. PAIC

To Sir Henry Wotton ("Sir, more than kisses letters mingle souls.") John Donne. TVS

To Sir Robert Wroth. Ben Jonson. TVS
"How bless'd art thou canst love the country, Wroth," *sel.* SCP-1

To Sleep. Keats. MBPR; OBP

To Sleep Sir Philip Sidney. *See* Astrophel and Stella, Sonnets, XXXIX.

To Sleep. Charlotte Smith. WPE

To Sleep. Wordsworth. MPBR

To Soar in Freedom and in Fullness of Power. Walt Whitman. RFM

To So-kin of Rakuyo, ancient friend, Chancellor of Gen. Exile's Letter. Li Po, *tr. by* Ezra Pound. TCP

To Some Ladies. Keats. MBPR

To Some Millions Who Survive Joseph E. Mander, Sr. Sarah E. Wright. PoBA

To speak in summer in a lecture hall. Lecture Hall. Patrick Kavanagh. NoAM

To speak of death is to deny it, is. Consolatio Nova: for Alan Swallow. J. V. Cunningham. PiAm

To speak of my influences. Jean Garrigue. LoAs

"To Speak of Woe That Is in Marriage." Robert Lowell. CAPP; NoAM

To speke of an unkinde man. Adrian and Bardus. John Gower. *Fr.* Confessio Amantis, V. OxBM

To Spring. Blake. LAuP; MBPR; PPP

To Spring. Charlotte Smith. WPE

To start the world of old. It Is Almost the Year Two Thousand. Robert Frost. TH

To Start With. J. S. Harry. CAAP

To steal from those that steal from you. Raffaele Minichiello. Sandra McPherson. CAAP

To stub an oar on a rock where none should be. Basking Shark. Norman MacCaig. BoAnP

To Summer. Blake. LAuP; MBPR

To Sylvia. An Imitation of Anacreon. *Unknown.* PiAm

To take the big gamble, leave the church. La Divina Commedia. David Malouf. CAAP

To tell the truth, I really am. The All-Night Waitress. Maura Stanton. AmPA

To the Accuser Who Is the God of This World. Blake. OBP

To the Age's Insanities. Marie Ponsot. VGW

To the Anxious Mother. Valente Malangatana, *tr. fr. Portuguese by* Dorothy Guedes *and* Philippa Rumsey. BBGO

To the Cambro-Britons and Their Harp, His Ballad of Agincourt. Michael Drayton. *See* Ballad of Agincourt, The.

To the Countess of Bedford ("Reason is our soul's left hand"). John Donne. PAIC
"Honour is so sublime perfection," *sel.* SCP-1

To the Countess of Salisbury, *sel.* John Donne.
"Fair, great, and good: since seeing you we see." SCP-1

To the Cuckoo. Wordsworth. MBPR

To the Daisy ("Sweet flower! belike one day to have"). Wordsworth. MBPR

To the Detractor. Robert Herrick. SCP-1

To the dim light and the large circle of shade. Sestina of the Lady Pietra degli Scrovigni. Dante, *tr. by* Dante Gabriel Rossetti. LoAs

To the edge of Europe, the eighteenth edge. John Berryman. *Fr.* Dream Songs. RRA

To the Evening Star. Blake. LAuP; MBPR; PPP

To the Fair Clarinda, Who Made Love to Me, Imagin'd More than Woman. Aphra Behn. SBG

To the Field Mice. Richard Eberhart. BoAnP

To the Film Industry in Crisis. Frank O'Hara. CAPP; NoAM; NOBA

To the Four Courts, Please. James Stephens. BIrV; PFIr

To the Fringed Gentian. Bryant. FSFS; PiAm

To the Garden the World. Walt Whitman. AmVN; GrRo

To the Ghost of Martial Ben Jonson. PAIC

To the Governor & Legislature of Massachusetts. Howard Nemerov. PPoD

To the hard-working miner whose dangers are great. The Hard-working Miner. *Unknown.* AmFP

To the Heart. Tadeusz Rozewicz, *tr. fr. Polish by* Victor Contoski. POL

To the Holy Spirit. Yvor Winters. PiAm; VGW

To the Immortal Memory and Friendship of That Noble Pair, Sir Lucius Cary and Sir Henry Morison. Ben Jonson. NOBE; PAIC
     *Sel.*
     Noble Nature, The, *sel.* VoPo
     ("It is not growing like a tree.") SoSe

To the Jews. Blake. *Fr.* Jerusalem MBPR

To the King, upon His Majesty's Happy Return, *sel.* Edmund Waller.
     "Rising sun complies with our weak sight, The." SCP-2

To the Ladies. Mary Lee, Lady Chudleigh. WPE

To the Ladies Who Saw Me Crown'd. Keats. MBPR

To the Lady May. Aurelian Townsend. GBL

To the Lairds o' Convention 'twas Claverhouse spoke. *See* To the Lords o' Convention...

To the legion of the lost ones, to the cohort of the damned. Gentlemen-Rankers. Kipling. BTTM

To the Lord Chancellor. Shelley. MBPR

To the Lord General Cromwell, May 1652. Milton. Epi
     (To Oliver Cromwell.) GBP

To the Lords [*or* Lairds] o' Convention 'twas Claverhouse [who] spoke. Bonnie Dundee. Sir Walter Scott. *Fr.* The Doom of Devergoil. BTTM; RDB

To the Man I Live With. Ann Menebroker. IHMS

To the Man-of-War Bird. Walt Whitman. BoAnP

To the Man Who Sidled Up to Me and Asked: "How Long You in fer, Buddy?" Etheridge Knight. NeAC

To the Memory of Lord Halifax, *sel.* Ambrose Philips.
     "Weeping o'er the sacred urn." FaBoCo

To the Memory of Mr. Oldham. Dryden. HeIP; InPK; InPS; NOBE; PAIC; PPoe; PPP; Prf

To the Memory of My Beloved, the Author, Mr. William Shakespeare, and What He Hath Left Us. Ben Jonson. HeIP; OBP
     "I, therefore, will begin. Soul of the age!" NOBE

To the Men of Kent. October, 1803. Wordsworth. MBPR

To the Men Who Hold the Line. W. F. Barron. SPo

To the Mocking Bird. Richard Henry Wilde. BoAnP

To the Moon. George Darley. Moon

To the Moon. Babette Deutsch. Moon

To the Moon. Goethe, *tr. fr. German by* John Frederick Nims. Moon

To the Moon. Shelley. MBPR; Moon; PBMP; PPP

To the Moon. Charlotte Smith. Moon

To the Moon. Yvor Winters. HeIP

To the Moon and Back. William Plomer. Moon

To the Most Excellent and Learned Shepheard Collin Cloute. William Smith. Chloris: Dedication. AAS

To the Most Fair and Lovely Mistress Anne Soame, Now Lady Abdie. Robert Herrick. NOBE

To the Mother from Scarsdale Who Asked About Publishing Her Daughter's Poems. Madeline Bass. WBN

To the much-tossed Ulysses, never done. Ulysses. Robert Graves. NoAM

To the Muses. Blake. HeIP; LAuP; MBPR; NOBE

To the New Annex to the Detroit County Jail. Richard W. Thomas. PoBA

To the Nightingale. Samuel Taylor Coleridge. MBPR

To the Nightingale. Countess of Winchilsea. PAIC; SBG; WPE

To the Nile. Keats. MBPR

To the Noble Sir Francis Drake. Thomas Beedome. SCP-2

To the Noblest and Best of Ladies [*or* Ladyes], the Countess of Denbigh. Richard Crashaw. MetP
     (Letter to the Countess of Denbigh against Irresolution and Delay in Matters of Religion, A.) BoReV
     "Astonished nymphs their flood's strange fate deplore, The." *sel.* OBP

To the north-east/ is the park of Mousseaux. Found Poem with Grafts 1866. Christopher Middleton. TwMBP

To the ocean now I fly. The Spirit Epiloguizes. Milton. *Fr.* Comus. NOBE

To the Other Side. T. Alan Broughton. FAF

To the Pious Memory of the Accomplished Young Lady Mrs. Anne Killigrew. Dryden. SCP-1

To the Reader. Baudelaire, *tr. fr. French by* Roy Campbell. GrRo

To the Reader. Edgar Bowers. PiAm

To the Reader. J. V. Cunningham. NoAM

To the Reader. Denise Levertov. VGW

To the Reader of These Sonnets. Michael Drayton. Idea, *introd.* AAS

To the Republicans of North America. Shelley. MBPR

To the Rev. W.L. Bowles, 2 *versions.* Samuel Taylor Coleridge. MBPR

To the Rt. Hon. the Lady C. Tufton. Countess of Winchilsea. SBG

To the Right Honourable the Lord High Treasurer. Ben Jonson. SCP-1

To the Right Honourable William, Earl of Dartmouth. Phillis Wheatley. SBG
     "Should you, my lord, while you pursue my song," *sel.* BPo

To the Rose upon the Rood of Time. W. B. Yeats. NoAM

To the Sad Moon. Sir Philip Sidney. *See* Astrophel and Stella, Sonnets, XXXI.

To the Same Flower. Wordsworth. MBPR

To the Sea. *Unknown, tr. fr. Anglo-Saxon by* Burton Raffel. *Fr.* Beowulf. OBP

To the Small Celandine. Wordsworth. MBPR

To the Snake. Denise Levertov. NMM; Psy; SFF

To the Snipe. John Clare. Epi

To the Spirit of Carlos Gardel. Victor Hernández Cruz. SA

To the State of Love, or the Senses' Festival. John Cleveland. SCP-2

To the Stone-Cutters. Robinson Jeffers. NOBA; PiAm

To the suburban house you return again. Portrait of a Marriage. Dannie Abse. NoAM

To the Thoughtful Reader. William Meredith. NoAM

To the University of Cambridge, in New-England. Phillis Wheatley. SBG

To the Upright. Stephen Dunn. NVAP

To the Veterans of the Abraham Lincoln Brigade. Genevieve Taggard. OFD

To the Virginian Voyage. Michael Drayton. Epi; NOBE

To the Virgins, to Make Much of Time. Robert Herrick. AnMo; BoLoP; GBL; HeIP; InPK; InPS; IPWM; NOBE; OLR; PAIC; PBMP; PPoe; SFF; SoSe; SpRo
     (Counsel to Girls, *st.* 1) AKE

To the Western World. Louis Simpson. ConAP; CoPAm; NOBA

To the White Critics. Carolyn M. Rodgers. SA

To the White Fiends. Claude McKay. PoBA

To the Wife of a Sick Friend. Edna St. Vincent Millay. SBG

To the Work, *with music.* Fanny Crosby. BLSH

To thee, fair freedom! I retire. Written at an Inn at Henley. William Shenstone. NOBE

To Theodora. *Unknown.* OxBChV

To Theon from His Son Theon. C. A. Trypanis. NCSH

To these whom death again did wed. An Epitaph upon Husband and Wife Who Died and Were Buried Together. Richard Crashaw. NOBE

To those who know the Lord I speak. Hymn. William Cowper. PAIC

To Tirzah. Blake. *Fr.* Songs of Experience. BoReV; MBPR; NOBE

To Toussaint L'Ouverture. Wordsworth. InPK; MBPR; NOBE; OBP; PBMP; PPP

To Turn Back. John Haines. ConAP

To Understand/ each other: anything. Their Attitudes Differ. Margaret Atwood. Psy

To V. S. Christopher Brennan. MAuV

To Vesta. Thomas Middleton. Moon

To Vietnam. Charlie Cobb. PoBA

To Vineyarders in cold Korea. Pinkletinks. Grace Elisabeth Allen. ECBV

To W. T. Scott. John Ciardi. NowV

To wade the Jordan, and not to believe! In Jerusalem. Elisavietta Ritchie. AATT

To Waken an Old Lady. William Carlos Williams. InPK; PSN

To western woods, and lonely plains. On the Emigration to America. Philip Freneau. PiAm

To what purpose, April, do you return again? Spring. Edna St. Vincent Millay. BuTh

To What Strangers, What Welcome. J. V. Cunningham. NoAM *Sels.*
    "Half hour for coffee, and at night, A," X. PiAm
    "Identity, that spectator," XV. PiAm
    "Innocent to innocent," IX. PiAm
    "Night is still, The. The unfailing surf," VIII. PiAm

To whom I owe the leaping delight. A Dedication to My Wife. T. S. Eliot. BoLoP

To whom none ever said scat. Epitaph for Bathsheba. Whittier. PCat

To William Hayley. Blake. FaBoCo

To William Wordsworth. Samuel Taylor Coleridge. MBPR

To William Wordsworth from Virginia. Julia Randall. NMM; WPE

To Wilt Chamberlain. Tom Meschery. SPo

To Winter. Blake. MBPR

To Women, as Far as I'm Concerned. D. H. Lawrence. InPS

To Wordsworth. Shelley. MBPR

To write in verse has been my pleasing choice. To the Rt. Hon. the Lady C. Tufton. Countess of Winchilsea. SBG

To X. Tom Scott. SLP

To You. Frank Horne. *Fr.* Letters Found near a Suicide. BPo

To You. Kenneth Koch. CAPP

To you I'll sing a good old song. Ye Ancient Yuba Miner of the Days of '49. Samuel C. Upham. AIW

To you [*or* yow], my purse, and to none other wight. The Complaint of Chaucer to His Purse. Chaucer. InPK; OxBM; PAIC; PPoD

To you, whose depth of soul measures the height. George Chapman. *Fr.* To My Admired and Soul-loved Friend, Master of All Essentials and True Knowledge, Mr. Harriots. SCP-2

To your left is the Gettysburg Address engraved on a medalion. Lecture before a Lecture on Pushkin. George M. Young, Jr. FAF

To Your Question. Duane Niatum. CDW

To youths, who hurry thus away. On a Painted Woman. Shelley. FaBoCo

Toad. John Cotton. BoAnP

Toad-Eater, The. Burns. POL

Toad School. Merle Meeter. AATT

Toad the power mower caught, A. The Death of a Toad. Richard Wilbur. AnMo; NoAM

Toads. Philip Larkin. NoAM; OxBTC

Tobacco. Robert Harris. CAAP

Toccata of Galuppi's, A. Robert Browning. NOBE; PAIC

Today. Langston Hughes. VGW

Today. Liz Lochhead. SLP

Today! Ella Wheeler Wilcox. SoSe

Today/ I am 24. January 3, 1970. Mae Jackson. PoBA

Today/I lost my temper. For Witches. Susan Sutheim. NMM

To-day, all day, I rode upon the Down. St. Valentine's Day. Wilfred Scawen Blunt. *Fr.* The Love Sonnets of Proteus. LoAs

Today as I passed through the market-place. A Sonnet Sequence, VIII. Robert Hillyer. TH

Today as well there seems to be something unfilled. A Transparent Autumn. Sadamu Fujiwara, *tr. by* Ichiro Kono *and* Rikutaro Fukuda. IPWM

Today at the Gateway. Butter. Tom Schmidt. NeAC

Today, autumn. The Fire of Despair Has Been Our Saviour. Robert Bly. CoPAm

Today between skirmishes. For Alan Blanchard. John Oliver Simon. NeAC

To-day, Cheng, I touched your face. The Prisoner. Keith Douglas. PSN

Today I am walking alone in a bare place. Late November in a Field. James Wright. CAPP

Today I have seen all I wish. At the Water Zoo. E. V. Knox. BoAnP

Today I love you so much I mistrust you. Fish and Swimmers and Lonely Birds Sweep Past Us. Mei Berssenbrugge. SA

Today I saw a woman wrapped in rags. At the Slackening of the Tide. James Wright. VGW

To-day I think. Digging. Edward Thomas. FSFS; OxBTC

Today I trade my last unwise. How It Goes On. Maxine W. Kumin. FiCP

Today I'll remember forever and ever. Counting. Harry Behn. ECBV

Today in Peru, this first day of summer. Pastoral. Lawrence Raab. AmPA

Today is a Day of Great Joy  Victor Hernandez Cruz. WIF

Today on the lip of a bowl in the backyard. The Caterpillar. Miller Williams. CoPAm

Today the birds are singing and. Pray in May. James J. Metcalfe. SoSe

Today the jailbird maple in the yard. For My Son on the Highways of His Mind. Maxine W. Kumin. CoPAm; MAT

Today the leaves cry, hanging on branches swept by wind. The Course of a Particular. Wallace Stevens. PPoe

To-day the lot caved in upon me. Page from a Diary. Desmond O'Grady. NoAM

To-day the woods are trembling through and through. Corn. Sidney Lanier. AmVN

Today they cut down the oak. The Stump. Donald Hall. MiP

To-day we have naming of parts. Yesterday. Naming of Parts. Henry Reed. Lessons of the War, I. HeIP; InPK; InPS; MPo; NOBE; OxBTC; PPoD; SoSe; VoPo; WIF

Today We've Moved. Jim Harrison. HeS

Tod's Hole, The. *Unknown.* GBP

Toe upon toe, a snowing flesh. Nude Descending a Staircase. X. J. Kennedy. ConAP; HeIP; POL; PPoD; WIF

Toe'osh: A Laguna Coyote Story. Leslie Silko. CDW

Together. Maxine W. Kumin. NMM; WBN

Toilet, The. Pope. *Fr.* The Rape of the Lock, I. NOBE

Token, A. Robert Creeley. VGW

Token, The. F. T. Prince. OxBTC

Tokens of Love, The ("I had four brothers over the sea"). *Unknown.* GBP

Tokens of Love, The ("I have a yong suster"). *Unknown. See* I Have a Young Sister.

Told me and told me. Where It's At. Carol Bergé. MMD

Toll for the brave. On the Loss of the Royal George. William Cowper. NOBE

Toll no bell for me, dear Father, dear Mother. The Changeling. Charlotte Mew. SoSe

Tollund Man, The. Seamus Heaney. BIrV

Tom Dooley. *Unknown.* AmFP; BLSo;*with music*

Tom, He Was a Piper's Son. *Unknown.* GBP; MG

Tom Jones's Plum Tree. *Unknown.* AmFP

Tom Matte. Ogden Nash. SPo

Tom O' Bedlam among the Sunflowers. Thomas James. HeS

Tom o' Bedlam's Song. *Unknown.* Moon; OBP (Loving Mad Tom.) NOBE

Tom, Tom, the piper's son. Mother Goose. MG

Tomb of Heracles, The. James McAuley. *Fr.* The Hero and the Hydra. MAuV

Tomb of Lieutenant John Learmonth, A. I. F., The. J. S. Manifold. MAuV

Tomb of Time, The. Albert Howard Carter. AATT

Tombstone told when she died, The. Dylan Thomas. OxBTC

Tom-Cat, The. Don Marquis. BoAnP; SS

Tommy. Kipling. BTTM; OxBTC

To-morowe ye shall on hunting fare. Diversions for an Unhappy Princess. *Unknown. Fr.* The Squyer of Lowe Degre. OxBM

Tomorrow afternoon. The Tragedy of Action. Dan Gerber. HeS

Tomorrow dawn that gathers up the night. The Tramp. Rayne Mackinnon. MIS

Tomorrow Is Saint Valentine's Day. Shakespeare. *Fr.* Hamlet, IV, v. LCL; OFD; WIF

Tomorrow let loveless, let lover tomorrow make love. The Vigil of Venus. *Unknown, tr. by* Allen Tate. GBL

"Tomorrow morn I'll be sixteen, and Billy Grimes the rover." Billy Grimes. *Unknown.* AmFP

Tomorrow morning, some poet will wake up. Modern Poetry. Anita Skeen. IHMS

Tomorrow the Heroes. A. B. Spellman. PoBA

To-Morrow's the Fair. *Unknown.* GBP

Tom's Angel. Walter de la Mare. AIW

Tonight. Iain Crichton Smith. SLP

Tonight/ the moon shines like a new ax. Everything Must Go. Tom Crawford. NVAP

Tonight a blackout. Twenty years ago. Christmas Eve under Hooker's Statue. Robert Lowell. CAPP; ConAP; PiAm

Tonight at Noon. Adrian Henri. MPo

Tonight, grave sir, both my poor house and I. Inviting a Friend to Supper. Ben Jonson, *after* Martial. NOBE; PPP; TVS

Tonight I am one of a number. Before the Frost. Harley Elliott. HeS

Tonight I can write the saddest line. Pablo Neruda, *tr. fr. Spanish by* W. S. Merwin. BoLoP; OLR

Tonight I could die as easily as the grass. In the Soul Hour. Robert Mezey. AmPA

Tonight I looked at the pale northern sky. Back. Robert Mezey. AmPA

Tonight I'll meet you: yes, tonight. I know. A Letter. Burns Singer. SLP

Tonight I've watched. Sappho, *tr. fr. Greek by* Mary Barnard. Moon

Tonight my children hunch. "It Out-Herods Herod. Pray You, Avoid It." Anthony Hecht. CoPAm; NCSH; NoAM; NOBA

Tonight Sally and I are making stuffed grapeleaves. Leaves. Sam Hamod. SA

Tonight, the barn is sitting under the rain. Exit, Pursued by a Bear. James Tipton. HeS

Tonight the brittle trees. Cold. Glyn Hughes. LP

Tonight the Famous Psychiatrist. Louis Simpson. SFF

To-night the winds began to rise. In Memoriam A. H. H., XV. Tennyson. FSFS; NOBE

Tonight you are a hundred miles away. Tonight. Iain Crichton Smith. SLP

Tonight you broke into my dreams. For Anne, Who Doesn't Know. Gail Fox. IHMS

Tonite, thriller was. Beware: Do Not Read This Poem. Ishmael Reed. BPo; Epi; IPWM; NCSH; PoBA

Tony Get the Boys. D. L. Graham. PoBA

Tony O. Colin Francis. FaBoCo

Tony the Turtle. E. V. Rieu. ECBV

Too Blue. Langston Hughes. SFF

Too dense to have a door. The Haystack. Andrew Young. POL

Too elementary. Reply. Victoria McCabe. POL

Too green the springing April grass. Spring in New Hampshire. Claude McKay. BPo

Too green. Too green. Marijuana Patch on the State Hospital's Former Grounds. Nathan Whiting. HeS

Too happy time dissolves itself. Emily Dickinson. NOBA

Too late for love, too late for joy. Bride Song Christina Rossetti. *Fr.* The Prince's Progress. WPE

Too long outside your door I have shivered. The Terrible Door. Harold Monro. BoLoP

Too many fucking mosquitoes under the blazing sun. Sonnet. Ted Berrigan. CAAP

Too many people scribbling on each others' tongues. Peace Prospect. Daniela Gioseffi. RiTi

Too poor for a bribe, and too proud to importune. Sketch of His Own Character. Thomas Gray. LAuP

Too tight, it is running over. Fence Wire. James Dickey. VGW

Tooten Out Blues. *Unknown.* BluL

Tops of the spruces here have always done, The. Jefferson Valley. John Hollander. PPP

Topsy-Turvy World. William Brighty Rands. ECBV; OxBChV

Torch of love dispels the gloom, The. Walter Savage Landor. GBL

Tornado. William Stafford. AnMo

Torrent, A/ of cobalt bullets. Lacrimas or There Is a Need to Scream. K. Curtis Lyle. PoBA

Tortoise, The. Cid Corman. InPK; VGW

Tortoise. Joanne de Longchamps. BoAnP

Tortoise Gallantry. D. H. Lawrence. NoAM

Tortoise Shout. D. H. Lawrence. NoAM

Tortoiseshell Cat, The. Patrick Reginald Chalmers. BoAnP; PCat

Tory Pledges. Thomas Moore. FaBoCo

Tory Poets, The: a Satire, *sel. At. to* Thomas Shadwell. "Shadwell and Settle are both fools to Bays." SCP-2

Tossing loneliness of many nights, The. Legende. Hart Crane. PSN

Total loss/ by physical severance. Injury to Insured. John Daniel. TwMBP

Total Revolution, A. Oscar Williams. WIF

Totem. Léopold Sédar Senghor, *tr. fr. French by* Gerald Moore *and* Ulli Beier. BuTh

Touch. Thom Gunn. LoAs; MPo

Touch. Erica Jong. RiTi

Touch. Octavio Paz, *tr. fr. Spanish by* Charles Tomlinson. BoLoP

Touch/ is what the eyes do, sometimes. From a Brother Dreaming in the Rye. James Cunningham. JB

Touch it: it won't shrink like an eyeball. A Life. Sylvia Plath. NOBA

Touch my hand as though it were an old coin. Sailing in Crosslight. Anita Skeen. IHMS

Touch of cold in the autumn night, A. Autumn. T. E. Hulme. Moon; PAIC

Touching me, you touch. The Wind. Charles Simic. NVAP

Tough./ Precise./ You/ move/ like/ a cougar. Movement. Gary Lawless. FAF

Toughest gal I ever did see. Kissie Lee. Margaret Walker. NMM

Tour 5. Robert Hayden. PPP

Touring the Hawkeye State. Gary Gildner. HeS

Touris', white man, wipin' his face. Song of the Banana Man. Evan Jones. MPo

Tourist came in from Orbitville, A. Southbound on the Freeway. May Swenson. BBGO

Tourist from Syracuse, The. Donald Justice. CoPAm

Tourist, spare the avid glance. The Attic Landscape. Herman Melville. NOBA

Toussaint, the most unhappy man of men! To Toussaint L'Ouverture. Wordsworth. InPK; MBPR; NOBE; OBP; PBMP; PPP

Toward the last in the morning she could not. Old Dog. William Stafford. BoAnP

Towards nightfall when the wind. Winter Mask. Allen Tate. Prf

Towards the evening of her splendid day. The Fragment. Hilaire Belloc. POL

Towards the Noel that morte saison. Villonaud for This Yule. Ezra Pound. PAIC

Towards the poem/ as towards. Projections for an Eagle Escaped in This City, March 1965. Nathaniel Tarn. TwMBP

Towards the Source, *sel.* Christopher Brennan.
"Yellow gas is fired from street to street, The." MAuV

Tower, The. Philip Booth. PAIC

Tower, The. W. B. Yeats. NoAM

Tower of Babel, The. Nathaniel Crouch. OxBChV

Towery city and branchy between towers. Duns Scotus's Oxford. Gerard Manley Hopkins. Epi; NoAM; OBP

Town Against Gown at Oxford. Robert of Gloucester. *Fr.* Chronicle. OxBM

Town does not exist, The. The Starry Night. Anne Sexton. NoAM

Town Dump, The. Howard Nemerov. MAT

Town grew, as with the lime-pits, The. A History of the Father. Charles Buckmaster. CAAP

Town I Left. Helen Sorrells. IHMS

Town is tilted toward the stream, The. A Sunday Dreamer's Guide to Yarrow, Missouri. Jim Barnes. HeS

Town of Bricked Pathways, The. Roger McDonald. CAAP

Town of Hill, The. Donald Hall. FiCP

Town remembers no such plenty, The. Lancashire Winter. Tony Connor. OxBTC

Town, the churchyard, and the setting sun, The. On Visiting the Tomb of Burns. Keats. MBPR

Towser Shall Be Tied Tonight, *parody. Unknown.* BoAnP

Toyland, *with music* Glen MacDonough. BLSo; FSN

Toys, The. Coventry Patmore. *Fr.* The Unknown Eros, I, x. BoReV; PAIC; SoSe; VPC

Tracing Back. Jane Mayhall. WBN

Track-lining Song. *Unknown.* AmFP

Tracking Rabbits: Night. Jim Barnes. CDW

Tracks. Peter Cooley. HeS

Tracks in the snow. Photograph of the Back of My House. Del Marie Rogers. NPW

Tract. William Carlos Williams. MiP; NoAM; NOBA; PPoD; TCP; VGW

Traded by my father in a drunken rage. Poem to a Mule, Dead Twenty Years. Guy Owen. BoAnP; POL

Trader. Jim Harrison. NoAM

Traditional Grammarian As Poet, The. Ted Hipple. POL

Traditional Red. Robert Huff. CoPAm

Traffic glitters towards dull junction, The. Vincent Buckley. *Fr.* Golden Builders. CAAP

Tragedy, A. Theophile Marzials. PPoD

Tragedy of Action, The. Dan Gerber. HeS

Tragedy of the Leaves, The. Charles Bukowski. CoPAm

Tragedy of Valentinian, The, *sels.* John Fletcher.
Hear, Ye Ladies, *fr.* II, v. NOBE
Love's Emblems, *fr.* II, iv. BoLoP; NOBE

Tragic Story, A. Adelbert von Chamisso, *tr. fr. German by* Thackeray. ECBV

Tragical History of Doctor Faustus. Christopher Marlowe. *See* Doctor Faustus.

Trahison des Clercs; Against the Perversion of Language. Ezra Pound. PAIC

Trail All Your Pikes. Countess of Winchelsea. WPE

Trail climbing/ you have to watch your footing. Finding a Poem. Eve Merriam. RFM

Trail to Mexico, The. *Unknown.* AmFP

Trailing her father, bearing his hand axe. Goose. Richard Emil Braun. NoAM

Trailing My Balloon. Stephen Stepanchev. SA

Train,The. Alan Brownjohn. OxBTC

Train/ run off/ nine mile, The. Chain Gang Trouble. *Unknown.* BluL

Train: Abstraction. Genevieve Taggard. WPE

Train Is Off the Track, The. *Unknown.* AmFP

Train of Religion, The, *sel.* Martin Tupper.
"How beautiful their feet." FaBoCo

Train Ride. John Wheelwright. VGW

Train Runs Late to Harlem, The. Conrad Kent Rivers. PoBA

Train shot through the dark, The. Return. Seamus Deane. BIrV

Train Tune. Louise Bogan. ECBV

Train will come tomorrow year, The. The Train. Alan Brownjohn. OxBTC

Trains Made of Stone. Ray A. Young Bear. CDW

"Tra la la la—See me dance the polka." Neptune—Polka. Edith Sitwell. NOBE

Trala Trala Trala La-le-la. William Carlos Williams. OFD

Tramp, The. Rayne Mackinnon. MIS

Tramp Miner's Song. *Unknown.* AmFP

Tramp! Tramp! Tramp! or, The Prisoner's Hope, *with music.* George Frederick Root. BLSo; PSoN

Tranquillity! thou better name. Ode to Tranquillity. Samuel Taylor Coleridge. MBPR

Transcontinent. Donald Hall. MiP

Transformations. Thomas Hardy. NoAM; PPP

Translated out of Martial. Martial, *tr. fr. Latin by* John Weever. PAIC

Translation. Roy Fuller. NOBE; OxBTC

Translation from, A. Fred Levinson. AmPA

Translation From Original. Joanne Casullo. NPW

Translations from the English. George Starbuck. VGW

Translucent green on the wall, a dance of leaves. The Green Afternoon. Henry Rago. VGW

Transparent Autumn, A. Sadamu Fujiwara, *tr. fr. Japanese by* Ichiro Kono *and* Rikutaro Fukuda. IPWM

Transparent Closet, The. Martha Shelley. WBN

Transplanting. Theodore Roethke. PiAm

Trap, The. William Beyer. PoTa

Trap doors take a Sunday afternoon drive. The Law of Falling and Catching Up. Cathleen Quirk. MMD

Traveller, The. John Berryman. VGW

Traveller, The. Goldsmith. LAuP
　"Remote, unfriended, melancholy, slow," *sel.* BIrV

Traveller, The. *Unknown.* AmFP

Traveler take heed for journeys undertaken in the dark of the year. October Journey. Margaret Walker. PoBA

Traveller who walks a temperate zone, A. Against Romanticism. Richard Wilbur. NoAM

Travelers, The. James Reeves. POL

Traveller's Curse after Misdirection. Robert Graves. NCSH

Travelin' Blues. *Unknown.* BluL

Traveling. Anne Waldman. RiTi

Travelling, a man met a tiger, so. Good Taste. Christopher Logue. RAE

Traveling Boy. William Meredith. NoAM

Traveling for days to reach you. Journey. Diane Wakoski. IHMS

Traveling North. John Woods. POL

Traveling Out, The. Lucile Adler. IHMS

Traveling Post Office, The. Andrew Barton Paterson. PoTa

Traveling Riverside Blues. *Unknown.* BluL

Traveling through the Dark. William Stafford. BoAnP; ConAP; InPK; NCSH; PoTa; SFF; TSWA

Travelling to My Second Marriage on the Day of the First Moonshot. Robert Nye. SLP

Traverse City Zoo. Jim Harrison. BoAnP

Travis, the Kid Was All Heart. Terry Stokes. AmPA

Treason. Sir John Harington. *See* Of Treason.

Treason doth never prosper; what's the reason? Of Treason [*or* Treason]. Sir John Harington. FaBoCo; InPK

Treat the woman tenderly, tenderly. *Unknown.* POL

Treating of songs. The Knight of the Sad Face. Rafael Jesús González. MIT

Treaty-trip from Shulus Reservation. Patrick Lane. NeAC

Treblinka Gas Chamber. Phyllis Webb. MMD

Tree, The. E. R. Cole. AATT

Tree. Daniel Hoffman. IPWM

Tree, The. Anna Madge Hopewell. RAE

Tree, The. Ezra Pound. PBMP; PiAm

Tree, The. Joel Sloman. VGW

Tree. A. J. M. Smith. IPWM

Tree Animals. Laurence Lieberman. CoPAm

Tree at My Window. Robert Frost. InPK; NoAM; PSN

Tree enters and says with a bow, A. The Lesson. Miroslav Holub, *tr. by* Ian Millner *and* George Theiner. LP

Tree in the Wood, The. *Unknown.* AmFP

Tree Is Father to the Man, The. Lou Lipsitz. NCSH

Tree outside the window. The Tree. Anna Madge Hopewell. RAE

Tree Party. Louis MacNeice. OxBTC

Tree, the Bird, The. Theodore Roethke. PiAm

Tree, too, wants to bend over, The. 3 Stanzas about a Tree. Marvin Bell. Prf

Tree will not ask for relief, The. From a Distance. Marvin Bell. HeS

Treehouse, The. James A. Emanuel. BPo; PoBA

Trees. Sara Coleridge. OxBChV

Trees, *abr.* Joyce Kilmer. AKE

Trees, The. Adrienne Rich. NOBA; PiAm; WPE

Trees, The. William Carlos Williams. TCP

Trees and Evening Sky. N. Scott Momaday. CDW

Trees are afraid to put forth buds, The. A Backward Spring. Thomas Hardy. PPP

Trees Are Down, The. Charlotte Mew. WPE

Trees are in their autumn beauty, The. The Wild Swans at Coole. W. B. Yeats. AnMo; BoAnP; FSFS; HeIP; IPWM; NoAM; PPP; PSN; TCP; VoPo

Trees ask me, The. Who Am I? Felice Holman. RFM

Trees—being trees, The. The Trees. William Carlos Williams. TCP

Trees in the garden rained flowers, The. War Is Kind, XXVI. Stephen Crane. SFF

Trees in the old days used to stand. Carentan O Carentan. Louis Simpson. MPo; NOBA

Trees inside are moving out into the forest, The. The Trees. Adrienne Rich. NOBA; PiAm; WPE

Tree's leaves may be ever so good, A. Leaves Compared with Flowers. Robert Frost. NOBA

Trees of Life, The. Jones Very. NOBA

Trees they do grow high, The. Still Growing. *Unknown.* InPK

Trees turn, The. Leaflight. Dorothy Donnelly. NCSH

Treetalk and windsong are. Sugarfields. Barbara Mahone. PoBA

Treetops. Marvin Bell. AmPA

Trembling, sand-dollar. Grunion. Wendy Rose. CDW

Triad. Adelaide Crapsey. PAIC; WPE

Triads. Swinburne. PBMP

Triads. *Unknown, tr. fr. Irish by* Thomas Kinsella. BIrV (Thirty-three Triads.) PFIr

Trial, A. Alan Dugan. NoAM

Trials of a Tourist. Anne Tibble. FaBoCo

Tribal Cemetery. Janet Campbell Hale. VW

Tribal Memories. Robert Duncan. *Fr.* Passages. NOBA; PiAm

Tribute. Al Young. NVAP; SA

Tribute to Kafka for Someone Taken. Alan Dugan. CAPP; CoPAm; NoAM

Tribute to the Angels, *sels.* Hilda Doolittle ("H.D.").
　"Not in our time, O Lord." NOBA
　"We have seen her/ the world over." RiTi; VGW

Tricks of the weather. Reeving. Michael Anania. HeS

Trico's Song: "What bird so sings, yet so does wail?" John Lyly. *Fr.* Alexander and Campaspe, V, i. OBP (Welcome to Spring.) NOBE

Trifles. William Everson. CoPAm

Trifling Women. *Unknown.* AmFP

Trilce: "In that corner, where we slept together." César Vallejo, *tr. fr. Spanish by* James Wright. LoAs

Trilobite, grapholite, nautilus pie. Rhyme for a Geological Baby. Joseph Cook. SpRo

Trilogy for X, *sel.* Louis MacNeice.
　"And love hung still as crystal over the bed." GBL

Trimming the Sails. Vassar Miller. NMM

Trinity, The. William Langland. *Fr.* The Vision of Piers Plowman. OxBM

Trinity Sunday. George Herbert. PAIC

Trio. Edwin Morgan. MPo

Triolet. G. K. Chesterton. LCL

Triolet Against Sisters. Phyllis McGinley. MiP

Trip, The.  Emmett Jarrett.  NeAC

Trip to Four or Five Towns, A.  John Logan.  ConAP

Trip to the Grand Banks, A.  Amos Hanson.  AmFP

Trip trap in a gap.  *Unknown.*  GBP

Triphammer Bridge.  A. R. Ammons.  NOBA

Triple Fool, The.  John Donne.  GBL

Triple Mirror, The.  Gloria C. Oden  IHMS

Trippers and askers surround me.  Walt Whitman.  *Fr.* Song of Myself, IV.  InPS

Tripping on sutures used to sew the wounds.  Low...the Violence Begins Low.  Ann Darr.  WBN

Triptych.  Luci Shaw.  AATT

Triumph of Charis, The.  Ben Jonson.  *Fr.* A Celebration of Charis.  InPS; NOBE
  (Her Triumph.)  LoAs

Triumph of Dullness, The.  Pope.  *Fr.* The Dunciad.  NOBE

Triumph of Life, The.  Shelley.  MBPR

Triumph of Time, The.  Swinburne.  VPC
  "I will go back to the great sweet mother,"  *sel.*  SoSe

Triumph of Vice, The.  Pope.  *Fr.* Epilogue to the Satires.  NOBE

Triumphs of the Prince D'Amour, The,  *sel.*  Sir William Davenant.
  "Unarm! unarm! No more your fights."  SCP-2

Trochee trips from long to short.  Metrical Feet.  Samuel Taylor Coleridge.  OxBChV

Troika, The.  Louis Simpson.  NoAM; NOBA

Troilus and Criseyde, *sels.*  Chaucer.
  Complaint of Troilus, The, *fr.* V.  NOBE
  Criseyde Sees Troilus Return from Battle, *fr.* II.  OxBM
  Go, Little Book ("Go, litel book, go litel myn tragedye"), *fr.* V.  OxBM
    ("Go little book, go, my little tragedy.")  OBP
  "If no love is, O God, what fele I so," *fr.* I.  LoAs
  "O cruel day, accusour of the joie," *fr.* III.  PAIC
  O Yonge Freshe Folkes, *fr.* V.  OxBM
    (Love Unfeigned.)  BoReV; NOBE
  Troilus Laments Criseyde's Absence, *fr.* V.  OxBM

Trolley has stopped long since, The.  The Dump.  Donald Hall.  TCP

Troll's Nosegay, The.  Robert Graves.  SoSe

Troop home to silent grots and caves!  The Mermaidens' Vesper-Hymn [*or* Siren Chorus].  George Darley.  Syren Songs, VI.  BIrV; GBL

Trooper and Maid, 2 *versions*.  *Unknown.*  AmFP

Tropics, The  Holly Prado.  NPW

Tropics in New York, The.  Claude McKay.  NoAM; PBMP; PoBA

Trouble.  James Wright.  InPK

Troubled was a house in Ealing.  The Widow's Plot: or, She Got What Was Coming to Her.  William Plomer.  NoAM

Troubled Woman.  Langston Hughes.  CTBA

Trout, The.  John Montague.  BoAnP; PFIr; SFF

Trout of the Well, The.  *Unknown, tr. fr. Gaelic by* G. R. D. McLean  SLP

Truant, The.  E. J. Pratt.  NoAM

Truckdriver.  Gary Sange.  NVAP

Truck Drivers.  Terri Haag.  CTBA

True Cat, A.  Anna Seward.  PCat

True Confession, A.  Jon Stallworthy.  NoAM

True ease in writing comes from art, not chance.  Sound and Sense.  Pope.  *Fr.* An Essay on Criticism.  SoSe

True genius, but true woman! dost deny.  To George Sand.  Elizabeth Barrett Browning.  SBG

True, I have always been happy that all the things that are inside the body.  To Persuade a Lady.  Michael Benedikt.  CAAP

True Import of Present Dialogue, Black vs. Negro, The.  Nikki Giovanni.  BPo; PoBA

True Is True.  Mark Van Doren.  LoAs

True Lent, A.  Robert Herrick.  *See* To Keep a True Lent.

True love is sweet and true love is pleasant.  William Hall.  *Unknown.*  AmFP

True love, true love, what have I done.  In the Pines.  *Unknown.*  AmFP

Truelove.  Mark Van Doren.  AIW

True Lover, The.  A. E. Housman.  LoAs

True Lovers Bold, The.  *Unknown.*  AmFP

True Maid, A.  Matthew Prior.  FaBoCo

True: nor love or loving is ultimate.  "A Taste of Honey."  King D. Kuka.  VW

True Picture Restored, A.  Vernon Watkins.  NoAM

True Religion.  Forrest Anderson.  AATT

True, the time, to one who does not love farce.  A Little Scraping.  Robinson Jeffers.  NoAM

True Thomas.  *Unknown.*  *See* Thomas the Rhymer.

True Thomas lay o'er yond grassy [*or* on Huntlie] bank.  Thomas the Rhymer [*or* Thomas Rymer *or* True Thomas].  *Unknown.*  AIW; InPK; InPS; NOBE; PeBB; PoTa; Prf

True to your might winds on dusky shores.  On the Death of William Edward Burghardt Du Bois by African Moonlight and Forgotten Shores.  Conrad Kent Rivers.  PoBA

Trueblue Gentleman, A.  Kenneth Patchen.  RAE

Truisms, The.  Louis MacNeice.  NOBE

Truly honoured lady, the Lady Venetia Digby, The.  Ben Jonson.  *Fr.* Eupheme.  SCP-1

Truly, my Satan, thou art but a dunce.  To the Accuser Who Is the God of This World.  Blake.  OBP

Trumpet's loud clangour, The.  Dryden.  *Fr.* A Song for St. Cecilia's Day.  RAE

Trumpet's voice, loud and authoritative, The.  Reasons for Attendance.  Philip Larkin.  NowV; OBP

Trust and Obey, *with music.*  J. H. Sammis.  BLSH

Truth.  Gwendolyn Brooks.  *Fr.* The Womanhood.  TH

Truth.  Chaucer.  BoReV; OxBM

Truth.  Claude McKay.  BPo

Truth.  Howard Nemerov.  CoPAm

Truth.  Susan Fromberg Schaeffer.  IHMS

Truth.  *Unknown.*  OxBM

Truth about My Sister and Me, The.  Anita Endrezze Probst.  CDW

Truth is not the secret of a few.  Lawrence Ferlinghetti.  WIF

Truth Kills Everybody.  Ted Hughes.  InPS

Truth-loving Persians do not dwell upon.  The Persian Version.  Robert Graves.  FaBoCo; NoAM

Truth the Best.  Elizabeth Turner.  OxBChV

Truth the Dead Know, The.  Anne Sexton.  CoPAm; NoAM; Psy

Truth, the whole truth always, The.  A True Confession.  Jon Stallworthy.  NoAM

Truth's Complaint over England.  Thomas Lodge.  TVS

Try Brillo on the Slimy Stove.  Phyllis Gotlieb.  BBGO

Trying to Forget.  John Wieners.  MIT

Trying to get the whiskey to do it and after that.  The Apparition.  Michael Heffernan.  HeS

Trying to open locked doors with a sword, threading.  Sojourn in the Whale.  Marianne Moore.  SBG

Trying to Talk with a Man.  Adrienne Rich.  RiTi; WBN

Tryptych for Jan Bockelson, A.  John Oliver Simon.  NeAC

Tryst, The.  Walter de la Mare.  AIW

Tryst.  Eve Merriam.  NMM

Tryst, The.  William Soutar.  SLP
  (Trysting Place, The.)  BoLoP

Tryst after Death, The. *Unknown, tr. fr. Old Irish by* Kuno Meyer. Epi

Trysting Bush, The. Joanna Baillie. WPE

Trysting Place, The. William Soutar. *See* Tryst, The.

Tu Non Se' in Terra, Si Come Tu Credi. Kathleen Raine. WPE

Tubes. Larry Mollin. NeAC

Tuft of Flowers, The. Robert Frost. IPWM

Tuft of Kelp, The. Herman Melville. SoSe

Tulips. Sylvia Plath. IPWM; PPP; PSN; Psy; WPE

Tumbleweed. Ramona Carden. VW

Tumbling. *Unknown.* OxBChV

Tumbling-hair. E. E. Cummings. BBGO

Tuna turn. A Fishy Square Dance. Eve Merriam. ECBV

Tundra, The. John Haines. ConAP

Tune, A. Arthur Symons. BoLoP

Tune in to a raga. Assassination Raga. Lawrence Ferlinghetti. CAPP

Tune is cowboy, The; the words, sentimental crap. D-Y Bar. James Welch. CDW

Tune thy musicke to thy hart. Thomas Campion. AAS

Tunnel, The. Hart Crane. *Fr.* The Bridge. MAT

Tunnel, The. Mark Strand. HeIP

Tunnyng of Elynour Rummyng, The. John Skelton. AAS

Tupelo Destruction, The. *Unknown.* AmFP

Turkey in the Straw. *Unknown.* BLSH, *with music, ad. by* James Morehead; BLSo, *with music;* GBP

*Turkish Revery,* The, *with music. Unknown.* RDB

Turn Again. *Unknown.* OxBM

Turn Back, O Man. Louis Bourgeois *and* Clifford Bax. PoRo

Turn on Your Side and Bear the Day to Me. George Barker. OxBTC

Turn Right Next Corner. Wichita Vortex Sutra. Allen Ginsberg. CAPP

Turn the Key Deftly. Edwin Brock. POL

Turn! Turn! Turn! Pete Seeger. WIF

Turner's Camp on the Chippewa. *Unknown.* AmFP

Turning, The. Philip Levine. VGW

Turning and turning in the widening gyre. The Second Coming. W. B. Yeats. AnMo; BIrV; GrRo; HeIP; InPK; InPS; IPWM; MAT; NoAM; NOBE; OBP; OxBTC; PBMP; PPoD; PPoe; PPP; PSN; TCP; VoPo; WIF

Turning it over, considering, like a madman. John Berryman. *Fr.* Dream Songs. NoAM; PiAm

Turning the nuts one at a time. Changing a Tire by the Missouri River. Harley Elliott. HeS

Turquoise and scarlet. Japan. Gavin Bantock. TwMBP

Turtle, The. Ogden Nash. SoSe

Turtle, The. Diane Wakoski. *Fr.* Greed. NoAM

Turtle lives 'twixt plated decks, The. The Turtle. Ogden Nash. SoSe

Turtle Soup. "Lewis Carroll." *Fr.* Alice's Adventures in Wonderland, *ch.* 10. SpRo

Turtle swims slowly, The. The Turtle. Diane Wakoski. *Fr.* Greed. NoAM

Turtle with eyes, The. Four Poems. Ray A. Young Bear. Epi

Turtle's Belly, The. Ellen Pearce. IHMS

Turtle's Song, The. *Unknown.* BPo

Tusked octopi the sign of. A Certain World. Ruth Herschberger. WBN

Tusks that clashed in mighty brawls, The. On the Vanity of Earthly Greatness. Arthur Guiterman. InPK

Tutivillus, the devil of hell. Chatterers in Church. *Unknown.* OxBM

Tutor who tooted the flute, A. Limerick. Carolyn Wells. SoSe

Tutsan. Charles Senior. MIS

Twa Corbies, The. *Unknown.* AIW; Epi; InPK; PAIC; PBMP; PoTa; PPP; SoSe

Two Magicians, The. *Unknown.* GBP; PeBB

'Twas a calm, still night. Lilly Dale. H. S. Thompson. BLSo

'Twas a long parting—but the time. Emily Dickinson. LoAs

'Twas a new feeling—something more. Did Not. Thomas Moore. BoLoP

'Twas a sunny day in June. Dear Old Girl. Richard Henry Buck. FSN

'Twas at the royal feast, for Persia won. Alexander's Feast; or, The Power of Music. Dryden. NOBE

'Twas autumn and 'round me the leaves were descending. The Banks of Champlain. *Unknown.* AmFP

'Twas brillig, and the slithy toves. Jabberwocky. "Lewis Carroll." *Fr.* Through the Looking-Glass. AnMo; FaBoCo; HeIP; InPK; InPS; NOBE; OBP; OxBChV; PPoe; PPP; SpRo; WIF

'Twas down at Aunty Jackson's. Walking for That Cake. Ed Harrigan. BLSo

'Twas down at Dan Mc Devitt's at the corner of this street. Throw Him Down M'Closkey; or, M'Closkey's Great Fight. John W. Kelly. FSN

'Twas down by the glenside. The Bold Fenian Men. *Unknown.* RDB

'Twas early one morning a fair maid arose. A Kiss in the Morning Early. *Unknown.* GBP

'Twas early one morning in the month of May. The Green Bushes. *Unknown.* AIW

'Twas earlye, earlye in the spring. Earlye, Earlye, in the Spring. *Unknown.* AmFP

'Twas Euclid, and the theorem pi. Plane Geometry. Emma Rounds. SpRo

'Twas Ever Thus. Henry Sambrooke Leigh. FaBoCo; SpRo

'Twas ever thus from childhood's hour! Disaster. Charles Stuart Calverley. SpRo

'Twas going to snow—'twas snowing! Curse his luck! The Drove-Road. W. W. Gibson. OxBTC

'Twas in Rosemary Lane, sirs. Neddy Nibble'm and Biddy Finn. *Unknown.* GBP

'Twas in the merry month of May. Barb'ry Allen. *Unknown.* BLSH

'Twas in the middle of the night. Mary's Ghost. Thomas Hood. PoTa

'Twas in the time when oranges surrender. The Man Who Prayed. John Shaw Neilson. MAuV

'Twas in the year of forty-nine. The Greenland Whale. *Unknown.* GBP; PeBB

'Twas just behind the woodshed. My First Cigar. Robert J. Burdette. PoTa

'Twas mercy brought me from my pagan land. On Being Brought from Africa to America. Phillis Wheatley. HeIP; IPWM; NOBA; PiAm; SBG; WPE

'Twas moonlight in the ripe barley. The Walking of the Moon-Woman. John Shaw Neilson. MAuV

'Twas more than a million years ago. Annabel Lee. Stanley Huntley. SpRo

'Twas my Belovèd spake. Canticle. John Norris. SCP-2

'Twas my last waking thought, how it could be. The Two Founts. Samuel Taylor Coleridge. MBPR

'Twas not for some calm blessing to receive. Her Muff. Richard Lovelace. SCP-2

'Twas of a brisk young sailor, as I have heard it said. Johnny German. *Unknown.* AmFP

'Twas of a nobleman's daughter. Caroline and Her Young Sailor Bold. *Unknown.* AmFP

'Twas on a Holy Thursday, their innocent faces clean.   Holy Thursday.   Blake.   *Fr.* Songs of Innocence.   BoReV; InPS; LAuP; MBPR; NOBE; OFD

'Twas on a lofty vase's side.   Ode on the Death of a Favourite Cat, Drowned in a Tub of Gold Fishes.   Thomas Gray.   Epi; FaBoCo; LAuP; NOBE; PBMP; PCat; PPP

'Twas on a Monday morning, just at the break of day.   *Maggie Mac.   Unknown.*   AmFP

'Twas on a Monday morning, right early in the year.   Charlie Is My Darling.   Lady Caroline Nairne.   RDB

'Twas on a summer's day—the sixth of June.   Byron.   *Fr.* Don Juan, I.   PPP

'Twas on the eighth of January, just at the dawn of day.   The Battle of New Orleans.   *Unknown.*   AmFP

'Twas on the field of Antietam where many's the soldier fell.   The Battle of Antietam Creek.   *Unknown.*   AmFP

'Twas on the shores that round our coast.   The Yarn of the *Nancy Bell.*   W. S. Gilbert.   FaBoCo; PeBB

'Twas out in California in the days of Forty-Nine.   How Bill Went East.   George S. Bryan.   PoTa

'Twas summer and the sun was mounted high.   The Ruined Cottage.   Wordsworth.   MBPR

'Twas sung of old in hut and hall.   Birthday Verses Written in a Child's Album.   James Russell Lowell.   OxBChV

'Twas the gray of early morning when the dreadful cry of "Fire!"   The Milwaukee Fire.   *Unknown.*   AmFP

'Twas the night before Christmas, when all through the house.   A Visit from St. Nicholas.   Clement Clarke Moore.   OxBChV

'Twas when the spousal time of May.   Coventry Patmore.   *Fr.* The Angel in the House, II, vii.   GBL

Tweed and Till.   *Unknown.*   GBP

Tweedle-dum and Tweedle-dee.   Mother Goose.   MG

Tweedside.   Lord Yester.   SLP

Twelfth Morning; or, What You Will.   Elizabeth Bishop.   PSN

Twelfth Night, *sels.*   Shakespeare.
   "Come away, come away death," *fr.* II, iv.   AIW; GBL; NOBE
   "O mistress mine, where are you roaming?" *fr.* II, iii.   GBL; HeIP; InPS; NOBE; OLR
   (Feste's Song.)  BoLoP
   (Sweet-and-Twenty.)  GrRo
   "When that I was and a little tiny boy," *fr.* V, i.   HeIP; NOBE; OBP; PPoe; WIF

Twelve and ugly.   Dresses.   Kathleen Fraser.   NMM

Twelve Days of Christmas, The.   *Unknown.*   AmFP; BLSH, *with music*

Twelve elements in slow orbit, The.   Upon Looking at a Book of Astrology.   David McFadden.   NeAC

Twelve Gates to the City.   Nikki Giovanni.   IHMS; PoBA

Twelve Hotels, The.   George MacBeth.   TwMBP

Twelve Huntsmen with Horns.   *Unknown.*   RAE

Twelve o'clock./ Along the reaches of the street.   Rhapsody on a Windy Night.   T. S. Eliot.   HeIP

Twelve o'clock—a misty night.   The Highwayman's Ghost.   Richard Garnett.   PoTa

XXth Century.   Robert Hillyer.   TH

Twentieth year is well nigh past, The.   To Mary.   William Cowper.   LAuP; PAIC

Twenty degrees below the normal for May.   On Lake Michigan—1972.   John Matthias.   HeS

28 VIII 69.   Laura Chester.   IHMS

Twenty-eight young men bathe by the shore.   Song of Myself, XI.   Walt Whitman.   LoAs

Twenty five years of the endless war.   Thomas Parkinson.   *Fr.* The New Antigone.   MIT

Twenty, forty, sixty, eighty.   Then.   Walter de la Mare.   RAE

24 December.   John Judson.   HeS

Twenty-four kilometers to the camp.   Atlas' Daughter.   Polly Mann.   NPW

Twenty-four Years.   Dylan Thomas.   MAT; NoAM

Twenty men stand watching the muckers.   Muckers.   Carl Sandburg.   CTBA

Twenty new sparrows.   Deep in Winter.   Ted Kooser.   HeS

Twenty nine years of stale cake and flat ale.   The Gorilla at Twenty Nine Years.   J. D. Reed.   NeAC

21.10.17/ left billet.   Excerpts from a Diary of a War (3).   John Daniel.   TwMBP

Twenty-one Years.   *Unknown.*   AmFP

Twenty-third Flight.   Earle Birney.   HeIP

Twenty-third Psalm, The.   Alan Simpson.   SFF

Twenty Words/ Twenty Days.   Gael Turnbull.   TwMBP

Twenty Year Marriage.   Ai.   CAAP

Twenty years, forty years, it's nothing.   The Cold Spring.   Denise Levertov.   CAAP; Psy

Twenty years hence my eyes may grow.   Walter Savage Landor.   GBL

'Twer when the busy birds did vlee.   Milken Time.   William Barnes.   VPC

Twice.   Christina Rossetti.   BoReV; GBL; NOBE

Twice during dinner.   To a Family Man in His Family Room.   Rosemary Danielle.   WBN

Twice I waked in the night.   Penelope.   Mary Gilmore.   MAuV

Twice of the Same Fever.   Robert Graves.   LoAs

Twice or thrice had I loved thee.   Air[e] and Angels.   John Donne.   LoAs; MetP; Prf; SCP-1

Twice Shy.   Seamus Heaney.   NCSH

Twice upon a time.   Duality.   Dannie Abse.   NoAM

Twicknam Garden.   John Donne.   SCP-1

Twilight.   John Masefield.   OxBTC

Twilight at the Zoo.   Alex Rodger.   NCSH

Twilight glitters on the fragmented glass.   Judeebug's Country.   Joe Johnson.   PoBA

Twilight in California.   Philip Dow.   AmPA

Twilight in Middle March, A.   Francis Ledwidge.   BIrV

Twilight is here, soft breezes bow the grass.   In Exile.   Emma Lazarus.   SBG

Twilight it is, and the far woods are dim, and the rooks cry.   Twilight.   John Masefield.   OxBTC

Twilight Man, A.   Harry Guest.   TwMBP

Twilight of Disquietude, The, *sel.*   Christopher Brennan.   "What do I know? myself alone."   MAuV

Twilight's Last Gleaming.   Arthur W. Monks.   OFD

Twin Brothers, The.   *Unknown.*   PBMP

Twin Lakes Hunter.   A. B. Guthrie, Jr.   PoTa

Twin streaks twice higher than cumulus.   Vapor Trails.   Gary Snyder.   CAPP

Twined together and, as is customary.   Never Such Love.   Robert Graves.   BoLoP

Twinkle, twinkle, little bat.   The Mad Hatter's Song.   "Lewis Carroll."   *Fr.* Alice's Adventures in Wonderland.   SpRo

Twinkle, twinkle, little star.   Paul Dehn.   SpRo

Twinkle, twinkle, little star.   The Star.   Jane Taylor.   ECBV; OxBChV; SpRo

Twirling your blue skirts, travelling the sward.   Blue Girls.   John Crowe Ransom.   GBL; NoAM; SS; VGW; VoPo

Twiss is a tidy bundle, chirped joyous Henry, The.   John Berryman.   *Fr.* Dream Songs.   RRA

Twist me a crown of windflowers.   A Crown of Windflowers.   Christina Rossetti.   OxBChV

Twist-Rime on Spring.   Arthur Guiterman.   ECBV

Twist thou and twine! in light and gloom.   Featherstone's Doom.   Robert Stephen Hawker.   VPC

Twitching in the cactus.  Deathwatch.  Michael S. Harper.  AmPA; PoBA

Twittingpan seized my arm, though I'd have gone.  The Encounter.  Edgell Rickword.  OxBTC

Two angels among the throng of angels.  A Vision.  Denise Levertov.  PiAm

Two April Mornings, The.  Wordsworth.  MBPR

Two Are Together.  Geoffrey Grigson.  GBL

Two Armies.  Stephen Spender.  OxBTC

Two athletes/ dancing in the cathedral.  Spring Images.  James Wright.  TH

Two baths in one day!  Man and Woman.  Don L. Lee.  NeAC

Two Beers in Argyle, Wisconsin.  Dave Etter.  ANTL

Two black heifers and a red.  Drinking Time.  D. J. O'Sullivan.  PFIr

Two boys from 4C who appeared, The.  Two Sec. Mods.  Zulfikar Ghose.  LP

Two boys uncoached are tossing a poem together.  Catch.  Robert Francis.  InPK; NCSH; WIF

Two bronzes, but they were passing bronze before.  Two Wrestlers.  Robert Francis.  SPo

Two Brothers, The.  *Unknown.*  AmFP

Two cats/ One up a tree.  Diamond Cut Diamond.  Ewart Milne.  ECBV; PCat

Two-Cent Coal.  *Unknown.*  AmFP

Two centuries ago Linnaeus said "nose frightful, tears pitiful" of you.  The Sloth.  Isabella Gardner.  BoAnP

Two Clocks.  John Daniel.  LP

Two coffees in the Español, the last.  Conrad Aiken.  Preludes for Memnon, II.  NoAM

Two college sophs of Cambridge growth.  Cassinus and Peter.  Swift.  PPP

Two days ago they were playing the piano.  Malvolio in San Francisco.  Jack Gilbert.  NowV

Two Deaths.  Elizabeth Jennings.  LP

Two Decisions.  Vernon Watkins.  OxBTC

Two Dedications, *sels.*      Gwendolyn Brooks.
  Chicago Picasso, The.  BPo; Psy
  Wall, The.  PoBA

Two drummers sat at dinner, in a grand hotel one day.  Mother Was a Lady; or, If Jack Were Only Here.  Edward B. Marks.  FSN

Two evils, monstrous either one apart.  Winter Remembered.  John Crowe Ransom.  NOBA; VGW

Two eyes, two hands.  Gemini.  Robert Creeley.  PiAm

Two Figures from the Movies.  William Meredith.  PPoD

Two for the Hampton Institute.  David Young.  CAAP

Two Founts, The.  Samuel Taylor Coleridge.  MBPR

Two Friends.  David Ignatow.  PBMP

Two Gentlemen of Verona, The, *sel.*  Shakespeare.
  "Thus have I shunned the fire for fear of burning," *fr.* I, iii.  GBL

Two Girls.  Howard Nemerov.  AnMo

Two girls discover.  The Secret.  Denise Levertov.  AnMo; PBMP; Psy; SFF

Two gray-winged farmers of the sea, they ride.  Maine Sea Gulls.  Russell Hoban.  BoAnP

225 days under grass.  For Jane.  Charles Bukowski.  CoPAm

Two in August.  John Crowe Ransom.  PPP

Two in the Campagna.  Robert Browning.  LoAs; NOBE

Two Invocations of Death.  Kathleen Raine.  OxBTC

Two Lean Cats.  Myron O'Higgins.  PoBA

Two leaps the water from its race.  A Mill.  William Allingham.  POL

Two legs sat upon three legs.  *Unknown.*  MG

Two Letters From Chang-Kan.  Li Po, *tr. fr. Chinese by* Shigeyoshi Obata.  OLR

Two liddle niggers all dressed in white.  Raise a "Rucus" To-Night.  *Unknown.*  BPo

Two Lines from the Brothers Grimm.  Gregory Orr.  AmPA

Two Lips.  Thomas Hardy.  BoLoP

Two little children one morning.  You Tell Me Your Dream, I'll Tell You Mine.  Seymour Rice *and* Albert H. Brown.  FSN

Two little creatures.  Monkeys.  Padraic Colum.  OxBTC

Two little girls, one fair, one dark.  The Lost Children.  Randall Jarrell.  PBMP; RRA

Two Little Kittens.  *Unknown.*  OxBChV

Two Little Miss Lloyds, The.  Elizabeth Turner.  OxBChV

Two little ships were sailing by.  Upon a Christmas Morning.  *Unknown.*  AmFP

2 little whos.  E. E. Cummings.  OLR

Two lofty ships of Eng-e-land set sail.  The Wild Barbaree.  *Unknown.*  AmFP

Two Loves.  Richard Eberhart.  LoAs

Two loves I have of comfort and despair.  Sonnets, CXLIV.  Shakespeare.  Epi

Two magpies under the cypresses, The.  What Birds Were There.  William Everson.  NoAM

Two Maidens Went Milking One Day, *with music.*  *Unknown.*  RDB

Two main diseases.  A Trial.  Alan Dugan.  NoAM

Two Mice, The.  Robert Henryson.  OxBM

Two Mornings.  Lawrence McGaugh.  PoBA

Two murders this month.  October.  Greg Pape.  AmPA

Two negro slaves.  The Sevier County Runaway.  Besmilr Brigham.  Psy

Two nights in Manchester: nothing much to do.  Mr. Cooper.  Anthony Thwaite.  OxBTC

Two Noble Kinsmen, The, *sel.*      At. to Shakespeare.
  Bridal Song, A: "Roses, their sharp spines being gone," *fr.* I, i.  NOBE

Two, of course there are two.  Death and Co.  Sylvia Plath.  ConAP

Two of Cups, The.  Emmett Jarrett.  NeAC

Two Old Ladies.  Siegfried Sassoon.  OxBTC

Two or Three: A Recipe [*or* Receipt] to Make a Cuckold.  Pope.  AnMo; BoLoP

Two Parents, The.  "Hugh MacDiarmid."  OxBTC

Two Pennies Found on the Gravel.  David Kherdian.  FAF

Two People.  E. V. Rieu.  ECBV

Two People in a room, speaking harshly.  Novella.  Adrienne Rich.  PPP

Two people live in Rosamund.  Two People.  E. V. Rieu.  ECBV

Two Pieces After Suetonius.  Robert Penn Warren.  NOBA

Two Poems about President Harding.  James Wright.  NoAM

2 Poems for Black Relocation Centers.  Etheridge Knight.  NoAM

2 Poems Written on Turning Around Too Quickly While Hiking.  Morton Marcus.  NVAP

Two-pointer by New York! Boryla leaps!  N.B.A. Prelim, Boston Garden.  Thomas Whitbread.  PPoD

Two policemen laughed, The.  Policemen Laughing.  Ray Fraser.  NeAC

Two Presentations.  Robert Duncan.  InPS

Two Pursuits.  Christina Rossetti.  WPE

Two Questions, The.  Alice Meynell.  WPE

Two Rain Songs.  *Unknown, tr. fr. Papago Indian.*  AKE

Two Rats, The.  *Unknown.*  ECBV
  (What Became of Them?)  OxBChV

Two Rivers.  Emerson.  NOBA

Two roads diverged in a yellow wood.  The Road Not Taken.
     Robert Frost.  HeIP; NoAM; RFM; SoSe; VoPo
Two Roads, Etc.  Dorothy Walters.  IHMS
Two Rural Sisters.  Charles Cotton.  *Fr.* Resolution in Four
     Sonnets, of a Poetical Question, Concerning Four Rural
     Sisters.  BoLoP
Two sculptors.  Four Translations from the English of Robert
     Hershon.  Robert Hershon.  NeAC
Two Sec. Mods.  Zulfikar Ghose.  LP
Two Selves, The.  Margaret Avison.  NoAM
Two separate divided silences.  Severed Selves.  Dante Gabriel
     Rossetti.  The House of Life, XL  BoLoP; VPC
Two Sisters, The.  *Unknown.*  AIW; AmFP; MAT
     (Binnorie.)  AIW
Two Songs.  C. Day Lewis.  NoAM
Two Songs.  Adrienne Rich.  NOBA; Psy
Two Songs from a Play.  W. B. Yeats.  *Fr.* The Resurrection.
     NOBE; OBP; PPoe; PPP
Two Sonnets.  John Ashbery.
     Dido.  CAPP; VGW
     Idiot, The.  VGW
Two Spirits, The: an Allegory.  Shelley.  MBPR; Prf
Two Summers in Moravia.  Roger McDonald.  CAAP
Two Takes from Love in Los Angeles.  Al Young.  CoPAm
Two that could not have lived their single lives.  Two in August.
     John Crowe Ransom.  PPP
2001: The Tennyson/Hardy Poem.  Gavin Ewart.  FaBoCo
Two Tramps in Mud Time.  Robert Frost.  NoAM
Two Travellers, The.  C. J. Boland.  PFIr
Two Variations.  Denise Levertov.  PPoe
     Enquiry, *sel.*  RiTi
Two Views of a Cadaver Room.  Sylvia Plath.  AnMo
Two Views of Two Ghost Towns.  Charles Tomlinson.  NoAM
Two voices are there: one is of the deep.  A Sonnet.  James
     Kenneth Stephen.  FaBoCo; PPoD; SpRo
Two voices are there; one is of the sea.  Thought of a Briton on
     the Subjugation of Switzerland.  Wordsworth.  MBPR;
     PBMP; SpRo
Two Voices in a Meadow.  Richard Wilbur.  PBMP
Two wedded hearts, if ere were such.  Samuel Taylor Coleridge.
     MBPR
Two White Horses in a Line.  *Unknown.*  BluL
Two wild duck of the upland spaces.  Duck.  John Lyle
     Donaghy.  BIrV
Two Witches, *sel.*  Robert Frost.
     Witch of Coös, The.  NoAM; NOBA; PAIC
Two Women.  Naomi Replansky.  NMM
Two Wrestlers.  Robert Francis.  SPo
'Twould ring the bells of Heaven.  The Bells of Heaven.  Ralph
     Hodgson.  NOBE; PPoD
Tyger, The.  Blake.  *See* Tiger, The.
Tyger! Tyger!  James Nolan.  AATT
Tyger! Tyger! burning bright.  *See* Tiger! Tiger! burning bright.
Tyndarus attempting too kis a fayre lasse with a long nose.  Of
     Tyndarus, That Frumped a Gentlewoman.  *Unknown, tr. by*
     Richard Stanyhurst.  BIrV
Type of the antique Rome! Rich reliquary.  The Coliseum.  Poe.
     NOBA
Tyson's Corner.  Primus St. John.  PoBA
Tywater.  Richard Wilbur.  ConAP

# U

U bet u wer.  To a Poet I Knew.  Jewel C. Latimore.  PoBA
U feel that way sometimes.  Mixed Sketches.  Don L. Lee.  BPo

U Name This One.  Carolyn M. Rodgers.  NMM; PoBA
U. S. A., The.  Grantland Rice.  SPo
U.S. Coast and Geodetic Survey Ship *Pioneer*, The.  Robert
     Hershon.  NeAC
Ubi Iam Sunt?  Richard L. Greene.  PAIC
Ubi Sunt Qui ante Nos Fuerunt?  *Unknown.*  PAIC
     (Ubi Sunt? *longer version.*)  OxBM
Ugly Child, The.  Elizabeth Jennings.  RAE
Ugly old man, An.  No Great Matter.  David Lawson.  VGW
Ulalume—a Ballad.  Poe.  NOBA; PiAm
Ulivfak's Song of the Caribou.  *Unknown, tr. fr. Caribou Eskimo.*
     AKE
Ultima Ratio Regum.  Stephen Spender.  LP; MPo; SFF
Ultima Thule.  Longfellow.  AmVN
Ultimate Anthology.  Martin Bell.  POL
Ultimate Antientropy, The.  Theodore Weiss.  NoAM
Ultimate Reality.  Ogden Nash.  FaBoCo
Ulysses.  Dante, *tr. fr. Italian by* Longfellow.  *Fr.* Divina
     Commedia: Inferno  Epi
Ulysses.  Robert Graves.  NoAM
Ulysses.  Tennyson.  AnMo; Epi; HeIP; InPK; InPS; IPWM;
     NOBE; PAIC; PPoe; PPP; SoSe
Ulysses and the Siren.  Samuel Daniel.  NOBE; PAIC
Ubaji Park.  David Kherdian.  SA
Umbilical. Eve Merriam.  CTBA
Umh——uhumh! Umh——uhumh/Get a breath of that country
     air.  Country Air.  Mike Love *and* Brian Wilson.  PoRo
Ummmmh oh ain't got no mama now.  That Black Snake Moan.
     *Unknown.*  BluL
Unaccustomed ripeness in the wood, An.  Elizabeth.  Robert
     Lowell.  *Fr.* Harriet.  CAPP; LoAs
Un-American Investigators.  Langston Hughes.  BPo
Unarm! unarm! No more your fights.  Sir William Davenant.
     *Fr.* The Triumphs of the Prince D'Amour.  SCP-2
Unbeliever, The.  Elizabeth Bishop.  NoAM
Unbounded is thy range; with varied style.  The Stormy Hebrides.
     William Collins.  *Fr.* An Ode on the Popular Superstitions.
     NOBE
Uncertainty.  Wordsworth.  *Fr.* Ecclesiastical Sonnets.  MBPR
Uncessant minutes, whilst you move you tell.  To His Watch
     When He Could Not Sleep.  Lord Herbert of Cherbury.
     NOBE
Uncle Bull-boy.  June Jordan.  PoBA
Uncle Death.  Walter Clark.  NCSH
Uncle Dog: the Poet at 9.  Robert Sward.  VGW
Uncle Roderick.  Norman MacCaig.  MPo
Uncle sent for O. T. told him we have to fight.  O. T.'s Blues.
     Waring Cuney.  MAT
Unclench Yourself.  Marge Piercy.  NeAC
Uncomly in cloistre I cowre ful of care.  Choristers Training.
     *Unknown.*  OxBM
Unconsumable material is everywhere.  The Square at Dawn.
     James Tate.  NoAM
Undead, The.  Richard Wilbur.  CAPP; ConAP
Undefined Tenderness, An.  Joel Oppenheimer.  VGW
Under.  George Bowering.  NeAC
Under a lawn, than skies more clear.  Upon Roses.  Robert
     Herrick.  SCP-1
Under a splintered mast.  A Talisman.  Marianne Moore.
     NCSH
Under a spreading chestnut-tree.  The Village Blacksmith.
     Longfellow.  AmVN
Under a swaying.  El Dorado.  Richard Ryan.  BIrV
Under Ben Bulben.  W. B. Yeats.  NoAM; OxBTC
Under cracking pieces of the moon, eelpout.  Spawning in
     Northern Minnesota.  David McElroy.  AmPA
Under great yellow flags and banners of the ancient cold.  The
     Shadow of Cain.  Edith Sitwell.  OxBTC

Under hawk-watch. Fisherman. Philip Booth. SPo

Under her deep plush roof. "Vierge Ouvrante." Miriam Palmer. NMM; RiTi

Under his careful crown he keeps. King Midas Has Asses' Ears. Donald Finkel. CoPAm

Under Milk Wood, *sel.* Dylan Thomas. "Johnnie Crack and Flossie Snail." LCL; RAE

Under my window. Letter in Winter. Raymond R. Patterson. PoBA

Under my window-ledge the waters race. Coole Park and Ballylee, 1931. W. B. Yeats. NoAM; PPP; PSN

Under our stillness fled the same low hooves. The Racetrack. Jane Cooper. LoAs

Under pressure only wood keeps its grain, spike and screw. Elective Affinities. David Malouf. CAAP

Under Seconal/ my apartment diminishes. Day Sleeper. James L. White. HeS

Under Sorrow's Sign. Gofraidh Fionn O'Dalaigh, *tr. fr. Irish by* John Montague. BIrV

Under the Bamboo Tree, *with music.* Bob Cole. BLSo; FSN

Under the big 500-watted lamps, in the huge sawdusted. The Slaughter-House. Alfred Hayes. NowV

Under the bronze crown. A Baroque Wall-Fountain in the Villa Sciarra. Richard Wilbur. CAPP; SoSe

Under the bronze-lipped Jesus bell. Bell at Midnight. May Miller. PPoD

Under the concrete benches. Weed Puller. Theodore Roethke. AnMo; PiAm

Under the dawn I wake my two-wheel friend. Yevgeny Yevtushenko, *tr. by* Robin Milner-Gulland *and* Peter Levi. *Fr.* On a Bicycle. SPo

Under the dusty print of hobnailed boot. Country Press. Rosemary Dobson. MAuV

Under the dying sun. The Reaper. L. H. Allen. MAuV

Under the forest, where the day is dark. The Manzanita. Yvor Winters. VGW

Under the Greenwood Tree. Shakespeare. *Fr.* As You Like It, II, v. ECBV; HeIP; InPS

Under the Greenwood Tree. *Unknown.* GBP

Under the hive-like dome the stooping haunted readers. The British Museum Reading Room. Louis MacNeice. NOBE

Under the Ladder to Heaven. Elizabeth Fenton. NMM

Under the Lime Tree. Walther von der Vogelweide, *tr. fr. German by* Thomas Lovell Beddoes. GBL

Under the lintel at midnight. Under the Sign of the Fisher. Bertram Higgins. MAuV

Under the Locust Blossoms. Frederick Goddard Tuckerman. NOBA

Under the long dark boughs, like jewels red. Cherry Robbers. D. H. Lawrence. OBP

Under the low dark sky and the sodden leaves. Wet Summer: Botanic Gardens. Nan McDonald. MAuV

Under the Maud Moon. Galway Kinnell. CAAP

Under the Mirabeau bridge the Seine. The Mirabeau Bridge. Guillaume Apollinaire. BoLoP

Under the mountain, as when first I knew. Sonnet. Frederick Goddard Tuckerman. *Fr.* Sonnets. PiAm

Under the olive trees, from the ground. The Coward. Stephen Spender. NoAM

Under the parabola of a ball. How to Kill. Keith Douglas. NOBE

Under the rusting elms his separate path. The Student. Dabney Stuart. NowV

Under the Sign of the Fisher. Bertram Higgins. MAuV

Under the sky's/ armpit. The Golden-eyed Crossbow. Claude Pélieu. MIT

Under the thick beams of that swirly smoking light. The Examination. W. D. Snodgrass. CAPP; ConAP

Under the too white marmorial Lincoln Memorial. The March. Robert Lowell. NowV

Under the trees. Running Water Music. Gary Snyder. PiAm

Under the Waterfall. Thomas Hardy. BoLoP

Under the wide and starry sky. Requiem. Robert Louis Stevenson. NOBE

Under the Willow-Shades. Sir William Davenant. BoLoP

Under the willow the willow. Recruiting Drive. Charles Causley. OxBTC

Under the willow whose roots are shallow. May-Fly. John Heath-Stubbs. SoSe

Under Way. Bruce Dawe. CAAP

Under yonder beech-tree single on the green-sward. Love in the Valley. George Meredith. NOBE; VPC

Under Your Voice, among Legends. Phyllis Beauvais. NMM

Underground grower, blind and a common brown, An. Potato. Richard Wilbur. CAPP

Underground Stream, The. James Dickey. NOBA

Underground System. Edna St. Vincent Millay. SBG

Underneath a cypress shade, the Queen of Love sat mourning. *Unknown.* GBL

Underneath my belt. When I Was Lost. Dorothy Aldis. CaYB

Underneath this sable [*or* marble] hearse [*or* herse]. On the Countess Dowager of Pembroke. William Browne. NOBE; OBP; SCP-2

Underneath this wooden cross there lies. Epitaph. Karl Shapiro. *Fr.* Elegy for a Dead Soldier. OFD

Underneath were the everlasting arms. I Looked Over Jordan. Lane Dunlop. NowV

Undertakers' Club, The. *Unknown.* GBP

Undertaking, The. John Donne. NOBE

Undertaking, The. Louis Glück. NVAP

Underwater. Michael Schmidt. SoSe

Underwater eyes, an eel's. An Otter. Ted Hughes. NoAM

Underwater, this is the cathedral. Underwater. Michael Schmidt. SoSe

Underworld. George Garrett. SS

Undo! *Unknown.* BoReV; OxBM

Undone, undone the lawyers are. The Downfall of Charing Cross. *Unknown.* FaBoCo

Unexpected, The. Ai. CAAP

Unexpected Pleasure, An. *Unknown.* FaBoCo

Unexpressible Love, The. William Cavendish, Duke of Newcastle. SCP-2

Unfaith and Faith. Robert Browning. *Fr.* Bishop Blougram's Apology. BoReV

Unfaithful Married Woman, The. Federico García Lorca, *tr. fr. Spanish by* Rolfe Humphries. LoAs

Unfelt, unheard, unseen. Lines. Keats. MBPR

Unfinished History. Archibald MacLeish. VGW

Unfold, unfold! take in His light. The Revival. Henry Vaughan. BoReV

Unfortunate Coincidence. Dorothy Parker. SBG

Unfortunate Lover, An. *Unknown.* OxBM

Unfortunate Lovers, The, *sel.* Sir William Davenant. "You fiends and furies, come along!" SCP-2

Unfortunate Miller, The. A. E. Coppard. PoTa

Unfortunate Miss Bailey. George Colman the Younger. GBP; PeBB

Unfurls in rain. The Newest Banana Plant Leaf. Ingrid Wendt. NMM

Unifying Principle, The. A. R. Ammons. NOBA

Unhappy dreamer, who outwinged in flight. On the Death of a Metaphysician. George Santayana. PAIC

Unhappy Schoolboy, The. *Unknown.* OxBChV

Unhappy summer you. This Summer and Last. Thomas Hardy. OxBTC

Unhappy verse, the witness of my unhappy state. Iambicum Trimetrum. Spenser. BoLoP

Unhatch you April butterflies. Ode to a Fat Cat. Annabel Farjeon. PCat

Unicorn. Nicholas Stuart Gray. ECBV

Unidentified Flying Object. Robert Hayden. NCSH

Union Man. Albert Morgan. AmFP

Unison, A. William Carlos Williams. Epi; NOBA

Unite, unite, let us all unite. The Padstow Night Song. *Unknown.* GBP

United States, The. William Carlos Williams. LoAs

United States Tony. David Kherdian. SA

Universal Explicator, The. Erica Jong. NVAP

Universal Passion, The. Edward Young. *See* Love of Fame, the Universal Passion.

Universality of things, The. The Eyeglasses. William Carlos Williams. NoAM

Universe, The. May Swenson. Psy

Universe expands and contracts like a great heart, The. The Great Explosion. Robinson Jeffers. IPWM

University. Karl Shapiro. NowV

University Curriculum. William Price Turner. POL

University Examinations in Egypt. D. J. Enright. NowV; OxBTC

Unknown, The. John Davidson. PAIC

Unknown, The. Edward Thomas. GBL

Unknown Citizen, The. W. H. Auden. BuTh; HeIP; InPK; IPWM; LP; PAIC; PPoD; SFF; SoSe; WIF

Unknown Color, The. Countee Cullen. ECBV

Unknown Dead, The. Henry Timrod. AmVN

Unknown Eros, The. Coventry Patmore. *Poems indexed separately by titles and first lines.*

Unknown faces in the street. The Turning. Philip Levine. VGW

Unknown Girl in the Maternity Ward. Anne Sexton. NoAM

Unknown Shores. D. M. Thomas, *after the French of* Théophile Gautier. MPo

Unknown Smoke. Archie Washburn. VW

Unknown Soldiers. Edgar Lee Masters. *Fr.* The New Spoon River. NoAM

Unlawful Assembly. D. J. Enright. OxBTC

Unless you remind me. Pavlov. Naomi Long Madgett. BPo

Unloading Rails. *Unknown.* AmFP

Unloved, The. Robert Canzoneri. CoPAm

Unmade girl on my bed, The. Easter Sunday: Not the Artist. Ralph Adamo. CoPAm

Unnatural Powers. Robinson Jeffers. PBMP

Unnoticed—/ The shriveled old woman in faded-flower print. Paso por Aqui. Wade Hall. AATT

Unnoticed Woman from Whose Kind Large Flesh. E. E. Cummings. Epi

Unpredicted, The. John Heath-Stubbs. BoLoP

Unpurged images of day recede, The. Byzantium. W. B. Yeats. InPS; NoAM; NOBE; OxBTC; PPP

Unquiet Grave, The. *Unknown.* AIW; AmFP, *shorter version*; Epi, *shorter version, with music*; GBP; HeIP; InPK; PeBB; SLP; WIF

Unquiet thought, whom at the first I bred. Amoretti, II. Spenser. PAIC

Unreal tall as a myth. The Bear on the Delhi Road. Earle Birney. BoAnP; HeIP

Unsaid. A. R. Ammons. NOBA

Unsaid Word, An. Adrienne Rich. NMM

Unseen Fire. R. N. Currey. MPo

"This is a damned inhuman sort of war," *sel.* OxBTC

Unstable dreame, accordyng to the place. The Lover Having Dreamed Enjoying of His Love, Complaineth That the Dreame Is Not either Longer or Truer. Sir Thomas Wyatt. AAS

Unsung Heroes, The. Paul Laurence Dunbar. BPo

Unthrifty loveliness, why dost thou spend. Sonnets, IV. Shakespeare. GrRo

Until that sun, which keeps. Trains Made of Stone. Ray A. Young Bear. CDW

Until the Cows Come Home. Michael McMahon. FAF

Until the desert knows. Emily Dickinson. NOBA

Until They Have Stopped. Sarah E. Wright. PoBA

Untitled. Daryl Hine. NoAM

Untitled. James A. Randall, Jr. BPo

Untitled. Michele Wallace. WBN

Untitled Requiem for Tomorrow. Conyus. PoBA

Unto this place when as the Elfin Knight. The Hill of the Graces. Spenser. *Fr.* The Faerie Queene, VI, 10. NOBE

Unto Us a Child Is Born. William Dunbar. BoReV

Unwanted. Edward Field. SS

Unwanted, The. Mary Gordon. IHMS

Unwelcome. Mary Elizabeth Coleridge. SS; WPE

Unwinding the spool of the morning. Invocation. Vassar Miller. NCSH

Unyielding in the pride of his defiance. The Flying Dutchman. E. A. Robinson. PiAM

Up against the wall. David Gitlin. MIT

Up and down the beach. The Skin Divers. George Starbuck. SPo

Up at a Villa—Down in the City. Robert Browning. NOBE; PPP

Up at La Serra. Charles Tomlinson. TwMBP

Up from Down Under. David McCord. ECBV

Up from the bronze, I saw. Roman Fountain. Louise Bogan. SBG

Up from the Egg: the Confessions of a Nuthatch Avoider. Ogden Nash. BoAnP

Up from the log cabin to the capitol. Edwin Markham. *Fr.* Lincoln, the Man of the People. OFD

Up from the meadows rich with corn. Barbara Frietchie. Whittier. BTTM; NOBA

Up from the south at break of day. Sheridan's Ride. Thomas Buchanan Read. BTTM

Up go the children, up the rungs. The Playground. Michael Bedard. BBGO

Up-Hill. *See* Uphill.

Up I Arose in Verno Tempore. *Unknown.* GBP

Up in the Air. James S. Tippett. ECBV

Up in the mountains, it's lonesome all the time. The Mountain Whippoorwill. Stephen Vincent Benét. PoTa

Up on the Downs. John Masefield. NOBE

Up, sun and mery wether! Sometime I Loved. *Unknown.* OxBM

Up Tailes All. Robert Herrick. LoAs

Up the airy mountain. The Fairies. William Allingham. ECBV; LCL; NOBE; OxBChV

Up the reputable walks of old established trees. The Campus on the Hill. W. D. Snodgrass. NoAM; NowV; WIF

Up There. W. H. Auden. OxBTC

Up to Date. "Hugh MacDiarmid." FaBoCo

Up to his shoulders. The Bird Fancier. James Kirkup. ECBV

Up to the bed by the window, where I be lyin'. Old Shepherd's Prayer. Charlotte Mew. OxBTC; WPE

Up! Up! my friend, and quit your books.  The Tables Turned. Wordsworth.  IPWM; MBPR

Up, up, old Benedict, the bard who would.  Wilder Bentley.  *Fr.* Six Reveilles to Match My Self-Indulgence.  MIT

Up where the world grows cold.  A North Pole Story.  Menella Bute Smedley.  OxBChV

Upasara, the heifer after first mating.  Sanskrit.  Les A. Murray. *Fr.* Walking to the Cattle-place.  CAAP

Up-Hill [*or* Uphill].  Christina Rossetti.  ECBV; IPWM; NOBE; PPP; SS; VPC; WPE

Upland.  A. R. Ammons.  NOBA

Upland farmers have all gone, The.  Above Penmaenmawr. Tony Connor.  MPo

Upon a Child.  Robert Herrick.  SCP-1

Upon a Child That Died.  Robert Herrick.  InPK; SCP-1

Upon a Christmas Morning.  *Unknown.*  AmFP

Upon a day, came sorrow in to me.  Sonnet.  Dante, *tr. by* Dante Gabriel Rossetti.  LoAs

Upon a gloomy night.  St. John of the Cross, *tr. fr. Spanish by* Roy Campbell.  BoLoP

Upon a great black horse-ily.  Song-ily.  *Unknown.*  ECBV

Upon a Mole in Celia's Bosom.  Thomas Carew.  SCP-2

Upon a Sabbath-day it fell.  The Eve of St. Mark.  Keats. MBPR

Upon a simmer Sunday morn.  The Holy Fair.  Burns.  LAuP

Upon a Snail.  John Bunyan.  *See* Upon the Snail.

Upon a Spider Catching a Fly.  Edward Taylor.  NOBA

Upon a stairway built of brick.  The Fearful Finale of the Irascible Mouse.  Guy Wetmore Carryl.  ECBV

Upon a sudden, as I gazing stood.  Rachel Speght.  *Fr.* A Dream.  WPE

Upon a time before the faery broods.  Lamia.  Keats.  MBPR

Upon a Wasp Child with Cold.  Edward Taylor.  NOBA; PiAm; SCP-2

Upon Appleton House.  Andrew Marvell.  SCP-1
  Garden of Appleton House, The, *sel.*  NOBE

Upon Boys Diverting Themselves in the River.  Thomas Foxton. OxBChV

Upon Christ's Nativity, or Christmas.  Rowland Watkyns.  SCP-2

Upon Easter Day.  Richard Crashaw.  *See* Easter Day.

Upon His Julia.  Robert Herrick.  SpRo

Upon His Leaving His Mistress.  Earl of Rochester.  GBL
  (Upon Leaving His Mistress.)  OBP

Upon His Picture.  Thomas Randolph.  NOBE

Upon Israel and upon the rabbis.  Kaddish.  Charles Reznikoff. *Fr.* Separate Way.  SA

Upon Julia's Breasts.  Robert Herrick.  SCP-1

Upon Julia's Clothes.  Robert Herrick.  AnMo; GBL; HeIP; InPS; IPWM; NOBE; PAIC; PPP; SCP-1; SpRo; SS; WIF

Upon Julia's Unlacing Herself.  Robert Herrick.  SCP-1

Upon Julia's Voice.  Robert Herrick.  AnMo; InPK; NOBE; SCP-1; SoSe

Upon Leaving His Mistress.  Earl of Rochester..  *See* Upon His Leaving His Mistress.

Upon Leaving the Parole Board Hearing.  Conyus.  PoBA

Upon Looking at a Book of Astrology.  David McFadden. NeAC

Upon Lucia Dabbled in the Dew.  Robert Herrick.  SCP-1

Upon Mr. Ben Jonson: Epigram.  Robert Herrick.  SCP-1

Upon Moon.  Robert Herrick.  Moon

Upon my right side I me lay.  Prayer for Good Dreams. *Unknown.*  OxBM

Upon my word and honour.  Mother Goose.  MG

Upon Nothing.  Earl of Rochester.  SCP-2

Upon Prew His Maid.  Robert Herrick.  InPK

Upon Roses.  Robert Herrick.  SCP-1

Upon the beach are thousands of crabs; they are.  Crustaceans. Roy Fuller.  NoAM

Upon the Book and Picture of the Seraphical Saint Teresa. Richard Crashaw.  *See* Flaming Heart, The.

Upon the Burning of Our House, July 10th, 1666.  Anne Bradstreet.  WPE
  (Some Verses upon the Burning of Our House July 10th, 1666.)  NOBA
  (Verses upon the Burning of Our House.)  PiAm; SBG

Upon the Death of a Gentleman.  Richard Crashaw.  MetP

Upon the Death of George Santayana.  Anthony Hecht. CoPAm

Upon the Death of Sir Albert Morton's Wife.  Sir Henry Wotton. BoLoP

Upon the Decease of My Infant Lady.  Clement Barksdale. SCP-2

Upon the Double Murther of King Charles I.  Katherine Philips. SBG

Upon the eyes, the lips, the feet.  Extreme Unction.  Ernest Dowson.  BoReV

Upon the hill my lover stands.  The House o' the Mirror.  Helen Adam.  MAT; NMM

Upon the hills new grass is seen.  Twist-Rime on Spring.  Arthur Guiterman.  ECBV

Upon the Horse and His Rider.  John Bunyan.  OxBChV

Upon the Image of Death.  Robert Southwell.  BoReV; NOBE

Upon the Infant Martyrs.  Richard Crashaw.  PAIC

Upon the Intimations of Love's Mortality.  Jean Garrigue.  LoAs

Upon the Nipples of Julia's Breasts.  Robert Herrick.  SCP-1

Upon the Saying That My Verses Were Made by Another.  Anne Killigrew.  WPE

Upon the Snail.  John Bunyan.  SCP-2
  (Upon a Snail.)  OxBChV

Upon the Sudden Restraint of the Earl of Somerset, Then Falling from [*or* out of] Favour.  Sir Henry Wotton.  NOBE; SCP-2

Upon the Swallow.  John Bunyan.  OxBChV

Upon the Weathercock.  John Bunyan.  OxBChV

Upon this greying page you wrote.  On Looking at a Copy of Alice Meynell's Poems.  Amy Lowell.  SBG

Upon this marble bust that is not I.  To Inez Milholland.  Edna St. Vincent Millay.  WPE

Upon this primrose hill.  The Primrose, Being at Montgomery Castle.  John Donne.  GBL

Upon Visiting His Lady by Moonlight.  "A. W."  Moon

Upon Westminster Bridge Sept. 3, 1802.  Wordsworth.  *See* Composed upon Westminster Bridge.

Upon Your Leaving.  Etheridge Knight.  NeAC

Upper chamber in a darkened house, An.  Frederick Goddard Tuckerman.  *Fr.* Sonnets.  AmVN; NOBA; PiAm

Upper Meadows, The.  Yvor Winters.  PiAm

Upper slopes are busy with the cricket, The.  Elegy on the Dust. Thom Gunn.  NoAM

Uppon a Deedmans Hed.  John Skelton.  AAS

Uprose the King of Men with speed.  The Descent of Odin; an Ode from the Norse Tongue.  Thomas Gray.  LAuP

Uprose, uprose, the stony fields uprose.  The Tree, the Bird. Theodore Roethke.  PiAm

Upstairs on the third floor.  Bottled: New York.  Helene Johnson.  PoBA

Upstate New York.  The House You Looked For.  William Pitt Root.  NVAP

Upstream.  Carl Sandburg.  MiP; PiAm

Uptown on Lenox Avenue.  Prime.  Langston Hughes.  PoBA

Upturning with a band.  Authentic Tidings.  Wordsworth.  *Fr.* The Prelude, VI.  BoReV

Urania, *sels.*  Mary Sidney Wroth, Countess of Montgomery. WPE

Duke's Song, The.
Lindamira's Complaint.
Morea's Sonnet.
Pamphilia to Amphilanthus.
Pamphilia's Sonnet.
Verses of the Talkative Knight, The
Urban Convalescence, An. James Merrill. NOBA; NowV
Urceus Exit. Austin Dobson. *Fr.* Rose-Leaves. PAIC
Urge to stroke the dead, The. Rabbits. Dennis Schmitz. FiCP
Uriel. Emerson. AmVN; NOBA; PiAm
Urizen. Blake. *See* Book of Urizen.
Ursula. David Ray. VGW
Ursula, in a garden, found. Cy Est Pourtraicte, Madame Ste. Ursule, et les Unze Mille Vierges. Wallace Stevens. LoAs
Us. Julius Lester. PoBA
Us. Anne Sexton. CAPP
Us Two. A. A. Milne. OxBChV
Us two was pals, the Kid and me. The Kid's Last Fight. *Unknown.* SPo
Useful these bowls may be. China Shop Vigil. Christopher Middleton. TwMBP
Useless./ Our shouts bounce off him. The Old Dog. Alasdair MacLean. LP
Useless Words. Carl Sandburg. PBMP; PPoD
Usual exquisite boredom of patrols, The. Hugh Popham. OxBTC
Usually they/ go, women like that. Women Like That. Lyn Lifshin. Psy
Utah. Anne Stevenson. NCSH
Utah Iron Horse, The. *Unknown.* AmFP
Utopia. Jewel C. Latimore. BPo
Utrillo on the wall. A nun is climbing. In a Mental Hospital Sitting Room. Elizabeth Jennings. LP

# V

V. B. Nimble, V. B. Quick ("V. B. Wigglesworth wakes at noon"). John Updike. CTBA
V. Innocentia Veritas Viat Fides Circumdederunt Me Inimici Mei. Sir Thomas Wyatt. AAS
V-Letter. Karl Shapiro. NoAM
Vacancy. Daniela Gioseffi. WBN
Vacant Lot, The. Gwendolyn Brooks. NoAM; NOBA
Vacation. William Stafford. POL; SFF
Vacation Trip. William Stafford. CTBA
Vachel, the stars are out. To Lindsay. Allen Ginsberg. ConAP
Vacillation. W. B. Yeats. NoAM
  *Sels.*
  "Although the summer sunlight gild." BoReV
  "Must we part, Von Hügel, though much alike, for we." BoReV
  "My fiftieth year had come and gone." BoReV
  "Seek out reality, leave things that seem." BoReV
Vacuum. Josephine Miles. Moon
Vain Gratuities. E. A. Robinson. SS
Vain Learning. Fulke Greville. *Fr.* Caelica. BoReV
Vain World Adieu. *Unknown.* AmFP
Vala, Night the Ninth Being the Last Judgment. Blake. *Fr.* The Four Zoas. MBPR
*Vale* from Carthage. Peter Viereck. CoPAm; SS
Valediction, A: "If we must part." Ernest Dowson. BoLoP
Valediction, A: Of Weeping. John Donne. HeIP; MetP; SCP-1

Valediction Forbidding Mourning, A. John Donne. AnMo; HeIP; InPK; InPS; MetP; NoAm; NOBE; PPoD; PPoe; PPP; SCP-1; SoSe; VoPo; WIF
Valediction to the River Duddon. Wordsworth. *See* After-Thought.
Valentine. Len Gasparini. NeAC
Valentine for a Lady, A. Lucilius, *tr. fr. Greek by* Dudley Fitts. OFD
Valentine for Marianne Moore, A. Elder Olson. PAIC
Valentines to My Mother, 1880. Christina Rossetti. OFD
Valiant Seaman's Happy Return to His Love, The. *Unknown.* GBP; PeBB
Valley floors. A Collage for Richard Davis—Two Short Forms. De Leon Harrison. PoBA
Valley of the Elwy, The. Gerard Manley Hopkins. LoAs
Valley Where I Don't Belong, A. Marge Piercy. IHMS
Valse Oubliée. John Heath-Stubbs. OxBTC
Valuable. Stevie Smith. OxBTC
Vampire's Aubade. W. D. Snodgrass. PAIC
Vandergast and the Girl. Louis Simpson. CoPAm
Vanessa Vanessa. Ewart Milne. BIrV
Van Gogh. Lynn Strongin. RiTi
Vanguard of liberty, ye men of Kent. To the Men of Kent. October, 1803. Wordsworth. MBPR
Vanish. John Oliver Simon. MIT
Vanished house that for an hour I knew, A. Souvenir. E. A. Robinson. NoAM
Vanishing Point. Peter Cooley. AmPA
Vanitas Vanitatum. John Webster. *Fr.* The Devil's Law Case. NOBE; OBP
Vanity of Human Wishes, The. John Leax. MiP
Vanity of Human Wishes, The: the Tenth Satire of Juvenal Imitated. Samuel Johnson. ESaP; HeIP; LAuP; *Sels.*
  Charles XII of Sweden. NOBE
  Power of Prayer, The. NOBE
  (Prayer: "Where then shall Hope and Fear their objects find?") BoReV
  Scholar's Life, The. NOBE
Vanity of Vanities. Ecclesiastes, Bible, *O. T.* PBMP
Vanity, saith the preacher, vanity! The Bishop Orders His Tomb at Saint Praxed's Church. Robert Browning. AnMo; Epi; GrRo; HeIP; IPWM; PPoe; PPP
Vanity, vanity, all is vanity. Ha! Original Sin. Ogden Nash. FaBoCo
Vantage. Brewster Ghiselin. PPoD
Van Winkle. Hart Crane. *Fr.* The Bridge: Powhatan's Daughter. PiAm
Vapor Trail Reflected in the Frog Pond. Galway Kinnell. VGW
Vapor Trails. Gary Snyder. CAPP
Variation on Heraclitus. Louis MacNeice. NoAM
Variations. Randall Jarrell. VGW
Variations Done for Gerald van de Wiele. Charles Olson. NoAM; NOBA
Variations: #21. James Stephens. WIF
Variations on a Theme. Mark Vinz. HeS
Variations on a Theme by William Carlos Williams. Kenneth Koch. CAPP; SpRo
Variations on a Time Theme, *sels.* Edwin Muir. NoAM
  "Child in Adam's field I dreamed away, A."
  "Now at the road's quick turn."
  "Ransomed from darkness and released in Time."
Variety is bewildering in its sameness, The. Letter from the North Atlantic. John Williams. CoPAm
Vase of Flowers, A. John Ashbery. ConAP
Vases of Wombs, The. Daniela Gioseffi. RiTi
Vassar, class of. Portrait of a Woman. Kathryn Ruby. WBN

Vast oceanic movements, the flux and reflux of immeasurable. Currents. Emma Lazarus. *Fr.* By the Waters of Babylon. WPE

Vaticide. Myron O'Higgins. PoBA

Vaudeville. Lincoln Kirstein. NoAM

Vaunting Oak. John Crowe Ransom. VGW

Vegetable, I Will Not Be, A. Donna Whitewing. ANTL; VW

Vehicle gives a lurch but seems, The. Foetal Song. Joyce Carol Oates. IHMS

Veiled in that light amazing. The Dispraise of Absalom. *Unknown, tr. by* Robin Flower. BIrV

Velvet Shoes. Elinor Wylie. FSFS

Vending myself. Investment. Norman Nathan. MiP

Venerable mother toothache. A Charm against the Toothache. John Heath-Stubbs. InPK

Veni Creator. Alice Meynell. WPE

Veni Creator Spiritus. *Unknown, paraphrased from Latin by* Dryden. BoReV

Venice and Sunset. Byron. *Fr.* Childe Harold's Pilgrimage, IV. PAIC

Venice, 182-. John Berryman. CoPAm

Venus and Adonis, *sels.* Shakespeare.
　Courser and Jennet. NOBE
　"Imperiously he leaps, he neighs, he bounds." BoAnP

Venus and Cupid. Mark Alexander Boyd. *See* Fra Bank to Bank, Fra Wood to Wood I Rin.

Venus and the Lute Player. Paul Engle. WIF

Venus glows in the east. Work to Do Toward Town. Gary Snyder. VGW

Venus of the Louvre. Emma Lazarus. SBG

Venus of the Salty Shell. Denis Devlin. BIrV

Venus, with young Adonis sitting by her. Bartholomew Griffin. *Fr.* The Passionate Pilgrim, XI. LoAs

Verdant meads are seen, The. Michael Drayton. *Fr.* The Shepherd's Sirena. SCP-2

Vergier. *Unknown, tr. fr. Provençal by* Ezra Pound. GBL

Vergissmeinicht. Keith Douglas. InPS; SoSe (Vergissmeinnicht.) OxBTC

Verifying the Dead. James Welch. CDW

Verigin, Moving in Alone. John Newlove. NeAC

Verigin 3. John Newlove. NeAC

Vermont Conversation. Patricia Hubbell. CTBA

Vernal Sentiment. Theodore Roethke. VoPo

Verona by the poet's pencil drawn. Gondibert, II, 1. Sir William Davenant. SCP-2

Veronica's lost in the garden. In the Sly Gardens. Sonya Dorman. RiTi

Vers de Société. Philip Larkin. PSN

Versatile Historian, The. James Welch. SA

Verse, a breeze mid blossoms straying. Youth and Age. Samuel Taylor Coleridge. MBPR

Verse in Praise of Lord Henry Howard, Earl of Surrey. George Turberville. PAIC

Verse: "What should we know." Oliver St. John Gogarty. WIF

Verses Made the Night before He Died. Michael Drayton. NOBE
　("So well I love thee, as without thee I.") GBL

Verses Made the Night before He Dyed. Sir Walter Ralegh. *See* Epitaph: "Even such is Times, which takes in trust."

Verses of the Talkative Knight, The. Mary Sidney Wroth, Countess of Montgomery. *Fr.* Urania. WPE

Verses on a Rose Street Muse. Charles Senior. MIS

Verses on the Death of Doctor Swift, *sels.* Swift. NOBE
　"Perhaps I may allow, the Dean."
　"Suppose me dead; and then suppose."
　"Time is not remote when I, The."

Verses on the Prospect of Planting Arts and Learning in America. George Berkeley. *See* On the Prospect of Planting...

Verses on the Snuff of a Candle, Made in Sickness. Anne Wharton. SCP-2

Verses upon the Burning of Our House. Anne Bradstreet. *See* Upon the Burning of Our House, July 10th, 1666.

Verses Written During the War, 1756-1763, *sel.* Thomas Osbert Mordaunt.
　Sound, Sound the Clarion. NOBE

Versions of Sunlight. James Applewhite. NVAP

Vertical Is Our New Sight. Daisy Aldan. AATT

Very dead of night: no noise, The. Ditty. Roger Hecht. NowV

Very earth will disown you, The. God Wills It. Gabriela Mistral, *tr. by* K. G. C. LoAs

Very first joy that Mary had, The. The Joys of Mary. *Unknown.* AmFP

Very Like a Whale. Ogden Nash. InPK

Very Odd Fish, A. D'Arcy Wentworth Thompson. OxBChV

Very old are the woods. All That's Past. Walter de la Mare. NOBE; OxBTC

Very Old Woman, A. Clayton Eshleman. MAT

Very personal truth is very hard to discuss, A. The Main Problem in Portraiture. Elisavietta Ritchie. AATT

Very portly crow, A. A Note on Master Crow. Jean Garrigue. BoAnP

Very small children in patched clothing, The. The Study in Aesthetics. Ezra Pound. InPS; NOBA

Very thin/ and opaque. Snake. David McCord. CaYB

Vespers. A. A. Milne. OxBChV; SpRo

Vessels of heavenly medicine! may the breeze. Sonnet on Launching Some Bottles Filled with Knowledge into the Bristol Channel. Shelley. MBPR

Vestal Lady on Brattle, The. Gregory Corso. NoAM

Vestiges. Basil Bunting. TwMBP

Vesture of the Soul, The. "Æ." PFIr

Vet, The. Guy Boas. BoAnP

Veteran. Lola Ridge. WPE

Veteran Sirens. E. A. Robinson. NoAM; NOBA; PiAm

Vet's Rehabilitation. Ray Durem. PoBA

Vicar of Bray, The. *Unknown.* AIW; ESaP; GBP; NOBE; RDB, *with music*

Vicar of Wakefield, The, *sels.* Goldsmith.
　Elegy on the Death of a Mad Dog, An, *fr. ch.* 17. AIW; FaBoCo; LAuP; SS
　Song: "When lovely woman stoops to folly," *fr. ch.* 24. BoLoP; LAuP; NOBE
　(When Lovely Woman Stoops to Folly.) HeIP

Vicious Winter finally yields, The. Heart's Needle, X. W. D. Snodgrass. PSN

Viciousness in the kitchen! Lesbos. Sylvia Plath. RiTi

Vickie. Marnie Walsh. VW

Victim of Aulis, The. Dannie Abse. NoAM

Victor Was a Little Baby. W. H. Auden. PeBB

Victories of Love, The, *sel.* Coventry Patmore.
　"Your love lacks joy, your letter says," II, v. GBL

Victory comes late. Emily Dickinson. InPK

"Vierge Ouvrante." Miriam Palmer. NMM; RiTi

Vietnam. Clarence Major. PoBA

Vietnam #4. Clarence Major. PoBA

View from an Attic Window, The. Howard Nemerov. ConAP

View from Here, The. William Stafford. RFM

View it, by day, from the back. Movie House. John Updike. PPoD

View of a Pig. Ted Hughes. BoAnP; OxBTC; SoSe

View of Vienna from Schonbrunn. Peggy Ruse. NPW

View Toward Wife Trading, A. Robert Gillespie. NVAP

Views from the High Camp.  W. S. Merwin.  ConAP

Views of Our Sphere.  Ernest Sandeen.  Moon

Vigil of Venus, The.  *Unknown, tr. fr. Latin by* Allen Tate.  GBL

Vigil Strange I Kept on the Field One Night.  Walt Whitman.  AmVN; NOBA

Viking Terror, The.  *Unknown, tr. fr. Old Irish by* Kuno Meyer.  PFIr
  (Vikings, The, *tr. by* John Montague.)  BIrV

Vile Stanhope, demons blush to tell.  On Lord Chesterfield and His Son.  *Unknown.*  FaBoCo

Village, The.  George Crabbe.  LAuP
  *Sels.*
  Oncoming Industrial Revolution, The.  OBP
  Rural Life.  NOBE

Village Blacksmith, The.  Longfellow.  AmVN

Village life, and every care that reigns, The.  The Village.  George Crabbe.  LAuP

Village of Balmaquhapple, The.  James Hogg.  FaBoCo

Village of the Presents, The.  James McMichael.  AmPA

Village pedagogue announced one day, A.  The Snuffboxes.  *Unknown.*  PoTa

Village Tale, A.  May Sarton.  BoAnP

Village Tudda, The.  Kenneth Patchen.  VGW

Villagers and Death, The.  Robert Graves.  HeIP

Villages, The.  R. E. Sebenthall.  HeS

Villain, The.  W. H. Davies.  OxBTC; SoSe

Villanelle: "Every day our bodies separate."  Marilyn Hacker.  AmPA

Villanelle: "It is the pain, it is the pain, endures."  William Empson.  LoAs; NoAM

Villanelle: "It's all a trick, quite easy when you know it."  W. W. Skeat.  FaBoCo

Villanelle of the Poet's Road.  Ernest Dowson.  PAIC

Villikins and His Dinah.  Sam Cowell.  PoTa

Villonaud for This Yule.  Ezra Pound.  PAIC

Villon's Straight Tip to All Cross Coves.  W. E. Henley, *after* Villon.  FaBoCo

Vinedresser Yearns over His Vineyard, The.  Irene Dayton.  AATT

Vines tougher than wrists.  Forcing House.  Theodore Roethke.  PiAm

Violence swaddles all (love-) acts before and after.  Peter Whigham.  *Fr. Astapovo, or What Are We to Do.*  TwMBP

Violent bear it away, The.  Question.  Lucille F. Travis.  AATT

Violent Space, The.  Etheridge Knight.  BPo

Virgidemiarum, *sels.*  Joseph Hall.  TVS
  "Great is the folly of a feeble brain," Bk. I, Satire VII.
  "I first adventure, with foolhardy might," Prologue, Bk.I.
  "I wot not how the world's degenerate," Bk. IV, Satire VI.
  "In the heavens' universal alphabet," Bk. II, Satire VII.
  Rome Ryme, Bk. IV, Satire VII.
  "When Gullion died (who knows not Gullion?)" Bk. III, Satire VI.

Virgin, The.  *Unknown.*  GBP

Virgin Jewess, Rising with a Cry, The.  Prentice Baker.  AATT

Virgin Mary, The.  Edgar Bowers.  PiAm

Virgin Mary, The.  Robert Herrick.  SCP-1

Virginal, A.  Ezra Pound.  NoAM; NOBA

Virginia.  Elouise Loftin.  PoBA

Virginia's Bloody Soil.  *Unknown.*  AmFP

Virgin's Song, The.  *Unknown.*  BoReV; NOBE; OxBM

Virtue.  George Herbert.  HeIP; NOBE; PPP; SCP-1; SoSe

Virtue may choose the high or low degree.  The Triumph of Vice.  Pope.  *Fr.* Epilogue to the Satires.  NOBE

Virtuous, witty, proud and gay.  The Romantic.  Colin Ellis.  POL

Virtus Vera Nobilitas.  Mildmay Fane, Earl of Westmorland.  SCP-2

Visible tallow of the hurricane night.  Saving Tallow.  Barbara Guest.  RiTi

Vision, A.  John Clare.  PPP

Vision, A.  Denise Levertov.  PiAm

Vision by Sweetwater.  John Crowe Ransom.  NOBA

Vision doesn't mean anything real.  American Poets.  Marvin Bell.  NVAP

Vision of a Queen of Fairyland, A.  Tadhg Dall O'Huiginn, *tr. by* the Earl of Longford.  *Fr.* The First Vision.  BIrV

Vision of Beulah, The.  Blake.  *Fr.* Milton, II.  NOBE

Vision of Felicity, The.  William Everson.  PiAm

Vision of Judgment, The.  Byron.  ESaP; MBPR

Vision of MacConglinne, The.  MacConglinne, *tr. fr. Middle Irish by* Kuno Meyer.  PFIr
  "Vision that appeared, The," *sel., tr. by* John Montague *after* Kuno Meyer.  BIrV

Vision of Piers Plowman, The, *sels.*  William Langland.
  Belling the Cat (C *text*).  OxBM
  Et Incarnatus Est, *fr.* Passus II (C *text*).  BoReV; NOBE
  Glutton in the Tavern (C *text*).  OxBM
  Jousting of Jesus, The, *fr.* Passus XVIII *and* XXI (B *and* C *texts*).  BoReV
  Long Will in London (C *text*).  OxBM
  Our Needy Neighbours (C *text*).  OxBM
  Poet, Rebuked, Responds, The, *fr.* Passus XII, *mod. by* Selden Rodman.  OBP
  Prologue: "In a summer season, when soft was the sun," *mod. by* Selden Rodman.  OBP
  (Field Full of Folk, The, A *text*.)  OxBM
  Trinity, The (C *text*).  OxBM

Vision of Rotterdam.  Gregory Corso.  NoAM

Vison of Sir Launfal, The, *sel.*  James Russell Lowell.  "And what is so rare as a day in June?"  FSFS

Vision of the Future; the Flood;  Milton.  *Fr.* Paradise Lost, XI.  SCP-1

Vision that appeared, The.  The Vision of MacConglinne.  MacConglinne, *tr. by* John Montague *after* Kuno Meyer.  BIrV

Vision that appeared to me, A.  The Vision of MacConglinne.  MacConglinne, *tr. by* Kuno Meyer.  PFIr

Vision to Electra, The.  Robert Herrick.  LoAs

Visionary, The.  Emily Brontë.  BoReV; NOBE

Visionary Hope, The.  Samuel Taylor Coleridge.  MBPR

Visions.  Kathleen Spivack.  AmPA

Visions of the Daughters of Albion.  Blake.  MBPR

Visions you never saw, The.  Grandfather.  Lance Henson.  CDW

Visit, The.  Emerson.  NOBA

Visit.  James Welch.  AmPA

Visit from St. Nicholas, A.  Clement Clarke Moore.  OxBChV

Visit Peru: Of Stoned Incas' Land.  Teresa McCarthy.  NPW

Visit to Bridge House, A.  Richard Weber.  BIrV

Visit to My Father-In-Law on Memorial Day, A.  Peggy Ruse.  NPW

Visitant, The.  Theodore Roethke.  PPoe

Visitant to our dumbly human home.  The Great Moth.  Robert Gittings.  OxBTC

Visitation.  Elisavietta Ritchie.  AATT

Visiting home to tell my people.  A Long Overdue Thankyou Note to the Girl Who Taught Me Loving.  Tom Schmidt.  NeAC

Visiting Hour.  Norman MacCaig.  LP

Visiting Poet.  John Frederick Nims.  InPK

Visiting the Oracle.  Lawrence Raab.  AmPA

Visitor, The.  W. H. Davies.  GBL

Visitors. Marie Harris. MMD

Visitors. Tu Fu, *tr. fr. Chinese by* Kenneth Rexroth. IPWM

Visits to St. Elizabeths. Elizabeth Bishop. VGW

Vita Nuova. Stanley Kunitz. VGW

Vita-Sheet. Ruth Weiss. MIT

Vitae Summa Brevis Spem Nos Vetat Incohare Longam. Ernest Dowson. NOBE

Vitaï Lampada. Sir Henry Newbolt. BTTM

Vitamins and Roughage. Kenneth Rexroth. NoAM

"Vive la Compagnie," *with music. Unknown.* PSoN

Vive Noir! Mari Evans. IHMS; PoBA; Psy

Vixen, The. John Clare. BoAnP

Vixi Puellis Nuper Idoneus. Sir Thomas Wyatt. *See* Lover Showeth How He Is Forsaken...

Vobiscum Est Iope. Thomas Campion. *See* Among the Shades.

Voice, The. Rupert Brooke. BuTh

Voice, The. George Chambers. HeS

Voice. Claudia Dobkins. NPW

Voice, The. Thomas Hardy. BoLoP; GBL; NoAM; PSN

Voice, The. Theodore Roethke. NowV; VGW

Voice from Danang. Thomas Dillon Redshaw. MAT

Voice from the Roses, A. Maxine W. Kumin. NMM

Voice from the Well, The. George Peele. *Fr.* The Old Wife's Tale. NOBE

Voice from under the Table, A. Richard Wilbur. NOBA

Voice in your chest speaks the language, The. Harold. Stephen Tudor. HeS

Voice of Caesar, The. W. H. Auden. *Fr.* For the Time Being. AnMo

Voice of my beloved, The! Song of Solomon, Bible, *O. T.* PBMP

Voice of the Ancient Bard, The. Blake. *Fr.* Songs Of Experience. MBPR

Voice of the Future, The. Michele Wallace. WBN

Voice of the glutton I heard with disdain, The. The Glutton. John Oakman. OxBChV

Voice of the last cricket, The. Splinter. Carl Sandburg. SoSe

Voice of the Surbahar, *sels.* Robin Fulton. MIS
  "It seems a frail mathematics, and ancient."
  "Spring was a month late, autumn a month early."

Voice peals in this end of night, A. A Thrush before Dawn. Alice Meynell. WPE

Voice, A, said, "Follow, follow": and I rose. Two Pursuits. Christina Rossetti. WPE

Voice, The, said, "Hurl her down!" The Lovely Shall Be Choosers. Robert Frost. NOBA

Voice, A, said, Look me in the stars. A Question. Robert Frost. TH

Voices Answering Back: The Vampires. Lawrence Raab. AmPA

Voices at the Window. Sir Philip Sidney. *See* Astrophel and Stella: Eleventh Song.

Voices from Things Growing in a Churchyard. Thomas Hardy. OxBTC

Voices Inescapable, The. Ann Stanford. IHMS

Voices move, The. they are walking. it is time. Not under Holly or Green Boughs. Tom Raworth. TwMBP

Voices moving about in the quiet house. Falling Asleep. Siegfried Sassoon. FSFS; OxBTC

Voices of birds are. Is Is Like Is. Adrien Stoutenburg. TSWA

Voices of Heroes. Horace Gregory. OFD

Voices of the Night, *sel.* Longfellow. Prelude: "Pleasant it was, when woods were green." FSFS

Volatile Kerryman, The. Owen Roe O'Sullivan, *tr. fr. Irish by* Sean O'Riada. BIrV

Volcanic Venus. D. H. Lawrence. InPS; POL

Volpone, *sels.* Ben Jonson.
  "Come, my Celia, let us prove," *fr.* III, vii. HeIP (Come, My Celia.) IPWM
  "Death of mine honor, with the city's fool!" *fr.* II, iii. SCP-1

Volunteer, The. Herbert Asquith. OxBTC

Voodoo on the Un-Assing of Janis Joplin. Carolyn M. Rodgers. JB

Votaries know. A Poem for Integration. Alvin Saxon. PoBA

Vote, The. Ralph Knevet. SCP-2

Vow, The. Anthony Hecht. ConAP; CoPAm; Prf

Vow to Love Faithfully, Howsoever He Be Rewarded, A. Petrarch, *tr. fr. Italian by* the Earl of Surrey. Sonnets to Laura: To Laura in Life, CXIII. PAIC ("Set me wheras the sonne dothe perche the grene.") AAS

Vowels. Peter West. AKE

Vox Populi. Dryden. *Fr.* The Medal. NOBE

"Voy wawm" said the dustman. Hymn to the Sun. Michael Roberts. OxBTC

Voyage. Stephen Stepanchev. SA

Voyage Itself, The. Ben Jonson. TVS

Voyage on the Thames, The. Pope. *Fr.* The Rape of the Lock, II. NOBE

Voyage to the Island of Love, A, *sel.* Aphra Behn. "Thousand gloomy walks the bower contains, A." SCP-2

Voyage to the Moon. William Dickey. CoPAm; Moon

Voyage to the Moon. Archibald MacLeish. Moon; PBMP

Voyage West. Archibald MacLeish. VGW

Voyages (I-VI). Hart Crane. NoAM; NOBA
  *Sels.*
  "Above the fresh ruffles of the surf," I. PSN; VGW
  "And yet this great wink of eternity," II. PAIC; PiAm; PPoe; PPP; VGW
  "Infinite consanguinity it bears," III. LoAs
  "Meticulous, past midnight in clear rime," V. PSN

Vulture, The. Hilaire Belloc. OxBChV

Vulture. Robinson Jeffers. BoAnP; NOBA; PiAm

Vulture and the Husbandman, The. A. C. HIlton. FaBoCo

Vulture eats between his meals, The. The Vulture. Hilaire Belloc. OxBChV

Vulture's very like a sack, The. Ecology. X. J. Kennedy. BoAnPoAS

# W

W. C. W. David Ray. POL

W. S. Landor. Marianne Moore. Psy

W. W. LeRoi Jones. HeIP; NOBA; PiAm; PoBA

Wabash Cannonball, *with music. Unknown.* BLSo

Wade/ through black jade. The Fish. Marianne Moore. NoAM; PBMP; PiAm

Wading upstream we bump his carcass. Raccoon Skeleton at Long Plain Creek. Helena Minton. FAF

Wae's Me for Prince Charlie. William Glen. BTTM

Wae's me, wae's me. Song of the Cauld Lad of Hylton. *Unknown.* GBP

Waggoner, The. *Unknown.* GBP

Wagoner's Lad, The. *Unknown.* AmFP

Wagons loom like blue caravans in the dusk, The. Harvest Home. Sir Herbert Read. RAE

Wagtail's Nest, The. Kenneth Mackenzie. MAuV

Wail, wail, ah for Adonis! He is lost to us, lovely Adonis. Lament for Adonis. Bion, *tr. by* John Addington Symonds. Epi

Wailing, wailing, wailing, the wind over land and sea. Rizpah. Tennyson. PAIC

Waily, Waily. *Unknown. See* Waly, Waly ("When cockle shells turn silver bells").

Waist up, I know. Mermaid. Helena Minton. FAF

Wait. P. D. Cummins. BuTh

Wait a Little! *Unknown.* BoReV; OxBM

Wait for Me. Robert Creeley. NOBA; PPP

Wait for the Wagon, *with music. Unknown, at. to* R. Bishop Buckley. BLSo; PSoN

Wait, Kate! You skate at such a rate. To Kate, Skating Better than Her Date. David Daiches. CTBA; SPo

Wait; the great horned owls. Owls. W. D. Snodgrass. BoAnP

Wait 'till the Sun Shines, Nellie, *with music.* Andrew B. Sterling. BLSH, *chorus only*; BLSo; FSN

Waiter waited, the cook ate, The. What Happened? What Do You Expect? Alan Dugan. NowV

Waiting. Robert Creeley. VGW

Waiting at the Church; or, My Wife Won't Let Me, *with music.* Fred W. Leigh. FSN

Waiting by the window. The Last Gangster. Gregory Corso. CoPAm; SA

Waiting for breakfast, while she brushed her hair. Philip Larkin. NoAM

Waiting for Her. Alden Nowlan. NeAC

Waiting for It. May Swenson. BoAnP

Waiting for the Bus. D. J. Enright. OxBTC

Waiting for the corpse. Shetland Funeral. James Rankin. MIS

Waiting for the Doctor. Colette Inez. IHMS

Waiting for the end, boys, waiting for the end. Just a Smack at Auden. William Empson. FaBoCo

Waiting for You to Come By. Simon J. Ortiz. CDW

Waiting in the Cafe. Stan Rice. MIT

Waiting rooms are full of "characters," The. Prentending Not to Sleep. Ian Hamilton. NoAM

Waiting, the Hallways under Her Skin Thick with Dreamchildren. Lyn Lifshin. FAF; NeAC

Waiting to Be Fed. Ray A. Young Bear. CDW

Wake, The. Madeline DeFrees. RiTi

Wake, The. Robert Herrick. PAIC

Wake All the Dead. Sir William Davenant. *Fr.* The Law against Lovers. OBP

Wake. And my eyes stun. I Wake, My Friend, I. Faye Kicknosway. IHMS

Wake at the Well, The. *Unknown.* GBP

Wake! For the sun, who scattered into flight. Omar Khayyám, *tr. fr. Persian by* Edward Fitzgerald. *Fr.* The Rubáiyát of Omar Khayyám of Naishápúr. OBP

Wake, friend, from forth thy lethargy! the drum. Ben Jonson. *Fr.* An Epistle to a Friend (Mr. Colby) to Persuade Him to the Wars. SCP-1

Wake Not for the World-Heard Thunder. A. E. Housman. NoAM

Wake, now my love, awake; for it is time. Spenser. *Fr.* Epithalamion: "Ye learned sisters which have oftentimes." GBL

Wake: the silver dusk returning. Reveille. A. E. Housman. SoSe

Wake up high up. Things to Do in New York (City). Ted Berrigan. NoAM

Wake up mama turn your lamp down lo-ow. Statesboro Blues. *Unknown.* BluL

Wake-Up Niggers. Don L. Lee. PoBA

Wake up, wake up, darlin' Cory. Darling Cory. *Unknown.* AmFP

Wakening pang had grown a sullen ache, The. Quem Queritis. Albert Howard Carter. AATT

Wakes, bluejean morning, sound of. Geography. Michael Dransfield. CAAP

Waking. Hugh Maxton. BIrV

Waking, The ("I strolled across/ An open field"). Theodore Roethke. RFM

Waking, The ("I wake to sleep, and take my waking slow"). Theodore Roethke. HeIP; InPS; NoAM; NOBA; PiAm; PPP; SoSe; TCP; VoPo

Waking at Night. Morton Marcus. MIT

Waking beside you I watch this night. Alba for Mélusine. Ramon Guthrie. LoAs

Waking, child, while you slept, your mother took. Ethel Anderson. *Fr.* Bucolic Eclogues. WPE

Waking close to the trees. In the Mountain Cabin. Del Marie Rogers. NPW

Waking Early Sunday Morning. Robert Lowell. NOBA

Waking from a Nap on the Beach. May Swenson. RFM

Waking from Sleep. Robert Bly. CAPP; InPS; NoAM; NOBA

Waking, I always waked you awake. Jean Garrigue. LoAs

Waking in the Blue. Robert Lowell. CoPAm; PiAm; PPP; PSN

Waking this morning. This Morning. Muriel Rukeyser. IPWM; NMM

Waking to Leopards. Nancy Mairs. NPW

Waking to Snowfall. Roderick Hartigh Jellema. AATT

Wakonda! Talako! deathonic turkey gobbling. Spontaneous Requiem for the American Indian. Gregory Corso. MAT

Waldeinsamkeit. Emerson. NOBA

Walden Pond/ All those noxious gases rising from it. Jack Spicer. *Fr.* "Graphemics." VGW

Waldheim Cemetery. Robert Sward. ANTL

Wale whyt as whalles bon, A. The White Beauty. *Unknown.* OxBM

Wales Visitation. Allen Ginsberg. CAPP; NOBA; Prf

Walk, The. Thomas Hardy. PSN

Walk. Frank Horne. BPo

Walk. Brian Merriman, *tr. fr. Modern Irish by* Brendan Behan. *Fr.* The Midnight Court. BIrV

Walk, A. Gary Snyder. NoAM; NOBA

Walk east. Dawn polishes the sky. Direction. Roberta Hill. CDW

Walk Home, The. Reed Whittemore. ConAP

Walk in March, A. Tim Reynolds. MAT

Walk on your heels. Achilles Tendon. Coleman Barks. *Fr.* Body Poems. NVAP

Walk out into your country. Who Shall Die. James A. Randall, Jr. BPo

Walk proud, walk straight, let your thoughts race. Musings. Patty Harjo. VW

Walk Together Children. *Unknown.* BPo

Walk with de Mayor of Harlem. David Henderson. PoBA

Walk with the sun. Dream Song. Lewis Alexander. PoBA

Walking at last by the tame little edge of the sea. Evening Before Rain. L. A. G. Strong. OxBTC

Walking at night on asphalt campus. Death News. Allen Ginsberg. NoAM

Walking Blues. *Unknown.* BluL

Walking by map, I chose unwonted ground. On the Hall at Stowey. Charles Tomlinson. NoAM

Walking for That Cake, *with music.* Ed Harrigan. BLSo

Walking from the killing place. Death and the Arkansas River. Frank Stanford. FiCP

Walking. I begin to notice.  Lost Country.  Warren Woessner. HeS

Walking, I heard the water dripping, running in the gutter.  Partly to My Cat.  Ellen Bass.  NMM

Walking in a meadow green.  *Unknown.*  BoLoP

Walking into a hall full of nurses.  A Poem for Richard Speck. Michael McMahon.  FAF

Walking into Love, *sel.*  Marge Piercy. Meditation in My Favorite Position.  RiTi

Walking of the Moon-Woman, The.  John Shaw Neilson. MAuV

Walking on the Green Grass.  *Unknown.*  AmFP

Walking out, I flushed some meadowlarks.  The Duck Pond at Mini's Pasture, a Dozen Years Later.  Philip Dow.  AmPA

Walking out of the "big E."  Before the Stuff Comes Down. Gary Snyder.  HeIP; PiAm

Walking Parker Home.  Bob Kaufman.  PoBA

Walking Song.  William E. Hickson.  OxBChV

Walking the Beach.  Sarah Youngblood.  IHMS

Walking the small oval of Gibbs Pond.  I Move to Random Consolations.  William Heyen.  AmPA

Walking the suburbs in the afternoon.  Suburban Dreams. Edwin Muir.  OxBTC

Walking through the Country.  Dennis Provisor.  PoRo

Walking thru Audley End Mansion Late Afternoon, *sels.*  Lyn Lifshin.  RiTi
"Down the hall a bookcase."
"In some places the color."
"Stuffed birds in a/ cage."
"Why her bedroom is a/ trip."

Walking to the Cattle-Place, *sels.*     Les A. Murray.  CAAP
Artery, The.
Birds in Their Title Work Freeholds of Straw.
Death Words.
Names of the Humble, The.
Sanskrit.

Walking up sands, offal is gaped from a tunnel seaward. Reclaimed Area.  Jon Silkin.  NoAM

Walking with God.  William Cowper.  BoReV

Walking without Snowshoes.  Elizabeth Hanson.  NPW

Wall, The.  Gwendolyn Brooks.  *Fr.* Two Dedications.  PoBA

Wall, The.  Raymond Carver.  NVAP

Wall, The.  David Jones.  TwMBP

Wallowing in this bloody sty.  The Drunken Fisherman.  Robert Lowell.  AnMo; CoPAm; NOBA; VGW

Walls Do Not Fall, The, *sels.*  Hilda Doolittle ("H.D.").  NoAM
"In me (the worm) clearly."
"Incident here and there, An."
"So we reveal our status."
"There is a spell, for instance."
"When in the company of the gods."

Walls. . .iridescent with eyes.  The Fifth-Floor Window.  Lola Ridge.  WPE

Walls, wire, fields, and a crumbly road.  Cape Cornwall.  Paul Mills.  MIS

Walnut bark, walnut sap.  Dogget Gap.  *Unknown.*  AmFP

Walnut-Leaf Scent.  Laurence Binyon.  BBGO

Walrus and the Carpenter, The.  "Lewis Carroll."  *Fr.* Through the Looking-Glass, *ch.* 4.  AKE; FaBoCo; OxBChV

Walsingham.  *Unknown, sometimes at. to* Sir Walter Ralegh. BoLoP; NOBE; PPP
("As you came from the holy land.")  AAS; GBL; LoAs
(As You Came from the Holy Land of Walsingham.)  InPS
(Ballad: "As you came...")  PAIC

Walt Whitman.  Edwin Honig.  PAIC

Walt Whitman, a kosmos, of Manhattan the son.  Song of Myself, XXIV.  Walt Whitman.  AnMo

Walt Whitman, an American, one of the roughs, a kosmos.  Walt Whitman.  *Fr.* Song of Myself, XXIV.  GrRo

Walt Whitman at Bear Mountain.  Louis Simpson.  ConAP

Walter Jenks' Bath.  William Meredith.  CoPAm

Walter Llywarch.  R. S. Thomas.  PSN

Walter Rawely of the Middle Temple, in Commendation of the Steele Glasse.  Sir Walter Ralegh.  AAS

Walter Spaggot.  Peter Wesley-Smith.  RAE

Waltz against the Mountains.  Thomas Hornsby Ferril.  VGW

Waltz in, waltz in, ye little kids, and gather round my knee.  The Spelling Bee at Angels.  Bret Harte.  PoTa

Waltz Me Around Again Willie; or, 'Round, 'Round, 'Round, *with music.*  Will D. Cobb.  FSN

Waltzing Matilda.  Andrew Barton Paterson.  GBP; PeBB; PoTa; RDB, *with music*

Waly, Waly ("O Waly, Waly up the bank").  *Unknown.*  SLP
(O Waly, Waly up the Bank.)  AIW; GBP

Waly, Waly ("When cockle shells turn silver bells").  *Unknown.* AmFP
(Cockleshells, *with music.*)  RDB
(Jamie Douglas.)  AIW
(Waily, Waily.)  AIW

Wan as pale thighs making apple belly strides.  Sonnet.  Ted Berrigan.  CAAP

Wand of that fisherman witching the waves, The.  Marlin. Brewster Ghiselin.  PPoD

Wanderer, The.  W. H. Auden.  NoAM

Wanderer, The, *sel.*  Christopher Brennan.
"Land I came thro' last was dumb with night, The."  MAuV

Wanderer, The.  *Unknown, tr. fr. Old English by* Andrew Hoyem. Epi

Wanderer, The: A Rococo Study, *sel.*  William Carlos Williams. Paterson—The Strike.  Epi

Wanderers, The.  William Morris.  *Fr.* The Earthly Paradise. VPC

Wandering minstrel I, A.  W. S. Gilbert.  *Fr.* The Mikado. AIW

Wandering oversea dreamer.  Prayer after World War.  Carl Sandburg.  VGW

Wandering through cold streets tangled like old string.  Brussels in Winter.  W. H. Auden.  OxBTC

Wand'ring in this place as a wilderness.  *Unknown.*  GBL

Waning Moon, The.  Shelley.  Moon

Wanted, Wanted: Dolores Haze.  Vladimir Nabokov.  RRA

Wanting a Mummy.  Sandra McPherson.  AmPA

Wanting to be myself, alone.  Cock Crow.  Rosemary Dobson. MAuV

Wanting to Die.  Anne Sexton.  ConAP; IHMS; NoAM

Wanton Merry Friar, A.  Chaucer.  *Fr.* The Canterbury Tales: Prologue.  BoReV

Wanton troopers riding by, The.  The Nymph Complaining for the Death of Her Fawn [*or* Faun].  Andrew Marvell.  Epi; HeIP; PAIC; SCP-1

Wanton with long delay the gay spring leaping cometh.  April 1885.  Robert Bridges.  OxBTC

Wants to be admired.  The Horse in the Drugstore.  Tess Gallagher.  AmPA

War.  Dryden.  *Fr.* Annus Mirabilis.  SCP-1

War ("Aged in the villages, The").  Miguel Hernández, *tr. fr. Spanish by* Edwin Honig.  IPWM

War ("All the mothers in the world").  Miguel Hernández, *tr. fr. Spanish by* James Wright.  Epi

War.  Joseph Langland.  IPWM

War.  Patricia Ramsey.  AATT

War Against the Trees, The.  Stanley Kunitz.  NoAM

War and Silence.  Robert Bly.  CAPP

War has begun, The.  The Root Eater.  Ai.  CAAP

War Horse, The.   Eavan Boland.   BIrV

War in Heaven.   Milton.   *Fr.* Paradise Lost, VI.   OBP

War Is Kind, *sels.*   Stephen Crane.
   "Fast rode the knight," VIII.   PiAm
   "Impact of a dollar upon the heart, The," XX.   PiAm
   Little Ink More or Less, A, IV.   VoPo
   "Man said to the universe, A," XXI.   AmVN; PiAm; SFF
   "Slant of sun on dull brown walls, A," XIV.   AmVN; PiAm
   "There was a man with tongue of wood," XVI.   PiAm
   "Trees in the garden rained flowers, The," XXVI.   SFF
   War Is Kind, I (title poem).   PAIC; PiAm; VoPo; WIF
    (Do Not Weep, Maiden, for War Is Kind.)   NOBA
   "Wayfarer, The," XIII.   PiAm

War Poet.   Sidney Keyes.   BuTh

War Requiem.   Del Marie Rogers.   NPW

War Song of Dinas Vawr, The.   Thomas Love Peacock.   *Fr.* The
   Misfortunes of Elphin.   NOBE; PoTa

War Summer.   James Applewhite.   NVAP

War Walking Near.   Ray A. Young Bear.   CDW

War War.   Michael Goode.   NowV

Ward, and still in bonds, one day, A.   Regeneration.   Henry
   Vaughan.   SCP-1

Ward X, *sel.*   Lola Ridge.
   "Salvation Army lass, The."   WPE

Wardour Street.   Humbert Wolfe.   OxBTC

Warm and savory sleep of sated desire, The.   Nightlines.   Paul
   Clause.   AATT

Warm sun is failing, the bleak wind is wailing, The.   Autumn; A
   Dirge.   Shelley.   FSFS

Warning, The.   Adelaide Crapsey.   WPE

Warning, The.   Robert Creeley.   CoPAm; VGW

Warning.   Langston Hughes.   BPo

Warning.   Jenny Joseph.   LP; MPo; OxBTC

Warning, The.   Longfellow.   PiAm

Warning ("My mother said").   *Unknown.*   ECBV

Warning and Reply.   Emily Brontë.   WPE

Warning to Beware, A.   *Unknown.*   OxBM

Warren Pryor.   Alden Nowlan.   BBGO

Warren's Address.   John Pierpont.   BTTM

Warrior Dreams.   Ray A. Young Bear.   VW

Wars of Santa Fe, The.   *Unknown.*   AmFP

Wars of the Roses, The.   *Unknown.*   GBP

Warship of 1812, The.   *Unknown.*   BTTM

Wartime Blues.   *Unknown.*   BluL

Wary of time O it seizes the soul tonight.   Easter Eve.   Muriel
   Rukeyser.   VGW

Was a Man.   Philip Booth.   NCSH; VGW

Was born obedient.   Robert.   Lucille Clifton.   CAAP

Was He Married?   Stevie Smith.   NoAM

Was I surprised!   Uncle Death.   Walter Clark.   NCSH

Was it a dream? We sailed, I thought we sailed.   A Dream.
   Matthew Arnold.   GBL

Was it for this I uttered prayers.   Grown-up.   Edna St. Vincent
   Millay.   NoAM; TH

Was It Not Curious?   Stevie Smith.   NoAM

Was it not the goddess of the moon.   Moon.   Elizabeth Brewster.
   MMD

Was it really you all the time?   Dream Sequence, Part 9.   Naomi
   Long Madgett.   BPo

Was she so chaste?   She rebukes Hippolyta.   Hilda Doolittle
   ("H.D.").   SBG

Was there ere sic a parish, a parish, a parish.   Little Dunkeld.
   *Unknown.*   GBP

Was this the daughter you bargained for.   The Mutant.   Anita
   Barrows.   RiTi

Was this the face that launched a thousand ships?   Christopher
   Marlowe.   *Fr.* Doctor Faustus.   GBL; HeIP

Was two sisters loved one man.   The Two Sisters.   *Unknown.*
   MAT

Was Worm.   May Swenson.   BoAnP

Wash.   Eilean Ni Chuilleanain.   BIrV

Wash.   John Updike.   TSWA

Wash Day.   Larry Mollin.   NeAC

Wash man out of the earth, shear off.   Wash.   Eilean Ni
   Chuilleanain.   BIrV

Washed in Silver.   James Stephens.   Moon

Washed in Water.   Rayne Mackinnon.   MIS

Washer-Windows, The.   Paul Clause.   AATT

Washing Windows.   Barry Spacks.   NCSH

Washington.   Nancy Byrd Turner.   ECBV

Washington Monument by Night.   Carl Sandburg.   OFD

Washington, the brave, the wise, the good.   Washington.
   *Unknown.*   OFD

Washington's Monument, February 1885.   Walt Whitman.   OFD

Wasn't it just that.   In More's Hotel.   Robert Nye.   SLP

Wasn't That a Mighty Storm?   *Unknown.*   AmFP

Wasp.   Alden Nowlan.   BoAnP

Waspish.   Robert Frost.   BoAnP

Wasps' Nest, The.   George MacBeth.   OxBTC

Wassail Song ("We have been a walking").   *Unknown.*   GBP

Waste.   Harry Graham.   FaBoCo

Waste Land, The.   T. S. Eliot.   NoAM; NOBA; NOBE;
   OxBTC; PiAm; PPoe

Watch, The.   Frances Cornford.   InPK; OxBTC

Watch.   John Daniel.   TwMBP

Watch, The.   May Swenson.   PoTa

Watch it. That's the body: what goes on.   The Body.   William
   Bronk.   VGW

Watch me/ I am moving through the cages of the animals.
   Animal Poems.   Gwendolyn MacEwen.   MMD

Watch me bruise the air with my hawk winged flutterings.
   Miracle Worker.   Claudia Dobkins.   NPW

Watch out for the bus.   Mercado.   Greg Pape.   AmPA

Watch that net drift. Grey tides.   How to Catch Tiddlers.   Brian
   Jones.   LP

Watch the Lights Fade.   Robinson Jeffers.   NoAM; NOBA

Watch upon my wrist, The.   Parable.   W. H. Auden.   FaBoCo

Watcher, The.   John Peck.   AmPA

Watchers, The.   Paul Blackburn.   PAIC

Watchdog.   Richard Armour.   ECBV

Watched clock never moves, they said, A.   The Slow Starter.
   Louis MacNeice.   MPo; PBMP

Watching Gymnasts.   Robert Francis.   SPo

Watching hands transplanting.   Transplanting.   Theodore
   Roethke.   PiAm

Watching Post.   C. Day Lewis.   MPo

Watching Salmon Jump.   Simon J. Ortiz.   CDW

Watching the iris.   Amy Lowell.   TH

Watching the light.   Morality Play.   Pat Lowther.   MMD

Watching the shied core.   As Bad as a Mile.   Philip Larkin.
   InPK

Watching the White Image, electric moon.   In a Moonlit Hermit's
   Cabin.   Allen Ginsberg.   Moon

Watching this dawn's mnemonic of old dawning.   Sestina in a
   Cantina.   Malcolm Lowry.   PAIC

Watching You Draw.   Carol Cox.   MMD

Watching You Walk.   Ruthven Todd.   SLP

Water.   Robert Lowell.   HeIP; NOBA; PiAm

Water and Light, Light and Water.   Mark Perlberg.   HeS

Water astonishing and difficult altogether. Water Raining. Gertrude Stein. *Fr.* Tender Buttons. RiTi

Water Babies, The, *sels.*      Charles Kingsley.
  Lost Doll, The. ECBV
    (Little Doll, The.) OxBChV
  Tide River, The. OxBChV
  Young and Old. OxBChV

Water clock of melting snow, The. For My Grandfather in Greenfield Center. Joseph Bruchac. FAF

Water closing, The. Together. Maxine W. Kumin. NMM; WBN

Watercolor of Grantchester Meadows. Sylvia Plath. SBG

Water Crowvoot, The. William Barnes. VPC

Water is H$_2$O, hydrogen two parts, oxygen one. The Third Thing. D. H. Lawrence. AKE

Water is heavy silver over stone. What Any Lover Learns. Archibald MacLeish. PiAm

Water Island. Howard Moss. Prf

Water like quartz, with the same kinds of strata, The. Nights Passed on Ward's Island, Toronto Harbour. Doug Fetherling. NeAC

Water Poems. Sandra McPherson. CAAP

Water Raining. Gertrude Stein. *Fr.* Tender Buttons. RiTi

Water-truck, The. Patrick Lane. NeAC

Water turns, The. You Are Happy. Margaret Atwood. MMD

Water was usually clean. Dead Man Creek. Van K. Brock. NVAP

Waterchew! Gregory Corso. VGW

Watercress Seller, The. Thomas Miller. OxBChV

Waterfall. Seamus Heaney. NoAM

Waterfall, The. Henry Vaughan. BoReV; NOBE

Waterfalls. Vernon Watkins. NoAM

Watering the Horse. Robert Bly. NCSH

Waterloo. Byron. *Fr.* Childe Harold's Pilgrimage. PPoD
  (Eve of Waterloo, The.) NOBE

Waters of the well of life, The. The Well of Life. Sir Herbert Read. NoAM

Waters of Tyne, The. *Unknown.* GBP

Watershed, The. Alice Meynell. SBG

Watts. Shirley Kaufman. NMM

Watts. Conrad Kent Rivers. PoBA

Watts. Alvin Saxon. PoBA

Wave, The. Daryl Hine. Prf

Wave, The. David Phillips. NeAC

Wavering planet most unstable, The. *Unknown.* Moon

Waving good-bye to mum. At the Airport. Evan Jones. MAuV

Way, The. Robert Creeley. BoLoP; PPP

Way a crow, The. Dust of Snow. Robert Frost. FSFS; IPWM; SoSe; SS; TSWA

Way at night these piping peepers, The. The Peepers in Our Meadow. Archibald MacLeish. NCSH

Way Down, The. Philip Levine. NOBA

Way down in the bottom. Poor Little Johnny. *Unknown.* AmFP

Way down in yonders low valley, in some lonesome place. Pretty Saro. *Unknown.* AmFP

Way down south in Dixie. Song for a Dark Girl. Langston Hughes. PoBA

Way down South where I was born. A Long time Ago. *Unknown.* AmFP

Way down upon the Swanee River [or de Swannee ribber]. The Old Folks at Home. Stephen Collins Foster. BLSH; BLSo; PSoN

'Way high up the Mogollons. The Glory Trail. Badger Clark. PoTa

Way I gained my titles, The. Champagne Charlie. *At. to* George Leybourne. BLSo

Way I read a letter's—this, The. Emily Dickinson. InPS; LoAs; WPE

Way I walked that Sunday night, I was one of them, The. Let's All Meet and Have a Party Sometime. John Birkby. BuTh

Way It Happens to You, The. Harold Bond. NVAP

Way It Is, The. Gloria C. Oden. IHMS

Way It Is, The. Mark Strand. CAAP

Way It Was, The. Lucille Clifton. WPE

Way of Keeping, A. Nancy WIllard. IHMS

Way out in California. The Santa Barbara Earthquake. *Unknown.* AmFP

Way Out in Idaho. *Unknown.* AmFP

Way Out West. LeRoi Jones. PoBA

Way Sun Keeps Falling Away from Every Window, The. Lyn Lifshin. NeAC

Way the Bird Sat, The. Ray A. Young Bear. CDW

Way Through, The. Denise Levertov. CoPAm

Way through the Woods, The. Kipling. NOBE; OxBChV; OxBTC; RFM

Way to call up quick wishes. On Seeing a Torn Out Coin Telephone. Martin Robbins. MAT

Way to Hump a Cow Is Not, The. E. E. Cummings. NoAM; NOBA

Way up in my tree I'm sitting by my fire. Gypsy Eyes. Jimi Hendrix. GrRo

Way We Wonder, The. Robert Pack. WIF

Wayfarer, The. War Is Kind, XIII. Stephen Crane. PiAm

Ways and Means. "Lewis Carroll." *See* White Knight's Song.

Ways of Day. Robert Penn Warren. *Fr.* Notes on a Life to Be Lived. NoAM

Ways of God, The. Milton. *Fr.* Samson Agonistes. BoReV

Wayside Station, The. Edwin Muir. PSN

Waz, adverse to thinking. No Bargains Today. Peggy Susberry Kenner. JB

We all have/ A bench in the park to reach. George Jonas. NeAC

We all have/ A new arm. The New Arm. Tom Hennen. HeS

We all have our faults. Mine is trying to write poems. Singing Aloud. Carolyn Kizer. IHMS

We all went to town one day. Bessie Dreaming Bear. Marnie Walsh. VW

We all were watching the quiz on television. A Singular Metamorphosis. Howard Nemerov. ConAP

We are/ sorry to have to. You Understand the Requirements. Lyn Lifshin. NeAC; RiTi

We Are. Maxine W. Kumin. WBN

We are a band of brothers, and native to the soil. The Bonnie Blue Flag. Harry Macarthy. BLSo; BTTM; PSoN

We are a meadow where the bees hum. Bedtime. Denise Levertov. AnMo; IHMS

We are already on the moon. Vacuum. Josephine Miles. Moon

We are approaching sleep: the chestnut blossoms in the mind. Awakening. Robert Bly. ConAP

We are as clouds that veil the midnight moon. Mutability. Shelley. MBPR

We are asleep under mirrors. What do I. Before the War. Marilyn Hacker. AmPA

We are burning/ in our heads. A Poet Recognizing the Echo of the Voice. Diane Wakoski. Psy

We are coming, Father Abraham, three hundred thousand more. Three Hundred Thousand More. James Sloan Gibbons. BTTM

We are coming from the cotton fields. Song of the Freeman. *Unknown.* PBMP

We are drowning now. Alienation (To My Son). Lucille F. Travis. AATT

We are going to see the rabbit. The Rabbit. Alan Brownjohn. MPo

We are in Chicago's Waldheim cemetery. Waldheim Cemetery. Robert Sward. ANTL

We are little airy creatures. The Five. Swift. ECBV

We are lovers/ after our fashion. The Dancer from the Dance. Suzanne Juhasz. IHMS

We are never free of the voices. The Voices Inescapable. Ann Stanford. IHMS

We are not come to wage a strife. The Day-breakers. Arna Bontemps. PoBA

We are not conceited. Coupling. Cynthia Macdonald. WBN

We are not going to steal the water tower. Stopping Near Highway 80. David Ray. HeS

We are not lovers. Man and Wife. Anne Sexton. CAPP

We are ourselves but carriers. Life. Epigram: For a Woman with Child. J. V. Cunningham. PiAm

We are prepared: we build our houses squat. Storm on the Island. Seamus Heaney. NCSH

We Are Seven. Wordsworth. MBPR; OxBChV; SpRo

We are singing for the face of cisco. Song for the Cisco Kid; or, Singing for the Face. K. Curtis Lyle. PoBA

We are so tired; my heart and I. Rest. Mathilde Blind. SBG

We are sorry we cannot use the enclosed. Form Rejection Letter. Philip Dacey. AmPA

We are squared off in the snow. Brothers Together in Winter. Harley Elliott. NeAC

We are standing facing each other. Margaret Atwood. NeAC

We are talking in bed. You show me snapshots. A Family Man. Maxine W. Kumin. CoPAm; IHMS

We are the hollow men. The Hollow Men. T. S. Eliot. AnMo; InPS; PBMP; TCP

We are the music-makers. Ode. Arthur O'Shaughnessy. PFIr; WIF

We are things of dry hours and the involuntary plan. Kitchenette Building. Gwendolyn Brooks. BPo

We Are Three Brethren Come from Spain. Unknown. GBP

We are three, clearly three. Beckoned in Dream to the Unconscious. David Kherdian. FAF

We Are Transmitters. D. H. Lawrence. OxBTC

We are unfair. We Own the Night. LeRoi Jones. PoBA

We are waltzing now into the moonlit morning. Waltz against the Mountains. Thomas Hornsby Ferril. VGW

We arrive like sunlight in winter: tentative. Pine Needles. Warren Slesinger. VGW

We artists have strange nerves! In a Hotel Writing-Room. John Cowper Powys. OxBTC

We Assume: On the Death of Our Son, Reuben Masai Harper. Michael S. Harper. AmPA

We ate our breakfast lying on our backs. Breakfast. W. W. Gibson. OxBTC

We Be Soldiers Three. Unknown. GBP

We Become New. Marge Piercy. WBN

We boogied when I was eight. Autobiography Part Two: Rock and Roll. Jessica Tarahata Hagedorn. MMD

We bought him for a watchdog. Watchdog. Richard Armour. ECBV

We brought them. Finally. Bruce Severy. HeS

We brushed our hair back and our. The Last Refuge. Augustus Young. BIrV

We but begin to hope to know, having known. Subject. Marie Ponsot. VGW

We came to the edge. A Pretty Woman. Simon J. Ortiz. CDW

We came to the outer light down a ramp in the dark. Westland Row. Thomas Kinsella. NoAM

We Can Be Together. Paul Kantner. GrRo

We can sclim up by words. Words. Duncan Glen. MIS

We cannot go to the country. Raleigh Was Right. William Carlos Williams. NoAM

We canoe a creek. Girl Friends. Rosemary Daniell. WBN

We can't grumble about accommodation. Song of the Battery Hen. Edwin Brock. LP; MPo

We carried you in our arms. Tears of Rage. Bob Dylan. RRA

We caught the tread of dancing feet. The Harlot's House. Oscar Wilde. InPK; PPoD

We chanced in passing by that afternoon. The Black Cottage. Robert Frost. VGW

We come!/ We come! Ben Jonson. Fr. The Golden Age Restored. SCP-1

We Continue. W. S. Merwin. CAPP

We couldn't even keep the furnace lit! To Delmore Schwartz. Robert Lowell. NoAM

We crave your condescension. The Mulligan Guard. Ned Harrigan. BLSo

We crossed by ferry to the bare island. By Ferry to the Island. Iain Crichton Smith. MPo

We Dance Like Ella Riffs. Carolyn M. Rodgers. PoBA

We dance round in a ring and suppose. The Secret Sits. Robert Frost. InPK; TH

We deserved that earth-shot from the. Views of Our Sphere. Ernest Sandeen. Moon

We Did It. Yehuda Amichai, tr. fr. Hebrew by Harold Schimmel. BoLoP

We didn't think/ nuthin. Poems about Playmates. Ronda Davis. JB

We died in Zortman on a Sunday. The Renegade Wants Words. James Welch. CDW; SA

We do lie beneath the grass. Sibilla's Dirge. Thomas Lovell Beddoes. Fr. Death's Jest Book. NOBE

We do not wish anything to happen. Chorus. T. S. Eliot. Fr. Murder in the Cathedral. OxBTC

We don't know the ins and outs. The Wall. David Jones. TwMBP

We don't lack people here on the Northern coast. Amusing Our Daughters. Carolyn Kizer. VGW

We drove south from Burwash Landing. At White River. John Haines. FiCP

We enter the darkened hall. The Physical Imperfections of Old Films. Paul Ramsey. PPoD

We finished clearing the last. Above Pate Valley. Gary Snyder. ConAP

We followed her unto the chamber-door. The Palace of Pleasant Regard. Lady of the Assembly. Fr. The Assembly of Ladies. WPE

We found a mouse in the chalk quarry today. Anne and the Field-Mouse. Ian Serraillier. RAE

We found the deer. The Lost Deer. Joseph Bruchac. FAF

We from childhood play'd together. Comrades. Felix McGlennon. FSN

We gather together to ask the Lord's blessing. Prayer of Thanksgiving. Unknown, tr. by Theodore Baker. BLSo

We go back. Proclamation/ From Sleep, Arise. Carolyn M. Rodgers. JB

We go no more to Calverly's. Calverly's. E. A. Robinson. NoAM

We got into the carriage. It was hot. Travelling to My Second Marriage on the Day of the First Moonshot. Robert Nye. SLP

We grew up in a time. What Lies on Us. Bruce Dawe. CAAP

We grid horns. A Talisman for the New Year. Deena Metzger. RiTi

We had a city also. Hand in hand. Decline and Fall. John Frederick Nims. CoPAm

We had a female passenger who came. September 1, 1802. Wordsworth. MBPR

We had known from the beginning this could happen. Robert Dana. *Fr.* Natural Odes/ American Elegies. HeS

We had the notion it was dawn. Five. Weldon Kees. PPP

We had to take the world as it was given. Ideal Landscape. Adrienne Rich. NoAM

We have a secret, just we three. The Secret. *Unknown.* ECBV

We have all been in rooms. Adultery. James Dickey. CAPP; PPoD

We have bathed, where none have seen us. Bridal Song. Thomas Lovell Beddoes. *Fr.* Death's Jest Book. GBL

We have been a walking. Wassail Song. *Unknown.* GBP

We Have Been Believers. Margaret Walker. PoBA

We have been shown. Six Variations. Denise Levertov. ConAP

We have climbed the mountain. Here in Katmandu. Donald Justice. ConAP; HeIP; RFM

We have come home here. Eyes of the Garden. Laura Chester. RiTi

We have done with dogma and divinity. After Trinity. John Meade Falkner. OxBTC

We have forgot, who safe in cities dwell. Sea-Sonnet. V. Sackville-West. SBG

We have gone out in boats upon the sea at night. Passage Over Water. Robert Duncan. NoAM; NOBA

We have little animals here. Robinson Jeffers. *Fr.* Skunks. BoAnP

We have loved each other in this time twenty years. Unfinished History. Archibald MacLeish. VGW

We have made hawks. Shaman Songs 12. Gene Fowler. MIT

We have met late—it is too late to meet. A Denial. Elizabeth Barrett Browning. GBL

We have not been happy, my Lord, we have not been too happy. Chorus. T. S. Eliot. *Fr.* Murder in the Cathedral. OxBTC

We have seen her/ the world over. Hilda Doolittle ("H.D."). *Fr.* Tribute to the Angels. RiTi; VGW

We have struck the regions wherein we are keel or reef. Zone. Louise Bogan. WPE

We have tangled together. Growing Together. Joyce Carol Oates. IHMS

We have turned together. Soundings. Jenne Andrews. HeS

We heard the thrushes by the shore and sea. In Kerry. J. M. Synge. GBL

We heard thunder. Nothing great—on high. Mouse Night: One of Our Games. William Stafford. NCSH

We hunted and we halloed. Cape Ann. *Unknown.* BLSo

We in the Fields. William Everson. PiAm

We is gathahed hyeah, my brothahs. An Ante-Bellum Sermon. Paul Laurence Dunbar. BPo

We killed a bat last night. A Bat in the Monastery. John L'Heureux. SFF

We kissed at the barrier; and passing through. On the Departure Platform. Thomas Hardy. NOBE; OxBTC

We knew the certain place of heaven above the loft. Death Insurance. Wade Hall. AATT

We knock red yellow blue. Croquet in Childhood. Helena Minton. FAF

We learned that you don't shoot. Statement on Our Higher Education. W. M. Ransom. CDW

We left the dusty. Taking Out Jim. John Walsh. RAE

We Let It Go That He Was a Perfect Man. Nicanor Parra, *tr. fr. Spanish by* Miller Williams. POL

We, like shades that were first conjured up. And through the Caribbean Sea. Margaret Danner. BPo

We Live in a Cage. William J. Harris. PoBA

We Love You the Way You Are. David McFadden. NeAC

We made castles of grass, green halls, enormous stem-lined rooms. The Riders. Ann Stanford. WPE

We make our meek adjustments. Chaplinesque. Hart Crane. NoAM; NOBA; VGW

We Manage Most When We Manage Small. Linda Gregg. AmPA

We marry our grandfathers. Extensions of Linear Mobility. Jeanine Hathaway. IHMS

We meet not as we parted. Lines. Shelley. MBPR

We met for supper in your flat-bottomed boat. Dream Barker. Jean Valentine. VGW

We move by means of our mud bumps. The Tall Figures of Giacometti. May Swenson. WIF

We move from one. The River. Sam Cornish. PoBA

We Must Be Polite, *sel.* Carl Sandburg. "If we meet a gorilla." CaYB

We must kill our gods before they kill us. Black Trumpeter. Henry Dumas. PoBA

We must not look for myths. Poetry and Revolution. William Pitt Root. NVAP

We must sit down. Councils. Marge Piercy. NeAC; RiTi; TSWA

We need a place much more than time. Sentimental Ode. Tom Buchan. MIS

We need no runners here. Booze is law. Harlem, Montana: Just off the Reservation. James Welch. CDW; SA; VW

We Never Said Farewell. Mary Elizabeth Coleridge. IPWM; WPE

We never spent time in the mountains. Interlude. Welton Smith. PoBA

We Own the Night. LeRoi Jones. PoBA

We outgrow love, like other things. Emily Dickinson. NOBA

We passed their graves. Peace. Langston Hughes. BPo

We praise Thee O God! Revive Us Again. William Paton Mackay. BLSH

We pulled for you when the wind was against us and the sails were low. Song of the Galley-Slaves. Kipling. OBP

We raise de wheat. Song. *Unknown.* BPo

We reach for destinies beyond. Beyond What. Alice Walker. WBN

We Real Cool. Gwendolyn Brooks. BuTh; CAPP; CoPAm; HeIP; InPK; PoBA; PPoD; Psy; SoSe; SS; TCP

We reden ofte and finde y-write. Sir Orfeo. *Unknown.* OxBM

We remove fifty brass screws. Bonded. Anne Hazlewood-Brady. WBN

We ride down the coast hwy through the rain. The Great Santa Barbara Oil Disaster OR. Conyus. AmPA

We rise to comb the fine mist from our hair. A Wish For Water. Laura Chester. RiTi

We rode updrafts to Bolivia. Canibolos de la Montana. Renée Roper. NPW

We run the dangercourse. We Walk the Way of the New World. Don L. Lee. BPo; NeAC; PoBA

We sail out of season into an oyster-gray wind. Crossing the Atlantic. Anne Sexton. NoAM

We sat across the table. The Friend. Marge Piercy. IPWM; NMM; RiTi

We sat together at one summer's end. Adam's Curse. W. B. Yeats. BIrV; LoAs; NoAM; PFIr; WIF

We sat within the farm-house old. The Fire of Drift Wood. Longfellow. NOBA; PiAm; VoPo

We save fish heads we don't know why. The Politician. Michael McMahon. FAF

We saw a bloody sunset over Courtland. Remembering Nat Turner. Sterling A. Brown. PoBA

We saw a town by the track in Colorado. Holding the Sky. William Stafford. RFM

We saw anchored worlds in a shallow stream. Lying On a Bridge. Van K. Brock. NVAP

We saw and wooed each others' eyes. To Castara: the Reward of Innocent Love. William Habington. SCP-2

"We saw reindeer." Rigorists. Marianne Moore. SBG

We saw the swallows gathering in the sky. Modern Love, XLVII. George Meredith. NOBE

We say the sea is lonely; better say. The Open Sea. William Meredith. CoPAm

We searched the wood again. The Writer Indulges a Hobby. Julia Randall. PPoD

We send you word of the Mother. Two Presentations. Robert Duncan. InPS

We shall have everything we want. Ode to Joy. Frank O'Hara. PPP

We shall have to force ourselves. "Terre des Hommes." Ruth Lisa Schechter. RiTi

We Shall Never Want. Sydney Goodsir Smith. SLP

We shall not always plant while others reap. From the Dark Tower. Countee Cullen. BPo; PoBA

We shall not ever meet them again in heaven. On the Death of Friends in Childhood. Donald Justice. ConAP; NCSH

We Shall Overcome. *Unknown.* BLSo, *with music*; PBMP

We shared not one idea in thirty years. A Reformer to His Father. James Simmons. BIrV

We should not worship suffering. What Wild-eyed Murderer. Peter Meinke. AATT

We sit indoors and talk of the cold outside. There are Roughly Zones. Robert Frost. PPP

We sit late, watching the dark slowly unfold. September. Ted Hughes. BoLoP; OLR

We sit nebulous in steam. Laundrette. Liz Lochhead. MIS

We sit outside. Death of Dr. King. Sam Cornish. OFD; PoBA

We sit, staring at books. Cut off from. Perspective. Adrianne Marcus. MIT

We sit watching the afternoon summer smell ripely. James Powell on Imagination. Larry Neal. BPo

We six pile in, the engine churning ink. Nigger Song: An Odyssey. Rita Dove. AmPA

We spoke like public saints. Call to Arms. James Welch. SA

We spray the fields and scatter. Harvest Hymn. John Betjeman. PAIC

We spurred our parents to the kiss. Children of Darkness. Robert Graves. NoAM

We stand here. Matthew Mead. *Fr.* Identities. TwMBP

We stand on the edge of the wounds, hugging canned meat. Dream of Rebirth. Roberta Hill. CDW

We stayed the night in the pathless gorge. Oh, Lovely Rock. Robinson Jeffers. NoAM

We stood by a pond that winter day. Neutral Tones. Thomas Hardy. HeIP; InPK; LoAs; NoAM; PPP; SS

We stood up before day. In the Dordogne. John Peale Bishop. VGW

We take place in what we believe. Elephant Rock. Primus St. John. PoBA

We take the children to the park. Stories In Kinsman's Park. Margaret Atwood. Psy

We talked with open heart, and tongue. The Fountain. Wordsworth. MBPR

We, the boys of Sanpete County, in obedience to the cause. The Boys of Sanpete County. *Unknown.* AmFP

We thought the grass. Photographs: A Vision of Massacre. Michael S. Harper. PoBA

We Three Kings of Orient Are, *with music.* John Henry Hopkins, Jr. BLSH

We Told You So. Nancy Keesing. MAuV

We tolerate closed doors by watching the sun. Father and Daughter. Joanne Casullo. NPW

We too, we too, descending once again. The Silent Slain. Archibald MacLeish. POL

We tore the green tree down. Verifying the Dead. James Welch. CDW

We turn out the light to undress by. Turn the Key Deftly. Edwin Brock. POL

We used to gather at the high window. When Mahalia Sings. Quandra Prettyman. MiP; PoBA

We waited for an omnibus. Walking Song. William E. Hickson. OxBChV

We wake entangled. Occasion. Roger. Pfingston. SFF

We Walk the Way of the New World. Don L. Lee. BPo; NeAC; PoBA

We walk tonight. The People Cannot Speak. T. Alan Broughton. FAF

We walked a mile from the road and with every step. Daisies. Alden Nowlan. NeAC

We walked along, while bright and red. The Two April Mornings. Wordsworth. MBPR

We watched/ a red rooster. William Carlos Williams. *Fr.* Calypsos. TH

We watched her breathing through the night. The Death-Bed. Thomas Hood. NOBE

We watched our love burn with the lumberyard. The Lumberyard. Ruth Herschberger. WPE

We Wear the Mask. Paul Laurence Dunbar. IPWM; PBMP; PoBA; PPoD

We went north/ to escape winter. Indian Song: Survival. Leslie Silko. CDW

We went out, early one morning. Out Fishing. Barbara Howes. PPoD; WPE

We went there on the train. Protocols. Randail Jarrell. VGW

We went to see the old church yard little left. Foveran Sands. Roderick Watson. MIS

We were alone and did your life. To Children. Lawrence McGaugh. PoBA

We were as tough as our glasses. Tyson's Corner. Primus St. John. PoBA

We were camped on the plains. The Zebra Dun. *Unknown.* PoTa

We were going single file. A Bummer. Michael Casey. TSWA

We were gone from each other. Farewell. Iain Crichton Smith. SLP

We were out in Arizona, on the Painted Desert ground. Arizona. *Unknown.* AmFP

We were parked on a hil.. Don 1958. Alta. MMD

We were up before anyone. Liard Hot Springs. Gordon Massman. CTBA

We were very tired, we were very merry. Recuerdo. Edna St. Vincent Millay. CTBA; NoAM

We were young, we were merry, we were very very wise. Unwelcome. Mary Elizabeth Coleridge. SS; WPE

We who are left, how shall we look again. Lament. W. W. Gibson. OxBTC

We who devour our unclean dead are now arisen. Letter to Robert. Mary Fabilli. IHMS

We who must act as handmaidens. A Muse of Water. Carolyn Kizer. NMM

We who strangely went astray. Richard Crashaw. *Fr.* In the Glorious Epiphany of Our Lord God. SCP-1

We who with songs beguile your pilgrimage. Prologue. James Elroy Flecker. *Fr.* The Golden Journey to Samarkand. OxBTC

We will pull, we will haul, hearty, healthy, and gay.　Blow the Man Down.　*Unknown.*　AmFP

We will watch the Northern Lights.　*Unknown, tr. fr. Abanaki.* RFM

We Won't Go Home Till Morning, *with music.*　*Unknown.*　PSoN

We worked in the kitchen.　The Function Room.　Patrice Phillips.　MAT

We would climb the highest dune.　With Kit, Age 7, at the Beach. William Stafford.　RFM

We zealots, made up of stiff clay.　Let Us All Be Unhappy on Sunday.　Lord Neaves.　FaBoCo

Weak, The.　Greg Kuzma.　HeS

Weak-winged is song.　Ode Recited at the Harvard Commemoration.　James Russell Lowell.　NOBA; PiAm

Wealth and wisdom.　*At. to* Alfred, King of England.　*Fr.* The Proverbs of Alfred.　OxBM

Weapons Training.　Bruce Dawe.　CAAP

Wear a dress.　An Answer to a Man's Question, "What Can I Do about Women's Liberation?"　Susan Griffin.　MMD

Wearin' o' the Green, The.　*Unknown.　See* Wearing of the Green, The.

Wearing Breasts.　Daniela Gioseffi.　RiTi

Wearing my familiar worry wrapped.　In the Penile Colony. Erica Jong.　MMD

Wearing of the Green, The.　*Unknown.*　BLSH, *with music;* BTTM; GBP
　(Wearin' o' the Green, The)　AIW

Weary Blues, The.　Langston Hughes.　InPK; NoAM; NOBA

Weary I was, and thought to sit at rest.　Elizabeth Melvill, Lady Culross.　*Fr.* A Godly Dream.　WPE

Weary lot is thine, fair maid, A.　The Rover's Farewell.　Sir Walter Scott.　*Fr.* Rokeby, III.　NOBE

Weary men, what reap ye?　The Famine Year.　Lady Wilde. PFIr

Weary of myself, and sick of asking.　Self-Dependence.　Matthew Arnold.　IPWM; PBMP

Weary on ye, sad waves!　On an Island.　"Ethna Carbery." WPE

Weary was when coming on a stream.　Aswelay.　Norman Henry Pritchard, II.　PoBA

Weary year his race now having run, The.　Amoretti, LXII. Spenser.　FSFS

Weary Will.　A. B. Paterson.　BoAnP

Weasel.　Sylvia Read.　RAE

Weather Ear.　Norman Nicholson.　MPo

Weather here is raw, The.　At Torrey Pines State Park.　Jerome Mazzaro.　FiCP

Weather of Six Mornings, The.　Jane Cooper.　IHMS

Weather of this winter night, The, my mistress.　Childlessness. James Merrill.　ConAP

Weather was fine, The.　They took away his teeth.　John Berryman.　*Fr.* Dream Songs.　CAPP

Weather Report.　Elaine H. Jennings.　NPW

Weathering the Depths.　Al Lee.　AmPA

Web, The.　Gregory O'Donoghue.　BIrV

Web, The.　Theodore Weiss.　NoAM

Webs.　Carl Sandburg.　TH

Webster was much possessed by death.　Whispers of Immortality. T. S. Eliot.　NoAM; NOBA

Wedding.　George Mackay Brown.　SLP

Wedding, The.　Roland Gant.　BuTh

Wedding and Funeral.　*Unknown.*　GBP

Wedding-Wind.　Philip Larkin.　BuTh; LoAs; MAT

Wedges/ slide/ into cracks.　Rail Splitting.　Gary Lawless.　FAF

Wednesbury Cocking, The.　*Unknown.*　PeBB

Wednesday morning at five o'clock as the day begins.　She's Leaving Home.　John Lennon *and* Paul McCartney.　RRA

Wednesday Night Prayer Meeting.　Jay Wright.　PoBA

Wednesdays at the bone orchard deliveries.　Memo.　Charles Lynch.　PoBA

Wee bird cam' to our ha' door, A.　Wae's Me for Prince Charlie. William Glen.　BTTM

Wee Davie Daylicht.　Robert Tennant.　OxBChV

Wee man o' leather.　*Unknown.*　GBP

Wee, sleeket, [*or* sleekit,] cow'rin', [*or* cowran,] tim'rous beastie. To a Mouse.　Burns.　HeIP; InPS; LAuP; PAIC; PPP

Wee Wee Man, The.　*Unknown.*　AIW; GBP; PeBB

Wee Willie Gray.　Burns.　OxBChV

Wee Willie Winkie rins through the town.　Willie Winkie. William Miller.　MG; OxBChV

Weed Puller.　Theodore Roethke.　AnMo; PiAm

Week in Paradise, A.　John Ridland.　NowV

Week of Che Guevara, hunted, hurt.　October and November. Robert Lowell.　MAT

Week on the Concord and Merrimack Rivers, A, *sels.*　　Henry David Thoreau.
　Conscience Is Instinct Bred in the House.　HeIP; PiAm
　Haze.　HeIP; PiAm

Week-end Naturalist, The.　Tom Buchan.　MIS

Weeksville Women.　Elouise Loftin.　PoBA

Weep [*or* Weepe] not, my wanton, smile upon my knee. Sephestia's Song to Her Childe.　Robert Greene.　*Fr.* Menaphon.　NOBE; OBP

Weep not, weep not.　Go Down Death.　James Weldon Johnson. PoBA

Weep with me, all you that read.　Epitaph on S. P., a Child of Queen Elizabeth's Chapel.　Ben Jonson.　HeIP; NOBE; PPP

Weep You No More, Sad Fountains.　*Unknown.*　GBL; SCP-2 (Tears.)　NOBE

Weepe not my wanton! smile upon my knee!　*See* Weep not, my wanton, . . .

*Weepers Tower* in Amsterdam, The.　Paul Goodman.　VGW

Weeping o'er the sacred urn.　Ambrose Philips.　*Fr.* To the Memory of Lord Halifax.　FaBoCo

Weeping Willow, The.　*Unknown.*　AmFP

Weevily Wheat.　*Unknown.*　AmFP

Weighing the steadfastness and state.　Man.　Henry Vaughan. MetP; NOBE; SCP-1

Weightless in water, swift as wind.　This Shell.　Mark Van Doren.　SPo

Weird sister.　In Salem.　Lucille Clifton.　AmPA

Weland from wounds underwent hardship.　Deor.　*Unknown, tr. by* Kemp Malone.　PAIC

Welcome, The.　Abraham Cowley.　*Fr.* The Mistress.　BoLoP

Welcome.　Harvey Feinberg.　POL

Welcome for Etheridge, A.　James Cunningham.　JB

Welcome home, driving downhill.　Lament City.　Thomas Lux. AmPA

Welcome home from the exhausting voyage.　Sea Legs.　Susan Feldman.　AmPA

Welcome joy, and welcome sorrow.　Fragment.　Keats.　MBPR

Welcome, old friend! These many years.　To Age.　Walter Savage Landor.　SoSe

Welcome, precious stone of the night.　Welcome to the Moon. *Unknown, tr. fr. Gaelic.*　Moon

Welcome, sulphur dioxide.　Air.　James Rado *and* Gerome Ragni.　PoRo

Welcome the Wrath.　Stanley Kunitz.　VGW

Welcome to Spring.　John Lyly.　*See* Trico's Song: "What bird so sings,..."

Welcome to the Moon.　*Unknown, tr. fr. Gaelic.*　Moon

Welcome to you rich autumn days. Rich Days. W. H. Davies. FSFS

Welfare Store. *Unknown.* BluL

Well/ black mama, what's the/ matter with you today. My Black Mama. *Unknown.* BluL

Well/ If I had my way. If I Had My Way. *Unknown.* BluL

Well/ I'm gonna run, I'm gonna run. I'm Gonna Run to the City of Refuge. *Unknown.* BluL

Well,/ When should she kill the child. The Abortion. Lucille Iverson. WBN

"We'll all be rooned," said Hanrahan. Said Hanrahan. P. J. Hartigan. MAuV

Well all you ladies gather 'round. Candy Man Blues. *Unknown.* BluL

Well, babbling philosophical rascal. Thomas Shadwell. *Fr.* Timon of Athens, the Man-hater. SCP-2

Well boss I met. Cheerio My Deario. Don Marquis. *Fr.* Archy and Mehitabel. FaBoCo

Well, Froggie went a-courting and he did ride. Froggie Went a-Courting. *Unknown.* AmFP

We'll Go No More a-Roving. Byron. *See* So We'll Go No More...

We'll Go to Sea No More. *Unknown.* GBP

Well, Heaven be thank'd my first-love fail'd. The County Ball. Coventry Patmore. *Fr.* The Angel in the House. VPC

Well, here I am and. Proteus. Kathleen Wiegner. MMD

Well, here we are; well, here we are! Yale Boola! A. M. Hirsh. FSN

Well, Honest John. John Clare. Epi

Well House, The. Robert Penn Warren. PiAm

Well I got up this morning. The Jinx Blues. *Unknown.* BluL

Well, I had an old hen and she had a wooden leg. Turkey in the Straw. *Unknown.* BLSH

Well, I may now receive, and die: my sin. Satires, IV. John Donne. TVS

Well I poisoned my man. Blood Hound Blues. *Unknown.* BluL

Well I remember how you smiled. Your Name upon the Sand. Walter Savage Landor. *Fr.* Ianthe. BuTh

Well I say I work in the Conoco station. Hottest Brand Goin'. *Unknown.* BluL

Well I think it's fine building jumbo planes. Where Do the Children Play? Cat Stevens. PoRo

Well I want all you women folks to fall in line. The Dirty Dozens. *Unknown.* BluL

Well, I was camped out on the draw at the head of Cimarron. The Zebra Dun. *Unknown.* AmFP

Well, I went to California in the year of Seventy-six. Root Hog or Die. *Unknown.* AmFP

Well I woke up this mornin'. Stamp Blues. *Unknown.* BluL

Well I woke up this mornin' it was Christmas Day. Adrian Henri's Talking after Christmas Blues. Adrian Henri. BuTh; LP; MPo

Well! If the Bard was weather-wise, who made. Dejection: An Ode. Samuel Taylor Coleridge. Epi; MBPR; NOBE; PPP

Well! I'm goin' home. Special Rider Blues. *Unknown.* AmFP

Well I'm going to Memphis, come to stop at Cincinnat'. On the Wall. *Unknown.* BluL

Well, I'm in love with a feller, a feller you have seen. Common Bill. *Unknown.* AmFP

Well, it's partly the shape of the thing. Limerick. *Unknown.* SoSe

Well, Jesus died to save me in all of my sin. The Rock Island Line. *Unknown.* AmFP

Well, Lizzie Anderson! seventeen men—and. To a Friend. William Carlos Williams. LoAs

Well look a-here, honey. Depot Blues. *Unknown.* AmFP

Well met, well met, my own true love. The House Carpenter. *Unknown.* AmFP; RDB; WIF

We'll Never Be the Same (Until Later). Grace Cavalieri. AATT

Well now you know my mama told me. Six Week Old Blues. *Unknown.* BluL

Well of Life, The. Sir Herbert Read. NoAM

Well, old spy. Award. Ray Durem. BPo; PoBA

Well-shadowed landscape, fare ye well! Farewell to Love. Sir John Suckling. SCP-2

Well, since you're from the other side of town. Public-House Confidence. Norman Cameron. BBGO

Well, some may hate, and some may scorn. Stanzas to ——. Emily Brontë. WPE

Well, son, I'll tell you. Mother to Son. Langston Hughes. CTBA; IPWM

Well the baby crying on up to his mama's knee. That Crawling Baby Blues. *Unknown.* BluL

Well the ugliest little thing. Killer Diller. *Unknown.* BluL

Well, then, I hate Thee, unrighteous picture. The Black Riders, XII. Stephen Crane. AmVN

Well then! I now do plainly see. The Wish. Abraham Cowley. *Fr.* The Mistress. NOBE

Well, they are gone, and here must I remain. This Lime-Tree Bower My Prison. Samuel Taylor Coleridge. HeIP; MBPR; PAIC

Well they'd made up their minds to be everywhere because why not. The Last One. W. S. Merwin. CoPAm; NoAM; VGW

Well, this bird comes, and under his wing is a crutch. The Bird. Moishe Leib Halpern, *tr. by* John Hollander. PPP

Well, to begin. What I Want in a Husband Besides a Mustache. Diane Wakoski. PPoD

Well tonight the damnfool sunset pitched. What Maisie Knew She Don't Want No. Judith Johnson Sherwin. NoAM

Well-Travelled Roadway, The. John Newlove. NeAC

Well Water. Randall Jarrell. NOBA; PPoD; VGW

Well we done told you. Jesus Is Coming Soon. *Unknown.* BluL

Well well well. Motherless Children. *Unknown.* BluL

Well when you can't see the forest. Orange Juice Song. David Phillips. NeAC

Well, whilst we here, sonny, having fun. Kentucky Blues. *Unknown.* BluL

Well-wishing to a Place of Pleasure, A. *Unknown.* GBL; SCP-2

Well, world, you have kept faith with me. He Never Expected Much. Thomas Hardy. NoAM; OxBTC

Well, you know the sun is going down. Lowdown Dirty Blues. *Unknown.* AmFP

Will-a come along boys and listen to my tale. The Old Chisholm Trail. *Unknown.* BLSH

Welsh Incident. Robert Graves. NOBE; OxBTC

Welsh Landscape. R. S. Thomas. LP; MPo

Welthistorische Perspektiven. Rodrick Watson. MIS

Wendigo, The. Ogden Nash. ECBV

Wenes King Edward with his longe shankes. The Scots in Berwick (1296). *Unknown.* OxBM

Wenest thou, usher, with thyn cointise. A Schoolboy's Lot. *Unknown.* OxBM

Wenne, wenne, wenchichenne. Charm against Wens. *Unknown.* OxBM

Went down on Johnson Street. Bob McKinney. *Unknown.* BluL

Went into a shoestore to buy a pair of shoes. Sale. Josephine Miles. POL; WPE

Went into the world like a shining knife. A Signature. F. Eugene Warren. AATT

Went out to plant some tomatoes. Humidity. R. P. Dickey. HeS

Went up on the hill, 'bout 12 o'clock. Fishing Blues. *Unknown.* BluL

We're All in the Dumps. *Unknown. See* In the Dumps.

We're all met here together. We Won't Go Home Till Morning. *Unknown.* PSoN

Were [*or* Where] beth they that biforen us weren. Ubi Sunt Qui ante Nos Fuerent? *Unknown.* OxBM; PAIC

We're connecting. Poems for the New. Kathleen Fraser. IHMS; NMM; RiTi

We're here to say goodbye. Beyond Silence (1). Andrew Taylor. CAAP

We're hoping to be arrested. Street Demonstration. Margaret Walker. BPo

Were I laid on Greenland's coast. Over the Hills and Far Away. John Gay. *Fr.* The Beggar's Opera. BLSo; NOBE

Were I (who to my cost already am). Homo Sapiens. Earl of Rochester. *Fr.* A Satire against Mankind. NOBE; PAIC; SCP-2

Were it undo that is y-do. He Is Far. *Unknown.* OxBM

We're marching 'round the levee. Marching 'round the Levee. *Unknown.* AmFP

We're Marching to Zion, *with music.* Isaac Watts. BLSH

Were my hart as some mens are, thy errours would not move me. Thomas Campion. AAS

We're not going to die. For My Daughter in Reply to a Question. David Ignatow. RRA

We're tenting tonight on the old camp ground. Tenting on the Old Camp Ground. Walter Kittredge. BLSo; PSoN

We're the hardrock men. Dynamite Song. *Unknown.* AmFP

Were ther outher in this town. His Sweetheart Slain. *Unknown.* OxBM

Were you ever in Quebec. Donkey Riding. *Unknown.* RAE

Were You There When They Crucified My Lord? *Unknown.* BPo

Werena My Heart Licht. Lady Grizel Baillie. SLP

Werther had a love for Charlotte. The Sorrows of Werther. Thackeray. FaBoCo

Wessex Heights. Thomas Hardy. IPWM

West Helena Blues. *Unknown.* BluL

West of Chicago. John Dimoff. RFM

West of the Sierras where. The California Phrasebook. Dennis Schmitz. AmPA

West Palm Beach Storm, The. *Unknown.* AmFP

West Ridge Is Menthol-cool, The. D. L. Graham. PoBA

West-running Brook. Robert Frost. NOBA; PAIC; PiAm; SoSe

West, so they say, is the home of the jay, The. Forty-five Minutes from Broadway. George M. Cohan. FSN

Western Star, *sel.* Stephen Vincent Benét.
"Oh, have you heard the gallant news." AIW

Western sun withdraws the shortened day, The. The Autumnal Moon. James Thomson. *Fr.* The Seasons: Autumn. NOBE

Western Wind. *Unknown.* GBP; HeIP; InPK; IPWM; MAT; NOBE; PPoD; PPP
(Lover in Winter Plaineth for the Spring, The.) SpRo
("Western wind, when will thou blow.") BoLoP; OLR
(Western Winde.) LoAs
(Westron Winde, When Will Thou Blow.) PPoe
("Westron wynd, when will thou blow.") GBL
(Westryn Wynde, *with music.*) RDB

Western wind has blown but a few days, The. The Cranes. Po Chü-i, *tr. by* Arthur Waley. ECBV

Western Wind, When Will Thou Blow. *Unknown. See* Western Wind.

Westland Row. Thomas Kinsella. NoAM

Westminster Drollery, 1671. Aphra Behn. SBG

Westron Winde, When Will Thou Blow. *Unknown. See* Western Wind.

Westward, hit a low note, for a roarer lost. A Strut for Roethke. John Berryman. NOBA

Wet August, A. Thomas Hardy. PPP

Wet dawn inks are doing their blue dissolve, The. Winter Trees. Sylvia Plath. NMM; SBG

Wet Day. James McAuley. MAuV

Wet gray day—rain falling slowly, mist over the valley, A. Morels. William Jay Smith. MAT; PPoD; RFM

Wet Hair: If Now His Mother Should Come. Robert Penn Warren. *Fr.* Penological Study: Southern Exposure. NoAM

Wet mirrors covering soft peat. At Rushy Lagoon. James McAuley. MAuV

Wet Sheet and a Flowing Sea, A. Allan Cunningham. BTTM

Wet Summer: Botanic Gardens. Nan McDonald. MAuV

Wet Time, A. Wendell Berry. PiAm

Wet Weather. Patricia Low. VGW

We've been here a week. Clydesdale New Town Walk. Duncan Glen. MIS

We've formed our band and are well manned. The Californian. *Unknown.* AmFP

We've fought with many men acrost the seas. Fuzzy-Wuzzy. Kipling. BTTM

We've seen some trees when they are seized by storms. Less than Love. Aileen Campbell Nye. SLP

We've taken our burlap sacks and entered. The Killigrew Wood. Norman Dubie. AmPA

Wexford Girl, The. *Unknown.* AmFP

Wha lies here? Johnny Dow. *Unknown.* FaBoCo

Wha wad na be in love. Maggie Lauder. *At. to* Francis Sempill of Beltrees. SLP

Wha wait if all that Chauceir wrait was trew? Robert Henryson. *Fr.* The Testament of Cresseid. SLP

"Wha you been, Lord Randal, my son?" Lord Randal. *Unknown.* AIW

Whack Fol the Diddle. Peadar Kearney. PFIr

Whale, The. John Donne. *Fr.* The Progresse of the Soule. OBP

Whale, The. *Unknown.* OxBM

Whale at Twilight. Elizabeth J. Coatsworth. BoAnP

Whale is killed as follows, A. Killing a Whale. David Gill. BoAnP

Whale Song. Francis Maguire. BoAnP; POL

Whales. Scott Bates. BoAnP

Whales, The. Marguerite Young. WPE

Whales have a tendency to move heavily. Whales. Scott Bates. BoAnP

Whales Weep Not! D. H. Lawrence. OBP; PPoe

Whan that April[l] with his shoures soote. Chaucer. The Canterbury Tales: Prologue. InPS; PPP

What/ has happened. Here. Robert Creeley. NOBA

What/ is it about. The Universe. May Swenson. Psy

What a beautiful day for a wedding in May! For Me and My Gal. Edgar Leslie *and* E. Ray Goetz. BLSo

What a Coincidence? *Unknown.* AKE

What a fellowship, what a joy divine. Leaning on the Everlasting Arms. Elisha Hoffman. BLSH

What a Friend We Have in Jesus, *with music.* Joseph Scriven. BLSH

What a girl called "the dailiness of life." Well Water. Randall Jarrell. NOBA; PPoD; VGW

What a Proud Dreamhorse. E. E. Cummings. VGW

What a relief, to find it in the *language.* Lapsus Linguae. Richard Howard. NoAM

What a thrill. Cut. Sylvia Plath. CAPP; InPK; PiAm

What a Way to Lose the War. Luís Omar Salinas. SA

What a wonderful bird the frog are. The Frog. *Unknown.* ECBV

What a wonderful change in my life has been wrought. Since Jesus Came into My Heart. R. H. McDaniel. BLSH

What about that bad short you saw last week. Black People! LeRoi Jones. BPo

What after all do we know of this terrible "matter." Diamond Body. "Hugh MacDiarmid." TwMBP

What! alive and so bold, o earth? Lines Written on Hearing the News of the Death of Napoleon. Shelley. MBPR

What am I? Nosing here, turning leaves over. Wodwo. Ted Hughes. NoAM; TwMBP

What Any Lover Learns. Archibald MacLeish. PiAm

What are days for? Days. Philip Larkin. LP; PSN

What Are Heavy? Christina Rossetti. OxBChV

What are little boys made of, made of. Mother Goose. MG

"What are ruins to us." At Lindos. May Sarton. WPE

"What are the bugles blowin' for?" said Files-on-Parade. Danny Deever. Kipling. AIW; BTTM; Epi; InPS; NOBE; OxBTC; PBMP; PeBB; SFF

What are the five dreams of the elders? The Five Dreams. John Woods. FiCP

What are we first? First, animals; and next. George Meredith. *Fr.* Modern Love. GBL; VPC

What Are Years? Marianne Moore. NoAM; NOBA; PiAm

What are you, then, my love, my friend, my father. The Quarry. Vassar Miller. WPE

What Became of Them? *Unknown. See* Two Rats, The.

What beckoning ghost, along the moonlight shade. Elegy to the Memory of an Unfortunate Lady. Pope. NObE; PAIC

What bird so sings, yet so does wail? Trico's Song [*or* Welcome to Spring]. John Lyly. *Fr.* Alexander and Campaspe. NOBE; OBP

What Birds Were There. William Everson. NoAM

What bring you, sailor, home from the sea? Luck. W. W. Gibson. ECBV; RAE

What can a man do that a beast cannot. In Shame and Humiliation. James Wright. CAPP

What can be wrong. Housewife. Susan Fromberg Schaeffer. IHMS; WBN

What can he want. The Panda. Harley Elliott. *Fr.* Animals That Stand in Dreams. NeAC

What can I do to drive away. To ——. Keats. MBPR

What can I give Him. Christina Rossetti. *Fr.* Christmas Carol: "In the bleak mid-winter." LCL

What Can I Tell My Bones? Theodore Roethke. NOBA

What can the spirit believe? The Young Girl. Theodore Roethke. AnMo; LoAs; NoAM

What can Tommy Onslow do? On Thomas, Second Earl of Onslow. *Unknown.* FaBoCo

What cannot be committed to memory, this can save. Photograph. Quandra Prettyman. PoBA

What Child Is This? *with music.* William Chatterton Dix. BLSH

What college kids we've grown up. For Randie. Geof Hewitt. NeAC

What Color Is Lonely. Carolyn M. Rodgers. BPo

What Could Be. John Gill. NeAC

What Could It Be? William Cole. BoAnP

What could she say to the fantastic foolybear. Lawrence Ferlinghetti. *Fr.* A Coney Island of the Mind. CAPP

What could we do, he and I. Opposites. Carolyn Stoloff. RiTi

What Counsel Has the Hooded Moon. James Joyce. Chamber Music, XII. Moon

What cry was that. Encounter. Geraldine Hammond. IHMS

What dawn is it? Aubade. Karl Shapiro. VGW

What Day Is. Robert Penn Warren. PiAm

What desperate nightmare rapts me to this land. Legacy: My South. Dudley Randall. PoBA

What did I find. A is for Abracadabra. Eleanor Farjeon. ECBV

What did we say to each other. Simile. N. Scott Momaday. CDW

What did you think when first. The Triple Mirror.Gloria C. Oden. IHMS

What dire offense from amorous causes springs. The Rape of the Lock. Pope. AnMo

What do a few crimes. Adultery. Alan Dugan. CAPP

What do hens say. Near and Far. Harry Behn. LCL

"What Do I Care." Sara Teasdale. VGW

What do I care. Pursuit. Hilda Doolittle ("H.D."). WPE

What do I know? myself alone. Christopher Brennan. *Fr.* The Twilight of Disquietude. MAuV

What do I stare at—not the colt. The White Horse. W. H. Davies. OxBTC

What do the people say, and what does the government do? Amours de Voyage, Canto II. Arthur Hugh Clough. VPC

What do you/ want, love. To be. Song. Robert Creeley. TCP

What Do You Do When It's Spring? John Woods. ConAP

What do you think. What Someone Told Me about Bobby Link. John Ciardi. CaYB

What do you think of us in fuzzy endeavor. A Catch of Shy Fish. Gwendolyn Brooks. CAPP

What Does it Mean? This Harmonica. Virginia Gilbert. NVAP

What does it mean to be born? The Point of Love. Alan Bold. SLP

What does little birdie say. Cradle Song. Tennyson. OxBChV

What does love look like? The Shape of Death. May Swenson. LoAs

What does not change? is the will to change. The Kingfishers. Charles Olson. NOBA; PiAm

What Does the Bee Do? Christina Rossetti. OxBChV

What does the cracker. Self. Norman Henry Pritchard, II. PoBA

What does the forest do monday through friday? Clerk's Song II. Norman H. Russell. VW

What does the hangman think about. The Hangman at Home. Carl Sandburg. AKE

What doth he get who ere prefers. Virtus Vera Nobilitas. Mildmay Fane, Earl of Westmorland. SCP-2

What else could we do, for the doors were guarded. Curfew. Paul Eluard, *tr. by* Quentin Stevenson. BoLoP

What face, in the water. Lament. William Carlos Williams. VGW

What face she put on it, we will not discuss. Conrad Aiken. *Fr.* Time in the Rock, LXXXIV. VGW

What Faire Pompe. Thomas Campion. Prf ("What fair pomp have I spied of glittering ladies.") GBL

What gall had he in him, so to begin Book VII. John Berryman. *Fr.* Dream Songs. RRA

What glories would we? Motions of the soul? The Renewal. Theodore Roethke. VGW

What God gives, and what we take. A Grace for Children. Robert Herrick. OxBChV

What goes on. Poem for Mother's Day. Stanley Kiesel. HeS

What great yoked brutes with briskets low. Crossing the Plains. Joaquin Miller. AmVN

What had you been thinking about. The Tennis Court Oath. John Ashbery. NoAM

What Happened. Dorothy Aldis. ECBV

What happened there, it was not much. The Well House. Robert Penn Warren. PiAm

What happened to Joey on our block. Of Kings and Things. Lillian Morrison. NCSH

What Happened? What Do You Expect? Alan Dugan. NowV

What Happens. June Jordan. BPo

What happens to a dream deferred? Harlem [or Dream Deferred]. Langston Hughes. Fr. Lenox Avenue Mural. CoPAm; HeIP; InPK; InPS; PBMP; PoBA; PPP; SoSe; WIF

What happens when the dog sits on a tiger. What Happens. June Jordan. BPo

What happens when the juice of the sun. Sunjuice. Erica Jong. MMD

What happiness you gave to me. The Yew-tree. Unknown, tr. by Geoffrey Grigson. GBL

What has become of our astonishment. The Way We Wonder. Robert Pack. WIF

What has happened in the world? Volcanic Venus. D. H. Lawrence. InPS; POL

What has want to give. Envoi. Kathleen Raine. WPE

What hath man done that man shall not undo. He Was Made Man. Giles Fletcher the Younger. Fr. Christ's Victory and Triumph, I. BoReV

What have I gilt, allace! or what deservit. Lancelot's Soliloquy in Prison. Unknown. Fr. Lancelot of the Laik. SLP

What have I made. The Children. Constance Urdang. IHMS

What, have I thus betrayed my liberty? Astrophel and Stella, XLVII. Sir Philip Sidney. GBL; LoAs

What Have They Done to the Rain. Malvina Reynolds. PoRo

What have we done? What cruel passion moved thee. Dialogue after Enjoyment. Abraham Cowley. BoLoP

"What have you there?" the great Panjandrum said. The Truant. E. J. Pratt. NoAM

What He Says. Robert Wallace. CoPAm

What heart could have thought you? To a Snow-flake. Francis Thompson. FSFS

What heartache—ne'er a hill! From the Flats. Sidney Lanier. NOBA

What heav'n-intreated [or heaven-besieged] heart is this. To the Noblest and Best of Ladyes [or Letter to the Countess of Denbigh, A]. Richard Crashaw. BoReV; MetP

What Holds the Universe Together. James Broughton. MIT

What hours I spent of precious time. Poetical Economy. Harry Graham. FaBoCo

What I am fashioning. After the Engraving. David Bromige. MIT

What I Expected. Stephen Spender. IPWM; NoAM; NOBE

What I fancy, I approve. No Loathsomeness in Love. Robert Herrick. GBL; PBMP

What I fancy, I approve. No Loathsomeness in Love. Robert Herrick. GBL; PBMP

What I Know. Morton Marcus. SFF

What I like most is when. Crimes of Passion: The Slasher. Terry Stokes. AmPA

What I remember. Memory of a Porch. Donald Justice. NCSH

What I remember about that day. The 1st. Lucille Clifton. CAAP; InPS; TSWA

What I Saw. Robert Duncan. NoAM; NOBA

What I shall leave thee none can tell. To His Son, Vincent Corbet. Richard Corbet. OxBChV

What I Tell Him. Simon J. Ortiz. CDW

What I Think of Hiawatha. J. W. Morris. SpRo

What I thought was love. The Liar. LeRoi Jones. NOBA; WIF

What I Want in a Husband Besides a Mustache. Diane Wakoski. PPoD

What I Wanted. In Weather. Robert Hass. AmPA

What I was would not work. Encounter in the Cage Country. James Dickey. CAPP

What if a day, or a month, or a yeare. Thomas Campion. AAS

What If a Much of a Which of a Wind. E. E. Cummings. NOBA; PPP; SoSe

What if I know, Liebknecht, who shot you dead. January 1919. Christopher Middleton. TwMBP

What if it was a. For Tinkers Who Travel on Foot. Margaret Avison. NoAM

What if jealousy is just a bad dream? Miriam Palmer. NMM

What if Orpheus,/ confident in the hard. Orpheus in Greenwich Village. Jack Gilbert. POL

What if these long races go on repeating themselves. Written in Dejection Near Rome. Robert Bly. CoPAm

What if this present were the world's last night? Holy Sonnets, XIII. John Donne. BoReV; HeIP; InPS

What in our lives is burnt. August 1914. Isaac Rosenberg. NOBE; OxBTC

What in the World. Eve Merriam. ECBV

What is Africa to me. Heritage. Countee Cullen. BPo; NoAM; PoBA; WIF

What is black. Canto 4: Gullfish. Tom Weatherly. PoBA

What is green in me. Stepping Westward. Denise Levertov. CAPP; NMM; Psy; VGW; WBN

What Is He? D. H. Lawrence. SFF

What is he buzzing in my ears? Confessions. Robert Browning. NOBE

What is he, this lordling, that cometh from the fight. Who Is This That Cometh from Edom? William Herebert. BoReV; OxBM

What is it about a Great Northern boxcar. Great Northern. Dave Etter. CoPAm

What is it men in women do require? The Question Answer'd. Blake. Fr. Several Questions Answered. GBL; MBPR

What is it more eyes doth wear. Unknown. GBP

What is it to grow old? Growing Old. Matthew Arnold. VoPo

"What is it you're mumbling, old Father, my Dad?" By the Exeter River. Donald Hall. AIW; MPo

What is Life? Samuel Taylor Coleridge. MBPR

What is more gentle than a wind in summer? Sleep and Poetry. Keats. FSFS; MBPR

What is more lovely than a day of sunshine. O Sole Mio. Eduardo di Capua. BLSH

What is our innocence. What Are Years? Marianne Moore. NoAM; NOBA; PiAm

What Is Our Life? A Play of Passion. Sir Walter Ralegh. InPK; PPoD
    (All the World's a Stage.) NOBE
    (On the Life of Man.) AAS

What Is Pink? Christina Rossetti. OxBChV

What Is Salt? John Vernon. PPoD

What Is She Trying to Do, to Pattern Love. Besmilr Brigham. RiTi

What is showed was always the same. The Night Mirror. John Hollander. Prf

What is so strange about a tree alone in an open field? Hunting Pheasants in a Cornfield. Robert Bly. ConAP

What is the beginning? Love. Start and Goal. Christina Rossetti. VoPo

What is the boy now, who has lost his ball. The Ball Poem. John Berryman. NoAM; NOBA; SoSe; SPo

What is the head. Some Last Questions. W. S. Merwin. CAPP

What is the use of the rule insane. The Solution. Brian Merriman, tr. by Arland Ussher. Fr. The Midnight Court. BIrV

"What is the world, o soldiers?" Napoleon. Walter de la Mare. NOBE

What Is There? Ruth Lisa Schechter. RiTi

What is there in the universal earth. To the Ladies Who Saw Me Crowned. Keats. MBPR

What is there they will not do to you? The First Test. Susan Fromberg Schaeffer. IHMS

What is this life if, full of care. Leisure. W. H. Davies. ECBV; NOBE; WIF

What is this that I can see. Oh! Death. *Unknown.* AmFP

What is this that roareth thus? Motor Bus. Alfred Denis Godley. FaBoCo

What Is This Why? *Unknown.* OxBM

What is to be done. Virginia Scott. NPW

What it is/ gold eyelids. Kayumangi. Jessica Tarahata Hagedorn. MMD

What it is, the literal size. The Riddle. Robert Creeley. PiAm

What It Means, Living in the City. William Dickey. POL

What joys attend the fisher's life! The Fisher's Life. *Unknown.* GBP

What jungles he swung out of into the imagination! Gorilla Gorilla. Bruce Dawe. CAAP

What just streamed outward from that midsummer center, not periphery? Snow in Summer. Daisy Aldan. RiTi

What! kill a partridge in the month of May. Epitaph for Mr. Partridge. *Unknown.* AKE

What Kind of War? Larry Rottman. POL

What lack you, sir? What seek you? What will you buy? Thomas Newbery. *Fr.* The Great Merchant, Dives Pragmaticus, Cries His Wares. OxBChV

What laid, I said. Rhyme. Louise Bogan. LoAs

What large, dark hands are these at the window. Love on the Farm. D. H. Lawrence. OBP

What Larkin bawled to hungry crowds. Inscription for a Headstone. Austin Clarke. BIrV

What lewd, naked, and revolting shape is this? Shopping for Meat in Winter. Oscar Williams. MiP

What Lies on Us. Bruce Dawe. CAAP

What lips my lips have kissed, and where, and why. Edna St. Vincent Millay. BoLoP

What little throat. The Blackbird by Belfast Lough. *Unknown, tr. by* Frank O'Connor. ECBV

What lively lad most pleasured me. A Last Confession. W. B. Yeats BoLoP

What love did. The beast sleeps. Brief Explanation. Claudia Dobkins. NPW

What love is this of thine, that cannot bee. Edward Taylor. *Fr.* Preparatory Meditations: First Series, I. PiAm

What Maisie Know She Don't Want No. Judith Johnson Sherwin. NoAM

What Makes Echo. Margaret Cavendish, Duchess of Newcastle. SCP-2

What makes thee, fool, so fat? Fool, thee so bare? Epigram. Francis Quarles. *Fr.* Emblems. SCP-2

What makes you write at this odd rate? Epigram on Miltonicks. Samuel Wesley. POL

What mean these dreams, and hideous forms that rise. George the Third's Soliloquy. Philip Freneau. NOBA

What meaneth this? When I lie alone. Sir Thomas Wyatt. GBL

What Might Pass a Man As a Survivor. J. S. Harry. CAAP

What My Child Learns of the Sea. Audre Lorde. PoBA

What mystery pervades a well! Emily Dickinson. AmVN

What need you, being come to sense. September 1913. W. B. Yeats. NoAM; PPoe

What needs complaints. Comfort to a Youth That Had Lost His Love. Robert Herrick. NOBE

What never filled? Be thy lips screwed so fast. Francis Quarles. *Fr.* Emblems. SCP-2

What News. Walter Savage Landor. BoLoP

What! no more favours? Not a ribband more. To a Lady that Forbade to Love before Company. Sir John Suckling. SCP-2

What no, perdy, ye may be sure! Sir Thomas Wyatt. AAS

What not one poem yet. Ah. Greg Kuzma. NVAP

What nudity is beautiful as this. Portrait of a Machine. Louis Untermeyer. MiP

What of earls with whom you have supped. The Toad-Eater. Burns. POL

What of her glass without her? The blank grey. Without Her. Dante Gabriel Rossetti. *Fr.* The House of Life. GBL

What opposite discoveries we have seen! Modern Discoveries. Byron. *Fr.* Don Juan, I. OBP

What our Dame bids us do. Ben Jonson. *Fr.* The Masque of Queens. OFD

What passing-bells for these who die as cattle? Anthem for Doomed Youth. Wilfred Owen. BuTh; HeIP; NoAM; NOBE; OxBTC; PPoD; PPP; PSN; SoSe; WIF

What pleasure have great princes. The Herdmen. *Unknown.* NOBE

What pleasures shall he ever find? Nil Pejus Est Caelibe Vita. Samuel Taylor Coleridge. MBPR

What profits it to me, though here allowed. Frederick Goddard Tuckerman. *Fr.* Sonnets. AmVN

What rage is this? what furour of what kynd? Sir Thomas Wyatt. AAS

What remains of summer. The Cold. Lance Henson. CDW

What Rider Spurs Him from the Darkening East. Edna St. Vincent Millay. WPE

What ruse of vision. The Bear. N. Scott Momaday. CDW; VW

What savage beast would willfully consent to ride jammed haunch to haunch. Bus Ride. Lenore Kandel. NMM

What Schoolmasters Say. Martin Seymour-Smith. OxBTC

What seas did you see. A Conversation. Dylan Thomas. RFM

What seas what shores what grey rocks and what islands. Marina. T. S. Eliot. BoReV; HeIP; NOBE; PiAm; PSN; RRA; TCP

What seems to us for us is true. Perspective. Coventry Patmore. *Fr.* The Angel in the House. GBL

What Semiramis Said. Vachel Lindsay. Moon

What shakes the eye but the invisible? The Decision. Theodore Roethke. VGW

What shall avail me. The Border. Edwin Muir. BoReV

What shall I do with this absurdity. The Tower. W. B. Yeats. NoAM

What Shall I Give? Edward Thomas. OxBChV

What Shall I Give My Children? Gwendolyn Brooks. BPo

What Shall I Pray for Today? *with music.* Albert Morehead *and* James Morehead. BLSH

What shall I say, because talk I must? The Yellow Flower. William Carlos Williams. PiAm

What shall the world do with its children? Romans Angry about the Inner World. Robert Bly. NoAM; NOBA; PPoe

What shall we do for timber? Kilcash. *Unknown, tr. by* Frank O'Connor. BIrV; PFIr

What She Said. Maturai Eruttalan Centamputan, *tr. fr. Tamil by* A. K. Ramanujan. BoLoP

What sholde I saye? but, at the monthes ende. The Wife's Fifth Husband. Chaucer. *Fr.* The Canterbury Tales: The Wife of Bath's Prologue. OxBM

What should I say. Farewell. Sir Thomas Wyatt. GBL; LoAs; NOBE

What should I speak in praise of Surrey's skill. Verse in Praise of Lord Henry Howard, Earl of Surrey. George Turberville. PAIC

What should one. The Picture of J. T. in a Prospect of Stone. Charles Tomlinson. PPP

What should we be without the sexual myth. Men Made Out of Words. Wallace Stevens. NOBA; VGW

What should we have taken. Provisions. Margaret Atwood. IHMS

What should we know. Verse. Oliver St. John Gogarty. WIF

What siren zooming is sounding our coming. The Exiles. W. H. Auden. OxBTC

What slender youth, bedew'd with liquid odors. To Pyrrha. Horace, *tr. by* Milton. Odes, I, 5. LoAs; SCP-1

What soft, cherubic creatures. Emily Dickinson. AmVN; WIF; WPE

What solemn sound the ear invades. Mount Vernon. *Unknown.* AmFP; OFD

What Someone Told Me about Bobby Link. John Ciardi. CaYB

What sort of man could inspire fear. Working for Dr. No. Valery Nash. PPoD

What soul would bargain for a cure that brings. Modern Love, XIV. George Meredith. PAIC

What sound awoke me? Dragon Skate. Gladys Cardiff. CDW

What sticks with me is the pit. Moonwalk. John Engels. MAT

What, Still Alive at Twenty-two. Hugh Kingsmill. FaBoCo; InPK; SpRo

What sugred termes, what all-perswading arte. Diella, IV. Richard Lynche. AAS

What tag or term long to remain. True Religion. Forrest Anderson. AATT

What the Birds Said. Whittier. NOBA

What the Chairman Told Tom. Basil Bunting. OxBTC; TwMBP

What the Thrush Said. Keats. OBP

What the wind harried, the fire worried. Deadfall. Martha Keller. ECBV

What Thing Is Love? George Peele. *Fr.* The Hunting of Cupid. LoAs; NOBE

What things are steadfast? Not the birds. We Manage Most When We Manage Small. Linda Gregg. AmPA

What thou lovest well remains. Ezra Pound. *Fr.* Cantos, LXXXI. InPS; NOBE

What though, for showing truth to flatter'd state. Written on the Day that Mr. Leigh Hunt Left Prison. Keats. MBPR

What though my penne wax faynt. To Maystres Jane Blenner-Haiset. John Skelton. *Fr.* The Garlande of Laurell. AAS

What though while the wonders of nature exploring. To Some Ladies. Keats. MBPR

What thoughts I have of you tonight, Walt Whitman. A Supermarket in California. Allen Ginsberg. ConAP; CoPAm; HeIP; NOBA; PBMP; PiAm; PPoD; TCP

What thwarts this fear I love. Sonnet. Ted Berrigan. CAAP

What Tidings? John Audelay. OxBM

What Tomas Said in a Pub. James Stephens. NoAM

What Train Will Come? William Jay Smith. PPoD

What vaileth trouth? or by it to take payn? Sir Thomas Wyatt. AAS

What was ashore, then? . . . Cargoed with forget. Sonnet. John Berryman. Epi

What was he doing, the great god Pan. A Musical Instrument. Elizabeth Barrett Browning. OBP; VPC; WPE

What was her beauty in our first estate. She. Richard Wilbur. AnMo; ConAP

What Was Her Name? John Ciardi. MiP

What was it/ that caught in our throats that day. The Greek Room. James W. Thompson. BPo

What was it? What was it? Woman as Market. Muriel Rukeyser. WBN

What was it you remember—the summer mornings. To Any Member of My Generation. George Barker. PAIC

What was most striking about them. Concerning the Dead Women: The Munitions Plant Explosion: June, 1918. Elizabeth Libbey. AmPA

What was that sound we heard. Why Must You Know? John Wheelwright. VGW

What was your war record, Prytherch? For the Record. R. S. Thomas. LP; MPo

What way does the Wind come? What way does he go? Address to a Child During a Boisterous Winter Evening. Dorothy Wordsworth. OxBChV

What weight of ancient witness can prevail. Revelation [*or* Confessio Fidei]. Dryden. *Fr.* The Hind and the Panther, I. BoReV; NOBE

What Were They Like? Denise Levertov. HeIP; PPoD; TCP; VGW; WPE

What were we playing? Was it prisoner's base? Running. Richard Wilbur. NCSH

What Wild Dawns There Were. Denise Levertov. NOBA

What Wild-eyed Murderer. Peter Meinke. AATT

What Will We Do for Linen? *Unknown.* GBP

"What will you have for your birthday?" Birthday Gifts. Herbert Asquith. OFD

What wonder strikes the curious, while he views. The Ants. John Clare. BoAnP

What wondrous life is this I lead! Andrew Marvell. *Fr.* The Garden. FSFS

What wondrous love is this! Oh, my soul! Oh, my soul! Wondrous Love. *Unknown, at. to* Alex Means. AmFP; BLSo

What wondrous pretty things I've seen. Young Master's Account of a Puppet Show. John Marchant. OxBChV

What worked/ for Donne. O My America. D. M. Thomas. TwMBP

What Would I Do White? June Jordan. NMM

What would I do without this world faceless incurious. Samuel Beckett. NoAM

What would this man? Now upward will he soar. Pope. *Fr.* An Essay on Man, Epistle I. HeIP

What wourde is that that chaungeth not. Sir Thomas Wyatt. AAS

What Yo' Gwine to Do When Yo' Lamp Burn Down? *Unknown.* BPo

"What, you are stepping westward?" Stepping Westward. Wordsworth. MBPR

What you gonna do. Wartime Blues. *Unknown.* BluL

What You Need. Kathleen Fraser. AmPA

What You Should Do Each Morning. Brian Patten. BuTh

What You Waited For. Marge Piercy. MMD

What You Will: a Comedy, *sel.* John Marston. "Now is Albano's marriage-bed new hung." SCP-2

What'd you get, black boy. Mr. Roosevelt Regrets. Pauli Murray. PoBA

Whate'er I be, old England is my dam! The Old Chartist. George Meredith. VPC

Whate'er is born of mortal birth. To Tirzah. Blake. *Fr.* Songs of Experience. BoReV; MBPR; NOBE

Whate'er thy countrymen have done. Written in the Beginning of Mezeray's History of France. Matthew Prior. NOBE

Whate'er we leave to God, God does. Inspiration. Henry David Thoreau. NOBA

Whatever it is, it must have. American Poetry. Louis Simpson. CoPAm; NoAM; NOBA; TH

Whatever it was that went wrong—the stove aflame. A Word to a Father, Dead. John Alexander Allen. PPoD

Whatever lies panting on its side. Field with Figurations. Warren Slesinger. HeS

Whatever sleeping in the world awakes. Creation of Anguish. Howard Nemerov. AnMo

Whatever story of their cruelty. On the Saviour's Wounds. Richard Crashaw. PAIC

Whatever we do, whether we light. Dilemma. David Ignatow. VGW

Whatever you have to say, leave. These Days. Charles Olsen. TSWA

Whatever your eye alights on this morning is yours. Years of Indiscretion. John Ashbery. NOBA

Whatever's good or bad or both. Nonsense Rhyme. Elinor Wylie. PBMP; Psy

Whatfor to 3 Who Stole My Shovel. Phyllis Gotlieb. BBGO

What's filling up the mirror? O, it is not I. The Fat Man in the Mirror. Robert Lowell. AnMo

What's in a Word? Carol Shine. NowV

What's in the Cupboard. *Unknown.* GBP

What's In There? *Unknown.* RAE

What's it like to be homeless. The Child's Umbrella. Raymond Souster. AKE

What's left of the sunset's watered blood. Working on Wall Street. May Swenson. NowV

What's love that's always strong? For Anybody's Martyr's Song. Jean Garrigue. LoAs

Whats My Name if Not Everyone Elses. Luís Omar Salinas. SA

What's sweeter than at the end of a summer's day. Thanksgiving. Kenneth Koch. VGW

What's that?/ An Egg. Whoroscope. Samuel Beckett. NoAM

What's that we see from far? the spring of day. A Nuptial Song, or Epithalamy, on Sir Clipesby Crew and His Lady. Robert Herrick. SCP-1

What's the balm. Poem. Alan Dugan. CAPP

What's up, today, with our lovers? The Lovers Go Fly a Kite. W. D. Snodgrass. NowV

Whaur are ye gaun. John Hielandman. *Unknown.* GBP

Wheat District, The. Ted Enslin. FAF

Wheel, The. Robert Hayden. BPo

Wheel, The. Rosalie Moore. RiTi

Wheel, The. Edwin Muir. NoAM

Wheel, oh wheel. Zekiel Saw the Wheel. *Unknown.* WIF

Wheel Revolves, The. Kenneth Rexroth. NoAM; RRA

Wheelchair Butterfly, The. James Tate. NoAM

Wheels. Vicki Viidikas. CAAP

Wheesht, Wheesht. "Hugh MacDiarmid." InPK; SLP

When. Dorothy Aldis. ECBV

When—/ Sir/ Beelzebub. Sir Beelzebub. Edith Sitwell. OBP; OxBTC

When a Beau Goes In. Gavin Ewart. OxBTC

When a fellow loves a maiden. La Cucaracha. *Unknown.* BLSH

When a friend calls to me from the road. A Time to Talk. Robert Frost. NCSH

When a lad, I stood one day by a cottage far away. She Was Bred in Old Kentucky. Harry Braisted. FSN

When a man gets troubled in mind. Sleepy Man Blues. *Unknown.* BluL

When a Man Hath No Freedom to Fight for at Home. Byron. PPoe; SS

When a player gets to thinking. Everlasting Teamwork in Basketball. H. Victory. SPo

When Abraham Lincoln was shoveled into the tombs. Cool Tombs. Carl Sandburg. HeIP; NoAM; NOBA; PAIC; PiAm

When Adam dalf and Eve span, go spire—if thou may spede. With I and E. *Unknown.* OxBM

When, after such a length of rolling years. Vergil, *tr. fr. Latin by* Dryden. *Fr.* Georgics, III. SCP-1

When age hath made me what I am not now. Upon His Picture. Thomas Randolph. NOBE

When Alexander Pope strolled in the city. Mr. Pope. Allen Tate. NoAM; NOBA; PAIC; VGW

When All My Five and Country Senses See. Dylan Thomas. NoAM; PAIC

When all of us wore smaller shoes. Ancient Lights. Austin Clarke. BIrV

When all the rubble of our fears was piled. Apocalypse in Black and White. Robert Pack. CoPAm

When all the world is young, lad. Young and Old. Charles Kingsley. *Fr.* The Water Babies. OxBChV

"When all this is over," said the swineherd. Swineherd. Eilean Ni Chuilleanain. BIrV; PFIr

When as man's life, the light of human lust. *See* Whenas man's life,...

When as the rye reach to the chin. A Summer Song. George Peele. *Fr.* The Old Wife's Tale. GBL; NOBE

When Aunt Emily died, her husband would not look at her. New England Protestant. Richard Eberhart. *Fr.* Attitudes. TH

When awful darkness and silence reign. The Dong with a Luminous Nose. Edward Lear. FaBoCo

When baby's cries grew hard to bear. L'Enfant Glacé. Harry Graham. FaBoCo

When bells stop ringing—church—begins. Emily Dickinson. PiAm

When Black People Are. A. B. Spellman. BPo; PoBA

When breezes are soft and skies are fair. Green River. Bryant. NOBA

When Britain first at Heaven's command. Rule, Britannia! James Thomson. *Fr.* Alfred, A Masque (*by* Thomson *and* David Mallett). BLSH; BTTM; VoPo

When Bunyan swung his whopping axe. Folk Tune. Richard Wilbur. AIW

When by mistake you miss. Your Own Image. Michael Ryan. HeS

When by my solitary hearth I sit. To Hope. Keats. MBPR

When by thy scorn, O murd'ress, I am dead. The Apparition. John Donne. GBL; HeIP; NOBE; PAIC; SCP-1

When by Zeus relenting the mandate was revoked. Phoebus with Admetus. George Meredith. NOBE

When Caesar decided to measure the world. Nathaniel Tarn. *Fr.* The Beautiful Contradictions. TwMBP

When cats run home and light is come. The Owl. Tennyson. ECBV

When Charlie Bowdre married Manuela, we carried them. Michael Ondaatje. POL

When children are born in Victoria. Life-Cycle. Bruce Dawe. MAuV

When civil fury first grew high. Presbyterian Knight. Samuel Butler. *Fr.* Hudibras, I, 1. NOBE; PAIC; SCP-2

When clerks and navvies fondle. For X. Louis MacNeice. BoLoP

When cockle shells turn silver bells. Waly, Waly [*or* Cockleshells]. *Unknown.* AIW; AmFP; RDB

When Cotton Haymes Walks Down the Street. Besmilr Brigham. RiTi

When curdling mists disturb the sight's. Midnight. Weldon Kees. NoAM

When Daddy Died. Duane Ackerson. POL

When daffodils begin to peer. Autolycus Sings. Shakespeare. *Fr.* The Winter's Tale, IV, ii. AIW; NOBE; OBP

When daisies pied and violets blue. Spring. Shakespeare. *Fr.* Love's Labour's Lost, V, ii. FSFS; HeIP; InPK; IPWM; NOBE; OBP; SoSe

When de Co'n Pone's Hot. Paul Laurence Dunbar. AmVN

When de night walks in, as black as a sheep. Pop Goes de Weasel. *Unknown.* PSoN

When despair for the world grows in me. The Peace of Wild Things. Wendell Berry. HeIP; IPWM; PiAm; VGW

When Dey 'Listed Colored Soldiers. Paul Laurence Dunbar. BPo

When did you begin your quest? Absences. James Tate. CAAP

When did you start your tricks. The Mosquito. D. H. Lawrence. BoAnP

When Dido found Aeneas would not come. A Note on the Latin Gerunds. Richard Porson. FaBoCo

When early morn walks forth in sober grey. Song. Blake. MBPR

When evening is come. Father is Home. *Unknown.* ECBV

When every one to pleasing pastime hies. Pamphilia to Amphilanthus. Mary Sidney Wroth, Countess of Montgomery. *Fr.* Urania. WPE

When every pencil meant a sacrifice. Warren Pryor. Alden Nowlan. BBGO

When father climbed the tabooed tree and shook. The Holy Eye Is Blind. Stephen Stepanchev. SA

When First. Edward Thomas. NoAM

When first, descending from the moorlands. Extempore Effusion upon the Death of James Hogg. Wordsworth. MBPR; NOBE

When first Diana leaves her bed. The Progress of Beauty. Swift. AnMo

When first I came here I had hope. When First. Edward Thomas. NoAM

When first I came to Louisville, some pleasure for to find. The Lily of the West. *Unknown.* AmFP

When first I knew this forest. The Forest. Judith Wright. MAuV

When first I saw the love-light in your eye. When You Were Sweet Sixteen. James Thornton. FSN

When first my beloved came to my bed. Epithalamium. John Peale Bishop. PAIC

When first my lines of heavenly joys made mention. Jordan. George Herbert. PPP

When First My Way to Fair I Took. A. E. Housman. POL

When first the college rolls receive his name. The Scholar's Life. Samuel Johnson. *Fr.* The Vanity of Human Wishes. NOBE

When first the peasant, long inclin'd to roam. The Young Author. Samuel Johnson. LAuP

When first thou didst entice to thee my heart. Affliction. George Herbert. BoReV; MetP; NOBE; SCP-1

When first thy sweet and gracious eye. The Glance. George Herbert. SCP-1

When Flora had ourfret the firth. May Poem. *Unknown.* SLP

When for eternal worlds we steer. Vain World Adieu. *Unknown.* AmFP

When for the thorns with which I long, too long. The Coronet. Andrew Marvell. BoReV; MetP

When fortune's blind goddess had shied my abode. Dick Turpin and Black Bess. *Unknown.* AmFP

When Freedom from her mountain height. The American Flag. Joseph Rodman Drake. BTTM

When gardens shone with flowery pride. On a Little Boy's Endeavouring to Catch a Snake. Thomas Foxton. OxBChV

When George the Third was reigning a hundred years ago. A Ballad for a Boy. William Cory. OxBChV

When getting my nose in a book. A Study of Reading Habits. Philip Larkin. PPP; SoSe

When God at first made man. The Pulley. George Herbert. HeIP; InPK; InPS; MetP; NOBE; PPP

When God Lets My Body Be. E. E. Cummings. NOBA

When gold was first discovered at Coloma, near the hill. The National Miner. *Unknown.* AmFP

When good King Arthur ruled this land. Mother Goose. MG

When Gullion died (who knows not Gullion?) Joseph Hall. *Fr.* Virgidemiarum. TVS

When he brings home a whale. Naughty Boy. Robert Creeley. NoAM; NOBA

When he came home. Poem. Sonia Sanchez. WBN

When he killed the Mudjokivis. *See* He killed the noble Mudjokivis.

When He Would Have His Verses Read. Robert Herrick. NOBE

When hearing tales of Bubba Smith. Bubba Smith. Ogden Nash. SPo

When He's at His Most Brawling. Patricia Goedicke. Psy

When I/ die/ I'm sure. The Rebel. Mari Evans. IHMS; PoBA

When I/ see you. Pressure. Anne Waldman. CAAP

When I/ took my. The Watch. May Swenson. PoTa

When I am almost awake in the morning. Curtain World. Heather Morse. CaYB

When I am an old woman I shall wear purple. Warning. Jenny Joseph. LP; MPo; OxBTC

When I Am Dead. George MacBeth. OxBTC

When I am dead, I hope it may be said. On His Books. Hilaire Belloc. FaBoCo

When I Am Dead, My Dearest. Christina Rossetti. *See* Song: "When I am dead, my dearest."

When I am grown to man's estate. Looking Forward. Robert Louis Stevenson. OxBChV

When I am in a great city, I know that I despair. City Life. D. H. Lawrence. SoSe

When I am most afraid, then I begin. The Fear. Margaret Reynolds. MIS

When I am old and long turned gray. 2001: The Tennyson/ Hardy Poem. Ewart Gavin. FaBoCo

When I Awoke. Raymond R. Patterson. PoBA

When I awoke this morning. The Blue Animals. Jon Anderson. AmPA

When I awoke with cold. Coffee. J. V. Cunningham. VGW

When I came back, he was gone. My Father's Leaving. Ira Sadoff. AmPA

When I Came from Colchis. W. S. Merwin. VGW

When I came to show you my summer cottage. Summer. Josephine Miles. WPE

When I can count the numbers far. Numbers. Elizabeth Madox Roberts. LCL

When I can hold a stone within my hand. Rumination. Richard Eberhart. CoPAm

When I can read my title clear. Ninety-fifth. Isaac Watts. AmFP

When I carefully consider the curious habits of dogs. Meditatio. Ezra Pound. PBMP

When I chanced to look over the wall in the glade. Bah! Walter de la Mare. BoAnP

When I consider how my life is spent. Reminiscent Reflection. Ogden Nash. FaBoCo

When I Consider How My Light Is Spent. Milton. *See* On His Blindness.

When I declared. Separation. Gary Sange. NVAP

When I Die, And. Laura Nyro. WIF

When I die choose a star. For My Daughter. David Ignatow. RRA

When I do count the clock that tells the time. Sonnets, XII. Shakespeare. InPS; VoPo

When I face north a lost Cree. Returned to Say. William Stafford. ConAP

When I faded back to pass. Ties. Dabney Stuart. CoPAm; SPo

When I fall asleep. Hands. Siv Cedering Fox. NVAP

When I fall asleep, and even during sleep. Baudelaire. Delmore Schwartz. VGW

When I finally read Genesis to the children. Genesis. Harold Witt. SFF

When I gaze at the sun. A Moment Please. Samuel Allen. PoBA; SS

When I get to heaven. Happy Day (or Independence Day). James Cunningham. JB

When I go musing all alone. Robert Burton. *Fr.* The Anatomy of Melancholy. SCP-2

When I go out to sow the wheat. To a Ground-Lark. David Campbell. *Fr.* Cocky's Calendar. MAuV

When I got to the field they were burning my biplane. Dreams of the Wars. David Young. CAAP

When I had firmly answered "No." The Last Ride Together. James Kenneth Stephen. FaBoCo

When I have been dead for several years. Poet's Wish. Valery Larbaud, *tr. by* William Jay Smith. LoAs

When I have borne in memory what has tamed. Wordsworth. MBPR

When I Have Fears That I May Cease to Be. Keats. HeIP; InPK; IPWM; MBPR; OBP; PAIC; PBMP; PPoe; VoPo

When I have seen by Time's fell hand defaced. Sonnets, LXIV. Shakespeare. HeIP; NOBE; PAIC; PPoe

When I have settled down in bed. The Attack. Leonard Clark. RAE

When I Heard at the Close of the Day. Walt Whitman. GBL

When I Heard Dat White Man Say. Zack Gilbert. PoBA

When I heard that. Regard to Neruda. Pat Lowther. MMD

When I Heard the Learn'd Astronomer. Walt Whitman. HeIP; IPWM; PBMP; PPoD; SFF; VoPo; WIF

When I Held You to My Chest, You Fit. Jack Myers. AmPA

When I hit her on the head, it was good. Herbert White. Frank Bidart AmPA

When I kiss Eve. Eden. D. M. Thomas. NCSH

When I last wrote. Letter to a Young Father in Exile. John Logan. CAPP

When I lay back in my chair last night. Eat 'Em Up Smith Tells All in South Africa. Judith Johnson Sherwin. NoAM

When I Learned to Whistle. Gordon Lea. AKE

When I leave this place. For the Far Edge. Mark Vinz. HeS

When I left the States for gold. Seeing the Elephant. *Unknown.* AIW

When I lie where shades of darkness. Fare Well. Walter de la Mare. NOBE

When I look forth at dawning, pool. Nature's Questioning. Thomas Hardy. IPWM; PBMP

When I looked at my poverty. Poverty. Charles Simic. MAT

When I put her out, once, by the garbage pail. The Geranium. Theodore Roethke. MPo

When I reached his place. It Was All Very Tidy. Robert Graves. OxBTC

When I Read Shakespeare. D. H. Lawrence. NoAM

When I recall your form and face. Recollection of First Love. William Soutar. SLP

When I returned at last from Paris hoofbeats pounded. Hobbes, 1651. John Hollander. NoAM

When I Roved a Young Highlander. Byron. SLP

When I ruled the world at six and would go to school in three weeks. Pigeons. James Mecklenburger. SFF

When I Saw Sweet Nelly Home, *with music.* John Fletcher. PSoN

When I saw that clumsy crow. Night Crow. Theodore Roethke. CoPAm; InPK; NCSH; VGW

When I saw your head bow, I knew I had beaten you. The Last Word. Peter Davison. InPK

When I see birches bend to left and right. Birches. Robert Frost. IPWM; NoAM

When I see hir forrow me. *Unknown, at. to* John Barbour. *Fr.* The Buik of Alexander. SLP

When I Set Out for Lyonnesse. Thomas Hardy. InPS

When I shall be without regret. Epitaph. J. V. Cunningham. InPK

When I survey the bright. Nox Nocti Indicat Scientiam. William Habington. NOBE

When I Survey the Wondrous Cross. Isaac Watts. AmFP; BLSH, *with music;* BoReV

When I think back to grammar school. P.S. 42. Gregory Corso. SA

When I took a job teaching in Massachusetts. To the Governor & Legislature of Massachusetts. Howard Nemerov. PPoD

When I veined that quick syrup. Glucose. Dabney Stuart. CoPAm

When I wake up. Remote House. Hans Enzenberger. LP

When I walk home from school. Oh, Joyous House. Richard Janzen. AKE

When I was/ thirteen I. Spring. Ruth Whitman. IHMS

When I was a bachelor bold and young. Bachelor Bold and Young. *Unknown.* AmFP

When I was a bachelor [*or* batchelor] I lived all alone [*or* early and young]. The Foggy, Foggy Dew. *Unknown.* BLSH; GBP; PeBB; RDB

When I was a bachelor, I lived by myself. Mother Goose. MG

When I was a bachelor, I lived by myself. Swapping Song. *Unknown.* RDB

When I was a batchelor early and young. *See* When I was a bachelor I lived all alone.

When I was a boy. The Piper's Progress. Francis Sylvester Mahony. PFIr

When I was a boy desiring the title of man. George. Dudley Randall. BPo; ConAP; NoAM

When I was a boy, I used to go to bed. The Remorse for Time. Howard Nemerov. NCSH

When I was a child. My People. Margery Himel. IHMS

When I was a child. Moon, Son of Heaven. Miyazawa Kenji, *tr. by* Gary Snyder. Moon

When I was a child. Sophistication. Vassar Miller. NCSH

When I was a child. Autobiographia Literaria. Frank O'Hara. NOBA

When I was a child/ I never smiled. The Truth about My Sister and Me. Anita Endrezze Probst. CDW

When I was a child I knew red miners. Childhood. Margaret Walker. IHMS; PoBA

When I was a child in Germany. Stiff Shirts. Derek Bowman. MIS

When I was a chile we used to play. Children's Rhymes. Langston Hughes. InPS

When I was a kid. The External Element. David McFadden. NeAC

When I was a kid I loved Shredded Wheat. Shredded Wheat. Louis Dudek. AKE

When I Was a Little Girl. Alice Milligan. PFIr

When I was a single girl, I went dressed very fine. Oh, I Wish I Were Single Again. *Unknown.* AmFP

When I was a wee thing. The Kirk of the Birds, Beasts and Fishes. *Unknown.* GBP

When I was a windy boy and a bit. Lament. Dylan Thomas. PPP

"When I was a young girl, I used to seek pleasure." One Morning in May; or, The Young Girl Cut Down in Her Prime. *Unknown.* AmFP

When I Was a Young Maid. *Unknown.* AmFP

When I was apprenticed in London. Blow the Candles Out. *Unknown.* RDB

When I was as high as that. A Memory. L. A. G. Strong. FaBoCo; PFIr

When I was born. The Day's Ration. Emerson. PiAm

When I was born on Amman hill. The Collier. Vernon Watkins. MPo

When I was bound apprentice. The Lincolnshire Poacher. *Unknown.* GBP

When I was but thirteen or so. Romance. Walter James Turner. NOBE

When I was christened. Perambulator Poem. David McCord. OFD

When I was down beside the sea. At the Seaside. Robert Louis Stevenson. LCL; OxBChV

When I was fair and young and favour graced me. Elizabeth I, Queen of England. BoLoP

When I Was Home Last Christmas. Randall Jarrell. AIW

When I was in Missouri, would not let me be. I Will Turn Your Money Green. *Unknown.* BluL

"When I was just as far as I could walk." The Telephone. Robert Frost. LoAs

When I Was Lost. Dorothy Aldis. CaYB

When I was lying in jail with my back turned to the wall. The Jailhouse Blues. *Unknown.* BluL

When I was once in Baltimore. Sheep W. H. Davies. PoTa; RAE

When I Was One-and-Twenty. A. E. Housman. BoLoP; HeIP; LoAs; MiP; NoAM; PBMP

When I was seventeen, a man in the Dakar Station. Objets d'Art. Cynthia Macdonald. NMM; WBN

When I was sick and lay abed. The Land of Counterpane. Robert Louis Stevenson. ECBV; OxBChV

When I was single. I Wish I Was Single. *Unknown.* AmFP

When I Was Soft as Ferns. Colette Inez. AATT

When I was the sissy of the block who nobody wanted on their team. The Sleeper. Edward Field. SPo

When I was 12. Nora. Fran Winant. WBN

When I was twelve I was kidnapped and sold as a slave. A Psalm of Onan for Harp, Flute and Tambourine. Alden Nowlan. NeAC

When I was twelve in that far land. Only for Me. Mark Van Doren. NCSH

When I was very very. Mama Knows. Sharon Scott. JB

When I was visiting a nephew of 10. Acrophobe and Lapidary. James Bonk. HeS

When I was wed. The Golden Witch. Alan Dienstag. MIT

When I was young and in my prime,/ I flourished like a vine. Thyme. *Unknown.* AmFP

When I was young and in my prime,/ I thought I never could marry. Devilish Mary. *Unknown.* AmFP

When I was young and in my prime, my age twenty-two. The Lightning Flash. *Unknown.* AmFP

When I was young and wanted to see the sights. On His Queerness. Christopher Isherwood. OxBTC

When I was young and we were poor. Modifications. Ron Koertge. MiP

When I was young I believed in intellectual conversation. In the Men's Room(s). Marge Piercy. MMD

When I was young I us'd to wait on Massa and hand him de plate. Jim Crack Corn [*or,* The Blue-tail Fly]. *Unknown.* BLSH; BLSo; GBP; PSoN

When I was young I woke gladly in the morning. Hoelderlin's Old Age. Stephen Spender. NoAM

When I Watch the Living Meet. A. E. Housman. VoPo

When I watch you. Miss Rosie. Lucille Clifton. AmPA; CAAP; NMM; PoBA; RiTi

When I went into my room, at mid-morning. Man and Bat. D. H. Lawrence. BoAnP

When I Went Off to Prospect. *Unknown.* AmFP

When I went out to kill myself, I caught. Saint Judas. James Wright. ConAP; NOBA; TCP

When I Went to the Circus. D. H. Lawrence. NoAM

When I would squat by holes and piles of dirt. The Unloved. Robert Canzoneri. CoPAm

When I wrote of the women in their dances and wildness, it was a mask. The Poem As Mask. Muriel Rukeyser. RiTi

When icicles hang by the wall. Winter. Shakespeare. *Fr.* Love's Labour's Lost, V, ii. AKE; FSFS; HeIP; InPK; InPS; IPWM; NOBE; OBP; SoSe

"When I'm alone"—the words tripped off his tongue. Siegfried Sassoon. OxBTC

"When I'm discharged in Liverpool 'n' draws my bit o' pay." Hell's Pavement. John Masefield. PoTa

When in disgrace with fortune and men's eyes. Sonnets, XXIX. Shakespeare. Epi; GBL; HeIP; NOBE; OBP; PAIC; PPoe; PPP; Prf

When in my youth I travelled. The Migration of the Grey Squirrels. William Howitt. OxBChV

When in nineteen-thirty-seven, Etta Moten, sweetheart. The Convert. Margaret Danner. BPo

When in Rome. Mari Evans. SoSe

When in that gold. Listening to Foxhounds. James Dickey. InPS; PPoD

When in the chronicle of wasted time. Sonnets, CVI. Shakespeare. NOBE; PPoe

When in the company of the gods. Hilda Doolittle ("H.D."). *Fr.* The Walls Do Not Fall. NoAM

When in the east the morning ray. The Garden of Appleton House. Andrew Marvell. *Fr.* Upon Appleton House. NOBE

When, in the middle of my life, the earth stalks me. Mona Van Duyn. *Fr.* Three Valentines to the Wide World. RiTi

When in your middle years. The Lights in the Sky Are Stars. Kenneth Rexroth. RRA

When Israel against Philistia. David and Goliath. Nathaniel Crouch. OxBChV

When Israel was in Egypt's land. Go Down, Moses. *Unknown.* NOBA; RDB

When it is all over. Lost Moment. Hoyt W. Fuller. PoBA

When it is finally ours, this freedom. Frederick Douglass. Robert Hayden. CoPAm; PBMP; PoBA

When it is not yet day. Looking for Mushrooms at Sunrise. W. S. Merwin. NOBA

When it is plucking time for my young son. Daisies. John Stevens Wade. FAF

When it rained five days and the skies turned dark as night. Back Water Blues. *Unknown.* BluL

When it stood, my town was small. A Beginning. David Steingass. CoPAm

When it's dull, or if the sun is gleaming. Going Fishing. Lexie Griffiths. RAE

When I've been warm. Realities. Shirley Kaufman. MIT

When I've outlived three plastic hearts, or four. D.O.M., A.D. 2167. John Frederick Nims. CoPAm

When Januar wind was blawin cauld. The Lass That Made the Bed to Me. Burns. OBP

When John Henry was a little babe [or fellow]. John Henry. *Unknown.* AmFP; BPo

When Johnny Comes Marching Home, *with music.* Patrick Sarsfield Gilmore. BLSo; PSoN

When Jones's Ale Was New. *Unknown.* AmFP

When Joseph was an old man. The Cherry-Tree Carol. *Unknown.* AmFP

When Kai is born. Not Leaving the House. Gary Snyder. IPWM

When Klopstock England defied. Blake. MBPR

When lads have done with labor. Humbert Wolfe. SpRo

When late I attempted your pity to move. An Expostulation. Isaac Bickerstaff. FaBoCo; PFIr

When lean Tom Paine blew on his thumbs. Citizen Paine. James Daugherty. ECBV

When Learning's triumph o'er her barb'rous foes. Prologue Spoken at the Opening of the Theatre in Drury-Lane, 1747. Samuel Johnson. LAuP

When Lilacs Last in the Dooryard Bloom'd. Walt Whitman. Epi; IPWM; NOBA; PAIC; PiAm; PPoe; PPP; VoPo *Sels.*
　"In the swamp in secluded recesses." RFM
　"When lilacs last in the dooryard bloom'd," 24 *ll.* OFD

When little people go abroad, wherever they may roam. To Henrietta, on Her Departure for Calais. Thomas Hood. OxBChV

When Louis came home to the flat. Meet Me in St. Louis, Louis. Andrew B. Sterling. FSN

When love with unconfined wings. To Althea, from Prison. Richard Lovelace. GBL; HeIP; InPS; MetP; NOBE

When Lovely Woman Stoops to Folly. Goldsmith *See* Song: "When lovely woman stoops to folly."

When lusty diet and the frolic cup. Francis Quarles. *Fr.* The History of Samson. SCP-2

When lyart leaves bestrow the yird. The Jolly Beggars. Burns. LAuP

When Maggie and I were acquaint. Tweedside. Lord Yester. SLP

When Mahalia Sings. Quandra Prettyman. MiP; PoBA

When Malindy Sings. Paul Laurence Dunbar. PoBA

When man and maiden meet, I like to see a drooping eye. The Modest Couple. W. S. Gilbert. PoTa

When man has conquered space. Earth's Bondman. Betty Page Dabney. ECBV

When Mary pulled the sorrel's reins from Stephen. Hoppy. Edwin S. Godsey. PPoD

When maukin bucks, at early fucks. Ode to Spring. Burns. OBP

When men beeth meriest at her mele. Think on Yesterday. *Unknown.* OxBM

When men discovered freedom first. The Ash and the Oak. Louis Simpson. ConAP

When men shall find thy flower, thy glory, pass. Samuel Daniel. *Fr.* To Delia. NOBE

When men turn mob. Music and Drum. Archibald MacLeish. TH

When men were all asleep the snow came flying. London Snow. Robert Bridges. FSFS; NoAM; NOBE; OxBTC

When Mrs. Gorm (Aunt Eloise). Opportunity. Harry Graham. FaBoCo

When music, heav'nly maid, was young. The Passions, an Ode to Music. William Collins. LAuP

When my devotions could not pierce. Denial. George Herbert. BoReV; NOBE

When my grandmother left the faces with Mr. Hughes. Deaths and Pretty Cousins. David Campbell. CAAP

When my grave is broke up again. The Relic. John Donne. GBL; MetP; NOBE; PPP; SCP-1

When my heart was the amorous worms' meat. The Amorous Worms' Meat. Petrarch, *tr. by* Anna Maria Armi. *Fr.* Sonnets to Laura: To Laura in Death. LoAs

When my love swears that she is made of truth. Sonnets, CXXXVIII. Shakespeare. Epi; LoAs; OBP; PPoD; PPP; SoSe

When my mother died I was very young. The Chimney Sweeper. Blake. *Fr.* Songs of Innocence. AnMo; HeIP; InPK; LAuP; MBPR; OxBChV; PPoe; PPP; SoSe

When My Uncle Willie Saw. Carole Freeman. NMM

When my young brother was killed. War. Joseph Langland. IPWM

When Nature dreamt of making bores. Epigram: On Sir Roger Phillimore. *Unknown.* FaBoCo

When Newton saw an apple fall, he found. Moon Shot. Byron. *Fr.* Don Juan, X. OBP

When night shadows slipped across the plain, I saw a man. A Nation Wrapped in Stone. Roberta Hill. CDW

When night stirred at sea. The Planter's Daughter. Austin Clarke. OxBTC; PFIr

When Noah, perceiving 'twas time to embark. The Dog's Cold Nose. Arthur Guiterman. ECBV; PoTa

When nothing is happening. How Everything Happens. May Swenson. Psy; RFM

When Oats Were Reaped. Thomas Hardy. OxBTC

When ocean-clouds over inland hills. Misgivings. Herman Melville. NOBA; PiAm

When Ogden his prosaic verse. On Dr. Samuel Ogden. R. P. Arden. FaBoCo

When old birds strangely-hearted strive to sing. The Sweetening of the Year. John Shaw Neilson. MAuV

When on they lip my soul I breathe. The Killing Kiss. Thomas Stanley. SCP-2

When once the scourging prophet, with his cry. The Disused Table. Norman Cameron. OxBTC

When one billion insurance. Going Home. Tim Reynolds. NowV

When other fair ones to the shades go down. On Certain Ladies. Pope. FaBoCo

When our brother Fire was having his dog's day. Brother Fire. Louis MacNeice. NoAM; NOBE

When our earth mother is replete with living waters. Prayer for Rain. *Unknown.* AKE

When our two souls stand up erect and strong. Sonnets from the Portuguese, XXII. Elizabeth Barrett Browning. NOBE; SBG; WPE

When over the flowery, sharp pasture's. Flowers by the Sea. William Carlos Williams. NoAM

When pails empty the last brightness. O You among Women. F. R. Higgins. BIrV

When passions's trance is overpast. To —— Shelley. MBPR

When Pat came o'er the hills his colleen for to see. The Whistling Thief. *Unknown.* PoTa

When Pelion wondering saw that rain, which fell. To Castara: of What We Were before Our Creation. William Habington. SCP-2

When people's ill they come to I. On Dr. Isaac Letsome. *Unknown.* FaBoCo

When periwigs came first in wear. The Bald Cavalier. *Unknown.* OxBChV

When raging [or raying] love with extreme pain [or payne]. Consolation. Earl of Surrey. AAS; NOBE

When Reason's ray shines over all. On the Triumph of Rationalism. Alfred Ainger. FaBoCo

When rising from the bed of death.  Addison.  BoReV

When roaring gloom surged inward and you cried.  To His Dead Body.  Siegfried Sassoon.  NoAM

When Robin Hood was about eighteen years old.  Robin Hood and Little John.  *Unknown.*  AmFP

When Ruth was left half desolate.  Ruth.  Wordsworth.  MBPR

When Serpents Bargain for the Right to Squirm.  E. E. Cummings.  InPK; SoSe

When she came on, straight.  Black Is Beautiful.  Philip Appleman.  SFF

When she carries food to the table and stoops down.  Part of Plenty.  Bernard Spencer.  GBL

When she looks out by night.  Michael Drayton.  *Fr.* The Shepherd's Sirena.  SCP-2

When she put her hand on me.  The First Time.  John Newlove.  NeAC

When she rises in the morning.  Gloire de Dijon.  D. H. Lawrence.  GBL; IPWM; LoAs; NoAM

When she was little.  Poem for Aretha.  Nikki Giovanni.  PoBA

When Sir Joshua Reynolds died.  Sir Joshua Reynolds.  Blake.  FaBoCo

When skies wer peale wi' twinklen stars.  Lydlinch Bells.  William Barnes.  VPC

When sly Jemmy Twitcher had smugged up his face.  The Candidate.  Thomas Gray.  PPP

When Smoke Stood Up from Ludlow.  A. E. Housman.  SoSe

When Snow Falls.  Katherine Hoskins.  TCP

When snow like sheep lay in the fold.  In Memory of Jane Fraser.  Geoffrey Hill.  NoAM; OxBTC

When Sol did cast no light.  The Valiant Seaman's Happy Return to His Love.  *Unknown.*  GBP; PeBB

When some beloveds, 'neath whose eyelids lay.  Bereavement.  Elizabeth Barrett Browning.  WPE

When some proud son of man returns to earth.  Inscription on the Monument of a Newfoundland Dog.  Bryon.  MBPR

When someone/ pulls down a blind.  Blindfold.  Luci Shaw.  AATT

When Something Happens.  James A. Randall, Jr.  BPo

When sommer toke in hand the winter to assail.  Earl of Surrey.  AAS

When Spoon River became a ganglion.  Marx the Sign Painter.  Edgar Lee Masters.  *Fr.* The New Spoon River.  NoAM

When Spring came.  *Unknown, tr. fr. Tlinglit Indian.*  RFM

When Statesmen gravely say "We must be realistic."  W. H. Auden.  FaBoCo

When summer was approaching.  First Love.  *Unknown, tr. by George F. Whicher.*  OLR

When supper time is almost come.  Milking Time.  Elizabeth Madox Roberts.  RAE

When sycamore leaves wer a-spreaden.  Woak Hill.  William Barnes.  VPC

When Tadlow walks the streets the paviours cry.  Tadlow.  Abel Evans.  FaBoCo

When that happens.  Resisting Each Other.  Anne Waldman.  RiTi

When that I was and a little tiny boy.  Shakespeare.  *Fr.* Twelfth Night, V, i.  HeIP; NOBE; OBP; PPoe; WIF

When the/ sun.  August 2.  Norman Jordan.  PoBA

When the *Alabama's* keel was laid.  Roll, *Alabama*, Roll.  *Unknown.*  AIW

When the alcoholic passed the crucial point.  Point of No Return.  Robert Graves.  BIrV

When the Animals Left the Ark.  *Unknown.*  RAE

When the black herds of the rain were gazing.  The Lost Heifer.  Austin Clarke.  BIrV

When the blackbird in the spring.  *See* As the blackbird in the spring.

When the bones walk out of me.  Never.  George Reavey.  BIrV

When the book is closed.  The Book Ends, Immortality Begins.  Adrianne Marcus.  NPW

When the boy undressed.  The Skull.  Ian Young.  NeAC

When the children had ferried across the river.  Children Visit the Island.  Diane Wakoski.  CAAP

When the clouds' swoln bosoms echo back the shouts.  In Tenebris, II.  Thomas Hardy.  NoAM; OxBTC

When the cold comes.  Where? When? Which?  Langston Hughes.  BPo

When the completely charming.  Bernard.  Raymond Souster.  POL

When the crowd has cheered the hostile teams.  Ballad of the Pigskin.  Horace Spencer Fiske.  SPo

When the dawn flames in the sky.  At Dawning.  Nelle Richmond Eberhart.  BLSo

When the Dumb Speak.  Robert Bly.  CAPP; NoAM; NOBA

When the eagle soared clear through a dawn distilling of emerald.  Crow and the Birds.  Ted Hughes.  OBP

When the earth is turned in spring.  The Worm.  Ralph Bergengren.  CaYB

When the fierce North-wind with his airy forces.  The Day of Judgement [*or* Judgment].  Isaac Watts.  NOBE; PAIC

When the flowers turn to husks.  Cells Breathe in the Emptiness.  Galway Kinnell.  VGW

When the forests have been destroyed their darkness remains.  The Asians Dying.  W. S. Merwin.  CAPP; NOBA

When the Frost is on the Punkin.  James Whitcomb Riley.  AmVN

When the giraffes left their silos in Iowa.  Giraffes: The American Version.  Stephen Dunn.  HeS

When the gnats dance at evening.  Gnat-Psalm.  Ted Hughes.  NoAM

When the gold fever raged I was doing very well.  The Miner's Lament.  *Unknown.*  AmFP

When the grass was closely mown.  The Dumb Soldier.  Robert Louis Stevenson.  OxBChV

When the green woods laugh with the voice of joy.  Laughing Song [*or* Laughter].  Blake.  *Fr.* Songs of Innocence.  ECBV; LAuP; MBPR; OxBChV

When the hounds of spring are on winter's traces.  Chorus.  Swinburne.  *Fr.* Atalanta in Calydon.  HeIP; NOBE; VPC

When the ice starts to shiver.  On Edges.  Adrienne Rich.  Psy

When the jet sprang into the sky.  Geography Lesson.  Zulfikar Ghose.  LP; MPo

When the lad for longing sighs.  A. E. Housman.  OLR

When the Lamp Is Shattered.  Shelley.  PPP
(Lines: "When the lamp is shattered.")  MBPR

When the master lived a king and I a starving hutted slave beneath the lash, and.  On Listening to the Spirituals.  Lance Jeffers.  PoBA

When the new alphabet soup of the earth.  Red Movie.  John Tranter.  CAAP

When the night falls silently, the night falls silently.  Glow Worm.  Lila Cayley Robinson.  BLSo

When the Nightingale Sings.  *Unknown.*  OxBM

When the nightingale to his mate.  Alba.  Ezra Pound.  VGW

When the norse.  Greenland, 850 A.D.  Lyn Lifshin.  MMD

When the old Cove Creek Dam first was started.  The Song of Cove Creek Dam.  *Unknown.*  AmFP

When the ox-horn sounds in the buried hills.  Second Psalm: The Signals.  W. S. Merwin.  CAAP

When the pine tosses its cones.  Woodnotes, I.  Emerson.  NOBA

When the pods went pop on the broom, green broom. A Runnable Stag. John Davidson. OxBTC

When the present has latched its postern behind my tremulous stay. Afterwards. Thomas Hardy. InPS; NOBE; OBP; SoSe

When the proficient poison of sure sleep. E. E. Cummings. LoAs

When the pumpkin yellows. Winter Soon Is Coming. Elizabeth J. Coatsworth. ECBV

When the rain comes tumbling down. The Story of Flying Robert. Heinrich Hoffmann, tr. fr. German. SpRo

When the Rain Raineth. Unknown. GBP

When the Revolution Really. Peter Michelson. HeS

When the ring gleamed white and your chair hugged the edge of it. Change of Address. Kathleen Fraser. WBN

When the Roll Is Called Up Yonder, with music. James M. Black. BLSH

When the rooster jumps up on the windowsill. Cuba, 1962. Ai. AmPA

When the Saints Come Marching In, with music. Edward C. Redding. BLSo

When the sea comes in at Horsey Gap. Horsey Gap. Unknown. GBP

When the sheep are in the fauld, and the kye at hame. Ault Robin Gray. Lady Anne Lindsay. WPE

When the speckled hen laid a white egg and. Racialism. John Blight. CAAP

When the spider dropped down from the ceiling. The Grandmother Came Down to Visit Us. Joseph Bruchac. CDW

When the summer fields are mown. Aftermath. Longfellow. NOBA; PiAm

When the sun/ falls behind the sumac. Loss. A. R. Ammons. ConAP

When the sun came, the rooster expanded to meet it. Josephine Miles. CoPAm

When the sun shouts and people abound. Summer Holiday. Robinson Jeffers. MiP

When the sun's perpendicular rays. Beginning of an Undergraduate Poem. Unknown. FaBoCo

When the swift-rolling brook, swollen deep. The Storm-Wind. William Barnes. NOBE

When the tea is brought at five o'clock. Milk for the Cat. Harold Monro. PCat

When the time has arrived. Trala Trala Trala Le-Le-La. William Carlos Williams. OFD

When the trial's in Belzoni. High Sheriff Blues. Unknown. BluL

When the trumpet of the Lord shall sound. When the Roll Is Called Up Yonder. James M. Black. BLSH

When the tv has been turned off. The Gift. J. D. Whitney. NVAP

When the voices of children are heard on the green/ And laughing is heard on the hill. Nurse's Song. Blake. Fr. Songs of Innocence. LAuP; MBPR; OxBChV

When the voices of children are heard on the green/ And whisprings are in the dale. Nurse's Song. Blake. Fr. Songs of Experience. LAuP; MBPR

When the war-cry of Liberty rang through the land. The Death of Warren. Epes Sargent. BTTM

When the War Is Over. W. S. Merwin. PPoD

When the ways are heavy with mire and rut. The Ballade of Prose and Rhyme. Austin Dobson. PAIC

When the white feet of the baby beat across the grass. Baby-Movements. D. H. Lawrence. RRA

When the white flame in us is gone. Dust. Rupert Brooke. OxBTC

When the wind blows loud and fearful. The Beggar Boy. Cecil Frances Alexander. OxBChV

When the wind is in the east. Unknown. MG

When the wind works against us in the dark. Storm Fear. Robert Frost. IPWM

When the world has lost. Containment. Howard Schwartz. HeS

When the world takes over for us. Lear. William Carlos Williams. NOBA

When the world turns completely upside down. Wild Peaches. Elinor Wylie. RiTi; SBG; WPE

When These Old Barns Lost Their Inhabitants. David Kherdian. FAF

When they ask your name. Children. Russell Edson. AmPA

When they had won the war. The Inner Part. Louis Simpson. InPS; PBMP; SFF

When they shot Malcolm Little down. At That Moment. Raymond R. Patterson. PoBA

When they stop poems. Today is a Day of Great Joy. Victor Hernandez Cruz. WIF

When they woke me. Coming Back. Joseph Bruchac. CDW

When thin-strewn memory I look through. Miss Loo. Walter de la Mare. OxBTC

When This Cruel War Is Over. Unknown. AmFP

When this troubled life is over, hide Thou me. Hide Thou Me. Unknown. AmFP

When thou and I are dead, my dear. Inseparable. Philip Bourke Marston. BoLoP

When thou hast spent the lingring day in pleasure and delight. Gascoygnes Good Night. George Gascoigne. AAS

When thou must home to shades of underground. Among the Shades. Thomas Campion, after Propertius. AAS; BoLoP; GBL; LoAs; NOBE

When thou, poor excommunicate. To My Inconstant Mistress. Thomas Carew. GBL; MetP; NOBE

When Thy King Is a Boy, sel. Ed Roberson. "You black out the sun." PoBA

When to her lute Corrina sings. Thomas Campion. AAS

When to the sessions of sweet silent thought. Sonnets, XXX. Shakespeare. Epi; GBL; InPS; NOBE; PAIC; PPP; VoPo; WIF

When trout swim down Great Ormond Street. Priapus and the Pool, III. Conrad Aiken. NoAM; NOBA

When two/ bodies meet. Radiant Heat. Rochelle Owens. WBN

When two men meet for the first time in all. Law in the Country of the Cats. Ted Hughes. NowV

When Two Suns Do Appear. Sir Philip Sidney. Fr. Arcadia. Moon

When Uncle Devereux died. Dunbarton. Robert Lowell. MPo

When up aloft. The Robin. Thomas Hardy. RAE

When warships anchored, spent in the Sound. Between Two Wars. R. P. Kingston. NVAP

When we are at last in that far heaven. The Birthday. Morley Jamieson. SLP

When we are dead, some hunting-boy will pass. The Statue. Hilaire Belloc. POL

When we are going toward someone we say. Simple Song. Marge Piercy. CTBA; Psy; TSWA

When we are in love, we love the grass. Love Poem. Robert Bly. InPS

When we are old and these rejoicing veins. Edna St, Vincent Millay. VGW

When we came home from school one day. Goat. Siddie Joe Johnson. ECBV

When we finally. There Is No Time. Elaine H. Jennings. NPW

When we first met we did not guess. Robert Bridges. POL

When we first rade down Ettrick. Ettrick. Lady John Scott. SLP; WPE

When we for age could neither read nor write. Of the Last Verses in the Book. Edmund Waller. MetP; PAIC; SCP-2

When we get a good day here. Young Couples Strolling By. Carl Rakosi. InPS

When we heard it announced. The Ambassadors. Paul Lawson. PPoD

When we in kind embracements had agre'd. *Unknown. Fr.* Zepheria. AAS

When we loved. Loving. Jane Stembridge. NMM

When we moved here, pulled. An Oregon Message. William Stafford. Moon

When we rolled up the three armored vehicles. One Morning We Brought Them Order. Al Lee. WIF

When we see/ the houses again. The Removal. W. S. Merwin. TCP

When we slept. Signature. Larry Mollin. NeAC

When we spurt off. Moving. William Matthews. POL

When we start breaking up in the wet darkness. Consolations of Philosophy. Derek Mahon. BIrV

When We Two Parted. Byron. BoLoP; NOBE; OLR; PBMP; VoPo

When we wake. After a Journey. Ken Smith. TwMBP

When we walk with the Lord. Trust and Obey. J.H. Sammis. BLSH

When we walked outside at sunset. Abortion. Mei Berssenbrugge. SA

When we were a soft amoeba. Ere You Were Queen of Sheba. Sir Arthur Shipley. FaBoCo

When we were children. The Key of the Kingdom. Ed Reed. BBGO

When we were children, clasping hands. But You, My Darling, Should Have Married the Prince. Kathleen Spivack. AmPA; NMM

When we were children old Nurse used to say. The Quiet House. Charlotte Mew. SBG

When we were married eight years. Tryst. Eve Merriam. NMM

When we'd make the rounds. Shazam. R. P. Dickey. HeS

When Westwell Downs I 'gan to tread. On Westwell Downs. William Strode. SCP-2

When, when and whenever death closes our eyelids. Ezra Pound. *Fr.* Homage to Sextus Propertius. NoAM

When whispering strains, with creeping wind. The Commendation of Music. William Strode. SCP-2

When Whistler's Mother's picture frame. To a Lost Sweetheart. Don Marquis. POL

When white people speak of being uptight. The Dancer. Al Young. PiAm; PoBA; SA

When will that war end? My whole house is still. On Seeing Films of the War. Louis Coxe. PPoD

When will the stream be aweary of flowing. Nothing Will Die. Tennyson. PBMP

When Windesor walles sustain'd my wearied arme. Earl of Surrey. AAS

When with staid mothers' milk and sunshine warmed. Alfred Austin. *Fr.* The Human Tragedy. FaBoCo

When world is water and all is flood, God said. Noah's Ark. Marguerite Young. WPE

When ye hunt at the roe, then shall ye see there. Julians Barnes. *Fr.* Book of Hunting. WPE

When Yon Full Moon. W. H. Davies. Moon

When you and I go down. Midnight Lamentation. Harold Monro. OxBTC

When You and I Must Part. *Unknown.* AmFP

When you and I on the Palos Verdes cliff. Shane O'Neill's Cairn. Robinson Jeffers. NoAM; NOBA

When You and I Were Young, Maggie, *with music.* George W. Johnson. BLSH; BLSo; PSoN

When You Are Old. W. B. Yeats. BoLoP; GBL; HeIP; IPWM; NoAM; OxBTC; SFF

When you begin, begin at the beginning. The Grass. Helen Wolfert. RiTi

When you come, as you soon must, to the streets of our city. Advice to a Prophet. Richard Wilbur. CAPP; MAT; PiAm; PPoD; PPP

When you come to the end of a perfect day. A Perfect Day. Carrie Jacobs Bond. BLSo

When you consider the radiance, that it does not withhold. The City Limits. A. R. Ammons. NoAM; NOBA

When you drive on the freeway, cars follow you. Paranoia. Michael Dennis Browne. AmPA

When you find yourself alone on the river island. Quechua Song. *Unknown, tr. by* Ruth Stephan. RRA

When you go through. Poem for a Goodbye. Norman MacCaig. SLP

When you grow up you learn better. Before You're a Stranger. Raymond Fraser. AKE

When You Have Forgotten Sunday: The Love Story. Gwendolyn Brooks. BPo; VoPo

When you have wearied of the valiant spires of this country town. Oxford Canal. James Elroy Flecker. OxBTC

When you hear me walking. Nappy Head Blues. *Unknown.* BluL

When you look down from the airplane you see lines. Field and Forest. Randall Jarrell. VGW

When you lose your money please don't lose your mind. Married Man Blues. *Unknown.* BluL

When you put on the feet be sure. Dr. Potatohead Talks to Mothers. Judith Johnson Sherwin. NoAM

When you reach to touch the markings. Indian Rock, Bainbridge Island, Washington. Duane Niatum. CDW

When you see a pretty maiden who has just turn'd seventeen. You're Not the Only Pebble on the Beach. Harry Braisted. FSN

When you shall see me in the toils of time. She, to Him. Thomas Hardy. OxBTC

When you show me. Colors for Mama. Barbara Mahone. PoBA

When you take your pill. The Pill Versus the Springhill Mine Disaster. Richard Brautigan. NowV

When you think of the distances. The Distances. W. S. Merwin. NOBA

When You Walk. James Stephens. ECBV

When you was down sick down on your bed. She's Gone Blues. *Unknown.* BluL

When you were. For Angela. Zack Gilbert. PoBA

When you were here in wonderful Detroit. Goodbye David Tamunoemi West. Margaret Danner. BPo

When You Were Sweet Sixteen, *with music.* James Thornton. BLSH; FSN

When you woke up among them. After Grief. Stanley Plumly. AmPA

When Young Ladies Get Married. *Unknown.* AmFP

When your eyes gaze seaward. Golden Moonrise. William Stanley Braithwaite. PoBA

When your hour was rung at last. Rendez-vous Manqué dans la Rue Racine. J. M. Synge. BIrV

When You're Away. Samuel Hoffenstein. POL

When you're lying awake with a dismal headache. Nightmare. W. S. Gilbert. *Fr.* Iolanthe. PBMP

When you're sailing in strange harbors, Cutty Sark, Cutty Sark. The Clipper *Dunbar* to the Clipper *Cutty Sark*. Ethel Anderson. PoTa

When you've grown up, my dears, and are as old as I. Toyland. Glen MacDonough. BLSo; FSN

Whenas in perfume Julia went. Herrick's Julia. Helen Bevington. SpRo

Whenas in silks my Julia goes. Upon Julia's Clothes. Robert Herrick. AnMo; GBL; HeIP; InPS; IPWM; NOBE; PAIC; PPP; SCP-1; SpRo; SS; WIF

Whenas [*or* When as] man's life, the light of human lust. Memento Mori. Fulke Greville. *Fr.* Caelica. BoReV; SCP-2

Whenas the mildest month. The Rose. Thomas Howell. FSFS

Whenas the nightingale chanted her vespers. Mark Antony. John Cleveland. SCP-2

Whence did all that fury come? A Stick of Incense. W. B. Yeats. AnMo

Whence Had They Come? W. B. Yeats. BoLoP

Whence hast thou then, thou witless puss. Tiger at Play. Joanna Baillie. PCat

Whene'er I come where ladies are. Love at Large. Coventry Patmore. *Fr.* The Angel in the House. VPC

Whenever I move. 2 Poems Written on Turning Around Too Quickly While Hiking. Morton Marcus. NVAP

Whenever I plunge my arm, like this. Under the Waterfall. Thomas Hardy. BoLoP

Whenever it rains. Telephones, Muzak. Vincent Buckley. *Fr.* Golden Builders. CAAP

Whenever Richard Cory went down town. Richard Cory. E. A. Robinson. AmVN; BBGO; InPK; IPWM; MiP; NOBA; PAIC; PoTa; SFF; SoSe; TH; WIF

Whenever the dark cloud horses galloped. And Jesus Don't Have Much Use for His Old Suitcase Anymore. Tom Kryss. NeAC

Whenever the days are cool and clear. The Sandhill Crane. Mary Austin. ECBV

Whenever the moon and stars are set. Windy Nights. Robert Louis Stevenson. ECBV; OxBChV

Whenne ich see on roode. On the Passion. *Unknown.* OxBM

Whenne mine eyen misteth. All Too Late. *Unknown.* OxBM

Wher is Paris and Heleine. Where is Paris and Helene? Thomas of Hales. OxBM

Where a safe hearth glows warm. Art and Civilization. Robert Conquest. NoAM

Where am I now? And what. A Song in Passing. Yvor Winters. VGW

Where am I? Sure I wander 'midst enchantment. Thomas Otway. *Fr.* The Orphan; or, The Unhappy Marriage. SCP-2

Where are all thy beauties now, all hearts enchaining? Thomas Campion. GBL

Where are Elmer, Herman, Bert, Tom and Charley. The Hill. Edgar Lee Masters. *Fr.* Spoon River Anthology. NoAM; NOBA

Where are the passions they essayed. Ballade of Dead Actors. W. E. Henley. PPoD

Where are the people. Question. Norma Craig. POL

Where are the swains, who, daily labour done. The Oncoming Industrial Revolution. George Crabbe. *Fr.* The Village. OBP

Where are the War Poets? C. Day Lewis. OxBTC

Where are we to go when this is done? Sonnet. Alfred A. Duckett. PoBA

Where are you going? asked Manny the Mayor. Jig Tune: Not for Love. Thomas McGrath. VGW

"Where are you going, my little pig?" Little Piggy. Thomas Hood. ECBV

"Where are you going?" said the knight in the road. The False Knight upon the Road. *Unknown.* AmFP

"Where are you going to, my pretty maid?" *Unknown.* MG

Where Are You Now? Mary Britton Miller. ECBV

Where are your heroes, my little black ones. Poem for Black Boys. Nikki Giovanni. BPo

Where art thou, God? or where is he. The Inquisition. Thomas Beedome. SCP-2

Where art thou, my beloved son. The Affliction of Margaret. Wordsworth. MBPR

Where be ye going, you Devon maid? Keats. MBPR

Where beeth they buforen us weren. *See* Were beth they that biforen us weren.

Where Cross the Crowded Ways of Life, *with music.* Frank Mason North. BLSH

Where did the voice come from? I hunted through the rooms. Bedtime Story for My Son. Peter Redgrove. BuTh

Where Did You Come from, Baby Dear? George MacDonald. OxBChV

Where Did You Get That Hat?, *with music.* Joseph J. Sullivan. FSN

Where do shadows live? Lectures on the Biology of the Shadow. George M. Young, Jr. FAF

Where Do the Children Play? Cat Stevens. PoRo

Where dost thou careless lie. An Ode to Himself. Ben Jonson. Epi; NOBE; PAIC; SCP-1

Where five old graves lay circled on a hill. The Graveyard. Jane Cooper. CoPAm

Where Go the Boats? Robert Louis Stevenson. LCL; OxBChV

Where has tenderness gone, he asked the mirror. Delirium in Vera Cruz. Malcolm Lowry. OxBTC

Where has ti been, maw canny hinny? Captain Bover. *Unknown.* GBP

Where hast 'te been, ma' canny hinny? Ma Canny Hinny. *Unknown.* GBP

Where Have All the Flowers Gone? Pete Seeger. PoRo

"Where have you been all day, Rendal my son?" Lord Rendal. *Unknown.* RDB

"Where have you been this while away." The Widow's Party. Kipling. PeBB

Where Have You Gone. Mari Evans. BPo; MiP

Where He Leads Me I Will Follow, *with music.* E. W. Blandy. BLSH

Where he really hung, there. One More Time. James Welch. VW

Where he stood and where. Jew. James A. Randall Jr. BPo

Where I lived the river. Eclogues. Dennis Schmitz. NVAP

Where I walk out. Song. Yvor Winters. BoAnP; POL

Where in what strange Elysium is now the *Literary Digest.* Ubi Iam Sunt? Richard L. Greene. PAIC

Where is my Chief, my master, this bleak night, mavrone! Ode to the Maguire. Eochaidh O'Hussey. BIrV

Where is Paris and Helene? Thomas of Hales. OxBM

Where is the grave of Sir Arthur O'Kellyn? The Knight's Tomb. Samuel Taylor Coleridge. MBPR

Where is the Jim Crow section. Merry-Go-Round. Langston Hughes. CTBA

Where is the star of Bethlehem? Christmas 1959 Et Cetera. Gerald William Barrax. OFD

Where is the world? not about. Merchant Marine. Josephine Miles. VGW

Where is the world we roved, Ned Bunn? To Ned. Herman Melville. NOBA

Where is this stupendous stranger? The Nativity of Our Lord and Saviour Jesus Christ. Christopher Smart. *Fr.* Hymns and Spiritual Songs. BoReV; LAuP; NOBE; OBP

Where It Appears. Robert Duncan. *Fr.* Passages. PiAm

Where it is. Robert Creeley. PiAm

Where it says snow. Errata. Charles Simic. NVAP

Where It's At. Carol Bergé. MMD

Where Knock Is Open Wide. Theodore Roethke. VGW

Where Lies the Land? Arthur Hugh Clough. BBGO; NOBE

Where lies the land to which yon ship must go? Wordsworth. MBPR

Where light is. To a Woman Who Wants Darkness and Time. Gerald W. Barrax. PoBA

Where, like a pillow on a bed. The Ecstasy [or Extasie]. John Donne. BoLoP; InPS; LoAs; MetP; NOBE; OBP; PPoe; SCP-1

Where London's column, pointing at the skies. A Sad Story. Pope. *Fr.* Moral Essays, Epistle III. BoReV

Where long the shadows of the wind had rolled. The Sheaves. E. A. Robinson. NoAM; NOBA; PiAm

Where marble stood and fell. Reflection in a Green Arena. Gregory Corso. VGW

Where might there be a refuge for me. Tell Me, Tell Me. Marianne Moore. Psy

Where my grandmother lived. Number Four. Doughtry Long. PoBA

Where now the high-rise-village highways. Out of the Past. Robert Wallace. POL

Where once we danced, where once we sang. An Ancient to Ancients. Thomas Hardy. OxBTC

Where others love and praise my verses, still. To The Detractor. Robert Herrick. SCP-1

Where peace goes whispering by. The Farm. Vassar Miller. NCSH

Where rivers tumble. The Shepherd. James K. Baxter. ECBV

Where shall we go? Where shall we go? June Fugue. Thomas Shapcott. CAAP

Where the acorn tumbles down. The Fieldmouse. Cecil Frances Alexander. OxBChV

Where the ball ran into the bushes. 1939. Alan Brownjohn. LP

Where the bee sucks, there suck I. Ariel's Song. Shakespeare. *Fr.* The Tempest. HeIP; LCL; NOBE; SoSe

Where the cedar leaf divides the sky. Passage. Hart Crane. NoAM; NOBA

Where the cities end. Transcontinent. Donald Hall. MiP

Where the city's ceaseless crowd moves on the livelong day. Sparkles from the Wheel. Walt Whitman. AmVN

Where the lizard ran to its little prey. The Range in the Desert. Randall Jarrell. NOBA

Where the Mind Meets the Moon in Revolt. Helen Wolfert. *Fr.* Woman Against the Moon. RiTi

Where the Moosatockmaguntic. The Ballad of Hiram Hover. Bayard Taylor. FaBoCo

Where the owl. Hunters. Sonya Dorman. RiTi

Where the Picnic Was. Thomas Hardy. OxBTC

Where the pools are bright and deep. A Boy's Song. James Hogg. OxBChV

Where the quiet-coloured end of evening smiles. Love among the Ruins. Robert Browning. NOBE

Where the Red Lion flaring o'er the way. A Description of an Author's Bedchamber. Goldsmith. BIrV

Where the remote Bermudas ride. Bermudas. Andrew Marvell. AnMo; BoReV; MetP; NOBE

Where the River Shannon Flows, *with music.* James I. Russell. FSN

Where the Slow Fig's Purple Sloth. Robert Penn Warren. PiAm

Where the waters gently flow. The Song of the Reed Sparrow. *Unknown.* OxBChV

Where the wind. Footprints on the Glacier. W. S. Merwin. NoAM

Where then shall hope and fear their objects find? The Power of Prayer [*or* Prayer] Samuel Johnson. *Fr.* The Vanity of Human Wishes. BoReV; NOBE

Where there is personal liking we go. The Hero. Marianne Moore. *Fr.* Part of a Novel, Part of a Poem, Part of a Play. NOBA

Where there's law, no woman gets justice. For Every Sister in the White Man's Jail. Rita Mae Brown. WBN

Where they came from once. The Cattle Ghosts. David Allan Evans. NVAP

Where to hide a leaf, he said. The Place. Robert Wallace. CoPAm

Where true love burns desire is love's pure flame. Desire. Samuel Taylor Coleridge. MBPR

Where two or three were heaped together, or fifty. The March. Robert Lowell. NowV

Where was the fault? You do not know nor can. The Garden. Stuart Silverman. CoPAm

Where was you last winter, boys. The Horse Trader's Song. *Unknown.* AmFP

Where we made the fire. Where the Picnic Was. Thomas Hardy. OxBTC

Where We Must Look for Help. Robert Bly. ConAP

Where we went in the boat was a long bay. The Mediterranean. Allen Tate. VGW

Where we were walking in the day's light, seeing. Time in the Rock, XXXVII. Conrad Aiken. VGW

Where were the greenhouses going. Big Wind. Theodore Roethke. AnMo; NCSH; PiAm; PPoe; VGW

Where? When? Which? Langston Hughes. BPo

Where, where but here have Pride and Truth. On Hearing That the Students of Our New University Have Joined the Agitation Against Immoral Literature. W. B. Yeats. NoAM

Wherefore peep'st thou, envious day? *Unknown.* GBL

Wherefore, unlaurelled boy. George Darley. NOBE

Wherefore, with this belief, held like a blade. Frederick Goddard Tuckerman. *Fr.* Sonnets. AmVN

Where's Babe Ruth, the King of Swat? The Ballad of Dead Yankees. Donald Petersen. HeIP

Where's the poet? show him! show him. Fragment. Keats. MBPR

Where's the winning without chocolate. The Chocolate Soldiers. Calvin Forbes. MAT

Wheresoe'er I turn my view. Lines [Written] in Ridicule of Certain Poems Published in 1777. Samuel Johnson. FaBoCo; PAIC; PPoD

Wheresoever ye fare by frith or by fell. Julians Barnes. *Fr.* Book of Hunting. WPE

Wherever I am, there's always Pooh. Us Two. A. A. Milne. OxBChV

Wherever I may be. The Absent One. Mary Queen of Scots, *tr. by* Antonia Fraser. SLP

Whether Firelocked. Mary Shumway. HeS

Whether on Ida's shady brow. To the Muses. Blake. HeIP; LAuP; MBPR; NOBE

Whether one paints five Helens. The Ultimate Antientropy. Theodore Weiss. NoAM

Whether or not I find the missing thing. But Not Forgotten. Luci Shaw. AATT

Whether the Turkish new-moon minded be. Astrophel and Stella, XXX. Sir Philip Sidney. Epi

Whether these lines do find you out. An Epistle. Sir John Suckling. PAIC

Whether what we sense of this world. William Bronk. VGW

Whether you strode from court to court. The Man, My Father. Marcia Lee Masters. HeS

Which I wish to remark. The Heathern Pass-ee. A. C. Hilton. FaBoCo

Which is man who wot, and what. This World Fares as a Fantasy. *Unknown.* OxBM

Which Is My Little Boy. Tennessee Williams. SS

Which is the best to hit your taste. Epigram on Two Ladies. Sophia Burrell. POL

Which is the Bow? *Unknown.* GBP

Which-a-way/ which-a-way. Bye Bye Baby Blues. *Unknown.* BluL

While an intrinsic ardor prompts to write. To the University of Cambridge, New-England. Phillis Wheatley. SBG

While Beast instructs his fair and innocent wife. On Sir Voluptuous Beast. Ben Jonson. SCP-1

While breaking the big rock. Stone Giant. Joseph Bruchac. CDW

While Cecil Snores: Mom Drinks Cold Milk. James Cunningham. JB

While duns were knocking at my door. The Ramble: an Anti-Heroic Poem. Alexander Radcliffe. SCP-2

While everyone else is laughing and drinking. Catullus, *tr. fr. Latin by* Peter Whigham. TwMBP

While going the road to sweet Athy. Johnny, I Hardly Knew Ye! *Unknown.* BIrV; GBP; InPK; OBP; PeBB

While he slept, I poured salt in his ears. Judith Recalls Holofernes. Maura Stanton. AmPA

While I stood here, in the open, lost in myself. Milkweed. James Wright. NOBA

While I was building neat. It Is Dangerous to Read Newspapers. Margaret Atwood. HeIP; Psy

While in the mask of night there shone that cut. Landing on the Moon. May Swenson. Moon

While in this cavernous place employed. A Civil Servant. Robert Graves. InPK

While joy gave clouds the light of stars. The Villain. W. H. Davies. OxBTC; SoSe

While many a noble name, to virtue dear. Epistle to Peter Pindar. William Gifford. ESaP

While my hair was still cut straight across my forehead. The River-Merchant's Wife: A Letter. Li Po, *tr. by* Ezra Pound. BoLoP; InPK; InPS; IPWM; LoAs; NoAM; NOBA; NOBE; PAIC; PPoe; PPP

While rain, with eve in partnership. Beyond the Last Lamp. Thomas Hardy. NOBE

While shepherds watched their flocks by night. Nahum Tate. AmFP

While some go dancing reels and some. Three Old Brothers. Frank O'Connor. PFIr

While sorrows encompass me round. Death-Bed Song. *Unknown.* AmFP

While strolling along with the city's vast throng. She May Have Seen Better Days. James Thornton. FSN

While strolling down the street one eve upon mere pleasure bent. Just Tell Them That You Saw Me. Paul Dresser. FSN

While Strolling Through the Park, *with music.* Ed Haley. BLSo (Fountain in the Park, The.) FSN

While that my soul repairs to her devotion. Church Monuments. George Herbert. SCP-1

While that the sun with his beams hot. Philon the Shepherd. *Unknown.* NOBE

While the blue noon above us arches. Annihilation. Conrad Aiken. GBL

While the cock with lively din. Milton. *Fr.* L'Allegro. SCP-1

While the leaves of the bamboo rustle. *Unknown, tr. fr. Japanese by* Geoffrey Bownas *and* Anthony Thwaite. BoLoP

While the Schools and the Teachers Are Teaching. Walt Whitman. AnMo

While the shot and shell were screaming upon the battlefield. Break the News to Mother. Charles Kassel Harris. FSN

While the storm clouds gather far across the sea. God Bless America. Irving Berlin. BLSo

While the TV Is Shut Off. Diane Kruchkow. FAF

While their hearts were jocund and sublime. Milton. *Fr.* Samson Agonistes. SCP-1

While this America settles in the mould of its vulgarity, heavily thickening to empire. Shine, Perishing Republic. Robinson Jeffers. IPWM; MAT; NoAM; NOBA; PiAm; PPoD; VGW; VoPo; WIF

While we were fearing it, it came. Emily Dickinson. PPP; Psy

While we were visiting David's grave. Despair. Denise Levertov. RiTi

While with a strong and yet a gentle hand. Edmund Waller. *Fr.* A Panegyric to My Lord Protector. SCP-2

While you read. The Cat. William Matthews. AmPA

Whiles I this standing lake. Sadness. William Cartwright. SCP-2

Whiles it can happen. Aince, I mind. Aiberdeen. Donald Campell. *Fr.* Sonnets frae Siberia. MIS

Whilom ther was dwellynge in my contree. The Friar's Tale. Chaucer. *Fr.* The Canterbury Tales. PAIC

Whilst Alexis lay pressed [*or* prest]. Song. Dryden. *Fr.* Marriage a-la-Mode. BoLoP; LoAs

Whilst eccho cryes, what shall become of mee. Henry Constable. *Fr.* Diana. AAS

Whilst I beheld the neck o' the dove. Hymn. Patrick Carey. SCP-2

Whilst pale anxiety, corrosive care. On the Prospect of Establishing a Pantisocracy in America. Samuel Taylor Coleridge. MBPR

Whilst thus my pen strives to eternize thee. Michael Drayton. *Fr.* Idea. AAS; PAIC

Whip, The. Robert Creeley. NoAM

Whipping, The. Robert Hayden. MiP; NCSH; PoBA; SFF

Whirl up, sea. Oread. Hilda Doolittle ("H.D."). NoAM; NOBA; PiAm; RiTi; SBG

Whirl'd off at last, for speech I sought. Coventry Patmore. *Fr.* The Angel in the House, II, xi. GBL

Whirr, The/ of the sewing machine. The Red Dress. James Bertolino. HeS

Whisker dripping bear grin. The Ainu Men. Gary Lawless. FAF

Whiskey on your breath, The. My Papa's Waltz. Theodore Roethke. AnMo; CTBA; HeIP; InPK; InPS; NCSH; NoAM; NOBA; NowV; PBMP; PPoe; PPP; PSN; VGW

Whisky Johnny. *Unknown.* AmFP

Whisky whipping g-string Jaguar megaton. Five Psalms of Common Man. Christopher Middleton. TwMBP

Whisper of the wind in, The. Idylls, I. Theocritus, *tr. by* William Carlos Williams. Epi

Whisper of yellow globes. Her Lips Are Copper Wire. Jean Toomer. NoAM

Whispering Hope, *with music.* Septimus Winner. PSoN

Whispers. Roberta Hill. CDW

Whispers. Myra Cohn Livingston. LCL

Whispers of Heavenly Death. Walt Whitman. NoAM

Whispers of Immortality. T. S. Eliot. NoAM; NOBA

Whistle, The/ of the bright. Belfast Lough. *Unknown, tr. by* John Montague. BIrV

Whistle, Daughter, Whistle. *Unknown.* AmFP

Which I wish to remark. The Heathen Chinee. Bret Harte. AmVN; FaBoCo

Whistle o'er the Lave o't. *Unknown.* GBP

Whistler's Father. Margaret Ryan. NPW

Whistling past this cemetery in the dark. In Memoriam: Gertrud Kolmar, 1943. A. D. Hope. CAAP

Whistling Thief, The. *Unknown.* PoTa

Whit was His nakede brest. White Was His Naked Breast. *Unknown.* OxBM

White an' Blue. William Barnes. GBL

White and blue my breathing lady leans. Venice, 182—. John Berryman. CoPAm

White as snow and snow it isn't. *Unknown.* GBP

White Beauty, The, *orig. and mod. English prose. Unknown.* OxBM

White bird featherless/ Flew from Paradise. *Unknown.* GBP

White bird featherless floats down through the air, A. *Unknown.* GBP

White Cat of Trenarren, The. A. L. Rowse. OxBTC; PCat

White chocolate jar full of petals, The Chez Jane. Frank O'Hara. NoAM; NOBA

White Christmas. W. R. Rodgers. PFIr

White City, The. Claude McKay. BPo; NoAM

White cock's tail, The. Ploughing on Sunday. Wallace Stevens. NCSH; RAE

White Collar Ballad. Weldon Kees. AnMo

White Crescents at the Bottoms of Fingernails. Coleman Barks. *Fr.* Body Poems. NVAP

White day, black river. The Predicter of Famine. William Carlos Williams. VGW

White Devil, The, *sels.* John Webster.
  Call for the Robin Redbreast and the Wren, *fr.* V, iv. HeIP (Cornelia's Song.) InPS
  (Dirge, A: "Call for the robin-redbreast and the wren.") NOBE; OBP
  "Do you hear, sir?" SCP-2

White doe appeared to me over green, A. Sonnets to Laura: To Laura in Life, CLVII. Petrarch, *tr. by.* R. G. Barnes. Epi

White Doe of Rylstone, The: or, The Fate of the Nortons. Wordsworth. MPBR

White Fields. James Stephens. ECBV

White fog lifting and falling on mountain-brow. Wales Visitation. Allen Ginsberg. CAPP; NOBA; Prf

White founts falling on the courts of the sun. Lepanto. G. K. Chesterton. BTTM

White Goddess, The. Robert Graves. OBP

White Hare, The. Lilian Bowes-Lyon. OxBTC

White Heliotrope. Arthur Symons. BoLoP; InPS

White Horse, The. W. H. Davies. OxBTC

White Horse, The. D. H. Lawrence. PSN

White horse came to our farm once, A. The White Stallion. Guy Owen. InPK

White horses galloping on the sand. The Black Cliffs, Ballybunion. Brendan Kennelly. PFIr

White-hot midday in the Snake Park, A. In the Snake Park. William Plomer. NoAM; OxBTC

White House, The. Claude McKay. PoBA

White Island, The; or, The Place of the Blest. Robert Herrick. BoReV; SCP-1

White Knight's Song, The. "Lewis Carroll." *Fr.* Through the Looking-Glass, *ch.* 8. FaBoCo; InPS; NOBE; OBP (Aged Aged Man, The.) OxBChV; SpRo (Ways and Means.) ECBV

White Lady has asked me to dance, The. Fourth Dance Poem. Gerald W. Barrax. PoBA

White man is, The. 12 Gates to the City. Nikki Giovanni. IHMS; PoBA

White man is a tiger at my throat, The. Tiger. Claude McKay. BPo

White Man Pressed the Locks, The. James C. Kilgore. InPK

White Man's Burden, The. Kipling. BTTM

White mares of the moon rush along the sky, The. Night Clouds. Amy Lowell. TH

White men's children spread over the earth. The Riddle. Georgia Douglas Johnson. PoBA

White Pass Ski Patrol. John Logan. CAPP

White Paternoster, The. *Unknown.* GBP ("Matthew, Mark, Luke, and John.") MG

White peacock roosting, The. What I Saw. Robert Duncan. NoAM; NOBA

White People. David Henderson. PoBA

White Piano, The. Ralph J. Mills, Jr. HeS

White Princess, The, *sel.* William Brighty Rands. Cat of Cats, The. OxBChV

White Room, The. Peter Cooley. NVAP

White Ropes. Franklin Brainard. HeS

White Rose, A. John Boyle O'Reilly. SoSe

White sagebrush desert, The. Noon. O'Pioneers! John Peale Bishop. VGW

White seed tossed on glass. Snow Chant. T. Alan Broughton. FAF

White sheep, white sheep, on a blue hill. *Unknown.* GBP

White sheer tieback curtains. Karen L. Kent. NPW

White sky, over the hemlocks bowed with snow. The Buck in the Snow. Edna St. Vincent Millay. BoAnP

White Stallion, The. Pete Morgan. SLP

White Stallion, The. Guy Owen. InPK

White sunshine on sweating skulls. May Mobilization. Allen Ginsberg. MIT

White Troops Had Their Orders, But the Negroes Looked Like Men, The. Gwendolyn Brooks. PBMP

White walls of the Institution, The. Now and Then. Ian Hamilton. NoAM

White Was His Naked Breast. *Unknown.* BoReV; OxBM

White woman have you heard. Montgomery. Sam Cornish. PoBA

White Worlds. Jane Marie Luecke. AATT

Whiter/ than the crust. The Wind Sleepers. Hilda Doolittle ("H.D."). WPE

Whither, indeed, midst falling dew. Poem Beginning with a Line Memorized at School. Roderick Hartigh Jellema. AATT

Whither, midst falling dew. To a Waterfowl. Bryant. AmVN; IPWM; NOBA; PiAm; SoSe

Whither, O splendid ship, thy white sails crowding. A Passer-By. Robert Bridges. OxBTC

Whither, say whither shall I fly. The Frozen Zone: or, Julia Disdainful. Robert Herrick. SCP-1

Whither shall I go. *Unknown, at. to* John Webster *and* William Rowley. *Fr.* The Thracian Wonder. GBL

Whitsun Weddings, The. Philip Larkin. NoAM; OxBTC; PSN

Whittier. James Russell Lowell. *Fr.* A Fable for Critics. AmVN; NOBA

Whittingham Fair. *Unknown.* AIW; GBP

Who Am I? Felice Holman. RFM

Who am I worthless that You spent such pains. A Prayer for the Self. John Berryman. *Fr.* Eleven Addresses to the Lord. PiAm; PPP

Who are these from the strange, ineffable places. Arabia. John Meade Falkner. OxBTC

Who are these people at the bridge to meet me? The Bee Meeting. Sylvia Plath. InPS; PPP; WPE

Who are these? Why sit they here in twilight? Mental Cases. Wilfred Owen. NoAM

Who are they talking to in the big temple? The Temple. C. H. Sisson. OxBTC

Who are they to be in their skin. The Subway Witnesses. Lorenzo Thomas. PoBA

Who are we to love. A Footnote to a Gray Bird's Pause. James Cunningham. JB

"Who are we waiting for?" "Soup burnt?" The Feckless Dinner Party. Walter de la Mare. PoTa

Who are you, listening to me, who are you. Poem for Half White College Students. LeRoi Jones. BPo; CAPP

Who are you, little I. E. E. Cummings. LCL

Who borrows all your ready cash. A Friend. Marguerite Power. FaBoCo

Who But the Lord? Langston Hughes. BPo

"Who called?" I said, and the words. Echo. Walter de la Mare. AKE

Who Calls? Frances Clarke. LCL

Who came to our door. Footprints in the Night. Elizabeth J. Coatsworth. CaYB

Who can say. Song. Tennyson. BBGO

Who can say now. The Old Codger's Lament. Carl Rakosi. HeS

Who cared enough for the town to take these pictures. The Taken Town. Constance Carrier. FAF

Who comes from far away, what old gray man. The Horse. A. E. Coppard. BoAnP

Who comes here? The Grenadier. *Unknown.* GBP

Who could believe an ant in theory? Credibility. John Ciardi. InPK; WIF

Who could have thought, but for eight days in space. Space. X. J. Kennedy. Moon

Who Doth Not See the Measure of the Moon? Sir John Davies. Moon

Who Drags the Fiery Artist Down? Clarence Day. FaBoCo

Who drowns an ocean. Proverbs. Morton Marcus. NVAP

Who even dead, yet hath his mind entire! Cantos, XLVII. Ezra Pound. PiAm; VGW

Who ever. *See* Whoever.

Who fed me from her gentle breast. My Mother. Ann Taylor. OxBChV

Who Goes Round My Pinfold Wall. *Unknown.* GBP

Who Goes with Fergus? W. B. Yeats. InPK; NoAM; NOBE

Who Has Seen the Wind. Christina Rossetti. ECBV; LCL (Wind, The.) OxBChV

Who hath desired the sea?—the sight of salt water unbounded. The Sea and the Hills. Kipling. OBP

Who hath herd of suche crueltye before? Sir Thomas Wyatt. AAS

Who have we here? Behold him and be mute. Samuel Rowlands. *Fr.* The Letting of Humour's Blood in the Head-Vein. TVS

Who having confused me with her mother. Beverly Fragments. Morgan Sanders. WBN

Who, in the garden-pony carrying skeps. Horses. Dorothy Wellesley. OxBTC

Who is it that this dark night. Voices at the Window. Sir Philip Sidney. Astrophel and Stella: Eleventh Song. NOBE

Who is my father is this world, in this house. The Irish Cliffs of Moher. Wallace Stevens. NOBA; VGW

Who is not a stranger still. Stephany Fuller. BPo

Who Is Sad? Elizabeth J. Coatsworth. ECBV

Who is she coming, whom all gaze upon. Sonnet: A Rapture Concerning His Lady. Guido Cavalcanti, *tr. by* Dante Gabriel Rossetti. LoAs

Who is the happy warrior? Who is he. Character of the Happy Warrior. Wordsworth. MBPR

Who Is This That Cometh from Edom? William Herebert. BoReV; OxBM

Who is this whose feet. The Swan's Feet. E. J. Scovell. OxBTC

Who killed Cock Robin? Mother Goose. MG; OBP; RDB

Who killed John Keats? John Keats. Byron. MBPR

Who Killed Lawless Lean? Stevie Smith. BBGO

Who Killed Poor Robin? *Unknown.* AmFP

Who knew her. On the Fifth Anniversary of Bluma Sach's Death. Vinnie-Marie D'Ambrosio. IHMS

Who knocks at the door? Pope. *Fr.* The Art of Sinking in Poetry. AnMo

"Who knocks?" "I, who was beautiful." The Ghost. Walter de la Mare. NOBE; OxBTC

Who knows if the moon's. E. E. Cummings. Moon

Who knows whether the sea heals or corrodes? Plague of Dead Sharks. Alan Dugan. NoAM

Who loves to peer up at the morning sun. On "The Story of Rimini." Keats. MBPR

Who lyst his welthe and eas Retayne. V. Innocentia Veritas Viat Fides Circumdederunt Me Inimici Mei. Sir Thomas Wyatt. AAS

Who on your breast pillows his head now. A Lost Jewel. Robert Graves. LoAs

Who or why, or which or what. The Akond of Swat. Edward Lear. FaBoCo

Who Points the Swallow. David Campbell. MAuV

Who prop, thou askest, in these bad days, my mind? To a Friend. Matthew Arnold. PAIC

Who rideth through the driving rain. The King's Son. Thomas Boyd. AIW

Who Said It Was Simple. Audré Lorde. WBN

Who said "Peacock Pie?" The Song of the Mad Prince. Walter de la Mare. NoAM; NOBE; OxBChV

Who (said the Moon). Edith Sitwell Assumes the Role of Luna. Robert Francis. Moon

Who says/ That it's by my desire. People Hide Their Love. Wu-ti, *tr. by* Arthur Waley. OLR

Who says [or sayes] that fictions only and false hair. Jordan. George Herbert. OBP; PAIC; PPP

Who says these Romish pageants been too high. Rome Ryme. Joseph Hall. *Fr.* Virgidemiarum. TVS

Who Shall Deliver Me? Christina Rossetti. BoReV; PFD

Who Shall Die? James A. Randall, Jr. BPo

Who Shall Doubt. George Oppen. CAAP

Who shall have my faire lady? *Unknown.* LoAs

Who shall tell the lady's grief. On the Death of a Cat. Christina Rossetti. PCat

Who shall thy gay buffoonery describe? To the Mocking Bird. Richard Henry Wilde. BoAnP

Who showed me. To Flossie. William Carlos Williams. TH

Who so list to hunt, I know where is an hind. *See* Whoso list to hunt...

"Who stuffed that white owl?" No one spoke in the shop. The Owl-Critic. James Thomas Fields. ECBV; PoTa

Who Threw the Overalls in Mistress Murphey's Chowder? *with music.* George L. Geifer. FSN

Who was he. Psalmen Gezangen. Irene Dayton. AATT

Who was this girl. Looking at Pictures to Be Put Away. Gary Snyder. CoPAm; InPS

Who wd. cope in this Quick. The Web. Gregory O'Donoghue. BIrV

Who were the builders? Question not the silence. The Nameless Doon. William Larminie. BIrV

Who, who will be the next man to entrust his girl to a friend? Ezra Pound. *Fr.* Homage to Sextus Propertius. NoAM

Who will endure. No Change of Place. W. H. Auden. OxBTC

Who will go drive with Fergus now. Who Goes with Fergus? W. B. Yeats. InPK; NoAM; NOBE

Who will in fairest book of Nature know. Astrophel and Stella, LXXI. Sir Philip Sidney. Epi

Who wins his love shall lose her. Lost Love. Andrew Lang. SLP

Who Wot Nowe That Ys Here. *Unknown.* InPS

Who would/ who could. Now Ain't That Love? Carolyn M. Rodgers. BPo

Who would be/ A mermaid fair. Tennyson. *Fr.* The Mermaid. LCL

Who would have thought that face of thine. Thomas Howell. *Fr.* The Lover Deceived Writes to His Lady. POL

Who would suspect, or even know. A Vegetable, I Will Not Be. Donna Whitewing. ANTL; VW

Who wrote *Who wrote Icon Basilike?* On Christopher Wordsworth, Master of Trinity. Benjamin Hall Kennedy. FaBoCo

Who'd believe me if. The Third Dimension. Denise Levertov. NoAM

Who'd ever think that Utah would stir the world so much? Marching to Utah. *Unknown.* AmFP

Whoe'er she be. Wishes to His Supposed Mistress. Richard Crashaw. BoLoP; SCP-1

Whoever comes to shroud me, do not harm. The Funeral. John Donne. BoLoP; HeIP

Whoever despises the clitoris despises the penis. The Speed of Darkness. Muriel Rukeyser. WBN

Whoever hath her wish, thou hast thy Will. Sonnets, CXXXV. Shakespeare. Epi

Whoever loves, if he do not propose. Love's Progress. John Donne. Elegies, XVIII. SCP-1

Who ever will find such fortune. Count Arnaldos. *Unknown, tr. by* W. S. Merwin. Epi

Whole day long, under the walking sun, The. The Sleeping Giant. Donald Hall. NCSH

Whole Duty of Children. Robert Louis Stevenson. OxBChV

Whole heap of nickles and a whole heap of dimes, A. Shout, Little Lulu. *Unknown.* AmFP

Whole Relentless Process, The. E. R. Cole. AATT

Whole World Is Coming, The. *Unknown, tr. fr. American Indian.* IPWM

Who'll take the coal from the mine? Don't Look Now. J. C. Fogerty. PoRo

Whoopee Blues. *Unknown.* BluL

Whoopee-Ti-Yi-Yo! *with music. Unknown, ad. by* James Morehead. BLSH

Whoroscope. Samuel Beckett. NoAM

Who's Most Afraid of Death? E. E. Cummings. VGW

Who's that knocking on the window. Innocent's Song. Charles Causley. MPo

Who's that ringing at our door-bell? That Little Black Cat. D'Arcy Wentworth Thompson. OxBChV

Who's There? Frances Frost. ECBV

Who's Who. W. H. Auden. BBGO; NoAM

Whose broken window is a cry of art. Boy Breaking Glass. Gwendolyn Brooks. NoAM; NowV

Whose Dog? Whose Cat? *Unknown.* ECBV

Whose gold you carry, camel. Timbuctu. Edward Brathwaite. MPo

Whose is that face? Three Riddles. Brian Swann. TSWA

Whose is this horrifying face. Ecce Homo. David Gascoyne. BoReV

Whose love is given over-well. Partial Comfort. Dorothy Parker. FaBoCo

Whose woods these are I think I know. Stopping by Woods on a Snowy Evening. Robert Frost. ECBV; FSFS; HeIP; InPK; InPS; IPWM; NoAM; NOBA; PiAm; PPoD; PSN; SoSe

Whoso in harvest mindeth to reap. To His Child. William Bullokar. OxBChV

Whoso list to hunt, I know where is an hind. Sir Thomas Wyatt, *after the Italian of* Petrarch. AAS; BoLoP; Epi; GBL; InPK

Whsst, and away, and over the green. Nothing. Walter de la Mare. ECBV

"Whu's aw thae fflag-poles ffur in Princess Street?" Heard in the Cougate. Robert Garioch. OxBTC

Why. Sonia Sanchez. WBN

Why are our ancestors. Ancestors. Dudley Randall. BPo

Why are the faces here so lined? Public Bar. D. J. Enright. LP

Why are the public buildings so high? W. H. Auden. FaBoCo

Why are the stamps adorned with kings. Power to the People. Howard Nemerov. POL

Why are women so energetic? Energetic Women. D. H. Lawrence. InPS

Why art thou silent and invisible. To Nobodaddy. Blake. MBPR

Why art thou silent! Is thy love a plant. Wordsworth. LoAs

Why call an anti-missile. For, Behold the Day Cometh. Rochelle Owens. Psy

Why canst thou not, as others do. The Appeal. Samuel Daniel. OLR

Why Can't I Leave You? Ai. AmPA

"Why, Colin, since thou found'st such grace." Spenser. *Fr.* Colin Clout's Come Home Again. TVS

Why come ye hither, Redcoats, your mind what madness fills? Riflemen's Song at Bennington. *Unknown.* BTTM

Why did I laugh to-night? No voice will tell. Keats. MBPR; OBP

Why did man leave the trees? How Man Learned to Walk—and Run. Louis Dudek. AKE

Why Did the Children Put Beans in Their Ears? Carl Sandburg. PBMP

Why did the Lord give us agility. Common Sense. Ogden Nash. SFF

Why did the woman want to kill one dog? A Village Tale. May Sarton. BoAnP

Why did you give no hint that night. The Going. Thomas Hardy. NOBE

Why Did You Go. E. E. Cummings. VGW

"Why do/ You thus devise." Susanna and the Elders. Adelaide Crapsey. PAIC; WPE

Why do I imagine the death of Mandelstam. Preparing for Exile. Derek Walcott. OBP

Why do some men want to create women? Pygmalion. Kathryn Ruby. WBN

Why Do the Graces. Walter Savage Landor. SoSe

Why do we labor at the poem. Reasons for Music. Archibald MacLeish. PiAm

Why do you hold the flag so high. Changing of the Guard. Charles G. Ballard. VW

Why do you rush through the field in trains. The Fat White Woman Speaks. G. K. Chesterton. SpRo

Why do you talk so much. For Robert Frost. Galway Kinnell. NOBA; VGW

"Why do you wear your hair like a man?" After Dilettante Concetti. Henry Duff Traill. FaBoCo

Why does the thin grey strand. Sorrow. D. H. Lawrence. PSN

Why does this pretty boy from Kong-po. Peter Whigham. *Fr.* Love Poems of the VIth Dalai Lama. TwMBP

"Why does [*or* dois] your brand sae drop wi' blude [*or* drap wi bluid]." Edward, Edward. *Unknown.* AIW;InPK; InPS; IPWM; NOBE; PeBB; PPoe; SoSe

Why don't we rock the casket here in the moonlight. The Pale Blue Casket. Oliver Pitcher. PoBA

Why don't you/ catch me a pony. The Pony Blues. *Unknown.* BluL

Why don't you go down Old Hannah. Ol' Hannah. *Unknown.* BluL

Why Dost Thou Shade Thy Lovely Face? Francis Quarles. Emblems, III, 7. BoReV

Why dost thou shade thy lovely face? O why. To His Mistress. Earl of Rochester. LoAs

Why doth the ear so tempt the voice. To Castara: of True Delight. William Habington. SCP-2

Why Fires Are Lit December 21st. Michael McMahon. FAF

Why first, you don't believe, you don't and can't. Unfaith and Faith. Robert Browning. Fr. Bishop Blougram's Apology. BoReV

Why from this her and him. E. E. Cummings. NoAM

Why hast thou nothing in thy face? Eros. Robert Bridges. NOBE

Why have such scores of lovely, gifted girls. A Slice of Wedding Cake. Robert Graves. BoLoP; BuTh; NOBE; OxBTC

Why have you risen, to stand with naked feet. With the Dawn. Thomas Caulfield Irwin. BIrV

Why He Was There. E. A. Robinson. NOBA

Why her bedroom is a/ trip. Lyn Lifshin. Fr. Walking thru Audley End Mansion Late Afternoon. RiTi

Why I Am Not a Painter. Frank O'Hara. ConAP; CoPAm; NoAM; NOBA

Why I Didn't Go to Delphi. James Welch. CDW

Why I Died. Erica Jong. RiTi

Why I Sing the Blues. B. B. King. MAT

Why I would bring a wagon into battle. Willie B (2). Lucille Clifton. InPS

Why is a Pump like V-sc--nt C-stl-r-gh? A Riddle. Thomas Moore. FaBoCo

Why is it said thou canst not live. Love. Shelley. MBPR

Why is the child so pale. Louise. Stevie Smith. SBG

Why must i string my hate. Why. Sonia Sanchez. WBN

Why Must You Know? John Wheelwright. VGW

Why not mark out the land. Hard Questions. Margaret Tsuda. RFM

Why not? The mouths of the ginger blooms slide open. Chinoiserie. Charles Wright. AmPA

Why say the idiot is not. The Locus. Cid Corman. VGW

Why seraphim like lutanists arranged. Evening without Angels. Wallace Stevens. VGW

Why Should a Foolish Marriage Vow. Dryden. Fr. Marriage à la Mode, I, i. HeIP
(Song: "Why should a foolish marriage vow.") BuTh; LoAs

Why should I be eaten by love. Untitled. James A. Randall, Jr. BPo

Why should I blame her that she filled my days. No Second Troy. W. B. Yeats. NoAM; NOBE; OxBTC; PPP

Why should I care for the men of Thames. Blake. MBPR

Why should I let the toad work. Toads. Philip Larkin. NoAM; OxBTC

Why should I seek for love or study it? Ribh Considers Christian Love Insufficient. W. B. Yeats. BoReV

Why should vain mortals tremble. Bunker Hill. Nathaniel Niles. BLSo

Why should we fear to melt away in death. To Castara. William Habington. SCP-2

Why should you believe in magic. Consumed. James Tate. MAT

Why should you swear I am forsworn. The Scrutiny [or Scrutinie]. Richard Lovelace. BoLoP; GBL; LoAs

Why should your face so please me. Song. Edwin Muir. SLP

Why sleeps the future, as a snake enrolled. Ecclesiastical Sonnets: Conclusion. Wordsworth. MBPR

Why so drawn, so worn. Vampire's Aubade. W. D. Snodgrass. PAIC

Why so Pale and Wan? Sir John Suckling. Fr. Aglaura, IV, ii. BuTh; NOBE

(Encouragement to a Lover.) PBMP
(Song: "Why so pale and wan, fond lover?") BoLoP; HeIP; InPS

Why, Some of My Best Friends Are Women. Phyllis McGinley. NMM

Why speak of memory and death. Two Views of Two Ghost Towns. Charles Tomlinson. NoAM

Why speak of the use. Hayden Carruth. VGW

Why that alarming sigh? Dialogue. Agathias Scholasticus, tr. by Dudley Fitts. OLR

Why the Soup Tastes like the Daily News. Marge Piercy. MAT

Why then did he make, at such cost, crazy sounds? John Berryman. Fr. Dream Songs. RRA

Why this girl has no fear. Carmen. Victor Hernandez Cruz. PoBA

Why were you born when the snow was falling. A Dirge. Christina Rossetti. SBG; VPC

Why, who makes much of a miracle? Miracles. Walt Whitman. PBMP

Why, why, what is this why. What Is This Why? Unknown. OxBM

Why will they never speak. The Grandfathers. Donald Justice. NCSH; PPoD

"Why William, on that old grey stone." Expostulation and Reply. Wordsworth. MBPR

Why without cease do I think of a bold youth. The Haunting. Irving Layton. NeAC

Why Would I Want. William J. Harris. PoBA

Whyles in the presence. Verses on a Rose Street Muse. Charles Senior. MIS

Wichita Vortex Sutra. Allen Ginsberg. CAPP

Wicked Tongues. Unknown. OxBM

Wicker Basket, A. Robert Creeley. CAPP; NoAM

Widest prairies have electric fences, The. Wires. Philip Larkin. MiP; SFF

Widow, The. W. S. Merwin. VGW

Widow, The/ met a big blk. Making Out. Leatrice W. Emeruwa. RiTi

Widow bird sate mourning for her love, A. Song. Shelley. NOBE

Widow of Drynam, The. Patrick MacDonogh. PFIr

Widow of Glencoe, The, sel. William Aytoun.
"Do not lift him from the bracken." SLP

Widow, Sapphics, The. Robert Southey. ESaP

Widow's Lament in Springtime, The. William Carlos Williams. IPWM; NoAM; NOBA; PSN

Widow's Old Broom, The. Unknown. AmFP

Widow's Party, The. Kipling. PeBB

Widow's Plot, The: or, She Got What Was Coming to Her. William Plomer. NoAM

Widow's Yard, The. Isabella Gardner. RiTi

Wife. Jenne Andrews. HeS

Wife, The. Robert Creeley. VGW

Wife a-Lost, The. William Barnes. BoLoP; VPC

Wife and servant are the same. To the Ladies. Mary Lee, Lady Chudleigh. WPE

Wife of Bath, The. Chaucer. Fr. The Canterbury Tales: Prologue. OxBM
("Good Wif was ther of biside Bathe, A.") InPS; PPoe

Wife of Bath's Prologue, The, sels. Chaucer. Fr. The Canterbury Tales.
"If there were no authority on earth," tr. fr. Middle English by Nevill Coghill. OBP

Wife's Fifth Husband. OxBM

Wife of Llew, The. Francis Ledwidge. PFIr

Wife of the Moon Man Who Never Came Back. Grace Butcher. RiTi

Wife of Usher's Well, The. *Unknown.* AIW, 2 *versions*; AmFP; Epi; NOBE; PeBB; SoSe

Wife was sitting at her reel ae night, A. The Strange Visitor. *Unknown.* GBP

Wife Who Would a Wanton Be, The. *Unknown.* FaBoCo

Wife-Woman, The. Anne Spencer. NoAM

Wife Wrapt in Wether's Skin, The. *Unknown.* AIW; AmFP

Wife's Complaint, The. *Unknown, tr. fr. Anglo-Saxon by* Michael Alexander. BoLoP

Wife's Fifth Husband, The. Chaucer. *Fr.* The Canterbury Tales: The Wife of Bath's Prologue. OxBM

Wife's Lament, The. *Unknown, tr. from Anglo-Saxon.* IPWM; WPE

Wiggling head-first from the egg. The Tiny Baby Lizard. Besmilr Brigham. RiTi

Wight in the Broom. *Unknown.* OxBM

Wild, The. Wendell Berry. VGW

Wild Colonial [*or* Colloina] Boy, The (*diff. versions*). *Unknown.* AIW; AmFP; PcBB

Wild Barbaree, The. *Unknown.* AmFP

Wild beauty of an eagle, once born to virgin sky, The. The Folding Fan. Grey Cohoe. VW

Wild Bill Jones. *Unknown.* AmFP

Wild Dog Rose, The. John Montague. BIrV

Wild Dreams of Summer What Is Your Grief. George Barker. OxBTC

Wild Geese   William Hart-Smith. BoAnP

Wild Geese, The. John Masefield. NoAM

Wild Honey Suckle, The. Philip Freneau. AmVN; NOBA; PiAm

Wild Lumberjack, The. *Unknown.* AIW

Wild Mustard River, The. *Unknown.* AmFP

Wild Negro Bill. *Unknown.* BPo

Wild nights!—Wild nights!   Emily Dickinson. AmVN; LoAs; NOBA; OLR; PiAm; SBG; WPE

Wild Oats. Philip Larkin. InPS

Wild Oats. Norman MacCaig. OxBTC

Wild Orphan. Allen Ginsberg. TCP

Wild Peaches. Elinor Wylie. RiTi; SBG; WPE

"Down to the Puritan marrow of my bones." IV. VoPo (Puritan Sonnet.) PAIC

Wild Strawberries. Robert Graves. FSFS

Wild Swans at Coole, The. W. B. Yeats. AnMo; BoAnP; FSFS; HeIP; IPWM; NoAM; PPP; PSN; TCP; VoPo

Wild winds weep, The. Mad Song. Blake. MBPR

Wild Woman's Resentment of Fakery. Rochelle Owens. RiTi

Wilderness. Ralph Mecklenburger. SFF

Wilderness, The. Kathleen Raine. WPE

Wilderness. Carl Sandburg. PiAm

Wildflowers, Smoke. Lyn Lifshin. MMD

Wildwood Flower, *with music. Unknown.* BLSo

Wilkes Booth came to Washington, an actor great was he. Booth Killed Lincoln. *Unknown.* AmFP; OFD

Will God forever cast off. Jesse Mercer. AmFP

Will he always love me? Lady Horikawa, *tr. fr. Japanese by* Kenneth Rexroth. OLR

Will the Weaver. *Unknown.* AmFP

Will There Be Any Stars in My Crown? *with music.* E. E. Hewitt. BLSH

Will there never come a season. To R. K. James Kenneth Stephen. FaBoCo

Will to Change, The. Adrienne Rich. NMM

Will ye heare, what I can say. Upon His Julia. Robert Herrick. SpRo

Will you come a boating, my gay old hag. The Gay Old Hag. *Unknown.* BIrV

Will you come with me, my Phyllis dear.   Wait for the Wagon. *Unknown, at. to* R. Bishop Buckley. BLSo; PSoN

Will you hear of a bloody Battle.   Teach the Rover. *Unknown.* PeBB

Will You Love Me in December as You Do in May? *with music.* James J. Walker. FSN

Will you perhaps consent to be. Delmore Schwartz. LoAs

"Will you walk a little faster?" said a whiting to a snail. The Lobster Quadrille. "Lewis Carroll." *Fr.* Alice's Adventures in Wonderland, *ch.* 10. OxBChV

"Will you walk into my parlor?" said the Spider to the Fly. The Spider and the Fly. Mary Howitt. ECBV; OxBChV

"Will you wear white, my dear, oh my dear." Jinnie Jinkins. *Unknown.* AmFP

Will You, Won't You. Mark Van Doren. NCSH

Willets, The. May Swenson. WPE

William and Mary. *Unknown.* AmFP

William Butler Yeats. A. D. Hope. MAuV

William Hall. *Unknown.* AmFP

William, my teacher, my friend! dear William and dear Dorothea! Hexameters. Samuel Taylor Coleridge. MBPR

William, the wild round plums are falling. The Dressing Stations. Norman Dubie. AmPA

William Was a Royal Lover. *Unknown.* AmFP

William Wordsworth. Sidney Keyes. OxBTC

Williams Avenue Zionist Church, The. Russia. William Carlos Williams. VGW

Williamsburg, *sel.* Linda Pastan.
  Governor's Palace, The. RiTi

Willie. *Unknown.* AmFP

Willie and Lady Margerie. *Unknown.* PeBB

Willie B (2). Lucille Clifton. InPS

Willie Fitzgibbons who used to sell ribbons. Waltz Me Around Again Willie; or, 'Round, 'Round, 'Round. Will D. Cobb. FSN

Willie had a purple monkey climbing on a yellow stick. In Memoriam. Max Adeler. FaBoCo

Willie Leonard; or, The Lake of Cold Finn. *Unknown.* AmFP

Willie Mays. Paul Ramsey. PPoD

Willie Metcalf. Edgar Lee Masters. *Fr.* Spoon River Anthology. IPWM

Willie O [*or* of] Winsbury. *Unknown.* AmFP; PeBB

Willie Taylor, *with music Unknown.* RDB

Willie was a widow's son. Willie and Lady Margerie. *Unknown.* PeBB

Willie Winkie. William Miller. OxBChV
  ("Wee Willie Winkie runs through the town.") MG

Willing Mistriss, The. Aphra Behn. *Fr.* The Dutch Lover. SBG

Willow-Man, The. Juliana Horatia Ewing. OxBChV

Willow Poem. William Carlos Williams. NCSH

Willow shining, The. The Knowledge of Light. Henry Rago. VGW

Willows carried a slow sound, The. Repose of Rivers. Hart Crane. NoAM; NOBA

Will's Love, The. Besmilr Brigham. IHMS

Willy, enormous Saskatchewan grizzly. Willy. Richard Moore. MAT

Willy the Weeper. *Unknown.* GBP; PeBB

Willy's rare, and Willy's fair. Rare Willie Drowned in Yarrow. *Unknown.* AIW; GBP; PeBB

Wilt thou be gone? it is not yet near day. Shakespeare. *Fr.* Romeo and Juliet, III, v. PAIC

Wilt thou forgive that sin where I begun. A Hymn to God the Father. John Donne. BoReV; InPK; MetP; NOBE; PAIC; PPoe; WIF

Wilt thou not visit me? The Prayer. Jones Very. AmVN

Wiltshire Downs. Andrew Young. OxBTC

Wind. Ted Hughes. LP; MPo; SoSe

Wind, The. James Reeves. ECBV

Wind, The. Christina Rossetti. *See* Who Has Seen the Wind.

Wind, The. Charles Simic. NVAP

Wind, The. James Stephens. CaYB; InPK; NoAM; PFIr

Wind and Silver. Amy Lowell. IPWM; Moon; RiTi; SoSe

Wind and the Moon, The, *sels.* George MacDonald. "Said the Wind to the Wind to the Moon, 'I will blow you out.'" CaYB; LCL

Wind at the Door, The. William Barnes. GBL

Wind begun to rock the grass, The. Emily Dickinson. ECBV

Wind billowing out the seat of my britches, The. Child on Top of a Greenhouse. Theodore Roethke. BuTh; NCSH; PiAm; VGW

Wind, bird, and tree. The Words. David Wagoner. TSWA

Wind blew all my wedding-day, The. Wedding-Wind. Philip Larkin. BuTh; LoAs; MAT

Wind comes from opposite poles, The. The Marriage. Mark Strand. NoAM

"Wind doth blow today, my love, The." The Unquiet Grave. *Unknown.* GBP; HeIP; InPK; PeBB; SLP

Wind flapped loose, the wind was still, The. The Woodspurge. Dante Gabriel Rossetti. HeIP; InPK; NOBE; PBMP; VPC

Wind has blown the rain away and blown, A. Sonnet. E. E. Cummings. PAIC

Wind has no voice, really, The. Day Time Sequence/ November. Dalene Stowe. NPW

Wind, heavy from the land, irons the surf, The. Offshore Breeze. Milton Acorn. NeAC

Wind in a Frolic, The. William Gowitt. OxBChV

Wind in the Willows, The, *sel.* Kenneth Grahame. Ducks' Ditty. OxBChV

Wind is blowing in the scent of formaldehyde, The. The Black Spring Becomes Anonymous. Sotère Torregian. MIT

Wind is blowing, A. The book being written. The Novel. Denise Levertov. NoAM

Wind is not nigh. Zone of Death. William Everson. VGW

Wind is ruffling the tawny pelt, A. A Far Cry from Africa. Derek Walcott. NoAM

Wind is shaking this house, The. The Storm House. Elizabeth Jennings. WPE

Wind is walking the tallest trees, The. Sudden Gale in Spring. Martha Banning Thomas. ECBV

Wind it blew from east to west, The. Get Up and Bar the Door. *Unknown.* AmFP

Wind moves above the wheat, The. Ezra Pound. *Fr.* A Song of the Degrees. AKE

Wind on the Corn. Charles Tennyson Turner. VPC

Wind one morning sprung up from sleep, The. The Wind in a Frolic. William Howitt. OxBChV

Wind rocks the car. Like This Together. Adrienne Rich. PiAm; VGW

Wind Secrets. Diane Wakoski. AmPA

Wind Sleepers, The. Hilda Doolittle ("H.D."). WPE

Wind Sou'west, The. *Unknown.* AmFP

Wind stood up, and gave a shout, The. The Wind. James Stephens. CaYB; InPK; NoAM; PFIr

Wind through the box-elder trees, The. Poem Against the British. Robert Bly. ConAP; InPS

Wind through the olive trees. Long, Long Ago. *Unknown.* RAE

Wind whines and whines the shingle. On the Beach at Fontana. James Joyce. SoSe

Windham Thaw, The. Arthur Guiterman. ECBV

Windhover, The. Gerard Manley Hopkins. AnMo; BoReV; Epi; InPK; InPS; NoAM; NOBE; PAIC; PPoD; PPoe; PPP; VoPo

Window, The. Robert Creeley. CAPP; CoPAm; NoAM; NOBA; VGW

Window in the Breast. *Unknown, tr. fr. Greek by* Walter Headlam. ECBV

Window insulates me from the street, The. Maternity Gown. David Holbrook. OxBTC

Window was made of ice with bears lumbering across it. Bad Dream. Louis MacNeice. NoAM

Windows, The. George Herbert. AnMo; SCP-1

Winds had hushed at last as by command, The. The Sower. Mathilde Blind. SBG; WPE

Winds of doctrine blow both ways at once, The. Conrad Aiken. *Fr.* A Letter from Li Po. VGW

Winds of the World, give answer! The English Flag. Kipling. BTTM

Winds snatch at the troll-tooth rocks. Lighthouse. Merle Meeter. AATT

Wind's spine is broken, The. Storm Tide on Mejit. *Unknown, tr. by* Augustin Kramer *and* Willard Trask. RFM

Wind's word, the Hebrew Hallelujah. Hallelujah: A Sestina. Robert Francis. PPoD

Windy Boy in a Windswept Tree. Geoffrey Summerfield. LP

Windy Nights. David Campbell. MAuV

Windy Nights. Robert Louis Stevenson. ECBV; OxBChV

Wine and Water. G. K. Chesterton. FaBoCo

Wine and woman and song. Villanelle of the Poet's Road. Ernest Dowson. PAIC

Wine comes in at the mouth. A Drinking Song. W. B. Yeats. BoLoP; POL; LoAs

Wine Cup, The. Meleager, *tr. fr.* Greek by Dudley Fitts. OLR

Wine Menagerie, The. Hart Crane. NoAM; NOBA; VGW

Winged bull trundles to the wired perimeter, The. C. Day Lewis. *Fr.* Flight to Italy. OxBTC

Wings, The. Denise Levertov. CAPP

Wings of Time are black and white, The. Compensation. Emerson. NOBA

Wings outstretched, a horned owl. Signatures. Daniel Hoffman. VGW

Wingwalking in Oregon. Robert Peterson. MIT; NeAC

Winifred Waters. William Brighty Rands. OxBChV

Winked too much and were afraid of snakes. The Monkeys. Marianne Moore. NoAM; NOBA

Winning way, a pleasant smile, A. Little Annie Rooney. Michael Nolan. FSN

Wino. Ted Hughes. NoAM

Wino Will. Eve Merriam. *Fr.* The Inner-City Mother Goose. IPWM

Winter. John Lyle Donaghy. BIrV

Winter. D. W. Donzella. FAF

Winter. Larry Levis. NVAP

Winter. Coventry Patmore. NOBE

Winter. Pope. *Fr.* Pastorals. PAIC

Winter. Shakespeare. *Fr.* Love's Labour's Lost, V, ii. AKE; FSFS; IPWM; SoSe

Winter. J. M. Synge. OxBTC; POL

Winter. Tennyson. FSFS

Winter. Katharine Tynan. FSFS

Winter. William Carlos Williams. NCSH

Winter, a Dirge. Burns. LAuP

Winter Bouquet. W. D. Snodgrass. NowV

Winter clenched its fist, The. The Redwing. Patric Dickinson. BoAnP

Winter Coming On. Martin Bell. OxBTC

Winter: East Anglia.  Edmund Blunden.  OxBTC

Winter Evening.  Harry Behn.  CaYB

Winter evening settles down, The.  Preludes.  T. S. Eliot.  HeIP; InPS; PPoD; PPP; PSN; VGW

Winter Excercise.  Howard Nemerov.  NowV

Winter fells.  Deathward.  John Lyle Donaghy.  BIrV

Winter Flowers.  Wade Hall.  AATT

Winter: For an Untenable Situation.  Alan Dugan.  NowV

Winter Holding Off the Coast of North America.  N. Scott Momaday.  CDW

Winter in Elwell.  James Tipton.  HeS

Winter Insomnia.  Raymond Carver.  NVAP

Winter is a far more fit.  Hens in Winter.  Robert P. Tristram Coffin.  TH

Winter Is Another Country.  Archibald MacLeish.  NCSH

Winter is cold-hearted.  Summer.  Christina Rossetti.  FSFS; PBMP

Winter is gone, and spring is over.  Alfred Austin.  FaBoCo

Winter is icummen in.  Ancient Music.  Ezra Pound.  FaBoCo; HeIP; PBMP; SpRo

Winter is long in this climate.  March.  William Carlos Williams.  NCSH

Winter Landscape.  John Berryman.  CoPAm; WIF

Winter Love.  Elizabeth Jennings.  BoLoP

Winter Mask.  Allen Tate.  Prf

Winter Memories.  Henry David Thoreau.  AmVN; VoPo (Within the Circuit of This Plodding Life.)  NOBA; PiAm

Winter Moon.  Langston Hughes.  PAIC

Winter Morning.  William Jay Smith.  HeS; NCSH

Winter Morning Walk, The.  William Cowper.  Fr. The Task.  LAuP

Winter Mornings.  Nancy Mairs.  NPW

Winter Night, A.  William Barnes.  NOBE

Winter Night, A.  James Thomson.  Fr. The Seasons: Winter.  NOBE

Winter Nightfall.  J. C. Squire.  OxBTC

Winter Nights.  Thomas Campion.  NOBE

Winter Ocean.  John Updike.  InPK; SoSe

Winter of my infancy being over-past, The.  Another Song.  Ann Collins.  SCP-2

Winter owl banked just in time to pass, The.  Questioning Faces.  Robert Frost.  NCSH

Winter-piece to a Friend Away, A.  John Berryman.  NOBA

Winter Pond.  Mary Logue.  NPW

Winter Remembered.  John Crowe Ransom.  NOBA; VGW

Winter Scene, A.  Reed Whittemore.  NCSH

Winter Scene.  Marguerite Young.  WPE

Winter Seascape.  John Betjeman.  SS

Winter Ship, A.  Sylvia Plath.  PSN

Winter-sky began to frown, The.  Stella at Wood-Park.  Swift.  BIrV

Winter sled, A.  Signs of the Seasons.  Unknown.  ECBV

Winter Sonnet.  Anne Waldman.  CAAP

Winter Soon Is Coming.  Elizabeth J. Coatsworth.  ECBV

Winter Storms, The.  Sir William Davenant.  SCP-2

Winter Sweetness.  Langston Hughes.  ECBV

Winter to spring; the west wind melts the frozen rancour.  Solvitur Acris Hiems.  Horace, tr. by Louis MacNeice.  Odes, I, 4.  Epi

Winter Trees.  Sylvia Plath.  NMM; SBG

Winter Twilight, A.  Angelina Weld Grimké.  PoBA

Winter Twilight, Glowing Black and Gold, The.  Delmore Schwartz.  NoAM

Winter wakeneth al my care.  Winter Wakens All My Care.  Unknown.  OxBM

Winter Warfare.  Edgell Rickword.  OxBTC

Winter will bar the swimmer soon.  Swimming Chenango Lake.  Charles Tomlinson.  NoAM

Winter Winds Cold and Blea.  John Clare.  GBL

Winter with the Gulf Stream  Gerard Manley Hopkins.  NoAM

Winterfall.  Unknown.  OxBM

Wintering.  Sylvia Plath.  NMM

Winters close, Springs open, no child stirs, The.  John Berryman.  Fr. Homage to Mistress Bradstreet.  NoAM

Winter's Tale, The, sels.  Shakespeare.
   Autolycus' Song ("Jog on, jog on the footpath way"), IV, ii.  SpRo
   "Here's flowers for you," fr. IV, iii.  GBL
   "When daffodils begin to peer," fr. IV, ii.  AIW; OBP (Autolycus Sings.)  NOBE

Winter Time.  Robert Louis Stevenson.  OxBChV

Winter time is coming.  Cold Wave Blues.  Unknown.  BluL

Wintertime nighs.  In Tenebris.  Thomas Hardy.  NOBE

Wintry west extends his blast, The.  Winter, a Dirge.  Burns.  LAuP

Winwick, Lancashire.  Unknown.  GBP

Wires.  Philip Larkin.  MiP; SFF

Wisconsin Farm Auction.  David Steingass.  NVAP

Wisdom.  Hy Sobiloff.  VGW

Wisdom and Spirit of the universe!  Wordsworth.  Fr. The Prelude, I.  NOBE

Wisdom has nothing to do with age.  Wisdom.  Hy Sobiloff.  VGW

Wise emblem of our politic world.  The Snail.  Richard Lovelace.  SCP-2

Wise Empty Landscape with a Death in the Foreground.  N. Scott Momaday.  CDW

Wise fish digs his silver in, The.  Night Catch.  Heather McHugh.  AmPA

Wise guys, The.  Kid Stuff.  Frank Horne.  PoBA

Wise Men and Shepherds.  Sidney Godolphin.  See Hymn: "Lord, when the wise men came from far."

Wish, The.  Abraham Cowley.  Fr. The Mistress.  NOBE

Wish.  Lance Henson.  CDW

Wish, A.  Fanny Kemble.  WPE

Wish, A.  Laurence Lerner.  OxBTC

Wish, A.  Samuel Rogers.  NOBE

Wish for a Young Wife.  Theodore Roethke.  AnMo; LoAs; NoAM

Wish for Water, A.  Laura Chester.  RiTi

Wish I was in Tennessee.  Tennessee.  Unknown.  AmFP

Wish, that of the living whole, The.  In Memoriam A.H.H., LV.  Tennyson.  BoReV

Wishbone, The.  Fred Bornhauser.  PPoD

Wishbone, The.  Rae Desmond Jones.  CAAP

Wished to have been milk.  Story.  Dennis Saleh.  NeAC

Wishes of an Elderly Man, The.  Sir Walter Alexander Raleigh.  FaBoCo

Wishes to His (Supposed) Mistress.  Richard Crashaw.  BoLoP; SCP-1

Wishing.  William Allingham.  OxBChV

Wispy cuttings lie in rows, The.  July in Indiana.  Robert Fitzgerald.  ANTL

Wistful,/ they speak of.  The People.  Robert Creeley.  VGW

Wistful Butch Poem.  Rochelle Owens.  WBN

Wit Wonders.  Unknown.  See God and Yet a Man, A?

Witch, The.  Mary Elizabeth Coleridge.  WPE

Witch?  Sam Reavin.  CaYB

Witch.  Jean Tepperman.  NMM

Witch Doctor.  Robert Hayden.  MAT; NoAM

Witch in the Wintry Wood, The, *sel.* Aileen Fisher. "This is the tale of how Tim one." CaYB

Witch of Atlas, The. Shelley. MBPR

Witch of Coös, The. Robert Frost. *Fr.* Two Witches. NoAM; NOBA; PAIC

Witch that came, The (the withered hag). Provide, Provide. Robert Frost. InPK; IPWM; NoAM; NOBA; PPP; SS

Witchcraft. Siddie Joe Johnson. ECBV

Witches' Charm, The. Ben Jonson. *Fr.* The Masque of Queens. NOBE
(Witches' 3rd Charm.) SCP-1

Witch's Broomstick Spell. *Unknown.* GBP

Witch's Milking Charm. *Unknown.* GBP

With. Carol Bergé. MMD

With a garland of thornes kene. The Seven Sins. *Unknown.* OxBM

With a Gift of Rings. Robert Graves. GBL

With a great working of elbows. Wedding. George Mackay Brown. SLP

With a Guitar, to Jane. Shelley. MBPR

With a lantern that wouldn't burn. The Draft Horse. Robert Frost. HeIP; PiAm

With a love a madness for Shelley. I am 25. Gregory Corso. CoPAm

With a whirl of thought oppres'd. The Day of Judgement. Swift. BIrV; ESaP; NOBE; PPP

With All Deliberate Speed. Don L. Lee. JB

With all its sinful doings, I must say. Italy and [or Versus] England. Byron. *Fr.* Beppo. NOBE; PAIC

With all my will, but much against my heart. A Farewell. Coventry Patmore. *Fr.* The Unknown Eros. BoLoP; NOBE

With all the heart in my body. Now Jentil Belly Down. *Unknown.* GBP

With an Antique Crystal Cup and Ring. John Sobieski Stuart. SLP

With Annie gone. For Anne. Leonard Cohen. TCP

With banners furled, and clarions mute. The Night-March. Herman Melville. PiAm

With blackest moss the flower-plots. Mariana. Tennyson. InPS; NOBE

With bodies bowed, with breath drawn in. The Cry of the High Hurdlers. Horace Spencer Fiske. SPo

With Child. Genevieve Taggard. LoAs

With death doomed to grapple. Epitaph for William Pitt. Byron. MBPR

With deathlace tickling my throat. Death-Lace. David Ray. MAT

With deep affection. The Shandon Bells. Francis Sylvester Mahony. PFIr

With Donne, whose muse on dromedary trots. On Donne's Poetry. Samuel Taylor Coleridge. MBPR; PAIC; PPoD

With every rising of the sun. Today! Ella Wheeler Wilcox. SoSe

With every soft gush of my feet. After Picking Rosehips. Harley Elliott. NeAC

With faith I trust in Christ the Lord. Mrs. Saunder's Experience. *Unknown.* AmFP

With favoring winds, o'er sunlit seas. Ultima Thule. Longfellow. AmVN

With Fifteen-ninety or Sixteen-sixteen. On an Anniversary. J. M. Synge. POL

With flintlocked guns and polished stocks. In Hardin County, 1809. Lul E. Thompson. PoTa

With focus sharp as Flemish-painted face. The Dome of Sunday. Karl Shapiro. NoAM

With Garments Flowing. John Clare. GBL

With gentleness/ his eyes filmed. Monument. Milton Acorn. NeAC

With great difficulty I managed to get out of my skin. Nanos Valaoritis. *Fr.* Birds of Hazard and Prey. MIT

With grenades of sumac fruit. Dinoland. Thomas Rieter. PPoD

With hay, with how, with hoy! My Twelve Oxen. *Unknown.* OxBM

With high-jeweled hair. Empress in the Mirror. Colette Inez. WBN

With horns and with hounds I waken the day. Dryden. *Fr.* The Secular Masque. NOBE

With how! fox, how! With hay! fox, hay! The False Fox. *Unknown.* OxBM

With How Sad Steps, O Moon, Thou Climb'st the Skies. Sir Philip Sidney. Astrophel and Stella, XXXI. BoLoP; Epi; GBL; HeIP; InPK; InPS; LoAs; MAT; Moon; OBP; PAIC; PBMP; PPoe; PPP
(To the Sad Moon.) NOBE

With huntis up, with huntis up. *Unknown.* TVS

With I and E, *orig. and mod. English prose. Unknown.* OxBM

With its baby rivers and little towns. England. Marianne Moore. Psy

With its cloud of skirmishers in advance. An Army Corps on the March. Walt Whitman. InPS; PiAm; PPoe

With joy all relics of the past I hail. Old Ruralities. Charles Tennyson Turner. VPC

With Kit, Age 7, at the Beach. William Stafford. RFM

With longing I am lad. A Maid Mars Me. *Unknown.* OxBM

With love so like fire they dared not. Parlour Piece. Ted Hughes. BuTh

With low thunder, with red bushes smooth. Red Rock Ceremonies. Anita Endrezze Probst. CDW

With lullay, lullay, like a child [or lyke a chylde]. My Darling Dear, My Daisy Flower. John Skelton. AAS; LoAs

With marjoram gentle. To Mistress Margery Wentworth. John Skelton. *Fr.* The Garlande of Laurell. NOBE

With Mercy for the Greedy. Anne Sexton. CAPP

With My Crowbar Key. William Stafford. ConAP

With my eyelids still squeezed. Waking to Leopards. Nancy Mairs. NPW

With my frailty don't upbraid me. Semele to Jupiter [or Song]. Congreve. LoAs; POL

With nets and kitchen sieves they raid the pond. The Pond. Anthony Thwaite. LP; MAT

With nought to hide or to betray. L'Amitié et l'Amour. John Swanick Drennan. BIrV

With one consuming roar along the shingle. Felixstowe, or The Last of Her Order. John Betjeman. OxBTC

With our banners and our smiles. Christopher St. Liberation Day, June 28, 1970. Fran Winant. MMD

With people conformed. Dear Girl. Gregory Corso. NoAM

With porcupine locks. The Katzenjammer Kids. James Reaney. AKE

With proud thanksgiving, a mother for her children. For the Fallen. Laurence Binyon. NOBE; OxBTC

With rope, knife, gun, brass knucks, and bloody laws. Simple Beast. Mark Van Doren. TH

With Rue My Heart Is Laden. A. E. Housman. HeIP; InPK; NoAM; VoPo

"With sacrifice before the rising morn." Laodamia. Wordsworth. MBPR

With Serving Still. Sir Thomas Wyatt. InPK

With songs and honors sounding loud. Isaac Watts. AmFP

With that he stripped him to the ivory skin. Amorous Neptune. Christopher Marlowe. *Fr.* Hero and Leander. NOBE

With the Dawn. Thomas Caulfield Irwin. BIrV

With the Door Open. David Ignatow. CTBA

With the Face. Laura Riding. NoAM

With the fierce rage of winter deep suffused. A Winter Night. James Thomson. *Fr.* The Seasons: Winter. NOBE

With the last whippoorwill call of evening. Birmingham. Margaret Walker. PoBA

With the motion of angels, out of. Skiers. Robert Penn Warren. *Fr.* In the Mountains. SPo; TCP

With the slightest sound. My Son. Rex Veeder. HeS

With the spring rains, small spiders. Vincent Buckley. *Fr.* Golden Builders. CAAP

With the stars. For the Coming Year. Peter Everwine. OFD

With the sun. Patricia Parker. MIT

With the thinking of winter. The Cook. Ray A. Young Bear. CDW

With thee conversing I forget all time. Eve Speaks to Adam. Milton. *Fr.* Paradise Lost. GBL

With thee, in the desert. Emily Dickinson. LoAs

With their harsh leaves old rhododendrons fill. The Mountain Cemetery. Edgar Bowers. ConAP

With their lithe, long, strong legs. Bullfrog. Ted Hughes. RFM; TSWA

With this ambiguous earth. Christ in the Universe. Alice Meynell. BoReV; NOBE

With torches I have wandered the dark poppy world. The Double Axe. Anne Hazlewood-Brady. IHMS

With two 60's stuck on the scoreboard. Foul Shot. Edwin A. Hoey. SPo

With Usura. Cantos, XLV. Ezra Pound. NOBA; PiAm

With what a glory comes and goes the year! Autumn. Longfellow. FSFS

With what attentive courtesy he bent. The Guitarist Tunes Up. Frances Cornford. SoSe

With what deep murmurs through time's silent stealth. The Waterfall. Henry Vaughan. BoReV; NOBE

With wine and words of love and every vow. Seduced Girl. Hedylos, *tr. by* Louis Untermeyer. BoLoP

Withal a meagre man was Aaron Stark. Aaron Stark. E. A. Robinson. AmVN

Withered leaves fly higher than dolls can see, The. Sonnet. Ted Berrigan. CAAP

Within a delicate grey ruin. The Vestal Lady on Brattle. Gregory Corso. NoAM

Within a greenwood sweet of myrtle savour. *Unknown, tr. fr. Italian.* GBL

Within a thick and spreading hawthorn bush. The Thrush's Nest. John Clare. BoAnP

Within our happy castle there dwelt one. Stanzas Written in My Pocket-Copy of Thomson's "Castle of Indolence." Wordsworth. MBPR

Within that porch, across the way. The Cat. W. H. Davies. NOBE; PCat

Within the Circuit of This Plodding Life. Henry David Thoreau. *See* Winter Memories.

Within the curved edge of quarter moon. The Path I Must Travel. Emerson Blackhorse Mitchell. VW

Within the Dream You Said. Philip Larkin. InPS

Within the mind strong fancies work. The Pass of Kirkstone. Wordsworth. MBPR

Within the oak a throb of pigeon wings. A Twilight in Middle March. Francis Ledwidge. BIrV

Within the purple graph of the Hokonuis, the dark. The Foxes. Janet Frame. WPE

Within this black hive to-night. Beehive. Jean Toomer. PoBA

Within this mindless vault. Epigram. J. V. Cunningham. VGW

Within this sober frame expect. Upon Appleton House. Andrew Marvell. SCP-1

Without Ceremony. Vassar Miller. CoPAm

Without expectation. Summer Oracle. Audre Lorde. PoBA

Without dressmakers to connect. Because of Clothes. Laura Riding. NoAM

Without flocks or cattle or the curved horns. A Time of Change. Egan O'Rahilly, *tr. by* Eavan Boland. BIrV

Without Her. Dante Gabriel Rossetti. The House of Life, LIII. GBL

Without Name. Pauli Murray. PoBA

Withouten you. Little Elegy. Elinor Wylie. LoAs

Witless gallant, a young wench that woo'd, A. Michael Drayton. *Fr.* Idea. AAS

Witness to Death. Richmond Lattimore. VGW

Wives in the Sere. Thomas Hardy. NOBE

Wives of Mafiosi, The. Erica Jong. AmPA

Wives of Spittal, The. *Unknown.* GBP

Woak Hill. William Barnes. VPC

Wo'd I see Lawn, clear as the Heaven, and thin? The Lawn. Robert Herrick. LoAs

Wodwo. Ted Hughes. NoAM; TwMBP

Woe is me! Woe is me! The Ghost's Song. *Unknown.* RAE

Woefully Arrayed. *Unknown.* BoReV

Woke—the old King of Cumberland. The Old King. Walter de la Mare. AIW

Woke up, it was a Chelsea morning. Chelsea Morning. Joni Mitchell. GrRo; PoRo; WIF

Woke up this morning. That Lonesome Train Took My Baby Away. *Unknown.* BluL

Woke up this morning, gal 'twixt mid night and day. Barbecue Blues. *Unknown.* BluL

Wolde God that it were so. Love Undeclared. *Unknown.* OxBM

Wolfram's Dirge. Thomas Lovell Beddoes. *Fr.* Death's Jest Book. NOBE

Wolsey, or possibly my John of Gaunt. Santa Claus. Christopher Hassall. OxBTC

Wolves. John Haines. BoAnP

Wolves. Louis MacNeice. NoAM; OxBTC

Wolves, The. Allen Tate. NoAM; NOBA; PiAm

Wolves for Company. *Unknown, tr. fr. Irish.* BIrV

Woman. Jane Chambers. IHMS

Woman. Randall Jarrell. NoAM; NOBA

Woman. Elouise Loftin. PoBA

Woman, A/ sleeps next to me on the earth. Night in the Forest. Galway Kinnell. CoPAm

Woman, A/ who loves a woman. Rapunzel. Anne Sexton. RiTi

Woman Against the Moon, *sels.* Helen Wolfert. RiTi
    Preparation of the Body, The.
    Where the Mind Meets the Moon in Revolt

Woman as Market. Muriel Rukeyser. WBN

Woman at the Washington Zoo, The. Randall Jarrell. PSN

Woman came to me, A. Michael Silverton. POL

Woman comes, A. Fisherman. William Pitt Root. NVAP

Woman coming down the snowy road, A. Grey Woman. Gladys Cardiff. CDW

Woman Crossing the Road. Rhyll McMaster. CAAP

Woman dressed in half brown shoes, The. Mistaken Identity. Joanne Casullo. NPW

Woman fears for man, he goes. Abel's Bride. Denise Levertov. WBN; VGW

"Woman for whom great gods might strive, A!" The Chosen. Thomas Hardy. LoAs

Woman gave me butter now, A. A Present of Butter. Tadhg Dall O'Huiginn, *tr. by* the Earl of Longford. BIrV

Woman I want, The. No More Than Five. Fred Levinson. AmPA

Woman in her room is standing at the mirror, The. The Importance of Mirrors. Helga Sandburg. IHMS

Woman in his belly stirs, The. When He's at His Most Brawling. Patricia Goedicke. Psy

Woman in the, The. Marge Piercy. NMM

Woman in the shape of a monster, A. Planetarium. Adrienne Rich. NoAM; NOBA; RiTi

Woman Is a Worthy Thing, A. *Unknown.* FaBoCo; GBP; OxBM

Woman is perfected, The. Edge. Sylvia Plath. PSN; RiTi

Woman is singing the song and summer. Sonnet. Ted Berrigan. CAAP

Woman Is Talking to Death, A. *sels.* Judy Grahn. WBN
   Death and Disfiguration.
   Dressed As I Am, a Young Man Once Called Me Names in Spanish.
   Mock Interrogation, A.

Woman Mourned by Daughters, A. Adrienne Rich. IHMS; NCSH; Psy

Woman much missed, how you call to me, call to me. The Voice. Thomas Hardy. BoLoP; GBL; NoAM; PSN

Woman named Tomorrow, The. Four Preludes on Playthings of the Wind. Carl Sandburg. NOBA; PAIC; PiAm

Woman never knows what a good man she's got, A. Silver Dollar. Kathleen Wiegner. MMD

Woman of Three Cows, The. *Unknown, tr. fr. Irish by* James Clarence Mangan. PFIr

Woman Poem. Nikki Giovanni. NMM; NoAM; Psy

Woman Sat Weeping, A. *Unknown.* OxBM

Woman Skating. Margaret Atwood. IHMS

Woman speaks, A. The Hour of Feeling. Louis Simpson. FiCP

Woman Thing, The. Audre Lorde. NMM

Woman to Child. Judith Wright. WPE

Woman to Man. Judith Wright. MAuV; WPE

Woman to man, they lie. In Bloemfontein. Alan Ross. BoLoP

Woman Waits for Me, A. Walt Whitman. NOBA

Woman! when I behold thee flippant, vain. Keats. MBPR

Woman who has grown old, The. The Crows. Louise Bogan. SBG

Woman who lived, A. The Moon. Donald Hall. NCSH

Woman Who Loved to Cook, The. Erica Jong. WBN

Woman Who Loved Worms, The. Colette Inez. AATT; NMM; RiTi; WBN

Woman who talks to death, A. Dressed as I Am, a Young Man Once Called Me Names in Spanish. Judy Grahn. *Fr.* A Woman Is Talking to Death. WBN

Woman who writes feels too much, A. The Black Art. Anne Sexton. Psy

Woman with a fine ironic face, A. Hypothesis. Jennifer Maiden. CAAP

Woman with Finger. Tom McKeown. NVAP

Woman with Girdle. Anne Sexton. NCSH; NoAM; SFF

Woman with no face walked into the light, A. Homage to Hieronymus Bosch. Thomas MacGreevy. BIrV

Woman with the caught fox. Plea for a Captive. W. S. Merwin. NoAM

Woman, women/ 1. An adult female person. The Dictionary Is an *Historian*: A Found Political Poem. Judith McCombs. IHMS

Woman, you'll never credit what. The Shepherd's Tale. Raoul Ponchon, *tr. by* James Kirkup. PoTa

Womanhod, wanton, ye want. *See* Womanhood, wanton...

Womanhood, The, *sels.* Gwendolyn Brooks.
   Children of the Poor, The, I. WPE
   "Exhaust the little moment. Soon it dies," X. TH
   Old Laughter, V. TH
   "One wants a Teller in a time like this," XI. WPE
   Rites for Cousin Vit, The, VI. BPo; WPE
   Truth, IX. TH

Womanhood [*or* Womanhod], wanton, ye want. John Skelton. AAS; LoAs

Womanisers. John Press. BoLoP

Woman's breasts, A. St. Valentine. William Carlos Williams. LoAs

Woman's Faith. Sir Walter Scott. SLP

Woman's Message, A. *Unknown, tr. fr. Anglo-Saxon by* Burton Raffel. OBP

Woman's pink body could be preserved, A. Little Yellow Leaf. James Tate. NoAM

Womb Is Ruins, The. Helena Minton. FAF

Womb Song. Susan Fromberg Schaeffer. IHMS

Women. Louise Bogan. SBG; VGW; WPE

Women. Adrienne Rich. NMM; Psy

Women/should be/pedestals. Women. May Swenson. NMM; Prf; RiTi

Women All Tell Me, The, *with music. Unknown.* BLSo

Women are dark and seem, The. Old Photographs. David Harsent. POL

Women are larger than I, The. Little League Women. Deena Metzger. RiTi

Women before were strangers. Dispatch Number Nine. Doug Fetherling. NeAC

Women Beware Women: a Tragedy, *sel.* Thomas Middleton. "Prithee forgive me,/ I did but chide in jest." SCP-2

Women don't travel in clubcars. George Jonas. NeAC

Women dream of, The. Mountains. Besmilr Brigham. RiTi

Women have no wilderness in them. Women. Louise Bogan. SBG; VGW; WPE

Women in Brooklyn. Paul Zweig. NowV

Women in uniform. Omen of Victory. Mina Loy. InPK

Women in Vietnam, The. Grace Paley. NMM

Women know how to wait here. Lines for Marking Time. Robert Hill. CDW

Women Like That. Lyn Lifshin. Psy

Women loving each other. Bad Girl Blues. *Unknown.* BluL

Women sit on a street in Brooklyn. Women in Brooklyn. Paul Zweig. NowV

"Women with Tongue in Cheek." Daniela Gioseffi. RiTi

Women Who Are Hard Inside. Phyllis Gotlieb. BBGO

Women women women women. A Fixture. May Swenson. RiTi

Womens ward. C44 Karen L. Kent. NPW

Won' you ring, old hammer? Hammer, Ring. *Unknown.* AmFP

Wonder. Thomas Traherne BoReV; PPoe; SCP-2

Wonderful bears that walked my room all night. Bears. Adrienne Rich. NCSH

Wonderful bird is the pelican, A. *Unknown.* FaBoCo

Wonderful Occupation, A. *Unknown, tr. fr. Canadian Eskimo.* AKE

Wonderful Words of Life, *with music.* Philip Paul Bliss. BLSH

Wonderful workings of the world, The: wonderful. Cut the Grass. A. R. Ammons. PPP

"Wondrous life!" cried Marvell at Appleton House. Round. Weldon Kees. NoAM

Wondrous Love. *Unknown, at. to* Alex Means. AmFP; BLSo, *with music*

Won't be rushed; will take. Old Men Working Concrete. Phil Hey. FiCP

Won't Go to School. James Rankin. MIS

Won't you be my chauffeur. Me and My Chauffeur Blues. *Unknown.* BluL

Wood Weasel, The. Marianne Moore. PiAm

Woodchuck Who Lives on Top of Mt. Ritter. John Oliver Simon. NeAC

Woodcock rises, The. Ornithology. Siv Cedering Fox. NVAP

Wooden Ships. David Crosby, Paul Kantner, *and* Stephen Stills. GrRo

Woodley. William Barnes. VPC

Woodman Spare That Tree, *with music.* George Pope Morris. BLSo; PSoN

Woodnotes I ("When the pine tosses its cones"). Emerson. NOBA

Woodnotes II ("As sunbeams stream through liberal space"). Emerson. NOBA

Woodpeckers here are redheaded, The. Ornithology in Florida. Arthur Guiterman. BoAnP

Wood-Pile, The. Robert Frost. AnMo; NoAM; VGW

Woods are overhead over everywhere, The. James Cunningham. *Fr.* The Narrator's Trance. JB

Woods decay, the woods decay and fall, The. Tithonus. Tennyson. NOBE; OBP; PPP

Woods of Arcady are dead, The. The Song of the Happy Shepherd. W. B. Yeats. NoAM

Woodspurge, The. Dante Gabriel Rossetti. HeIP; InPK; NOBE; PBMP; VPC

Woodstock. Joni Mitchell. GrRo; IPWM

Woody says, "Let's make our soap." Social Studies. Mary Neville. POL

Woodyards in the Rain. Anne Marriott. AKE

Woof of the sun, ethereal gauze. Haze. Henry David Thoreau. *Fr.* A Week on the Concord and Merrimack Rivers. HeIP; PiAm

Wooing in a Dream. Nicholas Breton. *See* Report Song in a Dream, A.

Wooing of Etain, The. *Unknown, tr. fr. Irish by* John Montague. BIrV

Woolward and wet-shod went I forth after. The Jousting of Jesus. William Langland. *Fr.* Vision of Piers Plowman. BoReV

Word Drunk. Jim Harrison. IPWM

Word has come from the kitchen. Mary Hamilton. *Unknown.* AmFP

Word has reached us here. The Magdalena Silver Mine. Gene Frumkin. CoPAm

Word made flesh is seldom, A. Emily Dickinson. PiAm

Word of the sun to the sky, The. Triads. Swinburne. PBMP

Word Poem. Nikki Giovanni. PoBA

Word to a Father, Dead, A. John Alexander Allen. PPoD

Word to Husbands, A. Ogden Nash. POL

Words. Duncan Glen. MIS

Words. David Phillips. NeAC

Words. Sylvia Plath. AnMo; ConAP

Words, The. David Wagoner. TSWA

Words and Music, *sel.* Samuel Beckett. "Age is when to a man." BIrV

Words are ciphers. Tree. A. J. M. Smith. IPWM

Words are flying out like endless rain into a paper cup. Across the Universe. John Lennon *and* Paul McCartney. PoRo

Words are sardines packed. Bell Too Heavy to Ring. Tom Kryss. NeAC

Words, for E. Tom Leonard. SLP

Words for his ugly mug his. Ludwig's Death Mask. Ted Hughes. NoAM

Words for the Wind. Theodore Roethke. LoAs; NoAM; NOBA

Words from Storms and Geese in the Morning. Jenne Andrews. HeS

Word's gane to the kitchen. Mary Hamilton. *Unknown.* AIW; PAIC

Words have all fled the country, The, they are not expected back. Emigration. Anita Barrows. NMM

Words Like Freedom. Langston Hughes. BPo

Words scored upon a bone. Meditation on a Bone. A. D. Hope. MAuV

Wordsworth, thou form almost divine, cried Henry. John Berryman. *Fr.* Dream Songs. CAPP

Wordsworth upon Helvellyn! Let the cloud. On a Portrait of Wordsworth by B. R. Haydon. Elizabeth Barrett Browning. HeIP

Work?/ I don't have to work. Necessity. Langston Hughes. NOBA

Work, for the Night Is Coming, *with music.* Anna Louise Walker. BLSH

Work of Artifice, A. Marge Piercy. IHMS

Work on the railroad. Roll on the Ground. *Unknown.* AmFP

Work-table, litter, books and standing lamp. Night Sweat. Robert Lowell. VGW

Work to Do Toward Town. Gary Snyder. VGW

Work Without Hope. Samuel Taylor Coleridge. AnMo; IPWM; MBPR; NOBE

Work—work—work. Thomas Hood. *Fr.* The Song of the Shirt. VoPo

Workbox, The. Thomas Hardy. InPK

Worker, The. Richard W. Thomas. PoBA

Workhouse Boy, The. *Unknown.* GBP; PeBB

Working/ in a stupor. Bruce Holsapple. FAF

Working against Time. David Wagoner. MAT

Working for Dr. No. Valery Nash. PPoD

Working in the Mines. *Unknown.* AIW

Working Man Blues. *Unknown.* BluL

Working on Wall Street. May Swenson. NowV

Working with Tools. A. R. Ammons. NoAM

Workman with a spade in half a day, A. New Excavations. Leonora Speyer. *Fr.* Pompeii. TH

Work-out, The. Geoffrey Movius. MAT

Works and Days, *sel.* David Campbell. Lambing. MAuV

World, The. Francis Bacon. *See* World's a Bubble, The.

World, The. Robert Creeley. NoAM

World, The. Kathleen Raine. OxBTC

World, The. William Brighty Rands. OxBChV

World, The. Henry Vaughan. BoReV; HeIP; MetP; NOBE; OBP; PPoe; PPP; SCP-1

World a Hunt, The. William Drummond of Hawthornden. NOBE

World and the Child, The. James Merrill. CoPAm; PAIC

World as Meditation, The. Wallace Stevens. HeIP; IPWM; PiAm; PPP

World below the Brine, The. Walt Whitman. InPS; MAT; PBMP

World cheats those who cannot read, The. A Mad Poem Addressed to My Nephews and Nieces. Po Chu-i, *tr. by* Arthur Waley. BBGO; BuTh

World Has Many Places Many Ways, The. Norman H. Russell. VW

World hath conquered, The. Tara Is Grass. *Unknown, tr. by* Padraic Pearse. POL

World, Hold Me Close. Virginia Floyd. AATT

World is, The/ not with us enough. O Taste and See. Denise Levertov. PiAm; PPP

World Is a Beautiful Place, The. Lawrence Ferlinghetti. BBGO; CAPP; MiP

World is a bundle of hay, The.  Epigram on John Bull.  Byron. FaBoCo

World is a wind, The.  Frames on Bright Faces.  Bruce Severy. HeS

World is charged with the grandeur of God, The.  God's Grandeur.  Gerard Manley Hopkins.  AnMo; BoReV; Epi; InPK; IPWM; NoAM; NOBE; OBP; PAIC; PPP; SoSe; VoPo

World is composed, The.  The Grass Is a Reasonable Colour. John Newlove.  NeAC

World is fast bound in the snares of Varuna, The.  "Hugh MacDiarmid."  Fr. In Memoriam James Joyce.  TwMBP

World is full of care, much like unto a bubble, The.  Epigram. Nathaniel Ward.  POL

World is full of mostly invisible things, The.  To David, about His Education.  Howard Nemerov.  NowV; SFF

World Is Really a Sugarplum House in the Forest, The.  Aram Boyajian.  NeAC

World is so full of a number of things, The.  Happy Thought. Robert Louis Stevenson.  OxBChV

World is the color of pumpkins, The.  Butterflies on an Illinois Road.  Helena Minton.  FAF

World Is Too Much with Us, The.  Wordsworth.  BBGo; Epi; HeIP; InPK; IPWM; MAT; MBPR; NOBE; OBP; PAIC; PBMP; PPoD; PPoe; PPP; VoPo; WIF

World Outside, The.  Denise Levertov.  ConAP

World so Wide, The.  Unknown.  OxBM

World, The—the clust'ring spheres he made.  Fruits of the Earth. Christopher Smart.  Fr. A Song to David.  OBP

World within World.  Peter Meinke.  AATT

"World without Objects Is a Sensible Emptiness, A."  Richard Wilbur.  ConAP; NoAM; NOBA; PiAm

World world world world.  Enueg II.  Samuel Beckett.  NoAM

Worlde so wide, th'air so remuable, The.  The World so Wide. Unknown.  OxBM

World's a Bubble, The.  Francis Bacon.  SCP-2 (World, The.)  PPoD

World's a stage, The.  The trifling entrance fee.  Hilaire Belloc. OxBTC

World's as the world is, The; the nations rearm and prepare to. Night without Sleep.  Robinson Jeffers.  PiAm

World's Bliss, Have Good Day!  Unknown.  OxBM

World's great age begins anew, The.  Shelley.  Fr. Hellas. HeIP; NOBE

World's great sould knows by protopathy, The.  Psychathanasia or the Second Part of the Song of the Soul, Bk. III.  Henry More.  SCP-2

Worlds on worlds are rolling ever.  Shelley.  Fr. Hellas.  HeIP

Worm, The.  Ralph Bergengren.  CaYB

Worm artist, The.  The Earth Worm.  Denise Levertov.  NOBA

Worms, The.  Carolyn Kizer.  IPWM

Worms would rather be worms.  Worms and the Wind.  Carl Sandburg.  RAE

Wormwood.  James E. Warren, Jr..  AATT

Worried Life Blues.  Unknown.  AmFP

Worsening Situation.  John Ashbery.  NOBA

Worship.  Elmer F. Suderman.  AATT

Would God I in that Golden City were.  Edward Taylor.  Fr. Preparatory Meditations: First Series, XXIII.  PiAm

Would I could cast a sail on the water.  The Collar-Bone of a Hare.  W. B. Yeats.  OxBTC

Would I might lie like this, without the pain.  In Hospital. James Elroy Flecker.  OxBTC

Would I were chang'd into that golden shower.  Sir Arthur Gorges.  GBL

"Would it had been the man of our wish!"  In the Room of the Bride-Elect.  Thomas Hardy.  BuTh

Would it please you if I strung my tears.  The Race Question. Naomi Long Madgett.  BPo

Would that the structure brave, the manifold music I build.  Abt Vogler.  Robert Browning.  BoReV

Would you believe some-/ one who said he.  Dance and Eye Me (Wicked)ly My Breath a Fixed Sphere.  Rochelle Owens. NMM

Wouldnt think/t look at m.  Panther Man.  James A. Emanuel. BPo

Would'st be happy, little child.  To Theodora.  Unknown. OxBChV

Wouldst thou hear what man can say.  Epitaph on Elizabeth, L. H.  Ben Jonson.  HeIP; SCP-1

Wound, The.  Thom Gunn.  PSN

Wound-Dresser, The.  Walt Whitman.  NOBA

Wounded Cupid, The.  Robert Herrick.  OFD

Wounded hare looks out, The.  Hare in Winter.  Marge Piercy. NeAC

Wounded Wildnerness of Morris Graves, The.  Lawrence Ferlinghetti.  A Coney Island of the Mind, 11.  WIF

Wrap up in a blanket in cold weather and just read.  Things to Do around a Lookout.  Gary Snyder.  CAPP

Wrathfull winter prochinge [or 'proaching] on a pace, The.  The Induction to "A Mirror for Magistrates."  Thomas Sackville. AAS; PAIC

Wreath, The.  Robert Graves.  BoLoP

Wreath of flowers as cold as snow, A.  The Birth.  Rosemary Dobson.  MAuV

Wreck of the Deutschland, The.  Gerard Manley Hopkins. BoReV; NoAM; NOBE; PFD

Wreck of the Julie Plante, The.  William Henry Drummond. PoTa

Wreck of the Royal Palm, The.  Unknown.  AmFP

Wreck of the Thresher, The.  William Meredith.  CoPAm

Wreckers/ Drilling and breaking rock.  Constructions: Upper East Side.  Sandra Hochman.  NowV

Wren, The.  Unknown.  OxBChV

Wrestling Jacob.  Charles Wesley.  BoReV; NOBE

Wretched Flavia on her couch reclined, The.  Saturday: The Small Pox.  Lady Mary Wortley Montagu.  WPE

Wretched lost rejected lover, The.  For the Moment.  Richard Weber.  PFIr

Wring the Swan's Neck.  Enrique Gonzáles Martínez, tr. fr. Spanish by Samuel Beckett.  Epi

Wrists.  Alberta Turner.  HeS

Writ on the Eve of My 32nd Birthday.  Gregory Corso.  SA

"Write a letter to Grandpa," my mother said, but he smelled old. A Memory.  Mona Van Duyn.  Fr. Recovery.  RiTi

Write as you will.  Young Poets.  Nicanor Parra, tr. by Miller Williams.  POL

Write! write! help! help, sweet Muse! and never cease! Parthenophil and Parthenophe, XVIII.  Barnabe Barnes. Epi

Writer, The.  Hildebrand Jacob.  FaBoCo

Writer Indulges a Hobby, The  Julia Randall.  PPoD

Writer's House, The.  Dick Allen.  FAF

Writing a letter he said.  Buffalo—Isle of Wight Power Cable. Anselm Hollo.  TwMBP

Writing, I crushed an insect with my nail.  Interlude.  Karl Shapiro.  PBMP

Writing in England Now.  Philip O'Connor.  OxBTC

Written after Swimming from Sestos to Abydos.  Byron.  MBPR

Written after the Death of Charles Lamb.  Wordsworth.  MBPR

Written at an Inn at Henley.  William Shenstone.  NOBE

Written in a Copy of Swift's Poems, for Wayne Burns.  James Wright.  NOBA

Written in a Lady's Prayer Book.  Earl of Rochester.  BoLoP

Written in Dejection Near Rome. Robert Bly. CoPAm

Written in Disgust of Vulgar Superstition. Keats. MBPR

Written in Exile. Kathleen Raine. WPE

Written in Her French Psalter. Elizabeth I, Queen of England. WPE

Written in London, September, 1802. Wordsworth. *See* O Friend! I Know Not Which Way I Must Look.

Written in March. Wordsworth. MBPR; PBMP

Written in Northampton County Asylum. John Clare. *See* I Am.

Written in Prison. John Clare. Epi

Written in the Album of a Child. Wordsworth. OxBChV

Written in the Beginning of Mezeray's History of France. Matthew Prior. NOBE

Written on a Blank Page in Shakespeare's Poems. Keats. *See* Bright Star! Would I Were Steadfast as Thou Art.

Written on a Paper Napkin. Len Gasparini. NeAC

Written on a Wall at Woodstock. Elizabeth I, Queen of England. WPE

Written on the Day that Mr. Leigh Hunt Left Prison. Keats. MBPR

Written on the Stub of the First Paycheck. William Stafford. *Fr.* The Move to California. AnMo; InPK

Written the Night Before His Execution. Chidiock Tichbourne. *See* Elegy: "My Prime of youth is but a frost of cares."

Written with a Diamond on Her Window at Woodstock. Elizabeth I, Queen of England. WPE

Wrong Kind of Love. Ray A. Young Bear. VW

Wuid-reek. Sydney Goodsir Smith. SLP

Wyat resteth here, that quicke coulde never rest. Earl of Surrey. AAS

Wykehamist's Address to Learning, A. P. N. Shuttleworth. FaBoCo

Wynken, Blynken, and Nod. Eugene Field. ECBV; Moon; OxBChV

Wynken De Worde. Frederick Von Ende. POL

Wyse men alwaye. A Mery Gest How a Sergeaunt Wolde Lerne to Be A Frere. Sir Thomas More. AASADSLP

# X

X. R. P. Dickey. HeS

X-Ray. David Ray. IPWM

Xenophanes. Emerson. NOBA

# Y

Y digamos que, pensamos que, like. Foreign Policy Commitments; or, You Get into the Catamaran First, Old Buddy. Paul Blackburn. NowV

Y M & V Blues. *Unknown.* BluL

Yachts, The. William Carlos Williams. HeIP; NoAM; NOBA; PiAm; PPP; SPo

Yahweh is my shepherd. Psalms, XXIII, Bible, *O.T.* SFF

Yak, The. Hilaire Belloc. OxBChV

Yak, The. Theodore Roethke. ECBV; LCL

Yale Boola!, *3 versions, with music.* A. M. Hirsh. FSN

Yall/ out there. A Chant for Young/Brothas and Sistuhs. Sonia Sanchez. BPo

Yankee Cradle. Robert P. Tristram Coffin. ECBV

Yankee Doodle. *Unknown, at. to* Richard Schuckburg. AIW; AmFP; BLSH, *with music;* BLSo, *with music;* BTTM; GBP

Yankee Doodle Boy, The, *with music.* George M. Cohan. BLSo; FSN

Yankee Man-of-War, The. *Unknown.* BTTM (*Stately Southerner,* The.) AmFP

Yankee ship and a Yankee crew, A. The *Constitution's* Last Fight. James Jeffrey Roche. BTTM

"Yap-yap, yap-yap!" the little dog barked at the moon. The Dog. A. Buttigieg. RAE

Yardbird's Skull. Owen Dodson. PoBA; TCP; VGW

Yarn of the *Loch Achray.* John Masefield. PoTa

Yarn of the *Nancy Bell,* The. W. S. Gilbert. FaBoCo; PeBB

Yarrow Unvisited. Wordsworth. MBPR

Yarrow Visited. Wordsworth. MBPR

Yawn, The. Paul Blackburn. CTBA

Yawning youth, scarce half awake, essays, The. Persius, *tr. fr. Latin by* Dryden. *Fr.* Satires, III. SCP-1

Ye Alps audacious, thro' the heavens that rise. The Hasty-Pudding, I. Joel Barlow. NOBA; PiAm

Ye angells bright, pluck from your wings a quill. Edward Taylor. *Fr.* Preparatory Meditations: Second Series, LX. PiAm

Ye are the temples of the Lord. The Exhortation of a Father to His Children. Robert Smith. OxBChV

Ye Banks and Braes. Burns. *See* Banks o' Doon, The.

Ye blushing virgins happy are. To Roses in the Bosom of Castara. William Habington. SCP-2

Ye cats that at midnight spit love at each other. An Appeal to Cats in the Business of Love. Thomas Flatman. GBL; PCat; SCP-2

Ye clouds! that far above me float and pause. France: an Ode. Samuel Taylor Coleridge. MBPR

Ye dayntye nymphs, that in this blessed brooke. The Lay to Eliza. Spenser. *Fr.* The Shepheardes Calendar: April. NOBE

Ye distant spires, ye antique towers. Ode on a Distant Prospect of Eton College. Thomas Gray. HeIP; LAuP; NOBE; PAIC

Ye elms that wave on Malvern Hill. Malvern Hill. Herman Melville. AmVN

Ye flippering soule. Let By Rain. Edward Taylor. NOBA

Ye flowery banks o' bonie Doon [*or* Ye banks and braes o' bonie Doon]. The Banks o' Doon [*or* Bonie Doon]. Burns. BoLoP; HeIP; NOBE; SLP

Ye gentlemen and ladies fair who grace this famous city. The Hunters of Kentucky. Samuel Woodworth. BLSo; BTTM

Ye goat-herd gods that love the grassy mountains. Sir Philip Sidney. *Fr.* Arcadia. NOBE

Ye green-rob'd Dryads, oft' at dusky eve. The Enthusiast; or, the Lover of Nature. Joseph Warton. LAuP

Ye groves (the statesman at his desk exclaims.) The Statesman in Retirement. William Cowper. *Fr.* Retirement. PPoD

Ye happy floods! that now must pass. Lucasta Taking the Waters at Tunbridge: Ode. Richard Lovelace. SCP-2

Ye Hasten to the Grave! Shelley. GrRo

Ye have been fresh and green. To Meadows. Robert Herrick. NOBE

"Ye have robbed," said he, "ye have slaughtered and made an end." He Fell Among Thieves. Sir Henry Newbolt. OxBTC

Ye Highlands [*or* Hielands] and ye Lawlands. The Bonny Earl of Murray. *Unknown.* AIW; RDB

Ye learned sisters which have oftentimes. Epithalamion. Spenser. AAS; BoLoP; Epi; InPS; LoAs; NOBE; PAIC

Ye living lamps, by whose dear light. The Mower to the Glow-worms. Andrew Marvell. AnMo; NOBE; PPP

Ye loyal Britons, I pray draw near. The Battle of Shiloh. *Unknown.* AmFP

Ye Mariners of England. Thomas Campbell. BTTM; NOBE

Ye Nuns and Capuchins, begin the song. John Courtenay. *Fr.* A Poetical and Philosophical Essay on the French Revolution.... ESaP

Ye nymphs! if e'er your eyes were red. On the Lamented Death of Mrs. Throckmorton's Bullfinch. William Cowper. LAuP; PPP

Ye old mule, that thinck your self so fayre. Sir Thomas Wyatt. AAS

Ye Parliament of England. *Unknown.* AmFP; BTTM

Ye people who delight in sin. The Hanging of Sam Archer. *Unknown.* AmFP

Ye saints who dwell on Europe's shore. The Handcart Song. *Unknown.* AmFP

Ye saw't floueran in my breist. The Mandrake Hairt. Sydney Goodsir Smith. SLP

Ye sons of Columbia, your attention I do crave. Fuller and Warren. *At. to* Moses Whitecotton. AmFP

Ye tender-hearted people, I pray you lend an ear. Samuel Allen. *Unknown.* AmFP

Ye tradefull merchants, that with weary toyle. Amoretti, XV. Spenser. HeIP

Ye true lovers bold, come listen unto me. The True Lovers Bold. *Unknown.* AmFP

Ye weary, heavy laden souls. The Lonesome Dove. *Unknown.* AmFP

Yea, but uncertain hopes are anchors feeble. Parthenophil and Parthenophe, XXI. Barnabe Barnes. Epi

Yeah./they hang you up. To All Brothers. Sonia Sanchez. BPo

Yeah./ you can really. Rebolushinary x-mas. Carolyn M. Rodgers. JB

Yeah, I Is Uh Shootin Off at the Mouth. Carolyn M. Rodgers. SA

"Yeah" she said "my man's gone too." Conversation. Nikki Giovanni. CTBA

Yeah, you know Katie May's a good girl. Katie May. *Unknown.* BluL

Year ago I fell in love with the functional ward, A. The Hospital. Patrick Kavanagh. BIrV

Year ago, on what was probably, A. Leaving the Flag Out All Night. Napoleon St. Cyr. FAF

Year ago you came, A. Pietà. James McAuley. MAuV

Year dies fiercely, The: out of the north the beating storms. Year's End. William Everson. NoAM

Year has come to us as though out of hiding, A. Early January. W. S. Merwin. VGW

Year of the Bird. Brian Swann. AmPA

Year Passes, A. Amy Lowell. Moon

Yearner for silence, believing in the quiet mind, The. Between the Electric Rhythm and the Melodic Mind. James Schevill. MIT

Years. Jon Anderson. AmPA

Years ago,/ he began dialing your number. The Obscene Caller. Philip Dacey. AmPA

Years ago, at a private school. An Ever-fixed Mark. Kingsley Amis. NoAM

Year's at the Spring, The. Robert Browning. *Fr.* Pippa Passes, sc. i. InPK
(Pippa's Song.) LCL
(Song: "Year's at the Spring, The.") GrRo

Year's Awakening, The. Thomas Hardy. OxBTC

Years creep slowly by, Lorena, The. Lorena. Henry De Lafayette Webster. PSoN

Year's End. Jim Barnes. HeS

Year's End. William Everson. NoAM

Year's End. Richard Wilbur. CAPP; HeIP

Years have gone, The. It is spring. Andrée Rexroth. Kenneth Rexroth. VGW

Years of Indiscretion. John Ashbery. NOBA

Years of love in a parked car, The. Sidewalk Restoration. Ron Ikan. NVAP

Years—years ago—ere yet my dreams. The Belle of the Ball Room. Winthrop Mackworth Praed. FaBoCo

Yeh./ billie. if someone. For Our Lady. Sonia Sanchez. IHMS

Yei-ie's Child. Charles C. Long. VW

Yell for Yellow, A. Eve Merriam. ECBV

Yellow. De Leon Harrison. PoBA

Yellow. Charles Wright. AmPA

Yellow Bird, The. James W. Thompson. PoBA

Yellow Bittern, The. Cathal Buidhe MacGiolla Gunna, *tr. fr. Irish by* Thomas MacDonagh. BIrV

Yellow chrysanthemums, The. Sequence for a Young Widow Passing. Deborah Munro. IHMS

Yellow Flower, The. William Carlos Williams. PiAm

Yellow gas is fired from street to street, The. Christopher Brennan. *Fr.* Towards the Source. MAuV

Yellow-haired Laddie, The. *Unknown.* GBP

Yellow is for regret, the distal, the second hand. Yellow. Charles Wright. ÀmPA

Yellow november/comes swaying. Rushing. Ray A. Young Bear. CDW

Yellow platform shoes, purple bell-bottoms, orange silk shirt. Saturday Night. Rubee Dreher Moxley. NPW

Yellow Rose of Texas, The, *with music. Unknown.* BLSo; PSoN

Yellow Submarine. John Lennon *and* Paul McCartney. PPoe

Yellow sun yellow. The Ballad of Red Fox. Melvin Walker LaFollette. BoAnP

Yellow, yellow, hello, yellow. A Yell for Yellow. Eve Merriam. ECBV

Yellowjacket breaks its throat, The Circling. Carole Oles. NPW

Yen's sorry. A Magpie Rhyme, Northumberland. *Unknown.* GBP

Yes,/ And in that month when Proserpine comes back. That Sharp Knife. Thomas Wolfe. NCSH

Yes, as I live, I'll do't.—Nay stay. The Oath. Joseph Beaumont. SCP-2

Yes brothers you invented jazz. Tribute. Al Young. NVAP; SA

Yes, contumelious fair, you scorn. The Author Apologizes to a Lady for His Being a Little Man. Christopher Smart. BoLoP

Yes, do you remember an inn. Lament for Lost Lodgings. Phyllis McGinley. SpRo

Yes, every poet is a fool. Another [Epigram]. Matthew Prior. FaBoCo

Yes, he said, darling, yes, of course you tried. The Appointment. L. A. G. Strong. OxBTC

Yes, I remember Adlestrop. Adlestrop. Edward Thomas. NOBE; OxBTC

Yes I rolled and I tumbled. Dough Roller Blues. *Unknown.* BluL

Yes; I Write Verses. Walter Savage Landor. SoSe

Yes, I'm in love, I feel it now. The "Je Ne Sais Quoi." William Whitehead. SoSe

Yes! in the sea of life enisled. To Marguerite—Continued. Matthew Arnold. *Fr.* Switzerland. BoLoP; NOBE; PFD; PPP

Yes, it was the mountain echo. Wordsworth. MBPR

Yes, lady, in the bright red suit. For the Woman Who Asked Me If I Believe in God and If I Pray. Kathleen Wiegner. MMD

Yes solid mountain mingle in my brain. Solid Mountain. George Bowering. NeAC

Yes, the candidate's a dodger. The Dodger. *Unknown.* AmFP; GBP

Yes, the Secret Mind Whispers. Al Young. PoBA

Yes, this is where I stood that day. Ballad of Hector in Hades. Edwin Muir. NoAM; NOBE

Yes, thou art gone! and never more. A Reminiscence. Anne Brontë. WPE

Yes, we'll rally 'round the flag, boys, we'll rally once again. The Battle-Cry of Freedom. George Frederick Root. BTTM; PSoN

Yes, yes/it's time. My Spring Thing. Everett Hoagland. BPo

Yes, yes, I grant the sons of earth. The Question. James Beattie. FaBoCo

Yes you never miss your water water water. You Never Miss the Water. *Unknown.* BluL

Yes, yours, my love, is the right human face. The Confirmation. Edwin Muir. SLP

Yesterday. Fran Winant. MMD

Yesterday I bought a penny fiddle. The Penny Fiddle. Robert Graves. ECBV

Yesterday I stood on the balcony. Not Often. Ray Fraser. NeAC

Yesterday I wanted to. For Love. Robert Creeley. ConAP; NOBA; PiAm

Yesterday I was told. Byron vs. DiMaggio. Peter Meinke. SPo

Yesterday Rebecca Mason. Truth the Best. Elizabeth Turner. OxBChV

Yesterday's December rain. White Ropes. Franklin Brainard. HeS

"Yet Chloe was formed without a spot." Chloe. Pope. *Fr.* Moral Essays. NOBE

Yet Do I Marvel. Countee Cullen. BPo; IPWM; NoAM; PBMP; PoBA; SS

Yet Gentle Will the Griffin Be. Vachel Lindsay. ECBV; Moon

Yet if His Majesty, our sovereign lord. Preparations. *Unknown.* NOBE

Yet is God a curteis lord. A Warning to Beware. *Unknown.* OxBM

Yet it was plain she struggled, and that salt. Modern Love, VIII. George Meredith. LoAs

Yet Nature, where the thunder leaves its trace. Frederick Goddard Tuckerman. *Fr.* Sonnets. AmVN

Yet once more, O ye laurels, and once more. Lycidas. Milton. AnMo; Epi; InPK; InPS; NOBE; OBP; PAIC; PPoD; PPoe; PPP; SCP-1

Yet there is no great problem in the world today. "Hugh MacDiarmid." *Fr.* Lament for the Great Music. OxBTC

Yet wear we on; the deep light disallowed. Frederick Goddard Tuckerman. *Fr.* Sonnets. AmVN

Yew-tree, The. *Unknown, tr. fr. Welsh by* Geoffrey Grigson. GBL

Yield. Ronald Gross. InPK

Yield Not to Temptation, *with music.* Horatio R. Palmer. BLSH

Yillow, yillow, yillow. Metamorphosis. Wallace Stevens. InPK; VGW

Yin and Yang. Kenneth Rexroth. MIT

Y'know/ even a cantaloupe has a cunt. Composition. Cathleen Quirk. MMD

Yo/ smile. Poem. Sonia Sanchez. WBN

Yolanthe. Dan Kenney. MIT

Yom Kippur: Fasting. Ruth Whitman. OFD

Yon spark's a poet, by my troth! The Difference. Tadhg Dall O'Huiginn, *tr. by* Robin Flower. BIrV

Yonder stands a pretty fair maiden. No, Sir, No. *Unknown.* AmFP

Yorunomado sat in. The Black Hat. Clayton Eshleman. VGW

You/ Refuse to see. Out. Riots and Rituals. Richard W. Thomas. PoBA

You a man, man, man, who knows the other word. Compozishun—to James Herndon and Others. Ronald J. Goba. NCSH

You agree/ With me. A Question. William Cole. BoAnP

You ain't part Indian. Wake-Up Niggers. Don L. Lee. PoBA

You All Know the Story of the Other Woman. Anne Sexton. InPK

You Also, Gaius Valerius Catullus. Archibald MacLeish. NoAM

You always know what to expect. The Country House. Louis Simpson. NOBA

You always read about it. Cinderella. Anne Sexton. Psy

You, Andrew Marvell. Archibald MacLeish. HeIP; NoAM; NOBA; PiAm; PPP; SoSe; VoPo

You are/ Getting free. Thoughts for You (When She Came back from the Mountains). Ranice Henderson Crosby. NMM

You are a tulip seen today. A Meditation for His Mistress. Robert Herrick. NOBE

You are all these people. To a Single Shadow Without Pity. Sam Cornish. PoBA

You Are Alms. James W. Thompson. PoBA

You are already/ asleep. Touch. Thomas Gunn. LoAs; MPo

You are barely able to walk. But What I'm Trying to Say Mother Is. Ai. CAAP

You are coming to me in the rain. Rodney Hall. *Fr.* The Owner of My Face. CAAP

You are coming toward us. Aunt Laura Moves Toward the Open Grave of Her Father. Joseph De Roche. HeIP

You are curious, you wish. Fishbowl. Margaret Atwood. MMD

You are falling asleep and I sit looking at you. After Dark. Adrienne Rich. VGW

You Are Happy. Margaret Atwood. MMD

You are here now. The Sleeping Fury. Louise Bogan. IHMS; RiTi

You are like a sun of the tropics. Luxury. Donald Justice. HeIP

You are made of a stone hard as its name is. Tiki. Forrest Anderson. AATT

You are made of almost nothing. The Dragonfly. Louise Bogan. HeIP

You are my friend. Lorine Niedecker. VGW

You are my shadow in the picture. Lines for Michael in the Picture. John Logan. CAPP

You are not here! the quaint witch Memory sees. To Maria Gisborne in England, from Italy. Shelley. *Fr.* Letter of Maria Gisborne. NOBE

You are not looked for through the smog. To the Moon. Babette Deutsch. Moon

"You are old, Father William," the young man cried. The Old Man's Comforts and How He Gained Them. Robert Southey. OxBChV; SpRo

"You are old, Father William," the young man said. Father William. "Lewis Carroll." *Fr.* Alice's Adventure's in Wonderland. FaBoCo; OxBChV; SpRo; SS

You are polishing me like old wood. Marriage Amulet. Nancy Willard. RiTi

You are right. In dreams I might well dance. Possession. Marie Ponsot. VGW

You are rumpled like a sweater. Nothing More Will Happen [or Different Persuasions]. Marge Piercy. InPK; NeAC

You are small and intense. To a Child Running with Outstretched Arms in Canyon de Chelly. N. Scott Momaday. CDW

You are so witty, profligate, and thin. Epigram on Voltaire. Edward Young. FaBoCo

You Are the Brave. Raymond R. Patterson. PoBA

You are the problem I propose. The Metaphysical Amorist. J. V. Cunningham. VGW

You are the town and we are the clock. Chorus. W. H. Auden. Fr. The Dog Beneath the Skin. OxBTC

You are tired. The Midnight Tennis Match. Thomas Lux. AmPA

"You are wise, Mr. Dodgson," the young child said. Lewis Carroll. Eleanor Farjeon. OxBChV

You ask me for a song, folks. Cousin Jack Song. At. to Charley Tregonning. AmFP

You ask me to sing, so I'll sing you a song. The Cranberry Song. Barney Reynolds. AmFP

You ask what I have found, and far and wide I go. The Curse of Cromwell. W. B. Yeats. BIrV

You better come on in my kitchen. Come On in My Kitchen. Unknown. BluL

You better learn how to treat everybody. You Got to Go Down. Unknown. BluL

You black out the sun. Ed Roberson. Fr. When Thy King Is a Boy. PoBA

You blame me that I do not write. Letter to a Friend. Jon Stallworthy. NoAM

You brave heroic minds. To the Virginian Voyage. Michael Drayton. Epi; NOBE

You bring me good news from the clinic. Face Lift. Sylvia Plath. InPK; PPoD

You build it where you will be heard only by chance. The Cabin North of It All. James McMichael. AmPA

You burst into the world with smiles wide as April. Sleeping with Foxes. Roberta Hill. CDW

You called yourself a dishwater blonde. What You Waited For. Marge Piercy. MMD

You came in out of the night. Francesca. Ezra Pound. PSN

You can have daughters, sons. Inventing a Family. Dennis Saleh. Fr. A Guide to Familiar American Incest. NeAC

You can look into my face. Poem. Mike Todachine. CTBA

You can make castles of it, construct. Sand. Charles Higham. LP

You can read my letter now sure don't know my mind. Ham Hound Crave. Unknown. BluL

You can say anything. The Art of Poetry. Dennis Trudell. NowV

You can take a tub with a rub and a scrub in a two-foot tank of tin. Pater's Bathe. Edward Abbott Parry. OxBChV

You can take away my mother. Umbilical. Eve Merriam. CTBA

You can talk about your farms and your Chinaman's charms. The Cowboy's Life Is a Very Dreary Life. Unknown. AmFP

You Cannot Go Down to the Spring. John Shaw Neilson. MAuV

You cannot hope. Humbert Wolfe. OxBTC

You can't keep it, I say. Civilizing the Child. Lisel Mueller. CTBA

You Can't Keep No Brown. Unknown. BluL

You captains brave and bold, hear our cries, hear our cries. Captain [Robert] Kidd. Unknown. AmFP; PeBB

You come forth/ the color of a stone cliff. To Insure Survival. Simon J. Ortiz. CDW

You come from some other forest. Little Horse. W. S. Merwin. TH

You come to fetch me from my work tonight. Putting in the Seed. Robert Frost. NoAM

You could be sitting now in a carrel. A Late Aubade. Richard Wilbur. PAIC; SoSe

You could not stop the snow the sky dumped down. Lines for a President. Robert Watson. PPoD

You could smell the river. For E. C. J. Emmett Jarrett. NeAC

You cut my passion back like a hedge, gardener. Tirade. Honor Moore. WBN

You darling girls of Bagaduce, who live along the shore. The Schooner Fred Dunbar. Amos Hanson. AmFP

You did not come. A Broken Appointment. Thomas Hardy. GBL; LoAS; NoAM

You did not see wood made pliable by rot, or rust-devoured iron. To a Proud Old Woman Watching the Tearing Down of The Hurricane Shed. Kay Boyle. MIT

You did not walk with me. The Walk. Thomas Hardy. PSN

You do not do, you do not do. Daddy. Sylvia Plath. AnMo; CAPP; InPK; InPS; NMM; NoAM; NOBA; PiAm; Psy; RiTi

You Do Not Have to Love Me. Leonard Cohen. NoAM

You do not know how beautiful you are. Ode to A Beautiful Woman. Carl Clark. JB

You, Doctor Martin. Anne Sexton. Psy

You don't find him in crowds. The Man Who Closes Himself. Peter Cooley. NVAP

You don't know I pretend my dumb. Plea to Those Who Matter. James Welch. AmPA; SA

You drop apprehensively—the sun gone out. David Jones. Fr. In Parenthesis. TwMBP

You earthly souls that court a wanton flame. La Belle Confidante. Thomas Stanley. SCP-2

You, Farrell O'Reilly, I feared as a boy. Farrell O'Reilly. Oliver St. John Gogarty. OxBTC

You fiends and furies, come along! Sir William Davenant. Fr. The Unfortunate Lovers. SCP-2

You fit into me. Margaret Atwood. POL

You gentlemen of England far and near. The Wind Sou'west. Unknown. AmFP

You gentlemen of England who live at home at ease. The Bay of Biscay. Unknown. AmFP

"You Get the Groceries, I'll Guard the Crib." Dennis Trudell. NVAP

You Get Used to It. Adrian Mitchell. NowV

You girls who were seeking. Girls. Pablo Neruda, tr. by Donald D. Walsh. OLR

You Got to Go Down. Unknown. BluL

You Got to Love Her with a Feeling. Unknown. BluL

You have come your way, I have come my way. Fronleichnam. D. H. Lawrence. GBL

You have gone through. Talks with Himself. Bruce Severy. HeS

You have just come in the door. The Confession. Peter Cooley. AmPA

You have only to wait, they will find you. Messengers. Louise Glück. CAAP

You have seen them. Above the freeways. Girls Who Wave at Cars from Bridges. Harold Bond. NVAP

You have taken our love and turned it into coins of silver. A Poet's Wife. Amy Lowell. RiTi

You have your shadow. Your Shadow. Mark Strand. Fr. Elegy for My Father. Prf

You Held the Air. Stephen Tudor. HeS

You, hiding there in your words. The Book. Adrienne Rich. RiTi

You hold your eager head.  To a Romantic.  Allen Tate.  PiAm

You in Anger.  James Reeves.  OxBTC

You jam your arm into the white air.  Poem.  Mira Fish.  FAF

You keep me waiting in a truck.  Twenty Year Marriage. Ai. CAAP

You kissed her, and I watched you for a moment. Metamorphoses.  Vassar Miller.  RiTi

You know her hustle.  Asking for Ruthie.  Judy Grahn.  NMM

You know I said to Mark that I'm furious at you.  The Quarrel. Diane Di Prima.  NMM; RiTi

You know it's April by the falling-off.  B Negative.  X. J. Kennedy.  ConAP

You know me.  Hypocrite.  Ann M. Craig.  PPoD

You know now mama.  Alley Blues.  *Unknown.*  BluL

"You know Orion always comes up sideways."  The Star-Splitter. Robert Frost.  PAIC

You know the records. They are there to read.  Willie Mays. Paul Ramsey.  PPoD

You know there is not much.  To a Friend Concerning Several Ladies.  William Carlos Williams.  VGW

You know this dream. You move.  The Owl.  David Young. CAAP

You know those windless summer evenings, swollen to stasis. Cigales.  Richard Wilbur.  NoAM; NOBA

You know, we French stormed Ratisbon.  Incident of the French Camp.  Robert Browning.  AKE; BTTM

You know what it is to be born alone.  Baby Tortoise.  D. H. Lawrence.  BoAnP

You landsmen and you seamen bold.  The Loss of the *Due Dispatch. Unknown.*  AmFP

You let the door sway open on its hinges.  A Figure of Plain Force.  Michael Heffernan.  HeS

You, Letting the Trees Stand as My Betrayer.  Diane Wakoski. NoAM

You lie in this Pittsburgh room.  Pittsburgh.  Peggy Ruse.  NPW

You lie now in many coffins.  For Malcolm: After Mecca. Gerald W. Barrax.  PoBA

You live here because there's no other place.  So Long Solon. Jack Myers.  AmPA

You look as though/ You know me.  The Moon Ground.  James Dickey.  Moon

You looked at me today.  For My Daughter's 20th Birthday. Walter Lowenfels.  RRA

You lousy bitch.  Wild Woman's Resentment of Fakery. Rochelle Owens.  RiTi

You, love, and I.  Counting the Beats.  Robert Graves.  GBL; OxBTC

You loved me because I brought you sugar cubes.  Timothy. Thomas James.  HeS

You loved me not at all, but let it go.  Edna St. Vincent Millay. VGW

You may not believe it.  The Pumpkin.  Robert Graves.  CaYB

You may search/ the ocean.  Searching for the Desert Blues. *Unknown.*  BluL

You may talk about me just as much as you please.  Hold the Wind.  *Unknown.*  GBP

You may talk o' gin and beer.  Gunga Din.  Kipling.  BTTM

You meaner beauties of the night.  On His Mistress, the Queen of Bohemia [*or* Elizabeth of Bohemia].  Sir Henry Wotton. BoLoP; GBL; MetP; NOBE

You must do as they do at Hoo.  Hoo, Suffolk.  *Unknown.*  GBP

You must live through the time when everything hurts.  The Double Shame.  Stephen Spender.  LoAs

You must remember structures beyond cotton plains.  If Blood Is Black Then Spirit Neglects My Unborn Son.  Conrad Kent Rivers.  PoBA

You Naughty, Naughty Men, *with music.*  T. Kennick.  BLSo

You need lightning.  To the Man Who Sidled Up to Me and Asked: "How Long You in fer, Buddy?"  Etheridge Knight. NeAC

You need not see what someone is doing.  Sext.  W. H. Auden. *Fr. Horae Canonica.*  TCP

You never asked to be a master.  Quotations from Charwoman Me.  Robin Morgan.  WBN

You Never Miss the Water.  *Unknown.*  BluL

You never saw my rib cage. I would lie next to you.  Farewell Poems.  Sandra Hochman.  RiTi

You Northern Girl.  Charles G. Ballard.  VW

You, once a belle in Shreveport.  Snapshots of a Daughter-in-Law.  Adrienne Rich.  NMM; NCSH

You only love/ when you love in vain.  Ode to Joy.  Miroslav Holub, *tr. by* Ian Milner *and* George Theiner.  BuTh

You ought to see my blue-eyed Sally.  Stay All Night, Stay a Little Longer.  *Unknown.*  AmFP

You ought to see my Cindy.  Cindy.  *Unknown.*  BLSo

You, passing along the path, if you see this tomb.  Epitaph on a Dog.  *Unknown, tr. by* Forrest Reid.  ECBV

You possess the sturdy elegance of a cannon.  For Natalya Correia.  Irving Layton.  NeAC

You praise the firm restraint with which they write.  On Some South African Novelists.  Roy Campbell.  FaBoCo; InPK; OxBTC

You promise heavens free from strife.  Mimnermus in Church. William Cory.  NOBE

You promised to send me some violets. Did you forget?  Letter from Town: The Almond Tree.  D. H. Lawrence.  PAIC

You raise the ax.  The Anniversary.  Ai.  CAAP

You read the New York Times.  Alfred Corning Clark.  Robert Lowell.  NoAM

You refuse to own.  Margaret Atwood.  NeAC

You replaced the Douglas firs.  You, Letting the Trees Stand as My Betrayer.  Diane Wakoski.  NoAM

You return home.  Homecoming.  Dan Gerber.  HeS

You said/ we will all.  The Sky.  Susan Griffin.  RiTi

You said it was just sex, we had.  After Swimming in the Pacific. Cathy Colman.  NPW

You said it went all the way.  Last Words, 1968.  Lance Henson. CDW

You said that your people.  To Richard Wright.  Conrad Kent Rivers.  PoBA

You sang round-dance songs.  Farewell.  Liz Sohappy Bahe. CDW

You sat with a bottle of beer.  After the Death of an Elder Klallam.  Duane Niatum.  CDW

You say, as I have often given tongue.  To a Poet, Who Would Have Me Praise Certain Bad Poets, Imitators of His and Mine.  W. B. Yeats.  PFIr

You say, "I will come."  Lady Otomo No Sakanoe, *tr. fr. Japanese by* Kenneth Rexroth.  OLR

You say that I take a good deal upon myself.  Monumentum Aere, Etc.  Ezra Pound.  NOBA

You say the king commands that I appear.  Diptych.  Velma West Sykes.  IHMS

You say, to me-wards your affection's strong.  Love Me Little, Love Me Long.  Robert Herrick.  LoAs

You say you love; but with a voice.  Stanzas.  Keats.  MBPR

You say you love me, nay, can swear it too.  Robert Heath. POL

"You say you love me truly."  True is True.  Mark Van Doren. LoAs

You scream, waking from a nightmare.  Little Sleep's-Head Sprouting Hair in the Moonlight.  Galway Kinnell.  RRA

You see, my whole life.  Woman Poem.  Nikki Giovanni. NMM; NoAM; Psy

You see, the problem is. Blue Like Death. James Welch. CDW

You see the worst of love, but not the best. Walter Savage Landor. GBL

You see this pebble-stone? The Cock and the Bull. Charles Stuart Calverley. FaBoCo

You send me a photograph. Porno Love. Philip Dacey. NVAP

You send them back to me. Letters, Returned. Adrianne Marcus. NPW

You Serve the Best Wines Always, My Dear Sir. Martial *tr. fr. Latin by* J. V. Cunningham. InPK

You Shall. *Unknown.* BluL

You Shall above All Things Be Glad and Young. E. E. Cummings. NOBA; NoAM

You shall not be overbold. The Titmouse. Emerson. PiAm

You shun me, Chloe, wild and shy. To Chloe. Horace, *tr. by* Austin Dobson. Odes, I, 23. LoAs

You sit on the porch steps. Possessions. Ai. CAAP

You sleeping child asleep, away. To Ping-Ku, Asleep. Lawrence Durrell. RRA

You smiled, you spoke, and I believed. Walter Savage Landor. BoLoP; GBL

You speed by with your camera and your spear. Interview with a Tourist. Margaret Atwood. IHMS

You spotted snakes with double tongue. Shakespeare. *Fr.* A Midsummer Night's Dream, II, ii. ECBV; NOBE

You stand behind the old black mare. Why Can't I Leave You? Ai. AmPA

You still sometimes sleep. Heron. Stanley Plumly. AmPA

You stood in our small boat. Friend with Spinning Rod. Napoleon St. Cyr. FAF

You, stranger, who only see us happy and free of care. Hunger. *Unknown, tr. by* Edward Field. IPWM

You take the dollar. For One Moment. David Ignatow. TCP

"You talk of snakes," said Jack the Rat. A Snake Yarn. W. T. Goodge. ECBV

You tell me that silence. Gift. Mark Strand. NoAM

You Tell Me Your Dream, I'll Tell You Mine, *with music.* Seymour Rice *and* Albert H. Brown. FSN

You that are sprung of northern stock. To a Calvinist in Bali. Edna St. Vincent Millay. NoAM

You, that decipher out the fate. Mourning. Andrew Marvell. SCP-1

You that have spent the silent night. Gascoignes Good Morrow. George Gascoigne. AAS

You that in love finde lucke and habundance. Sir Thomas Wyatt. AAS

You that know the way. Lemuel's Blessing. W. S. Merwin. CAPP; TCP

You that with allegory's curious frame. Astrophel and Stella, XXVIII. Sir Philip Sidney. InPK

You, the one woman that could have me all. To V. S. Christopher Brennan. MAuV

You, the woman; I, the man; this, the world. The Character of Love Seen as a Search for the Lost. Kenneth Patchen. VGW

You there, ain't your mamma never. Poem for Blackboys in Floppy Tie-Dye Hats. Jodi Braxton. WBN

You think it horrible that lust and rage. The Spur. W. B. Yeats. SoSe

You think they might come. Riding Double. Peter Wild. AmPA

You thought the leaden winter. Tales of Brave Ulysses. Eric Clapton *and* Martin Sharp. GrRo

You thunder at my side. The Snoring Bedmate. *Unknown, tr. by* John V. Kelleher. BIrV

You told me, early last fall, you never had no man at all. Fare Thee Well Blues. *Unknown.* BluL

You track for days. Hunting Dragons with Fire Tongues and Deep Smoky Throats. J. S. Harry. CAAP

You travel across the room. Distances. Linda Pastan. RiTi

You tried so hard to make me believe in this day. To My Father on Pearl Harbor Day. D. W. Donzella. FAF

You Understand the Requirements. Lyn Lifshin. NeAC; RiTi

You used to be my sugar, but. Tooten Out Blues. *Unknown.* BluL

You virgins that did late despair. Piping Peace. James Shirley. *Fr.* The Imposture. NOBE; SCP-2

You wake up feeling. Ripeness. Ruth Whitman. TSWA

You want coins? Roman? Greek? Nice vase? Head of god, goddess. Ali Ben Shufti. Anthony Thwaite. OxBTC

You want to go back. Margaret Atwood. NeAC

You want to integrate me into your anonymity. Black Narcissus. Gerald W. Barrax. PoBA

You want to know what's the matter with me, do yer? Reaping. Amy Lowell. SBG

You wanted the perfect setting. For Anna. Irving Layton. NeAC

You watched out for him or. Travis, the Kid Was All Heart. Terry Stokes. AmPA

You Went Away. Norman MacCaig. SLP

You were a girl of satin and gauze. The Wheel Revolves. Kenneth Rexroth. NoAM; RRA

You were being driven down to Prague. Polemical Elegy for Reinhardt Heydrich. Tom Buchan. MIS

You were brought up. Coming Up and Falling Down. Stephen Vincent. NeAC

You were lying on top of me. Night of Dreams. Laura Beausoleil. NPW

You were praised, my books. Salutation the Second. Ezra Pound. NOBA

You were up early. Sunday. Laura Beausoleil. NPW

You Were Wearing. Kenneth Koch. NoAM

You Were Wearing Blue. Tom Raworth. TwMBP

You were wearing your Edgar Allan Poe printed cotton blouse. You Were Wearing. Kenneth Koch. NoAM

You were writing a long poem, yes. Residue of Song. Marvin Bell. AmPA

You were young—but that was scarcely to your credit. Gerald Gould. *Fr.* Monogamy. OxBTC

You were't even a. To L. Julianne Perry. PoBA

You, who/ Are more like/ A little girl. Serene Art. Lewis Warsh. MIT

You who desired so much—in vain to ask. To Emily Dickinson. Hart Crane. NoAM; NOBA

You who dump the beer cans in the lake. Malediction. Barry Spacks. InPK

You who go every Sunday to the Botanical Garden. Song for Afterwards. Francisco Lopez Merino, *tr. by* Richard O'Connell. LoAs

You who go out on schedule. Two Variations. Denise Levertov. PPoe; RiTi

You who were darkness warmed my flesh. Woman to Child. Judith Wright. WPE

You who would sorrow even for a token. Reciprocity. Vassar Miller. IHMS

You, Whose Mother's Lover Was Grass. Gregory Corso. NoAM

You will be aware of an absence, presently. For a Fatherless Son. Sylvia Plath. TSWA

You will be beautiful now. The Piercing. Pat Lowther. MMD

You will have the road gate open, the front door ajar. In Memory of My Mother. Patrick Kavanagh. BIrV

You worry me whoever you are.  Badman of the Guest Professor.  Ishmael Reed.  BPo

You would extend the mind beyond the act.  The Moralists.  Yvor Winters.  PiAm

You would have understood me, had you waited.  Paul Verlaine, *tr. fr. French by* Ernest Dowson.  BoLoP

You would not recognize me.  The Tourist from Syracuse.  Donald Justice.  CoPAm

You would sleep with the moon.  Alternatives.  Peter Cooley.  AmPA

You would take/everything.  At Times.  Kathleen Wiegner.  MMD

You would think the fury of aerial bombardment.  The Fury of Aerial Bombardment.  Richard Eberhart.  CoPAm; HeIP; InPK; IPWM; NoAM; PPoD; PSN; TCP; VGW; VoPo; WIF

You'd Better Believe Him.  Brian Patten.  LP

You'd think that at 3:00 A.M.  L'Elisir d'Amore.  Dallas E. Wiebe.  MAT

You'll know it—as you know—tis noon.  Emily Dickinson.  PiAm

You'll Love Me Yet!  Robert Browning.  *Fr.* Pippa Passes, sc. iii.  OLR

You'll Never Miss Your Jelly.  *Unknown.*  BluL

Young.  Anne Sexton.  MPo; NCSH

Young and Old.  Charles Kingsley.  *Fr.* The Water Babies.  OxBChV

Young are quick of speech, The.  On Teaching the Young.  Yvor Winters.  NoAM; NOBA

Young Author, The.  Samuel Johnson.  LAuP

Young Ben he was a nice young man.  Sally Brown.  Thomas Hood.  FaBoCo

Young bloods come round less often now, The.  Horace, *tr. by* James Michie.  Odes, I, 25.  BoLoP

Young boys forget about cars awhile, The.  Results of the Polo Game.  Grace Butcher.  RiTi

Young Calidore is paddling o'er the lake.  Calidore.  Keats.  MBPR

Young cat knew enough to lick her firstborn, but, The.  Dill.  Marie Harris.  MMD

Young Charlottie; or, The Frozen Girl.  *Unknown.*  AmFP

Young Corydon [or Coridon] and Phyllis [or Phillis].  On the Happy Corydon and Phyllis.  Sir Charles Sedley.  BoLoP; SCP-2; SFF

Young Couples Strolling By.  Carl Rakosi.  InPS

Young Dead Soldiers, The.  Archibald MacLeish.  OFD

Young Deputy, The.  James Whitehead.  CoPAm

Young Edward came to Emily his gold all for to show.  Edwin in the Lowlands Low.  *Unknown.*  AmFP

Young fellow walks about, The.  Charles Reznikoff.  CTBA

Young Fenians, The.  Padraic Fallon.  BIrV

Young flowers were whispering in melody.  Song.  Poe.  *Fr.* Al Aaraaf.  NOBA

Young Girl.  Menzies McKillop.  SLP

Young Girl, The.  Theodore Roethke.  AnMo; LoAs; NoAM

Young girl stood beside me, The.  The Orange Tree.  John Shaw Neilson.  MAuV

Young Girl's Song, The.  Alvin J. Gordon.  MiP

Young, groomed sullen men of boyless purpose.  Highway 101, Seal Beach.  Curtis Zahn.  NowV

Young Heroes.  Gwendolyn Brooks.  BPo

Young heroes, the generous young men, The.  Young Girl.  Menzies McKillop.  SLP

Young Housewife, The.  William Carlos Williams.  HeIP; NoAM; PiAm

Young Hunting (" 'Get down, get down, lovin' Henry,' she cried").  *Unknown.*  AmFP

Young Hunting ("O lady, rock never your young son young").  *Unknown.*  PeBB

Young in Fall I said: the birds.  Lorine Niedecker.  VGW

Young Johnnie Steele has an Oldsmobile.  In My Merry Oldsmobile.  Vincent Bryan.  FSN

Young Johnny sails the sea, young Johnny sails the shore.  The Green Bed.  *Unknown.*  AmFP

Young Johnny the miller he courted of late.  The Gray Mare.  *Unknown.*  AmFP

Young Johnstone.  *Unknown.*  PeBB

Young Juan wandered by the glassy brooks.  The Seduction of Juan.  Byron.  *Fr.* Don Juan, I.  OBP

Young lords o' the north country, The.  Lady Maisery.  *Unknown.*  Epi

Young Love.  Andrew Marvell.  RRA

Young Lover, A.  E. N. Sargent.  WBN

Young man and maid, pray lend attention.  The Silver Dagger.  *Unknown.*  AmFP

Young man and the miller's lass they set out on the hill, The.  The Miller's Daughter.  *Unknown.*  PeBB

Young man of twenty, A.  Lost Picture.  Ray Fraser.  NeAC

Young man, wearing a loose jacket of light brown, A.  Puerto Ricans in New York, II.  Charles Reznikoff.  CTBA

Young Man Who Loved the Girl Who Took Care of Her Aging Father, The.  Greg Kuzma.  AmPA

Young Man's Epigram on Existence, A.  Thomas Hardy.  NoAM

Young Master's Account of a Puppet Show.  John Marchant.  OxBChV

Young May Moon, The.  Thomas Moore.  Moon

Young Molly Ban.  *Unknown.*  PeBB

Young mouth laughs at a gift, A.  Her Words.  Theodore Roethke.  LoAs

Young niggers/ die old.  Dedication to the Final Confrontation.  Lloyd M. Corbin, Jr.  PoBA

Young Ones, The.  Elizabeth Jennings.  OxBTC

Young Ones, Flip Side, The.  James A. Emanuel.  SS

Young Palmus was a ferryman.  Shackley-Hay.  *Unknown.*  GBP

Young people all, attention give.  Liverpool.  *Unknown.*  AmFP

Young people, all attention give.  Mission.  *Unknown.*  AmFP

Young People Who Delight in Sin.  *Unknown.*  AmFP

Young Poet.  Myron O'Higgins.  PoBA

Young Poets.  Nicanor Parra, *tr. fr. Spanish by* Miller Williams.  POL

Young Prince and the Young Princess, The.  John Ashbery.  ConAP

Young Soul.  LeRoi Jones.  BPo; TSWA

Young Stock.  V. Sackville-West.  OxBTC

Young Training.  Lawrence McGaugh.  PoBA

Young Wife, A.  D. H. Lawrence.  PBMP; VoPo

Young Woman in Apathy.  Christopher Middleton.  TwMBP

Young Woman of Beare, The.  Austin Clarke.  NoAM

Young women are obsessed with beauty, The.  The Clothes Pit.  Douglas Dunn.  OxBTC

Youngest Schizophrene, The.  Katherine Hoskins.  TCP

Your Absence Has Not Taught Me.  Doug Fetherling.  NeAC

Your Attention Please.  Peter Porter.  LP; OxBTC

Your back is rough all.  Margaret Atwood.  NeAC

Your bare white legs.  The Beach at Veracruz.  George Bowering.  NeAC

Your beauty, ripe and calm, and fresh.  The Philosopher and the Lover: To a Mistress Dying.  Sir William Davenant.  NOBE; Prf

Your blonde beard crushes ice into.  Departure.  Elizabeth Hanson.  NPW

Your blood does not flow, not even a little. A Poem for Diane Wakoski. Ray A. Young Bear. CDW

Your bones left out all night. Beginning Again As Morning. Eugene Ruggles. MIT

Your bottoms are not purple. Horror Comic. Robert Conquest. OxBTC

Your cheekbones live. Cathy Colman. NPW

Your children are not your children. On Children. Kahlil Gibran. *Fr.* The Prophet. SFF

Your closed eyes bulge like mushrooms. Letter to Kafka. Maura Stanton. AmPA

Your correspondent must be kidding when he says. Americana IX. Carl Rakosi. InPS

Your door is shut against my tightened face. The White House. Claude McKay. PoBA

Your elephant adolescence in sandlots Brooklyn. 16/53. Marge Piercy. NeAC

Your eyebrows are splotched on like market flies. The Prostitutes at Les Halles. Jane Mayhall. WBN

Your eyen [or yen] two will slay me suddenly. Merciless Beauty. Chaucer. BoLoP; OxBM; PAIC

Your eyes are just. Four-Word Lines. May Swenson. WPE

Your eyes are open. Carious Exposure. Gladys Cardiff. CDW

Your Eyes Have Their Silence. Gerald W. Barrax. PoBA

Your Eyes, Your Name. William Matthews. NVAP

Your face/ half blue. Homage to Chagall. Kathleen Teague. MIT

Your face,/ so pale now it is blue. Poem. David St. John. AmPA

Your face broods from my table, Suicide. John Berryman. *Fr.* Dream Songs. CAPP

Your face scrapes my sleep tonight. Letter to Be Disguised As a Gas Bill. Marge Piercy. MMD; WPE

"Your father's gone," my bald headmaster said. The Lesson. Edward Lucie-Smith. BuTh; LP; MPo; NCSH; OxBTC

Your foe in war to overrate. Porson on His Majesty's Government. Richard Porson. FaBoCo

Your Friend. Anselm Hollo. TwMBP

Your friends come fondly to your living room. Birthday Card for a Psychiatrist. Mona Van Duyn. IHMS

Your ghost will walk, you lover of trees. "De Gustibus." Robert Browning. InPS

Your hair all wrinkled and you full of sweat, your. I Can Tell by the Way You Smell. *Unknown.* BluL

Your Hands. Angelina Weld Grimké. PoBA

Your hands lie open in the long fresh grass. Silent Noon. Dante Gabriel Rossetti. *Fr.* The House of Life. OBP

Your head is so fragrant tonight that only the sky is above it. Only the Sky. Pete Winslow. MIT

Your health, Master Willow. Contrive me a bat. Tree Party. Louis MacNeice. OxBTC

Your husband will be with us at the treat. To His Mistress. Ovid, *tr. by* Dryden. BoLoP

Your learning, James, in classics and romance. A Letter to a Teacher of English. Robert Hillyer. PAIC

Your leaves bound up compact and fair. To an Author. Philip Freneau. AmVN; NOBA

Your letter came.—Glutted the earth and cold. A Winter-piece to a Friend Away. John Berryman. NOBA

Your little voice, E. E. Cummings. OLR

Your love is dead, lady, your love is dead. Madrigal. R. S. Thomas. BoLoP

Your love lacks joy, your letter says. Coventry Patmore. *Fr.* The Victories of Love. GBL

Your love, love. The Lover to Himself. David Phillips. NeAC

Your midriff sags toward your knees. Woman with Girdle. Anne Sexton. NCSH; NoAM; SFF

Your mind and you are our Sargasso Sea. Portrait d'une Femme. Ezra Pound. NoAM; NOBA; PPP; SoSe

Your Name upon the Sand. Walter Savage Landor. *Fr.* Ianthe. BuTh

Your nurse could only speak Italian. Sailing Home from Rapallo. Robert Lowell. NoAM

Your Own Image. Michael Ryan. HeS

Your parents don't like me. Farewell, Sweet Mary. *Unknown.* AmFP

Your smiles are not, as other women's be. To the Lady May. Aurelian Townsend. GBL

Your smiling, or the hope, the thought of it. A Simile for Her Smile. Richard Wilbur. InPK; OLR; WIF

Your soul is a sealed garden. Clair de Lune. Paul Verlaine, *tr. by* Arthur Symons. Moon

Your tears, Niobe. Hayden Carruth. VGW

Your thighs are appletrees. Portrait of a Lady. William Carlos Williams. NoAM; NOBA

Your turn. Grass of confusion. Journal for My Daughter. Stanley Kunitz. RRA

Your voice always whacked me right on the funny bone. Burying Blues for Janis. Marge Piercy. NeAC; WBN

Your voice at times a fist. To a Husband. Maya Angelou. IHMS

Your voice is the color of a robin's breast. To O.E.A. Claude McKay. BPo

Your wand,/ the flowering stalk of the radish. The Magician. Diane Wakoski. Psy

Your yen two will slay me suddenly. *See* Your eyen two...

You're. Sylvia Plath. NCSH

Your're a Grand Old Flag, *with music.* George M. Cohan. FSN

Your're a mean mistreating mama. Mean Mistreater Mama. *Unknown.* BluL

"You're fired, Lane." The Water-Truck. Patrick Lane. NeAC

You're going into play? An instant more. To a Baseball. *Unknown.* SPo

You're Going to Reap Just What You Sow. *Unknown.* AmFP

You're having a helluva good time. Girl with Car and Guitar. Ralph Mecklenburger. SFF

You're In the Army Now, *with music. Unknown.* BLSo

You're Not the Only Pebble on the Beach, *with music.* Harry Braisted. FSN

You're Nothing But a Spanish Colored Kid. Felipe Luciano. PoBA

You're probably wondering. Little Keats' Soliloquy. Leon Stokesbury. NVAP

You're the Flower of My Heart. Richard H. Gerard. *See* Sweet Adeline.

You're too late. The Blues: a Literary Eclogue. Byron. MBPR

Youre ugly tokyn. Uppon a Deedmans Hed. John Skelton. AAS

Yours is a benison. Pregnancy. Mira Fish. FAF

Yourself. Jones Very. AmVN; NOBA

Youth and Age. Samuel Taylor Coleridge. MBPR

Youth and Beauty. Aurelian Townsend. GBL

Youth and Beauty. William Carlos Williams. RRA

Youth and Love. John Gay. *Fr.* The Beggar's Opera, II, i. NOBE

Youth and Love. Robert Louis Stevenson. SLP

Youth and the Northwind, The. John Godfrey Saxe. PoTa

Youth gone, and beauty gone if ever there. Christina Rossetti. *Fr.* Monna Innominata. GBL

Youth in apparel that glittered, A. The Black Riders, XXVII. Stephen Crane. PiAm

Youth Mowing, A. D. H. Lawrence. NoAM

Youth of delight come hither. The Voice of the Ancient Bard. Blake. *Fr.* Songs of Experience. MBPR

Youth one day in a garden fair, A. The Story of the Rose. "Alice." FSN

Youth walks up to the white horse, to put its halter on, The. The White Horse. D. H. Lawrence. PSN

Youth's the season made for joys. Youth and Love. John Gay. *Fr.* The Beggar's Opera, II, i. NOBE

You've got nice knees. Love Song. Gavin Ewart. OxBTC

You've got to cross that lonesome valley. The Lonesome Valley. *Unknown.* RDB

You've gotten in through the transom. To a Child Trapped in a Barber Shop. Philip Levine. InPK; NoAM; NOBA; VGW

You've heard of the Gresford disaster. The Gresford Disaster. *Unknown.* AIW; GBP; PeBB

You've plucked a curlew, drawn a hen. On an Island. J. M. Synge. BIrV

You've seen coalminers coming up. Underworld. George Garrett. SS

Ys yt possyble. *See* Is it possible.

Yucca clump, The/ is blooming. The Yucca Moth. A. R. Ammons. NOBA

Yugoslav Cemetery. Celeste Turner Wright. WPE

Yuh Lookin Good. Carolyn M. Rodgers. BPo

Yule Days, The. *Unknown.* GBP

Yule's Come, and Yule's Gane. *Unknown.* GBP

# Z

Zalka Peetruza. Ray Garfield Dandridge. PoBA

Zapata and the Landlord. A. B. Spellman. PoBA

Zebra. "Isak Dinesen." MiP; RFM

Zebra, born both black and white, The. The Miscegenous Zebra. Roland Young. BoAnP

Zebra Dun, The, *diff. versions.* *Unknown.* AmFP; PoTa

Zeenty, peenty, heathery, mithery. *Unknown.* GBP

Zekiel Saw the Wheel. *Unknown.* WIF

Zepheria, *sel.* *Unknown.*
   "When we in kind embracements had agre'd." AAS

Zero/ zero/ zero/ the museum of modern art. The Story of the Zeros. Victor Hernandez Cruz. PoBA

Zeus lies in Ceres' bosom. Cantos, LXXXI. Ezra Pound. NoAM; NOBA; VGW

Zimmer Drunk and Alone, Dreaming of Old Football Games. Paul Zimmer. MAT

Zimri: the Duke of Buckingham. Dryden. *Fr.* Absalom and Achitophel, Pt. I. NOBE

Zion's Sons and Daughters. *Unknown.* AmFP

Zip Coon, *with music.* *Unknown.* PSoN

Zizi's Lament. Gregory Corso. Epi; VGW

Zodiac Rhyme, The. *Unknown.* GBP

Zolgotz. *Unknown.* AmFP

Zone. Louise Bogan. WPE

Zone of Death. William Everson. VGW

Zong, A: "O Jenny, don't sobby! vor I shall be true." William Barnes. BoLoP

Zoo day, today. And How It Goes. Anselm Hollo. TwMBP

Zooming across the sky. Up in the Air. James S. Tippett. ECBV

# Author Index

"A. N." *See* "N., A."

**Aaron, Jonathan**
Death of the Sports-car Driver, The.

**Abbe, George**
I Saw an Army.
Last Patch of Snow.
My Friend, the Doctor.
Skill in Killing, A.

**Abercrombie, Lascelles**
Epitaph: "Sir, you should notice me: I am the Man."

**Abse, Dannie**
Duality.
French Master, The.
Night Out, A.
Portrait of a Marriage.
Second Coming, The.
Victim of Aulis, The.

**Acconci, Vito Hannibal**
Re.

**Ackerson, Duane**
When Daddy Died.

**Acorn, Milton**
Blackfish Poem.
Ghostly Story.
I'd Like to Mark Myself.
I've Gone and Stained with the Color of Love.
Lover That I Hope You Are.
Monument.
Offshore Breeze.
On Saint-Urbain Street.
Poem for a Singer.
Saint-Henri Spring.

**Adam, Helen**
House o' the Mirror, The.
I Love My Love.

**Adamo, Ralph**
Easter Sunday: Not the Artist.
Low along the River.

**Adams, Bob, Paul Schindler** *and* **David Lewis.** *See* **Lewis, David, Paul Schindler** *and* **Bob Adams**

**Adams, Elijah**
Ashland Tragedy, The, 2 *versions.*

**Adams, Franklin Pierce ("F. P.A.")**
Rich Man, The.
Such Stuff as Dreams.

**Adams, Herbert R.**
He Don't Know the Inside Feel.

**Adams, Léonie**
Caryatid.
Figurehead, The.

**Adams, Sarah Flower (Mrs. William Bridges Adams)**
Nearer, My God, to Thee, *with music.*

**Adamson, Robert**
Final Solstice, The.
Sail Away.
Sonnets to Be Written from Prison.

**Adcock, Fleur**
Note on Propertius 1.5.

**Addison, Joseph**
Ode: "Spacious firmament on high, The."
When rising from the bed of death.

**"Adeler, Max" (Charles Heber Clark)**
In Memoriam.
Sacred to the Memory of Maria (To Say Nothing of Jane and Martha) Sparks.

**Adler, Lucile**
Traveling Out, The.

**"Æ" (George William Russell)**
Exiles.
Germinal.
Vesture of the Soul, The.

**Aesop (6th century B. C.)**
Ass in the Lion's Skin, The.

**Agathias Scholasticus**
Dialogue.

**Ai (Florence Anthony)**
Anniversary, The.
But What I'm Trying to Say Mother Is.
Country Midwife, The: A Day.
Cuba, 1962.
Everything: Eloy, Arizona, 1956
Hangman.
Possessions.
Root Eater, The.
Twenty Year Marriage.
Unexpected, The.
Why Can't I Leave You?

**Aiken, Conrad**
Accomplices, The.
And in the Hanging Gardens.
Annihilation.
Bread and Music.
Crab, The.
Dear Uncle Stranger.
Discordants, *sel.*
Hatteras Calling.
Herman Melville.
Letter from Li Po, A, *sel.*
Lovers, The.
Morning Dialogue.
Morning Song.
Preludes for Memnon, *sels.*
Priapus and the Pool, *sels.*
Quarrel, The.
Rimbaud and Verlaine, precious pair of poets.
Room, The.
Senlin; a Biography, *sel.*
Sonnet: "Imprimis: I forgot all day your face."
Sonnet: "My love, I have betrayed you seventy times."
Summer.
Time in the Rock; or, Preludes to Definition,*sels.*

**Aikin, John**
Tit for Tat: A Tale.

**Aikin, Lucy**
Beggar Man, The.
Swallow, The.

**Ainger, Alfred**
On the Triumph of Rationalism.

**Akahito (Yamabe no Akahito)**
I wish I were close.

**Akhmadulina, Bella**
Fifteen Boys.

**"Akhmatova, Anna" (Anna Andreyevna Gorenko)**
Guest, The.
I wrung my hands under my dark veil.

**Alabaster, William**
Incarnatio Est Maximum Dei Donum.

**Alba, Nanina**
Be Daedalus.
For Malcolm X.

**Albert, Richard E.**
Malfunction.

**Albright, Rachel**
LaSalle Street.
Steel Mills.

**Aldan, Daisy**
Christmas.
Everywhere in constancy, He is intoning, Look! Look!
Green at Colmar.
I Am Moved by a Necessity from Within.
No longer will I close an opaque door.
Snow in Summer.
Vertical Is Our New Sight.

**Alderson, A. F.**
Montezuma.

**Aldington, Richard**
Evening.

**Aldis, Dorothy**
Blum.
Island, The.
Supper for a Lion.
What Happened.
When.
When I Was Lost.

**Aldrich, Henry**
Five Reasons, The.

**Alexander, Cecil Frances (Mrs. William Alexander)**
All Things Bright and Beautiful.
Beggar Boy, The.
Fieldmouse, The.
Jesus Calls Us, *with music.*
Once in Royal David's City.
There Is a Green Hill.

**Alexander, Lewis**
Dream Song.
Enchantment.
Negro Woman.
Nocturne Varial.

**Alexander, Sir William.** *See* **Stirling, William Alexander, Earl of**

**Ali, Muhammed (Cassius Clay)**
Clay Comes Out to Meet Terrell.
I Dance and I Have a Fast Hook.

**"Alice"**
Story of the Rose, The, *with music.*

**Alighieri, Dante.** *See* **Dante Alighieri**

**Allcock, John**
Death Is a Door.
Looking Up.

**Allen, Dick**
American Gothic, An.
Depression: My Father Speaks to My Mother.
Normal Lives.
Podunk, 1941.

Present, The.
Staying Married.
To a Woman Half a World Away.
Writer's House, The.
**Allen, Edward**
Best Line Yet, The.
**Allen, Grace Elisabeth**
Pinkletinks.
**Allen, James B.**
Homecoming, The.
Night Shift at the Plating Division of
　Keeler Brass.
**Allen, John Alexander**
Word to a Father, Dead, A.
**Allen, Leslie Holdsworth**
Reaper, The.
**Allen, Paula Gunn**
Lament of My Father, Lakota.
**Allen, Samuel ("Paul Vesey")**
Dylan, Who Is Dead.
If the Stars Should Fall.
Moment Please, A.
Staircase, The ("Stairs mount to his
　eternity, The").
To Satch.
**Allingham, William**
Dream, The [or A].
Eviction, The.
Fairies, The.
Laurence Bloomfield in Ireland, *sel.*
Memory, A.
Mill, A.
Riding.
Robin Redbreast.
Wishing.
**Allison, Drummond**
No Remedy.
**Allott, Kenneth**
Lament for a Cricket Eleven.
**Alma-Tadema, Laurence**
If No One Ever Marries Me.
**Alpaugh, Ern** *and* **Dewey G. Pell**
Swinging Chick.
**Alta**
After Reading Sylvia Plath.
And Why Are All the Voices I Hear
　Divided into Colors?
Anybody Could Write This Poem. All
　You Have to Say Is Yes.
Art of Enforced Deprivation, The.
Car has pulled up outside, A.
Don 1958.
Euridice.
Fight my dependency.
Firebird.
First Pregnancy.
He asked me what was I fantasizing.
How can people stand to be around me?
　I'm always babbling.
I slept alone last nite but when you
　know you dont have to.
Penus envy, they call it.
Stockton State Mental Hospital 1962.
**Ames, Bernice**
Country of Water.
**Amichai, Yehuda**
Pity, A; We Were Such a Good
　Invention.
Quick and Bitter.
We Did It.
**Amini, Johari.** *See* **Latimore, Jewel C.**

**Amis, Kingsley**
Aberdarcy: the Main Square.
After Goliath.
Against Romanticism.
Beowulf.
Bookshop Idyll, A.
Dream of Fair Women, A.
Ever-fixed Mark, An.
New Approach Needed.
St. Asaph's.
**Ammons, Archie Randolph**
After Yesterday.
Apologia pro Vita Sua.
Arc Inside and Out, The.
Auto Mobile.
Cascadilla Falls.
City Limits, The.
Classic.
Conserving the Magnitude of Uselessness
Coon Song.
Corsons Inlet.
Cut the Grass.
Dark Song.
Diner.
Gravelly Run.
Hardweed Path Going.
He Held Radical Light.
Hymn: "I know if I find you I will have
　to leave the earth."
Identity.
Laser.
Loss.
Periphery.
Plunder.
Prospecting.
Runoff.
Saying.
Small Song.
So I Said I Am Ezra.
Spring Coming.
Terrain.
Triphammer Bridge.
Unifying Principle, The.
Unsaid.
Upland.
Working with Tools.
**Amorosi, Ray**
Nothing Inside and Nothing Out.
**Anania, Michael**
Reeving.
Return.
Riversong.
**Andersen, Hans Christian**
Pearl, The.
**Anderson, Bill**
Letter from a Black Soldier.
Outbreak.
**Anderson, Ethel Louisa Mason**
Bucolic Eclogues, *sel.*
Clipper *Dunbar* to the clipper *Cutty
　Sark*, The.
**Anderson, Forrest**
Metropole.
Tiki.
True Religion.
**Anderson, Jack**
Aesthetics of the Moon.
Invention of New Jersey, The.
**Anderson, Jon**
Blue Animals, The.
Campaign for Peace in Our Time, The.
In Autumn.

John Clare.
Lives of the Saints.
Mouths of the Poor, The.
Parachutist, The.
Photograph of Myself, The.
Rosebud.
Stories.
Years.
**Anderson, S. E.**
Junglegrave.
Sound of Afroamerican History Chapt I,
　The.
Sound of Afroamerican History Chapt
　II, The.
**Anderson, Sherwood**
Evening Song.
**Andrewes, Francis**
Shepherdess' Valentine, *sel.*
**Andrews, Jenne**
Autumn Horses.
In Pursuit of the Family.
Reach of Winter, The.
Sounding.
Wife.
Words from Storms and Geese in the
　Morning.
**Angelou, Maya**
They Went Home.
To a Husband.
**Angus, Marion**
Anemones.
Mary's Song.
**Anthony Florence.** *See* **Ai**
**Antoninus, Brother.** *See* **Everson, William.**
**Apollinaire, Guillaume**
Mirabeau Bridge, The.
Moonlight.
**Applegarth, George S.**
Charge of the Grid Brigade.
**Appleman, Philip**
Black Is Beautiful.
Memo to the 21st Century.
**Applewhite, James**
Dream of Ascent.
My Grandfather's Funeral.
Versions of Sunlight.
War Summer.
**Arberg, H. W.** *and* **Edmund L. Gruber.**
　*See* **Gruber, Edmund L.** *and* **H. W.**
　**Arberg**
**Archilochos**
On the Daughter of Lykambes.
**Arden, R. P.**
On Dr. Samuel Ogden.
**Armour, Richard**
Common Carrier.
Copy.
Enticer.
Fish Story.
Good Sportsmanship.
High Chair and Low Spirits.
Library.
Seasonal Phenomenon.
Watchdog.
**"Armytage, R."** *See* **Watson, Rosamund
　Marriot**
**Arnold, Lila**
Paisley Ceiling, The.
**Arnold, Matthew**
Buried Life, The.
Cruel, but composed and bland.
Dover Beach.

Dream, A.
Empedocles on Etna, *sel.*
Growing Old
In Harmony with Nature.
Last Word, The.
Matthias,*sels.*
Palladium.
Philomela.
Requiescat.
Scholar-Gipsy, The.
Self-Dependence.
So, some tempestuous morn in early
  June.
Sohrab and Rustum, *sel.*
Song of Callicles, The.
Switzerland, *sel.*
Thyrsis.
To a Friend.
To a Republican Friend, 1848.
To Marguerite ("Yes! in the sea
  enisled").

**Arraya, Hailu**
Marital Journey, The.

**Arundel, Anne Howard, Duchess of.** *See*
  **Howard, Anne, Duchess of Arundel**

**Asbaje, Juana de.** *See* **Juana Inés de la**
  **Cruz, Sister**

**Asbery, John**
Civilization and Its Discontents.
Definition of Blue.
Dido.
Forties Flick.
How much longer will I be able to
  inhabit the divine sepulcher.
Idiot, The.
Instruction Manual, The.
Last Month.
Leaving the Atocha Station.
Märchenbilder.
No Way of Knowing.
One Thing That Can Save America,
  The.
Our Youth.
Painter, The.
Picture of Little J. A. in a Prospect of
  Flowers, The.
Rivers and Mountains.
Some Trees.
Soonest Mended.
Spring Day.
Task, The.
Tennis Court Oath, The.
Tenth Symphony.
These Lacustrine Cities.
They Dream Only of America.
Thoughts of a Young Girl.
Two Sonnets.
Vase of Flowers, A.
Worsening Situation.
Years of Indiscretion.
Young Prince and the Young Princess,
  The.

**Asheron, Sara**
Echo.
How Come?

**Ashmore, John**
Ex M. Antonio Flaminio, Ad Agellum
  Suum.

**Askew, Anne**
Ballad Which Anne Askew Made and
  Sang When She Was in Newgate, The.

**Asquith, Herbert**

Birthday Gifts.
Hairy Dog, The.
Volunteer, The.

**Asturias, Miguel Angel**
Indians Come Down from Mixco, The.

**Atkins, Russell**
It's Here in The.
Narrative.
Night and a Distant Church.
On the Fine Arts Garden, Cleveland.

**Atwood, Margaret**
Accident Has Occurred, The.
After All You Are Quiet.
After the agony in the guest/ bedroom.
Against Still Life.
At first I was given centuries.
Carrying Food Home in Winter.
Eden Is a Zoo.
First Element.
First Prayer.
Fishbowl.
Game After Supper.
I can change my-/ self more easily.
Interview with a Tourist.
It Is Dangerous to Read Newspapers.
Landlady, The.
Late August.
Midwinter, Presolstice.
Provisions.
Revenant, The.
Stories In Kinsman's Park.
Their Attitudes Differ.
There Is Only One of Everything.
They Eat Out.
This year I intended children.
We are standing facing each other.
Woman Skating.
You Are Happy.
You fit into me.
You refuse to own.
You want to go back.
Your back is rough all.

**Aubert, Alvin**
Bessie Smith's Funeral.
Codicil.
Last Will and Testament.
Nat Turner in the Clearing.

**Audelay, John**
Dread of Death.
Fairest Flower, The.
Love of God, The.
Passion of Christ Strengthen Me.
What Tidings?

**Auden, Wystan Hugh**
As I Walked Out One Evening.
At the Manger Mary Sings.
Average, The.
Brussels in Winter.
Casino.
Chorus: "Summer holds, The: upon its
  glittering lake."
Chorus: "You are the town and we are
  the clock."
Consider ("Consider this and in our
  time.").
Dear, though the night is gone.
Dog Beneath the Skin, The, *sels.*
Epitaph for the Unknown Soldier.
Epitaph on a Tyrant.
Exiles, The.
Fairground.
Fall of Rome, The.

Fish in the unruffled lakes.
Gare du Midi.
Good-Bye to the Mezzogiorno.
Horae Canonica, *sel.*
If I Could Tell You.
In Due Season.
In Memory of W. B. Yeats.
In Praise of Limestone.
James Watt.
Lady Weeping at the Crossroads.
Law Like Love.
Letter, The.
Love Feast, The.
Lullaby: "Lay your sleeping head, my
  love."
Miss Gee.
Missing.
Moon Landing.
Musée des Beaux Arts.
New Year Letter, *sel.*
Night Mail.
No Change of Place.
O What Is That Sound.
O Where Are You Going?
On the Circuit.
On This Island.
Orators, The, *sel.*
Our Bias.
Our Hunting Fathers.
Parable.
Prologue: "By landscape reminded once
  of his mother's figure."
Quarry, The.
Sea and the Mirror, *sel.*
Sext.
Shield of Achilles, The.
Since.
Sir Rider Haggard.
Song: "Deftly, admiral, cast your fly."
Song of the Master and Boatswain.
Sonnets from China, *sel.*
Summer Night, A.
That Night When Joy Began.
This Lunar Beauty.
Unknown Citizen, The.
Up There.
Victor Was a Little Baby.
Voice of Caesar, The.
Wanderer, The.
When Statesmen gravely say "We must
  be realistic."
Who's Who.
Why are the public buildings so high?

**Audiberti, Jacques**
If I die let my widow go.

**"Aunt Effie."** *See* **Browne, Jane Euphemia**

**Austin, Alfred**
Human Tragedy, The, *sel.*
Winter is gone, and spring is over.

**Austin, Mary**
Grizzly Bear.
Sandhill Crane, The.

**Avison, Margaret**
For Tinkers Who Travel on Foot.
Nameless One, A.
Tennis.
Two Selves, The.

**Axelrod, Susan**
Home, The.

**Ayton, Sir Robert**
Inconstancy Reproved.

**Aytoun, William Edmonstoune**

Execution of Montrose, The.
Massacre of the Macpherson, The.
Old Scottish Cavalier, The.
Sonnet to Britain.
Widow of Glencoe, The, *sel.*

**Aytoun, William E.** *and* **Sir Theodore Martin**
Lay of the Lovelorn, The.

# B

**"B. V." ("Bysshe Vanolis").** *See* **Thomson, James (1834-1882)**

**Babcock, Maltbie Davenport**
Be Strong.

**Bacon, Francis**
World, The.
World's a Bubble, The.

**Bacon, Leonard**
Richard Tolman's Universe.

**Bahe, Liz Sohappy**
And What of Me?
Farewell: "You sang round-dance songs."
Grandmother Sleeps.
Once Again.
Parade, The.
Printed Words.
Ration Card, The.
Talking Designs.

**Baillie, Joanna**
Tiger at Play.
Trysting Bush, The.

**Baker, Donald W.**
Formal Application.

**Baker, Prentice**
Moth, The.
Pine Assessor, The.
Virgin Jewess, Rising with a Cry, The.

**Baker, Verna Tomlinson**
Bird ecstatic with the spring, A.
Clarity of spring, The.
Night filled, A:/ Light pinning the dark.

**Ballard, Charles G.**
Changing of the Guard.
During the Pageant at Medicine Lodge.
Man of Property, The.
Navajo Girl of Many Farms.
Now the People Have the Light.
Time Was the Trail Went Deep.
You Northern Girl.

**Bantock, Gavin**
Bard.
Blame.
Christ, *sel.*
Dirge: "Body lies under the ground."
Hiroshima, *sel.*
Ichor, *sel.*
Japan.
Joy.
Person, *sel.*

**Baraka, Imamu Amiri.** *See* **Jones, LeRoi**

**Barba, Sharon**
Cycle of Women, A.
Dropping Toward Stillness.
Letter Reaching Out to My Sister, 1600 Miles.
Thanksgiving.

**Barbauld, Anna Laetitia**
Mouse's Petition, The.

**Barbour, John**
Bruce, The, *sel.*

**Barham, Richard Harris.** *See* **"Ingoldsby, Thomas"**

**Baring-Gould, Sabine**
Now the Day Is Over.
Onward, Christian Soldiers, *with music.*

**Barker, George**
In Memory of a Friend.
On a Friend's Escape from Drowning off the Norfolk Coast.
Secular Elegies, *sel.*
Sonnet to My Mother.
To Any Member of My Generation.
To My Mother.
Turn on Your Side and Bear the Day to Me.
Wild Dreams of Summer What Is Your Grief.

**Barker, Jane**
Coming from —— in a Dark Night.
Epitaph on the Secretary to the Muses.
In Commendation of the Female Sex.
Parting with——.

**Barks, Coleman**
Achilles Tendon
Adam's Apple.
Back Just Below the Shoulder Blades.
Body Poems, *sels.*
Brain.
Bruises.
Cheek.
Dimple.
Downy Hair in the Shape of a Flame.
Genitals.
Hair on the Chest.
Liver.
Mule, The.
Scar.
Semen.
Skeleton.
Skull.
Tic.
White Crescents at the Bottoms of Fingernails.

**Barksdale, Clement**
Upon the Decease of My Infant Lady.

**Barlow, Joel**
Advice to a Raven in Russia.
Columbiad, The, *sel.*
Hasty Pudding, The.

**Barnes, Barnabe**
Parthenophil and Parthenophe, *sels.*

**Barnes, Jim**
Autobiography: Last Chapter.
Bone Yard.
Camping Out on Rainy Mountain.
Captive Stone, The.
Halcyon Days.
Last Look at La Plata, Missouri.
Lying in a Yuma Saloon.
Paiute Ponies.
Sunday dreamer's Guide to Yarrow, Missouri, A.
Sweating It Out on Winding Stair Mountain.
These Damned Trees Crouch.
Tracking Rabbits: Night.
Year's End.

**Barnes, Julians**

Book of Hunting, *sels.*

**Barnes, William**
Day's Work a-Done.
Eclogue: The Common a-Took In.
Evenen in the Village.
Father Out, an' Mother Hwome, A.
Grammer's Shoes.
Hallowed Pleaces.
Heedless o' My Love.
In the Spring.
Lydlinch Bells.
Milken Time.
Mother's Dream, The.
Musings.
My Love's Guardian Angel.
Naighbour Playmeates.
Sonnet: "In every dream thy lovely features rise."
Storm-Wind, The.
Water Crowvoot, The.
White an' Blue.
Wife a-Lost, The.
Wind at the Door, The.
Winter Night, A.
Woak Hill.
Woodley.
Zong, A: "O Jenny, don't sobby! vor I shall be true."

**Barnfield, Richard**
If musique and sweet poetrie agree.
Philomel.

**Baron, Robert**
To Eliza, with a Tulip-fashioned Watch.

**Barrax, Gerald William**
Black Narcissus.
Christmas 1959 Et Cetera
Efficiency Apartment.
For Malcolm: After Mecca.
Fourth Dance Poem.
To a Woman Who Wants Darkness and Time.
Your Eyes Have Their Silence.

**Barron, W. F.**
To the Men Who Hold the Line.

**Barrows, Anita**
Emigration.
Fire.
Letter to a Friend in an Unknown Place.
Mutant, The.
Reflections.

**Bart-Williams, Gaston**
God Bless Us.

**Barton, Joan**
Mistress, The.

**Basho (Matsuo Basho)**
Haiku: "Lightning gleam, A."
Haiku: "New moon in the sky."

**Bass, Ellen**
Celia.
I am the sorrow in the wheat fields.
In Celebration.
Partly to My Cat.
September 7.

**Bass, Madeline**
Continuing.
To My Former Student on the Occasion of Birth.
To the Mother from Scarsdale Who Asked About Publishing Her Daughter's Poems.

**Baster, Andrew**
Judas.

**Bastian, Richard**
Good Friday.
Night Thoughts.
Poem for One Who Bares a Pome, A.
**Bates, David**
Speak Gently.
**Bates, G. E.**
Pentagonia.
**Bates, Katherine Lee**
America the Beautiful.
**Bates, Scott**
Fable of the Talented Mockingbird.
Fable of the Transcendent Tannenbaum.
Whales.
**Baudelaire, Charles**
Abyss, The.
Damned Women.
Injured Moon, The.
Inward Conversation.
Meditation.
Peace, Be at Peace, O Thou My
    Heaviness.
Sadness of the Moon, The.
To the Reader.
**Baxter, James Keir**
Old Man Jeremy.
Shepherd, The.
Spring-Heeled Jack.
**Baxter, Lydia**
Take the Name of Jesus with You, *with
    music.*
**Bayes, Nora** and **Jack Norworth**
Shine on, Harvest Moon, *with music.*
**Bayly, Thomas Haynes**
Gaily the Troubadour, *with music.*
Long, Long Ago, *with music.*
**"Beachcomber."** *See* **Morton, John
    Bingham**
**Beattie, James**
Question, The.
**Beattie, James Hay**
On the Author of the *Treatise of Human
    Nature.*
**Beaumont, Francis**
On the Tombs in Westminster Abbey.
    *At. to*
Pining for Love.
**Beaumont, Francis** and **John Fletcher**
Maid's Tragedy, The, *sels.*
**Beaumont, Sir John**
Of My Dear Son, Gervase Beaumont.
Relish of the Muse, The.
**Beaumont, Joseph**
Gnat, The.
Home ("Home's home, although it
    reachèd be").
Honour ("Ambitious sir, take heed!").
Jesus Inter Ubera Mariae.
Oath, The.
Psyche or Love's Mystery, *sels.*
**Beausoleil, Laura**
Night of Dreams.
On the Border of Impossibility.
Sunday.
**Beauvais, Phyllis (Phyllis Harris)**
Outside.
Under Your Voice, among Legends.
**Beaver, Bruce**
Lauds and Plaints, *sels.*
Letters to Live Poets, *sel.*
**Beckett, Samuel**
Age is when to a man.

Alba.
Enueg II.
Gnome.
I would like my love to die.
What would I do without this world
    faceless incurious.
Whoroscope.
Words and Music, *sel.*
**Bedard, Michael**
Playground, The.
**Beddoes, Thomas Lovell**
Bridal Song.
Death's Jest Book, *sels.*
Dream-Pedlary.
Resurrection Song.
Sibilla's Dirge.
Song: "Old Adam, the carrion crow."
Song from the Waters.
Wolfram's Dirge.
**Beebe, Lucius**
Quid Restat, *abr.*
**Beedome, Thomas**
Inquisition, The.
To the Noble Sir Francis Drake.
**Beer, Patricia**
Dream of Hanging, A.
Lion Hunts.
Pardoner's Tale Blues.
**Beerbohm, Max**
Luncheon, A.
On the Imprint of the First English
    Edition of "The Works of Max
    Beerbohm."
**Beers, Ethel Lynn**
All Quiet Along the Potomac To-Night,
    *with music.*
**Behn, Aphra**
Abdelazer, *sel.*
Disappointment, The.
Dutch Lover, The, *sels.*
Emperor of the Moon,*sels.*
Lucky Chance, The, *sel.*
Ode to Love, An.
On Her Loving Two Equally.
Song: "Ah false Amyntas, can that
    hour."
Song: "All joy to mortals, joy and
    mirth."
Song: "Curse upon that faithless maid,
    A."
Song: "Love in fantastic triumph sate."
Song: "Oh! Love, that stronger art than
    wine."
Song by the Wavering Nymph.
Thousand Martyrs I Have Made, A.
To the Fair Clarinda, Who Made Love
    to Me, Imagin'd More than Woman.
Voyage to the Island of Love, A, *sel.*
Westminster Drollery, 1671.
Willing Mistriss, The.
**Behn, Harry**
Circles.
Counting.
Near and Far.
New Little Boy, The.
Tea Party.
Winter Evening.
**"Belasco, F."** *See* **Rosenfeld, Monroe F.**
**Belford, Ken**
Beside the Road
Blueline.
Branches Back Into.

Dusk.
For Kelley.
Glove Glue.
Hunchbacked and corrected.
In spots/ it is warm enough.
New Potatoes.
Peanuts.
Stove.
**Belitt, Ben**
Moon Walk.
Spool, The.
**Bell, DeWitt**
Motorcyclist's Song, The.
**Bell, Martin**
Ultimate Anthology.
Winter Coming On.
**Bell, Marvin**
About That.
Acceptance Speech.
American Poets.
Delicate Bird Who Is Flying Up Our
    Asses, The.
From a Distance.
Gemwood.
Her Dream House.
Here.
Impotence.
In the Home.
On Returning to Teach.
Perfection of Dentistry, The.
Residue of Song.
Song: Organic Years, The.
3 Stanzas about a Tree.
Treetops.
**Bell, William**
On a Dying Boy.
To a Lady on Her Marriage.
**Bellamy, Francis**
Pledge to the Flag, The, *with music.*
**Bellerby, Frances**
Bereft Child's First Night.
**Belloc, Hilaire**
Birds in their little nests agree.
Early Morning, The.
Fatigue.
Fragment, The: "Towards the evening of
    her splendid day."
Frog, The.
Gnu, The.
Godolphin Horne.
Ha'nacker Mill.
Hippopotamus, The.
I am a sundial, turned the wrong way
    round.
Is There Any Reward?
Jack and His Pony, Tom.
Jim, Who Ran Away from His Nurse,
    and Was Eaten by a Lion.
Juliet.
Lines for a Christmas Card.
Lines to a Don.
Lord Finchley.
Lord Lundy.
Matilda Who Told Lies, and Was
    Burned to Death.
On a General Election.
On a Sundial.
On His Books.
On Lady Poltagrue, a Public Peril.
On Mundane Acquaintances.
On Paunch, a Parasite.
On Vital Statistics.

Python, The.
Scorpion, The.
Statesman, The.
Statue, The.
Tarantella.
Vulture, The.
World's a stage, The. The trifling entrance fee.
Yak, The.

**Benedikt, Michael**
Clement Attlee.
Divine Love.
European Shoe, The.
Eye, The.
Going and Coming: Two Poems.
Grand Guignols of Love, The.
Let Me Out.
Meat Epitaph, The.
Some Feelings.
Thoughts.
To Persuade a Lady.

**Benét, Rosemary** and Stephen Vincent Benét
Nancy Hanks.

**Benét, Stephen Vincent**
Invocation: "American muse, whose strong and diverse heart."
John Brown's Body, sels.
Melora's Song.
Metropolitan Nightmare.
Mountain Whippoorwill, The.
Nightmare, with Angels.
Western Star, sel.

**Benét, William Rose**
Jesse James.

**Benlowes, Edward**
Cynthia.
Theophila; or, Love's Sacrifice, sels.

**Benn, Gottfried**
Beautiful Youth.

**Bennard, George**
Old Rugged Cross, The, with music.

**Bennett, Arnold**
Love Affair, A.

**Bennett, Benjamin K.**
Paradox.

**Bennett, Gwendolyn B.**
Hatred.
Heritage.
Sonnet: "He came in silvern armor, trimmed with black."
Sonnet: "Some things are very dear to me."
To a Dark Girl.

**Bennett, Henry Holcomb**
Flag Goes By, The.

**Bennett, John**
"He Killed Many of My Men."

**Bennett, Lerone, Jr.**
And Was Not Improved.
Blues and Bitterness.

**Bennett, Sanford Fillmore**
In the Sweet Bye-and-bye, with music.

**Benson, Stella**
Frost.
Now I Have Nothing.

**Bentley, Beth**
Birthing, The.

**Bentley, Edmund Clerihew**
Adam Smith.
Ballade of Liquid Refreshment.
Clerihews, sels.

George the Third.
John Stuart Mill.
Sir Christopher Wren.
Sir Humphry Davy.

**Bentley, Nelson**
Spouting Horn, The.

**Bentley, Wilder**
Six Reveilles to Match My Self-Indulgence, sel.

**Beresford, Anne**
Romanies in Town, The.
Saturday in New York.

**Bergé, Carol**
Blues for a Cello Man.
Lying Down Hungry.
Madonna and Daughter.
Poem for Explorers.
Position.
Rested near Nefertete.
Textures.
Third Day in a Strange City.
Where It's At.
With.

**Bergengren, Ralph Wilhelm**
Worm, The.

**Berger, Art**
March on the Delta.

**Berkeley, George**
On the Prospect of Planting Arts and Learning in America.

**Berlin, Irving**
God Bless America, with music.

**Bernard, Sidney**
Paraders for the Bomb.

**Berrigan, Daniel**
Great God Paused among Men.

**Berrigan, Ted**
Living with Chris.
Mess Occupations.
Real Life.
Resolution.
Sonnet: "Banging around in a cigarette she isn't 'in love.'"
Sonnet: "Beware of Benjamin Franklin, he is totally lacking in grace."
Sonnet: "Dear Ron: hello. Your name is now a household name."
Sonnet: "Francis Marion nudges himself gently into the big blue sky."
Sonnet: "Gray his head goes his feet green."
Sonnet: "Harum-scarum haze on the Pollock streets."
Sonnet: "How strange to be gone in a minute."
Sonnet: "How strange to be gone in a minute! A man!"
Sonnet: "I like to beat people up."
Sonnet: "I wake up back aching from soft bed Pat."
Sonnet: "In Joe Brainard's collage its white arrows."
Sonnet: "In my paintings for they are present."
Sonnet: "It is a human universe: and I."
Sonnet: "It is night. You are asleep. And beautiful tears."
Sonnet: "It's 8:54 a.m. Brooklyn it's the 28th of July and."
Sonnet: "Joyful ants nest on the roof of my tree."

Sonnet: "My dream a drink with Lonnie Johnson."
Sonnet: "Oh the 15th day of November in the year of the motorcar."
Sonnet: "Sleep half sleep half silence and with reasons."
Sonnet: "Summer so histrionic, marvelous dirty days."
Sonnet: "They basted his caption on top of the fat sheriff, 'The Pig.'"
Sonnet: "Too many fucking mosquitoes under the blazing sun."
Sonnet: "Wan as pale thighs making apple belly strides."
Sonnet: "What thwarts this fear I love."
Sonnet: "Withered leaves fly higher than dolls can see, The."
Sonnet: "Woman is singing the song and summer."
Things to Do in New York (City).

**Berry, Chuck**
Memphis, Tennessee.

**Berry, D. C.**
On Reading Poems to a Senior Class at South High.

**Berry, Wendell**
Dead Calf, The.
Enriching the Earth.
Independence Day.
Music, A.
My Great-Grandfather's Slaves.
Peace of Wild Things, The.
Satisfactions of the Mad Farmer, The.
Wet Time, A.
Wild, The.

**Berryman, John**
Again, his friend's death made the man sit still.
Animal moment, when he sorted out her tail, The.
Apollo 8.
As a kid I believed in democracy: I.
At Henry's bier let some thing fall out well.
Ball Poem, The.
Black Book, The, sel.
Canto Amor.
Come touch me baby in his waking dream.
Deprived of his enemy, shrugged to a standstill.
Dinch me, dark God, having smoked me out.
Dispossessed, The.
Dooms menace from tumults. Who's immune.
Eleven Addresses to the Lord, sels.
Filling her compact and delicious body.
Go, ill-sped book, and whisper to her or.
God bless Henry. He lived like a rat.
Governor your husband lived so long, The.
Grandfather, sleepless in a room upstairs.
He Resigns.
He yelled at me in Greek.
Henry in transition, transient Henry.
Henry's Confession.
Henry's mind grew blacker the more he thought.
Henry's pelt was put on sundry walls.
Henry's Understanding.

Map, The.
Monument, The.
Over 2000 Illustrations and a Complete
   Concordance.
Prodigal, The.
Questions of Travel.
Roosters.
Sandpiper.
Seascape.
Some Dreams They Forgot.
Twelfth Morning; or, What You Will.
Unbeliever, The.
Visits to St. Elizabeths.

**Bishop, John Peale**
Always, from My First Boyhood.
Epithalamium: "When first my beloved
   came to my bed."
Fiametta.
In the Dordogne.
O, Pioneers!
Recollection, A.

**Bishop, Morris**
For the Opening of the Hunting Season.
Melody For Lute and Ocarina.
Ozymandias Revisited.
Perforated Spirit, The.
Settling Some Old Football Scores.

**Black, D. M.**
Educators, The.

**Black, James M.**
When the Roll Is Called Up Yonder,
   *with music.*

**Black, Peter**
Man in the Bowler Hat, The.

**Blackburn, Paul**
Clickety-Clack.
Foreign Policy Commitments; or, You
   Get Into the Catamaran First, Old
   Buddy.
Good Morning Love!
Hot Afternoons Have Been in West 15th
   Street.
Invitation Standing.
Phone Call to Rutherford.
Plaza Reál with Palmtrees.
Sunflower Rock.
Watchers, The.
Yawn, The.

**Blackburn, Thomas**
Felo De Se.
Hospital for Defectives.

**Blacker, Captain**
Battle of the Boyne, The.

**Blacklock, Thomas**
Happy Marriage.

**Blades, Leslie B.**
Out of Blindness.

**Blaikley, Howard**
From the Underworld.

**Blair, Eric.**   *See* **Orwell, George**

**Blake, James W.**
Sidewalks of New York, The, *with music.*

**Blake, William**
Abstinence sows sand all over.
Ah! Sun-flower.
America a Prophecy.
Ancient Proverb, An.
And Did Those Feet in Ancient Time.
Angel, The.
Angel That Presided o'er My Birth, The.
Auguries of Innocence.
Blossom, The.

Book of Thel, The.
Book of Urizen, The.
Chimney Sweeper, The ("A little black
   thing among the snow").
Chimney Sweeper, The ("When my
   mother died I was very young").
Clod and the Pebble, The.
Cradle Song, A: "Sweet dreams form a
   shade."
Crystal Cabinet, The.
Divine Image, A ("Cruelty has a human
   heart").
Divine Image, The ("To mercy pity
   peace and love").
Dream, A.
Earth's Answer.
Echoing [*or* Ecchoing] Green, The.
Eternity ("He who binds [*or* bends] to
   himself a joy").
Fairy, The.
Fly, The.
Four Zoas, The,*sels.*
French Revolution, The.
Garden of Love, The.
Golden Net, The.
Hear the Voice of the Bard (*Introd. to
   Songs of Experience*).
Her Whole Life Is an Epigram.
Holy Thursday ("Is this a holy thing to
   see").
Holy Thursday ("'Twas on a Holy
   Thursday").
I asked a thief to steal me a peach
I feared the fury of my wind.
I laid me down upon a bank.
I Saw a Chapel All of Gold.
Infant Joy.
Infant Sorrow.
Lamb, The.
Laughing Song.
Laughter.
Let the Brothels of Paris Be Opened.
Lilly, The.
Little Black Boy, The.
Little Boy Found, The.
Little Boy Lost, A ("Nought loves
   another as itself").
Little Boy Lost, The ("Father, father,
   where are you going").
Little Girl Found, The.
Little Girl Lost, A ("Children of the
   future age").
Little Girl Lost, The ("In futurity/ I
   prophetic see").
Little Vagabond, The.
Long John Brown and Little Mary Bell.
Love's Secret.
Mad Song.
Marriage of Heaven and Hell, The.
Mary.
Mental Traveller, The.
Milton.
Mock On, Mock On, Voltaire, Rousseau.
Motto to the Songs of Innocence and of
   Experience.
My Pretty Rose Tree.
Nakedness of women, The.
Never pain to tell thy love.
Night.
Nurse's Song ("When the voices of
   children are heard on the green/ And
   laughing is heard on the hill")

Nurse's Song ("When the voices of
   children are heard on the green/ And
   whisprings are in the dale").
O why was I born with a different face?
Of the sleep of Ulro! and of the passage
   through.
On Anothers Sorrow.
On Cromek
Piper, The.
Piping Down the Valleys Wild (*Introd.* to
   Songs of Innocence).
Poison Tree, The.
Prince of Love, The.
Question Answer'd, The.
Robin Redbreast in a Cage, A, *abr.*
School Boy, The.
Secrets of the Earth, The.
Shepherd, The.
Sick Rose, The.
Silent silent night.
Sir Joshua Reynolds.
Smile, The.
Soft Snow.
Song: "Fresh from the dewy hill, the
   merry year."
Song: "How sweet I roamed [*or* roam'd]
   from field to field."
Song: "I love the jocund dance."
Song: "Love and harmony combine."
Song: "Memory, hither come."
Song: "My silks and fine array."
Song: "When early morn walks forth in
   sober grey."
Song of Liberty.
Songs of Experience, *sels.*
Songs of Innocence, *sels.*
Spring.
Tiger, The.
Tiriel, *sel.*
To Autumn.
To Nobodaddy.
To Spring.
To Summer.
To the Accuser Who Is the God of This
   World.
To the Evening Star.
To the Jews.
To the Muses.
To Tirzah.
To William Hayley.
To Winter.
Vala, Night the Ninth Being the Last
   Judgment.
Vision of Beulah, The.
Visions of the Daughters of Albion.
Voice of the Ancient Bard, The.
When Klopstock England defied.

**Bland, James A.**
Carry Me Back to Old Virginny, *with
   music.*
In the Evening by the Moonlight, *with
   music.*
Oh, Dem Golden Slippers!, *with music.*

**Blandy, E. W.**
Where He Leads Me I Will Follow, *with
   music.*

**Blight, John**
Doctor Black.
Gold Watch, The.
Home.

Larder.
Lowson.
Racialism.

**Blind, Mathilde**
Dead, The.
Lassitude.
Manchester by Night.
Mourning Women.
Reapers.
Rest.
Sakiyeh, The.
Soul-drift.
Sower, The.

**Bliss, Paul Southworth**
Lucas Park (Saint Louis).

**Bliss, Philip Paul**
Almost Persuaded, *with music.*
Wonderful Words of Life, *with music.*

**Blixen, Karen.** *See* **"Dinesen, Isak"**

**Block, Allan**
Animal, The.
Child's Drawing.
46 and Recalling.
Four Homages.
High Tension Wires.
In Noah's Wake.
In the Glue Factory.
January Thaw.
Tarzan, Old.
Through Old Farmhouse Windows.

**Blok, Alexander**
Little Catkins.

**Bloom, Robert**
Achromatic Bear, The.
As If Trooth.
Hawk, The.
In the Evening as from a Cradle.
Regenerate.

**Blossom, Henry**
Because You're You, *with music.*
Kiss Me Again, *with music.*
Streets of New York, The, *with music.*

**Blunden, Edmund**
Almswomen.
Forefathers.
Lonely Love.
Midnight Skaters, The.
Report on Experience.
Winter: East Anglia.

**Blunt, Wilfred Scawen**
Farewell to Juliet.
Love Sonnets of Proteus, The,*sels.*
St. Valentine's Day.

**Bly, Robert**
After the Industrial Revolution, All
    Things Happen at Once.
Andrew Jackson's Speech.
Asian Peace Offers Rejected without
    Publication.
Awakening.
Busy Man Speaks, A.
Clear Air of October, The.
Come with Me.
Counting Small-Boned Bodies.
Driving to Town Late to Mail a Letter.
Driving toward the Lac Qui Parle River.
Evolution from the Fish.
Fire of Despair Has Been Our Saviour,
    The.
Great Society, The.
Hearing Men Shout at Night on
    Macdougal Street.

Hunting Pheasants in a Cornfield.
Hurrying Away from the Earth.
In a Mountain Cabin in Norway.
In a Train.
In Danger from the Outer World.
Johnson's Cabinet Watched by Ants.
Late Spring Day in My Life, A.
Laziness and Silence.
Looking at Some Flowers.
Looking into a Face.
Looking into a Tide Pool.
Love Poem: "When we are in love, we
    love the grass."
Old Boards.
Poem Against the British.
Poem Against the Rich.
Poem in Three Parts.
Possibility of New Poetry, The.
Romans Angry about the Inner World.
Sleet Storm on the Merritt Parkway.
Snowfall in the Afternoon.
Solitude Late at Night in the Woods.
Summer, 1960, Minnesota.
Sunday in Glastonbury.
Surprised by Evening.
Teeth Mother Naked at Last, The.
Those Being Eaten By America.
Three Kinds of Pleasures.
Waking from Sleep.
War and Silence.
Watering the Horse.
When the Dumb Speak.
Where We Must Look for Help.
Written in Dejection Near Rome.

**Boas, Guy**
Vet, The.

**Bodet, Jaime Torres**
Love.

**Bogan, Louise**
Animal, Vegetable and Mineral.
Cassandra.
Crossed Apple, The.
Crows, The.
Dragonfly, The.
Dream, The.
Evening in the Sanitarium.
Frightened Man, The.
Henceforth, from the Mind.
Hypocrite Swift.
Late.
Medusa.
Men Loved Wholly Beyond Wisdom.
Old Countryside.
Question in a Field.
Rhyme.
Roman Fountain.
Sleeping Fury, The.
Song for the Last Act.
Spirit's Song.
To Be Sung on the Water.
Train Tune.
Women.
Zone.

**Bogardus, Edgar**
Eastward to Eden.

**Boland, C. J.**
Two Travellers, The.

**Boland, Eavan**
Requiem for a Personal Friend.
War Horse, The.

**Bold, Alan**
I drink to forget, but whenever I think.

Point of Love, The.

**Bold, Henry**
Song: "Chloris, forbear a while."
Song: "Fire, fire."

**Bolton, Edmund**
Canzone Pastoral in Honor of Her
    Majesty, A.
Palinode, A.

**Bond, Carrie Jacobs**
I Love You Truly, *with music.*
Perfect Day, A, *with music.*

**Bond, Harold**
Girls Who Wave at Cars from Bridges.
It Is Oregon, The Highway Looms.
Way It Happens to You, The.

**Bonk, James**
Acrophobe and Lapidary
Elegy for a Polish Grandaunt.
Painting an Old Apartment.

**Bontemps, Arna**
Black Man Talks of Reaping, A.
Close Your Eyes!
Day-breakers, The.
God Give to Men ("God give the yellow
    man").
Nocturne of the Wharves.
Reconnaissance.
Return, The.
Southern Mansion.

**Booth, Philip**
Big Dog.
Cold Water Flat.
Deer Isle.
Dreamscape.
Elegy for a Diver.
First Lesson.
Fisherman.
If It Comes.
Misery of Mechanics, The.
One Man's Wife.
Original Sequence.
Round, The.
Thanksgiving 1963.
Tower, The.
Was a Man.

**Boothroyd, Basil**
Best of Two Worlds.

**Bornhauser, Fred**
Wishbone, The.

**Bosley, Keith**
Number 14.

**Bossidy, John Collins**
Boston ("I come from the city of
    Boston").

**Bourdillon, Francis William**
Night has a thousand eyes, The.

**Bowering, George**
Beach at Veracruz, The.
Egg, The.
Grass, Grass.
My Atlas Poet.
Smoking Drugs with Strangers.
Solid Mountain.
Under.

**Bowers, Edgar**
Adam's Song to Heaven.
Afternoon at the Beach, An.
Amor Vincit Omnia.
Autumn Shade, *sels.*
Centaur Overheard, The.
Le Rêve.
Mountain Cemetery, The.

Prince, The.
Stoic, The: for Laura von Courten.
To the Reader.
Virgin Mary, The.
**Bowes-Lyon, Lilian**
White Hare, The.
**Bowles, William Lisle**
Bells, Ostend, The.
**Bowman, Derek**
Members of the Family.
Old Sinner.
Peeled Wand.
Root-Crops.
Slicing Button Mushrooms.
Stiff Shirts.
**Boyajian, Aram**
American Commencement.
Blok: Let Me Learn the Poem.
Death of the Epileptic Poet Yesenin, The.
George Washington Goes to a Girlie Movie.
Hairs in My Nose, The.
Poetry is in the Darkness.
World Is Really a Sugarplum House in the Forest, The.
**Boyd, Mark Alexander**
Cupid and Venus.
Fra Bank to Bank, Fra Wood to Wood I Rin.
**"Boyd, Nancy."** *See* **Millay, Edna St. Vincent**
**Boyd, Thomas**
King's Son, The.
**Boyle, Kay**
American Citizen, *sel.*
For James Baldwin.
For Marianne Moore's Birthday.
Invitation in It, The.
New Emigration, The.
October 1954.
Thunderstorm in South Dakota.
To a Proud Old Woman Watching the Tearing Down of the Hurricane Shed.
**Bradford, Walter**
Poem for Foster, A.
Poem with a Conclusion, A.
T. C.
**Bradley, Katherine** *and* **Edith Cooper.**
*See* **"Field, Michael"**
**Bradstreet, Anne**
As Weary Pilgrim, Now at Rest.
Author to Her Book, The.
Before the Birth of One of Her Children.
Childhood.
Contemplations, *abr.*
Flesh and the Spirit, The.
Four Ages of Man, The, *sel.*
In Honour of That High and Mighty Princess Queen Elizabeth of Happy Memory.
In Memory of My Dear Grandchild Elizabeth Bradstreet.
In Reference to Her Children, 23 June, 1656.
Letter to Her Husband, Absent upon Public Employment, A ("As loving hind...").
Letter to Her Husband, Absent upon Publick Employment, A ("My head, my heart, mine eyes,...").

Prologue, The: "To sing of wars, of captain[e]s, and of kings."
Upon the Burning of Our House, July 10th, 1666.
**Brady, Anne Hazlewood**
Anonymous.
Bonded.
Justice Had Become a Woman.
**Brainard, Franklin**
Inland Sea.
Raingatherer.
Roubaix Cemetery.
White Ropes.
**Braisted, Harry**
She Was Bred in Old Kentucky, *with music.*
You're Not the Only Pebble on the Beach, *with music.*
**Braithwaite, William Stanley**
Golden Moonrise.
In a Grave-Yard.
To——: "Half in the dim light from the hall."
**Brame, Terence**
Black Clouds.
No Meaning.
**Bramston, James**
Man of Taste, The, *sel.*
**Brand, Marian Frances**
Apple-Logia.
Ebony: Contemporary.
Homily: Contemporary.
**Brant, Sebastian**
Foote-Ball.
**Brathwaite, Edward**
Chad.
Mmenson.
Timbuctu.
**Brathwaite, Richard**
I Am Not as I Wish.
Nature's Embassy, *sel.*
**Braun, Richard Emil**
Domestic Duties.
Goose.
Niagara.
**Brautigan, Richard**
All Watched Over by Machines of Loving Grace.
Curiously Young Like a Freshly-dug Grave.
Day They Busted the Grateful Dead, The.
Haiku Ambulance.
Have You Ever Had a Witch Bloom Like a Highway.
Karma Repair Kit: Items 1-4.
On Pure Sudden Days Like Innocence.
Pill Versus the Springhill Mine Disaster, The.
**Braxton, Jodi**
Black Sheba.
Miss Maime.
Poem for Blackboys in Floppy Tie-Dye Hats.
**"Breitmann, Hans."** *See* **Leland, Charles Godfrey**
**Brennan, Christopher John**
Burden of Tyre, The, *sel.*
Epilogue: "O life, O radiance, love, delight."
Lilith, *sel.*
Quest of Silence, The, *sel.*

To V. S.
Towards the Source, *sel.*
Twilight of Disquietude, The, *sel.*
Wanderer, The, *sel.*
**Brennan, Eileen**
One Kingfisher and One Yellow Rose.
**Brennan, John Michael**
Air Is.
**Brennan, Joseph Payne**
Raccoon on the Road.
**Brenner, Summer**
Dede's Return to New Mexico.
For Paige.
**Brereton, Jane**
On Mr. Nash's Picture at Full Length.
**Breton, André**
Always for the first time.
Dreams.
**Breton, Nicholas**
Come, Little Babe.
Cradle Song, A: "Come, little babe, come, silly soul."
Honourable Entertainment Given to the Queen's Majesty in Progress at Elvetham, The, 1591, *sel.*
Pastoral of Phillis and Coridon, A.
Ploughman's Song, The.
Report Song in a Dream, A.
Solemn Farewell to the World, A.
**Brewster, Elizabeth**
Disqualification.
For the Unknown Goddess.
Moon.
On Reading Another Poet.
Princess Addresses the Frog Prince, The.
**Bridges, Robert**
April 1885.
Awake, my heart, to be loved, awake, awake!
Eros.
Ethick.
Growth of Love, The,*sels.*
Johannes Milton, Senex.
London Snow.
Low Barometer.
My delight and thy delight.
Nightingales.
North Wind in October.
On a Dead Child.
Passer-By, A.
Philosopher to His Mistress, The.
Poor Poll.
Screaming Tarn.
Snow Lies Sprinkled on the Beach, The.
Spring Goeth All in White.
Testament of Beauty, The, *sel.*
When we first met we did not guess.
**Bridges-Adams, W.**
Fragment from the Elizabethans.
**Brigham, Besmilr**
Dream in Cold, A.
Heaved from the Earth.
Mountains.
Rain Sleets Flat.
Sevier County Runaway, The.
State in Indian Language Was Called "Running Water," The.
Tell Our Daughters.
Tiny Baby Lizard, The.
What Is She Trying to Do, to Pattern Love.

When Cotton Haymes Walks Down the
    Street.
Will's Love, The.
**Brine, Mary Dow**
Hearts and Flowers, *with music.*
**Brinnin, John Malcolm**
Hotel Paradiso e Commerciale.
John Without Heaven.
Nuns at Eve.
Roethke Plain.
Saul, Afterward, Riding East.
**Brock, Edwin**
Clutter of Mothers, A.
D-day Minus.
Evolution.
Five Ways to Kill a Man.
Life Style, The.
Song of the Battery Hen.
To My Wife.
Turn the Key Deftly.
**Brock, Van K.**
Dead Man Creek.
Evidence, The.
Lying On a Bridge.
Sea Birds, The.
**Bromige, David**
After the Engraving.
**Bronk, William**
Aspects of the World Like Coral Reefs.
Body, The.
Feeling, The.
Metonymy as an Approach to a Real
    world.
Postcard to Send to Sumer, A.
Whether what we sense of this world.
**Brontë, Anne ("Acton Bell")**
Reminiscence, A.
**Brontë, Charlotte ("Currer Bell")**
On the Death of Anne Brontë.
**Brontë, Emily ("Ellis Bell")**
Fall, Leaves, Fall.
How Still, How Happy.
I Am the Only Being Whose Doom.
I Gazed upon the Cloudless Moon.
Last Lines.
Last Words.
Night Is Darkening Round Me.
Night-Wind, The.
Old Stoic, The.
Prisoner, The.
Remembrance.
Stanza: "I'll not weep that thou art
    going to leave me."
Stanzas to ——: "Well, some may hate,
    and some may scorn."
Visionary, The.
Warning and Reply.
**Brooke, Fulke Greville, 1st Baron.** *See*
    **Greville, Fulke, 1st Baron Brooke**
**Brooke, Rupert**
Clouds.
Dust.
Heaven.
Hill, The.
1914, *sels.*
Old Vicarage, Grantchester, The.
Peace.
Soldier, The.
Sonnet: "I said I splendidly loved you;
    it's not true."
Success.
Voice, The.

**Brooks, Fred Emerson**
Pat's Opinion of Flags.
**Brooks, Gwendolyn**
Aspect of Love, Alive in the Ice and
    Fire, An.
Ballad of Chocolate Mabbie, The.
Bean Eaters, The.
Beverly Hills, Chicago.
Big Bessie Throws Her Son into the
    Street.
Blackstone Rangers, The.
Boy Breaking Glass.
Bronzeville Man with a Belt in the Back.
Catch of Shy Fish, A.
Chicago *Defender* Sends a Man to Little
    Rock, The.
Chicago Picasso, The.
Children of the Poor, The.
Cynthia in the Snow.
Egg Boiler, The.
Empty Woman, The.
First Fight. Then Fiddle. Ply the
    Slipping String.
Jessie Mitchell's Mother.
Kitchenette Building.
Last Quatrain of the Ballad of Emmet
    Till, The.
Lovely Love, A.
Lovers of the Poor, The.
Malcolm X.
Martin Luther King, Jr.
Medgar Evers.
Mother, The.
Negro Hero.
Of De Witt Williams on His Way to
    Lincoln Cemetery.
Of Robert Frost.
Old Laughter.
Old-Marrieds, The.
Old Mary.
Paul Robeson.
Penitent Considers Another Coming of
    Mary, A.
Pete at the Zoo.
Preacher, The: Ruminates behind the
    Sermon.
Riot.
Rites for Cousin Vit, The.
Sadie and Maud.
Second Sermon on the Warpland, The.
Sermon on the Warpland, The.
Song in the Front Yard, A.
Street in Bronzeville, A: Southeast
    Corner.
Strong Men, Riding Horses.
Third Sermon on the Warpland, The.
To Be in Love.
Truth.
Two Dedications,*sels.*
Vacant Lot, The.
Wall, The.
We Real Cool.
What Shall I Give My Children?
When You Have Forgotten Sunday: The
    Love Story.
White Troops Had Their Orders, But the
    Negroes Looked Like Men, The.
Womanhood, The, *sels.*
Young Heroes.
**Brooks, Phillips**
O Little Town of Bethlehem, *with music.*
**Brooks, Shirley**

For A' That and A' That, *parody.*
"Prize" Poem, A.
**Broughton, James Richard**
Birds of America, The.
What Holds the Universe Together.
**Broughton, T. Alan**
Cave Where Night Sleeps, The.
Gift for Mary MacLane, A.
People Cannot Speak, The.
Planet Dream.
Snow Chant.
To the Other Side.
**Brown, Albert H.** *See* **Rice, Seymour** *and*
    **Albert H. Brown**
**Brown, George Mackay**
Country Girl.
Fiddler's Song.
Lord of the Mirrors, *sel.*
Shipwreck.
Wedding.
**Brown, Michael R.**
Brown Bug, The.
**Brown, Rita Mae**
Aristophanes' Symposium.
Dancing the Shout to the True Gospel;
    or, The Song Movement Sisters Don't
    Want Me to Sing.
Disconnection, The.
Fire Island.
For Every Sister in the White Man's
    Jail.
Hymn to the 10,000 Who Die Each Year
    on the Abortionist's Table in Amerika.
New Lost Feminist, The.
**Brown, Rosalie Moore.** *See* **Moore,**
    **Rosalie**
**Brown, Sterling Allen**
After Winter.
Crispus Attucks McCoy.
Foreclosure.
Long Gone.
Old Lem.
Old Woman Remembers, An.
Remembering Nat Turner.
Sister Lou.
Slim in Hell ("Slim Greer went to
    heaven").
Southern Cop.
Southern Road.
Strange Legacies.
Strong Men.
**Brown, Sydney**
Maple Leaf Rag, *with music.*
**Brown, Thomas (Tom)**
Doctor Fell.
**Brown, Thomas Edward**
My Garden.
**Browne, Jane Euphemia ("Aunt Effie")**
Great Brown Owl, The.
Little Raindrops.
Pleasant Changes.
Rooks, The.
**"Browne, Matthew."** *See* **Rands, William**
    **Brighty**
**Browne, Michael Dennis**
Hallowe'en 1971.
Iowa.
Iowa, June.
Paranoia.
Power Failure.
Roof of the World, The.
**Browne, William**

Britannia's Pastorals,*sels.*
Epigram: "King to Oxford sent a troop of horse, The."
Glide soft, ye silver floods.
In Obitum M. S. x Maij, 1614.
Inner Temple Masque, *sel.*
On the Countess Dowager of Pembroke.
On the Death of Mary, Countess of Pembroke.
Sirens' Song, The.
Song: "Choose now among this fairest number."

**Browning, Elizabeth Barrett**
Adequacy.
Bereavement.
Cry of the Children, The.
Curse for a Nation, A.
Denial, A.
Grief.
Hiram Powers' "Greek Slave."
Mother and Poet.
Musical Instrument, A.
On a Portrait of Wordsworth by B. R. Haydon.
Runaway Slave at Pilgrim's Point, The.
Song for the Ragged Schools of London, A.
Sonnets from the Portuguese,*sels.*
Tears.
To George Sand.

**Browning, Robert**
Abt Vogler.
Apparent Failure.
Asolando, *sel.*
Bishop Blougram's Apology.
Bishop Orders His Tomb at Saint Praxed's Church, The.
Cavalier Tunes.
"Childe Roland to the Dark Tower Came."
Confessional, The ("It is a lie—their Priests, their Pope").
Confessions ("What is he buzzing in my ears?").
"De Gustibus."
Epilogue: "At the midnight in the silence of the sleep-time."
Epistle, An, Containing the Strange Medical Experience of Karshish, the Arab Physician.
Face, A.
Fra Lippo Lippi, *sel.*
Garden Fancies, *sel.*
Home Thoughts from Abroad.
Home Thoughts from the Sea.
How They Brought the Good News from Ghent to Aix.
In a Gondola, *sel.*
Incident of the French Camp.
Laboratory, The: Ancien Régime.
Last Ride Together, The.
Likeness, A.
Lost Leader, The.
Lost Mistress, The.
Love among the Ruins.
Love in a Life.
May and Death.
Meeting at Night.
Moth's kiss, first, The!
My Last Duchess.
My Star.
One Word More, *sel.*

Parting at Morning.
Patriot, The.
Phases of the Moon.
Pied Piper of Hamelin, The.
Pippa Passes, *sels.*
Porphyria's Lover.
Prospice.
Rabbi Ben Ezra.
Saul.
Sibrandus Schafnaburgensis.
Soliloquy of the Spanish Cloister.
Song: "Nay but you, who do not love her."
Toccata of Galuppi's, A.
Two in the Campagna.
Unfaith and Faith.
Up at a Villa—Down in the City.
Year's at the Spring, The.
You'll Love Me Yet!

**Brownjohn, Alan**
Class Incident from Graves.
Farmer's Point of View.
For My Son.
1939.
Rabbit, The.
Railings, The.
Train,The.

**Bruce, George**
Three Love Poems for My Wife.

**Bruce, Lennart**
Hunger.
Photo, The.
Poem: "I meet Mother on the street."

**Bruchac, Joseph**
City.
Coming Back.
Drum Songs.
Elegy for Jack Bowman.
For a Winnebago Brave.
For My Grandfather in Greenfield Center.
Frozen Hands.
Grandmother Came Down to Visit Us, The.
Hiking.
How I Cancelled My Life Insurance.
Leaving the Prison.
Lost Deer, The.
Near the Old Slave Fort.
Poem for Jan.
Second Skins—A Peyote Song.
Stone Giant.
There is a stream which rises.
Three Poems for the Indian Steelworkers.

**Brush, Thomas**
Falling In Love with Tygers.
Gerard de Nerval.
Mailman, The.
Problem With Dreams, The.

**Bryan, George S.**
How Bill Went East.

**Bryan, Vincent**
In My Merry Oldsmobile, *with music.*

**Bryant, Frederick J., Jr.**
Cathexis.

**Bryant, William Cullen**
Green River.
Hymn of the City.
Indian at the Burial-Place of His Fathers, An.
Inscription for the Entrance to a Wood.

Prairies, The.
Scene on the Banks of the Hudson, A.
Song of Marion's Men.
Thanatopsis.
To a Waterfowl.
To Cole, the Painter, Departing for Europe.
To the Fringed Gentian.

**Buchan, Tom**
Camas Tuath.
Fighting Talk.
Loch Ness Monster, The.
Low Road, The.
Polemical Elegy for Reinhardt Heydrich.
Sentimental Ode.
Subversive Sublime.
Week-end Naturalist, The.

**Buchanan, Robert Williams**
Green Gnome, The.

**Buck, Richard Henry**
Dear Old Girl, *with music.*
Kentucky Babe, *with music.*

**Buckley, Tim**
Goodbye and Hello.

**Buckley, Vincent**
Fitzroy, Carlton.
Golden Builders, *sels.*
No New Thing.
Puritan Poet Reel.
Stroke,*sels.*
Telephones, Muzak.

**Buckmaster, Charles**
History of the Father, A.

**Bukowski, Charles**
Footnote upon the Construction of the Masses.
For Jane.
Loser, The.
Singular Self, The.
Sun Wields Mercy, The.
Tragedy of the Leaves, The.

**Bullett, Gerald**
Church Mouse, The.

**Bullokar, William**
To His Child.

**Bulwer-Lytton, Edward Robert, 1st Earl of Lytton.** *See* "Meredith, Owen"

**Bunner, Henry Cuyler**
Grandfather Watts's Private Fourth.

**Bunting, Basil**
Briggflatts,*sels.*
Chomei at Toyama.
Coda.
Darling of Gods and Men, beneath the gliding stars.
On the Fly-Leaf of Pound's Cantos.
Orotava Road, The.
Poet appointed dare not decline.
Vestiges.
What the Chairman Told Tom.

**Bunyan, John**
Of the Boy and Butterfly.
Of the Child with the Bird on the Bush.
Pilgrim's Progress, The, *sel.*
Shepherd Boy Sings in th Valley of Humiliation.
Upon the Horse and His Rider.
Upon the Swallow.
Upon the Weathercock.
Upon the Snail.

**Burden, Jean**
Poem before Departure.

**Burdette, Robert Jones**
  My First Cigar.
  Sisyphus.
**Burford, William**
  Christmas Tree, A.
**Burgess, Anthony**
  Lines: Inspired by the Controversy on
    the Value or Otherwise of Old English
    Studies.
**Burgess, Gelett**
  Purple Cow, The.
  Sequel to the Purple Cow.
**Burke, Kenneth**
  Conspirators, The.
  Heavy, Heavy—What Hangs Over?
**Burns, Robert**
  Address to the Deil.
  Address to the Unco Guid.
  Ae Fond Kiss.
  Afton Water.
  Auld Lang Syne.
  Banks o' Doon, The.
  Bannockburn.
  Bonnie Lesley.
  Cares o' Love, The.
  Comin' Thro' the Rye.
  Corn Rigs Are Bonie.
  Cotter's Saturday Night, The.
  Epitaph on a Schoolmaster.
  Epitaph on Holy Willie
  Epitaph on John Dove.
  For A' That, and A' That.
  Green Grow the Rashes[ or Rushes], O.
  Hey for a Lass wi'a Tocher.
  Holy Fair, The.
  Holy Willie's Prayer.
  How Can I Keep My Maidenhead.
  I Hae a Wife o' My Ain.
  I Love My Jean.
  I murder hate by field or flood.
  I'm Owre Young to Marry Yet.
  It Is Na, Jean, Thy Bonie Face.
  It Was A' for Our Rightfu' King.
  John Anderson, My Jo ("John Ander-
    son my jo, John,/ When we were first
    acquent")
  Jolly Beggars, The.
  Lass That Made the Bed to Me, The.
  Love and Liberty (The Jolly Beggars),
    sel.
  My Heart's in the Highlands.
  O, Were I on Parnassus Hill
  O, Wert Thou in the Cauld Blast.
  O Were My Love Yon Lilac Fair.
  O Whistle, and I'll Come to You, My
    Lad.
  Ode to Spring.
  On Elphinston's Translation of Martial.
  Once Fondly Lov'd.
  Poet's Welcome to His Love-Begotten
    Daughter, A.
  Rantin Dog the Daddie O't, The.
  Red, Red Rose, A.
  Rigs o' Barley, The.
  See the smoking bowl before us!
  Silver Tassie, The.
  Song: "Ae fond kiss, and then we sever."
  Thine Am I.
  To a Louse.
  To a Mouse [on Turning Her Up in Her
    Nest, with the Plough, November
    1785].

To an Artist.
Toad-Eater, The.
Wee Willie Gray.
Winter, a Dirge.
**Burr, Gray**
  Robin Hood.
  Sailing, Sailing.
**Burrell, Sophia**
  Epigram on Two Ladies.
**Burroway, Janet**
  Scientist, The.
**Burton, Robert**
  Anatomy of Melancholy, The, sel.
  Author's Abstract of Melancholy, The.
**Buson (Taniguchi Bunson)**
  Haiku: "Halo of the moon, The."
  Piercing Chill I Feel, The.
  Short Night, The.
**Butcher, Grace**
  Assignment.
  On Driving Behind a School Bus for
    Mentally Retarded Children.
  Results of the Polo Game.
  Wife of the Moon Man Who Never
    Came Back.
**Butler, Lynne**
  Man in the Dream Is Death, The.
**Butler, Samuel (1612-80)**
  Arts and Sciences, sels.
  Elephant in the Moon, The: a Satire,
    sel.
  Hudibras,sels.
  Independent Squire.
  Presbyterian Knight.
  Sir Hudibras, His Passing Worth.
**Butler, Samuel (1835-1902)**
  O God! O Montreal!
**Butterworth, Hezekiah**
  Thanksgiving in Boston Harbor, The.
**Buttigieg, A.**
  Cock, The.
  Dog, The.
  Lamp, The.
**Byers, Margaretta**
  South American Sway.
**Bynner, Witter ("Emanuel Morgan")**
  Spectra, sel.
**Byrom, John**
  Hymn for Christmas Day, A.
  Jacobite Toast, A.
  My Spirit Longeth for Thee.
  On Two Monopolists.
**Byron, George Gordon Noel Byron, 6th
  Baron**
  And I Have Loved Thee, Ocean!
  Beppo: a Venetian Story.
  Blues, The: a Literary Eclogue.
  Childe Harold's Pilgrimage, sels.
  Dedication: "Bob Southey! You're a
    poet—poet-laureate."
  Destruction of Sennacherib, The.
  Don Juan, abr.
  Dream, The, sel.
  Dying Gladiator, The.
  English Bards, and Scotch Reviewers.
  Epigram: "In digging up your bones,
    Tom Paine."
  Epigram on John Bull.
  Epilogue: "There's something in a stupid
    ass."
  Epistle to Augusta.

Epitaph, An: Inscription on a
  Monument at Newstead Abbey.
Epitaph for William Pitt.
Fare Thee well.
Farewell! If Ever Fondest Prayer.
Field of Waterloo, The.
First Kiss of Love, The.
Fragment: "I would to heaven that I
  were so much clay."
Giaour, The: a Fragment of a Turkish
  Tale.
Growing Old.
Inscription on the Monument of a
  Newfoundland Dog.
Isles of Greece, The.
Italy and England.
John Keats.
Lake Leman woos me with its crystal
  face.
Lines Addressed to a Young Lady.
Lines Inscribed upon a Cup Formed
  from a Skull.
Lines on Hearing that Lady Byron Was
  Ill.
Lines to Mr. Hodgson.
Lines Written Beneath an Elm in the
  Churchyard of Harrow.
Love and Death.
Maid of Athens Ere We Part.
Manfred: A Dramatic Poem.
Modern Discoveries.
Moon Shot.
Ode to Napoleon Buonaparte.
On Leaving Newstead Abbey.
On My Thirty-third Birthday.
On the Death of a Young Lady, Cousin
  to the Author.
On the Death of Mr. Fox.
On This Day I Complete My Thirty-
  Sixth Year.
Prisoner of Chillon, The.
Prometheus.
Race.
Remember thee! remember Thee!
Seduction of Juan, The.
She Walks in Beauty.
So We'll Go No More a-Roving.
Song for the Luddites.
Sonnet on Chillon.
Sonnet to the Prince Regent.
Stanzas: "I heard thy fate without a
  tear."
Stanzas to a Lady, on Leaving England.
Sun of the Sleepless!
Sun Set, and Up Rose the Yellow Moon,
  The.
To Caroline ("Oh— when shall the
  grave hide for ever my sorrow").
To Caroline ("Think'st thou I saw thy
  beauteous eyes").
To Mr. Murray.
To our theme—The man who has stood
  on the Acropolis.
Venice and Sunset.
Vision of Judgment, The.
Waterloo.
When a Man Hath No Freedom to
  Fight for at Home.
When I Roved a Young Highlander.
When We Two Parted.
Written after Swimming from Sestos to
  Abydos.

# C

**Cabral, Olga**
Life and Death Among the Xerox
    People.
Occupation: Spinster.
Sappho.
**Caeiro, Alberto (Fernando Pessoa)**
I don't bother with rhymes.
**Caesar, Irving**
Tea for Two, *with music.*
**Callimachus**
Elegy on Herakleitos.
**Calverley, Charles Stuart**
Ballad: "Auld wife sat at her ivied door,
    The."
Beer.
Cock and the Bull, The.
Companions.
Disaster.
Lines on Hearing the Organ.
Lovers, and a Reflection.
Ode to Tobacco.
Proverbial Philosophy: Of Reading.
**Cameron, Norman**
Compassionate Fool, The.
Disused Temple, The.
Green, Green Is El Aghir.
In the Queen's Room.
Public-House Confidence.
Shepherdess.
Three Love Poems, *sel.*
**Camoës [or Camoëns], Luís**
Dear gentle soul, who went so soon
    away.
**Camp, James**
Bruckner.
**Campbell, Alistair**
Images.
O Catch Miss Daisy Pinks.
**Campbell, David**
Cocky's Calendar, *sel.*
Deaths and Pretty Cousins.
Delivering Lambs.
Lambing.
Love who points the swallow home.
    Who Points the Swallow.
Mothers and Daughters.
Night Sowing.
Starting from Central Station.
To a Ground-Lark.
Who Points the Swallow.
Windy Nights.
Works and Days, *sel.*
**Campbell, Donald**
Ablow the Mune.
Aiberdeen.
Betrayal in Morninside.
Cougait Revisited.
Laneliet Place in the Warld, The.
Minding.
Sonnets frae Siberia, *sel.*
**Campbell, Joseph ("Seosamh
    MacCathmhaoil")**
Ad Limina.
Antiquary, The.
Blanaid's Song ("Blanaid loves roses").
Butterfly in the Fields.
Darkness.
Gombeen, The.

Harvest Song.
I Will Go with My Father a-Ploughing.
Ideal and Reality.
Old Woman, The.
Three Colts Exercising in a Six-Acre.
**Campbell, Roy**
Autumn.
Georgiad, The, *sel.*
Golden Shower, The, *sel.*
Heartbreak Camp.
On Some South African Novelists.
On the Same.
Sisters, The.
**Campbell, Thomas**
Battle of the Baltic.
Gilderoy, *sel.*
Hohenlinden.
Ye Mariners of England.
**Campion, Thomas**
Among the Shades.
Are you what your faire lookes expresse?
Author of light, revive my dying spright.
Be thou then my beauty named.
Blame not my cheeks, though pale with
    love they be.
Breake now my heart and dye! Oh no,
    she may relent.
Cherry-ripe.
Come, chearfull day, part of my life, to
    mee.
De Profundis.
Devotion
Elegye, An: "Constant to none, but ever
    false to me."
Follow Thy Fair Sun.
Give beauty all her right.
Harden now thy tyred hart with more
    then flinty rage.
Hark, All You Ladies.
I care not for these ladies.
I must complain, yet doe enjoy my love.
In Praise of Neptune.
Integer Vitae.
Jacke and Jone, they thinke no ill.
Kind[e] are her answers [or answeres].
Lover's Plea, A.
My Sweetest Lesbia [Let Us Live and
    Love].
Never love unlesse you can.
Now Winter Nights Enlarge.
O Come Quickly!
Raving warre, begot.
Rose-cheeked Laura, Come.
Secret love or two, I must confesse, A.
Seek the Lord!
Shall I then hope when faith is fled?
Silly boy 'tis full moon yet, thy night as
    day shines clearly.
So Tired Are All My Thoughts.
There Is a Garden in Her Face.
Thou art not faire, for all thy red and
    white.
Though your strangenesse frets my hart.
Thrice Toss These Oaken Ashes in the
    Air.
To musicke bent is my retyred minde.
Tune thy musicke to thy hart.
Vobiscum Est Iope.
Were my hart as some mens are, thy
    errours would not move me.
What Faire Pompe.
What if a day, or a month, or a yeare.

When to her lute Corrina sings.
Where are all thy beauties now, all
    hearts enchaining?
Winter Nights.
**Campos, Haroldo de**
If.
**Canfield, Harry Clifford**
On the Loss of U.S. Submarine S4, *sel.*
**Cannan, May Wedderburn**
Rouen.
**Canning, Effie I.**
Baby Mine, *with music.*
Rock-a-Bye Baby, *with music.*
**Canning, George**
Ballynahinch.
Cat and the Bird, The.
Elderly Gentleman, The.
Political Despatch, A.
**Canning, George and John Hookham Frere**
Friend of Humanity and the Knife-
    Grinder, The.
Inscription.
New Morality, *sel.*
**Cannon, Hughie**
Bill Bailey Won't You Pleases Come
    Home, *with music.*
**Canzoneri, Robert**
One Lion, Once.
Unloved, The.
**Capua, Eduardo di**
O Sole Mio, *with music.*
**"Carbery, Ethna" (Anna Johnston
    MacManus)**
Brian Boy Magee.
King of Ireland's Cairn, The, *abr.*
Love-Talker, The.
On an Island, *abr.* "
**Carden, Ramona**
Moccasins of an Old Man, The.
Tumbleweed.
**Cardenal, Ernesto**
Epitaph for the Tomb of Adolfo Baez
    Bone.
**Cardiff, Gladys**
Carious Exposure.
Combing.
Grey Woman.
Leaves Like Fish.
Long Person.
O nuclear wind, when wilt thou blow.
Swimmer.
Tlanusi' yi, the Leech Place.
To Frighten a Storm.
**Carew, Thomas**
Celia Bleeding: to the Surgeon.
Epitaph on the Lady Mary Villiers.
Hymeneal Dialogue, An.
Love's Force.
Maria Wentworth.
On the Death of Donne.
On the Lady Mary Villiers.
On the Marriage of T. K. and C. C., the
    Morning Stormy.
Pastoral Dialogue, A.
Persuasions to Enjoy.
Rapture, A.
Song, A: "Ask me no more where Jove
    bestows."
Song: Mediocrity in Love Rejected.
Spring, The.
To My Inconstant Mistris[s].
Upon a Mole in Celia's Bosom.

**Carey, Lady Elizabeth**
Mariam, *sel.*
**Carey, Henry**
Sally in Our Alley.
**Carey [or Cary], Patrick**
Crucifixus Pro Nobis.
Hymn: "Whilst I beheld the neck o' the
dove."
Nulla Fides.
**Carleton, Will M.**
Doctor's Story, The.
**Carman, Bliss**
Marigolds.
**Carney, Julia A. Fletcher**
Little Things.
**Carolan, Turlough.** *See* O'Carolan,
Turlough
**Carrier, Constance**
At Tripolis.
Commencement.
Elegy: "Here where the elm trees were."
Intimations of Immortality, Cuttingsville,
Vermont, 1880.
Pro Patria, *abr.*
Taken Town, The.
**"Carroll, Lewis" (Charles Lutwidge
Dodson)**
Aged Aged Man, The.
Alice's Adventures in Wonderland, *sels.*
Alice's Recitation.
Duchess's Lullaby, The.
Evidence Read at the Trial of the Knave
of Hearts.
Father William.
Hiawatha's Photographing.
How Doth the Little Crocodile.
Humpty Dumpty's Song [or Recitation].
Jabberwocky.
Lobster, The.
Lobster Quadrille, The.
Mad Gardener's Song, The.
Mad Hatter's Song.
My Fancy.
Pig Tale, The, *abr.*
Sylvie and Bruno,*sels.*
Tèma Con Variazioni.
Through the Looking-Glass,*sels.*
Turtle Soup.
Walrus and the Carpenter, The.
White Knight's Song, The.
**Carroll, Wallace**
Cried the Lip.
**Carruth, Hayden**
Ah, you beast of love.
Hard Journey, A. Yes.
Loneliness.
So be it. I am.
Why speak of the use.
Your tears, Niobe.
**Carryl, Charles Edward**
Camel's Complaint, The.
Davy and the Goblin, *sel.*
Robinson Crusoe's Story.
**Carryl, Guy Wetmore**
Embarrassing Episode of Little Miss
Muffet, The.
Fearful Finale of the Irascible Mouse,
The.
Harmonious Heedlessness of Little Boy
Blue, The.

Sycophantic Fox and the Gullible
Raven, The.
**Carson, Ciaran**
Insular Celts, The.
**Carter, Albert Howard**
Christmas Needles.
Crack of Doom.
Critique for Our Times.
For the Spring Being.
In the Wilderness.
Peter.
Quem Queritis.
Reflections on Limitations.
Tomb of Time, The.
**Carter, Hodding**
In the Jury Room.
**Carter, Sydney**
Friday Morning.
Lord of the Dance.
**Cartwright, William**
Bill of Fare, A, *sel.*
Dead Sparrow, The.
No Platonic Love.
On the Circumcision: for the King's
Music.
Royal Slave, The, *sel.*
Sadness.
Siege; or, Love's Convert, The, *sel.*
To Chloe Who Wish'd Her Self Young
Enough for Me.
**Carver, Raymond**
Deschutes River.
Drinking While Driving.
Hunter.
Wall, The.
Winter Insomnia.
**Cary, Patrick.** *See* Carey
**Case, Mose**
Arkansas Traveller, The, *with music.*
**Casey, Michael**
Bummer, A.
**Cassel, Irwin M.**
I Love Life, *with music.*
**Castiello, Jaime**
Partners.
**Castiglione, Jack**
Noisy Boys.
**Casto, Robert Clayton**
Salt Pork, The.
**Casullo, Jóanne**
Father and Daughter.
Mistaken Identity.
Suicide, The.
Translation From Original.
**Cather, Willa Sibert**
Dedicatory: "Somewhere, sometime, in
an April twilight."
Grandmither, Think Not I Forget.
**Cato, Nancy**
Independence.
**Catullus, Caius [or Gaius] Valerius**
Break off/ fallen Catullus.
Dianae Sumus in Fide.
From the quarters of the compass.
Lesbia loads me night and day with her
curses.
Lesbia's sparrow.
Phyllis Corydon clutched to him.
**"Caudwell, Christopher" (Christopher St.
John Sprigg)**
Classic Encounter.
Progress of Poetry, The.

**Causley, Charles**
Ballad of the Bread Man.
Betjeman, 1984.
Chief Petty Officer.
Cowboy Song.
Death of a Poet.
Hawthorn White.
I Am the Great Sun.
I Saw a Jolly Hunter.
Innocent's Song.
Nursery Rhyme of Innocence and
Experience.
Recruiting Drive.
Song of the Dying Gunner A.A.1.
Timothy Winters.
**Cavafy, Constantine P.**
On the Street.
Return.
To Remain.
**Cavalcanti, Guido**
Sonnet: Rapture Concerning His Lady,
A.
**Cavalieri, Grace**
After the Fact.
Black in Virginia.
Christmas.
Come to a Wedding.
Cry, The.
Novus Ordo Seclorum.
Our Sobbing Must Be Heard.
We'll Never Be the Same (Until Later).
**Cavanass, J. M.**
By the Waters of Minnetonka, *with
music.*
**Cavendish, Margaret, Duchess of
Newcastle.** *See* Newcastle, Margaret
Cavendish, Duchess of
**Cavendish, William, Duke of Newcastle.**
*See* Newcastle, William Cavendish,
Duke of
**Centamputan, Maturai Eruttalan**
What She Said.
**Chalmers, Patrick Reginald**
Cuckoo, The.
Tortoiseshell Cat, The.
**Chamberlain, Brenda**
Dead Ponies.
Lament: "My man is a bone ringed with
weed."
**Chambers, George**
Life, The.
Voice, The.
**Chambers, Henry·Tim**
Beforehand and Afterward
("Beforehand, liars studied how to
lie").
God Walks among the Dust.
Prophet.
They Slept While Jesus Prayed.
**Chambers, Jane**
Woman.
**Chamisso, Adelbert von**
Tragic Story, A.
**Chapin, Edwin H.**
Ocean Burial, The, *with music.*
**Chapman, George (1559?-1634)**
Bridal Song.
Conspiracy of Charles, Duke of Byron,
The, *sel.*
Hero and Leader, *sel.*
Ovid's Banquet of Sense, *sel.*
To My Admired and Soul-loved Friend,

Master of All Essentials and True Knowledge, Mr. Harriots, *sel.*

**Chappell, Fred**
Skin Flick.
Spitballer.

**Char, René**
Basket-weaver's Love, The.

**Charles, Dorthi**
Concrete Cat.

**Charles, Ed**
Athlete's Prayer, An.

**Chartier, Alain**
I turn you out of doors.

**Chasin, Helen**
Falling Out.
Looking Out.
Mythics.
Photograph at the Cloisters: April 1972.
Poetess Kō Ōgimi, The.
Recovery Room, The: Lying-in.

**Chatterton, Thomas**
Aella, *sel.*
Elinoure and Juga
Excelente Balade of Charitie, An.
Minstrel's Song, The.

**Chaucer, Geoffrey**
Balade: "Hide, Absalon, thy gilte tresses clear."
Canterbury Tales, The, *sels.*
Clerk of Oxford, The.
Complaint of Chaucer to His Purse, The.
Complaint of Troilus, The.
Controlling the Tongue.
Criseyde Sees Troilus Return from Battle.
Eagle Converses with Chaucer, The.
Former Age, The.
Friar's Tale, The.
Go, Little Book ("Go, litel book, go, litel myn tragedy").
House of Fame, The, *sels.*
Jove's Eagle Carries Chaucer into Space.
Knight's Tale, The, *sel.*
Lack of Steadfastness.
Love Unfeigned.
Manciple's Tale, The, *sel.*
Merciless Beauty.
Mice before Milk.
Mill at Trumpington, The.
O Yonge Freshe Folkes.
Old Books.
Parliament of Fowls, The, *sel.*
Persons of the Prologue.
Poor Parson, A.
Prioress, The.
Prologue: "Whan that April with his showres soote."
Reeve, The.
Three Revellers Search for Death.
To Adam, His Scribe.
Troilus and Criseyde, *sels.*
Truth.
Wanton Merry Friar, A.
Wife of Bath, The.
Wife's Fifth Husband, The.

**Chear, Abraham**
To My Youngest Kinsman, R. L.

**Cherbury, Edward Herbert, 1st Baron.** *See* **Herbert of Cherbury**

**Cherry, Kelly**
Song for Sigmund Freud, A.

**Chesham, Sallie**
Aside to Julie.
Into the Sky.
Mark This.
Thoughts on Pain.

**Chester, Laura**
Eyes of the Garden.
Hibernating in an Old Lost Neighbourhood.
House Guest, The.
Pavane for the Passing of a Child.
28 VIII 69
Wish for Water, A.

**Chesterton, Gilbert Keith**
Antichrist, or the Reunion of Christendom: an Ode.
Ballade of Suicide, A.
Fat White Woman Speaks, The.
For the Crèche.
Gold Leaves.
Lepanto.
Rolling English Road, The.
Secret People, The.
Song Against Grocers, The.
Songs of Education, *sel.*
Triolet.
Wine and Water.

**Chettle, Henry**
Diaphenia.

**Child, Lydia Maria**
Thanksgiving Day.

**Childress, William**
Metamorphosis of Aunt Jemima, The.

**Chilgren, Delia**
Big Sur Summer.
Letter to My Father.
Nightwalker.

**Chosa, Martha**
Drums.

**Chudleigh, Mary Lee, Lady**
Offering, The: Part One.
Resolve, The.
To the Ladies.

**Chukovsky, Kornei**
Crocodile ("Once a haughty crocodile left his home upon the Nile").
Crocodile ("Once there was a crocodile.")

**Church, Richard**
Alchemist, The.
Be Frugal.
Cat, The.

**Churchill, Charles**
Apology Addressed to the Critical Reviewers, The.
Author, The.
Pains of Education, The.

**Ciardi, John**
About the Teeth of Sharks.
Benefits of an Education, The.
Box Comes Home, A.
Boy.
Cat Heard the Cat-bird, The.
Chorus: "They were singing Old MacDonald in the schoolbus."
Credibility.
Dragons.
Evil Eye, The.
Get Up or You'll Be Late for School, Silly!
I Wouldn't.
In Place of a Curse.

Letter from a Death Bed.
Magus, A.
On a Photo of Sgt. Ciardi a Year Later.
On Flunking a Nice Boy Out of School.
Polo Match.
Romping.
Shark, The.
Summer Song.
To W. T. Scott.
What Someone Told Me about Bobby Link.

**Cibber, Colley**
Blind Boy, The.

**Clancy, Joseph P.**
Boxer.

**Clapton, Eric *and* Martin Sharp**
Tales of Brave Ulysses.

**Clare, John**
Ants, The.
Autumn ("The thistle down's flying . . .")
Badger, The.
Clock-a-clay (The Ladybird).
February.
First Love.
Fox, The.
Gipsies ("The snow falls deep; the forest lies alone").
Hen's Nest.
I Am.
I Hid My Love.
Ladybird, The, *sel.*
Love lives beyond.
Mouse's Nest.
November.
Red Robin, The.
Sea Boy on the Giddy Mast, A.
Secret, The.
Sheep in Winter.
Shepherd's Calendar, The, *sels.*
Signs of Winter.
Spring Morning, A.
Sudden Shower.
Thrush's Nest, The.
To Mary: I Sleep with Thee, and Wake with Thee.
To Mary: It Is the Evening Hour.
To the Snipe.
Vision, A.
Vixen, The.
Well, Honest John.
Winter Winds Cold and Blea.
With Garments Flowing.
Written in Northampton County Asylum.
Written in Prison.

**Clark, Badger**
Glory Trail, The.

**Clark, Carl**
Allegory in Black.
Conundrum.
No More.
Ode to a Beautiful Woman.
Second Coming, The.
Thoughts from a Bottle.

**Clark, Charles Heber.** *See* **"Adeler, Max"**

**Clark, Leonard**
Attack, The.
Our Family.
Silver Screen.

**Clark, Thomas**
And Our Gifts to the Seasons.

**Clark, Tom**
Doors.
Eyeglasses.
Going to School in France or America.
Like Musical Instruments.
Poem: "Tiny new emotions, The."
Sonnet: "Five A.M. on East Fourteenth
  I'm out to eat."
Sonnet: "Orgasm completely, The."
**Clark, Walter**
After Snow.
Free Will.
Morning After, The.
Uncle Death.
**Clarke, Austin**
Ancient Lights.
Burial of an Irish President.
Fair at Windgap, The.
Inscription for a Headstone.
Irish-American Dignitary.
Jest, The.
Lost Heifer, The.
Marriage.
Night and Morning.
Penal Law.
Planter's Daughter, The.
Sermon on Swift, A.
Straying Student, The.
Strong Wind, A.
Tenebrae.
Young Woman of Beare, The.
**Clarke, Frances (Frances Clarke Sayers)**
Who Calls?
**Clarke, John Henrik**
Determination.
Sing Me a New Song.
**Clarkson, E. Margaret**
First Frost.
Hummingbird.
Pond Lily.
Prayer from a Stryker Frame.
**Clause, Paul**
Burial in the Country, A.
Loftiest spirit that ever flamed in flesh,
  The.
Nightlines.
Washer-Windows, The.
**Clemmons, Carole Gregory**
Ghetto Lovesong—Migration.
I'm Just a Stranger Here, Heaven Is My
  Home.
Love from My Father.
Spring.
**Clemo, Jack R.**
Calvinist in Love, A.
**Clephane, Elizabeth Cecilia**
Ninety and Nine, The, *with music.*
**Clerk, John**
Fane Wald I Luve.
**Clerk-Maxwell, James.** *See* **Maxwell,
  James Clerk**
**Cleveland, John**
Antiplatonick, The.
Epitaph on the Earl of Strafford.
Fuscara; or, the Bee-Errant.
Mark Anthony.
On the Memory of Mr. Edward King,
  Drowned in the Irish Seas.
To the State of Love, or the Senses'
  Festival.
**Clifton, Lucille**
Admonitions.

Discoveries of Fire, The.
1st, The.
For de Lawd.
Good Times.
If I Stand in My Window.
If Something Should Happen.
In Salem.
In the inner city.
Lane Is the Pretty One.
Listen Children.
Lost Baby Poem, The.
Love Rejected.
Miss Rosie.
My daddy's fingers move among the
  couplers.
My Mama Moved among the Days.
Robert.
Running across to the lot.
Still.
Stops.
Thirty eighth year, The.
Those Boys That Ran Together.
Way It Was, The.
Willie B (2).
**Clinton, D.**
Breathing, at Last, in the Wichita Art
  Museum.
**Close, John**
In Respectful Memory of Mr. Yarker,
  *sel.*
**Clough, Arthur Hugh**
Amours de Voyage.
Dipsychus, *sels.*
Duty.
Easter Day, Naples, 1849.
Easter Day II.
Epi-Strauss-ium.
How Pleasant It Is to Have Money.
In the Great Metropolis.
Is it true, ye gods, who treat us.
Latest Decalogue, The.
Natura Naturans.
Qua Cursum Ventus.
Qui Laborat, Orat.
Reply to Dipsychus.
Say Not the Struggle Nougth Availeth.
Spectator Ab Extra.
"There is no God," the wicked saith.
Where Lies the Land?
**Coatsworth, Elizabeth Jane (Mrs. Henry
  Beston)**
All Goats.
Calling in the Cat.
Footprint in the Night.
Lady Comes to an Inn, A.
Open Door, The.
Rain Poem.
Swallows, The.
Whale at Twilight.
Who Is Sad?
Winter Soon Is Coming.
**Cobb, Charlie**
"Containing Communism."
For Sammy Younge.
Nation.
To Vietnam.
**Cobb, Will D.**
School Days, *with music.*
Somebody's Sweetheart I Want To Be,
  *with music.*
Waltz Me Around Again Willie; or,
  'Round, 'Round, 'Round, *with music.*

**Coffey, Brian**
Muse, June, Related, *sel.*
**Coffin, Robert Peter Tristram**
Christening-Day Wishes for My
  God-child.
Crystal Moment.
Hens in Winter.
Pheasant, The.
Sacrament, The.
Secret, The.
Thief Jones.
Yankee Cradle.
**Cohan, George M.**
Forty-five Minutes from Broadway, *with
  music.*
Give My Regards to Broadway, *with
  music.*
Mary's a Grand Old Name, *with music.*
Yankee Doodle Boy, The, *with music.*
Your're a Grand Old Flag, *with music.*
**Cohen, Leonard**
Bus, The.
Elegy: "Do not look for him."
For Anne.
For E .J. P.
Gift.
Kite Is a Victim, A.
Only Tourist in Havana Turns His
  Thoughts Homeward, The.
Queen Victoria and Me.
Stories of the Street.
Story of Isaac.
Suit, The.
Summer Night.
Suzanne Takes You Down.
You Do Not Have to Love Me.
**Cohoe, Grey**
Folding Fan, The.
**Cole, Barry**
Men Are Coming Back, The.
**Cole, Bob**
Under the Bamboo Tree, *with music.*
**Cole, E. R.**
Apology for the Fall.
**Cole, Eugene Roger**
Good Friday Explosives.
Tree, The.
Whole Relentless Process, The.
**Cole, G. D. H.**
Civil Riot, *sel.*
**Cole, William**
Hypnopompic Poem.
Just Dropped In.
Lost Contact.
Mutual Problem.
Question, A.
What Could It Be?
**Coleridge, Hartley**
He Lived amidst th' Untrodden Ways.
November.
On the Death of Echo.
Sonnets on the Seasons, *sel.*
There Lived among the Untrodden
  Ways.
**Coleridge, Mary Elizabeth**
At a Friends' Meeting.
Deserted House, The.
In Dispraise of the Moon.
In London Town.
Jealousy.
"My True Love Hath My Heart and I
  Have His."

Our Lady.
Salus Mundi.
September.
There.
Unwelcome.
We Never Said Farewell.
Witch, The.

**Coleridge, Samuel Taylor**
Ad Vilmum Axiologum.
Answer [or Answers] to a Child's
  Question.
Apologia pro Vita Sua.
Ballad of the Dark Ladie, The.
Burke.
Character, A.
Christabel.
Cologne.
Constancy to an Ideal Object.
Day-Dream, A.
Day-Dream from an Emigrant to His
  Absent Wife, The.
Dejection; an Ode.
Desire.
Destruction of the Bastille.
Eolian Harp, The.
Epitaph on an Infant.
Epitaph: "Stop, Christian passer-by!—
  Stop, child of God."
Fears in solitude.
Foster-Mother's Tale, The.
France: an Ode.
Frost at Midnight.
Hexameters.
Human Life: on the Denial of
  Immortality.
Hymn before Sunrise in the Vale of
  Chamouni.
Inscription for a Fountain on a Heath.
Knight's Tomb, The.
Kubla Kahn; or, A Vision in a Dream.
La Fayette.
Lewti; or, The Circassian Love-Chaunt.
Limbo.
Lines Written in the Album at
  Elbingerode.
Love.
Love's Apparition and Evanishment.
Mad Monk, The.
Metrical Feet.
Monody on a Tea-Kettle.
Monody on the Death of Chatterton.
Ne Plus Ultra.
New Moon, The.
Nightingale, The.
Nil Pejus Est Caelibe Vita.
Ode to the Departing Year.
Ode to the Rain, An.
Ode to Tranquillity.
On a Lord
On a Ruined House in a Romantic
  Country.
On Donne's Poetry.
On My Joyful Departure.
On the Prospect of Establishing a
  Pantisocracy in America.
Pains of Sleep, The.
Pantisocracy.
Phantom.
Phantom or Fact.
Picture, The; or, the Lover's Resolution.
Priestley.
Psyche.

Recantation Illustrated in the Story of
  the Mad Ox.
Reflections on Having Left a Place of
  Retirement.
Religious Musings.
Rime of the Ancient Mariner, The.
Self-Knowledge.
Separation.
Silence of a city, how awful at midnight,
  The.
Sonnet to the River Otter.
Sonnets Attempted in the Manner of
  Contemporary Writers,*sels.*
Sonnets on Eminent Characters,*sels.*
Swans Sing before They Die.
Therefore all seasons shall be sweet to
  thee.
This Lime-Tree Bower My Prison.
Time, Real and Imaginary.
To a Young Ass.
To a Young Lady with a Poem on the
  French Revolution.
To Asra.
To Fortune on Buying a Ticket in the
  Irish Lottery.
To Nature
To Simplicity.
To the Nightingale.
To the Rev. W.L. Bowles, 2 *versions.*
To William Wordsworth.
Two Founts, The.
Two wedded hearts, if ere were such.
Visionary Hope, The.
What is Life?
Work Without Hope.
Youth and Age.

**Coleridge, Samuel Taylor and Robert**
  **Southey.** *See* **Southey, Robert** *and*
  **Samuel Taylor Coleridge**

**Coleridge, Sara**
Months, The.
Trees.

**Collins, Ann [or Anne]**
Another Song ("The winter of my
  infancy being over-past").
Song: "My straying thoughts, reduced
  stay."

**Collins, Judy**
Albatross.
My Father.

**Collins, Mortimer**
King Arthur Growing Very Tired
  Indeed.
My Aunt's Spectre.

**Collins, William**
How Sleep the Brave.
Ode Occasion'd by the Death of Mr.
  Thomson.
Ode on the Poetical Character.
Ode on the Popular Superstitions of the
  Highlands of Scotland, An.
Ode to Evening.
Ode to Fear.
Ode to Mercy.
Ode to Pity.
Ode to Simplicity.
Passions, The; an Ode to Music.
Song from Shakespear's Cymbelyne, A.
Stormy Hebrides, The.

**Colman, Cathy**
After Swimming in the Pacific.
Fox Court, Winter.

**Colman, George, the Younger**
Sir Marmaduke.
Unfortunate Miss Bailey.

**Colombo, John Robert**
Riverdale Lion.

**Colum, Padraic**
Ballad Maker, A.
Book of Kells, The.
Drover, A.
I Saw the Wind Today.
Interior.
Monkeys.
Reminiscence, *sel.*
Rive-Mates.
She Moved through the Fair.

**Columcille [or Columba], Saint**
Clamour of the wind making music.
On some island I long to be.

**Comfort, Alex**
Letter to an American Visitor.
There is a white mare that my love
  keeps.

**Congreve, William**
Semele to Jupiter.
Song: "Pious Selinda goes to prayers."

**Conn, Stuart**
Arrivals.

**Connor, Tony**
Above Penmaenmawr.
Apologue.
Child Half-Asleep, A.
Elegy for Alfred Hubbard.
Fashionable Poet Reading.
Lancashire Winter.

**Conquest, Robert**
Art and Civilization.
By Rail Through Istria.
Horror Comic.
Man and Woman.
Near the Death of Ovid.
Poem about a Poem about a Poem.
Rokeby Venus, The.

**Constable, Henry**
Diana, *sels.*
My lady's presence makes the roses red.

**Contoski, Victor**
Kansa, The.

**Conyus**
Great Santa Barbara Oil Disaster OR,
  The.
He's Doing Natural Life.
Untitled Requiem for Tomorrow.
Upon Leaving the Parole Board
  Hearing.

**Cook, Eliza**
Mouse and the Cake, The.
Old Arm-Chair, The.

**Cook, Joseph**
Rhyme for a Chemical Baby.
Rhyme for a Geological Baby.
Rhyme for Astronomical Baby.
Rhyme for Botanical Baby.

**Cook, Mike**
Bootie Black and the Seven Giants.

**Cooley, Peter**
Ah, Wilderness.
Alternatives.
Confession, The.
Floating Coathangers.
Man Who Closes Himself, The.
Packer City Poem.
Revenant, The.

Tracks.
Vanishing Point.
White Room, The.
**"Coolidge, Susan" (Susan Chauncey Woolsey)**
Measles in the Ark.
**Cooney, Ellen**
From four walls of/ ivory.
Monday Night in Winter.
So you dance with me.
**Cooper, Charles**
Dreams.
Honky.
Rubin.
**Cooper, Edith** and **Katherine Bradley.** *See* **"Field, Michael"**
**Cooper, George**
Sweet Genevieve, *with music.*
**Cooper, Jane**
Faithful, The.
Graveyard, The.
In the House of the Dying.
In the Last Few Moments Came the Old German Cleaning Woman.
Knowledge That Comes through Experience, The.
My Young Mother.
Racetrack, The.
Rock Climbing.
Weather of Six Mornings, The.
**Cooper, Leonard**
Rhyming Prophecy for a New Year.
**Coppard, Alfred Edgar**
Horse, The.
Unfortunate Miller, The.
**Corbet, Richard**
Fairies' Farewell, The.
Iter Boreale, *sel.*
To His Son, Vincent Corbet.
**Corbett, Elizabeth T.**
Three Wise Old Women.
**Corbin, Lloyd M., Jr. (Djangatolum)**
Ali.
Dedication to the Final Confrontation.
**Corman, Cid**
Call it a louse—I'm.
Container, The.
Deceased.
Desk, The.
I have come far to have found nothing.
La Selva.
Locus, The.
Tortoise, The.
**Cornford, Frances (Darwin)**
All Souls' Night.
Childhood.
Coast, The: Norfolk.
Country Bedroom, The, *sel.*
Guitarist Tunes Up, The.
On the Beach.
Princess and the Gypsies, The.
To a Fat Lady Seen from the Train.
Watch, The.
**Cornford, John**
Huesca.
**Cornish, Sam**
Black Man, A.
Death of Dr. King.
Forecast.
Frederick Douglass.
Generations 1.
Generations 2.

Montgomery.
One Eyed Black Man in Nebraska.
Panther.
Ray Charles.
River, The.
To a Single Shadow Without Pity.
**Cornish, William**
Knight and the Lady, The.
**Corrington, John William**
For a Woodscolt Miscarried.
Grand Inquisitor Continues, The.
Guevara with Minutes to Go.
Mr. Clean.
On My 18th Birthday.
**Corso, Gregory**
Birthplace Revisited.
But I Do Not Need Kindness.
Dear Girl.
Difference of Zoos, A.
Dream of a Baseball Star.
Dreamed Realization, A.
Eastside Incidents.
Hair.
I am 25.
I Held a Shelley Manuscript.
In the Fleeting Hand of Time.
Italian Extravaganza.
Last Gangster, The.
Last Warmth of Arnold, The.
Mad Yak, The.
Marriage.
Paris.
Poets Hitchhiking on the Highway.
P.S. 42.
Reflection in a Green Arena.
Second Night in N.Y.C. after 3 Years.
Seed Journey.
Spontaneous Requiem for the American Indian.
Three.
Vestal Lady on Brattle, The.
Vision of Rotterdam.
Waterchew!
Writ on the Eve of My 32nd Birthday.
You, Whose Mother's Lover Was Grass.
Zizi's Lament.
**Cortez, Jayne**
For Real.
Initiation.
Lead.
**Cory, William Johnson**
Ballad for a Boy, A.
Heraclitus.
Mimnermus in Church.
**Cott, Jonathan**
He Spends Time in Southern California.
**Cotter, Joseph Seamon, Jr.**
And What Shall You Say?
Sonnet to Negro Soldiers.
**Cotton, Charles**
Burlesque upon the Great Frost, *sel.*
Evening.
Resolution in Four Sonnets, of a Poetical Question Put to Me by a Friend. Concerning Four Rural Sisters.
See how like twilight slumber falls.
Two Rural Sisters.
**Cotton, John**
Pigs.
Toad.
**Cotton, Nathaniel**
Bee, the Ant, and the Sparrow, The.
Contentment.

Early Thoughts of Marriage.
To a Child Five Years Old.
**Cottrau, Teodoro**
Santa Lucia, *with music.*
**Coulette, Henri**
Blue-eyed Precinct Worker, The.
Family Goldschmitt, The.
**Courtenay, John**
Poetical and Philosophical Essay on the French Revolution . . ., A, *sel.*
**Cousins, James H.**
Corncrake, The.
**Coward, Noel**
Boy Actor, The.
**Cowell, Sam**
Villikins and His Dinah.
**Cowley, Abraham** and **Richard Crashaw**
Answer to an Invitation to Cambridge, An.
Davideis, *sel.*
Dialogue after Enjoyment.
Drinking.
Ecstasy, The.
Hell.
Honour.
Mistress, The, *sels.*
Music.
Ode: Of Wit.
On the Death of Mr. William Harvey, *sel.*
Spring, The.
Welcome, The.
Wish, The.
**Cowley, Abraham and Richard Crashaw**
On Hope by Way of Question and Answer between Abraham Cowley and Richard Crashaw.
**Cowley, Malcolm**
Blown Door, The.
Long Voyage, The.
Smoke of Birds, A.
**Cowper, William**
Castaway, The.
Contrite Heart, The.
Diverting History of John Gilpin, The.
Epitaph: "Here Johnson lies—a sage by all allow'd."
Epitaph on a Hare
Hymn: "To those who know the Lord I speak."
Light Shining Out of Darkness.
Lines Written During a Period of Insanity.
Lines Written on a Window Shutter at Weston.
Lovest Thou Me?
On the Death of Mrs. Throckmorton's Bullfinch.
On the Loss of the Royal George.
Poplar-Field, The ("The poplars are felled, farewell to the shade").
Retired Cat, The.
Retirement, *sel.*
Robin in Winter, The, *sel.*
Shrubbery, The.
Sofa, The.
Squirrel in Sunshine.
Statesman in Retirement, The.
Task, The, *sels.*
To Mary.
Walking with God.
Winter Morning Walk, The.

**Cox, Carol**
All Three of Us.
From the Direction of the State Mental
  Institution.
He Left the Pine Ridge Reservation.
How the Indians Lost the Hot Springs.
Papa Doc Is Dead.
**Coxe, Louis**
On Seeing Films of the War.
**Crabbe, Chris Wallace-.** *See*
  **Wallace-Crabbe, Chris**
**Crabbe, George**
Borough, The, *sel.*
Frenzy.
Lady of the Manor, The.
Marriage Ring, A.
Oncoming Industrial Revolution, The.
Parish Register, The, *sel.*
Peter Grimes; the Outcast.
Rural Life.
Sir Eustace Grey, *sel.*
Village, The.
**Craig, Ann M.**
Hypocrite.
**Craig, Maurice James**
Ballad to a Traditional Refrain.
Poem: "High on a ridge of tiles."
**Craig, Norma**
Question.
**Crane, Hart**
At Melville's Tomb.
Ave Maria.
Black Tambourine.
Bridge, The, *sels.*
Broken Tower, The.
Cape Hatteras.
Carrier Letter.
Chaplinesque.
Dance, The.
For the Marriage of Faustus and Helen.
Garden Abstract.
Harbor Dawn, The.
In Shadow.
Indiana.
Island Quarry.
Legend.
Legende.
My Grandmother's Love Letters.
Name for All, A.
National Winter Garden.
North Labrador.
O Carib Isle!
October-November.
Passage.
Pastorale: "No more violets."
Powhatan's Daughter.
Praise for an Urn.
Repose of Rivers.
River, The.
Royal Palm.
To Brooklyn Bridge.
To Emily Dickinson.
Tunnel, The.
Van Winkle.
Voyages (I-VI).
Wine Menagerie, The.
**Crane, Stephen**
Black Riders, The, *sels.*
God in Wrath, A.
I Saw a Man Pursuing the Horizon.
If I Should Cast Off This Tattered Coat.
In the Desert.

Little Ink More or Less, A.
Man adrift on a slim spar, A.
Tell me not in joyous numbers.
War Is Kind, *sels.*
**Crapsey, Adelaide**
Guarded Wound, The.
November Night.
Susanna and the Elders.
Triad.
Warning, The.
**Crashaw, Richard**
Charitas Nimia; or, The Dear Bargain.
Easter Day.
Epitaph upon Husband and Wife Who
  Died and Were Buried Together, An.
Flaming Heart, The, *sels.*
Hymn of the Nativity, Sung as by the
  Shepherds, An.
Hymn to the Name and Honour of the
  Admirable Saint Teresa, A.
In the Glorious Epiphany of Our Lord
  God, *sel.*
In the Holy Nativity of Our Lord God,
  *sel.*
Luke XI: Blessed Be the Paps Which
  Thou Hast Sucked.
Luke VII: She Began to Wash His Feet
  with Tears.
Music's Duel.
On Our Crucified Lord, Naked and
  Bloody.
On the Saviour's Wounds.
Saint Mary Magdalene; or, The Weeper.
Shepherds' Hymn, The.
Song, A: "Lord, when the sense of thy
  sweet grace."
To the Noblest and Best of Ladies [*or*
  Ladyes], the Countess of Denbigh.
Upon the Death of a Gentleman.
Upon the Infant Martyrs.
Wishes to His (Supposed) Mistress.
**Crashaw, Richard** *and* **Abraham Cowley.**
  *See* **Cowley** *and* **Crashaw**
**Crawford, Tom**
Enormous Sleep.
Everything Must Go.
Feeding Cycle of the Catfish, The.
**Creeley, Robert**
After Lorca.
Air: "Cat bird singing."
Air: "Love of a woman, The."
America.
Business, The.
Counterpoint, A.
Cracks, The.
Crisis, The.
Death of Venus, The.
Dishonest Mailmen, The.
Door, The.
Fancy.
Fire, The.
Flower, The.
For Fear.
For Love.
For No Clear Reason.
For Some Weeks.
Form of Women, A.
Friends, The.
Gemini.
Gift, The.
Here.
Heroes.

Hill, The.
I keep to myself such.
I Know a Man.
If You.
Immoral Proposition, The.
In secret/ the out's in.
Innocence, The.
Invoice, The.
Joy.
Kore.
Language, The.
Memory, The.
Moon, The.
Name, The.
Naughty Boy.
Not Now.
Oh No.
Pattern, The.
People, The.
Quick-Step.
Rain, The.
Rescue, The.
Riddle, The: "What it is, the literal
  size."
Signboard, The.
Sitting Here.
Somewhere.
Song: "Those rivers run from that land."
Song: "What do you/ want, love. To
  be."
Token, A.
Wait for Me.
Waiting.
Warning, The.
Way, The.
Where it is.
Whip, The.
Wicker Basket, A.
Wife, The.
Window, The.
World, The.
**Croffut, William Augustus**
Simon Soggs' Thanksgiving.
**Cronin, Anthony**
Baudelaire in Brussels.
On the bog road the blackthorn flowers,
  the turf-stacks.
R.M.S. *Titanic,* sel.
**Cros, Charles**
Smoked Herring, The.
**Crosby, David**
Long Time Gone.
**Crosby, David, Paul Kantner** *and* **Stephen
  Stills**
Wooden Ships.
**Crosby, Fanny (Frances Jane Crosby)**
All the Way My Saviour Leads Me, *with
  music.*
Blessed Assurance, *with music.*
Pass Me Not, O Gentle Saviour, *with
  music.*
There's Music in the Air, *with music.*
To the Work, *with music.*
**Crosby, Ranice Henderson**
Poem about a Seashell.
Thoughts for You (When She Came
  Back from the Mountains).
**Crossman, Samuel**
My Song Is Love Unknown.
**Crouch, Nathaniel**
David and Goliath.
Tower of Babel, The.

**Crouch, Stanley**
Albert Ayler: Eulogy for a Decomposed
 Saxophone Player.
Blackie Thinks of His Brothers.
No New Music.
Riding Across John Lee's Finger.
**Cruickshank, Helen B.**
There Was a Sang.
**Cruz, Juana Inés de la.** *See Juana Inés de*
*la Cruz*
**Cruz, Victor Hernández**
African Things
Alone/ December/ Night.
Bronxomania.
Carmen.
Chicago/ 3 Hours.
Electric Cop, The.
Energy.
Going Uptown to Visit Miriam.
Group, The.
Los New Yorks.
Megalopolis.
Poem: "Greater cities are, The."
Sonsito.
Spirits.
Story of the Zeros, The.
To the Spirit of Carlos Gardel.
Today is a Day of Great Joy
**Cudmore, Daniel**
If could some Delius with divided hands.
**Cullen, Countee**
Black Majesty.
Brown Boy to Brown Girl.
For a Lady I Know.
For a Mouthy Woman.
For My Grandmother.
Four Epitaphs.
From the Dark Tower.
Heritage.
In Memory of Colonel Charles Young.
Incident.
Magnets.
Only the Polished Skeleton.
Saturday's Child.
Scottsboro, Too, Is Worth Its Song.
Simon the Cyrenian Speaks.
Tableau.
To Certain Critics.
Unknown Color, The.
Yet Do I Marvel.
**Cummings, Edward Estlin**
All Ignorance Toboggans into Know.
All in Green Went My Love Riding.
All Which Isn't Singing Is Mere Talking.
All worlds have halfsight, seeing either
 with.
Anyone Lived in a Pretty How Town.
As Freedom Is a Breakfastfood.
Buffalo Bill's.
But/ he" i/ staring.
Buy me an ounce and I'll sell you a
 pound.
Cambridge Ladies Who Live in
 Furnished Souls, The.
Chansons Innocentes, *sels.*
Come, gaze with me upon this dome.
Dirty Colours of Her Kiss Have Just,
 The.
Dive for dreams.
First of All My Dreams Was of, The.
Flotsam and Jetsam.
For Prodigal Read Generous.

Greedy the People, The.
He as O, A.
Helves Surling Out of Eakspeasies Per
 (Reel) hapsingly.
Here Is Little Effie's Head.
Hist Whist.
I carry your heart with me (I carry it in).
I Like My Body When It Is with Your
 Body.
I Sing of Olaf Glad and Big.
I Thank You God for Most This
 Amazing.
I was sitting in mcsorley's.
I Will Be.
If Everything Happens That Can't Be
 Done.
If I Have Made, My Lady, Intricate.
If I Should Sleep with a Lady Called
 Death.
In Heavenly Realms of Hellas Dwelt.
In Just-/ Spring.
Is 5, *sel.*
It is so long since my heart has been
 with yours.
It may not always be so; and I say.
It's Over a (See Just).
Jake Hates All the Girls.
L(a.
Little joe gould has lost his teeth and
 doesn't know where.
Love is a place.
Love Is More Thicker than Forget.
Maggie and Milly and Molly and May.
Man Who Had Fallen among Thieves,
 A.
May I Feel Said He.
Mr. U Will Not Be Missed.
My Father Moved Through Dooms of
 Love.
My Love.
My Specialty Is Living Said.
My Sweet Old Etcetera.
Next to of Course God America I.
No Man, If Men Are Gods.
Nobody Loses All the Time.
Nothing False and Possible Is Love.
Notice the Convulsed Orange Inch of
 Moon.
Now air is air and thing is thing: no
 bliss.
Now I lay (with everywhere around).
O It's Nice to Get Up in, the Slipshod
 Mucous Kiss.
O Sweet Spontaneous Earth.
Old Age.
Old Age Sticks.
One winter afternoon.
Pity This Busy Monster, Manunkind.
Plato Told Him.
Poem, or Beauty Hurts Mr. Vinal.
Politician, A.
Ponder, darling, these busted statues.
R-P-O-P-H-E-S-S-A-G-R.
Raise the Shade.
Salesman is an it that stinks Excuse, A.
She Being Brand.
Since feeling is first.
Sky Was Candy Luminous, The.
Somewhere I Have Never Travelled,
 Gladly Beyond.
Sonnet: "Wind has blown the rain away
 and blown, A."

Sonnets—Actualities, *sel.*
Sonnets—Realities,*sel.*
Sonnets—Unrealities, *sel.*
Space Being (Don't Forget to
 Remember) Curved.
Spring Is Like a Perhaps Hand.
"Sweet spring is your."
Than (By Yon Sunset's Wintry Glow).
This little bride and groom are.
Thou in Whose Swordgreat Story Shine
 the Deeds.
Thy fingers make early flowers of.
Tumbling-hair.
2 little whos.
Unnoticed Woman from Whose Kind
 Large Flesh.
Way to Hump a Cow Is Not, The.
What a Proud Dreamhorse.
What If a Much of a Which of a Wind.
When God Lets My Body Be.
When Serpents Bargain for the Right to
 Squirm.
When the proficient poison of sure sleep.
Who are you, little I.
Who knows if the moon's.
Who's Most Afraid of Death?
Why Did You Go.
Why from this her and him.
You Shall above All Things Be Glad
 and Young.
Your little voice.
**Cummins, P. D.**
Wait.
**Cuney, Waring**
No Images.
O. T.'s Blues.
**Cunningham, Allan**
Wet Sheet and a Flowing Sea, A.
**Cunningham, James**
City Rises, The.
Covenant, The.
Footnote to a Gray Bird's Pause, A.
For Cal.
From a Brother Dreaming in the Rye.
Happy Day (or Independence Day).
High-cool/ 2.
Incidental Pieces to a Walk.
Lee-ers of Hew.
Leg-acy of a Blue Capricorn.
Narrator's Trance, The,*sels.*
Plea to My Sister, A.
Rapping Along with Rhonda Davis.
Slow Riff for Billy.
Solitary Visions of Kaufmanoid.
St. Julien's Eve.
Street in Kaufman-ville, A.
Tambourine.
· Welcome for Etheridge, A.
While Cecil Snores: Mom Drinks Cold
 Milk.
**Cunningham, James Vincent**
Aged Lover Discourses In the Flat Style,
 The.
Agnosco Veteris Vestigia Flammae.
And what is love? Misunderstanding,
 pain.
Apology.
Chase, The.
Choice.
Coffee.
Consolatio Nova: for Alan Swallow.
Convalescence.

Dream Vision.
Elegy for a Cricket.
Envoi: "Hear me, whom I betrayed."
Epigram: "Dark thoughts are my companions. I have wined."
Epigram: "Dear, if unsocial privacies obsess me."
Epigram: For a Woman with Child.
Epigram: "Homer was poor. His scholars live at ease."
Epigram: "How we desire desire! Joy of surcease."
Epigram: "If wisdom, as it seems it is."
Epigram: "In whose will is our peace? Thou happiness."
Epigram: "Life flows to death as rivers to the sea."
Epigram: "Naked I came, naked I leave the scene."
Epigram: Night-piece.
Epigram: "This Humanist whom no beliefs constrained."
Epigram: "Time heals not: it extends a sorrow's scope."
Epigram: "Within this mindless vault."
Epitaph: "When I shall be without regret."
For a College Yearbook.
For My Contemporaries.
Friend, on this scaffold Thomas More lies dead.
In the thirtieth year of life.
Interview with Doctor Drink.
Lady, of anonymous flesh and face.
Meditation on Statistical Method.
Metaphysical Amorist, The.
Modern Love.
Montana Fifty Years Ago.
Montana Pastoral.
Moral Poem, A.
Motto for a Sun Dial.
Phoenix, The.
Reason and Nature.
Ripeness Is All.
Some twenty years of marital agreement.
To a Friend, on Her Examination for the Doctorate in English.
To My Wife.
To the Reader.
To What Strangers, What Welcome.
**Cunninghame-Graham, Robert.** *See* **Graham, Robert**
**Currey, Ralph Nixon**
Jersey Cattle.
Unseen Fire.
**Curry, David**
I Am of These.
Thinking Back Seven Years and Being Here Now.
**Cuscaden, R. R.**
Derricks.
Sold.
**Czerkawska, Catherine Lucy**
Thread.

# D

"**D., H.**" *See* **Doolittle, Hilda**
**Dabney, Betty Page**

Earth's Bondman.
**Dacey, Philip**
Amputee Soldier, The.
Animals' Christmas, The.
Anniversary.
Birthday, The.
Form Rejection Letter.
How I Escaped from the Labyrinth.
Looking at Models in the Sears Catalogue.
Obscene Caller, The.
Perfectionist, The.
Porno Love.
Thumb.
**Dacre, Harry**
Daisy Bell; or, A Bicycle Built for Two, *with music.*
**Daiches, David**
To Kate, Skating Better Than Her Date.
**D'Ambrosio, Vinnie-Marie**
Grace of Cynthia's Maidenhood, The.
Moon as Medusa.
On the Fifth Anniversary of Bluma Sach's Death.
**Dammers, Kim**
MANICdepressant.
**Dana, Robert**
Natural Odes/ American Elegies, *sel.*
**Dandridge, Ray Garfield**
Time to Die.
Zalka Peetruza.
"**Dane, Barry.**" *See* **Logan, John Edward**
**Daniel, John**
Auto Icon.
Excerpts from a Diary of a War (1-3).
Injury to Insured.
My Wife Who Is American.
Of 91 Men Leaving an Underground Station.
Phrases for Everyday Use by the British in India.
Two Clocks.
Watch.
**Daniel, Samuel**
Appeal, The.
Beauty, sweet love, is like the morning dew.
Care-Charmer Sleep.
First Flame.
Heavenly Eloquence.
Hymen's Triumph, *sels.*
Love Is a Sickness.
Musophilus, *sel.*
None other fame mine unambitious muse.
Secrecy.
Sonnet: "I must not grieve my love, whose eyes would read."
Tethys' Festival, *sel.*
To Delia, *sels.*
Ulysses and the Siren.
**Daniell, Rosemary**
Before the Fall.
Girl Friends.
I Want.
To a Family Man in His Family Room.
**Danner, Margaret**
And through the Caribbean Sea.
Best Loved of Africa.
Convert, The.
Elevator Man Adheres to Form, The.
Far from Africa: Four Poems.

Garnishing the Aviary.
Goodbye David Tamunoemi West.
Painted Lady, The.
Sadies's Playhouse.
Slave and the Iron Lace, The.
This Is an African Worm.
**Dante Alighieri**
Divina Commedia, *sels.*
Guido da Montefeltro.
Inferno, The, *sel.*
Sonnet: "Upon a day, came sorrow in to me."
Ulysses.
**Darion, Joe**
Impossible Dream, The, *with music*
**Darley, George**
Ethelstan, *sel.*
Hundred-gated Thebes.
Mermaidens' Vesper-Hymn, The.
Nepenthe, *sels.*
Phoenix, The.
Runilda's Chant.
Sea-Ritual, The.
Serenade of a Loyal Martyr.
Syren Songs, *sels.*
To the Moon.
Wherefore, unlaurelled boy.
**Darnley, Henry Stuart [or Stewart], Lord**
If Langour Makis Men Licht.
**Darr, Ann**
Before Dawn.
Dear Oedipus.
Hangar Nine.
Love Is.
Low...the Violence Begins Low.
**Daryush, Elizabeth**
Still-Life.
**Daugherty, James**
Citizen Paine.
**Davenant [or D'Avenant], Sir William**
Aubade: "Lark now leaves his watery nest, The."
Endimion Porter and Olivia.
Gondibert, *sels.*
Just Italian, The, *sel.*
Law Against Lovers, The, *sel.*
Luminalia, *sel.*
Night's Song.
Philosopher and the Lover, The: To a Mistress Dying.
Siege of Rhodes, The, *sel.*
Soldier [or Souldier] Going to the Field, The.
Song: "Come, melt thy soul in mine, that when unite."
Temple of Love, The, *sel.*
Triumphs of the Prince D'Amour, The, *sel.*
Under the Willow-Shades.
Unfortunate Lovers, The, *sel.*
Wake All the Dead.
Winter Storms, The.
**Davidson, John**
Ballad of a Nun, A.
In Romney Marsh.
London.
Runnable Stag, A.
Thirty Bob a Week.
Unknown, The.
**Davie, Donald**
Across the Bay.
Forests of Lithuania, The, *sel.*

Fountain, The.
Heigh-ho on a Winter Afternoon.
Remembering the 'Thirties.
Thanks to Industrial Essex.
Time Passing, Beloved.
**Davies, Idris**
High Summer on the Mountain.
Lay Preacher Ponders, The.
**Davies, Idris** *and* **Pete Seeger**
Bells of Rhymney.
**Davies, J. R. S.**
Cranes.
**Davies, Sir John**
Affliction.
Gulling Sonnets, *sels.*
Hymns of Astraea, *sel.*
Kate Being Pleased.
Nosce Teipsum,*sels.*
Of Astraea.
Orchestra, or A Poeme of Dauncing, *sels.*
Praise of Dancing, The.
Soul and the Body, The.
Who Doth Not See the Measure of the Moon?
**Davies, William Henry**
Beautiful, The.
Cat, The.
Dumb World, The.
Inquest, The.
Kingfisher, The.
Leisure.
Rabbit, The.
Rain, The.
Rat, The.
Rich Days.
Sailor to His Parrot, The.
School's Out.
Sheep.
Villain, The.
Visitor, The.
When Yon Full Moon.
White Horse, The.
**Davis, Frank Marshall**
Arthur Ridgewood, M.D.
Flowers of Darkness.
Four Glimpses of Night.
Giles Johnson, Ph.D.
I Sing No New Songs.
Robert Whitmore.
Snapshots of the Cotton South.
**Davis, Gussie L.**
In the Baggage Coach Ahead, *with music.*
**Davis, Ronda**
Invitation (To the Night and All Other Things Dark).
Parasitosis.
Personality Sketch, A: Bill.
Poems about Playmates.
Spacin.
**Davis, Thomas Osborne**
Geraldines, The.
Girl I Left behind Me, The ("Dames of France are fond and free, The").
Lament for the Death of Eoghan Ruadh O'Neill.
**Davison, Peter**
Last Word, The.
**Davison, Walter**
Ode: "At her fair hands how have I grace entreated."

**Dawe, Bruce**
Drifters.
Frog Plague, The.
Gorilla Gorilla.
Katrina.
Life-Cycle.
Sleight-of-Hand.
Somewhere Friendly.
Under Way.
Weapons Training.
What Lies on Us.
**Dawson, William**
Lay of Oliver Gogarty, The.
**Day, Clarence**
Who Drags the Fiery Artist Down?
**Day, James William**
Rowan County Crew, The.
**Day Lewis, Cecil**
Album, The.
Almost Human.
Circus Lion.
Come, live with me and be my love.
Do Not Expect Again.
Double Vision, The.
Failure, A.
Flight to Italy, *sel.*
Fox, The.
Is It Far to Go?
Jig.
My Mother's Sister.
Newsreel.
Reconciliation.
Sheepdog Trials in Hyde Park.
Two Songs.
Watching Post.
Where are the War Poets?
**Dayre, Sydney (Mrs. Cochran)**
Lesson for Mamma, A.
Morning Compliments.
**Dayton, Irene**
His Coming.
Psalmen Gezangen.
Vinedresser Yearns over His Vineyard, The.
**Deane, Seamus**
Return.
**DeBruhl, Melvin**
At Last.
Brown Circles.
**DeFrees, Madeline**
Letter to an Absent Son.
Pendant Watch.
Wake, The.
**Dehn, Paul**
Armistice.
At the Dark Hour.
Come unto these yellow sands.
Geiger, geiger, ticking slow.
I wandered angry as a cloud.
Leaden Treasury of English Verse, A, *sel.*
Ring-a-ring o' neutrons.
Twinkle, twinkle, little star.
**Dekker, Thomas**
Art thou poor, yet hast thou golden slumbers?
Cradle Song, A: "Golden slumbers kiss your eyes."
Death Terrible in Countenance.
Dekker His Dream, *sels.*
Extremities of Cold in Hell, The.

London's Tempe; or, The Field of Happiness, *sel.*
Noble Soldier, The, *sel.*
Pleasant Comedy of Patient Grissell, The, *sels.*
Thwick-a-thwack.
**De la Mare, Walter ("Walter Ramal")**
Alas, Alack!
All That's Past.
At the Zoo.
Autumn.
Bah!
Brueghel's Winter.
Bunches of Grapes.
Echo.
Fare Well.
Feckless Dinner Party, The.
Five Eyes.
Full Moon.
Ghost, The.
Hunt, The.
John Mouldy.
Listeners, The.
Miss Loo.
Napoleon.
Nod.
Nothing.
Off the Ground.
Old King, The.
Old Shellover.
Old Tailor, The.
Portrait, A.
Railway Junction, The.
Rats.
Revenant, The.
Scarecrow, The.
Scholars.
Silver.
Silver Penny, The.
Snow-flake, The.
Some One.
Song of the Mad Prince, The.
Tartary.
Then.
Thomas Hardy.
Tired Tim.
Tom's Angel.
Tryst, The.
**Delany, Clarissa Scott**
Solace.
**De la Selva, Salomon**
Elegy: "My comrade is dead."
**De Longchamps, Joanne**
Tortoise.
**De Morgan, Augustus**
Fleas, The.
**DenBoer, James**
Casting a Vote
Charming the Moon.
**Denham, Sir John**
Cooper's Hill, *sel.*
Progress of Learning, The, *sel.*
**Dennis, C. J.**
Swagman, The.
**Dennis, Nigel**
Desperate Measure, A.
**De Pietro, Albert**
Colossi.
Dog talk.
Meditations on Frost's "Stopping by Woods."
Rejoinder.

**Derleth, August**
  Planetary Arc-Light, The.
**De Roche, Joseph**
  Aunt Laura Moves Toward the Open
    Grave of Her Father.
  Blond.
**Derricotte, Toi**
  Boxes.
  Doll Poem ("Doll is sitting in a box").
  Face as It Might Be of Love, The.
  This Woman Will Not Bear Children.
**Derwood, Gene**
  After Reading St. John the Divine.
**Desmond, Gerald, Earl of**
  Against Blame of Woman.
**Desnos, Robert**
  Poem to the Mysterious Woman.
**De Tabley, John Byrne Leicester Warren,
    3d Baron**
  Churchyard on the Sands, The.
**Deutsch, Babette**
  Barges on the Hudson.
  Bull, A.
  Destruction of Letters.
  Fireworks.
  Mother, The.
  Natural Law.
  Stranger Than the Worst.
  To the Moon.
**De Vere, Aubrey Thomas**
  In Ruin Reconciled.
  Little Black Rose, The.
**Devlin, Denis**
  Ank'hor Vat.
  Ascension.
  Encounter.
  Lough Derg.
  Venus of the Salty Shell.
**Dewey, A. A.**
  At the Drive-In: "John Wayne vs. God."
  Blizzard, The.
  Coyote, The.
**Dickey, James**
  Adultery.
  Bee, The.
  Between Two Prisoners.
  Birth, A.
  Buckdancer's Choice.
  Bums, on Waking.
  Celebration, The.
  Chenille.
  Cherrylog Road.
  Deer among Cattle.
  Driver, The.
  Encounter in the Cage Country.
  Falling.
  Fence Wire.
  Fiend, The.
  Firebombing, The.
  Heaven of Animals, The.
  Hospital Window, The.
  Hunting Civil War Relics at Nimblewill
    Creek.
  In the Mountain Tent.
  In the Pocket.
  Inside the River.
  Lifeguard, The.
  Listening to Foxhounds.
  Moon Ground, The.
  Movement of Fish, The.
  On Giving a Son to the Sea.
  On the Hill Below the Lighthouse.

  Performance, The.
  Pursuit from Under.
  Reincarnation (I).
  Reincarnation (II).
  Shark's Parlor, The.
  Sheep Child, The.
  Slave Quarters.
  Springer Mountain.
  Sun.
  Them, Crying.
  Underground Stream, The.
**Dickey, R. P.**
  Humidity.
  Shazam.
  Takes All Kinds.
  X.
**Dickey, William**
  Exploration Over the Rim.
  Hope.
  Lesson of the Master.
  Memoranda.
  Resolving Doubts.
  Spectrum.
  Voyage to the Moon.
  What It Means, Living in the City.
**Dickinson, Emily**
  After great pain, a formal feeling comes.
  Ah, necromancy sweet!
  Ah, Teneriffe!
  Alter! When the hills do.
  Altered look about the hills, An.
  Apparently with no surprise.
  "Arcturus" is his other name.
  As imperceptibly as grief.
  Because I could not stop for Death.
  Bee his burnished carriage, A.
  Bee! I'm expecting you!
  Bird came down the walk, A.
  Birthday of but a single pang.
  Brain, within its groove, The.
  Brain is wider than the sky, The.
  Bustle in a house, The.
  Circumference thou bride of awe.
  Clock stopped, A.
  Color—caste—denomination.
  Conscious am I in my chamber.
  Crisis is a hair.
  Crumbling is not an instant's act.
  Dear March, come in.
  Death is the supple suitor.
  Did our best moment last.
  Did the harebell loose her girdle.
  Difference between despair, The.
  Drama's vitallest expression is the
    common day.
  Drunkard cannot meet a cork, A.
  Elysium is as far as to.
  Essential oils are wrung.
  Everywhere of silver, An.
  Exultation is the going.
  "Faith" is a fine invention.
  Farther in summer than the birds.
  Finding is the first act.
  First day's night had come, The.
  Forever—is composed of nows.
  Further in summer than the birds.
  God is indeed a jealous God.
  He outstripped Time with but a bout.
  He preached upon "breadth" till it
    argued him narrow.
  Heart asks pleasure first, The.
  Heart! We will forget him!

  Heaven is so far of the mind.
  "Heavenly Father"—take to thee.
  Her—"last poems."
  Hope is a strange invention.
  Hope is a subtle glutton.
  "Hope" is the thing with feathers.
  How brittle are the piers.
  How the waters closed above him.
  I am afraid to own a body.
  I am alive—I guess.
  I asked no other thing.
  I breathed enough to take the trick.
  I can wade grief.
  I cannot live with you.
  I died for beauty—but was scarce.
  I dreaded that first robin, so.
  I dwell in Possibility.
  I envy seas, whereon he rides.
  I felt a cleaving in my mind.
  I felt a funeral, in my brain.
  I found the phrase to every thought.
  I had been hungry, all the years.
  I heard a fly buzz—when I died.
  I know that He exists.
  I like a look of agony.
  I like to see it lap the miles.
  I meant to have but modest needs.
  I never hear the word "escape."
  I never lost as much but twice.
  I never saw a moor.
  I read my sentence—steadily.
  I reckon—when I count at all.
  I saw no way—the heavens were
    stitched.
  I shall know why—when time is over.
  I started early, took my dog.
  I stepped from plank to plank.
  I taste a liquor never brewed.
  I watched the moon around the house.
  I would not paint—a picture.
  I years had been from home.
  If you were coming in the fall.
  I'm ceded—I've stopped being theirs.
  I'm nobody! Who are you?
  I'm "wife"—I've finished that.
  In winter in my room.
  It dropped so low—in my regard.
  It sifts from leaden sieves.
  It struck me every day.
  It was not death, for I stood up.
  It would have starved a gnat.
  I've seen a dying eye.
  Just lost, when I was saved!
  Light exists in spring, A.
  Lightning is a yellow fork, The.
  Like trains of cars on tracks of plush.
  Me from myself—to banish.
  Mine—by the right of the white election.
  Mine enemy is growing old.
  Moon was but a chin of gold, The.
  Morns are meeker than they were, The.
  Much madness is divinest sense.
  My life closed twice before its close.
  My life had stood—a loaded gun.
  Name—of it—is "Autumn," The.
  Narrow fellow in the grass, A.
  No crowd that has occurred.
  Of all the souls that stand create.
  Of bronze and blaze.
  One need not be a chamber—to be
    haunted.
  Our journey had advanced.

Our lives are Swiss.
Over the fence.
Pain—expands the time.
Pain has an element of blank.
Papa above!
Pedigree of honey, The.
Perception of an object costs.
Poets light but lamps, The.
Remorse is memory awake.
Renunciation—is a piercing virtue.
Reportless subjects, to the quick.
Revolution is the pod.
Route of evanescence, A.
Safe in their alabaster chambers.
Satisfaction—is the agent.
Sepal, petal, and a thorn, A.
She staked her feathers—gained an arc.
Single clover plank, A.
Sky is low, the clouds are mean, The.
Snow that never drifts, The.
So proud she was to die.
Softened by time's consummate plush.
Some keep the Sabbath going to church.
Soul has bandaged moments, The.
Soul selects her own society, The.
Spider as an artist, The.
Spider holds a silver ball, The.
Spider sewed at night, A.
Success is counted sweetest.
Tell all the truth but tell it slant.
That it will never come again.
That love is all there is.
There are two Mays.
There came a day at summer's full.
There is a pain—so utter.
There is no frigate like a book.
There's a certain slant of light.
There's been a death in the opposite
  house.
These are the days when birds come
  back.
They shut me up in prose.
This is my letter to the world.
This was a poet—it is that.
This world is not conclusion.
Time feels so vast that were it not.
'Tis true—they shut me in the cold.
Title divine—is mine!
To be alive—is power.
To die—takes just a little while.
To fight aloud is very brave.
To make a prairie it takes a clover and
  one bee.
Too happy time dissolves itself.
'Twas a long parting—but the time.
Until the desert knows.
Victory comes late.
Way I read a letter's—this, The.
We outgrow love, like other things.
What mystery pervades a well!
What soft, cherubic creatures.
When bells stop ringing—church—
  begins.
While we were fearing it, it came.
Wild nights!—Wild nights!
Wind begun to rock the grass, The.
With thee, in the desert.
Word made flesh is seldom, A.
You'll know it—as you know—tis noon.

**Dickinson, John**
Liberty Song, The, with music.

**Dickinson, Patric**

Dam, The.
New Block.
Redwing, The.

**Dienstag, Alan**
Golden Witch, The.

**Dillard, Annie**
Arches and Shadows.

**Dillard, R. H. W.**
America Is Darken'd.
Day I Stopped Dreaming About
  Barbara Steele, The.
Downtown Roanoke.
Hats.
Looking for Asia.
Meditation for a Pickle Suite.

**Dimoff, John**
West of Chicago.

**"Dinesen, Isak" (Karen Blixen)**
Zebra.

**DiPasquale, Emanuel**
Rain.

**DiPrima, Diane**
Prayer to the Mothers.
Quarrel, The.
Revolutionary Letter # 1.
Revolutionary Letter # 4.
Revolutionary Letter # 19.
Revolutionary Letter # 21.

**Dix, William Chatterton**
What Child Is This? with music.

**Dixon, Alan**
Chops.

**Dixon, Henry**
Description of a Good Boy, The.

**Dixon, Richard Watson**
Song: "Feathers of the willow, The."

**Djangatolum.** See **Corbin, Lloyd M., Jr.**

**Doak, Katherine**
Fox Song.
Nunnery.
Sea Otter, Dream Poem to My Mother.
Song of Ceres.

**Doane, William Croswell**
Ancient of Days, with music.

**Dobkins, Claudia**
Brief Explanation.
Miracle Worker.
Still Life.
Voice.

**Dobson, Austin**
Ballade of Prose and Rhyme, The.
July.
Kiss, A.
Rondel; The Wanderer.
Rose-Leaves, sels.
Urceus Exit.

**Dobson, Rosemary**
Birth, The.
Cock Crow.
Country Morning.
Country Press.
Martyrdom of Saint Sebastian, The.
Still Life.

**"Doc Long."** See **Long, Doughtry, Jr.**

**Dodat, François**
Dromedary.
Ladybug.

**Doddridge, Philip**
O Happy Day, with music.

**Dodge, Mary Mapes**
Buttercup.
Farmer in Bungleton, A.

**Dodge, Ossian E.**
Ho! Westward Ho! with music.

**Dodgson, Charles Lutwidge.** See **"Carroll, Lewis"**

**Dodson, Owen**
Hymn Written after Jeremiah Preached
  to Me in a Dream.
I Break the Sky.
Mary Passed This Morning.
Poems for My Brother Kenneth, sel.
Sorrow Is the Only Faithful One.
Yardbird's Skull.

**Donaghy, John Lyle**
Deathward.
Duck.
Portrait.
Winter.

**Donne, John**
Air and Angels.
Anagram, The.
Anatomy of the World, An, sel.
Anniversary [or Anniversarie], The.
Annunciation.
Antiquary.
Apparition, The.
Autumnal, The.
Bait, The.
Blossom, The.
Break of Day.
Burnt Ship, A.
Canonization, The.
Death, Be Not Proud.
Dreame, The.
Ecstasy, The.
Elegies, sels.
Elegy: "Nature's lay idiot, I taught thee
  to love."
Elephant, The.
Epithalamion, An; or, Marriage-Song on
  the Lady Elizabeth and Count
  Palatine Being Married on St.
  Valentine's Day, abr.
Epithalamion Made at Lincoln's Inn.
Epithalamion: "Thou art reprieved old
  year, thou shalt not die," abr.
Expiration, The.
Flea, The.
Funeral, The.
Good Friday, 1613. Riding Westward.
Good Lord, Deliver Us!
Good-Morrow, The.
Holy Sonnets, sels.
Hymn to Christ, at the Author's Last
  Going into Germany, A.
Hymn to God My God, in My Sickness.
Hymn to God the Father, A.
In Eundem Macaronicon.
Indifferent, The.
Lecture Upon the Shadow, A.
Letter to the Lady Carey and Mrs. Essex
  Rich, A, sel.
Litany, A, sels.
Love's Alchemy.
Love's Deity [or Deitie].
Love's Growth; or, Spring.
Love's Progress.
Message, The.
Nativity.
Nocturnal[l] upon St Lucy's [or S.
  Lucies] Day, Being the Shortest Day,
  A.

Of the Progress of the Soul; the Second
  Anniversary, *sels.*
On His Mistress [*or* Mistris].
Primrose, Being at Montgomery Castle,
  The.
Progresse of the Soule, The ("I sing the
  progress of a deathless soul"), *sels.*
Relic, The.
Satire: "Kind pity chokes my spleen;
  brave scorn forbids.
Satire: "Well, I may now receive, and
  die: my sin."
Satires, *sels.*
Seek True Religion!
Song: "Go and catch a falling star."
Song: "Sweetest love, I do not go."
Sonnet: "Batter my heart, three-personed
  God; for you."
Storm, The, *sel.*
Storm at Sea, A.
Sun [*or* Sunne] Rising, The.
Take heed of loving me.
To Mr. Rowland Woodward.
To Mrs. Magdalen Herbert, *sel.*
To Sir Henry Wotton ("Here's no more
  news than virtue").
To Sir Henry Wotton ("Sir, more than
  kisses letters mingle souls.")
To the Countess of Bedford ("Reason is
  our soul's left hand").
To the Countess of Salisbury, *sel.*
Triple Fool, The.
Twicknam Garden.
Undertaking, The.
Valediction, A: Of Weeping.
Valediction Forbidding Mourning, A.
Whale, The.
**Donnelly, Charles**
Last Poem.
**Donnelly, Dorothy**
Chinese Baby Asleep.
Glass World.
Leaflight.
Recollection.
Serenade: "Tin-type tune the locusts
  make, The."
**"Donovan."** *See* **Leitch, Donovan**
**Donzella, D. W.**
To My Father on Pearl Harbor Day.
Winter.
**Dooley, Ebon**
Easter Bunny Blues Or All I Want for
  Xmas Is the Loop, The.
Prophet's Warning or Shoot to Kill, The.
Query.
**Doolittle, Hilda ("H. D.")**
Acon.
At Baia.
At Ithaca.
Callypso Speaks.
Centaur Song.
Evening.
Eurydice
Evadne.
Flowering of the Rod, The. *sel.*
Fragment 113.
Fragment Thirty-Six.
Garden, The, *sel.*
Good Frend, *sel.*
Heat.
Helen.
Helen in Egypt, *sels.*

Hermes of the Ways.
Hippolytus Temporizes.
Lethe.
Mysteries Remain, The.
Oread.
Pear Tree.
Pursuit.
Sea Poppies.
Sea Rose.
She Contrasts with Herself Hippolyta.
She Rebukes Hippolyta.
Sigil.
Stars Wheel in Purple.
Time has an end, they say.
Tribute to the Angels, *sels.*
Walls Do Not Fall, The, *sel.*
Wind Sleepers, The.
**Dorman, Sonya**
Burglar, The.
Decorating Problem.
Hunters.
In the Sly Gardens.
Surfer and Others.
**Dorn, Edward**
Biggest Killing, The.
Comforted by Limestone.
Eugene Delacroix Says.
From Gloucester Out.
Gunslinger, *sels.*
Idle Visitation, An.
Morning to Remember, A; or, E
  Pluribus Unum.
Mourning Letter, March 29 1963.
On the Debt My Mother Owed to Sears
  Roebuck.
Oxford, *sel.*
Song, A: "There is a blue sky."
Song, The: "So light no one noticed."
Thesis.
**Dorset, Catherine Ann**
Peacock "At Home," The.
**Dorset, Charles Sackville, 6th Earl of.** *See*
  **Sackville, Charles, 6th Earl of Dorset**
Dorset, Thomas Sackville, 1st Earl of. *See*
  **Sackville, Thomas, 1st Earl of Dorset**
**Douglas, Lord Alfred Bruce**
Lion, The.
**Douglas, Keith**
How to Kill.
John Anderson.
Knife, The.
Prisoner, The.
Russians.
Simplify Me When I'm Dead.
Syria.
Vergissmeinicht.
**Douglas, William** *and* **Lady John Scott**
Annie Laurie, *with music.*
**Doulis, Thomas**
Honored Dead, The.
**Dove, Rita**
Adolescence—II.
Nigger Song: An Odyssey.
This Life.
**Dow, Philip**
Duck Pond at Mini's Pasture, a Dozen
  Years Later, The.
Life, The.
Playing.
Twilight in California.
**Dowson, Ernest Christopher**
Exile.

Extreme Unction.
Non Sum Qualis Eram Bonae Sub
  Regno Cynarae.
Valediction, A: "If we must part."
Villanelle of the Poet's Road.
Vitae Summa Brevis Spem Nos Vetat
  Incohare Longam.
**Drake, Joseph Rodman**
American Flag, The.
**Dransfield, Michael**
Change, The.
Geograpy.
**Drayton, Michael**
As love and I, late harbour'd in one inn.
Ballad of Agincourt, The.
Calling to mind since first my love
  begun.
Crier, The.
Dear, why should you command me to
  my rest.
Farewell to Love.
First Steps Up Parnassus.
His Remedie for Love.
Idea, *sels.*
Idea's Mirror.
Shepherd's Sirena, The,*sels.*
To His Coy Love.
To Master George Sandys, Treasurer for
  the English Colony in Virginia, *sel.*
To My Most Dearly Loved Henry
  Reynolds, *sel.*
To My Noble Friend Master William
  Browne: of the Evil Time,*sels.*
To the Reader of These Sonnets.
To the Virginian Voyage.
Verses Made the Night before He Died.
**Drennan, John Swanick**
Epigram: "Golden casket I designed,
  A."
Epigram: "Love signed the contract
  blithe and leal."
On the Telescopic Moon.
**Dresbach, Glenn Ward**
Cave, The.
**Dresser, Paul**
Just Tell Them That You Saw Me, *with
  music.*
My Gal Sal, *with music.*
On the Banks of the Wabash, Far Away,
  *with music.*
**"Drinan, Adam."** *See* **Macleod, Joseph
  Gordon**
**Drinkwater, John**
Birthright.
Moonlit Apples.
Snail.
Sun, The.
Symbols.
**Drouet, Minou**
Garden.
**Drummond, William, of Hawthornden**
Inexorable.
Madrigal: "Like the Idalian queen."
Nativity, The.
Saint John Baptist.
This life which seems so fair.
This world a hunting is.
World a Hunt, The.
**Drummond, William Henry**
Wreck of the *Julie Plante*, The.
**Dryden, John**
Absalom and Achitophel, Pt. I., *sels.*

Achitophel: the Earl of Shaftesbury.
Alexander's Feast: or, The Power of
  Music.
All, All of a Piece.
Amphitryon, sel.
Annus Mirabilis, sels.
Crown Prince of Dullness, The.
Cymon and Iphigenia, sel.
Farewell, Ungrateful Traitor.
Fire of London, sel.
Hind and the Panther, The, sel.
Incantation to Oedipus.
Let him rail on, let his invective Muse.
Lines on a Paid Militia.
Lines Printed under the Engraved
  Portrait of Milton.
London after the Great Fire, 1666.
MacFlecknoe; or, A Satire upon the
  True-Blue Protestant Poet T. S.
Marriage à la Mode,sels.
Medal, The, sel.
Mercury's Song to Phaedra.
Oedipus, sel.
Of these the false Achitophel was first.
Prologue to His Royal Highness.
Reason and Religion.
Religio Laici, sel.
Revelation.
Rondelay, A: "Chloe found Amyntas
  lying."
Secular Masque, The.
Shadwell Anatomized.
Song for Saint Cecilia's Day, 1687, A.
Song: "Whilst Alexis lay pressed."
Spanish Friar, The, sel.
To the Memory of Mr. Oldham.
To the Pious Memory of the
  Accomplished Young Lady Mrs. Anne
  Killigrew.
War.
Why Should a Foolish Marriage Vow.
Zimri: the Duke of Buckingham.
**Dryden, John and Nahum Tate.** *See* **Tate,**
  **Nahum** *and* **John Dryden**
**Dubie, Norman**
Balalaika.
Dressing Stations, The.
In the Dead of the Night.
Killigrew Wood, The.
Monologue of Two Moons, Nudes with
  Crests. 1938.
Pastoral: "It all happened so fast. Fenya
  was in the straight chair."
**DuBois, William Edward Burghardt**
Song of the Smoke, The.
**Duckett, Alfred A.**
Sonnet: "Where are we to go when this
  is done?"
**Dudek, Louis**
How Man Learned to Walk—and Run.
Shredded Wheat.
**Dufferin, Lady.** *See* **Sheridan, Helen Selina**
**Duffield, George**
Stand Up! Stand Up for Jesus, *with*
  *music.*
**Dugan, Alan**
Actual Vision of Morning's Extrusion.
Adultery.
American against Solitude.
Elegy for a Puritan Conscience.
Elegy: "I know but will not tell."
Fabrication of Ancestors.

For Masturbation.
From Rome, for More Public Fountains
  in New York City.
Funeral Oration for a Mouse.
Holiday.
How We Heard the Name.
Let Heroes Account to Love.
Letter to Eve.
Love Song: I and Thou.
Morning Song.
On Alexander and Aristotle, on a Black-
  on-Red Greek Plate.
On Finding the Meaning of "Radiance."
On Hurricane Jackson.
On Rape Unattempted.
Plague of Dead Sharks.
Poem: "In the old days either the
  plaintiff or the defendant won or lost."
Poem: "Person who can do, The."
Poem: "What's the balm."
Stability before Departure.
Stutterer.
Thesis, Antithesis, and Nostalgia.
To a Red-headed Do-good Waitress.
Trial, A.
Tribute to Kafka for Someone Taken.
What Happened? What Do You Expect?
Winter: For an Untenable Situation.
**Dugdale, Norman**
Anarchist.
**Duguid, Sandra Ruth**
Bee, A/ Interestingly.
If it is a poem.
Maze of the Magi, A.
On Restoring Verticals.
Plato.
Rabbinic/ The cynic.
**Duke, Richard**
After the fiercest pangs of hot desire.
**Dumas, Henry**
America.
Black Star Line.
Black Trumpeter.
Buffalo.
Knock on Wood.
**Dunbar, Paul Laurence**
Ante-Bellum Sermon, An.
Compensation.
Corn-Song, A.
Debt, The.
Frederick Douglass.
Harriet Beecher Stowe.
In the Morning.
Misapprehension.
Paradox, The.
Philosophy.
Poet, The.
Soliloquy of a Turkey.
Spiritual, A.
Sympathy.
Then and Now.
To a Captious Critic.
Unsung Heroes, The.
We Wear the Mask.
When de Co'n Pone's Hot.
When Dey 'Listed Colored Soldiers.
When Malindy Sings.
**Dunbar, William**
Lord Is Risen, The.
Of the Changes of Life.
Timor Mortis Conturbat Me.
To a Lady [*or* Ladye].

Unto Us a Child Is Born.
**Duncan, Robert**
African Elegy, An.
Answering.
At Christmas.
At the Loom.
Ballad of Mrs. Noah, The.
Dante Etudes, *sel.*
Envoy.
Etude from the Third Epistle.
Fire, The.
Fourth Song the Night Nurse Sang.
Homage and Lament for Ezra Pound in
  Captivity.
Law I Love Is Major Mover, The.
Moon, The.
My Mother Would Be a Falconress.
Night Scenes.
Often I Am Permitted to Return to a
  Meadow.
Orders, Passages 24.
Part-Sequence for Change, A.
Passage over Water.
Passages, *sels*
Persephone.
Poem Beginning with a Line by Pindar,
  A.
Poetry, a Natural Thing.
Roots and Branches.
Tears of St. Francis.
Temple of the Animals, The.
This Place Rumord to Have Been
  Sodom.
Tribal Memories.
Two Presentations.
What I Saw.
Where It Appears.
**Dunn, Douglas**
Clothes Pit, The.
From the Night-Window.
Hunched, The.
On Roofs of Terry Street.
Removal from Terry Street, A.
**Dunn, Stephen**
At Every Gas Station There Are
  Mechanics.
Biography in the First Person.
City Boy, The.
Cycle, The.
Day and Night Handball.
Dream, The.
For the Sleepless.
Giraffes: The American Version.
If I Were in Charge of Epiphanies.
Looking for a Rest Area.
Loss, The.
On Hearing the Airlines Will Use a
  Psychological Profile to Catch
  Potential Skyjackers.
Rapist, The.
Small Town: The Friendly.
To the Upright.
**Dunsany, Edward John Moreton Drax**
  **Plunkett, 18th Baron**
Call to the Wild, A.
**Durem, Ray**
Award.
Friends.
I Know I'm Not Sufficiently Obscure.
Problem in Social Geometry—The
  Inverted Square!
Vet's Rehabilitation.

**Durfey, Thomas**
Bee-hive, The.
Don Quixote, *sel.*
Early in the Dawning.
Gentle Breeze, A.
I'll Sail Upon the Dog-star.
Mountebank Song, The.
New Dialogue, Sung by a Boy and Girl at the Playhouse, A.
New Song Made in Honour of His Grace the Duke of Marlborough, A.
**Durrell, Lawrence**
Ballad of the Oedipus Complex.
Bitter Lemons.
Coptic Poem.
Epitaph: "Stavro's dead. A truant vine."
Mythology.
Poggio.
This Unimportant Morning.
To Ping-Ku, Asleep.
**Dyer, Lady Catherine**
Epitaph on the Monument of Sir William Dyer At Colmworth, 1641.
If a large heart joined with a noble mind.
Sir William Dyer, Knight,*sels.*
**Dyer, Sir Edward**
My Mind to Me a Kingdom Is.
Silent Love, A.
**Dyer, John**
Grongar Hill.
**Dylan, Bob**
Dear Mister Congressman.
Desolation Row.
Father of Night.
Hard Rain's a-Gonna Fall, A.
Masters of War.
New Morning.
Subterranean Homesick Blues.
Tears of Rage.
**Dyment, Clifford**
As a boy with a richness of needs I wandered.
Man and Beast.
Sea Shanty.
Swans, The.

# E

**"Eagle, Solomon."** *See* **Squire, Sir John Collings**
**Earley, Tom**
Jackdaw.
Moorhen Pond, The.
**"Eastaway, Edward."** *See* **Thomas, Edward**
**Eberhart, Nelle Richmond**
At Dawning, *with music.*
**Eberhart, Richard**
Analogue of Unity in Multeity.
At Night.
Attitudes, *sel.*
Ball Game.
Cold Fall.
Cover me over, clover.
Flux.
Forms of the Human.
Fury of Aerial Bombardment, The.
Groundhog, The.

Horse Chestnut Tree, The.
I walked over the grave of Henry James.
If I Could Only Live at the Pitch That Is Near Madness.
Kaire.
"Mysticism Has Not the Patience to Wait for God's Revelation."
New England Bachelor, A.
New England Protestant.
New Hampshire, February.
On a Squirrel Crossing the Road in Autumn, in New England.
Rumination.
Sea-Hawk.
Snowfall, A.
To the Field Mice.
Two Loves.
**Eckman, Frederick**
Old Man, Phantom Dog.
Student, The.
**Economou, George**
Seventh Georgic.
**Edelman, Elaine**
How Beautiful You Are: 3.
**Edson, Russell**
Childhood of an Equestrian, The.
Children.
Counting Sheep.
In All the Days of My Childhood.
Performance at Hog Theater, A.
Retirement of the Elephant, The.
**Eigner, Larry**
All Intents.
Elysee.
Fleche.
**"Eliot, George" (Mary Ann [or Marian] Evans Lewes Cross)**
O May I Join the Choir Invisible.
**Eliot, Thomas Stearns**
Ash-Wednesday.
*Boston Evening Transcript*, The.
Burnt Norton.
Chorus: "We do not wish anything to happen."
Chorus: "We have not been happy, my Lord, we have not been too happy."
Cultivation of Christmas Trees, The.
Dedication to My Wife, A.
Dry Salvages, The.
East Coker.
Eyes that last I saw in tears.
Four Quartets,*sels.*
Gerontion.
Gus: the Theatre Cat.
Hippopotamus, The.
Hollow Men, The.
Journey of the Magi.
La Figlia Che Piange.
Lines for Cuscuscaraway and Mirza Murad Ali Beg.
Little Gidding.
Love Song of J. Alfred Prufrock, The.
Macavity: The Mystery Cat.
Marina.
Morning at the Window.
Murder in the Cathedral,*sels.*
Naming of Cats, The.
Portrait of a Lady.
Preludes (I–IV).
Rhapsody on a Windy Night.
Skimbleshanks: The Railway Cat.
Song for Simeon, A.

Song of the Jellicles, The.
Sweeney Among the Nightingales.
Sweeney Erect.
Waste Land, The.
Whispers of Immortality.
**Elizabeth I, Queen of England**
Doubt of Future Foes, The.
On Fortune.
On Monsieur's Departure.
When I was fair and young and favour graced me.
Written in Her French Psalter.
Written on a Wall at Woodstock.
Written with a Diamond on Her Window at Woodstock.
**Elizabeth of York, Queen**
My Heart Is Set upon a Lusty Pin.
**Ellerton, John Lodge**
Day Thou Gavest, Lord, Is Ended, The, *with music.*
**Elliot, Charlotte**
Just as I Am, *with music.*
**Elliot, Jane [or Jean] (1727–1805)**
Flowers of the Forest, The; or, The Battle of Flodden.
**Elliott, George P.**
Her Dwarf.
**Elliott, Harley**
After Picking Rosehips.
Animals That Stand in Dreams.
Before the Frost.
Blessed and Resting Uncle.
Brothers Together in Winter.
Changing a Tire by the Missouri River.
Crazy Horse Returns to South Dakota.
Natural Order of Things, The.
On a Country Road.
Outside Abilene.
Panda, The.
Passing Stockyards Where They Killed the Buffalo.
Planting, The.
Resident Stranger, The.
Thinking Twice in the Laundromat.
**Ellis, Colin**
Epitaph, An: "He worshipped at the altar of Romance."
Old Ladies, The.
Romantic, The.
**Ellis, George**
Rondeau: "Of Eden lost, in ancient days."
**Eluard, Paul**
Curfew.
One for All Time, The.
**Emanuel, James A.**
Church Burning: Mississippi.
Emmett Till.
For "Mr. Dudley," a Black Spy.
Get Up, Blues.
Negritude.
Nightmare.
Old Black Men Say.
Panther Man.
Small Discovery, A.
Treehouse, The.
Young Ones, Flip Side, The.
**Emerson, Ralph Waldo**
Alphonso of Castile.
Apology, The.
Bacchus.
Blight.

Brahma.
Compensation.
Concord Hymn.
Days.
Day's Ration, The.
Each and All.
Fable: "Mountain and the squirrel,
    The."
Give All to Love.
Guy.
Hamatreya.
Humble-Bee, The.
Mithridates.
Nemesis.
Ode Inscribed to W. H. Channing.
Pan.
Problem, The.
Rhodora, The.
Snow-Storm, The.
Song of Seyd Nimetollah of Kuhistan.
Sphinx, The.
Stars, the stars everlasting are fugitives
    also, The.
Terminus.
Thine Eyes Still Shined.
Threnody: "South-wind brings, The."
Titmouse, The.
Two Rivers.
Uriel.
Visit, The.
Waldeinsamkeit.
Woodnotes I ("When the pine tosses its
    cones").
Woodnotes II ("As sunbeams stream
    through liberal space").
Xenophanes.
**Emerson, Ida** and **Joseph E. Howard.** *See*
    **Howard, Joseph E.** and **Ida Emerson**
**Emeruwa, Leatrice W.**
Making Out.
"Personals."
**Emig, Janet**
Avalanche.
**Emmett, Daniel Decatur**
Dixie ("I wish I was in the land of
    cotton"), *with music.*
Old Dan Tucker, *with music.*
**Empson, William**
Aubade: "Hours before dawn we were
    woken by the quake."
Bacchus.
Camping Out.
Ignorance of Death.
Just a Smack at Auden.
Legal Fiction.
Let It Go.
Missing Dates.
Note on Local Flora.
Success.
Teasers, The.
This Last Pain.
To an Old Lady.
Villanelle: "It is the pain, it is the pain,
    endures."
**Engels, John**
Moonwalk.
**Engle, Paul**
In a Bar Near Shibuya Station, Tokyo.
Venus and the Lute Player.
**English, Thomas Dunn**
Ben Bolt; or, Ah! Don't You
    Remember, *with music.*

**Enright, Dennis Joseph**
Dreaming in the Shanghai Restaurant.
Names.
No Offence.
Quagga, The.
Terminal.
University Examinations in Egypt.
Unlawful Assembly.
Waiting for the Bus.
**Enslin, Ted**
District, The: Both Sides of Chandler
    River.
Wheat District, The.
**Enzenberger, Hans**
Remote House.
**"Ephelia" (Joan Philips)**
Maidenhead.
To Philocles [or Phylocles], Inviting Him
    to Friendship.
**Erskine, Thomas, Erskine, 1st Baron**
On Scott's "The Field of Waterloo."
**Eshleman, Clayton**
Black Hat, The.
Very Old Woman, A.
**Etter, Dave**
Autumn on the Wabash.
Chicken.
Great Northern.
Old Dubuque.
Snow Country.
Two Beers in Argyle, Wisconsin.
**Evans, Abel**
On Sir John Vanbrugh, Architect.
Tadlow.
**Evans, David Allan**
Cattle Ghosts, The.
Citizens' Complaint, The.
Ford Pickup.
Neighbors.
Poem without a Metaphor.
Pole Vaulter.
Some lines after the Razing of the Sioux
    City Armour's Plant.
**Evans, Frances**
Colours.
**Evans, H. A. C.**
Egotist, The.
Liftman, The.
**Evans, Mari E.**
Alarm Clock, The.
And the Old Women Gathered.
Black Jam for Dr. Negro.
I Am a Black Woman.
If There Be Sorrow.
Into Blackness Softly.
Marrow of My Bone.
Rebel, The.
Spectrum.
To Mother and Steve.
Vive Noir!
When in Rome.
Where Have You Gone.
**Evans, Mary Ann [or Marian].** *See* **"Eliot,
    George"**
**Everson, William (Brother Antoninus)**
August.
Bard.
Canticle to the Waterbirds, A.
Flight in the Desert, The.
In All These Acts.
Lava Bed.
Making of the Cross, The.

One Fragment for God.
Poet is Dead, The.
Raid, The.
Rose of Solitude, The.
San Joaquin.
Song the Body Dreamed in the Spirit's
    Mad Behest, The.
South Coast, The.
Stranger, The.
Trifles.
Vision of Felicity, The.
We in the Fields.
What Birds Were There.
Year's End.
Zone of Death.
**Everwine, Peter**
For the Coming Year.
Routes.
**Evtushenko, Evgeny.** *See* **Yevtushenko,
    Yevgeny**
**Ewart, Gavin**
Love Song.
New Poet Arrives, A.
Officers' Mess.
2001: The Tennyson/ Hardy Poem.
When a Beau Goes In.
**Ewing, Juliana Horatia**
Burial of the Linnet, The.
Dolls' Wash, The.
Friend in the Garden, A.
Garden Lore.
Willow-Man, The.

# F

**Faber, Frederick William**
Faith of Our Fathers, *with music.*
**Fabilli, Mary**
Letter to Robert.
**Fabio, Sarah Webster**
Black Man's Feast.
Evil Is No Black Thing.
**Fahy, Francis A.**
Queen of Connemara, The.
**Fainlight, Harry**
Bride, A.
Morning.
**Fainlight, Ruth**
Sleep-Learning.
**Fairbairn, Nicholas**
Love in Edinburgh.
**Falconer, Ross**
It Is Impossible.
**Falkner, John Meade**
After Trinity.
Arabia.
Christmas Day.
**Fallon, Padraic**
Assumption.
Mary Hines.
Young Fenians, The.
**Fane, Mildmay, Earl of Westmorland.** *See*
    **Westmorland, Mildmay Fane, 2nd Earl
    of**
**Fanshawe, Sir Richard**
Ode, An, upon Occasion of His
    Majesty's Proclamation in the Year
    1630.

Of Beauty.

**Farber, Allan D.**
Skipping Stones.

**Farber, Norma**
Crooked Carol.

**Farina, Richard**
Birmingham Sunday.

**Farjeon, Annabel**
Ode to a Fat Cat.

**Farjeon, Eleanor**
A is for Abracadabra.
Argus and Ulysses ("Argus was a puppy").
Blackfriars.
Cat.
Cats.
In the Week When Christmas Comes.
Kitten, A.
Lewis Carrol.
Mrs. Malone.
Night Will Never Stay, The.
Tailor.

**Farjeon, Eleanor** and **Herbert**
Henry VIII.

**Farley, Hilary-Anne**
This Is a Poem.

**Farley, Jean**
Night Riders.

**Farren, Robert (Roibéard O'Faracháin)**
Pets, The.
Rich Morning.

**Fauset, Jessie Redmond**
Oriflamme.

**Fawcett, John**
Blest Be the Tie That Binds, *with music.*

**Fearing, Kenneth**
American Rhapsody (4).
Cracked Record Blues.
Dirge: "1-2-3 was the number he played but today the number came 3-2-1."
Green Light.
Obituary.

**Federman, Raymond**
Lune Concrete.

**Feinberg, Harvey**
Welcome.

**Feinstein, Elaine**
Our Vegetable Love Shall Grow.

**Feldman, Irving**
My Olson Elegy.
No-Night, The.
"Portrait de Femme."
Pripet Marshes, The.

**Feldman, Susan**
How the Invalids Make Love.
Intruder.
Lamentations of an Au Pair Girl.
Sea Legs.

**Felltham, Owen**
Sympathy, The.

**Fenton, Elizabeth**
Masks.
Under the Ladder to Heaven.

**Ferguson, David**
Norman Morrison.

**Ferguson, James**
Auld Daddy Darkness.

**Ferguson, John**
Cock Crowing in a Poulterer's Shop, A.

**Ferguson, Sir Samuel**
Lament for the Death of Thomas Davis.

**Ferlinghetti, Lawrence**

After the Cries of the Birds.
Assassination Raga.
Away above a Harborful.
Christ Climbed Down.
Coney Island of the Mind, A, *sels.*
Crazy/ to be alive in such a strange.
Dog.
Don't Let That Horse.
Fortune.
Frightened/ by the sound of my own voice.
I Am Waiting.
In Golden Gate Park That Day.
In Goya's Greatest Scenes.
In Woods Where Many Rivers Run.
Junkman's Obbligato.
One Thousand Fearful Words for Fidel Castro.
Oral Messages, *sel.*
Pennycandystore beyond the El, The.
Salute!
Starting from San Francisco.
Terrible/ a horse at night.
Third World, The.
This life is not a circus where.
Truth is not the secret of a few.
World Is a Beautiful Place, The.
Wounded Wildnerness of Morris Graves, The.

**Fernandez, Carlos**
Cielito Lindo, *with music.*

**Ferril, Thomas Hornsby**
Always Begin Where You Are.
Morning Star.
Swallows.
Waltz against the Mountains.

**Ferriter, Pierce**
Lay Your Arms Aside.

**Fetherling, Doug**
Bathing with Father.
Dialogue 4 1 Voice Only.
Diseases of the Moon.
Dispatch Number Nine.
Dispatch Number Sixteen.
Dispatch Number Sixty.
Genius Loci of the Morning.
Nights Passed on Ward's Island, Toronto Harbour.
Sex Play in Four Acts.
Shacked Up at the Ritz.
She Employed the Familiar "Tu" Form.
Your Absence Has Not Taught Me.

**Fethy, Sir John**
My Trewth is Plicht.

**Fey, Isabella**
Bad Example.

**Fiacc, Padraic**
Boy and the Geese, The.
Deranged.

**Field, Edward**
Bride of Frankenstein, The.
Donkeys.
My Polish Grandma.
Sleeper, The.
Unwanted.

**Field, Eugene**
Boy, The.
Coquetry.
Death of Robin Hood, The.
Duel, The.
Little Boy Blue.
Sugar-Plum Tree, The.

Wynken, Blynken, and Nod.

**"Field, Michael" (Katherine Bradley** and **Edith Cooper)**
After Mass.
Macrinus against Trees.

**Field, Rachel Lyman (Mrs. Arthur Pederson)**
City Rain.
Green Fiddler, The.
Hills, The.
Peabody Bird, The.
Skyscrapers.
Snow in the City.

**Fields, Dorothy**
I Can't Give You Anything But Love, *with music.*

**Fields, James Thomas**
Owl-Critic, The.

**Fields, Julia**
Aardvark.
Alabama.
Poems: Birmingham 1962-1964.

**Finch, Anne, Countess of Winchilsea.** *See* Winchilsea, Anne Finch, Countess of

**Finch, Francis Miles**
Blue and the Gray, The.
Nathan Hale.

**Finkel, Donald**
Cross-eyed Lover, The.
Gesture.
Great Wave, The: Hokusai.
Hands.
Hunting Song.
King Midas Has Asses' Ears.
They.

**Finlay, Ian Hamilton**
Black Tomintoul.
Horizon of Holland, The.

**Finnigan, Joan**
May Day Rounds: Renfrew County, *sel.*
Noon Hour.

**Fish, Mira**
Cape Code Murders, 1968.
Oh, Say, Mr. Toffler.
Poem: "Four miles out the tide curls in."
Poem: "You jam your arm into the white air."
Pregnancy.

**Fishback, Margaret**
Babies: Just Babies.

**Fisher, Aileen**
Shivers.
Witch in the Wintry Wood, The, *sel.*

**Fisher, Roy**
City.

**Fiske, Horace Spencer**
Ballad of the Pigskin.
Cry of the High Hurdlers, The.

**Fitton, Molly**
Linger longer, Olga.

**Fitzgerald, F. Scott**
Football.

**Fitzgerald, Robert**
July in Indiana.
Mise en Scène.
Shore of Life, The.
Song for September.

**Fitzgerald, Robert David**
Beginnings.
Fifth Day.
Song in Autumn.

**Flaccus, Aulus Persius.** *See* Persius

**Flaccus, Quintus Horatius.** *See* **Horace**
**Flaherty, Doug**
Coming on to Winter.
Lake Flies of Winnebago, The.
Raspberries.
**Flanagan, Robert**
Atlas.
Heirloom.
State Message: A Midwestern Small
Town.
**Flanner, Hildegarde**
Hawk Is a Woman.
Let Us Believe.
Sonnets in Quaker Language,*sels.*
Swift Love, Sweet Motor.
This Day.
**Flatman, Thomas**
Appeal to Cats in the Business of Love,
An.
Nudus Redibo.
On Mrs. E. Montague's Blushing in the
Cross-bath.
Song on New Year's Day before the
King, A.
**Flecker, James Elroy**
Epilogue: "Away, for we are ready to a
man!"
Golden Journey to Samarkand, The, *sels.*
In Hospital.
Lord Arnaldos.
Oxford Canal.
Prologue: "We who with songs beguile
your pilgrimage.
**Flecknoe, Richard**
Stillborn Silence.
**Fleming, Marjory**
Sonnet, A: "O lovely O most charming
pug."
**Fletcher, Giles, the Elder**
Licia, *sels.*
**Fletcher, Giles, the Younger**
Celestial City, The.
Christ's Victory and Triumph, *sels.*
He Was Made Man.
Palm Sunday: Good Friday.
**Fletcher, John**
Aspatia's Song.
Away, Delights.
Captain, The, *sel.*
Chances, The, *sel.*
Faithful Shepherdess, The,*sels.*
Hear, Ye Ladies.
Hymn to Pan.
Love's Emblems.
Mad Lover, The, *sels.*
Sweet Music's Power.
Tragedy of Valentinian, The,*sels.*
**Fletcher, John** and **Francis Beaumont.**
*See* **Beaumont, Francis** and **John
Fletcher**
**Fletcher, John** and **William Rowley**
Maid in the Mill, *sel.*
**Fletcher, John** and **others**
Bloody Brother, The, *sel.*
Drink Today.
**Fletcher, John** (19th century)
When I Saw Sweet Nelly Home, *with
music.*
**Fletcher, John Gould**
Arizona Poems, *sel.*
Lincoln, *sel.*
Rain in the Desert.

**Fletcher, Julia A.** *See* **Carney, Julia A.
Fletcher**
**Fletcher, Phineas**
Divine Lover, The.
Divine Wooer, The, *sel.*
Drop, Drop, Slow Tears.
Locusts or Appolyonists, The, *sel.*
To My Soul in Its Blindness.
**Flint, Francis Stewart**
Eau-Forte.
**Flocos, Nicholas**
Allegiance to Aphrodite.
Bogart.
Coin from B.C.
Comfort From Arcadia.
Garden Blooms.
Gossip.
In the Gazebo.
Old Upright I Did Not Learn to Play,
The.
Salt.
**Flower, Robin**
Passage at Night, The—The Blaskets.
**Flower, Sarah.** *See* **Adams, Sarah Flower**
**Floyd, Virginia**
Life, the Eternal Sacrament.
Street Where I Live, The.
World, Hold Me Close.
**Flynn, Joseph**
Down Went McGinty, *with music.*
**Fogerty, John C.**
Bad Moon Rising.
Don't Look Now.
Have You Ever Seen the Rain?
**Folk, Pat**
Empty Holds a Question.
Senile.
**Foot, Edward Edwin**
On the Inauguration of the Memorial
Statue, *sel.*
**Foote, Samuel**
Great Panjandrum, The.
**Forbes, Calvin**
Chocolate Soldiers, The.
Hours, The.
Lullaby for Ann-Lucian.
My Father's House.
Reading Walt Whitman.
**Forché, Carolyn**
Burning the Tomato Worms.
Kalaloch.
Taking Off My Clothes.
**Ford, Ford Madox** (*formerly* **Ford Madox
Hueffer**)
Cat of the House, The.
**Ford, Gena**
Legacy.
Lines for a Hard Time.
Nude on the Bathroom Wall, The.
**Ford, John**
Broken Heart, The, *sels.*
Love's Martyrs.
**Ford, Walter H.**
Sunshine of Paradise Alley, The, *with
music.*
**Forgotson, E. S.**
Elderly Nobody Erases Self in Central
Park.
**Forman, Nicole**
Labour of the Brain, Ballad of the Body.
**Fosdick, W. W.**
Aura Lea [*or* Lee], *with music.*

**Foster, Stephen Collins**
Beautiful Dreamer, *with music.*
Camptown Races, The [*or* De], *with
music.*
Jeanie with the Light Brown Hair, *with
music.*
My Old Kentucky Home, *with music.*
Oh! Susanna, *with music.*
Old Black Joe, *with music.*
Old Folks at Home, The, *with music.*
**Fowler, Gene**
Shaman Songs 12.
**Fowles, John**
Barbarians.
**Fox, Gail**
For Anne, Who Doesn't Know.
**Fox, Siv Cedering**
Hands.
Ornithology.
Poem: "From what strange country do
you come, then?"
River and Light.
**Fox-Smith, C.**
Mules.
**Foxton, Thomas**
On a Little Boy's Endeavouring to Catch
a Snake
Upon Boys Diverting Themselves in the
River.
**Frame, Janet**
Footballer in the Small Room, The.
Foxes, The.
Telephonist.
**Francis, Colin**
Tony O.
**Francis, Robert**
Base Stealer, The.
Burial.
By Night.
Catch.
Diver.
Edith Sitwell Assumes the Role of Luna.
Fair and Unfair.
Fall.
Farm Boy after Summer.
Hallelujah: A Sestina.
Hound, The.
Juniper.
Pitcher.
Seagulls.
Silent Poem.
Sing a Song of Juniper.
Skier.
That Dark Other Mountain.
Two Wrestlers.
Watching Gymnasts.
**Frankau, Gilbert**
Gun Teams.
**Franklin, Benjamin**
Quatrain: "Jack, eating rotten cheese,
did say."
**Fraser, Antonia**
My Mind to Me a Kingdom Is.
**Fraser, George S.**
Christmas Letter Home.
**Fraser, Kathleen**
Agnes.
Casa de Pollos.
Change of Address.
Dresses.
History of My Feeling, The.
How Tuesday Began.

Loving.
Poem for a Hustler.
Poem in which My Legs Are Accepted.
Poem Wondering If I'm Pregnant.
Poems for the New.
What You Need.

**Fraser, Ray**
Before You're a Stranger.
Cry of an Aged One, The.
Ecole St. Luc.
Flora.
Grotto, The.
In an Empty Window.
Lost Picture.
Not Often.
On Learning to Play the Guitar.
Policemen Laughing.
Souster.

**Freebairn, A. L.**
Ride 'Im Cowboy.

**Freedgood, Laura**
Ruth.

**Freeman, Arthur**
Cat, Caged and Shrunken, The.

**Freeman, Carole [or Carol]**
Christmas Morning, I.
I Saw Them Lynch.
When My Uncle Willie Saw.

**French, Percy**
Come Back, Paddy Reilly.
Mountains of Mourne, The.

**Freneau, Philip**
Eutaw Springs.
George the Third's Soliloquy.
Indian Burying Ground, The.
Literary Importation.
On the Emigration to America.
On the Uniformity and Perfection of
    Nature.
Picture of the Times, A.
Republican Genius of Europe, The.
Rising Glory of America, The, sel.
To an Author.
Wild Honey Suckle, The.

**Frere, John Hookham**
Boy and the Parrot, The.
Fable, A: "Dingy donkey, formal and
    unchanged, A."
Fable of the Piece of Glass and the Piece
    of Ice, The.

**Frere, John Hookham and George Canning**
See **Canning, George** and **John
    Hookham Frere**

**Friebert, Stuart**
Apron, The.

**Fripp, Robert and Peter Sinfield**
Pictures of a City.

**Frost, Frances Mary**
Apples to Keep.
Who's There?

**Frost, Robert**
Acquainted with the Night.
After Apple-picking.
Aim Was Song, The.
All Revelation.
Away!
Bear, The.
Bearer of Evil Tidings, The.
Birches.
Birthplace, The.
Black Cottage, The.
Blue-Butterfly Day.

Brown's Descent.
Cabin in the Clearing, A.
Carpe Diem.
Code, The.
Come In.
Considerable Speck, A.
Cow in Apple Time, The.
Death of the Hired Man, The.
Departmental
Desert Places.
Design.
Directive.
Draft Horse, The.
Drumlin Woodchuck, A.
Dust of Snow.
Empty Threat, An.
Fire and Ice.
For Once, Then, Something.
Forgive, O Lord.
Fountain, a bottle, a Donkey's Ears and
    Some Books, A.
Freedom of the Moon, The.
Gathering Leaves.
Gift Outright, The.
Hardship of Accounting, The.
HIll Wife, The,sels.
Home Burial.
Importer, An.
Impulse, The.
In Dives' Dive.
In Neglect.
In White.
In Winter in the Woods Alone.
It Is Almost the Year Two Thousand.
Last Word of a Bluebird, The.
Leaf Treader, A.
Leaves Compared with Flowers.
Lockless Door, The.
Love and a Question.
Lovely Shall Be Choosers, The.
Mending Wall.
Middleness of the Road, The.
Moon Compasses.
Most of It, The.
Mowing.
Need of Being Versed in Country
    Things, The.
Neither Out Far nor In Deep.
Never Again Would Birds' Song Be the
    Same.
Not All There.
Nothing Gold Can Stay.
Old Man's Winter Night, An.
Once by the Pacific.
Onset, The.
"Out, Out."
Oven Bird, The.
Pasture, The.
Prayer in Spring, A.
Provide, Provide.
Putting in the Seed.
Question, A.
Questioning Faces.
Rabbit Hunter, The.
Range-Finding.
Reluctance.
Road Not Taken, The.
Rose Family, The.
Runaway, The.
Sand Dunes.
Secret Sits, The.
Semi-Revolution, A.

Servant to Servants, A.
Silken Tent, The.
Soldier, The.
Sound of Trees, The.
Span of Life, The.
Spring Pools.
Star-Splitter, The.
Stopping by Woods on a Snowy
    Evening.
Storm Fear.
Strong Are Saying Nothing, The.
Subverted Flower, The.
Telephone, The.
There are Roughly Zones.
Time to Talk, A.
To a Young Wretch.
To Earthward.
Tree at My Window.
Tuft of Flowers, The.
Two Tramps in Mud Time.
Two Witches, sel.
Waspish.
West-running Brook.
Witch of Coös, The.
Wood-Pile, The.

**Frumkin, Gene**
Magdalene Silver Mine, The.
On a Windy Day.
Some Days the Blood is Warm and
    Certain.
Some Kind of Toughguy.

**Fujiwara, Sadamu**
Transparent Autumn, A.

**Fuller, Hoyt W.**
Lost Moment.
Seravazza.

**Fuller, John**
Girl with Coffee Tray.
Owls.

**Fuller, Roy**
Autobiography of a Lungworm.
Barber, The.
Crustaceans.
Day, The.
Death.
Faust's Servant.
Giraffes, The.
Image, The.
In Memory of My Cat Domino:
    1951–1966.
Metamorphoses.
Shore Leave Lorry.
Spring 1942.
Statue, The.
Translation.

**Fuller, Stephany**
In the Silence.
Let Me Be Held When the Longing
    Comes.
My Love When This Is Past.
That We Head Towards.
Who is not a stranger still.

**Fullerton, Mary Elizabeth ("E.")**
Emus.

**Fulton, Robin**
Hung Red, sel.
Northern Habitat, A.
Quiet Days in Sutherland.
Voice of the Surbahar,sels.

**Fyleman, Rose**
Fairies.

Fairies Have Never a Penny to Spend,
   The.
Fairy Went A-Marketing, A.
I Don't Like Beetles.
Mrs. Brown.
Temper.

# G

**Gallagher, Joseph**
   John J. Curtis.
**Gallagher, Tess**
   Breasts.
   Horse in the Drugstore, The.
   Kidnaper.
   Stepping Outside.
**Gant, Roland**
   Wedding, The.
**Garcia, Luis**
   Passport, The.
**Garcia Lorca, Federico**
   Ballad of the Moon, Moon.
   Ballad of the Sleepwalker, The.
   Faithless Wife, The.
   Guitar.
   Half Moon.
   It Is True.
   Poem of Solitude at Columbia
      University.
   Somnambulistic Ballad.
   Unfaithful Married Woman, The.
**Gardner, Carl**
   Dead Man Dragged from the Sea, The.
   Reflections.
**Gardner, Isabella**
   At a Summer Hotel.
   Cock-a-Hoop.
   Fall in Massachusetts.
   Part of the Darkness.
   Sloth, The.
   That "Craning of the Neck."
   Widow's Yard, The.
**Garioch, Robert (Robert Sutherland)**
   Heard in the Cougate.
   I Was Fair Beat.
**Garneau, Saint-Denys**
   My House.
**Garner, Alan**
   RIP.
   Summer Solstice.
**Garnett, Richard**
   Fair Circassian.
   Highwayman's Ghost, The.
   Marigold.
**Garrett, George**
   After Bad Dreams.
   Cage, The.
   Goodbye, Old Paint, I'm Leaving
      Cheyenne.
   Romantic.
   Salome.
   Snapshot of a Pedant.
   Tiresias.
   Underworld.
**Garrick, David**
   On Sir John Hill, M.D., Playwright.
**Garrigue, Jean**
   Beside a fall there is a round wood pipe.

Catch What You Can.
Cracked Looking Glass.
For Anybody's Martyr's Song.
Forest.
From Venice Was That Afternoon.
Incantatory Poem.
Last Letter to the Scholar.
Note on Master Crow, A.
Now Snow Descends.
Old Haven.
Primer of Plato.
Remember That Country.
Stranger, The.
To speak of my influences.
Upon the Intimations of Love's
   Mortality.
Waking, I always waked you awake.
**Garstin, Crosbie**
   Figurehead, The.
**Gascoigne, George**
   Adventures of Master F. I., The, *sel.*
   All were to little for the merchauntes
      hande.
   And every yeare a worlde my will did
      deeme.
   Arraignment of a Lover, The.
   Before mine eye to feede my greedy will.
   Councell Given to Master Bartholmew
      Withipoll.
   Divorce of a Lover, The ("Divorce me
      nowe good death").
   Farewell, A: "And if I did, what then?"
   Farewell with a Mischeife.
   For why? the gaines doth seldome quitte
      the charge.
   Gascoignes Good Morrow.
   Gascoignes Woodmanship.
   Gascoygnes Good Night.
   Lullabie of a Lover, The.
   Memories, *sel.*
   No haste but good, where wisdome
      makes the waye.
   Sonet Written in Prayse of the Browne
      Beautie, A.
   Steel Glass [or Steele Glas], The.
   Straunge Passion of a Lover, A.
   To prinke me up and make me higher
      plaste.
**Gascoyne, David**
   Ecce Homo.
   Salvador Dali.
   Snow in Europe.
**Gasparini, Len**
   Accident, The.
   Greasy Spoon Blues.
   Kafka's Other Metamorphosis.
   Niagara Falls Nocturne.
   Valentine.
   Written on a Paper Napkin.
**Gatty, Sir Alfred Scott**
   Three Little Pigs, The.
**Gavronsky, Serge**
   Testimonies for a School Prayer.
**Gay, John**
   Acis and Galatea, *sel.*
   All in the Downs.
   Beggar's Opera, The, *sels.*
   Fables, *sel.*
   New Song of New Similies, A.
   Over the Hills and Far Away.
   Poet and the Rose, The.
   Song: "O ruddier than the cherry."

Sweet William's Farewell to Black-eyed
   Susan.
Youth and Love.
**Gaye, Marvin**
   Mercy Mercy Me.
**Geifer, George L.**
   Who Threw the Overalls in Mistress
      Murphey's Chowder? *with music.*
**Genestet, Petrus Augustus de**
   Such Is Holland!
**Geoghegan, J. B.**
   Down in a Coal Mine.
**Georgakas, Dan**
   19??.
**George, Phil**
   Ask the Mountains.
   Battle Won Is Lost.
   Night Blessing.
   Old Man, the Sweat Lodge.
**Gerard, Richard H.**
   Sweet Adeline, *with music.*
**"Geraud, Saint."** See **Knott, William**
**Gerber, Dan**
   Homecoming.
   Line, The.
   Tragedy of Action, The.
**Gershwin, Ira**
   Embraceable You, *with music.*
**Ghiselin, Brewster**
   Marlin.
   Vantage.
**Ghose, Zulfikar**
   Crows, The.
   Geography Lesson.
   This Landscape, These People.
   Two Sec. Mods.
**Gibbon, Monk**
   Discovery, The.
   I Tell Her She Is Lovely.
**Gibbons, James Sloan**
   Three Hundred Thousand More.
**Gibran, Kahlil**
   On Children.
   Prophet, The, *sel.*
**Gibson, Wilfrid Wilson**
   All Being Well.
   Breakfast.
   Drove-Road, The.
   Flannan Isle.
   Ice, The.
   Lament: "We who are left, how shall we
      look again."
   Long Tom.
   Luck.
**Gibson, Walter**
   In Memory of the Circus Ship *Euzkera.*
**Gidlow, Elsa**
   Invocation to Sappho.
**Gifford, William**
   Epistle to Peter Pindar.
**Gilbert, Fred**
   Man Who Broke the Bank at Monte
      Carlo, The, *with music.*
**Gilbert, Jack**
   Bay Bridge from Portrero Hill, the.
   Malvolio in San Francisco.
   Orpheus in Greenwich Village.
**Gilbert, Virginia**
   Becket.
   Finding You.
   For John Berryman.
   Pax Romana.

What Does it Mean? This Harmonica.

**Gilbert, Sir William Schwenck**
Banquet Song.
Etiquette.
Ferdinando and Elvira.
Flowers That Bloom in the Spring.
Gentle Alice Brown.
Gondoliers, The, *sel.*
Iolanthe, *sel.*
Merryman Sings, The.
Mikado, The, *sels.*
Modest Couple, The.
Nightmare.
Patience, *sel.*
Perils of Invisibility, The.
Story of Prince Agib, The.
There Lived a King.
To Phoebe.
Yarn of the *Nancy Bell,* The.

**Gilbert, Zack**
For Angela.
For Stephen Dixon.
My Own Hallelujahs.
When I Heard Dat White Man Say.

**Gilboa, Amir**
Birth.

**Gildner, Gary**
Digging for Indians.
First Practice.
Geisha.
Life of the Wolf, The.
Meeting the Reincarnation Analyst.
Then.
Touring the Hawkeye State.

**Gill, Brendan**
Girls' Voices.

**Gill, David**
Killing a Whale.

**Gill, John**
As a Child Seeing a Cardinal.
Before the Thaw.
First Hymn.
"I Don't Hear Any Melody Breathing I Hear."
Late Spring: a Heaving, a Turning.
Poem: "Something broke the dream."
What Could Be.

**Gillespie, Robert**
Shawano Lake, Wisconsin.
Snow White.
View Toward Wife Trading, A.

**Gillies, Valerie**
Straits, The.

**Gilmore, Joseph Henry**
He Leadeth Me, *with music.*

**Gilmore, Mary**
Nationality.
Nurse No Long Grief.
Out on the Hillside.
Penelope.
Tenancy, The.

**Gilmore, Patrick Sarsfield ("Louis Lambert")**
When Johnny Comes Marching Home, *with music.*

**"Ginger."** *See* **Irwin, Wallace**

**Ginsberg, Allen**
America.
Cézanne's Ports.
Death News.
Death to Van Gogh's Ear!
Dream Record: June 8, 1955.

Ecologue.
End, The.
First Party at Ken Keseys with Hell's Angels.
Footnote to Howl.
Howl.
Hymmnn.
In a Moonlit Hermit's Cabin.
In Back of the Real.
Kaddish, *sel.*
Kral Majales.
Last Night in Calcutta.
Love Poem on Theme by Whitman.
May Mobilization.
Message.
My Alba.
My Sad Self.
Night-Apple, The.
On Burroughs' Work.
Poem Rocket.
Psalm III: "To God: to illuminate all men. Beginning with Skid Row."
Shrouded Stranger, The.
Sunflower Sutra.
Supermarket in California, A.
To Aunt Rose.
To Lindsay.
Wales Visitation.
Wichita Vortex Sutra.
Wild Orphan.

**Ginsberg, Louis**
Morning in Spring.

**Gioseffi, Daniela**
After Drinking Water.
Paradise Is Not a Place.
Peace Prospect.
Some Slippery Afternoon.
Vacancy.
Vases of Wombs, The.
Wearing Breasts.
"Women with Tongue in Cheek."

**Giovanni, Nikki**
Adulthood.
Beautiful Black Men.
Black Power.
Concerning One Responsible Negro with Too Much Power.
Conversation.
Dreams.
Ego Tripping.
For Saundra.
Funeral of Martin Luther King, Jr., The.
Kidnap Poem.
Knoxville, Tennessee.
Legacies.
Mothers.
My Poem.
Nikki-Rosa.
Poem for Aretha.
Poem for Black Boys.
Poem for Flora.
Poem of Angela Yvonne Davis.
Seduction.
True Import of Present Dialogue, Black vs. Negro, The.
Twelve Gates to the City.
Woman Poem.
Word Poem.

**Gitlin, David**
Up against the wall.

**Gittings, Robert**
Great Moth, The.

**Gladish, David**
If Only.

**Glaser, Elton**
Asides and Memoranda.
General's Wife, The.
Meal Piece.
Sacred Heart of Jesus Bleeds for You, The.

**Gleason, Madeline**
Starface, The.

**Glen, Duncan**
Clydesdale New Town Walk.
Gullion, The.
My Faither.
Psychology.
Room, The.
Words.

**Glen, William**
Wae's Me for Prince Charlie.

**Glück, Louise**
All Hallows.
Fire, The.
Flowering Plum.
For Jane Myers.
For My Mother.
Fortress, The.
Garden, The.
Gratitude.
Gretel in Darkness.
Messengers.
Phenomenal Survivals of Death in Nantucket.
Pond, The.
Racer's Widow, The.
School Children, The.
Shad-Blow Tree, The.
Undertaking, The.

**Goba, Ronald J.**
Compozishun—to James Herndon and Others.

**Godley, Alfred Denis**
Motor Bus.

**Godolphin, Sidney**
Hymn: "Lord, when the wise men came from far."
'Tis affection but dissembled.

**Godoy Alcayaga, Lucila**   *See* **"Mistral, Gabriela"**

**Godsey, Edwin S.**
Hoppy.

**Goedicke, Patricia**
My Mother's/ My/ Death/ Birthday.
Slabs of Her Eyes, The.
Sprinkle Me, Just.
When He's at His Most Brawling.

**Goethe, Johann Wolfgang von**
To the Moon.

**Goetz, E. Ray and Edgar Leslie.**   *See* **Leslie, Edgar and E. Ray Goetz**

**Goffin, Gerry and Carole King**
Child of Mine.

**Gogarty, Oliver St. John**
Back from the Country.
Farrell O'Reilly.
Hay Hotel, The.
Kingdoms.
O Boys! O Boys!
Ringsend.
Verse: "What should we know."

**Goldbarth, Albert**
Body Mechanics.
From the Bridge.

Letter Back to Oregon.
On Sunday, the Beginning of the Week,
　I Make a Religion.
Survival.
**Goldman, Michael**
Orpheus.
**Goldsmith, Oliver**
Description of an Author's Bedchamber,
　A.
Deserted Village, The.
Elegy on That Glory of Her Sex, Mrs.
　Mary Blaize, An.
Elegy on the Death of a Mad Dog, An.
O luxury! Thou curst by Heaven's
　decree.
Retaliation.
She Stoops to Conquer, sel.
Song: "Let school-masters puzzle their
　brain."
Song: "When lovely woman stoops to
　folly."
Traveller, The.
Vicar of Wakefield, The,sels.
**González, Rafael Jesús**
Knight of the Sad Face, The.
**Goodchild, Keighley**
Nautical Ballad.
**Goode, Michael**
Shot with a Hot Rot Gun.
War War.
**Goodge, W. T.**
Snake Yarn, A.
**Goodman, Mitchell**
Coming and Going.
Man and Wife.
**Goodman, Paul**
April 1962.
Classical Quatrain, A.
Don Larsen's Perfect Game.
Handball Players.
I planned to have a border of lavender.
Kent State, May 4, 1970.
Long Lines.
Lordly Hudson, The.
My Daughter Very Ill.
Saint Harmony my patroness.
Sonnet 21.
Surfers at Santa Cruz.
Weepers Tower in Amsterdam, The.
**Googe, Barnabe**
Out of Sight, Out of Mind.
To Doctor Bale.
**Gordon, Alvin J.**
Young Girl's Song, The.
**Gordon, Giles**
Between Appointments.
Former Love, A.
**Gordon, Mary**
Unwanted, The.
**Gorenko, Anna Andreyevna** See
　"Akhmatova, Anna"
**Gorges, Sir Arthur**
Henceforth I will not set my love.
She that holds me under the laws of
　love.
**Gotlieb, Phyllis**
First Person Demonstrative.
Try Brillo on the Slimy Stove.
Whatfor to 3 Who Stole My Shovel.
Women Who Are Hard Inside.
**Gottlieb, Ann**
Lady Luck.

**Gough, Irene**
Lost—A Lizard.
Possum Tree, The.
**Gould, Gerald**
Monogamy, sel.
**Gower, John**
Adrian and Bardus.
Confessio Amantis, sels.
Medea's Magic.
**Gowitt, William**
Wind in a Frolic, The.
**Graham, Al**
Casey's Daughter at the Bat.
**Graham, D. L.**
Soul.
Tony Get the Boys.
West Ridge Is Menthol-cool, The.
**Graham, Harry ("Col. D. Streamer")**
Billy.
L'Enfant Glacé.
Lord Gorbals.
Mr. Jones.
Necessity.
Opportunity.
Poetical Economy.
Waste.
**Graham, Henry**
Good Luck to You Kafka/ You'll Need
　It Boss.
**Graham, James, Marquess of Montrose**
Epitaph on Charles I.
I" Never Love Thee More.
On Himself, upon Hearing What Was
　His Sentence.
**Graham, Robert (Robert**
　**Cunninghame-Graham)**
O Tell Me How to Woo Thee.
**Graham, William Sydney**
I leave this at your ear for when you
　wake.
Letter V.
**Grahame, Kenneth**
Ducks' Ditty.
Wind in the Willows, The, sel.
**Grahn, Judy**
Asking for Ruthie.
Common Woman, The.
Death and Disfiguration.
Dressed As I Am, a Young Man Once
　Called Me Names in Spanish.
Ella, in a Square Apron, along Highway
　80.
I have come to claim.
Mock Interrogation, A.
Woman Is Talking to Death, A.sels.
**Grandsen, K. W.**
Interview, An.
**Grant, Richard E.**
Broken Heart, Broken Machine.
**Granville [or Grenville, George, Baron**
　**Lansdowne]**
Cloë.
Love.
**Graves, Alfred Perceval**
Father O'Flynn.
Herring Is King.
**Graves, Benny**
Boy, A.
**Graves, Robert**
Acrobats.
Blue-Fly, The.
Broken Girth, The.

Call It a Good Marriage
Change.
Children of Darkness.
Civil Servant, A.
Cool Web, The.
Counting the Beats.
Devil's Advice to Story-Tellers, The.
Down, Wanton, Down!
Face in the Mirror, The.
Falcon Woman, The.
Foreboding, The.
Frosty Night, A.
Full Moon.
Hag-ridden.
Hedges Freaked with Snow.
In Broken Images.
In Her Praise.
It Was All Very Tidy.
Laureate, The.
Legs, The.
Lost Acres.
Lost Jewel, A.
Love without Hope.
Mark, The.
My Name and I.
Naked and the Nude, The.
Never Such Love.
Not to Sleep.
Ogres and Pygmies.
Penny Fiddle, The.
Persian Version, The.
Philatelist Royal.
Pier-Glass, The.
Point of No Return.
Portrait, The.
Pumpkin, The.
Quiet Glades of Eden, The.
Recalling War.
Rocky Acres.
Second-fated, The.
She tells Her Love While Half Asleep.
Sick Love.
Six Badgers, The.
Slice of Wedding Cake, A.
Song: How can I Care?
Star-Talk.
Starred Coverlet, The.
Straw, The.
Symptoms of Love.
Thieves, The.
To Juan at the Winter Solstice.
Traveller's Curse after Misdirection.
Troll's Nosegay, The.
Twice of the Same Fever.
Ulysses.
Villagers and Death, The.
Welsh Incident.
White Goddess, The.
Wild Strawberries.
With a Gift of Rings.
Wreath, The.
**Graves, Steven**
Rendezvous, The.
**Gray, John**
Odiham.
**Gray, Nicholas Stuart**
Unicorn.
**Gray, Robert**
Greyhounds.
Landscape 4.
Meat Works, The.
North Coast Town.

**Gray, Thomas**
Bard, The.
Candidate, The.
Descent of Odin, The; an Ode from the Norse Tongue.
Elegy Written in a Country Churchyard.
Fatal Sisters, The.
Ode on a Distant Prospect of Eton College.
Ode on the Death of a Favourite Cat, Drowned in a Tub of Gold Fishes.
Ode on the Pleasure Arising from Vicissitude.
Ode on the Spring.
On Lord Holland's Seat near Margate, Kent.
Progress of Poesy, The.
Satire upon the Heads.
Sketch of His Own Character.
Sonnet on the Death of [Mr.] Richard West.

**Gray, William B.**
She Is More To Be Pitied, Than Censured, *with music.*

**Green, F. Pratt**
Old Couple, The.

**Greenaway, Kate**
Little Wind.

**Greenberg, Barbara L.**
Husband, The.
Just after the Widow's Death.
Poem for Susan.
Survival.

**Greenberg, Eliezer**
Dog and Tiger.

**Greene, Richard L.**
Autolycus' Song (In Basic English).
Ubi Iam Sunt?

**Greene, Robert**
Greene's Mourning Garment, *sel.*
Hexametra Alexis in Laudem Rosamundi.
Menaphon, *sels.*
Samela.
Sephestia's Song to Her Childe.

**Greenwell, Dora**
Sun-flower, The.

**Greenwood, Theresa**
Here I sit in my infested cubicle.

**Gregg, Linda**
Beckett Kit, The.
Girl I Call Alma, The.
Sigismundo.
We Manage Most When We Manage Small.

**Gregor, Arthur**
Elements of Night
Late Last Night.
Likeness, The.
Poem: "So many pigeons at Columbus."
Spirits, Dancing.

**Gregory, Horace**
And of Columbus.
Chorus for Survival, *sel.*
Longface Mahoney Discusses Heaven.
Night-Walker, The.
Prisoner's Song.
Rehearsal, The.
Stanzas for My Daughter.
Voices of Heroes.

**Greig, Andrew**
Marry the Lass?

**Grenfell, Julian**
Into Battle.

**Grenville, George.** *See* **Granville, George, Baron Lansdowne**

**Greville, Fulke, 1st Baron Brooke**
Caelica, *sels.*
Chorus Sacerdotum.
Cynthia, because your horns look diverse ways.
Downe in the depth of mine iniquity.
Earth with thunder torne, with fire blasted, The.
Epitaph upon the Right Honorable Sir Philip Sidney, An.
I offer wrong to my beloved saint.
Love, the delight of all well-thinking minds.
Memento Mori.
Mustapha, *sels.*
Myra.
Vain Learning.

**Grierson, Constantia**
To Miss Laetitia Van Lewen.

**Grieve, Christopher Murray.** *See* **"MacDiarmid, Hugh"**

**Griffin, Bartholomew**
Fidessa, More Chaste than Kind, *sels.*
Venus, with young Adonis sitting by her.

**Griffin, Ellen McEvilley**
Confession of a Young Hegelian.
Good Harbor Bay, Leland, Michigan.
If I Ask Whether the Islands.
Rimbaud in Abyssinia.

**Griffin, Jonathan**
Storm End.

**Griffin, Margaret Johnston**
To My Son.

**Griffin, "Sin-Killer"**
Man of Calvary, The, *sel.*

**Griffin, Susan**
Answer to a Man's Question, An, "What Can I Do about Women's Liberation?"
Grenadine.
I Like to Think of Harriet Tubman.
Love should grow up like a wild iris in the fields.
Revolution.
Sky, The.
Song My.

**Griffiths, Lexie**
Going Fishing.

**Grigson, Geoffrey**
Bibliotheca Bodleiana.
By the Road.
End of the Affair.
Heart Burial.
May Trees in a Storm.
Two Are Together.

**Grimké, Angelina Weld**
Black Finger, The.
Tenebris.
Winter Twilight, A.
Your Hands.

**Gross, Ronald**
Hero.
Yield.

**Gruber, Edmund L.**
Caissons Go Rolling Along, The.

**Gruber, Edmund L.** *and* **H. W. Arberg**
Army Goes Rolling Along, The, *with music.*

**Guarini, Giovanni Battista**
Faith, Hope, and Charity.
Il Pastor Fido, *sel.*
Microcosm, The.
Thus saith my Chloris bright.

**Guest, Barbara**
Direction.
Safe Flights.
Saving Tallow.

**Guest, Harry**
Matsushima.
Montage.
Twilight Man, A.

**Guevara, Miguel de**
Raise Me Up, Lord.

**Guilpin, Everard**
Let me alone, I prithee, in this cell.
Skialetheia, *sel.*

**Guiterman, Arthur**
Dog Parade, The.
Dog's Cold Nose, The.
Dorlan's Home Walk.
Eight Oars and a Coxswain.
Everything in Its Place.
Habits of the Hippopotamus.
Kag the Porcupine (The Misanthrope).
Mavrone.
Nesting Time.
Nocturne: "Three-toed tree toad, The."
Ode of Odium on Aquariums.
On the Vanity of Earthly Greatness.
Ornithology in Florida.
Sleepy Song.
Three Ponies.
Twist-Rime on Spring.
Windham Thaw, The.

**Gunderson, Keith**
Gypsy Motorcycle Club of South Minneapolis, The.
Naming the State Bird.

**Gunn, Thom**
Annihilation of Nothing, The.
Autumn Chapter in a Novel.
Black Jackets.
Byrnies, The.
Carnal Knowledge.
Corridor, The.
Discovery of the Pacific, The.
Elegy on the Dust.
Feel of Hands, The.
In the Tank.
Incident on a Journey.
Innocence.
Jesus and His Mother.
Modes of Pleasure.
Moly.
My Sad Captains.
No Speech from the Scaffold.
On the Move.
Street Song.
Touch.
Wound, The.

**Guri, Chaim**
Piyyut for Rosh Hashana.

**Gurney, Ivor**
Strange Hells.

**Gustafson, Ingemar**
Locked In.

**Guthrie, A. B., Jr.**
Twin Lakes Hunter.

**Guthrie, Ramon**
Alba for Mélusine.

Guthrie, Woody
  Plane Wreck at Los Gatos (Deportee).

# H

"H. D."  *See* Doolittle, Hilda
Haag, Terri
  Truck Drivers.
Habington, William
  Against Them Who Lay Unchastity to
    the Sex of Women.
  Dialogue between Araphil and Castara,
    A.
  Nox Nocti Indicat Scientiam.
  Pretty Sport.
  Quoniam Ego in Flagella Paratus Sum.
    David, *sel.*
  To Castara ("Why should we fear to
    melt away in death").
  To Castara: of True Delight.
  To Castara: of What We Were before
    Our Creation.
  To Castara: the Reward of Innocent
    Love.
  To Roses in the Bosom of Castara.
Hacker, Marilyn
  After the Revolution.
  Aube Provençale.
  Before the War.
  Presentation Piece.
  Villanelle: "Every day our bodies
    separate."
Hackett, J. W.
  Haiku: "Bitter morning, A,"
Hafiz
  Lips of the one I love are my perpetual
    pleasure, The.
Hagedorn, Jessica Tarahata
  Autobiography Part Two: Rock and
    Roll.
  Kayumangi.
  Smokey's Gettin' Old.
Hagthorpe, John
  Elegy upon the Death of the Most
    Illustrious Prince Henry, An, *sel.*
Haines, John
  And When the Green Man Comes.
  At White River.
  Cauliflower, The.
  Denali Road.
  Foreboding.
  If the Owl Calls Again.
  Legend of Paper Plates, The.
  Marigold.
  Mole, The.
  Prayer to the Snowy Owl.
  Snowy Night.
  To Turn Back.
  Tundra, The.
  Wolves.
Hajime, Kamimura
  Firefly.
Haldane, J. B. S.
  Cancer's a Funny Thing.
Haldane, Sean
  I Meant to Tell You.
Hale, Janet Campbell
  Tribal Cemetery.

Hale, Sarah Josepha Buell
  Mary's Lamb.
Hales, Thomas.  *See* Thomas of Hales
Haley, Bruce
  Rime of the Ancient Mariner, The.
Haley, Ed
  While Strolling Through the Park, *with
    music.*
Hall, Donald
  Airstrip in Essex, 1960, An.
  Alligator Bride, The.
  Blue Wing, The.
  By the Exeter River.
  Child, The.
  Cold Water.
  Crew-cuts.
  Days, The.
  Detroit.
  Dump, The.
  Gold.
  In the Kitchen of the Old House.
  Long River, The.
  Man in the Dead Machine, The.
  Moon, The.
  My Son, My Executioner.
  Old Pilot's Death, The.
  Reclining Figure.
  Repeated Shapes, The.
  Six Poets in Search of a Lawyer.
  Sleeping Giant, The.
  Stump, The.
  Three Movements, The.
  Town of Hill, The.
  Transcontinent.
Hall, James Baker
  Song of the Mean Mary Jean Machine,
    The.
Hall, John (1627-56)
  Dithyramb, A.
  On an Hour-glass.
Hall, Joseph
  Great is the folly of a feeble brain.
  Prologue: "I first adventure, with
    foolhardy might."
  Rome Ryme.
  Virgidemiarum, *sels.*
Hall, Katie V.
  Old, Filthy Beer Pail, The.
Hall, Owen
  Tell Me Pretty Maiden; or, English Girls
    and Clerks, *with music.*
Hall, Rodney
  Owner of My Face, The, *sel.*
Hall, Wade
  Dark Hope.
  Death Insurance.
  Eschatology
  Paso por Aqui.
  Winter Flowers.
Halley, Anne
  Against Dark's Harm.
  Autograph Book/ Prophecy.
  Dear God, the Day Is Grey.
  Housewife's Letter: to Mary.
  O Doctor Dear My Love.
  Pride of Ladies, A.
Halpern, Daniel
  Clove As Ego.
  Endings.
  Ethnic Life, The.
  Fish.
  Landing, The.

Nebraskan Childhood.
  Street Fire.
  Summer, 1970.
Halpern, Max
  Epigram: "In the neat parlor of their
    honeymoon."
Halpern, Moishe-Leib
  Bird, The.
Hamburger, Michael
  Dual Site, The.
  London Tom-Cat.
  Memory.
  Poet's Progress, A.
Hamilton, Eugene Lee-.  *See*
    Leé-Hamilton, Eugene
Hamilton, George Rostrevor ("George
    Rostrevor")
  Don's Holiday.
  On a Distant Prospect of an Absconding
    Bookmaker.
  On a Statue of Sir Arthur Sullivan.
Hamilton, Ian
  Complaint.
  Now and Then.
  Pretending Not to Sleep.
  Recruits, The.
Hammerstein, Oscar, II
  All the Things You Are, *with music.*
  June Is Bustin' Out All Over, *with music.*
  Ol' Man River, *with music.*
Hammond, Geraldine
  Encounter.
Hammond, Jerry
  Feature Time.
Hamod, Sam
  After the Funeral of Assam Hamady.
  Famous Hot Pepper Eating Contest,
    The.
  Fight, The.
  Leaves.
  Lines to My Father.
  Loss of Black Camels, The.
  Mother's Day.
Hanby, Benjamin Russel
  Darling Nelly Gray, *with music.*
Handy, William Christopher
  Saint Louis Blues, *with music.*
Hanes, Leigh
  Old Fence Post.
Hankey, Katherine
  I Love to Tell the Story, *with music.*
Hannigan, Paul
  Carnation, The.
Hans, Marcie
  Fueled.
Hanson, Amos
  Schooner *Fred Dunbar*, The.
  Trip to the Grand Banks, A.
Hanson, Elizabeth
  Departure.
  Summer's Darkness.
  Walking without Snowshoes.
Hanson, Pauline
  Love.
Harburg, E. Y.
  Brother, Can You Spare a Dime?
Harding, Samuel
  Sicily and Naples; or, The Fatal Union:
    a Tragedy, *sel.*
Hardy, Thomas
  After a Journey.
  After the Visit.

Afterwards.
Ah, Are You Digging on My Grave?
Ancient to Ancients, An.
Anniversary, An.
At a Hasty Wedding.
At Casterbridge Fair, *sel.*
At Castle Boterel.
Backward Spring, A.
Bags of Meat.
Ballad-Singer, The.
Beeny Cliff.
Bereft.
Beyond the Last Lamp.
Blinded Bird, The.
Broken Appointment, A.
Brother, The.
By Her Aunt's Grave
Channel Firing.
Chosen, The.
Christmas: 1924.
Church Romance, A.
Comet at Yell'ham, The.
Convergence of the Twain, The.
Copying Architecture in an Old Minster.
Darkling Thrush, The.
Drummer Hodge.
During Wind and Rain.
Echo Elf Answers, The.
Fallow Deer at the Lonely House, The.
For Life I Had Never Cared Greatly.
Former Beauties.
God's Education.
Going, The.
Going and Staying.
Great Things.
Hap.
Haunter, The.
He Never Expected Much.
Heredity.
Horses Aboard ("Horses in horsecloths
   stand in a row").
House of Hospitalities, The.
I Am the One.
I Found Her Out There.
I look into my glass.
I Need Not Go.
I Said to Love.
If It's Ever Spring Again.
If You Had Known.
In Church.
In Tenebris.
In the Moonlight.
In the Room of the Bride-Elect.
In the Vaulted Way.
In Time of "The Breaking of Nations."
In Weatherbury Stocks.
Last Look Round St. Martin's Fair.
Last Words to a Dumb Friend.
Let Me Enjoy.
Levelled Churchyard, The.
Man He Killed, The.
Midnight on the Great Western.
Mound, The.
Nature's Questioning.
Near Lanivet, 1872.
Neutral Tones.
New Year's Eve.
Newcomer's Wife, The.
Night of the Dance, The.
1967.
Old Furniture.
On the Departure Platform.

Oxen, The.
Phantom Horsewoman, The.
Poet, A.
Proud Songsters.
Rain on a Grave.
Refusal, A.
Respectable Burgher, The.
Robin, The.
Roman Road, The.
Ruined Maid, The.
Satires of Circumstance, *sel.*
Schreckhorn, The.
Self-Unseeing, The.
She, to Him.
Sheep Fair, A.
Shut Out That Moon.
Snow in the Suburbs.
Subalterns, The.
Sunshade, The.
This Summer and Last.
Thoughts of Phena.
Thunderstorm in Town, A.
Transformations.
Two Lips.
Under the Waterfall.
Voice, The.
Voices from Things Growing in a
   Churchyard.
Walk, The.
Wessex Heights.
Wet August, A.
When I Set Out for Lyonnesse.
When Oats Were Reaped.
Where the Picnic Was.
Wives in the Sere.
Workbox, The.
Year's Awakening, The.
Young Man's Epigram on Existence, A.
**Harington, Sir John (1561-1612)**
Author to His Wife, of a Woman's
   Eloquence, The.
Comparison of the Sonnet and the
   Epigram.
Of an Heroical Answer of a Great
   Roman Lady to Her Husband.
Of Treason.
**Harington, Lucy, Countess of Bedford**
Elegy: "Death be not proud, thy hand
   gave not this blow."
**Harjo, Joy**
Creek Mother Poem.
Hopi Woman Talking, A.
Ignacio, Colorado, for You That Time.
Lame Deer.
Lost Weekend Bar, The.
People, The.
Snake Poem I.
**Harjo, Patty**
Musings.
**Harper, Frances E. W.**
Bury Me in a Free Land.
Slave Auction, The.
**Harper, Michael S.**
American History.
Barricades.
"Bird Lives": Charles Parker in St.
   Louis.
Black Angel, The.
Blue Ruth: America.
Breaded Meat, Breaded Hands.
Come Back Blues.
Dear John, Dear Coltrane.

Deathwatch.
Effendi.
Elvin's Blues.
Grandfather.
Here Where Coltrane Is.
Madimba: Gwendolyn Brooks.
Martin's Blues.
Mother Speaks, A: The Algiers Motel
   Incident, Detroit.
Newsletter from My Mother.
Photographs: A Vision of Massacre.
We Assume: On the Death of Our Son,
   Reuben Masai Harper.
**Harrigan, Ned [*or* Ed]**
Mulligan Guard, The, *with music.*
Walking for That Cake, *with music.*
**Harrington, Edward**
Bushrangers, The.
**Harrington, Sir John (1561-1612).** *See*
   **Harington, Sir John**
**Harris, Charles Kassell**
After the Ball, *with music.*
Break the News to Mother, *with music.*
**Harris, Marie**
Dill.
Facts of Winter.
Learning.
Lemon Balm.
Luxury Apt.
Monkshood.
Song: "Hair/ like heather, father would
   boast."
Visitors.
**Harris, Phyllis.** *See* **Beauvais, Phyllis**
**Harris, Robert**
That Bad Music.
Tobacco.
**Harris, William J.**
For Bill Hawkins, a Black Militant.
Grandfather Poem, A.
Practical Concerns.
We Live in a Cage.
Why Would I Want.
**Harrison, De Leon**
Collage for Richard Davis, A—Two
   Short Forms.
Room, The.
Seed of Nimrod, The.
Some Days/ Out Walking Above.
Yellow.
**Harrison, James**
Bellevue.
Moving.
Sequence.
Sequence of Women, A.
**Harrison, Jim**
After Reading Takahashi.
After the Anonymous Swedish.
After the "invitation" by the preacher
   she collapsed in the.
Fair/ Boy Christian Takes a Break.
Ghazals, *sels.*
Horse.
I Was Proud.
Locations.
Poem: "Form is the woods: the beast."
Returning at Night.
Sketch for a Job Application Blank.
Sound.
Suite to Fathers.
Today We've Moved.
Trader.

Traverse City Zoo.
Word Drunk.
**Harrison, Tony**
Schwiegermutterlieder.
**Harrold, William**
Another Load.
Flowers for the Grangerford Girl.
Small Tribute, A.
**Harry, J. S.**
Hunting Dragons with Fire Tongues and Deep Smoky Throats.
Little Grenade, The.
Outposts.
To Start With.
What Might Pass a Man As a Survivor.
**Harsent, David**
Old Photographs.
Rag Doll to the Heedless Child, The.
**Hart, Elizabeth Anna**
Mother Tabbyskins.
**Hart, John**
Confrontation.
**Hart, Joseph**
Come Ye Sinners, Poor and Needy, *with music.*
**Hart, Lorenz**
My Heart Stood Still, *with music.*
**Hart-Smith, William**
Beach, The.
Otters.
Rhinoceros.
Wild Geese
**Harte, Bret (Francis Bret Harte)**
Caldwell of Springfield.
Dow's Flat.
Further Language from Truthful James.
Heathen Chinee, The.
Plain Language from Truthful James ("I reside at Table Mountain").
Plain Language from Truthful James ("Which I wish to remark").
Spelling Bee at Angels, The.
**Hartford, John**
Poor Old Prurient Interest Blues, The.
**Hartigan, Patrick Joseph ("John O'Brien")**
Said Hanrahan.
**Hartnett, Michael**
Domestic Scene.
Enamoured of the Miniscule.
For My Grandmother, Bridgid Halpin.
Sonnet: "I saw magic on a green country road."
**Harvey, Frederick William**
November.
**Harwood, Gwen**
Barn Owl.
David's Harp.
Father and Child.
In the Park.
Night Thoughts.
**Harwood, Lee**
Animal Days.
Blue Mosque, The.
Plato Was Right Though.
**Hass, Robert**
Against Botticelli.
Fall.
In Weather.
Maps.
Nineteenth Century as a Song, The.
Politics of a Pornographer.
Pornographer, The.

Return of Robinson Jeffers, The.
Song: "Afternoon cooking in the fall sun."
Songs to Survive the Summer.
**Hassall, Christopher Vernon**
Santa Claus.
**Hathaway, Jeanine**
Extensions of Linear Mobility.
Reflections on a Womb Which Is Called "Vacant."
**Hausman, Gerald**
Poem for Lorry.
**Havergal, Frances Ridley**
Take My Life and Let It Be, *with music.*
**Hawker, Robert Stephen**
Burial Hour, The.
Fatal Ship, The.
Featherstone's Doom.
Legend of the Hive, A.
Poor Man and His Parish Church, The.
Silent Tower of Bottreau, The.
Song of the Western Men, The.
**Hawkins, Walter Everette**
Death of Justice, The.
Spade Is Just a Spade, A.
**"Hawthore, Alice."** *See* **Winner, Septimus**
**Hay, John (1838–1905)**
Enchanted Shirt, The.
**Hayden, Joe**
Hot Time in the Old Town, A, *with music.*
**Hayden, Robert Earl**
Aunt Jemima of the Ocean Waves.
Baha'u'llah in the Garden of Ridwan.
Ballad for Sue Ellen Westerfield, The.
Ballad of Nat Turner, The.
Ballad of Remembrance, A.
Diver, The.
El-Hajj Malik El-Shabazz.
Frederick Douglass.
Full Moon.
Homage to the Empress of the Blues.
In the Mourning Time.
Kid.
Middle Passage.
Mourning Poem for the Queen of Sunday.
" 'Mystery boy' Looks for Kin in Nashville."
Night, Death, Mississippi.
O Daedalus, Fly Away Home.
Road in Kentucky, A.
Runagate Runagate.
"Summertime and the Living."
Those Winter Sundays.
Tour 5.
Unidentified Flying Object.
Wheel, The.
Whipping, The.
Witch Doctor.
**Hayes, Alfred**
Death of the Craneman, The.
Slaughter-House, The.
**Hayes, Donald Jeffrey**
Appoggiatura.
**Hayman, Robert**
Mad Answer of a Madman, A.
**Hays, H. R.**
Age?
**Hazlewood-Brady, Anne**
Closer First to Earth.

Double Axe, The.
**Hazo, Samuel**
Day They Ate the Baritone, The.
Parachutist.
**Heaney, Seamus**
Advancement of Learning, An.
Boy Driving His Father to Confession.
Death of a Naturalist.
Digging.
Docker.
Early Purges, The.
Follower.
Forge, The.
Given Note, The.
Gravities.
In Small Townlands.
Mid-term Break.
Mossbawn Sunlight.
Outlaw, The.
Requiem for the Croppies.
Scaffolding.
Storm on the Island.
Tollund Man, The.
Twice Shy.
Waterfall.
**Heath, ——**
These Women All.
**Heath-Stubbs, John**
Beggar's Serenade.
Charm against the Toothache, A.
Epitaph: "Mr. Heath-Stubbs as you must understand."
History of the Flood, The.
May-Fly.
Poet in Need, A.
Poetry Today.
Starling, The.
Unpredicted, The.
Valse Oubliée.
**Heber, Reginald**
From Greenland's Icy Mountains, *with music.*
Holy, Holy, Holy! *with music.*
**Hecht, Anthony**
Alceste in the Wilderness.
Birdwatchers of America.
Dover Bitch, The.
End of the Weekend, The.
Epitaph: "Here lies a poet, briefly known as Hecht."
Epitaph: "Here lies fierce Strephon, whose poetic rage."
Going the Rounds: A Sort of Love Poem.
"It Out-Herods Herod. Pray You, Avoid It."
Japan.
La Condition Botanique.
Letter, A.
Lizards and Snakes.
"More Light! More Light!"
Samuel Sewall.
Third Avenue in Sunlight.
Upon the Death of George Santayana.
Vow, The.
**Hecht, Roger**
Ditty.
**Hedley, Leslie Woolf**
On Seeing a Stamp from the Democratic Republic of Vietnam.
**Hedylos**
Seduced Girl.

**Heffernan, Michael**
  Apparition, The.
  Figure of Plain Force, A.
  In Blessed Weather.
**Heginbothom, Ottiwell**
  Great God, let all my tuneful pow'rs.
**Heguri, Lady**
  Parting.
**Heine, Cincinnatus.**  *See* **Miller, Joaquin**
**Heine, Heinrich**
  Grave of Love, The.
  Lorelei, The, *with music.*
**Hellyer, Jill**
  Calculating Female.
**Hemans, Felicia Dorothea**
  Graves of a Household, The.
  Homes of England, The.
  Indian Woman's Death-Song.
  Landing of the Pilgrim Fathers in New
    England, The.
  Memorial Pillar, The.
  Properzia Rossi.
**Hemensley, Kris**
  Melancholy Summer.
  Mile from Poetry, A,  *sel.*
  Mr. Whitman to His Friends in the
    Antipodes.
  Poem of the Clear Eye, The, *sel.*
**Henderson, David**
  Do Nothing Till You Hear from Me.
  Documentary on Airplane Glue, A.
  Egyptian Book of the Dead
  Keep on Pushing.
  Louisiana Weekly # 4, The.
  Sketches of Harlem.
  They Are Killing All the Young Men.
  Walk with de Mayor of Harlem.
  White People.
**Henderson, Peggy**
  Serpent Muses, The.
**Hendrix, Jimi**
  Gypsy Eyes.
**Hendry, J. F.**
  Constant North, The.
  Ship, The.
**Henley, Patricia**
  Days of Re-entry.
  Near Caledonia.
  Returning from the Funeral.
  Time Out.
**Henley, William Ernest**
  Ballade Made in Hot weather.
  Ballade of Dead Actors.
  In Hospital.
  Madam Life's a Piece in Bloom.
  Margaritae Sorori.
  Out of the night that covers me.
  To A. D.
  Villon's Straight Tip to All Cross Coves.
**Hennen, Tom**
  Dirt Road.
  Going into the Woods.
  Job Hunting.
  Minneapolis.
  New Arm, The.
  Old Folks Home.
  Smelling a Stone in the Middle of
    Winter.
**Henri, Adrian**
  Adrian Henri's Talking after Christmas
    Blues.

  Mrs. Albion You've Got a Lovely
    Daughter.
  Tonight at Noon.
**Henryson, Robert**
  Robene and Makyne ("Robene sat on
    gud grene hill").
  Testament of Cresseid, The,  *sel.*
  Two Mice, The.
**Henson, Lance**
  Cold, The.
  Dawn in January.
  Grandfather.
  Last Words, 1968.
  Moon at Three A.M.
  Our Smoke Has Gone Four Ways.
  Wish.
**Herbert, Sir Alan Patrick**
  Less Nonsense.
  Racing-Man, The.
  Snail, The.
**Herbert, Edward.**  *See* **Herbert of
    Cherbury, Edward Herbert, 1st Baron**
**Herbert, George**
  Affliction ("Broken in pieces all
    asunder").
  Affliction ("When first thou didst entice
    to thee my heart").
  Agony, The.
  Altar, The.
  Answer, The.
  Artillery.
  Bitter-Sweet.
  Bunch of Grapes, The.
  Church Monuments.
  Collar, The.
  Content.
  Death.
  Denial.
  Dialogue.
  Discipline.
  Easter ("I got me flowers to straw thy
    way").
  Easter ("Rise, heart! thy Lord is risen").
  Easter Wings.
  Flower, The.
  Forerunners, The.
  Glance, The.
  Holdfast, The.
  Holy Baptism ("Since, Lord, to thee/ A
    narrow way and little gate").
  Holy Scriptures, The, I.
  Jordan ("When first my lines of heavenly
    joy made mention").
  Jordan ("Who says that fictions only and
    false hair").
  Love ("Love bade me welcome; yet my
    soul drew back").
  Love Unknown.
  Man.
  Mortification.
  Paradise.
  Pearl, The.
  Pilgrimage, The.
  Posy, The.
  Prayer: "Prayer the church's [*or*
    churches] banquet, angels' age."
  Pulley, The.
  Quip, The.
  Redemption.
  Sacrifice, The, *much abr.*
  Sepulchre.
  Sin.

  Tempest, The ("How should I praise
    thee, Lord!").
  Trinity Sunday.
  Virtue.
  Windows, The.
**Herbert, Mary, Countess of Pembroke.**
    *See* **Penbroke, Mary Sidney Herbert,
    Countess of**
**Herbert, Zbigniew**
  I Would Like to Describe.
  Our Fear.
**Herbert of Cherbury, Edward Herbert, 1st
    Baron**
  Echo to a Rock.
  Elegy over a Tomb.
  Idea, The. Made of Alnwick, in His
    Expedition to Scotland with the Army,
    1639.
  Ode upon a Question Moved, Whether
    Love Should Continue Forever?
  Platonic Love.
  Sonnet of Black Beauty.
**Herder, Johann Gottfried von**
  Erl-King's Daughter, The.
**Herebert, William**
  My Folk, What Have I Done Thee?
  Orison to the Blessed Virgin, An.
  Who Is This That Cometh from Edom?
**Herford, Oliver**
  Earth.
  Fall of J. W. Beane, The.
  I Heard a Bird Sing.
  Song: "Gather kittens while you may."
**Hernández, Miguel**
  War ("Aged in the villages, The").
  War ("All the mothers in the world").
**Hernton, Calvin C.**
  D Blues.
  Distant Drum, The.
  Fall Down.
  Jitterbugging in the Streets.
  Madhouse.
  Patient, The: Rockland County
    Sanitarium.
**Herrick, Robert**
  Another on Her.
  Argument of His Book, The.
  Bag of the Bee, The.
  Captived Bee, The: or, the Little Filcher.
  Cat, A/ I keep, that plays about my.
  Child's Present, A.
  Comfort to a Youth That Had Lost His
    Love.
  Conjuration, to Electra, A.
  Corinna's Going a-Maying.
  Counsel to Girls.
  Delight in Disorder.
  Discontents in Devon.
  Dream, The.
  Frozen Zone, The; or Julia Disdainful.
  God to Be First Served.
  Good Luck.
  Grace for a Child.
  Grace for Children, A.
  Her Leg [*or* Legs].
  His Litany to the Holy Spirit.
  His Prayer for Absolution.
  Hock-Cart, or Harvest Home, The.
  Ill Government.
  Impossibilities to His Friend.
  Julia's Petticoat.
  Kiss, The: A Dialogue.

Kissing and Bussing.
Lawn, The.
Love Me Little, Love Me Long.
Love What It Is.
Lovers How They Come and Part.
Mad Maid's Song, The.
Meditation for His Mistress, A.
Mr. Robert Herrick, His Farewell unto
  Poetry.
My Daughter's Dowry.
No Loath[e]someness in Love.
Nuptial Song, or Epithalamy, on Sir
  Clipesby Crew and His Lady, A.
Oberon's Feast.
Ode to Master Endymion Porter, upon
  His Brother's Death, An.
Slavery.
Star Song, The: A Carol to the King.
Ternarie of Littles, upon a Pipkin of
  Jelly Sent to a Lady, A.
Thanksgiving.
Thanksgiving to God, for His House, A.
This Cross-Tree Here.
To a Gentlewoman Objecting to Him
  His Grey Hairs.
To Anthea.
To Anthea, Who May Command Him
  Anything.
To Anthea Lying in Bed.
To Daffodils [or Daffadills].
To Daisies, Not To Shut So Soon.
To Dianeme.
To His Mistresse.
To His Mistresses.
To Keep a True Lent.
To Meadows.
To Music, to Becalm a Sweet-Sick
  Youth.
To Phillis to Love, and Live with Him.
To the Detractor.
To the Most Fair and Lovely Mistress
  Anne Soame, Now Lady Abdie.
To the Virgins, to Make Much of Time.
Up Tailes All.
Upon a Child.
Upon a Child That Died.
Upon His Julia.
Upon Julia's Breasts.
Upon Julia's Clothes.
Upon Julia's Unlacing Herself.
Upon Julia's Voice.
Upon Lucia Dabbled in the Dew.
Upon Moon.
Upon Mr. Ben Jonson: Epigram.
Upon Prew His Maid.
Upon Roses.
Upon the Nipples of Julia's Breasts.
Virgin Mary, The.
Vision to Electra, The.
Wake, The.
When He Would Have His Verses Read.
White Island, The; or, The Place of the
  Blest.
Wounded Cupid, The.
**Herrstrom, David Sten**
Afternoon.
Canto del Señor Segovia.
**Herschberger, Ruth**
Certain World, A.
Displays of Skill: The Bat.
First Walk in the Park.
Huron, The.

In a Bar.
Lumberyard, The.
O Terry why is sex so quick.
**Hershon, Robert**
Boy Who Smells Like Cocoa, A.
Cooper & Bailey Great London Circus,
  The.
Four Translations from the English of
  Robert Hershon.
Ireland Lake.
Kelly.
Responses.
Spitting on Ira Rosenblatt.
Swimming Lesson, The.
U.S. Coast and Geodetic Survey Ship
  *Pioneer*, The.
**Herzog, Arthur, Jr.,** *and* **Billie Holiday**
God Bless the Child.
**Hesketh, Phoebe**
Ducks.
**Hesse, Hermann**
Glorious World.
**Hewitt, E. E.**
Will There Be Any Stars in My Crown?
  *with music.*
**Hewitt, Geof**
Behind That Wall My Roomate Fucks
  His Girl.
Conversion.
Emergency at 8.
Explanation.
For Bill.
For Randie.
Rip-off # 1: Hippie Capitalism.
**Hewitt, John**
From a Museum Man's Album.
Frontier, The.
In this Year of Grace.
Irishman in Coventry, An.
O Country People.
Ram's Horn, The.
**Hey, Phillip**
Epigrams.
Gunfighter.
Lines Written in Objection, or the
  Limpopo Express.
Old Men Working Concrete.
Thank You Poem for the Andersons,
  The.
**Heyen, William**
Dog Sacrifice at Lake Ronkonkoma.
I Move to Random Consolations.
Snapper, The.
Spirit of Wrath, The.
**Heyrick, Thomas**
On a Mandrake.
On an Indian Tomineios, the Least of
  Birds.
Submarine Voyage, The: a Pindaric
  Poem in Four Parts,*sels.*
**Heywood, John**
Of Late and Never.
Of Loving a Dog.
On Botching.
**Heywood, Thomas**
Love's Good-morrow.
Rape of Lucrece, The.*sels.*
**Hickson, William E.**
Walking Song.
**Higgins, Bertram**
Under the Sign of the Fisher.
**Higgins, Brian**

Corrupt Man in the French Pub, The.
**Higgins, Dick**
Teechur.
**Higgins, Frederick Robert**
At Flock Mass.
Chinese Winter.
Father and Son.
O You among Women.
Old Jockey, The.
Padraic O'Conaire, Gaelic Storyteller.
**Higginson, Nesta.** *See* **"O'Neill, Moira"**
**Higham, Charles**
Kelly Show, The.
Sand.
**Hilberry, Conrad**
Poet.
Sleeping Out in Vermont.
**Hill, Donald L.**
Buzzing Doubt, The.
**Hill, Geoffrey**
Imaginative Life, The.
In Memory of Jane Fraser.
Love, oh my love, it will come.
Mercian Hymns, *sel.*
Merlin.
Of Commerce and Society.
Offa's Laws.
Ovid in the Third Reich.
Picture of a Nativity.
Requiem for the Plantagenet Kings.
Songbook of Sebastian Arrurruz, The,
  *sel.*
**Hill, Leslie Pinckney**
So Quietly.
**Hill, Roberta**
Beginning the Year at Rosebud, S.D.
Direction.
Dream of Rebirth.
Falling Moon.
In the Madison Zoo.
Lines for Marking Time.
Midnight on Front Street.
Nation Wrapped in Stone, A.
Night along the Mackinac Bridge.
Sleeping with Foxes.
Song for Healing.
Star Quilt.
Whispers.
**Hillyer, Robert Silliman**
Assassination, The.
Letter to a Teacher of English, A.
Moo!
Pastorals, *sel.*
Sonnet Sequence, A, *sel.*
Sonnet: "Today as I passed through the
  market-place."
XXth Century.
**Hilton, Arthur Clement**
Heathen Pass-ee, The, *parody.*
Octopus.
Vulture and the Husbandman, The.
**Hilton, David**
In Praise of BIC Pens.
Poet Tries to Turn in His Jock, The.
**Himel, Margery**
My People.
**Hinde, Gertrude**
Donkey, The.
**Hine, Daryl**
Bluebeard's Wife.
English Elegy, An.
Untitled.

Wave, The.
**Hinkson, Katharine Tynan.** *See* **Tynan, Katharine**
**Hippisley, John**
Sweet Is the Budding Spring of Love, *with music.*
**Hipple, Ted**
Traditional Grammarian As Poet, The.
**Hirsh, A. M.**
Yale Boola!, *3 versions, with music.*
**Hitchcock, George**
Figures in a Ruined Balloon.
May All Earth Be Clothed in Light.
Song of Expectancy.
Three Portraits.
**Hitomaro (Kakinomoto no Hitomaro)**
Gossip grows like weeds.
**Hoagland, Everett**
Anti-Semanticist, The.
It's a Terrible Thing!
Love Child—a Black Aesthetic.
My Spring Thing.
**Hoban, Russell**
Maine Sea Gulls.
**Hoberman, Mary Ann**
I Was Riding to Poughkeepsie.
**Hobsbaum, Philip**
Astigmatic, The.
Lesson in Love, A.
Place's Fault, The.
**Hoccleve, Thomas**
Anxious Thought.
De Regimine Principum, *sels.*
Lament for Chaucer and Gower.
**Hochman, Sandra**
Constructions: Upper East Side.
Couple, The.
Elephant, The.
Eyes of Flesh, The.
Farewell Poem.
Goldfish Wife, The.
Grief.
History of the Opera, A.
Postscript.
Swimming Pool, The.
**Hodgson, Ralph**
Bells of Heaven, The.
Bull, The.
Eve.
Gently, years, gently!
Hammers, The.
Hymn to Moloch.
Past comes back, The.
Silver Wedding.
Stupidity Street.
**Hoey, Edwin A.**
Foul Shot.
**Hoffenstein, Samuel**
I'd rather listen to a flute.
Mr. Walter de la Mare makes the Little Ones Dizzy, *sel.*
Poem Intended to Incite the Utmost Depression, A.
When You're Away.
**Hoffman, Daniel Gerard**
Ballad of No Proper Man.
City of Satisfactions, The.
È, the Feasting Florentines.
Old Photo in an Old Life, An.
Signatures.
Tree.
**Hoffman, Elisha A.**

Leaning on the Everlasting Arms, *with music.*
**Hoffmann, Heinrich**
Cruel Frederick.
Story of Augustus Who Would Not Have Any Soup, The.
Story of Fidgety Philip, The.
Story of Flying Robert, The.
Story of Johnny Head-in-Air, The.
Story of Little Suck-a-Thumb, The.
**Hogg, James ("The Ettrick Shepherd")**
Boy's Song, A.
Love Is Like a Dizziness.
Moon Was Waning, The.
Queen's Wake, The, *sel.*
Song, The: "O! Lady dear, fair is thy noon."
Village of Balmaquhapple, The.
**Holahan, Pamela Crawford**
Song to the Ninth Grade.
**Holbrook, David**
Drought.
Maternity Gown.
**Holden, Molly**
Giant Decorative Dahlia.
Photograph of Haymaker, 1890.
**Hölderlin, Friedrich**
Socrates and Alcibiades.
To Diotima.
**Holiday, Billie and Arthur Herzog, Jr.** *See* **Herzog, Arthur, Jr., and Billie Holiday**
**Holland, Barbara A.**
Apples of Sodom and Gomorrah, The.
Leavings.
**Hollander, John**
Adam's Task.
Altarpiece Finished, The.
Great Bear, The.
Helicon.
Hobbes, 1651.
Jefferson Valley.
Last Quarter.
Movie-Going.
Night Mirror, The.
Ninth of July, The.
Skeleton Key.
**Hollo, Anselm**
And How It Goes.
Bison Flower Days.
Bouzouki Music.
Buffalo—Isle of Wight Power Cable.
Charge, The.
He She Because How.
Instances.
On the Occasion of Becoming an Echo.
Your Friend.
**Holman, Felice**
Who Am I?
**Holman, M. Carl**
And on This Shore.
Mr. Z.
Notes for a Movie Script.
Picnic: The Liberated.
**Holmes, Oliver Wendell**
At the "Atlantic" Dinner.
Autocrat of the Breakfast-Table, The, *sels.*
Chambered Nautilus, The.
Deacon's Masterpiece, The; or, The Wonderful "One-Hoss Shay."
Dorothy Q.
Last Leaf, The.

Nearing the Snow-line.
Old Ironsides.
**Holmes, R. Ernest**
Black Lady in an Afro Hairdo Cheers for Cassius.
**Holsapple, Bruce**
I send these wild roses.
Quiet faces.
**Holt, Ray**
My Morose Master-Sergeants.
**Holub, Miroslav**
Dog in the Quarry, A, *sel.*
Door, The.
History Lesson, A.
Lesson, The.
Ode to Joy.
Dog in the Quarry, A, *sel.*
**Homer**
Odyssey, The, *sel.*
Sirens' Song, The.
**Honig, Edwin**
As a Great Prince.
November Through a Giant Copper Beech.
Now, My Usefulness Over.
Some Knots.
Tête-à-Tête.
Walt Whitman.
**Hood, Thomas**
Athol Brose.
Choosing Their Names.
Death-bed, The.
Faithless Nellie Gray.
I Remember, I Remember.
Little Piggy.
Mary's Ghost.
No!
Nocturnal Sketch, A.
Ode: Autumn.
Ruth.
Sally Brown.
Song of the Shirt, The, *sel.*
To Henrietta, on Her Departure for Calais.
To Minerva.
Work—work—work.
**Hood, Tom (Thomas Hood, Jr.)**
Cannibal Flea, The.
**Hook, Theodore**
Cautionary Verses to Youth of Both Sexes.
**Hope, Alec Derwent**
Advice to Young Ladies
Agony Column.
Ascent into Hell.
Bed, The.
Brides, The.
Circe.
Conquistador.
Coup de Grâce.
Death of the Bird, The.
Gateway, The.
Gauguin's Menhir, Tahiti ("Gauguin's Museum in Papeari bay").
Imperial Adam.
In Memoriam: Gertrud Kolmar, 1943.
Invaders, The.
Lingam and the Yoni, The.
Meditation on a Bone.
Moschus Moschiferus.
Observation Car.
Sportsfield.

William Butler Yeats.
**Hope, Francis**
Live Man's Epitaph.
**Hopewell, Anna Madge**
Tree, The.
**Hopkins, Gerard Manley**
Alchemist in the City, The.
At the Wedding March.
Binsey Poplars.
Bugler's First Communion, The ("A
bugler boy from barrack").
Caged Skylark, The.
Carrion Comfort.
"Child Is Father to the Man, The."
Duns Scotus's Oxford.
Easter Communion.
Felix Randal.
Fragment: "Strike, churl; hurl, cheerless
wind, then; heltering hail."
God's Grandeur.
Habit of Perfection, The.
Heaven-haven.
Hurrahing in Harvest.
I Wake and Feel the Fell of Dark, Not
Day.
Inversnaid.
Lantern Out of Doors, The.
Leaden Echo and the Golden Echo, The.
Moonrise.
My Own Heart Let Me More Have Pity
On.
No Worst, There Is None.
Patience Hard Thing.
Pied Beauty.
Spring.
Spring and Fall.
Starlight Night, The.
That Nature Is a Heraclitean Fire and
of the Comfort of the Resurrection.
Thou Art Indeed Just, Lord, If I
Contend.
To Margaret.
Valley of the Elwy, The.
Windhover, The.
Winter with the Gulf Stream
Wreck of the *Deutschland*, The.
**Hopkins, John Henry, Jr.**
We Three Kings of Orient Are, *with
music.*
**Hopkinson, Francis**
Enraptured I Gaze,*with music.*
**Hopkinson, Joseph**
Hail, Columbia.
**Hopper, Nora**
March.
**Horace (Quintus Horatius Flaccus)**
Odes, *sels.*
Praise of Pindar, The.
Preference Declared, The ("Persicos
odi").
Ribald Romeos Less and Less Berattle.
Satires, *sel.*
Solvitur Acris Hiems.
This Monument Will Outlast.
To Chloe ("Vitas hinnuleo").
To Pyrrha ("Quis multa gracilis").
**Horne, Frank**
Kid Stuff.
Letters [*or* Notes] Found near a Suicide.
Mamma!
On Seeing Two Brown Boys in a
Catholic Church.

Patience.
Resurrection.
To "Chick"
To James.
To Mother.
To You.
Walk.
**Hoskins, Katherine**
When Snow Falls.
Youngest Schizophrene, The.
**Hoskyns, John**
To His Little Son Benedict from the
Tower of London.
**Hough, Lindy**
Portrait of the Father.
**Houghton, Richard Monckton Milnes, 1st
Baron.** *See* Milnes, Richard
Monckton, 1st Baron Houghton
**Housman, Alfred Edward**
As Into the Garden.
Because I liked you better.
Carpenter's Son, The.
Chestnut Casts His Flambeaux, The.
Could Man Be Drunk For Ever.
Crossing alone the nighted ferry.
Culprit, The.
Easter Hymn.
Eight O'Clock.
1887.
Epitaph on an Army of Mercenaries
Fairies Break Their Dances, The.
"Farewell to barn and stack and tree."
For My Funeral.
Fragment of a Greek Tragedy.
From Far, from Eve and Morning.
From the Wash the Laundress Sends.
Hell Gate.
Her Strong Enchantments Failing.
I Did Not Lose My Heart.
I Promise Nothing.
In the Morning, in the Morning.
Infant Innocence.
Into My Heart an Air That Kills.
Is Football Playing?
Is My Team Ploughing?
Lads in their hundreds to Ludlow come
in for the fair, The.
Laws of God, The.
Loitering with a Vacant Eye.
Loveliest of Trees.
Mill-stream, now that noises cease, The.
New Mistress, The.
O have you caught the tiger?
Oh, When I Was in Love with You.
Olive, The.
On Forelands High in Heaven.
On moonlit heath and lonesome bank.
On the idle hill of summer.
On Wenlock Edge the wood's in trouble.
Oracles, The.
Others, I am not the first.
Parta Quies.
Rainy Pleiads Wester, The.
Reveille.
Shades of night were falling fast, The.
Street Sounds to the Soldiers' Tread,
The.
Tell me not here, it needs not saying.
Terence, This Is Stupid Stuff.
They Say My Verse Is Sad: No Wonder.
To an Athlete Dying Young.
True Lover, The.

Wake Not for the World-Heard
Thunder.
When First My Way to Fair I Took.
When I Was One-and-Twenty.
When I Watch the Living Meet.
When Smoke Stood Up from Ludlow.
When the lad for longing sighs.
With Rue My Heart Is Laden.
**Howard, Anne, Duchess of Arundel**
Elegy on the the Death of Husband.
**Howard, Frances Minturn**
Sampler from Haworth.
**Howard, Henry.** *See* Surrey, Henry
Howard, Earl of
**Howard, Joseph E.**
Good Bye, My Lady Love, *with music.*
**Howard, Joseph E. and Ida Emerson**
Hello, Ma Baby, *with music*
**Howard, Richard**
Giovanni Da Fiesole on the Sublime; or,
Fra Angelico's "Last Judgment."
Lapsus Linguae.
1907, A Proposal from Paris.

Oystering.
**Howe, Julia Ward**
Battle Hymn of the Republic, The.
**Howell, Thomas**
Lover Deceived Writes to His Lady,
The, *sel.*
Rose, The.
**Howes, Barbara**
At 79th and Park.
Cat on Couch.
City Afternoon.
Conversation, A.
Danäe.
Death of a Vermont Farm Woman.
Early Supper.
Gulls.
Indian Summer.
Landscape, Deer Season.
Light and Dark.
Mercedes.
New Leda, The.
Out Fishing.
Portrait of an Artist.
**Howitt, Mary**
Buttercups and Daisies.
Seagull, The.
Spider and the Fly, The.
**Howitt, William**
Migration of the Grey Squirrels, The.
**Hoyem, Andrew**
Filtres.
**Hoyt, Charles Hale**
Bowery, The, *with music.*
**Hsieh, Chen**
Number One Daughter of the Wang
Family, The.
**Hsü Pên**
Hermit, The.
**Huang-fu Jan**
Spring Thoughts.
**Hubbell, Patricia**
Lemons.
Mag.
Vermont Conversation.
**Hueffer, Ford Madox.** *See* Ford, Ford
Madox
**Huff, Robert**
Getting Drunk with Daughter.

Porcupines.
Rainbow.
Traditional Red.
**Hughes, Glyn**
Cold.
Diggle Mill.
Epitaphs
**Hughes, Langston**
Afro-American Fragment.
American Heartbreak.
Angola Question Mark.
April Rain Song.
Backlash Blues, The.
Bad Morning.
Ballad of the Landlord.
Ballad of the Man Who's Gone.
Beale Street.
Black Pierrot, A.
Brass Spittoons.
Carol of the Brown King.
Catch.
Children's Rhymes.
Christ in Alabama.
City.
Cross.
Cultural Exchange.
Death in Yorkville.
Dinner Guest: Me.
Down and Out.
Dream Variation [or Variations].
Epigram: "Oh, God of dust and
    rainbows."
Esthete in Harlem
50-50.
Fire.
Florida Road Workers.
Frederick Douglass: 1817-1895.
Freedom.
Good Morning.
Harlem ("Here on the edge of hell").
Harlem ("What happens to a dream
    defferred").
Heaven.
I, Too.
Jazzonia.
Juke Box Love Song.
Junior Addict.
Justice.
Ku Klux.
Late Last Night.
Lenox Avenue Mural.
Lincoln Monument: Washington.
Madam and the Minister.
Madam's Past History.
Merry-Go-Round.
Midnight Raffle.
Militant.
Morning After.
Mother to Son.
Motto.
Mulatto.
Necessity.
Negro Servant.
Negro Speaks of Rivers, The.
Night Funeral in Harlem.
October 16: The Raid.
Old Walt.
Peace.
Personal.
Preference.
Prime.
Question and Answer.

Sailor.
Same in Blues.
Sea Calm.
Song for a Dark Girl.
Special Bulletin.
Still Here.
Stony Lonesome.
Sylvester's Dying Bed.
Theme for English B.
Third Degree.
Today.
Too Blue.
Troubled Woman.
Un-American Investigators.
Warning.
Weary Blues, The.
Where? When? Which?
Who But the Lord?
Winter Moon.
Winter Sweetness.
Words Like Freedom.
**Hughes, Ted**
Bullfrog.
Crow and the Birds.
Crow's First Lesson.
Crow's Last Stand.
Esther's Tomcat.
Ghost Crabs.
Gnat-Psalm.
Hawk Roosting.
Horses, The.
Howling of Wolves, The.
In Laughter.
Law in the Country of the Cats.
Lovesong.
Ludwig's Death Mask.
New Year's Song.
October Dawn.
Otter, An.
Out.
Parlour Piece.
Pennines in April.
Pibroch.
Pike.
Reveille.
Second Glance at a Jaguar.
Secretary.
September.
Stations.
Theology.
Thistles.
Thought-Fox, The.
Thrushes.
Truth Kills Everybody.
View of a Pig.
Wind.
Wino.
Wodwo.
**Hughes, Thomas**
Dolgelley Hotel, The.
**Hugo, Richard**
Church on Comiaken Hill, The.
Maratea Porto: Saying Goodbye to the
    Vitolos.
**Huidobro, Vincente**
She.
**Hulme, Thomas Ernest**
Autumn.
Embankment, The.
Image.
**Humphries, Rolfe**
Around Thanksgiving.

Looking Up at Airplanes, Always.
Sad Song, This Time, A.
**Hunt, Leigh**
Abou Ben Adhem.
Jenny Kiss'd [or Kissed] Me.
Nile, The.
**Hunter, Robert**
Casey Jones ("Driving that train, high
    on cocaine").
**Huntley, Stanley**
Annabel Lee, *parody*.
**Hutchinson, Pearse**
Gaeltacht.
Malaga.
**Hutchinson, Robert**
Drifting, A.
**"Hyde, Robin" (Iris Guiver Wilkinson)**
Deserted Village, The.
Pihsien Road.

**I**

**Ian, Janis**
Society's Child.
**Ibn Ezra, Abraham**
My Stars.
**Icaza, Francisco A. de**
Responding Voice.
**Idley, Peter**
Covetousness.
Sources of Good Counsel.
**Ignacio, Bruce**
Lost.
**Ignatow, David**
All Quiet.
Allegory, An.
Bagel, The.
Bowery.
Brooding.
Dilemma.
Dream, The.
East Bronx.
Europe and America.
For My Daughter.
For My Daughter in Reply to a
    Question.
For One Moment.
Get the Gasworks.
He Puts Me to Rest.
Last Night.
Paper Cutter, The.
Rescue the Dead.
Ritual Three.
Simultaneously.
To Nowhere.
Two Friends.
With the Door Open.
**Ikan, Ron**
American Saturday Afternoon.
Babylon.
Sidewalk Restoration.
**Illot, Percy H.**
Lost Egg, The.
**Imamu Amiri Baraka.** *See* **Jones, LeRoi**
**Iman, Yusef**
Love Your Enemy.
**Inada, Lawson Fusao**
Asian Brother, Asian Sister.

From Our Album.
Plucking Out a Rhythm.
**Inez, Colette**
Colette, Poor Clare.
Empress in the Mirror.
For Mama Streek.
Good news! Nilda Is Back.
Instructions for the Erection of a Statue
  to Myself in Central Park.
Mercedes, Her Aloneness.
Snapshot.
Waiting for the Doctor.
When I Was Soft as Ferns.
Woman Who Loved Worms, The.
**Ingelow, Jean**
Divided.
One Morning, Oh, So Early!
**"Ingoldsby, Thomas" (Richard Harris
  Barham)**
Ingoldsby Legends, The, *sels.*
Jackdaw of Rheims, The.
Not a Sous Had He Got.
**Iremonger, Valentin**
Dog, The.
Icarus.
Invocation: "Ten bloody years with this
  quill lying."
Spring Stops Me Suddenly.
This Houre Her Vigill.
**Irwin, Thomas Caulfield**
Swift, *sel.*
With the Dawn.
**Irwin, Wallace ("Ginger"; "Hashimura
  Togo")**
Ballad of Hagensack, The.
Nautical Extravaganza, A.
Powerful Eyes o' Jeremy Tait, The.
**Isherwood, Christopher**
Common Cormorant, The.
On His Queerness
**Issa (Kobayashi Issa)**
Buddha's Birthday: April 8, 1819.
Buddha's Death Day: February 15,
  1815.
Crawl, laugh.
New Moon, The.
Oraga Haru, *sels.*
**Ivens, Michael**
First Day at School
**Iverson, Lucille**
Abortion, The.
Man, The.
Outrage.

# J

**Jackson, Mae**
Blues Today, The.
For Some Poets.
I Remember.
I Used to Wrap My White Doll Up in.
January 3, 1970.
Reincarnation.
**Jacob, Hildebrand**
Writer, The.
**Jacob, Max**
It may that a strange dream.
**Jacob, Violet**

Tam i' the Kirk.
**Jacobsen, Josephine**
Destinations.
Reason of Numbers, A.
Reindeer and Engine.
Thief, The.
**Jagger, Mick *and* Keith Richard**
Live with Me.
**Jago, Richard**
Hamlet's Soliloquy Imitated.
**James, Thomas (1593-1635?)**
Lines on His Companions who Died in
  the Northern Seas.
**James, Thomas (1946-74)**
Hunting for Blueberries.
Letter to a Mute.
Letters to a Stranger.
Mummy of a Lady Named
  Jemutesonekh XXI Dynasty.
Spider in the Grapes.
Timothy.
Tom O' Bedlam among the Sunflowers.
**James I, King of England**
Ane Metaphoricall Invention of a
  Tragedie Called Phoenix, *sel.*
Constant Love in All Conditions.
For I complaine not of sic common cace.
**James I, King of Scotland**
Kingis Quair, The, *sels.*
**Jamieson, Morley**
Birthday, The.
Swans.
**Janik, Phyllis**
In the Field.
Story of Good, The.
**Janosco, Beatrice**
Garden Hose, The.
**Janzen, Richard**
Oh, Joyous House.
**Jarrell, Randall**
Bats.
Bird of Night, The.
Bronze David of Donatello, The.
Burning the Letters.
Camp in the Prussian Forest, A.
Chipmunk's Day, The.
Come to the Stone.
Death of the Ball Turret Gunner, The.
Eighth Air Force.
Field and Forest.
Forsaken Girl, The.
Front, A.
Game at Salzburg, A.
Girl in a Library, A.
Gunner.
In Montecito.
Jerome.
Jonah.
Lonely Man, The.
Lost Children, The.
Mockingbird, The.
Next Day.
"Night before the Night before
  Christmas," *sel.*
90 North.
Old and the New Masters, The.
Orient Express, The.
Protocols.
Range in the Desert, The.
Sick Child, A.
Thinking of the Lost World.
Variations.

Well Water.
When I Was Home Last Christmas.
Woman.
Woman at the Washington Zoo, The.
**Jarrett, Emmett**
Dear Mother.
For E. C. J.
"Hamlet."
Human Relations.
Song: "Help me now."
Trip, The.
Two of Cups, The.
**Jeffers, Lance**
Grief Streams Down My Chest.
How High the Moon.
My Blackness Is the Beauty of This
  Land.
On Listening to the Spirituals.
**Jeffers, Robinson**
Antrim.
Apology for Bad Dreams.
Artist, An.
Ave Caesar.
Beaks of Eagles, The.
Bed by the Window, The.
Birds.
Birds and Fishes.
Broken Promise.
But I Am Growing Old and Indolent.
Carmel Point.
Cassandra.
Compensation.
Continent's End.
Deer Lay Down Their Bones, The.
Divinely Superfluous Beauty.
Evening Ebb.
Eye, The.
Fawn's Foster-Mother.
Gray Weather.
Great Explosion, The.
Hurt Hawks.
Little Scraping, A.
Love the Wild Swan.
New Mexican Mountain.
Night.
Night without Sleep.
Oh, Lovely Rock.
Original Sin.
Phenomena.
Post Mortem.
Purse-Seine, The.
Rearmament.
Rock and Hawk.
Science.
Shane O'Neill's Cairn.
Shine, Perishing Republic.
Shiva.
Signpost.
Skunks, *sel.*
Summer Holiday.
To the Stone-Cutters.
Unnatural Powers.
Vulture.
Watch the Lights Fade.
We have little animals here.
**Jeffrey, Francis, Lord Jeffrey**
On Peter Robinson.
**Jellema, Roderick Hartigh**
Four-square Gospel.
In Imago Dei: Fiat Lux.
On the Death of God.

Poem Beginning with a Line Memorized at School.
Sixes and Sevens.
To a Student Poet, Hospitalized, Having "Broken with Reality."
Waking to Snowfall.
**Jenkins, Brooks**
Loneliness.
**Jenkins, Louis**
Library.
Medicine.
Portage Poem.
Quiet Place, A.
**Jenks, Orville**
Dying Mine Brakeman, The.
**Jennings, Elaine H.**
Each night/ just before dusk.
I am riding a lion.
There Is No Time.
Weather Report.
**Jennings, Elizabeth**
Answers.
Clothes.
Delay.
Doubts.
Fountain.
Friends.
In a Mental Hospital Sitting Room.
Interrogator, The.
My Grandmother.
Old Woman.
One Flesh.
Song at the Beginning of Autumn.
Storm House, The.
Two Deaths.
Ugly Child, The.
Winter Love.
Young Ones, The.
**Jensen, Laura**
After I Have Voted.
In the Hospital.
Indian.
Sleep in the Heat.
Talking to the Mule.
**Jenyns, Soame**
Modern Fine Gentleman, The.
**Jerome, Judson**
At the Dancing School of the Sisters Schwarz.
Deer Hunt.
Eve: Night Thoughts.
**Jerome, William**
Bedelia, *with music.*
**Jewsbury, Maria Jane**
Partings.
To a Young Brother.
**Jiménez, Juan Ramón**
New Spring.
Nudes.
Poetry.
**Joad, C. E. M.**
Materialism.
**Joans, Ted**
It Is Time.
Its Curtains.
Protective Grigri, The.
Scenery.
**Johari Amini.** *See* **Latimore, Jewel C.**
**John of the Cross, Saint**
Upon a gloomy night.
**Johnson, Dan**
Stray Things.

**Johnson, Fenton**
Aunt Jane Allen.
Old Repair Man, The.
Scarlet Woman, The.
Tired.
**Johnson, Fred**
Arabesque.
Fire, Hair, Meat and Bone.
**Johnson, George W.**
When You and I Were Young, Maggie, *with music.*
**Johnson, Georgia Douglas**
Common Dust.
Credo.
Escape.
Old Black Men.
Prejudice.
Riddle, The: "White men's children spread over the earth."
Suppliant, The.
**Johnson, Helene**
Bottled: New York.
Magalu.
Poem: "Little brown boy."
**Johnson, James Weldon**
Creation, The.
Glory of the Day Was in Her Face, The.
Go down Death.
Listen, Lord—a Prayer.
O Black and Unknown Bards.
**Johnson, Joe**
If I Ride This Train.
Judeebug's Country.
**Johnson, Lionel Pigot**
By the Statue of King Charles at Charing Cross.
Dark Angel, The.
**Johnson, Ronald**
Letters to Walt Whitman,*sels.*
**Johnson, Samuel (1709-84)**
Burlesque of Lope De Vega.
Charles XII of Sweden.
Imitation of the Style of * * * *.
Lines Written in Ridicule of Certain Poems Published in 1777.
London: a Poem in Imitation of the Third Satire of Juvenal.
On the Death of Mr. [or Dr.] Robert Levet, a Practiser in Physic.
Power of Prayer, The.
Prologue Spoken at the Opening of the Theatre in Drury-Lane, 1747.
Scholar's Life, The.
Short Song of Congratulation, A.
Vanity of Human Wishes, The: the Tenth Satire of Juvenal Imitated.
Young Author, The.
**Johnson, Siddie Joe**
Goat.
I Did Not See a Mermaid?
Witchcraft.
**Johnston, Anna.** *See* **"Carbery, Ethna"**
**Johnston, Laughton**
Love Poem 3.
**Johnstone, Henry, Lord Johnstone**
Fastidious Serpent, The.
**Jonas, George**
Eight Lines for a Script Girl.
Exit Lines
Glass Eaters, The.
Let me put it this way.
Once More.

Peace.
Portrait: The Freedom Fighter.
Sleep only with strangers.
To Christian Montpelier, *sel.*
We all have/ A bench in the park to reach.
**Jones, Brian**
Death of a Cat.
How to Catch Tiddlers.
**Jones, David**
Anathemata, The, *sels.*
Angle-Land
Five Unmistakable Marks, The.
In Parenthesis,*sels.*
King Pellam's Launde.
Redriff.
Wall, The.
**Jones, Evan**
At the Airport.
Generations.
Lament of the Banana Man.
Song of the Banana Man.
**Jones, Jeanetta**
Involuntary flex.
**Jones, L. E.**
Death.
Epigram on the Unknown Inventor of Scissors.
**Jones, LeRoi (Imamu Amiri Baraka)**
Agony, An. As Now.
Audubon, Drafted.
Babylon Revisited.
Balboa, the Entertainer.
Beautiful Black Women.
Black Art.
Black Bourgeoisie.
Black People!
Black People: This Is Our Destiny.
Bumi.
Cold Term.
Dance, The.
Dead Lady Canonized, The.
Duncan Spoke of a Process.
Each Morning.
Evil Nigger Waits for Lightnin'.
For Hettie.
Guerrilla Handbook, A.
Hymn for Lanie Poo, *sel.*
I Substitute for the Dead Lecturer.
Incident.
Invention of Comics, The.
Ka 'Ba.
Legacy.
Leroy.
Letter to E. Franklin Frazier.
Liar, The.
Lines to García Lorca.
New World, The.
Numbers, Letters.
Part of the Doctrine.
Poem for Black Hearts, A.
Poem for Democrats, A.
Poem for Half White College Students.
Poem for Speculative Hipsters, A.
Poem for Willie Best, A.
Poem Some People Will Have to Understand, A.
Political Poem.
Politics of Rich Painters, The.
Preface to a Twenty Volume Suicide Note.
Pressures, The.

Return of the Native.
Scenario VI.
Snake Eyes.
Song Form.
SOS.
Spell, THe.
Study Peace.
Three Modes of History and Culture.
W. W.
Way Out West.
We Own the Night.
Young Soul.
**Jones, Rae Desmond**
Generator, The.
New Year 1974.
Poems to My Father.
Wishbone, The.
**Jong, Erica**
Aging.
Alcestis on the Poetry Circuit.
Back to Africa.
Becoming a Nun.
Bitter Pills for the Dark Ladies.
Colder.
Dear Colette.
Dear Man-in-the-Moon.
For a Marriage.
Fruit and Vegetables.
Here Comes.
Hook.
In Sylvia Plath Country.
In the Penile Colony.
Man Under the Bed, The.
Seminar.
Seventeen Warnings in Search of a
    Feminist Poem.
Sunjuice.
Touch.
Universal Explicator, The.
Why I Died.
Wives of Mafiosi, The.
Woman Who Loved to Cook, The.
**Jonson, Ben**
Celebration of Charis, A, *sel.*
Charles Cavendish to His Posterity.
Come, My Celia.
Cynthia's Revels, *sels.*
Death and Love.
Dream, The.
Echo's Lament of Narcissus.
Elegy, An: "Let me be what I am, as
    Virgil cold," *abr.*
Epicoene; or, The Silent Woman, *sel.*
Epistle to a Friend (Mr. Colby) to
    Persuade Him to the Wars, An, *sel.*
Epistle to Katherine, Lady Aubigny,
    *sel.*
Epitaph on Elizabeth, L. H.
Epitaph on S. P., a Child of Queen
    Elizabeth's Chapel.
Eupheme,*sels.*
Fit of Rime against Rime, A.
Fortunate Isles, and Their Union, The,
    *sel.*
Golden Age Restored, The, *sel.*
Hymenaei, *sel.*
Hymn to Diana.
Hymn to God the Father, A.
Inviting a Friend to Supper.
Masque of Queens, The,*sels.*
Noble Nature, The.
Oberon the Fairy Prince, *sel.*

Ode, An: "High spirited friend."
Ode to Himself, An ("Where dost thou
    careless lie").
On Courtworm.
On Gut.
On My First Daughter.
On My First Son [*or* Sonne].
On Sir Voluptuous Beast.
On Something That Walks Somewhere.
On the Famous Voyage.
Pindaric Ode, A.
Praises of a Country Life, The.
Return of Astraea, The.
Sad Shepherd, The,*sels.*
Simplex Munditiis.
Song, A: "Oh do not wanton with those
    eyes."
That Women Are but Men's Shadows.
To Celia ("Drink to me only with thine
    eyes").
To Fool, or Knave.
To Heaven.
To Penshurst.
To Sir Robert Wroth.
To the Ghost of Martial
To the Immortal Memory and
    Friendship of That Noble Pair, Sir
    Lucius Cary and Sir Henry Morison.
To the Memory of My Beloved, the
    Author, Mr. William Shakespeare, and
    What He Hath Left Us.
To the Right Honourable the Lord High
    Treasurer.
Triumph of Charis, The.
Volpone, *sels.*
Voyage Itself, The.
Witches' Charm, The.
**Jordan, June**
All the World Moved.
And Who Are You?
Cameo No. II.
For My Mother.
If You Saw a Negro Lady.
In Memoriam: Martin Luther King, Jr.
May 27, 1971: No Poem.
Maybe the Birds.
My Sadness Sits around Me.
Nobody Riding the Roads Today.
Okay "Negroes."
Poem for My Family.
Poem from the Empire State.
Poem to My Sister, Ethel Ennis, Who
    Sang "The Star-spangled Banner" at
    the Second Inauguration of Richard
    Milhous Nixon.
Reception, The.
Uncle Bull-boy.
What Happens.
What Would I Do White?
**Jordan, Norman**
August 2.
Black Warrior.
Feeding the Lions.
July 31.
**Jordan, Thomas**
Epicure, The, Sung by One in the Habit
    of a Town Gallant.
**Joseph, Jenny**
Warning.
**Joseph, Michael Kennedy**
Girl, Boy, Flower, Bicycle.
**Joseph, Rosemary**

Baking Day.
**Joyce, J.**
Soil Searcher.
**Joyce, James**
All Day I Hear the Noise of Waters.
Bahnhofstrasse.
Because your voice was at my side.
Ecce Puer.
Finnegans Wake,  *sel.*
Flower Given to My Daughter, A.
Gentle lady, do not sing.
Holy Office, The.
I Hear an Army Charging upon the
    Land.
Memory of the Players in a Mirror at
    Midnight, A.
Nightpiece.
O sweetheart, hear you.
On the Beach at Fontana.
Ondt and the Gracehoper, The.
Sleep now, O sleep now.
Though I Thy Mithridates Were.
What Counsel Has the Hooded Moon.
**Juana Inés de la Cruz, Sister (originally
    Juana de Asbaje)**
Crimson lute that comest in the dawn.
**Judson, John**
Finding Words in Winter.
24 December.
**Juhász, Ferenc**
Birth of the Foal.
**Juhasz, Suzanne**
Dancer from the Dance, The.
Saying Goodbye.
**Justice, Donald**
Anonymous Drawing.
Another Song ("Merry the green, the
    green hill shall be merry").
Beyond the Hunting Woods.
Bus Stop.
But That Is Another Story.
Counting the Mad.
Crossing Kansas by Train.
First Death.
Grandfathers, The.
Here in Katmandu.
In Bertram's Garden.
Incident in a Rose Garden.
Local Storm, A.
Luxury.
Memory of a Porch.
Men at Forty.
On a Painting by Patient B of the
    Independence State Hospital for the
    Insane.
On the Death of Friends in Childhood.
Poem to Be Read at 3 A.M.
Snowfall, The.
Song: "Morning opened/ Like a rose.
Tourist from Syracuse, The.
**Juvenal**
Jove, grant me length of life, and years'
    good store.
Satires, *sel.*

# K

**Kahn, Hannah**
Signature.

**Kalidasa**
Is poetry always worthy when it's old.
**Kandel, Lenore**
Blues for Sister Sally.
Bus Ride.
Circus, *sels.*
Freak Show and Finale.
Love in the Middle of the Air.
**Kantner, Paul**
We Can Be Together.
**Kantner, Paul, David Crosby** *and* **Stephen Stills** *See* **Crosby, David, Paul Kantner** *and* **Stephen Stills**
**Kaplan, Allan**
Marvelous.
**Kariuki, Joseph**
Come Away, My Love.
**Katzin, Olga.** *See* **"Sagittarius"**
**Kaufman, Bob**
African Dream.
Afterwards, They Shall Dance.
Benediction.
Blues Note.
Come.
Falling.
I Have Folded My Sorrows.
Mingus.
Patriotic Ode on the Fourteenth Anniversary of the Persecution of Charlie Chaplin.
To My Son Parker, Asleep in the Next Room.
Walking Parker Home.
**Kaufman, Shirley**
Always She Moves from Me.
Apples.
Beetle on the Shasta Daylight.
Dinosaur Tracks in Beit Zayit.
Her Going.
Hunger Artist, The.
Mothers, Daughters.
Realities.
Room.
Watts.
**Kavanagh, P. J.**
Temperance Billiards Rooms, The.
**Kavanagh, Patrick**
Canal Bank Walk.
Come Dance with Kitty Stobling.
Epic.
Great Hunger, The, *sels.*
Hospital, The.
I Had a Future.
If Ever You Go to Dublin Town.
In Memory of My Mother.
Inniskeen Road: July Evening.
Lecture Hall.
Lines Written on a Seat on the Grand Canal.
Pegasus.
Prelude: "Give us another poem, he said."
Sanctity.
Shancoduff.
Spraying the Potatoes.
Tinker's Wife.
To a Late Poplar.

**Kay, Billy**
Furst Snaw.
Glencoe.
**Kay, W. Lowrie**
Lancaster County Tragedy.
**Kearney, Peadar**
Whack Fol the Diddle.
**Keating, Geoffrey**
Mourn for Yourself.
**Keats, John**
Acrostic of My Sister's Name.
Addressed to Haydon ("Great spirits now on earth are sojourning").
Addressed to Haydon ("Highmindedness, a jealousy for good").
After dark vapours have oppress'd our plains.
Ah! who can e'er forget so fair a being?
Answer to a Sonnet Ending Thus.
Are Then Regalities All Gilded Masks?
As from the darkening gloom a silver dove.
Asleep! O sleep a little while, white pearl!
Bright Star! Would I Were Steadfast as Thou Art.
Calidore.
Cancelled Stanza of the Ode on Melancholy.
Character of Charles Brown.
Day is gone, and all its sweets are gone, The!
Death.
Dedication to Leigh Hunt, Esq.
Endymion [a Poetic Romance],*sels.*
Eve of Saint Mark, The.
Eve of St. Agnes, The.
Fall of Hyperion, The: a Dream.
Fancy.
Four seasons fill the measure of the year.
Fragment of an Ode to Maia.
Fragment: "Welcome joy, and welcome sorrow."
Fragment: "Where's the poet? show him! show him."
Gadfly, The.
Give me women, wine and snuff.
God of the Meridian.
Happy is England! I could be content.
How many bards gild the lapses of time!
Hymn to Apollo.
Hyperion; a Fragment.
Imitation of Spenser.
In a Drear-Nighted December.
Isabella; or, the Pot of Basil.
King Stephen: a Fragment of a Tragedy.
La Belle Dame sans Merci.
Lamia.
Last Sonnet.
Lines on Seeing a Lock of Milton's Hair.
Lines on the Mermaid Tavern.
Lines Rhymed in a Letter Received from Oxford.
Lines: "Unfelt, unheard, unseen."
Lines Written in the Highlands after a Visit to Burns's Country.

Meg Merrilies.
Modern Love.
O solitude! if I must with thee dwell.
Ode: "Bards of passion and of mirth."
Ode on a Grecian Urn.
Ode on Indolence.
Ode on Melancholy.
Ode to a Nightingale.
Ode to Apollo.
Ode to Fanny.
Ode to Psyche.
Oh, how I love, on a fair summer's eve.
On a Dream.
On a Leander Gem.
On a Summer's Day.
On Fame ("Fame, like a wayward girl, will still be coy").
On Fame ("How fever'd is the man, who cannot look").
On First Looking into Chapman's Homer.
On Peace.
On Receiving a Curious Shell, and a Copy of Verses.
On Receiving a Laurel Crown from Leigh Hunt.
On Seeing the Elgin Marbles.
She Walked Unaware.
On Sitting Down to Read King Lear Once Again.
On the Grasshopper and Cricket.
On the Sea.
On the Sonnet.
On "The Story of Rimini."
On Visiting Staffa.
On Visiting the Tomb of Burns.
Over the hill and over the dale.
Pensive they sit, and roll their languid eyes.
Robin Hood.
Sleep and Poetry.
Song About Myself.
Song: "Hence burgundy, claret, and port."
Song: "Hush, hush! tread softly! hush, hush, my dear!"
Song: "O blush not so! O blush not so!
Song: "Stranger lighted from his steed, The."
Song of the Indian Maid, The.
Sonnet Written in the Cottage Where Burns Was Born.
Sonnet Written upon Ben Bevis.
Specimen of an Induction to a Poem.
Spenser! a jealous honourer of thine.
Sweet, sweet is the greeting of eyes.
This Living Hand, Now Warm and Capable.
This pleasant tale is like a little copse.
'Tis "the witching time of night."
To a Cat.
To a Friend Who Sent Me Some Roses.
To Ailsa Rock.

To Autumn.
To B. R. Haydon.
To Charles Cowden Clarke.
To Chatterton.
To Fanny.
To G. A. W.
To George Felton Mathew.
To——: "Had I a man's fair form, then might my sighs."
To——: "Hadst thou liv'd in days of old."
To——: "Time's sea hath been five years at its slow ebb."
To——: "What can I do to drive away."
To Homer.
To Hope.
To J. H. Reynolds, Esq.
To Kosciusko.
To Lord Byron.
To My Brother George ("Full many a dreary hour have I past").
To My Brother George ("Many the wonders I this day have seen").
To My Brothers.
To One Who Has Been Long in City Pent.
To Sleep.
To Some Ladies.
To the Ladies Who Saw Me Crown'd.
To the Nile.
What the Thrush Said.
When I Have Fears That I May Cease to Be.
Where be ye going, you Devon maid?
Why did I laugh to-night? No voice will tell.
Woman! when I behold thee flippant, vain.
Written in Disgust of Vulgar Superstition.
Written on the Day that Mr. Leigh Hunt Left Prison.

**Keble, John**
Evening Hymn.
Fill High the Bowl.

**Kees, Weldon**
Aspects of Robinson.
Beach in August, The.
Coming of the Plague, The.
Crime Club.
Distance from the Sea, A.
Five.
For My Daughter.
Guide to the Symphony.
La Vita Nuova.
Midnight.
Obituary.
Patient Is Rallying, The.
Relating to Robinson.
River Song.
Robinson.
Robinson at Home.
Round.
Saratoga Ending.
Small Prayer.
White Collar Ballad.

**Keesing, Nancy**
We Told You So.

**Kell, Richard**
Citadels.
Fishing Harbour towards Evening.
Makers, The.

Pay Is Good, The.
Pigeons.

**Keller, Martha**
Brady's Bend.
Deadfall.

**Kelly, Dave**
And Then What.

**Kelly, John W.**
Throw Him Down M'Closkey; or, M'Closkey's Great Fight, *with music.*

**Kelly, M.**
Last Week I Took a Wife, *with music.*

**Kelly, Robert**
Last Light.
Moonshot.
Poem for Easter.

**Kelso, Peter**
Poems.

**Kemble, Fanny (Frances Anne)**
Wish, A.

**Ken, Thomas**
All Praise to Thee, My God, This Night.

**Kendall, Timothy**
To a Married Couple That Could Not Agree.

**Kennedy, Benjamin Hall**
On Christopher Wordsworth, Master of Trinity.

**Kennedy, Harry**
Say "Au Revoir," but not "Good-Bye," *with music.*

**Kennedy, X. J.**
B. Negative.
Consumer's Report.
Cross Ties.
Down in Dallas.
Ecology
Edgar's Story, *sel.*
First Confession.
In a Prominent Bar in Secaucus One Day.
Little Elegy.
National Shrine.
Nothing in Heaven Functions As It Ought.
Nude Descending a Staircase.
Space.

**Kennelly, Brendan**
Black Cliffs, Ballybunion, The.
Light Dying.
Moloney Remembers the Resurrection of Kate Finucane.
My Dark Fathers.

**Kenner, Peggy Susberry**
Black Taffy.
Comments.
Image in the Mirror.
No Bargains Today.
Round Table, The.

**Kenney, Dan**
Yolanthe.

**Kennick, T.**
You Naughty, Naughty Men, *with music.*

**Kent, Karen L.**
C44.
White sheer tieback curtains.

**Kent, Louis**
Hunt, The.

**Kenyon, Theda**
City Bird.

**Kerouac, Jack**
Chorus: "Dharma law"

Chorus: "Praised be man, he is existing in milk."
Chorus: "Songs that erupt, The."
Mexico City Blues, *sels.*
Pun for Al Gelpi, A.

**Kerr, Alexander**
Mary and Her Dead Canary.

**"Kerr, Orpheus C." (Robert Henry Newell)**
American Traveller, The.

**Kessler, Edward**
Dodo, The.

**Kessler, Milton**
Beyond Anguish.
Lynching, The.
Route 40—Ohio, U.S.A.

**Kethe, William**
Old Hundredth, *with music.*

**Key, Francis Scott**
Star-Spangled Banner, The.

**Keyes, Sidney**
Death and the Plowman.
Hope for Those Separated by War, A.
War Poet.
William Wordsworth.

**Keys, William**
Duo.

**Kgositsile, Keorapetse**
For Eusi, Ayi Kwei and Gwen Brooks.
Ivory Masks in Orbit.
My Name Is Afrika.
Origins.

**Kherdian, David**
Beckoned in Dream to the Unconscious.
Dtah Dtah.
Kato's Poem.
Lake Michigan.
My Father.
My Mother and the Americans.
My Mother Takes My Wife's Side.
Squirrels in Wind Pine.
To My Sister.
Two Pennies Found on the Gravel.
Ubaji Park.
United States Tony.
When These Old Barns Lost Their Inhabitants.

**Kickham, Charles Joseph**
My Ulick.

**Kicknosway, Faye**
Cigarette Poem, The.
Crystal.
Gracie.
I Wake, My Friend, I.

**Kiesel, Stanley**
Don't Put Me.
Farewell, A: "Partner in the corner bar is high, a grin."
Kindergarten Teacher.
Poem for Mother's Day.

**Kilgore, James C.**
White Man Pressed the Locks, The.

**Killigrew, Anne**
Chloris' Charms Dissolved by Eudora, *sel.*
On the Soft and Gentle Motions of Eudora.
Upon the Saying That My Verses Were Made by Another.

**Kilmer, Joyce**
Trees, *abr.*

**Kilner, Dorothy**
Henry's Secret.

**Kim Yo-sop**
  Shooting at the Moon.
**King, B. B.**
  Why I Sing the Blues.
**King, Ben**
  But Then.
  Cow Slips Away, The.
  Pessimist, The.
**King, Carole and Gerry Goffin.** *See*
  **Goffin, Gerry and Carole King**
**King, Henry, Bishop of Chicester**
  Exequy, The.
  Sic Vita.
  Surrender, The.
**Kingsley, Charles**
  Farewell, A: "My fairest child, I have no
    song to give you."
  Knight's Leap, The.
  Little Doll, The.
  Lost Doll, The.
  Tide River, The.
  Water Babies, The,*sels.*
  Young and Old.
**Kingsmill, Hugh (Hugh Kingsmill Lunn)**
  What, Still Alive at Twenty-two.
**Kingston, R. P.**
  Between Two Wars.
  He's Known His Lesson for Years.
  Mystic Lake.
  Stateside.
**Kinnell, Galway**
  Avenue Bearing the Initial of Christ into
    the New World, The, *sel.*
  Bear, The.
  Burning.
  Cells Breathe in the Emptiness.
  Correspondence School Instructor Says
    Goodbye to His Poetry Students, The.
  Dead Shall Be Raised Incorruptible,
    The.
  Duck-Chasing.
  First Song.
  Flower Herding on Mount Monadnock.
  For Robert Frost.
  Garbage Disposal Truck, The.
  Hen Flower, The.
  How Many Nights.
  In Fields of Summer.
  Little Sleep's-Head Sprouting Hair in the
    Moonlight.
  Night in the Forest.
  On Hardscrabble Mountain
  Path among the Stones, The.
  Poems of Night.
  Porcupine, The.
  Promontory Moon.
  Ruins Under the Stars, *sel.*
  Spindrift.
  Supper after the Last, The.
  To Christ Our Lord.
  Under the Maud Moon.
  Vapor Trail Reflected in the Frog Pond.
**Kinsella, Thomas**
  Ancestor.
  Another September.
  Ballydavid Pier.
  Chrysalides.
  First Light.
  Je t'adore.
  Mirror in February.
  Nightwalker, *sel.*
  Scylla and Charybdis.

  Westland Row.
**Kipling, Rudyard**
  Ballad of East and West, The.
  Ballad of Minepit Shaw, The.
  Beasts Are Very Wise, The.
  Cities and Thrones and Powers.
  Code of Morals, A.
  Dane-Geld.
  Danny Deever.
  'Eathen, The.
  English Flag, The.
  Fuzzy-Wuzzy.
  Gentlemen-Rankers.
  Gods of the Copybook Headings, The.
  Horses.
  Hump, The.
  If.
  Jane Smith.
  Last Lap, The.
  Last of the Light Brigade, The.
  Mandalay.
  McAndrew's Hymn.
  My Rival.
  Power of the Dog, The.
  Puck of Pook's Hill, *sels.*
  Puck's Song ("See you the ferny ride
    that steals").
  Recessional.
  Sea and the Hills, The.
  Sergeant's Weedin', The.
  Sestina of the Tramp-Royal.
  Smuggler's Song, A.
  Song of the Galley-Slaves.
  Song to Mithras, A.
  Storm Cone,The.
  Sussex.
  Tommy.
  Way through the Woods, The.
  White Man's Burden, The.
  Widow's Party, The.
**Kirkup, James**
  All-In Wrestlers.
  Bird Fancier, The.
  Correct Compassion, A.
  Cosy Cat Nap.
  Dripping Tap, The.
  Japanese Children.
  Lonely Scarecrow, The.
  Love in a Space-suit.
  Tea in a Space-ship.
**Kirstein, Lincoln**
  Bath.
  Das Schloss.
  Fall In.
  Foresight.
  Vaudeville.
**Kittredge, Walter**
  Tenting on the Old Camp Ground, *with
    music.*
**Kizer, Carolyn**
  Amusing Our Daughters.
  Columns and Caryatids.
  Copulating Gods, The.
  Dying Goddess, The.
  For Jan, in Bar Maria.
  Great Blue Heron, The.
  Hera, Hung from the sky.
  Intruder, The.
  Muse of Water, A.
  Poet's Household, A.
  Pro Femina, *sels.*
  Semele Recycled.

  Singing Aloud.
  Skein, The.
  Summer Near the River.
  Worms, The.
**Kizer, Gary**
  For Laurence Jones.
**Klappert, Peter**
  Invention of the Telephone, The.
  Lord's Chameleons, The.
  O'Connor the Bad Traveler.
  Poem for L. C.
**Klein, Abraham Moses**
  Commercial Bank.
  Pastoral of the City Streets.
**Knevet, Ralph**
  Deliverance, The.
  Progress, The.
  Vote, The.
**Knight, Etheridge**
  Apology for Apostasy?
  As You Leave Me.
  Cell Song.
  For Black Poets Who Think of Suicide.
  For Dan Berrigan.
  For Freckle-faced Gerald.
  Haiku: "Eastern guard tower."
  Hard Rock Returns to Prison from the
    Hospital for the Criminal Insane.
  He Sees Through Stone.
  I Sing of Shine.
  Idea of Ancestry, The.
  It Was a Funky Deal.
  Portrait of Malcolm X.
  Sun Came, The.
  To Dinah Washington.
  To the Man Who Sidled Up to Me and
    Asked: "How Long You in fer,
    Buddy?"
  2 Poems for Black Relocation Centers.
  Upon Your Leaving.
  Violent Space, The.
**Knister, Raymond**
  Colt, The.
**Knoepfle, John**
  "Ten-Fifteen Community Poems, The,"
    *sel.*
**Knott, William ("Saint Geraud")**
  Hair Poem.
  Poem: "Only response, The."
  Song: "She was lyin face down in her
    face."
**Knox, E. V.**
  At the Water Zoo.
**Knox, Ronald Arbuthnott**
  Absolute and Abitofhell.
  Idealism.
**Knudson, R. R.**
  Grand Slammer.
**Kobayashi Issa.** *See* **Issa**
**Koch, Kenneth**
  Down at the Docks.
  Fresh Air.
  Geograpy.
  In Love with You.
  Mending Sump.
  Permanently.
  Poem: "Thing, The/ To do/ Is
    organize."
  Sleeping with Women.
  Taking a Walk with You.
  Thanksgiving.
  To You.

Variations on a Theme by William
  Carlos Williams.
You Were Wearing.
**Koehler, Ted**
I've Got the World on a String, *with
  music.*
**Koertge, Ron**
Modifications.
**Konek, Carol**
Daring.
**Kooser, Ted**
Blind Always Come As Such a Surprise,
  The.
Deep in Winter.
Goldfish Floats, The.
History Lesson for My Son.
I Put My Hand on His Head.
Phoning My Son Long Distance.
Place in Kansas, A.
Poem: "Get your tongue."
Rooming House.
Themes for Country-Western Singers,
  *sel.*
**Körte, Mary Norbert**
Ghost Poem Five.
Lines on the Back of a Leary Bailfund
  Card.
**Koster, Gloria Bussel**
Diner, The.
Early Morning Song: The Snowstorm.
Interpretation.
**Krapf, Norbert**
Darkness Comes to the Woods.
Skinning a Rabbit.
**Kroll, Judith**
Dick and Jane.
Not Thinking of America.
Sestina.
**Kruchkow, Diane**
City Is Falling Apart, The.
Poem: "Camera records, The."
Poem: "For the 5th time."
Poem: "She didn't know it yet."
Putting the Croutons Back into the Jar.
Sabinas Hidalgo.
While the TV Is Shut Off.
**Krysl, Marilyn**
Dreams from War.
Lecture with Slides, Film Clips and
  Tape.
Summer Solstice.
**Kryss, Tom**
And Jesus Don't Have Much Use for
  His Old Suitcase Anymore.
Ballad of an Empty Table.
Bell Too Heavy to Ring.
Breaking Ground in Me.
Nothing Strange.
Suicide, A.
This Wind.
**Kuka, King D.**
"Taste of Honey, A."
**Küken, Friedrich Wilhelm**
How Can I Leave Thee? *with music.*
**Kumalo, Peter**
Play Song.
**Kumin, Maxine W.**
After Love.
Appointment, The.
At the End of the Affair.
Creatures.
Family Man, A.

For My Son on the Highways of His
  Mind.
400-Meter Freestyle.
Fräulein Reads Instructive Rhymes.
Hermit Picks Berries, The.
How It Goes On.
Lunar Probe, The.
Masochist, The.
May 10th.
Microscope, The.
Morning Swim.
Mother Rosarine.
Nightmare Factory, The.
Pawnbroker, The.
Presence, The.
Purgatory.
Riding in the Rain.
Song for Seven Parts of the Body,*sels.*
Sound of Night, The.
Together.
Voice from the Roses, A.
We Are.
**Kunitz, Stanley Jasspon**
Benediction.
Choice of Weapons, A.
Dark and the Fair, The.
End of Summer.
Father and Son.
Flight of Apollo, The.
For Proserpine.
For the Word Is Flesh.
He.
Journal for My Daughter.
Last Picnic, The.
Portrait, The.
River Road.
Robin Redbreast.
She Wept, She Railed.
Spark of Laurel, A.
Testing-Tree, The.
Thief, The.
Vita Nuova.
War Against the Trees, The.
Welcome the Wrath.
**Kürenberg, The Knight of**
Falcon, The.
**Kuzma, Greg**
Ah.
First Camp.
Garden Report.
Greens.
Hose and Iron.
I Visit My Brother.
Journal of the Storm.
Melons.
Monster, The.
Peace, So That.
Pelican, The.
Poppies.
Sleep.
Weak, The.
Young Man Who Loved the Girl Who
  Took Care of Her Aging Father, The.
**Kyger, Joanne**
From this moment/ and hence
  backwards.
In the high/ clear air.
Time Is Open, The.
**Kynaston, Sir Francis**
To Cynthia.
To Cynthia, on Her Looking-glass.

To Cynthia, on Sugar and Her
  Sweetness.
To Cynthia: Learn'd Lapidaries.
To Cynthia: On Concealment of Her
  Beauty.

# L

**Labé, Louise**
Sonnet: "And so one sees all living
  matter perish."
Sonnet: "O kiss me yet again, O kiss me
  over."
**Lady of the Arbour**
Flower and the Leaf, The,   *sel.*
**Lady of the Assembly**
Assembly of Ladies, The, *sel.*
Palace of Pleasant Regard, The.
**La Farge, Peter**
Ballad of Ira Hayes
**La Follette, Melvin Walker**
All the Dead Birds.
Ballad of Red Fox, The.
**La Farge, Peter**
Ballad of Ira Hayes.
**La Fontaine, Jean de**
Cat into Lady.
Fox and the Crow, The.
Fox and the Goat, The.
**Laforgue, Jules**
For the Book of Love.
Legend.
**Laing, Ronald David**
Finger Points to the Moon, A.
**Lake, Richard**
Atavism.
**Lamantia, Philip**
Hermetic Bird.
She Speaks the Morning's Filigree.
**Lamb, Arthur J.**
Asleep in the Deep, *with music.*
Bird in a Gilded Cage, A, *with music.*
Bird on Nellie's Hat, The, *with music.*
**Lamb, Charles**
Free Thoughts on Several Eminent
  Composers.
Old Familiar Faces, The.
**Lamb, Charles and Mary**
Boy and the Snake, The.
Choosing a Name.
Cleanliness.
Envy.
Feigned Courage.
First Tooth, The.
Going into Breeches.
**"Lambert, Louis."** *See* **Gilmore, Patrick
  Sarsfield**
**Lampman, Archibald**
Midnight.
**Lancaster, Osbert**
Afternoons with Baedeker.
French.
**Landor, Walter Savage**
Age.
Art thou afraid the adorer's prayer.
Before a Saint's Picture.
Called Proud.
Corinna, to Tanagra, from Athens.

Dirce.
Dying Speech of an Old Philosopher.
Have I, this moment, led thee from the beach.
Hellenics, The, *sel.*
I can not tell, not I, why she.
Ianthe, *sels.*
Ireland Never Was Contented.
Is it no dream that I am he.
Last Fruit off an Old Tree, The, *sel.*
Love and Age.
Loves who many years held all my mind, The.
Mother, I Cannot Mind My Wheel.
My hopes retire; my wishes as before.
No, thou hast never griev'd but I griev'd too.
O fond, but fickle and untrue.
O friends! who have accompanied thus far.
O Friendship! Friendship! the shell of Aphrodite.
On Death.
On His Seventy-Fifth Birthday.
On Seeing a Hair of Lucretia Borgia.
On the Four Georges.
On the smooth brow and clustering hair.
Past Ruined [*or* Ruin'd] Ilion Helen Lives.
Pericles and Aspasia, *sels.*
Retired this hour from wondering crowds.
Rose Aylmer.
Silent, you say, I'm grown of late.
Ternissa.
To Age.
To Alfred Tennyson.
To My Daughter.
To My Ninth Decade.
To Our House-Dog Captain.
Torch of love dispels the gloom, The.
Twenty years hence my eyes may grow.
What News.
Why Do the Graces.
Yes; I Write Verses.
You see the worst of love, but not the best.
You smiled, you spoke, and I believed.
Your Name upon the Sand.

**Lane, Patrick**
Beware the Months of Fire.
Elephants.
Gray Silk Twisting.
Love.
Loving She Stood Apart.
Mountain Oysters.
Sleep on the Fraser.
Surcease.
Treaty-trip from Shulus Reservation.
Water-truck, The.

**Lang, Andrew**
Brahma.
Lost Love.
O Joy of Love's Renewing.

**Langhorne, John**
Owen of Carron, *sel.*

**Langland, Joseph**
Hunters in the Snow: Brueghel.
War.

**Langland, William**
Belling the Cat.
Et Incarnatus Est.

Field Full of Folk, The.
Glutton in the Tavern.
Jousting of Jesus, The.
Long Will in London.
Our Needy Neighbours.
Poet, Rebuked, Responds, The.
Prologue: "In a summer season, when soft was the sun."
Trinity, The.
Vision of Piers Plowman, The, *sels.*

**Langley, Eve**
Native Born.

**Langton, Daniel J.**
Land's End.

**Lanier, Sidney**
Corn.
From the Flats.
Into the Woods My Master Went.
Marsh Song—At Sunset.
Marshes of Glynn, The.
Sunrise.
Thar's More in the Man Than Thar Is in the Land.

**Lape, Fred**
Lambs Frolicking Home.
Laughing Faces of Pigs, The.
Old Grey.
Puppy.

**Lapidus, Jacqueline**
Coming Out.

**Larbaud, Valery**
Poet's Wish.

**Larkin, Philip**
Afternoons.
Arundel Tomb, An.
As Bad as a Mile.
At Grass.
Born Yesterday.
Building, The.
Church Going.
Coming.
Days.
Dockery and Son (" 'Dockery was junior to you' ").
Essential Beauty.
Faith Healing.
First Sight.
Going.
Home Is So Sad.
Lines on a Young Lady's Photograph Album.
Love Songs in Age.
Mr. Bleaney.
Myxomatosis.
Next, Please.
Night-Music.
Nothing to Be Said.
Poetry of Departures.
Reasons for Attendance.
So through that unripe day you bore your head.
Study of Reading Habits, A.
Sunny Prestatyn.
Take One Home for the Kiddies.
Talking in Bed.
Toads.
Vers de Société.
Waiting for breakfast, while she brushed her hair.
Wedding-Wind.
Whitsun Weddings, The.
Wild Oats.

Wires.
Within the Dream You Said.

**Larminie, William**
Nameless Doon, The.

**Lathum, William**
Prosopopoeia-Corporis Animae Valedicturi: Adios: Arrivederci.

**Latimer, Bette Darcie**
For William Edward Burghardt Du Bois on His Eightieth Birthday.

**Latimore, Jewel C. (Johari Amini)**
Before/ and After.
Brother.
Childhood.
Positives.
Saint Malcolm.
Signals.
Sun Heals, A.
To a Poet I Knew.
Utopia.

**Lattimore, Richmond**
Dolphin See Alone.
February Loves.
Game Resumed.
Siding Near Chillicothe, A.
Sky Diving.
Witness to Death.

**Laughlin, James**
Mountain Afterglow, The.
Step on His Head.
Swarming Bees, The.

**Laurance, Annabel**
My Brain.

**LaVoie, Kent**
Me and You and a Dog Named Boo.

**Lawless, Gary**
Ainu Men, The.
Confession, The.
Hunting Fragment.
Movement.
Rail Splitting.

**Lawner, Lynne**
Rino's Song.

**Lawrence, David Herbert**
All I ask of a woman is that she.
Andraitx—Pomegranate Flowers.
Baby-Movements.
Baby Tortoise.
Bavarian Gentians.
Birds.
Bride, The.
Cherry Robbers.
City Life.
Collier's Wife, The.
Death Is Not Evil, Evil is Mechanical.
Deepest Sensuality, The.
Dog-Tired.
Don'ts.
Elephant Is Slow to Mate, The.
Elephants in the Circus.
Energetic Women.
Enkindled Spring, The.
Fronleichnam.
Gazelle Calf, The.
Giorno dei Morti.
Gloire de Dijon.
Green.
How Beastly the Bourgeois Is.
Hummingbird.
Intimates.
It's No Good!
Kangeroo.

Kisses in the Train.
Letter from Town: The Almond Tree.
Little Fish.
Living, A.
Lizard.
Love on the Farm.
Man and Bat.
Moonrise.
Mosquito, The.
Mosquito Knows, The.
Mountain Lion.
New Houses, New Clothes.
New Year's Eve.
Now It's Happened.
On the Balcony
Pax.
Piano.
Red-Herring.
River Roses.
Salt of the Earth.
Sane Revloution, A.
Self-Pity.
Seven Seals.
Shadows.
Ship of Death, The.
Snake.
Song of a Man Who Has Come
    Through, The.
Sorrow.
Stand Up! ("Stand up, but not for
    Jesus").
Terra Incognita.
Things Made by Iron.
Things Men Have Made.
Third Thing, The.
To Women, as Far as I'm Concerned.
Tortoise Gallantry.
Tortoise Shout.
Volcanic Venus.
We Are Transmitters.
Whales Weep Not!
What Is He?
When I Read Shakespeare.
When I Went to the Circus.
White Horse, The.
Young Wife, A.
Youth Mowing, A.

**Lawson, David**
No Great Matter.

**Lawson, Henry**
Middleton's Rouseabout.
Sweeney.

**Lawson, Paul**
Ambassadors, The.

**Layamon**
Brut, The, *sel.*
Death of Arthur, The.

**Layton, Irving**
Aran Islands.
Bull Calf, The.
For Anna.
For Natalya Correia.
Haunting, The.
Icarus
Innocence.
Letter to a Librarian.
Ohms.
Osip Mandelshtam.

**Lazarus, Emma**
By the Waters of Babylon,*sels.*
Currents.
Echoes.

Epochs.
Exodus, The (August 3, 1492).
1492.
In Exile.
In Memoriam: Rev. J. J. Lyons, *sel.*
Magnetism.
New Colossus, The.
Success.
Venus of the Louvre.

**Lea, Gordon**
When I Learned to Whistle.

**Leach, Christopher**
Blackbird.

**Leadbelly (Huddie Ledbetter)**
T.B. Blues.

**Leaf, Walter**
Better Way, The.

**Lear, Edward**
A Was Once an Apple Pie.
Akond of Swat, The.
C was papa's gray cat.
Calico Pie.
Cold Are the Crabs.
Dong with a Luminous Nose, The.
Duck and the Kangaroo, The.
How Pleasant to Know Mr. Lear.
Incidents in the Life of My Uncle Arly.
Jumblies, The.
Limerick: "There was an Old Man of
    Hong Kong."
Limerick: "There was an old man who
    said, 'Hush!' "
Limerick: "There was an old man with a
    beard,/ Who said, 'It is just as I
    feared!' "
Limerick: "There was an Old Person of
    Anerley."
Love Song.
Mr. and Mrs. Spikky Sparrow.
New Vestments, The.
Owl and the Pussy-cat, The.
Pobble Who Has No Toes, The.
There is a young lady, whose nose.
There was an old lady of Chertsey.
There was an old lady of France.
There was an old man in a tree.
There was an old man of Dumbree.
There was an old man on the Border.
There was an old man who said, "How."
There was an old person of Gretna.
There was an old person of Ware.

**Leax, John**
Cycle, A.
Grandfather.
Grocery Shopping.
That Day.
Vanity of Human Wishes, The.

**Lechlitner, Ruth**
Kansas Boy.

**Ledbetter, Huddie.** *See* **Leadbelly**

**Ledwidge, Francis**
Had I a Golden Pound.
June.
Lament for Thomas MacDonagh.
Twilight in Middle March, A.
Wife of Llew, The.

**Lee, Al**
Among Sharks.
Karl Marx.
Lie, The.
One Morning We Brought Them Order.
Poem for the Year Twenty Twenty.

Weathering the Depths.

**Lee, Don L.**
Afterword, An: for Gwen Brooks.
Assassination.
Awareness.
Back Again, Home.
Big Momma.
Black Sketches.
But He Was Cool; or, He Even Stopped
    for Green Lights.
Change-Up.
Communication in Whi-te.
Gwendolyn Brooks.
Man and Woman.
Man Thinking about Woman.
Mixed Sketches.
Mwilu/ or Poem for the Living.
Nigerian Unity/ or Little Niggers Killing
    Little Niggers.
One Sided Shoot-out.
Poem for a Poet, A.
Poem to Complement Other Poems, A.
Positives for Sterling Plumpp.
Primitive, The.
Re-act for Action ("Re-act to Animals").
Self-Hatred of Don L. Lee, The.
Stereo.
To Be Quicker.
Wake-Up Niggers.
We Walk the Way of the New World.
With All Deliberate Speed.

**Lee, Laurie**
April Rise.
Field of Autumn.
Long War, The.
Milkmaid.

**Lee, Mary.** *See* **Chudleigh, Mary Lee,**
    **Lady**

**Lee-Hamilton, Eugene**
Sea-Shell Murmurs.

**Legler, Philip**
Love and an Old Western at the Starlite
    Drive-In Theater.

**Lehmann, Geoffrey**
For J. A. R. McKellar.
Roses.
Saving the Harvest.

**Lehmann, John**
Sphere of Glass, The.
This Excellent Machine.

**Lehrer, Tom**
Pollution.

**Leifer, Jay**
Six-forty-two Farm Commune Struggle
    Poem.

**Leigh, Fred W.**
Waiting at the Church; or, My Wife
    Won't Let Me, *with music.*

**Leigh, Henry Sambrooke**
Only Seven.
Saragossa.
'Twas Ever Thus.

**Leitch, Donovan ("Donovan")**
Observation, The.

**Leland, Charles Godfrey ("Hans**
    **Breitmann")**
Hans Breitmann's Barty.
Story of Samuel Jackson, The.

**Leland, John**
Ecstasy.
Evening Shade.

**L'Engle, Madeleine**

From St. Luke's Hospital.
**Lennon, John** and **Paul McCartney**
Across the Universe.
Continuing Story of Bungalow Bill, The.
Day in the Life, A.
Eleanor Rigby.
Fool on the Hill, The.
I Am the Walrus.
In My Life.
Norwegian Wood.
She's Leaving Home.
Strawberry Fields Forever.
Yellow Submarine.
**Lenox, Jean**
I Don't Care, *with music.*
**Leonard, Eddie**
Ida, Sweet as Apple Cider, *with music.*
**Leonard, Tom**
Words, for E.
**Leopardi, Giacomo**
Setting of the Moon, The.
Terror by Night, The.
**Lerner, Laurence David**
Wish, A.
**Leslie, Edgar** and **E. Ray Goetz**
For Me and My Gal.
**Leslie, Kenneth**
Knife and Sap.
Sudden Assertion.
**Leslie, Shane**
Muckish Mountain (The Pig's Back).
Prayer for Fine Weather.
**Lester, Julius**
In the Time of Revolution, *sels.*
On the Birth of My Son, Malcolm
Coltrane.
Us.
**Letts, Winifrid M. (Mrs. W. H. Foster Verschoyle)**
Bold Unbiddable Child, The.
Choice, The.
Fantasia.
**Levenberg, Diane**
After Selecting the Wedding Invitations.
Alchemy.
Dreaming of Conn-Eda.
Out of the Desert.
**Lever, Charles James**
It's Little for Glory I Care.
Pope He Leads a Happy Life, The.
**Leverant, Robert**
Figures and Ground.
In His Poems Are El Greco's Hands.
**Levertov, Denise**
Abel's Bride.
About Marriage.
Ache of Marriage, The.
Advent 1966.
Altars in the Street, The.
Art.
Bedtime.
Beyond the End.
Breathing, The.
Cat as Cat, The.
City Psalm.
Claritas.
Cold Spring, The.
Come into Animal Presence.
Coming Fall, The, *sel.*
Day Begins, A.
Despair.
Dog of Art, The.

During the Eichmann Trial, *sel.*
Earth Psalm.
Earth Worm, The.
"Else a Great Prince in Prison Lies."
Embroidery, An.
Enquiry.
Everything That Acts Is Actual.
February Evening in New York.
Garden Wall, The.
Goddess, The.
Grace-note, The.
Ground-Mist, The.
Hypocrite Women.
Illustrious Ancestors.
In Mind.
Jacob's Ladder, The.
Lamentation, A: "Grief, have I denied thee?"
Life at War.
Living.
Losing Track.
Mad Song.
Map of the Western Part of he County of Essex in England, A.
Martins.
Moon Tiger.
Mutes, The.
Night on Hatchet Cove.
90th Year, The.
Note to Olga (1966), A.
Novel, The.
O Taste and See.
Obsessions.
One A. M.
Our Bodies.
Overland to the Islands.
Partial Resemblance.
Peachtree, The.
Pleasures.
Psalm Concerning the Castle.
Psalm Praising the Hair of Man's Body, A.
Quarry Pool, The.
Rainwalkers, The.
Recognition, The.
Relearning the Alpahabet.
Resolve, The.
Resting Figure.
Secret, The.
Shalom.
Shlup, shlup, the dog.
Six Variations.
Song for Ishtar.
Springtime, The.
Stepping Westward.
Sunday Afternoon.
Third Dimension, The.
To the Reader.
To the Snake.
Two Variations.
Vision, A.
Way Through, The.
What Were They Like?
What Wild Dawns There Were.
Wings, The.
World Outside, The.
**Levine, Philip**
Above It All.
Animals Are Passing from Our Lives.
Distant Winter, The.
Gangrene.
Lost Angel, The.
Midget, The.

Salami.
They Feed They Lion.
To a Child Trapped in a Barber Shop.
Turning, The.
Way Down, The.
**Levinson, Fred**
No More Than Five.
Poem: "Country, The/ was back in the hands of the patriots."
Poem against Rats, A.
Sharks in Shallow Water.
Translation from, A.
**Levis, Larry**
Bat Angels.
Fish.
For the Country.
Poem You Asked For, The.
Winter.
**Lewis, Alun**
All Day It Has Rained.
Dawn on the East Coast.
Goodbye.
Peasants, The.
Postscript: For Gweno.
Public Gardens, The.
Sentry, The.
**Lewis, Angelo**
America Bleeds.
Clear.
**Lewis, Cecil Day.** *See* **Day Lewis, Cecil**
**Lewis, Clive Staples**
On a Vulgar Error.
**Lewis, Dominic Bevan Wyndham ("Timothy Shy")**
Shot at Random, A.
**Lewis, Janet (Mrs. Yvor Winters)**
Remembered Morning.
**Lewis, Michael Arthur**
Caulker, The.
**Lewis, Percy Wyndham**
Song of the Militant Romance, The.
**Lewis, David, Paul Schindler** and **Bob Adams**
Mother Pin a Rose on Me, *with music.*
**Leybourne, George**
Man on the Flying Trapeze, The.
**L'Heureux, John**
Bat in the Monastery, A.
St. Ignatius Loyola, Founder of the Jesuits: His Autobiography.
**Libbey, Elizabeth**
Before the Mountain.
Concerning the Dead Women: The Munitions Plant Explosion: June, 1918.
Marceline, to Her Husband.
To Her Dead Mate: Montana, 1966.
**Libera, Sharon Mayer**
Mother.
Patty, 1949–1961.
**Lieberman, Laurence**
Dream of Lakes, A.
My Father Dreams of Baseball.
No One to Blame.
Skin Song.
Tree Animals.
**Lifshin, Lyn**
Arizona Ruins.
Beryl.
Blue Bowl of Plums Invention, The.
Ceremony.

Developing Curious Survival Patterns against Winter Saltwinds The.
Downstairs Two Old Lovers Meet.
Drifting The.
Even There.
Family 8.
For a Friend.
Greenland, 850 A.D.
In Spite of His Dangling Pronoun.
Leaving Them, Letting the Farm Swallow.
Monet's Les Nymphéas.
Names.
Nice.
Not Quite Spring.
On the New Road.
Origin of Hot and Cold According to the Delawares, The.
Pulling Out.
Sedna.
Snake Dance.
Tentacles, Leaves.
Thaw.
To Poem.
Waiting, the Hallways under Her Skin Thick with Dreamchildren.
Walking thru Audley End Mansion Late Afternoon, sel.
Way Sun Keeps Falling Away from Every Window, The.
Wildflowers, Smoke.
Women Like That.
You Understand the Requirements.

**Lightfoot, Gordon**
Black Day in July.

**Liliuokalani, Queen Lydia**
Aloha Oe, with music.

**Lindon, J. A.**
London Sparrow's If, A.
My Garden, parody.

**Lindop, Grevel**
Perplexed by the Sunlight.

**Lindsay, John Vliet**
Ode to the New York Mets.

**Lindsay, Lady Anne (Lady Anne Lindsay Barnard)**
Auld Robin Gray.

**Lindsay, Maurice**
Ballad of Orpheus, A.

**Lindsay, T.**
Theological Limerick.

**Lindsay, Vachel**
Abraham Lincoln Walks at Midnight.
At Mass.
Blacksmith's Serenade, The.
Congo, The.
Eagle That Is Forgotten, The.
Euclid.
Flower-fed Buffaloes, The.
General William Booth Enters into Heaven.
Indian Summer Day on the Prairie, An.
Leaden-eyed, The.
Little Turtle, The.
Moon's the North Wind's Cooky, The.
Spider and the Ghost of the Fly, The.
What Semiramis Said.
Yet Gentle Will the Griffin Be.

**Lingard, William Horace**
Captain Jinks, with music.

**Linklater, Eric**
Memory, Now Distant, A.

Song for an Able Bastard, A.

**Li Po [or Li Tai Po or in Japanese Rihaku]**
Exile's Letter.
I Am a Peach Tree.
Jewel Stairs' Grievance, The ("The jewelled steps are already quite white with dew").
Lament of the Fronter Guard.
River-Merchant's Wife, The: a Letter.
Two Letters From Chang-Kan.

**Lipsitz, Lou**
Bedtime Story.
Conjugation of the Verb, "To Hope."
Pancho Villa.
Prospect Beach.
Thaw in the City.
To a Fighter Killed in the Ring.
Tree Is Father to the Man, The.

**Lisle, Rouget de.**  See **Rouget de Lisle, Claude Joseph**

**Lister, Richard Percival**
Cuckoo.
Postscript to Die Schöne Müllerin.
Target.

**Li Tai Po.**  See **Li Po**

**"Littlebird."**  See **Bird, Harold**

**Livingston, Myra Cohn**
Conversation with Washington.
Cooking.
Discovery.
German Shepherd
Grunion.
Halloween.
Mill Valley.
Mourning Dove, The.
Old People.
74th Street.
Whispers.

**Livingstone, Douglas**
Conversation with a Giraffe at Dusk in the Zoo.
King, The.
Sunstrike.

**Lloyd, Noel**
Gecko

**Lloyd-Evans, L. Paul**
Crowsfeet Splaying Round His Eyes.

**Lochhead, Liz**
Fourth of July Fireworks.
Laundrette.
Rainbow.
Three Women.
Today.

**Lodge, Thomas**
Discontented Satyre, The.
Fig for Momus, A,  sel.
In Commendation of a Solitary Life.
Phillis, sels.
Rosalynde; or, Euphues' Golden Legacy, sel.
Truth's Complaint over England.

**Loesser, Frank**
Once in Love With Amy, with music.

**Loftin, Elouise**
Virginia.
Weeksville Women.
Woman.

**Logan, John (b. 1923)**
Concert Scene.
Letter to a Young Father in Exile.
Lines for Michael in the Picture.
Lines on His Birthday.

Lines to His Son on Reaching Adolescence.
Love Poem: "Last night you would not come."
On the Death of Keats.
Picnic, The.
Spring of the Thief.
Thirteen Preludes for Pioneer Square.
Three Moves.
To a Young Poet Who Fled.
Trip to Four or Five Towns, A.
White Pass Ski Patrol.

**Logan, Robert**
On a Prize Crucifix by a Student Sculptor.

**Logue, Christopher**
Epitaph: "I am old."
Foreword to New Numbers.
Friday. Wet Dusk.
Good Taste.
Letters from an Irishman to a Rat.

**Logue, Mary**
Indian Warrior.
South Wind.
Winter Pond.

**Lomax, Pearl Cleage**
Glimpse.

**Long, Charles C.**
Yei-ie's Child.

**Long, Doughtry ("Doc Long")**
Ginger Bread Mama.
Negro Dreams.
Number Four.
One Time Henry Dreamed the Number.

**Longfellow, Henry Wadsworth**
Aftermath.
Autumn ("With what a glory comes and goes the year!").
Building of the Ship, The, sel.
Challenge, The.
Chaucer.
Chimes.
Cross of Snow, The.
Day Is Done, The.
Evangeline, sel.
Excelsior
Fire of Drift-wood, The.
Hiawatha and Mudjekeewis.
Hymn to the Night.
Introduction: "Should you ask me, whence these stories?"
Luck of Edenhall, The.
Mezzo Cammin.
Moonlight.
My Cathedral.
My Lost Youth.
Old Nokomis Sings.
Paul Revere's Ride.
Prelude: "Pleasant it was, when woods were green."
Psalm of Life, A.
Rain in Summer.
Republic, The.
Ropewalk, The.
Serenade: "Stars of the summer night."
Snow-flakes.
Song of Hiawatha, The, sels.
Spanish Student, The, sel.
Tales of a Wayside Inn, sel.
Tide Rises, the Tide Falls, The.
Ultima Thule.

Village Blacksmith, The.
Voices of the Night, sel.
Warning, The.
**Longley, Michael**
Letter to Three Irish Poets, A.
Miscarriage.
**Lopez, Alonzo**
Direction.
I Am Crying from Thirst.
Lavender Kitten, The.
**Lorca, Federico García.** *See* **García Lorca, Federico**
**Lorde, Audre**
And What About the Children.
Black Mother Woman.
Coal.
Father, the Year Is Fallen.
Father Son and Holy Ghost.
Now That I Am Forever with Child.
Poem for a Poet, A.
Rites of Passage.
Suffer the Children.
Summer Oracle.
To a Girl Who Lives in a Tree.
What My Child Learns of the Sea.
Who Said It Was Simple.
Woman Thing, The.
**Loudermilk, John D.**
Lament of the Cherokee Reservation Indian, The.
**Lourie, Dick**
Dream about Junior High School in America, The.
Getting a Poem in the Rain.
Gift, The.
Pearl Harbor Day 1970.
September 30.
Sharks.
Stumbling.
Telegram.
Thinking of You.
**Love, Mike** *and* **Brian Wilson**
Country Air.
**Lovelace, Richard**
Black Patch on Lucasta's Face, A.
Elinda's Glove.
Grasshopper, The.
Her Muff.
La Bella Bona Roba.
Love Made in the First Age: to Chloris.
Lucasta Taking the Waters at Tunbridge: Ode.
Lucasta's Fan, With a Looking-glass in It.
On Sannazar's Being Honoured, sel.
Scrutiny [or Scrutinie], The.
Snail, The.
Strive not, vain lover, to be fine.
To Althea, from Prison.
To Amarantha, That She Would Dishevel Her Hair.
To Lucasta, [on] Going to the Wars.
**Lover, Samuel**
Lanty Leary.
Paddy O'Rafther.
**Low, Patricia**
First Day of the Hunting Moon, The.
Wet Weather.
**Lowell, Amy**
Cyclists, The.
Dog-Days.
Last night it rained.

Lilacs, sel.
Madonna of the Evening Flowers.
Meeting-House Hill.
Music.
Night Clouds.
Night lies beside me.
On Looking at a Copy of Alice Meynell's Poems.
Patterns.
Poet's Wife, A.
Reaping.
Sea Shell.
Sisters, The.
Streets.
Watching the iris.
Wind and Silver.
Year Passes, A.
**Lowell, James Russell**
American Literature.
Biglow Papers, The,sels.
Birthday Verses Written in a Child's Album.
Bryant.
Cooper.
Courtin', The.
Emerson.
Fable for Critics, A,sels.
Freedom ("Men! whose boast it is that ye").
Hawthorne.
Holmes.
Letter from a Candidate for the Presidency, A.
Lowell.
Ode Recited at the Harvard Commemoration.
Pious Editor's Creed, The.
Poe and Longfellow.
Vison of Sir Launfal, The, sel.
Whittier.
**Lowell, Robert (1917-77)**
After the Surprising Conversions.
Alfred Corning Clark.
As a Plane Tree by the Water.
At a Bible House.
At the Altar.
At the Indian Killer's Grave.
Between the Porch and the Altar,sels.
Beyond the Alps.
Christmas Eve under Hooker's Statue.
Cistercians in Germany.
Colloquy in Black Rock.
Commander Lowell.
Crucifix, The.
Dolphin.
Drinker, The.
Drunken Fisherman, The.
Dunbarton.
Elizabeth.
Eye and Tooth.
Ezra Pound.
Fall 1961.
Falling Asleep over the Aeneid.
Fat Man in the Mirror, The.
For George Santayana.
For John Berryman, I.
For Sale.
For the Union Dead.
Fourth of July in Maine.
Grandparents.
Harriet, sel.
Holy Innocents, The.

Home after Three Months Away.
In Memory of Arthur Winslow.
In the Cage.
July in Washington.
Katherine's Dream.
Last Things, Black Pines at 4 a.m.
Long Summer, sel.
Man and Wife.
March, The ("Under the too white marmorial Lincoln Memorial").
March, The ("Where two or three were heaped together, or fifty").
Mary Winslow.
Memories of West Street and Lepke.
Mouth of the Hudson, The.
Mr. Edwards and the Spider.
My Last Afternoon with Uncle Devereux Winslow.
Near the Ocean.
New Year's Day.
Night Sweat.
October and November.
Old Flame, The.
Picture, The.
Quaker Graveyard in Nantucket, The.
Robert Frost.
Sailing Home from Rapallo.
Skunk Hour.
T. S. Eliot.
Teminal Days at Beverly Farms.
To Delmore Schwartz.
"To Speak of Woe That Is in Marriage."
Waking Early Sunday Morning.
Waking in the Blue.
Water.
**Lowell, Robert Traill Spence (1816-91)**
Relief of Lucknow, The.
**Lowenfels, Walter**
For My Daughter's 20th Birthday.
**Lowry, Malcolm**
Delirium in Vera Cruz.
He Liked the Dead.
Sestina in a Cantina.
**Lowry, Robert**
Beautiful River, *with music*.
**Lowther, Pat**
Earth Sings Mi-fa-mi, The.
Morality Play.
Piercing, The.
Regard to Neruda.
Remembering How.
**Loy, Mina**
Love Songs.
Lunar Baedeker.
Omen of Victory
**Lubeck, Kathleen**
Sons, sel.
**Luciano, Felipe**
You're Nothing But a Spanish Colored Kid.
**Lucie-Smith, Edward**
Dodo, The.
Giant Tortoise, The.
Imperialists in Retirement.
Ladybirds, The.
Lesson, The.
Lime-Tree, The.
Parrot, The.
Silence.
**Lucilius [or Lucillius]**
Valentine for a Lady, A.
**Luecke, Jane Marie**

On Christ's Birth (To Sisters).
Sixth Station, The.
"Strength of That Food, The."
White Worlds.

**Lueders, Edward**
Rodeo.

**Lummis, Charles Fletcher**
Cannibalee: A Po'em of Passion.

**Lunn, Hugh Kingsmill.** *See* **Kingsmill, Hugh**

**Luther, Martin**
Mighty Fortress, A, *with music.*

**Lux, Thomas**
Five Men I Know.
Going Home.
History and Abstraction.
How to Cure Your Fever.
If You See This Man
Lament City.
Midnight Tennis Match, The.
Some Oral Stanzas.
This Is a Poem for the Fathers and for Michael Ryan.

**Lu Yu**
I Walk Out into the Country at Night.

**Lydgate, John**
Balade Simple.
Boy Serving at Table, The.
Fall of Princes, The, *sel.*
Froward Maymond ("Froward knave plainly to descrive, A").
Inordinate Love.
Like a Midsummer Rose.

**Lyle, K. Curtis**
Lacrimas or There Is a Need to Scream.
Sometimes I Go to Camarillo and Sit in the Lounge.
Song for the Cisco Kid; or, Singing for the Face.
Songs for the Cisco Kid; or, Singing: Song # 2.

**Lyly, John**
Alexander and Campaspe, *sels.*
Cards and Kisses.
Cupid and My Campaspe.
Serving-Men's Song, A.
Trico's Song: "What bird so sings, yet so does wail?"

**Lynch, Charles**
If We Cannot Live As People.
Memo.

**Lynche, Richard**
Diella, *sels.*

**Lynn, Ethel.** *See* **Beers, Ethel Lynn**

**Lyon, Lilian Bowes.** *See* **Bowes-Lyon, Lilian**

**Lyons, Richard**
Loyal Citizen.
Medora, N.D.

**Lyte, Henry Francis**
Abide with Me, *with music.*

**Lytton, Edward Robert Bulwer-Lytton, 1st Earl of.** *See* **"Meredith, Owen"**

# M

**"M., T."**
Cheating Droone.

Micro-Cynicon, *sel.*

**Macadam, George**
Gentle Ambush, The.

**Mac an Bhaird, Laoiseach**
Man of Experience, A.

**Macarthy [*or* McCarthy], Harry**
Bonnie Blue Flag, The.

**Macaulay, Thomas Babington Macaulay, 1st Baron**
Battle of Naseby, The.
Horatius.
Ivry.
Jacobite's Epitaph, A.
Lays of Ancient Rome, *sel.*

**McAuley, James Phillip**
At Rushy Lagoon.
Because.
Hero and the Hydra, the, *sel.*
In Aeternum.
In Northern Tasmania.
In the Huon Valley.
Incarnation of Sirius, The.
Mating Swans.
Merry-Go-Round.
Morning Voluntary.
Pietás.
Six Days of Creation, The.
St. John's Park.
Tomb of Heracles, The.
Wet Day.

**MacBeth [*or* Macbeth], George**
Against the Sun.
At Hunegg.
Bats.
Bedtime Story.
Drop.
Early Warning.
Marshall.
Miner's Helmet, The.
Owl.
Poem Before Birth.
Riddle, A, (for Ponge). *sel.*
Shell, The.
Suicides, The.
Twelve Hotels, The.
Wasps' Nest, The.
When I Am Dead.

**Macbride, Hamish**
For Bonny Elspeth.

**McCabe, Angela**
Back.
Blind Adolphus.
Bloom Street.
From Lois in London.
Inside History.

**McCabe, Victoria**
Reply.

**MacCaig, Norman**
Aunt Julia.
Basking Shark.
Byre.
Fetching Cows.
Frogs.
Moorings.
Near Midnight.
Ordinary Day, An.
Poem for a Goodbye.
Starlings.
Summer Farm.
Uncle Roderick.
Visiting Hour.
Wild Oats.

You Went Away.

**McCarthy, Eugene**
Bicycle Rider.
Dogs of Santiago.

**McCarthy, Harry.** *See* **Macarthy**

**McCarthy, Teresa A.**
Anita, la Maldita.
Misericordia.
Visit Peru: Of Stoned Incas Land.

**McCartney, Paul.** *See* **Lennon, John** *and* **Paul McCartney**

**"MacCathmhaoil, Seosamh."** *See* **Campbell, Joseph**

**McClintock, Charles W.**
Everybody Works but Father, *with music.*

**McClure, Michael**
It is not youth that intrigues me but suppleness.

**McCombs, Judith**
Dictionary Is an *His*torian, The: A Found Political Poem.
Hilda Lay in Hospital.
Hilda's Pelt.
Joe Was the Best of Them.
Seat Was Up, The.

**MacConglinne**
Vision of MacConglinne, The.

**"MacDiarmid, Hugh" (Christopher Murray Grieve)**
Another Epitaph on an Army of Mercenaries.
At the Cenotaph.
Birth of a Genius Among Men.
Bonnie Broukit Bairn, The.
British Leftish Poetry, 1930-40.
Cloudburst and Soaring Moon.
Cophetua.
Crystals like Blood.
Diamond Body.
Empty Vessel.
Esplumeoir.
First Love.
Harry Semen.
I Heard Christ Sing.
In Memoriam James Joyce, *sel.*
In the Pantry.
Kind of Poetry I Want, The,*sels.*
Lament for the Great Music, *sel.*
My Love Is to the Light of Lights.
O Wha's the Bride?
Of My First Love.
Old Wife in High Spirits.
Parley of Beasts.
Sauchs in the Reuch Heuch Hauch, The.
Scarlet Woman, The.
Second Hymn to Lenin.
Storm-Cock's Song, The.
Two Parents, The.
Up to Date.
Wheesht, Wheesht.

**MacDonagh, Donagh**
Dublin Made Me.
Going to Mass Last Sunday.
Hungry Grass.
Prothalamium.
Revel, A.

**MacDonagh, Thomas**
John-John.
Man Upright, The.
Night Hunt, The.

**McDonald, Barry**

Ingestion.

**Macdonald, Cynthia**
Another Attempt at the Trick.
Coupling.
Insatiable Baby, The.
Instruction from Bly.
Objets d'Art.
Stained Glass Man, The.

**MacDonald, George**
Baby-Sermon, A.
Mammon-Marriage, A.
Where Did You Come from, Baby
    Dear?
Wind and the Moon, The,*sels.*

**McDonald, Nan**
Photograph of an Actress, c. 1860.
Wet Summer: Botanic Gardens.

**McDonald, Roger**
Consequence, The.
Flights.
Grasshopper.
Hollow Thesaurus, The.
Town of Bricked Pathways, The.
Two Summers in Moravia.

**MacDonald, Susan**
Children, The.

**MacDonogh, Patrick**
Dodona's Oaks Were Still.
Escape to Love, *sel.*
No Mean City.
Now the Holy Lamp of Love.
She Walked Unaware.
Song: "She spoke to me gently with
    words of sweet meaning."
Widow of Drynam, The.

**MacDonough, Glen**
Toyland, *with music*

**McElroy, David**
Dragging in Winter.
Making It Simple December 8, 1969.
Ode to a Dead Dodge.
Report from the Correspondent They
    Fired.
Spawning in Northern Minnesota.

**MacEwen, Gwendolyn**
Animal Poems.

**McFadden, David**
Art's Variety.
Day of the Pancreas, The.
External Element, The.
Fiddlehead, The.
It's a Different Story When You're
    Going into the Wind.
Kicking from Centre Field.
Pop.
Upon Looking at a Book of Astrology.
We Love You the Way You Are.

**McGahey, Jeanne**
Lines for a Fifty-fifth Birthday.

**McGaugh, Lawrence**
To Children.
Two Mornings.
Young Training.

**McGinley, Phyllis**
Almost Any Evening.
Ballad of Befana, The.
Choice of Weapons, A.
Conquerors, The.
Country Club Sunday.
Customs of the Country, The.
Daniel at Breakfast.
Death at Suppertime.

5:32, The.
Giveaway, The.
Homework for Annabelle.
I Know a Village, *sel.*
Lament for Lost Lodgings.
Launcelot with Bicycle.
New England Pilgrimage, *sel.*
Occupation: Housewife.
Portrait of a Girl with Comic Book.
Reflections Dental.
Speaking of Television,*sels.*
Triolet Against Sisters.
Why, Some of My Best Friends Are
    Women.

**MacGiolla Gunna, Cathal Buidhe**
Yellow Bittern, The.

**McGlennon, Felix**
Comrades, *with music.*

**McGonagall, William**
Address to the New Tay Bridge, An,
    *Abr.*
Railway Bridge of the Silvery Tay, The.
Tay Bridge Disaster, The, *abr.*

**McGough, Roger**
40-Love.
Goodbat Nightman.
If Life's a Lousy Picture, Why Not
    Leave Before the End.
Let Me Die a Youngman's Death.
Mother the Wardrobe Is Full of
    Infantrymen.
My Busconductor.
My Cat and I.
Newly Pressed Suit, The.
P. C. Plod Versus the Dale St. Dog
    Strangler.

**MacGowran, Hugh**
O'Rourke's Feast ("O'Rourke's revel
    rout let no person forget").

**McGrath, Thomas**
Death for the Dark Stranger.
Jig Tune: Not for Love.
Letter for Marian, A.
Long Way Outside Yellowstone, A.
Ode for the American dead in Korea.
Song: "Lovers in ladies' magazines."

**MacGreevy, Thomas**
Homage to Hieronymus Bosch.
Nocturne of the Self-evident Presence.

**McGregor, Bruce**
Teacher,A.

**Macgregor, Forbes**
Herberie.
Jezebel.
Lammermuir Lilt, The.
On Cementing Level the Stable Floor at
    the Old Manse.
Snawdon Woods.

**McHugh, Heather**
Corps d'Esprit.
Night Catch.
Note Delivered by a Female
    Impersonator.

**McHugh, Vincent**
Mutabilities, The.

**McIntosh, Stewart**
Diane.

**MacIntyre, Lorn M.**
At Kilbryde Castle.

**McIntyre, Philip, Jr.**
Rabbit, The.

**MacIntyre, Tom**
On Sweet Killen Hill.

**Mack, Cecil**
Teasing; or, I Was Only, Only Teasing
    You, *with music.*

**Mack, L. V.**
Biafra.
Death Songs.

**McKay, Claude**
After the Winter.
America.
Enslaved.
Harlem Dancer, The.
I Know My Soul.
If We Must Die.
In Bondage.
Lynching, The.
Negro's Tragedy, Th.
Outcast.
Pagan Isms, The.
Spring in New Hampshire.
St. Isaac's Church, Petrograd.
Tiger.
Tired Worker, The.
To O. E. A.
To the White Fiends.
Tropics in New York, The.
Truth.
White City, The.
White House, The.

**Mackay, William Paton**
Revive Us Again, *with music.*

**MacKellar, Dorothea**
Once When She Thought Aloud.

**McKellar, John Alexander Ross**
Nominis Umbra.

**Mackenzie, Compton**
Bridal Day.

**Mackenzie, Kenneth**
Night Duty.
Spider, The.
Wagtail's Nest, The.

**McKeown, Tom**
Buffalo, Our Sacred Beast, The.
Graveyard Road, The.
1937 Ford Convertible.
November on Lake Michigan.
Woman with Finger.

**McKillop, Menzies**
Young Girl.

**Mackinnon, Rayne**
Reilly.
Tramp, The.
Washed in Water.

**Mackintosh, E. A.**
Cha Till Maccruimein.

**Mackintosh, Newton**
Lucy Lake.

**McKuen, Rod**
Cowboys: One ("Brave/ they straddle
    the animals").
Cowboys: Three ("They wade through
    beer cans").
Cowboys: Two ("Huddled in the pits").
Plan.
Thoughts on Capital Punishment.

**McLean, Alan**
Lizard.

**MacLean, Alasdair**
Hen Dying.
Old Dog, The.

**McLean, Albert, Jr.**

Petty Murder.
**MacLean, Sorley**
Dogs and Wolves.
Shores
**MacLeish, Archibald**
Ars Poetica.
Black Humor.
Boy in the Roman Zoo.
Brave New World.
Calypso's Island.
Conquistador, *sel.*
Crossing.
Dr. Sigmund Freud Discovers the Sea
Shell.
Eleven.
End of the World, The.
Epistle to Be Left in the Earth.
Ezry.
Hurricane.
L'An Trentiesme de Mon Eage [*or* Age].
Late Abed.
Lines for an Interment.
Memorial Rain.
Music and Drum.
"Not Marble nor the Gilded
Monuments."
Old Man to the Lizard, The.
Peepers in Our Meadow, The.
Prologue: "And the way goes on in the
worn earth."
Reasons for Music.
Seafarer.
Signature for Tempo.
Silent Slain, The.
Spring in These Hills.
Survivor.
Unfinished History.
Voyage to the Moon.
Voyage West.
What Any Lover Learns.
Winter Is Another Country.
You, Andrew Marvell.
You Also, Gaius Valerius Catullus.
Young Dead Soldiers, The.
**McLellan, Robert**
Sang: "There's a reid lowe in your
cheek.
**Macleod, Joseph Gordon ("Adam Drinan")**
Love Song.
**McMahon, Michael**
Birth of My Drinking Problem, The.
Dossier, The.
Maidenhead.
Poem for Richard Speck, A.
Politician, The.
Stranger in Your Town, A.
Until the Cows Come Home.
Why Fires are Lit December 21st.
**MacManus, Anna Johnston.** *See*
"Carbery, Ethna"
**MacManus, Seumas**
Health to the Birds, A.
**MacMarcuis, Aindrais**
This Night Sees Ireland Desolate.
**McMaster, Guy Humphreys**
Carmen Bellicosum.
**McMaster, Rhyll**
Discovering Parts of a Body.
Dream of Washed Hair, A.
Here's Death.
One for the Album.
Sleep.

Starer, The.
Woman Crossing the Road.
**McMichael, James**
Cabin North of It All, The.
Great Garret, or 100 Wheels, The.
Inland Lighthouse, The.
Lutra, The Fisher.
Village of the Presents, The.
**MacMuireadach, Niall Mor**
Soraidh Slan Don Oidhche Areir.
**McNair, Wesley**
Characters of Forgotten Dirty Jokes,
The.
Fire in Enfield.
Fitz Hugh Lane Goes to the Masthead.
Leaving the Country House to the
Landlord, Five Years Later.
Little Lovey Comic, the.
Memory of Kuhre.
Thinking about Carnevale's Wife.
**McNally, Leonard**
Lass of Richmond Hill, The, *with music.*
**MacNamee, Giolla Brighde**
Childless.
**MacNeice, Louis**
And love hung still as crystal over the
bed.
As in Their Time.
Aubade! "Having bitten on life like a
sharp apple."
Autobiography.
Autumn Journal, *sels.*
Bad Dream.
Bagpipe Music.
Bottleneck.
British Museum Reading Room, The.
Brother Fire.
Carrickfergus.
Christina.
Death of a Cat, The, *sels.*
Didymus.
Dublin.
Eclogue for Christmas, An.
Fanfare for the Makers, A, *abr.*
For X.
Glass Falling ("Glass is going down,
The").
June Thunder ("Junes were free and
full").
Les Sylphides.
Libertine, The.
London Rain.
Mahabalipuram.
Nature Morte.
Old Story, The.
Pet Shop.
Prayer before Birth.
Prayer in Mid-Passage.
Prognosis.
Slow Starter, The.
Snow.
Streets of Laredo, The.
Sunday Morning.
Sunlight on the Garden, The.
Taxis, The.
Thalassa.
This Is the Life.
Tree Party.
Trilogy for X, *sel.*
Truisms, The.
Variation on Heraclitus.
Wolves.

**Macpherson, James ("Ossian")**
Oithona: a Poem.
Songs of Selma, The, *sel.*
**McPherson, Sandra**
Coconut for Katerina, A.
Elegies for the Hot Season.
Gift of Trilliums, A.
His Body.
Holding Pattern.
Lions.
Marlow and Nancy.
Pisces Child.
Pregnancy.
Raffaele Minichiello.
Seaweeds.
Sisters.
Three from the Market.
Wanting a Mummy.
Water Poems.
**McRoberts, Robert L.**
Photo of a Retired Farmer, Big Bend,
Wisconsin.
Poem for My Students.
**MacSweeney, Barry**
If It Were Winter.
**Madge, Charles**
Solar Creation.
**Madgett, Naomi Long (Naomi Long
Witherspoon)**
Alabama Centennial.
Black Woman.
Dream Sequence, Part 9.
Her Story.
Midway.
Morality.
Pavlov.
Quest.
Race Question, The.
Simple.
Star Journey.
**Magid, Margo**
Night Watch.
**Maglow, T. O.**
Dylan Thomas.
**Maguire, Francis**
Whale Song.
**Mahon, Derek**
Consolations of Philosophy.
Dark Country, A.
Ecclesiastes
Exit Molloy.
Girls in their Seasons.
Grandfather.
Prisoner, The.
**Mahone, Barbara**
Colors for Mama.
Poem for Positive Thinkers, A.
Sugarfields.
**Mahony, Francis Sylvester ("Father
Prout")**
Piper's Progress, The.
Shandon Bells, The.
**Maiden, Jennifer**
Dew.
Hypothesis.
Over Coffee.
Strawberry-bright.
Table, The.
**Mairs, Nancy**
Departure of the Women, The.
Poison.
Waking to Leopards.

Winter Mornings.
**Maisel, Carolyn**
Dream of Women, A.
Girl in the Willow Tree, The.
Letter from a Friend, A.
**Major, Clarence**
Blind Old Woman.
Design, The.
New Pietà, The: For the Mothers and
Children of Detroit.
Swallow the Lake.
Vietnam.
Vietnam #4.
**Major, Nadine**
Agatha.
**Malangatana, Valente**
To the Anxious Mother.
**Mallarmé, Stéphane**
Fan for His Daughter, A.
**Mallet, David**
Birks of Invermay, The.
**Mallet, David** and **James Thomson.** *See*
**Thomson, James** and **David Mallet**
**Mally, E. Louise**
Moon Rock.
**Malouf, David**
Elective Affinities.
Elements of Geometry, The.
Fables, The.
Gray's Anatomy.
La Divina Commedia.
L'Education Sentimentale.
Theologia Germanica.
**Mangan, James Clarence**
Nameless One, The.
Rest Only in the Grave.
Shapes and Signs.
Siberia.
**Manifold, John Streeter**
Griesly Wife, The.
Tomb of Lieutenant John Learmonth, A.
I. F., The.
**Mann, Polly**
Atlas' Daughter.
Museum Item 237.
Smile at the Birdie.
**Mannyng, Robert**
Dancers of Colbek, The.
Handlyng Synne, *sel.*
**Marchant, John**
Little Miss and Her Parrot.
Young Master's Account of a Puppet
Show.
**Marcus, Adrianne**
Beyond Logic.
Book Ends, Immortality Begins, The.
In a Dream, the Automobile.
Letters, Returned.
Lines Found on an Envelope.
Perspective.
**Marcus, Morton**
Family Game.
Hand.
Look Closely.
Proverbs.
2 Poems Written on Turning Around
Too Quickly While Hiking.
Waking at Night.
What I Know.
**Margolis, Gary**
Keep It under Your Hat.
Rearrangement for the Brain.

**Marion, David**
Her Eyes Don't Shine Like Diamonds,
*with music.*
**Markham, Edwin**
Lincoln, the Man of the People, *sel.*
Man with the Hoe, The.
**Marks, Edward B.**
Mother Was a Lady; or, If Jack Were
Only Here, *with music.*
**Marlowe, Christopher**
Ah, Faustus,/ Now hast thou but one
bare hour [*or* hower] to live.
Amorous Neptune.
Doctor Faustus, *sels.*
Hero and Leander.
Hero Feels the Shaft of Love.
Love at First Sight.
Passionate Shepherd to His Love, The.
Was this the face that launched a
thousand ships?
**Marquis, Don**
Archy and Mehitabel, *sels.*
Cheerio My Deario.
Freddy the Rat Perishes.
Honey Bee, The.
Old Trouper, The.
Small Talk.
To a Lost Sweetheart.
Tom-Cat, The.
**Marriott, Anne**
Woodyards in the Rain.
**Marryat, Frederick**
Old Navy, The.
**Marston, John**
Antonio's Revenge, *sel.*
Cynic Satyre, A.
Inamorato Curio.
Scourge of Villainy, The,*sels.*
What You Will: a Comedy, *sel.*
**Marston, Philip Bourke**
Inseparable.
**Martial (Marcus Valerius Martialis)**
Happy Life, The.
Lycoris darling, once I burned for you.
Translated out of Martial.
You Serve the Best Wines Always, My
Dear Sir.
**Martin, Mrs. C.D.**
God Will Take Care of You, *with music.*
**Martin, Herbert**
Antigone I.
Antigone VI.
Lines: "Singularly and in pairs the
decade has been ripped by bullets."
Negro Soldier's Viet Nam Diary, A.
**Martin, Robert A.**
At Poetry Workshop, Winter Semester.
Beggar and Poet.
In Memory of G. K., for 50 Years the
College Carpenter.
**Martin, Sarah Catherine**
Comic Adventures of Old Mother
Hubbard and Her Dog, The.
**Martinez, David W.**
New Way, Old Way.
This Is Today.
**Martinez, Enrique Gonzales**
Last Journey.
Wring the Swan's Neck.
**Marvell, Andrew**
Bermudas.
Clorinda and Damon.

Coronet, The.
Damon the Mower.
Definition of Love, The.
Dialogue between the Resolved Soul and
Created Pleasure, A.
Dialogue between the Soul and Body, A.
Eyes and Tears.
Fair Singer, The.
Garden, The ("How vainly men
themselves amaze").
Garden of Appleton House, The.
Horatian Ode upon Cromwell's Return
from Ireland, An.
Last Instructions to a Painter, The,*sels.*
Mourning.
Mower Against Gardens, The.
Mower to the Glow-Worms, The.
Mower's Song, The.
Nymph Complaining for the Death of
Her Fawn, The.
On a Drop of Dew.
Picture of Little T. C. in a Prospect of
Flowers, The.
To His Coy Mistress.
Upon Appleton House.
Young Love.
**Mary Queen of Scots**
Absent One, The.
**Marzials, Théophile Julius Henry**
Tragedy, A.
**Masaoka Shiki**
Haiku: "All the hot night."
**Masefield, John**
Biography, *sel.*
C. L. M.
Cape Horn Gospel—1 (" 'I was in a
hooker once,' said Karlssen").
Cargoes.
Consecration, A.
Crowd, The.
Epilogue, An: "I have seen flowers come
in stony places."
Everlasting Mercy, The, *sel.*
From the Gallows Hill to the Tineton
Copse.
Hell's Pavement.
Lemmings, The.
Old Song Re-sung, A.
Partridges.
Reynard the Fox, *sels.*
Sea Change.
Sea-Fever.
Tarry Buccaneer, The.
Twilight.
Up on the Downs.
Wild Geese, The.
Yarn of the *Loch Achray.*
**Mason, John**
General Song of Praise to Almighty
God, A.
**Mason, Walt**
Football.
**Massman, Gordon**
Liard Hot Springs.
**Master, Thomas**
Cat and the Lute, The.
**Masters, Edgar Lee**
Amanda Barker.
Anne Rutledge.
Arlo Will.
Butch Weldy.
Cassius Hueffer.

Cooney Potter.
Editor Whedon.
Elsa Wertman.
Fiddler Jones.
Frank Drummer.
Hamilton Greene.
Hill, The.
Lucinda Matlock.
Marx the Sign Painter.
New Spoon River, The,*sels.*
Petit, the Poet.
Rhoda Pitkin.
Spoon River Anthology,*sels.*
Unknown Soldiers.
Willie Metcalf.
**Masters, Marcia Lee**
At My Mother's Bedside.
Figure.
House in Chicago, The.
Man, My Father, The.
**Masterson, Dan**
Cook-out.
One-Eleven Grape Street.
**Matchett, William H.**
Aunt Alice in April.
**Matheson, George**
O Love That Wilt Not Let Me Go, *with music.*
**Mathews, Richard**
Blood and My Brother.
Griffin.
Oh, Do You Know the Muffin Man?
Seal in the Lowry Park Zoo, The.
**Matsuo Basho.** *See Basho*
**Matthews, T. S.**
Invisible Man, The.
**Matthews, William**
Blues for John Coltrane, Dead at 41.
Cat, The.
Directions.
Invention of Astronomy, The.
Moving.
Nurse Sharks.
Oh Yes.
Oscar Robertson: Peripheral Vision.
Praise.
Your Eyes, Your Name.
**Matthias, John**
On Lake Michigan—1972.
**Maxton, Hugh**
Waking.
**Maxwell, James Clerk**
Rigid Body Sings.
**Mayer, Gerda**
Dandelions.
**Mayhall, Jane**
Prostitutes at Les Halles, The.
Tracing Back.
**Mazzaro, Jerome**
At Torrey Pines State Park.
**Mead, Matthew**
Administration of Things, The, *sels.*
Barbarians, The.
Identities,*sels.*
To Redistort a Weltanschauung.
**Mecklenburger, James**
No Matter How Her Thighs.
Pigeons.
**Mecklenburger, Ralph**
Girl with Car and Guitar.
Idolatry.
Poem at Semester's End.

Still Life.
Wilderness.
**Meeter, Merle**
Birth Day.
Exigent Gymnastic, An.
Horseplay by Reverse Descartes.
Knell for Insularity.
Lighthouse.
Toad School.
**Meidhre, Brian MacGiolla.** *See Merriman, Brian*
**Meinke, Peter**
Byron vs. DiMaggio.
Candles.
Necessary Bucket, A.
Preacher, Said the General.
Progress.
Revelation.
Third Child.
To an Athlete Turned Poet.
What Wild-eyed Murderer.
World within World.
**Meleager**
Busy with love, the bumble bee.
Lost Desire.
Love's night and a lamp.
Wine Cup, The.
**Meltzer, David**
Forte: for Tina.
**Meltzer, Richard**
Poem moves down a page, A.
**Melvill, Elizabeth, Lady Culross**
Godly Dream, A, *sels.*
**Melville, Herman**
After the Pleasure Party.
Art.
Attic Landscape, The.
Battle Picture, A.
Bench of Boors, The.
Berg, The.
Billy Budd, Foretopman, *sel.*
Billy in the Darbies.
Blue-Bird, The.
Buddha.
Conflict of Convictions, The.
Fragments of a Lost Gnostic Poem of the 12th Century.
House-Top, The.
In a Bye-Canal.
In the Desert.
Maldive Shark, The.
Malvern Hill.
March into Virginia, The.
Martyr, The.
Misgivings.
Night-March, The.
Pebbles.
Pontoosuce.
Portent, The.
Ravaged Villa, The.
Return of the Sire de Nesle A. D. 16—, The.
Shiloh; a Requiem.
To Ned.
Tuft of Kelp, The.
**Menebroker, Ann**
To the Man I Live With.
**Menzies, G. K.**
Poaching *in Excelsis.*
**Meogo, Pero**
Cossante.
**Meredith, George**

Love in the Valley.
Lucifer in Starlight.
Modern Love, *sels.*
Old Chartist, The.
Phoebus with Admetus.
Seed-Time.
What are we first? First, animals; and next.
**"Meredith, Owen" (Edward Robert Bulwer-Lytton, 1st Earl of Lytton)**
Check to Song.
**Meredith, William**
Bachelor.
Battle Problem
Consequences.
Couple Overhead, The.
Earth Walk.
Effort at Speech.
Last Things.
Old Field Mowed For Appearances' Sake, An.
On Falling Asleep by Firelight.
Open Sea, The.
Preponderance, The.
Ritual Mouse, A.
To the Thoughtful Reader.
Traveling Boy.
Two Figures from the Movies.
Walter Jenks' Bath.
Wreck of the *Thresher*, The.
**Merina, Francisco Lopez**
Song for Afterwards.
**Merriam, Eve**
Cheers.
Ding, Dong, Bell.
Fee, Fi, Fo, Fum.
Fertile Valley of the Nile, The.
Finding a Poem.
Fishy Square Dance, A.
Inner-City Mother Goose, The,*sels.*
Jamboree for J, A.
Martian.
Mean Song.
Tryst.
Umbilical.
What in the World.
Wino Will.
Yell for Yellow, A.
**Merrill, James**
About the Phoenix.
After Greece.
Angel.
Another Angel.
Broken Home, The.
Childlessness.
Foliage of Vision.
Furnished Room, The.
Laboratory Poem.
Mad Scene, The.
Matinees.
Parrot Fish, The.
Part of the Vigil.
Power Station, The.
Preface to the Memoirs, A.
Renewal, A.
Swimming By Night.
Timepiece, A.
Urban Convalescence, An.
World and the Child, The.
**Merriman, Brian [or Brian MacGiolla Meidhre]**
Country's Crisis, The.

Irish Marriage Night, An.
Maiden's Plight, The.
Midnight Court, The,*sels.*
Now God Stand Up for Bastards.
Old Man's Tale, The.
Solution, The.
Walk.

**Merton, Thomas**
Elegy for the Monastery Barn.
Responsory, 1948, A.
St. Malachy.
There Has to Be a Jail for Ladies.

**Merwin, William Stanley**
Air: "Naturally it is night."
Another Year Come.
Approaches, The.
Asians Dying, The.
Avoiding News by the River.
Ballad of John Cable and Three
    Gentlemen.
Birds Waking.
Black Plateau, The.
Bones, The.
Caesar.
Chaff, The.
Child, The.
Cold before the Moonrise, The.
Dead Hand.
December Night.
Departure's Girl-Friend.
Dictum: For a Masque of Deluge.
Distances, The.
Drunk in the Furnace, The.
Early January.
Exercise.
Fly.
Fog-Horn.
Footprints on the Glacier.
For a Coming Extinction.
For the Anniversary of My Death.
Fourth Psalm: The Cerements.
Full Moonlight in Spring.
Grandfather in the Old Men's Home.
Grandmother Watching at Her Window.
Home for Thanksgiving.
I Live Up Here.
In the Winter of My Thirty-Eighth Year.
Last One, The.
Lemuel's Blessing.
Leviathan.
Little Horse.
Looking for Mushrooms at Sunrise.
Low Fields and Light.
Moths, The.
Mountain, The.
Odysseus.
Old Boast, The.
Owl, The.
Pens, The.
Plea for a Captive.
Removal, The.
River of Bees, The.
Room, The.
Second Psalm: The Signals.
Sire.
Small Woman on Swallow Street.
Some Last Questions.
Song of Three Smiles.
Surf-Casting.
Tale.
Views from the High Camp.
We Continue.

When I Came from Colchis.
When the War Is Over.
Widow, The.

**Meschery, Tom**
As It Should Be.
Pro Basketball Players.
To Wilt Chamberlain.

**Messenger, Bill**
Carol Took Her Clothes Off.

**Metcalfe, James J.**
Pray in May.

**Metzger, Deena**
Little League Women.
Talisman for the New Year, A.

**Mew, Charlotte**
A Quoi Bon Dire.
Beside the Bed.
Cenotaph, The.
Changeling, The.
Fame.
Farmer's Bride, The.
I So Liked Spring.
In the Fields.
Madeleine in Church.
Monsieur qui Passe.
Narrow Door, The.
Old Shepherd's Prayer.
Quiet House, The.
Saturday Market.
Sea Love.
Smile, Death.
Trees Are Down, The.

**Meyers, Bert**
Stars Climb Girders of Light.

**Meynell, Alice**
Chimes.
Christ in the Universe.
Easter Night.
Father of Women, A.
General Communion, A.
In Manchester Square.
Launch, The.
Letter from a Girl to Her Own Old Age,
    A.
Maternity.
Parentage.
Poet of One Mood, A.
Rainy Summer, The.
Renouncement.
Roaring Frost, The.
Shepherdess, The.
Singers to Come.
Summer in England, 1914.
Threshing-Machine, The.
Thrush before Dawn, A.
Two Questions, The.
Veni Creator.
Watershed, The.

**Mezey, Robert**
Back.
Confession, A.
In the Soul Hour.
Night on Clinton.
There.

**Mheic Cailein, Iseabal Ni**
Alas for Him Whose Sickness Is Love.

**Michelson, Peter**
Parable for Our Time.
When the Revolution Really.

**Michie, James**
Dooley Is a Traitor.

**Middleton, Christopher**

China Shop Vigil.
Disturbing the Tarantula.
Five Psalms of Common Man.
For a Junior School Poetry Book.
Found Poem with Grafts 1866.
Historian, The.
January 1919.
Jindrichuv Hradec.
Octobers.
Poem Written after Contemplating the
    Adverb "Primarily."
Thousand Things, The.
Young Woman in Apathy.

**Middleton, Richard**
On a Dead Child.
Time's Metamorphosis.

**Middleton, Thomas**
Blurt, Master Constable, *sel.*
Night Sounds.
To Vesta.
Women Beware Women: a Tragedy, *sel.*

**Midlane, Albert**
Above the Bright Blue Sky, *sel.*

**Miles, Alfred H.**
Anchors Aweigh, *with music.*

**Miles, C. Austin**
In the Garden, *with music.*

**Miles, Josephine**
After I come home from the meeting
    with friends.
As difference blends into identity.
Belief.
Bounty.
Campaign, The.
Civilian.
David.
Doctor Who Sits at the Bedside of a
    Rat, The.
Entrepreneur chicken shed his tail
    feathers, surplus, The.
Find.
Forecast.
Gypsy.
Housewife.
In the town where every man is king.
I've been going around everywhere
    without any skin.
Made Shine.
Maxim.
Merchant Marine.
Midweek.
None.
Oedipus.
On Inhabiting an Orange.
Opal.
Players.
Preliminary to Classroom Lecture.
Reason.
Ride.
Sale.
So Graven.
Summer.
Tally.
Vacuum.
When the sun came, the rooster
    expanded to meet it.

**Miles, Susan (Ursula Roberts)**
Microcosmos.

**Millay, Edna St. Vincent ("Nancy Boyd")**
Admetus, from my marrow's core I do.
Afternoon on a Hill.
Apostrophe to Man.

Ballad of the Harp-Weaver, The.
Buck in the Snow, The.
Cameo, The.
Conscientious Objector.
Dirge without Music.
Elegy: "Let them bury your big eyes."
Even in the moment of our earliest kiss.
First Fig.
Fitting, The.
Gazing upon him now, severe and dead.
God's World.
Grown-up.
Hearing your words, and not a word
    among them.
Huntsman, What Quarry?
I, being a woman and distressed.
Intention to Escape from Him.
Justice Denied in Massachusetts.
Love is not all; it is not meat nor drink.
Love is not blind. I see with single eye.
Memorial to D. C.,    sel.
My most distinguished guest and learnèd
    friend.
Never May the Fruit Be Plucked.
Not in a silver casket cool with pearls.
Oh, sleep forever in the Latmian cave.
On Hearing a Symphony of Beethoven.
On the Wide Heath.
Passer Mortuus Est.
Plum Gatherer, The.
Portrait by a Neighbor.
Recuerdo.
Rendezvous.
Return, The.
Say that We Saw Spain Die.
Second Fig.
Since of no creature living the last
    breath.
Spring.
Theme and Variations.
Think not, nor for a moment let your
    mind.
This beast that rends me in the sight of
    all.
To a Calvinist in Bali.
To Inez Milholland.
To Jesus on His Birthday.
To the Wife of a Sick Friend.
Underground System.
What Rider Spurs Him from the
    Darkening East.
When we are old and these rejoicing
    veins.
You loved me not at all, but let it go.
**Miller, Adam David**
Crack in the Wall Holds Flowers.
Hungry Black Child, The.
**Miller, Harry S.**
Cat Came Back, The, *with music.*
**Miller, Heather Ross**
Quail Walk.
**Miller, Joaquin (Cincinnatus Heine [or
    Hiner] Miller)**
Columbus.
Crossing the Plains.
Cuba Libre.
Defence of the Alamo, The.
**Miller, Mary Britton**
Cat.
This Wonderful World.
Where Are You Now?
**Miller, May**

Bell at Midnight.
Direction, The.
**Miller, Thomas**
Evening.
Watercress Seller, The.
**Miller, Vassar**
Accepting.
Beat Poem by an Academic Poet.
Bout with Burning.
Christmas Mourning.
Farm, The.
Invocation: "Unwinding the spool of the
    morning."
Judas.
Love Song for the Future.
Metamorphoses.
On Approaching My Birthday.
Paradox.
Quarry, The.
Reciprocity.
Regret.
Song for a Marriage.
Sophistication.
Spinster's Lullaby.
Trimming the Sails.
Without Ceremony.
**Miller, Wayne**
For Kenneth Patchen.
**Miller, William**
Willie Winkie.
**Milligan, Alice**
When I Was a Little Girl.
**Mills, Kerry**
At a Georgia Camp Meeting, *with music.*
**Mills, Paul**
Acorns.
Beinn Damph
Cape Cornwall.
Cerne Giant, The.
Cromwell.
Fish, The.
Green Room, The.
Lizard.
**Mills, Ralph J., Jr.**
Door to the Sun.
White Piano, The.
**Mills, William**
I Know a Spot Just over the Hill.
Pity.
**Milne, Alan Alexander**
Buckingham Palace.
Halfway Down.
King's Breakfast, The.
Mirror, The.
Solitude.
Three Foxes, The.
Us Two.
Vespers.
**Milne, Ewart**
Diamond Cut Diamond.
Martyred Earth, The.
Vanessa Vanessa.
**Milnes, Richard Monckton, 1st Baron
    Houghton**
Good Night and Good Morning.
Lady Moon.
**Milton, John**
Adam and Eve in Paradise.
Arcades, *sel.*
At a Solemn Music.
Banishment, The.

Beneath him with new wonder now he
    views.
Comus, *sels.*
Conclusion: "High in front advanc'd/
    The brandisht sword of God before
    them blaz'd."
Creation: the Fifth Day, Fishes and
    Birds.
Cyriack, Whose Grandsire on the Royal
    Beach.
Eve Contemplates Sharing Her Sin.
Eve Speaks to Adam ("With thee
    conversing I forget all time").
Evening in Eden.
He ended; and thus Adam last replied.
Holy Light.
How Soon Hath Time the Subtle Thief
    of Youth.
Hymn on the Morning of Christ's
    Nativity.
Il Penseroso.
Immortal Hate.
Invocation: "Of mans first disobedience,
    and the fruit."
Lady Sings, The.
L'Allegro.
Light the prime work of God to me is
    extinct.
Lycidas.
Moon and the Nightingale, The.
Ode on the Morning of Christ's Nativity.
On His Blindness.
On His Deceased Wife.
On the Detraction Which Followed
    upon My Writing Certain Treatises.
On the Forcers of Conscience.
On the Late Massacre in Piedmont.
On the Morning of Christ's Nativity.
On the New Forcers of Conscience.
On Time.
Paradise Lost, *sels.*
Paradise Regained, *sels.*
Poet's Blindness, The.
Political Power.
Rivers Arise; Whether Thou Be the Son.
Sabrina.
Satan and the Fallen Angels.
Satan as Rebel-Liberator.
Satan Flies to the Sun.
Song: "Nymphs and shepherds dance no
    more."
Song on May Morning.
Spirit Epiloguizes, The.
Temptation of the Magic Banquet.
To Mr. Cyriac Skinner upon His
    Blindness.
To the Lord General Cromwell, May
    1652.
Vision of the Future; the Flood;
War in Heaven.
Ways of God, The.
**Minot, Laurence**
Halidon Hill.
**Minton, Helena**
Befriending the Weather.
Butterflies on an Illinois Road.
Croquet in Childhood.
God, Woman, Egg.
Intimations at the Lake, 1963.
Mermaid.
Raccoon Skeleton at Long Plain Creek.
Womb Is Ruins, The.

**Minty, Judith**
Boundaries.
End of Summer, The.
Finding Roots.
**Mirikitani, Janice**
First Generation, The.
**"Mistral, Gabriela" (Lucila Godoy Alcayaga)**
Ballad: "He passed by with another."
God Wills It.
To See Him Again.
**Mitchell, Adrian**
Calypso's Song to Ulysses.
Child Is Singing, A.
Fifteen Million Plastic Bags.
Leaflets.
Norman Morrison.
Remember Suez?
Riddle: "Their tongues are knives, their forks are hands and feet."
Song About Mary.
You Get Used to It.
**Mitchell, Emerson Blackhorse**
Four Directions, The.
Miracle Hill.
New Direction, The.
Path I Must Travel, The.
**Mitchell, Joni**
Cactus Tree.
Chelsea Morning.
I Think I Understand.
Michael from Mountains.
Woodstock.
**Mitchell, Matthew**
Printing Jenny ("Printing Bibles is Jenny's daily chore").
**Mitchell, Roger**
Riding with Some North Vietnamese Students in a Polish Elevator, 1966.
**Mitchell, William R.**
Aboriginal Sin.
Benediction.
Benediction for Danny.
Christmas Prayer, A.
Epiphany on a Plot of Moonlight
Had I but gone some forty days or more.
Requiem for Innocence, A.
Theoria in Early Morning.
**Miyazawa, Kenji**
Moon, Son of Heaven.
Snow on Saddle Mountain, The.
**Moffitt, John**
To Look at Any Thing.
**Mohr, Joseph**
Silent Night! Holy Night! *with music.*
**Moll, Ernest G.**
Eagles Over the Lambing Paddock
Robbing the Tree Hive.
**Mollin, Larry**
As the World Turns.
Bunky Boy Bunky Boy Who's My Little Bunky Boy.
My Elbow Ancestry.
Signature.
Tubes.
Wash Day.
**Momaday, N. Scott**
Angle of Geese.
Bear, The.
But Then and There the Sun Bore Down.
Buteo Regalis.

Carriers of the Dream Wheel.
Delight Song of Tsoai-Talee, The.
Eagle-feather Fan, The ("The Eagle is my power").
Earth and I Gave You Turquoise.
Forms of the Earth at Abiquiu.
Gourd Dancer, The.
Pit Viper.
Plainview: 3.
Rainy Mountain Cemetery.
Simile.
Story of a Well-made Shield, The.
To a Child Running with Outstretched Arms in the Canyon de Chelly.
Trees and Evening Sky.
Winter Holding Off the Coast of North America.
Wise Empty Landscape with a Death in the Foreground.
**Monette, Paul**
Bathing the Aged.
Degas.
Into the Dark.
**Monks, Arthur W.**
Twilight's Last Gleaming.
**Monro, Harold**
Midnight Lamentation.
Milk for the Cat.
Overheard in a Saltmarsh.
Terrible Door, The.
Thistledown.
**Montagu, Lady Mary Wortley**
Farewell to Bath.
Good Advice.
Saturday: The Small Pox.
**Montague, John**
All Legendary Obstacles.
Beginnings ("Beginnings of a language").
Beyond the Liss.
Chosen Light, The.
Country Fiddler, The.
Grafted Tongue, A.
Hymn to the New Omagh Road.
Last Monster, The.
Murphy in Manchester.
Road's End, The.
Same Gesture, The.
Sentence for Konarak.
Time Out.
Trout, The.
Wild Dog Rose, The.
**Montgomerie, Alexander**
Evin Dead Behold I Breathe, *sel.*
To His Mistress [*or* Maistres].
**Montgomerie, William**
Epitaph: "My brother is skull and skeleton now."
**Montgomery, Countess of.** *See* **Wroth, Mary Sidney**
**Montoya, José**
Forgive?
**Moody, William Vaughn**
Gloucester Moors.
On a Soldier Fallen in the Philippines.
**Moore, Clement Clarke**
Visit from St. Nicholas, A.
**Moore, Daniel**
Diamond, The.
**Moore, Honor**
Conversation in the Eighth Street Bookstore.
My Mother's Moustache.

Tirade.
**Moore, John**
Broken Gull, A.
Dingman's Marsh.
Squall.
**Moore, Julia A.**
And now, kind friends, what I have wrote.
**Moore, Lilian**
All Kinds of Shivers.
**Moore, Marianne**
Arthur Mitchell.
Baseball and Writing.
Carriage from Sweden, A.
Critics and Connoisseurs.
Egyptian Pulled Glass Bottle in the Shape of a Fish, An.
England.
Enough.
Face, A.
Fish, The.
Frigate Pelican, The.
Granite and Steel.
Grave, A.
He "Digesteth Harde Yron."
Hero, The.
I May, I Might, I Must.
In Distrust of Merits.
In the Days of Prismatic Color.
In the Public Garden.
Like a Bulwark.
Marriage.
Melchoir Vulpius.
Mind, Intractable Thing, The.
Mind Is an Enchanting Thing, The.
Monkeys, The.
Pangolin, The.
Paper Nautilus, The.
Part of a Novel, Part of a Poem, Part of a Play, *sels.*
Poetry.
Rigorists.
Saint Nicholas.
Silence.
Sojourn in the Whale.
Spenser's Ireland.
St. Valentine.
Steeple-Jack, The.
Student, The.
Sun.
Talisman, A.
Tell Me, Tell Me.
To a Snail.
To a Steam Roller.
W. S. Landor.
What Are Years?
Wood Weasel, The.
**Moore, Mary**
In the Cabin of Lost Fir Smells.
Li Po.
Salesman, The.
Seeding.
**Moore, Rosalie (Rosalie Moore Brown)**
After the Storm.
Imprecation for an Aesthetics Society with Newts, Warts, Waxes and Pins.
Letter to Belden.
Wheel, The.
**Moore, Thomas**
Argument, An.
At the Mid Hour of Night.

Believe Me, If All Those Endearing
Young Charms, *with music.*
Child's Song.
Did Not.
Epitaph on a Tuft-Hunter.
Epitaph on Robert Southey.
Fly to the desert, fly with me.
Fragment of a Character.
Fudge Family in Paris, The, *sel.*
Harp That Once through Tara's Halls,
The.
"I never nursed a dear gazelle."
I Saw from the Beach.
Joke Versified, A.
Lying.
Oft, in the Stilly Night.
On a Squinting Poetess.
Pastoral Ballad by John Bull, A.
Riddle, A: "Why is a pump like V-sc--
nt C--stl-r-gh?"
Song of Fionnuala, The.
Thee, Thee, Only Thee.
Time I've Lost in Wooing, The.
Tory Pledges.
Young May Moon, The.
**Moore, Thomas Sturge**
On Harting Down.
**Moraes, Dom**
John Nobody.
Letter to My Mother.
Santa Claus.
**Moraff, Barbara**
Let us suppose the mind.
**Moran, Michael ("Zozimus")**
Pharao's Daughter.
**Mordaunt, Thomas Osbert**
Sound, Sound the Clarion.
Verses Written During the War,
1756–1763, *sel.*
**More, Henry**
Psychathanasia; or, the Second Part of
the Song of the Soul, *sel.*
Psychozoia; or, the First Part of the
Song of the Soul, *sels.*
**More, Sir Thomas (Saint Thomas Moore)**
Measure of Love, The.
Mery Gest How a Sergeaunt Wolde
Lerne to Be a Frere, A.
Pageant Verses.
Prayer, A: "Grant, I thee pray, such
heat into mine heart."
Rueful Lamentation, A.
**Morehead, Albert** *and* **James Morehead**
What Shall I Pray for Today? *with
music.*
**Moreland, Wayne**
Sunday Morning.
**Morgan, Albert**
Union Man.
**Morgan, Edwin**
Addition to the Family, An.
Canedolia.
Computer's First Christmas Card, The.
Floating off to Timor.
French Persian Cats Having a Ball.
In Glasgow.
Siesta of a Hungarian Snake.
Strawberries.
Trio.
**Morgan, James Appleton**
Malum Opus.
**Morgan, Pete**

Big Hat or What, A?
White Stallion, The.
**Morgan, Robin**
Invisible Woman, The.
Lesbian Poem.
Matrilineal Descent.
News.
Quotations from Charwoman Me.
**Morgenstern, Christian**
Moonsheep, The.
Snail's Monologue, The.
**Moritake, Arakida**
Haiku: "Falling flower, The."
**Morley, Thomas**
Sing We and Chant It.
**Morris, George Pope**
Woodman Spare That Tree, *with music.*
**Morris, J. W.**
What I Think of Hiawatha.
**Morris, John N.**
Thanksgiving.
**Morris, William**
Apology, An.
August.
Defence of Guenevere, The.
Earthly Paradise, The,*sels.*
February.
Garden by the Sea, A.
Haystack in the Floods, The.
L'Envoi: "Here we are for the last time
face to face."
Life and Death of Jason, The, *sel.*
October.
Outlanders, The.
Riding Together.
Scenes from the Fall of Troy.
Summer Dawn.
Wanderers, The.
**Morrison, Lillian ("Lee Murchison")**
In the beginning was the/ Kickoff.
Of Kings and Things.
**Morse, Heather**
Curtain World.
**Mortimer, Charlotte**
Pioneers, The.
Spring Revue.
**Morton, John Bingham ("Beachcomber")**
Health and Fitness.
Lovely Big Cow.
Now We Are Sick.
To a Lady.
**Moses, W. R.**
Angina Pectoris.
Impulse of October, The.
Little-League Baseball Fan.
Nature of Jungles, The.
Night Wind in Fall.
Sitting in the Woods: A Contemplation.
**Moss, Howard**
Adolescent's Song.
Gift to be Simple, The.
Going to Sleep in the Country.
Horror Movie.
Roof Garden, The.
Water Island.
**Moss, Stanley**
God Poem.
Hangman's Love Song, The.
Prayer: "Give me a death like Buddha's,
let me fall."
Return, The.
Sailing from the United States.

**Mother Goose**
A Apple-pie.
A was an apple-pie.
All of a row.
As I was going to St. Ives.
As Tommy Snooks and Bessy Brooks.
Baa, baa, black sheep, have you any
wool?
Barber, barber, shave a pig.
Bye, baby bunting./ Daddy's gone a-
hunting.
Carrion crow sat on an oak, A.
Cock-a-doodle-doo!
Cock doth crow, the wind doth blow,
The.
Come, let's to bed.
Come when you're called.
Cross Patch/ Lift the latch.
Cry, baby, cry,/ Put your finger in your
eye.
Curly locks! curly locks! wilt thou be
mine?
Daffy-Down-Dilly has come up to town.
Dance to your daddy.
Danty, baby, diddy.
Deedle, deedle, dumpling, my son John.
Dillar, a dollar, A,/ A ten o'clock
scholar.
Ding, dong, bell/ Pussy's in the well!
Doctor Faustus was a good man.
Doctor Foster went to Glo'ster.
Elizabeth, Elspeth, Betsy, and Bess.
Fair maid who, the first of May, The.
Farmer went riding [*or* trotting] upon his
gray mare, A.
For want of a nail, the shoe was lost.
Four and twenty tailors went to kill a
snail.
Georgie Porgie, pudding and pie.
Girls and boys, come out to play.
Goosey, goosey, gander,/ Whither shall I
wander?
Great A, little a.
Hark, hark, the dogs do bark.
Hector Protector was dressed all in
green.
Here am I, little jumping Joan.
Here we go round the mulberry bush.
Hey! diddle, diddle,/ The cat and the
fiddle.
Hickety, Pickety,/ My black hen.
Hot cross buns!
How many days has my baby to play?
How many miles to Babylon.
Humpty Dumpty sat on a wall.
Hush-a-bye, baby, on the tree top.
I had a little nut tree.
I had a little pony.
I love sixpence, pretty little sixpence.
I saw a ship a-sailing.
I saw three ships come sailing by.
If all the seas were one sea.
If all the world was apple-pie.
If I'd as much money as I could spend.
If wishes were horses.
I'll tell you a story.
Intry, mintry, cutry corn.
Jack and Jill went up the hill.
Jack be nimble.
Jack Sprat could eat no fat.
Johnny shall have a new bonnet.
Lady bird, lady bird, fly away home.

Lion and the unicorn, The.
Little Betty Blue.
Little Bo-Peep has lost her sheep.
Little boy blue, come, blow up your horn.
Little cock-sparrow sat on a green tree, A.
Little Jack Horner/ Sat in a corner.
Little Miss Muffett.
Little Nancy Etticoat.
Little Polly Flinders.
Little Tom Tucker.
Long legs, crooked thighs.
Man in the wilderness asked me, The.
Mary, Mary, quite contrary.
Monday's child [or bairn] is fair of face.
North wind doth blow, The.
O, the grand old Duke of York.
Old King Cole.
Old Mother Goose, when.
"Old woman, old woman, shall we go shearing?"
One, two/ Buckle my shoe.
One, two, three, four.
One misty, moisty morning.
Pat-a-cake, pat-a-cake, baker's man!
Pease-pudding hot.
Peter Piper picked a peck of pickled pepper.
Polly put the kettle on.
Poor old Robinson Crusoe!
Pussy-cat, pussy-cat, where have you been?
Queen of Hearts, The/ She made some tarts.
Ride a cock-horse to Banbury Cross.
Robin and Richard were two pretty men.
Rock-a-bye, baby, thy cradle is green.
Rub a dub dub,/ Three men in a tub.
Rule of the road is a paradox quite, The.
See, saw, Margery Daw,/ Johnny shall have a new master.
See-saw sacradown,/ which is the way to London town?
Simple Simon met a pieman.
Sing, sing, what shall I sing?
Sing a song of sixpence.
Smiling girls, rosy boys.
Sneeze on a Monday, sneeze for danger.
Solomon Grundy.
Some little mice sat in a barn to spin.
Taffy was a Welshman, Taffy was a thief.
Tell tale, tit!
There was a crooked man, and he went a crooked mile.
There was a little boy and a little girl.
There was a little man/ And he had a little gun.
There was an old woman/ Lived under a hill.
There was an old woman, and what do you think?
There was an old woman, as I've heard tell.
There was an old woman called Nothing-at-all.
There was an old woman tossed up in a basket.

There was an old woman who lived in a shoe.
Thirty days hath September.
This is the house that Jack built.
This is the way the ladies ride:/ Tri, tre, tre, tree.
This little pig went to market.
Three blind mice.
To market, to market/ To buy a plum cake.
To market, to market, to buy a fat pig.
Tweedle-dum and Tweedle-dee.
Upon my word and honour.
What are little boys made of, made of.
When good King Arthur ruled this land.
When I was a bachelor, I lived by myself.
Who killed Cock Robin?

**Movius, Geoffrey**
Work-out, The.

**Moxley, Rubee Dreher**
6th and Walnut Street.
Ol' Tim Legion.
Saturday Night.

**Mozeen, Thomas**
Kilruddery Hunt, The.

**Mudie, Ian**
This Land.

**Mueller, Lisel**
Alive Together.
Blind Leading the Blind, The.
Childhood.
Civilizing the Child.
Farewell, a Welcome, A.
Flight, The.
Gift of Fire, The.
Mermaid, The.
Nude by Edward Hopper, A.
Palindrome.
Recluse, The.

**Muir, Alexander**
Maple Leaf Forever, The, *with music.*

**Muir, E. A.**
Gulls.

**Muir, Edwin**
Absent, The.
Animals, The.
Annunciation, The.
Ballad of Hector in Hades.
Birthday, A.
Border, The.
Brothers, The.
Childhood.
Combat, The.
Commemoration, The.
Confirmation, The.
Horses, The ("Barely a twelvemonth after").
In Love for Long.
Labyrinth, The.
Love's Remorse.
Mythical Journey, The.
One Foot in Eden.
Refugees, The.
Scotland's Winter.
Song: "Why should your face so please me."
Suburban Dream.
Three Mirrors, The.
Variations on a Time Theme, *sels.*
Wayside Station, The.

Wheel, The.

**Muir, John**
From garden to garden, ridge to ridge.

**Muldoon, Paul**
Dancers at the Moy.
Hedgehog.

**Munday, Anthony**
Beauty Bathing.
I serve a mistress whiter than the snow.
Primaleon of Greece, *sel.*

**Munkittrick, Richard Kendall**
Bulb, A.

**Munro, Deborah**
Sequence for a Young Widow Passing.
Song of the Strange Young Duckling.

**Murano, Shiro**
Diving.

**"Murchison, Lee."** *See* **Morrison, Lillian**

**Murphy, Richard**
Battle of Aughrim, The, *sels.*
Droit de Seigneur.
Girl at the Seaside.
Little Hunger.
Planter.
Rapparees.
Sailing to an Island.

**Murray, G. E.**
Driving Wheels, The.
Pavement Artist, A.
Plant Rhythms, The.

**Murray, Les A.**
Artery, The.
Birds in Their Title Work Freeholds of Straw.
Blood.
Death Words.
Names of the Humble, The.
Princes' Land, The.
Sanskrit.
Smle.
Walking to the Cattle-Place, *sels.*

**Murray, Paul**
Rain.

**Murray, Pauli**
Death of a Friend.
For Mack C. Parker.
Harlem Riot, 1943.
Mr. Roosevelt Regrets.
Ruth.
Without Name.

**Murray, Philip**
Heron, The.

**Murray, Robert Fuller**
Andrew M'Crie.
Every critic in the town.

**Murray, Susan**
Sailing.

**Murry, Ann**
Familiar Epistle, A.

**Muske, Carol**
Child with Six Fingers.
Found.
Hyena.
Rice.
Swansong.

**Myers, Jack**
Apprentice Painter, The.
Mirror for the Barnyard.
So Long Solon.
When I Held You to My Chest, You Fit.

# N

"N., A."
  Ascent of T. J. Jackson: a Soldier's Tale.
Nabokov, Vladimir
  Ode to a Model.
  Wanted, Wanted: Dolores Haze.
Nairne, Carolina Oliphant, Baroness
  Charlie Is My Darling, *with music.*
  Laird o' Cockpen, The.
  Land o' the Leal, The.
Naone, Dana
  Girl with the Green Skirt.
  I make all the poetic pauses.
  Long Distance.
  Presence, The.
  Sleep.
Narihira (Ariwara no Narihira)
  I Have Always Known.
Nash, Ogden
  Abominable Snowman, The.
  Adventures of Isabel.
  Anatomy of Happiness, The.
  Boy Who Laughed at Santa Claus, The.
  Bubba Smith.
  Calling Spring VII-MMMC.
  Columbus.
  Common Sense.
  Dick Szymanski.
  Dog's Best Friend Is His Illiteracy, A.
  Duck, The.
  First Families Move Over!
  Ha! Original Sin.
  Handsome young rodent named Gratian, A.
  Hearts of Gold.
  Horrors, The.
  Hunter, The.
  Lama, The.
  Love under the Republicans (or Democrats.)
  Mel Allen, Mel Allen, Lend Me Your Cliché.
  Morning Prayer.
  Mr. Artesian's Conscientiousness.
  Old Men.
  Porcupine, The.
  Portrait of the Artist as a Prematurely Old Man.
  Poultries, The.
  Reflection on a Wicked World.
  Reflections on Ice-Breaking.
  Reminiscent Reflection.
  Romantic Age, The.
  Sea-Gull, The.
  Song of the Open Road.
  Tom Matte.
  Turtle, The.
  Ultimate Reality.
  Up from the Egg: the Confessions of a Nuthatch Avoider.
  Very Like a Whale.
  Wendigo, The.
  Word to Husbands, A.
Nash, Valery
  Working for Dr. No.
Nashe [or Nash], Thomas
  Adieu, Farewell Earth's Bliss.
  Choice of Valentines: or, The Merry Ballad of Nashe His Dildo, The. *sels.*

Spring.
Summer's Last Will and Testament, *sels.*
Nathan, Leonard E.
  Short Pastoral.
Nathan, Norman
  Investment.
Neal, Larry
  Harlem Gallery: From the Inside.
  James Powell on Imagination.
  Malcolm X—An Autobiography.
Neaves, Lord Charles
  Let Us All be Unhappy on Sunday.
Neilson, John Shaw
  Beauty Imposes.
  Crane Is My Neighbour, The.
  Hour of the Parting, The.
  Little Militant, The.
  Man Who Prayed, The.
  May.
  Old Man in the Autumn, The.
  Orange Tree, The.
  Poor, Poor Country, The.
  Poor Can Feed the Birds, The.
  Smoker Parrot, The.
  Song Be Delicate.
  Sweetening of the Year, The.
  Walking of the Moon-Woman, The.
  You Cannot Go Down to the Spring.
Nelson, Alice Dunbar Moore
  Sonnet: "I had no thought of violets of late."
Nemerov, Howard
  Absent-Minded Professor.
  Blue Swallows, The.
  Boom!
  Brainstorm.
  Brief Journey West, The.
  Creation of Anguish.
  Dial Tone, The.
  Distances They Keep, The.
  Elegy for a Nature Poet.
  Fall Again, The.
  First Day, The.
  Flame of a Candle, The.
  Goldfish.
  Goose Fish, The.
  Grace to Be Said at the Supermarket.
  Great Society, Mark X, The.
  History of a Literary Movement.
  Human Condition, The.
  I Only Am Escaped Alone to Tell Thee.
  Icehouse in Summer, The.
  Learning By Doing.
  Life, A.
  Life Cycle of Common Man.
  Lobsters.
  Lot Later.
  Make Love Not War.
  May Day Dancing, The.
  Moment.
  Mousemeal.
  Picture, A.
  Power to the People.
  Remorse for Time, The.
  Santa Claus.
  Scales of the Eyes, The, *sel.*
  September, the First Day of School.
  Singular Metamorphosis, A.
  Sparrow in the Zoo, The.
  Statues in the Public Gardens, The.
  Storm Windows.
  Style.

Tapestry, The.
This, That and the Other.
To David, about His Education.
To the Governor & Legislature of Massachusetts.
Town Dump, The.
Truth.
Two Girls.
View from an Attic Window, The.
Winter Excercise.
"Neruda, Pablo" (Neftalí Ricardo Reyes Basualto)
  Always.
  Body of a woman, white hills, white thigh.
  Drunk as drunk on turpentine.
  Fable of the Mermaid and the Drunks.
  Fear.
  Fickle One, The.
  Girls.
  I remember you as you were that final autumn.
  Love.
  Ode to My Socks.
  Queen, The
Nerval, Gérard de (Gérard Labrunie)
  Golden
  Spook Sheep.
Nesbit, Edith (Edith Nesbit Bland)
  Child's Song in Spring.
  Things That Matter, The.
Neville, Mary
  Social Studies.
Newbery, John
  Base-Ball.
Newbery, Thomas
  Great Merchant, Dives Pragmaticus, Cries His Wares, The, *sel.*
Newbolt, Sir Henry
  He Fell Among Thieves.
  Master and Man.
  Vitaï Lampada.
Newcastle, Margaret Cavendish, Duchess of
  Bigness of Atoms, The.
  Convent of Pleasure, The, *sel.*
  Epigraph to the Theme of Love.
  Fort or Castle of Hope, The, *sel.*
  Hunting of th Hare, Th, *sel.*
  Mirth and Melancholy.
  Nature's Cook, *sel.*
  Nature's Dessert, *sel.*
  Nature's Landskip, *sel.*
  Nature's Prospect.
  Of Loose Atoms.
  On a Melting Beauty.
  Song: "My cabinets are oyster-shells."
  Soul's Garment, The.
  Sweet marmalade of kisses newly gathered.
  What Makes Echo.
Newcastle, William Cavendish, Duke of
  Love's Commission.
  Love's Flowers.
  Love's Matrimony.
  Love's Preparation.
  Love's Vision.
  Unexpressible Love, The.
Newcomb, Bobby
  Big Sunflower, The, *with music.*
Newcombe, Rosemarie
  At last I bless the hours.

**Newell, Robert Henry.** *See* "Kerr, Orpheus C."
**Newlove, John**
First Time, The.
Grass Is a Reasonable Colour, The.
Succubi.
Verigin, Moving in Alone.
Verigin 3.
Well-Travelled Roadway, The.
**Newman, Edward**
Insect Hunter, The, *sel.*
**Newman, John Henry, Cardinal**
Angel ("Softly and gently, dearly-ransomed soul").
Dream of Gerontius, The, *sel.*
Pillar of the Cloud, The.
**Newsome, Mary Effie Lee**
Morning Light (The Dew-Drier).
Sassafras Tea.
**Newton, John**
Amazing Grace, *with music.*
Name of Jesus, The.
**Niatum, Duane**
After the Death of an Elder Klallam.
Ascending Red Cedar Moon.
Chief Leschi of the Nisqually.
Crow's Way.
Elegy for Chief Sealth.
Homage to Chagall.
Indian Rock, Bainbridge Island, Washington.
No One Remembers Abandoning the Village of White Fir.
Novelty Shop, The.
Old Woman Awaiting the Greyhound Bus.
On Hearing the Marsh Bird's Water Cry.
On Leaving Baltimore.
On Visiting My Son, Port Angeles, Washington.
Owl Seen In Rearview Mirror.
Separation.
Slow Dancer That No One Hears but You.
Songs from the Maker of Totems.
To Your Question.
**Nichols, Jeanette**
Kind of Love, A.
Mostly People.
My Father Toured the South.
Same Lady, The.
Someone Gone Away Downstairs.
**Nicholson, Norman**
Cleator Moor.
Rising Five.
Weather Ear.
**Ni Chuilleanain, Eilean**
Swineherd.
Wash.
**Niedecker, Lorine**
As praiseworthy/ the power of breathing.
In the great snowfall before the bomb.
My mother saw the green tree toad.
Paean to Place.
River-march-drowse.
Young in Fall I said: the birds.
**Niles, Nathaniel**
Bunker Hill, *with music.*
**Nims, John Frederick**
Decline and Fall.
D.O.M., A.D. 2167.

Girl Marcher.
Love and Death.
Love Poem: "My clumsiest dear, whose hands shipwreck vases."
Midwest.
Nature Lover.
Visiting Poet.
**Noel, Henry**
Beauty's Excellency.
**Noin Hoshi**
Tanka: "In the evening/ Quiet of the country town."
**Nolan, James**
Cross and the Weathercock, The.
Locked in a Home for Les Enfants Dérangés en Dieu.
Tyger! Tyger!
**Nolan, Michael**
Little Annie Rooney, *with music.*
**Noll, Bink**
Divorce.
June.
Landscape with Pervert.
Picador Bit, The.
Quaker Hero, Burning.
**Norris, John**
Canticle.
Meditation, The.
**Norris, Kathleen**
Evaporation Poems.
Her Application to Elysium.
Running through Sleep.
**Norris, Leslie**
Elegy for David Beynon.
One Leaf, The.
**North, Frank Mason**
Where Cross the Crowded Ways of Life, *with music.*
**Norton, Caroline Elizabeth Sarah Sheridan**
Juanita, *with music.*
**Norworth, Jack**
Take Me Out to the Ball Game, *with music.*
**Norworth, Jack,** *and* **Nora Bayes.** *See* **Bayes, Nora,** *and* **Jack Norworth**
**Nowlan, Alden**
Baptism.
Beginning.
Daisies.
Golden Pyramids of the Sun, The.
Gypsies.
Hens.
I, Icarus.
Kyran's Christening.
Letter to a Young Friend.
Palomino Stallion, The.
Party at Bannon Brook.
Porch.
Psalm of Onan for Harp, Flute and Tambourine, A.
Rivalry.
Semi-Private Room.
Stars.
Therese.
Waiting for Her.
Warren Pryor.
Wasp.
**Noyes, Alfred**
Barrel-Organ, The, *abr.*
Rustling of Grass, The.
Spring, and the Blind Children.
**Nugent, Maude**

Sweet Rosie O'Grady, *with music.*
**Nye, Aileen Campbell**
Less than Love.
**Nye, Robert**
In More's Hotel.
Travelling to My Second Marriage on the Day of the First Moonshot.
**Nyro, Laura**
And When I Die.

# O

**Oakman, John**
Glutton, The.
**Oates, Joyce Carol**
American City.
Foetal Song.
Girl at the Center of Her Life, A.
Growing Together.
Lines for Those to Whom Tragedy Is Denied.
**Ober, Don**
Contemporary Fear.
**O'Bolger, T. D.**
Counsels of O'Riordan, the Rann Maker, The.
**"O'Brien, John."** *See* **Hartigan, Patrick Joseph**
**O'Bruadair, David**
Change, The.
Eire.
New Style, The.
O'Bruadair.
**O'Carolan, Turlough**
Mabel Kelly.
Peggy Browne.
**Ochester, Ed**
Farewell to the Moon, A.
**Ochs, Phil**
Draft Dodger Rag.
Outside of a Small Circle of Friends.
**O'Connell, Eibhlin Dubh**
Lament for Art O'Leary.
**O'Connor, Frank (originally Michael O'Donovan)**
Three Old Brothers.
**O'Connor, Philip**
Writing in England Now.
**O'Connor, Tony**
Last of the Poet's Car.
**O'Críadáin, Seán**
Great-Aunts.
**O'Dalaigh, Gofraidh Fionn**
Under Sorrow's Sign.
**O'Dalaigh, Muireadach**
On the Death of His Wife.
**Oden, Gloria Catherine**
Carousel, The.
Man White, Brown Girl and All That Jazz.
Review from Staten Island.
Riven Quarry, The.
Triple Mirror, The.
Way It Is, The.
**O'Donoghue, Gregory**
Web, The.
**O'Donovan, Michael.** *See* **O'Connor, Frank**

**O'Egan, Gerry**
1867: Last Sounds.
**Oerke, Andrew**
Serengeti Sunset.
**O'Faracháin, Roibéard.** *See* **Farren, Robert**
**Ogilvie, Will H.**
Death of Ben Hall, The.
**Ogilvie-Laing, Galina V.**
I Saw the Light Yesterday.
**Og MacWard, Fearghal**
Flight of the Earls, The, 1607. *sel.*
**O'Grady, Desmond**
Afternoon.
Dying Gaul, The.
Father, The.
Page from a Diary.
Poet Loves from Afar, The.
Professor Kelleher and the Charles
   River.
**O'Hara, Frank**
Abortion, An.
Autobiographia Literaria.
Biotherm (For Bill Berkson).
Chez Jane.
Day Lady Died, The.
Homosexuality.
Les Etiquettes Jaunes.
Les Luths.
Ode on Lust.
Ode to Joy.
Ode to Willem de Kooning.
On Rachmaninoff's Birthday.
Personal Poem
Poem: "At night Chinamen jump."
Poem: "Eager note, The, on my door
   said, 'Call me'."
Poem: "Lana Turner has collapsed!"
Rhapsody.
Should We Legalize Abortion?
Step Away from Them, A.
Steps.
To the Film Industry in Crisis.
Why I Am Not a Painter.
**O'Hare, Felix**
Shoofly, The.
**O'Heffernan, Mahon**
My Son, Forsake Your Art.
**O'Higgins, Myron**
Two Lean Cats.
Vaticide.
Young Poet.
**O'Huiginn, Tadhg Dall**
Difference, The.
First Vision, *sel.*
Present of Butter, A.
**O'Hussey, Eochaidh**
Ode to the Maguire.
**Ojenke.** *See* **Saxon, Alvin**
**O'John, Calvin**
Dancing Teepees.
**O'Keefe, John**
Amo, Amas.
**O'Keeffe, Adelaide**
Beasts and Birds.
Kite, The.
**Olcott, Chauncey**
My Wild Irish Rose, *with music.*
**Oldmixon, John**
Song: "I lately vow'd, but 'twas in
   haste."
**Oldys, William**

Fly, The.
**Oles, Carole**
Brother at One Week.
Circling.
Poem for my Hands.
· Price of Beast in Las Vegas, The
**Oliphant, Carolina.** *See* **Nairne, Carolina Oliphant, Baroness**
**Oliver, Mary**
Diviners, The.
Grandmothers, The.
Through Ruddy Orchards.
**Olson, Charles**
Distances, The.
I, Maximus of Gloucester, to You.
Kingfishers, The.
La Chute.
Letter 6.
Maximus, to Gloucester, Letter 19.
Maximus, to Gloucester, Letter 6.
Maximus, to Gloucester, Letter 27.
Maximus, to Gloucester, Letter 2.
Maximus, to Himself.
Newly Discovered "Homeric". Hymn, A.
Praises, The.
Ring Of, The.
Songs of Maximus, The.
These Days.
Variations Done for Gerald van de
   Wiele.
**Olson, Elder**
Valentine for Marianne Moore, A.
**Omar Khayyám**
Book of verses underneath the bough, A.
Rubáiyát of Omar Khayyám of
   Naishápúr, The.
**Ondaatje, Michael**
When Charlie Bowdre married Manuela,
   we carried them.
**Oneil, Henrietta**
Ode to the Poppy.
**"O'Neill, Moira" (Nesta Higginson Skrine)**
Her Sister.
Rachray Man, The.
**Oppen, George**
Exodus
Latitude, Longitude.
Myth of the Blaze.
Who Shall Doubt.
**Oppenheimer, Joel**
Leave It to Me Blues.
Undefined Tenderness, An.
**O'Rahilly [or O'Reilly], Egan**
Brightest of the Bright, The.
Egan O Rahilly.
Inis Fal.
More Power.
Time of Change, A.
**O'Reilly, John Boyle**
White Rose, A.
**"Orinda."** *See* **Philips, Katherine**
**Orléans, Charles, Duc d'**
Lost.
My Ghostly Father, I Me Confess.
**Orr, Gregory**
Dinner, The.
Doll, The.
Gathering the Bones Together.
Girl with 18 Nightgowns, The.
Love Poem: "Black biplane crashes into
   the window, The."
Poem: "This life like no other."

Two Lines from the Brothers Grimm.
**Orred, Meta**
In the Gloaming, *with music.*
**Ortiz, Simon J.**
Bony.
Creation, The: According to Coyote.
Forming Child Poems.
Pretty Woman, A.
Relocation.
San Diego Poem, A.
Serenity in Stones, The.
Smoking Prayers.
Survival This Way.
Ten O'Clock News.
This Preparation.
To Insure Survival.
Waiting for You to Come By.
Watching Salmon Jump.
What I Tell Him.
**Orwell, George (Eric Blair)**
As One Non-Combatant to Another.
**O'Shaughnessy, Arthur William Edgar**
Ode: "We are the music-makers."
**"Ossian."** *See* **Macpherson, James**
**Ostrander, Fred**
Tides.
**Ostroff, Anthony**
Sunday, Guadalajara.
**O'Sullivan, Daniel James**
Drinking Time.
**O'Sullivan, Owen Roe**
His Request.
Volatile Kerryman, The.
**"O'Sullivan, Seumas" (James Starkey)**
Blessing on the Cows, A.
Convent, The.
Cottage.
In North Great George's Street.
Lamplighter, The.
Piper, A.
Rain.
**Otway, Thomas**
Orphan, or the Unhappy Marriage, The,
   *sels.*
Poet's Complaint of His Muse, The, *sel.*
**Outram, George**
Strictures on the Economy of Nature.
**Ovid (Publius Ovidius Naso)**
Amores, *sel.*
Constant Penelope sends to thee, careless
   Ulysses.
Corinnae Concubitus.
Medea Casts a Spell to Make Aeson
   Young Again.
Orpheus and Eurydice.
Ovid's Fifth Elegy.
To His Mistress ("Your husband will be
   with us at the treat").
**Owen, David**
All through the Night, *with music.*
**Owen, Guy**
Poem to a Mule, Dead Twenty Years.
White Stallion, The.
**Owen, Wilfred**
A Terre.
Anthem for Doomed Youth.
Arms and the Boy.
Chances, The.
Disabled.
Dulce et Decorum Est.
Exposure
Futility.

Greater Love.
Insensibility.
Mental Cases.
Miners.
Parable of the Old Man [*or* Men] and the Young, The.
Send-off, The.
Show, The.
Song of Songs.
Strange Meeting.
To My Friend.

**Owens, Rochelle**
All Owners of Meat Are Hospitable.
Dance and Eye Me (Wicked)ly My Breath a Fixed Sphere.
For, Behold the Day Cometh.
Let Us Honor Them.
Never in This World You Will Drop a Yellow Sponge.
Power of Love He Wants Shih (Everything), The.
Radiant Heat.
Sky-Splitting Pink Rubber Bistro, The.
Wild Woman's Resentment of Fakery.
Wistful Butch Poem.

**P**

**Pack, Robert**
Apocalypse in Black and White.
Bird in Search of a Cage, A.
Everything Is Possible.
In a Field.
Love.
My Daughter.
Pack Rat, The.
Way We Wonder, The.

**Packard, William**
Teacher of Poetry, The.

**Padgett, Ron**
After the Broken Arm.
Sandwich Man, The.

**Page, Edgar**
Beulah Land, *with music*

**Pain, Philip**
Meditation 8 ("Scarce do I pass a day but that I hear").
Meditation 9 ("Man's life is like a rose, that in the spring").
Meditation 62 ("How is it that I am so careless here").
Meditation 10 ("Alas, what is the world? A sea of glass").
Meditation 29 ("How mutable is every thing that here").
Porch, The.

**Paine, Thomas**
Liberty Tree.

**Paley, Grace**
One day when I was a child, long ago.
Women in Vietnam, The.

**Palmer, E. Harriet**
Parterre, The.

**Palmer, Herbert Edward**
Rock Pilgrim.

**Palmer, Horatio R.**
Yield Not to Temptation, *with music*.

**Palmer, John F.**
Band Played On, The, *with music*.

**Palmer, John Williamson**
Maryland Battalion, The.
Stonewall Jackson's Way.

**Palmer, Miriam**
Getting into Focus.
Raccoon Poem.
"Vierge Ouvrante."
What if jealousy is just a bad dream?

**Palmer, Ray**
My Faith Looks Up to Thee, *with music*.

**Pape, Greg**
For Rosa Yen, Who Lived Here.
La Llorona.
Mercado.
October.

**Parish, Mitchell**
Star Dust, *with music*.

**Parker, Dorothy**
Chant for Dark Hours.
Coda.
Fair Weather.
Interior.
Of a Woman, Dead Young.
One Perfect Rose.
Partial Comfort.
Résumé.
Symptom Recital.
Theory.
Unfortunate Coincidence.

**Parker, Patricia**
With the sun.

**Parker-Silverman, Linda**
Advice to the Lovelorn
Nursing Home.

**Parkhurst, John**
Of Alphus.

**Parkinson, Thomas**
New Antigone, The, *sel.*

**Parks, Lorine**
Person to Person.

**Parra, Nicanor**
Manifesto, *sel.*
Seven.
We Let It Go That He Was a Perfect Man.
Young Poets.

**Parrot, Henry**
In Obitum Promi.

**Parry, David Fisher**
Miniver Cheevy, Jr.

**Parry, Edward Abbott**
I Would Like You for a Comrade.
Jam Fish, The.
Pater's Bathe.

**Parvin, Betty**
Edwardian Hat

**Pastan, Linda**
After X-Ray.
At the Gynecologist's.
Distances.
Governor's Palace, The.
Notes from the Delivery Room.
Old Woman.
Williamsburg, *sel.*

**Pasternak, Boris Leonidovich**
Hops.

**Patchen, Kenneth**
And With the Sorrows of This Joyousness.
Animal I wanted, The.
Because He Liked to Be at Home.

Biography of Southern Rain.
Character of Love Seen as a Search for the Lost, The.
Do the Dead Know What Time It Is?
Easy Decision, An.
Fox, The.
In Judgment of the Leaf.
In Order to.
Lions of fire, The.
May I Ask You a Question.
Midnight Special.
Mirru.
O terrible is the highest thing.
Orange Bears, The.
Origin of Baseball, The.
Peter's Little Daughter Dies.
Trueblue Gentleman, A.
Village Tudda, The.

**Paterson, Andrew Barton**
Clancy of the Overflow.
Man from Snowy River, The.
Old Man Platypus.
Traveling Post Office, The.
Waltzing Matilda.
Weary Will.

**Patmore, Coventry Kersey Dighton**
Across the sky the daylight crept.
Angel in the House, The, *sels.*
Azalea, The.
Barren Shore, The.
Cathedral Close, The.
County Ball, The.
Departure.
1867.
Faint Yet Pursuing.
Farewell, A: "With all my will, but much against my heart."
Kiss, The.
London Fete, A.
Love at Large.
Magna Est Veritas.
Night and Sleep.
Perspective.
Revelation, The.
Spirit's Epochs, The.
Toys, The.
Victories of Love, The, *sel.*
Whirl'd off at last, for speech I sought.
Winter.

**Patten, Brian**
Interruption at the Opera House.
Little Johnny's Final Letter.
Little Johnny's Foolish Invention.
No Matter If You Remain Unaffected by.
Ode on Celestial Music.
Party Piece.
Portrait of a Young Girl Raped at a Suburban Party.
Projectionist's Nightmare, The.
Seen through the Trees behind Which You're Walking.
Small Dragon, A.
What You Should Do Each Morning.
You'd Better Believe Him.

**Patterson, Raymond Richard**
At That Moment.
Birmingham 1963.
Black All Day.
I've Got a Home in That Rock.
Letter in Winter.
Night-Piece.

When I Awoke.
You Are the Brave.
**Paulus Silentiarius**
Tantalos.
**Paxton, Tom**
Bishop Cody's Last Request.
**Payne, Basil**
Angry Old Men.
**Payne, Gerrye**
Claritas.
There was a time when we all were
dancers.
**Payne, John Howard**
Clari, the Maid of Milan, *sel.*
Home, Sweet Home, *with music.*
**Paz, Octavio**
Dawn.
Touch.
**Peacock, Thomas Love**
Crotchet Castle, *sel.*
Friar of Rubygill, The.
Maid Marian, *sel.*
Merry Jest of Robin Hood, A.
Misfortune of Elphin, The, *sel.*
Newark Abbey.
Priest and the Mulberry Tree, The.
Rich and Poor; or, Saint and Sinner.
War Song of Dinas Vawr, The.
**Peake, Mervyn Laurence**
Is There No Love Can Link Us?
**Pearce, Ellen**
Orange Tree, The.
Turtle's Belly, The.
**Pearse, Padraic**
Last Lines—1916.
**Peck, John**
Cider and Vesalius.
Colophon for Lan-t'ing Hsiu-Hsi.
Ringers, The.
Spring Festival on the River, The.
Watcher, The.
**Peck, Richard**
Jump Shot.
Mission Uncontrolled.
TKO.
**Peele, George**
Arraignment of Paris, The, *sel.*
Bethsabe's Song.
David and Bethsabe, *sel.*
His Golden Locks Time Hath to Silver
Turned.
Hunting of Cupid, The, *sel.*
Oenone and Paris.
Old Wife's Tale, The.
Old Wives' [or Wife's] Tale, The, *sels.*
Polyhymnia, *sels.*
Summer Song, A.
Voice from the Well, The.
What Thing Is Love?
**Pélieu, Claude**
Golden-eyed Crossbow, The.
**Pell, Dewey G.**   *See* **Alpaugh, Ern** *and*
**Dewey G. Pell**
**Pellicer, Carlos**
Etude.
**Pembroke, Mary Sidney Herbert, Countess**
**of**
If Ever Hapless Woman Had a Cause.
**Penkethman, John**
Schoolmaster's Precepts, A.
Some Boys.
**Penny, Rob**

And We Conquered.
Be Cool, Baby.
I Remember How She Sang.
Real People Loves One Another, The.
**Percy, William**
Coelia, *sels.*
**Perkins, David**
Blue Gift, The.
Falling in Love.
"How Long Hast Thou Been a
Gravemaker?"
**Perkins, Michael**
Carpenter, The.
**Perlberg, Mark**
In Praise of Lichen.
Water and Light, Light and Water.
**Perronet, Edward**
All Hail the Power of Jesus' Name.
Coronation, *with music.*
**Perry, Julianne**
No Dawns.
To L.
**Persius (Aulus Persius Flaccus)**
Satires, *sel.*
Thus fares the drudge; but thou, whose
life's a dream.
Yawning youth, scarce half awake,
essays, The.
**Pessoa, Fernando.**   *See* **Caeiro, Alberto**
**Peter, Robert**
O! Wherefore.
**Petersen, Donald**
Ballad of Dead Yankees, The.
**Peterson, Robert**
At Veronica's.
Dear America.
For the Minority.
Groom's Lament, The.
Hands folded like napkins in my lap.
Highway Patrol Stops Me, Going Too
Slow.
In the 2 A.M. Club, a working man's
bar.
To Myself, Late, in a Myrtle Grove.
Wingwalking in Oregon.
**Peterson, Ruth De Long**
Midwest Town.
**Petrarch (Francesco Petrarca)**
Amorous Worms' Meat, The.
Description of the Contrarious Passions
in a Lover.
He Understands the Great Cruelty of
Death.
Love That Doth Reign and Live within
My Thought.
Lover Compareth His State to a Ship in
Perilous Storm Tossed on the Sea,
The.
Lover for Shamefastnesse Hideth His
Desire within His Faithfull Hart, The.
Sonnets to Laura, *sels.*
Vow to Love Faithfully, Howsoever He
Be Rewarded, A.
**Petrie, Paul**
Old Pro's Lament, The.
**Petronius Arbiter (Caius Petronius Arbiter)**
Doing, a Filthy Pleasure Is, and Short.
Good God, what a night that was.
**Pfingston, Roger**
Occasion.
**Phair, George E.**
Old-Fashioned Pitcher, The.

**Philips, Ambrose**
To the Memory of Lord Halifax, *sel.*
**Philips, Joan**   *See* **"Ephelia"**
**Philips, John**
Splendid Shilling, The.
**Philips, Katherine ("Orinda")**
Against Love.
Dialogue of Absence 'twixt Lucasia and
Orinda, A.
Friendship's Mystery, to My Dearest
Lucasia.
Orinda to Lucasia Parting, October 1661,
at London.
Sea-Voyage from Tenby to Bristol, A.
To Antenor.
To Mr. Henry Lawes.
To My Excellent Lucasia, on Our
Friendship.
Upon the Double Murther of King
Charles I.
**Phillips, David**
Fighting Her.
Lover to Himself, The.
Notes on a Long Evening.
Old Storm.
Orange Juice Song.
Things of Late.
Wave, The.
Words.
**Phillips, Rodney**
Out of You.
**Phillpotts, Eden**
Houses, The.
Man's Days.
**Philodemos the Epicurean**
Remonstrance.
**Piercy, Marge**
Agitprop.
Burying Blues for Janis.
Cold and Married War, A.
Councils.
Death Dance, The.
Different Persuasions.
Embryos.
Friend, The.
Gracious Goodness.
Hare in Winter.
High Frequency.
I Awoke with the Room Cold.
I Still Feel You.
In the Men's Room(s).
Kneeling Here, I Feel Good.
Letter to Be Disguised As a Gas Bill.
Meditation in My Favorite Position.
Morning Half-Life Blues, The.
Night Letter.
Noon of the Sunbather.
Nothing More Will Happen.
Organizer's Bogeymen, The.
Right Thinking Man.
Riptide.
Ritual, The.
Seedlings in the Mail.
Sign.
Simple-Song.
16/53.
Someplace Else.
Song of the Fucked Duck.
Spring Offensive of the Snail, The.
Three Weeks in the State of Loneliness.
Unclench Yourself.
Valley Where I Don't Belong, A.

Walking into Love, *sel.*
We Become New.
What You Waited For.
Why the Soup Tastes like the Daily
  News.
Woman in the, The.
Work of Artifice, A.
**Pierpont, James S.**
Jingle Bells, *with music.*
One Horse Open Sleigh, The.
**Pierpont, John**
Pilgrim Fathers, The.
Warren's Address.
**Pike, Albert**
Dixie ("Southrons, hear your country
  call you!").
**Pilkington, Laetitia**
Song: "Lying is an occupation."
**Pindar**
Odes, *sel.*
Seventh Olympic Hymn.
**"Pindar, Peter" (John Wolcott)**
Poetical and Congratulatory Epistle to
  James Boswell, Esq., A.
**Pinder, Mike**
Dawn is a Feeling.
**Pitcher, Oliver**
Pale Blue Casket, The.
Salute.
**Pitt, William**
Sailor's Consolation, The.
**Pitter, Ruth**
But for Lust.
Eternal Image, The.
Hen Under Bay-Tree.
O where is the dwelling I love the most.
Old Woman Speaks of the Moon, An.
Swan Bathing, The.
Three Cheers for the Black, White and
  Blue.
Time's Fool.
**Pitts, William S.**
Little Brown Church in the Vale, The,
  *with music.*
**Plath, Sylvia**
Aftermath.
All the Dead Dears.
Appearance, An.
Applicant, The.
Ariel.
Arrival of the Bee Box, The.
Balloons.
Bee Meeting, The.
Beekeeper's Daughter, The.
Black Rook In Rainy Weather.
Blackberrying.
By Candlelight.
Candles.
Colossus, The.
Cut.
Daddy.
Death and Co.
Disquieting Muses, The.
Edge.
Elm.
Event.
Face Lift.
Fever 103°.
For a Fatherless Son.
Gulliver.
Kindness.
Lady Lazarus.

Last Words.
Lesbos.
Life, A.
Love Letter.
Mary's Song.
Medallion.
Medusa.
Metaphors.
Mirror.
Moon and the Yew Tree, The.
Morning Song.
Mushrooms.
Nick and the Candlestick.
Poppies in October.
Rabbit Catcher, The.
Sheep in Fog.
Sow.
Spinster.
Stones, The.
Suicide Off Egg Rock.
Tulips.
Two Views of a Cadaver Room.
Watercolor of Grantchester Meadows.
Winter Ship, A.
Winter Trees.
Wintering.
Words.
You're.
**Plomer, William**
Father and Son: 1939.
Headline History.
In the Snake Park.
Playboy of the Demi-World, The: 1938.
Positive, a Coxcomb.
Scorpion, The.
Seven Rainy Months.
To the Moon and Back.
Widow's Plot, The: or, She Got What
  Was Coming to Her.
**Plumly, Stanley**
After Grief.
Fungo.
Giraffe.
Heron.
One Song.
Out-of-the-Body Travel.
Porches.
Pull of the Earth.
**Plumpp, Sterling**
Beyond the Nigger ("Beyond the
  outstretched hands").
Half Black, Half Blacker.
I Told Jesus.
Living Truth, The.
**Plunkett, Joseph Mary**
1867.
**Plutzik, Hyam**
I Am Disquieted when I See Many
  Hills.
Jim Desterland.
Of Objects Considered as Fortresses in a
  Baleful Place.
**Plymell, Charles**
Baltimore Eclipse.
For Cynara.
**Po Chü-i**
Cranes, The.
**Poe, Edgar Allan**
Al Aaraaf, *sels.*
Alone.
Annabel Lee.
Bells, The, *sel.*

City in the Sea, The.
Coliseum, The.
Conqueror Worm, The.
Dream-Land.
Dream within a Dream, A.
Eldorado.
Fall of the House of Usher, The, *sel.*
For Annie.
Haunted Palace, The.
Introduction: "Romance, who loves to
  nod and sing."
Israfel.
Lenore, 3 *versions.*
Ligeia, *prose tale, sel.*
Raven, The.
Sleeper, The.
Song: "Young flowers were whispering
  in melody."
Sonnet—Silence.
Sonnet—To Science.
To Helen ("Helen, thy beauty is to me").
To One in Paradise.
Ulalume—a Ballad.
**Pollak, Felix**
Historical Society Exhibit: Old
  Programme.
How I Got Myself Trapped.
Nofretete.
Speaking: the Hero.
Stone and the Obliging Pond.
**Pollard, Adelaide A.**
Have Thine Own Way, Lord! *with music.*
**Pomeroy, Marnie**
News.
**Ponchon, Raoul**
Shepherd's Tale, The.
**Ponsot, Marie**
Communion of Saints: the Poor Bastard
  under the Bridge.
Multipara: Gravida 5.
Possession.
Subject.
To the Age's Insanities.
**Popa, Vasko**
Donkey.
**Pope, Alexander**
Apologia pro Vita Sua.
Art of Sinking in Poetry, The, *sel.*
Atticus.
Chloe.
Dialogue, A.
Duke of Buckingham, The.
Duke upon Duke.
Dunciad, The, *sel.*
Elegy to the Memory of an Unfortunate
  Lady.
Epigram Engraved on the Collar of a
  Dog Given to His Royal Highness.
Epilogue to the Satires,*sels.*
Epistle to Dr. Arbuthnot.
Epistle to Miss Blount, on Her Leaving
  the Town after the Coronation.
Essay on Man, An,*sels.*
First Satire of the Second Book of
  Horace, The.
For forms of government let fools
  contest.
Know Thyself.
Lamentation of Glumdalclitch, The.
Lines on Swift's Ancestors.
Little Learning, A.
Lock, The.

Moral Essays,*sels.*
Ode on Solitude.
Ode on St. Cecilia's Day, *sel.*
Of all the causes which conspire to blind.
On a Certain Lady at Court
On Certain Ladies.
Pastorals, *sels.*
Power of Ridicule, The.
Rape of the Lock, The.
Sad Story, A.
Sound and Sense.
Sporus.
Sylvan Delights.
To Richard Boyle, Earl of Burlington: Of the Use of Riches.
Toilet, The.
Triumph of Dullness, The.
Triumph of Vice, The.
Two or Three: A Recipe [*or* Receipt] to Make a Cuckold.
Voyage on the Thames, The.
What would this man? Now upward will he soar.
Who knocks at the door?
Winter.

**Popham, Hugh**
Usual exquisite boredom of patrols, The.

**Porson, Richard**
Note on the Latin Gerunds, A.
On a Doctor of Divinity.
Porson on German Scholarship.
Porson on His Majesty's Government.
Porson's Visit to the Continent.
To Dr. Kipling.

**Porter, Cole**
Night and Day, *with music.*
So In Love, *with music.*

**Porter, Peter**
Affair of the Heart.
Annotations of Auschwitz, *sel.*
Consumer's Report, A.
London is full of chickens, on electric spits.
Metamorphosis.
Mort Aux Chats.
Nine O'Clock Thoughts on the 73 Bus.
Notes to a Biographer.
Sex and the Over Forties.
Story Which Should Have Happened.
Your Attention Please.

**Pound, Ezra**
Alba.
Ancient Music.
Ancient Wisdom, Rather Cosmic.
And the Days Are Not Full Enough.
And Thus in Nineveh.
Ballad of the Goodly Fere.
Ballatetta.
Cantos, *sels.*
Cino.
Coda.
Commission.
Dance Figure.
De Aegypto.
E. P. Ode pour l'Election de Son Sepulchre.
Eleanor (she spoiled in a British climate).
Elegy: "Me happy, night, night full of brightness."
Envoi (1919).

Francesca.
"From the colour the nature."
Garden, The.
Garret, The.
Hang it all, Robert Browning.
Homage to Sextus Propertius,*sels.*
Hugh Selwyn Mauberley (Life and Contacts).
Immorality, An.
In a Station of the Metro.
Lake Isle, The.
L'Art, 1910.
Liu Ch'e.
Marvoil.
Medallion.
Meditatio.
Mr. Housman's Message.
Monumentum Aere, Etc.
New Cake of Soap, The.
Pact, A.
Paracelsus In Excelsis.
Portrait d'une Femme.
Rest, The.
Return, The.
Salutation.
Salutation the Second.
Sestina: Altaforte.
Sketch 48b.11.
Song of the Degrees, A, *sel.*
Study in Aesthetics, The.
Tea Shop, The.
Temperaments, The.
Trahison des Clercs; Against the Perversion of Language.
Tree, The.
Villonaud for This Yule.
Virginal, A.
What thou lovest well remains.
When, when and whenever death closes our eyelids.

**Pounds, Jessie B.**
Beautiful Isle of Somewhere, *with music.*

**Power, Marguerite (Countess of Blessington)**
Friend, A.

**Powys, John Cowper**
In a Hotel Writing-Room.

**Prado, Holly**
Mouth That Is a Wound, The.
Night You Got Back from the Mountains, The.
Tropics, The

**Prados, Emilio**
Dream.

**Praed, Winthrop Mackworth**
Belle of the Ball Room, The.
Good-night to the Season.

**Pratt, Agnes**
Death Takes Only a Minute.
Empathy.

**Pratt, Edwin John**
Prize Cat, The.
Ritual, The.
Truant, The.

**Press, John**
Womanisers.

**Prettyman, Quandra**
Mood, The.
Photograph.
Still Life: Lady with Birds.
When Mahalia Sings.

**Prévert, Jacques**

Alicante.

**Price, E. Curmie**
Ballad of Bigger Thomas, The.

**Price, Jonathan**
* Considered Reply to a Child, A.
Ezra Pound.
Glaze, The. You try to see.
Nine meshes of the net enclose.
Test.

**Price, Nancy**
Harbor.

**Primrose, Lady Diana**
Chain of Pearl, A, *sel.*
Fourth Pearl, The: Temperance.

**Prince, Alison**
Dog howled and howled, The.

**Prince, Frank Templeton**
Question, The.
Soldiers Bathing.
Token, The.

**Prior, Matthew**
Another ("Yes, every poet is a fool").
Answer to Chloe Jealous.
Chaste Florimel.
Dutch Proverb, A.
Epigram: "To John I ow'd great obligation."
Fatal Love.
Great Bacchus: from the Greek.
Jinny the Just.
Letter to the Honourable Lady Miss Margaret Cavendish Holles-Harley, A.
To a Child of Quality [Five Years Old].
To Cloe Weeping.
True Maid, A.
Written in the Beginning of Mezeray's History of France.

**Pritchard, Norman Henry, II**
Aswelay.
Gyre's Galax.
Self.

**Pritchard, Sheila**
Some Kind of Giant.

**Pritzkow, Louis W.**
Take Back Your Gold, *with music.*

**Probst, Anita Endrezze**
Canto Llano.
Eclipse.
Exodus
In the Flight of the Blue Heron: To Montezuma.
Learning the Spells: A Diptych.
Manifest Destiny.
Notes from an Analyst's Couch.
Red Rock Ceremonies.
Stripper, The.
Truth about My Sister and Me, The.

**"Prout, Father."** *See* **Mahony, Francis Sylvester**

**Provisor, Dennis**
Walking through the Country.

**Pudney, John**
Aunts Watching Television.
Missing.

**Purdy, Alfred Wellington**
Cariboo Horses, The
Dead Seal.
Girl.
Nine Bean-Rows on the Moon.

**Pushkin, Aleksandr Sergeyevich**
I loved you; even now I may confess.

# Q

**Quarles, Francis**
Emblems,*sels.*
Epigram: "My Soul, sit thou a patient
  looker-on."
Epigram; "My soul, thy love is dear:
  'twas thought a good."
Epigram: "What makes thee, fool, so
  fat? Fool, thee so bare?"
History of Samson, The, *sel.*
My Beloved Is Mine and I Am His.
On the Infancy of Our Saviour.
On Those That Deserve It.
On Zacheus.
Why Dost Thou Shade Thy Lovely
  Face?
**Queremel, Angel Miguel**
Ballad of Love and Blood.
**Quirk, Cathleen**
Another Night on the Porch Swing.
Bird Calls.
Collaborations.
Composition.
"Hold Back the Edges of Your Gowns,
  Ladies, We Are Going through Hell."
Law of Falling and Catching Up, The.
Poem: "Crow flies between your phone
  and mine, The."

# R

**Raab, Lawrence**
Assassin's Fatal Error, The.
Attack of the Crab Monsters.
Pastoral: "Today in Peru, this first day
  of summer."
Visiting the Oracle.
Voices Answering Back: The Vampires.
**Radcliffe, Alexander**
Ramble, The: an Anti-Heroic Poem,
  *much abr.*
**Radcliffe, Anne**
Night.
Sonnet: "Now the bat circles on the
  breeze of eve."
Stanzas: "How smooth that lake expands
  its ample breast!"
**Rado, James and Gerome Ragni**
Air.
**Raftery, Anthony**
County Mayo, The.
I Am Raftery.
Lass from Bally-na-Lee, The.
**Raftery, Gerald**
Apartment House.
**Ragni, Gerome and James Rado.** *See*
  **Rado, James and Gerome Ragni**
**Rago, Henry**
Green Afternoon, The.
Knowledge of Light, The.
Summer Countries, The.
**Raine, Kathleen Jessie**
End of Love, The.
Envoi: "Take of me what is not my
  own."

Envoi: "What has want to give."
Human Form Divine, The ("The human
  contours are so easily lost.").
In Time.
Message from Home.
Rose.
To My Mountain.
Tu Non Se' in Terra, Si Come Tu Credi.
Two Invocations of Death.
Wilderness, The.
World, The.
Written in Exile.
**Rakosi, Carl**
Americana IX: "Your correspondent
  must be kidding when he says."
Americana XIII: "Captain Patterson, the
  folks back home."
Americana XV: Simplicity.
Americana XVII: Reminder of William
  Carlos Williams, A.
Country Singer, The.
Experiment with a Rat, The.
Medium IV, The: Sights.
Old Codger's Lament, The.
Young Couples Strolling By.
**Ralegh, Sir Walter**
Advice, The.
Epitaph: "Even such is Time, which
  takes in trust."
Excuse, The.
Farewell to False Love, A.
Heaven's Queene.
Lie, The.
Nymph's Reply to the Shepherd, The.
On the Life of Man.
Passionate Man's Pilgrimage, The.
Poem of Sir Walter Rawleighs, A.
Sir Walter Ralegh to the Queen.
To His Son.
Walter Rawely of the Middle Temple, in
  Commendation of the Steele Glasse.
What Is Our Life? A Play of Passion.
**Raleigh, Sir Walter Alexander (1861-1922)**
Wishes of an Elderly Man, The.
**"Ramal, Walter."** *See* **De la Mare, Walter**
**Ramanujan, A. K.**
River, A.
**Ramón Jiménez, Juan.** *See* **Jiménez, Juan
  Ramón**
**Ramsay, Allan**
Generous Gentleman, The.
**Ramsey, Patricia**
Anomie.
Creation, The.
Time, A: A Season.
War.
**Ramsey, Paul**
Marilyn Monroe.
Physical Imperfections of Old Films,
  The.
Willie Mays.
**Ranaivo, Flavien**
Song of a Common Lover.
**Randall, Dudley**
Abu.
Analysands.
Ancestors.
Ballad of Birmingham.
Black Magic.
Black Poet, White Critic.
Blackberry Sweet.
Booker T. and W. E. B.

Different Image, A.
George.
Hail, Dionysos.
Idiot, The.
Intellectuals, The.
Legacy: My South.
Melting Pot, The.
Memorial Wreath.
Old Witherington.
On Getting a Natural.
Pacific Epitaphs.
Primitives.
Profile on the Pillow, The.
Roses and Revolutions.
Southern Road, The.
Souvenirs.
**Randall, James A., Jr.**
Don't Ask Me Who I Am.
Execution.
Jew.
Untitled.
When Something Happens.
Who Shall Die?
**Randall, James Ryder**
Maryland, My Maryland!
**Randall, Julia**
For a Homecoming.
Rockland.
To William Wordsworth from Virginia.
Writer Indulges a Hobby, The
**Randolph, Thomas**
Invocation: "Come from thy palace,
  beauteous Queen of Greece."
Milkmaid's Epithalamium, The.
Phyllis.
Poet, The.
Upon His Picture.
**Rands, William Brighty**
Cat of Cats, The.
Dream of a Boy Who Lived at Nine
  Elms, The.
Dream of a Girl Who Lived at
  Sevenoaks, The.
Pedlar's Caravan, The.
Shooting Song, A.
Topsy-Turvy World.
White Princess, The, *sel.*
Winifred Waters.
World, The.
**Rankin, James**
Dustless Chalk.
Fair Isle Pattern.
Glasgow Botanic Gardens.
Grandpa.
Lamb.
Shetland funeral.
Won't Go to School.
**Rankin, Jeremiah Eames**
God Be with You Till We Meet Again,
  *with music.*
**Ransom, John Crowe**
Blue Girls.
Captain Carpenter.
Dead Boy.
Dog.
Equilibrists, The.
Here Lies a Lady.
Janet Waking.
Judith of Bethulia.
Master's in the Garden Again.

Necrological.
Old Mansion.
Painted Head.
Parting, without a Sequel.
Parting at Dawn.
Persistent Explorer.
Philomela.
Piazza Piece.
Spectral Lovers.
Survey of Literature.
Two in August.
Vaunting Oak.
Vision by Sweetwater.
Winter Remembered.

**Ransom, W. M.**
Catachism, 1958.
Critter.
Grandpa's .45.
Indian Summer: Montana, 1956.
Message from Ohanapecosh Glacier.
On the Morning of the Third Night
    above Nisqually.
Statement on Our Higher Education.

**Raphael, Lennox**
Mike 65.

**Ratcliffe, Dorothy Una**
Rake.

**Ratner, Rochelle**
Captive, The.
Tightrope Walker, The.

**Raven, John**
Assailant.
Inconvenience, An.
Roach, The.

**Ravenel, Beatrice**
Alligator, The.

**Raworth, Tom**
Here in Polynia.
Hot Day at the Races.
North Africa Breakdown.
Not under Holly or Green Boughs.
Six Days.
Sliding Two Mirrors.
There Are Lime Trees in Leaf on the
    Promenade.
You Were Wearing Blue.

**Ray, David**
Blue Duck, The.
Card-Players, The.
Death-Lace.
Greens.
Orphans.
Ravenna.
Stopping Near Highway 80.
Ursula.
W. C. W.
X-Ray.

**Read, Sir Herbert**
Execution of Cornelius Vane, The.
Harvest Home.
1945.
Waters of the well of life, The.    The
    Well of Life.
Well of Life, The.

**Read, Sylvia**
Monkey.
Weasel.

**Read, Thomas Buchanan**
Sheridan's Ride.

**Reaney, James**
Crow, The.
Katzenjammer Kids, The.

**Reavey, George**
Bridge of Heraclitus, The.
Never.

**Reavin, Sam**
Octopus.
Someone.
Witch?

**Rechter, Judith**
Fay Wray to the King.

**Red Cloud, Fred**
Machu Picchu, Peru.
Tale of Last Stands, A.

**Redding, Edward C.**
When the Saints Come Marching In,
    *with music.*

**Redgrove, Peter**
Bedtime Story for My Son.
Corposant.
Force, The.
Secretary, The.

**Redmond, Eugene**
Definition of Nature.
Gods in Vietnam.

**Redshaw, Thomas Dillon**
Voice from Danang.

**Reece, Byron Herbert**
Beetle in the Wood, The.

**Reed, Ed**
Key of the Kingdom, The.

**Reed, Henry**
Chard Whitlow.
Judging Distances.
Lessons of the War.
Morning.
Naming of Parts.

**Reed, Ishmael**
Al Capone in Alaska.
Badman of the Guest Professor.
Beware: Do Not Read This Poem.
Black Power Poem.
Feral Pioneers, The.
.05 (Five Cents).
Gangster's Death, The.
I Am a Cowboy in the Boat of Ra.
Instructions to a Princess.
Rain Rain on the Splintered Girl.
Sermonette.

**Reed, J. D.**
Cripples.
Gorilla at Twenty Nine Years, The.
Organ Transplant.
Out from Lobster Cove.
Stony Brook Tavern.
Strange Kind (II).

**Reeves, James**
Academic.
Bagatelle, A.
Beech Leaves.
Bobadil.
Castles and Candlelight.
Little Brother, The.
Magic Seeds, The.
Mick.
Old Wife and the Ghost, The.
Seeds.
Snail, The.
Spicer's Instant Poetry.
Stocking and Shirt.
Travelers, The.
Wind, The.
You in Anger.

**Reid, Alastair**

At First Sight.
Curiosity.
Daedalus.
Day the Weather Broke, The.
Figures on the Frieze, The.
Tale the Hermit Told, The.

**Reid, Christopher**
Gladstone gave his name to the
    gladstone bag.

**Reid, Keith**
She Wandered Through the Garden
    Fence.

**Reingold, Paula**
And This Is Love.

**Reiss, James**
Breathers, The.
First Poem, The.
Green Tree, The.
Habla Usted Español?
In One Battle.
Macy's Poem, The.
Morningside Hights: Fragment of a
    Film.
On Hot Days.
Slight Confusion, A.
Something Like an Apple.
Sueños.

**Reiter, Thomas**
Dinoland.

**Remaly, Nancy**
August Afternoon.

**Rendall, Robert**
Angle of Vision.

**Replansky, Naomi**
Brick not used in building, A.
Housing Shortage.
Two Women.

**Rexford, Eben Eugene**
Silver Threads among the Gold, *with
    music*

**Rexroth, Kenneth**
Andrée Rexroth.
Bad Old Days, The.
Dialogue of Watching, A.
Education.
For Mary.
Great Canzon, The.
Inversely, as the Square of Their
    Distances Apart.
Lights in the Sky Are Stars, The.
Lyell's Hypothesis Again.
Oh, who will shoe your pretty little foot.
Proust's Madeleine.
Strength Through Joy.
Time Is the Mercy of Eternity.
Vitamins and Roughage.
Wheel Revolves, The.
Yin and Yang.

**Reyes Basualto, Neftalí Ricardo.**  *See*
    "**Neruda, Pablo**"

**Reynolds, Barney**
Cranberry Song, The.

**Reynolds, Malvina**
What Have They Done to the Rain.

**Reynolds, Margaret**
Acceptance.
Eruption
Fear, The.
Naturalist, The.
Old Tiger and the God of the Water-
    hole, The.
Poverty.

Seventy.
**Reynolds, Tim**
  Going Home.
  Walk in March, A.
**Rezmerski, John Calvin**
  Driving at Night.
  Pettigrew Museum.
  Some Good Things Left after the War
    with the Sioux.
**Reznikoff, Charles**
  About an Excavation.
  After I Had Worked All Day.
  Autobiography: Hollywood.
  Citizen, A.
  Depression, *sel.*
  Five Groups of Verse,*sels.*
  Ghetto Funeral.
  Going To and Fro and Walking Up and
    Down, *sels.*
  Hebrew of Your Poets, Zion, The.
  How difficult for me is Hebrew.
  How Shall We Mourn You Who Are
    Killed and Wasted.
  I Will Go into the Ghetto.
  I Will Write Songs Against you.
  Kaddish: "In her last sickness, my
    mother took my hand in hers."
  Kaddish: "Upon Israel and upon the
    rabbis."
  Let Other People Come as Streams.
  New Year's.
  Puerto Ricans in New York, I.
  Puerto Ricans in New York, II.
  Samuel.
  Separate Way, *sel.*
  Showing a torn sleeve, with stiff and
    shaking fingers the old man.
  Simple soul, who so early in the
    morning.
  These Days the Papers in the Street.
  This Subway Station.
  Young fellow walks about, The
**Rhodes, Hugh**
  Rising in the Morning.
**Rice, Grantland**
  Any Golf Championship.
  Game Called.
  U. S. A., The.
**Rice, Seymour and Albert H. Brown**
  You Tell Me Your Dream, I'll Tell You
    Mine, *with music.*
**Rice, Stan**
  Waiting in the Cafe.
**Rice, Thomas D.**
  Jump Jim Crow, *with music.*
**Rich, Adrienne Cecile**
  Abnegation.
  After Dark.
  Afterwake, The.
  At a Bach Concert.
  Aunt Jennifer's Tigers.
  Autumn Sequence.
  Bears.
  Book, The.
  Burning of Paper Instead of Children,
    The.
  Clock in the Square, A.
  Demon Lover, The.
  Diving into the Wreck.

Double Monologue.
5:30 A.M.
Focus.
From a Survivor.
Gabriel.
Ghazals: Homage to Ghalib.
"I Am in Danger—Sir."
I Dream I'm the Death of Orpheus.
Ideal Landscape.
In the Woods.
Insusceptibles, The.
Knight, The.
Leaflets.
Like This Together.
Living in Sin.
Merced.
Mirror in Which Two Are Seen As One,
  The.
Necessities of Life.
Nightbreak.
Not Like That.
Novella.
November 1968.
On Edges.
Orion.
Picnic.
Pierrot le Fou.
Planetarium.
Primary Ground, A.
Prospective Immigrants Please Note.
Readings of History.
Roofwalker, The.
Side by Side.
Sisters.
Snapshots of a Daughter-in-Law.
Trees, The.
Trying to Talk with a Man.
Two Songs.
Unsaid Word, An.
Will to Change, The.
Woman Mourned by Daughters, A.
Women.
**Richard, Keith**   *See* **Jagger, Mick** *and*
  **Keith Richard**
**Richards, Laura Elizabeth**
  Bobbily Boo and Wollypotump.
  Eletelephony.
  Legend of Lake Okeefinokee, The.
  Mrs. Snipkin and Mrs. Wobblechin.
  My Uncle Jehoshaphat.
**Richardson, Justin**
  Oocuck, The.
**Rickword, Edgell**
  Encounter, The.
  Winter Warfare.
**Riddell, Alan**
  Circle, The.
**Riddell, Elizabeth**
  Letter, The.
**Ridge, Lola**
  Electrocution.
  Fifth-Floor Window, The.
  Reveille.
  Saint's Bridge.
  Song, The: "That day, in the slipping of
    torsos and straining flanks."
  Spring.
  Veteran.
  Ward X, *sel.*
**Riding, Laura (Laura Riding Jackson)**
  Auspice of Jewels.
  Because of Clothes.

Forgiven Past, The.
Map of Places, The.
Opening of Eyes.
With the Face.
**Ridland, John**
  Assassination Poems.
  Light Year, The.
  Week in Paradise, A.
**Ridler, Anne**
  Backgrounds to Italian Paintings:
    Fifteenth Century.
  Choosing a Name.
  For a Child Expected.
  Nothing Is Lost.
**Rieu, Emile Victor**
  Castaways, The.
  Cat's Funeral.
  Happy Hedgehog, The.
  Snake and the Snake-Charmer, The.
  Tony the Turtle.
  Two People.
**Rihaku.**   *See* **Li Po**
**Riley, James Whitcomb**
  Extremes.
  Little Orphant Annie.
  Old Man and Jim, The.
  Raggedy Man, The.
  When the Frost is on the Punkin.
**Rilke, Rainer Maria**
  Christ's Descent into Hell.
  Do you know, I would quietly.
  Foreboding.
  Last Supper, The.
  Lovesong.
  Pieta.
  Slumbersong.
**Rimbaud, Arthur**
  Dark and Wrinkled.
  Dreamed-Up for Winter.
**Rioff, Suzanne Berger**
  Cycles, Cycles.
  Seduction, A.
**Ritchie, Elisavietta**
  Curriculum Vitae: Incomplete.
  Dachau, Now: "Roses Grow There, Fat
    with Blood."
  Goals.
  Haiku: "This broken bottle."
  In Answer to a Request to Write a Poem
    on World Peace.
  In Jerusalem.
  Main Problem in Portraiture, The.
  Most Days.
  Search.
  Street Scenes from All Over.
  Tarred Gull.
  Visitation.
**Ritsos, Yannis**
  After the Rain.
  Motionless Swaying.
**Rivers, Conrad Kent**
  Death of a Negro Poet, The.
  Four Sheets to the Wind and a One-
    Way Ticket to France.
  If Blood Is Black Then Spirit Neglects
    My Unborn Son.
  In Defense of Black Poets.
  Mourning Letter from Paris, A.
  On the Death of William Edward

Burghardt Du Bois by African
   Moonlight and Forgotten Shores.
Prelude: "Night and the hood."
Still Voice of Harlem, The.
To Richard Wright.
Train Runs Late to Harlem, The.
Watts.
**Robbins, Martin**
On Seeing a Torn Out Coin Telephone.
**Roberson, Ed**
Blue Horses.
If the Black Frog Will Not Ring.
Mayday.
Othello Jones Dresses for Dinner.
Poll.
Seventh Son.
When Thy King Is a Boy, *sel.*
**Robert of Gloucester**
Chronicle, *sel.*
Town Against Gown at Oxford.
**Roberts, Elizabeth Madox**
Autumn.
Cold Fear.
Firefly.
Hens, The.
Little Bush.
Milking Time.
Numbers.
**Roberts, Michael**
H. M. S. *Hero.*
Hymn to the Sun.
**Roberts, Ursula.** *See* **Miles, Susan**
**Robertson, Robbie**
All La Glory.
**Robinson, Barbara B.**
Foreign Student.
**Robinson, Edwin Arlington**
Aaron Stark.
As It Looked Then.
Bewick Finzer.
Calvary.
Calverly's.
Cassandra.
Clerks, The.
Cliff Klingenhagen.
Companion, The.
Credo.
Dark Hills, The.
Eros Turannos.
Firelight.
Flammonde.
Flying Dutchman, The.
For a Dead Lady.
George Crabbe.
Hillcrest.
House on the Hill, The.
How Annandale Went Out.
John Gorham.
Karma.
Lost Anchors.
Luke Havergal.
Many Are Called.
Maya.
Mill, The.
Miniver Cheevy.
Mr. Flood's Party.
New England.
New Tenants, The.
Old Story, An.
Reuben Bright.
Reunion.
Richard Cory.

Sheaves, The.
Souvenir.
Supremacy.
Tact.
Vain Gratuities.
Veteran Sirens.
Why He Was There.
**Robinson, Lila Cayley**
Glow Worm, *with music.*
**Robinson, Robert**
Come, Thou Fount of Every Blessing,
   *with music.*
**Roche, James Jeffrey**
*Constitution's* Last Fight, The.
**Rochester, John Wilmot, 2nd Earl of**
Against Constancy.
Commons' Petition to Charles II, The.
Disabled Debauchee, The.
Epitaph on Charles II.
Fall, The: a Song.
Homo Sapiens.
Imperfect Enjoyment, The.
Impromptu on Charles II.
Letter from Artemisia in the Town to
   Cloe in the Country, A.
Love and Life.
Mistress, The.
Satire against Mankind, A.
Song, A: "Absent from thee, I languish
   still."
Song: "Give me leave to rail at you."
Song: "Love a woman? You're an ass!"
Song of a Young Lady to Her Ancient
   Lover, A.
To His Mistress.
Upon His Leaving His Mistress.
Upon Nothing.
Written in a Lady's Prayer Book.
**Rodger, Alex**
Twilight at the Zoo.
**Rodgers, Carolyn M.**
And While We Are Waiting.
Breakthrough.
For H. W. Fuller.
Greek Crazeology.
It Is Deep.
Jazz.
Jesus Was Crucified or: It Must Be
   Deep.
Look at My face, a Collage.
Me, in Kulu Se and Karma.
Missing Beat.
Newark, for Now (68).
Non Poem About Vietnam, A.
Now Ain't That Love?
One.
Phoenix.
Poem/ Ditty-Bop.
Proclamation/ From Sleep, Arise.
Rebolushinary X-mas.
Remember Times for Sandy.
Setting/ Slow Drag.
Somebody Call.
Testimony.
To the White Critics.
U Name This One.
Voodoo on the Un-Assing of Janis
   Joplin.
We Dance Like Ella Riffs.
What Color Is Lonely.
Yeah, I Is Uh Shootin Off at the Mouth.
Yuh Lookin Good.

**Rodgers, William Robert**
Armagh.
Christ Walking on the Water.
Field Day.
Fountains, The.
Irish Lake, An.
Last Word, A.
Lovers, The.
Net, The.
Party, The.
Swan, The.
White Christmas.
**Roethke, Theodore**
Another woman: a change of tears.
Apparition, The.
Bat, The.
Big Wind.
Ceiling, The.
Chair, The.
Child on Top of a Greenhouse.
Chums, The.
Cuttings ("Sticks-in-a-drowse droop over
   sugary loam").
Cuttings ("This urge, wrestle,
   resurrection of dry sticks").
Decision.
Deep in their roots, all flowers keep the
   light.
Dolor.
Donkey, The.
Elegy for Jane.
Elegy: "Her face like a rain-beaten stone
   on the day she rolled off."
Epidermal Macabre.
Exorcism, The.
Field of Light, A.
First Meditation.
Flower Dump.
Forcing House.
Four for Sir John Davies.
Frau Bauman, Frau Schmidt, and Frau
   Schwartze.
Geranium The.
Gnu, The.
Grandeurs of the crazy man alone, The.
Heard in a Violent Ward.
Her Reticence.
Her Words.
Heron, The.
Hippo, The.
I Knew a Woman.
I rasp like a sick dog.
I would be with the wind.
I'm Here.
I'm lost in my name.
In a Dark Time.
Journey to the Interior.
Lady and the Bear, The.
Lamb, The.
Light Listened.
Long Live the Weeds.
Longing, The.
Lost Son, The.
Meadow Mouse, The.
Meditations of an Old Woman, *sels.*
Minimal, The.
Moss-Gathering.
My Papa's Waltz.
Myrtle.
Night Crow.
Night Journey.
Old Florist.

Open House.
Orchids.
Pickle Belt.
Renewal, The.
Root Cellar.
Rose, The.
Serpent, The.
She.
Sloth, The.
Snake.
Song: "From whence cometh song?"
Storm, The.
Swan, The.
Transplanting.
Tree, the Bird, The.
Vernal Sentiment.
Visitant, The.
Voice, The.
Waking, The ("I strolled across/ An
    open field").
Waking, The ("I wake to sleep, and take
    my waking slow").
Weed Puller.
What Can I Tell My Bones?
Where Knock Is Open Wide.
Wish for a Young Wife.
Words for the Wind.
Yak, The.
Young Girl, The.
**Rogers, Del Marie**
Desert.
In the Mountain Cabin.
Photograph of the Back of My House.
War Requiem.
**Rogers, Robert Cameron**
Rosary, The, *with music.*
**Rogers, Ronald**
Kindergarten.
Taking Off.
**Rogers, Samuel**
Wish, A.
**Rolle of Hampole, Richard**
Love Is Life, *orig. and mod. English
    prose.*
**Ronksley, William**
To Cheer Our Minds.
**Ronsard, Pierre de**
Corinna in Vendome.
**Root, George Frederick**
Battle-Cry of Freedom, The.
Just Before the Battle, Mother, *with
    music.*
Rosalie, the Prairie Flower, *with music.*
Tramp! Tramp! Tramp! or, The
    Prisoner's Hope, *with music.*
**Root, William Pitt**
Fisherman.
House You Looked For, The.
Jellyfish, The.
Poetry and Revolution.
Stoplight.
**Roper, Renée**
Canibolos de la Montana.
Emma in My Third Eye.
Going Home.
**Roscoe, William**
Butterfly's Ball, The.
**Rose, Sir George**
Chancery Suit, A.
**Rose, Sir George and James Smith.** *See*
    **Smith, James and Sir George Rose**
**Rose, Wendy**

America.
Celebration for My Mother.
Epitaph: "Roots of mankind are tangled
    in my hair, The."
For My People.
For Steph.
For Walter Lowenfels.
Grunion.
Oh Father.
Oh My People I Remember.
Poem to a Redskin.
Saint Patrick's Day, 1973.
Self Dirge.
They Sometimes Call Me.
To an Imaginary Father.
**Rosen, Kenneth**
Abstinence.
Act, An.
Confab.
Girls.
**Rosenberg, Isaac**
August 1914.
Break of Day in the Trenches.
Louse Hunting.
**Rosenberg, Jim**
Richard Hofstadter and Michael
    Wallace, a Documentary History of
    American Violence.
**Rosenfeld, Monroe H. ("F. Belasco")**
Johnny Get Your Gun, *with music.*
Those Wedding Bells Shall Not Ring
    Out! *with music.*
**Rosenthal, Macha Louis**
Blue Boy on Skates (Twilight).
**Ross, Alan**
In Bloemfontein.
Koala.
Radar.
Stanley Matthews.
**Ross, Charles Henry**
Jack.
John, Tom, and James ("John was a bad
    boy").
Old Woman, An.
**Rossetti, Christina Georgina**
After Death.
All the bells were ringing.
Apple Gathering, An.
Birthday, A.
Bitter for Sweet.
Bride Song.
Caterpillar.
Christmas Carol, A: "In the bleak mid-
    winter."
Comparisons.
Crown of Windflowers, A.
Dirge, A: "Why were you born when the
    snow was falling?"
Echo.
End, An.
Ferry Me across the Water.
First Day, The.
Flint.
Frog and the Toad, The.
Frog's Fate, A.
From Sunset to Star Rise.
Fruits.
Goblin Market.
Good Friday.
Green Cornfield, A.
Half Moon Shows a Face of Plaintive
    Sweetness, The.

Hope and Joy.
Horses of the sea, The.
Hurt No Living Thing.
I do not look for love that is a dream.
In an Artist's Studio.
In Progress.
Irresponsive silence of the land, The.
Is the Moon Tired?
Italia, Io Ti Saluto.
Last Rites.
Marvel of Marvels.
Maude Clare.
May.
Meeting.
Mirage.
Mix a pancake.
Mona Innominata, *sels.*
None Other Lamb, None Other Name.
O Lady Moon.
Oh, Fair to See.
Old-World Thicket, An.
On the Death of a Cat.
On the Wing.
Passing Away.
Pause of Thought, A.
Poor Ghost, The.
Prince's Progress, The, *sel.*
Rainbow, The.
Remember.
Rest.
Riddle, A: "There is one that has a head
    without an eye."
Safe where I cannot lie yet.
Sleeping at Last.
Somewhere or Other.
Song: "She sat and sang alway."
Song: "When I am dead, my dearest."
Spring Quiet.
Start and Goal.
Summer.
Thread of Life, The, *sel.*
Twice.
Two Pursuits.
Up-Hill [*or* Uphill].
Valentines to My Mother, 1880.
What Are Heavy?
What Does the Bee Do?
What Is Pink?
Who Has Seen the Wind.
Who Shall Deliver Me?
Youth gone, and beauty gone if ever
    there.
**Rossetti, Dante Gabriel**
Alas, So Long!
Autumn Idleness.
Barren Spring.
Blessed Damozel, The.
Dark Glass, The.
Even So.
for "Our Lady of the Rocks."
Heart's Compass.
House of Life, The, *sels.*
Jenny.
Old Song Ended, An.
Paris Railway-Station, The.
Severed Selves.
Silent Noon.
Sonnet, A: "Sonnet is a moment's
    monument, A."
Sudden Light.
Superscription, A.
To Art.

Without Her.
Woodspurge, The.
**Rostand, Edmond**
Cyrano De Bergerac, *sel.*
**Rosten, Norman**
Nobody Dies Like Humphrey Bogart.
**"Rostrevor, George."**   See **Hamilton, George Rostrevor**
**Rothenberg, Jerome**
Poland/ 1931.
**Rottman, Larry**
What Kind of War?
**Rouget de Lisle, Claude Joseph**
Marseillaise, La, *with music.*
**Rounds, Emma**
Plane Geometry.
**Routhier, Adolphe**
O Canada! *with music.*
**Rowbotham, Colin**
Relative Sadness.
**Rowbotham, David**
Cliff, The.
E=mc²: Einstein at Princeton.
Los Alamos: Manhattan.
**Rowe, James**
Love Lifted Me, *with music.*
**Rowe, James Wilton**
Lake Chemo.
**Rowland, J. R.**
Cairo Hotel.
**Rowlands, Samuel**
Letting of Humour's Blood in the Head-Vein, The, *sels.*
Like Mistress, Like Maid.
Sir Eglamour.
**Rowley, Francis H.**
I Will Sing the Wondrous Story, *with music.*
**Rowley, William.**   See **Fletcher, John** *and* **William Rowley**
**Rowse, Alfred Leslie**
White Cat of Trenarren, The.
**Royde-Smith, Naomi Gwladys**
Horse, The.
**Rozewicz, Tadeusz**
Leave Us Alone.
To the Heart.
**Ruark, Gibbons**
Finding the Pistol.
1965.
Slowness ("Slowness, says Rodin, is beauty").
**Ruby, Kathryn**
Banker's Daughter, The.
Portrait of a Woman.
Pygmalion.
**Rückert, Friedrich ("Freimund Raimar")**
And Then No More.
**Rudnick, Raphael**
Penny Trumpet.
**Rufinus Domesticus**
Aut Neutrum . . . Vel Duos.
Complaint.
**Ruggles, Eugene**
Beginning Again As Morning.
God.
**Ruggles, William B.**
Pioneer, The.
**Rukeyser, Muriel**
Are You Born?—I.
Boy with His Hair Cut Short.
Despisals.

Easter Eve.
Effort at Speech between Two People.
Käthe Kollwitz.
Little Stone in the Middle of the Road, in Florida, A.
Mrs. Walpurga.
More Clues.
More of a Corpse Than a Woman. .
Myth.
Night Feeding.
Poem as Mask, The.
Poem Out of Childhood.
Question, The.
Speaking Tree, The.
Speed of Darkness, The.
This Morning.
Woman as Market.
**Runyon, Damon (Alfred Damon Runyon)**
Babe Ruth.
Pool-Shootin' Roy.
**Ruse, Peggy**
Pittsburgh.
View of Vienna from Schonbrunn.
Visit to My Father-In-Law on Memorial Day, A.
**Russell, Ethel Green**
Gathering Gems.
Hunchback Pine.
Letter to Her Son's Commanding Officer.
Maple in November.
**Russell, George William.**   See **Æ**
**Russell, James I.**
Where the River Shannon Flows, *with music.*
**Russell, Norman H.**
Clerk's Song II.
Eyes of the Child Do Not See Me, The.
Great Way of the Man, The.
Indian School.
World Has Many Places Many Ways, The.
**Ryan, Margaret**
Dreams of Eurydice.
Whistler's Father.
**Ryan, Michael**
Barren Poem.
Hitting Fungoes.
Letter from an Institution: III.
Prothalamion.
Speaking.
This Is a Poem for the Dead.
Your Own Image.
**Ryan, Richard**
Deafness.
El Dorado.
Thrush's Nest, The.

# S

**Sackville, Charles, 6th Earl of Dorset**
Dainty young heiress of Lincoln's Inn Fields, The.
Song Written at Sea in the First Dutch War.
To Mr. Edward Howard, on His Plays.
**Sackville, Thomas, 1st Earl of Dorset**
Shield of War, The.

Thomas Sackevyll in Commendation of the Worke to the Reader.
**Sackville-West, Victoria Mary (Mrs. Harold Nicolson)**
Aquarium, San Francisco, The.
Black Tarn.
Bull, The.
Craftsmen.
On the Lake.
Owl, The.
Persia.
Sea-Sonnet.
Sometimes When Night.
To Any M. F. H.
Young Stock.
**Sadoff, Ira**
Concise History of the World, A.
Fifties, The.
My Father's Leaving.
Poem after Apollinaire.
**Safka, Melanie**
I Don't Eat Animals (And They Don't Eat Me.)
**"Sagittarius" (Olga Katzin)**
Nerves.
**St. Cyr, Napoleon**
All Men Are . . . Socrates Is.
Artery of the Sea.
Friend with Spinning Rod.
Leaving the Flag Out All Night.
Oriental.
**"Saint Geraud."**   See **Knott, William.**
**St. John, David**
For Lerida.
Poem: "Your face,/so pale now it is blue."
Slow Dance.
**St. John, Justin**
Hard Chesse.
**St. John, Primus**
Benign Neglect/ Mississippi, 1970.
Elephant Rock.
Lynching and Burning.
Morning Star, The.
Tyson's Corner.
**St. Leger, Warham**
False Gallop of Analogies, A.
**Sainte-Marie, Buffy**
My Country 'Tis of Thy People You're Dying.
Now That the Buffalo's Gone.
**Sakanoe, Lady Otomo No**
You say, "I will come."
**Saleh, Dennis**
Bed, The.
Furniture of the Poem, The.
Guide to Familiar American Incest, A, *sel.*
Inventing a Family.
Nesting.
Return, The.
Story.
Thumb, The.
**Salinas, Luis Omar**
Barefoot.
For the Waiter at Jhonny Pavlovs.
Happiness Is a Charlie Chaplin Movie.
Ode to a Violin.
Ode to Mexican Experience.
Señor Torres.
This is Not a Poem.
Tihuitkli.

What a Way to Lose the War.
Whats My Name if Not Everyone Elses.
**Sammis, J. H.**
Trust and Obey, *with music.*
**Sanchez, Sonia**
Answer to Yo/ Question.
Black Magic.
Chant for Young/Brothas and Sistuhs, A.
Definition for Blk/ Children.
For Our Lady.
Homecoming.
Hospital/ Poem.
Listenen to Big Black at S. F. State.
Nigger.
Now Poem. For Us.
Personal Letter No. 2.
Poem at Thirty.
Poem for Etheridge.
Poem for My Father, A.
Poem: "I've been a woman."
Poem: "Look at me 8th."
Poem: "When he came home."
Poem: "Yo/ smile."
Right On: White America.
Summary.
Summer Words of a Sistuh Addict.
Three X Three.
To All Brothers.
To All Sisters.
Why.
**Sandburg, Carl**
Aprons of Silence.
Baby Toes.
Bilbea
Buffalo Dusk.
Cheap Rent.
Cheer Leader, The.
Chicago.
Child of the Romans.
Cool Tombs.
Crapshooters.
Death Snips Proud Men.
Dinosaur Bones, The.
Early Copper.
Elm Buds.
Explanations of Love.
Finale.
Fog ("The fog comes/ on little cat feet").
Four Preludes on Playthings of the Wind.
Fourth of July Night.
Gargoyle.
Gone.
Good Morning America, sel.
Grass.
Grassroots.
Hangman at Home, The.
Happiness.
Harbor, The.
Hits and Runs.
Illinois Farmer.
Improved Farm Land.
Laughing Child.
Limited.
Little Girl Saw Her First Troop Parade, The.
Losers.
Love in Labrador.
Muckers.
Mysterious Biography.

New Farm Tractor.
Old Timers.
On a Flimmering Floom You Shall Ride.
Paper II.
People, Yes, The, sels.
Potomac Town in February.
Prairie, sel.
Prayer after World War.
Primer Lesson.
River Roads.
Sins of Kalamazoo, The.
Skyscrapers Stand Proud.
Soup.
Splinter.
Street Window.
Summer Stars.
Ten Definitions of Poetry.
Theme in Yellow.
They All Want To Play Hamlet.
Upstream.
Useless Words.
Washington Monument by Night.
We Must Be Polite, sel.
Webs.
Why Did the Children Put Beans in Their Ears?
Wilderness.
**Sandburg, Helga**
Importance of Mirrors, The.
**Sandeen, Ernest**
Mail from Home in the Sky.
Views of Our Sphere.
**Sanders, Morgan**
Beverly Fragments.
Looking for Lola.
"Many Brave Hearts Are Asleep in the Deep."
**Sandy, Stephen**
Ballad of Mary Baldwin, The.
**Sange, Gary**
Drive In Movie.
Lighthouse Keeper.
Separation.
Truckdriver.
**Sangster, Margaret Elizabeth Munson (1838-1912)**
Sin of Omission, The.
**Sannazaro, Jacopo (Actius Sincerus Sannazarius)**
Like to these unmesurable montayns.
**Sansom, Clive**
Butterflies.
"Dorset Nose," The.
Font, The.
Schoolmistress.
**Santayana, George**
On the Death of a Metaphysician.
**Sappho**
I begin with words of air but delightful ones.
Ode to Anactoria.
Sleep, Darling.
Tonight I've watched.
**Sarett, Lew**
Four Little Foxes.
**Sargent, Elizabeth Nancy**
Sailor at Midnight, A.
Young Lover, A.
**Sargent, Epes**
Death of Warren, The.
Life on the Ocean Wave, A, *with music.*

**Saroyan, Aram**
Crickets.
**Sarton, May**
At Lindos.
Baroque Image.
Invocation to Kali, The, sels.
Kingdom of Kali, The.
Summer Music.
Village Tale, A.
**Sassoon, Siegfried**
At Max Gate.
Attack.
Base Details.
Does It Matter?
Dreamers.
Effect, The.
Everyone Sang ("Everyone suddenly burst out singing").
Faith Unfaithful.
Falling Asleep.
Fathers, The.
General, The.
In the National Gallery.
Investiture, The.
Post-Mortem, A.
Rear-Guard, The.
Repression of War Experience.
Sporting Acquaintances.
To His Dead Body.
Two Old Ladies.
**Sawyer, C. P.**
I Used to Love My Garden.
**Saxe, John Godfrey**
Blind Men and the Elephant, The.
Puzzled Census Taker, The.
Sonnet to a Clam.
Youth and the Northwind, The.
**Sáxon, Alvin (Ojenke)**
Black Power.
Poem for Integration, A.
Watts.
**Sayers, Henry J.**
Ta-ra-ra Boom-der-é, *with music.*
**Sayles, James M.**
Star of the Evening.
**Scannell, Vernon**
Act of Love
Ageing Schoolmaster, An.
Any Complaints?
Autobiographical Note.
Autumn.
Gunpowder Plot.
Hide and Seek.
Tightrope Walker.
**Scarfe, Francis**
Cats.
Cat's Eyes.
**Schaeffer, Susan Fromberg**
First Test, The.
Housewife.
Truth.
Womb Song.
**Schaff, David**
Memoir.
**Schechter, Ruth Lisa**
And We Are Strangers to Each Other.
"Terre des Hommes."
What Is There?
**Schevill, James**
Between the Electric Rhythm and the Melodic Mind.
**Schiller, Johann Christoph Friedrich von**

Columbus.
Homeric Hexameter Described and
Exemplified, The.
Ovidian Elegiac Metre Described and
Exemplified, The.
**Schindler, Paul, Bob Adams** and **David
Lewis.** *See* **Lewis, David, Paul
Schindler** and **Bob Adams**
**Schjeldahl, Peter**
Citizen.
Flower.
La Vie En Rose.
**Schmidt, Michael**
Underwater.
**Schmidt, Tom**
Black and White.
Butcherboy.
Butter.
Civilization.
Creeper, The.
Drowning in Spanish.
In the Garden.
Long Overdue Thankyou Note to the
Girl Who Taught Me Loving, A.
Seven Mexican Children.
**Schmitz, Dennis**
California Phrasebook, The.
Chicago: Near West-Side Renewal.
Eclogues.
Goodwill, Inc.
If I Could Meet God.
Mole, The.
Name of Our Country, The.
Poke-Pole Fishing.
Rabbit Leaves, The.
Rabbits.
**Schuyler, James**
December.
Head, A.
Quick, Henry, the Flit!
Sorting, Wrapping, Packing, Stuffing.
Stun.
**Schwartz, Delmore**
Baudelaire.
Beautiful American Word, Sure, The.
Dogs Are Shakespearean, Children Are
Strangers.
Far Rockaway.
For the One Who Would Take Man's
Life in His Hands.
Heavy Bear Who Goes with Me, The.
In the Naked Bed, in Plato's Cave.
Journey of a Poem Compared to all the
Sad Variety of Travel, The.
Mind Is an Ancient and Famous
Capital, The.
Small Score, A.
Time's Dedication.
Will you perhaps consent to be.
Winter Twilight, Glowing Black and
Gold, The.
**Schwartz, Howard**
Containment.
Love Poem: "She coils her body around
me."
Maps.
**Scott, Alexander (1520? - 1590?)**
Lament of the Master of Erskine.
Returne Thee, Hairt.
Rondel of Love [or Luve], A.
To Luve Unluvit.
**Scott, Alexander (b. 1920)**

Continent o Venus.
**Scott, Clement William**
Oh, Promise Me, *with music.*
**Scott, Dennis**
Epitaph: "They hanged him on a
clement morning, swung."
**Scott, Duncan Campbell**
Forsaken, The.
**Scott, Francis Reginald**
MD Sewed Wrong Section of Colon.
**Scott, Herbert**
That summer nothing would do.
**Scott, John, of Amwell.** *See* **Scott of
Amwell, John**
**Scott, Lady John**
Ettrick.
**Scott, Lady John** and **William Douglass.**
*See* **Douglass, William** and **Lady John
Scott**
**Scott, Sharon**
Between Me and Anyone Who Can
Understand.
Come on Home.
Discovering.
For Both of Us at Fisk.
Just Taking Note.
Little More About the Brothers and
Sisters, A.
Mama Knows.
Oh---Yeah!
Okay.
On My Stand.
Our Lives.
Sharon Will Be No/ Where on Nobody's
Best-Selling List.
**Scott, Tom**
To X.
**Scott, Virginia**
Elegy: "My mother in the witness box."
President says, The/eat fish.
What is to be done.
**Scott, Sir Walter**
Allen-a-Dale.
Bonnie Dundee.
Bride of Lammermoor, The, *sel.*
Doom of Devergoil, The, *sel.*
From the French.
Gathering Song of Donald the Black.
Heart of Midlothian, The, *sel.*
Hour with Thee, An.
Lady of the Lake, The, *sel.*
Lay of the Last Minstrel, The, *sel.*
Lochinvar.
Lord of the Isles, The, *sel.*
Lucy Ashton's Song.
Lullaby of an Infant Chief.
Maid of Neidpath, The.
Marmion, *sel.*
Nora's Vow.
Patriotism.
Proud Maisie.
Rokeby,*sels.*
Rover's Farewell, The.
Soldier, Rest!
Then Strip Lads, and To It.
This Is My Own, My Native Land.
Woman's Faith.
**Scott, Winfield Townley**
Five for the Grace of Man.
Mr. Whittier.
O Lyric Love.
**Scott** and **Textor**

Air Force Blue, The, *with music.*
**Scott-Gatty, Sir Alfred.** *See* **Gatty, Sir
Alfred Scott**
**Scott of Amwell, John**
Drum, The.
**Scovell, E. J.**
After Midsummer.
Alone.
Betrothal, A.
In a Wood.
Love's Immaturity.
Swan's Feet, The.
**Scriven, Joseph**
What a Friend We Have in Jesus, *with
music.*
**Seager, Francis**
Prayer to Be Said When Thou Goest to
Bed, A.
**Sears, Edmund Hamilton**
It Came upon a Midnight Clear, *with
music.*
**Seay, James**
No Man's Good Bull.
**Sebenthall, R. E.**
Old Ones, The.
Villages, The.
**Sedley, Sir Charles**
Advice to the Old Beaux
On a Cock at Rochester.
Phyllis Knotting.
Song: "Love still has something of the
sea."
To Celia.
To Cloris ("Cloris, I cannot say your
eyes").
**Sedulius Scottus**
Apologia pro Vita Sua.
Easter Sunday.
**Seeger, Alan**
I Have a Rendezvous with Death.
**Seeger, Pete**
Turn! Turn! Turn!
Where Have All the Flowers Gone?
**Seeger, Pete** and **Idris Davies.** *See* **Davies**
**Seferis, George**
Mythistorema.
**Seibert, T. Lawrence**
Casey Jones ("Come, all you rounders, if
you want to hear").
**Seidman, Hugh**
Drop the Wires.
Great Nebula in Andromeda, The.
Making of Color, The.
Science As Art.
Tale of Genji.
**Sellar, Walter Carruthers** and **Robert
Julian Yeatman.** *See*Yeatman, Robert
Julian** and **Walter Carruthers Sellar**
**Sen, Pradip**
Man on My Back, The.
**Seneca (Lucius Annaeus Seneca)**
Thyestes, *sel.*
**Senghor, Léopold Sédar**
Totem.
**Senior, Charles**
Island Letter.
Poem: "Always loving or blithe."
Poem While Reading "The Naked
Lunch" by William Burroughs.
Primula Scotica.
Tutsan.
Verses on a Rose Street Muse.

**Serin, Judith**
Orange Tree Dream.
Sheep on these hills, The.
Sock left by the road, A.
**Serraillier, Ian**
After Ever Happily.
Anne and the Field-Mouse.
Helicopter, The.
**Serrano, Nina**
To R——Before Leaving to Fight in
Unknown Terrain.
**Service, Robert William**
Cremation of Sam McGee, The.
Ordinary Man, The.
Reckoning, The.
**Severy, Bruce**
Crossing into the Prairies.
Deserted Farms Poem.
Finally.
First and Last.
Frames on Bright Faces.
Opening Day.
Poems.
Struggle for the Roads.
Talks with Himself.
**Seward, Anna**
True Cat, A.
**Sexton, Anne**
Abortion, The.
Addict, The
All My Pretty Ones.
Barefoot.
Black Art, The.
Christmas Eve.
Cinderella.
Consorting with Angels.
Crossing the Atlantic.
December 18th.
Eighteen Days without You, sel.
Farmer's Wife, The.
For Eleanor Boylan Talking with God.
For God while Sleeping.
For My Lover, Returning to His Wife.
Her Kind.
Housewife.
In Celebration of My Uterus.
In the Beach House.
In the Deep Museum.
Knee Song.
Lament: "Someone is dead."
Little Girl, My String Bean, My Lovely
Woman.
Love Song.
Lullaby: "It is a summer evening."
Man and Wife.
Menstruation at Forty.
Moon Song, Woman Song.
Moss of His Skin, The.
Mothers.
Mr. Mine.
Nude Swim, The.
Rapunzel.
Ringing the Bells.
Said the Poet to the Analyst.
Starry Night, The.
Sylvia's Death.
That Day.
Truth the Dead Know, The.
Unknown Girl in the Maternity Ward.
Us.
Wanting to Die.
With Mercy for the Greedy.

Woman with Girdle.
You, Doctor Martin.
You All Know the Story of the Other
Woman.
Young.
**Seymour-Smith, Martin**
What Schoolmasters Say.
**Shadwell, Thomas**
Medal of John Bays, The: A Satire
against Folly and Knavery, sel.
Timon of Athens, the Man-hater, sel.
**Shakespeare, William**
All the world's a stage.
Anthony and Cleopatra, sel.
Ariel's Song: "Come unto these yellow
sands."
Ariel's Song: "Where the bee sucks,
there suck I."
As You Like It, sels.
At the Moated Grange.
Autolycus Sings.
Autolycus' Song ("Jog on, jog on . . .").
Blow, Blow, Thou Winter Wind!
Come away, come away, death.
Courser and Jennet.
Crabbed Age and Youth.
Cymbeline, sels.
Death of Kings, The.
Dirge for Fidele.
Fear No More the Heat o' the Sun.
Feste's Song ("O mistress mine").
Full Fathom Five Thy Father Lies.
Hamlet, sels.
Hark! hark! the lark at heaven's gate
sings.
It Was a Lover, and His Lass.
King Henry V, sels.
Let it be so; thy truth then be thy
dower.
Lover's eyes will gaze an eagle blind, A.
Love's Labour's Lost, sels.
Lunatic, the Lover, and the Poet, The.
Macbeth, sels.
Measure for Measure, sel.
Merchant of Venice, The, sels.
Midsummer Night's Dream, A, sel.
Much Ado about Nothing, sel.
Ophelia's Song.
Othello, sels.
Outcry upon Opportunity, An.
Phoenix and the Turtle, The.
Puck's Night Song ("Now the hungry
lion").
Quality of Mercy, The.
Romeo and Juliet, sels.
She should have died hereafter.
Sigh no more, ladies, sigh no more.
Some say that ever 'gainst that season
comes.
Song: "Hark, hark!/ Bow-wow."
Sonnet: "As an unperfect actor on the
stage."
Sonnet: "Being your slave, what should
I do but tend."
Sonnet: "Devouring Time, blunt thou
the lion's paws."
Sonnet: "Expense of spirit in a waste of
shame, The."
Sonnet: "Farewell! thou art too dear for
my possessing."
Sonnet: "From you have I been absent
in the spring."

Sonnet: "Full many a glorious morning
have I seen."
Sonnet: "How like a winter hath my
absence been."
Sonnet: "How oft when thou, my music,
music play'st."
Sonnet: "If thy soul check thee that I
come so near."
Sonnet: "Let me not to the marriage of
true minds."
Sonnet: "Like as the waves make
towards the pebbled shore."
Sonnet: "Lo, as a careful housewife runs
to catch."
Sonnet: "Love is too young to know
what conscience is."
Sonnet: "My mistress' eyes are nothing
like the sun."
Sonnet: "No longer mourn for me when
I am dead."
Sonnet: "Not marble, not the gilded
monuments."
Sonnet: "Not mine own fears nor the
prophetic soul."
Sonnet: "O! Never say that I was false
of heart."
Sonnet: "Poor soul, the center of my
sinful earth."
Sonnet: "Shall I compare thee to a
summer's day?"
Sonnet: "Since brass, nor stone, nor
earth, nor boundless sea."
Sonnet: "That time of year thou mayst
in me behold."
Sonnet: "Then hate me when thou wilt;
if ever, now."
Sonnet: "They that have power to hurt
and will do none."
Sonnet: "Thy bosom is endearèd with all
hearts."
Sonnet: "Tired with all these, for restful
death I cry."
Sonnet: "To me, fair friend, you never
can be old."
Sonnet: "Two loves have I of comfort
and despair."
Sonnet: "Unthrifty loveliness, why dost
thou spend."
Sonnet: "When I do count the clock that
tells the time."
Sonnet: "When I have seen by Time's
fell hand defaced."
Sonnet: "When in disgrace with fortune
and men's eyes."
Sonnet: "When in the chronicle of
wasted time."
Sonnet: "When my love swears that she
is made of truth."
Sonnet: "When to the sessions of sweet
silent thought."
Sonnet: "Whoever hath her wish, thou
hast thy Will."
Sonnets, sel.
Spring.
This England ("This royal throne of
kings, this sceptered isle").
Thrice the brinded cat hath mew'd.
Thus have I shunned the fire for fear of
burning.
Tomorrow Is Saint Valentine's Day.
Twelfth Night, sels.
Two Gentlemen of Verona, The, sel.

Under the Greenwood Tree.
Venus and Adonis,*sels.*
When that I was and a little tiny boy.
Winter.
You spotted snakes with double tongue.
**Shakespeare, William** *and others.*
Passionate Pilgrim, The, *sels.*
**Shanks, Edward**
Going in to Dinner.
**Shapcott, Thomas William**
August Fugue.
Finches, The.
In Memory of Francis Webb.
June Fugue.
March Fugue.
**Shapiro, Harvey**
Feast of the Ram's Horn.
Glory.
Mountain, Fire, Thornbush.
National Cold Storage Company.
Past Time.
**Shapiro, Karl**
All Tropic Places Smell of Mold.
Alphabet, The.
Aubade: "What dawn is it?"
Auto Wreck.
Boy-Man.
Dark Exciting Days, The.
Dirty Word, The.
Dome of Sunday, The.
Drug Store.
Elegy for a Dead Soldier, *sel.*
Epitaph: "Underneath this wooden cross
   there lies."
First Time, The.
Fly, The.
Hospital.
In the Second-Best Hotel in Tokyo.
Interlude.
Jew at Christmas Eve, The.
Lower the Standard: That's My Motto.
Manhole Covers.
My Grandmother.
Poet.
Quintana Lay in the Shallow Grave of
   Coral.
There is Gray in My Eyebrows.
University.
V-Letter.
**Sharp, Martin.** *See* **Clapton, Eric** *and*
   **Martin Sharp**
**Sharpe, Richard Scrafton**
Country Mouse and the City Mouse,
   The.
**Shaw, David T.**
Columbia, the Gem of the Ocean.
**Shaw, Dorothy Stott**
Caprice.
**Shaw, Knowles**
Bringing in the Sheaves, *with music.*
**Shaw, Luci**
Blindfold.
But Not Forgotten.
Of Consolation.
Royalty.
Tithes.
Triptych.
**Shegonee, Loyal**
Loneliness.
**Shelley, Martha**
After Reading *The First Circle.*
Note to a New Lesbian.

Round Trip to Chicago.
Transparent Closet, The.
**Shelley, Percy Bysshe**
Adonais: an Elegy on the Death of John
   Keats.
Alastor; or, The Spirit of Solitude.
Arethusa.
Asia's Song.
Autumn; A Dirge.
Cenci, The.
Cloud, The.
Dirge, A: "Rough wind, that moanest
   loud."
Dirge for the Year.
England in 1819.
Epipsychidion.
Evening: Ponte a Mare, Pisa.
Evening: to Harriet
Exhortation, An.
Feelings of a Republican on the Fall of
   Bonaparte.
Fragment: To Byron.
Hate-Song, A.
Hell is a city much like London.
Hellas, *sels.*
Hymn of Apollo.
Hymn of Pan.
Hymn to Intellectual Beauty.
I met Murder on the way.
Indian Serenade, The.
Julian and Maddalo.
Lament, A: "O world! O life! O time!"
Letter to Maria Gisborne.
Liberty.
Life Rounded with Sleep.
Lines to a Critic.
Lines: "We meet not as we parted."
Lines Written Among the Euganean
   Hills.
Lines Written in the Bay of Lerici.
Lines Written on Hearing the News of
   the Death of Napoleon.
Love.
Love's Philosophy.
Mask of Anarchy, The.
Monarch's Funeral, The.
Mont Blanc.
Mourn Not for Adonais.
Mutability ("The flower that smiles to-
   day").
Mutability ("We are as clouds that veil
   the midnight moon.")
Ode to a Skylark.
Ode to Liberty.
Ode to Naples.
Ode to the West Wind.
Oedipus Tyrannus; or, Swellfoot the
   Tyrant.
On a Painted Woman.
On Keats.
On Leaving London for Wales.
Ozymandias.
Peter Bell the Third.
Prometheus Unbound.
Question, The ("I dream'd that, as I
   wander'd by the way").
Rain.
Sensitive Plant, The.
Similes for Two Political Characters of
   1819.
Solitary, The.
Song: "Rarely, rarely, comest thou."

Song: "Widow bird sate mourning for
   her love, A."
Song to the Men of England.
Sonnet: "Lift not the painted veil which
   those who live."
Sonnet on Launching Some Bottles
   Filled with Knowledge into the Bristol
   Channel.
Sonnet: Political Greatness.
Sonnet To Byron.
Sonnet to Harriet on Her Birthday.
Stanzas, Written in Dejection, near
   Naples.
To——: "Cold earth slept below, The."
To——: "Music, when soft voices die."
To——: "Oh! There are spirits of the
   air."
To——: "One word is too often
   profaned."
To——: "When passions's trance is
   overpast."
To a Skylark.
To Constantia Singing.
To Death.
To Edward Williams.
To Harriet ("Harriet! thy kiss to my soul
   is dear").
To Harriett ("Thy look of love has
   power to calm").
To Jane: the Invitation.
To Jane: the Recollection.
To Maria Gisborne in England, from
   Italy.
To Night.
To the Lord Chancellor.
To the Moon.
To the Republicans of North America.
To Wordsworth.
Triumph of Life, The.
Two Spirits, The: an Allegory.
Waning Moon, The.
When the Lamp Is Shattered.
Witch of Atlas, The.
With a Guitar, to Jane.
World's great age begins anew, The.
Worlds on worlds are rolling ever.
Ye Hasten to the Grave!
**Shelton, Peter**
Singing.
**Shelton, Richard**
Children of Night.
**Shenstone, William**
School-Mistress, The.
Written at an Inn at Henley.
**Sheridan, Caroline Elizabeth Sarah.** *See*
   **Norton, Caroline Elizabeth Sarah**
   **Sheridan**
**Sheridan, Helen Selina, Lady Dufferin**
Charming Woman, The.
**Sheridan, Michael**
Grace.
**Sheridan, Richard Brinsley**
Geranium, The.
**Sherman, Jane**
Night Storm.
**Sherwin, Judith Johnson**
Construction #13.
Dr. Potatohead Talks to Mothers.
Earth, The: To Marilyn.
Eat 'Em Up Smith Tells All in South
   Africa.
Lights, Flowers.

Nightpiece.
What Maisie Know She Don't Want No.
**Shields, Ren**
In the Good Old Summertime, *with music.*
**Shiffert, Edith Marcombe**
Manners.
Monkeys on Mt. Hiei.
Shadow of a Branch, The.
**Shine, Carol**
What's in a Word?
**Shipley, Sir Arthur**
Ere You Were Queen of Sheba.
**Shipman, Thomas**
Resolute Courtier, The.
**Shirley, James**
Contention of Ajax and Ulysses, The, *sel.*
Cupid's Call.
Death the Leveller.
Glories of Our Blood and State, The.
Imposture, The, *sel.*
Piping Peace.
**Sholé, Mba**
Fish Does . . . Hip! The.
**Short, Clarice**
Imperfect Sympathies.
Old One and the Wind, The.
Taking Leave of the Old.
**Short, John**
Carol: "There was a boy bedded in bracken."
**Shumway, Mary**
Before the Dark is Down.
Cattails for Bennett.
Flight.
Gooseberry Wine.
Passage.
River Road.
Whether Firelocked.
**Shuttleworth, P. N.**
Wykehamist's Address to Learning, A.
**"Shy, Timothy."** *See* **Lewis, Dominic Bevan Wyndham**
**Sidney, Mary, Countess of Pembroke.** *See* **Pembroke, Mary Sidney Herbert, Countess of**
**Sidney, Sir Philip**
Arcadia, *sels.*
Astrophel and Stella.
Bargain, The.
Desire.
Farewell, A: "Oft have I mused, but now at length I find."
Fourth Song.
Lady My Treasure.
Leave Me, O Love.
Philomela.
Ring out your bells, let mourning shows be spread.
Sestina: "Farewell, Oh sun, Arcadia's clearest light."
Sleep, baby mine, Desire, nurse Beauty singeth.
Thou Blind Man's Mark.
To the Sad Moon.
Voices at the Window.
When Two Suns Do Appear.
With How Sad Steps, O Moon, Thou Climb'st the Skies.
Ye goat-herd gods that love the grassy mountains.

**Siegel, Robert**
Ego.
Mad Dog.
Nude.
Poet.
**Silbert, Layle**
Breathe In Breathe Out.
Good Morning.
Relicts.
**Silkin, Jon**
Death of a Bird.
Death of a Son.
Furnished Lives.
Light.
Lilies of the Valley.
Reclaimed Area.
Respectabilities.
Shirt, The.
**Silko, Leslie**
Indian Song: Survival.
Poem for Ben Barney.
Prayer to the Pacific.
Toe'osh: A Laguna Coyote Story.
**Sillitoe, Alan**
Picture of Loot.
**Sills, Stephen, David Crosby** *and* **Paul Kantner.** *See* **Crosby, David, Paul Kantner** *and* **Stephen Sills**
**Silverman, Stuart**
Game, The.
Garden, The.
**Silvers, Frances**
Frankie Silvers.
**Silverstein, Shel**
Beware, My Child.
Boa Constrictor.
For Sale.
Hector the Collector.
Jimmy Jet and His TV Set.
**Silverton, Michael**
Adorable paratroopess alights, The.
I am yours and you are mine so.
**Simcock, Jack**
To My Wife.
**Simic, Charles**
Bestiary for the Fingers of My Right Hand.
Bird, The.
Bones.
Brooms.
Butcher Shop.
Errata
Fork.
George Simic.
Partial Explanation, The.
Poem: "Every morning I forget how it is."
Poverty.
Psalm.
Starry Sky.
Tale, The.
Tapestry.
Wind, The.
**Simmons, Gary**
Some Thoughts.
**Simmons, James**
Cavalier Lyric.
Experience.
For Delphine.
Goodbye, Sally.
Reformer to His Father, A.
Summing Up, The.

**Simon, John Oliver**
Don't Tell Bad Dreams Says Tita's Mother.
For Alan Blanchard.
Living in the Boneyard.
Tryptych for Jan Bockelson, A.
Vanish.
Woodchuck Who Lives on Top of Mt. Ritter.
**Simon, Paul**
Dangling Conversation.
59th Street Bridge Song, The.
Richard Cory.
Sounds of Silence, The.
**Simone, Nina**
Four Women.
**Simpson, Alan**
Twenty-third Psalm, The.
**Simpson, Louis**
After Midnight.
American Poetry.
As Birds Are Fitted to the Boughs.
Ash and the Oak, The.
Big Dream, Little Dream.
Birch ("Birch tree, you remind me").
Carentan O Carentan.
Climate of Paradise, The.
Columbus.
Country House, The.
Custom of the World, The.
Dvonya.
Early in the Morning.
Frogs.
Goodnight, The.
Green Shepherd, The.
Hot Night on Water Street.
Hour of Feeling, The.
In California.
In the Suburbs.
Inner Part, The.
Love and Poetry.
Man Who Married Magdalene, The.
Memories of a Lost War.
Morning Light, The.
My Father in the Night Commanding No.
On the Lawn at the Villa.
Port Jefferson.
Redwoods, The.
Simplicity.
Song: "Rough Winds Do Shake the Darling Buds of May."
Story about Chicken Soup, A.
Stumpfoot on 42nd Street.
There Is.
Things.
To the Western World.
Tonight the Famous Psychiatrist.
Troika, The.
Vandergast and the Girl.
Walt Whitman at Bear Mountain.
**Simpson, R. A.**
Sea Variations.
**Sinfield, Peter.** *See* **Fripp, Robert** *and* **Peter Sinfield**
**Singer, Burns**
Letter, A.
**Sissman, Louis Edward**
New York Woman, The.
Safety at Forty; or, An Abecedarian Takes a Walk.
**Sisson, C. H.**

Human Relations.
Money.
Temple, The.
**Sitwell, Edith**
Aubade: "Jane, Jane,/ Tall as a crane."
Canticle of the Rose, The.
Country Dance.
Evening.
Four in the Morning.
Heart and Mind.
Innocent Spring, The.
King of China's Daughter, The.
Neptune—Polka.
Poet Laments the Coming of Old Age, The.
Shadow of Cain, The.
Sir Beelzebub.
Sleeping Beauty, The, *sel.*
Still Falls the Rain.
Swans, The.
**Sitwell, Sir Osbert**
Mrs. Busk.
**Sizemore, George**
Drill Man Blues.
**Skeat, Walter William**
Villanelle: "It's all a trick, quite easy when you know it."
**Skeen, Anita**
Instructions.
Letter to My Mother.
Modern Poetry.
Sailing in Crosslight.
**Skelton, John**
Anathema of Cats.
Auncient acquaintance, madam, betwen us twayn, The.
Bowge of Courte, The.
Colin Clout, *abr.*
Garlande of Laurell, The,*sels.*
Gup, Scot.
Knolege, aquayntance, resort, favour with grace.
Manerly Margery Mylk and Ale.
My Darling Dear, My Daisy Flower.
Phyllyp Sparowe [*or* Philip Sparrow].
To Maystres Jane Blenner-Haiset.
To Mistress Margery Wentworth.
To Mistress [*or* Maystres] Isabel[l] Pennell.
To Mistress [*or* Maystres] Margaret Hussey.
Tunnyng of Elynour Rummyng, The.
Uppon a Deedmans Hed.
Womanhood [*or* Womanhod], wanton, ye want.
**Skinner, Knute**
Cold Irish Earth, The.
Location.
**Skipsey, Joseph**
Get Up!
**Skrine, Nesta Higginson.** *See* "O'Neill, Moira"
**Skrzynecki, Peter**
Feliks Skrzynecki.
Kornelia Woloszczuk.
Migrant Hostel.
**Slavitt, David R.**
Day Sailing.
Epitaph for Goliath
Jonah: A Report.
Ride the High Country.
Seals.

**Slesinger, Warren**
Field with Figurations.
Green Beginning, The.
Passage.
Pine Needles.
**Slessor, Kenneth**
Beach Burial.
Cock-Crow.
Country Towns.
Five Bells.
Night-Ride, The.
Nuremberg.
Serenade: "Thou moon, like a white Christus hanging."
South Country.
**Sloman, Joel**
In a Remote Cloister Bordering the Empyrean.
Tree, The.
**Smart, Christopher**
Adoremus.
Author Apologizes to a Lady for His Being a Little Man, The.
Consideration for Others.
For I will consider my cat Jeoffry.
For Saturday.
Fruits of the Earth.
Gloria.
Gratitude.
Hymns and Spiritual Songs,*sels.*
Hymns for the Amusement of Children,*sels.*
Jubilate Agno,*sels.*
Long-Suffering of God.
Mirth.
Miser and the Mouse, The.
Morning Hymn, A.
Nativity of Our Lord and Saviour Jesus Praise.
Song to David, A.
St. Mark.
St. Matthias.
**Smedley, Menella Bute**
North Pole Story, A.
**Smith, Adrian Keith**
Rain.
**Smith, Alexander**
Glasgow.
**Smith, Arthur James Marshall**
Tree.
**Smith, Charlotte**
Beachy Head, *sels.*
He May Be Envied, Who with Tranquil Breast.
Invitation to the Bee.
Montalbert, *sel.*
Mute Is Thy Wild Harp, Now, O Bard Sublime!
Press'd by the Moon, Mute Arbitress of Tides.
Thirty-Eight.
To Sleep.
To Spring.
To the Moon.
**Smith, David**
Closet, The.
Dying Off Egg Island Bar.
High Are the Winter Rivers.
How One Thing Leads to Another.
Mean Rufus Thrown-Down.
Pietas: The Petrified Wood.

**Smith, Edward Lucie-.** *See* Lucie-Smith, Edward
**Smith, Florence Margaret.** *See* Smith, Stevie
**Smith, Harry B.**
Gypsy Love Song, *with music.*
**Smith, Horace**
Tale of Drury Lane, A.
**Smith, Iain Crichton**
By Ferry to the Island.
Farewell: "We were gone from each other."
Old Woman.
Rythm.
Shadows, The.
Tonight.
**Smith, James** *and* **Sir George Rose**
Conversation in Craven Street, Strand.
**Smith, John (b. 1924)**
Colin Barnes, Drums.
First, Goodbye.
Jazz for Five,*sels.*
Shake Keane, Trumpet.
**Smith, Ken**
After a Journey.
Amana Colonies, The.
Beyond Breath.
Facts.
Inventory/ Itinerary.
Old Mill, Newton St. Cyres.
Persistent Narrative.
Stone Poems, The.
Street, The.
**Smith, Margoret J.**
Cataract.
**Smith, Naomi Gwladys Royde-.** *See* Royde-Smith, Naomi Gwladys
**Smith, Patrick**
In Flight.
**Smith, Robert (d. 1555)**
Exhortation of a Father to His Children, The.
**Smith, Robert Paul**
Song For Everybody.
Tie Your Tongue, Sir?
Time Upon a Once.
**Smith, Samuel Francis**
America.
**Smith, Stevie (Florence Margaret Smith)**
Admire Cranmer! ("Admire the old man, admire him, admire him").
Avondale.
Away, Melancholy.
Conventionalist, The.
Dedicated Dancing Bull and the Water Maid, The, *sel.*
Edmonton, thy cemetery.
Exeat.
I Love.
I Remember.
Jungle Husband, The.
Louise.
Major Macroo.
Monsieur Pussy-cat, Blackmailer.
Not Waving but Drowning.
Papa Love Baby.
Seymour and Chantelle or Un Peu de Vice.
Singing Cat, The.
Some Are Born.
Tenuous and Precarious.

Thoughts about the Person from Porlock.
To Carry the Child.
Valuable.
Was It Not Curious?
Who Killed Lawless Lean?

**Smith, Sydney Goodsir**
Mandrake Hairt, The.
There is a Tide.
We Shall Never Want.
Wuid-reek.

**Smith, Vivian**
At an Exhibition of Historical Paintings, Hobart.
Effect of Light, An.

**Smith, Welton**
Beast Section, The.
Interlude.
Malcolm.
Nigga Section, The.
Strategies.

**Smith, William**
Chloris, *sels.*
To the Most Excellent and Learned Shepheard Collin Cloute.

**Smith, William Hart-.** *See* **Hart-Smith, William**

**Smith, William Jay**
American Primitive.
Closing of the Rodeo, The.
Elegy: "I stood between two mirrors when you died."
Massacre of the Innocents, The.
Moon.
Morels.
Mr. Smith/ (With Nods to Mr. Lear and Mr. Eliot.)
Seal.
Tin Can, The.
What Train Will Come?
Winter Morning.

**Smyth, Florida Watts**
Green Mountain Boy.

**Smythe, Daniel**
Driftwood.

**Snodgrass, William DeWitt**
After experience taught me that all the ordinary.
April Inventory.
Campus on the Hill, The.
Examination, The.
Flat One, A.
Friend, A.
Heart's Needle.
Home Town.
Leaving the Motel.
Lobsters in the Window.
Lovers Go Fly a Kite, The.
Marsh, The.
Matisse: "The Red Studio."
Mementos, 1 ("Sorting out letters and piles of my old").
Mementos, 2 ("I found them there today").
Men's Room in the College Chapel, The.
Monet: "Les Nymphéas."
No Use.
Operation, The.
Owls.
Partial Eclipse.
Planting a Magnolia.
September.

Song: "Sweet beast, I have gone prowling."
These Trees Stand.
Vampire's Aubade.
Winter Bouquet.

**Snyder, Gary**
Above Pate Valley.
After weeks of watching the roof leak.
After Work.
Again the ancient, meaningless.
All through the Rains.
Before the Stuff Comes Down.
Burning the Small Dead.
December.
Dry Day just before the Rainy Season, A.
Elwha River, The.
First Shaman Song.
Four Poems for Robin.
Hay for the Horses.
Heifer Clambers Up, A.
Hitch Haiku, *sels.*
How rare to be born a human being!
I Went into the Maverick Bar.
John Muir on Mt. Ritter.
Kyoto Born in Spring Song.
Kyoto: March.
Long Hair.
Looking at Pictures to Be Put Away.
Manichaeans, The.
Meeting the Mountains.
Mid-August at Sourdough Mountain Lookout.
Milton by Firelight.
Myths and Texts, *sels.*
Nansen.
Not Leaving the House.
Once Only.
Pine Tree Tops.
Piute Creek.
Prayer for the Great Family.
Regarding Wave, II.
Revolution in the Revolution in the Revolution.
Riprap.
Running Water Music.
Sappa Creek, The.
Second Shaman Song.
Some Good Things to Be Said for the Iron Age.
Spring Night in Shokoku-Ji, A.
Text, The.
Things to Do around a Lookout.
Things to Do around a Ship at Sea.
This Poem Is for Bear.
This Poem Is for Deer.
This Tokyo.
To Hell With Your Fertility Cult.
Vapor Trails.
Walk, A.
Work to Do Toward Town.

**Sobiloff, Hy**
Child's Sight, The.
Wisdom.

**Sobin, A. G.**
December Sky, The.
January Sky, The.
March Rite: Getting It Up.

**Sohappy, Liz.** *See* **Bahe, Liz Sohappy**

**Sophocles**
Colonus' Praise.
Oedipus at Colonus, *sel.*

**Sorrells, Helen**
From a Correct Address in a Suburb of a Major City.
Mountain Corral.
To a Child Born in Time of Small War.
Town I Left.

**Sorrentino, Gilbert**
Anatomy.

**Souster, Raymond**
Bernard.
Child's Umbrella, The.
Flight of the Roller Coaster.
Lift, The.
Man Who Finds That His Son Has Become a Thief, The.

**Soutar, William**
Recollection of First Love.
Sleeper, The.
Tryst, The.

**South, Joe**
So the Seeds Are Growing.

**Southey, Robert**
Battle of Blenheim, The.
Bishop Hatto
Cataract of Lodore, The.
March to Moscow, The.
Old Man's Comforts and How He Gained Them, The.
Widow, Sapphics, The.

**Southey, Robert** *and* **Samuel Taylor Coleridge**
Devil's Thoughts, The.

**Southgate, Margaret**
Pale faced, tight laced.

**Southwell, Robert**
Burning Babe, The.
Nativity of Christ, The.
New Heaven, New War.
New Prince, New Pomp.
Upon the Image of Death.

**Soyinka, Wole**
Koko Oloro.
Telephone Conversation.

**Spacks, Barry**
Emblem of Two Foxes, An
Freshmen.
Malediction.
Muse, The.
Outrageously Blessed, The.
Washing Windows.

**Spear, Roberta**
August/ Fresno 1973.
Bat, The.
Bringing Flowers.
Sale of Smoke, A.

**Spector, Albert**
Eastside Chick with Drive.

**Speght, Rachel**
Dream, A, *sels.*

**Spellman, Alfred B.**
For My Unborn and Wretched Children.
In Orangeburg My Brothers Did.
John Coltrane: an Impartial Review.
Tomorrow the Heroes.
When Black People Are.
Zapata and the Landlord.

**Spence, Skip**
Motorcycle Irene.

**Spencer, Anne**
At the Carnival.
Lady, Lady.
Letter to My Sister.

Wife-Woman, The.

**Spencer, Bernard**
Allotments: April.
Boat Poem.
Part of Plenty.

**Spencer, C. Mordaunt**
Rose of Tralee, The, *with music.*

**Spencer, Theodore**
Escapist's Song.

**Spender, Stephen**
Acts passed beyond the boundary of
mere wishing.
Beethoven's Death Mask.
Boy, Cat, Canary.
Chalk Blue Butterfly, The.
Coward, The.
Daybreak.
Double Shame, The.
Elementary School Classroom [*or* Class
Room ]in a Slum, An.
Express, The.
Funeral, The.
Hoelderlin's Old Age.
I Think Continually of Those Who Were
Truly Great.
Icarus.
Landscape near an Aerodrome, The.
Missing My Daughter.
Moving through the Silent Crowd.
My Parents Kept Me.
Not Palaces.
One More New Botched Beginning.
Perhaps.
Polar Exploration.
Pylons, The.
Room above the Square, The.
To My Daughter.
Two Armies.
Ultima Ratio Regum.
What I Expected.

**Spenser, Edmund**
Amoretti
August.
Bower of Bliss, The.
Care in Heaven.
Cave of Despair, The.
Colin Clout's Come Home Again, *sel.*
Epithalamion: "Ye learned sisters which
have oftentimes."
Faerie Queen, The, *sel.*
Garden of Adonis, The.
Guyon's Temptation.
Hill of the Graces, The.
Iambicum Trimetrum.
June.
Lay to Eliza, The.
Masque of Cupid, The.
Mother Hubberd's Tale, *sel.*
Nature's Reply to Mutability.
November.
Prothalamion.
Sonnet: "One day I wrote her name
upon the strand."
Sonnet: "Weary year his race now
having run, The."

**"Speranza."** *See* **Wilde, Lady Jane
Francesca**

**Speyer, Leonora**
Cantares, *sels.*
Gulls.
New Excavations.
Pompeii, *sel.*

Sad-pipings, *sel.*
Storm's End.

**Spicer, Jack**
"Graphemics," *sels.*

**Spinnanger, Ruthe T.**
Criteria.
Insight.
Label, The.
Last View, The.
Love at Stress-Point.
New York Skyline.
Profile of a Day.
Prophecy of the Grecian Urn.
Queen Anne's Lace.

**Spivack, Kathleen**
But You, My Darling, Should Have
Married the Prince.
Child's Visit to the Biology Lab, A.
Cripples.
Drifting.
Meeting, The.
Mythmaking.
Private Pain in Time of Trouble.
Visions.

**Sprigg, Christopher St. John.** *See*
**"Caudwell, Christopher"**

**Squire, Sir John Collings ("Solomon
Eagle")**
Discovery, The.
It Did Not Last.
Numerous Celts.
Stockyard, The.
Winter Nightfall.

**Stafford, William**
Animal That Drank Up Sound, The.
Ask Me.
At Cove on the Crooked River.
At Our House.
At the Bomb Testing Site.
At the Chairman's Housewarming.
At the Un-National Monument along
the Canadian Border.
Aunt Mabel.
Behind the Falls.
Believing What I Know.
Concealment, The: Ishi, the Last Wild
Indian.
Farm on the Great Plains, The.
Father's voice.
Found in a Storm.
Freedom.
Holding the Sky.
In Fur.
Late at Night.
Listening.
Long Distance.
Moles.
Mouse Night: One of Our Games.
Move to California, The, *sel.*
My father: October 1942.
Near.
Old Dog.
One Home.
Oregon Message, An.
Our City Is Guarded by Automatic
Rockets.
Prairie Town.
Quiet Town.
Reporting Back.
Returned to Say.
So Long.
Sound from the Earth, A.

Star in the Hills, The.
Stories from Kansas.
Story, A.
Strokes.
Summons in Indiana, The.
Thinking for Berky.
Tornado.
Traveling through the Dark.
Vacation.
Vacation Trip.
View from Here, The.
With Kit, Age 7, at the Beach.
With My Crowbar Key.
Written on the Stub of the First
Paycheck.

**Stallworthy, Jon**
Camel.
First Blood.
Here and There.
Letter from Berlin, A.
Letter to a Friend.
Poem about Poems about Vietnam, A.
True Confession, A.

**Stanford, Ann**
Beating, The.
Edward Hicks: "The Peaceable
Kingdom."
Late Visitor, The.
Night of Souls.
Rider, The.
Voices Inescapable, The.

**Stanford, Frank**
Death and the Arkansas River.

**Stanley, George**
Attis.

**Stanley, Thomas**
Killing Kiss, The.
La Belle Confidante.
Magnet, The.
Repulse, The.

**Stanton, Frank Lebby**
Mighty Lak' a Rose, *with music.*

**Stanton, Maura**
All-Night Waitress, The.
Extracts: from the Journal of Elisa
Lynch.
Judith Recalls Holofernes.
Letter to Kafka.

**Starbird, Kaye**
Ann.

**Starbuck, George**
Cora Punctuated with Strawberries.
Esthetique du Machiavel.
Margaret Are You Drug.
Of Late.
Skin Divers, The.
Translations from the English.

**Stark, Irwin**
Poets of My Epoch.

**Starkey, James.** *See* **"O'Sullivan,
Seumas"**

**Stedman, Edmund Clarence**
Aaron Burr's Wooing.
Kearney at Seven Pines.

**Steele, Silas S.**
Kiss me Quick and Go, *with music.*

**Steele, Timothy**
Epitaph: "Here lies Sir Tact, a
diplomatic fellow."

**Stein, Gertrude**
Blue Coat, A.
Celery.

Cooking.
Pastry.
Petticoat, A.
Susie Asado.
Tender Buttons, *sels.*
Water Raining.
**Steingass, David**
Beginning, A.
Love Poem Beginning with I.
Midwest U. F. O.
Seven-Year Body Cycle, The: To My
  Cells Replacing Themselves for the
  Fourth Time.
Slaughter-Room Picture, The.
Songs.
Wisconsin Farm Auction
**Stembridge, Jane**
City.
Loving.
Mrs. Hamer.
**Stennett, Samuel**
Promised Land, The.
**Stepanchev, Stephen**
Buying Lilies.
Holy Eye Is Blind, The.
In Split: Diocletian's Palace.
Irondale.
Roads, The.
Trailing My Balloon.
Voyage.
**Stephen, James Kenneth**
Last Ride Together, The.
Sincere Flattery of W. W. (Americanus)
Sonnet, A: "Two voices are there: one is
  of the deep."
To R. K.
**Stephens, James**
Bessie Bobtail.
Breakfast Time.
Cage, The.
Centaurs, The.
Cow, The.
Deirdre.
Devil's Bag, The.
Glass of Beer, A.
Hate.
Hesperus, *sel.*
Little Things.
Market, The.
Nora Criona.
Paps of Dana, The.
Psychometrist.
Rivals, The.
River, The.
Sarasvati.
Sensible People.
Seumas Beg.
Snare, The.
To the Four Courts, Please.
Variations: #21.
Washed in Silver.
What Tomas Said in a Pub.
When You Walk.
White Fields.
Wind, The.
**Sterling, Andrew B.**
Coax Me, *with music.*
Meet Me in St. Louis, Louis, *with music.*
On a Sunday Afternoon, *with music.*
Wait 'till the Sun Shines, Nellie, *with
  music.*
**Stevens, Cat**

Where Do the Children Play?
**Stevens, Wallace**
Anecdote of the Jar.
Angel Surrounded by Paysans.
Bantams in Pine-Woods.
Beginning, The.
Brave Man, The.
Course of a Particular, The.
Cy Est Pourtraicte, Madame Ste. Ursule,
  et les Unze Mille Vierges.
Dance of the Macabre Mice.
Death of a Soldier, The.
Disillusionment of Ten O'Clock.
Domination of Black.
Dry Loaf.
Earthy Anecdote.
Emperor of Ice-Cream, The.
Esthétique du Mal, *sels.*
Evening without Angels.
Final Soliloquy of the Interior
  Paramour.
Hibiscus on the Sleeping Shores.
High-Toned Old Christian Woman, A.
House Was Quiet and the World Was
  Calm, The.
Idea of Order at Key West, The.
In the Carolinas.
Irish Cliffs of Moher, The.
It feels good as it is without the giant.
Le Monocle de Mon Oncle.
Less and Less Human, O Savage Spirit.
Lunar Paraphrase.
Man Whose Pharynx Was Bad, The.
Man with the Blue Guitar, The, *sel.*
Martial Cadenza.
Men Made Out of Words.
Metamorphosis.
Mrs. Alfred Uruguay.
No Possum, No Sop, No Taters.
Notes toward a Supreme Fiction, *sels.*
Of Modern Poetry.
Peter Quince at the Clavier.
Plain Sense of Things, The.
Pleasures of Merely Circulating, The.
Ploughing on Sunday.
Poem That Took the Place of a
  Mountain, The.
Primitive Like an Orb, A.
Rabbit as King of the Ghosts, A.
River of Rivers in Connecticut, The.
Sea Surface Full of clouds.
Sense of the Sleight-of-hand Man, The.
Snow Man, The.
So-and-so Reclining on Her Couch.
Song of Fixed Accord.
Study of Two Pears.
Sunday Morning.
Thirteen Ways of Looking at a
  Blackbird.
This Solitude of Cataracts.
To an Old Philosopher in Rome.
World as Meditation, The.
**Stevenson, Anne**
Indian Summer: Vermont.
Love.
Stabilities.
Suburb, The.
Utah.
**Stevenson, Robert Louis**
At the Seaside.
Bed in Summer.
Careful Angler, The.

Christmas at Sea.
Cow, The.
Dumb Soldier, The.
From a Railway Carriage.
Good and Bad Children.
Happy Thought.
Heather Ale.
House Beautiful, The.
How to Sing or Read.
I Will Make You Brooches.
Lamplighter, The.
Land of Counterpane, The.
Looking Forward.
My Shadow.
Plain as the Glistering Planets Shine.
Rain.
Requiem.
Sing Me a Song.
Swing, The.
Time to Rise.
To Minnie.
To S. R. Crockett.
Where Go the Boats?
Whole Duty of Children.
Windy Nights.
Winter Time.
Youth and Love.
**Stewart, Douglas**
B Flat.
Gully, The.
Kindred.
Lady Feeding the Cats,   *sel.*
Nesting Time.
Silkworms, The.
Snow-Gum, The.
Sunflowers, The.
Terra Australis.
**Stewart, Harold**
Flight of Wild Geese, A,   *sel.*
**Stickney, Trumbull**
In the Past.
Mnemosyne.
Sir, say no more.
Six O'Clock.
**Stills, Stephen**
For What It's Worth.
Four and Twenty.
Suite: Judy Blue Eyes.
**Stills, Stephen, David Crosby and Paul
  Kantner.   See Crosby, David, Paul
  Kantner and Stephen Stills**
**Stirling, William Alexander, Earl of**
Aurora, *sel.*
Sonnet: "Ile give thee leave my love, in
  beauties field."
**Stokes, Terry**
All Morning.
Crimes of Passion: The Phone Caller.
Crimes of Passion: The Slasher.
Farmer, The.
Giving the Moon a New Chance.
Man All Grown Up Is Supposed To, A.
Travis, the Kid Was All Heart.
**Stokesbury, Leon**
Back Behind the Eyes.
Graduate Assistant Tells about His Visit,
  The.
Little Keats' Soliloquy.
Summer in Fairbanks.
To Laura Phelan: 1880-1906.
**Stoloff, Carolyn**
Bearing It.

For the Suicide's Daughter.
Opposites.
Short Subjects.
**Stone, John**
Cadaver.
Linda.
Living with a Voodoo Doll.
To a 14 Year Old Girl in Labor and
Delivery.
**Stone, John A.**
Coming around the Horn.
**Stone, Ruth**
Advice.
Burned Bridge, The.
I Have Three Daughters.
My Son.
Salt.
**Stone, Samuel John**
Church's One Foundation, The, *with
music.*
**Stoutenburg, Adrien**
Affinities.
Ants and Others.
Cicada.
Is Is Like Is.
Jack Rabbit.
Model T.
Reel One.
Rhinoceros.
Sky Diver.
**Stow, Randolph**
As He Lay Dying.
**Stowe, Dalene**
Day Time Sequence/ November.
Muscle Building.
Poem to My Twin Possibility.
**Strachey, Lytton**
Cat.
**Strand, Mark**
Dead, The.
Door, The.
"Dreadful Has Already Happened,
The."
Eating Poetry.
Elegy for My Father.
From a Litany.
Keeping Things Whole.
Letter.
Marriage, The.
My Death.
My Life.
My Life by Somebody Else.
Prediction, The.
Remains, The.
Tunnel, The.
Way It Is, The.
**"Streamer, Col. D."**   *See* **Graham, Harry**
**Strode, William**
Commendation of Music, The.
On a Great Hollow Tree
On Chloris Walking in the Snow.
On the Bible.
On Westwell Downs.
**Stroh, Mary Swanson**
Excuses.
Farmer's Wife, The.
Liberation.
November Birthday.
**Strong, George A.**
Modern Hiawatha, The, *parody.*
**Strong, Leonard Alfred George**
Appointment, The.

Brewer's Man, The.
Coroner's Jury.
Evening Before Rain.
Knowledgeable Child, The.
Mad-Woman, The.
Memory, A.
**Strongin, Lynn**
Ascent.
Emily Dickinson Postage Stamp.
First Aspen, *sels.*
Miniatures IV.
Ready.
Sayre.
Van Gogh.
**Struthers, Eleanor**
Cat's Life, A.
**Stuart, Dabney**
Fall Practice.
Fisherman, The.
Glucose.
His Third Decade.
Hunter, Prey.
Power Failure.
Soup Jar, The.
Student, The.
Ties.
**Stuart, Floyd C.**
Balances.
Hard Edge of Beauty.
Pilot.
Six Statues in a Park.
Stone Age.
**Stuart, John Sobieski**
With an Antique Crystal Cup and Ring.
**Stuart, Mary [or Marie].**   *See* **Mary Queen
of Scots**
**Stuart, Muriel**
In the Orchard.
**Stubbs, Marcia**
In a Mirror.
**Stults, Robert Morrison**
Sweetest Story Ever Told, The, *with
music.*
**Stutsman, Rebecca**
Honorable Mention.
**Suckling, Sir John**
Aglaura, *sel.*
Ballad upon a Wedding, A.
Constant Lover, The.
Doubt of Martyrdom, A.
Encouragement to a Lover.
Epistle An: "Whether these lines do find
you out."
Farewell to Love.
Out Upon It! I Have Loved.
To a Lady that Forbade to Love before
Company.
Why so Pale and Wan?
**Suderman, Elmer F.**
Adam in the Garden.
On Listening to a Death-of-God
Theologian Lecture in the Chapel.
Placid Pew, The.
Preacher Considers His Sermon, The.
Thy Kingdom Come.
Worship.
**Suffolk, Peter**
Street Scene.
**Sukenick, Lynn**
Death.
Early Ella
Parting: A Game.

Poster, The.
That Life, on Film.
**Sullivan, Frank**
September Valentine.
**Sullivan, Joseph J.**
Where Did You Get That Hat?, *with
music.*
**Sullivan, Nancy**
Number 1 by Jackson Pollock (1948).
Six Kisses.
**Summerfield, Geoffrey**
Windy Boy in a Windswept Tree.
**Summers, Hal**
My Old Cat.
Rescue, The.
**Summers, Hollis**
At the Wax Museum.
Delivery, The.
Peddler, The.
Song to Be Attached.
**Sund, Robert**
Afternoon,/ with just enough of a breeze
for him to ride it.
Dusty black beetle, A.
**Sun-Ra**
Plane, The: Earth.
Primary Lesson: The Second Class
Citizens.
**Surrey, Henry Howard, Earl of**
Brittle beautie, that nature made so
fraile.
Complaint by Night of the Lover Not
Beloved, A.
Complaint of the Absence of Her Lover
Being upon the Sea.
Consolation.
From Tuscan cam my ladies worthi race.
Geve place, ye lovers, here before.
Golden gift that nature did thee geve,
The.
I never saw you, madam, lay apart.
In Cipres springes (wheras dame Venus
dwelt).
In the rude age when scyence was not so
rife.
In Windsor Castle.
In winters just returne, when Boreas gan
his raigne.
Laid in My Quiet Bed.
London, hast thow accused me.
My Ratclif, when thy retchlesse youth
offendes.
Norfolk sprang thee, Labeth holds thee
dead.
Sonne hath twyse brought forthe the
tender grene, The.
Soote Season, The.
Thassyryans king, in peas with fowle
desyre.
Though I regarded not.
Wyat resteth here, that quicke coulde
never rest.
**Sutheim, Susan**
For Witches.
**Sutherland, Robert.**   *See* **Garioch, Robert**
**Su Tung p'o [or Tung-po]**
At the Washing of My Son.
On the Birth of His Son.
Spring Night.
Thoughts in Exile.
**Swan, Jon**
Nebraska.

**Swann, Brian**
Desert in the Sea.
Paradigms of Fire.
Quiet.
Three Riddles.
Year of the Bird.
**Sward, Robert**
By the Swimming.
Concert.
How totally unpredictable we are to one
another.
In Mexico.
Uncle Dog: the Poet at 9.
Waldheim Cemetery.
**Swenson, Karen**
Evening Gown, The.
Lovers, The.
Quilt, The.
**Swenson, May**
All That Time.
Analysis of Baseball.
At Breakfast.
Beginning to Squall.
Cardinal Ideograms.
Cat and the Weather.
Centaur, The.
Couple, A.
Death Invited.
Evolution.
Fable for When There's No Way Out.
Feel Like a Bird.
Fixture, A.
Flying Home from Utah.
Four-Word Lines.
Frontispiece.
Green Red Brown and White.
How Everything Happens.
How to Be Old.
Key to Everything, The.
Landing on the Moon.
Living Tenderly.
Lowering, The.
On Its Way.
Out of the Sea, Early.
Pair, A.
Question.
Shape of Death, The.
Southbound on the Freeway.
Stone Gullets.
Tall Figures of Giacometti, The.
3 Models of the Universe.
To Make a Play.
Universe, The.
Waiting for It.
Waking from a Nap on the Beach.
Was Worm.
Watch, The.
Willets, The.
Working on Wall Street.
**Swift, Joan**
Line-Up, The.
**Swift, Jonathan**
Beautiful Young Nymph Going to Bed,
A.
Cassinus and Peter.
Cat and the Rain, The.
Day of Judgement, The.
Description of a City Shower, A.
Description of the Morning, A.
Epigram: "As Thomas was cudgeled one
day by his wife."
Five, The.

Furniture of a Woman's Mind, The.
Gentle Echo on Woman, A.
Holyhead, Sept. 25th, 1727.
Humble Petition of Frances Harris, The.
Lady's Dressing Room, The.
Market Women's Cries.
On Dreams.
On Himself.
On His Own Deafness
On Stella's Birthday.
Onyons.
Progress of Beauty, The.
Satirical Elegy on the Death of a Late
Famous General, A.
Stella at Wood-Park.
Time is not remote when I, The.
Verses on the Death of Doctor Swift, *sels.*
**Swinburne, Algernon Charles**
Atalanta in Calydon, *sels.*
Ave atque Vale.
Before Parting.
Cameo, A.
Chorus: "When the hounds of spring are
on winter's traces."
Dead Love.
Forsaken Garden, A.
Garden of Proserpine, The.
Higher Pantheism in a Nutshell, The,
*parody.*
Hymn to Proserpine.
In the Orchard.
Lake of Gaube, The.
Leave-taking, A.
Leper, The.
Love and Sleep.
Nephelidia.
Rondel: "Kissing her hair I sat against
her feet."
Sapphics.
To a Cat.
Triads.
Triumph of Time, The.
**Sykes, Velma West**
Diptych.
**Sylvester, Joshua**
Du Bartas His Divine Weeks and
Works, *sels.*
1st Week 5th Day.
1st Week 6th Day.
**Symons, Arthur**
Amends to Nature.
Tune, A.
White Heliotrope.
**Synge, John Millington**
Curse, The.
Dread.
In Glencullen.
In Kerry.
Is It a Month.
On a Birthday.
On an Anniversary.
On an Island.
Passing of the Shee, The.
Patch-Shaneen.
Queens.
Question, A.
Rendez-vous Manqué dans la Rue
Racine.
Winter.
**Syrett, Lesley**
My Cat.

**T**

"T. M." *See* "M., T."
**Tabb, John Banister**
Hospitality.
**Tablada, José Juan**
Haiku: "Although he never stirs from
home."
Haiku: "Ants on inert cricket crawling."
Haiku: "Dragon-fly strives patiently,
The."
Haiku: "Lumps of mud, the toads."
Haiku: "Red cold."
Haiku: "Tiny monkey looks at me,
The."
**Tabley, Lord De.** *See* **De Tabley, John
Byrne Leicester Warren, 3rd Baron**
**Tadema, Laurence Alma-.** *See* **Alma-
Tadema, Laurence**
**Taft, Margo**
I have been my arm.
**Taggard, Genevieve (Mrs. Kenneth Durant)**
American Farm, 1934.
Geraniums, The.
In the Tail of the Scorpion.
Little Girl with Bands on Her Teeth,
The.
Squirrel near Library.
To the Veterans of the Abraham Lincoln
Brigade.
Train: Abstraction.
With Child.
**Taggart, George**
Moth and the Flame, The, *with music.*
**Tagore, Rabindranath**
Paper Boats, *sel.*
**Tait, Margaret**
To Anybody At All.
**Tait, Robert**
Cold Snap, A.
No You.
**Takamura, Kotaro**
My Poetry.
**Tamura, Ryuichi**
Invisible Tree.
**Tarn, Nathaniel**
Beautiful Contradictions, The, *sels.*
Bring a Child Flowers.
Last of the Chiefs.
Nowhere for Vallejo, A, *sels.*
Projections for an Eagle Escaped in This
City, March 1965.
**Tasso, Torquato**
Happiness of a Flea, The.
**Tate, Allen**
Aeneas at Washington.
Buried Lake, The.
Emblems.
Last Days of Alice.
Mediterranean, The.
Mother and Son.
Mr. Pope.
Oath, The.
Ode to Fear.
Ode to the Confederate Dead.
Paradigm, The.
Shadow and Shade.
Sonnets at Christmas (I-II).
Subway, The.
Swimmers, The.

To a Romantic.
Winter Mask.
Wolves, The.
**Tate, James**
Absences.
Blue Booby, The.
Book of Lies, The.
Box for Tom, A.
Coda.
Coming Down Cleveland Avenue.
Consumed.
Distant Orgasm, The.
Flight.
It's Not the Heat So Much as the
  Humidity.
Little Yellow Leaf.
Pity Ascending with the Fog.
Shadowboxing.
Soup of Venus, The.
Square at Dawn, The.
Stray Animals.
Wheelchair Butterfly, The.
**Tate, Nahum**
On Sight of Some Martyrs' Sepulchres.
Sliding on Skates in Very Hard Frost.
While shepherds watched their flocks by
  night.
**Tate, Nahum and John Dryden**
Absalom and Achitophel, Pt. II, *sels.*
**Taupin, Bernie**
King Must Die, The.
**Taylor, Alexander**
On the Knowledge of Things.
**Taylor, Ann**
Baby's Dance, The.
Meddlesome Matty.
My Mother.
Notorious Glutton, The.
Pin, The.
**Taylor, Ann or Jane**
Cow, The.
Sheep, The.
**Taylor, Bayard**
Ballad of Hiram Hover, The.
Bison Track, The.
Camerados.
Ode on a Jar of Pickles.
On Leaving California.
Promissory Note, The.
Quaker Widow, The.
Song of the Camp, The.
Three Songs, The.
**Taylor, Edward**
Am I thy gold? Or purse, Lord, for thy
  wealth.
Did ever lord such noble house
  maintain.
God's Determinations,*sels.*
How sweet a Lord is mine? If any
  should.
Huswifery.
I kening through astronomy divine.
Let By Rain.
Lord, dub my tongue with a new tier of
  words.
My blessed Lord, art thou a lilly flower?
My dear, deare, Lord I do thee Saviour
  call.
My gracious Lord, I would thee glory
  doe.
My shattred phancy stole away from
  mee.

Oh! Good, good, good, my Lord. What
  more love yet.
Oh Leaden heeld. Lord, give, forgive I
  pray.
Oh! What a thing is man? Lord, who am
  I?
Our Insufficiency to Praise God Suitably,
  for His Mercy.
Preface, The: "Infinity, when all things it
  beheld."
Preparatory Meditations, *sels.*
Thy humane frame, my glorious Lord, I
  spy.
Upon a Spider Catching a Fly.
Upon a Wasp Child with Cold.
What love is this of thine, that cannot
  bee.
Would God I in that Golden City were.
Ye angells bright, pluck from your wings
  a quill.
**Taylor, Henry**
Hughsville Scythe, The.
Remembering Kevan MacKenzie.
Speech.
**Taylor, James**
Country Road.
Fire and Rain.
**Taylor, James O.**
Broken Promise.
These Dreamings Mine.
**Taylor, Jane**
Gleaner, The.
Greedy Richard.
Star, The.
**Taylor, John**
Carmen Saeculare.
Dick Swash.
**Taylor, R. Dean**
Ain't It a Sad Thing?
**Teague, Kathleen**
Homage to Chagall.
**Teasdale, Sara**
Barter.
"I Am Not Yours."
Moonlight.
Moon's Ending.
Morning Song.
New Moon, The.
Night.
Solitary, The.
"What Do I Care."
**Teitoku**
Both my child.
**Tennant, Robert**
Wee Davie Daylicht.
**Tennyson, Alfred Tennyson, 1st Baron**
Becket,*sels.*
Blow, Bugle, Blow.
Break, Break, Break.
Charge of the Heavy Brigade, The.
Charge of the Light Brigade, The.
City Child, The.
Columbus, *sel.*
Come into the garden, Maud.
Come Not, When I Am Dead.
Cradle Song: "What does little birdie
  say."
Crossing the Bar.
Duet.
Eagle, The.
Flower in the Crannied Wall.
"Frater Ave atque Vale."

Goose, The.
Hendescasyllabics.
Higher Pantheism, The.
Idylls of the King, *sel.*
In the Valley of Cauteretz.
June Bracken and Heather.
Lady Clare.
Lady of Shalott, The.
Lo! in the middle of the wood.
Locksley Hall.
Locksley Hall, Sixty Years After.
Lotos-Eaters, The, *sels.*
Mariana.
Marriage Morning.
Maud,*sels.*
Mechanophilus, *sel.*
Mermaid, The, *sel.*
Milton.
Minnie and Winnie.
Morte D'Arthur.
Nothing Will Die.
Now Sleeps the Crimson Petal.
Oak, The.
Owl, The.
Princess, The, *sels.*
Prologue: "Over! the sweet summer
  closes."
*Revenge,* The.
Rizpah.
Sailor Boy, The.
Snowdrop, The.
Song of the Lotos-Eaters.
Song: "Spirit haunts the year's last
  hours, A."
Song: "Who can say."
Splendor Falls on Castle Walls, The.
Sweet and Low.
Tears, Idle Tears.
Tithonus.
Ulysses.
Winter.
**Tennyson, Charles.** *See* **Turner, Charles**
  **Tennyson**
**Tepperman, Jean**
Going Through Changes.
Witch.
**Terry, Lucy**
Bar's Fight, August 28, 1746.
**Teschemacher, Edward**
Because, *with music.*
**Tessimond, Arthur Seymour John**
Cats.
Epitaph on Any Man
Jamaican Bus Ride.
La Marche des Machines.
Middle-aged Conversation.
**Thackeray, William Makepeace**
At the Zoo.
Little Billee.
Sorrows of Werther, The.
**Thaxter, Celia**
Sandpiper, The.
**Thayer, Ernest Lawrence**
Casey at the Bat.
**Theocritus**
Daphnis.
Idylls, *sels*
**Thomas, Donald Michael**
Eden.
Elegy for an Android.
Missionary.
O My America.

Unknown Shores.

**Thomas, Dylan**
After the Funeral.
Altarwise by Owl-Light, *sels.*
And Death Shall Have No Dominion.
Ballad of the Long-legged Bait.
Conversation, A.
Countryman's Return, The.
Do Not Go Gentle into That Good
 Night.
Especially when the October wind.
Fern Hill.
Force That Through the Green Fuse
 Drives the Flower, The.
Hunchback in the Park, The.
I Have Longed to Move Away.
If My Head Hurt a Hair's Foot.
In My Craft or Sullen Art.
It is the sinners' dust-tongued bell claps
 me to churches.
Johnnie Crack and Flossie Snail.
Lament: "When I was a windy boy and
 a bit."
Light Breaks Where No Sun Shines.
Love in the Asylum.
Poem in October.
Refusal to Mourn the Death, by Fire, of
 a Child in London, A.
Twenty-four Years.
Under Milk Wood, *sel.*
When All My Five and Country Senses
 See.

**Thomas, Edward ("Edward Eastaway")**
Adlestrop.
After Rain.
And You, Helen.
As the Team's Head-Brass.
Aspens.
Birds' Nest.
Cat, A.
Celandine.
Digging.
February Afternoon.
Gallows, The.
Glory, The.
Green Roads, The.
Gypsy, The.
Hollow Wood, The.
If I Should Ever by Chance.
In Memoriam (Easter, 1915).
It Rains.
Lights Out.
Like the Touch of Rain.
New House, The.
No One So Much as You.
October.
Old Man.
Out in the Dark.
Owl, The.
Path, The.
Rain.
Some Eyes Condemn.
Thaw.
Unknown, The.
What Shall I Give?
When First.

**Thomas, Lorenzo**
Onion Bucket.
Subway Witnesses, The.

**Thomas, Martha Banning**
Sudden Gale in Spring.

**Thomas, Richard W.**

Amen.
Life After Death.
Martyrdom.
Riots and Rituals.
To the New Annex to the Detroit
 County Jail.
Worker, The.

**Thomas, Ronald Stuart**
Alpine.
Ap Huw's Testament.
Blackbird Singing, A.
Country Clergy, The.
Cynddylan on a Tractor.
Evacuee, The.
For the Record.
Here.
Hill Farmer Speaks, The.
Invasion on the Farm.
Madrigal: "Your love is dead, lady, your
 love is dead."
Mother and Son.
Musician, The.
On the Farm.
Sorry.
They.
Walter Llywarch.
Welsh Landscape.

**Thomas More, Saint.** *See* **More, Sir**
 **Thomas**

**Thomas of Hales**
Where is Paris and Helene?

**Thompson, D'Arcy Wentworth**
Crazy Arithmetic.
That Little Black Cat.
Very Odd Fish, A.

**Thompson, Francis**
Ex Ore Infantium.
In No Strange Land.
To a Snow-flake.

**Thompson, H. S.**
Lilly Dale, *with music.*

**Thompson, James W.**
Constant Labor, A.
Greek Room, The.
Plight, The.
Spawn of Slums, The.
Yellow Bird, The.
You Are Alms.

**Thompson, John**
Homecoming.

**Thompson, Larry**
Black Is Best.

**Thompson, Lulu E.**
In Hardin County, 1809.

**Thompson, Samuel**
April.
To a Hedgehog.

**Thompson, Will L.**
Softly and Tenderly Jesus Is Calling,
 *with music.*

**Thomson, Barbara Earl**
Celebration for a Young Priest.
From Thursday.
Lesson from Jim Crane.

**Thomson, James (1700-1748)**
Autumnal Moon, The.
Castle of Indolence, The, *sel.*
Hymn on the Seasons, A.
Rule, Britannia.
Seasons, The,*sels.*
Spring.
Spring Flowers.

Winter Night, A.

**Thomson, James** *and* **David Mallet**
Alfred, a Masque, *sel.*

**Thomson, James (1834-1882; "B.V." or**
 **Bysshe Vanolis)**
City, The.
City of Dreadful Night, The.
City's Queen, The.

**Thoreau, Henry David**
Conscience Is Instinct Bred in the
 House.
Epitaph on the World.
Great God! I Ask Thee for No Meaner
 Pelf.
Haze.
I Am a Parcel of Vain Strivings Tied.
Inspiration.
Inward Morning, The.
My Love Must Be As Free.
Respectable Folks, The.
River Swelleth More and More, The.
Smoke.
Week on the Concord and Merrimack
 Rivers, A,*sels.*
Winter Memories.

**Thornbury, George Walter**
Sally from Coventry, The.
Three Troopers, The.

**Thornton, James**
She May Have Seen Better Days, *with*
 *music.*
Streets of Cairo; or, The Poor Little
 Country Maid, *with music.*
When You Were Sweet Sixteen, *with*
 *music.*

**Thrupp, Dorothy Ann**
Saviour, Like a Shepherd Lead Us, *with*
 *music.*

**Thwaite, Anthony**
Ali Ben Shufti.
At Dunwich.
Boys, The.
Disturbances.
Mr. Cooper.
Pond, The.
Sense of Property, A.
Sunday Afternoons.

**Tibble, Anne**
Trials of a Tourist.

**Tichborne [*or* Tichbourne], Chidiock**
Elegy: "My prime of youth is but a frost
 of cares."

**Timrod, Henry**
Charleston.
Ethnogenesis
Ode: "Sleep sweetly in your humble
 graves."
Unknown Dead, The.

**Ting, Walasse**
Pepsi Generation.

**Tippett, James Sterling**
Sunning.
Up in the Air.

**Tipping, Richard**
Soursobs.

**Tipton, James**
Dialogue.
Exit, Pursued by a Bear.
February I Turn off the Porch Light and
 Go Outside.
Now Everyone Is Writing Poems about
 Indians.

Pastoral: "Shuddering geography pulls the dead sentences, A."
Winter in Elwell.
**Todachine, Mike**
Poem: "You can look into my face."
**Todd, Barbara Euphan**
Sing a Song of Honey.
**Todd, Ruthven**
To a Very Beautiful Lady.
Watching You Walk.
**Todhunter, John**
Aghadoe.
**Tolkien, J. R. R.**
Cat.
Old Walking Song, The.
Oliphaunt.
**Tolson, Melvin B.**
African China.
Birth of John Henry, The.
Harlem Gallery, *sels.*
Legend of Versailles, A.
PSI.
Satchmo.
Sea-Turtle and the Shark, The.
**Tomlinson, Charles**
At Barstow.
Death in the Desert, A.
Fiascherino.
Idyll: "A door:/ Per L'Universo."
Las Trampas U.S.A.
Mr. Brodsky.
Observation of Facts.
On the Hall at Stowey.
Oxen: Ploughing at Fiesole.
Paring the Apple.
Picture of J. T. in a Prospect of Stone, The.
Swimming Chenango Lake.
Two Views of Two Ghost Towns.
Up at La Serra.
**Tonks, Rosemary**
Farewell to Kurdistan.
Story of a Hotel Room.
**Toomer, Jean**
Beehive.
Brown River, Smile.
Cotton Song.
Evening Song.
Five Vignettes.
Georgia Dusk.
Her Lips Are Copper Wire.
Lost Dancer, The.
November Cotton Flower.
Reapers.
Song of the Son.
**Toplady, Augustus Montague**
Rock of Ages, *with music.*
**Torgerson, Eric**
One Year Later.
**Torneol, Nuño Fernández**
Lady's Farewell, The.
**Torregian, Sotère**
Back Spring Becomes Anonymous, The.
**Touré, Askia Muhammad**
Floodtide.
JuJu
Tauhid.
**Tourneur, Cyril**
Age and bare bone/ Are e'er allied in action.
And now methinks I could e'en chide myself.

Awake, oh Heaven, for (lo) the heavens conspire.
Revenger's Tragedy, The, *sel.*
**Towne, Charles Hanson**
Messed Damozel, The.
**Townsend [or Townshend], Aurelian**
Dialogue betwixt [or between] Time and a Pilgrim, A.
To the Lady May.
Youth and Beauty.
**Track, Soge**
Indian Love Letter.
**Traherne, Thomas**
Demonstration, The, *sel.*
Dreams.
News.
On Leaping over the Moon.
On News
Poverty.
Preparative, The.
Salutation, The.
Shadows in the Water.
Third Century, The, *sel.*
**Traill, Henry Duff**
After Dilettante Concetti.
**Trakl, Georg**
At the Eastern Front.
**Tranter, John**
Red Movie.
**Trapp, Joseph**
Epigram: "King George, observing with judicious eyes."
**Travis, Lucille F.**
Alienation (To My Son).
Bells, The.
Judas Before.
Negrun.
Question.
To Sing the People.
**Treasone, Grace**
Life.
**Treece, Henry**
Conquerors.
**Trench, Herbert**
Jean Richepin's Song.
**Trevathan, Charles E.**
Bully Song, The, *with music.*
**Trevisa, John**
Prologue to a Translation.
**Tropp, Stephen**
My Wife Is My Shirt.
**Troupe, Quincy**
Dirge: "It is the endless dance of the dead."
For Malcolm Who Walks in the Eyes of Our Children.
In Texas Grass.
Poem for Friends.
Sense of Coolness, A.
**Trowbridge, John Townsend**
Darius Green and His Flying-Machine.
**Trudell, Dennis**
Art of Poetry, The.
Epilogue: "I have just joined a raggedy line."
I Was Driving across the Island.
Thirty-nine thousand.
"You Get the Groceries, I'll Guard the Crib."
**Trypanis, Constantine A.**
To Theon from His Son Theon.
**Tsuda, Margaret**

Commitment in a City.
Hard Questions.
**Ts'uei Tu**
On New Year's Eve.
**Tuckerman, Frederick Goddard**
All men,—the preacher saith,—whate'er or whence.
And borne with theirs, my proudest thoughts do seem.
And she—her beauty never made her cold.
And so the day drops by; the horizon draws.
As when, down some broad river dropping, we.
By this low fire I often sit to woo.
Cricket, The.
For Nature daily through her grand design.
Hast thou seen reversed the prophet's miracle.
Here, where the red man swept the leaves away.
Nor looks that backward life so bare to me.
November.
Sonnet: "And change with hurried has swept these scenes."
Sonnet: "But man finds means, grant him but place and room."
Sonnet: "For Nature daily through her grand design."
Sonnet: "Not the round natural world, not the deep mind."
Sonnet: "One still dark night I sat alone and wrote."
Sonnet: "Roll on, sad world! not Mercury or Mars."
Sonnet: "Sometimes I walk where the deep water dips."
Sonnet: "Under the mountain, as when first I knew."
Sonnets, *sels.*
Under the Locust Blossoms.
Upper chamber in a darkened house, An.
**Tudor, Stephen**
Augur, The.
Harold.
Poem for Nancy.
You Held the Air.
**Tu Fu**
Road to Pengya, The.
Visitors.
**Tupper, Martin**
Train of Religion, The, *sel.*
**Turberville, George**
That No Man Should Write But Such As Do Excel.
Verse in Praise of Lord Henry Howard, Earl of Surrey.
**Turco, Lewis**
Door, The.
Forest beyond the Glass, The.
Love Poem: "These words are all of me."
Old Acquaintance, An.
Ordinary Evening in Cleveland, An.
Pilot, The.
**Turnbull, Gael**
Twenty Words/ Twenty Days.
**Turner, Alberta**

Sisters.
Structure.
To Leonard and Kerstin, With a Gift of
Books.
Wrists.
**Turner, Charles Tennyson**
After the School-Feast.
Country Dance, The.
Drunkard's Last Market, The.
Eustace and Edith.
Evening in Harvest Time, An.
Mary—A Reminiscence.
Old Ruralities.
Old Stephen.
On the Eclipse of the Moon of October
1865.
Quiet Tide near Ardrossan, The.
Seaside, The.
Steam Threshing-Machine, The.
To a Red-Wheat Field.
To a Scarecrow; or, Malkin, Left Long
after Harvest.
To a "Tenting" Boy.
Wind on the Corn.
**Turner, Doris**
Fragment Reflection I.
Reckoning A. M. Thursday.
**Turner, Elizabeth**
Canary, The.
How to Write a Letter.
Truth the Best.
Two Little Miss Lloyds, The.
**Turner, Nancy Byrd**
Washington.
**Turner, Walter James**
Romance.
Silence.
**Turner, William Price**
Personal Column.
Reproaches.
University Curriculum.
**Tynan, Katharine (Katharine Tynan
Hinkson)**
August Weather.
Slow Spring.
Winter.
**Tyutchev, Fyodor Ivanovich**
Last Love.

**U**

**Untermeyer, Louis**
Dog at Night.
Edna St. Vincent Millay Exhorts Little
Boy Blue.
Portrait of a Machine.
**Updike, John**
Amish, The.
Cloud Shadows.
Ex-Basketball Player.
From a Cheerful Alphabet.
Hoeing.
Mosquito.
Movie House.
Pendulum.
Report of Health.
Some Frenchmen.
Stunt Flier, The.

Superman.
Tao in the Yankee Stadium Bleachers.
V. B. Nimble, V. B. Quick ("V. B.
Wigglesworth wakes at noon").
Wash.
Winter Ocean.
**Upham, Samuel C.**
Ancient Yuba Miner of the Days of '49,
Ye.
**Upton, Charles**
Moon, The.
**Urdang, Constance**
Because the Three Moirai Have Become
the Three Maries.
Children, The.
Day the Houses Sank, The.
One-Eyed Bridegroom, The.
**Usborne, Richard**
Casanova.

**V**

**"V., B."**  *See* **Thomson, James (1834-1882)**
**Valaoritis, Nanos**
Birds of Hazard and Prey, *sel.*
**Valentine, Jean**
Dream Barker.
Moon Man.
Sasha and the Poet.
**Valéry, Paul**
Footsteps, The.
**Vallejo, César**
Eternal Dice, The.
Poem to Be Read and Sung.
To My Brother Miguel: In Memoriam.
Trilce: "In that corner, where we slept
together."
**Van Arsdale, H.**
Lucky Louie Makes a Goal.
**Van Doren, Mark**
Afterward.
Ancient Couple on Lu Mountain, The.
And Did the Animals?
Child at Winter Sunset, The.
Envy the Old.
Family Prime.
First Snow of the Year, The.
King Wind.
Morning Worship.
Only for Me.
Rapunzel, Rapunzel.
Simple Beast.
Spring Thunder.
Story-Teller, The.
This Shell.
True Is True.
Truelove.
Will You, Won't You.
**Van Duyn, Mona**
Birthday Card for a Psychiatrist.
Death by Aesthetics.
Fear of Flying, The.
Gardener to His God, The.
Leda.
Leda Reconsidered.
Memory, A.
Pieta, The, Rhenish, 14th C., The
Cloisters.

Recovery, *sel.*
Relationships.
Talker, The.
Three Valentines to the Wide World,
*sel.*
**Van Dyke, Henry**
America for Me.
**"Vanolis, Bysshe."**  *See* **Thomson, James
(1834-1882)**
**Van Walleghen, Michael**
Poem for My Great Grandfather.
**Vas Dias, Robert**
Impossibility, An.
Petoskey Stone.
Salvaging Spikes.
**Vaughan, Henry**
Bird, The.
Charnel-House, The.
Childhood.
Cock-Crowing.
Corruption.
Dawning, The.
Man.
Morning-Watch, The.
Night, The ("Through that pure virgin
shrine").
Peace.
Quickness.
Regeneration.
Relapse, The.
Religion.
Resurrection and Immortality.
Retreat[e], The.
Revival, The.
Since Thou Art Gone.
Tempest, The.
They Are All Gone into the World of
Light.
To Etesia Looking from Her Casement
at the Full Moon.
Waterfall, The.
World, The.
**Veeder, Rex**
Magic.
My Son.
**Vergil [*or* Virgil] (Publius Vergilius Maro)**
Aeneid, The, *sel.*
Georgics, *sel.*
Tenth Pastoral, The; or, Gallus.
**Verlaine, Paul**
Clair de Lune.
You would have understood me, had
you waited.
**Vernon, John**
Not Having a History.
What Is Salt?
**Very, Jones**
Clouded Morning, The.
Columbine, The.
Created, The.
Day of Denial, The.
Dead, The.
Fair Morning, The.
Garden, The.
Grave-Yard, The.
Hand and Foot, The.
I Was Sick and in Prison.
Lament of the Flowers, The.
Lost, The.
New Birth, The.
New Man, The.
New World, The.

Prayer, The: "Wilt thou not visit me?"
Sumach Leaves, The.
Thy Brother's Blood.
Trees of Life, The.
Yourself.
**"Vesey, Paul."** *See* **Allen, Samuel**
**Victory, H.**
Everlasting Teamwork in Basketball.
**Viereck, Peter**
Mary, Mary.
Poet.
To Helen (of Troy, N.Y.).
*Vale* from Carthage.
**Viidikas, Vicki**
Wheels.
**Villa, José Garcia**
There came you wishing me.
**Villon, Francois**
Ballad of Dead Ladies, The.
Ballad of Villon and Fat Madge, The.
Old Lady's Lament for Her Youth, The.
**Vincent, Stephen**
Basketball.
Coming Up and Falling Down.
Elevator Landscapes,*sels.*
Floor: Five.
Floor: O.
Jealousy.
Mother.
Relationship, The.
Requiem.
Song of This House, The.
**Vincent, W. G.**
Moonlight, *sel.*
**Vinograd, Julia**
Investigation.
**Vinz, Mark**
For the Far Edge.
North Dakota Gothic.
Variations on a Theme.
**Vliet, R. G.**
Love's own form.
**Vogelweide, Walther von der.** *See* **Walther von der Vogelweide**
**Von Ende, Frederick**
Wynken De Worde.
**Voznesensky, Andrei**
Dead Still.
Give Me Peace ("Give me quietness and peace").
Soccer.
Someone Is Beating a Woman.

# W

**"W., A."**
Upon Visiting His Lady by Moonlight.
**Wade, John Stevens**
Clothesline, The.
Daisies.
Days Like This.
Smell of Wood, The.
**Wagoner, David**
Burglar, The.
Leaving Something Behind.
Looking for Mountain Beavers.
Making Up for a Soul.

Poets Agree to Be Quiet by the Swamp, The.
Song to Accompany the Bearer of Bad News.
Staying Alive.
To My Friend Whose Parachute Did Not Open.
Words, The.
Working against Time.
**Wain, John**
Apology for Understatement.
Au Jardin des Plantes.
Bad Thing, The.
Brooklyn Heights.
Reason for Not Writing Orthodox Nature Poetry.
Song about Major Eatherly, A.
**Wakoski, Diane**
Anticipation of Sharks.
Children Visit the Island.
Duchess Potatoes, The.
Father of My Country, The.
Greed, *sel.*
Ice Eagle, The.
In Gratitude to Beethoven.
In Place of a Phone Call to Arabia.
Journey.
Justice Is Reason Enough.
Love to My Electric Handmixer.
Magician, The.
Mechanic, The.
My Knees Go before the Firing Squad at Dawn.
My Mother Tries to Visit Me in the Dead of Night.
Night a Sailor Came to Me in a Dream, The.
No More Soft Talk.
Overweight Poem.
Patriotic Poem.
Poet Recognizing the Echo of the Voice, A.
Ringless.
Sestina from the Home Gardener.
Smudging.
Summer.
Thank You for the Valentine.
To Bed.
Turtle, The.
What I Want in a Husband Besides a Mustache.
Wind Secrets.
You, Letting the Trees Stand as My Betrayer.
**Walcott, Derek**
Another Life, *sel.*
Blues.
Codicil.
Crusoe's Island.
Elegy: "Our hammock swung between Americas."
Far Cry from Africa, A.
Letter from Brooklyn, A.
Moon.
Nights in the Gardens of Port of Spain.
Pocomania.
Polish Rider, The.
Preparing for Exile.
Runner at Sauteurs, The.
Tales of the Islands.
**Waldman, Anne**
Holy City.

Lines: "Lines which are the imitation of imagined veins."
Over Asia.
Pressure.
Resisting Each Other.
Romantic Poem.
Traveling.
Winter Sonnet.
**Waldrop, Keith**
Before Bed.
Song: Paper.
**Waldrop, Rosemarie**
Morning Has No House.
**Waley, Arthur**
Censorship.
**Walford, William W.**
Sweet Hour of Prayer, *with music.*
**Walker, Alice**
Beyond What.
Black Mail.
Burial.
Chic Freedom's Reflection.
Expect Nothing.
For My Sister Molly Who in the Fifties.
Green lawn/ a picket fence.
In These Dissenting Times.
Love, *sel.*
Medicine.
Mornings/ of an Impossible Love.
Old Warrior Terror, The.
Once, *sels.*
So We've Come at Last to Freud.
**Walker, Anna Louise**
Work, for the Night Is Coming, *with music.*
**Walker, Charlie**
St. George.
**Walker, E. M.**
Anno Domini.
**Walker, James J.**
Will You Love Me in December as You Do in May? *with music.*
**Walker, Kath**
Then and Now.
**Walker, Margaret Abigail**
Big John Henry.
Birmingham.
Childhood.
For Andy Goodman—Michael Schwerner—and James Chaney.
For Malcolm X.
For My People.
Girl Held without Bail.
Kissie Lee.
Lineage.
Molly Means.
October Journey.
Prophets for a New Day.
Street Demonstration.
We Have Been Believers.
**Wailace, Michele**
Untitled.
Voice of the Future, The.
**Wallace, Robert**
Aubade: N.Y.C.
In a Spring Still Not Written of.
Out of the Past.
Place, The.
Star-nosed Mole, The.
Swimmer in the Rain.
What He Says.
**Wallace, William Ross**

Sword of Bunker Hill, The.
**Wallace-Crabbe, Chris**
Apparition, The.
Going to Cythera.
Star Quality.
Terra Australia.
**Waller, Edmund**
Fall, The.
Go, Lovely Rose.
Of English Verse.
Of the Last Verses in the Book.
Old Age.
On a Girdle.
Panegyric to My Lord Protector, A, *sel.*
To the King, upon His Majesty's Happy
Return, *sel.*
**Waller, John Francis**
Spinning Wheel, The.
**Walsh, John**
Taking Out Jim.
**Walsh, Marnie**
Bessie Dreaming Bear.
Charlie Two-Head.
Emmet Kills-Warrior Turtle Mountain
Reservation.
Seth Dismounts Thrice.
Thomas Iron-Eyes.
Vickie.
**Walsh, William (1663-1708)**
Love and Jealousy.
Lyce.
**Walter, Beatrice**
Photograph the Cat Licks, The.
**Walters, Dorothy**
Cinéma Vérité.
Flannery O'Connor.
Two Roads, Etc.
**Walters, Winifred Fields**
Navajo Signs.
**Walther von der Vogelweide**
Under the Lime Tree.
**Walton, John**
God, the Port of Peace.
**Wanley, Nathaniel**
Felled at a Word?
Invitation, The.
Resurrection, The.
**Ward, Christopher**
Ballad of Benjamin Bones, The.
**Ward, Nathaniel**
Epigram: "World is full of care, much
like unto a bubble, The."
**Warner, Sylvia Townsend**
Dear Girl, The.
**Warren, F. Eugene**
Angry Sermon for Any Day in the
Week, An.
Bareback in Kansas.
Customarily Autumn.
Signature, A.
**Warren, James Edward, Jr.**
Alston Chapel.
I Musk Ask.
Perfect Poem Trumpets, The.
Somewhere.
Wormwood.
**Warren, John Byrne Leicester, Baron de
Tabley.** *See* De Tabley, John Byrne
Leicester Warren, Baron
**Warren, Robert Penn**
Ballad of Billie Potts, The.
Bearded Oaks.

Blow, West Wind.
Child Next Door, The.
Debate: Question, Quarry, Dream.
Dragon Country: To Jacob Boehme.
Fall Comes in Back-Country Vermont.
Founding Fathers, Nineteenth-Century
Style.
History.
In Italian They Call the Bird Civetta.
In the Mountains, *sel.*
Jet Must Be Hunting for Something,
The.
Mango on the Mango Tree, The.
Mexico Is a Foreign Country: Four
Studies in Naturalism, *sel.*
Mortmain, *sel.*
Notes on a Life to Be Lived,*sels.*
Original Sin: A Short Story.
Owl, The.
Penological Study: Southern Exposure,
*sel.*
Promises, *sel.*
Pursuit.
Real Question Calling for Solution, A.
Revelation.
Skiers.
Small White House.
Two Pieces After Suetonius.
Ways of Day.
Well House, The.
Wet Hair: If Now His Mother Should
Come.
What Day Is.
Where the Slow Fig's Purple Sloth.
**Warsh, Lewis**
Serene Art.
**Warton, Joseph**
Enthusiast, The; or, The Lover of
Nature.
Ode to Fancy.
**Warton, Thomas, the Younger**
Pleasures of Melancholy, The.
**Washburn, Archie**
Hogan.
Unknown Smoke.
**Watkins, Vernon**
Ballad of the Three Coins.
Collier, The.
Foal.
For a Wine Festival.
Peace in the Welsh Hills.
True Picture Restored, A.
Two Decisions.
Waterfalls.
**Watkyns, Rowland**
Upon Christ's Nativity, or Christmas.
**Watson, Robert**
Blue Whale, The.
Do You Love Me?
Lines for a President.
**Watson, Roderick**
Black Forest.
Director of the Museum, The.
Foveran Sands.
New Kelso.
3 Stones.
Welthistorische Perspektiven.
**Watson, Rosamund Marriott ("Graham R.
Tomson"; "R. Armytage")**
To My Cat.
**Watson, Thomas**

Hekatompathia; or, Passionate Century
of Love,*sels.*
**Watton, Joan**
Requiem of a War-Baby.
**Watts, Alaric Alexander**
Austrian Army, An.
**Watts, Isaac**
Against Idleness and Mischief.
Against Quarrelling and Fighting.
Broad is the road that leads to death.
Cradle Hymn.
Day of Judgement, The.
Early, my God, without delay.
For the Lord's Day Evening.
Give to Our God Immortal Praise, *with
music.*
Great God, attend while Zion sings.
How long, dear Savior, O how long.
Joy to the World, *with music.*
Ninety-fifth.
Our God, Our Help in Ages Past.
Our Saviour's Golden Rule.
Sluggard, The.
Sweet Muse, Descend.
There is a land of pure delight.
Through every age, eternal God.
We're Marching to Zion, *with music.*
When I Survey the Wondrous Cross.
With songs and honors sounding loud.
**Wayman, Tom**
Poem Composed in Rogue River
Park. . .
**Weatherly, Frederick E.**
Nancy Lee, *with music.*
**Weatherly, Tom**
Arroyo.
Cantos, *sels.*
First Monday Scottsboro Alabama.
Imperial Thumbprint.
**Webb, Francis**
Death at Winson Green, A.
Eyre All Alone.
Five Days Old.
**Webb, Phyllis**
Antisong.
Ezra Pound.
For Fyodor.
Kropotkin Poems, The, *sel.*
Solitary Confinement.
Treblinka Gas Chamber.
**Weber, Richard**
Elizabeth in Italy
For the Moment.
Observation.
Stephen's Green Revisited.
Visit to Bridge House, A.
**Weber, Tom**
"I'm 92," Joe said.
**Webster, Henry De Lafayette**
Lorena, *with music.*
**Webster, John**
Call for the Robin Redbreast and the
Wren.
Cornelia's Song.
Devil's Law-Case, The. *sel.*
Duchess of Malfi, The, *sels.*
Hark, Now Everything Is Still.
I am come to make thy tomb.
Vanitas Vanitatum.
White Devil, The,*sels.*
**Weever, John**
Prophecy of this Present Year 1600, A.

**Weever, Robert.** *See* **Wever, Robert**
**Weingarten, Roger**
Blue Bog Children.
Ethan Boldt.
Her Apron through the Trees.
These Obituaries of Rattlesnakes Being
Eaten by the Hogs.
**Weismiller, Edward**
Soliloquies, The.
**Weiss, Neil**
Roman Candle.
**Weiss, Ruth**
Vita-Sheet.
**Weiss, Theodore**
Clothes Maketh the Man.
Dab of Color, A.
Last Day and the First, The.
Letter from the Pygmies, A.
Moral, The.
Preface: " 'Sonja Henie,' the young girl."
Sow's Ear, A.
This Narrow Stage.
Ultimate Antientropy, The.
Web, The.
**Welburn, Ron**
Avoidances.
Cecil County.
Eulogy for Populations.
**Welch, James**
Across to the Peloponnese.
Arizona Highways.
Blackfeet, Blood and Piegan Hunters.
Blue Like Death.
Call to Arms.
Christmas Comes to Moccasin Flat.
D-Y Bar.
Directions to the Nomad.
Dreaming Winter.
Going to Remake This World.
Harlem, Montana: Just Off the
Reservation.
In My First Hard Springtime.
In My Lifetime.
Lady in a Distant Face.
Magic Fox.
Man from Washington, The.
One More Time.
Only Bar in Dixon, The.
Plea to Those Who Matter.
Please Forward.
Renegade Wants Words, The.
Snow Country Weavers.
Spring for All Seasons.
Surviving.
Verifying the Dead.
Versatile Historian, The.
Visit.
Why I Didn't Go to Delphi.
**Welch, Lew**
Song Mt. Tamalpais Sings, The.
**Welch, Marie de L.**
Mus Ridiculus Non.
**Wellesley, Dorothy, Duchess of Wellington**
Horses.
Lighthouses.
Lost Lane.
**Wells, Carolyn**
How to Tell the Wild Animals, *sel.*
Limerick: "Tutor who tooted the flute,
A."
**Wendt, Ingrid**
Newest Banana Plant Leaf, The.

Personal Poem.
**Wesley, Charles**
Free Grace.
Gentle Jesus, Meek and Mild.
Hark, the Herald Angels Sing, *with
music.*
I Know That My Redeemer Lives, *with
music.*
Jesus, Lover of My Soul, *with music.*
Love Divine, *with music.*
Morning Hymn.
Wrestling Jacob.
**Wesley, Samuel (1662-1735)**
Boys and the Bubble, The.
To My Gingerbread Mistress, *sel.*
**Wesley, Samuel (1691-1739)**
Epigram on Miltonicks.
**Wesley-Smith, Peter**
Walter Spaggot.
**West, Peter**
Vowels.
**Westendorf, Thomas P.**
I'll Take You Home Again, Kathleen,
*with music.*
**Westmorland, Mildmay Fane, 2d Earl of**
Virtus Vera Nobilitas.
**Weston, Elizabeth**
Alphabet of Christmas Cheer.
**Weston, Mildred**
Central Park Tourney.
Query.
**Westwood, Thomas**
Mine Host of the "Golden Apple."
**Wever, Robert**
In Youth Is Pleasure.
Lusty Juventus, *sel.*
**Whalen, Philip**
For C.
Further Notice.
**Wharton, Anne**
Verses on the Snuff of a Candle, Made
in Sickness.
**Wheatley, Phillis**
Hymn to the Evening, An.
Liberty and Peace.
On Being Brought from Africa to
America.
Should you, my lord, while you pursue
my song.
To His Excellency George Washington.
To the Right Honourable William, Earl
of Dartmouth.
To the University of Cambridge, in
New-England.
**Wheelock, John Hall**
Ballad: "I dreamed I passed a
doorway."
Bonac.
Dear Men and Women.
Divine Insect, The.
Earth (" 'A planet doesn't explode' ").
Song: "Oh, with the hunger of the sea,
forever born anew."
**Wheelwright, John**
Train Ride.
Why Must You Know?
**Whigham, Peter**
Astapovo, or What Are We to Do, *sels.*
Erotion's Death.
Ingathering of Love, The, *sel.*
Love Poems of the VIth Dalai
Lama, *sels.*

Orchard Is Not Cut Down, The ("The
orchard is gone. A space").
**Whitbread, Thomas**
N. B. A. Prelim, Boston Garden.
**White, Elwyn Brooks**
Classic Waits for Me, A.
Commuters.
**White, James L.**
Anderson, Indiana.
Day Sleeper.
Minneapolis White Castle, Winter '72.
Mover.
**White, Joseph Blanco**
Black Is a Soul.
To Night.
**Whitehead, James**
First Lecture.
Local Man Remembers the Killing
Ground, A.
Statement and Vision, Two Signs of
History.
Young Deputy, The.
**Whitehead, William**
"Je Ne Sais Quoi," The.
**Whitehill, Karen**
Magdalene, Afterward.
Morning in Gainesville.
Penelope.
**Whitewing, Donna**
August 24, 1963—1:00 A.M.—Omaha.
Vegetable, I Will Not Be, A.
**Whitfield, James M.**
From America.
**Whiting, Nathan**
Good-By on an All Day Bean Planter.
Marijuana Patch on the State Hospital's
Former Grounds.
**Whiting, William**
Navy Hymn, The, *with music.*
**Whitman, Ruth**
Castoff Skin.
Cutting the Jewish Bride's Hair.
In the Smoking Car.
Marriage Wig, The.
Ripeness.
She Doesn't Want to Bring the Tides in
Any More.
Sister Pharaoh.
Spring.
Yom Kippur: Fasting.
**Whitman, Walt**
Aboard at a Ship's Helm.
Among the Multitude ("Among the men
and women the multitude").
Animals.
Are You the New Person Drawn
Toward Me?
Army Corps on the March, An.
As Adam Early in the Morning.
As I Ebb'd with the Ocean of Life.
As I Lay with My Head in Your Lap
Camerado.
As If a Phantom Caress'd Me.
As Toilsome I Wandered Virginia's
Woods.
Beat! Beat! Drums!
Bivouac on a Mountain Side.
By Blue Ontario's Shore, *sels.*
By the Bivouac's Fitful Flame.
Cavalry Crossing a Ford.
City Dead-House, The.
Come, Said My Soul.

Come Up from the Fields Father.
Crossing Brooklyn Ferry.
Dalliance of the Eagles, The.
Darest Thou Now O Soul.
Dismantled Ship, The.
Facing West From California's Shore.
Farm Picture, A.
From Montauk Point.
From Pent-up Aching Rivers.
Give Me the Splendid Silent Sun.
Glimpse, A.
Had I the Choice.
I Hear America Singing.
I Hear It Was Charged against Me.
I Saw in Louisiana a Live-Oak Growing.
I Sit and Look Out.
In Paths Untrodden.
Joy, Shipmate, Joy.
Long, Too Long America.
Long I Thought That Knowledge Alone
  Would Suffice.
Look down Fair Moon.
Me Imperturbe.
Miracles ("Why, who makes much of a
  miracle?").
My lovers suffocate me.
Night on the Prairies, sel.
Noiseless Patient Spider, A.
O Captain! My Captain!
O Living Always, Always Dying.
Old War-Dreams.
On the Beach at Night.
Once I Pass'd through a Populous City.
One's-Self I Sing.
Out of the Cradle Endlessly Rocking.
Out of the rolling ocean the crowd came
  a drop gently to me."
Prairie Sunset, A.
Respondez!
Runner, The.
Shut Not Your Doors.
Sight in Camp in the Daybreak Gray
  and Dim, A.
Sometimes with One I Love.
Song of Myself.
Song of the Open Road.
Sparkles from the Wheel.
Starting from Paumanok, sel.
There Was a Child Went Forth.
To a Locomotive in Winter.
To a Stranger.
To Soar in Freedom and in Fullness of
  Power.
To the Garden the World.
To the Man-of-War Bird.
Trippers and askers surround me.
Vigil Strange I Kept on the Field One
  Night.
Washington's Monument, February
  1885.
When I Heard at the Close of the Day.
When I Heard the Learn'd Astronomer.
When Lilacs Last in the Dooryard
  Bloom'd.
While the Schools and the Teachers Are
  Teaching.
Whispers of Heavenly Death.
Woman Waits for Me, A.
World below the Brine, The.
Wound-Dresser, The.
**Whitney, Isabella**
Sweet Nosegay, A, or Pleasant Posy, sels.

**Whitney, J. D.**
Bedtime.
Gift, The.
Here.
**Whittemore, Reed**
Clamming.
Day with the Foreign Legion, A.
Fall of the House of Usher, The.
High School Band, The.
On the Suicide of a Friend.
Party, The.
Projection, A.
Still Life.
Teacher, A.
Walk Home, The.
Winter Scene, A.
**Whittier, John Greenleaf**
Barbara Frietchie.
Cable Hymn, The.
Centennial Hymn.
Dear Lord and Father of Mankind, with
  music.
Epitaph: "Bathsheba! to whom none
  ever said scat."
First-Day Thoughts.
Ichabod.
In School Days.
Lost Occasion, The.
My Playmate.
My Triumph.
Proem: "I love the old melodious lays."
Skipper Ireson's Ride.
Snow-Bound; a Winter Idyl.
Telling the Bees.
To My Old Schoolmaster.
What the Birds Said.
**Whur, Cornelius**
Female Friend, The.
**Wickham, Anna (Mrs. Patrick Hepburn)**
Conscience, The.
Fired Pot, The.
Meditation at Kew.
**Widerberg, Siv**
Divorce.
**Wiebe, Dallas E.**
L'Elisir d'Amore.
**Wieber, Wendy**
One, The Other, And.
**Wiegner, Kathleen**
At Times.
For the Woman Who Asked Me If I
  Believed in God and If I Pray.
Four Untitled Poems.
No Dice.
Proteus.
Silver Dollar.
**Wieners, John**
Le Chariot.
Moon Poems.
Trying to Forget.
**Wilbur, Richard**
Advice to a Prophet.
After the Last Bulletins.
All These Birds.
Baroque Wall-Fountain in the Villa
  Sciarra, A.
Beasts.
Beautiful Changes, The.
Black November Turkey, A.
Boy at the Window.
Ceremony.
Christmas Hymn, A.

Cigales.
Death of a Toad, The.
Digging for China.
Dubious Night, A.
Epistemology
Event, An.
Exeunt.
Eye, The.
Fire-Truck, A.
Folk Tune.
For Ellen.
Grasse: The Olive Trees.
Grasshopper, A.
He Was.
Hole in the Floor, A.
In a Churchyard.
In the Elegy Season.
In the Smoking Car.
Juggler.
Junk.
Late Aubade, A.
Looking into History.
Love Calls Us to the Things of This
  World.
Loves of the Puppets.
Miltonic Sonnet for Mr. Johnson on His
  Refusal of Peter Hurd's Official
  Portrait, A.
Mind.
Museum Piece.
My Father Paints the Summer.
On the Marginal Way.
Pangloss's Song.
Pardon, The.
Piazza di Spagna, Early Morning.
Place Pigalle.
Playboy.
Potato.
Praise in Summer.
Running.
Seed Leaves.
Shame.
She.
Simile for Her Smile, A.
Still, Citizen Sparrow.
Two Voices in a Meadow.
Tywater.
Undead, The.
Voice from under the Table, A.
"World without Objects Is a Sensible
  Emptiness, A."
Year's End.
**Wilcox, Ella Wheeler**
Today!
**Wild, Peter**
Dog Hospital.
For the El Paso Weather Bureau.
Riding Double.
Snakes.
Thomas and Charlie.
**Wilde, Lady Jane Francesca ("Speranza")**
Famine Year, The.
**Wilde, Oscar**
Ballad of Reading Gaol, The, sel.
Harlot's House, The.
Preface to the Picture of Dorian Gray.
Theocritus.
**Wilde, Richard Henry**
To the Mocking Bird.
**Wilkinson, Iris Guiver.** See "Hyde,
  Robin"
**Willard, Emma Hart**

Rock'd in the Cradle of the Deep, *with music.*

**Willard, Nancy**
Angels in Winter.
Clearing the Air.
For You, Who Didn't Know.
Foxfire.
Freak Show, The.
In the Hospital of the Holy Physician.
Marriage Amulet.
Poet's Wife Makes Him a Door So He Can Find the Way Home, The.
Way of Keeping, A.

**Williams, Charles Kenneth**
Hood.

**Williams, Harry H.**
In the Shade of the Old Apple Tree, *with music.*

**Williams, Hugo**
Butcher, The.
Couple Upstairs, The.
Some Kisses from "The Kama Sutra."

**Williams, John (b. 1922)**
At the Theatre.
Cold Coffee.
Letter form the North Atlantic.
Skaters, The.

**Williams, John A.**
Safari West.

**Williams, Jonathan**
Mahler, *sel.*
Symphony No. 3, in D Minor.

**Williams, Kim**
Requiem for a River.

**Williams, Miller**
Caterpillar, The.
Let Me Tell You.
Love Poem: "Six o'clock and/ the sun rises..."

**Williams, Oscar**
Shopping for Meat in Winter.
Total Revolution, A.

**Williams, Tennessee**
Heavenly Grass.
Paper Lantern, The.
Recuerdo, *sel.*
Which Is My Little Boy.

**Williams, Ursula Vaughan**
Memorial Service.

**Williams, William**
Guide Me, O Thou Great Jehovah, *with music.*

**Williams, William Carlos**
Act, The.
Artist, The.
At Kenneth Burke's Place.
At the Ball Game.
Between Walls.
Burning the Christmas Greens.
Calypsos, *sels.*
Catholic Bells, The.
Children, The.
Clouds, The.
Coda.
Complaint.
Corn Harvest, The.
Dance, The.
Danse Russe.
Death.
Delineaments of the Giants, The.
Descent, The.
Descent of Winter, The (Section 10/30).

Elegy for D. H. Lawrence, An.
Exercise No. 2.
Eyeglasses, The.
First Praise.
Fish.
Flowers by the Sea.
Folded Skyscraper, A, *sel.*
For Eleanor and Bill Monahan.
Gift, The.
Great Figure, The.
Hemmed-in Males.
History of Love, A.
Horse Show, The.
House, The.
Iris.
January Morning.
Lament: "What face, in the water."
Landscape with the Fall of Icarus.
Lear.
Locust Tree in Flower, The.
Loving Dexterity, The.
March.
Marriage.
Mental Hospital Garden, The.
Metric Figure.
Negro Woman, A.
Ol' Bunk's Band.
Paterson, *sels.*
Paterson ("Before the grass is out the people are out").
Paterson—The Strike.
Pictures from Brueghel, *sels.*
Poem: "As the cat."
Poem: "On getting a card."
Poor, The.
Portrait of a Lady.
Pot of Flowers, The.
Predicter of Famine, The.
Preface: "To make a start."
Proletarian Portrait.
Queen-Ann's-Lace.
Raleigh Was Right.
Red Wheelbarrow, The.
Return to Work, The.
Rose, The.
Russia.
Semblables, The.
Sonnet in Search of an Author.
Sparrow, The.
Spring and All ("By the road to the contagious hospital").
St. Valentine.
Term, The.
These.
This Is Just to Say.
To a Friend.
To a Friend Concerning Several Ladies.
To a Solitary Disciple.
To Be Recited to Flossie on Her Birthday.
To Elsie.
To Flossie.
To Ford Madox Ford in Heaven.
To Mark Anthony in Heaven.
To Waken an Old Lady.
Tract.
Trala Trala Trala La-le-la.
Trees, The.
Unison, A.
United States, The.
Wanderer, The: A Rococo Study, *sel.*
Widow's Lament in Springtime, The.

Willow Poem.
Winter.
Yachts, The.
Yellow Flower, The.
Young Housewife, The.
Youth and Beauty.

**Wilmot, John, Earl of Rochester.** *See* **Rochester, John Wilmot, 2d Earl of**

**Wilson, August**
Theme One: The Variations.

**Wilson, Brian.** *See* **Love, Mike** *and* **Brian Wilson**

**Wilson, Charles G.**
Ballad of New Orleans.

**Wilson, Fred**
How Do You Do, *Alabama*!

**Wilson, John (1588-1677)**
Armada, 1588, The.

**Wilson, Keith**
Classes.

**Wilson, Meredith**
Seventy Six Trombones, *with music.*

**Wilson, Robert Noble Denison**
Elegy in a Presbyterian Burying-Ground.

**Wilson, Robley, Jr.**
At Night.

**Winant, Fran**
Christopher St. Liberation Day, June 28, 1970.
Nora.
Poem to My New Jacket.
Yesterday.

**Winchilsea, Anne Finch, Countess of**
Appology, The.
Clarinda's Indifference at Parting with Her Beauty.
Introduction, The: "Did I, my lines intend for publick view."
Letter to Dafnis, A.
Nocturnal Reverie, A.
On Myselfe.
Petition for an Absolute Retreat, The.
To Melancholy.
To the Nightingale.
To the Rt. Hon. the Lady C. Tufton.
Trail All Your Pikes.

**Wingate, Philip**
I Don't Want to Play in Your Yard, *with music.*

**Winner, Septimus ("Alice Hawthorne")**
Der Deitcher's Dog, *with music.*
Listen to the Mocking Bird, *with music.*
Whispering Hope, *with music.*

**Winslow, Pete**
Only the Sky.

**Winters, Yvor**
Apollo and Daphne.
April.
Aspen's Song, The.
At the San Francisco Airport.
Castle of Thorns, The.
Elegy, An: "Noon is beautiful, The: the perfect wheel."
Grave, The.
Invaders, The.
John Sutter.
Manzanita, The.
Moralists, The.
On Teaching the Young.
Orpheus.
Rows of Cold Trees, The.
Shadow's Song, The.

Sir Gawaine and the Green Knight.
Sleep.
Slow Pacific Swell, The.
Song: "Where I walk out."
Song in Passing, A.
Theseus: a Trilogy.
Time and the Garden.
To Emily Dickinson.
To My Infant Daughter: "Alas, that I should be."
To the Holy Spirit.
To the Moon.
Upper Meadows, The.

**Wither, George**
Fair Virtue, *sel.*
For Scholars and Pupils.
I Loved a Lass.
Lover's Resolution, A.
Rhomboidal Dirge, *sel.*
Rocking Hymn, A.
Shall I Wasting in Despair.

**Witherspoon, Naomi Long.** *See* **Madgett, Naomi Long**

**Witherup, William**
Crows.
Depression.

**Witt, Harold**
Dog Alive.
Genesis.

**Woessner, Warren**
Flitcraft's Woods.
Lost Country.
Navajo Poem.

**Wolcott, John.** *See* **"Pindar, Peter"**

**Wolfe, Charles**
Burial of Sir John Moore after [*or* at] Corunna, The.

**Wolfe, Humbert**
Autumn.
Blackbird, The.
Child Unborn, The.
Wardour Street.
When lads have done with labor.

**Wolfe, Thomas**
Ben.
That Sharp Knife.

**Wolfert, Helen**
Cat, The.
Grass, The.
Preparation of the Body, The.
Where the Mind Meets the Moon in Revolt.
Woman Against the Moon, *sels.*

**Wood, Peggy**
My Aunt.

**Woodford, Bruce P.**
Going Through.

**Woods, John**
Deaths of Paragon, The.
Five Dreams, The.
Lie Closed, My Lately Loved.
Looking Both Ways before Crossing.
Traveling North.
What Do You Do When It's Spring?

**Woods, Nancy**
I Read a Tight-Fisted Poem Once.

**Woodworth, Samuel**
Hunters of Kentucky, The.
Old Oaken Bucket, The, *with music.*

**Woolsey, Sarah Chauncey.** *See* **"Coolidge, Susan"**

**Woolson, Constance Fenimore**

Kentucky Belle.

**Wordsworth, Dorothy**
Address to a Child During a Boisterous Winter Evening.
Cottager to Her Infant, The.
Loving and Liking.

**Wordsworth, Elizabeth**
Good and Clever.

**Wordsworth, William**
Affliction of Margaret, The.
After-Thought.
Alice Fell; or, Poverty.
Anecdote for Fathers.
At the Grave of Burns, 1803.
Authentic Tidings.
Brothers, The.
Calais, August, 1802.
Calais, August 15, 1802.
Character of the Happy Warrior.
Characteristics of a Child Three Years Old.
Childhood and School-Time.
Complaint, A.
Complaint of a Forsaken Indian Woman, The.
Composed by the Sea-Side, near Calais, August 1802.
Composed by the Side of Grasmere Lake.
Composed in the Valley near Dover, on the Day of Landing.
Composed near Calais, on the Road Leading to Ardres.
Composed on a May Morning, 1838.
Composed Upon Westminster Bridge, September 3, 1802.
Convict, The.
Daffodils.
Dedication: "Memory of one particular hour, The."
Elegiac Verses.
Even as a dragon's eye that feels the stress.
Evening Walk, An.
Expostulation and Reply.
Extempore Effusion upon the Death of James Hogg.
Farewell, A: "Farewell, thou little nook of mountain-ground."
Female Vagrant, The.
Fountain, The.
Glow-Worm, The.
Goody Blake, and Harry Gill.
Great men have been among us; hands that penned.
Guilt.
I grieved for Buonaparté, with a vain.
I Traveled among Unknown Men.
I Wandered Lonely As a Cloud.
Idiot Boy, The.
It Is a Beauteous Evening, Calm and Free.
It is not to be thought of that the flood.
Laodamia.
Last of the Flock, The.
Liberty, *sel.*
Lines Composed a Few Miles above Tintern Abbey.
Lines Left upon a Seat in a Yew-Tree.
Lines Written in Early Spring.
London, 1802 ("Milton! thou shouldst be living...").

Longest Day, The.
Louisa.
Lucy, *complete, in 5 parts.*
Lucy Gray; or, Solitude.
Mad Mother, The.
Matthew.
Michael: A Pastoral Poem.
Mutability.
My Heart Leaps Up When I Behold.
Night-Piece, A.
Nuns fret not at their convent's narrow room.
Nutting.
O Friend! I Know Not Which Way I Must Look.
Ode: Intimations of Immortality from Recollections of Early Childhood.
Ode on the Installation of His Royal Highness Prince Albert.
Ode to Duty.
Old Cumberland Beggar, The.
Old Man Travelling; Animal Tranquillity and Decay, a Sketch.
On the Extinction of the Venetian Republic.
One Summer Evening.
Pass of Kirkstone, The.
Personal Talk.
Pet Lamb, The.
Peter Bell.
Poet's Epitaph, A.
Power of armies is a visible thing, The.
Prelude, The [or, Growth of a Poet's Mind].
Recluse, The; or, Home at Grasmere.
Resolution and Independence.
Reverie of Poor Susan, The.
Ruined Cottage, The.
Ruth.
Scorn Not the Sonnet.
September, 1819.
September 1, 1802.
September 1802. Near Dover.
She Dwelt among the Untrodden Way.
She Was a Phantom of Delight.
Simon Lee.
Skaters, The.
Slumber Did My Spirit Seal, A.
Small Celandine, The.
Solitary Reaper, The.
Song at the Feast of Bougham Castle.
Sonnet in Allusion to Various Recent Histories and Notices of the French Revolution.
Sonnet on the Projected Kendal and Windermere Railway.
Stanzas Written in My Pocket-Copy of Thomson's "Castle of Indolence."
Stepping Westward.
Strange Fits of Passion I Have Known.
Sun has long been set, The.
Surprised by Joy—Impatient as the Wind.
Tables Turned, The.
These chairs they have no words to utter.
Thorn, The.
Thought of a Briton on the Subjugation of Switzerland.
Three Years She Grew in Sun and Shower.

Thus did my days pass on, and now at length.

'Tis said, that some have died for love.

To a Butterfly ("I've watched you now a full half-hour").

To a Butterfly ("Stay near me—do not take thy flight!").

To a Highland Girl.

To a Skylark.

To a Young Lady.

To B. R. Haydon.

To H. C.

To Joanna.

To My Sister.

To Sleep.

To the Cuckoo.

To the Men of Kent. October, 1803.

To the Same Flower.

To the Small Celandine.

To Toussaint L'Ouverture.

Two April Mornings, The.

Uncertainty.

We Are Seven.

When I have borne in memory what has tamed.

Where lies the land to which yon ship must go?

White Doe of Rylstone, The: or, The Fate of the Nortons.

Why art thou silent! Is thy love a plant.

Wisdom and Spirit of the universe!

World Is Too Much with Us, The.

Written after the Death of Charles Lamb.

Written in March.

Written in the Album of a Child.

Yarrow Unvisited.

Yarrow Visited.

Yes, it was the mountain echo.

**Work, Henry Clay**

Grandfather's Clock, *with music.*

Kingdom Coming, *with music.*

Marching Through Georgia, *with music.*

**Wotton, Sir Henry**

Character of a Happy Life, The.

Hymn to My God in a Night of My Late Sickness, A.

On His Mistress, [*or* Mistris], the Queen of Bohemia.

Upon the Death of Sir Albert Morton's Wife.

Upon the Sudden Restraint of the Earl of Somerset, Then Falling from [*or* out of] Favour.

**Wratislaw, Theodore**

Eros d' aute.

**Wrench, Margaret Stanley**

In the Radiotherapy Unit.

**Wright, Bruce McM.**

African Affair, The.

**Wright, Celeste Turner**

Yugoslav Cemetery.

**Wright, Charles**

Chinoiserie.

Death.

Delta Traveller.

Dog Creek Mainline.

Epithalamion: "Kingfisher falls through the dry air, The."

Fever Toy, The.

New Poem, The.

Yellow.

**Wright, David**

Grasmere Sonnets.

Invocation to the Goddess, An.

Kleomedes.

Monologue of a Deaf Man.

**Wright, James**

Ars Poetica: Some Recent Criticism.

As I Step over a Puddle at the End of Winter, I Think of an Ancient Chinese Governor.

At the Slackening of the Tide.

At Thomas Hardy's Birthplace, 1953.

Autumn Begins in Martins Ferry, Ohio.

Before a Cashier's Window in a Department Store.

Blessing, A.

Blue Teal's Mother.

Breath of Air, A.

Centenary Ode, A: Inscribed to Little Crow, Leader of the Sioux Rebellion.

Complaint.

Confession to J. Edgar Hoover.

Depressed by a Book of Bad Poetry, I Walk Toward an Unused Pasture and Invite the Insects to Join Me.

Eisenhower's Visit to Franco, 1959.

Evening.

Gesture by a Lady with an Assumed Name, A.

I Try to Waken and Greet the World Once Again.

In Response to a Rumor That the Oldest Whorehouse In Wheeling, West Virginia, Has Been Condemned.

In Shame and Humiliation.

Jewel, The.

Last November in a Field.

Lights in the Hallway, The.

Lying in a Hammock at William Duffy's Farm.

March.

Milkweed.

Miners.

Minneapolis Poem, The.

Mutterings over the Crib of a Deaf Child.

Northern Pike.

October Ghosts.

On Minding One's Own Business.

Paul.

Poem about Breasts, A.

Presentation of Two Birds to My Son, A.

Saint Judas.

Spring Images.

Three Sentences for a Dead Swan.

To a Fugitive.

To Flood Stage Again.

Trouble.

Two Poems about President Harding.

Written in a Copy of Swift's Poems, for Wayne Burns.

**Wright, Jay**

Death As History.

Homecoming Singer, The.

Invitation to Madison County, An.

This morning I threw the windows.

Wednesday Night Prayer Meeting.

**Wright, Judith**

Bull, The.

Bullocky.

Cycads, The.

Document, A.

Egrets.

Eve to Her Daughters.

Extinct Birds

Forest, The.

Hawthorn Hedge, The.

Legend.

Lyrebirds.

Night Herons.

Old Prison, The.

Sanctuary.

Some Words.

South of My Days.

Sports Field.

Storm.

Surfer, The.

Woman to Child.

Woman to Man.

**Wright, Richard**

Between the World and Me.

Four Haiku.

Hokku Poems.

I Have Seen Black Hands.

**Wright, Sarah E.**

To Some Millions Who Survive Joseph E. Mander, Sr.

Until They Have Stopped.

**Wroth, Mary Sidney (Countess of Montgomery)**

Duke's Song, The.

Lindamira's Complaint.

Pamphilia to Amphilanthus.

Pamphilia's Sonnet.

Urania,*sels.*

Verses of the Talkative Knight, The.

**Wu Ti, Emperor**

People Hide Their Love.

**Wyatt, Sir Thomas**

Alas, madam, for stealing of a kiss.

Appeal, An.

Behold, love, thy power how she despiseth!

Blame not my lute for he must sownde.

Dyvers dother use as I have hard and kno.

Eche man me telleth I chaunge moost my devise.

Farewell, all my welfare.

Farewell: "What should I say."

Forget Not Yet.

He is not ded that somtyme hath a fall.

How oft have I, my dere and cruell foo.

I abide and abide and better abide.

If fansy would favor.

If waker care, if sodayne pale coulor.

In Eternum.

Is it possible [*or* Ys yt possyble].

It may be good, like it who list.

Lament my losse, my labor, and my payne.

Lover Complaineth the Unkindness of His Love, The.

Lover Having Dreamed Enjoying of His Love, Complaineth That the Dream Is Not either Longer or Truer.

Lover Showeth [*or* Sheweth] How He Is Forsaken of Such as He Sometime Enjoyed, The.

Luckes, my faire falcon, and your fellowes all.

Madame, withouten many wordes.

Me list no more to sing.

Mye love toke skorne my servise to retaine.
Myne owne John Poyntz, sins ye delight to know.
Now must I lerne to lyve at rest.
Once as methought Fortune me kissed.
Piller pearisht is whearto I lent, The.
Quondam was I in my leady's grace.
Renouncing of Love, A.
Resound my voyse, ye wodes that here me plain.
Robyn, A/ Joly Robyn.
Rondeau: "Help me to seek, for I lost it there."
Satires, *sels.*
Some tyme I fled the fyre that me brent.
Tagus, fare well, that westward with thy stremes.
Tanglid I was yn loves snare.
There was never nothing more me pained [*or* payned].
Throughout the World If It Were Sought.
To cause accord or to aggre.
To Rail or Jest, Ye Know I Use It Not.
V. Innocentia Veritas Viat Fides Circumdederunt Me Inimici Mei.
Vixi Puellis Nuper Idoneus.
What meaneth this? When I lie alone.
What no, perdy, ye may be sure!
What rage is this? what furour of what kynd?
What vaileth truth? or by it to take payn?
What wourde is that that chaungeth not.
Who hath herd of suche crueltye before?
Whoso list to hunt, I know where is an hind.
With Serving Still.
Ye old mule, that thinck your self so fayre.
You that in love finde lucke and habundance.

**Wylie, Elinor**
Atavism.
Cold-blooded Creatures.
Confession of Faith.
Eagle and the Mole,The.
Epitaph: "For this she starred her eyes with salt."
Full Moon.
Hughie at the Inn.
Let No Charitable Hope.
Little Elegy.
Madman's Song.
Nebuchadnezzar.
Nonsense Rhyme.
Preference.
Prophecy.
Proud Lady, A.
Puritan Sonnet.
Sanctuary.
Sea Lullaby.
This Hand.
Velvet Shoes.
Wild Peaches.

**Wyndham, Harald**
Anarchist's Letter, An.

**Wynne, John Huddlestone**
Horse and the Mule, The.
Time.

**Wyse, Louis**
Did You See the *Times* Today?

# Y

**Yeatman, Robert Julian** *and* **Walter Carruthers Sellar**
How I Brought the Good News from Aix to Ghent.

**Yeats, William Butler**
Acre of Grass, An.
Adam's Curse.
Aedh Thinks of Those Who Have Spoken Evil of His Beloved.
Aedh Wishes for the Cloths of Heaven.
After Long Silence.
All Things Can Tempt Me.
Among School Children.
Ballad of Father Gilligan, The.
Balloon of the Mind, The.
Beggar to Beggar Cried.
Black Tower, The.
Broken Dreams.
Brown Penny.
Byzantium.
Cap and Bells, The.
Cat and the Moon, The.
Chambermaid's First Song, The.
Chambermaid's Second Song, The.
Choice, The.
Chosen.
Circus Animals' Desertion, The.
Coat, The.
Cold Heaven, The.
Collar-Bone of a Hare, The.
Colonel Martin.
Coming of Wisdom with Time, The.
Coole Park and Ballylee, 1931.
Cradle Song, A: "Angels are stooping, The."
Crazed Girl, The.
Crazed Moon, The ("Crazed through much child-bearing").
Crazy Jane and the Bishop.
Crazy Jane on God.
Crazy Jane Talks with the Bishop.
Curse of Cromwell, The.
Dawn, The.
Dedication to a Book of Stories Selected from the Irish Novelists, The.
Deep-Sworn Vow, The.
Dialogue of Self and Soul, A.
Dolls, The.
Down by the Salley Gardens.
Dream of Death, A.
Drinking Song, A.
Easter 1916.
Fascination of What's Difficult, The.
Father and Child.
Father Gilligan.
Fisherman, The.
Folly of Being Comforted, The.
For Anne Gregory.
Four Ages of Man, The.
Fragment: "Locke sank into a swoon."
Friends.
Girl's Song.
Great Day, The.

Gyres, The.
He Hears the Cry of the Sedge.
Hosting of the Sidhe, The ("The host is riding from Knocknarea").
"I Am of Ireland."
In Memory of Eva Gore-Booth and Con Markiewicz.
In the Seven Woods.
Indian to His Love, The.
Indian upon God, The.
Irish Airman Foresees His Death, An.
Lady's First Song, The.
Lake Isle of Innisfree, The.
Lamentation of the Old Pensioner, The.
Lapis Lazuli.
Last Confession, A.
Leaders of the Crowd, The.
Leda and the Swan.
Long-legged Fly.
Lover Tells of the Rose in His Heart, The.
Lover's Song, The.
Lullaby: "Beloved, may your sleep be sound."
Magi, The.
Man Who Dreamed of Faeryland, The.
Meditations in Time of Civil War,*sels.*
Memory.
Meru.
Michael Robartes Bids His Beloved Be at Peace.
Mohini Chatterjee.
Municipal Gallery Revisited, The.
Never Give All the Heart.
News for the Delphic Oracle.
Nineteen Hundred and Nineteen.
No Second Troy.
Old Men Admiring Themselves in the Water, The.
Old Pensioner, The.
Old Stone Cross, The.
On Being Asked for a War Poem
On Hearing That the Students of Our New University Have Joined the Agitation Against Immoral Literature.
Paudeen.
Pity of Love, The.
Politics.
Prayer for My Daughter, A.
Purgatory.
Ragged Wood, The.
Resurrection, The, *sel.*
Ribh Considers Christian Love Insufficient.
Road at My Door, The.
Scholars, The.
Second Coming, The.
September 1913.
Solomon and the Witch.
Song of the Happy Shepherd, The.
Song of the Old Mother, The.
Song of Wandering Aengus, The.
Sorrow of Love, The.
Spur, The.
Stare's Nest by My Window, The.
Statesman's Holiday, The.
Statues, The.
Stick of Incense, A.
Sweet Dancer.
To a Child Dancing in the Wind.
To a Poet, Who Would Have Me Praise

Certain Bad Poets, Imitators of His
  and Mine.
To a Squirrel at Kyle-Na-No.
To a Young Girl.
To Be Carved on a Stone at Thoor
  Ballylee.
To Ireland in the Coming Times.
To the Rose upon the Rood of Time.
Tower, The.
Two Songs from a Play.
Under Ben Bulben.
Vacillation.
When You Are Old.
Whence Had They Come?
Who Goes with Fergus?
Wild Swans at Coole, The.
**Yester, Lord**
Tweedside.
**Yevtushenko, Yevgeny**
Lies.
**Yoak, Martha**
Mother and I.
Mother and the Moon.
Sunday Evening with Elizabeth, Age 5.
**Yosano, Akiko No**
Tanka: "Once, far over the breakers."
Tanka: "Swifter than hail."
**Young, Al**
Dance for Ma Rainey, A.
Dance for Militant Dilettantes, A.
Dance of the Infidels.
Dancer, The.
Dancing in the Street.
For Kenneth and Miriam Patchen.
For Poets.
Groupie.
Kiss.
Lemons, Lemons.
Loneliness.
Lonesome in the Country.
Move Continuing, The.
Myself When I Am Real.
Paris.
Poem Found Emptying Out My Pockets.
Prestidigitator, The.
Song Turning Back into Itself, The.
Squirrels.
Tribute.
Two Takes from Love in Los Angeles.
Yes, the Secret Mind Whispers.
**Young, Andrew**
Beauty and Love.
Culbin Sands.
Haystack, The.
Last Snow.
Shepherd's Hut, The.
Song for Autumn.
Stockdoves, The.
Wiltshire Downs.
**Young, Augustus**
After Five Years.
Last Refuge, The.
School-Friend.
**Young, David**
August at the Lake.
Boxcar Poem, The. ("Boxcars drift by,
  The").
Death of the Novel, The.
Dreams of the Wars.
Man Who Swallowed a Bird, The.

Mandelstam.
Occupational Hazards.
Owl, The.
Thoughts of Chairman Mao.
Two for the Hampton Institute.
**Young, Douglas**
Last Lauch.
Shepherd's Dochter, The.
**Young, E. R.**
Railroad Reverie.
**Young, Edward (1683-1765)**
Art of Happiness, The.
Complaint, The.
Epigram on Voltaire.
Instalment, The, *sel.*
Lavinia at Church.
Love of Fame, The Universal Passion,
  *sel.*
Night Thoughts [The Complaint],*sels.*
Satire III: "Long, Dodington, in debt, I
  long have sought."
Satire on Women, *sel.*
Tir'd nature's sweet restorer, balmy
  sleep!
**Young, Francis Brett**
Seascape.
**Young, George M., Jr.**
Lecture before a Lecture on Pushkin.
Lecturer seeks a Wife, The.
Lectures on the Biology of the Shadow.
Polar Expedition.
Three Lectures on the Skeleton.
**Young, Ian**
At Rochdale.
Double Exposure.
Elephants from the Sea.
It's no good/ being an actor.
Skull, The.
Sugar-Candy Bird, A.
**Young, Marguerite**
Angels, The.
Noah's Ark.
Whales, The.
Winter Scene.
**Young, Neil**
Here We Are in the Years.
**Young, Roland**
Goat, The.
Miscegenous Zebra, The.
**Young Bear, Ray A.**
Another Face.
Black Dog.
Celebration.
Coming Back Home.
Cook, The.
Crow-Children Walk My Circles in the
  Snow, The.
Empty Streams of Autumn
Four Poems.
In Dream: The Privacy of Sequence.
In Missing.
Listening Rock, The.
One Chip of Human Bone.
Poem for Diane Wakoski, A.
Remembrance of a Color inside a
  Forest, A.
Rushing.
Star Blanket.
These Horses Came.
This House.

Trains Made of Stone.
Waiting to Be Fed.
War Walking Near.
Warrior Dreams.
Way the Bird Sat, The.
Wrong Kind of Love.
**Youngblood, Sarah**
At the Western Shore.
Walking the Beach.
**Yradier, Sebastian**
La Paloma, *with music.*
**Yvonne**
Rachel and the Truth (c.1945).
Rachel at Thirteen.
Rachel at Twenty-three.

## Z

**Zach, Natan**
Do Not Dream.
**Zachariou, Paulette Dusdall**
In the Embers at Midnight.
In the Morning.
Sticks and Stones.
**Zahn, Curtis**
Highway 101, Seal Beach.
**Zaturenska, Marya Alexandrovna (Mrs.
  Horace Gregory)**
All Is Well with the Child.
Daisy, The.
Descent of the Vulture, The.
Girl's Song.
Hymn to Artemis, the Destroyer.
Intruder, The.
Lunar Tides, The.
Ophelia's Song.
**Zavatsky, Bill**
Being Adult.
**Zimmer, Paul**
Apple Blight.
Lord Fluting Dreams of America on the
  Eve of His Departure from Liverpool.
Phineas Within and Without.
Zimmer Drunk and Alone, Dreaming of
  Old Football Games.
**"Zozimus."** *See* **Moran, Michael**
**Zukofsky, Louis**
"A" (1–12), *sels.*
"A 11."
"A 4."
Ask of the sun.
Cars once steel and green, now old.
For you I have emptied the meaning.
Green leaf that will outlast the winter,
  The.
I walk in the old street.
In Arizona/ (how many years in the
  mountains).
It's hard to see but think of a sea.
Lights, *sels.*
Lines of this new song are nothing, The.
Non Ti Fidar.
Reading and Talking.
Tall and singularly dark you pass among
  the breakers.
**Zweig, Paul**
Women in Brooklyn.

# SUBJECT INDEX

**Abolitionists**
Runagate Runagate. Hayden.
**Abominable Snowman**
Abominable Snowman, The. Nash.
**Abortion**
Abortion, The. Iverson.
Abortion, An. O'Hara.
Abortion, The. Sexton.
Inquest, The. Davies.
Lost Baby Poem, The. Clifton.
Mother, The. Brooks.
Should We Legalize Abortion? O'Hara.
Unwanted, The. Gordon.
Vow, The. Hecht.
**Abraham**
Parable of the Old Man and the Young, The. Owen.
**Absence**
Letter to Her Husband, Absent upon Public Employment, A.
   Bradstreet.
Talking after Christmas Blues. Henri.
**Accidents**
Accident, The. Gasparini.
At 79th and Park. Howes.
Blue-tailed Fly, The. *Unknown.*
Cut. Plath.
Death of the Sports-Car Driver, The. Aaron.
Down Went McGinty. Flynn.
Dying Mine Brakeman, The. Jenks.
George Allen. *Unknown.*
Henry K. Sawyer. *Unknown.*
It's Here in The. Atkins.
Out, Out. Frost.
Poems about Playmates. Davis.
Tay Bridge Disaster, The. McGonagall.
Worker, The. Thomas.
Wreck of the Royal Palm, The. *Unknown.*
**Acorns**
Acorns. Mills.
**Acting and Actors**
Ballade of Dead Actors. Henley.
Boy Actor, The. Coward.
If I Were on the Stage. Blossom
Old Trouper, The.*Fr.* Archy and Mehitabel. Marquis.
Santa Claus. Hassall.
They All Want to Play Hamlet. Sandburg.
**Adam**
Adam Driven from Eden. *Unknown.*
Adam in the Garden. Suderman.
Adam Lay Y-Bounden. *Unknown.*
Adam's Task. Hollander.
Banishment, The. *Fr.* Paradise Lost. Milton.
Discovery, The. Gibbon.
Garden, The. Silverman.
Imperial Adam. Hope.
Original Sequence. Booth.
Reveille. Hughes.
**Adams, John Quincy**
Twilight's Last Gleaming. Monks.
**Adlestrop, England**
Adlestrop. Thomas.
**Adolescence**
Adolescence II. Dove.
Conventionalist, The. Smith.
Girl Friends. Daniell.
Homework for Annabelle. McGinley.
I Remember How She Sang. Penny.

Impossibility, An. Vas Dias.
Lines to His Son on Reaching Adolescence. Logan.
Little Girl, My String Bean, My Lovely Woman. Sexton.
Pennycandystore beyond the El, The.*Fr.* A Coney Island of the
   Mind. Ferlinghetti.
Portrait of Girl with Comic Book. McGinley.
September 7. Bass.
16/53. Piercy.
Triolet against Sisters. McGinley.
Young. Sexton.
Young Ones, The. Jennings.
**Adultery.** *See* **Infidelity.**
**Advent**
Advent. *Unknown.*
**Aeneas**
Aeneas at Washington. Tate.
Falling Asleep over the Aeneid. Lowell.
**Africa**
African Affair, The. Wright.
African Dream. Kaufman.
African Elegy, An. Duncan.
Bedtime Story. MacBeth.
Blue Tanganyika. Bethune.
Bwagamoyo. Bethune.
Chad. Brathwaite.
Coptic Poem. Durrell.
Far Cry from Africa, A. Walcott.
Heritage. Bennett.
Heritage. Cullen.
Heritage. Hughes.
Into the Dark. Monette.
Mmenson. Brathwaite.
Near the Old Slave Fort. Bruchac.
Old Laughter. Brooks.
Scorpion, The. Plomer.
Timbuctu. Brathwaite.
**Afton (river) Scotland**
Afton Water. Burns.
**Age** *See* **Middle Age; Old Age.**
**Agincourt, Battle of**
Agincourt Carol, The. *Unknown.*
Ballad of Agincourt, The. Drayton.
King Henry the Fifth before Agincourt.*Fr.* King Henry V.
   Shakespeare.
**Aging**
Aging. Jong.
Key of the Kingdom, The. Reed.
Loveliest of Trees, the Cherry Now. Housman.
Ode: Intimations of Immortality from Recollections of Early
   Childhood. Wordsworth.
Tonight I've watched. Sappho.
What I Expected. Spender.
Will You Love Me in December as You Do in May? Walker.
**Ailsa Craig, Scotland**
To Ailsa Rock. Keats.
**Air Warfare**
Americana XIII. Rakosi.
Brother Fire. MacNeice.
Crack of Doom. Carter.
Death of the Ball Turret Gunner, The. Jarrell.
Firebombing, The. Dickey.
Front, A. Jarrell.
Fury of Aerial Bombardment, The. Eberhart.
Gods in Vietnam. Redmond.
Irish Airman Foresees His Death, An. Yeats.
Man in the Dead Machine, The. Hall.

Pilot, The. Turco.
Raid, The. Everson.
Still Falls the Rain. Sitwell.
Usual exquisite boredom of patrols, The. Popham.
When a Beau Goes In. Ewart.

**Airline Stewardesses**
Falling. Dickey.

**Airplanes.** *See* **Aviation and Aviators.**

**Airports**
At the Airport. Jones.
At the San Francisco Airport. Winters.

**Alabama (ship)**
How Do You Do, *Alabama!* Wilson.
Roll, *Alabama,* Roll. *Unknown.*

**Alamo**
Defence of the Alamo, The. Miller.

**Alaska**
Denali Road. Haines.
Summer in Fairbanks. Stokesbury.

**Albert Hall (London)**
Poem about Poems about Vietnam, A. Stallworthy.

**Alchemy and Alchemists**
Paracelsus in Excelsis. Pound.

**Alcoholism.** *See* **Drunkards.**

**Ale**
Back and Side Go Bare.*Fr.* Gammer Gurton's Needle. *At. to*
Stevenson.
Bring Us in Good Ale. *Unknown.*
Doll Thy Ale. *Unknown.*
When Jones's Ale Was New. *Unknown.*

**Alexander the Great**
Alexander and Gymnosophists. *Unknown.*
On Alexander and Aristotle, on a Black-on-Red Greek Plate.
Dugan.
Speaking Tree, The. Rukeyser.

**Alfonso X, King of Castile and Leon**
Alphonso of Castile. Emerson.

**Ali, Muhammed (Cassius Clay)**
Ali. Corbin.
Black Lady in an Afro Hairdo Cheers for Cassius. Holmes.
Clay Comes out to Meet Terrell. Ali.
I Dance and I Have a Fast Hook. Ali.

**Alice in Wonderland**
Last Days of Alice. Tate.

**Alienation**
Alienation (To My Son). Travis.
Alone/December/Night. Cruz.
American Rhapsody (4). Fearing.
Anomie. Ramsey.
Average, The. Auden.
Back Again, Home. Lee.
Between Me and Anyone Who Can Understand. Scott.
Blight. Emerson.
Brooding. Ignatow.
Dangling Conversation. Simon.
Desolation Row. Dylan.
Dirge: "1-2-3 was the number he played." Fearing.
Howl. Ginsberg.
In a Dark Time. Roethke.
Invention of the Comics, The. Jones.
It is Oregon, the Highway Looms. Bond.
Looking Up. Allcock.
Love Song of J. Alfred Prufrock, The. Eliot.
Mr. Flood's Party. Robinson.
No Bargains Today. Kenner.
Not Waving But Drowning. Smith
Personality Sketch, A: Bill. Davis.
Pressure. Waldman.
Sound of Silence, The. Simon.
Unwanted. Field.
Useless Words. Sandburg.
Warren Pryor. Nowlan.

Waste Land, The. Eliot.
World Is Too Much with Us, The. Wordsworth.
Writer's House, The. Allen.
Written in Northampton County Asylum. Clare.

**All Saints' Eve.** *See* **Halloween.**

**All Souls' Night**
All Souls' Night. Cornford.

**Allen, Ethan**
Green Mountain Boy. Smyth.

**Alligators**
Alligator, The. Ravenel.

**Alphabet Poems**
ABC, An. *Unknown.*
A B C Objects. *Unknown.*
A Is for Abracadabra. Farjeon.
A was an apple-pie. Mother Goose.
A Was an Archer. *Unknown.*
A Was Once an Apple Pie. Lear.
Alphabet of Christmas Cheer. Weston.
And with the Sorrows of This Joyousness. Patchen.
Animal Alphabet, An. *Unknown.*
Austrian Army, An. Watts.
From a Cheerful Alphabet. Updike.
Jamboree for J, A. Merriam.
Lumberman's Alphabet, The. *Unknown.*
Nursery Rhyme Alphabet, A. *Unknown.*
Sailors'Alphabet, The. *Unknown.*

**Alps**
Authentic Tidings.*Fr.* The Prelude. Wordsworth.
Hymn Before Sunrise in the Vale of Chamouni. Coleridge.
Nocturne of the Self-Evident Presence. MacGreevy.
On the Fly-Leaf of Pound's Cantos. Bunting.

**Altgeld, John Peter**
Eagle That Is Forgotten, The. Lindsay.

**Amana Colonies**
Amana Colonies, The. Smith.

**America (United States of).** *See* **United States.**

**American Revolution**
America Is Darken'd. Dillard.
Ballad of Benjamin Jones, The. Ward.
Ballad of Bunker Hill, The. *Unknown.*
Bombardment of Bristol, R.I., The. *Unknown.*
Caldwell of Springfield. Harte.
Capture of Major André, The. *Unknown.*
Carmen Bellicosum. McMaster.
Concord Hymn. Emerson.
Cornwallis' Country Dance. *Unknown.*
Death of Warren, The. Sargent.
Dying Sergeant, The. *Unknown.*
Eutaw Springs. Freneau.
Farewell to Kingsbridge. *Unknown.*
Maryland Battalion, The. Palmer.
Nathan Hale. Finch.
Nathan Hale. *Unknown.*
Paul Revere's Ride*Fr.* Tales of a Wayside Inn. Longfellow.
Picture of the Times, A. Freneau.
Rich Lady over the Sea, The. *Unknown.*
Riflemen's Song at Bennington. *Unknown.*
Song of Marion's Men. Bryant.
Sons of Liberty, The. *Unknown.*
Sword of Bunker Hill, The. Wallace.
Warren's Address. Pierpont.
Yankee Doodle. *Unknown.*
Yankee Man-of-War, The. *Unknown.*
Ye Parliament of England. *Unknown.*

**Americans**
Ave Caesar. Jeffers.
Boy-Man. Shapiro.
Byron vs. DiMaggio. Mienke.
I Hear America Singing. Whitman.
My Wife Who Is American. Daniel.
*See also* **United States.**

**Amish, The (Mennonite Christians)**
Amish, The. Updike.
**Amusement Parks**
Dinoland. Rieter.
**Anatomy**
Cider and Vesalius. Peck.
**Ancestors and Ancestry**
Ancestors. Randall.
Cycle of Women, A. Barba.
Forefathers. Blunden.
Heritage. Bennett.
Heritage. Cullen.
Idea of Ancestry, The. Knight.
Illustrious Ancestors. Levertov.
Lineage. Walker.
Lost. Ignacio.
**André, John**
Capture of Major André, The. *Unknown.*
Major André. *Unknown.*
**Angels**
Air and Angels. Donne.
Angel. Merrill.
Angels, The. Young.
Angels in Winter. Willard.
How Grand and How Bright. *Unknown.*
Propeller Sleep. Berssenbrugge.
Tom's Angel. De la Mare.
Vision, A. Levertov.
**Anger**
Death Dance, The. Piercy.
My Mother Takes My Wife's Side. Kherdian.
Poison Tree, A.*Fr.* Songs of Experience: Blake.
Temper. Fyleman.
**Angkor Wat**
Ank'hor Vat. Devlin.
**Animals**
Ad limina. Campbell.
And Did the Animals? Van Doren.
Animals, The. Muir.
Animals.*Fr.* Song of Myself. Whitman.
Animals' Christmas, The. Dacey.
At the Zoo. Thackeray.
Barnyard, The. *Unknown.*
Beasts. Wilbur.
Beasts and Birds. O'Keeffe.
Bells of Heaven, The. Hodgson.
Burial of the Linnet, The. Ewing.
Butterfly's Ball, The. Roscoe.
Byre. MacCaig.
Cage, The. Stephens.
Chenille. Dickey.
Come into Animal Presence. Levertov.
Creatures. Kumin.
Dog and Tiger. Greenberg.
Dumb World, The. Davies.
Eau-Forte. Flint.
Fiddle-I-Fee. *Unknown.*
Fish Does . . . Hip! The. Mba Sholé.
Gallows, The. Thomas.
Heaven of Animals. Dickey.
Mirror for the Barnyard. Myers.
Mrs. Malone. Farjeon.
Mouse's Courting Song, The. *Unknown.*
My Father Kept a Horse. *Unknown.*
Peacock "At Home," The. Dorset.
Pet Shop. MacNiece.
Robin Redbreast in a Cage, A.*Fr.* Auguries of Innocence.
Blake.
Self-Pity. Lawrence.
Stockyard, The. Squire.
Take One Home for the Kiddies. Larkin.
Temple of the Animals, The. Duncan.

Tree in the Wood, The. *Unknown.*
When the Animals Left the Ark. *Unknown.*
Young Stock. Sackville-West.
**Antietam Campaign**
Battle of Antietam Creek, The. *Unknown.*
**Ants**
Ants, The. Clare.
Ants and Others. Stoutenberg.
Departmental. Frost.
Ondt and the Gracehoper, The. Joyce.
**Apes**
Best Loved of Africa. Danner.
**Aphrodite**
Ring of, The. Olson.
Sapphics. Swinburne.
*See also* **Venus.**
**Apollo**
Hymn of Apollo. Shelley.
Many Are Called. Robinson.
Metric Figure. Williams.
Ode to Apollo. Keats.
**Apostles**
They Slept While Jesus Prayed. Chambers.
**Apple Trees**
Mine Host of the "Golden Apple." Westwood.
Old Sinner. Bowman.
Saving the Harvest. Lehmann.
**Apples**
After Apple-Picking. Frost.
Apple-Logia. Brand.
Apples. Kaufman.
Apples to Keep. F. Frost.
Crossed Apple, The. Bogan.
Moonlit Apples. Drinkwater.
**April**
Allotments: April. Spencer.
April 1885. Bridges.
April Inventory. Snodgrass.
April Rise. Lee.
Same Lady, The. Nichols.
Spring. Millay.
**Aquariums**
At the Water Zoo. Knox.
Ode of Odium on Aquariums. Guiterman.
**Arabia**
Arabia. Falkner.
**Aran Islands, Ireland**
Aran Islands. Layton.
**Arcadia**
Comfort from Arcadia. Flocos.
**Archaeology**
Digging for Indians. Gildner.
**Arethusa**
Arethusa. Shelley.
**Arkansas**
Sanford Barney. *Unknown.*
**Armada.** *See* **Spanish Armada.**
**Armagh, Ireland**
Armagh. Rodgers.
**Armies**
Epitaph on an Army of Mercenaries. Housman.
**Armstrong, Louis ("Satchmo")**
Satchmo. Tolson.
**Army Life**
Base Details. Sassoon.
By the Bivouac's Fitful Flame. Whitman.
Cavalry Crossing a Ford. Whitman.
Class Incident from Graves. Brownjohn.
Danny Deever. Kipling.
'Eathen, The. Kipling.
Execution of Cornelius Vane, The. Read.
Going in to Dinner. Shanks.

Lessons of the War. Reed.
Officers' Mess. Ewart.
Spring 1942. Fuller.
Tenting on the Old Camp Ground. Kittredge.
Weapons Training. Dawe.
Vaudeville. Kirstein.

**Art and Artists**
Against Botticelli. Hass.
Anecdote of the Jar. Stevens.
Anonymous Drawing. Justice.
Art. Levertov.
Art. Melville.
Artist, An. Jeffers.
Chicago Picasso, The. Brooks.
Dab of Color, A. Weiss.
Dog of Art, The. Levertov.
Egyptian Pulled Glass Bottle in the Shape of a Fish, An.
   Moore.
I would not paint—a picture. Dickinson.
In the National Gallery. Sassoon.
Martyrdom of Saint Sebastian, The. Dobson.
Miltonic Sonnet for Mr. Johnson on His Refusal of Peter Hurd's
   Official Portrait, A. Wilbur.
Musée des Beaux Arts. Auden.
Museum Piece. Wilbur.
Nature Morte. MacNeice.
Ode on a Grecian Urn. Keats.
Paring the Apple. Tomlinson.
Preface to the Picture of Dorian Gray. Wilde.
Primitives. Randall.
That No Man Should Write But Such as Do Excel.
   Turberville.
To an Artist. Burns.
To B. R. Haydon. Wordsworth.
To My Son Parker, Asleep in the Next Room. Kaufman.
Why I Am Not a Painter. O'Hara.
   *See also* **Painting and Painters; Portraits; Sculpture and
      Sculptors; Statues.**

**Artemis**
Hymn to Artemis, the Destroyer. Zaturenska.
   *See also* **Diana.**

**Arthurian Legend**
Death of Arthur, The.*Fr.* The Brut. Layamon.
Sir Gawaine and the Green Knight. Winters.

**Aspen Trees**
Aspens. Thomas.

**Assassinations and Assassins**
Assassination. Lee.
Assassination Poems. Ridland.
Assassination Raga. Ferlinghetti.
Booth Killed Lincoln. *Unknown.*
Ceremony. Lifshin.
Charles Guiteau. *Unknown.*
Down in Dallas. Kennedy.
For Malcolm: After Mecca. Barrax.
Zolgotz. *Unknown.*

**Asses.** *See* **Donkeys.**
**Assumption of the Virgin.** *See* **Mary, the Virgin.**
**Assyrians**
Destruction of Sennacherib, The. Byron.

**Astrology**
Upon Looking at a Book of Astrology. McFadden.
Zodiac Rhyme, The. *Unknown.*

**Astronomers and Astronomy**
Great Bear, The. Hollander.
Planetarium. Rich.
Stargazer, The. *Unknown.*
3 Models of the Universe. Swenson.
When I Heard the Learn'd Astronomer. Whitman.

**Atheism**
There Is No God.*Fr.* Dipsychus. Clough.

**Athletes**

Athlete's Prayer, An. Charles.
Boxer. Clancy.
Everlasting Teamwork in Basketball. Victory.
Ex-Basketball Player. Updike.
Kleomedes. Wright.
Old Pro's Lament, The. Petrie.
Pole-Vaulter, The. *Unknown.*
Pro Basketball Players. Meschery.
Runner, The. Whitman.
To an Athlete Dying Young. Housman.
To an Athlete Turned Poet. Meinke.
To James.*Fr.* Letters Found Near a Suicide. Horne.

**Atomic Bomb**
Actual Vision of Morning's Extrusion. Dugan.
Little Johnny's Foolish Invention. Patten.
   *See also* **Hiroshima; Nuclear War.**

**Atoms**
Bigness of Atoms, The. Newcastle.
Our Insufficiency to Praise God Suitably, for His Mercy.*Fr.*
   God's Determinations. Taylor.
Third Thing, The. Lawrence.
Walter Jenks' Bath. Meredith.

**Attics**
Up There. Auden.

**Attis**
Attis. Stanley.

**Auctions**
Wisconsin Farm Auction. Steingass.

**Auden, Wystan Hugh**
Certain World, A. Herschberger.
Just a Smack at Auden. Empson.

**August**
August Weather. Tynan.
Mid-August at Sourdough Mountain Lookout. Snyder.

**Auschwitz, Poland**
London is full of chickens on electric spits.*Fr.* Annotations of
   Auschwitz. Porter.

**Australia**
Eyre All Alone. Webb.
History of the Father, A. Buckmaster.
Middleton's Rouseabout. Lawson.
South Country. Slessor.
Terra Australis. Stewart.
This Land. Mudie.
Waltzing Matilda. *Unknown.*
*Contemporary American and Australian Poetry* (CAAP).
   Thomas Shapcott, ed.
*Map of Australian Verse, A* (MAuV). James McAuley, ed.

**Authors and Authorship**
Absolute and Abitofhell. Knox.
After Dilettante Concetti. Traill.
Author, The. Churchill.
Author to Her Book. The. Bradstreet.
Black Art, The. Sexton.
Country House, The. Simpson.
Dear Colette. Jong.
Form Rejection Letter. Dacey.
Great men have been among us; hands that penned.
   Wordsworth.
Hamlet's Soliloquy Imitated. Jago.
History of a Literary Movement. Nemerov.
In Praise of BIC Pens. Hilton.
Novel, The. Levertov.
On Some South African Novelists. Campbell.
On the Same. Campbell.
This Monument Will Outlast.*Fr.* Odes. Horace.
To an Author. Freneau.
To Mr. Edward Howard, on His Plays. Sackville.
2001: Tennyson/Hardy Poem, The. Gavin.
Upon the Saying that My Verses Were Made by Another.
   Killigrew.
Young Author, The. Johnson.

**Autism**
Death of a Son. Silkin.
**Automation**
All Watched Over by Machines of Loving Grace. Brautigan.
**Automobiles**
"As a boy with a richness of needs I wandered." Dyment.
Auto Wreck. Shapiro.
Brides, The. Hope.
In a Dream, the Automobile. Marcus.
In My Merry Oldsmobile. Bryan.
Last of the Poet's Car. Connor.
Meditation on the A30. Betjeman.
1937 Ford Convertible. McKeown.
Ode to a Dead Dodge. McElroy.
She being brand. Cummings.
Southbound on the Freeway. Swenson.
Terraplane Blues. *Unknown.*
Tête-à-Tête. Honig.
**Autumn**
Autumn. Campbell.
Autumn. Clare.
Autumn. Hulme.
Autumn. Longfellow.
Autumn. Scannell.
Autumn. Wolfe.
Autumn; a Dirge. Shelley.
Autumn Horses. Andrews.
Before the Frost. Elliott.
Burning of the Leaves, The. Binyon.
Clear Air of October, The. Bly.
Digging. Thomas.
End of Summer, The. Minty.
Fall. Francis.
Falling Asleep. Sasson.
Field of Autumn. Lee.
Fire of Despair Has Been Our Saviour, The. Bly.
Gold Leaves. Chesterton.
Indian Summer: Vermont. Stevenson.
Leaflight. Donnelly.
Morns are meeker than they were, The. Dickinson.
Name—of it—is "Autumn," The. Dickinson.
Night Wind in Fall. Moses.
North Wind in October. Bridges.
October-November. Crane.
Ode: Autumn. Hood.
Rich Days. Davies.
Seed-Time. Meredith.
September. Snodgrass.
Song at the Beginning of Autumn. Jennings.
Song for Autumn. Young.
Song in Autumn. Fitzgerald.
Survivor. MacLeish.
That time of year thou may'st in me behold.*Fr.* Sonnets. Shakespeare.
To Autumn. Blake.
To Autumn. Keats.
To the Fringed Gentian. Bryant.
Tonight the winds begin to rise.*Fr.* In Memoriam, A.H.H. Tennyson.
When the Frost Is on the Punkin. Riley.
Wild Swans at Coole, The. Yeats.
Winter Is Another Country. MacLeish.
**Aviation and Aviators**
As a boy with a richness of needs I wandered. Dyment.
Flights. McDonald.
Flying Home from Utah. Swenson.
Hangar Nine. Darr.
In Flight. Smith.
Irish Airman Foresees His Death, An. Yeats.
Landscape Near an Aerodrome, The. Spender.
Old Pilot's Death, The. Hall.
Pilot. Stuart.

Pilot, The. Turco.
San Diego Poem, A. Ortiz.
Up in the Air. Tippett.
Vapor Trails. Snyder.
When a Beau Goes In. Ewart.
Winged bull trundles to the wired perimeter, The.*Fr.* Flight to Italy. Day Lewis.
*See also* **Air Warfare.**

# B

**Babel, Tower of**
Tower of Babel, The. Crouch.
**Babies**
Baby-Movements. Lawrence.
Baby's Dance, The. Taylor.
Breathers, The. Reiss.
Chinese Baby Asleep. Donnelly.
Copy. Armour.
Cradle Hymn. Watts.
Cradle Song, A: 'Sweet dreams form a shade.'*Fr.* Songs of Innocence. Blake.
Deathwatch. Harper.
Dolls, The. Yeats.
Ecce Puer. Joyce.
High Chair and Low Spirits. Armour.
Infant Joy.*Fr.* Songs of Innocence. Blake.
Infant Sorrow.*Fr.* Songs of Experience. Blake.
Katrina. Dawe.
Make Love Not War. Nemerov.
Morning Song. Plath.
Night Feeding. Rukeyser.
Perambulator Poem. McCord.
Rock-a-Bye Baby. Canning.
Song for the Newborn. *Unknown.*
Stunt Flier, The. Updike.
To the White Critics. Rodgers.
Unknown Girl in the Maternity Ward. Sexton.
We Assume: On the Death of Our Son, Reuben Masai Harper. Harper.
**Baboons**
At the Zoo. De la Mare.
**Bacchus**
Bacchus. Emerson.
Bacchus. Empson.
Great Bacchus: from the Greek. Prior.
**Bachelors**
After the Ball. Harris.
Bachelor's Life, A. *Unknown.*
I Don't Let the Girls Worry My Mind. *Unknown.*
New England Bachelor, A. Eberhart.
Nil Pejus Est Caelibe Vita. Coleridge.
**Badgers**
Badger, The. Clare.
Six Badgers, The. Graves.
**Baldness**
Bald Cavalier, The. *Unknown.*
**Baldwin, James**
For James Baldwin. Boyle.
**Bale, John**
To Doctor Bale. Googe.
**Ballads and Folk Songs**
*American Folk Poetry* (AmFP). Duncan Emrich, ed.
*As I Walked Out One Evening* (AIW). Helen Plotz, comp.
*Penguin Book of Ballads, The* (PeBB). Geoffrey Grigson, ed.
*Richard Dyer-Bennet Folk Song Book, The* (RDB). Richard Dyer-Bennet, ed.
**Ballet**

Les Sylphides.  MacNeice.
**Balloons**
   Armadillo, The.  Bishop.
   Balloons.  Plath.
   Pop.  McFadden.
**Bands**
   High School Band, The.  Whittemore.
**Banking and Bankers**
   My Alba.  Ginsberg.
**Banners.**  *See* **Flags.**
**Bannockburn, Battle of**
   Robert Bruce's March to Bannockburn.  Burns.
**Baptism**
   Baptism.  Nowlan.
   Holy Baptism.  Herbert.
**Barbers**
   Barber, The.  Fuller.
**Bards**
   Bard.  Everson.
   Bard, The.  Gray.
   *See also*  **Poetry and Poets.**
**Barley**
   Ripe and Bearded Barley, The.  *Unknown.*
**Barns**
   Byre.  MacCaig.
   When These Old Barns Lost Their Inhabitants.  Kherdian.
**Baseball**
   Analysis of Baseball.  Swenson.
   At the Ball Game.  Williams.
   Athlete's Prayer, An.  Charles.
   Ball Game.  Eberhart.
   Ballad of Dead Yankees, The.  Petersen.
   Base Stealer, The.  Francis.
   Baseball and Writing.  Moore.
   Casey at the Bat.  Thayer.
   Catch.  Francis.
   Cried the Lip.  Carroll.
   Don Larsen's Perfect Game.  Goodman.
   Dorlan's Home Walk.  Guiterman.
   Hero.  Gross.
   Hits and Runs.  Sandburg.
   Little-League Baseball.  Moses.
   Mel Allen, Mel Allen, Lend Me Your Cliché.  Nash.
   My Father Dreams of Baseball.  Lieberman.
   Nuns at Eve.  Brinnin.
   Ode to the New York Mets.  Lindsay.
   Of Kings and Things.  Morrison.
   Old-Fashioned Pitcher, The.  Phair.
   Pitcher.  Francis.
   September Valentine.  Sullivan.
   Spitballer.  Chappell.
   Take Me Out to the Ball Game.  Norworth.
   To a Baseball.  *Unknown.*
   To Satch (or American Gothic).  Allen.
   Willie Mays.  Ramsey.
**Basketball**
   As It Should Be.  Meschery.
   Basketball.  Vincent.
   Ex-Basketball Player.  Updike.
   Foul Shot.  Hoey.
   Jump Shot.  Peck.
   Lucky Louie Makes a Goal.  Van Arsdale.
   N.B.A. Prelim, Boston Garden.  Whitbread.
   Oscar Robertson: Peripheral Vision.  Matthews.
   Poet Tries to Turn in His Jock, The.  Hilton.
   To Wilt Chamberlain.  Meschery.
**Basset Hounds**
   Addition to the Family, An.  Morgan.
**Baths and Bathing**
   Bath.  Kirstein.
   Gloire de Dijon.  Lawrence.
   Pater's Bathe.  Parry.

**Batman and Robin**
   Goodbat Nightman.  McGough.
**Bats**
   Bat, The.  Roethke.
   Bat, The.  Spear.
   Bat Angels.  Levis.
   Bat in the Monastery, A.  L'Heureux.
   Bats.  Jarrell.
   Bats.  Macbeth.
   Displays of Skill: The Bat.  Herschberger.
   Intruder, The.  Kizer.
   Mad Hatter's Song, The.*Fr.* Alice's Adventures in Wonderland.  "Carroll."
   Man and Bat.  Lawrence.
   Seven Mexican Children.  Schmidt.
**Baudelaire, Charles**
   Ave Atque Vale.  Swinburne.
   Baudelaire.  Schwartz.
   Baudelaire in Brussels.  Cronin.
**Bazille, Frederic**
   Ceremony.  Wilbur.
**Beaches**
   Beach, The.  Hart-Smith.
   Beach in August, The.  Kees.
   By the Swimming.  Sward.
   Fiascherino.  Tomlinson.
   German Shepherd.  Livingston.
   On the Marginal Way.  Wilbur.
   Prospect Beach.  Lipsitz.
   Skin Divers, The.  Starbuck.
   With Kit, Age 7, at the Beach.  Stafford.
**Beagles**
   On the Death of Echo.  Coleridge.
**Bears**
   Achromatic Bear, The.  Bloom.
   Bad Example.  Fey.
   Bear, The.  Frost.
   Bear, The.  Kinnell.
   Bear, The.  Momaday.
   Bear on the Delhi Road, The.  Birney.
   Bears.  Rich.
   Grizzly Bear.  Austin.
   Part of the Darkness.  Gardner.
   This Poem Is for Bear.  Snyder.
   Willy.  Moore.
**Beaumont, Sir George**
   Elegiac Stanzas.  Wordsworth.
**Beauty**
   Alabama.  Fields.
   Beautiful, The.  Davies.
   Beautiful Changes, The.  Wilbur.
   Beauty Imposes.  Neilson.
   Beauty, sweet love, is like the morning dew.*Fr.* To Delia.  Daniel.
   Beauty's Excellency.  Noel.
   Clarinda's Indifference at Parting with Her Beauty.  Countess of Winchilsea.
   Divinely Superfluous Beauty.  Jeffers.
   Glory, The.  Thomas.
   Hymn to Intellectual Beauty.  Shelley.
   July 31.  Jordan.
   Merciless Beauty.  Chaucer.
   Ode on a Grecian Urn.  Keats.
   Of Beauty.  Fanshawe.
   Old Lady's Lament for Her Youth, The.  Villon.
   Peter Quince at the Clavier.  Stevens.
   Pied Beauty.  Hopkins.
   Question in a Field.  Bogan.
   Saturday: The Small Pox.  Wortley.
   She Walks in Beauty.  Byron.
   Study in Aesthetics, The.  Pound.
   To Cynthia: On Concealment of Her Beauty.  Kynaston.

To me, fair friend, you never can be old.*Fr.* Sonnets.
    Shakespeare.
Valentine for a Lady, A.  Lucillius.
**Beavers**
Looking for Mountain Beavers.  Wagoner.
**Bedford, Countess of.**  *See* **Russell, Lucy, Countess of Bedford.**
**Beds**
Bed, The.  Hope.
Land of Counterpane, The.  Stevenson.
**Beech Trees**
November Through a Giant Copper Beech.  Honig.
**Beer**
Beer.  Calverley.
Glass of Beer, A.  Stephens.
**Bees**
Animal, Vegetable and Mineral.  Bogan.
Arrival of the Bee Box, The.  Plath.
As I went owre the Hill o' Hoos.  *Unknown..*
Bee, The.  Dickey.
Bee, The.  *Unknown..*
Bee his burnished carriage, A.  Dickinson.
Bee, the Ant and the Sparrow, The.  Cotton.
Beehive.  Toomer.
Captived Bee, The: or, The Little Filcher.  Herrick.
Couple, A.  Swenson.
Fuscara; or, The Bee-Errant.  Cleveland.
Honey Bee, The.  Marquis.
Humble-Bee, The.  Emerson.
Invitation to the Bee.  Smith.
Legend of the Hive, A.  Hawker.
Life of a Queen.  Mueller.
Like trains of cars on tracks of plush.  Dickinson.
Single clover plank, A.  Dickinson.
Some Kind of Giant.  Pritchard.
Swarming Bees, The.  Laughlin.
Telling the Bees.  Whittier.
**Beethoven, Ludwig van**
Beethoven's Death Mask.  Spender.
Dooms menace from tumults. Who's immune.  Berryman.
In Gratitude to Beethoven.  Wakoski.
Ludwig's Death Mask.  Hughes.
**Beetles**
Dusty black beetle, A.  Sund.
Wee man o' leather.  *Unknown..*
**Begging and Beggars**
Beggar and Poet.  Martin.
Beggar Boy, The.  Alexander.
Beggar Man, The.  L. Aikin.
Beggarman, The.  *Unknown..*
Beggars Are Coming to Town, The.  *Unknown..*
Blind Old Woman.  Major.
Jolly Beggars, The.  Burns.
Old Cumberland Beggar, The.  Wordsworth.
**Belfast, Ireland**
Ballad to a Traditional Refrain.  Craig.
**Bells**
Bells, The.  Travis.
Bells Ostend, The.  Bowles.
Broken Tower, The.  Crane.
Catholic Bells, The.  Williams.
Chimes.  Meynell.
Shandon Bells, The.  Mahony.
**Ben Bulben, Ireland**
Deserted Mountain, The.  *Unknown..*
Under Ben Bulben.  Yeats.
**Benbow, Admiral John**
Death of Admiral Benbow, The.  *Unknown..*
**Bennington, Battle of**
Riflemen's Song at Bennington.  *Unknown..*
**Beowulf**
Beowulf.  Amis.
**Berkeley, George**

Fountain, The.  Davie.
**Bermuda**
Bermudas.  Marvell.
**Berrigan, Daniel**
For Dan Berrigan.  Knight.
**Berryman, John**
For John Berryman.  Gilbert.
For John Berryman I.  Lowell.
**Bethlehem**
Long, Long Ago.  *Unknown..*
**Betjeman, Sir John**
Betjeman, 1984.  Causley.
**Bible**
Genesis.  Witt.
Holy Scriptures, The.  Herbert.
On the Bible.  Strode.
**Bicycles and Bicycling**
Bicycle Rider.  McCarthy.
Daisy Bell; or, A Bicycle Built for Two.  Dacre.
Under the dawn I wake my two-wheel friend.*Fr.* On a Bicycle.
    Yevtushenko.
**Bigamy**
Moth and the Flame, The.  Taggart.
Those Wedding Bells Shall Not Ring Out!  Rosenfeld.
**Birch Trees**
Birch.  Simpson.
Birches.  Frost.
**Birds**
All These Birds.  Wilbur.
Beat Poem by an Academic Poet.  Miller.
Belfast Lough.  *Unknown..*
Bird came down the walk, A.  Dickinson.
Birds.  Jeffers.
Birds.  Lawrence.
Birds and Fishes.  Jeffers.
Birds of America, The.  Broughton.
Birds Waking.  Merwin.
Blinded Bird, The.  Hardy.
Cage, The.  Garrett.
City Bird.  Kenyon.
Corncrake, The.  Cousins.
Death of a Bird.  Silkin.
Death of the Bird, The.  Hope.
Distances They Keep, The.  Nemerov.
Dream in Cold, A.  Brigham.
Event, An.  Wilbur.
Feel Like a Bird.  Swenson.
Garnishing the Aviary.  Danner.
Health to the Birds, A.  MacManus.
I Hear a Bird Sing.  Herford.
Illustrious Ancestors.  Levertov.
In Glencullen.  Synge.
Jackdaw of Rheims, The.  "Ingoldsby."
Never Again Would Birds' Song Be the Same.  Frost.
No One to Blame.  Lieberman.
Of the Child with the Bird on the Bush.  Bunyan.
On an Indian Tomineios, the Least of Birds.  Heyrick.
On the Death of Mrs. Throckmorton's Bullfinch.  Cowper.
Ornithology.  Fox.
Ornithology in Florida.  Guiterman.
Oven Bird, The.  Frost.
Philip Sparrow.  Skelton.
Poem: "You jam your arm into the white air."  Fish.
Presentation of Two Birds to My Son, A.  Wright.
Proud Songsters.  Hardy.
Reincarnation (II).  Dickey.
Rivals, The.  Stephens.
Robin, Wren, Martin, Swallow.  *Unknown..*
Rooks, The.  *Unknown..*
Sea Birds, The.  Brock.
She staked her feathers—gained an arc.  Dickinson.
Still Life: Lady with Birds.  Prettyman.

Storm-Cock's Song, The. "MacDiarmid."
Sympathy. Dunbar.
To a Ground-Lark. Campbell.
To a Waterfowl. Bryant.
Up from the Egg: The Confessions of a Nuthatch Avoider. Nash.
Visitation. Ritchie.
Wagtail's Nest, The. MacKenzie.
What Birds Were There. Everson.
See also *names of birds* (e.g. **Canaries**).

**Birds' Nests**
Birds' Nests. Thomas.
Nesting Time. Guiterman.
Nesting Time. Stewart.

**Birds of Paradise**
In London Town M. Coleridge.

**Bird-watching**
Up from the Egg: The Confessions of a Nuthatch Avoider. Nash.

**Birmingham, Alabama**
Ballad of Birmingham. Randall.
Birmingham 1963. Patterson.

**Birth**
Before the Birth on One of Her Children. Bradstreet.
Birth Day. Meeter.
Birthing, The. Bentley.
Country Midwife, The: A Day. Ai.
Crooked Carol. Farber.
D-Day Minus. Brock.
Infant Sorrow.*Fr.* Songs of Experience. Blake.
Night Was Smooth, The. Bertolino.
Notes from the Delivery Room. Pastan.
Our Sobbing Must Be Heard. Cavalieri.
Poem to Ease Birth. *Unknown..*
Prayer before Birth. MacNiece.
Recovery Room, The: Lying-In. Chasin.
To a 14 Year Old Girl in Labor and Delivery. Stone.
To Insure Survival. Ortiz.
To the Anxious Mother. Malangatana.

**Birth Control**
Pill Versus the Springhill Mine Disaster, The. Brautigan.

**Birthdays**
Birthday of but a single pang. Dickinson.
Monday's child is fair of face. Mother Goose.
Poem in October. Thomas.
Trala Trala Trala La-Le-La. Williams.
Writ on the Eve of My 32nd Birthday. Corso.

**Bison.** *See* **Buffaloes.**

**Black Verse.** *See* **Negro Verse.**

**Blackberries**
Blackberrying. Plath.

**Blackbirds**
Best of Two Worlds. Boothroyd.
Blackbird. Leach.
Blackbird, The. Wolfe.
Blackbird by Belfast Lough, The. *Unknown..*
Blackbird Singing, A. Thomas.
Blackbird's Song. *Unknown..*
Redwing, The. P. Dickinson.
Thirteen Ways of Looking at a Blackbird. Stevens.

**Blackout**
Power Failure. Browne.

**Blacks.** *See* **Negroes.**

**Blacksmiths**
Blacksmiths, The. *Unknown..*
Blacksmith's Song, The. *Unknown..*
Forge, The. Heaney.
Village Blacksmith, The. Longfellow.

**Blenheim, Battle of**
Battle of Blenheim, The. Southey.

**Blindness**
Blind Always Come as Such a Surprise, The. Kooser.

Blind Boy, The. Cibber.
On His Blindness. Milton.
Spring, and the Blind Children. Noyes.
To Mr. Cyriac Skinner upon His Blindness. Milton.

**Bluebeard**
Bluebeard's Wife. Hine.

**Blueberries**
Hermit Picks Blueberries, The. Kumin.
Secret, The. Coffin.

**Bluebirds**
Blue-Bird, The. Melville.
Last Word of a Bluebird, The. Frost.

**Blues (mood)**
D Blues. Hernton.
Death Sting Me Blues. *Unknown..*
Get Up, Blues. Emanuel.
Good Mornin' Blues. *Unknown..*
It was not death, for I stood up. Dickinson.
Talking after Christmas Blues. Henri.
Too Blue. Hughes.

**Blues (music)**
Blues and Bitterness. Bennett.
Blues Today, The. Jackson.
Coal Loadin' Blues. *Unknown..*
Depot Blues. *Unknown..*
East St. Louis Blues. *Unknown..*
Four O'Clock Flower Blues. *Unknown..*
Gonna Lay My Head Down on Some Railroad Line. *Unknown..*
Homage to the Empress of the Blues. Hayden.
I Remember How She Sang. Penny.
I Rode Southern, I Rode L & N. *Unknown..*
Lowdown Dirty Blues. *Unknown..*
Mississippi Blues. *Unknown..*
Ragged and Dirty. *Unknown..*
Railroad Blues, The. *Unknown..*
Special Rider Blues. *Unknown..*
To Dinah Washington. Knight.
Train Is off the Track, The. *Unknown..*
Weary Blues, The. Hughes.
Why I Sing the Blues. B. B. King.
Worried Life Blues. *Unknown..*

**Boarding Houses**
Mr. Bleaney. Larkin.

**Boats**
Barges on the Hudson. Deutsch.
Beginning to Squall. Swenson.
Boat Poem Spencer.
Bonded. Brady.
Paper Boats, *sel.* Tagore.
Queen of Connemara, The. Fahy.
Where Go the Boats? Stevenson.
Yachts, The. Williams.
See also **Ships.**

**Bodies**
Body Poems, *sels.* Barks.
First Prayer. Atwood.
His Body. McPherson.
I Like My Body When It Is with Yours. Cummings.
Praise. Matthews.
Question. Swenson.
Seven-Year Body Cycle, The. Steingass.
Soul's Garment, The. Duchess of Newcastle.
Vases of Wombs, The. Gioseffi.

**Bogart, Humphrey**
Bogart. Flocos.
Nobody Dies Like Humphrey Bogart. Rosten.

**Bogs**
Gullion, The. Glen.

**Bohemia and Bohemians**
For Hettie. Jones.
Helicon. Hollander.

Little Joe Gould has lost his teeth and doesn't know where. Cummings.
Problem in Social Geometry—The Inverted Square! Durem.
**Boll Weevils**
Ballit of de Boll Weevil, De. *Unknown..*
Boll Weevil Song, The. *Unknown..*
**Bones**
After X-Ray. Pastan.
Raccoon Skeleton at Long Plain Creek. Minton.
Three Lectures on the Skeleton. Young.
***Bonhomme Richard (ship)***
Ballad of Benjamin Bones, The. Ward.
**Bonnie Prince Charlie.** *See* **Stuart, Charles Edward.**
**Books**
Bookshop Idyll, A. Amis.
Fire at Alexandria, The. Weiss.
House Was Quiet and the World Was Calm, The. Stevens.
On His Books. Belloc.
Over 2000 Illustrations and a Complete Concordance. Bishop.
Study of Reading Habits, A. Larkin.
Style. Nemerov.
There is no frigate like a book. Dickinson.
**Booth, John Wilkes**
Booth Killed Lincoln. *Unknown..*
**Booth, William**
General William Booth Enters into Heaven. Lindsay.
**Borden, Lizzie**
Crimes of Lizzie Borden The. *Unknown..*
**Boredom**
Dolor. Roethke.
**Borgia, Lucrezia**
On Seeing a Hair of Lucretia Borgia. Landor.
**Bosch, Hieronymus**
Homage to Hieronymus Bosch. MacGreevy.
**Boston, Massachusetts**
As a Plane Tree by the Water. Lowell.
Boston. Bossidy.
For the Union Dead. Lowell.
Thanksgiving in Boston Harbor, The. Butterworth.
***Boston Evening Transcript (newspaper)***
*Boston Evening Transcript,* The. Eliot.
**Boswell, James**
Poetical and Congratulatory Epistle to James Boswell Esq., A. "Pindar."
**Bourgeoisie**
How Beastly the Bourgeois Is. Lawrence.
Red-Herring. Lawrence.
Salesman is an it that stinks excuse, A. Cummings.
Subaltern's Love Song, A. Betjeman.
Unknown Citizen, The. Auden.
**Bowery, The (New York CIty)**
Bowery. Ignatow.
**Bowles, William Lisle**
To the Rev. W. L. Bowles. Coleridge.
**Boxer Rebellion**
Old Photo in an Old Life, An. Hoffman.
**Boxing and Boxers**
Black Lady in an Afro Hairdo Cheers for Cassius. Holmes.
Boxer. Clancy.
Clay Comes Out to Meet Terrell. Ali.
Kid's Last Fight, The. *Unknown..*
Loser, The. Bukowski.
On Hurricane Jackson. Dugan.
Throw Him Down M'Closkey. Kelly.
TKO. Peck.
To a Fighter Killed in the Ring. Lipsitz.
**Boyne, Battle of the**
Battle of the Boyne, The. Blacker.
**Boys.** *See* **Childhood and Children; Youth.**
**Brahma**
Brahma. Emerson.
**Bread**

Baking Day. Joseph.
**Brendan, Saint**
Fish at Mass, The. *Unknown..*
**Bridges**
Address to the New Tay Bridge, An. McGonagall.
Burned Bridge, The. Stone.
Railway Bridge of the Silvery Tay, The. McGonagall.
**Bridget, Saint**
Giveaway, The. McGinley.
**Bristol, Rhode Island**
Bombardment of Bristol, R.I., The. *Unknown..*
**British Empire**
English Flag, The. Kipling.
Fuzzy-Wuzzy. Kipling.
Recessional. Kipling.
**Broadway, New York City**
Give My Regards to Broadway. Cohan.
**Brontë, Anne**
On the Death of Anne Brontë. C. Brontë.
**Brontë, Charlotte**
Sampler from Haworth. Howard.
**Bronx, New York City**
Bronxomania. Cruz.
East Bronx. Ignatow.
**Brooklyn, New York City**
Brooklyn Heights. Wain.
Clickety-Clack. Blackburn.
Crossing Brooklyn Ferry. Whitman.
It's 8:54 a.m. Brooklyn it's the 28th of July and. Berrigan.
**Brooklyn Bridge**
Granite and Steel. Moore.
To Brooklyn Bridge.*Fr.* The Bridge. Crane.
**Brooks, Gwendolyn**
Afterword, An: for Gwen Brooks. Lee.
Gwendolyn Brooks. Lee.
Madimba: Gwendolyn Brooks. Harper.
**Brooks and Streams**
Inversnaid. Hopkins.
Resolve, The. Levertov.
Runoff Ammons.
There is a stream which rises. Bruchac.
West-running Brook. Frost.
**Brotherhood**
As It Should Be. Meschery.
Blest Be the Tie That Binds. Fawcett.
Dual Site, The. Hamburger.
In the Mourning Time. Hayden.
Round Table, The. Kenner.
To Some Millions Who Survive Joseph E. Mander, Sr. Wright.
**Brown, John**
John Brown's Body. *Unknown..*
October 16: The Raid. Hughes.
Portent, The. Melville.
**Browning, Elizabeth Barrett**
Her—"last poems." Dickinson.
Sisters, The. A. Lowell.
**Browning, Robert**
Last Ride Together, The. Stephen.
**Bruce, Robert**
Bruce Meets Three Men with a Wether. Barbour.
Robert Bruce's March to Bannockburn. Burns.
**Bruckner, Anton**
Bruckner. Camp.
**Bruegel, Pieter**
Brueghel's Winter. De la Mare.
Dance The. Williams.
Hunters in the Snow: Brueghel. Langland.
Landscape with the Fall of Icarus. Williams.
Musée des Beaux Arts. Auden.
Winter Landscape. Berryman.
**Brunanburh, Battle of**
Battle of Brunanburh. *Unknown..*

**Bryan, William Jennings**
  Bryan's Last Battle.  *Unknown.*.
  Free Silver.  *Unknown.*.
**Bryant, William Cullen**
  Bryant.*Fr.* A Fable for Critics.  Lowell.
**Buddha**
  Buddha.  Melville.
  Buddha's Birthday: April 8, 1819.*Fr.* Oraga Haru.  Issa.
  Buddha's Death Day: February l5, 1815.*Fr.* Oraga Haru.  Issa.
**Buffalo Bill (William Frederick Cody)**
  Buffalo Bill's.  Cummings.
**Buffaloes**
  Bison Track, The.  Taylor.
  Bone Yard.  Barnes.
  Buffalo Dusk.  Sandburg.
  Buffalo, Our Sacred Beast, The.  McKeown.
  Crossing the Plains.  Miller.
  Flower-Fed Buffaloes, The.  Lindsay.
  I rise, I rise/ I who makes the earth to tremble.  *Unknown.*.
  Rising of the Buffalo Men, The.  *Unknown.*.
**Bull Run, Battle of**
  Battle of Bull Run, The.  *Unknown.*.
  March into Virginia, The.  Melville.
**Bullfights and Bullfighters**
  Death Invited.  Swenson.
  Laneliest Place in the World, The.  Campbell.
  Picador Bit, The.  Noll.
  Black Tomintoul.  Finlay.
  Bull, A.  Deutsch.
  Bull, The.  Sackville-West.
  Bull, The.  Wright.
  No Man's Good Bull.  Seay.
  Outlaw, The.  Heaney.
  Seventh Georgic.  Economou.
**Bunker Hill, Battle of**
  Ballad of Bunker Hil, The.  *Unknown.*.
  Death of Warren, The.  Sargent.
  Sword of Bunker Hill, The.  Wallace.
  Warren's Address.  Pierpont.
**Bunyan, John**
  For Tinkers Who Travel on Foot.  Avison.
**Bureaucracy**
  Sharks in Shallow Water.  Levinson.
**Burke, Edmund**
  Burke.*Fr.* Sonnets on Eminent Characters.  Coleridge.
**Burlesque**
  Stripper, The.  Probst.
**Burns, Robert**
  At the Grave of Burns, 1803.  Wordsworth.
  Mute Is Thy Wild Harp, Now, O Bard Sublime.  Smith.
  On Visiting the Tomb of Burns.  Keats.
  Sonnet Written in the Cottage Where Burns Was Born.  Keats.
**Burr, Aaron**
  Aaron Burr's Wooing.  Stedman.
**Burroughs, William**
  On Burroughs' Work.  Ginsberg.
**Buses**
  Bus, The.  Cohen.
  Bus Ride.  Kandel.
  Motor Bus.  Godley.
  My Busconductor.  McGough.
**Butchers and Butchering**
  Blood.  Murray.
  Butcherboy.  Schmidt.
  Cock Crowing in a Poulterer's Shop, A.  Ferguson.
  Kicking from Centre Field.  McFadden.
  Meat Works, The.  Gray.
  Skill in Killing, A.  Abbe.
  Slaughter-House, The.  Hayes.
  Slaughter-Room Picture, The.  Steingass.
  Stockyard, The.  Squire.
**Buttercups**

  Buttercup.  Dodge.
**Butterflies**
  Blue-Butterfly Day.  Frost.
  Butterflies.  Sansom.
  Butterflies on an Illinois Road.  Minton.
  Butterfly in the Fields.  Campbell.
  Chalk Blue Butterfly, The.  Spender.
  I was round and small like a pearl.  *Unknown.*.
  Of the Boy and Butterfly.  Bunyan.
  Roots and Branches.  Duncan.
  To a Butterfly ("I've watched you now a full half hour").
    Wordsworth.
  To a Butterfly ("Stay near me—do not take thy flight!").
    Wordsworth.
  Was Worm.  Swenson.
**Byron, George Gordon Noel Byron, 6th Baron**
  Byron vs. DiMaggio.  Meinke.
  Fragment: To Byron.  Shelley.
  Sonnet to Byron.  Shelley.
  To Lord Byron.  Keats.
**Byzantium**
  Byzantium.  Yeats.
  Sailing to Byzantium  Yeats.

# C

**Caesar, Julius**
  Julius Caesar.  *Unknown.*.
  Voice of Caesar, The.*Fr.* For the Time Being.  Auden.
**California**
  Before the Stuff Comes Down.  Snyder.
  California Phrasebook, The.  Schmitz.
  Vitamins and Roughage.  Rexroth.
**Calvary.**  *See* **Crucifixion, The.**
**Calves**
  Bull Calf, The.  Layton.
  I Would Like You for a Comrade.  Parry.
**Calvinism**
  After the Surprising Conversions.  Lowell.
  McAndrew's Hymn.  Kipling.
  Mr. Edwards and the Spider.  Lowell.
  To a Calvinist in Bali.  Millay.
  Words.  Glen.
**Calypso (mythology)**
  Callypso Speaks.  Doolittle ("H.D.").
  Calypso's Island.  MacLeish.
**Cambridge, England**
  Old Vicarage, Grantchester, The.  Brooke.
**Cambridge, Massachusetts**
  Professor Kelleher and the Charles River.  O'Grady.
**Cambridge University**
  Answer to an Invitation to Cambridge, An.  Cowley.
  Satire Upon the Heads.  Gray.
**Camels**
  Camel.  Stallworthy.
  Camel's Complaint, The.  Carryl.
  Dromedary.  Dodat.
**Camping**
  First Camp.  Kuzma.
  Sleeping Out in Vermont.  Hilberry.
  Staying Alive.  Wagoner.
  To Myself, Late, in a Myrtle Grove.  Peterson.
**Canada**
  Let me put is this way.  Jonas.
  Only Tourist in Havana Turns His Thoughts Homeward, The.
    Cohen.
  *New American and Canadian Poetry* (NeAC).  John Gill, ed.
**Canals**

Lines Written on a Seat on the Grand Canal. Kavanagh.

**Canaries**
Boy, Cat, Canary. Spender.
Canary, The. Turner.

**Cancer (disease)**
Cancer's a Funny Thing. Haldane.
In the Radiotherapy Unit. Wrench.
Miss Gee. Auden.

**Candles**
Even as a dragon's eye that feels the stress. Wordsworth.

**Candy**
Girtonian Funeral, A. *Unknown.*.
Pennycandystore Beyond the El, The.*Fr.* A Coney Island of the Mind. Ferlinghetti.

**Cardinals (birds)**
As a Child Seeing a Cardinal. Gill.

**Caribbean islands**
O Carib Isle! Crane.

**Carmel, California**
Carmel Point. Jeffers.

**Carpe Diem**
Beauty. Guarini.
Blue Girls. Ransom.
Carpe Diem. Frost.
Come, my Celia, let us prove.*Fr.* Volpone. Jonson.
Corinna in Vendome. Ronsard.
Dream within a Dream, A. Poe.
Drink Today.*Fr.* The Bloody Brother. Fletcher.
Give me women, wine and snuff. Keats.
Go, Lovely Rose. Waller.
Lines Written at a Small Distance from My House. Wordsworth.
Loveliest of Trees, the Cherry Now. Housman.
My Sweetest Lesbia. Campion.
Passionate Shepherd to His Love, The. Marlowe.
Persuasions to Enjoy. Carew.
Reckoning, The. Service.
Rubáiyát of Omar Khayyám of Naishápúr, The. Omar Khayyám.
Sing We and Chant It. Morley.
To His Coy Mistress. Marvell.
To the Virgins, to Make Much of Time. Herrick.
Vive La Compagnie. *Unknown.*.
Youth and Love.*Fr.* The Beggar's Opera. Gay.

**Carpenters**
Four-square Gospel. Jellema.
In Memory of G.K., for 50 Years the College Carpenter. Martin.

**"Carroll, Lewis"**
Lewis Carroll. Farjeon.

**Cars.** *See* **Automobiles.**

**Carson, Kit**
Imperfect Sympathies. Short.

**Cary, Sir Lucius**
To the Immortal Memory and Friendship of That Noble Pair, Sir Lucius Cary and Sir H. Morison. Jonson.

**Casanova, Giovann**
Casanova. Usborne.

**Cassandra**
Cassandra. Bogan.
Cassandra. Jeffers.
Cassandra. Robinson.

**Castlereagh, Robert Stewart, 2nd Viscount**
Riddle, A: "Why is a pump like V-sc--nt C-stl-r--gh? Moore.
To Sidmouth and Castlereagh. Shelley.

**Castles**
Psalm Concerning the Castle. Levertov.

**Castro, Fidel**
One Thousand Fearful Words for Fidel Castro. Ferlinghetti.

**Catbirds**
Air: Cat Bird Singing. Creeley.

**Caterpillars**

Caterpillar. C. Rossetti.
Caterpillar, The. Williams.
Elegies for the Hot Season. McPherson.

**Catfish**
Feeding Cycle of the Catfish, The. Crawford.

**Catholicism**
First Confession. Kennedy.
Habit of Perfection, The. Hopkins.

**Cats**
Affinities. Stoutenberg.
Appeal to Cats in the Business of Love, An: A Song. Flatman.
Auld Seceder Cat, The. *Unknown.*.
Belling the Cat.*Fr.* The Vision of Piers Plowman. Langland.
Bird Fancier, The. Kirkup.
Calling in the Cat. Coatsworth.
Cat, The. Church.
Cat, The. Davies.
Cat. Farjeon.
Cat, The. Matthews.
Cat. Miller.
Cat, A. Thomas.
Cat. Tolkien.
Cat and the Bird, The. Canning.
Cat and the Moon, The. Yeats.
Cat as Cat, The. Levertov.
Cat at the Cream. *Unknown.*.
Cat, Caged and Shrunken, The. Freeman.
Cat Came Back, The. Miller.
Cat Heard the Cat-Bird, The. Ciardi.
Cat of Cats, The. Rands.
Cat on Couch. Howes.
Cats. Farjeon.
Cats. Scarfe.
Cats. Tessimond.
Cats and the Weather. Swenson.
Cat's Funeral. Rieu.
Cat's Life, A. Struthers.
Cheerio My Deario.*Fr.* Archy and Mehitabel. Marquis.
Chops. Dixon.
Civilization. Schmidt.
Cosy Cat Nap. Kirkup.
Cruel, but composed and bland.*Fr.* Matthias. Arnold.
Death of a Cat. Jones.
Diamond Cut Diamond. Milne.
Fiddling Cat, The. *Unknown.*.
For a Little Girl Mourning Her Favorite Cat. Whittier.
For I Will Consider My Cat Jeoffry.*Fr.* Jubilate Agno. Smart.
Gus: The Theatre Cat. Eliot.
I Wouldn't. Ciardi.
In Memory of My Cat Domino: l951-1966. Fuller.
Intruder. Feldman.
Kitten, A. Farjeon.
Lavender Kitten, The. Lopez.
London Tom-Cat. Hamburger.
Macavity: The Mystery Cat. Eliot.
Man and Beast. Dyment.
Moon. Smith.
Mort aux Chats. Porter.
Mother Tabbyskins. Hart.
My Cat. Syrett.
My Old Cat. Summers.
Naming of Cats, The. Eliot.
Nansen. Snyder.
Ode on the Death of a Favourite Cat, Drowned in a Tub of Gold Fishes. Gray.
Old Trouper, The.*Fr.* Archy and Mehitabel. Marquis.
Open Door, The. Coatsworth.
Owl and the Pussy-Cat, The. Lear.
Pangur Ban. *Unknown.*.
Poem: "As the cat." Williams.
Poem: "High on a ridge of tiles." Craig.
Prize Cat, The. Pratt.

Pussy. *Unknown.*.
Rescue, The. Summers.
Shuffling along in her broken shoes from the slums.*Fr.* Lady
　Feeding the Cats. Stewart.
Singing Cat, The. Smith.
Skimbleshanks: The Railway Cat. Eliot.
Song of the Jellicles, The. Eliot.
Three Cheers for the Black, White and Blue. Pitter.
To Mrs. Reynolds's Cat. Keats.
Tom-Cat, The. Marquis.
Tortoiseshell Cat, The. Chalmers.
Two Little Kittens. *Unknown.*.
Waiting for IT. Swenson.
What Could It Be? Cole.
Why Did You Go? Cummings.
*Poetry of Cats, The* (PCat). Samuel Carr, ed.
**Cattle**
Bags of Meat. Hardy
Deer Among Cattle. Dickey.
Drove-Road, The. Gibson.
Jersey Cattle. Currey.
Upasara, the heifer after first mating.*Fr.* Walking to the Cattle-
　Place. Murray.
Wires. Larkin.
See also **Bulls; Calves; Cows; Oxen.**
**Catullus**
You Also, Gaius Valerius Catullus. MacLeish.
**Cauteretz Valley, France**
In the Valley of Cauteretz. Tennyson.
**Cavalry**
Cavalry Crossing a Ford. Whitman.
**Caves**
Cave Where Night Sleeps, The. Broughton.
**Cecilia, Saint**
Song for St. Cecilia's Day, 1687, A. Dryden.
**Celandine**
Celandine. Thomas.
Small Celandine, The. Wordsworth.
To the Same Flower. Wordsworth.
To the Small Celandine. Wordsworth.
**Cemeteries**
Dead at Clonmacnoise, The. *Unknown.*.
Elegy in a Presbyterian Burying-Ground. Wilson.
Elegy Written in a Country Churchyard. Gray.
Epitaphs. Hughes.
Grave-Yard, The. Very.
In a Churchyard. Wilbur.
In a Grave-Yard. Braithwaite.
Indian at the Burial-Place of His Fathers, An. Bryant.
Indian Burying Ground, The. Freneau.
Jewish Cemetery at Newport, The. Longfellow.
Mistress, The. Barton.
Mountain Cemetery, The. Bowers.
Not Like That. Rich.
RIP. Garner.
Roubaix Cemetery. Brainard.
Voices from Things Growing in a Churchyard. Hardy.
Yugoslav Cemetery. Wright.
See also **Graves.**
**Censorship**
Letter to a Librarian. Layton.
Penal Law. Clarke.
**Centaurs**
Centaurs, The. Stephens.
**Ceres.** *See* **Demeter.**
**Cézanne, Paul**
Cézanne's Ports. Ginsberg.
**Chad, Lake**
Chad. Brathwaite.
**Chagall, Marc**
Don't Let That Horse. Ferlinghetti.
Homage to Chagall. Niatum.

Homage to Chagall. Teague.
**Chamberlain, Wilt**
To Wilt Chamberlain. Meschery.
**Chameleons**
Lord's Chameleon, The. Klappert.
**Chamonix, France**
Hymn Before Sunrise in the Vale of Chamouni. Coleridge.
**Change**
Ancient to Ancients, An. Hardy.
Lack of Steadfastness. Chaucer.
Mutability ("Flower that smiles to-day, The"). Shelley.
Mutability ("We are as clouds that veil the midnight moon").
　Shelley.
Mutability.*Fr.* Ecclesiastical Sonnets. Wordsworth.
Nothing Gold Can Stay. Frost.
**Channing, William Henry**
Ode: Inscribed to W. H. Channing. Emerson.
**Chaplin, Charlie**
Chaplinesque. Crane.
Patriotic Ode on the Fourteenth Anniversary of the Persecution
　of Charlie Chaplin. Kaufman.
**Chapman, George**
On First Looking into Chapman's Homer. Keats.
**Charity**
Faith, Hope and Charity. Guarini.
Karma. Robinson.
Lovers of the Poor, The. Brooks.
My House. Garneau.
**Charles, Ray**
Blues Note. Kaufman.
Ray Charles. Cornish.
**Charles I, King of England**
Cavalier Tunes. Browning.
Epitaph on Charles I, King of England. Graham.
**Charles II, King of England**
Commons' Petition to Charles II, The. Earl of Rochester.
Epitaph on Charles II. Earl of Rochester.
**Charles XII, King of Sweden**
Charles XII of Sweden.*Fr.* The Vanity of Human Wishes.
　Johnson.
**Charleston, South Carolina**
Charleston. Timrod.
**Chatterton, Thomas**
Monody on the Death of Chatterton. Coleridge.
To Chatterton. Keats.
**Chaucer, Geoffrey**
Chaucer. Longfellow.
**Chenango Lake**
Swimming Chenango Lake. Tomlinson.
**Cherry Trees**
Loveliest of Trees, the Cherry Now. Housman.
Oh, Fair to See. C. Rossetti.
**Chesterton, Gilbert Keith**
Lines to a Don. Belloc.
**Chevy Chase, Battle of.** *See* **Otterburn, Battle of.**
**Chicago, Illinois**
Chicago. Sandburg.
Chicago/ 3 Hours. Cruz.
LaSalle Street. Albright.
Sold. Cuscaden.
Stockyard, The. Squire.
**Chickadees**
Titmouse, The. Emerson.
**Chickens**
Casa de Pollos. Fraser.
Chickens, The. *Unknown.*.
Poultries, The. Nash.
**Child Abuse**
Inquest, The. Davies.
**Child Labor**
Chimney Sweeper, The.*Fr.* Songs of Innocence. Blake.
**Childhood and Children**

Anecdote for Fathers. Wordsworth.
Assignment. Butcher.
Autobiographical Note. Scannell.
Before You're a Stranger. Fraser.
Bells for John Whiteside's Daughter. Ransom.
Bold Unbiddable Child, The. Letts.
Boy. Ciardi.
Boy, The. Field.
Boy, A. Graves.
Boy with His Hair Cut Short. Rukeyser.
Centaur, The. Swenson.
Characteristics of a Child Three Years Old. Wordsworth.
Child, The. Hall.
Child Half-Asleep, A. Connor.
Child on Top of a Greenhouse. Roethke.
Childhood. Vaughan.
Children, The. MacDonald.
Children, The. Williams.
Child's Drawing. Block.
Child's Sight, The. Sobiloff.
Common Carrier. Armour.
Croquet in Childhood. Minton.
Dead Boy. Ransom.
Dead Man Creek. Brock.
Dinoland. Reiter.
Dogs Are Shakespearean, Children Are Strangers. Schwartz.
Early Supper. Howes.
Ecce Puer. Joyce.
Efficiency Apartment. Barrax.
Eleven. MacLeish.
Evening. Wright.
Ex Ore Infantium. Thompson.
Eyes of the Child Do Not See Me, The. Russell.
False Security. Betjeman.
Farm Boy after Summer. Francis.
Father and Child. Harwood.
Fern Hill. Thomas.
First Song. Kinnell.
For a Junior School Poetry Book. Middleton.
For the Crêche.*Fr.* Songs of Education. Chesterton.
Game after Supper. Atwood.
Germinal. "AE."
Goodbat Nightman. McGough.
Hard Cheese. St. John.
Heart's Needle. Snodgrass.
I Don't Like Beetles. Fyleman.
I Don't Want to Play in Your Yard. Wingate.
I Remember, I Remember. Hood.
I Would Like You for a Comrade. Parry.
In Reference to Her Children, 23 June, 1656. Bradstreet.
In Woods Where Many Rivers Run.*Fr.* A Coney Island of the Mind. Ferlinghetti.
Incident in the Early Life of Ebenezer Jones, Poet, 1828, An. Betjeman.
It Is Impossible. Falconer.
It Out-Herods Herod. Pray You, Avoid It. Hecht.
Janet Waking. Ransom.
Jim, Who Ran Away from His Nurse, and Was Eaten by a Lion. Belloc.
Judeebug's Country. Johnson.
Key of the Kingdom, The. Reed.
Kindergarten. Rogers.
Knock on Wood. Dumas.
Little Boy Blue. Field.
Little Brother, The. Reeves.
Little Dancers, The. Binyon.
Little Girl with Bands on Her Teeth, The. Taggard.
Lost Children, The. Jarrell.
Love. Lane.
Mama! Horne.
Mighty Lak' a Rose. Stanton.
My Father in the Night Commanding No. Simpson.

My Parents Kept Me. Spender.
Nikki-Rosa. Giovanni.
Noisy Boys. Castiglione.
Nurse's Song.*Fr.* Songs of Innocence. Blake.
On a Dead Child. Bridges.
On Children.*Fr.* The Prophet. Gibran.
On My First Son. Jonson.
Original Sin on the Sussex Coast. Betjeman.
Paean to Place. Niedecker.
Party, The. Whittemore.
Pastoral of the City Streets. Klein.
Pennycandystore Beyond the El, The.*Fr.* A Coney Island of the Mind. Ferlinghetti.
Piano. Lawrence.
Picnic, The. Logan.
Playground, The. Bedard.
Retreat, The. Vaughan.
Romping. Ciardi.
Rough. Spender.
September, the First Day of School. Nemerov.
Sick Child, A. Jarrell.
Sleeper, The. Field.
Song about Myself. Keats.
Spitting on Ira Rosenblatt. Hershon.
There Was a Child Went Forth. Whitman.
There Was a Little Girl. Longfellow.
To a Child Dancing in the Wind. Yeats.
To a Child Five Years Old. Cotton.
To a Child Trapped a Barber Shop. Levine.
To H. C. Wordsworth.
To My Former Student on the Occasion of Birth. Bass.
Toyland. MacDonough.
Tumbling. *Unknown.*
Verigin, Moving in Alone. Newlove.
Walnut-Leaf Scent. Binyon.
When I Learned to Whistle. Lea.
Why Did the Chidren Put Beans in Their Ears? Sandburg.
Windy Boy in a Windswept Tree. Summerfield.
Won't Go to School. Rankin.
World and the Child, The. Merrill.
Worms, The. Kizer.
*See also* **Babies; Youth.**

**Children's Verse**
*Every Child's Book of Verse* (ECBV). Sarah Chokla Gross, comp.
*Listen, Children, Listen* (LCL). Myra Cohn Livingston, ed.
*Mother Goose Nursery Rhymes* (MG). Arthur Rackham, illus.
*Oxford Book of Children's Verse, The* (OxBChV). Iona and Peter Opie, eds.

**Chillon Castle, Switzerland**
Prisoner of Chillon, The. Byron.

**Chimney Sweepers**
Chimney Sweeper, The.*Fr.* Songs of Experience. Blake.
Chimney Sweeper, The.*Fr.* Songs of Innocence. Blake.

**China**
Old Photo in an Old Life, An. Hoffman.

**Chipmunks**
Chipmunk's Day, The. Jarrell.

**Christ.** *See* **Jesus Christ.**

**Christenings**
Kyran's Christening. Nowlan.

**Christmas**
Advent 1966. Levertov.
Alphabet of Christmas Cheer. Weston.
Animals' Christmas, The. Dacey.
Away in a Manger. *Unknown.*
Ballad of Befana, The. McGinley.
Burning Babe, The. Southwell.
Burning the Christmas Greens. Williams.
Carol: "There was a boy bedded in bracken." Short.
Christ Climbed Down. Ferlinghetti.
Christmas. Betjeman.

Christmas. Cavalieri.
Christmas at Sea. Stevenson.
Christmas Comes to Moccasin Flat. Welch.
Christmas Day. Falkner.
Christmas Eve under Hooker's Statue. Lowell.
Christmas 1959 Et Cetera. Barrax.
Christmas Tree, A. Burford.
Computer's First Christmas Card, The. Morgan.
Cultivation of Christmas Trees, The. Eliot.
December. Schuyler.
Deck the Halls. *Unknown.*
Farewell Advent! Ryman.
First Nowell, The. *Unknown.*
God Rest You Merry, Gentleman. *Unknown.*
Hark, the Herald Angels Sing. Wesley.
Holly and the Ivy, The. *Unknown.*
Hymn for Christmas Day, A. Byrom.
I Am Christmas. *Unknown.*
In the Week When Christmas Comes. Farjeon.
It Came upon a Midnight Clear. Sears.
Jew at Christmas Eve, The. Shapiro.
Jolly Shepherd Wat, The. *Unknown.*
Joy to the World. Watts.
Lines for a Christmas Card. Belloc.
Little tree. Cummings.
Nativity, The. Drummond of Hawthornden.
Nativity of Christ, The. Southwell.
Nativity of Our Lord and Saviour, The.*Fr.* Hymns and Spiritual
   Songs. Smart.
New Heaven, New War. Southwell.
New Prince, New Pomp. Southwell.
Now Is Yule Come. *Unknown.*
O Come, All Ye Faithful. *Unknown.*
O Little Town of Bethlehem. Brooks.
On the Morning of Christ's Nativity. Milton.
Oxen, The. Hardy.
Silent Night! Holy Night! Mohr.
Song Bewailing the Time of Christmas, A. *Unknown.*
Sonnets at Christmas. Tate.
Sunny Bank. *Unknown.*
To a Young Wretch. Frost.
Twelve Days of Christmas, The. *Unknown.*
Unto Us a Child Is Born. Dunbar.
Upon a Christmas Morning. *Unknown.*
Upon Christ's Nativity, or Christmas. Watkyns.
What Child Is This? Dix.
What Tidings? Audelay.
White Christmas. Rodgers.
Yule Days, The. *Unknown.*

**Churches**
Church Going. Larkin.
Church on Comiaken Hill, The. Hugo.
Diary of a Church Mouse. Betjeman.
Eighteen-Forty-Three. *Unknown.*
For the Lord's Day Evening. Watts.
Little Brown Church in the Vale, The. Pitts.
Loftiest spirit that ever flamed in flesh, The. Clause.
Manners. Shiffert.
Placid Pew, The. Suderman.
St. Isaac's Church, Petrograd. McKay.
Wednesday Night Prayer Meeting. Wright.

**Cicadas**
Cicada. Stoutenberg.
Cigales. Wilbur.
Invocation: "Unwinding the spool of the morning." Miller.

**Cigars**
My First Cigar. Burdette.

**Cinderella**
Cinderella. Sexton.

**Circe**
Circe. Hope.
Moly. Gunn.

To a Lady. Morton.

**Circus**
Flying Trapeze, The. Leybourne.
Freak Show, The. Willard.
Tightrope Walker. Scannell.
What Happens. Jordan.
When I Went to the Circus. Lawrence.

**Cities**
American City. Oates.
Apartment House. Raftery.
City. Fisher.
City. Hughes.
City. Stembridge.
City Afternoon. Howes.
City of Dreadful Night, The. Thomson ("B.V.").
City Psalm. Levertov.
City Rises, The. Cunningham.
Cold Water Flat. Booth.
Commitment in a City. Tsuda.
Composed upon Westminster Bridge. Wordsworth.
Constructions: Upper East Side. Hochman.
Countryman's Return, The. Thomas.
Driving at Night. Rezmerski.
Get the Gasworks. Ignatow.
Give Me the Splendid Silent Sun. Whitman.
Glasgow. Smith.
Going and Coming: Two Poems. Benedikt.
Honored Dead, The. Doulis.
In the inner city. Clifton.
Lines. Waldman.
Lost. Ignacio.
Manchester by Night. Blind.
Megalopolis. Cruz.
Metropole. Anderson.
Nature of Jungles, The. Moses.
New block. P. Dickinson.
Pastoral of the City Streets. Klein.
Pictures of a City. Fripp.
Poem: "The greater cities are." Cruz.
Poem for Democrats, A. Jones.
Romanies in Town, the. Beresford.
Roof Garden, The. Moss.
Silence of a city, how awful at midnight, The! Coleridge.
Thaw in the City. Lipsitz.
Thirteen Preludes for Pioneer Square. Logan.
To Nowhere. Ignatow.
Up at a Villa—Down in the City. Browning.
Urban Convalescence, An. Merrill.
Vita-Sheet. Weiss.
What It Means, Living in the City. Dickey.
What Train Will Come? Smith.
White City, The. McKay.
World Outside, The. Levertov.

**Civil Rights.** *See* **Protest, Social.**

**Civil War, American**
Ascent of T. J. Jackson: A Soldier's Tale. "A. N."
Barbara Frietchie. Whittier.
Battle-Cry of Freedom, The. Root.
Battle-Hymn of the Republic. Howe.
Battle of Shiloh, The. *Unknown.*
Blue and the Gray, The. Finch.
Bonnie Blue Flag, The. Macarthy.
Break the News to Mother. Harris.
Brother Green. *Unknown.*
Charleston. Timrod.
Cripple for Life, The. *Unknown.*
*Cumberland* and the *Merrimac*, The. *Unknown.*
*Cumberland*'s Crew, The. *Unknown.*
Dan Ellis's Boys. *Unknown.*
Dixie. Emmett
Dixie (Battle Hymn). Pike.
Fabrication of Ancestors. Dugan.

Fare You Well, My Darling. *Unknown.*
For the Union Dead. Lowell.
Goin' 'Cross the Mountain. *Unknown.*
Goober Peas. *Unknown.*
How Do You Do, *Alabama*! Wilson.
John Brown's Body. *Unknown.*
Just Before the Battle Mother. Root.
Kearney at Seven Pines. Stedman.
Last Fierce Charge, The. *Unknown.*
Malvern Hill. Melville.
Marching through Georgia. Work.
Maryland, My Maryland! Randall.
Memorial Wreath. Randall.
Negro Soldier's Civil War Chant. *Unknown.*
Ode: "Sleep sweetly in your humble graves." Timrod.
Ode Recited at the Harvard Commemoration. Lowell.
Ode to the Confederate Dead. Tate.
Portent, The. Melville.
Red, White and Red, The. *Unknown.*
Roll, *Alabama*, Roll. *Unknown.*
Sheridan's Ride. Read.
Shiloh; a Requiem. Melville.
Stonewall Jackson's Way. Palmer.
Tenting on the Old Camp Ground. Kittredge.
Three Hundred Thousand More. Gibbons.
Unsung Heroes, The. Dunbar.
Vigil Strange I Kept on the Field One Night. Whitman.
When Dey 'Listed Colored Soldiers. Dunbar.
When Johnny Comes Marching Home. Gilmore.
When This Cruel War Is Over. *Unknown.*
Wound-Dresser, The. Whitman.
**Civil War, Nigerian**
Nigerian Unity; or, Little Niggers Killing Little Niggers. Lee.
**Civil War, Spanish**
Say That We Saw Spain Die. Millay.
**Civil Wars, English**
Battle of Naseby, The. Macaulay.
Bonne Dundee.*Fr.* The Doom of Devergoil. Scott.
Cavalier Tunes. Browning.
Do not lift him from the bracken.*Fr.* The Widow of Glencoe.
   Aytoun.
Execution of Montrose, The. Aytoun.
It Was A' for Our Rightfu' King. Burns.
O What's the Rhyme to Porringer. *Unknown.*
Parliament Soldiers, The. *Unknown.*
Sally from Coventry, The. Thornbury.
Song of the Western Men, The. Hawker.
Three Troopers, The. Thornbury.
Vicar of Bray, The. *Unknown.*
**Civilization**
Long-Legged Fly. Yeats.
Marx the Sign Painter.*Fr.* The New Spoon River. Masters.
Meru. Yeats.
**Clams and Clamming**
Clamming. Whittemore.
Sonnet to a Clam. Saxe.
**Clare, John**
John Clare. Anderson.
**Clark, Alfred Corning**
Alfred Corning Clark. Lowell.
**Clarke, Austin**
Visit to Bridge House, A. Weber.
**Clarke, Charles Cowden**
To Charles Cowden Clarke. Keats.
**Clay, Cassius.** *See* **Ali, Muhammed.**
**Clergy**
Auld Seceder Cat, The. *Unknown.*
Colin Clout. Skelton.
Collar, The. Herbert.
Country Clergy, The. Thomas.
Father O'Flynn. Graves.
Gentle Alice Brown. Gilbert.

Habit of Perfection, The. Hopkins.
Irish-American Dignitary. Clarke.
Jackdaw of Rheims, The. "Ingoldsby."
Madam and the Minister. Hughes.
Ol' Tim Legion. Moxley.
On a Clergyman's Horse Biting Him. *Unknown.*
On the Forcers of Conscience. Milton.
Poor Parson, A.*Fr.* Canterbury Tales: Prologue. Chaucer.
Prayer of Holy Willie, The. Burns.
Preacher Considers His Sermon, The. Suderman.
Soliloquy of the Spanish Cloister. Browning.
Vicar of Bray, The. *Unknown.*
You Shall. *Unknown.*
**Clerks**
What Was Her Name? Ciardi.
**Cleveland, Ohio**
Ordinary Evening in Cleveland, An. Turco.
**Clocks and Watches**
Clock in the Square, A. Rich.
Gold Watch, The. Blight.
Grandfather's Clock. Work.
Watch, The. Cornford.
**Clonmacnoise, Ireland**
Dead at Clonmacnoise, The. *Unknown.*
**Clothing**
Because of Clothes. Riding.
Box for Tom, A. Tate.
Clothes. Jennings.
Clothes Maketh the Man. Weiss.
Delight in Disorder. Herrick.
Dresses. Fraser.
Evening Gown, The. Swenson.
Goodwill, Inc. Schmitz.
Shirt, The. Silkin.
Stiff Shirts. Bowman.
Upon Julia's Clothes. Herrick.
**Clouds**
Clouds. Brooke.
Clouds, The. Williams.
Job Hunting. Hennen.
**Clough, Arthur Hugh**
Thyrsis. Arnold.
**Coal Mining and Miners**
Avondale Mine Disaster, The. *Unknown.*
Blue Monday. *Unknown.*
Cleator Moor. Nicholson.
Coal Diggin' Blues. *Unknown.*
Coal Miner's Goodbye, A. *Unknown.*
Collier, The. Watkins.
Collier's Wife, The. Lawrence.
Down in a Coal Mine. Geoghegan.
Dying Mine Brakeman, The. Jenks.
Gresford Disaster, The. *Unknown.*
John J. Curtis. Gallagher.
Miner's Doom, The. *Unknown.*
Miner's Helmet, The. MacBeth.
Mourning Letter, March 29, 1963. Dorn.
Old Miner's Refrain, The. *Unknown.*
Payday at Coal Creek. *Unknown.*
That Little Lump of Coal. *Unknown.*
Two-Cent Coal. *Unknown.*
Working in the Mines. *Unknown.*
**Cockaigne, Land of**
Land of Cockaigne, The. *Unknown.*
**Cockroaches**
Roach, The. Raven.
**Cocks.** *See* **Roosters.**
**Cody, William Frederick.** *See* **Buffalo Bill.**
**Cold**
Cold. Hughes.
**Colds (illness)**
Winter Scene, A. Whittemore.

**Cole, Thomas**
To Cole, the Painter, Departing for Europe.   Bryant.
**Coleridge, Samuel Taylor**
Thoughts about the Person from Porlock.   Smith.
**Colette (Sidonie Gabrielle Colette)**
Dear Colette.   Jong.
**Coliseum.**   *See* **Colosseum.**
**Colleges and Universities**
Campus on the Hill, The.   Snodgrass.
Fisk is.   Scott.
For a College Yearbook.   Cunningham.
Town Against Gown at Oxford.   *Unknown.*
University Curriculum.   Turner.
You Understand the Requirements.   Lifshin.
**Cologne, Germany**
Cologne.   Coleridge.
**Colonus, Greece**
Colonus' Praise.*Fr.* Oedipus at Colonus.   Sophocles.
**Colors**
Answer to a Sonnet Ending Thus.   Keats.
Colours.   Evans.
Making of Color, The.   Seidman.
No Meaning.   Brame.
What Is Pink?   C. Rossetti.
**Colosseum**
Coliseum, The.   Poe.
**Coltrane, John**
Blues for John Coltrane, Dead at 41.   Matthews.
Dear John, Dear Coltrane.   Harper.
Here Where Coltrane Is.   Harper.
John Coltrane: An Impartial Review.   Spellman.
JuJu.   Touré.
**Columbia University**
Poem of Solitude at Columbia University.   García Lorca.
**Columbines**
Columbine, The.   Very.
**Columbus, Christopher**
And of Columbus.   Gregory.
Ave Maria.*Fr.* The Bridge.   Crane.
Columbus.   Miller.
Columbus.   Nash.
Columbus.   Simpson.
Columbus.   Von Schiller.
Discovery, The.   Squire.
Mysterious Biography.   Sandburg.
**Comic Books**
Shazam.   Dickey.
**Comic Verse.**   *See* **Humorous Verse.**
**Commencement Day**
Commencement.   Carrier.
**Communes**
Six-forty-two Farm Communes Struggle Poem.   Leifer.
**Communion.**   *See* **Eucharist.**
**Communism**
Reveille.   Ridge.
**Commuters**
Commuters.   White.
**Computers**
All Watched Over by Machines of Loving Grace.   Brautigan.
Computer's First Christmas Card, The.   Morgan.
Reason of Numbers, A.   Jacobsen.
**Concentration Camps**
After the Fact.   Cavalieri.
Camp in the Prussian Forest, A.   Jarrell.
Dachau, Now: "Roses Grow There, Fat with Blood."   Ritchie.
Treblinka Gas Chamber.   Webb.
**Concord, Massachusetts**
Concord Hymn.   Emerson.
**Confederacy**
Bonnie Blue Flag.   Macarthy.
Dixie.   Emmett.
Dixie (Battle Hymn).   Pike.
Maryland, My Maryland.   Randall.
Ode: "Sleep sweetly in your humble graves."   Timrod.

**Conformity**
At the Chariman's Housewarming.   Stafford.
Man in the Bowler Hat, The.   Black.
Much madness is divinest sense.   Dickinson.
Unknown Citizen, The.   Auden.
**Connecticut River**
River of Rivers in Connecticut, The.   Stevens.
**Conquistadors**
El Dorado.   Ryan.
**Conscience**
Conscience, The.   Wickham.
Conscience Is Instinct Bred in the House.*Fr.* A Week on the Concord and Merrimack Rivers.   Thoreau.
**Conscientious Objectors.**   *See* **Pacifism and Pacifists.**
**Conservation.**   *See* **Ecology.**
**Constitution (ship)**
*Constitution* and the *Guerrière*, The.   *Unknown.*
*Constitution*'s Last Fight, The.   Roche.
Old Ironsides.   Holmes.
**Contentment**
Character of a Happy Life, The.   Wotton.
Contentment.   Cotton.
Integer Vitae.   Campion.
My Mind to Me a Kingdom Is.   Dyer.
**Convents**
Convent, The.   O'Sullivan.
**Conversion**
Mr. Davis's Experience.   *Unknown.*
Mrs. Saunder's Experience.   *Unknown.*
**Cooking and Cooks**
Clove as Ego.   Halpern.
**Cooper, James Fenimore**
Cooper.*Fr.* A Fable for Critics.   Lowell.
**Corn**
Garden Report.   Kuzma.
**Corncrakes**
Corncrake, The.   Cousins.
**Cornwall, England**
Cape Cornwall.   Mills.
Cornish Cliffs.   Betjeman.
**Cornwallis, Charles Cornwallis, 1st Marquis**
Cornwallis' Country Dance.   *Unknown.*
**Coruña, La, Spain**
Burial of Sir John Moore at Corunna, The.   Wolfe.
**Cosmetics**
Empress in the Mirror.   Inez.
My Mother's Moustache.   Moore.
Progress of Beauty, The.   Swift.
Rachel and the Truth (c. 1945).   Yvonne.
Valentine for a Lady, A.   Lucillius.
**Cotton**
Cotton Song.   Toomer.
November Cotton Flower.   Toomer.
Poor Little Johnny.   *Unknown.*
Roll the Cotton Down.   *Unknown.*
Snapshots of the Cotton South.   Davis.
**Country Life**
Above Penmaenmawr.   Connor.
At Rushy Lagoon.   McAuley.
Before the Thaw.   Gill.
Bull, The.   Sackville-West.
Cotter's Saturday Night, The.   Burns.
Cranberry Song, The.   Reynolds.
Digging.   Thomas.
Farm Picture, A.   Whitman.
Farm, The.   Miller.
Farrell O'Reilly.   Gogarty.
For E. C. J.   Jarrett.
Going to Sleep in the Country.   Moss.
He May Be Envied Who with Tranquil Breast.   Smith.

Knoxville, Tennessee. Giovanni.
Need of Being Versed in Country Things, The. Frost.
O Country People. Hewitt.
Ode to Master Anthony Stafford to Hasten Him into the
   Country, An. Randolph.
Pass of Kirkstone, The. Wordsworth.
Pasture, The. Frost.
Raleigh Was Right. Williams.
Short Pastoral. Nathan.
Silent Poem. Francis.
Solitary Reaper, The. Wordsworth.
Spraying the Potatoes. Kavanagh.
To Miss Laetitia Van Lewen (Afterwards Mrs. Pilkington), at a
   Country Assize. Grierson.
Up at a Villa—Down in the City. Browning.
Village, The. Crabbe.
Walking through the Country. Provisor.
Wish, A. Rogers.

**Courage**
Any Complaints? Scannell.
Feigned Courage. Lamb.
Strong Men, Riding Horses. Brooks.

**Coventry, England**
Sally from Coventry, The. Thornbury.

**Cowboys**
As I Walked Out in the Streets of Laredo. *Unknown.*
Bucking Bronco. *Unknown.*
Buffalo Skinners, The. *Unknown.*
Clancy of the Overflow. *Unknown.*
Closing of the Rodeo, The. Smith.
Cowboy Song. Causley.
Cowboy's Lament, The. *Unknown.*
Cowboy's Life Is a Very Dreary Life, The. *Unknown.*
Cowboys: One ("Brave/ they straddle the animals"). McKuen.
Cowboys: Two ("Huddled in the pits"). McKuen.
Cowboys: Three ("They wade through beer cans"). McKuen.
Goodbye, Old Paint, I'm Leaving Cheyenne. Garrett.
Hoppy. Godsey.
I Am a Cowboy in the Boat of Ra. Reed.
I Ride an Old Paint. *Unknown.*
I've Got No Use for the Women. *Unknown.*
Love and an Old Western at the Starlite Drive-in Theater.
   Legler.
O Bury Me Not on the Lone Prairie. *Unknown.*
Old Chisholm Trail, The. *Unknown.*
Old Dolores. *Unknown.*
Red Whiskey. *Unknown.*
Ride 'Im Cowboy. Freebairn.
Ride the High Country. Slavitt.
Rodeo. Lueders.
Sandy Maranoa, The. Davis.
Silver Screen. Clark.
Streets of Laredo, The. *Unknown.*
Texas Cowboy, The. *Unknown.*
Whoopee-Ti-Yi-Yo! *Unknown.*
Zebra Dun, The. *Unknown.*

**Cows**
Blessing on the Cows, A. O'Sullivan.
Cow, The. Stephens.
Cow, The. Stevenson.
Cow, The. Taylor.
Cow in Apple Time, The. Frost.
Cushy Cow, Bonny. *Unknown.*
Drinking Time. O'Sullivan.
Fetching Cows. MacCaig.
Going Home. Lux.
Harmonious Heedlessness of Little Boy Blue, The. Carryl.
Lovely Big Cow. Morton.
Milking Time. Roberts.
Moo! Hillyer.
Purple Cow, The. Burgess.
*See also* **Cattle.**

**Coyotes**
Coyote, The. Dewey.
Toe'osh: A Laguna Coyote Story. Silko.

**Crabbe, George**
George Crabbe. Robinson.

**Crabs**
Crab, The. Aiken.
Crustaceans. Fuller.
Ghost Crabs. Hughes.

**Cradle Songs.** *See* **Cradle Song** *and* **Lullaby** *in Title and First
   Line Index.*

**Craftmanship**
Correct Compassion, A. Kirkup.
Craftsmen. Sackville-West.

**Crane, Hart**
Orpheus. Winters.

**Cranes (birds)**
Crane Is My Neighbour, The. Neilson.
Cranes, The. *Unknown.*
Sandhill Crane, The. Austin.

**Cranmer, Thomas**
Admire Cranmer! Smith.

**Crazy Horse (Indian Chief)**
Crazy Horse Returns to South Dakota. Elliott.
Sound from the Earth, A. Stafford.

**Creation**
Assignment. Butcher.
Creation, The. Johnson.
Creation, The: According to Coyote. Ortiz.
Six Days of Creation, The. McAuley.

**Crew Racing**
Eight Oars and a Coxswain. Guiterman.
This Shell. Van Doren.

**Crickets**
Animal That Drank Up Sound, The. Stafford.
Cricket, The. Tuckerman.
Crickets. Saroyan.
On the Grasshopper and the Cricket. Keats.

**Crime and Criminals**
Act, An. Rosen.
Bold Jack Donahue. *Unknown.*
Boston Burglar, The. *Unknown.*
Bowery, The. Hoyt.
Burglar, The. Dorman.
Captain Hall. *Unknown.*
Claude Allen. *Unknown.*
Cole Younger. *Unknown.*
Convict of Clonmel, The. Callanan.
Crafty Farmer, The. *Unknown.*
Crimes of Passion: The Slasher. Stokes.
Effort at Speech. Meredith.
Frank James, the Roving Gambler. *Unknown.*
Frankie Silvers. Silvers.
Gentle Alice Brown. Gilbert.
He Fell Among Thieves. Newbolt.
Jim Jones at Botany Bay. *Unknown.*
Johnson-Jinkson. *Unknown.*
Last Gangster, The. Corso.
Musgrove. *Unknown.*
Peddler and His Wife, The. *Unknown.*
Robbing and Stealing Blues. *Unknown.*
Sam Bass. *Unknown.*
Sam Hall. *Unknown.*
Somebody Call. Rogers.
Thief, The. Jacobsen.
Thief, The. Kunitz.
To a Fugitive. Wright.
Twenty-One Years. *Unknown.*
Wild Colonial Boy, The. *Unknown.*

**Crimean War**
Charge of the Heavy Brigade, The. Tennyson.
Charge of the Light Brigade, The. Tennyson.

**Cripples**
  Cripples.  Spivak.
  Disabled.  Owen.
**Criticism and Critics**
  Apology Addressed to the Critical Reviewer, The.   Churchill.
  Black Poet, White Critic.  Randall.
  Choice of Weapons, A.  Kunitz.
  English Bards and Scotch Reviewers.  Byron.
  Essay on Criticism, An.  Pope.
  Lines to a Critic.  Shelley.
  Owl-Critic, The.  Fields.
  To a Captious Critic.  Dunbar.
  To Certain Critics.  Cullen.
**Crocodiles**
  Be Careful!  *Unknown.*
  Crocodile.  Chukovsky.
  How Doth the Little Crocodile. *Fr.* Alice's Adventures in
    Wonderland.  "Carroll."
  If you should meet a crocodile.  *Unknown.*
**Crocuses**
  For the Spring Being.  Carter.
**Cromwell, Oliver**
  Horatian Ode upon Cromwell's Return from Ireland, An.
    Marvell.
  More Power.  O'Rahilly.
  To the Lord General Cromwell.  Milton.
**Cross, The**
  Dream of the Rood, The.  *Unknown.*
  Ebony: Contemporary.  Brand.
  Making of the Cross, The.  Everson.
  Old Rugged Cross, The.  Bennard.
**Crowds**
  At the Ball Game.  Williams.
**Crows**
  Craw's Killed the Poussie, O, The!  *Unknown.*
  Crow, The.  Reaney.
  Crows, The.  Ghose.
  Crows.  McCord.
  Crows.  Witherup.
  Crow's First Lesson.  Hughes.
  Frog and the Crow, The.  *Unknown.*
  Night Crow.  Roethke.
  Note on Master Crow, A.  Garrigue.
  Rooks, The.  Browne.
  Three Ravens, The.  *Unknown.*
  To Be or Not to Be.  *Unknown.*
**Crucifixion**
  At the Crucifixion.  *Unknown.*
  Calvary.  Robinson.
  Crucifixion.  *Unknown.*
  Ebony: Contemporary.  Brand.
  Ecce Homo.  Gascoyne.
  I Sigh When I Sing.  *Unknown.*
  On our Crucified Lord, Naked and Bloody.  Crashaw.
  On the Passion.  *Unknown.*
  Palm Sunday: Good Friday.  Fletcher.
  Signature, A.  Warren.
  This crosse-tree here.  Herrick.
  Were You There When They Crucified My Lord?  *Unknown.*
  When I Survey the Wondrous Cross.  Watts.
  Zone of Death.  Everson.
**Cruelty to Animals**
  Barn Owl.*Fr.* Father and Child.  Harwood.
  Beasts Are Very Wise, The.  Kipling.
  Blinded Bird, The.  Hardy.
  Coyote, The.  Dewey.
  Elephant, The.  Hochman.
  Seven Mexican Children.  Schmidt.
  Thoughts on Capital Punishment.  McKuen.
  Traverse City Zoo.  Harrison.
  Village Tale, A.  Sarton.
**Cuba**
  Cuba Libre.  Miller.
**Cuckoos**
  Cuckoo, The.  Chalmers.
  Cuckoo.  Lister.
  Cuckoo, The.  *Unknown.*
  Koocoo, The.  *Unknown.*
  Oocuck, The.  Richardson.
  To the Cuckoo.  Wordsworth.
**Cupid**
  Cupid's Call.  Shirley.
  Love Arm'd.  Behn.
  Ode to Love, An.  Behn.
  Wounded Cupid, The.  Herrick.
**Curses**
  Bruadar and Smith and Glinn.  *Unknown.*
  Curse for a Nation, A.  E. Browning.
  Curse on a Closed Gate, A.  *Unknown.*
  Glass of Beer, A.  Stephens.
  Goblin Market.  C. Rossetti.
  Goody Blake, and Harry Gill.  Wordsworth.
  Irish Curse on the Occupying English.   *Unknown.*
  Skin the Goat's Curse on Carey.  *Unknown.*
  When Klopstock England defied.  Blake.
**Custer, George Armstrong**
  Tale of Last Stands, A.  Red Cloud.
**Cybele**
  Mother, The.  Deutsch.

# D

**Da Vince, Leonardo**   *See* **Leonardo Da Vinci.**
**Daedalus**
  Be Daedalus.  Alba.
**Daffodils**
  Lent Lily, The.  Housman.
  To Daffodills.  Herrick.
**Dahlias**
  Autumn.  A. Lowell.
  Giant Decorative Dahlia.  Holden.
**Daisies**
  Daisies.  Nowlan.
  Diasies.  Wade.
  Daisy, The.  Zaturenska.
  Loss.  Ammons.
**Dali, Salvador**
  Salvador Dali.  Gascoyne.
**Dancing and Dancers**
  Artist, The.  Williams.
  At the Dancing School of the Sisters Schwarz.  Jerome.
  Band Played On, The.  Palmer.
  Bottled: New York.  Johnson.
  Dance Steps.  *Unknown.*
  Harlem Dancer, The.  McKay.
  Lost Dancer, The.  Toomer.
  Morris Dance, The.  *Unknown.*
  Praise of Dancing, The.*Fr.* Orchestra; or, A Poem of Dancing.
    Davies.
  Quick-Step.  Creeley.
  Swansong.  Muske.
  Waltz Me Around Again Willie; or, Round, Round, Round.
    Cobb.
**Dandelions**
  American XVII: A Reminder of William Carlos Williams.
    Rakosi.
**Daphne**
  Apollo and Daphne.  Winters.
**Daughters**
  At a Summer Hotel.  Gardner.

First Lesson.  Booth.
Goodnight, The.  Simpson.
I Have Three Daughters.  Stone.
Little Girl, My String Bean, My Lovely Woman.  Sexton.
Madonna and Daughter.  Bergé.
Mothers, Daughters.  Kaufman.
Mutant, The.  Barrows.
Name, The.  Creeley.
On My First Daughter.  Jonson.
Prayer for My Daughter, A.  Yeats.
Sleep Darling.  Sappho.
To My Infant Daughter: "Alas, that I Should Be."  Winters.
*Roses Race Around Her Name, The* (RRA).  Jonathan Cott, ed.

**David (Bible)**
After Goliath.  Amis.
David.  Miles.
David and Goliath.  Crouch.
Song to David, A.  Smart.

**David (statue)**
Bronze David of Donatello, The.  Jarrell.

**Davies, Sir John**
Four for Sir John Davies.  Roethke.

**Davy, Sir Humphrey**
Sir Humphry Davy*Fr.* Clerihews.  Bentley.

**Dawn**
Dawn, The.  Yeats.
Dew.  Maiden.
First Light.  Kinsella.
Harbor Dawn, The.  Crane.
I dreamed I saw the crescent moon.  *Unknown.*
Square at Dawn, The.  Tate.
Sun-Rising, The.  Donne.
*See also* **Morning; Sunrise.**

**Day**
Curiously Young Like a Freshly-Dug Grave.  Brautigan.
Days.  Emerson.
Days.  Larkin.
Wee Davie Daylicht.  Tennant.

**Daydreams.**  *See* **Dreaming and Dreams.**

**Deafness**
Deafness.  Ryan.
Monologue of a Deaf Man.  Wright.
Mutterings over the Crib of a Deaf Child.  Wright.
On His Own Deafness.  Swift.
On a Portrait of a Deaf Man.  Betjeman.

**Death and the Dead**
Adieu, Farewell Earth's Bliss.*Fr.* Summer's Last Will and Testament.  Nashe.
After Death.  C. Rossetti.
After Lorca.  Creeley.
Afterwards.  Hardy.
Age.  Landor.
Ah, Are You Digging on My Grave?  Hardy.
All Being Well.  Gibson.
All the Dead Dears.  Plath.
And Death Shall Have No Dominion.  Thomas.
And When I Die.  Nyro.
Angel of Death, The.  *Unknown.*
Angina Pectoris.  Moses.
Annabel Lee.  Poe.
Anthem for Doomed Youth.  Owen.
Arundel Tomb, An.  Larkin.
As from the darkening gloom a silver dove.  Keats.
As I Ebb'd with the Ocean of Life.  Whitman.
Autumn.  De la Mare.
Ballad of Dead Yankees, The.  Petersen.
Beautiful Youth.  Benn.
Because I could not stop for Death.  Dickinson.
Bed by the Window, The.  Jeffers.
Before the Birth of One of Her Children.  Bradstreet.
Bells for John Whiteside's Daughter.  Ransom.
Bereft Child's First Night.  Bellerby.

Beside the Bed.  Mew.
Book of the Dead, Prayer l4.  Berssenbrugge.
Breathers, The.  Reiss.
Bride, The.  Lawrence.
Broken Gull, A.  Moore.
Burial.  Francis.
Burial.  Walker.
Channel Firing.  Hardy.
Charge, The.  Hollo.
City Dead-House, The.  Whitman.
Coming and Going.  Goodman.
Conqueror Worm, The.  Poe.
Consolatio Nova: for Alan Swallow.  Cunningham.
Cool Tombs.  Sandburg.
Creek Mother Poem.  Harjo.
Crossing the Bar.  Tennyson.
Darest Thou Now O Soul.  Whitman.
Dead, The.  Blind.
Dead, The.  Very.
Dead Boy.  Ransom.
Dead Ponies.  Chamberlain.
Death.  Jones.
Death.  Williams.
Death.  Wright.
Death and the Arkansas River.  Stanford.
Death and the Plowman.  Keyes.
Death, Be Not Proud.*Fr.* Holy Sonnets.  Donne.
Death Bells.  *Unknown.*
Death Is a Door.  Allcock.
Death Is Awful.  *Unknown.*
Death is the cook of nature, and we find.*Fr.* Nature's Cook.  Duchess of Newcastle.
Death is the supple suitor.  Dickinson.
Death of a Poet.  Causley.
Death of a Son.  Silkin.
Death of the Ball Turret Gunner, The.  Jarrell.
Death of the Craneman, The.  Hayes.
Death Snips Proud Men.  Sandburg.
Death stands above me, whispering low.  Landor.
Death Takes Only a Minute.  Pratt.
Death Valley Blues.  *Unknown.*
Death-Bed, The.  Hood.
Death-Bed Song.  *Unknown.*
Deathwatch.  Harper.
Deer Lay Down Their Bones, The.  Jeffers.
Dirge, A: "Why were you born when the snow was falling."  C. Rossetti.
Dirge without Music.  Millay.
Do Not Go Gentle into That Good Night.  Thomas.
Do the Dead Know What Time It Is?  Patchen.
Dream, A.  Allingham.
During Wind and Rain.  Hardy.
Dying Californian, The.  *Unknown.*
Dying Father's Farewell, The.  *Unknown.*
Dying Gaul, The.  O'Grady.
Early Purges, The.  Heaney.
Edmonton, thy cemetery.  Smith.
Egyptian Book of the Dead.  Henderson.
Elegy: "Death be not proud, thy hand gave not this blow."  Harington.
Elegy: "My prime of youth is but a frost of cares."  Tichborne.
Elegy for a School-Friend.  Young.
Elegy for Alfred Hubbard.  Connor.
Elegy for Jack Bowman.  Bruchac.
Elegy for Jane.  Roethke.
Elegy for My Father.  Strand.
Elegy over a Tomb.  Herbert of Cherbury.
Elegy Written in a Country Churchyard.  Gray.
Epitaph: "My brother is skull and skeleton now."  Montgomerie.
Epitaph: "Sir, you should notice me: I am the Man."  Abercrombie.

Epitaph on an Infant.  Coleridge.

Epitaph on the Lady Mary Villiers.  Carew.

Erotion's Death.  Whigham.

Exequy, The.  King.

Exit Molloy.  Mahon.

Fall Comes in Back-Country Vermont.  Warren.

Fear No More the Heat o' the Sun.*Fr.* Cymbeline.
  Shakespeare.

Felix Randal.  Hopkins.

First Death.  Justice.

First Death in Nova Scotia.  Bishop.

Fixing to Die.  *Unknown.*

Flat One, A.  Snodgrass.

For a Dead Lady.  Robinson.

For the Moment.  Weber.

Force That through the Green Fuse Drives the Flower, The.
  Thomas.

Forsaken Garden, A.  Swinburne.

Fox, The.  Patchen.

Funeral Oration for a Mouse.  Dugan.

Futility.  Owen.

Game Called.  Rice.

Glories of Our Blood and State, The.*Fr.* The Contention of Ajax
  and Ulysses.  Shirley.

Glory of the Day Was in Her Face, The.  Johnson.

Go Down Death.  Johnson.

Graves of a Household, The.  Hemans.

Hearse Song, The.  *Unknown.*

Heart Burial.  Grigson.

Heaven and Hell.  *Unknown.*

Here's Death.  McMaster.

Home Burial.  Frost.

How Annandale Went Out.  Robinson.

Hungry Grass.  MacDonagh.

Hymn to God My God, in My Sickness.  Donne.

I heard a fly buzz when I died.  Dickinson.

I Thank God I'm Free at Las'.  *Unknown.*

I Went to Death.  *Unknown.*

In a Grave-Yard.  Braithwaite.

In Memoriam (Easter 1915).  Thomas.

In Memory of a Friend.  Barker.

In Memory of G. K., for 50 Years the College Carpenter.
  Martin.

In Memory of My Cat Domino: 1951-1966.  Fuller.

In Memory of My Dear Grandchild Elizabeth Bradstreet.
  Bradstreet.

In Tenebris.  Hardy.

In the Desert.  Melville.

In the House of the Dying.  Cooper.

In the thirtieth year of life.  Cunningham.

Incident in a Rose Garden.  Justice.

Inseperable.  Marston.

Interlude.  Shapiro.

Intimations of Immortality, Cuttingsville, Vermont, 1880.
  Carrier.

Invocations of Death, The.  Raine.

Is It Far to Go?  Day Lewis.

Is My Team Ploughing.  Housman.

I've seen a dying eye.  Dickinson.

Janet Waking.  Ranson.

Lads in their hundreds to Ludlow come in for the fair, The.
  Housman.

Lady Lazarus.  Plath.

Last Journey.  Martinez.

Last Lines—1916.  Pearse.

Last Quatrain of the Ballad of Emmett Till, The.  Brooks.

Last Word, A.  Rodgers.

Last Words.  Plath.

Lesson, The.  Lucie-Smith.

Let Me Die a Youngman's Death.  McGough.

Letter from a Death Bed.  Ciardi.

Life flows to death as rivers to the sea.  Cunningham.

Little Elegy.  Kennedy.

Luke Havergal.  Robinson.

Lycidas.  Milton.

Madam Life's a Piece in Bloom.  Henley.

Madrigal.  Thomas.

Malfunction.  Albert.

Margaritae Sorori.  Henley.

Maria Wentworth.  Carew.

Meditation, The.  Norris.

Memorial Service.  Williams.

Merlin.  Hill.

Midnight Lamentation.  Monro.

Mid-Term Break.  Heaney.

Missing.  Pudney.

Mother, they say you looked Irish.  Brenner.

Mourn for Yourself.  Keating.

My life closed twice before its close.  Dickinson.

Nature.  Longfellow.

Nearer, My God to Thee.  Adams.

Necrological.  Ransom.

New England Protestant.*Fr.* Attitudes.  Eberhart.

Newly Discovered "Homeric" Hymn, A.  Olson.

News.  Pomeroy.

O Bury Me Not on the Lone Prairie.  *Unknown.*

Oh! Death.  *Unknown.*

O Death, Rock Me Asleep.  Boleyn.

Oath, The.  Tate.

Ocean Burial, The.  Chapin.

Of De Witt Williams on His Way to Lincoln Cemetery.
  Brooks.

Old King, The.  De la Mare.

On a Dead Child.  Bridges.

On a Dead Child.  Middleton.

On a Dying Boy.  Bell.

On Death.  Landor.

On My First Daughter.  Jonson.

On My First Son.  Jonson.

On Solomon Pavy, a Child of Queen Elizabeth's Chapel.
  Jonson.

On the Death of a Young Lady, Cousin to the Author.  Byron.

On the Death of Friends in Childhood.  Justice.

On the Death of His Wife.  O'Dalaigh.

One Morning in May; or, The Young Girl Cut Down in Her
  Prime.  *Unknown.*

Our journey had advanced.  Dickinson.

Out of the Cradle Endlessly Rocking.  Whitman.

Pale Blue Casket, The.  Pitcher.

Pardon, The.  Wilbur.

Pardoner's Tale Blues.  Beer.

Paul.  Wright.

Peace.  Hughes.

Peter's Little Daughter Dies.  Patchen.

Piazza Piece.  Ransom.

Poor Ghost, The.  C. Rossetti.

Poor soul, the center of my sinful earth.*Fr.* Sonnets.
  Shakespeare.

Porch, The.  Pain.

Prayer: "Give me a death like Buddha's, let me fall."  Moss.

Primary Ground, A.  Rich.

Prosopopoeia Corporis Animae Valedicturi: Adios: Arrivederci.
  Lathum.

Prospice.  Browning.

Quaker Graveyard in Nantucket, The.  Lowell.

Rain.  Thomas.

Reconciliation.  Lewis.

Refusal to Mourn the Death, by Fire, of a Child in London, A.
  Thomas.

Remember.  C. Rossetti.

Remembrance.  E. Brontë.

Reminiscence, A.  A. Brontë.

Requiescat.  Arnold.

Responsory, 1948, A.  Merton.

Rumination. Eberhart.
Safe in their alabaster chambers. Dickinson.
Sailing Home from Rapallo. Lowell.
St. James Infirmary. *Unknown.*
Sea Shanty. Dyment.
Shape of Death, The. Swenson.
Ship of Death, The. Lawrence.
Simplify Me When I'm Dead. Douglas.
Sister Lou. Brown.
Smile, Death. Mew.
Sonnet 21. Goodman.
Sparrow-Hawk's Complaint, The. *Unknown.*
Springfield Mountain. *Unknown.*
Staircase, The. Allen.
Stanzas: "I'll not weep that thou art going to leave me." E. Brontë.
Stanzas to——: "Well, some may hate, and some may scorn." E. Brontë.
Statue, The. Belloc.
Stony Lonesome. Hughes.
Streets of Laredo, The. *Unknown.*
Tenancy, The. Gilmore.
Thanatopsis. Bryant.
That Dark Other Mountain. Francis.
That time of year thou mayst in me behold.*Fr.* Sonnets. Shakespeare.
There's been a death in the opposite house. Dickinson.
They are all gone into the world of light! Vaughan.
This Houre Her Vigill. Iremonger.
Thoughts of Phena. Hardy.
Three. Corso.
Threnody: "The south-wind brings." Emerson.
Timor Mortis Conturbat Me. Dunbar.
To——: "The cold earth slept below." Shelley.
To an Athlete Dying Young. Housman.
To Death. Shelley.
To die—takes just a little while. Dickinson.
To My Friend Whose Parachute Did Not Open. Wagoner.
To My Ninth Decade. Landor.
To Night. White.
To the Holy Spirit. Winters.
To the Thoughtful Reader. Meredith.
Transformations. Hardy.
Trifles. Everson.
Truth the Dead Know, The. Sexton.
Two Deaths. Jennings.
Two Views of a Cadaver Room. Plath.
Two White Horses in a Line. *Unknown.*
Uncle Death. Clark.
Uphill. C. Rossetti.
Upon the Death of a Gentleman. Crashaw.
Upon the Image of Death. Southwell.
*Vale* from Carthage. Viereck.
Valediction, A: Forbidding Mourning. Donne.
Vegetable, I Will Not Be, A. Whitewing.
Villagers and Death, The. Graves.
Visit to My Father-in-Law on Memorial Day, A. Ruse.
Voice of Heroes. Gregory.
Wake Not for the World-Heard Thunder. Housman.
Waking to Snowfall. Jellema.
Warning and Reply. E. Brontë.
Watch, The. Cornford.
Water Island. Moss.
We Are Seven. Wordsworth.
We Assume: On the Death of Our Son, Reuben Masai Harper. Harper.
We slowly drove, he knew no haste. Dickinson.
When I Am Dead, My Dearest. C. Rossetti.
When I Have Fears That I May Cease to Be. Keats.
When I Was Home Last Christmas. Jarrell.
Who's Most Afraid of Death? Cummings.
Wild Mustard River, The. *Unknown.*

Witness to Death. Lattimore.
Woman Mourned by Daughters, A. Rich.
Written in Disgust of Vulgar Superstition. Keats.
**Death of God**
On Listening to a Death-of-God Theologian Lecture in Chapel. Suderman.
On the Death of God. Jellema.
**Debussy, Claude**
1907: A Proposal from Paris. Howard.
**Decay**
Hammers, The. Hodgson.
**Deer**
Buck in the Snow, The. Millay.
Deer among Cattle. Dickey.
Deer Isle. Booth.
Deer Lay Down Their Bones, The. Jeffers.
Fallow Deer at the Lonely House, The. Hardy.
Landscape, Deer Season. Howes.
Long Hair. Snyder.
Lost Deer, The. Bruchac.
Moschus Moschiferus. Hope.
Nymph Complaining for the Death of Her Fawn, The. Marvell.
Poacher, The. *Unknown.*
Runnable Stag, A. Davidson.
This Poem Is for Deer.*Fr.* Myths and Texts: Hunting. Snyder.
Traveling through the Dark. Stafford.
**Degas, Edgar**
Degas. Monette.
**Dierdre**
Deirdre. Stephens.
**Dejection**
Dejection; an Ode. Coleridge.
Here I sit in my infested cubicle. Greenwood.
Stanzas Written in Dejection Near Naples. Shelley.
**De Kooning, Willem**
Ode to Willem de Kooning. O'Hara.
**Demeter**
Song of Ceres. Doak.
**Democracy**
As a kid I believed in democracy: I. Berryman.
Councils. Piercy.
**Dentists**
Hands folded like napkins in my lap. Peterson.
**Denver, Colorado**
Waltz Against the Mountains. Ferril.
**Depression (economic). See Great Depression.**
**Depression (psychological). See Dejection; Mental Illness.**
**Descartes, René**
Whoroscope. Beckett.
**Deserts**
Rain in the Desert. Fletcher.
**Desire**
I turn you out of doors. Chartier.
Thou Blind Man's Mark.*Fr.* Astrophel and Stella. Sidney.
**Despair**
Carrion Comfort. Hopkins.
City of Dreadful Night, The. Thomson ("B.V.").
Delirium in Vera Cruz. Lowry.
Divorce of a Lover, The. Gascoigne.
I cannot live with you. Dickinson.
I Wake and Feel the Fell of Dark. Hopkins.
No Worst, There Is None. Hopkins.
Old-World Thicket, An. C. Rossetti.
She May Have Seen Better Days. Thornton.
Thou Art Indeed Just, Lord. Hopkins.
Warren Pryor. Nowlan.
**Destiny. See Fate.**
**Detroit, Michigan**
Black Day in July. Lightfoot.
Detroit. Hall.
In Detroit, I walk out Woodward Avenue. Cuscaden.

**Devil.** *See* **Satan.**

**Dew**
On a Drop of Dew. Marvell.

**Diabetes**
Day of the Pancreas, The. McFadden.

**Diana**
Dianae Sumus in Fide. Catullus.
Hymn to Diana.*Fr.* Cynthia's Revels. Jonson.

**Dickinson, Emily**
Emily Dickinson Postage Stamp. Strongin.
I Am in Danger—Sir. Rich.
Occupation: Spinster. Cabral.
Sisters, The. A. Lowell.
To Emily Dickinson. Crane.
To Emily Dickinson. Winters.

**Dictators**
Epitaph on a Tyrant. Auden.

**Dietrich, Marlene**
Welthistoriche Perspektiven. Watson.

**DiMaggio, Joe**
Byron vs. DiMaggio. Meinke.

**Dinosaurs**
Dinosaur Bones, The. Sandburg.
Dinosaurs Tracks in Beit Zayit. Kaufman.

**Dionysus**
Hail, Dionysos. Randall.

**Dirigibles**
Elegy for the U. S. N. Dirigible, Macon, The. Winters.

**Disarmament**
This Excellent Machine. Lehmann.

**Diving and Divers**
Diver. Francis.
Diver, The. Hayden.
Diving. Murano.
Diving into the Wreck. Rich.
Elegy for a Diver. Booth.
Skin Song. Lieberman.
Underwater. Schmidt.

**Divorce**
Divorce. Noll.
Divorce. Widerberg.

**Doctors.** *See* **Physicians.**

**Dodoes**
Dodo, The. Kessler.
Dodo, The. Lucie-Smith.

**Dogs**
Ah, Are You Digging on My Grave? Hardy.
Argus and Ulysses. Farjeon.
Big Dog. Booth.
Bony. Ortiz.
Der Deitcher's Dog. Winner.
Dog. Ferlinghetti.
Dog, The. Iremonger.
Dog. Ransom.
Dog Alive. Witt.
Dog at Night. Untermeyer.
Dog Hospital. Wild.
Dog in the Quarry, A, *sel.* Holub.
Dog Parade, The. Guiterman.
Dog Talk. De Pietro.
Dogs Are Shakespearean, Children Are Strangers. Schwartz.
Dog's Best Friend Is His Illiteracy, A. Nash.
Dog's Cold Nose, The. Guiterman.
Dogs of Santiago. McCarthy.
Elegy on the Death of a Mad Dog, An.*Fr.* The Vicar of Wakefield. Goldsmith.
Epitaph, An: Inscription on a Monument at Newstead Abbey. Byron.
Epitaph on a Dog. *Unknown.*
German Shepherd. Livingston.
Hairy Dog, The. Asquith.
Hope. Dickey.

Inscription on the Monument of a Newfoundland Dog. Byron.
Mad Dog. Siegel.
Maltese Dog, The. *Unknown.*
Night Hunt, The. MacDonagh.
Old Dog, The. MacLean.
Old Dog. Stafford.
Old Dog Blue. *Unknown.*
Overland to the Islands. Levertov.
P. C. Plod Versus the Dale St Dog Strangler. McGough.
Pardon, The. Wilbur.
Power of the Dog, The. Kipling.
Puppy. Lape.
Rake. Ratcliffe.
Sheepdog Trials in Hyde Park. Day Lewis.
Span of Life, The. Frost.
Sudden Assertion. Leslie.
Sunning. Tippett.
To Our House-Dog Captain. Landor.
Towser Shall Not Be Tied Tonight. *Unknown.*
Unloved, The. Canzoneri.
Village Tale, A. Sarton.
Watchdog. Armour.
*See also* **individual breeds of dogs (e.g. Basset Hounds).**

**Dolls**
Dolls, The. Yeats.
Lost Doll, The.*Fr.* The Water Babies. Kingsley.

**Dolphins**
Dolphin Seen Alone. Lattimore.

**Don Quixote**
Bridge of Heraclitus, The. Reavey.

**Donatello**
Bronze David of Donatello, The. Jarrell.

**Donkeys**
Donkey, The. Hinde.
Donkey, The. Roethke.
Donkey Riding. *Unknown.*
Donkeys. Field.
Time Out. Montague.
To a Young Ass. Coleridge.

**Donne, John**
On Donne's Poetry. Coleridge.
On the Death of Donne. Carew.

**Dorsetshire, England**
Dorset. Betjeman.
"Dorset Nose," The. Sansom.

**Dostoyevsky, Feodor**
For Fyodor. Webb.
Now It's Happened. Lawrence.
Buzzing Doubt, The. Hill.
Respectable Burgher, The. Hardy.
Will You, Won't You? Van Doren.

**Douglass, Frederick**
Frederick Douglass. Cornish.
Frederick Douglass. Dunbar.
Frederick Douglass. Hayden.
Frederick Douglass: 1817-1895. Hughes.

**Doves**
Mourning Dove, The. Livingston.
Stockdoves, The. Young.

**Dragonflies**
Dragonfly, The. Bogan.

**Dragons**
Dragons. Ciardi.
O To Be a Dragon. Moore.

**Drake, Sir Francis**
Sir Francis Drake; or Eighty-Eight. *Unknown.*
To the Noble Sir Francis Drake. Beedome.

**Dreaming and Dreams**
African Dream. Kaufman.
Back Behind the Eyes. Stokesbury.
Beale Street. Hughes.
Big Dream, Little Dream. Simpson.

Day-Dream from an Emigrant to His Absent Wife, The. Coleridge.
Do Not Dream. Zach.
Dream Deferred. Hughes.
Dream Record: June 8, 1955. Ginsberg.
Dream-Pedlary. Beddoes.
Dreams. Traherne.
Dreamscape. Booth.
First of All My Dreams Was Of, The. Cummings.
Five Dreams, The. Woods.
Le Rêve. Bowers.
Lenox Avenue Mural. Hughes.
Lime-Tree, The. Lucie-Smith.
Mad Scene, the. Merrill.
Night a Sailor Came to Me in a Dream, The. Wakoski.
On Dreams. Swift.
On His Deceased Wife. Milton.
Rain. Murray.
Salome. Garrett.
Sleep-Learning. Fainlight.

**Dress.** *See* **Clothing.**

**Driftwood**
Driftwood. Smythe.

**Drinking**
At the Tavern. *Unknown.*
Back and Side Go Bare. *Unknown.*
Ballade of Liquid Refreshment. Bentley.
Drinking. Cowley.
Drinking Song. *Unknown.*
Drinking Song, A. Yeats.
Drinking While Driving. Brush.
Fill the Bowl, Butler. *Unknown.*
I drink to forget, but whenever I think. Bold.
Ignacio, Colorado, for You That Time. Harjo.
In the 2 A.M. Club, a working man's bar. Peterson.
Interview with Doctor Drink. Cunningham.
Last Drink, A. *Unknown.*
Little Brown Jug, The. Winner.
Midget, The. Levine.
Moonshine. *Unknown.*
Morning After. Hughes.
Revenue Man Blues. *Unknown.*
Rubáyát of Omar Khayyám of Naishápúr, The. Omar Khayyám.
Song: "Let school-masters puzzle their brain."*Fr.* She Stoops to Conquer. Goldsmith.
Stony Brook Tavern. Reed.
To Laura Phelan: 1880-1906. Stokesbury.
Wassail Song. *Unknown.*
We Be Soldiers Three. *Unknown.*
Yellow Bittern, The. Gunna.
*See also* **Drunkards.**

**Drought**
I Am Crying from Thirst. Lopez.

**Drowning**
Dead Man Dragged from the Sea, The. Gardner.
Dying off Egg Island Bar. Smith.
Floating Bridge. *Unknown.*
Jimmy Judge. *Unknown.*
On a Friend's Escape from Drowning off the Norfolk Coast. Barker.
Samuel Allen. *Unknown.*
Sir Patrick Spens. *Unknown.*
To Some Millions Who Survive Joseph E. Mander, Sr. Wright.

**Drug Addiction**
Addict, The. Sexton.
Answer to Yo/ Question of Am I Not Yo/ Woman. Sanchez.
Blues for Sister Sally. Kandel.
Cocaine Lil and Morphine Sue. *Unknown.*
Documetary on Airplane Glue, A. Henderson.
Idea of Ancestry, The. Knight.
Junior Addict. Hughes.

Street Song. Gunn.
Summer Words of a Sistuh Addict. Sanchez.
Take a Whiff on Me. *Unknown.*
Willy the Weeper. *Unknown.*

**Drugstores**
Drug Store. Shapiro.

**Drunkards**
A he as o. Cummings.
Bowery. Ignatow.
Canned Heat Blues. *Unknown.*
Cliff, The. Rowbotham.
Dead Drunk Blues. *Unknown.*
Drunk in the Furnace, The. Merwin.
Drunkard, A. *Unknown.*
Eclipse. Probst.
Epitaph: "Stavro's dead. A truant vine." Durrell.
Helves Surling Out of Eakspeasies Per (Reel) Hapsingly. Cummings.
John Adkins' Farewell. *Unknown.*
Little Brown Jug, The. Winner.
Love ("There's the wonderful love of a beautiful maid"). *Unknown.*
Lying in a Yuma Saloon. Barnes.
My Papa's Waltz. Roethke.
Old Witherington. Randall.
Point of No Return. Graves.
Red Whiskey. *Unknown.*
Rolling English Road, The. Chesterton.
Whisky Johnny. *Unknown.*
Wino. Hughes.
Zimmer Drunk and Alone, Dreaming of Old Football Games. Zimmer.

**Dryden, John**
How long shall I endure without reply.*Fr.* .The Medal of John Bays: A Satire against Folly and Knavery. Shadwell.
Shadwell and Settle are both fools to Bays.*Fr.* The Tory Poets: A Satire. *At. to* Shadwell.

**Dublin, Ireland**
Dublin. MacNeice.
Dublin Made Me. MacDonagh.

**Du Bois, William Edward Burghardt**
Booker T. and W. E. B. Randall.
For William Edward Burghardt Du Bois on His Eightieth Birthday. Latimer.
On the Death of William Edward Burghardt Du Bois by African Moonlight and Forgotten Shores. Rivers.

**Duchamp, Marcel**
Nude Descending a Staricase. Kennedy.

**Ducks**
Duck. Donaghy.
Duck, The. Nash.
Duck and the Kangaroo, The. Lear.
Duck-Chasing. Kinnell.
Ducks. Hesketh.
Ducks' Ditty. Grahame.
Notorious Glutton, The. Taylor.
Three Moves. Logan.
Trueblue Gentleman, A. Patchen.

**Duddon River, England**
River Duddon, The, *sels.* Wordsworth.

**Dundee, John Graham of Claverhouse, 1st Viscount (Bonnie Dundee)**
Bonnie Dundee.*Fr.* The Doom of Devergoil. Scott.

**Dunes**
Sand Dunes. Frost.

**Dunwich, England**
At Dunwich. Thwaite.

**Dürer, Albrecht**
Nuremberg. Slessor.

**Dusk.** *See* **Twilight.**

**Duty**
Duty. Clough.

Ode to Duty. Wordsworth.
Stopping by Woods on a Snowy Evening. Frost.

# E

**Eagles**
Dalliance of Eagles, The. Whitman.
Eagle, The. Tennyson.
Eagle and the Mole, The. Wylie.
Folding Fan, The. Cohoe.
**Ear Piercing**
Piercing, The. Lowther.
**Earth**
Aspects of the World Like Coral Reefs. Bronk.
Bonnie Broukit Bairn, The. "MacDiarmid."
Earth. Herford.
God's World. Millay.
Hamatreya. Emerson.
O Sweet Spontaneous Earth. Cummings.
Views of Our Sphere. Sandeen.
World, The. Raine.
World, The. Rands.
**Earthquakes**
Crack in the Wall Holds Flowers. Emanuel.
Santa Barbara Earthquake, The. *Unknown.*
**Easter**
Easter. Herbert.
Easter.*Fr.* Amoretti. Spenser.
Easter Communion. Hopkins.
Easter Day. Crashaw.
Easter Hymn. Housman.
Easter Sunday. Sedulius Scottus.
Easter Wings. Herbert.
Lord Is Risen, The. Dunbar.
**Eatherly, Claude R.**
Song about Major Eatherly, A. Wain.
**Echoes**
Echo. Asheron.
Echo. De la Mare.
Echo to a Rock. Herbert.
Gentle Echo on Woman, A. Swift.
What Makes Echo. Duchess of Newcastle.
**Eclipses**
Baltimore Eclipse. Plymell.
**Ecology**
Ain't It a Sad Thing. Taylor.
Air. Rado *and* Ragni.
Al Capone in Alaska. Reed.
Bedtime Story. Macbeth.
Binsey Poplars. Hopkins.
Don't Look Now. Fogerty.
Ecologue. Ginsberg.
Hamatreya. Emerson.
Hard Questions. Tsuda.
Hymn to Moloch. Hodgson.
Inexpensive Progress. Betjeman.
Malediction. Spacks.
Martyred Earth, The. Milne.
Memo to the 21st Century. Appleman.
Moorhen Pond, The. Earley.
Moss-Gathering. Roethke.
Mower against Gardens, The. Marvell.
Poem for the Year Twenty Twenty. Lee.
Pollution. Lehrer.
Poplar-Field, The. Cowper.
Pylons, The. Spender.
Rabbit, The. Brownjohn.
Requiem for a River. Williams.

Rip Tide. Piercy.
Smokey the Bear Sutra. *Unknown.*
Song of Cove Creek Dam, The. *Unknown.*
Statement on Our Higher Education. Ransom.
To a Young Wretch. Frost.
Transcontinent. Hall.
Vantage. Ghiselin.
Why the Soup Tastes Like the Daily News. Piercy.
Wilderness. Mecklenburger.
Working against Time. Wagoner.
**Eden, William**
Rondeau: "Of Eden lost, in ancient days." Ellis.
**Eden**
Garden, The. Very.
**Editors**
Editor Whedon.*Fr.* Spoon River Anthology. Masters.
**Education**
Homework for Annabelle. McGinley.
Lines to a Don. Belloc.
Pains of Education, The. Churchill.
Student, The. Moore.
To David, about His Education. Nemerov.
University Examinations in Egypt. Enright.
*See also* **Teaching and Teachers; Scholars and Scholarship.**
**Edward I, King of England**
Bard, The. Gray.
Scots in Berwick, The. *Unknown.*
**Edward II, King of England**
Four Wise Men on Edward II's Reign. *Unknown.*
**Edward III, King of England**
On the Death of Edward III. *Unknown.*
**Edward IV, King of England**
King Edward the Fourth and a Tanner of Tamworth.
*Unknown.*
**Edwards, Jonathan**
After the Surprising Conversions. Lowell.
Mr. Edwards and the Spider. Lowell.
**Eggs**
At Breadfast. Swenson.
Egg, The. Bowering.
Egg Boiler, The. Brooks.
In marble halls as white as milk. *Unknown.*
Long white barn, A. *Unknown.*
**Egotism**
Ego. Siegel.
Egotist, The. Evans.
Immoral Proposition, The. Creeley.
Talker, The. Van Duyn.
**Egrets**
Egrets. Wright.
**Egypt**
I Am a Cowboy in the Boat of Ra. Reed.
Ozymandias. Shelley.
This Is the Life. MacNeice.
**Eichmann, Adol**
Peachtree, The. Levertov.
**Einstein, Albert**
$E = mc^2$. D. Rowbotham.
Gift to Be Simple, The. Moss.
Relative Sadness. C. Rowbotham.
**Eisenhower, Dwight D.**
Eisenhower's Visit to Franco, 1959. Wright.
**El Dorado**
Eldorado. Poe.
**Electricity**
High Tension Wires. Block.
Ohms. Layton.
Pylons, The. Spender.
**Elephants**
Elephant, The.*Fr.* The Progresse of the Soule. Donne.
Elephant, The. Hochman.
Elephant Is Slow to Mate, The. Lawrence.

Elephants in the Circus. Lawrence.
Eletelephony. Richards.
Pete at the Zoo. Brooks.
Retirement of the Elephant, The. Edson.
Tit for Tat: A Tale. Aikin.

**Elgin Marbles**
On Seeing the Elgin Marbles. Keats.

**Eliot, Thomas Stearns**
Lines for Cuscuscaraway and Mirza Murad Ali Beg. Eliot.
T. S. Eliot. Lowell.

**Elizabeth I, Queen of England**
In Honour of That High and Mighty Princess Queen Elizabeth
    of Happy Memory. Bradstreet.
Of Astraea.*Fr.* Hymns of Astraea. Davies.

**Elm Trees**
Elegy: "Here where the elm trees were." Carrier.
Elm Buds. Sandburg.

**Embryos**
Embryos. Piercy.

**Emerson, Ralph Waldo**
Emerson.*Fr.* A Fable for Critics. Lowell.
In the Garden. Schmidt.

**Emus**
Emus. Fullerton.

**Endymion**
Oh, sleep forever in the Latmian cave. Millay.

**England**
Composed by the Sea-Side, near Calais, August, 1802.
    Wordsworth.
Compsed in the Valley near Dover, on the Day of Landing.
    Wordsworth.
England.*Fr.* King Richard II. Shakespeare.
England in 1819. Shelley.
English Counties. *Unknown.*
English Succession, The. *Unknown.*
Happy is England! I could be content. Keats.
Home-Thoughts, from Abroad. Browning.
Homes of England, The. Hemans.
It is not to be thought of that the flood. Wordsworth.
Italy versus England.*Fr.* Beppo. Byron.
Lines Written in the Album at Elbingerode. Coleridge.
Properties of the Shires of England, The. *Unknown.*
Recessional. Kipling.
Rhyming Prophecy for a New Year. Cooper.
Rolling English Road, The. Chesterton.
Soldier, The. Brooke.
Summer in England, 1914. Meynell.
This Landscape, These People. Ghose.
When I have borne in memory what has tamed. Wordsworth.

**English, The**
English, The. *Unknown.*
Old England Forever and Do It No More. *Unknown.*
Secret People, The. Chesterton.

**Epictetus**
To a Friend. Arnold.

**Epstein, Sir Jacob**
Jacob Epstein. *Unknown.*

**Erie Canal**
Erie Canal, The. *Unknown.*

**Erotic Love**
After Love. Kumin.
Anybody Could Write This Poem. All You Have to Say Is Yes.
    Alta.
Before the Fall. Daniell.
Candy Man Blues. *Unknown.*
December 18th.*Fr.* Eighteen Days Without You. Sexton.
Desire. Coleridge.
Dirty Colours of Her Kiss Have Just, The. Cummings.
Drunk as drunk on turpentine. Neruda.
Firebird. Alta.
Fragment of Petronius Translated, A. Petronius Arbiter.
From pent-up, arching rivers. Whitman.

Geranium, The. Sheridan.
Goodbye, Sally. Simmons.
I gently touched her hand: she gave. *Unknown.*
I like my body when it is with your. Cummings.
Imperfect Enjoyment, The. Earl of Rochester.
Love and Sleep. Swinburne.
Love Poem on Theme by Walt Whitman. Ginsberg.
Man and Woman. Lee.
May I Feel Said He. Cummings.
Meditation in My Favorite Position.*Fr.* Walking into Love.
    Piercy.
Net, The. Rodgers.
New Year's Eve. Lawrence.
Nice. Lifshin.
Now Ain't That Love? Rodgers.
O It's Nice to Get Up in, the Slipshod Mucous Kiss.
    Cummings.
Oh! the time that is past. *Unknown.*
On the Happy Corydon and Phyllis. Sedley.
Our Bodies. Levertov.
Over the hill and over the dale. Keats.
Paradise Is Not a Place. Gioseffi.
Power of Love He Wants Shih, The. Owens.
Radiant Heat. Owens.
Rapping Along with Ronda Davis. Cunningham.
Seen through the Trees behind Which You're Walking. Patten.
Sex and the Over Forties. Porter.
Song: "O blush not so!" Keats.
Terraplane Blues. *Unknown.*
That Day. Sexton.
To His Mistress Going to Bed. Donne.
To the Fair Clarinda, Who Made Love to Me, Imagin'd More
    than Woman. Behn.
Tubes. Mollin.
Two Songs. Rich.
Us. Sexton.
Where be ye going, you Devon maid? Keats.
Woman Waits for Me, A. Whitman.

**Eschatology**
End of the World, The. MacLeish.
Eschatology. Hall.
Fire and Ice. Frost.

**Eskimos**
Hunger. *Unknown.*

**Essex, England**
Map of the Western Part of the County of Essex in England, A.
    Levertov.

**Eternity**
Eternity. Blake.

**Etiquette**
Boy Serving at the Table, The. Lydgate.
Eitquette. Gilbert.
How to Get on in Society. Betjeman.
Manners at Table When away from Home. *Unknown.*
Story of Fidgity Philip, The. Hoffman.
Table Rules for Little Folks. *Unknown.*

**Eton College**
Ode on a Distant Prospect of Eton College. Gray.

**Eucharist**
Bugler's First Communion, The. Hopkins.

**Europe**
Beyond the Alps. Lowell.

**Eurydice**
Dreams of Eurydice. Ryan.
Euridice. Alta.
Eurydice. Doolittle ("H.D.").

**Eutaw Springs, South Carolina**
Eutaw Springs. Freneau.

**Eve**
Banishment, The.*Fr.* Paradise Lost. Milton
Eve. Hodgson.
Eve. *Unknown.*

Eve to Her Daughters. Wright.
Eve's Lament. *Unknown.*
Garden, The. Silverman.
Letter to Eve. Dugan.
Never Again Would Birds' Song Be the Same. Frost.
Reveille. Hughes.
She. Wilbur.

**Evening**
Evening. Aldington.
Evening. Cotton.
Evening. Doolittle ("H. D.").
Evening. Miller.
Evening in Paradise.*Fr.* Paradise Lost. Milton.
Evening: Ponte a Mare, Pisa. Shelley.
Evening without Angels. Stevens.
Georgia Dusk. Toomer.
It Is a Beauteous Evening. Wordsworth.
Night. Teasdale.
Ode to Evening. Collins.
Six O'Clock. Stickney.
Surprised by Evening. Bly.
*See also* **Sunset; Twilight.**

**Evening Star**
To the Evening Star. Blake.

**Evers, Medgar**
Medgar Evers. Brooks.

**Evolution**
Evolution. Brock.
Evolution. Swenson.
Evolution from the Fish. Bly.
Wearing Breasts. Gioseffi.

**Executions**
Croppy Boy, The. *Unknown.*
Culprit, The. Housman.
Danny Deever. Kipling.
Droit de Seigneur. Murphy.
Electrocution. Ridge.
Elegy: "My prime of youth is but a frost of cares." Tichborne.
Epitaph: "They hanged him on a clement morning, swung." Scott.
Execution of Cornelius Vane, The. Read.
Execution of Montrose, The. Aytoun.
Mary Hamilton. *Unknown.*
More Light! More Light! Hecht.
Night Before Larry Was Stretched, The. *Unknown.*
No Speech from the Scaffold. Gunn.
Romans Angry about the Inner World. Bly.
*See also* **Hanging.**

**Exile**
Girl I Left Behind Me, The. *Unknown.*
Thoughts in Exile. Su Tung-Po.

**Explorers and Exploring**
Arabia. Falkner.
Into the Dark. Monette.
North Pole Story, A. Smedley.
O Pioneers! Bishop.
Terra Australis. Stewart.
To the Virginian Voyage. Drayton.
Voyage West. MacLeish.

**Eyes**
Astigmatic, The. Hobsbaum.
Dark Eyes. *Unknown.*
Eye, The. Benedikt.
For Sore Eyes. *Unknown.*

# F

**Fairies**
Fairies' Farewell, The. Corbet.

Fairies Never Have a Penny to Spend, The. Fyleman.
Fairy Went a-Marketing, A. Fyleman.
Hosting of the Sidhe, The. Yeats.
Little Orphant Annie. Riley.
Tam Lin. *Unknown.*
Thomas the Rhymer. *Unknown.*
Thomas Rymer. *Unknown.*
Wee Wee Man, The. *Unknown.*

**Fairs**
Fair at Windgap, The. Clarke.

**Faith**
Amazing Grace. Newton.
Ballad Which Anne Askew Made and Sang When She Was in Newgate, The. Askew.
Carrion Comfort. Hopkins.
Discipline. Herbert.
Doubts. Jennings.
Dover Beach. Arnold.
Faith, Hope and Charity. Guarini.
"Faith" is a fine invention. Dickinson.
Faith of Our Fathers. Faber.
Great God! I Ask Thee for No Meaner Pelf. Thoreau.
How brittle are the piers. Dickinson.
My Faith Looks Up to Thee. Palmer.
No Coward Soul Is Mine. E. Brontë.
Pagan Isms, The. McKay.
Sunday Morning. Stevens.
Thou Art Indeed Just, Lord, if I Contend. Hopkins.
Trust and Obey. Sammis.

**Falcons**
Sparrow-Hawk's Complaint, The. *Unknown.*
Windhover, The: To Christ Our Lord. Hopkins.

**Fall.** *See* **Autumn.**

**Fame**
Cool Tombs. Sandburg.
I'm nobody! Who are you? Dickinson.
On Fame ("Fame, like a wayward girl, will still be coy"). Keats.
On Fame ("How fever'd is the man, who cannot look"). Keats.
Resolve, The. Chudleigh.
Soup. Sandburg.
To an Athlete Dying Young. Housman.
Transparent Closet, The. M. Shelley.
Wish, A. Kemble.

**Family Life**
Because. McAuley.
Generations. Jones.
Life Style, The. Brock.
My Father in the Night Commanding No. Simpson.
Nikki-Rosa. Giovanni.
To My Sister. Kherdian.

**Famine**
Famine Year, The. Wilde.
Hunger. Binyon.

**Fans**
Eagle-Feather Fan, The. Momaday.
Fan for His Daughter, A. Mallarmé.
Folding Fan, The. Cohoe.

**Farming and Farmers**
After Winter. Brown.
Black Man Talks of Reaping, A. Bontemps.
Blown Door, The. Cowley.
Cooney Potter.*Fr.* Spoon River Anthology. Masters.
Drumdelgie. *Unknown.*
Enriching the Earth. Berry.
Ex M. Antonio Flaminio, Ad Agellum Suum. Ashmore.
Farm Picture. Whitman.
Farmer, The. Stokes.
Farmer's Life, A. *Unknown.*
Field and Forest. Jarrell.
Floodtide. Touré.
Follower. Heaney.

For the Record.  Thomas.
Hill Farmer Speaks, The.  Thomas.
Hoeing.  Updike.
I Will Go with My Father a-Ploughing.  Campbell.
Illinois Farmer.  Sandburg.
Improved Farm Land.  Sandburg.
Memory of Kuhre.  McNair.
Mowing.  Frost.
New Farm Tractor.  Sandburg.
Old Field Mowed for Appearances' Sake, An.  Meredith.
On the Debt My Mother Owed to Sears Roebuck.  Dorn.
Ploughman, The.  *Unknown.*
Pretty Ploughboy, The.  *Unknown.*
Prodigal, The.  Bishop.
Reapers.  Blind.
Reapers.  Toomer.
Said Hanrahan.  Hartigan.
Satisfactions of the Mad Farmer, The.  Berry.
Sower, The.  Blind.
Spraying the Potatoes.  Kavanagh.
Thank You Poem for the Andersons, A.  Hey.
Through Old Farmhouse Windows.  Block.
Vermont Conversation.  Hubbell.
Warren Pryor.  Nowlan.
*See also*  **Fields and Pastures.**

**Fate**
Day's Ration, The.  Emerson.
Eros Turannos.  Robinson.
Flux.  Eberhart.
Hap.  Hardy.
Karma.  Robinson.
New Year's Eve.  Hardy.
Subalterns, The.  Hardy.
*See also*  **Fortune.**

**Fathers**
All My Pretty Ones.  Sexton.
Au Tombeau de Mon Père.  McCuaig.
Beryl.  Lifshin.
Boy.  Ciardi.
Boy Driving His Father to Confession.  Heaney.
Colossus, The.  PLath.
Commander Lowell.  Lowell.
Daddy.  Plath.
Efficiency Apartment.  Barrax.
Elegy for My Father.  Strand.
Europe and America.  Ignatow.
Everybody Works but Father.  McClintock.
Eyes of Flesh, The.  Hochman.
Father and Son.  Higgins.
Father and Son.  Kunitz.
Father Is Home.  *Unknown.*
Father of My Country, The.  Wakoski.
Father Son and Holy Ghost.  Lorde.
Feliks Skrzynecki.  Skrzynecki.
Follower.  Heaney.
Game, The.  Silverman.
Hallelujah: A Sestina.  Francis.
House You Looked For, The.  Root.
I Put My Hand on His Head.  Kooser.
Irish Cliffs of Moher, The.  Stevens.
Leaves.  Hamod.
Letter to a Young Father in Exile.  Logan.
Lines to His Son on Reaching Adolescence.  Logan.
Lines to My Father.  Hamod.
My Faither.  Glen.
My Father.  Collins.
My Father.  Kherdian.
My Father Dreams of Baseball.  Lieberman.
My Father Moved through Dooms of Love.  Cummings.
My Father Toured the South.  Nichols.
My Papa's Waltz.  Roethke.
On My First Son.  Jonson.

Paean to Place.  Niedecker.
Pawnbroker, The.  Kumin.
Phoning My Son Long Distance.  Kooser.
Portrait, The.  Kunitz.
Portrait of the Father.  Hough.
Reformer to His Father, A.  Simmons.
Requiem of a War-Baby.  Watton.
Terminal Days at Beverly Farms.  Lowell.
Those Winter Sundays.  Hayden.
Toys, The.  Patmore.
Word to a Father, Dead, A.  Allen.

**Faust**
Doctor Faustus, *sel.*  Marlowe.

**Fawn.**  *See* **Deer.**

**Fear**
Animal, The.  Block.
Fear, The.  Reynolds.
Garden, The.  Glück.
Ode to Fear.  Collins.
Ode to Fear.  Tate.
With the sun fear leaves me.  Parker.

**February**
February.*Fr.* The Shepherd's Calendar.  Clare.
When.  Aldis.

**Fences**
Fence Wire.  Dickey.
Wires.  Larkin.

**Ferlinghetti, Lawrence**
Clickety-Clack.  Blackburn.

**Ferns**
Japanese Fold-Song from Hyogo.  *Unknown.*

**Ferry Boats**
Crossing Brooklyn Ferry.  Whitman.

**Feuds**
Massacre of the MacPhersons, The.  Aytoun.
Rowan County Crew, The.  Day.

**Fidelity**
Lover Beseecheth His Mistress Not to Forget His Steadfast
   Faith and True Intent, The.  Wyatt.

**Fields and Pastures**
Low Fields and Light.  Merwin.
Pasture, The.  Frost.
To Meadows.  Herrick.
*See also*  **Farming and Farmers.**

**Figs**
Where the Slow Fig's Purple Sloth.  Warren.

**Films.**  *See* **Motion Pictures.**

**Finches**
Finches, The.  Shapcott.
On the Lamented Death of Mrs. Throckmorton's Bullfinch.
   Cowper.
Song: "Where I walk out."  Winters.

**Fire**
Aftermath.  Plath.
Armadillo, The.  Bishop.
Brooklyn Theater Fire, The.  *Unknown.*
Brother Fire.  MacNeice.
Burning the Christmas Greens.  Williams.
Burning the Small Dead.  Snyder.
Fire.  Barrows.
Fire and Ice.  Frost.
Fire at Alexandria, The.  Weiss.
Fire in Enfield.  McNair.
Fire of Drift-wood, The.  Longfellow.
Lumberyard, The.  Herschberger.
Milwaukee Fire, The.  *Unknown.*
Miramichi Fire, The.  *Unknown.*
Mister Charlie.  *Unknown.*
Some Verses upon the Burning of Our House July 10th, 1666.
   Bradstreet.
Street Fire.  Halpern.
Streets of Laredo, The.  MacNeice.

**Fire**
Summer Oracle. Lorde.
**Fire Engines**
Fire-Truck, A. Wilbur.
Great Figure, The. Williams.
**Fireflies**
Fireflies. Minton.
Firefly. Hajime.
Firefly. Roberts.
Flattered Lightning Bug, The. Marquis.
Glowworm. McCord.
Glow-Worm, The. Wordsworth.
Mower to the Glowworms, The. Marvell.
**Fireworks**
Fireworks. Deutsch.
Fourth of July Night. Sandburg.
**Fish**
Alas, Alack! De la Mare.
Although it's cold no clothes I wear. *Unknown.*
Aquarium, San Francisco, The. Sackville-West.
Beginning of an Undergraduate Poem. *Unknown.*
Birds and Fishes. Jeffers.
Egyptian Pulled Glass Bottle in the Shape of a Fish, An.
  Moore.
Fish, The. Bishop.
Fish, The. Moore.
Fish. Williams.
Fish Story. Armour.
Fishes, The. *Unknown.*
Fishy Square Dance, A. Merriam.
Grunion. Livingston.
Heaven. Brooke.
Little Fish. Lawrence.
Mrs. Busk. Sitwell.
Movement of Fish, The. Dickey.
Pike. Hughes.
Robbers came to our house, The. *Unknown.*
**Fishing and Fishermen**
Blackfriars. Farjeon.
Careful Angler, The. Stevenson.
Caulker, The. Lewis.
Don's Holiday. Hamilton.
Dragging in Winter. McElroy.
Drunken Fisherman, The. Lowell.
Fish, The. Bishop.
Fish. Williams.
Fisherman. Booth.
Fisherman. Root.
Fisherman, The. Stuart.
Fisherman, The. Yeats.
Fisher's Life, The. *Unknown.*
Fishing Blues. *Unknown.*
Fishing Harbour towards Evening. Kell.
Friend with Spinning Rod. St. Cyr.
Going Fishing. Griffiths.
How to Catch Tiddlers. Jones.
Marlin. Ghiselin.
Master and Man. Newbolt.
Northern Pike. Wright.
Old Man Let's Go Fishing in the Yellow Reeds of the Bay.
  Berssenbrugge.
Out Fishing. Howes.
Out from Lobster Cove. Reed.
Paean to Place. Niedecker.
Poke-Pole Fishing. Schmitz.
Purse-Seine, The. Jeffers.
Trip to the Grand Banks, A. Hanson.
Trout, The. Montague.
Uncle Roderick. MacCaig.
**Fitzgerald, Ella**
Early Ella. Sukenick.
**Fitzgeralds, The**
Geraldines, The. Davis.

**Flags**
Foreboding. Rilke.
**Flags, Confederacy**
Bonnie Blue Flag, The. Macarthy.
**Flags, Great Britain**
English Flag, The. Kipling.
**Flags, United States**
American Flag, The. Drake.
Flag Goes By, The. Bennett.
Leaving the Flag Out All Night. St. Cyr.
Lowering, The. Swenson.
Star-spangled Banner, The. Key.
You're a Grand Old Flag. Cohan.
**Flamingos**
Boy in the Roman Zoo. MacLeish.
**Fleas**
Cannibal Flea, The. Hood.
Flea, The. Donne.
Fleas, The. De Morgan.
**Flies**
Blue-Fly, The. Graves.
Blue-tailed Fly, The. *Unknown.*
Fly, The.*Fr.* Songs of Experience. Blake.
Fly, The. Oldys.
Fly, The. Shapiro.
Lake Flies of Winnebago, The. Flaherty.
Spider and the Fly, The. Howitt.
**Flirtation**
Song in the Same Play by the Wavering Nymph. Behn.
Teasing; or, I Was Only, Only Teasing You. Mack.
**Flodden Field, England**
Flowers of the Forest, The: or, Battle of Floden, The. Elliot.
**Floods**
Back Water Blues. *Unknown.*
Cabin Creek Flood, The. *Unknown.*
High Water Everywhere ("The back water done rose around
  Sumner, now"). *Unknown.*
Rising High Water Blues. *Unknown.*
River, A. Ramanujan.
River Swelleth More and More, The. Thoreau.
**Florence, Italy**
E, the Feasting Florentines. Hoffman.
Elements of Geometry, The. Malouf.
**Florida**
Morning in Gainesville. Whitehill.
**Florists**
Old Florist. Roethke.
**Flowers**
Blossom, The.*Fr.* Songs of Innocence. Blake.
Buttercups and Daisies. Howitt.
Buying Lilies. Stepanchev.
Cuttings ("Sticks-in-a-drowse over sugary loam"). Roethke.
Cuttings ("This urge, wrestle, resurrection of dry sticks").
  Roethke.
Cuttings (Later). Roethke.
Flower. Schjeldahl.
Flower Dump. Roethke.
Flower in the Crannied Wall. Tennyson.
Garden Blooms. Flocos.
Gift of Trilliums, A. McPherson.
In Back of the Real. Ginsberg.
Lament of the Flowers, The. Very.
Leaves Compared with Flowers. Frost.
Morning Compliments. Dayre.
Pot of Flowers, The. Williams.
Rhodora, The. Emerson.
Spring Flowers.*Fr.* The Seasons. Thomson.
Thrice happy flowers.*Fr.* The Masque of Flowers. *Unknown.*
Troll's Nosegay, The. Graves.
Yellow Flower, The. Williams.
*See also* **names of flowers (e.g. Lilies).**
**Flutes**

Musical Instrument, A.   E. Browning.

**Flying Dutchman (ship)**
Flying Dutchman, The.   Robinson.

**Flying Saucers.**   *See* **UFO's.**

**Fog**
Breathing, The.   Levertov.
Fog.   Sandburg.
Fog-Horn.   Merwin.
Ground-Mist, The.   Levertov.
Haze.   Thoreau.
Plaint Against the Fog.   *Unknown.*

**Folk Songs.**   *See* **Ballads and Folk Songs.**

**Food**
Breaded Meat, Breaded Hands.   Harper.
Expect no strange or puzzling meat, no pie. *Fr.* A Bill of Fare.
    Cartwright.
Famous Hot Pepper Eating Contest, The.   Hamod.
Grace to Be Said at the Supermarket.   Nemerov.
Oberon's Feast.   Herrick.
Poem to My New Jacket.   Winant.
Rice.   Muske.
Shopping for Meat in Winter.   Williams.
Shredded Wheat.   Dudek.
Soup of Venus, The.   Tate.
Spectator Ab Extra.   Clough.
This Is Just to Say.   Williams.
When De Co'n Pone's Hot.   Dunbar.
When in Rome.   Evans.

**Football**
Autumn Begins in Martins Ferry, Ohio.   Wright.
Ballad of the Pigskin.   Fiske.
Bee, The.   Dickey.
Bubba Smith.   Nash.
Charge of the Grid Brigade.   Applegarth.
Dick Szymanski.   Nash.
Fall Practice.   Stuart.
First Practice.   Gildner.
Football.   Fitzgerald.
Football.   Mason.
In the beginning was the.   Morrison.
In the Pocket.   Dickey.
To the Men Who Hold the Line.   Barron.
Tom Matte.   Nash.

**Ford, Ford Madox**
To Ford Madox Ford in Heaven.   Williams.

**Forest Rangers**
Jolly Forester, The.   *Unknown.*

**Forests**
Black Forest.   Watson.
Breathing, The.   Levertov.
Darkness Comes to the Woods.   Krapf.
Forest.   Garrigue.
Forest, The.   Wright.
Hollow Wood, The.   Thomas.
Inscription for the Entrance to a Wood.   Bryant.
Path, The.   Thomas.
Sitting in the Woods: A Contemplation.   Moses.
Solitude Late at Night in the Woods.   Bly.
Waldeinsamkeit.   Emerson.
Way through the Woods, The.   Kipling.
Woodnotes I ("When the pine tosses its cones").   Emerson.
Woodnotes II ("As sunbeams stream through liberal space").
    Emerson.

**Forgiveness**
Forgive?   Montoya.
'Tis true—they shut me in the cold.   Dickinson.

**Fortune**
Good Luck.   Herrick.
Hap.   Hardy.
Hughie at the Inn.   Wylie.
Lady Fortune, The.   *Unknown.*
My Stars.   Ibn Ezra.

To Fortune on Buying a Ticket in the Irish Lottery.   Coleridge.
*See also* **Fate; Luck.**

**Fountains**
Baroque Wall-Fountain in the Villa Sciarra.   Wilbur.
Fountain, The.   Davie.
Fountains, The.   Rodgers.
From Rome. For More Public Fountains in New York City.
    Dugan.
Inscription for a Fountain on a Heath.   Coleridge.
Roman Fountain.   Bogan.

**Fourth of July**
Concord Hymn.   Emerson.
Independence Day.   Berry.

**Fox, Charles James**
On the Death of Mr. Fox.   Byron.

**Foxes**
Abnegation.   Rich.
Ballad of Red Fox, The.   La Follette.
Emblem of Two Foxes, An.   Spacks.
False Fox, The.   *Unknown.*
Four Little Foxes.   Sarett.
Fox, The.   Clare.
Fox, The.   Day Lewis.
Fox, The.   Patchen.
Fox, The.   *Unknown.*
Fox and the Geese, The.   *Unknown.*
Fox and the Goose, The.   *Unknown.*
Fox and the Wolf, The.   *Unknown.*
Hunt, The.   De la Mare.
Hunting Song.   Finkel.
Kilruddery Hunt, The.   Mozeen.
Listening to Foxhounds.   Dickey
Plea for a Captive.   Merwin.
Thought-Fox, The.   Hughes.
Trap, The.   Beyer.
Vixen, The.   Clare.

**France**
Four Sheets to the Wind and a One-Way Ticket to France.
    Rivers.
France: An Ode.   Coleridge.
September, 1802, Near Dover.   Wordsworth.

**Francis of Assisi, Saint**
Mental Hospital Garden, The.   Williams.
Tears of Saint Francis.   Duncan.

**Franco, Francisco**
Eisenhower's Visit to Franco, 1959.   Wright.

**Frankenstein**
Bride of Frankenstein, The.   Field.

**Franklin, Aretha**
Poem for Aretha.   Giovanni.

**Frederick Louis, Prince of Wales**
On Prince Frederick.   *Unknown.*

**Free Will**
Free Will.   Clark.

**Freedom**
Ante-Bellum Sermon, An.   Dunbar.
Brave New World.   MacLeish.
Frederick Douglass.   Hayden.
Freedom.   Hughes.
Freedom.   Lowell.
Freedom.   Stafford.
If We Must Die.   McKay.
In Exile.   Lazarus.
Liberty.   Shelley
Liberty Tree.   Paine.
Ode to Liberty.   Shelley.
Of the Child with the Bird on the Bush.   Bunyan.
So the Seeds Are Growing.   South.
They shut me up in prose.   Dickinson.
To the Republicans of North America.   Shelley.
Wires.   Larkin.
Words Like Freedom.   Hughes.

**French, The**
To Henrietta, on Her Departure for Calais. Hood
**French Revolution**
Character, A. Coleridge.
Destruction of the Bastille. Coleridge.
French Revolution, The, *sel.* Blake.
Let the brothels of Paris be opened. Blake.
Poetical and Philosophical Essay on the French Revolution, A. Courtenay.
**Freud, Sigmund**
Psychology. Glen.
Song for Sigmund Freud, A. Cherry.
**Friars**
Against the Friars. *Unknown.*
Friar's Retort, The. *Unknown.*
Wanton Merry Friar, A.*Fr.* The Canterbury Tales. Chaucer.
**Friends, Society of**
At a Friends' Meeting. M. Coleridge.
First-Day Thoughts. Whittier.
Quaker Widow, The. Taylor.
**Friendship**
Auld Lang Syne. Burns.
But. Cummings.
Comrades. McGlennon.
Female Friend, The. Whur.
Fire of Drift Wood, The. Longfellow.
Friend, The. Piercy.
Friend, A. Power.
Friends. Durem.
Friends. Jennings.
Friendship's Mystery, to My Dearest Lucasia. Philips.
Grasshopper, The: To My Noble Friend, Mr. Charles Cotton. Lovelace.
Interlude. Smith.
I've Gone and Stained with the Color of Love. Acorn.
La Belle Confidante. Stanley.
My Gal Sal. Dresser.
O! Wherefore. Peter.
Old Familiar Faces, The. Lamb.
Time to Talk, A. Frost.
To Edward Williams. Shelley.
To My Excellent Lucasia and Our Friendship. Philips.
To Phylocles, Inviting Him to Friendship. "Ephelia."
When to the sessions of sweet silent thought.*Fr.* Sonnets. Shakespeare.
**Frietchie, Barbara**
Barbara Frietchie. Whittier.
**Frogs**
Bullfrog. Hughes.
Cheers, Merriam.
Death of a Naturalist. Heaney.
Frog, The. Belloc.
Frog, The. *Unknown.*
Frog and the Crow, The. *Unknown.*
Frog and the Toad, The. C. Rossetti.
Frog Plague, The. Dawe.
Frog Went a-Courting. *Unknown.*
Frogs. MacCaig.
Frogs. Simpson.
Frog's Fate, A. C. Rossetti.
Kato's Poem. Kherdian.
Padda Song, The. *Unknown.*
Peepers in our Meadow, The. MacLeish.
Princess Addresses the Frog Prince, The. Brewster.
**Frost, Robert**
For Robert Frost. Kinnell.
Mending Sump. Koch.
Of Robert Frost. Brooks.
Robert Frost. Lowell.
**Fruit**
Fruit and Vegetables. Jong.
Fruits. C. Rossetti.

This Is Just to Say. Williams.
Three from the Market. McPherson.
**Funerals**
Agony Column. Hope.
Burial in the Country, A. Clause.
Come Not, When I Am Dead. Tennyson.
Dirge without Music. Millay.
Do Nothing Till You Hear from Me. Henderson.
Elegy for a Polish Grandaunt. Bonk.
First Death. Justice.
Funeral, The. Donne.
Italian Extravaganza. Corso.
Lowering, The. Swenson.
My Grandfather's Funeral. Applewhite.
Night Funeral in Harlem. Hughes.
Question, A. Synge.
Returning from the Funeral. Henley.
Shetland Funeral. Rankin.
Tract. Williams.
**Furniture**
Heirloom. Flanigan.

## G

**Gadflies**
Gadfly, The. Keats.
**Gambling and Gamblers**
Camptown Races, De. Foster.
Casino. Auden.
Crapshooters. Sandburg.
Gambler, The. *Unknown.*
Heathen Chinee, The. Harte.
Man Who Broke the Bank at Monte Carlo, The. Gilbert.
Midweek. Miles.
On a Distant Prospect of an Absconding Bookmaker. Hamilton
Root Hog or Die. *Unknown.*
To Fortune on Buying a Ticket in the Irish Lottery. Coleridge.
**Gandhi, Mohandas Karamchand**
Vaticide. O'Higgins.
**Gangs**
Black Jackets. Gunn.
Blackstone Rangers, The. Brooks.
**Gangsters**
Last Gangster, The. Corso.
**Gannets**
Blue Booby, The. Tate.
**García Lorca, Federico**
Lines to Garcia Lorca. Jones.
**Garda, Lake, Italy**
"Frater Ave Atque Vale." Tennyson.
**Gardens**
Forsaken Garden, A. Swinburne.
Garden, The. Marvell.
Garden, The. Very.
Garden by Moonlight, The. A. Lowell.
Garden Lore. Ewing.
Garden of Appleton House, The.*Fr.* Upon Appleton House. Marvell.
Glasgow Botanic Gardens. Rankin.
My Garden. Brown.
My Garden. Lindon.
Old Florist. Roethke.
Transplanting. Roethke.
Weed Puller. Roethke.
**Garfield, James Abram**
Charles Guiteau. *Unknown.*
**Gasoline Stations**

At Every Gas Station There Are Mechanics.  Dunn.
Hottest Brand Goin'.  *Unknown.*

**Gauguin, Paul**
Gauguin's Menhir, Tahiti.  Hope.

**Gawain, Sir**
Sir Gawaine and the Green Knight.  Winters.

**Gazelles**
Gazelle Calf, The.  Lawrence.

**Geese**
Boy and the Geese, The.  Fiacc.
Fox and the Goose, The.  *Unknown.*
Goose.  Braun.
Late at Night.  Stafford.
Wild Geese.  Hart-Smith.
Wild Geese, The.  Masefield.

**Gentians**
Bavarian Gentians.  Lawrence.
To the Fringed Gentian.  Bryant.

**Geography**
Geography Lesson.  Ghose.

**Geology**
Lyell's Hypothesis Again.  Rexroth.

**George I, King of England**
Epigram: "King George, observing with judicious eyes."
  Trapp.

**George III, King of England**
George the Third.*Fr.* Clerihews.  Bentley.
George the Third's Soliloquy.  Freneau.
Monarch's Funeral, The.  Shelley.

**Georgia**
Georgia Dusk.  Toomer.

**Geraniums**
Geranium, The.  Roethke.

**Germany**
No Offence.  Enright.

**Ghost Towns**
Two Views of Two Ghost Towns.  Tomlinson.

**Ghosts**
All Souls' Night.  Cornford.
Apparition, The.  Donne.
Ghost, The.  De la Mare.
Highwayman's Ghost, The.  Garnett.
Lost Weekend Bar, The.  Harjo.
Low Barometer.  Bridges.
Mary's Ghost.  Hood.
Molly Means.  Walker.
My Aunt's Spectre.  Collins.
Old Wife and the Ghost, The.  Reeves.
Sweet William's Ghost.  *Unknown.*
Unfortunate Miss Bailey.  *Unknown.*
Wife of Usher's Well, The.  *Unknown.*

**Giacometti, Alberto**
Tall Figures of Giacometti, The.  Swenson.

**Gipsies.  See Gypsies.**

**Giraffes**
Conversation with a Giraffe at Dusk in the Zoo.  Livingstone.
Giraffe, The.  Fuller.
Giraffe.  Plumly.
Giraffes: The American Version.  Dunn.

**Girdles**
Woman with Girdle.  Sexton.

**Girls.  See Childhood and Children; Youth.**

**Gloucester, Massachusetts**
Gloucester Moors.  Moody.

**Glowworms.  See Fireflies.**

**Gluttony and Gluttons**
Glutton, The.  Oakman.
Greedy Jane.  *Unknown.*
Mouse and the Cake, The.  Cook.
Notorious Glutton, The.  Taylor.
On Gut.  Jonson.

**Gnats**

Gnat, The.  Beaumont.
Gnat-Psalm.  Hughes.

**Gnus**
Gnu, The.  Belloc.
Gnu, The.  Roethke.

**Goats**
All Goats.  Coatsworth.
April.  Winters.
Goat.  Johnson.
Goat, The.  Young.

**God**
Accepting.  Miller.
All the Way My Saviour Leads Me.  Crosby.
Bermudas.  Marvell.
Black Cliffs, Ballybunion, The.  Kennelly.
Canticle to the Waterbirds, A.  Everson.
Counsels of O'Riordan, The Rann Maker, The.  O'Bolger.
Creation, The.  Johnson.
Design.  Frost.
Divine Image, The.*Fr.* Songs of Innocence.  Blake.
Edom.  Watts.
Eternal Dice, The.  Vallejo.
Flower in the Crannied Wall.  Tennyson.
For Eleanor Boylan Talking with God.  Sexton.
Forgive, O Lord.  Frost.
Fury of Aerial Bombardment, The.  Eberhart.
Genesis.  Witt.
Give to Our God Immortal Praise.  Watts.
God.  Ruggles.
God Don't Never Change.  *Unknown.*
God is indeed a jealous God.  Dickinson.
God Poem.  Moss.
God, That Madest All Things.  *Unknown.*
God Walks Among the Dust.  Chambers.
God's Grandeur.  Hopkins.
Hand and Foot, The.  Very.
He Leadeth Me.  Gilmore.
He Puts Me to Rest.  Ignatow.
Here Follows Some Verses Upon the Burning of Our House.
  Bradstreet.
He's Got the Whole World in His Hands.  *Unknown.*
Higher Pantheism, The.  Tennyson.
Hymn of the City.  Bryant.
Hypnopompic Poem.  Cole.
I Am the Great Sun.  Causley.
I know that He exists.  Dickinson.
Indian upon God, The.  Yeats.
Law I Love Is Major Mover, The.  Duncan.
Less and Less Human, O Savage Spirit.  Stevens.
Mighty Fortress, A.  Luther.
My Garden.  Brown.
Noah's Ark.  Young.
Old Repair Man, The.  Johnson.
On a Squirrel Crossing the Road in Autumn, in New England.
  Eberhart.
Preacher, The: Ruminates behind the Sermon.  Brooks.
Search.  Ritchie.
Song: "My straying thoughts, reduced stay."  Collins.
South Coast, The.  Everson.
Star Quality.  Wallace-Crabbe.
Testimony.  Rodgers.
To a Waterfowl.  Bryant.
What Tomas Said in a Pub.  Stephens.
Written in Exile.  Raine.
Yet Do I Marvel.  Cullen.

**Gods and Goddesses**
For the Unknown Goddess.  Brewster.
God in Wrath, A. *Fr.* The Black Riders.  Crane.

**Goethe, Johann Wolfgang von**
Sorrows of Werther, The.  Thackeray.

**Gogarty, Oliver St. John**
Lay of Oliver Gogarty, The.  Dawson.

**Gold Mining and Miners**
Californian, The. *Unknown.*
Clementine. *Unknown.*
Dreary Black Hills, The. *Unknown.*
Joe Bowers. *Unknown.*
Lousy Miner. *Unknown.*
Miner's Lament, The. *Unknown.*
National Miner, The. *Unknown.*
Prospecting Dream. *Unknown.*
San Francisco Company, The. *Unknown.*
Seeing the Elephant. *Unknown.*
Sweet Jane. *Unknown.*
When I Went Off to Prospect. *Unknown.*
**Goldfinches**
Crimson lute that comest in the dawn. Asbaje.
Song: "Where I walk out." Winters.
**Goldfish**
Goldfish. Nemerov.
**Golf**
Any Golf Championship. Rice.
Seaside Golf. Betjeman.
**Goliath**
David and Goliath. Crouch.
Epitaph for Goliath. Slavitt.
**Gonne, Maud**
No Second Troy. Yeats.
Good Friday
Tenebrae. Clarke.
*See also* **Crucifixion, The.**
**Gore-Booth, Eva**
In Memory of Eva Gore-Booth and Con Markiewicz. Yeats.
**Gorillas**
Au Jardin des Plantes. Wain.
Gorilla Gorilla. Dawe.
**Government**
Ill Government. Herrick.
**Goya y Lucientes, Francisco José de**
In Goya's greatest scenes we seem to see.*Fr.* A Coney Island of the Mind. Ferlinghetti.
**Graffiti**
Sunny Prestatyn. Larkin.
**Granada, Spain**
Moorish King Who Lost Granada, The. *Unknown.*
**Grandfathers**
Dunbarton. Lowell.
Grandfather. Harper.
Grandfather. Leax.
Grandfather. Mahon.
Grandfather in the Old Men's Home. Merwin.
Grandpa. Rankin.
Grandparents. Lowell.
Two Clocks. Daniel.
"Write a letter to Grandpa," my mother said, but he smelled old.*Fr.* Recovery. Van Duyn.
**Grandmothers**
Black Sheba. Braxton.
First Generation, The. Mirikitani.
Foxfire. Willard.
Grammer's Shoes. Barnes.
Grandmother Sleeps. Bahe.
Grandmothers, The. Oliver.
Grandparents. Lowell.
Legacies. Giovanni.
My Grandmother. Jennings.
My Grandmother. Shapiro.
My Grandmother's Love Letters. Crane.
**Grantchester, England**
Old Vicarage, Grantchester, The. Brooke.
**Grapes**
Father and His Children, The. *Unknown.*
**Grasmere, England**
Grasmere Sonnets. Wright.

Recluse, The. Wordsworth.
**Grass**
Grass. Sandburg.
Grassroots. Sandburg.
Heavenly Grass. Williams.
Rustling of Grass, The. Noyes.
**Grasshoppers**
Grasshopper, The. Lovelace.
Grasshopper. McDonald.
On the Grasshopper and the Cricket. Keats.
Ondt and the Gracehoper, The. Joyce.
R-p-o-p-h-e-s-s-a-g-r. Cummings.
**Graves**
Arundel Tomb, An. Larkin.
At White River. Haines.
Burial. Walker.
Bury Me in a Free Land. Harper.
Cover me over, clover. Eberhart.
Dig My Grave. *Unknown.*
Father Son and Holy Ghost. Lorde.
Grave, The. Winters.
Lord Cozens Hardy. Betjeman.
On the Tombs in Westminster Abbey. Beaumont.
Sonnet Written in the Church-Yard at Middleton, in Sussex. Smith.
Stranger, The. De la Mare.
To——: "The cold earth slept below." Shelley.
To Laura Phelan: 1880-1906. Stokesbury.
Tribal Cemetery. Hale.
Way of Keeping, A. Willard.
Yugoslav Cemetery. Wright.
**Graveyards.** *See* **Cemeteries.**
**Gray, Thomas**
Sketch of His Own Character. Gray.
**Great Depression**
Arizona. *Unknown.*
Brother, Can You Spare a Dime? Harburg.
Depression: My Father Speaks to My Mother. Allen.
34 Blues. *Unknown.*
Working Man Blues. *Unknown.*
**Greece**
At Lindos. Sarton.
Isles of Greece, The.*Fr.* Don Juan. Byron.
**Greed**
Bird on Nellie's Hat, The. Lamb.
Covetousness. Idley.
Greedy Richard. Taylor
Greedy the People, The. Cummings.
Mother Pin a Rose on Me. *Unknown.*
On a Favourite Cat Drowned in a Tub of Goldfishes. Gray.
**Greenhouses**
Big Wind. Roethke.
Forcing House. Roethke.
**Gregory, Lady Augusta**
Municipal Gallery Revisited, The. Yeats.
**Grenville, Sir Richard**
*Revenge*, The. Tennyson.
**Greyhounds**
Greyhounds. Gray.
How a Good Greyhound Is Shaped. *Unknown.*
**Grief**
After great pain, a formal feeling comes. Dickinson.
Aunt Laura Moves toward the Open Grave of Her Father. De Roche.
Bereavement. E. Browning.
Bereft. Hardy.
Carousel, The. Oden.
Cross of Snow, The. Longfellow.
Despair. Levertov.
Dirge: "I make this dirge for you Miss Mary Binning I miss you." *Unknown.*

Do not lift him from the bracken.*Fr.* The Widow of Glencoe. Aytoun.
Elegy for Jane.  Roethke.
Elegy on the Death of Her Husband.  Howard.
Exequy, The.  King.
Glory of the Day Was in Her Face, The.  Johnson.
Grief.  E. Browning.
If Ever Hapless Woman Had a Cause.  Pembroke.
Lament for Art O'Leary.  O'Connell.
Lament of the Border Widow, The.  *Unknown.*
Lamentation, A: "Grief, have I denied thee?"  Levertov.
Lycidas.  Milton.
Mad Song.  Blake.
Mourning Women.  Blind.
My Buried Friends.  *Unknown.*
"My True Love Hath My Heart and I Have His."  M. Coleridge.
Nurse No Long Grief.  Gilmore.
Old Familiar Faces, The.  Lamb.
Poet Is Dead, The.  Everson.
Sonnet on the Death of Mr. Richard West.  Gray.
Spring and Fall: To a Young Child.  Hopkins.
Story about Chicken Soup, A.  Simpson.
Surprised by Joy—Impatient As the Wind.  Wordsworth.
To Margaret.  Hopkins.
Widow's Lament in Springtime, The.  Williams.
With Rue My Heart Is Laden.  Housman.
**Griffins**
Griffin.  Matthews.
**Grocers**
Song Against Grocers, The.  Chesterton.
**Grongar Hill, Wales**
Grongar Hill.  Dyer.
**Groundhogs**
Drumlin Woodchuck, A.  Frost.
Groundhog, The.  Eberhart.
Woodchuck Who Lives on Top of Mt. Ritter, The.  Simon.
**Grünewald, Mathias**
Green at Colmar.  Aldan.
**Guerrière (ship)**
*Constitution* and the *Guerrière*, The.  *Unknown.*
**Guevara, Ernesto ("Che")**
Guevara with Minutes to Go.  Corrington.
**Guilt**
Christina.  MacNeice.
First Frost.  Clarkson.
Song about Major Eatherly, A.  Wain.
**Guinea Pigs**
Guinea-Pig Song, A.  *Unknown.*
**Guitars**
Guitar.  García Lorca.
Guitarist Tunes Up, The.  Cornford.
**Gulls**
Gulls.  Howes.
Gulls.  Muir.
Maine Sea Gulls.  Hoban.
On the Beach.  Cornford.
Predictor of Famine, The.  Williams.
Seagull, The.  Howitt.
Sea-Gull, The.  Nash.
Sea-Gull, The.  *Unknown.*
Seagulls.  Francis.
Storm's End.  Speyer.
Tarred Gull.  Ritchie.
**Gunpowder Plot**
Now they are met: this armèd with a spade.*Fr.* The Locusts, or Appolyonists.  Fletcher.
**Guns**
Grandpa's .45.  Ransom.
Naming of Parts.*Fr.* Lessons of the War.  Reed.
**Gymnastics**
Watching Gymnasts.  Francis.

**Gypsies**
Gipsies.  Clare.
Gypsies.  Nowlan.
Gypsy.  Miles.
Gypsy, The.  Thomas.
Gypsy Davy, The.  *Unknown.*
Gypsy Laddie, The.  *Unknown.*
Meg Merrilies.  Keats.
Romanies in Town, The.  Beresford.
Scholar-Gypsy, The.  Arnold.

# H

**Hair**
Boy with His Hair Cut Short.  Rukeyser.
For Anne Gregory.  Yeats.
Hair.  Corso.
Hair Poem.  Knott.
On Getting a Natural.  Randall.
W. W. Jones.
**Hale, Nathan**
Nathan Hale.  Finch.
Nathan Hale.  *Unknown.*
**Halloween**
Halloween.  Livingston.
Hist whist.  Cummings.
Shivers.  Fisher.
Witch?  Reavin.
**Hamlet**
They All Want to Play Hamlet.  Sandburg.
**Handball**
Day and Night Handball.  Dunn.
Game Resumed.  Lattimore.
Handball Players.  Goodman.
**Hands**
Bestiary for the Fingers of My Right Hand.  Simic.
Hand.  Marcus.
Hands.  Fox.
Poem for My Hands.  Oles.
This Hand.  Wylie.
This Living Hand.  Keats.
Your Hands.  Grimké.
**Hanging**
Captain Hall.  *Unknown.*
Danny Deever.  Kipling.
Dream of Hanging, A.  Beer.
Eight O'Clock.  Housman.
Epitaph: "They hanged him on a clement morning, swung." Scott.
Hang Me, O Hang Me, and I'll Be Dead and Gone.  *Unknown.*
Hanging Johnny.  *Unknown.*
Hanging of Sam Archer, The.  *Unknown.*
Hangman at Home, The.  Sandburg.
Maid Freed from the Gallows, The.  *Unknown.*
Night before Larry Was Stretched, The.  *Unknown.*
River Song.  Kees.
Sam Hall.  *Unknown.*
Song of the Death of Mr. Thewlis, The.  *Unknown.*
To His Son.  Ralegh.
*See also* **Executions; Lynching.**
**Hanks, Nancy**
Nancy Hanks.  R. *and* S. V. Benét.
**Happiness**
Anatomy of Happiness, The.  Nash.
Art of Happiness, The.  Young.
Breathing, The.  Levertov.
Happiness.  Sandburg.
Happy Life, The.  Martial.

**Harbors**

Running.  Wilbur.

**Harbors and Ports**

Harbor Dawn, The. *Fr.* The Bridge.  Crane.

Winter Ship, A.  Plath.

**Harding, Warren Gamaliel**

Two Poems About President Harding.  Wright.

**Hardy, Thomas**

At Max Gate.  Sassoon.

At Thomas Hardy's Birthplace, 1953.  Wright.

Luncheon, A.  Beerbohm.

Thomas Hardy.  De la Mare.

**Hares**

Epitaph on a Hare.  Cowper.

Hare, The.  *Unknown.*

Hare in Winter.  Piercy.

White Hare, The.  Lyon.

*See also*  **Rabbits.**

**Harfleur, France, Battle of**

King Henry the Fifth before Harfleur. *Fr.* King Henry V. Shakespeare.

**Harlem, New York City**

Esthete in Harlem.  Hughes.

Good Morning.  Hughes.

Harlem.  Hughes.

Harlem Freeze Frame.  Bethune.

Harlem Gallery: From the Inside.  Neal.

Jitterbugging in the Streets.  Hernton.

Juke Box Love Song.  Hughes.

Keep on Pushing.  Henderson.

Night Funeral in Harlem.  Hughes.

Prime.  Hughes.

Sketches of Harlem.  Henderson.

Still Voice of Harlem, The.  Rivers.

Train Runs Late to Harlem, The.  Rivers.

Walk with de Mayor of Harlem.  Henderson.

**Harper's Ferry, West Virginia**

Narrative.  Atkins.

**Harps**

Harper, The.  *Unknown.*

**Harvest**

Evening in Harvest Time, An.  Turner.

Harvest Song.  Campbell.

Hock-Cart, or Harvest Home, The.  Herrick.

Hurrahing in Harvest.  Hopkins.

In the Huon Valley.  McAuley.

Reaper, The.  Allen.

Reapers.  Blind.

Reapers.  Toomer.

Solitary Reaper, The.  Wordsworth.

Threshing-Machine, The.  Meynell.

**Harvey, William**

On the Death of Mr. William Harvey.  Cowley.

**Hastings, Warren**

Fifth Day.  Fitzgerald.

**Hasty Pudding**

Hasty Pudding, The.  Barlow.

**Hate**

Consequence, The.  McDonald.

Enslaved.  McKay.

Hatred.  Bennett.

Immortal Hate. *Fr.* Paradise Lost.  Milton.

Poison Tree, A. *Fr.* Songs of Experience.  Blake.

**Hats**

Where Did You Get That Hat?  Sullivan.

**Hawaii**

Twenty-Third Flight.  Birney.

**Hawks**

Afternoon.  Sund.

Balances.  Stuart.

Buteo Regalis.  Momaday.

Fieldmouse crouches low, A.  Sund.

Hawk, The.  Bloom.

Hawk Is a Woman.  Flanner.

Hawk Roosting.  Hughes.

Hurt Hawks.  Jeffers.

Rock and Hawk,  Jeffers.

Shiva.  Jeffers.

**Hawthorne, Nathaniel**

Hawthorne. *Fr.* A Fable for Cirtics.  Lowell.

**Haydon, Benjamin Robert**

Addressed to Haydon ("Great spirits are now on earth sojourning").  Keats.

Addressed to Haydon ("Highmindedness, a jealousy for good").  Keats.

To B. R. Haydon with the Foregoing Sonnet on the Elgin Marbles.  Keats.

**Haze.**  *See* **Fog.**

**Heat**

Heat. *Fr.* The Garden.  Doolittle ("H. D.").

**Heaven**

Celestial City, The. *Fr.* Christ's Victory and Triumph.  Fletcher.

Evening in Paradise. *Fr.* Paradise Lost.  Milton.

Heaven.  Hughes.

Heaven is so far of the mind.  Dickinson.

Hierusalem, My Happy Home.  *Unknown.*

I never saw a moor.  Dickinson.

In the Sweet Bye-and-Bye.  Bennett.

There is a land of pure delight.  Watts.

To Ford Madox Ford in Heaven.  Williams.

White Island: Or the Place of the Blest, The.  Herrick.

**Hebrides**

Stormy Hebrides, The. *Fr.* An Ode on the Popular Superstitions.  Collins.

**Hector**

Ballad of Hector in Hades.  Muir.

**Hedgehogs**

Happy Hedgehog, The.  Rieu.

Hedgehog.  Muldoon.

To a Hedgehog.  Thompson.

**Helen of Troy**

Helen.  Doolittle ("H. D.").

Mythmaking.  Spivack.

To Helen.  Poe.

Ultimate Antientropy, The.  Weiss.

**Helicopters**

Helicopter, The.  Serraillier.

Street Scene.  Suffolk.

**Hell**

Ascent into Hell.  Hope.

Hell Gate.  Housman.

Slim in Hell.  Brown.

Strange Meeting.  Owen.

Supremacy.  Robinson.

Underworld.  Garrett.

**Hell's Angels**

Black Jackets.  Gunn.

**Henry VIII, King of England**

Henry VIII.  E. *and* H. Farjeon.

**Henry IV, King of France**

Ivry.  Macaulay.

**Hens**

Hen Dying.  Maclean.

Hen Flower, The.  Kinnell.

Hen Under Bay-Tree.  Pitter.

Hens.  Nowlan.

Hens, The.  Roberts.

Hens in Winter.  Coffin.

Hen's Nest.  Clare.

Janet Waking.  Ransom.

Near and Far.  Behn.

Song of the Battery Hen.  Brock.

**Heraclitus**

Variation on Heraclitus.  MacNeice.

**Hermits**

Hermit, The.  Hsü Pên.
Hermit's Song, A.  *Unknown.*
Marban, a Hermit Speaks.  *Unknown.*
**Hero and Leander**
On a Leander Gem.  Keats.
Written after swimming from Sestos to Abydos.  Byron.
**Herod the Great**
Innocent's Song.  Causley.
**Heroes and Heriones**
Babe Ruth.  Runyon.
Casey at the Bat.  Thayer.
Casey's Daughter at the Bat.  Graham.
Heroes.  Creeley.
Settling Some Old Football Scores.  Bishop.
Tom Matte.  Nash.
**Heroin.**  *See* **Drug Addiction.**
**Herons**
Great Blue Heron, The.  Kizer.
Heron, The.  Murray.
Heron.  Plumly.
Heron, The.  Roethke.
Night Herons.  Wright.
**Herrick, Robert**
Mr. Robert Herrick, His Farewell unto Poetry.  Herrick.
**Herring**
Herring Is King.  Graves.
**Heydrich, Reinhard**
Polemical Elegy for Reinhardt Heydrich.  Buchan.
**Hiawatha**
Hiawaths's Photographing.  "Carroll."
Modern Hiawatha, The.  Strong.
**Hicks, Edward**
Edward Hicks: The Peaceable Kingdom.  Stanford.
**Highwaymen**
Bold Jack Donahue.  *Unknown.*
Brennan on the Moor.  *Unknown.*
Dick Turpin and Black Bess.  *Unknown.*
Mulberry Mountain.  *Unknown.*
Wild Colloina boy, The.  *Unknown.*
**Hills and Mountains**
Alpine.  Thomas.
Fable: "The mountain and the squirrel."  Emerson.
Here in Katmandu.  Justice.
Hills, The.  Field.
Muckish Mountain (The Pig's Back).  Leslie.
Nocturne of the Self-Evident Presence.  MacGreevy.
Paps of Dana, The.  Stephens.
Pennines in April.  Hughes.
Pilgrimage Song.  *Unknown.*
Rocky Acres.  Graves.
Sleeping Giant, The.  Hall.
Snow on Saddle Mountain, The.  Miyazawa.
**Hinduism**
Mahabalipuram.  MacNeice.
**Hippopotamuses**
Habits of the Hippopotamus.  Guiterman.
Hippo, The.  Roethke.
Hippopotamus, The.  Eliot.
**Hiroshima**
There were many of us at that time.*Fr.* Hiroshima.  Bantock.
**History and Historians**
Concise History of the World, A.  Sadoff.
How many bards gild the lapses of time!  Keats.
Living Truth, The.  Plumpp.
Readings of History.  Rich.
Written in the Beginning of Mezeray's History of France.  Prior.
**Hobbes, Thomas**
Hobbes, 1651.  Hollander.
**Hogg, James**
Extempore Effusion upon the Death of James Hogg.  Wordsworth.

**Hohenlinden, Battle of**
Battle of Hohenlinden, The.  Campbell.
**Hokusai, Katsushika.**
Great Wave: Hokusai, The.  Finkel.
**Holiday, Billie (Eleanora Fagan McKay)**
Blues and Bitterness.  Bennett.
Day Lady Died, The.  O'Hara.
For Our Lady.  Sanchez.
**Holidays**
Adrian Henri's Talking After Christmas Blues.  Henri.
Conversation with Washington.  Livingston.
Rebolushinary X-mas.  Rodgers.
*O Frabjous Day*! (OFD).  Myra Cohn Livingston, ed.
*See also* **specific holidays.**
**Holly**
Holly and the Ivy, The.  *Unknown.*
Itum Paradisum all clothed in green.  *Unknown.*
**Hollywood, California**
Trying to Forget.  Wieners.
**Holmes, Oliver Wendell (1809-94)**
Holmes.*Fr.* A Fable for Critics.  Lowell.
**Holy Family**
Cherry-Tree Carol, The.  *Unknown.*
**Home**
Disturbances.  Thwaite.
Family Prime.  Van Doren.
Home ("Home's home, although it reached be").  Beaumont.
Home on the Range.  *Unknown.*
Home! Sweet Home!  Payne.
Homecoming.  Thompson.
I've Got a Home in That Rock.  Patterson.
Oh, Joyous House.  Janzen.
On the Wide Heath.  Millay.
One Home.  Stafford.
**Homer**
On First Looking into Chapman's Homer.  Keats.
To a Friend.  Arnold.
To Homer.  Keats.
**Homesickness**
Lament of the Banana Man.  Jones.
Tropics in New York, The.  McKay.
**Homesteaders**
Little Old Sod Shanty.  *Unknown.*
Starving to Death on a Government Claim.  *Unknown.*
**Homosexuality and Homosexuals**
Art of Enforced Deprivation, The.  Alta.
Christopher St. Liberation Day, June 28, 1970.  Winant.
Coming Out.  Lapidus.
For Freckle-faced Gerald.  Knight.
Homosexuality.  O'Hara.
Lesbian Poem.  Morgan.
Note to a New Lesbian.  M. Shelley.
Playboy of the Demi-World: 1938, The.  Plomer.
Poem to My New Jacket.  Winant.
Song: "Love a woman? You're an ass!"  Earl of Rochester.
**Honesty**
Truth the Best.  Turner.
**Honey**
Sing a Song of Honey.  Todd.
**Honey Eaters**
Nesting Time.  Stewart.
**Honeysuckle**
Wild Honey Suckle, The.  Freneau.
**Honor**
Honour ("Ambitious sir, take heed!").  Beaumont.
To Lucasta, Going to the Wars.  Lovelace.
**Hope**
Faith, Hope and Charity.  Guarini.
Hope is a strange invention.  Dickinson.
Hope is a subtle glutton.  Dickinson.
Hope is the thing with feathers.  Dickinson.
On Himself, upon Hearing What Was His Sentence.  Graham.

On Hope, by Way of Question and Answer between Abraham Cowley and Richard Crashaw.  Crashaw.
Plan.  McKuen.
To Hope.  Keats.
Visionary Hope, The.  Coleridge.

**Horatius**
Horatius.*Fr.* Lays of Ancient Rome.  Macaulay.

**Horseradish**
Consumer's Report.  Kennedy.

**Horses**
All through the Rains.  Snyder.
At Grass.  Larkin.
Birth of the Foal.  Juhász.
Blessing, The.  Wright.
Cariboo Horses, The.  Purdy.
Colt, The.  Knister.
Dead Ponies.  Chamberlain.
Draft Horse, The.  Frost.
Foal.  Watkins.
Ghostly Story.  Acorn.
Gun Teams.  Frankau.
Horse, The.  Coppard.
Horse.  Harrison.
Horse, The.  Smith.
Horses, The.  Hughes.
Horses.  Kipling.
Horses, The.  Muir.
Horses.  Wellesley.
Horses Aboard.  Hardy.
Imperiously he leaps, he nieghs, he bounds.*Fr.* Venus and Adonis.  Shakespeare.
Jack and His Pony, Tom.  Belloc.
Lyarde Is an Old Horse.  *Unknown.*
Mountain Corral.  Sorrells.
Old Gray Mare.  *Unknown.*
Old Timbrook Blues.  *Unknown.*
Paiute Ponies.  Barnes.
Palomino Stallion, The.  Nowlan.
Pony Blues, The.  *Unknown.*
Racing-Man, The.  Herbert.
Riding in the Rain.  Kumin.
Runaway, The.  Frost.
Tête-à-Tête.  Honig.
Three Colts Exercising in a Six-Acre.  Campbell.
Three Ponies.  Guiterman.
Timothy.  James.
To the Four Courts, Please.  Stephens.
War Horse, The.  Boland.
White Horse, The.  Lawrence.
White Stallion, The.  Owen.

**Hospitals**
And We Are Strangers to Each Other.  Schechter.
Building, The.  Larkin.
C44.  Kent.
Hospital, The.  Kavanagh.
Hospital.  Shapiro.
Hospital Window, The.  Dickey.
In Hospital.  Flecker.
In Hospital.  Henley.
Katrina.  Dawe.
Lullaby.  Sexton.
Microcosmos.  Miles.
Recovery Room, The: Lying-In.  Chasin.
Saratoga Ending.  Kees.
Semi-Private Room.  Nowlan.
Stones, The.  Plath.
Them, Crying.  Dickey.
Tulips.  Plath.
Visiting Hour.  MacCaig.

**Hotels**
Cairo Hotel.  Rowland.
Dolgelley Hotel, The.  Hughes.

Stirling's Hotel.  *Unknown.*
Up-Hill.  Rossetti.

**Houses**
Deserted House, The.  M. Coleridge.
House, The.  Williams.
New House, The.  Thomas.
*See also* **Home.**

**Hudson, Henry**
Weepers Tower in Amsterdam, The.  Goodman.

**Hudson River**
Lordly Hudson, The.  Goodman.
Scene on the Banks of the Hudson, A.  Bryant.

**Hughes, Langston**
Do Nothing Till You Hear from Me.  Henderson.
Reading Walt Whitman.  Forbes.

**Hume, David**
On the Author of the *Treatise of Human Nature.*  Beattie.

**Humility**
Nudus Redibo.  Flatman.
Nulla Fides.  Carey.
Resolve, The.  Chudleigh.

**Hummingbirds**
Container, The.  Corman.
Hummingbird.  Clarkson.
Hummingbird.  Lawrence.
Route of evanescence, A.  Dickinson.

**Humorous Verse**
*Faber Book of Comic Verse, The* (FaBoCo).  Michael Roberts and Janet Adam Smith, eds.
*Poems One Line and Longer* (POL).  William Cole, ed.
*Speak Roughly to Your Little Boy* (SpRo).  Myra Cohn Livingston, ed.

**Hundred Years War**
Ballad of Agincourt, The.  Drayton.
King Henry the Fifth before Agincourt.*Fr.* Henry V.  Shakespeare.

**Hunger**
Hunger.  Binyon.
Hunger.  *Unknown.*

**Hunt, Leigh**
Addressed to Haydon ("Great spirits are now on earth sojourning").  Keats.
Written on the Day That Mr. Leigh Left Prison.  Keats.

**Hunting and Hunters**
All in Green Went My Love Riding.  Cummings.
Ballad of Red Fox, The.  LaFollette.
Bear, The.  Kinnell.
Buffalo Skinners, The.  *Unknown.*
Chase, The.  Cunningham.
Coon Song.  Ammons.
Deer Hunt.  Jerome.
Deer Lay Down Their Bones, The.  Jeffers.
Duck.  Donaghy.
First Blood.  Stallworthy.
For the Opening of the Hunting Season.  Bishop.
Gallows, The.  Thomas.
Hunt, The.  De la Mare.
Hunt, The.  Kent.
Hunter, The.  Nash.
Hunting Fragment.  Lawless.
Hunting Song.  Finkel.
I Saw a Jolly Hunter.  Causley.
Kilruddery Hunt, The.  Mozeen.
Lion Hunts.  Beer.
Listening to Foxhounds.  Dickey.
Lost Deer, The.  Bruchac.
Moschus Moschiferus.  Hope.
Opening Day.  Severy.
Partridges.  Masefield.
Petty Murder.  MacLean.
Poacher, The.  *Unknown.*
Rabbit, The.  Davies.

Rabbit Hunter, The.  Frost.
Raid, The.  Everson.
Rainbow.  Huff.
Runnable Stag, A.  Davidson.
Sportsman, The.  McCord.
Springer Mountain.  Dickey.
Stag-Hunt.  *Unknown.*
This Poem Is for Deer.*Fr.* Myths and Texts: Hunting.  Snyder.
To Christ Our Lord.  Kinnell.
Tracking Rabbits: Night.  Barnes.
Ulivfak's Song of the Caribou.  *Unknown.*
Winter: East Anglia.  Blunden.

**Huron, Lake**
Huron, The.  Herschberger.

**Hurricanes**
Hurricane.  MacLeish.
Wasn't That a Mighty Storm?  *Unknown.*

**Husbands**
Henpecked Husband, A.  *Unknown.*
Slice of Wedding Cake, A.  Graves.
What I Want in a Husband Besides a Mustache.  Wakoski.
*See also*  **Marriage.**

**Hussey, Margaret**
To Mistress Margaret Hussey.  Skelton.

**Hyde, Douglas**
Burial of an Irish President.  Clarke.

**Hyenas**
Hyena.  Muske.

**Hypocrisy**
American Heartbreak.  Hughes.
Holy Willie's Prayer.  Burns.
Hypocrite Women.  Levertov.
Johnson's Cabinet Watched by Ants.  Bly.
On Flunking a Nice Boy Out of School.  Ciardi.
Vicar of Bray, The.  *Unknown.*

# I

**Icarus**
I, Icarus.  Nowlan.
Icarus.  Iremonger.
Icarus.  Layton.
Icarus.  Spender.
Landscape with the Fall of Icarus.  Williams.

**Ice**
Fire and Ice.  Frost.
Icehouse in Summer, The.  Nemerov.

**Ice-Skating.**  *See* **Skating and Skaters.**

**Icebergs**
Berg, The.  Melville.
Convergence of the Twain, The.  Hardy.
*Titanic* Blues.  *Unknown.*

**Idaho**
Idaho.  *Unknown.*

**Identity Crisis**
After Love.  Kumin.
Had I but gone some forty days or more.  Mitchell.
Main Problem in Portraiture, The.  Ritchie.
My Son.  Stone.
Self-Dependence.  Arnold.
To a Family Man in His Family Room.  Daniell.
Vacancy.  Gioseffi.

**Illinois**
First Song.  Kinnell.
Illinois Farmer.  Sandburg.

**Illness**
As I lie alone.  *Unknown.*
Bout with Burning.  Miller.

Fever 103°.  Plath.
Flat One, A.  Snodgrass.
For Kenneth and Miriam Patchen.  Young.
Hymn to God, My God, in My Sickness.  Donne.
Katrina.  Dawe.
Litany in Time of Plague, A.  Nashe.
Memphis Minnie-Jitis Blues.  *Unknown.*
My Daughter Very Ill.  Goodman.
To Mary.  Cowper.
Visionary Hope, The.  Coleridge.
Watch, The.  Cornford.

**Imagination**
Digging for China.  Wilbur.
Fancy.  Keats.
I saw in a poet's song.  Drinkwater.
Ode to Fancy.  Warton.
Sick Child, A.  Jarrell.
This Last Pain.  Empson.
Woman with Finger.  McKeown.

**Immigrants**
Canadian Boat-Song.  *Unknown.*
Europe and America.  Ignatow.
Feliks Skrzynecki.  Skrzynecki.
In Exile.  Lazarus.
In the Gazebo.  Flocos.
Lament of the Banana Man.  Jones.
Migrant Hostel.  Skrzynecki.
My Polish Grandma.  Field.
New Colossus, The.  Lazarus.
Schwiegermutterlieder.  Harrison.

**Immortality**
Because I could not stop for death.  Dickinson.
Death Be Not Proud.*Fr.* Holy Sonnets.  Donne.
Mohini Chatterjee.  Yeats.
Not marble, nor the gilded monuments.*Fr.* Sonnets.
    Shakespeare.
O May I Join the Choir Invisible.  "Eliot."
Ode: "Bards of passion and of mirth."  Keats.
Ode: Intimations of Immortality from Recollections of Early
    Childhood.  Wordsworth.
On the Beach, at Night.  Whitman.
One day I wrote her name upon the strand.*Fr.* Amoretti.
    Spenser.
Poem in Three Parts.  Bly.
Sailing to Byzantium.  Yeats.
This Monument Will Outlast.  Horace.
To Inez Milholland.  Millay.
To the Stone-cutters.  Jeffers.
Whilst thus my pen strives to eternize thee.*Fr.* Idea.  Drayton.
Wish, A.  Kemble.

**Imperialism**
Recessional.  Kipling.
Remember Suez?  Mitchell.
White Man's Burden, The.  Kipling.

**Impotence**
Carnation, The.  Hannigan.
Disappointment, The.  Behn.
Imperfect Enjoyment, The.  Earl of Rochester.
Impotence.  Bell.

**Independence Day.**  *See* **Fourth of July.**

**India**
Phrases for Everyday Use by the British in India.  Daniel.
Relief of Lucknow, The.  R. T. S. Lowell.
This Landscape, These People.  Ghose.

**Indian Summer**
Indian Summer: Vermont.  Stevenson.

**Indiana**
Anderson, Indiana.  White.
July In Indiana.  Fitzgerald.
Midwest.  Nims.

**Indians, American**
American Indian, The.  *Unknown.*

Ballad of Ira Hayes. La Farge.
Bar's Fight, August 28, 1746. Terry.
Blackfeet, Blood and Piegan Hunters. Welch.
Centenary Ode, A: Inscribed to Little Crow, Leader of the Sioux Rebellion in Minnesota, 1862. Wright.
Christmas Comes to Moccasin Flat. Welch.
Citizens' Complaint, The. Evans.
Concealment, The: Ishi, the Last Wild Indian. Stafford.
Crazy Horse Returns to South Dakota. Elliott.
Ignacio, Colorado, for You That Time. Harjo.
In My First Hard Springtime. Welch.
Indian at the Burial-Place of His Fathers, An. Bryant.
Indian Burying Ground, The. Freneau.
Indian School. Russell.
Indian Woman's Death-Song. Hemans.
Kansa, The. Contoski.
Lament of the Cherokee Reservation Indian, The. Loudermilk.
My Country 'Tis of Thy People You're Dying. Sainte-Marie.
Navajo Poem. Woessner.
New Mexican Mountain. Jeffers.
Now That the Buffalo's Gone. Sainte-Marie.
Prairies, The. Bryant.
Returned to Say. Stafford.
Rosebud. Anderson.
Shaman Songs 12. Fowler.
Sioux Indians, The. *Unknown.*
Spontaneous Requiem for the American Indian. Corso.
*Carriers of the Dream Wheel* (CDW). Duane Niatum, ed.
*Voices from Wah'Kon-Tah* (VW). Robert K. Dodge *and* Joseph B. McCullough, eds.

**Individualism**
Dual Site, The. Hamburger.
For My Son. Brownjohn.
I Don't Care. Lenox.
Letter to a Young Friend. Nowlan.
Ode: Inscribed to W. H. Channing. Emerson.
On Myselfe. Countess of Winchilsea.
Self-Dependence. Arnold.
Silence. Moore.
Solitary, The. Teasdale.

**Industrial Revolution**
Factory Girl's Come-All-Ye, The. *Unknown.*

**Infants.** *See* **Babies.**

**Infidelity**
Adultery. Dickey.
Adultery. Dugan.
Bird on Nellie's Hat, The. Lamb.
Black Snake. *Unknown.*
Bold Trooper, The. *Unknown.*
Clever Skipper, The. *Unknown.*
Don't Fish in My Sea. *Unknown.*
Early in the Spring. *Unknown.*
Faithless Wife, The. García Lorca.
First Lawcase, The. *Unknown.*
Good Bye, My Lady Love. Howard.
Gypsy Davy. *Unknown.*
Gypsy Laddie, The. *Unknown.*
I'm Gonna Move to the Outskirts of Town. *Unknown.*
Little Musgrave and Lady Barnard. *Unknown.*
Little Sparrow. *Unknown.*
Message, The. Donne.
Mind Reader Blues. *Unknown.*
Modern Love. Cunningham.
Newcomer's Wife, The. Hardy.
Of a Heroical Answer of a Great Romantic Lady to Her Husband. Harington.
Old Devil. *Unknown.*
Old Farmer and His Young Wife, The. *Unknown.*
Only Jealousy of Emer, The. *Unknown.*
Our Goodman. *Unknown.*
Peach Orchard Mama. *Unknown.*
Pneumonia Blues. *Unknown.*

Poem: "When he came home." Sanchez.
Reaping. Lowell.
Song: "Go and catch a falling star." Donne.
Take Back Your Gold. Pritzkow.
Temperaments, The. Pound.
To His Mistress. Ovid.
Trail to Mexico, The. *Unknown.*
Two or Three a Recipe to Make a Cuckold. Pope.
Unfaithful Married Woman, The. García Lorca.
When Daisies Pied and Violets Blue.*Fr.* Love's Labour's Lost. Shakespeare.
Whoopee Blues. *Unknown.*
Why So Pale and Wan. Suckling.
You All Know the Story of the Other Woman. Sexton.

**Innisfree, Ireland**
Lake Isle of Innisfree, The. Yeats.

**Inns.** *See* **Hotels.**

**Insanity.** *See* **Madness; Mental Illness.**

**Insects**
Brown Bug, The. Brown.
Creatures. Kumin.
Depressed by a Book of Bad Poetry, I Walk Toward an Unused Pasture and Invite the Insects to Join Me. Wright.
Minimal, The. Roethke.
Take thy hat, my little Laura.*Fr.* The Insect Hunters. Newman.

**Insomnia**
For the Sleepless. Dunn.
Winter Insomnia. Carver.

**Insurance**
Injury to Insured. Daniel.

**Intellect**
Mind. Wilbur.
Mind, Intractable Thing, The. Moore.
Mind Is an Ancient and Famous Capital, The. Schwartz.
Mind Is an Enchanting Thing, The. Moore.
My Brain. Laurance.
On the Birth of His Son. Su Tung-Po.

**Inventors**
Darius Green and His Flying-Machine. Trowbridge.
Invention of the Telephone, The. Klappert.

**Iowa**
Iowa. Browne.
Touring the Hawkeye State. Gildner.

**Iphigenia**
Victim of Aulis, The. Abse.

**Ireland**
Antrim. Jeffers.
Battle of the Boyne, The. Blacker.
Bold Fenian Men, The. *Unknown.*
Carrickfergus. MacNeice.
Change, The. O'Bruadair.
Clay is the word and clay is the flesh.*Fr.* The Great Hunger. Kavanagh.
Dublin Made Me. MacDonagh.
Easter 1916. Yeats.
Eire. O'Bruadair.
Go to Old Ireland. *Unknown.*
Grafted Tongue, A. Montague.
Harp That Once through Tara's Halls, The. Moore.
I Am of Ireland. *Unknown.*
"I Am of Ireland." Yeats.
In Ruin Reconciled. De Vere.
Inis Fal. O'Rahilly.
Ireland Never Was Contented. Landor.
Ireland with Emily. Betjeman.
Irish Airman Foresees His Death, An. Yeats.
Irish Cliffs of Moher, The. Stevens.
Irish Dancer, The. *Unknown.*
Kilcash. *Unknown.*
Lament for the Death of Thomas Davis. Ferguson.
Lilli Burlero. *Unknown.*

Municipal Gallery Revisited, The.  Yeats.
My Son, Forsake Your Art.  O'Heffernan.
New Style, The.  O'Bruadair.
Old Orange Flute.  *Unknown.*
On some island I long to be.  Saint Columcille.
Orange Lily, The.  *Unknown.*
Passage at Night—The Blaskets.  Flower.
Pastoral Ballad by John Bull, A.  Moore.
Requiem for the Croppies.  Heaney.
Rising of the Moon, The.  *Unknown.*
September 1913.  Yeats.
Shan Van Vocht, The.  *Unknown.*
Shancoduff.  Kavanagh.
Spenser's Ireland.  Moore.
This Night Sees Ireland Desolate.  MacMarcuis.
Time of Change, A.  O'Rahilly.
To Colman Returning.  Colman.
To Ireland in the Coming Times.  Yeats.
Wearing of the Green, The.  *Unknown.*
Where the River Shannon Flows.  Russell.
Young Fenians, The.  Fallon.
*Poems from Ireland* (PFIr).  William Cole, comp.

**Iris (flower)**
Iris.  Williams.

**Irish**
Gaeltacht.  Hutchinson.
Insular Celts, The.  Carson.
Irishman in Coventry, An.  Hewitt.
Spenser's Ireland.  Moore.

**Ironsides (ship).  *See* Constitution.**

**Isaac**
Parable of the Old Man and the Young, The.  Owen.
Story of Isaac, The.  Cohen.

**Ishtar**
Song for Ishtar.  Levertov.

**Islands**
By Ferry to the Island.  Smith.
On This Island.  Auden.

**Israel**
Reclaimed Area.  Silkin.

**Italy**
Good-Bye to the Mezzogiorno.  Auden.
Italia, Io Ti Saluto.  C. Rossetti.
Italy Versus England.*Fr.* Beppo.  Byron.
Poem: "So many pigeons at Columbus."  Gregor.

**Ivry-La-Bataille, France**
Ivry.  Macauley.

**Ivy**
Holly and Ivy.  *Unknown.*
Ivy, Chief of Trees.  *Unknown.*

**J**

**Jackdaws**
Jackdaw.  Earley.

**Jackrabbits**
Jack Rabbit.  Stoutenberg.

**Jackson, Mahalia**
When Mahalia Sings.  Prettyman.

**Jackson, Thomas Jonathan (Stonewall)**
Ascent of T. J. Jackson: A Soldier's Tale.  "A. N."
Stonewall Jackson's Way.  Palmer.

**Jacobites**
It Was A' For Our Rightfu' King.  Burns.

**Jagger, Mick**
Going Home.  Reynolds.

**Jaguars**
Second Glance at a Jaguar.  Hughes.

**James, Henry**
Old Mansion.  Ransom.

**James, Jesse**
Jesse James.  W. R. Benét.
Jesse James ("Jesse James was a lad that killed many a man").
*Unknown.*

**Jamestown, Virginia**
Enough.  Moore.

**Japan**
In the Second-Best Hotel in Tokyo.  Shapiro.
Japan.  Hecht.

**Japanese**
Asian Brother, Asian Sister.  Inada.
Japanese Children.  Kirkup.

**Jazz**
"Bird Lives": Charles Parker in St. Louis.  Harper.
Jazz.  Rogers.
Jazzonia.  Hughes.
Mingus.  Kaufman.
Satchmo.  Tolson.
Song thumbed down a cruiser for a ride, A.  Cunningham.
There were blood spots on the skirt.  Cunningham.
Voodoo on the Un-Assing of Janis Joplin.  Rogers.
Walking Parker Home.  Kaufman.

**Jealousy**
Lily of the West, The.  *Unknown.*
Sheffield 'Prentice, The.  *Unknown.*
Those Wedding Bells Shall Not Ring Out!  Rosenfeld.
What if jealousy is just a bad dream.  Palmer.
Widow's Old Broom, The.  *Unknown.*
Wild Bill Jones.  *Unknown.*

**Jeffers, Robinson.**
Poet Is Dead, The.  Everson.
Return of Robinson Jeffers, The.  Hass.

**Jefferson, Thomas**
Brave New World.  MacLeish.
Twilight's Last Gleaming.  Monks.

**Jellyfish**
Jellyfish, The.  Root.

**Jerome, Saint**
Jerome.  Jarrell.

**Jerusalem**
Hierusalem, My Happy Home.  *Unknown.*
In Jerusalem.  Ritchie.

**Jesus Christ**
Advent 1966.  Levertov.
All Hail the Power of Jesus' Name.  Perronet.
Away in a Manger.  *Unknown.*
Ballad of the Bread Man.  Causley.
Ballad of the Goodly Fere.  Pound.
Ballad of Trees and the Master, A.  Lanier.
Bambino.  Bird.
Bitter Withy, The.  *Unknown.*
Blessed Assurance.  Crosby.
Burning Babe, The.  Southwell.
Calvary.  Robinson.
Carpenter's Son, The.  Housman.
Cherry-Tree Carol, The.  *Unknown.*
Child's Present, A.  Herrick.
Christ Climbed Down.  Ferlinghetti.
Christ in the Universe.  Meynell.
Christ Walking on the Water.  Rodgers.
Christmas Hymn, A.  Wilbur.
Christ's Descent into Hell.  Rilke.
Christ's Love Song.  *Unknown.*
Church's One Foundation, The.  Stone.
Corpus Christi Carol, The: "Heron flew east, the heron flew
west, The."  *Unknown.*
Corpus Christi Carol, The: "Lully, lulley, lully, Lulley."
*Unknown.*
Corpus Christi Carol, The: "Over yonder's a park, which is
newly begun."  *Unknown.*

Coventry Carol. *Unknown.*
Cradle Hymn. Watts.
Crucifixus pro Nobis. Carey.
Deep Spring. *Unknown.*
Easter Hymn. Housman.
Easter Song, An. *Unknown.*
Ex Ore Infantium. Thompson.
Fairest Lord Jesus. *Unknown.*
For God While Sleeping. Sexton.
Friday Morning. Carter.
Friendly Beasts, The. *Unknown.*
Gentle Jesus, Meek and Mild. Wesley.
Gift, The. Williams.
Give Me Jesus. *Unknown.*
God, That Madest All Things. *Unknown.*
Good Friday. Bastian.
Good Friday. C. Rossetti.
He Was Made Man. Fletcher.
Holly and the Ivy, The. *Unknown.*
Holy Well, The. *Unknown.*
I Heard Christ Sing. "MacDiarmid."
I Told Jesus. Plumpp.
I Will Sing the Wondrous Story. Rowley.
If Christ/ Had lept from the cross. Duguid.
Into the Woods My Master Went. Lanier.
Jesu Christ, My Leman Swete. *Unknown.*
Jesus and His Mother. Gunn.
Jesus Borned in Bethlea. *Unknown.*
Jesus, Lover of My Soul. Wesley.
Jesus Make Up My Dying Bed. *Unknown.*
Jolly Shepherd Wat, The. *Unknown.*
Joys of Mary. *Unknown.*
Just as I Am. Elliot.
Last Supper, The. Rilke.
Little Cradle Rocks Tonight in Glory, The. *Unknown.*
Lord of the Dance. Carter.
Mary and Her Son Alone. Ryman.
My Heart Is Woe. *Unknown.*
My Song Is Love Unknown. Crossman.
Name of Jesus, The. Newton.
Never Said a Mumbalin' Word. *Unknown.*
New Approach Needed. Amis.
New Heaven, New War. Southwell.
On the Infancy of Our Saviour. Quarles.
On the Morning of Christ's Nativity. Milton.
Once in Royal David's City. Alexander.
Paradox. Miller.
Pieta, The, Rhenish, 14th C., the Cloisters. Van Duyn.
Pun for Al Gelpi, A. Kerouac.
Redemption. Herbert.
Revive Us Again. MacKay.
Royalty. Shaw.
Second Coming, The. Clark.
Seven Virgins, The. *Unknown.*
Softly and Tenderly Jesus Is Calling. Thompson.
Sometime During Eternity.*Fr.* A Coney Island of the Mind. Ferlinghetti.
Sweet Jesu. *Unknown.*
Take the Name of Jesus with You. Baxter.
There Is a Green Hill. Alexander.
To Jesus on His birthday. Millay.
Under Sorrow's Sign. O'Dalaigh.
Was He Married? Smith.
When I Survey the Wondrous Cross. Watts.
White Was His Naked Breast. *Unknown.*
Young Poet. O'Higgins.
**Jewelry**
With a Gift of Rings. Graves.
**Jews**
Hebrew of Your Poets, Zion, The. Reznikoff.
Jew. Randall.
Jewish Cemetery at Newport, The. Longfellow.

Let Other People Come As Streams. Reznikoff.
**Jezebel**
Jezebel. Forbes.
**John Bull**
Epigram on John Bull. Byron.
**John Henry (folk hero)**
Birth of John Henry, The. Tolson.
John Henry ("John Henry was a li'l baby, uh-huh"). *Unknown.*
Spike Driver Blues. *Unknown.*
**John the Baptist, Saint**
Prophet. Chambers.
Saint John Baptist. Drummond of Hawthornden.
**Johnson, Lyndon Baines**
Miltonic Sonnet for Mr. Johnson on His Refusal of Peter Hurd's Official Portrait, A. Wilbur.
**Johnson, Samuel**
Epitaph: "Here Johnson lies—a sage by all allow'd." Cowper.
**Jokes**
Characters of Forgotten Dirty Jokes, The. McNair.
**Jonah**
Jonah Is Cast into the Sea. *Unknown.*
**Jones, Casey (John Luther Jones)**
Casey Jones. Seibert.
Kassie Jones. *Unknown.*
**Jones, John Paul**
Ballad of Benjamin Bones, The. Ward.
Paul Jones's Victory. *Unknown.*
*Stately Southerner,* The. *Unknown.*
Yankee Man-of-War, The. *Unknown.*
**Jonson, Ben**
Ode, An: To Himself. Jonson.
Upon Mr. Ben Jonson: Epigram. Herrick.
**Joplin, Janis**
Burying Blues for Janis. Piercy.
Voodoo on the Un-Assing of Janis Joplin. Rodgers.
**Joshua**
Joshua Fit de Battle ob Jerico. *Unknown.*
**Joy**
59th Street Bridge Song, The. Simon.
Joy. Creeley.
What Are Years? Moore.
**Judas Iscariot**
Judas. Miller.
Judas. *Unknown.*
Judas Before. Travis.
Saint Judas. Wright.
**Judgment Day**
Blow Gabriel. *Unknown.*
Crowdieknowe. "MacDiarmid."
Day of Judgment, The. Swift.
Day of Judgment, The. Watts.
How long, dear Saviour, O how long. Watts.
Jesus Is Coming Soon. *Unknown.*
Revelation. Meinke.
Second Coming, The. Yeats.
When the Roll Is Called Up Yonder. Black.
**Judith (Apocrypha)**
Judith of Bethulia. Ransom.
Judith Recalls Holofernes. Stanton.
**Jugglers**
Juggler. Wilbur.
Juggler and the Baron's Daughter, The. *Unknown.*
**July**
July in Indiana. Fitzgerald.
Loud is the summer's busy song.*Fr.* The Shepherd's Calender: July. Clare.
**June**
June. Ledwidge.
June Is Bustin' Out All Over. Hammerstein.
**Juniper**
Juniper. Francis.
Juniper. *Unknown.*

Sing a Song of Juniper. Francis.

**Justice**
Death of Justice, The. Hawkins.
Justice. Hughes.
Poem: "In the old days either the plaintiff or the defendant won or lost." Dugan.

# K

**Kafka, Franz**
Letter to Kafka. Stanton.
Tribute to Kafka for Someone Taken. Dugan.

**Kalamazoo, Mighigan**
Sins of Kalamazoo, The. Sandburg.

**Kali**
Invocation to Kali, The, *sels.* Sarton.

**Kangaroos**
Duck and the Kangaroo, The. Lear.
Kangaroo. Lawrence.
Kangaroo, The. *Unknown.*

**Kansas**
Crossing Kansas by Train. Justice.
Kansas Boy. Lechlitner.
Outside Abilene. Elliott.
Place in Kansas, A. Kooser.
Wichita Vortex Sutra. Ginsberg.

**Katmandu, Nepal**
Here in Katmandu. Justice.

**Katzenjammer Kids**
Katzenjammer Kids, The. Reaney.

**Kearney, Phillip**
Kearney at Seven Pines. Stedman.

**Kearsarge (ship)**
How Do You Do, *Alabama*! Wilson.

**Keats, John**
Adonais: An Elegy on the Death of John Keats. Shelley.
John Keats. Byron.
On Keats. Shelley.
On the Death of Keats. Logan.

**Kells, Book of**
Book of Kells, The. Colum.

**Kennedy, John Fitzgerald**
Assassination Raga. Ferlinghetti.
Down in Dallas. Kennedy.
Lines for a President. Watson.
Thanksgiving 1963. Booth.

**Kennedy, Robert Francis**
Assassination Raga. Ferlinghetti.
Lowering, The. Swenson.

**Kent, England**
In Romney Marsh. Davidson.
To the Men of Kent. October, 1803. Wordsworth.

**Kent State University, Ohio**
Kent State, May 4, 1970. Goodman.

**Kentucky**
Hunters of Kentucky, The. Woodworth.
My Old Kentucky Home. Foster.

**Kesey, Ken**
First Party at Ken Keseys with Hell's Angels. Ginsberg.

**Kew Gardens, London**
Barrel-Organ, The. Noyes.

**Keys**
Skeleton Key. Hollander.

**Kidd, William**
Captain Kidd. *Unknown.*

**Kilcash, Ireland**
Kilcash. *Unknown.*

**King, Edward**
Lycidas. Milton.

**King, Martin Luther, Jr.**
Alabama Bus. *Unknown.*
Assassination. Lee.
Death of Dr. King. Cornish.
Funeral of Martin Luther King, Jr., The. Giovanni.
In Memoriam: Martin Luther King, Jr. Jordan.
Martin Luther King, Jr. Brooks.
Martin's Blues. Harper.
Shot with a Hot Rot Gun. Goode.
War War. Goode.

**King Kong**
Fay Wray to the King. Rechter.

**Kingfishers**
Kingfisher, The. Davies.
Kingfishers, The. Olson.
One Kingfisher and One Yellow Rose. Brennan.

**Kings**
English Succession, The. *Unknown.*
Ill Government. Herrick.
On the Four Georges. Landor.

**Kipling, Rudyard**
To R. K. Stephen.

**Kisses**
Did Not. Moore.
Kiss, The. Patmore.
Love's Philosophy. Shelley.
Mark, The. Graves.
Moth's kiss, first, The!*Fr.* In a Gondola. Browning.
Some Kisses from *The Kama Sutra*. Williams.
To Dianeme. Herrick.

**Kites**
Kite, The. O'Keeffe.
Kite is a Victim, A. Cohen.

**Knight, Etheridge**
Hospital/Poem. Sanchez.

**Knighthood and Knights**
Fast rode the knight.*Fr.* War Is Kind. Crane.
Knight, The. Rich.

**Koalas**
Koala. Ross.

**Kollwitz, Kathë**
Kathë Kollwitz. Rukeyser.

**Korea**
Ode for the American Dead in Korea. McGrath.

**Kosciusko, Thaddeus**
To Kosciusko. Keats.

**Ku Klux Klan**
Ku Klux. Hughes.
Special Bulletin. Hughes.

# L

**Labor and Laborers**
Apprentice Painter, The. Myers.
Captain Captain. *Unknown.*
Cynddylan on a Tractor. Thomas.
Docker. Heaney.
Drill, Ye Tarriers, Drill! *Unknown.*
Drover, A. Colum.
Florida Road Workers. Hughes.
Freighting from Wilcox to Globe. *Unknown.*
George. Randall.
Go Down, Old Hannah. *Unknown.*
Going Up the River. *Unknown.*
Grinders, The; or, The Saddle on the Right Horse. *Unknown.*
Hay for the Horses. Snyder.
I've Been Workin' on the Railroad. *Unknown.*
John Henry *Unknown.*

Life and Death Among the Xerox People. Cabral.
Liftman, The. Evans.
Lining Track. *Unknown.*
Man with the Hoe, The. Markham.
May I Ask You a Question, Mr. Youngtown Sheet & Tube? Patchen.
Muckers. Sandburg.
Night Shift at the Plating Division of Keeler Brass. Allen.
Old Men Working Concrete. Hey.
Paper Cutter, The. Ignatow.
Pas Por Aqui. Hall.
Public-House Confidence. Cameron.
Shovelling Iron Ore. *Unknown.*
So Handy, Me Boys, So Handy. *Unknown.*
Song of the Banana Man. Jones.
Song of the Shirt, The. Hood.
Tamping Ties. *Unknown.*
This Sun Is Hot. *Unknown.*
Tired Worker, The. MaKay.
Track-Lining Song. *Unknown.*
Train Runs Late to Harlem, The. Rivers
Unloading Rails. *Unknown.*
Way Out in Idaho. *Unknown.*
Worker, The. Thomas.

**Labor Unions**
Union Man. Morgan.

**Labrador**
North Labrador. Crane.

**Ladybirds**
Clock-a-clay (The Ladybird). Clare.
Ladybird, The, *sel.* Clare.
Ladybirds, The. Lucie-Smith.
Ladybug. Dodat.

**La Fayette, Marie Joseph, Marquis de**
La Fayette,*Fr.* Sonnets on Eminent Characters. Coleridge.
Let the brothels of Paris be opened. Blake.

**Lakes and Ponds**
Imitation of Spenser. Keats.
Pond, The Thwaite.
Reason and Nature. Cunningham.
Spring Pools. Frost.
Water and Light, Light and Water. Perlberg.

**Lamb, Charles**
This Lime-Tree Bower My Prison. Coleridge.
Written after the Death of Charles Lamb. Wordsworth.

**Lambs**
Composed on a May Morning, 1838. Wordsworth.
Delivering Lambs. Campbell.
Lamb, The.*Fr.* Songs of Innocence. Blake.
Lamb. Rankin.
Lambs Frolicking Home. Lape.
Mary's Lamb. Hale.
Pet Lamb, The. Wordsworth.

**Lamplighters**
Lamplighter, The. O'Sullivan.
Lamplighter, The. Stevenson.

**Lancashire, England**
Lancashire Winter. Connor.

**Lancelot du Lac**
Lanzarote. *Unknown.*

**Landlords and Landladies**
Landlady, The. Atwood.
Leaving the Country House to the Landlord, Five Years Later. McNair.
Scenery. Joans.
Telephone Conversation. Soyinka.

**Landor, Walter Savage**
Fable, A. Frere.
W. S. Landor. Moore.

**Language**
Americana IX. Rakosi.
Change, The. O'Bruadair.

Cool Web, The. Graves.
Crow's First Lesson. Hughes.
Goose, Moose, & Spruce. McCord.
Grafted Tongue, A. Montague.
Habla Usted Español? Reiss.
How One Thing Leads to Another. Smith.
Just Because... McCord.
Lapsus Linguae. Howard.
Logical English *Unknown.*
Loving and Liking. D. Wordsworth.
New Style, The. O'Bruadair.
Nigger. Sanchez.
Nine Parts of Speech, The. *Unknown.*
Permanently. Koch.
Scat! Scitten! McCord.
Test. Price.
What's in a Word? Shine.
Word made flesh is seldom, A. Dickinson.

**Laodamia**
Laodamia. Wordsworth.

**La Plata, Missouri**
Last Look at La Plata, Missouri. Barnes.

**Larkin, James**
Inscription for a Headstone. Clarke.

**Larks**
Caged Skylark, The. Hopkins.
To a Skylark. Shelley.
To a Skylark. Wordsworth.

**Laughter**
Laughing Song. *Fr.* Songs of Innocence. Blake.
Why did I laugh to-night? No voice will tell. Keats.

**Laundry and Laundering**
Clothesline, The. Wade.
Dolls' Wash, The. Ewing.
Laundrette. Lochhead.
Love Calls Us to the Things of This World Wilbur.
Mad Scene, The. Merrill.
Shepherd's Hut, The. Young.
Stocking and Shirt. Reeves.
Thinking Twice in the Laundromat. Elliott.
Wash. Updike.
Wash Day. Mollin.

**Lavender**
I planned to have a border of lavender. Goodman.

**Lawes, Henry**
To Mr. Henry Lawes. Philips.

**Lawrence, David Herbert**
An Elegy for D. H. Lawrence. Williams.

**Lawyers and Law**
Conversation in Craven Street, Strand. Smith *and* Rose
Law I Love Is Major Mover, The. Duncan
Law Like Love. Auden.
Lawyer Clark Blues. *Unknown.*
Legal Fiction. Empson.

**Lazarus**
Come Out, Lazarus! *Unknown.*
Dives and Lazarus. *Unknown.*

**Lear, King**
Lear. Williams.

**Learning**
He That Never Read a Line. *Unknown.*
Little Learning, A.*Fr.* An Essay on Criticism. Pope.
To David, About His Education. Nemerov.
Vain Learning,*Fr.* Caelica. Greville.

**Leaves**
Gathering Leaves. Frost.
Invitation Standing. Blackburn.
Leaf Treader, A. Frost.
Leaves Compared with Flowers. Frost.
Les Etiquettes Jaunes. O'Hara.
One Leaf, The. Norris.

**Leda**

Leda. Van Duyn.
Leda and the Swan. Yeats.
Leda Reconsidered. Van Duyn.
New Leda, The. Howes.

**Leeuwenhoek, Anton**
Microscope, The. Kumin.

**Legs**
Her Leg. Herrick.
Legs, The. Graves.
Poem in Which My Legs Are Accepted. Fraser.
Vet's Rehabilitation. Durem.

**Leisure**
Leisure. Davies.

**Lemmings**
Lemmings, The. Masefield.

**Lemons**
Lemons. Hubbell.
Lemons, Lemons. Young.

**Lenin, Vladimir Ilyich**
Second Hymn to Lenin. "MacDiarmid."

**Lent**
To Keep a True Lent. Herrick.

**Leonardo da Vinc**
For "Our Lady of the Rocks." D. G. Rossetti.

**Leopold III, King of the Belgians**
Moon and the Night and the Men, The. Berryman.

**Lepanto, Battle of**
Lepanto. Chesterton.

**Lesbianism.** *See* **Homosexuality.**

**Letters**
Destruction of Letters. Deutsch.
How to Write a Letter. Turner.
Letter to a Conceivable Great-Grandson. Birney.
Way I read a letter's—this, The. Dickinson.

**Levett, Robert**
On the Death of Mr. Robert Levet, a Practiser in Physic. Johnson.

**Liberalism and Liberals**
Respectabilities. Silkin.

**Libraries**
Fire at Alexandria, The. Weiss.
Girl in a Library, A. Jarrell.
Library. Armour.
Rhoda Pitkin.*Fr.* The New Spoon River. Masters.

**Lice**
Louse Hunting. Rosenberg.

**Lichen**
In Praise of Lichen. Perlberg.

**Lies and Lying**
Book of Lies, The. Tate.
Lying. Moore.
Matilda, Who Told Lies, and Was Burned to Death. Belloc.
Song: "Lying is an occupation." Pilkington.

**Life**
Anyone Lived in a Pretty How Town. Cummings.
April Inventory. Snodgrass.
Barter. Teasdale.
Beach in August, The. Kees.
Cold Spring, The. Levertov.
Consumer's Report, A. Porter.
Curiosity. Reid.
Elegy, Written with His Own Hand in the Tower before His Execution. Tichborne.
Esthete in Harlem. Hughes.
Flux. Eberhart.
Fly, The.*Fr.* Songs of Experience. Blake.
For Life I Had Never Cared Greatly. Hardy.
Force That through the Green Fuse Drives the Flower, The. Thomas.
He Never Expected Much. Hardy.
Hound, The. Francis.
Hughie at the Inn. Wylie.

Human Life: On the Denial of Immortality. Coleridge.
Into My Heart an Air That Kills. Housman.
Leaf Treader, A. Frost.
Lies. Yevtushenko.
Life, A. Nemerov.
Life. Treasone.
Life flows to death as rivers to the sea. Cunningham.
Life, friends, is boring. We must not say so. Berryman.
Lying in a Hammock at William Duffy's Farm in Pine Island, Minnesota. Wright.
Mean Old Twister. *Unknown.*
Men Made Out of Words. Stevens.
Mother to Son. Hughes.
Nature's Questioning. Hardy.
On the Life of Man. Ralegh.
On Wenlock Edge the wood's in trouble. Housman.
Our lives are Swiss. Dickinson.
Pale Blue Casket, The. Pitcher.
Postscript. Hochman.
Psalm of Life, A. Longfellow.
Responding Voice. Icaza.
Sea Boy on the Giddy Mast, A. Clare.
Secret, The. Levertov.
Sestina of the Tramp-Royal. Kipling.
Shut Out That Moon. Hardy.
Sic Vita. King.
Sic Vita. Thoreau.
Sower, The. Blind.
Still Here. Hughes.
These chairs they have no words to utter. Wordsworth.
This life which seems so fair. Drummond of Hawthornden.
Triumph of Life, The. Shelley.
Under Sorrow's Sign. O'Dalaigh.
Up-Hill. C. Rossetti.
We Are Transmitters. Lawrence.
What Is Life? Coleridge.
Woman Poem. Giovanni.
World, The. Bacon.

**Lifeguards**
Lifeguard, The. Dickey.
Seasonal Phenomenon. Armour.

**Light**
Holy Light.*Fr.* Paradise Lost. Milton.

**Lighthouses**
Eddystone Light, The. *Unknown.*
Inland Lighthouse, The. McMichael.
Lighthouse. Meeter.
Lighthouse Keeper. Sange.
Lighthouses. Wellesley.
Lightning is a yellow fork, The. Dickinson.

**Lilies**
Bulb, A. Munkittrick.
Lilly, The.*Fr.* Songs of Experience. Blake.

**Lilies of the Valley**
Lilies of the Valley. Silkin.

**Limbo**
Limbo. Coleridge.

**Lincoln, Abraham**
Abraham Lincoln Walks at Midnight. Lindsay.
Booth Killed Lincoln. *Unknown.*
In Hardin County, 1909. Thompson.
Lincoln, *sel.* Fletcher.
Lincoln Monument: Washington. Hughes.
Lincoln, the Man of the People, *sel.* Markham.
Martyr, The. Melville.
O Captain! My Captain! Whitman.
When Lilacs Last in the Dooryard Bloom'd. Whitman.

**Lindbergh, Charles**
Lindbergh. *Unknown.*

**Lindsay, Vachel**
To Lindsay. Ginsberg.

**Lions**

Circus Lions.   Day Lewis.
Glory Trail, The.   Clark.
Jim, Who Ran Away from His Nurse, and Was Eaten by a
   Lion.   Belloc.
King, The.   Livingstone.
Lion, The.   Douglas.
Lion Hunts.   Beer.
Lions.   McPherson.
One Lion, Once.   Canzoneri.
Riverdale Lion.   Colombo.
Sunt Leones.   Smith.
Supper for a Lion.   Aldis.
**Li Po**
Li Po.   Moore.
**Lippi, Fra Filippo**
Fra Lippo Lippi, *sel.*   Browning.
**Little Big Horn, Battle of**
Tale of Last Stands, A.   Red Cloud.
**Little Red Riding Hood**
Coup de Grâce.   Hope.
**Little Rock, Arkansas**
Chicago *Defender* Sends a Man to Little Rock, The.   Brooks
**Livingstone, David**
Into the Dark.   Monette.
**Lizards**
Gecko.   Lloyd
Lizard.   Lawrence.
Lizard.   McLean.
Lizard.   Mills.
Lizards and Snakes.   Hecht.
Old Man to the Lizard, The.   MacLeish.
Tiny Baby Lizard, The.   Brigham.
**Lloyd George, David, 1st Earl Lloyd-George of Dwyfor**
Lloyd George.   *Unknown.*
**Lobsters**
Lobsters.   Nemerov.
Lobsters in the Window.   Snodgrass.
**Locusts**
Serenade: "The tin-type tune the locusts make."   Donnelly.
**London, England**
Composed upon Westminster Bridge, September 3, 1802.
   Wordsworth.
Countryman's Return, The.   Thomas.
Description of the Morning, A.   Swift.
Farewell to Kurdistan.   Tonks.
London.*Fr.* Songs of Experience.   Blake.
London   Davidson.
London: A Poem in Imitation of the Third Satire of Juvenal.
   Johnson.
London after the Great Fire, 1666.*Fr.* Annus Mirabilis.
   Dryden.
London Rain.   MacNeice.
London Snow.   Bridges.
Mountains of Mourne, The.   French.
**Loneliness**
Acquainted with the Night.   Frost.
Alone.   Poe.
Bachelor.   Meredith.
Bad Thing, The.   Wain.
Bereft.   Hardy.
Crowsfeet Splaying Round His Eyes.   Lloyd-Evans.
Desert Places   Frost.
Eleanor Rigby.   Lennon *and* McCartney.
I Saw in Louisiana a Live-Oak Growing.   Whitman.
Interior.   Parker.
Little Ecologue.   Wylie.
Loneliness.   Carruth.
Loneliness.   Jenkins.
Loneliness.   Shegonee.
Lonely Man, The.   Jarrell.
Missing My Daughter.   Spender.
Mr. Flood's Party.   Robinson.

On the Wide Heath.   Millay.
One.   Rodgers.
Poem: "I've been a woman."   Sanchez.
Suite: Judy Blue Eyes.   Stills.
Summary.   Sanchez.
Talking after Christmas Blues.   Henri.
These.   Williams.
Third Day in a Strange City.   Berge.
Three Weeks in the State of Loneliness.   Piercy.
To Marguerite—Continued.*Fr.* Switzerland.   Arnold.
Tonight I've watched.   Sappho.
What Color Is Lonely.   Rodgers.
"When I'm alone"-the words tripped off his tongue.   Sassoon.
Wife A-Lost, The.   Barnes.
**Long Island, New York**
Bonac.   Wheelock.
**Longfellow, Henry Wadsworth**
Poe and Longfellow.*Fr.* A Fable for Critics.   Lowell.
**Lorelei**
Lorelei, The.   Heine.
**Louisburg, Nova Scotia**
Louisburg.   *Unknown.*
**Love**
Book of Love Poetry, A (BoLoP).   Jon Stallworthy, ed.
*Gambit Book of Love Poems* (GBL).   Geoffrey Grigson, ed.
*Love's Aspects* (LoAs).   Jean Garrigue, comp.
*One Little Room, an Everywhere* (OLR).   Myra Cohn Livingston,
   ed.
*Scottish Love Poems* (SLP).   Antonia Fraser, ed.
**Lowell, James Russell**
Lowell.*Fr.* A Fable for Critics.   Lowell.
**Lucifer.**   *See* **Satan.**
**Luck**
Luck.   Gibson.
**Lucknow, India**
Relief of Lucknow, The.   R.T.S. Lowell.
**Luddites**
Song for the Luddites.   Byron.
**Lullabies.**   *See* **Cradle Song** *and* **Lullaby** in **Title and First Line
Index.**
**Lumbering and Lumbermen**
Colley's Run-I-O.   *Unknown.*
Farmer and the Shanty Boy, The.   *Unknown.*
In Winter in the Woods Alone.   Frost.
Jam on Gerry's Rocks, The.   *Unknown.*
Johnny Carroll's Camp.   *Unknown.*
Little Brown Bulls, The.   *Unknown.*
Lumberman's Alphabet, The.   *Unknown.*
Michigan I-O.   *Unknown.*
Once More A-Lumbering Go.   *Unknown.*
Peter Amberley.   *Unknown.*
Roving Shanty Boy, The.   *Unknown.*
Shanty Boys and the Pine, The.   *Unknown.*
Shanty Man's Life, A.   *Unknown.*
Turner's Camp on the Chippewa.   *Unknown.*
Wild Lumberjack, The.   *Unknown.*
Wild Mustard River, The.   *Unknown.*
Woodman Spare That Tree.   Morris.
**Lust**
At Times.   Wiegner.
Becoming a Nun.   Jong.
Conversion.   Hewitt.
Desire.   Coleridge.
Don 1958.   Alta.
Down, Wanton, Down!   Graves.
Expense of spirit in a waste of shame, Th'.*Fr.* Sonnets.
   Shakespeare.
Filling her compact and delicious body.   Berryman.
Gentle Breeze, A.   Durfey.
Late-Flowering Lust.   Betjeman.
Mutes, The.   Levertov.
On Sir Voluptuous Beast.   Jonson.

Playboy. Wilbur.
Twenty-Third Flight. Birney.
**Lutes**
Cat and the Lute, The. Master.
**Lynching**
Between the World and Me. Wright.
I Saw Them Lynching. Freeman.
Lynching, The. McKay.
Lynching and Burning. St. John.
So Quietly. Hill.
Swimmers, The. Tate.
**Lyonesse**
When I Set Out for Lyonesse. Hardy.
**Lyrebirds**
Lyrebirds. Wright.

# M

**Machado, Antonio**
Street, The. Smith.
**McHenry, Fort**
Star-spangled Banner, The. Key.
**Machines**
Garbage Disposal Truck, The. Kinnell.
La Marche des Machines. Tessimond.
Love to My Electric Handmixer. Wakoski.
Portrait of a Machine. Untermeyer.
**McKinley, William**
Zolgotz. *Unknown.*
**MacNeice, Louis**
Last Word, A. Rodgers.
**McSorley's Bar (New York City)**
I was sitting in McSorley's Cummings.
**Macy's (department store)**
Macy's Poem, The. Reiss.
**Madness**
Birdwatchers of America. Hecht.
Counting the Mad. Justice.
Curriculum Vitae: Incomplete. Ritchie.
Evening in the Sanitarium. Bogan.
First day's night had come, The. Dickinson.
First Lecture. Whitehead.
Going Home. Roper.
Heard in a Violent Ward. Roethke.
Howl. Ginsberg.
Kaddish, *sel.* Ginsberg.
Locked in a Home for Les Enfants Dérangés en Dieu. Nolan.
Mad Mother, The. Wordsworth.
Mad Song. Blake.
Mad Song. Levertov.
Mad Tom of Bedlam. *Unknown.*
Madhouse. Hernton.
Mad-Woman, The. Strong.
Much madness is divinest sense. Dickinson.
Ringing the Bells. Sexton.
Song of the Mad Prince, The. De la Mare.
Three anti-depressants and one diuretic a day.*Fr.* Letters to Live Poets. Beaver.
Time Out. Henley.
To a Student Poet, Hospitalized, Having "Broken with Reality." Jellema.
Tom o' Bedlam's Song. *Unknown.*
Tyger! Tyger! Nolan.
Visits to St. Elizabeths. Bishop.
Waking in the Blue. Lowell.
Whats My Name If Not Everyone Elses. Salinas.
You, Doctor Martin. Sexton.
**Magi**

Ballad of Befana, The. McGinley.
Carol of the Brown King. Hughes.
Gift, The. Williams.
Journey of the Magi, The. Eliot.
Magi, The. Yeats.
We Three Kings of Orient Are. Hopkins.
Wise Men and Shepherds. Godolphin
**Magic**
For the El Paso Weather Bureau. Wild.
Sermonette. Reed.
Testing-Tree, The. Kunitz.
**Magnolia Trees**
Planting a Magnolia. Snodgrass.
**Maia**
Ode to May, Fragment. Keats.
**Mail and Mailmen**
Mailman, The Brush.
Night Mail. Auden.
**Maine (state)**
District, The: Both Sides of Chandler River. Enslin.
**Majorca**
Andraitx-Pomegranate Flowers. Lawrence.
**Malachy, Saint**
St. Malachy. Merton.
**Malaga, Spain**
Malaga. Hutchinson.
**Malcolm X (Malcolm Little)**
Aardvark. Fields.
At That Moment. Patterson.
El-Hajj Malik El-Shabazz. Hayden.
For Malcolm: After Mecca. Barrax.
For Malcolm Who Walks in the Eyes of Our Children. Troupe.
For Malcolm X. Alba.
For Malcolm X. Walker.
I Remember. Jackson.
Malcolm X. Brooks.
Malcolm X—An Autobiography. Neal.
Poem for Black Hearts, A. Jones.
Portrait of Malcolm X. Knight.
Sun Came, The. Knight.
They Are Killing All the Young Men. Henderson.
**Manassas, Battles of.** *See* **Bull Run, Battles of.**
**Manchester, England**
Murphy in Manchester. Montague.
**Mandalay, Burma**
Mandalay. Kipling.
**Mandelstam, Osip**
Mandelstam. Young.
Osip Mandelshtam. Layton.
**Manhattan.** *See* **New York City.**
**Mankind**
Apostrophe to Man. Millay.
Awake, my St. John! leave all meaner things.*Fr.* An Essay on Man. Pope.
Away, Melancholy. Smith.
Chorus Sacerdotum. Greville.
Common Dust. Johnson.
Corruption. Vaughan.
Dead, The. Very.
For A' That and A' That. Burns.
Four seasons fill the measure of the year. Keats.
Great Way of the Man, The. Russell.
Here. Thomas.
Hollow Men, The. Eliot.
Homo Sapiens.*Fr.* A Satire Against Mankind. Earl of Rochester.
Horror Comic. Conquest.
Human Abstract, The.*Fr.* Songs of Experience. Blake.
Human Form Divine, The. Raine.
Human Life: On the Denial of Immortality. Coleridge.
If. Kipling.

In Shame and Humiliation.  Wright.
Inscription on the Monument of a Newfoundland Dog.  Byron.
Know then thyself, presume not God to scan.*Fr.* An Essay on
  Man.  Pope.
Lines Written in Early Spring.  Wordsworth.
Man.  Herbert.
Man.  Vaughan.
Meditatio.  Pound.
Mostly People.  Nichols.
Pity This Busy Monster, Manunkind.  Cummings.
Prayer before Birth.  MacNeice.
Progress.  Meinke.
Psyche.  Coleridge.
Pulley, The.  Herbert.
Self-Knowledge.  Coleridge.
Sic Vita.  King.
That Nature Is a Heraclitean Fire.  Hopkins.
To My Son Parker, Asleep in the Next Room.  Kaufman.
Truant, The.  Pratt.
Unnatural Powers.  Jeffers.
What Is He?  Lawrence.
When Serpents Bargain for the Right to Squirm.  Cummings.
Windows, The.  Herbert.

**Man-of-War Birds**
To The Man-of-War Bird.  Whitman.

**Mao Tse-Tung**
Thoughts of Chairman Mao.  Young.

**Maps**
Map of Places, The.  Riding.

**Marathon, Battle of**
Persian Version, The.  Graves.

**Marc Antony**
To Mark Anthony in Heaven.  Williams.

**March**
Dear March, come in!  Dickinson.
March.  Hopper.
March.  *Unknown.*
March.  Williams.
March.  Wright
Twilight in Middle March, A.  Ledwidge.

**Marigolds**
Marigolds.  Carman.
Marigold.  Haines.

**Marijuana**
Marijuana Patch on the State Hospital's Former Grounds.
  Whiting.
Smoking Drugs with Strangers.  Bowering.

**Marines.  *See* United States Marine Corps.**

**Marion, Francis**
Song of Marion's Men.  Bryant.

**Mark Antony.  *See* Marc Antony.**

**Markiewicz, Constance Georgine, Countess**
In Memory of Eva Gore-Booth and Con Markiewicz.  Yeats.

**Marlborough, John Churchill, 1st Duke of**
New Song Made in Honour of His Grace the Duke of
  Marlborough, A.  Durfey.
Satirical Elegy on the Death of a Late Famous General, A.
  Swift.

**Marriage**
About Marriage.  Levertov.
Ache of Marriage, The.  Levertov.
After Selecting the Wedding Invitations.  Levenberg.
Anniversary, The.  Ai.
Bachelor Bold and Young.  *Unknown.*
Bed, The.  Saleh.
Birthday, The.  Dacey.
Bon Mot, A.  *Unknown.*
Brewer's Man, The.  Strong.
Call It a Good Marriage.  Graves.
Conspirators, The.  Burke.
Crisis, The.  Creeley.
Daisy Bell; or, A Bicycle Built for Two.  Dacre.

Early Thoughts of Marriage.  Cotton.
Enticer.  Armour.
Epigram: "As Thomas was cudgeled one day by his wife."
  Swift.
Epigram: "In the neat parlor of their honeymoon."  Halpern.
Epitaph upon Husband and Wife Who Died and Were Buried
  Together, An.  Crashaw.
Epithalamion: "The kingfisher falls through the dry air."
  Wright.
Epithalamion: "Ye learned sisters which have oftentimes."
  Spenser.
Epithalamion Made at Lincoln's Inn.  Donne.
Exequy upon His Wife.  King.
Farmer's Bride, The.  Mew.
First Snow of the Year, The.  Van Doren.
For a Marriage.  Jong.
For three days.  Payne.
Griesly Wife, The.  Manifold.
Groom's Lament, The.  Peterson.
Happy Marriage.  Blacklock.
Here Comes.  Jong.
Home Burial  Frost.
I Am of These.  Curry.
In the Last Few Moments Came the Old German Cleaning
  Woman.  Cooper.
In the Room of the Bride-Elect.  Hardy.
Late Abed.  MacLeish.
Les Sylphides.  MacNeice.
Letter to Dafnis, A.  Countess of Winchilsea.
Lines for Those to Whom Tragedy Is Denied.  Oates.
Live Man's Epitaph.  Hope.
Love ("She stood in her snood and arasaid").  *Unknown.*
Love's Matrimony.  Duke of Newcastle.
Mad Answer to a Madman, A.  Hayman.
Major Macroo.  Smith.
Man and Wife.  Goodman.
Man and Wife.  Sexton.
Marital Journey, The.  Araaya.
Marriage, The.  Bertolino.
Marriage.  Clarke.
Marriage.  Corso.
Marriage.  Moore.
Marriage.  *Unknown.*
Married and Single Life.  *Unknown.*
Married Man Blues.  *Unknown.*
Maternity Gown.  Holbrook.
Meditation at Kew.  Wickham.
Nesting.  Saleh.
Old Flame, The.  Lowell.
Old-Marrieds, The.  Brooks.
Packin' Trunk Blues.  *Unknown.*
Portrait of a Marriage.  Abse.
Prothalamium.  MacDonagh.
Robertin Tush.  *Unknown.*
Rosy Apple, Lemon or Pear.  *Unknown.*
She Vowed Him This.  Box.
Silver Wedding.  Hodgson.
Slave Marriage Ceremony Supplement.  *Unknown.*
Slice of Wedding Cake, A.  Graves.
Some twenty years of marital agreement.  Cunningham.
Song Ballet.  *Unknown.*
Song for a Marriage.  Miller.
Staying Married.  Allen.
Stumbling.  Lourie.
To a Friend, Who Recommended a Wife to Him.  *Unknown.*
To a Lady on Her Marriage.  Bell.
To My Dear and Loving Husband.  Bradstreet.
"To Speak of Woe That Is in Marriage."  Lowell.
To the Ladies.  Chudleigh.
Twenty Year Marriage.  Ai.
Wait for Me.  Creeley.
Waiting at the Church; or, My Wife Won't Let Me.  Leigh.

Way Sun Keeps Falling Away from Every Window, The. Lifshin.
Wedding. Brown.
Wedding-Wind. Larkin.
Westminster Drollery, 1671. Behn.
When Charlie Bowdre married Manuela, we carried them. Ondaatje.
Whitsun Weddings, The. Larkin.
Who Drags the Fiery Artist Down? Day.
Why Should a Foolish Marriage Vow.*Fr.* Marriage à la Mode. Dryden.
Wife Who Would a Wanton Be, The. *Unknown.*
Wife Wrapt in Wether's Skin, The. *Unknown.*
Word to Husbands, A. Nash.
World Is Really a Sugarplum House in the Forest, The. Boyajian.
You were young—but that was scarcely to your credit.*Fr.* Monogamy. Gould.

**Marshes**
Dingman's Marsh. Moore.
Marsh, The. Snodgrass.
Marsh Song—At Sunset. Lanier.
Marshes of Glynn, The. Lanier.
Paean to Place. Niedecker.
Sunrise. Lanier.
Winter Pond. Logue.

**Martyrs**
Admire Cranmer! Smith.
Gift of Fire, The. Mueller.
Norman Morrison. Ferguson.
Norman Morrison. Mitchell.
Of Late. Starbuck.
On the Late Massacre in Piedmont. Milton.
Sunt Leones. Smith.

**Marvell, Andrew**
You, Andrew Marvell. MacLeish.

**Mary, The Virgin**
Annunciation, The. *Unknown.*
Assumption. Fallon.
Assumption, The. *Unknown.*
God, Woman, Egg. Minton.
Hymn to the Virgin. William of Shoreham.
I Sing of a Maiden. *Unknown.*
In Praise of Mary. *Unknown.*
M and A, R and I. *Unknown.*
Maiden That Is Makeless, A. *Unknown.*
Mary and Her Son Alone. Ryman.
O, My Heart Is Woe! *Unknown.*
Of One that is so Fair and Bright. *Unknown.*
Orison to the Blessed Virgin, An. Herebert.
Our Lady. M. Coleridge.
Penitent Considers Another Coming of Mary, A. Brooks.
Song about Mary. Mitchell.
Star Song, The: A Carol to the King. Herrick.
Virgin Jewess, Rising with a Cry, The. Baker.
Virgin Mary, The. Bowers.
Virgin's Song, The. *Unknown.*

**Mary Magdalene**
Magdalene, Afterward. Whitehill.
Saint Mary Magdalene; or, The Weeper. Crashaw.

**Maryland**
Maryland, My Maryland! Randall.

**Massachusetts**
To the Governor and Legislature of Massachusetts. Nemerov.

**Masters, Edgar Lee**
Figure. M. L. Masters.
House in Chicago, The. M. L. Masters.
Man, My Father, The. M. L. Masters.

**Mathematics**
Euclid. Lindsay.

**Matisse, Henri**
Matisse: "The Red Studio." Snodgrass.

**May**
Composed on a May Morning, 1838. Wordsworth.
Corinna's Going a-Maying. Herrick.
Fountain in the Park, The. Haley.
May. Neilson.
May. C. Rossetti.
May Day Carol, A. *Unknown.*
May Day Dancing, The. Nemerov.
May Poem. *Unknown.*
Mayers' Song, The. *Unknown.*
Padstow Night Song, The. *Unknown.*
Pray in May. Metcalfe.
Same Lady, The. Nichols.
Song on May Morning. Milton.
Spring in These Hills. MacLeish.
To the Lady May. Townsend.
You that in love finde lucke and habundance. Wyatt.

**Mayo, Ireland**
County Mayo, The. Raftery.

**Mechanics**
Misery of Mechanics, The. Booth.

**Mediterranean Sea**
Mediterranean, The. Tate.

**Medusa**
Medusa. Bogan.

**Melancholy**
City of Dreadful Night, The. Thomson ("B. V.").
Dejection; An Ode. Coleridge.
Mirth and Melancholy. Duchess of Newcastle.
Ode on Melancholy. Keats.
Pleasures of Melancholy, The. Warton.
Sadness. Cartwright.
Stanzas, Written in Dejection, near Naples. Shelley.
To Melancholy. Countess of Winchelsea.

**Melville, Herman**
At Melville's Tomb. Crane.
Herman Melville. Aiken.

**Memory**
Celandine. Thomas.
Crossing. MacLeish.
Crystals Like Blood. "MacDiarmid."
Dear Men and Women. Wheelock.
Home. Blight.
House of Hospitalities, The. Hardy.
Legende. Crane.
Lines Written a Few Miles above Tintern Abbey. Wordsworth.
Mementos, 1. Snodgrass.
Memory, A. Allingham.
Mnemosyne. Stickney.
Oft, in the Stilly Night. Moore.
Old Upright I Did Not Learn to Play, The. Flocos.
People, The. Creeley.
Piano. Lawrence.
Proust's Madeleine. Rexroth.
Remember. C. Rossetti.
Rustling of Grass, The. Noyes.
Since. Auden.
Song: "Memory, hither come." Blake.
Stanzas: "In a drear-nighted December." Keats.
Stephen's Green Revisited Weber.
Thinking of the Lost World. Jarrell.
Two Old Ladies. Sassoon.
When to the sessions of sweet silent thought.*Fr.* Sonnets. Shakespeare.
Within the Circuit of This Plodding Life. Thoreau.

**Men**
Man, Man, Man Is for the Woman Made. *Unknown.*
Ordinary Man, The. Service.
Psalm Praising the Hair of Man's Body, A. Levertov.
Resting Figure. Levertov.
Stew Meat Blues. *Unknown.*
Three Men. *Unknown.*

Tired As I Can Be. *Unknown.*
*See also* **Mankind.**
**Menageries.** *See* **Zoos.**
**Mental Illness**
Death of a Son. Silkin.
Dropping Toward Stillness. Barba.
Evening in the Sanitarium. Bogan.
Frank Drummer.*Fr.* Spoon River Anthology. Masters.
Grandeurs of the crazy man alone, The. Roethke.
Hard Rock Returns to Prison from the Hospital for the Criminal Insane. Knight.
Hour of Feeling, The. Simpson.
In a Mental Hospital Sitting Room. Jennings.
Invisible Woman, The. Morgan.
Lines Written During a Period of Insanity. Cowper.
Manic Depressant. Dammers.
Mental Cases. Owen.
Mental Hospital Garden, The. Williams.
Patient, The: Rockland County Sanitarium. Hernton.
Repression of War Experience. Sassoon.
Ringing the Bells. Sexton.
Simplicity. Simpson.
Waking in the Blue. Lowell.
What Is There? Schechter.
*See also* **Madness.**
**Mental Retardation**
Hospital for Defectives. Blackburn.
**Mercy**
Mercy. *Unknown.*
Ode to Mercy. Collins.
Quality of Mercy, The.*Fr.* The Merchant of Venice. Shakespeare.
**Merlin**
Merlin. Emerson.
Merlin, They Say. Greville.
**Mermaid Tavern**
Lines on the Mermaid Tavern. Keats.
**Mermaids and Mermen**
Catch. Hughes.
Fable of the Mermaid and the Drunks. Neruda.
I Did Not See a Mermaid? Johnson.
Keeper of the Eddystone Light, The. *Unknown.*
Mermaid, The. Mueller.
Mermaid, The, *sel.* Tennyson.
Mermaid, The. *Unknown.*
Mermaidens' Vesper-Hymn, The.*Fr.* Syren Songs. Darley.
Sailor Boy, The. Tennyson.
**Merrimac (ship)**
*Cumberland* and the *Merrimac,* The. *Unknown.*
**Merry-go-rounds**
Carousel, The. Oden.
Merry-Go-Round. McAuley.
**Mets, New York (baseball team)**
Ode to the New York Mets. Lindsay.
September Valentine. Sullivan.
**Mexican War**
Defence of the Alamo, The. Miller.
Maid of Monterey, The. *Unknown.*
**Mexico**
Sunday, Guadalajara. Ostroff.
**Meynell, Alice**
On Looking at a Copy of Alice Meynell's Poems. A. Lowell.
**Mice**
Anne and the Field-Mouse. Serraillier.
Church Mouse, The. Bullett.
Country Mouse and the City Mouse, The. Sharpe.
Diary of a Church Mouse. Betjeman.
Fearful Finale of the Irascible Mouse, The. Carryl.
Fieldmouse crouches low, A. Sund.
Frog Went A-Courting. *Unknown.*
Funeral Oration for a Mouse. Dugan.
Meadow Mouse, The. Roethke.

Mouse and the Cake, The. Cook.
Mouse Night: One of Our Games. Stafford.
Mouse's Nest. Clare.
Mouse's Petition, The. Barbauld.
Mus Ridiculus Non. Welch.
My mother's maids, when they did sew and spin.*Fr.* Satires. Wyatt.
Ritual Mouse, A. Meredith.
To a Mouse. Burns.
To the Field Mice. Eberhart.
Two Mice, The. Henryson.
**Michigan, Lake**
Lake Michigan. Kherdian.
November on Lake Michigan. McKeown.
**Middle Age**
Aging. Jong.
Birthday Card for a Psychiatrist. Van Duyn.
Face in the Mirror, The. Graves.
For My Daughter's 20th Birthday. Lowenfels.
From a Correct Address in a Suburb of a Major City. Sorrells.
Hunger Artist, The. Kaufman.
In the Smoking Car. Whitman.
Libertine, The. MacNeice.
Love Song of J. Alfred Prufrock, The. Eliot.
Men at Forty. Justice.
Menstruation at Forty. Sexton.
Mezzo Cammin. Longfellow.
Middle-Aged Conversation. Tessimond.
Next Day. Jarrell.
Ode on Celestial Music. Patten.
Some Slippery Afternoon. Gioseffi.
Tea Shop, The. Pound.
There Is Grey in My Eyebrows. Shapiro.
Thirty-Eight. Smith.
Thirty eighth year, The. Clifton.
**Middlesex, England**
Middlesex. Betjeman.
**Midwifery and Midwives**
Country Midwife, The: A Day. Ai.
**Milk**
Milkmaid. Lee.
**Mill, John Stuart**
John Stuart Mill.*Fr.* Clerihews. Bentley.
**Millennium**
It Is Almost the Year Two Thousand. Frost.
**Mills and Millers**
Dishonest Miller, The. *Unknown.*
Miller of Dee, The. *Unknown.*
Song: "There was a jolly miller once."*Fr.* Love in a Village. Bickerstaffe.
**Milton, John**
Johannes Milton, Senex. Bridges.
Lines on Seeing a Lock of Milton's Hair. Keats.
Lines Printed under the Engraved Portrait of Milton. Dryden.
London, 1802 ("Milton! Thou shouldst be living at this hour"). Wordsworth.
Milton. Blake.
Milton. Tennyson.
On His Blindness. Milton.
**Mind.** *See* **Intellect.**
**Minerals**
Crystals Like Blood. "MacDiarmid."
*See also* **Mining and Miners.**
**Minerva**
To Minerva. Hood.
**Mining and Miners**
Blackleg Miners, The. *Unknown.*
Casey Jones ("Come all you muckers and gather here"). *Unknown.*
Cousin Jack Song. *At. to* Tregonning.
Drill Man Blues. Sizemore.
Dynamite Song. *Unknown.*

For Laurence Jones. Kizer.
Hard-Working Miner, The. *Unknown.*
I'm Only a Broken-Down Miner. *Unknown.*
Lament While Descending a Shaft. *Unknown.*
Miner Boy, The. *Unknown.*
Miners. Wright.
Oh, Give Me the Hills. *Unknown.*
Only a Miner. *Unknown.*
Prospecting. Ammons.
Tramp Miner's Song. *Unknown.*
Working in the Mines. *Unknown.*
Ye Ancient Yuba Miner of the Days of '49. Upham.
**Ministers.** *See* **Clergy.**
**Minneapolis, Minnesota**
Minneapolis. Hennen.
Minneapolis Poem, The. Wright.
**Minnesota**
Driving toward the Lac Qui Parle River. Bly.
**Miracles**
Distance from the Sea, A. Kees.
Epistle Containing the Strange Medical Experience of Karshish, the Arab Physician, An. Browning.
**Mirrors**
Mirror. Plath.
To Cynthia, on Her Looking-Glass. Kynaston.
With the Face. Riding.
**Misanthropy**
Wishes of an Elderly Man, The. Ralegh.
**Missionaries**
From Greenland's Icy Mountains. Heber.
**Mississippi River**
Brown River, Smile. Toomer.
**Missouri**
Last Look at La Plata Missouri. Barnes.
**Missouri River**
Foreclosure. Brown.
**Mithra**
Song to Mithras, A. Kipling.
**Mithridates the Great**
Mithridates. Emerson.
**Moccasins**
Moccasins of an Old Man, The. Carden.
**Mockingbirds**
Fable of the Talented Mockingbird. Bates.
Mockingbird, The. Jarrell.
To the Mocking Bird. Wilde.
**Models**
Looking at Models in Sears Catalogue. Dacey.
Ode to a Model. Nabokov.
**Moles**
Anarchist. Dugdale.
Eagle and the Mole, The. Wylie.
Mole, The. Haines.
Moles. Stafford.
Star-Nosed Mole, The. Wallace.
**Monasteries**
December. Snyder.
**Monet, Claude**
Monet: "Les Nymphéas." Snodgrass.
**Money**
America. Dumas.
Complaint of Chaucer to His Purse, The. Chaucer.
Fatigue. Belloc.
Hardship of Accounting, The. Frost.
How Pleasant It Is to Have Money.*Fr.* Dipsychus. Clough.
Impact of a dollar upon the heart, The.*Fr.* War Is Kind. Crane.
Money. Sisson.
My Purse. *Unknown.*
Splendid Shilling, The. Philips.
**Monkeys**
Monkey. Read.

Monkeys. Colum.
Monkeys on Mt. Hiei. Shiffert.
**Monks**
Soliloquy of the Spanish Cloister. Browning.
**Monroe, Marilyn**
I have come to claim. Grahn.
Marilyn Monroe. Ramsey.
**Mont Blanc**
Hymn before Sun-Rise, in the Vale of Chamouni. Coleridge.
Mont Blanc. Shelley.
**Montana**
Montana Pastoral. Cunningham.
**Months**
Labours of the Months. *Unknown.*
Months, The. S. Coleridge.
Months, The. *Unknown.*
**Montreal, Canada**
O God! O Montreal. Butler.
**Montrose, James Graham, 5th Earl of**
Execution of Montrose, The. Aytoun.
**Moon**
Ablow the Mune. Campbell.
All Other Love Is Like the Moon. *Unknown.*
Autumnal Moon, The.*Fr.* The Seasons. Thomson.
Ballad of the Moon, Moon. García Lorca.
Cat and the Moon, The. Yeats.
Charming the Moon. Den Boer.
Epiphany on a Plot of Moonlight. Mitchell.
Full Moon. De la Mare.
Full Moon. Hayden.
Full Moonlight in Spring. Merwin.
Golden Moonrise. Braithwaite.
Half Moon. García Lorca.
Lady Moon. Milnes.
Learn'd society of late, A.*Fr.* The Elephant in the Moon: A Satire. Butler.
Lunar Baedeker. Loy.
Man in the Moon, The ("Man in the moone stand and strit"). *Unknown.*
Moon, The. Creeley.
Moon, The.*Fr.* Passages. Duncan.
Moon, The. Upton.
Moon and the Yew Tree, The. Plath.
Moon Rock. Mally.
Moon's the North Wind's Cooky, The. Lindsay.
On the Telescopic Moon. Drennan.
Once Only. Snyder.
Partial Eclipse. Snodgrass.
Silver. De la Mare.
Song for Ishtar. Levertov.
Sonnet of the Moon, A. Best.
Target. Lister.
To a Solitary Disciple. Williams.
To the Moon ("Art thou pale for weariness"). Shelley.
To the Moon. Winters.
Voyage to the Moon. MacLeish.
Where the Mind Meets the Moon in Revolt.*Fr.* Woman Against the Moon. Wolfert.
Wind and Silver. Lowell.
Winter Moon. Hughes.
With How Sad Steps, O Moon, Thou Climb'st the Skies.*Fr.* Astrophel and Stella. Sidney.
*Moonstruck* (Moon). Robert Phillips, ed.
**Moore, Sir John**
Burial of Sir John Moore at Corunna, The. Wolfe.
**Moore, Marianne**
For Marianne Moore's Birthday. Boyle.
Valentine for Marianne Moore, A. Olson.
**Moore, Thomas**
On T. Moore's Poems. *Unknown.*
**Morison, Sir Henry**

To the Immortal Memory and Friendship of That Noble Pair, Sir Lucius Cary and Sir H. Morison. Jonson.

**Mormons**

Marching to Utah. *Unknown.*

**Morning**

Aubade: "The lark now leaves his watery nest." Davenant.
Breakfast Time. Stephens.
Chelsea Morning. Mitchell.
Clouded Morning, The. Very.
Description of the Morning, A. Swift.
Early Morning, The. Belloc.
Fair Morning, The. Very.
Fairies Break Their Dances, The. Housman.
Good Morning Love! Blackburn.
In the Nake Bed, in Plato's Cave. Schwartz.
May All Earth Be Clothed in Light. Hitchcock.
Morning. Fainlight.
Morning at the Window. Eliot.
New Morning. Dylan.
Removal from Terry Street, A. Dunn.
Song: "Year's at the spring, The." Browning.
This morning I threw the windows. Wright.
Waking from Sleep. Bly.
*See also* **Dawn; Sunrise.**

**Morris, William**

1915: A Pre-Raphaelite Ending, London. Howard.

**Morrison, Norman**

Norman Morrison. Ferguson.
Norman Morrison. Mitchell.
Of Late. Starbuck.

**Moses**

Go Down, Moses. *Unknown.*
Last View, The. Spinnanger.
Pharao's Daughter. Moran.

**Mosquitoes**

Mosquito, The. Lawrence.
Mosquito. Updike.
Mosquito Knows, The. Lawrence.

**Motels**

Leaving the Motel. Snodgrass.

**Mothers**

Affliction of Margaret, The. Wordsworth.
Apples. Kaufman.
At My Mother's Bedside. M. L. Masters.
Black Mother Woman. Lorde.
C. L. M. Masefield.
Child of Mine. Goffin *and* King.
Children, The. MacDonald.
Children, The. Urdang.
Christmas Eve. Sexton.
Clutter of Mothers, A. Brock.
Creek Mother Poem. Harjo.
Disquieting Muses, The. Plath.
Doll Poem. Derricotte.
Elegy: "My mother in the witness box." Scott.
External Element, The. Mc Fadden.
For Mama Streek. Inez.
Her Eyes Don't Shine Like Diamonds. Marion.
Homework for Annabelle. McGinley.
In Memory of My Mother. Kavanagh.
It Is Deep. Rodgers.
Jessie Mitchell's Mother. Brooks.
Jesus Was Crucified, or, It Must Be Deep. Rodgers.
Kornelia Woloszczuk. Skrzynecki.
Leroy. Jones.
Letter to My Mother. Moraes.
Mad Mother, The. Wordsworth.
Madonna and Daughter. Bergé.
Maternity. Meynell.
Matrilineal Descent. Morgan.
Metamorphoses. Fuller.
Morning Song. Plath.

Mother. Libera.
Mother. Vincent.
Mother and I. Yoak.
Mother and Poet. E. Browning.
Mother to Son. Hughes.
Mother, they say you looked Irish. Brenner.
Mothers. Giovanni.
Mothers. Sexton.
Mothers, Daughters. Kaufman.
Mother's Day. Hamod.
My Mother. Taylor.
My Mother and the Americans. Kherdian.
My Mother Would Be a Falconress. Duncan.
My Young Mother. Cooper.
Night Feeding. Rukeyser.
90th Year, The. Levertov.
Old Arm-Chair, The. Cook.
Old Mother turns blue and from us. Niedecker.
Paean to Place. Niedecker.
Pavane for the Passing of a Child. Chester.
Poem: "I meet Mother on the street." Bruce.
Reflections. Barrows.
Snapshot. Inez.
Song of the Old Mother, The. Yeats.
Sonnet to My Mother. Barker.
To My Son. Griffin.
Unknown Girl in the Maternity Ward. Sexton.
Vacation Trip. Stafford.
Way It Is, The. Oden.
Widow's Plot, The: or, She Got What Was Coming to Her. Plomer.
Woman Mourned by Daughters. Rich.

**Mothers-in-law**

Prince Robert. *Unknown.*
Unexpected Pleasure, An. *Unknown.*

**Moths**

Great Moth, The. Gittings.
Moth, The. Baker.
Yucca Moth, The. Ammons.

**Motion Pictures**

As a Great Prince. Honig.
At the Drive-In: "John Wayne vs. God." Dewey.
Attack of the Crab Monsters. Raab.
Autobiographical Note. Scannell.
Bogart. Flocos.
Bride of Frankenstein, The. Field.
Day I Stopped Dreaming about Barbara Steele, The. Dillard.
Day with the Foreign Legion, A. Whittemore.
Drive In Movie. Sange.
Feature Time. Hammond.
Forties Flick. Ashbery.
Grenadine. Griffin.
Hoppy. Godsey.
Horror Movie. Moss.
If Life's a Lousy Picture, Why Not Leave Before the End. McGough.
Movie House. Updike.
Movie-Going. Hollander.
Newsreel. Day Lewis.
Nobody Dies Like Humphrey Bogart. Rosten.
Physical Imperfections of Old Films, The. Ramsey.
Projectionist's Nightmare, The. Patten.
Reel One. Stoutenburg.
Ride the High Country. Slavitt.
Skin Flick. Chappell.
Spool, The. Belitt.
To the Film Industry in Crisis. O'Hara.
Two Figures from the Movies. Meredith.
While Cecil Snores: Mom Drinks Cold Milk. Cunningham.
Working for Dr. No. Nash.

**Motorcycles**

Gypsy Motorcycle Club of South Minneapolis, The. Gunderson.
Motorcycle Irene. Spence.
Motorcyclist's Song, The. Bell.
Stoplight. Root.
**Mountain Climbing**
Alpine. Thomas.
Finding a Poem. Merriam.
Here in Katmandu. Justice.
John Muir on Mt. Ritter. Snyder.
Schreckhorn, The. Hardy.
Story, A. Stafford.
Summer Solstice. Garner.
Wingwalking in Oregon. Peterson.
**Mountain Lions**
Mountain Lion. Lawrence.
**Mountains.** *See* **Hills and Mountains.**
**Movies.** *See* **Motion Pictures.**
**Moving Day**
Drifters. Dawe.
Moving. Matthews.
Removal from Terry Street, A. Dunn.
**Mowing and Mowers**
Damon the Mower. Marvell.
Mower, Against Gardens, The. Marvell.
Mower to the Glo-Worms, The. Marvell.
Mower's Song, The. Marvell.
Mowing. Frost.
Photograph of Haymaker, 1890. Holden.
**Muhammed Ali.** *See* **Ali, Muhammed.**
**Mules**
Kicking Mule, The. *Unknown.*
Mule, The. Barks.
Mules. Fox-Smith.
My Sweetie's a Mule in the Mine. *Unknown.*
Poem to a Mule, Dead Twenty Years. Owen.
**Mummies**
Breathing, at Last, in the Wichita Art Museum. Clinton.
Mummy of a Lady Named Jemutesonekh XXI Dynasty. James.
Wanting a Mummy. McPherson.
**Munch, Edvard**
God, Woman, Egg. Minton.
**Murder and Murderers**
Ashland Tragedy, The. Adams.
Babylon; or, The Bonnie Banks 'o Fordie. *Unknown.*
Bad Luck Blues. *Unknown.*
Bad Man Ballad. *Unknown.*
Billy Lyons and Stack O'Lee. *Unknown.*
Blood Hound Blues. *Unknown.*
Brother, The. Hardy.
Check to Song. Meredith.
Coroner's Jury. Strong.
Cruel Mother, The. *Unknown.*
Death of Samuel Adams, The. *Unknown.*
Delia Holmes. *At. to.* Ruff.
Earl Richard. *Unknown.*
Edward. *Unknown.*
Edward, Edward. *Unknown.*
Ella Speed. *Unknown.*
Ellen Flannery. *Unknown.*
Farewell to barn and stack and tree. Housman.
Fine Flowers in the Valley. *Unknown.*
Florella. *Unknown.*
For Andy Goodman — Michael Schwerner — and James Chaney. Walker.
For the One Who Would Take Man's Life in His Hands. Schwartz.
Fragment from the Elizabethans. Bridges-Adams.
Frankie and Johnnie. *Unknown.*
Fuller and Warren. *At. to* Whitecotton.
Gosport Tragedy, The. *Unknown.*

He Fell Among Thieves. Newbolt.
Herbert White. Bidart.
Incident. Jones.
Inquest, The. Davies.
John Adkins' Farewell. *Unknown.*
John Hardy. *Unknown.*
Johnson-Jinkson. *Unknown.*
Lady Isabella's Tragedy, The. *Unknown.*
Little Musgrave and Lady Barnard. *Unknown.*
Local Man Remembers the Killing Ground, A. Whitehead.
Lord Randal. *Unknown.*
Lula Vires. *Unknown.*
Lynching, The. Kessler.
McAfee's Confession. *Unknown.*
Mary Wyatt and Henry Green. *Unknown.*
Murder of Goins, The. *Unknown.*
Naomi Wise. *Unknown.*
Oxford Girl, The. *Unknown.*
Paris Railway-Station, The. D. G. Rossetti.
Pearl Bryan. *Unknown.*
Peddler and His Wife, The. *Unknown.*
Poem for Richard Speck, A. McMahon.
Poor Ellen Smith. *Unknown.*
Pretty Polly. *Unknown.*
Prince Robert. *Unknown.*
Robin and Gandelein. *Unknown.*
Rose Connoley. *Unknown.*
Salute! Ferlinghetti.
Scenery. Joans.
Seth Dismounts Thrice. Walsh.
Silvery Tide, The. *Unknown.*
Tom Dooley. *Unknown.*
Two Sisters, The. *Unknown.*
Upon the Double Murther of King Charles I in Answer to. Philips.
Wexford Girl, The. *Unknown.*
Wild Bill Jones. *Unknown.*
Willie Taylor. *Unknown.*
Young Hunting. *Unknown.*
**Muses**
Saint Harmony my patroness. Goodman.
To the Muses. Blake.
**Museums**
Museum Item 237. Mann.
Museum Piece. Wilbur.
**Mushrooms**
Morels. Smith.
Mushrooms. Plath.
Slicing Button Mushrooms. Bowman.
**Music and Musicians**
Alexander's Feast: or, The Power of Music. Dryden.
At a Solemn Music. Milton.
Autobiography Part Two: Rock and Roll Dedicated to the Poet Victor Hernandez Cruz. Hagedorn.
Day They Ate the Baritone, The. Hazo.
Free Thoughts on Several Eminent Composers. Lamb.
Group, The. Cruz.
Guide to the Symphony. Kees.
Guitar. García Lorca.
Here Where Coltrane Is. Harper.
I Was Fair Beat. Garioch.
Impossibility, An. Vas Dias.
Juke Box Love Song. Hughes.
Music. A. Lowell.
Music and Drum. MacLeish.
Musical Instrument, A. E. Browning.
Musician, The. Thomas.
Music's Duel. Crashaw.
1907: A Proposal from Paris. Howard.
Ode: "We are the music-makers." O'Shaughnessy.
On Hearing a Symphony of Beethoven. Millay.
Passions, an Ode to Music, The. Collins.

Peter Quince at the Clavier. Stevens.
Piper, A. O'Sullivan.
Piper's Progress, The. Mahony.
Piping down the Valleys Wild.*Fr.* Songs of Innocence. Blake.
Seventy Six Trombones. Willson.
Singers to Come. Meynell.
Song for St. Cecilia's Day, 1687, A. Dryden.
Sonsito. Cruz.
Soul. Graham.
Spirits Unchained. Kgositsile.
To——: "Half in the dim light from the hall." Braithwaite.
We Dance Like Ella Riffs. Rodgers.

**Mysticism**
"Mysticism Has Not the Patience to Wait for God's Revelation." Eberhart.

**Mythology**
In Heavenly Realms of Hellas. Cummings.
To Juan at the Winter Solstice. Graves.

# N

**Names**
Choosing a Name. Lamb.
Hallelujah: A Sestina. Francis.
Mary's a Grand Old Name. Cohan.
Mutual Problem. Cole.
My Mother Takes My Wife's Side. Kherdian.
My Name and I. Graves.
Names. Lifshin.
Naming of Cats, The. Eliot.
Reason of Numbers, A. Jacobsen.
United States Tony. Kherdian.

**Nantucket, Massachusetts**
Phenomenal Survivals of Death in Nantucket. Glück.
Quaker Graveyard in Nantucket, The. Lowell.

**Naples, Italy**
Ode to Naples. Shelley.

**Napoleon I**
Advice to a Raven in Russia. Barlow.
Calais, August 15, 1802. Wordsworth.
Feelings of a Republican on the Fall of Bonaparte. Shelley.
Lines Written on Hearing the News of the Death of Napoleon. Shelley.
March to Moscow, The. Southey.
Napoleon I. De la Mare.
Ode to Napoleon Buonaparte. Byron.

**Napoleonic Wars**
Battle of the Baltic. Campbell.
Burial of Sir John Moore at Corunna, The. Wolfe.
Field of Waterloo, The.*Fr.* Childe Harold's Pilgrimage. Byron.
Incident of the French Camp. Browning.

**Narcotics.** *See* **Drug Addiction.**

**Naseby, Battle of**
Battle of Naseby, The. Macaulay.

**Nash, Richard (Beau Nash)**
On Mr. Nash's Picture at Full Length. Brereton.

**Nativity**
Hymn of the Nativity, Sung as by the Shepherds, An. Crashaw.
Nativity of Our Lord and Saviour Jesus Christ, The. Smart.
Ode on the Morning of Christ's Nativity. Milton.
Salus Mundi. Coleridge.
*See also* **Christmas.**

**Naturalists**
Naturalist, The. Reynolds.

**Nature**
Amends to Nature. Symons.
Animal, Vegetable and Mineral. Bogan.

Apology, The. Emerson.
Apparently with no surprise. Dickinson.
Birds and Fishes. Jeffers.
Blue Horses. Roberson.
Chorus Sacerdotum. Greville.
Composed by the Side of Grasmere Lake. Wordsworth.
Design. Frost.
Each and All. Emerson.
Enthusiast, The; or, The Lover of Nature. Warton.
Evening Walk, An. Wordsworth.
Expostulation and Reply. Wordsworth.
Gravelly Run. Ammons.
Great Way of the Man, The. Russell.
Gully, The. Stewart.
Heaven of Animals, The. Dickey.
Hymn before Sun-rise, in the Vale of Chamouni. Coleridge.
I stood tip-toe upon a little hill. Keats.
I taste a liquor never brewed. Dickinson.
In All These Acts. Everson.
In Harmony with Nature. Arnold.
Innocence. Layton.
Inscription for the Entrance to a Wood. Bryant.
Kindred. Stewart.
Line Written a Few Miles above Tintern Abbey. Wordsworth.
Lines Written in Early Spring. Wordsworth.
Loving and Liking. D. Wordsworth.
Marban, a Hermit Speaks. *Unknown.*
Me Imperturbe. Whitman.
Miracles("Why, who makes much of a miracle"). Whitman.
Nature Lover. Nims.
Nature's Questioning. Hardy.
Nocturnal Reverie, A. Countess of Winchilsea.
Nothing Will Die. Tennyson.
On the Grasshopper and the Cricket. Keats.
On the Uniformity and Perfection of Nature. Freneau.
On thy stupendous summit, rock sublime!*Fr.* Beachy Head. Smith.
One Fragment for God. Everson.
Onset, The. Frost.
Peace of Wild Things, The. Berry.
Pied Beauty. Hopkins.
Poor, Poor Country, The. Neilson.
Rainy Summer, The. Meynell.
Sky is low, the clouds are mean, The. Dickinson.
Song of the Sky Loom. *Unknown.*
For Nature daily through her grand design.*Fr.* Sonnets. Tuckerman.
Spring Pools. Frost.
Stars, I have seen them fall. Housman.
Tables Turned, The. Wordsworth.
To Mr. Henry Lawes. Philips.
To Nature. Coleridge.
Unison, A. Williams.
Waking, The. Roethke.
What mystery pervades a well! Dickinson.
Wilderness, The. Raine.
Work without Hope. Coleridge.
World Has Many Places Many Ways, The. Russell.
Writer Indulges a Hobby, The. Randall.
Written in March. Wordsworth.
*Room for Me and a Mountain Lion* (RFM). Nancy Larrick, comp.

**Nautilus (shell)**
Chambered Nautilus, The. Holmes.

**Navy, France**
Ballad for a Boy, A. Cory.

**Navy, Great Britain**
Ballad for a Boy, A. Cory.
Battle of Sole Bay, The. *Unknown.*
Battle of the Baltic. Campbell.
Chief Petty Officer. Causley.
Death of Admiral Benbow, The. *Unknown.*

Old Navy, The.  Marryat.
Ye Mariners of England.  Cambell.
**Navy, United States**
Anchors Aweigh.  Miles.
Ballad of Benjamin Bones, The.  Ward.
*Constitution's* Last Fight, The.  Roche.
How Do You Do, *Alabama*!  Wilson.
Navy Hymn, The.  Whiting.
Warship of 1812, The.  *Unknown.*
Yankee Man-of-War, The.  *Unknown.*
**Nazis**
Construction #13.  Sherwin.
Family Goldschmitt, The.  Coulette.
In Memoriam: Gertrud Kolmar, 1943.  Hope.
"More Light! More Light!"  Hecht.
Peachtree, The.  Levertov.
**Nefertiti**
Nofretete.  Pollak.
**Negro Verse**
*Black Poets, The* (BPo).  Dudley Randall, ed.
*Blues Lines, The* (BluL).  Eric Sackheim, Comp.
*Jump Bad: A New Chicago Anthology* (JB).  Gwendolyn Brooks,
  ed.
*Poetry of Black America, The* (PoBA).  Arnold Adoff, ed.
**Negroes**
Allegory in Black.  Clark.
Black Art.  Jones.
Black Jam for Dr. Negro.  Evans.
Black Majesty.  Cullen.
Black Mother Woman.  Lorde.
Black Tambourine.  Crane.
Blackberry Street.  Randall.
Blackstone Rangers, The.  Brooks.
Blue-eyed Precinct Worker, The.  Coulette.
But He Was Cool or: He Even Stopped for Green Lights.  Lee.
Congo, The.  Lindsay.
Dab of Color, A.  Weiss.
Dance for Militant Dilettantes, A.  Young.
Dinner Guest: Me.  Hughes.
Dream Variation.  Hughes.
For a Lady I Know.  Cullen.
For Both of Us at Fisk.  Scott.
For de Lawd.  Clifton.
For My People.  Walker.
Good Morning.  Hughes.
Her Story.  Madgett.
Heritage.  Cullen.
I, Too.  Hughes.
I was five.  Lee.
Image in the Mirror.  Kenner.
Incident.  Cullen.
Ka 'Ba.  Jones.
Little Black Boy, The.*Fr.* Songs of Innocence.  Blake.
Madimba: Gwendolyn Brooks.  Harper.
Making Out.  Emeruwa.
Merry-go-Round.  Hughes.
Metamorphosis of Aunt Jemima, The.  Childress.
Missing Beat.  Rogers.
Mr. Z.  Holman.
Mulatto.  Hughes.
Necessity.  Hughes.
Negro Servant.  Hughes.
Negro Speaks of Rivers, The.  Hughes.
Nikki-Rosa.  Giovanni.
Of De Witt Williams on His Way to Lincoln Cemetery.
  Brooks.
Old Black Joe.  Foster.
On Being Brought from Africa to America.  Wheatley.
Poem for Halfwhite College Students.  Jones.
Remember Times for Sandy.  Rogers.
Robert.  Clifton.
September 1, 1802.  Wordsworth.

Sermon on the Warpland, The.  Brooks.
Sevier County Runaway, The.  Brigham.
Southern Cop.  Brown.
Stereo.  Lee.
Theme for English B.  Hughes.
2 Takes from Love in Los Angeles.  Young.
Vive Noir!  Evans.
Way It Is, The.  Oden.
Way It Was, The.  Clifton.
We Real Cool.  Brooks.
Where It's At.  Bergé.
White Troops Had Their Orders But the Negroes Looked Like
  Men, The.  Brooks.
Woman Poem.  Giovanni.
Yet Do I Marvel.  Cullen.
**Neighbors**
Body, The.  Bronk.
**Nepal**
Here in Katmandu.  Justice.
**Neptune (god)**
In Praise of Neptune.  Campion.
**Neruda, Pablo**
Regard to Neruda.  Lowther.
**Nerval, Gérard de**
Gerard de Nerval.  Brush.
**Netherlands**
Such Is Holland!  Genestet.
**New England**
New England.  Robinson.
**New Jersey**
Invention of New Jersey, The.  Anderson.
**New Orleans, Battle of**
Ballad of New Orleans.  Wilson.
Hunters of Kentucky.  Woodworth.
**New Year**
Both my child.  Teitoku.
For a fresh start.*Fr.* Oraga Haru.  Issa.
New Year 1974.  Jones.
New Year's Day.  Lowell.
New Year's Water.  *Unknown.*
Year's End.  Wilbur.
**New York City**
B Negative.  Kennedy.
Crossing Brooklyn Ferry.  Whitman.
Give Me Splendid Silent Sun.  Whitman.
Give My Regards to Broadway.  Cohan.
Hymn of the City.  Bryant.
I Awoke with the Room Cold.  Piercy.
Letter to N.Y.  Bishop.
Metropolitan Nightmare.  Benét.
Mouth of the Hudson, The.  Lowell.
My Sad Self.  Ginsberg.
New York Skyline.  Spinnanger.
Ode to the New York Mets.  Lindsay.
Review from Staten Island.  Oden.
Saturday in New York.  Beresford.
Sidewalks of New York, The.  Lawlor *and* Blake.
Sonnet: "Five A.M. on East Fourteenth I'm out to eat."  Clark.
Step Away from Them, A.  O'Hara.
Steps.  O'Hara.
Things to Do in New York (City).  Berrigan.
Tropics in New York, The.  McKay.
Under.  Bowering.
**Newark, New Jersey**
Newark, for Now (68).  Rodgers.
**News**
Ten O'Clock News.  Ortiz.
**Newspapers**
After the Last Bulletin.  Wilbur.
Country Press.  Dobson.
Depression.  Witherup.
Editor Whedon.*Fr.* Spoon River Anthology.  Masters.

Headline History.  Plomer.
You cannot hope.  Wolfe.
**Newton, Sir Isaac**
Intended for Sir Isaac Newton in Westminster Abbey.  Pope.
**Niagara Falls**
Niagara.  Braun.
Niagara Falls Nocturne.  Gasparini.
**Night**
Acquainted with the Night.  Frost.
Auld Daddy Darkness.  Ferguson.
Children of Night.  Shelton.
Day Is Done, The.  Longfellow.
Domination of Black.  Stevens.
Driving to Town Late to Mail a Letter.  Bly.
Evening.  Doolittle ("H.D.")
Four Glimpses of Night.  Davis.
Hymn to the Evening, An.  Wheatley.
Hymn to the Night.  Longfellow.
Midnight.  Lampman.
Moonlit Apples.  Drinkwater.
Night.*Fr.* Songs of Innocence.  Blake.
Night.  Radcliffe.
Night, The ("Through that pure Virgin-shrine").  Vaughan.
Night and Sleep.  Patmore.
Night Clouds.  A. Lowell.
Night Is Darkening Round Me, The.  E. Brontë.
Night-Piece, A.  Wordsworth.
Night Sounds.*Fr.* Blunt, Master Constable.  Middleton.
Night Will Never Stay, The.  Farjeon.
Nocturnal Reverie, The.  Countess of Winchelsea.
Nocturnal Sketch, A.  Hood.
Nocturne: "Three-toed tree toad, The."  Guiterman.
Now Winter Nights Enlarge.  Campion.
Pine Tree Tops.  Snyder.
Puck's Night Song.*Fr.* A Midsummer Night's Dream.  Shakespeare.
She is the night: all horror of her.*Fr.* Lilith.  Brennan.
Short Night, The.  Buson.
Sound of Night, The.  Kumin.
Spring Night.  Su Tung-P'o.
Still Life.  Whittemore.
Sun has long been set, The.  Wordsworth.
To Night.  Shelley.
To Night.  *Unknown.*
To Night.  White.
Winter Night, A.  Barnes.
You, Andrew Marvell.  MacLeish.
**Nightingale**
Happy Nightingale, The.  *Unknown.*
Nightingale, The.  Coleridge.
Nightingales.  Bridges.
Ode to a Nightingale.  Keats.
Owl Against Nightingale.  *Unknown.*
Philomel.  Barnfield.
Philomela.  Arnold.
Philomela.  Ransom.
Philomela.  Sidney.
To the Nightingale.  Coleridge.
To the Nightingale.  Countess of Winchelsea.
**Nile (river)**
Nile, The.  Hunt.
To the Nile.  Keats.
**Noah**
And Did the Animals?  Van Doren.
Animals in the Ark, The.  *Unknown.*
Ballad of Mrs. Noah, The.  Duncan.
Hammer, Ring.  *Unknown.*
History of the Flood, The.  Heath-Stubbs.
In Noah's Wake.  Block.
Noah's Ark.  Young.
Parley of Beasts.  "MacDiarmid."
Still, Citizen Sparrow.  Wilbur.

**Norfolk, England**
Coast: Norfolk, The.  Cornford.
**North Dakota**
North Dakota Gothic.  Vinz.
**North Pole**
90 North.  Jarrell.
Polar Exploration.  Spender.
**Northwest Passage**
Looking for Asia.  Dillard.
**Noses**
"Dorset Nose,"The.  Sansom.
Hairs in My Nose, The.  Boyajian.
Of Tyndarus.  *Unknown.*
**Nostalgia**
Ballad of Dead Yankees, The.  Petersen.
Fifties, The.  Sadoff.
Miniver Cheevy.  Robinson.
Old Furniture.  Hardy.
Old Ruralities.  Turner.
Old-fashioned Pitcher, The.  Phair.
One day when I was a child, long ago.  Paley.
Piano.  Lawrence.
TKO.  Peck.
Tropics in New York, The.  McKay.
**November**
Late November in a Field.  Wright.
November.  Clare.
November.*Fr.* Sonnets on the Seasons.  H. Coleridge.
November.  Harvey.
November.  Tuckerman.
November Through a Giant Copper Beech.  Honig.
**Nuclear War**
Canticle of the Rose, The.  Sitwell.
Earth.  Wheelock.
Fall 1961.  Lowell.
Fifteen Million Plastic Bags.  Mitchell.
Horses, The.  Muir.
I Saw an Army.  Abbe.
Mother the Wardrobe Is Full of Infantrymen.  McGough.
Relative Sadness.  Rowbotham.
Song about Major Eatherly, A.  Wain.
What Have They Done to the Rain?  Reynolds.
Your Attention Please.  Porter.
*See also* **Atomic Bombs.**
**Nudity**
Naked and the Nude, The.  Graves.
Nude Descending a Staircase.  Kennedy.
**Nuns**
Ballad of a Nun, A.  Davidson.
Convent, The.  O'Sullivan.
Felixstowe, or The Last of Her Order.  Betjeman.
Heaven-Haven.  Hopkins.
Holding Pattern.  McPherson.
Mother Rosarine.  Kumin.
Nuns at Eve.  Brinnin.
On Christ's Birth (To Sisters).  Luecke.
Wreck of the *Deutschland*, The.  Hopkins.
**Nurses**
Night Duty.  MacKenzie.
Rivalry.  Nowlan.

**O**

**Oak Trees**
Bearded Oaks.  Warren.
I Saw in Louisiana a Live-Oak Growing.  Whitman.
Oak, The.  Tennyson.
**Oases**

Green, Green is El Aghir.  Cameron.
**Ocean.**  *See* **Sea.**
**O'Connor, Flannery**
  Flannery O'Connor.  Walters.
**O'Connor, Frank**
  Light Dying.  Kennelly.
**October**
  Impulse of October, The.  Moses.
  October Dawn.  Hughes.
  October 1954.  Boyle.
  Poem in October.  Thomas.
  Poppies in October.  Plath.
**Octopuses**
  Octopus.  Hilton.
  Octopus.  Reavin.
  Underwater.  Schmidt.
**Odin**
  Descent of Odin, The; an Ode from the Norse Tongue.  Gray.
**Odysseus.**  *See* **Ulysses.**
**Oklahoma**
  Captive Stone, The.  Barnes.
**Old Age**
  Acre of Grass, An.  Yeats.
  Age.  Landor.
  Almswomen.  Blunden.
  Ancient to Ancients, An.  Hardy.
  Angry Old Men.  Payne.
  Aunt Alice in April.  Matchett.
  Bean Eaters, The.  Brooks.
  Broken Dreams.  Yeats.
  But I Am Growing Old and Indolent.  Jeffers.
  Childhood.  Wolfe.
  Coming of Wisdom with Time, The.  Yeats.
  Complaint.  Hamilton.
  Conversation.  Giovanni.
  Crabbed Age and Youth.  *Unknown.*
  Crows, The.  Bogan.
  Crowsfeet Splaying Round His Eyes.  Lloyd-Evans.
  Cry of an Aged One, The.  Fraser.
  Dear Men and Women.  Wheelock.
  Death of a Vermont Farm Woman.  Howes.
  Do Not Go Gentle into That Good Night.  Thomas.
  Envy the Old.  Van Doren.
  Fair Isle Pattern.  Rankin.
  Father William.*Fr.* Alice's Adventure in Wonderland.  "Carroll."
  Fountain, The.  Wordsworth.
  George.  Randall.
  Gold Leaves.  Chesterton.
  Grandfathers, The.  Justice.
  Growing Old.  Arnold.
  Growing Old.*Fr.* Don Juan.  Byron.
  Heavy, Heavy — What Hangs Over?  Burke.
  His Golden Locks Time Hath to Silver Turned.*Fr.* Polyhymnia.  Peele.
  How to Be Old.  Swenson.
  I'm Here.*Fr.* Meditations of an Old Woman.  Roethke.
  "I'm 92," Joe said.  Weber.
  I Saw from the Beach.  Moore.
  Ice, The.  Gibson.
  Imperialists in Retirement.  Lucie-Smith.
  Invisible Man, The.  Matthews.
  John Anderson, My Jo.  Burns.
  Lament of the Old Woman of Beare, The.  *Unknown.*
  Lamentation of the Old Pensioner, The.  Yeats.
  Last Leaf, The.  Holmes.
  Letter from a Girl to Her Own Old Age, A.  Meynell.
  Light and Dark.  Howes.
  Little Old Women, The.  Baudelaire.
  Mad Poem Addressed to My Nephews and Nieces, A.  Po Chu-i.
  Missing Dates.  Empson.

  Moccasins of an Old Man, The.  Carden.
  Model T.  Stoutenburg.
  Moonlight.  Teasdale.
  90th Year, The.  Levertov.
  Niño Leading an Old Man to Market.  Nathan.
  Norfolk.  Betjeman.
  Nursing Home.  Parker-Silverman.
  Of the Last Verses in the Book.  Waller.
  Old Age.  Cummings.
  Old Black Men.  Johnson.
  Old Couple, The.  Green.
  Old Folks Home.  Hennen.
  Old Jockey, The.  Higgins.
  Old Lady's Lament For Her Youth, The.  Villon.
  Old Man, Phantom Dog.  Eckman.
  Old Man's Comforts and How He Gained Them, The.  Southey.
  Old Man's Winter Night, An.  Frost.
  Old Men.  Nash.
  Old Men Admiring Themselves in the Water, The.  Yeats.
  Old Mother turns blue and from us.  Niedecker.
  Old Pensioner, The.  Yeats.
  Old People.  Livingston.
  Old Wife in High Spirits.  "MacDiarmid."
  Old Woman, The.  Campbell.
  Old Woman.  Jennings.
  Old Woman.  Smith.
  Old Woman Awaiting the Greyhound Bus.  Niatum.
  Old woman sits, The.  Davis.
  On His Seventy-Fifth Birthday.*Fr.* The Last Fruit off an Old Tree.  Landor.
  On Living Too Long.  Landor.
  One Flesh.  Jennings.
  Phone Call to Rutherford.  Blackburn.
  Provide, Provide.  Frost.
  Sair Fyel'd, Hinny.  *Unknown.*
  Senile.  Folk.
  Seventy.  Reynolds.
  Sex and the Over Forties.  Porter.
  She, to Him.  Hardy.
  Silver Threads among the Gold.  Rexford.
  Simon Lee.  Wordsworth.
  Something Like an Apple.  Reiss.
  Song for September.  Fitzgerald.
  Song of a Woman Abandoned by the Tribe.  *Unknown.*
  Spur, The.  Yeats.
  Strokes.  Stafford.
  Survival.  Greenberg.
  Tarzan, Old.  Block.
  Terminus.  Emerson.
  Three Old Brothers.  O'Connor.
  To Age.  Landor.
  To an Old Lady.  Empson.
  To My Ninth Decade.  Landor.
  To Waken an Old Lady.  Williams.
  Very Old Woman, A.  Eshleman.
  Veteran Sirens.  Robinson.
  Warning.  Joseph.
  Weeksville Women.  Loftin.
  When You and I Were Young Maggie.  Johnson.
  When You Are Old.  Yeats.
  Young and Old.*Fr.* The Water Babies.  Kingsley.
  Youth and Age.  Coleridge.
**Old Ironsides.**  *See* **Constitution (ship).**
**Oldham, John**
  To the Memory of Mr. Oldham.  Dryden.
**O'Leary, Arthur**
  Lament for Arthur O'Leary.  O'Connell.
**Olson, Charles**
  From Gloucester Out.  Dorn.
**O'Neill, Owen Roe**
  Lament for the Death of Eoghan Ruadh O'Neill.  Davis.

**O'Neill, Shane**
  Shane O'Neill's Cairn.   Jeffers.
**Onions**
  Onyons.*Fr.* Market Women's Cries.   Swift.
**Opals**
  Opal.   Miles.
**Opera**
  Matinees.   Merrill.
**Ophelia**
  Ophelia's Song.   Zaturenska.
**Opossums**
  Possum Tree, The.   Gough.
**Optimism**
  Pangloss's Song.   Wilbur.
  When the clouds' swoln bosoms echo back the shouts.*Fr.* In
    Tenebris.   Hardy.
**Oracles**
  Oracles, The.   Housman.
**O'Rahilly, Egan**
  Egan O Rahilly.   O'Rahilly.
**Oranges**
  Orange Tree Dream.   Serin.
  Smudging.   Wakoski.
**Orchards**
  Through Ruddy Orchards.   Oliver.
**Orchids**
  Orchids.   Roethke.
**Original Sin**
  Fall, The: a Song.   Earl of Rochester.
**Orion (constellation)**
  Orion.   Rich.
**Orphans**
  Child's Umbrella, The.   Souster.
  Little Oprhant Annie.   Riley.
  Motherless Children.   *Unknown.*
  Orphans.   Ray.
**Orpheus**
  Ballad of Orpheus, A.   Lindsay.
  Orpheus.   Winters.
  Orpheus in Greenwich Village.   Gilbert.
  Thus sung Orpheus to his strings.   *Unknown.*
**Ostriches**
  He "Digesteth Harde Yron."   Moore.
**Othello**
  At the Theatre.   Williams.
**Otter (river), Devon, England**
  Sonnet to the River Otter.   Coleridge.
**Otterburn, Battle**
  Battle of Otterbourne, The.   *Unknown.*
  Chevy Chase.   *Unknown.*
**Otters**
  Lutra, the Fisher.   McMichael.
  Otter, An.   Hughes.
  Otters.   Hart-Smith.
  River-Mates.   Colum.
**Outlaws.**   *See* **Crime and Criminals.**
**Ovenbirds**
  Oven Bird, The.   Frost.
**Ovid (Publius Ovidius Naso)**
  Near the Death of Ovid.   Conquest.
**Owls**
  Barn Owl.*Fr.* Father and Child.   Harwood.
  Bird of Night, The.   Jarrell.
  Great Brown Owl, The.   Browne.
  If the Owl Calls Again.   Haines.
  Owl.   MacBeth.
  Owl, The.   Sackville-West.
  Owl, The.   Tennyson.
  Owl, The.   Thomas.
  Owl Against Nightingale.   *Unknown.*
  Owl and the Pussy-Cat, The.   Lear.
  Owl Critic, The.   Fields.

  Owl Seen In Rearview Mirror.   Niatum.
  Owls.   Snodgrass.
  Prayer to the Snowy Owl.   Haines.
  Questioning Faces.   Frost.
  Tree Animals.   Lieberman.
  Wring the Swan's Neck.   Martínez.
**Oxen**
  Beasts Are Very Wise, The.   Kipling.
  I Have Twelve Oxen.   *Unknown.*
  Oxen, The.   Hardy.
  Oxen: Ploughing at the Fiesole.   Tomlinson.
  Recantation Illustrated in the Story of the Mad Ox.   Coleridge.
**Oxford, England**
  Duns Scotus's Oxford.   Hopkins.
  Oxford Canal.   Flecker.
  Town Against Gown at Oxford.   Robert of Gloucester.
**Oysters**
  Oystering.   Howard.

## P

**Pacific Ocean**
  Eye, The.   Jeffers.
  Facing West from California's Shores.   Whitman.
  Once by the Pacific.   Frost.
  Prayer to the Pacific.   Silko.
  Slow Pacific Swell, The.   Winters.
**Pacifism and Pacifists**
  Advent 1966.   Levertov.
  Conscientious Objector.   Millay.
  Dooley Is a Traitor.   Michie.
  For the Minority.   Peterson.
  For the One Who Would Take Man's Life in His Hands.
    Schwartz.
  I Sing of Olaf Glad and Big.   Cummings.
  Memories of West Street and Lepke.   Lowell.
**Paganism**
  Plain of Adoration, The.   *Unknown.*
**Paige, Leroy ("Satchel")**
  To Satch.   Allen.
**Pain**
  After great pain, a formal feeling comes.   Dickinson.
  Flower, The.   Creeley.
  For Kenneth Patchen.   Miller.
  Horrors, The.   Nash.
  My Knees Go before the Firing Squad at Dawn.   Wakoski.
  Pain — has an element of blank.   Dickinson.
  Prayer from a Stryker Frame.   Clarkson.
  Thoughts on Pain.   Chesham.
  Two Founts, The.   Coleridge.
  Villanelle: "It is the pain, it is the pain, endures."   Empson.
**Paine, Thomas**
  Citizen Paine.   Daugherty.
  Epigram: "In digging up your bones, Tom Paine."   Byron.
**Painting and Painters**
  At an Exhibition of Historical Paintings, Hobart.   Smith.
  Backgrounds to Italian Paintings: Fifteenth Century.   Ridler.
  Dance, The.   Williams.
  Giovanni da Fiesole on the Sublime; or, Fra Angelico's "Last
    Judgement."   Howard.
  In Goya's Greatest Scenes.*Fr.* A Coney Island of the Mind.
    Ferlinghetti.
  Landscape with Pervert.   Noll.
  On a Painting by Patient B of the Independence State Hospital
    for the Insane.   Justice.
  Still Life.   Dobson.
  Ultimate Antientropy, The.   Weiss.
  Why I Am Not a Painter.   O'Hara.

**Palm Trees**
Royal Palm.  Crane.
**Pan (god)**
Hymn of Pan.  Shelley.
Hymn to Pan.*Fr.* The Faithful Shepherdess.  Fletcher.
Musical Instrument, A.  E. Browning.
Pan.  Emerson.
**Pandas**
Panda, The.*Fr.* Animals That Stand in Dreams.  Elliott.
**Parachuting**
Drop.  MacBeth.
**Paradise.**  *See* **Heaven.**
**Paranoia**
Dossier, The.  McMahon.
Paranoia.  Browne.
Tryst.  Merriam.
Tunnel, The.  Strand.
**Parenthood**
And How It Goes.  Hollo.
At the Washing of My Son.  Su Tung P'o.
Bring a Child Flowers.  Tarn.
Childless.  MacNamee.
Children, The.  Urdang.
For a Child Expected.  Ridler.
For My Son on the Highways of His Mind.  Kumin.
Goodnight, The.  Simpson.
Heart's Needle.  Snodgrass.
Journal for My Daughter.  Kunitz.
Lost Children, The.  Jarrell.
Man Who Finds That His Son Has Become a Thief, The.
    Souster.
On Giving a Son to the Sea.  Dickey.
She's Leaving Home.  Lennon *and* McCartney.
Sitting Here.  Creeley.
Sons, *sel.* Lubeck.
What My Child Learns of the Sea.  Lorde.
Wheel Revolves, The.  Rexroth.
**Paris, France**
Four Sheets to the Wind.  Rivers.
Mourning Letter from Paris, A.  Rivers.
Paris.  Young.
**Parker, Charlie**
"Bird Lives": Charles Parker in St. Louis.  Harper.
Sidewalk Restoration.  Ikan.
Walking Parker Home.  Kaufman.
Yardbird's Skull.  Dodson.
**Parks**
Central Park Tourney.  Weston.
Definition of Nature.  Redmond.
Fountain in the Park, The.  Haley.
In Golden Gate Park that day.*Fr.* A Coney Island of the Mind.
    Ferlinghetti.
On the Fine Arts Garden, Cleveland.  Atkins.
Public Gardens, The.  Lewis.
St. John's Park.  McAuley.
Umbaji Park.  Kherdian.
**Parodies**
*Faber Book of Comic Verse, The* (FaBoCo).  Michael Roberts *and*
Janet Adam Smith, eds.
*Speak Roughly to Your Little Boy* (SpRo).  Myra Cohn Livingston,
ed.
*See also*  **the special parody sections in:** *Poetry and Its Conventions*
(PAIC).  Frederick R. Lapides *and* John T. Shawcross, eds.
**Parrots**
Little Miss and Her Parrot.  Marchant.
Obituary.  Kees.
Parrot, The.  Lucie-Smith.
Poor Poll.  Bridges.
Sailor to His Parrot, The.  Davies.
Who Killed Lawless Lean?  Smith.
**Parties**
Saturday Night.  Moxley.

**Parthenon**
On Seeing the Elgin Marbles.  Keats.
**Partridges**
Partridges.  Masefield.
**Patience**
Patience.  Horne.
Patience, Hard Thing.  Hopkins.
**Patriotic Songs, American**
America.  Smith.
America the Beautiful.  Bates.
Army Goes Rolling Along, The.  Gruber and Arberg.
Battle-Cry of Freedom, The.  Root.
Battle-Hymn of the Republic.  Howe.
Bunker Hill.  Niles.
Chester.  Billings.
God Bless America.  Berlin.
Hail, Columbia.  Hopkinson.
Liberty Song, The.  J. Dickinson.
Marines' Hymn, The.  *Unknown.*
Pledge to the Flag, The.  Bellamy.
Star-spangled Banner, The.  Key.
Tenting Tonight.  Kittredge.
Tramp! Tramp! Tramp!  Root.
When Johnny Comes Marching Home.  Gilmore.
Yankee Doodle Boy, The.  Cohan.
**Patriotic Songs, Canadian**
Maple Leaf Forever, The.  Muir.
O Canada!  Weir.
**Patriotic Songs, Confederate**
Bonnie Blue Flag, The.  Macarthy.
Dixie.  Emmett.
Dixie (Battle-Hymn).  Pike.
Maryland, My Maryland!  Randall.
**Patriotic Songs, English**
God Save the King.  *At. to* Carey.
Rule Britannia.*Fr.* Alfred, a Masque.  Thomson.
**Patriotic Songs, French**
La Marseillaise.  De Lisle.
**Patriotic Songs, Scottish**
Campbells are Comin', The.  *Unknown.*
**Patriotism**
As One Non-Combatant to Another.  Orwell.
Barbara Frietchie.  Whittier.
Columbia.  *Unknown.*
Dulce et Decorum Est.  Owen.
Great men have been among us; hands that penned.
    Wordsworth.
Hail, Columbia.  Hopkinson.
Homes of England, The.  Hemans.
Long Voyage, The.  Cowley.
Pat's Opinion of Flags.  Brooks.
Sussex.  Kipling.
These Fought in Any Case.*Fr.* Hugh Selwyn Mauberley.
    Pound.
This Is My Own, My Native Land.*Fr.* The Lay of the Last
    Minstrel.  Scott.
To the Men of Kent, October, 1803.  Wordsworth.
Yankee Doodle Boy, The.  Cohan.
*Breathes There the Man* (BTTM).  Frank S. Meyer, ed.
**Paul, Saint**
Saul, Afterward Riding East.  Brinnin.
**Pawnbrokers**
Pawnbroker, The.  Kumin.
**Peace**
At the Un-National Monument along the Canadian Border.
    Stafford.
Legend of Versailles, A.  Tolson.
On Peace.  Keats.
Peace.  Jonas.
Peace, So That.  Kuzma.
**Peacocks**
Domination of Black.  Stevens.

What is it more eyes doth wear.  *Unknown.*
**Pear Trees**
Pear Tree.  Doolittle ("H.D.").
Study of Two Pears.  Stevens.
**Peasants**
Exiles.  "AE."
**Peeping Toms**
Fiend, The.  Dickey.
**Pegasus**
Pegasus.  Kavanagh.
**Pelicans**
Frigate Pelican, The.  Moore.
Pelican, The.  Kuzma.
**Pembroke, Mary Sidney Herbert, Countess of**
On the Death of Mary, Countess of Pembroke.  Browne.
**Penelope (mythology)**
Ancient Gesture, An.  Millay.
Penelope.  Gilmore.
World as Meditation, The.  Stevens.
**Penguins**
View from Here, The.  Stafford.
**Penshurst, England**
To Penshurst.  Jonson.
**Persephone**
Garden of Proserpine, The.  Swinburne.
Kore.  Creeley.
Persephone.  Duncan.
**Pessimism**
Pessimist, The.  King.
Said Hanrahan.  Hartigan.
World's a Bubble, The.  Bacon.
**Peterloo Massacre**
Mask of Anarchy, The.  Shelley.
Song: To the Men of England.  Shelley.
Sonnet: England in 1819.
**Pets**
Ode of Odium on Aquariums.  Guiterman.
Pet Shop.  MacNeice.
**Pheasants**
Pheasant, The.  Coffin.
**Philately**
Philatelist Royal.  Graves.
**Philippine Islands**
On a Soldier Fallen in the Philippines.  Moody.
White Man's Burden, The.  Kipling.
**Philosophy and Philosophers**
Alexander and the Gymnosophists.  *Unknown.*
Epistemology.  Wilbur.
Ignorance of Death.  Empson.
Maya.  Robinson.
Metaphysical Amorist, The.  Cunningham.
Mock On, Mock On, Voltaire, Rousseau.  Blake.
Moralists, The.  Winters.
On the Death of a Metaphysician.  Santayana.
Philosopher and the Lover to a Mistress Dying, The.
    Davenant.
Reading and Talking.  Zukofsky.
This, That & the Other.  Nemerov.
Variation on Heraclitus.  MacNeice.
Words.  Glen.
**Phoenix**
About the Phoenix.  Merrill.
Phoenix, The.  Cunningham.
**Photographs**
Lines on a Young Lady's Photograph Album.  Larkin.
Mementos, I.  Snodgrass.
Old Photographs.  Harsent.
Photo, The.  Bruce.
Photograph.  Prettyman.
**Physicians**
Arthur Ridgewood, M.D.  Davis.
Bed, The.  Hope.

Better Way, The.  Leaf.
Correct Compassion, A.  Kirkup.
Doctor Black.  Blight.
Doctor Who Sits at the Bedside of a Rat, The.  Miles.
Football.  Mason.
MD Sewed Wrong Section of Colon.  Scott.
My Friend, The Doctor.  Abbe.
On Dr. Isaac Letsome.  *Unknown.*
On the Death of Dr. Robert Levet.  Johnson.
Scientist, The.  Burroway.
**Pianos**
Old Upright I Did Not Learn to Play, The.  Flocos.
Piano.  Lawrence.
**Picasso, Pablo**
"Portrait de Femme."  Feldman.
**Pickles**
Meditation for a Pickle Suite.  Dillard.
**Picnics**
Georgia Dusk.  Toomer.
Picnic, The.  Logan.
Picnic: The Liberated.  Holman.
**Piedmont, Italy**
On the Late Massacre in Piedmont.  Milton.
**Pigeons**
Fly.  Merwin.
Pigeons.  Kell.
Wild Oats.  MacCaig.
**Pigs**
Animals Are Passing from Our Lives.  Levine.
Blood.  Murray.
Ego.  Siegel.
Lady Who Loved a Swine, The.  *Unknown.*
Laughing Faces of Pigs, The.  Lape.
Little Piggy.  Hood.
Little Pigs Lie in the Best of Straw.  *Unknown.*
Pigs.  Cotton.
Sow.  Plath.
Three Little Pigs, The.  Gatty.
View of a Pig.  Hughes.
**Pike**
Pike.  Hughes.
**Pilgrim Fathers**
Landing of the Pilgrim Fathers in New England, The.
    Hemans.
Pilgrim Fathers, The.  Pierpont.
**Pilgrims and Pilgrimages**
Passionate Mans Pilgrimage, The.  Ralegh.
Pilgrimage, The.  Herbert.
**Pindar**
Praise of Pindar, The.  Horace.
**Pine Trees**
At Torrey Pines State Park.  Mazzaro.
Developing Curious Survival Patterns Against Winter Saltwinds,
    The.  Lifshin.
Hunchback Pine.  Russell.
My Cathedral.  Longfellow.
Pine Assessor, The.  Baker.
**Pioneers**
Boys of Sanpete County, The.  *Unknown.*
Handcart Song, The.  *Unknown.*
Once I Lived in Cottonwood.  *Unknown.*
Pioneer, The.  Ruggles.
St. George.  Walker.
Sioux Indians, The.  *Unknown.*
Sweet Betsy from Pike.  *Unknown.*
Tittery-Irie-Aye.  *Unknown.*
**Pirates and Piracy**
Bounty.  Miles.
Captain Kidd.  *Unknown.*
*Flying Cloud,* The.  *Unknown.*
Salcombe Seaman's Flaunt to the Proud Pirate, The.  *Unknown.*
Sir Andrew Barton.  *Unknown.*

Tarry Buccaneer, The. Masefield.
Teach the Rover. *Unknown.*
Wild Barbaree, The. *Unknown.*

**Pisa, Italy**
Evening: Ponte a Mare, Pisa. Shelley.

**Pitt, William**
Epitaph for William Pitt. Byron.

**Pity**
Expostulation, An. Bickerstaffe.
Ode to Pity. Collins.
Pity. Mills.

**Place Names**
Yankee Cradle. Coffin.

**Plague**
Coming of the Plague, The. Kees.

**Plants**
Cuttings ("Sticks-in-a-drowse droop over sugary loam").
   Roethke.
Cuttings ("This urge, wrestle, resurrection of dry sticks").
   Roethke.
Giant Decorative Dahlia. Holden.
La Condition Botanique. Hecht.
Moss-Gathering. Roethke.
Old Man. Thomas.
Root Cellar. Roethke.
Seed Leaves. Wilbur.
Seedlings in the Mail. Piercy.
*See also* **Flowers, Trees,** *etc.*

**Plath, Sylvia**
After Reading Sylvia Plath. Alta.
Bitter Pills for the Dark Ladies. Jong.
Closer First to Earth. Hazlewood-Brady.
In Sylvia Plath Country. Jong.
Sylvia's Death. Sexton.
Your face broods from my table, Suicide. Berryman.

**Plato**
Plato. Duguid.

**Platonic Love**
La Belle Confidante. Stanley.

**Platonism**
Idea, The. Made of Alnwick, in His Expedition to Scotland with
   the Army, 1639. Herbert.
No Platonic Love. Cartwright.
Platonic Love. Herbert.

**Platypuses**
Old Man Platypus. Paterson.

**Play**
Romping. Ciardi.

**Plum Trees**
Plum Gatherer, The. Millay.
This Is Just to Say. Williams.

**Plumbing and Plumbers**
Elegy for Alfred Hubbard. Connor.

**Po Chu -i**
As I Step Over a Puddle at the End of Winter, I Think of an
   Ancient Chinese Governor. Wright.

**Poaching and Poachers**
Lincolnshire Poacher, The. *Unknown.*
Poaching in Excelsis. Menzies.

**Poe, Edgar Allan**
Fall of the House of Usher, The. Whittemore.
Poe and Longfellow.*Fr.* A Fable for Critics. Lowell.

**Poetry and Poets**
Acrophobe and Lapidary. Bonk.
Adam's Curse. Yeats.
Ah. Kuzma.
All Things Can Tempt Me. Yeats.
American Poetry. Simpson.
American Saturday Afternoon. Ikan.
And Thus in Nineveh. Pound.
Another. Prior.
Apologia Pro Vita Sua. Coleridge.

Apology: "Simplicity assuages." Cunningham.
Apology for Apostasy? Knight.
Appology, The. Countess of Winchilsea.
Ars Poetica. MacLeish.
Arthur Ridgewood, M.D. Davis.
As One Non-Combatant to Another. Orwell.
At Poetry Workshop, Winter Semester. Martin.
At the "Atlantic" Dinner. Holmes.
Author to Her Book, The. Bradstreet.
Ballad Maker, A. Colum.
Ballade of Prose and Rhyme, The. Dobson.
Bard. Everson.
Bell Too Heavy to Ring. Kryss.
Betjeman, 1984. Causley.
Beware: Do Not Read This Poem. Reed.
Bitter Pills for the Dark Ladies. Jong.
Black Art. Jones.
Bookshop Idyll, A. Amis.
Breakthrough. Rodgers.
British Leftish Poetry, 1930-40. "MacDiarmid."
By Rail Through Istria. Conquest.
Catch. Francis.
Choice, The. Yeats.
Choice of Weapons, A. Kunitz.
Circus Animals' Desertion, The. Yeats.
Coat, A. Yeats.
Codicil. Walcott.
Colophon for Lan-t'ing Hsiu-Hsi. Peck.
Come, Said My Soul. Whitman.
Comparison of the Sonnet and the Epigram. Harington.
Constantly risking absurdity.*Fr.* A Coney Island of the Mind.
   Ferlinghetti.
Correspondence School Instructor Says Goodbye to his Poetry
   Students, The. Kinnell.
Craftsmen. Sackville-West.
Cycle, A. Leax.
Dance for Militant Dilettantes, A. Young.
Digging. Heaney.
Discontents in Devon. Herrick.
Distant Drum, The. Hernton.
Eating Poetry. Strand.
Echoes. Lazarus.
Egg Boiler, The. Brooks.
Elegy for a Nature Poet. Nemerov.
Elegy in a Presbyterian Burying-Ground. Wilson.
Emerson.*Fr.* A Fable for Critics. Lowell.
Enamoured of the Miniscule. Hartnett.
Epigram on Miltonicks. Wesley.
Epistle from Mr. Pope to Dr. Abuthnot, An. Pope.
Epitaph: "Here lies a poet, briefly known as Hecht." Hecht.
Esthetique du Machiavel. Starbuck.
Every critic in the town. Murray.
Exhortation, An. Shelley.
Fashionable Poet Reading. Connor.
Father, The. O'Grady.
First Steps up Parnassus.*Fr.* To My Most Dearly Loved Henry
   Reynolds. Drayton.
Fit of Rime Against Rime, A. Jonson.
For Black Poets Who Think of Suicide. Knight.
For J. A. R. McKellar. Lehmann.
For My Contemporaries. Cunningham.
For Poets. Young.
For Saundra. Giovanni.
For Some Poets. Jackson.
Foreword to New Numbers. Logue.
Fragment, The. Belloc.
Fragment: "Where's the poet? Show him! Show him!" Keats.
Fresh Air. Koch.
Gesture. Finkel.
Gift, The. Lourie.
Had I the Choice. Whitman.
Hands. Finkel.

Hebrew of Your Poets, Zion, The.   Reznikoff.
Hendecasyllabics.   Tennyson.
Hexameters.   Coleridge.
High-Toned Old Christian Woman, A.   Stevens.
Holding Pattern.   McPherson.
Holy Office, The.   Joyce.
I Am Raftery.   Raftery.
I Am 25.   Corso.
I don't bother with rhymes.   Caeiro.
I Know I'm Not Sufficiently Obscure.   Durem.
I polish, cook or clean my nest.   Holsapple.
I reckon when I count at all.   Dickinson.
I Would Like to Describe.   Herbert.
I would not paint a picture.   Dickinson.
If it is a poem.   Duguid.
Illustrious Ancestors.   Levertov.
In a Spring Still Not Written Of.   Wallace.
In Defense of Black Poets.   Rivers.
In My Craft or Sullen Art.   Thomas.
In the great snowfall before the bomb.   Niedecker.
Instruction from Bly.   Macdonald.
Introduction, The.   Countess of Winchilsea.
Invocation: "Ten bloody years with this quill lying."
   Iremonger.
Israfel.   Poe.
It is difficult now to speak of poetry.*Fr.* Of Being Numerous.
   Oppen.
Jacob's Ladder, The.   Levertov.
Jordan ("Who says that fictions only and false hair.").   Herbert.
Journey of a Poem Compared to All the Sad Variety of Travel,
   The.   Schwartz.
Kidnap Poem.   Giovanni.
Ladies and gentlemen/ This is our final word.*Fr.* Manifesto.
   Parra.
Lake Isle, The.   Pound.
Lamentations of an Au Pair Girl.   Feldman.
Laureate, The.   Graves.
Let Me Tell You.   Williams.
Let Us Honor Them.   Owens.
Letter to a Friend.   Stallworthy.
Letter to an American Visitor.   Comfort.
Lines Written in Ridicule of Certain Poems Published in 1777.
   Johnson.
Loneliness.   Young.
Loss of Black Camels, The.   Hamod.
Love and Poetry.   Simpson.
Love the Wild Swan.   Jeffers.
Makers, The.   Kell.
Metre Columbian, The.   *Unknown.*
Metrical Feet.   Coleridge.
Milton by Firelight.   Snyder.
Modern Poetry.   Skeen.
Moon.   Walcott.
Most Days.   Ritchie.
Muse, The.   Spacks.
Muse of Amergin, The.   *Unknown.*
My Olson Elegy.   Feldman.
My Poem.   Hewell.
My Poetry.   Takamura.
My Son, Forsake Your Art.   O'Heffernan.
Nameless One, The.   Mangan.
New Poem, The.   Wright.
New Poet Arrives, A.   Ewart.
New Simile in the Manner of Swift, A.   Goldsmith.
Newly Pressed Suit, The.   McGough.
Not marble, nor the gilded monuments.*Fr.* Sonnets.
   Shakespeare.
O Black and Unknown Bard.   Johnson.
O'Bruadair.   O'Bruadair.
Ode: "Bards of passion and of mirth."   Keats.
Ode: "We are the music-makers."   O'Shaughnessy.
Ode on the Poetical Character.   Collins.

Ode to Apollo.   Keats.
Ode to Himself, An.   Jonson.
Of English Verse.   Waller.
Of Modern Poetry.   Stevens.
On an Anniversary.   Synge.
On Learning to Play the Guitar.   Fraser.
On Reading Another Poet.   Brewster.
On Teaching the Youth.   Winters.
On the New Laureate.   *Unknown.*
On the Sonnet.   Keats.
Pact, A.   Pound.
Paradox.   Bennett.
Past Ruin'd Illion Helen Lives.   Landor.
Pegasus.   Kavanagh.
Petit, the Poet.*Fr.* Spoon River Anthology.   Masters.
Piping down the Valleys Wild.*Fr.* Songs of Innocence.   Blake.
Pitcher.   Francis.
Poem: "On getting a card."   Williams.
Poem about a Poem about a Poem.   Conquest.
Poem About Poems About Vietnam, A.   Stallworthy.
Poem moves down a page, A.   Meltzer.
Poem, or Beauty Hurts Mr. Vinal.   Cummings.
Poem: Rocket.   Ginsberg.
Poem That Took the Place of a Mountain, The.   Stevens.
Poem You Asked For, The.   Levis.
Poems.   Kelso.
Poems.   Severy.
Poet, A.   Hardy.
Poet.   Hilberry.
Poet, The.   Randolph.
Poet.   Siegel.
Poet.   Viereck.
Poet and the Rose, The.*Fr.* Fables.   Gay.
Poet in Need, A.   Heath-Stubbs.
Poet of One Mood, A.   Meynell.
Poetical Economy.   Graham.
Poetry.   Moore.
Poetry, a Natural Thing.   Duncan.
Poetry Is in the Darkness.   Boyajian.
Poetry of one the Russians call "a broad nature," The.*Fr.* The
   Kind of Poetry I Want.   "MacDiarmid."
Poetry Today.   Heath-Stubbs.
Poets Agree To Be Quiet by the Swamp, The   Wagoner.
Poets Hitchhiking on the Highway.   Corso.
Poet's Household, A.   Kizer.
Poets light but lamps, The.   Dickinson.
Poets of My Epoch.   Stark.
Poet's Progress, A.   Hamburger.
Poet's Wife, A.   A. Lowell.
Poet's Wife Makes Him a Door So He Can Find the Way
   Home, The.   Willard.
Preface.   Weiss.
Prelude: "Give us another poem, he said."   Kavanagh.
Prestidigitator, The.   Young.
Proem: "I love the old melodious lays."   Whittier.
Progress of Poesy, The.   Gray.
Prologue, The: "To sing of wars, of captains, and of kings."
   Bradstreet.
Reading and Talking.   Zukofsky.
Reading Walt Whitman.   Forbes.
Reason for Not Writing Orthodox Nature Poetry.   Wain.
Reasons for Music.   MacLeish.
Relish of the Muse, The.   Beaumont.
Said the Poet to the Analyst.   Sexton.
Sarasvati.   Stephens.
Sasha and the Poet.   Valentine.
Scottsboro, Too, Is Worth Its Song.   Cullen.
Secret, The.   Levertov.
Seven.   Parra.
Sharon Will Be No/Where on Nobody's Best-Selling List.
   Scott.
Singing Aloud.   Kizer.

Sisters, The.  A. Lowell.
Six Poets in Search of a Lawyer.  Hall.
Sleep and Poetry.  Keats.
Sometimes/ the poems.  Scott.
Song to Accompany the Bearer of Bad News.  Wagoner.
Song's Eternity.  Clare.
Sonnet: "Nuns fret not at their convent's narrow room." Wordsworth.
Sonnet, The ("Sonnet is a moment's monument, A").*Fr.* The House of Life.  D.G. Rossetti.
Sonnet, A: "Two voices are there: one is of the deep." Stephen.
Sonnets to Be Written from Prison.  Adamson.
Souster.  Fraser.
Spenser! a jealous honourer of thine.  Keats.
Spicer's Instant Poetry.  Reeves.
Spur, The.  Yeats.
Strike Among the Poets, A.  *Unknown.*
Survey of Literature.  Ransom.
Teacher of Poetry, The.  Packard.
Ten Definitions of Poetry.  Sandburg.
Terence, This Is Stupid Stuff.  Housman.
Terminus.  Emerson.
Thinking of You.  Lourie.
This was a poet — it is that.  Dickinson.
Thoughts from a Bottle.  Clark.
Throughout the World If It Were Sought.  Wyatt.
Tin Can, The.  Smith.
To a Poet, Who Would Have Me Praise Certain Bad Poets, Imitators of His and Mine.  Yeats.
To a Young Poet Who Fled.  Logan.
To an Athlete Turned Poet.  Meinke.
To Ireland in the Coming Times.  Yeats.
To My Brother George.  Keats.
To Poem.  Lifshin.
To the Mother from Scarsdale Who Asked About Publishing Her Daughter's Poems.  Bass.
To the Nightingale.  Countess of Winchilsea.
To the Reader.  Bowers.
To the Rt. Hon. the Lady C. Tufton.  Countess of Winchilsea.
To the Stone-Cutters.  Jeffers.
Today Is a Day of Great Joy.  Cruz.
Traditional Grammarian as Poet, The.  Hipple.
Ultimate Anthology.  Bell.
Up, up old Benedict, the bard who would.*Fr.* Six Reveilles to Match My Self-Indulgence.  Bentley.
Valentine for Marianne Moore, A.  Olson.
Variations: #21.  Stephens.
Verse: "What should we know."  Gogarty.
Very Like a Whale.  Nash.
Villanelle: "It's all a trick, quite easy when you know it." Skeat.
Visiting Poet.  Nims.
W. C. W.  Ray.
What the Chairman Told Tom.  Bunting.
Whats My Name If Not Everyone Elses.  Salinas.
When He Would Have His Verses Read.  Herrick.
Where Are the War Poets?  Day Lewis.
Why I Am Not a Painter.  O'Hara.
With Mercy for the Greedy.  Sexton.
Witness to Death.  Lattimore.
Word Drunk.  Harrison.
Words, The.  Wagoner.
Writing in England Now.  O'Connor.
Yes; I Write Verses.  Landor.
Yes the Secret Mind Whispers.  Young.
Yet Do I Marvel.  Cullen.
Young Poets.  Parra.
*See also  names of individual poets.*

**Poland**
Poland/1931.  Rothenberg.

**Policemen**

Definition for Blk/Children.  Sanchez.
Fish.  Levis.
Idiot, The.  Randall.
Knock on Wood.  Dumas.
Negro Hero.  Brooks.
P.C. Plod Versus the Dale St Dog Strangler.  McGough.
Southern Cop.  Brown.
Third Degree.  Hughes.
When Cotton Haymes Walks down the Street.  Brigham.
Who But the Lord?  Hughes.

**Politics and Politicians**
As a kid I believed in democracy: I.  Berryman.
As I strole the city, oft I.*Fr.* The Legion Club.  Swift.
Campaign, The.  Miles.
Dodger, The.  *Unknown.*
Hand That Signed the Paper, The.  Thomas.
Legend of Versailles, A.  Tolson.
Letter from a Candidate for the Presidency.*Fr.* The Biglow Papers.  Lowell.
Next to of course God America I.  Cummings.
On a General Election.  Belloc.
Politician, A.  Cummings.
Politics.  Yeats.
Similes for Two Political Characters of 1819.  Shelley.
Statesman, The.  Belloc.
To Antenor.  Philips.
Tory Pledges.  Moore.

**Pollock, Jackson**
Number 1 by Jackson Pollock (1948).  Sullivan.

**Pollution.**  *See* **Ecology.**

**Polo**
Polo Match.  Ciardi.

**Pompeii, Italy**
New Excavations.*Fr.* Pompeii.  Speyer.

**Ponds.**  *See* **Lakes and Ponds.**

**Pool (game)**
Kelley.  Hershon.
Pool-Shootin' Roy.  Runyon.

**Pope, Alexander**
Mr. Pope.  Tate.

**Poplar Trees**
Poplar-Field, The.  Cowper.
To a Late Poplar.  Kavanagh.

**Poppies**
Ode to the Poppy.  Oneil.

**Porcupines**
Kag the Porcupine (the Misanthrope).  Guiterman.
Pretty Murder.  MacLean.
Porcupine, The.  Kinnell.
Porcupine, The.  Nash.
Porcupines.  Huff.

**Port Jefferson, New York**
Port Jefferson.  Simpson.

**Portraits**
Dorothy Q.  Holmes.
Recollection, A.  Bishop.

**Ports.**  *See* **Harbors and Ports.**

**Poseidon.**  *See* **Neptune.**

**Potatoes**
Potato.  Wilbur.

**Pound, Ezra**
Ezra Pound.  Lowell.
Ezra Pound.  Price.
Ezra Pound.  Webb.
Ezry.  MacLeish.
Homage and Lament for Ezra Pound in Captivity.  Duncan.
On the Fly-Leaf of Pound's Cantos.  Bunting.

**Poverty**
Alice Fell.  Wordsworth.
Art thou poor, yet hast thou golden slumbers?*Fr.* The Pleasant Comedy of Patient Grissell.  Dekker.
Ballad of the Man Who's Gone.  Hughes.

Bean Eaters, The. Brooks.
City Life. Lawrence.
Come, live with me and be my love. Day Lewis.
Eugene Delacroix Says. Dorn.
Furnished Lives. Silkin.
Gleaner, The. Taylor.
Hard Time Killin' Floor Blues. *Unknown.*
Last of The Flock, The. Wordsworth.
Leaden-Eyed, The. Lindsay.
Miss Rosie. Clifton.
Moving through the Silent Crowd. Spender.
Nikki-Rosa. Giovanni.
No New Music. Crouch.
Orphan Girl, The. *Unknown.*
Poor, The. Williams.
Poor Girl's Meditation, The. *Unknown.*
Poor Man, The. *Unknown.*
Poverty. Simic.
Proletarian Portrait. Williams.
Rich and Poor. Hunt.
Rich and Poor; or, Saint and Sinner. Peacock.
Saturday's Child. Cullen.
Shoofly, The. O'Hare.
Street Window. Sandburg.
Thirty Bob a Week. Davidson.
Tin Cup Blues. *Unknown.*
Tinker's Wife. Kavanagh.
To a Fighter Killed in the Ring. Lipsitz.
To a Red-headed Do-good Waitress. Dugan.
To the Four Courts, Please. Stephens.
Winter. Synge.
Woman Poem. Giovanni.

**Prairies**
Nebraska. Swan.
Prairie Town. Stafford.
Prairies, The. Bryant.
Stories from Kansas. Stafford.
West of Chicago. Dimoff.

**Prayer**
After the Funeral of Assam Hamady. Hamod.
And yet hath prayer, the heav'n breathing foliage of faith.*Fr.*
   The Testament of Beauty. Bridges.
For the Woman Who Asked Me If I Believe in God and If I
   Pray. Wiegner.
Great God, let all by tuneful pow'rs. Heginbothom.
How the Ploughman Learned His Paternoster. *Unknown.*
Letter to the Child Lady Margaret Cavendish Holles-Harley, A.
   Prior.
Oft have I seen at some cathedral door.*Fr.* Divina Commedia.
   Longfellow.
Our Insufficiency to Praise God Suitably, for His Mercy.*Fr.*
   God's Determinations. Taylor.
Power of Prayer, The.*Fr.* Vanity of Human Wishes. Johnson.
Pray in May. Metcalfe.
Prayer: "Prayer the Church's banquet, angels' age." Herbert.
Sweet Hour of Prayer. Walford.
Temple, The. Sisson.
What a Friend We Have in Jesus. Scriven.
What Shall I Pray For Today? Morehead.
Without Ceremony. Miller.
Worship. Suderman.

**Praying Mantis**
Confrontation. Hart.

**Pregnancy**
Birthing, The. Bentley.
D-Day Minus. Brock.
Emergency at 8. Hewitt.
Epigram: for a Woman with Child. Cunningham.
First Pregnancy. Alta.
Foetal Song. Oates.
For a Woodscolt Miscarried. Corrington.
For You, Who Didn't Know. Willard.

Kind of Love, A. Nichols.
Labour of the Brain, Ballad of the Body. Forman.
Maternity Gown. Holbrook.
Meeting, The. Spivack.
Night Watch. Magid.
Now Jentil Belly Down. *Unknown.*
Now That I Am Forever with Child. Lorde.
Poem Wondering If I'm Pregnant. Fraser.
Pregnancy. Fish.
Pregnancy. McPherson.
Timepiece, A. Merrill.
To a Child Born in Time of Small War. Sorrells.
Unexpected, The. Ai.
Vow, The. Hecht.
Waiting for the Doctor. Inez.
With Child. Taggard.
Woman to Child. Wright.
Woman to Man. Wright.

**Prejudice.** *See* **Racial Prejudice.**

**Pride**
Postive, a Coxcomb. Plomer.
Primer Lesson. Sandburg.

**Priestly, Joseph**
Priestly.*Fr.* Sonnets on Eminent Characters. Coleridge.

**Priests.** *See* **Clergy.**

**Primroses**
Primrose, Being at Montgomery Castle, The. Donne.
Primula Scotica. Senior.

**Printing and Printers**
Printing Jenny. Mitchell.

**Prisoners of War**
Between Two Prisoners. Dickey.
Tramp! Tramp! Tramp! or, The Prisoner's Hope. Root.

**Prisons and Prisoners**
Cell Song. Knight.
Chain Gang Trouble. *Unknown.*
Clonmel Jail. *Unknown.*
Convict, The. Wordsworth.
For Freckle-faced Gerald. Knight.
Gaol Song, The. *Unknown.*
Girl Held Without Bail. Walker.
Hand Me Down My Walking Cane. *Unknown.*
Hard Rock Returns to Prison from the Hospital for the Criminal
   Insane. Knight.
He Sees Through Stone. Knight.
High Sheriff Blues. *Unknown.*
Idea of Ancestry, The. Knight.
In the Cage. Lowell.
In the Tank. Gunn.
Jailhouse Blues, The. *Unknown.*
Jim Jones at Botany Bay. *Unknown.*
Judge Harsh Blues. *Unknown.*
Kind of change came in my fate, A.*Fr.* The Prisoner of Chillon.
   Byron.
Leaving the Prison. Bruchac.
Line-up, The. Swift.
Memories of West Street and Lepke. Lowell.
My Crime. *Unknown.*
Nashville Stonewall Blues. *Unknown.*
O Death, Rock Me Asleep. Boleyn.
Ol' Hannah. *Unknown.*
Parchman Farm Blues. *Unknown.*
Prison Cell Blues. *Unknown.*
Prisoner, The. Mahon.
San Francisco County Jail Cell B-6. Conyus.
Solitary Confinement.*Fr.* The Kropotkin Poems. Webb.
Sonnets to Be Written from Prison. Adamson.
Sympathy. Dunbar.
To Althea, from Prison. Lovelace.
Written in Her French Psalter. Elizabeth I, Queen of England.
Written on a Wall at Woodstock. Elizabeth I, Queen of
   England.

Written With a Diamond on Her Window at Woodstock. Elizabeth I, Queen of England.

**Prometheus**
Prometheus. Byron.
Prometheus Unbound. Shelley.

**Prophets and Prophecy**
Advice to a Prophet. Wilbur.
Cassandra. Robinson.
Prophet. Chambers.
Prophets for a New Day. Walker.

**Proserpina** *or* **Proserpine.** *See* **Persephone**
**Prospectors.** *See* **Gold Mining and Miners.**
**Prostitution and Prostitutes**
As You Leave Me. Knight.
Cavalier Lyric. Simmons.
Greasy Spoon Blues. Gasparini.
In Response to a Rumor That the Oldest Whorehouse in Wheeling, West Virginia, Has Been Condemned. Wright.
Old Lady's Lament for Her Youth, The. Villon.
Place Pigalle. Wilbur.
Prostitutes at Les Halles, The. Mayhall.
Ruined Maid, The. Hardy.
Scarlet Woman, The. Johnson.
She Is More to Be Pitied, than Censured. Gray.
Stranger, The. Everson.
Violent Space, The. Knight.
Young Woman of Beare, The. Clarke.

**Protest, Social**
Adultery. Dugan.
Advent 1966. Levertov.
Advice to a Prophet. Wilbur.
Advice to Young Ladies. Hope.
After the Industrial Revolution, All Things Happen At Once. Bly.
Alabama Bus. *Unknown.*
Alabama Centennial. Madgett.
America. Ginsberg.
Americana XV: Simplicity. Rakosi.
And you'll say a nation totters.*Fr.* Civil Riot. Cole.
Apostrophe to Man. Millay.
April 1962. Goodman.
Bad Old Days, The. Rexroth.
Ballad of the Landlord. Hughes.
Benediction. Kaufman.
Benediction. Mitchell.
Blighters. Sassoon.
Burning of Paper Instead of Children, The. Rich.
Chic Freedom's Reflection. Walker.
Child of the Romans. Sandburg.
Childhood. Walker.
Christmas Prayer, A. Mitchell.
Comments. Kenner.
Covenant, The. Cunningham.
Dance for Militant Dilettantes, A. Young.
Death to Van Gogh's Ear! Ginsberg.
Don't Want No Hungry Woman. *Unknown.*
Draft Dodger Rag. Ochs.
Ecologue. Ginsberg.
First Fight. Then Fiddle. Ply the Slipping String. Brooks.
Florida Road Workers. Hughes.
For My People. Walker.
Foreign Policy Commitments; or, You Get Into the Catamaran First, Old Buddy. Blackburn.
Free Silver. *Unknown.*
Girl Held Without Bail. Walker.
Gloucester Moors. Moody.
Great Society, Mark X, The. Nemerov.
Harlem. Hughes.
Home on the Range, February 1962. Dorn.
How Beastly the Bourgeois Is. Lawrence.
I Am Waiting. Ferlinghetti.
I Have Seen Black Hands. Wright.

I Sing of Olaf Glad and Big. Cummings.
If We Must Die. McKay.
In Goya's greatest scenes we seem to see.*Fr.* A Coney Island of the Mind. Ferlinghetti.
In Mexico. Sward.
Johnson's Cabinet Watched by Ants. Bly.
Just Taking Note. Scott.
Kent State, May 4, 1970. Goodman.
Last of the Light Brigade, The. Kipling.
Latest Decalogue, The. Clough.
Let Us All Be Unhappy on Sunday. Neaves.
Man of Property, The. Ballard.
March, The ("Under the too white marmorial Lincoln Memorial"). Lowell.
March, The ("Where two or three were heaped together, or fifty"). Lowell.
Masters of War. Dylan.
May Mobilization. Ginsberg.
Montgomery. Cornish.
Much madness is divinest sense. Dickinson.
Necessary Bucket, A. Meinke.
No More. Clark.
Norman Morrison. Ferguson.
Norman Morrison. Mitchell.
Note to Olga (1966), A. Levertov.
Ode: Inscribed to W. H. Channing. Emerson.
Of Late. Starbuck.
Outside of a Small Circle of Friends. Ochs.
Pull Off Your Old Coat. *Unknown.*
Quaker Hero, Burning. Noll.
Revolution in the Revolution in the Revolution. Snyder.
Revolutionary Letter #19. Di Prima.
Rich and Poor; or, Saint and Sinner. Peacock.
Riot. Brooks.
Same in Blues. Hughes.
Secret People, The. Chesterton.
She Was Poor, but She Was Honest. *Unknown.*
Song for the Ragged Schools of London, A. E. Browning.
Song of the Militant Romance, The. Lewis.
Song to the Men of England. Shelley.
Sonnet on the Projected Kendal and Windermere Railway. Wordsworth.
Stand Up! Lawrence.
Strange Hells. Gurney.
Street Demonstration. Walker.
Superman. Updike.
"Terres des Hommes." Schechter.
Thanks to Industrial Essex. Davie.
Thirty Bob a Week. Davidson.
To the Governor and Legislature of Massachusetts. Nemerov.
Un-American Investigators. Hughes.
Unlawful Assembly. Enright.
Until They Have Stopped. Wright.
Vacation. Stafford.
We Can Be Together. Kantner.
We Real Cool. Brooks.
We Shall Overcome. *Unknown.*
Wack Fol the Diddle. Kearney.
What a Way to Lose the War. Salinas.
What Have They Done to the Rain? Reynolds.
Where Do the Children Play? Stevens.
World Is a Beautiful Place, The. Ferlinghetti.
You Get Used to It. Mitchell.

**Psyche**
Ode to Psyche. Keats.

**Psychiatry**
Birthday Card for a Psychiatrist. Van Duyn.

**Psychoanalysis**
Analysands. Randall.
Ballad of the Oedipus Complex. Durrell.
Interrogator, The. Jennings.
Note from an Analyst's Couch. Probst.

**Puerto Ricans**
Puerto Ricans in New York.  Reznikoff.
Puerto Ricans in New York II.  Reznikoff.
You're Nothing But a Spanish Colored Kid.  Luciano.
**Pumpkins**
How Come?  Asheron.
Mr.Macklin's Jack-o'-Lantern.  McCord.
Pumpkin, The.  Graves.
Theme in Yellow.  Sandburg.
Young Master's Account of a Puppet Show.  Marchant.
**Purcell, Henry**
Bounty.  Miles.
**Purgatory**
Negrun.  Travis.
**Pygmalion**
Pygmalion.  Ruby.
**Pythons**
Python, The.  Belloc.

# Q

**Quaggas**
Quagga, The.  Enright.
**Quail**
Quail Walk.  Miller.
**Quakers.**  *See* **Friends, Society of.**
**Quarrels**
Wife.  Andrews.
**Queen Anne's Lace**
Quiet faces.  Holsapple.
Queen Anne's Lace.  Spinnanger.
Queen-Ann's-Lace.  Williams.

# R

**Ra (Egyptian sun god)**
I Am a Cowboy in the Boat of Ra.  Reed.
**Rabbits**
Myxomatosis.  Larkin.
Rabbit, The.  Brownjohn.
Rabbit, The.  Davies.
Rabbit, The.  McIntyre.
Rabbit, The.  *Unknown.*
Snare, The.  Stephens.
*See also*  **Hares.**
**Rabies**
Elegy on the Death of a Mad Dog, An.*Fr.* The Vicar of
Wakefield.  Goldsmith.
Mad Dog.  Siegal.
**Raccoons**
Babies: Just Babies.  Fishback.
Coon Song.  Ammons.
Mill Valley.  Livingston.
Raccoon on the Road.  Brennan.
Raccoon Poem.  Palmer.
**Racial Prejudice**
Alarm Clock, The.  Evans.
Backlash Blues, The.  Hughes.
Birmingham Sunday.  Farina.
Black Poet, White Critic.  Randall.
Cameo No. 11.  Jordan.
Chicago *Defender* Sends a Man to Little Rock, The.  Brooks.
Children's Rhymes.  Hughes.
Cripus Attacks McCoy.  Brown.
In Bloemfontein.  Ross.

Incident.  Cullen.
Mark This.  Chesham.
May 27, 1971: No Poem.  Jordan.
Moment Please, A.  Allen.
Montgomery.  Cornish.
Necessary Bucket, A.  Meinke.
Non Poem about Vietnam, A.  Rodgers.
Old Lem.  Brown.
On Seeing Two Brown Boys in a Catholic Church.  Horne.
Parasitosis.  Davis.
Prejudice.  Johnson.
Racialism.  Blight.
Runaway Slave at Pilgrim's Point, The.  E. Browning.
Society's Child.  Ian.
Telephone Conversation.  Soyinka.
Tiger.  McKay.
Vietnam #4.  Major.
Where? When? Which?  Hughes.
White City, The.  McKay.
With All Deliberate Speed.  Lee.
Yet Do I Marvel.  Cullen.
**Radar**
Radar.  Ross.
**Radio**
Umbilical.  Merriam.
**Railroads**
Calling Trains.  *Unknown.*
Casey Jones.  Seibert.
Echo Canyon.  *Unknown.*
Express, The.  Spender.
From a Railway Carriage.  Stevenson.
George Allen.  *Unknown.*
Great Northern.  Etter.
Henry K. Sawyer.  *Unknown.*
I like to see it lap the miles.  Dickinson.
I Rode Southern, I Rode L & N.  *Unknown.*
In Texas Grass.  Troupe.
I've Been Working on the Railroad.  *Unknown.*
Lining Track.  *Unknown.*
Metropolitan Railway, The.  Betjeman.
Old Section Boss, The.  *Unknown.*
Railroad Blues, The.  *Unknown.*
Railroad Reverie.  Young.
Railway Junction, The.  De la Mare.
Rock Island Line, The.  *Unknown.*
Salvaging Spikes.  Vas Dias.
Siding near Chillicothe, A.  Lattimore.
Tay Bridge Disaster, The.  McGonagall.
To a Locomotive in Winter.  Whitman.
Unloading Rails.  *Unknown.*
Utah Iron Horse, The.  *Unknown.*
Wreck of the Royal Palm, The.  *Unknown.*
*See also*  **Trains; Subways; Trolleys.**
**Rain**
After Rain.  Thomas.
April Rain Song.  Hughes.
Atavism.  Lake.
Biography of Southern Rain.  Patchen.
Cat and the Rain, The.  Swift.
City Rain.  Field.
Cold Irish Earth, The.  Skinner.
Description of a City Shower, A.  Swift.
Drums.  Chosa.
Glass Falling.  MacNeice.
Have You Ever Seen the Rain?  Fogerty.
It Rains.  Thomas.
Little Raindrops.  Browne.
London Rain.  MacNeice.
Ode to the Rain, An.  Coleridge.
Prayer for Fine Weather.  Leslie.
Prayer for Rain.  *Unknown.*
Rain, The.  Creeley.

**Rain, The.** Davies.
Rain. DiPasquale.
Rain. O'Sullivan.
Rain. Smith.
Rain. Stevenson.
Rain. Thomas.
Rain. *Unknown.*
Rain in Summer. Longfellow.
Rain in the Desert. Fletcher.
Rain Poem. Coatsworth.
Rain Sleets Flat. Brigham.
Rainy Summer, The. Meynell.
Seven Rainy Months. Plomer.
Sophistication. Miller.
Sudden Shower. Clare.
Thunderstorm in South Dakota. Boyle.
Way Through, The. Levertov.
Wet Day. McAuley.
Wet Time, A. Berry.
Wet Weather. Low.
What Have They Done to the Rain? Reynolds.

**Rainbows**
Epigram: "Oh, God of dust and rainbows, help us see."
   Hughes.
My Heart Leaps Up When I Behold. Wordsworth.
Rainbow. Lochhead.
Rainbow, The. *Unknown.*
Red and blue and delicate green. *Unknown.*

**Rape**
Exodus. Probst.
On Rape Unattempted. Dugan.

**Rats**
Advancement of Learning, An. Heaney.
Assailant. Raven.
Experiment with a Rat, The. Rakosi.
Freddy the Rat Perishes. Marquis.
Letters from an Irishman to a Rat. Logue.
Pack Rat, The. Pack.
Pied Piper of Hamelin, The. Browning.
Poem against Rats, A. Levinson.
Rat, The. Davies.
Rats. De la Mare.
Reapers. Toomer.
Three Young Rats. *Unknown.*
What Became of Them? *Unknown.*

**Raven**
Raven, The. Poe.
Three Ravens, The. *Unknown.*
Twa Corbies, The. *Unknown.*

**Reading**
Proverbial Philosophy: of Reading. Calverley.
Study of Reading Habits, A. Larkin.

**Reason**
On the Triumph of Rationalism. Ainger.
Reason. Miles.

**Rebirth**
New Birth, The. Very.

**Redemption**
Amazing Grace. Newton.
Come Ye Sinners, Poor and Needy. Hart.
Love Lifted Me. Rowe.
O Happy Day. Doddridge.
Redemption. Herbert.
Since Jesus Came into My Heart. McDaniel.

**Redwings**
Redwing, The. P. Dickinson.

**Refugees**
Epilogue: "I have just joined a raggedy line." Trudell.
My Polish Grandma. Field.
Refugees, The. Muir.
Road to Pengya. Tu Fu.

**Reincarnation**

Book of the Dead, Prayer 14. Berssenbrugge.
Meeting the Reincarnation Analyst. Gildner.
Mohini Chatterjee. Yeats.

**Reindeer**
Reindeer and Engine. Jacobsen.

**Religion**
After Lorca. Creeley.
At a Bible House. Lowell.
Boom! Nemerov.
Church Going. Larkin.
Holy Willie's Prayer. Burns.
I'm ceded — I've stopped being theirs. Dickinson.
I'm Gonna Run to the City of Refuge. *Unknown.*
Latest Decalogue, The. Clough.
Lay Preacher Ponders, The. Davies.
Little Vagabond, The.*Fr.* Songs of Experience. Blake.
Madam and the Minister. Hughes.
Pie in the Sky. *Unknown.*
Pocomania. Walcott.
Poor Can Feed the Birds, The. Neilson.
Religion. Vaughan.
Religious Musings. Coleridge.
Signpost. Jeffers.
Some keep the Sabbath going to church. Dickinson.
That Old Time Religion. *Unknown.*
True Religion. Anderson.
Vicar of Bray, The. *Unknown.*
Wednesday Night Prayer Meeting. Wright.
When Mahalia Sings. Prettyman.
With huntis up, with huntis up. *Unknown.*
With Mercy for the Greedy. Sexton.
Written in Exile. Raine.

**Religious Life**
December. Snyder.

**Religious Verse**
*Adam Among the Television Trees* (AATT). Virginia R.
   Mollenkott, ed.
*Book of Religious Verse, A.* (BoReV). Helen Gardner, ed.
*Poems of Faith and Doubt* (PFD). R. L. Brett, ed.

**Rembrandt Harmenszoon van Rijn**
Polish Rider, The. Walcott.

**Remorse**
When Oats Were Reaped. Hardy.

**Restaurants**
Geraniums, The. Taggard.
Partial Explanation, The. Simic.

**Resurrection, The**
Quem Queritis. Carter.
*See also* **Easter**

**Retirement**
Swineherd. Chuilleanáin.

**Revenge (ship)**
*Revenge*, The. Tennyson.

**Revenge**
Brian Boy Magee. Carbery.
Enslaved. McKay.
Mine enemy is growing old. Dickinson.

**Revere, Paul**
Paul Revere's Ride.*Fr.* Tales of a Wayside Inn. Longfellow.

**Revolution**
Abu. Randall.
Black People! Jones.
Easter 1916. Yeats.
For Saundra. Giovanni.
Great Day, The. Yeats.
Greek Crazeology. Rodgers.
Last Poem. Donnelly.
Liberty. Shelley.
Militant. Hughes.
Republican Genius of Europe, The. Freneau.
Revolution is the pod. Dickinson.
Roses and Revolutions. Randall.

Sane Revolution, A. Lawrence.
Semi-Revolution, A. Frost.
Total Revolution, A. Williams.
Tryptych for Jan Bockelson, A. Simon.
Warning. Hughes.
When the Revolution Really. Michelson.
Yeah, I Is Uh Shootin off at the Mouth. Rodgers.
*See also* **American Revolution; French Revolution.**

**Reynolds, Sir Joshua**
Sir Joshua Reynolds. Blake.

**Rhinoceroses**
Rhinoceros. Hart-Smith.
Rhinoceros. Stoutenburg.

**Rhodora**
Rhodora, The. Emerson.

**Riddles**
Bishop of Canterbury, The. *Unknown.*
Captain Wedderburn's Courtship. *Unknown.*

**Rifles**
Naming of Parts.*Fr.* Lessons of the War. Reed.

**Rilke, Rainer Maria**
Visions. Spivack.

**Rimbaud, Arthur**
Rimbaud in Abyssinia. Griffin.

**Riots**
Black Day in July. Lightfoot.
For What It's Worth. Stills.
Harlem Riot, 1943. Murray.
In This Year of Grace. Hewitt.
Mr. Roosevelt regrets. Murray.
Old Woman Remembers, An. Brown.
Richard Hofstadter and Michael Wallace: A Documentary
    History of American Violence. Rosenberg.
Riot. Brooks.
Willie B. Clifton.

**Rivers**
Green River. Bryant.
Negro Speaks of Rivers, The. Hughes.
Not envying Latian shades—if yet they throw.*Fr.* The River
    Duddon. Wordsworth.
Repose of Rivers. Crane.
River of Rivers in Connecticut, The. Stevens.
River Roads. Sandburg.
River Swelleth More and More, The. Thoreau.
Rivers Arise; Whether Thou Be the Son. Milton.
Riversong. Anania.
Tide River, The.*Fr.* The Water Babies. Kingsley.
Watershed, The. Meynell.

**Roads**
Florida Road Workers. Hughes.
Middleness of the Road, The. Frost.
Rolling English Road, The. Chesterton.
Roman Road, The. Hardy.
Song of the Open Road. Whitman.
Southern Road, The. Randall.

**Roanoke, Virginia**
Downtown Roanoke. Dillard.

**Robeson, Paul**
Paul Robeson. Brooks.

**Robin Hood**
Bold Peddlar and Robin Hood, The. *Unknown.*
Death of Robin Hood, The. Field.
How Robin Hood Rescued the Widow's Sons. *Unknown.*
Merry Jest of Robin Hood, A. Peacock.
Robin Hood. Burr.
Robin Hood. Keats.
Robin Hood and Allen a Dale. *Unknown.*
Robin Hood and Little John. *Unknown.*
Robin Hood and the Bishop of Hereford. *Unknown.*
Robin Hood and the Sheriff. *Unknown.*

**Robins**
Call for the Robin Redbreast and the Wren. Webster.

I am called by name of man. *Unknown.*
No noise is here, or none that hinders thought.*Fr.* The Robin in
    Winter. Cowper.
Red Robin, The. Clare.
Robin, The Hardy.
Robin Redbreast. Allingham.
Robin Redbreast. Kunitz.
Robin Redbreast's Testament. *Unknown.*

**Rocks.** *See* **Stones and Rocks.**

**Roethke, Theodore**
Roethke Plain. Brinnin.
Strut for Roethke, A. Berryman.

**Roland.**
Silent Slain, The. MacLeish.

**Roman Catholic Church.** *See* **Catholicism.**

**Rome**
Amours de Voyage, *sels.* Clough.
Piazza di Spagna, Early Morning. Wilbur.
Thief, The. Kunitz.
To an Old Philosopher in Rome. Stevens.

**Romeo and Juliet**
Silver Dagger, The. *Unknown.*

**Romney Marsh, England**
In Romney Marsh. Davidson.

**Ronkonkoma, Lake**
Dog Sacrifice at Lake Ronkonkoma. Heyen.

**Roosevelt, Franklin Delano**
President Roosevelt. *Unknown.*

**Roosters**
Bonny Grey, The. *Unknown.*
Cock Crowing in a Poulterer's Shop, A. Ferguson.
I Have a Gentle Cock. *Unknown.*
Old Grey. Lape.
On a Cock at Rochester. Sedley.
Roosters. Bishop.
To Be or Not to Be. *Unknown.*
When the sun came, the rooster expanded to meet it. Miles.

**Rosemary**
Time has an end, they say. Doolittle ("H.D.").

**Roses**
Act, The. Williams.
Of a Rose, a Lovely Rose. *Unknown.*
Rose, The. Howell.
Rose, The. Roethke.
Rose, The. Williams.
Rose Family, The. Frost.
Roses. *Unknown.*
Sea Rose. Doolittle ("H.D.").
Sepal, petal, and a thorn, A. Dickinson.
Sick Rose, The.*Fr.* Songs of Experience. Blake.
Song: "Go lovely rose." Waller.
To a Friend Who Sent Me Some Roses. Keats.
To Flossie. Williams.
White Rose, A. O'Reilly.

**Rosh Hashanah**
Feast of the Ram's Horn. Shapiro.
This is the autumn and our harvest.*Fr.* New Years's. Reznikoff.

**Rotterdam, Netherlands**
Vision of Rotterdam. Corso.

**Rouen, France**
Rouen. Cannan.

**Rousseau, Jean Jacques**
Mock on mock on Voltaire Rousseau. Blake.

**Royal George (ship)**
On the Loss of the *Royal George.* Cowper.

**Rugby**
Is Football Playing?*Fr.* Is My Team Plowing? Housman.

**Rugs**
Oriental. St. Cyr.

**Running.** *See* **Track Athletics.**

**Russell, Lucy, Countess of Bedford**
To the Countess of Bedford. Donne.

**Russia**
  "Less Nonsense." Herbert.
  Russia. Williams.
**Ruth (Bible)**
  Ruth. Hood.
**Ruth, George Herman (Babe)**
  Babe Ruth. Runyon.
**Rutledge, Ann**
  Anne Rutledge. *Fr.* Spoon River Anthology. Masters.


# S


**Sailing and Sailors**
  Banks of Newfoundland, The. *Unknown.*
  Battle Problem. Meredith.
  Bay of Biscay, The. *Unknown.*
  Blow the Man Down. *Unknown.*
  Blow, Ye Winds. *Unknown.*
  Brown Robyn's Confession. *Unknown.*
  Canada-I-O. *Unknown.*
  Cape Horn Gospel — 1. Masefield.
  Captain Bunker. *Unknown.*
  Chief Petty Officer. Causley.
  Christmas at Sea. Stevenson.
  Clipper *Dunbar* to the Clipper *Cutty Sark*, The. Anderson.
  Codfish Shanty, The. *Unknown.*
  Coming around the Horn. Stone.
  Crowd, The. Masefield.
  Day Sailing. Slavitt.
  *Dom Pedro*, The. *Unknown.*
  *Dreadnought*, The. *Unknown.*
  Earlye, Earlye, in the Spring. *Unknown.*
  Fifteen Ships on Georges Banks. *Unknown.*
  Figurehead, The. Garstin.
  Girls around Cape Horn, The. *Unknown.*
  *Golden Vanity*, The. *Unknown.*
  Greenland Whale Fishery, The. *Unknown.*
  Haul Away, My Rosy. *Unknown.*
  Heaving the Lead Line. *Unknown.*
  Hell's Pavement. Masefield.
  Jolly Soldier. *Unknown.*
  Life on the Ocean Wave, A. Sargent.
  Lightning Flash, The. *Unknown.*
  Lines to Mr. Hodgson. Byron.
  Lord Arnaldos. Flecker.
  Lowson. Blight.
  Luck. Gibson.
  McAndrew's Hymn. Kipling.
  Nautical Extravaganza, A. Irwin.
  Navy Hymn, The. Whiting.
  Ocean Burial, The. Chapin.
  Paddy, Get Back. *Unknown.*
  Powerful Eyes o' Jeremy Tait, The. Irwin.
  Reuben Ranzo. *Unknown.*
  Rime of the Ancient Mariner, The. Coleridge.
  Sailing Home from Rapallo. Lowell.
  Sailing, Sailing. Burr.
  Sailing to an Island. Murphy.
  Sailor. Hughes.
  Sailor Boy, The. Tennyson.
  Sailors' Alphabet, The. *Unknown.*
  Sailor's Consolation, The. Dibdin.
  Schooner *Fred Dunbar*, The. Hanson.
  Sea Change. Masefield.
  Sea Fever. Masefield.
  Seafarer. MacLeish.
  Seafarer, The. *Unknown.*
  Sea-Voyage from Tenby to Bristol, A. Philips.

  Seumas Beg. Stephens.
  Skipper Ireson's Ride. Whittier.
  Song: "To all you ladies now at land." Sackville.
  Stony Brook Tavern. Reed.
  Tempest, The. *Unknown.*
  Things to Do Around a Ship at Sea. Snyder.
  Uncle Roderick. MacCaig.
  We'll Go to Sea No More. *Unknown.*
  Wet Sheet and a Flowing Sea, A. Cunningham.
  Where Lies the Land. Clough.
  Wind Sou'west, The. *Unknown.*
  Yachts, The. Williams.
  Yarn of the *Loch Achray*, The. Masefield.
  Yarn of the *Nancy Bell*, The. Gilbert.
  Ye Mariners of England. Campbell.
**St. Agnes Eve**
  Eve of St. Agnes, The. Keats.
**St. Cecilia's Day.** *See* **Cecilia, Saint.**
**St. Louis, Missouri**
  Letter to Belden. Moore.
  Lucas Park (St. Louis). Bliss.
**St. Mark's Eve**
  Eve of St. Mark, The. Keats.
**Saints**
  Mrs. Malone. Farjeon.
**Sales Clerks**
  Sale. Miles.
**Salt**
  What Is Salt? Vernon.
**Salvation Army**
  General William Booth Enters into Heaven. Lindsay.
**Samaritan, Good**
  Man Who Had Fallen Among Thieves, A. Cummings.
**Samson (Bible)**
  History of Samson, The, *sel.* Quarles.
  If I Had My Way. *Unknown.*
  Warning, The. Longfellow.
**San Francisco, California**
  After the Cries of the Birds. Ferlinghetti.
  Idyll: "San Francisco, California". Tomlinson.
  In Golden Gate Park that day. *Fr.* A Coney Island of the Mind.
    Ferlinghetti.
**San Joaquin, California**
  San Joaquin. Everson.
**Sand, George**
  To George Sand. E. Browning.
**Sand**
  Sand. Higham.
**Sandpipers**
  Sandpiper. Bishop.
  Sandpiper, The. Thaxter.
**Santa Claus**
  Boy Who Laughed at Santa Claus, The. Nash.
  Saint Nicholas. Moore.
  Santa Claus. Moraes.
  Santa Claus. Nemerov.
  Visit from St. Nicholas, A. Moore.
**Santayana, George**
  For George Santayana. Lowell.
  To an Old Philosopher in Rome. Stevens.
  Upon the Death of George Santayana. Hecht.
**Sappho**
  Invocation to Sappho. Gidlow.
  Sapphics. Swinburne.
  Sappho. Cabral.
  Sisters, The. A. Lowell.
**Sassafras Tea**
  Sassafras Tea. Newsome.
**Satan**
  Address to the Deil. Burns.
  Citadels. Kell.
  Devil's Bag, The. Stephens.

Devil's Thoughts, The. Coleridge *and* Southey.
False Knight upon the Road, The. *Unknown.*
Lucifer in Starlight. Meredith.
Riddles Wisely Expounded. *Unknown.*
Whale, The. *Unknown.*
**Satie, Erik**
Angel. Merrill.
**Satiric Verse**
Art. Bierce.
Best Line Yet, The. Allen.
Boom! Nemerov.
Cavalier Lyric. Simmons.
Charming Woman, The. Sheridan.
Dover Bitch, The: A Criticism of Life. Hecht.
Epistle to Dr. Arbuthnot.
"Faith"is a fine invention. Dickinson.
First Satire of the Second Book of Horace, The. Pope.
Friends. Durem.
Furniture of a Woman's Mind, The. Swift.
Giles Johnson, Ph.D. Davis.
Latest Decalogue, The. Clough.
Letter from a Candidate for the Presidency in Answer to Suttin Questions Proposed by Mr. Hosea Biglow, A.*Fr.* The Biglow Papers. Lowell.
Little Vagabond, The.*Fr.* Songs of Experience. Blake.
Lovers of the Poor, The. Brooks.
Of Alphus. *Unknown.*
Old, Filthy Beer Pail, The. Hall.
On the Vanity of Earthly Greatness. Guiterman.
Outside of a Small Circle of Friends. Ochs.
Pioneers, The. Mortimer.
Pious Editor's Creed, The.*Fr.* The Biglow Papers. Lowell.
Poem, Or Beauty Hurts Mr. Vinal. Cummings.
Prayer of Holy Willie, The. Burns.
Rape of the Lock, The. Pope.
Résumé. Parker.
Santa Claus. Nemerov.
Satirical Elegy on the Death of a Late Famous General, A. Swift.
Spade Is Just a Spade, A. Hawkins.
Teacher of Poetry, The. Packard.
Twenty-Third Psalm, The. Simpson.
Unknown Citizen, The. Auden.
*English Satiric Poetry: Dryden to Byron* (ESaP). James Kinsley *and* James T. Boulton, eds.
**Saul (Bible)**
Saul. Browning.
**Scarecrows**
Lonely Scarecrow, The. Kirkup.
Scarecrow, The. De la Mare.
To a Scarecrow, or Malkin, Left Long after Harvest. Turner.
**Scholars and Scholarship**
Academic. Reeves.
Antiquary, The. Campbell.
April Inventory. Snodgrass.
Desperate Measure, A. Dennis.
For Scholars and Pupils. Wither.
Giles Johnson, Ph.D. Davis.
Lecture Hall. Kavanagh.
Plain Language from Truthful James. Harte.
Professor Kelleher and the Charles River. O'Grady.
Scholars. De la Mare.
Scholars, The. Yeats.
Scholar's Life, The.*Fr.* Vanity of Human Wishes. Johnson.
Snapshot of a Pedant. Garrett.
To a Friend, on Her Examination for the Doctorate in English. Cunningham.
Young Man's Epigram on Existence, A. Hardy.
*See also* **Teaching and Teachers; Students.**
**School**
Description of a Good Boy, A. Dixon.
Ecole St. Luc. Fraser.

Elementary School Class Room in a Slum, An. Spender.
I wake up in a morning. *Unknown.*
Kindergarten. Rogers.
P.S. 42. Corso.
Poem Beginning with a Line Memorized at School. Jellema.
Schoolboy's Lot, A. *Unknown.*
September, the First Day of School. Nemerov.
Unhappy Schoolboy, The. *Unknown.*
University. Shapiro.
University Examinations in Egypt. Enright.
*See also* **Colleges and Universities.**
**Schwartz, Delmore**
This world is gradually becoming a place. Berryman.
To Delmore Schwartz. Lowell.
**Science**
And, constantly, I seek/ A poetry of facts.*Fr.* The Kind of Poetry I Want. "MacDiarmid."
"Arcturus" is his other name. Dickinson.
Blight. Emerson.
Counting Sheep. Edson.
Credibility. Ciardi.
Dr. Sigmund Freud Discovers the Sea Shell. MacLeish.
Laboratory Poem. Merrill.
Last Monster, The. Montague.
Los Alamos: Manhattan. Rowbotham.
Poem: "The thing/ to do/ is organize." Koch.
Projection, A. Whittemore.
Richard Tolman's Universe. Bacon.
Science. Jeffers.
Science as Art. Seidman.
Sonnet — To Science. Poe.
Space being (don't forget to remember) curved. Cummings.
V. B. Nimble, V. B. Quick. Updike.
**Science Fiction**
Missionary. Thomas.
**Scopes Trial**
Bryan's Last Battle. *Unknown.*
**Scorpions**
Scorpion, The. Belloc.
**Scotland**
My Heart's in the Highlands. Burns.
Robert Bruce's March to Bannockburn. Burns.
Scotland's Winter. Muir.
This Is My Own, My Native Land.*Fr.* The Lay of the Last Minstrel. Scott.
*Made in Scotland* (MIS). Robert Garioch, ed.
**Scots, The**
Gup, Scot. Skelton.
**Scott, Sir Walter**
On Scott's "The Field of Waterloo." Erskine.
**Scottish Border**
Battle of Otterbourne, The. *Unknown.*
Flowers of the Forest, The: or, The Battle of Flodden. Elliot.
**Scottsboro Case**
Communication to Nancy Cunard, A. Boyle.
Scottsboro, Too, Is Worth Its Song. Cullen.
**Sculpture and Sculptors**
Arundel Tomb, An. Larkin.
Convert, The. Danner.
Hiram Powers' "Greek Slave." E. Browning.
On a Prize Crucifix by a Student Sculptor. Logan.
On Seeing the Elgin Marbles. Keats.
Statues, The. Yeats.
**Sea**
And I Have Loved Thee, Ocean!*Fr.* Childe Harold's Pilgrimage. Byron.
At Dunwich. Thwaite.
At Melville's Tomb. Crane.
At the Seaside. Stevenson.
At the Western Shore. Youngblood.
Ayii, Ayii,/ I walked on the ice of the sea. *Unknown.*
Ayii, Ayii/ The great sea has set me in motion. *Unknown.*

Continent's End. Jeffers.
Crossing the Atlantic. Sexton.
Evening Ebb. Jeffers.
Fish, The. Moore.
Four Homages. Block.
Garden. Drouet.
Grave, A. Moore.
I started early, took my dog. Dickinson.
I will go back to the great sweet mother. *Fr.* The Triumph of
　Time. Swinburne.
Idea of Order at Key West, The. Stevens.
Land's End. Langton.
Letter from the North Atlantic. Williams.
Maggie and Milly and Molly and May. Cummings.
Neither Out Far nor In Deep. Frost.
Offshore Breeze. Acorn.
On the Sea. Keats.
On This Island. Auden.
Oread. Doolittle. ("H.D.")
Pebbles. Melville.
Plague of Dead Sharks. Dugan.
Prayer to the Pacific. Silko.
Quaker Graveyard in Nantucket, The. Lowell.
Sea Calm. Hughes.
Sea Fever. Masefield.
Sea Lullaby. Wylie.
Sea Surface Full of Clouds. Stevens.
Sea Variations. Simpson.
Seafarer, The. *Unknown.*
Seascape. Bishop.
Seascape. Young.
Slow Pacific Swell, The. Winters.
Sonnet Written in the Church-Yard at Middleton, in Sussex.
　Smith.
Spindrift. Kinnell.
Storm Tide on Mejit. *Unknown.*
Thalassa. MacNeice.
Tide Rises, the Tide Falls, The. Longfellow.
Traveling Boy. Meredith.
Waking from a Nap on the Beach. Swenson.
Winter Ocean. Updike.
Winter Seascape. Betjeman.
World below the Brine, The. Whitman.
**Sea Gulls.** *See* **Gulls.**
**Sea Serpents**
Loch Ness Monster, The. Buchan.
**Sea Shells.** *See* **Shells.**
**Sea Voyages.** *See* **Voyages.**
**Seals**
Dead Seal. Purdy.
Great Silkie of Sule Skerry, The. *Unknown.*
Question, A. Cole.
Seal. Smith.
Sealchie Song. *Unknown.*
Seals. Slavitt.
**Seasons**
Eskimo Chant. *Unknown.*
Four seasons fill the measure of the year. Keats.
Hymn on the Seasons, A. *Fr.* The Seasons. Thomson.
In Due Season. Auden.
In the Elegy Season. Wilbur.
Insight. Spinnanger.
Metamorphosis. Stevens.
Origin of Hot and Cold According to the Delawares, The.
　Lifshin.
Seasons, The. *Unknown.*
Signs of the Seasons. *Unknown.*
Winter Flowers. Hall.
*Four Seasons Five Senses* (FSFS). Elinor Parker, ed.
**Seattle, Washington**
Thirteen Preludes for Pioneer Square. Logan.
**Sebastian, Saint**

Martyrdom of Saint Sebastian, The. Dobson.
**Second World War.** *See* **World War, Second.**
**Secretaries**
Secretary. Hughes.
Secretary, The. Redgrove.
**Seduction**
Disappointment, The. Behn.
Seduced Girl. Hedylos.
Seduction. Giovanni.
Volatile Kerryman, The. O'Sullivan.
Willing Mistriss, The. Behn.
**Seeds**
Seeds. Reeves.
**Segovia, Andrés**
Canto del Señor Segovia. Herrstrom.
**Semele**
Semele Recycled. Kizer.
**Sennacherib, King of Assyria**
Destruction of Sennacherib, The. Byron.
**Separation**
Ancient Couple on Lu Mountain, The. Van Doren.
Exile. Dowson.
Exile's Letter. Li Po.
First, Goodbye. Smith.
Frisco Whistle Blues. *Unknown.*
Goodbye. Lewis.
In the Vaulted Way. Hardy.
Into the Sky. Chesham.
Lake Michigan Blues. *Unknown.*
Letter to Her Husband Absent on Public Employment, A.
　Bradstreet.
Long Distance Moan. *Unknown.*
Message. Ginsberg.
Missing My Daughter. Spender.
My life closed twice before its close. Dickinson.
Never Let Your Left Hand Know. *Unknown.*
New Spring. Jiménez.
O! Wherefore. Peter.
On the Departure Platform. Hardy.
Parting. Herguri.
Partings. Jewsbury.
Reproaches. Turner.
River-Merchant's Wife, The: A Letter. Li Po.
Separation. Sange.
Since there's no help, come, let us kiss and part. *Fr.* Idea.
　Drayton.
Starface, The. Gleason.
Terrible Door, The. Monro.
That Lonesome Train Took My Baby Away. *Unknown.*
Three Weeks in the State of Loneliness. Piercy.
Two Letters from Chang-Kan. Li Po.
Upon Your Leaving. Knight.
Valediction, A: Forbidding Mourning. Donne.
Voyage. Stepanchev.
When We Two Parted. Byron.
Within the Dream You Said. Larkin.
You Never Miss the Water. *Unknown.*
You'll Never Miss Your Jelly. *Unknown.*
**September**
September. M. Coleridge.
**Sequoia Trees**
Redwoods, The. Simpson.
**Sewell, Samuel**
Samuel Sewell. Hecht.
**Sewing**
Red Dress, The. Bertolino.
What Is She Trying to Do, to Pattern Love. Brigham.
**Seymour, Jane**
Death of Queen Jane, The. *Unknown.*
**Shadows**
Escape. Johnson.
Lectures on the Biology of the Shadow. Young.

**Shadwell**
My Shadow. Stevenson.
Nocturne Varial. Alexander.
Tenebris. Grimké.

**Shadwell, Thomas**
MacFlecknoe. Dryden.

**Shakespeare, William**
On Sitting Down to Read "King Lear" Once Again. Keats.
To the Memory of My Beloved, the Author, Mr. William
   Shakespeare, and What He Hath Left Us. Jonson.
When I Read Shakespeare. Lawrence.

**Shaped Poetry**
Altar, The. Herbert.
Diamond Cut Diamond. Milne.
Easter Wings. Herbert.
Out of the Sea, Early. Swenson.
Seal. Smith.
Skeleton Key. Hollander.
This crosse-tree here. Herrick.

**Sharks**
About the Teeth of Sharks. Ciardi.
Among Sharks. Lee.
Basking Shark. MacCaig.
Maldive Shark, The. Melville.
Nurse Sharks. Matthews.
Plague of Dead Sharks. Dugan.
Sea-Turtle and the Shark, The. Tolson.
Shark, The. Ciardi.
Shark's Parlor, The. Dickey.

**Shaw, George Bernard**
Last words of Shaw, The: "I'm going to die." Bold.

**Shaw, Robert Gould**
For the Union Dead. Lowell.

**Sheep**
Bah! De la Mare.
Derby Ram, The. *Unknown.*
First Sight. Larkin.
Lambs Frolicking Home. Lape.
Little Bo-Peep. *Unknown.*
Sheep. Davies.
Sheep, The. Taylor.
Sheep Fair, A. Hardy.
Sheep in Winter. Clare.

**Sheep Shearing**
Banks of the Condamine, The. *Unknown.*
Click Go the Shears, Boys. *Unknown.*

**Shells**
Poem about a Seashell. Crosby.
Sea Shell. A. Lowell.
Sea-Shell Murmurs. Lee-Hamilton.
Shell, The. McCord.

**Shenandoah River**
Shenandoah. *Unknown.*

**Shepherds and Shepherdesses**
Jolly Shepherd Wat, The. *Unknown.*
Nod. De la Mare.
Nymph's Reply to the Shepherd, The. Ralegh.
Passionate Shepherd to His Love, The. Marlowe.
Shepherd, The. Baxter.
Shepherd, The.*Fr.* Songs of Innocence. Blake.
Shepherd Boy Sings in the Valley of Humiliation, The.*Fr.* The
   Pilgrim's Progress. Bunyan.
Shepherdess. Cameron.
Wise Men and Shepherds. Godolphin.

**Sheridan, Philip Henry**
Sheridan's Ride. Read.

**Shiloh, Battle of**
Battle of Shiloh, The. *Unknown.*
Drummer Boy of Shiloh, The. *Unknown.*
Shiloh; A Requiem. Melville.

**Ships**
Cargoes. Masefield.
Dismantled Ship, The. Whitman.

H.M.S. *Hero.* Roberts.
Lines to Mr. Hodgson. Byron.
Nocturne of the Wharves. Bontemps.
Passer-By, A. Bridges.
Ritual, The. Pratt.
Where lies the land to which yon ship must go? Wordsworth.
Winter Ship, A. Plath.
*See also* **Boats; Yachts.**

**Shipwrecks**
Asleep in the Deep. Lamb.
Berg, The. Melville.
Castaway, The. Cowper.
Convergence of the Twain, The. Hardy.
Great *Titanic.* *Unknown.*
In Memory of the Circus Ship *Euzkera.* Gibson.
Isle of Man Shore, The. *Unknown.*
Loss of the *Due Dispatch*, The. *Unknown.*
Loss of the *New Columbia*, The. *Unknown.*
Mermaid, The. *Unknown.*
Ritual, The. Pratt.
Sinking of the *Titanic.* *Unknown.*
Sir Patrick Spens. *Unknown.*
*Titanic*, The. *Unknown.*
*Titanic* Blues. *Unknown.*
Wreck of the *Deutschland*, The. Hopkins.
Wreck of the *Julie Plante*, The. Drummond.

**Shiva.** *See* **Siva.**

**Shoes**
Sale. Miles.
On Hot Days. Reiss.

**Shopping**
Grocery Shopping. Leax.
Poem to My New Jacket. Winant.

**Siberia**
Siberia. Mangan.

**Sickness.** *See* **Illness.**

**Sidmouth, Henry Addington, Viscount**
To Sidmouth and Castlereagh. Shelley.

**Sidney, Sir Philip**
Epitaph upon the Right Honorable Sir Philip Sidney, An.
   Greville.

**Silence**
Aprons of Silence. Sandburg.
Between the Electric Rhythm and the Melodic Mind. Schevill.
Choice of Weapons, A. McGinley.
On The Eclipse of the Moon of October 1865. Turner.
Silence. Hood.
Silence. Lucie-Smith.
Silence. Moore.
Silence. Turner.
Silence of a city, how awful at midnight, The! Coleridge.
Sonnet—Silence. Poe.
Sound of Silence, The. Simon.

**Silkworms**
Silkworms, The. Stewart.

**Simon of Cyrene**
Simon the Cyrenian Speaks. Cullen.

**Simplicity**
Familiar Epistle, A. Murry.
Ode to Simplicity. Collins.

**Sin**
Adam Lay Y-Bounden. *Unknown.*
As a Plane Tree by the Water. Lowell.
Attend, Young Friends, While I Relate. *Unknown.*
Elegy for a Puritan Conscience. Dugan.
Fire. Hughes.
Going to Hell. *Unknown.*
Good Lord, what a wicked world is this. *Unknown.*
Ha! Original Sin. Nash.
Hymne to God the Father, A. Donne.
If poisonous minerals, and if that tree.*Fr.* Holy Sonnets.
   Donne.

My Ghostly Father, I Me Confess. Orléans.
Portrait of the Artist As a Prematurely Old Man. Nash.
Seven Sins, The. *Unknown.*
Sin. Herbert.
Sin of Omission, The. Sangster.
Two Questions, The. Meynell.
Yield Not to Temptation. Palmer.
Young People Who Delight in Sin. *Unknown.*

**Singing and Singers**
Aim Was Song, The. Frost.
Alabama. Fields.
All Which Isn't Singing Is Mere Talking. Cummings.
And the Old Women Gathered. Evans.
Buckdancer's Choice. Dickey.
Choristers Training. *Unknown.*
Cino. Pound.
Everyone Sang. Sasson.
Fair Singer,The. Marvell.
I Remember How She Sang. Penny.
Idea of Order at Key West, The. Stevens.
Piano. Lawrence.
Poem for a Singer. Acorn.
Poem for Aretha. Giovanni.
Rivals, The. Stephens.
Singers to Come. Meynell.
Singing. Shelton.
Solitary Reaper, The. Wordsworth.
There was a man with tongue of wood.*Fr.* War Is Kind. Crane.
To Constantia Singing. Shelley.
When Malindy Sings. Dunbar.

**Sirens (mythology)**
Sirens' Song, The. Browne.

**Sisters**
Letter Reaching out to My Sister 1600 Miles. Barba.
Sisters. Turner.

**Siva**
Shiva. Jeffers.

**Skating and Skaters**
Blue Boy on Skates (Twilight). Rosenthal.
Midnight Skaters, The. Blunden.
74th Street. Livingston.
Skaters, The. Williams.
Skaters, The.*Fr.* The Prelude. Wordsworth.
To Kate, Skating Better Than Her Date. Daiches.
Woman Skating. Atwood.

**Skiing**
Avalanche. Emig.
Hunger. Bruce.
Skier. Francis.
Skiers.*Fr.* In the Mountains. Warren.
White Pass Ski Patrol. Logan.

**Skulls**
Lines Inscribed upon a Cup Formed from a Skull. Byron.
Scientist, The. Burroway.
Uppon a Deedmans Hed. Skelton.
Yardbird's Skull. Dodson.

**Skunks**
Skunk Hour. Lowell.
Skunks, *sel.* Jeffers.
Wood Weasel, The. Moore.

**Sky**
Sky was candy luminous, The. Cummings.
We will watch the Northern lights. *Unknown.*

**Sky Diving**
Parachutist. Hazo.
Sky Diver. Stoutenburg.
Sky Diving. Lattimore.

**Skyjackers**
Raffaele Minichiello. McPherson.

**Skylarks.** *See* **Larks.**

**Skyscrapers**

Skyscrapers. Field.
Skyscrapers Stand Proud. Sandburg.

**Slavery**
Alcestis on the Poetry Circuit. Jong.
*Flying Cloud*, The. *Unknown.*
From America. Whitfield.
In Bondage. McKay.
Jack and Dinah Want Freedom. *Unknown.*
Jim Crack Corn; or, The Blue Tail Fly. *Unknown.*
John Cherokee. *Unknown.*
Middle Passage. Hayden.
My Great-Grandfather's Slaves. Berry.
No More Auction Block. *Unknown.*
On Being Brought from Africa to America. Wheatley.
Poem for My Family: Hazel Griffin and Victor Hernandez Cruz. Jordan.
Primitive, The. Lee.
Promises of Freedom. *Unknown.*
Runagate Runagate. Hayden.
Runaway Slave at Pilgrim's Point, The. E. Browning.
Safari West. Williams.
Sevier County Runaway, The. Brigham.
Slave Auction, The. Harper.
Slavery. Herrick.
Song to the Runaway Slave. *Unknown.*
Was It Not Curious? Smith.
Wild Negro Bill. *Unknown.*

**Sleep**
After I come home from the meeting with friends. Miles.
Care-charmer sleep, son of the sable night.*Fr.* To Delia. Daniel.
Come Sleep! O Sleep.*Fr.* Astrophel and Stella. Sidney.
Country of Water. Ames.
Disillusionment of Ten O'Clock. Stevens.
Falling Asleep. Sassoon.
Insomnia. Bishop.
Night and Sleep. Patmore.
Night Blessing. George.
Now i lay (with everywhere around). Cummings.
Serenade: "Stars of the summer night!" Longfellow.
Slumber Did My Spirit Seal, A. Wordsworth.
To Sleep. Clare.
To Sleep. Keats.
To Sleep. Smith.
To Sleep. Wordsworth.
Waking From Sleep. Bly.
What is more gentle than a wind in summer?*Fr.* Sleep and Poetry. Keats.
Willie Winkie. Miller.
Wynken, Blynken, and Nod. Field.

**Sleighs**
Jingle Bells. Pierpont.

**Sloth**
Sluggard, The. Watts.

**Sloths**
Sloth, The. Gardner.
Sloth, The. Roethke.

**Slums**
Childhood. Latimore.
East Bronx. Ignatow.
Elementary School Class Room in a Slum, An. Spender.
Feeding the Lions. Jordan.
Get the Gasworks. Ignatow.
Judeebug's Country. Johnson.
Letter in Winter. Patterson.
Lovers of the Poor, The. Brooks.
On Saint-Urbain Street. Acorn.
Rat, The. Davies.
Reckoning A.M. Thursday after an Encounter between a Sawdust Sack and a Silly. Turner.
Scenery. Joans.
6th and Walnut Street. Moxley.

Summertime and the Living. Hayden.
To the New Annex to the Detroit County Jail. Thomas.

**Smiles**
Simile for Her Smile, A. Wilbur.
Smile, The. Blake.
Philosophy. Dunbar.

**Smith, Adam**
Adam, Smith.*Fr.* Clerihews. Bentley.

**Smith, Bessie.**
Bessie Smith's Funeral. Aubert.
Homage to the Empress of the Blues. Hayden.

**Smoke**
Light-Winged Smoke, Icarian Bird. Thoreau.
Song of the Smoke, The. Du Bois.

**Smugglers**
Smuggler's Song, A.*Fr.* Puck of Pook's Hill. Kipling.

**Snails**
Elegies for the Hot Season. McPherson.
My Garden. Lindon.
Snail. Drinkwater.
Snail, The. Herbert.
Snail, The. Lovelace.
Snail, The. Reeves.
Snail, The. *Unknown.*
Snail's Monologue, The. Morgenstern.
To a Snail. Moore.
Upon a Snail. Bunyan.
Widow's Yard, The. Gardner.

**Snakes**
Boa Constrictor. Silverstein.
Boy and His Snake, The. Lamb.
Cheers. Merriam.
Fastidious Serpent, The. Johnstone.
Garden Hose, The. Janosco.
Heaved from the Earth. Brigham.
In the Snake Park. Plomer.
Lizards and Snakes. Hecht.
Medallion. Plath.
Narrow fellow in the grass, A. Dickinson.
On a Little Boy's Endeavouring to Catch a Snake. Foxton.
Pit Viper. Momaday.
Python, The. Belloc.
Reveille. Hughes.
Serpent, The. Roethke.
Silent Snake, The. *Unknown.*
Snake. Lawrence.
Snake. McCord.
Snake. Roethke.
Snake and the Snake-Charmer, The. Rieu.
Snake Poem I. Harjo.
Snakes. Wild.
Springfield Mountain. *Unknown.*
Summer. Wakoski.
To the Snake. Levertov.

**Snipes**
To the Snipe. Clare.

**Snobbery**
Epitaph on a Tuft-Hunter. Moore.

**Snoring**
Snoring Bedmate, The. *Unknown.*

**Snow**
After Snow. Clark.
Angels in Winter. Willard.
Boy at the Window. Wilbur.
Cynthia in the Snow. Brooks.
Driving to Town Late to Mail a Letter. Bly.
Drove-Road, The. Gibson.
Dust of Snow. Frost.
Feathers of Snow. *Unknown.*
First Snow. Kay.
Going to Remake This World. Welch.
It sifts from leaden sieves. Dickinson.

Last Patch of Snow. Abbe.
London Snow. Bridges.
Long Lines. Goodman.
Riddles of the Weather. *Unknown.*
Snow Chant. Broughton.
Snow in the City. Field.
Snow in the Suburbs. Hardy.
Snow on Saddle Mountain, The. Miyazawa.
Snow that never drifts, The. Dickinson.
Snow-bound; a Winter Idyl. Whittier.
Snowfall, A. Eberhart.
Snowfall in the Afternoon. Bly.
Snowflake, The. De la Mare.
Snow-Flakes. Longfellow.
Snow-Storm, The. Emerson.
Soft Snow. Blake.
Stopping by Woods on a Snowy Evening. Frost.
There was a young man of Quebec. *Unknown.*
To a Snow-Flake. Thompson.
Velvet Shoes. Wylie.
White Fields. Stephens.
White Worlds. Luecke.

**Snowdrops**
Snowdrop, The. Tennyson.

**Snowflakes**
Snowflakes, The. De la Mare.
Watering the Horse. Bly.

**Soccer**
Rythm. Smith.
Soccer. Voznesensky.
Stanley Matthews. Ross.
Then Strip Lads, and To It. Scott.

**Social Protest.** *See* **Protest, Social.**

**Social Workers**
Feeding the Lions. Jordan.

**Sodom**
This Place Rumord to Have Been Sodom. Duncan.

**Softball**
Casey's Daughter at the Bat. Graham.

**Soldiers**
Another Epitaph on an Army of Mercenaries. "MacDiarmid."
Anthem for Doomed Youth. Owens.
Army Corps on the March, An. Whitman.
Arthur McBride. *Unknown.*
Box Comes Home, A. Ciardi.
Breakfast. Gibson.
British Grenadiers, The. *Unknown.*
Bugler's First Communion, The. Hopkins.
Cavalry Crossing a Ford. Whitman.
Character of the Happy Warrior. Wordsworth.
Comrades. McGlennon.
Coward, The. Spender.
Danny Deever. Kipling.
Defeated Victor, The. Bienek.
Disabled. Owen.
Does It Matter? Sassoon.
Dreamers. Sassoon.
1887. Housman.
Eighth Air Force. Jarrell.
Epitaph on an Army of Mercenaries. Housman.
For the Fallen. Binyon.
Fuzzy-Wuzzy. Kipling.
Gentlemen-Rankers. Kipling.
Gunga Din. Kipling.
How Sleep the Brave. Collins.
How We Heard the Name. Dugan.
Incident of the French Camp. Browning.
Innocence. Gunn.
Into Battle. Grenfell.
Kerry Recruit, The. *Unknown.*
Last of the Light Brigade, The. Kipling.
Lessons of the War. Reed.

Letter to Her Son's Commanding Officer.  Russell.
Lines on a Paid Militia.*Fr.* Cymon and Iphigenia.  Dryden.
Little Girl Saw Her First Troop Parade, The.  Sandburg.
My Morose Master-Sergeants.  Holt.
New Mistress, The.  Housman.
O What Is That Sound.  Auden.
Old Timers.  Sandburg.
On a Soldier Fallen in the Philippines.  Moody.
Peasants, The.  Lewis.
Place Pigalle.  Wilbur.
Recruiting Drive.  Causley.
Satirical Elegy, A.  Swift.
Send-off, The.  Owen.
Soldier, The.*Fr.* 1914.  Brooke.
Soldier Going to the Field, The.  Davenant.
Soldier, Rest!*Fr.* The Lady of the Lake.  Scott.
Soldiers Bathing.  Prince.
Song of the Freedman.  *Unknown.*
Sonnet to Negro Soldiers.  Cotter.
Speaking: The Hero.  Pollak.
Strange Meeting.  Owen.
Street Sounds to the Soldiers' Tread, The.  Housman.
To the Veterans of the Abraham Lincoln Brigade.  Taggard.
Tommy.  Kipling.
Vale from Carthage.  Viereck.
Volunteer, The.  Asquith.
When Johnny Comes Marching Home.  Gilmore.
*See also* **War.**
**Solitude**
Acre of Grass, An.  Yeats.
Anticipation of Sharks.  Wakoski.
Compensation.  Jeffers.
Desert Places.  Frost.
In Commendation of a Solitary Life.  Lodge.
Little Ecologue.  Wylie.
Most of It, The.  Frost.
O solitude! if I must with thee dwell.  Keats.
Ode on Solitude.  Pope.
Petition for an Absolute Retreat, The.  Countess of Winchilsea.
Poem of Solitude at Columbia University.  García Lorca.
Solitary Reaper, The.  Wordsworth.
Solitude.  Milne.
Solitude Late at Night in the Woods.  Bly.
Tin Can, The.  Smith.
To Any M.F.H.  Sackville-West.
To Marguerite — Continued.*Fr.* Switzerland.  Arnold.
**Solomon**
Solomon and the Witch.  Yeats.
**Somerset, Robert, Earl of**
Upon the Sudden Restraint of the Earl of Somerset, Then Falling Out of Favor.  Wotton.
**Sonnets**
On the Sonnet.  Keats.
Scorn not the sonnet; critic, you have frowned.  Wordsworth.
Sonnet, The.*Fr.* The House of Life.  D. G. Rossetti.
**Sons**
Ancient Couple on Lu Mountain, The.  Van Doren.
Death of a Son.  Silkin.
I Walk out into the Country at Night.  Lu Yu.
On My First Son.  Jonson.
To My Son.  Griffin.
**Sophocles**
Kaire.  Eberhart.
To a Friend.  Arnold.
**Sorrow**
Dark Song.  Ammons.
Dolor.  Roethke.
O Sorrow, Sorrow, say where dost thou dwell?*Fr.* The Noble Soldier.  Dekker.
Sorrow Is the Only Faithful One.  Dodson.
Troubled Woman.  Hughes.
With Rue My Heart Is Laden.  Housman.

*See also* **Grief.**
**Soul**
Caged Skylark, The.  Hopkins.
Dialogue between the Soul and Body, A.  Marvell.
Dialogue of Self and Soul, A.  Yeats.
I Know My Soul.  McKay.
Invention of Comics, The.  Jones.
Maya.  Robinson.
Noiseless Patient Spider, A.  Whitman.
Ode: "Bards of passion and of mirth."  Keats.
Pegasus.  Kavanagh.
Poor soul, the center of my sinful earth.*Fr.* Sonnets.  Shakespeare.
Soul and the Body, The.*Fr.* Nosce Teipsum.  Davies.
Soul has bandaged moments, The.  Dickinson.
Terrain.  Ammons.
**Sound**
Animal That Drank Up Sound, The.  Stafford.
**South, The**
Dixie.  Emmett.
First Families Move Over!  Nash.
Georgia Dusk.  Toomer.
Invitation to Madison County, An.  Wright.
Legacy: My South.  Randall.
Snapshots of the Cotton South.  Davis.
Southern Mansion.  Bontemps.
Southern Road, The.  Randall.
**South America**
South American Sway.  Byers.
**Southey, Robert**
Epitaph on Robert Southey.  Moore.
Vision of Judgment, The.  Byron.
**Space and Space Travel**
Beginnings.  Fitzgerald.
Christmas 1959 Et Cetera.  Barrax.
Earth's Bondman.  Dabney.
Love in a Space-Suit.  Kirkup.
Mission Uncontrolled.  Peck.
Missionary.  Thomas.
Moon Walk.  Belitt.
Moonwalk.  Engels.
Space.  Kennedy.
Tea in a Space-Ship.  Kirkup.
Unknown Shores.  Thomas.
**Spanish Armada**
Armada, 1588, The.  Wilson.
Sir Francis Drake; or Eighty-Eight.  *Unknown.*
**Spanish Civil War.  See Civil War, Spanish.**
**Sparrows**
Bee, the Ant and the Sparrow, The.  Cotton.
Dead Sparrow, The.  Cartwright.
Haiku: "Bitter morning, A."  Hackett.
London Sparrow's If, A.  Lindon.
Mr. and Mrs. Spikky Sparrow.  Lear.
Phyllyp Sparrowe.  Skelton.
Song of the Reed Sparrow, The.  *Unknown.*
Sparrow, The.  Williams.
Sparrow in the Zoo, The.  Nemerov.
**Spenser, Edmund**
Spenser! a jealous honourer of thine.  Keats.
**Sphinx**
Sphinx, The.  Emerson.
**Spiders**
Design.  Frost.
Identity.  Ammons.
Mr. Edwards and the Spider.  Lowell.
Noiseless Patient Spider, A.  Whitman.
Spider, The.  MacKenzie.
Spider and the Fly, The.  Howitt.
Spider and the Ghost of the Fly, The.  Lindsay.
Spider as an artist, The.  Dickinson.
Spider holds a silver ball, The.  Dickinson.

Spider in the Grapes. James.
Spider sewed at night, A. Dickinson.
**Spinsters**
Eleanor Rigby. Lennon *and* McCartney.
I'll Not Marry at All. *Unknown.*
Miss Gee. Auden.
Miss Loo. De la Mare.
My Mother's Sister. Day Lewis.
Old Ladies, The. Ellis.
Old Maid's Song. *Unknown.*
Spinster. Plath.
Waiting, the Hallways under Her Skin Thick with
   Dreamchildren. Lifshin.
Woman Who Loved Worms, The. Inez.
**Sports**
Life-Cycle. Dawe.
*Sports Poems* (SPo). R. R. Knudson *and* P. K. Ebert, eds.
*See also* **Athletes** *and* **individual games.**
**Spring**
After dark vapours have oppress'd our plains. Keats.
Allotments: April. Spencer.
And When the Green Man Comes. Haines.
April. Thompson.
April 1885. Bridges.
Aunt Alice in April. Matchett.
Backward Spring, A. Hardy.
Bee! I'm expecting you. Dickinson.
Canzone Pastoral in Honor of Her Majesty, A. Bolton.
Coming. Larkin.
Cuckoo Song. *Unknown.*
Echoing Green, The.*Fr.* Songs of Innocence. Blake.
Elm Buds. Sandburg.
Enkindled Spring, The. Lawrence.
First Sight. Larkin.
First Walk in the Park. Herschberger.
For Jane Myers. Gluck.
From you I have been absent in the spring.*Fr.* Sonnets.
   Shakespeare.
In a Spring Still Not Written Of. Wallace.
In Just-/ Spring.*Fr.* Chansons Innocentes. Cummings.
Innocent Spring, The. Sitwell.
June. Ledwidge.
Last Snow. Young.
Late Spring: a Heaving, a Turning. Gill.
Late Spring Day in My Life, A. Bly.
Lent Lily, The. Housman.
Light exists in spring, A. Dickinson.
Lines Written at a Small Distance from My House.
   Wordsworth.
Loveliest of Trees, the Cherry Now. Housman.
May 10th. Kumin.
Morning in Spring. Ginsberg.
Now fades the last long streak of snow.*Fr.* In Memoriam
   A.H.H. Tennyson.
Ode on the Spring. Gray.
Prayer in Spring, A. Frost.
Question, The ("I dream'd that, as I wander'd by the way").
   Shelley.
Rich Morning. Farren.
Sailing. Murray.
Saint-Henri Spring. Acorn.
Same Lady, The. Nichols.
Seed Leaves. Wilbur.
Slow Spring. Tynan.
Solvitur Acris Hiems. Horace.
Spring.*Fr.* Songs of Innocence. Blake.
Spring, The. Carew.
Spring. Hopkins.
Spring. Nashe.
Spring. Ridge.
Spring. Surrey.
Spring.*Fr.* The Seasons. Thomson.

Spring ("Lenten is come with love to towne"). *Unknown.*
Spring and All. Williams.
Spring Coming. Ammons.
Spring Goeth All in White. Bridges.
Spring Images. Wright.
Spring in New Hampshire. McKay.
Spring is like a perhaps hand. Cummings.
Spring Morning, A. Clare.
Spring Pools. Frost.
Spring Quiet. C. Rossetti.
Spring Stops Me Suddenly. Iremonger.
Spring, the Sweet Spring.*Fr.* Summer's Last Will and Testament.
   Nashe.
Spring Thunder. Van Doren.
Sweet spring is your. Cummings.
That Sharp Knife. Wolfe.
Thaw. Lifshin.
Thaw in the City. Lipsitz.
These are the days when birds come back. Dickinson.
Time, A: A Season. Ramsey.
To Spring. Blake.
To Spring. Smith.
Twilight in Middle March, A. Ledwidge.
Twist-Rime on Spring. Guiterman.
Vernal Sentiment. Roethke.
When daisies pied and violets blue.*Fr.* Love's Labour's Lost.
   Shakespeare.
When Spring came,/ Leaves grew with a green fresh.
   *Unknown.*
Who Calls? Clarke.
Written in March. Wordsworth.
Year's Awakening, The. Hardy.
Yin and Yang. Rexroth.
**Squirrels**
Fable: "The mountain and the squirrel." Emerson.
Migration of the Grey Squirrels, The. Howitt.
On a Squirrel Crossing the Road in Autumn, in New England.
   Eberhart.
Squirrel in Sunshine. Cowper.
Squirrel Near Library. Taggard.
Squirrels. Young.
**Stalin, Joseph**
"Less Nonsense." Herbert.
**Stanley, Sir Henry Morton**
Into the Dark. Monette.
**Starlings**
Smoke of Birds, A. Cowley.
Starling, The. Heath-Stubbs.
Starlings. MacCaig.
**Stars**
Awake, oh Heaven, for (lo) the Heavens Conspire. Tourneur.
Bright Star! Would I Were As Steadfast As Thou Art. Keats.
Darkness. Campbell.
First Star. *Unknown.*
Great Bear, The. Hollander.
If the Stars Should Fall. Allen.
Little Star, The. *Unknown.*
Lost Lane. Wellesley.
Martial Cadenza. Stevens.
My Star. Browning.
Star, The. Taylor.
Star-Talk. Graves.
Stars. Nowlan.
Stars Wheel in Purple. Doolittle ("H.D.").
Summer Stars. Sandburg.
To the Evening Star. Blake.
Twinkle, twinkle, little star. Dehn.
When I Heard the Learn'd Astronomer. Whitman.
**Statistics**
Meditation on Statistical Method. Cunningham.
**Statues**
By the Statue of King Charles at Charing Cross. Johnson.

Cheap Rent. Sandburg.
Instructions for the Erection of a Statue of Myself in Central Park. Inez.
On a Statue of Sir Arthur Sullivan. Hamilton.
Ponder, darling, these busted statues. Cummings.
Six Statues in a Park. Stuart.
Statue, The. Fuller.
Statues in the Public Gardens, The. Nemerov.
Tiki. Anderson.

**Steeples**
Steeple-Jack, The. Moore.
To a Solitary Disciple. Williams.

**Stein, Gertrude**
Yesterday. Winant.

**Stevens, Wallace**
In His Poems Are El Greco's Hands. Leverant.
So Long? Stevens. Berryman.

**Stinkbugs**
Dusty black beetle, A. Sund.

**Stones and Rocks**
Forecast. Miles.
I've Got a Home in That Rock. Patterson.
Petoskey Stone. Vas Dias.
Rock and Hawk. Jeffers.
Rock Climbing. Cooper.
Serenity in Stones, The. Ortiz.
Skipping Stones. Farber.
Stone Poems, The. Smith.
Three Stones. Watson.
To the Stone-Cutters. Jeffers.
What Any Lover Learns. MacLeish.

**Storms**
Beginning to Squall. Swenson.
Big Wind. Roethke.
Blizzard, The. Dewey.
Brainstorm. Nemerov.
Found in a Storm. Stafford.
Hatteras Calling. Aiken.
June Thunder. MacNeice.
Little Exercise. Bishop.
Local Storm, A. Justice.
Low Barometer. Bridges.
Misgivings. Melville.
Snow-bound; a Winter Idyl. Whittier.
Snow-Storm, The. Emerson.
Squall. Moore.
Storm, The. Roethke.
Storm. Wright.
Storm at Sea, A. Donne.
Storm Cone, The. Kipling.
Storm Fear. Frost.
Storm on the Island. Heaney.
Storm Tide on Mejit. *Unknown.*
Storm-Wind, The. Barnes.
Tempest, The. *Unknown.*
Thunderstorm in Town, A. Hardy.
West Palm Beach Storm, The. *Unknown.*
Wind begun to rock the grass, The. Dickinson.

**Story Poems**
*The Poet's Tales; A New Book of Story Poems* (PoTa). William Cole, ed.

**Storytelling and Storytellers**
Story-Teller, The. Van Doren.

**Stowe, Harriet Beecher**
Harriet Beecher Stowe. Dunbar.

**Strauss, Richard**
1907: A Proposal from Paris. Howard.

**Strawberries**
Wild Strawberries. Graves.

**Streams.** *See* **Brooks and Streams.**

**Stuart, Charles Edward, the Young Pretender**
Charlie Is My Darling. Nairne.

Old Scottish Cavalier, The. Aytoun.
Wae's Me for Prince Charlie. Glen.

**Students**
Foreign Student. Robinson.
Freshmen. Spacks.
Heathen Pass-ee, The. Hilton.
On Hearing That the Students of Our New University Have Joined the Agitation Against Immoral Literature. Yeats.
Straying Student, The. Clarke.
Student, The. Stuart.
Theme for English B. Hughes.
Two Sec. Mods. Ghose.
University Examinations in Egypt. Enright.
Vulture and the Husbandman, The. Hilton.
You Understand the Requirements. Lifshin.
*See also* **Education; Scholars and Scholarship; School.**

**Stuttering**
Mister Charlie. *Unknown.*
Stutterer. Dugan.

**Suburbs**
Before the Stuff Comes Down. Snyder.
5:32, The. McGinley.
In the Suburbs. Simpson.
Middlesex. Betjeman.
Suburb, The. Stevenson.
Suburban Dream. Muir.
We Told You So. Keesing.

**Subways**
Boy Who Smells Like Cocoa, A. Hershon.
City Afternoon. Howes.
Clickety-Clack. Blackburn.
In a Station of the Metro. Pound.
Metropolitan Railway, The. Betjeman.
Subway, The. Tate.
This Subway Station. Reznikoff.
Tubes. Mollin.

**Success**
Names. Enright.
Robert Whitmore. Davis.
Success is counted sweetest. Dickinson.

**Suicide**
After the Surprising Conversions. Lowell.
Butcher Boy, The. *Unknown.*
Call It a Good Marriage. Graves.
Caroline of Edinboro' Town. *Unknown.*
Dear Girl, The. Warner.
Elderly Nobody Erases Self in Central Park. Forgotson.
Exeat. Smith.
Felo De Se. Blackburn.
For Black Poets Who Think of Suicide. Knight.
Henry's Understanding. Berryman.
Justice Is Reason Enough. Wakoski.
Lady Lazarus. Plath.
Mill, The. Robinson.
Newcomer's Wife, The. Hardy.
Notes Found Near a Suicide. Horne.
Of Late. Starbuck.
Of Suicide. Berryman.
On the Suicide of a Friend. Whittemore.
Quaker Hero, Burning. Noll.
Résumé. Parker.
Richard Cory. Robinson.
Richard Cory. Simon.
Singular Self, The. Bukowski.
Sportsman, The. McCord.
Suicide Off Egg Rock. Plath.
Wanting to Die. Sexton.
Wedding, The. Gant.
Why I Died. Jong.

**Sumac**
Sumach Leaves, The. Very.

**Summer**

As imperceptibly as grief. Dickinson.
August Fugue. Shapcott.
Beginning, The. Stevens.
Cuckoo Song. *Unknown.*
Dog-Days. A. Lowell.
End of Summer. Kunitz.
Exeunt. Wilbur.
Fortune. Ferlinghetti.
High Summer on the Mountains. Davies.
Hymn to the Sun. Roberts.
In Fields of Summer. Kinnell.
In the Good Old Summer Time. Shields.
Knoxville, Tennessee. Giovanni.
Late August. Atwood.
Loud is the summer's busy song.*Fr.* The Shepherd's Calender:
   July. Clare.
Musings. Barnes.
My Father Paints the Summer. Wilbur.
Rainy Summer, The. Meynell.
School Boy, The.*Fr.* Songs of Experience. Blake.
Songs to Survive the Summer. Hass.
Soote Season, The. Surrey.
Summer. C. Rossetti.
Summer Countries, The. Rago.
Summer Is Gone. *Unknown.*
Summer Music. Sarton.
Summer Song. Ciardi.
Summertime and the Living. Hayden.
These are the days when birds come back. Dickinson.
To Summer. Blake.

**Sun**
Ask of the sun. Zukofsky.
Indian Summer Day on the Prairie, An. Lindsay.
Metric Figure. Williams.
November. Harvey.
Ol' Hannah. *Unknown.*
Prayer, A: "Sun my relative." *Unknown.*
Sun. Dickey.
Sun, The. Drinkwater.
Sun. Moore.
Sun Rising, The. Donne.
Sun-flower, The. Greenwell.
Versions of Sunlight. Applewhite.

**Sunday**
On a Sunday Afternoon. Sterling.

**Sundials**
Epigram: "I who by day am function of the light."
   Cunningham.
I am a sundial, turned the wrong way round. Belloc.
On a Sundial. Belloc.

**Sunflowers**
Ah! Sun-Flower.*Fr.* Songs of Experience. Blake.
Sun-flower, The. Greenwell.
Sunflower Sutra. Ginsberg.
Sunflowers, The. Stewart.
Tom O'Bedlam among the Sunflowers. James.

**Sunrise**
Out of the Sea, Early. Swenson.
Plainview: 3. Momaday.
Sunrise. Lanier.
*See also* **Dawn; Morning.**

**Sunset**
Evening: to Harriet. Shelley.
Mise en Scene. Fitzgerald.
On Its Way. Swenson.
Prairie Sunset, A. Whitman.
We in the Fields. Everson.
*See also* **Evening; Twilight.**

**Supermarkets**
Grace to Be Said at the Supermarket. Nemerov.
Supermarket in California, A. Ginsberg.

**Supernatural**

*Catch Your Breath: A Book of Shivery Poems* (CaYB). Lilian
   Moore *and* Lawrence Webster, comps.

**Surfers and Surfing**
Surfer, The. Wright.
Surfer and Others. Dorman.
Surfers at Santa Cruz. Goodman.

**Surrealism**
Salvador Dali. Gascoyne.

**Surrey, Henry Howard, Earl of**
Verse in Praise of Lord Henry Howard, Earl of Surrey.
   Turberville.

**Susanna (Bible)**
Peter Quince at the Clavier. Stevens.
Susannah and the Elders. *Unknown.*

**Sussex, England**
Puck's Song.*Fr.* Puck of Pook's Hill. Kipling.
Sussex. Kipling.

**Swallows**
Swallow, The. Aikin.
Swallows, The. Coatsworth.
Swallows. Ferril.
Upon the Swallow. Bunyan.

**Swamps**
Alligator, The. Ravenel.

**Swan**
Hard Edge of Beauty. Stuart.
Love the Wild Swan. Jeffers.
Mating Swans. McAuley.
Mirror, The. Milne.
Silver Swan, The. *Unknown.*
Swan Bathing, The. Pitter.
Swans, The. Dyment.
Swans, The. Sitwell.
Swan's Feet, The. Scovell.
Three Sentences for a Dead Swan. Wright.
Wild Swans at Coole, The. Yeats.
Wring the Swan's Neck. Martinez.

**Sweden**
Carriage from Sweden, A. Moore.

**Swift, Jonathan**
Hypocrite Swift. Bogan.
Lamentation of Glumdalclitch, The. Pope.
Lines on Swift's Ancestors. Pope.
On Himself. Swift.
Sermon on Swift, A. Clarke.
Verses on the Death of Doctor Swift, *sels.* Swift.
Written in a Copy of Swift's Poems for Wayne Burns. Wright.

**Swimming and Swimmers**
And I Have Loved Thee, Ocean!*Fr.* Childe Harold's Pilgrimage.
   Byron.
Dead Man Creek. Brock.
Fall In. Kirstein.
First Lesson. Booth.
400-Meter Freestyle. Kumin.
Inside the River. Dickey.
Intimations at the Lake, 1963. Minton.
Morning Swim. Kumin.
On a Friend's Escape from Drowning off the Norfolk Coast.
   Barker.
Swimmer in the Rain. Wallace.
Swimming by Night. Merrill.
Swimming Chenango Lake. Tomlinson.
Upon Boys Diverting Themselves in the River. Foxton.
Written after Swimming from Sestos to Abydos. Byron.

**Swings**
Swing, The. Stevenson.

**Switzerland**
Thought of a Briton on the Subjugation of Switzerland.
   Wordsworth.

**Synge, John Millington**
Memory, A. Strong.
Municipal Gallery Revisited, The. Yeats.

## T

**Tailors**
Tailor. Farjeon.
**Tapestry**
Tapestry, The. Nemerov.
**Tasmania**
In Northern Tasmania. McAuley.
**Taxis**
Taxis, The. MacNeice.
**Tea**
Monody on a Tea-Kettle. Coleridge.
**Teaching and Teachers**
Absent-Minded Professor. Nemerov.
Ageing Schoolmaster, An. Scannell.
April Inventory. Snodgrass.
Correspondence School Instructor Says Goodbye to His Poetry
   Students, The. Kinnell.
Dustless Chalk. Rankin.
Educators, The. Black.
French Master, The. Abse.
Freshmen. Spacks.
He Don't Know the Inside Feel. Adams.
Kindergarten Teacher. Kiesel.
Letter to a Teacher of English, A. Hillyer.
On Reading Poems to a Senior Class at South High. Berry.
Pay Is Good, The. Kell.
Place's Fault, The. Hobsbaum.
Preliminary to Classroom Lecture. Miles.
Professor's Song, A. Berryman.
Schoolmistress. Sansom.
School-Mistress, The. Shenstone.
Student, The. Eckman.
Teacher, A. McGregor.
Teacher, A. Whittemore.
Teacher of Poetry, The. Packard.
Teechur. Higgins.
To My Old Schoolmaster. Whittier.
What Schoolmasters Say. Seymour-Smith.
Year's End. Barnes.
**Tears**
Eyes and Tears. Marvell.
My Lady's Tears. *Unknown.*
Tears. E. Browning.
Tears. *Unknown.*
Tears, Idle Tears.*Fr.* The Princess. Tennyson.
Valediction, A: of Weeping. Donne.
**Telegraph**
Cable Hymn, The. Whittier.
**Telephones**
Crimes of Passion: The Phone Caller. Stokes.
Dial Tone, The. Nemerov.
Eletelephony. Richards.
Obscene Caller, The. Dacey.
On Seeing a Torn Out Coin Telephone. Robbins.
Slight Confusion, A. Reiss.
**Television**
Aunts Watching Television. Pudney.
Electric Cop, The. Cruz.
Goodbye, Old Paint, I'm Leaving Cheyenne. Garrett.
Jimmy Jet and His TV Set. Silverstein.
Mousemeal. Nemerov.
Speaking of Television, *sels.* McGinley.
When Daddy Died. Ackerson.
**Teniers, David, the Younger.**
Bench of Boors, The. Melville.
**Tennis**
40—Love. McGough.
Midnight Tennis Match, The. Lux.
Old Pro's Lament, The. Petrie.

Subaltern's Love Song, A. Betjeman.
Tennis. Avison.
**Tennyson, Alfred Tennyson, 1st Baron**
To Alfred Tennyson. Landor.
**Termites**
Tree Animals. Lieberman.
**Terns**
Gracious Goodness. Piercy.
**Terrorists**
Montage. Guest.
**Thames (river), England.**
Lines Written near Richmond, upon the Thames, at Evening.
   Wordsworth.
Voyage on the Thames, The.*Fr.* The Rape of the Lock. Pope.
**Thanksgiving**
Prayer for the Great Family. Snyder.
Thanksgiving. Herrick.
Thanksgiving. Morris.
**Thanksgiving Day**
Thanksgiving Day. Child.
Thanksgiving in Boston Harbor, The. Butterworth.
Thanksgiving to God, for His House, A. Herrick.
**Theater**
Prologue Spoken at the Opening of the Theatre in Drury-Lane,
   1747. Johnson.
Rehearsal, The. Gregory.
**Theresa, Saint, of Avila**
Flaming Heart, The, *sels.* Crashaw.
Hymn to the Name and Honor of the Admirable St. Theresa, A.
   Crashaw.
**Thermopylae, Battle of**
Oracles, The. Housman.
**Theseus**
Theseus: A Trilogy. Winters.
**Thistles**
Thistledown. Monro.
Thistles. Hughes.
**Thomas, Dylan**
True Picture Restored, A. Watkins.
**Thomas à Becket, Saint**
Becket. Gilbert.
**Thomas the Rhymer (Thomas of Erceldoune)**
Thomas Rymer. *Unknown.*
**Thomson, James (1700-1748)**
Ode Occasion'd by the Death of Mr. Thomson. Collins.
**Thrushes**
Darkling Thrush, The. Hardy.
Thrush Before Dawn, A. Meynell.
Thrushes. Hughes.
Thrush's Nest, The. Clare.
Thrush's Nest, The. Ryan.
What the Thrush Said. Keats.
**Thunder**
Spring Thunder. Van Doren.
**Tides**
Tide Rises, the Tide Falls, The. Longfellow.
**Tigers**
O have you caught the tiger? Housman.
Tyger, The.*Fr.* Songs of Experience. Blake.
**Timbuktu**
Timbuctu. Brathwaite.
**Time**
And the Days Are Not Full Enough. Pound.
Birthday, The. Dacey.
Birthday Verses Written in a Child's Album. Lowell.
Cat's Eyes. Scarfe.
Cities and Thrones and Powers.*Fr.* Puck of Pook's Hill.
   Kipling.
Clerks, The. Robinson.
Cold Fall. Eberhart.
Confession of a Young Hegelian. Griffin.
Days. Emerson.

Days, The.  Hall.

Dear Men and Women.  Wheelock.

Devouring time blunt thou the lion's paws.*Fr.* Sonnets.
  Shakespeare.

Dialogue betwixt Time and a Pilgrim, A.  Townsend.

Dream within a Dream, A.  Poe.

During Wind and Rain.  Hardy.

Even Such Is Tyme.  Ralegh.

Forever is composed of nows.  Dickinson.

Four Preludes on Playthings of the Wind.  Sandburg.

Four seasons fill the measure of the year.  Keats.

God's Education.  Hardy.

Going and Staying.  Hardy.

Her Reply.  Ralegh.

How Soon Hath Time the Subtle Thief of Youth.  Milton.

In Italian They Call the Bird Civetta.  Warren.

In the Fleeting Hand of Time.  Corso.

Lamentation of the Old Pensioner, The.  Yeats.

Light Year, The.  Ridland.

Like as the waves make towards the pebbled shore.*Fr.* Sonnets.
  Shakespeare.

Maple in November.  Russell.

Mutability.*Fr.* Ecclesiastical Sonnets.  Wordsworth.

Next, Please.  Larkin.

1967.  Hardy.

Nothing Gold Can Stay.  Frost.

Old Furniture.  Hardy.

On an Hour-Glass.  Hall.

On Time.  Milton.

Our Bias.  Auden.

Poet Laments the Coming of Old Age, The.  Sitwell.

Rising Five.  Nicholson.

Roll on, sad world! not Mercury or Mars.*Fr.* Sonnets.
  Tuckerman.

Scene on the Banks of the Hudson, A.  Bryant.

Sheep Fair, A.  Hardy.

Shut Out That Moon.  Hardy.

Signature for Tempo.  MacLeish.

Since brass, nor stone, nor earth, nor boundless sea.*Fr.* Sonnets.
  Shakespeare.

Slow Starter, The.  MacNeice.

Song: "Who can say."  Tennyson.

Sunshade, The.  Hardy.

Tide Rises, the Tide Falls, The.  Longfellow.

Time.  Wynne.

Time Is the Mercy of Eternity.  Rexroth.

Time, Real and Imaginary.  Coleridge.

Time's Dedication.  Schwartz.

To Daffodils.  Herrick.

XXth Century.  Hillyer.

Wheel Revolves, The.  Rexroth.

When I have seen by Time's fell hand defaced.*Fr.* Sonnets.
  Shakespeare.

Where it is.  Creeley.

You, Andrew Marvell.  MacLeish.

**Titanic (ship)**

Convergence of the Twain, The.  Hardy.

Great *Titanic*.  *Unknown.*

I Sing of Shine.  Knight.

Sinking of the *Titanic*.  *Unknown.*

*Titanic*, The.  *Unknown.*

*Titanic* Blues.  *Unknown.*

**Tithonus**

Tithonus.  Tennyson.

**Titian**

Venus and the Lute Player.  Engle.

**Toads**

Death of a Toad, The.  Wilbur.

Friend in the Garden, A.  Ewing.

History Lesson for My Son.  Kooser.

Toad.  Cotton.

Toad School.  Meeter.

**Tobacco**

Ode to Tobacco.  Calverley.

Says the Miner to the Mucker.  *Unknown.*

Tobacco.  Harris.

**Toledo, Ohio**

Atlas.  Flanagan.

**Tolstoy, Leo**

Now It's Happened.  Lawrence.

**Tools**

His Request.  O'Sullivan.

**Toothaches**

Charm against the Toothache, A.  Heath-Stubbs.

**Tornadoes**

Sherman Cyclone, The.  *Unknown.*

Tornado.  Stafford.

Tupelo Destruction, The.  *Unknown.*

**Toronto, Ontario**

Nights Passed on Ward's Island, Toronto Harbour.  Fetherling.

**Tortoises**

Baby Tortoise.  Lawrence.

Giant Tortoise, The.  Lucie-Smith.

Tortoise.  De Longchamps.

Tortoise Gallantry.  Lawrence.

Tortoise Shout.  Lawrence.

**Tourists**

Afternoons with Baedeker.  Lancaster.

Importer, An.  Frost.

Manners.  Shiffert.

This Is the Life.  MacNeice.

Trials of a Tourist.  Tibble.

Twenty-Third Flight.  Birney.

**Toussaint L'Overture, François Dominique**

To Toussaint L'Ouverture.  Wordsworth.

**Towns**

Anderson, Indiana.  White.

Midwest Town.  Peterson.

Sunday Dreamer's Guide to Yarrow, Missouri, A.  Barnes.

X.  Dickey.

**Toys**

Little Boy Blue.  Field.

Toys, The.  Patmore.

**Track Athletics**

Cry of the High Hurdlers, The.  Fiske.

High Jump, The.  *Unknown.*

Pole Vaulter.  Evans.

Pole-Vaulter, The.  *Unknown.*

Runner, The.  Whitman.

Sports Field.  Wright.

**Tractors**

Cynddylan on a Tractor.  Thomas.

**Traffic**

Meditations on Frost's "Stopping by Woods."  De Pietro.

**Traffic Accidents**

Auto Wreck.  Shapiro.

Chorus: "They were singing Old MacDonald in the schoolbus."
  Ciardi.

Obituary.  Fearing.

**Trains**

Boxcar Poem, The.  Young.

By Rail Through Istria.  Conquest.

Express, The.  Spender.

Evening Song.  Anderson.

Flying Crow.  *Unknown.*

I like to see it lap the miles.  Dickinson.

In a Train.  Bly.

Limited.  Sandburg.

Lines Written in Objection; or, the Limpopo Express.  Hey.

Midnight on the Great Western.  Hardy.

Night Journey.  Roethke.

Night Mail.  Auden.

Number 29.  *Unknown.*

Observation Car.  Hope.

Panama Limited, The. *Unknown.*
Railroad Reverie. Young.
Smokestack Lightin'. *Unknown.*
Starting from San Francisco. Ferlinghetti.
To a Locomotive in Winter. Whitman.
Train, The. Brownjohn.
Train: Abstraction. Taggard.
Train Tune. Bogan.
Women don't travel in clubcars. Jonas.
*See also* **Railroads.**

**Trappers and Trapping**
Hare in Winter. Piercy.
Rabbit, The. Davies.

**Trash**
Junk. Wilbur.

**Travel**
Crossing the Atlantic. Sexton.
Farewell to Kurdistan. Tonks.
Frontier, The. Hewitt.
I Am Going to California. Jace.
Lines to Mr. Hodgson. Byron.
Louise. Smith.
Old Walking Song, The. Tolkien.
On the Circuit. Auden.
Over 2000 Illustrations and a Complete Concordance. Bishop.
Questions of Travel. Bishop.
Railway Junction, The. De la Mare.
Starting from San Francisco. Ferlinghetti.
Traveller, The. Berryman.
Travelers, The. Reeves.
Two Travellers, The. Boland.

**Treason**
Treason. Harington.

**Trees**
All That Time. Swenson.
And When the Green Man Comes. Haines.
Ballad of Trees and the Master, A. Lanier.
Binsey Poplars. Hopkins.
Child's Song in Spring. Nesbit.
Cycads, The. Wright.
He Praises the Trees. *Unknown.*
Knife and Sap. Leslie.
Learning by Doing. Nemerov.
Legend of Paper Plates, The. Haines.
Loveliest of Trees, the Cherry Now. Housman.
On a Great Hollow Tree. Strode.
Snow-Gum, The. Stewart.
Some Knots. Honig.
Song: "Love and harmony combine." Blake.
Song of the Open Road. Nash.
Sound of Trees, The. Frost.
Stump, The. Hall.
Tenebris. Grimké.
They. Finkel.
3 Stanzas About a Tree. Bell.
Tree. Hoffman.
Tree, The. Hopewell.
Tree, The. Pound.
Tree. Smith.
Tree at My Window. Frost.
Tree Is Father to the Man, The. Lipsitz.
Tree Party. MacNeice.
Trees. S. Coleridge.
Trees. Kilmer.
Trees, The. Rich.
Trees, The. Williams.
Trees and Evening Sky. Momaday.
Trees Are Down, The. Mew.
Walnut-Leaf Scent. Binyon.
War Against the Trees, The. Kunitz.
Willow-Man, The. Ewing.
Winter Trees. Plath.

Woodman Spare That Tree. Morris.
*See also* **names of trees** *(e.g.,* **Poplars***).*

**Trojan War**
Palladium. Arnold.
Scenes from the Fall of Troy. Morris.

**Trolleys**
Burned Bridge, The. Stone.
Dump, The. Hall.

**Trout**
Trout, The. Montague.
Trout of the Well, The. *Unknown.*

**Troy, New York**
Going and Coming: Two Poems. Benedikt.

**Trucks and Truckers**
Pancho Villa. Lipsitz.
Truck Drivers. Haag.
Truckdriver. Sange.
Water-Truck, The. Lane.

**Trumpets**
How High the Moon. L. Jeffers.

**Truth**
Tell all the truth but tell it slant. Dickinson.
True Confession, A. Stallworthy.
Truth. McKay.
Wayfarer, The. *Fr.* War is Kind. Crane.
When my love swears that she is made of truth. *Fr.* Sonnets. Shakespeare.

**Truth, Sojourner**
Oriflamme. Fauset.

**Tuberculosis**
T.B. Blues. *Unknown.*

**Tubman, Harriet**
I Like to Think of Harriet Tubman. Griffin.
Runagate Runagate. Hayden.

**Tulips**
Tulips. Plath.

**Turkeys**
Black November Turkey, A. Wilbur.
Soliloquy of a Turkey. Dunbar.

**Turner, Lana**
Poem: "Lana Turner has collapsed." O'Hara.

**Turner, Nat**
Ballad of Nat Turner, The. Hayden.
Nat Turner in the Clearing. Aubert.
Remembering Nat Turner. Brown.

**Turtles**
Little Turtle, The. Lindsay.
Living Tenderly. Swenson.
Sea-Turtle and the Shark, The. Tolson.
Snapper, The. Heyen.
Tony the Turtle. Rieu.
Turtle, The. Nash.
Turtle, The. *Fr.* Greed. Wakoski.
Turtle's Song, The. *Unknown.*

**Tutsan (plant)**
Tutsan. Senior.

**Twilight**
Georgia Dusk. Toomer.
If the Owl Calls Again. Haines.
Winter Twilight, A. Grimké.
*See also* **Evening; Sunset.**

**Twins**
Gemini. Creeley.

**Tyranny**
Epitaph on a Tyrant. Auden.
Song to the Men of England. Shelley.

# U

**UFO's**
Midwest U.F.O. Steingass.

**Ulysses**
Callypso Speaks.  Doolittle ("H.D.").
Canto I: "And then went down to the ship."  Pound.
Odysseus.  Merwin.
Tales of Brave Ulysses.  Clapton *and* Sharp.
Ulysses.*Fr.* Divina Commedia: Inferno.  Dante.
Ulysses.  Graves.
Ulysses.  Tennyson.
Ulysses and the Siren.  Daniel.
World as Meditation, The.  Stevens.
**Underground Railroad**
Runagate Runagate.  Hayden.
**Undertakers**
Undertaker's Club, The.  *Unknown.*
**Unemployment**
Moving through the Silent Crowd.  Spender.
Young fellow walks about, The.  Reznikoff.
**Unicorns**
Talisman for the New Year, A.  Metzger.
Unicorn.  Gray.
**Unions.**  *See* **Labor Unions.**
**United States**
America.  Creeley.
America.  Ginsberg.
America.  McKay.
America.  Smith.
America a Prophecy.  Blake.
America Bleeds.  Lewis.
America for Me.  Van Dyke.
America the Beautiful.  Bates.
Brooklyn Heights.  Wain.
Brown River, Smile.  Toomer.
Centennial Hymn.  Whittier.
Columbia.  *Unknown.*
Columbia, the Gem of the Ocean.  Shaw.
Dear America.  Peterson.
England.  Moore.
Flag Goes By, The.  Bennett.
1492.  Lazarus.
Free America.  Warren.
Gift Outright, The.  Frost.
Hail, Columbia.  Hopkinson.
I Hear America Singing.  Whitman.
In Goya's greatest scenes we seem to see.*Fr.* A Coney Island of
the Mind.  Ferlinghetti.
Inner Part, The.  Simpson.
Invocation: "American muse, whose strong and diverse
heart."*Fr.* John Brown's Body.  Benét.
Long, Too Long America.  Whitman.
My Blackness Is the Beauty of This Land.  L. Jeffers.
New Colossus, The.  Lazarus.
On the Emigration to America.  Freneau.
On the Prospect of Planting Arts and Learning in America.
Berkeley.
Poem, or Beauty Hurts Mr. Vinal.  Cummings.
Republic, The.  Longfellow.
Sailing from the United States.  Moss.
Shine, Perishing Republic.  Jeffers.
Starting from San Francisco.  Ferlinghetti.
To Cole, the Painter, Departing for Europe.  Bryant.
To My Son Parker, Asleep in the Next Room.  Kaufman.
To the Republicans of North America.  Shelley.
U.S.A., The.  Rice.
Watch the Lights Fade.  Jeffers.
**United States Air Force**
Air Force Blue, The.  *Unknown.*
**United States Army**
Caissons Go Rolling Along, The.  Gruber.
**United States Marine Corps**
Marine Hymn, The.  *Unknown.*
**Universe**
3 Models of the Universe.  Swenson.

Universe, The.  Swenson.
**Universities.**  *See* **Colleges and Universities.**
**Unknown Soldier**
Unknown Dead, The.  Timrod.
**Unwin, Mary**
To Mary.  Cowper.
**Uriel**
Uriel.  Emerson.
**Ursa Major**
Great Bear, The.  Hollander.
**Usury**
Canto XLV: "With Usura."  Pound.
Gombeen, The.  Campbell.
**Utah**
Marching to Utah.  *Unknown.*
Utah.  Stevenson.

# V

**Vacation**
I'm Going to Rocky Island.  *Unknown.*
Lake Chemo.  Rowe.
School's Out.  Davies.
Vacation.  Stafford.
**Vagabonds**
Bums, on Waking.  Dickey.
Communion of Saints: The Poor Bastard under the Bridge.
Ponsot.
Dying Hobo, The.  *Unknown.*
Hallelujah, Bum Again.  *Unknown.*
Me and You and a Dog Named Boo.  LaVoie.
Sunflower Rock.  Blackburn.
Taking Off.  Rogers.
**Valentine's Day**
February Loves.  Lattimore.
Hail, Bishop Valentine, whose day this is.*Fr.* An Epithalamion.
Donne.
St. Valentine.  Moore.
Thank You for the Valentine.  Wakoski.
To My Valentine.  *Unknown.*
To-morrow is Saint Valentine's Day.*Fr.* Hamlet.  Shakespeare.
Valentines to My Mother, 1880.  C. Rossetti.
**Vampires**
Undead, The.  Wilbur.
Voices Answering Back: The Vampires.  Raab.
**Vanbrugh, Sir John**
On Sir John Vanbrugh, Architect.  Evans.
**Vanity**
Four Preludes on Playthings of the Wind.  Sandburg.
On the Death of a Metaphysician.  Santayana.
Ozymandias.  Shelley.
Palinode, A.  Bolton.
Vanitas Vanitatum.*Fr.* The Devil's Law Case.  Webster.
**Vegetables**
Cauliflower, The.  Haines.
Fruit and Vegetables.  Jong.
Marshall.  Macbeth.
Root-crops.  Bowman.
Three from the Market.  McPherson.
**Vegetarians**
I Don't Eat Animals (and They Don't Eat Me).  Safka.
**Velázquez, Diego Rodríguez de Silva y**
Portrait, A.  De la Mare.
Rokeby Venus, The.  Conquest.
**Venereal Disease**
Cadaver.  Stone.
Pangloss's song.  Wilbur.
**Venice, Italy**

On the Extinction of the Venetian Republic. Wordsworth.
Venice and Sunset. *Fr.* Childe Harold's Pilgrimage. Byron.

**Venus (goddess)**
Death of Venus, The. Creeley.
Invocation to the Goddess, An. Wright.
Venus of the Salty Shell. Devlin.
*See also* **Aphrodite.**

**Venus (planet).** *See* **Evening Star.**

**Venus of Milo (statue)**
Venus of the Louvre. Lazarus.

**Veracruz, Mexico**
Beach at Veracruz, The. Bowering.

**Vermont**
Indian Summer: Vermont. Stevenson.
Windham Thaw, The. Guiterman.

**Vesalius, Andreas**
Cider and Vesalius. Peck.

**Vesta**
To Vesta. Middleton.

**Veterinarians**
Vet, The. Boas.

**Victoria, Queen of England**
1887. Housman.
Ode on the Installation of His Royal Highness Prince Albert. Wordsworth.
Queen Victoria and Me. Cohen.

**Vienna, Austria**
View of Vienna from Schonbrunn. Ruse.

**Vietnam.**
Advent 1966. Levertov.
Altars in the Street, The. Levertov.
Americana XV: Simplicity. Rakosi.
Asian Peace Offers Rejected Without Publication. Bly.
Atlas' Daughter. Mann.
Bummer, A. Casey.
Butter. Schmidt.
Containing Communism. Cobb.
Earth Sings Mi-Fa-Mi, The. Lowther.
Epitaph: "Here lies fierce Strephon, whose poetic rage." Hecht.
Foreign Policy Commitments; or, You Get Into the Catamaran First, Old Buddy. Blackburn.
Hallowe'en 1971. Browne.
In the Mourning Time. Hayden.
Junglegrave. Anderson.
Lost, The. Dunn.
Memo. Lynch.
Negro Soldier's Viet Nam Diary, A. Martin.
Non Poem about Vietnam, A. Rodgers.
Norman Morrison. Mitchell.
Of Late. Starbuck.
Paraders for the Bomb. Bernard.
Poem About Poems About Vietnam, A. Stallworthy.
Teeth Mother Naked at Last, The. Bly.
Third World, The. Ferlinghetti.
Thirty-nine thousand/five hundred and seventy-two. Trudell.
Vietnam. Major.
Vietnam #4. Major.
Voice from Danang. Redshaw.
What Were They Like? Levertov.
Wichita Vortex Sutra. Ginsberg.
Women in Vietnam, The. Paley.

**Vikings**
Battle of Brunanburh. *Unknown.*
Runilda's Chant. *Fr.* Ethelstan. Darley.
Viking Terror, The. *Unknown.*
Vikings, The. *Unknown.*

**Vinci, Leonardo da.** *See* **Leonardo da Vinci.**

**Violence**
Beating, The. Stanford.
Formal Application. Baker.
Mousemeal. Nemerov.

**Violets**

Sonnet: "I had no thought of violets of late." Nelson.

**Violins**
Country Fiddler, The. Montague.
Ode to a Violin. Salinas.

**Virgin Mary.** *See* **Mary, the Virgin.**

**Virginia**
Carry Me Back to Old Virginny. Bland.

**Virginity**
All Night by the Rose. *Unknown.*
Best Line Yet, The. Allen.
Broomfield Hill, The. *Unknown.*
Dialogue After Enjoyment. Cowley.
First Time, The. Newlove.
Honour. Cowley.
How Can I Keep My Maidenhead. Burns.
In Bertram's Garden. Justice.
Maidenhead. Philips.
To the Virgins, to Make Much of Time. Herrick.
Twa Magicians, The. *Unknown.*

**Vogler, Georg Joseph**
Abt Vogler. Browning.

**Voltaire, François Marie Arouet de**
Epigram on Voltaire. Young.
Mock on mock on Voltaire Rousseau. Blake.

**Voters and Voting**
Poll. Roberson.

**Vowels**
Five, The. Swift.
Vowels. West.

**Voyages**
Crossing the Atlantic. Sexton.
Voyages, *sels.* Crane.

**Vulpius, Melchoir**
Melchior Vulpius. Moore.

**Vultures**
Ecology. Kennedy.
Vulture, The. Belloc.
Vulture. Jeffers.

# W

**Wabash River**
Autumn on the Wabash. Etter.

**Waiters and Waitresses**
All-Night Waitress, The. Stanton.
What You Waited For. Piercy.

**Wales**
Above Penmaenmawr. Connor.
On Leaving London for Wales. Shelley.
Wales Visitation. Ginsberg.
Walter Llywarch. Thomas.
Welsh Landscape. Thomas.

**Wall Street**
Working on Wall Street. Swenson.

**Walls**
Mending Wall. Frost.

**Wanderlust**
Long Gone. Brown.

**War**
A Terre. Owens.
Advent 1966. Levertov.
All Day It Has Rained. Lewis.
Anthem for Doomed Youth. Owen.
As One Non-Combatant to Another. Orwell.
Ash and the Oak, The. Simpson.
Attack. Sassoon.
August 1914. Rosenberg.
Base Details. Sassoon.

Battle Picture, A. Melville.
Battle Won Is Lost. George.
Beat! Beat! Drums! Whitman.
Break of Day in the Trenches. Rosenberg.
Breakfast. Gibson.
Broken Promise. Taylor.
Carentan O Carentan. Simpson.
Censorship. Waley.
Chances, The. Owen.
Channel Firing. Hardy.
Charge of the Light Brigade, The. Tennyson.
Christmas Letter Home. Fraser.
Come to the Stone. Jarrell.
Conquerors, The. McGinley.
Conquerors. Treece.
Counting Small-Boned Bodies. Bly.
Das Schloss. Kirstein.
Dead Shall Be Raised Incorruptible, The. Kinnell.
Death of the Ball Turret Gunner, The. Jarrell.
Defeated Victor, The. Bienek.
Disabled. Owen.
Dreams from War. Krysl.
Drum, The. Scott.
Dulce et Decorum Est. Owen.
Eighth Air Force. Jarrell.
Exposure. Owen.
Flowers of the Forest, The. Elliot.
For the Record. Thomas.
Foresight. Kirstein.
Fortunes of War, The. *Unknown.*
Fury of Aerial Bombardment, The. Eberhart.
Futility. Owen.
General, The. Sassoon.
Greater Love. Owen.
Gun Teams. Frankau.
Gunpowder Plot. Scannell.
Hand That Signed the Paper Felled a City, The. Thomas.
Hope for Those Separated by War, A. Keyes.
I Did Not Lose My Heart. Housman.
I Have a Rendezvous with Death. Seeger.
In Distrust of Merits. Moore.
In Flanders Fields. McCrae.
In the Dordogne. Bishop.
In Time of "The Breaking of Nations." Hardy.
Insensibility. Owen.
Into Battle. Grenfell.
It Is Dangerous to Read Newspapers. Atwood.
Johnny, I Hardly Knew Ye. *Unknown.*
Lament of the Frontier Guard. Pound.
Letter to an American Visitor. Comfort.
Life at War. Levertov.
Little Girl Saw Her First Troop Parade, The. Sandburg.
Long War, The. Lee.
Malvern Hill. Melville.
Man He Killed, The. Hardy.
March into Virginia, The. Melville.
Maryland Battalion, The. Palmer.
Masters of War. Dylan.
Memories of a Lost War. Simpson.
Mental Cases. Owen.
Montcalm and Wolfe. *Unknown.*
Mother and Poet. E. Browning.
My Sweet Old Etcetera.*Fr.* Is 5. Cummings.
Noon Hour. Finnigan.
Oh, It's Nine Years Ago I Was Digging in the Land. *Unknown.*
O.T.'s Blues. Cuney.
Ode for the American Dead in Korea. McGrath.
Ode upon the Occasion of His Majesty's Proclamation in the Year 1630, An. Fanshawe.
Ode Written in the Beginning of the Year 1746. Collins.
Old War-Dreams. Whitman.
On Being Asked for a War Poem. Yeats.

One-and-Twenty. *Unknown.*
One Morning We Brought Them Order. Lee.
Peace. Brooke.
Peasants, The. Lewis.
Preformance, The. Dickey.
Perplexed by the Sunlight. Lindop.
Plato told. Cummings.
Poem to My Sister, Ethel Ennis, Who Sang "The Star-spangled Banner" at the Second Inauguration of Richard Milhous Nixon. Jordan.
Portrait: The Freedom Fighter. Jonas.
Prayer after World War. Sandburg.
Preacher, Said the General. Meinke.
Quintana Lay in the Shallow Grave of Coral. Shapiro.
Recalling War. Graves.
Repression of War Experience. Sassoon.
Russians. Douglas.
Send-Off, The. Owen.
Show, The. Owen.
Smile at the Birdie. Mann.
Snow in Europe. Gascoyne.
Soldiers Bathing. Prince.
Song of the Camp, The. Taylor.
Song of the Freedman. *Unknown.*
Sonnet to Britain. Aytoun.
Spool, The. Belitt.
Spring 1942. Fuller.
Strange Hells. Gurney.
Strength through Joy. Rexroth.
Ten Thousand Miles. *Unknown.*
Tenting Tonight. Kittredge.
Tewa Song of War. *Unknown.*
These. Williams.
To Lucasta, Going to the Wars. Lovelace.
To R — Before Leaving to Fight in Unknown Terrain. Serrano.
Twenty five years of the endless war.*Fr.* The New Antigone. Parkinson.
Two Armies. Spender.
Ultima Ratio Regum. Spender.
Unseen Fire. Currey.
Vale from Carthage. Viereck.
Vergissmeinnicht. Douglas.
Vigil Strange I Kept on the Field One Night. Whitman.
Vitai Lampada. Newbolt.
Voices of Heroes. Gregory.
War. Ramsey.
War Is Kind. Crane.
Watching Post. Day Lewis.
What Kind of War? Rottman.
When the War Is Over. Merwin.
Widow's Party, The. Kipling.
Winter Warfare. Rickword.
*See also* **Soldiers; World War, First; World War, Second.**

**War Dead**
Anthem for Doomed Youth. Owen.
Armistice. Dehn.
Cenotaph, The. Mew.
Classic Encounter. Caudwell.
Counting Small-Boned Bodies. Bly.
Death of a Soldier, A. Stevens.
Death of the Ball Turret Gunner, The. Jarrell.
Drummer Hodge. Hardy.
Dulce et Decorum Est. Owen.
Elegy for a Dead Soldier, *sel.* Shapiro.
Futility. Owen.
Grass. Sandburg.
Greater Love. Owen.
Hunting Civil War Relics at Nimblewill Creek. Dickey.
Investiture, The. Sassoon.
John Anderson. Douglas.
Johnny, I Hardly Knew Ye. *Unknown.*

Lines for an Interment. MacLeish.
Memo. Lynch.
Memorial Rain. MacLeish.
Memorial Wreath. Randall.
Ode to the Confederate Dead. Tate.
Ode, Written in the Beginning of the Year 1746. Collins.
Olive, The. Housman.
Pacific Epitaphs. Randall.
Performance, The. Dickey.
Photographs: A Vision of Massacre. Harper.
Pro Patria. Carrier.
Show, The. Owen.
Sight in Camp in the Daybreak Gray and Dim, A. Whitman.
Soldier, The. Brooke.
Song of the Dying Gunner A.A.1. Causley.
Strange Meeting. Owen.
To His Dead Body. Sassoon.
Tomb of Lieutenant John Learmonth, A.I.F., The. Manifold.
Unknown Soldiers.*Fr.* The New Spoon River. Masters.
Vergissmeinicht. Douglas.
Volunteer, The. Asquith.
War. Langland.
Young Dead Soldiers, The. MacLeish.

**War of 1812**
Ballad of New Orleans. Wilson.
Banks of Champlain, The. *Unknown.*
Battle of New Orleans, The. *Unknown.*
*Constitution's* Last Fight, The. Roche.
Hunters of Kentucky. Woodworth.
James Bird. *Unknown.*
Warship of 1812, The. *Unknown.*
Ye Parliament of England. *Unknown.*

**Warren, Joseph**
Death of Warren, The. Sargent.

**Warren, Robert Penn**
To a Romantic. Tate.

**Wars of the Roses**
Song at the Feast of Brougham Castle. Wordsworth.
War of the Roses, The. *Unknown.*

**Washington, Booker T.**
Booker T. and W.E.B. Randall.

**Washington, George**
Cameo No. II. Jordan.
Mount Vernon. *Unknown.*
Patriotic Poem. Wakoski.
To His Excellency, General Washington. Wheatley.
Washington. *Unknown.*
Washington Monument by Night. Sandburg.
Washington's Monument, February 1885. Whitman.

**Washington, D.C.**
July in Washington. Lowell.

**Wasps**
Upon a Wasp Chilled with Cold. Taylor.
Wasp. Nowlan.
Waspish. Frost.
Wasps' Nest, The. MacBeth.

**Water**
All Day I Hear. Joyce.
Diviners, The. Oliver.
Third Thing, The. Lawrence.
Well Water. Jarrell.
What Any Lover Learns. MacLeish.

**Water Lilies**
Monet: "Les Nympheas." Snodgrass.
Pond Lily. Clarkson.

**Water Wheels**
Force, The. Redgrove.

**Waterfalls**
Cascadilla Falls. Ammons.
Cataract of Lodore, The. Southey.
Persistent Explorer. Ransom.
Waterfall. Heaney.

Waterfall, The. Vaughan.
Waterfalls. Watkins.

**Waterfowl**
Canticle to the Waterbirds, A. Everson.
Little Militant, The. Neilson.
Pair, A. Swenson.
To a Waterfowl. Bryant.
Willets, The. Swenson.

**Waterloo, Battle of**
Field of Waterloo, The.*Fr.* Childe Harold's Pilgrimage. Byron.

**Watts, Los Angeles, California**
Watts. Kaufman.
Watts. Rivers.

**Waves**
How Everything Happens. Swenson.
Surfer and Others. Dorman.

**Wealth**
Art thou poor, yet hast thou golden slumbers?*Fr.* The Pleasant Comedy of Patient Grisell. Dekker.
Beverly Hills, Chicago. Brooks.
For A' That and A' That. Brooks.
Short Song of Congratulation, A. Johnson.
Spectator Ab Extra. Clough.
To Richard Boyle, Earl of Burlington: Of the Use of Riches. Pope.
Wealth and Wisdom. *Unknown.*

**Weasels**
Weasel. Read.

**Weather**
Gray Weather. Jeffers.
Rainbow at Night. *Unknown.*

**Weathervanes**
Upon the Weathercock. Bunyan.

**Webster, Daniel**
Ichabod. Whittier.

**Wedding Songs**
Bridal Song.*Fr.* Hero and Leander. Chapman.
Bridal Song, A.*Fr.* The Two Noble Kinsmen. Shakespeare.
Epithalamion: "Ye learned sisters which have oftentimes." Spenser.
Sergeant's Weddin', The. Kipling.

**Welfare State**
Stamp Blues. *Unknown.*

**Wenceslaus, Saint**
Good King Wenceslas. Neale.

**Wendigos**
Wendigo, The. Nash.

**Werewolves**
Beasts. Wilbur.

**Wessex, England**
Wessex Heights. Hardy.

**West, Richard**
Sonnet on the Death of Richard West. Gray.

**West (United States)**
Home on the Range. *Unknown.*
Hoppy. Godsey.
Love and an Old Western at the Starlite Drive-in Theater. Legler.
O Bury Me Not on the Lone Prairie. *Unknown.*
Song Mt. Tamalpais Sings, The. Welch.
Whoopee-Ti-Yi-Yo! *Unknown.*

**West Indies**
Jamaican Bus Ride. Tessimond.
O Carib Isle! Crane.
Tales of the Islands. Walcott.

**Westminster Abbey**
On the Tombs in Westminster Abbey. Beaumont.
Refusal, A. Hardy.

**Whales and Whaling**
Blackfish Poem. Acorn.
Blue Whale, The. Watson.
Greenland Whale, The. *Unknown.*

Greenland Whale Fishery, The. *Unknown.*
Killing a Whale. Gill.
Leviathan. Merwin.
Quaker Graveyard in Nantucket, The. Lowell.
Suicides, The. Macbeth.
Whale, The.*Fr.* The Progresse of the Soule. Donne.
Whale, The. *Unknown.*
Whale at Twilight. Coatsworth.
Whale Song. Maguire.
Whale. Bates.
Whales, The. Young.
Whales Weep Not! Lawrence.

**Wheat**
Sheaves, The. Robinson.
To a Red-Wheat Field. Turner.

**Wheelbarrows**
Red Wheelbarrow, The. Williams.

**Whistler, James Abbot McNeill**
Whistler's Father. Ryan.

**Whitman, Walt**
Letters to Walt Whitman. Johnson.
Old Walt. Hughes.
Pact, A. Pound.
Reading Walt Whitman. Forbes.
Supermarket in California, A. Ginsberg.
Walt Whitman. Honig.
Walt Whitman at Bear Mountain. Simpson.

**Whittier, John Greenleaf**
Mr. Whittier. Scott.
Whittier.*Fr.* A Fable for Critics. Lowell.

**Widows and Widowers**
Dear Old Girl. Buck.
Sequence for a Young Widow Passing. Munro.
Stony Lonesome. Hughes.
Widow of Drynam, The. MacDonogh.

**Wigs**
Bald Cavalier, The. *Unknown.*

**Wilde, Oscar**
Arrest of Oscar Wilde at the Cadogan Hotel, The. Betjeman.

**Williams, William Carlos**
Death News. Ginsberg.

**Willow Trees**
Hunting Pheasants in a Cornfield. Bly.
Sauchs in the Reuch Heuch Hauch, The. "MacDiarmid."
Willow Poem. Williams.

**Wiltshire, England**
Wiltshire Downs. Young.

**Winchester, England**
In Praise of Winchester. *Unknown.*

**Wind**
Address to a Child During a Boisterous Winter Evening. D. Wordsworth.
Aim Was Song, The. Frost.
Big Wind. Roethke.
Blow, Blow Thou Winter Wind.*Fr.* As You Like It. Shakespeare.
Cars once steel and green, now old. Zukofsky.
Dirge, A: "Rough wind, that moanest loud." Shelley.
I Saw the Wind Today. Colum.
King Wind. Van Doren.
Little Wind. Greenaway.
My Lady Wind. *Unknown.*
Night-Wind, The. E. Bronte.
North Wind in October. Bridges.
Nothing. De la Mare.
Ode to the West Wind. Shelley.
Old Prison, The. Wright.
Reminiscence II. Colum.
Snow-Storm, The. Emerson.
Sonnet: "A wind has blown the rain away and blown." Cummings.
Strong Wind, A. Clarke.

Sudden Gale in Spring. Thomas.
Term, The. Williams.
Tumbleweed. Carden.
Unknown Color, The. Cullen.
Villain, The. Davies.
Western Wind. *Unknown.*
Who Has Seen the Wind? C. Rossetti.
Wind. Hughes.
Wind, The. Reeves.
Wind, The. Stephens.
Wind in a Frolic, The. Howitt.
Wind Secrets. Wakoski.
Windy Nights. Stevenson.

**Windhovers.** *See* **Falcons.**

**Wine**
Gooseberry Wine. Shumway.
Song: "Hence burgundy, claret, and port." Keats.
Wine Menagerie, The. Crane.

**Winter**
Ancient Music. Pound.
Beyond Anguish. Kessler.
Blow, Blow, Thou Winter Wind.*Fr.* As You Like It. Shakespeare.
Blue Horses. Roberson.
Cold Fear. Roberts.
Cold Wave Blues. *Unknown.*
Coming on to Winter. Flaherty.
Darkling Thrush, The. Hardy.
Deep in Winter. Kooser.
Dirge for the Year. Shelley.
Exposure. Owen.
Facts of Winter. Harris.
Frost is here, The. Tennyson.
Glass World. Donnelly.
How Still, How Happy. E. Bronte.
In Winter in the Woods Alone. Frost.
Induction to "A Mirror for Magistrates." Sackville.
January Thaw. Block.
London Snow. Bridges.
New Year's Song. Hughes.
No Possum, No Sop, No Taters. Stevens.
Now Winter Nights Enlarge. Campion.
Old Man's Winter Night, An. Frost.
One Horse Open Sleigh, The. Pierpont.
Persia. Sackville-West.
Reach of Winter, The. Andrews.
Sky is low, the clouds are mean, The. Dickinson.
Snow Country. Etter.
Snow Man, The. Stevens.
Snow-bound; a Winter Idyl. Whittier.
Snowy Night. Haines.
Song of Winter, A. Meyer.
Star-Talk. Graves.
Stopping by Woods on a Snowy Evening. Frost.
Thaw. Thomas.
There's a certain slant of light. Dickinson.
To Winter. Blake.
Weary year his race now having run, The.*Fr.* Amoretti. Spenser.
White Ropes. Brainard.
Why Fires Are Lit December 21st. McMahon.
Winter. Donaghy.
Winter. Donzella.
Winter. Patmore.
Winter.*Fr.* Love's Labour's Lost. Shakespeare.
Winter. Synge.
Winter. Tynan.
Winter. Williams.
Winter; a Dirge. Burns.
Winter Evening. Behn.
Winter Memories. Thoreau.
Winter Morning. Smith.

Winter Night, A.  Barnes.
Winter Night, A.*Fr.* The Seasons.  Thomson.
Winter Nights.  Campion.
Winter Pond.  Logue.
Winter Scene, A.  Whittemore.
Winter Scene.  Young.
Winter Seascape.  Betjeman.
Winter Sonnet.  Waldman.
Winter Soon is Coming.  Coatsworth.
Winter Time.  Stevenson.
Winterfall.  *Unknown.*
Wintering.  Plath.

**Wisdom**
Art of Happiness, The.  Young.
Coming of Wisdom with Time, The.  Yeats.
Wealth and Wisdom.  *Unknown.*
Wisdom.  Sobiloff.

**Wise Men.**  *See* **Magi.**

**Wishes**
Wishing.  Allingham.

**Wit**
Ode: Of Wit.  Cowley.

**Witchcraft and Witches**
Against Witches.  *Unknown.*
Allison Gross.  *Unknown.*
Apples of Sodom and Gomorrah, The.  Holland.
Demon Lover, The.  *Unknown.*
Hag-ridden.  Graves.
Her Kind.  Sexton.
Her Strong Enchantments Failing.  Housman.
In Salem.  Clifton.
Laily Worm and the Machrel of the Sea, The.  *Unknown.*
Molly Means.  Walker.
Old Woman on a Broom.  *Unknown.*
Song of Wandering Aengus, The.  Yeats.
Thrice Toss These Oaken Ashes in the Air.  Campion.
Witch of Atlas, The.  Shelley.
Witch of Coös, The.*Fr.* Two Witches.  Frost.
Witchcraft.  Johnson.
Witch's Broomstick Spell.  *Unknown.*
Witches' Charm, The.*Fr.* The Masque of Queens.  Jonson.
Witch's Milking Charm.  *Unknown.*

**Wives**
At Flock Mass.  Higgins.
Breaded Meat, Breaded Hands.  Harper.
On His Dead Wife.  Milton.
To the Ladies.  Chudleigh.
Wish for a Young Wife.  Roethke.
Wives of Mafiosi, The.  Jong.
Young Housewife, The.  Williams.
*See also* **Marriage.**

**Wolsey, Thomas, Cardinal**
On Cardinal Wolsey.  *Unknown.*

**Wolves**
Fox and the Wolf, The.  *Unknown.*
Howling of Wolves, The.  Hughes.
Life of the Wolf, The.  Gildner.
Wolves.  Haines.
Wolves, The.  Tate.

**Wombats**
Weary Will.  Paterson.

**Women**
Against Blame of Women.  Desmond.
Ah! who can e'er forget so fair a being?  Keats.
Bad Girl Blues.  *Unknown.*
Beautiful Black Women.  Jones.
Before Bed.  Waldrop.
Birthday, The.  Dacey.
Bookshop Idyll, A.  Amis.
Broken Dreams.  Yeats.
C. L. M.  Masefield.
Charming Woman.  Sheridan.

Childhood.*Fr.* The Four Ages of Man.  Bradstreet.
Combing.  Cardiff.
Common Woman, The.  Grahn.
Dear Colette.  Jong.
Dispraise of Absalom, The.  *Unknown.*
Energetic Women.  Lawrence.
Evil Devil Woman.  *Unknown.*
Farmer's Curst Wife, The.  *Unknown.*
Father of Women, A.  Meynell.
Female Friend, The.  Whur.
Four Women.  Simone.
Frau Bauman, Frau Schmidt, and Frau Schwartze.  Roethke.
Furniture of a Woman's Mind, The.  Swift.
Gentle Echo on Woman, A.  Swift.
Her Sister.  O'Neill.
Housewife.  Sexton.
Hypocrite Women.  Levertov.
I Dream I'm the Death of Orpheus.  Rich.
I Know a Spot Just Over the Hill.  Mills.
In Celebration of My Uterus.  Sexton.
In Her Praise.  Graves.
In Mind.  Levertov.
In the Park.  Harwood.
Introduction, The.  Countess of Winchilsea.
It's No Good!  Lawrence.
James Alley.  *Unknown.*
Katie May.  *Unknown.*
Lay Your Arms Aside.  Ferriter.
Letter to My Sister.  Spencer.
Light feet, dark violet eyes, and parted hair.  Keats.
Little League Women.  Metzger.
Little Old Women, The.  Baudelaire.
Looking Out.  Chasin.
Mabel Kelly.  O'Carolan.
Man, Man, Man is for the Woman Made.  *Unknown.*
Metamorphoses.  Fuller.
Mutes, The.  Levertov.
My Mother's Sister.  Day Lewis.
Nakedness of women is the work of God, The.  Blake.
Negro Women.  Alexander.
Nehi Blues.  *Unknown.*
New York Woman, The.  Sissman.
No Images.  Cuney.
No Second Troy.  Yeats.
O Woman, Shapely As the Swan.  *Unknown.*
Ode to a Beautiful Woman.  Clark.
On the Debt My Mother Owed to Sears Roebuck.  Dorn.
Out on Santa-Fe—Blues.  *Unknown.*
Peggy Browne.  O'Carolan.
Planetarium.  Rich.
Poem: "The person who can do."  Dugan.
Portrait, The.  Graves.
Prayer for My Daughter, A.  Yeats.
Pro Femina, *sels.*  Kizer.
Prologue, The.  Bradstreet.
Robbing and Stealing Blues.  *Unknown.*
Sadie and Maud.  Brooks.
Saturday Blues.  *Unknown.*
Saying Goodbye.  Juhasz.
Short Haired Woman.  *Unknown.*
Sisters, The.  A. Lowell.
Someone Is Beating a Woman.  Voznesensky.
Song: "With my frailty don't upbraid Me."  Congreve.
Streets.  A. Lowell.
Streets of New York, The.  Blossom.
That Women Are but Men's Shadows.  Jonson.
There Has to Be a Jail for Ladies.  Merton.
These Women All.  Heath.
Thirty eighth year, The.  Clifton.
This Pretty Woman.  *Unknown.*
To a Young Lady.  Wordsworth.
To Women, As Far As I'm Concerned.  Lawrence.

Treat the woman tenderly, tenderly. *Unknown.*
Two Parents, The. "MacDiarmid."
Ultimate Antientropy, The. Weiss.
Vierge Ouvrante. Palmer.
Volcanic Venus. Lawrence.
W.W. Jones.
Way It Was, The. Clifton.
Weeksville Women. Loftin.
What You Waited For. Piercy.
Why, Some of My Best Friends Are Women. McGinley.
Wish, A. Lerner.
Woman. Jarrell.
Woman Is a Worthy Thing, A. *Unknown.*
Woman Poem. Giovanni.
Woman! when I behold thee flippant, vain. Keats.
Woman with Girdle. Sexton.
Women. Bogan.
Women. Swenson.
Women in Brooklyn. Zweig.
Women in Vietnam, The. Paley.
Women Who Are Hard Inside. Gotlieb.
*Mountain Moving Day: Poems by Women.* (MMD). Elaine Gill, ed.
*New Poets: Women* (NPW). Terry Wetherby, ed.
*Psyche: the Feminine Poetic Consciousness* (Psy). Barbara Segnitz *and* Carol Rainey, eds.
*Rising Tides: 20th Century American Women Poets* (RiTi). Laura Chester *and* Sharon Barba, eds.
*Salt and Bitter and Good: Three Centuries of English and American Women Poets* (SBG). Cora Kaplan, ed.
*We Become New* (WBN). Lucille Iverson *and* Kathryn Ruby, eds.
*Women Poets in English, The.* (WPE). Ann Stanford, ed.
**Women's Liberation**
Advice to Young Ladies. Hope.
After Drinking Water. Gioseffi.
Alcestis on the Poetry Circuit. Jong.
Answer to a Man's Question, "What Can I Do About Women's Liberation?" Griffin.
Back to Africa. Jong.
Beyond What. Walker.
Cactus Tree. Mitchell.
Conversation in the Eighth Street Bookshop. Moore.
Councils. Piercy.
Departure of the Women, The. Mairs.
From Sappho to myself, consider the fate of women.*Fr.* Pro Femina. Kizer.
Her Sister. O'Neill.
Housewife. Schaeffer.
Housewife's Lament, The. *Unknown.*
Hypocrite Women. Levertov.
I Like to Think of Harriet Tubman. Griffin.
I take as my theme, "The Independent Woman."*Fr.* Pro Femina. Kizer.
In the Men's Room(s). Piercy.
Interpretation. Koster
Justice Has Become a Woman. Brady.
Morning Half-Life Blues, The. Piercy.
Mountain moving day is coming, The. Akiko *and* Weisstein.
My People. Himel.
Myth. Rukeyser.
New Lost Feminist, The. Brown.
No More Soft Talk. Wakoski.
Out of the Desert. Levenberg.
Over the fence. Dickinson.
Personal Letter No. 2. Sanchez.
Quarrel, The. Di Prima.
Seventeen Warnings in Search of a Feminist Poem. Jong.
Someone Is Beating a Woman. Voznesensky.
Soul-Drift. Blind.
Spring Offensive of the Snail, The. Piercy.
Three X Three. Sanchez.

Tirade. Moore.
To Kate, Skating Better Than Her Date. Daiches.
To the Ladies. Chudleigh.
Try Brillo on the Slimy Stove. Gotlieb.
Winter Mornings. Mairs.
*I Hear My Sisters Saying* (IHMS). Carol Konek *and* Dorothy Walters, eds.
*No More Masks!* (NMM). Florence Howe *and* Ellen Bass, eds.
**Wood**
Anniversary. Dacey.
Old Boards. Bly.
Rail Splitting. Lawless.
Woodyards in the Rain. Marriott.
**Woodchucks.** *See* **Groundhogs.**
**Woods.** *See* **Forests.**
**Woodstock, New York**
Woodstock. Mitchell.
**Wordsworth, William**
Addressed to Haydon ("Great spirits are now on earth sojourning"). Keats.
Epilogue: "There's something in a stupid ass." Byron.
Lost Leader, The. Browning.
On a Portrait of Wordsworth by B.R. Haydon. E. Browning.
Sonnet, A: "Two voices are there: one is of the deep." Stephen.
To William Wordsworth. Coleridge.
To Wordsworth. Shelley.
William Wordsworth. Keyes.
**Work.** *See* **Labor and Laborers.**
**Work Songs**
Corn-Song, A. Dunbar.
Drill, Ye Tarriers, Drill! *Unknown.*
I've Been Workin' on the Railroad. *Unknown.*
*American Folk Poetry* (AmFP). Duncan Emrich, ed.
*Blues Line, The* (BluL). Eric Sackheim, ed.
**World.** *See* **Earth.**
**World War, First**
At the Eastern Front. Trakl.
Break of Day in the Trenches. Rosenberg.
Channel Firing. Hardy.
Dulce et Decorum Est. Owen.
Exposure. Owen.
Fathers, The. Sassoon.
Gun Teams. Frankau.
I Have a Rendezvous with Death. Seeger.
In Flanders Fields. McCrae.
In Time of "The Breaking of Nations." Hardy.
Rear-Guard, The. Sassoon.
Rouen. Cannan.
Show, The. Owen.
Summer in England, 1914. Meynell.
**World War, Second**
Carentan O Carentan. Simpson.
Firebombing, The. Dickey.
In Westminster Abbey. Betjeman.
"Less Nonsense." Herbert.
Moon and the Night and the Men, The. Berryman.
Nerves. "Sagittarius."
On Seeing Films of the War. Coxe.
Stoic, The: For Laura von Courten. Bowers.
To My Father on Pearl Harbor Day. Donzella.
Watch the Lights Fade. Jeffers.
What Lies on Us. Dawe.
**Worms**
Autobiography of a Lungworm. Fuller.
Fish, The. Mills.
Old Shellover. De la Mare.
This Is an African Worm. Danner.
Worm, The. Bergengren.
Worms and the Wind. Sandburg.
**Wren, Sir Christopher**
Sir Christopher Wren.*Fr.* Clerihews. Bentley.

**Wrens**
  Call for the Robin Redbreast and the Wren.   Webster.
  Wren, The.   *Unknown.*
**Wrestling and Wrestlers**
  All-In Wrestlers.   Kirkup.
  Two Wrestlers.   Francis.
**Wright, Richard**
  Mourning Letter from Paris, A.   Rivers.
  To Richard Wright.   Rivers.
**Wyoming**
  Snow Country.   Etter.

# X

**X-Rays**
  After X-Ray.   Pastan.
**Xenophanes**
  Xenophanes.   Emerson.

# Y

**Yachts**
  Yachts, The.   Williams.
**Yaks**
  Mad Yak, The.   Corso.
  Yak, The.   Belloc.
  Yak, The.   Roethke.
**Yale University**
  Yale Boola!   Hirsh.
**Yankee Stadium**
  Tao in the Yankee Stadium Bleachers.   Updike.
**Yankees, New York (baseball team)**
  Baseball and Writing.   Moore.
**Yarrow or Yarrow Water, Scotland**
  Yarrow Unvisited.   Wordsworth.
  Yarrow Visited.   Wordsworth.
**Yeats, William Butler**
  I have moved to Dublin to have it out with you.   Berryman.
  If I Ask Whether the Islands.   Griffin.
  In Memory of W.B.Yeats.   Auden.
  William Buttler Yeats.   Hope.
**Yellow.**
  Yell for Yellow, A.   Merriam.
**Yesenin, Sergey**

  Death of the Epileptic Poet Yesenin, The.   Boyajian.
**Yew Trees**
  Moon and the Yew Trees, The.   Plath.
**Yom Kippur**
  Yom Kippur: Fasting.   R. Whitman.
**Young Pretender, The.**   *See* **Stuart, Charles Edward, the Young Pretender.**
**Youth**
  Boys, The.   Thwaite.
  Crabbed Age and Youth.   Shakespeare.
  Daedalus.   Reid.
  Fern Hill.   Thomas.
  For My Son on the Highways of His Mind.   Kumin.
  Great-Aunts.   O'Críadáin.
  In Youth Is Pleasure.   Wever.
  Linda.   Stone.
  Little Johnny's Final Letter.   Patten.
  My Lost Youth.   Longfellow.
  My Rival.   Kipling.
  Old age sticks.   Cummings.
  On My 18th Birthday.   Corrington.
  Portrait of a Girl with Comic Book   McGinley.
  Young.   Sexton.
  Young and Old.*Fr.* The Water Babies.   Kingsley.
  Young Ones, Flip Side, The.   Emanuel.
  Youth and Age.   Coleridge.
  Youth and Love.*Fr.* The Beggar's Opera.   Gay.

# Z

**Zebras**
  Miscegenous Zebra, The.   Young.
  Zebra.   "Isak Dinesen."
**Zen**
  December.   Snyder.
**Zoos**
  At the Zoo.   Thackeray.
  Au Jardin des Plantes.   Wain.
  Elephant, The.   Hochman.
  Invitation to the Zoological Gardens, An.   *Unknown.*
  Monkeys, The.   Moore.
  Traverse City Zoo.   Harrison.
  Twilight at the Zoo.   Rodger.